PRESENTED

TO:

BY:

ON:

NEW KING JAMES VERSION

COLOR CODE BIBLE

FOR KIDS

NEW KING JAMES VERSION

COLOR CODE BIBLE

FOR KIDS

THOMAS NELSON
Since 1798

www.ThomasNelson.com

Color Code Bible for Kids

Published in Nashville, TN, by Thomas Nelson. Thomas Nelson is a registered trademark of HarperCollins Christian Publishing, Inc.

Library of Congress Control Number: 2024931259

HarperCollins Publishers, Macken House, 39/40 Mayor Street Upper, Dublin 1, D01 C9W8, Ireland (https://www.harpercollins.com)

Printed in India

26 27 28 29 30 31 32 /BPI/ 15 14 13 12 11 10 9 8 7 6 5 4 3

CONTENTS

BOOK ABBREVIATIONS

In Alphabetical Order by Abbreviation

OT = Old Testament
NT = New Testament

WHAT IS THE BIBLE?

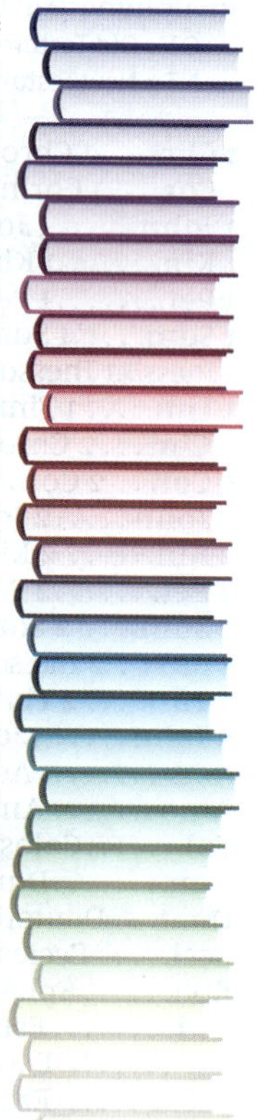

The word *bible* simply means "book" or "books." The Bible is a collection of sixty-six books written by over forty people on three continents over fifteen hundred years. These books are divided into two sections: thirty-nine books make up the Old Testament, and twenty-seven books make up the New Testament. All these books, though, work together to tell one big, true story.

The Old Testament begins the story by telling how God created everything, including people. God made us to be in a relationship with Him—to know Him, worship Him, and obey Him. But the first people, Adam and Eve, disobeyed God and sin entered creation. From that moment on, our relationship with God was broken and there was nothing we could do about it. But God could, and He did. The Old Testament continues telling this story with God promising to provide a rescuer. Beginning with a man named Abraham, God formed a special people whom He would use to bring this rescuer into the world. The Old Testament tells the story of this group of people and how God continued to love them and provide for them even when they continued to sin.

The New Testament picks up the story about four hundred years after the Old Testament ends. It describes how God provided this rescuer in Jesus, the Son of God. Jesus lived a perfect life of about thirty years, not even sinning once, and then gave up His life to pay the punishment for sin. But Jesus did not stay dead. He rose from the dead on the third day, and now all who trust in Him are forgiven of their sins and can be in a relationship with God. The New Testament continues this story by describing how Jesus' first followers formed the church and continued to tell others about Him. It ends with the promise that Jesus will return one day and defeat sin and death for good.

AN INSPIRED BOOK

The Bible is completely true—every part of the story that makes up the big story, every fact, every verse. Because of this, we can trust what the Bible says. The reason is that the Bible is different from other books in an important way.

While the Bible has about forty different authors, they did not write the Bible on their own. Second Timothy 3:16 tells us that "all Scripture is given by inspiration of God." The word "inspiration" means "breathed out." God is the source of every word of Scripture. The authors wrote what God wanted them to write in their own words and in their own way, but God made sure that every word they wrote was true and what He wanted to be said. God has provided and protected the Bible so that we can be confident that it is true.

A LIFE-CHANGING BOOK

The Bible tells one big story, but unlike many other books we read, we are part of this one. God gave us the Bible so that we can trust in Jesus and be in a relationship with Him. God wants us to read the Bible and see how loving and good He is and how much He cares for us. He also wants us to read the Bible so we can understand the best way to live—the way that shows others how great God is and gives us the most meaning and joy.

God doesn't want us to stumble through life with no idea of why we are here or what we should be doing. He wants us to know His plan and purpose for our lives. The Bible is for everyone, but it's also very personal. It's just for you. Remember, God created you as a special and unique person. The Bible can speak to your heart like no other book in the world because it's God's Word especially for you.

As you read the Bible, then, you will find that you will begin to change. You will grow to love God more and to live more like Jesus. You will learn to see things differently and care for other people more. This will not happen immediately. Change takes time. It happens slowly, but surely. Likewise, change also isn't automatic. This is why it's important to keep reading the Bible. Even if you don't understand it all at first, in time, you will understand more. It is through regular reading—even if it's just a few verses at a time—that you will grow and change.

OLD TESTAMENT (39 BOOKS)

BOOKS OF LAW

1 GENESIS
2 EXODUS
3 LEVITICUS
4 NUMBERS
5 DEUTERONOMY

Moses wrote these books when he was leading God's people, the Israelites. This group of books is also called the Pentateuch, which means "five books." The Pentateuch begins telling the story of God's people. In these books, we learn about God creating the world, sin entering the world, the beginning of God's plan to forgive people, and the early history of the Israelites. The Pentateuch also contains the laws God gave to His people through Moses. These laws explain what God expects of people, how to worship God and love others, and how to be pure and holy.

BOOKS OF HISTORY

6 JOSHUA
7 JUDGES
8 RUTH
9 10 1, 2 SAMUEL
11 12 1, 2 KINGS
13 14 1, 2 CHRONICLES
15 EZRA
16 NEHEMIAH
17 ESTHER

The twelve books of history continue the story of Israel where the Pentateuch leaves off. Moses had died and Joshua had become the leader of the Israelites. In these books, we learn about the people of Israel returning to the land God had given Abraham, and how they settled in that land and were led by judges and kings. We also read of how God's people rebelled against Him, mostly by worshiping false gods and treating one another poorly. As a result, God disciplined His people by sending mighty nations to defeat Israel and take many of the people away into captivity. But we also see that God is always loving and forgiving. Eventually, He brought His people back to their land.

BOOKS OF POETRY

- 18 JOB
- 19 PSALMS
- 20 PROVERBS
- 21 ECCLESIASTES
- 22 SONG OF SONGS
- 23 LAMENTATIONS

These books of poetry and wisdom provide wonderful examples of prayer and praise from people who loved God and enjoyed a close relationship with Him. They also provide insight into how we are to live. These books tell about hope and failure, trust and fear, sorrow and joy. Often used by the Israelites during special times of celebration, these books provided examples for expressing love to God. Even today, we can often hear the words of these treasured books set to music and sung by Christians in worship.

BOOKS OF PROPHECY

MAJOR PROPHETS

- 24 ISAIAH
- 25 JEREMIAH
- 26 EZEKIEL
- 27 DANIEL

MINOR PROPHETS

- 28 HOSEA
- 29 JOEL
- 30 AMOS
- 31 OBADIAH
- 32 JONAH
- 33 MICAH
- 34 NAHUM
- 35 HABAKKUK
- 36 ZEPHANIAH
- 37 HAGGAI
- 38 ZECHARIAH
- 39 MALACHI

The books of prophecy were written by prophets, men who heard God's voice and faithfully told God's people what He wanted them to know and do. The messages God sent were words of love, correction, and warning. These messengers of God were sent to remind people about God's law and promises, and to help them make right choices about how to live.

Although these books are called "major" and "minor" prophets, all are of the same importance. The minor books of prophecy are simply shorter than the major books of prophecy. All the words of God are of incredible value; no one portion is greater than another.

NEW TESTAMENT (27 BOOKS)

THE GOSPELS

1 MATTHEW
2 MARK
3 LUKE
4 JOHN

The word *gospel* means "good news." The first four books of the New Testament are called Gospels because they tell the story and good news of Jesus. He is the Son of God. He was born to a woman by the power of the Holy Spirit and grew to be a man. He taught people about God's love and helped them understand how to live a life that pleases God. He died on a cross for our sins. He rose from the dead on the third day. And He gave His followers a mission to tell others about Him.

The main purpose of the Gospels is to show how Jesus is the fulfillment of what God promised in the Old Testament and that everyone can believe in Him to be forgiven of their sins. Each Gospel tells this same story of Jesus, but each one tells it in a slightly different way.

CHURCH HISTORY

5 ACTS

Only one book makes up this section of church history: the Acts of the Apostles. Acts begins with Jesus returning to be with God the Father and His first followers obeying the mission He had given them. The church began in Jerusalem but soon grew into the surrounding Judea, nearby Samaria, and the rest of the world just as Jesus had commanded. Acts describes this growth and how the church began to understand the gospel more clearly.

THE LETTERS

6 ROMANS
7 8 1, 2 CORINTHIANS
9 GALATIANS
10 EPHESIANS
11 PHILIPPIANS
12 COLOSSIANS
13 14 1, 2 THESSALONIANS
15 16 1, 2 TIMOTHY
17 TITUS
18 PHILEMON
19 HEBREWS
20 JAMES
21 22 1, 2 PETER
23 24 25 1, 2, 3 JOHN
26 JUDE

The early church grew quickly. The Bible tells us that three thousand people came to believe in Jesus in just one day (see Acts 2:41). As the church grew in numbers, it also needed to grow in its understanding of the gospel. The early believers needed to know what it meant to live for Jesus and what was required of them. In addition, Christians continued (and continue) to sin, which caused some problems in the churches. So, leaders like Paul, Peter, and John wrote letters to different churches and individuals to help them learn how to keep the Christian faith pure and healthy and love one another. These letters help us do that today, too.

THE BOOK OF PROPHECY

27 REVELATION

The last book of the Bible talks about Jesus' return. The apostle John described a vision Jesus gave him during a time when Christians were being treated like criminals—they were hunted, imprisoned, and even put to death for their faith. Jesus allowed John to see and understand that no matter what horrible things happened to His people, we should never lose hope. Jesus is the King of kings and the Lord of lords. When the final battle has been fought, there will be one winner. While we may not understand exactly how or when it will happen, Jesus will return, and when He does, He will win the final victory. Sin, death, and evil will be destroyed for all time.

WHY DID GOD GIVE US THE BIBLE?

The Bible is a book of sixty-six smaller books full of different stories, people, places, and events. But every story in the Bible works with the others to tell one big, true story of Jesus. God the Father provided His Son, Jesus, as the only way we can be forgiven of our sins and be friends with Him. Here is what you need to know about this story of God's good news so that you can have a friendship with God:

God

1. GOD CREATED THE WORLD. God made everything to show how good He is. Whatever you can see, feel, touch, hear, and smell (and so much more that you cannot) was made by God. And it all shows how amazing, big, and wonderful He is. There are millions and billions of stars and other planets in the universe, and God made each one. And God made you. You are special. God made you because He loves you, and He wants to be your friend. (See Gen. 1–2; Ps. 19:1–6; Col. 1:16–17.)

Sin

2. WE DISOBEYED GOD. Because God created everything, He is in charge of everything. He has the right to say how the world works and how you are to live. For a time, everything worked just as God wanted. But then Adam and Eve disobeyed what God had told them to do. This is sin. And from that moment on, everyone has sinned against God. Even you. We all do and think wrong things at times. And we don't do the right things at other times. Because of sin, we cannot have friendship with God. But worse than that, Adam's sin against God and our sin, too, comes at a very high cost. The Bible says that the punishment we all deserve is death. (See Gen. 3:1–19; Rom. 3:23; 6:23; James 4:17.)

Jesus

3. GOD PROVIDED JESUS. No matter how hard we try, we cannot do enough good things to make up for the times we have sinned against God. But God had an amazing solution. He provided Jesus, His own Son, to do what we could not do. Jesus came to earth from heaven and lived a perfect life, not sinning even once. Then He gave up His perfect, sinless life and died on the cross to pay the punishment of death we all deserve. But Jesus did not stay dead. On the third day, He rose from the dead, fully alive, defeating sin and death. (See John 3:16; 14:6; Rom. 5:8.)

Salvation

4. WE RESPOND IN FAITH. Just because Jesus died and rose again doesn't mean we are forgiven and are friends with God. He has given you a great gift, but you still have to accept it. If you agree with God that you have sinned, want to turn from your sin and become friends with God, and believe who Jesus is and trust in what He has done, you will be saved. (See John 3:17–18; Rom. 10:9–10; Eph. 2:8–9.)

Heaven

5. GOD FORGIVES US. Once you respond to God in faith, you are forgiven. Completely. Totally. All the way. But it gets even better than that. Jesus took all your sin from you, but He gave you something in its place: His own perfect obedience. When God looks at you, He does not see any sin (because it is gone), but what He does see is perfect obedience, which the Bible calls righteousness. It is as if you took a test and got a score of 0 percent and someone else got a score of 100 percent but then switched tests with you. You get the credit for the perfect life that Jesus lived. In short, you are now the person God created you to be and in the friendship with Him that He has always wanted. This friendship begins now and will last forever. (See 2 Cor. 5:21; Eph. 1:7; 1 John 1:9.)

Growth

6. WE LIVE FOR GOD. Jesus did much more than save you from the punishment of sin and give you eternal life. He has also made it so that you can do what God made you to do: show others how great God is. This is called glorifying Him. You can glorify God by developing your friendship with Jesus and loving Him more. You can glorify God by reading the Bible, worshiping Him, and enjoying His creation. And you can glorify Him by loving other people and telling them about the Bible's good news. Trusting in Jesus isn't the end of the story; it's only the beginning of a great new story. (See 1 Cor. 6:19–20; Phil. 1:21; Col. 3:17.)

WHAT NOW? Have you responded to the Bible's good news? If so, here are four things you can do starting today:

1. TELL SOMEONE. It's hard to keep good news to yourself. So, don't. Tell someone about how you responded to the Bible's good news. Maybe that person is a parent, grandparent, uncle, or aunt. Maybe that person is a teacher or leader at your church. Whoever it is would love to hear your good news and help you know what to do next.

2. TALK WITH GOD. The way that you become better friends with someone is by spending time together. The same is true with your friendship with God. Remember, He made you to be His friend, so He wants to spend time with you. He wants to hear from you. The Bible calls this prayer. You can pray about anything. There is no right way to pray. Just tell God what you are thinking and feeling. Share about what you need and any concerns you might have. Tell Him about what makes you happy and the good things you experience each day.

3. READ YOUR BIBLE. There is so much more to understand about the Bible's good news. The Bible is a big book, but you don't have to rush to finish it. Take your time and read a little bit at a time. Look up any words you don't know, or ask an adult to help you with them. Write down any questions you have. Remember that God wants you to understand what you read. If you don't know where to begin, try the Gospel of Mark.

4. TURN FROM SIN. Once you have trusted in Jesus, all your sins are forgiven, but you will still sin. When you do, confess that sin to God. To confess is to agree with God that you did something wrong. Then celebrate that God has already forgiven that sin because Jesus died for it. Ask God to help you not to sin again so that you can glorify Him the best you can.

WHO WROTE THE BIBLE?

God guided about forty people to write the Bible. In one sense, each author was quite ordinary. Some were fishermen, soldiers, and farmers. But each of these ordinary people was used by God in an extraordinary way because each was willing to listen to God and do what He said. We don't have space to talk about every one of the writers of the Bible, but here are a few of the more well-known ones.

MOSES

Moses wrote the first five books of the Bible: Genesis, Exodus, Leviticus, Numbers, and Deuteronomy. He was a Hebrew born in Egypt when God's people were slaves there. But Moses was taken in by Pharaoh's daughter when he was a baby and raised like a prince. When Moses was older, he saw an Egyptian hurting a Hebrew slave, and Moses killed the Egyptian. As a result, he ran away and lived in another land for many years.

One day, Moses was on a mountain tending his sheep when he saw a bush burning without it being damaged. When he went to look closer at the bush, God called to him. God told Moses to go back to Egypt where He would use him to deliver the Hebrews from captivity.

Moses obeyed God, and after a series of miracles and signs, Pharaoh let the Hebrews leave Egypt. As the Hebrews traveled toward the Promised Land—the land God had given to Abraham and his descendants—God spoke to Moses and gave him the law to share with the people so they would know how to live. God also gave instructions for constructing the tabernacle, a tent where the people could worship God.

When the Hebrew people arrived at the edge of the Promised Land, they became afraid of the people living there and failed to trust and obey God and enter. As a result, God disciplined them by having them wander in the wilderness for forty years while most of the grown-ups died off. During that time, Moses wrote the Books of the Law so that God's people would know what God had done.

You can read Moses' story in the books of Exodus and Numbers.

JOSHUA

Joshua wrote the Old Testament book named after him: the Book of Joshua. It tells the story of how the Hebrews finally entered the Promised Land after forty years of wandering in the wilderness.

After leaving Egypt, Joshua became a soldier and Moses' assistant. When the Hebrews reached the border of the Promised Land the first time and Moses sent twelve spies into the land, Joshua was one of them. All the spies except Joshua and Caleb gave a bad report, which caused the people to become afraid and refuse to enter the land. Because of their faithfulness, Joshua and Caleb were the only adults God allowed to enter the land forty years later.

When Moses died just before it was time for the Hebrews to enter the land, Joshua became their new leader. Like Moses, Joshua was a good leader. He was strong and courageous, like God had told him to be, and he did his best to obey God.

You can read Joshua's story in the books of Exodus, Numbers, and Joshua.

SAMUEL

Samuel wrote the Book of Judges and may have written all or parts of three other books: Ruth, 1 Samuel, and 2 Samuel. Some think that Samuel may not have written these other books directly; other writers—perhaps Nathan and Gad—may have used Samuel's records to write them instead. These books are historical accounts of the nation of Israel under the leadership of several judges and its first kings. They tell of many triumphs of God's people but also many of their sins and failures.

Samuel was a judge and a prophet of God. This means he heard from God and told the people what God wanted him to share. Samuel was just a child when he first heard God speak. Throughout his life, Samuel spoke to kings and priests, telling them the words God spoke. Samuel spoke to the people when they were choosing sin instead of God; he warned them of the consequences of their sin. God also used Samuel to anoint Israel's first two kings: Saul and David.

You can read Samuel's story in the books of 1 Samuel and 2 Samuel.

DAVID

David wrote a large portion of the Book of Psalms. A psalm is a song used by God's people in worship. David wrote about eighty of these songs.

When David was young, there was a war between Israel and the Philistines. One large Philistine warrior named Goliath challenged Israel's army. He wanted the top warrior of the Israelites to face him in battle. Whoever won would win the battle for his people. But no Israelite soldier was brave enough to face Goliath.

David was too young to be a soldier, but one day he came to the battlefield to visit his brothers. He couldn't believe that no Israelite would stand up for God and face Goliath. So, David said he would face Goliath. The size of Goliath didn't matter because God was on the Israelites' side. David took a slingshot and a stone, aimed, and hit Goliath right in the forehead. The giant fell at David's feet. When the Philistines saw this, they ran, and the Israelites chased after them.

After this, David became known for his courage. He later became Israel's king after Saul. David was a good king, but not a perfect one. He sinned like everyone else. But he was also quick to repent of his sins, which is why God said David was a man after His own heart.

You can read David's story in 1 Samuel, 2 Samuel, 1 Kings, and 1 Chronicles.

SOLOMON

Solomon wrote Ecclesiastes, most of Proverbs, and the Song of Solomon. He was King David's son and became king of Israel after David died.

When Solomon became king, God asked him what gift he would like to have. Solomon could have asked for anything, but he asked God to make him wise. God granted Solomon's request. Because of this, Solomon is known to be the wisest man who ever lived. This made him a great king. Solomon expanded the kingdom, built a palace and the temple, and was very rich. But he, too, wasn't perfect. One of Solomon's biggest sins was worshiping false gods while also trying to worship God still. Because of this sin, God told Solomon that the kingdom of Israel would break into two, which it did after Solomon died and his son Rehoboam became king.

You can read Solomon's story in 1 Kings and 1 Chronicles.

JOHN

John wrote five books of the New Testament: the Gospel of John; 1, 2, and 3 John; and the Book of Revelation. One of John's main ideas throughout all his writings is Jesus' love for us.

John was a young fisherman when he met Jesus. John and his brother, James, dropped everything to follow Jesus and learn from Him. John became one of Jesus' closest friends. He traveled with Jesus, heard Him teach about God, and saw Him perform amazing miracles.

Of all the books in the Bible, Revelation is one of the hardest to understand. It is all about a vision John saw near the end of his life, when he was being held prisoner on an island. Jesus gave John a vision of what His return will look like. While we don't know when Jesus will return and the events around it are hard to understand, we know for sure that Jesus is returning and when He does, He will defeat sin and death for good. All who have trusted in Him will then be gathered together to live with Him forever.

You can read John's story in Matthew, Mark, Luke, John, and Acts.

PAUL

Paul wrote much of the New Testament: the letters of Romans, 1 Corinthians, 2 Corinthians, Galatians, Ephesians, Philippians, Colossians, 1 Thessalonians, 2 Thessalonians, 1 Timothy, 2 Timothy, Titus, and Philemon. Some people believe he may have written Hebrews too.

Paul, who was also called Saul, was not one of Jesus' original followers. He was a Pharisee who believed the early Christians were wrong for following Jesus as God. He did all he could to stop them, including throwing them into prison and even having them killed.

One day, Jesus appeared to Paul in a vision and told him to stop mistreating Christians. Jesus made Paul blind for a short time while Paul learned the truth of Jesus' identity and the power of His teachings. Through this experience, Paul trusted in Jesus.

Once Paul knew the truth, he went from being one of the strongest opponents of the church to one of its main teachers and missionaries. Paul spent the rest of his life traveling from town to town, telling everyone he met about Jesus and starting new churches. He faced unbelievable dangers: he was shipwrecked, bitten by a poisonous snake, arrested many times, and kept in chains and under arrest; he often faced death by stoning. But nothing could make him stop telling others about the good news of Jesus.

Paul's writings in the Bible are letters he wrote to churches he helped start, churches he wasn't able to visit in person yet, or to leaders of the churches. In these letters, he explained the gospel in greater detail, how believers are to live out the gospel, and how churches should operate.

You can read Paul's story in the Book of Acts.

PETER

Peter wrote two letters that are now books of the New Testament: 1 Peter and 2 Peter. He was a close friend of Jesus. Just like John, Peter worked as a fisherman before Jesus invited him to become a disciple. Peter's brother, Andrew, was also a follower of Jesus.

Peter was bold—he was the only disciple to get out of a boat and walk on water to Jesus—and he often acted as the spokesperson for the disciples. But Peter's faith was far from perfect. At times he misspoke, and while Jesus was on trial, he denied even knowing Jesus three times.

Jesus, of course, forgave His friend for his mistakes, including Peter's denial of Him. After Jesus rose from the dead, He asked Peter if he loved Him three times. Three times, Peter assured Jesus of his love, making up for the three times he had denied Him.

After Jesus returned to heaven, Peter became the key leader of the early church. He preached the sermon at Pentecost where three thousand people trusted in Jesus. He performed miracles in Jesus' name. And he helped the early church resolve a conflict about what was needed to follow Jesus.

You can read Peter's story in Matthew, Mark, Luke, John, and Acts.

HOW SHOULD YOU READ THE BIBLE?

Before we talk about some helpful ways to read the Bible, let's first take a look around your Bible and get a feel for how it's put together. This will also help you find what you are looking for and recognize some of its helpful tools.

- **TABLE OF CONTENTS:** This is on one of the first pages of your Bible. You can use it to find what you need. All the books of the Bible are listed in the order they appear and then later in alphabetical order. The *Color Code Bible* table of contents also provides a list of the articles, like this one, an explanation of the color codes used, and a listing of the coded verses.

- **TESTAMENTS:** The books of the Bible are grouped into two main parts called the Old Testament and the New Testament. The Old Testament is thirty-nine books covering the time from God creating everything up until about four hundred years before Jesus' birth. The New Testament is twenty-seven books that begin with Jesus' birth and cover His life, death, and resurrection and then the beginning of the church.

- **BOOKS:** There are sixty-six total books written by forty different authors over a period of about fifteen hundred years. These books are different types, called genres, and were written for different reasons, to different people, at different times, but they all work together to tell the story of God's good news.

- **CHAPTERS:** Each book is divided into chapters to help you find what you are looking for. Some books are only one chapter long, like Philemon in the New Testament. Psalms has the most chapters: 150. The chapter numbers are the larger numbers.

- **VERSES:** Every chapter is then divided into verses. These are the smaller numbers. A Bible reference (like an address) will indicate the book, then the chapter, followed by a colon (:), and then the verse. John 3:16, for example, is the address for the Book of John, chapter 3 and verse 16. When saying a reference, you generally don't say the colon. John 3:16 is said as "John three sixteen."

- **BOOK INTRODUCTIONS:** Each book of the Bible plays a part in telling one big story, but each has a story of its own too. Book introductions provide background information to the books so you can better understand their smaller stories.

THREE WAYS TO PREPARE

Now, it's time to talk about how to read your Bible. Before you even open the Bible, there are a few important things you can do to help you read and understand.

1. CHOOSE A GOOD TIME AND PLACE TO READ. Make sure you are comfortable and get rid of any distractions, like electronic devices.

2. ASK GOD TO HELP YOU. You never read your Bible alone. God is always with you. Remember, He wants you to understand the Bible. Ask Him to help you focus on what you are reading, understand it, and be changed by it.

3. TAKE YOUR TIME. There is no need to rush, so read slowly. It does no good to read a lot of words if you don't understand what they say and mean. It is better to read a little bit and understand it.

THREE STEPS TO TAKE

Imagine you come across a group of friends playing a game you don't know. Everyone seems to be having fun, and you think you might want to join them. But you don't want to jump in before trying to figure the game out. So, what would you do?

1. OBSERVE—TAKE A LOOK AROUND. The first thing you would likely do, perhaps even without thinking about it, would be to get a closer look at the game. You would simply watch what is happening for a while. This is called *observation*. You watch and gather facts. When reading the Bible, this is the first thing to do too. Notice as much as you can about what you are reading. Who is in the story? Where are they? What are they doing? What was said? Are there any words you need to look up?

2. INTERPRET—MAKE SENSE OF WHAT YOU SEE. After observing the game for a while, you probably would begin to make sense of what you were seeing. At this point, you could take a good guess at how to play. This step is called *interpretation*. You are figuring out the meaning of the facts you observed. After observing as much as you can in a Bible passage, you would do the same thing and start figuring out what it all means. Why is this passage in the Bible? What does God want to teach us about Him or ourselves from it? What can we learn about the gospel? If you have trouble with this step, don't hesitate to ask a parent, teacher, or friend for help.

3. APPLY—FIGURE OUT WHAT TO DO. Finally, after observing and interpreting the game, you would be ready to play. Why do all that simply to walk away, right? This is called *application*. You are doing something based on what you have learned. Many times, people reading the Bible will do a great job with the first two steps but then stop. But everything you read in the Bible should help you to live differently, to be more like Jesus in some way. Are there any commands to obey? Warnings to watch for? Ways you can live more like Jesus?

THREE WAYS TO READ

Now that you know your way around the Bible and have a plan for how to read it each time, how do you begin? Where do you start? You could open to any random page and read, and it would be helpful, but it's best to have a plan.

1. READ THROUGH A BOOK OF THE BIBLE. One of the best and most common ways to read the Bible is through a book at a time. This is the same way you would read a book from the library; you would start at the beginning and read straight through it. Genesis, Ruth, 1 and 2 Samuel, Jonah, the Gospels of Mark and John, and Acts are good books to start with.

2. FOLLOW A READING PLAN. Reading straight through a book of the Bible might be one of the best ways to read, but that doesn't mean it's wrong to read the Bible other ways. The *Color Code Bible* includes three reading plans that you can try:

a. 365 DAYS THROUGH THE BIBLE: This plan guides you through the whole Bible in one year by reading about three chapters a day. You can begin this reading at any time, and it's OK if it takes longer than a year.

b. 60 DAYS THROUGH THE STORY OF SCRIPTURE: This plan guides you through the Bible by reading highlights of its one main story of Jesus. You can begin this reading at any time, and it's OK if it takes longer than sixty days.

C. 30 DAYS OF GETTING TO KNOW JESUS: This plan guides you through the highlights of Jesus' life and ministry recorded in the Gospels. You can begin this reading at any time, and it's OK if it takes longer than thirty days.

3. EXPLORE THE *COLOR CODE BIBLE* HIGHLIGHTED SCRIPTURE INDEX. The main purpose of the *Color Code Bible* is to show you what the Bible teaches about some of its biggest and most important ideas. These color-coded verses are helpful no matter how you read the Bible, but they also provide a way to read it. Choose one of the colors and take your time reading all those verses. Then choose another and keep going until you are finished.

WHAT IS SPECIAL ABOUT THE BIBLE?

40	Human writers of the Bible
1,600	Years it took to write the Bible (~1500 BC to ~ AD 100)
3	Languages the Bible was written in (Hebrew, Aramaic, and Greek)
3	Continents the Bible was written on (Asia, Africa, and Europe)
1,200+	Languages the Bible has been translated into
5,000,000,000+	Bibles that have been sold[1]

SIGNIFICANT YEARS IN BIBLE PUBLISHING

1228	Chapter numbers added to the Bible
1388	First Bible in English published
1448	Old Testament verse numbers added to the Bible
1551	New Testament verse numbers added to the Bible
1752	First Bible in America published
1901	Red letters of Jesus' words added to the Bible
1982	New King James Version published

BOOKS, CHAPTERS, AND VERSES OF THE BIBLE

WHOLE BIBLE
66 BOOKS

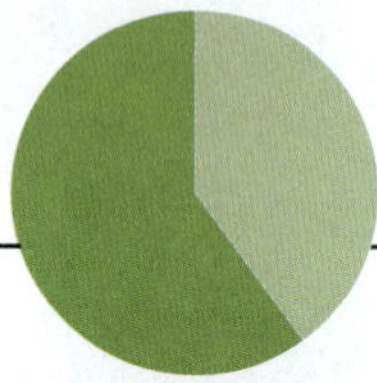

OLD TESTAMENT
39 BOOKS

NEW TESTAMENT
27 BOOKS

WHOLE BIBLE
1,189 CHAPTERS

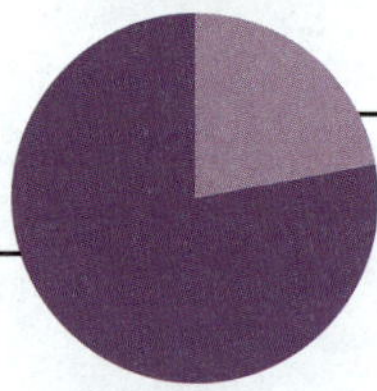

NEW TESTAMENT
260 CHAPTERS

OLD TESTAMENT
929 CHAPTERS

WHOLE BIBLE
31,102 VERSES

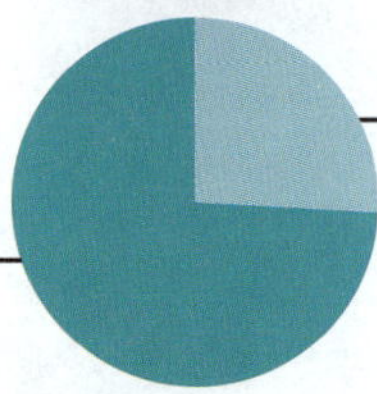

NEW TESTAMENT
7,957 VERSES

OLD TESTAMENT
23,145 VERSES

1 Guinness World Records, "Best selling book of non-fiction," Guinness World Records, http://www.guinnessworldrecords.com/world-records/best-selling-book-of-non-fiction/.

	BOOK	CHAPTER	VERSE
MIDDLE			
Whole Bible	Micah/Nahum	Psalm 117	Psalm 103:1–2
Old Testament	Proverbs	Job 29	2 Chronicles 18:30
New Testament	2 Thessalonians	Romans 13–14	Acts 7:7
SHORTEST			
Old Testament	Obadiah (646 words)	Psalm 117 (30 words)	Gen. 10:27 + 90 others (3 words)
New Testament	3 John (296 words)	Revelation 15 (244 words)	John 11:35; 1 Thessalonians 5:16 (2 words)
LONGEST			
Old Testament	Psalms (42,023 words)	Psalm 119 (2,386 words)	Esther 8:9 (81 words)
New Testament	Luke (25,412 words)	Matthew 26 (1,619 words)	Revelation 20:4 (70 words)

WORDS IN THE BIBLE

WHOLE BIBLE
769,296 WORDS

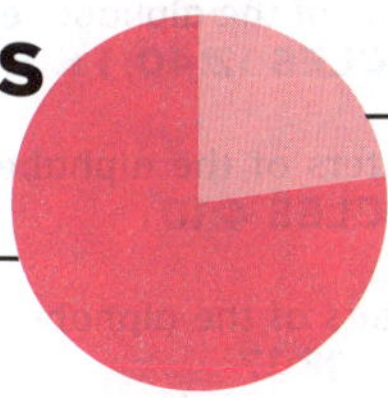

NEW TESTAMENT
177,976 WORDS

OLD TESTAMENT
591,320 WORDS

MIDDLE

Whole Bible	"the inward" (Ps. 64:6)
Old Testament	"soldiers of" (1 Chr. 19:18)
New Testament	"me, that" (Acts 8:24)

MAHER-SHALAL-HASH-BAZ	Longest word (18 letters)
9,706	Appearances of *a*/*an*
61,650	Appearances of *the*
4,425	Appearances of *God* or *god*
7,909	Appearances of *lord*, *Lord*, or Lord
981	Appearances of *Jesus*
361	Appearances of *love*
158	Appearances of *joy*

LETTERS IN THE BIBLE

WHOLE BIBLE
3,124,782 LETTERS

OLD TESTAMENT
2,402,942 LETTERS

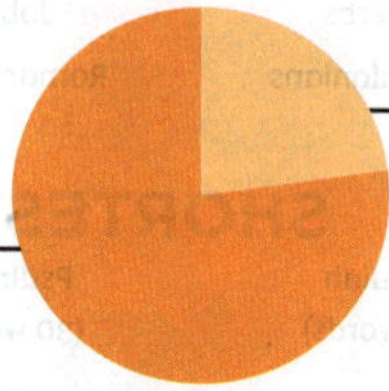

NEW TESTAMENT
721,840 LETTERS

MIDDLE

Whole Bible	*fl* in "flesh" (Ps. 63:1)
Old Testament	*at* in "that" (1 Chr. 22:12)
New Testament	*N a* in "heaven again" (Acts 10:16)

Verse that contains all the letters of the alphabet: **EZEKIEL 28:13**

Verse that contains all the letters of the alphabet except "j": **EZRA 7:21**

Verses that contain all the letters of the alphabet except "q": **GENESIS 34:30**; **JOSHUA 7:24**; **1 CHRONICLES 12:40**; **1 KINGS 1:9**; **HAGGAI 1:1**

Verses that contain all the letters of the alphabet except "x": **2 KINGS 1:2**; **2 KINGS 16:15**; **1 CHRONICLES 4:10**

Verses that contain all the letters of the alphabet except "z": **1 KINGS 19:21**; **JEREMIAH 21:12**; **EZEKIEL 18:17**

THE COLOR CODE BIBLE OVERVIEW

The *Color Code Bible* is designed to help you trace nine of the more important ideas, or themes, of the Bible: **GOD**, **JESUS**, **SIN**, **SALVATION**, **LOVE**, **WORSHIP**, **GROWTH**, **HEAVEN**, and **FAMILY**. Each of these themes is central to what the Bible is all about—God's plan to forgive you through your coming to faith in Jesus Christ. Each of these themes has been assigned a color, and verses that speak to that theme are highlighted in that color throughout the Bible.

GOD

GOLD
God

God has always existed and is the creator of everything. He made us so that we could be in a relationship with Him. When people sinned and that relationship was broken, God put a plan in motion to restore that relationship through Jesus Christ. This is what the Bible is all about.

The Bible doesn't just tell us about God's plan to forgive us. It also shares quite a bit about who God is—how amazing and great He is. While we cannot know everything about God, we can know plenty.

We can know that God is three Persons in one. This is called the Trinity and is one of the more difficult truths about God to understand. God is one, but He has always existed in three Persons: Father, Son, and Spirit. God the Father is fully God. Jesus, the Son, is fully God. The Holy Spirit is fully God. The Father, Son, and Spirit are not three different Gods or each one-third part of God. They are the three Persons of our one God. While the word Trinity does not appear in the Bible, we can see it demonstrated in Jesus' baptism when the Father spoke and the Spirit descended while the Son came up out of the water (see Luke 3:21–22). Furthermore, Jesus commanded that people be baptized in the name of the Father, the Son, and the Holy Spirit (see Matt. 28:19). The Trinity is taught in several other passages (e.g., 2 Cor. 1:21–22; Eph. 4:4; 1 Pet. 1:2).

We can know that God is Spirit. Another important truth about God is that He is Spirit; He has no physical body (see John 4:24). When we think of a person, we think of a body first because that is what we see. But a body isn't what makes you a person. The inner part of you that is often called a spirit, or a soul, is. This is where your thoughts, emotions, decisions, likes, and dislikes come from. When the Bible tells us that God is Spirit, it means He has thoughts, emotions, decisions, likes, and dislikes too. However, unlike us, all that God thinks, feels, and does is perfect. And He has no body like we have to limit Him. We can only be in one place at a time. God is everywhere. We get sick and die. God does not.

We can know that God is holy. The word *holy* means to be set apart or different. God is completely separate from sin and evil (see Lev. 19:2). All He is and all He does is good and perfect. And just as God is separate from sin, He also cannot accept people who are sinful. This is why He could not just look the other way at our sins but must judge us for it. This is where the beauty of the gospel shines. God did not just ignore sin; He judged it when Jesus took it upon Himself and died on the cross.

We can know that God is love. Because God is holy, He could have left us to face the punishment for our sins against Him. But He is also love (see 1 John 4:8). He isn't just loving. He is the source and definition of love. And God pours out His amazing, perfect love freely on us. The Bible tells us that nothing can separate those who trust in Jesus from God's love—ever (see Rom. 8:38–39).

There are many other attributes of God that are just as important—He is infinite, unchanging, righteous, and true, for example. You can learn about these, too, by exploring the highlighted verses.

The *Color Code Bible* highlights verses about God in gold. Job 37:22 says God "comes from the north as golden splendor." When we think of gold, we think of something of great worth. Because nothing is more valuable than God, gold is the perfect color to assign to the verses about Him. As you read the *Color Code Bible*, watch for the gold-colored verses. They will help you get to know your amazing heavenly Father.

JESUS

RED
Jesus

Jesus is the Son of God. Just like God the Father and God the Holy Spirit, the Son of God has always existed and always will. He was present and active in creating the world (see Col. 1:16), and He will be present to bring in the new heaven and earth (see Rev. 21). Unlike God the Father and God the Holy Spirit, though, the Son of God came to earth as a human, being born in Bethlehem two thousand years ago. Jesus grew up and lived like any other person, except He never sinned. He obeyed God the Father completely.

Jesus came to earth for several reasons. He came to show us who God is and what He is like. We can learn much about God by what is written in the Bible—that He is loving and good, for example. But seeing Jesus' love and goodness in action helps us understand God that much more.

Jesus also came to teach about God's kingdom. God is our Creator and our perfect Ruler. God wants us to live according to His ways, and when we do, we bring Him glory and experience joyful living. This is what many of Jesus' parables are about.

Jesus also came to earth to die for our sins. Even though Jesus was completely sinless, He willingly took the sins of people upon Himself. And in its place, He gives His own perfect obedience, or righteousness. Second Corinthians 5:21 puts it this way: "For He [the Father] made Him [Jesus] who knew no sin to be sin for us, that we might become the righteousness of God in Him." This means that when you trust in Jesus, all your sin is taken by Him—every sin you have committed and every sin you will commit—and in its place, Jesus gives you His perfect righteousness. When God the Father sees you, then, He sees you looking just like Jesus. You are fully forgiven and pleasing to God no matter what.

While we learn most about Jesus in the New Testament, especially in the four Gospels, all the Bible tells His story, so we can learn about Him in all sixty-six books. Just because the name Jesus is not found in the Old Testament doesn't mean He isn't there. The Old Testament includes God's many promises that He would provide Jesus and what Jesus would be like. These are called prophecies. God promised He would send someone to defeat Satan way back in the Garden of Eden (see Gen. 3:15). We also learn that Jesus would be part of Abraham's family (see Gen. 12:3), be born in Bethlehem (Mic. 5:2), perform great miracles (see Is. 42), be the Suffering Servant (see Is. 53), ride into Jerusalem on a donkey (see Zech. 9:9), and much more.

We also see many pictures of Jesus and what He would do throughout the Old Testament. For example, when God was freeing His people from captivity in Egypt, He sent ten plagues so that the Egyptian pharaoh would let them go. The tenth plague was the most severe—the death of the firstborn male in every home. God, however, provided a way for His people to be spared from this plague. Each Hebrew family was to take the blood of a spotless lamb and place it around their door. Then, when God went through Egypt, He passed over the homes marked by blood. You can read more about this in Exodus 11–12. This true story looks forward to what Jesus did for us. Because Jesus gave up His life, all who trust in Him are spared from God's judgment too.

Another clear picture of Jesus is the Day of Atonement, which you can read about in Leviticus 16. After God brought His people out of Egypt, He gave them instructions for how they were to live and worship Him. But they still had the problem of sin to deal with. So, God commanded that they celebrate the Day of Atonement each year. On this day, the high priest would take two goats before the people. He would pray over the first and symbolically place the sins of the people on it. He would then sacrifice that goat, providing a picture of that goat dying in the people's place. The high priest would then take the second goat, pray over it, and symbolically place the sins of the people on it too. Only this time, he would release the goat into the wilderness, symbolizing how the people's sins had been removed far away from them. Both of these goats picture what Jesus would do with our sin, perfectly, once and for all.

The *Color Code Bible* highlights verses about Jesus in red. This color reminds us how Jesus shed His blood when He died on the cross. As you read through the *Color Code Bible*, watch for these red verses about Jesus. By reading them, you will discover how amazing Jesus is and what an incredible, undeserved gift He is to us.

SIN

NAVY
Sin

Sin is thinking or doing anything that goes against what God has commanded. All people sin. There is no one living on this earth who is perfectly good and never disobeys God. But that was not how God created us.

When God made the first people—Adam and Eve—they were sinless. They lived in a beautiful garden called Eden and had a very close friendship with God. They had everything they needed or could ever want. But they had one rule to obey: they were not to eat from the tree of the knowledge of good and evil. One day, Satan used a serpent to trick Adam and Eve. He told them that God had lied when He said they would die if they ate from that tree and that if they did eat from it, they would become wise like God. Adam and Eve ended up believing Satan's lies rather than God's truth, and they ate from that tree in rebellion against God.

Because of what Adam and Eve did, sin entered the world, and everyone is now a sinner. The Bible says that the punishment for sin is death, and everyone must face that punishment too. We are all separated from the holy God. And all that goes wrong in the world is ultimately because of sin.

The *Color Code Bible* uses the dark color navy for sin because it reminds us of the dark sky at night. When it is completely dark, it's impossible to find your way around. You get lost easily and can trip, fall, and get hurt. This reminds us of what sin does in our lives. Instead of walking safely and confidently in God's light, we turn away from Him and stumble in the darkness of sin. So, all the verses about sin will be this greyish navy color. As you read through the *Color Code Bible*, watch for the grayish navy verses. They aren't fun or comforting verses to read, but we need to face this problem of sin. When we do, the other colors that follow will appear brighter and more beautiful.

SALVATION

ORANGE
Salvation

When you work at a job, the pay you earn for your work is called a "wage." This is money that you deserve. The Bible tells us that "the wages of sin is death" (Rom. 6:23). Our sins have earned us separation from God. And because God is holy and righteous, He cannot simply ignore our sins or withhold the punishment due to us. Our sin is a barrier between us and God that we can do nothing about. But while we cannot do anything, God can. And He did.

Because sin deserves death, the only way for a person to be forgiven is through another's death. Put simply: there can be no forgiveness of sin "without shedding of blood" (Heb. 9:22). In the Old Testament, God's people performed animal sacrifices as a means of receiving forgiveness. But God never meant for the blood of bulls and goats to save people (see Heb. 10:4). These sacrifices pointed toward the sacrifice Jesus would make. Jesus was the one-time, perfect sacrifice for the sins of the world. Now, all who trust in Him are forgiven completely by His blood that was shed (see Eph. 1:7).

Being forgiven of sin is far more than just escaping judgment, though. Salvation is not just about what we are saved *from* but also about what we are saved *to*. When we trust in Christ, we are fully forgiven of all our sin, which takes care of our disobedience, and we are also declared fully righteous, which takes care of our obedience (see 2 Cor. 5:21). This means that God accepts us no matter what. We are perfectly pleasing to Him. God makes us to be new people (see 2 Cor. 5:17), and He adopts us as His children (see Eph. 1:4–5). This means that we are in perfect relationship with God as He made us to be, and we can do the things that God made us to do—we can show others how great God is.

In the *Color Code Bible*, the verses about salvation are highlighted in orange, a vibrant, happy color. The gospel of Jesus Christ is called that because *gospel* means "good news." That we are forgiven and accepted by God in Christ is indeed good news. It is *great* news that gives us joy. As you read through the *Color Code Bible*, watch for these orange verses about salvation. As you read them, if you have trusted in Christ, let them fill your heart with joy. If you have not trusted in Christ and experienced this forgiveness, why not do that today?

LOVE

PINK
Love

While it is important to talk about God's holiness and righteousness when we think about the gospel of Jesus Christ, talking about God's love is just as important. Part of the reason that God did not leave us to face the judgment for sin that we deserve is His amazing, unfailing love for us (see Jer. 31:3; John 3:16). Even though we were rebels who sinned against God, His love stayed fixed on us. And that love led Him to give His own Son to pay for our sins.

The Bible teaches that God made us in His image (see Gen. 1:26) and that God is love (see 1 John 4:8). This means that we are like Him in many ways (but not in every way) and that one way we are to be like Him is in how we love. We are to love Him and love other people like He does (see Matt. 22:36–40). This means that we are to care about others and put them first whenever we can. It also means that we should want the best for them, and the absolute best thing for them is that they come to know Jesus, trust in Him, and be forgiven by Him. So, there are many ways we can love people, but the greatest way we can love them is by telling them about Jesus.

In the *Color Code Bible*, the verses about love are highlighted in magenta, a color that might remind you of hearts and love. This color reminds us of how God loves us and how we can love God and other people. As you read through the *Color Code Bible*, watch for these magenta verses about love. Hopefully, seeing how much God loves you will make it easier to love Him and others.

WORSHIP

BLUE Worship

In many ways, we can sum up the reason we exist as worship. To worship God is to declare His great worth. Worship is to express how great God is, how much we love Him, and how much we need Him. It is to tell God how thankful we are for Him and that we want to obey Him.

Just as sin messed everything else up, it also ruined our worship of God. Instead of worshiping Him, we found other things to worship. We see this in the Bible in how people worshiped idols. But we experience it in how people worship money, fame, power, and even themselves. When we trust in Jesus, we are able to worship God as we were designed to do.

In Christ, we can worship by rejoicing in God. God created our emotions, and joy is one that He wants us to feel about Him. While life is hard at times, we know that God is always good and in control. Remembering this can comfort us and fill us with joy too.

In Christ, we can worship by thanking God. We recognize that everything good we have is from God and that Christ is our greatest good. We understand that we did nothing to deserve or earn these good gifts, but God gives them to us because of His love for us.

In Christ, we can worship by talking with God. The Bible calls talking with God *prayer*. We might think that prayer is a formal, rigid thing we do with our eyes closed. Prayer can be more organized, and it's OK to pray with our eyes closed, but prayer is also talking with God and listening to Him as we live each day. We can always be in prayer this way. God is always there, wanting to hear from us and share with us.

These are just a few of the ways that we can worship God as followers of Jesus. Now, when we think of worship, we often think of music and singing. And that is a great way to worship, but it's not the only way. As we have seen, we can worship simply by talking with God. We can worship by how we feel. We can worship by obeying God and living for Him. We can worship by telling others about Jesus.

In the *Color Code Bible*, the verses about worship are highlighted in blue. This is the color of the sky, which we can only see when we look up. This reminds us of our need for and privilege of looking up to God in worship. As you read through the *Color Code Bible*, look for these verses that teach us what worship is and how we can worship. Let these verses prompt you to worship God today and every day.

GROWTH

GREEN Growth

We are all born helpless, unable even to feed ourselves. We cannot do anything on our own. But we don't stay that way; we grow. We get bigger and stronger. We learn how to walk and talk. We learn how to think. And in time, we are able to do more and more on our own.

The same is true of us spiritually. When we trust in Jesus, we are like newborn babies. There is so much we haven't learned about God, Jesus, and the gospel. We likely struggle to obey God. We might not even want to obey Him very much at first. But the good thing is that we don't have to stay there.

God has given us the Bible so that we can read it and grow. He has given us the church and other believers to help us grow. And He has given us the Holy Spirit to help us grow. Like physical growth, spiritual growth is a long, slow process. You might not see much growth from day to day, week to week, or even month to month. But that doesn't mean you are not growing.

The *Color Code Bible* highlights verses that will help your spiritual growth in green. When we see the color green, we likely think of grass, plants, and trees. We might think of the springtime when these begin to grow. This reminds us of what God is doing in us. As you read through the *Color Code Bible*, watch for these green verses about growth. Learn how you can grow and be encouraged that God is helping you grow. But also, be patient with yourself; understand that growth takes time.

PURPLE **Heaven**

HEAVEN

Put simply, heaven is God's dwelling place (see Matt. 5:16), where He rules sitting on His throne (see Ps. 11:4). It is not as simple as that though. Remember that God is Spirit, which means He is not only in one place; He is everywhere. This is another truth about God that might be hard for us to understand. Thankfully, God often speaks to us in the Bible in ways to make it easier for us to understand. It might be better to think of heaven as where people who trust in Jesus go when they die. They go to heaven, where they are with God.

The apostle John saw heaven in a vision given to him by Jesus, which he recorded as the Book of Revelation. John described heaven as a wonderfully beautiful place where everything is perfect. Jesus had returned to heaven after He was crucified and rose again (see Acts 1:9–11), and John saw Him there (see Rev. 5:6).

But Jesus will not stay in heaven. One day, He will return to defeat sin and death for good. And when Jesus returns, He will bring with Him a new heaven and earth, where all of us who trust in Him will live together forevermore. Like Eden in Genesis 1–2, the new heaven and earth will be a perfect place. Sin and death will not be part of it. Neither will pain and tears (see Rev. 21:3–4).

The *Color Code Bible* highlights verses about heaven in purple. Purple is a color that kings and queens often use. This makes purple the perfect color to identify heaven, where God rules from His throne. As you read through the *Color Code Bible*, watch for these purple verses about heaven. While we have a lot of questions about heaven that the Bible doesn't answer, we can learn quite a bit about it still. So be encouraged and filled with hope that God has a perfect plan and a perfect place in store for us.

TEAL **Family**

FAMILY

The family is important to God. One of the first things God did was make a family in Eden (see Gen. 2). Then, the family was a critical part of God's plan to forgive people through Jesus (see Gen. 12:1–3). Furthermore, God often describes His relationship with His people in terms of the family. God is our Father (see Matt. 6:9), we are His children (John 1:12), and we are reminded that we are brothers and sisters in Christ.

Because God cares about families so much, He wants to help us be in families that show love for one another, others, and God. While no family is perfect, and many are far from it, God's heart is for each to be as loving, honoring, and joyful as possible. These same lessons help us understand how we are to live as church families too.

As you know, children are an important part of the family. In addition to the Bible giving instructions for how children are to honor and obey their parents, it also speaks to the value that children bring to God's kingdom. Some of the godly kings of Judah were children when they began ruling. Jesus used a boy's lunch to feed over five thousand people (see John 6:9–10). When Jesus' followers tried to keep children from coming to see Him, He stood up for them, saying, "Let the little children come to Me, and do not forbid them; for of such is the kingdom of heaven" (Matt. 19:14). Families matter to God, and so do children.

The *Color Code Bible* highlights verses about the family in teal, a color that combines the blue of worship and green of growth. While we often think of worship happening at church, God also wants us to worship Him in our homes with our families. God also designed the family to be a key way of helping us grow physically, mentally, emotionally, and spiritually. As you read through the *Color Code Bible*, watch for these teal verses about family. These verses will help you understand the family and what you, as a child, can do for God and His kingdom.

HIGHLIGHTED SCRIPTURE INDEX

GOD

OLD TESTAMENT VERSES

Genesis 1:26
Genesis 16:13
Genesis 50:20
Exodus 3:14–15
Exodus 15:3
Exodus 20:5
Exodus 33:14
Numbers 14:18
Numbers 23:19
Deuteronomy 4:39
Deuteronomy 5:9–10
Deuteronomy 7:9–10
Deuteronomy 10:17–18
Deuteronomy 32:4
Deuteronomy 33:27
Joshua 23:3
Judges 14:19
Judges 15:14b
Judges 16:20b
1 Samuel 2:2
1 Samuel 2:6–8
2 Samuel 22:9–13
2 Samuel 22:15–16
1 Chronicles 16:34
1 Chronicles 29:12
2 Chronicles 1:5–6
2 Chronicles 6:18
2 Chronicles 16:9
Ezra 9:15
Nehemiah 9:6
Job 9:4
Job 11:7–11
Job 21:22
Job 28:23–27
Job 31:15
Job 32:8
Job 36:5
Job 37:23–24
Job 42:2
Psalm 1:6
Psalm 4:2–5
Psalm 7:9–13
Psalm 9:7–9
Psalm 11:7
Psalm 18:2
Psalm 19:9–11
Psalm 22:3
Psalm 25:8–10
Psalm 28:8
Psalm 33:6–9
Psalm 36:7–9
Psalm 46:10–11
Psalm 50:6
Psalm 53:2
Psalm 56:8
Psalm 65:5–7
Psalm 68:34
Psalm 69:5
Psalm 74:16–17
Psalm 77:13–15
Psalm 83:18
Psalm 84:11
Psalm 89:8–11
Psalm 90:1–4
Psalm 92:5
Psalm 95:3
Psalm 97:9
Psalm 98:9b
Psalm 99:1–2
Psalm 102:12
Psalm 103:6–11
Psalm 108:4
Psalm 110:5–7
Psalm 113:4–6
Psalm 116:5–6
Psalm 117:2
Psalm 119:11
Psalm 119:137–138
Psalm 121:3–6
Psalm 125:2
Psalm 130:7
Psalm 135:13–14
Psalm 139:1–12
Psalm 147:15–18
Psalm 148:13
Proverbs 3:19–20
Proverbs 10:29
Proverbs 15:25–26
Proverbs 16:4–5
Proverbs 16:33
Proverbs 17:3
Proverbs 19:21
Proverbs 20:27
Proverbs 21:1–3
Proverbs 26:10
Proverbs 29:26
Proverbs 30:5
Ecclesiastes 3:11
Ecclesiastes 11:5
Isaiah 6:1
Isaiah 14:26–27
Isaiah 26:4
Isaiah 33:21–22
Isaiah 40:12–14
Isaiah 42:5–8
Isaiah 45:12
Isaiah 46:9b–10
Isaiah 47:4
Isaiah 48:12–13
Isaiah 51:15–16
Isaiah 54:5
Isaiah 55:8–11
Isaiah 57:15–16
Isaiah 64:6
Isaiah 66:1–2
Jeremiah 10:6–7
Jeremiah 10:10
Jeremiah 17:10
Jeremiah 18:5–6
Jeremiah 23:23–24
Jeremiah 27:5
Jeremiah 32:27
Jeremiah 51:15–16
Jeremiah 51:56b
Lamentations 3:22–23
Lamentations 5:19
Ezekiel 1:26–28
Ezekiel 39:29
Ezekiel 43:2b

NEW TESTAMENT VERSES

JESUS

OLD TESTAMENT VERSES

NEW TESTAMENT VERSES

SIN

OLD TESTAMENT VERSES

NEW TESTAMENT VERSES

SALVATION

OLD TESTAMENT VERSES

NEW TESTAMENT VERSES

LOVE

OLD TESTAMENT VERSES

NEW TESTAMENT VERSES

WORSHIP

OLD TESTAMENT VERSES

NEW TESTAMENT VERSES

GROWTH

OLD TESTAMENT VERSES

NEW TESTAMENT VERSES

HEAVEN

OLD TESTAMENT VERSES

NEW TESTAMENT VERSES

FAMILY

OLD TESTAMENT VERSES

NEW TESTAMENT VERSES

ABOUT THE NEW KING JAMES VERSION

The Bible was originally written in three languages. Most of the Old Testament was written in Hebrew, most of the New Testament was written in Greek, and a few parts of each were written in Aramaic. Bibles in all other languages are translated from these three languages.

The first Bible translations in English were published in the 1500s. Although several different ones existed, in 1604 King James of England wanted to make a new translation in English. While the existing translations were all good, he believed a better translation could be made using the original languages and these other translations. So, a skilled team of translators was formed, and work began in 1607. The King James Version of the Bible was finished and published in 1611.

The King James Version has been published ever since and is not only one of the most loved and read Bible translations, but it is also one of the most loved and read books of all time. But because language can change over time, in 1975 and 1976 Thomas Nelson Publishers invited church leaders to meetings in Chicago, Illinois; Nashville, Tennessee; and London, England to ask if the King James Version Bible should be revised. The church leaders decided a revision was needed.

Work began immediately on what would become known as the New King James Version. Similar to the purpose of the King James Version, the purpose of this revision was not to make an all-new translation, but to make a good one better. Biblical scholars from different churches were selected to work on this major project. They came from England, Scotland, Canada, New Zealand, Australia, the Netherlands, and the United States, so that the New King James Version would use internationally accepted English.

Each translator worked independently and recommended changes that would improve the King James text for today's use. The translators' work was then submitted to the Executive Editor for the Old Testament or New Testament. Using the original Hebrew, Greek, and Aramaic texts, the King James Bible, and carefully established guidelines, the Executive Editors then reviewed each scholar's work. They either accepted the changes, recommended further changes, or declined to make the changes and restored the King James reading.

Each finished book was then submitted to an English Editor who checked for grammatical accuracy, literary beauty, and effective communication.

Throughout the entire process, the work was regularly reviewed by church advisors who served on the British and North American Overview Committees.

The final review process was carried out by a separate Executive Review Committee for each Testament over a four-year period. All proposed changes by translators, editors, and reviewers were considered during this time, including final changes proposed by the Review Committees themselves. The review process was completed in July 1981 at St. Andrews University in northeast Scotland, not far from Stirling Castle, King James's historic residence.

The New King James Version was thus prepared with reverence for the Word of God and with a deep appreciation of the work of the King James Version translators in 1611. It was the prayer of the revisers that the work they did indeed made a good translation better. And it is the prayer of the publishers at Thomas Nelson that the New King James Version Bible you hold helps you draw close to God through His Son, Jesus Christ.

THE OLD TESTAMENT

THE FIRST BOOK OF MOSES CALLED
GENESIS

The Book of Genesis is about beginnings: the beginning of the universe, the beginning of people, the beginning of sin, and the beginning of God's plan to forgive people of their sin. The first eleven chapters cover a period of hundreds or even thousands of years, but then the book slows down, and the last thirty-nine chapters cover God making a special people through one family. God begins with a man named Abraham and promises to use him to bless the entire world. This blessing would later come through Jesus being born through Abraham's family. Abraham is followed by Isaac who is followed by Jacob, who is followed by his twelve sons who would become leaders of the twelve tribes of Israel.

- **GENRE:** Law
- **AUTHOR:** Moses
- **TIME:** c. 4000–1804 BC (written c. 1445–1406 BC)
- **PURPOSE:** To tell how God made everything, including people, and about the beginning of God's plan to rescue people from sin.

The History of Creation

1 In the beginning God created the
heavens and the earth. 2The earth
was without form, and void; and dark-
ness *was*[a] on the face of the deep. And
the Spirit of God was hovering over the
face of the waters.
3Then God said, "Let there be light";
and there was light. 4And God saw the
light, that *it was* good; and God divid-
ed the light from the darkness. 5God
called the light Day, and the darkness
He called Night. So the evening and the
morning were the first day.
6Then God said, "Let there be a firma-
ment in the midst of the waters, and let
it divide the waters from the waters."
7Thus God made the firmament, and
divided the waters which *were* under the
firmament from the waters which *were*
above the firmament; and it was so.
8And God called the firmament Heaven.
So the evening and the morning were
the second day.
9Then God said, "Let the waters under
the heavens be gathered together into
one place, and let the dry *land* appear";
and it was so. 10And God called the dry
land Earth, and the gathering together
of the waters He called Seas. And God
saw that *it was* good.
11Then God said, "Let the earth bring
forth grass, the herb *that* yields seed,
and the fruit tree *that* yields fruit ac-
cording to its kind, whose seed *is* in
itself, on the earth"; and it was so. 12And
the earth brought forth grass, the herb
that yields seed according to its kind,
and the tree *that* yields fruit, whose
seed *is* in itself according to its kind.
And God saw that *it was* good. 13So the
evening and the morning were the third
day.
14Then God said, "Let there be lights in
the firmament of the heavens to divide
the day from the night; and let them be
for signs and seasons, and for days and
years; 15and let them be for lights in the
firmament of the heavens to give light
on the earth"; and it was so. 16Then God
made two great lights: the greater light
to rule the day, and the lesser light to
rule the night. *He made* the stars also.
17God set them in the firmament of the
heavens to give light on the earth, 18and
to rule over the day and over the night,
and to divide the light from the dark-
ness. And God saw that *it was* good. 19So

1:2 [a] Words in italic type have been added for clarity. They are not found in the original Hebrew or Aramaic.

the evening and the morning were the
fourth day.
20Then God said, "Let the waters
abound with an abundance of living
creatures, and let birds fly above the
earth across the face of the firmament
of the heavens." 21So God created great
sea creatures and every living thing
that moves, with which the waters
abounded, according to their kind,
and every winged bird according to
its kind. And God saw that *it was* good.
22And God blessed them, saying, "Be
fruitful and multiply, and fill the waters
in the seas, and let birds multiply on
the earth." 23So the evening and the
morning were the fifth day.

24Then God said, "Let the earth bring
forth the living creature according to
its kind: cattle and creeping thing and
beast of the earth, *each* according to its
kind"; and it was so. 25And God made
the beast of the earth according to its
kind, cattle according to its kind, and
everything that creeps on the earth
according to its kind. And God saw that
it was good.

26Then God said, "Let Us make man in
Our image, according to Our likeness;
let them have dominion over the fish
of the sea, over the birds of the air, and
over the cattle, over all[a] the earth and
over every creeping thing that creeps
on the earth." 27So God created man
in His *own* image; in the image of God
He created him; male and female He
created them. 28Then God blessed them,
and God said to them, "Be fruitful and
multiply; fill the earth and subdue it;
have dominion over the fish of the sea,
over the birds of the air, and over every
living thing that moves on the earth."
29And God said, "See, I have given
you every herb *that* yields seed which
is on the face of all the earth, and every
tree whose fruit yields seed; to you it
shall be for food. 30Also, to every beast
of the earth, to every bird of the air,
and to everything that creeps on the
earth, in which *there is* life, *I have given*
every green herb for food"; and it was
so. 31Then God saw everything that He
had made, and indeed *it was* very good.
So the evening and the morning were
the sixth day.

2 Thus the heavens and the earth, and
all the host of them, were finished.
2And on the seventh day God ended
His work which He had done, and He
rested on the seventh day from all His
work which He had done. 3Then God
blessed the seventh day and sanctified
it, because in it He rested from all His
work which God had created and made.
4This *is* the history[a] of the heavens and
the earth when they were created, in the
day that the LORD God made the earth
and the heavens, 5before any plant of
the field was in the earth and before any
herb of the field had grown. For the LORD
God had not caused it to rain on the
earth, and *there was* no man to till the
ground; 6but a mist went up from
the earth and watered the whole face
of the ground.

7And the LORD God formed man *of* the
dust of the ground, and breathed into
his nostrils the breath of life; and man
became a living being.

Life in God's Garden

8The LORD God planted a garden east-
ward in Eden, and there He put the man
whom He had formed. 9And out of the
ground the LORD God made every tree
grow that is pleasant to the sight and
good for food. The tree of life *was* also in
the midst of the garden, and the tree of
the knowledge of good and evil.

10Now a river went out of Eden to water
the garden, and from there it parted and
became four riverheads. 11The name of
the first *is* Pishon; it *is* the one which
skirts the whole land of Havilah, where
there is gold. 12And the gold of that land
is good. Bdellium and the onyx stone *are*
there. 13The name of the second river *is*
Gihon; it *is* the one which goes around
the whole land of Cush. 14The name of
the third river *is* Hiddekel;[a] it *is* the one
which goes toward the east of Assyria.
The fourth river *is* the Euphrates.

15Then the LORD God took the man and
put him in the garden of Eden to tend
and keep it. 16And the LORD God com-
manded the man, saying, "Of every tree

1:26 [a] Syriac reads *all the wild animals of.* **2:4** [a] Hebrew *toledoth,* literally *generations* **2:14** [a] Or *Tigris*

of the garden you may freely eat; 17but
of the tree of the knowledge of good
and evil you shall not eat, for in the day
that you eat of it you shall surely die."
18And the LORD God said, "*It is* not good
that man should be alone; I will make
him a helper comparable to him." 19Out
of the ground the LORD God formed every
beast of the field and every bird of the air,
and brought *them* to Adam to see what
he would call them. And whatever Adam
called each living creature, that *was* its
name. 20So Adam gave names to all cat-
tle, to the birds of the air, and to every
beast of the field. But for Adam there was
not found a helper comparable to him.
21And the LORD God caused a deep
sleep to fall on Adam, and he slept;
and He took one of his ribs, and closed
up the flesh in its place. 22Then the rib
which the LORD God had taken from
man He made into a woman, and He
brought her to the man.
23And Adam said:

"This *is* now bone of my bones
And flesh of my flesh;
She shall be called Woman,
Because she was taken out of Man."

24Therefore a man shall leave his father
and mother and be joined to his wife,
and they shall become one flesh.
25And they were both naked, the man
and his wife, and were not ashamed.

The Temptation and Fall of Man

3 Now the serpent was more cunning
than any beast of the field which
the LORD God had made. And he said
to the woman, "Has God indeed said,
'You shall not eat of every tree of the
garden'?"
2And the woman said to the serpent,
"We may eat the fruit of the trees of
the garden; 3but of the fruit of the tree
which *is* in the midst of the garden, God
has said, 'You shall not eat it, nor shall
you touch it, lest you die.' "
4Then the serpent said to the woman,
"You will not surely die. 5For God knows
that in the day you eat of it your eyes
will be opened, and you will be like God,
knowing good and evil."
6So when the woman saw that the tree
was good for food, that it *was* pleasant
to the eyes, and a tree desirable to make
one wise, she took of its fruit and ate. She
also gave to her husband with her, and
he ate. 7Then the eyes of both of them
were opened, and they knew that they
were naked; and they sewed fig leaves to-
gether and made themselves coverings.
8And they heard the sound of the LORD
God walking in the garden in the cool
of the day, and Adam and his wife hid
themselves from the presence of the
LORD God among the trees of the garden.
9Then the LORD God called to Adam
and said to him, "Where *are* you?"
10So he said, "I heard Your voice in the
garden, and I was afraid because I was
naked; and I hid myself."
11And He said, "Who told you that you
were naked? Have you eaten from the
tree of which I commanded you that
you should not eat?"
12Then the man said, "The woman
whom You gave *to be* with me, she gave
me of the tree, and I ate."
13And the LORD God said to the wom-
an, "What *is* this you have done?"
The woman said, "The serpent de-
ceived me, and I ate."
14So the LORD God said to the serpent:

"Because you have done this,
You *are* cursed more than all
cattle,
And more than every beast of the
field;
On your belly you shall go,
And you shall eat dust
All the days of your life.
15 And I will put enmity
Between you and the woman,
And between your seed and her
Seed;
He shall bruise your head,
And you shall bruise His heel."

16To the woman He said:

"I will greatly multiply your sorrow
and your conception;
In pain you shall bring forth
children;
Your desire *shall be* for your
husband,
And he shall rule over you."

17Then to Adam He said, "Because you have heeded the voice of your wife, and have eaten from the tree of which I commanded you, saying, 'You shall not eat of it':

"Cursed *is* the ground for your
 sake;
In toil you shall eat *of* it
All the days of your life.
18 Both thorns and thistles it shall
 bring forth for you,
And you shall eat the herb of the
 field.
19 In the sweat of your face you
 shall eat bread
Till you return to the ground,
For out of it you were taken;
For dust you *are,*
And to dust you shall return."

20And Adam called his wife's name Eve, because she was the mother of all living.

21Also for Adam and his wife the LORD God made tunics of skin, and clothed them.

22Then the LORD God said, "Behold, the man has become like one of Us, to know good and evil. And now, lest he put out his hand and take also of the tree of life, and eat, and live forever"—23therefore the LORD God sent him out of the garden of Eden to till the ground from which he was taken. 24So He drove out the man; and He placed cherubim at the east of the garden of Eden, and a flaming sword which turned every way, to guard the way to the tree of life.

Cain Murders Abel

4 Now Adam knew Eve his wife, and she conceived and bore Cain, and said, "I have acquired a man from the LORD." 2Then she bore again, this time his brother Abel. Now Abel was a keeper of sheep, but Cain was a tiller of the ground. 3And in the process of time it came to pass that Cain brought an offering of the fruit of the ground to the LORD. 4Abel also brought of the firstborn of his flock and of their fat. And the LORD respected Abel and his offering, 5but He did not respect Cain and his offering. And Cain was very angry, and his countenance fell.

6So the LORD said to Cain, "Why are you angry? And why has your countenance fallen? 7If you do well, will you not be accepted? And if you do not do well, sin lies at the door. And its desire *is* for you, but you should rule over it."

8Now Cain talked with Abel his brother;[a] and it came to pass, when they were in the field, that Cain rose up against Abel his brother and killed him.

9Then the LORD said to Cain, "Where *is* Abel your brother?"

He said, "I do not know. *Am* I my brother's keeper?"

10And He said, "What have you done? The voice of your brother's blood cries out to Me from the ground. 11So now you *are* cursed from the earth, which has opened its mouth to receive your brother's blood from your hand. 12When you till the ground, it shall no longer yield its strength to you. A fugitive and a vagabond you shall be on the earth."

13And Cain said to the LORD, "My punishment *is* greater than I can bear! 14Surely You have driven me out this day from the face of the ground; I shall be hidden from Your face; I shall be a fugitive and a vagabond on the earth, and it will happen *that* anyone who finds me will kill me."

15And the LORD said to him, "Therefore,[a] whoever kills Cain, vengeance shall be taken on him sevenfold." And the LORD set a mark on Cain, lest anyone finding him should kill him.

The Family of Cain

16Then Cain went out from the presence of the LORD and dwelt in the land of Nod on the east of Eden. 17And Cain knew his wife, and she conceived and bore Enoch. And he built a city, and called the name of the city after the name of his son—Enoch. 18To Enoch was born Irad; and Irad begot Mehujael, and Mehujael begot Methushael, and Methushael begot Lamech.

19Then Lamech took for himself two wives: the name of one *was* Adah, and

4:8 [a] Samaritan Pentateuch, Septuagint, Syriac, and Vulgate add *"Let us go out to the field."*
4:15 [a] Following Masoretic Text and Targum; Septuagint, Syriac, and Vulgate read *Not so.*

the name of the second *was* Zillah. 20And Adah bore Jabal. He was the father of those who dwell in tents and have livestock. 21His brother's name *was* Jubal. He was the father of all those who play the harp and flute. 22And as for Zillah, she also bore Tubal-Cain, an instructor of every craftsman in bronze and iron. And the sister of Tubal-Cain *was* Naamah.

23Then Lamech said to his wives:

"Adah and Zillah, hear my voice;
Wives of Lamech, listen to my
speech!
For I have killed a man for
wounding me,
Even a young man for hurting me.
24 If Cain shall be avenged
sevenfold,
Then Lamech seventy-sevenfold."

A New Son

25And Adam knew his wife again, and she bore a son and named him Seth, "For God has appointed another seed for me instead of Abel, whom Cain killed." 26And as for Seth, to him also a son was born; and he named him Enosh.[a] Then *men* began to call on the name of the LORD.

The Family of Adam

5 This is the book of the genealogy of Adam. In the day that God created man, He made him in the likeness of God. 2He created them male and female, and blessed them and called them Mankind in the day they were created. 3And Adam lived one hundred and thirty years, and begot *a son* in his own likeness, after his image, and named him Seth. 4After he begot Seth, the days of Adam were eight hundred years; and he had sons and daughters. 5So all the days that Adam lived were nine hundred and thirty years; and he died.

6Seth lived one hundred and five years, and begot Enosh. 7After he begot Enosh, Seth lived eight hundred and seven years, and had sons and daughters. 8So all the days of Seth were nine hundred and twelve years; and he died.

9Enosh lived ninety years, and begot Cainan.[a] 10After he begot Cainan, Enosh lived eight hundred and fifteen years, and had sons and daughters. 11So all the days of Enosh were nine hundred and five years; and he died.

12Cainan lived seventy years, and begot Mahalalel. 13After he begot Mahalalel, Cainan lived eight hundred and forty years, and had sons and daughters. 14So all the days of Cainan were nine hundred and ten years; and he died.

15Mahalalel lived sixty-five years, and begot Jared. 16After he begot Jared, Mahalalel lived eight hundred and thirty years, and had sons and daughters. 17So all the days of Mahalalel were eight hundred and ninety-five years; and he died.

18Jared lived one hundred and sixty-two years, and begot Enoch. 19After he begot Enoch, Jared lived eight hundred years, and had sons and daughters. 20So all the days of Jared were nine hundred and sixty-two years; and he died.

21Enoch lived sixty-five years, and begot Methuselah. 22After he begot Methuselah, Enoch walked with God three hundred years, and had sons and daughters. 23So all the days of Enoch were three hundred and sixty-five years. 24And Enoch walked with God; and he *was* not, for God took him.

25Methuselah lived one hundred and eighty-seven years, and begot Lamech. 26After he begot Lamech, Methuselah lived seven hundred and eighty-two years, and had sons and daughters. 27So all the days of Methuselah were nine hundred and sixty-nine years; and he died.

28Lamech lived one hundred and eighty-two years, and had a son. 29And he called his name Noah, saying, "This *one* will comfort us concerning our work and the toil of our hands, because of the ground which the LORD has cursed." 30After he begot Noah, Lamech lived five hundred and ninety-five years, and had sons and daughters. 31So all the days of Lamech were seven hundred and seventy-seven years; and he died.

32And Noah was five hundred years old, and Noah begot Shem, Ham, and Japheth.

4:26 [a] Greek *Enos* **5:9** [a] Hebrew *Qenan*

The Wickedness and Judgment of Man

6 Now it came to pass, when men be-
gan to multiply on the face of the
earth, and daughters were born to them,
2that the sons of God saw the daughters
of men, that they *were* beautiful; and
they took wives for themselves of all
whom they chose.
3And the LORD said, "My Spirit shall
not strive[a] with man forever, for he *is*
indeed flesh; yet his days shall be one
hundred and twenty years." 4There were
giants on the earth in those days, and
also afterward, when the sons of God
came in to the daughters of men and
they bore *children* to them. Those *were*
the mighty men who *were* of old, men
of renown.
5Then the LORD[a] saw that the wicked-
ness of man *was* great in the earth, and
that every intent of the thoughts of his
heart *was* only evil continually. 6And
the LORD was sorry that He had made
man on the earth, and He was grieved
in His heart. 7So the LORD said, "I will
destroy man whom I have created from
the face of the earth, both man and
beast, creeping thing and birds of the
air, for I am sorry that I have made
them." 8But Noah found grace in the
eyes of the LORD.

Noah Pleases God

9This is the genealogy of Noah. Noah
was a just man, perfect in his gener-
ations. Noah walked with God. 10And
Noah begot three sons: Shem, Ham,
and Japheth.
11The earth also was corrupt before
God, and the earth was filled with vio-
lence. 12So God looked upon the earth,
and indeed it was corrupt; for all flesh
had corrupted their way on the earth.

The Ark Prepared

13And God said to Noah, "The end of
all flesh has come before Me, for the
earth is filled with violence through
them; and behold, I will destroy them
with the earth. 14Make yourself an ark
of gopherwood; make rooms in the ark,
and cover it inside and outside with
pitch. 15And this is how you shall make
it: The length of the ark *shall be* three
hundred cubits, its width fifty cubits,
and its height thirty cubits. 16You shall
make a window for the ark, and you
shall finish it to a cubit from above; and
set the door of the ark in its side. You
shall make it *with* lower, second, and
third *decks*. 17And behold, I Myself am
bringing floodwaters on the earth, to
destroy from under heaven all flesh in
which *is* the breath of life; everything
that *is* on the earth shall die. 18But I will
establish My covenant with you; and
you shall go into the ark—you, your
sons, your wife, and your sons' wives
with you. 19And of every living thing of
all flesh you shall bring two of every *sort*
into the ark, to keep *them* alive with you;
they shall be male and female. 20Of the
birds after their kind, of animals after
their kind, and of every creeping thing
of the earth after its kind, two of every
kind will come to you to keep *them* alive.
21And you shall take for yourself of all
food that is eaten, and you shall gather
it to yourself; and it shall be food for
you and for them."
22Thus Noah did; according to all that
God commanded him, so he did.

The Great Flood

7 Then the LORD said to Noah, "Come
into the ark, you and all your house-
hold, because I have seen *that* you *are*
righteous before Me in this generation.
2You shall take with you seven each
of every clean animal, a male and his
female; two each of animals that *are*
unclean, a male and his female; 3also
seven each of birds of the air, male and
female, to keep the species alive on the
face of all the earth. 4For after seven
more days I will cause it to rain on the
earth forty days and forty nights, and
I will destroy from the face of the earth
all living things that I have made." 5And
Noah did according to all that the LORD
commanded him. 6Noah *was* six hun-
dred years old when the floodwaters
were on the earth.
7So Noah, with his sons, his wife, and
his sons' wives, went into the ark be-
cause of the waters of the flood. 8Of

6:3 [a] Septuagint, Syriac, Targum, and Vulgate read *abide*. 6:5 [a] Following Masoretic Text and Targum; Vulgate reads *God;* Septuagint reads LORD *God*.

clean animals, of animals that *are* un-
clean, of birds, and of everything that
creeps on the earth, 9two by two they
went into the ark to Noah, male and
female, as God had commanded Noah.
10And it came to pass after seven days
that the waters of the flood were on
the earth. 11In the six hundredth year
of Noah's life, in the second month, the
seventeenth day of the month, on that
day all the fountains of the great deep
were broken up, and the windows of
heaven were opened. 12And the rain was
on the earth forty days and forty nights.
13On the very same day Noah and No-
ah's sons, Shem, Ham, and Japheth, and
Noah's wife and the three wives of his
sons with them, entered the ark— 14they
and every beast after its kind, all cattle
after their kind, every creeping thing
that creeps on the earth after its kind,
and every bird after its kind, every bird
of every sort. 15And they went into the
ark to Noah, two by two, of all flesh in
which *is* the breath of life. 16So those
that entered, male and female of all
flesh, went in as God had commanded
him; and the LORD shut him in.
17Now the flood was on the earth forty
days. The waters increased and lifted up
the ark, and it rose high above the earth.
18The waters prevailed and greatly in-
creased on the earth, and the ark moved
about on the surface of the waters. 19And
the waters prevailed exceedingly on the
earth, and all the high hills under the
whole heaven were covered. 20The wa-
ters prevailed fifteen cubits upward,
and the mountains were covered. 21And
all flesh died that moved on the earth:
birds and cattle and beasts and every
creeping thing that creeps on the earth,
and every man. 22All in whose nostrils
was the breath of the spirit[a] of life, all
that *was* on the dry *land,* died. 23So He
destroyed all living things which were
on the face of the ground: both man and
cattle, creeping thing and bird of the air.
They were destroyed from the earth.
Only Noah and those who *were* with
him in the ark remained *alive.* 24And
the waters prevailed on the earth one
hundred and fifty days.

Noah's Deliverance

8 Then God remembered Noah, and
every living thing, and all the an-
imals that *were* with him in the ark.
And God made a wind to pass over the
earth, and the waters subsided. 2The
fountains of the deep and the windows
of heaven were also stopped, and the
rain from heaven was restrained. 3And
the waters receded continually from the
earth. At the end of the hundred and
fifty days the waters decreased. 4Then
the ark rested in the seventh month, the
seventeenth day of the month, on the
mountains of Ararat. 5And the waters
decreased continually until the tenth
month. In the tenth *month,* on the first
day of the month, the tops of the moun-
tains were seen.
6So it came to pass, at the end of forty
days, that Noah opened the window of
the ark which he had made. 7Then he
sent out a raven, which kept going to
and fro until the waters had dried up
from the earth. 8He also sent out from
himself a dove, to see if the waters had
receded from the face of the ground.
9But the dove found no resting place for
the sole of her foot, and she returned
into the ark to him, for the waters *were*
on the face of the whole earth. So he put
out his hand and took her, and drew her
into the ark to himself. 10And he waited
yet another seven days, and again he
sent the dove out from the ark. 11Then
the dove came to him in the evening,
and behold, a freshly plucked olive leaf
was in her mouth; and Noah knew that
the waters had receded from the earth.
12So he waited yet another seven days
and sent out the dove, which did not
return again to him anymore.
13And it came to pass in the six hun-
dred and first year, in the first *month,*
the first *day* of the month, that the wa-
ters were dried up from the earth; and
Noah removed the covering of the ark
and looked, and indeed the surface of
the ground was dry. 14And in the second
month, on the twenty-seventh day of
the month, the earth was dried.
15Then God spoke to Noah, saying,
16"Go out of the ark, you and your wife,

7:22 [a] Septuagint and Vulgate omit *of the spirit.*

and your sons and your sons' wives with
you. 17Bring out with you every living
thing of all flesh that *is* with you: birds
and cattle and every creeping thing that
creeps on the earth, so that they may
abound on the earth, and be fruitful and
multiply on the earth." 18So Noah went
out, and his sons and his wife and his
sons' wives with him. 19Every animal,
every creeping thing, every bird, *and*
whatever creeps on the earth, according
to their families, went out of the ark.

God's Covenant with Creation

20Then Noah built an altar to the LORD,
and took of every clean animal and
of every clean bird, and offered burnt
offerings on the altar. 21And the LORD
smelled a soothing aroma. Then the
LORD said in His heart, "I will never
again curse the ground for man's sake,
although the imagination of man's
heart *is* evil from his youth; nor will
I again destroy every living thing as
I have done.

22 "While the earth remains,
Seedtime and harvest,
Cold and heat,
Winter and summer,
And day and night
Shall not cease."

9 So God blessed Noah and his sons,
and said to them: "Be fruitful and
multiply, and fill the earth.[a] 2And the
fear of you and the dread of you shall
be on every beast of the earth, on every
bird of the air, on all that move *on* the
earth, and on all the fish of the sea.
They are given into your hand. 3Every
moving thing that lives shall be food for
you. I have given you all things, even
as the green herbs. 4But you shall not
eat flesh with its life, *that is,* its blood.
5Surely for your lifeblood I will demand
a reckoning; from the hand of every
beast I will require it, and from the hand
of man. From the hand of every man's
brother I will require the life of man.

6 "Whoever sheds man's blood,
By man his blood shall be shed;
For in the image of God
He made man.
7 And as for you, be fruitful and
multiply;
Bring forth abundantly in the
earth
And multiply in it."

8Then God spoke to Noah and to his
sons with him, saying: 9"And as for Me,
behold, I establish My covenant with
you and with your descendants[a] after
you, 10and with every living creature
that *is* with you: the birds, the cattle, and
every beast of the earth with you, of all
that go out of the ark, every beast of the
earth. 11Thus I establish My covenant
with you: Never again shall all flesh be
cut off by the waters of the flood; never
again shall there be a flood to destroy
the earth."
12And God said: "This *is* the sign of the
covenant which I make between Me and
you, and every living creature that *is*
with you, for perpetual generations: 13I
set My rainbow in the cloud, and it shall
be for the sign of the covenant between
Me and the earth. 14It shall be, when I
bring a cloud over the earth, that the
rainbow shall be seen in the cloud; 15and
I will remember My covenant which *is*
between Me and you and every living
creature of all flesh; the waters shall
never again become a flood to destroy
all flesh. 16The rainbow shall be in the
cloud, and I will look on it to remember
the everlasting covenant between God
and every living creature of all flesh
that *is* on the earth." 17And God said to
Noah, "This *is* the sign of the covenant
which I have established between Me
and all flesh that *is* on the earth."

Noah and His Sons

18Now the sons of Noah who went out
of the ark were Shem, Ham, and Ja-
pheth. And Ham *was* the father of Ca-
naan. 19These three *were* the sons of
Noah, and from these the whole earth
was populated.
20And Noah began *to be* a farmer, and
he planted a vineyard. 21Then he drank
of the wine and was drunk, and became

9:1 [a] Compare Genesis 1:28 9:9 [a] Literally *seed*

uncovered in his tent. 22And Ham, the
father of Canaan, saw the nakedness
of his father, and told his two brothers
outside. 23But Shem and Japheth took a
garment, laid *it* on both their shoulders,
and went backward and covered the
nakedness of their father. Their faces
were turned away, and they did not see
their father's nakedness.
24So Noah awoke from his wine, and
knew what his younger son had done
to him. 25Then he said:

"Cursed *be* Canaan;
A servant of servants
He shall be to his brethren."

26And he said:

"Blessed *be* the LORD,
The God of Shem,
And may Canaan be his servant.
27 May God enlarge Japheth,
And may he dwell in the tents of
Shem;
And may Canaan be his servant."

28And Noah lived after the flood three
hundred and fifty years. 29So all the
days of Noah were nine hundred and
fifty years; and he died.

Nations Descended from Noah

10 Now this *is* the genealogy of the
sons of Noah: Shem, Ham, and
Japheth. And sons were born to them
after the flood.
2The sons of Japheth *were* Gomer,
Magog, Madai, Javan, Tubal, Meshech,
and Tiras. 3The sons of Gomer *were* Ash-
kenaz, Riphath,[a] and Togarmah. 4The
sons of Javan *were* Elishah, Tarshish,
Kittim, and Dodanim.[a] 5From these the
coastland *peoples* of the Gentiles were
separated into their lands, everyone
according to his language, according
to their families, into their nations.
6The sons of Ham *were* Cush, Miz-
raim, Put,[a] and Canaan. 7The sons of
Cush *were* Seba, Havilah, Sabtah, Ra-
amah, and Sabtechah; and the sons of
Raamah *were* Sheba and Dedan.
8Cush begot Nimrod; he began to be
a mighty one on the earth. 9He was a
mighty hunter before the LORD; there-
fore it is said, "Like Nimrod the mighty
hunter before the LORD." 10And the
beginning of his kingdom was Babel,
Erech, Accad, and Calneh, in the land
of Shinar. 11From that land he went to
Assyria and built Nineveh, Rehoboth
Ir, Calah, 12and Resen between Nineveh
and Calah (that *is* the principal city).
13Mizraim begot Ludim, Anamim,
Lehabim, Naphtuhim, 14Pathrusim,
and Casluhim (from whom came the
Philistines and Caphtorim).
15Canaan begot Sidon his firstborn,
and Heth; 16the Jebusite, the Amorite,
and the Girgashite; 17the Hivite, the
Arkite, and the Sinite; 18the Arvadite,
the Zemarite, and the Hamathite. Af-
terward the families of the Canaanites
were dispersed. 19And the border of the
Canaanites was from Sidon as you go
toward Gerar, as far as Gaza; then as you
go toward Sodom, Gomorrah, Admah,
and Zeboiim, as far as Lasha. 20These
were the sons of Ham, according to their
families, according to their languages,
in their lands *and* in their nations.
21And *children* were born also to Shem,
the father of all the children of Eber, the
brother of Japheth the elder. 22The sons
of Shem *were* Elam, Asshur, Arphaxad,
Lud, and Aram. 23The sons of Aram *were*
Uz, Hul, Gether, and Mash.[a] 24Arphaxad
begot Salah,[a] and Salah begot Eber. 25To
Eber were born two sons: the name of
one *was* Peleg, for in his days the earth
was divided; and his brother's name *was*
Joktan. 26Joktan begot Almodad, She-
leph, Hazarmaveth, Jerah, 27Hadoram,
Uzal, Diklah, 28Obal,[a] Abimael, Sheba,
29Ophir, Havilah, and Jobab. All these
were the sons of Joktan. 30And their
dwelling place was from Mesha as you
go toward Sephar, the mountain of the
east. 31These *were* the sons of Shem,
according to their families, according
to their languages, in their lands, ac-
cording to their nations.

10:3 [a] Spelled *Diphath* in 1 Chronicles 1:6 **10:4** [a] Spelled *Rodanim* in Samaritan Pentateuch and 1 Chronicles 1:7 **10:6** [a] Or *Phut* **10:23** [a] Called *Meshech* in Septuagint and 1 Chronicles 1:17 **10:24** [a] Following Masoretic Text, Vulgate, and Targum; Septuagint reads *Arphaxad begot Cainan, and Cainan begot Salah* (compare Luke 3:35, 36). **10:28** [a] Spelled *Ebal* in 1 Chronicles 1:22

32These *were* the families of the sons
of Noah, according to their generations,
in their nations; and from these the
nations were divided on the earth after
the flood.

The Tower of Babel

11 Now the whole earth had one
language and one speech. 2And
it came to pass, as they journeyed from
the east, that they found a plain in the
land of Shinar, and they dwelt there.
3Then they said to one another, "Come,
let us make bricks and bake *them* thor-
oughly." They had brick for stone, and
they had asphalt for mortar. 4And they
said, "Come, let us build ourselves a city,
and a tower whose top *is* in the heavens;
let us make a name for ourselves, lest
we be scattered abroad over the face of
the whole earth."
5But the LORD came down to see the
city and the tower which the sons of
men had built. 6And the LORD said,
"Indeed the people *are* one and they
all have one language, and this is
what they begin to do; now nothing
that they propose to do will be with-
held from them. 7Come, let Us go down
and there confuse their language, that
they may not understand one another's
speech." 8So the LORD scattered them
abroad from there over the face of all
the earth, and they ceased building
the city. 9Therefore its name is called
Babel, because there the LORD confused
the language of all the earth; and from
there the LORD scattered them abroad
over the face of all the earth.

Shem's Descendants

10This *is* the genealogy of Shem: Shem
was one hundred years old, and begot
Arphaxad two years after the flood.
11After he begot Arphaxad, Shem lived
five hundred years, and begot sons and
daughters.
12Arphaxad lived thirty-five years,
and begot Salah. 13After he begot Salah,
Arphaxad lived four hundred and three
years, and begot sons and daughters.
14Salah lived thirty years, and begot
Eber. 15After he begot Eber, Salah lived
four hundred and three years, and be-
got sons and daughters.
16Eber lived thirty-four years, and be-
got Peleg. 17After he begot Peleg, Eber
lived four hundred and thirty years,
and begot sons and daughters.
18Peleg lived thirty years, and begot
Reu. 19After he begot Reu, Peleg lived
two hundred and nine years, and begot
sons and daughters.
20Reu lived thirty-two years, and be-
got Serug. 21After he begot Serug, Reu
lived two hundred and seven years, and
begot sons and daughters.
22Serug lived thirty years, and begot
Nahor. 23After he begot Nahor, Serug
lived two hundred years, and begot
sons and daughters.
24Nahor lived twenty-nine years, and
begot Terah. 25After he begot Terah,
Nahor lived one hundred and nineteen
years, and begot sons and daughters.
26Now Terah lived seventy years, and
begot Abram, Nahor, and Haran.

Terah's Descendants

27This *is* the genealogy of Terah: Terah
begot Abram, Nahor, and Haran. Haran
begot Lot. 28And Haran died before his
father Terah in his native land, in Ur
of the Chaldeans. 29Then Abram and
Nahor took wives: the name of Abram's
wife *was* Sarai, and the name of Nahor's
wife, Milcah, the daughter of Haran the
father of Milcah and the father of Iscah.
30But Sarai was barren; she had no child.
31And Terah took his son Abram and
his grandson Lot, the son of Haran,
and his daughter-in-law Sarai, his son
Abram's wife, and they went out with
them from Ur of the Chaldeans to go to
the land of Canaan; and they came to
Haran and dwelt there. 32So the days of
Terah were two hundred and five years,
and Terah died in Haran.

Promises to Abram

12 Now the LORD had said to Abram:

"Get out of your country,
From your family
And from your father's house,
To a land that I will show you.
2 I will make you a great nation;
I will bless you
And make your name great;
And you shall be a blessing.

GOD SIN JESUS SALVATION LOVE

3 I will bless those who bless you,
And I will curse him who curses
you;
And in you all the families of the
earth shall be blessed."

4So Abram departed as the LORD had
spoken to him, and Lot went with him.
And Abram *was* seventy-five years old
when he departed from Haran. 5Then
Abram took Sarai his wife and Lot his
brother's son, and all their possessions
that they had gathered, and the peo-
ple whom they had acquired in Haran,
and they departed to go to the land of
Canaan. So they came to the land of
Canaan. 6Abram passed through the
land to the place of Shechem, as far as
the terebinth tree of Moreh.[a] And the
Canaanites *were* then in the land.
7Then the LORD appeared to Abram
and said, "To your descendants I will
give this land." And there he built an
altar to the LORD, who had appeared to
him. 8And he moved from there to the
mountain east of Bethel, and he pitched
his tent *with* Bethel on the west and Ai
on the east; there he built an altar to
the LORD and called on the name of the
LORD. 9So Abram journeyed, going on
still toward the South.[a]

Abram in Egypt

10Now there was a famine in the land,
and Abram went down to Egypt to dwell
there, for the famine *was* severe in the
land. 11And it came to pass, when he was
close to entering Egypt, that he said to
Sarai his wife, "Indeed I know that you
are a woman of beautiful countenance.
12Therefore it will happen, when the
Egyptians see you, that they will say,
'This *is* his wife'; and they will kill me,
but they will let you live. 13Please say
you *are* my sister, that it may be well
with me for your sake, and that I[a] may
live because of you."
14So it was, when Abram came into
Egypt, that the Egyptians saw the wom-
an, that she *was* very beautiful. 15The
princes of Pharaoh also saw her and
commended her to Pharaoh. And the
woman was taken to Pharaoh's house.
16He treated Abram well for her sake. He
had sheep, oxen, male donkeys, male
and female servants, female donkeys,
and camels.
17But the LORD plagued Pharaoh and
his house with great plagues because
of Sarai, Abram's wife. 18And Pharaoh
called Abram and said, "What *is* this
you have done to me? Why did you not
tell me that she *was* your wife? 19Why
did you say, 'She *is* my sister'? I might
have taken her as my wife. Now there-
fore, here is your wife; take *her* and go
your way." 20So Pharaoh commanded
his men concerning him; and they sent
him away, with his wife and all that
he had.

Abram Inherits Canaan

13 Then Abram went up from Egypt,
he and his wife and all that he
had, and Lot with him, to the South.[a]
2Abram *was* very rich in livestock, in
silver, and in gold. 3And he went on his
journey from the South as far as Bethel,
to the place where his tent had been at
the beginning, between Bethel and Ai,
4to the place of the altar which he had
made there at first. And there Abram
called on the name of the LORD.
5Lot also, who went with Abram, had
flocks and herds and tents. 6Now the
land was not able to support them, that
they might dwell together, for their
possessions were so great that they
could not dwell together. 7And there
was strife between the herdsmen of
Abram's livestock and the herdsmen
of Lot's livestock. The Canaanites
and the Perizzites then dwelt in the
land.
8So Abram said to Lot, "Please let there
be no strife between you and me, and
between my herdsmen and your herds-
men; for we *are* brethren. 9*Is* not the
whole land before you? Please separate
from me. If *you take* the left, then I will
go to the right; or, if *you go* to the right,
then I will go to the left."
10And Lot lifted his eyes and saw all
the plain of Jordan, that it *was* well
watered everywhere (before the LORD
destroyed Sodom and Gomorrah) like

12:6 [a] Hebrew *Alon Moreh* 12:9 [a] Hebrew *Negev* 12:13 [a] Literally *my soul* 13:1 [a] Hebrew *Negev*

the garden of the LORD, like the land of
Egypt as you go toward Zoar. [11]Then Lot
chose for himself all the plain of Jordan,
and Lot journeyed east. And they sepa-
rated from each other. [12]Abram dwelt in
the land of Canaan, and Lot dwelt in the
cities of the plain and pitched *his* tent
even as far as Sodom. [13]But the men of
Sodom *were* exceedingly wicked and
sinful against the LORD.
[14]And the LORD said to Abram, after
Lot had separated from him: "Lift your
eyes now and look from the place where
you are—northward, southward, east-
ward, and westward; [15]for all the land
which you see I give to you and your
descendants[a] forever. [16]And I will make
your descendants as the dust of the
earth; so that if a man could number the
dust of the earth, *then* your descendants
also could be numbered. [17]Arise, walk
in the land through its length and its
width, for I give it to you."
[18]Then Abram moved *his* tent, and
went and dwelt by the terebinth trees
of Mamre,[a] which *are* in Hebron, and
built an altar there to the LORD.

Lot's Captivity and Rescue

14 And it came to pass in the days
of Amraphel king of Shinar, Ari-
och king of Ellasar, Chedorlaomer king
of Elam, and Tidal king of nations,[a]
[2]*that* they made war with Bera king of
Sodom, Birsha king of Gomorrah, Shi-
nab king of Admah, Shemeber king of
Zeboiim, and the king of Bela (that is,
Zoar). [3]All these joined together in the
Valley of Siddim (that is, the Salt Sea).
[4]Twelve years they served Chedorla-
omer, and in the thirteenth year they
rebelled.
[5]In the fourteenth year Chedorlaomer
and the kings that *were* with him came
and attacked the Rephaim in Ashteroth
Karnaim, the Zuzim in Ham, the Emim
in Shaveh Kiriathaim, [6]and the Horites
in their mountain of Seir, as far as El
Paran, which *is* by the wilderness. [7]Then
they turned back and came to En Mish-
pat (that *is,* Kadesh), and attacked all the
country of the Amalekites, and also the
Amorites who dwelt in Hazezon Tamar.
[8]And the king of Sodom, the king of Go-
morrah, the king of Admah, the king of
Zeboiim, and the king of Bela (that *is,*
Zoar) went out and joined together in
battle in the Valley of Siddim [9]against
Chedorlaomer king of Elam, Tidal king of
nations,[a] Amraphel king of Shinar, and
Arioch king of Ellasar—four kings against
five. [10]Now the Valley of Siddim *was full of*
asphalt pits; and the kings of Sodom and
Gomorrah fled; *some* fell there, and the
remainder fled to the mountains. [11]Then
they took all the goods of Sodom and Go-
morrah, and all their provisions, and went
their way. [12]They also took Lot, Abram's
brother's son who dwelt in Sodom, and
his goods, and departed.
[13]Then one who had escaped came and
told Abram the Hebrew, for he dwelt by
the terebinth trees of Mamre[a] the Am-
orite, brother of Eshcol and brother of
Aner; and they *were* allies with Abram.
[14]Now when Abram heard that his
brother was taken captive, he armed
his three hundred and eighteen trained
servants who were born in his own house,
and went in pursuit as far as Dan. [15]He
divided his forces against them by night,
and he and his servants attacked them
and pursued them as far as Hobah, which
is north of Damascus. [16]So he brought
back all the goods, and also brought back
his brother Lot and his goods, as well as
the women and the people.
[17]And the king of Sodom went out to
meet him at the Valley of Shaveh (that
is, the King's Valley), after his return
from the defeat of Chedorlaomer and
the kings who *were* with him.

Abram and Melchizedek

[18]Then Melchizedek king of Salem
brought out bread and wine; he *was*
the priest of God Most High. [19]And he
blessed him and said:

"Blessed be Abram of God Most High,
Possessor of heaven and earth;
[20] And blessed be God Most High,
Who has delivered your enemies
into your hand."

And he gave him a tithe of all.

13:15 [a] Literally *seed,* and so throughout the book 13:18 [a] Hebrew *Alon Mamre* 14:1 [a] Hebrew *goyim* 14:9 [a] Hebrew *goyim* 14:13 [a] Hebrew *Alon Mamre*

21Now the king of Sodom said to
Abram, "Give me the persons, and take
the goods for yourself."
22But Abram said to the king of Sodom,
"I have raised my hand to the LORD, God
Most High, the Possessor of heaven and
earth, 23that I *will take* nothing, from a
thread to a sandal strap, and that I will
not take anything that *is* yours, lest you
should say, 'I have made Abram rich'—
24except only what the young men have
eaten, and the portion of the men who
went with me: Aner, Eshcol, and Mamre;
let them take their portion."

God's Covenant with Abram

15 After these things the word of the
LORD came to Abram in a vision,
saying, "Do not be afraid, Abram. I *am*
your shield, your exceedingly great
reward."
2But Abram said, "Lord GOD, what will
You give me, seeing I go childless, and
the heir of my house *is* Eliezer of Da-
mascus?" 3Then Abram said, "Look, You
have given me no offspring; indeed one
born in my house is my heir!"
4And behold, the word of the LORD
came to him, saying, "This one shall
not be your heir, but one who will come
from your own body shall be your heir."
5Then He brought him outside and said,
"Look now toward heaven, and count
the stars if you are able to number
them." And He said to him, "So shall
your descendants be."
6And he believed in the LORD, and He
accounted it to him for righteousness.
7Then He said to him, "I *am* the LORD,
who brought you out of Ur of the Chal-
deans, to give you this land to inherit it."
8And he said, "Lord GOD, how shall I
know that I will inherit it?"
9So He said to him, "Bring Me a three-
year-old heifer, a three-year-old female
goat, a three-year-old ram, a turtledove,
and a young pigeon." 10Then he brought
all these to Him and cut them in two,
down the middle, and placed each piece
opposite the other; but he did not cut
the birds in two. 11And when the vultures
came down on the carcasses, Abram
drove them away.
12Now when the sun was going down, a
deep sleep fell upon Abram; and behold,
horror *and* great darkness fell upon
him. 13Then He said to Abram: "Know
certainly that your descendants will
be strangers in a land *that is* not theirs,
and will serve them, and they will afflict
them four hundred years. 14And also the
nation whom they serve I will judge; af-
terward they shall come out with great
possessions. 15Now as for you, you shall
go to your fathers in peace; you shall
be buried at a good old age. 16But in
the fourth generation they shall return
here, for the iniquity of the Amorites *is*
not yet complete."
17And it came to pass, when the sun
went down and it was dark, that behold,
there appeared a smoking oven and a
burning torch that passed between those
pieces. 18On the same day the LORD
made a covenant with Abram, saying:
"To your descendants I have given
this land, from the river of Egypt to the
great river, the River Euphrates— 19the
Kenites, the Kenezzites, the Kadmonites,
20the Hittites, the Perizzites, the Repha-
im, 21the Amorites, the Canaanites, the
Girgashites, and the Jebusites."

Hagar and Ishmael

16 Now Sarai, Abram's wife, had
borne him no *children.* And she
had an Egyptian maidservant whose
name was Hagar. 2So Sarai said to
Abram, "See now, the LORD has restrained
me from bearing *children.* Please, go in to
my maid; perhaps I shall obtain children
by her." And Abram heeded the voice of
Sarai. 3Then Sarai, Abram's wife, took
Hagar her maid, the Egyptian, and gave
her to her husband Abram to be his wife,
after Abram had dwelt ten years in the
land of Canaan. 4So he went in to Hagar,
and she conceived. And when she saw
that she had conceived, her mistress
became despised in her eyes.
5Then Sarai said to Abram, "My wrong
be upon you! I gave my maid into your
embrace; and when she saw that she
had conceived, I became despised in
her eyes. The LORD judge between you
and me."
6So Abram said to Sarai, "Indeed your
maid *is* in your hand; do to her as you
please." And when Sarai dealt harshly
with her, she fled from her presence.

7Now the Angel of the LORD found her
by a spring of water in the wilderness,
by the spring on the way to Shur. 8And
He said, "Hagar, Sarai's maid, where
have you come from, and where are
you going?"
She said, "I am fleeing from the pres-
ence of my mistress Sarai."
9The Angel of the LORD said to her, "Re-
turn to your mistress, and submit your-
self under her hand." 10Then the Angel
of the LORD said to her, "I will multiply
your descendants exceedingly, so that
they shall not be counted for multitude."
11And the Angel of the LORD said to her:

"Behold, you *are* with child,
And you shall bear a son.
You shall call his name Ishmael,
Because the LORD has heard your
affliction.
12 He shall be a wild man;
His hand *shall be* against every
man,
And every man's hand against
him.
And he shall dwell in the presence
of all his brethren."

13Then she called the name of the
LORD who spoke to her, You-Are-the-
God-Who-Sees; for she said, "Have I also
here seen Him who sees me?" 14There-
fore the well was called Beer Lahai Roi;[a]
observe, *it is* between Kadesh and Bered.
15So Hagar bore Abram a son; and
Abram named his son, whom Hagar
bore, Ishmael. 16Abram *was* eighty-six
years old when Hagar bore Ishmael
to Abram.

The Sign of the Covenant

17 When Abram was ninety-nine
years old, the LORD appeared to
Abram and said to him, "I *am* Almighty
God; walk before Me and be blameless.
2And I will make My covenant between
Me and you, and will multiply you ex-
ceedingly." 3Then Abram fell on his face,
and God talked with him, saying: 4"As
for Me, behold, My covenant is with you,
and you shall be a father of many na-
tions. 5No longer shall your name be
called Abram, but your name shall be
Abraham; for I have made you a fa-
ther of many nations. 6I will make you
exceedingly fruitful; and I will make
nations of you, and kings shall come
from you. 7And I will establish My cov-
enant between Me and you and your
descendants after you in their gener-
ations, for an everlasting covenant, to
be God to you and your descendants
after you. 8Also I give to you and your
descendants after you the land in which
you are a stranger, all the land of Ca-
naan, as an everlasting possession; and
I will be their God."
9And God said to Abraham: "As for you,
you shall keep My covenant, you and
your descendants after you throughout
their generations. 10This *is* My covenant
which you shall keep, between Me and
you and your descendants after you:
Every male child among you shall be
circumcised; 11and you shall be circum-
cised in the flesh of your foreskins, and it
shall be a sign of the covenant between
Me and you. 12He who is eight days old
among you shall be circumcised, ev-
ery male child in your generations, he
who is born in your house or bought
with money from any foreigner who is
not your descendant. 13He who is born
in your house and he who is bought
with your money must be circumcised,
and My covenant shall be in your flesh
for an everlasting covenant. 14And the
uncircumcised male child, who is not
circumcised in the flesh of his foreskin,
that person shall be cut off from his
people; he has broken My covenant."
15Then God said to Abraham, "As for
Sarai your wife, you shall not call her
name Sarai, but Sarah *shall be* her
name. 16And I will bless her and also
give you a son by her; then I will bless
her, and she shall be *a mother of* nations;
kings of peoples shall be from her."
17Then Abraham fell on his face and
laughed, and said in his heart, "Shall
a child be born to a man who is one
hundred years old? And shall Sarah,
who is ninety years old, bear *a child?*"
18And Abraham said to God, "Oh, that
Ishmael might live before You!"

16:14 [a] Literally *Well of the One Who Lives and Sees Me*

GOD SIN JESUS SALVATION LOVE

19Then God said: "No, Sarah your wife
shall bear you a son, and you shall call
his name Isaac; I will establish My cov-
enant with him for an everlasting cov-
enant, *and* with his descendants after
him. 20And as for Ishmael, I have heard
you. Behold, I have blessed him, and
will make him fruitful, and will multiply
him exceedingly. He shall beget twelve
princes, and I will make him a great na-
tion. 21But My covenant I will establish
with Isaac, whom Sarah shall bear to
you at this set time next year." 22Then
He finished talking with him, and God
went up from Abraham.

23So Abraham took Ishmael his son, all
who were born in his house and all who
were bought with his money, every male
among the men of Abraham's house,
and circumcised the flesh of their fore-
skins that very same day, as God had
said to him. 24Abraham *was* ninety-nine
years old when he was circumcised in
the flesh of his foreskin. 25And Ishmael
his son *was* thirteen years old when he
was circumcised in the flesh of his fore-
skin. 26That very same day Abraham
was circumcised, and his son Ishmael;
27and all the men of his house, born in
the house or bought with money from
a foreigner, were circumcised with him.

The Son of Promise

18 Then the LORD appeared to him
by the terebinth trees of Mamre,[a]
as he was sitting in the tent door in the
heat of the day. 2So he lifted his eyes
and looked, and behold, three men were
standing by him; and when he saw *them,*
he ran from the tent door to meet them,
and bowed himself to the ground, 3and
said, "My Lord, if I have now found favor
in Your sight, do not pass on by Your ser-
vant. 4Please let a little water be brought,
and wash your feet, and rest yourselves
under the tree. 5And I will bring a mor-
sel of bread, that you may refresh your
hearts. After that you may pass by, inas-
much as you have come to your servant."

They said, "Do as you have said."

6So Abraham hurried into the tent to
Sarah and said, "Quickly, make ready
three measures of fine meal; knead *it*
and make cakes." 7And Abraham ran to
the herd, took a tender and good calf,
gave *it* to a young man, and he hastened
to prepare it. 8So he took butter and milk
and the calf which he had prepared, and
set *it* before them; and he stood by them
under the tree as they ate.

9Then they said to him, "Where *is*
Sarah your wife?"

So he said, "Here, in the tent."

10And He said, "I will certainly return
to you according to the time of life, and
behold, Sarah your wife shall have a
son."

(Sarah was listening in the tent door
which *was* behind him.) 11Now Abra-
ham and Sarah were old, well advanced
in age; *and* Sarah had passed the age
of childbearing.[a] 12Therefore Sarah
laughed within herself, saying, "After
I have grown old, shall I have pleasure,
my lord being old also?"

13And the LORD said to Abraham,
"Why did Sarah laugh, saying, 'Shall
I surely bear *a child,* since I am old?'
14Is anything too hard for the LORD?
At the appointed time I will return to
you, according to the time of life, and
Sarah shall have a son."

15But Sarah denied *it,* saying, "I did
not laugh," for she was afraid.

And He said, "No, but you did laugh!"

Abraham Intercedes for Sodom

16Then the men rose from there and
looked toward Sodom, and Abraham
went with them to send them on the
way. 17And the LORD said, "Shall I hide
from Abraham what I am doing, 18since
Abraham shall surely become a great
and mighty nation, and all the nations
of the earth shall be blessed in him?
19For I have known him, in order that
he may command his children and his
household after him, that they keep
the way of the LORD, to do righteous-
ness and justice, that the LORD may
bring to Abraham what He has spoken
to him." 20And the LORD said, "Because
the outcry against Sodom and Gomor-
rah is great, and because their sin is
very grave, 21I will go down now and
see whether they have done altogether

18:1 [a] Hebrew *Alon Mamre* 18:11 [a] Literally *the manner of women had ceased to be with Sarah*

according to the outcry against it that
has come to Me; and if not, I will know."
22Then the men turned away from
there and went toward Sodom, but Abra-
ham still stood before the LORD. 23And
Abraham came near and said, "Would
You also destroy the righteous with the
wicked? 24Suppose there were fifty righ-
teous within the city; would You also
destroy the place and not spare *it* for
the fifty righteous that were in it? 25Far
be it from You to do such a thing as this,
to slay the righteous with the wicked,
so that the righteous should be as the
wicked; far be it from You! Shall not the
Judge of all the earth do right?"
26So the LORD said, "If I find in Sodom
fifty righteous within the city, then I
will spare all the place for their sakes."
27Then Abraham answered and said,
"Indeed now, I who *am but* dust and ash-
es have taken it upon myself to speak
to the Lord: 28Suppose there were five
less than the fifty righteous; would You
destroy all of the city for *lack of* five?"
So He said, "If I find there forty-five, I
will not destroy *it*."
29And he spoke to Him yet again and
said, "Suppose there should be forty
found there?"
So He said, "I will not do *it* for the sake
of forty."
30Then he said, "Let not the Lord be
angry, and I will speak: Suppose thirty
should be found there?"
So He said, "I will not do *it* if I find
thirty there."
31And he said, "Indeed now, I have tak-
en it upon myself to speak to the Lord:
Suppose twenty should be found there?"
So He said, "I will not destroy *it* for the
sake of twenty."
32Then he said, "Let not the Lord be
angry, and I will speak but once more:
Suppose ten should be found there?"
And He said, "I will not destroy *it* for
the sake of ten." 33So the LORD went
His way as soon as He had finished
speaking with Abraham; and Abraham
returned to his place.

Sodom's Depravity

19 Now the two angels came to
Sodom in the evening, and Lot
was sitting in the gate of Sodom. When
Lot saw *them*, he rose to meet them, and
he bowed himself with his face toward
the ground. 2And he said, "Here now, my
lords, please turn in to your servant's
house and spend the night, and wash
your feet; then you may rise early and
go on your way."
And they said, "No, but we will spend
the night in the open square."
3But he insisted strongly; so they
turned in to him and entered his house.
Then he made them a feast, and baked
unleavened bread, and they ate.
4Now before they lay down, the men of
the city, the men of Sodom, both old and
young, all the people from every quar-
ter, surrounded the house. 5And they
called to Lot and said to him, "Where
are the men who came to you tonight?
Bring them out to us that we may know
them *carnally*."
6So Lot went out to them through the
doorway, shut the door behind him,
7and said, "Please, my brethren, do not
do so wickedly! 8See now, I have two
daughters who have not known a man;
please, let me bring them out to you,
and you may do to them as you wish;
only do nothing to these men, since this
is the reason they have come under the
shadow of my roof."
9And they said, "Stand back!" Then
they said, "This one came in to stay
here, and he keeps acting as a judge;
now we will deal worse with you than
with them." So they pressed hard
against the man Lot, and came near
to break down the door. 10But the men
reached out their hands and pulled Lot
into the house with them, and shut the
door. 11And they struck the men who
were at the doorway of the house with
blindness, both small and great, so
that they became weary *trying* to find
the door.

Sodom and Gomorrah Destroyed

12Then the men said to Lot, "Have you
anyone else here? Son-in-law, your sons,
your daughters, and whomever you
have in the city—take *them* out of this
place! 13For we will destroy this place,
because the outcry against them has
grown great before the face of the LORD,
and the LORD has sent us to destroy it."

GOD SIN JESUS SALVATION LOVE

14So Lot went out and spoke to his sons-in-law, who had married his daughters, and said, "Get up, get out of this place; for the LORD will destroy this city!" But to his sons-in-law he seemed to be joking.

15When the morning dawned, the angels urged Lot to hurry, saying, "Arise, take your wife and your two daughters who are here, lest you be consumed in the punishment of the city." 16And while he lingered, the men took hold of his hand, his wife's hand, and the hands of his two daughters, the LORD being merciful to him, and they brought him out and set him outside the city. 17So it came to pass, when they had brought them outside, that he[a] said, "Escape for your life! Do not look behind you nor stay anywhere in the plain. Escape to the mountains, lest you be destroyed."

18Then Lot said to them, "Please, no, my lords! 19Indeed now, your servant has found favor in your sight, and you have increased your mercy which you have shown me by saving my life; but I cannot escape to the mountains, lest some evil overtake me and I die. 20See now, this city *is* near *enough* to flee to, and it *is* a little one; please let me escape there (*is* it not a little one?) and my soul shall live."

21And he said to him, "See, I have favored you concerning this thing also, in that I will not overthrow this city for which you have spoken. 22Hurry, escape there. For I cannot do anything until you arrive there."

Therefore the name of the city was called Zoar.

23The sun had risen upon the earth when Lot entered Zoar. 24Then the LORD rained brimstone and fire on Sodom and Gomorrah, from the LORD out of the heavens. 25So He overthrew those cities, all the plain, all the inhabitants of the cities, and what grew on the ground.

26But his wife looked back behind him, and she became a pillar of salt.

27And Abraham went early in the morning to the place where he had stood before the LORD. 28Then he looked toward Sodom and Gomorrah, and toward all the land of the plain; and he saw, and behold, the smoke of the land which went up like the smoke of a furnace. 29And it came to pass, when God destroyed the cities of the plain, that God remembered Abraham, and sent Lot out of the midst of the overthrow, when He overthrew the cities in which Lot had dwelt.

The Descendants of Lot

30Then Lot went up out of Zoar and dwelt in the mountains, and his two daughters were with him; for he was afraid to dwell in Zoar. And he and his two daughters dwelt in a cave. 31Now the firstborn said to the younger, "Our father *is* old, and *there is* no man on the earth to come in to us as is the custom of all the earth. 32Come, let us make our father drink wine, and we will lie with him, that we may preserve the lineage of our father." 33So they made their father drink wine that night. And the firstborn went in and lay with her father, and he did not know when she lay down or when she arose.

34It happened on the next day that the firstborn said to the younger, "Indeed I lay with my father last night; let us make him drink wine tonight also, and you go in *and* lie with him, that we may preserve the lineage of our father." 35Then they made their father drink wine that night also. And the younger arose and lay with him, and he did not know when she lay down or when she arose.

36Thus both the daughters of Lot were with child by their father. 37The firstborn bore a son and called his name Moab; he *is* the father of the Moabites to this day. 38And the younger, she also bore a son and called his name Ben-Ammi; he *is* the father of the people of Ammon to this day.

Abraham and Abimelech

20 And Abraham journeyed from there to the South, and dwelt between Kadesh and Shur, and stayed in Gerar. 2Now Abraham said of Sarah his wife, "She *is* my sister." And Abimelech king of Gerar sent and took Sarah.

19:17 [a] Septuagint, Syriac, and Vulgate read *they*.

3But God came to Abimelech in a
dream by night, and said to him, "In-
deed you *are* a dead man because of
the woman whom you have taken, for
she *is* a man's wife."
4But Abimelech had not come near
her; and he said, "Lord, will You slay a
righteous nation also? 5Did he not say
to me, 'She *is* my sister'? And she, even
she herself said, 'He *is* my brother.' In
the integrity of my heart and innocence
of my hands I have done this."
6And God said to him in a dream, "Yes,
I know that you did this in the integrity
of your heart. For I also withheld you
from sinning against Me; therefore I
did not let you touch her. 7Now there-
fore, restore the man's wife; for he *is* a
prophet, and he will pray for you and
you shall live. But if you do not restore
her, know that you shall surely die, you
and all who *are* yours."
8So Abimelech rose early in the morn-
ing, called all his servants, and told all
these things in their hearing; and the
men were very much afraid. 9And Abim-
elech called Abraham and said to him,
"What have you done to us? How have
I offended you, that you have brought
on me and on my kingdom a great sin?
You have done deeds to me that ought
not to be done." 10Then Abimelech said
to Abraham, "What did you have in view,
that you have done this thing?"
11And Abraham said, "Because I
thought, surely the fear of God *is* not
in this place; and they will kill me on
account of my wife. 12But indeed *she is*
truly my sister. She *is* the daughter of
my father, but not the daughter of my
mother; and she became my wife. 13And
it came to pass, when God caused me to
wander from my father's house, that I
said to her, 'This *is* your kindness that
you should do for me: in every place,
wherever we go, say of me, "He *is* my
brother." ' "
14Then Abimelech took sheep, oxen,
and male and female servants, and
gave *them* to Abraham; and he restored
Sarah his wife to him. 15And Abime-
lech said, "See, my land *is* before you;
dwell where it pleases you." 16Then to
Sarah he said, "Behold, I have given
your brother a thousand *pieces* of silver;
indeed this vindicates you[a] before all
who *are* with you and before every-
body." Thus she was rebuked.
17So Abraham prayed to God; and
God healed Abimelech, his wife, and
his female servants. Then they bore
children; 18for the LORD had closed up
all the wombs of the house of Abime-
lech because of Sarah, Abraham's wife.

Isaac Is Born

21 And the LORD visited Sarah as He
had said, and the LORD did for
Sarah as He had spoken. 2For Sarah con-
ceived and bore Abraham a son in his
old age, at the set time of which God had
spoken to him. 3And Abraham called
the name of his son who was born to
him—whom Sarah bore to him—Isaac.
4Then Abraham circumcised his son
Isaac when he was eight days old, as God
had commanded him. 5Now Abraham
was one hundred years old when his
son Isaac was born to him. 6And Sarah
said, "God has made me laugh, *and* all
who hear will laugh with me." 7She also
said, "Who would have said to Abraham
that Sarah would nurse children? For I
have borne *him* a son in his old age."

Hagar and Ishmael Depart

8So the child grew and was weaned.
And Abraham made a great feast on
the same day that Isaac was weaned.
9And Sarah saw the son of Hagar the
Egyptian, whom she had borne to Abra-
ham, scoffing. 10Therefore she said to
Abraham, "Cast out this bondwoman
and her son; for the son of this bond-
woman shall not be heir with my son,
namely with Isaac." 11And the matter
was very displeasing in Abraham's sight
because of his son.
12But God said to Abraham, "Do not
let it be displeasing in your sight be-
cause of the lad or because of your
bondwoman. Whatever Sarah has said
to you, listen to her voice; for in Isaac
your seed shall be called. 13Yet I will
also make a nation of the son of the
bondwoman, because he *is* your seed."

20:16 a Literally *it is a covering of the eyes for you*

14So Abraham rose early in the morn-
ing, and took bread and a skin of water;
and putting *it* on her shoulder, he gave
it and the boy to Hagar, and sent her
away. Then she departed and wandered
in the Wilderness of Beersheba. 15And
the water in the skin was used up, and
she placed the boy under one of the
shrubs. 16Then she went and sat down
across from *him* at a distance of about
a bowshot; for she said to herself, "Let
me not see the death of the boy." So she
sat opposite *him*, and lifted her voice
and wept.

17And God heard the voice of the lad.
Then the angel of God called to Hagar
out of heaven, and said to her, "What
ails you, Hagar? Fear not, for God has
heard the voice of the lad where he *is*.
18Arise, lift up the lad and hold him
with your hand, for I will make him a
great nation."

19Then God opened her eyes, and she
saw a well of water. And she went and
filled the skin with water, and gave the
lad a drink. 20So God was with the lad;
and he grew and dwelt in the wilderness,
and became an archer. 21He dwelt in the
Wilderness of Paran; and his mother
took a wife for him from the land of
Egypt.

A Covenant with Abimelech

22And it came to pass at that time
that Abimelech and Phichol, the com-
mander of his army, spoke to Abraham,
saying, "God *is* with you in all that you
do. 23Now therefore, swear to me by God
that you will not deal falsely with me,
with my offspring, or with my posterity;
but that according to the kindness that I
have done to you, you will do to me and
to the land in which you have dwelt."

24And Abraham said, "I will swear."

25Then Abraham rebuked Abimelech
because of a well of water which Abime-
lech's servants had seized. 26And Abim-
elech said, "I do not know who has done
this thing; you did not tell me, nor had
I heard *of it* until today." 27So Abraham
took sheep and oxen and gave them to
Abimelech, and the two of them made
a covenant. 28And Abraham set seven
ewe lambs of the flock by themselves.

29Then Abimelech asked Abraham,
"What *is the meaning of* these seven
ewe lambs which you have set by them-
selves?"

30And he said, "You will take *these* sev-
en ewe lambs from my hand, that they
may be my witness that I have dug this
well." 31Therefore he called that place
Beersheba,[a] because the two of them
swore an oath there.

32Thus they made a covenant at Beer-
sheba. So Abimelech rose with Phichol,
the commander of his army, and they
returned to the land of the Philistines.
33Then *Abraham* planted a tamarisk
tree in Beersheba, and there called on
the name of the LORD, the Everlasting
God. 34And Abraham stayed in the land
of the Philistines many days.

Abraham's Faith Confirmed

22 Now it came to pass after these
things that God tested Abraham,
and said to him, "Abraham!"

And he said, "Here I am."

2Then He said, "Take now your son,
your only *son* Isaac, whom you love,
and go to the land of Moriah, and offer
him there as a burnt offering on one of
the mountains of which I shall tell you."

3So Abraham rose early in the morn-
ing and saddled his donkey, and took
two of his young men with him, and
Isaac his son; and he split the wood
for the burnt offering, and arose and
went to the place of which God had told
him. 4Then on the third day Abraham
lifted his eyes and saw the place afar
off. 5And Abraham said to his young
men, "Stay here with the donkey; the
lad[a] and I will go yonder and worship,
and we will come back to you."

6So Abraham took the wood of the
burnt offering and laid *it* on Isaac his
son; and he took the fire in his hand,
and a knife, and the two of them went
together. 7But Isaac spoke to Abraham
his father and said, "My father!"

And he said, "Here I am, my son."

Then he said, "Look, the fire and the
wood, but where *is* the lamb for a burnt
offering?"

21:31 [a] Literally *Well of the Oath* or *Well of the Seven*

22:5 [a] Or *young man*

[8]And Abraham said, "My son, God
will provide for Himself the lamb for
a burnt offering." So the two of them
went together.
[9]Then they came to the place of which
God had told him. And Abraham built
an altar there and placed the wood in
order; and he bound Isaac his son and
laid him on the altar, upon the wood.
[10]And Abraham stretched out his hand
and took the knife to slay his son.
[11]But the Angel of the LORD called to
him from heaven and said, "Abraham,
Abraham!"
So he said, "Here I am."
[12]And He said, "Do not lay your hand
on the lad, or do anything to him; for
now I know that you fear God, since you
have not withheld your son, your only
son, from Me."
[13]Then Abraham lifted his eyes and
looked, and there behind *him was* a ram
caught in a thicket by its horns. So Abra-
ham went and took the ram, and offered
it up for a burnt offering instead of his
son. [14]And Abraham called the name of
the place, The-LORD-Will-Provide;[a] as it
is said *to* this day, "In the Mount of the
LORD it shall be provided."
[15]Then the Angel of the LORD called to
Abraham a second time out of heaven,
[16]and said: "By Myself I have sworn,
says the LORD, because you have done
this thing, and have not withheld your
son, your only *son*— [17]blessing I will
bless you, and multiplying I will mul-
tiply your descendants as the stars of
the heaven and as the sand which *is* on
the seashore; and your descendants
shall possess the gate of their enemies.
[18]In your seed all the nations of the
earth shall be blessed, because you
have obeyed My voice." [19]So Abraham
returned to his young men, and they
rose and went together to Beersheba;
and Abraham dwelt at Beersheba.

The Family of Nahor

[20]Now it came to pass after these things
that it was told Abraham, saying, "In-
deed Milcah also has borne children to
your brother Nahor: [21]Huz his firstborn,
Buz his brother, Kemuel the father of
Aram, [22]Chesed, Hazo, Pildash, Jidlaph,
and Bethuel." [23]And Bethuel begot Re-
bekah.[a] These eight Milcah bore to Nahor,
Abraham's brother. [24]His concubine,
whose name was Reumah, also bore
Tebah, Gaham, Thahash, and Maachah.

Sarah's Death and Burial

23 Sarah lived one hundred and
twenty-seven years; *these were*
the years of the life of Sarah. [2]So Sarah
died in Kirjath Arba (that *is,* Hebron) in
the land of Canaan, and Abraham came
to mourn for Sarah and to weep for her.
[3]Then Abraham stood up from before
his dead, and spoke to the sons of Heth,
saying, [4]"I *am* a foreigner and a visitor
among you. Give me property for a
burial place among you, that I may
bury my dead out of my sight."
[5]And the sons of Heth answered Abra-
ham, saying to him, [6]"Hear us, my lord:
You *are* a mighty prince among us;
bury your dead in the choicest of our
burial places. None of us will withhold
from you his burial place, that you may
bury your dead."
[7]Then Abraham stood up and bowed
himself to the people of the land, the sons
of Heth. [8]And he spoke with them, saying,
"If it is your wish that I bury my dead
out of my sight, hear me, and meet with
Ephron the son of Zohar for me, [9]that he
may give me the cave of Machpelah which
he has, which *is* at the end of his field.
Let him give it to me at the full price, as
property for a burial place among you."
[10]Now Ephron dwelt among the sons of
Heth; and Ephron the Hittite answered
Abraham in the presence of the sons of
Heth, all who entered at the gate of his
city, saying, [11]"No, my lord, hear me: I
give you the field and the cave that *is*
in it; I give it to you in the presence of
the sons of my people. I give it to you.
Bury your dead!"
[12]Then Abraham bowed himself down
before the people of the land; [13]and he
spoke to Ephron in the hearing of the
people of the land, saying, "If you *will*
give it, please hear me. I will give you
money for the field; take *it* from me and
I will bury my dead there."

22:14 [a] Hebrew *YHWH Yireh* 22:23 [a] Spelled *Rebecca* in Romans 9:10

14And Ephron answered Abraham,
saying to him, 15"My lord, listen to me;
the land *is worth* four hundred shekels
of silver. What *is* that between you and
me? So bury your dead." 16And Abra-
ham listened to Ephron; and Abraham
weighed out the silver for Ephron which
he had named in the hearing of the sons
of Heth, four hundred shekels of silver,
currency of the merchants.
17So the field of Ephron which *was* in
Machpelah, which *was* before Mamre,
the field and the cave which *was* in it,
and all the trees that *were* in the field,
which *were* within all the surrounding
borders, were deeded 18to Abraham
as a possession in the presence of the
sons of Heth, before all who went in at
the gate of his city.
19And after this, Abraham buried
Sarah his wife in the cave of the field
of Machpelah, before Mamre (that *is*,
Hebron) in the land of Canaan. 20So
the field and the cave that *is* in it were
deeded to Abraham by the sons of Heth
as property for a burial place.

A Bride for Isaac

24 Now Abraham was old, well ad-
vanced in age; and the LORD
had blessed Abraham in all things. 2So
Abraham said to the oldest servant of
his house, who ruled over all that he
had, "Please, put your hand under my
thigh, 3and I will make you swear by the
LORD, the God of heaven and the God of
the earth, that you will not take a wife
for my son from the daughters of the
Canaanites, among whom I dwell; 4but
you shall go to my country and to my
family, and take a wife for my son Isaac."
5And the servant said to him, "Perhaps
the woman will not be willing to follow
me to this land. Must I take your son
back to the land from which you came?"
6But Abraham said to him, "Beware
that you do not take my son back there.
7The LORD God of heaven, who took me
from my father's house and from the
land of my family, and who spoke to me
and swore to me, saying, 'To your de-
scendants[a] I give this land,' He will send
His angel before you, and you shall take
a wife for my son from there. 8And if the
woman is not willing to follow you, then
you will be released from this oath; only
do not take my son back there." 9So the
servant put his hand under the thigh of
Abraham his master, and swore to him
concerning this matter.
10Then the servant took ten of his mas-
ter's camels and departed, for all his mas-
ter's goods *were in* his hand. And he arose
and went to Mesopotamia, to the city of
Nahor. 11And he made his camels kneel
down outside the city by a well of water
at evening time, the time when women go
out to draw *water*. 12Then he said, "O LORD
God of my master Abraham, please give
me success this day, and show kindness
to my master Abraham. 13Behold, *here* I
stand by the well of water, and the daugh-
ters of the men of the city are coming
out to draw water. 14Now let it be that the
young woman to whom I say, 'Please let
down your pitcher that I may drink,' and
she says, 'Drink, and I will also give your
camels a drink'—*let* her *be the one* You
have appointed for Your servant Isaac.
And by this I will know that You have
shown kindness to my master."
15And it happened, before he had fin-
ished speaking, that behold, Rebekah,
who was born to Bethuel, son of Milcah,
the wife of Nahor, Abraham's brother,
came out with her pitcher on her shoul-
der. 16Now the young woman *was* very
beautiful to behold, a virgin; no man
had known her. And she went down to
the well, filled her pitcher, and came up.
17And the servant ran to meet her and
said, "Please let me drink a little water
from your pitcher."
18So she said, "Drink, my lord." Then
she quickly let her pitcher down to her
hand, and gave him a drink. 19And when
she had finished giving him a drink,
she said, "I will draw *water* for your
camels also, until they have finished
drinking." 20Then she quickly emptied
her pitcher into the trough, ran back to
the well to draw *water*, and drew for all
his camels. 21And the man, wondering
at her, remained silent so as to know
whether the LORD had made his journey
prosperous or not.

24:7 [a] Literally *seed*

22So it was, when the camels had
finished drinking, that the man took
a golden nose ring weighing half a
shekel, and two bracelets for her wrists
weighing ten *shekels* of gold, 23and said,
"Whose daughter *are* you? Tell me,
please, is there room *in* your father's
house for us to lodge?"

24So she said to him, "I *am* the daugh-
ter of Bethuel, Milcah's son, whom she
bore to Nahor." 25Moreover she said
to him, "We have both straw and feed
enough, and room to lodge."

26Then the man bowed down his head
and worshiped the LORD. 27And he said,
"Blessed *be* the LORD God of my master
Abraham, who has not forsaken His
mercy and His truth toward my mas-
ter. As for me, being on the way, the
LORD led me to the house of my mas-
ter's brethren." 28So the young woman
ran and told her mother's household
these things.

29Now Rebekah had a brother whose
name *was* Laban, and Laban ran out
to the man by the well. 30So it came to
pass, when he saw the nose ring, and the
bracelets on his sister's wrists, and when
he heard the words of his sister Rebekah,
saying, "Thus the man spoke to me," that
he went to the man. And there he stood
by the camels at the well. 31And he said,
"Come in, O blessed of the LORD! Why do
you stand outside? For I have prepared
the house, and a place for the camels."

32Then the man came to the house.
And he unloaded the camels, and pro-
vided straw and feed for the camels,
and water to wash his feet and the feet
of the men who *were* with him. 33*Food*
was set before him to eat, but he said,
"I will not eat until I have told about
my errand."

And he said, "Speak on."

34So he said, "I *am* Abraham's ser-
vant. 35The LORD has blessed my mas-
ter greatly, and he has become great;
and He has given him flocks and herds,
silver and gold, male and female ser-
vants, and camels and donkeys. 36And
Sarah my master's wife bore a son to my
master when she was old; and to him
he has given all that he has. 37Now my
master made me swear, saying, 'You
shall not take a wife for my son from the
daughters of the Canaanites, in whose
land I dwell; 38but you shall go to my
father's house and to my family, and
take a wife for my son.' 39And I said to
my master, 'Perhaps the woman will
not follow me.' 40But he said to me, 'The
LORD, before whom I walk, will send His
angel with you and prosper your way;
and you shall take a wife for my son
from my family and from my father's
house. 41You will be clear from this oath
when you arrive among my family; for
if they will not give *her* to you, then you
will be released from my oath.'

42"And this day I came to the well and
said, 'O LORD God of my master Abra-
ham, if You will now prosper the way
in which I go, 43behold, I stand by the
well of water; and it shall come to pass
that when the virgin comes out to draw
water, and I say to her, "Please give me
a little water from your pitcher to drink,"
44and she says to me, "Drink, and I will
draw for your camels also,"—*let* her *be*
the woman whom the LORD has ap-
pointed for my master's son.'

45"But before I had finished speaking
in my heart, there was Rebekah, coming
out with her pitcher on her shoulder;
and she went down to the well and drew
water. And I said to her, 'Please let me
drink.' 46And she made haste and let
her pitcher down from her *shoulder,* and
said, 'Drink, and I will give your camels
a drink also.' So I drank, and she gave
the camels a drink also. 47Then I asked
her, and said, 'Whose daughter *are* you?'
And she said, 'The daughter of Bethu-
el, Nahor's son, whom Milcah bore to
him.' So I put the nose ring on her nose
and the bracelets on her wrists. 48And
I bowed my head and worshiped the
LORD, and blessed the LORD God of my
master Abraham, who had led me in the
way of truth to take the daughter of my
master's brother for his son. 49Now if
you will deal kindly and truly with my
master, tell me. And if not, tell me, that I
may turn to the right hand or to the left."

50Then Laban and Bethuel answered
and said, "The thing comes from the
LORD; we cannot speak to you either bad
or good. 51Here *is* Rebekah before you;
take *her* and go, and let her be your mas-
ter's son's wife, as the LORD has spoken."

52And it came to pass, when Abra-
ham's servant heard their words, that
he worshiped the LORD, *bowing himself*
to the earth. 53Then the servant brought
out jewelry of silver, jewelry of gold, and
clothing, and gave *them* to Rebekah. He
also gave precious things to her brother
and to her mother.
54And he and the men who *were* with
him ate and drank and stayed all night.
Then they arose in the morning, and
he said, "Send me away to my master."
55But her brother and her mother said,
"Let the young woman stay with us *a
few* days, at least ten; after that she
may go."
56And he said to them, "Do not hinder
me, since the LORD has prospered my
way; send me away so that I may go
to my master."
57So they said, "We will call the young
woman and ask her personally." 58Then
they called Rebekah and said to her,
"Will you go with this man?"
And she said, "I will go."
59So they sent away Rebekah their
sister and her nurse, and Abraham's ser-
vant and his men. 60And they blessed
Rebekah and said to her:

"Our sister, *may* you *become*
The mother of thousands of ten
thousands;
And may your descendants
possess
The gates of those who hate them."

61Then Rebekah and her maids arose,
and they rode on the camels and fol-
lowed the man. So the servant took Re-
bekah and departed.
62Now Isaac came from the way of
Beer Lahai Roi, for he dwelt in the South.
63And Isaac went out to meditate in the
field in the evening; and he lifted his
eyes and looked, and there, the camels
were coming. 64Then Rebekah lifted
her eyes, and when she saw Isaac she
dismounted from her camel; 65for she
had said to the servant, "Who *is* this
man walking in the field to meet us?"
The servant said, "It *is* my master."
So she took a veil and covered herself.
66And the servant told Isaac all the
things that he had done. 67Then Isaac
brought her into his mother Sarah's
tent; and he took Rebekah and she be-
came his wife, and he loved her. So Isaac
was comforted after his mother's *death*.

Abraham and Keturah

25 Abraham again took a wife, and
her name *was* Keturah. 2And
she bore him Zimran, Jokshan, Medan,
Midian, Ishbak, and Shuah. 3Jokshan
begot Sheba and Dedan. And the sons
of Dedan were Asshurim, Letushim, and
Leummim. 4And the sons of Midian
were Ephah, Epher, Hanoch, Abidah,
and Eldaah. All these *were* the children
of Keturah.
5And Abraham gave all that he had to
Isaac. 6But Abraham gave gifts to the
sons of the concubines which Abraham
had; and while he was still living he sent
them eastward, away from Isaac his
son, to the country of the east.

Abraham's Death and Burial

7This *is* the sum of the years of Abra-
ham's life which he lived: one hundred
and seventy-five years. 8Then Abraham
breathed his last and died in a good old
age, an old man and full *of years*, and
was gathered to his people. 9And his
sons Isaac and Ishmael buried him in
the cave of Machpelah, which *is* before
Mamre, in the field of Ephron the son
of Zohar the Hittite, 10the field which
Abraham purchased from the sons of
Heth. There Abraham was buried, and
Sarah his wife. 11And it came to pass,
after the death of Abraham, that God
blessed his son Isaac. And Isaac dwelt
at Beer Lahai Roi.

The Families of Ishmael and Isaac

12Now this *is* the genealogy of Ishma-
el, Abraham's son, whom Hagar the
Egyptian, Sarah's maidservant, bore to
Abraham. 13And these *were* the names
of the sons of Ishmael, by their names,
according to their generations: The first-
born of Ishmael, Nebajoth; then Kedar,
Adbeel, Mibsam, 14Mishma, Dumah,
Massa, 15Hadar,[a] Tema, Jetur, Naphish,

25:15 [a] Masoretic Text reads *Hadad*.

and Kedemah. 16These *were* the sons of Ishmael and these *were* their names, by their towns and their settlements, twelve princes according to their nations. 17These *were* the years of the life of Ishmael: one hundred and thirty-seven years; and he breathed his last and died, and was gathered to his people. 18(They dwelt from Havilah as far as Shur, which *is* east of Egypt as you go toward Assyria.) He died in the presence of all his brethren.

19This *is* the genealogy of Isaac, Abraham's son. Abraham begot Isaac. 20Isaac was forty years old when he took Rebekah as wife, the daughter of Bethuel the Syrian of Padan Aram, the sister of Laban the Syrian. 21Now Isaac pleaded with the LORD for his wife, because she *was* barren; and the LORD granted his plea, and Rebekah his wife conceived. 22But the children struggled together within her; and she said, "If *all is* well, why *am I like* this?" So she went to inquire of the LORD.

23And the LORD said to her:

"Two nations *are* in your womb,
Two peoples shall be separated
from your body;
One people shall be stronger than
the other,
And the older shall serve the
younger."

24So when her days were fulfilled *for her* to give birth, indeed *there were* twins in her womb. 25And the first came out red. *He was* like a hairy garment all over; so they called his name Esau.[a] 26Afterward his brother came out, and his hand took hold of Esau's heel; so his name was called Jacob.[a] Isaac *was* sixty years old when she bore them.

27So the boys grew. And Esau was a skillful hunter, a man of the field; but Jacob was a mild man, dwelling in tents. 28And Isaac loved Esau because he ate *of his* game, but Rebekah loved Jacob.

Esau Sells His Birthright

29Now Jacob cooked a stew; and Esau came in from the field, and he *was* weary. 30And Esau said to Jacob, "Please feed me with that same red *stew,* for I *am* weary." Therefore his name was called Edom.[a]

31But Jacob said, "Sell me your birthright as of this day."

32And Esau said, "Look, I *am* about to die; so what *is* this birthright to me?"

33Then Jacob said, "Swear to me as of this day."

So he swore to him, and sold his birthright to Jacob. 34And Jacob gave Esau bread and stew of lentils; then he ate and drank, arose, and went his way. Thus Esau despised *his* birthright.

Isaac and Abimelech

26 There was a famine in the land, besides the first famine that was in the days of Abraham. And Isaac went to Abimelech king of the Philistines, in Gerar.

2Then the LORD appeared to him and said: "Do not go down to Egypt; live in the land of which I shall tell you. 3Dwell in this land, and I will be with you and bless you; for to you and your descendants I give all these lands, and I will perform the oath which I swore to Abraham your father. 4And I will make your descendants multiply as the stars of heaven; I will give to your descendants all these lands; and in your seed all the nations of the earth shall be blessed; 5because Abraham obeyed My voice and kept My charge, My commandments, My statutes, and My laws."

6So Isaac dwelt in Gerar. 7And the men of the place asked about his wife. And he said, "She *is* my sister"; for he was afraid to say, "*She is* my wife," *because he thought,* "lest the men of the place kill me for Rebekah, because she *is* beautiful to behold." 8Now it came to pass, when he had been there a long time, that Abimelech king of the Philistines looked through a window, and saw, and there was Isaac, showing endearment to Rebekah his wife. 9Then Abimelech called Isaac and said, "Quite obviously she *is* your wife; so how could you say, 'She *is* my sister'?"

Isaac said to him, "Because I said, 'Lest I die on account of her.' "

25:25 [a] Literally *Hairy* **25:26** [a] Literally *Supplanter* **25:30** [a] Literally *Red*

10And Abimelech said, "What *is* this
you have done to us? One of the people
might soon have lain with your wife,
and you would have brought guilt on
us." 11So Abimelech charged all *his* peo-
ple, saying, "He who touches this man
or his wife shall surely be put to death."
12Then Isaac sowed in that land, and
reaped in the same year a hundredfold;
and the LORD blessed him. 13The man
began to prosper, and continued pros-
pering until he became very prosper-
ous; 14for he had possessions of flocks
and possessions of herds and a great
number of servants. So the Philistines
envied him. 15Now the Philistines had
stopped up all the wells which his fa-
ther's servants had dug in the days of
Abraham his father, and they had filled
them with earth. 16And Abimelech said
to Isaac, "Go away from us, for you are
much mightier than we."
17Then Isaac departed from there and
pitched his tent in the Valley of Gerar,
and dwelt there. 18And Isaac dug again
the wells of water which they had dug
in the days of Abraham his father, for
the Philistines had stopped them up
after the death of Abraham. He called
them by the names which his father
had called them.
19Also Isaac's servants dug in the val-
ley, and found a well of running water
there. 20But the herdsmen of Gerar
quarreled with Isaac's herdsmen, say-
ing, "The water *is* ours." So he called
the name of the well Esek,[a] because
they quarreled with him. 21Then they
dug another well, and they quarreled
over that *one* also. So he called its name
Sitnah.[a] 22And he moved from there
and dug another well, and they did not
quarrel over it. So he called its name
Rehoboth,[a] because he said, "For now
the LORD has made room for us, and we
shall be fruitful in the land."
23Then he went up from there to Be-
ersheba. 24And the LORD appeared to
him the same night and said, "I *am* the
God of your father Abraham; do not
fear, for I *am* with you. I will bless you
and multiply your descendants for My
servant Abraham's sake." 25So he built
an altar there and called on the name of
the LORD, and he pitched his tent there;
and there Isaac's servants dug a well.
26Then Abimelech came to him from
Gerar with Ahuzzath, one of his friends,
and Phichol the commander of his
army. 27And Isaac said to them, "Why
have you come to me, since you hate
me and have sent me away from you?"
28But they said, "We have certainly
seen that the LORD is with you. So we
said, 'Let there now be an oath between
us, between you and us; and let us make
a covenant with you, 29that you will do
us no harm, since we have not touched
you, and since we have done nothing to
you but good and have sent you away
in peace. You *are* now the blessed of
the LORD.' "
30So he made them a feast, and they
ate and drank. 31Then they arose early
in the morning and swore an oath with
one another; and Isaac sent them away,
and they departed from him in peace.
32It came to pass the same day that
Isaac's servants came and told him
about the well which they had dug, and
said to him, "We have found water."
33So he called it Shebah.[a] Therefore
the name of the city *is* Beersheba[b] to
this day.
34When Esau was forty years old, he
took as wives Judith the daughter of
Beeri the Hittite, and Basemath the
daughter of Elon the Hittite. 35And they
were a grief of mind to Isaac and Re-
bekah.

Isaac Blesses Jacob

27 Now it came to pass, when Isaac
was old and his eyes were so dim
that he could not see, that he called
Esau his older son and said to him, "My
son."
And he answered him, "Here I am."
2Then he said, "Behold now, I am old. I
do not know the day of my death. 3Now
therefore, please take your weapons,
your quiver and your bow, and go out
to the field and hunt game for me. 4And
make me savory food, such as I love,
and bring *it* to me that I may eat, that
my soul may bless you before I die."

26:20 [a] Literally *Quarrel* **26:21** [a] Literally *Enmity* **26:22** [a] Literally *Spaciousness*
26:33 [a] Literally *Oath* or *Seven* [b] Literally *Well of the Oath* or *Well of the Seven*

5 Now Rebekah was listening when
Isaac spoke to Esau his son. And Esau
went to the field to hunt game and to
bring *it.* 6 So Rebekah spoke to Jacob her
son, saying, "Indeed I heard your father
speak to Esau your brother, saying,
7 'Bring me game and make savory food
for me, that I may eat it and bless you
in the presence of the LORD before my
death.' 8 Now therefore, my son, obey
my voice according to what I command
you. 9 Go now to the flock and bring me
from there two choice kids of the goats,
and I will make savory food from them
for your father, such as he loves. 10 Then
you shall take *it* to your father, that he
may eat *it,* and that he may bless you
before his death."

11 And Jacob said to Rebekah his
mother, "Look, Esau my brother *is* a
hairy man, and I *am* a smooth-*skinned*
man. 12 Perhaps my father will feel me,
and I shall seem to be a deceiver to him;
and I shall bring a curse on myself and
not a blessing."

13 But his mother said to him, "*Let* your
curse *be* on me, my son; only obey my
voice, and go, get *them* for me." 14 And
he went and got *them* and brought *them*
to his mother, and his mother made
savory food, such as his father loved.
15 Then Rebekah took the choice clothes
of her elder son Esau, which *were* with
her in the house, and put them on Jacob
her younger son. 16 And she put the skins
of the kids of the goats on his hands and
on the smooth part of his neck. 17 Then
she gave the savory food and the bread,
which she had prepared, into the hand
of her son Jacob.

18 So he went to his father and said,
"My father."

And he said, "Here I am. Who *are* you,
my son?"

19 Jacob said to his father, "I *am* Esau
your firstborn; I have done just as you
told me; please arise, sit and eat of my
game, that your soul may bless me."

20 But Isaac said to his son, "How *is it* that
you have found *it* so quickly, my son?"

And he said, "Because the LORD your
God brought *it* to me."

21 Isaac said to Jacob, "Please come
near, that I may feel you, my son,
whether you *are* really my son Esau
or not." 22 So Jacob went near to Isaac
his father, and he felt him and said, "The
voice *is* Jacob's voice, but the hands *are*
the hands of Esau." 23 And he did not
recognize him, because his hands were
hairy like his brother Esau's hands; so
he blessed him.

24 Then he said, "*Are* you really my
son Esau?"

He said, "I *am.*"

25 He said, "Bring *it* near to me, and I
will eat of my son's game, so that my
soul may bless you." So he brought *it*
near to him, and he ate; and he brought
him wine, and he drank. 26 Then his fa-
ther Isaac said to him, "Come near now
and kiss me, my son." 27 And he came
near and kissed him; and he smelled
the smell of his clothing, and blessed
him and said:

"Surely, the smell of my son
Is like the smell of a field
Which the LORD has blessed.
28 Therefore may God give you
Of the dew of heaven,
Of the fatness of the earth,
And plenty of grain and wine.
29 Let peoples serve you,
And nations bow down to you.
Be master over your brethren,
And let your mother's sons bow
down to you.
Cursed *be* everyone who curses
you,
And blessed *be* those who bless
you!"

Esau's Lost Hope

30 Now it happened, as soon as Isaac
had finished blessing Jacob, and Jacob
had scarcely gone out from the presence
of Isaac his father, that Esau his brother
came in from his hunting. 31 He also had
made savory food, and brought it to his
father, and said to his father, "Let my
father arise and eat of his son's game,
that your soul may bless me."

32 And his father Isaac said to him,
"Who *are* you?"

So he said, "I *am* your son, your first-
born, Esau."

33 Then Isaac trembled exceedingly,
and said, "Who? Where *is* the one who
hunted game and brought *it* to me?

I ate all *of it* before you came, and I
have blessed him—*and* indeed he shall
be blessed."
34When Esau heard the words of his
father, he cried with an exceedingly
great and bitter cry, and said to his fa-
ther, "Bless me—me also, O my father!"
35But he said, "Your brother came
with deceit and has taken away your
blessing."
36And *Esau* said, "Is he not rightly
named Jacob? For he has supplanted
me these two times. He took away my
birthright, and now look, he has taken
away my blessing!" And he said, "Have
you not reserved a blessing for me?"
37Then Isaac answered and said to
Esau, "Indeed I have made him your
master, and all his brethren I have given
to him as servants; with grain and wine
I have sustained him. What shall I do
now for you, my son?"
38And Esau said to his father, "Have
you only one blessing, my father? Bless
me—me also, O my father!" And Esau
lifted up his voice and wept.
39Then Isaac his father answered and
said to him:

"Behold, your dwelling shall be of
the fatness of the earth,
And of the dew of heaven from
above.
40 By your sword you shall live,
And you shall serve your brother;
And it shall come to pass, when
you become restless,
That you shall break his yoke
from your neck."

Jacob Escapes from Esau

41So Esau hated Jacob because of the
blessing with which his father blessed
him, and Esau said in his heart, "The
days of mourning for my father are at
hand; then I will kill my brother Jacob."
42And the words of Esau her older son
were told to Rebekah. So she sent and
called Jacob her younger son, and said
to him, "Surely your brother Esau com-
forts himself concerning you *by intend-
ing* to kill you. 43Now therefore, my son,
obey my voice: arise, flee to my brother
Laban in Haran. 44And stay with him a
few days, until your brother's fury turns
away, 45until your brother's anger turns
away from you, and he forgets what you
have done to him; then I will send and
bring you from there. Why should I be
bereaved also of you both in one day?"
46And Rebekah said to Isaac, "I am
weary of my life because of the daugh-
ters of Heth; if Jacob takes a wife of the
daughters of Heth, like these *who are*
the daughters of the land, what good
will my life be to me?"

28 Then Isaac called Jacob and
blessed him, and charged him,
and said to him: "You shall not take a
wife from the daughters of Canaan.
2Arise, go to Padan Aram, to the house
of Bethuel your mother's father; and
take yourself a wife from there of the
daughters of Laban your mother's
brother.

3 "May God Almighty bless you,
And make you fruitful and
multiply you,
That you may be an assembly of
peoples;
4 And give you the blessing of
Abraham,
To you and your descendants
with you,
That you may inherit the land
In which you are a stranger,
Which God gave to Abraham."

5So Isaac sent Jacob away, and he went
to Padan Aram, to Laban the son of
Bethuel the Syrian, the brother of Re-
bekah, the mother of Jacob and Esau.

Esau Marries Mahalath

6Esau saw that Isaac had blessed Ja-
cob and sent him away to Padan Aram
to take himself a wife from there, *and
that* as he blessed him he gave him a
charge, saying, "You shall not take a
wife from the daughters of Canaan,"
7and that Jacob had obeyed his father
and his mother and had gone to Padan
Aram. 8Also Esau saw that the daugh-
ters of Canaan did not please his father
Isaac. 9So Esau went to Ishmael and
took Mahalath the daughter of Ishmael,
Abraham's son, the sister of Nebajoth,
to be his wife in addition to the wives
he had.

Jacob's Vow at Bethel

10 Now Jacob went out from Beersheba
and went toward Haran. 11 So he came
to a certain place and stayed there all
night, because the sun had set. And he
took one of the stones of that place and
put it at his head, and he lay down in
that place to sleep. 12 Then he dreamed,
and behold, a ladder *was* set up on the
earth, and its top reached to heaven;
and there the angels of God were as-
cending and descending on it.
13 And behold, the LORD stood above it
and said: "I *am* the LORD God of Abra-
ham your father and the God of Isaac;
the land on which you lie I will give
to you and your descendants. 14 Also
your descendants shall be as the dust
of the earth; you shall spread abroad
to the west and the east, to the north
and the south; and in you and in your
seed all the families of the earth shall
be blessed. 15 Behold, I *am* with you and
will keep you wherever you go, and will
bring you back to this land; for I will
not leave you until I have done what I
have spoken to you."
16 Then Jacob awoke from his sleep and
said, "Surely the LORD is in this place,
and I did not know *it*." 17 And he was
afraid and said, "How awesome *is* this
place! This *is* none other than the house
of God, and this *is* the gate of heaven!"
18 Then Jacob rose early in the morning,
and took the stone that he had put at his
head, set it up as a pillar, and poured oil
on top of it. 19 And he called the name of
that place Bethel;[a] but the name of that
city had been Luz previously. 20 Then Ja-
cob made a vow, saying, "If God will be
with me, and keep me in this way that I
am going, and give me bread to eat and
clothing to put on, 21 so that I come back
to my father's house in peace, then the
LORD shall be my God. 22 And this stone
which I have set as a pillar shall be God's
house, and of all that You give me I will
surely give a tenth to You."

Jacob Meets Rachel

29 So Jacob went on his journey
and came to the land of the peo-
ple of the East. 2 And he looked, and saw
a well in the field; and behold, there *were*
three flocks of sheep lying by it; for out
of that well they watered the flocks. A
large stone *was* on the well's mouth.
3 Now all the flocks would be gathered
there; and they would roll the stone
from the well's mouth, water the sheep,
and put the stone back in its place on
the well's mouth.
4 And Jacob said to them, "My breth-
ren, where *are* you from?"
And they said, "We *are* from Haran."
5 Then he said to them, "Do you know
Laban the son of Nahor?"
And they said, "We know him."
6 So he said to them, "Is he well?"
And they said, "*He is* well. And look,
his daughter Rachel is coming with
the sheep."
7 Then he said, "Look, *it is* still high day;
it is not time for the cattle to be gathered
together. Water the sheep, and go and
feed *them*."
8 But they said, "We cannot until all the
flocks are gathered together, and they
have rolled the stone from the well's
mouth; then we water the sheep."
9 Now while he was still speaking with
them, Rachel came with her father's
sheep, for she was a shepherdess. 10 And
it came to pass, when Jacob saw Ra-
chel the daughter of Laban his mother's
brother, and the sheep of Laban his
mother's brother, that Jacob went near
and rolled the stone from the well's
mouth, and watered the flock of Laban
his mother's brother. 11 Then Jacob kissed
Rachel, and lifted up his voice and wept.
12 And Jacob told Rachel that he *was* her
father's relative and that he *was* Rebek-
ah's son. So she ran and told her father.
13 Then it came to pass, when Laban
heard the report about Jacob his sister's
son, that he ran to meet him, and em-
braced him and kissed him, and brought
him to his house. So he told Laban all
these things. 14 And Laban said to him,
"Surely you *are* my bone and my flesh."
And he stayed with him for a month.

Jacob Marries Leah and Rachel

15 Then Laban said to Jacob, "Be-
cause you *are* my relative, should you

28:19 [a] Literally *House of God*

GOD SIN JESUS SALVATION LOVE

therefore serve me for nothing? Tell
me, what *should* your wages *be?*" 16Now
Laban had two daughters: the name of
the elder *was* Leah, and the name of
the younger *was* Rachel. 17Leah's eyes
were delicate, but Rachel was beautiful
of form and appearance.
18Now Jacob loved Rachel; so he said,
"I will serve you seven years for Rachel
your younger daughter."
19And Laban said, "*It is* better that I
give her to you than that I should give
her to another man. Stay with me." 20So
Jacob served seven years for Rachel,
and they seemed *only* a few days to
him because of the love he had for her.
21Then Jacob said to Laban, "Give *me*
my wife, for my days are fulfilled, that
I may go in to her." 22And Laban gath-
ered together all the men of the place
and made a feast. 23Now it came to pass
in the evening, that he took Leah his
daughter and brought her to Jacob; and
he went in to her. 24And Laban gave his
maid Zilpah to his daughter Leah *as* a
maid. 25So it came to pass in the morn-
ing, that behold, it *was* Leah. And he said
to Laban, "What is this you have done to
me? Was it not for Rachel that I served
you? Why then have you deceived me?"
26And Laban said, "It must not be done
so in our country, to give the younger
before the firstborn. 27Fulfill her week,
and we will give you this one also for
the service which you will serve with
me still another seven years."
28Then Jacob did so and fulfilled her
week. So he gave him his daughter Ra-
chel as wife also. 29And Laban gave his
maid Bilhah to his daughter Rachel as
a maid. 30Then *Jacob* also went in to
Rachel, and he also loved Rachel more
than Leah. And he served with Laban
still another seven years.

The Children of Jacob

31When the LORD saw that Leah *was* un-
loved, He opened her womb; but Rachel
was barren. 32So Leah conceived and
bore a son, and she called his name Reu-
ben;[a] for she said, "The LORD has surely
looked on my affliction. Now therefore,
my husband will love me." 33Then she
conceived again and bore a son, and
said, "Because the LORD has heard that
I *am* unloved, He has therefore given me
this *son* also." And she called his name
Simeon.[a] 34She conceived again and
bore a son, and said, "Now this time my
husband will become attached to me,
because I have borne him three sons."
Therefore his name was called Levi.[a]
35And she conceived again and bore
a son, and said, "Now I will praise the
LORD." Therefore she called his name
Judah.[a] Then she stopped bearing.

30 Now when Rachel saw that she
bore Jacob no children, Rachel
envied her sister, and said to Jacob,
"Give me children, or else I die!"
2And Jacob's anger was aroused
against Rachel, and he said, "*Am* I in
the place of God, who has withheld from
you the fruit of the womb?"
3So she said, "Here is my maid Bilhah;
go in to her, and she will bear *a child* on
my knees, that I also may have children
by her." 4Then she gave him Bilhah her
maid as wife, and Jacob went in to her.
5And Bilhah conceived and bore Jacob a
son. 6Then Rachel said, "God has judged
my case; and He has also heard my voice
and given me a son." Therefore she called
his name Dan.[a] 7And Rachel's maid Bil-
hah conceived again and bore Jacob a
second son. 8Then Rachel said, "With
great wrestlings I have wrestled with my
sister, *and* indeed I have prevailed." So
she called his name Naphtali.[a]
9When Leah saw that she had stopped
bearing, she took Zilpah her maid and
gave her to Jacob as wife. 10And Leah's
maid Zilpah bore Jacob a son. 11Then
Leah said, "A troop comes!"[a] So she
called his name Gad.[b] 12And Leah's
maid Zilpah bore Jacob a second son.
13Then Leah said, "I am happy, for the
daughters will call me blessed." So she
called his name Asher.[a]
14Now Reuben went in the days of
wheat harvest and found mandrakes
in the field, and brought them to his

29:32 [a] Literally *See, a Son* **29:33** [a] Literally *Heard* **29:34** [a] Literally *Attached* **29:35** [a] Literally *Praise* **30:6** [a] Literally *Judge* **30:8** [a] Literally *My Wrestling* **30:11** [a] Following Qere, Syriac, and Targum; Kethib, Septuagint, and Vulgate read *in fortune.* [b] Literally *Troop* or *Fortune*
30:13 [a] Literally *Happy*

mother Leah. Then Rachel said to Leah,
"Please give me *some* of your son's man-
drakes."
15But she said to her, "*Is it* a small
matter that you have taken away my
husband? Would you take away my
son's mandrakes also?"
And Rachel said, "Therefore he will lie
with you tonight for your son's man-
drakes."
16When Jacob came out of the field in
the evening, Leah went out to meet him
and said, "You must come in to me, for I
have surely hired you with my son's man-
drakes." And he lay with her that night.
17And God listened to Leah, and she
conceived and bore Jacob a fifth son.
18Leah said, "God has given me my
wages, because I have given my maid
to my husband." So she called his name
Issachar.[a] 19Then Leah conceived again
and bore Jacob a sixth son. 20And Leah
said, "God has endowed me *with* a good
endowment; now my husband will dwell
with me, because I have borne him six
sons." So she called his name Zebulun.[a]
21Afterward she bore a daughter, and
called her name Dinah.
22Then God remembered Rachel, and
God listened to her and opened her
womb. 23And she conceived and bore
a son, and said, "God has taken away
my reproach." 24So she called his name
Joseph,[a] and said, "The LORD shall add
to me another son."

Jacob's Agreement with Laban

25And it came to pass, when Rachel
had borne Joseph, that Jacob said to
Laban, "Send me away, that I may go
to my own place and to my country.
26Give *me* my wives and my children
for whom I have served you, and let
me go; for you know my service which
I have done for you."
27And Laban said to him, "Please *stay,*
if I have found favor in your eyes, *for*
I have learned by experience that the
LORD has blessed me for your sake."
28Then he said, "Name me your wages,
and I will give *it.*"
29So *Jacob* said to him, "You know
how I have served you and how your
livestock has been with me. 30For what
you had before I *came was* little, and it
has increased to a great amount; the
LORD has blessed you since my coming.
And now, when shall I also provide for
my own house?"
31So he said, "What shall I give you?"
And Jacob said, "You shall not give
me anything. If you will do this thing
for me, I will again feed and keep your
flocks: 32Let me pass through all your
flock today, removing from there all
the speckled and spotted sheep, and
all the brown ones among the lambs,
and the spotted and speckled among
the goats; and *these* shall be my wages.
33So my righteousness will answer for
me in time to come, when the subject of
my wages comes before you: every one
that *is* not speckled and spotted among
the goats, and brown among the lambs,
will be considered stolen, if *it is* with me."
34And Laban said, "Oh, that it were
according to your word!" 35So he re-
moved that day the male goats that
were speckled and spotted, all the fe-
male goats that were speckled and spot-
ted, every one that had *some* white in
it, and all the brown ones among the
lambs, and gave *them* into the hand
of his sons. 36Then he put three days'
journey between himself and Jacob,
and Jacob fed the rest of Laban's flocks.
37Now Jacob took for himself rods of
green poplar and of the almond and
chestnut trees, peeled white strips in
them, and exposed the white which *was*
in the rods. 38And the rods which he had
peeled, he set before the flocks in the
gutters, in the watering troughs where
the flocks came to drink, so that they
should conceive when they came to
drink. 39So the flocks conceived before
the rods, and the flocks brought forth
streaked, speckled, and spotted. 40Then
Jacob separated the lambs, and made
the flocks face toward the streaked and
all the brown in the flock of Laban; but
he put his own flocks by themselves and
did not put them with Laban's flock.
41And it came to pass, whenever the
stronger livestock conceived, that Ja-
cob placed the rods before the eyes of

30:18 [a] Literally *Wages* 30:20 [a] Literally *Dwelling* 30:24 [a] Literally *He Will Add*

the livestock in the gutters, that they might conceive among the rods. 42But when the flocks were feeble, he did not put *them* in; so the feebler were Laban's and the stronger Jacob's. 43Thus the man became exceedingly prosperous, and had large flocks, female and male servants, and camels and donkeys.

Jacob Flees from Laban

31 Now *Jacob* heard the words of Laban's sons, saying, "Jacob has taken away all that was our father's, and from what was our father's he has acquired all this wealth." 2And Jacob saw the countenance of Laban, and indeed it *was* not *favorable* toward him as before. 3Then the LORD said to Jacob, "Return to the land of your fathers and to your family, and I will be with you."

4So Jacob sent and called Rachel and Leah to the field, to his flock, 5and said to them, "I see your father's countenance, that it *is* not *favorable* toward me as before; but the God of my father has been with me. 6And you know that with all my might I have served your father. 7Yet your father has deceived me and changed my wages ten times, but God did not allow him to hurt me. 8If he said thus: 'The speckled shall be your wages,' then all the flocks bore speckled. And if he said thus: 'The streaked shall be your wages,' then all the flocks bore streaked. 9So God has taken away the livestock of your father and given *them* to me.

10"And it happened, at the time when the flocks conceived, that I lifted my eyes and saw in a dream, and behold, the rams which leaped upon the flocks *were* streaked, speckled, and gray-spotted. 11Then the Angel of God spoke to me in a dream, saying, 'Jacob.' And I said, 'Here I am.' 12And He said, 'Lift your eyes now and see, all the rams which leap on the flocks *are* streaked, speckled, and gray-spotted; for I have seen all that Laban is doing to you. 13I *am* the God of Bethel, where you anointed the pillar *and* where you made a vow to Me. Now arise, get out of this land, and return to the land of your family.' "

14Then Rachel and Leah answered and said to him, "Is there still any portion or inheritance for us in our father's house? 15Are we not considered strangers by him? For he has sold us, and also completely consumed our money. 16For all these riches which God has taken from our father are *really* ours and our children's; now then, whatever God has said to you, do it."

17Then Jacob rose and set his sons and his wives on camels. 18And he carried away all his livestock and all his possessions which he had gained, his acquired livestock which he had gained in Padan Aram, to go to his father Isaac in the land of Canaan. 19Now Laban had gone to shear his sheep, and Rachel had stolen the household idols that were her father's. 20And Jacob stole away, unknown to Laban the Syrian, in that he did not tell him that he intended to flee. 21So he fled with all that he had. He arose and crossed the river, and headed toward the mountains of Gilead.

Laban Pursues Jacob

22And Laban was told on the third day that Jacob had fled. 23Then he took his brethren with him and pursued him for seven days' journey, and he overtook him in the mountains of Gilead. 24But God had come to Laban the Syrian in a dream by night, and said to him, "Be careful that you speak to Jacob neither good nor bad."

25So Laban overtook Jacob. Now Jacob had pitched his tent in the mountains, and Laban with his brethren pitched in the mountains of Gilead.

26And Laban said to Jacob: "What have you done, that you have stolen away unknown to me, and carried away my daughters like captives *taken* with the sword? 27Why did you flee away secretly, and steal away from me, and not tell me; for I might have sent you away with joy and songs, with timbrel and harp? 28And you did not allow me to kiss my sons and my daughters. Now you have done foolishly in *so* doing. 29It is in my power to do you harm, but the God of your father spoke to me last night, saying, 'Be careful that you speak to Jacob neither good nor bad.' 30And now you have surely gone because you greatly long for your father's house, *but* why did you steal my gods?"

31Then Jacob answered and said to
Laban, "Because I was afraid, for I said,
'Perhaps you would take your daugh-
ters from me by force.' 32With whom-
ever you find your gods, do not let him
live. In the presence of our brethren,
identify what I have of yours and take
it with you." For Jacob did not know that
Rachel had stolen them.

33And Laban went into Jacob's tent,
into Leah's tent, and into the two maids'
tents, but he did not find *them*. Then
he went out of Leah's tent and entered
Rachel's tent. 34Now Rachel had taken
the household idols, put them in the
camel's saddle, and sat on them. And
Laban searched all about the tent but
did not find *them*. 35And she said to her
father, "Let it not displease my lord that
I cannot rise before you, for the manner
of women *is* with me." And he searched
but did not find the household idols.

36Then Jacob was angry and rebuked
Laban, and Jacob answered and said to
Laban: "What *is* my trespass? What *is*
my sin, that you have so hotly pursued
me? 37Although you have searched all
my things, what part of your household
things have you found? Set *it* here be-
fore my brethren and your brethren,
that they may judge between us both!
38These twenty years I *have been* with
you; your ewes and your female goats
have not miscarried their young, and I
have not eaten the rams of your flock.
39That which was torn *by beasts* I did
not bring to you; I bore the loss of it.
You required it from my hand, *wheth-
er* stolen by day or stolen by night.
40*There* I was! In the day the drought
consumed me, and the frost by night,
and my sleep departed from my eyes.
41Thus I have been in your house twenty
years; I served you fourteen years for
your two daughters, and six years for
your flock, and you have changed my
wages ten times. 42Unless the God of
my father, the God of Abraham and
the Fear of Isaac, had been with me,
surely now you would have sent me
away empty-handed. God has seen my
affliction and the labor of my hands,
and rebuked *you* last night."

Laban's Covenant with Jacob

43And Laban answered and said to Ja-
cob, "*These* daughters *are* my daughters,
and *these* children *are* my children, and
this flock *is* my flock; all that you see
is mine. But what can I do this day to
these my daughters or to their children
whom they have borne? 44Now there-
fore, come, let us make a covenant, you
and I, and let it be a witness between
you and me."

45So Jacob took a stone and set it up
as a pillar. 46Then Jacob said to his
brethren, "Gather stones." And they took
stones and made a heap, and they ate
there on the heap. 47Laban called it
Jegar Sahadutha,[a] but Jacob called it
Galeed.[b] 48And Laban said, "This heap *is*
a witness between you and me this day."
Therefore its name was called Galeed,
49also Mizpah,[a] because he said, "May
the LORD watch between you and me
when we are absent one from another.
50If you afflict my daughters, or if you
take *other* wives besides my daughters,
although no man *is* with us—see, God *is*
witness between you and me!"

51Then Laban said to Jacob, "Here is
this heap and here is *this* pillar, which
I have placed between you and me.
52This heap *is* a witness, and *this* pillar
is a witness, that I will not pass beyond
this heap to you, and you will not pass
beyond this heap and this pillar to me,
for harm. 53The God of Abraham, the
God of Nahor, and the God of their father
judge between us." And Jacob swore by
the Fear of his father Isaac. 54Then Ja-
cob offered a sacrifice on the mountain,
and called his brethren to eat bread.
And they ate bread and stayed all night
on the mountain. 55And early in the
morning Laban arose, and kissed his
sons and daughters and blessed them.
Then Laban departed and returned to
his place.

Esau Comes to Meet Jacob

32 So Jacob went on his way, and
the angels of God met him.
2When Jacob saw them, he said, "This
is God's camp." And he called the name
of that place Mahanaim.[a]

31:47 [a] Literally, in Aramaic, *Heap of Witness* [b] Literally, in Hebrew, *Heap of Witness*
31:49 [a] Literally *Watch* 32:2 [a] Literally *Double Camp*

3Then Jacob sent messengers before
him to Esau his brother in the land of
Seir, the country of Edom. 4And he com-
manded them, saying, "Speak thus to
my lord Esau, 'Thus your servant Ja-
cob says: "I have dwelt with Laban and
stayed there until now. 5I have oxen,
donkeys, flocks, and male and female
servants; and I have sent to tell my lord,
that I may find favor in your sight." ' "

6Then the messengers returned to Ja-
cob, saying, "We came to your brother
Esau, and he also is coming to meet
you, and four hundred men *are* with
him." 7So Jacob was greatly afraid and
distressed; and he divided the people
that *were* with him, and the flocks and
herds and camels, into two companies.
8And he said, "If Esau comes to the one
company and attacks it, then the other
company which is left will escape."

9Then Jacob said, "O God of my father
Abraham and God of my father Isaac,
the LORD who said to me, 'Return to
your country and to your family, and I
will deal well with you': 10I am not wor-
thy of the least of all the mercies and
of all the truth which You have shown
Your servant; for I crossed over this
Jordan with my staff, and now I have
become two companies. 11Deliver me, I
pray, from the hand of my brother, from
the hand of Esau; for I fear him, lest he
come and attack me *and* the mother
with the children. 12For You said, 'I will
surely treat you well, and make your de-
scendants as the sand of the sea, which
cannot be numbered for multitude.' "

13So he lodged there that same night,
and took what came to his hand as a
present for Esau his brother: 14two hun-
dred female goats and twenty male
goats, two hundred ewes and twenty
rams, 15thirty milk camels with their
colts, forty cows and ten bulls, twenty
female donkeys and ten foals. 16Then
he delivered *them* to the hand of his ser-
vants, every drove by itself, and said to
his servants, "Pass over before me, and
put some distance between successive
droves." 17And he commanded the first
one, saying, "When Esau my brother
meets you and asks you, saying, 'To
whom do you belong, and where are
you going? Whose *are* these in front
of you?' 18then you shall say, 'They *are*
your servant Jacob's. It *is* a present sent
to my lord Esau; and behold, he also *is*
behind us.' " 19So he commanded the
second, the third, and all who followed
the droves, saying, "In this manner you
shall speak to Esau when you find him;
20and also say, 'Behold, your servant
Jacob *is* behind us.' " For he said, "I will
appease him with the present that goes
before me, and afterward I will see his
face; perhaps he will accept me." 21So the
present went on over before him, but he
himself lodged that night in the camp.

Wrestling with God

22And he arose that night and took
his two wives, his two female servants,
and his eleven sons, and crossed over
the ford of Jabbok. 23He took them, sent
them over the brook, and sent over what
he had. 24Then Jacob was left alone;
and a Man wrestled with him until the
breaking of day. 25Now when He saw
that He did not prevail against him, He
touched the socket of his hip; and the
socket of Jacob's hip was out of joint as
He wrestled with him. 26And He said,
"Let Me go, for the day breaks."

But he said, "I will not let You go unless
You bless me!"

27So He said to him, "What *is* your
name?"

He said, "Jacob."

28And He said, "Your name shall no
longer be called Jacob, but Israel;[a] for
you have struggled with God and with
men, and have prevailed."

29Then Jacob asked, saying, "Tell *me*
Your name, I pray."

And He said, "Why *is* it *that* you ask
about My name?" And He blessed him
there.

30So Jacob called the name of the
place Peniel:[a] "For I have seen God
face to face, and my life is preserved."
31Just as he crossed over Penuel[a] the
sun rose on him, and he limped on his
hip. 32Therefore to this day the chil-
dren of Israel do not eat the muscle
that shrank, which *is* on the hip socket,

32:28 [a] Literally *Prince with God* **32:30** [a] Literally *Face of God* **32:31** [a] Same as *Peniel*, verse 30

because He touched the socket of Ja-
cob's hip in the muscle that shrank.

Jacob and Esau Meet

33 Now Jacob lifted his eyes and
looked, and there, Esau was
coming, and with him were four hun-
dred men. So he divided the children
among Leah, Rachel, and the two maid-
servants. 2And he put the maidservants
and their children in front, Leah and her
children behind, and Rachel and Joseph
last. 3Then he crossed over before them
and bowed himself to the ground seven
times, until he came near to his brother.
4But Esau ran to meet him, and em-
braced him, and fell on his neck and
kissed him, and they wept. 5And he
lifted his eyes and saw the women and
children, and said, "Who *are* these with
you?"
So he said, "The children whom God
has graciously given your servant."
6Then the maidservants came near,
they and their children, and bowed
down. 7And Leah also came near with
her children, and they bowed down.
Afterward Joseph and Rachel came
near, and they bowed down.
8Then Esau said, "What *do* you *mean*
by all this company which I met?"
And he said, "*These are* to find favor in
the sight of my lord."
9But Esau said, "I have enough, my
brother; keep what you have for yourself."
10And Jacob said, "No, please, if I have
now found favor in your sight, then
receive my present from my hand, in-
asmuch as I have seen your face as
though I had seen the face of God, and
you were pleased with me. 11Please,
take my blessing that is brought to you,
because God has dealt graciously with
me, and because I have enough." So he
urged him, and he took *it.*
12Then Esau said, "Let us take our jour-
ney; let us go, and I will go before you."
13But Jacob said to him, "My lord
knows that the children *are* weak, and
the flocks and herds which are nursing
are with me. And if the men should drive
them hard one day, all the flock will die.
14Please let my lord go on ahead before
his servant. I will lead on slowly at a
pace which the livestock that go before
me, and the children, are able to endure,
until I come to my lord in Seir."
15And Esau said, "Now let me leave with
you *some* of the people who *are* with me."
But he said, "What need is there? Let
me find favor in the sight of my lord."
16So Esau returned that day on his way
to Seir. 17And Jacob journeyed to Suc-
coth, built himself a house, and made
booths for his livestock. Therefore the
name of the place is called Succoth.[a]

Jacob Comes to Canaan

18Then Jacob came safely to the city
of Shechem, which *is* in the land of
Canaan, when he came from Padan
Aram; and he pitched his tent before
the city. 19And he bought the parcel
of land, where he had pitched his tent,
from the children of Hamor, Shechem's
father, for one hundred pieces of mon-
ey. 20Then he erected an altar there and
called it El Elohe Israel.[a]

The Dinah Incident

34 Now Dinah the daughter of Leah,
whom she had borne to Jacob,
went out to see the daughters of the land.
2And when Shechem the son of Hamor
the Hivite, prince of the country, saw her,
he took her and lay with her, and violat-
ed her. 3His soul was strongly attracted
to Dinah the daughter of Jacob, and he
loved the young woman and spoke kind-
ly to the young woman. 4So Shechem
spoke to his father Hamor, saying, "Get
me this young woman as a wife."
5And Jacob heard that he had defiled
Dinah his daughter. Now his sons were
with his livestock in the field; so Jacob
held his peace until they came. 6Then
Hamor the father of Shechem went out
to Jacob to speak with him. 7And the
sons of Jacob came in from the field
when they heard *it;* and the men were
grieved and very angry, because he
had done a disgraceful thing in Is-
rael by lying with Jacob's daughter,
a thing which ought not to be done.
8But Hamor spoke with them, saying,
"The soul of my son Shechem longs for

33:17 [a] Literally *Booths* 33:20 [a] Literally *God, the God of Israel* your daughter. Please give her to him as a wife. 9And make marriages with us; give your daughters to us, and take our daughters to yourselves. 10So you shall dwell with us, and the land shall be before you. Dwell and trade in it, and acquire possessions for yourselves in it."

11Then Shechem said to her father and her brothers, "Let me find favor in your eyes, and whatever you say to me I will give. 12Ask me ever so much dowry and gift, and I will give according to what you say to me; but give me the young woman as a wife."

13But the sons of Jacob answered Shechem and Hamor his father, and spoke deceitfully, because he had defiled Dinah their sister. 14And they said to them, "We cannot do this thing, to give our sister to one who is uncircumcised, for that *would be* a reproach to us. 15But on this *condition* we will consent to you: If you will become as we *are,* if every male of you is circumcised, 16then we will give our daughters to you, and we will take your daughters to us; and we will dwell with you, and we will become one people. 17But if you will not heed us and be circumcised, then we will take our daughter and be gone."

18And their words pleased Hamor and Shechem, Hamor's son. 19So the young man did not delay to do the thing, because he delighted in Jacob's daughter. He *was* more honorable than all the household of his father.

20And Hamor and Shechem his son came to the gate of their city, and spoke with the men of their city, saying: 21"These men *are* at peace with us. Therefore let them dwell in the land and trade in it. For indeed the land *is* large enough for them. Let us take their daughters to us as wives, and let us give them our daughters. 22Only on this *condition* will the men consent to dwell with us, to be one people: if every male among us is circumcised as they *are* circumcised. 23*Will* not their livestock, their property, and every animal of theirs *be* ours? Only let us consent to them, and they will dwell with us." 24And all who went out of the gate of his city heeded Hamor and Shechem his son; every male was circumcised, all who went out of the gate of his city.

25Now it came to pass on the third day, when they were in pain, that two of the sons of Jacob, Simeon and Levi, Dinah's brothers, each took his sword and came boldly upon the city and killed all the males. 26And they killed Hamor and Shechem his son with the edge of the sword, and took Dinah from Shechem's house, and went out. 27The sons of Jacob came upon the slain, and plundered the city, because their sister had been defiled. 28They took their sheep, their oxen, and their donkeys, what *was* in the city and what *was* in the field, 29and all their wealth. All their little ones and their wives they took captive; and they plundered even all that *was* in the houses.

30Then Jacob said to Simeon and Levi, "You have troubled me by making me obnoxious among the inhabitants of the land, among the Canaanites and the Perizzites; and since I *am* few in number, they will gather themselves together against me and kill me. I shall be destroyed, my household and I."

31But they said, "Should he treat our sister like a harlot?"

Jacob's Return to Bethel

35 Then God said to Jacob, "Arise, go up to Bethel and dwell there; and make an altar there to God, who appeared to you when you fled from the face of Esau your brother."

2And Jacob said to his household and to all who *were* with him, "Put away the foreign gods that *are* among you, purify yourselves, and change your garments. 3Then let us arise and go up to Bethel; and I will make an altar there to God, who answered me in the day of my distress and has been with me in the way which I have gone." 4So they gave Jacob all the foreign gods which *were* in their hands, and the earrings which *were* in their ears; and Jacob hid them under the terebinth tree which *was* by Shechem.

5And they journeyed, and the terror of God was upon the cities that *were* all around them, and they did not pursue the sons of Jacob. 6So Jacob came to Luz (that *is,* Bethel), which *is* in the land of

Canaan, he and all the people who *were*
with him. 7And he built an altar there
and called the place El Bethel,[a] because
there God appeared to him when he fled
from the face of his brother.
8Now Deborah, Rebekah's nurse, died,
and she was buried below Bethel under
the terebinth tree. So the name of it was
called Allon Bachuth.[a]
9Then God appeared to Jacob again,
when he came from Padan Aram, and
blessed him. 10And God said to him,
"Your name *is* Jacob; your name shall
not be called Jacob anymore, but Israel
shall be your name." So He called his
name Israel. 11Also God said to him:
"I *am* God Almighty. Be fruitful and
multiply; a nation and a company of
nations shall proceed from you, and
kings shall come from your body. 12The
land which I gave Abraham and Isaac
I give to you; and to your descendants
after you I give this land." 13Then God
went up from him in the place where
He talked with him. 14So Jacob set up a
pillar in the place where He talked with
him, a pillar of stone; and he poured a
drink offering on it, and he poured oil
on it. 15And Jacob called the name of the
place where God spoke with him, Bethel.

Death of Rachel

16Then they journeyed from Bethel.
And when there was but a little dis-
tance to go to Ephrath, Rachel labored
in childbirth, and she had hard labor.
17Now it came to pass, when she was
in hard labor, that the midwife said
to her, "Do not fear; you will have this
son also." 18And so it was, as her soul
was departing (for she died), that she
called his name Ben-Oni;[a] but his father
called him Benjamin.[b] 19So Rachel died
and was buried on the way to Ephrath
(that *is,* Bethlehem). 20And Jacob set a
pillar on her grave, which *is* the pillar
of Rachel's grave to this day.
21Then Israel journeyed and pitched
his tent beyond the tower of Eder. 22And
it happened, when Israel dwelt in that
land, that Reuben went and lay with
Bilhah his father's concubine; and Is-
rael heard *about it.*

Jacob's Twelve Sons

Now the sons of Jacob were twelve:
23the sons of Leah *were* Reuben, Jacob's
firstborn, and Simeon, Levi, Judah, Issa-
char, and Zebulun; 24the sons of Rachel
were Joseph and Benjamin; 25the sons
of Bilhah, Rachel's maidservant, *were*
Dan and Naphtali; 26and the sons of
Zilpah, Leah's maidservant, *were* Gad
and Asher. These *were* the sons of Jacob
who were born to him in Padan Aram.

Death of Isaac

27Then Jacob came to his father Isaac
at Mamre, or Kirjath Arba[a] (that *is,* He-
bron), where Abraham and Isaac had
dwelt. 28Now the days of Isaac were
one hundred and eighty years. 29So
Isaac breathed his last and died, and
was gathered to his people, *being* old
and full of days. And his sons Esau and
Jacob buried him.

The Family of Esau

36 Now this *is* the genealogy of
Esau, who is Edom. 2Esau took
his wives from the daughters of Canaan:
Adah the daughter of Elon the Hittite;
Aholibamah the daughter of Anah, the
daughter of Zibeon the Hivite; 3and
Basemath, Ishmael's daughter, sister
of Nebajoth. 4Now Adah bore Eliphaz to
Esau, and Basemath bore Reuel. 5And
Aholibamah bore Jeush, Jaalam, and
Korah. These *were* the sons of Esau who
were born to him in the land of Canaan.
6Then Esau took his wives, his sons,
his daughters, and all the persons of
his household, his cattle and all his an-
imals, and all his goods which he had
gained in the land of Canaan, and went
to a country away from the presence
of his brother Jacob. 7For their posses-
sions were too great for them to dwell
together, and the land where they were
strangers could not support them be-
cause of their livestock. 8So Esau dwelt
in Mount Seir. Esau *is* Edom.
9And this *is* the genealogy of Esau the
father of the Edomites in Mount Seir.
10These *were* the names of Esau's sons:
Eliphaz the son of Adah the wife of Esau,
and Reuel the son of Basemath the wife

35:7 [a] Literally *God of the House of God* 35:8 [a] Literally *Terebinth of Weeping* 35:18 [a] Literally *Son of My Sorrow* [b] Literally *Son of the Right Hand* 35:27 [a] Literally *Town of Arba*

of Esau. 11And the sons of Eliphaz were
Teman, Omar, Zepho,[a] Gatam, and Kenaz.
12Now Timna was the concubine of
Eliphaz, Esau's son, and she bore Am-
alek to Eliphaz. These *were* the sons of
Adah, Esau's wife.
13These *were* the sons of Reuel: Nahath,
Zerah, Shammah, and Mizzah. These
were the sons of Basemath, Esau's wife.
14These were the sons of Aholibamah,
Esau's wife, the daughter of Anah, the
daughter of Zibeon. And she bore to
Esau: Jeush, Jaalam, and Korah.

The Chiefs of Edom

15These *were* the chiefs of the sons of
Esau. The sons of Eliphaz, the firstborn
son of Esau, were Chief Teman, Chief
Omar, Chief Zepho, Chief Kenaz, 16Chief
Korah,[a] Chief Gatam, *and* Chief Amalek.
These *were* the chiefs of Eliphaz in the
land of Edom. They *were* the sons of Adah.
17These *were* the sons of Reuel, Esau's
son: Chief Nahath, Chief Zerah, Chief
Shammah, and Chief Mizzah. These
were the chiefs of Reuel in the land of
Edom. These *were* the sons of Basemath,
Esau's wife.
18And these *were* the sons of Aholi-
bamah, Esau's wife: Chief Jeush, Chief
Jaalam, and Chief Korah. These *were* the
chiefs *who descended* from Aholibamah,
Esau's wife, the daughter of Anah.
19These *were* the sons of Esau, who is
Edom, and these *were* their chiefs.

The Sons of Seir

20These *were* the sons of Seir the Horite
who inhabited the land: Lotan, Sho-
bal, Zibeon, Anah, 21Dishon, Ezer, and
Dishan. These *were* the chiefs of the
Horites, the sons of Seir, in the land
of Edom.
22And the sons of Lotan were Hori
and Hemam.[a] Lotan's sister *was* Timna.
23These *were* the sons of Shobal:
Alvan,[a] Manahath, Ebal, Shepho,[b] and
Onam.
24These *were* the sons of Zibeon: both
Ajah and Anah. This *was the* Anah who
found the water[a] in the wilderness as he
pastured the donkeys of his father Zibeon.
25These *were* the children of Anah: Dishon
and Aholibamah the daughter of Anah.
26These *were* the sons of Dishon:[a]
Hemdan,[b] Eshban, Ithran, and Cheran.
27These *were* the sons of Ezer: Bilhan,
Zaavan, and Akan.[a] 28These *were* the
sons of Dishan: Uz and Aran.
29These *were* the chiefs of the Horites:
Chief Lotan, Chief Shobal, Chief Zibeon,
Chief Anah, 30Chief Dishon, Chief Ezer,
and Chief Dishan. These *were* the chiefs
of the Horites, according to their chiefs
in the land of Seir.

The Kings of Edom

31Now these *were* the kings who reigned
in the land of Edom before any king
reigned over the children of Israel: 32Bela
the son of Beor reigned in Edom, and the
name of his city *was* Dinhabah. 33And
when Bela died, Jobab the son of Zerah
of Bozrah reigned in his place. 34When
Jobab died, Husham of the land of the Te-
manites reigned in his place. 35And when
Husham died, Hadad the son of Bedad,
who attacked Midian in the field of Moab,
reigned in his place. And the name of
his city *was* Avith. 36When Hadad died,
Samlah of Masrekah reigned in his place.
37And when Samlah died, Saul of Reho-
both-*by*-the-River reigned in his place.
38When Saul died, Baal-Hanan the son of
Achbor reigned in his place. 39And when
Baal-Hanan the son of Achbor died, Ha-
dar[a] reigned in his place; and the name
of his city *was* Pau.[b] His wife's name *was*
Mehetabel, the daughter of Matred, the
daughter of Mezahab.

The Chiefs of Esau

40And these *were* the names of the
chiefs of Esau, according to their families
and their places, by their names: Chief
Timnah, Chief Alvah,[a] Chief Jetheth,

36:11 [a] Spelled *Zephi* in 1 Chronicles 1:36 **36:16** [a] Samaritan Pentateuch omits *Chief Korah.* **36:22** [a] Spelled *Homam* in 1 Chronicles 1:39 **36:23** [a] Spelled *Alian* in 1 Chronicles 1:40 [b] Spelled *Shephi* in 1 Chronicles 1:40 **36:24** [a] Following Masoretic Text and Vulgate (*hot springs*); Septuagint reads *Jamin;* Targum reads *mighty men;* Talmud interprets as *mules.* **36:26** [a] Hebrew *Dishan* [b] Spelled *Hamran* in 1 Chronicles 1:41 **36:27** [a] Spelled *Jaakan* in 1 Chronicles 1:42 **36:39** [a] Spelled *Hadad* in Samaritan Pentateuch, Syriac, and 1 Chronicles 1:50 [b] Spelled *Pai* in 1 Chronicles 1:50 **36:40** [a] Spelled *Aliah* in 1 Chronicles 1:51

[41]Chief Aholibamah, Chief Elah, Chief
Pinon, [42]Chief Kenaz, Chief Teman, Chief
Mibzar, [43]Chief Magdiel, and Chief Iram.
These *were* the chiefs of Edom, according
to their dwelling places in the land of
their possession. Esau *was* the father
of the Edomites.

Joseph Dreams of Greatness

37 Now Jacob dwelt in the land
where his father was a strang-
er, in the land of Canaan. [2]This *is* the
history of Jacob.
Joseph, *being* seventeen years old, was
feeding the flock with his brothers. And
the lad *was* with the sons of Bilhah and
the sons of Zilpah, his father's wives;
and Joseph brought a bad report of
them to his father.
[3]Now Israel loved Joseph more than
all his children, because he *was* the
son of his old age. Also he made him
a tunic of *many* colors. [4]But when his
brothers saw that their father loved
him more than all his brothers, they
hated him and could not speak peace-
ably to him.
[5]Now Joseph had a dream, and he told
it to his brothers; and they hated him
even more. [6]So he said to them, "Please
hear this dream which I have dreamed:
[7]There we were, binding sheaves in the
field. Then behold, my sheaf arose and
also stood upright; and indeed your
sheaves stood all around and bowed
down to my sheaf."
[8]And his brothers said to him, "Shall
you indeed reign over us? Or shall you
indeed have dominion over us?" So they
hated him even more for his dreams
and for his words.
[9]Then he dreamed still another dream
and told it to his brothers, and said,
"Look, I have dreamed another dream.
And this time, the sun, the moon, and
the eleven stars bowed down to me."
[10]So he told *it* to his father and his
brothers; and his father rebuked him
and said to him, "What *is* this dream
that you have dreamed? Shall your
mother and I and your brothers in-
deed come to bow down to the earth
before you?" [11]And his brothers envied
him, but his father kept the matter *in
mind.*

Joseph Sold by His Brothers

[12]Then his brothers went to feed their
father's flock in Shechem. [13]And Israel
said to Joseph, "Are not your brothers
feeding *the flock* in Shechem? Come, I
will send you to them."
So he said to him, "Here I am."
[14]Then he said to him, "Please go and
see if it is well with your brothers and
well with the flocks, and bring back
word to me." So he sent him out of the
Valley of Hebron, and he went to She-
chem.
[15]Now a certain man found him, and
there he was, wandering in the field.
And the man asked him, saying, "What
are you seeking?"
[16]So he said, "I am seeking my
brothers. Please tell me where they are
feeding *their flocks.*"
[17]And the man said, "They have depart-
ed from here, for I heard them say, 'Let
us go to Dothan.' " So Joseph went after
his brothers and found them in Dothan.
[18]Now when they saw him afar off,
even before he came near them, they
conspired against him to kill him.
[19]Then they said to one another, "Look,
this dreamer is coming! [20]Come there-
fore, let us now kill him and cast him
into some pit; and we shall say, 'Some
wild beast has devoured him.' We shall
see what will become of his dreams!"
[21]But Reuben heard *it,* and he deliv-
ered him out of their hands, and said,
"Let us not kill him." [22]And Reuben said
to them, "Shed no blood, *but* cast him
into this pit which *is* in the wilderness,
and do not lay a hand on him"—that
he might deliver him out of their hands,
and bring him back to his father.
[23]So it came to pass, when Joseph had
come to his brothers, that they stripped
Joseph *of* his tunic, the tunic of *many*
colors that *was* on him. [24]Then they took
him and cast him into a pit. And the
pit *was* empty; *there was* no water in it.
[25]And they sat down to eat a meal.
Then they lifted their eyes and looked,
and there was a company of Ishmael-
ites, coming from Gilead with their cam-
els, bearing spices, balm, and myrrh, on
their way to carry *them* down to Egypt.
[26]So Judah said to his brothers, "What
profit *is there* if we kill our brother and

conceal his blood? 27Come and let us sell
him to the Ishmaelites, and let not our
hand be upon him, for he *is* our brother
and our flesh." And his brothers listened.
28Then Midianite traders passed by; so
the brothers pulled Joseph up and lifted
him out of the pit, and sold him to the
Ishmaelites for twenty *shekels* of silver.
And they took Joseph to Egypt.

29Then Reuben returned to the pit, and
indeed Joseph *was* not in the pit; and
he tore his clothes. 30And he returned
to his brothers and said, "The lad *is* no
more; and I, where shall I go?"

31So they took Joseph's tunic, killed a
kid of the goats, and dipped the tunic
in the blood. 32Then they sent the tunic
of *many* colors, and they brought *it* to
their father and said, "We have found
this. Do you know whether it *is* your
son's tunic or not?"

33And he recognized it and said, "*It*
is my son's tunic. A wild beast has de-
voured him. Without doubt Joseph is
torn to pieces." 34Then Jacob tore his
clothes, put sackcloth on his waist, and
mourned for his son many days. 35And
all his sons and all his daughters arose
to comfort him; but he refused to be
comforted, and he said, "For I shall
go down into the grave to my son in
mourning." Thus his father wept for
him.

36Now the Midianites[a] had sold him in
Egypt to Potiphar, an officer of Pharaoh
and captain of the guard.

Judah and Tamar

38 It came to pass at that time
that Judah departed from his
brothers, and visited a certain Adul-
lamite whose name *was* Hirah. 2And
Judah saw there a daughter of a cer-
tain Canaanite whose name *was* Shua,
and he married her and went in to her.
3So she conceived and bore a son, and
he called his name Er. 4She conceived
again and bore a son, and she called
his name Onan. 5And she conceived
yet again and bore a son, and called his
name Shelah. He was at Chezib when
she bore him.

6Then Judah took a wife for Er his
firstborn, and her name *was* Tamar.
7But Er, Judah's firstborn, was wicked
in the sight of the LORD, and the LORD
killed him. 8And Judah said to Onan,
"Go in to your brother's wife and mar-
ry her, and raise up an heir to your
brother." 9But Onan knew that the heir
would not be his; and it came to pass,
when he went in to his brother's wife,
that he emitted on the ground, lest he
should give an heir to his brother. 10And
the thing which he did displeased the
LORD; therefore He killed him also.

11Then Judah said to Tamar his
daughter-in-law, "Remain a widow in
your father's house till my son Shelah
is grown." For he said, "Lest he also die
like his brothers." And Tamar went and
dwelt in her father's house.

12Now in the process of time the
daughter of Shua, Judah's wife, died;
and Judah was comforted, and went up
to his sheepshearers at Timnah, he and
his friend Hirah the Adullamite. 13And
it was told Tamar, saying, "Look, your
father-in-law is going up to Timnah to
shear his sheep." 14So she took off her
widow's garments, covered *herself* with
a veil and wrapped herself, and sat in
an open place which *was* on the way to
Timnah; for she saw that Shelah was
grown, and she was not given to him
as a wife. 15When Judah saw her, he
thought she *was* a harlot, because she
had covered her face. 16Then he turned
to her by the way, and said, "Please let
me come in to you"; for he did not know
that she *was* his daughter-in-law.

So she said, "What will you give me,
that you may come in to me?"

17And he said, "I will send a young
goat from the flock."

So she said, "Will you give *me* a pledge
till you send *it?*"

18Then he said, "What pledge shall I
give you?"

So she said, "Your signet and cord,
and your staff that *is* in your hand."
Then he gave *them* to her, and went in
to her, and she conceived by him. 19So
she arose and went away, and laid aside
her veil and put on the garments of her
widowhood.

37:36 [a] Masoretic Text reads *Medanites.*

20And Judah sent the young goat by
the hand of his friend the Adullamite,
to receive *his* pledge from the woman's
hand, but he did not find her. 21Then he
asked the men of that place, saying,
"Where is the harlot who *was* openly
by the roadside?"

And they said, "There was no harlot
in this *place*."

22So he returned to Judah and said,
"I cannot find her. Also, the men of the
place said there was no harlot in this
place."

23Then Judah said, "Let her take *them*
for herself, lest we be shamed; for I sent
this young goat and you have not found
her."

24And it came to pass, about three
months after, that Judah was told, say-
ing, "Tamar your daughter-in-law has
played the harlot; furthermore she *is*
with child by harlotry."

So Judah said, "Bring her out and let
her be burned!"

25When she *was* brought out, she sent
to her father-in-law, saying, "By the man
to whom these belong, I *am* with child."
And she said, "Please determine whose
these *are*—the signet and cord, and staff."

26So Judah acknowledged *them* and
said, "She has been more righteous than
I, because I did not give her to Shelah
my son." And he never knew her again.

27Now it came to pass, at the time for
giving birth, that behold, twins *were* in
her womb. 28And so it was, when she
was giving birth, that *the one* put out
his hand; and the midwife took a scarlet
thread and bound it on his hand, saying,
"This one came out first." 29Then it hap-
pened, as he drew back his hand, that
his brother came out unexpectedly; and
she said, "How did you break through?
This breach *be* upon you!" Therefore his
name was called Perez.[a] 30Afterward his
brother came out who had the scarlet
thread on his hand. And his name was
called Zerah.

Joseph a Slave in Egypt

39 Now Joseph had been taken down
to Egypt. And Potiphar, an officer
of Pharaoh, captain of the guard, an
Egyptian, bought him from the Ishma-
elites who had taken him down there.
2The LORD was with Joseph, and he was
a successful man; and he was in the
house of his master the Egyptian. 3And
his master saw that the LORD *was* with
him and that the LORD made all he did
to prosper in his hand. 4So Joseph found
favor in his sight, and served him. Then
he made him overseer of his house, and
all *that* he had he put under his author-
ity. 5So it was, from the time *that* he had
made him overseer of his house and all
that he had, that the LORD blessed the
Egyptian's house for Joseph's sake; and
the blessing of the LORD was on all that
he had in the house and in the field.
6Thus he left all that he had in Joseph's
hand, and he did not know what he had
except for the bread which he ate.

Now Joseph was handsome in form
and appearance.

7And it came to pass after these things
that his master's wife cast longing eyes
on Joseph, and she said, "Lie with me."

8But he refused and said to his mas-
ter's wife, "Look, my master does not
know what *is* with me in the house, and
he has committed all that he has to
my hand. 9*There is* no one greater in
this house than I, nor has he kept back
anything from me but you, because
you *are* his wife. How then can I do this
great wickedness, and sin against God?"

10So it was, as she spoke to Joseph day
by day, that he did not heed her, to lie
with her *or* to be with her.

11But it happened about this time,
when Joseph went into the house to do
his work, and none of the men of the
house *was* inside, 12that she caught him
by his garment, saying, "Lie with me."
But he left his garment in her hand,
and fled and ran outside. 13And so it
was, when she saw that he had left his
garment in her hand and fled outside,
14that she called to the men of her house
and spoke to them, saying, "See, he has
brought in to us a Hebrew to mock us. He
came in to me to lie with me, and I cried
out with a loud voice. 15And it happened,
when he heard that I lifted my voice and
cried out, that he left his garment with

38:29 [a] Literally *Breach* or *Breakthrough*

me, and fled and went outside."
16 So she kept his garment with her
until his master came home. 17 Then
she spoke to him with words like these,
saying, "The Hebrew servant whom you
brought to us came in to me to mock
me; 18 so it happened, as I lifted my voice
and cried out, that he left his garment
with me and fled outside."
19 So it was, when his master heard the
words which his wife spoke to him, say-
ing, "Your servant did to me after this
manner," that his anger was aroused.
20 Then Joseph's master took him and
put him into the prison, a place where
the king's prisoners *were* confined. And
he was there in the prison. 21 But the
LORD was with Joseph and showed him
mercy, and He gave him favor in the
sight of the keeper of the prison. 22 And
the keeper of the prison committed to
Joseph's hand all the prisoners who
were in the prison; whatever they did
there, it was his doing. 23 The keeper of
the prison did not look into anything
that was under *Joseph's* authority,[a] be-
cause the LORD was with him; and what-
ever he did, the LORD made *it* prosper.

The Prisoners' Dreams

40 It came to pass after these things
that the butler and the baker of
the king of Egypt offended their lord,
the king of Egypt. 2 And Pharaoh was
angry with his two officers, the chief
butler and the chief baker. 3 So he put
them in custody in the house of the
captain of the guard, in the prison, the
place where Joseph *was* confined. 4 And
the captain of the guard charged Joseph
with them, and he served them; so they
were in custody for a while.
5 Then the butler and the baker of the
king of Egypt, who *were* confined in
the prison, had a dream, both of them,
each man's dream in one night *and* each
man's dream with its *own* interpreta-
tion. 6 And Joseph came in to them in
the morning and looked at them, and
saw that they *were* sad. 7 So he asked
Pharaoh's officers who *were* with him in
the custody of his lord's house, saying,
"Why do you look *so* sad today?"
8 And they said to him, "We each have
had a dream, and *there is* no interpreter
of it."
So Joseph said to them, "Do not inter-
pretations belong to God? Tell *them* to
me, please."
9 Then the chief butler told his dream
to Joseph, and said to him, "Behold, in
my dream a vine *was* before me, 10 and
in the vine *were* three branches; it *was*
as though it budded, its blossoms shot
forth, and its clusters brought forth ripe
grapes. 11 Then Pharaoh's cup *was* in my
hand; and I took the grapes and pressed
them into Pharaoh's cup, and placed
the cup in Pharaoh's hand."
12 And Joseph said to him, "This *is* the
interpretation of it: The three branches
are three days. 13 Now within three days
Pharaoh will lift up your head and re-
store you to your place, and you will put
Pharaoh's cup in his hand according to
the former manner, when you were his
butler. 14 But remember me when it is
well with you, and please show kindness
to me; make mention of me to Pharaoh,
and get me out of this house. 15 For in-
deed I was stolen away from the land
of the Hebrews; and also I have done
nothing here that they should put me
into the dungeon."
16 When the chief baker saw that the
interpretation was good, he said to
Joseph, "I also *was* in my dream, and
there *were* three white baskets on my
head. 17 In the uppermost basket *were*
all kinds of baked goods for Pharaoh,
and the birds ate them out of the basket
on my head."
18 So Joseph answered and said, "This
is the interpretation of it: The three bas-
kets *are* three days. 19 Within three days
Pharaoh will lift off your head from you
and hang you on a tree; and the birds
will eat your flesh from you."
20 Now it came to pass on the third day,
which was Pharaoh's birthday, that he
made a feast for all his servants; and he
lifted up the head of the chief butler and
of the chief baker among his servants.
21 Then he restored the chief butler to his
butlership again, and he placed the cup
in Pharaoh's hand. 22 But he hanged the

39:23 [a] Literally *his hand*

chief baker, as Joseph had interpreted
to them. 23Yet the chief butler did not
remember Joseph, but forgot him.

Pharaoh's Dreams

41 Then it came to pass, at the end
of two full years, that Pharaoh
had a dream; and behold, he stood by
the river. 2Suddenly there came up out
of the river seven cows, fine looking
and fat; and they fed in the meadow.
3Then behold, seven other cows came
up after them out of the river, ugly and
gaunt, and stood by the *other* cows on
the bank of the river. 4And the ugly and
gaunt cows ate up the seven fine looking
and fat cows. So Pharaoh awoke. 5He
slept and dreamed a second time; and
suddenly seven heads of grain came up
on one stalk, plump and good. 6Then
behold, seven thin heads, blighted by
the east wind, sprang up after them.
7And the seven thin heads devoured the
seven plump and full heads. So Phar-
aoh awoke, and indeed, *it was* a dream.
8Now it came to pass in the morning
that his spirit was troubled, and he
sent and called for all the magicians
of Egypt and all its wise men. And Phar-
aoh told them his dreams, but *there
was* no one who could interpret them
for Pharaoh.

9Then the chief butler spoke to Phar-
aoh, saying: "I remember my faults
this day. 10When Pharaoh was angry
with his servants, and put me in cus-
tody in the house of the captain of the
guard, *both* me and the chief baker,
11we each had a dream in one night, he
and I. Each of us dreamed according to
the interpretation of his *own* dream.
12Now there *was* a young Hebrew man
with us there, a servant of the captain
of the guard. And we told him, and he
interpreted our dreams for us; to each
man he interpreted according to his
own dream. 13And it came to pass, just
as he interpreted for us, so it happened.
He restored me to my office, and he
hanged him."

14Then Pharaoh sent and called Jo-
seph, and they brought him quickly
out of the dungeon; and he shaved,
changed his clothing, and came to
Pharaoh. 15And Pharaoh said to Joseph,
"I have had a dream, and *there is* no one
who can interpret it. But I have heard
it said of you *that* you can understand
a dream, to interpret it."

16So Joseph answered Pharaoh, say-
ing, "*It is* not in me; God will give Phar-
aoh an answer of peace."

17Then Pharaoh said to Joseph: "Be-
hold, in my dream I stood on the bank
of the river. 18Suddenly seven cows
came up out of the river, fine looking
and fat; and they fed in the meadow.
19Then behold, seven other cows came
up after them, poor and very ugly and
gaunt, such ugliness as I have never
seen in all the land of Egypt. 20And the
gaunt and ugly cows ate up the first sev-
en, the fat cows. 21When they had eaten
them up, no one would have known that
they had eaten them, for they *were* just
as ugly as at the beginning. So I awoke.
22Also I saw in my dream, and suddenly
seven heads came up on one stalk, full
and good. 23Then behold, seven heads,
withered, thin, *and* blighted by the east
wind, sprang up after them. 24And the
thin heads devoured the seven good
heads. So I told *this* to the magicians,
but *there was* no one who could explain
it to me."

25Then Joseph said to Pharaoh, "The
dreams of Pharaoh *are* one; God has
shown Pharaoh what He *is* about to
do: 26The seven good cows *are* seven
years, and the seven good heads *are*
seven years; the dreams *are* one. 27And
the seven thin and ugly cows which
came up after them *are* seven years,
and the seven empty heads blighted by
the east wind are seven years of famine.
28This *is* the thing which I have spoken
to Pharaoh. God has shown Pharaoh
what He *is* about to do. 29Indeed seven
years of great plenty will come through-
out all the land of Egypt; 30but after
them seven years of famine will arise,
and all the plenty will be forgotten in
the land of Egypt; and the famine will
deplete the land. 31So the plenty will
not be known in the land because of
the famine following, for it *will be* very
severe. 32And the dream was repeated
to Pharaoh twice because the thing *is*
established by God, and God will shortly
bring it to pass.

33“Now therefore, let Pharaoh select a
discerning and wise man, and set him
over the land of Egypt. 34Let Pharaoh
do *this,* and let him appoint officers
over the land, to collect one-fifth *of the*
produce of the land of Egypt in the seven
plentiful years. 35And let them gather
all the food of those good years that
are coming, and store up grain under
the authority of Pharaoh, and let them
keep food in the cities. 36Then that food
shall be as a reserve for the land for the
seven years of famine which shall be in
the land of Egypt, that the land may not
perish during the famine.”

Joseph’s Rise to Power

37So the advice was good in the eyes
of Pharaoh and in the eyes of all his
servants. 38And Pharaoh said to his
servants, “Can we find *such a one* as this,
a man in whom *is* the Spirit of God?”
39Then Pharaoh said to Joseph, “In-
asmuch as God has shown you all this,
there is no one as discerning and wise
as you. 40You shall be over my house,
and all my people shall be ruled ac-
cording to your word; only in regard to
the throne will I be greater than you.”
41And Pharaoh said to Joseph, “See, I
have set you over all the land of Egypt.”
42Then Pharaoh took his signet ring off
his hand and put it on Joseph’s hand;
and he clothed him in garments of fine
linen and put a gold chain around his
neck. 43And he had him ride in the sec-
ond chariot which he had; and they
cried out before him, “Bow the knee!”
So he set him over all the land of Egypt.
44Pharaoh also said to Joseph, “I *am*
Pharaoh, and without your consent no
man may lift his hand or foot in all the
land of Egypt.” 45And Pharaoh called
Joseph’s name Zaphnath-Paaneah.
And he gave him as a wife Asenath,
the daughter of Poti-Pherah priest of
On. So Joseph went out over *all* the land
of Egypt.
46Joseph was thirty years old when
he stood before Pharaoh king of Egypt.
And Joseph went out from the presence
of Pharaoh, and went throughout all
the land of Egypt. 47Now in the seven
plentiful years the ground brought forth
abundantly. 48So he gathered up all the
food of the seven years which were in the
land of Egypt, and laid up the food in
the cities; he laid up in every city the food
of the fields which surrounded them.
49Joseph gathered very much grain,
as the sand of the sea, until he stopped
counting, for *it was* immeasurable.
50And to Joseph were born two sons
before the years of famine came, whom
Asenath, the daughter of Poti-Pherah
priest of On, bore to him. 51Joseph called
the name of the firstborn Manasseh:[a]
“For God has made me forget all my toil
and all my father’s house.” 52And the
name of the second he called Ephraim:[a]
“For God has caused me to be fruitful
in the land of my affliction.”
53Then the seven years of plenty which
were in the land of Egypt ended, 54and
the seven years of famine began to
come, as Joseph had said. The famine
was in all lands, but in all the land of
Egypt there was bread. 55So when all
the land of Egypt was famished, the
people cried to Pharaoh for bread. Then
Pharaoh said to all the Egyptians, “Go
to Joseph; whatever he says to you, do.”
56The famine was over all the face of
the earth, and Joseph opened all the
storehouses[a] and sold to the Egyptians.
And the famine became severe in the
land of Egypt. 57So all countries came
to Joseph in Egypt to buy *grain,* because
the famine was severe in all lands.

Joseph’s Brothers Go to Egypt

42 When Jacob saw that there was
grain in Egypt, Jacob said to his
sons, “Why do you look at one another?”
2And he said, “Indeed I have heard that
there is grain in Egypt; go down to that
place and buy for us there, that we may
live and not die.”
3So Joseph’s ten brothers went down to
buy grain in Egypt. 4But Jacob did not
send Joseph’s brother Benjamin with
his brothers, for he said, “Lest some
calamity befall him.” 5And the sons of
Israel went to buy *grain* among those
who journeyed, for the famine was in
the land of Canaan.

41:51 [a] Literally *Making Forgetful* **41:52** [a] Literally *Fruitfulness* **41:56** [a] Literally *all that was in them*

6Now Joseph *was* governor over the
land; and it was he who sold to all
the people of the land. And Joseph's
brothers came and bowed down before
him with *their* faces to the earth. 7Jo-
seph saw his brothers and recognized
them, but he acted as a stranger to them
and spoke roughly to them. Then he said
to them, "Where do you come from?"
And they said, "From the land of Ca-
naan to buy food."
8So Joseph recognized his brothers,
but they did not recognize him. 9Then
Joseph remembered the dreams which
he had dreamed about them, and said
to them, "You *are* spies! You have come
to see the nakedness of the land!"
10And they said to him, "No, my lord,
but your servants have come to buy
food. 11We *are* all one man's sons; we
are honest *men;* your servants are not
spies."
12But he said to them, "No, but you
have come to see the nakedness of the
land."
13And they said, "Your servants *are*
twelve brothers, the sons of one man
in the land of Canaan; and in fact, the
youngest *is* with our father today, and
one *is* no more."
14But Joseph said to them, "It *is* as I
spoke to you, saying, 'You *are* spies!'
15In this *manner* you shall be tested: By
the life of Pharaoh, you shall not leave
this place unless your youngest brother
comes here. 16Send one of you, and let
him bring your brother; and you shall
be kept in prison, that your words may
be tested to see whether *there is* any
truth in you; or else, by the life of Phar-
aoh, surely you *are* spies!" 17So he put
them all together in prison three days.
18Then Joseph said to them the third
day, "Do this and live, *for* I fear God:
19If you *are* honest *men,* let one of your
brothers be confined to your prison
house; but you, go and carry grain for
the famine of your houses. 20And bring
your youngest brother to me; so your
words will be verified, and you shall not
die."
And they did so. 21Then they said to
one another, "We *are* truly guilty con-
cerning our brother, for we saw the an-
guish of his soul when he pleaded with
us, and we would not hear; therefore
this distress has come upon us."
22And Reuben answered them, saying,
"Did I not speak to you, saying, 'Do not
sin against the boy'; and you would not
listen? Therefore behold, his blood is
now required of us." 23But they did not
know that Joseph understood *them,* for
he spoke to them through an interpret-
er. 24And he turned himself away from
them and wept. Then he returned to
them again, and talked with them. And
he took Simeon from them and bound
him before their eyes.

The Brothers Return to Canaan

25Then Joseph gave a command to fill
their sacks with grain, to restore every
man's money to his sack, and to give
them provisions for the journey. Thus
he did for them. 26So they loaded their
donkeys with the grain and departed
from there. 27But as one *of them* opened
his sack to give his donkey feed at the
encampment, he saw his money; and
there it was, in the mouth of his sack.
28So he said to his brothers, "My money
has been restored, and there it is, in my
sack!" Then their hearts failed *them* and
they were afraid, saying to one another,
"What *is* this *that* God has done to us?"
29Then they went to Jacob their father
in the land of Canaan and told him all
that had happened to them, saying:
30"The man *who is* lord of the land spoke
roughly to us, and took us for spies of
the country. 31But we said to him, 'We
are honest *men;* we are not spies. 32We
are twelve brothers, sons of our father;
one *is* no *more,* and the youngest *is* with
our father this day in the land of Ca-
naan.' 33Then the man, the lord of the
country, said to us, 'By this I will know
that you *are* honest *men:* Leave one of
your brothers *here* with me, take *food*
for the famine of your households, and
be gone. 34And bring your youngest
brother to me; so I shall know that you
are not spies, but *that* you *are* honest
men. I will grant your brother to you,
and you may trade in the land.' "
35Then it happened as they emptied
their sacks, that surprisingly each
man's bundle of money *was* in his sack;
and when they and their father saw the

bundles of money, they were afraid.
36And Jacob their father said to them,
"You have bereaved me: Joseph is no
more, Simeon is no *more,* and you want
to take Benjamin. All these things are
against me."
37Then Reuben spoke to his father,
saying, "Kill my two sons if I do not
bring him *back* to you; put him in my
hands, and I will bring him back to you."
38But he said, "My son shall not go
down with you, for his brother is dead,
and he is left alone. If any calamity
should befall him along the way in which
you go, then you would bring down my
gray hair with sorrow to the grave."

Joseph's Brothers Return with Benjamin

43 Now the famine *was* severe in
the land. 2And it came to pass,
when they had eaten up the grain which
they had brought from Egypt, that their
father said to them, "Go back, buy us a
little food."
3But Judah spoke to him, saying,
"The man solemnly warned us, say-
ing, 'You shall not see my face unless
your brother *is* with you.' 4If you send
our brother with us, we will go down
and buy you food. 5But if you will not
send *him,* we will not go down; for the
man said to us, 'You shall not see my
face unless your brother *is* with you.' "
6And Israel said, "Why did you deal *so*
wrongfully with me *as* to tell the man
whether you had still *another* brother?"
7But they said, "The man asked us
pointedly about ourselves and our fam-
ily, saying, '*Is* your father still alive?
Have you *another* brother?' And we told
him according to these words. Could we
possibly have known that he would say,
'Bring your brother down'?"
8Then Judah said to Israel his father,
"Send the lad with me, and we will arise
and go, that we may live and not die,
both we and you *and* also our little ones.
9I myself will be surety for him; from
my hand you shall require him. If I do
not bring him *back* to you and set him
before you, then let me bear the blame
forever. 10For if we had not lingered,
surely by now we would have returned
this second time."
11And their father Israel said to them,
"If *it must be* so, then do this: Take some
of the best fruits of the land in your
vessels and carry down a present for the
man—a little balm and a little honey,
spices and myrrh, pistachio nuts and
almonds. 12Take double money in your
hand, and take back in your hand the
money that was returned in the mouth
of your sacks; perhaps it was an over-
sight. 13Take your brother also, and
arise, go back to the man. 14And may
God Almighty give you mercy before
the man, that he may release your other
brother and Benjamin. If I am bereaved,
I am bereaved!"
15So the men took that present and
Benjamin, and they took double mon-
ey in their hand, and arose and went
down to Egypt; and they stood before
Joseph. 16When Joseph saw Benjamin
with them, he said to the steward of his
house, "Take *these* men to my home,
and slaughter an animal and make
ready; for *these* men will dine with me
at noon." 17Then the man did as Joseph
ordered, and the man brought the men
into Joseph's house.
18Now the men were afraid because
they were brought into Joseph's house;
and they said, "*It is* because of the mon-
ey, which was returned in our sacks the
first time, that we are brought in, so
that he may make a case against us
and seize us, to take us as slaves with
our donkeys."
19When they drew near to the steward
of Joseph's house, they talked with him
at the door of the house, 20and said,
"O sir, we indeed came down the first
time to buy food; 21but it happened,
when we came to the encampment, that
we opened our sacks, and there, *each*
man's money *was* in the mouth of his
sack, our money in full weight; so we
have brought it back in our hand. 22And
we have brought down other money in
our hands to buy food. We do not know
who put our money in our sacks."
23But he said, "Peace *be* with you, do
not be afraid. Your God and the God of
your father has given you treasure in
your sacks; I had your money." Then he
brought Simeon out to them.
24So the man brought the men into
Joseph's house and gave *them* water,

and they washed their feet; and he gave
their donkeys feed. 25Then they made
the present ready for Joseph's coming
at noon, for they heard that they would
eat bread there.
26And when Joseph came home, they
brought him the present which *was* in
their hand into the house, and bowed
down before him to the earth. 27Then he
asked them about *their* well-being, and
said, "*Is* your father well, the old man
of whom you spoke? *Is* he still alive?"
28And they answered, "Your servant
our father *is* in good health; he *is* still
alive." And they bowed their heads
down and prostrated themselves.
29Then he lifted his eyes and saw his
brother Benjamin, his mother's son, and
said, "*Is* this your younger brother of
whom you spoke to me?" And he said,
"God be gracious to you, my son." 30Now
his heart yearned for his brother; so Jo-
seph made haste and sought *somewhere*
to weep. And he went into *his* chamber
and wept there. 31Then he washed his
face and came out; and he restrained
himself, and said, "Serve the bread."
32So they set him a place by himself,
and them by themselves, and the Egyp-
tians who ate with him by themselves;
because the Egyptians could not eat
food with the Hebrews, for that *is* an
abomination to the Egyptians. 33And
they sat before him, the firstborn ac-
cording to his birthright and the youn-
gest according to his youth; and the men
looked in astonishment at one another.
34Then he took servings to them from
before him, but Benjamin's serving was
five times as much as any of theirs. So
they drank and were merry with him.

Joseph's Cup

44 And he commanded the stew-
ard of his house, saying, "Fill
the men's sacks with food, as much as
they can carry, and put each man's
money in the mouth of his sack. 2Also
put my cup, the silver cup, in the mouth
of the sack of the youngest, and his
grain money." So he did according to
the word that Joseph had spoken. 3As
soon as the morning dawned, the men
were sent away, they and their donkeys.
4When they had gone out of the city,
and were not *yet* far off, Joseph said to
his steward, "Get up, follow the men;
and when you overtake them, say to
them, 'Why have you repaid evil for
good? 5*Is* not this *the one* from which my
lord drinks, and with which he indeed
practices divination? You have done
evil in so doing.' "
6So he overtook them, and he spoke
to them these same words. 7And they
said to him, "Why does my lord say
these words? Far be it from us that your
servants should do such a thing. 8Look,
we brought back to you from the land
of Canaan the money which we found
in the mouth of our sacks. How then
could we steal silver or gold from your
lord's house? 9With whomever of your
servants it is found, let him die, and we
also will be my lord's slaves."
10And he said, "Now also *let* it *be* ac-
cording to your words; he with whom it
is found shall be my slave, and you shall
be blameless." 11Then each man speed-
ily let down his sack to the ground, and
each opened his sack. 12So he searched.
He began with the oldest and left off
with the youngest; and the cup was
found in Benjamin's sack. 13Then they
tore their clothes, and each man loaded
his donkey and returned to the city.
14So Judah and his brothers came to
Joseph's house, and he *was* still there;
and they fell before him on the ground.
15And Joseph said to them, "What deed
is this you have done? Did you not know
that such a man as I can certainly prac-
tice divination?"
16Then Judah said, "What shall we say
to my lord? What shall we speak? Or how
shall we clear ourselves? God has found
out the iniquity of your servants; here
we are, my lord's slaves, both we and
he also with whom the cup was found."
17But he said, "Far be it from me that I
should do so; the man in whose hand the
cup was found, he shall be my slave. And
as for you, go up in peace to your father."

Judah Intercedes for Benjamin

18Then Judah came near to him and
said: "O my lord, please let your servant
speak a word in my lord's hearing, and
do not let your anger burn against your
servant; for you *are* even like Pharaoh.

19My lord asked his servants, saying,
'Have you a father or a brother?' 20And
we said to my lord, 'We have a father,
an old man, and a child of *his* old age,
who is young; his brother is dead, and he
alone is left of his mother's children, and
his father loves him.' 21Then you said to
your servants, 'Bring him down to me,
that I may set my eyes on him.' 22And we
said to my lord, 'The lad cannot leave his
father, for *if* he should leave his father,
his father would die.' 23But you said to
your servants, 'Unless your youngest
brother comes down with you, you shall
see my face no more.'

24"So it was, when we went up to your
servant my father, that we told him the
words of my lord. 25And our father said,
'Go back *and* buy us a little food.' 26But we
said, 'We cannot go down; if our youngest
brother is with us, then we will go down;
for we may not see the man's face unless
our youngest brother *is* with us.' 27Then
your servant my father said to us, 'You
know that my wife bore me two sons;
28and the one went out from me, and
I said, "Surely he is torn to pieces"; and
I have not seen him since. 29But if you
take this one also from me, and calamity
befalls him, you shall bring down my
gray hair with sorrow to the grave.'

30"Now therefore, when I come to your
servant my father, and the lad *is* not
with us, since his life is bound up in the
lad's life, 31it will happen, when he sees
that the lad *is* not *with us,* that he will
die. So your servants will bring down the
gray hair of your servant our father with
sorrow to the grave. 32For your servant
became surety for the lad to my father,
saying, 'If I do not bring him *back* to you,
then I shall bear the blame before my
father forever.' 33Now therefore, please
let your servant remain instead of the
lad as a slave to my lord, and let the lad
go up with his brothers. 34For how shall
I go up to my father if the lad *is* not with
me, lest perhaps I see the evil that would
come upon my father?"

Joseph Revealed to His Brothers

45 Then Joseph could not restrain
himself before all those who
stood by him, and he cried out, "Make
everyone go out from me!" So no one
stood with him while Joseph made him-
self known to his brothers. 2And he wept
aloud, and the Egyptians and the house
of Pharaoh heard *it.*

3Then Joseph said to his brothers, "I
am Joseph; does my father still live?"
But his brothers could not answer him,
for they were dismayed in his presence.
4And Joseph said to his brothers, "Please
come near to me." So they came near.
Then he said: "I *am* Joseph your brother,
whom you sold into Egypt. 5But now, do
not therefore be grieved or angry with
yourselves because you sold me here;
for God sent me before you to preserve
life. 6For these two years the famine
has been in the land, and *there are* still
five years in which *there will be* neither
plowing nor harvesting. 7And God sent
me before you to preserve a posterity
for you in the earth, and to save your
lives by a great deliverance. 8So now
it was not you *who* sent me here, but
God; and He has made me a father to
Pharaoh, and lord of all his house, and
a ruler throughout all the land of Egypt.

9"Hurry and go up to my father, and
say to him, 'Thus says your son Joseph:
"God has made me lord of all Egypt;
come down to me, do not tarry. 10You
shall dwell in the land of Goshen, and
you shall be near to me, you and your
children, your children's children, your
flocks and your herds, and all that you
have. 11There I will provide for you, lest
you and your household, and all that
you have, come to poverty; for *there are*
still five years of famine." '

12"And behold, your eyes and the eyes
of my brother Benjamin see that *it is*
my mouth that speaks to you. 13So you
shall tell my father of all my glory in
Egypt, and of all that you have seen;
and you shall hurry and bring my fa-
ther down here."

14Then he fell on his brother Benja-
min's neck and wept, and Benjamin
wept on his neck. 15Moreover he kissed
all his brothers and wept over them, and
after that his brothers talked with him.

16Now the report of it was heard in Phar-
aoh's house, saying, "Joseph's brothers
have come." So it pleased Pharaoh and
his servants well. 17And Pharaoh said
to Joseph, "Say to your brothers, 'Do

this: Load your animals and depart;
go to the land of Canaan. 18Bring your
father and your households and come
to me; I will give you the best of the land
of Egypt, and you will eat the fat of the
land. 19Now you are commanded—do
this: Take carts out of the land of Egypt
for your little ones and your wives; bring
your father and come. 20Also do not be
concerned about your goods, for the
best of all the land of Egypt *is* yours.' "
21Then the sons of Israel did so; and
Joseph gave them carts, according to
the command of Pharaoh, and he gave
them provisions for the journey. 22He
gave to all of them, to each man, chang-
es of garments; but to Benjamin he gave
three hundred *pieces* of silver and five
changes of garments. 23And he sent
to his father these *things:* ten donkeys
loaded with the good things of Egypt,
and ten female donkeys loaded with
grain, bread, and food for his father for
the journey. 24So he sent his brothers
away, and they departed; and he said
to them, "See that you do not become
troubled along the way."
25Then they went up out of Egypt, and
came to the land of Canaan to Jacob their
father. 26And they told him, saying, "Jo-
seph *is* still alive, and he *is* governor over
all the land of Egypt." And Jacob's heart
stood still, because he did not believe
them. 27But when they told him all the
words which Joseph had said to them,
and when he saw the carts which Joseph
had sent to carry him, the spirit of Jacob
their father revived. 28Then Israel said,
"*It is* enough. Joseph my son *is* still alive.
I will go and see him before I die."

Jacob's Journey to Egypt

46 So Israel took his journey with
all that he had, and came to Be-
ersheba, and offered sacrifices to the
God of his father Isaac. 2Then God spoke
to Israel in the visions of the night, and
said, "Jacob, Jacob!"
And he said, "Here I am."
3So He said, "I *am* God, the God of
your father; do not fear to go down to
Egypt, for I will make of you a great
nation there. 4I will go down with you
to Egypt, and I will also surely bring
you up *again;* and Joseph will put his
hand on your eyes."
5Then Jacob arose from Beersheba;
and the sons of Israel carried their fa-
ther Jacob, their little ones, and their
wives, in the carts which Pharaoh had
sent to carry him. 6So they took their
livestock and their goods, which they
had acquired in the land of Canaan,
and went to Egypt, Jacob and all his
descendants with him. 7His sons and his
sons' sons, his daughters and his sons'
daughters, and all his descendants he
brought with him to Egypt.
8Now these *were* the names of the
children of Israel, Jacob and his sons,
who went to Egypt: Reuben *was* Jacob's
firstborn. 9The sons of Reuben *were* Ha-
noch, Pallu, Hezron, and Carmi. 10The
sons of Simeon *were* Jemuel,[a] Jamin,
Ohad, Jachin,[b] Zohar,[c] and Shaul, the
son of a Canaanite woman. 11The sons of
Levi *were* Gershon, Kohath, and Merari.
12The sons of Judah *were* Er, Onan, She-
lah, Perez, and Zerah (but Er and Onan
died in the land of Canaan). The sons of
Perez were Hezron and Hamul. 13The
sons of Issachar *were* Tola, Puvah,[a] Job,[b]
and Shimron. 14The sons of Zebulun
were Sered, Elon, and Jahleel. 15These
were the sons of Leah, whom she bore to
Jacob in Padan Aram, with his daughter
Dinah. All the persons, his sons and his
daughters, *were* thirty-three.
16The sons of Gad *were* Ziphion,[a]
Haggi, Shuni, Ezbon,[b] Eri, Arodi,[c] and
Areli. 17The sons of Asher *were* Jimnah,
Ishuah, Isui, Beriah, and Serah, their
sister. And the sons of Beriah *were*
Heber and Malchiel. 18These *were* the
sons of Zilpah, whom Laban gave to
Leah his daughter; and these she bore
to Jacob: sixteen persons.
19The sons of Rachel, Jacob's wife, *were*
Joseph and Benjamin. 20And to Joseph
in the land of Egypt were born Manasseh
and Ephraim, whom Asenath, the daugh-
ter of Poti-Pherah priest of On, bore to

46:10 [a] Spelled *Nemuel* in 1 Chronicles 4:24 [b] Called *Jarib* in 1 Chronicles 4:24 [c] Called *Zerah* in 1 Chronicles 4:24 **46:13** [a] Spelled *Puah* in 1 Chronicles 7:1 [b] Same as *Jashub* in Numbers 26:24 and 1 Chronicles 7:1 **46:16** [a] Spelled *Zephon* in Samaritan Pentateuch, Septuagint, and Numbers 26:15 [b] Called *Ozni* in Numbers 26:16 [c] Spelled *Arod* in Numbers 26:17

him. 21The sons of Benjamin *were* Belah,
Becher, Ashbel, Gera, Naaman, Ehi, Rosh,
Muppim, Huppim,[a] and Ard. 22These
were the sons of Rachel, who were born
to Jacob: fourteen persons in all.
23The son of Dan *was* Hushim.[a] 24The
sons of Naphtali *were* Jahzeel,[a] Guni,
Jezer, and Shillem.[b] 25These *were* the
sons of Bilhah, whom Laban gave to
Rachel his daughter, and she bore these
to Jacob: seven persons in all.
26All the persons who went with Jacob
to Egypt, who came from his body, be-
sides Jacob's sons' wives, *were* sixty-six
persons in all. 27And the sons of Joseph
who were born to him in Egypt *were* two
persons. All the persons of the house of
Jacob who went to Egypt were seventy.

Jacob Settles in Goshen

28Then he sent Judah before him to
Joseph, to point out before him *the way*
to Goshen. And they came to the land
of Goshen. 29So Joseph made ready
his chariot and went up to Goshen to
meet his father Israel; and he presented
himself to him, and fell on his neck and
wept on his neck a good while.
30And Israel said to Joseph, "Now let
me die, since I have seen your face,
because you *are* still alive."
31Then Joseph said to his brothers and
to his father's household, "I will go up
and tell Pharaoh, and say to him, 'My
brothers and those of my father's house,
who *were* in the land of Canaan, have
come to me. 32And the men *are* shep-
herds, for their occupation has been to
feed livestock; and they have brought
their flocks, their herds, and all that they
have.' 33So it shall be, when Pharaoh calls
you and says, 'What is your occupation?'
34that you shall say, 'Your servants' oc-
cupation has been with livestock from
our youth even till now, both we *and* also
our fathers,' that you may dwell in the
land of Goshen; for every shepherd *is* an
abomination to the Egyptians."

47 Then Joseph went and told Phar-
aoh, and said, "My father and
my brothers, their flocks and their herds
and all that they possess, have come
from the land of Canaan; and indeed
they *are* in the land of Goshen." 2And he
took five men from among his brothers
and presented them to Pharaoh. 3Then
Pharaoh said to his brothers, "What *is*
your occupation?"
And they said to Pharaoh, "Your ser-
vants *are* shepherds, both we *and* also our
fathers." 4And they said to Pharaoh, "We
have come to dwell in the land, because
your servants have no pasture for their
flocks, for the famine *is* severe in the land
of Canaan. Now therefore, please let your
servants dwell in the land of Goshen."
5Then Pharaoh spoke to Joseph, saying,
"Your father and your brothers have
come to you. 6The land of Egypt *is* before
you. Have your father and brothers dwell
in the best of the land; let them dwell in
the land of Goshen. And if you know *any*
competent men among them, then make
them chief herdsmen over my livestock."
7Then Joseph brought in his father
Jacob and set him before Pharaoh; and
Jacob blessed Pharaoh. 8Pharaoh said
to Jacob, "How old *are* you?"
9And Jacob said to Pharaoh, "The days
of the years of my pilgrimage *are* one
hundred and thirty years; few and evil
have been the days of the years of my
life, and they have not attained to the
days of the years of the life of my fa-
thers in the days of their pilgrimage."
10So Jacob blessed Pharaoh, and went
out from before Pharaoh.
11And Joseph situated his father and his
brothers, and gave them a possession in
the land of Egypt, in the best of the land,
in the land of Rameses, as Pharaoh had
commanded. 12Then Joseph provided his
father, his brothers, and all his father's
household with bread, according to the
number in *their* families.

Joseph Deals with the Famine

13Now *there was* no bread in all the land;
for the famine *was* very severe, so that
the land of Egypt and the land of Canaan
languished because of the famine. 14And
Joseph gathered up all the money that
was found in the land of Egypt and in the
land of Canaan, for the grain which they
bought; and Joseph brought the money
into Pharaoh's house.

46:21 [a] Called *Hupham* in Numbers 26:39 **46:23** [a] Called *Shuham* in Numbers 26:42 **46:24** [a] Spelled *Jahziel* in 1 Chronicles 7:13 [b] Spelled *Shallum* in 1 Chronicles 7:13

15So when the money failed in the land
of Egypt and in the land of Canaan, all
the Egyptians came to Joseph and said,
"Give us bread, for why should we die in
your presence? For the money has failed."
16Then Joseph said, "Give your live-
stock, and I will give you *bread* for
your livestock, if the money is gone."
17So they brought their livestock to Jo-
seph, and Joseph gave them bread *in
exchange* for the horses, the flocks, the
cattle of the herds, and for the donkeys.
Thus he fed them with bread *in exchange*
for all their livestock that year.
18When that year had ended, they
came to him the next year and said to
him, "We will not hide from my lord that
our money is gone; my lord also has our
herds of livestock. There is nothing left in
the sight of my lord but our bodies and
our lands. 19Why should we die before
your eyes, both we and our land? Buy
us and our land for bread, and we and
our land will be servants of Pharaoh;
give *us* seed, that we may live and not
die, that the land may not be desolate."
20Then Joseph bought all the land of
Egypt for Pharaoh; for every man of
the Egyptians sold his field, because the
famine was severe upon them. So the
land became Pharaoh's. 21And as for
the people, he moved them into the
cities,[a] from *one* end of the borders of
Egypt to the *other* end. 22Only the land
of the priests he did not buy; for the
priests had rations *allotted to them* by
Pharaoh, and they ate their rations
which Pharaoh gave them; therefore
they did not sell their lands.
23Then Joseph said to the people,
"Indeed I have bought you and your
land this day for Pharaoh. Look, *here
is* seed for you, and you shall sow the
land. 24And it shall come to pass in the
harvest that you shall give one-fifth to
Pharaoh. Four-fifths shall be your own,
as seed for the field and for your food,
for those of your households and as
food for your little ones."
25So they said, "You have saved our
lives; let us find favor in the sight of my
lord, and we will be Pharaoh's servants."
26And Joseph made it a law over the
land of Egypt to this day, *that* Pharaoh
should have one-fifth, except for the
land of the priests only, *which* did not
become Pharaoh's.

Joseph's Vow to Jacob

27So Israel dwelt in the land of Egypt,
in the country of Goshen; and they had
possessions there and grew and multi-
plied exceedingly. 28And Jacob lived in
the land of Egypt seventeen years. So the
length of Jacob's life was one hundred
and forty-seven years. 29When the time
drew near that Israel must die, he called
his son Joseph and said to him, "Now if
I have found favor in your sight, please
put your hand under my thigh, and deal
kindly and truly with me. Please do not
bury me in Egypt, 30but let me lie with
my fathers; you shall carry me out of
Egypt and bury me in their burial place."
And he said, "I will do as you have said."
31Then he said, "Swear to me." And he
swore to him. So Israel bowed himself
on the head of the bed.

Jacob Blesses Joseph's Sons

48 Now it came to pass after these
things that Joseph was told, "In-
deed your father *is* sick"; and he took
with him his two sons, Manasseh and
Ephraim. 2And Jacob was told, "Look,
your son Joseph is coming to you"; and
Israel strengthened himself and sat up
on the bed. 3Then Jacob said to Joseph:
"God Almighty appeared to me at Luz
in the land of Canaan and blessed me,
4and said to me, 'Behold, I will make you
fruitful and multiply you, and I will make
of you a multitude of people, and give
this land to your descendants after you
as an everlasting possession.' 5And now
your two sons, Ephraim and Manasseh,
who were born to you in the land of Egypt
before I came to you in Egypt, *are* mine;
as Reuben and Simeon, they shall be
mine. 6Your offspring whom you beget
after them shall be yours; they will be
called by the name of their brothers in
their inheritance. 7But as for me, when
I came from Padan, Rachel died beside
me in the land of Canaan on the way,
when *there was* but a little distance to

47:21 [a] Following Masoretic Text and Targum; Samaritan Pentateuch, Septuagint, and Vulgate read *made the people virtual slaves.*

go to Ephrath; and I buried her there on the way to Ephrath (that is, Bethlehem)."

[8]Then Israel saw Joseph's sons, and said, "Who *are* these?"

[9]Joseph said to his father, "They *are* my sons, whom God has given me in this *place*."

And he said, "Please bring them to me, and I will bless them." [10]Now the eyes of Israel were dim with age, *so that* he could not see. Then Joseph brought them near him, and he kissed them and embraced them. [11]And Israel said to Joseph, "I had not thought to see your face; but in fact, God has also shown me your offspring!"

[12]So Joseph brought them from beside his knees, and he bowed down with his face to the earth. [13]And Joseph took them both, Ephraim with his right hand toward Israel's left hand, and Manasseh with his left hand toward Israel's right hand, and brought *them* near him. [14]Then Israel stretched out his right hand and laid *it* on Ephraim's head, who *was* the younger, and his left hand on Manasseh's head, guiding his hands knowingly, for Manasseh *was* the firstborn. [15]And he blessed Joseph, and said:

"God, before whom my fathers
Abraham and Isaac walked,
The God who has fed me all my
life long to this day,
16 The Angel who has redeemed me
from all evil,
Bless the lads;
Let my name be named upon them,
And the name of my fathers
Abraham and Isaac;
And let them grow into a multitude
in the midst of the earth."

[17]Now when Joseph saw that his father laid his right hand on the head of Ephraim, it displeased him; so he took hold of his father's hand to remove it from Ephraim's head to Manasseh's head. [18]And Joseph said to his father, "Not so, my father, for this *one is* the firstborn; put your right hand on his head."

[19]But his father refused and said, "I know, my son, I know. He also shall become a people, and he also shall be great; but truly his younger brother shall be greater than he, and his descendants shall become a multitude of nations."

[20]So he blessed them that day, saying, "By you Israel will bless, saying, 'May God make you as Ephraim and as Manasseh!'" And thus he set Ephraim before Manasseh.

[21]Then Israel said to Joseph, "Behold, I am dying, but God will be with you and bring you back to the land of your fathers. [22]Moreover I have given to you one portion above your brothers, which I took from the hand of the Amorite with my sword and my bow."

Jacob's Last Words to His Sons

49 And Jacob called his sons and said, "Gather together, that I may tell you what shall befall you in the last days:

2 "Gather together and hear, you
sons of Jacob,
And listen to Israel your father.

3 "Reuben, you are my firstborn,
My might and the beginning of
my strength,
The excellency of dignity and the
excellency of power.
4 Unstable as water, you shall not
excel,
Because you went up to your
father's bed;
Then you defiled *it*—
He went up to my couch.

5 "Simeon and Levi *are* brothers;
Instruments of cruelty *are in* their
dwelling place.
6 Let not my soul enter their
council;
Let not my honor be united to
their assembly;
For in their anger they slew a man,
And in their self-will they
hamstrung an ox.
7 Cursed *be* their anger, for *it is* fierce;
And their wrath, for it is cruel!
I will divide them in Jacob
And scatter them in Israel.

8 "Judah, you *are he* whom your
brothers shall praise;
Your hand *shall be* on the neck of
your enemies;

Your father's children shall bow
down before you.
9 Judah *is* a lion's whelp;
From the prey, my son, you have
gone up.
He bows down, he lies down as a
lion;
And as a lion, who shall rouse him?
10 The scepter shall not depart from
Judah,
Nor a lawgiver from between his
feet,
Until Shiloh comes;
And to Him *shall be* the obedience
of the people.
11 Binding his donkey to the vine,
And his donkey's colt to the
choice vine,
He washed his garments in wine,
And his clothes in the blood of
grapes.
12 His eyes *are* darker than wine,
And his teeth whiter than milk.

13 "Zebulun shall dwell by the haven
of the sea;
He *shall become* a haven for ships,
And his border shall adjoin Sidon.

14 "Issachar is a strong donkey,
Lying down between two burdens;
15 He saw that rest *was* good,
And that the land *was* pleasant;
He bowed his shoulder to bear *a
burden,*
And became a band of slaves.

16 "Dan shall judge his people
As one of the tribes of Israel.
17 Dan shall be a serpent by the way,
A viper by the path,
That bites the horse's heels
So that its rider shall fall
backward.
18 I have waited for your salvation,
O LORD!

19 "Gad, a troop shall tramp upon him,
But he shall triumph at last.

20 "Bread from Asher *shall be* rich,
And he shall yield royal dainties.

21 "Naphtali *is* a deer let loose;
He uses beautiful words.

22 "Joseph *is* a fruitful bough,
A fruitful bough by a well;
His branches run over the wall.
23 The archers have bitterly grieved
him,
Shot *at him* and hated him.
24 But his bow remained in strength,
And the arms of his hands were
made strong
By the hands of the Mighty *God* of
Jacob
(From there *is* the Shepherd, the
Stone of Israel),
25 By the God of your father who will
help you,
And by the Almighty who will
bless you
With blessings of heaven above,
Blessings of the deep that lies
beneath,
Blessings of the breasts and of the
womb.
26 The blessings of your father
Have excelled the blessings of my
ancestors,
Up to the utmost bound of the
everlasting hills.
They shall be on the head of Joseph,
And on the crown of the head of
him who was separate from
his brothers.

27 "Benjamin is a ravenous wolf;
In the morning he shall devour
the prey,
And at night he shall divide the
spoil."

28 All these *are* the twelve tribes of Isra-
el, and this *is* what their father spoke to
them. And he blessed them; he blessed
each one according to his own blessing.

Jacob's Death and Burial

29 Then he charged them and said to
them: "I am to be gathered to my people;
bury me with my fathers in the cave that
is in the field of Ephron the Hittite, 30 in
the cave that *is* in the field of Machpelah,
which *is* before Mamre in the land of Ca-
naan, which Abraham bought with the
field of Ephron the Hittite as a possession
for a burial place. 31 There they buried
Abraham and Sarah his wife, there they
buried Isaac and Rebekah his wife, and

there I buried Leah. 32The field and the
cave that *is* there *were* purchased from
the sons of Heth." 33And when Jacob had
finished commanding his sons, he drew
his feet up into the bed and breathed
his last, and was gathered to his people.

50 Then Joseph fell on his father's
face and wept over him, and
kissed him. 2And Joseph commanded
his servants the physicians to embalm
his father. So the physicians embalmed
Israel. 3Forty days were required for
him, for such are the days required for
those who are embalmed; and the Egyp-
tians mourned for him seventy days.

4Now when the days of his mourning
were past, Joseph spoke to the house-
hold of Pharaoh, saying, "If now I have
found favor in your eyes, please speak
in the hearing of Pharaoh, saying, 5'My
father made me swear, saying, "Behold,
I am dying; in my grave which I dug for
myself in the land of Canaan, there you
shall bury me." Now therefore, please
let me go up and bury my father, and
I will come back.' "

6And Pharaoh said, "Go up and bury
your father, as he made you swear."

7So Joseph went up to bury his father;
and with him went up all the servants of
Pharaoh, the elders of his house, and all
the elders of the land of Egypt, 8as well as
all the house of Joseph, his brothers, and
his father's house. Only their little ones,
their flocks, and their herds they left in
the land of Goshen. 9And there went up
with him both chariots and horsemen,
and it was a very great gathering.

10Then they came to the threshing floor
of Atad, which *is* beyond the Jordan, and
they mourned there with a great and
very solemn lamentation. He observed
seven days of mourning for his father.
11And when the inhabitants of the land,
the Canaanites, saw the mourning at the
threshing floor of Atad, they said, "This
is a deep mourning of the Egyptians."
Therefore its name was called Abel Miz-
raim,[a] which *is* beyond the Jordan.

12So his sons did for him just as he had
commanded them. 13For his sons carried
him to the land of Canaan, and buried
him in the cave of the field of Machpelah,
before Mamre, which Abraham bought
with the field from Ephron the Hittite as
property for a burial place. 14And after
he had buried his father, Joseph returned
to Egypt, he and his brothers and all
who went up with him to bury his father.

Joseph Reassures His Brothers

15When Joseph's brothers saw that
their father was dead, they said, "Per-
haps Joseph will hate us, and may ac-
tually repay us for all the evil which we
did to him." 16So they sent *messengers* to
Joseph, saying, "Before your father died
he commanded, saying, 17'Thus you
shall say to Joseph: "I beg you, please
forgive the trespass of your brothers
and their sin; for they did evil to you." '
Now, please, forgive the trespass of the
servants of the God of your father." And
Joseph wept when they spoke to him.

18Then his brothers also went and fell
down before his face, and they said,
"Behold, we *are* your servants."

19Joseph said to them, "Do not be
afraid, for *am* I in the place of God?
20But as for you, you meant evil against
me; *but* God meant it for good, in order
to bring it about as *it is* this day, to save
many people alive. 21Now therefore,
do not be afraid; I will provide for you
and your little ones." And he comforted
them and spoke kindly to them.

Death of Joseph

22So Joseph dwelt in Egypt, he and his
father's household. And Joseph lived
one hundred and ten years. 23Joseph
saw Ephraim's children to the third *gen-
eration.* The children of Machir, the son
of Manasseh, were also brought up on
Joseph's knees.

24And Joseph said to his brethren, "I
am dying; but God will surely visit you,
and bring you out of this land to the
land of which He swore to Abraham,
to Isaac, and to Jacob." 25Then Joseph
took an oath from the children of Israel,
saying, "God will surely visit you, and
you shall carry up my bones from here."
26So Joseph died, *being* one hundred
and ten years old; and they embalmed
him, and he was put in a coffin in Egypt.

50:11 [a] Literally *Mourning of Egypt*

THE SECOND BOOK OF MOSES CALLED

EXODUS

The Book of Exodus continues the story of God's people who had gone to Egypt to escape a severe famine during Joseph's lifetime. Hundreds of years later, they are still in Egypt but now as slaves. When the people cry out for help, God hears them and sends Moses to rescue them. The Egyptian Pharaoh, however, refuses to let God's people, known as the Hebrews or Israelites, go. God shows Pharaoh how powerful He is by sending a series of plagues upon Egypt, and Pharaoh finally lets the Hebrews leave. Once they are free, God stays with them and leads them on a journey through the wilderness. Along the way, God provides for them and begins teaching them what it means to be in a relationship with Him. The Hebrews are traveling toward the land God had given Abraham in Genesis.

- **GENRE:** Law
- **AUTHOR:** Moses
- **TIME:** c. 1875–1445 BC (written c. 1445–1406 BC)
- **PURPOSE:** To tell how God's people escaped captivity in Egypt and how he gave them rules for how they were to live with Him and each other.

Israel's Suffering in Egypt

1 Now these *are* the names of the chil-
dren of Israel who came to Egypt;
each man and his household came
with Jacob: 2Reuben, Simeon, Levi, and
Judah; 3Issachar, Zebulun, and Benja-
min; 4Dan, Naphtali, Gad, and Asher.
5All those who were descendants[a] of
Jacob were seventy[b] persons (for Joseph
was in Egypt *already*). 6And Joseph died,
all his brothers, and all that generation.
7But the children of Israel were fruitful
and increased abundantly, multiplied
and grew exceedingly mighty; and the
land was filled with them.

8Now there arose a new king over
Egypt, who did not know Joseph. 9And
he said to his people, "Look, the people
of the children of Israel *are* more and
mightier than we; 10come, let us deal
shrewdly with them, lest they multiply,
and it happen, in the event of war, that
they also join our enemies and fight
against us, and *so* go up out of the land."
11Therefore they set taskmasters over
them to afflict them with their burdens.
And they built for Pharaoh supply cit-
ies, Pithom and Raamses. 12But the
more they afflicted them, the more they
multiplied and grew. And they were in
dread of the children of Israel. 13So the
Egyptians made the children of Israel
serve with rigor. 14And they made their
lives bitter with hard bondage—in mor-
tar, in brick, and in all manner of service
in the field. All their service in which
they made them serve *was* with rigor.

15Then the king of Egypt spoke to the
Hebrew midwives, of whom the name of
one *was* Shiphrah and the name of the
other Puah; 16and he said, "When you do
the duties of a midwife for the Hebrew
women, and see *them* on the birthstools,
if it *is* a son, then you shall kill him; but if
it *is* a daughter, then she shall live." 17But
the midwives feared God, and did not do
as the king of Egypt commanded them,
but saved the male children alive. 18So the
king of Egypt called for the midwives and
said to them, "Why have you done this
thing, and saved the male children alive?"

19And the midwives said to Pharaoh,
"Because the Hebrew women *are* not
like the Egyptian women; for they *are*
lively and give birth before the mid-
wives come to them."

1:5 [a] Literally *who came from the loins of* [b] Dead Sea Scrolls and Septuagint read *seventy-five* (compare Acts 7:14).

20Therefore God dealt well with the
midwives, and the people multiplied
and grew very mighty. 21And so it was,
because the midwives feared God, that
He provided households for them.
22So Pharaoh commanded all his peo-
ple, saying, "Every son who is born[a]
you shall cast into the river, and every
daughter you shall save alive."

Moses Is Born

2 And a man of the house of Levi
went and took *as wife* a daughter
of Levi. 2So the woman conceived and
bore a son. And when she saw that he
was a beautiful *child,* she hid him three
months. 3But when she could no longer
hide him, she took an ark of bulrushes
for him, daubed it with asphalt and
pitch, put the child in it, and laid *it* in
the reeds by the river's bank. 4And his
sister stood afar off, to know what would
be done to him.
5Then the daughter of Pharaoh came
down to bathe at the river. And her
maidens walked along the riverside;
and when she saw the ark among the
reeds, she sent her maid to get it. 6And
when she opened *it,* she saw the child,
and behold, the baby wept. So she had
compassion on him, and said, "This is
one of the Hebrews' children."
7Then his sister said to Pharaoh's
daughter, "Shall I go and call a nurse
for you from the Hebrew women, that
she may nurse the child for you?"
8And Pharaoh's daughter said to her,
"Go." So the maiden went and called the
child's mother. 9Then Pharaoh's daugh-
ter said to her, "Take this child away and
nurse him for me, and I will give *you*
your wages." So the woman took the
child and nursed him. 10And the child
grew, and she brought him to Pharaoh's
daughter, and he became her son. So
she called his name Moses,[a] saying,
"Because I drew him out of the water."

Moses Flees to Midian

11Now it came to pass in those days,
when Moses was grown, that he went out
to his brethren and looked at their bur-
dens. And he saw an Egyptian beating
a Hebrew, one of his brethren. 12So he
looked this way and that way, and when
he saw no one, he killed the Egyptian
and hid him in the sand. 13And when he
went out the second day, behold, two
Hebrew men were fighting, and he said
to the one who did the wrong, "Why are
you striking your companion?"
14Then he said, "Who made you a
prince and a judge over us? Do you in-
tend to kill me as you killed the Egyp-
tian?"
So Moses feared and said, "Surely this
thing is known!" 15When Pharaoh heard
of this matter, he sought to kill Moses.
But Moses fled from the face of Pharaoh
and dwelt in the land of Midian; and he
sat down by a well.
16Now the priest of Midian had seven
daughters. And they came and drew
water, and they filled the troughs to
water their father's flock. 17Then the
shepherds came and drove them away;
but Moses stood up and helped them,
and watered their flock.
18When they came to Reuel their fa-
ther, he said, "How *is it that* you have
come so soon today?"
19And they said, "An Egyptian deliv-
ered us from the hand of the shepherds,
and he also drew enough water for us
and watered the flock."
20So he said to his daughters, "And
where *is* he? Why *is* it *that* you have
left the man? Call him, that he may
eat bread."
21Then Moses was content to live with
the man, and he gave Zipporah his
daughter to Moses. 22And she bore *him*
a son. He called his name Gershom,[a]
for he said, "I have been a stranger in
a foreign land."
23Now it happened in the process of
time that the king of Egypt died. Then
the children of Israel groaned because
of the bondage, and they cried out; and
their cry came up to God because of the
bondage. 24So God heard their groan-
ing, and God remembered His covenant
with Abraham, with Isaac, and with
Jacob. 25And God looked upon the chil-
dren of Israel, and God acknowledged
them.

1:22 [a] Samaritan Pentateuch, Septuagint, and Targum add *to the Hebrews.* **2:10** [a] Literally *Drawn Out* **2:22** [a] Literally *Stranger There*

Moses at the Burning Bush

3 Now Moses was tending the flock of
Jethro his father-in-law, the priest of
Midian. And he led the flock to the back
of the desert, and came to Horeb, the
mountain of God. 2And the Angel of the
LORD appeared to him in a flame of fire
from the midst of a bush. So he looked,
and behold, the bush was burning with
fire, but the bush *was* not consumed.
3Then Moses said, "I will now turn aside
and see this great sight, why the bush
does not burn."
4So when the LORD saw that he turned
aside to look, God called to him from
the midst of the bush and said, "Moses,
Moses!"
And he said, "Here I am."
5Then He said, "Do not draw near this
place. Take your sandals off your feet,
for the place where you stand *is* holy
ground." 6Moreover He said, "I *am* the
God of your father—the God of Abra-
ham, the God of Isaac, and the God of
Jacob." And Moses hid his face, for he
was afraid to look upon God.
7And the LORD said: "I have surely
seen the oppression of My people who
are in Egypt, and have heard their cry
because of their taskmasters, for I know
their sorrows. 8So I have come down
to deliver them out of the hand of the
Egyptians, and to bring them up from
that land to a good and large land, to
a land flowing with milk and honey,
to the place of the Canaanites and the
Hittites and the Amorites and the Periz-
zites and the Hivites and the Jebusites.
9Now therefore, behold, the cry of the
children of Israel has come to Me, and
I have also seen the oppression with
which the Egyptians oppress them.
10Come now, therefore, and I will send
you to Pharaoh that you may bring
My people, the children of Israel, out
of Egypt."
11But Moses said to God, "Who *am* I
that I should go to Pharaoh, and that I
should bring the children of Israel out
of Egypt?"
12So He said, "I will certainly be with
you. And this *shall be* a sign to you that I
have sent you: When you have brought
the people out of Egypt, you shall serve
God on this mountain."
13Then Moses said to God, "Indeed,
when I come to the children of Israel
and say to them, 'The God of your fa-
thers has sent me to you,' and they say
to me, 'What *is* His name?' what shall
I say to them?"
14And God said to Moses, "I AM WHO I
AM." And He said, "Thus you shall say to
the children of Israel, 'I AM has sent me
to you.' " 15Moreover God said to Moses,
"Thus you shall say to the children of Is-
rael: 'The LORD God of your fathers, the
God of Abraham, the God of Isaac, and
the God of Jacob, has sent me to you. This
is My name forever, and this *is* My memo-
rial to all generations.' 16Go and gather
the elders of Israel together, and say to
them, 'The LORD God of your fathers, the
God of Abraham, of Isaac, and of Jacob,
appeared to me, saying, "I have surely
visited you and *seen* what is done to you
in Egypt; 17and I have said I will bring
you up out of the affliction of Egypt to the
land of the Canaanites and the Hittites
and the Amorites and the Perizzites and
the Hivites and the Jebusites, to a land
flowing with milk and honey." ' 18Then
they will heed your voice; and you shall
come, you and the elders of Israel, to the
king of Egypt; and you shall say to him,
'The LORD God of the Hebrews has met
with us; and now, please, let us go three
days' journey into the wilderness, that
we may sacrifice to the LORD our God.'
19But I am sure that the king of Egypt will
not let you go, no, not even by a mighty
hand. 20So I will stretch out My hand and
strike Egypt with all My wonders which I
will do in its midst; and after that he will
let you go. 21And I will give this people
favor in the sight of the Egyptians; and it
shall be, when you go, that you shall not
go empty-handed. 22But every woman
shall ask of her neighbor, namely, of her
who dwells near her house, articles of
silver, articles of gold, and clothing; and
you shall put *them* on your sons and on
your daughters. So you shall plunder
the Egyptians."

Miraculous Signs for Pharaoh

4 Then Moses answered and said, "But
suppose they will not believe me or
listen to my voice; suppose they say,
'The LORD has not appeared to you.' "

2So the LORD said to him, "What *is* that in your hand?"

He said, "A rod."

3And He said, "Cast it on the ground." So he cast it on the ground, and it became a serpent; and Moses fled from it. 4Then the LORD said to Moses, "Reach out your hand and take *it* by the tail" (and he reached out his hand and caught it, and it became a rod in his hand), 5"that they may believe that the LORD God of their fathers, the God of Abraham, the God of Isaac, and the God of Jacob, has appeared to you."

6Furthermore the LORD said to him, "Now put your hand in your bosom." And he put his hand in his bosom, and when he took it out, behold, his hand *was* leprous, like snow. 7And He said, "Put your hand in your bosom again." So he put his hand in his bosom again, and drew it out of his bosom, and behold, it was restored like his *other* flesh. 8"Then it will be, if they do not believe you, nor heed the message of the first sign, that they may believe the message of the latter sign. 9And it shall be, if they do not believe even these two signs, or listen to your voice, that you shall take water from the river[a] and pour *it* on the dry *land.* The water which you take from the river will become blood on the dry *land.*"

10Then Moses said to the LORD, "O my Lord, I *am* not eloquent, neither before nor since You have spoken to Your servant; but I *am* slow of speech and slow of tongue."

11So the LORD said to him, "Who has made man's mouth? Or who makes the mute, the deaf, the seeing, or the blind? *Have* not I, the LORD? 12Now therefore, go, and I will be with your mouth and teach you what you shall say."

13But he said, "O my Lord, please send by the hand of whomever *else* You may send."

14So the anger of the LORD was kindled against Moses, and He said: "Is not Aaron the Levite your brother? I know that he can speak well. And look, he is also coming out to meet you. When he sees you, he will be glad in his heart. 15Now you shall speak to him and put the words in his mouth. And I will be with your mouth and with his mouth, and I will teach you what you shall do. 16So he shall be your spokesman to the people. And he himself shall be as a mouth for you, and you shall be to him as God. 17And you shall take this rod in your hand, with which you shall do the signs."

Moses Goes to Egypt

18So Moses went and returned to Jethro his father-in-law, and said to him, "Please let me go and return to my brethren who *are* in Egypt, and see whether they are still alive."

And Jethro said to Moses, "Go in peace."

19Now the LORD said to Moses in Midian, "Go, return to Egypt; for all the men who sought your life are dead." 20Then Moses took his wife and his sons and set them on a donkey, and he returned to the land of Egypt. And Moses took the rod of God in his hand.

21And the LORD said to Moses, "When you go back to Egypt, see that you do all those wonders before Pharaoh which I have put in your hand. But I will harden his heart, so that he will not let the people go. 22Then you shall say to Pharaoh, 'Thus says the LORD: "Israel *is* My son, My firstborn. 23So I say to you, let My son go that he may serve Me. But if you refuse to let him go, indeed I will kill your son, your firstborn." ' "

24And it came to pass on the way, at the encampment, that the LORD met him and sought to kill him. 25Then Zipporah took a sharp stone and cut off the foreskin of her son and cast *it* at *Moses'*[a] feet, and said, "Surely you *are* a husband of blood to me!" 26So He let him go. Then she said, "*You are* a husband of blood!"—because of the circumcision.

27And the LORD said to Aaron, "Go into the wilderness to meet Moses." So he went and met him on the mountain of God, and kissed him. 28So Moses told Aaron all the words of the LORD who had sent him, and all the signs which He had commanded him. 29Then Moses and Aaron went and gathered together all the elders of the children of Israel.

4:9 [a] That is, the Nile **4:25** [a] Literally *his*

30 And Aaron spoke all the words which
the LORD had spoken to Moses. Then he
did the signs in the sight of the people.
31 So the people believed; and when they
heard that the LORD had visited the chil-
dren of Israel and that He had looked
on their affliction, then they bowed their
heads and worshiped.

First Encounter with Pharaoh

5 Afterward Moses and Aaron went
in and told Pharaoh, "Thus says
the LORD God of Israel: 'Let My people
go, that they may hold a feast to Me in
the wilderness.' "
2 And Pharaoh said, "Who *is* the LORD,
that I should obey His voice to let Israel
go? I do not know the LORD, nor will I
let Israel go."
3 So they said, "The God of the Hebrews
has met with us. Please, let us go three
days' journey into the desert and sacri-
fice to the LORD our God, lest He fall upon
us with pestilence or with the sword."
4 Then the king of Egypt said to them,
"Moses and Aaron, why do you take the
people from their work? Get *back* to your
labor." 5 And Pharaoh said, "Look, the
people of the land *are* many now, and
you make them rest from their labor!"
6 So the same day Pharaoh command-
ed the taskmasters of the people and
their officers, saying, 7 "You shall no
longer give the people straw to make
brick as before. Let them go and gather
straw for themselves. 8 And you shall
lay on them the quota of bricks which
they made before. You shall not reduce
it. For they are idle; therefore they cry
out, saying, 'Let us go *and* sacrifice to
our God.' 9 Let more work be laid on the
men, that they may labor in it, and let
them not regard false words."
10 And the taskmasters of the people
and their officers went out and spoke
to the people, saying, "Thus says Phar-
aoh: 'I will not give you straw. 11 Go, get
yourselves straw where you can find it;
yet none of your work will be reduced.' "
12 So the people were scattered abroad
throughout all the land of Egypt to
gather stubble instead of straw. 13 And
the taskmasters forced *them* to hurry,
saying, "Fulfill your work, *your* daily
quota, as when there was straw." 14 Also
the officers of the children of Israel,
whom Pharaoh's taskmasters had set
over them, were beaten *and* were asked,
"Why have you not fulfilled your task
in making brick both yesterday and
today, as before?"
15 Then the officers of the children of
Israel came and cried out to Pharaoh,
saying, "Why are you dealing thus with
your servants? 16 There is no straw given
to your servants, and they say to us,
'Make brick!' And indeed your servants
are beaten, but the fault *is* in your *own*
people."
17 But he said, "You *are* idle! Idle! There-
fore you say, 'Let us go *and* sacrifice to
the LORD.' 18 Therefore go now *and* work;
for no straw shall be given you, yet you
shall deliver the quota of bricks." 19 And
the officers of the children of Israel saw
that they *were* in trouble after it was
said, "You shall not reduce *any* bricks
from your daily quota."
20 Then, as they came out from Phar-
aoh, they met Moses and Aaron who
stood there to meet them. 21 And they
said to them, "Let the LORD look on
you and judge, because you have made
us abhorrent in the sight of Pharaoh
and in the sight of his servants, to put
a sword in their hand to kill us."

Israel's Deliverance Assured

22 So Moses returned to the LORD and
said, "Lord, why have You brought trou-
ble on this people? Why *is* it You have
sent me? 23 For since I came to Pharaoh
to speak in Your name, he has done
evil to this people; neither have You
delivered Your people at all."
6 Then the LORD said to Moses, "Now
you shall see what I will do to Phar-
aoh. For with a strong hand he will let
them go, and with a strong hand he will
drive them out of his land."
2 And God spoke to Moses and said to
him: "I *am* the LORD. 3 I appeared to
Abraham, to Isaac, and to Jacob, as
God Almighty, but *by* My name LORD[a]
I was not known to them. 4 I have also
established My covenant with them,

6:3 [a] Hebrew *YHWH,* traditionally *Jehovah*

to give them the land of Canaan, the
land of their pilgrimage, in which they
were strangers. 5And I have also heard
the groaning of the children of Israel
whom the Egyptians keep in bondage,
and I have remembered My covenant.
6Therefore say to the children of Israel:
'I *am* the LORD; I will bring you out from
under the burdens of the Egyptians, I
will rescue you from their bondage, and
I will redeem you with an outstretched
arm and with great judgments. 7I will
take you as My people, and I will be
your God. Then you shall know that
I *am* the LORD your God who brings
you out from under the burdens of the
Egyptians. 8And I will bring you into
the land which I swore to give to Abra-
ham, Isaac, and Jacob; and I will give
it to you *as* a heritage: I *am* the LORD.' "
9So Moses spoke thus to the children
of Israel; but they did not heed Moses,
because of anguish of spirit and cruel
bondage.

10And the LORD spoke to Moses, say-
ing, 11"Go in, tell Pharaoh king of Egypt
to let the children of Israel go out of
his land."

12And Moses spoke before the LORD,
saying, "The children of Israel have not
heeded me. How then shall Pharaoh
heed me, for I *am* of uncircumcised
lips?"

13Then the LORD spoke to Moses and
Aaron, and gave them a command for
the children of Israel and for Pharaoh
king of Egypt, to bring the children of
Israel out of the land of Egypt.

The Family of Moses and Aaron

14These *are* the heads of their fathers'
houses: The sons of Reuben, the first-
born of Israel, *were* Hanoch, Pallu, Hez-
ron, and Carmi. These are the families
of Reuben. 15And the sons of Simeon
were Jemuel,[a] Jamin, Ohad, Jachin,
Zohar, and Shaul the son of a Canaan-
ite woman. These *are* the families of
Simeon. 16These *are* the names of the
sons of Levi according to their gener-
ations: Gershon, Kohath, and Merari.
And the years of the life of Levi *were*
one hundred and thirty-seven. 17The
sons of Gershon *were* Libni and Shimi
according to their families. 18And the
sons of Kohath *were* Amram, Izhar, He-
bron, and Uzziel. And the years of the
life of Kohath *were* one hundred and
thirty-three. 19The sons of Merari *were*
Mahli and Mushi. These *are* the families
of Levi according to their generations.

20Now Amram took for himself Joche-
bed, his father's sister, as wife; and she
bore him Aaron and Moses. And the
years of the life of Amram *were* one
hundred and thirty-seven. 21The sons of
Izhar *were* Korah, Nepheg, and Zichri.
22And the sons of Uzziel *were* Mishael,
Elzaphan, and Zithri. 23Aaron took to
himself Elisheba, daughter of Ammina-
dab, sister of Nahshon, as wife; and she
bore him Nadab, Abihu, Eleazar, and
Ithamar. 24And the sons of Korah *were*
Assir, Elkanah, and Abiasaph. These are
the families of the Korahites. 25Eleazar,
Aaron's son, took for himself one of the
daughters of Putiel as wife; and she
bore him Phinehas. These *are* the heads
of the fathers' houses of the Levites
according to their families.

26These *are the same* Aaron and Moses
to whom the LORD said, "Bring out the
children of Israel from the land of Egypt
according to their armies." 27These *are*
the ones who spoke to Pharaoh king
of Egypt, to bring out the children of
Israel from Egypt. These *are the same*
Moses and Aaron.

Aaron Is Moses' Spokesman

28And it came to pass, on the day the
LORD spoke to Moses in the land of
Egypt, 29that the LORD spoke to Moses,
saying, "I *am* the LORD. Speak to Phar-
aoh king of Egypt all that I say to you."

30But Moses said before the LORD,
"Behold, I *am* of uncircumcised lips, and
how shall Pharaoh heed me?"

7 So the LORD said to Moses: "See,
I have made you *as* God to Phar-
aoh, and Aaron your brother shall be
your prophet. 2You shall speak all that I
command you. And Aaron your brother
shall tell Pharaoh to send the children
of Israel out of his land. 3And I will
harden Pharaoh's heart, and multiply

6:15 [a] Spelled *Nemuel* in Numbers 26:12

My signs and My wonders in the land of
Egypt. 4But Pharaoh will not heed you,
so that I may lay My hand on Egypt
and bring My armies *and* My people,
the children of Israel, out of the land
of Egypt by great judgments. 5And the
Egyptians shall know that I *am* the
LORD, when I stretch out My hand on
Egypt and bring out the children of Is-
rael from among them."

6Then Moses and Aaron did *so;* just as
the LORD commanded them, so they
did. 7And Moses *was* eighty years old
and Aaron eighty-three years old when
they spoke to Pharaoh.

Aaron's Miraculous Rod

8Then the LORD spoke to Moses and
Aaron, saying, 9"When Pharaoh speaks
to you, saying, 'Show a miracle for your-
selves,' then you shall say to Aaron,
'Take your rod and cast *it* before Phar-
aoh, *and* let it become a serpent.' " 10So
Moses and Aaron went in to Pharaoh,
and they did so, just as the LORD com-
manded. And Aaron cast down his rod
before Pharaoh and before his servants,
and it became a serpent.

11But Pharaoh also called the wise men
and the sorcerers; so the magicians of
Egypt, they also did in like manner with
their enchantments. 12For every man
threw down his rod, and they became
serpents. But Aaron's rod swallowed up
their rods. 13And Pharaoh's heart grew
hard, and he did not heed them, as the
LORD had said.

The First Plague: Waters Become Blood

14So the LORD said to Moses: "Phar-
aoh's heart *is* hard; he refuses to let
the people go. 15Go to Pharaoh in the
morning, when he goes out to the wa-
ter, and you shall stand by the river's
bank to meet him; and the rod which
was turned to a serpent you shall take
in your hand. 16And you shall say to
him, 'The LORD God of the Hebrews has
sent me to you, saying, "Let My peo-
ple go, that they may serve Me in the
wilderness"; but indeed, until now you
would not hear! 17Thus says the LORD:
"By this you shall know that I *am* the
LORD. Behold, I will strike the waters
which *are* in the river with the rod that
is in my hand, and they shall be turned
to blood. 18And the fish that *are* in the
river shall die, the river shall stink, and
the Egyptians will loathe to drink the
water of the river." ' "

19Then the LORD spoke to Moses, "Say
to Aaron, 'Take your rod and stretch out
your hand over the waters of Egypt, over
their streams, over their rivers, over
their ponds, and over all their pools of
water, that they may become blood.
And there shall be blood throughout
all the land of Egypt, both in *buckets
of* wood and *pitchers of* stone.' " 20And
Moses and Aaron did so, just as the
LORD commanded. So he lifted up the
rod and struck the waters that *were* in
the river, in the sight of Pharaoh and
in the sight of his servants. And all the
waters that *were* in the river were turned
to blood. 21The fish that *were* in the river
died, the river stank, and the Egyptians
could not drink the water of the river.
So there was blood throughout all the
land of Egypt.

22Then the magicians of Egypt did so
with their enchantments; and Phar-
aoh's heart grew hard, and he did
not heed them, as the LORD had said.
23And Pharaoh turned and went into
his house. Neither was his heart moved
by this. 24So all the Egyptians dug all
around the river for water to drink, be-
cause they could not drink the water of
the river. 25And seven days passed after
the LORD had struck the river.

The Second Plague: Frogs

8 And the LORD spoke to Moses, "Go
to Pharaoh and say to him, 'Thus
says the LORD: "Let My people go, that
they may serve Me. 2But if you refuse to
let *them* go, behold, I will smite all your
territory with frogs. 3So the river shall
bring forth frogs abundantly, which
shall go up and come into your house,
into your bedroom, on your bed, into
the houses of your servants, on your
people, into your ovens, and into your
kneading bowls. 4And the frogs shall
come up on you, on your people, and
on all your servants." ' "

5Then the LORD spoke to Moses, "Say
to Aaron, 'Stretch out your hand with
your rod over the streams, over the rivers,

and over the ponds, and cause frogs to
come up on the land of Egypt.' " 6So Aaron
stretched out his hand over the waters of
Egypt, and the frogs came up and covered
the land of Egypt. 7And the magicians did
so with their enchantments, and brought
up frogs on the land of Egypt.

8Then Pharaoh called for Moses and
Aaron, and said, "Entreat the LORD that
He may take away the frogs from me
and from my people; and I will let the
people go, that they may sacrifice to
the LORD."

9And Moses said to Pharaoh, "Accept
the honor of saying when I shall inter-
cede for you, for your servants, and for
your people, to destroy the frogs from
you and your houses, *that* they may
remain in the river only."

10So he said, "Tomorrow." And he said,
"*Let it be* according to your word, that
you may know that *there is* no one like
the LORD our God. 11And the frogs shall
depart from you, from your houses,
from your servants, and from your peo-
ple. They shall remain in the river only."

12Then Moses and Aaron went out
from Pharaoh. And Moses cried out to
the LORD concerning the frogs which
He had brought against Pharaoh. 13So
the LORD did according to the word of
Moses. And the frogs died out of the
houses, out of the courtyards, and out
of the fields. 14They gathered them to-
gether in heaps, and the land stank.
15But when Pharaoh saw that there was
relief, he hardened his heart and did
not heed them, as the LORD had said.

The Third Plague: Lice

16So the LORD said to Moses, "Say to
Aaron, 'Stretch out your rod, and strike
the dust of the land, so that it may be-
come lice throughout all the land of
Egypt.' " 17And they did so. For Aaron
stretched out his hand with his rod and
struck the dust of the earth, and it be-
came lice on man and beast. All the dust
of the land became lice throughout all
the land of Egypt.

18Now the magicians so worked with
their enchantments to bring forth lice,
but they could not. So there were lice on
man and beast. 19Then the magicians
said to Pharaoh, "This *is* the finger of
God." But Pharaoh's heart grew hard,
and he did not heed them, just as the
LORD had said.

The Fourth Plague: Flies

20And the LORD said to Moses, "Rise
early in the morning and stand before
Pharaoh as he comes out to the water.
Then say to him, 'Thus says the LORD:
"Let My people go, that they may serve
Me. 21Or else, if you will not let My peo-
ple go, behold, I will send swarms *of flies*
on you and your servants, on your peo-
ple and into your houses. The houses of
the Egyptians shall be full of swarms
of flies, and also the ground on which
they *stand.* 22And in that day I will set
apart the land of Goshen, in which My
people dwell, that no swarms *of flies*
shall be there, in order that you may
know that I *am* the LORD in the midst
of the land. 23I will make a difference[a]
between My people and your people.
Tomorrow this sign shall be." ' " 24And
the LORD did so. Thick swarms *of flies*
came into the house of Pharaoh, *into*
his servants' houses, and into all the
land of Egypt. The land was corrupted
because of the swarms *of flies.*

25Then Pharaoh called for Moses and
Aaron, and said, "Go, sacrifice to your
God in the land."

26And Moses said, "It is not right to
do so, for we would be sacrificing the
abomination of the Egyptians to the
LORD our God. If we sacrifice the abom-
ination of the Egyptians before their
eyes, then will they not stone us? 27We
will go three days' journey into the wil-
derness and sacrifice to the LORD our
God as He will command us."

28So Pharaoh said, "I will let you go,
that you may sacrifice to the LORD your
God in the wilderness; only you shall
not go very far away. Intercede for me."

29Then Moses said, "Indeed I am going
out from you, and I will entreat the
LORD, that the swarms *of flies* may de-
part tomorrow from Pharaoh, from his
servants, and from his people. But let
Pharaoh not deal deceitfully anymore

8:23 [a] Literally *set a ransom* (compare Exodus 9:4 and 11:7)

in not letting the people go to sacrifice
to the LORD."
30So Moses went out from Pharaoh
and entreated the LORD. 31And the LORD
did according to the word of Moses;
He removed the swarms *of flies* from
Pharaoh, from his servants, and from
his people. Not one remained. 32But
Pharaoh hardened his heart at this time
also; neither would he let the people go.

The Fifth Plague: Livestock Diseased

9 Then the LORD said to Moses, "Go in
to Pharaoh and tell him, 'Thus says
the LORD God of the Hebrews: "Let My
people go, that they may serve Me. 2For
if you refuse to let *them* go, and still hold
them, 3behold, the hand of the LORD
will be on your cattle in the field, on the
horses, on the donkeys, on the camels,
on the oxen, and on the sheep—a very
severe pestilence. 4And the LORD will
make a difference between the livestock
of Israel and the livestock of Egypt. So
nothing shall die of all *that* belongs to
the children of Israel." ' " 5Then the LORD
appointed a set time, saying, "Tomorrow
the LORD will do this thing in the land."
6So the LORD did this thing on the next
day, and all the livestock of Egypt died;
but of the livestock of the children of
Israel, not one died. 7Then Pharaoh
sent, and indeed, not even one of the
livestock of the Israelites was dead. But
the heart of Pharaoh became hard, and
he did not let the people go.

The Sixth Plague: Boils

8So the LORD said to Moses and Aaron,
"Take for yourselves handfuls of ashes
from a furnace, and let Moses scatter
it toward the heavens in the sight of
Pharaoh. 9And it will become fine dust
in all the land of Egypt, and it will cause
boils that break out in sores on man and
beast throughout all the land of Egypt."
10Then they took ashes from the furnace
and stood before Pharaoh, and Moses
scattered *them* toward heaven. And *they*
caused boils that break out in sores on
man and beast. 11And the magicians
could not stand before Moses because
of the boils, for the boils were on the
magicians and on all the Egyptians.
12But the LORD hardened the heart of
Pharaoh; and he did not heed them,
just as the LORD had spoken to Moses.

The Seventh Plague: Hail

13Then the LORD said to Moses, "Rise
early in the morning and stand before
Pharaoh, and say to him, 'Thus says
the LORD God of the Hebrews: "Let My
people go, that they may serve Me, 14for
at this time I will send all My plagues to
your very heart, and on your servants
and on your people, that you may know
that *there is* none like Me in all the earth.
15Now if I had stretched out My hand
and struck you and your people with
pestilence, then you would have been
cut off from the earth. 16But indeed for
this *purpose* I have raised you up, that I
may show My power *in* you, and that My
name may be declared in all the earth.
17As yet you exalt yourself against My
people in that you will not let them go.
18Behold, tomorrow about this time I will
cause very heavy hail to rain down, such
as has not been in Egypt since its found-
ing until now. 19Therefore send now *and*
gather your livestock and all that you
have in the field, for the hail shall come
down on every man and every animal
which is found in the field and is not
brought home; and they shall die." ' "
20He who feared the word of the LORD
among the servants of Pharaoh made
his servants and his livestock flee to the
houses. 21But he who did not regard the
word of the LORD left his servants and
his livestock in the field.
22Then the LORD said to Moses,
"Stretch out your hand toward heaven,
that there may be hail in all the land of
Egypt—on man, on beast, and on every
herb of the field, throughout the land of
Egypt." 23And Moses stretched out his
rod toward heaven; and the LORD sent
thunder and hail, and fire darted to the
ground. And the LORD rained hail on
the land of Egypt. 24So there was hail,
and fire mingled with the hail, so very
heavy that there was none like it in all
the land of Egypt since it became a na-
tion. 25And the hail struck throughout
the whole land of Egypt, all that *was* in
the field, both man and beast; and the
hail struck every herb of the field and
broke every tree of the field. 26Only in

the land of Goshen, where the children
of Israel *were,* there was no hail.
27 And Pharaoh sent and called for
Moses and Aaron, and said to them, "I
have sinned this time. The LORD *is* righ-
teous, and my people and I *are* wicked.
28 Entreat the LORD, that there may be
no *more* mighty thundering and hail,
for *it is* enough. I will let you go, and
you shall stay no longer."
29 So Moses said to him, "As soon as I
have gone out of the city, I will spread
out my hands to the LORD; the thunder
will cease, and there will be no more
hail, that you may know that the earth
is the LORD's. 30 But as for you and your
servants, I know that you will not yet
fear the LORD God."
31 Now the flax and the barley were
struck, for the barley *was* in the head
and the flax *was* in bud. 32 But the wheat
and the spelt were not struck, for they
are late crops.
33 So Moses went out of the city from
Pharaoh and spread out his hands to
the LORD; then the thunder and the hail
ceased, and the rain was not poured on
the earth. 34 And when Pharaoh saw
that the rain, the hail, and the thunder
had ceased, he sinned yet more; and he
hardened his heart, he and his servants.
35 So the heart of Pharaoh was hard; nei-
ther would he let the children of Israel
go, as the LORD had spoken by Moses.

The Eighth Plague: Locusts

10 Now the LORD said to Moses,
"Go in to Pharaoh; for I have
hardened his heart and the hearts of his
servants, that I may show these signs
of Mine before him, 2 and that you may
tell in the hearing of your son and your
son's son the mighty things I have done
in Egypt, and My signs which I have
done among them, that you may know
that I *am* the LORD."
3 So Moses and Aaron came in to Phar-
aoh and said to him, "Thus says the
LORD God of the Hebrews: 'How long will
you refuse to humble yourself before
Me? Let My people go, that they may
serve Me. 4 Or else, if you refuse to let
My people go, behold, tomorrow I will
bring locusts into your territory. 5 And
they shall cover the face of the earth,
so that no one will be able to see the
earth; and they shall eat the residue of
what is left, which remains to you from
the hail, and they shall eat every tree
which grows up for you out of the field.
6 They shall fill your houses, the houses
of all your servants, and the houses of
all the Egyptians—which neither your
fathers nor your fathers' fathers have
seen, since the day that they were on
the earth to this day.' " And he turned
and went out from Pharaoh.
7 Then Pharaoh's servants said to him,
"How long shall this man be a snare to
us? Let the men go, that they may serve
the LORD their God. Do you not yet know
that Egypt is destroyed?"
8 So Moses and Aaron were brought
again to Pharaoh, and he said to them,
"Go, serve the LORD your God. Who *are*
the ones that are going?"
9 And Moses said, "We will go with our
young and our old; with our sons and
our daughters, with our flocks and our
herds we will go, for we must hold a
feast to the LORD."
10 Then he said to them, "The LORD had
better be with you when I let you and
your little ones go! Beware, for evil is
ahead of you. 11 Not so! Go now, you *who
are* men, and serve the LORD, for that is
what you desired." And they were driven
out from Pharaoh's presence.
12 Then the LORD said to Moses, "Stretch
out your hand over the land of Egypt for
the locusts, that they may come upon
the land of Egypt, and eat every herb
of the land—all that the hail has left."
13 So Moses stretched out his rod over the
land of Egypt, and the LORD brought an
east wind on the land all that day and
all *that* night. When it was morning, the
east wind brought the locusts. 14 And
the locusts went up over all the land of
Egypt and rested on all the territory of
Egypt. *They were* very severe; previously
there had been no such locusts as they,
nor shall there be such after them. 15 For
they covered the face of the whole earth,
so that the land was darkened; and they
ate every herb of the land and all the
fruit of the trees which the hail had left.
So there remained nothing green on
the trees or on the plants of the field
throughout all the land of Egypt.

16Then Pharaoh called for Moses
and Aaron in haste, and said, “I have
sinned against the LORD your God and
against you. 17Now therefore, please
forgive my sin only this once, and en-
treat the LORD your God, that He may
take away from me this death only.”
18So he went out from Pharaoh and
entreated the LORD. 19And the LORD
turned a very strong west wind, which
took the locusts away and blew them
into the Red Sea. There remained not
one locust in all the territory of Egypt.
20But the LORD hardened Pharaoh’s
heart, and he did not let the children
of Israel go.

The Ninth Plague: Darkness

21Then the LORD said to Moses, “Stretch
out your hand toward heaven, that
there may be darkness over the land
of Egypt, darkness *which* may even be
felt.” 22So Moses stretched out his hand
toward heaven, and there was thick
darkness in all the land of Egypt three
days. 23They did not see one another;
nor did anyone rise from his place for
three days. But all the children of Israel
had light in their dwellings.

24Then Pharaoh called to Moses and
said, “Go, serve the LORD; only let your
flocks and your herds be kept back. Let
your little ones also go with you.”

25But Moses said, “You must also give
us sacrifices and burnt offerings, that
we may sacrifice to the LORD our God.
26Our livestock also shall go with us; not a
hoof shall be left behind. For we must take
some of them to serve the LORD our God,
and even we do not know with what we
must serve the LORD until we arrive there.”

27But the LORD hardened Pharaoh’s
heart, and he would not let them go.
28Then Pharaoh said to him, “Get away
from me! Take heed to yourself and see
my face no more! For in the day you see
my face you shall die!”

29So Moses said, “You have spoken
well. I will never see your face again.”

Death of the Firstborn Announced

11 And the LORD said to Moses,
“I will bring one more plague
on Pharaoh and on Egypt. Afterward
he will let you go from here. When he
lets *you* go, he will surely drive you out
of here altogether. 2Speak now in the
hearing of the people, and let every
man ask from his neighbor and every
woman from her neighbor, articles of
silver and articles of gold.” 3And the
LORD gave the people favor in the sight
of the Egyptians. Moreover the man
Moses *was* very great in the land of
Egypt, in the sight of Pharaoh’s servants
and in the sight of the people.

4Then Moses said, “Thus says the
LORD: ‘About midnight I will go out
into the midst of Egypt; 5and all the
firstborn in the land of Egypt shall die,
from the firstborn of Pharaoh who sits
on his throne, even to the firstborn of
the female servant who *is* behind the
handmill, and all the firstborn of the
animals. 6Then there shall be a great
cry throughout all the land of Egypt,
such as was not like it *before,* nor shall
be like it again. 7But against none of the
children of Israel shall a dog move its
tongue, against man or beast, that you
may know that the LORD does make a
difference between the Egyptians and
Israel.’ 8And all these your servants
shall come down to me and bow down
to me, saying, ‘Get out, and all the peo-
ple who follow you!’ After that I will go
out.” Then he went out from Pharaoh
in great anger.

9But the LORD said to Moses, “Phar-
aoh will not heed you, so that My won-
ders may be multiplied in the land of
Egypt.” 10So Moses and Aaron did all
these wonders before Pharaoh; and the
LORD hardened Pharaoh’s heart, and
he did not let the children of Israel go
out of his land.

The Passover Instituted

12 Now the LORD spoke to Moses
and Aaron in the land of Egypt,
saying, 2“This month *shall be* your be-
ginning of months; it *shall be* the first
month of the year to you. 3Speak to all
the congregation of Israel, saying: ‘On
the tenth of this month every man shall
take for himself a lamb, according to the
house of *his* father, a lamb for a house-
hold. 4And if the household is too small
for the lamb, let him and his neighbor
next to his house take *it* according to

the number of the persons; according
to each man's need you shall make your
count for the lamb. 5 Your lamb shall be
without blemish, a male of the first year.
You may take *it* from the sheep or from
the goats. 6 Now you shall keep it until
the fourteenth day of the same month.
Then the whole assembly of the congre-
gation of Israel shall kill it at twilight.
7 And they shall take *some* of the blood
and put *it* on the two doorposts and on
the lintel of the houses where they eat
it. 8 Then they shall eat the flesh on that
night; roasted in fire, with unleavened
bread *and* with bitter *herbs* they shall eat
it. 9 Do not eat it raw, nor boiled at all
with water, but roasted in fire—its head
with its legs and its entrails. 10 You shall
let none of it remain until morning, and
what remains of it until morning you
shall burn with fire. 11 And thus you shall
eat it: *with* a belt on your waist, your
sandals on your feet, and your staff in
your hand. So you shall eat it in haste.
It *is* the LORD's Passover.

12 'For I will pass through the land of
Egypt on that night, and will strike all
the firstborn in the land of Egypt, both
man and beast; and against all the gods
of Egypt I will execute judgment: I *am*
the LORD. 13 Now the blood shall be a
sign for you on the houses where you
are. And when I see the blood, I will pass
over you; and the plague shall not be
on you to destroy *you* when I strike the
land of Egypt.

14 'So this day shall be to you a memori-
al; and you shall keep it as a feast to the
LORD throughout your generations. You
shall keep it as a feast by an everlasting
ordinance. 15 Seven days you shall eat
unleavened bread. On the first day you
shall remove leaven from your houses.
For whoever eats leavened bread from
the first day until the seventh day, that
person shall be cut off from Israel. 16 On
the first day *there shall be* a holy con-
vocation, and on the seventh day there
shall be a holy convocation for you. No
manner of work shall be done on them;
but *that* which everyone must eat—that
only may be prepared by you. 17 So you
shall observe *the Feast of* Unleavened
Bread, for on this same day I will have
brought your armies out of the land
of Egypt. Therefore you shall observe
this day throughout your generations
as an everlasting ordinance. 18 In the
first *month,* on the fourteenth day of
the month at evening, you shall eat
unleavened bread, until the twenty-
first day of the month at evening. 19 For
seven days no leaven shall be found in
your houses, since whoever eats what
is leavened, that same person shall be
cut off from the congregation of Israel,
whether *he is* a stranger or a native of
the land. 20 You shall eat nothing leav-
ened; in all your dwellings you shall
eat unleavened bread.' "

21 Then Moses called for all the elders
of Israel and said to them, "Pick out and
take lambs for yourselves according
to your families, and kill the Passover
lamb. 22 And you shall take a bunch of
hyssop, dip *it* in the blood that *is* in the
basin, and strike the lintel and the two
doorposts with the blood that *is* in the
basin. And none of you shall go out of
the door of his house until morning.
23 For the LORD will pass through to
strike the Egyptians; and when He sees
the blood on the lintel and on the two
doorposts, the LORD will pass over the
door and not allow the destroyer to
come into your houses to strike *you.*
24 And you shall observe this thing as
an ordinance for you and your sons
forever. 25 It will come to pass when you
come to the land which the LORD will
give you, just as He promised, that you
shall keep this service. 26 And it shall be,
when your children say to you, 'What
do you mean by this service?' 27 that you
shall say, 'It *is* the Passover sacrifice of
the LORD, who passed over the houses
of the children of Israel in Egypt when
He struck the Egyptians and delivered
our households.' " So the people bowed
their heads and worshiped. 28 Then the
children of Israel went away and did
so; just as the LORD had commanded
Moses and Aaron, so they did.

The Tenth Plague: Death of the Firstborn

29 And it came to pass at midnight
that the LORD struck all the firstborn
in the land of Egypt, from the firstborn
of Pharaoh who sat on his throne to
the firstborn of the captive who *was*

in the dungeon, and all the firstborn of livestock. 30So Pharaoh rose in the night, he, all his servants, and all the Egyptians; and there was a great cry in Egypt, for *there was* not a house where *there was* not one dead.

The Exodus

31Then he called for Moses and Aaron by night, and said, "Rise, go out from among my people, both you and the children of Israel. And go, serve the LORD as you have said. 32Also take your flocks and your herds, as you have said, and be gone; and bless me also."

33And the Egyptians urged the people, that they might send them out of the land in haste. For they said, "We *shall* all *be* dead." 34So the people took their dough before it was leavened, having their kneading bowls bound up in their clothes on their shoulders. 35Now the children of Israel had done according to the word of Moses, and they had asked from the Egyptians articles of silver, articles of gold, and clothing. 36And the LORD had given the people favor in the sight of the Egyptians, so that they granted them *what they requested.* Thus they plundered the Egyptians.

37Then the children of Israel journeyed from Rameses to Succoth, about six hundred thousand men on foot, besides children. 38A mixed multitude went up with them also, and flocks and herds—a great deal of livestock. 39And they baked unleavened cakes of the dough which they had brought out of Egypt; for it was not leavened, because they were driven out of Egypt and could not wait, nor had they prepared provisions for themselves.

40Now the sojourn of the children of Israel who lived in Egypt[a] *was* four hundred and thirty years. 41And it came to pass at the end of the four hundred and thirty years—on that very same day—it came to pass that all the armies of the LORD went out from the land of Egypt. 42It *is* a night of solemn observance to the LORD for bringing them out of the land of Egypt. This *is* that night of the LORD, a solemn observance for all the children of Israel throughout their generations.

Passover Regulations

43And the LORD said to Moses and Aaron, "This *is* the ordinance of the Passover: No foreigner shall eat it. 44But every man's servant who is bought for money, when you have circumcised him, then he may eat it. 45A sojourner and a hired servant shall not eat it. 46In one house it shall be eaten; you shall not carry any of the flesh outside the house, nor shall you break one of its bones. 47All the congregation of Israel shall keep it. 48And when a stranger dwells with you *and wants* to keep the Passover to the LORD, let all his males be circumcised, and then let him come near and keep it; and he shall be as a native of the land. For no uncircumcised person shall eat it. 49One law shall be for the native-born and for the stranger who dwells among you."

50Thus all the children of Israel did; as the LORD commanded Moses and Aaron, so they did. 51And it came to pass, on that very same day, that the LORD brought the children of Israel out of the land of Egypt according to their armies.

The Firstborn Consecrated

13 Then the LORD spoke to Moses, saying, 2"Consecrate to Me all the firstborn, whatever opens the womb among the children of Israel, *both* of man and beast; it is Mine."

The Feast of Unleavened Bread

3And Moses said to the people: "Remember this day in which you went out of Egypt, out of the house of bondage; for by strength of hand the LORD brought you out of this *place.* No leavened bread shall be eaten. 4On this day you are going out, in the month Abib. 5And it shall be, when the LORD brings you into the land of the Canaanites and the Hittites and the Amorites and the Hivites and the Jebusites, which He swore to your fathers to give you, a land flowing with milk and honey, that you shall keep this service in this month. 6Seven days you

12:40 [a] Samaritan Pentateuch and Septuagint read *Egypt and Canaan.*

shall eat unleavened bread, and on the
seventh day *there shall be* a feast to the
LORD. 7 Unleavened bread shall be eaten
seven days. And no leavened bread shall
be seen among you, nor shall leaven be
seen among you in all your quarters.
8 And you shall tell your son in that day,
saying, '*This is done* because of what the
LORD did for me when I came up from
Egypt.' 9 It shall be as a sign to you on
your hand and as a memorial between
your eyes, that the LORD's law may be
in your mouth; for with a strong hand
the LORD has brought you out of Egypt.
10 You shall therefore keep this ordinance
in its season from year to year.

The Law of the Firstborn

11 "And it shall be, when the LORD brings
you into the land of the Canaanites, as
He swore to you and your fathers, and
gives it to you, 12 that you shall set apart
to the LORD all that open the womb, that
is, every firstborn that comes from an
animal which you have; the males *shall*
be the LORD's. 13 But every firstborn of a
donkey you shall redeem with a lamb;
and if you will not redeem *it,* then you
shall break its neck. And all the firstborn
of man among your sons you shall re-
deem. 14 So it shall be, when your son
asks you in time to come, saying, 'What
is this?' that you shall say to him, 'By
strength of hand the LORD brought us
out of Egypt, out of the house of bond-
age. 15 And it came to pass, when Phar-
aoh was stubborn about letting us go,
that the LORD killed all the firstborn in
the land of Egypt, both the firstborn of
man and the firstborn of beast. There-
fore I sacrifice to the LORD all males that
open the womb, but all the firstborn of
my sons I redeem.' 16 It shall be as a sign
on your hand and as frontlets between
your eyes, for by strength of hand the
LORD brought us out of Egypt."

The Wilderness Way

17 Then it came to pass, when Pharaoh
had let the people go, that God did not
lead them *by* way of the land of the
Philistines, although that *was* near;
for God said, "Lest perhaps the people
change their minds when they see war,
and return to Egypt." 18 So God led the
people around *by* way of the wilderness
of the Red Sea. And the children of Is-
rael went up in orderly ranks out of the
land of Egypt.
19 And Moses took the bones of Joseph
with him, for he had placed the children
of Israel under solemn oath, saying,
"God will surely visit you, and you shall
carry up my bones from here with you."[a]
20 So they took their journey from Suc-
coth and camped in Etham at the edge
of the wilderness. 21 And the LORD went
before them by day in a pillar of cloud
to lead the way, and by night in a pillar
of fire to give them light, so as to go by
day and night. 22 He did not take away
the pillar of cloud by day or the pillar
of fire by night *from* before the people.

The Red Sea Crossing

14 Now the LORD spoke to Moses,
saying: 2 "Speak to the children
of Israel, that they turn and camp be-
fore Pi Hahiroth, between Migdol and
the sea, opposite Baal Zephon; you shall
camp before it by the sea. 3 For Phar-
aoh will say of the children of Israel,
'They *are* bewildered by the land; the
wilderness has closed them in.' 4 Then I
will harden Pharaoh's heart, so that he
will pursue them; and I will gain honor
over Pharaoh and over all his army,
that the Egyptians may know that I *am*
the LORD." And they did so.
5 Now it was told the king of Egypt that
the people had fled, and the heart of
Pharaoh and his servants was turned
against the people; and they said, "Why
have we done this, that we have let Is-
rael go from serving us?" 6 So he made
ready his chariot and took his people
with him. 7 Also, he took six hundred
choice chariots, and all the chariots
of Egypt with captains over every one
of them. 8 And the LORD hardened the
heart of Pharaoh king of Egypt, and
he pursued the children of Israel; and
the children of Israel went out with
boldness. 9 So the Egyptians pursued
them, all the horses *and* chariots of
Pharaoh, his horsemen and his army,

13:19 [a] Genesis 50:25

and overtook them camping by the sea
beside Pi Hahiroth, before Baal Zephon.
10 And when Pharaoh drew near, the
children of Israel lifted their eyes, and
behold, the Egyptians marched after
them. So they were very afraid, and the
children of Israel cried out to the LORD.
11 Then they said to Moses, "Because
there were no graves in Egypt, have you
taken us away to die in the wilderness?
Why have you so dealt with us, to bring
us up out of Egypt? 12 *Is* this not the word
that we told you in Egypt, saying, 'Let
us alone that we may serve the Egyp-
tians'? For *it would have been* better for
us to serve the Egyptians than that we
should die in the wilderness."
13 And Moses said to the people, "Do not
be afraid. Stand still, and see the salva-
tion of the LORD, which He will accom-
plish for you today. For the Egyptians
whom you see today, you shall see again
no more forever. 14 The LORD will fight
for you, and you shall hold your peace."
15 And the LORD said to Moses, "Why do
you cry to Me? Tell the children of Israel
to go forward. 16 But lift up your rod, and
stretch out your hand over the sea and di-
vide it. And the children of Israel shall go
on dry *ground* through the midst of the
sea. 17 And I indeed will harden the hearts
of the Egyptians, and they shall follow
them. So I will gain honor over Pharaoh
and over all his army, his chariots, and
his horsemen. 18 Then the Egyptians shall
know that I *am* the LORD, when I have
gained honor for Myself over Pharaoh,
his chariots, and his horsemen."
19 And the Angel of God, who went
before the camp of Israel, moved and
went behind them; and the pillar of
cloud went from before them and stood
behind them. 20 So it came between the
camp of the Egyptians and the camp of
Israel. Thus it was a cloud and darkness
to the one, and it gave light by night *to
the other,* so that the one did not come
near the other all that night.
21 Then Moses stretched out his hand
over the sea; and the LORD caused the
sea to go *back* by a strong east wind
all that night, and made the sea into
dry *land,* and the waters were divided.
22 So the children of Israel went into the
midst of the sea on the dry *ground,* and
the waters *were* a wall to them on their
right hand and on their left. 23 And the
Egyptians pursued and went after them
into the midst of the sea, all Pharaoh's
horses, his chariots, and his horsemen.
24 Now it came to pass, in the morning
watch, that the LORD looked down upon
the army of the Egyptians through the
pillar of fire and cloud, and He troubled
the army of the Egyptians. 25 And He
took off[a] their chariot wheels, so that
they drove them with difficulty; and
the Egyptians said, "Let us flee from
the face of Israel, for the LORD fights
for them against the Egyptians."
26 Then the LORD said to Moses,
"Stretch out your hand over the sea,
that the waters may come back upon
the Egyptians, on their chariots, and
on their horsemen." 27 And Moses
stretched out his hand over the sea;
and when the morning appeared,
the sea returned to its full depth, while the
Egyptians were fleeing into it. So the
LORD overthrew the Egyptians in
the midst of the sea. 28 Then the waters
returned and covered the chariots, the
horsemen, *and* all the army of Phar-
aoh that came into the sea after them.
Not so much as one of them remained.
29 But the children of Israel had walked
on dry *land* in the midst of the sea, and
the waters *were* a wall to them on their
right hand and on their left.
30 So the LORD saved Israel that day
out of the hand of the Egyptians, and
Israel saw the Egyptians dead on the
seashore. 31 Thus Israel saw the great
work which the LORD had done in Egypt;
so the people feared the LORD, and be-
lieved the LORD and His servant Moses.

The Song of Moses

15 Then Moses and the children
of Israel sang this song to the
LORD, and spoke, saying:

"I will sing to the LORD,
For He has triumphed gloriously!
The horse and its rider
He has thrown into the sea!

14:25 [a] Samaritan Pentateuch, Septuagint, and Syriac read *bound.*

2 The LORD *is* my strength and song,
And He has become my salvation;
He *is* my God, and I will praise Him;
My father's God, and I will exalt Him.
3 The LORD *is* a man of war;
The LORD *is* His name.
4 Pharaoh's chariots and his army He has cast into the sea;
His chosen captains also are drowned in the Red Sea.
5 The depths have covered them;
They sank to the bottom like a stone.

6 "Your right hand, O LORD, has become glorious in power;
Your right hand, O LORD, has dashed the enemy in pieces.
7 And in the greatness of Your excellence
You have overthrown those who rose against You;
You sent forth Your wrath;
It consumed them like stubble.
8 And with the blast of Your nostrils
The waters were gathered together;
The floods stood upright like a heap;
The depths congealed in the heart of the sea.
9 The enemy said, 'I will pursue,
I will overtake,
I will divide the spoil;
My desire shall be satisfied on them.
I will draw my sword,
My hand shall destroy them.'
10 You blew with Your wind,
The sea covered them;
They sank like lead in the mighty waters.

11 "Who *is* like You, O LORD, among the gods?
Who *is* like You, glorious in holiness,
Fearful in praises, doing wonders?
12 You stretched out Your right hand;
The earth swallowed them.
13 You in Your mercy have led forth
The people whom You have redeemed;
You have guided *them* in Your strength
To Your holy habitation.

14 "The people will hear *and* be afraid;
Sorrow will take hold of the inhabitants of Philistia.
15 Then the chiefs of Edom will be dismayed;
The mighty men of Moab,
Trembling will take hold of them;
All the inhabitants of Canaan will melt away.
16 Fear and dread will fall on them;
By the greatness of Your arm
They will be *as* still as a stone,
Till Your people pass over, O LORD,
Till the people pass over
Whom You have purchased.
17 You will bring them in and plant them
In the mountain of Your inheritance,
In the place, O LORD, *which* You have made
For Your own dwelling,
The sanctuary, O Lord, *which* Your hands have established.

18 "The LORD shall reign forever and ever."

19For the horses of Pharaoh went with
his chariots and his horsemen into
the sea, and the LORD brought back
the waters of the sea upon them. But the
children of Israel went on dry *land* in
the midst of the sea.

The Song of Miriam

20Then Miriam the prophetess, the
sister of Aaron, took the timbrel in her
hand; and all the women went out af-
ter her with timbrels and with dances.
21And Miriam answered them:

"Sing to the LORD,
For He has triumphed gloriously!
The horse and its rider
He has thrown into the sea!"

Bitter Waters Made Sweet

22So Moses brought Israel from the
Red Sea; then they went out into the
Wilderness of Shur. And they went
three days in the wilderness and found
no water. 23Now when they came to
Marah, they could not drink the waters
of Marah, for they *were* bitter. Therefore
the name of it was called Marah.[a] 24And
the people complained against Moses,
saying, "What shall we drink?" 25So he
cried out to the LORD, and the LORD
showed him a tree. When he cast *it* into
the waters, the waters were made sweet.

There He made a statute and an ordinance for them, and there He tested
them, 26and said, "If you diligently heed
the voice of the LORD your God and do
what is right in His sight, give ear to His
commandments and keep all His statutes, I will put none of the diseases on
you which I have brought on the Egyptians. For I *am* the LORD who heals you."

27Then they came to Elim, where there
were twelve wells of water and seventy
palm trees; so they camped there by
the waters.

Bread from Heaven

16 And they journeyed from Elim,
and all the congregation of the
children of Israel came to the Wilderness of Sin, which is between Elim and
Sinai, on the fifteenth day of the second month after they departed from
the land of Egypt. 2Then the whole
congregation of the children of Israel
complained against Moses and Aaron
in the wilderness. 3And the children of
Israel said to them, "Oh, that we had
died by the hand of the LORD in the land
of Egypt, when we sat by the pots of
meat *and* when we ate bread to the full!
For you have brought us out into this
wilderness to kill this whole assembly
with hunger."

4Then the LORD said to Moses, "Behold,
I will rain bread from heaven for you.
And the people shall go out and gather
a certain quota every day, that I may
test them, whether they will walk in My
law or not. 5And it shall be on the sixth
day that they shall prepare what they
bring in, and it shall be twice as much
as they gather daily."

6Then Moses and Aaron said to all
the children of Israel, "At evening you
shall know that the LORD has brought
you out of the land of Egypt. 7And in
the morning you shall see the glory of
the LORD; for He hears your complaints
against the LORD. But what *are* we, that
you complain against us?" 8Also Moses
said, "*This shall be seen* when the LORD
gives you meat to eat in the evening,
and in the morning bread to the full; for
the LORD hears your complaints which
you make against Him. And what *are*
we? Your complaints *are* not against us
but against the LORD."

9Then Moses spoke to Aaron, "Say to
all the congregation of the children of
Israel, 'Come near before the LORD, for
He has heard your complaints.' " 10Now
it came to pass, as Aaron spoke to the
whole congregation of the children of
Israel, that they looked toward the wilderness, and behold, the glory of the
LORD appeared in the cloud.

11And the LORD spoke to Moses, saying, 12"I have heard the complaints of
the children of Israel. Speak to them,
saying, 'At twilight you shall eat meat,
and in the morning you shall be filled
with bread. And you shall know that I
am the LORD your God.' "

13So it was that quail came up at evening and covered the camp, and in the
morning the dew lay all around the
camp. 14And when the layer of dew lifted, there, on the surface of the wilderness, was a small round substance, *as*
fine as frost on the ground. 15So when
the children of Israel saw *it*, they said
to one another, "What is it?" For they
did not know what it *was*.

And Moses said to them, "This *is* the
bread which the LORD has given you to
eat. 16This is the thing which the LORD
has commanded: 'Let every man gather
it according to each one's need, one
omer for each person, *according to the*
number of persons; let every man take
for *those* who *are* in his tent.' "

17Then the children of Israel did so
and gathered, some more, some less.

15:23 [a] Literally *Bitter*

18So when they measured *it* by omers,
he who gathered much had nothing
left over, and he who gathered little
had no lack. Every man had gathered
according to each one's need. 19And
Moses said, "Let no one leave any of it
till morning." 20Notwithstanding they
did not heed Moses. But some of them
left part of it until morning, and it bred
worms and stank. And Moses was angry
with them. 21So they gathered it every
morning, every man according to his
need. And when the sun became hot,
it melted.

22And so it was, on the sixth day, *that*
they gathered twice as much bread, two
omers for each one. And all the rulers
of the congregation came and told
Moses. 23Then he said to them, "This *is*
what the LORD has said: 'Tomorrow *is*
a Sabbath rest, a holy Sabbath to the
LORD. Bake what you will bake *today,*
and boil what you will boil; and lay up
for yourselves all that remains, to be
kept until morning.' " 24So they laid it
up till morning, as Moses commanded;
and it did not stink, nor were there any
worms in it. 25Then Moses said, "Eat
that today, for today *is* a Sabbath to
the LORD; today you will not find it in
the field. 26Six days you shall gather it,
but on the seventh day, the Sabbath,
there will be none."

27Now it happened *that some* of the
people went out on the seventh day
to gather, but they found none. 28And
the LORD said to Moses, "How long do
you refuse to keep My commandments
and My laws? 29See! For the LORD has
given you the Sabbath; therefore He
gives you on the sixth day bread for
two days. Let every man remain in his
place; let no man go out of his place on
the seventh day." 30So the people rested
on the seventh day.

31And the house of Israel called its
name Manna.[a] And it *was* like white
coriander seed, and the taste of it *was*
like wafers *made* with honey.

32Then Moses said, "This *is* the thing
which the LORD has commanded: 'Fill
an omer with it, to be kept for your gen-
erations, that they may see the bread
with which I fed you in the wilderness,
when I brought you out of the land of
Egypt.' " 33And Moses said to Aaron,
"Take a pot and put an omer of manna
in it, and lay it up before the LORD, to
be kept for your generations." 34As the
LORD commanded Moses, so Aaron
laid it up before the Testimony, to be
kept. 35And the children of Israel ate
manna forty years, until they came to
an inhabited land; they ate manna until
they came to the border of the land of
Canaan. 36Now an omer *is* one-tenth
of an ephah.

Water from the Rock

17 Then all the congregation of
the children of Israel set out on
their journey from the Wilderness of
Sin, according to the commandment
of the LORD, and camped in Rephidim;
but *there was* no water for the people to
drink. 2Therefore the people contended
with Moses, and said, "Give us water,
that we may drink."

So Moses said to them, "Why do you
contend with me? Why do you tempt
the LORD?"

3And the people thirsted there for wa-
ter, and the people complained against
Moses, and said, "Why *is* it you have
brought us up out of Egypt, to kill us
and our children and our livestock with
thirst?"

4So Moses cried out to the LORD, say-
ing, "What shall I do with this people?
They are almost ready to stone me!"

5And the LORD said to Moses, "Go on
before the people, and take with you
some of the elders of Israel. Also take
in your hand your rod with which you
struck the river, and go. 6Behold, I will
stand before you there on the rock in
Horeb; and you shall strike the rock,
and water will come out of it, that the
people may drink."

And Moses did so in the sight of the
elders of Israel. 7So he called the name
of the place Massah[a] and Meribah,[b] be-
cause of the contention of the children
of Israel, and because they tempted
the LORD, saying, "Is the LORD among
us or not?"

16:31 [a] Literally *What?* (compare Exodus 16:15) **17:7** [a] Literally *Tempted* [b] Literally *Contention*

Victory over the Amalekites

8Now Amalek came and fought with
Israel in Rephidim. 9And Moses said
to Joshua, "Choose us some men and
go out, fight with Amalek. Tomorrow I
will stand on the top of the hill with the
rod of God in my hand." 10So Joshua did
as Moses said to him, and fought with
Amalek. And Moses, Aaron, and Hur
went up to the top of the hill. 11And so it
was, when Moses held up his hand, that
Israel prevailed; and when he let down
his hand, Amalek prevailed. 12But Mo-
ses' hands *became* heavy; so they took
a stone and put *it* under him, and he sat
on it. And Aaron and Hur supported his
hands, one on one side, and the other
on the other side; and his hands were
steady until the going down of the sun.
13So Joshua defeated Amalek and his
people with the edge of the sword.

14Then the LORD said to Moses, "Write
this *for* a memorial in the book and
recount *it* in the hearing of Joshua, that
I will utterly blot out the remembrance
of Amalek from under heaven." 15And
Moses built an altar and called its name,
The-LORD-Is-My-Banner;[a] 16for he said,
"Because the LORD has sworn: the LORD
will have war with Amalek from gener-
ation to generation."

Jethro's Advice

18 And Jethro, the priest of Midian,
Moses' father-in-law, heard of all
that God had done for Moses and for
Israel His people—that the LORD had
brought Israel out of Egypt. 2Then Jeth-
ro, Moses' father-in-law, took Zipporah,
Moses' wife, after he had sent her back,
3with her two sons, of whom the name
of one *was* Gershom (for he said, "I have
been a stranger in a foreign land")[a] 4and
the name of the other *was* Eliezer[a] (for
he said, "The God of my father *was* my
help, and delivered me from the sword
of Pharaoh"); 5and Jethro, Moses' father-
in-law, came with his sons and his wife
to Moses in the wilderness, where he was
encamped at the mountain of God. 6Now
he had said to Moses, "I, your father-in-
law Jethro, am coming to you with your
wife and her two sons with her."

7So Moses went out to meet his father-
in-law, bowed down, and kissed him.
And they asked each other about *their*
well-being, and they went into the tent.
8And Moses told his father-in-law all that
the LORD had done to Pharaoh and to
the Egyptians for Israel's sake, all the
hardship that had come upon them on
the way, and *how* the LORD had deliv-
ered them. 9Then Jethro rejoiced for all
the good which the LORD had done for
Israel, whom He had delivered out of
the hand of the Egyptians. 10And Jethro
said, "Blessed *be* the LORD, who has de-
livered you out of the hand of the Egyp-
tians and out of the hand of Pharaoh,
and who has delivered the people from
under the hand of the Egyptians. 11Now I
know that the LORD *is* greater than all the
gods; for in the very thing in which they
behaved proudly, *He was* above them."
12Then Jethro, Moses' father-in-law, took[a]
a burnt offering and *other* sacrifices *to
offer* to God. And Aaron came with all the
elders of Israel to eat bread with Moses'
father-in-law before God.

13And so it was, on the next day, that
Moses sat to judge the people; and the
people stood before Moses from morning
until evening. 14So when Moses' father-
in-law saw all that he did for the people,
he said, "What *is* this thing that you are
doing for the people? Why do you alone
sit, and all the people stand before you
from morning until evening?"

15And Moses said to his father-in-
law, "Because the people come to me
to inquire of God. 16When they have a
difficulty, they come to me, and I judge
between one and another; and I make
known the statutes of God and His laws."

17So Moses' father-in-law said to him,
"The thing that you do *is* not good. 18Both
you and these people who *are* with you
will surely wear yourselves out. For this
thing *is* too much for you; you are not
able to perform it by yourself. 19Listen
now to my voice; I will give you counsel,
and God will be with you: Stand before
God for the people, so that you may
bring the difficulties to God. 20And you
shall teach them the statutes and the
laws, and show them the way in which

17:15 [a] Hebrew *YHWH Nissi* **18:3** [a] Compare Exodus 2:22 **18:4** [a] Literally *My God Is Help*
18:12 [a] Following Masoretic Text and Septuagint; Syriac, Targum, and Vulgate read *offered.*

they must walk and the work they must
do. 21Moreover you shall select from
all the people able men, such as fear
God, men of truth, hating covetousness;
and place *such* over them *to be* rulers of
thousands, rulers of hundreds, rulers of
fifties, and rulers of tens. 22And let them
judge the people at all times. Then it will
be *that* every great matter they shall
bring to you, but every small matter
they themselves shall judge. So it will
be easier for you, for they will bear *the*
burden with you. 23If you do this thing,
and God *so* commands you, then you will
be able to endure, and all this people will
also go to their place in peace."

24So Moses heeded the voice of his
father-in-law and did all that he had
said. 25And Moses chose able men out
of all Israel, and made them heads over
the people: rulers of thousands, rulers
of hundreds, rulers of fifties, and rulers
of tens. 26So they judged the people at
all times; the hard cases they brought
to Moses, but they judged every small
case themselves.

27Then Moses let his father-in-law de-
part, and he went his way to his own land.

Israel at Mount Sinai

19 In the third month after the
children of Israel had gone out
of the land of Egypt, on the same day,
they came *to* the Wilderness of Sinai.
2For they had departed from Rephidim,
had come *to* the Wilderness of Sinai,
and camped in the wilderness. So Isra-
el camped there before the mountain.

3And Moses went up to God, and the
LORD called to him from the mountain,
saying, "Thus you shall say to the house
of Jacob, and tell the children of Israel:
4'You have seen what I did to the Egyp-
tians, and *how* I bore you on eagles'
wings and brought you to Myself. 5Now
therefore, if you will indeed obey My
voice and keep My covenant, then you
shall be a special treasure to Me above
all people; for all the earth *is* Mine. 6And
you shall be to Me a kingdom of priests
and a holy nation.' These *are* the words
which you shall speak to the children
of Israel."

7So Moses came and called for the
elders of the people, and laid before
them all these words which the LORD
commanded him. 8Then all the people
answered together and said, "All that
the LORD has spoken we will do." So
Moses brought back the words of the
people to the LORD. 9And the LORD said
to Moses, "Behold, I come to you in the
thick cloud, that the people may hear
when I speak with you, and believe you
forever."

So Moses told the words of the people
to the LORD.

10Then the LORD said to Moses, "Go to
the people and consecrate them today
and tomorrow, and let them wash their
clothes. 11And let them be ready for the
third day. For on the third day the LORD
will come down upon Mount Sinai in
the sight of all the people. 12You shall
set bounds for the people all around,
saying, 'Take heed to yourselves *that*
you do *not* go up to the mountain or
touch its base. Whoever touches the
mountain shall surely be put to death.
13Not a hand shall touch him, but he
shall surely be stoned or shot *with an*
arrow; whether man or beast, he shall
not live.' When the trumpet sounds long,
they shall come near the mountain."

14So Moses went down from the moun-
tain to the people and sanctified the
people, and they washed their clothes.
15And he said to the people, "Be ready
for the third day; do not come near
your wives."

16Then it came to pass on the third day,
in the morning, that there were thunder-
ings and lightnings, and a thick cloud
on the mountain; and the sound of the
trumpet was very loud, so that all the
people who *were* in the camp trembled.
17And Moses brought the people out of
the camp to meet with God, and they
stood at the foot of the mountain. 18Now
Mount Sinai *was* completely in smoke,
because the LORD descended upon it in
fire. Its smoke ascended like the smoke
of a furnace, and the whole mountain[a]
quaked greatly. 19And when the blast of
the trumpet sounded long and became
louder and louder, Moses spoke, and

19:18 a Septuagint reads *all the people.*

God answered him by voice. 20 Then the
LORD came down upon Mount Sinai, on
the top of the mountain. And the LORD
called Moses to the top of the mountain,
and Moses went up.
21 And the LORD said to Moses, "Go
down and warn the people, lest they
break through to gaze at the LORD, and
many of them perish. 22 Also let the
priests who come near the LORD con-
secrate themselves, lest the LORD break
out against them."
23 But Moses said to the LORD, "The
people cannot come up to Mount Sinai;
for You warned us, saying, 'Set bounds
around the mountain and consecrate it.'"
24 Then the LORD said to him, "Away!
Get down and then come up, you and
Aaron with you. But do not let the
priests and the people break through
to come up to the LORD, lest He break
out against them." 25 So Moses went
down to the people and spoke to them.

The Ten Commandments

20 And God spoke all these words, saying:

2 "I *am* the LORD your God, who
brought you out of the land of
Egypt, out of the house of bond-
age.
3 "You shall have no other gods be-
fore Me.
4 "You shall not make for yourself a
carved image—any likeness *of*
anything that *is* in heaven above,
or that *is* in the earth beneath,
or that *is* in the water under the
earth; 5 you shall not bow down
to them nor serve them. For I, the
LORD your God, *am* a jealous God,
visiting the iniquity of the fathers
upon the children to the third and
fourth *generations* of those who
hate Me, 6 but showing mercy to
thousands, to those who love Me
and keep My commandments.
7 "You shall not take the name of the
LORD your God in vain, for the
LORD will not hold *him* guiltless
who takes His name in vain.
8 "Remember the Sabbath day, to keep
it holy. 9 Six days you shall labor
and do all your work, 10 but the
seventh day *is* the Sabbath of the
LORD your God. *In it* you shall do
no work: you, nor your son, nor
your daughter, nor your male ser-
vant, nor your female servant, nor
your cattle, nor your stranger who
is within your gates. 11 For *in* six
days the LORD made the heavens
and the earth, the sea, and all that
is in them, and rested the seventh
day. Therefore the LORD blessed
the Sabbath day and hallowed it.
12 "Honor your father and your mother,
that your days may be long upon
the land which the LORD your
God is giving you.
13 "You shall not murder.
14 "You shall not commit adultery.
15 "You shall not steal.
16 "You shall not bear false witness
against your neighbor.
17 "You shall not covet your neighbor's
house; you shall not covet your
neighbor's wife, nor his male
servant, nor his female servant,
nor his ox, nor his donkey, nor
anything that *is* your neighbor's."

The People Afraid of God's Presence

18 Now all the people witnessed the
thunderings, the lightning flashes, the
sound of the trumpet, and the mountain
smoking; and when the people saw *it*,
they trembled and stood afar off. 19 Then
they said to Moses, "You speak with us,
and we will hear; but let not God speak
with us, lest we die."
20 And Moses said to the people, "Do
not fear; for God has come to test you,
and that His fear may be before you, so
that you may not sin." 21 So the people
stood afar off, but Moses drew near the
thick darkness where God *was*.

The Law of the Altar

22 Then the LORD said to Moses, "Thus
you shall say to the children of Israel:
'You have seen that I have talked with
you from heaven. 23 You shall not make
anything to be with Me—gods of silver
or gods of gold you shall not make for
yourselves. 24 An altar of earth you shall
make for Me, and you shall sacrifice on
it your burnt offerings and your peace
offerings, your sheep and your oxen. In

every place where I record My name I
will come to you, and I will bless you.
25And if you make Me an altar of stone,
you shall not build it of hewn stone;
for if you use your tool on it, you have
profaned it. 26Nor shall you go up by
steps to My altar, that your nakedness
may not be exposed on it.'

The Law Concerning Servants

21 "Now these *are* the judgments
which you shall set before them:
2If you buy a Hebrew servant, he shall
serve six years; and in the seventh he
shall go out free and pay nothing. 3If he
comes in by himself, he shall go out by
himself; if he *comes in* married, then his
wife shall go out with him. 4If his master
has given him a wife, and she has borne
him sons or daughters, the wife and
her children shall be her master's, and
he shall go out by himself. 5But if the
servant plainly says, 'I love my master,
my wife, and my children; I will not go
out free,' 6then his master shall bring
him to the judges. He shall also bring
him to the door, or to the doorpost, and
his master shall pierce his ear with an
awl; and he shall serve him forever.

7"And if a man sells his daughter to
be a female slave, she shall not go out
as the male slaves do. 8If she does not
please her master, who has betrothed
her to himself, then he shall let her be
redeemed. He shall have no right to
sell her to a foreign people, since he
has dealt deceitfully with her. 9And if
he has betrothed her to his son, he shall
deal with her according to the custom of
daughters. 10If he takes another *wife,* he
shall not diminish her food, her cloth-
ing, and her marriage rights. 11And if he
does not do these three for her, then she
shall go out free, without *paying* money.

The Law Concerning Violence

12"He who strikes a man so that he dies
shall surely be put to death. 13However,
if he did not lie in wait, but God delivered
him into his hand, then I will appoint for
you a place where he may flee.

14"But if a man acts with premedita-
tion against his neighbor, to kill him by
treachery, you shall take him from My
altar, that he may die.

15"And he who strikes his father or his
mother shall surely be put to death.

16"He who kidnaps a man and sells
him, or if he is found in his hand, shall
surely be put to death.

17"And he who curses his father or his
mother shall surely be put to death.

18"If men contend with each other,
and one strikes the other with a stone
or with *his* fist, and he does not die but
is confined to *his* bed, 19if he rises again
and walks about outside with his staff,
then he who struck *him* shall be acquit-
ted. He shall only pay *for* the loss of his
time, and shall provide *for him* to be
thoroughly healed.

20"And if a man beats his male or
female servant with a rod, so that he
dies under his hand, he shall surely
be punished. 21Notwithstanding, if he
remains alive a day or two, he shall
not be punished; for he *is* his property.

22"If men fight, and hurt a woman
with child, so that she gives birth pre-
maturely, yet no harm follows, he shall
surely be punished accordingly as the
woman's husband imposes on him;
and he shall pay as the judges *deter-
mine.* 23But if *any* harm follows, then
you shall give life for life, 24eye for eye,
tooth for tooth, hand for hand, foot for
foot, 25burn for burn, wound for wound,
stripe for stripe.

26"If a man strikes the eye of his male
or female servant, and destroys it, he
shall let him go free for the sake of his
eye. 27And if he knocks out the tooth
of his male or female servant, he shall
let him go free for the sake of his tooth.

Animal Control Laws

28"If an ox gores a man or a woman
to death, then the ox shall surely be
stoned, and its flesh shall not be eat-
en; but the owner of the ox *shall be* ac-
quitted. 29But if the ox tended to thrust
with its horn in times past, and it has
been made known to his owner, and he
has not kept it confined, so that it has
killed a man or a woman, the ox shall
be stoned and its owner also shall be
put to death. 30If there is imposed on
him a sum of money, then he shall pay
to redeem his life, whatever is imposed
on him. 31Whether it has gored a son

or gored a daughter, according to this
judgment it shall be done to him. 32If
the ox gores a male or female servant,
he shall give to their master thirty shek-
els of silver, and the ox shall be stoned.
33"And if a man opens a pit, or if a man
digs a pit and does not cover it, and an
ox or a donkey falls in it, 34the owner
of the pit shall make *it* good; he shall
give money to their owner, but the dead
animal shall be his.
35"If one man's ox hurts another's, so
that it dies, then they shall sell the live
ox and divide the money from it; and
the dead *ox* they shall also divide. 36Or
if it was known that the ox tended to
thrust in time past, and its owner has
not kept it confined, he shall surely pay
ox for ox, and the dead animal shall
be his own.

Responsibility for Property

22 "If a man steals an ox or a sheep,
and slaughters it or sells it, he
shall restore five oxen for an ox and
four sheep for a sheep. 2If the thief is
found breaking in, and he is struck so
that he dies, *there shall be* no guilt for his
bloodshed. 3If the sun has risen on him,
there shall be guilt for his bloodshed.
He should make full restitution; if he
has nothing, then he shall be sold for
his theft. 4If the theft is certainly found
alive in his hand, whether it is an ox or
donkey or sheep, he shall restore double.
5"If a man causes a field or vineyard
to be grazed, and lets loose his animal,
and it feeds in another man's field, he
shall make restitution from the best of
his own field and the best of his own
vineyard.
6"If fire breaks out and catches in
thorns, so that stacked grain, stand-
ing grain, or the field is consumed, he
who kindled the fire shall surely make
restitution.
7"If a man delivers to his neighbor
money or articles to keep, and it is sto-
len out of the man's house, if the thief
is found, he shall pay double. 8If the
thief is not found, then the master of
the house shall be brought to the judges
to see whether he has put his hand into
his neighbor's goods.
9"For any kind of trespass, *whether it*
concerns an ox, a donkey, a sheep, or
clothing, *or* for any kind of lost thing
which *another* claims to be his, the cause
of both parties shall come before the
judges; *and* whomever the judges con-
demn shall pay double to his neighbor.
10If a man delivers to his neighbor a
donkey, an ox, a sheep, or any animal
to keep, and it dies, is hurt, or driven
away, no one seeing *it,* 11*then* an oath of
the LORD shall be between them both,
that he has not put his hand into his
neighbor's goods; and the owner of it
shall accept *that,* and he shall not make
it good. 12But if, in fact, it is stolen from
him, he shall make restitution to the
owner of it. 13If it is torn to pieces *by a*
beast, then he shall bring it as evidence,
and he shall not make good what was
torn.
14"And if a man borrows *anything* from
his neighbor, and it becomes injured or
dies, the owner of it not *being* with it, he
shall surely make *it* good. 15If its owner
was with it, he shall not make *it* good; if
it *was* hired, it came for its hire.

Moral and Ceremonial Principles

16"If a man entices a virgin who is not
betrothed, and lies with her, he shall
surely pay the bride-price for her *to be*
his wife. 17If her father utterly refuses
to give her to him, he shall pay money
according to the bride-price of virgins.
18"You shall not permit a sorceress
to live.
19"Whoever lies with an animal shall
surely be put to death.
20"He who sacrifices to *any* god, except
to the LORD only, he shall be utterly
destroyed.
21"You shall neither mistreat a strang-
er nor oppress him, for you were strang-
ers in the land of Egypt.
22"You shall not afflict any widow or
fatherless child. 23If you afflict them in
any way, *and* they cry at all to Me, I will
surely hear their cry; 24and My wrath
will become hot, and I will kill you with
the sword; your wives shall be widows,
and your children fatherless.
25"If you lend money to *any of* My
people *who are* poor among you, you
shall not be like a moneylender to him;
you shall not charge him interest. 26If

you ever take your neighbor's garment
as a pledge, you shall return it to him
before the sun goes down. 27For that *is*
his only covering, it *is* his garment for
his skin. What will he sleep in? And it
will be that when he cries to Me, I will
hear, for I *am* gracious.
28"You shall not revile God, nor curse
a ruler of your people.
29"You shall not delay *to offer* the first
of your ripe produce and your juices.
The firstborn of your sons you shall give
to Me. 30Likewise you shall do with your
oxen *and* your sheep. It shall be with its
mother seven days; on the eighth day
you shall give it to Me.
31"And you shall be holy men to Me:
you shall not eat meat torn *by beasts* in
the field; you shall throw it to the dogs.

Justice for All

23 "You shall not circulate a false
report. Do not put your hand
with the wicked to be an unrighteous
witness. 2You shall not follow a crowd to
do evil; nor shall you testify in a dispute
so as to turn aside after many to pervert
justice. 3You shall not show partiality to
a poor man in his dispute.
4"If you meet your enemy's ox or his
donkey going astray, you shall surely
bring it back to him again. 5If you see
the donkey of one who hates you lying
under its burden, and you would refrain
from helping it, you shall surely help
him with it.
6"You shall not pervert the judgment
of your poor in his dispute. 7Keep your-
self far from a false matter; do not kill
the innocent and righteous. For I will
not justify the wicked. 8And you shall
take no bribe, for a bribe blinds the dis-
cerning and perverts the words of the
righteous.
9"Also you shall not oppress a strang-
er, for you know the heart of a stranger,
because you were strangers in the land
of Egypt.

The Law of Sabbaths

10"Six years you shall sow your land
and gather in its produce, 11but the sev-
enth *year* you shall let it rest and lie
fallow, that the poor of your people may
eat; and what they leave, the beasts of
the field may eat. In like manner you
shall do with your vineyard *and* your
olive grove. 12Six days you shall do your
work, and on the seventh day you shall
rest, that your ox and your donkey may
rest, and the son of your female servant
and the stranger may be refreshed.
13"And in all that I have said to you,
be circumspect and make no mention
of the name of other gods, nor let it be
heard from your mouth.

Three Annual Feasts

14"Three times you shall keep a feast
to Me in the year: 15You shall keep the
Feast of Unleavened Bread (you shall
eat unleavened bread seven days, as I
commanded you, at the time appointed
in the month of Abib, for in it you came
out of Egypt; none shall appear before
Me empty); 16and the Feast of Harvest,
the firstfruits of your labors which you
have sown in the field; and the Feast
of Ingathering at the end of the year,
when you have gathered in *the fruit of*
your labors from the field.
17"Three times in the year all your
males shall appear before the Lord
GOD.[a]
18"You shall not offer the blood of
My sacrifice with leavened bread; nor
shall the fat of My sacrifice remain until
morning. 19The first of the firstfruits of
your land you shall bring into the house
of the LORD your God. You shall not boil
a young goat in its mother's milk.

The Angel and the Promises

20"Behold, I send an Angel before you
to keep you in the way and to bring you
into the place which I have prepared.
21Beware of Him and obey His voice; do
not provoke Him, for He will not pardon
your transgressions; for My name *is*
in Him. 22But if you indeed obey His
voice and do all that I speak, then I will
be an enemy to your enemies and an
adversary to your adversaries. 23For My
Angel will go before you and bring you
in to the Amorites and the Hittites and
the Perizzites and the Canaanites and

23:17 [a] Hebrew *YHWH,* usually translated LORD

the Hivites and the Jebusites; and I will cut them off. 24You shall not bow down to their gods, nor serve them, nor do according to their works; but you shall utterly overthrow them and completely break down their *sacred* pillars.

25"So you shall serve the LORD your God, and He will bless your bread and your water. And I will take sickness away from the midst of you. 26No one shall suffer miscarriage or be barren in your land; I will fulfill the number of your days.

27"I will send My fear before you, I will cause confusion among all the people to whom you come, and will make all your enemies turn *their* backs to you. 28And I will send hornets before you, which shall drive out the Hivite, the Canaanite, and the Hittite from before you. 29I will not drive them out from before you in one year, lest the land become desolate and the beasts of the field become too numerous for you. 30Little by little I will drive them out from before you, until you have increased, and you inherit the land. 31And I will set your bounds from the Red Sea to the sea, Philistia, and from the desert to the River.[a] For I will deliver the inhabitants of the land into your hand, and you shall drive them out before you. 32You shall make no covenant with them, nor with their gods. 33They shall not dwell in your land, lest they make you sin against Me. For *if* you serve their gods, it will surely be a snare to you."

Israel Affirms the Covenant

24 Now He said to Moses, "Come up to the LORD, you and Aaron, Nadab and Abihu, and seventy of the elders of Israel, and worship from afar. 2And Moses alone shall come near the LORD, but they shall not come near; nor shall the people go up with him."

3So Moses came and told the people all the words of the LORD and all the judgments. And all the people answered with one voice and said, "All the words which the LORD has said we will do." 4And Moses wrote all the words of the LORD. And he rose early in the morning, and built an altar at the foot of the mountain, and twelve pillars according to the twelve tribes of Israel. 5Then he sent young men of the children of Israel, who offered burnt offerings and sacrificed peace offerings of oxen to the LORD. 6And Moses took half the blood and put *it* in basins, and half the blood he sprinkled on the altar. 7Then he took the Book of the Covenant and read in the hearing of the people. And they said, "All that the LORD has said we will do, and be obedient." 8And Moses took the blood, sprinkled *it* on the people, and said, "This is the blood of the covenant which the LORD has made with you according to all these words."

On the Mountain with God

9Then Moses went up, also Aaron, Nadab, and Abihu, and seventy of the elders of Israel, 10and they saw the God of Israel. And *there was* under His feet as it were a paved work of sapphire stone, and it was like the very heavens in *its* clarity. 11But on the nobles of the children of Israel He did not lay His hand. So they saw God, and they ate and drank.

12Then the LORD said to Moses, "Come up to Me on the mountain and be there; and I will give you tablets of stone, and the law and commandments which I have written, that you may teach them."

13So Moses arose with his assistant Joshua, and Moses went up to the mountain of God. 14And he said to the elders, "Wait here for us until we come back to you. Indeed, Aaron and Hur *are* with you. If any man has a difficulty, let him go to them." 15Then Moses went up into the mountain, and a cloud covered the mountain.

16Now the glory of the LORD rested on Mount Sinai, and the cloud covered it six days. And on the seventh day He called to Moses out of the midst of the cloud. 17The sight of the glory of the LORD *was* like a consuming fire on the top of the mountain in the eyes of the children of Israel. 18So Moses went into the midst of the cloud and went up into the mountain. And Moses was on the mountain forty days and forty nights.

23:31 [a] Hebrew *Nahar,* the Euphrates

Offerings for the Sanctuary

25 Then the LORD spoke to Moses,
saying: 2"Speak to the children
of Israel, that they bring Me an offering.
From everyone who gives it willingly
with his heart you shall take My of-
fering. 3And this *is* the offering which
you shall take from them: gold, silver,
and bronze; 4blue, purple, and scarlet
thread, fine linen, and goats' *hair;* 5ram
skins dyed red, badger skins, and aca-
cia wood; 6oil for the light, and spices
for the anointing oil and for the sweet
incense; 7onyx stones, and stones to be
set in the ephod and in the breastplate.
8And let them make Me a sanctuary,
that I may dwell among them. 9Ac-
cording to all that I show you, *that is,*
the pattern of the tabernacle and the
pattern of all its furnishings, just so
you shall make *it.*

The Ark of the Testimony

10"And they shall make an ark of aca-
cia wood; two and a half cubits *shall be*
its length, a cubit and a half its width,
and a cubit and a half its height. 11And
you shall overlay it with pure gold, in-
side and out you shall overlay it, and
shall make on it a molding of gold all
around. 12You shall cast four rings of
gold for it, and put *them* in its four cor-
ners; two rings *shall be* on one side, and
two rings on the other side. 13And you
shall make poles *of* acacia wood, and
overlay them with gold. 14You shall put
the poles into the rings on the sides of
the ark, that the ark may be carried by
them. 15The poles shall be in the rings
of the ark; they shall not be taken from
it. 16And you shall put into the ark the
Testimony which I will give you.

17"You shall make a mercy seat of
pure gold; two and a half cubits *shall
be* its length and a cubit and a half its
width. 18And you shall make two cher-
ubim of gold; of hammered work you
shall make them at the two ends of the
mercy seat. 19Make one cherub at one
end, and the other cherub at the other
end; you shall make the cherubim at
the two ends of it *of one piece* with the
mercy seat. 20And the cherubim shall
stretch out *their* wings above, covering
the mercy seat with their wings, and
they shall face one another; the faces of
the cherubim *shall be* toward the mercy
seat. 21You shall put the mercy seat
on top of the ark, and in the ark you
shall put the Testimony that I will give
you. 22And there I will meet with you,
and I will speak with you from above
the mercy seat, from between the two
cherubim which *are* on the ark of the
Testimony, about everything which I
will give you in commandment to the
children of Israel.

The Table for the Showbread

23"You shall also make a table of aca-
cia wood; two cubits *shall be* its length,
a cubit its width, and a cubit and a half
its height. 24And you shall overlay it
with pure gold, and make a molding of
gold all around. 25You shall make for it
a frame of a handbreadth all around,
and you shall make a gold molding for
the frame all around. 26And you shall
make for it four rings of gold, and put
the rings on the four corners that *are* at
its four legs. 27The rings shall be close
to the frame, as holders for the poles to
bear the table. 28And you shall make the
poles of acacia wood, and overlay them
with gold, that the table may be carried
with them. 29You shall make its dishes,
its pans, its pitchers, and its bowls for
pouring. You shall make them of pure
gold. 30And you shall set the showbread
on the table before Me always.

The Gold Lampstand

31"You shall also make a lampstand
of pure gold; the lampstand shall be of
hammered work. Its shaft, its branches,
its bowls, its *ornamental* knobs, and
flowers shall be *of one piece.* 32And six
branches shall come out of its sides:
three branches of the lampstand out
of one side, and three branches of the
lampstand out of the other side. 33Three
bowls *shall be* made like almond *blos-
soms* on one branch, *with* an *ornamen-
tal* knob and a flower, and three bowls
made like almond *blossoms* on the other
branch, *with* an *ornamental* knob and
a flower—and so for the six branches
that come out of the lampstand. 34On
the lampstand itself four bowls *shall be*
made like almond *blossoms, each with*

its *ornamental* knob and flower. 35And *there shall be* a knob under the *first* two branches of the same, a knob under the *second* two branches of the same, and a knob under the *third* two branches of the same, according to the six branches that extend from the lampstand. 36Their knobs and their branches *shall be of one piece;* all of it *shall be* one hammered piece of pure gold. 37You shall make seven lamps for it, and they shall arrange its lamps so that they give light in front of it. 38And its wick-trimmers and their trays *shall be* of pure gold. 39It shall be made of a talent of pure gold, with all these utensils. 40And see to it that you make *them* according to the pattern which was shown you on the mountain.

The Tabernacle

26 "Moreover you shall make the tabernacle *with* ten curtains *of* fine woven linen and blue, purple, and scarlet *thread;* with artistic designs of cherubim you shall weave them. 2The length of each curtain *shall be* twenty-eight cubits, and the width of each curtain four cubits. And every one of the curtains shall have the same measurements. 3Five curtains shall be coupled to one another, and *the other* five curtains *shall be* coupled to one another. 4And you shall make loops of blue *yarn* on the edge of the curtain on the selvedge of *one* set, and likewise you shall do on the outer edge of *the other* curtain of the second set. 5Fifty loops you shall make in the one curtain, and fifty loops you shall make on the edge of the curtain that *is* on the end of the second set, that the loops may be clasped to one another. 6And you shall make fifty clasps of gold, and couple the curtains together with the clasps, so that it may be one tabernacle.

7"You shall also make curtains of goats' *hair,* to be a tent over the tabernacle. You shall make eleven curtains. 8The length of each curtain *shall be* thirty cubits, and the width of each curtain four cubits; and the eleven curtains shall all have the same measurements. 9And you shall couple five curtains by themselves and six curtains by themselves, and you shall double over the sixth curtain at the forefront of the tent. 10You shall make fifty loops on the edge of the curtain that is outermost in *one* set, and fifty loops on the edge of the curtain of the second set. 11And you shall make fifty bronze clasps, put the clasps into the loops, and couple the tent together, that it may be one. 12The remnant that remains of the curtains of the tent, the half curtain that remains, shall hang over the back of the tabernacle. 13And a cubit on one side and a cubit on the other side, of what remains of the length of the curtains of the tent, shall hang over the sides of the tabernacle, on this side and on that side, to cover it.

14"You shall also make a covering of ram skins dyed red for the tent, and a covering of badger skins above that.

15"And for the tabernacle you shall make the boards of acacia wood, standing upright. 16Ten cubits *shall be* the length of a board, and a cubit and a half *shall be* the width of each board. 17Two tenons *shall be* in each board for binding one to another. Thus you shall make for all the boards of the tabernacle. 18And you shall make the boards for the tabernacle, twenty boards for the south side. 19You shall make forty sockets of silver under the twenty boards: two sockets under each of the boards for its two tenons. 20And for the second side of the tabernacle, the north side, *there shall be* twenty boards 21and their forty sockets of silver: two sockets under each of the boards. 22For the far side of the tabernacle, westward, you shall make six boards. 23And you shall also make two boards for the two back corners of the tabernacle. 24They shall be coupled together at the bottom and they shall be coupled together at the top by one ring. Thus it shall be for both of them. They shall be for the two corners. 25So there shall be eight boards with their sockets of silver—sixteen sockets—two sockets under each of the boards.

26"And you shall make bars of acacia wood: five for the boards on one side of the tabernacle, 27five bars for the boards on the other side of the tabernacle, and five bars for the boards of the side of the tabernacle, for the far side westward.

28The middle bar shall pass through
the midst of the boards from end to
end. 29You shall overlay the boards with
gold, make their rings of gold *as* holders
for the bars, and overlay the bars with
gold. 30And you shall raise up the tab-
ernacle according to its pattern which
you were shown on the mountain.
31"You shall make a veil woven of
blue, purple, and scarlet *thread,* and
fine woven linen. It shall be woven with
an artistic design of cherubim. 32You
shall hang it upon the four pillars of
acacia *wood* overlaid with gold. Their
hooks *shall be* gold, upon four sockets
of silver. 33And you shall hang the veil
from the clasps. Then you shall bring
the ark of the Testimony in there, be-
hind the veil. The veil shall be a divider
for you between the holy *place* and the
Most Holy. 34You shall put the mercy
seat upon the ark of the Testimony in
the Most Holy. 35You shall set the table
outside the veil, and the lampstand
across from the table on the side of the
tabernacle toward the south; and you
shall put the table on the north side.
36"You shall make a screen for the door
of the tabernacle, *woven of* blue, purple,
and scarlet *thread,* and fine woven lin-
en, made by a weaver. 37And you shall
make for the screen five pillars of acacia
wood, and overlay them with gold; their
hooks *shall be* gold, and you shall cast
five sockets of bronze for them.

The Altar of Burnt Offering

27 "You shall make an altar of
acacia wood, five cubits long
and five cubits wide—the altar shall be
square—and its height *shall be* three
cubits. 2You shall make its horns on its
four corners; its horns shall be of one
piece with it. And you shall overlay it
with bronze. 3Also you shall make its
pans to receive its ashes, and its shovels
and its basins and its forks and its fire-
pans; you shall make all its utensils of
bronze. 4You shall make a grate for it, a
network of bronze; and on the network
you shall make four bronze rings at its
four corners. 5You shall put it under
the rim of the altar beneath, that the
network may be midway up the altar.
6And you shall make poles for the altar,
poles of acacia wood, and overlay them
with bronze. 7The poles shall be put in
the rings, and the poles shall be on the
two sides of the altar to bear it. 8You
shall make it hollow with boards; as
it was shown you on the mountain, so
shall they make *it.*

The Court of the Tabernacle

9"You shall also make the court of the
tabernacle. For the south side *there shall
be* hangings for the court *made of* fine
woven linen, one hundred cubits long
for one side. 10And its twenty pillars and
their twenty sockets *shall be* bronze. The
hooks of the pillars and their bands *shall
be* silver. 11Likewise along the length
of the north side *there shall be* hang-
ings one hundred *cubits* long, with its
twenty pillars and their twenty sockets
of bronze, and the hooks of the pillars
and their bands of silver.
12"And along the width of the court on
the west side *shall be* hangings of fifty
cubits, with their ten pillars and their
ten sockets. 13The width of the court on
the east side *shall be* fifty cubits. 14The
hangings on *one* side *of the gate shall
be* fifteen cubits, *with* their three pillars
and their three sockets. 15And on the
other side *shall be* hangings of fifteen
cubits, with their three pillars and their
three sockets.
16"For the gate of the court *there shall
be* a screen twenty cubits long, *woven of*
blue, purple, and scarlet *thread,* and fine
woven linen, made by a weaver. It *shall
have* four pillars and four sockets. 17All
the pillars around the court shall have
bands of silver; their hooks *shall be* of
silver and their sockets of bronze. 18The
length of the court *shall be* one hundred
cubits, the width fifty throughout, and
the height five cubits, *made of* fine wo-
ven linen, and its sockets of bronze. 19All
the utensils of the tabernacle for all its
service, all its pegs, and all the pegs of
the court, *shall be* of bronze.

The Care of the Lampstand

20"And you shall command the chil-
dren of Israel that they bring you pure
oil of pressed olives for the light, to cause
the lamp to burn continually. 21In the
tabernacle of meeting, outside the veil

which *is* before the Testimony, Aaron
and his sons shall tend it from evening
until morning before the LORD. *It shall*
be a statute forever to their generations
on behalf of the children of Israel.

Garments for the Priesthood

28 "Now take Aaron your brother,
and his sons with him, from
among the children of Israel, that he
may minister to Me as priest, Aaron
and Aaron's sons: Nadab, Abihu, Elea-
zar, and Ithamar. 2And you shall make
holy garments for Aaron your brother,
for glory and for beauty. 3So you shall
speak to all *who are* gifted artisans,
whom I have filled with the spirit of
wisdom, that they may make Aaron's
garments, to consecrate him, that he
may minister to Me as priest. 4And these
are the garments which they shall make:
a breastplate, an ephod,[a] a robe, a skill-
fully woven tunic, a turban, and a sash.
So they shall make holy garments for
Aaron your brother and his sons, that
he may minister to Me as priest.

The Ephod

5"They shall take the gold, blue, purple,
and scarlet *thread,* and the fine linen,
6and they shall make the ephod of gold,
blue, purple, *and* scarlet *thread,* and
fine woven linen, artistically worked. 7It
shall have two shoulder straps joined at
its two edges, and *so* it shall be joined
together. 8And the intricately woven
band of the ephod, which *is* on it, shall
be of the same workmanship, *made of*
gold, blue, purple, and scarlet *thread,*
and fine woven linen.
9"Then you shall take two onyx stones
and engrave on them the names of the
sons of Israel: 10six of their names on
one stone and six names on the other
stone, in order of their birth. 11With the
work of an engraver in stone, *like* the
engravings of a signet, you shall en-
grave the two stones with the names
of the sons of Israel. You shall set them
in settings of gold. 12And you shall
put the two stones on the shoulders
of the ephod *as* memorial stones for
the sons of Israel. So Aaron shall bear
their names before the LORD on his two
shoulders as a memorial. 13You shall
also make settings of gold, 14and you
shall make two chains of pure gold like
braided cords, and fasten the braided
chains to the settings.

The Breastplate

15"You shall make the breastplate of
judgment. Artistically woven according
to the workmanship of the ephod you
shall make it: of gold, blue, purple, and
scarlet *thread,* and fine woven linen, you
shall make it. 16It shall be doubled into
a square: a span *shall be* its length, and
a span *shall be* its width. 17And you shall
put settings of stones in it, four rows of
stones: *The first* row *shall be* a sardius,
a topaz, and an emerald; *this shall be*
the first row; 18the second row *shall be* a
turquoise, a sapphire, and a diamond;
19the third row, a jacinth, an agate, and
an amethyst; 20and the fourth row, a
beryl, an onyx, and a jasper. They shall
be set in gold settings. 21And the stones
shall have the names of the sons of Is-
rael, twelve according to their names,
like the engravings of a signet, each
one with its own name; they shall be
according to the twelve tribes.
22"You shall make chains for the
breastplate at the end, like braided cords
of pure gold. 23And you shall make two
rings of gold for the breastplate, and
put the two rings on the two ends of
the breastplate. 24Then you shall put
the two braided *chains* of gold in the
two rings which are on the ends of the
breastplate; 25and the *other* two ends of
the two braided *chains* you shall fasten
to the two settings, and put them on the
shoulder straps of the ephod in the front.
26"You shall make two rings of gold,
and put them on the two ends of the
breastplate, on the edge of it, which is on
the inner side of the ephod. 27And two
other rings of gold you shall make, and
put them on the two shoulder straps,
underneath the ephod toward its front,
right at the seam above the intricately
woven band of the ephod. 28They shall
bind the breastplate by means of its
rings to the rings of the ephod, using a

28:4 [a] That is, an ornamented vest

blue cord, so that it is above the intri-
cately woven band of the ephod, and
so that the breastplate does not come
loose from the ephod.
29“So Aaron shall bear the names of
the sons of Israel on the breastplate of
judgment over his heart, when he goes
into the holy *place,* as a memorial before
the LORD continually. 30And you shall
put in the breastplate of judgment the
Urim and the Thummim,[a] and they shall
be over Aaron's heart when he goes in
before the LORD. So Aaron shall bear the
judgment of the children of Israel over
his heart before the LORD continually.

Other Priestly Garments

31“You shall make the robe of the
ephod all of blue. 32There shall be an
opening for his head in the middle of it;
it shall have a woven binding all around
its opening, like the opening in a coat
of mail, so that it does not tear. 33And
upon its hem you shall make pome-
granates of blue, purple, and scarlet,
all around its hem, and bells of gold
between them all around: 34a golden
bell and a pomegranate, a golden bell
and a pomegranate, upon the hem of
the robe all around. 35And it shall be
upon Aaron when he ministers, and
its sound will be heard when he goes
into the holy *place* before the LORD and
when he comes out, that he may not die.
36“You shall also make a plate of pure
gold and engrave on it, *like* the engrav-
ing of a signet:

HOLINESS TO THE LORD.

37And you shall put it on a blue cord,
that it may be on the turban; it shall
be on the front of the turban. 38So it
shall be on Aaron's forehead, that Aaron
may bear the iniquity of the holy things
which the children of Israel hallow in
all their holy gifts; and it shall always
be on his forehead, that they may be
accepted before the LORD.
39“You shall skillfully weave the tunic
of fine linen *thread,* you shall make the
turban of fine linen, and you shall make
the sash of woven work.
40“For Aaron's sons you shall make
tunics, and you shall make sashes for
them. And you shall make hats for them,
for glory and beauty. 41So you shall put
them on Aaron your brother and on his
sons with him. You shall anoint them,
consecrate them, and sanctify them, that
they may minister to Me as priests. 42And
you shall make for them linen trousers to
cover their nakedness; they shall reach
from the waist to the thighs. 43They shall
be on Aaron and on his sons when they
come into the tabernacle of meeting, or
when they come near the altar to minister
in the holy *place,* that they do not incur
iniquity and die. *It shall be* a statute forev-
er to him and his descendants after him.

Aaron and His Sons Consecrated

29 “And this is what you shall do to
them to hallow them for minis-
tering to Me as priests: Take one young
bull and two rams without blemish, 2and
unleavened bread, unleavened cakes
mixed with oil, and unleavened wafers
anointed with oil (you shall make them
of wheat flour). 3You shall put them in
one basket and bring them in the basket,
with the bull and the two rams.
4“And Aaron and his sons you shall
bring to the door of the tabernacle of
meeting, and you shall wash them with
water. 5Then you shall take the gar-
ments, put the tunic on Aaron, and the
robe of the ephod, the ephod, and the
breastplate, and gird him with the intri-
cately woven band of the ephod. 6You
shall put the turban on his head, and
put the holy crown on the turban. 7And
you shall take the anointing oil, pour
it on his head, and anoint him. 8Then
you shall bring his sons and put tunics
on them. 9And you shall gird them with
sashes, Aaron and his sons, and put the
hats on them. The priesthood shall be
theirs for a perpetual statute. So you
shall consecrate Aaron and his sons.
10“You shall also have the bull brought
before the tabernacle of meeting, and
Aaron and his sons shall put their hands
on the head of the bull. 11Then you shall
kill the bull before the LORD, *by* the door
of the tabernacle of meeting. 12You shall

28:30 [a] Literally *the Lights and the Perfections* (compare Leviticus 8:8)

take *some* of the blood of the bull and
put *it* on the horns of the altar with your
finger, and pour all the blood beside
the base of the altar. 13 And you shall
take all the fat that covers the entrails,
the fatty lobe *attached* to the liver, and
the two kidneys and the fat that *is* on
them, and burn *them* on the altar. 14 But
the flesh of the bull, with its skin and its
offal, you shall burn with fire outside
the camp. It *is* a sin offering.
15 "You shall also take one ram, and
Aaron and his sons shall put their hands
on the head of the ram; 16 and you shall
kill the ram, and you shall take its blood
and sprinkle *it* all around on the altar.
17 Then you shall cut the ram in pieces,
wash its entrails and its legs, and put
them with its pieces and with its head.
18 And you shall burn the whole ram
on the altar. It *is* a burnt offering to the
LORD; it *is* a sweet aroma, an offering
made by fire to the LORD.
19 "You shall also take the other ram,
and Aaron and his sons shall put their
hands on the head of the ram. 20 Then
you shall kill the ram, and take some
of its blood and put *it* on the tip of the
right ear of Aaron and on the tip of the
right ear of his sons, on the thumb of
their right hand and on the big toe of
their right foot, and sprinkle the blood
all around on the altar. 21 And you shall
take some of the blood that is on the
altar, and some of the anointing oil,
and sprinkle *it* on Aaron and on his
garments, on his sons and on the gar-
ments of his sons with him; and he and
his garments shall be hallowed, and his
sons and his sons' garments with him.
22 "Also you shall take the fat of the ram,
the fat tail, the fat that covers the entrails,
the fatty lobe *attached to* the liver, the two
kidneys and the fat on them, the right
thigh (for it *is* a ram of consecration),
23 one loaf of bread, one cake *made with*
oil, and one wafer from the basket of the
unleavened bread that *is* before the LORD;
24 and you shall put all these in the hands
of Aaron and in the hands of his sons, and
you shall wave them *as* a wave offering
before the LORD. 25 You shall receive them
back from their hands and burn *them* on
the altar as a burnt offering, as a sweet
aroma before the LORD. It *is* an offering
made by fire to the LORD.
26 "Then you shall take the breast of the
ram of Aaron's consecration and wave
it *as* a wave offering before the LORD;
and it shall be your portion. 27 And from
the ram of the consecration you shall
consecrate the breast of the wave of-
fering which is waved, and the thigh
of the heave offering which is raised,
of *that* which *is* for Aaron and of *that*
which is for his sons. 28 It shall be from
the children of Israel *for* Aaron and
his sons by a statute forever. For it is a
heave offering; it shall be a heave of-
fering from the children of Israel from
the sacrifices of their peace offerings,
that is, their heave offering to the LORD.
29 "And the holy garments of Aaron
shall be his sons' after him, to be anoint-
ed in them and to be consecrated in
them. 30 That son who becomes priest
in his place shall put them on for seven
days, when he enters the tabernacle of
meeting to minister in the holy *place.*
31 "And you shall take the ram of the
consecration and boil its flesh in the
holy place. 32 Then Aaron and his sons
shall eat the flesh of the ram, and the
bread that *is* in the basket, *by* the door
of the tabernacle of meeting. 33 They
shall eat those things with which the
atonement was made, to consecrate
and to sanctify them; but an outsider
shall not eat *them,* because they *are*
holy. 34 And if any of the flesh of the
consecration offerings, or of the bread,
remains until the morning, then you
shall burn the remainder with fire. It
shall not be eaten, because it *is* holy.
35 "Thus you shall do to Aaron and
his sons, according to all that I have
commanded you. Seven days you shall
consecrate them. 36 And you shall offer
a bull every day *as* a sin offering for
atonement. You shall cleanse the altar
when you make atonement for it, and
you shall anoint it to sanctify it. 37 Seven
days you shall make atonement for
the altar and sanctify it. And the altar
shall be most holy. Whatever touches
the altar must be holy.[a]

29:37 [a] Compare Numbers 4:15 and Haggai 2:11–13

The Daily Offerings

38“Now this *is* what you shall offer
on the altar: two lambs of the first
year, day by day continually. 39One
lamb you shall offer in the morning,
and the other lamb you shall offer at
twilight. 40With the one lamb shall be
one-tenth *of an ephah* of flour mixed
with one-fourth of a hin of pressed oil,
and one-fourth of a hin of wine *as* a
drink offering. 41And the other lamb
you shall offer at twilight; and you shall
offer with it the grain offering and the
drink offering, as in the morning, for a
sweet aroma, an offering made by fire
to the LORD. 42*This shall be* a continual
burnt offering throughout your generations
at the door of the tabernacle of
meeting before the LORD, where I will
meet you to speak with you. 43And there
I will meet with the children of Israel,
and *the tabernacle* shall be sanctified
by My glory. 44So I will consecrate the
tabernacle of meeting and the altar. I
will also consecrate both Aaron and
his sons to minister to Me as priests.
45I will dwell among the children of
Israel and will be their God. 46And they
shall know that I *am* the LORD their God,
who brought them up out of the land of
Egypt, that I may dwell among them. I
am the LORD their God.

The Altar of Incense

30 “You shall make an altar to burn
incense on; you shall make it
of acacia wood. 2A cubit *shall be* its
length and a cubit its width—it shall
be square—and two cubits *shall be* its
height. Its horns *shall be* of one piece
with it. 3And you shall overlay its top,
its sides all around, and its horns with
pure gold; and you shall make for it a
molding of gold all around. 4Two gold
rings you shall make for it, under the
molding on both its sides. You shall
place *them* on its two sides, and they
will be holders for the poles with which
to bear it. 5You shall make the poles of
acacia wood, and overlay them with
gold. 6And you shall put it before the
veil that *is* before the ark of the Testimony,
before the mercy seat that *is* over the
Testimony, where I will meet with you.
7“Aaron shall burn on it sweet incense
every morning; when he tends the
lamps, he shall burn incense on it. 8And
when Aaron lights the lamps at twilight,
he shall burn incense on it, a perpetual
incense before the LORD throughout
your generations. 9You shall not offer
strange incense on it, or a burnt
offering, or a grain offering; nor shall
you pour a drink offering on it. 10And
Aaron shall make atonement upon its
horns once a year with the blood of
the sin offering of atonement; once a
year he shall make atonement upon it
throughout your generations. It *is* most
holy to the LORD.”

The Ransom Money

11Then the LORD spoke to Moses, saying:
12“When you take the census of
the children of Israel for their number,
then every man shall give a ransom for
himself to the LORD, when you number
them, that there may be no plague
among them when *you* number them.
13This is what everyone among those
who are numbered shall give: half a
shekel according to the shekel of the
sanctuary (a shekel *is* twenty gerahs).
The half-shekel *shall be* an offering to
the LORD. 14Everyone included among
those who are numbered, from twenty
years old and above, shall give an
offering to the LORD. 15The rich shall
not give more and the poor shall not
give less than half a shekel, when *you*
give an offering to the LORD, to make
atonement for yourselves. 16And you
shall take the atonement money of the
children of Israel, and shall appoint
it for the service of the tabernacle of
meeting, that it may be a memorial for
the children of Israel before the LORD,
to make atonement for yourselves.”

The Bronze Laver

17Then the LORD spoke to Moses, saying:
18“You shall also make a laver of bronze,
with its base also of bronze, for washing.
You shall put it between the tabernacle
of meeting and the altar. And you shall
put water in it, 19for Aaron and his sons
shall wash their hands and their feet in
water from it. 20When they go into the
tabernacle of meeting, or when they
come near the altar to minister, to burn

an offering made by fire to the LORD, they shall wash with water, lest they die. 21So they shall wash their hands and their feet, lest they die. And it shall be a statute forever to them—to him and his descendants throughout their generations."

The Holy Anointing Oil

22Moreover the LORD spoke to Moses, saying: 23"Also take for yourself quality spices—five hundred *shekels* of liquid myrrh, half as much sweet-smelling cinnamon (two hundred and fifty *shekels*), two hundred and fifty *shekels* of sweet-smelling cane, 24five hundred *shekels* of cassia, according to the shekel of the sanctuary, and a hin of olive oil. 25And you shall make from these a holy anointing oil, an ointment compounded according to the art of the perfumer. It shall be a holy anointing oil. 26With it you shall anoint the tabernacle of meeting and the ark of the Testimony; 27the table and all its utensils, the lampstand and its utensils, and the altar of incense; 28the altar of burnt offering with all its utensils, and the laver and its base. 29You shall consecrate them, that they may be most holy; whatever touches them must be holy.[a] 30And you shall anoint Aaron and his sons, and consecrate them, that *they* may minister to Me as priests.

31"And you shall speak to the children of Israel, saying: 'This shall be a holy anointing oil to Me throughout your generations. 32It shall not be poured on man's flesh; nor shall you make *any other* like it, according to its composition. It *is* holy, *and* it shall be holy to you. 33Whoever compounds *any* like it, or whoever puts *any* of it on an outsider, shall be cut off from his people.' "

The Incense

34And the LORD said to Moses: "Take sweet spices, stacte and onycha and galbanum, and pure frankincense with *these* sweet spices; there shall be equal amounts of each. 35You shall make of these an incense, a compound according to the art of the perfumer, salted, pure, *and* holy. 36And you shall beat *some* of it very fine, and put some of it before the Testimony in the tabernacle of meeting where I will meet with you. It shall be most holy to you. 37But *as for* the incense which you shall make, you shall not make any for yourselves, according to its composition. It shall be to you holy for the LORD. 38Whoever makes *any* like it, to smell it, he shall be cut off from his people."

Artisans for Building the Tabernacle

31 Then the LORD spoke to Moses, saying: 2"See, I have called by name Bezalel the son of Uri, the son of Hur, of the tribe of Judah. 3And I have filled him with the Spirit of God, in wisdom, in understanding, in knowledge, and in all *manner of* workmanship, 4to design artistic works, to work in gold, in silver, in bronze, 5in cutting jewels for setting, in carving wood, and to work in all *manner of* workmanship.

6"And I, indeed I, have appointed with him Aholiab the son of Ahisamach, of the tribe of Dan; and I have put wisdom in the hearts of all the gifted artisans, that they may make all that I have commanded you: 7the tabernacle of meeting, the ark of the Testimony and the mercy seat that *is* on it, and all the furniture of the tabernacle— 8the table and its utensils, the pure *gold* lampstand with all its utensils, the altar of incense, 9the altar of burnt offering with all its utensils, and the laver and its base— 10the garments of ministry,[a] the holy garments for Aaron the priest and the garments of his sons, to minister as priests, 11and the anointing oil and sweet incense for the holy *place*. According to all that I have commanded you they shall do."

The Sabbath Law

12And the LORD spoke to Moses, saying, 13"Speak also to the children of Israel, saying: 'Surely My Sabbaths you shall keep, for it *is* a sign between Me and you throughout your generations, that *you* may know that I *am* the LORD who sanctifies you. 14You shall keep the Sabbath, therefore, for *it is* holy to you. Everyone who profanes it shall surely

30:29 [a] Compare Numbers 4:15 and Haggai 2:11–13 **31:10** [a] Or *woven garments*

be put to death; for whoever does *any*
work on it, that person shall be cut off
from among his people. 15Work shall be
done for six days, but the seventh *is* the
Sabbath of rest, holy to the LORD. Who-
ever does *any* work on the Sabbath day,
he shall surely be put to death. 16There-
fore the children of Israel shall keep
the Sabbath, to observe the Sabbath
throughout their generations *as* a per-
petual covenant. 17It *is* a sign between
Me and the children of Israel forever; for
in six days the LORD made the heavens
and the earth, and on the seventh day
He rested and was refreshed.' "
18And when He had made an end of
speaking with him on Mount Sinai, He
gave Moses two tablets of the Testimo-
ny, tablets of stone, written with the
finger of God.

The Gold Calf

32 Now when the people saw that
Moses delayed coming down
from the mountain, the people gath-
ered together to Aaron, and said to
him, "Come, make us gods that shall
go before us; for *as for* this Moses, the
man who brought us up out of the land
of Egypt, we do not know what has be-
come of him."
2And Aaron said to them, "Break
off the golden earrings which *are* in
the ears of your wives, your sons, and
your daughters, and bring *them* to me."
3So all the people broke off the gold-
en earrings which *were* in their ears,
and brought *them* to Aaron. 4And he
received *the gold* from their hand, and
he fashioned it with an engraving tool,
and made a molded calf.
Then they said, "This *is* your god, O Is-
rael, that brought you out of the land
of Egypt!"
5So when Aaron saw *it,* he built an altar
before it. And Aaron made a procla-
mation and said, "Tomorrow *is* a feast
to the LORD." 6Then they rose early on
the next day, offered burnt offerings,
and brought peace offerings; and the
people sat down to eat and drink, and
rose up to play.
7And the LORD said to Moses, "Go,
get down! For your people whom you
brought out of the land of Egypt have
corrupted *themselves.* 8They have
turned aside quickly out of the way
which I commanded them. They have
made themselves a molded calf, and
worshiped it and sacrificed to it, and
said, 'This *is* your god, O Israel, that
brought you out of the land of Egypt!' "
9And the LORD said to Moses, "I have
seen this people, and indeed it *is* a stiff-
necked people! 10Now therefore, let Me
alone, that My wrath may burn hot
against them and I may consume them.
And I will make of you a great nation."
11Then Moses pleaded with the LORD
his God, and said: "LORD, why does Your
wrath burn hot against Your people
whom You have brought out of the land
of Egypt with great power and with a
mighty hand? 12Why should the Egyp-
tians speak, and say, 'He brought them
out to harm them, to kill them in the
mountains, and to consume them from
the face of the earth'? Turn from Your
fierce wrath, and relent from this harm
to Your people. 13Remember Abraham,
Isaac, and Israel, Your servants, to whom
You swore by Your own self, and said to
them, 'I will multiply your descendants as
the stars of heaven; and all this land that
I have spoken of I give to your descen-
dants, and they shall inherit *it* forever.' "[a]
14So the LORD relented from the harm
which He said He would do to His people.
15And Moses turned and went down
from the mountain, and the two tablets
of the Testimony *were* in his hand. The
tablets *were* written on both sides; on
the one *side* and on the other they were
written. 16Now the tablets *were* the work
of God, and the writing *was* the writing
of God engraved on the tablets.
17And when Joshua heard the noise
of the people as they shouted, he said
to Moses, "*There is* a noise of war in the
camp."
18But he said:

"*It is* not the noise of the shout of
victory,
Nor the noise of the cry of defeat,
But the sound of singing I hear."

32:13 [a] Genesis 13:15 and 22:17

19So it was, as soon as he came near
the camp, that he saw the calf *and* the
dancing. So Moses' anger became hot,
and he cast the tablets out of his hands
and broke them at the foot of the moun-
tain. 20Then he took the calf which they
had made, burned *it* in the fire, and
ground *it* to powder; and he scattered
it on the water and made the children
of Israel drink *it*. 21And Moses said to
Aaron, "What did this people do to you
that you have brought *so* great a sin
upon them?"
22So Aaron said, "Do not let the anger
of my lord become hot. You know the
people, that they *are set* on evil. 23For
they said to me, 'Make us gods that shall
go before us; *as for* this Moses, the man
who brought us out of the land of Egypt,
we do not know what has become of
him.' 24And I said to them, 'Whoever
has any gold, let them break *it* off.' So
they gave *it* to me, and I cast it into the
fire, and this calf came out."
25Now when Moses saw that the peo-
ple *were* unrestrained (for Aaron had
not restrained them, to *their* shame
among their enemies), 26then Moses
stood in the entrance of the camp, and
said, "Whoever *is* on the LORD's side—
come to me!" And all the sons of Levi
gathered themselves together to him.
27And he said to them, "Thus says the
LORD God of Israel: 'Let every man put
his sword on his side, and go in and out
from entrance to entrance throughout
the camp, and let every man kill his
brother, every man his companion,
and every man his neighbor.' " 28So the
sons of Levi did according to the word of
Moses. And about three thousand men
of the people fell that day. 29Then Moses
said, "Consecrate yourselves today to
the LORD, that He may bestow on you
a blessing this day, for every man has
opposed his son and his brother."
30Now it came to pass on the next day
that Moses said to the people, "You have
committed a great sin. So now I will go
up to the LORD; perhaps I can make
atonement for your sin." 31Then Moses
returned to the LORD and said, "Oh,
these people have committed a great
sin, and have made for themselves a
god of gold! 32Yet now, if You will forgive
their sin—but if not, I pray, blot me out
of Your book which You have written."
33And the LORD said to Moses, "Who-
ever has sinned against Me, I will blot
him out of My book. 34Now therefore,
go, lead the people to *the place* of which
I have spoken to you. Behold, My Angel
shall go before you. Nevertheless, in
the day when I visit for punishment,
I will visit punishment upon them for
their sin."
35So the LORD plagued the people
because of what they did with the calf
which Aaron made.

The Command to Leave Sinai

33 Then the LORD said to Moses,
"Depart *and* go up from here,
you and the people whom you have
brought out of the land of Egypt, to the
land of which I swore to Abraham, Isaac,
and Jacob, saying, 'To your descendants
I will give it.' 2And I will send *My* Angel
before you, and I will drive out the Ca-
naanite and the Amorite and the Hittite
and the Perizzite and the Hivite and the
Jebusite. 3*Go up* to a land flowing with
milk and honey; for I will not go up in
your midst, lest I consume you on the
way, for you *are* a stiff-necked people."
4And when the people heard this bad
news, they mourned, and no one put on
his ornaments. 5For the LORD had said
to Moses, "Say to the children of Israel,
'You *are* a stiff-necked people. I could
come up into your midst in one moment
and consume you. Now therefore, take
off your ornaments, that I may know
what to do to you.' " 6So the children
of Israel stripped themselves of their
ornaments by Mount Horeb.

Moses Meets with the LORD

7Moses took his tent and pitched it
outside the camp, far from the camp,
and called it the tabernacle of meeting.
And it came to pass *that* everyone who
sought the LORD went out to the tab-
ernacle of meeting which *was* outside
the camp. 8So it was, whenever Moses
went out to the tabernacle, *that* all the
people rose, and each man stood *at*
his tent door and watched Moses until
he had gone into the tabernacle. 9And
it came to pass, when Moses entered

the tabernacle, that the pillar of cloud
descended and stood *at* the door of the
tabernacle, and *the* LORD talked with
Moses. 10All the people saw the pillar of
cloud standing *at* the tabernacle door,
and all the people rose and worshiped,
each man *in* his tent door. 11So the LORD
spoke to Moses face to face, as a man
speaks to his friend. And he would re-
turn to the camp, but his servant Joshua
the son of Nun, a young man, did not
depart from the tabernacle.

The Promise of God's Presence

12Then Moses said to the LORD, "See,
You say to me, 'Bring up this people.'
But You have not let me know whom
You will send with me. Yet You have said,
'I know you by name, and you have
also found grace in My sight.' 13Now
therefore, I pray, if I have found grace
in Your sight, show me now Your way,
that I may know You and that I may
find grace in Your sight. And consider
that this nation *is* Your people."

14And He said, "My Presence will go
with you, and I will give you rest."

15Then he said to Him, "If Your Pres-
ence does not go *with us,* do not bring
us up from here. 16For how then will it
be known that Your people and I have
found grace in Your sight, except You go
with us? So we shall be separate, Your
people and I, from all the people who
are upon the face of the earth."

17So the LORD said to Moses, "I will also
do this thing that you have spoken; for
you have found grace in My sight, and
I know you by name."

18And he said, "Please, show me Your
glory."

19Then He said, "I will make all My
goodness pass before you, and I will
proclaim the name of the LORD before
you. I will be gracious to whom I will be
gracious, and I will have compassion on
whom I will have compassion." 20But
He said, "You cannot see My face; for
no man shall see Me, and live." 21And
the LORD said, "Here is a place by Me,
and you shall stand on the rock. 22So it
shall be, while My glory passes by, that
I will put you in the cleft of the rock,
and will cover you with My hand while
I pass by. 23Then I will take away My
hand, and you shall see My back; but
My face shall not be seen."

Moses Makes New Tablets

34 And the LORD said to Moses, "Cut
two tablets of stone like the first
ones, and I will write on *these* tablets
the words that were on the first tablets
which you broke. 2So be ready in the
morning, and come up in the morning
to Mount Sinai, and present yourself to
Me there on the top of the mountain.
3And no man shall come up with you,
and let no man be seen throughout all
the mountain; let neither flocks nor
herds feed before that mountain."

4So he cut two tablets of stone like the
first *ones.* Then Moses rose early in the
morning and went up Mount Sinai, as
the LORD had commanded him; and he
took in his hand the two tablets of stone.

5Now the LORD descended in the
cloud and stood with him there, and
proclaimed the name of the LORD.
6And the LORD passed before him and
proclaimed, "The LORD, the LORD God,
merciful and gracious, longsuffering,
and abounding in goodness and truth,
7keeping mercy for thousands, forgiv-
ing iniquity and transgression and sin,
by no means clearing *the guilty,* visit-
ing the iniquity of the fathers upon the
children and the children's children to
the third and the fourth generation."

8So Moses made haste and bowed his
head toward the earth, and worshiped.
9Then he said, "If now I have found
grace in Your sight, O Lord, let my Lord,
I pray, go among us, even though we
are a stiff-necked people; and pardon
our iniquity and our sin, and take us as
Your inheritance."

The Covenant Renewed

10And He said: "Behold, I make a cov-
enant. Before all your people I will do
marvels such as have not been done
in all the earth, nor in any nation; and
all the people among whom you *are*
shall see the work of the LORD. For it *is*
an awesome thing that I will do with
you. 11Observe what I command you
this day. Behold, I am driving out from
before you the Amorite and the Canaan-
ite and the Hittite and the Perizzite and

the Hivite and the Jebusite. 12 Take heed
to yourself, lest you make a covenant
with the inhabitants of the land where
you are going, lest it be a snare in your
midst. 13 But you shall destroy their al-
tars, break their *sacred* pillars, and cut
down their wooden images 14 (for you
shall worship no other god, for the LORD,
whose name *is* Jealous, *is* a jealous God),
15 lest you make a covenant with the
inhabitants of the land, and they play
the harlot with their gods and make
sacrifice to their gods, and *one of them*
invites you and you eat of his sacrifice,
16 and you take of his daughters for your
sons, and his daughters play the harlot
with their gods and make your sons play
the harlot with their gods.
17 "You shall make no molded gods for
yourselves.
18 "The Feast of Unleavened Bread you
shall keep. Seven days you shall eat
unleavened bread, as I commanded
you, in the appointed time of the month
of Abib; for in the month of Abib you
came out from Egypt.
19 "All that open the womb *are* Mine,
and every male firstborn among your
livestock, *whether* ox or sheep. 20 But
the firstborn of a donkey you shall re-
deem with a lamb. And if you will not
redeem *him,* then you shall break his
neck. All the firstborn of your sons you
shall redeem.

"And none shall appear before Me
empty-handed.
21 "Six days you shall work, but on the
seventh day you shall rest; in plowing
time and in harvest you shall rest.
22 "And you shall observe the Feast of
Weeks, of the firstfruits of wheat har-
vest, and the Feast of Ingathering at
the year's end.
23 "Three times in the year all your men
shall appear before the Lord, the LORD
God of Israel. 24 For I will cast out the
nations before you and enlarge your
borders; neither will any man covet
your land when you go up to appear
before the LORD your God three times
in the year.
25 "You shall not offer the blood of
My sacrifice with leaven, nor shall the
sacrifice of the Feast of the Passover be
left until morning.
26 "The first of the firstfruits of your
land you shall bring to the house of
the LORD your God. You shall not boil a
young goat in its mother's milk."
27 Then the LORD said to Moses, "Write
these words, for according to the tenor
of these words I have made a covenant
with you and with Israel." 28 So he was
there with the LORD forty days and forty
nights; he neither ate bread nor drank
water. And He wrote on the tablets the
words of the covenant, the Ten Com-
mandments.[a]

The Shining Face of Moses

29 Now it was so, when Moses came
down from Mount Sinai (and the two
tablets of the Testimony *were* in Mo-
ses' hand when he came down from the
mountain), that Moses did not know that
the skin of his face shone while he talked
with Him. 30 So when Aaron and all the
children of Israel saw Moses, behold,
the skin of his face shone, and they were
afraid to come near him. 31 Then Moses
called to them, and Aaron and all the
rulers of the congregation returned to
him; and Moses talked with them. 32 Af-
terward all the children of Israel came
near, and he gave them as command-
ments all that the LORD had spoken with
him on Mount Sinai. 33 And when Moses
had finished speaking with them, he put
a veil on his face. 34 But whenever Moses
went in before the LORD to speak with
Him, he would take the veil off until he
came out; and he would come out and
speak to the children of Israel whatever
he had been commanded. 35 And when-
ever the children of Israel saw the face
of Moses, that the skin of Moses' face
shone, then Moses would put the veil
on his face again, until he went in to
speak with Him.

Sabbath Regulations

35 Then Moses gathered all the
congregation of the children
of Israel together, and said to them,
"These *are* the words which the LORD has
commanded *you* to do: 2 Work shall be

34:28 [a] Literally *Ten Words*

done for six days, but the seventh day
shall be a holy day for you, a Sabbath
of rest to the LORD. Whoever does any
work on it shall be put to death. 3You
shall kindle no fire throughout your
dwellings on the Sabbath day."

Offerings for the Tabernacle

4And Moses spoke to all the congre-
gation of the children of Israel, saying,
"This *is* the thing which the LORD com-
manded, saying: 5'Take from among
you an offering to the LORD. Whoever
is of a willing heart, let him bring it as
an offering to the LORD: gold, silver,
and bronze; 6blue, purple, and scarlet
thread, fine linen, and goats' *hair;* 7ram
skins dyed red, badger skins, and aca-
cia wood; 8oil for the light, and spices
for the anointing oil and for the sweet
incense; 9onyx stones, and stones to be
set in the ephod and in the breastplate.

Articles of the Tabernacle

10'All *who are* gifted artisans among
you shall come and make all that the
LORD has commanded: 11the taber-
nacle, its tent, its covering, its clasps,
its boards, its bars, its pillars, and its
sockets; 12the ark and its poles, *with* the
mercy seat, and the veil of the covering;
13the table and its poles, all its utensils,
and the showbread; 14also the lamp-
stand for the light, its utensils, its lamps,
and the oil for the light; 15the incense al-
tar, its poles, the anointing oil, the sweet
incense, and the screen for the door at
the entrance of the tabernacle; 16the
altar of burnt offering with its bronze
grating, its poles, all its utensils, *and*
the laver and its base; 17the hangings of
the court, its pillars, their sockets, and the
screen for the gate of the court; 18the
pegs of the tabernacle, the pegs of
the court, and their cords; 19the gar-
ments of ministry,[a] for ministering in
the holy *place*—the holy garments for
Aaron the priest and the garments of
his sons, to minister as priests.' "

The Tabernacle Offerings Presented

20And all the congregation of the
children of Israel departed from the
presence of Moses. 21Then everyone
came whose heart was stirred, and ev-
eryone whose spirit was willing, *and*
they brought the LORD's offering for
the work of the tabernacle of meeting,
for all its service, and for the holy gar-
ments. 22They came, both men and
women, as many as had a willing heart,
and brought earrings and nose rings,
rings and necklaces, all jewelry of gold,
that is, every man who *made* an offering
of gold to the LORD. 23And every man,
with whom was found blue, purple, and
scarlet *thread,* fine linen, and goats' *hair,*
red skins of rams, and badger skins,
brought *them.* 24Everyone who offered
an offering of silver or bronze brought
the LORD's offering. And everyone with
whom was found acacia wood for any
work of the service, brought *it.* 25All the
women *who were* gifted artisans spun
yarn with their hands, and brought
what they had spun, of blue, purple,
and scarlet, and fine linen. 26And all
the women whose hearts stirred with
wisdom spun yarn of goats' *hair.* 27The
rulers brought onyx stones, and the
stones to be set in the ephod and in
the breastplate, 28and spices and oil
for the light, for the anointing oil, and
for the sweet incense. 29The children of
Israel brought a freewill offering to the
LORD, all the men and women whose
hearts were willing to bring *material*
for all kinds of work which the LORD,
by the hand of Moses, had commanded
to be done.

The Artisans Called by God

30And Moses said to the children of Is-
rael, "See, the LORD has called by name
Bezalel the son of Uri, the son of Hur, of
the tribe of Judah; 31and He has filled
him with the Spirit of God, in wisdom
and understanding, in knowledge and
all manner of workmanship, 32to design
artistic works, to work in gold and sil-
ver and bronze, 33in cutting jewels for
setting, in carving wood, and to work
in all manner of artistic workmanship.
34"And He has put in his heart the abil-
ity to teach, *in* him and Aholiab the
son of Ahisamach, of the tribe of Dan.

35:19 [a] Or *woven garments*

35He has filled them with skill to do all
manner of work of the engraver and
the designer and the tapestry maker, in
blue, purple, and scarlet *thread,* and fine
linen, and of the weaver—those who
do every work and those who design
artistic works.

36 "And Bezalel and Aholiab, and
every gifted artisan in whom the
LORD has put wisdom and understand-
ing, to know how to do all manner of
work for the service of the sanctuary,
shall do according to all that the LORD
has commanded."

The People Give More than Enough

2Then Moses called Bezalel and Aho-
liab, and every gifted artisan in whose
heart the LORD had put wisdom, every-
one whose heart was stirred, to come
and do the work. 3And they received
from Moses all the offering which the
children of Israel had brought for the
work of the service of making the sanc-
tuary. So they continued bringing to
him freewill offerings every morning.
4Then all the craftsmen who were doing
all the work of the sanctuary came,
each from the work he was doing, 5and
they spoke to Moses, saying, "The peo-
ple bring much more than enough for
the service of the work which the LORD
commanded *us* to do."

6So Moses gave a commandment,
and they caused it to be proclaimed
throughout the camp, saying, "Let
neither man nor woman do any more
work for the offering of the sanctuary."
And the people were restrained from
bringing, 7for the material they had was
sufficient for all the work to be done—
indeed too much.

Building the Tabernacle

8Then all the gifted artisans among
them who worked on the tabernacle
made ten curtains woven of fine linen,
and of blue, purple, and scarlet *thread;*
with artistic designs of cherubim they
made them. 9The length of each cur-
tain *was* twenty-eight cubits, and the
width of each curtain four cubits; the
curtains *were* all the same size. 10And
he coupled five curtains to one another,
and *the other* five curtains he coupled
to one another. 11He made loops of blue
yarn on the edge of the curtain on the
selvedge of one set; likewise he did on
the outer edge of *the other* curtain of
the second set. 12Fifty loops he made on
one curtain, and fifty loops he made on
the edge of the curtain on the end of the
second set; the loops held one *curtain* to
another. 13And he made fifty clasps of
gold, and coupled the curtains to one
another with the clasps, that it might
be one tabernacle.

14He made curtains of goats' *hair* for
the tent over the tabernacle; he made
eleven curtains. 15The length of each
curtain *was* thirty cubits, and the width
of each curtain four cubits; the elev-
en curtains *were* the same size. 16He
coupled five curtains by themselves
and six curtains by themselves. 17And
he made fifty loops on the edge of the
curtain that is outermost in one set,
and fifty loops he made on the edge
of the curtain of the second set. 18He
also made fifty bronze clasps to couple
the tent together, that it might be one.
19Then he made a covering for the tent
of ram skins dyed red, and a covering
of badger skins above *that.*

20For the tabernacle he made boards
of acacia wood, standing upright. 21The
length of each board *was* ten cubits, and
the width of each board a cubit and a
half. 22Each board had two tenons for
binding one to another. Thus he made
for all the boards of the tabernacle.
23And he made boards for the taber-
nacle, twenty boards for the south side.
24Forty sockets of silver he made to go
under the twenty boards: two sockets
under each of the boards for its two
tenons. 25And for the other side of the
tabernacle, the north side, he made
twenty boards 26and their forty sock-
ets of silver: two sockets under each of
the boards. 27For the west side of the
tabernacle he made six boards. 28He
also made two boards for the two back
corners of the tabernacle. 29And they
were coupled at the bottom and coupled
together at the top by one ring. Thus he
made both of them for the two corners.
30So there were eight boards and their
sockets—sixteen sockets of silver—two
sockets under each of the boards.

31And he made bars of acacia wood:
five for the boards on one side of the
tabernacle, 32five bars for the boards on
the other side of the tabernacle, and five
bars for the boards of the tabernacle on
the far side westward. 33And he made
the middle bar to pass through the
boards from one end to the other. 34He
overlaid the boards with gold, made
their rings of gold *to be* holders for the
bars, and overlaid the bars with gold.

35And he made a veil of blue, purple,
and scarlet *thread,* and fine woven linen;
it was worked *with* an artistic design of
cherubim. 36He made for it four pillars
of acacia *wood,* and overlaid them with
gold, with their hooks of gold; and he
cast four sockets of silver for them.

37He also made a screen for the taber-
nacle door, of blue, purple, and scarlet
thread, and fine woven linen, made by
a weaver, 38and its five pillars with their
hooks. And he overlaid their capitals
and their rings with gold, but their five
sockets *were* bronze.

Making the Ark of the Testimony

37 Then Bezalel made the ark of
acacia wood; two and a half cu-
bits *was* its length, a cubit and a half its
width, and a cubit and a half its height.
2He overlaid it with pure gold inside and
outside, and made a molding of gold all
around it. 3And he cast for it four rings
of gold *to be set* in its four corners: two
rings on one side, and two rings on the
other side of it. 4He made poles of aca-
cia wood, and overlaid them with gold.
5And he put the poles into the rings at
the sides of the ark, to bear the ark. 6He
also made the mercy seat of pure gold;
two and a half cubits *was* its length and
a cubit and a half its width. 7He made
two cherubim of beaten gold; he made
them of one piece at the two ends of the
mercy seat: 8one cherub at one end on
this side, and the other cherub at the
other end on that side. He made the
cherubim at the two ends *of one piece*
with the mercy seat. 9The cherubim
spread out *their* wings above, *and* cov-
ered the mercy seat with their wings.
They faced one another; the faces of
the cherubim were toward the mercy
seat.

Making the Table for the Showbread

10He made the table of acacia wood;
two cubits *was* its length, a cubit its
width, and a cubit and a half its height.
11And he overlaid it with pure gold, and
made a molding of gold all around it.
12Also he made a frame of a hand-
breadth all around it, and made a mold-
ing of gold for the frame all around it.
13And he cast for it four rings of gold,
and put the rings on the four corners
that *were* at its four legs. 14The rings
were close to the frame, as holders for
the poles to bear the table. 15And he
made the poles of acacia wood to bear
the table, and overlaid them with gold.
16He made of pure gold the utensils
which were on the table: its dishes,
its cups, its bowls, and its pitchers for
pouring.

Making the Gold Lampstand

17He also made the lampstand of pure
gold; of hammered work he made the
lampstand. Its shaft, its branches, its
bowls, its *ornamental* knobs, and its
flowers were of the same piece. 18And
six branches came out of its sides:
three branches of the lampstand out
of one side, and three branches of
the lampstand out of the other side.
19There were three bowls made like
almond *blossoms* on one branch, with
an *ornamental* knob and a flower, and
three bowls made like almond *blos-
soms* on the other branch, with an
ornamental knob and a flower—and
so for the six branches coming out of
the lampstand. 20And on the lamp-
stand itself *were* four bowls made like
almond *blossoms, each with* its *orna-
mental* knob and flower. 21*There was*
a knob under the *first* two branches
of the same, a knob under the *sec-
ond* two branches of the same, and
a knob under the *third* two branch-
es of the same, according to the six
branches extending from it. 22Their
knobs and their branches were of one
piece; all of it *was* one hammered
piece of pure gold. 23And he made its
seven lamps, its wick-trimmers, and
its trays of pure gold. 24Of a talent
of pure gold he made it, with all its
utensils.

Making the Altar of Incense

25He made the incense altar of acacia wood. Its length *was* a cubit and its width a cubit—*it was* square—and two cubits *was* its height. Its horns were *of one piece* with it. 26And he overlaid it with pure gold: its top, its sides all around, and its horns. He also made for it a molding of gold all around it. 27He made two rings of gold for it under its molding, by its two corners on both sides, as holders for the poles with which to bear it. 28And he made the poles of acacia wood, and overlaid them with gold.

Making the Anointing Oil and the Incense

29He also made the holy anointing oil and the pure incense of sweet spices, according to the work of the perfumer.

Making the Altar of Burnt Offering

38 He made the altar of burnt offering of acacia wood; five cubits *was* its length and five cubits its width—*it was* square—and its height *was* three cubits. 2He made its horns on its four corners; the horns were *of one piece* with it. And he overlaid it with bronze. 3He made all the utensils for the altar: the pans, the shovels, the basins, the forks, and the firepans; all its utensils he made of bronze. 4And he made a grate of bronze network for the altar, under its rim, midway from the bottom. 5He cast four rings for the four corners of the bronze grating, *as* holders for the poles. 6And he made the poles of acacia wood, and overlaid them with bronze. 7Then he put the poles into the rings on the sides of the altar, with which to bear it. He made the altar hollow with boards.

Making the Bronze Laver

8He made the laver of bronze and its base of bronze, from the bronze mirrors of the serving women who assembled at the door of the tabernacle of meeting.

Making the Court of the Tabernacle

9Then he made the court on the south side; the hangings of the court *were of* fine woven linen, one hundred cubits long. 10There *were* twenty pillars for them, with twenty bronze sockets. The hooks of the pillars and their bands *were* silver. 11On the north side *the hangings were* one hundred cubits *long*, with twenty pillars and their twenty bronze sockets. The hooks of the pillars and their bands *were* silver. 12And on the west side *there were* hangings of fifty cubits, with ten pillars and their ten sockets. The hooks of the pillars and their bands *were* silver. 13For the east side *the hangings were* fifty cubits. 14The hangings of one side *of the gate were* fifteen cubits *long, with* their three pillars and their three sockets, 15and the same for the other side of the court gate; on this side and that *were* hangings of fifteen cubits, *with* their three pillars and their three sockets. 16All the hangings of the court all around *were of* fine woven linen. 17The sockets for the pillars *were* bronze, the hooks of the pillars and their bands *were* silver, and the overlay of their capitals *was* silver; and all the pillars of the court had bands of silver. 18The screen for the gate of the court *was* woven of blue, purple, and scarlet *thread,* and of fine woven linen. The length *was* twenty cubits, and the height along its width *was* five cubits, corresponding to the hangings of the court. 19And *there were* four pillars *with* their four sockets of bronze; their hooks *were* silver, and the overlay of their capitals and their bands *was* silver. 20All the pegs of the tabernacle, and of the court all around, *were* bronze.

Materials of the Tabernacle

21This is the inventory of the tabernacle, the tabernacle of the Testimony, which was counted according to the commandment of Moses, for the service of the Levites, by the hand of Ithamar, son of Aaron the priest.

22Bezalel the son of Uri, the son of Hur, of the tribe of Judah, made all that the LORD had commanded Moses. 23And with him *was* Aholiab the son of Ahisamach, of the tribe of Dan, an engraver and designer, a weaver of blue, purple, and scarlet *thread,* and of fine linen.

24All the gold that was used in all the work of the holy *place,* that is, the gold of the offering, was twenty-nine talents and seven hundred and thirty shekels,

according to the shekel of the sanctu-
ary. 25And the silver from those who
were numbered of the congregation *was*
one hundred talents and one thousand
seven hundred and seventy-five shekels,
according to the shekel of the sanctu-
ary: 26a bekah for each man (*that is,* half
a shekel, according to the shekel of the
sanctuary), for everyone included in
the numbering from twenty years old
and above, for six hundred and three
thousand, five hundred and fifty *men.*
27And from the hundred talents of silver
were cast the sockets of the sanctuary
and the bases of the veil: one hundred
sockets from the hundred talents, one
talent for each socket. 28Then from
the one thousand seven hundred and
seventy-five *shekels* he made hooks for
the pillars, overlaid their capitals, and
made bands for them.
29The offering of bronze *was* seventy
talents and two thousand four hun-
dred shekels. 30And with it he made the
sockets for the door of the tabernacle
of meeting, the bronze altar, the bronze
grating for it, and all the utensils for
the altar, 31the sockets for the court all
around, the bases for the court gate, all
the pegs for the tabernacle, and all the
pegs for the court all around.

Making the Garments of the Priesthood

39 Of the blue, purple, and scarlet
thread they made garments of
ministry,[a] for ministering in the holy
place, and made the holy garments for
Aaron, as the LORD had commanded
Moses.

Making the Ephod

2He made the ephod of gold, blue,
purple, and scarlet *thread,* and of fine
woven linen. 3And they beat the gold
into thin sheets and cut *it into* threads,
to work *it* in *with* the blue, purple, and
scarlet *thread,* and the fine linen, *into*
artistic designs. 4They made shoulder
straps for it to couple *it* together; it was
coupled together at its two edges. 5And
the intricately woven band of his ephod
that *was* on it *was* of the same work-
manship, *woven of* gold, blue, purple,
and scarlet *thread,* and *of* fine woven
linen, as the LORD had commanded
Moses.
6And they set onyx stones, enclosed in
settings of gold; they were engraved, as
signets are engraved, with the names
of the sons of Israel. 7He put them on
the shoulders of the ephod *as* memorial
stones for the sons of Israel, as the LORD
had commanded Moses.

Making the Breastplate

8And he made the breastplate, artis-
tically woven like the workmanship of
the ephod, of gold, blue, purple, and
scarlet *thread,* and of fine woven lin-
en. 9They made the breastplate square
by doubling it; a span *was* its length
and a span its width when doubled.
10And they set in it four rows of stones:
a row with a sardius, a topaz, and an
emerald was the first row; 11the second
row, a turquoise, a sapphire, and a di-
amond; 12the third row, a jacinth, an
agate, and an amethyst; 13the fourth
row, a beryl, an onyx, and a jasper.
They were enclosed in settings of gold
in their mountings. 14*There were* twelve
stones according to the names of the
sons of Israel: according to their names,
engraved like a signet, each one with
its own name according to the twelve
tribes. 15And they made chains for the
breastplate at the ends, like braided
cords of pure gold. 16They also made
two settings of gold and two gold rings,
and put the two rings on the two ends
of the breastplate. 17And they put the
two braided *chains* of gold in the two
rings on the ends of the breastplate.
18The two ends of the two braided *chains*
they fastened in the two settings, and
put them on the shoulder straps of the
ephod in the front. 19And they made
two rings of gold and put *them* on the
two ends of the breastplate, on the edge
of it, which *was* on the inward side of
the ephod. 20They made two *other* gold
rings and put them on the two shoulder
straps, underneath the ephod toward
its front, right at the seam above the
intricately woven band of the ephod.
21And they bound the breastplate by

39:1 [a] Or *woven garments*

means of its rings to the rings of the
ephod with a blue cord, so that it would
be above the intricately woven band
of the ephod, and that the breastplate
would not come loose from the ephod,
as the LORD had commanded Moses.

Making the Other Priestly Garments

22He made the robe of the ephod of
woven work, all of blue. 23And *there was*
an opening in the middle of the robe,
like the opening in a coat of mail, *with* a
woven binding all around the opening,
so that it would not tear. 24They made
on the hem of the robe pomegranates
of blue, purple, and scarlet, and of fine
woven *linen.* 25And they made bells of
pure gold, and put the bells between the
pomegranates on the hem of the robe
all around between the pomegranates:
26a bell and a pomegranate, a bell and
a pomegranate, all around the hem of
the robe to minister in, as the LORD had
commanded Moses.

27They made tunics, artistically woven
of fine linen, for Aaron and his sons, 28a
turban of fine linen, exquisite hats of
fine linen, short trousers of fine woven
linen, 29and a sash of fine woven linen
with blue, purple, and scarlet *thread,*
made by a weaver, as the LORD had
commanded Moses.

30Then they made the plate of the
holy crown of pure gold, and wrote on
it an inscription *like* the engraving of
a signet:

HOLINESS TO THE LORD.

31And they tied to it a blue cord, to fas-
ten *it* above on the turban, as the LORD
had commanded Moses.

The Work Completed

32Thus all the work of the tabernacle
of the tent of meeting was finished. And
the children of Israel did according
to all that the LORD had commanded
Moses; so they did. 33And they brought
the tabernacle to Moses, the tent and all
its furnishings: its clasps, its boards, its
bars, its pillars, and its sockets; 34the
covering of ram skins dyed red, the
covering of badger skins, and the veil
of the covering; 35the ark of the Tes-
timony with its poles, and the mercy
seat; 36the table, all its utensils, and
the showbread; 37the pure *gold* lamp-
stand with its lamps (the lamps set in
order), all its utensils, and the oil for
light; 38the gold altar, the anointing oil,
and the sweet incense; the screen for
the tabernacle door; 39the bronze altar,
its grate of bronze, its poles, and all its
utensils; the laver with its base; 40the
hangings of the court, its pillars and its
sockets, the screen for the court gate,
its cords, and its pegs; all the utensils
for the service of the tabernacle, for the
tent of meeting; 41and the garments of
ministry,[a] to minister in the holy *place:*
the holy garments for Aaron the priest,
and his sons' garments, to minister as
priests.

42According to all that the LORD had
commanded Moses, so the children of
Israel did all the work. 43Then Moses
looked over all the work, and indeed
they had done it; as the LORD had com-
manded, just so they had done it. And
Moses blessed them.

The Tabernacle Erected and Arranged

40 Then the LORD spoke to Moses,
saying: 2"On the first day of the
first month you shall set up the taberna-
cle of the tent of meeting. 3You shall put
in it the ark of the Testimony, and parti-
tion off the ark with the veil. 4You shall
bring in the table and arrange the things
that are to be set in order on it; and
you shall bring in the lampstand and
light its lamps. 5You shall also set the
altar of gold for the incense before the
ark of the Testimony, and put up
the screen for the door of the taber-
nacle. 6Then you shall set the altar of
the burnt offering before the door of
the tabernacle of the tent of meeting.
7And you shall set the laver between
the tabernacle of meeting and the altar,
and put water in it. 8You shall set up
the court all around, and hang up the
screen at the court gate.

9"And you shall take the anointing oil,
and anoint the tabernacle and all that

39:41 [a] Or *woven garments*

is in it; and you shall hallow it and all
its utensils, and it shall be holy. 10You
shall anoint the altar of the burnt offer-
ing and all its utensils, and consecrate
the altar. The altar shall be most holy.
11And you shall anoint the laver and its
base, and consecrate it.

12"Then you shall bring Aaron and
his sons to the door of the tabernacle
of meeting and wash them with wa-
ter. 13You shall put the holy garments
on Aaron, and anoint him and con-
secrate him, that he may minister to
Me as priest. 14And you shall bring his
sons and clothe them with tunics. 15You
shall anoint them, as you anointed their
father, that they may minister to Me as
priests; for their anointing shall surely
be an everlasting priesthood through-
out their generations."

16Thus Moses did; according to all
that the LORD had commanded him,
so he did.

17And it came to pass in the first
month of the second year, on the first
day of the month, *that* the tabernacle
was raised up. 18So Moses raised up
the tabernacle, fastened its sockets,
set up its boards, put in its bars, and
raised up its pillars. 19And he spread
out the tent over the tabernacle and put
the covering of the tent on top of it, as
the LORD had commanded Moses. 20He
took the Testimony and put *it* into the
ark, inserted the poles through the rings
of the ark, and put the mercy seat on
top of the ark. 21And he brought the ark
into the tabernacle, hung up the veil of
the covering, and partitioned off the
ark of the Testimony, as the LORD had
commanded Moses.

22He put the table in the tabernacle of
meeting, on the north side of the taber-
nacle, outside the veil; 23and he set the
bread in order upon it before the LORD,
as the LORD had commanded Moses.
24He put the lampstand in the taberna-
cle of meeting, across from the table, on
the south side of the tabernacle; 25and
he lit the lamps before the LORD, as the
LORD had commanded Moses. 26He
put the gold altar in the tabernacle of
meeting in front of the veil; 27and he
burned sweet incense on it, as the LORD
had commanded Moses. 28He hung up
the screen *at* the door of the tabernacle.
29And he put the altar of burnt offering
before the door of the tabernacle of the
tent of meeting, and offered upon it
the burnt offering and the grain of-
fering, as the LORD had commanded
Moses. 30He set the laver between the
tabernacle of meeting and the altar,
and put water there for washing; 31and
Moses, Aaron, and his sons would wash
their hands and their feet *with water*
from it. 32Whenever they went into the
tabernacle of meeting, and when they
came near the altar, they washed, as the
LORD had commanded Moses. 33And
he raised up the court all around the
tabernacle and the altar, and hung up
the screen of the court gate. So Moses
finished the work.

The Cloud and the Glory

34Then the cloud covered the taber-
nacle of meeting, and the glory of the
LORD filled the tabernacle. 35And Moses
was not able to enter the tabernacle of
meeting, because the cloud rested above
it, and the glory of the LORD filled the
tabernacle. 36Whenever the cloud was
taken up from above the tabernacle, the
children of Israel would go onward in
all their journeys. 37But if the cloud was
not taken up, then they did not journey
till the day that it was taken up. 38For
the cloud of the LORD *was* above the
tabernacle by day, and fire was over it
by night, in the sight of all the house of
Israel, throughout all their journeys.

THE THIRD BOOK OF MOSES CALLED

LEVITICUS

The Book of Leviticus continues where Exodus leaves off. The Israelites have made the tabernacle, their place of worship, and now God gives them rules for how to use it properly. God selects some of the people, called the Levites, to be priests who would serve Him and the people in the tabernacle. He gives rules for how the Levites are to be holy, or different, and what their work would be. God also gives rules to all of His people, like what food they could not eat, what offerings to give, what feast days to celebrate, and how to be clean and pure. God promises that those who obey Him will be blessed, but those who disobey will be disciplined.

- **GENRE:** Law
- **AUTHOR:** Moses
- **TIME:** c. 1444 BC (written: c. 1444–1406 BC)
- **PURPOSE:** To teach the Israelites how to worship God the right way and how to live as a holy people.

The Burnt Offering

1 Now the LORD called to Moses, and
spoke to him from the tabernacle
of meeting, saying, 2“Speak to the chil-
dren of Israel, and say to them: ‘When
any one of you brings an offering to the
LORD, you shall bring your offering of the
livestock—of the herd and of the flock.
3‘If his offering *is* a burnt sacrifice
of the herd, let him offer a male with-
out blemish; he shall offer it of his own
free will at the door of the tabernacle
of meeting before the LORD. 4Then he
shall put his hand on the head of the
burnt offering, and it will be accepted
on his behalf to make atonement for
him. 5He shall kill the bull before the
LORD; and the priests, Aaron’s sons,
shall bring the blood and sprinkle the
blood all around on the altar that *is by*
the door of the tabernacle of meeting.
6And he shall skin the burnt offering
and cut it into its pieces. 7The sons of
Aaron the priest shall put fire on the
altar, and lay the wood in order on the
fire. 8Then the priests, Aaron’s sons,
shall lay the parts, the head, and the
fat in order on the wood that *is* on the
fire upon the altar; 9but he shall wash
its entrails and its legs with water. And
the priest shall burn all on the altar as
a burnt sacrifice, an offering made by
fire, a sweet aroma to the LORD.
10‘If his offering *is* of the flocks—of
the sheep or of the goats—as a burnt
sacrifice, he shall bring a male without
blemish. 11He shall kill it on the north
side of the altar before the LORD; and
the priests, Aaron’s sons, shall sprinkle
its blood all around on the altar. 12And
he shall cut it into its pieces, with its
head and its fat; and the priest shall lay
them in order on the wood that *is* on the
fire upon the altar; 13but he shall wash
the entrails and the legs with water. Then
the priest shall bring *it* all and burn *it* on the
altar; it *is* a burnt sacrifice, an offering
made by fire, a sweet aroma to the LORD.
14‘And if the burnt sacrifice of his of-
fering to the LORD *is* of birds, then he
shall bring his offering of turtledoves
or young pigeons. 15The priest shall
bring it to the altar, wring off its head,
and burn *it* on the altar; its blood shall
be drained out at the side of the altar.
16And he shall remove its crop with its
feathers and cast it beside the altar on
the east side, into the place for ashes.
17Then he shall split it at its wings, *but*
shall not divide *it* completely; and the
priest shall burn it on the altar, on the
wood that *is* on the fire. It *is* a burnt
sacrifice, an offering made by fire, a
sweet aroma to the LORD.

GOD SIN JESUS SALVATION LOVE

The Grain Offering

2 'When anyone offers a grain offer-
ing to the LORD, his offering shall
be *of* fine flour. And he shall pour oil on
it, and put frankincense on it. 2He shall
bring it to Aaron's sons, the priests, one
of whom shall take from it his handful
of fine flour and oil with all the frank-
incense. And the priest shall burn *it as*
a memorial on the altar, an offering
made by fire, a sweet aroma to the LORD.
3The rest of the grain offering *shall be*
Aaron's and his sons'. *It is* most holy of
the offerings to the LORD made by fire.
4'And if you bring as an offering a
grain offering baked in the oven, *it shall*
be unleavened cakes of fine flour mixed
with oil, or unleavened wafers anointed
with oil. 5But if your offering *is* a grain
offering *baked* in a pan, *it shall be of* fine
flour, unleavened, mixed with oil. 6You
shall break it in pieces and pour oil on
it; it *is* a grain offering.
7'If your offering *is* a grain offering
baked in a covered pan, it shall be made
of fine flour with oil. 8You shall bring
the grain offering that is made of these
things to the LORD. And when it is pre-
sented to the priest, he shall bring it
to the altar. 9Then the priest shall take
from the grain offering a memorial
portion, and burn *it* on the altar. *It is* an
offering made by fire, a sweet aroma to
the LORD. 10And what is left of the grain
offering *shall be* Aaron's and his sons'.
It is most holy of the offerings to the
LORD made by fire.
11'No grain offering which you bring
to the LORD shall be made with leaven,
for you shall burn no leaven nor any
honey in any offering to the LORD made
by fire. 12As for the offering of the first-
fruits, you shall offer them to the LORD,
but they shall not be burned on the altar
for a sweet aroma. 13And every offering
of your grain offering you shall season
with salt; you shall not allow the salt of
the covenant of your God to be lacking
from your grain offering. With all your
offerings you shall offer salt.
14'If you offer a grain offering of your
firstfruits to the LORD, you shall offer
for the grain offering of your firstfruits
green heads of grain roasted on the fire,
grain beaten from full heads. 15And you
shall put oil on it, and lay frankincense
on it. It *is* a grain offering. 16Then the
priest shall burn the memorial portion:
part of its beaten grain and *part* of its
oil, with all the frankincense, as an of-
fering made by fire to the LORD.

The Peace Offering

3 'When his offering *is* a sacrifice of
a peace offering, if he offers *it* of
the herd, whether male or female, he
shall offer it without blemish before
the LORD. 2And he shall lay his hand on
the head of his offering, and kill it *at* the
door of the tabernacle of meeting; and
Aaron's sons, the priests, shall sprinkle
the blood all around on the altar. 3Then
he shall offer from the sacrifice of the
peace offering an offering made by
fire to the LORD. The fat that covers the
entrails and all the fat that *is* on the
entrails, 4the two kidneys and the fat
that *is* on them by the flanks, and the
fatty lobe *attached* to the liver above the
kidneys, he shall remove; 5and Aaron's
sons shall burn it on the altar upon the
burnt sacrifice, which *is* on the wood
that *is* on the fire, *as* an offering made
by fire, a sweet aroma to the LORD.
6'If his offering as a sacrifice of a peace
offering to the LORD *is* of the flock,
whether male or female, he shall offer
it without blemish. 7If he offers a lamb
as his offering, then he shall offer it
before the LORD. 8And he shall lay his
hand on the head of his offering, and
kill it before the tabernacle of meeting;
and Aaron's sons shall sprinkle its blood
all around on the altar.
9'Then he shall offer from the sacri-
fice of the peace offering, as an offering
made by fire to the LORD, its fat *and* the
whole fat tail which he shall remove
close to the backbone. And the fat that
covers the entrails and all the fat that *is*
on the entrails, 10the two kidneys and
the fat that *is* on them by the flanks,
and the fatty lobe *attached* to the liver
above the kidneys, he shall remove; 11and
the priest shall burn *them* on the altar *as*
food, an offering made by fire to the LORD.
12'And if his offering *is* a goat, then he
shall offer it before the LORD. 13He shall
lay his hand on its head and kill it be-
fore the tabernacle of meeting; and the

sons of Aaron shall sprinkle its blood all
around on the altar. 14Then he shall offer
from it his offering, as an offering made
by fire to the LORD. The fat that covers
the entrails and all the fat that *is* on the
entrails, 15the two kidneys and the fat
that *is* on them by the flanks, and the
fatty lobe *attached* to the liver above
the kidneys, he shall remove; 16and
the priest shall burn them on the altar
as food, an offering made by fire for a
sweet aroma; all the fat *is* the LORD's.
17'*This shall be* a perpetual statute
throughout your generations in all
your dwellings: you shall eat neither
fat nor blood.' "

The Sin Offering

4 Now the LORD spoke to Moses, say-
ing, 2"Speak to the children of Israel,
saying: 'If a person sins unintentionally
against any of the commandments of
the LORD *in anything* which ought not to
be done, and does any of them, 3if the
anointed priest sins, bringing guilt on
the people, then let him offer to the LORD
for his sin which he has sinned a young
bull without blemish as a sin offering.
4He shall bring the bull to the door of
the tabernacle of meeting before the
LORD, lay his hand on the bull's head,
and kill the bull before the LORD. 5Then
the anointed priest shall take some of
the bull's blood and bring it to the tab-
ernacle of meeting. 6The priest shall
dip his finger in the blood and sprinkle
some of the blood seven times before the
LORD, in front of the veil of the sanctu-
ary. 7And the priest shall put some of the
blood on the horns of the altar of sweet
incense before the LORD, which is in the
tabernacle of meeting; and he shall pour
the remaining blood of the bull at the
base of the altar of the burnt offering,
which is at the door of the tabernacle
of meeting. 8He shall take from it all
the fat of the bull as the sin offering.
The fat that covers the entrails and all
the fat which *is* on the entrails, 9the two
kidneys and the fat that *is* on them by
the flanks, and the fatty lobe *attached*
to the liver above the kidneys, he shall
remove, 10as it was taken from the bull
of the sacrifice of the peace offering; and
the priest shall burn them on the altar
of the burnt offering. 11But the bull's
hide and all its flesh, with its head and
legs, its entrails and offal— 12the whole
bull he shall carry outside the camp
to a clean place, where the ashes are
poured out, and burn it on wood with
fire; where the ashes are poured out it
shall be burned.
13'Now if the whole congregation of Is-
rael sins unintentionally, and the thing
is hidden from the eyes of the assembly,
and they have done *something against*
any of the commandments of the LORD
in anything which should not be done,
and are guilty; 14when the sin which
they have committed becomes known,
then the assembly shall offer a young
bull for the sin, and bring it before the
tabernacle of meeting. 15And the elders
of the congregation shall lay their hands
on the head of the bull before the LORD.
Then the bull shall be killed before the
LORD. 16The anointed priest shall bring
some of the bull's blood to the taberna-
cle of meeting. 17Then the priest shall
dip his finger in the blood and sprinkle
it seven times before the LORD, in front
of the veil. 18And he shall put *some* of the
blood on the horns of the altar which
is before the LORD, which *is* in the tab-
ernacle of meeting; and he shall pour
the remaining blood at the base of the
altar of burnt offering, which is at the
door of the tabernacle of meeting. 19He
shall take all the fat from it and burn
it on the altar. 20And he shall do with
the bull as he did with the bull as a sin
offering; thus he shall do with it. So the
priest shall make atonement for them,
and it shall be forgiven them. 21Then he
shall carry the bull outside the camp,
and burn it as he burned the first bull. It
is a sin offering for the assembly.
22'When a ruler has sinned, and done
something unintentionally *against* any
of the commandments of the LORD his
God *in anything* which should not be
done, and is guilty, 23or if his sin which
he has committed comes to his knowl-
edge, he shall bring as his offering a kid
of the goats, a male without blemish.
24And he shall lay his hand on the head
of the goat, and kill it at the place where
they kill the burnt offering before the
LORD. It *is* a sin offering. 25The priest

shall take some of the blood of the sin of-
fering with his finger, put *it* on the horns
of the altar of burnt offering, and pour
its blood at the base of the altar of burnt
offering. 26And he shall burn all its fat
on the altar, like the fat of the sacrifice
of the peace offering. So the priest shall
make atonement for him concerning his
sin, and it shall be forgiven him.
27'If anyone of the common people
sins unintentionally by doing *something*
against any of the commandments of
the LORD *in anything* which ought not
to be done, and is guilty, 28or if his sin
which he has committed comes to his
knowledge, then he shall bring as his
offering a kid of the goats, a female
without blemish, for his sin which he
has committed. 29And he shall lay his
hand on the head of the sin offering,
and kill the sin offering at the place of
the burnt offering. 30Then the priest
shall take *some* of its blood with his
finger, put *it* on the horns of the altar of
burnt offering, and pour all *the remain-*
ing blood at the base of the altar. 31He
shall remove all its fat, as fat is removed
from the sacrifice of the peace offering;
and the priest shall burn it on the altar
for a sweet aroma to the LORD. So the
priest shall make atonement for him,
and it shall be forgiven him.
32'If he brings a lamb as his sin of-
fering, he shall bring a female without
blemish. 33Then he shall lay his hand on
the head of the sin offering, and kill it
as a sin offering at the place where they
kill the burnt offering. 34The priest shall
take *some* of the blood of the sin offering
with his finger, put *it* on the horns of the
altar of burnt offering, and pour all *the*
remaining blood at the base of the altar.
35He shall remove all its fat, as the fat of
the lamb is removed from the sacrifice
of the peace offering. Then the priest
shall burn it on the altar, according to
the offerings made by fire to the LORD.
So the priest shall make atonement for
his sin that he has committed, and it
shall be forgiven him.

The Trespass Offering

5 'If a person sins in hearing the ut-
terance of an oath, and *is* a witness,
whether he has seen or known *of the*
matter—if he does not tell *it*, he bears
guilt.
2'Or if a person touches any unclean
thing, whether *it is* the carcass of an
unclean beast, or the carcass of unclean
livestock, or the carcass of unclean
creeping things, and he is unaware of
it, he also shall be unclean and guilty.
3Or if he touches human uncleanness—
whatever uncleanness with which a
man may be defiled, and he is unaware
of it—when he realizes *it*, then he shall
be guilty.
4'Or if a person swears, speaking
thoughtlessly with *his* lips to do evil or
to do good, whatever *it is* that a man
may pronounce by an oath, and he is
unaware of it—when he realizes *it*, then
he shall be guilty in any of these *matters*.
5'And it shall be, when he is guilty in
any of these *matters*, that he shall con-
fess that he has sinned in that *thing;*
6and he shall bring his trespass offering
to the LORD for his sin which he has
committed, a female from the flock, a
lamb or a kid of the goats as a sin offer-
ing. So the priest shall make atonement
for him concerning his sin.
7'If he is not able to bring a lamb,
then he shall bring to the LORD, for his
trespass which he has committed, two
turtledoves or two young pigeons: one
as a sin offering and the other as a burnt
offering. 8And he shall bring them to the
priest, who shall offer *that* which *is* for
the sin offering first, and wring off its
head from its neck, but shall not divide
it completely. 9Then he shall sprinkle
some of the blood of the sin offering on
the side of the altar, and the rest of the
blood shall be drained out at the base
of the altar. It *is* a sin offering. 10And he
shall offer the second *as* a burnt offering
according to the prescribed manner.
So the priest shall make atonement
on his behalf for his sin which he has
committed, and it shall be forgiven him.
11'But if he is not able to bring two
turtledoves or two young pigeons, then
he who sinned shall bring for his offer-
ing one-tenth of an ephah of fine flour
as a sin offering. He shall put no oil on it,
nor shall he put frankincense on it, for
it *is* a sin offering. 12Then he shall bring
it to the priest, and the priest shall take

his handful of it as a memorial portion,
and burn *it* on the altar according to the
offerings made by fire to the LORD. It *is*
a sin offering. 13The priest shall make
atonement for him, for his sin that he
has committed in any of these matters;
and it shall be forgiven him. *The rest*
shall be the priest's as a grain offering.' "

Offerings with Restitution

14Then the LORD spoke to Moses, saying:
15"If a person commits a trespass, and
sins unintentionally in regard to the holy
things of the LORD, then he shall bring to
the LORD as his trespass offering a ram
without blemish from the flocks, with
your valuation in shekels of silver ac-
cording to the shekel of the sanctuary, as
a trespass offering. 16And he shall make
restitution for the harm that he has done
in regard to the holy thing, and shall add
one-fifth to it and give it to the priest. So
the priest shall make atonement for him
with the ram of the trespass offering, and
it shall be forgiven him.

17"If a person sins, and commits any
of these things which are forbidden to
be done by the commandments of the
LORD, though he does not know *it*, yet
he is guilty and shall bear his iniquity.
18And he shall bring to the priest a ram
without blemish from the flock, with
your valuation, as a trespass offering.
So the priest shall make atonement for
him regarding his ignorance in which
he erred and did not know *it*, and it
shall be forgiven him. 19It is a trespass
offering; he has certainly trespassed
against the LORD."

6 And the LORD spoke to Moses, say-
ing: 2"If a person sins and commits
a trespass against the LORD by lying
to his neighbor about what was deliv-
ered to him for safekeeping, or about
a pledge, or about a robbery, or if he
has extorted from his neighbor, 3or if
he has found what was lost and lies
concerning it, and swears falsely—in
any one of these things that a man may
do in which he sins: 4then it shall be,
because he has sinned and is guilty,
that he shall restore what he has sto-
len, or the thing which he has extort-
ed, or what was delivered to him for
safekeeping, or the lost thing which
he found, 5or all that about which he
has sworn falsely. He shall restore its
full value, add one-fifth more to it, *and*
give it to whomever it belongs, on the
day of his trespass offering. 6And he
shall bring his trespass offering to the
LORD, a ram without blemish from the
flock, with your valuation, as a trespass
offering, to the priest. 7So the priest
shall make atonement for him before
the LORD, and he shall be forgiven for
any one of these things that he may
have done in which he trespasses."

The Law of the Burnt Offering

8Then the LORD spoke to Moses, say-
ing, 9"Command Aaron and his sons,
saying, 'This *is* the law of the burnt of-
fering: The burnt offering *shall be* on
the hearth upon the altar all night until
morning, and the fire of the altar shall
be kept burning on it. 10And the priest
shall put on his linen garment, and his
linen trousers he shall put on his body,
and take up the ashes of the burnt of-
fering which the fire has consumed on
the altar, and he shall put them beside
the altar. 11Then he shall take off his
garments, put on other garments, and
carry the ashes outside the camp to a
clean place. 12And the fire on the altar
shall be kept burning on it; it shall not
be put out. And the priest shall burn
wood on it every morning, and lay the
burnt offering in order on it; and he
shall burn on it the fat of the peace of-
ferings. 13A fire shall always be burning
on the altar; it shall never go out.

The Law of the Grain Offering

14'This *is* the law of the grain offering:
The sons of Aaron shall offer it on the altar
before the LORD. 15He shall take from it
his handful of the fine flour of the grain
offering, with its oil, and all the frank-
incense which *is* on the grain offering,
and shall burn *it* on the altar *for* a sweet
aroma, as a memorial to the LORD. 16And
the remainder of it Aaron and his sons
shall eat; with unleavened bread it shall
be eaten in a holy place; in the court of
the tabernacle of meeting they shall eat it.
17It shall not be baked with leaven. I have
given it *as* their portion of My offerings
made by fire; it *is* most holy, like the sin

offering and the trespass offering. 18All
the males among the children of Aaron
may eat it. *It shall be* a statute forever in
your generations concerning the offer-
ings made by fire to the LORD. Everyone
who touches them must be holy.' "[a]
19And the LORD spoke to Moses, say-
ing, 20"This *is* the offering of Aaron and
his sons, which they shall offer to the
LORD, *beginning* on the day when he
is anointed: one-tenth of an ephah of
fine flour as a daily grain offering, half
of it in the morning and half of it at
night. 21It shall be made in a pan with
oil. *When it is* mixed, you shall bring it
in. The baked pieces of the grain offer-
ing you shall offer *for* a sweet aroma
to the LORD. 22The priest from among
his sons, who is anointed in his place,
shall offer it. *It is* a statute forever to the
LORD. It shall be wholly burned. 23For
every grain offering for the priest shall
be wholly burned. It shall not be eaten."

The Law of the Sin Offering

24Also the LORD spoke to Moses, say-
ing, 25"Speak to Aaron and to his sons,
saying, 'This *is* the law of the sin of-
fering: In the place where the burnt
offering is killed, the sin offering shall
be killed before the LORD. It *is* most
holy. 26The priest who offers it for sin
shall eat it. In a holy place it shall be
eaten, in the court of the tabernacle of
meeting. 27Everyone who touches its
flesh must be holy.[a] And when its blood
is sprinkled on any garment, you shall
wash that on which it was sprinkled, in
a holy place. 28But the earthen vessel in
which it is boiled shall be broken. And
if it is boiled in a bronze pot, it shall be
both scoured and rinsed in water. 29All
the males among the priests may eat
it. It *is* most holy. 30But no sin offering
from which *any* of the blood is brought
into the tabernacle of meeting, to make
atonement in the holy *place*,[a] shall be
eaten. It shall be burned in the fire.

The Law of the Trespass Offering

7 'Likewise this *is* the law of the tres-
pass offering (it *is* most holy): 2In
the place where they kill the burnt
offering they shall kill the trespass of-
fering. And its blood he shall sprinkle
all around on the altar. 3And he shall
offer from it all its fat. The fat tail and
the fat that covers the entrails, 4the two
kidneys and the fat that *is* on them by
the flanks, and the fatty lobe *attached*
to the liver above the kidneys, he shall
remove; 5and the priest shall burn them
on the altar *as* an offering made by fire
to the LORD. It *is* a trespass offering.
6Every male among the priests may
eat it. It shall be eaten in a holy place.
It *is* most holy. 7The trespass offering
is like the sin offering; *there is* one law
for them both: the priest who makes
atonement with it shall have *it*. 8And
the priest who offers anyone's burnt of-
fering, that priest shall have for himself
the skin of the burnt offering which he
has offered. 9Also every grain offering
that is baked in the oven and all that is
prepared in the covered pan, or in a pan,
shall be the priest's who offers it. 10Ev-
ery grain offering, *whether* mixed with
oil or dry, shall belong to all the sons
of Aaron, to one *as much* as the other.

The Law of Peace Offerings

11'This *is* the law of the sacrifice of
peace offerings which he shall offer to
the LORD: 12If he offers it for a thanks-
giving, then he shall offer, with the
sacrifice of thanksgiving, unleavened
cakes mixed with oil, unleavened wafers
anointed with oil, or cakes of blended
flour mixed with oil. 13Besides the cakes,
as his offering he shall offer leavened
bread with the sacrifice of thanksgiving
of his peace offering. 14And from it he
shall offer one cake from each offering
as a heave offering to the LORD. It shall
belong to the priest who sprinkles the
blood of the peace offering.
15'The flesh of the sacrifice of his peace
offering for thanksgiving shall be eaten
the same day it is offered. He shall not
leave any of it until morning. 16But if
the sacrifice of his offering *is* a vow or
a voluntary offering, it shall be eaten
the same day that he offers his sacrifice;
but on the next day the remainder of
it also may be eaten; 17the remainder

6:18 [a] Compare Numbers 4:15 and Haggai 2:11–13
6:30 [a] The Most Holy Place when capitalized
6:27 [a] Compare Numbers 4:15 and Haggai 2:11–13

of the flesh of the sacrifice on the third
day must be burned with fire. 18And if
any of the flesh of the sacrifice of his
peace offering is eaten at all on the
third day, it shall not be accepted, nor
shall it be imputed to him; it shall be an
abomination *to* him who offers it, and
the person who eats of it shall bear guilt.
19"The flesh that touches any unclean
thing shall not be eaten. It shall be
burned with fire. And as for the *clean*
flesh, all who are clean may eat of it.
20But the person who eats the flesh of
the sacrifice of the peace offering that
belongs to the LORD, while he is unclean,
that person shall be cut off from his peo-
ple. 21Moreover the person who touches
any unclean thing, *such as* human un-
cleanness, *an* unclean animal, or any
abominable unclean thing,[a] and who
eats the flesh of the sacrifice of the peace
offering that *belongs* to the LORD, that
person shall be cut off from his people.' "

Fat and Blood May Not Be Eaten

22And the LORD spoke to Moses, saying,
23"Speak to the children of Israel, saying:
'You shall not eat any fat, of ox or sheep
or goat. 24And the fat of an animal that
dies *naturally*, and the fat of what is torn
by wild beasts, may be used in any other
way; but you shall by no means eat it.
25For whoever eats the fat of the animal
of which men offer an offering made by
fire to the LORD, the person who eats *it*
shall be cut off from his people. 26More-
over you shall not eat any blood in any of
your dwellings, *whether* of bird or beast.
27Whoever eats any blood, that person
shall be cut off from his people.' "

The Portion of Aaron and His Sons

28Then the LORD spoke to Moses, say-
ing, 29"Speak to the children of Israel,
saying: 'He who offers the sacrifice of his
peace offering to the LORD shall bring his
offering to the LORD from the sacrifice
of his peace offering. 30His own hands
shall bring the offerings made by fire to
the LORD. The fat with the breast he shall
bring, that the breast may be waved *as* a
wave offering before the LORD. 31And the
priest shall burn the fat on the altar, but
the breast shall be Aaron's and his sons'.
32Also the right thigh you shall give to
the priest *as* a heave offering from the
sacrifices of your peace offerings. 33He
among the sons of Aaron, who offers the
blood of the peace offering and the fat,
shall have the right thigh for *his* part.
34For the breast of the wave offering
and the thigh of the heave offering I
have taken from the children of Israel,
from the sacrifices of their peace offer-
ings, and I have given them to Aaron the
priest and to his sons from the children
of Israel by a statute forever.' "
35This *is* the consecrated portion for
Aaron and his sons, from the offerings
made by fire to the LORD, on the day
when *Moses* presented them to minis-
ter to the LORD as priests. 36The LORD
commanded this to be given to them by
the children of Israel, on the day that
He anointed them, *by* a statute forever
throughout their generations.
37This *is* the law of the burnt offering,
the grain offering, the sin offering, the
trespass offering, the consecrations,
and the sacrifice of the peace offering,
38which the LORD commanded Moses
on Mount Sinai, on the day when He
commanded the children of Israel to
offer their offerings to the LORD in the
Wilderness of Sinai.

Aaron and His Sons Consecrated

8 And the LORD spoke to Moses, say-
ing: 2"Take Aaron and his sons with
him, and the garments, the anointing
oil, a bull as the sin offering, two rams,
and a basket of unleavened bread; 3and
gather all the congregation together at
the door of the tabernacle of meeting."
4So Moses did as the LORD commanded
him. And the congregation was gath-
ered together at the door of the taberna-
cle of meeting. 5And Moses said to the
congregation, "This *is* what the LORD
commanded to be done."
6Then Moses brought Aaron and his
sons and washed them with water. 7And
he put the tunic on him, girded him with
the sash, clothed him with the robe, and
put the ephod on him; and he girded
him with the intricately woven band

7:21 [a] Following Masoretic Text, Septuagint, and Vulgate; Samaritan Pentateuch, Syriac, and Targum read *swarming thing* (compare 5:2).

of the ephod, and with it tied *the ephod* on him. 8Then he put the breastplate on him, and he put the Urim and the Thummim[a] in the breastplate. 9And he put the turban on his head. Also on the turban, on its front, he put the golden plate, the holy crown, as the LORD had commanded Moses.

10Also Moses took the anointing oil, and anointed the tabernacle and all that *was* in it, and consecrated them. 11He sprinkled some of it on the altar seven times, anointed the altar and all its utensils, and the laver and its base, to consecrate them. 12And he poured some of the anointing oil on Aaron's head and anointed him, to consecrate him.

13Then Moses brought Aaron's sons and put tunics on them, girded them with sashes, and put hats on them, as the LORD had commanded Moses.

14And he brought the bull for the sin offering. Then Aaron and his sons laid their hands on the head of the bull for the sin offering, 15and Moses killed *it*. Then he took the blood, and put *some* on the horns of the altar all around with his finger, and purified the altar. And he poured the blood at the base of the altar, and consecrated it, to make atonement for it. 16Then he took all the fat that *was* on the entrails, the fatty lobe *attached to* the liver, and the two kidneys with their fat, and Moses burned *them* on the altar. 17But the bull, its hide, its flesh, and its offal, he burned with fire outside the camp, as the LORD had commanded Moses.

18Then he brought the ram as the burnt offering. And Aaron and his sons laid their hands on the head of the ram, 19and Moses killed *it*. Then he sprinkled the blood all around on the altar. 20And he cut the ram into pieces; and Moses burned the head, the pieces, and the fat. 21Then he washed the entrails and the legs in water. And Moses burned the whole ram on the altar. It *was* a burnt sacrifice for a sweet aroma, an offering made by fire to the LORD, as the LORD had commanded Moses.

22And he brought the second ram, the ram of consecration. Then Aaron and his sons laid their hands on the head of the ram, 23and Moses killed *it*. Also he took *some* of its blood and put it on the tip of Aaron's right ear, on the thumb of his right hand, and on the big toe of his right foot. 24Then he brought Aaron's sons. And Moses put *some* of the blood on the tips of their right ears, on the thumbs of their right hands, and on the big toes of their right feet. And Moses sprinkled the blood all around on the altar. 25Then he took the fat and the fat tail, all the fat that *was* on the entrails, the fatty lobe *attached to* the liver, the two kidneys and their fat, and the right thigh; 26and from the basket of unleavened bread that was before the LORD he took one unleavened cake, a cake of bread *anointed with* oil, and one wafer, and put *them* on the fat and on the right thigh; 27and he put all *these* in Aaron's hands and in his sons' hands, and waved them *as* a wave offering before the LORD. 28Then Moses took them from their hands and burned *them* on the altar, on the burnt offering. They *were* consecration offerings for a sweet aroma. That *was* an offering made by fire to the LORD. 29And Moses took the breast and waved it *as* a wave offering before the LORD. It was Moses' part of the ram of consecration, as the LORD had commanded Moses.

30Then Moses took some of the anointing oil and some of the blood which *was* on the altar, and sprinkled *it* on Aaron, on his garments, on his sons, and on the garments of his sons with him; and he consecrated Aaron, his garments, his sons, and the garments of his sons with him.

31And Moses said to Aaron and his sons, "Boil the flesh *at* the door of the tabernacle of meeting, and eat it there with the bread that *is* in the basket of consecration offerings, as I commanded, saying, 'Aaron and his sons shall eat it.' 32What remains of the flesh and of the bread you shall burn with fire. 33And you shall not go outside the door of the tabernacle of meeting *for* seven days, until the days of your consecration are ended. For seven days he shall consecrate you. 34As he has done this day, *so* the LORD has commanded to do, to make atonement for you. 35Therefore

8:8 [a] Literally *the Lights and the Perfections* (compare Exodus 28:30)

you shall stay *at* the door of the tab-
ernacle of meeting day and night for
seven days, and keep the charge of the
LORD, so that you may not die; for so
I have been commanded." 36So Aaron
and his sons did all the things that the
LORD had commanded by the hand
of Moses.

The Priestly Ministry Begins

9 It came to pass on the eighth day
that Moses called Aaron and his sons
and the elders of Israel. 2And he said to
Aaron, "Take for yourself a young bull
as a sin offering and a ram as a burnt
offering, without blemish, and offer *them*
before the LORD. 3And to the children
of Israel you shall speak, saying, 'Take
a kid of the goats as a sin offering, and
a calf and a lamb, *both* of the first year,
without blemish, as a burnt offering,
4also a bull and a ram as peace offerings,
to sacrifice before the LORD, and a grain
offering mixed with oil; for today the
LORD will appear to you.' "
5So they brought what Moses com-
manded before the tabernacle of meet-
ing. And all the congregation drew near
and stood before the LORD. 6Then Moses
said, "This *is* the thing which the LORD
commanded you to do, and the glory
of the LORD will appear to you." 7And
Moses said to Aaron, "Go to the altar,
offer your sin offering and your burnt
offering, and make atonement for your-
self and for the people. Offer the offer-
ing of the people, and make atonement
for them, as the LORD commanded."
8Aaron therefore went to the altar
and killed the calf of the sin offering,
which *was* for himself. 9Then the sons
of Aaron brought the blood to him. And
he dipped his finger in the blood, put *it*
on the horns of the altar, and poured the
blood at the base of the altar. 10But the
fat, the kidneys, and the fatty lobe from
the liver of the sin offering he burned on
the altar, as the LORD had command-
ed Moses. 11The flesh and the hide he
burned with fire outside the camp.
12And he killed the burnt offering;
and Aaron's sons presented to him the
blood, which he sprinkled all around
on the altar. 13Then they presented the
burnt offering to him, with its pieces
and head, and he burned *them* on the
altar. 14And he washed the entrails and
the legs, and burned *them* with the burnt
offering on the altar.
15Then he brought the people's offer-
ing, and took the goat, which *was* the
sin offering for the people, and killed
it and offered it for sin, like the first
one. 16And he brought the burnt of-
fering and offered it according to the
prescribed manner. 17Then he brought
the grain offering, took a handful of it,
and burned *it* on the altar, besides the
burnt sacrifice of the morning.
18He also killed the bull and the ram
as sacrifices of peace offerings, which
were for the people. And Aaron's sons
presented to him the blood, which he
sprinkled all around on the altar, 19and
the fat from the bull and the ram—the
fatty tail, what covers *the entrails* and
the kidneys, and the fatty lobe *attached*
to the liver; 20and they put the fat on
the breasts. Then he burned the fat on
the altar; 21but the breasts and the right
thigh Aaron waved *as* a wave offering
before the LORD, as Moses had com-
manded.
22Then Aaron lifted his hand toward
the people, blessed them, and came
down from offering the sin offering,
the burnt offering, and peace offerings.
23And Moses and Aaron went into the
tabernacle of meeting, and came out
and blessed the people. Then the glory
of the LORD appeared to all the people,
24and fire came out from before the
LORD and consumed the burnt offering
and the fat on the altar. When all the
people saw *it*, they shouted and fell on
their faces.

The Profane Fire of Nadab and Abihu

10 Then Nadab and Abihu, the sons
of Aaron, each took his censer
and put fire in it, put incense on it, and
offered profane fire before the LORD,
which He had not commanded them.
2So fire went out from the LORD and
devoured them, and they died before
the LORD. 3And Moses said to Aaron,
"This is what the LORD spoke, saying:

'By those who come near Me
I must be regarded as holy;

And before all the people
I must be glorified.' "

So Aaron held his peace.
4Then Moses called Mishael and El-
zaphan, the sons of Uzziel the uncle of
Aaron, and said to them, "Come near,
carry your brethren from before the
sanctuary out of the camp." 5So they
went near and carried them by their tu-
nics out of the camp, as Moses had said.
6And Moses said to Aaron, and to Ele-
azar and Ithamar, his sons, "Do not un-
cover your heads nor tear your clothes,
lest you die, and wrath come upon all
the people. But let your brethren, the
whole house of Israel, bewail the burn-
ing which the LORD has kindled. 7You
shall not go out from the door of the
tabernacle of meeting, lest you die, for
the anointing oil of the LORD *is* upon
you." And they did according to the
word of Moses.

Conduct Prescribed for Priests

8Then the LORD spoke to Aaron, say-
ing: 9"Do not drink wine or intoxicat-
ing drink, you, nor your sons with you,
when you go into the tabernacle of
meeting, lest you die. *It shall be* a statute
forever throughout your generations,
10that you may distinguish between
holy and unholy, and between unclean
and clean, 11and that you may teach
the children of Israel all the statutes
which the LORD has spoken to them by
the hand of Moses."
12And Moses spoke to Aaron, and to
Eleazar and Ithamar, his sons who
were left: "Take the grain offering that
remains of the offerings made by fire
to the LORD, and eat it without leaven
beside the altar; for it *is* most holy. 13You
shall eat it in a holy place, because it *is*
your due and your sons' due, of the sac-
rifices made by fire to the LORD; for so
I have been commanded. 14The breast
of the wave offering and the thigh of
the heave offering you shall eat in a
clean place, you, your sons, and your
daughters with you; for *they are* your
due and your sons' due, *which* are given
from the sacrifices of peace offerings
of the children of Israel. 15The thigh of
the heave offering and the breast of the
wave offering they shall bring with the
offerings of fat made by fire, to offer *as*
a wave offering before the LORD. And it
shall be yours and your sons' with you,
by a statute forever, as the LORD has
commanded."
16Then Moses made careful inquiry
about the goat of the sin offering, and
there it was—burned up. And he was an-
gry with Eleazar and Ithamar, the sons
of Aaron *who were* left, saying, 17"Why
have you not eaten the sin offering in a
holy place, since it *is* most holy, and *God*
has given it to you to bear the guilt of
the congregation, to make atonement
for them before the LORD? 18See! Its
blood was not brought inside the holy
place;[a] indeed you should have eaten
it in a holy *place*, as I commanded."
19And Aaron said to Moses, "Look, this
day they have offered their sin offer-
ing and their burnt offering before the
LORD, and such things have befallen
me! *If* I had eaten the sin offering today,
would it have been accepted in the sight
of the LORD?" 20So when Moses heard
that, he was content.

Foods Permitted and Forbidden

11 Now the LORD spoke to Moses
and Aaron, saying to them,
2"Speak to the children of Israel, say-
ing, 'These *are* the animals which you
may eat among all the animals that
are on the earth: 3Among the animals,
whatever divides the hoof, having clo-
ven hooves *and* chewing the cud—that
you may eat. 4Nevertheless these you
shall not eat among those that chew the
cud or those that have cloven hooves:
the camel, because it chews the cud
but does not have cloven hooves, is un-
clean to you; 5the rock hyrax, because it
chews the cud but does not have cloven
hooves, *is* unclean to you; 6the hare,
because it chews the cud but does not
have cloven hooves, *is* unclean to you;
7and the swine, though it divides the
hoof, having cloven hooves, yet does
not chew the cud, *is* unclean to you.
8Their flesh you shall not eat, and their

10:18 [a] The Most Holy Place when capitalized

carcasses you shall not touch. They *are*
unclean to you.
9'These you may eat of all that *are* in
the water: whatever in the water has
fins and scales, whether in the seas or
in the rivers—that you may eat. 10But
all in the seas or in the rivers that do
not have fins and scales, all that move
in the water or any living thing which *is*
in the water, they *are* an abomination
to you. 11They shall be an abomination
to you; you shall not eat their flesh, but
you shall regard their carcasses as an
abomination. 12Whatever in the water
does not have fins or scales—that *shall*
be an abomination to you.
13'And these you shall regard as an
abomination among the birds; they
shall not be eaten, they *are* an abomi-
nation: the eagle, the vulture, the buz-
zard, 14the kite, and the falcon after its
kind; 15every raven after its kind, 16the
ostrich, the short-eared owl, the sea gull,
and the hawk after its kind; 17the little
owl, the fisher owl, and the screech owl;
18the white owl, the jackdaw, and the
carrion vulture; 19the stork, the heron
after its kind, the hoopoe, and the bat.
20'All flying insects that creep on *all*
fours *shall be* an abomination to you.
21Yet these you may eat of every flying
insect that creeps on *all* fours: those
which have jointed legs above their
feet with which to leap on the earth.
22These you may eat: the locust after
its kind, the destroying locust after its
kind, the cricket after its kind, and the
grasshopper after its kind. 23But all
other flying insects which have four feet
shall be an abomination to you.

Unclean Animals

24'By these you shall become unclean;
whoever touches the carcass of any of
them shall be unclean until evening;
25whoever carries part of the carcass
of any of them shall wash his clothes
and be unclean until evening: 26*The*
carcass of any animal which divides
the foot, but is not cloven-hoofed or
does not chew the cud, *is* unclean to
you. Everyone who touches it shall be
unclean. 27And whatever goes on its
paws, among all kinds of animals that
go on *all* fours, those *are* unclean to you.
Whoever touches any such carcass shall
be unclean until evening. 28Whoever
carries *any such* carcass shall wash his
clothes and be unclean until evening.
It *is* unclean to you.
29'These also *shall be* unclean to you
among the creeping things that creep
on the earth: the mole, the mouse, and
the large lizard after its kind; 30the
gecko, the monitor lizard, the sand
reptile, the sand lizard, and the cha-
meleon. 31These *are* unclean to you
among all that creep. Whoever touch-
es them when they are dead shall be
unclean until evening. 32Anything on
which *any* of them falls, when they are
dead shall be unclean, whether *it is* any
item of wood or clothing or skin or sack,
whatever item *it is*, in which *any* work
is done, it must be put in water. And it
shall be unclean until evening; then it
shall be clean. 33Any earthen vessel
into which *any* of them falls you shall
break; and whatever *is* in it shall be
unclean: 34in such a vessel, any edible
food upon which water falls becomes
unclean, and any drink that may be
drunk from it becomes unclean. 35And
everything on which *a part* of *any such*
carcass falls shall be unclean; *whether*
it is an oven or cooking stove, it shall
be broken down; *for* they *are* unclean,
and shall be unclean to you. 36Never-
theless a spring or a cistern, *in which*
there is plenty of water, shall be clean,
but whatever touches any such carcass
becomes unclean. 37And if a part of *any*
such carcass falls on any planting seed
which is to be sown, it *remains* clean.
38But if water is put on the seed, and if
a part of *any such* carcass falls on it, it
becomes unclean to you.
39'And if any animal which you may
eat dies, he who touches its carcass shall
be unclean until evening. 40He who eats
of its carcass shall wash his clothes and
be unclean until evening. He also who
carries its carcass shall wash his clothes
and be unclean until evening.
41'And every creeping thing that
creeps on the earth *shall be* an abomi-
nation. It shall not be eaten. 42Whatever
crawls on its belly, whatever goes on
all fours, or whatever has many feet
among all creeping things that creep

on the earth—these you shall not eat,
for they *are* an abomination. 43You
shall not make yourselves abominable
with any creeping thing that creeps;
nor shall you make yourselves unclean
with them, lest you be defiled by them.
44For I *am* the LORD your God. You shall
therefore consecrate yourselves, and
you shall be holy; for I *am* holy. Nei-
ther shall you defile yourselves with
any creeping thing that creeps on the
earth. 45For I *am* the LORD who brings
you up out of the land of Egypt, to be
your God. You shall therefore be holy,
for I *am* holy.

46'This *is* the law of the animals and
the birds and every living creature that
moves in the waters, and of every crea-
ture that creeps on the earth, 47to dis-
tinguish between the unclean and the
clean, and between the animal that may
be eaten and the animal that may not
be eaten.' "

The Ritual After Childbirth

12 Then the LORD spoke to Moses,
saying, 2"Speak to the children
of Israel, saying: 'If a woman has con-
ceived, and borne a male child, then
she shall be unclean seven days; as in
the days of her customary impurity she
shall be unclean. 3And on the eighth
day the flesh of his foreskin shall be
circumcised. 4She shall then continue in
the blood of *her* purification thirty-three
days. She shall not touch any hallowed
thing, nor come into the sanctuary until
the days of her purification are fulfilled.

5'But if she bears a female child, then
she shall be unclean two weeks, as in
her customary impurity, and she shall
continue in the blood of *her* purification
sixty-six days.

6'When the days of her purification are
fulfilled, whether for a son or a daugh-
ter, she shall bring to the priest a lamb
of the first year as a burnt offering, and
a young pigeon or a turtledove as a sin
offering, to the door of the tabernacle of
meeting. 7Then he shall offer it before
the LORD, and make atonement for her.
And she shall be clean from the flow of
her blood. This *is* the law for her who has
borne a male or a female.

8'And if she is not able to bring a lamb,
then she may bring two turtledoves or
two young pigeons—one as a burnt
offering and the other as a sin offering.
So the priest shall make atonement for
her, and she will be clean.' "

The Law Concerning Leprosy

13 And the LORD spoke to Moses
and Aaron, saying: 2"When
a man has on the skin of his body a
swelling, a scab, or a bright spot, and it
becomes on the skin of his body *like* a
leprous[a] sore, then he shall be brought
to Aaron the priest or to one of his sons
the priests. 3The priest shall examine the
sore on the skin of the body; and if
the hair on the sore has turned white,
and the sore appears *to be* deeper than
the skin of his body, it *is* a leprous sore.
Then the priest shall examine him, and
pronounce him unclean. 4But if the
bright spot *is* white on the skin of his
body, and does not appear *to be* deep-
er than the skin, and its hair has not
turned white, then the priest shall iso-
late *the one who has* the sore seven days.
5And the priest shall examine him on
the seventh day; and indeed *if* the sore
appears to be as it was, *and* the sore has
not spread on the skin, then the priest
shall isolate him another seven days.
6Then the priest shall examine him
again on the seventh day; and indeed
if the sore has faded, *and* the sore has
not spread on the skin, then the priest
shall pronounce him clean; it *is only* a
scab, and he shall wash his clothes and
be clean. 7But if the scab should at all
spread over the skin, after he has been
seen by the priest for his cleansing, he
shall be seen by the priest again. 8And *if*
the priest sees that the scab has indeed
spread on the skin, then the priest shall
pronounce him unclean. It *is* leprosy.

9"When the leprous sore is on a person,
then he shall be brought to the priest.
10And the priest shall examine *him;*
and indeed *if* the swelling on the skin *is*
white, and it has turned the hair white,
and *there is* a spot of raw flesh in the
swelling, 11it *is* an old leprosy on the skin

13:2 a Hebrew *saraath,* disfiguring skin diseases, including leprosy, and so in verses 2–46 and 14:2–32

of his body. The priest shall pronounce
him unclean, and shall not isolate him,
for he *is* unclean.
12“And if leprosy breaks out all over
the skin, and the leprosy covers all the
skin of *the one who has* the sore, from
his head to his foot, wherever the priest
looks, 13then the priest shall consider;
and indeed *if* the leprosy has covered
all his body, he shall pronounce *him*
clean *who has* the sore. It has all turned
white. He *is* clean. 14But when raw flesh
appears on him, he shall be unclean.
15And the priest shall examine the raw
flesh and pronounce him to be unclean;
for the raw flesh *is* unclean. It *is* leprosy.
16Or if the raw flesh changes and turns
white again, he shall come to the priest.
17And the priest shall examine him; and
indeed *if* the sore has turned white, then
the priest shall pronounce *him* clean
who has the sore. He *is* clean.
18“If the body develops a boil in the
skin, and it is healed, 19and in the place
of the boil there comes a white swelling
or a bright spot, reddish-white, then it
shall be shown to the priest; 20and *if,*
when the priest sees it, it indeed appears
deeper than the skin, and its hair has
turned white, the priest shall pronounce
him unclean. It *is* a leprous sore which
has broken out of the boil. 21But if the
priest examines it, and indeed *there are*
no white hairs in it, and it *is* not deep-
er than the skin, but has faded, then
the priest shall isolate him seven days;
22and if it should at all spread over the
skin, then the priest shall pronounce him
unclean. It *is* a leprous sore. 23But if the
bright spot stays in one place, *and* has
not spread, it *is* the scar of the boil; and
the priest shall pronounce him clean.
24“Or if the body receives a burn on its
skin by fire, and the raw *flesh* of the burn
becomes a bright spot, reddish-white or
white, 25then the priest shall examine it;
and indeed *if* the hair of the bright spot
has turned white, and it appears deeper
than the skin, it *is* leprosy broken out
in the burn. Therefore the priest shall
pronounce him unclean. It *is* a leprous
sore. 26But if the priest examines it, and
indeed *there are* no white hairs in the
bright spot, and it *is* not deeper than
the skin, but has faded, then the priest
shall isolate him seven days. 27And the
priest shall examine him on the seventh
day. If it has at all spread over the skin,
then the priest shall pronounce him
unclean. It *is* a leprous sore. 28But if the
bright spot stays in one place, *and* has
not spread on the skin, but has faded,
it *is* a swelling from the burn. The priest
shall pronounce him clean, for it *is* the
scar from the burn.
29“If a man or woman has a sore on
the head or the beard, 30then the priest
shall examine the sore; and indeed if it
appears deeper than the skin, *and there*
is in it thin yellow hair, then the priest
shall pronounce him unclean. It *is* a
scaly leprosy of the head or beard. 31But
if the priest examines the scaly sore,
and indeed it does not appear deep-
er than the skin, and *there is* no black
hair in it, then the priest shall isolate
the one who has the scale seven days.
32And on the seventh day the priest
shall examine the sore; and indeed *if*
the scale has not spread, and there is no
yellow hair in it, and the scale does not
appear deeper than the skin, 33he shall
shave himself, but the scale he shall not
shave. And the priest shall isolate *the*
one who has the scale another seven
days. 34On the seventh day the priest
shall examine the scale; and indeed *if*
the scale has not spread over the skin,
and does not appear deeper than the
skin, then the priest shall pronounce
him clean. He shall wash his clothes and
be clean. 35But if the scale should at all
spread over the skin after his cleansing,
36then the priest shall examine him;
and indeed *if* the scale has spread over
the skin, the priest need not seek for
yellow hair. He *is* unclean. 37But if the
scale appears to be at a standstill, and
there is black hair grown up in it, the
scale has healed. He *is* clean, and the
priest shall pronounce him clean.
38“If a man or a woman has bright
spots on the skin of the body, *specifically*
white bright spots, 39then the priest
shall look; and indeed *if* the bright spots
on the skin of the body *are* dull white,
it *is* a white spot *that* grows on the skin.
He *is* clean.
40“As for the man whose hair has fall-
en from his head, he *is* bald, *but* he *is*

clean. 41He whose hair has fallen from
his forehead, he *is* bald on the forehead,
but he *is* clean. 42And if there is on the
bald head or bald forehead a reddish-
white sore, it *is* leprosy breaking out
on his bald head or his bald forehead.
43Then the priest shall examine it;
and indeed *if* the swelling of the sore
is reddish-white on his bald head or on
his bald forehead, as the appearance of
leprosy on the skin of the body, 44he is
a leprous man. He *is* unclean. The priest
shall surely pronounce him unclean;
his sore *is* on his head.

45"Now the leper on whom the sore *is*,
his clothes shall be torn and his head
bare; and he shall cover his mustache,
and cry, 'Unclean! Unclean!' 46He shall
be unclean. All the days he has the sore
he shall be unclean. He *is* unclean, and
he shall dwell alone; his dwelling *shall*
be outside the camp.

The Law Concerning Leprous Garments

47"Also, if a garment has a leprous
plague[a] in it, *whether it is* a woolen gar-
ment or a linen garment, 48whether *it*
is in the warp or woof of linen or wool,
whether in leather or in anything made
of leather, 49and if the plague is green-
ish or reddish in the garment or in the
leather, whether in the warp or in the
woof, or in anything made of leather, it
is a leprous plague and shall be shown
to the priest. 50The priest shall examine
the plague and isolate *that which has*
the plague seven days. 51And he shall
examine the plague on the seventh day.
If the plague has spread in the garment,
either in the warp or in the woof, in the
leather *or* in anything made of leath-
er, the plague *is* an active leprosy. It
is unclean. 52He shall therefore burn
that garment in which is the plague,
whether warp or woof, in wool or in
linen, or anything of leather, for it *is*
an active leprosy; *the garment* shall be
burned in the fire.

53"But if the priest examines *it*, and
indeed the plague has not spread in
the garment, either in the warp or in
the woof, or in anything made of leath-
er, 54then the priest shall command
that they wash *the thing* in which *is* the
plague; and he shall isolate it anoth-
er seven days. 55Then the priest shall
examine the plague after it has been
washed; and indeed *if* the plague has
not changed its color, though the plague
has not spread, it *is* unclean, and you
shall burn it in the fire; it continues
eating away, *whether* the damage *is*
outside or inside. 56If the priest exam-
ines *it*, and indeed the plague has faded
after washing it, then he shall tear it
out of the garment, whether out of the
warp or out of the woof, or out of the
leather. 57But if it appears again in
the garment, either in the warp or in the
woof, or in anything made of leather,
it *is* a spreading *plague;* you shall burn
with fire that in which is the plague.
58And if you wash the garment, either
warp or woof, or whatever is made of
leather, if the plague has disappeared
from it, then it shall be washed a second
time, and shall be clean.

59"This *is* the law of the leprous plague
in a garment of wool or linen, either in
the warp or woof, or in anything made
of leather, to pronounce it clean or to
pronounce it unclean."

The Ritual for Cleansing Healed Lepers

14 Then the LORD spoke to Moses,
saying, 2"This shall be the law of
the leper for the day of his cleansing: He
shall be brought to the priest. 3And the
priest shall go out of the camp, and the
priest shall examine *him;* and indeed, *if*
the leprosy is healed in the leper, 4then
the priest shall command to take for
him who is to be cleansed two living
and clean birds, cedar wood, scarlet,
and hyssop. 5And the priest shall com-
mand that one of the birds be killed in
an earthen vessel over running water.
6As for the living bird, he shall take it,
the cedar wood and the scarlet and the
hyssop, and dip them and the living bird
in the blood of the bird *that was* killed
over the running water. 7And he shall
sprinkle it seven times on him who is
to be cleansed from the leprosy, and
shall pronounce him clean, and shall
let the living bird loose in the open field.

13:47 [a] A mold, fungus, or similar infestation, and so in verses 47–59

8He who is to be cleansed shall wash his clothes, shave off all his hair, and wash himself in water, that he may be clean. After that he shall come into the camp, and shall stay outside his tent seven days. 9But on the seventh day he shall shave all the hair off his head and his beard and his eyebrows—all his hair he shall shave off. He shall wash his clothes and wash his body in water, and he shall be clean.

10"And on the eighth day he shall take two male lambs without blemish, one ewe lamb of the first year without blemish, three-tenths *of an ephah* of fine flour mixed with oil as a grain offering, and one log of oil. 11Then the priest who makes *him* clean shall present the man who is to be made clean, and those things, before the LORD, *at* the door of the tabernacle of meeting. 12And the priest shall take one male lamb and offer it as a trespass offering, and the log of oil, and wave them *as* a wave offering before the LORD. 13Then he shall kill the lamb in the place where he kills the sin offering and the burnt offering, in a holy place; for as the sin offering *is* the priest's, so *is* the trespass offering. It *is* most holy. 14The priest shall take *some* of the blood of the trespass offering, and the priest shall put *it* on the tip of the right ear of him who is to be cleansed, on the thumb of his right hand, and on the big toe of his right foot. 15And the priest shall take *some* of the log of oil, and pour *it* into the palm of his own left hand. 16Then the priest shall dip his right finger in the oil that *is* in his left hand, and shall sprinkle some of the oil with his finger seven times before the LORD. 17And of the rest of the oil in his hand, the priest shall put *some* on the tip of the right ear of him who is to be cleansed, on the thumb of his right hand, and on the big toe of his right foot, on the blood of the trespass offering. 18The rest of the oil that *is* in the priest's hand he shall put on the head of him who is to be cleansed. So the priest shall make atonement for him before the LORD.

19"Then the priest shall offer the sin offering, and make atonement for him who is to be cleansed from his uncleanness. Afterward he shall kill the burnt offering. 20And the priest shall offer the burnt offering and the grain offering on the altar. So the priest shall make atonement for him, and he shall be clean.

21"But if he *is* poor and cannot afford it, then he shall take one male lamb *as* a trespass offering to be waved, to make atonement for him, one-tenth *of an ephah* of fine flour mixed with oil as a grain offering, a log of oil, 22and two turtledoves or two young pigeons, such as he is able to afford: one shall be a sin offering and the other a burnt offering. 23He shall bring them to the priest on the eighth day for his cleansing, to the door of the tabernacle of meeting, before the LORD. 24And the priest shall take the lamb of the trespass offering and the log of oil, and the priest shall wave them *as* a wave offering before the LORD. 25Then he shall kill the lamb of the trespass offering, and the priest shall take *some* of the blood of the trespass offering and put *it* on the tip of the right ear of him who is to be cleansed, on the thumb of his right hand, and on the big toe of his right foot. 26And the priest shall pour some of the oil into the palm of his own left hand. 27Then the priest shall sprinkle with his right finger *some* of the oil that *is* in his left hand seven times before the LORD. 28And the priest shall put *some* of the oil that *is* in his hand on the tip of the right ear of him who is to be cleansed, on the thumb of the right hand, and on the big toe of his right foot, on the place of the blood of the trespass offering. 29The rest of the oil that *is* in the priest's hand he shall put on the head of him who is to be cleansed, to make atonement for him before the LORD. 30And he shall offer one of the turtledoves or young pigeons, such as he can afford—31such as he is able to afford, the one *as* a sin offering and the other *as* a burnt offering, with the grain offering. So the priest shall make atonement for him who is to be cleansed before the LORD. 32This *is* the law *for one* who had a leprous sore, who cannot afford the usual cleansing."

The Law Concerning Leprous Houses

33And the LORD spoke to Moses and Aaron, saying: 34"When you have come into the land of Canaan, which I give you as a possession, and I put the leprous plague[a] in a house in the land of your possession, 35and he who owns the house comes and tells the priest, saying, 'It seems to me that *there is* some plague in the house,' 36then the priest shall command that they empty the house, before the priest goes *into it* to examine the plague, that all that *is* in the house may not be made unclean; and afterward the priest shall go in to examine the house. 37And he shall examine the plague; and indeed *if* the plague *is* on the walls of the house with ingrained streaks, greenish or reddish, which appear to be deep in the wall, 38then the priest shall go out of the house, to the door of the house, and shut up the house seven days. 39And the priest shall come again on the seventh day and look; and indeed *if* the plague has spread on the walls of the house, 40then the priest shall command that they take away the stones in which *is* the plague, and they shall cast them into an unclean place outside the city. 41And he shall cause the house to be scraped inside, all around, and the dust that they scrape off they shall pour out in an unclean place outside the city. 42Then they shall take other stones and put *them* in the place of *those* stones, and he shall take other mortar and plaster the house.

43"Now if the plague comes back and breaks out in the house, after he has taken away the stones, after he has scraped the house, and after it is plastered, 44then the priest shall come and look; and indeed *if* the plague has spread in the house, it *is* an active leprosy in the house. It *is* unclean. 45And he shall break down the house, its stones, its timber, and all the plaster of the house, and he shall carry *them* outside the city to an unclean place. 46Moreover he who goes into the house at all while it is shut up shall be unclean until evening. 47And he who lies down in the house shall wash his clothes, and he who eats in the house shall wash his clothes.

48"But if the priest comes in and examines *it,* and indeed the plague has not spread in the house after the house was plastered, then the priest shall pronounce the house clean, because the plague is healed. 49And he shall take, to cleanse the house, two birds, cedar wood, scarlet, and hyssop. 50Then he shall kill one of the birds in an earthen vessel over running water; 51and he shall take the cedar wood, the hyssop, the scarlet, and the living bird, and dip them in the blood of the slain bird and in the running water, and sprinkle the house seven times. 52And he shall cleanse the house with the blood of the bird and the running water and the living bird, with the cedar wood, the hyssop, and the scarlet. 53Then he shall let the living bird loose outside the city in the open field, and make atonement for the house, and it shall be clean.

54"This *is* the law for any leprous sore and scale, 55for the leprosy of a garment and of a house, 56for a swelling and a scab and a bright spot, 57to teach when *it is* unclean and when *it is* clean. This *is* the law of leprosy."

The Law Concerning Bodily Discharges

15 And the LORD spoke to Moses and Aaron, saying, 2"Speak to the children of Israel, and say to them: 'When any man has a discharge from his body, his discharge *is* unclean. 3And this shall be his uncleanness in regard to his discharge—whether his body runs with his discharge, or his body is stopped up by his discharge, it *is* his uncleanness. 4Every bed is unclean on which he who has the discharge lies, and everything on which he sits shall be unclean. 5And whoever touches his bed shall wash his clothes and bathe in water, and be unclean until evening. 6He who sits on anything on which he who has the discharge sat shall wash his clothes and bathe in water, and be unclean until evening. 7And he who touches the body of him who has the discharge shall wash his clothes and bathe in water, and be unclean until evening. 8If he who has the discharge spits on him who is clean, then he shall

14:34 [a] Decomposition by mildew, mold, dry rot, etc., and so in verses 34–53

wash his clothes and bathe in water, and be unclean until evening. [9]Any saddle on which he who has the discharge rides shall be unclean. [10]Whoever touches anything that was under him shall be unclean until evening. He who carries *any of* those things shall wash his clothes and bathe in water, and be unclean until evening. [11]And whomever the one who has the discharge touches, and has not rinsed his hands in water, he shall wash his clothes and bathe in water, and be unclean until evening. [12]The vessel of earth that he who has the discharge touches shall be broken, and every vessel of wood shall be rinsed in water.

[13]'And when he who has a discharge is cleansed of his discharge, then he shall count for himself seven days for his cleansing, wash his clothes, and bathe his body in running water; then he shall be clean. [14]On the eighth day he shall take for himself two turtledoves or two young pigeons, and come before the LORD, to the door of the tabernacle of meeting, and give them to the priest. [15]Then the priest shall offer them, the one *as* a sin offering and the other *as* a burnt offering. So the priest shall make atonement for him before the LORD because of his discharge.

[16]'If any man has an emission of semen, then he shall wash all his body in water, and be unclean until evening. [17]And any garment and any leather on which there is semen, it shall be washed with water, and be unclean until evening. [18]Also, when a woman lies with a man, and *there is* an emission of semen, they shall bathe in water, and be unclean until evening.

[19]'If a woman has a discharge, *and* the discharge from her body is blood, she shall be set apart seven days; and whoever touches her shall be unclean until evening. [20]Everything that she lies on during her impurity shall be unclean; also everything that she sits on shall be unclean. [21]Whoever touches her bed shall wash his clothes and bathe in water, and be unclean until evening. [22]And whoever touches anything that she sat on shall wash his clothes and bathe in water, and be unclean until evening. [23]If *anything* is on *her* bed or on anything on which she sits, when he touches it, he shall be unclean until evening. [24]And if any man lies with her at all, so that her impurity is on him, he shall be unclean seven days; and every bed on which he lies shall be unclean.

[25]'If a woman has a discharge of blood for many days, other than at the time of her *customary* impurity, or if it runs beyond her *usual time of* impurity, all the days of her unclean discharge shall be as the days of her *customary* impurity. She *shall be* unclean. [26]Every bed on which she lies all the days of her discharge shall be to her as the bed of her impurity; and whatever she sits on shall be unclean, as the uncleanness of her impurity. [27]Whoever touches those things shall be unclean; he shall wash his clothes and bathe in water, and be unclean until evening.

[28]'But if she is cleansed of her discharge, then she shall count for herself seven days, and after that she shall be clean. [29]And on the eighth day she shall take for herself two turtledoves or two young pigeons, and bring them to the priest, to the door of the tabernacle of meeting. [30]Then the priest shall offer the one *as* a sin offering and the other *as* a burnt offering, and the priest shall make atonement for her before the LORD for the discharge of her uncleanness.

[31]'Thus you shall separate the children of Israel from their uncleanness, lest they die in their uncleanness when they defile My tabernacle that *is* among them. [32]This *is* the law for one who has a discharge, and *for him* who emits semen and is unclean thereby, [33]and for her who is indisposed because of her *customary* impurity, and for one who has a discharge, either man or woman, and for him who lies with her who is unclean.' "

The Day of Atonement

16 Now the LORD spoke to Moses after the death of the two sons of Aaron, when they offered *profane fire* before the LORD, and died; [2]and the LORD said to Moses: "Tell Aaron your brother not to come at *just* any time into the Holy *Place* inside the veil,

before the mercy seat which *is* on the
ark, lest he die; for I will appear in the
cloud above the mercy seat.
3“Thus Aaron shall come into the Holy
Place: with *the blood of* a young bull as
a sin offering, and *of* a ram as a burnt
offering. 4He shall put the holy linen
tunic and the linen trousers on his body;
he shall be girded with a linen sash, and
with the linen turban he shall be attired.
These *are* holy garments. Therefore he
shall wash his body in water, and put
them on. 5And he shall take from the
congregation of the children of Israel
two kids of the goats as a sin offering,
and one ram as a burnt offering.
6“Aaron shall offer the bull as a sin
offering, which *is* for himself, and
make atonement for himself and for
his house. 7He shall take the two goats
and present them before the LORD *at*
the door of the tabernacle of meeting.
8Then Aaron shall cast lots for the two
goats: one lot for the LORD and the other
lot for the scapegoat. 9And Aaron shall
bring the goat on which the LORD’s lot
fell, and offer it *as* a sin offering. 10But
the goat on which the lot fell to be the
scapegoat shall be presented alive be-
fore the LORD, to make atonement upon
it, *and* to let it go as the scapegoat into
the wilderness.
11“And Aaron shall bring the bull of the
sin offering, which is for himself, and
make atonement for himself and for his
house, and shall kill the bull as the sin
offering which *is* for himself. 12Then he
shall take a censer full of burning coals
of fire from the altar before the LORD,
with his hands full of sweet incense
beaten fine, and bring *it* inside the veil.
13And he shall put the incense on the
fire before the LORD, that the cloud of
incense may cover the mercy seat that
is on the Testimony, lest he die. 14He
shall take some of the blood of the bull
and sprinkle *it* with his finger on the
mercy seat on the east *side;* and before
the mercy seat he shall sprinkle some
of the blood with his finger seven times.
15“Then he shall kill the goat of the
sin offering, which *is* for the people,
bring its blood inside the veil, do with
that blood as he did with the blood of
the bull, and sprinkle it on the mercy
seat and before the mercy seat. 16So
he shall make atonement for the Holy
Place, because of the uncleanness of
the children of Israel, and because of
their transgressions, for all their sins;
and so he shall do for the tabernacle of
meeting which remains among them in
the midst of their uncleanness. 17There
shall be no man in the tabernacle of
meeting when he goes in to make atone-
ment in the Holy *Place,* until he comes
out, that he may make atonement for
himself, for his household, and for all
the assembly of Israel. 18And he shall go
out to the altar that *is* before the LORD,
and make atonement for it, and shall
take some of the blood of the bull and
some of the blood of the goat, and put
it on the horns of the altar all around.
19Then he shall sprinkle some of the
blood on it with his finger seven times,
cleanse it, and consecrate it from the
uncleanness of the children of Israel.
20“And when he has made an end of
atoning for the Holy *Place,* the taber-
nacle of meeting, and the altar, he shall
bring the live goat. 21Aaron shall lay
both his hands on the head of the live
goat, confess over it all the iniquities of
the children of Israel, and all their trans-
gressions, concerning all their sins, put-
ting them on the head of the goat, and
shall send *it* away into the wilderness by
the hand of a suitable man. 22The goat
shall bear on itself all their iniquities
to an uninhabited land; and he shall
release the goat in the wilderness.
23“Then Aaron shall come into the
tabernacle of meeting, shall take off the
linen garments which he put on when
he went into the Holy *Place,* and shall
leave them there. 24And he shall wash
his body with water in a holy place, put
on his garments, come out and offer his
burnt offering and the burnt offering
of the people, and make atonement
for himself and for the people. 25The
fat of the sin offering he shall burn on
the altar. 26And he who released the
goat as the scapegoat shall wash his
clothes and bathe his body in water, and
afterward he may come into the camp.
27The bull *for* the sin offering and the
goat *for* the sin offering, whose blood
was brought in to make atonement in

the Holy *Place*, shall be carried outside
the camp. And they shall burn in the
fire their skins, their flesh, and their
offal. 28Then he who burns them shall
wash his clothes and bathe his body
in water, and afterward he may come
into the camp.
29"*This* shall be a statute forever for
you: In the seventh month, on the tenth
day of the month, you shall afflict your
souls, and do no work at all, *whether* a
native of your own country or a strang-
er who dwells among you. 30For on that
day *the priest* shall make atonement
for you, to cleanse you, *that* you may
be clean from all your sins before the
LORD. 31It *is* a sabbath of solemn rest
for you, and you shall afflict your souls.
It is a statute forever. 32And the priest,
who is anointed and consecrated to
minister as priest in his father's place,
shall make atonement, and put on the
linen clothes, the holy garments; 33then
he shall make atonement for the Holy
Sanctuary,[a] and he shall make atone-
ment for the tabernacle of meeting
and for the altar, and he shall make
atonement for the priests and for all the
people of the assembly. 34This shall be
an everlasting statute for you, to make
atonement for the children of Israel, for
all their sins, once a year." And he did
as the LORD commanded Moses.

The Sanctity of Blood

17 And the LORD spoke to Moses,
saying, 2"Speak to Aaron, to his
sons, and to all the children of Isra-
el, and say to them, 'This *is* the thing
which the LORD has commanded, say-
ing: 3"Whatever man of the house of
Israel who kills an ox or lamb or goat
in the camp, or who kills *it* outside the
camp, 4and does not bring it to the
door of the tabernacle of meeting to
offer an offering to the LORD before
the tabernacle of the LORD, the guilt
of bloodshed shall be imputed to that
man. He has shed blood; and that man
shall be cut off from among his people,
5to the end that the children of Israel
may bring their sacrifices which they
offer in the open field, that they may
bring them to the LORD at the door of
the tabernacle of meeting, to the priest,
and offer them *as* peace offerings to the
LORD. 6And the priest shall sprinkle
the blood on the altar of the LORD *at* the
door of the tabernacle of meeting, and
burn the fat for a sweet aroma to the
LORD. 7They shall no more offer their
sacrifices to demons, after whom they
have played the harlot. This shall be a
statute forever for them throughout
their generations." '
8"Also you shall say to them: 'What-
ever man of the house of Israel, or of
the strangers who dwell among you,
who offers a burnt offering or sacrifice,
9and does not bring it to the door of the
tabernacle of meeting, to offer it to the
LORD, that man shall be cut off from
among his people.
10'And whatever man of the house of Is-
rael, or of the strangers who dwell among
you, who eats any blood, I will set My face
against that person who eats blood, and
will cut him off from among his people.
11For the life of the flesh *is* in the blood,
and I have given it to you upon the altar
to make atonement for your souls; for it
is the blood *that* makes atonement for the
soul.' 12Therefore I said to the children
of Israel, 'No one among you shall eat
blood, nor shall any stranger who dwells
among you eat blood.'
13"Whatever man of the children of
Israel, or of the strangers who dwell
among you, who hunts and catches
any animal or bird that may be eaten,
he shall pour out its blood and cover it
with dust; 14for *it is* the life of all flesh. Its
blood sustains its life. Therefore I said
to the children of Israel, 'You shall not
eat the blood of any flesh, for the life
of all flesh is its blood. Whoever eats it
shall be cut off.'
15"And every person who eats what
died *naturally* or what was torn *by
beasts*, *whether he is* a native of your
own country or a stranger, he shall both
wash his clothes and bathe in water,
and be unclean until evening. Then he
shall be clean. 16But if he does not wash
them or bathe his body, then he shall
bear his guilt."

16:33 [a] That is, *the Most Holy Place*

Laws of Sexual Morality

18 Then the LORD spoke to Moses,
saying, 2"Speak to the children
of Israel, and say to them: 'I am the
LORD your God. 3According to the do-
ings of the land of Egypt, where you
dwelt, you shall not do; and according to
the doings of the land of Canaan, where
I am bringing you, you shall not do; nor
shall you walk in their ordinances. 4You
shall observe My judgments and keep
My ordinances, to walk in them: I *am*
the LORD your God. 5You shall therefore
keep My statutes and My judgments,
which if a man does, he shall live by
them: I *am* the LORD.
6'None of you shall approach anyone
who is near of kin to him, to uncover his
nakedness: I *am* the LORD. 7The naked-
ness of your father or the nakedness of
your mother you shall not uncover. She
is your mother; you shall not uncover
her nakedness. 8The nakedness of your
father's wife you shall not uncover; it *is*
your father's nakedness. 9The naked-
ness of your sister, the daughter of your
father, or the daughter of your mother,
whether born at home or elsewhere, their
nakedness you shall not uncover. 10The
nakedness of your son's daughter or your
daughter's daughter, their nakedness
you shall not uncover; for theirs *is* your
own nakedness. 11The nakedness of your
father's wife's daughter, begotten by
your father—she *is* your sister—you
shall not uncover her nakedness. 12You
shall not uncover the nakedness of
your father's sister; she *is* near of kin
to your father. 13You shall not uncover
the nakedness of your mother's sister,
for she *is* near of kin to your mother.
14You shall not uncover the nakedness
of your father's brother. You shall not
approach his wife; she *is* your aunt. 15You
shall not uncover the nakedness of your
daughter-in-law—she *is* your son's wife—
you shall not uncover her nakedness.
16You shall not uncover the nakedness
of your brother's wife; it *is* your brother's
nakedness. 17You shall not uncover the
nakedness of a woman and her daughter,
nor shall you take her son's daughter or
her daughter's daughter, to uncover her
nakedness. They *are* near of kin to her.
It *is* wickedness. 18Nor shall you take a
woman as a rival to her sister, to uncover
her nakedness while the other is alive.
19'Also you shall not approach a wom-
an to uncover her nakedness as long as
she is in her *customary* impurity. 20More-
over you shall not lie carnally with your
neighbor's wife, to defile yourself with
her. 21And you shall not let any of your
descendants pass through *the fire* to
Molech, nor shall you profane the name
of your God: I *am* the LORD. 22You shall
not lie with a male as with a woman. It
is an abomination. 23Nor shall you mate
with any animal, to defile yourself with
it. Nor shall any woman stand before an
animal to mate with it. It *is* perversion.
24'Do not defile yourselves with any
of these things; for by all these the na-
tions are defiled, which I am casting
out before you. 25For the land is defiled;
therefore I visit the punishment of its
iniquity upon it, and the land vomits
out its inhabitants. 26You shall therefore
keep My statutes and My judgments,
and shall not commit *any* of these abom-
inations, *either* any of your own nation
or any stranger who dwells among you
27(for all these abominations the men
of the land have done, who *were* before
you, and thus the land is defiled), 28lest
the land vomit you out also when you
defile it, as it vomited out the nations
that *were* before you. 29For whoever
commits any of these abominations,
the persons who commit *them* shall be
cut off from among their people.
30'Therefore you shall keep My ordi-
nance, so that *you* do not commit *any*
of these abominable customs which
were committed before you, and that
you do not defile yourselves by them:
I *am* the LORD your God.' "

Moral and Ceremonial Laws

19 And the LORD spoke to Moses,
saying, 2"Speak to all the con-
gregation of the children of Israel, and
say to them: 'You shall be holy, for I the
LORD your God *am* holy.
3'Every one of you shall revere his
mother and his father, and keep My
Sabbaths: I *am* the LORD your God.
4'Do not turn to idols, nor make for
yourselves molded gods: I *am* the LORD
your God.

5‘And if you offer a sacrifice of a peace
offering to the LORD, you shall offer it
of your own free will. 6It shall be eaten
the same day you offer *it,* and on the
next day. And if any remains until the
third day, it shall be burned in the fire.
7And if it is eaten at all on the third
day, it *is* an abomination. It shall not
be accepted. 8Therefore *everyone* who
eats it shall bear his iniquity, because
he has profaned the hallowed *offering*
of the LORD; and that person shall be
cut off from his people.
9‘When you reap the harvest of your
land, you shall not wholly reap the cor-
ners of your field, nor shall you gather
the gleanings of your harvest. 10And
you shall not glean your vineyard, nor
shall you gather *every* grape of your
vineyard; you shall leave them for the
poor and the stranger: I *am* the LORD
your God.
11‘You shall not steal, nor deal falsely,
nor lie to one another. 12And you shall
not swear by My name falsely, nor shall
you profane the name of your God: I
am the LORD.
13‘You shall not cheat your neighbor,
nor rob *him.* The wages of him who is
hired shall not remain with you all
night until morning. 14You shall not
curse the deaf, nor put a stumbling
block before the blind, but shall fear
your God: I *am* the LORD.
15‘You shall do no injustice in judg-
ment. You shall not be partial to the
poor, nor honor the person of the
mighty. In righteousness you shall
judge your neighbor. 16You shall not go
about *as* a talebearer among your peo-
ple; nor shall you take a stand against
the life of your neighbor: I *am* the LORD.
17‘You shall not hate your brother in
your heart. You shall surely rebuke your
neighbor, and not bear sin because of
him. 18You shall not take vengeance,
nor bear any grudge against the chil-
dren of your people, but you shall love
your neighbor as yourself: I *am* the
LORD.
19‘You shall keep My statutes. You shall
not let your livestock breed with an-
other kind. You shall not sow your field
with mixed seed. Nor shall a garment of
mixed linen and wool come upon you.
20‘Whoever lies carnally with a woman
who *is* betrothed to a man as a con-
cubine, and who has not at all been
redeemed nor given her freedom, for
this there shall be scourging; *but* they
shall not be put to death, because she
was not free. 21And he shall bring his
trespass offering to the LORD, to the
door of the tabernacle of meeting, a
ram as a trespass offering. 22The priest
shall make atonement for him with the
ram of the trespass offering before the
LORD for his sin which he has commit-
ted. And the sin which he has committed
shall be forgiven him.
23‘When you come into the land, and
have planted all kinds of trees for food,
then you shall count their fruit as un-
circumcised. Three years it shall be as
uncircumcised to you. *It* shall not be
eaten. 24But in the fourth year all its
fruit shall be holy, a praise to the LORD.
25And in the fifth year you may eat its
fruit, that it may yield to you its in-
crease: I *am* the LORD your God.
26‘You shall not eat *anything* with the
blood, nor shall you practice divination
or soothsaying. 27You shall not shave
around the sides of your head, nor shall
you disfigure the edges of your beard.
28You shall not make any cuttings in
your flesh for the dead, nor tattoo any
marks on you: I *am* the LORD.
29‘Do not prostitute your daughter, to
cause her to be a harlot, lest the land
fall into harlotry, and the land become
full of wickedness.
30‘You shall keep My Sabbaths and
reverence My sanctuary: I *am* the LORD.
31‘Give no regard to mediums and famil-
iar spirits; do not seek after them, to be
defiled by them: I *am* the LORD your God.
32‘You shall rise before the gray head-
ed and honor the presence of an old
man, and fear your God: I *am* the LORD.
33‘And if a stranger dwells with you in
your land, you shall not mistreat him.
34The stranger who dwells among you
shall be to you as one born among you,
and you shall love him as yourself; for
you were strangers in the land of Egypt:
I *am* the LORD your God.
35‘You shall do no injustice in judg-
ment, in measurement of length,
weight, or volume. 36You shall have

honest scales, honest weights, an honest ephah, and an honest hin: I *am* the LORD your God, who brought you out of the land of Egypt.

37"Therefore you shall observe all My statutes and all My judgments, and perform them: I *am* the LORD.' "

Penalties for Breaking the Law

20 Then the LORD spoke to Moses, saying, 2"Again, you shall say to the children of Israel: 'Whoever of the children of Israel, or of the strangers who dwell in Israel, who gives *any* of his descendants to Molech, he shall surely be put to death. The people of the land shall stone him with stones. 3I will set My face against that man, and will cut him off from his people, because he has given *some* of his descendants to Molech, to defile My sanctuary and profane My holy name. 4And if the people of the land should in any way hide their eyes from the man, when he gives *some* of his descendants to Molech, and they do not kill him, 5then I will set My face against that man and against his family; and I will cut him off from his people, and all who prostitute themselves with him to commit harlotry with Molech.

6'And the person who turns to mediums and familiar spirits, to prostitute himself with them, I will set My face against that person and cut him off from his people. 7Consecrate yourselves therefore, and be holy, for I *am* the LORD your God. 8And you shall keep My statutes, and perform them: I *am* the LORD who sanctifies you.

9'For everyone who curses his father or his mother shall surely be put to death. He has cursed his father or his mother. His blood *shall be* upon him.

10'The man who commits adultery with *another* man's wife, *he* who commits adultery with his neighbor's wife, the adulterer and the adulteress, shall surely be put to death. 11The man who lies with his father's wife has uncovered his father's nakedness; both of them shall surely be put to death. Their blood *shall be* upon them. 12If a man lies with his daughter-in-law, both of them shall surely be put to death. They have committed perversion. Their blood *shall be* upon them. 13If a man lies with a male as he lies with a woman, both of them have committed an abomination. They shall surely be put to death. Their blood *shall be* upon them. 14If a man marries a woman and her mother, it *is* wickedness. They shall be burned with fire, both he and they, that there may be no wickedness among you. 15If a man mates with an animal, he shall surely be put to death, and you shall kill the animal. 16If a woman approaches any animal and mates with it, you shall kill the woman and the animal. They shall surely be put to death. Their blood *is* upon them.

17'If a man takes his sister, his father's daughter or his mother's daughter, and sees her nakedness and she sees his nakedness, it *is* a wicked thing. And they shall be cut off in the sight of their people. He has uncovered his sister's nakedness. He shall bear his guilt. 18If a man lies with a woman during her sickness and uncovers her nakedness, he has exposed her flow, and she has uncovered the flow of her blood. Both of them shall be cut off from their people.

19'You shall not uncover the nakedness of your mother's sister nor of your father's sister, for that would uncover his near of kin. They shall bear their guilt. 20If a man lies with his uncle's wife, he has uncovered his uncle's nakedness. They shall bear their sin; they shall die childless. 21If a man takes his brother's wife, it *is* an unclean thing. He has uncovered his brother's nakedness. They shall be childless.

22'You shall therefore keep all My statutes and all My judgments, and perform them, that the land where I am bringing you to dwell may not vomit you out. 23And you shall not walk in the statutes of the nation which I am casting out before you; for they commit all these things, and therefore I abhor them. 24But I have said to you, "You shall inherit their land, and I will give it to you to possess, a land flowing with milk and honey." I *am* the LORD your God, who has separated you from the peoples. 25You shall therefore distinguish between clean animals and unclean, between unclean birds and clean, and you shall not make yourselves abominable

by beast or by bird, or by any kind of
living thing that creeps on the ground,
which I have separated from you as
unclean. 26And you shall be holy to
Me, for I the LORD *am* holy, and have
separated you from the peoples, that
you should be Mine.
27'A man or a woman who is a medium,
or who has familiar spirits, shall surely
be put to death; they shall stone them
with stones. Their blood *shall be* upon
them.' "

Regulations for Conduct of Priests

21 And the LORD said to Moses,
"Speak to the priests, the sons
of Aaron, and say to them: 'None shall
defile himself for the dead among his
people, 2except for his relatives who are
nearest to him: his mother, his father,
his son, his daughter, and his brother;
3also his virgin sister who is near to him,
who has had no husband, for her he
may defile himself. 4*Otherwise* he shall
not defile himself, *being* a chief man
among his people, to profane himself.
5'They shall not make any bald *place*
on their heads, nor shall they shave
the edges of their beards nor make any
cuttings in their flesh. 6They shall be
holy to their God and not profane the
name of their God, for they offer the
offerings of the LORD made by fire, *and*
the bread of their God; therefore they
shall be holy. 7They shall not take a wife
who is a harlot or a defiled woman, nor
shall they take a woman divorced from
her husband; for *the priest*[a] is holy to his
God. 8Therefore you shall consecrate
him, for he offers the bread of your God.
He shall be holy to you, for I the LORD,
who sanctify you, *am* holy. 9The daugh-
ter of any priest, if she profanes herself
by playing the harlot, she profanes her
father. She shall be burned with fire.
10'*He who is* the high priest among his
brethren, on whose head the anointing
oil was poured and who is consecrated
to wear the garments, shall not uncover
his head nor tear his clothes; 11nor shall
he go near any dead body, nor defile
himself for his father or his mother;
12nor shall he go out of the sanctuary,
nor profane the sanctuary of his God;
for the consecration of the anointing oil
of his God *is* upon him: I *am* the LORD.
13And he shall take a wife in her vir-
ginity. 14A widow or a divorced woman
or a defiled woman *or* a harlot—these
he shall not marry; but he shall take a
virgin of his own people as wife. 15Nor
shall he profane his posterity among
his people, for I the LORD sanctify him.' "
16And the LORD spoke to Moses, say-
ing, 17"Speak to Aaron, saying: 'No man
of your descendants in *succeeding* gen-
erations, who has *any* defect, may ap-
proach to offer the bread of his God.
18For any man who has a defect shall
not approach: a man blind or lame,
who has a marred *face* or any *limb* too
long, 19a man who has a broken foot or
broken hand, 20or is a hunchback or a
dwarf, or *a man* who has a defect in his
eye, or eczema or scab, or is a eunuch.
21No man of the descendants of Aaron
the priest, who has a defect, shall come
near to offer the offerings made by fire
to the LORD. He has a defect; he shall not
come near to offer the bread of his God.
22He may eat the bread of his God, *both*
the most holy and the holy; 23only he
shall not go near the veil or approach
the altar, because he has a defect, lest
he profane My sanctuaries; for I the
LORD sanctify them.' "
24And Moses told *it* to Aaron and his
sons, and to all the children of Israel.

22 Then the LORD spoke to Moses,
saying, 2"Speak to Aaron and
his sons, that they separate themselves
from the holy things of the children of
Israel, and that they do not profane My
holy name *by* what they dedicate to Me:
I *am* the LORD. 3Say to them: 'Whoever
of all your descendants throughout your
generations, who goes near the holy
things which the children of Israel ded-
icate to the LORD, while he has unclean-
ness upon him, that person shall be cut
off from My presence: I *am* the LORD.
4'Whatever man of the descendants of
Aaron, who *is* a leper or has a discharge,
shall not eat the holy offerings until he
is clean. And whoever touches anything
made unclean *by* a corpse, or a man

21:7 [a] Literally *he*

who has had an emission of semen, 5or
whoever touches any creeping thing by
which he would be made unclean, or
any person by whom he would become
unclean, whatever his uncleanness may
be— 6the person who has touched any
such thing shall be unclean until evening, and shall not eat the holy *offerings*
unless he washes his body with water.
7And when the sun goes down he shall
be clean; and afterward he may eat
the holy *offerings*, because it *is* his food.
8Whatever dies *naturally* or is torn *by beasts* he shall not eat, to defile himself
with it: I *am* the LORD.

9'They shall therefore keep My ordinance, lest they bear sin for it and die
thereby, if they profane it: I the LORD
sanctify them.

10'No outsider shall eat the holy *offering*; one who dwells with the priest, or
a hired servant, shall not eat the holy
thing. 11But if the priest buys a person
with his money, he may eat it; and one
who is born in his house may eat his
food. 12If the priest's daughter is married to an outsider, she may not eat of
the holy offerings. 13But if the priest's
daughter is a widow or divorced, and has
no child, and has returned to her father's
house as in her youth, she may eat her
father's food; but no outsider shall eat it.

14'And if a man eats the holy *offering*
unintentionally, then he shall restore
a holy *offering* to the priest, and add
one-fifth to it. 15They shall not profane
the holy *offerings* of the children of Israel, which they offer to the LORD, 16or
allow them to bear the guilt of trespass
when they eat their holy *offerings*; for I
the LORD sanctify them.' "

Offerings Accepted and Not Accepted

17And the LORD spoke to Moses, saying,
18"Speak to Aaron and his sons, and to all
the children of Israel, and say to them:
'Whatever man of the house of Israel, or
of the strangers in Israel, who offers his
sacrifice for any of his vows or for any
of his freewill offerings, which they offer
to the LORD as a burnt offering— 19*you shall offer* of your own free will a male
without blemish from the cattle, from the
sheep, or from the goats. 20Whatever has
a defect, you shall not offer, for it shall
not be acceptable on your behalf. 21And
whoever offers a sacrifice of a peace
offering to the LORD, to fulfill *his* vow, or
a freewill offering from the cattle or the
sheep, it must be perfect to be accepted;
there shall be no defect in it. 22Those
that are blind or broken or maimed, or
have an ulcer or eczema or scabs, you
shall not offer to the LORD, nor make an
offering by fire of them on the altar to
the LORD. 23Either a bull or a lamb that
has any limb too long or too short you
may offer *as* a freewill offering, but for
a vow it shall not be accepted.

24'You shall not offer to the LORD what
is bruised or crushed, or torn or cut;
nor shall you make *any offering of them*
in your land. 25Nor from a foreigner's
hand shall you offer any of these as
the bread of your God, because their
corruption *is* in them, *and* defects *are*
in them. They shall not be accepted on
your behalf.' "

26And the LORD spoke to Moses, saying: 27"When a bull or a sheep or a goat
is born, it shall be seven days with its
mother; and from the eighth day and
thereafter it shall be accepted as an
offering made by fire to the LORD.
28*Whether it is* a cow or ewe, do not kill
both her and her young on the same
day. 29And when you offer a sacrifice
of thanksgiving to the LORD, offer *it* of
your own free will. 30On the same day
it shall be eaten; you shall leave none
of it until morning: I *am* the LORD.

31"Therefore you shall keep My commandments, and perform them: I *am*
the LORD. 32You shall not profane
My holy name, but I will be hallowed
among the children of Israel. I *am* the
LORD who sanctifies you, 33who brought
you out of the land of Egypt, to be your
God: I *am* the LORD."

Feasts of the LORD

23 And the LORD spoke to Moses,
saying, 2"Speak to the children
of Israel, and say to them: 'The feasts of
the LORD, which you shall proclaim *to be*
holy convocations, these *are* My feasts.

The Sabbath

3'Six days shall work be done, but the
seventh day *is* a Sabbath of solemn

rest, a holy convocation. You shall do
no work *on it;* it *is* the Sabbath of the
LORD in all your dwellings.

The Passover and Unleavened Bread

4"These *are* the feasts of the LORD, holy
convocations which you shall proclaim
at their appointed times. 5On the four-
teenth *day* of the first month at twilight
is the LORD's Passover. 6And on the fif-
teenth day of the same month *is* the
Feast of Unleavened Bread to the LORD;
seven days you must eat unleavened
bread. 7On the first day you shall have
a holy convocation; you shall do no
customary work on it. 8But you shall
offer an offering made by fire to the
LORD for seven days. The seventh day
shall be a holy convocation; you shall
do no customary work *on it.*' "

The Feast of Firstfruits

9And the LORD spoke to Moses, saying,
10"Speak to the children of Israel, and
say to them: 'When you come into the
land which I give to you, and reap its
harvest, then you shall bring a sheaf
of the firstfruits of your harvest to the
priest. 11He shall wave the sheaf before
the LORD, to be accepted on your be-
half; on the day after the Sabbath the
priest shall wave it. 12And you shall offer
on that day, when you wave the sheaf,
a male lamb of the first year, without
blemish, as a burnt offering to the LORD.
13Its grain offering *shall be* two-tenths *of
an ephah* of fine flour mixed with oil, an
offering made by fire to the LORD, for a
sweet aroma; and its drink offering *shall
be* of wine, one-fourth of a hin. 14You
shall eat neither bread nor parched
grain nor fresh grain until the same
day that you have brought an offering
to your God; *it shall be* a statute forever
throughout your generations in all your
dwellings.

The Feast of Weeks

15'And you shall count for yourselves
from the day after the Sabbath, from the
day that you brought the sheaf of the
wave offering: seven Sabbaths shall be
completed. 16Count fifty days to the day
after the seventh Sabbath; then you shall
offer a new grain offering to the LORD.
17You shall bring from your dwellings
two wave *loaves* of two-tenths *of an ephah.*
They shall be of fine flour; they shall be
baked with leaven. *They are* the firstfruits
to the LORD. 18And you shall offer with
the bread seven lambs of the first year,
without blemish, one young bull, and
two rams. They shall be *as* a burnt offer-
ing to the LORD, with their grain offering
and their drink offerings, an offering
made by fire for a sweet aroma to the
LORD. 19Then you shall sacrifice one
kid of the goats as a sin offering, and
two male lambs of the first year as a
sacrifice of a peace offering. 20The priest
shall wave them with the bread of the
firstfruits *as* a wave offering before the
LORD, with the two lambs. They shall be
holy to the LORD for the priest. 21And you
shall proclaim on the same day *that* it
is a holy convocation to you. You shall
do no customary work *on it. It shall be*
a statute forever in all your dwellings
throughout your generations.
22'When you reap the harvest of your
land, you shall not wholly reap the cor-
ners of your field when you reap, nor
shall you gather any gleaning from
your harvest. You shall leave them for
the poor and for the stranger: I *am* the
LORD your God.' "

The Feast of Trumpets

23Then the LORD spoke to Moses, say-
ing, 24"Speak to the children of Israel,
saying: 'In the seventh month, on the
first *day* of the month, you shall have
a sabbath-*rest,* a memorial of blowing
of trumpets, a holy convocation. 25You
shall do no customary work *on it;* and
you shall offer an offering made by fire
to the LORD.' "

The Day of Atonement

26And the LORD spoke to Moses, say-
ing: 27"Also the tenth *day* of this seventh
month *shall be* the Day of Atonement.
It shall be a holy convocation for you;
you shall afflict your souls, and offer an
offering made by fire to the LORD. 28And
you shall do no work on that same day,
for it *is* the Day of Atonement, to make
atonement for you before the LORD
your God. 29For any person who is not
afflicted *in soul* on that same day shall

be cut off from his people. 30And any
person who does any work on that same
day, that person I will destroy from
among his people. 31You shall do no
manner of work; *it shall be* a statute
forever throughout your generations
in all your dwellings. 32It *shall be* to you
a sabbath of *solemn* rest, and you shall
afflict your souls; on the ninth *day* of
the month at evening, from evening
to evening, you shall celebrate your
sabbath."

The Feast of Tabernacles

33Then the LORD spoke to Moses, say-
ing, 34"Speak to the children of Israel,
saying: 'The fifteenth day of this seventh
month *shall be* the Feast of Tabernacles
for seven days to the LORD. 35On the
first day *there shall be* a holy convoca-
tion. You shall do no customary work
on it. 36*For* seven days you shall offer
an offering made by fire to the LORD.
On the eighth day you shall have a holy
convocation, and you shall offer an
offering made by fire to the LORD. It *is*
a sacred assembly, *and* you shall do no
customary work *on it*.

37'These *are* the feasts of the LORD
which you shall proclaim *to be* holy
convocations, to offer an offering made
by fire to the LORD, a burnt offering and
a grain offering, a sacrifice and drink
offerings, everything on its day— 38be-
sides the Sabbaths of the LORD, besides
your gifts, besides all your vows, and
besides all your freewill offerings which
you give to the LORD.

39'Also on the fifteenth day of the sev-
enth month, when you have gathered
in the fruit of the land, you shall keep
the feast of the LORD *for* seven days; on
the first day *there shall be* a sabbath-*rest*,
and on the eighth day a sabbath-*rest*.
40And you shall take for yourselves on
the first day the fruit of beautiful trees,
branches of palm trees, the boughs of
leafy trees, and willows of the brook; and
you shall rejoice before the LORD your
God for seven days. 41You shall keep it
as a feast to the LORD for seven days in
the year. *It shall be* a statute forever in
your generations. You shall celebrate it
in the seventh month. 42You shall dwell
in booths for seven days. All who are
native Israelites shall dwell in booths,
43that your generations may know that
I made the children of Israel dwell in
booths when I brought them out of the
land of Egypt: I *am* the LORD your God.' "

44So Moses declared to the children of
Israel the feasts of the LORD.

Care of the Tabernacle Lamps

24 Then the LORD spoke to Moses,
saying: 2"Command the chil-
dren of Israel that they bring to you
pure oil of pressed olives for the light,
to make the lamps burn continually.
3Outside the veil of the Testimony, in
the tabernacle of meeting, Aaron shall
be in charge of it from evening until
morning before the LORD continual-
ly; *it shall be* a statute forever in your
generations. 4He shall be in charge of
the lamps on the pure *gold* lampstand
before the LORD continually.

The Bread of the Tabernacle

5"And you shall take fine flour and
bake twelve cakes with it. Two-tenths
of an ephah shall be in each cake. 6You
shall set them in two rows, six in a row,
on the pure *gold* table before the LORD.
7And you shall put pure frankincense on
each row, that it may be on the bread for
a memorial, an offering made by fire to
the LORD. 8Every Sabbath he shall set
it in order before the LORD continually,
being taken from the children of Israel by
an everlasting covenant. 9And it shall be
for Aaron and his sons, and they shall
eat it in a holy place; for it *is* most holy
to him from the offerings of the LORD
made by fire, by a perpetual statute."

The Penalty for Blasphemy

10Now the son of an Israelite wom-
an, whose father *was* an Egyptian,
went out among the children of Isra-
el; and this Israelite *woman's* son and
a man of Israel fought each other in
the camp. 11And the Israelite woman's
son blasphemed the name *of the LORD*
and cursed; and so they brought him to
Moses. (His mother's name *was* Shelo-
mith the daughter of Dibri, of the tribe
of Dan.) 12Then they put him in custody,
that the mind of the LORD might be
shown to them.

13And the LORD spoke to Moses, say-
ing, 14"Take outside the camp him who
has cursed; then let all who heard *him*
lay their hands on his head, and let all
the congregation stone him.
15"Then you shall speak to the children
of Israel, saying: 'Whoever curses his
God shall bear his sin. 16And whoever
blasphemes the name of the LORD shall
surely be put to death. All the congre-
gation shall certainly stone him, the
stranger as well as him who is born
in the land. When he blasphemes the
name *of the LORD*, he shall be put to
death.
17'Whoever kills any man shall sure-
ly be put to death. 18Whoever kills an
animal shall make it good, animal for
animal.
19'If a man causes disfigurement of his
neighbor, as he has done, so shall it be
done to him— 20fracture for fracture,
eye for eye, tooth for tooth; as he has
caused disfigurement of a man, so shall
it be done to him. 21And whoever kills
an animal shall restore it; but whoever
kills a man shall be put to death. 22You
shall have the same law for the stranger
and for one from your own country; for
I *am* the LORD your God.' "
23Then Moses spoke to the children of
Israel; and they took outside the camp
him who had cursed, and stoned him
with stones. So the children of Israel
did as the LORD commanded Moses.

The Sabbath of the Seventh Year

25 And the LORD spoke to Moses on
Mount Sinai, saying, 2"Speak to
the children of Israel, and say to them:
'When you come into the land which
I give you, then the land shall keep a
sabbath to the LORD. 3Six years you
shall sow your field, and six years you
shall prune your vineyard, and gather
its fruit; 4but in the seventh year there
shall be a sabbath of solemn rest for the
land, a sabbath to the LORD. You shall
neither sow your field nor prune your
vineyard. 5What grows of its own accord
of your harvest you shall not reap, nor
gather the grapes of your untended vine,
for it is a year of rest for the land. 6And
the sabbath *produce* of the land shall
be food for you: for you, your male and
female servants, your hired man, and the
stranger who dwells with you, 7for your
livestock and the beasts that *are* in your
land—all its produce shall be for food.

The Year of Jubilee

8'And you shall count seven sabbaths
of years for yourself, seven times seven
years; and the time of the seven sab-
baths of years shall be to you forty-nine
years. 9Then you shall cause the trum-
pet of the Jubilee to sound on the tenth
day of the seventh month; on the Day
of Atonement you shall make the trum-
pet to sound throughout all your land.
10And you shall consecrate the fiftieth
year, and proclaim liberty throughout
all the land to all its inhabitants. It shall
be a Jubilee for you; and each of you
shall return to his possession, and each
of you shall return to his family. 11That
fiftieth year shall be a Jubilee to you; in
it you shall neither sow nor reap what
grows of its own accord, nor gather *the*
grapes of your untended vine. 12For it
is the Jubilee; it shall be holy to you;
you shall eat its produce from the field.
13'In this Year of Jubilee, each of you
shall return to his possession. 14And if
you sell anything to your neighbor or
buy from your neighbor's hand, you
shall not oppress one another. 15Ac-
cording to the number of years after
the Jubilee you shall buy from your
neighbor, and according to the number
of years of crops he shall sell to you.
16According to the multitude of years
you shall increase its price, and accord-
ing to the fewer number of years you
shall diminish its price; for he sells to
you *according* to the number *of the years*
of the crops. 17Therefore you shall not
oppress one another, but you shall fear
your God; for I *am* the LORD your God.

Provisions for the Seventh Year

18'So you shall observe My statutes
and keep My judgments, and perform
them; and you will dwell in the land
in safety. 19Then the land will yield its
fruit, and you will eat your fill, and dwell
there in safety.
20'And if you say, "What shall we eat
in the seventh year, since we shall not
sow nor gather in our produce?" 21Then

I will command My blessing on you in
the sixth year, and it will bring forth
produce enough for three years. 22And
you shall sow in the eighth year, and eat
old produce until the ninth year; until
its produce comes in, you shall eat *of*
the old *harvest*.

Redemption of Property

23'The land shall not be sold perma-
nently, for the land *is* Mine; for you
are strangers and sojourners with Me.
24And in all the land of your possession
you shall grant redemption of the land.

25'If one of your brethren becomes
poor, and has sold *some* of his pos-
session, and if his redeeming relative
comes to redeem it, then he may redeem
what his brother sold. 26Or if the man
has no one to redeem it, but he himself
becomes able to redeem it, 27then let
him count the years since its sale, and
restore the remainder to the man to
whom he sold it, that he may return to
his possession. 28But if he is not able
to have *it* restored to himself, then what
was sold shall remain in the hand of him
who bought it until the Year of Jubilee;
and in the Jubilee it shall be released,
and he shall return to his possession.

29'If a man sells a house in a walled
city, then he may redeem it within a
whole year after it is sold; *within* a full
year he may redeem it. 30But if it is not
redeemed within the space of a full year,
then the house in the walled city shall
belong permanently to him who bought
it, throughout his generations. It shall
not be released in the Jubilee. 31However
the houses of villages which have no wall
around them shall be counted as the
fields of the country. They may be re-
deemed, and they shall be released in the
Jubilee. 32Nevertheless the cities of the
Levites, *and* the houses in the cities of
their possession, the Levites may redeem
at any time. 33And if a man purchases a
house from the Levites, then the house
that was sold in the city of his possession
shall be released in the Jubilee; for the
houses in the cities of the Levites *are* their
possession among the children of Israel.
34But the field of the common-land of
their cities may not be sold, for it *is* their
perpetual possession.

Lending to the Poor

35'If one of your brethren becomes
poor, and falls into poverty among you,
then you shall help him, like a stranger
or a sojourner, that he may live with
you. 36Take no usury or interest from
him; but fear your God, that your
brother may live with you. 37You shall
not lend him your money for usury, nor
lend him your food at a profit. 38I *am*
the LORD your God, who brought you
out of the land of Egypt, to give you
the land of Canaan *and* to be your God.

The Law Concerning Slavery

39'And if *one of* your brethren *who
dwells* by you becomes poor, and sells
himself to you, you shall not compel
him to serve as a slave. 40As a hired
servant *and* a sojourner he shall be with
you, *and* shall serve you until the Year of
Jubilee. 41And *then* he shall depart from
you—he and his children with him—
and shall return to his own family. He
shall return to the possession of his fa-
thers. 42For they *are* My servants, whom
I brought out of the land of Egypt; they
shall not be sold as slaves. 43You shall
not rule over him with rigor, but you
shall fear your God. 44And as for your
male and female slaves whom you may
have—from the nations that are around
you, from them you may buy male and
female slaves. 45Moreover you may
buy the children of the strangers who
dwell among you, and their families
who are with you, which they beget in
your land; and they shall become your
property. 46And you may take them as
an inheritance for your children after
you, to inherit *them as* a possession;
they shall be your permanent slaves.
But regarding your brethren, the chil-
dren of Israel, you shall not rule over
one another with rigor.

47'Now if a sojourner or stranger close
to you becomes rich, and *one of* your
brethren *who dwells* by him becomes
poor, and sells himself to the stranger *or*
sojourner close to you, or to a member
of the stranger's family, 48after he is
sold he may be redeemed again. One
of his brothers may redeem him; 49or
his uncle or his uncle's son may redeem
him; or *anyone* who is near of kin to him

in his family may redeem him; or if he
is able he may redeem himself. 50Thus
he shall reckon with him who bought
him: The price of his release shall be
according to the number of years, from
the year that he was sold to him until
the Year of Jubilee; *it shall be* according
to the time of a hired servant for him.
51If *there are* still many years *remaining*,
according to them he shall repay the
price of his redemption from the money
with which he was bought. 52And if there
remain but a few years until the Year
of Jubilee, then he shall reckon with
him, *and* according to his years he shall
repay him the price of his redemption.
53He shall be with him as a yearly hired
servant, and he shall not rule with rigor
over him in your sight. 54And if he is not
redeemed in these *years*, then he shall be
released in the Year of Jubilee—he and
his children with him. 55For the children
of Israel *are* servants to Me; they *are*
My servants whom I brought out of the
land of Egypt: I *am* the LORD your God.

Promise of Blessing and Retribution

26 'You shall not make idols for
yourselves;
neither a carved image nor a *sacred*
pillar shall you rear up for yourselves;
nor shall you set up an engraved
stone in your land, to bow down
to it;
for I *am* the LORD your God.
2 You shall keep My Sabbaths and
reverence My sanctuary:
I *am* the LORD.

3 'If you walk in My statutes and keep
My commandments, and perform them,
4 then I will give you rain in its season,
the land shall yield its produce,
and the trees of the field
shall yield their fruit.
5 Your threshing shall last till the time
of vintage, and the vintage shall
last till the time of sowing;
you shall eat your bread to the full,
and dwell in your land safely.
6 I will give peace in the land, and
you shall lie down, and none will
make *you* afraid;
I will rid the land of evil beasts,
and the sword will not go through
your land.
7 You will chase your enemies, and
they shall fall by the sword before
you.
8 Five of you shall chase a hundred,
and a hundred of you shall put
ten thousand to flight;
your enemies shall fall by the sword
before you.

9 'For I will look on you favorably and
make you fruitful, multiply you
and confirm My covenant with
you.
10 You shall eat the old harvest, and clear
out the old because of the new.
11 I will set My tabernacle among you,
and My soul shall not abhor you.
12 I will walk among you and be your
God, and you shall be My people.
13 I *am* the LORD your God, who
brought you out of the land of
Egypt, that *you* should not be
their slaves;
I have broken the bands of your
yoke and made you walk upright.

14 'But if you do not obey Me, and do
not observe all these commandments,
15 and if you despise My statutes, or if
your soul abhors My judgments,
so that you do not perform all
My commandments, *but* break
My covenant,
16 I also will do this to you:
I will even appoint terror over
you, wasting disease and fever
which shall consume the eyes
and cause sorrow of heart.
And you shall sow your seed in vain,
for your enemies shall eat it.
17 I will set My face against you, and
you shall be defeated by your enemies.
Those who hate you shall reign over
you, and you shall flee when no
one pursues you.

18 'And after all this, if you do not obey
Me, then I will punish you seven
times more for your sins.
19 I will break the pride of your power;

I will make your heavens like iron
and your earth like bronze.
20 And your strength shall be spent in
vain;
for your land shall not yield its produce,
nor shall the trees of the
land yield their fruit.

21 'Then, if you walk contrary to Me,
and are not willing to obey Me,
I will bring on you seven times
more plagues, according to your
sins.
22 I will also send wild beasts among
you, which shall rob you of your
children, destroy your livestock,
and make you few in number;
and your highways shall be desolate.

23 'And if by these things you are not
reformed by Me, but walk contrary
to Me,
24 then I also will walk contrary to you,
and I will punish you yet seven
times for your sins.
25 And I will bring a sword against you
that will execute the vengeance
of the covenant;
when you are gathered together
within your cities I will send pestilence
among you;
and you shall be delivered into the
hand of the enemy.
26 When I have cut off your supply
of bread, ten women shall bake
your bread in one oven, and they
shall bring back your bread by
weight, and you shall eat and
not be satisfied.

27 'And after all this, if you do not obey
Me, but walk contrary to Me,
28 then I also will walk contrary to you
in fury;
and I, even I, will chastise you seven
times for your sins.
29 You shall eat the flesh of your sons,
and you shall eat the flesh of
your daughters.
30 I will destroy your high places, cut
down your incense altars, and
cast your carcasses on the lifeless
forms of your idols;
and My soul shall abhor you.
31 I will lay your cities waste and bring
your sanctuaries to desolation,
and I will not smell the fragrance
of your sweet aromas.
32 I will bring the land to desolation,
and your enemies who dwell in
it shall be astonished at it.
33 I will scatter you among the nations
and draw out a sword after you;
your land shall be desolate and
your cities waste.
34 Then the land shall enjoy its sabbaths
as long as it lies desolate
and you *are* in your enemies'
land;
then the land shall rest and enjoy
its sabbaths.
35 As long as *it* lies desolate it shall
rest—
for the time it did not rest on your
sabbaths when you dwelt in it.

36 'And as for those of you who are left, I
will send faintness into their hearts
in the lands of their enemies;
the sound of a shaken leaf shall
cause them to flee;
they shall flee as though fleeing
from a sword, and they shall fall
when no one pursues.
37 They shall stumble over one another,
as it were before a sword, when
no one pursues;
and you shall have no *power* to
stand before your enemies.
38 You shall perish among the nations,
and the land of your enemies
shall eat you up.
39 And those of you who are left shall
waste away in their iniquity in
your enemies' lands;
also in their fathers' iniquities,
which are with them, they shall
waste away.

40 '*But* if they confess their iniquity and
the iniquity of their fathers, with
their unfaithfulness in which
they were unfaithful to Me, and
that they also have walked contrary
to Me,
41 and *that* I also have walked contrary
to them and have brought them
into the land of their enemies;
if their uncircumcised hearts are humbled,
and they accept their guilt—

42 then I will remember My covenant
with Jacob, and My covenant
with Isaac and My covenant with
Abraham I will remember;
I will remember the land.
43 The land also shall be left empty by
them, and will enjoy its sabbaths
while it lies desolate without them;
they will accept their guilt, because
they despised My judgments and
because their soul abhorred My
statutes.
44 Yet for all that, when they are in
the land of their enemies, I will
not cast them away, nor shall I
abhor them, to utterly destroy
them and break My covenant
with them;
for I *am* the LORD their God.
45 But for their sake I will remember
the covenant of their ancestors,
whom I brought out of the land of
Egypt in the sight of the nations,
that I might be their God:
I *am* the LORD.' "

46These *are* the statutes and judg-
ments and laws which the LORD made
between Himself and the children of
Israel on Mount Sinai by the hand of
Moses.

Redeeming Persons and Property Dedicated to God

27 Now the LORD spoke to Moses,
saying, 2"Speak to the children
of Israel, and say to them: 'When a man
consecrates by a vow certain persons to
the LORD, according to your valuation,
3if your valuation is of a male from
twenty years old up to sixty years old,
then your valuation shall be fifty shek-
els of silver, according to the shekel of
the sanctuary. 4If it *is* a female, then
your valuation shall be thirty shekels;
5and if from five years old up to twenty
years old, then your valuation for a
male shall be twenty shekels, and for
a female ten shekels; 6and if from a
month old up to five years old, then
your valuation for a male shall be
five shekels of silver, and for a female
your valuation shall be three shekels
of silver; 7and if from sixty years old
and above, if *it is* a male, then your
valuation shall be fifteen shekels, and
for a female ten shekels.
8'But if he is too poor to pay your val-
uation, then he shall present himself
before the priest, and the priest shall
set a value for him; according to the
ability of him who vowed, the priest
shall value him.
9'If *it is* an animal that men may bring
as an offering to the LORD, all that *any-
one* gives to the LORD shall be holy. 10He
shall not substitute it or exchange it,
good for bad or bad for good; and if he
at all exchanges animal for animal,
then both it and the one exchanged
for it shall be holy. 11If *it is* an unclean
animal which they do not offer as a sac-
rifice to the LORD, then he shall present
the animal before the priest; 12and the
priest shall set a value for it, whether it
is good or bad; as you, the priest, value
it, so it shall be. 13But if he *wants* at all
to redeem it, then he must add one-fifth
to your valuation.
14'And when a man dedicates his house
to be holy to the LORD, then the priest
shall set a value for it, whether it is good
or bad; as the priest values it, so it shall
stand. 15If he who dedicated it *wants to*
redeem his house, then he must add
one-fifth of the money of your valuation
to it, and it shall be his.
16'If a man dedicates to the LORD *part*
of a field of his possession, then your
valuation shall be according to the seed
for it. A homer of barley seed *shall be
valued* at fifty shekels of silver. 17If he
dedicates his field from the Year of Jubi-
lee, according to your valuation it shall
stand. 18But if he dedicates his field after
the Jubilee, then the priest shall reckon
to him the money due according to the
years that remain till the Year of Jubi-
lee, and it shall be deducted from your
valuation. 19And if he who dedicates
the field ever wishes to redeem it, then
he must add one-fifth of the money of
your valuation to it, and it shall be-
long to him. 20But if he does not want
to redeem the field, or if he has sold
the field to another man, it shall not
be redeemed anymore; 21but the field,
when it is released in the Jubilee, shall
be holy to the LORD, as a devoted field;
it shall be the possession of the priest.

22'And if a man dedicates to the LORD
a field which he has bought, which is not
the field of his possession, 23then the
priest shall reckon to him the worth of
your valuation, up to the Year of Jubilee,
and he shall give your valuation on that
day *as* a holy *offering* to the LORD. 24In
the Year of Jubilee the field shall return
to him from whom it was bought, to the
one who *owned* the land as a possession.
25And all your valuations shall be ac-
cording to the shekel of the sanctuary:
twenty gerahs to the shekel.

26'But the firstborn of the animals,
which should be the LORD's firstborn,
no man shall dedicate; whether *it is*
an ox or sheep, it *is* the LORD's. 27And
if *it is* an unclean animal, then he shall
redeem *it* according to your valuation,
and shall add one-fifth to it; or if it is not
redeemed, then it shall be sold accord-
ing to your valuation.

28'Nevertheless no devoted *offering*
that a man may devote to the LORD of
all that he has, *both* man and beast, or
the field of his possession, shall be sold
or redeemed; every devoted *offering is*
most holy to the LORD. 29No person un-
der the ban, who may become doomed
to destruction among men, shall be
redeemed, *but* shall surely be put to
death. 30And all the tithe of the land,
whether of the seed of the land *or* of the
fruit of the tree, *is* the LORD's. It *is* holy
to the LORD. 31If a man wants at all to
redeem *any* of his tithes, he shall add
one-fifth to it. 32And concerning the
tithe of the herd or the flock, of whatev-
er passes under the rod, the tenth one
shall be holy to the LORD. 33He shall
not inquire whether it is good or bad,
nor shall he exchange it; and if he ex-
changes it at all, then both it and the
one exchanged for it shall be holy; it
shall not be redeemed.' "

34These *are* the commandments which
the LORD commanded Moses for the
children of Israel on Mount Sinai.

THE FOURTH BOOK OF MOSES CALLED

NUMBERS

The Book of Numbers continues the story of God's people heading toward the Promised Land after leaving Egypt. After leaving Mount Sinai, where God gave Moses the Law described in Exodus and Leviticus, the Hebrews reach the outskirts of the Promised Land. Moses then sends twelve spies into the land. The spies report that the land is wonderful, but ten of the spies are afraid of the strong people living there. Moses and two of the spies named Joshua and Caleb encourage the Hebrews to trust in God, but the people don't listen. Instead of entering the land, the people turn around and wander in the wilderness for forty years. Numbers ends with the next generation—children when the spies went into the land—grown up and heading back toward the land as Moses warns them to be faithful to God.

- **GENRE:** Law
- **AUTHOR:** Moses
- **TIME:** c. 1444–1406 BC (written: c. 1406 BC)
- **PURPOSE:** To continue the history of God's people and show how God takes sin seriously, but He still loves and cares for His people.

The First Census of Israel

1 Now the LORD spoke to Moses in
the Wilderness of Sinai, in the tab-
ernacle of meeting, on the first *day* of
the second month, in the second year
after they had come out of the land of
Egypt, saying: 2"Take a census of all the
congregation of the children of Israel,
by their families, by their fathers' hous-
es, according to the number of names,
every male individually, 3from twenty
years old and above—all who *are able
to* go to war in Israel. You and Aaron
shall number them by their armies.
4And with you there shall be a man
from every tribe, each one the head of
his father's house.
5"These are the names of the men who
shall stand with you: from Reuben, Eli-
zur the son of Shedeur; 6from Simeon,
Shelumiel the son of Zurishaddai; 7from
Judah, Nahshon the son of Ammina-
dab; 8from Issachar, Nethanel the son
of Zuar; 9from Zebulun, Eliab the son of
Helon; 10from the sons of Joseph: from
Ephraim, Elishama the son of Ammi-
hud; from Manasseh, Gamaliel the son
of Pedahzur; 11from Benjamin, Abidan
the son of Gideoni; 12from Dan, Ahiezer
the son of Ammishaddai; 13from Asher,
Pagiel the son of Ocran; 14from Gad, Eli-
asaph the son of Deuel;[a] 15from Naph-
tali, Ahira the son of Enan." 16These
were chosen from the congregation,
leaders of their fathers' tribes, heads
of the divisions in Israel.
17Then Moses and Aaron took these
men who had been mentioned by name,
18and they assembled all the congre-
gation together on the first *day* of the
second month; and they recited their
ancestry by families, by their fathers'
houses, according to the number of
names, from twenty years old and
above, each one individually. 19As the
LORD commanded Moses, so he num-
bered them in the Wilderness of Sinai.
20Now the children of Reuben, Israel's
oldest son, their genealogies by their
families, by their fathers' house, ac-
cording to the number of names, every
male individually, from twenty years
old and above, all who *were able to* go to
war: 21those who were numbered of the
tribe of Reuben *were* forty-six thousand
five hundred.
22From the children of Simeon, their
genealogies by their families, by their
fathers' house, of those who were num-
bered, according to the number of

1:14 [a] Spelled *Reuel* in 2:14

names, every male individually, from
twenty years old and above, all who
were able to go to war: 23those who were
numbered of the tribe of Simeon *were*
fifty-nine thousand three hundred.
24From the children of Gad, their ge-
nealogies by their families, by their
fathers' house, according to the num-
ber of names, from twenty years old
and above, all who *were able to* go to
war: 25those who were numbered of the
tribe of Gad *were* forty-five thousand
six hundred and fifty.
26From the children of Judah, their
genealogies by their families, by their
fathers' house, according to the number
of names, from twenty years old and
above, all who *were able to* go to war:
27those who were numbered of the tribe
of Judah *were* seventy-four thousand
six hundred.
28From the children of Issachar, their
genealogies by their families, by their
fathers' house, according to the number
of names, from twenty years old and
above, all who *were able to* go to war:
29those who were numbered of the tribe
of Issachar *were* fifty-four thousand
four hundred.
30From the children of Zebulun, their
genealogies by their families, by their
fathers' house, according to the number
of names, from twenty years old and
above, all who *were able to* go to war:
31those who were numbered of the tribe
of Zebulun *were* fifty-seven thousand
four hundred.
32From the sons of Joseph, the chil-
dren of Ephraim, their genealogies by
their families, by their fathers' house,
according to the number of names,
from twenty years old and above, all
who *were able to* go to war: 33those who
were numbered of the tribe of Ephraim
were forty thousand five hundred.
34From the children of Manasseh, their
genealogies by their families, by their
fathers' house, according to the number
of names, from twenty years old and
above, all who *were able to* go to war:
35those who were numbered of the tribe
of Manasseh *were* thirty-two thousand
two hundred.
36From the children of Benjamin, their
genealogies by their families, by their
fathers' house, according to the number
of names, from twenty years old and
above, all who *were able to* go to war:
37those who were numbered of the tribe
of Benjamin *were* thirty-five thousand
four hundred.
38From the children of Dan, their ge-
nealogies by their families, by their
fathers' house, according to the number
of names, from twenty years old and
above, all who *were able to* go to war:
39those who were numbered of the tribe
of Dan *were* sixty-two thousand seven
hundred.
40From the children of Asher, their
genealogies by their families, by their
fathers' house, according to the number
of names, from twenty years old and
above, all who *were able to* go to war:
41those who were numbered of the tribe
of Asher *were* forty-one thousand five
hundred.
42From the children of Naphtali, their
genealogies by their families, by their
fathers' house, according to the number
of names, from twenty years old and
above, all who *were able to* go to war:
43those who were numbered of the tribe
of Naphtali *were* fifty-three thousand
four hundred.
44These are the ones who were num-
bered, whom Moses and Aaron num-
bered, with the leaders of Israel, twelve
men, each one representing his father's
house. 45So all who were numbered of
the children of Israel, by their fathers'
houses, from twenty years old and
above, all who *were able to* go to war
in Israel— 46all who were numbered
were six hundred and three thousand
five hundred and fifty.
47But the Levites were not numbered
among them by their fathers' tribe;
48for the LORD had spoken to Moses,
saying: 49"Only the tribe of Levi you
shall not number, nor take a census
of them among the children of Israel;
50but you shall appoint the Levites over
the tabernacle of the Testimony, over
all its furnishings, and over all things
that belong to it; they shall carry the
tabernacle and all its furnishings; they
shall attend to it and camp around the
tabernacle. 51And when the tabernacle
is to go forward, the Levites shall take

it down; and when the tabernacle is to
be set up, the Levites shall set it up. The
outsider who comes near shall be put
to death. 52The children of Israel shall
pitch their tents, everyone by his own
camp, everyone by his own standard,
according to their armies; 53but the Le-
vites shall camp around the tabernacle
of the Testimony, that there may be
no wrath on the congregation of the
children of Israel; and the Levites shall
keep charge of the tabernacle of the
Testimony."

54Thus the children of Israel did; ac-
cording to all that the LORD command-
ed Moses, so they did.

The Tribes and Leaders by Armies

2 And the LORD spoke to Moses and
Aaron, saying: 2"Everyone of the
children of Israel shall camp by his own
standard, beside the emblems of his fa-
ther's house; they shall camp some dis-
tance from the tabernacle of meeting.
3On the east side, toward the rising of the
sun, those of the standard of the forces
with Judah shall camp according to their
armies; and Nahshon the son of Ammin-
adab *shall be* the leader of the children
of Judah." 4And his army was numbered
at seventy-four thousand six hundred.

5"Those who camp next to him *shall
be* the tribe of Issachar, and Nethanel
the son of Zuar *shall be* the leader of the
children of Issachar." 6And his army
was numbered at fifty-four thousand
four hundred.

7"Then *comes* the tribe of Zebulun,
and Eliab the son of Helon *shall be* the
leader of the children of Zebulun." 8And
his army was numbered at fifty-seven
thousand four hundred. 9"All who were
numbered according to their armies of
the forces with Judah, one hundred and
eighty-six thousand four hundred—
these shall break camp first.

10"On the south side *shall be* the stan-
dard of the forces with Reuben accord-
ing to their armies, and the leader of
the children of Reuben *shall be* Elizur
the son of Shedeur." 11And his army
was numbered at forty-six thousand
five hundred.

12"Those who camp next to him *shall
be* the tribe of Simeon, and the leader
of the children of Simeon *shall be* She-
lumiel the son of Zurishaddai." 13And
his army was numbered at fifty-nine
thousand three hundred.

14"Then *comes* the tribe of Gad, and
the leader of the children of Gad *shall
be* Eliasaph the son of Reuel."[a] 15And
his army was numbered at forty-five
thousand six hundred and fifty. 16"All
who were numbered according to their
armies of the forces with Reuben, one
hundred and fifty-one thousand four
hundred and fifty—they shall be the
second to break camp.

17"And the tabernacle of meeting shall
move out with the camp of the Levites in
the middle of the camps; as they camp,
so they shall move out, everyone in his
place, by their standards.

18"On the west side *shall be* the standard
of the forces with Ephraim according to
their armies, and the leader of the chil-
dren of Ephraim *shall be* Elishama the son
of Ammihud." 19And his army was num-
bered at forty thousand five hundred.

20"Next to him *comes* the tribe of Ma-
nasseh, and the leader of the children
of Manasseh *shall be* Gamaliel the
son of Pedahzur." 21And his army was
numbered at thirty-two thousand two
hundred.

22"Then *comes* the tribe of Benjamin,
and the leader of the children of Ben-
jamin *shall be* Abidan the son of Gid-
eoni." 23And his army was numbered
at thirty-five thousand four hundred.
24"All who were numbered according to
their armies of the forces with Ephra-
im, one hundred and eight thousand
one hundred—they shall be the third
to break camp.

25"The standard of the forces with Dan
shall be on the north side according
to their armies, and the leader of the
children of Dan *shall be* Ahiezer the son
of Ammishaddai." 26And his army was
numbered at sixty-two thousand seven
hundred.

27"Those who camp next to him *shall be*
the tribe of Asher, and the leader of the
children of Asher *shall be* Pagiel the son

2:14 [a] Spelled *Deuel* in 1:14 and 7:42

of Ocran." 28And his army was numbered
at forty-one thousand five hundred.
29"Then *comes* the tribe of Naphtali,
and the leader of the children of Naph-
tali *shall be* Ahira the son of Enan."
30And his army was numbered at fifty-
three thousand four hundred. 31"All who
were numbered of the forces with Dan,
one hundred and fifty-seven thousand
six hundred—they shall break camp
last, with their standards."
32These *are* the ones who were num-
bered of the children of Israel by their
fathers' houses. All who were numbered
according to their armies of the forces
were six hundred and three thousand five
hundred and fifty. 33But the Levites were
not numbered among the children of Is-
rael, just as the LORD commanded Moses.
34Thus the children of Israel did ac-
cording to all that the LORD commanded
Moses; so they camped by their stan-
dards and so they broke camp, each
one by his family, according to their
fathers' houses.

The Sons of Aaron

3 Now these *are* the records of Aaron
and Moses when the LORD spoke
with Moses on Mount Sinai. 2And these
are the names of the sons of Aaron:
Nadab, the firstborn, and Abihu, El-
eazar, and Ithamar. 3These *are* the
names of the sons of Aaron, the anoint-
ed priests, whom he consecrated to
minister as priests. 4Nadab and Abihu
had died before the LORD when they
offered profane fire before the LORD in
the Wilderness of Sinai; and they had
no children. So Eleazar and Ithamar
ministered as priests in the presence
of Aaron their father.

The Levites Serve in the Tabernacle

5And the LORD spoke to Moses, say-
ing: 6"Bring the tribe of Levi near, and
present them before Aaron the priest,
that they may serve him. 7And they
shall attend to his needs and the needs
of the whole congregation before the
tabernacle of meeting, to do the work of
the tabernacle. 8Also they shall attend
to all the furnishings of the tabernacle of
meeting, and to the needs of the children
of Israel, to do the work of the taberna-
cle. 9And you shall give the Levites to
Aaron and his sons; they *are* given en-
tirely to him[a] from among the children
of Israel. 10So you shall appoint Aaron
and his sons, and they shall attend to
their priesthood; but the outsider who
comes near shall be put to death."
11Then the LORD spoke to Moses, say-
ing: 12"Now behold, I Myself have taken
the Levites from among the children of
Israel instead of every firstborn who
opens the womb among the children
of Israel. Therefore the Levites shall
be Mine, 13because all the firstborn *are*
Mine. On the day that I struck all the
firstborn in the land of Egypt, I sancti-
fied to Myself all the firstborn in Israel,
both man and beast. They shall be Mine:
I *am* the LORD."

Census of the Levites Commanded

14Then the LORD spoke to Moses in the
Wilderness of Sinai, saying: 15"Number
the children of Levi by their fathers'
houses, by their families; you shall
number every male from a month old
and above."
16So Moses numbered them accord-
ing to the word of the LORD, as he was
commanded. 17These were the sons of
Levi by their names: Gershon, Kohath,
and Merari. 18And these *are* the names
of the sons of Gershon by their fami-
lies: Libni and Shimei. 19And the sons
of Kohath by their families: Amram,
Izehar, Hebron, and Uzziel. 20And the
sons of Merari by their families: Mahli
and Mushi. These *are* the families of the
Levites by their fathers' houses.
21From Gershon *came* the family of the
Libnites and the family of the Shimites;
these *were* the families of the Gershon-
ites. 22Those who were numbered, ac-
cording to the number of all the males
from a month old and above—of those
who were numbered *there were* seven
thousand five hundred. 23The families of
the Gershonites were to camp behind the
tabernacle westward. 24And the leader
of the father's house of the Gershon-
ites *was* Eliasaph the son of Lael. 25The

3:9 [a] Samaritan Pentateuch and Septuagint read *Me.*

duties of the children of Gershon in the tabernacle of meeting *included* the tabernacle, the tent with its covering, the screen for the door of the tabernacle of meeting, 26the screen for the door of the court, the hangings of the court which *are* around the tabernacle and the altar, and their cords, according to all the work relating to them.

27From Kohath *came* the family of the Amramites, the family of the Izharites, the family of the Hebronites, and the family of the Uzzielites; these *were* the families of the Kohathites. 28According to the number of all the males, from a month old and above, *there were* eight thousand six[a] hundred keeping charge of the sanctuary. 29The families of the children of Kohath were to camp on the south side of the tabernacle. 30And the leader of the fathers' house of the families of the Kohathites *was* Elizaphan the son of Uzziel. 31Their duty *included* the ark, the table, the lampstand, the altars, the utensils of the sanctuary with which they ministered, the screen, and all the work relating to them.

32And Eleazar the son of Aaron the priest *was to be* chief over the leaders of the Levites, *with* oversight of those who kept charge of the sanctuary.

33From Merari *came* the family of the Mahlites and the family of the Mushites; these *were* the families of Merari. 34And those who were numbered, according to the number of all the males from a month old and above, *were* six thousand two hundred. 35The leader of the fathers' house of the families of Merari *was* Zuriel the son of Abihail. These *were* to camp on the north side of the tabernacle. 36And the appointed duty of the children of Merari *included* the boards of the tabernacle, its bars, its pillars, its sockets, its utensils, all the work relating to them, 37and the pillars of the court all around, with their sockets, their pegs, and their cords.

38Moreover those who were to camp before the tabernacle on the east, before the tabernacle of meeting, *were* Moses, Aaron, and his sons, keeping charge of the sanctuary, to meet the needs of the children of Israel; but the outsider who came near was to be put to death. 39All who were numbered of the Levites, whom Moses and Aaron numbered at the commandment of the LORD, by their families, all the males from a month old and above, *were* twenty-two thousand.

Levites Dedicated Instead of the Firstborn

40Then the LORD said to Moses: "Number all the firstborn males of the children of Israel from a month old and above, and take the number of their names. 41And you shall take the Levites for Me—I *am* the LORD—instead of all the firstborn among the children of Israel, and the livestock of the Levites instead of all the firstborn among the livestock of the children of Israel." 42So Moses numbered all the firstborn among the children of Israel, as the LORD commanded him. 43And all the firstborn males, according to the number of names from a month old and above, of those who were numbered of them, were twenty-two thousand two hundred and seventy-three.

44Then the LORD spoke to Moses, saying: 45"Take the Levites instead of all the firstborn among the children of Israel, and the livestock of the Levites instead of their livestock. The Levites shall be Mine: I *am* the LORD. 46And for the redemption of the two hundred and seventy-three of the firstborn of the children of Israel, who are more than the number of the Levites, 47you shall take five shekels for each one individually; you shall take *them* in the currency of the shekel of the sanctuary, the shekel of twenty gerahs. 48And you shall give the money, with which the excess number of them is redeemed, to Aaron and his sons."

49So Moses took the redemption money from those who were over and above those who were redeemed by the Levites. 50From the firstborn of the children of Israel he took the money, one thousand three hundred and sixty-five *shekels*, according to the shekel of the sanctuary. 51And Moses gave their redemption money to Aaron and his sons, according to the word of the LORD, as the LORD commanded Moses.

3:28 [a] Some manuscripts of the Septuagint read *three*.

GOD SIN JESUS SALVATION LOVE

Duties of the Sons of Kohath

4 Then the LORD spoke to Moses and Aaron, saying: 2“Take a census of the sons of Kohath from among the children of Levi, by their families, by their fathers' house, 3from thirty years old and above, even to fifty years old, all who enter the service to do the work in the tabernacle of meeting.

4“This *is* the service of the sons of Kohath in the tabernacle of meeting, *relating to* the most holy things: 5When the camp prepares to journey, Aaron and his sons shall come, and they shall take down the covering veil and cover the ark of the Testimony with it. 6Then they shall put on it a covering of badger skins, and spread over *that* a cloth entirely of blue; and they shall insert its poles.

7“On the table of showbread they shall spread a blue cloth, and put on it the dishes, the pans, the bowls, and the pitchers for pouring; and the showbread[a] shall be on it. 8They shall spread over them a scarlet cloth, and cover the same with a covering of badger skins; and they shall insert its poles. 9And they shall take a blue cloth and cover the lampstand of the light, with its lamps, its wick-trimmers, its trays, and all its oil vessels, with which they service it. 10Then they shall put it with all its utensils in a covering of badger skins, and put *it* on a carrying beam.

11“Over the golden altar they shall spread a blue cloth, and cover it with a covering of badger skins; and they shall insert its poles. 12Then they shall take all the utensils of service with which they minister in the sanctuary, put *them* in a blue cloth, cover them with a covering of badger skins, and put *them* on a carrying beam. 13Also they shall take away the ashes from the altar, and spread a purple cloth over it. 14They shall put on it all its implements with which they minister there—the firepans, the forks, the shovels, the basins, and all the utensils of the altar—and they shall spread on it a covering of badger skins, and insert its poles. 15And when Aaron and his sons have finished covering the sanctuary and all the furnishings of the sanctuary, when the camp is set to go, then the sons of Kohath shall come to carry *them;* but they shall not touch any holy thing, lest they die.

“These *are* the things in the tabernacle of meeting which the sons of Kohath are to carry.

16“The appointed duty of Eleazar the son of Aaron the priest *is* the oil for the light, the sweet incense, the daily grain offering, the anointing oil, the oversight of all the tabernacle, of all that *is* in it, with the sanctuary and its furnishings.”

17Then the LORD spoke to Moses and Aaron, saying: 18“Do not cut off the tribe of the families of the Kohathites from among the Levites; 19but do this in regard to them, that they may live and not die when they approach the most holy things: Aaron and his sons shall go in and appoint each of them to his service and his task. 20But they shall not go in to watch while the holy things are being covered, lest they die.”

Duties of the Sons of Gershon

21Then the LORD spoke to Moses, saying: 22“Also take a census of the sons of Gershon, by their fathers' house, by their families. 23From thirty years old and above, even to fifty years old, you shall number them, all who enter to perform the service, to do the work in the tabernacle of meeting. 24This *is* the service of the families of the Gershonites, in serving and carrying: 25They shall carry the curtains of the tabernacle and the tabernacle of meeting *with* its covering, the covering of badger skins that *is* on it, the screen for the door of the tabernacle of meeting, 26the screen for the door of the gate of the court, the hangings of the court which *are* around the tabernacle and altar, and their cords, all the furnishings for their service and all that is made for these things: so shall they serve.

27“Aaron and his sons shall assign all the service of the sons of the Gershonites, all their tasks and all their service. And you shall appoint to them all their tasks as their duty. 28This *is* the service of the families of the sons of Gershon

4:7 [a] Literally *the continual bread*

in the tabernacle of meeting. And their duties *shall be* under the authority[a] of Ithamar the son of Aaron the priest.

Duties of the Sons of Merari

29"*As for* the sons of Merari, you shall number them by their families and by their fathers' house. 30From thirty years old and above, even to fifty years old, you shall number them, everyone who enters the service to do the work of the tabernacle of meeting. 31And this *is* what they must carry as all their service for the tabernacle of meeting: the boards of the tabernacle, its bars, its pillars, its sockets, 32and the pillars around the court with their sockets, pegs, and cords, with all their furnishings and all their service; and you shall assign *to each man* by name the items he must carry. 33This *is* the service of the families of the sons of Merari, as all their service for the tabernacle of meeting, under the authority[a] of Ithamar the son of Aaron the priest."

Census of the Levites

34And Moses, Aaron, and the leaders of the congregation numbered the sons of the Kohathites by their families and by their fathers' house, 35from thirty years old and above, even to fifty years old, everyone who entered the service for work in the tabernacle of meeting; 36and those who were numbered by their families were two thousand seven hundred and fifty. 37These *were* the ones who were numbered of the families of the Kohathites, all who might serve in the tabernacle of meeting, whom Moses and Aaron numbered according to the commandment of the LORD by the hand of Moses.

38And those who were numbered of the sons of Gershon, by their families and by their fathers' house, 39from thirty years old and above, even to fifty years old, everyone who entered the service for work in the tabernacle of meeting— 40those who were numbered by their families, by their fathers' house, were two thousand six hundred and thirty. 41These *are* the ones who were numbered of the families of the sons of Gershon, of all who might serve in the tabernacle of meeting, whom Moses and Aaron numbered according to the commandment of the LORD.

42Those of the families of the sons of Merari who were numbered, by their families, by their fathers' house, 43from thirty years old and above, even to fifty years old, everyone who entered the service for work in the tabernacle of meeting— 44those who were numbered by their families were three thousand two hundred. 45These *are* the ones who were numbered of the families of the sons of Merari, whom Moses and Aaron numbered according to the word of the LORD by the hand of Moses.

46All who were numbered of the Levites, whom Moses, Aaron, and the leaders of Israel numbered, by their families and by their fathers' houses, 47from thirty years old and above, even to fifty years old, everyone who came to do the work of service and the work of bearing burdens in the tabernacle of meeting— 48those who were numbered were eight thousand five hundred and eighty.

49According to the commandment of the LORD they were numbered by the hand of Moses, each according to his service and according to his task; thus were they numbered by him, as the LORD commanded Moses.

Ceremonially Unclean Persons Isolated

5 And the LORD spoke to Moses, saying: 2"Command the children of Israel that they put out of the camp every leper, everyone who has a discharge, and whoever becomes defiled by a corpse. 3You shall put out both male and female; you shall put them outside the camp, that they may not defile their camps in the midst of which I dwell." 4And the children of Israel did so, and put them outside the camp; as the LORD spoke to Moses, so the children of Israel did.

Confession and Restitution

5Then the LORD spoke to Moses, saying, 6"Speak to the children of Israel:

4:28 [a] Literally *hand* 4:33 [a] Literally *hand*

'When a man or woman commits any sin that men commit in unfaithfulness against the LORD, and that person is guilty, 7then he shall confess the sin which he has committed. He shall make restitution for his trespass in full, plus one-fifth of it, and give *it* to the one he has wronged. 8But if the man has no relative to whom restitution may be made for the wrong, the restitution for the wrong *must go* to the LORD for the priest, in addition to the ram of the atonement with which atonement is made for him. 9Every offering of all the holy things of the children of Israel, which they bring to the priest, shall be his. 10And every man's holy things shall be his; whatever any man gives the priest shall be his.' "

Concerning Unfaithful Wives

11And the LORD spoke to Moses, saying, 12"Speak to the children of Israel, and say to them: 'If any man's wife goes astray and behaves unfaithfully toward him, 13and a man lies with her carnally, and it is hidden from the eyes of her husband, and it is concealed that she has defiled herself, and *there was* no witness against her, nor was she caught— 14if the spirit of jealousy comes upon him and he becomes jealous of his wife, who has defiled herself; or if the spirit of jealousy comes upon him and he becomes jealous of his wife, although she has not defiled herself— 15then the man shall bring his wife to the priest. He shall bring the offering required for her, one-tenth of an ephah of barley meal; he shall pour no oil on it and put no frankincense on it, because it *is* a grain offering of jealousy, an offering for remembering, for bringing iniquity to remembrance.

16'And the priest shall bring her near, and set her before the LORD. 17The priest shall take holy water in an earthen vessel, and take some of the dust that is on the floor of the tabernacle and put *it* into the water. 18Then the priest shall stand the woman before the LORD, uncover the woman's head, and put the offering for remembering in her hands, which *is* the grain offering of jealousy. And the priest shall have in his hand the bitter water that brings a curse. 19And the priest shall put her under oath, and say to the woman, "If no man has lain with you, and if you have not gone astray to uncleanness *while* under your husband's *authority,* be free from this bitter water that brings a curse. 20But if you have gone astray *while* under your husband's *authority,* and if you have defiled yourself and some man other than your husband has lain with you"— 21then the priest shall put the woman under the oath of the curse, and he shall say to the woman—"the LORD make you a curse and an oath among your people, when the LORD makes your thigh rot and your belly swell; 22and may this water that causes the curse go into your stomach, and make *your* belly swell and *your* thigh rot."

'Then the woman shall say, "Amen, so be it."

23'Then the priest shall write these curses in a book, and he shall scrape *them* off into the bitter water. 24And he shall make the woman drink the bitter water that brings a curse, and the water that brings the curse shall enter her *to become* bitter. 25Then the priest shall take the grain offering of jealousy from the woman's hand, shall wave the offering before the LORD, and bring it to the altar; 26and the priest shall take a handful of the offering, as its memorial portion, burn *it* on the altar, and afterward make the woman drink the water. 27When he has made her drink the water, then it shall be, if she has defiled herself and behaved unfaithfully toward her husband, that the water that brings a curse will enter her *and become* bitter, and her belly will swell, her thigh will rot, and the woman will become a curse among her people. 28But if the woman has not defiled herself, and is clean, then she shall be free and may conceive children.

29'This *is* the law of jealousy, when a wife, *while* under her husband's *authority,* goes astray and defiles herself, 30or when the spirit of jealousy comes upon a man, and he becomes jealous of his wife; then he shall stand the woman before the LORD, and the priest shall execute all this law upon her. 31Then the man shall be free from iniquity, but that woman shall bear her guilt.' "

The Law of the Nazirite

6 Then the LORD spoke to Moses,
saying, 2"Speak to the children of
Israel, and say to them: 'When either a
man or woman consecrates an offering
to take the vow of a Nazirite, to separate
himself to the LORD, 3he shall separate
himself from wine and *similar* drink; he
shall drink neither vinegar made from
wine nor vinegar made from *similar*
drink; neither shall he drink any grape
juice, nor eat fresh grapes or raisins.
4All the days of his separation he shall
eat nothing that is produced by the
grapevine, from seed to skin.

5'All the days of the vow of his separa-
tion no razor shall come upon his head;
until the days are fulfilled for which he
separated himself to the LORD, he shall
be holy. *Then* he shall let the locks of
the hair of his head grow. 6All the days
that he separates himself to the LORD
he shall not go near a dead body. 7He
shall not make himself unclean even for
his father or his mother, for his brother
or his sister, when they die, because his
separation to God *is* on his head. 8All
the days of his separation he shall be
holy to the LORD.

9'And if anyone dies very suddenly be-
side him, and he defiles his consecrated
head, then he shall shave his head on the
day of his cleansing; on the seventh day
he shall shave it. 10Then on the eighth
day he shall bring two turtledoves or
two young pigeons to the priest, to the
door of the tabernacle of meeting; 11and
the priest shall offer one as a sin offer-
ing and *the* other as a burnt offering,
and make atonement for him, because
he sinned in regard to the corpse; and
he shall sanctify his head that same
day. 12He shall consecrate to the LORD
the days of his separation, and bring a
male lamb in its first year as a trespass
offering; but the former days shall be
lost, because his separation was defiled.

13'Now this *is* the law of the Nazirite:
When the days of his separation are
fulfilled, he shall be brought to the door
of the tabernacle of meeting. 14And he
shall present his offering to the LORD:
one male lamb in its first year without
blemish as a burnt offering, one ewe
lamb in its first year without blemish as
a sin offering, one ram without blem-
ish as a peace offering, 15a basket of
unleavened bread, cakes of fine flour
mixed with oil, unleavened wafers
anointed with oil, and their grain of-
fering with their drink offerings.

16'Then the priest shall bring *them* be-
fore the LORD and offer his sin offering
and his burnt offering; 17and he shall
offer the ram as a sacrifice of a peace
offering to the LORD, with the basket of
unleavened bread; the priest shall also
offer its grain offering and its drink
offering. 18Then the Nazirite shall shave
his consecrated head *at* the door of the
tabernacle of meeting, and shall take
the hair from his consecrated head and
put *it* on the fire which is under the sac-
rifice of the peace offering.

19'And the priest shall take the boiled
shoulder of the ram, one unleavened
cake from the basket, and one un-
leavened wafer, and put *them* upon
the hands of the Nazirite after he has
shaved his consecrated *hair,* 20and the
priest shall wave them as a wave offer-
ing before the LORD; they *are* holy for
the priest, together with the breast of
the wave offering and the thigh of the
heave offering. After that the Nazirite
may drink wine.'

21"This is the law of the Nazirite who
vows to the LORD the offering for his
separation, and besides that, what-
ever else his hand is able to provide;
according to the vow which he takes,
so he must do according to the law of
his separation."

The Priestly Blessing

22And the LORD spoke to Moses, say-
ing: 23"Speak to Aaron and his sons,
saying, 'This is the way you shall bless
the children of Israel. Say to them:

24 "The LORD bless you and keep you;
25 The LORD make His face shine
upon you,
And be gracious to you;
26 The LORD lift up His countenance
upon you,
And give you peace." '

27"So they shall put My name on the
children of Israel, and I will bless them."

Offerings of the Leaders

7 Now it came to pass, when Moses had finished setting up the tabernacle, that he anointed it and consecrated it and all its furnishings, and the altar and all its utensils; so he anointed them and consecrated them. 2Then the leaders of Israel, the heads of their fathers' houses, who *were* the leaders of the tribes and over those who were numbered, made an offering. 3And they brought their offering before the LORD, six covered carts and twelve oxen, a cart for *every* two of the leaders, and for each one an ox; and they presented them before the tabernacle.

4Then the LORD spoke to Moses, saying, 5"Accept *these* from them, that they may be used in doing the work of the tabernacle of meeting; and you shall give them to the Levites, *to* every man according to his service." 6So Moses took the carts and the oxen, and gave them to the Levites. 7Two carts and four oxen he gave to the sons of Gershon, according to their service; 8and four carts and eight oxen he gave to the sons of Merari, according to their service, under the authority[a] of Ithamar the son of Aaron the priest. 9But to the sons of Kohath he gave none, because theirs *was* the service of the holy things, *which* they carried on their shoulders.

10Now the leaders offered the dedication *offering* for the altar when it was anointed; so the leaders offered their offering before the altar. 11For the LORD said to Moses, "They shall offer their offering, one leader each day, for the dedication of the altar."

12And the one who offered his offering on the first day *was* Nahshon the son of Amminadab, from the tribe of Judah. 13His offering *was* one silver platter, the weight of which *was* one hundred and thirty *shekels,* and one silver bowl of seventy shekels, according to the shekel of the sanctuary, both of them full of fine flour mixed with oil as a grain offering; 14one gold pan of ten *shekels,* full of incense; 15one young bull, one ram, and one male lamb in its first year, as a burnt offering; 16one kid of the goats as a sin offering; 17and for the sacrifice of peace offerings: two oxen, five rams, five male goats, and five male lambs in their first year. This *was* the offering of Nahshon the son of Amminadab.

18On the second day Nethanel the son of Zuar, leader of Issachar, presented *an offering.* 19*For* his offering he offered one silver platter, the weight of which *was* one hundred and thirty *shekels,* and one silver bowl of seventy shekels, according to the shekel of the sanctuary, both of them full of fine flour mixed with oil as a grain offering; 20one gold pan of ten *shekels,* full of incense; 21one young bull, one ram, and one male lamb in its first year, as a burnt offering; 22one kid of the goats as a sin offering; 23and as the sacrifice of peace offerings: two oxen, five rams, five male goats, and five male lambs in their first year. This *was* the offering of Nethanel the son of Zuar.

24On the third day Eliab the son of Helon, leader of the children of Zebulun, *presented an offering.* 25His offering *was* one silver platter, the weight of which *was* one hundred and thirty *shekels,* and one silver bowl of seventy shekels, according to the shekel of the sanctuary, both of them full of fine flour mixed with oil as a grain offering; 26one gold pan of ten *shekels,* full of incense; 27one young bull, one ram, and one male lamb in its first year, as a burnt offering; 28one kid of the goats as a sin offering; 29and for the sacrifice of peace offerings: two oxen, five rams, five male goats, and five male lambs in their first year. This *was* the offering of Eliab the son of Helon.

30On the fourth day Elizur the son of Shedeur, leader of the children of Reuben, *presented an offering.* 31His offering *was* one silver platter, the weight of which *was* one hundred and thirty *shekels,* and one silver bowl of seventy shekels, according to the shekel of the sanctuary, both of them full of fine flour mixed with oil as a grain offering; 32one gold pan of ten *shekels,* full of incense; 33one young bull, one ram, and one male lamb in its first year, as a burnt offering; 34one kid of the goats as a sin offering; 35and as the sacrifice of peace

7:8 [a] Literally *hand*

offerings: two oxen, five rams, five male
goats, and five male lambs in their first
year. This *was* the offering of Elizur the
son of Shedeur.
36On the fifth day Shelumiel the son
of Zurishaddai, leader of the children of
Simeon, *presented an offering.* 37His of-
fering *was* one silver platter, the weight
of which *was* one hundred and thirty
shekels, and one silver bowl of seventy
shekels, according to the shekel of the
sanctuary, both of them full of fine flour
mixed with oil as a grain offering; 38one
gold pan of ten *shekels,* full of incense;
39one young bull, one ram, and one male
lamb in its first year, as a burnt offering;
40one kid of the goats as a sin offer-
ing; 41and as the sacrifice of peace
offerings: two oxen, five rams, five male
goats, and five male lambs in their first
year. This *was* the offering of Shelumiel
the son of Zurishaddai.
42On the sixth day Eliasaph the son
of Deuel,[a] leader of the children of Gad,
presented an offering. 43His offering *was*
one silver platter, the weight of which
was one hundred and thirty *shekels,* and
one silver bowl of seventy shekels, ac-
cording to the shekel of the sanctuary,
both of them full of fine flour mixed with
oil as a grain offering; 44one gold pan of
ten *shekels,* full of incense; 45one young
bull, one ram, and one male lamb in
its first year, as a burnt offering; 46one
kid of the goats as a sin offering; 47and
as the sacrifice of peace offerings: two
oxen, five rams, five male goats, and
five male lambs in their first year. This
was the offering of Eliasaph the son
of Deuel.
48On the seventh day Elishama the
son of Ammihud, leader of the chil-
dren of Ephraim, *presented an offering.*
49His offering *was* one silver platter, the
weight of which *was* one hundred and
thirty *shekels,* and one silver bowl of
seventy shekels, according to the shekel
of the sanctuary, both of them full of
fine flour mixed with oil as a grain of-
fering; 50one gold pan of ten *shekels,* full
of incense; 51one young bull, one ram,
and one male lamb in its first year, as
a burnt offering; 52one kid of the goats
as a sin offering; 53and as the sacrifice
of peace offerings: two oxen, five rams,
five male goats, and five male lambs in
their first year. This *was* the offering of
Elishama the son of Ammihud.
54On the eighth day Gamaliel the son
of Pedahzur, leader of the children of
Manasseh, *presented an offering.* 55His
offering *was* one silver platter, the
weight of which *was* one hundred and
thirty *shekels,* and one silver bowl of
seventy shekels, according to the shekel
of the sanctuary, both of them full of
fine flour mixed with oil as a grain of-
fering; 56one gold pan of ten *shekels,* full
of incense; 57one young bull, one ram,
and one male lamb in its first year, as
a burnt offering; 58one kid of the goats
as a sin offering; 59and as the sacrifice
of peace offerings: two oxen, five rams,
five male goats, and five male lambs in
their first year. This *was* the offering of
Gamaliel the son of Pedahzur.
60On the ninth day Abidan the son of
Gideoni, leader of the children of Ben-
jamin, *presented an offering.* 61His of-
fering *was* one silver platter, the weight
of which *was* one hundred and thirty
shekels, and one silver bowl of seventy
shekels, according to the shekel of the
sanctuary, both of them full of fine flour
mixed with oil as a grain offering; 62one
gold pan of ten *shekels,* full of incense;
63one young bull, one ram, and one
male lamb in its first year, as a burnt
offering; 64one kid of the goats as a sin
offering; 65and as the sacrifice of peace
offerings: two oxen, five rams, five male
goats, and five male lambs in their first
year. This *was* the offering of Abidan the
son of Gideoni.
66On the tenth day Ahiezer the son of
Ammishaddai, leader of the children of
Dan, *presented an offering.* 67His offering
was one silver platter, the weight of which
was one hundred and thirty *shekels,* and
one silver bowl of seventy shekels, ac-
cording to the shekel of the sanctuary,
both of them full of fine flour mixed with
oil as a grain offering; 68one gold pan of
ten *shekels,* full of incense; 69one young
bull, one ram, and one male lamb in
its first year, as a burnt offering; 70one

7:42 [a] Spelled *Reuel* in 2:14

kid of the goats as a sin offering; 71and
as the sacrifice of peace offerings: two
oxen, five rams, five male goats, and
five male lambs in their first year. This
was the offering of Ahiezer the son of
Ammishaddai.
72On the eleventh day Pagiel the son of
Ocran, leader of the children of Asher,
presented an offering. 73His offering *was*
one silver platter, the weight of which
was one hundred and thirty *shekels,* and
one silver bowl of seventy shekels, ac-
cording to the shekel of the sanctuary,
both of them full of fine flour mixed with
oil as a grain offering; 74one gold pan of
ten *shekels,* full of incense; 75one young
bull, one ram, and one male lamb in
its first year, as a burnt offering; 76one
kid of the goats as a sin offering; 77and
as the sacrifice of peace offerings: two
oxen, five rams, five male goats, and five
male lambs in their first year. This *was*
the offering of Pagiel the son of Ocran.
78On the twelfth day Ahira the son of
Enan, leader of the children of Naphtali,
presented an offering. 79His offering *was*
one silver platter, the weight of which
was one hundred and thirty *shekels,* and
one silver bowl of seventy shekels, ac-
cording to the shekel of the sanctuary,
both of them full of fine flour mixed with
oil as a grain offering; 80one gold pan of
ten *shekels,* full of incense; 81one young
bull, one ram, and one male lamb in
its first year, as a burnt offering; 82one
kid of the goats as a sin offering; 83and
as the sacrifice of peace offerings: two
oxen, five rams, five male goats, and five
male lambs in their first year. This *was*
the offering of Ahira the son of Enan.
84This *was* the dedication *offering*
for the altar from the leaders of Isra-
el, when it was anointed: twelve silver
platters, twelve silver bowls, and twelve
gold pans. 85Each silver platter *weighed*
one hundred and thirty *shekels* and each
bowl seventy *shekels.* All the silver of
the vessels *weighed* two thousand four
hundred *shekels,* according to the shek-
el of the sanctuary. 86The twelve gold
pans full of incense *weighed* ten *shek-
els* apiece, according to the shekel of
the sanctuary; all the gold of the pans
weighed one hundred and twenty *shek-
els.* 87All the oxen for the burnt offering
were twelve young bulls, the rams
twelve, the male lambs in their first year
twelve, with their grain offering, and the
kids of the goats as a sin offering twelve.
88And all the oxen for the sacrifice of
peace offerings were twenty-four bulls,
the rams sixty, the male goats sixty,
and the lambs in their first year sixty.
This *was* the dedication *offering* for the
altar after it was anointed.
89Now when Moses went into the tab-
ernacle of meeting to speak with Him,
he heard the voice of One speaking to
him from above the mercy seat that
was on the ark of the Testimony, from
between the two cherubim; thus He
spoke to him.

Arrangement of the Lamps

8 And the LORD spoke to Moses, say-
ing: 2"Speak to Aaron, and say to
him, 'When you arrange the lamps, the
seven lamps shall give light in front of
the lampstand.' " 3And Aaron did so;
he arranged the lamps to face toward
the front of the lampstand, as the LORD
commanded Moses. 4Now this work-
manship of the lampstand *was* ham-
mered gold; from its shaft to its flowers
it *was* hammered work. According to
the pattern which the LORD had shown
Moses, so he made the lampstand.

Cleansing and Dedication of the Levites

5Then the LORD spoke to Moses, say-
ing: 6"Take the Levites from among
the children of Israel and cleanse them
ceremonially. 7Thus you shall do to them
to cleanse them: Sprinkle water of pu-
rification on them, and let them shave
all their body, and let them wash their
clothes, and *so* make themselves clean.
8Then let them take a young bull with its
grain offering of fine flour mixed with
oil, and you shall take another young
bull as a sin offering. 9And you shall
bring the Levites before the taberna-
cle of meeting, and you shall gather
together the whole congregation of the
children of Israel. 10So you shall bring
the Levites before the LORD, and the
children of Israel shall lay their hands
on the Levites; 11and Aaron shall offer
the Levites before the LORD *like* a wave
offering from the children of Israel, that

they may perform the work of the LORD.
12 Then the Levites shall lay their hands
on the heads of the young bulls, and you
shall offer one as a sin offering and the
other as a burnt offering to the LORD, to
make atonement for the Levites.
13 "And you shall stand the Levites be-
fore Aaron and his sons, and then offer
them *like* a wave offering to the LORD.
14 Thus you shall separate the Levites
from among the children of Israel, and
the Levites shall be Mine. 15 After that
the Levites shall go in to service the
tabernacle of meeting. So you shall
cleanse them and offer them *like* a wave
offering. 16 For they *are* wholly given to
Me from among the children of Israel; I
have taken them for Myself instead of
all who open the womb, the firstborn of
all the children of Israel. 17 For all the
firstborn among the children of Israel
are Mine, *both* man and beast; on the
day that I struck all the firstborn in the
land of Egypt I sanctified them to My-
self. 18 I have taken the Levites instead of
all the firstborn of the children of Israel.
19 And I have given the Levites as a gift
to Aaron and his sons from among the
children of Israel, to do the work for the
children of Israel in the tabernacle of
meeting, and to make atonement for
the children of Israel, that there be no
plague among the children of Israel
when the children of Israel come near
the sanctuary."
20 Thus Moses and Aaron and all the
congregation of the children of Israel
did to the Levites; according to all that
the LORD commanded Moses concern-
ing the Levites, so the children of Israel
did to them. 21 And the Levites purified
themselves and washed their clothes;
then Aaron presented them *like* a wave
offering before the LORD, and Aaron
made atonement for them to cleanse
them. 22 After that the Levites went in to
do their work in the tabernacle of meet-
ing before Aaron and his sons; as the
LORD commanded Moses concerning
the Levites, so they did to them.
23 Then the LORD spoke to Moses,
saying, 24 "This *is* what *pertains* to the
Levites: From twenty-five years old
and above one may enter to perform
service in the work of the tabernacle
of meeting; 25 and at the age of fifty
years they must cease performing this
work, and shall work no more. 26 They
may minister with their brethren in
the tabernacle of meeting, to attend to
needs, but they *themselves* shall do no
work. Thus you shall do to the Levites
regarding their duties."

The Second Passover

9 Now the LORD spoke to Moses in
the Wilderness of Sinai, in the first
month of the second year after they had
come out of the land of Egypt, saying:
2 "Let the children of Israel keep the
Passover at its appointed time. 3 On the
fourteenth day of this month, at twi-
light, you shall keep it at its appointed
time. According to all its rites and cer-
emonies you shall keep it." 4 So Moses
told the children of Israel that they
should keep the Passover. 5 And they
kept the Passover on the fourteenth
day of the first month, at twilight, in
the Wilderness of Sinai; according to
all that the LORD commanded Moses,
so the children of Israel did.
6 Now there were *certain* men who were
defiled by a human corpse, so that they
could not keep the Passover on that day;
and they came before Moses and Aaron
that day. 7 And those men said to him,
"We *became* defiled by a human corpse.
Why are we kept from presenting the
offering of the LORD at its appointed
time among the children of Israel?"
8 And Moses said to them, "Stand still,
that I may hear what the LORD will com-
mand concerning you."
9 Then the LORD spoke to Moses, saying,
10 "Speak to the children of Israel, say-
ing: 'If anyone of you or your posterity
is unclean because of a corpse, or *is* far
away on a journey, he may still keep the
LORD's Passover. 11 On the fourteenth day
of the second month, at twilight, they
may keep it. They shall eat it with un-
leavened bread and bitter herbs. 12 They
shall leave none of it until morning, nor
break one of its bones. According to all
the ordinances of the Passover they
shall keep it. 13 But the man who *is* clean
and is not on a journey, and ceases to
keep the Passover, that same person
shall be cut off from among his people,

because he did not bring the offering
of the LORD at its appointed time; that
man shall bear his sin.
14'And if a stranger dwells among you,
and would keep the LORD's Passover,
he must do so according to the rite of
the Passover and according to its cer-
emony; you shall have one ordinance,
both for the stranger and the native of
the land.' "

The Cloud and the Fire

15Now on the day that the tabernacle
was raised up, the cloud covered the
tabernacle, the tent of the Testimony;
from evening until morning it was
above the tabernacle like the appear-
ance of fire. 16So it was always: the cloud
covered it *by day,* and the appearance of
fire by night. 17Whenever the cloud was
taken up from above the tabernacle,
after that the children of Israel would
journey; and in the place where the
cloud settled, there the children of Israel
would pitch their tents. 18At the com-
mand of the LORD the children of Israel
would journey, and at the command of
the LORD they would camp; as long as
the cloud stayed above the tabernacle
they remained encamped. 19Even when
the cloud continued long, many days
above the tabernacle, the children of
Israel kept the charge of the LORD and
did not journey. 20So it was, when the
cloud was above the tabernacle a few
days: according to the command of the
LORD they would remain encamped,
and according to the command of the
LORD they would journey. 21So it was,
when the cloud remained only from
evening until morning: when the cloud
was taken up in the morning, then they
would journey; whether by day or by
night, whenever the cloud was taken up,
they would journey. 22*Whether it was*
two days, a month, or a year that the
cloud remained above the tabernacle,
the children of Israel would remain
encamped and not journey; but when
it was taken up, they would journey.
23At the command of the LORD they
remained encamped, and at the com-
mand of the LORD they journeyed; they
kept the charge of the LORD, at the com-
mand of the LORD by the hand of Moses.

Two Silver Trumpets

10 And the LORD spoke to Moses,
saying: 2"Make two silver trum-
pets for yourself; you shall make them
of hammered work; you shall use them
for calling the congregation and for
directing the movement of the camps.
3When they blow both of them, all the
congregation shall gather before you
at the door of the tabernacle of meet-
ing. 4But if they blow *only* one, then the
leaders, the heads of the divisions of
Israel, shall gather to you. 5When you
sound the advance, the camps that lie
on the east side shall then begin their
journey. 6When you sound the advance
the second time, then the camps that
lie on the south side shall begin their
journey; they shall sound the call for
them to begin their journeys. 7And
when the assembly is to be gathered
together, you shall blow, but not sound
the advance. 8The sons of Aaron, the
priests, shall blow the trumpets; and
these shall be to you as an ordinance
forever throughout your generations.
9"When you go to war in your land
against the enemy who oppresses you,
then you shall sound an alarm with the
trumpets, and you will be remembered
before the LORD your God, and you will
be saved from your enemies. 10Also in
the day of your gladness, in your ap-
pointed feasts, and at the beginning of
your months, you shall blow the trum-
pets over your burnt offerings and over
the sacrifices of your peace offerings;
and they shall be a memorial for you be-
fore your God: I *am* the LORD your God."

Departure from Sinai

11Now it came to pass on the twentieth
day of the second month, in the second
year, that the cloud was taken up from
above the tabernacle of the Testimo-
ny. 12And the children of Israel set out
from the Wilderness of Sinai on their
journeys; then the cloud settled down
in the Wilderness of Paran. 13So they
started out for the first time according to
the command of the LORD by the hand
of Moses.
14The standard of the camp of the chil-
dren of Judah set out first according
to their armies; over their army was

Nahshon the son of Amminadab. 15Over
the army of the tribe of the children of
Issachar *was* Nethanel the son of Zuar.
16And over the army of the tribe of the
children of Zebulun *was* Eliab the son
of Helon.

17Then the tabernacle was taken down;
and the sons of Gershon and the sons of
Merari set out, carrying the tabernacle.

18And the standard of the camp of Reu-
ben set out according to their armies;
over their army *was* Elizur the son of
Shedeur. 19Over the army of the tribe of
the children of Simeon *was* Shelumiel
the son of Zurishaddai. 20And over the
army of the tribe of the children of Gad
was Eliasaph the son of Deuel.

21Then the Kohathites set out, carrying
the holy things. (The tabernacle would
be prepared for their arrival.)

22And the standard of the camp of the
children of Ephraim set out according
to their armies; over their army *was*
Elishama the son of Ammihud. 23Over
the army of the tribe of the children
of Manasseh *was* Gamaliel the son of
Pedahzur. 24And over the army of the
tribe of the children of Benjamin *was*
Abidan the son of Gideoni.

25Then the standard of the camp of
the children of Dan (the rear guard of
all the camps) set out according to their
armies; over their army *was* Ahiezer the
son of Ammishaddai. 26Over the army
of the tribe of the children of Asher *was*
Pagiel the son of Ocran. 27And over
the army of the tribe of the children
of Naphtali *was* Ahira the son of Enan.

28Thus *was* the order of march of the
children of Israel, according to their
armies, when they began their journey.

29Now Moses said to Hobab the son
of Reuel[a] the Midianite, Moses' father-
in-law, "We are setting out for the place
of which the LORD said, 'I will give it to
you.' Come with us, and we will treat
you well; for the LORD has promised
good things to Israel."

30And he said to him, "I will not go,
but I will depart to my *own* land and
to my relatives."

31So *Moses* said, "Please do not leave,
inasmuch as you know how we are to
camp in the wilderness, and you can be
our eyes. 32And it shall be, if you go with
us—indeed it shall be—that whatever
good the LORD will do to us, the same
we will do to you."

33So they departed from the mountain
of the LORD on a journey of three days;
and the ark of the covenant of the LORD
went before them for the three days'
journey, to search out a resting place
for them. 34And the cloud of the LORD
was above them by day when they went
out from the camp.

35So it was, whenever the ark set out,
that Moses said:

"Rise up, O LORD!
Let Your enemies be scattered,
And let those who hate You flee
before You."

36And when it rested, he said:

"Return, O LORD,
To the many thousands of Israel."

The People Complain

11 Now *when* the people com-
plained, it displeased the LORD;
for the LORD heard *it,* and His anger was
aroused. So the fire of the LORD burned
among them, and consumed *some* in
the outskirts of the camp. 2Then the
people cried out to Moses, and when
Moses prayed to the LORD, the fire was
quenched. 3So he called the name of the
place Taberah,[a] because the fire of the
LORD had burned among them.

4Now the mixed multitude who were
among them yielded to intense crav-
ing; so the children of Israel also wept
again and said: "Who will give us meat
to eat? 5We remember the fish which
we ate freely in Egypt, the cucumbers,
the melons, the leeks, the onions, and
the garlic; 6but now our whole being *is*
dried up; *there is* nothing at all except
this manna *before* our eyes!"

7Now the manna *was* like coriander
seed, and its color like the color of bdel-
lium. 8The people went about and gath-
ered *it,* ground *it* on millstones or beat
it in the mortar, cooked *it* in pans, and

10:29 [a] Septuagint reads *Raguel* (compare Exodus 2:18). **11:3** [a] Literally *Burning*

made cakes of it; and its taste was like
the taste of pastry prepared with oil.
9And when the dew fell on the camp in
the night, the manna fell on it.

10Then Moses heard the people weep-
ing throughout their families, everyone
at the door of his tent; and the anger of
the LORD was greatly aroused; Moses
also was displeased. 11So Moses said
to the LORD, "Why have You afflicted
Your servant? And why have I not found
favor in Your sight, that You have laid
the burden of all these people on me?
12Did I conceive all these people? Did
I beget them, that You should say to
me, 'Carry them in your bosom, as a
guardian carries a nursing child,' to the
land which You swore to their fathers?
13Where am I to get meat to give to all
these people? For they weep all over me,
saying, 'Give us meat, that we may eat.'
14I am not able to bear all these people
alone, because the burden *is* too heavy
for me. 15If You treat me like this, please
kill me here and now—if I have found
favor in Your sight—and do not let me
see my wretchedness!"

The Seventy Elders

16So the LORD said to Moses: "Gather to
Me seventy men of the elders of Israel,
whom you know to be the elders of the
people and officers over them; bring
them to the tabernacle of meeting, that
they may stand there with you. 17Then I
will come down and talk with you there.
I will take of the Spirit that *is* upon you
and will put *the same* upon them; and
they shall bear the burden of the peo-
ple with you, that you may not bear *it*
yourself alone. 18Then you shall say
to the people, 'Consecrate yourselves
for tomorrow, and you shall eat meat;
for you have wept in the hearing of the
LORD, saying, "Who will give us meat to
eat? For *it was* well with us in Egypt."
Therefore the LORD will give you meat,
and you shall eat. 19You shall eat, not
one day, nor two days, nor five days,
nor ten days, nor twenty days, 20but
for a whole month, until it comes out of
your nostrils and becomes loathsome
to you, because you have despised the
LORD who is among you, and have wept
before Him, saying, "Why did we ever
come up out of Egypt?" ' "

21And Moses said, "The people whom
I *am* among *are* six hundred thousand
men on foot; yet You have said, 'I will
give them meat, that they may eat *for* a
whole month.' 22Shall flocks and herds
be slaughtered for them, to provide
enough for them? Or shall all the fish of
the sea be gathered together for them,
to provide enough for them?"

23And the LORD said to Moses, "Has
the LORD's arm been shortened? Now
you shall see whether what I say will
happen to you or not."

24So Moses went out and told the
people the words of the LORD, and he
gathered the seventy men of the elders
of the people and placed them around
the tabernacle. 25Then the LORD came
down in the cloud, and spoke to him,
and took of the Spirit that *was* upon him,
and placed *the same* upon the seventy
elders; and it happened, when the Spirit
rested upon them, that they prophesied,
although they never did *so* again.[a]

26But two men had remained in the
camp: the name of one *was* Eldad, and
the name of the other Medad. And the
Spirit rested upon them. Now they *were*
among those listed, but who had not
gone out to the tabernacle; yet they
prophesied in the camp. 27And a young
man ran and told Moses, and said, "El-
dad and Medad are prophesying in the
camp."

28So Joshua the son of Nun, Moses' as-
sistant, *one* of his choice men, answered
and said, "Moses my lord, forbid them!"

29Then Moses said to him, "Are you
zealous for my sake? Oh, that all the
LORD's people were prophets *and* that
the LORD would put His Spirit upon
them!" 30And Moses returned to the
camp, he and the elders of Israel.

The LORD Sends Quail

31Now a wind went out from the LORD,
and it brought quail from the sea and
left *them* fluttering near the camp, about
a day's journey on this side and about
a day's journey on the other side, all

11:25 [a] Targum and Vulgate read *did not cease.*

around the camp, and about two cubits
above the surface of the ground. 32And
the people stayed up all that day, all
night, and all the next day, and gathered
the quail (he who gathered least gath-
ered ten homers); and they spread *them*
out for themselves all around the camp.
33But while the meat *was* still between
their teeth, before it was chewed, the
wrath of the LORD was aroused against
the people, and the LORD struck the
people with a very great plague. 34So
he called the name of that place Kibroth
Hattaavah,[a] because there they buried
the people who had yielded to craving.
35From Kibroth Hattaavah the people
moved to Hazeroth, and camped at
Hazeroth.

Dissension of Aaron and Miriam

12 Then Miriam and Aaron spoke
against Moses because of the
Ethiopian woman whom he had mar-
ried; for he had married an Ethiopian
woman. 2So they said, "Has the LORD
indeed spoken only through Moses?
Has He not spoken through us also?"
And the LORD heard *it.* 3(Now the man
Moses *was* very humble, more than all
men who *were* on the face of the earth.)
4Suddenly the LORD said to Moses,
Aaron, and Miriam, "Come out, you
three, to the tabernacle of meeting!"
So the three came out. 5Then the LORD
came down in the pillar of cloud and
stood *in* the door of the tabernacle, and
called Aaron and Miriam. And they both
went forward. 6Then He said,

"Hear now My words:
If there is a prophet among you,
I, the LORD, make Myself known
to him in a vision;
I speak to him in a dream.
7 Not so with My servant Moses;
He *is* faithful in all My house.
8 I speak with him face to face,
Even plainly, and not in dark
sayings;
And he sees the form of the LORD.
Why then were you not afraid
To speak against My servant
Moses?"

9So the anger of the LORD was aroused
against them, and He departed. 10And
when the cloud departed from above
the tabernacle, suddenly Miriam *be-
came* leprous, as *white as* snow. Then
Aaron turned toward Miriam, and
there she was, a leper. 11So Aaron said
to Moses, "Oh, my lord! Please do not
lay *this* sin on us, in which we have done
foolishly and in which we have sinned.
12Please do not let her be as one dead,
whose flesh is half consumed when he
comes out of his mother's womb!"
13So Moses cried out to the LORD, say-
ing, "Please heal her, O God, I pray!"
14Then the LORD said to Moses, "If her
father had but spit in her face, would she
not be shamed seven days? Let her be
shut out of the camp seven days, and af-
terward she may be received *again.*" 15So
Miriam was shut out of the camp seven
days, and the people did not journey till
Miriam was brought in *again.* 16And af-
terward the people moved from Hazeroth
and camped in the Wilderness of Paran.

Spies Sent into Canaan

13 And the LORD spoke to Moses,
saying, 2"Send men to spy out
the land of Canaan, which I am giving
to the children of Israel; from each tribe
of their fathers you shall send a man,
every one a leader among them."
3So Moses sent them from the Wilder-
ness of Paran according to the com-
mand of the LORD, all of them men who
were heads of the children of Israel.
4Now these *were* their names: from the
tribe of Reuben, Shammua the son of
Zaccur; 5from the tribe of Simeon, Sha-
phat the son of Hori; 6from the tribe
of Judah, Caleb the son of Jephunneh;
7from the tribe of Issachar, Igal the son
of Joseph; 8from the tribe of Ephraim,
Hoshea[a] the son of Nun; 9from the tribe
of Benjamin, Palti the son of Raphu;
10from the tribe of Zebulun, Gaddiel
the son of Sodi; 11from the tribe of Jo-
seph, *that is,* from the tribe of Manasseh,
Gaddi the son of Susi; 12from the tribe of
Dan, Ammiel the son of Gemalli; 13from
the tribe of Asher, Sethur the son of
Michael; 14from the tribe of Naphtali,

11:34 [a] Literally *Graves of Craving* 13:8 [a] Septuagint and Vulgate read *Oshea.*

Nahbi the son of Vophsi; 15from the tribe of Gad, Geuel the son of Machi.

16These *are* the names of the men whom Moses sent to spy out the land. And Moses called Hoshea[a] the son of Nun, Joshua.

17Then Moses sent them to spy out the land of Canaan, and said to them, "Go up this *way* into the South, and go up to the mountains, 18and see what the land is like: whether the people who dwell in it *are* strong or weak, few or many; 19whether the land they dwell in *is* good or bad; whether the cities they inhabit *are* like camps or strongholds; 20whether the land *is* rich or poor; and whether there are forests there or not. Be of good courage. And bring some of the fruit of the land." Now the time *was* the season of the first ripe grapes.

21So they went up and spied out the land from the Wilderness of Zin as far as Rehob, near the entrance of Hamath. 22And they went up through the South and came to Hebron; Ahiman, Sheshai, and Talmai, the descendants of Anak, *were* there. (Now Hebron was built seven years before Zoan in Egypt.) 23Then they came to the Valley of Eshcol, and there cut down a branch with one cluster of grapes; they carried it between two of them on a pole. *They* also *brought* some of the pomegranates and figs. 24The place was called the Valley of Eshcol,[a] because of the cluster which the men of Israel cut down there. 25And they returned from spying out the land after forty days.

26Now they departed and came back to Moses and Aaron and all the congregation of the children of Israel in the Wilderness of Paran, at Kadesh; they brought back word to them and to all the congregation, and showed them the fruit of the land. 27Then they told him, and said: "We went to the land where you sent us. It truly flows with milk and honey, and this *is* its fruit. 28Nevertheless the people who dwell in the land *are* strong; the cities *are* fortified *and* very large; moreover we saw the descendants of Anak there. 29The Amalekites dwell in the land of the South; the Hittites, the Jebusites, and the Amorites dwell in the mountains; and the Canaanites dwell by the sea and along the banks of the Jordan."

30Then Caleb quieted the people before Moses, and said, "Let us go up at once and take possession, for we are well able to overcome it."

31But the men who had gone up with him said, "We are not able to go up against the people, for they *are* stronger than we." 32And they gave the children of Israel a bad report of the land which they had spied out, saying, "The land through which we have gone as spies *is* a land that devours its inhabitants, and all the people whom we saw in it *are* men of *great* stature. 33There we saw the giants[a] (the descendants of Anak came from the giants); and we were like grasshoppers in our own sight, and so we were in their sight."

Israel Refuses to Enter Canaan

14 So all the congregation lifted up their voices and cried, and the people wept that night. 2And all the children of Israel complained against Moses and Aaron, and the whole congregation said to them, "If only we had died in the land of Egypt! Or if only we had died in this wilderness! 3Why has the LORD brought us to this land to fall by the sword, that our wives and children should become victims? Would it not be better for us to return to Egypt?" 4So they said to one another, "Let us select a leader and return to Egypt."

5Then Moses and Aaron fell on their faces before all the assembly of the congregation of the children of Israel.

6But Joshua the son of Nun and Caleb the son of Jephunneh, *who were* among those who had spied out the land, tore their clothes; 7and they spoke to all the congregation of the children of Israel, saying: "The land we passed through to spy out *is* an exceedingly good land. 8If the LORD delights in us, then He will bring us into this land and give it to us, 'a land which flows with milk and honey.'[a] 9Only do not rebel against the LORD, nor fear the people of the land,

13:16 [a] Septuagint and Vulgate read *Oshea*. **13:24** [a] Literally *Cluster* **13:33** [a] Hebrew *nephilim*
14:8 [a] Exodus 3:8

for they *are* our bread; their protection
has departed from them, and the LORD
is with us. Do not fear them."
10And all the congregation said to
stone them with stones. Now the glory of
the LORD appeared in the tabernacle of
meeting before all the children of Israel.

Moses Intercedes for the People

11Then the LORD said to Moses: "How
long will these people reject Me? And
how long will they not believe Me, with
all the signs which I have performed
among them? 12I will strike them with
the pestilence and disinherit them, and
I will make of you a nation greater and
mightier than they."
13And Moses said to the LORD: "Then
the Egyptians will hear *it,* for by Your
might You brought these people up from
among them, 14and they will tell *it* to the
inhabitants of this land. They have heard
that You, LORD, *are* among these people;
that You, LORD, are seen face to face and
Your cloud stands above them, and You
go before them in a pillar of cloud by day
and in a pillar of fire by night. 15Now *if*
You kill these people as one man, then
the nations which have heard of Your
fame will speak, saying, 16'Because the
LORD was not able to bring this people
to the land which He swore to give them,
therefore He killed them in the wilder-
ness.' 17And now, I pray, let the power
of my Lord be great, just as You have
spoken, saying, 18'The LORD is longsuf-
fering and abundant in mercy, forgiving
iniquity and transgression; but He by
no means clears *the guilty,* visiting the
iniquity of the fathers on the children to
the third and fourth *generation.*'[a] 19Par-
don the iniquity of this people, I pray,
according to the greatness of Your mer-
cy, just as You have forgiven this people,
from Egypt even until now."
20Then the LORD said: "I have pardoned,
according to your word; 21but truly, as
I live, all the earth shall be filled with
the glory of the LORD— 22because all
these men who have seen My glory and
the signs which I did in Egypt and in the
wilderness, and have put Me to the test
now these ten times, and have not heeded
My voice, 23they certainly shall not see
the land of which I swore to their fathers,
nor shall any of those who rejected Me
see it. 24But My servant Caleb, because
he has a different spirit in him and has
followed Me fully, I will bring into the land
where he went, and his descendants shall
inherit it. 25Now the Amalekites and the
Canaanites dwell in the valley; tomorrow
turn and move out into the wilderness by
the Way of the Red Sea."

Death Sentence on the Rebels

26And the LORD spoke to Moses and
Aaron, saying, 27"How long *shall I*
bear with this evil congregation who
complain against Me? I have heard
the complaints which the children of
Israel make against Me. 28Say to them,
'As I live,' says the LORD, 'just as you
have spoken in My hearing, so I will
do to you: 29The carcasses of you who
have complained against Me shall fall
in this wilderness, all of you who were
numbered, according to your entire
number, from twenty years old and
above. 30Except for Caleb the son of
Jephunneh and Joshua the son of Nun,
you shall by no means enter the land
which I swore I would make you dwell
in. 31But your little ones, whom you
said would be victims, I will bring in,
and they shall know the land which you
have despised. 32But *as for* you, your
carcasses shall fall in this wilderness.
33And your sons shall be shepherds in
the wilderness forty years, and bear the
brunt of your infidelity, until your car-
casses are consumed in the wilderness.
34According to the number of the days
in which you spied out the land, forty
days, for each day you shall bear your
guilt one year, *namely* forty years, and
you shall know My rejection. 35I the
LORD have spoken this. I will surely do
so to all this evil congregation who are
gathered together against Me. In this
wilderness they shall be consumed, and
there they shall die.'"
36Now the men whom Moses sent to spy
out the land, who returned and made
all the congregation complain against
him by bringing a bad report of the

14:18 [a] Exodus 34:6, 7

land, 37those very men who brought the
evil report about the land, died by the
plague before the LORD. 38But Joshua
the son of Nun and Caleb the son of
Jephunneh remained alive, of the men
who went to spy out the land.

A Futile Invasion Attempt

39Then Moses told these words to all
the children of Israel, and the people
mourned greatly. 40And they rose early
in the morning and went up to the top
of the mountain, saying, "Here we are,
and we will go up to the place which the
LORD has promised, for we have sinned!"
41And Moses said, "Now why do you
transgress the command of the LORD?
For this will not succeed. 42Do not go
up, lest you be defeated by your ene-
mies, for the LORD *is* not among you.
43For the Amalekites and the Canaanites
are there before you, and you shall fall
by the sword; because you have turned
away from the LORD, the LORD will not
be with you."
44But they presumed to go up to the
mountaintop. Nevertheless, neither the
ark of the covenant of the LORD nor
Moses departed from the camp. 45Then
the Amalekites and the Canaanites who
dwelt in that mountain came down and
attacked them, and drove them back as
far as Hormah.

Laws of Grain and Drink Offerings

15 And the LORD spoke to Moses,
saying, 2"Speak to the children
of Israel, and say to them: 'When you
have come into the land you are to in-
habit, which I am giving to you, 3and
you make an offering by fire to the
LORD, a burnt offering or a sacrifice,
to fulfill a vow or as a freewill offering
or in your appointed feasts, to make a
sweet aroma to the LORD, from the herd
or the flock, 4then he who presents his
offering to the LORD shall bring a grain
offering of one-tenth *of an ephah* of fine
flour mixed with one-fourth of a hin
of oil; 5and one-fourth of a hin of wine
as a drink offering you shall prepare
with the burnt offering or the sacrifice,
for each lamb. 6Or for a ram you shall
prepare as a grain offering two-tenths
of an ephah of fine flour mixed with one-
third of a hin of oil; 7and as a drink
offering you shall offer one-third of
a hin of wine as a sweet aroma to the
LORD. 8And when you prepare a young
bull as a burnt offering, or as a sacrifice
to fulfill a vow, or as a peace offering to
the LORD, 9then shall be offered with the
young bull a grain offering of three-
tenths *of an ephah* of fine flour mixed
with half a hin of oil; 10and you shall
bring as the drink offering half a hin
of wine as an offering made by fire, a
sweet aroma to the LORD.
11'Thus it shall be done for each young
bull, for each ram, or for each lamb or
young goat. 12According to the number
that you prepare, so you shall do with
everyone according to their number.
13All who are native-born shall do these
things in this manner, in presenting
an offering made by fire, a sweet aro-
ma to the LORD. 14And if a stranger
dwells with you, or whoever *is* among
you throughout your generations, and
would present an offering made by fire,
a sweet aroma to the LORD, just as you
do, so shall he do. 15One ordinance
shall be for you of the assembly and
for the stranger who dwells *with you,*
an ordinance forever throughout your
generations; as you are, so shall the
stranger be before the LORD. 16One law
and one custom shall be for you and for
the stranger who dwells with you.' "[a]
17Again the LORD spoke to Moses, say-
ing, 18"Speak to the children of Israel,
and say to them: 'When you come into
the land to which I bring you, 19then it
will be, when you eat of the bread of the
land, that you shall offer up a heave of-
fering to the LORD. 20You shall offer up
a cake of the first of your ground meal
as a heave offering; as a heave offering
of the threshing floor, so shall you offer
it up. 21Of the first of your ground meal
you shall give to the LORD a heave of-
fering throughout your generations.

Laws Concerning Unintentional Sin

22'If you sin unintentionally, and do
not observe all these commandments

15:16 [a] Compare Exodus 12:49

which the LORD has spoken to Moses—
23all that the LORD has commanded you
by the hand of Moses, from the day the
LORD gave commandment and onward
throughout your generations— 24then
it will be, if it is unintentionally com-
mitted, without the knowledge of the
congregation, that the whole congre-
gation shall offer one young bull as
a burnt offering, as a sweet aroma to
the LORD, with its grain offering and
its drink offering, according to the or-
dinance, and one kid of the goats as a
sin offering. 25So the priest shall make
atonement for the whole congregation
of the children of Israel, and it shall be
forgiven them, for it was unintentional;
they shall bring their offering, an offer-
ing made by fire to the LORD, and their
sin offering before the LORD, for their
unintended sin. 26It shall be forgiven
the whole congregation of the children
of Israel and the stranger who dwells
among them, because all the people
did it unintentionally.

27'And if a person sins unintentionally,
then he shall bring a female goat in
its first year as a sin offering. 28So the
priest shall make atonement for the
person who sins unintentionally, when
he sins unintentionally before the LORD,
to make atonement for him; and it shall
be forgiven him. 29You shall have one
law for him who sins unintentionally,
for him who is native-born among the
children of Israel and for the stranger
who dwells among them.

Law Concerning Presumptuous Sin

30'But the person who does *anything*
presumptuously, *whether he is* native-
born or a stranger, that one brings re-
proach on the LORD, and he shall be cut
off from among his people. 31Because
he has despised the word of the LORD,
and has broken His commandment,
that person shall be completely cut off;
his guilt *shall be* upon him.' "

Penalty for Violating the Sabbath

32Now while the children of Israel were
in the wilderness, they found a man
gathering sticks on the Sabbath day.
33And those who found him gathering
sticks brought him to Moses and Aaron,
and to all the congregation. 34They put
him under guard, because it had not
been explained what should be done
to him.

35Then the LORD said to Moses, "The
man must surely be put to death; all
the congregation shall stone him
with stones outside the camp." 36So,
as the LORD commanded Moses, all
the congregation brought him outside
the camp and stoned him with stones,
and he died.

Tassels on Garments

37Again the LORD spoke to Moses,
saying, 38"Speak to the children of Is-
rael: Tell them to make tassels on the
corners of their garments throughout
their generations, and to put a blue
thread in the tassels of the corners.
39And you shall have the tassel, that
you may look upon it and remember
all the commandments of the LORD and
do them, and that you *may* not follow
the harlotry to which your own heart
and your own eyes are inclined, 40and
that you may remember and do all My
commandments, and be holy for your
God. 41I *am* the LORD your God, who
brought you out of the land of Egypt, to
be your God: I *am* the LORD your God."

Rebellion Against Moses and Aaron

16 Now Korah the son of Izhar, the
son of Kohath, the son of Levi,
with Dathan and Abiram the sons of
Eliab, and On the son of Peleth, sons of
Reuben, took *men;* 2and they rose up be-
fore Moses with some of the children of
Israel, two hundred and fifty leaders of
the congregation, representatives of the
congregation, men of renown. 3They
gathered together against Moses and
Aaron, and said to them, "*You take* too
much upon yourselves, for all the con-
gregation *is* holy, every one of them,
and the LORD *is* among them. Why then
do you exalt yourselves above the as-
sembly of the LORD?"

4So when Moses heard *it,* he fell on
his face; 5and he spoke to Korah and
all his company, saying, "Tomorrow
morning the LORD will show who *is* His
and *who is* holy, and will cause *him* to
come near to Him. That one whom He

GOD SIN JESUS SALVATION LOVE

chooses He will cause to come near to
Him. 6Do this: Take censers, Korah and
all your company; 7put fire in them and
put incense in them before the LORD
tomorrow, and it shall be *that* the man
whom the LORD chooses *is* the holy one.
You take too much upon yourselves, you
sons of Levi!"

8Then Moses said to Korah, "Hear now,
you sons of Levi: 9*Is it* a small thing to
you that the God of Israel has separat-
ed you from the congregation of Isra-
el, to bring you near to Himself, to do
the work of the tabernacle of the LORD,
and to stand before the congregation to
serve them; 10and that He has brought
you near *to Himself,* you and all your
brethren, the sons of Levi, with you? And
are you seeking the priesthood also?
11Therefore you and all your company
are gathered together against the LORD.
And what *is* Aaron that you complain
against him?"

12And Moses sent to call Dathan and
Abiram the sons of Eliab, but they said,
"We will not come up! 13*Is it* a small
thing that you have brought us up out
of a land flowing with milk and honey,
to kill us in the wilderness, that you
should keep acting like a prince over
us? 14Moreover you have not brought
us into a land flowing with milk and
honey, nor given us inheritance of fields
and vineyards. Will you put out the eyes
of these men? We will not come up!"

15Then Moses was very angry, and
said to the LORD, "Do not respect their
offering. I have not taken one donkey
from them, nor have I hurt one of them."

16And Moses said to Korah, "Tomor-
row, you and all your company be pres-
ent before the LORD—you and they, as
well as Aaron. 17Let each take his censer
and put incense in it, and each of you
bring his censer before the LORD, two
hundred and fifty censers; both you and
Aaron, each *with* his censer." 18So every
man took his censer, put fire in it, laid
incense on it, and stood at the door of
the tabernacle of meeting with Moses
and Aaron. 19And Korah gathered all
the congregation against them at the
door of the tabernacle of meeting. Then
the glory of the LORD appeared to all
the congregation.

20And the LORD spoke to Moses and
Aaron, saying, 21"Separate yourselves
from among this congregation, that
I may consume them in a moment."

22Then they fell on their faces, and
said, "O God, the God of the spirits of
all flesh, shall one man sin, and You
be angry with all the congregation?"

23So the LORD spoke to Moses, saying,
24"Speak to the congregation, saying,
'Get away from the tents of Korah, Da-
than, and Abiram.' "

25Then Moses rose and went to Dathan
and Abiram, and the elders of Israel fol-
lowed him. 26And he spoke to the con-
gregation, saying, "Depart now from
the tents of these wicked men! Touch
nothing of theirs, lest you be consumed
in all their sins." 27So they got away
from around the tents of Korah, Dathan,
and Abiram; and Dathan and Abiram
came out and stood at the door of their
tents, with their wives, their sons, and
their little children.

28And Moses said: "By this you shall
know that the LORD has sent me to do
all these works, for *I have* not *done them*
of my own will. 29If these men die nat-
urally like all men, or if they are visited
by the common fate of all men, *then*
the LORD has not sent me. 30But if the
LORD creates a new thing, and the earth
opens its mouth and swallows them up
with all that belongs to them, and they
go down alive into the pit, then you
will understand that these men have
rejected the LORD."

31Now it came to pass, as he finished
speaking all these words, that the
ground split apart under them, 32and
the earth opened its mouth and swal-
lowed them up, with their households
and all the men with Korah, with all
their goods. 33So they and all those with
them went down alive into the pit; the
earth closed over them, and they per-
ished from among the assembly. 34Then
all Israel who *were* around them fled at
their cry, for they said, "Lest the earth
swallow us up *also!*"

35And a fire came out from the LORD
and consumed the two hundred and
fifty men who were offering incense.

36Then the LORD spoke to Moses, say-
ing: 37"Tell Eleazar, the son of Aaron the

priest, to pick up the censers out of the
blaze, for they are holy, and scatter the
fire some distance away. 38The censers
of these men who sinned against their
own souls, let them be made into ham-
mered plates as a covering for the altar.
Because they presented them before
the LORD, therefore they are holy; and
they shall be a sign to the children of
Israel." 39So Eleazar the priest took the
bronze censers, which those who were
burned up had presented, and they were
hammered out as a covering on the
altar, 40*to be* a memorial to the children
of Israel that no outsider, who *is* not a
descendant of Aaron, should come near
to offer incense before the LORD, that
he might not become like Korah and
his companions, just as the LORD had
said to him through Moses.

Complaints of the People

41On the next day all the congregation
of the children of Israel complained
against Moses and Aaron, saying, "You
have killed the people of the LORD."
42Now it happened, when the congre-
gation had gathered against Moses
and Aaron, that they turned toward the
tabernacle of meeting; and suddenly
the cloud covered it, and the glory of
the LORD appeared. 43Then Moses and
Aaron came before the tabernacle of
meeting.
44And the LORD spoke to Moses, say-
ing, 45"Get away from among this con-
gregation, that I may consume them
in a moment."
And they fell on their faces.
46So Moses said to Aaron, "Take a
censer and put fire in it from the altar,
put incense *on it,* and take it quickly
to the congregation and make atone-
ment for them; for wrath has gone
out from the LORD. The plague has
begun." 47Then Aaron took *it* as Moses
commanded, and ran into the midst of
the assembly; and already the plague
had begun among the people. So he
put in the incense and made atone-
ment for the people. 48And he stood
between the dead and the living; so the
plague was stopped. 49Now those who
died in the plague were fourteen thou-
sand seven hundred, besides those
who died in the Korah incident. 50So
Aaron returned to Moses at the door
of the tabernacle of meeting, for the
plague had stopped.

The Budding of Aaron's Rod

17 And the LORD spoke to Moses,
saying: 2"Speak to the children
of Israel, and get from them a rod from
each father's house, all their leaders ac-
cording to their fathers' houses—twelve
rods. Write each man's name on his rod.
3And you shall write Aaron's name on
the rod of Levi. For there shall be one
rod for the head of *each* father's house.
4Then you shall place them in the taber-
nacle of meeting before the Testimony,
where I meet with you. 5And it shall be
that the rod of the man whom I choose
will blossom; thus I will rid Myself of
the complaints of the children of Israel,
which they make against you."
6So Moses spoke to the children of Is-
rael, and each of their leaders gave him
a rod apiece, for each leader according
to their fathers' houses, twelve rods;
and the rod of Aaron *was* among their
rods. 7And Moses placed the rods before
the LORD in the tabernacle of witness.
8Now it came to pass on the next day
that Moses went into the tabernacle of
witness, and behold, the rod of Aaron,
of the house of Levi, had sprouted and
put forth buds, had produced blossoms
and yielded ripe almonds. 9Then Moses
brought out all the rods from before the
LORD to all the children of Israel; and
they looked, and each man took his rod.
10And the LORD said to Moses, "Bring
Aaron's rod back before the Testimony,
to be kept as a sign against the reb-
els, that you may put their complaints
away from Me, lest they die." 11Thus did
Moses; just as the LORD had command-
ed him, so he did.
12So the children of Israel spoke to
Moses, saying, "Surely we die, we perish,
we all perish! 13Whoever even comes
near the tabernacle of the LORD must
die. Shall we all utterly die?"

Duties of Priests and Levites

18 Then the LORD said to Aaron:
"You and your sons and your
father's house with you shall bear

the iniquity *related to* the sanctuary,
and you and your sons with you shall
bear the iniquity *associated with* your
priesthood. 2Also bring with you your
brethren of the tribe of Levi, the tribe
of your father, that they may be joined
with you and serve you while you and
your sons *are* with you before the tab-
ernacle of witness. 3They shall attend
to your needs and all the needs of the
tabernacle; but they shall not come
near the articles of the sanctuary and
the altar, lest they die—they and you
also. 4They shall be joined with you and
attend to the needs of the tabernacle of
meeting, for all the work of the taber-
nacle; but an outsider shall not come
near you. 5And you shall attend to the
duties of the sanctuary and the duties
of the altar, that there *may* be no more
wrath on the children of Israel. 6Behold,
I Myself have taken your brethren the
Levites from among the children of Is-
rael; *they are* a gift to you, given by the
LORD, to do the work of the tabernacle of
meeting. 7Therefore you and your sons
with you shall attend to your priesthood
for everything at the altar and behind
the veil; and you shall serve. I give your
priesthood *to you* as a gift for service,
but the outsider who comes near shall
be put to death."

Offerings for Support of the Priests

8And the LORD spoke to Aaron: "Here,
I Myself have also given you charge of
My heave offerings, all the holy gifts of
the children of Israel; I have given them
as a portion to you and your sons, as an
ordinance forever. 9This shall be yours
of the most holy things *reserved* from
the fire: every offering of theirs, every
grain offering and every sin offering
and every trespass offering which they
render to Me, *shall be* most holy for you
and your sons. 10In a most holy *place*
you shall eat it; every male shall eat it.
It shall be holy to you.

11"This also *is* yours: the heave offering
of their gift, with all the wave offerings
of the children of Israel; I have given
them to you, and your sons and daugh-
ters with you, as an ordinance forever.
Everyone who is clean in your house
may eat it.

12"All the best of the oil, all the best
of the new wine and the grain, their
firstfruits which they offer to the LORD,
I have given them to you. 13Whatever
first ripe fruit is in their land, which
they bring to the LORD, shall be yours.
Everyone who is clean in your house
may eat it.

14"Every devoted thing in Israel shall
be yours.

15"Everything that first opens the
womb of all flesh, which they bring to
the LORD, whether man or beast, shall
be yours; nevertheless the firstborn of
man you shall surely redeem, and the
firstborn of unclean animals you shall
redeem. 16And those redeemed of the
devoted things you shall redeem when
one month old, according to your valu-
ation, for five shekels of silver, accord-
ing to the shekel of the sanctuary, which
is twenty gerahs. 17But the firstborn of
a cow, the firstborn of a sheep, or the
firstborn of a goat you shall not redeem;
they *are* holy. You shall sprinkle their
blood on the altar, and burn their fat
as an offering made by fire for a sweet
aroma to the LORD. 18And their flesh
shall be yours, just as the wave breast
and the right thigh are yours.

19"All the heave offerings of the holy
things, which the children of Israel offer
to the LORD, I have given to you and
your sons and daughters with you as
an ordinance forever; it *is* a covenant
of salt forever before the LORD with you
and your descendants with you."

20Then the LORD said to Aaron: "You
shall have no inheritance in their land,
nor shall you have any portion among
them; I *am* your portion and your in-
heritance among the children of Israel.

Tithes for Support of the Levites

21"Behold, I have given the children of
Levi all the tithes in Israel as an inheri-
tance in return for the work which they
perform, the work of the tabernacle of
meeting. 22Hereafter the children of
Israel shall not come near the taber-
nacle of meeting, lest they bear sin and
die. 23But the Levites shall perform the
work of the tabernacle of meeting, and
they shall bear their iniquity; *it shall
be* a statute forever, throughout your

generations, that among the children of Israel they shall have no inheritance. 24For the tithes of the children of Israel, which they offer up *as* a heave offering to the LORD, I have given to the Levites as an inheritance; therefore I have said to them, 'Among the children of Israel they shall have no inheritance.' "

The Tithe of the Levites

25Then the LORD spoke to Moses, saying, 26"Speak thus to the Levites, and say to them: 'When you take from the children of Israel the tithes which I have given you from them as your inheritance, then you shall offer up a heave offering of it to the LORD, a tenth of the tithe. 27And your heave offering shall be reckoned to you as though *it were* the grain of the threshing floor and as the fullness of the winepress. 28Thus you shall also offer a heave offering to the LORD from all your tithes which you receive from the children of Israel, and you shall give the LORD's heave offering from it to Aaron the priest. 29Of all your gifts you shall offer up every heave offering due to the LORD, from all the best of them, the consecrated part of them.' 30Therefore you shall say to them: 'When you have lifted up the best of it, then *the rest* shall be accounted to the Levites as the produce of the threshing floor and as the produce of the winepress. 31You may eat it in any place, you and your households, for it *is* your reward for your work in the tabernacle of meeting. 32And you shall bear no sin because of it, when you have lifted up the best of it. But you shall not profane the holy gifts of the children of Israel, lest you die.' "

Laws of Purification

19 Now the LORD spoke to Moses and Aaron, saying, 2"This *is* the ordinance of the law which the LORD has commanded, saying: 'Speak to the children of Israel, that they bring you a red heifer without blemish, in which there *is* no defect *and* on which a yoke has never come. 3You shall give it to Eleazar the priest, that he may take it outside the camp, and it shall be slaughtered before him; 4and Eleazar the priest shall take some of its blood with his finger, and sprinkle some of its blood seven times directly in front of the tabernacle of meeting. 5Then the heifer shall be burned in his sight: its hide, its flesh, its blood, and its offal shall be burned. 6And the priest shall take cedar wood and hyssop and scarlet, and cast *them* into the midst of the fire burning the heifer. 7Then the priest shall wash his clothes, he shall bathe in water, and afterward he shall come into the camp; the priest shall be unclean until evening. 8And the one who burns it shall wash his clothes in water, bathe in water, and shall be unclean until evening. 9Then a man *who is* clean shall gather up the ashes of the heifer, and store *them* outside the camp in a clean place; and they shall be kept for the congregation of the children of Israel for the water of purification;[a] it *is* for purifying from sin. 10And the one who gathers the ashes of the heifer shall wash his clothes, and be unclean until evening. It shall be a statute forever to the children of Israel and to the stranger who dwells among them.

11'He who touches the dead body of anyone shall be unclean seven days. 12He shall purify himself with the water on the third day and on the seventh day; *then* he will be clean. But if he does not purify himself on the third day and on the seventh day, he will not be clean. 13Whoever touches the body of anyone who has died, and does not purify himself, defiles the tabernacle of the LORD. That person shall be cut off from Israel. He shall be unclean, because the water of purification was not sprinkled on him; his uncleanness *is* still on him.

14'This *is* the law when a man dies in a tent: All who come into the tent and all who *are* in the tent shall be unclean seven days; 15and every open vessel, which has no cover fastened on it, *is* unclean. 16Whoever in the open field touches one who is slain by a sword or who has died, or a bone of a man, or a grave, shall be unclean seven days.

19:9 [a] Literally *impurity*

17'And for an unclean *person* they shall
take some of the ashes of the heifer burnt
for purification from sin, and running
water shall be put on them in a vessel.
18A clean person shall take hyssop and
dip *it* in the water, sprinkle *it* on the tent,
on all the vessels, on the persons who
were there, or on the one who touched a
bone, the slain, the dead, or a grave. 19The
clean *person* shall sprinkle the unclean
on the third day and on the seventh day;
and on the seventh day he shall purify
himself, wash his clothes, and bathe in
water; and at evening he shall be clean.
20'But the man who is unclean and
does not purify himself, that person
shall be cut off from among the assem-
bly, because he has defiled the sanctuary
of the LORD. The water of purification
has not been sprinkled on him; he *is*
unclean. 21It shall be a perpetual statute
for them. He who sprinkles the water of
purification shall wash his clothes; and
he who touches the water of purification
shall be unclean until evening. 22What-
ever the unclean *person* touches shall be
unclean; and the person who touches *it*
shall be unclean until evening.' "

Moses' Error at Kadesh

20 Then the children of Israel, the
whole congregation, came into
the Wilderness of Zin in the first month,
and the people stayed in Kadesh; and
Miriam died there and was buried there.
2Now there was no water for the con-
gregation; so they gathered together
against Moses and Aaron. 3And the peo-
ple contended with Moses and spoke,
saying: "If only we had died when our
brethren died before the LORD! 4Why
have you brought up the assembly of
the LORD into this wilderness, that we
and our animals should die here? 5And
why have you made us come up out of
Egypt, to bring us to this evil place? It
is not a place of grain or figs or vines or
pomegranates; nor *is* there any water to
drink." 6So Moses and Aaron went from
the presence of the assembly to the door
of the tabernacle of meeting, and they
fell on their faces. And the glory of the
LORD appeared to them.
7Then the LORD spoke to Moses, saying,
8"Take the rod; you and your brother
Aaron gather the congregation togeth-
er. Speak to the rock before their eyes,
and it will yield its water; thus you shall
bring water for them out of the rock, and
give drink to the congregation and their
animals." 9So Moses took the rod from
before the LORD as He commanded him.
10And Moses and Aaron gathered the
assembly together before the rock;
and he said to them, "Hear now, you
rebels! Must we bring water for you out
of this rock?" 11Then Moses lifted his
hand and struck the rock twice with
his rod; and water came out abun-
dantly, and the congregation and
their animals drank.
12Then the LORD spoke to Moses and
Aaron, "Because you did not believe Me,
to hallow Me in the eyes of the children
of Israel, therefore you shall not bring
this assembly into the land which I have
given them."
13This *was* the water of Meribah,[a] be-
cause the children of Israel contended
with the LORD, and He was hallowed
among them.

Passage Through Edom Refused

14Now Moses sent messengers from
Kadesh to the king of Edom. "Thus says
your brother Israel: 'You know all the
hardship that has befallen us, 15how
our fathers went down to Egypt, and
we dwelt in Egypt a long time, and the
Egyptians afflicted us and our fathers.
16When we cried out to the LORD, He
heard our voice and sent the Angel and
brought us up out of Egypt; now here we
are in Kadesh, a city on the edge of your
border. 17Please let us pass through
your country. We will not pass through
fields or vineyards, nor will we drink
water from wells; we will go along the
King's Highway; we will not turn aside
to the right hand or to the left until we
have passed through your territory.' "
18Then Edom said to him, "You shall
not pass through my *land*, lest I come
out against you with the sword."
19So the children of Israel said to him,
"We will go by the Highway, and if I or

20:13 [a] Literally *Contention*

my livestock drink any of your water, then I will pay for it; let me only pass through on foot, nothing *more.*"

20Then he said, "You shall not pass through." So Edom came out against them with many men and with a strong hand. 21Thus Edom refused to give Israel passage through his territory; so Israel turned away from him.

Death of Aaron

22Now the children of Israel, the whole congregation, journeyed from Kadesh and came to Mount Hor. 23And the LORD spoke to Moses and Aaron in Mount Hor by the border of the land of Edom, saying: 24"Aaron shall be gathered to his people, for he shall not enter the land which I have given to the children of Israel, because you rebelled against My word at the water of Meribah. 25Take Aaron and Eleazar his son, and bring them up to Mount Hor; 26and strip Aaron of his garments and put them on Eleazar his son; for Aaron shall be gathered *to his people* and die there." 27So Moses did just as the LORD commanded, and they went up to Mount Hor in the sight of all the congregation. 28Moses stripped Aaron of his garments and put them on Eleazar his son; and Aaron died there on the top of the mountain. Then Moses and Eleazar came down from the mountain. 29Now when all the congregation saw that Aaron was dead, all the house of Israel mourned for Aaron thirty days.

Canaanites Defeated at Hormah

21 The king of Arad, the Canaanite, who dwelt in the South, heard that Israel was coming on the road to Atharim. Then he fought against Israel and took *some* of them prisoners. 2So Israel made a vow to the LORD, and said, "If You will indeed deliver this people into my hand, then I will utterly destroy their cities." 3And the LORD listened to the voice of Israel and delivered up the Canaanites, and they utterly destroyed them and their cities. So the name of that place was called Hormah.[a]

The Bronze Serpent

4Then they journeyed from Mount Hor by the Way of the Red Sea, to go around the land of Edom; and the soul of the people became very discouraged on the way. 5And the people spoke against God and against Moses: "Why have you brought us up out of Egypt to die in the wilderness? For *there is* no food and no water, and our soul loathes this worthless bread." 6So the LORD sent fiery serpents among the people, and they bit the people; and many of the people of Israel died.

7Therefore the people came to Moses, and said, "We have sinned, for we have spoken against the LORD and against you; pray to the LORD that He take away the serpents from us." So Moses prayed for the people.

8Then the LORD said to Moses, "Make a fiery *serpent,* and set it on a pole; and it shall be that everyone who is bitten, when he looks at it, shall live." 9So Moses made a bronze serpent, and put it on a pole; and so it was, if a serpent had bitten anyone, when he looked at the bronze serpent, he lived.

From Mount Hor to Moab

10Now the children of Israel moved on and camped in Oboth. 11And they journeyed from Oboth and camped at Ije Abarim, in the wilderness which *is* east of Moab, toward the sunrise. 12From there they moved and camped in the Valley of Zered. 13From there they moved and camped on the other side of the Arnon, which *is* in the wilderness that extends from the border of the Amorites; for the Arnon *is* the border of Moab, between Moab and the Amorites. 14Therefore it is said in the Book of the Wars of the LORD:

"Waheb in Suphah,[a]
The brooks of the Arnon,
15 And the slope of the brooks
That reaches to the dwelling of Ar,
And lies on the border of Moab."

16From there *they went* to Beer, which *is* the well where the LORD said to Moses, "Gather the people together, and I will

21:3 [a] Literally *Utter Destruction* 21:14 [a] Ancient unknown places; Vulgate reads *What He did in the Red Sea.*

give them water." 17Then Israel sang
this song:

"Spring up, O well!
All of you sing to it—
18 The well the leaders sank,
Dug by the nation's nobles,
By the lawgiver, with their staves."

And from the wilderness *they went* to
Mattanah, 19from Mattanah to Naha-
liel, from Nahaliel to Bamoth, 20and
from Bamoth, *in* the valley that *is* in the
country of Moab, to the top of Pisgah
which looks down on the wasteland.[a]

King Sihon Defeated

21Then Israel sent messengers to Sihon
king of the Amorites, saying, 22"Let me pass
through your land. We will not turn aside
into fields or vineyards; we will not drink
water from wells. We will go by the King's
Highway until we have passed through
your territory." 23But Sihon would not al-
low Israel to pass through his territory. So
Sihon gathered all his people together and
went out against Israel in the wilderness,
and he came to Jahaz and fought against
Israel. 24Then Israel defeated him with the
edge of the sword, and took possession of
his land from the Arnon to the Jabbok, as
far as the people of Ammon; for the border
of the people of Ammon *was* fortified. 25So
Israel took all these cities, and Israel dwelt
in all the cities of the Amorites, in Hesh-
bon and in all its villages. 26For Heshbon
was the city of Sihon king of the Amorites,
who had fought against the former king
of Moab, and had taken all his land from
his hand as far as the Arnon. 27Therefore
those who speak in proverbs say:

"Come to Heshbon, let it be built;
Let the city of Sihon be repaired.

28 "For fire went out from Heshbon,
A flame from the city of Sihon;
It consumed Ar of Moab,
The lords of the heights of the
Arnon.
29 Woe to you, Moab!
You have perished, O people of
Chemosh!
He has given his sons as fugitives,
And his daughters into captivity,
To Sihon king of the Amorites.

30 "But we have shot at them;
Heshbon has perished as far as
Dibon.
Then we laid waste as far as
Nophah,
Which *reaches* to Medeba."

31Thus Israel dwelt in the land of the
Amorites. 32Then Moses sent to spy out
Jazer; and they took its villages and
drove out the Amorites who *were* there.

King Og Defeated

33And they turned and went up by
the way to Bashan. So Og king of Ba-
shan went out against them, he and
all his people, to battle at Edrei. 34Then
the LORD said to Moses, "Do not fear
him, for I have delivered him into your
hand, with all his people and his land;
and you shall do to him as you did to
Sihon king of the Amorites, who dwelt
at Heshbon." 35So they defeated him,
his sons, and all his people, until there
was no survivor left him; and they took
possession of his land.

Balak Sends for Balaam

22 Then the children of Isra-
el moved, and camped in the
plains of Moab on the side of the Jordan
across from Jericho.

2Now Balak the son of Zippor saw all
that Israel had done to the Amorites.
3And Moab was exceedingly afraid of
the people because they *were* many,
and Moab was sick with dread because
of the children of Israel. 4So Moab said
to the elders of Midian, "Now this com-
pany will lick up everything around us,
as an ox licks up the grass of the field."
And Balak the son of Zippor *was* king
of the Moabites at that time. 5Then he
sent messengers to Balaam the son of
Beor at Pethor, which *is* near the River[a]
in the land of the sons of his people,[b]
to call him, saying: "Look, a people has
come from Egypt. See, they cover the
face of the earth, and are settling next

21:20 [a] Hebrew *Jeshimon* 22:5 [a] That is, the Euphrates [b] Or *the people of Amau*

to me! 6Therefore please come at once,
curse this people for me, for they *are*
too mighty for me. Perhaps I shall be
able to defeat them and drive them out
of the land, for I know that he whom
you bless *is* blessed, and he whom you
curse is cursed."
7So the elders of Moab and the elders
of Midian departed with the diviner's
fee in their hand, and they came to Ba-
laam and spoke to him the words of
Balak. 8And he said to them, "Lodge
here tonight, and I will bring back word
to you, as the LORD speaks to me." So the
princes of Moab stayed with Balaam.
9Then God came to Balaam and said,
"Who *are* these men with you?"
10So Balaam said to God, "Balak the
son of Zippor, king of Moab, has sent to
me, *saying,* 11'Look, a people has come
out of Egypt, and they cover the face
of the earth. Come now, curse them for
me; perhaps I shall be able to overpower
them and drive them out.' "
12And God said to Balaam, "You shall
not go with them; you shall not curse
the people, for they *are* blessed."
13So Balaam rose in the morning and
said to the princes of Balak, "Go back
to your land, for the LORD has refused
to give me permission to go with you."
14And the princes of Moab rose and
went to Balak, and said, "Balaam re-
fuses to come with us."
15Then Balak again sent princes, more
numerous and more honorable than
they. 16And they came to Balaam and
said to him, "Thus says Balak the son of
Zippor: 'Please let nothing hinder you
from coming to me; 17for I will certainly
honor you greatly, and I will do what-
ever you say to me. Therefore please
come, curse this people for me.' "
18Then Balaam answered and said to
the servants of Balak, "Though Balak
were to give me his house full of silver
and gold, I could not go beyond the
word of the LORD my God, to do less or
more. 19Now therefore, please, you also
stay here tonight, that I may know what
more the LORD will say to me."
20And God came to Balaam at night
and said to him, "If the men come to
call you, rise *and* go with them; but only
the word which I speak to you—that
you shall do." 21So Balaam rose in the
morning, saddled his donkey, and went
with the princes of Moab.

Balaam, the Donkey, and the Angel

22Then God's anger was aroused be-
cause he went, and the Angel of the
LORD took His stand in the way as an
adversary against him. And he was
riding on his donkey, and his two ser-
vants *were* with him. 23Now the donkey
saw the Angel of the LORD standing in
the way with His drawn sword in His
hand, and the donkey turned aside out
of the way and went into the field. So Ba-
laam struck the donkey to turn her back
onto the road. 24Then the Angel of the
LORD stood in a narrow path between
the vineyards, *with* a wall on this side
and a wall on that side. 25And when the
donkey saw the Angel of the LORD, she
pushed herself against the wall and
crushed Balaam's foot against the wall;
so he struck her again. 26Then the Angel
of the LORD went further, and stood
in a narrow place where there *was* no
way to turn either to the right hand or
to the left. 27And when the donkey saw
the Angel of the LORD, she lay down
under Balaam; so Balaam's anger was
aroused, and he struck the donkey with
his staff.
28Then the LORD opened the mouth
of the donkey, and she said to Balaam,
"What have I done to you, that you have
struck me these three times?"
29And Balaam said to the donkey,
"Because you have abused me. I wish
there were a sword in my hand, for now
I would kill you!"
30So the donkey said to Balaam, "*Am*
I not your donkey on which you have
ridden, ever since *I became* yours, to
this day? Was I ever disposed to do this
to you?"
And he said, "No."
31Then the LORD opened Balaam's
eyes, and he saw the Angel of the LORD
standing in the way with His drawn
sword in His hand; and he bowed his
head and fell flat on his face. 32And the
Angel of the LORD said to him, "Why
have you struck your donkey these
three times? Behold, I have come out
to stand against you, because *your* way

is perverse before Me. 33The donkey saw
Me and turned aside from Me these
three times. If she had not turned aside
from Me, surely I would also have killed
you by now, and let her live."
34And Balaam said to the Angel of
the LORD, "I have sinned, for I did not
know You stood in the way against me.
Now therefore, if it displeases You, I will
turn back."
35Then the Angel of the LORD said to
Balaam, "Go with the men, but only
the word that I speak to you, that you
shall speak." So Balaam went with the
princes of Balak.
36Now when Balak heard that Balaam
was coming, he went out to meet him
at the city of Moab, which *is* on the bor-
der at the Arnon, the boundary of the
territory. 37Then Balak said to Balaam,
"Did I not earnestly send to you, calling
for you? Why did you not come to me?
Am I not able to honor you?"
38And Balaam said to Balak, "Look,
I have come to you! Now, have I any
power at all to say anything? The word
that God puts in my mouth, that I must
speak." 39So Balaam went with Balak,
and they came to Kirjath Huzoth.
40Then Balak offered oxen and sheep,
and he sent *some* to Balaam and to the
princes who *were* with him.

Balaam's First Prophecy

41So it was, the next day, that Balak
took Balaam and brought him up to the
high places of Baal, that from there he
might observe the extent of the people.
23 Then Balaam said to Balak,
"Build seven altars for me here,
and prepare for me here seven bulls
and seven rams."
2And Balak did just as Balaam had
spoken, and Balak and Balaam offered
a bull and a ram on *each* altar. 3Then Ba-
laam said to Balak, "Stand by your burnt
offering, and I will go; perhaps the LORD
will come to meet me, and whatever He
shows me I will tell you." So he went to a
desolate height. 4And God met Balaam,
and he said to Him, "I have prepared
the seven altars, and I have offered on
each altar a bull and a ram."
5Then the LORD put a word in Balaam's
mouth, and said, "Return to Balak, and
thus you shall speak." 6So he returned
to him, and there he was, standing by
his burnt offering, he and all the princes
of Moab.
7And he took up his oracle and said:

"Balak the king of Moab has
brought me from Aram,
From the mountains of the east.
'Come, curse Jacob for me,
And come, denounce Israel!'

8 "How shall I curse whom God has
not cursed?
And how shall I denounce
whom the LORD has not
denounced?
9 For from the top of the rocks I see
him,
And from the hills I behold him;
There! A people dwelling alone,
Not reckoning itself among the
nations.

10 "Who can count the dust[a] of Jacob,
Or number one-fourth of Israel?
Let me die the death of the
righteous,
And let my end be like his!"

11Then Balak said to Balaam, "What
have you done to me? I took you to
curse my enemies, and look, you have
blessed *them* bountifully!"
12So he answered and said, "Must I not
take heed to speak what the LORD has
put in my mouth?"

Balaam's Second Prophecy

13Then Balak said to him, "Please come
with me to another place from which
you may see them; you shall see only
the outer part of them, and shall not
see them all; curse them for me from
there." 14So he brought him to the field
of Zophim, to the top of Pisgah, and
built seven altars, and offered a bull
and a ram on *each* altar.
15And he said to Balak, "Stand here
by your burnt offering while I meet[a]
the LORD over there."

23:10 [a] Or *dust cloud* **23:15** [a] Following Masoretic Text, Targum, and Vulgate; Syriac reads *call;* Septuagint reads *go and ask God.*

16Then the LORD met Balaam, and put a
word in his mouth, and said, "Go back to
Balak, and thus you shall speak." 17So he
came to him, and there he was, standing
by his burnt offering, and the princes of
Moab were with him. And Balak said to
him, "What has the LORD spoken?"
18Then he took up his oracle and said:

"Rise up, Balak, and hear!
Listen to me, son of Zippor!

19 "God *is* not a man, that He should lie,
Nor a son of man, that He should repent.
Has He said, and will He not do?
Or has He spoken, and will He not make it good?
20 Behold, I have received *a* *command* to bless;
He has blessed, and I cannot reverse it.

21 "He has not observed iniquity in Jacob,
Nor has He seen wickedness in Israel.
The LORD his God *is* with him,
And the shout of a King *is* among them.
22 God brings them out of Egypt;
He has strength like a wild ox.

23 "For *there is* no sorcery against Jacob,
Nor any divination against Israel.
It now must be said of Jacob
And of Israel, 'Oh, what God has done!'
24 Look, a people rises like a lioness,
And lifts itself up like a lion;
It shall not lie down until it devours the prey,
And drinks the blood of the slain."

25Then Balak said to Balaam, "Neither
curse them at all, nor bless them at all!"
26So Balaam answered and said to
Balak, "Did I not tell you, saying, 'All
that the LORD speaks, that I must do'?"

Balaam's Third Prophecy

27Then Balak said to Balaam, "Please
come, I will take you to another place;
perhaps it will please God that you may
curse them for me from there." 28So
Balak took Balaam to the top of Peor,
that overlooks the wasteland.[a] 29Then
Balaam said to Balak, "Build for me
here seven altars, and prepare for me
here seven bulls and seven rams." 30And
Balak did as Balaam had said, and offered a bull and a ram on *every* altar.

24 Now when Balaam saw that it
pleased the LORD to bless Israel,
he did not go as at other times, to seek
to use sorcery, but he set his face toward
the wilderness. 2And Balaam raised his
eyes, and saw Israel encamped according to their tribes; and the Spirit of God
came upon him.
3Then he took up his oracle and said:

"The utterance of Balaam the son of Beor,
The utterance of the man whose eyes are opened,
4 The utterance of him who hears the words of God,
Who sees the vision of the Almighty,
Who falls down, with eyes wide open:

5 "How lovely are your tents, O Jacob!
Your dwellings, O Israel!
6 Like valleys that stretch out,
Like gardens by the riverside,
Like aloes planted by the LORD,
Like cedars beside the waters.
7 He shall pour water from his buckets,
And his seed *shall be* in many waters.

"His king shall be higher than Agag,
And his kingdom shall be exalted.

8 "God brings him out of Egypt;
He has strength like a wild ox;
He shall consume the nations, his enemies;
He shall break their bones
And pierce *them* with his arrows.
9 'He bows down, he lies down as a lion;
And as a lion, who shall rouse him?'[a]

23:28 [a] Hebrew *Jeshimon* 24:9 [a] Genesis 49:9

"Blessed *is* he who blesses you,
And cursed *is* he who curses you."

10Then Balak's anger was aroused
against Balaam, and he struck his
hands together; and Balak said to Ba-
laam, "I called you to curse my enemies,
and look, you have bountifully blessed
them these three times! 11Now therefore,
flee to your place. I said I would greatly
honor you, but in fact, the LORD has
kept you back from honor."
12So Balaam said to Balak, "Did I not
also speak to your messengers whom
you sent to me, saying, 13'If Balak were to
give me his house full of silver and gold, I
could not go beyond the word of the LORD,
to do good or bad of my own will. What
the LORD says, that I must speak'? 14And
now, indeed, I am going to my people.
Come, I will advise you what this people
will do to your people in the latter days."

Balaam's Fourth Prophecy

15So he took up his oracle and said:

"The utterance of Balaam the son of Beor,
And the utterance of the man whose eyes are opened;
16 The utterance of him who hears the words of God,
And has the knowledge of the Most High,
Who sees the vision of the Almighty,
Who falls down, with eyes wide open:

17 "I see Him, but not now;
I behold Him, but not near;
A Star shall come out of Jacob;
A Scepter shall rise out of Israel,
And batter the brow of Moab,
And destroy all the sons of tumult.[a]

18 "And Edom shall be a possession;
Seir also, his enemies, shall be a possession,
While Israel does valiantly.
19 Out of Jacob One shall have dominion,
And destroy the remains of the city."

20Then he looked on Amalek, and he
took up his oracle and said:

"Amalek *was* first among the nations,
But *shall be* last until he perishes."

21Then he looked on the Kenites, and
he took up his oracle and said:

"Firm is your dwelling place,
And your nest is set in the rock;
22 Nevertheless Kain shall be burned.
How long until Asshur carries you away captive?"

23Then he took up his oracle and said:

"Alas! Who shall live when God does this?
24 But ships *shall come* from the coasts of Cyprus,[a]
And they shall afflict Asshur and afflict Eber,
And so shall *Amalek*,[b] until he perishes."

25So Balaam rose and departed and
returned to his place; Balak also went
his way.

Israel's Harlotry in Moab

25 Now Israel remained in Acacia
Grove,[a] and the people began
to commit harlotry with the women of
Moab. 2They invited the people to the
sacrifices of their gods, and the peo-
ple ate and bowed down to their gods.
3So Israel was joined to Baal of Peor,
and the anger of the LORD was aroused
against Israel.
4Then the LORD said to Moses, "Take
all the leaders of the people and hang
the offenders before the LORD, out in the
sun, that the fierce anger of the LORD
may turn away from Israel."
5So Moses said to the judges of Israel,
"Every one of you kill his men who were
joined to Baal of Peor."

24:17 [a] Hebrew *Sheth* (compare Jeremiah 48:45)
25:1 [a] Hebrew *Shittim*
24:24 [a] Hebrew *Kittim* [b] Literally *he* or *that one*

6And indeed, one of the children of Israel came and presented to his brethren a Midianite woman in the sight of Moses and in the sight of all the congregation of the children of Israel, who *were* weeping at the door of the tabernacle of meeting. 7Now when Phinehas the son of Eleazar, the son of Aaron the priest, saw *it,* he rose from among the congregation and took a javelin in his hand; 8and he went after the man of Israel into the tent and thrust both of them through, the man of Israel, and the woman through her body. So the plague was stopped among the children of Israel. 9And those who died in the plague were twenty-four thousand.

10Then the LORD spoke to Moses, saying: 11"Phinehas the son of Eleazar, the son of Aaron the priest, has turned back My wrath from the children of Israel, because he was zealous with My zeal among them, so that I did not consume the children of Israel in My zeal. 12Therefore say, 'Behold, I give to him My covenant of peace; 13and it shall be to him and his descendants after him a covenant of an everlasting priesthood, because he was zealous for his God, and made atonement for the children of Israel.' "

14Now the name of the Israelite who was killed, who was killed with the Midianite woman, *was* Zimri the son of Salu, a leader of a father's house among the Simeonites. 15And the name of the Midianite woman who was killed *was* Cozbi the daughter of Zur; he *was* head of the people of a father's house in Midian.

16Then the LORD spoke to Moses, saying: 17"Harass the Midianites, and attack them; 18for they harassed you with their schemes by which they seduced you in the matter of Peor and in the matter of Cozbi, the daughter of a leader of Midian, their sister, who was killed in the day of the plague because of Peor."

The Second Census of Israel

26 And it came to pass, after the plague, that the LORD spoke to Moses and Eleazar the son of Aaron the priest, saying: 2"Take a census of all the congregation of the children of Israel from twenty years old and above, by their fathers' houses, all who are able to go to war in Israel." 3So Moses and Eleazar the priest spoke with them in the plains of Moab by the Jordan, *across from* Jericho, saying: 4"*Take a census of the people* from twenty years old and above, just as the LORD commanded Moses and the children of Israel who came out of the land of Egypt."

5Reuben *was* the firstborn of Israel. The children of Reuben *were: of* Hanoch, the family of the Hanochites; *of* Pallu, the family of the Palluites; 6*of* Hezron, the family of the Hezronites; *of* Carmi, the family of the Carmites. 7These *are* the families of the Reubenites: those who were numbered of them were forty-three thousand seven hundred and thirty. 8And the son of Pallu *was* Eliab. 9The sons of Eliab *were* Nemuel, Dathan, and Abiram. These *are* the Dathan and Abiram, representatives of the congregation, who contended against Moses and Aaron in the company of Korah, when they contended against the LORD; 10and the earth opened its mouth and swallowed them up together with Korah when that company died, when the fire devoured two hundred and fifty men; and they became a sign. 11Nevertheless the children of Korah did not die.

12The sons of Simeon according to their families *were: of* Nemuel,[a] the family of the Nemuelites; *of* Jamin, the family of the Jaminites; *of* Jachin,[b] the family of the Jachinites; 13*of* Zerah,[a] the family of the Zarhites; *of* Shaul, the family of the Shaulites. 14These *are* the families of the Simeonites: twenty-two thousand two hundred.

15The sons of Gad according to their families *were: of* Zephon,[a] the family of the Zephonites; *of* Haggi, the family of the Haggites; *of* Shuni, the family of the Shunites; 16*of* Ozni,[a] the family of the Oznites; *of* Eri, the family of the Erites; 17*of* Arod,[a] the family of the Arodites; *of* Areli, the family of the Arelites. 18These *are* the families of the sons

26:12 [a] Spelled *Jemuel* in Genesis 46:10 and Exodus 6:15 [b] Called *Jarib* in 1 Chronicles 4:24
26:13 [a] Called *Zohar* in Genesis 46:10 **26:15** [a] Called *Ziphion* in Genesis 46:16 **26:16** [a] Called *Ezbon* in Genesis 46:16 **26:17** [a] Spelled *Arodi* in Samaritan Pentateuch, Syriac, and Genesis 46:16

of Gad according to those who were numbered of them: forty thousand five hundred.

19 The sons of Judah *were* Er and Onan; and Er and Onan died in the land of Canaan. 20 And the sons of Judah according to their families were: *of* Shelah, the family of the Shelanites; *of* Perez, the family of the Parzites; *of* Zerah, the family of the Zarhites. 21 And the sons of Perez were: *of* Hezron, the family of the Hezronites; *of* Hamul, the family of the Hamulites. 22 These *are* the families of Judah according to those who were numbered of them: seventy-six thousand five hundred.

23 The sons of Issachar according to their families *were: of* Tola, the family of the Tolaites; of Puah,[a] the family of the Punites;[b] 24 of Jashub, the family of the Jashubites; of Shimron, the family of the Shimronites. 25 These *are* the families of Issachar according to those who were numbered of them: sixty-four thousand three hundred.

26 The sons of Zebulun according to their families *were:* of Sered, the family of the Sardites; of Elon, the family of the Elonites; of Jahleel, the family of the Jahleelites. 27 These *are* the families of the Zebulunites according to those who were numbered of them: sixty thousand five hundred.

28 The sons of Joseph according to their families, by Manasseh and Ephraim, *were:* 29 The sons of Manasseh: of Machir, the family of the Machirites; and Machir begot Gilead; of Gilead, the family of the Gileadites. 30 These *are* the sons of Gilead: *of* Jeezer,[a] the family of the Jeezerites; of Helek, the family of the Helekites; 31 *of* Asriel, the family of the Asrielites; *of* Shechem, the family of the Shechemites; 32 *of* Shemida, the family of the Shemidaites; *of* Hepher, the family of the Hepherites. 33 Now Zelophehad the son of Hepher had no sons, but daughters; and the names of the daughters of Zelophehad *were* Mahlah, Noah, Hoglah, Milcah, and Tirzah. 34 These *are* the families of Manasseh; and those who were numbered of them *were* fifty-two thousand seven hundred.

35 These *are* the sons of Ephraim according to their families: of Shuthelah, the family of the Shuthalhites; of Becher,[a] the family of the Bachrites; of Tahan, the family of the Tahanites. 36 And these *are* the sons of Shuthelah: of Eran, the family of the Eranites. 37 These *are* the families of the sons of Ephraim according to those who were numbered of them: thirty-two thousand five hundred.

These *are* the sons of Joseph according to their families.

38 The sons of Benjamin according to their families were: of Bela, the family of the Belaites; of Ashbel, the family of the Ashbelites; of Ahiram, the family of the Ahiramites; 39 of Shupham,[a] the family of the Shuphamites; of Hupham,[b] the family of the Huphamites. 40 And the sons of Bela were Ard[a] and Naaman: *of Ard,* the family of the Ardites; of Naaman, the family of the Naamites. 41 These *are* the sons of Benjamin according to their families; and those who were numbered of them *were* forty-five thousand six hundred.

42 These *are* the sons of Dan according to their families: of Shuham,[a] the family of the Shuhamites. These *are* the families of Dan according to their families. 43 All the families of the Shuhamites, according to those who were numbered of them, *were* sixty-four thousand four hundred.

44 The sons of Asher according to their families *were:* of Jimna, the family of the Jimnites; of Jesui, the family of the Jesuites; of Beriah, the family of the Beriites. 45 Of the sons of Beriah: of Heber, the family of the Heberites; of Malchiel, the family of the Malchielites. 46 And the name of the daughter of Asher *was* Serah. 47 These *are* the families of the sons of Asher according to those who were numbered of them: fifty-three thousand four hundred.

26:23 [a] Hebrew *Puvah* (compare Genesis 46:13 and 1 Chronicles 7:1); Samaritan Pentateuch, Septuagint, Syriac, and Vulgate read *Puah.* [b] Samaritan Pentateuch, Septuagint, Syriac, and Vulgate read *Puaites.* **26:30** [a] Called *Abiezer* in Joshua 17:2 **26:35** [a] Called *Bered* in 1 Chronicles 7:20 **26:39** [a] Masoretic Text reads *Shephupham,* spelled *Shephuphan* in 1 Chronicles 8:5. [b] Called *Huppim* in Genesis 46:21 **26:40** [a] Called *Addar* in 1 Chronicles 8:3 **26:42** [a] Called *Hushim* in Genesis 46:23

48The sons of Naphtali according to
their families *were:* of Jahzeel,[a] the fam-
ily of the Jahzeelites; of Guni, the family
of the Gunites; 49of Jezer, the family of
the Jezerites; of Shillem, the family of
the Shillemites. 50These *are* the families
of Naphtali according to their families;
and those who were numbered of them
were forty-five thousand four hundred.
51These *are* those who were numbered
of the children of Israel: six hundred
and one thousand seven hundred and
thirty.
52Then the LORD spoke to Moses,
saying: 53"To these the land shall be
divided as an inheritance, according
to the number of names. 54To a large
tribe you shall give a larger inheritance,
and to a small *tribe* you shall give a
smaller inheritance. Each shall be given
its inheritance according to those who
were numbered of them. 55But the land
shall be divided by lot; they shall inherit
according to the names of the tribes of
their fathers. 56According to the lot their
inheritance shall be divided between
the larger and the smaller."
57And these *are* those who were num-
bered of the Levites according to their
families: of Gershon, the family of the
Gershonites; of Kohath, the family of
the Kohathites; of Merari, the family
of the Merarites. 58These *are* the fam-
ilies of the Levites: the family of the
Libnites, the family of the Hebronites,
the family of the Mahlites, the family
of the Mushites, and the family of the
Korathites. And Kohath begot Amram.
59The name of Amram's wife *was* Joche-
bed the daughter of Levi, who was born
to Levi in Egypt; and to Amram she
bore Aaron and Moses and their sister
Miriam. 60To Aaron were born Nadab
and Abihu, Eleazar and Ithamar. 61And
Nadab and Abihu died when they of-
fered profane fire before the LORD.
62Now those who were numbered of
them were twenty-three thousand, ev-
ery male from a month old and above;
for they were not numbered among
the other children of Israel, because
there was no inheritance given to them
among the children of Israel.
63These *are* those who were numbered
by Moses and Eleazar the priest, who
numbered the children of Israel in the
plains of Moab by the Jordan, *across
from* Jericho. 64But among these there
was not a man of those who were num-
bered by Moses and Aaron the priest
when they numbered the children of
Israel in the Wilderness of Sinai. 65For
the LORD had said of them, "They shall
surely die in the wilderness." So there
was not left a man of them, except Caleb
the son of Jephunneh and Joshua the
son of Nun.

Inheritance Laws

27 Then came the daughters of Ze-
lophehad the son of Hepher, the
son of Gilead, the son of Machir, the son
of Manasseh, from the families of Ma-
nasseh the son of Joseph; and these *were*
the names of his daughters: Mahlah,
Noah, Hoglah, Milcah, and Tirzah. 2And
they stood before Moses, before Eleazar
the priest, and before the leaders and
all the congregation, *by* the doorway
of the tabernacle of meeting, saying:
3"Our father died in the wilderness; but
he was not in the company of those who
gathered together against the LORD,
in company with Korah, but he died in
his own sin; and he had no sons. 4Why
should the name of our father be re-
moved from among his family because
he had no son? Give us a possession
among our father's brothers."
5So Moses brought their case before
the LORD.
6And the LORD spoke to Moses, saying:
7"The daughters of Zelophehad speak
what is right; you shall surely give them
a possession of inheritance among their
father's brothers, and cause the inher-
itance of their father to pass to them.
8And you shall speak to the children
of Israel, saying: 'If a man dies and
has no son, then you shall cause his
inheritance to pass to his daughter.
9If he has no daughter, then you shall
give his inheritance to his brothers. 10If
he has no brothers, then you shall give
his inheritance to his father's brothers.
11And if his father has no brothers, then

26:48 [a] Spelled *Jahziel* in 1 Chronicles 7:13

GOD SIN JESUS SALVATION LOVE

you shall give his inheritance to the rel-
ative closest to him in his family, and he
shall possess it.' " And it shall be to the
children of Israel a statute of judgment,
just as the LORD commanded Moses.

Joshua the Next Leader of Israel

12 Now the LORD said to Moses: "Go
up into this Mount Abarim, and see
the land which I have given to the chil-
dren of Israel. 13 And when you have
seen it, you also shall be gathered to
your people, as Aaron your brother was
gathered. 14 For in the Wilderness of Zin,
during the strife of the congregation,
you rebelled against My command to
hallow Me at the waters before their
eyes." (These *are* the waters of Meribah,
at Kadesh in the Wilderness of Zin.)
15 Then Moses spoke to the LORD, say-
ing: 16 "Let the LORD, the God of the
spirits of all flesh, set a man over the
congregation, 17 who may go out before
them and go in before them, who may
lead them out and bring them in, that
the congregation of the LORD may not
be like sheep which have no shepherd."
18 And the LORD said to Moses: "Take
Joshua the son of Nun with you, a man
in whom *is* the Spirit, and lay your hand
on him; 19 set him before Eleazar the
priest and before all the congregation,
and inaugurate him in their sight.
20 And you shall give *some* of your au-
thority to him, that all the congregation
of the children of Israel may be obe-
dient. 21 He shall stand before Eleazar
the priest, who shall inquire before the
LORD for him by the judgment of the
Urim. At his word they shall go out, and
at his word they shall come in, he and
all the children of Israel with him—all
the congregation."
22 So Moses did as the LORD command-
ed him. He took Joshua and set him
before Eleazar the priest and before
all the congregation. 23 And he laid his
hands on him and inaugurated him,
just as the LORD commanded by the
hand of Moses.

Daily Offerings

28 Now the LORD spoke to Moses,
saying, 2 "Command the chil-
dren of Israel, and say to them, 'My
offering, My food for My offerings made
by fire as a sweet aroma to Me, you
shall be careful to offer to Me at their
appointed time.'
3 "And you shall say to them, 'This *is*
the offering made by fire which you
shall offer to the LORD: two male lambs
in their first year without blemish, day
by day, as a regular burnt offering. 4 The
one lamb you shall offer in the morning,
the other lamb you shall offer in the
evening, 5 and one-tenth of an ephah
of fine flour as a grain offering mixed
with one-fourth of a hin of pressed oil.
6 *It is* a regular burnt offering which was
ordained at Mount Sinai for a sweet
aroma, an offering made by fire to the
LORD. 7 And its drink offering *shall be*
one-fourth of a hin for each lamb; in a
holy *place* you shall pour out the drink
to the LORD as an offering. 8 The other
lamb you shall offer in the evening; as
the morning grain offering and its drink
offering, you shall offer *it* as an offering
made by fire, a sweet aroma to the LORD.

Sabbath Offerings

9 'And on the Sabbath day two lambs
in their first year, without blemish, and
two-tenths *of an ephah* of fine flour as
a grain offering, mixed with oil, with
its drink offering— 10 *this is* the burnt
offering for every Sabbath, besides the
regular burnt offering with its drink
offering.

Monthly Offerings

11 'At the beginnings of your months
you shall present a burnt offering to the
LORD: two young bulls, one ram, and
seven lambs in their first year, without
blemish; 12 three-tenths *of an ephah* of
fine flour as a grain offering, mixed
with oil, for each bull; two-tenths *of an
ephah* of fine flour as a grain offering,
mixed with oil, for the one ram; 13 and
one-tenth *of an ephah* of fine flour,
mixed with oil, as a grain offering for
each lamb, as a burnt offering of sweet
aroma, an offering made by fire to the
LORD. 14 Their drink offering shall be half
a hin of wine for a bull, one-third of a
hin for a ram, and one-fourth of a hin
for a lamb; this *is* the burnt offering for
each month throughout the months of

the year. 15Also one kid of the goats as a
sin offering to the LORD shall be offered,
besides the regular burnt offering and
its drink offering.

Offerings at Passover

16'On the fourteenth day of the first
month *is* the Passover of the LORD.
17And on the fifteenth day of this month
is the feast; unleavened bread shall be
eaten for seven days. 18On the first day
you shall have a holy convocation. You
shall do no customary work. 19And you
shall present an offering made by fire
as a burnt offering to the LORD: two
young bulls, one ram, and seven lambs
in their first year. Be sure they are with-
out blemish. 20Their grain offering shall
be of fine flour mixed with oil: three-
tenths *of an ephah* you shall offer for
a bull, and two-tenths for a ram; 21you
shall offer one-tenth *of an ephah* for
each of the seven lambs; 22also one goat
as a sin offering, to make atonement for
you. 23You shall offer these besides the
burnt offering of the morning, which *is*
for a regular burnt offering. 24In this
manner you shall offer the food of the
offering made by fire daily for seven
days, as a sweet aroma to the LORD;
it shall be offered besides the regular
burnt offering and its drink offering.
25And on the seventh day you shall
have a holy convocation. You shall do
no customary work.

Offerings at the Feast of Weeks

26'Also on the day of the firstfruits,
when you bring a new grain offering
to the LORD at your *Feast of* Weeks,
you shall have a holy convocation.
You shall do no customary work. 27You
shall present a burnt offering as a sweet
aroma to the LORD: two young bulls,
one ram, and seven lambs in their first
year, 28with their grain offering of fine
flour mixed with oil: three-tenths *of an*
ephah for each bull, two-tenths for the
one ram, 29and one-tenth for each of
the seven lambs; 30*also* one kid of the
goats, to make atonement for you. 31Be
sure they are without blemish. You shall
present *them* with their drink offerings,
besides the regular burnt offering with
its grain offering.

Offerings at the Feast of Trumpets

29 'And in the seventh month,
on the first *day* of the month,
you shall have a holy convocation.
You shall do no customary work. For
you it is a day of blowing the trumpets.
2You shall offer a burnt offering as a
sweet aroma to the LORD: one young
bull, one ram, *and* seven lambs in their
first year, without blemish. 3Their grain
offering *shall be* fine flour mixed with
oil: three-tenths *of an ephah* for the bull,
two-tenths for the ram, 4and one-tenth
for each of the seven lambs; 5also one
kid of the goats *as* a sin offering, to
make atonement for you; 6besides the
burnt offering with its grain offering
for the New Moon, the regular burnt
offering with its grain offering, and
their drink offerings, according to their
ordinance, as a sweet aroma, an offer-
ing made by fire to the LORD.

Offerings on the Day of Atonement

7'On the tenth *day* of this seventh
month you shall have a holy convoca-
tion. You shall afflict your souls; you
shall not do any work. 8You shall pre-
sent a burnt offering to the LORD *as* a
sweet aroma: one young bull, one ram,
and seven lambs in their first year. Be
sure they are without blemish. 9Their
grain offering *shall be of* fine flour mixed
with oil: three-tenths *of an ephah* for
the bull, two-tenths for the one ram,
10and one-tenth for each of the seven
lambs; 11also one kid of the goats *as* a
sin offering, besides the sin offering for
atonement, the regular burnt offering
with its grain offering, and their drink
offerings.

Offerings at the Feast of Tabernacles

12'On the fifteenth day of the seventh
month you shall have a holy convoca-
tion. You shall do no customary work,
and you shall keep a feast to the LORD
seven days. 13You shall present a burnt
offering, an offering made by fire as
a sweet aroma to the LORD: thirteen
young bulls, two rams, *and* fourteen
lambs in their first year. They shall be
without blemish. 14Their grain offer-
ing *shall be of* fine flour mixed with oil:
three-tenths *of an ephah* for each of the

thirteen bulls, two-tenths for each of the
two rams, [15]and one-tenth for each of
the fourteen lambs; [16]also one kid of
the goats *as* a sin offering, besides the
regular burnt offering, its grain offer-
ing, and its drink offering.

[17]'On the second day *present* twelve
young bulls, two rams, fourteen lambs
in their first year without blemish, [18]and
their grain offering and their drink of-
ferings for the bulls, for the rams, and
for the lambs, by their number, accord-
ing to the ordinance; [19]also one kid of
the goats *as* a sin offering, besides the
regular burnt offering with its grain
offering, and their drink offerings.

[20]'On the third day *present* eleven
bulls, two rams, fourteen lambs in their
first year without blemish, [21]and their
grain offering and their drink offerings
for the bulls, for the rams, and for the
lambs, by their number, according to
the ordinance; [22]also one goat *as* a sin
offering, besides the regular burnt of-
fering, its grain offering, and its drink
offering.

[23]'On the fourth day *present* ten bulls,
two rams, *and* fourteen lambs in their
first year, without blemish, [24]and their
grain offering and their drink offerings
for the bulls, for the rams, and for the
lambs, by their number, according to
the ordinance; [25]also one kid of the
goats *as* a sin offering, besides the reg-
ular burnt offering, its grain offering,
and its drink offering.

[26]'On the fifth day *present* nine bulls,
two rams, *and* fourteen lambs in their
first year without blemish, [27]and their
grain offering and their drink offerings
for the bulls, for the rams, and for the
lambs, by their number, according to
the ordinance; [28]also one goat *as* a sin
offering, besides the regular burnt of-
fering, its grain offering, and its drink
offering.

[29]'On the sixth day *present* eight bulls,
two rams, *and* fourteen lambs in their
first year without blemish, [30]and their
grain offering and their drink offerings
for the bulls, for the rams, and for the
lambs, by their number, according to the
ordinance; [31]also one goat *as* a sin offer-
ing, besides the regular burnt offering,
its grain offering, and its drink offering.

[32]'On the seventh day *present* seven
bulls, two rams, *and* fourteen lambs in
their first year without blemish, [33]and
their grain offering and their drink of-
ferings for the bulls, for the rams, and
for the lambs, by their number, accord-
ing to the ordinance; [34]also one goat
as a sin offering, besides the regular
burnt offering, its grain offering, and
its drink offering.

[35]'On the eighth day you shall have
a sacred assembly. You shall do no
customary work. [36]You shall present
a burnt offering, an offering made by
fire as a sweet aroma to the LORD: one
bull, one ram, seven lambs in their
first year without blemish, [37]and their
grain offering and their drink offer-
ings for the bull, for the ram, and for
the lambs, by their number, accord-
ing to the ordinance; [38]also one goat
as a sin offering, besides the regular
burnt offering, its grain offering, and
its drink offering.

[39]'These you shall present to the LORD
at your appointed feasts (besides your
vowed offerings and your freewill offer-
ings) as your burnt offerings and your
grain offerings, as your drink offerings
and your peace offerings.' "

[40]So Moses told the children of Israel
everything, just as the LORD command-
ed Moses.

The Law Concerning Vows

30 Then Moses spoke to the heads
of the tribes concerning the chil-
dren of Israel, saying, "This *is* the thing
which the LORD has commanded: [2]If a
man makes a vow to the LORD, or swears
an oath to bind himself by some agree-
ment, he shall not break his word; he
shall do according to all that proceeds
out of his mouth.

[3]"Or if a woman makes a vow to the
LORD, and binds *herself* by some agree-
ment while in her father's house in her
youth, [4]and her father hears her vow
and the agreement by which she has
bound herself, and her father holds his
peace, then all her vows shall stand,
and every agreement with which she
has bound herself shall stand. [5]But if
her father overrules her on the day that
he hears, then none of her vows nor her

agreements by which she has bound
herself shall stand; and the LORD will
release her, because her father over-
ruled her.
6“If indeed she takes a husband,
while bound by her vows or by a rash
utterance from her lips by which she
bound herself, 7and her husband hears
it, and makes no response to her on the
day that he hears, then her vows shall
stand, and her agreements by which
she bound herself shall stand. 8But if
her husband overrules her on the day
that he hears *it,* he shall make void her
vow which she took and what she ut-
tered with her lips, by which she bound
herself, and the LORD will release her.
9“Also any vow of a widow or a di-
vorced woman, by which she has bound
herself, shall stand against her.
10“If she vowed in her husband’s house,
or bound herself by an agreement with
an oath, 11and her husband heard *it,*
and made no response to her *and* did
not overrule her, then all her vows shall
stand, and every agreement by which
she bound herself shall stand. 12But if
her husband truly made them void on
the day he heard *them,* then whatever
proceeded from her lips concerning
her vows or concerning the agreement
binding her, it shall not stand; her hus-
band has made them void, and the
LORD will release her. 13Every vow and
every binding oath to afflict her soul,
her husband may confirm it, or her
husband may make it void. 14Now if her
husband makes no response whatever
to her from day to day, then he confirms
all her vows or all the agreements that
bind her; he confirms them, because he
made no response to her on the day that
he heard *them.* 15But if he does make
them void after he has heard *them,* then
he shall bear her guilt.”
16These *are* the statutes which the
LORD commanded Moses, between a
man and his wife, and between a father
and his daughter in her youth in her
father’s house.

Vengeance on the Midianites

31 And the LORD spoke to Moses,
saying: 2“Take vengeance on
the Midianites for the children of Israel.
Afterward you shall be gathered to your
people.”
3So Moses spoke to the people, saying,
“Arm some of yourselves for war, and
let them go against the Midianites to
take vengeance for the LORD on Mid-
ian. 4A thousand from each tribe of
all the tribes of Israel you shall send
to the war.”
5So there were recruited from the divi-
sions of Israel one thousand from *each*
tribe, twelve thousand armed for war.
6Then Moses sent them to the war, one
thousand from *each* tribe; he sent them
to the war with Phinehas the son of El-
eazar the priest, with the holy articles
and the signal trumpets in his hand.
7And they warred against the Midi-
anites, just as the LORD commanded
Moses, and they killed all the males.
8They killed the kings of Midian with
the rest of those who were killed—Evi,
Rekem, Zur, Hur, and Reba, the five
kings of Midian. Balaam the son of Beor
they also killed with the sword.
9And the children of Israel took the
women of Midian captive, with their
little ones, and took as spoil all their cat-
tle, all their flocks, and all their goods.
10They also burned with fire all the cities
where they dwelt, and all their forts.
11And they took all the spoil and all the
booty—of man and beast.

Return from the War

12Then they brought the captives, the
booty, and the spoil to Moses, to Elea-
zar the priest, and to the congregation
of the children of Israel, to the camp in
the plains of Moab by the Jordan, *across
from* Jericho. 13And Moses, Eleazar the
priest, and all the leaders of the congre-
gation, went to meet them outside the
camp. 14But Moses was angry with the
officers of the army, *with* the captains
over thousands and captains over hun-
dreds, who had come from the battle.
15And Moses said to them: “Have you
kept all the women alive? 16Look, these
women caused the children of Israel,
through the counsel of Balaam, to tres-
pass against the LORD in the incident
of Peor, and there was a plague among
the congregation of the LORD. 17Now
therefore, kill every male among the

little ones, and kill every woman who
has known a man intimately. 18But keep
alive for yourselves all the young girls
who have not known a man intimately.
19And as for you, remain outside the
camp seven days; whoever has killed
any person, and whoever has touched
any slain, purify yourselves and your
captives on the third day and on the
seventh day. 20Purify every garment,
everything made of leather, everything
woven of goats' *hair*, and everything
made of wood."
21Then Eleazar the priest said to the
men of war who had gone to the battle,
"This *is* the ordinance of the law which
the LORD commanded Moses: 22Only the
gold, the silver, the bronze, the iron, the
tin, and the lead, 23everything that can
endure fire, you shall put through the
fire, and it shall be clean; and it shall
be purified with the water of purifica-
tion. But all that cannot endure fire you
shall put through water. 24And you shall
wash your clothes on the seventh day
and be clean, and afterward you may
come into the camp."

Division of the Plunder

25Now the LORD spoke to Moses, say-
ing: 26"Count up the plunder that was
taken—of man and beast—you and
Eleazar the priest and the chief fathers
of the congregation; 27and divide the
plunder into two parts, between those
who took part in the war, who went
out to battle, and all the congregation.
28And levy a tribute for the LORD on the
men of war who went out to battle: one
of every five hundred of the persons,
the cattle, the donkeys, and the sheep;
29take *it* from their half, and give *it* to
Eleazar the priest as a heave offering
to the LORD. 30And from the children
of Israel's half you shall take one of
every fifty, drawn from the persons,
the cattle, the donkeys, and the sheep,
from all the livestock, and give them
to the Levites who keep charge of the
tabernacle of the LORD." 31So Moses
and Eleazar the priest did as the LORD
commanded Moses.
32The booty remaining from the plun-
der, which the men of war had taken, was
six hundred and seventy-five thousand
sheep, 33seventy-two thousand cattle,
34sixty-one thousand donkeys, 35and
thirty-two thousand persons in all, of
women who had not known a man inti-
mately. 36And the half, the portion for
those who had gone out to war, was in
number three hundred and thirty-seven
thousand five hundred sheep; 37and
the LORD's tribute of the sheep was six
hundred and seventy-five. 38The cattle
were thirty-six thousand, of which the
LORD's tribute *was* seventy-two. 39The
donkeys *were* thirty thousand five hun-
dred, of which the LORD's tribute *was*
sixty-one. 40The persons *were* sixteen
thousand, of which the LORD's tribute
was thirty-two persons. 41So Moses gave
the tribute *which was* the LORD's heave
offering to Eleazar the priest, as the
LORD commanded Moses.
42And from the children of Israel's
half, which Moses separated from the
men who fought— 43now the half be-
longing to the congregation was three
hundred and thirty-seven thousand five
hundred sheep, 44thirty-six thousand
cattle, 45thirty thousand five hundred
donkeys, 46and sixteen thousand per-
sons— 47and from the children of Isra-
el's half Moses took one of every fifty,
drawn from man and beast, and gave
them to the Levites, who kept charge of
the tabernacle of the LORD, as the LORD
commanded Moses.
48Then the officers who *were* over
thousands of the army, the captains
of thousands and captains of hundreds,
came near to Moses; 49and they said
to Moses, "Your servants have taken a
count of the men of war who *are* under
our command, and not a man of us is
missing. 50Therefore we have brought
an offering for the LORD, what every
man found of ornaments of gold: arm-
lets and bracelets and signet rings and
earrings and necklaces, to make atone-
ment for ourselves before the LORD."
51So Moses and Eleazar the priest re-
ceived the gold from them, all the fash-
ioned ornaments. 52And all the gold
of the offering that they offered to the
LORD, from the captains of thousands
and captains of hundreds, was sixteen
thousand seven hundred and fifty shek-
els. 53(The men of war had taken spoil,

every man for himself.) 54And Moses
and Eleazar the priest received the gold
from the captains of thousands and of
hundreds, and brought it into the tab-
ernacle of meeting as a memorial for
the children of Israel before the LORD.

The Tribes Settling East of the Jordan

32 Now the children of Reuben and
the children of Gad had a very
great multitude of livestock; and when
they saw the land of Jazer and the land
of Gilead, that indeed the region *was* a
place for livestock, 2the children of Gad
and the children of Reuben came and
spoke to Moses, to Eleazar the priest,
and to the leaders of the congregation,
saying, 3"Ataroth, Dibon, Jazer, Nim-
rah, Heshbon, Elealeh, Shebam, Nebo,
and Beon, 4the country which the LORD
defeated before the congregation of
Israel, *is* a land for livestock, and your
servants have livestock." 5Therefore
they said, "If we have found favor in
your sight, let this land be given to your
servants as a possession. Do not take
us over the Jordan."

6And Moses said to the children of Gad
and to the children of Reuben: "Shall
your brethren go to war while you sit
here? 7Now why will you discourage
the heart of the children of Israel from
going over into the land which the LORD
has given them? 8Thus your fathers did
when I sent them away from Kadesh
Barnea to see the land. 9For when they
went up to the Valley of Eshcol and saw
the land, they discouraged the heart of
the children of Israel, so that they did
not go into the land which the LORD had
given them. 10So the LORD's anger was
aroused on that day, and He swore an
oath, saying, 11'Surely none of the men
who came up from Egypt, from twenty
years old and above, shall see the land
of which I swore to Abraham, Isaac, and
Jacob, because they have not wholly
followed Me, 12except Caleb the son of
Jephunneh, the Kenizzite, and Joshua
the son of Nun, for they have wholly
followed the LORD.' 13So the LORD's an-
ger was aroused against Israel, and He
made them wander in the wilderness
forty years, until all the generation
that had done evil in the sight of the
LORD was gone. 14And look! You have
risen in your fathers' place, a brood of
sinful men, to increase still more the
fierce anger of the LORD against Israel.
15For if you turn away from following
Him, He will once again leave them in
the wilderness, and you will destroy all
these people."

16Then they came near to him and
said: "We will build sheepfolds here for
our livestock, and cities for our little
ones, 17but we ourselves will be armed,
ready *to go* before the children of Isra-
el until we have brought them to their
place; and our little ones will dwell in
the fortified cities because of the inhab-
itants of the land. 18We will not return
to our homes until every one of the
children of Israel has received his in-
heritance. 19For we will not inherit with
them on the other side of the Jordan
and beyond, because our inheritance
has fallen to us on this eastern side of
the Jordan."

20Then Moses said to them: "If you
do this thing, if you arm yourselves
before the LORD for the war, 21and all
your armed men cross over the Jordan
before the LORD until He has driven out
His enemies from before Him, 22and
the land is subdued before the LORD,
then afterward you may return and be
blameless before the LORD and before
Israel; and this land shall be your pos-
session before the LORD. 23But if you
do not do so, then take note, you have
sinned against the LORD; and be sure
your sin will find you out. 24Build cities
for your little ones and folds for your
sheep, and do what has proceeded out
of your mouth."

25And the children of Gad and the
children of Reuben spoke to Moses,
saying: "Your servants will do as my
lord commands. 26Our little ones, our
wives, our flocks, and all our livestock
will be there in the cities of Gilead; 27but
your servants will cross over, every man
armed for war, before the LORD to battle,
just as my lord says."

28So Moses gave command con-
cerning them to Eleazar the priest, to
Joshua the son of Nun, and to the chief
fathers of the tribes of the children of
Israel. 29And Moses said to them: "If

the children of Gad and the children of
Reuben cross over the Jordan with you,
every man armed for battle before the
LORD, and the land is subdued before
you, then you shall give them the land
of Gilead as a possession. 30But if they
do not cross over armed with you, they
shall have possessions among you in
the land of Canaan."
31Then the children of Gad and the
children of Reuben answered, saying:
"As the LORD has said to your servants,
so we will do. 32We will cross over armed
before the LORD into the land of Canaan,
but the possession of our inheritance
shall remain with us on this side
of the Jordan."
33So Moses gave to the children of
Gad, to the children of Reuben, and
to half the tribe of Manasseh the son
of Joseph, the kingdom of Sihon king
of the Amorites and the kingdom of
Og king of Bashan, the land with its
cities within the borders, the cities of
the surrounding country. 34And the
children of Gad built Dibon and Ataroth
and Aroer, 35Atroth and Shophan
and Jazer and Jogbehah, 36Beth Nimrah
and Beth Haran, fortified cities,
and folds for sheep. 37And the children
of Reuben built Heshbon and Elealeh
and Kirjathaim, 38Nebo and Baal Meon
(*their* names being changed) and Shibmah;
and they gave *other* names to the
cities which they built.
39And the children of Machir the son
of Manasseh went to Gilead and took it,
and dispossessed the Amorites who *were*
in it. 40So Moses gave Gilead to Machir
the son of Manasseh, and he dwelt in
it. 41Also Jair the son of Manasseh went
and took its small towns, and called
them Havoth Jair.[a] 42Then Nobah went
and took Kenath and its villages, and
he called it Nobah, after his own name.

Israel's Journey from Egypt Reviewed

33 These *are* the journeys of the
children of Israel, who went out
of the land of Egypt by their armies under
the hand of Moses and Aaron. 2Now
Moses wrote down the starting points
of their journeys at the command of
the LORD. And these *are* their journeys
according to their starting points:
3They departed from Rameses in the
first month, on the fifteenth day of the
first month; on the day after the Passover
the children of Israel went out with
boldness in the sight of all the Egyptians.
4For the Egyptians were burying
all *their* firstborn, whom the LORD had
killed among them. Also on their gods
the LORD had executed judgments.
5Then the children of Israel moved
from Rameses and camped at Succoth.
6They departed from Succoth
and camped at Etham, which *is* on the
edge of the wilderness. 7They moved
from Etham and turned back to Pi Hahiroth,
which *is* east of Baal Zephon;
and they camped near Migdol. 8They
departed from before Hahiroth[a] and
passed through the midst of the sea
into the wilderness, went three days'
journey in the Wilderness of Etham, and
camped at Marah. 9They moved from
Marah and came to Elim. At Elim *were*
twelve springs of water and seventy
palm trees; so they camped there.
10They moved from Elim and camped
by the Red Sea. 11They moved from the
Red Sea and camped in the Wilderness
of Sin. 12They journeyed from the Wilderness
of Sin and camped at Dophkah.
13They departed from Dophkah
and camped at Alush. 14They moved
from Alush and camped at Rephidim,
where there was no water for the people
to drink.
15They departed from Rephidim and
camped in the Wilderness of Sinai.
16They moved from the Wilderness of
Sinai and camped at Kibroth Hattaavah.
17They departed from Kibroth
Hattaavah and camped at Hazeroth.
18They departed from Hazeroth and
camped at Rithmah. 19They departed
from Rithmah and camped at Rimmon
Perez. 20They departed from Rimmon
Perez and camped at Libnah. 21They
moved from Libnah and camped at
Rissah. 22They journeyed from Rissah
and camped at Kehelathah. 23They
went from Kehelathah and camped at
Mount Shepher. 24They moved from

32:41 [a] Literally *Towns of Jair* **33:8** [a] Many Hebrew manuscripts, Samaritan Pentateuch, Syriac, Targum, and Vulgate read *from Pi Hahiroth* (compare verse 7).

Mount Shepher and camped at Hara-
dah. 25They moved from Haradah and
camped at Makheloth. 26They moved
from Makheloth and camped at Ta-
hath. 27They departed from Tahath
and camped at Terah. 28They moved
from Terah and camped at Mithkah.
29They went from Mithkah and camped
at Hashmonah. 30They departed from
Hashmonah and camped at Mose-
roth. 31They departed from Moseroth
and camped at Bene Jaakan. 32They
moved from Bene Jaakan and camped
at Hor Hagidgad. 33They went from Hor
Hagidgad and camped at Jotbathah.
34They moved from Jotbathah and
camped at Abronah. 35They departed
from Abronah and camped at Ezion
Geber. 36They moved from Ezion Geber
and camped in the Wilderness of Zin,
which *is* Kadesh. 37They moved from
Kadesh and camped at Mount Hor, on
the boundary of the land of Edom.

38Then Aaron the priest went up to
Mount Hor at the command of the
LORD, and died there in the fortieth
year after the children of Israel had
come out of the land of Egypt, on the
first *day* of the fifth month. 39Aaron *was*
one hundred and twenty-three years
old when he died on Mount Hor.

40Now the king of Arad, the Canaan-
ite, who dwelt in the South in the land
of Canaan, heard of the coming of the
children of Israel.

41So they departed from Mount Hor
and camped at Zalmonah. 42They de-
parted from Zalmonah and camped at
Punon. 43They departed from Punon and
camped at Oboth. 44They departed from
Oboth and camped at Ije Abarim, at the
border of Moab. 45They departed from
Ijim[a] and camped at Dibon Gad. 46They
moved from Dibon Gad and camped
at Almon Diblathaim. 47They moved
from Almon Diblathaim and camped in
the mountains of Abarim, before Nebo.
48They departed from the mountains
of Abarim and camped in the plains of
Moab by the Jordan, *across from* Jeri-
cho. 49They camped by the Jordan, from
Beth Jesimoth as far as the Abel Acacia
Grove[a] in the plains of Moab.

Instructions for the Conquest of Canaan

50Now the LORD spoke to Moses in the
plains of Moab by the Jordan, *across
from* Jericho, saying, 51"Speak to the
children of Israel, and say to them:
'When you have crossed the Jordan
into the land of Canaan, 52then you
shall drive out all the inhabitants of
the land from before you, destroy all
their engraved stones, destroy all their
molded images, and demolish all their
high places; 53you shall dispossess *the
inhabitants of* the land and dwell in it,
for I have given you the land to pos-
sess. 54And you shall divide the land
by lot as an inheritance among your
families; to the larger you shall give a
larger inheritance, and to the smaller
you shall give a smaller inheritance;
there everyone's *inheritance* shall be
whatever falls to him by lot. You shall
inherit according to the tribes of your
fathers. 55But if you do not drive out
the inhabitants of the land from before
you, then it shall be that those whom
you let remain *shall be* irritants in your
eyes and thorns in your sides, and they
shall harass you in the land where you
dwell. 56Moreover it shall be *that* I will
do to you as I thought to do to them.' "

The Appointed Boundaries of Canaan

34 Then the LORD spoke to Moses,
saying, 2"Command the chil-
dren of Israel, and say to them: 'When
you come into the land of Canaan, this
is the land that shall fall to you as an
inheritance—the land of Canaan to
its boundaries. 3Your southern bor-
der shall be from the Wilderness of Zin
along the border of Edom; then your
southern border shall extend eastward
to the end of the Salt Sea; 4your border
shall turn from the southern side of the
Ascent of Akrabbim, continue to Zin,
and be on the south of Kadesh Barnea;
then it shall go on to Hazar Addar, and
continue to Azmon; 5the border shall
turn from Azmon to the Brook of Egypt,
and it shall end at the Sea.

6'As for the western border, you shall
have the Great Sea for a border; this
shall be your western border.

33:45 [a] Same as *Ije Abarim*, verse 44 33:49 [a] Hebrew *Abel Shittim*

7'And this shall be your northern
border: From the Great Sea you shall
mark out your *border* line to Mount
Hor; 8from Mount Hor you shall mark
out *your border* to the entrance of Ha-
math; then the direction of the border
shall be toward Zedad; 9the border shall
proceed to Ziphron, and it shall end at
Hazar Enan. This shall be your north-
ern border.
10'You shall mark out your eastern
border from Hazar Enan to Shepham;
11the border shall go down from She-
pham to Riblah on the east side of Ain;
the border shall go down and reach
to the eastern side of the Sea of Chin-
nereth; 12the border shall go down
along the Jordan, and it shall end at
the Salt Sea. This shall be your land with
its surrounding boundaries.' "
13Then Moses commanded the chil-
dren of Israel, saying: "This *is* the land
which you shall inherit by lot, which
the LORD has commanded to give to the
nine tribes and to the half-tribe. 14For the
tribe of the children of Reuben accord-
ing to the house of their fathers, and the
tribe of the children of Gad according to
the house of their fathers, have received
their inheritance; and the half-tribe of
Manasseh has received its inheritance.
15The two tribes and the half-tribe have
received their inheritance on this side
of the Jordan, *across from* Jericho east-
ward, toward the sunrise."

The Leaders Appointed to Divide the Land

16And the LORD spoke to Moses, say-
ing, 17"These *are* the names of the men
who shall divide the land among you
as an inheritance: Eleazar the priest
and Joshua the son of Nun. 18And you
shall take one leader of every tribe to
divide the land for the inheritance.
19These *are* the names of the men: from
the tribe of Judah, Caleb the son of
Jephunneh; 20from the tribe of the
children of Simeon, Shemuel the son
of Ammihud; 21from the tribe of Ben-
jamin, Elidad the son of Chislon; 22a
leader from the tribe of the children of
Dan, Bukki the son of Jogli; 23from the
sons of Joseph: a leader from the tribe
of the children of Manasseh, Hanniel
the son of Ephod, 24and a leader from
the tribe of the children of Ephraim,
Kemuel the son of Shiphtan; 25a leader
from the tribe of the children of Zebu-
lun, Elizaphan the son of Parnach; 26a
leader from the tribe of the children of
Issachar, Paltiel the son of Azzan; 27a
leader from the tribe of the children
of Asher, Ahihud the son of Shelomi;
28and a leader from the tribe of the
children of Naphtali, Pedahel the son
of Ammihud."
29These *are* the ones the LORD com-
manded to divide the inheritance
among the children of Israel in the
land of Canaan.

Cities for the Levites

35 And the LORD spoke to Moses in
the plains of Moab by the Jordan
across from Jericho, saying: 2"Command
the children of Israel that they give
the Levites cities to dwell in from the
inheritance of their possession, and you
shall *also* give the Levites common-land
around the cities. 3They shall have the
cities to dwell in; and their common-
land shall be for their cattle, for their
herds, and for all their animals. 4The
common-land of the cities which you
will give the Levites *shall extend* from
the wall of the city outward a thousand
cubits all around. 5And you shall mea-
sure outside the city on the east side two
thousand cubits, on the south side
two thousand cubits, on the west side
two thousand cubits, and on the north
side two thousand cubits. The city *shall
be* in the middle. This shall belong to
them as common-land for the cities.
6"Now among the cities which you will
give to the Levites *you shall appoint* six
cities of refuge, to which a manslayer
may flee. And to these you shall add
forty-two cities. 7So all the cities you
will give to the Levites *shall be* forty-
eight; these *you shall give* with their
common-land. 8And the cities which
you will give *shall be* from the posses-
sion of the children of Israel; from the
larger *tribe* you shall give many, from
the smaller you shall give few. Each
shall give some of its cities to the Le-
vites, in proportion to the inheritance
that each receives."

Cities of Refuge

9Then the LORD spoke to Moses, saying,
10"Speak to the children of Israel,
and say to them: 'When you cross the
Jordan into the land of Canaan, 11then
you shall appoint cities to be cities of
refuge for you, that the manslayer who
kills any person accidentally may flee
there. 12They shall be cities of refuge
for you from the avenger, that the
manslayer may not die until he stands
before the congregation in judgment.
13And of the cities which you give, you
shall have six cities of refuge. 14You
shall appoint three cities on this side
of the Jordan, and three cities you shall
appoint in the land of Canaan, *which*
will be cities of refuge. 15These six cities
shall be for refuge for the children
of Israel, for the stranger, and for the
sojourner among them, that anyone
who kills a person accidentally may
flee there.

16'But if he strikes him with an iron
implement, so that he dies, he *is* a murderer;
the murderer shall surely be put
to death. 17And if he strikes him with a
stone in the hand, by which one could
die, and he does die, he *is* a murderer;
the murderer shall surely be put
to death. 18Or *if* he strikes him with a
wooden hand weapon, by which one
could die, and he does die, he *is* a murderer;
the murderer shall surely be put
to death. 19The avenger of blood himself
shall put the murderer to death; when
he meets him, he shall put him to death.
20If he pushes him out of hatred or,
while lying in wait, hurls something
at him so that he dies, 21or in enmity
he strikes him with his hand so that he
dies, the one who struck *him* shall surely
be put to death. He *is* a murderer. The
avenger of blood shall put the murderer
to death when he meets him.

22'However, if he pushes him suddenly
without enmity, or throws anything at
him without lying in wait, 23or uses a
stone, by which a man could die, throwing
it at him without seeing *him,* so that
he dies, while he was not his enemy or
seeking his harm, 24then the congregation
shall judge between the manslayer
and the avenger of blood according to
these judgments. 25So the congregation
shall deliver the manslayer from the
hand of the avenger of blood, and
the congregation shall return him to
the city of refuge where he had fled, and
he shall remain there until the death of
the high priest who was anointed with
the holy oil. 26But if the manslayer at
any time goes outside the limits of the
city of refuge where he fled, 27and the
avenger of blood finds him outside
the limits of his city of refuge, and the
avenger of blood kills the manslayer, he
shall not be guilty of blood, 28because
he should have remained in his city of
refuge until the death of the high priest.
But after the death of the high priest
the manslayer may return to the land
of his possession.

29'And these *things* shall be a statute of
judgment to you throughout your generations
in all your dwellings. 30Whoever
kills a person, the murderer shall
be put to death on the testimony of
witnesses; but one witness is not *sufficient*
testimony against a person for
the death *penalty.* 31Moreover you shall
take no ransom for the life of a murderer
who *is* guilty of death, but he shall
surely be put to death. 32And you shall
take no ransom for him who has fled to
his city of refuge, that he may return
to dwell in the land before the death of
the priest. 33So you shall not pollute the
land where you *are;* for blood defiles the
land, and no atonement can be made
for the land, for the blood that is shed
on it, except by the blood of him who
shed it. 34Therefore do not defile the
land which you inhabit, in the midst
of which I dwell; for I the LORD dwell
among the children of Israel.' "

Marriage of Female Heirs

36 Now the chief fathers of the families
of the children of Gilead the
son of Machir, the son of Manasseh, of
the families of the sons of Joseph, came
near and spoke before Moses and before
the leaders, the chief fathers of the
children of Israel. 2And they said: "The
LORD commanded my lord *Moses* to
give the land as an inheritance by lot to
the children of Israel, and my lord was
commanded by the LORD to give the inheritance
of our brother Zelophehad to

his daughters. 3Now if they are married
to any of the sons of the *other* tribes of
the children of Israel, then their inheri-
tance will be taken from the inheritance
of our fathers, and it will be added to
the inheritance of the tribe into which
they marry; so it will be taken from the
lot of our inheritance. 4And when the
Jubilee of the children of Israel comes,
then their inheritance will be added to
the inheritance of the tribe into which
they marry; so their inheritance will be
taken away from the inheritance of the
tribe of our fathers."

5Then Moses commanded the children
of Israel according to the word of the
LORD, saying: "What the tribe of the
sons of Joseph speaks is right. 6This *is*
what the LORD commands concerning
the daughters of Zelophehad, saying,
'Let them marry whom they think best,
but they may marry only within the
family of their father's tribe.' 7So the
inheritance of the children of Israel
shall not change hands from tribe to
tribe, for every one of the children of
Israel shall keep the inheritance of the
tribe of his fathers. 8And every daughter
who possesses an inheritance in any
tribe of the children of Israel shall be
the wife of one of the family of her fa-
ther's tribe, so that the children of Israel
each may possess the inheritance of
his fathers. 9Thus no inheritance shall
change hands from *one* tribe to another,
but every tribe of the children of Israel
shall keep its own inheritance."

10Just as the LORD commanded Moses,
so did the daughters of Zelophehad;
11for Mahlah, Tirzah, Hoglah, Milcah,
and Noah, the daughters of Zelophe-
had, were married to the sons of their
father's brothers. 12They were married
into the families of the children of Ma-
nasseh the son of Joseph, and their in-
heritance remained in the tribe of their
father's family.

13These *are* the commandments and
the judgments which the LORD com-
manded the children of Israel by the
hand of Moses in the plains of Moab by
the Jordan, *across from* Jericho.

THE FIFTH BOOK OF MOSES CALLED

DEUTERONOMY

The Book of Deuteronomy is Moses's goodbye to the Hebrew people, who are now just outside of the Promised Land. Moses is older and God had told him he would not enter the land. As Moses prepares for Joshua to become the next leader, he gives a series of speeches to the people, reminding them of their history and what God had done. Moses first tells about what has happened since leaving Egypt. Then he reminds the people of the rules God had given and how they have agreed to obey God. Finally, he guides the people to promise again to obey God. The Book of Deuteronomy ends with Moses making Joshua leader, blessing the people, and then dying on Mount Nebo.

- **GENRE:** Law
- **AUTHOR:** Moses, with perhaps Joshua writing the final chapter
- **TIME:** c. 1406 BC
- **PURPOSE:** To remind the Hebrews of their history and all that God had done for them. Moses wanted the people to remember that God is faithful to them so they would be faithful to Him in the Promised Land.

The Previous Command to Enter Canaan

1 These *are* the words which Moses
spoke to all Israel on this side of the
Jordan in the wilderness, in the plain[a]
opposite Suph,[b] between Paran, Tophel,
Laban, Hazeroth, and Dizahab. 2*It is*
eleven days' *journey* from Horeb by way
of Mount Seir to Kadesh Barnea. 3Now it
came to pass in the fortieth year, in the
eleventh month, on the first *day* of the
month, *that* Moses spoke to the children
of Israel according to all that the LORD
had given him as commandments to
them, 4after he had killed Sihon king
of the Amorites, who dwelt in Heshbon,
and Og king of Bashan, who dwelt at
Ashtaroth in[a] Edrei.
5On this side of the Jordan in the
land of Moab, Moses began to explain
this law, saying, 6"The LORD our God
spoke to us in Horeb, saying: 'You have
dwelt long enough at this mountain.
7Turn and take your journey, and go
to the mountains of the Amorites, to all
the neighboring *places* in the plain,[a] in
the mountains and in the lowland, in the
South and on the seacoast, to the land of
the Canaanites and to Lebanon, as far
as the great river, the River Euphrates.
8See, I have set the land before you; go
in and possess the land which the LORD
swore to your fathers—to Abraham,
Isaac, and Jacob—to give to them and
their descendants after them.'

Tribal Leaders Appointed

9"And I spoke to you at that time, say-
ing: 'I alone am not able to bear you.
10The LORD your God has multiplied
you, and here you *are* today, as the stars
of heaven in multitude. 11May the LORD
God of your fathers make you a thou-
sand times more numerous than you
are, and bless you as He has promised
you! 12How can I alone bear your prob-
lems and your burdens and your com-
plaints? 13Choose wise, understanding,
and knowledgeable men from among
your tribes, and I will make them heads
over you.' 14And you answered me and
said, 'The thing which you have told *us*
to do *is* good.' 15So I took the heads of
your tribes, wise and knowledgeable
men, and made them heads over you,
leaders of thousands, leaders of hun-
dreds, leaders of fifties, leaders of tens,
and officers for your tribes.
16"Then I commanded your judges
at that time, saying, 'Hear *the cases*
between your brethren, and judge

1:1 [a] Hebrew *arabah* [b] One manuscript of the Septuagint, also Targum and Vulgate, read *Red Sea.*
1:4 [a] Septuagint, Syriac, and Vulgate read *and* (compare Joshua 12:4). **1:7** [a] Hebrew *arabah*

righteously between a man and his
brother or the stranger who is with him.
17You shall not show partiality in judg-
ment; you shall hear the small as well
as the great; you shall not be afraid in
any man's presence, for the judgment *is*
God's. The case that is too hard for you,
bring to me, and I will hear it.' 18And I
commanded you at that time all the
things which you should do.

Israel's Refusal to Enter the Land

19"So we departed from Horeb, and
went through all that great and terrible
wilderness which you saw on the way
to the mountains of the Amorites, as
the LORD our God had commanded
us. Then we came to Kadesh Barnea.
20And I said to you, 'You have come to
the mountains of the Amorites, which
the LORD our God is giving us. 21Look, the
LORD your God has set the land before
you; go up *and* possess *it*, as the LORD
God of your fathers has spoken to you;
do not fear or be discouraged.'

22"And every one of you came near to
me and said, 'Let us send men before us,
and let them search out the land for us,
and bring back word to us of the way by
which we should go up, and of the cities
into which we shall come.'

23"The plan pleased me well; so I took
twelve of your men, one man from *each*
tribe. 24And they departed and went up
into the mountains, and came to the
Valley of Eshcol, and spied it out. 25They
also took *some* of the fruit of the land
in their hands and brought *it* down to
us; and they brought back word to us,
saying, '*It is* a good land which the LORD
our God is giving us.'

26"Nevertheless you would not go up,
but rebelled against the command of
the LORD your God; 27and you com-
plained in your tents, and said, 'Because
the LORD hates us, He has brought us
out of the land of Egypt to deliver us into
the hand of the Amorites, to destroy us.
28Where can we go up? Our brethren
have discouraged our hearts, saying,
"The people *are* greater and taller than
we; the cities *are* great and fortified up
to heaven; moreover we have seen the
sons of the Anakim there." '

29"Then I said to you, 'Do not be
terrified, or afraid of them. 30The LORD
your God, who goes before you, He will
fight for you, according to all He did for
you in Egypt before your eyes, 31and
in the wilderness where you saw how
the LORD your God carried you, as a
man carries his son, in all the way that
you went until you came to this place.'
32Yet, for all that, you did not believe
the LORD your God, 33who went in the
way before you to search out a place for
you to pitch your tents, to show you the
way you should go, in the fire by night
and in the cloud by day.

The Penalty for Israel's Rebellion

34"And the LORD heard the sound of
your words, and was angry, and took an
oath, saying, 35'Surely not one of these
men of this evil generation shall see that
good land of which I swore to give to
your fathers, 36except Caleb the son of
Jephunneh; he shall see it, and to him
and his children I am giving the land
on which he walked, because he wholly
followed the LORD.' 37The LORD was also
angry with me for your sakes, saying,
'Even you shall not go in there. 38Joshua
the son of Nun, who stands before you,
he shall go in there. Encourage him, for
he shall cause Israel to inherit it.

39'Moreover your little ones and your
children, who you say will be victims,
who today have no knowledge of good
and evil, they shall go in there; to them
I will give it, and they shall possess it.
40But *as for* you, turn and take your
journey into the wilderness by the Way
of the Red Sea.'

41"Then you answered and said to me,
'We have sinned against the LORD; we
will go up and fight, just as the LORD our
God commanded us.' And when every-
one of you had girded on his weapons
of war, you were ready to go up into
the mountain.

42"And the LORD said to me, 'Tell
them, "Do not go up nor fight, for I *am*
not among you; lest you be defeated
before your enemies." ' 43So I spoke
to you; yet you would not listen, but
rebelled against the command of the
LORD, and presumptuously went up
into the mountain. 44And the Amorites
who dwelt in that mountain came out

against you and chased you as bees
do, and drove you back from Seir to
Hormah. 45Then you returned and wept
before the LORD, but the LORD would not
listen to your voice nor give ear to you.
46"So you remained in Kadesh many
days, according to the days that you
spent *there.*

The Desert Years

2 "Then we turned and journeyed into
the wilderness of the Way of the
Red Sea, as the LORD spoke to me, and
we skirted Mount Seir for many days.
2"And the LORD spoke to me, saying:
3'You have skirted this mountain long
enough; turn northward. 4And com-
mand the people, saying, "You *are about
to* pass through the territory of your
brethren, the descendants of Esau, who
live in Seir; and they will be afraid of
you. Therefore watch yourselves care-
fully. 5Do not meddle with them, for I
will not give you *any* of their land, no,
not so much as one footstep, because
I have given Mount Seir to Esau *as* a
possession. 6You shall buy food from
them with money, that you may eat;
and you shall also buy water from them
with money, that you may drink.
7"For the LORD your God has blessed
you in all the work of your hand. He
knows your trudging through this great
wilderness. These forty years the LORD
your God *has been* with you; you have
lacked nothing." '
8"And when we passed beyond our
brethren, the descendants of Esau who
dwell in Seir, away from the road of
the plain, away from Elath and Ezion
Geber, we turned and passed by way of
the Wilderness of Moab. 9Then the LORD
said to me, 'Do not harass Moab, nor
contend with them in battle, for I will
not give you *any* of their land *as* a pos-
session, because I have given Ar to the
descendants of Lot *as* a possession.' "
10(The Emim had dwelt there in times
past, a people as great and numerous
and tall as the Anakim. 11They were also
regarded as giants,[a] like the Anakim,
but the Moabites call them Emim. 12The
Horites formerly dwelt in Seir, but the
descendants of Esau dispossessed them
and destroyed them from before them,
and dwelt in their place, just as Israel
did to the land of their possession which
the LORD gave them.)
13" 'Now rise and cross over the Valley
of the Zered.' So we crossed over the
Valley of the Zered. 14And the time we
took to come from Kadesh Barnea until
we crossed over the Valley of the Zered
was thirty-eight years, until all the gen-
eration of the men of war was consumed
from the midst of the camp, just as the
LORD had sworn to them. 15For indeed
the hand of the LORD was against them,
to destroy them from the midst of the
camp until they were consumed.
16"So it was, when all the men of war
had finally perished from among the
people, 17that the LORD spoke to me,
saying: 18'This day you are to cross over
at Ar, the boundary of Moab. 19And *when*
you come near the people of Ammon, do
not harass them or meddle with them,
for I will not give you *any* of the land of
the people of Ammon *as* a possession,
because I have given it to the descen-
dants of Lot *as* a possession.' "
20(That was also regarded as a land of
giants;[a] giants formerly dwelt there. But
the Ammonites call them Zamzummim,
21a people as great and numerous and tall
as the Anakim. But the LORD destroyed
them before them, and they dispossessed
them and dwelt in their place, 22just as He
had done for the descendants of Esau,
who dwelt in Seir, when He destroyed the
Horites from before them. They dispos-
sessed them and dwelt in their place, even
to this day. 23And the Avim, who dwelt in
villages as far as Gaza—the Caphtorim,
who came from Caphtor, destroyed them
and dwelt in their place.)
24" 'Rise, take your journey, and cross
over the River Arnon. Look, I have giv-
en into your hand Sihon the Amorite,
king of Heshbon, and his land. Begin
to possess *it,* and engage him in battle.
25This day I will begin to put the dread
and fear of you upon the nations under
the whole heaven, who shall hear the
report of you, and shall tremble and
be in anguish because of you.'

2:11 [a] Hebrew *rephaim* **2:20** [a] Hebrew *rephaim*

King Sihon Defeated

26“And I sent messengers from the Wil-
derness of Kedemoth to Sihon king of
Heshbon, with words of peace, saying,
27‘Let me pass through your land; I will
keep strictly to the road, and I will turn
neither to the right nor to the left. 28You
shall sell me food for money, that I may
eat, and give me water for money, that I
may drink; only let me pass through on
foot, 29just as the descendants of Esau
who dwell in Seir and the Moabites who
dwell in Ar did for me, until I cross the
Jordan to the land which the LORD our
God is giving us.’
30“But Sihon king of Heshbon would
not let us pass through, for the LORD
your God hardened his spirit and made
his heart obstinate, that He might deliv-
er him into your hand, as *it is* this day.
31“And the LORD said to me, ‘See, I have
begun to give Sihon and his land over to
you. Begin to possess *it,* that you may
inherit his land.’ 32Then Sihon and all
his people came out against us to fight
at Jahaz. 33And the LORD our God de-
livered him over to us; so we defeated
him, his sons, and all his people. 34We
took all his cities at that time, and we
utterly destroyed the men, women, and
little ones of every city; we left none
remaining. 35We took only the live-
stock as plunder for ourselves, with the
spoil of the cities which we took. 36From
Aroer, which *is* on the bank of the River
Arnon, and *from* the city that *is* in the
ravine, as far as Gilead, there was not
one city too strong for us; the LORD our
God delivered all to us. 37Only you did
not go near the land of the people of
Ammon—anywhere along the River
Jabbok, or to the cities of the moun-
tains, or wherever the LORD our God
had forbidden us.

King Og Defeated

3 “Then we turned and went up the
road to Bashan; and Og king of Ba-
shan came out against us, he and all
his people, to battle at Edrei. 2And the
LORD said to me, ‘Do not fear him, for
I have delivered him and all his people
and his land into your hand; you shall
do to him as you did to Sihon king of
the Amorites, who dwelt at Heshbon.’
3“So the LORD our God also delivered
into our hands Og king of Bashan, with
all his people, and we attacked him until
he had no survivors remaining. 4And
we took all his cities at that time; there
was not a city which we did not take
from them: sixty cities, all the region
of Argob, the kingdom of Og in Bashan.
5All these cities *were* fortified with high
walls, gates, and bars, besides a great
many rural towns. 6And we utterly de-
stroyed them, as we did to Sihon king of
Heshbon, utterly destroying the men,
women, and children of every city. 7But
all the livestock and the spoil of the
cities we took as booty for ourselves.
8“And at that time we took the land
from the hand of the two kings of the
Amorites who *were* on this side of the
Jordan, from the River Arnon to Mount
Hermon 9(the Sidonians call Hermon
Sirion, and the Amorites call it Senir),
10all the cities of the plain, all Gilead, and
all Bashan, as far as Salcah and Edrei,
cities of the kingdom of Og in Bashan.
11“For only Og king of Bashan re-
mained of the remnant of the giants.[a]
Indeed his bedstead *was* an iron bed-
stead. (*Is* it not in Rabbah of the people
of Ammon?) Nine cubits *is* its length and
four cubits its width, according to the
standard cubit.

The Land East of the Jordan Divided

12“And this land, *which* we possessed
at that time, from Aroer, which *is* by the
River Arnon, and half the mountains of
Gilead and its cities, I gave to the Reu-
benites and the Gadites. 13The rest of
Gilead, and all Bashan, the kingdom of
Og, I gave to half the tribe of Manasseh.
(All the region of Argob, with all Ba-
shan, was called the land of the giants.[a]
14Jair the son of Manasseh took all the
region of Argob, as far as the border of
the Geshurites and the Maachathites,
and called Bashan after his own name,
Havoth Jair,[a] to this day.)
15“Also I gave Gilead to Machir. 16And
to the Reubenites and the Gadites I gave
from Gilead as far as the River Arnon, the

3:11 [a] Hebrew *rephaim* 3:13 [a] Hebrew *rephaim* 3:14 [a] Literally *Towns of Jair*

middle of the river as *the* border, as far as
the River Jabbok, the border of the people
of Ammon; 17the plain also, with the Jor-
dan as *the* border, from Chinnereth as far
as the east side of the Sea of the Arabah
(the Salt Sea), below the slopes of Pisgah.
18“Then I commanded you at that time,
saying: ‘The LORD your God has given
you this land to possess. All you men
of valor shall cross over armed before
your brethren, the children of Israel.
19But your wives, your little ones, and
your livestock (I know that you have
much livestock) shall stay in your cit-
ies which I have given you, 20until the
LORD has given rest to your brethren as
to you, and they also possess the land
which the LORD your God is giving them
beyond the Jordan. Then each of you
may return to his possession which I
have given you.’
21“And I commanded Joshua at that
time, saying, ‘Your eyes have seen all
that the LORD your God has done to
these two kings; so will the LORD do to
all the kingdoms through which you
pass. 22You must not fear them, for the
LORD your God Himself fights for you.’

Moses Forbidden to Enter the Land

23“Then I pleaded with the LORD at
that time, saying: 24‘O Lord GOD, You
have begun to show Your servant Your
greatness and Your mighty hand, for
what god *is there* in heaven or on earth
who can do *anything* like Your works
and Your mighty *deeds?* 25I pray, let
me cross over and see the good land
beyond the Jordan, those pleasant
mountains, and Lebanon.’
26“But the LORD was angry with me on
your account, and would not listen to
me. So the LORD said to me: ‘Enough of
that! Speak no more to Me of this mat-
ter. 27Go up to the top of Pisgah, and lift
your eyes toward the west, the north, the
south, and the east; behold *it* with your
eyes, for you shall not cross over this
Jordan. 28But command Joshua, and
encourage him and strengthen him;
for he shall go over before this people,
and he shall cause them to inherit the
land which you will see.’
29“So we stayed in the valley opposite
Beth Peor.

Moses Commands Obedience

4 “Now, O Israel, listen to the statutes
and the judgments which I teach
you to observe, that you may live, and
go in and possess the land which the
LORD God of your fathers is giving you.
2You shall not add to the word which I
command you, nor take from it, that you
may keep the commandments of the
LORD your God which I command you.
3Your eyes have seen what the LORD did
at Baal Peor; for the LORD your God has
destroyed from among you all the men
who followed Baal of Peor. 4But you who
held fast to the LORD your God *are* alive
today, every one of you.
5“Surely I have taught you statutes
and judgments, just as the LORD my
God commanded me, that you should
act according *to them* in the land which
you go to possess. 6Therefore be careful
to observe *them;* for this *is* your wisdom
and your understanding in the sight of
the peoples who will hear all these stat-
utes, and say, ‘Surely this great nation
is a wise and understanding people.’
7“For what great nation *is there* that
has God *so* near to it, as the LORD our
God *is* to us, for whatever *reason* we may
call upon Him? 8And what great na-
tion *is there* that has *such* statutes and
righteous judgments as are in all this
law which I set before you this day?
9Only take heed to yourself, and dil-
igently keep yourself, lest you forget
the things your eyes have seen, and lest
they depart from your heart all the days
of your life. And teach them to your
children and your grandchildren, 10*es-
pecially concerning* the day you stood
before the LORD your God in Horeb,
when the LORD said to me, ‘Gather the
people to Me, and I will let them hear
My words, that they may learn to fear
Me all the days they live on the earth,
and *that* they may teach their children.’
11“Then you came near and stood
at the foot of the mountain, and the
mountain burned with fire to the midst
of heaven, with darkness, cloud, and
thick darkness. 12And the LORD spoke
to you out of the midst of the fire. You
heard the sound of the words, but saw
no form; *you* only *heard* a voice. 13So He
declared to you His covenant which He

commanded you to perform, the Ten
Commandments; and He wrote them
on two tablets of stone. 14And the LORD
commanded me at that time to teach
you statutes and judgments, that you
might observe them in the land which
you cross over to possess.

Beware of Idolatry

15"Take careful heed to yourselves, for
you saw no form when the LORD spoke
to you at Horeb out of the midst of the
fire, 16lest you act corruptly and make
for yourselves a carved image in the
form of any figure: the likeness of male
or female, 17the likeness of any animal
that *is* on the earth or the likeness of any
winged bird that flies in the air, 18the
likeness of anything that creeps on the
ground or the likeness of any fish that
is in the water beneath the earth. 19And
take heed, lest you lift your eyes to heav-
en, and *when* you see the sun, the moon,
and the stars, all the host of heaven,
you feel driven to worship them and
serve them, which the LORD your God
has given to all the peoples under the
whole heaven as a heritage. 20But the
LORD has taken you and brought you
out of the iron furnace, out of Egypt, to
be His people, an inheritance, as you
are this day. 21Furthermore the LORD
was angry with me for your sakes, and
swore that I would not cross over the
Jordan, and that I would not enter the
good land which the LORD your God is
giving you as an inheritance. 22But I
must die in this land, I must not cross
over the Jordan; but you shall cross
over and possess that good land. 23Take
heed to yourselves, lest you forget the
covenant of the LORD your God which
He made with you, and make for your-
selves a carved image in the form of
anything which the LORD your God has
forbidden you. 24For the LORD your
God *is* a consuming fire, a jealous God.

25"When you beget children and
grandchildren and have grown old in
the land, and act corruptly and make a
carved image in the form of anything,
and do evil in the sight of the LORD your
God to provoke Him to anger, 26I call
heaven and earth to witness against
you this day, that you will soon utterly
perish from the land which you cross
over the Jordan to possess; you will
not prolong *your* days in it, but will be
utterly destroyed. 27And the LORD will
scatter you among the peoples, and
you will be left few in number among
the nations where the LORD will drive
you. 28And there you will serve gods, the
work of men's hands, wood and stone,
which neither see nor hear nor eat nor
smell. 29But from there you will seek the
LORD your God, and you will find *Him*
if you seek Him with all your heart and
with all your soul. 30When you are in
distress, and all these things come upon
you in the latter days, when you turn to
the LORD your God and obey His voice
31(for the LORD your God *is* a merciful
God), He will not forsake you nor de-
stroy you, nor forget the covenant of
your fathers which He swore to them.

32"For ask now concerning the days
that are past, which were before you,
since the day that God created man on
the earth, and *ask* from one end of heav-
en to the other, whether *any* great *thing*
like this has happened, or *anything* like
it has been heard. 33Did *any* people *ever*
hear the voice of God speaking out of
the midst of the fire, as you have heard,
and live? 34Or did God *ever* try to go *and*
take for Himself a nation from the midst
of *another* nation, by trials, by signs,
by wonders, by war, by a mighty hand
and an outstretched arm, and by great
terrors, according to all that the LORD
your God did for you in Egypt before
your eyes? 35To you it was shown, that
you might know that the LORD Himself
is God; *there is* none other besides Him.
36Out of heaven He let you hear His
voice, that He might instruct you; on
earth He showed you His great fire, and
you heard His words out of the midst of
the fire. 37And because He loved your
fathers, therefore He chose their de-
scendants after them; and He brought
you out of Egypt with His Presence,
with His mighty power, 38driving out
from before you nations greater and
mightier than you, to bring you in, to
give you their land *as* an inheritance, as
it is this day. 39Therefore know this day,
and consider *it* in your heart, that the
LORD Himself *is* God in heaven above

and on the earth beneath; *there is* no
other. [40]You shall therefore keep His
statutes and His commandments which
I command you today, that it may go
well with you and with your children
after you, and that you may prolong
your days in the land which the LORD
your God is giving you for all time."

Cities of Refuge East of the Jordan

[41]Then Moses set apart three cities
on this side of the Jordan, toward the
rising of the sun, [42]that the manslayer
might flee there, who kills his neighbor
unintentionally, without having hated
him in time past, and that by fleeing to
one of these cities he might live: [43]Bezer
in the wilderness on the plateau for
the Reubenites, Ramoth in Gilead for
the Gadites, and Golan in Bashan for the
Manassites.

Introduction to God's Law

[44]Now this *is* the law which Moses set
before the children of Israel. [45]These *are*
the testimonies, the statutes, and the
judgments which Moses spoke to the
children of Israel after they came out of
Egypt, [46]on this side of the Jordan, in the
valley opposite Beth Peor, in the land of
Sihon king of the Amorites, who dwelt at
Heshbon, whom Moses and the children
of Israel defeated after they came out of
Egypt. [47]And they took possession of his
land and the land of Og king of Bashan,
two kings of the Amorites, who *were* on
this side of the Jordan, toward the rising
of the sun, [48]from Aroer, which *is* on the
bank of the River Arnon, even to Mount
Sion[a] (that is, Hermon), [49]and all the
plain on the east side of the Jordan as
far as the Sea of the Arabah, below the
slopes of Pisgah.

The Ten Commandments Reviewed

5 And Moses called all Israel, and said
to them: "Hear, O Israel, the statutes
and judgments which I speak in your
hearing today, that you may learn them
and be careful to observe them. [2]The
LORD our God made a covenant with us
in Horeb. [3]The LORD did not make this
covenant with our fathers, but with us,
those who *are* here today, all of us who
are alive. [4]The LORD talked with you
face to face on the mountain from the
midst of the fire. [5]I stood between the
LORD and you at that time, to declare to
you the word of the LORD; for you were
afraid because of the fire, and you did
not go up the mountain. *He* said:

6 'I *am* the LORD your God who brought
you out of the land of Egypt, out
of the house of bondage.

7 'You shall have no other gods
before Me.

8 'You shall not make for yourself a
carved image—any likeness *of
anything* that *is* in heaven above,
or that *is* in the earth beneath,
or that *is* in the water under the
earth; [9]you shall not bow down
to them nor serve them. For I, the
LORD your God, *am* a jealous God,
visiting the iniquity of the fathers
upon the children to the third and
fourth *generations* of those who
hate Me, [10]but showing mercy to
thousands, to those who love Me
and keep My commandments.

11 'You shall not take the name of the
LORD your God in vain, for the
LORD will not hold *him* guiltless
who takes His name in vain.

12 'Observe the Sabbath day, to keep it
holy, as the LORD your God com-
manded you. [13]Six days you shall
labor and do all your work, [14]but
the seventh day *is* the Sabbath
of the LORD your God. *In it* you
shall do no work: you, nor your
son, nor your daughter, nor your
male servant, nor your female
servant, nor your ox, nor your
donkey, nor any of your cattle,
nor your stranger who *is* within
your gates, that your male ser-
vant and your female servant
may rest as well as you. [15]And re-
member that you were a slave in
the land of Egypt, and the LORD
your God brought you out from
there by a mighty hand and by
an outstretched arm; therefore
the LORD your God commanded
you to keep the Sabbath day.

4:48 [a] Syriac reads *Sirion* (compare 3:9).

16 'Honor your father and your mother,
as the LORD your God has commanded you, that your days may
be long, and that it may be well
with you in the land which the
LORD your God is giving you.
17 'You shall not murder.
18 'You shall not commit adultery.
19 'You shall not steal.
20 'You shall not bear false witness
against your neighbor.
21 'You shall not covet your neighbor's
wife; and you shall not desire
your neighbor's house, his field,
his male servant, his female servant, his ox, his donkey, or any-
thing that *is* your neighbor's.'
22"These words the LORD spoke to all
your assembly, in the mountain from
the midst of the fire, the cloud, and the
thick darkness, with a loud voice; and He
added no more. And He wrote them on
two tablets of stone and gave them to me.

The People Afraid of God's Presence

23"So it was, when you heard the voice
from the midst of the darkness, while
the mountain was burning with fire,
that you came near to me, all the heads
of your tribes and your elders. 24And
you said: 'Surely the LORD our God has
shown us His glory and His greatness,
and we have heard His voice from the
midst of the fire. We have seen this day
that God speaks with man; yet he *still*
lives. 25Now therefore, why should we
die? For this great fire will consume us;
if we hear the voice of the LORD our God
anymore, then we shall die. 26For who
is there of all flesh who has heard the
voice of the living God speaking from
the midst of the fire, as we *have,* and
lived? 27You go near and hear all that
the LORD our God may say, and tell us
all that the LORD our God says to you,
and we will hear and do *it.*'
28"Then the LORD heard the voice of
your words when you spoke to me, and
the LORD said to me: 'I have heard the
voice of the words of this people which
they have spoken to you. They are right
in all that they have spoken. 29Oh, that
they had such a heart in them that they
would fear Me and always keep all My
commandments, that it might be well
with them and with their children forever! 30Go and say to them, "Return to
your tents." 31But as for you, stand here
by Me, and I will speak to you all the
commandments, the statutes, and the
judgments which you shall teach them,
that they may observe *them* in the land
which I am giving them to possess.'
32"Therefore you shall be careful to do
as the LORD your God has commanded
you; you shall not turn aside to the right
hand or to the left. 33You shall walk in
all the ways which the LORD your God
has commanded you, that you may live
and *that it may be* well with you, and
that you may prolong *your* days in the
land which you shall possess.

The Greatest Commandment

6 "Now this *is* the commandment,
and these are the statutes and judgments which the LORD your God has
commanded to teach you, that you may
observe *them* in the land which you are
crossing over to possess, 2that you may
fear the LORD your God, to keep all His
statutes and His commandments which
I command you, you and your son and
your grandson, all the days of your life,
and that your days may be prolonged.
3Therefore hear, O Israel, and be careful
to observe *it,* that it may be well with
you, and that you may multiply greatly
as the LORD God of your fathers has
promised you—'a land flowing with
milk and honey.'[a]
4"Hear, O Israel: The LORD our God, the
LORD *is* one![a] 5You shall love the LORD
your God with all your heart, with all
your soul, and with all your strength.
6"And these words which I command
you today shall be in your heart. 7You
shall teach them diligently to your children, and shall talk of them when you
sit in your house, when you walk by
the way, when you lie down, and when
you rise up. 8You shall bind them as a
sign on your hand, and they shall be
as frontlets between your eyes. 9You
shall write them on the doorposts of
your house and on your gates.

6:3 [a] Exodus 3:8 6:4 [a] Or *The LORD is our God, the LORD alone* (that is, the only one)

Caution Against Disobedience

10"So it shall be, when the LORD your
God brings you into the land of which
He swore to your fathers, to Abraham,
Isaac, and Jacob, to give you large and
beautiful cities which you did not build,
11houses full of all good things, which
you did not fill, hewn-out wells which
you did not dig, vineyards and olive
trees which you did not plant—when
you have eaten and are full— 12*then*
beware, lest you forget the LORD who
brought you out of the land of Egypt,
from the house of bondage. 13You shall
fear the LORD your God and serve Him,
and shall take oaths in His name. 14You
shall not go after other gods, the gods
of the peoples who *are* all around you
15(for the LORD your God *is* a jealous God
among you), lest the anger of the LORD
your God be aroused against you and
destroy you from the face of the earth.
16"You shall not tempt the LORD your
God as you tempted *Him* in Massah.
17You shall diligently keep the com-
mandments of the LORD your God, His
testimonies, and His statutes which He
has commanded you. 18And you shall do
what is right and good in the sight of the
LORD, that it may be well with you, and
that you may go in and possess the good
land of which the LORD swore to your
fathers, 19to cast out all your enemies
from before you, as the LORD has spoken.
20"When your son asks you in time to
come, saying, 'What *is the meaning of*
the testimonies, the statutes, and the
judgments which the LORD our God has
commanded you?' 21then you shall say
to your son: 'We were slaves of Pharaoh
in Egypt, and the LORD brought us out
of Egypt with a mighty hand; 22and the
LORD showed signs and wonders be-
fore our eyes, great and severe, against
Egypt, Pharaoh, and all his household.
23Then He brought us out from there,
that He might bring us in, to give us
the land of which He swore to our fa-
thers. 24And the LORD commanded us
to observe all these statutes, to fear the
LORD our God, for our good always, that
He might preserve us alive, as *it is* this
day. 25Then it will be righteousness for
us, if we are careful to observe all these
commandments before the LORD our
God, as He has commanded us.'

A Chosen People

7 "When the LORD your God brings you
into the land which you go to pos-
sess, and has cast out many nations be-
fore you, the Hittites and the Girgashites
and the Amorites and the Canaanites
and the Perizzites and the Hivites and
the Jebusites, seven nations greater and
mightier than you, 2and when the LORD
your God delivers them over to you, you
shall conquer them *and* utterly destroy
them. You shall make no covenant with
them nor show mercy to them. 3Nor shall
you make marriages with them. You
shall not give your daughter to their
son, nor take their daughter for your
son. 4For they will turn your sons away
from following Me, to serve other gods;
so the anger of the LORD will be aroused
against you and destroy you sudden-
ly. 5But thus you shall deal with them:
you shall destroy their altars, and break
down their *sacred* pillars, and cut down
their wooden images,[a] and burn their
carved images with fire.
6"For you *are* a holy people to the
LORD your God; the LORD your God has
chosen you to be a people for Himself,
a special treasure above all the peoples
on the face of the earth. 7The LORD did
not set His love on you nor choose you
because you were more in number than
any other people, for you were the least
of all peoples; 8but because the LORD
loves you, and because He would keep
the oath which He swore to your fathers,
the LORD has brought you out with a
mighty hand, and redeemed you from
the house of bondage, from the hand
of Pharaoh king of Egypt.
9"Therefore know that the LORD your
God, He *is* God, the faithful God who
keeps covenant and mercy for a thou-
sand generations with those who love
Him and keep His commandments;
10and He repays those who hate Him to
their face, to destroy them. He will not
be slack with him who hates Him; He
will repay him to his face. 11Therefore

7:5 [a] Hebrew *Asherim,* Canaanite deities

you shall keep the commandment, the
statutes, and the judgments which I
command you today, to observe them.

Blessings of Obedience

12“Then it shall come to pass, because
you listen to these judgments, and keep
and do them, that the LORD your God
will keep with you the covenant and the
mercy which He swore to your fathers.
13And He will love you and bless you
and multiply you; He will also bless the
fruit of your womb and the fruit of your
land, your grain and your new wine and
your oil, the increase of your cattle and
the offspring of your flock, in the land of
which He swore to your fathers to give
you. 14You shall be blessed above all
peoples; there shall not be a male or fe-
male barren among you or among your
livestock. 15And the LORD will take away
from you all sickness, and will afflict
you with none of the terrible diseases
of Egypt which you have known, but
will lay *them* on all those who hate you.
16Also you shall destroy all the peoples
whom the LORD your God delivers over
to you; your eye shall have no pity on
them; nor shall you serve their gods, for
that *will be* a snare to you.

17“If you should say in your heart,
‘These nations are greater than I; how
can I dispossess them?’— 18you shall not
be afraid of them, *but* you shall remem-
ber well what the LORD your God did to
Pharaoh and to all Egypt: 19the great
trials which your eyes saw, the signs and
the wonders, the mighty hand and the
outstretched arm, by which the LORD
your God brought you out. So shall the
LORD your God do to all the peoples of
whom you are afraid. 20Moreover the
LORD your God will send the hornet
among them until those who are left,
who hide themselves from you, are de-
stroyed. 21You shall not be terrified of
them; for the LORD your God, the great
and awesome God, *is* among you. 22And
the LORD your God will drive out those
nations before you little by little; you
will be unable to destroy them at once,
lest the beasts of the field become *too*
numerous for you. 23But the LORD your
God will deliver them over to you, and
will inflict defeat upon them until they
are destroyed. 24And He will deliver their
kings into your hand, and you will de-
stroy their name from under heaven; no
one shall be able to stand against you
until you have destroyed them. 25You
shall burn the carved images of their
gods with fire; you shall not covet the
silver or gold *that is* on them, nor take *it*
for yourselves, lest you be snared by it;
for it *is* an abomination to the LORD your
God. 26Nor shall you bring an abomina-
tion into your house, lest you be doomed
to destruction like it. You shall utterly
detest it and utterly abhor it, for it *is* an
accursed thing.

Remember the LORD Your God

8 “Every commandment which I
command you today you must be
careful to observe, that you may live
and multiply, and go in and possess
the land of which the LORD swore to
your fathers. 2And you shall remember
that the LORD your God led you all the
way these forty years in the wilder-
ness, to humble you *and* test you, to
know what *was* in your heart, whether
you would keep His commandments
or not. 3So He humbled you, allowed
you to hunger, and fed you with manna
which you did not know nor did your
fathers know, that He might make you
know that man shall not live by bread
alone; but man lives by every *word* that
proceeds from the mouth of the LORD.
4Your garments did not wear out on
you, nor did your foot swell these forty
years. 5You should know in your heart
that as a man chastens his son, *so* the
LORD your God chastens you.

6“Therefore you shall keep the com-
mandments of the LORD your God, to
walk in His ways and to fear Him. 7For
the LORD your God is bringing you into
a good land, a land of brooks of water,
of fountains and springs, that flow out
of valleys and hills; 8a land of wheat
and barley, of vines and fig trees and
pomegranates, a land of olive oil and
honey; 9a land in which you will eat
bread without scarcity, in which you
will lack nothing; a land whose stones
are iron and out of whose hills you can
dig copper. 10When you have eaten and
are full, then you shall bless the LORD

your God for the good land which He has given you.

11“Beware that you do not forget the LORD your God by not keeping His commandments, His judgments, and His statutes which I command you today, 12lest—*when* you have eaten and are full, and have built beautiful houses and dwell *in them;* 13and *when* your herds and your flocks multiply, and your silver and your gold are multiplied, and all that you have is multiplied; 14when your heart is lifted up, and you forget the LORD your God who brought you out of the land of Egypt, from the house of bondage; 15who led you through that great and terrible wilderness, *in which were* fiery serpents and scorpions and thirsty land where there was no water; who brought water for you out of the flinty rock; 16who fed you in the wilderness with manna, which your fathers did not know, that He might humble you and that He might test you, to do you good in the end— 17then you say in your heart, ‘My power and the might of my hand have gained me this wealth.’

18“And you shall remember the LORD your God, for *it is* He who gives you power to get wealth, that He may establish His covenant which He swore to your fathers, as *it is* this day. 19Then it shall be, if you by any means forget the LORD your God, and follow other gods, and serve them and worship them, I testify against you this day that you shall surely perish. 20As the nations which the LORD destroys before you, so you shall perish, because you would not be obedient to the voice of the LORD your God.

Israel’s Rebellions Reviewed

9 “Hear, O Israel: You *are* to cross over the Jordan today, and go in to dispossess nations greater and mightier than yourself, cities great and fortified up to heaven, 2a people great and tall, the descendants of the Anakim, whom you know, and *of whom* you heard *it said,* ‘Who can stand before the descendants of Anak?’ 3Therefore understand today that the LORD your God *is* He who goes over before you *as* a consuming fire. He will destroy them and bring them down before you; so you shall drive them out and destroy them quickly, as the LORD has said to you.

4“Do not think in your heart, after the LORD your God has cast them out before you, saying, ‘Because of my righteousness the LORD has brought me in to possess this land’; but *it is* because of the wickedness of these nations *that* the LORD is driving them out from before you. 5*It is* not because of your righteousness or the uprightness of your heart *that* you go in to possess their land, but because of the wickedness of these nations *that* the LORD your God drives them out from before you, and that He may fulfill the word which the LORD swore to your fathers, to Abraham, Isaac, and Jacob. 6Therefore understand that the LORD your God is not giving you this good land to possess because of your righteousness, for you *are* a stiff-necked people.

7“Remember! Do not forget how you provoked the LORD your God to wrath in the wilderness. From the day that you departed from the land of Egypt until you came to this place, you have been rebellious against the LORD. 8Also in Horeb you provoked the LORD to wrath, so that the LORD was angry *enough* with you to have destroyed you. 9When I went up into the mountain to receive the tablets of stone, the tablets of the covenant which the LORD made with you, then I stayed on the mountain forty days and forty nights. I neither ate bread nor drank water. 10Then the LORD delivered to me two tablets of stone written with the finger of God, and on them *were* all the words which the LORD had spoken to you on the mountain from the midst of the fire in the day of the assembly. 11And it came to pass, at the end of forty days and forty nights, *that* the LORD gave me the two tablets of stone, the tablets of the covenant.

12“Then the LORD said to me, ‘Arise, go down quickly from here, for your people whom you brought out of Egypt have acted corruptly; they have quickly turned aside from the way which I commanded them; they have made themselves a molded image.’

13“Furthermore the LORD spoke to me, saying, ‘I have seen this people, and

indeed they are a stiff-necked people.
14Let Me alone, that I may destroy them
and blot out their name from under
heaven; and I will make of you a nation
mightier and greater than they.'
15"So I turned and came down from the
mountain, and the mountain burned
with fire; and the two tablets of the cov-
enant *were* in my two hands. 16And I
looked, and behold, you had sinned
against the LORD your God—had made
for yourselves a molded calf! You had
turned aside quickly from the way which
the LORD had commanded you. 17Then
I took the two tablets and threw them
out of my two hands and broke them
before your eyes. 18And I fell down be-
fore the LORD, as at the first, forty days
and forty nights; I neither ate bread
nor drank water, because of all your sin
which you committed in doing wickedly
in the sight of the LORD, to provoke Him
to anger. 19For I was afraid of the anger
and hot displeasure with which the LORD
was angry with you, to destroy you. But
the LORD listened to me at that time
also. 20And the LORD was very angry
with Aaron *and* would have destroyed
him; so I prayed for Aaron also at the
same time. 21Then I took your sin, the
calf which you had made, and burned
it with fire and crushed it *and* ground *it*
very small, until it was as fine as dust;
and I threw its dust into the brook that
descended from the mountain.
22"Also at Taberah and Massah and
Kibroth Hattaavah you provoked the
LORD to wrath. 23Likewise, when the
LORD sent you from Kadesh Barnea,
saying, 'Go up and possess the land
which I have given you,' then you re-
belled against the commandment of
the LORD your God, and you did not
believe Him nor obey His voice. 24You
have been rebellious against the LORD
from the day that I knew you.
25"Thus I prostrated myself before
the LORD; forty days and forty nights
I kept prostrating myself, because the
LORD had said He would destroy you.
26Therefore I prayed to the LORD, and
said: 'O Lord GOD, do not destroy Your
people and Your inheritance whom You
have redeemed through Your greatness,
whom You have brought out of Egypt
with a mighty hand. 27Remember Your
servants, Abraham, Isaac, and Jacob; do
not look on the stubbornness of this peo-
ple, or on their wickedness or their sin,
28lest the land from which You brought
us should say, "Because the LORD was
not able to bring them to the land which
He promised them, and because He
hated them, He has brought them out to
kill them in the wilderness." 29Yet they
are Your people and Your inheritance,
whom You brought out by Your mighty
power and by Your outstretched arm.'

The Second Pair of Tablets

10 "At that time the LORD said to
me, 'Hew for yourself two tablets
of stone like the first, and come up to
Me on the mountain and make yourself
an ark of wood. 2And I will write on the
tablets the words that were on the first
tablets, which you broke; and you shall
put them in the ark.'
3"So I made an ark of acacia wood,
hewed two tablets of stone like the first,
and went up the mountain, having
the two tablets in my hand. 4And He
wrote on the tablets according to the
first writing, the Ten Commandments,
which the LORD had spoken to you in
the mountain from the midst of the
fire in the day of the assembly; and the
LORD gave them to me. 5Then I turned
and came down from the mountain,
and put the tablets in the ark which I
had made; and there they are, just as
the LORD commanded me."
6(Now the children of Israel journeyed
from the wells of Bene Jaakan to Mo-
serah, where Aaron died, and where he
was buried; and Eleazar his son minis-
tered as priest in his stead. 7From there
they journeyed to Gudgodah, and from
Gudgodah to Jotbathah, a land of rivers
of water. 8At that time the LORD sepa-
rated the tribe of Levi to bear the ark
of the covenant of the LORD, to stand
before the LORD to minister to Him
and to bless in His name, to this day.
9Therefore Levi has no portion nor in-
heritance with his brethren; the LORD
is his inheritance, just as the LORD your
God promised him.)
10"As at the first time, I stayed in the
mountain forty days and forty nights;

the LORD also heard me at that time,
and the LORD chose not to destroy you.
11Then the LORD said to me, 'Arise, begin
your journey before the people, that they
may go in and possess the land which
I swore to their fathers to give them.'

The Essence of the Law

12"And now, Israel, what does the LORD
your God require of you, but to fear the
LORD your God, to walk in all His ways
and to love Him, to serve the LORD your
God with all your heart and with all your
soul, 13*and* to keep the commandments
of the LORD and His statutes which I
command you today for your good?
14Indeed heaven and the highest heav-
ens belong to the LORD your God, *also*
the earth with all that *is* in it. 15The LORD
delighted only in your fathers, to love
them; and He chose their descendants
after them, you above all peoples, as
it is this day. 16Therefore circumcise
the foreskin of your heart, and be stiff-
necked no longer. 17For the LORD your
God *is* God of gods and Lord of lords,
the great God, mighty and awesome,
who shows no partiality nor takes a
bribe. 18He administers justice for the
fatherless and the widow, and loves the
stranger, giving him food and clothing.
19Therefore love the stranger, for you
were strangers in the land of Egypt.
20You shall fear the LORD your God; you
shall serve Him, and to Him you shall
hold fast, and take oaths in His name.
21He *is* your praise, and He *is* your God,
who has done for you these great and
awesome things which your eyes have
seen. 22Your fathers went down to Egypt
with seventy persons, and now the LORD
your God has made you as the stars of
heaven in multitude.

Love and Obedience Rewarded

11 "Therefore you shall love the
LORD your God, and keep His
charge, His statutes, His judgments,
and His commandments always. 2Know
today that *I do* not *speak* with your chil-
dren, who have not known and who
have not seen the chastening of the
LORD your God, His greatness and His
mighty hand and His outstretched
arm— 3His signs and His acts which
He did in the midst of Egypt, to Phar-
aoh king of Egypt, and to all his land;
4what He did to the army of Egypt, to
their horses and their chariots: how He
made the waters of the Red Sea overflow
them as they pursued you, and *how* the
LORD has destroyed them to this day;
5what He did for you in the wilderness
until you came to this place; 6and what
He did to Dathan and Abiram the sons
of Eliab, the son of Reuben: how the
earth opened its mouth and swallowed
them up, their households, their tents,
and all the substance that *was* in their
possession, in the midst of all Israel—
7but your eyes have seen every great
act of the LORD which He did.

8"Therefore you shall keep every com-
mandment which I command you to-
day, that you may be strong, and go in
and possess the land which you cross
over to possess, 9and that you may
prolong *your* days in the land which
the LORD swore to give your fathers,
to them and their descendants, 'a land
flowing with milk and honey.'[a] 10For
the land which you go to possess *is*
not like the land of Egypt from which
you have come, where you sowed your
seed and watered *it* by foot, as a vege-
table garden; 11but the land which you
cross over to possess *is* a land of hills
and valleys, which drinks water from
the rain of heaven, 12a land for which
the LORD your God cares; the eyes of the
LORD your God *are* always on it, from
the beginning of the year to the very
end of the year.

13'And it shall be that if you earnestly
obey My commandments which I com-
mand you today, to love the LORD your
God and serve Him with all your heart
and with all your soul, 14then I[a] will give
you the rain for your land in its season,
the early rain and the latter rain, that
you may gather in your grain, your
new wine, and your oil. 15And I will send
grass in your fields for your livestock,
that you may eat and be filled.' 16Take
heed to yourselves, lest your heart be
deceived, and you turn aside and serve

11:9 [a] Exodus 3:8 **11:14** [a] Following Masoretic Text and Targum; Samaritan Pentateuch, Septuagint, and Vulgate read *He.*

GOD SIN JESUS SALVATION LOVE

other gods and worship them, 17lest the
LORD's anger be aroused against you,
and He shut up the heavens so that there
be no rain, and the land yield no pro-
duce, and you perish quickly from the
good land which the LORD is giving you.
18"Therefore you shall lay up these
words of mine in your heart and in your
soul, and bind them as a sign on your
hand, and they shall be as frontlets be-
tween your eyes. 19You shall teach them
to your children, speaking of them when
you sit in your house, when you walk by
the way, when you lie down, and when
you rise up. 20And you shall write them
on the doorposts of your house and on
your gates, 21that your days and the
days of your children may be multiplied
in the land of which the LORD swore to
your fathers to give them, like the days
of the heavens above the earth.
22"For if you carefully keep all these
commandments which I command you
to do—to love the LORD your God, to
walk in all His ways, and to hold fast to
Him— 23then the LORD will drive out all
these nations from before you, and you
will dispossess greater and mightier
nations than yourselves. 24Every place
on which the sole of your foot treads
shall be yours: from the wilderness and
Lebanon, from the river, the River Eu-
phrates, even to the Western Sea,[a] shall
be your territory. 25No man shall be
able to stand against you; the LORD
your God will put the dread of you and
the fear of you upon all the land where
you tread, just as He has said to you.
26"Behold, I set before you today a
blessing and a curse: 27the blessing,
if you obey the commandments of
the LORD your God which I command
you today; 28and the curse, if you do
not obey the commandments of the
LORD your God, but turn aside from
the way which I command you today,
to go after other gods which you have
not known. 29Now it shall be, when the
LORD your God has brought you into
the land which you go to possess, that
you shall put the blessing on Mount
Gerizim and the curse on Mount Ebal.
30*Are* they not on the other side of the
Jordan, toward the setting sun, in the
land of the Canaanites who dwell in
the plain opposite Gilgal, beside the
terebinth trees of Moreh? 31For you will
cross over the Jordan and go in to pos-
sess the land which the LORD your God
is giving you, and you will possess it and
dwell in it. 32And you shall be careful to
observe all the statutes and judgments
which I set before you today.

A Prescribed Place of Worship

12 "These *are* the statutes and
judgments which you shall be
careful to observe in the land which the
LORD God of your fathers is giving you
to possess, all the days that you live on
the earth. 2You shall utterly destroy all
the places where the nations which you
shall dispossess served their gods, on
the high mountains and on the hills
and under every green tree. 3And you
shall destroy their altars, break their
sacred pillars, and burn their wooden
images with fire; you shall cut down
the carved images of their gods and
destroy their names from that place.
4You shall not worship the LORD your
God *with* such *things*.
5"But you shall seek the place where
the LORD your God chooses, out of all
your tribes, to put His name for His
dwelling place; and there you shall
go. 6There you shall take your burnt
offerings, your sacrifices, your tithes,
the heave offerings of your hand, your
vowed offerings, your freewill offer-
ings, and the firstborn of your herds
and flocks. 7And there you shall eat
before the LORD your God, and you
shall rejoice in all to which you have
put your hand, you and your house-
holds, in which the LORD your God has
blessed you.
8"You shall not at all do as we are
doing here today—every man doing
whatever *is* right in his own eyes— 9for
as yet you have not come to the rest and
the inheritance which the LORD your
God is giving you. 10But *when* you cross
over the Jordan and dwell in the land
which the LORD your God is giving you
to inherit, and He gives you rest from

11:24 a That is, the Mediterranean

all your enemies round about, so that
you dwell in safety, 11then there will
be the place where the LORD your God
chooses to make His name abide. There
you shall bring all that I command
you: your burnt offerings, your sacri-
fices, your tithes, the heave offerings of
your hand, and all your choice offerings
which you vow to the LORD. 12And you
shall rejoice before the LORD your God,
you and your sons and your daughters,
your male and female servants, and the
Levite who *is* within your gates, since
he has no portion nor inheritance with
you. 13Take heed to yourself that you do
not offer your burnt offerings in every
place that you see; 14but in the place
which the LORD chooses, in one of your
tribes, there you shall offer your burnt
offerings, and there you shall do all that
I command you.
15"However, you may slaughter and
eat meat within all your gates, whatever
your heart desires, according to the
blessing of the LORD your God which
He has given you; the unclean and the
clean may eat of it, of the gazelle and
the deer alike. 16Only you shall not eat
the blood; you shall pour it on the earth
like water. 17You may not eat within
your gates the tithe of your grain or
your new wine or your oil, of the first-
born of your herd or your flock, of any
of your offerings which you vow, of your
freewill offerings, or of the heave offer-
ing of your hand. 18But you must eat
them before the LORD your God in the
place which the LORD your God chooses,
you and your son and your daughter,
your male servant and your female
servant, and the Levite who *is* within
your gates; and you shall rejoice before
the LORD your God in all to which you
put your hands. 19Take heed to yourself
that you do not forsake the Levite as
long as you live in your land.
20"When the LORD your God enlarges
your border as He has promised you,
and you say, 'Let me eat meat,' because
you long to eat meat, you may eat as
much meat as your heart desires. 21If
the place where the LORD your God
chooses to put His name is too far from
you, then you may slaughter from your
herd and from your flock which the
LORD has given you, just as I have com-
manded you, and you may eat within
your gates as much as your heart de-
sires. 22Just as the gazelle and the deer
are eaten, so you may eat them; the
unclean and the clean alike may eat
them. 23Only be sure that you do not
eat the blood, for the blood *is* the life;
you may not eat the life with the meat.
24You shall not eat it; you shall pour it
on the earth like water. 25You shall not
eat it, that it may go well with you and
your children after you, when you do
what is right in the sight of the LORD.
26Only the holy things which you have,
and your vowed offerings, you shall
take and go to the place which the LORD
chooses. 27And you shall offer your
burnt offerings, the meat and the blood,
on the altar of the LORD your God; and
the blood of your sacrifices shall be
poured out on the altar of the LORD your
God, and you shall eat the meat. 28Ob-
serve and obey all these words which I
command you, that it may go well with
you and your children after you forever,
when you do *what is* good and right in
the sight of the LORD your God.

Beware of False Gods

29"When the LORD your God cuts off
from before you the nations which you
go to dispossess, and you displace them
and dwell in their land, 30take heed to
yourself that you are not ensnared to
follow them, after they are destroyed
from before you, and that you do not
inquire after their gods, saying, 'How
did these nations serve their gods? I also
will do likewise.' 31You shall not worship
the LORD your God in that way; for ev-
ery abomination to the LORD which He
hates they have done to their gods; for
they burn even their sons and daugh-
ters in the fire to their gods.
32"Whatever I command you, be care-
ful to observe it; you shall not add to it
nor take away from it.

Punishment of Apostates

13 "If there arises among you a
prophet or a dreamer of dreams,
and he gives you a sign or a wonder,
2and the sign or the wonder comes
to pass, of which he spoke to you,

saying, 'Let us go after other gods'—
which you have not known—'and let
us serve them,' 3you shall not listen
to the words of that prophet or that
dreamer of dreams, for the LORD your
God is testing you to know whether you
love the LORD your God with all your
heart and with all your soul. 4You shall
walk after the LORD your God and fear
Him, and keep His commandments and
obey His voice; you shall serve Him and
hold fast to Him. 5But that prophet or
that dreamer of dreams shall be put to
death, because he has spoken in order
to turn *you* away from the LORD your
God, who brought you out of the land
of Egypt and redeemed you from the
house of bondage, to entice you from
the way in which the LORD your God
commanded you to walk. So you shall
put away the evil from your midst.

6"If your brother, the son of your
mother, your son or your daughter, the
wife of your bosom, or your friend who
is as your own soul, secretly entices you,
saying, 'Let us go and serve other gods,'
which you have not known, neither you
nor your fathers, 7of the gods of the peo-
ple which *are* all around you, near to
you or far off from you, from *one* end of
the earth to the *other* end of the earth,
8you shall not consent to him or listen
to him, nor shall your eye pity him, nor
shall you spare him or conceal him; 9but
you shall surely kill him; your hand shall
be first against him to put him to death,
and afterward the hand of all the people.
10And you shall stone him with stones
until he dies, because he sought to entice
you away from the LORD your God, who
brought you out of the land of Egypt,
from the house of bondage. 11So all Is-
rael shall hear and fear, and not again
do such wickedness as this among you.

12"If you hear someone in one of your
cities, which the LORD your God gives
you to dwell in, saying, 13'Corrupt men
have gone out from among you and
enticed the inhabitants of their city,
saying, "Let us go and serve other
gods" '—which you have not known—
14then you shall inquire, search out, and
ask diligently. And *if it is* indeed true
and certain *that* such an abomination
was committed among you, 15you shall
surely strike the inhabitants of that
city with the edge of the sword, utter-
ly destroying it, all that is in it and its
livestock—with the edge of the sword.
16And you shall gather all its plunder
into the middle of the street, and com-
pletely burn with fire the city and all
its plunder, for the LORD your God. It
shall be a heap forever; it shall not be
built again. 17So none of the accursed
things shall remain in your hand, that
the LORD may turn from the fierceness
of His anger and show you mercy, have
compassion on you and multiply you,
just as He swore to your fathers, 18be-
cause you have listened to the voice
of the LORD your God, to keep all His
commandments which I command you
today, to do *what is* right in the eyes of
the LORD your God.

Improper Mourning

14 "You *are* the children of the LORD
your God; you shall not cut your-
selves nor shave the front of your head
for the dead. 2For you *are* a holy people
to the LORD your God, and the LORD has
chosen you to be a people for Himself,
a special treasure above all the peoples
who *are* on the face of the earth.

Clean and Unclean Meat

3"You shall not eat any detestable
thing. 4These *are* the animals which
you may eat: the ox, the sheep, the goat,
5the deer, the gazelle, the roe deer, the
wild goat, the mountain goat,[a] the an-
telope, and the mountain sheep. 6And
you may eat every animal with cloven
hooves, having the hoof split into two
parts, *and that* chews the cud, among
the animals. 7Nevertheless, of those that
chew the cud or have cloven hooves, you
shall not eat, *such as* these: the camel,
the hare, and the rock hyrax; for they
chew the cud but do not have cloven
hooves; they *are* unclean for you. 8Also
the swine is unclean for you, because
it has cloven hooves, yet *does* not *chew*
the cud; you shall not eat their flesh or
touch their dead carcasses.

14:5 [a] Or *addax*

9"These you may eat of all that *are* in
the waters: you may eat all that have
fins and scales. 10And whatever does
not have fins and scales you shall not
eat; it *is* unclean for you.
11"All clean birds you may eat. 12But
these you shall not eat: the eagle, the
vulture, the buzzard, 13the red kite, the
falcon, and the kite after their kinds;
14every raven after its kind; 15the os-
trich, the short-eared owl, the sea gull,
and the hawk after their kinds; 16the
little owl, the screech owl, the white owl,
17the jackdaw, the carrion vulture, the
fisher owl, 18the stork, the heron after
its kind, and the hoopoe and the bat.
19"Also every creeping thing that flies is
unclean for you; they shall not be eaten.
20"You may eat all clean birds.
21"You shall not eat anything that dies
of itself; you may give it to the alien who
is within your gates, that he may eat it,
or you may sell it to a foreigner; for you
are a holy people to the LORD your God.
"You shall not boil a young goat in its
mother's milk.

Tithing Principles

22"You shall truly tithe all the increase
of your grain that the field produces
year by year. 23And you shall eat before
the LORD your God, in the place where
He chooses to make His name abide,
the tithe of your grain and your new
wine and your oil, of the firstborn of
your herds and your flocks, that you
may learn to fear the LORD your God
always. 24But if the journey is too long
for you, so that you are not able to carry
the tithe, or if the place where the LORD
your God chooses to put His name is
too far from you, when the LORD your
God has blessed you, 25then you shall
exchange *it* for money, take the money
in your hand, and go to the place which
the LORD your God chooses. 26And you
shall spend that money for whatever
your heart desires: for oxen or sheep,
for wine or similar drink, for whatever
your heart desires; you shall eat there
before the LORD your God, and you
shall rejoice, you and your household.
27You shall not forsake the Levite who
is within your gates, for he has no part
nor inheritance with you.
28"At the end of *every* third year you
shall bring out the tithe of your produce
of that year and store *it* up within your
gates. 29And the Levite, because he has
no portion nor inheritance with you,
and the stranger and the fatherless and
the widow who *are* within your gates,
may come and eat and be satisfied, that
the LORD your God may bless you in all
the work of your hand which you do.

Debts Canceled Every Seven Years

15 "At the end of *every* seven years
you shall grant a release *of
debts.* 2And this *is* the form of the re-
lease: Every creditor who has lent *any-
thing* to his neighbor shall release *it;* he
shall not require *it* of his neighbor or his
brother, because it is called the LORD's
release. 3Of a foreigner you may require
it; but you shall give up your claim to
what is owed by your brother, 4except
when there may be no poor among
you; for the LORD will greatly bless you
in the land which the LORD your God
is giving you to possess *as* an inheri-
tance— 5only if you carefully obey the
voice of the LORD your God, to observe
with care all these commandments
which I command you today. 6For the
LORD your God will bless you just as He
promised you; you shall lend to many
nations, but you shall not borrow; you
shall reign over many nations, but they
shall not reign over you.

Generosity to the Poor

7"If there is among you a poor man of
your brethren, within any of the gates
in your land which the LORD your God
is giving you, you shall not harden your
heart nor shut your hand from your poor
brother, 8but you shall open your hand
wide to him and willingly lend him suf-
ficient for his need, whatever he needs.
9Beware lest there be a wicked thought in
your heart, saying, 'The seventh year, the
year of release, is at hand,' and your eye
be evil against your poor brother and
you give him nothing, and he cry out
to the LORD against you, and it become
sin among you. 10You shall surely give
to him, and your heart should not be
grieved when you give to him, because
for this thing the LORD your God will

bless you in all your works and in all to
which you put your hand. 11For the poor
will never cease from the land; therefore
I command you, saying, 'You shall open
your hand wide to your brother, to your
poor and your needy, in your land.'

The Law Concerning Bondservants

12"If your brother, a Hebrew man, or
a Hebrew woman, is sold to you and
serves you six years, then in the seventh
year you shall let him go free from you.
13And when you send him away free
from you, you shall not let him go away
empty-handed; 14you shall supply him
liberally from your flock, from your
threshing floor, and from your wine-
press. *From what* the LORD your God has
blessed you with, you shall give to him.
15You shall remember that you were a
slave in the land of Egypt, and the LORD
your God redeemed you; therefore I
command you this thing today. 16And
if it happens that he says to you, 'I will
not go away from you,' because he loves
you and your house, since he prospers
with you, 17then you shall take an awl
and thrust *it* through his ear to the door,
and he shall be your servant forever.
Also to your female servant you shall
do likewise. 18It shall not seem hard to
you when you send him away free from
you; for he has been worth a double
hired servant in serving you six years.
Then the LORD your God will bless you
in all that you do.

The Law Concerning Firstborn Animals

19"All the firstborn males that come
from your herd and your flock you shall
sanctify to the LORD your God; you shall
do no work with the firstborn of your
herd, nor shear the firstborn of your
flock. 20You and your household shall
eat *it* before the LORD your God year by
year in the place which the LORD choos-
es. 21But if there is a defect in it, *if it is*
lame or blind *or has* any serious defect,
you shall not sacrifice it to the LORD
your God. 22You may eat it within your
gates; the unclean and the clean *person*
alike *may eat it,* as *if it were* a gazelle or a
deer. 23Only you shall not eat its blood;
you shall pour it on the ground like
water.

The Passover Reviewed

16 "Observe the month of Abib,
and keep the Passover to the
LORD your God, for in the month of Abib
the LORD your God brought you out of
Egypt by night. 2Therefore you shall
sacrifice the Passover to the LORD your
God, from the flock and the herd, in the
place where the LORD chooses to put
His name. 3You shall eat no leavened
bread with it; seven days you shall eat
unleavened bread with it, *that is,* the
bread of affliction (for you came out
of the land of Egypt in haste), that you
may remember the day in which you
came out of the land of Egypt all the
days of your life. 4And no leaven shall
be seen among you in all your territory
for seven days, nor shall *any* of the meat
which you sacrifice the first day at twi-
light remain overnight until morning.
5"You may not sacrifice the Passover
within any of your gates which the LORD
your God gives you; 6but at the place
where the LORD your God chooses to
make His name abide, there you shall
sacrifice the Passover at twilight, at the
going down of the sun, at the time you
came out of Egypt. 7And you shall roast
and eat *it* in the place which the LORD
your God chooses, and in the morning
you shall turn and go to your tents. 8Six
days you shall eat unleavened bread,
and on the seventh day there *shall be* a
sacred assembly to the LORD your God.
You shall do no work *on it.*

The Feast of Weeks Reviewed

9"You shall count seven weeks for
yourself; begin to count the seven weeks
from *the time* you begin *to put* the sickle
to the grain. 10Then you shall keep the
Feast of Weeks to the LORD your God
with the tribute of a freewill offering
from your hand, which you shall give
as the LORD your God blesses you. 11You
shall rejoice before the LORD your God,
you and your son and your daughter,
your male servant and your female
servant, the Levite who *is* within your
gates, the stranger and the fatherless
and the widow who *are* among you,
at the place where the LORD your God
chooses to make His name abide. 12And
you shall remember that you were a

slave in Egypt, and you shall be careful to observe these statutes.

The Feast of Tabernacles Reviewed

13“You shall observe the Feast of Tabernacles seven days, when you have gathered from your threshing floor and from your winepress. 14And you shall rejoice in your feast, you and your son and your daughter, your male servant and your female servant and the Levite, the stranger and the fatherless and the widow, who *are* within your gates. 15Seven days you shall keep a sacred feast to the LORD your God in the place which the LORD chooses, because the LORD your God will bless you in all your produce and in all the work of your hands, so that you surely rejoice.

16“Three times a year all your males shall appear before the LORD your God in the place which He chooses: at the Feast of Unleavened Bread, at the Feast of Weeks, and at the Feast of Tabernacles; and they shall not appear before the LORD empty-handed. 17Every man *shall give* as he is able, according to the blessing of the LORD your God which He has given you.

Justice Must Be Administered

18“You shall appoint judges and officers in all your gates, which the LORD your God gives you, according to your tribes, and they shall judge the people with just judgment. 19You shall not pervert justice; you shall not show partiality, nor take a bribe, for a bribe blinds the eyes of the wise and twists the words of the righteous. 20You shall follow what is altogether just, that you may live and inherit the land which the LORD your God is giving you.

21“You shall not plant for yourself any tree, as a wooden image, near the altar which you build for yourself to the LORD your God. 22You shall not set up a *sacred* pillar, which the LORD your God hates.

17 “You shall not sacrifice to the LORD your God a bull or sheep which has any blemish *or* defect, for that *is* an abomination to the LORD your God.

2“If there is found among you, within any of your gates which the LORD your God gives you, a man or a woman who has been wicked in the sight of the LORD your God, in transgressing His covenant, 3who has gone and served other gods and worshiped them, either the sun or moon or any of the host of heaven, which I have not commanded, 4and it is told you, and you hear *of it,* then you shall inquire diligently. And if *it is* indeed true *and* certain that such an abomination has been committed in Israel, 5then you shall bring out to your gates that man or woman who has committed that wicked thing, and shall stone to death that man or woman with stones. 6Whoever is deserving of death shall be put to death on the testimony of two or three witnesses; he shall not be put to death on the testimony of one witness. 7The hands of the witnesses shall be the first against him to put him to death, and afterward the hands of all the people. So you shall put away the evil from among you.

8“If a matter arises which is too hard for you to judge, between degrees of guilt for bloodshed, between one judgment or another, or between one punishment or another, matters of controversy within your gates, then you shall arise and go up to the place which the LORD your God chooses. 9And you shall come to the priests, the Levites, and to the judge *there* in those days, and inquire *of them;* they shall pronounce upon you the sentence of judgment. 10You shall do according to the sentence which they pronounce upon you in that place which the LORD chooses. And you shall be careful to do according to all that they order you. 11According to the sentence of the law in which they instruct you, according to the judgment which they tell you, you shall do; you shall not turn aside *to* the right hand or *to* the left from the sentence which they pronounce upon you. 12Now the man who acts presumptuously and will not heed the priest who stands to minister there before the LORD your God, or the judge, that man shall die. So you shall put away the evil from Israel. 13And all the people shall hear and fear, and no longer act presumptuously.

Principles Governing Kings

14“When you come to the land which
the LORD your God is giving you, and
possess it and dwell in it, and say, ‘I will
set a king over me like all the nations
that *are* around me,’ 15you shall surely
set a king over you whom the LORD your
God chooses; *one* from among your
brethren you shall set as king over you;
you may not set a foreigner over you,
who *is* not your brother. 16But he shall
not multiply horses for himself, nor
cause the people to return to Egypt to
multiply horses, for the LORD has said
to you, ‘You shall not return that way
again.’ 17Neither shall he multiply wives
for himself, lest his heart turn away;
nor shall he greatly multiply silver and
gold for himself.

18“Also it shall be, when he sits on the
throne of his kingdom, that he shall
write for himself a copy of this law in
a book, from *the one* before the priests,
the Levites. 19And it shall be with him,
and he shall read it all the days of his
life, that he may learn to fear the LORD
his God and be careful to observe all the
words of this law and these statutes,
20that his heart may not be lifted above
his brethren, that he may not turn aside
from the commandment *to* the right
hand or *to* the left, and that he may
prolong *his* days in his kingdom, he
and his children in the midst of Israel.

The Portion of the Priests and Levites

18 “The priests, the Levites—all the
tribe of Levi—shall have no part
nor inheritance with Israel; they shall
eat the offerings of the LORD made by
fire, and His portion. 2Therefore they
shall have no inheritance among their
brethren; the LORD is their inheritance,
as He said to them.

3“And this shall be the priest’s due from
the people, from those who offer a sac-
rifice, whether *it is* bull or sheep: they
shall give to the priest the shoulder, the
cheeks, and the stomach. 4The firstfruits
of your grain and your new wine and
your oil, and the first of the fleece of your
sheep, you shall give him. 5For the LORD
your God has chosen him out of all your
tribes to stand to minister in the name
of the LORD, him and his sons forever.

6“So if a Levite comes from any of your
gates, from where he dwells among
all Israel, and comes with all the de-
sire of his mind to the place which the
LORD chooses, 7then he may serve in
the name of the LORD his God as all his
brethren the Levites *do,* who stand there
before the LORD. 8They shall have equal
portions to eat, besides what comes
from the sale of his inheritance.

Avoid Wicked Customs

9“When you come into the land which
the LORD your God is giving you, you
shall not learn to follow the abomina-
tions of those nations. 10There shall not
be found among you *anyone* who makes
his son or his daughter pass through
the fire, *or one* who practices witchcraft,
or a soothsayer, or one who interprets
omens, or a sorcerer, 11or one who con-
jures spells, or a medium, or a spiritist,
or one who calls up the dead. 12For all
who do these things *are* an abomina-
tion to the LORD, and because of these
abominations the LORD your God drives
them out from before you. 13You shall
be blameless before the LORD your God.
14For these nations which you will dis-
possess listened to soothsayers and
diviners; but as for you, the LORD your
God has not appointed such for you.

A New Prophet Like Moses

15“The LORD your God will raise up for
you a Prophet like me from your midst,
from your brethren. Him you shall hear,
16according to all you desired of the LORD
your God in Horeb in the day of the as-
sembly, saying, ‘Let me not hear again
the voice of the LORD my God, nor let me
see this great fire anymore, lest I die.’

17“And the LORD said to me: ‘What they
have spoken is good. 18I will raise up for
them a Prophet like you from among
their brethren, and will put My words in
His mouth, and He shall speak to them
all that I command Him. 19And it shall
be *that* whoever will not hear My words,
which He speaks in My name, I will re-
quire *it* of him. 20But the prophet who
presumes to speak a word in My name,
which I have not commanded him to
speak, or who speaks in the name of
other gods, that prophet shall die.’ 21And

if you say in your heart, 'How shall we
know the word which the LORD has not
spoken?'— 22when a prophet speaks in
the name of the LORD, if the thing does
not happen or come to pass, that *is* the
thing which the LORD has not spoken;
the prophet has spoken it presumptu-
ously; you shall not be afraid of him.

Three Cities of Refuge

19 "When the LORD your God has
cut off the nations whose land
the LORD your God is giving you, and
you dispossess them and dwell in their
cities and in their houses, 2you shall
separate three cities for yourself in the
midst of your land which the LORD your
God is giving you to possess. 3You shall
prepare roads for yourself, and divide
into three parts the territory of your
land which the LORD your God is giving
you to inherit, that any manslayer may
flee there.

4"And this *is* the case of the manslayer
who flees there, that he may live: Who-
ever kills his neighbor unintentionally,
not having hated him in time past— 5as
when *a man* goes to the woods with his
neighbor to cut timber, and his hand
swings a stroke with the ax to cut down
the tree, and the head slips from the
handle and strikes his neighbor so that
he dies—he shall flee to one of these cit-
ies and live; 6lest the avenger of blood,
while his anger is hot, pursue the man-
slayer and overtake him, because the
way is long, and kill him, though he
was not deserving of death, since he
had not hated the victim in time past.
7Therefore I command you, saying, 'You
shall separate three cities for yourself.'

8"Now if the LORD your God enlarges
your territory, as He swore to your fa-
thers, and gives you the land which He
promised to give to your fathers, 9and if
you keep all these commandments and
do them, which I command you today,
to love the LORD your God and to walk
always in His ways, then you shall add
three more cities for yourself besides
these three, 10lest innocent blood be
shed in the midst of your land which
the LORD your God is giving you *as* an
inheritance, and *thus* guilt of bloodshed
be upon you.

11"But if anyone hates his neighbor,
lies in wait for him, rises against him
and strikes him mortally, so that he
dies, and he flees to one of these cities,
12then the elders of his city shall send
and bring him from there, and deliver
him over to the hand of the avenger of
blood, that he may die. 13Your eye shall
not pity him, but you shall put away *the
guilt of* innocent blood from Israel, that
it may go well with you.

Property Boundaries

14"You shall not remove your neigh-
bor's landmark, which the men of old
have set, in your inheritance which you
will inherit in the land that the LORD
your God is giving you to possess.

The Law Concerning Witnesses

15"One witness shall not rise against
a man concerning any iniquity or any
sin that he commits; by the mouth of
two or three witnesses the matter shall
be established. 16If a false witness ris-
es against any man to testify against
him of wrongdoing, 17then both men in
the controversy shall stand before the
LORD, before the priests and the judg-
es who serve in those days. 18And the
judges shall make careful inquiry, and
indeed, *if* the witness *is* a false witness,
who has testified falsely against his
brother, 19then you shall do to him as
he thought to have done to his brother;
so you shall put away the evil from
among you. 20And those who remain
shall hear and fear, and hereafter they
shall not again commit such evil among
you. 21Your eye shall not pity: life *shall
be* for life, eye for eye, tooth for tooth,
hand for hand, foot for foot.

Principles Governing Warfare

20 "When you go out to battle
against your enemies, and see
horses and chariots *and* people more
numerous than you, do not be afraid
of them; for the LORD your God *is* with
you, who brought you up from the land
of Egypt. 2So it shall be, when you are
on the verge of battle, that the priest
shall approach and speak to the peo-
ple. 3And he shall say to them, 'Hear,
O Israel: Today you are on the verge

of battle with your enemies. Do not let
your heart faint, do not be afraid, and
do not tremble or be terrified because of
them; 4for the LORD your God *is* He who
goes with you, to fight for you against
your enemies, to save you.'
5"Then the officers shall speak to the
people, saying: 'What man *is there* who
has built a new house and has not ded-
icated it? Let him go and return to his
house, lest he die in the battle and an-
other man dedicate it. 6Also what man
is there who has planted a vineyard and
has not eaten of it? Let him go and re-
turn to his house, lest he die in the battle
and another man eat of it. 7And what
man *is there* who is betrothed to a wom-
an and has not married her? Let him go
and return to his house, lest he die in
the battle and another man marry her.'
8"The officers shall speak further to the
people, and say, 'What man *is there who*
is fearful and fainthearted? Let him go
and return to his house, lest the heart
of his brethren faint[a] like his heart.'
9And so it shall be, when the officers
have finished speaking to the people,
that they shall make captains of the
armies to lead the people.
10"When you go near a city to fight
against it, then proclaim an offer of peace
to it. 11And it shall be that if they accept
your offer of peace, and open to you, then
all the people *who are* found in it shall be
placed under tribute to you, and serve
you. 12Now if *the city* will not make peace
with you, but war against you, then you
shall besiege it. 13And when the LORD
your God delivers it into your hands, you
shall strike every male in it with the edge
of the sword. 14But the women, the little
ones, the livestock, and all that is in the
city, all its spoil, you shall plunder for
yourself; and you shall eat the enemies'
plunder which the LORD your God gives
you. 15Thus you shall do to all the cities
which are very far from you, which *are*
not of the cities of these nations.
16"But of the cities of these peoples
which the LORD your God gives you *as*
an inheritance, you shall let nothing
that breathes remain alive, 17but you
shall utterly destroy them: the Hittite
and the Amorite and the Canaanite
and the Perizzite and the Hivite and the
Jebusite, just as the LORD your God has
commanded you, 18lest they teach you
to do according to all their abominations
which they have done for their gods,
and you sin against the LORD your God.
19"When you besiege a city for a long
time, while making war against it to
take it, you shall not destroy its trees by
wielding an ax against them; if you can
eat of them, do not cut them down to
use in the siege, for the tree of the field
is man's *food.* 20Only the trees which
you know *are* not trees for food you
may destroy and cut down, to build
siegeworks against the city that makes
war with you, until it is subdued.

The Law Concerning Unsolved Murder

21 "If *anyone* is found slain, lying
in the field in the land which the
LORD your God is giving you to pos-
sess, *and* it is not known who killed him,
2then your elders and your judges shall
go out and measure *the distance* from
the slain man to the surrounding cities.
3And it shall be *that* the elders of the
city nearest to the slain man will take
a heifer which has not been worked
and which has not pulled with a yoke.
4The elders of that city shall bring the
heifer down to a valley with flowing
water, which is neither plowed nor sown,
and they shall break the heifer's neck
there in the valley. 5Then the priests,
the sons of Levi, shall come near, for
the LORD your God has chosen them
to minister to Him and to bless in the
name of the LORD; by their word every
controversy and every assault shall be
settled. 6And all the elders of that city
nearest to the slain *man* shall wash
their hands over the heifer whose neck
was broken in the valley. 7Then they
shall answer and say, 'Our hands have
not shed this blood, nor have our eyes
seen *it.* 8Provide atonement, O LORD, for
Your people Israel, whom You have re-
deemed, and do not lay innocent blood
to the charge of Your people Israel.' And
atonement shall be provided on their
behalf for the blood. 9So you shall put

20:8 a Following Masoretic Text and Targum; Samaritan Pentateuch, Septuagint, Syriac, and Vulgate read *lest he make his brother's heart faint.*

away the *guilt of* innocent blood from
among you when you do *what is* right
in the sight of the LORD.

Female Captives

10“When you go out to war against
your enemies, and the LORD your God
delivers them into your hand, and you
take them captive, 11and you see among
the captives a beautiful woman, and
desire her and would take her for your
wife, 12then you shall bring her home
to your house, and she shall shave her
head and trim her nails. 13She shall put
off the clothes of her captivity, remain
in your house, and mourn her father
and her mother a full month; after that
you may go in to her and be her hus-
band, and she shall be your wife. 14And
it shall be, if you have no delight in
her, then you shall set her free, but you
certainly shall not sell her for money;
you shall not treat her brutally, because
you have humbled her.

Firstborn Inheritance Rights

15“If a man has two wives, one loved
and the other unloved, and they have
borne him children, *both* the loved and
the unloved, and *if* the firstborn son is
of her who is unloved, 16then it shall
be, on the day he bequeaths his pos-
sessions to his sons, *that* he must not
bestow firstborn status on the son of
the loved wife in preference to the son
of the unloved, the *true* firstborn. 17But
he shall acknowledge the son of the
unloved wife *as* the firstborn by giving
him a double portion of all that he has,
for he *is* the beginning of his strength;
the right of the firstborn *is* his.

The Rebellious Son

18“If a man has a stubborn and rebel-
lious son who will not obey the voice of
his father or the voice of his mother, and
who, when they have chastened him,
will not heed them, 19then his father
and his mother shall take hold of him
and bring him out to the elders of his
city, to the gate of his city. 20And they
shall say to the elders of his city, ‘This
son of ours is stubborn and rebellious;
he will not obey our voice; he is a glutton
and a drunkard.’ 21Then all the men of
his city shall stone him to death with
stones; so you shall put away the evil
from among you, and all Israel shall
hear and fear.

Miscellaneous Laws

22“If a man has committed a sin de-
serving of death, and he is put to death,
and you hang him on a tree, 23his body
shall not remain overnight on the tree,
but you shall surely bury him that day,
so that you do not defile the land which
the LORD your God is giving you *as* an
inheritance; for he who is hanged *is*
accursed of God.

22 “You shall not see your brother’s
ox or his sheep going astray, and
hide yourself from them; you shall cer-
tainly bring them back to your brother.
2And if your brother *is* not near you, or
if you do not know him, then you shall
bring it to your own house, and it shall
remain with you until your brother seeks
it; then you shall restore it to him. 3You
shall do the same with his donkey, and
so shall you do with his garment; with
any lost thing of your brother’s, which he
has lost and you have found, you shall
do likewise; you must not hide yourself.

4“You shall not see your brother’s don-
key or his ox fall down along the road,
and hide yourself from them; you shall
surely help him lift *them* up again.

5“A woman shall not wear anything
that pertains to a man, nor shall a man
put on a woman’s garment, for all who
do so *are* an abomination to the LORD
your God.

6“If a bird’s nest happens to be before
you along the way, in any tree or on the
ground, with young ones or eggs, with
the mother sitting on the young or on
the eggs, you shall not take the mother
with the young; 7you shall surely let
the mother go, and take the young for
yourself, that it may be well with you
and *that* you may prolong *your* days.

8“When you build a new house, then you
shall make a parapet for your roof, that
you may not bring guilt of bloodshed on
your household if anyone falls from it.

9“You shall not sow your vineyard with
different kinds of seed, lest the yield of
the seed which you have sown and the
fruit of your vineyard be defiled.

10"You shall not plow with an ox and a donkey together.

11"You shall not wear a garment of different sorts, *such as* wool and linen mixed together.

12"You shall make tassels on the four corners of the clothing with which you cover *yourself*.

Laws of Sexual Morality

13"If any man takes a wife, and goes
in to her, and detests her, 14and charges
her with shameful conduct, and brings a bad name on her, and says, 'I took this woman, and when I came to her I
found she *was* not a virgin,' 15then the
father and mother of the young woman shall take and bring out *the evidence of* the young woman's virginity to the
elders of the city at the gate. 16And
the young woman's father shall say to the elders, 'I gave my daughter to this
man as wife, and he detests her. 17Now
he has charged her with shameful conduct, saying, "I found your daughter *was* not a virgin," and yet these *are the evidences of* my daughter's virginity.' And they shall spread the cloth before
the elders of the city. 18Then the elders
of that city shall take that man and
punish him; 19and they shall fine him one hundred *shekels* of silver and give *them* to the father of the young woman, because he has brought a bad name on a virgin of Israel. And she shall be his wife; he cannot divorce her all his days.

20"But if the thing is true, *and evidences of* virginity are not found for the young
woman, 21then they shall bring out the young woman to the door of her father's house, and the men of her city shall stone her to death with stones, because she has done a disgraceful thing in Israel, to play the harlot in her father's house. So you shall put away the evil from among you.

22"If a man is found lying with a woman married to a husband, then both of them shall die—the man that lay with the woman, and the woman; so you shall put away the evil from Israel.

23"If a young woman *who is* a virgin is betrothed to a husband, and a man finds her in the city and lies with her,
24then you shall bring them both out to the gate of that city, and you shall stone them to death with stones, the young woman because she did not cry out in the city, and the man because he humbled his neighbor's wife; so you shall put away the evil from among you.

25"But if a man finds a betrothed young woman in the countryside, and the man forces her and lies with her, then only the man who lay with her
shall die. 26But you shall do nothing to
the young woman; *there is* in the young woman no sin *deserving* of death, for just as when a man rises against his neighbor and kills him, even so *is* this matter.
27For he found her in the countryside, *and* the betrothed young woman cried out, but *there was* no one to save her.

28"If a man finds a young woman *who is* a virgin, who is not betrothed, and he seizes her and lies with her, and they are
found out, 29then the man who lay with
her shall give to the young woman's father fifty *shekels* of silver, and she shall be his wife because he has humbled her; he shall not be permitted to divorce her all his days.

30"A man shall not take his father's wife, nor uncover his father's bed.

Those Excluded from the Congregation

23 "He who is emasculated by crushing or mutilation shall not enter the assembly of the LORD.

2"One of illegitimate birth shall not enter the assembly of the LORD; even to the tenth generation none of his *descendants* shall enter the assembly of the LORD.

3"An Ammonite or Moabite shall not enter the assembly of the LORD; even to the tenth generation none of his *descendants* shall enter the assembly of
the LORD forever, 4because they did
not meet you with bread and water on the road when you came out of Egypt, and because they hired against you Balaam the son of Beor from Pethor
of Mesopotamia,[a] to curse you. 5Nev-
ertheless the LORD your God would not listen to Balaam, but the LORD your God turned the curse into a blessing for you,

23:4 [a] Hebrew *Aram Naharaim*

because the LORD your God loves you. 6You shall not seek their peace nor their prosperity all your days forever.

7"You shall not abhor an Edomite, for he *is* your brother. You shall not abhor an Egyptian, because you were an alien in his land. 8The children of the third generation born to them may enter the assembly of the LORD.

Cleanliness of the Campsite

9"When the army goes out against your enemies, then keep yourself from every wicked thing. 10If there is any man among you who becomes unclean by some occurrence in the night, then he shall go outside the camp; he shall not come inside the camp. 11But it shall be, when evening comes, that he shall wash with water; and when the sun sets, he may come into the camp.

12"Also you shall have a place outside the camp, where you may go out; 13and you shall have an implement among your equipment, and when you sit down outside, you shall dig with it and turn and cover your refuse. 14For the LORD your God walks in the midst of your camp, to deliver you and give your enemies over to you; therefore your camp shall be holy, that He may see no unclean thing among you, and turn away from you.

Miscellaneous Laws

15"You shall not give back to his master the slave who has escaped from his master to you. 16He may dwell with you in your midst, in the place which he chooses within one of your gates, where it seems best to him; you shall not oppress him.

17"There shall be no *ritual* harlot[a] of the daughters of Israel, or a perverted[b] one of the sons of Israel. 18You shall not bring the wages of a harlot or the price of a dog to the house of the LORD your God for any vowed offering, for both of these *are* an abomination to the LORD your God.

19"You shall not charge interest to your brother—interest on money *or* food *or* anything that is lent out at interest. 20To a foreigner you may charge interest, but to your brother you shall not charge interest, that the LORD your God may bless you in all to which you set your hand in the land which you are entering to possess.

21"When you make a vow to the LORD your God, you shall not delay to pay it; for the LORD your God will surely require it of you, and it would be sin to you. 22But if you abstain from vowing, it shall not be sin to you. 23That which has gone from your lips you shall keep and perform, for you voluntarily vowed to the LORD your God what you have promised with your mouth.

24"When you come into your neighbor's vineyard, you may eat your fill of grapes at your pleasure, but you shall not put *any* in your container. 25When you come into your neighbor's standing grain, you may pluck the heads with your hand, but you shall not use a sickle on your neighbor's standing grain.

Law Concerning Divorce

24 "When a man takes a wife and marries her, and it happens that she finds no favor in his eyes because he has found some uncleanness in her, and he writes her a certificate of divorce, puts *it* in her hand, and sends her out of his house, 2when she has departed from his house, and goes and becomes another man's *wife,* 3*if* the latter husband detests her and writes her a certificate of divorce, puts *it* in her hand, and sends her out of his house, or if the latter husband dies who took her as his wife, 4*then* her former husband who divorced her must not take her back to be his wife after she has been defiled; for that *is* an abomination before the LORD, and you shall not bring sin on the land which the LORD your God is giving you *as* an inheritance.

Miscellaneous Laws

5"When a man has taken a new wife, he shall not go out to war or be charged with any business; he shall be free at home one year, and bring happiness to his wife whom he has taken.

23:17 [a] Hebrew *qedeshah,* feminine of *qadesh* (see next note) [b] Hebrew *qadesh,* that is, one practicing sodomy and prostitution in religious rituals

6"No man shall take the lower or the
upper millstone in pledge, for he takes
one's living in pledge.
7"If a man is found kidnapping any
of his brethren of the children of Isra-
el, and mistreats him or sells him, then
that kidnapper shall die; and you shall
put away the evil from among you.
8"Take heed in an outbreak of lepro-
sy, that you carefully observe and do
according to all that the priests, the
Levites, shall teach you; just as I com-
manded them, *so* you shall be careful
to do. 9Remember what the LORD your
God did to Miriam on the way when you
came out of Egypt!
10"When you lend your brother any-
thing, you shall not go into his house to
get his pledge. 11You shall stand outside,
and the man to whom you lend shall
bring the pledge out to you. 12And if
the man *is* poor, you shall not keep his
pledge overnight. 13You shall in any
case return the pledge to him again
when the sun goes down, that he may
sleep in his own garment and bless you;
and it shall be righteousness to you
before the LORD your God.
14"You shall not oppress a hired ser-
vant *who is* poor and needy, *whether*
one of your brethren or one of the aliens
who *is* in your land within your gates.
15Each day you shall give *him* his wages,
and not let the sun go down on it, for
he *is* poor and has set his heart on it;
lest he cry out against you to the LORD,
and it be sin to you.
16"Fathers shall not be put to death for
their children, nor shall children be put
to death for *their* fathers; a person shall
be put to death for his own sin.
17"You shall not pervert justice due
the stranger or the fatherless, nor take
a widow's garment as a pledge. 18But
you shall remember that you were a
slave in Egypt, and the LORD your God
redeemed you from there; therefore I
command you to do this thing.
19"When you reap your harvest in your
field, and forget a sheaf in the field,
you shall not go back to get it; it shall
be for the stranger, the fatherless, and
the widow, that the LORD your God may
bless you in all the work of your hands.
20When you beat your olive trees, you
shall not go over the boughs again; it
shall be for the stranger, the fatherless,
and the widow. 21When you gather the
grapes of your vineyard, you shall not
glean *it* afterward; it shall be for the
stranger, the fatherless, and the widow.
22And you shall remember that you
were a slave in the land of Egypt; there-
fore I command you to do this thing.

25 "If there is a dispute between
men, and they come to court,
that *the judges* may judge them, and
they justify the righteous and condemn
the wicked, 2then it shall be, if the wick-
ed man deserves to be beaten, that the
judge will cause him to lie down and
be beaten in his presence, according
to his guilt, with a certain number of
blows. 3Forty blows he may give him
and no more, lest he should exceed this
and beat him with many blows above
these, and your brother be humiliated
in your sight.
4"You shall not muzzle an ox while it
treads out *the grain.*

Marriage Duty of the Surviving Brother

5"If brothers dwell together, and one
of them dies and has no son, the widow
of the dead man shall not be *married* to
a stranger outside *the family;* her hus-
band's brother shall go in to her, take
her as his wife, and perform the duty
of a husband's brother to her. 6And it
shall be *that* the firstborn son which she
bears will succeed to the name of his
dead brother, that his name may not be
blotted out of Israel. 7But if the man does
not want to take his brother's wife, then
let his brother's wife go up to the gate
to the elders, and say, 'My husband's
brother refuses to raise up a name to
his brother in Israel; he will not perform
the duty of my husband's brother.' 8Then
the elders of his city shall call him and
speak to him. But *if* he stands firm and
says, 'I do not want to take her,' 9then
his brother's wife shall come to him in
the presence of the elders, remove his
sandal from his foot, spit in his face,
and answer and say, 'So shall it be done
to the man who will not build up his
brother's house.' 10And his name shall
be called in Israel, 'The house of him
who had his sandal removed.'

Miscellaneous Laws

11"If *two* men fight together, and the
wife of one draws near to rescue her
husband from the hand of the one at-
tacking him, and puts out her hand and
seizes him by the genitals, 12then you
shall cut off her hand; your eye shall
not pity *her.*

13"You shall not have in your bag dif-
fering weights, a heavy and a light.
14You shall not have in your house dif-
fering measures, a large and a small.
15You shall have a perfect and just
weight, a perfect and just measure,
that your days may be lengthened in
the land which the LORD your God is
giving you. 16For all who do such things,
all who behave unrighteously, *are* an
abomination to the LORD your God.

Destroy the Amalekites

17"Remember what Amalek did to
you on the way as you were coming
out of Egypt, 18how he met you on the
way and attacked your rear ranks, all
the stragglers at your rear, when you
were tired and weary; and he did not
fear God. 19Therefore it shall be, when
the LORD your God has given you rest
from your enemies all around, in the
land which the LORD your God is giving
you to possess *as* an inheritance, *that*
you will blot out the remembrance of
Amalek from under heaven. You shall
not forget.

Offerings of Firstfruits and Tithes

26 "And it shall be, when you come
into the land which the LORD
your God is giving you *as* an inheri-
tance, and you possess it and dwell in
it, 2that you shall take some of the first
of all the produce of the ground, which
you shall bring from your land that
the LORD your God is giving you, and
put *it* in a basket and go to the place
where the LORD your God chooses to
make His name abide. 3And you shall
go to the one who is priest in those days,
and say to him, 'I declare today to the
LORD your[a] God that I have come to
the country which the LORD swore to
our fathers to give us.'

4"Then the priest shall take the basket
out of your hand and set it down before
the altar of the LORD your God. 5And
you shall answer and say before the
LORD your God: 'My father *was* a Syri-
an,[a] about to perish, and he went down
to Egypt and dwelt there, few in number;
and there he became a nation, great,
mighty, and populous. 6But the Egyp-
tians mistreated us, afflicted us, and
laid hard bondage on us. 7Then we cried
out to the LORD God of our fathers, and
the LORD heard our voice and looked
on our affliction and our labor and our
oppression. 8So the LORD brought us out
of Egypt with a mighty hand and with
an outstretched arm, with great terror
and with signs and wonders. 9He has
brought us to this place and has given
us this land, "a land flowing with milk
and honey";[a] 10and now, behold, I have
brought the firstfruits of the land which
you, O LORD, have given me.'

"Then you shall set it before the LORD
your God, and worship before the LORD
your God. 11So you shall rejoice in every
good *thing* which the LORD your God
has given to you and your house, you
and the Levite and the stranger who *is*
among you.

12"When you have finished laying
aside all the tithe of your increase in
the third year—the year of tithing—and
have given *it* to the Levite, the stranger,
the fatherless, and the widow, so that
they may eat within your gates and be
filled, 13then you shall say before the
LORD your God: 'I have removed the
holy *tithe* from *my* house, and also have
given them to the Levite, the stranger,
the fatherless, and the widow, accord-
ing to all Your commandments which
You have commanded me; I have not
transgressed Your commandments,
nor have I forgotten *them.* 14I have not
eaten any of it when in mourning, nor
have I removed *any* of it for an unclean
use, nor given *any* of it for the dead. I
have obeyed the voice of the LORD my
God, and have done according to all
that You have commanded me. 15Look
down from Your holy habitation, from
heaven, and bless Your people Israel

26:3 [a] Septuagint reads *my.* 26:5 [a] Or *Aramean* 26:9 [a] Exodus 3:8

GOD SIN JESUS SALVATION LOVE

and the land which You have given us,
just as You swore to our fathers, “a land
flowing with milk and honey.” ’[a]

A Special People of God

16“This day the LORD your God com-
mands you to observe these statutes
and judgments; therefore you shall be
careful to observe them with all your
heart and with all your soul. 17Today
you have proclaimed the LORD to be
your God, and that you will walk in
His ways and keep His statutes, His
commandments, and His judgments,
and that you will obey His voice. 18Also
today the LORD has proclaimed you to
be His special people, just as He prom-
ised you, that *you* should keep all His
commandments, 19and that He will
set you high above all nations which
He has made, in praise, in name, and
in honor, and that you may be a holy
people to the LORD your God, just as He
has spoken.”

The Law Inscribed on Stones

27 Now Moses, with the elders of
Israel, commanded the people,
saying: “Keep all the commandments
which I command you today. 2And it
shall be, on the day when you cross over
the Jordan to the land which the LORD
your God is giving you, that you shall
set up for yourselves large stones, and
whitewash them with lime. 3You shall
write on them all the words of this law,
when you have crossed over, that you
may enter the land which the LORD your
God is giving you, ‘a land flowing with
milk and honey,’[a] just as the LORD God
of your fathers promised you. 4There-
fore it shall be, when you have crossed
over the Jordan, *that* on Mount Ebal
you shall set up these stones, which
I command you today, and you shall
whitewash them with lime. 5And there
you shall build an altar to the LORD
your God, an altar of stones; you shall
not use an iron *tool* on them. 6You shall
build with whole stones the altar of the
LORD your God, and offer burnt offer-
ings on it to the LORD your God. 7You
shall offer peace offerings, and shall eat
there, and rejoice before the LORD your
God. 8And you shall write very plainly
on the stones all the words of this law.”
9Then Moses and the priests, the Le-
vites, spoke to all Israel, saying, “Take
heed and listen, O Israel: This day you
have become the people of the LORD
your God. 10Therefore you shall obey
the voice of the LORD your God, and
observe His commandments and His
statutes which I command you today.”

Curses Pronounced from Mount Ebal

11And Moses commanded the people
on the same day, saying, 12“These shall
stand on Mount Gerizim to bless the
people, when you have crossed over the
Jordan: Simeon, Levi, Judah, Issachar,
Joseph, and Benjamin; 13and these shall
stand on Mount Ebal to curse: Reuben,
Gad, Asher, Zebulun, Dan, and Naphtali.
14“And the Levites shall speak with
a loud voice and say to all the men of
Israel: 15‘Cursed *is* the one who makes
a carved or molded image, an abom-
ination to the LORD, the work of the
hands of the craftsman, and sets *it* up
in secret.’

“And all the people shall answer and
say, ‘Amen!’

16‘Cursed *is* the one who treats his fa-
ther or his mother with contempt.’

“And all the people shall say, ‘Amen!’

17‘Cursed *is* the one who moves his
neighbor’s landmark.’

“And all the people shall say, ‘Amen!’

18‘Cursed *is* the one who makes the
blind to wander off the road.’

“And all the people shall say, ‘Amen!’

19‘Cursed *is* the one who perverts the
justice due the stranger, the fatherless,
and widow.’

“And all the people shall say, ‘Amen!’

20‘Cursed *is* the one who lies with his
father’s wife, because he has uncovered
his father’s bed.’

“And all the people shall say, ‘Amen!’

21‘Cursed *is* the one who lies with any
kind of animal.’

“And all the people shall say, ‘Amen!’

22‘Cursed *is* the one who lies with his
sister, the daughter of his father or the
daughter of his mother.’

26:15 [a] Exodus 3:8 **27:3** [a] Exodus 3:8

"And all the people shall say, 'Amen!'
23'Cursed *is* the one who lies with his
mother-in-law.'
"And all the people shall say, 'Amen!'
24'Cursed *is* the one who attacks his
neighbor secretly.'
"And all the people shall say, 'Amen!'
25'Cursed *is* the one who takes a bribe
to slay an innocent person.'
"And all the people shall say, 'Amen!'
26'Cursed *is* the one who does not con-
firm *all* the words of this law by observ-
ing them.'
"And all the people shall say, 'Amen!'"

Blessings on Obedience

28 "Now it shall come to pass, if you
diligently obey the voice of the
LORD your God, to observe carefully all
His commandments which I command
you today, that the LORD your God will
set you high above all nations of the
earth. 2And all these blessings shall
come upon you and overtake you, be-
cause you obey the voice of the LORD
your God:
3"Blessed *shall* you *be* in the city, and
blessed *shall* you *be* in the country.
4"Blessed *shall be* the fruit of your
body, the produce of your ground and
the increase of your herds, the increase
of your cattle and the offspring of your
flocks.
5"Blessed *shall be* your basket and your
kneading bowl.
6"Blessed *shall* you *be* when you come
in, and blessed *shall* you *be* when you
go out.
7"The LORD will cause your enemies
who rise against you to be defeated
before your face; they shall come out
against you one way and flee before
you seven ways.
8"The LORD will command the blessing
on you in your storehouses and in all
to which you set your hand, and He will
bless you in the land which the LORD
your God is giving you.
9"The LORD will establish you as a holy
people to Himself, just as He has sworn
to you, if you keep the commandments
of the LORD your God and walk in His
ways. 10Then all peoples of the earth
shall see that you are called by the
name of the LORD, and they shall be
afraid of you. 11And the LORD will grant
you plenty of goods, in the fruit of your
body, in the increase of your livestock,
and in the produce of your ground, in
the land of which the LORD swore to
your fathers to give you. 12The LORD
will open to you His good treasure, the
heavens, to give the rain to your land
in its season, and to bless all the work
of your hand. You shall lend to many
nations, but you shall not borrow. 13And
the LORD will make you the head and
not the tail; you shall be above only,
and not be beneath, if you heed the
commandments of the LORD your God,
which I command you today, and are
careful to observe *them*. 14So you shall
not turn aside from any of the words
which I command you this day, *to* the
right or the left, to go after other gods
to serve them.

Curses on Disobedience

15"But it shall come to pass, if you do
not obey the voice of the LORD your God,
to observe carefully all His command-
ments and His statutes which I com-
mand you today, that all these curses
will come upon you and overtake you:
16"Cursed *shall* you *be* in the city, and
cursed *shall* you *be* in the country.
17"Cursed *shall be* your basket and your
kneading bowl.
18"Cursed *shall be* the fruit of your body
and the produce of your land, the in-
crease of your cattle and the offspring
of your flocks.
19"Cursed *shall* you *be* when you come
in, and cursed *shall* you *be* when you
go out.
20"The LORD will send on you cursing,
confusion, and rebuke in all that you set
your hand to do, until you are destroyed
and until you perish quickly, because of
the wickedness of your doings in which
you have forsaken Me. 21The LORD will
make the plague cling to you until He
has consumed you from the land which
you are going to possess. 22The LORD
will strike you with consumption, with
fever, with inflammation, with severe
burning fever, with the sword, with
scorching, and with mildew; they shall
pursue you until you perish. 23And your
heavens which *are* over your head shall

be bronze, and the earth which is un-
der you *shall be* iron. 24The LORD will
change the rain of your land to powder
and dust; from the heaven it shall come
down on you until you are destroyed.
25"The LORD will cause you to be de-
feated before your enemies; you shall
go out one way against them and flee
seven ways before them; and you shall
become troublesome to all the king-
doms of the earth. 26Your carcasses
shall be food for all the birds of the air
and the beasts of the earth, and no one
shall frighten *them* away. 27The LORD
will strike you with the boils of Egypt,
with tumors, with the scab, and with the
itch, from which you cannot be healed.
28The LORD will strike you with madness
and blindness and confusion of heart.
29And you shall grope at noonday, as
a blind man gropes in darkness; you
shall not prosper in your ways; you
shall be only oppressed and plundered
continually, and no one shall save *you.*
30"You shall betroth a wife, but an-
other man shall lie with her; you shall
build a house, but you shall not dwell in
it; you shall plant a vineyard, but shall
not gather its grapes. 31Your ox *shall be*
slaughtered before your eyes, but you
shall not eat of it; your donkey *shall be*
violently taken away from before you,
and shall not be restored to you; your
sheep *shall be* given to your enemies,
and you shall have no one to rescue
them. 32Your sons and your daughters
shall be given to another people, and
your eyes shall look and fail *with long-
ing* for them all day long; and *there shall
be* no strength in your hand. 33A nation
whom you have not known shall eat
the fruit of your land and the produce
of your labor, and you shall be only op-
pressed and crushed continually. 34So
you shall be driven mad because of the
sight which your eyes see. 35The LORD
will strike you in the knees and on the
legs with severe boils which cannot be
healed, and from the sole of your foot
to the top of your head.
36"The LORD will bring you and the
king whom you set over you to a nation
which neither you nor your fathers have
known, and there you shall serve other
gods—wood and stone. 37And you shall
become an astonishment, a proverb,
and a byword among all nations where
the LORD will drive you.
38"You shall carry much seed out to
the field but gather little in, for the lo-
cust shall consume it. 39You shall plant
vineyards and tend *them,* but you shall
neither drink *of* the wine nor gather the
grapes; for the worms shall eat them.
40You shall have olive trees through-
out all your territory, but you shall not
anoint *yourself* with the oil; for your
olives shall drop off. 41You shall beget
sons and daughters, but they shall not
be yours; for they shall go into captivity.
42Locusts shall consume all your trees
and the produce of your land.
43"The alien who *is* among you shall
rise higher and higher above you, and
you shall come down lower and lower.
44He shall lend to you, but you shall not
lend to him; he shall be the head, and
you shall be the tail.
45"Moreover all these curses shall
come upon you and pursue and over-
take you, until you are destroyed, be-
cause you did not obey the voice of
the LORD your God, to keep His com-
mandments and His statutes which He
commanded you. 46And they shall be
upon you for a sign and a wonder, and
on your descendants forever.
47"Because you did not serve the LORD
your God with joy and gladness of
heart, for the abundance of everything,
48therefore you shall serve your ene-
mies, whom the LORD will send against
you, in hunger, in thirst, in nakedness,
and in need of everything; and He will
put a yoke of iron on your neck until
He has destroyed you. 49The LORD will
bring a nation against you from afar,
from the end of the earth, *as swift* as the
eagle flies, a nation whose language
you will not understand, 50a nation
of fierce countenance, which does not
respect the elderly nor show favor to the
young. 51And they shall eat the increase
of your livestock and the produce of
your land, until you are destroyed; they
shall not leave you grain or new wine
or oil, *or* the increase of your cattle or
the offspring of your flocks, until they
have destroyed you.
52"They shall besiege you at all your

gates until your high and fortified walls,
in which you trust, come down through-
out all your land; and they shall besiege
you at all your gates throughout all
your land which the LORD your God
has given you. 53You shall eat the fruit
of your own body, the flesh of your sons
and your daughters whom the LORD
your God has given you, in the siege and
desperate straits in which your enemy
shall distress you. 54The sensitive and
very refined man among you will be
hostile toward his brother, toward the
wife of his bosom, and toward the rest
of his children whom he leaves behind,
55so that he will not give any of them
the flesh of his children whom he will
eat, because he has nothing left in the
siege and desperate straits in which
your enemy shall distress you at all your
gates. 56The tender and delicate woman
among you, who would not venture to
set the sole of her foot on the ground
because of her delicateness and sensi-
tivity, will refuse[a] to the husband of her
bosom, and to her son and her daughter,
57her placenta which comes out from
between her feet and her children whom
she bears; for she will eat them secretly
for lack of everything in the siege and
desperate straits in which your enemy
shall distress you at all your gates.
58"If you do not carefully observe all
the words of this law that are written
in this book, that you may fear this
glorious and awesome name, THE
LORD YOUR GOD, 59then the LORD will
bring upon you and your descendants
extraordinary plagues—great and
prolonged plagues—and serious and
prolonged sicknesses. 60Moreover He
will bring back on you all the diseases
of Egypt, of which you were afraid, and
they shall cling to you. 61Also every
sickness and every plague, which *is*
not written in this Book of the Law, will
the LORD bring upon you until you are
destroyed. 62You shall be left few in
number, whereas you were as the stars
of heaven in multitude, because you
would not obey the voice of the LORD
your God. 63And it shall be, *that* just as
the LORD rejoiced over you to do you
good and multiply you, so the LORD
will rejoice over you to destroy you and
bring you to nothing; and you shall be
plucked from off the land which you
go to possess.
64"Then the LORD will scatter you
among all peoples, from one end of the
earth to the other, and there you shall
serve other gods, which neither you
nor your fathers have known—wood
and stone. 65And among those nations
you shall find no rest, nor shall the sole
of your foot have a resting place; but
there the LORD will give you a trem-
bling heart, failing eyes, and anguish
of soul. 66Your life shall hang in doubt
before you; you shall fear day and
night, and have no assurance of life.
67In the morning you shall say, 'Oh,
that it were evening!' And at evening
you shall say, 'Oh, that it were morning!'
because of the fear which terrifies your
heart, and because of the sight which
your eyes see.
68"And the LORD will take you back
to Egypt in ships, by the way of which
I said to you, 'You shall never see it
again.' And there you shall be offered
for sale to your enemies as male and
female slaves, but no one will buy *you.*"

The Covenant Renewed in Moab

29 These *are* the words of the cov-
enant which the LORD com-
manded Moses to make with the
children of Israel in the land of Moab,
besides the covenant which He made
with them in Horeb.
2Now Moses called all Israel and said
to them: "You have seen all that the
LORD did before your eyes in the land of
Egypt, to Pharaoh and to all his servants
and to all his land— 3the great trials
which your eyes have seen, the signs,
and those great wonders. 4Yet the LORD
has not given you a heart to perceive
and eyes to see and ears to hear, to this
very day. 5And I have led you forty years
in the wilderness. Your clothes have not
worn out on you, and your sandals have
not worn out on your feet. 6You have not
eaten bread, nor have you drunk wine or
similar drink, that you may know that I

28:56 [a] Literally *her eye shall be evil toward*

am the LORD your God. 7And when you
came to this place, Sihon king of Hesh-
bon and Og king of Bashan came out
against us to battle, and we conquered
them. 8We took their land and gave it
as an inheritance to the Reubenites,
to the Gadites, and to half the tribe of
Manasseh. 9Therefore keep the words
of this covenant, and do them, that you
may prosper in all that you do.

10"All of you stand today before the
LORD your God: your leaders and your
tribes and your elders and your offi-
cers, all the men of Israel, 11your little
ones and your wives—also the stranger
who *is* in your camp, from the one who
cuts your wood to the one who draws
your water— 12that you may enter into
covenant with the LORD your God, and
into His oath, which the LORD your God
makes with you today, 13that He may
establish you today as a people for
Himself, and *that* He may be God to
you, just as He has spoken to you, and
just as He has sworn to your fathers, to
Abraham, Isaac, and Jacob.

14"I make this covenant and this oath,
not with you alone, 15but with *him* who
stands here with us today before the
LORD our God, as well as with *him* who
is not here with us today 16(for you know
that we dwelt in the land of Egypt and
that we came through the nations which
you passed by, 17and you saw their
abominations and their idols which
were among them—wood and stone and
silver and gold); 18so that there may not
be among you man or woman or family
or tribe, whose heart turns away today
from the LORD our God, to go *and* serve
the gods of these nations, and that there
may not be among you a root bearing
bitterness or wormwood; 19and so it may
not happen, when he hears the words
of this curse, that he blesses himself in
his heart, saying, 'I shall have peace,
even though I follow the dictates[a] of my
heart'—as though the drunkard could
be included with the sober.

20"The LORD would not spare him;
for then the anger of the LORD and His
jealousy would burn against that man,
and every curse that is written in this
book would settle on him, and the LORD
would blot out his name from under
heaven. 21And the LORD would separate
him from all the tribes of Israel for ad-
versity, according to all the curses of the
covenant that are written in this Book
of the Law, 22so that the coming gener-
ation of your children who rise up after
you, and the foreigner who comes from
a far land, would say, when they see the
plagues of that land and the sicknesses
which the LORD has laid on it:

23'The whole land *is* brimstone, salt,
and burning; it is not sown, nor does it
bear, nor does any grass grow there, like
the overthrow of Sodom and Gomorrah,
Admah, and Zeboiim, which the LORD
overthrew in His anger and His wrath.'
24All nations would say, 'Why has the
LORD done so to this land? What does the
heat of this great anger mean?' 25Then
people would say: 'Because they have
forsaken the covenant of the LORD God
of their fathers, which He made with
them when He brought them out of the
land of Egypt; 26for they went and served
other gods and worshiped them, gods
that they did not know and that He had
not given to them. 27Then the anger of
the LORD was aroused against this land,
to bring on it every curse that is written
in this book. 28And the LORD uprooted
them from their land in anger, in wrath,
and in great indignation, and cast them
into another land, as *it is* this day.'

29"The secret *things belong* to the LORD
our God, but those *things which are* re-
vealed *belong* to us and to our children
forever, that *we* may do all the words
of this law.

The Blessing of Returning to God

30 "Now it shall come to pass, when
all these things come upon you,
the blessing and the curse which I have
set before you, and you call *them* to
mind among all the nations where the
LORD your God drives you, 2and you re-
turn to the LORD your God and obey His
voice, according to all that I command
you today, you and your children, with
all your heart and with all your soul,
3that the LORD your God will bring you

29:19 [a] Or *stubbornness*

back from captivity, and have compas-
sion on you, and gather you again from
all the nations where the LORD your God
has scattered you. 4If *any* of you are
driven out to the farthest *parts* under
heaven, from there the LORD your God
will gather you, and from there He will
bring you. 5Then the LORD your God will
bring you to the land which your fathers
possessed, and you shall possess it. He
will prosper you and multiply you more
than your fathers. 6And the LORD your
God will circumcise your heart and the
heart of your descendants, to love the
LORD your God with all your heart and
with all your soul, that you may live.
7"Also the LORD your God will put all
these curses on your enemies and on
those who hate you, who persecuted you.
8And you will again obey the voice of the
LORD and do all His commandments
which I command you today. 9The LORD
your God will make you abound in all the
work of your hand, in the fruit of your
body, in the increase of your livestock,
and in the produce of your land for good.
For the LORD will again rejoice over you
for good as He rejoiced over your fathers,
10if you obey the voice of the LORD your
God, to keep His commandments and
His statutes which are written in this
Book of the Law, *and* if you turn to the
LORD your God with all your heart and
with all your soul.

The Choice of Life or Death

11"For this commandment which I
command you today *is* not *too* mys-
terious for you, nor *is* it far off. 12It *is*
not in heaven, that you should say,
'Who will ascend into heaven for us
and bring it to us, that we may hear it
and do it?' 13Nor *is* it beyond the sea,
that you should say, 'Who will go over
the sea for us and bring it to us, that we
may hear it and do it?' 14But the word
is very near you, in your mouth and in
your heart, that you may do it.
15"See, I have set before you today life
and good, death and evil, 16in that I
command you today to love the LORD
your God, to walk in His ways, and to
keep His commandments, His statutes,
and His judgments, that you may live
and multiply; and the LORD your God
will bless you in the land which you
go to possess. 17But if your heart turns
away so that you do not hear, and are
drawn away, and worship other gods
and serve them, 18I announce to you
today that you shall surely perish; you
shall not prolong *your* days in the land
which you cross over the Jordan to go in
and possess. 19I call heaven and earth as
witnesses today against you, *that* I have
set before you life and death, blessing
and cursing; therefore choose life, that
both you and your descendants may
live; 20that you may love the LORD your
God, that you may obey His voice, and
that you may cling to Him, for He *is* your
life and the length of your days; and
that you may dwell in the land which
the LORD swore to your fathers, to Abra-
ham, Isaac, and Jacob, to give them."

Joshua the New Leader of Israel

31 Then Moses went and spoke
these words to all Israel. 2And
he said to them: "I *am* one hundred
and twenty years old today. I can no
longer go out and come in. Also the
LORD has said to me, 'You shall not cross
over this Jordan.' 3The LORD your God
Himself crosses over before you; He will
destroy these nations from before you,
and you shall dispossess them. Joshua
himself crosses over before you, just as
the LORD has said. 4And the LORD will
do to them as He did to Sihon and Og,
the kings of the Amorites and their land,
when He destroyed them. 5The LORD will
give them over to you, that you may
do to them according to every com-
mandment which I have commanded
you. 6Be strong and of good courage,
do not fear nor be afraid of them; for
the LORD your God, He *is* the One who
goes with you. He will not leave you nor
forsake you."
7Then Moses called Joshua and said to
him in the sight of all Israel, "Be strong
and of good courage, for you must go
with this people to the land which the
LORD has sworn to their fathers to give
them, and you shall cause them to in-
herit it. 8And the LORD, He *is* the One
who goes before you. He will be with
you, He will not leave you nor forsake
you; do not fear nor be dismayed."

GOD | SIN | JESUS | SALVATION | LOVE

The Law to Be Read Every Seven Years

9So Moses wrote this law and deliv-
ered it to the priests, the sons of Levi,
who bore the ark of the covenant of the
LORD, and to all the elders of Israel.
10And Moses commanded them, saying:
"At the end of *every* seven years, at the
appointed time in the year of release,
at the Feast of Tabernacles, 11when all
Israel comes to appear before the LORD
your God in the place which He chooses,
you shall read this law before all Israel
in their hearing. 12Gather the people
together, men and women and little
ones, and the stranger who *is* within
your gates, that they may hear and that
they may learn to fear the LORD your
God and carefully observe all the words
of this law, 13and *that* their children,
who have not known it, may hear and
learn to fear the LORD your God as long
as you live in the land which you cross
the Jordan to possess."

Prediction of Israel's Rebellion

14Then the LORD said to Moses, "Be-
hold, the days approach when you must
die; call Joshua, and present yourselves
in the tabernacle of meeting, that I may
inaugurate him."

So Moses and Joshua went and pre-
sented themselves in the tabernacle of
meeting. 15Now the LORD appeared at
the tabernacle in a pillar of cloud, and
the pillar of cloud stood above the door
of the tabernacle.

16And the LORD said to Moses: "Behold,
you will rest with your fathers; and this
people will rise and play the harlot with
the gods of the foreigners of the land,
where they go *to be* among them, and
they will forsake Me and break My cov-
enant which I have made with them.
17Then My anger shall be aroused
against them in that day, and I will
forsake them, and I will hide My face
from them, and they shall be devoured.
And many evils and troubles shall be-
fall them, so that they will say in that
day, 'Have not these evils come upon
us because our God *is* not among us?'
18And I will surely hide My face in that
day because of all the evil which they
have done, in that they have turned to
other gods.

19"Now therefore, write down this
song for yourselves, and teach it to
the children of Israel; put it in their
mouths, that this song may be a wit-
ness for Me against the children of
Israel. 20When I have brought them to
the land flowing with milk and honey,
of which I swore to their fathers, and
they have eaten and filled themselves
and grown fat, then they will turn to
other gods and serve them; and they
will provoke Me and break My cov-
enant. 21Then it shall be, when many
evils and troubles have come upon
them, that this song will testify against
them as a witness; for it will not be
forgotten in the mouths of their de-
scendants, for I know the inclination
of their behavior today, even before I
have brought them to the land of which
I swore *to give them*."

22Therefore Moses wrote this song
the same day, and taught it to the chil-
dren of Israel. 23Then He inaugurated
Joshua the son of Nun, and said, "Be
strong and of good courage; for you
shall bring the children of Israel into
the land of which I swore to them, and
I will be with you."

24So it was, when Moses had complet-
ed writing the words of this law in a
book, when they were finished, 25that
Moses commanded the Levites, who
bore the ark of the covenant of the
LORD, saying: 26"Take this Book of
the Law, and put it beside the ark of the
covenant of the LORD your God, that
it may be there as a witness against
you; 27for I know your rebellion and
your stiff neck. *If* today, while I am
yet alive with you, you have been re-
bellious against the LORD, then how
much more after my death? 28Gath-
er to me all the elders of your tribes,
and your officers, that I may speak
these words in their hearing and call
heaven and earth to witness against
them. 29For I know that after my death
you will become utterly corrupt, and
turn aside from the way which I have
commanded you. And evil will befall
you in the latter days, because you
will do evil in the sight of the LORD,
to provoke Him to anger through the
work of your hands."

The Song of Moses

30 Then Moses spoke in the hearing of all the assembly of Israel the words of this song until they were ended:

32 "Give ear, O heavens, and I will speak;
And hear, O earth, the words of my mouth.
2 Let my teaching drop as the rain,
My speech distill as the dew,
As raindrops on the tender herb,
And as showers on the grass.
3 For I proclaim the name of the LORD:
Ascribe greatness to our God.
4 *He is* the Rock, His work *is* perfect;
For all His ways *are* justice,
A God of truth and without injustice;
Righteous and upright *is* He.

5 "They have corrupted themselves;
They are not His children,
Because of their blemish:
A perverse and crooked generation.
6 Do you thus deal with the LORD,
O foolish and unwise people?
Is He not your Father, *who* bought you?
Has He not made you and established you?

7 "Remember the days of old,
Consider the years of many generations.
Ask your father, and he will show you;
Your elders, and they will tell you:
8 When the Most High divided their inheritance to the nations,
When He separated the sons of Adam,
He set the boundaries of the peoples
According to the number of the children of Israel.
9 For the LORD's portion *is* His people;
Jacob *is* the place of His inheritance.

10 "He found him in a desert land
And in the wasteland, a howling wilderness;
He encircled him, He instructed him,
He kept him as the apple of His eye.
11 As an eagle stirs up its nest,
Hovers over its young,
Spreading out its wings, taking them up,
Carrying them on its wings,
12 *So* the LORD alone led him,
And *there was* no foreign god with him.

13 "He made him ride in the heights of the earth,
That he might eat the produce of the fields;
He made him draw honey from the rock,
And oil from the flinty rock;
14 Curds from the cattle, and milk of the flock,
With fat of lambs;
And rams of the breed of Bashan, and goats,
With the choicest wheat;
And you drank wine, the blood of the grapes.

15 "But Jeshurun grew fat and kicked;
You grew fat, you grew thick,
You are obese!
Then he forsook God *who* made him,
And scornfully esteemed the Rock of his salvation.
16 They provoked Him to jealousy with foreign *gods;*
With abominations they provoked Him to anger.
17 They sacrificed to demons, not to God,
To gods they did not know,
To new *gods,* new arrivals
That your fathers did not fear.
18 Of the Rock *who* begot you, you are unmindful,
And have forgotten the God who fathered you.

19 "And when the LORD saw *it,* He spurned *them,*
Because of the provocation of His sons and His daughters.
20 And He said: 'I will hide My face from them,

I will see what their end *will be,*
For they *are* a perverse
generation,
Children in whom *is* no faith.
21 They have provoked Me to
jealousy by *what* is not God;
They have moved Me to anger by
their foolish idols.
But I will provoke them to
jealousy by *those who are* not
a nation;
I will move them to anger by a
foolish nation.
22 For a fire is kindled in My anger,
And shall burn to the lowest hell;
It shall consume the earth with
her increase,
And set on fire the foundations of
the mountains.

23 'I will heap disasters on them;
I will spend My arrows on them.
24 *They shall be* wasted with hunger,
Devoured by pestilence and bitter
destruction;
I will also send against them the
teeth of beasts,
With the poison of serpents of the
dust.
25 The sword shall destroy outside;
There shall be terror within
For the young man and virgin,
The nursing child with the man of
gray hairs.
26 I would have said, "I will dash
them in pieces,
I will make the memory of them
to cease from among men,"
27 Had I not feared the wrath of the
enemy,
Lest their adversaries should
misunderstand,
Lest they should say, "Our hand *is*
high;
And it is not the LORD who has
done all this." '

28 "For they *are* a nation void of
counsel,
Nor *is there any* understanding in
them.
29 Oh, that they were wise, *that* they
understood this,
That they would consider their
latter end!
30 How could one chase a thousand,
And two put ten thousand to
flight,
Unless their Rock had sold them,
And the LORD had surrendered
them?
31 For their rock *is* not like our Rock,
Even our enemies themselves
being judges.
32 For their vine *is* of the vine of
Sodom
And of the fields of Gomorrah;
Their grapes *are* grapes of gall,
Their clusters *are* bitter.
33 Their wine *is* the poison of
serpents,
And the cruel venom of cobras.

34 '*Is* this not laid up in store with Me,
Sealed up among My treasures?
35 Vengeance is Mine, and
recompense;
Their foot shall slip in *due* time;
For the day of their calamity *is* at
hand,
And the things to come hasten
upon them.'

36 "For the LORD will judge His people
And have compassion on His
servants,
When He sees that *their* power is
gone,
And *there is* no one *remaining,*
bond or free.
37 He will say: 'Where *are* their gods,
The rock in which they sought
refuge?
38 Who ate the fat of their sacrifices,
And drank the wine of their drink
offering?
Let them rise and help you,
And be your refuge.

39 'Now see that I, *even* I, *am* He,
And *there is* no God besides Me;
I kill and I make alive;
I wound and I heal;
Nor *is there any* who can deliver
from My hand.
40 For I raise My hand to heaven,
And say, "As I live forever,
41 If I whet My glittering sword,
And My hand takes hold on
judgment,

I will render vengeance to My enemies,
And repay those who hate Me.
42 I will make My arrows drunk with blood,
And My sword shall devour flesh,
With the blood of the slain and the captives,
From the heads of the leaders of the enemy." '

43 "Rejoice, O Gentiles, *with* His people;[a]
For He will avenge the blood of His servants,
And render vengeance to His adversaries;
He will provide atonement for His land *and* His people."

44So Moses came with Joshua[a] the
son of Nun and spoke all the words of
this song in the hearing of the people.
45Moses finished speaking all these
words to all Israel, 46and he said to them:
"Set your hearts on all the words which I
testify among you today, which you shall
command your children to be careful to
observe—all the words of this law. 47For
it *is* not a futile thing for you, because it
is your life, and by this word you shall
prolong *your* days in the land which you
cross over the Jordan to possess."

Moses to Die on Mount Nebo

48Then the LORD spoke to Moses that
very same day, saying: 49"Go up this
mountain of the Abarim, Mount Nebo,
which *is* in the land of Moab, across
from Jericho; view the land of Canaan,
which I give to the children of Israel as a
possession; 50and die on the mountain
which you ascend, and be gathered to
your people, just as Aaron your brother
died on Mount Hor and was gathered
to his people; 51because you trespassed
against Me among the children of Israel
at the waters of Meribah Kadesh, in the
Wilderness of Zin, because you did not
hallow Me in the midst of the children
of Israel. 52Yet you shall see the land
before *you,* though you shall not go
there, into the land which I am giving
to the children of Israel."

Moses' Final Blessing on Israel

33 Now this *is* the blessing with
which Moses the man of God
blessed the children of Israel before his
death. 2And he said:

"The LORD came from Sinai,
And dawned on them from Seir;
He shone forth from Mount Paran,
And He came with ten thousands of saints;
From His right hand
Came a fiery law for them.
3 Yes, He loves the people;
All His saints *are* in Your hand;
They sit down at Your feet;
Everyone receives Your words.
4 Moses commanded a law for us,
A heritage of the congregation of Jacob.
5 And He was King in Jeshurun,
When the leaders of the people were gathered,
All the tribes of Israel together.

6 "Let Reuben live, and not die,
Nor let his men be few."

7And this he said of Judah:

"Hear, LORD, the voice of Judah,
And bring him to his people;
Let his hands be sufficient for him,
And may You be a help against his enemies."

8And of Levi he said:

"*Let* Your Thummim and Your Urim *be* with Your holy one,
Whom You tested at Massah,
And with whom You contended at the waters of Meribah,
9 Who says of his father and mother,
'I have not seen them';
Nor did he acknowledge his brothers,
Or know his own children;
For they have observed Your word
And kept Your covenant.

32:43 [a] A Dead Sea Scroll fragment adds *And let all the gods (angels) worship Him* (compare Septuagint and Hebrews 1:6). 32:44 [a] Hebrew *Hoshea* (compare Numbers 13:8, 16)

10 They shall teach Jacob Your
judgments,
And Israel Your law.
They shall put incense before You,
And a whole burnt sacrifice on
Your altar.
11 Bless his substance, LORD,
And accept the work of his hands;
Strike the loins of those who rise
against him,
And of those who hate him, that
they rise not again."

12Of Benjamin he said:

"The beloved of the LORD shall dwell
in safety by Him,
Who shelters him all the day long;
And he shall dwell between His
shoulders."

13And of Joseph he said:

"Blessed of the LORD *is* his land,
With the precious things of
heaven, with the dew,
And the deep lying beneath,
14 With the precious fruits of the sun,
With the precious produce of the
months,
15 With the best things of the
ancient mountains,
With the precious things of the
everlasting hills,
16 With the precious things of the
earth and its fullness,
And the favor of Him who dwelt
in the bush.
Let *the blessing* come 'on the head
of Joseph,
And on the crown of the head of
him *who was* separate from
his brothers.'[a]
17 His glory *is like* a firstborn bull,
And his horns *like* the horns of the
wild ox;
Together with them
He shall push the peoples
To the ends of the earth;
They *are* the ten thousands of
Ephraim,
And they *are* the thousands of
Manasseh."

18And of Zebulun he said:

"Rejoice, Zebulun, in your going
out,
And Issachar in your tents!
19 They shall call the peoples *to* the
mountain;
There they shall offer sacrifices of
righteousness;
For they shall partake *of* the
abundance of the seas
And *of* treasures hidden in the
sand."

20And of Gad he said:

"Blessed *is* he who enlarges
Gad;
He dwells as a lion,
And tears the arm and the crown
of his head.
21 He provided the first *part* for
himself,
Because a lawgiver's portion was
reserved there.
He came *with* the heads of the
people;
He administered the justice of the
LORD,
And His judgments with Israel."

22And of Dan he said:

"Dan *is* a lion's whelp;
He shall leap from Bashan."

23And of Naphtali he said:

"O Naphtali, satisfied with favor,
And full of the blessing of the
LORD,
Possess the west and the south."

24And of Asher he said:

"Asher *is* most blessed of sons;
Let him be favored by his
brothers,
And let him dip his foot in oil.
25 Your sandals *shall be* iron and
bronze;
As your days, *so shall* your
strength *be*.

33:16 [a] Genesis 49:26

26 "*There is* no one like the God of
Jeshurun,
Who rides the heavens to help
you,
And in His excellency on the
clouds.
27 The eternal God *is your* refuge,
And underneath *are* the
everlasting arms;
He will thrust out the enemy from
before you,
And will say, 'Destroy!'
28 Then Israel shall dwell in safety,
The fountain of Jacob alone,
In a land of grain and new wine;
His heavens shall also drop dew.
29 Happy *are* you, O Israel!
Who *is* like you, a people saved by
the LORD,
The shield of your help
And the sword of your majesty!
Your enemies shall submit to you,
And you shall tread down their
high places."

Moses Dies on Mount Nebo

34 Then Moses went up from the
plains of Moab to Mount Nebo,
to the top of Pisgah, which is across
from Jericho. And the LORD showed him
all the land of Gilead as far as Dan, 2all
Naphtali and the land of Ephraim and
Manasseh, all the land of Judah as far
as the Western Sea,[a] 3the South, and the
plain of the Valley of Jericho, the city
of palm trees, as far as Zoar. 4Then the
LORD said to him, "This *is* the land of
which I swore to give Abraham, Isaac,
and Jacob, saying, 'I will give it to your
descendants.' I have caused you to see *it*
with your eyes, but you shall not cross
over there."
5So Moses the servant of the LORD died
there in the land of Moab, according to
the word of the LORD. 6And He buried
him in a valley in the land of Moab,
opposite Beth Peor; but no one knows
his grave to this day. 7Moses *was* one
hundred and twenty years old when
he died. His eyes were not dim nor his
natural vigor diminished. 8And the
children of Israel wept for Moses in the
plains of Moab thirty days. So the days
of weeping *and* mourning for Moses
ended.
9Now Joshua the son of Nun was full
of the spirit of wisdom, for Moses had
laid his hands on him; so the children
of Israel heeded him, and did as the
LORD had commanded Moses.
10But since then there has not arisen
in Israel a prophet like Moses, whom
the LORD knew face to face, 11in all the
signs and wonders which the LORD sent
him to do in the land of Egypt, before
Pharaoh, before all his servants, and
in all his land, 12and by all that mighty
power and all the great terror which
Moses performed in the sight of all
Israel.

34:2 [a] That is, the Mediterranean

THE BOOK OF

JOSHUA

The Book of Joshua tells how God brought His people into the Promised Land, the land He had given their ancestor Abraham in the Book of Genesis. Joshua is the new leader. His challenge is to lead the Hebrews into a land filled with strong people living in walled cities. Their hope is not in themselves, though, but in God who has promised to go before them in battle and win the victories for them. It all begins with God stopping the waters of the Jordan River, letting the people cross into the land on dry ground. Then, God topples the walls of Jericho, the first city the Hebrews reach. Despite some setbacks, in time, the Hebrews' enemies are defeated, and they settle in the land as God had promised.

- **GENRE:** History
- **AUTHOR:** Joshua
- **TIME:** c. 1406–1391 BC
- **PURPOSE:** To tell how God gave His people the land He had promised to them starting with Abraham. God goes before His people in battle and wins the victory.

God's Commission to Joshua

1 After the death of Moses the servant
of the LORD, it came to pass that the
LORD spoke to Joshua the son of Nun,
Moses' assistant, saying: 2"Moses My
servant is dead. Now therefore, arise, go
over this Jordan, you and all this people,
to the land which I am giving to them—
the children of Israel. 3Every place that
the sole of your foot will tread upon
I have given you, as I said to Moses.
4From the wilderness and this Lebanon
as far as the great river, the River Eu-
phrates, all the land of the Hittites, and
to the Great Sea toward the going down
of the sun, shall be your territory. 5No
man shall *be able to* stand before you
all the days of your life; as I was with
Moses, *so* I will be with you. I will not
leave you nor forsake you. 6Be strong
and of good courage, for to this people
you shall divide as an inheritance the
land which I swore to their fathers to
give them. 7Only be strong and very
courageous, that you may observe to
do according to all the law which Moses
My servant commanded you; do not
turn from it to the right hand or to the
left, that you may prosper wherever
you go. 8This Book of the Law shall
not depart from your mouth, but you
shall meditate in it day and night, that
you may observe to do according to all
that is written in it. For then you will
make your way prosperous, and then
you will have good success. 9Have I
not commanded you? Be strong and
of good courage; do not be afraid, nor
be dismayed, for the LORD your God *is*
with you wherever you go."

The Order to Cross the Jordan

10Then Joshua commanded the of-
ficers of the people, saying, 11"Pass
through the camp and command the
people, saying, 'Prepare provisions for
yourselves, for within three days you
will cross over this Jordan, to go in to
possess the land which the LORD your
God is giving you to possess.' "
12And to the Reubenites, the Gadites,
and half the tribe of Manasseh Joshua
spoke, saying, 13"Remember the word
which Moses the servant of the LORD
commanded you, saying, 'The LORD
your God is giving you rest and is giving
you this land.' 14Your wives, your little
ones, and your livestock shall remain in
the land which Moses gave you on this
side of the Jordan. But you shall pass
before your brethren armed, all your
mighty men of valor, and help them,

15until the LORD has given your breth-
ren rest, as He *gave* you, and they also
have taken possession of the land which
the LORD your God is giving them. Then
you shall return to the land of your
possession and enjoy it, which Moses
the LORD's servant gave you on this
side of the Jordan toward the sunrise."
16So they answered Joshua, saying, "All
that you command us we will do, and
wherever you send us we will go. 17Just
as we heeded Moses in all things, so we
will heed you. Only the LORD your God be
with you, as He was with Moses. 18Who-
ever rebels against your command and
does not heed your words, in all that you
command him, shall be put to death.
Only be strong and of good courage."

Rahab Hides the Spies

2 Now Joshua the son of Nun sent
out two men from Acacia Grove[a] to
spy secretly, saying, "Go, view the land,
especially Jericho."
So they went, and came to the house
of a harlot named Rahab, and lodged
there. 2And it was told the king of Jer-
icho, saying, "Behold, men have come
here tonight from the children of Israel
to search out the country."
3So the king of Jericho sent to Rahab,
saying, "Bring out the men who have
come to you, who have entered your
house, for they have come to search
out all the country."
4Then the woman took the two men
and hid them. So she said, "Yes, the men
came to me, but I did not know where
they *were* from. 5And it happened as
the gate was being shut, when it was
dark, that the men went out. Where the
men went I do not know; pursue them
quickly, for you may overtake them."
6(But she had brought them up to the
roof and hidden them with the stalks of
flax, which she had laid in order on the
roof.) 7Then the men pursued them by
the road to the Jordan, to the fords. And
as soon as those who pursued them had
gone out, they shut the gate.
8Now before they lay down, she came
up to them on the roof, 9and said to the
men: "I know that the LORD has given
you the land, that the terror of you has
fallen on us, and that all the inhabitants
of the land are fainthearted because of
you. 10For we have heard how the LORD
dried up the water of the Red Sea for you
when you came out of Egypt, and what
you did to the two kings of the Amorites
who *were* on the other side of the Jor-
dan, Sihon and Og, whom you utterly
destroyed. 11And as soon as we heard
these things, our hearts melted; neither
did there remain any more courage in
anyone because of you, for the LORD
your God, He *is* God in heaven above
and on earth beneath. 12Now therefore,
I beg you, swear to me by the LORD,
since I have shown you kindness, that
you also will show kindness to my fa-
ther's house, and give me a true token,
13and spare my father, my mother, my
brothers, my sisters, and all that they
have, and deliver our lives from death."
14So the men answered her, "Our lives
for yours, if none of you tell this busi-
ness of ours. And it shall be, when the
LORD has given us the land, that we will
deal kindly and truly with you."
15Then she let them down by a rope
through the window, for her house
was on the city wall; she dwelt on the
wall. 16And she said to them, "Get to
the mountain, lest the pursuers meet
you. Hide there three days, until the
pursuers have returned. Afterward you
may go your way."
17So the men said to her: "We *will be*
blameless of this oath of yours which
you have made us swear, 18unless, *when*
we come into the land, you bind this line
of scarlet cord in the window through
which you let us down, and unless you
bring your father, your mother, your
brothers, and all your father's household
to your own home. 19So it shall be *that*
whoever goes outside the doors of your
house into the street, his blood *shall be*
on his own head, and we *will be* guiltless.
And whoever is with you in the house,
his blood *shall be* on our head if a hand
is laid on him. 20And if you tell this busi-
ness of ours, then we will be free from
your oath which you made us swear."
21Then she said, "According to your

2:1 [a] Hebrew *Shittim*

words, so *be* it." And she sent them away,
and they departed. And she bound the
scarlet cord in the window.

22They departed and went to the
mountain, and stayed there three days
until the pursuers returned. The pursu-
ers sought *them* all along the way, but
did not find *them*. 23So the two men
returned, descended from the moun-
tain, and crossed over; and they came
to Joshua the son of Nun, and told him
all that had befallen them. 24And they
said to Joshua, "Truly the LORD has
delivered all the land into our hands,
for indeed all the inhabitants of the
country are fainthearted because of us."

Israel Crosses the Jordan

3 Then Joshua rose early in the morn-
ing; and they set out from Acacia
Grove[a] and came to the Jordan, he and
all the children of Israel, and lodged
there before they crossed over. 2So it
was, after three days, that the officers
went through the camp; 3and they com-
manded the people, saying, "When you
see the ark of the covenant of the LORD
your God, and the priests, the Levites,
bearing it, then you shall set out from
your place and go after it. 4Yet there
shall be a space between you and it,
about two thousand cubits by measure.
Do not come near it, that you may know
the way by which you must go, for you
have not passed *this* way before."

5And Joshua said to the people, "Sanc-
tify yourselves, for tomorrow the LORD
will do wonders among you." 6Then
Joshua spoke to the priests, saying,
"Take up the ark of the covenant and
cross over before the people."

So they took up the ark of the covenant
and went before the people.

7And the LORD said to Joshua, "This day
I will begin to exalt you in the sight of all
Israel, that they may know that, as I was
with Moses, *so* I will be with you. 8You
shall command the priests who bear the
ark of the covenant, saying, 'When you
have come to the edge of the water of the
Jordan, you shall stand in the Jordan.' "

9So Joshua said to the children of Is-
rael, "Come here, and hear the words
of the LORD your God." 10And Joshua
said, "By this you shall know that the
living God *is* among you, and *that* He will
without fail drive out from before you
the Canaanites and the Hittites and the
Hivites and the Perizzites and the Gir-
gashites and the Amorites and the Jeb-
usites: 11Behold, the ark of the covenant
of the Lord of all the earth is crossing
over before you into the Jordan. 12Now
therefore, take for yourselves twelve
men from the tribes of Israel, one man
from every tribe. 13And it shall come to
pass, as soon as the soles of the feet of
the priests who bear the ark of the LORD,
the Lord of all the earth, shall rest in the
waters of the Jordan, *that* the waters of
the Jordan shall be cut off, the waters
that come down from upstream, and
they shall stand as a heap."

14So it was, when the people set out
from their camp to cross over the Jor-
dan, with the priests bearing the ark of
the covenant before the people, 15and
as those who bore the ark came to the
Jordan, and the feet of the priests who
bore the ark dipped in the edge of the
water (for the Jordan overflows all its
banks during the whole time of harvest),
16that the waters which came down
from upstream stood *still, and* rose in
a heap very far away at Adam, the city
that *is* beside Zaretan. So the waters that
went down into the Sea of the Arabah,
the Salt Sea, failed, *and* were cut off;
and the people crossed over opposite
Jericho. 17Then the priests who bore the
ark of the covenant of the LORD stood
firm on dry ground in the midst of the
Jordan; and all Israel crossed over on
dry ground, until all the people had
crossed completely over the Jordan.

The Memorial Stones

4 And it came to pass, when all the
people had completely crossed over
the Jordan, that the LORD spoke to Josh-
ua, saying: 2"Take for yourselves twelve
men from the people, one man from ev-
ery tribe, 3and command them, saying,
'Take for yourselves twelve stones from
here, out of the midst of the Jordan,
from the place where the priests' feet

3:1 a Hebrew *Shittim*

stood firm. You shall carry them over with you and leave them in the lodging place where you lodge tonight.' "

[4]Then Joshua called the twelve men whom he had appointed from the children of Israel, one man from every tribe; [5]and Joshua said to them: "Cross over before the ark of the LORD your God into the midst of the Jordan, and each one of you take up a stone on his shoulder, according to the number of the tribes of the children of Israel, [6]that this may be a sign among you when your children ask in time to come, saying, 'What do these stones *mean* to you?' [7]Then you shall answer them that the waters of the Jordan were cut off before the ark of the covenant of the LORD; when it crossed over the Jordan, the waters of the Jordan were cut off. And these stones shall be for a memorial to the children of Israel forever."

[8]And the children of Israel did so, just as Joshua commanded, and took up twelve stones from the midst of the Jordan, as the LORD had spoken to Joshua, according to the number of the tribes of the children of Israel, and carried them over with them to the place where they lodged, and laid them down there. [9]Then Joshua set up twelve stones in the midst of the Jordan, in the place where the feet of the priests who bore the ark of the covenant stood; and they are there to this day.

[10]So the priests who bore the ark stood in the midst of the Jordan until everything was finished that the LORD had commanded Joshua to speak to the people, according to all that Moses had commanded Joshua; and the people hurried and crossed over. [11]Then it came to pass, when all the people had completely crossed over, that the ark of the LORD and the priests crossed over in the presence of the people. [12]And the men of Reuben, the men of Gad, and half the tribe of Manasseh crossed over armed before the children of Israel, as Moses had spoken to them. [13]About forty thousand prepared for war crossed over before the LORD for battle, to the plains of Jericho. [14]On that day the LORD exalted Joshua in the sight of all Israel; and they feared him, as they had feared Moses, all the days of his life.

[15]Then the LORD spoke to Joshua, saying, [16]"Command the priests who bear the ark of the Testimony to come up from the Jordan." [17]Joshua therefore commanded the priests, saying, "Come up from the Jordan." [18]And it came to pass, when the priests who bore the ark of the covenant of the LORD had come from the midst of the Jordan, *and* the soles of the priests' feet touched the dry land, that the waters of the Jordan returned to their place and overflowed all its banks as before.

[19]Now the people came up from the Jordan on the tenth *day* of the first month, and they camped in Gilgal on the east border of Jericho. [20]And those twelve stones which they took out of the Jordan, Joshua set up in Gilgal. [21]Then he spoke to the children of Israel, saying: "When your children ask their fathers in time to come, saying, 'What *are* these stones?' [22]then you shall let your children know, saying, 'Israel crossed over this Jordan on dry land'; [23]for the LORD your God dried up the waters of the Jordan before you until you had crossed over, as the LORD your God did to the Red Sea, which He dried up before us until we had crossed over, [24]that all the peoples of the earth may know the hand of the LORD, that it *is* mighty, that you may fear the LORD your God forever."

The Second Generation Circumcised

5 So it was, when all the kings of the Amorites who *were* on the west side of the Jordan, and all the kings of the Canaanites who *were* by the sea, heard that the LORD had dried up the waters of the Jordan from before the children of Israel until we[a] had crossed over, that their heart melted; and there was no spirit in them any longer because of the children of Israel.

[2]At that time the LORD said to Joshua, "Make flint knives for yourself, and circumcise the sons of Israel again the second time." [3]So Joshua made flint knives for himself, and circumcised the sons of

5:1 [a] Following Kethib; Qere, some Hebrew manuscripts and editions, Septuagint, Syriac, Targum, and Vulgate read *they*.

Israel at the hill of the foreskins.[a] 4And
this *is* the reason why Joshua circum-
cised them: All the people who came out
of Egypt *who were* males, all the men of
war, had died in the wilderness on the
way, after they had come out of Egypt.
5For all the people who came out had
been circumcised, but all the people
born in the wilderness, on the way as
they came out of Egypt, had not been
circumcised. 6For the children of Israel
walked forty years in the wilderness,
till all the people *who were* men of war,
who came out of Egypt, were consumed,
because they did not obey the voice of
the LORD—to whom the LORD swore
that He would not show them the land
which the LORD had sworn to their fa-
thers that He would give us, "a land
flowing with milk and honey."[a] 7Then
Joshua circumcised their sons *whom* He
raised up in their place; for they were
uncircumcised, because they had not
been circumcised on the way.
8So it was, when they had finished
circumcising all the people, that they
stayed in their places in the camp till
they were healed. 9Then the LORD said
to Joshua, "This day I have rolled away
the reproach of Egypt from you." There-
fore the name of the place is called Gil-
gal[a] to this day.
10Now the children of Israel camped
in Gilgal, and kept the Passover on the
fourteenth day of the month at twilight
on the plains of Jericho. 11And they ate
of the produce of the land on the day
after the Passover, unleavened bread
and parched grain, on the very same
day. 12Then the manna ceased on the
day after they had eaten the produce
of the land; and the children of Israel
no longer had manna, but they ate the
food of the land of Canaan that year.

The Commander of the Army of the LORD

13And it came to pass, when Joshua
was by Jericho, that he lifted his eyes
and looked, and behold, a Man stood
opposite him with His sword drawn in
His hand. And Joshua went to Him and
said to Him, "*Are* You for us or for our
adversaries?"
14So He said, "No, but *as* Commander
of the army of the LORD I have now
come."
And Joshua fell on his face to the earth
and worshiped, and said to Him, "What
does my Lord say to His servant?"
15Then the Commander of the LORD's
army said to Joshua, "Take your sandal
off your foot, for the place where you
stand *is* holy." And Joshua did so.

The Destruction of Jericho

6 Now Jericho was securely shut up be-
cause of the children of Israel; none
went out, and none came in. 2And the
LORD said to Joshua: "See! I have given
Jericho into your hand, its king, *and* the
mighty men of valor. 3You shall march
around the city, all *you* men of war; you
shall go all around the city once. This
you shall do six days. 4And seven priests
shall bear seven trumpets of rams' horns
before the ark. But the seventh day you
shall march around the city seven times,
and the priests shall blow the trumpets.
5It shall come to pass, when they make a
long *blast* with the ram's horn, *and* when
you hear the sound of the trumpet, that
all the people shall shout with a great
shout; then the wall of the city will fall
down flat. And the people shall go up
every man straight before him."
6Then Joshua the son of Nun called the
priests and said to them, "Take up the
ark of the covenant, and let seven priests
bear seven trumpets of rams' horns be-
fore the ark of the LORD." 7And he said to
the people, "Proceed, and march around
the city, and let him who is armed ad-
vance before the ark of the LORD."
8So it was, when Joshua had spoken to
the people, that the seven priests bear-
ing the seven trumpets of rams' horns
before the LORD advanced and blew
the trumpets, and the ark of the cov-
enant of the LORD followed them. 9The
armed men went before the priests who
blew the trumpets, and the rear guard
came after the ark, while *the priests* con-
tinued blowing the trumpets. 10Now
Joshua had commanded the people,
saying, "You shall not shout or make
any noise with your voice, nor shall a

5:3 [a] Hebrew *Gibeath Haaraloth* 5:6 [a] Exodus 3:8 5:9 [a] Literally *Rolling* word proceed out of your mouth, until the day I say to you, 'Shout!' Then you shall shout." 11So he had the ark of the LORD circle the city, going around *it* once. Then they came into the camp and lodged in the camp.

12And Joshua rose early in the morning, and the priests took up the ark of the LORD. 13Then seven priests bearing seven trumpets of rams' horns before the ark of the LORD went on continually and blew with the trumpets. And the armed men went before them. But the rear guard came after the ark of the LORD, while *the priests* continued blowing the trumpets. 14And the second day they marched around the city once and returned to the camp. So they did six days.

15But it came to pass on the seventh day that they rose early, about the dawning of the day, and marched around the city seven times in the same manner. On that day only they marched around the city seven times. 16And the seventh time it happened, when the priests blew the trumpets, that Joshua said to the people: "Shout, for the LORD has given you the city! 17Now the city shall be doomed by the LORD to destruction, it and all who *are* in it. Only Rahab the harlot shall live, she and all who *are* with her in the house, because she hid the messengers that we sent. 18And you, by all means abstain from the accursed things, lest you become accursed when you take of the accursed things, and make the camp of Israel a curse, and trouble it. 19But all the silver and gold, and vessels of bronze and iron, *are* consecrated to the LORD; they shall come into the treasury of the LORD."

20So the people shouted when *the priests* blew the trumpets. And it happened when the people heard the sound of the trumpet, and the people shouted with a great shout, that the wall fell down flat. Then the people went up into the city, every man straight before him, and they took the city. 21And they utterly destroyed all that *was* in the city, both man and woman, young and old, ox and sheep and donkey, with the edge of the sword.

22But Joshua had said to the two men who had spied out the country, "Go into the harlot's house, and from there bring out the woman and all that she has, as you swore to her." 23And the young men who had been spies went in and brought out Rahab, her father, her mother, her brothers, and all that she had. So they brought out all her relatives and left them outside the camp of Israel. 24But they burned the city and all that *was* in it with fire. Only the silver and gold, and the vessels of bronze and iron, they put into the treasury of the house of the LORD. 25And Joshua spared Rahab the harlot, her father's household, and all that she had. So she dwells in Israel to this day, because she hid the messengers whom Joshua sent to spy out Jericho.

26Then Joshua charged *them* at that time, saying, "Cursed *be* the man before the LORD who rises up and builds this city Jericho; he shall lay its foundation with his firstborn, and with his youngest he shall set up its gates."

27So the LORD was with Joshua, and his fame spread throughout all the country.

Defeat at Ai

7 But the children of Israel committed a trespass regarding the accursed things, for Achan the son of Carmi, the son of Zabdi,[a] the son of Zerah, of the tribe of Judah, took of the accursed things; so the anger of the LORD burned against the children of Israel.

2Now Joshua sent men from Jericho to Ai, which *is* beside Beth Aven, on the east side of Bethel, and spoke to them, saying, "Go up and spy out the country." So the men went up and spied out Ai. 3And they returned to Joshua and said to him, "Do not let all the people go up, but let about two or three thousand men go up and attack Ai. Do not weary all the people there, for *the people of Ai are* few." 4So about three thousand men went up there from the people, but they fled before the men of Ai. 5And the men of Ai struck down about thirty-six men, for they chased them *from* before

7:1 [a] Called *Zimri* in 1 Chronicles 2:6

the gate as far as Shebarim, and struck them down on the descent; therefore the hearts of the people melted and became like water.

6 Then Joshua tore his clothes, and fell to the earth on his face before the ark of the LORD until evening, he and the elders of Israel; and they put dust on their heads. 7 And Joshua said, "Alas, Lord GOD, why have You brought this people over the Jordan at all—to deliver us into the hand of the Amorites, to destroy us? Oh, that we had been content, and dwelt on the other side of the Jordan! 8 O Lord, what shall I say when Israel turns its back before its enemies? 9 For the Canaanites and all the inhabitants of the land will hear *it,* and surround us, and cut off our name from the earth. Then what will You do for Your great name?"

The Sin of Achan

10 So the LORD said to Joshua: "Get up! Why do you lie thus on your face? 11 Israel has sinned, and they have also transgressed My covenant which I commanded them. For they have even taken some of the accursed things, and have both stolen and deceived; and they have also put *it* among their own stuff. 12 Therefore the children of Israel could not stand before their enemies, *but* turned *their* backs before their enemies, because they have become doomed to destruction. Neither will I be with you anymore, unless you destroy the accursed from among you. 13 Get up, sanctify the people, and say, 'Sanctify yourselves for tomorrow, because thus says the LORD God of Israel: "*There is* an accursed thing in your midst, O Israel; you cannot stand before your enemies until you take away the accursed thing from among you." 14 In the morning therefore you shall be brought according to your tribes. And it shall be *that* the tribe which the LORD takes shall come according to families; and the family which the LORD takes shall come by households; and the household which the LORD takes shall come man by man. 15 Then it shall be *that* he who is taken with the accursed thing shall be burned with fire, he and all that he has, because he has transgressed the covenant of the LORD, and because he has done a disgraceful thing in Israel.' "

16 So Joshua rose early in the morning and brought Israel by their tribes, and the tribe of Judah was taken. 17 He brought the clan of Judah, and he took the family of the Zarhites; and he brought the family of the Zarhites man by man, and Zabdi was taken. 18 Then he brought his household man by man, and Achan the son of Carmi, the son of Zabdi, the son of Zerah, of the tribe of Judah, was taken.

19 Now Joshua said to Achan, "My son, I beg you, give glory to the LORD God of Israel, and make confession to Him, and tell me now what you have done; do not hide *it* from me."

20 And Achan answered Joshua and said, "Indeed I have sinned against the LORD God of Israel, and this is what I have done: 21 When I saw among the spoils a beautiful Babylonian garment, two hundred shekels of silver, and a wedge of gold weighing fifty shekels, I coveted them and took them. And there they are, hidden in the earth in the midst of my tent, with the silver under it."

22 So Joshua sent messengers, and they ran to the tent; and there it was, hidden in his tent, with the silver under it. 23 And they took them from the midst of the tent, brought them to Joshua and to all the children of Israel, and laid them out before the LORD. 24 Then Joshua, and all Israel with him, took Achan the son of Zerah, the silver, the garment, the wedge of gold, his sons, his daughters, his oxen, his donkeys, his sheep, his tent, and all that he had, and they brought them to the Valley of Achor. 25 And Joshua said, "Why have you troubled us? The LORD will trouble you this day." So all Israel stoned him with stones; and they burned them with fire after they had stoned them with stones.

26 Then they raised over him a great heap of stones, still there to this day. So the LORD turned from the fierceness of His anger. Therefore the name of that place has been called the Valley of Achor[a] to this day.

7:26 a Literally *Trouble*

The Fall of Ai

8 Now the LORD said to Joshua: "Do
not be afraid, nor be dismayed; take
all the people of war with you, and arise,
go up to Ai. See, I have given into your
hand the king of Ai, his people, his city,
and his land. 2And you shall do to Ai
and its king as you did to Jericho and
its king. Only its spoil and its cattle you
shall take as booty for yourselves. Lay
an ambush for the city behind it."
3So Joshua arose, and all the people
of war, to go up against Ai; and Joshua
chose thirty thousand mighty men of
valor and sent them away by night. 4And
he commanded them, saying: "Behold,
you shall lie in ambush against the city,
behind the city. Do not go very far from
the city, but all of you be ready. 5Then I
and all the people who *are* with me will
approach the city; and it will come about,
when they come out against us as at the
first, that we shall flee before them. 6For
they will come out after us till we have
drawn them from the city, for they will
say, '*They are* fleeing before us as at the
first.' Therefore we will flee before them.
7Then you shall rise from the ambush
and seize the city, for the LORD your God
will deliver it into your hand. 8And it will
be, when you have taken the city, *that*
you shall set the city on fire. According
to the commandment of the LORD you
shall do. See, I have commanded you."
9Joshua therefore sent them out; and
they went to lie in ambush, and stayed
between Bethel and Ai, on the west side
of Ai; but Joshua lodged that night
among the people. 10Then Joshua rose
up early in the morning and mustered
the people, and went up, he and the el-
ders of Israel, before the people to Ai.
11And all the people of war who *were*
with him went up and drew near; and
they came before the city and camped
on the north side of Ai. Now a valley *lay*
between them and Ai. 12So he took about
five thousand men and set them in am-
bush between Bethel and Ai, on the west
side of the city. 13And when they had set
the people, all the army that *was* on the
north of the city, and its rear guard on
the west of the city, Joshua went that
night into the midst of the valley.
14Now it happened, when the king of Ai
saw *it,* that the men of the city hurried
and rose early and went out against Is-
rael to battle, he and all his people, at an
appointed place before the plain. But he
did not know that *there was* an ambush
against him behind the city. 15And Josh-
ua and all Israel made as if they were
beaten before them, and fled by the way
of the wilderness. 16So all the people who
were in Ai were called together to pursue
them. And they pursued Joshua and
were drawn away from the city. 17There
was not a man left in Ai or Bethel who
did not go out after Israel. So they left
the city open and pursued Israel.
18Then the LORD said to Joshua,
"Stretch out the spear that *is* in your
hand toward Ai, for I will give it into
your hand." And Joshua stretched out
the spear that *was* in his hand toward
the city. 19So *those in* ambush arose
quickly out of their place; they ran as
soon as he had stretched out his hand,
and they entered the city and took it,
and hurried to set the city on fire. 20And
when the men of Ai looked behind them,
they saw, and behold, the smoke of the
city ascended to heaven. So they had
no power to flee this way or that way,
and the people who had fled to the wil-
derness turned back on the pursuers.
21Now when Joshua and all Israel saw
that the ambush had taken the city and
that the smoke of the city ascended,
they turned back and struck down the
men of Ai. 22Then the others came out
of the city against them; so they were
caught in the midst of Israel, some on
this side and some on that side. And
they struck them down, so that they
let none of them remain or escape.
23But the king of Ai they took alive,
and brought him to Joshua.
24And it came to pass when Israel had
made an end of slaying all the inhab-
itants of Ai in the field, in the wilderness
where they pursued them, and when
they all had fallen by the edge of the
sword until they were consumed, that all
the Israelites returned to Ai and struck
it with the edge of the sword. 25So it was
that all who fell that day, both men and
women, *were* twelve thousand—all the
people of Ai. 26For Joshua did not draw
back his hand, with which he stretched

out the spear, until he had utterly destroyed all the inhabitants of Ai. 27 Only the livestock and the spoil of that city Israel took as booty for themselves, according to the word of the LORD which He had commanded Joshua. 28 So Joshua burned Ai and made it a heap forever, a desolation to this day. 29 And the king of Ai he hanged on a tree until evening. And as soon as the sun was down, Joshua commanded that they should take his corpse down from the tree, cast it at the entrance of the gate of the city, and raise over it a great heap of stones *that remains* to this day.

Joshua Renews the Covenant

30 Now Joshua built an altar to the LORD God of Israel in Mount Ebal, 31 as Moses the servant of the LORD had commanded the children of Israel, as it is written in the Book of the Law of Moses: "an altar of whole stones over which no man has wielded an iron *tool.*"[a] And they offered on it burnt offerings to the LORD, and sacrificed peace offerings. 32 And there, in the presence of the children of Israel, he wrote on the stones a copy of the law of Moses, which he had written. 33 Then all Israel, with their elders and officers and judges, stood on either side of the ark before the priests, the Levites, who bore the ark of the covenant of the LORD, the stranger as well as he who was born among them. Half of them *were* in front of Mount Gerizim and half of them in front of Mount Ebal, as Moses the servant of the LORD had commanded before, that they should bless the people of Israel. 34 And afterward he read all the words of the law, the blessings and the cursings, according to all that is written in the Book of the Law. 35 There was not a word of all that Moses had commanded which Joshua did not read before all the assembly of Israel, with the women, the little ones, and the strangers who were living among them.

The Treaty with the Gibeonites

9 And it came to pass when all the kings who *were* on this side of the Jordan, in the hills and in the lowland and in all the coasts of the Great Sea toward Lebanon—the Hittite, the Amorite, the Canaanite, the Perizzite, the Hivite, and the Jebusite—heard *about it,* 2 that they gathered together to fight with Joshua and Israel with one accord.

3 But when the inhabitants of Gibeon heard what Joshua had done to Jericho and Ai, 4 they worked craftily, and went and pretended to be ambassadors. And they took old sacks on their donkeys, old wineskins torn and mended, 5 old and patched sandals on their feet, and old garments on themselves; and all the bread of their provision was dry *and* moldy. 6 And they went to Joshua, to the camp at Gilgal, and said to him and to the men of Israel, "We have come from a far country; now therefore, make a covenant with us."

7 Then the men of Israel said to the Hivites, "Perhaps you dwell among us; so how can we make a covenant with you?"

8 But they said to Joshua, "We *are* your servants."

And Joshua said to them, "Who *are* you, and where do you come from?"

9 So they said to him: "From a very far country your servants have come, because of the name of the LORD your God; for we have heard of His fame, and all that He did in Egypt, 10 and all that He did to the two kings of the Amorites who *were* beyond the Jordan—to Sihon king of Heshbon, and Og king of Bashan, who was at Ashtaroth. 11 Therefore our elders and all the inhabitants of our country spoke to us, saying, 'Take provisions with you for the journey, and go to meet them, and say to them, "We *are* your servants; now therefore, make a covenant with us." ' 12 This bread of ours we took hot *for* our provision from our houses on the day we departed to come to you. But now look, it is dry and moldy. 13 And these wineskins which we filled *were* new, and see, they are torn; and these our garments and our sandals have become old because of the very long journey."

14 Then the men of Israel took some of their provisions; but they did not ask counsel of the LORD. 15 So Joshua made peace with them, and made a covenant

8:31 [a] Deuteronomy 27:5, 6

with them to let them live; and the rulers of the congregation swore to them.

16And it happened at the end of three days, after they had made a covenant with them, that they heard that they *were* their neighbors who dwelt near them. 17Then the children of Israel journeyed and came to their cities on the third day. Now their cities *were* Gibeon, Chephirah, Beeroth, and Kirjath Jearim. 18But the children of Israel did not attack them, because the rulers of the congregation had sworn to them by the LORD God of Israel. And all the congregation complained against the rulers.

19Then all the rulers said to all the congregation, "We have sworn to them by the LORD God of Israel; now therefore, we may not touch them. 20This we will do to them: We will let them live, lest wrath be upon us because of the oath which we swore to them." 21And the rulers said to them, "Let them live, but let them be woodcutters and water carriers for all the congregation, as the rulers had promised them."

22Then Joshua called for them, and he spoke to them, saying, "Why have you deceived us, saying, 'We *are* very far from you,' when you dwell near us? 23Now therefore, you *are* cursed, and none of you shall be freed from being slaves—woodcutters and water carriers for the house of my God."

24So they answered Joshua and said, "Because your servants were clearly told that the LORD your God commanded His servant Moses to give you all the land, and to destroy all the inhabitants of the land from before you; therefore we were very much afraid for our lives because of you, and have done this thing. 25And now, here we are, in your hands; do with us as it seems good and right to do to us." 26So he did to them, and delivered them out of the hand of the children of Israel, so that they did not kill them. 27And that day Joshua made them woodcutters and water carriers for the congregation and for the altar of the LORD, in the place which He would choose, even to this day.

The Sun Stands Still

10 Now it came to pass when Adoni-Zedek king of Jerusalem heard how Joshua had taken Ai and had utterly destroyed it—as he had done to Jericho and its king, so he had done to Ai and its king—and how the inhabitants of Gibeon had made peace with Israel and were among them, 2that they feared greatly, because Gibeon *was* a great city, like one of the royal cities, and because it *was* greater than Ai, and all its men *were* mighty. 3Therefore Adoni-Zedek king of Jerusalem sent to Hoham king of Hebron, Piram king of Jarmuth, Japhia king of Lachish, and Debir king of Eglon, saying, 4"Come up to me and help me, that we may attack Gibeon, for it has made peace with Joshua and with the children of Israel." 5Therefore the five kings of the Amorites, the king of Jerusalem, the king of Hebron, the king of Jarmuth, the king of Lachish, *and* the king of Eglon, gathered together and went up, they and all their armies, and camped before Gibeon and made war against it.

6And the men of Gibeon sent to Joshua at the camp at Gilgal, saying, "Do not forsake your servants; come up to us quickly, save us and help us, for all the kings of the Amorites who dwell in the mountains have gathered together against us."

7So Joshua ascended from Gilgal, he and all the people of war with him, and all the mighty men of valor. 8And the LORD said to Joshua, "Do not fear them, for I have delivered them into your hand; not a man of them shall stand before you." 9Joshua therefore came upon them suddenly, having marched all night from Gilgal. 10So the LORD routed them before Israel, killed them with a great slaughter at Gibeon, chased them along the road that goes to Beth Horon, and struck them down as far as Azekah and Makkedah. 11And it happened, as they fled before Israel *and* were on the descent of Beth Horon, that the LORD cast down large hailstones from heaven on them as far as Azekah, and they died. *There were* more who died from the hailstones than the children of Israel killed with the sword.

12Then Joshua spoke to the LORD in the day when the LORD delivered up the Amorites before the children of Israel, and he said in the sight of Israel:

"Sun, stand still over Gibeon;
And Moon, in the Valley of
Aijalon."
13 So the sun stood still,
And the moon stopped,
Till the people had revenge
Upon their enemies.

Is this not written in the Book of Jasher?
So the sun stood still in the midst of
heaven, and did not hasten to go *down*
for about a whole day. 14 And there has
been no day like that, before it or after
it, that the LORD heeded the voice of a
man; for the LORD fought for Israel.
15 Then Joshua returned, and all Israel
with him, to the camp at Gilgal.

The Amorite Kings Executed

16 But these five kings had fled and
hidden themselves in a cave at Makke-
dah. 17 And it was told Joshua, saying,
"The five kings have been found hidden
in the cave at Makkedah."
18 So Joshua said, "Roll large stones
against the mouth of the cave, and set
men by it to guard them. 19 And do not
stay *there* yourselves, *but* pursue your
enemies, and attack their rear *guard.*
Do not allow them to enter their cities,
for the LORD your God has delivered
them into your hand." 20 Then it hap-
pened, while Joshua and the children
of Israel made an end of slaying them
with a very great slaughter, till they
had finished, that those who escaped
entered fortified cities. 21 And all the
people returned to the camp, to Joshua
at Makkedah, in peace.
No one moved his tongue against any
of the children of Israel.
22 Then Joshua said, "Open the mouth
of the cave, and bring out those five
kings to me from the cave." 23 And they
did so, and brought out those five kings
to him from the cave: the king of Jeru-
salem, the king of Hebron, the king of
Jarmuth, the king of Lachish, *and* the
king of Eglon.
24 So it was, when they brought out
those kings to Joshua, that Joshua
called for all the men of Israel, and said
to the captains of the men of war who
went with him, "Come near, put your
feet on the necks of these kings." And
they drew near and put their feet on
their necks. 25 Then Joshua said to them,
"Do not be afraid, nor be dismayed; be
strong and of good courage, for thus
the LORD will do to all your enemies
against whom you fight." 26 And after-
ward Joshua struck them and killed
them, and hanged them on five trees;
and they were hanging on the trees
until evening. 27 So it was at the time of
the going down of the sun *that* Joshua
commanded, and they took them down
from the trees, cast them into the cave
where they had been hidden, and laid
large stones against the cave's mouth,
which remain until this very day.

Conquest of the Southland

28 On that day Joshua took Makke-
dah, and struck it and its king with the
edge of the sword. He utterly destroyed
them[a]—all the people who *were* in it.
He let none remain. He also did to the
king of Makkedah as he had done to
the king of Jericho.
29 Then Joshua passed from Makke-
dah, and all Israel with him, to Libnah;
and they fought against Libnah. 30 And
the LORD also delivered it and its king
into the hand of Israel; he struck it and
all the people who *were* in it with the
edge of the sword. He let none remain
in it, but did to its king as he had done
to the king of Jericho.
31 Then Joshua passed from Libnah,
and all Israel with him, to Lachish; and
they encamped against it and fought
against it. 32 And the LORD delivered La-
chish into the hand of Israel, who took
it on the second day, and struck it and
all the people who *were* in it with the
edge of the sword, according to all that
he had done to Libnah. 33 Then Horam
king of Gezer came up to help Lachish;
and Joshua struck him and his people,
until he left him none remaining.
34 From Lachish Joshua passed to
Eglon, and all Israel with him; and
they encamped against it and fought
against it. 35 They took it on that day
and struck it with the edge of the sword;

10:28 [a] Following Masoretic Text and most authorities; many Hebrew manuscripts, some manuscripts of the Septuagint, and some manuscripts of the Targum read *it.*

all the people who *were* in it he utterly
destroyed that day, according to all
that he had done to Lachish.
36So Joshua went up from Eglon, and
all Israel with him, to Hebron; and they
fought against it. 37And they took it and
struck it with the edge of the sword—its
king, all its cities, and all the people
who *were* in it; he left none remaining,
according to all that he had done to
Eglon, but utterly destroyed it and all
the people who *were* in it.
38Then Joshua returned, and all Isra-
el with him, to Debir; and they fought
against it. 39And he took it and its king
and all its cities; they struck them with
the edge of the sword and utterly de-
stroyed all the people who *were* in it. He
left none remaining; as he had done to
Hebron, so he did to Debir and its king, as
he had done also to Libnah and its king.
40So Joshua conquered all the land:
the mountain country and the South[a]
and the lowland and the wilderness
slopes, and all their kings; he left none
remaining, but utterly destroyed all
that breathed, as the LORD God of Is-
rael had commanded. 41And Joshua
conquered them from Kadesh Barnea
as far as Gaza, and all the country of
Goshen, even as far as Gibeon. 42All
these kings and their land Joshua took
at one time, because the LORD God of
Israel fought for Israel. 43Then Joshua
returned, and all Israel with him, to the
camp at Gilgal.

The Northern Conquest

11 And it came to pass, when Jabin
king of Hazor heard *these things,*
that he sent to Jobab king of Madon,
to the king of Shimron, to the king of
Achshaph, 2and to the kings who *were*
from the north, in the mountains, in
the plain south of Chinneroth, in the
lowland, and in the heights of Dor on
the west, 3to the Canaanites in the east
and in the west, the Amorite, the Hittite,
the Perizzite, the Jebusite in the moun-
tains, and the Hivite below Hermon in
the land of Mizpah. 4So they went out,
they and all their armies with them,
as many people *as* the sand that *is* on
the seashore in multitude, with very
many horses and chariots. 5And when
all these kings had met together, they
came and camped together at the wa-
ters of Merom to fight against Israel.
6But the LORD said to Joshua, "Do not
be afraid because of them, for tomorrow
about this time I will deliver all of them
slain before Israel. You shall hamstring
their horses and burn their chariots
with fire." 7So Joshua and all the people
of war with him came against them
suddenly by the waters of Merom, and
they attacked them. 8And the LORD
delivered them into the hand of Israel,
who defeated them and chased them
to Greater Sidon, to the Brook Misre-
photh,[a] and to the Valley of Mizpah
eastward; they attacked them until they
left none of them remaining. 9So Joshua
did to them as the LORD had told him:
he hamstrung their horses and burned
their chariots with fire.
10Joshua turned back at that time and
took Hazor, and struck its king with the
sword; for Hazor was formerly the head
of all those kingdoms. 11And they struck
all the people who *were* in it with the
edge of the sword, utterly destroying
them. There was none left breathing.
Then he burned Hazor with fire.
12So all the cities of those kings, and
all their kings, Joshua took and struck
with the edge of the sword. He utterly
destroyed them, as Moses the servant of
the LORD had commanded. 13But *as for*
the cities that stood on their mounds,[a]
Israel burned none of them, except
Hazor only, *which* Joshua burned. 14And
all the spoil of these cities and the live-
stock, the children of Israel took as boo-
ty for themselves; but they struck every
man with the edge of the sword until
they had destroyed them, and they left
none breathing. 15As the LORD had com-
manded Moses His servant, so Moses
commanded Joshua, and so Joshua did.
He left nothing undone of all that the
LORD had commanded Moses.

Summary of Joshua's Conquests

16Thus Joshua took all this land: the
mountain country, all the South, all

10:40 [a] Hebrew *Negev,* and so throughout this book 11:8 [a] Hebrew *Misrephoth Maim*
11:13 [a] Hebrew *tel,* a heap of successive city ruins

the land of Goshen, the lowland, and
the Jordan plain[a]—the mountains of
Israel and its lowlands, 17from Mount
Halak and the ascent to Seir, even as
far as Baal Gad in the Valley of Leba-
non below Mount Hermon. He captured
all their kings, and struck them down
and killed them. 18Joshua made war a
long time with all those kings. 19There
was not a city that made peace with the
children of Israel, except the Hivites,
the inhabitants of Gibeon. All *the others*
they took in battle. 20For it was of the
LORD to harden their hearts, that they
should come against Israel in battle,
that He might utterly destroy them,
and that they might receive no mercy,
but that He might destroy them, as the
LORD had commanded Moses.

21And at that time Joshua came and cut
off the Anakim from the mountains: from
Hebron, from Debir, from Anab, from all
the mountains of Judah, and from all
the mountains of Israel; Joshua utterly
destroyed them with their cities. 22None
of the Anakim were left in the land of the
children of Israel; they remained only in
Gaza, in Gath, and in Ashdod.

23So Joshua took the whole land, ac-
cording to all that the LORD had said
to Moses; and Joshua gave it as an in-
heritance to Israel according to their
divisions by their tribes. Then the land
rested from war.

The Kings Conquered by Moses

12 These *are* the kings of the land
whom the children of Israel de-
feated, and whose land they possessed
on the other side of the Jordan toward
the rising of the sun, from the River
Arnon to Mount Hermon, and all the
eastern Jordan plain: 2*One king was*
Sihon king of the Amorites, who dwelt
in Heshbon *and* ruled half of Gilead,
from Aroer, which is on the bank of the
River Arnon, from the middle of that
river, even as far as the River Jabbok,
which is the border of the Ammonites,
3and the eastern Jordan plain from the
Sea of Chinneroth as far as the Sea of
the Arabah (the Salt Sea), the road to
Beth Jeshimoth, and southward below
the slopes of Pisgah. 4*The other king was*
Og king of Bashan and his territory,
who was of the remnant of the giants,
who dwelt at Ashtaroth and at Edrei,
5and reigned over Mount Hermon,
over Salcah, over all Bashan, as far as
the border of the Geshurites and the
Maachathites, and over half of Gilead
to the border of Sihon king of Heshbon.

6These Moses the servant of the LORD
and the children of Israel had con-
quered; and Moses the servant of the
LORD had given it *as* a possession to
the Reubenites, the Gadites, and half
the tribe of Manasseh.

The Kings Conquered by Joshua

7And these *are* the kings of the country
which Joshua and the children of Israel
conquered on this side of the Jordan, on
the west, from Baal Gad in the Valley
of Lebanon as far as Mount Halak and
the ascent to Seir, which Joshua gave
to the tribes of Israel *as* a possession
according to their divisions, 8in the
mountain country, in the lowlands, in
the *Jordan* plain, in the slopes, in the
wilderness, and in the South—the Hit-
tites, the Amorites, the Canaanites, the
Perizzites, the Hivites, and the Jebusites:
9the king of Jericho, one; the king of Ai,
which *is* beside Bethel, one; 10the king
of Jerusalem, one; the king of Hebron,
one; 11the king of Jarmuth, one; the king
of Lachish, one; 12the king of Eglon,
one; the king of Gezer, one; 13the king
of Debir, one; the king of Geder, one;
14the king of Hormah, one; the king of
Arad, one; 15the king of Libnah, one;
the king of Adullam, one; 16the king of
Makkedah, one; the king of Bethel, one;
17the king of Tappuah, one; the king of
Hepher, one; 18the king of Aphek, one;
the king of Lasharon, one; 19the king
of Madon, one; the king of Hazor, one;
20the king of Shimron Meron, one; the
king of Achshaph, one; 21the king of Ta-
anach, one; the king of Megiddo, one;
22the king of Kedesh, one; the king of
Jokneam in Carmel, one; 23the king of
Dor in the heights of Dor, one; the king
of the people of Gilgal, one; 24the king
of Tirzah, one—all the kings, thirty-one.

11:16 [a] Hebrew *arabah*

Remaining Land to Be Conquered

13 Now Joshua was old, advanced in years. And the LORD said to him: "You are old, advanced in years, and there remains very much land yet to be possessed. 2This is the land that yet remains: all the territory of the Philistines and all *that of* the Geshurites, 3from Sihor, which *is* east of Egypt, as far as the border of Ekron northward (*which* is counted as Canaanite); the five lords of the Philistines—the Gazites, the Ashdodites, the Ashkelonites, the Gittites, and the Ekronites; also the Avites; 4from the south, all the land of the Canaanites, and Mearah that belongs to the Sidonians as far as Aphek, to the border of the Amorites; 5the land of the Gebalites,[a] and all Lebanon, toward the sunrise, from Baal Gad below Mount Hermon as far as the entrance to Hamath; 6all the inhabitants of the mountains from Lebanon as far as the Brook Misrephoth,[a] *and* all the Sidonians—them I will drive out from before the children of Israel; only divide it by lot to Israel as an inheritance, as I have commanded you. 7Now therefore, divide this land as an inheritance to the nine tribes and half the tribe of Manasseh."

The Land Divided East of the Jordan

8With the other half-tribe the Reubenites and the Gadites received their inheritance, which Moses had given them, beyond the Jordan eastward, as Moses the servant of the LORD had given them: 9from Aroer which *is* on the bank of the River Arnon, and the town that *is* in the midst of the ravine, and all the plain of Medeba as far as Dibon; 10all the cities of Sihon king of the Amorites, who reigned in Heshbon, as far as the border of the children of Ammon; 11Gilead, and the border of the Geshurites and Maachathites, all Mount Hermon, and all Bashan as far as Salcah; 12all the kingdom of Og in Bashan, who reigned in Ashtaroth and Edrei, who remained of the remnant of the giants; for Moses had defeated and cast out these.

13Nevertheless the children of Israel did not drive out the Geshurites or the Maachathites, but the Geshurites and the Maachathites dwell among the Israelites until this day.

14Only to the tribe of Levi he had given no inheritance; the sacrifices of the LORD God of Israel made by fire *are* their inheritance, as He said to them.

The Land of Reuben

15And Moses had given to the tribe of the children of Reuben *an inheritance* according to their families. 16Their territory was from Aroer, which *is* on the bank of the River Arnon, and the city that *is* in the midst of the ravine, and all the plain by Medeba; 17Heshbon and all its cities that *are* in the plain: Dibon, Bamoth Baal, Beth Baal Meon, 18Jahaza, Kedemoth, Mephaath, 19Kirjathaim, Sibmah, Zereth Shahar on the mountain of the valley, 20Beth Peor, the slopes of Pisgah, and Beth Jeshimoth—21all the cities of the plain and all the kingdom of Sihon king of the Amorites, who reigned in Heshbon, whom Moses had struck with the princes of Midian: Evi, Rekem, Zur, Hur, and Reba, who *were* princes of Sihon dwelling in the country. 22The children of Israel also killed with the sword Balaam the son of Beor, the soothsayer, among those who were killed by them. 23And the border of the children of Reuben was the bank of the Jordan. This *was* the inheritance of the children of Reuben according to their families, the cities and their villages.

The Land of Gad

24Moses also had given *an inheritance* to the tribe of Gad, to the children of Gad according to their families. 25Their territory was Jazer, and all the cities of Gilead, and half the land of the Ammonites as far as Aroer, which *is* before Rabbah, 26and from Heshbon to Ramath Mizpah and Betonim, and from Mahanaim to the border of Debir, 27and in the valley Beth Haram, Beth Nimrah, Succoth, and Zaphon, the rest of the kingdom of Sihon king of Heshbon, with the Jordan as *its* border, as far as the edge of the Sea of Chinnereth, on the other side of the Jordan eastward.

13:5 [a] Or *Giblites* 13:6 [a] Hebrew *Misrephoth Maim*

28This *is* the inheritance of the children
of Gad according to their families, the
cities and their villages.

Half the Tribe of Manasseh (East)

29Moses also had given *an inheritance*
to half the tribe of Manasseh; it was for
half the tribe of the children of Manas-
seh according to their families: 30Their
territory was from Mahanaim, all Ba-
shan, all the kingdom of Og king of Ba-
shan, and all the towns of Jair which are
in Bashan, sixty cities; 31half of Gilead,
and Ashtaroth and Edrei, cities of the
kingdom of Og in Bashan, *were* for the
children of Machir the son of Manas-
seh, for half of the children of Machir
according to their families.
32These *are the areas* which Moses
had distributed as an inheritance in
the plains of Moab on the other side of
the Jordan, by Jericho eastward. 33But
to the tribe of Levi Moses had given no
inheritance; the LORD God of Israel *was*
their inheritance, as He had said to them.

The Land Divided West of the Jordan

14 These *are the areas* which the
children of Israel inherited in
the land of Canaan, which Eleazar the
priest, Joshua the son of Nun, and
the heads of the fathers of the tribes of
the children of Israel distributed as an
inheritance to them. 2Their inheritance
was by lot, as the LORD had command-
ed by the hand of Moses, for the nine
tribes and the half-tribe. 3For Moses
had given the inheritance of the two
tribes and the half-tribe on the other
side of the Jordan; but to the Levites
he had given no inheritance among
them. 4For the children of Joseph were
two tribes: Manasseh and Ephraim.
And they gave no part to the Levites in
the land, except cities to dwell *in*, with
their common-lands for their livestock
and their property. 5As the LORD had
commanded Moses, so the children of
Israel did; and they divided the land.

Caleb Inherits Hebron

6Then the children of Judah came to
Joshua in Gilgal. And Caleb the son of
Jephunneh the Kenizzite said to him:
"You know the word which the LORD said
to Moses the man of God concerning
you and me in Kadesh Barnea. 7I *was*
forty years old when Moses the servant
of the LORD sent me from Kadesh Bar-
nea to spy out the land, and I brought
back word to him as *it was* in my heart.
8Nevertheless my brethren who went up
with me made the heart of the people
melt, but I wholly followed the LORD
my God. 9So Moses swore on that day,
saying, 'Surely the land where your foot
has trodden shall be your inheritance
and your children's forever, because you
have wholly followed the LORD my God.'
10And now, behold, the LORD has kept
me alive, as He said, these forty-five
years, ever since the LORD spoke this
word to Moses while Israel wandered
in the wilderness; and now, here I am
this day, eighty-five years old. 11As yet
I *am as* strong this day as on the day
that Moses sent me; just as my strength
was then, so now *is* my strength for war,
both for going out and for coming in.
12Now therefore, give me this mountain
of which the LORD spoke in that day; for
you heard in that day how the Anakim
were there, and *that* the cities *were* great
and fortified. It may be that the LORD
will be with me, and I shall be able to
drive them out as the LORD said."
13And Joshua blessed him, and gave
Hebron to Caleb the son of Jephunneh
as an inheritance. 14Hebron therefore
became the inheritance of Caleb the son
of Jephunneh the Kenizzite to this day,
because he wholly followed the LORD
God of Israel. 15And the name of Hebron
formerly was Kirjath Arba (*Arba was*
the greatest man among the Anakim).
Then the land had rest from war.

The Land of Judah

15 So *this* was the lot of the tribe of
the children of Judah according
to their families:
The border of Edom at the Wilder-
ness of Zin southward *was* the extreme
southern boundary. 2And their south-
ern border began at the shore of the Salt
Sea, from the bay that faces southward.
3Then it went out to the southern side of
the Ascent of Akrabbim, passed along to
Zin, ascended on the south side of Ka-
desh Barnea, passed along to Hezron,

went up to Adar, and went around to Karkaa. 4*From there* it passed toward Azmon and went out to the Brook of Egypt; and the border ended at the sea. This shall be your southern border.

5The east border *was* the Salt Sea as far as the mouth of the Jordan.

And the border on the northern quarter *began* at the bay of the sea at the mouth of the Jordan. 6The border went up to Beth Hoglah and passed north of Beth Arabah; and the border went up to the stone of Bohan the son of Reuben. 7Then the border went up toward Debir from the Valley of Achor, and it turned northward toward Gilgal, which *is* before the Ascent of Adummim, which *is* on the south side of the valley. The border continued toward the waters of En Shemesh and ended at En Rogel. 8And the border went up by the Valley of the Son of Hinnom to the southern slope of the Jebusite *city* (which *is* Jerusalem). The border went up to the top of the mountain that *lies* before the Valley of Hinnom westward, which *is* at the end of the Valley of Rephaim[a] northward. 9Then the border went around from the top of the hill to the fountain of the water of Nephtoah, and extended to the cities of Mount Ephron. And the border went around to Baalah (which *is* Kirjath Jearim). 10Then the border turned westward from Baalah to Mount Seir, passed along to the side of Mount Jearim on the north (which *is* Chesalon), went down to Beth Shemesh, and passed on to Timnah. 11And the border went out to the side of Ekron northward. Then the border went around to Shicron, passed along to Mount Baalah, and extended to Jabneel; and the border ended at the sea.

12The west border *was* the coastline of the Great Sea. This *is* the boundary of the children of Judah all around according to their families.

Caleb Occupies Hebron and Debir

13Now to Caleb the son of Jephunneh he gave a share among the children of Judah, according to the commandment of the LORD to Joshua, *namely,* Kirjath Arba, which *is* Hebron (*Arba was* the father of Anak). 14Caleb drove out the three sons of Anak from there: Sheshai, Ahiman, and Talmai, the children of Anak. 15Then he went up from there to the inhabitants of Debir (formerly the name of Debir *was* Kirjath Sepher).

16And Caleb said, "He who attacks Kirjath Sepher and takes it, to him I will give Achsah my daughter as wife." 17So Othniel the son of Kenaz, the brother of Caleb, took it; and he gave him Achsah his daughter as wife. 18Now it was so, when she came *to him,* that she persuaded him to ask her father for a field. So she dismounted from *her* donkey, and Caleb said to her, "What do you wish?" 19She answered, "Give me a blessing; since you have given me land in the South, give me also springs of water." So he gave her the upper springs and the lower springs.

The Cities of Judah

20This *was* the inheritance of the tribe of the children of Judah according to their families:

21The cities at the limits of the tribe of the children of Judah, toward the border of Edom in the South, were Kabzeel, Eder, Jagur, 22Kinah, Dimonah, Adadah, 23Kedesh, Hazor, Ithnan, 24Ziph, Telem, Bealoth, 25Hazor, Hadattah, Kerioth, Hezron (which *is* Hazor), 26Amam, Shema, Moladah, 27Hazar Gaddah, Heshmon, Beth Pelet, 28Hazar Shual, Beersheba, Bizjothjah, 29Baalah, Ijim, Ezem, 30Eltolad, Chesil, Hormah, 31Ziklag, Madmannah, Sansannah, 32Lebaoth, Shilhim, Ain, and Rimmon: all the cities *are* twenty-nine, with their villages.

33In the lowland: Eshtaol, Zorah, Ashnah, 34Zanoah, En Gannim, Tappuah, Enam, 35Jarmuth, Adullam, Socoh, Azekah, 36Sharaim, Adithaim, Gederah, and Gederothaim: fourteen cities with their villages; 37Zenan, Hadashah, Migdal Gad, 38Dilean, Mizpah, Joktheel, 39Lachish, Bozkath, Eglon, 40Cabbon, Lahmas,[a] Kithlish, 41Gederoth, Beth Dagon, Naamah, and Makkedah: sixteen cities with their villages; 42Libnah, Ether, Ashan, 43Jiphtah, Ashnah, Nezib, 44Keilah, Achzib, and Mareshah: nine

15:8 [a] Literally *Giants* 15:40 [a] Or *Lahmam*

cities with their villages; 45Ekron, with
its towns and villages; 46from Ekron to
the sea, all that *lay* near Ashdod, with
their villages; 47Ashdod with its towns
and villages, Gaza with its towns and
villages—as far as the Brook of Egypt
and the Great Sea with *its* coastline.
48And in the mountain country: Sha-
mir, Jattir, Sochoh, 49Dannah, Kirjath
Sannah (which *is* Debir), 50Anab, Esh-
temoh, Anim, 51Goshen, Holon, and
Giloh: eleven cities with their villages;
52Arab, Dumah, Eshean, 53Janum, Beth
Tappuah, Aphekah, 54Humtah, Kirjath
Arba (which *is* Hebron), and Zior: nine
cities with their villages; 55Maon, Car-
mel, Ziph, Juttah, 56Jezreel, Jokdeam,
Zanoah, 57Kain, Gibeah, and Timnah:
ten cities with their villages; 58Halhul,
Beth Zur, Gedor, 59Maarath, Beth Anoth,
and Eltekon: six cities with their villages;
60Kirjath Baal (which *is* Kirjath Jearim)
and Rabbah: two cities with their villages.
61In the wilderness: Beth Arabah, Mid-
din, Secacah, 62Nibshan, the City of
Salt, and En Gedi: six cities with their
villages.
63As for the Jebusites, the inhabitants
of Jerusalem, the children of Judah
could not drive them out; but the Jeb-
usites dwell with the children of Judah
at Jerusalem to this day.

Ephraim and West Manasseh

16 The lot fell to the children of
Joseph from the Jordan, by Jer-
icho, to the waters of Jericho on the
east, to the wilderness that goes up
from Jericho through the mountains
to Bethel, 2then went out from Beth-
el to Luz,[a] passed along to the border
of the Archites at Ataroth, 3and went
down westward to the boundary of the
Japhletites, as far as the boundary of
Lower Beth Horon to Gezer; and it ended
at the sea.
4So the children of Joseph, Manasseh
and Ephraim, took their inheritance.

The Land of Ephraim

5The border of the children of Ephraim,
according to their families, was *thus:*
The border of their inheritance on the
east side was Ataroth Addar as far as
Upper Beth Horon.
6And the border went out toward the
sea on the north side of Michmethath;
then the border went around eastward
to Taanath Shiloh, and passed by it on
the east of Janohah. 7Then it went down
from Janohah to Ataroth and Naarah,[a]
reached to Jericho, and came out at
the Jordan.
8The border went out from Tappuah
westward to the Brook Kanah, and it
ended at the sea. This *was* the inher-
itance of the tribe of the children of
Ephraim according to their families.
9The separate cities for the children of
Ephraim *were* among the inheritance of
the children of Manasseh, all the cities
with their villages.
10And they did not drive out the Ca-
naanites who dwelt in Gezer; but the
Canaanites dwell among the Ephra-
imites to this day and have become
forced laborers.

The Other Half-Tribe of Manasseh (West)

17 There was also a lot for the tribe
of Manasseh, for he *was* the
firstborn of Joseph: *namely* for Machir
the firstborn of Manasseh, the father of
Gilead, because he was a man of war;
therefore he was given Gilead and Ba-
shan. 2And there was *a lot* for the rest of
the children of Manasseh according to
their families: for the children of Abie-
zer,[a] the children of Helek, the children
of Asriel, the children of Shechem, the
children of Hepher, and the children of
Shemida; these *were* the male children
of Manasseh the son of Joseph accord-
ing to their families.
3But Zelophehad the son of Hepher,
the son of Gilead, the son of Machir, the
son of Manasseh, had no sons, but only
daughters. And these *are* the names of
his daughters: Mahlah, Noah, Hoglah,
Milcah, and Tirzah. 4And they came
near before Eleazar the priest, before
Joshua the son of Nun, and before the
rulers, saying, "The LORD commanded
Moses to give us an inheritance among
our brothers." Therefore, according to
the commandment of the LORD, he gave

16:2 [a] Septuagint reads *Bethel* (that is, Luz). 16:7 [a] Or *Naaran* (compare 1 Chronicles 7:28)
17:2 [a] Called *Jeezer* in Numbers 26:30

them an inheritance among their fa-
ther's brothers. 5Ten shares fell to Ma-
nasseh, besides the land of Gilead and
Bashan, which *were* on the other side
of the Jordan, 6because the daughters
of Manasseh received an inheritance
among his sons; and the rest of Ma-
nasseh's sons had the land of Gilead.
7And the territory of Manasseh was
from Asher to Michmethath, that *lies*
east of Shechem; and the border went
along south to the inhabitants of En
Tappuah. 8Manasseh had the land of
Tappuah, but Tappuah on the border
of Manasseh *belonged* to the children
of Ephraim. 9And the border descend-
ed to the Brook Kanah, southward to
the brook. These cities of Ephraim *are*
among the cities of Manasseh. The bor-
der of Manasseh *was* on the north side
of the brook; and it ended at the sea.
10Southward *it was* Ephraim's, north-
ward *it was* Manasseh's, and the sea
was its border. Manasseh's territory
was adjoining Asher on the north and
Issachar on the east. 11And in Issachar
and in Asher, Manasseh had Beth Shean
and its towns, Ibleam and its towns, the
inhabitants of Dor and its towns, the
inhabitants of En Dor and its towns,
the inhabitants of Taanach and its
towns, and the inhabitants of Megiddo
and its towns—three hilly regions. 12Yet
the children of Manasseh could not
drive out *the inhabitants of* those cities,
but the Canaanites were determined to
dwell in that land. 13And it happened,
when the children of Israel grew strong,
that they put the Canaanites to forced
labor, but did not utterly drive them out.

More Land for Ephraim and Manasseh

14Then the children of Joseph spoke to
Joshua, saying, "Why have you given
us *only* one lot and one share to inherit,
since we *are* a great people, inasmuch
as the LORD has blessed us until now?"
15So Joshua answered them, "If you
are a great people, *then* go up to the for-
est *country* and clear a place for your-
self there in the land of the Perizzites
and the giants, since the mountains
of Ephraim are too confined for you."
16But the children of Joseph said, "The
mountain country is not enough for
us; and all the Canaanites who dwell in
the land of the valley have chariots of
iron, *both those* who *are* of Beth Shean
and its towns and *those* who *are* of the
Valley of Jezreel."
17And Joshua spoke to the house of
Joseph—to Ephraim and Manasseh—
saying, "You *are* a great people and
have great power; you shall not have
only one lot, 18but the mountain country
shall be yours. Although it *is* wooded,
you shall cut it down, and its farthest
extent shall be yours; for you shall drive
out the Canaanites, though they have
iron chariots *and* are strong."

The Remainder of the Land Divided

18 Now the whole congregation of
the children of Israel assembled
together at Shiloh, and set up the tab-
ernacle of meeting there. And the land
was subdued before them. 2But there
remained among the children of Israel
seven tribes which had not yet received
their inheritance.
3Then Joshua said to the children of
Israel: "How long will you neglect to go
and possess the land which the LORD
God of your fathers has given you? 4Pick
out from among you three men for *each*
tribe, and I will send them; they shall
rise and go through the land, survey
it according to their inheritance, and
come *back* to me. 5And they shall di-
vide it into seven parts. Judah shall
remain in their territory on the south,
and the house of Joseph shall remain in
their territory on the north. 6You shall
therefore survey the land in seven parts
and bring *the survey* here to me, that I
may cast lots for you here before the
LORD our God. 7But the Levites have no
part among you, for the priesthood of
the LORD *is* their inheritance. And Gad,
Reuben, and half the tribe of Manasseh
have received their inheritance beyond
the Jordan on the east, which Moses the
servant of the LORD gave them."
8Then the men arose to go away; and
Joshua charged those who went to sur-
vey the land, saying, "Go, walk through
the land, survey it, and come back to
me, that I may cast lots for you here
before the LORD in Shiloh." 9So the men
went, passed through the land, and

wrote the survey in a book in seven parts by cities; and they came to Joshua at the camp in Shiloh. 10 Then Joshua cast lots for them in Shiloh before the LORD, and there Joshua divided the land to the children of Israel according to their divisions.

The Land of Benjamin

11 Now the lot of the tribe of the children of Benjamin came up according to their families, and the territory of their lot came out between the children of Judah and the children of Joseph. 12 Their border on the north side began at the Jordan, and the border went up to the side of Jericho on the north, and went up through the mountains westward; it ended at the Wilderness of Beth Aven. 13 The border went over from there toward Luz, to the side of Luz (which *is* Bethel) southward; and the border descended to Ataroth Addar, near the hill that *lies* on the south side of Lower Beth Horon.

14 Then the border extended around the west side to the south, from the hill that *lies* before Beth Horon southward; and it ended at Kirjath Baal (which *is* Kirjath Jearim), a city of the children of Judah. This *was* the west side.

15 The south side *began* at the end of Kirjath Jearim, and the border extended on the west and went out to the spring of the waters of Nephtoah. 16 Then the border came down to the end of the mountain that *lies* before the Valley of the Son of Hinnom, which *is* in the Valley of the Rephaim[a] on the north, descended to the Valley of Hinnom, to the side of the Jebusite *city* on the south, and descended to En Rogel. 17 And it went around from the north, went out to En Shemesh, and extended toward Geliloth, which is before the Ascent of Adummim, and descended to the stone of Bohan the son of Reuben. 18 Then it passed along toward the north side of Arabah,[a] and went down to Arabah. 19 And the border passed along to the north side of Beth Hoglah; then the border ended at the north bay at the Salt Sea, at the south end of the Jordan. This *was* the southern boundary.

20 The Jordan was its border on the east side. This *was* the inheritance of the children of Benjamin, according to its boundaries all around, according to their families.

21 Now the cities of the tribe of the children of Benjamin, according to their families, were Jericho, Beth Hoglah, Emek Keziz, 22 Beth Arabah, Zemaraim, Bethel, 23 Avim, Parah, Ophrah, 24 Chephar Haammoni, Ophni, and Gaba: twelve cities with their villages; 25 Gibeon, Ramah, Beeroth, 26 Mizpah, Chephirah, Mozah, 27 Rekem, Irpeel, Taralah, 28 Zelah, Eleph, Jebus (which *is* Jerusalem), Gibeath, *and* Kirjath: fourteen cities with their villages. This was the inheritance of the children of Benjamin according to their families.

Simeon's Inheritance with Judah

19 The second lot came out for Simeon, for the tribe of the children of Simeon according to their families. And their inheritance was within the inheritance of the children of Judah. 2 They had in their inheritance Beersheba (Sheba), Moladah, 3 Hazar Shual, Balah, Ezem, 4 Eltolad, Bethul, Hormah, 5 Ziklag, Beth Marcaboth, Hazar Susah, 6 Beth Lebaoth, and Sharuhen: thirteen cities and their villages; 7 Ain, Rimmon, Ether, and Ashan: four cities and their villages; 8 and all the villages that *were* all around these cities as far as Baalath Beer, Ramah of the South. This *was* the inheritance of the tribe of the children of Simeon according to their families.

9 The inheritance of the children of Simeon *was included* in the share of the children of Judah, for the share of the children of Judah was too much for them. Therefore the children of Simeon had *their* inheritance within the inheritance of that people.

The Land of Zebulun

10 The third lot came out for the children of Zebulun according to their families, and the border of their inheritance was as far as Sarid. 11 Their border went toward the west and to Maralah, went to Dabbasheth, and extended along the

18:16 [a] Literally *Giants* 18:18 [a] Or *Beth Arabah* (compare 15:6 and 18:22)

brook that is east of Jokneam. 12Then from Sarid it went eastward toward the sunrise along the border of Chisloth Tabor, and went out toward Daberath, bypassing Japhia. 13And from there it passed along on the east of Gath Hepher, toward Eth Kazin, and extended to Rimmon, which borders on Neah. 14Then the border went around it on the north side of Hannathon, and it ended in the Valley of Jiphthah El. 15Included were Kattath, Nahallal, Shimron, Idalah, and Bethlehem: twelve cities with their villages. 16This *was* the inheritance of the children of Zebulun according to their families, these cities with their villages.

The Land of Issachar

17The fourth lot came out to Issachar, for the children of Issachar according to their families. 18And their territory went to Jezreel, and *included* Chesulloth, Shunem, 19Haphraim, Shion, Anaharath, 20Rabbith, Kishion, Abez, 21Remeth, En Gannim, En Haddah, and Beth Pazzez. 22And the border reached to Tabor, Shahazimah, and Beth Shemesh; their border ended at the Jordan: sixteen cities with their villages. 23This *was* the inheritance of the tribe of the children of Issachar according to their families, the cities and their villages.

The Land of Asher

24The fifth lot came out for the tribe of the children of Asher according to their families. 25And their territory included Helkath, Hali, Beten, Achshaph, 26Alammelech, Amad, and Mishal; it reached to Mount Carmel westward, along *the Brook* Shihor Libnath. 27It turned toward the sunrise to Beth Dagon; and it reached to Zebulun and to the Valley of Jiphthah El, then northward beyond Beth Emek and Neiel, bypassing Cabul *which was* on the left, 28including Ebron,[a] Rehob, Hammon, and Kanah, as far as Greater Sidon. 29And the border turned to Ramah and to the fortified city of Tyre; then the border turned to Hosah, and ended at the sea by the region of Achzib. 30Also Ummah, Aphek, and Rehob *were included:* twenty-two cities with their villages. 31This *was* the inheritance of the tribe of the children of Asher according to their families, these cities with their villages.

The Land of Naphtali

32The sixth lot came out to the children of Naphtali, for the children of Naphtali according to their families. 33And their border began at Heleph, enclosing the territory from the terebinth tree in Zaanannim, Adami Nekeb, and Jabneel, as far as Lakkum; it ended at the Jordan. 34From Heleph the border extended westward to Aznoth Tabor, and went out from there toward Hukkok; it adjoined Zebulun on the south side and Asher on the west side, and ended at Judah by the Jordan toward the sunrise. 35And the fortified cities *are* Ziddim, Zer, Hammath, Rakkath, Chinnereth, 36Adamah, Ramah, Hazor, 37Kedesh, Edrei, En Hazor, 38Iron, Migdal El, Horem, Beth Anath, and Beth Shemesh: nineteen cities with their villages. 39This *was* the inheritance of the tribe of the children of Naphtali according to their families, the cities and their villages.

The Land of Dan

40The seventh lot came out for the tribe of the children of Dan according to their families. 41And the territory of their inheritance was Zorah, Eshtaol, Ir Shemesh, 42Shaalabbin, Aijalon, Jethlah, 43Elon, Timnah, Ekron, 44Eltekeh, Gibbethon, Baalath, 45Jehud, Bene Berak, Gath Rimmon, 46Me Jarkon, and Rakkon, with the region near Joppa. 47And the border of the children of Dan went beyond these, because the children of Dan went up to fight against Leshem and took it; and they struck it with the edge of the sword, took possession of it, and dwelt in it. They called Leshem, Dan, after the name of Dan their father. 48This *is* the inheritance of the tribe of the children of Dan according to their families, these cities with their villages.

Joshua's Inheritance

49When they had made an end of dividing the land as an inheritance

19:28 [a] Following Masoretic Text, Targum, and Vulgate; a few Hebrew manuscripts read *Abdon* (compare 21:30 and 1 Chronicles 6:74).

according to their borders, the children
of Israel gave an inheritance among
them to Joshua the son of Nun. 50Ac-
cording to the word of the LORD they
gave him the city which he asked for,
Timnath Serah in the mountains of
Ephraim; and he built the city and dwelt
in it.
51These *were* the inheritances which
Eleazar the priest, Joshua the son of
Nun, and the heads of the fathers of the
tribes of the children of Israel divided
as an inheritance by lot in Shiloh before
the LORD, at the door of the tabernacle
of meeting. So they made an end of
dividing the country.

The Cities of Refuge

20 The LORD also spoke to Joshua,
saying, 2"Speak to the children
of Israel, saying: 'Appoint for your-
selves cities of refuge, of which I spoke
to you through Moses, 3that the slayer
who kills a person accidentally *or* un-
intentionally may flee there; and they
shall be your refuge from the avenger
of blood. 4And when he flees to one of
those cities, and stands at the entrance
of the gate of the city, and declares his
case in the hearing of the elders of that
city, they shall take him into the city
as one of them, and give him a place,
that he may dwell among them. 5Then
if the avenger of blood pursues him,
they shall not deliver the slayer into
his hand, because he struck his neigh-
bor unintentionally, but did not hate
him beforehand. 6And he shall dwell
in that city until he stands before the
congregation for judgment, *and* until
the death of the one who is high priest in
those days. Then the slayer may return
and come to his own city and his own
house, to the city from which he fled.'"
7So they appointed Kedesh in Gali-
lee, in the mountains of Naphtali, She-
chem in the mountains of Ephraim, and
Kirjath Arba (which *is* Hebron) in the
mountains of Judah. 8And on the other
side of the Jordan, by Jericho eastward,
they assigned Bezer in the wilderness
on the plain, from the tribe of Reuben,
Ramoth in Gilead, from the tribe of Gad,
and Golan in Bashan, from the tribe
of Manasseh. 9These were the cities
appointed for all the children of Israel
and for the stranger who dwelt among
them, that whoever killed a person ac-
cidentally might flee there, and not die
by the hand of the avenger of blood
until he stood before the congregation.

Cities of the Levites

21 Then the heads of the fathers'
houses of the Levites came near
to Eleazar the priest, to Joshua the son
of Nun, and to the heads of the fathers'
houses of the tribes of the children of
Israel. 2And they spoke to them at
Shiloh in the land of Canaan, saying,
"The LORD commanded through Moses
to give us cities to dwell in, with their
common-lands for our livestock." 3So
the children of Israel gave to the Le-
vites from their inheritance, at the com-
mandment of the LORD, these cities and
their common-lands:
4Now the lot came out for the families
of the Kohathites. And the children of
Aaron the priest, *who were* of the Le-
vites, had thirteen cities by lot from the
tribe of Judah, from the tribe of Simeon,
and from the tribe of Benjamin. 5The
rest of the children of Kohath had ten
cities by lot from the families of the
tribe of Ephraim, from the tribe of Dan,
and from the half-tribe of Manasseh.
6And the children of Gershon had thir-
teen cities by lot from the families of the
tribe of Issachar, from the tribe of Asher,
from the tribe of Naphtali, and from
the half-tribe of Manasseh in Bashan.
7The children of Merari according to
their families had twelve cities from the
tribe of Reuben, from the tribe of Gad,
and from the tribe of Zebulun.
8And the children of Israel gave these
cities with their common-lands by lot
to the Levites, as the LORD had com-
manded by the hand of Moses.
9So they gave from the tribe of the
children of Judah and from the tribe
of the children of Simeon these cities
which are designated by name, 10which
were for the children of Aaron, one of
the families of the Kohathites, *who were*
of the children of Levi; for the lot was
theirs first. 11And they gave them Kir-
jath Arba (*Arba was* the father of Anak),
which *is* Hebron, in the mountains of

Judah, with the common-land sur-
rounding it. 12But the fields of the city
and its villages they gave to Caleb the
son of Jephunneh as his possession.

13Thus to the children of Aaron
the priest they gave Hebron with its
common-land (a city of refuge for the
slayer), Libnah with its common-land,
14Jattir with its common-land, Eshtemoa
with its common-land, 15Holon with its
common-land, Debir with its common-
land, 16Ain with its common-land, Jut-
tah with its common-land, and Beth
Shemesh with its common-land: nine
cities from those two tribes; 17and from
the tribe of Benjamin, Gibeon with its
common-land, Geba with its common-
land, 18Anathoth with its common-land,
and Almon with its common-land: four
cities. 19All the cities of the children of
Aaron, the priests, *were* thirteen cities
with their common-lands.

20And the families of the children of
Kohath, the Levites, the rest of the chil-
dren of Kohath, even they had the cities
of their lot from the tribe of Ephraim.
21For they gave them Shechem with
its common-land in the mountains of
Ephraim (a city of refuge for the slayer),
Gezer with its common-land, 22Kibza-
im with its common-land, and Beth
Horon with its common-land: four cit-
ies; 23and from the tribe of Dan, Elte-
keh with its common-land, Gibbethon
with its common-land, 24Aijalon with
its common-land, *and* Gath Rimmon
with its common-land: four cities; 25and
from the half-tribe of Manasseh, Tanach
with its common-land and Gath Rim-
mon with its common-land: two cities.
26All the ten cities with their common-
lands were for the rest of the families
of the children of Kohath.

27Also to the children of Gershon, of
the families of the Levites, from the
other half-tribe of Manasseh, *they gave*
Golan in Bashan with its common-land
(a city of refuge for the slayer), and Be
Eshterah with its common-land: two
cities; 28and from the tribe of Issachar,
Kishion with its common-land, Dabe-
rath with its common-land, 29Jarmuth
with its common-land, *and* En Gannim
with its common-land: four cities; 30and
from the tribe of Asher, Mishal with its
common-land, Abdon with its common-
land, 31Helkath with its common-land,
and Rehob with its common-land: four
cities; 32and from the tribe of Naphtali,
Kedesh in Galilee with its common-land
(a city of refuge for the slayer), Ham-
moth Dor with its common-land, and
Kartan with its common-land: three
cities. 33All the cities of the Gershonites
according to their families *were* thirteen
cities with their common-lands.

34And to the families of the children
of Merari, the rest of the Levites, from
the tribe of Zebulun, Jokneam with its
common-land, Kartah with its common-
land, 35Dimnah with its common-land,
and Nahalal with its common-land: four
cities; 36and from the tribe of Reuben,
Bezer with its common-land, Jahaz with
its common-land, 37Kedemoth with its
common-land, and Mephaath with its
common-land: four cities;[a] 38and from
the tribe of Gad, Ramoth in Gilead with
its common-land (a city of refuge for the
slayer), Mahanaim with its common-
land, 39Heshbon with its common-land,
and Jazer with its common-land: four
cities in all. 40So all the cities for the
children of Merari according to their
families, the rest of the families of the
Levites, were *by* their lot twelve cities.

41All the cities of the Levites within the
possession of the children of Israel *were*
forty-eight cities with their common-
lands. 42Every one of these cities had
its common-land surrounding it; thus
were all these cities.

The Promise Fulfilled

43So the LORD gave to Israel all the
land of which He had sworn to give to
their fathers, and they took possession
of it and dwelt in it. 44The LORD gave
them rest all around, according to all
that He had sworn to their fathers. And
not a man of all their enemies stood
against them; the LORD delivered all
their enemies into their hand. 45Not a
word failed of any good thing which
the LORD had spoken to the house of
Israel. All came to pass.

21:37 [a] Following Septuagint and Vulgate (compare 1 Chronicles 6:78, 79); Masoretic Text, Bomberg, and Targum omit verses 36 and 37.

Eastern Tribes Return to Their Lands

22 Then Joshua called the Reubenites, the Gadites, and half the tribe of Manasseh, 2and said to them: "You have kept all that Moses the servant of the LORD commanded you, and have obeyed my voice in all that I commanded you. 3You have not left your brethren these many days, up to this day, but have kept the charge of the commandment of the LORD your God. 4And now the LORD your God has given rest to your brethren, as He promised them; now therefore, return and go to your tents *and* to the land of your possession, which Moses the servant of the LORD gave you on the other side of the Jordan. 5But take careful heed to do the commandment and the law which Moses the servant of the LORD commanded you, to love the LORD your God, to walk in all His ways, to keep His commandments, to hold fast to Him, and to serve Him with all your heart and with all your soul." 6So Joshua blessed them and sent them away, and they went to their tents.

7Now to half the tribe of Manasseh Moses had given a possession in Bashan, but to the *other* half of it Joshua gave *a possession* among their brethren on this side of the Jordan, westward. And indeed, when Joshua sent them away to their tents, he blessed them, 8and spoke to them, saying, "Return with much riches to your tents, with very much livestock, with silver, with gold, with bronze, with iron, and with very much clothing. Divide the spoil of your enemies with your brethren."

9So the children of Reuben, the children of Gad, and half the tribe of Manasseh returned, and departed from the children of Israel at Shiloh, which *is* in the land of Canaan, to go to the country of Gilead, to the land of their possession, which they had obtained according to the word of the LORD by the hand of Moses.

An Altar by the Jordan

10And when they came to the region of the Jordan which *is* in the land of Canaan, the children of Reuben, the children of Gad, and half the tribe of Manasseh built an altar there by the Jordan—a great, impressive altar. 11Now the children of Israel heard *someone* say, "Behold, the children of Reuben, the children of Gad, and half the tribe of Manasseh have built an altar on the frontier of the land of Canaan, in the region of the Jordan—on the children of Israel's side." 12And when the children of Israel heard *of it,* the whole congregation of the children of Israel gathered together at Shiloh to go to war against them.

13Then the children of Israel sent Phinehas the son of Eleazar the priest to the children of Reuben, to the children of Gad, and to half the tribe of Manasseh, into the land of Gilead, 14and with him ten rulers, one ruler each from the chief house of every tribe of Israel; and each one *was* the head of the house of his father among the divisions[a] of Israel. 15Then they came to the children of Reuben, to the children of Gad, and to half the tribe of Manasseh, to the land of Gilead, and they spoke with them, saying, 16"Thus says the whole congregation of the LORD: 'What treachery *is* this that you have committed against the God of Israel, to turn away this day from following the LORD, in that you have built for yourselves an altar, that you might rebel this day against the LORD? 17*Is* the iniquity of Peor not enough for us, from which we are not cleansed till this day, although there was a plague in the congregation of the LORD, 18but that you must turn away this day from following the LORD? And it shall be, if you rebel today against the LORD, that tomorrow He will be angry with the whole congregation of Israel. 19Nevertheless, if the land of your possession *is* unclean, *then* cross over to the land of the possession of the LORD, where the LORD's tabernacle stands, and take possession among us; but do not rebel against the LORD, nor rebel against us, by building yourselves an altar besides the altar of the LORD our God. 20Did not Achan the son of Zerah commit a trespass in the accursed thing, and wrath

22:14 [a] Literally *thousands*

fell on all the congregation of Israel? And that man did not perish alone in his iniquity.' "

21Then the children of Reuben, the children of Gad, and half the tribe of Manasseh answered and said to the heads of the divisions[a] of Israel: 22"The LORD God of gods, the LORD God of gods, He knows, and let Israel itself know—if *it is* in rebellion, or if in treachery against the LORD, do not save us this day. 23If we have built ourselves an altar to turn from following the LORD, or if to offer on it burnt offerings or grain offerings, or if to offer peace offerings on it, let the LORD Himself require *an account.* 24But in fact we have done it for fear, for a reason, saying, 'In time to come your descendants may speak to our descendants, saying, "What have you to do with the LORD God of Israel? 25For the LORD has made the Jordan a border between you and us, *you* children of Reuben and children of Gad. You have no part in the LORD." So your descendants would make our descendants cease fearing the LORD.' 26Therefore we said, 'Let us now prepare to build ourselves an altar, not for burnt offering nor for sacrifice, 27but *that* it *may be* a witness between you and us and our generations after us, that we may perform the service of the LORD before Him with our burnt offerings, with our sacrifices, and with our peace offerings; that your descendants may not say to our descendants in time to come, "You have no part in the LORD." ' 28Therefore we said that it will be, when they say *this* to us or to our generations in time to come, that we may say, 'Here is the replica of the altar of the LORD which our fathers made, though not for burnt offerings nor for sacrifices; but it *is* a witness between you and us.' 29Far be it from us that we should rebel against the LORD, and turn from following the LORD this day, to build an altar for burnt offerings, for grain offerings, or for sacrifices, besides the altar of the LORD our God which *is* before His tabernacle."

30Now when Phinehas the priest and the rulers of the congregation, the heads of the divisions[a] of Israel who *were* with him, heard the words that the children of Reuben, the children of Gad, and the children of Manasseh spoke, it pleased them. 31Then Phinehas the son of Eleazar the priest said to the children of Reuben, the children of Gad, and the children of Manasseh, "This day we perceive that the LORD *is* among us, because you have not committed this treachery against the LORD. Now you have delivered the children of Israel out of the hand of the LORD."

32And Phinehas the son of Eleazar the priest, and the rulers, returned from the children of Reuben and the children of Gad, from the land of Gilead to the land of Canaan, to the children of Israel, and brought back word to them. 33So the thing pleased the children of Israel, and the children of Israel blessed God; they spoke no more of going against them in battle, to destroy the land where the children of Reuben and Gad dwelt.

34The children of Reuben and the children of Gad[a] called the altar, *Witness,* "For *it is* a witness between us that the LORD *is* God."

Joshua's Farewell Address

23 Now it came to pass, a long time after the LORD had given rest to Israel from all their enemies round about, that Joshua was old, advanced in age. 2And Joshua called for all Israel, for their elders, for their heads, for their judges, and for their officers, and said to them:

"I am old, advanced in age. 3You have seen all that the LORD your God has done to all these nations because of you, for the LORD your God *is* He who has fought for you. 4See, I have divided to you by lot these nations that remain, to be an inheritance for your tribes, from the Jordan, with all the nations that I have cut off, as far as the Great Sea westward. 5And the LORD your God will expel them from before you and drive them out of your sight. So you shall possess their land, as the LORD your God promised you. 6Therefore be very courageous to keep and to do all

22:21 [a] Literally *thousands* **22:30** [a] Literally *thousands* **22:34** [a] Septuagint adds *and half the tribe of Manasseh.*

that is written in the Book of the Law
of Moses, lest you turn aside from it to
the right hand or to the left, 7and lest
you go among these nations, these who
remain among you. You shall not make
mention of the name of their gods, nor
cause *anyone* to swear *by them;* you
shall not serve them nor bow down to
them, 8but you shall hold fast to the
LORD your God, as you have done to this
day. 9For the LORD has driven out from
before you great and strong nations;
but *as for* you, no one has been able to
stand against you to this day. 10One
man of you shall chase a thousand, for
the LORD your God *is* He who fights for
you, as He promised you. 11Therefore
take careful heed to yourselves, that
you love the LORD your God. 12Or else,
if indeed you do go back, and cling to
the remnant of these nations—these
that remain among you—and make
marriages with them, and go in to them
and they to you, 13know for certain that
the LORD your God will no longer drive
out these nations from before you. But
they shall be snares and traps to you,
and scourges on your sides and thorns
in your eyes, until you perish from this
good land which the LORD your God
has given you.

14"Behold, this day I *am* going the
way of all the earth. And you know in
all your hearts and in all your souls
that not one thing has failed of all the
good things which the LORD your God
spoke concerning you. All have come to
pass for you; not one word of them has
failed. 15Therefore it shall come to pass,
that as all the good things have come
upon you which the LORD your God
promised you, so the LORD will bring
upon you all harmful things, until He
has destroyed you from this good land
which the LORD your God has given
you. 16When you have transgressed the
covenant of the LORD your God, which
He commanded you, and have gone
and served other gods, and bowed down
to them, then the anger of the LORD will
burn against you, and you shall perish
quickly from the good land which He
has given you."

The Covenant at Shechem

24 Then Joshua gathered all the
tribes of Israel to Shechem and
called for the elders of Israel, for their
heads, for their judges, and for their
officers; and they presented themselves
before God. 2And Joshua said to all the
people, "Thus says the LORD God of Is-
rael: 'Your fathers, *including* Terah, the
father of Abraham and the father of
Nahor, dwelt on the other side of the Riv-
er[a] in old times; and they served other
gods. 3Then I took your father Abraham
from the other side of the River, led him
throughout all the land of Canaan, and
multiplied his descendants and gave
him Isaac. 4To Isaac I gave Jacob and
Esau. To Esau I gave the mountains of
Seir to possess, but Jacob and his chil-
dren went down to Egypt. 5Also I sent
Moses and Aaron, and I plagued Egypt,
according to what I did among them.
Afterward I brought you out.

6'Then I brought your fathers out of
Egypt, and you came to the sea; and
the Egyptians pursued your fathers
with chariots and horsemen to the Red
Sea. 7So they cried out to the LORD; and
He put darkness between you and the
Egyptians, brought the sea upon them,
and covered them. And your eyes saw
what I did in Egypt. Then you dwelt
in the wilderness a long time. 8And I
brought you into the land of the Am-
orites, who dwelt on the other side of
the Jordan, and they fought with you.
But I gave them into your hand, that
you might possess their land, and I
destroyed them from before you. 9Then
Balak the son of Zippor, king of Moab,
arose to make war against Israel, and
sent and called Balaam the son of Beor
to curse you. 10But I would not listen
to Balaam; therefore he continued to
bless you. So I delivered you out of his
hand. 11Then you went over the Jordan
and came to Jericho. And the men of
Jericho fought against you—*also* the
Amorites, the Perizzites, the Canaanites,
the Hittites, the Girgashites, the Hivites,
and the Jebusites. But I delivered them
into your hand. 12I sent the hornet be-
fore you which drove them out from

24:2 [a] Hebrew *Nahar,* the Euphrates, and so in verses 3, 14, and 15

before you, *also* the two kings of the
Amorites, *but* not with your sword or
with your bow. 13I have given you a land
for which you did not labor, and cities
which you did not build, and you dwell
in them; you eat of the vineyards and
olive groves which you did not plant.'

14"Now therefore, fear the LORD, serve
Him in sincerity and in truth, and put
away the gods which your fathers
served on the other side of the River
and in Egypt. Serve the LORD! 15And if
it seems evil to you to serve the LORD,
choose for yourselves this day whom
you will serve, whether the gods which
your fathers served that *were* on the
other side of the River, or the gods of
the Amorites, in whose land you dwell.
But as for me and my house, we will
serve the LORD."

16So the people answered and said:
"Far be it from us that we should for-
sake the LORD to serve other gods; 17for
the LORD our God *is* He who brought
us and our fathers up out of the land
of Egypt, from the house of bondage,
who did those great signs in our sight,
and preserved us in all the way that we
went and among all the people through
whom we passed. 18And the LORD drove
out from before us all the people, in-
cluding the Amorites who dwelt in the
land. We also will serve the LORD, for
He *is* our God."

19But Joshua said to the people, "You
cannot serve the LORD, for He *is* a holy
God. He *is* a jealous God; He will not
forgive your transgressions nor your
sins. 20If you forsake the LORD and
serve foreign gods, then He will turn
and do you harm and consume you,
after He has done you good."

21And the people said to Joshua, "No,
but we will serve the LORD!"

22So Joshua said to the people, "You
are witnesses against yourselves that
you have chosen the LORD for your-
selves, to serve Him."

And they said, "*We are* witnesses!"

23"Now therefore," *he said,* "put away
the foreign gods which *are* among you,
and incline your heart to the LORD God
of Israel."

24And the people said to Joshua, "The
LORD our God we will serve, and His
voice we will obey!"

25So Joshua made a covenant with the
people that day, and made for them a
statute and an ordinance in Shechem.

26Then Joshua wrote these words in
the Book of the Law of God. And he took
a large stone, and set it up there under
the oak that *was* by the sanctuary of
the LORD. 27And Joshua said to all the
people, "Behold, this stone shall be a
witness to us, for it has heard all the
words of the LORD which He spoke to
us. It shall therefore be a witness to you,
lest you deny your God." 28So Joshua
let the people depart, each to his own
inheritance.

Death of Joshua and Eleazar

29Now it came to pass after these
things that Joshua the son of Nun, the
servant of the LORD, died, *being* one
hundred and ten years old. 30And they
buried him within the border of his in-
heritance at Timnath Serah, which *is*
in the mountains of Ephraim, on the
north side of Mount Gaash.

31Israel served the LORD all the days
of Joshua, and all the days of the elders
who outlived Joshua, who had known
all the works of the LORD which He had
done for Israel.

32The bones of Joseph, which the chil-
dren of Israel had brought up out of
Egypt, they buried at Shechem, in the
plot of ground which Jacob had bought
from the sons of Hamor the father of
Shechem for one hundred pieces of
silver, and which had become an inher-
itance of the children of Joseph.

33And Eleazar the son of Aaron died.
They buried him in a hill *belonging to*
Phinehas his son, which was given to
him in the mountains of Ephraim.

THE BOOK OF
JUDGES

The Book of Judges is quite different from the Book of Joshua that comes right before it. In Joshua, God's people are mostly obedient and experience victory after victory over their enemies to conquer the Promised Land. They are not perfect, of course, but they trust in God for the most part. In Judges, though, the people living in the Promised Land are disobedient and experience defeat after defeat by their enemies. Each time, the Israelites cry out to God for help, and He answers by sending a leader called a judge to rescue and lead them. After each judge dies the people disobey God once again, though, and the pattern repeats itself.

- **GENRE:** History
- **AUTHOR:** Samuel, possibly
- **TIME:** c. 1380–1045 BC (written c. 1040–1020 BC)
- **PURPOSE:** To tell about how God's people continued to disobey Him for over 300 years after Joshua's death. God disciplined His people for their own good, but He also continued to love them, forgive them, and rescue them.

The Continuing Conquest of Canaan

1 Now after the death of Joshua it
came to pass that the children of
Israel asked the LORD, saying, "Who
shall be first to go up for us against
the Canaanites to fight against them?"
2And the LORD said, "Judah shall go
up. Indeed I have delivered the land
into his hand."
3So Judah said to Simeon his brother,
"Come up with me to my allotted terri-
tory, that we may fight against the Ca-
naanites; and I will likewise go with you
to your allotted territory." And Simeon
went with him. 4Then Judah went up, and
the LORD delivered the Canaanites and
the Perizzites into their hand; and they
killed ten thousand men at Bezek. 5And
they found Adoni-Bezek in Bezek, and
fought against him; and they defeated
the Canaanites and the Perizzites. 6Then
Adoni-Bezek fled, and they pursued him
and caught him and cut off his thumbs
and big toes. 7And Adoni-Bezek said,
"Seventy kings with their thumbs and
big toes cut off used to gather *scraps*
under my table; as I have done, so God
has repaid me." Then they brought him
to Jerusalem, and there he died.
8Now the children of Judah fought
against Jerusalem and took it; they
struck it with the edge of the sword and
set the city on fire. 9And afterward the
children of Judah went down to fight
against the Canaanites who dwelt in
the mountains, in the South,[a] and in the
lowland. 10Then Judah went against
the Canaanites who dwelt in Hebron.
(Now the name of Hebron *was* formerly
Kirjath Arba.) And they killed Sheshai,
Ahiman, and Talmai.
11From there they went against the
inhabitants of Debir. (The name of Debir
was formerly Kirjath Sepher.)
12Then Caleb said, "Whoever attacks
Kirjath Sepher and takes it, to him I
will give my daughter Achsah as wife."
13And Othniel the son of Kenaz, Caleb's
younger brother, took it; so he gave him
his daughter Achsah as wife. 14Now it
happened, when she came *to him,* that
she urged him[a] to ask her father for
a field. And she dismounted from *her*
donkey, and Caleb said to her, "What do
you wish?" 15So she said to him, "Give
me a blessing; since you have given me
land in the South, give me also springs
of water."
And Caleb gave her the upper springs
and the lower springs.

1:9 [a] Hebrew *Negev,* and so throughout this book
1:14 [a] Septuagint and Vulgate read *he urged her.*

16Now the children of the Kenite, Mo-
ses' father-in-law, went up from the City
of Palms with the children of Judah into
the Wilderness of Judah, which *lies* in
the South *near* Arad; and they went and
dwelt among the people. 17And Judah
went with his brother Simeon, and they
attacked the Canaanites who inhabited
Zephath, and utterly destroyed it. So
the name of the city was called Hor-
mah. 18Also Judah took Gaza with its
territory, Ashkelon with its territory,
and Ekron with its territory. 19So the
LORD was with Judah. And they drove
out the mountaineers, but they could
not drive out the inhabitants of the low-
land, because they had chariots of iron.
20And they gave Hebron to Caleb, as
Moses had said. Then he expelled from
there the three sons of Anak. 21But the
children of Benjamin did not drive out
the Jebusites who inhabited Jerusalem;
so the Jebusites dwell with the children
of Benjamin in Jerusalem to this day.

22And the house of Joseph also went
up against Bethel, and the LORD *was*
with them. 23So the house of Joseph sent
men to spy out Bethel. (The name of the
city *was* formerly Luz.) 24And when the
spies saw a man coming out of the city,
they said to him, "Please show us the
entrance to the city, and we will show
you mercy." 25So he showed them the
entrance to the city, and they struck
the city with the edge of the sword; but
they let the man and all his family go.
26And the man went to the land of the
Hittites, built a city, and called its name
Luz, which *is* its name to this day.

Incomplete Conquest of the Land

27However, Manasseh did not drive
out *the inhabitants of* Beth Shean and its
villages, or Taanach and its villages, or
the inhabitants of Dor and its villages,
or the inhabitants of Ibleam and its
villages, or the inhabitants of Megid-
do and its villages; for the Canaanites
were determined to dwell in that land.
28And it came to pass, when Israel was
strong, that they put the Canaanites
under tribute, but did not completely
drive them out.

29Nor did Ephraim drive out the Ca-
naanites who dwelt in Gezer; so the Ca-
naanites dwelt in Gezer among them.

30Nor did Zebulun drive out the inhab-
itants of Kitron or the inhabitants of Na-
halol; so the Canaanites dwelt among
them, and were put under tribute.

31Nor did Asher drive out the inhab-
itants of Acco or the inhabitants of Sidon,
or of Ahlab, Achzib, Helbah, Aphik, or
Rehob. 32So the Asherites dwelt among
the Canaanites, the inhabitants of the
land; for they did not drive them out.

33Nor did Naphtali drive out the inhab-
itants of Beth Shemesh or the inhab-
itants of Beth Anath; but they dwelt
among the Canaanites, the inhabitants
of the land. Nevertheless the inhab-
itants of Beth Shemesh and Beth Anath
were put under tribute to them.

34And the Amorites forced the children
of Dan into the mountains, for they
would not allow them to come down
to the valley; 35and the Amorites were
determined to dwell in Mount Heres, in
Aijalon, and in Shaalbim;[a] yet when the
strength of the house of Joseph became
greater, they were put under tribute.

36Now the boundary of the Amorites
was from the Ascent of Akrabbim, from
Sela, and upward.

Israel's Disobedience

2 Then the Angel of the LORD came
up from Gilgal to Bochim, and said:
"I led you up from Egypt and brought
you to the land of which I swore to your
fathers; and I said, 'I will never break
My covenant with you. 2And you shall
make no covenant with the inhabitants
of this land; you shall tear down their
altars.' But you have not obeyed My
voice. Why have you done this? 3There-
fore I also said, 'I will not drive them
out before you; but they shall be *thorns*
in your side,[a] and their gods shall be
a snare to you.' " 4So it was, when the
Angel of the LORD spoke these words to
all the children of Israel, that the people
lifted up their voices and wept.

5Then they called the name of that
place Bochim;[a] and they sacrificed
there to the LORD. 6And when Joshua

1:35 [a] Spelled *Shaalabbin* in Joshua 19:42 2:3 [a] Septuagint, Targum, and Vulgate read *enemies to you.* 2:5 [a] Literally *Weeping*

had dismissed the people, the children of Israel went each to his own inheritance to possess the land.

Death of Joshua

7So the people served the LORD all the days of Joshua, and all the days of the elders who outlived Joshua, who had seen all the great works of the LORD which He had done for Israel. 8Now Joshua the son of Nun, the servant of the LORD, died *when he was* one hundred and ten years old. 9And they buried him within the border of his inheritance at Timnath Heres, in the mountains of Ephraim, on the north side of Mount Gaash. 10When all that generation had been gathered to their fathers, another generation arose after them who did not know the LORD nor the work which He had done for Israel.

Israel's Unfaithfulness

11Then the children of Israel did evil in the sight of the LORD, and served the Baals; 12and they forsook the LORD God of their fathers, who had brought them out of the land of Egypt; and they followed other gods from *among* the gods of the people who *were* all around them, and they bowed down to them; and they provoked the LORD to anger. 13They forsook the LORD and served Baal and the Ashtoreths.[a] 14And the anger of the LORD was hot against Israel. So He delivered them into the hands of plunderers who despoiled them; and He sold them into the hands of their enemies all around, so that they could no longer stand before their enemies. 15Wherever they went out, the hand of the LORD was against them for calamity, as the LORD had said, and as the LORD had sworn to them. And they were greatly distressed.

16Nevertheless, the LORD raised up judges who delivered them out of the hand of those who plundered them. 17Yet they would not listen to their judges, but they played the harlot with other gods, and bowed down to them. They turned quickly from the way in which their fathers walked, in obeying the commandments of the LORD; they did not do so. 18And when the LORD raised up judges for them, the LORD was with the judge and delivered them out of the hand of their enemies all the days of the judge; for the LORD was moved to pity by their groaning because of those who oppressed them and harassed them. 19And it came to pass, when the judge was dead, that they reverted and behaved more corruptly than their fathers, by following other gods, to serve them and bow down to them. They did not cease from their own doings nor from their stubborn way.

20Then the anger of the LORD was hot against Israel; and He said, "Because this nation has transgressed My covenant which I commanded their fathers, and has not heeded My voice, 21I also will no longer drive out before them any of the nations which Joshua left when he died, 22so that through them I may test Israel, whether they will keep the ways of the LORD, to walk in them as their fathers kept *them*, or not." 23Therefore the LORD left those nations, without driving them out immediately; nor did He deliver them into the hand of Joshua.

The Nations Remaining in the Land

3 Now these *are* the nations which the LORD left, that He might test Israel by them, *that is,* all who had not known any of the wars in Canaan 2(*this was* only so that the generations of the children of Israel might be taught to know war, at least those who had not formerly known it), 3*namely,* five lords of the Philistines, all the Canaanites, the Sidonians, and the Hivites who dwelt in Mount Lebanon, from Mount Baal Hermon to the entrance of Hamath. 4And they were *left, that He might* test Israel by them, to know whether they would obey the commandments of the LORD, which He had commanded their fathers by the hand of Moses.

5Thus the children of Israel dwelt among the Canaanites, the Hittites, the Amorites, the Perizzites, the Hivites, and the Jebusites. 6And they took their daughters to be their wives, and gave their daughters to their sons; and they served their gods.

2:13 [a] Canaanite goddesses

Othniel

7So the children of Israel did evil in
the sight of the LORD. They forgot the
LORD their God, and served the Baals
and Asherahs.[a] 8Therefore the anger of
the LORD was hot against Israel, and He
sold them into the hand of Cushan-Rish-
athaim king of Mesopotamia; and the
children of Israel served Cushan-Risha-
thaim eight years. 9When the children
of Israel cried out to the LORD, the LORD
raised up a deliverer for the children of
Israel, who delivered them: Othniel the
son of Kenaz, Caleb's younger brother.
10The Spirit of the LORD came upon
him, and he judged Israel. He went out
to war, and the LORD delivered Cushan-
Rishathaim king of Mesopotamia into
his hand; and his hand prevailed over
Cushan-Rishathaim. 11So the land had
rest for forty years. Then Othniel the
son of Kenaz died.

Ehud

12And the children of Israel again
did evil in the sight of the LORD. So
the LORD strengthened Eglon king
of Moab against Israel, because they
had done evil in the sight of the LORD.
13Then he gathered to himself the peo-
ple of Ammon and Amalek, went and
defeated Israel, and took possession
of the City of Palms. 14So the children
of Israel served Eglon king of Moab
eighteen years.

15But when the children of Israel
cried out to the LORD, the LORD raised
up a deliverer for them: Ehud the son
of Gera, the Benjamite, a left-handed
man. By him the children of Israel sent
tribute to Eglon king of Moab. 16Now
Ehud made himself a dagger (it was
double-edged and a cubit in length)
and fastened it under his clothes on his
right thigh. 17So he brought the tribute
to Eglon king of Moab. (Now Eglon *was*
a very fat man.) 18And when he had
finished presenting the tribute, he sent
away the people who had carried the
tribute. 19But he himself turned back
from the stone images that *were* at Gil-
gal, and said, "I have a secret message
for you, O king."
He said, "Keep silence!" And all who
attended him went out from him.

20So Ehud came to him (now he was
sitting upstairs in his cool private
chamber). Then Ehud said, "I have a
message from God for you." So he arose
from *his* seat. 21Then Ehud reached with
his left hand, took the dagger from his
right thigh, and thrust it into his belly.
22Even the hilt went in after the blade,
and the fat closed over the blade, for
he did not draw the dagger out of his
belly; and his entrails came out. 23Then
Ehud went out through the porch and
shut the doors of the upper room behind
him and locked them.

24When he had gone out, *Eglon's*[a]
servants came to look, and *to their*
surprise, the doors of the upper room
were locked. So they said, "He is prob-
ably attending to his needs in the cool
chamber." 25So they waited till they
were embarrassed, and still he had not
opened the doors of the upper room.
Therefore they took the key and opened
them. And there was their master, fallen
dead on the floor.

26But Ehud had escaped while they
delayed, and passed beyond the stone
images and escaped to Seirah. 27And
it happened, when he arrived, that he
blew the trumpet in the mountains of
Ephraim, and the children of Israel
went down with him from the moun-
tains; and he led them. 28Then he said
to them, "Follow *me,* for the LORD has
delivered your enemies the Moabites
into your hand." So they went down
after him, seized the fords of the Jor-
dan leading to Moab, and did not allow
anyone to cross over. 29And at that
time they killed about ten thousand
men of Moab, all stout men of valor;
not a man escaped. 30So Moab was
subdued that day under the hand of
Israel. And the land had rest for eighty
years.

Shamgar

31After him was Shamgar the son of
Anath, who killed six hundred men of
the Philistines with an ox goad; and he
also delivered Israel.

3:7 [a] Name or symbol for Canaanite goddesses

3:24 [a] Literally *his*

Deborah

4 When Ehud was dead, the children
of Israel again did evil in the sight
of the LORD. 2So the LORD sold them
into the hand of Jabin king of Canaan,
who reigned in Hazor. The commander
of his army *was* Sisera, who dwelt in
Harosheth Hagoyim. 3And the children
of Israel cried out to the LORD; for Jabin
had nine hundred chariots of iron, and
for twenty years he had harshly op-
pressed the children of Israel.
4Now Deborah, a prophetess, the wife
of Lapidoth, was judging Israel at that
time. 5And she would sit under the palm
tree of Deborah between Ramah and
Bethel in the mountains of Ephraim.
And the children of Israel came up to
her for judgment. 6Then she sent and
called for Barak the son of Abinoam
from Kedesh in Naphtali, and said to
him, "Has not the LORD God of Israel
commanded, 'Go and deploy *troops* at
Mount Tabor; take with you ten thou-
sand men of the sons of Naphtali and of
the sons of Zebulun; 7and against you
I will deploy Sisera, the commander of
Jabin's army, with his chariots and his
multitude at the River Kishon; and I will
deliver him into your hand'?"
8And Barak said to her, "If you will go
with me, then I will go; but if you will
not go with me, I will not go!"
9So she said, "I will surely go with you;
nevertheless there will be no glory for
you in the journey you are taking, for
the LORD will sell Sisera into the hand
of a woman." Then Deborah arose and
went with Barak to Kedesh. 10And Barak
called Zebulun and Naphtali to Kedesh;
he went up with ten thousand men un-
der his command,[a] and Deborah went
up with him.
11Now Heber the Kenite, of the children
of Hobab the father-in-law of Moses,
had separated himself from the Kenites
and pitched his tent near the terebinth
tree at Zaanaim, which *is* beside Kedesh.
12And they reported to Sisera that
Barak the son of Abinoam had gone
up to Mount Tabor. 13So Sisera gathered
together all his chariots, nine hundred
chariots of iron, and all the people who
were with him, from Harosheth Hagoy-
im to the River Kishon.
14Then Deborah said to Barak, "Up! For
this *is* the day in which the LORD has
delivered Sisera into your hand. Has
not the LORD gone out before you?" So
Barak went down from Mount Tabor
with ten thousand men following him.
15And the LORD routed Sisera and all
his chariots and all *his* army with the
edge of the sword before Barak; and
Sisera alighted from *his* chariot and
fled away on foot. 16But Barak pursued
the chariots and the army as far as Ha-
rosheth Hagoyim, and all the army of
Sisera fell by the edge of the sword; not
a man was left.
17However, Sisera had fled away on
foot to the tent of Jael, the wife of Heber
the Kenite; for *there was* peace between
Jabin king of Hazor and the house of
Heber the Kenite. 18And Jael went out
to meet Sisera, and said to him, "Turn
aside, my lord, turn aside to me; do not
fear." And when he had turned aside
with her into the tent, she covered him
with a blanket.
19Then he said to her, "Please give me
a little water to drink, for I am thirsty."
So she opened a jug of milk, gave him a
drink, and covered him. 20And he said
to her, "Stand at the door of the tent,
and if any man comes and inquires of
you, and says, 'Is there any man here?'
you shall say, 'No.' "
21Then Jael, Heber's wife, took a tent
peg and took a hammer in her hand,
and went softly to him and drove the
peg into his temple, and it went down
into the ground; for he was fast asleep
and weary. So he died. 22And then, as
Barak pursued Sisera, Jael came out to
meet him, and said to him, "Come, I will
show you the man whom you seek." And
when he went into her *tent,* there lay
Sisera, dead with the peg in his temple.
23So on that day God subdued Jabin
king of Canaan in the presence of the
children of Israel. 24And the hand of
the children of Israel grew stronger and
stronger against Jabin king of Canaan,
until they had destroyed Jabin king of
Canaan.

4:10 [a] Literally *at his feet*

The Song of Deborah

5 Then Deborah and Barak the son of Abinoam sang on that day, saying:

2 "When leaders lead in Israel,
When the people willingly offer themselves,
Bless the LORD!

3 "Hear, O kings! Give ear, O princes!
I, *even* I, will sing to the LORD;
I will sing praise to the LORD God of Israel.

4 "LORD, when You went out from Seir,
When You marched from the field of Edom,
The earth trembled and the heavens poured,
The clouds also poured water;
5 The mountains gushed before the LORD,
This Sinai, before the LORD God of Israel.

6 "In the days of Shamgar, son of Anath,
In the days of Jael,
The highways were deserted,
And the travelers walked along the byways.
7 Village life ceased, it ceased in Israel,
Until I, Deborah, arose,
Arose a mother in Israel.
8 They chose new gods;
Then *there was* war in the gates;
Not a shield or spear was seen among forty thousand in Israel.
9 My heart *is* with the rulers of Israel
Who offered themselves willingly with the people.
Bless the LORD!

10 "Speak, you who ride on white donkeys,
Who sit in judges' attire,
And who walk along the road.
11 Far from the noise of the archers, among the watering places,
There they shall recount the righteous acts of the LORD,
The righteous acts *for* His villagers in Israel;
Then the people of the LORD shall go down to the gates.

12 "Awake, awake, Deborah!
Awake, awake, sing a song!
Arise, Barak, and lead your captives away,
O son of Abinoam!

13 "Then the survivors came down, the people against the nobles;
The LORD came down for me against the mighty.
14 From Ephraim *were* those whose roots were in Amalek.
After you, Benjamin, with your peoples,
From Machir rulers came down,
And from Zebulun those who bear the recruiter's staff.
15 And the princes of Issachar[a] *were* with Deborah;
As Issachar, so *was* Barak
Sent into the valley under his command;[b]
Among the divisions of Reuben
There were great resolves of heart.
16 Why did you sit among the sheepfolds,
To hear the pipings for the flocks?
The divisions of Reuben have great searchings of heart.
17 Gilead stayed beyond the Jordan,
And why did Dan remain on ships?[a]
Asher continued at the seashore,
And stayed by his inlets.
18 Zebulun *is* a people *who* jeopardized their lives to the point of death,
Naphtali also, on the heights of the battlefield.

19 "The kings came *and* fought,
Then the kings of Canaan fought
In Taanach, by the waters of Megiddo;
They took no spoils of silver.
20 They fought from the heavens;

5:15 [a] Following Septuagint, Syriac, Targum, and Vulgate; Masoretic Text reads *And my princes in Issachar.* [b] Literally *at his feet* 5:17 [a] Or *at ease*

The stars from their courses
fought against Sisera.
21 The torrent of Kishon swept them
away,
That ancient torrent, the torrent
of Kishon.
O my soul, march on in strength!
22 Then the horses' hooves pounded,
The galloping, galloping of his
steeds.
23 'Curse Meroz,' said the angel[a] of the
LORD,
'Curse its inhabitants bitterly,
Because they did not come to the
help of the LORD,
To the help of the LORD against
the mighty.'

24 "Most blessed among women is
Jael,
The wife of Heber the Kenite;
Blessed is she among women in
tents.
25 He asked for water, she gave
milk;
She brought out cream in a lordly
bowl.
26 She stretched her hand to the tent
peg,
Her right hand to the workmen's
hammer;
She pounded Sisera, she pierced
his head,
She split and struck through his
temple.
27 At her feet he sank, he fell, he lay
still;
At her feet he sank, he fell;
Where he sank, there he fell dead.

28 "The mother of Sisera looked
through the window,
And cried out through the lattice,
'Why is his chariot *so* long in
coming?
Why tarries the clatter of his
chariots?'
29 Her wisest ladies answered her,
Yes, she answered herself,
30 'Are they not finding and dividing
the spoil:
To every man a girl *or* two;
For Sisera, plunder of dyed
garments,
Plunder of garments embroidered
and dyed,
Two pieces of dyed embroidery
for the neck of the looter?'

31 "Thus let all Your enemies perish,
O LORD!
But *let* those who love Him *be* like
the sun
When it comes out in full strength."

So the land had rest for forty years.

Midianites Oppress Israel

6 Then the children of Israel did evil
in the sight of the LORD. So the LORD
delivered them into the hand of Midian
for seven years, 2and the hand of Mid-
ian prevailed against Israel. Because
of the Midianites, the children of Isra-
el made for themselves the dens, the
caves, and the strongholds which *are*
in the mountains. 3So it was, whenever
Israel had sown, Midianites would come
up; also Amalekites and the people of
the East would come up against them.
4Then they would encamp against them
and destroy the produce of the earth as
far as Gaza, and leave no sustenance for
Israel, neither sheep nor ox nor don-
key. 5For they would come up with their
livestock and their tents, coming in as
numerous as locusts; both they and
their camels were without number; and
they would enter the land to destroy it.
6So Israel was greatly impoverished
because of the Midianites, and the chil-
dren of Israel cried out to the LORD.
7And it came to pass, when the children
of Israel cried out to the LORD because
of the Midianites, 8that the LORD sent
a prophet to the children of Israel, who
said to them, "Thus says the LORD God
of Israel: 'I brought you up from Egypt
and brought you out of the house of
bondage; 9and I delivered you out of
the hand of the Egyptians and out
of the hand of all who oppressed you,
and drove them out before you and gave
you their land. 10Also I said to you, "I
am the LORD your God; do not fear the
gods of the Amorites, in whose land
you dwell." But you have not obeyed
My voice.' "

5:23 [a] Or *Angel*

Gideon

11Now the Angel of the LORD came and sat under the terebinth tree which *was* in Ophrah, which *belonged* to Joash the Abiezrite, while his son Gideon threshed wheat in the winepress, in order to hide *it* from the Midianites. 12And the Angel of the LORD appeared to him, and said to him, "The LORD *is* with you, you mighty man of valor!"

13Gideon said to Him, "O my lord,[a] if the LORD is with us, why then has all this happened to us? And where *are* all His miracles which our fathers told us about, saying, 'Did not the LORD bring us up from Egypt?' But now the LORD has forsaken us and delivered us into the hands of the Midianites."

14Then the LORD turned to him and said, "Go in this might of yours, and you shall save Israel from the hand of the Midianites. Have I not sent you?"

15So he said to Him, "O my Lord,[a] how can I save Israel? Indeed my clan *is* the weakest in Manasseh, and I *am* the least in my father's house."

16And the LORD said to him, "Surely I will be with you, and you shall defeat the Midianites as one man."

17Then he said to Him, "If now I have found favor in Your sight, then show me a sign that it is You who talk with me. 18Do not depart from here, I pray, until I come to You and bring out my offering and set *it* before You."

And He said, "I will wait until you come back."

19So Gideon went in and prepared a young goat, and unleavened bread from an ephah of flour. The meat he put in a basket, and he put the broth in a pot; and he brought *them* out to Him under the terebinth tree and presented *them*. 20The Angel of God said to him, "Take the meat and the unleavened bread and lay *them* on this rock, and pour out the broth." And he did so.

21Then the Angel of the LORD put out the end of the staff that *was* in His hand, and touched the meat and the unleavened bread; and fire rose out of the rock and consumed the meat and the unleavened bread. And the Angel of the LORD departed out of his sight.

22Now Gideon perceived that He *was* the Angel of the LORD. So Gideon said, "Alas, O Lord GOD! For I have seen the Angel of the LORD face to face."

23Then the LORD said to him, "Peace *be* with you; do not fear, you shall not die." 24So Gideon built an altar there to the LORD, and called it The-LORD-*Is*-Peace.[a] To this day it *is* still in Ophrah of the Abiezrites.

25Now it came to pass the same night that the LORD said to him, "Take your father's young bull, the second bull of seven years old, and tear down the altar of Baal that your father has, and cut down the wooden image[a] that *is* beside it; 26and build an altar to the LORD your God on top of this rock in the proper arrangement, and take the second bull and offer a burnt sacrifice with the wood of the image which you shall cut down." 27So Gideon took ten men from among his servants and did as the LORD had said to him. But because he feared his father's household and the men of the city too much to do *it* by day, he did *it* by night.

Gideon Destroys the Altar of Baal

28And when the men of the city arose early in the morning, there was the altar of Baal, torn down; and the wooden image that *was* beside it was cut down, and the second bull was being offered on the altar *which had been* built. 29So they said to one another, "Who has done this thing?" And when they had inquired and asked, they said, "Gideon the son of Joash has done this thing." 30Then the men of the city said to Joash, "Bring out your son, that he may die, because he has torn down the altar of Baal, and because he has cut down the wooden image that *was* beside it."

31But Joash said to all who stood against him, "Would you plead for Baal? Would you save him? Let the one who would plead for him be put to death by morning! If he *is* a god, let him plead for himself, because his altar has been torn down!" 32Therefore on that day he called him Jerubbaal,[a] saying, "Let Baal

6:13 [a] Hebrew *adoni,* used of man **6:15** [a] Hebrew *Adonai,* used of God **6:24** [a] Hebrew *YHWH Shalom* **6:25** [a] Hebrew *Asherah,* a Canaanite goddess **6:32** [a] Literally *Let Baal Plead*

plead against him, because he has torn
down his altar."
33Then all the Midianites and Ama-
lekites, the people of the East, gath-
ered together; and they crossed over
and encamped in the Valley of Jezreel.
34But the Spirit of the LORD came upon
Gideon; then he blew the trumpet, and
the Abiezrites gathered behind him.
35And he sent messengers throughout
all Manasseh, who also gathered behind
him. He also sent messengers to Asher,
Zebulun, and Naphtali; and they came
up to meet them.

The Sign of the Fleece

36So Gideon said to God, "If You will
save Israel by my hand as You have
said— 37look, I shall put a fleece of wool
on the threshing floor; if there is dew on
the fleece only, and *it is* dry on all the
ground, then I shall know that You will
save Israel by my hand, as You have
said." 38And it was so. When he rose
early the next morning and squeezed
the fleece together, he wrung the dew
out of the fleece, a bowlful of water.
39Then Gideon said to God, "Do not be
angry with me, but let me speak just
once more: Let me test, I pray, just once
more with the fleece; let it now be dry
only on the fleece, but on all the ground
let there be dew." 40And God did so that
night. It was dry on the fleece only, but
there was dew on all the ground.

Gideon's Valiant Three Hundred

7 Then Jerubbaal (that *is,* Gideon)
and all the people who *were* with
him rose early and encamped beside
the well of Harod, so that the camp of
the Midianites was on the north side of
them by the hill of Moreh in the valley.
2And the LORD said to Gideon, "The
people who *are* with you *are* too many
for Me to give the Midianites into their
hands, lest Israel claim glory for itself
against Me, saying, 'My own hand has
saved me.' 3Now therefore, proclaim
in the hearing of the people, saying,
'Whoever *is* fearful and afraid, let him
turn and depart at once from Mount
Gilead.' " And twenty-two thousand of
the people returned, and ten thousand
remained.
4But the LORD said to Gideon, "The
people *are* still *too* many; bring them
down to the water, and I will test them
for you there. Then it will be, *that* of
whom I say to you, 'This one shall go
with you,' the same shall go with you;
and of whomever I say to you, 'This one
shall not go with you,' the same shall
not go." 5So he brought the people down
to the water. And the LORD said to Gide-
on, "Everyone who laps from the water
with his tongue, as a dog laps, you shall
set apart by himself; likewise everyone
who gets down on his knees to drink."
6And the number of those who lapped,
putting their hand to their mouth, was
three hundred men; but all the rest of
the people got down on their knees to
drink water. 7Then the LORD said to Gid-
eon, "By the three hundred men who
lapped I will save you, and deliver the
Midianites into your hand. Let all the
other people go, every man to his place."
8So the people took provisions and their
trumpets in their hands. And he sent
away all *the rest of* Israel, every man
to his tent, and retained those three
hundred men. Now the camp of Midian
was below him in the valley.
9It happened on the same night that
the LORD said to him, "Arise, go down
against the camp, for I have delivered it
into your hand. 10But if you are afraid
to go down, go down to the camp with
Purah your servant, 11and you shall
hear what they say; and afterward your
hands shall be strengthened to go down
against the camp." Then he went down
with Purah his servant to the outpost of
the armed men who *were* in the camp.
12Now the Midianites and Amalekites,
all the people of the East, were lying in
the valley as numerous as locusts; and
their camels *were* without number, as
the sand by the seashore in multitude.
13And when Gideon had come, there
was a man telling a dream to his com-
panion. He said, "I have had a dream:
To my surprise, a loaf of barley bread
tumbled into the camp of Midian; it
came to a tent and struck it so that it fell
and overturned, and the tent collapsed."
14Then his companion answered and
said, "This *is* nothing else but the sword
of Gideon the son of Joash, a man of

Israel! Into his hand God has delivered
Midian and the whole camp."
15And so it was, when Gideon heard the
telling of the dream and its interpre-
tation, that he worshiped. He returned
to the camp of Israel, and said, "Arise,
for the LORD has delivered the camp of
Midian into your hand." 16Then he di-
vided the three hundred men *into* three
companies, and he put a trumpet into
every man's hand, with empty pitchers,
and torches inside the pitchers. 17And
he said to them, "Look at me and do
likewise; watch, and when I come to
the edge of the camp you shall do as
I do: 18When I blow the trumpet, I and
all who *are* with me, then you also blow
the trumpets on every side of the whole
camp, and say, '*The sword of* the LORD
and of Gideon!' "
19So Gideon and the hundred men
who *were* with him came to the outpost
of the camp at the beginning of the
middle watch, just as they had posted
the watch; and they blew the trumpets
and broke the pitchers that *were* in their
hands. 20Then the three companies blew
the trumpets and broke the pitchers—
they held the torches in their left hands
and the trumpets in their right hands
for blowing—and they cried, "The sword
of the LORD and of Gideon!" 21And every
man stood in his place all around the
camp; and the whole army ran and
cried out and fled. 22When the three
hundred blew the trumpets, the LORD
set every man's sword against his com-
panion throughout the whole camp;
and the army fled to Beth Acacia,[a] to-
ward Zererah, as far as the border of
Abel Meholah, by Tabbath.
23And the men of Israel gathered to-
gether from Naphtali, Asher, and all
Manasseh, and pursued the Midianites.
24Then Gideon sent messengers
throughout all the mountains of Ephra-
im, saying, "Come down against the
Midianites, and seize from them the
watering places as far as Beth Barah
and the Jordan." Then all the men of
Ephraim gathered together and seized
the watering places as far as Beth Barah
and the Jordan. 25And they captured
two princes of the Midianites, Oreb and
Zeeb. They killed Oreb at the rock of
Oreb, and Zeeb they killed at the wine-
press of Zeeb. They pursued Midian and
brought the heads of Oreb and Zeeb to
Gideon on the other side of the Jordan.

Gideon Subdues the Midianites

8 Now the men of Ephraim said to
him, "Why have you done this
to us by not calling us when you went
to fight with the Midianites?" And they
reprimanded him sharply.
2So he said to them, "What have I done
now in comparison with you? *Is* not the
gleaning *of the grapes* of Ephraim better
than the vintage of Abiezer? 3God has
delivered into your hands the princes
of Midian, Oreb and Zeeb. And what was
I able to do in comparison with you?"
Then their anger toward him subsided
when he said that.
4When Gideon came to the Jordan,
he and the three hundred men who
were with him crossed over, exhausted
but still in pursuit. 5Then he said to the
men of Succoth, "Please give loaves of
bread to the people who follow me, for
they are exhausted, and I am pursuing
Zebah and Zalmunna, kings of Midian."
6And the leaders of Succoth said, "*Are*
the hands of Zebah and Zalmunna now
in your hand, that we should give bread
to your army?"
7So Gideon said, "For this cause, when
the LORD has delivered Zebah and Zal-
munna into my hand, then I will tear
your flesh with the thorns of the wilder-
ness and with briers!" 8Then he went
up from there to Penuel and spoke to
them in the same way. And the men
of Penuel answered him as the men
of Succoth had answered. 9So he also
spoke to the men of Penuel, saying,
"When I come back in peace, I will tear
down this tower!"
10Now Zebah and Zalmunna *were* at
Karkor, and their armies with them,
about fifteen thousand, all who were left
of all the army of the people of the East;
for one hundred and twenty thousand
men who drew the sword had fallen.
11Then Gideon went up by the road of

7:22 [a] Hebrew *Beth Shittah*

those who dwell in tents on the east of Nobah and Jogbehah; and he attacked the army while the camp felt secure. 12When Zebah and Zalmunna fled, he pursued them; and he took the two kings of Midian, Zebah and Zalmunna, and routed the whole army.

13Then Gideon the son of Joash returned from battle, from the Ascent of Heres. 14And he caught a young man of the men of Succoth and interrogated him; and he wrote down for him the leaders of Succoth and its elders, seventy-seven men. 15Then he came to the men of Succoth and said, "Here are Zebah and Zalmunna, about whom you ridiculed me, saying, '*Are* the hands of Zebah and Zalmunna now in your hand, that we should give bread to your weary men?'" 16And he took the elders of the city, and thorns of the wilderness and briers, and with them he taught the men of Succoth. 17Then he tore down the tower of Penuel and killed the men of the city.

18And he said to Zebah and Zalmunna, "What kind of men *were they* whom you killed at Tabor?"

So they answered, "As you *are*, so *were* they; each one resembled the son of a king."

19Then he said, "They *were* my brothers, the sons of my mother. *As* the LORD lives, if you had let them live, I would not kill you." 20And he said to Jether his firstborn, "Rise, kill them!" But the youth would not draw his sword; for he was afraid, because he *was* still a youth.

21So Zebah and Zalmunna said, "Rise yourself, and kill us; for as a man *is, so is* his strength." So Gideon arose and killed Zebah and Zalmunna, and took the crescent ornaments that *were* on their camels' necks.

Gideon's Ephod

22Then the men of Israel said to Gideon, "Rule over us, both you and your son, and your grandson also; for you have delivered us from the hand of Midian."

23But Gideon said to them, "I will not rule over you, nor shall my son rule over you; the LORD shall rule over you." 24Then Gideon said to them, "I would like to make a request of you, that each of you would give me the earrings from his plunder." For they had golden earrings, because they *were* Ishmaelites.

25So they answered, "We will gladly give *them*." And they spread out a garment, and each man threw into it the earrings from his plunder. 26Now the weight of the gold earrings that he requested was one thousand seven hundred *shekels* of gold, besides the crescent ornaments, pendants, and purple robes which *were* on the kings of Midian, and besides the chains that *were* around their camels' necks. 27Then Gideon made it into an ephod and set it up in his city, Ophrah. And all Israel played the harlot with it there. It became a snare to Gideon and to his house.

28Thus Midian was subdued before the children of Israel, so that they lifted their heads no more. And the country was quiet for forty years in the days of Gideon.

Death of Gideon

29Then Jerubbaal the son of Joash went and dwelt in his own house. 30Gideon had seventy sons who were his own offspring, for he had many wives. 31And his concubine who *was* in Shechem also bore him a son, whose name he called Abimelech. 32Now Gideon the son of Joash died at a good old age, and was buried in the tomb of Joash his father, in Ophrah of the Abiezrites.

33So it was, as soon as Gideon was dead, that the children of Israel again played the harlot with the Baals, and made Baal-Berith their god. 34Thus the children of Israel did not remember the LORD their God, who had delivered them from the hands of all their enemies on every side; 35nor did they show kindness to the house of Jerubbaal (Gideon) in accordance with the good he had done for Israel.

Abimelech's Conspiracy

9 Then Abimelech the son of Jerubbaal went to Shechem, to his mother's brothers, and spoke with them and with all the family of the house of his mother's father, saying, 2"Please speak in the hearing of all the men of Shechem: 'Which is better for you, that

all seventy of the sons of Jerubbaal
reign over you, or that one reign over
you?' Remember that I *am* your own
flesh and bone."
3And his mother's brothers spoke all
these words concerning him in the hear-
ing of all the men of Shechem; and their
heart was inclined to follow Abimelech,
for they said, "He is our brother." 4So they
gave him seventy *shekels* of silver from
the temple of Baal-Berith, with which
Abimelech hired worthless and reckless
men; and they followed him. 5Then he
went to his father's house at Ophrah and
killed his brothers, the seventy sons of
Jerubbaal, on one stone. But Jotham
the youngest son of Jerubbaal was left,
because he hid himself. 6And all the men
of Shechem gathered together, all of Beth
Millo, and they went and made Abime-
lech king beside the terebinth tree at the
pillar that *was* in Shechem.

The Parable of the Trees

7Now when they told Jotham, he went
and stood on top of Mount Gerizim, and
lifted his voice and cried out. And he
said to them:

"Listen to me, you men of Shechem,
That God may listen to you!

8 "The trees once went forth to anoint
a king over them.
And they said to the olive tree,
'Reign over us!'
9 But the olive tree said to them,
'Should I cease giving my oil,
With which they honor God and
men,
And go to sway over trees?'

10 "Then the trees said to the fig tree,
'You come *and* reign over us!'
11 But the fig tree said to them,
'Should I cease my sweetness and
my good fruit,
And go to sway over trees?'

12 "Then the trees said to the vine,
'You come *and* reign over us!'
13 But the vine said to them,
'Should I cease my new wine,
Which cheers *both* God and men,
And go to sway over trees?'

14 "Then all the trees said to the
bramble,
'You come *and* reign over us!'
15 And the bramble said to the trees,
'If in truth you anoint me as king
over you,
Then come *and* take shelter in my
shade;
But if not, let fire come out of the
bramble
And devour the cedars of
Lebanon!'

16"Now therefore, if you have acted in
truth and sincerity in making Abime-
lech king, and if you have dealt well
with Jerubbaal and his house, and have
done to him as he deserves— 17for my
father fought for you, risked his life, and
delivered you out of the hand of Midi-
an; 18but you have risen up against my
father's house this day, and killed his
seventy sons on one stone, and made
Abimelech, the son of his female ser-
vant, king over the men of Shechem,
because he is your brother— 19if then
you have acted in truth and sincerity
with Jerubbaal and with his house this
day, *then* rejoice in Abimelech, and let
him also rejoice in you. 20But if not, let
fire come from Abimelech and devour
the men of Shechem and Beth Millo;
and let fire come from the men of She-
chem and from Beth Millo and devour
Abimelech!" 21And Jotham ran away
and fled; and he went to Beer and dwelt
there, for fear of Abimelech his brother.

Downfall of Abimelech

22After Abimelech had reigned over
Israel three years, 23God sent a spirit of
ill will between Abimelech and the men
of Shechem; and the men of Shechem
dealt treacherously with Abimelech,
24that the crime *done* to the seventy
sons of Jerubbaal might be settled and
their blood be laid on Abimelech their
brother, who killed them, and on the
men of Shechem, who aided him in
the killing of his brothers. 25And the
men of Shechem set men in ambush
against him on the tops of the moun-
tains, and they robbed all who passed
by them along that way; and it was told
Abimelech.

26Now Gaal the son of Ebed came with
his brothers and went over to Shechem;
and the men of Shechem put their confi-
dence in him. 27So they went out into the
fields, and gathered *grapes* from their
vineyards and trod *them,* and made
merry. And they went into the house
of their god, and ate and drank, and
cursed Abimelech. 28Then Gaal the son
of Ebed said, "Who *is* Abimelech, and
who *is* Shechem, that we should serve
him? *Is he* not the son of Jerubbaal,
and *is not* Zebul his officer? Serve the
men of Hamor the father of Shechem;
but why should we serve him? 29If only
this people were under my authority![a]
Then I would remove Abimelech." So
he[b] said to Abimelech, "Increase your
army and come out!"

30When Zebul, the ruler of the city,
heard the words of Gaal the son of Ebed,
his anger was aroused. 31And he sent
messengers to Abimelech secretly, say-
ing, "Take note! Gaal the son of Ebed
and his brothers have come to She-
chem; and here they are, fortifying the
city against you. 32Now therefore, get
up by night, you and the people who
are with you, and lie in wait in the field.
33And it shall be, as soon as the sun is
up in the morning, *that* you shall rise
early and rush upon the city; and *when*
he and the people who are with him
come out against you, you may then
do to them as you find opportunity."

34So Abimelech and all the people who
were with him rose by night, and lay in
wait against Shechem in four compa-
nies. 35When Gaal the son of Ebed went
out and stood in the entrance to the city
gate, Abimelech and the people who
were with him rose from lying in wait.
36And when Gaal saw the people, he
said to Zebul, "Look, people are coming
down from the tops of the mountains!"

But Zebul said to him, "You see the
shadows of the mountains as *if they
were* men."

37So Gaal spoke again and said, "See,
people are coming down from the cen-
ter of the land, and another company is
coming from the Diviners'[a] Terebinth
Tree."

38Then Zebul said to him, "Where in-
deed *is* your mouth now, with which you
said, 'Who is Abimelech, that we should
serve him?' *Are* not these the people
whom you despised? Go out, if you will,
and fight with them now."

39So Gaal went out, leading the men of
Shechem, and fought with Abimelech.
40And Abimelech chased him, and he
fled from him; and many fell wounded,
to the *very* entrance of the gate. 41Then
Abimelech dwelt at Arumah, and Zebul
drove out Gaal and his brothers, so that
they would not dwell in Shechem.

42And it came about on the next
day that the people went out into the
field, and they told Abimelech. 43So
he took his people, divided them into
three companies, and lay in wait in the
field. And he looked, and there were the
people, coming out of the city; and he
rose against them and attacked them.
44Then Abimelech and the company
that *was* with him rushed forward and
stood at the entrance of the gate of
the city; and the *other* two companies
rushed upon all who *were* in the fields
and killed them. 45So Abimelech fought
against the city all that day; he took the
city and killed the people who *were* in it;
and he demolished the city and sowed
it with salt.

46Now when all the men of the tower of
Shechem had heard *that,* they entered
the stronghold of the temple of the god
Berith. 47And it was told Abimelech that
all the men of the tower of Shechem
were gathered together. 48Then Abim-
elech went up to Mount Zalmon, he
and all the people who *were* with him.
And Abimelech took an ax in his hand
and cut down a bough from the trees, and
took it and laid *it* on his shoulder; then
he said to the people who were with
him, "What you have seen me do, make
haste *and* do as I *have done.*" 49So each
of the people likewise cut down his own
bough and followed Abimelech, put
them against the stronghold, and set
the stronghold on fire above them, so
that all the people of the tower of She-
chem died, about a thousand men and
women.

9:29 [a] Literally *hand* [b] Following Masoretic Text and Targum; Dead Sea Scrolls read *they;* Septuagint reads *I.* **9:37** [a] Hebrew *Meonenim*

50Then Abimelech went to Thebez, and
he encamped against Thebez and took it.
51But there was a strong tower in the city,
and all the men and women—all the
people of the city—fled there and shut
themselves in; then they went up to the
top of the tower. 52So Abimelech came
as far as the tower and fought against it;
and he drew near the door of the tower to
burn it with fire. 53But a certain woman
dropped an upper millstone on Abime-
lech's head and crushed his skull. 54Then
he called quickly to the young man, his
armorbearer, and said to him, "Draw
your sword and kill me, lest men say of
me, 'A woman killed him.' " So his young
man thrust him through, and he died.
55And when the men of Israel saw that
Abimelech was dead, they departed,
every man to his place.

56Thus God repaid the wickedness of
Abimelech, which he had done to his
father by killing his seventy brothers.
57And all the evil of the men of Shechem
God returned on their own heads, and
on them came the curse of Jotham the
son of Jerubbaal.

Tola

10 After Abimelech there arose to
save Israel Tola the son of Puah,
the son of Dodo, a man of Issachar; and
he dwelt in Shamir in the mountains
of Ephraim. 2He judged Israel twenty-
three years; and he died and was buried
in Shamir.

Jair

3After him arose Jair, a Gileadite; and
he judged Israel twenty-two years. 4Now
he had thirty sons who rode on thirty
donkeys; they also had thirty towns,
which are called "Havoth Jair"[a] to this
day, which *are* in the land of Gilead.
5And Jair died and was buried in Camon.

Israel Oppressed Again

6Then the children of Israel again did
evil in the sight of the LORD, and served
the Baals and the Ashtoreths, the gods
of Syria, the gods of Sidon, the gods of
Moab, the gods of the people of Ammon,
and the gods of the Philistines; and they
forsook the LORD and did not serve Him.
7So the anger of the LORD was hot against
Israel; and He sold them into the hands
of the Philistines and into the hands of
the people of Ammon. 8From that year
they harassed and oppressed the chil-
dren of Israel for eighteen years—all the
children of Israel who *were* on the other
side of the Jordan in the land of the Am-
orites, in Gilead. 9Moreover the people of
Ammon crossed over the Jordan to fight
against Judah also, against Benjamin,
and against the house of Ephraim, so
that Israel was severely distressed.

10And the children of Israel cried out
to the LORD, saying, "We have sinned
against You, because we have both for-
saken our God and served the Baals!"

11So the LORD said to the children of
Israel, "*Did I* not *deliver you* from the
Egyptians and from the Amorites and
from the people of Ammon and from
the Philistines? 12Also the Sidonians
and Amalekites and Maonites[a] op-
pressed you; and you cried out to Me,
and I delivered you from their hand.
13Yet you have forsaken Me and served
other gods. Therefore I will deliver you
no more. 14Go and cry out to the gods
which you have chosen; let them deliver
you in your time of distress."

15And the children of Israel said to the
LORD, "We have sinned! Do to us what-
ever seems best to You; only deliver us
this day, we pray." 16So they put away
the foreign gods from among them and
served the LORD. And His soul could
no longer endure the misery of Israel.
17Then the people of Ammon gathered
together and encamped in Gilead. And
the children of Israel assembled togeth-
er and encamped in Mizpah. 18And the
people, the leaders of Gilead, said to
one another, "Who *is* the man who will
begin the fight against the people of
Ammon? He shall be head over all the
inhabitants of Gilead."

Jephthah

11 Now Jephthah the Gileadite was
a mighty man of valor, but he
was the son of a harlot; and Gilead be-
got Jephthah. 2Gilead's wife bore sons;

10:4 [a] Literally *Towns of Jair* (compare Numbers 32:41 and Deuteronomy 3:14) **10:12** [a] Some Septuagint manuscripts read *Midianites.*

and when his wife's sons grew up, they
drove Jephthah out, and said to him,
"You shall have no inheritance in our
father's house, for you *are* the son of an-
other woman." 3Then Jephthah fled from
his brothers and dwelt in the land of Tob;
and worthless men banded together with
Jephthah and went out *raiding* with him.
4It came to pass after a time that the
people of Ammon made war against
Israel. 5And so it was, when the people
of Ammon made war against Israel,
that the elders of Gilead went to get
Jephthah from the land of Tob. 6Then
they said to Jephthah, "Come and be our
commander, that we may fight against
the people of Ammon."
7So Jephthah said to the elders of Gil-
ead, "Did you not hate me, and expel
me from my father's house? Why have
you come to me now when you are in
distress?"
8And the elders of Gilead said to Jeph-
thah, "That is why we have turned again
to you now, that you may go with us
and fight against the people of Ammon,
and be our head over all the inhabitants
of Gilead."
9So Jephthah said to the elders of Gil-
ead, "If you take me back home to fight
against the people of Ammon, and the
LORD delivers them to me, shall I be
your head?"
10And the elders of Gilead said to
Jephthah, "The LORD will be a witness
between us, if we do not do according
to your words." 11Then Jephthah went
with the elders of Gilead, and the people
made him head and commander over
them; and Jephthah spoke all his words
before the LORD in Mizpah.
12Now Jephthah sent messengers to
the king of the people of Ammon, say-
ing, "What do you have against me,
that you have come to fight against
me in my land?"
13And the king of the people of Ammon
answered the messengers of Jephthah,
"Because Israel took away my land
when they came up out of Egypt, from
the Arnon as far as the Jabbok, and to
the Jordan. Now therefore, restore those
lands peaceably."
14So Jephthah again sent messengers
to the king of the people of Ammon,
15and said to him, "Thus says Jephthah:
'Israel did not take away the land of
Moab, nor the land of the people of
Ammon; 16for when Israel came up
from Egypt, they walked through the
wilderness as far as the Red Sea and
came to Kadesh. 17Then Israel sent mes-
sengers to the king of Edom, saying,
"Please let me pass through your land."
But the king of Edom would not heed.
And in like manner they sent to the king
of Moab, but he would not *consent.* So
Israel remained in Kadesh. 18And they
went along through the wilderness and
bypassed the land of Edom and the
land of Moab, came to the east side of
the land of Moab, and encamped on the
other side of the Arnon. But they did not
enter the border of Moab, for the Arnon
was the border of Moab. 19Then Israel
sent messengers to Sihon king of the
Amorites, king of Heshbon; and Israel
said to him, "Please let us pass through
your land into our place." 20But Sihon
did not trust Israel to pass through his
territory. So Sihon gathered all his peo-
ple together, encamped in Jahaz, and
fought against Israel. 21And the LORD
God of Israel delivered Sihon and all his
people into the hand of Israel, and they
defeated them. Thus Israel gained pos-
session of all the land of the Amorites,
who inhabited that country. 22They took
possession of all the territory of the
Amorites, from the Arnon to the Jabbok
and from the wilderness to the Jordan.
23'And now the LORD God of Israel
has dispossessed the Amorites from
before His people Israel; should you
then possess it? 24Will you not possess
whatever Chemosh your god gives you
to possess? So whatever the LORD our
God takes possession of before us, we
will possess. 25And now, *are* you any
better than Balak the son of Zippor,
king of Moab? Did he ever strive against
Israel? Did he ever fight against them?
26While Israel dwelt in Heshbon and its
villages, in Aroer and its villages, and
in all the cities along the banks of the
Arnon, for three hundred years, why did
you not recover *them* within that time?
27Therefore I have not sinned against
you, but you wronged me by fighting
against me. May the LORD, the Judge,

render judgment this day between the children of Israel and the people of Ammon.' " 28However, the king of the people of Ammon did not heed the words which Jephthah sent him.

Jephthah's Vow and Victory

29Then the Spirit of the LORD came upon Jephthah, and he passed through Gilead and Manasseh, and passed through Mizpah of Gilead; and from Mizpah of Gilead he advanced *toward* the people of Ammon. 30And Jephthah made a vow to the LORD, and said, "If You will indeed deliver the people of Ammon into my hands, 31then it will be that whatever comes out of the doors of my house to meet me, when I return in peace from the people of Ammon, shall surely be the LORD's, and I will offer it up as a burnt offering."

32So Jephthah advanced toward the people of Ammon to fight against them, and the LORD delivered them into his hands. 33And he defeated them from Aroer as far as Minnith—twenty cities—and to Abel Keramim,[a] with a very great slaughter. Thus the people of Ammon were subdued before the children of Israel.

Jephthah's Daughter

34When Jephthah came to his house at Mizpah, there was his daughter, coming out to meet him with timbrels and dancing; and she *was his* only child. Besides her he had neither son nor daughter. 35And it came to pass, when he saw her, that he tore his clothes, and said, "Alas, my daughter! You have brought me very low! You are among those who trouble me! For I have given my word to the LORD, and I cannot go back on it."

36So she said to him, "My father, *if* you have given your word to the LORD, do to me according to what has gone out of your mouth, because the LORD has avenged you of your enemies, the people of Ammon." 37Then she said to her father, "Let this thing be done for me: let me alone for two months, that I may go and wander on the mountains and bewail my virginity, my friends and I."

38So he said, "Go." And he sent her away *for* two months; and she went with her friends, and bewailed her virginity on the mountains. 39And it was so at the end of two months that she returned to her father, and he carried out his vow with her which he had vowed. She knew no man.

And it became a custom in Israel 40*that* the daughters of Israel went four days each year to lament the daughter of Jephthah the Gileadite.

Jephthah's Conflict with Ephraim

12 Then the men of Ephraim gathered together, crossed over toward Zaphon, and said to Jephthah, "Why did you cross over to fight against the people of Ammon, and did not call us to go with you? We will burn your house down on you with fire!"

2And Jephthah said to them, "My people and I were in a great struggle with the people of Ammon; and when I called you, you did not deliver me out of their hands. 3So when I saw that you would not deliver *me,* I took my life in my hands and crossed over against the people of Ammon; and the LORD delivered them into my hand. Why then have you come up to me this day to fight against me?" 4Now Jephthah gathered together all the men of Gilead and fought against Ephraim. And the men of Gilead defeated Ephraim, because they said, "You Gileadites *are* fugitives of Ephraim among the Ephraimites *and* among the Manassites." 5The Gileadites seized the fords of the Jordan before the Ephraimites *arrived.* And when *any* Ephraimite who escaped said, "Let me cross over," the men of Gilead would say to him, "*Are* you an Ephraimite?" If he said, "No," 6then they would say to him, "Then say, 'Shibboleth'!" And he would say, "Sibboleth," for he could not pronounce *it* right. Then they would take him and kill him at the fords of the Jordan. There fell at that time forty-two thousand Ephraimites.

7And Jephthah judged Israel six years. Then Jephthah the Gileadite died and was buried among the cities of Gilead.

11:33 [a] Literally *Plain of Vineyards*

Ibzan, Elon, and Abdon

8After him, Ibzan of Bethlehem judged
Israel. 9He had thirty sons. And he gave
away thirty daughters in marriage,
and brought in thirty daughters from
elsewhere for his sons. He judged Israel
seven years. 10Then Ibzan died and was
buried at Bethlehem.
11After him, Elon the Zebulunite judged
Israel. He judged Israel ten years. 12And
Elon the Zebulunite died and was buried
at Aijalon in the country of Zebulun.
13After him, Abdon the son of Hillel
the Pirathonite judged Israel. 14He had
forty sons and thirty grandsons, who
rode on seventy young donkeys. He
judged Israel eight years. 15Then Abdon
the son of Hillel the Pirathonite died
and was buried in Pirathon in the land
of Ephraim, in the mountains of the
Amalekites.

The Birth of Samson

13 Again the children of Israel did
evil in the sight of the LORD, and
the LORD delivered them into the hand
of the Philistines for forty years.
2Now there was a certain man from
Zorah, of the family of the Danites,
whose name *was* Manoah; and his wife
was barren and had no children. 3And
the Angel of the LORD appeared to the
woman and said to her, "Indeed now, you
are barren and have borne no children,
but you shall conceive and bear a son.
4Now therefore, please be careful not
to drink wine or *similar* drink, and not
to eat anything unclean. 5For behold,
you shall conceive and bear a son. And
no razor shall come upon his head, for
the child shall be a Nazirite to God from
the womb; and he shall begin to deliver
Israel out of the hand of the Philistines."
6So the woman came and told her husband, saying, "A Man of God came to
me, and His countenance *was* like the
countenance of the Angel of God, very
awesome; but I did not ask Him where
He *was* from, and He did not tell me
His name. 7And He said to me, 'Behold,
you shall conceive and bear a son. Now
drink no wine or *similar* drink, nor eat
anything unclean, for the child shall be
a Nazirite to God from the womb to the
day of his death.' "
8Then Manoah prayed to the LORD,
and said, "O my Lord, please let the
Man of God whom You sent come to us
again and teach us what we shall do for
the child who will be born."
9And God listened to the voice of Manoah, and the Angel of God came to the
woman again as she was sitting in the
field; but Manoah her husband *was* not
with her. 10Then the woman ran in haste
and told her husband, and said to him,
"Look, the Man who came to me the
other day has just now appeared to me!"
11So Manoah arose and followed his
wife. When he came to the Man, he said
to Him, "Are You the Man who spoke to
this woman?"
And He said, "I *am.*"
12Manoah said, "Now let Your words
come *to pass!* What will be the boy's rule
of life, and his work?"
13So the Angel of the LORD said to Manoah, "Of all that I said to the woman
let her be careful. 14She may not eat
anything that comes from the vine, nor
may she drink wine or *similar* drink,
nor eat anything unclean. All that I
commanded her let her observe."
15Then Manoah said to the Angel of
the LORD, "Please let us detain You, and
we will prepare a young goat for You."
16And the Angel of the LORD said to
Manoah, "Though you detain Me, I will
not eat your food. But if you offer a
burnt offering, you must offer it to the
LORD." (For Manoah did not know He
was the Angel of the LORD.)
17Then Manoah said to the Angel of the
LORD, "What *is* Your name, that when
Your words come *to pass* we may honor
You?"
18And the Angel of the LORD said to
him, "Why do you ask My name, seeing
it *is* wonderful?"
19So Manoah took the young goat
with the grain offering, and offered it
upon the rock to the LORD. And He did a
wondrous thing while Manoah and his
wife looked on— 20it happened as the
flame went up toward heaven from the
altar—the Angel of the LORD ascended
in the flame of the altar! When Manoah
and his wife saw *this,* they fell on their
faces to the ground. 21When the Angel of
the LORD appeared no more to Manoah

and his wife, then Manoah knew that
He *was* the Angel of the LORD.
22And Manoah said to his wife, "We
shall surely die, because we have seen
God!"
23But his wife said to him, "If the LORD
had desired to kill us, He would not have
accepted a burnt offering and a grain
offering from our hands, nor would
He have shown us all these *things*, nor
would He have told us *such things* as
these at this time."
24So the woman bore a son and called
his name Samson; and the child grew,
and the LORD blessed him. 25And the
Spirit of the LORD began to move upon
him at Mahaneh Dan[a] between Zorah
and Eshtaol.

Samson's Philistine Wife

14 Now Samson went down to Tim-
nah, and saw a woman in Timnah
of the daughters of the Philistines. 2So he
went up and told his father and mother,
saying, "I have seen a woman in Timnah
of the daughters of the Philistines; now
therefore, get her for me as a wife."
3Then his father and mother said to
him, "*Is there* no woman among the
daughters of your brethren, or among
all my people, that you must go and
get a wife from the uncircumcised Phi-
listines?"
And Samson said to his father, "Get her
for me, for she pleases me well."
4But his father and mother did not
know that it was of the LORD—that
He was seeking an occasion to move
against the Philistines. For at that time
the Philistines had dominion over Israel.
5So Samson went down to Timnah with
his father and mother, and came to the
vineyards of Timnah.
Now *to his* surprise, a young lion *came*
roaring against him. 6And the Spirit of
the LORD came mightily upon him, and
he tore the lion apart as one would have
torn apart a young goat, though *he had*
nothing in his hand. But he did not tell his
father or his mother what he had done.
7Then he went down and talked with
the woman; and she pleased Samson
well. 8After some time, when he returned
to get her, he turned aside to see the
carcass of the lion. And behold, a swarm
of bees and honey *were* in the carcass of
the lion. 9He took some of it in his hands
and went along, eating. When he came
to his father and mother, he gave *some*
to them, and they also ate. But he did not
tell them that he had taken the honey
out of the carcass of the lion.
10So his father went down to the wom-
an. And Samson gave a feast there, for
young men used to do so. 11And it hap-
pened, when they saw him, that they
brought thirty companions to be with
him.
12Then Samson said to them, "Let me
pose a riddle to you. If you can correctly
solve and explain it to me within the
seven days of the feast, then I will give
you thirty linen garments and thirty
changes of clothing. 13But if you cannot
explain *it* to me, then you shall give
me thirty linen garments and thirty
changes of clothing."
And they said to him, "Pose your rid-
dle, that we may hear it."
14So he said to them:

"Out of the eater came something
to eat,
And out of the strong came
something sweet."

Now for three days they could not ex-
plain the riddle.
15But it came to pass on the seventh[a]
day that they said to Samson's wife,
"Entice your husband, that he may
explain the riddle to us, or else we will
burn you and your father's house with
fire. Have you invited us in order to take
what is ours? *Is that* not *so?*"
16Then Samson's wife wept on him,
and said, "You only hate me! You do
not love me! You have posed a riddle
to the sons of my people, but you have
not explained *it* to me."
And he said to her, "Look, I have not
explained *it* to my father or my mother;
so should I explain *it* to you?" 17Now she
had wept on him the seven days while
their feast lasted. And it happened on the
seventh day that he told her, because she

13:25 [a] Literally *Camp of Dan* (compare 18:12)
14:15 [a] Following Masoretic Text, Targum, and Vulgate; Septuagint and Syriac read *fourth*.

pressed him so much. Then she explained
the riddle to the sons of her people. 18So
the men of the city said to him on the
seventh day before the sun went down:

"What *is* sweeter than honey?
And what *is* stronger than a lion?"

And he said to them:

"If you had not plowed with my
heifer,
You would not have solved my
riddle!"

19Then the Spirit of the LORD came upon
him mightily, and he went down to Ash-
kelon and killed thirty of their men, took
their apparel, and gave the changes *of*
clothing to those who had explained the
riddle. So his anger was aroused, and
he went back up to his father's house.
20And Samson's wife was *given* to his
companion, who had been his best man.

Samson Defeats the Philistines

15 After a while, in the time of
wheat harvest, it happened that
Samson visited his wife with a young
goat. And he said, "Let me go in to my
wife, into *her* room." But her father
would not permit him to go in.
2Her father said, "I really thought that
you thoroughly hated her; therefore I
gave her to your companion. *Is* not her
younger sister better than she? Please,
take her instead."
3And Samson said to them, "This time
I shall be blameless regarding the Phi-
listines if I harm them!" 4Then Samson
went and caught three hundred foxes;
and he took torches, turned *the foxes* tail
to tail, and put a torch between each pair
of tails. 5When he had set the torches on
fire, he let *the foxes* go into the standing
grain of the Philistines, and burned up
both the shocks and the standing grain,
as well as the vineyards *and* olive groves.
6Then the Philistines said, "Who has
done this?"
And they answered, "Samson, the
son-in-law of the Timnite, because he
has taken his wife and given her to his
companion." So the Philistines came up
and burned her and her father with fire.
7Samson said to them, "Since you
would do a thing like this, I will surely
take revenge on you, and after that I
will cease." 8So he attacked them hip
and thigh with a great slaughter; then
he went down and dwelt in the cleft of
the rock of Etam.
9Now the Philistines went up, encamped
in Judah, and deployed themselves
against Lehi. 10And the men of Judah
said, "Why have you come up against us?"
So they answered, "We have come up
to arrest Samson, to do to him as he
has done to us."
11Then three thousand men of Judah
went down to the cleft of the rock of
Etam, and said to Samson, "Do you
not know that the Philistines rule over
us? What *is* this you have done to us?"
And he said to them, "As they did to
me, so I have done to them."
12But they said to him, "We have come
down to arrest you, that we may deliver
you into the hand of the Philistines."
Then Samson said to them, "Swear to
me that you will not kill me yourselves."
13So they spoke to him, saying, "No, but
we will tie you securely and deliver you
into their hand; but we will surely not kill
you." And they bound him with two new
ropes and brought him up from the rock.
14When he came to Lehi, the Philistines
came shouting against him. Then the
Spirit of the LORD came mightily upon
him; and the ropes that *were* on his
arms became like flax that is burned
with fire, and his bonds broke loose
from his hands. 15He found a fresh jaw-
bone of a donkey, reached out his hand
and took it, and killed a thousand men
with it. 16Then Samson said:

"With the jawbone of a donkey,
Heaps upon heaps,
With the jawbone of a donkey
I have slain a thousand men!"

17And so it was, when he had finished
speaking, that he threw the jawbone
from his hand, and called that place
Ramath Lehi.[a]

15:17 [a] Literally *Jawbone Height*

18Then he became very thirsty; so he cried out to the LORD and said, "You have given this great deliverance by the hand of Your servant; and now shall I die of thirst and fall into the hand of the uncircumcised?" 19So God split the hollow place that *is* in Lehi,[a] and water came out, and he drank; and his spirit returned, and he revived. Therefore he called its name En Hakkore,[b] which is in Lehi to this day. 20And he judged Israel twenty years in the days of the Philistines.

Samson and Delilah

16 Now Samson went to Gaza and saw a harlot there, and went in to her. 2*When* the Gazites *were told,* "Samson has come here!" they surrounded *the place* and lay in wait for him all night at the gate of the city. They were quiet all night, saying, "In the morning, when it is daylight, we will kill him." 3And Samson lay *low* till midnight; then he arose at midnight, took hold of the doors of the gate of the city and the two gateposts, pulled them up, bar and all, put *them* on his shoulders, and carried them to the top of the hill that faces Hebron.

4Afterward it happened that he loved a woman in the Valley of Sorek, whose name *was* Delilah. 5And the lords of the Philistines came up to her and said to her, "Entice him, and find out where his great strength *lies,* and by what *means* we may overpower him, that we may bind him to afflict him; and every one of us will give you eleven hundred *pieces* of silver."

6So Delilah said to Samson, "Please tell me where your great strength *lies,* and with what you may be bound to afflict you."

7And Samson said to her, "If they bind me with seven fresh bowstrings, not yet dried, then I shall become weak, and be like any *other* man."

8So the lords of the Philistines brought up to her seven fresh bowstrings, not yet dried, and she bound him with them. 9Now *men were* lying in wait, staying with her in the room. And she said to him, "The Philistines *are* upon you, Samson!" But he broke the bowstrings as a strand of yarn breaks when it touches fire. So the secret of his strength was not known.

10Then Delilah said to Samson, "Look, you have mocked me and told me lies. Now, please tell me what you may be bound with."

11So he said to her, "If they bind me securely with new ropes that have never been used, then I shall become weak, and be like any *other* man."

12Therefore Delilah took new ropes and bound him with them, and said to him, "The Philistines *are* upon you, Samson!" And *men were* lying in wait, staying in the room. But he broke them off his arms like a thread.

13Delilah said to Samson, "Until now you have mocked me and told me lies. Tell me what you may be bound with."

And he said to her, "If you weave the seven locks of my head into the web of the loom"—

14So she wove *it* tightly with the batten of the loom, and said to him, "The Philistines *are* upon you, Samson!" But he awoke from his sleep, and pulled out the batten and the web from the loom.

15Then she said to him, "How can you say, 'I love you,' when your heart *is* not with me? You have mocked me these three times, and have not told me where your great strength *lies.*" 16And it came to pass, when she pestered him daily with her words and pressed him, *so* that his soul was vexed to death, 17that he told her all his heart, and said to her, "No razor has ever come upon my head, for I *have been* a Nazirite to God from my mother's womb. If I am shaven, then my strength will leave me, and I shall become weak, and be like any *other* man."

18When Delilah saw that he had told her all his heart, she sent and called for the lords of the Philistines, saying, "Come up once more, for he has told me all his heart." So the lords of the Philistines came up to her and brought the money in their hand. 19Then she lulled him to sleep on her knees, and called for a man and had him shave off the seven locks of his head. Then she began to torment him,[a] and his strength left

15:19 [a] Literally *Jawbone* (compare verse 14) [b] Literally *Spring of the Caller* 16:19 [a] Following Masoretic Text, Targum, and Vulgate; Septuagint reads *he began to be weak.*

him. 20And she said, "The Philistines *are* upon you, Samson!" So he awoke from his sleep, and said, "I will go out as before, at other times, and shake myself free!" But he did not know that the LORD had departed from him.

21Then the Philistines took him and put out his eyes, and brought him down to Gaza. They bound him with bronze fetters, and he became a grinder in the prison. 22However, the hair of his head began to grow again after it had been shaven.

Samson Dies with the Philistines

23Now the lords of the Philistines gathered together to offer a great sacrifice to Dagon their god, and to rejoice. And they said:

> "Our god has delivered into our
> hands
> Samson our enemy!"

24When the people saw him, they praised their god; for they said:

> "Our god has delivered into our
> hands our enemy,
> The destroyer of our land,
> And the one who multiplied our
> dead."

25So it happened, when their hearts were merry, that they said, "Call for Samson, that he may perform for us." So they called for Samson from the prison, and he performed for them. And they stationed him between the pillars. 26Then Samson said to the lad who held him by the hand, "Let me feel the pillars which support the temple, so that I can lean on them." 27Now the temple was full of men and women. All the lords of the Philistines *were* there—about three thousand men and women on the roof watching while Samson performed.

28Then Samson called to the LORD, saying, "O Lord GOD, remember me, I pray! Strengthen me, I pray, just this once, O God, that I may with one *blow* take vengeance on the Philistines for my two eyes!" 29And Samson took hold of the two middle pillars which supported the temple, and he braced himself against them, one on his right and the other on his left. 30Then Samson said, "Let me die with the Philistines!" And he pushed with *all his* might, and the temple fell on the lords and all the people who *were* in it. So the dead that he killed at his death were more than he had killed in his life.

31And his brothers and all his father's household came down and took him, and brought *him* up and buried him between Zorah and Eshtaol in the tomb of his father Manoah. He had judged Israel twenty years.

Micah's Idolatry

17 Now there was a man from the mountains of Ephraim, whose name *was* Micah. 2And he said to his mother, "The eleven hundred *shekels* of silver that were taken from you, and on which you put a curse, even saying it in my ears—here *is* the silver with me; I took it."

And his mother said, "*May you be* blessed by the LORD, my son!" 3So when he had returned the eleven hundred *shekels* of silver to his mother, his mother said, "I had wholly dedicated the silver from my hand to the LORD for my son, to make a carved image and a molded image; now therefore, I will return it to you." 4Thus he returned the silver to his mother. Then his mother took two hundred *shekels* of silver and gave them to the silversmith, and he made it into a carved image and a molded image; and they were in the house of Micah.

5The man Micah had a shrine, and made an ephod and household idols;[a] and he consecrated one of his sons, who became his priest. 6In those days *there was* no king in Israel; everyone did *what was* right in his own eyes.

7Now there was a young man from Bethlehem in Judah, of the family of Judah; he *was* a Levite, and was staying there. 8The man departed from the city of Bethlehem in Judah to stay wherever he could find *a place*. Then he came to

17:5 a Hebrew *teraphim*

the mountains of Ephraim, to the house
of Micah, as he journeyed. 9And Micah
said to him, "Where do you come from?"
So he said to him, "I *am* a Levite from
Bethlehem in Judah, and I am on my
way to find *a place* to stay."
10Micah said to him, "Dwell with me,
and be a father and a priest to me, and
I will give you ten *shekels* of silver per
year, a suit of clothes, and your suste-
nance." So the Levite went in. 11Then
the Levite was content to dwell with
the man; and the young man became
like one of his sons to him. 12So Micah
consecrated the Levite, and the young
man became his priest, and lived in
the house of Micah. 13Then Micah said,
"Now I know that the LORD will be good
to me, since I have a Levite as priest!"

The Danites Adopt Micah's Idolatry

18 In those days *there was* no king
in Israel. And in those days the
tribe of the Danites was seeking an in-
heritance for itself to dwell in; for until
that day *their* inheritance among the
tribes of Israel had not fallen to them.
2So the children of Dan sent five men of
their family from their territory, men
of valor from Zorah and Eshtaol, to spy
out the land and search it. They said
to them, "Go, search the land." So they
went to the mountains of Ephraim, to
the house of Micah, and lodged there.
3While they *were* at the house of Micah,
they recognized the voice of the young
Levite. They turned aside and said to
him, "Who brought you here? What
are you doing in this *place?* What do
you have here?"
4He said to them, "Thus and so Micah
did for me. He has hired me, and I have
become his priest."
5So they said to him, "Please inquire
of God, that we may know whether the
journey on which we go will be pros-
perous."
6And the priest said to them, "Go in
peace. The presence of the LORD *be* with
you on your way."
7So the five men departed and went
to Laish. They saw the people who
were there, how they dwelt safely, in
the manner of the Sidonians, quiet and
secure. *There were* no rulers in the land
who might put *them* to shame for any-
thing. They *were* far from the Sidonians,
and they had no ties with anyone.[a]
8Then *the spies* came back to their
brethren at Zorah and Eshtaol, and
their brethren said to them, "What *is*
your *report?*"
9So they said, "Arise, let us go up
against them. For we have seen the
land, and indeed it *is* very good. *Would*
you *do* nothing? Do not hesitate to go,
and enter to possess the land. 10When
you go, you will come to a secure people
and a large land. For God has given it
into your hands, a place where *there is*
no lack of anything that *is* on the earth."
11And six hundred men of the family of
the Danites went from there, from Zorah
and Eshtaol, armed with weapons of
war. 12Then they went up and encamped
in Kirjath Jearim in Judah. (Therefore
they call that place Mahaneh Dan[a] to
this day. There *it is,* west of Kirjath Je-
arim.) 13And they passed from there to
the mountains of Ephraim, and came
to the house of Micah.
14Then the five men who had gone to
spy out the country of Laish answered
and said to their brethren, "Do you know
that there are in these houses an ephod,
household idols, a carved image, and a
molded image? Now therefore, consider
what you should do." 15So they turned
aside there, and came to the house of
the young Levite man—to the house
of Micah—and greeted him. 16The six
hundred men armed with their weapons
of war, who *were* of the children of Dan,
stood by the entrance of the gate. 17Then
the five men who had gone to spy out
the land went up. Entering there, they
took the carved image, the ephod, the
household idols, and the molded image.
The priest stood at the entrance of the
gate with the six hundred men *who were*
armed with weapons of war.
18When these went into Micah's house
and took the carved image, the ephod,
the household idols, and the molded
image, the priest said to them, "What
are you doing?"

18:7 a Following Masoretic Text, Targum, and Vulgate; Septuagint reads *with Syria.*
18:12 a Literally *Camp of Dan*

19And they said to him, "Be quiet, put your hand over your mouth, and come with us; be a father and a priest to us. *Is it* better for you to be a priest to the household of one man, or that you be a priest to a tribe and a family in Israel?" 20So the priest's heart was glad; and he took the ephod, the household idols, and the carved image, and took his place among the people.

21Then they turned and departed, and put the little ones, the livestock, and the goods in front of them. 22When they were a good way from the house of Micah, the men who *were* in the houses near Micah's house gathered together and overtook the children of Dan. 23And they called out to the children of Dan. So they turned around and said to Micah, "What ails you, that you have gathered such a company?"

24So he said, "You have taken away my gods which I made, and the priest, and you have gone away. Now what more do I have? How can you say to me, 'What ails you?' "

25And the children of Dan said to him, "Do not let your voice be heard among us, lest angry men fall upon you, and you lose your life, with the lives of your household!" 26Then the children of Dan went their way. And when Micah saw that they *were* too strong for him, he turned and went back to his house.

Danites Settle in Laish

27So they took *the things* Micah had made, and the priest who had belonged to him, and went to Laish, to a people quiet and secure; and they struck them with the edge of the sword and burned the city with fire. 28*There was* no deliverer, because it *was* far from Sidon, and they had no ties with anyone. It was in the valley that belongs to Beth Rehob. So they rebuilt the city and dwelt there. 29And they called the name of the city Dan, after the name of Dan their father, who was born to Israel. However, the name of the city formerly *was* Laish.

30Then the children of Dan set up for themselves the carved image; and Jonathan the son of Gershom, the son of Manasseh,[a] and his sons were priests to the tribe of Dan until the day of the captivity of the land. 31So they set up for themselves Micah's carved image which he made, all the time that the house of God was in Shiloh.

The Levite's Concubine

19 And it came to pass in those days, when *there was* no king in Israel, that there was a certain Levite staying in the remote mountains of Ephraim. He took for himself a concubine from Bethlehem in Judah. 2But his concubine played the harlot against him, and went away from him to her father's house at Bethlehem in Judah, and was there four whole months. 3Then her husband arose and went after her, to speak kindly to her *and* bring her back, having his servant and a couple of donkeys with him. So she brought him into her father's house; and when the father of the young woman saw him, he was glad to meet him. 4Now his father-in-law, the young woman's father, detained him; and he stayed with him three days. So they ate and drank and lodged there.

5Then it came to pass on the fourth day that they arose early in the morning, and he stood to depart; but the young woman's father said to his son-in-law, "Refresh your heart with a morsel of bread, and afterward go your way."

6So they sat down, and the two of them ate and drank together. Then the young woman's father said to the man, "Please be content to stay all night, and let your heart be merry." 7And when the man stood to depart, his father-in-law urged him; so he lodged there again. 8Then he arose early in the morning on the fifth day to depart, but the young woman's father said, "Please refresh your heart." So they delayed until afternoon; and both of them ate.

9And when the man stood to depart—he and his concubine and his servant—his father-in-law, the young woman's father, said to him, "Look, the day is now drawing toward evening; please spend the night. See, the day is coming to an

18:30 [a] Septuagint and Vulgate read *Moses.*

end; lodge here, that your heart may be merry. Tomorrow go your way early, so that you may get home."

10However, the man was not willing to spend that night; so he rose and departed, and came opposite Jebus (that *is,* Jerusalem). With him were the two saddled donkeys; his concubine *was* also with him. 11They *were* near Jebus, and the day was far spent; and the servant said to his master, "Come, please, and let us turn aside into this city of the Jebusites and lodge in it."

12But his master said to him, "We will not turn aside here into a city of foreigners, who *are* not of the children of Israel; we will go on to Gibeah." 13So he said to his servant, "Come, let us draw near to one of these places, and spend the night in Gibeah or in Ramah." 14And they passed by and went their way; and the sun went down on them near Gibeah, which belongs to Benjamin. 15They turned aside there to go in to lodge in Gibeah. And when he went in, he sat down in the open square of the city, for no one would take them into *his* house to spend the night.

16Just then an old man came in from his work in the field at evening, who also *was* from the mountains of Ephraim; he was staying in Gibeah, whereas the men of the place *were* Benjamites. 17And when he raised his eyes, he saw the traveler in the open square of the city; and the old man said, "Where are you going, and where do you come from?"

18So he said to him, "We *are* passing from Bethlehem in Judah toward the remote mountains of Ephraim; I *am* from there. I went to Bethlehem in Judah; *now* I am going to the house of the LORD. But there *is* no one who will take me into his house, 19although we have both straw and fodder for our donkeys, and bread and wine for myself, for your female servant, and for the young man *who is* with your servant; *there is* no lack of anything."

20And the old man said, "Peace *be* with you! However, *let* all your needs *be* my responsibility; only do not spend the night in the open square." 21So he brought him into his house, and gave fodder to the donkeys. And they washed their feet, and ate and drank.

Gibeah's Crime

22As they were enjoying themselves, suddenly certain men of the city, perverted men,[a] surrounded the house *and* beat on the door. They spoke to the master of the house, the old man, saying, "Bring out the man who came to your house, that we may know him *carnally!*"

23But the man, the master of the house, went out to them and said to them, "No, my brethren! I beg you, do not act *so* wickedly! Seeing this man has come into my house, do not commit this outrage. 24Look, *here is* my virgin daughter and *the man's*[a] concubine; let me bring them out now. Humble them, and do with them as you please; but to this man do not do such a vile thing!" 25But the men would not heed him. So the man took his concubine and brought *her* out to them. And they knew her and abused her all night until morning; and when the day began to break, they let her go.

26Then the woman came as the day was dawning, and fell down at the door of the man's house where her master *was,* till it was light.

27When her master arose in the morning, and opened the doors of the house and went out to go his way, there was his concubine, fallen *at* the door of the house with her hands on the threshold. 28And he said to her, "Get up and let us be going." But there was no answer. So the man lifted her onto the donkey; and the man got up and went to his place.

29When he entered his house he took a knife, laid hold of his concubine, and divided her into twelve pieces, limb by limb,[a] and sent her throughout all the territory of Israel. 30And so it was that all who saw it said, "No such deed has been done or seen from the day that the children of Israel came up from the land of Egypt until this day. Consider it, confer, and speak up!"

19:22 [a] Literally *sons of Belial* 19:24 [a] Literally *his* 19:29 [a] Literally *with her bones*

Israel's War with the Benjamites

20 So all the children of Israel came
out, from Dan to Beersheba, as
well as from the land of Gilead, and
the congregation gathered together as
one man before the LORD at Mizpah.
2And the leaders of all the people, all the
tribes of Israel, presented themselves
in the assembly of the people of God,
four hundred thousand foot soldiers
who drew the sword. 3(Now the children
of Benjamin heard that the children of
Israel had gone up to Mizpah.)

Then the children of Israel said, "Tell
us, how did this wicked deed happen?"
4So the Levite, the husband of the
woman who was murdered, answered
and said, "My concubine and I went into
Gibeah, which belongs to Benjamin, to
spend the night. 5And the men of Gib-
eah rose against me, and surrounded
the house at night because of me. They
intended to kill me, but instead they
ravished my concubine so that she died.
6So I took hold of my concubine, cut her
in pieces, and sent her throughout all
the territory of the inheritance of Israel,
because they committed lewdness and
outrage in Israel. 7Look! All of you *are*
children of Israel; give your advice and
counsel here and now!"

8So all the people arose as one man,
saying, "None *of us* will go to his tent,
nor will any turn back to his house; 9but
now this *is* the thing which we will do to
Gibeah: *We will go up* against it by lot.
10We will take ten men out of *every* hun-
dred throughout all the tribes of Israel,
a hundred out of *every* thousand, and
a thousand out of *every* ten thousand,
to make provisions for the people, that
when they come to Gibeah in Benjamin,
they may repay all the vileness that
they have done in Israel." 11So all the
men of Israel were gathered against
the city, united together as one man.

12Then the tribes of Israel sent men
through all the tribe of Benjamin, say-
ing, "What *is* this wickedness that has
occurred among you? 13Now there-
fore, deliver up the men, the perverted
men[a] who *are* in Gibeah, that we may
put them to death and remove the evil
from Israel!" But the children of Benja-
min would not listen to the voice of their
brethren, the children of Israel. 14In-
stead, the children of Benjamin gathered
together from their cities to Gibeah, to go
to battle against the children of Israel.
15And from their cities at that time the
children of Benjamin numbered twenty-
six thousand men who drew the sword,
besides the inhabitants of Gibeah, who
numbered seven hundred select men.
16Among all this people *were* seven hun-
dred select men *who were* left-handed;
every one could sling a stone at a hair's
breadth and not miss. 17Now besides Ben-
jamin, the men of Israel numbered four
hundred thousand men who drew the
sword; all of these *were* men of war.

18Then the children of Israel arose and
went up to the house of God[a] to inquire
of God. They said, "Which of us shall go
up first to battle against the children of
Benjamin?"

The LORD said, "Judah first!"

19So the children of Israel rose in the
morning and encamped against Gib-
eah. 20And the men of Israel went out
to battle against Benjamin, and the
men of Israel put themselves in battle
array to fight against them at Gibeah.
21Then the children of Benjamin came
out of Gibeah, and on that day cut down
to the ground twenty-two thousand
men of the Israelites. 22And the people,
that is, the men of Israel, encouraged
themselves and again formed the battle
line at the place where they had put
themselves in array on the first day.
23Then the children of Israel went up
and wept before the LORD until eve-
ning, and asked counsel of the LORD,
saying, "Shall I again draw near for bat-
tle against the children of my brother
Benjamin?"

And the LORD said, "Go up against
him."

24So the children of Israel approached
the children of Benjamin on the second
day. 25And Benjamin went out against
them from Gibeah on the second day,
and cut down to the ground eighteen
thousand more of the children of Israel;
all these drew the sword.

20:13 [a] Literally *sons of Belial* **20:18** [a] Or *Bethel*

26 Then all the children of Israel, that is, all the people, went up and came to the house of God[a] and wept. They sat there before the LORD and fasted that day until evening; and they offered burnt offerings and peace offerings before the LORD. 27 So the children of Israel inquired of the LORD (the ark of the covenant of God *was* there in those days, 28 and Phinehas the son of Eleazar, the son of Aaron, stood before it in those days), saying, "Shall I yet again go out to battle against the children of my brother Benjamin, or shall I cease?"

And the LORD said, "Go up, for tomorrow I will deliver them into your hand."

29 Then Israel set men in ambush all around Gibeah. 30 And the children of Israel went up against the children of Benjamin on the third day, and put themselves in battle array against Gibeah as at the other times. 31 So the children of Benjamin went out against the people, *and* were drawn away from the city. They began to strike down *and* kill some of the people, as at the other times, in the highways (one of which goes up to Bethel and the other to Gibeah) and in the field, about thirty men of Israel. 32 And the children of Benjamin said, "They *are* defeated before us, as at first."

But the children of Israel said, "Let us flee and draw them away from the city to the highways." 33 So all the men of Israel rose from their place and put themselves in battle array at Baal Tamar. Then Israel's men in ambush burst forth from their position in the plain of Geba. 34 And ten thousand select men from all Israel came against Gibeah, and the battle was fierce. But *the Benjamites*[a] did not know that disaster *was* upon them. 35 The LORD defeated Benjamin before Israel. And the children of Israel destroyed that day twenty-five thousand one hundred Benjamites; all these drew the sword.

36 So the children of Benjamin saw that they were defeated. The men of Israel had given ground to the Benjamites, because they relied on the men in ambush whom they had set against Gibeah. 37 And the men in ambush quickly rushed upon Gibeah; the men in ambush spread out and struck the whole city with the edge of the sword. 38 Now the appointed signal between the men of Israel and the men in ambush was that they would make a great cloud of smoke rise up from the city, 39 whereupon the men of Israel would turn in battle. Now Benjamin had begun to strike *and* kill about thirty of the men of Israel. For they said, "Surely they are defeated before us, as *in* the first battle." 40 But when the cloud began to rise from the city in a column of smoke, the Benjamites looked behind them, and there was the whole city going up *in smoke* to heaven. 41 And when the men of Israel turned back, the men of Benjamin panicked, for they saw that disaster had come upon them. 42 Therefore they turned *their backs* before the men of Israel in the direction of the wilderness; but the battle overtook them, and whoever *came* out of the cities they destroyed in their midst. 43 They surrounded the Benjamites, chased them, *and* easily trampled them down as far as the front of Gibeah toward the east. 44 And eighteen thousand men of Benjamin fell; all these *were* men of valor. 45 Then they[a] turned and fled toward the wilderness to the rock of Rimmon; and they cut down five thousand of them on the highways. Then they pursued them relentlessly up to Gidom, and killed two thousand of them. 46 So all who fell of Benjamin that day were twenty-five thousand men who drew the sword; all these *were* men of valor.

47 But six hundred men turned and fled toward the wilderness to the rock of Rimmon, and they stayed at the rock of Rimmon for four months. 48 And the men of Israel turned back against the children of Benjamin, and struck them down with the edge of the sword—from *every* city, men and beasts, all who were found. They also set fire to all the cities they came to.

Wives Provided for the Benjamites

21 Now the men of Israel had sworn an oath at Mizpah, saying, "None of us shall give his daughter to Benjamin as a wife." 2 Then the people came to the house of God,[a] and

20:26 [a] Or *Bethel* **20:34** [a] Literally *they* **20:45** [a] Septuagint reads *the rest.* **21:2** [a] Or *Bethel*

remained there before God till evening.
They lifted up their voices and wept bit-
terly, 3and said, "O LORD God of Israel,
why has this come to pass in Israel,
that today there should be one tribe
missing in Israel?"
4So it was, on the next morning, that
the people rose early and built an altar
there, and offered burnt offerings and
peace offerings. 5The children of Israel
said, "Who *is there* among all the tribes
of Israel who did not come up with the
assembly to the LORD?" For they had
made a great oath concerning anyone
who had not come up to the LORD at
Mizpah, saying, "He shall surely be put
to death." 6And the children of Isra-
el grieved for Benjamin their brother,
and said, "One tribe is cut off from Is-
rael today. 7What shall we do for wives
for those who remain, seeing we have
sworn by the LORD that we will not give
them our daughters as wives?"
8And they said, "What one *is there*
from the tribes of Israel who did not
come up to Mizpah to the LORD?" And, in
fact, no one had come to the camp from
Jabesh Gilead to the assembly. 9For
when the people were counted, indeed,
not one of the inhabitants of Jabesh
Gilead *was* there. 10So the congregation
sent out there twelve thousand of their
most valiant men, and commanded
them, saying, "Go and strike the inhab-
itants of Jabesh Gilead with the edge of
the sword, including the women and
children. 11And this *is* the thing that
you shall do: You shall utterly destroy
every male, and every woman who has
known a man intimately." 12So they
found among the inhabitants of Ja-
besh Gilead four hundred young virgins
who had not known a man intimately;
and they brought them to the camp at
Shiloh, which is in the land of Canaan.
13Then the whole congregation sent
word to the children of Benjamin who
were at the rock of Rimmon, and an-
nounced peace to them. 14So Benjamin
came back at that time, and they gave
them the women whom they had saved
alive of the women of Jabesh Gilead; and
yet they had not found enough for them.
15And the people grieved for Benjamin,
because the LORD had made a void in
the tribes of Israel.
16Then the elders of the congregation
said, "What shall we do for wives for those
who remain, since the women of Benja-
min have been destroyed?" 17And they
said, "*There must be* an inheritance for the
survivors of Benjamin, that a tribe may
not be destroyed from Israel. 18Howev-
er, we cannot give them wives from our
daughters, for the children of Israel have
sworn an oath, saying, 'Cursed *be* the one
who gives a wife to Benjamin.' " 19Then
they said, "In fact, *there is* a yearly feast
of the LORD in Shiloh, which *is* north of
Bethel, on the east side of the highway
that goes up from Bethel to Shechem,
and south of Lebonah."
20Therefore they instructed the chil-
dren of Benjamin, saying, "Go, lie in
wait in the vineyards, 21and watch;
and just when the daughters of Shiloh
come out to perform their dances, then
come out from the vineyards, and every
man catch a wife for himself from the
daughters of Shiloh; then go to the land
of Benjamin. 22Then it shall be, when
their fathers or their brothers come
to us to complain, that we will say to
them, 'Be kind to them for our sakes,
because we did not take a wife for any
of them in the war; for *it is* not *as though*
you have given the *women* to them at
this time, making yourselves guilty of
your oath.' "
23And the children of Benjamin did so;
they took enough wives for their num-
ber from those who danced, whom they
caught. Then they went and returned
to their inheritance, and they rebuilt
the cities and dwelt in them. 24So the
children of Israel departed from there
at that time, every man to his tribe and
family; they went out from there, every
man to his inheritance.
25In those days *there was* no king in
Israel; everyone did *what was* right in
his own eyes.

THE BOOK OF RUTH

The Book of Ruth takes place during the time of the Book of Judges. Ruth is from the land of Moab but becomes the daughter-in-law of Naomi, who is from Israel. When both women face hard times in Moab, Naomi plans to return to the town of Bethlehem in Israel. Naomi tells Ruth to stay in Moab, but Ruth chooses to go with Naomi to help take care of her mother-in-law. In Bethlehem, the women are not sure how they will even eat. So, Ruth goes into the fields to work hard collecting grain. A man named Boaz notices Ruth's faithfulness to help care for Naomi and ends up marrying Ruth. They have a son named Obed, who would have a son named Jesse, who would have a son named David. This David would become king of Israel and an ancestor of Jesus.

- **GENRE:** History
- **AUTHOR:** Samuel, possibly
- **TIME:** c. 1370–1041 BC (written c. 1050–1010 BC)
- **PURPOSE:** To show the amazing faithfulness of Ruth during a time when most of God's people were unfaithful and to show God's faithfulness to her.

Elimelech's Family Goes to Moab

1 Now it came to pass, in the days
when the judges ruled, that there
was a famine in the land. And a certain
man of Bethlehem, Judah, went to dwell
in the country of Moab, he and his wife
and his two sons. 2The name of the man
was Elimelech, the name of his wife *was*
Naomi, and the names of his two sons
were Mahlon and Chilion—Ephrathites
of Bethlehem, Judah. And they went
to the country of Moab and remained
there. 3Then Elimelech, Naomi's hus-
band, died; and she was left, and her
two sons. 4Now they took wives of the
women of Moab: the name of the one
was Orpah, and the name of the other
Ruth. And they dwelt there about ten
years. 5Then both Mahlon and Chilion
also died; so the woman survived her
two sons and her husband.

Naomi Returns with Ruth

6Then she arose with her daughters-
in-law that she might return from the
country of Moab, for she had heard in
the country of Moab that the LORD had
visited His people by giving them bread.
7Therefore she went out from the place
where she was, and her two daughters-
in-law with her; and they went on the
way to return to the land of Judah. 8And
Naomi said to her two daughters-in-law,
"Go, return each to her mother's house.
The LORD deal kindly with you, as you
have dealt with the dead and with me.
9The LORD grant that you may find
rest, each in the house of her husband."
So she kissed them, and they lifted up
their voices and wept. 10And they said
to her, "Surely we will return with you
to your people."

11But Naomi said, "Turn back, my
daughters; why will you go with me? *Are*
there still sons in my womb, that they
may be your husbands? 12Turn back,
my daughters, go—for I am too old to
have a husband. If I should say I have
hope, *if* I should have a husband tonight
and should also bear sons, 13would you
wait for them till they were grown?
Would you restrain yourselves from
having husbands? No, my daughters;
for it grieves me very much for your
sakes that the hand of the LORD has
gone out against me!"
14Then they lifted up their voices and
wept again; and Orpah kissed her
mother-in-law, but Ruth clung to her.

15And she said, "Look, your sister-in-
law has gone back to her people and to
her gods; return after your sister-in-law."

GOD SIN JESUS SALVATION LOVE

16 But Ruth said:

"Entreat me not to leave you,
Or to turn back from following
after you;
For wherever you go, I will go;
And wherever you lodge, I will
lodge;
Your people *shall be* my people,
And your God, my God.
17 Where you die, I will die,
And there will I be buried.
The LORD do so to me, and more
also,
If *anything but* death parts you
and me."

18 When she saw that she was deter-
mined to go with her, she stopped
speaking to her.
19 Now the two of them went until they
came to Bethlehem. And it happened,
when they had come to Bethlehem, that
all the city was excited because of them;
and the women said, "*Is* this Naomi?"
20 But she said to them, "Do not call
me Naomi;[a] call me Mara,[b] for the
Almighty has dealt very bitterly with
me. 21 I went out full, and the LORD has
brought me home again empty. Why do
you call me Naomi, since the LORD has
testified against me, and the Almighty
has afflicted me?"
22 So Naomi returned, and Ruth the
Moabitess her daughter-in-law with
her, who returned from the country of
Moab. Now they came to Bethlehem at
the beginning of barley harvest.

Ruth Meets Boaz

2 There was a relative of Naomi's
husband, a man of great wealth,
of the family of Elimelech. His name
was Boaz. 2 So Ruth the Moabitess said
to Naomi, "Please let me go to the field,
and glean heads of grain after *him* in
whose sight I may find favor."
And she said to her, "Go, my daughter."
3 Then she left, and went and gleaned
in the field after the reapers. And she
happened to come to the part of the
field *belonging* to Boaz, who *was* of the
family of Elimelech.
4 Now behold, Boaz came from Bethle-
hem, and said to the reapers, "The LORD
be with you!"
And they answered him, "The LORD
bless you!"
5 Then Boaz said to his servant who
was in charge of the reapers, "Whose
young woman *is* this?"
6 So the servant who was in charge of
the reapers answered and said, "It *is* the
young Moabite woman who came back
with Naomi from the country of Moab.
7 And she said, 'Please let me glean and
gather after the reapers among the
sheaves.' So she came and has contin-
ued from morning until now, though
she rested a little in the house."
8 Then Boaz said to Ruth, "You will lis-
ten, my daughter, will you not? Do not
go to glean in another field, nor go from
here, but stay close by my young wom-
en. 9 *Let* your eyes *be* on the field which
they reap, and go after them. Have I
not commanded the young men not to
touch you? And when you are thirsty,
go to the vessels and drink from what
the young men have drawn."
10 So she fell on her face, bowed down
to the ground, and said to him, "Why
have I found favor in your eyes, that
you should take notice of me, since I
am a foreigner?"
11 And Boaz answered and said to her,
"It has been fully reported to me, all that
you have done for your mother-in-law
since the death of your husband, and
how you have left your father and your
mother and the land of your birth, and
have come to a people whom you did
not know before. 12 The LORD repay your
work, and a full reward be given you by
the LORD God of Israel, under whose
wings you have come for refuge."
13 Then she said, "Let me find favor
in your sight, my lord; for you have
comforted me, and have spoken kindly
to your maidservant, though I am not
like one of your maidservants."
14 Now Boaz said to her at mealtime,
"Come here, and eat of the bread, and
dip your piece of bread in the vinegar."
So she sat beside the reapers, and he
passed parched *grain* to her; and she ate

1:20 [a] Literally *Pleasant* [b] Literally *Bitter*

and was satisfied, and kept some back.
15And when she rose up to glean, Boaz
commanded his young men, saying,
"Let her glean even among the sheaves,
and do not reproach her. 16Also let *grain*
from the bundles fall purposely for her;
leave *it* that she may glean, and do not
rebuke her."
17So she gleaned in the field until
evening, and beat out what she had
gleaned, and it was about an ephah of
barley. 18Then she took *it* up and went
into the city, and her mother-in-law saw
what she had gleaned. So she brought
out and gave to her what she had kept
back after she had been satisfied.
19And her mother-in-law said to her,
"Where have you gleaned today? And
where did you work? Blessed be the one
who took notice of you."
So she told her mother-in-law with
whom she had worked, and said, "The
man's name with whom I worked today
is Boaz."
20Then Naomi said to her daughter-
in-law, "Blessed *be* he of the LORD, who
has not forsaken His kindness to the
living and the dead!" And Naomi said
to her, "This man *is* a relation of ours,
one of our close relatives."
21Ruth the Moabitess said, "He also
said to me, 'You shall stay close by my
young men until they have finished all
my harvest.' "
22And Naomi said to Ruth her
daughter-in-law, "*It is* good, my daugh-
ter, that you go out with his young
women, and that people do not meet
you in any other field." 23So she stayed
close by the young women of Boaz, to
glean until the end of barley harvest
and wheat harvest; and she dwelt with
her mother-in-law.

Ruth's Redemption Assured

3 Then Naomi her mother-in-law said
to her, "My daughter, shall I not seek
security for you, that it may be well with
you? 2Now Boaz, whose young women
you were with, *is he* not our relative? In
fact, he is winnowing barley tonight
at the threshing floor. 3Therefore wash
yourself and anoint yourself, put on
your *best* garment and go down to the
threshing floor; *but* do not make yourself
known to the man until he has finished
eating and drinking. 4Then it shall be,
when he lies down, that you shall notice
the place where he lies; and you shall go
in, uncover his feet, and lie down; and he
will tell you what you should do."
5And she said to her, "All that you say
to me I will do."
6So she went down to the threshing
floor and did according to all that her
mother-in-law instructed her. 7And af-
ter Boaz had eaten and drunk, and his
heart was cheerful, he went to lie down
at the end of the heap of grain; and she
came softly, uncovered his feet, and
lay down.
8Now it happened at midnight that the
man was startled, and turned himself;
and there, a woman was lying at his
feet. 9And he said, "Who *are* you?"
So she answered, "I *am* Ruth, your
maidservant. Take your maidservant
under your wing,[a] for you are a close
relative."
10Then he said, "Blessed *are* you of
the LORD, my daughter! For you have
shown more kindness at the end than
at the beginning, in that you did not go
after young men, whether poor or rich.
11And now, my daughter, do not fear. I
will do for you all that you request, for
all the people of my town know that
you *are* a virtuous woman. 12Now it is
true that I *am* a close relative; however,
there is a relative closer than I. 13Stay
this night, and in the morning it shall
be *that* if he will perform the duty of a
close relative for you—good; let him do
it. But if he does not want to perform
the duty for you, then I will perform
the duty for you, *as* the LORD lives! Lie
down until morning."
14So she lay at his feet until morning,
and she arose before one could recog-
nize another. Then he said, "Do not let it
be known that the woman came to the
threshing floor." 15Also he said, "Bring
the shawl that *is* on you and hold it."
And when she held it, he measured six
ephahs of barley, and laid *it* on her. Then
she[a] went into the city.

3:9 [a] Or *Spread the corner of your garment over your maidservant* 3:15 [a] Many Hebrew manuscripts, Syriac, and Vulgate read *she;* Masoretic Text, Septuagint, and Targum read *he.*

16When she came to her mother-in-law,
she said, "*Is* that you, my daughter?"
Then she told her all that the man had
done for her. 17And she said, "These six
ephahs of barley he gave me; for he said
to me, 'Do not go empty-handed to your
mother-in-law.' "
18Then she said, "Sit still, my daughter,
until you know how the matter will turn
out; for the man will not rest until he has
concluded the matter this day."

Boaz Redeems Ruth

4 Now Boaz went up to the gate and
sat down there; and behold, the
close relative of whom Boaz had spo-
ken came by. So Boaz said, "Come aside,
friend,[a] sit down here." So he came aside
and sat down. 2And he took ten men
of the elders of the city, and said, "Sit
down here." So they sat down. 3Then
he said to the close relative, "Naomi,
who has come back from the country
of Moab, sold the piece of land which
belonged to our brother Elimelech. 4And
I thought to inform you, saying, 'Buy *it*
back in the presence of the inhabitants
and the elders of my people. If you will
redeem *it,* redeem *it;* but if you[a] will not
redeem *it, then* tell me, that I may know;
for *there is* no one but you to redeem *it,*
and I *am* next after you.' "
And he said, "I will redeem *it.*"
5Then Boaz said, "On the day you buy
the field from the hand of Naomi, you
must also buy *it* from Ruth the Moab-
itess, the wife of the dead, to perpetu-
ate[a] the name of the dead through his
inheritance."
6And the close relative said, "I cannot
redeem *it* for myself, lest I ruin my own
inheritance. You redeem my right of
redemption for yourself, for I cannot
redeem *it.*"
7Now this *was the custom* in former
times in Israel concerning redeeming
and exchanging, to confirm anything:
one man took off his sandal and gave
it to the other, and this *was* a confirma-
tion in Israel.
8Therefore the close relative said to
Boaz, "Buy *it* for yourself." So he took off
his sandal. 9And Boaz said to the elders
and all the people, "You *are* witnesses
this day that I have bought all that was
Elimelech's, and all that *was* Chilion's
and Mahlon's, from the hand of Naomi.
10Moreover, Ruth the Moabitess, the
widow of Mahlon, I have acquired as
my wife, to perpetuate the name of the
dead through his inheritance, that the
name of the dead may not be cut off
from among his brethren and from his
position at the gate.[a] You *are* witnesses
this day."
11And all the people who *were* at the
gate, and the elders, said, "*We are* wit-
nesses. The LORD make the woman who
is coming to your house like Rachel
and Leah, the two who built the house
of Israel; and may you prosper in Eph-
rathah and be famous in Bethlehem.
12May your house be like the house of
Perez, whom Tamar bore to Judah, be-
cause of the offspring which the LORD
will give you from this young woman."

Descendants of Boaz and Ruth

13So Boaz took Ruth and she became
his wife; and when he went in to her,
the LORD gave her conception, and she
bore a son. 14Then the women said to
Naomi, "Blessed *be* the LORD, who has
not left you this day without a close
relative; and may his name be famous
in Israel! 15And may he be to you a
restorer of life and a nourisher of your
old age; for your daughter-in-law, who
loves you, who is better to you than
seven sons, has borne him." 16Then
Naomi took the child and laid him on
her bosom, and became a nurse to him.
17Also the neighbor women gave him
a name, saying, "There is a son born
to Naomi." And they called his name
Obed. He *is* the father of Jesse, the fa-
ther of David.
18Now this *is* the genealogy of Perez:
Perez begot Hezron; 19Hezron begot
Ram, and Ram begot Amminadab;
20Amminadab begot Nahshon, and
Nahshon begot Salmon;[a] 21Salmon be-
got Boaz, and Boaz begot Obed; 22Obed
begot Jesse, and Jesse begot David.

4:1 [a] Hebrew *peloni almoni;* literally *so and so* 4:4 [a] Following many Hebrew manuscripts, Septuagint, Syriac, Targum, and Vulgate; Masoretic Text reads *he.* 4:5 [a] Literally *raise up* 4:10 [a] Probably his civic office 4:20 [a] Hebrew *Salmah*

THE FIRST BOOK OF

SAMUEL

The Book of 1 Samuel describes how the Israelites change from being led by judges to kings. The book begins with Israel being led by Samuel, a prophet, priest, and the last of the judges. But in time, the people want to be led by a king instead so they can be like the nations around them. God tells Samuel to warn the people that this would be a mistake, but the people insist. God gives the people what they want, and Saul becomes the first king of Israel. It does not take long before Saul proves God right. He disobeys God, and God rejects him as king. A new king would take his place, a young man by the name of David.

- **GENRE:** History
- **AUTHOR:** Unknown
- **TIME:** c. 1105–1011 BC
- **PURPOSE:** To record Israel's change from being led by judges to being led by kings.

The Family of Elkanah

1 Now there was a certain man of Ramathaim Zophim, of the mountains of Ephraim, and his name *was* Elkanah the son of Jeroham, the son of Elihu,[a] the son of Tohu,[b] the son of Zuph, an Ephraimite. 2And he had two wives: the name of one *was* Hannah, and the name of the other Peninnah. Peninnah had children, but Hannah had no children. 3This man went up from his city yearly to worship and sacrifice to the LORD of hosts in Shiloh. Also the two sons of Eli, Hophni and Phinehas, the priests of the LORD, *were* there. 4And whenever the time came for Elkanah to make an offering, he would give portions to Peninnah his wife and to all her sons and daughters. 5But to Hannah he would give a double portion, for he loved Hannah, although the LORD had closed her womb. 6And her rival also provoked her severely, to make her miserable, because the LORD had closed her womb. 7So it was, year by year, when she went up to the house of the LORD, that she provoked her; therefore she wept and did not eat.

Hannah's Vow

8Then Elkanah her husband said to her, "Hannah, why do you weep? Why do you not eat? And why is your heart grieved? *Am* I not better to you than ten sons?"

9So Hannah arose after they had finished eating and drinking in Shiloh. Now Eli the priest was sitting on the seat by the doorpost of the tabernacle[a] of the LORD. 10And she *was* in bitterness of soul, and prayed to the LORD and wept in anguish. 11Then she made a vow and said, "O LORD of hosts, if You will indeed look on the affliction of Your maidservant and remember me, and not forget Your maidservant, but will give Your maidservant a male child, then I will give him to the LORD all the days of his life, and no razor shall come upon his head."

12And it happened, as she continued praying before the LORD, that Eli watched her mouth. 13Now Hannah spoke in her heart; only her lips moved, but her voice was not heard. Therefore Eli thought she was drunk. 14So Eli said to her, "How long will you be drunk? Put your wine away from you!"

15But Hannah answered and said, "No, my lord, I *am* a woman of sorrowful spirit. I have drunk neither wine nor intoxicating drink, but have poured out my soul before the LORD. 16Do not

1:1 [a] Spelled *Eliel* in 1 Chronicles 6:34 [b] Spelled *Toah* in 1 Chronicles 6:34 1:9 [a] Hebrew *heykal*, palace or temple

consider your maidservant a wicked
woman,[a] for out of the abundance of
my complaint and grief I have spoken
until now."
17Then Eli answered and said, "Go in
peace, and the God of Israel grant your
petition which you have asked of Him."
18And she said, "Let your maidservant
find favor in your sight." So the woman
went her way and ate, and her face was
no longer *sad.*

Samuel Is Born and Dedicated

19Then they rose early in the morning
and worshiped before the LORD, and
returned and came to their house at
Ramah. And Elkanah knew Hannah his
wife, and the LORD remembered her.
20So it came to pass in the process of
time that Hannah conceived and bore
a son, and called his name Samuel,[a]
saying, "Because I have asked for him
from the LORD."
21Now the man Elkanah and all his
house went up to offer to the LORD the
yearly sacrifice and his vow. 22But Han-
nah did not go up, for she said to her
husband, "*Not* until the child is weaned;
then I will take him, that he may ap-
pear before the LORD and remain there
forever."
23So Elkanah her husband said to her,
"Do what seems best to you; wait until
you have weaned him. Only let the LORD
establish His[a] word." Then the woman
stayed and nursed her son until she
had weaned him.
24Now when she had weaned him, she
took him up with her, with three bulls,[a]
one ephah of flour, and a skin of wine, and
brought him to the house of the LORD in
Shiloh. And the child *was* young. 25Then
they slaughtered a bull, and brought the
child to Eli. 26And she said, "O my lord! As
your soul lives, my lord, I *am* the woman
who stood by you here, praying to the
LORD. 27For this child I prayed, and the
LORD has granted me my petition which
I asked of Him. 28Therefore I also have
lent him to the LORD; as long as he lives
he shall be lent to the LORD." So they wor-
shiped the LORD there.

Hannah's Prayer

2 And Hannah prayed and said:

"My heart rejoices in the LORD;
My horn[a] is exalted in the LORD.
I smile at my enemies,
Because I rejoice in Your
salvation.

2 "No one is holy like the LORD,
For *there is* none besides You,
Nor *is there* any rock like our God.

3 "Talk no more so very proudly;
Let no arrogance come from your
mouth,
For the LORD *is* the God of
knowledge;
And by Him actions are weighed.

4 "The bows of the mighty men *are*
broken,
And those who stumbled are
girded with strength.
5 *Those who were* full have hired
themselves out for bread,
And the hungry have ceased *to*
hunger.
Even the barren has borne seven,
And she who has many children
has become feeble.

6 "The LORD kills and makes alive;
He brings down to the grave and
brings up.
7 The LORD makes poor and makes
rich;
He brings low and lifts up.
8 He raises the poor from the dust
And lifts the beggar from the ash
heap,
To set *them* among princes
And make them inherit the
throne of glory.

"For the pillars of the earth *are* the
LORD's,
And He has set the world upon
them.
9 He will guard the feet of His saints,
But the wicked shall be silent in
darkness.

1:16 [a] Literally *daughter of Belial* 1:20 [a] Literally *Heard by God* 1:23 [a] Following Masoretic Text, Targum, and Vulgate; Dead Sea Scrolls, Septuagint, and Syriac read *your.* 1:24 [a] Dead Sea Scrolls, Septuagint, and Syriac read *a three-year-old bull.* 2:1 [a] That is, strength

"For by strength no man shall
prevail.
10 The adversaries of the LORD shall
be broken in pieces;
From heaven He will thunder
against them.
The LORD will judge the ends of
the earth.

"He will give strength to His king,
And exalt the horn of His
anointed."

11Then Elkanah went to his house at
Ramah. But the child ministered to the
LORD before Eli the priest.

The Wicked Sons of Eli

12Now the sons of Eli *were* corrupt;[a]
they did not know the LORD. 13And the
priests' custom with the people *was*
that when any man offered a sacrifice,
the priest's servant would come with a
three-pronged fleshhook in his hand
while the meat was boiling. 14Then he
would thrust *it* into the pan, or kettle,
or caldron, or pot; and the priest would
take for himself all that the fleshhook
brought up. So they did in Shiloh to all
the Israelites who came there. 15Also,
before they burned the fat, the priest's
servant would come and say to the man
who sacrificed, "Give meat for roasting
to the priest, for he will not take boiled
meat from you, but raw."
16And *if* the man said to him, "They
should really burn the fat first; *then*
you may take *as much* as your heart
desires," he would then answer him,
"*No,* but you must give *it* now; and if
not, I will take *it* by force."
17Therefore the sin of the young men
was very great before the LORD, for men
abhorred the offering of the LORD.

Samuel's Childhood Ministry

18But Samuel ministered before the
LORD, *even as* a child, wearing a linen
ephod. 19Moreover his mother used to
make him a little robe, and bring *it* to
him year by year when she came up
with her husband to offer the yearly
sacrifice. 20And Eli would bless Elkanah
and his wife, and say, "The LORD give
you descendants from this woman for
the loan that was given to the LORD."
Then they would go to their own home.
21And the LORD visited Hannah, so
that she conceived and bore three sons
and two daughters. Meanwhile the child
Samuel grew before the LORD.

Prophecy Against Eli's Household

22Now Eli was very old; and he heard
everything his sons did to all Israel,[a]
and how they lay with the women who
assembled at the door of the tabernacle
of meeting. 23So he said to them, "Why
do you do such things? For I hear of
your evil dealings from all the people.
24No, my sons! For *it is* not a good re-
port that I hear. You make the LORD's
people transgress. 25If one man sins
against another, God will judge him.
But if a man sins against the LORD,
who will intercede for him?" Never-
theless they did not heed the voice of
their father, because the LORD desired
to kill them.
26And the child Samuel grew in stat-
ure, and in favor both with the LORD
and men.
27Then a man of God came to Eli and
said to him, "Thus says the LORD: 'Did
I not clearly reveal Myself to the house
of your father when they were in Egypt
in Pharaoh's house? 28Did I not choose
him out of all the tribes of Israel *to be*
My priest, to offer upon My altar, to
burn incense, and to wear an ephod
before Me? And did I not give to the
house of your father all the offerings
of the children of Israel made by fire?
29Why do you kick at My sacrifice and
My offering which I have commanded
in My dwelling place, and honor your
sons more than Me, to make yourselves
fat with the best of all the offerings
of Israel My people?' 30Therefore the
LORD God of Israel says: 'I said indeed
that your house and the house of your
father would walk before Me forever.'
But now the LORD says: 'Far be it from
Me; for those who honor Me I will hon-
or, and those who despise Me shall be
lightly esteemed. 31Behold, the days are

2:12 [a] Literally *sons of Belial* 2:22 [a] Following Masoretic Text, Targum, and Vulgate; Dead Sea Scrolls and Septuagint omit the rest of this verse.

GOD SIN JESUS SALVATION LOVE

coming that I will cut off your arm and the arm of your father's house, so that there will not be an old man in your house. 32And you will see an enemy *in My* dwelling place, *despite* all the good which God does for Israel. And there shall not be an old man in your house forever. 33But any of your men *whom* I do not cut off from My altar shall consume your eyes and grieve your heart. And all the descendants of your house shall die in the flower of their age. 34Now this *shall be* a sign to you that will come upon your two sons, on Hophni and Phinehas: in one day they shall die, both of them. 35Then I will raise up for Myself a faithful priest *who* shall do according to what *is* in My heart and in My mind. I will build him a sure house, and he shall walk before My anointed forever. 36And it shall come to pass that everyone who is left in your house will come *and* bow down to him for a piece of silver and a morsel of bread, and say, "Please, put me in one of the priestly positions, that I may eat a piece of bread." ' "

Samuel's First Prophecy

3 Now the boy Samuel ministered to the LORD before Eli. And the word of the LORD was rare in those days; *there was* no widespread revelation. 2And it came to pass at that time, while Eli *was* lying down in his place, and when his eyes had begun to grow so dim that he could not see, 3and before the lamp of God went out in the tabernacle[a] of the LORD where the ark of God *was,* and while Samuel was lying down, 4that the LORD called Samuel. And he answered, "Here I am!" 5So he ran to Eli and said, "Here I am, for you called me."

And he said, "I did not call; lie down again." And he went and lay down.

6Then the LORD called yet again, "Samuel!"

So Samuel arose and went to Eli, and said, "Here I am, for you called me." He answered, "I did not call, my son; lie down again." 7(Now Samuel did not yet know the LORD, nor was the word of the LORD yet revealed to him.)

8And the LORD called Samuel again the third time. So he arose and went to Eli, and said, "Here I am, for you did call me."

Then Eli perceived that the LORD had called the boy. 9Therefore Eli said to Samuel, "Go, lie down; and it shall be, if He calls you, that you must say, 'Speak, LORD, for Your servant hears.' " So Samuel went and lay down in his place.

10Now the LORD came and stood and called as at other times, "Samuel! Samuel!"

And Samuel answered, "Speak, for Your servant hears."

11Then the LORD said to Samuel: "Behold, I will do something in Israel at which both ears of everyone who hears it will tingle. 12In that day I will perform against Eli all that I have spoken concerning his house, from beginning to end. 13For I have told him that I will judge his house forever for the iniquity which he knows, because his sons made themselves vile, and he did not restrain them. 14And therefore I have sworn to the house of Eli that the iniquity of Eli's house shall not be atoned for by sacrifice or offering forever."

15So Samuel lay down until morning,[a] and opened the doors of the house of the LORD. And Samuel was afraid to tell Eli the vision. 16Then Eli called Samuel and said, "Samuel, my son!"

He answered, "Here I am."

17And he said, "What *is* the word that *the LORD* spoke to you? Please do not hide *it* from me. God do so to you, and more also, if you hide anything from me of all the things that He said to you." 18Then Samuel told him everything, and hid nothing from him. And he said, "It *is* the LORD. Let Him do what seems good to Him."

19So Samuel grew, and the LORD was with him and let none of his words fall to the ground. 20And all Israel from Dan to Beersheba knew that Samuel *had been* established as a prophet of the LORD. 21Then the LORD appeared again in Shiloh. For the LORD revealed Himself to Samuel in Shiloh by the word of the LORD.

3:3 [a] Hebrew *heykal,* palace or temple 3:15 [a] Following Masoretic Text, Targum, and Vulgate; Septuagint adds *and he arose in the morning.*

4

And the word of Samuel came to all Israel.[a]

The Ark of God Captured

Now Israel went out to battle against the Philistines, and encamped beside Ebenezer; and the Philistines encamped in Aphek. 2 Then the Philistines put themselves in battle array against Israel. And when they joined battle, Israel was defeated by the Philistines, who killed about four thousand men of the army in the field. 3 And when the people had come into the camp, the elders of Israel said, "Why has the LORD defeated us today before the Philistines? Let us bring the ark of the covenant of the LORD from Shiloh to us, that when it comes among us it may save us from the hand of our enemies." 4 So the people sent to Shiloh, that they might bring from there the ark of the covenant of the LORD of hosts, who dwells *between* the cherubim. And the two sons of Eli, Hophni and Phinehas, *were* there with the ark of the covenant of God.

5 And when the ark of the covenant of the LORD came into the camp, all Israel shouted so loudly that the earth shook. 6 Now when the Philistines heard the noise of the shout, they said, "What *does* the sound of this great shout in the camp of the Hebrews *mean?*" Then they understood that the ark of the LORD had come into the camp. 7 So the Philistines were afraid, for they said, "God has come into the camp!" And they said, "Woe to us! For such a thing has never happened before. 8 Woe to us! Who will deliver us from the hand of these mighty gods? These *are* the gods who struck the Egyptians with all the plagues in the wilderness. 9 Be strong and conduct yourselves like men, you Philistines, that you do not become servants of the Hebrews, as they have been to you. Conduct yourselves like men, and fight!"

10 So the Philistines fought, and Israel was defeated, and every man fled to his tent. There was a very great slaughter, and there fell of Israel thirty thousand foot soldiers. 11 Also the ark of God was captured; and the two sons of Eli, Hophni and Phinehas, died.

Death of Eli

12 Then a man of Benjamin ran from the battle line the same day, and came to Shiloh with his clothes torn and dirt on his head. 13 Now when he came, there was Eli, sitting on a seat by the wayside watching,[a] for his heart trembled for the ark of God. And when the man came into the city and told *it,* all the city cried out. 14 When Eli heard the noise of the outcry, he said, "What *does* the sound of this tumult *mean?*" And the man came quickly and told Eli. 15 Eli was ninety-eight years old, and his eyes were so dim that he could not see.

16 Then the man said to Eli, "I *am* he who came from the battle. And I fled today from the battle line."

And he said, "What happened, my son?"

17 So the messenger answered and said, "Israel has fled before the Philistines, and there has been a great slaughter among the people. Also your two sons, Hophni and Phinehas, are dead; and the ark of God has been captured."

18 Then it happened, when he made mention of the ark of God, that Eli fell off the seat backward by the side of the gate; and his neck was broken and he died, for the man was old and heavy. And he had judged Israel forty years.

Ichabod

19 Now his daughter-in-law, Phinehas' wife, was with child, *due* to be delivered; and when she heard the news that the ark of God was captured, and that her father-in-law and her husband were dead, she bowed herself and gave birth, for her labor pains came upon her. 20 And about the time of her death the women who stood by her said to her, "Do not fear, for you have borne a son." But she did not answer, nor did she regard *it.* 21 Then she named the child Ichabod,[a] saying, "The glory has departed from Israel!" because the ark of God had been

4:1 [a] Following Masoretic Text and Targum; Septuagint and Vulgate add *And it came to pass in those days that the Philistines gathered themselves together to fight;* Septuagint adds further *against Israel.*
4:13 [a] Following Masoretic Text and Vulgate; Septuagint reads *beside the gate watching the road.*
4:21 [a] Literally *Inglorious*

captured and because of her father-in-
law and her husband. 22And she said,
"The glory has departed from Israel,
for the ark of God has been captured."

The Philistines and the Ark

5 Then the Philistines took the ark of
God and brought it from Ebenezer
to Ashdod. 2When the Philistines took
the ark of God, they brought it into the
house of Dagon[a] and set it by Dagon.
3And when the people of Ashdod arose
early in the morning, there was Dagon,
fallen on its face to the earth before the
ark of the LORD. So they took Dagon and
set it in its place again. 4And when they
arose early the next morning, there was
Dagon, fallen on its face to the ground
before the ark of the LORD. The head of
Dagon and both the palms of its hands
were broken off on the threshold; only
Dagon's *torso*[a] was left of it. 5Therefore
neither the priests of Dagon nor any who
come into Dagon's house tread on the
threshold of Dagon in Ashdod to this day.
6But the hand of the LORD was heavy
on the people of Ashdod, and He rav-
aged them and struck them with tu-
mors,[a] *both* Ashdod and its territory.
7And when the men of Ashdod saw how
it was, they said, "The ark of the God of
Israel must not remain with us, for His
hand is harsh toward us and Dagon our
god." 8Therefore they sent and gathered
to themselves all the lords of the Philis-
tines, and said, "What shall we do with
the ark of the God of Israel?"

And they answered, "Let the ark of the
God of Israel be carried away to Gath."
So they carried the ark of the God of
Israel away. 9So it was, after they had
carried it away, that the hand of the
LORD was against the city with a very
great destruction; and He struck the
men of the city, both small and great,
and tumors broke out on them.

10Therefore they sent the ark of God to
Ekron. So it was, as the ark of God came
to Ekron, that the Ekronites cried out,
saying, "They have brought the ark of
the God of Israel to us, to kill us and our
people!" 11So they sent and gathered
together all the lords of the Philistines,
and said, "Send away the ark of the God
of Israel, and let it go back to its own
place, so that it does not kill us and our
people." For there was a deadly destruc-
tion throughout all the city; the hand
of God was very heavy there. 12And the
men who did not die were stricken with
the tumors, and the cry of the city went
up to heaven.

The Ark Returned to Israel

6 Now the ark of the LORD was in the
country of the Philistines seven
months. 2And the Philistines called for
the priests and the diviners, saying,
"What shall we do with the ark of the
LORD? Tell us how we should send it to
its place."

3So they said, "If you send away the
ark of the God of Israel, do not send it
empty; but by all means return *it* to Him
with a trespass offering. Then you will
be healed, and it will be known to you
why His hand is not removed from you."
4Then they said, "What *is* the trespass
offering which we shall return to Him?"

They answered, "Five golden tumors
and five golden rats, *according to* the
number of the lords of the Philistines.
For the same plague *was* on all of you
and on your lords. 5Therefore you shall
make images of your tumors and im-
ages of your rats that ravage the land,
and you shall give glory to the God of
Israel; perhaps He will lighten His hand
from you, from your gods, and from
your land. 6Why then do you harden
your hearts as the Egyptians and Phar-
aoh hardened their hearts? When He
did mighty things among them, did
they not let the people go, that they
might depart? 7Now therefore, make
a new cart, take two milk cows which
have never been yoked, and hitch the
cows to the cart; and take their calves
home, away from them. 8Then take the
ark of the LORD and set it on the cart;
and put the articles of gold which you
are returning to Him *as* a trespass of-
fering in a chest by its side. Then send
it away, and let it go. 9And watch: if it

5:2 [a] A Philistine idol **5:4** [a] Following Septuagint, Syriac, Targum, and Vulgate; Masoretic Text reads *Dagon.* **5:6** [a] Probably bubonic plague. Septuagint and Vulgate add here *And in the midst of their land rats sprang up, and there was a great death panic in the city.*

goes up the road to its own territory, to Beth Shemesh, *then* He has done us this great evil. But if not, then we shall know that *it is* not His hand *that* struck us—it happened to us by chance."

10Then the men did so; they took two milk cows and hitched them to the cart, and shut up their calves at home. 11And they set the ark of the LORD on the cart, and the chest with the gold rats and the images of their tumors. 12Then the cows headed straight for the road to Beth Shemesh, *and* went along the highway, lowing as they went, and did not turn aside to the right hand or the left. And the lords of the Philistines went after them to the border of Beth Shemesh.

13Now *the people of* Beth Shemesh *were* reaping their wheat harvest in the valley; and they lifted their eyes and saw the ark, and rejoiced to see *it.* 14Then the cart came into the field of Joshua of Beth Shemesh, and stood there; a large stone *was* there. So they split the wood of the cart and offered the cows as a burnt offering to the LORD. 15The Levites took down the ark of the LORD and the chest that *was* with it, in which *were* the articles of gold, and put *them* on the large stone. Then the men of Beth Shemesh offered burnt offerings and made sacrifices the same day to the LORD. 16So when the five lords of the Philistines had seen *it,* they returned to Ekron the same day.

17These *are* the golden tumors which the Philistines returned *as* a trespass offering to the LORD: one for Ashdod, one for Gaza, one for Ashkelon, one for Gath, one for Ekron; 18and the golden rats, *according to* the number of all the cities of the Philistines *belonging* to the five lords, *both* fortified cities and country villages, even as far as the large *stone of* Abel on which they set the ark of the LORD, *which stone remains* to this day in the field of Joshua of Beth Shemesh.

19Then He struck the men of Beth Shemesh, because they had looked into the ark of the LORD. He struck fifty thousand and seventy men[a] of the people, and the people lamented because the LORD had struck the people with a great slaughter.

The Ark at Kirjath Jearim

20And the men of Beth Shemesh said, "Who is able to stand before this holy LORD God? And to whom shall it go up from us?" 21So they sent messengers to the inhabitants of Kirjath Jearim, saying, "The Philistines have brought back the ark of the LORD; come down *and* take it up with you."

7 Then the men of Kirjath Jearim came and took the ark of the LORD, and brought it into the house of Abinadab on the hill, and consecrated Eleazar his son to keep the ark of the LORD.

Samuel Judges Israel

2So it was that the ark remained in Kirjath Jearim a long time; it was there twenty years. And all the house of Israel lamented after the LORD.

3Then Samuel spoke to all the house of Israel, saying, "If you return to the LORD with all your hearts, *then* put away the foreign gods and the Ashtoreths[a] from among you, and prepare your hearts for the LORD, and serve Him only; and He will deliver you from the hand of the Philistines." 4So the children of Israel put away the Baals and the Ashtoreths,[a] and served the LORD only.

5And Samuel said, "Gather all Israel to Mizpah, and I will pray to the LORD for you." 6So they gathered together at Mizpah, drew water, and poured *it* out before the LORD. And they fasted that day, and said there, "We have sinned against the LORD." And Samuel judged the children of Israel at Mizpah.

7Now when the Philistines heard that the children of Israel had gathered together at Mizpah, the lords of the Philistines went up against Israel. And when the children of Israel heard *of it,* they were afraid of the Philistines. 8So the children of Israel said to Samuel, "Do not cease to cry out to the LORD our God for us, that He may save us from the hand of the Philistines."

9And Samuel took a suckling lamb and offered *it as* a whole burnt offering to the LORD. Then Samuel cried out to the LORD for Israel, and the LORD answered him. 10Now as Samuel was offering up the

6:19 [a] Or *He struck seventy men of the people and fifty oxen of a man* **7:3** [a] Canaanite goddesses
7:4 [a] Canaanite goddesses

burnt offering, the Philistines drew near
to battle against Israel. But the LORD
thundered with a loud thunder upon
the Philistines that day, and so confused
them that they were overcome before
Israel. 11And the men of Israel went out
of Mizpah and pursued the Philistines,
and drove them back as far as below
Beth Car. 12Then Samuel took a stone
and set *it* up between Mizpah and Shen,
and called its name Ebenezer,[a] saying,
"Thus far the LORD has helped us."
13So the Philistines were subdued,
and they did not come anymore into
the territory of Israel. And the hand of
the LORD was against the Philistines
all the days of Samuel. 14Then the cities
which the Philistines had taken from Is-
rael were restored to Israel, from Ekron
to Gath; and Israel recovered its terri-
tory from the hands of the Philistines.
Also there was peace between Israel
and the Amorites.
15And Samuel judged Israel all the
days of his life. 16He went from year
to year on a circuit to Bethel, Gilgal,
and Mizpah, and judged Israel in all
those places. 17But he always returned
to Ramah, for his home *was* there. There
he judged Israel, and there he built an
altar to the LORD.

Israel Demands a King

8 Now it came to pass when Samuel
was old that he made his sons judg-
es over Israel. 2The name of his firstborn
was Joel, and the name of his second,
Abijah; *they were* judges in Beersheba.
3But his sons did not walk in his ways;
they turned aside after dishonest gain,
took bribes, and perverted justice.
4Then all the elders of Israel gath-
ered together and came to Samuel at
Ramah, 5and said to him, "Look, you are
old, and your sons do not walk in your
ways. Now make us a king to judge us
like all the nations."
6But the thing displeased Samuel
when they said, "Give us a king to judge
us." So Samuel prayed to the LORD. 7And
the LORD said to Samuel, "Heed the
voice of the people in all that they say
to you; for they have not rejected you,
but they have rejected Me, that I should
not reign over them. 8According to all
the works which they have done since
the day that I brought them up out of
Egypt, even to this day—with which
they have forsaken Me and served other
gods—so they are doing to you also.
9Now therefore, heed their voice. How-
ever, you shall solemnly forewarn them,
and show them the behavior of the king
who will reign over them."
10So Samuel told all the words of the
LORD to the people who asked him for
a king. 11And he said, "This will be the
behavior of the king who will reign over
you: He will take your sons and appoint
them for his own chariots and *to be* his
horsemen, and *some* will run before his
chariots. 12He will appoint captains over
his thousands and captains over his
fifties, *will set some* to plow his ground
and reap his harvest, and *some* to make
his weapons of war and equipment for
his chariots. 13He will take your daugh-
ters *to be* perfumers, cooks, and bakers.
14And he will take the best of your fields,
your vineyards, and your olive groves,
and give *them* to his servants. 15He will
take a tenth of your grain and your
vintage, and give it to his officers and
servants. 16And he will take your male
servants, your female servants, your
finest young men,[a] and your donkeys,
and put *them* to his work. 17He will take
a tenth of your sheep. And you will be
his servants. 18And you will cry out in
that day because of your king whom
you have chosen for yourselves, and
the LORD will not hear you in that day."
19Nevertheless the people refused to
obey the voice of Samuel; and they
said, "No, but we will have a king over
us, 20that we also may be like all the
nations, and that our king may judge
us and go out before us and fight our
battles."
21And Samuel heard all the words of
the people, and he repeated them in
the hearing of the LORD. 22So the LORD
said to Samuel, "Heed their voice, and
make them a king."
And Samuel said to the men of Israel,
"Every man go to his city."

7:12 [a] Literally *Stone of Help* 8:16 [a] Septuagint reads *cattle*.

Saul Chosen to Be King

9 There was a man of Benjamin whose
name *was* Kish the son of Abiel, the
son of Zeror, the son of Bechorath, the
son of Aphiah, a Benjamite, a mighty
man of power. 2And he had a choice
and handsome son whose name *was*
Saul. *There was* not a more handsome
person than he among the children of
Israel. From his shoulders upward *he*
was taller than any of the people.
3Now the donkeys of Kish, Saul's fa-
ther, were lost. And Kish said to his son
Saul, "Please take one of the servants
with you, and arise, go and look for the
donkeys." 4So he passed through the
mountains of Ephraim and through
the land of Shalisha, but they did not
find *them*. Then they passed through the
land of Shaalim, and *they were* not *there*.
Then he passed through the land of the
Benjamites, but they did not find *them*.
5When they had come to the land of
Zuph, Saul said to his servant who *was*
with him, "Come, let us return, lest my
father cease *caring* about the donkeys
and become worried about us."
6And he said to him, "Look now, *there*
is in this city a man of God, and *he is* an
honorable man; all that he says surely
comes to pass. So let us go there; per-
haps he can show us the way that we
should go."
7Then Saul said to his servant, "But
look, *if* we go, what shall we bring the
man? For the bread in our vessels is all
gone, and *there is* no present to bring
to the man of God. What do we have?"
8And the servant answered Saul again
and said, "Look, I have here at hand one-
fourth of a shekel of silver. I will give *that*
to the man of God, to tell us our way."
9(Formerly in Israel, when a man went to
inquire of God, he spoke thus: "Come, let
us go to the seer"; for *he who is* now *called*
a prophet was formerly called a seer.)
10Then Saul said to his servant, "Well
said; come, let us go." So they went to
the city where the man of God *was*.
11As they went up the hill to the city,
they met some young women going
out to draw water, and said to them, "Is
the seer here?"
12And they answered them and said,
"Yes, there he is, just ahead of you. Hur-
ry now; for today he came to this city,
because there is a sacrifice of the people
today on the high place. 13As soon as
you come into the city, you will surely
find him before he goes up to the high
place to eat. For the people will not eat
until he comes, because he must bless
the sacrifice; afterward those who are
invited will eat. Now therefore, go up,
for about this time you will find him."
14So they went up to the city. As they
were coming into the city, there was
Samuel, coming out toward them on
his way up to the high place.
15Now the LORD had told Samuel in his
ear the day before Saul came, saying,
16"Tomorrow about this time I will send
you a man from the land of Benjamin,
and you shall anoint him commander
over My people Israel, that he may save
My people from the hand of the Philis-
tines; for I have looked upon My people,
because their cry has come to Me."
17So when Samuel saw Saul, the LORD
said to him, "There he is, the man of
whom I spoke to you. This one shall reign
over My people." 18Then Saul drew near
to Samuel in the gate, and said, "Please
tell me, where *is* the seer's house?"
19Samuel answered Saul and said, "I
am the seer. Go up before me to the
high place, for you shall eat with me
today; and tomorrow I will let you go
and will tell you all that *is* in your heart.
20But as for your donkeys that were lost
three days ago, do not be anxious about
them, for they have been found. And on
whom *is* all the desire of Israel? *Is it* not
on you and on all your father's house?"
21And Saul answered and said, "*Am*
I not a Benjamite, of the smallest of
the tribes of Israel, and my family the
least of all the families of the tribe[a] of
Benjamin? Why then do you speak like
this to me?"
22Now Samuel took Saul and his ser-
vant and brought them into the hall,
and had them sit in the place of honor
among those who were invited; there
were about thirty persons. 23And Sam-
uel said to the cook, "Bring the portion

9:21 [a] Literally *tribes*

which I gave you, of which I said to you, 'Set it apart.' " 24So the cook took up the thigh with its upper part and set *it* before Saul. And *Samuel* said, "Here it is, what was kept back. *It* was set apart for you. Eat; for until this time it has been kept for you, since I said I invited the people." So Saul ate with Samuel that day.

25When they had come down from the high place into the city, *Samuel* spoke with Saul on the top of the house.[a] 26They arose early; and it was about the dawning of the day that Samuel called to Saul on the top of the house, saying, "Get up, that I may send you on your way." And Saul arose, and both of them went outside, he and Samuel.

Saul Anointed King

27As they were going down to the outskirts of the city, Samuel said to Saul, "Tell the servant to go on ahead of us." And he went on. "But you stand here awhile, that I may announce to you the word of God."

10 Then Samuel took a flask of oil and poured *it* on his head, and kissed him and said: "*Is it* not because the LORD has anointed you commander over His inheritance?[a] 2When you have departed from me today, you will find two men by Rachel's tomb in the territory of Benjamin at Zelzah; and they will say to you, 'The donkeys which you went to look for have been found. And now your father has ceased caring about the donkeys and is worrying about you, saying, "What shall I do about my son?" ' 3Then you shall go on forward from there and come to the terebinth tree of Tabor. There three men going up to God at Bethel will meet you, one carrying three young goats, another carrying three loaves of bread, and another carrying a skin of wine. 4And they will greet you and give you two *loaves* of bread, which you shall receive from their hands. 5After that you shall come to the hill of God where the Philistine garrison *is.* And it will happen, when you have come there to the city, that you will meet a group of prophets coming down from the high place with a stringed instrument, a tambourine, a flute, and a harp before them; and they will be prophesying. 6Then the Spirit of the LORD will come upon you, and you will prophesy with them and be turned into another man. 7And let it be, when these signs come to you, *that* you do as the occasion demands; for God *is* with you. 8You shall go down before me to Gilgal; and surely I will come down to you to offer burnt offerings *and* make sacrifices of peace offerings. Seven days you shall wait, till I come to you and show you what you should do."

9So it was, when he had turned his back to go from Samuel, that God gave him another heart; and all those signs came to pass that day. 10When they came there to the hill, there was a group of prophets to meet him; then the Spirit of God came upon him, and he prophesied among them. 11And it happened, when all who knew him formerly saw that he indeed prophesied among the prophets, that the people said to one another, "What *is* this *that* has come upon the son of Kish? *Is* Saul also among the prophets?" 12Then a man from there answered and said, "But who *is* their father?" Therefore it became a proverb: "*Is* Saul also among the prophets?" 13And when he had finished prophesying, he went to the high place.

14Then Saul's uncle said to him and his servant, "Where did you go?"

So he said, "To look for the donkeys. When we saw that *they were* nowhere *to be found,* we went to Samuel."

15And Saul's uncle said, "Tell me, please, what Samuel said to you."

16So Saul said to his uncle, "He told us plainly that the donkeys had been found." But about the matter of the kingdom, he did not tell him what Samuel had said.

9:25 [a] Following Masoretic Text and Targum; Septuagint omits *He spoke with Saul on the top of the house;* Septuagint and Vulgate add *And he prepared a bed for Saul on the top of the house, and he slept.*
10:1 [a] Following Masoretic Text, Targum, and Vulgate; Septuagint reads *His people Israel; and you shall rule the people of the Lord;* Septuagint and Vulgate add *And you shall deliver His people from the hands of their enemies all around them. And this shall be a sign to you, that God has anointed you to be a prince.*

Saul Proclaimed King

17 Then Samuel called the people to-
gether to the LORD at Mizpah, 18 and said
to the children of Israel, "Thus says the
LORD God of Israel: 'I brought up Israel
out of Egypt, and delivered you from
the hand of the Egyptians *and* from the
hand of all kingdoms and from those
who oppressed you.' 19 But you have
today rejected your God, who Himself
saved you from all your adversities and
your tribulations; and you have said
to Him, 'No, set a king over us!' Now
therefore, present yourselves before the
LORD by your tribes and by your clans."[a]
20 And when Samuel had caused all
the tribes of Israel to come near, the
tribe of Benjamin was chosen. 21 When
he had caused the tribe of Benjamin to
come near by their families, the family
of Matri was chosen. And Saul the son of
Kish was chosen. But when they sought
him, he could not be found. 22 Therefore
they inquired of the LORD further, "Has
the man come here yet?"

And the LORD answered, "There he is,
hidden among the equipment."

23 So they ran and brought him from
there; and when he stood among the
people, he was taller than any of the
people from his shoulders upward.
24 And Samuel said to all the people,
"Do you see him whom the LORD has
chosen, that *there is* no one like him
among all the people?"

So all the people shouted and said,
"Long live the king!"

25 Then Samuel explained to the people
the behavior of royalty, and wrote *it* in
a book and laid *it* up before the LORD.
And Samuel sent all the people away,
every man to his house. 26 And Saul also
went home to Gibeah; and valiant *men*
went with him, whose hearts God had
touched. 27 But some rebels said, "How
can this man save us?" So they despised
him, and brought him no presents. But
he held his peace.

Saul Saves Jabesh Gilead

11 Then Nahash the Ammonite
came up and encamped against
Jabesh Gilead; and all the men of Jabesh
said to Nahash, "Make a covenant with
us, and we will serve you."
2 And Nahash the Ammonite answered
them, "On this *condition* I will make *a
covenant* with you, that I may put out
all your right eyes, and bring reproach
on all Israel."

3 Then the elders of Jabesh said to him,
"Hold off for seven days, that we may
send messengers to all the territory of
Israel. And then, if *there is* no one to save
us, we will come out to you."

4 So the messengers came to Gibeah of
Saul and told the news in the hearing of
the people. And all the people lifted up
their voices and wept. 5 Now there was
Saul, coming behind the herd from the
field; and Saul said, "What *troubles* the
people, that they weep?" And they told
him the words of the men of Jabesh.
6 Then the Spirit of God came upon Saul
when he heard this news, and his anger
was greatly aroused. 7 So he took a yoke
of oxen and cut them in pieces, and
sent *them* throughout all the territory
of Israel by the hands of messengers,
saying, "Whoever does not go out with
Saul and Samuel to battle, so it shall be
done to his oxen."

And the fear of the LORD fell on the
people, and they came out with one
consent. 8 When he numbered them
in Bezek, the children of Israel were
three hundred thousand, and the men
of Judah thirty thousand. 9 And they
said to the messengers who came, "Thus
you shall say to the men of Jabesh Gil-
ead: 'Tomorrow, by *the time* the sun is
hot, you shall have help.' " Then the
messengers came and reported *it* to
the men of Jabesh, and they were glad.
10 Therefore the men of Jabesh said,
"Tomorrow we will come out to you, and
you may do with us whatever seems
good to you."

11 So it was, on the next day, that Saul
put the people in three companies; and
they came into the midst of the camp
in the morning watch, and killed Am-
monites until the heat of the day. And
it happened that those who survived
were scattered, so that no two of them
were left together.

10:19 [a] Literally *thousands*

12Then the people said to Samuel,
"Who *is* he who said, 'Shall Saul reign
over us?' Bring the men, that we may
put them to death."
13But Saul said, "Not a man shall be
put to death this day, for today the LORD
has accomplished salvation in Israel."
14Then Samuel said to the people,
"Come, let us go to Gilgal and renew
the kingdom there." 15So all the people
went to Gilgal, and there they made Saul
king before the LORD in Gilgal. There
they made sacrifices of peace offerings
before the LORD, and there Saul and all
the men of Israel rejoiced greatly.

Samuel's Address at Saul's Coronation

12 Now Samuel said to all Isra-
el: "Indeed I have heeded your
voice in all that you said to me, and
have made a king over you. 2And now
here is the king, walking before you;
and I am old and grayheaded, and look,
my sons *are* with you. I have walked
before you from my childhood to this
day. 3Here I am. Witness against me
before the LORD and before His anoint-
ed: Whose ox have I taken, or whose
donkey have I taken, or whom have I
cheated? Whom have I oppressed, or
from whose hand have I received *any*
bribe with which to blind my eyes? I will
restore *it* to you."
4And they said, "You have not cheated
us or oppressed us, nor have you taken
anything from any man's hand."
5Then he said to them, "The LORD *is*
witness against you, and His anointed
is witness this day, that you have not
found anything in my hand."
And they answered, "*He is* witness."
6Then Samuel said to the people, "*It is*
the LORD who raised up Moses and Aaron,
and who brought your fathers up from
the land of Egypt. 7Now therefore, stand
still, that I may reason with you before
the LORD concerning all the righteous
acts of the LORD which He did to you
and your fathers: 8When Jacob had gone
into Egypt,[a] and your fathers cried out
to the LORD, then the LORD sent Moses
and Aaron, who brought your fathers
out of Egypt and made them dwell in
this place. 9And when they forgot the
LORD their God, He sold them into the
hand of Sisera, commander of the army
of Hazor, into the hand of the Philistines,
and into the hand of the king of Moab;
and they fought against them. 10Then
they cried out to the LORD, and said, 'We
have sinned, because we have forsaken
the LORD and served the Baals and Ashto-
reths;[a] but now deliver us from the hand
of our enemies, and we will serve You.'
11And the LORD sent Jerubbaal,[a] Bedan,[b]
Jephthah, and Samuel,[c] and delivered
you out of the hand of your enemies on
every side; and you dwelt in safety. 12And
when you saw that Nahash king of the
Ammonites came against you, you said
to me, 'No, but a king shall reign over us,'
when the LORD your God *was* your king.
13"Now therefore, here is the king
whom you have chosen *and* whom
you have desired. And take note, the
LORD has set a king over you. 14If you
fear the LORD and serve Him and obey
His voice, and do not rebel against the
commandment of the LORD, then both
you and the king who reigns over you
will continue following the LORD your
God. 15However, if you do not obey the
voice of the LORD, but rebel against
the commandment of the LORD, then
the hand of the LORD will be against
you, as *it was* against your fathers.
16"Now therefore, stand and see this
great thing which the LORD will do be-
fore your eyes: 17*Is* today not the wheat
harvest? I will call to the LORD, and He
will send thunder and rain, that you
may perceive and see that your wick-
edness *is* great, which you have done in
the sight of the LORD, in asking a king
for yourselves."
18So Samuel called to the LORD, and
the LORD sent thunder and rain that
day; and all the people greatly feared
the LORD and Samuel.
19And all the people said to Samuel,
"Pray for your servants to the LORD
your God, that we may not die; for we
have added to all our sins the evil of
asking a king for ourselves."

12:8 [a] Following Masoretic Text, Targum, and Vulgate; Septuagint adds *and the Egyptians afflicted them.* 12:10 [a] Canaanite goddesses 12:11 [a] Syriac reads *Deborah;* Targum reads *Gideon.* [b] Septuagint and Syriac read *Barak;* Targum reads *Simson.* [c] Syriac reads *Simson.*

20Then Samuel said to the people, "Do not fear. You have done all this wickedness; yet do not turn aside from following the LORD, but serve the LORD with all your heart. 21And do not turn aside; for *then you would go* after empty things which cannot profit or deliver, for they *are* nothing. 22For the LORD will not forsake His people, for His great name's sake, because it has pleased the LORD to make you His people. 23Moreover, as for me, far be it from me that I should sin against the LORD in ceasing to pray for you; but I will teach you the good and the right way. 24Only fear the LORD, and serve Him in truth with all your heart; for consider what great things He has done for you. 25But if you still do wickedly, you shall be swept away, both you and your king."

Saul's Unlawful Sacrifice

13 Saul reigned one year; and when he had reigned two years over Israel,[a] 2Saul chose for himself three thousand *men* of Israel. Two thousand were with Saul in Michmash and in the mountains of Bethel, and a thousand were with Jonathan in Gibeah of Benjamin. The rest of the people he sent away, every man to his tent.

3And Jonathan attacked the garrison of the Philistines that *was* in Geba, and the Philistines heard *of it*. Then Saul blew the trumpet throughout all the land, saying, "Let the Hebrews hear!" 4Now all Israel heard it said *that* Saul had attacked a garrison of the Philistines, and *that* Israel had also become an abomination to the Philistines. And the people were called together to Saul at Gilgal.

5Then the Philistines gathered together to fight with Israel, thirty[a] thousand chariots and six thousand horsemen, and people as the sand which *is* on the seashore in multitude. And they came up and encamped in Michmash, to the east of Beth Aven. 6When the men of Israel saw that they were in danger (for the people were distressed), then the people hid in caves, in thickets, in rocks, in holes, and in pits. 7And *some of* the Hebrews crossed over the Jordan to the land of Gad and Gilead.

As for Saul, he *was* still in Gilgal, and all the people followed him trembling. 8Then he waited seven days, according to the time set by Samuel. But Samuel did not come to Gilgal; and the people were scattered from him. 9So Saul said, "Bring a burnt offering and peace offerings here to me." And he offered the burnt offering. 10Now it happened, as soon as he had finished presenting the burnt offering, that Samuel came; and Saul went out to meet him, that he might greet him.

11And Samuel said, "What have you done?"

Saul said, "When I saw that the people were scattered from me, and *that* you did not come within the days appointed, and *that* the Philistines gathered together at Michmash, 12then I said, 'The Philistines will now come down on me at Gilgal, and I have not made supplication to the LORD.' Therefore I felt compelled, and offered a burnt offering."

13And Samuel said to Saul, "You have done foolishly. You have not kept the commandment of the LORD your God, which He commanded you. For now the LORD would have established your kingdom over Israel forever. 14But now your kingdom shall not continue. The LORD has sought for Himself a man after His own heart, and the LORD has commanded him *to be* commander over His people, because you have not kept what the LORD commanded you."

15Then Samuel arose and went up from Gilgal to Gibeah of Benjamin.[a] And Saul numbered the people present with him, about six hundred men.

No Weapons for the Army

16Saul, Jonathan his son, and the people present with them remained in Gibeah of Benjamin. But the Philistines encamped in Michmash. 17Then raiders

13:1 [a] The Hebrew is difficult (compare 2 Samuel 5:4; 2 Kings 14:2; see also 2 Samuel 2:10; Acts 13:21).
13:5 [a] Following Masoretic Text, Septuagint, Targum, and Vulgate; Syriac and some manuscripts of the Septuagint read *three*. 13:15 [a] Following Masoretic Text and Targum; Septuagint and Vulgate add *And the rest of the people went up after Saul to meet the people who fought against them, going from Gilgal to Gibeah in the hill of Benjamin.*

came out of the camp of the Philistines
in three companies. One company
turned onto the road to Ophrah, to
the land of Shual, 18another company
turned to the road *to* Beth Horon, and
another company turned *to* the road of
the border that overlooks the Valley of
Zeboim toward the wilderness.
19Now there was no blacksmith to be
found throughout all the land of Israel,
for the Philistines said, "Lest the He-
brews make swords or spears." 20But
all the Israelites would go down to the
Philistines to sharpen each man's plow-
share, his mattock, his ax, and his sickle;
21and the charge for a sharpening was
a pim[a] for the plowshares, the mat-
tocks, the forks, and the axes, and to
set the points of the goads. 22So it came
about, on the day of battle, that there
was neither sword nor spear found in
the hand of any of the people who *were*
with Saul and Jonathan. But they were
found with Saul and Jonathan his son.
23And the garrison of the Philistines
went out to the pass of Michmash.

Jonathan Defeats the Philistines

14 Now it happened one day that
Jonathan the son of Saul said
to the young man who bore his armor,
"Come, let us go over to the Philistines'
garrison that *is* on the other side." But
he did not tell his father. 2And Saul was
sitting in the outskirts of Gibeah under a
pomegranate tree which *is* in Migron. The
people who *were* with him *were* about six
hundred men. 3Ahijah the son of Ahitub,
Ichabod's brother, the son of Phinehas,
the son of Eli, the LORD's priest in Shiloh,
was wearing an ephod. But the people
did not know that Jonathan had gone.
4Between the passes, by which Jona-
than sought to go over to the Philistines'
garrison, *there was* a sharp rock on
one side and a sharp rock on the other
side. And the name of one *was* Bozez,
and the name of the other Seneh. 5The
front of one faced northward opposite
Michmash, and the other southward
opposite Gibeah.
6Then Jonathan said to the young
man who bore his armor, "Come, let
us go over to the garrison of these uncir-
cumcised; it may be that the LORD will
work for us. For nothing restrains the
LORD from saving by many or by few."
7So his armorbearer said to him, "Do
all that is in your heart. Go then; here I
am with you, according to your heart."
8Then Jonathan said, "Very well, let
us cross over to *these* men, and we will
show ourselves to them. 9If they say
thus to us, 'Wait until we come to you,'
then we will stand still in our place and
not go up to them. 10But if they say thus,
'Come up to us,' then we will go up. For
the LORD has delivered them into our
hand, and this *will be* a sign to us."
11So both of them showed themselves
to the garrison of the Philistines. And
the Philistines said, "Look, the Hebrews
are coming out of the holes where they
have hidden." 12Then the men of the
garrison called to Jonathan and his
armorbearer, and said, "Come up to
us, and we will show you something."
Jonathan said to his armorbearer,
"Come up after me, for the LORD has
delivered them into the hand of Is-
rael." 13And Jonathan climbed up on
his hands and knees with his armor-
bearer after him; and they fell before
Jonathan. And as he came after him,
his armorbearer killed them. 14That
first slaughter which Jonathan and his
armorbearer made was about twenty
men within about half an acre of land.[a]
15And there was trembling in the
camp, in the field, and among all the
people. The garrison and the raiders
also trembled; and the earth quaked,
so that it was a very great trembling.
16Now the watchmen of Saul in Gibe-
ah of Benjamin looked, and *there* was
the multitude, melting away; and they
went here and there. 17Then Saul said
to the people who *were* with him, "Now
call the roll and see who has gone from
us." And when they had called the roll,
surprisingly, Jonathan and his armor-
bearer *were* not *there*. 18And Saul said
to Ahijah, "Bring the ark[a] of God here"
(for at that time the ark[b] of God was with

13:21 [a] About two-thirds shekel weight 14:14 [a] Literally *half the area plowed by a yoke* (of oxen in a day) 14:18 [a] Following Masoretic Text, Targum, and Vulgate; Septuagint reads *ephod*. [b] Following Masoretic Text, Targum, and Vulgate; Septuagint reads *ephod*.

the children of Israel). 19Now it happened, while Saul talked to the priest, that the noise which *was* in the camp of the Philistines continued to increase; so Saul said to the priest, "Withdraw your hand." 20Then Saul and all the people who *were* with him assembled, and they went to the battle; and indeed every man's sword was against his neighbor, *and there was* very great confusion. 21Moreover the Hebrews *who* were with the Philistines before that time, who went up with them into the camp *from the* surrounding *country,* they also joined the Israelites who *were* with Saul and Jonathan. 22Likewise all the men of Israel who had hidden in the mountains of Ephraim, *when* they heard that the Philistines fled, they also followed hard after them in the battle. 23So the LORD saved Israel that day, and the battle shifted to Beth Aven.

Saul's Rash Oath

24And the men of Israel were distressed that day, for Saul had placed the people under oath, saying, "Cursed *is* the man who eats *any* food until evening, before I have taken vengeance on my enemies." So none of the people tasted food. 25Now all *the people* of the land came to a forest; and there was honey on the ground. 26And when the people had come into the woods, there was the honey, dripping; but no one put his hand to his mouth, for the people feared the oath. 27But Jonathan had not heard his father charge the people with the oath; therefore he stretched out the end of the rod that *was* in his hand and dipped it in a honeycomb, and put his hand to his mouth; and his countenance brightened. 28Then one of the people said, "Your father strictly charged the people with an oath, saying, 'Cursed *is* the man who eats food this day.'" And the people were faint.

29But Jonathan said, "My father has troubled the land. Look now, how my countenance has brightened because I tasted a little of this honey. 30How much better if the people had eaten freely today of the spoil of their enemies which they found! For now would there not have been a much greater slaughter among the Philistines?"

31Now they had driven back the Philistines that day from Michmash to Aijalon. So the people were very faint. 32And the people rushed on the spoil, and took sheep, oxen, and calves, and slaughtered *them* on the ground; and the people ate *them* with the blood. 33Then they told Saul, saying, "Look, the people are sinning against the LORD by eating with the blood!"

So he said, "You have dealt treacherously; roll a large stone to me this day." 34Then Saul said, "Disperse yourselves among the people, and say to them, 'Bring me here every man's ox and every man's sheep, slaughter *them* here, and eat; and do not sin against the LORD by eating with the blood.'" So every one of the people brought his ox with him that night, and slaughtered *it* there. 35Then Saul built an altar to the LORD. This was the first altar that he built to the LORD.

36Now Saul said, "Let us go down after the Philistines by night, and plunder them until the morning light; and let us not leave a man of them."

And they said, "Do whatever seems good to you."

Then the priest said, "Let us draw near to God here."

37So Saul asked counsel of God, "Shall I go down after the Philistines? Will You deliver them into the hand of Israel?" But He did not answer him that day. 38And Saul said, "Come over here, all you chiefs of the people, and know and see what this sin was today. 39For *as* the LORD lives, who saves Israel, though it be in Jonathan my son, he shall surely die." But not a man among all the people answered him. 40Then he said to all Israel, "You be on one side, and my son Jonathan and I will be on the other side."

And the people said to Saul, "Do what seems good to you."

41Therefore Saul said to the LORD God of Israel, "Give a perfect *lot.*"[a] So Saul

14:41 [a] Following Masoretic Text and Targum; Septuagint and Vulgate read *Why do You not answer Your servant today? If the injustice is with me or Jonathan my son, O LORD God of Israel, give proof; and if You say it is with Your people Israel, give holiness.*

and Jonathan were taken, but the peo-
ple escaped. 42And Saul said, "Cast *lots*
between my son Jonathan and me." So
Jonathan was taken. 43Then Saul said to
Jonathan, "Tell me what you have done."
And Jonathan told him, and said, "I
only tasted a little honey with the end
of the rod that *was* in my hand. So now
I must die!"
44Saul answered, "God do so and more
also; for you shall surely die, Jonathan."
45But the people said to Saul, "Shall
Jonathan die, who has accomplished
this great deliverance in Israel? Certainly
not! *As* the LORD lives, not one hair of his
head shall fall to the ground, for he has
worked with God this day." So the people
rescued Jonathan, and he did not die.
46Then Saul returned from pursuing
the Philistines, and the Philistines went
to their own place.

Saul's Continuing Wars

47So Saul established his sovereignty
over Israel, and fought against all his
enemies on every side, against Moab,
against the people of Ammon, against
Edom, against the kings of Zobah, and
against the Philistines. Wherever he
turned, he harassed *them*.[a] 48And he
gathered an army and attacked the
Amalekites, and delivered Israel from
the hands of those who plundered them.
49The sons of Saul were Jonathan, Ji-
shui,[a] and Malchishua. And the names of
his two daughters *were these:* the name
of the firstborn Merab, and the name
of the younger Michal. 50The name of
Saul's wife *was* Ahinoam the daughter
of Ahimaaz. And the name of the com-
mander of his army *was* Abner the son
of Ner, Saul's uncle. 51Kish *was* the father
of Saul, and Ner the father of Abner *was*
the son of Abiel.
52Now there was fierce war with the
Philistines all the days of Saul. And
when Saul saw any strong man or any
valiant man, he took him for himself.

Saul Spares King Agag

15 Samuel also said to Saul, "The
LORD sent me to anoint you
king over His people, over Israel. Now
therefore, heed the voice of the words
of the LORD. 2Thus says the LORD of
hosts: 'I will punish Amalek *for* what he
did to Israel, how he ambushed him on
the way when he came up from Egypt.
3Now go and attack Amalek, and ut-
terly destroy all that they have, and do
not spare them. But kill both man and
woman, infant and nursing child, ox
and sheep, camel and donkey.' "
4So Saul gathered the people together
and numbered them in Telaim, two
hundred thousand foot soldiers and
ten thousand men of Judah. 5And Saul
came to a city of Amalek, and lay in
wait in the valley.
6Then Saul said to the Kenites, "Go,
depart, get down from among the Am-
alekites, lest I destroy you with them.
For you showed kindness to all the
children of Israel when they came up
out of Egypt." So the Kenites departed
from among the Amalekites. 7And Saul
attacked the Amalekites, from Havi-
lah all the way to Shur, which is east of
Egypt. 8He also took Agag king of the
Amalekites alive, and utterly destroyed
all the people with the edge of the sword.
9But Saul and the people spared Agag
and the best of the sheep, the oxen, the
fatlings, the lambs, and all *that was*
good, and were unwilling to utterly de-
stroy them. But everything despised and
worthless, that they utterly destroyed.

Saul Rejected as King

10Now the word of the LORD came to
Samuel, saying, 11"I greatly regret that
I have set up Saul *as* king, for he has
turned back from following Me, and has
not performed My commandments."
And it grieved Samuel, and he cried out
to the LORD all night. 12So when Sam-
uel rose early in the morning to meet
Saul, it was told Samuel, saying, "Saul
went to Carmel, and indeed, he set up
a monument for himself; and he has
gone on around, passed by, and gone
down to Gilgal." 13Then Samuel went to
Saul, and Saul said to him, "Blessed *are*
you of the LORD! I have performed the
commandment of the LORD."
14But Samuel said, "What then *is* this

14:47 [a] Septuagint and Vulgate read *prospered*. **14:49** [a] Called *Abinadab* in 1 Chronicles 8:33 and 9:39

bleating of the sheep in my ears, and
the lowing of the oxen which I hear?"
15And Saul said, "They have brought
them from the Amalekites; for the peo-
ple spared the best of the sheep and the
oxen, to sacrifice to the LORD your God;
and the rest we have utterly destroyed."
16Then Samuel said to Saul, "Be quiet!
And I will tell you what the LORD said
to me last night."
And he said to him, "Speak on."
17So Samuel said, "When you *were* little
in your own eyes, *were* you not head of
the tribes of Israel? And did not the LORD
anoint you king over Israel? 18Now the
LORD sent you on a mission, and said,
'Go, and utterly destroy the sinners, the
Amalekites, and fight against them until
they are consumed.' 19Why then did you
not obey the voice of the LORD? Why did
you swoop down on the spoil, and do
evil in the sight of the LORD?"
20And Saul said to Samuel, "But I have
obeyed the voice of the LORD, and gone
on the mission on which the LORD sent
me, and brought back Agag king of
Amalek; I have utterly destroyed the
Amalekites. 21But the people took of
the plunder, sheep and oxen, the best
of the things which should have been
utterly destroyed, to sacrifice to the
LORD your God in Gilgal."
22So Samuel said:

"Has the LORD *as great* delight
in burnt offerings and
sacrifices,
As in obeying the voice of the
LORD?
Behold, to obey is better than
sacrifice,
And to heed than the fat of rams.
23 For rebellion *is as* the sin of
witchcraft,
And stubbornness *is as* iniquity
and idolatry.
Because you have rejected the
word of the LORD,
He also has rejected you from
being king."

24Then Saul said to Samuel, "I have
sinned, for I have transgressed the
commandment of the LORD and your
words, because I feared the people and
obeyed their voice. 25Now therefore,
please pardon my sin, and return with
me, that I may worship the LORD."
26But Samuel said to Saul, "I will not
return with you, for you have rejected
the word of the LORD, and the LORD has
rejected you from being king over Israel."
27And as Samuel turned around to go
away, *Saul* seized the edge of his robe,
and it tore. 28So Samuel said to him,
"The LORD has torn the kingdom of Is-
rael from you today, and has given it to
a neighbor of yours, *who is* better than
you. 29And also the Strength of Israel
will not lie nor relent. For He *is* not a
man, that He should relent."
30Then he said, "I have sinned; *yet*
honor me now, please, before the elders
of my people and before Israel, and
return with me, that I may worship the
LORD your God." 31So Samuel turned
back after Saul, and Saul worshiped
the LORD.
32Then Samuel said, "Bring Agag king
of the Amalekites here to me." So Agag
came to him cautiously.
And Agag said, "Surely the bitterness
of death is past."
33But Samuel said, "As your sword has
made women childless, so shall your
mother be childless among women."
And Samuel hacked Agag in pieces be-
fore the LORD in Gilgal.
34Then Samuel went to Ramah, and Saul
went up to his house at Gibeah of Saul.
35And Samuel went no more to see Saul
until the day of his death. Nevertheless
Samuel mourned for Saul, and the LORD
regretted that He had made Saul king
over Israel.

David Anointed King

16 Now the LORD said to Samuel,
"How long will you mourn for
Saul, seeing I have rejected him from
reigning over Israel? Fill your horn with
oil, and go; I am sending you to Jesse
the Bethlehemite. For I have provided
Myself a king among his sons."
2And Samuel said, "How can I go? If
Saul hears *it*, he will kill me."
But the LORD said, "Take a heifer with
you, and say, 'I have come to sacrifice
to the LORD.' 3Then invite Jesse to the
sacrifice, and I will show you what you

shall do; you shall anoint for Me the one
I name to you."
4So Samuel did what the LORD said,
and went to Bethlehem. And the elders
of the town trembled at his coming, and
said, "Do you come peaceably?"
5And he said, "Peaceably; I have come
to sacrifice to the LORD. Sanctify your-
selves, and come with me to the sacri-
fice." Then he consecrated Jesse and his
sons, and invited them to the sacrifice.
6So it was, when they came, that he
looked at Eliab and said, "Surely the
LORD's anointed *is* before Him!"
7But the LORD said to Samuel, "Do not
look at his appearance or at his physical
stature, because I have refused him. For
the LORD *does* not *see* as man sees;[a] for
man looks at the outward appearance,
but the LORD looks at the heart."
8So Jesse called Abinadab, and made
him pass before Samuel. And he said,
"Neither has the LORD chosen this one."
9Then Jesse made Shammah pass by.
And he said, "Neither has the LORD cho-
sen this one." 10Thus Jesse made seven of
his sons pass before Samuel. And Sam-
uel said to Jesse, "The LORD has not cho-
sen these." 11And Samuel said to Jesse,
"Are all the young men here?" Then he
said, "There remains yet the youngest,
and there he is, keeping the sheep."
And Samuel said to Jesse, "Send and
bring him. For we will not sit down[a] till
he comes here." 12So he sent and brought
him in. Now he *was* ruddy, with bright
eyes, and good-looking. And the LORD
said, "Arise, anoint him; for this *is* the
one!" 13Then Samuel took the horn of
oil and anointed him in the midst of his
brothers; and the Spirit of the LORD came
upon David from that day forward. So
Samuel arose and went to Ramah.

A Distressing Spirit Troubles Saul

14But the Spirit of the LORD departed
from Saul, and a distressing spirit from
the LORD troubled him. 15And Saul's
servants said to him, "Surely, a distress-
ing spirit from God is troubling you.
16Let our master now command your
servants, *who are* before you, to seek
out a man *who is* a skillful player on the
harp. And it shall be that he will play
it with his hand when the distressing
spirit from God is upon you, and you
shall be well."
17So Saul said to his servants, "Provide
me now a man who can play well, and
bring *him* to me."
18Then one of the servants answered
and said, "Look, I have seen a son of
Jesse the Bethlehemite, *who is* skillful
in playing, a mighty man of valor, a
man of war, prudent in speech, and
a handsome person; and the LORD *is*
with him."
19Therefore Saul sent messengers to
Jesse, and said, "Send me your son
David, who *is* with the sheep." 20And
Jesse took a donkey *loaded with* bread,
a skin of wine, and a young goat, and
sent *them* by his son David to Saul. 21So
David came to Saul and stood before
him. And he loved him greatly, and he
became his armorbearer. 22Then Saul
sent to Jesse, saying, "Please let David
stand before me, for he has found favor
in my sight." 23And so it was, whenever
the spirit from God was upon Saul, that
David would take a harp and play *it*
with his hand. Then Saul would become
refreshed and well, and the distressing
spirit would depart from him.

David and Goliath

17 Now the Philistines gathered
their armies together to battle,
and were gathered at Sochoh, which
belongs to Judah; they encamped be-
tween Sochoh and Azekah, in Ephes
Dammim. 2And Saul and the men of
Israel were gathered together, and
they encamped in the Valley of Elah,
and drew up in battle array against
the Philistines. 3The Philistines stood
on a mountain on one side, and Israel
stood on a mountain on the other side,
with a valley between them.
4And a champion went out from the
camp of the Philistines, named Goliath,
from Gath, whose height *was* six cubits
and a span. 5*He had* a bronze helmet on
his head, and he *was* armed with a coat

16:7 [a] Septuagint reads *For God does not see as man sees;* Targum reads *It is not by the appearance of a man;* Vulgate reads *Nor do I judge according to the looks of a man.* **16:11** [a] Following Septuagint and Vulgate; Masoretic Text reads *turn around;* Targum and Syriac read *turn away.*

of mail, and the weight of the coat *was*
five thousand shekels of bronze. 6And
he had bronze armor on his legs and a
bronze javelin between his shoulders.
7Now the staff of his spear *was* like a
weaver's beam, and his iron spearhead
weighed six hundred shekels; and a
shield-bearer went before him. 8Then
he stood and cried out to the armies
of Israel, and said to them, "Why have
you come out to line up for battle? *Am* I
not a Philistine, and you the servants of
Saul? Choose a man for yourselves, and
let him come down to me. 9If he is able
to fight with me and kill me, then we will
be your servants. But if I prevail against
him and kill him, then you shall be our
servants and serve us." 10And the Phi-
listine said, "I defy the armies of Israel
this day; give me a man, that we may
fight together." 11When Saul and all Is-
rael heard these words of the Philistine,
they were dismayed and greatly afraid.
12Now David *was* the son of that Eph-
rathite of Bethlehem Judah, whose
name *was* Jesse, and who had eight
sons. And the man was old, advanced
in years, in the days of Saul. 13The three
oldest sons of Jesse had gone to follow
Saul to the battle. The names of his three
sons who went to the battle *were* Eliab
the firstborn, next to him Abinadab, and
the third Shammah. 14David *was* the
youngest. And the three oldest followed
Saul. 15But David occasionally went and
returned from Saul to feed his father's
sheep at Bethlehem.

16And the Philistine drew near and
presented himself forty days, morning
and evening.

17Then Jesse said to his son David,
"Take now for your brothers an ephah
of this dried *grain* and these ten loaves,
and run to your brothers at the camp.
18And carry these ten cheeses to the
captain of *their* thousand, and see how
your brothers fare, and bring back news
of them." 19Now Saul and they and all
the men of Israel *were* in the Valley of
Elah, fighting with the Philistines.

20So David rose early in the morning,
left the sheep with a keeper, and took *the
things* and went as Jesse had command-
ed him. And he came to the camp as the
army was going out to the fight and
shouting for the battle. 21For Israel and
the Philistines had drawn up in battle
array, army against army. 22And David
left his supplies in the hand of the sup-
ply keeper, ran to the army, and came
and greeted his brothers. 23Then as he
talked with them, there was the cham-
pion, the Philistine of Gath, Goliath by
name, coming up from the armies of the
Philistines; and he spoke according to
the same words. So David heard *them.*
24And all the men of Israel, when they
saw the man, fled from him and were
dreadfully afraid. 25So the men of Israel
said, "Have you seen this man who has
come up? Surely he has come up to defy
Israel; and it shall be *that* the man who
kills him the king will enrich with great
riches, will give him his daughter, and
give his father's house exemption *from
taxes* in Israel."

26Then David spoke to the men who
stood by him, saying, "What shall be
done for the man who kills this Phi-
listine and takes away the reproach
from Israel? For who *is* this uncircum-
cised Philistine, that he should defy the
armies of the living God?"

27And the people answered him in this
manner, saying, "So shall it be done for
the man who kills him."

28Now Eliab his oldest brother heard
when he spoke to the men; and Eliab's
anger was aroused against David, and
he said, "Why did you come down here?
And with whom have you left those
few sheep in the wilderness? I know
your pride and the insolence of your
heart, for you have come down to see
the battle."

29And David said, "What have I done
now? *Is there* not a cause?" 30Then he
turned from him toward another and
said the same thing; and these people
answered him as the first ones *did.*

31Now when the words which David
spoke were heard, they reported *them*
to Saul; and he sent for him. 32Then
David said to Saul, "Let no man's heart
fail because of him; your servant will go
and fight with this Philistine."

33And Saul said to David, "You are not
able to go against this Philistine to fight
with him; for you *are* a youth, and he a
man of war from his youth."

34 But David said to Saul, "Your servant used to keep his father's sheep, and when a lion or a bear came and took a lamb out of the flock, 35 I went out after it and struck it, and delivered *the lamb* from its mouth; and when it arose against me, I caught *it* by its beard, and struck and killed it. 36 Your servant has killed both lion and bear; and this uncircumcised Philistine will be like one of them, seeing he has defied the armies of the living God." 37 Moreover David said, "The LORD, who delivered me from the paw of the lion and from the paw of the bear, He will deliver me from the hand of this Philistine."

And Saul said to David, "Go, and the LORD be with you!"

38 So Saul clothed David with his armor, and he put a bronze helmet on his head; he also clothed him with a coat of mail. 39 David fastened his sword to his armor and tried to walk, for he had not tested *them*. And David said to Saul, "I cannot walk with these, for I have not tested *them*." So David took them off.

40 Then he took his staff in his hand; and he chose for himself five smooth stones from the brook, and put them in a shepherd's bag, in a pouch which he had, and his sling was in his hand. And he drew near to the Philistine. 41 So the Philistine came, and began drawing near to David, and the man who bore the shield *went* before him. 42 And when the Philistine looked about and saw David, he disdained him; for he was *only* a youth, ruddy and good-looking. 43 So the Philistine said to David, "*Am* I a dog, that you come to me with sticks?" And the Philistine cursed David by his gods. 44 And the Philistine said to David, "Come to me, and I will give your flesh to the birds of the air and the beasts of the field!"

45 Then David said to the Philistine, "You come to me with a sword, with a spear, and with a javelin. But I come to you in the name of the LORD of hosts, the God of the armies of Israel, whom you have defied. 46 This day the LORD will deliver you into my hand, and I will strike you and take your head from you. And this day I will give the carcasses of the camp of the Philistines to the birds of the air and the wild beasts of the earth, that all the earth may know that there is a God in Israel. 47 Then all this assembly shall know that the LORD does not save with sword and spear; for the battle *is* the LORD's, and He will give you into our hands."

48 So it was, when the Philistine arose and came and drew near to meet David, that David hurried and ran toward the army to meet the Philistine. 49 Then David put his hand in his bag and took out a stone; and he slung *it* and struck the Philistine in his forehead, so that the stone sank into his forehead, and he fell on his face to the earth. 50 So David prevailed over the Philistine with a sling and a stone, and struck the Philistine and killed him. But *there was* no sword in the hand of David. 51 Therefore David ran and stood over the Philistine, took his sword and drew it out of its sheath and killed him, and cut off his head with it.

And when the Philistines saw that their champion was dead, they fled. 52 Now the men of Israel and Judah arose and shouted, and pursued the Philistines as far as the entrance of the valley[a] and to the gates of Ekron. And the wounded of the Philistines fell along the road to Shaaraim, even as far as Gath and Ekron. 53 Then the children of Israel returned from chasing the Philistines, and they plundered their tents. 54 And David took the head of the Philistine and brought it to Jerusalem, but he put his armor in his tent.

55 When Saul saw David going out against the Philistine, he said to Abner, the commander of the army, "Abner, whose son *is* this youth?"

And Abner said, "As your soul lives, O king, I do not know."

56 So the king said, "Inquire whose son this young man *is*."

57 Then, as David returned from the slaughter of the Philistine, Abner took him and brought him before Saul with the head of the Philistine in his hand. 58 And Saul said to him, "Whose son *are* you, young man?"

So David answered, "*I am* the son of your servant Jesse the Bethlehemite."

17:52 [a] Following Masoretic Text, Syriac, Targum, and Vulgate; Septuagint reads *Gath*.

Saul Resents David

18 Now when he had finished speaking to Saul, the soul of Jonathan was knit to the soul of David, and Jonathan loved him as his own soul. 2 Saul took him that day, and would not let him go home to his father's house anymore. 3 Then Jonathan and David made a covenant, because he loved him as his own soul. 4 And Jonathan took off the robe that *was* on him and gave it to David, with his armor, even to his sword and his bow and his belt.

5 So David went out wherever Saul sent him, *and* behaved wisely. And Saul set him over the men of war, and he was accepted in the sight of all the people and also in the sight of Saul's servants. 6 Now it had happened as they were coming *home,* when David was returning from the slaughter of the Philistine, that the women had come out of all the cities of Israel, singing and dancing, to meet King Saul, with tambourines, with joy, and with musical instruments. 7 So the women sang as they danced, and said:

"Saul has slain his thousands,
And David his ten thousands."

8 Then Saul was very angry, and the saying displeased him; and he said, "They have ascribed to David ten thousands, and to me they have ascribed *only* thousands. Now *what* more can he have but the kingdom?" 9 So Saul eyed David from that day forward.

10 And it happened on the next day that the distressing spirit from God came upon Saul, and he prophesied inside the house. So David played *music* with his hand, as at other times; but *there was* a spear in Saul's hand. 11 And Saul cast the spear, for he said, "I will pin David to the wall!" But David escaped his presence twice.

12 Now Saul was afraid of David, because the LORD was with him, but had departed from Saul. 13 Therefore Saul removed him from his presence, and made him his captain over a thousand; and he went out and came in before the people. 14 And David behaved wisely in all his ways, and the LORD *was* with him. 15 Therefore, when Saul saw that he behaved very wisely, he was afraid of him. 16 But all Israel and Judah loved David, because he went out and came in before them.

David Marries Michal

17 Then Saul said to David, "Here is my older daughter Merab; I will give her to you as a wife. Only be valiant for me, and fight the LORD's battles." For Saul thought, "Let my hand not be against him, but let the hand of the Philistines be against him."

18 So David said to Saul, "Who *am* I, and what *is* my life *or* my father's family in Israel, that I should be son-in-law to the king?" 19 But it happened at the time when Merab, Saul's daughter, should have been given to David, that she was given to Adriel the Meholathite as a wife.

20 Now Michal, Saul's daughter, loved David. And they told Saul, and the thing pleased him. 21 So Saul said, "I will give her to him, that she may be a snare to him, and that the hand of the Philistines may be against him." Therefore Saul said to David a second time, "You shall be my son-in-law today."

22 And Saul commanded his servants, "Communicate with David secretly, and say, 'Look, the king has delight in you, and all his servants love you. Now therefore, become the king's son-in-law.' "

23 So Saul's servants spoke those words in the hearing of David. And David said, "Does it seem to you *a* light *thing* to be a king's son-in-law, seeing I *am* a poor and lightly esteemed man?" 24 And the servants of Saul told him, saying, "In this manner David spoke."

25 Then Saul said, "Thus you shall say to David: 'The king does not desire any dowry but one hundred foreskins of the Philistines, to take vengeance on the king's enemies.' " But Saul thought to make David fall by the hand of the Philistines. 26 So when his servants told David these words, it pleased David well to become the king's son-in-law. Now the days had not expired; 27 therefore David arose and went, he and his men, and killed two hundred men of the Philistines. And David brought their foreskins, and they gave them in full count

to the king, that he might become the
king's son-in-law. Then Saul gave him
Michal his daughter as a wife.
28Thus Saul saw and knew that the
LORD *was* with David, and *that* Michal,
Saul's daughter, loved him; 29and Saul
was still more afraid of David. So Saul
became David's enemy continually.
30Then the princes of the Philistines
went out *to war.* And so it was, whenever
they went out, *that* David behaved more
wisely than all the servants of Saul, so
that his name became highly esteemed.

Saul Persecutes David

19 Now Saul spoke to Jonathan his
son and to all his servants, that
they should kill David; but Jonathan,
Saul's son, delighted greatly in David.
2So Jonathan told David, saying, "My
father Saul seeks to kill you. Therefore
please be on your guard until morning,
and stay in a secret *place* and hide. 3And
I will go out and stand beside my father
in the field where you *are,* and I will
speak with my father about you. Then
what I observe, I will tell you."
4Thus Jonathan spoke well of David to
Saul his father, and said to him, "Let not
the king sin against his servant, against
David, because he has not sinned
against you, and because his works
have been very good toward you. 5For
he took his life in his hands and killed
the Philistine, and the LORD brought
about a great deliverance for all Israel.
You saw *it* and rejoiced. Why then will
you sin against innocent blood, to kill
David without a cause?"
6So Saul heeded the voice of Jonathan,
and Saul swore, "*As* the LORD lives, he
shall not be killed." 7Then Jonathan
called David, and Jonathan told him
all these things. So Jonathan brought
David to Saul, and he was in his pres-
ence as in times past.
8And there was war again; and David
went out and fought with the Philistines,
and struck them with a mighty blow,
and they fled from him.
9Now the distressing spirit from the
LORD came upon Saul as he sat in his
house with his spear in his hand. And
David was playing *music* with *his* hand.
10Then Saul sought to pin David to the
wall with the spear, but he slipped away
from Saul's presence; and he drove the
spear into the wall. So David fled and
escaped that night.
11Saul also sent messengers to David's
house to watch him and to kill him in
the morning. And Michal, David's wife,
told him, saying, "If you do not save
your life tonight, tomorrow you will
be killed." 12So Michal let David down
through a window. And he went and
fled and escaped. 13And Michal took
an image and laid *it* in the bed, put a
cover of goats' *hair* for his head, and
covered *it* with clothes. 14So when Saul
sent messengers to take David, she said,
"He *is* sick."
15Then Saul sent the messengers *back*
to see David, saying, "Bring him up
to me in the bed, that I may kill him."
16And when the messengers had come
in, there was the image in the bed, with
a cover of goats' *hair* for his head. 17Then
Saul said to Michal, "Why have you de-
ceived me like this, and sent my enemy
away, so that he has escaped?"
And Michal answered Saul, "He said to
me, 'Let me go! Why should I kill you?' "
18So David fled and escaped, and went
to Samuel at Ramah, and told him all
that Saul had done to him. And he and
Samuel went and stayed in Naioth.
19Now it was told Saul, saying, "Take
note, David *is* at Naioth in Ramah!"
20Then Saul sent messengers to take
David. And when they saw the group
of prophets prophesying, and Samuel
standing *as* leader over them, the Spirit
of God came upon the messengers of
Saul, and they also prophesied. 21And
when Saul was told, he sent other mes-
sengers, and they prophesied likewise.
Then Saul sent messengers again the
third time, and they prophesied also.
22Then he also went to Ramah, and
came to the great well that *is* at Sechu.
So he asked, and said, "Where *are* Sam-
uel and David?"
And *someone* said, "Indeed *they are* at
Naioth in Ramah." 23So he went there
to Naioth in Ramah. Then the Spirit of
God was upon him also, and he went on
and prophesied until he came to Nai-
oth in Ramah. 24And he also stripped
off his clothes and prophesied before

Samuel in like manner, and lay down
naked all that day and all that night.
Therefore they say, "*Is* Saul also among
the prophets?"[a]

Jonathan's Loyalty to David

20 Then David fled from Naioth in
Ramah, and went and said to
Jonathan, "What have I done? What *is*
my iniquity, and what *is* my sin before
your father, that he seeks my life?"
2 So Jonathan said to him, "By no
means! You shall not die! Indeed, my
father will do nothing either great or
small without first telling me. And why
should my father hide this thing from
me? It *is* not *so!*"
3 Then David took an oath again, and
said, "Your father certainly knows that
I have found favor in your eyes, and
he has said, 'Do not let Jonathan know
this, lest he be grieved.' But truly, *as* the
LORD lives and *as* your soul lives, *there*
is but a step between me and death."
4 So Jonathan said to David, "Whatever
you yourself desire, I will do *it* for you."
5 And David said to Jonathan, "Indeed
tomorrow *is* the New Moon, and I should
not fail to sit with the king to eat. But
let me go, that I may hide in the field
until the third *day* at evening. 6 If your
father misses me at all, then say, 'David
earnestly asked *permission* of me that
he might run over to Bethlehem, his
city, for *there is* a yearly sacrifice there
for all the family.' 7 If he says thus: '*It is*
well,' your servant will be safe. But if he
is very angry, be sure that evil is deter-
mined by him. 8 Therefore you shall deal
kindly with your servant, for you have
brought your servant into a covenant of
the LORD with you. Nevertheless, if there
is iniquity in me, kill me yourself, for why
should you bring me to your father?"
9 But Jonathan said, "Far be it from
you! For if I knew certainly that evil
was determined by my father to come
upon you, then would I not tell you?"
10 Then David said to Jonathan, "Who
will tell me, or what *if* your father an-
swers you roughly?"
11 And Jonathan said to David, "Come,
let us go out into the field." So both of
them went out into the field. 12 Then Jon-
athan said to David: "The LORD God of
Israel *is witness!* When I have sounded
out my father sometime tomorrow, *or*
the third *day,* and indeed *there is* good
toward David, and I do not send to you
and tell you, 13 may the LORD do so and
much more to Jonathan. But if it pleases
my father *to do* you evil, then I will re-
port it to you and send you away, that
you may go in safety. And the LORD be
with you as He has been with my father.
14 And you shall not only show me the
kindness of the LORD while I still live,
that I may not die; 15 but you shall not
cut off your kindness from my house
forever, no, not when the LORD has cut
off every one of the enemies of David
from the face of the earth." 16 So Jona-
than made *a covenant* with the house
of David, *saying,* "Let the LORD require
it at the hand of David's enemies."
17 Now Jonathan again caused David to
vow, because he loved him; for he loved
him as he loved his own soul. 18 Then
Jonathan said to David, "Tomorrow *is*
the New Moon; and you will be missed,
because your seat will be empty. 19 And
when you have stayed three days, go
down quickly and come to the place
where you hid on the day of the deed;
and remain by the stone Ezel. 20 Then I
will shoot three arrows to the side, as
though I shot at a target; 21 and there
I will send a lad, *saying,* 'Go, find the
arrows.' If I expressly say to the lad,
'Look, the arrows *are* on this side of you;
get them and come'—then, as the LORD
lives, *there is* safety for you and no harm.
22 But if I say thus to the young man,
'Look, the arrows *are* beyond you'—go
your way, for the LORD has sent you
away. 23 And as for the matter which
you and I have spoken of, indeed the
LORD *be* between you and me forever."
24 Then David hid in the field. And
when the New Moon had come, the king
sat down to eat the feast. 25 Now the king
sat on his seat, as at other times, on a
seat by the wall. And Jonathan arose,[a]
and Abner sat by Saul's side, but David's
place was empty. 26 Nevertheless Saul
did not say anything that day, for he

19:24 [a] Compare 1 Samuel 10:12 **20:25** [a] Following Masoretic Text, Syriac, Targum, and Vulgate; Septuagint reads *he sat across from Jonathan.*

thought, "Something has happened to
him; he *is* unclean, surely he *is* unclean."
27And it happened the next day, the sec-
ond *day* of the month, that David's place
was empty. And Saul said to Jonathan
his son, "Why has the son of Jesse not
come to eat, either yesterday or today?"
28So Jonathan answered Saul, "David
earnestly asked *permission* of me *to go* to
Bethlehem. 29And he said, 'Please let me
go, for our family has a sacrifice in the
city, and my brother has commanded
me *to be there.* And now, if I have found
favor in your eyes, please let me get
away and see my brothers.' Therefore
he has not come to the king's table."
30Then Saul's anger was aroused
against Jonathan, and he said to him,
"You son of a perverse, rebellious *wom-
an!* Do I not know that you have chosen
the son of Jesse to your own shame
and to the shame of your mother's na-
kedness? 31For as long as the son of
Jesse lives on the earth, you shall not
be established, nor your kingdom. Now
therefore, send and bring him to me, for
he shall surely die."
32And Jonathan answered Saul his fa-
ther, and said to him, "Why should he be
killed? What has he done?" 33Then Saul
cast a spear at him to kill him, by which
Jonathan knew that it was determined
by his father to kill David.
34So Jonathan arose from the table in
fierce anger, and ate no food the second
day of the month, for he was grieved for
David, because his father had treated
him shamefully.
35And so it was, in the morning, that
Jonathan went out into the field at the
time appointed with David, and a little
lad *was* with him. 36Then he said to his
lad, "Now run, find the arrows which I
shoot." As the lad ran, he shot an arrow
beyond him. 37When the lad had come
to the place where the arrow was which
Jonathan had shot, Jonathan cried out
after the lad and said, "*Is* not the arrow
beyond you?" 38And Jonathan cried
out after the lad, "Make haste, hurry,
do not delay!" So Jonathan's lad gath-
ered up the arrows and came back to
his master. 39But the lad did not know
anything. Only Jonathan and David
knew of the matter. 40Then Jonathan
gave his weapons to his lad, and said to
him, "Go, carry *them* to the city."
41As soon as the lad had gone, David
arose from *a place* toward the south, fell
on his face to the ground, and bowed
down three times. And they kissed one
another; and they wept together, but
David more so. 42Then Jonathan said
to David, "Go in peace, since we have
both sworn in the name of the LORD,
saying, 'May the LORD be between you
and me, and between your descendants
and my descendants, forever.' " So he
arose and departed, and Jonathan went
into the city.

David and the Holy Bread

21 Now David came to Nob, to
Ahimelech the priest. And Ahim-
elech was afraid when he met David,
and said to him, "Why *are* you alone,
and no one is with you?"
2So David said to Ahimelech the priest,
"The king has ordered me on some busi-
ness, and said to me, 'Do not let any-
one know anything about the business
on which I send you, or what I have
commanded you.' And I have direct-
ed *my* young men to such and such a
place. 3Now therefore, what have you
on hand? Give *me* five *loaves of* bread
in my hand, or whatever can be found."
4And the priest answered David and
said, "*There is* no common bread on
hand; but there is holy bread, if the
young men have at least kept them-
selves from women."
5Then David answered the priest, and
said to him, "Truly, women *have been*
kept from us about three days since I
came out. And the vessels of the young
men are holy, and *the bread is* in effect
common, even though it was consecrat-
ed in the vessel this day."
6So the priest gave him holy *bread;*
for there was no bread there but the
showbread which had been taken from
before the LORD, in order to put hot
bread *in its place* on the day when it
was taken away.
7Now a certain man of the servants of
Saul *was* there that day, detained before
the LORD. And his name *was* Doeg, an
Edomite, the chief of the herdsmen who
belonged to Saul.

8And David said to Ahimelech, "Is there
not here on hand a spear or a sword? For
I have brought neither my sword nor my
weapons with me, because the king's
business required haste."
9So the priest said, "The sword of Go-
liath the Philistine, whom you killed in
the Valley of Elah, there it is, wrapped
in a cloth behind the ephod. If you will
take that, take *it.* For *there is* no other
except that one here."
And David said, "*There is* none like it;
give it to me."

David Flees to Gath

10Then David arose and fled that day
from before Saul, and went to Achish
the king of Gath. 11And the servants of
Achish said to him, "*Is* this not David
the king of the land? Did they not sing
of him to one another in dances, saying:

'Saul has slain his thousands,
And David his ten thousands'?"[a]

12Now David took these words to heart,
and was very much afraid of Achish
the king of Gath. 13So he changed his
behavior before them, pretended mad-
ness in their hands, scratched on the
doors of the gate, and let his saliva fall
down on his beard. 14Then Achish said
to his servants, "Look, you see the man
is insane. Why have you brought him
to me? 15Have I need of madmen, that
you have brought this *fellow* to play the
madman in my presence? Shall this
fellow come into my house?"

David's Four Hundred Men

22 David therefore departed from
there and escaped to the cave of
Adullam. So when his brothers and all
his father's house heard *it,* they went
down there to him. 2And everyone *who
was* in distress, everyone who *was* in
debt, and everyone *who was* discontent-
ed gathered to him. So he became cap-
tain over them. And there were about
four hundred men with him.
3Then David went from there to Miz-
pah of Moab; and he said to the king of
Moab, "Please let my father and mother
come here with you, till I know what God
will do for me." 4So he brought them
before the king of Moab, and they dwelt
with him all the time that David was in
the stronghold.
5Now the prophet Gad said to David,
"Do not stay in the stronghold; depart,
and go to the land of Judah." So David
departed and went into the forest of
Hereth.

Saul Murders the Priests

6When Saul heard that David and
the men who *were* with him had been
discovered—now Saul was staying in
Gibeah under a tamarisk tree in Ramah,
with his spear in his hand, and all his
servants standing about him— 7then
Saul said to his servants who stood
about him, "Hear now, you Benjamites!
Will the son of Jesse give every one of
you fields and vineyards, *and* make you
all captains of thousands and captains
of hundreds? 8All of you have conspired
against me, and *there is* no one who
reveals to me that my son has made
a covenant with the son of Jesse; and
there is not one of you who is sorry for
me or reveals to me that my son has
stirred up my servant against me, to
lie in wait, as *it is* this day."
9Then answered Doeg the Edomite,
who was set over the servants of Saul,
and said, "I saw the son of Jesse going
to Nob, to Ahimelech the son of Ahitub.
10And he inquired of the LORD for him,
gave him provisions, and gave him the
sword of Goliath the Philistine."
11So the king sent to call Ahimelech the
priest, the son of Ahitub, and all his fa-
ther's house, the priests who *were* in Nob.
And they all came to the king. 12And
Saul said, "Hear now, son of Ahitub!"
He answered, "Here I am, my lord."
13Then Saul said to him, "Why have
you conspired against me, you and the
son of Jesse, in that you have given him
bread and a sword, and have inquired of
God for him, that he should rise against
me, to lie in wait, as it is this day?"
14So Ahimelech answered the king and
said, "And who among all your servants
is as faithful as David, who is the king's

21:11 [a] Compare 1 Samuel 18:7

son-in-law, who goes at your bidding,
and is honorable in your house? 15Did I
then begin to inquire of God for him? Far
be it from me! Let not the king impute
anything to his servant, *or* to any in the
house of my father. For your servant
knew nothing of all this, little or much."
16And the king said, "You shall surely
die, Ahimelech, you and all your father's house!" 17Then the king said to
the guards who stood about him, "Turn
and kill the priests of the LORD, because
their hand also *is* with David, and because they knew when he fled and did
not tell it to me." But the servants of
the king would not lift their hands to
strike the priests of the LORD. 18And
the king said to Doeg, "You turn and
kill the priests!" So Doeg the Edomite
turned and struck the priests, and killed
on that day eighty-five men who wore a
linen ephod. 19Also Nob, the city of the
priests, he struck with the edge of the
sword, both men and women, children
and nursing infants, oxen and donkeys
and sheep—with the edge of the sword.
20Now one of the sons of Ahimelech the
son of Ahitub, named Abiathar, escaped
and fled after David. 21And Abiathar told
David that Saul had killed the LORD's
priests. 22So David said to Abiathar, "I
knew that day, when Doeg the Edomite
was there, that he would surely tell Saul.
I have caused *the death* of all the persons
of your father's house. 23Stay with me; do
not fear. For he who seeks my life seeks
your life, but with me you *shall be* safe."

David Saves the City of Keilah

23 Then they told David, saying,
"Look, the Philistines are fighting against Keilah, and they are robbing the threshing floors."
2Therefore David inquired of the LORD,
saying, "Shall I go and attack these
Philistines?"
And the LORD said to David, "Go and
attack the Philistines, and save Keilah."
3But David's men said to him, "Look,
we are afraid here in Judah. How much
more then if we go to Keilah against the
armies of the Philistines?" 4Then David
inquired of the LORD once again.
And the LORD answered him and said,
"Arise, go down to Keilah. For I will deliver the Philistines into your hand."
5And David and his men went to Keilah
and fought with the Philistines, struck
them with a mighty blow, and took
away their livestock. So David saved
the inhabitants of Keilah.
6Now it happened, when Abiathar the
son of Ahimelech fled to David at Keilah, *that* he went down *with* an ephod
in his hand.
7And Saul was told that David had gone
to Keilah. So Saul said, "God has delivered him into my hand, for he has shut
himself in by entering a town that has
gates and bars." 8Then Saul called all
the people together for war, to go down
to Keilah to besiege David and his men.
9When David knew that Saul plotted
evil against him, he said to Abiathar the
priest, "Bring the ephod here." 10Then
David said, "O LORD God of Israel, Your
servant has certainly heard that Saul
seeks to come to Keilah to destroy the
city for my sake. 11Will the men of Keilah deliver me into his hand? Will Saul
come down, as Your servant has heard?
O LORD God of Israel, I pray, tell Your
servant."
And the LORD said, "He will come
down."
12Then David said, "Will the men of
Keilah deliver me and my men into the
hand of Saul?"
And the LORD said, "They will deliver
you."
13So David and his men, about six
hundred, arose and departed from Keilah and went wherever they could go.
Then it was told Saul that David had
escaped from Keilah; so he halted the
expedition.

David in Wilderness Strongholds

14And David stayed in strongholds
in the wilderness, and remained in the
mountains in the Wilderness of Ziph.
Saul sought him every day, but God did
not deliver him into his hand. 15So David
saw that Saul had come out to seek his
life. And David *was* in the Wilderness
of Ziph in a forest.[a] 16Then Jonathan,

23:15 [a] Or *in Horesh*

Saul's son, arose and went to David in
the woods and strengthened his hand in
God. 17And he said to him, "Do not fear,
for the hand of Saul my father shall not
find you. You shall be king over Isra-
el, and I shall be next to you. Even my
father Saul knows that." 18So the two
of them made a covenant before the
LORD. And David stayed in the woods,
and Jonathan went to his own house.
19Then the Ziphites came up to Saul at
Gibeah, saying, "Is David not hiding with
us in strongholds in the woods, in the hill
of Hachilah, which *is* on the south of Je-
shimon? 20Now therefore, O king, come
down according to all the desire of your
soul to come down; and our part *shall
be* to deliver him into the king's hand."
21And Saul said, "Blessed *are* you of
the LORD, for you have compassion on
me. 22Please go and find out for sure,
and see the place where his hideout is,
and who has seen him there. For I am
told he is very crafty. 23See therefore,
and take knowledge of all the lurking
places where he hides; and come back
to me with certainty, and I will go with
you. And it shall be, if he is in the land,
that I will search for him throughout
all the clans[a] of Judah."
24So they arose and went to Ziph be-
fore Saul. But David and his men *were*
in the Wilderness of Maon, in the plain
on the south of Jeshimon. 25When Saul
and his men went to seek *him,* they told
David. Therefore he went down to the
rock, and stayed in the Wilderness of
Maon. And when Saul heard *that,* he
pursued David in the Wilderness of
Maon. 26Then Saul went on one side of
the mountain, and David and his men
on the other side of the mountain. So
David made haste to get away from
Saul, for Saul and his men were encir-
cling David and his men to take them.
27But a messenger came to Saul, say-
ing, "Hurry and come, for the Philistines
have invaded the land!" 28Therefore
Saul returned from pursuing David,
and went against the Philistines; so they
called that place the Rock of Escape.[a]
29Then David went up from there and
dwelt in strongholds at En Gedi.

David Spares Saul

24 Now it happened, when Saul
had returned from following
the Philistines, that it was told him,
saying, "Take note! David *is* in the Wil-
derness of En Gedi." 2Then Saul took
three thousand chosen men from all
Israel, and went to seek David and his
men on the Rocks of the Wild Goats. 3So
he came to the sheepfolds by the road,
where there *was* a cave; and Saul went
in to attend to his needs. (David and his
men were staying in the recesses of the
cave.) 4Then the men of David said to
him, "This is the day of which the LORD
said to you, 'Behold, I will deliver your
enemy into your hand, that you may
do to him as it seems good to you.' "
And David arose and secretly cut off a
corner of Saul's robe. 5Now it happened
afterward that David's heart troubled
him because he had cut Saul's robe.
6And he said to his men, "The LORD
forbid that I should do this thing to my
master, the LORD's anointed, to stretch
out my hand against him, seeing he *is*
the anointed of the LORD." 7So David
restrained his servants with *these* words,
and did not allow them to rise against
Saul. And Saul got up from the cave and
went on *his* way.
8David also arose afterward, went out
of the cave, and called out to Saul, say-
ing, "My lord the king!" And when Saul
looked behind him, David stooped with
his face to the earth, and bowed down.
9And David said to Saul: "Why do you
listen to the words of men who say, 'In-
deed David seeks your harm'? 10Look,
this day your eyes have seen that the
LORD delivered you today into my hand
in the cave, and *someone* urged *me* to kill
you. But *my eye* spared you, and I said,
'I will not stretch out my hand against
my lord, for he *is* the LORD's anointed.'
11Moreover, my father, see! Yes, see the
corner of your robe in my hand! For in
that I cut off the corner of your robe,
and did not kill you, know and see that
there is neither evil nor rebellion in my
hand, and I have not sinned against
you. Yet you hunt my life to take it. 12Let
the LORD judge between you and me,

23:23 [a] Literally *thousands* **23:28** [a] Hebrew *Sela Hammahlekoth*

and let the LORD avenge me on you.
But my hand shall not be against you.
13As the proverb of the ancients says,
'Wickedness proceeds from the wick-
ed.' But my hand shall not be against
you. 14After whom has the king of Israel
come out? Whom do you pursue? A dead
dog? A flea? 15Therefore let the LORD be
judge, and judge between you and me,
and see and plead my case, and deliver
me out of your hand."

16So it was, when David had finished
speaking these words to Saul, that Saul
said, "*Is* this your voice, my son David?"
And Saul lifted up his voice and wept.
17Then he said to David: "You *are* more
righteous than I; for you have rewarded
me with good, whereas I have rewarded
you with evil. 18And you have shown this
day how you have dealt well with me;
for when the LORD delivered me into
your hand, you did not kill me. 19For if a
man finds his enemy, will he let him get
away safely? Therefore may the LORD
reward you with good for what you have
done to me this day. 20And now I know
indeed that you shall surely be king,
and that the kingdom of Israel shall be
established in your hand. 21Therefore
swear now to me by the LORD that you
will not cut off my descendants after me,
and that you will not destroy my name
from my father's house."

22So David swore to Saul. And Saul
went home, but David and his men went
up to the stronghold.

Death of Samuel

25 Then Samuel died; and the Is-
raelites gathered together and
lamented for him, and buried him at his
home in Ramah. And David arose and
went down to the Wilderness of Paran.[a]

David and the Wife of Nabal

2Now *there was* a man in Maon whose
business *was* in Carmel, and the man
was very rich. He had three thousand
sheep and a thousand goats. And he
was shearing his sheep in Carmel. 3The
name of the man *was* Nabal, and the
name of his wife Abigail. And *she was*
a woman of good understanding and
beautiful appearance; but the man *was*
harsh and evil in *his* doings. He *was of
the house of* Caleb.

4When David heard in the wilderness
that Nabal was shearing his sheep, 5Da-
vid sent ten young men; and David said
to the young men, "Go up to Carmel, go
to Nabal, and greet him in my name.
6And thus you shall say to him who lives
in prosperity: 'Peace *be* to you, peace to
your house, and peace to all that you
have! 7Now I have heard that you have
shearers. Your shepherds were with us,
and we did not hurt them, nor was there
anything missing from them all the while
they were in Carmel. 8Ask your young
men, and they will tell you. Therefore let
my young men find favor in your eyes,
for we come on a feast day. Please give
whatever comes to your hand to your
servants and to your son David.' "

9So when David's young men came,
they spoke to Nabal according to all
these words in the name of David, and
waited.

10Then Nabal answered David's ser-
vants, and said, "Who *is* David, and
who *is* the son of Jesse? There are many
servants nowadays who break away
each one from his master. 11Shall I then
take my bread and my water and my
meat that I have killed for my shearers,
and give *it* to men when I do not know
where they *are* from?"

12So David's young men turned on
their heels and went back; and they
came and told him all these words.
13Then David said to his men, "Every
man gird on his sword." So every man
girded on his sword, and David also
girded on his sword. And about four
hundred men went with David, and
two hundred stayed with the supplies.
14Now one of the young men told Abi-
gail, Nabal's wife, saying, "Look, David
sent messengers from the wilderness to
greet our master; and he reviled them.
15But the men *were* very good to us, and
we were not hurt, nor did we miss any-
thing as long as we accompanied them,
when we were in the fields. 16They were
a wall to us both by night and day, all
the time we were with them keeping the

25:1 [a] Following Masoretic Text, Syriac, Targum, and Vulgate; Septuagint reads *Maon.*

sheep. 17Now therefore, know and con-
sider what you will do, for harm is deter-
mined against our master and against
all his household. For he *is such* a scoun-
drel[a] that *one* cannot speak to him."
18Then Abigail made haste and took
two hundred *loaves* of bread, two skins
of wine, five sheep already dressed, five
seahs of roasted *grain,* one hundred clus-
ters of raisins, and two hundred cakes of
figs, and loaded *them* on donkeys. 19And
she said to her servants, "Go on before
me; see, I am coming after you." But she
did not tell her husband Nabal.
20So it was, *as* she rode on the donkey,
that she went down under cover of the
hill; and there were David and his men,
coming down toward her, and she met
them. 21Now David had said, "Surely in
vain I have protected all that this *fellow*
has in the wilderness, so that nothing
was missed of all that *belongs* to him.
And he has repaid me evil for good.
22May God do so, and more also, to the
enemies of David, if I leave one male of
all who *belong* to him by morning light."
23Now when Abigail saw David, she
dismounted quickly from the donkey,
fell on her face before David, and bowed
down to the ground. 24So she fell at his
feet and said: "On me, my lord, *on* me
let this iniquity *be!* And please let your
maidservant speak in your ears, and
hear the words of your maidservant.
25Please, let not my lord regard this
scoundrel Nabal. For as his name *is,*
so *is* he: Nabal[a] *is* his name, and folly
is with him! But I, your maidservant,
did not see the young men of my lord
whom you sent. 26Now therefore, my
lord, *as* the LORD lives and *as* your
soul lives, since the LORD has held you
back from coming to bloodshed and
from avenging yourself with your own
hand, now then, let your enemies and
those who seek harm for my lord be as
Nabal. 27And now this present which
your maidservant has brought to my
lord, let it be given to the young men
who follow my lord. 28Please forgive the
trespass of your maidservant. For the
LORD will certainly make for my lord
an enduring house, because my lord
fights the battles of the LORD, and evil
is not found in you throughout your
days. 29Yet a man has risen to pursue
you and seek your life, but the life of my
lord shall be bound in the bundle of the
living with the LORD your God; and the
lives of your enemies He shall sling out,
as from the pocket of a sling. 30And it
shall come to pass, when the LORD has
done for my lord according to all the
good that He has spoken concerning
you, and has appointed you ruler over
Israel, 31that this will be no grief to you,
nor offense of heart to my lord, either
that you have shed blood without cause,
or that my lord has avenged himself.
But when the LORD has dealt well with
my lord, then remember your maid-
servant."
32Then David said to Abigail: "Blessed
is the LORD God of Israel, who sent you
this day to meet me! 33And blessed *is*
your advice and blessed *are* you, be-
cause you have kept me this day from
coming to bloodshed and from aveng-
ing myself with my own hand. 34For
indeed, *as* the LORD God of Israel lives,
who has kept me back from hurting
you, unless you had hurried and come
to meet me, surely by morning light no
males would have been left to Nabal!"
35So David received from her hand what
she had brought him, and said to her,
"Go up in peace to your house. See, I
have heeded your voice and respected
your person."
36Now Abigail went to Nabal, and there
he was, holding a feast in his house, like
the feast of a king. And Nabal's heart
was merry within him, for he *was* very
drunk; therefore she told him nothing,
little or much, until morning light. 37So
it was, in the morning, when the wine
had gone from Nabal, and his wife had
told him these things, that his heart
died within him, and he became *like* a
stone. 38Then it happened, *after* about
ten days, that the LORD struck Nabal,
and he died.
39So when David heard that Nabal was
dead, he said, "Blessed *be* the LORD, who
has pleaded the cause of my reproach
from the hand of Nabal, and has kept

25:17 [a] Literally *son of Belial* 25:25 [a] Literally *Fool*

His servant from evil! For the LORD has
returned the wickedness of Nabal on
his own head."
And David sent and proposed to Abi-
gail, to take her as his wife. 40When the
servants of David had come to Abigail
at Carmel, they spoke to her saying,
"David sent us to you, to ask you to
become his wife."
41Then she arose, bowed her face to
the earth, and said, "Here is your maid-
servant, a servant to wash the feet of
the servants of my lord." 42So Abigail
rose in haste and rode on a donkey,
attended by five of her maidens; and
she followed the messengers of David,
and became his wife. 43David also took
Ahinoam of Jezreel, and so both of them
were his wives.
44But Saul had given Michal his
daughter, David's wife, to Palti[a] the son
of Laish, who *was* from Gallim.

David Spares Saul a Second Time

26 Now the Ziphites came to Saul
at Gibeah, saying, "Is David not
hiding in the hill of Hachilah, opposite
Jeshimon?" 2Then Saul arose and went
down to the Wilderness of Ziph, having
three thousand chosen men of Israel
with him, to seek David in the Wilder-
ness of Ziph. 3And Saul encamped in the
hill of Hachilah, which *is* opposite Je-
shimon, by the road. But David stayed
in the wilderness, and he saw that Saul
came after him into the wilderness.
4David therefore sent out spies, and
understood that Saul had indeed come.
5So David arose and came to the place
where Saul had encamped. And David
saw the place where Saul lay, and Abner
the son of Ner, the commander of his
army. Now Saul lay within the camp,
with the people encamped all around
him. 6Then David answered, and said
to Ahimelech the Hittite and to Abish-
ai the son of Zeruiah, brother of Joab,
saying, "Who will go down with me to
Saul in the camp?"
And Abishai said, "I will go down with
you."
7So David and Abishai came to the
people by night; and there Saul lay
sleeping within the camp, with his spear
stuck in the ground by his head. And
Abner and the people lay all around
him. 8Then Abishai said to David, "God
has delivered your enemy into your
hand this day. Now therefore, please,
let me strike him at once with the spear,
right to the earth; and I will not *have to*
strike him a second time!"
9But David said to Abishai, "Do not
destroy him; for who can stretch out his
hand against the LORD's anointed, and
be guiltless?" 10David said furthermore,
"*As* the LORD lives, the LORD shall strike
him, or his day shall come to die, or he
shall go out to battle and perish. 11The
LORD forbid that I should stretch out my
hand against the LORD's anointed. But
please, take now the spear and the jug of
water that *are* by his head, and let us go."
12So David took the spear and the jug of
water *by* Saul's head, and they got away;
and no man saw or knew *it* or awoke.
For they *were* all asleep, because a deep
sleep from the LORD had fallen on them.
13Now David went over to the other
side, and stood on the top of a hill afar
off, a great distance *being* between
them. 14And David called out to the
people and to Abner the son of Ner,
saying, "Do you not answer, Abner?"
Then Abner answered and said, "Who
are you, calling out to the king?"
15So David said to Abner, "*Are* you not
a man? And who *is* like you in Israel?
Why then have you not guarded your
lord the king? For one of the people
came in to destroy your lord the king.
16This thing that you have done *is* not
good. *As* the LORD lives, you deserve
to die, because you have not guarded
your master, the LORD's anointed. And
now see where the king's spear *is*, and
the jug of water that *was* by his head."
17Then Saul knew David's voice, and
said, "*Is* that your voice, my son David?"
David said, "*It is* my voice, my lord,
O king." 18And he said, "Why does my
lord thus pursue his servant? For what
have I done, or what evil *is* in my hand?
19Now therefore, please, let my lord the
king hear the words of his servant: If
the LORD has stirred you up against

25:44 [a] Spelled *Paltiel* in 2 Samuel 3:15

me, let Him accept an offering. But if
it is the children of men, *may* they *be*
cursed before the LORD, for they have
driven me out this day from sharing
in the inheritance of the LORD, saying,
'Go, serve other gods.' 20 So now, do not
let my blood fall to the earth before the
face of the LORD. For the king of Israel
has come out to seek a flea, as when one
hunts a partridge in the mountains."
21 Then Saul said, "I have sinned. Re-
turn, my son David. For I will harm you
no more, because my life was precious
in your eyes this day. Indeed I have
played the fool and erred exceedingly."
22 And David answered and said, "Here
is the king's spear. Let one of the young
men come over and get it. 23 May the
LORD repay every man *for* his righ-
teousness and his faithfulness; for the
LORD delivered you into *my* hand today,
but I would not stretch out my hand
against the LORD's anointed. 24 And in-
deed, as your life was valued much this
day in my eyes, so let my life be valued
much in the eyes of the LORD, and let
Him deliver me out of all tribulation."
25 Then Saul said to David, "*May* you *be*
blessed, my son David! You shall both
do great things and also still prevail."
So David went on his way, and Saul
returned to his place.

David Allied with the Philistines

27 And David said in his heart,
"Now I shall perish someday
by the hand of Saul. *There is* nothing
better for me than that I should speedily
escape to the land of the Philistines;
and Saul will despair of me, to seek
me anymore in any part of Israel. So
I shall escape out of his hand." 2 Then
David arose and went over with the
six hundred men who *were* with him
to Achish the son of Maoch, king of
Gath. 3 So David dwelt with Achish at
Gath, he and his men, each man with
his household, *and* David with his two
wives, Ahinoam the Jezreelitess, and
Abigail the Carmelitess, Nabal's widow.
4 And it was told Saul that David had
fled to Gath; so he sought him no more.
5 Then David said to Achish, "If I have
now found favor in your eyes, let them
give me a place in some town in the
country, that I may dwell there. For why
should your servant dwell in the royal
city with you?" 6 So Achish gave him
Ziklag that day. Therefore Ziklag has
belonged to the kings of Judah to this
day. 7 Now the time that David dwelt in
the country of the Philistines was one
full year and four months.
8 And David and his men went up and
raided the Geshurites, the Girzites,[a] and
the Amalekites. For those *nations* were
the inhabitants of the land from of old,
as you go to Shur, even as far as the land
of Egypt. 9 Whenever David attacked the
land, he left neither man nor woman
alive, but took away the sheep, the oxen,
the donkeys, the camels, and the appar-
el, and returned and came to Achish.
10 Then Achish would say, "Where have
you made a raid today?" And David
would say, "Against the southern *area* of
Judah, or against the southern *area* of
the Jerahmeelites, or against the south-
ern *area* of the Kenites." 11 David would
save neither man nor woman alive, to
bring *news* to Gath, saying, "Lest they
should inform on us, saying, 'Thus Da-
vid did.' " And thus *was* his behavior all
the time he dwelt in the country of the
Philistines. 12 So Achish believed David,
saying, "He has made his people Israel
utterly abhor him; therefore he will be
my servant forever."

28 Now it happened in those days
that the Philistines gathered
their armies together for war, to fight
with Israel. And Achish said to David,
"You assuredly know that you will go out
with me to battle, you and your men."
2 So David said to Achish, "Surely you
know what your servant can do."
And Achish said to David, "Therefore
I will make you one of my chief guard-
ians forever."

Saul Consults a Medium

3 Now Samuel had died, and all Israel
had lamented for him and buried him
in Ramah, in his own city. And Saul had
put the mediums and the spiritists out
of the land.

27:8 [a] Or *Gezrites*

4Then the Philistines gathered togeth-
er, and came and encamped at Shunem.
So Saul gathered all Israel together, and
they encamped at Gilboa. 5When Saul
saw the army of the Philistines, he was
afraid, and his heart trembled greatly.
6And when Saul inquired of the LORD,
the LORD did not answer him, either by
dreams or by Urim or by the prophets.
7Then Saul said to his servants, "Find
me a woman who is a medium, that I
may go to her and inquire of her."
And his servants said to him, "In fact,
there is a woman who is a medium at
En Dor."
8So Saul disguised himself and put on
other clothes, and he went, and two men
with him; and they came to the woman
by night. And he said, "Please conduct
a séance for me, and bring up for me
the one I shall name to you."
9Then the woman said to him, "Look,
you know what Saul has done, how he
has cut off the mediums and the spirit-
ists from the land. Why then do you lay
a snare for my life, to cause me to die?"
10And Saul swore to her by the LORD,
saying, "*As* the LORD lives, no pun-
ishment shall come upon you for this
thing."
11Then the woman said, "Whom shall
I bring up for you?"
And he said, "Bring up Samuel for me."
12When the woman saw Samuel, she
cried out with a loud voice. And the wom-
an spoke to Saul, saying, "Why have you
deceived me? For you *are* Saul!"
13And the king said to her, "Do not be
afraid. What did you see?"
And the woman said to Saul, "I saw
a spirit[a] ascending out of the earth."
14So he said to her, "What *is* his form?"
And she said, "An old man is coming
up, and he *is* covered with a mantle."
And Saul perceived that it *was* Sam-
uel, and he stooped with *his* face to the
ground and bowed down.
15Now Samuel said to Saul, "Why have
you disturbed me by bringing me up?"
And Saul answered, "I am deeply dis-
tressed; for the Philistines make war
against me, and God has departed from
me and does not answer me anymore,
neither by prophets nor by dreams.
Therefore I have called you, that you
may reveal to me what I should do."
16Then Samuel said: "So why do you
ask me, seeing the LORD has departed
from you and has become your enemy?
17And the LORD has done for Himself[a] as
He spoke by me. For the LORD has torn
the kingdom out of your hand and given
it to your neighbor, David. 18Because
you did not obey the voice of the LORD
nor execute His fierce wrath upon Am-
alek, therefore the LORD has done this
thing to you this day. 19Moreover the
LORD will also deliver Israel with you
into the hand of the Philistines. And
tomorrow you and your sons *will be* with
me. The LORD will also deliver the army
of Israel into the hand of the Philistines."
20Immediately Saul fell full length on
the ground, and was dreadfully afraid
because of the words of Samuel. And
there was no strength in him, for he
had eaten no food all day or all night.
21And the woman came to Saul and
saw that he was severely troubled, and
said to him, "Look, your maidservant
has obeyed your voice, and I have put
my life in my hands and heeded the
words which you spoke to me. 22Now
therefore, please, heed also the voice
of your maidservant, and let me set
a piece of bread before you; and eat,
that you may have strength when you
go on *your* way."
23But he refused and said, "I will not
eat."
So his servants, together with the
woman, urged him; and he heeded their
voice. Then he arose from the ground
and sat on the bed. 24Now the woman
had a fatted calf in the house, and she
hastened to kill it. And she took flour
and kneaded *it,* and baked unleavened
bread from it. 25So she brought *it* before
Saul and his servants, and they ate. Then
they rose and went away that night.

The Philistines Reject David

29 Then the Philistines gathered to-
gether all their armies at Aphek,
and the Israelites encamped by a foun-
tain which *is* in Jezreel. 2And the lords

28:13 [a] Hebrew *elohim* 28:17 [a] Or *him,* that is, David

of the Philistines passed in review by
hundreds and by thousands, but David
and his men passed in review at the
rear with Achish. 3Then the princes of
the Philistines said, "What *are* these
Hebrews *doing here?*"

And Achish said to the princes of the
Philistines, "*Is* this not David, the ser-
vant of Saul king of Israel, who has been
with me these days, or these years? And
to this day I have found no fault in him
since he defected *to me.*"

4But the princes of the Philistines were
angry with him; so the princes of the
Philistines said to him, "Make this fel-
low return, that he may go back to the
place which you have appointed for
him, and do not let him go down with
us to battle, lest in the battle he become
our adversary. For with what could he
reconcile himself to his master, if not
with the heads of these men? 5*Is* this
not David, of whom they sang to one
another in dances, saying:

'Saul has slain his thousands,
And David his ten thousands'?"[a]

6Then Achish called David and said to
him, "Surely, *as* the LORD lives, you have
been upright, and your going out and
your coming in with me in the army *is*
good in my sight. For to this day I have
not found evil in you since the day of
your coming to me. Nevertheless the
lords do not favor you. 7Therefore return
now, and go in peace, that you may not
displease the lords of the Philistines."

8So David said to Achish, "But what
have I done? And to this day what have
you found in your servant as long as I
have been with you, that I may not go
and fight against the enemies of my
lord the king?"

9Then Achish answered and said to
David, "I know that you *are* as good in
my sight as an angel of God; neverthe-
less the princes of the Philistines have
said, 'He shall not go up with us to the
battle.' 10Now therefore, rise early in the
morning with your master's servants
who have come with you.[a] And as soon
as you are up early in the morning and
have light, depart."

11So David and his men rose early to
depart in the morning, to return to the
land of the Philistines. And the Philis-
tines went up to Jezreel.

David's Conflict with the Amalekites

30 Now it happened, when David
and his men came to Ziklag, on
the third day, that the Amalekites had
invaded the South and Ziklag, attacked
Ziklag and burned it with fire, 2and had
taken captive the women and those who
were there, from small to great; they
did not kill anyone, but carried *them*
away and went their way. 3So David and
his men came to the city, and there it
was, burned with fire; and their wives,
their sons, and their daughters had
been taken captive. 4Then David and
the people who *were* with him lifted up
their voices and wept, until they had no
more power to weep. 5And David's two
wives, Ahinoam the Jezreelitess, and
Abigail the widow of Nabal the Car-
melite, had been taken captive. 6Now
David was greatly distressed, for the
people spoke of stoning him, because
the soul of all the people was grieved,
every man for his sons and his daugh-
ters. But David strengthened himself
in the LORD his God.

7Then David said to Abiathar the priest,
Ahimelech's son, "Please bring the ephod
here to me." And Abiathar brought the
ephod to David. 8So David inquired of
the LORD, saying, "Shall I pursue this
troop? Shall I overtake them?"

And He answered him, "Pursue, for you
shall surely overtake *them* and without
fail recover *all.*"

9So David went, he and the six hun-
dred men who *were* with him, and came
to the Brook Besor, where those stayed
who were left behind. 10But David pur-
sued, he and four hundred men; for
two hundred stayed *behind,* who were
so weary that they could not cross the
Brook Besor.

11Then they found an Egyptian in the
field, and brought him to David; and

29:5 [a] Compare 1 Samuel 18:7 **29:10** [a] Following Masoretic Text, Targum, and Vulgate; Septuagint adds *and go to the place which I have selected for you there; and set no bothersome word in your heart, for you are good before me. And rise on your way.*

they gave him bread and he ate, and they let him drink water. 12And they gave him a piece of a cake of figs and two clusters of raisins. So when he had eaten, his strength came back to him; for he had eaten no bread nor drunk water for three days and three nights. 13Then David said to him, "To whom do you *belong,* and where *are* you from?"

And he said, "I *am* a young man from Egypt, servant of an Amalekite; and my master left me behind, because three days ago I fell sick. 14We made an invasion of the southern *area* of the Cherethites, in the *territory* which *belongs* to Judah, and of the southern *area* of Caleb; and we burned Ziklag with fire."

15And David said to him, "Can you take me down to this troop?"

So he said, "Swear to me by God that you will neither kill me nor deliver me into the hands of my master, and I will take you down to this troop."

16And when he had brought him down, there they were, spread out over all the land, eating and drinking and dancing, because of all the great spoil which they had taken from the land of the Philistines and from the land of Judah. 17Then David attacked them from twilight until the evening of the next day. Not a man of them escaped, except four hundred young men who rode on camels and fled. 18So David recovered all that the Amalekites had carried away, and David rescued his two wives. 19And nothing of theirs was lacking, either small or great, sons or daughters, spoil or anything which they had taken from them; David recovered all. 20Then David took all the flocks and herds they had driven before those *other* livestock, and said, "This *is* David's spoil."

21Now David came to the two hundred men who had been so weary that they could not follow David, whom they also had made to stay at the Brook Besor. So they went out to meet David and to meet the people who *were* with him. And when David came near the people, he greeted them. 22Then all the wicked and worthless men[a] of those who went with David answered and said, "Because they did not go with us, we will not give them *any* of the spoil that we have recovered, except for every man's wife and children, that they may lead *them* away and depart."

23But David said, "My brethren, you shall not do so with what the LORD has given us, who has preserved us and delivered into our hand the troop that came against us. 24For who will heed you in this matter? But as his part *is* who goes down to the battle, so *shall* his part *be* who stays by the supplies; they shall share alike." 25So it was, from that day forward; he made it a statute and an ordinance for Israel to this day.

26Now when David came to Ziklag, he sent *some* of the spoil to the elders of Judah, to his friends, saying, "Here is a present for you from the spoil of the enemies of the LORD"— 27to *those* who *were* in Bethel, *those* who *were* in Ramoth of the South, *those* who *were* in Jattir, 28*those* who *were* in Aroer, *those* who *were* in Siphmoth, *those* who *were* in Eshtemoa, 29*those* who *were* in Rachal, *those* who *were* in the cities of the Jerahmeelites, *those* who *were* in the cities of the Kenites, 30*those* who *were* in Hormah, *those* who *were* in Chorashan,[a] *those* who *were* in Athach, 31*those* who *were* in Hebron, and to all the places where David himself and his men were accustomed to rove.

The Tragic End of Saul and His Sons

31 Now the Philistines fought against Israel; and the men of Israel fled from before the Philistines, and fell slain on Mount Gilboa. 2Then the Philistines followed hard after Saul and his sons. And the Philistines killed Jonathan, Abinadab, and Malchishua, Saul's sons. 3The battle became fierce against Saul. The archers hit him, and he was severely wounded by the archers.

4Then Saul said to his armorbearer, "Draw your sword, and thrust me through with it, lest these uncircumcised men come and thrust me through and abuse me."

30:22 [a] Literally *men of Belial* **30:30** [a] Or *Borashan*

But his armorbearer would not, for he
was greatly afraid. Therefore Saul took
a sword and fell on it. 5And when his
armorbearer saw that Saul was dead,
he also fell on his sword, and died with
him. 6So Saul, his three sons, his armor-
bearer, and all his men died together
that same day.
7And when the men of Israel who *were*
on the other side of the valley, and *those*
who *were* on the other side of the Jor-
dan, saw that the men of Israel had fled
and that Saul and his sons were dead,
they forsook the cities and fled; and
the Philistines came and dwelt in them.
8So it happened the next day, when the
Philistines came to strip the slain, that
they found Saul and his three sons fallen
on Mount Gilboa. 9And they cut off his
head and stripped off his armor, and
sent *word* throughout the land of the
Philistines, to proclaim *it in* the temple
of their idols and among the people.
10Then they put his armor in the temple
of the Ashtoreths, and they fastened his
body to the wall of Beth Shan.[a]
11Now when the inhabitants of Jabesh
Gilead heard what the Philistines had
done to Saul, 12all the valiant men arose
and traveled all night, and took the
body of Saul and the bodies of his sons
from the wall of Beth Shan; and they
came to Jabesh and burned them there.
13Then they took their bones and buried
them under the tamarisk tree at Jabesh,
and fasted seven days.

31:10 [a] Spelled *Beth Shean* in Joshua 17:11 and elsewhere

THE SECOND BOOK OF
SAMUEL

The Book of 2 Samuel continues the story of the kingdom of Israel. It begins with David learning of the deaths of King Saul and Jonathan. David becomes the second king of Israel and is a much better king than Saul was, but he is not perfect. David commits a series of terrible sins, but when the prophet Nathan confronts him, David confesses his sin to God and asks forgiveness. God forgives David, but the last part of David's reign as king is filled with trouble.

- **GENRE:** History
- **AUTHOR:** Unknown
- **TIME:** c. 1011–971 BC
- **PURPOSE:** To continue telling the story of Israel being led by kings and how even the best of human kings would not be good enough.

The Report of Saul's Death

1 Now it came to pass after the death
of Saul, when David had returned
from the slaughter of the Amalekites,
and David had stayed two days in Zik-
lag, 2 on the third day, behold, it hap-
pened that a man came from Saul's
camp with his clothes torn and dust
on his head. So it was, when he came
to David, that he fell to the ground and
prostrated himself.
3 And David said to him, "Where have
you come from?"
So he said to him, "I have escaped from
the camp of Israel."
4 Then David said to him, "How did the
matter go? Please tell me."
And he answered, "The people have
fled from the battle, many of the people
are fallen and dead, and Saul and Jon-
athan his son are dead also."
5 So David said to the young man who
told him, "How do you know that Saul
and Jonathan his son are dead?"
6 Then the young man who told him
said, "As I happened by chance *to be* on
Mount Gilboa, there was Saul, leaning on
his spear; and indeed the chariots and
horsemen followed hard after him. 7 Now
when he looked behind him, he saw me
and called to me. And I answered, 'Here
I am.' 8 And he said to me, 'Who *are* you?'
So I answered him, 'I *am* an Amalekite.'
9 He said to me again, 'Please stand over
me and kill me, for anguish has come
upon me, but my life still *remains* in
me.' 10 So I stood over him and killed
him, because I was sure that he could
not live after he had fallen. And I took
the crown that *was* on his head and the
bracelet that *was* on his arm, and have
brought them here to my lord."
11 Therefore David took hold of his own
clothes and tore them, and *so did* all
the men who *were* with him. 12 And they
mourned and wept and fasted until
evening for Saul and for Jonathan his
son, for the people of the LORD and for
the house of Israel, because they had
fallen by the sword.
13 Then David said to the young man
who told him, "Where *are* you from?"
And he answered, "I *am* the son of an
alien, an Amalekite."
14 So David said to him, "How was it
you were not afraid to put forth your
hand to destroy the LORD's anointed?"
15 Then David called one of the young
men and said, "Go near, *and* execute
him!" And he struck him so that he died.
16 So David said to him, "Your blood *is*
on your own head, for your own mouth
has testified against you, saying, 'I have
killed the LORD's anointed.'"

The Song of the Bow

17 Then David lamented with this lam-
entation over Saul and over Jonathan

his son, 18and he told *them* to teach the
children of Judah *the Song of* the Bow;
indeed *it is* written in the Book of Jasher:

19 "The beauty of Israel is slain on your high places!
How the mighty have fallen!
20 Tell *it* not in Gath,
Proclaim *it* not in the streets of Ashkelon—
Lest the daughters of the Philistines rejoice,
Lest the daughters of the uncircumcised triumph.

21 "O mountains of Gilboa,
Let there be no dew nor rain upon you,
Nor fields of offerings.
For the shield of the mighty is cast away there!
The shield of Saul, not anointed with oil.
22 From the blood of the slain,
From the fat of the mighty,
The bow of Jonathan did not turn back,
And the sword of Saul did not return empty.

23 "Saul and Jonathan *were* beloved and pleasant in their lives,
And in their death they were not divided;
They were swifter than eagles,
They were stronger than lions.

24 "O daughters of Israel, weep over Saul,
Who clothed you in scarlet, with luxury;
Who put ornaments of gold on your apparel.

25 "How the mighty have fallen in the midst of the battle!
Jonathan *was* slain in your high places.
26 I am distressed for you, my brother Jonathan;
You have been very pleasant to me;
Your love to me was wonderful,
Surpassing the love of women.

27 "How the mighty have fallen,
And the weapons of war perished!"

David Anointed King of Judah

2 It happened after this that David
inquired of the LORD, saying, "Shall
I go up to any of the cities of Judah?"
And the LORD said to him, "Go up."
David said, "Where shall I go up?"
And He said, "To Hebron."
2So David went up there, and his two
wives also, Ahinoam the Jezreelitess, and
Abigail the widow of Nabal the Carmelite.
3And David brought up the men who *were*
with him, every man with his household.
So they dwelt in the cities of Hebron.
4Then the men of Judah came, and
there they anointed David king over the
house of Judah. And they told David,
saying, "The men of Jabesh Gilead *were*
the ones who buried Saul." 5So David sent
messengers to the men of Jabesh Gil-
ead, and said to them, "You *are* blessed
of the LORD, for you have shown this
kindness to your lord, to Saul, and have
buried him. 6And now may the LORD
show kindness and truth to you. I also
will repay you this kindness, because
you have done this thing. 7Now there-
fore, let your hands be strengthened,
and be valiant; for your master Saul is
dead, and also the house of Judah has
anointed me king over them."

Ishbosheth Made King of Israel

8But Abner the son of Ner, commander
of Saul's army, took Ishbosheth[a] the son
of Saul and brought him over to Ma-
hanaim; 9and he made him king over
Gilead, over the Ashurites, over Jezreel,
over Ephraim, over Benjamin, and over
all Israel. 10Ishbosheth, Saul's son, *was*
forty years old when he began to reign
over Israel, and he reigned two years.
Only the house of Judah followed David.
11And the time that David was king in
Hebron over the house of Judah was
seven years and six months.

Israel and Judah at War

12Now Abner the son of Ner, and the
servants of Ishbosheth the son of Saul,

2:8 [a] Called *Esh-Baal* in 1 Chronicles 8:33 and 9:39

went out from Mahanaim to Gibeon.
13And Joab the son of Zeruiah, and the
servants of David, went out and met
them by the pool of Gibeon. So they sat
down, one on one side of the pool and
the other on the other side of the pool.
14Then Abner said to Joab, “Let the young
men now arise and compete before us.”
And Joab said, “Let them arise.”
15So they arose and went over by num-
ber, twelve from Benjamin, *followers* of
Ishbosheth the son of Saul, and twelve
from the servants of David. 16And each
one grasped his opponent by the head
and *thrust* his sword in his opponent’s
side; so they fell down together. There-
fore that place was called the Field of
Sharp Swords,[a] which *is* in Gibeon. 17So
there was a very fierce battle that day,
and Abner and the men of Israel were
beaten before the servants of David.
18Now the three sons of Zeruiah were
there: Joab and Abishai and Asahel.
And Asahel *was as* fleet of foot as a wild
gazelle. 19So Asahel pursued Abner, and
in going he did not turn to the right
hand or to the left from following Abner.
20Then Abner looked behind him and
said, “*Are* you Asahel?”
He answered, “I *am*.”
21And Abner said to him, “Turn aside
to your right hand or to your left, and
lay hold on one of the young men and
take his armor for yourself.” But Asahel
would not turn aside from following
him. 22So Abner said again to Asahel,
“Turn aside from following me. Why
should I strike you to the ground? How
then could I face your brother Joab?”
23However, he refused to turn aside.
Therefore Abner struck him in the stom-
ach with the blunt end of the spear, so
that the spear came out of his back;
and he fell down there and died on the
spot. So it was *that* as many as came to
the place where Asahel fell down and
died, stood still.
24Joab and Abishai also pursued
Abner. And the sun was going down
when they came to the hill of Ammah,
which *is* before Giah by the road to the
Wilderness of Gibeon. 25Now the chil-
dren of Benjamin gathered together
behind Abner and became a unit, and
took their stand on top of a hill. 26Then
Abner called to Joab and said, “Shall
the sword devour forever? Do you not
know that it will be bitter in the latter
end? How long will it be then until you
tell the people to return from pursuing
their brethren?”
27And Joab said, “*As* God lives, unless
you had spoken, surely then by morn-
ing all the people would have given
up pursuing their brethren.” 28So Joab
blew a trumpet; and all the people
stood still and did not pursue Israel
anymore, nor did they fight anymore.
29Then Abner and his men went on all
that night through the plain, crossed
over the Jordan, and went through all
Bithron; and they came to Mahanaim.
30So Joab returned from pursuing
Abner. And when he had gathered all
the people together, there were missing
of David’s servants nineteen men and
Asahel. 31But the servants of David had
struck down, of Benjamin and Abner’s
men, three hundred and sixty men who
died. 32Then they took up Asahel and
buried him in his father’s tomb, which
was in Bethlehem. And Joab and his
men went all night, and they came to
Hebron at daybreak.
3 Now there was a long war between
the house of Saul and the house of
David. But David grew stronger and
stronger, and the house of Saul grew
weaker and weaker.

Sons of David

2Sons were born to David in Hebron:
His firstborn was Amnon by Ahinoam
the Jezreelitess; 3his second, Chileab,
by Abigail the widow of Nabal the Car-
melite; the third, Absalom the son of
Maacah, the daughter of Talmai, king
of Geshur; 4the fourth, Adonijah the son
of Haggith; the fifth, Shephatiah the
son of Abital; 5and the sixth, Ithream,
by David’s wife Eglah. These were born
to David in Hebron.

Abner Joins Forces with David

6Now it was so, while there was war be-
tween the house of Saul and the house

2:16 [a] Hebrew *Helkath Hazzurim*

of David, that Abner was strengthening
his hold on the house of Saul.
7And Saul had a concubine, whose
name *was* Rizpah, the daughter of Aiah.
So *Ishbosheth* said to Abner, "Why have
you gone in to my father's concubine?"
8Then Abner became very angry at
the words of Ishbosheth, and said, "*Am*
I a dog's head that belongs to Judah?
Today I show loyalty to the house of
Saul your father, to his brothers, and to
his friends, and have not delivered you
into the hand of David; and you charge
me today with a fault concerning this
woman? 9May God do so to Abner, and
more also, if I do not do for David as the
LORD has sworn to him— 10to transfer
the kingdom from the house of Saul,
and set up the throne of David over Isra-
el and over Judah, from Dan to Beershe-
ba." 11And he could not answer Abner
another word, because he feared him.
12Then Abner sent messengers on his
behalf to David, saying, "Whose *is* the
land?" saying *also,* "Make your covenant
with me, and indeed my hand *shall be*
with you to bring all Israel to you."
13And *David* said, "Good, I will make
a covenant with you. But one thing I
require of you: you shall not see my
face unless you first bring Michal, Saul's
daughter, when you come to see my
face." 14So David sent messengers to
Ishbosheth, Saul's son, saying, "Give
me my wife Michal, whom I betrothed
to myself for a hundred foreskins of
the Philistines." 15And Ishbosheth sent
and took her from *her* husband, from
Paltiel[a] the son of Laish. 16Then her
husband went along with her to Bahu-
rim, weeping behind her. So Abner said
to him, "Go, return!" And he returned.
17Now Abner had communicated with
the elders of Israel, saying, "In time
past you were seeking for David *to be*
king over you. 18Now then, do *it!* For the
LORD has spoken of David, saying, 'By
the hand of My servant David, I[a] will
save My people Israel from the hand of
the Philistines and the hand of all their
enemies.' " 19And Abner also spoke in
the hearing of Benjamin. Then Abner
also went to speak in the hearing of
David in Hebron all that seemed good to
Israel and the whole house of Benjamin.
20So Abner and twenty men with him
came to David at Hebron. And David
made a feast for Abner and the men
who *were* with him. 21Then Abner said
to David, "I will arise and go, and gather
all Israel to my lord the king, that they
may make a covenant with you, and
that you may reign over all that your
heart desires." So David sent Abner
away, and he went in peace.

Joab Murders Abner

22At that moment the servants of Da-
vid and Joab came from a raid and
brought much spoil with them. But
Abner *was* not with David in Hebron,
for he had sent him away, and he had
gone in peace. 23When Joab and all the
troops that *were* with him had come,
they told Joab, saying, "Abner the son
of Ner came to the king, and he sent him
away, and he has gone in peace." 24Then
Joab came to the king and said, "What
have you done? Look, Abner came to
you; why *is* it *that* you sent him away,
and he has already gone? 25Surely you
realize that Abner the son of Ner came
to deceive you, to know your going out
and your coming in, and to know all
that you are doing."
26And when Joab had gone from Da-
vid's presence, he sent messengers after
Abner, who brought him back from the
well of Sirah. But David did not know
it. 27Now when Abner had returned to
Hebron, Joab took him aside in the gate
to speak with him privately, and there
stabbed him in the stomach, so that he
died for the blood of Asahel his brother.
28Afterward, when David heard *it,* he
said, "My kingdom and I *are* guiltless
before the LORD forever of the blood
of Abner the son of Ner. 29Let it rest on
the head of Joab and on all his father's
house; and let there never fail to be in the
house of Joab one who has a discharge or
is a leper, who leans on a staff or falls by
the sword, or who lacks bread." 30So Joab
and Abishai his brother killed Abner,
because he had killed their brother As-
ahel at Gibeon in the battle.

3:15 [a] Spelled *Palti* in 1 Samuel 25:44 **3:18** [a] Following many Hebrew manuscripts, Septuagint, Syriac, and Targum; Masoretic Text reads *he.*

David's Mourning for Abner

31Then David said to Joab and to all the
people who were with him, "Tear your
clothes, gird yourselves with sackcloth,
and mourn for Abner." And King David
followed the coffin. 32So they buried
Abner in Hebron; and the king lifted up
his voice and wept at the grave of Abner,
and all the people wept. 33And the king
sang *a lament* over Abner and said:

"Should Abner die as a fool dies?
34 Your hands were not bound
Nor your feet put into fetters;
As a man falls before wicked men,
so you fell."

Then all the people wept over him again.
35And when all the people came to
persuade David to eat food while it was
still day, David took an oath, saying,
"God do so to me, and more also, if I
taste bread or anything else till the sun
goes down!" 36Now all the people took
note *of it,* and it pleased them, since
whatever the king did pleased all the
people. 37For all the people and all Is-
rael understood that day that it had
not been the king's *intent* to kill Abner
the son of Ner. 38Then the king said to
his servants, "Do you not know that a
prince and a great man has fallen this
day in Israel? 39And I *am* weak today,
though anointed king; and these men,
the sons of Zeruiah, *are* too harsh for
me. The LORD shall repay the evildoer
according to his wickedness."

Ishbosheth Is Murdered

4 When Saul's son[a] heard that Abner
had died in Hebron, he lost heart,
and all Israel was troubled. 2Now Saul's
son *had* two men *who were* captains of
troops. The name of one *was* Baanah
and the name of the other Rechab, the
sons of Rimmon the Beerothite, of the
children of Benjamin. (For Beeroth also
was *part* of Benjamin, 3because the Be-
erothites fled to Gittaim and have been
sojourners there until this day.)
4Jonathan, Saul's son, had a son *who
was* lame in *his* feet. He was five years
old when the news about Saul and
Jonathan came from Jezreel; and his
nurse took him up and fled. And it hap-
pened, as she made haste to flee, that
he fell and became lame. His name *was*
Mephibosheth.[a]
5Then the sons of Rimmon the Be-
erothite, Rechab and Baanah, set out
and came at about the heat of the day
to the house of Ishbosheth, who was
lying on his bed at noon. 6And they
came there, all the way into the house,
as though to get wheat, and they stabbed
him in the stomach. Then Rechab and
Baanah his brother escaped. 7For when
they came into the house, he was lying
on his bed in his bedroom; then they
struck him and killed him, beheaded
him and took his head, and were all
night escaping through the plain. 8And
they brought the head of Ishbosheth to
David at Hebron, and said to the king,
"Here is the head of Ishbosheth, the
son of Saul your enemy, who sought
your life; and the LORD has avenged
my lord the king this day of Saul and
his descendants."
9But David answered Rechab and Ba-
anah his brother, the sons of Rimmon
the Beerothite, and said to them, "*As* the
LORD lives, who has redeemed my life
from all adversity, 10when someone told
me, saying, 'Look, Saul is dead,' thinking
to have brought good news, I arrested
him and had him executed in Ziklag—
the one who *thought* I would give him a
reward for *his* news. 11How much more,
when wicked men have killed a righ-
teous person in his own house on his
bed? Therefore, shall I not now require
his blood at your hand and remove you
from the earth?" 12So David commanded
his young men, and they executed them,
cut off their hands and feet, and hanged
them by the pool in Hebron. But they
took the head of Ishbosheth and buried
it in the tomb of Abner in Hebron.

David Reigns over All Israel

5 Then all the tribes of Israel came to
David at Hebron and spoke, saying,
"Indeed we *are* your bone and your
flesh. 2Also, in time past, when Saul was
king over us, you were the one who led

4:1 [a] That is, Ishbosheth 4:4 [a] Called *Merib-Baal* in 1 Chronicles 8:34 and 9:40

Israel out and brought them in; and the
LORD said to you, 'You shall shepherd
My people Israel, and be ruler over Is-
rael.' " 3Therefore all the elders of Is-
rael came to the king at Hebron, and
King David made a covenant with them
at Hebron before the LORD. And they
anointed David king over Israel. 4David
was thirty years old when he began to
reign, *and* he reigned forty years. 5In
Hebron he reigned over Judah seven
years and six months, and in Jerusa-
lem he reigned thirty-three years over
all Israel and Judah.

The Conquest of Jerusalem

6And the king and his men went to
Jerusalem against the Jebusites, the
inhabitants of the land, who spoke to
David, saying, "You shall not come in
here; but the blind and the lame will
repel you," thinking, "David cannot
come in here." 7Nevertheless David took
the stronghold of Zion (that *is,* the City
of David).

8Now David said on that day, "Whoev-
er climbs up by way of the water shaft
and defeats the Jebusites (the lame
and the blind, *who are* hated by David's
soul), *he shall be chief and captain.*"[a]
Therefore they say, "The blind and the
lame shall not come into the house."

9Then David dwelt in the stronghold,
and called it the City of David. And Da-
vid built all around from the Millo[a] and
inward. 10So David went on and became
great, and the LORD God of hosts *was*
with him.

11Then Hiram king of Tyre sent mes-
sengers to David, and cedar trees, and
carpenters and masons. And they built
David a house. 12So David knew that the
LORD had established him as king over
Israel, and that He had exalted His king-
dom for the sake of His people Israel.

13And David took more concubines
and wives from Jerusalem, after he had
come from Hebron. Also more sons and
daughters were born to David. 14Now
these *are* the names of those who were
born to him in Jerusalem: Shammua,[a]
Shobab, Nathan, Solomon, 15Ibhar, El-
ishua,[a] Nepheg, Japhia, 16Elishama,
Eliada, and Eliphelet.

The Philistines Defeated

17Now when the Philistines heard that
they had anointed David king over Isra-
el, all the Philistines went up to search
for David. And David heard *of it* and
went down to the stronghold. 18The Phi-
listines also went and deployed them-
selves in the Valley of Rephaim. 19So
David inquired of the LORD, saying,
"Shall I go up against the Philistines?
Will You deliver them into my hand?"

And the LORD said to David, "Go up, for
I will doubtless deliver the Philistines
into your hand."

20So David went to Baal Perazim, and
David defeated them there; and he said,
"The LORD has broken through my en-
emies before me, like a breakthrough
of water." Therefore he called the name
of that place Baal Perazim.[a] 21And they
left their images there, and David and
his men carried them away.

22Then the Philistines went up once
again and deployed themselves in the
Valley of Rephaim. 23Therefore David
inquired of the LORD, and He said, "You
shall not go up; circle around behind
them, and come upon them in front of
the mulberry trees. 24And it shall be,
when you hear the sound of marching
in the tops of the mulberry trees, then
you shall advance quickly. For then the
LORD will go out before you to strike the
camp of the Philistines." 25And David
did so, as the LORD commanded him;
and he drove back the Philistines from
Geba[a] as far as Gezer.

The Ark Brought to Jerusalem

6 Again David gathered all *the* choice
men of Israel, thirty thousand.
2And David arose and went with all
the people who *were* with him from
Baale Judah to bring up from there
the ark of God, whose name is called
by the Name,[a] the LORD of Hosts, who
dwells *between* the cherubim. 3So they

5:8 [a] Compare 1 Chronicles 11:6 **5:9** [a] Literally *The Landfill* **5:14** [a] Spelled *Shimea* in 1 Chronicles 3:5 **5:15** [a] Spelled *Elishama* in 1 Chronicles 3:6 **5:20** [a] Literally *Master of Breakthroughs* **5:25** [a] Following Masoretic Text, Targum, and Vulgate; Septuagint reads *Gibeon.* **6:2** [a] Septuagint, Targum, and Vulgate omit *by the Name;* many Hebrew manuscripts and Syriac read *there.*

set the ark of God on a new cart, and
brought it out of the house of Abinadab,
which *was* on the hill; and Uzzah and
Ahio, the sons of Abinadab, drove the
new cart.[a] 4And they brought it out of
the house of Abinadab, which *was* on
the hill, accompanying the ark of God;
and Ahio went before the ark. 5Then
David and all the house of Israel played
music before the LORD on all kinds of
instruments of fir wood, on harps, on
stringed instruments, on tambourines,
on sistrums, and on cymbals.

6And when they came to Nachon's
threshing floor, Uzzah put out *his hand*
to the ark of God and took hold of it, for
the oxen stumbled. 7Then the anger of
the LORD was aroused against Uzzah,
and God struck him there for *his* error;
and he died there by the ark of God.
8And David became angry because of
the LORD's outbreak against Uzzah; and
he called the name of the place Perez
Uzzah[a] to this day.

9David was afraid of the LORD that
day; and he said, "How can the ark of
the LORD come to me?" 10So David would
not move the ark of the LORD with him
into the City of David; but David took it
aside into the house of Obed-Edom the
Gittite. 11The ark of the LORD remained
in the house of Obed-Edom the Gittite
three months. And the LORD blessed
Obed-Edom and all his household.

12Now it was told King David, saying,
"The LORD has blessed the house of
Obed-Edom and all that *belongs* to him,
because of the ark of God." So David
went and brought up the ark of God
from the house of Obed-Edom to the
City of David with gladness. 13And so
it was, when those bearing the ark of
the LORD had gone six paces, that he
sacrificed oxen and fatted sheep. 14Then
David danced before the LORD with
all *his* might; and David *was* wearing
a linen ephod. 15So David and all the
house of Israel brought up the ark of
the LORD with shouting and with the
sound of the trumpet.

16Now as the ark of the LORD came
into the City of David, Michal, Saul's
daughter, looked through a window and
saw King David leaping and whirling
before the LORD; and she despised him
in her heart. 17So they brought the ark
of the LORD, and set it in its place in
the midst of the tabernacle that David
had erected for it. Then David offered
burnt offerings and peace offerings
before the LORD. 18And when David had
finished offering burnt offerings and
peace offerings, he blessed the people
in the name of the LORD of hosts. 19Then
he distributed among all the people,
among the whole multitude of Israel,
both the women and the men, to everyone a loaf of bread, a piece *of meat,*
and a cake of raisins. So all the people
departed, everyone to his house.

20Then David returned to bless his
household. And Michal the daughter
of Saul came out to meet David, and
said, "How glorious was the king of Israel today, uncovering himself today
in the eyes of the maids of his servants,
as one of the base fellows shamelessly
uncovers himself!"

21So David said to Michal, "*It was* before the LORD, who chose me instead of
your father and all his house, to appoint
me ruler over the people of the LORD,
over Israel. Therefore I will play *music*
before the LORD. 22And I will be even
more undignified than this, and will
be humble in my own sight. But as for
the maidservants of whom you have
spoken, by them I will be held in honor."

23Therefore Michal the daughter of
Saul had no children to the day of her
death.

God's Covenant with David

7 Now it came to pass when the king
was dwelling in his house, and the
LORD had given him rest from all his
enemies all around, 2that the king said
to Nathan the prophet, "See now, I dwell
in a house of cedar, but the ark of God
dwells inside tent curtains."

3Then Nathan said to the king, "Go, do
all that *is* in your heart, for the LORD *is*
with you."

4But it happened that night that the
word of the LORD came to Nathan, saying, 5"Go and tell My servant David,

6:3 [a] Septuagint adds *with the ark.* 6:8 [a] Literally *Outburst Against Uzzah*

'Thus says the LORD: "Would you build
a house for Me to dwell in? 6For I have
not dwelt in a house since the time
that I brought the children of Israel
up from Egypt, even to this day, but
have moved about in a tent and in a
tabernacle. 7Wherever I have moved
about with all the children of Israel,
have I ever spoken a word to anyone
from the tribes of Israel, whom I com-
manded to shepherd My people Israel,
saying, 'Why have you not built Me
a house of cedar?'" ' 8Now therefore,
thus shall you say to My servant David,
'Thus says the LORD of hosts: "I took
you from the sheepfold, from following
the sheep, to be ruler over My people,
over Israel. 9And I have been with you
wherever you have gone, and have cut
off all your enemies from before you,
and have made you a great name, like
the name of the great men who *are* on
the earth. 10Moreover I will appoint
a place for My people Israel, and will
plant them, that they may dwell in a
place of their own and move no more;
nor shall the sons of wickedness oppress
them anymore, as previously, 11since
the time that I commanded judges *to be*
over My people Israel, and have caused
you to rest from all your enemies. Also
the LORD tells you that He will make
you a house.[a]

12"When your days are fulfilled and
you rest with your fathers, I will set
up your seed after you, who will come
from your body, and I will establish
his kingdom. 13He shall build a house
for My name, and I will establish the
throne of his kingdom forever. 14I will
be his Father, and he shall be My son. If
he commits iniquity, I will chasten him
with the rod of men and with the blows
of the sons of men. 15But My mercy
shall not depart from him, as I took *it*
from Saul, whom I removed from before
you. 16And your house and your king-
dom shall be established forever before
you.[a] Your throne shall be established
forever." ' "

17According to all these words and
according to all this vision, so Nathan
spoke to David.

David's Thanksgiving to God

18Then King David went in and sat be-
fore the LORD; and he said: "Who *am* I,
O Lord GOD? And what is my house, that
You have brought me this far? 19And
yet this was a small thing in Your sight,
O Lord GOD; and You have also spoken
of Your servant's house for a great while
to come. *Is* this the manner of man,
O Lord GOD? 20Now what more can
David say to You? For You, Lord GOD,
know Your servant. 21For Your word's
sake, and according to Your own heart,
You have done all these great things, to
make Your servant know *them*. 22There-
fore You are great, O Lord GOD.[a] For
there is none like You, nor *is there any*
God besides You, according to all that
we have heard with our ears. 23And who
is like Your people, like Israel, the one
nation on the earth whom God went to
redeem for Himself as a people, to make
for Himself a name—and to do for
Yourself great and awesome deeds for
Your land—before Your people whom
You redeemed for Yourself from Egypt,
the nations, and their gods? 24For You
have made Your people Israel Your very
own people forever; and You, LORD,
have become their God.

25"Now, O LORD God, the word which
You have spoken concerning Your ser-
vant and concerning his house, estab-
lish *it* forever and do as You have said.
26So let Your name be magnified forev-
er, saying, 'The LORD of hosts *is* the God
over Israel.' And let the house of Your
servant David be established before
You. 27For You, O LORD of hosts, God of
Israel, have revealed *this* to Your ser-
vant, saying, 'I will build you a house.'
Therefore Your servant has found it in
his heart to pray this prayer to You.

28"And now, O Lord GOD, You are God,
and Your words are true, and You have
promised this goodness to Your servant.
29Now therefore, let it please You to
bless the house of Your servant, that it
may continue before You forever; for
You, O Lord GOD, have spoken *it*, and
with Your blessing let the house of Your
servant be blessed forever."

7:11 [a] That is, a royal dynasty **7:16** [a] Septuagint reads *Me*. **7:22** [a] Targum and Syriac read *O LORD God*.

David's Further Conquests

8 After this it came to pass that David
attacked the Philistines and sub-
dued them. And David took Metheg
Ammah from the hand of the Philis-
tines.
2Then he defeated Moab. Forcing them
down to the ground, he measured them
off with a line. With two lines he mea-
sured off those to be put to death, and
with one full line those to be kept alive.
So the Moabites became David's ser-
vants, *and* brought tribute.
3David also defeated Hadadezer the
son of Rehob, king of Zobah, as he went to
recover his territory at the River Euphra-
tes. 4David took from him one thousand
chariots, seven hundred[a] horsemen, and
twenty thousand foot soldiers. Also Da-
vid hamstrung all the chariot *horses,*
except that he spared *enough* of them
for one hundred chariots.
5When the Syrians of Damascus came
to help Hadadezer king of Zobah, David
killed twenty-two thousand of the Syri-
ans. 6Then David put garrisons in Syria
of Damascus; and the Syrians became
David's servants, *and* brought tribute.
So the LORD preserved David wherever
he went. 7And David took the shields of
gold that had belonged to the servants
of Hadadezer, and brought them to Je-
rusalem. 8Also from Betah[a] and from
Berothai, cities of Hadadezer, King
David took a large amount of bronze.
9When Toi[a] king of Hamath heard that
David had defeated all the army of Had-
adezer, 10then Toi sent Joram[a] his son to
King David, to greet him and bless him,
because he had fought against Hadad-
ezer and defeated him (for Hadadezer
had been at war with Toi); and *Joram*
brought with him articles of silver, ar-
ticles of gold, and articles of bronze.
11King David also dedicated these to
the LORD, along with the silver and gold
that he had dedicated from all the na-
tions which he had subdued— 12from
Syria,[a] from Moab, from the people
of Ammon, from the Philistines, from
Amalek, and from the spoil of Hadad-
ezer the son of Rehob, king of Zobah.
13And David made *himself* a name
when he returned from killing eigh-
teen thousand Syrians[a] in the Valley of
Salt. 14He also put garrisons in Edom;
throughout all Edom he put garrisons,
and all the Edomites became David's
servants. And the LORD preserved David
wherever he went.

David's Administration

15So David reigned over all Israel; and
David administered judgment and justice
to all his people. 16Joab the son of Zeruiah
was over the army; Jehoshaphat the son
of Ahilud *was* recorder; 17Zadok the son of
Ahitub and Ahimelech the son of Abiathar
were the priests; Seraiah[a] *was* the scribe;
18Benaiah the son of Jehoiada *was over*
both the Cherethites and the Pelethites;
and David's sons were chief ministers.

David's Kindness to Mephibosheth

9 Now David said, "Is there still any-
one who is left of the house of Saul,
that I may show him kindness for Jon-
athan's sake?"
2And *there was* a servant of the house
of Saul whose name *was* Ziba. So when
they had called him to David, the king
said to him, "*Are* you Ziba?"
He said, "At your service!"
3Then the king said, "*Is* there not still
someone of the house of Saul, to whom
I may show the kindness of God?"
And Ziba said to the king, "There is still
a son of Jonathan *who is* lame in *his* feet."
4So the king said to him, "Where *is* he?"
And Ziba said to the king, "Indeed he
is in the house of Machir the son of Am-
miel, in Lo Debar."
5Then King David sent and brought
him out of the house of Machir the son
of Ammiel, from Lo Debar.
6Now when Mephibosheth the son of
Jonathan, the son of Saul, had come to
David, he fell on his face and prostrated
himself. Then David said, "Mephibo-
sheth?"

8:4 [a] Or *seven thousand* (compare 1 Chronicles 18:4) **8:8** [a] Spelled *Tibhath* in 1 Chronicles 18:8 **8:9** [a] Spelled *Tou* in 1 Chronicles 18:9 **8:10** [a] Spelled *Hadoram* in 1 Chronicles 18:10 **8:12** [a] Septuagint, Syriac, and some Hebrew manuscripts read *Edom.* **8:13** [a] Septuagint, Syriac, and some Hebrew manuscripts read *Edomites* (compare 1 Chronicles 18:12). **8:17** [a] Spelled *Shavsha* in 1 Chronicles 18:16

And he answered, "Here is your servant!"
7So David said to him, "Do not fear,
for I will surely show you kindness for
Jonathan your father's sake, and will
restore to you all the land of Saul your
grandfather; and you shall eat bread
at my table continually."
8Then he bowed himself, and said,
"What *is* your servant, that you should
look upon such a dead dog as I?"
9And the king called to Ziba, Saul's
servant, and said to him, "I have given
to your master's son all that belonged
to Saul and to all his house. 10You there-
fore, and your sons and your servants,
shall work the land for him, and you
shall bring in *the harvest,* that your
master's son may have food to eat. But
Mephibosheth your master's son shall
eat bread at my table always." Now Ziba
had fifteen sons and twenty servants.
11Then Ziba said to the king, "Accord-
ing to all that my lord the king has
commanded his servant, so will your
servant do."
"As for Mephibosheth," *said the king,*
"he shall eat at my table[a] like one of
the king's sons." 12Mephibosheth had
a young son whose name *was* Micha.
And all who dwelt in the house of Ziba
were servants of Mephibosheth. 13So
Mephibosheth dwelt in Jerusalem, for
he ate continually at the king's table.
And he was lame in both his feet.

The Ammonites and Syrians Defeated

10 It happened after this that the
king of the people of Ammon
died, and Hanun his son reigned in his
place. 2Then David said, "I will show
kindness to Hanun the son of Nahash,
as his father showed kindness to me."
So David sent by the hand of his ser-
vants to comfort him concerning his
father. And David's servants came into
the land of the people of Ammon. 3And
the princes of the people of Ammon
said to Hanun their lord, "Do you think
that David really honors your father
because he has sent comforters to you?
Has David not *rather* sent his servants
to you to search the city, to spy it out,
and to overthrow it?"
4Therefore Hanun took David's ser-
vants, shaved off half of their beards,
cut off their garments in the middle,
at their buttocks, and sent them away.
5When they told David, he sent to meet
them, because the men were greatly
ashamed. And the king said, "Wait at
Jericho until your beards have grown,
and *then* return."
6When the people of Ammon saw that
they had made themselves repulsive to
David, the people of Ammon sent and
hired the Syrians of Beth Rehob and
the Syrians of Zoba, twenty thousand
foot soldiers; and from the king of Ma-
acah one thousand men, and from Ish-
Tob twelve thousand men. 7Now when
David heard *of it,* he sent Joab and all
the army of the mighty men. 8Then
the people of Ammon came out and
put themselves in battle array at the
entrance of the gate. And the Syrians of
Zoba, Beth Rehob, Ish-Tob, and Maacah
were by themselves in the field.
9When Joab saw that the battle line
was against him before and behind, he
chose some of Israel's best and put *them*
in battle array against the Syrians. 10And
the rest of the people he put under the
command of Abishai his brother, that he
might set *them* in battle array against
the people of Ammon. 11Then he said, "If
the Syrians are too strong for me, then
you shall help me; but if the people of
Ammon are too strong for you, then I will
come and help you. 12Be of good courage,
and let us be strong for our people and for
the cities of our God. And may the LORD
do *what is* good in His sight."
13So Joab and the people who *were*
with him drew near for the battle
against the Syrians, and they fled be-
fore him. 14When the people of Ammon
saw that the Syrians were fleeing, they
also fled before Abishai, and entered the
city. So Joab returned from the people
of Ammon and went to Jerusalem.
15When the Syrians saw that they had
been defeated by Israel, they gathered
together. 16Then Hadadezer[a] sent and
brought out the Syrians who *were*
beyond the River,[b] and they came to
Helam. And Shobach the commander

9:11 [a] Septuagint reads *David's table.* **10:16** [a] Hebrew *Hadarezer* [b] That is, the Euphrates

of Hadadezer's army *went* before them. 17When it was told David, he gathered all Israel, crossed over the Jordan, and came to Helam. And the Syrians set themselves in battle array against David and fought with him. 18Then the Syrians fled before Israel; and David killed seven hundred charioteers and forty thousand horsemen of the Syrians, and struck Shobach the commander of their army, who died there. 19And when all the kings *who were* servants to Hadadezer[a] saw that they were defeated by Israel, they made peace with Israel and served them. So the Syrians were afraid to help the people of Ammon anymore.

David, Bathsheba, and Uriah

11 It happened in the spring of the year, at the time when kings go out *to battle,* that David sent Joab and his servants with him, and all Israel; and they destroyed the people of Ammon and besieged Rabbah. But David remained at Jerusalem.

2Then it happened one evening that David arose from his bed and walked on the roof of the king's house. And from the roof he saw a woman bathing, and the woman *was* very beautiful to behold. 3So David sent and inquired about the woman. And *someone* said, "*Is* this not Bathsheba, the daughter of Eliam, the wife of Uriah the Hittite?" 4Then David sent messengers, and took her; and she came to him, and he lay with her, for she was cleansed from her impurity; and she returned to her house. 5And the woman conceived; so she sent and told David, and said, "I *am* with child."

6Then David sent to Joab, *saying,* "Send me Uriah the Hittite." And Joab sent Uriah to David. 7When Uriah had come to him, David asked how Joab was doing, and how the people were doing, and how the war prospered. 8And David said to Uriah, "Go down to your house and wash your feet." So Uriah departed from the king's house, and a gift *of food* from the king followed him. 9But Uriah slept at the door of the king's house with all the servants of his lord, and did not go down to his house. 10So when they told David, saying, "Uriah did not go down to his house," David said to Uriah, "Did you not come from a journey? Why did you not go down to your house?"

11And Uriah said to David, "The ark and Israel and Judah are dwelling in tents, and my lord Joab and the servants of my lord are encamped in the open fields. Shall I then go to my house to eat and drink, and to lie with my wife? *As* you live, and *as* your soul lives, I will not do this thing."

12Then David said to Uriah, "Wait here today also, and tomorrow I will let you depart." So Uriah remained in Jerusalem that day and the next. 13Now when David called him, he ate and drank before him; and he made him drunk. And at evening he went out to lie on his bed with the servants of his lord, but he did not go down to his house.

14In the morning it happened that David wrote a letter to Joab and sent *it* by the hand of Uriah. 15And he wrote in the letter, saying, "Set Uriah in the forefront of the hottest battle, and retreat from him, that he may be struck down and die." 16So it was, while Joab besieged the city, that he assigned Uriah to a place where he knew there *were* valiant men. 17Then the men of the city came out and fought with Joab. And *some* of the people of the servants of David fell; and Uriah the Hittite died also.

18Then Joab sent and told David all the things concerning the war, 19and charged the messenger, saying, "When you have finished telling the matters of the war to the king, 20if it happens that the king's wrath rises, and he says to you: 'Why did you approach so near to the city when you fought? Did you not know that they would shoot from the wall? 21Who struck Abimelech the son of Jerubbesheth?[a] Was it not a woman who cast a piece of a millstone on him from the wall, so that he died in Thebez? Why did you go near the wall?'—then you shall say, 'Your servant Uriah the Hittite is dead also.' "

22So the messenger went, and came and told David all that Joab had sent by

10:19 [a] Hebrew *Hadarezer* **11:21** [a] Same as *Jerubbaal* (Gideon), Judges 6:32ff

him. 23And the messenger said to David,
"Surely the men prevailed against us
and came out to us in the field; then we
drove them back as far as the entrance
of the gate. 24The archers shot from
the wall at your servants; and *some* of
the king's servants are dead, and your
servant Uriah the Hittite is dead also."
25Then David said to the messenger,
"Thus you shall say to Joab: 'Do not
let this thing displease you, for the
sword devours one as well as another.
Strengthen your attack against the city,
and overthrow it.' So encourage him."
26When the wife of Uriah heard
that Uriah her husband was dead,
she mourned for her husband. 27And
when her mourning was over, David
sent and brought her to his house, and
she became his wife and bore him a
son. But the thing that David had done
displeased the LORD.

Nathan's Parable and David's Confession

12 Then the LORD sent Nathan to
David. And he came to him, and
said to him: "There were two men in
one city, one rich and the other poor.
2The rich *man* had exceedingly many
flocks and herds. 3But the poor *man*
had nothing, except one little ewe lamb
which he had bought and nourished;
and it grew up together with him and
with his children. It ate of his own food
and drank from his own cup and lay in
his bosom; and it was like a daughter to
him. 4And a traveler came to the rich
man, who refused to take from his own
flock and from his own herd to prepare
one for the wayfaring man who had
come to him; but he took the poor man's
lamb and prepared it for the man who
had come to him."
5So David's anger was greatly aroused
against the man, and he said to Nathan,
"*As* the LORD lives, the man who
has done this shall surely die! 6And
he shall restore fourfold for the lamb,
because he did this thing and because
he had no pity."
7Then Nathan said to David, "You *are*
the man! Thus says the LORD God of
Israel: 'I anointed you king over Israel,
and I delivered you from the hand of
Saul. 8I gave you your master's house
and your master's wives into your keeping,
and gave you the house of Israel
and Judah. And if *that had been* too little,
I also would have given you much more!
9Why have you despised the commandment
of the LORD, to do evil in His sight?
You have killed Uriah the Hittite with the
sword; you have taken his wife *to be* your
wife, and have killed him with the sword
of the people of Ammon. 10Now therefore,
the sword shall never depart from
your house, because you have despised
Me, and have taken the wife of Uriah the
Hittite to be your wife.' 11Thus says the
LORD: 'Behold, I will raise up adversity
against you from your own house; and
I will take your wives before your eyes
and give *them* to your neighbor, and he
shall lie with your wives in the sight of
this sun. 12For you did *it* secretly, but I
will do this thing before all Israel, before
the sun.'"
13So David said to Nathan, "I have
sinned against the LORD."
And Nathan said to David, "The LORD
also has put away your sin; you shall
not die. 14However, because by this deed
you have given great occasion to the
enemies of the LORD to blaspheme,
the child also *who is* born to you shall
surely die." 15Then Nathan departed to
his house.

The Death of David's Son

And the LORD struck the child that Uriah's
wife bore to David, and it became
ill. 16David therefore pleaded with God
for the child, and David fasted and went
in and lay all night on the ground. 17So
the elders of his house arose *and went* to
him, to raise him up from the ground.
But he would not, nor did he eat food
with them. 18Then on the seventh day
it came to pass that the child died. And
the servants of David were afraid to tell
him that the child was dead. For they
said, "Indeed, while the child was alive,
we spoke to him, and he would not heed
our voice. How can we tell him that the
child is dead? He may do some harm!"
19When David saw that his servants
were whispering, David perceived that
the child was dead. Therefore David
said to his servants, "Is the child dead?"
And they said, "He is dead."

20So David arose from the ground,
washed and anointed himself, and
changed his clothes; and he went into
the house of the LORD and worshiped.
Then he went to his own house; and
when he requested, they set food before
him, and he ate. 21Then his servants
said to him, "What *is* this that you have
done? You fasted and wept for the child
while he was alive, but when the child
died, you arose and ate food."
22And he said, "While the child was
alive, I fasted and wept; for I said, 'Who
can tell *whether* the LORD[a] will be gra-
cious to me, that the child may live?'
23But now he is dead; why should I fast?
Can I bring him back again? I shall go
to him, but he shall not return to me."

Solomon Is Born

24Then David comforted Bathsheba
his wife, and went in to her and lay with
her. So she bore a son, and he[a] called
his name Solomon. Now the LORD loved
him, 25and He sent *word* by the hand of
Nathan the prophet: So he[a] called his
name Jedidiah,[b] because of the LORD.

Rabbah Is Captured

26Now Joab fought against Rabbah of
the people of Ammon, and took the roy-
al city. 27And Joab sent messengers to
David, and said, "I have fought against
Rabbah, and I have taken the city's wa-
ter *supply.* 28Now therefore, gather the
rest of the people together and encamp
against the city and take it, lest I take the
city and it be called after my name." 29So
David gathered all the people together
and went to Rabbah, fought against it,
and took it. 30Then he took their king's
crown from his head. Its weight *was*
a talent of gold, with precious stones.
And it was *set* on David's head. Also he
brought out the spoil of the city in great
abundance. 31And he brought out the
people who *were* in it, and put *them to*
work with saws and iron picks and iron
axes, and made them cross over to the
brick works. So he did to all the cities of
the people of Ammon. Then David and
all the people returned to Jerusalem.

Amnon and Tamar

13 After this Absalom the son of
David had a lovely sister, whose
name *was* Tamar; and Amnon the son
of David loved her. 2Amnon was so
distressed over his sister Tamar that
he became sick; for she *was* a virgin.
And it was improper for Amnon to do
anything to her. 3But Amnon had a
friend whose name *was* Jonadab the
son of Shimeah, David's brother. Now
Jonadab *was* a very crafty man. 4And
he said to him, "Why *are* you, the king's
son, becoming thinner day after day?
Will you not tell me?"
Amnon said to him, "I love Tamar, my
brother Absalom's sister."
5So Jonadab said to him, "Lie down
on your bed and pretend to be ill. And
when your father comes to see you,
say to him, 'Please let my sister Tamar
come and give me food, and prepare the
food in my sight, that I may see *it* and
eat it from her hand.' " 6Then Amnon
lay down and pretended to be ill; and
when the king came to see him, Amnon
said to the king, "Please let Tamar my
sister come and make a couple of cakes
for me in my sight, that I may eat from
her hand."
7And David sent home to Tamar, say-
ing, "Now go to your brother Amnon's
house, and prepare food for him." 8So
Tamar went to her brother Amnon's
house; and he was lying down. Then she
took flour and kneaded *it,* made cakes in
his sight, and baked the cakes. 9And she
took the pan and placed *them* out before
him, but he refused to eat. Then Amnon
said, "Have everyone go out from me."
And they all went out from him. 10Then
Amnon said to Tamar, "Bring the food
into the bedroom, that I may eat from
your hand." And Tamar took the cakes
which she had made, and brought *them*
to Amnon her brother in the bedroom.
11Now when she had brought *them* to
him to eat, he took hold of her and said
to her, "Come, lie with me, my sister."
12But she answered him, "No, my
brother, do not force me, for no such
thing should be done in Israel. Do not

12:22 [a] A few Hebrew manuscripts and Syriac read *God.* **12:24** [a] Following Kethib, Septuagint, and Vulgate; Qere, a few Hebrew manuscripts, Syriac, and Targum read *she.* **12:25** [a] Qere, some Hebrew manuscripts, Syriac, and Targum read *she.* [b] Literally *Beloved of the LORD*

do this disgraceful thing! 13And I, where
could I take my shame? And as for you,
you would be like one of the fools in Is-
rael. Now therefore, please speak to the
king; for he will not withhold me from
you." 14However, he would not heed her
voice; and being stronger than she, he
forced her and lay with her.
15Then Amnon hated her exceedingly,
so that the hatred with which he hated
her *was* greater than the love with which
he had loved her. And Amnon said to
her, "Arise, be gone!"
16So she said to him, "No, indeed! This
evil of sending me away *is* worse than
the other that you did to me."
But he would not listen to her. 17Then
he called his servant who attended him,
and said, "Here! Put this *woman* out,
away from me, and bolt the door behind
her." 18Now she had on a robe of many
colors, for the king's virgin daughters
wore such apparel. And his servant put
her out and bolted the door behind her.
19Then Tamar put ashes on her head,
and tore her robe of many colors that
was on her, and laid her hand on her
head and went away crying bitterly.
20And Absalom her brother said to
her, "Has Amnon your brother been
with you? But now hold your peace,
my sister. He *is* your brother; do not
take this thing to heart." So Tamar re-
mained desolate in her brother Absa-
lom's house.
21But when King David heard of all
these things, he was very angry. 22And
Absalom spoke to his brother Amnon
neither good nor bad. For Absalom hat-
ed Amnon, because he had forced his
sister Tamar.

Absalom Murders Amnon

23And it came to pass, after two full
years, that Absalom had sheepshearers
in Baal Hazor, which *is* near Ephraim;
so Absalom invited all the king's sons.
24Then Absalom came to the king and
said, "Kindly note, your servant has
sheepshearers; please, let the king and
his servants go with your servant."
25But the king said to Absalom, "No,
my son, let us not all go now, lest we be a
burden to you." Then he urged him, but
he would not go; and he blessed him.
26Then Absalom said, "If not, please let
my brother Amnon go with us."
And the king said to him, "Why should
he go with you?" 27But Absalom urged
him; so he let Amnon and all the king's
sons go with him.
28Now Absalom had commanded his
servants, saying, "Watch now, when
Amnon's heart is merry with wine, and
when I say to you, 'Strike Amnon!' then
kill him. Do not be afraid. Have I not
commanded you? Be courageous and
valiant." 29So the servants of Absalom
did to Amnon as Absalom had com-
manded. Then all the king's sons arose,
and each one got on his mule and fled.
30And it came to pass, while they
were on the way, that news came to
David, saying, "Absalom has killed all
the king's sons, and not one of them
is left!" 31So the king arose and tore
his garments and lay on the ground,
and all his servants stood by with their
clothes torn. 32Then Jonadab the son
of Shimeah, David's brother, answered
and said, "Let not my lord suppose they
have killed all the young men, the king's
sons, for only Amnon is dead. For by
the command of Absalom this has been
determined from the day that he forced
his sister Tamar. 33Now therefore, let
not my lord the king take the thing to
his heart, to think that all the king's
sons are dead. For only Amnon is dead."

Absalom Flees to Geshur

34Then Absalom fled. And the young
man who was keeping watch lifted his
eyes and looked, and there, many peo-
ple were coming from the road on the
hillside behind him.[a] 35And Jonadab
said to the king, "Look, the king's sons
are coming; as your servant said, so it
is." 36So it was, as soon as he had fin-
ished speaking, that the king's sons
indeed came, and they lifted up their
voice and wept. Also the king and all
his servants wept very bitterly.
37But Absalom fled and went to Talmai
the son of Ammihud, king of Geshur.
And *David* mourned for his son every

13:34 [a] Septuagint adds *And the watchman went and told the king, and said, "I see men from the way of Horonaim, from the regions of the mountains."*

day. 38 So Absalom fled and went to Ge-
shur, and was there three years. 39 And
King David[a] longed to go to[b] Absalom.
For he had been comforted concerning
Amnon, because he was dead.

Absalom Returns to Jerusalem

14 So Joab the son of Zeruiah per-
ceived that the king's heart *was*
concerned about Absalom. 2 And Joab
sent to Tekoa and brought from there a
wise woman, and said to her, "Please pre-
tend to be a mourner, and put on mourn-
ing apparel; do not anoint yourself with
oil, but act like a woman who has been
mourning a long time for the dead. 3 Go
to the king and speak to him in this man-
ner." So Joab put the words in her mouth.
4 And when the woman of Tekoa spoke[a]
to the king, she fell on her face to the
ground and prostrated herself, and
said, "Help, O king!"
5 Then the king said to her, "What trou-
bles you?"
And she answered, "Indeed I *am* a
widow, my husband is dead. 6 Now your
maidservant had two sons; and the two
fought with each other in the field, and
there was no one to part them, but the
one struck the other and killed him.
7 And now the whole family has risen
up against your maidservant, and
they said, 'Deliver him who struck his
brother, that we may execute him for
the life of his brother whom he killed;
and we will destroy the heir also.' So
they would extinguish my ember that
is left, and leave to my husband *neither*
name nor remnant on the earth."
8 Then the king said to the woman, "Go
to your house, and I will give orders
concerning you."
9 And the woman of Tekoa said to the
king, "My lord, O king, *let* the iniquity
be on me and on my father's house, and
the king and his throne *be* guiltless."
10 So the king said, "Whoever says *any-
thing* to you, bring him to me, and he
shall not touch you anymore."
11 Then she said, "Please let the king re-
member the LORD your God, and do not
permit the avenger of blood to destroy
anymore, lest they destroy my son."
And he said, "As the LORD lives, not one
hair of your son shall fall to the ground."
12 Therefore the woman said, "Please,
let your maidservant speak *another*
word to my lord the king."
And he said, "Say on."
13 So the woman said: "Why then have
you schemed such a thing against the
people of God? For the king speaks this
thing as one who is guilty, *in that* the
king does not bring his banished one
home again. 14 For we will surely die and
become like water spilled on the ground,
which cannot be gathered up again. Yet
God does not take away a life; but He
devises means, so that His banished
ones are not expelled from Him. 15 Now
therefore, I have come to speak of this
thing to my lord the king because the
people have made me afraid. And your
maidservant said, 'I will now speak to
the king; it may be that the king will
perform the request of his maidservant.
16 For the king will hear and deliver his
maidservant from the hand of the man
who would destroy me and my son to-
gether from the inheritance of God.'
17 Your maidservant said, 'The word of
my lord the king will now be comforting;
for as the angel of God, so *is* my lord the
king in discerning good and evil. And
may the LORD your God be with you.' "
18 Then the king answered and said to
the woman, "Please do not hide from
me anything that I ask you."
And the woman said, "Please, let my
lord the king speak."
19 So the king said, "*Is* the hand of Joab
with you in all this?" And the woman
answered and said, "*As* you live, my
lord the king, no one can turn to the
right hand or to the left from anything
that my lord the king has spoken. For
your servant Joab commanded me, and
he put all these words in the mouth of
your maidservant. 20 To bring about
this change of affairs your servant Joab
has done this thing; but my lord *is* wise,
according to the wisdom of the angel

13:39 [a] Following Masoretic Text, Syriac, and Vulgate; Septuagint reads *the spirit of the king;* Targum reads *the soul of King David.* [b] Following Masoretic Text and Targum; Septuagint and Vulgate read *ceased to pursue after.* **14:4** [a] Many Hebrew manuscripts, Septuagint, Syriac, and Vulgate read *came.*

of God, to know everything that *is* in
the earth."
21And the king said to Joab, "All right,
I have granted this thing. Go therefore,
bring back the young man Absalom."
22Then Joab fell to the ground on his
face and bowed himself, and thanked the
king. And Joab said, "Today your servant
knows that I have found favor in your
sight, my lord, O king, in that the king
has fulfilled the request of his servant."
23So Joab arose and went to Geshur, and
brought Absalom to Jerusalem. 24And
the king said, "Let him return to his own
house, but do not let him see my face."
So Absalom returned to his own house,
but did not see the king's face.

David Forgives Absalom

25Now in all Israel there was no one
who was praised as much as Absalom
for his good looks. From the sole of his
foot to the crown of his head there was
no blemish in him. 26And when he cut
the hair of his head—at the end of every
year he cut *it* because it was heavy on
him—when he cut it, he weighed the
hair of his head at two hundred shekels
according to the king's standard. 27To
Absalom were born three sons, and one
daughter whose name *was* Tamar. She
was a woman of beautiful appearance.
28And Absalom dwelt two full years
in Jerusalem, but did not see the king's
face. 29Therefore Absalom sent for Joab,
to send him to the king, but he would
not come to him. And when he sent
again the second time, he would not
come. 30So he said to his servants, "See,
Joab's field is near mine, and he has
barley there; go and set it on fire." And
Absalom's servants set the field on fire.
31Then Joab arose and came to Ab-
salom's house, and said to him, "Why
have your servants set my field on fire?"
32And Absalom answered Joab, "Look,
I sent to you, saying, 'Come here, so that
I may send you to the king, to say, "Why
have I come from Geshur? *It would be*
better for me *to be* there still."' Now there-
fore, let me see the king's face; but if there
is iniquity in me, let him execute me."
33So Joab went to the king and told
him. And when he had called for Ab-
salom, he came to the king and bowed
himself on his face to the ground before
the king. Then the king kissed Absalom.

Absalom's Treason

15 After this it happened that Ab-
salom provided himself with
chariots and horses, and fifty men to
run before him. 2Now Absalom would
rise early and stand beside the way to the
gate. *So* it was, whenever anyone who had
a lawsuit came to the king for a decision,
that Absalom would call to him and say,
"What city *are* you from?" And he would
say, "Your servant *is* from such and such
a tribe of Israel." 3Then Absalom would
say to him, "Look, your case *is* good and
right; but *there is* no deputy of the king to
hear you." 4Moreover Absalom would say,
"Oh, that I were made judge in the land,
and everyone who has any suit or cause
would come to me; then I would give him
justice." 5And *so* it was, whenever anyone
came near to bow down to him, that he
would put out his hand and take him
and kiss him. 6In this manner Absalom
acted toward all Israel who came to the
king for judgment. So Absalom stole the
hearts of the men of Israel.
7Now it came to pass after forty[a] years
that Absalom said to the king, "Please,
let me go to Hebron and pay the vow
which I made to the LORD. 8For your ser-
vant took a vow while I dwelt at Geshur
in Syria, saying, 'If the LORD indeed
brings me back to Jerusalem, then I
will serve the LORD.'"
9And the king said to him, "Go in
peace." So he arose and went to Hebron.
10Then Absalom sent spies throughout
all the tribes of Israel, saying, "As soon
as you hear the sound of the trumpet,
then you shall say, 'Absalom reigns in
Hebron!'" 11And with Absalom went two
hundred men invited from Jerusalem,
and they went along innocently and did
not know anything. 12Then Absalom sent
for Ahithophel the Gilonite, David's coun-
selor, from his city—from Giloh—while
he offered sacrifices. And the conspiracy
grew strong, for the people with Absalom
continually increased in number.

15:7 [a] Septuagint manuscripts, Syriac, and Josephus read *four.*

David Escapes from Jerusalem

13Now a messenger came to David,
saying, "The hearts of the men of Israel
are with Absalom."
14So David said to all his servants who
were with him at Jerusalem, "Arise, and
let us flee, or we shall not escape from
Absalom. Make haste to depart, lest he
overtake us suddenly and bring disaster
upon us, and strike the city with the
edge of the sword."
15And the king's servants said to the
king, "We *are* your servants, *ready to do*
whatever my lord the king commands."
16Then the king went out with all his
household after him. But the king left
ten women, concubines, to keep the
house. 17And the king went out with all
the people after him, and stopped at the
outskirts. 18Then all his servants passed
before him; and all the Cherethites, all
the Pelethites, and all the Gittites, six
hundred men who had followed him
from Gath, passed before the king.
19Then the king said to Ittai the Gittite,
"Why are you also going with us? Return
and remain with the king. For you *are* a
foreigner and also an exile from your
own place. 20In fact, you came *only* yes-
terday. Should I make you wander up
and down with us today, since I go I know
not where? Return, and take your breth-
ren back. Mercy and truth *be* with you."
21But Ittai answered the king and said,
"*As* the LORD lives, and *as* my lord the
king lives, surely in whatever place my
lord the king shall be, whether in death or
life, even there also your servant will be."
22So David said to Ittai, "Go, and cross
over." Then Ittai the Gittite and all his
men and all the little ones who *were*
with him crossed over. 23And all the
country wept with a loud voice, and all
the people crossed over. The king him-
self also crossed over the Brook Kidron,
and all the people crossed over toward
the way of the wilderness.
24There was Zadok also, and all the
Levites with him, bearing the ark of
the covenant of God. And they set down
the ark of God, and Abiathar went up
until all the people had finished cross-
ing over from the city. 25Then the king
said to Zadok, "Carry the ark of God
back into the city. If I find favor in the
eyes of the LORD, He will bring me back
and show me *both* it and His dwelling
place. 26But if He says thus: 'I have no
delight in you,' here I am, let Him do to
me as seems good to Him." 27The king
also said to Zadok the priest, "*Are* you
not a seer? Return to the city in peace,
and your two sons with you, Ahimaaz
your son, and Jonathan the son of Abia-
thar. 28See, I will wait in the plains of the
wilderness until word comes from you
to inform me." 29Therefore Zadok and
Abiathar carried the ark of God back to
Jerusalem. And they remained there.
30So David went up by the Ascent of
the *Mount of* Olives, and wept as he
went up; and he had his head covered
and went barefoot. And all the peo-
ple who *were* with him covered their
heads and went up, weeping as they
went up. 31Then *someone* told David,
saying, "Ahithophel *is* among the con-
spirators with Absalom." And David
said, "O LORD, I pray, turn the counsel
of Ahithophel into foolishness!"
32Now it happened when David had
come to the top *of the mountain,* where
he worshiped God—there was Hushai
the Archite coming to meet him with his
robe torn and dust on his head. 33David
said to him, "If you go on with me, then
you will become a burden to me. 34But if
you return to the city, and say to Absa-
lom, 'I will be your servant, O king; *as* I
was your father's servant previously, so
I *will* now also *be* your servant,' then you
may defeat the counsel of Ahithophel
for me. 35And *do* you not *have* Zadok
and Abiathar the priests with you there?
Therefore it will be *that* whatever you
hear from the king's house, you shall
tell to Zadok and Abiathar the priests.
36Indeed *they have* there with them their
two sons, Ahimaaz, Zadok's *son,* and
Jonathan, Abiathar's *son;* and by them
you shall send me everything you hear."
37So Hushai, David's friend, went into
the city. And Absalom came into Je-
rusalem.

Mephibosheth's Servant

16 When David was a little past
the top *of the mountain,* there
was Ziba the servant of Mephibosheth,
who met him with a couple of saddled

donkeys, and on them two hundred *loaves* of bread, one hundred clusters of raisins, one hundred summer fruits, and a skin of wine. 2And the king said to Ziba, "What do you mean to do with these?"

So Ziba said, "The donkeys *are* for the king's household to ride on, the bread and summer fruit for the young men to eat, and the wine for those who are faint in the wilderness to drink."

3Then the king said, "And where *is* your master's son?"

And Ziba said to the king, "Indeed he is staying in Jerusalem, for he said, 'Today the house of Israel will restore the kingdom of my father to me.' "

4So the king said to Ziba, "Here, all that *belongs* to Mephibosheth *is* yours."

And Ziba said, "I humbly bow before you, *that* I may find favor in your sight, my lord, O king!"

Shimei Curses David

5Now when King David came to Bahurim, there was a man from the family of the house of Saul, whose name *was* Shimei the son of Gera, coming from there. He came out, cursing continuously as he came. 6And he threw stones at David and at all the servants of King David. And all the people and all the mighty men *were* on his right hand and on his left. 7Also Shimei said thus when he cursed: "Come out! Come out! You bloodthirsty man, you rogue! 8The LORD has brought upon you all the blood of the house of Saul, in whose place you have reigned; and the LORD has delivered the kingdom into the hand of Absalom your son. So now you *are caught* in your own evil, because you are a bloodthirsty man!"

9Then Abishai the son of Zeruiah said to the king, "Why should this dead dog curse my lord the king? Please, let me go over and take off his head!"

10But the king said, "What have I to do with you, you sons of Zeruiah? So let him curse, because the LORD has said to him, 'Curse David.' Who then shall say, 'Why have you done so?' "

11And David said to Abishai and all his servants, "See how my son who came from my own body seeks my life. How much more now *may this* Benjamite? Let him alone, and let him curse; for so the LORD has ordered him. 12It may be that the LORD will look on my affliction,[a] and that the LORD will repay me with good for his cursing this day." 13And as David and his men went along the road, Shimei went along the hillside opposite him and cursed as he went, threw stones at him and kicked up dust. 14Now the king and all the people who *were* with him became weary; so they refreshed themselves there.

The Advice of Ahithophel

15Meanwhile Absalom and all the people, the men of Israel, came to Jerusalem; and Ahithophel *was* with him. 16And so it was, when Hushai the Archite, David's friend, came to Absalom, that Hushai said to Absalom, "*Long* live the king! *Long* live the king!"

17So Absalom said to Hushai, "*Is* this your loyalty to your friend? Why did you not go with your friend?"

18And Hushai said to Absalom, "No, but whom the LORD and this people and all the men of Israel choose, his I will be, and with him I will remain. 19Furthermore, whom should I serve? *Should I* not *serve* in the presence of his son? As I have served in your father's presence, so will I be in your presence."

20Then Absalom said to Ahithophel, "Give advice as to what we should do."

21And Ahithophel said to Absalom, "Go in to your father's concubines, whom he has left to keep the house; and all Israel will hear that you are abhorred by your father. Then the hands of all who are with you will be strong." 22So they pitched a tent for Absalom on the top of the house, and Absalom went in to his father's concubines in the sight of all Israel.

23Now the advice of Ahithophel, which he gave in those days, *was* as if one had inquired at the oracle of God. So *was* all the advice of Ahithophel both with David and with Absalom.

16:12 [a] Following Kethib, Septuagint, Syriac, and Vulgate; Qere reads *my eyes;* Targum reads *tears of my eyes.*

17 Moreover Ahithophel said to
Absalom, "Now let me choose
twelve thousand men, and I will arise
and pursue David tonight. 2I will come
upon him while he *is* weary and weak,
and make him afraid. And all the peo-
ple who *are* with him will flee, and I
will strike only the king. 3Then I will
bring back all the people to you. When
all return except the man whom you
seek, all the people will be at peace."
4And the saying pleased Absalom and
all the elders of Israel.

The Advice of Hushai

5Then Absalom said, "Now call Hushai
the Archite also, and let us hear what
he says too." 6And when Hushai came
to Absalom, Absalom spoke to him,
saying, "Ahithophel has spoken in this
manner. Shall we do as he says? If not,
speak up."

7So Hushai said to Absalom: "The ad-
vice that Ahithophel has given *is* not
good at this time. 8For," said Hushai,
"you know your father and his men, that
they *are* mighty men, and they *are* en-
raged in their minds, like a bear robbed
of her cubs in the field; and your father
is a man of war, and will not camp with
the people. 9Surely by now he is hidden
in some pit, or in some *other* place. And
it will be, when some of them are over-
thrown at the first, that whoever hears *it*
will say, 'There is a slaughter among the
people who follow Absalom.' 10And even
he *who is* valiant, whose heart *is* like the
heart of a lion, will melt completely.
For all Israel knows that your father *is*
a mighty man, and *those* who *are* with
him *are* valiant men. 11Therefore I advise
that all Israel be fully gathered to you,
from Dan to Beersheba, like the sand
that *is* by the sea for multitude, and that
you go to battle in person. 12So we will
come upon him in some place where he
may be found, and we will fall on him
as the dew falls on the ground. And of
him and all the men who *are* with him
there shall not be left so much as one.
13Moreover, if he has withdrawn into
a city, then all Israel shall bring ropes
to that city; and we will pull it into the
river, until there is not one small stone
found there."

14So Absalom and all the men of Israel
said, "The advice of Hushai the Archite
is better than the advice of Ahithophel."
For the LORD had purposed to defeat the
good advice of Ahithophel, to the intent
that the LORD might bring disaster on
Absalom.

Hushai Warns David to Escape

15Then Hushai said to Zadok and Abi-
athar the priests, "Thus and so Ahitho-
phel advised Absalom and the elders
of Israel, and thus and so I have ad-
vised. 16Now therefore, send quickly and
tell David, saying, 'Do not spend this
night in the plains of the wilderness,
but speedily cross over, lest the king
and all the people who *are* with him be
swallowed up.' " 17Now Jonathan and
Ahimaaz stayed at En Rogel, for they
dared not be seen coming into the city;
so a female servant would come and tell
them, and they would go and tell King
David. 18Nevertheless a lad saw them,
and told Absalom. But both of them went
away quickly and came to a man's house
in Bahurim, who had a well in his court;
and they went down into it. 19Then the
woman took and spread a covering over
the well's mouth, and spread ground
grain on it; and the thing was not known.
20And when Absalom's servants came
to the woman at the house, they said,
"Where *are* Ahimaaz and Jonathan?"

So the woman said to them, "They have
gone over the water brook."

And when they had searched and could
not find *them,* they returned to Jerusa-
lem. 21Now it came to pass, after they
had departed, that they came up out of
the well and went and told King David,
and said to David, "Arise and cross over
the water quickly. For thus has Ahitho-
phel advised against you." 22So David
and all the people who *were* with him
arose and crossed over the Jordan. By
morning light not one of them was left
who had not gone over the Jordan.

23Now when Ahithophel saw that his
advice was not followed, he saddled a
donkey, and arose and went home to
his house, to his city. Then he put his
household in order, and hanged him-
self, and died; and he was buried in his
father's tomb.

24Then David went to Mahanaim. And
Absalom crossed over the Jordan, he
and all the men of Israel with him.
25And Absalom made Amasa captain
of the army instead of Joab. This Amasa
was the son of a man whose name *was*
Jithra,[a] an Israelite,[b] who had gone
in to Abigail the daughter of Nahash,
sister of Zeruiah, Joab's mother. 26So
Israel and Absalom encamped in the
land of Gilead.
27Now it happened, when David had
come to Mahanaim, that Shobi the son
of Nahash from Rabbah of the people
of Ammon, Machir the son of Ammiel
from Lo Debar, and Barzillai the Gilead-
ite from Rogelim, 28brought beds and
basins, earthen vessels and wheat, bar-
ley and flour, parched *grain* and beans,
lentils and parched *seeds,* 29honey and
curds, sheep and cheese of the herd, for
David and the people who *were* with
him to eat. For they said, "The people
are hungry and weary and thirsty in
the wilderness."

Absalom's Defeat and Death

18 And David numbered the peo-
ple who *were* with him, and set
captains of thousands and captains of
hundreds over them. 2Then David sent
out one third of the people under the
hand of Joab, one third under the hand
of Abishai the son of Zeruiah, Joab's
brother, and one third under the hand
of Ittai the Gittite. And the king said to
the people, "I also will surely go out
with you myself."
3But the people answered, "You shall
not go out! For if we flee away, they
will not care about us; nor if half of us
die, will they care about us. But *you are*
worth ten thousand of us now. For you
are now more help to us in the city."
4Then the king said to them, "Whatever
seems best to you I will do." So the king
stood beside the gate, and all the people
went out by hundreds and by thou-
sands. 5Now the king had commanded
Joab, Abishai, and Ittai, saying, "*Deal*
gently for my sake with the young man
Absalom." And all the people heard
when the king gave all the captains
orders concerning Absalom.
6So the people went out into the field of
battle against Israel. And the battle was
in the woods of Ephraim. 7The people of
Israel were overthrown there before the
servants of David, and a great slaughter
of twenty thousand took place there that
day. 8For the battle there was scattered
over the face of the whole countryside,
and the woods devoured more people
that day than the sword devoured.
9Then Absalom met the servants of
David. Absalom rode on a mule. The
mule went under the thick boughs of
a great terebinth tree, and his head
caught in the terebinth; so he was left
hanging between heaven and earth.
And the mule which *was* under him
went on. 10Now a certain man saw *it* and
told Joab, and said, "I just saw Absalom
hanging in a terebinth tree!"
11So Joab said to the man who told
him, "You just saw *him!* And why did
you not strike him there to the ground?
I would have given you ten *shekels* of
silver and a belt."
12But the man said to Joab, "Though
I were to receive a thousand *shekels* of
silver in my hand, I would not raise
my hand against the king's son. For in
our hearing the king commanded you
and Abishai and Ittai, saying, 'Beware
lest anyone *touch* the young man Ab-
salom!'[a] 13Otherwise I would have dealt
falsely against my own life. For there
is nothing hidden from the king, and
you yourself would have set yourself
against *me.*"
14Then Joab said, "I cannot linger with
you." And he took three spears in his
hand and thrust them through Absa-
lom's heart, while he was *still* alive in
the midst of the terebinth tree. 15And
ten young men who bore Joab's armor
surrounded Absalom, and struck and
killed him.
16So Joab blew the trumpet, and the
people returned from pursuing Israel.
For Joab held back the people. 17And

17:25 [a] Spelled *Jether* in 1 Chronicles 2:17 and elsewhere [b] Following Masoretic Text, some manuscripts of the Septuagint, and Targum; some manuscripts of the Septuagint read *Ishmaelite* (compare 1 Chronicles 2:17); Vulgate reads *of Jezrael.* **18:12** [a] The ancient versions read *'Protect the young man Absalom for me!'*

they took Absalom and cast him into a
large pit in the woods, and laid a very
large heap of stones over him. Then all
Israel fled, everyone to his tent.
18Now Absalom in his lifetime had
taken and set up a pillar for himself,
which *is* in the King's Valley. For he
said, "I have no son to keep my name
in remembrance." He called the pillar
after his own name. And to this day it
is called Absalom's Monument.

David Hears of Absalom's Death

19Then Ahimaaz the son of Zadok said,
"Let me run now and take the news to
the king, how the LORD has avenged
him of his enemies."
20And Joab said to him, "You shall not
take the news this day, for you shall
take the news another day. But today
you shall take no news, because the
king's son is dead." 21Then Joab said
to the Cushite, "Go, tell the king what
you have seen." So the Cushite bowed
himself to Joab and ran.
22And Ahimaaz the son of Zadok said
again to Joab, "But whatever happens,
please let me also run after the Cushite."
So Joab said, "Why will you run, my
son, since you have no news ready?"
23"But whatever happens," *he said,*
"let me run."
So he said to him, "Run." Then Ahima-
az ran by way of the plain, and outran
the Cushite.
24Now David was sitting between the
two gates. And the watchman went up
to the roof over the gate, to the wall,
lifted his eyes and looked, and there
was a man, running alone. 25Then the
watchman cried out and told the king.
And the king said, "If he *is* alone, *there*
is news in his mouth." And he came
rapidly and drew near.
26Then the watchman saw *another*
man running, and the watchman called
to the gatekeeper and said, "There is
another man, running alone!"
And the king said, "He also brings
news."
27So the watchman said, "I think the
running of the first is like the running
of Ahimaaz the son of Zadok."
And the king said, "He *is* a good man,
and comes with good news."
28So Ahimaaz called out and said to
the king, "All is well!" Then he bowed
down with his face to the earth before
the king, and said, "Blessed *be* the LORD
your God, who has delivered up the men
who raised their hand against my lord
the king!"
29The king said, "Is the young man
Absalom safe?"
Ahimaaz answered, "When Joab sent
the king's servant and *me* your servant,
I saw a great tumult, but I did not know
what *it was about.*"
30And the king said, "Turn aside *and*
stand here." So he turned aside and
stood still.
31Just then the Cushite came, and
the Cushite said, "There is good news,
my lord the king! For the LORD has
avenged you this day of all those who
rose against you."
32And the king said to the Cushite, "Is
the young man Absalom safe?"
So the Cushite answered, "May the
enemies of my lord the king, and all
who rise against you to do harm, be
like *that* young man!"

David's Mourning for Absalom

33Then the king was deeply moved,
and went up to the chamber over the
gate, and wept. And as he went, he said
thus: "O my son Absalom—my son, my
son Absalom—if only I had died in your
place! O Absalom my son, my son!"
19 And Joab was told, "Behold, the
king is weeping and mourning
for Absalom." 2So the victory that day
was *turned* into mourning for all the
people. For the people heard it said that
day, "The king is grieved for his son."
3And the people stole back into the city
that day, as people who are ashamed
steal away when they flee in battle. 4But
the king covered his face, and the king
cried out with a loud voice, "O my son
Absalom! O Absalom, my son, my son!"
5Then Joab came into the house to
the king, and said, "Today you have
disgraced all your servants who today
have saved your life, the lives of your
sons and daughters, the lives of your
wives and the lives of your concubines,
6in that you love your enemies and hate
your friends. For you have declared

today that you regard neither princes
nor servants; for today I perceive that
if Absalom had lived and all of us had
died today, then it would have pleased
you well. 7Now therefore, arise, go out
and speak comfort to your servants.
For I swear by the LORD, if you do not
go out, not one will stay with you this
night. And that will be worse for you
than all the evil that has befallen you
from your youth until now." 8Then the
king arose and sat in the gate. And they
told all the people, saying, "There is
the king, sitting in the gate." So all the
people came before the king.

For everyone of Israel had fled to his
tent.

David Returns to Jerusalem

9Now all the people were in a dispute
throughout all the tribes of Israel, say-
ing, "The king saved us from the hand of
our enemies, he delivered us from the
hand of the Philistines, and now he has
fled from the land because of Absalom.
10But Absalom, whom we anointed over
us, has died in battle. Now therefore,
why do you say nothing about bringing
back the king?"

11So King David sent to Zadok and
Abiathar the priests, saying, "Speak to
the elders of Judah, saying, 'Why are
you the last to bring the king back to
his house, since the words of all Israel
have come to the king, to his *very* house?
12You *are* my brethren, you *are* my bone
and my flesh. Why then are you the last
to bring back the king?' 13And say to
Amasa, '*Are* you not my bone and my
flesh? God do so to me, and more also,
if you are not commander of the army
before me continually in place of Joab.'"
14So he swayed the hearts of all the men
of Judah, just as *the heart of* one man,
so that they sent *this word* to the king:
"Return, you and all your servants!"

15Then the king returned and came to
the Jordan. And Judah came to Gilgal,
to go to meet the king, to escort the king
across the Jordan. 16And Shimei the
son of Gera, a Benjamite, who *was* from
Bahurim, hurried and came down with
the men of Judah to meet King David.
17*There were* a thousand men of Benja-
min with him, and Ziba the servant of
the house of Saul, and his fifteen sons
and his twenty servants with him; and
they went over the Jordan before the
king. 18Then a ferryboat went across to
carry over the king's household, and to
do what he thought good.

David's Mercy to Shimei

Now Shimei the son of Gera fell down
before the king when he had crossed the
Jordan. 19Then he said to the king, "Do
not let my lord impute iniquity to me,
or remember what wrong your servant
did on the day that my lord the king
left Jerusalem, that the king should
take *it* to heart. 20For I, your servant,
know that I have sinned. Therefore here
I am, the first to come today of all the
house of Joseph to go down to meet my
lord the king."

21But Abishai the son of Zeruiah an-
swered and said, "Shall not Shimei be
put to death for this, because he cursed
the LORD's anointed?"

22And David said, "What have I to do
with you, you sons of Zeruiah, that you
should be adversaries to me today?
Shall any man be put to death today
in Israel? For do I not know that today
I *am* king over Israel?" 23Therefore the
king said to Shimei, "You shall not die."
And the king swore to him.

David and Mephibosheth Meet

24Now Mephibosheth the son of Saul
came down to meet the king. And he had
not cared for his feet, nor trimmed his
mustache, nor washed his clothes, from
the day the king departed until the day
he returned in peace. 25So it was, when
he had come to Jerusalem to meet the
king, that the king said to him, "Why
did you not go with me, Mephibosheth?"

26And he answered, "My lord, O king,
my servant deceived me. For your ser-
vant said, 'I will saddle a donkey for
myself, that I may ride on it and go to
the king,' because your servant *is* lame.
27And he has slandered your servant
to my lord the king, but my lord the
king *is* like the angel of God. Therefore
do *what is* good in your eyes. 28For all
my father's house were but dead men
before my lord the king. Yet you set your
servant among those who eat at your

own table. Therefore what right have I
still to cry out anymore to the king?"
29So the king said to him, "Why do you
speak anymore of your matters? I have
said, 'You and Ziba divide the land.' "
30Then Mephibosheth said to the king,
"Rather, let him take it all, inasmuch
as my lord the king has come back in
peace to his own house."

David's Kindness to Barzillai

31And Barzillai the Gileadite came
down from Rogelim and went across
the Jordan with the king, to escort him
across the Jordan. 32Now Barzillai was
a very aged man, eighty years old. And
he had provided the king with supplies
while he stayed at Mahanaim, for he
was a very rich man. 33And the king
said to Barzillai, "Come across with me,
and I will provide for you while you are
with me in Jerusalem."
34But Barzillai said to the king, "How
long have I to live, that I should go
up with the king to Jerusalem? 35I *am*
today eighty years old. Can I discern
between the good and bad? Can your
servant taste what I eat or what I drink?
Can I hear any longer the voice of sing-
ing men and singing women? Why then
should your servant be a further burden
to my lord the king? 36Your servant
will go a little way across the Jordan
with the king. And why should the king
repay me *with* such a reward? 37Please
let your servant turn back again, that I
may die in my own city, near the grave
of my father and mother. But here is
your servant Chimham; let him cross
over with my lord the king, and do for
him what seems good to you."
38And the king answered, "Chimham
shall cross over with me, and I will do
for him what seems good to you. Now
whatever you request of me, I will do for
you." 39Then all the people went over the
Jordan. And when the king had crossed
over, the king kissed Barzillai and blessed
him, and he returned to his own place.

The Quarrel About the King

40Now the king went on to Gilgal, and
Chimham[a] went on with him. And all
the people of Judah escorted the king,
and also half the people of Israel. 41Just
then all the men of Israel came to the
king, and said to the king, "Why have
our brethren, the men of Judah, stolen
you away and brought the king, his
household, and all David's men with
him across the Jordan?"
42So all the men of Judah answered
the men of Israel, "Because the king *is*
a close relative of ours. Why then are
you angry over this matter? Have we
ever eaten at the king's *expense?* Or has
he given us any gift?"
43And the men of Israel answered the
men of Judah, and said, "We have ten
shares in the king; therefore we also
have more *right* to David than you. Why
then do you despise us—were we not the
first to advise bringing back our king?"
Yet the words of the men of Judah
were fiercer than the words of the men
of Israel.

The Rebellion of Sheba

20 And there happened to be there
a rebel,[a] whose name *was* Sheba
the son of Bichri, a Benjamite. And he
blew a trumpet, and said:

"We have no share in David,
Nor do we have inheritance in the
son of Jesse;
Every man to his tents, O Israel!"

2So every man of Israel deserted David,
and followed Sheba the son of Bichri.
But the men of Judah, from the Jordan
as far as Jerusalem, remained loyal to
their king.
3Now David came to his house at
Jerusalem. And the king took the ten
women, his concubines whom he had
left to keep the house, and put them in
seclusion and supported them, but did
not go in to them. So they were shut
up to the day of their death, living in
widowhood.
4And the king said to Amasa, "Assem-
ble the men of Judah for me within three
days, and be present here yourself."
5So Amasa went to assemble *the men of*
Judah. But he delayed longer than the

19:40 [a] Masoretic Text reads *Chimhan.* **20:1** [a] Literally *man of Belial*

set time which David had appointed
him. 6And David said to Abishai, "Now
Sheba the son of Bichri will do us more
harm than Absalom. Take your lord's
servants and pursue him, lest he find for
himself fortified cities, and escape us."
7So Joab's men, with the Cherethites, the
Pelethites, and all the mighty men, went
out after him. And they went out of Jeru-
salem to pursue Sheba the son of Bich-
ri. 8When they *were* at the large stone
which *is* in Gibeon, Amasa came before
them. Now Joab was dressed in battle
armor; on it was a belt *with* a sword fas-
tened in its sheath at his hips; and as he
was going forward, it fell out. 9Then Joab
said to Amasa, "*Are* you in health, my
brother?" And Joab took Amasa by the
beard with his right hand to kiss him.
10But Amasa did not notice the sword
that *was* in Joab's hand. And he struck
him with it in the stomach, and his en-
trails poured out on the ground; and he
did not *strike* him again. Thus he died.

Then Joab and Abishai his brother pur-
sued Sheba the son of Bichri. 11Meanwhile
one of Joab's men stood near Amasa, and
said, "Whoever favors Joab and whoever
is for David—follow Joab!" 12But Amasa
wallowed in *his* blood in the middle of the
highway. And when the man saw that all
the people stood still, he moved Amasa
from the highway to the field and threw
a garment over him, when he saw that
everyone who came upon him halted.
13When he was removed from the high-
way, all the people went on after Joab to
pursue Sheba the son of Bichri.

14And he went through all the tribes of
Israel to Abel and Beth Maachah and
all the Berites. So they were gathered
together and also went after *Sheba*.[a]
15Then they came and besieged him in
Abel of Beth Maachah; and they cast up
a siege mound against the city, and it
stood by the rampart. And all the people
who *were* with Joab battered the wall to
throw it down.

16Then a wise woman cried out from
the city, "Hear, hear! Please say to Joab,
'Come nearby, that I may speak with
you.'" 17When he had come near to her,
the woman said, "*Are* you Joab?"

He answered, "I *am*."

Then she said to him, "Hear the words
of your maidservant."

And he answered, "I am listening."

18So she spoke, saying, "They used to
talk in former times, saying, 'They shall
surely seek *guidance* at Abel,' and so
they would end *disputes*. 19I *am among*
the peaceable *and* faithful in Israel. You
seek to destroy a city and a mother in
Israel. Why would you swallow up the
inheritance of the LORD?"

20And Joab answered and said, "Far
be it, far be it from me, that I should
swallow up or destroy! 21That *is* not
so. But a man from the mountains of
Ephraim, Sheba the son of Bichri by
name, has raised his hand against the
king, against David. Deliver him only,
and I will depart from the city."

So the woman said to Joab, "Watch,
his head will be thrown to you over the
wall." 22Then the woman in her wisdom
went to all the people. And they cut off
the head of Sheba the son of Bichri,
and threw *it* out to Joab. Then he blew
a trumpet, and they withdrew from the
city, every man to his tent. So Joab re-
turned to the king at Jerusalem.

David's Government Officers

23And Joab *was* over all the army of
Israel; Benaiah the son of Jehoiada *was*
over the Cherethites and the Pelethites;
24Adoram *was* in charge of revenue;
Jehoshaphat the son of Ahilud *was*
recorder; 25Sheva *was* scribe; Zadok
and Abiathar *were* the priests; 26and
Ira the Jairite was a chief minister un-
der David.

David Avenges the Gibeonites

21 Now there was a famine in the
days of David for three years,
year after year; and David inquired of
the LORD. And the LORD answered, "*It*
is because of Saul and *his* bloodthirsty
house, because he killed the Gibeonites."
2So the king called the Gibeonites and
spoke to them. Now the Gibeonites *were*
not of the children of Israel, but of the
remnant of the Amorites; the children
of Israel had sworn protection to them,

20:14 [a] Literally *him*

but Saul had sought to kill them in his zeal for the children of Israel and Judah.

[3]Therefore David said to the Gibeonites, "What shall I do for you? And with what shall I make atonement, that you may bless the inheritance of the LORD?"

[4]And the Gibeonites said to him, "We will have no silver or gold from Saul or from his house, nor shall you kill any man in Israel for us."

So he said, "Whatever you say, I will do for you."

[5]Then they answered the king, "As for the man who consumed us and plotted against us, *that* we should be destroyed from remaining in any of the territories of Israel, [6]let seven men of his descendants be delivered to us, and we will hang them before the LORD in Gibeah of Saul, *whom* the LORD chose."

And the king said, "I will give *them.*"

[7]But the king spared Mephibosheth the son of Jonathan, the son of Saul, because of the LORD's oath that *was* between them, between David and Jonathan the son of Saul. [8]So the king took Armoni and Mephibosheth, the two sons of Rizpah the daughter of Aiah, whom she bore to Saul, and the five sons of Michal[a] the daughter of Saul, whom she brought up for Adriel the son of Barzillai the Meholathite; [9]and he delivered them into the hands of the Gibeonites, and they hanged them on the hill before the LORD. So they fell, *all* seven together, and were put to death in the days of harvest, in the first *days,* in the beginning of barley harvest.

[10]Now Rizpah the daughter of Aiah took sackcloth and spread it for herself on the rock, from the beginning of harvest until the late rains poured on them from heaven. And she did not allow the birds of the air to rest on them by day nor the beasts of the field by night.

[11]And David was told what Rizpah the daughter of Aiah, the concubine of Saul, had done. [12]Then David went and took the bones of Saul, and the bones of Jonathan his son, from the men of Jabesh Gilead who had stolen them from the street of Beth Shan,[a] where the Philistines had hung them up, after the Philistines had struck down Saul in Gilboa. [13]So he brought up the bones of Saul and the bones of Jonathan his son from there; and they gathered the bones of those who had been hanged. [14]They buried the bones of Saul and Jonathan his son in the country of Benjamin in Zelah, in the tomb of Kish his father. So they performed all that the king commanded. And after that God heeded the prayer for the land.

Philistine Giants Destroyed

[15]When the Philistines were at war again with Israel, David and his servants with him went down and fought against the Philistines; and David grew faint. [16]Then Ishbi-Benob, who *was* one of the sons of the giant, the weight of whose bronze spear *was* three hundred *shekels,* who was bearing a new *sword,* thought he could kill David. [17]But Abishai the son of Zeruiah came to his aid, and struck the Philistine and killed him. Then the men of David swore to him, saying, "You shall go out no more with us to battle, lest you quench the lamp of Israel."

[18]Now it happened afterward that there was again a battle with the Philistines at Gob. Then Sibbechai the Hushathite killed Saph,[a] who *was* one of the sons of the giant. [19]Again there was war at Gob with the Philistines, where Elhanan the son of Jaare-Oregim[a] the Bethlehemite killed *the brother of* Goliath the Gittite, the shaft of whose spear *was* like a weaver's beam.

[20]Yet again there was war at Gath, where there was a man of *great* stature, who had six fingers on each hand and six toes on each foot, twenty-four in number; and he also was born to the giant. [21]So when he defied Israel, Jonathan the son of Shimea,[a] David's brother, killed him.

[22]These four were born to the giant in Gath, and fell by the hand of David and by the hand of his servants.

21:8 [a] Or *Merab* (compare 1 Samuel 18:19 and 25:44; 2 Samuel 3:14 and 6:23) **21:12** [a] Spelled *Beth Shean* in Joshua 17:11 and elsewhere **21:18** [a] Spelled *Sippai* in 1 Chronicles 20:4 **21:19** [a] Spelled *Jair* in 1 Chronicles 20:5 **21:21** [a] Spelled *Shammah* in 1 Samuel 16:9 and elsewhere

Praise for God's Deliverance

22 Then David spoke to the LORD the words of this song, on the day when the LORD had delivered him from the hand of all his enemies, and from the hand of Saul. 2And he said:[a]

"The LORD *is* my rock and my
fortress and my deliverer;
3 The God of my strength, in whom
I will trust;
My shield and the horn of my
salvation,
My stronghold and my refuge;
My Savior, You save me from
violence.
4 I will call upon the LORD, *who is*
worthy to be praised;
So shall I be saved from my
enemies.

5 "When the waves of death
surrounded me,
The floods of ungodliness made
me afraid.
6 The sorrows of Sheol
surrounded me;
The snares of death confronted me.
7 In my distress I called upon the
LORD,
And cried out to my God;
He heard my voice from His
temple,
And my cry *entered* His ears.

8 "Then the earth shook and
trembled;
The foundations of heaven[a]
quaked and were shaken,
Because He was angry.
9 Smoke went up from His nostrils,
And devouring fire from His mouth;
Coals were kindled by it.
10 He bowed the heavens also, and
came down
With darkness under His feet.
11 He rode upon a cherub, and flew;
And He was seen[a] upon the wings
of the wind.
12 He made darkness canopies
around Him,
Dark waters *and* thick clouds of
the skies.
13 From the brightness before Him
Coals of fire were kindled.

14 "The LORD thundered from
heaven,
And the Most High uttered His
voice.
15 He sent out arrows and scattered
them;
Lightning bolts, and He
vanquished them.
16 Then the channels of the sea were
seen,
The foundations of the world were
uncovered,
At the rebuke of the LORD,
At the blast of the breath of His
nostrils.

17 "He sent from above, He took me,
He drew me out of many waters.
18 He delivered me from my strong
enemy,
From those who hated me;
For they were too strong for me.
19 They confronted me in the day of
my calamity,
But the LORD was my support.
20 He also brought me out into a
broad place;
He delivered me because He
delighted in me.

21 "The LORD rewarded me according
to my righteousness;
According to the cleanness of my
hands
He has recompensed me.
22 For I have kept the ways of the
LORD,
And have not wickedly departed
from my God.
23 For all His judgments *were* before
me;
And *as for* His statutes, I did not
depart from them.
24 I was also blameless before Him,
And I kept myself from my
iniquity.

22:2 [a] Compare Psalm 18 22:8 [a] Following Masoretic Text, Septuagint, and Targum; Syriac and Vulgate read *hills* (compare Psalm 18:7). 22:11 [a] Following Masoretic Text and Septuagint; many Hebrew manuscripts, Syriac, and Vulgate read *He flew* (compare Psalm 18:10); Targum reads *He spoke with power*.

25 Therefore the LORD has
recompensed me according
to my righteousness,
According to my cleanness in His
eyes.[a]

26 "With the merciful You will show
Yourself merciful;
With a blameless man You will
show Yourself blameless;
27 With the pure You will show
Yourself pure;
And with the devious You will
show Yourself shrewd.
28 You will save the humble people;
But Your eyes *are* on the haughty,
that You may bring *them*
down.

29 "For You *are* my lamp, O LORD;
The LORD shall enlighten my
darkness.
30 For by You I can run against a
troop;
By my God I can leap over a wall.
31 *As for* God, His way *is* perfect;
The word of the LORD *is* proven;
He *is* a shield to all who trust in
Him.

32 "For who *is* God, except the LORD?
And who *is* a rock, except our God?
33 God *is* my strength *and* power,[a]
And He makes my[b] way perfect.
34 He makes my[a] feet like the *feet* of
deer,
And sets me on my high places.
35 He teaches my hands to make
war,
So that my arms can bend a bow
of bronze.

36 "You have also given me the shield
of Your salvation;
Your gentleness has made me
great.
37 You enlarged my path under me;
So my feet did not slip.

38 "I have pursued my enemies and
destroyed them;
Neither did I turn back again till
they were destroyed.
39 And I have destroyed them and
wounded them,
So that they could not rise;
They have fallen under my feet.
40 For You have armed me with
strength for the battle;
You have subdued under me
those who rose against me.
41 You have also given me the necks
of my enemies,
So that I destroyed those who
hated me.
42 They looked, but *there was* none to
save;
Even to the LORD, but He did not
answer them.
43 Then I beat them as fine as the
dust of the earth;
I trod them like dirt in the streets,
And I spread them out.

44 "You have also delivered me from
the strivings of my people;
You have kept me as the head of
the nations.
A people I have not known shall
serve me.
45 The foreigners submit to me;
As soon as they hear, they obey me.
46 The foreigners fade away,
And come frightened[a] from their
hideouts.

47 "The LORD lives!
Blessed *be* my Rock!
Let God be exalted,
The Rock of my salvation!
48 *It is* God who avenges me,
And subdues the peoples under me;
49 He delivers me from my enemies.
You also lift me up above those
who rise against me;
You have delivered me from the
violent man.

22:25 [a] Septuagint, Syriac, and Vulgate read *the cleanness of my hands in His sight* (compare Psalm 18:24); Targum reads *my cleanness before His word.* **22:33** [a] Dead Sea Scrolls, Septuagint, Syriac, and Vulgate read *It is God who arms me with strength* (compare Psalm 18:32); Targum reads *It is God who sustains me with strength.* [b] Following Qere, Septuagint, Syriac, Targum, and Vulgate (compare Psalm 18:32); Kethib reads *His.* **22:34** [a] Following Qere, Septuagint, Syriac, Targum, and Vulgate (compare Psalm 18:33); Kethib reads *His.* **22:46** [a] Following Septuagint, Targum, and Vulgate (compare Psalm 18:45); Masoretic Text reads *gird themselves.*

50 Therefore I will give thanks to You,
O LORD, among the Gentiles,
And sing praises to Your name.

51 "*He is* the tower of salvation to His
king,
And shows mercy to His anointed,
To David and his descendants
forevermore."

David's Last Words

23 Now these *are* the last words
of David.

Thus says David the son of Jesse;
Thus says the man raised up on
high,
The anointed of the God of Jacob,
And the sweet psalmist of Israel:

2 "The Spirit of the LORD spoke by me,
And His word *was* on my tongue.
3 The God of Israel said,
The Rock of Israel spoke to me:
'He who rules over men *must be*
just,
Ruling in the fear of God.
4 And *he shall be* like the light of the
morning *when* the sun rises,
A morning without clouds,
Like the tender grass *springing* out
of the earth,
By clear shining after rain.'

5 "Although my house *is* not so with
God,
Yet He has made with me an
everlasting covenant,
Ordered in all *things* and secure.
For *this is* all my salvation and all
my desire;
Will He not make *it* increase?
6 But *the sons* of rebellion *shall* all
be as thorns thrust away,
Because they cannot be taken
with hands.
7 But the man *who* touches them
Must be armed with iron and the
shaft of a spear,
And they shall be utterly burned
with fire in *their* place."

David's Mighty Men

8 These *are* the names of the mighty
men whom David had: Josheb-
Basshebeth[a] the Tachmonite, chief
among the captains.[b] He was called
Adino the Eznite, because he had killed
eight hundred men at one time. 9 And
after him *was* Eleazar the son of Dodo,[a]
the Ahohite, *one* of the three mighty
men with David when they defied the
Philistines *who* were gathered there for
battle, and the men of Israel had retreat-
ed. 10 He arose and attacked the Phi-
listines until his hand was weary, and
his hand stuck to the sword. The LORD
brought about a great victory that day;
and the people returned after him only
to plunder. 11 And after him *was* Sham-
mah the son of Agee the Hararite. The
Philistines had gathered together into a
troop where there was a piece of ground
full of lentils. So the people fled from the
Philistines. 12 But he stationed himself
in the middle of the field, defended it,
and killed the Philistines. So the LORD
brought about a great victory.
13 Then three of the thirty chief men went
down at harvest time and came to David
at the cave of Adullam. And the troop of
Philistines encamped in the Valley of
Rephaim. 14 David *was* then in the strong-
hold, and the garrison of the Philistines
was then *in* Bethlehem. 15 And David said
with longing, "Oh, that someone would
give me a drink of the water from the
well of Bethlehem, which *is* by the gate!"
16 So the three mighty men broke through
the camp of the Philistines, drew water
from the well of Bethlehem that *was* by
the gate, and took it and brought *it* to
David. Nevertheless he would not drink
it, but poured it out to the LORD. 17 And he
said, "Far be it from me, O LORD, that I
should do this! Is *this not* the blood of the
men who went in *jeopardy of* their lives?"
Therefore he would not drink it.
These things were done by the three
mighty men.
18 Now Abishai the brother of Joab,
the son of Zeruiah, was chief of *another*
three.[a] He lifted his spear against three

23:8 [a] Literally *One Who Sits in the Seat* (compare 1 Chronicles 11:11) [b] Following Masoretic Text and Targum; Septuagint and Vulgate read *the three*. 23:9 [a] Spelled *Dodai* in 1 Chronicles 27:4
23:18 [a] Following Masoretic Text, Septuagint, and Vulgate; some Hebrew manuscripts and Syriac read *thirty*; Targum reads *the mighty men*.

hundred *men,* killed *them,* and won a
name among *these* three. 19Was he not
the most honored of three? Therefore he
became their captain. However, he did
not attain to the *first* three.
20Benaiah *was* the son of Jehoiada, the
son of a valiant man from Kabzeel, who
had done many deeds. He had killed two
lion-like heroes of Moab. He also had gone
down and killed a lion in the midst of a
pit on a snowy day. 21And he killed an
Egyptian, a spectacular man. The Egyp-
tian *had* a spear in his hand; so he went
down to him with a staff, wrested the spear
out of the Egyptian's hand, and killed him
with his own spear. 22These *things* Bena-
iah the son of Jehoiada did, and won a
name among three mighty men. 23He
was more honored than the thirty, but he
did not attain to the *first* three. And David
appointed him over his guard.
24Asahel the brother of Joab *was* one
of the thirty; Elhanan the son of Dodo
of Bethlehem, 25Shammah the Harodite,
Elika the Harodite, 26Helez the Paltite,
Ira the son of Ikkesh the Tekoite, 27Abi-
ezer the Anathothite, Mebunnai the Hu-
shathite, 28Zalmon the Ahohite, Maharai
the Netophathite, 29Heleb the son of Ba-
anah (the Netophathite), Ittai the son of
Ribai from Gibeah of the children of Ben-
jamin, 30Benaiah a Pirathonite, Hiddai
from the brooks of Gaash, 31Abi-Albon
the Arbathite, Azmaveth the Barhumite,
32Eliahba the Shaalbonite (of the sons
of Jashen), Jonathan, 33Shammah the
Hararite, Ahiam the son of Sharar the
Hararite, 34Eliphelet the son of Ahasbai,
the son of the Maachathite, Eliam the
son of Ahithophel the Gilonite, 35Hezrai[a]
the Carmelite, Paarai the Arbite, 36Igal
the son of Nathan of Zobah, Bani the
Gadite, 37Zelek the Ammonite, Naharai
the Beerothite (armorbearer of Joab
the son of Zeruiah), 38Ira the Ithrite,
Gareb the Ithrite, 39*and* Uriah the Hittite:
thirty-seven in all.

David's Census of Israel and Judah

24 Again the anger of the LORD was
aroused against Israel, and He
moved David against them to say, "Go,
number Israel and Judah."
2So the king said to Joab the com-
mander of the army who *was* with him,
"Now go throughout all the tribes of Is-
rael, from Dan to Beersheba, and count
the people, that I may know the number
of the people."
3And Joab said to the king, "Now may
the LORD your God add to the people
a hundred times more than there are,
and may the eyes of my lord the king
see *it.* But why does my lord the king
desire this thing?" 4Nevertheless the
king's word prevailed against Joab and
against the captains of the army. There-
fore Joab and the captains of the army
went out from the presence of the king
to count the people of Israel.
5And they crossed over the Jordan
and camped in Aroer, on the right side
of the town which *is* in the midst of the
ravine of Gad, and toward Jazer. 6Then
they came to Gilead and to the land of
Tahtim Hodshi; they came to Dan Jaan
and around to Sidon; 7and they came
to the stronghold of Tyre and to all the
cities of the Hivites and the Canaanites.
Then they went out to South Judah *as far
as* Beersheba. 8So when they had gone
through all the land, they came to Je-
rusalem at the end of nine months and
twenty days. 9Then Joab gave the sum
of the number of the people to the king.
And there were in Israel eight hundred
thousand valiant men who drew the
sword, and the men of Judah were five
hundred thousand men.

The Judgment on David's Sin

10And David's heart condemned him
after he had numbered the people. So
David said to the LORD, "I have sinned
greatly in what I have done; but now,
I pray, O LORD, take away the iniquity
of Your servant, for I have done very
foolishly."
11Now when David arose in the morn-
ing, the word of the LORD came to the
prophet Gad, David's seer, saying, 12"Go
and tell David, 'Thus says the LORD: "I
offer you three *things;* choose one of
them for yourself, that I may do *it* to
you." ' " 13So Gad came to David and
told him; and he said to him, "Shall

23:35 [a] Spelled *Hezro* in 1 Chronicles 11:37

seven[a] years of famine come to you
in your land? Or shall you flee three
months before your enemies, while
they pursue you? Or shall there be
three days' plague in your land? Now
consider and see what answer I should
take back to Him who sent me."
14And David said to Gad, "I am in great
distress. Please let us fall into the hand
of the LORD, for His mercies *are* great;
but do not let me fall into the hand of
man."
15So the LORD sent a plague upon Isra-
el from the morning till the appointed
time. From Dan to Beersheba seventy
thousand men of the people died. 16And
when the angel[a] stretched out His hand
over Jerusalem to destroy it, the LORD
relented from the destruction, and said
to the angel who was destroying the
people, "It is enough; now restrain your
hand." And the angel of the LORD was
by the threshing floor of Araunah[b] the
Jebusite.
17Then David spoke to the LORD when
he saw the angel who was striking the
people, and said, "Surely I have sinned,
and I have done wickedly; but these
sheep, what have they done? Let Your
hand, I pray, be against me and against
my father's house."

The Altar on the Threshing Floor

18And Gad came that day to David and
said to him, "Go up, erect an altar to the
LORD on the threshing floor of Araunah
the Jebusite." 19So David, according to
the word of Gad, went up as the LORD
commanded. 20Now Araunah looked,
and saw the king and his servants com-
ing toward him. So Araunah went out
and bowed before the king with his face
to the ground.
21Then Araunah said, "Why has my
lord the king come to his servant?"
And David said, "To buy the threshing
floor from you, to build an altar to the
LORD, that the plague may be with-
drawn from the people."
22Now Araunah said to David, "Let my
lord the king take and offer up what-
ever *seems* good to him. Look, *here are*
oxen for burnt sacrifice, and threshing
implements and the yokes of the oxen
for wood. 23All these, O king, Araunah
has given to the king."
And Araunah said to the king, "May
the LORD your God accept you."
24Then the king said to Araunah, "No,
but I will surely buy *it* from you for a
price; nor will I offer burnt offerings
to the LORD my God with that which
costs me nothing." So David bought
the threshing floor and the oxen for
fifty shekels of silver. 25And David built
there an altar to the LORD, and offered
burnt offerings and peace offerings.
So the LORD heeded the prayers for the
land, and the plague was withdrawn
from Israel.

24:13 [a] Following Masoretic Text, Syriac, Targum, and Vulgate; Septuagint reads *three* (compare 1 Chronicles 21:12). **24:16** [a] Or *Angel* [b] Spelled *Ornan* in 1 Chronicles 21:15

GOD SIN JESUS SALVATION LOVE

THE FIRST BOOK OF THE

KINGS

This book continues where 2 Samuel leaves off and records about one hundred twenty years of Israel's history. After David dies, his son Solomon becomes the third king of Israel. Like Saul and David before him, Solomon begins his rule well. He grows the kingdom and builds a palace and the temple in Jerusalem. But Solomon also sins against God by beginning to worship false gods. Because of this sin, the kingdom of Israel splits into two kingdoms after Solomon's death. The northern kingdom of Israel is led by evil kings who continue to worship false gods. The southern kingdom of Judah also is led by evil kings, but at times it is led by good kings. God does not let His people continue in sin without warning them, though. He begins sending prophets, like Elijah, to call on the people to return to God.

- **GENRE:** History
- **AUTHOR:** Jeremiah, possibly
- **TIME:** c. 971–851 BC (written c. 561–538 BC)
- **PURPOSE:** To continue recording Israel's history and to show what happened when the kings and people disobeyed God.

Adonijah Presumes to Be King

1 Now King David was old, advanced
in years; and they put covers on him,
but he could not get warm. 2 Therefore
his servants said to him, "Let a young
woman, a virgin, be sought for our lord
the king, and let her stand before the
king, and let her care for him; and let
her lie in your bosom, that our lord the
king may be warm." 3 So they sought for a
lovely young woman throughout all the
territory of Israel, and found Abishag
the Shunammite, and brought her to the
king. 4 The young woman *was* very lovely;
and she cared for the king, and served
him; but the king did not know her.

5 Then Adonijah the son of Haggith
exalted himself, saying, "I will be king";
and he prepared for himself chariots
and horsemen, and fifty men to run
before him. 6 (And his father had not re-
buked him at any time by saying, "Why
have you done so?" He *was* also very
good-looking. *His mother* had borne
him after Absalom.) 7 Then he conferred
with Joab the son of Zeruiah and with
Abiathar the priest, and they followed
and helped Adonijah. 8 But Zadok the
priest, Benaiah the son of Jehoiada,
Nathan the prophet, Shimei, Rei, and
the mighty men who *belonged* to David
were not with Adonijah.

9 And Adonijah sacrificed sheep and
oxen and fattened cattle by the stone of
Zoheleth, which *is* by En Rogel; he also
invited all his brothers, the king's sons,
and all the men of Judah, the king's
servants. 10 But he did not invite Nathan
the prophet, Benaiah, the mighty men,
or Solomon his brother.

11 So Nathan spoke to Bathsheba the
mother of Solomon, saying, "Have you
not heard that Adonijah the son of Hag-
gith has become king, and David our
lord does not know *it?* 12 Come, please,
let me now give you advice, that you
may save your own life and the life of
your son Solomon. 13 Go immediate-
ly to King David and say to him, 'Did
you not, my lord, O king, swear to your
maidservant, saying, "Assuredly your
son Solomon shall reign after me, and
he shall sit on my throne"? Why then
has Adonijah become king?' 14 Then,
while you are still talking there with
the king, I also will come in after you
and confirm your words."

15 So Bathsheba went into the cham-
ber to the king. (Now the king was very
old, and Abishag the Shunammite was

serving the king.) 16And Bathsheba
bowed and did homage to the king.
Then the king said, "What is your wish?"
17Then she said to him, "My lord, you
swore by the LORD your God to your
maidservant, *saying,* 'Assuredly Sol-
omon your son shall reign after me,
and he shall sit on my throne.' 18So now,
look! Adonijah has become king; and
now, my lord the king, you do not know
about *it.* 19He has sacrificed oxen and
fattened cattle and sheep in abundance,
and has invited all the sons of the king,
Abiathar the priest, and Joab the com-
mander of the army; but Solomon your
servant he has not invited. 20And as
for you, my lord, O king, the eyes of all
Israel *are* on you, that you should tell
them who will sit on the throne of my
lord the king after him. 21Otherwise it
will happen, when my lord the king
rests with his fathers, that I and my son
Solomon will be counted as offenders."
22And just then, while she was still
talking with the king, Nathan the proph-
et also came in. 23So they told the king,
saying, "Here is Nathan the prophet."
And when he came in before the king,
he bowed down before the king with his
face to the ground. 24And Nathan said,
"My lord, O king, have you said, 'Adoni-
jah shall reign after me, and he shall sit
on my throne'? 25For he has gone down
today, and has sacrificed oxen and fat-
tened cattle and sheep in abundance,
and has invited all the king's sons, and
the commanders of the army, and Abia-
thar the priest; and look! They are eating
and drinking before him; and they say,
'*Long* live King Adonijah!' 26But he has
not invited me—me your servant—nor
Zadok the priest, nor Benaiah the son
of Jehoiada, nor your servant Solomon.
27Has this thing been done by my lord
the king, and you have not told your
servant who should sit on the throne of
my lord the king after him?"

David Proclaims Solomon King

28Then King David answered and
said, "Call Bathsheba to me." So she
came into the king's presence and stood
before the king. 29And the king took
an oath and said, "*As* the LORD lives,
who has redeemed my life from every
distress, 30just as I swore to you by the
LORD God of Israel, saying, 'Assuredly
Solomon your son shall be king after
me, and he shall sit on my throne in my
place,' so I certainly will do this day."
31Then Bathsheba bowed with *her* face
to the earth, and paid homage to the
king, and said, "Let my lord King David
live forever!"
32And King David said, "Call to me
Zadok the priest, Nathan the prophet,
and Benaiah the son of Jehoiada." So
they came before the king. 33The king
also said to them, "Take with you the
servants of your lord, and have Sol-
omon my son ride on my own mule,
and take him down to Gihon. 34There
let Zadok the priest and Nathan the
prophet anoint him king over Israel;
and blow the horn, and say, '*Long* live
King Solomon!' 35Then you shall come
up after him, and he shall come and sit
on my throne, and he shall be king in
my place. For I have appointed him to
be ruler over Israel and Judah."
36Benaiah the son of Jehoiada an-
swered the king and said, "Amen! May
the LORD God of my lord the king say
so *too.* 37As the LORD has been with my
lord the king, even so may He be with
Solomon, and make his throne greater
than the throne of my lord King David."
38So Zadok the priest, Nathan the
prophet, Benaiah the son of Jehoiada,
the Cherethites, and the Pelethites went
down and had Solomon ride on King
David's mule, and took him to Gihon.
39Then Zadok the priest took a horn of
oil from the tabernacle and anointed
Solomon. And they blew the horn, and
all the people said, "*Long* live King Sol-
omon!" 40And all the people went up
after him; and the people played the
flutes and rejoiced with great joy, so that
the earth *seemed to* split with their sound.
41Now Adonijah and all the guests who
were with him heard *it* as they finished
eating. And when Joab heard the sound
of the horn, he said, "Why *is* the city in
such a noisy uproar?" 42While he was
still speaking, there came Jonathan, the
son of Abiathar the priest. And Adoni-
jah said to him, "Come in, for you *are* a
prominent man, and bring good news."
43Then Jonathan answered and said

to Adonijah, "No! Our lord King David
has made Solomon king. 44The king has
sent with him Zadok the priest, Nathan
the prophet, Benaiah the son of Jehoi-
ada, the Cherethites, and the Pelethites;
and they have made him ride on the
king's mule. 45So Zadok the priest and
Nathan the prophet have anointed him
king at Gihon; and they have gone up
from there rejoicing, so that the city is
in an uproar. This *is* the noise that you
have heard. 46Also Solomon sits on the
throne of the kingdom. 47And moreover
the king's servants have gone to bless
our lord King David, saying, 'May God
make the name of Solomon better than
your name, and may He make his throne
greater than your throne.' Then the king
bowed himself on the bed. 48Also the
king said thus, 'Blessed *be* the LORD God
of Israel, who has given *one* to sit on my
throne this day, while my eyes see *it!*' "

49So all the guests who were with Ado-
nijah were afraid, and arose, and each
one went his way.

50Now Adonijah was afraid of Sol-
omon; so he arose, and went and took
hold of the horns of the altar. 51And
it was told Solomon, saying, "Indeed
Adonijah is afraid of King Solomon;
for look, he has taken hold of the horns
of the altar, saying, 'Let King Solomon
swear to me today that he will not put
his servant to death with the sword.' "

52Then Solomon said, "If he proves
himself a worthy man, not one hair of
him shall fall to the earth; but if wicked-
ness is found in him, he shall die." 53So
King Solomon sent them to bring him
down from the altar. And he came and
fell down before King Solomon; and Sol-
omon said to him, "Go to your house."

David's Instructions to Solomon

2 Now the days of David drew near
that he should die, and he charged
Solomon his son, saying: 2"I go the way
of all the earth; be strong, therefore, and
prove yourself a man. 3And keep the
charge of the LORD your God: to walk
in His ways, to keep His statutes, His
commandments, His judgments, and
His testimonies, as it is written in the Law
of Moses, that you may prosper in all
that you do and wherever you turn; 4that
the LORD may fulfill His word which He
spoke concerning me, saying, 'If your
sons take heed to their way, to walk be-
fore Me in truth with all their heart and
with all their soul,' He said, 'you shall
not lack a man on the throne of Israel.'

5"Moreover you know also what Joab
the son of Zeruiah did to me, *and* what
he did to the two commanders of the
armies of Israel, to Abner the son of
Ner and Amasa the son of Jether, whom
he killed. And he shed the blood of war
in peacetime, and put the blood of war
on his belt that *was* around his waist,
and on his sandals that *were* on his
feet. 6Therefore do according to your
wisdom, and do not let his gray hair
go down to the grave in peace.

7"But show kindness to the sons of
Barzillai the Gileadite, and let them be
among those who eat at your table, for
so they came to me when I fled from
Absalom your brother.

8"And see, *you have* with you Shimei
the son of Gera, a Benjamite from Ba-
hurim, who cursed me with a malicious
curse in the day when I went to Maha-
naim. But he came down to meet me
at the Jordan, and I swore to him by
the LORD, saying, 'I will not put you to
death with the sword.' 9Now therefore,
do not hold him guiltless, for you *are* a
wise man and know what you ought to
do to him; but bring his gray hair down
to the grave with blood."

Death of David

10So David rested with his fathers, and
was buried in the City of David. 11The
period that David reigned over Israel
was forty years; seven years he reigned
in Hebron, and in Jerusalem he reigned
thirty-three years. 12Then Solomon sat
on the throne of his father David; and
his kingdom was firmly established.

Solomon Executes Adonijah

13Now Adonijah the son of Haggith came
to Bathsheba the mother of Solomon. So
she said, "Do you come peaceably?"

And he said, "Peaceably." 14Moreover
he said, "I have something *to say* to you."

And she said, "Say it."

15Then he said, "You know that the king-
dom was mine, and all Israel had set their

expectations on me, that I should reign.
However, the kingdom has been turned
over, and has become my brother's; for
it was his from the LORD. 16 Now I ask one
petition of you; do not deny me."
And she said to him, "Say it."
17 Then he said, "Please speak to King
Solomon, for he will not refuse you, that
he may give me Abishag the Shunam-
mite as wife."
18 So Bathsheba said, "Very well, I will
speak for you to the king."
19 Bathsheba therefore went to King
Solomon, to speak to him for Adonijah.
And the king rose up to meet her and
bowed down to her, and sat down on
his throne and had a throne set for the
king's mother; so she sat at his right
hand. 20 Then she said, "I desire one
small petition of you; do not refuse me."
And the king said to her, "Ask it, my
mother, for I will not refuse you."
21 So she said, "Let Abishag the Shu-
nammite be given to Adonijah your
brother as wife."
22 And King Solomon answered and said
to his mother, "Now why do you ask Abi-
shag the Shunammite for Adonijah? Ask
for him the kingdom also—for he *is* my
older brother—for him, and for Abiathar
the priest, and for Joab the son of Zerui-
ah." 23 Then King Solomon swore by the
LORD, saying, "May God do so to me, and
more also, if Adonijah has not spoken this
word against his own life! 24 Now there-
fore, *as* the LORD lives, who has confirmed
me and set me on the throne of David my
father, and who has established a house[a]
for me, as He promised, Adonijah shall
be put to death today!"
25 So King Solomon sent by the hand
of Benaiah the son of Jehoiada; and he
struck him down, and he died.

Abiathar Exiled, Joab Executed

26 And to Abiathar the priest the king
said, "Go to Anathoth, to your own
fields, for you *are* deserving of death;
but I will not put you to death at this
time, because you carried the ark of the
Lord GOD before my father David, and
because you were afflicted every time
my father was afflicted." 27 So Solomon
removed Abiathar from being priest to
the LORD, that he might fulfill the word
of the LORD which He spoke concerning
the house of Eli at Shiloh.
28 Then news came to Joab, for Joab
had defected to Adonijah, though he
had not defected to Absalom. So Joab
fled to the tabernacle of the LORD, and
took hold of the horns of the altar. 29 And
King Solomon was told, "Joab has fled
to the tabernacle of the LORD; there *he*
is, by the altar." Then Solomon sent Be-
naiah the son of Jehoiada, saying, "Go,
strike him down." 30 So Benaiah went to
the tabernacle of the LORD, and said to
him, "Thus says the king, 'Come out!' "
And he said, "No, but I will die here."
And Benaiah brought back word to the
king, saying, "Thus said Joab, and thus
he answered me."
31 Then the king said to him, "Do as
he has said, and strike him down and
bury him, that you may take away from
me and from the house of my father
the innocent blood which Joab shed.
32 So the LORD will return his blood on
his head, because he struck down two
men more righteous and better than he,
and killed them with the sword—Abner
the son of Ner, the commander of the
army of Israel, and Amasa the son of
Jether, the commander of the army of
Judah—though my father David did
not know *it.* 33 Their blood shall there-
fore return upon the head of Joab and
upon the head of his descendants forev-
er. But upon David and his descendants,
upon his house and his throne, there
shall be peace forever from the LORD."
34 So Benaiah the son of Jehoiada went
up and struck and killed him; and he
was buried in his own house in the wil-
derness. 35 The king put Benaiah the son
of Jehoiada in his place over the army,
and the king put Zadok the priest in the
place of Abiathar.

Shimei Executed

36 Then the king sent and called for
Shimei, and said to him, "Build yourself
a house in Jerusalem and dwell there,
and do not go out from there anywhere.
37 For it shall be, on the day you go out

2:24 [a] That is, a royal dynasty

and cross the Brook Kidron, know for
certain you shall surely die; your blood
shall be on your own head."
38And Shimei said to the king, "The
saying *is* good. As my lord the king has
said, so your servant will do." So Shimei
dwelt in Jerusalem many days.
39Now it happened at the end of three
years, that two slaves of Shimei ran
away to Achish the son of Maachah,
king of Gath. And they told Shimei, say-
ing, "Look, your slaves *are* in Gath!" 40So
Shimei arose, saddled his donkey, and
went to Achish at Gath to seek his slaves.
And Shimei went and brought his slaves
from Gath. 41And Solomon was told
that Shimei had gone from Jerusalem
to Gath and had come back. 42Then
the king sent and called for Shimei,
and said to him, "Did I not make you
swear by the LORD, and warn you, say-
ing, 'Know for certain that on the day
you go out and travel anywhere, you
shall surely die'? And you said to me,
'The word I have heard *is* good.' 43Why
then have you not kept the oath of the
LORD and the commandment that I
gave you?" 44The king said moreover
to Shimei, "You know, as your heart
acknowledges, all the wickedness that
you did to my father David; therefore
the LORD will return your wickedness
on your own head. 45But King Solomon
shall be blessed, and the throne of David
shall be established before the LORD
forever."
46So the king commanded Benaiah
the son of Jehoiada; and he went out
and struck him down, and he died. Thus
the kingdom was established in the
hand of Solomon.

Solomon Requests Wisdom

3 Now Solomon made a treaty
with Pharaoh king of Egypt, and
married Pharaoh's daughter; then he
brought her to the City of David until
he had finished building his own house,
and the house of the LORD, and the wall
all around Jerusalem. 2Meanwhile the
people sacrificed at the high places,
because there was no house built for
the name of the LORD until those days.
3And Solomon loved the LORD, walk-
ing in the statutes of his father David,
except that he sacrificed and burned
incense at the high places.
4Now the king went to Gibeon to sac-
rifice there, for that *was* the great high
place: Solomon offered a thousand
burnt offerings on that altar. 5At Gib-
eon the LORD appeared to Solomon in
a dream by night; and God said, "Ask!
What shall I give you?"
6And Solomon said: "You have shown
great mercy to Your servant David my
father, because he walked before You
in truth, in righteousness, and in up-
rightness of heart with You; You have
continued this great kindness for him,
and You have given him a son to sit on
his throne, as *it is* this day. 7Now, O LORD
my God, You have made Your servant
king instead of my father David, but I
am a little child; I do not know *how* to
go out or come in. 8And Your servant
is in the midst of Your people whom
You have chosen, a great people, too
numerous to be numbered or count-
ed. 9Therefore give to Your servant an
understanding heart to judge Your peo-
ple, that I may discern between good
and evil. For who is able to judge this
great people of Yours?"
10The speech pleased the Lord, that Sol-
omon had asked this thing. 11Then God
said to him: "Because you have asked
this thing, and have not asked long life
for yourself, nor have asked riches for
yourself, nor have asked the life of your
enemies, but have asked for yourself
understanding to discern justice, 12be-
hold, I have done according to your
words; see, I have given you a wise and
understanding heart, so that there has
not been anyone like you before you, nor
shall any like you arise after you. 13And
I have also given you what you have not
asked: both riches and honor, so that
there shall not be anyone like you among
the kings all your days. 14So if you walk
in My ways, to keep My statutes and My
commandments, as your father David
walked, then I will lengthen your days."
15Then Solomon awoke; and indeed
it had been a dream. And he came to
Jerusalem and stood before the ark of
the covenant of the LORD, offered up
burnt offerings, offered peace offerings,
and made a feast for all his servants.

Solomon's Wise Judgment

16Now two women *who were* harlots came to the king, and stood before him. 17And one woman said, "O my lord, this woman and I dwell in the same house; and I gave birth while she *was* in the house. 18Then it happened, the third day after I had given birth, that this woman also gave birth. And we *were* together; no one *was* with us in the house, except the two of us in the house. 19And this woman's son died in the night, because she lay on him. 20So she arose in the middle of the night and took my son from my side, while your maidservant slept, and laid him in her bosom, and laid her dead child in my bosom. 21And when I rose in the morning to nurse my son, there he was, dead. But when I had examined him in the morning, indeed, he was not my son whom I had borne."

22Then the other woman said, "No! But the living one *is* my son, and the dead one *is* your son."

And the first woman said, "No! But the dead one *is* your son, and the living one *is* my son."

Thus they spoke before the king.

23And the king said, "The one says, 'This *is* my son, who lives, and your son *is* the dead one'; and the other says, 'No! But your son *is* the dead one, and my son *is* the living one.' " 24Then the king said, "Bring me a sword." So they brought a sword before the king. 25And the king said, "Divide the living child in two, and give half to one, and half to the other."

26Then the woman whose son *was* living spoke to the king, for she yearned with compassion for her son; and she said, "O my lord, give her the living child, and by no means kill him!"

But the other said, "Let him be neither mine nor yours, *but* divide *him*."

27So the king answered and said, "Give the first woman the living child, and by no means kill him; she *is* his mother."

28And all Israel heard of the judgment which the king had rendered; and they feared the king, for they saw that the wisdom of God *was* in him to administer justice.

Solomon's Administration

4 So King Solomon was king over all Israel. 2And these *were* his officials: Azariah the son of Zadok, the priest; 3Elihoreph and Ahijah, the sons of Shisha, scribes; Jehoshaphat the son of Ahilud, the recorder; 4Benaiah the son of Jehoiada, over the army; Zadok and Abiathar, the priests; 5Azariah the son of Nathan, over the officers; Zabud the son of Nathan, a priest *and* the king's friend; 6Ahishar, over the household; and Adoniram the son of Abda, over the labor force.

7And Solomon had twelve governors over all Israel, who provided food for the king and his household; each one made provision for one month of the year. 8These *are* their names: Ben-Hur,[a] in the mountains of Ephraim; 9Ben-Deker,[a] in Makaz, Shaalbim, Beth Shemesh, and Elon Beth Hanan; 10Ben-Hesed,[a] in Arubboth; to him *belonged* Sochoh and all the land of Hepher; 11Ben-Abinadab,[a] *in* all the regions of Dor; he had Taphath the daughter of Solomon as wife; 12Baana the son of Ahilud, *in* Taanach, Megiddo, and all Beth Shean, which *is* beside Zaretan below Jezreel, from Beth Shean to Abel Meholah, as far as the other side of Jokneam; 13Ben-Geber,[a] in Ramoth Gilead; to him *belonged* the towns of Jair the son of Manasseh, in Gilead; to him *also belonged* the region of Argob in Bashan—sixty large cities with walls and bronze gate-bars; 14Ahinadab the son of Iddo, *in* Mahanaim; 15Ahimaaz, in Naphtali; he also took Basemath the daughter of Solomon as wife; 16Baanah the son of Hushai, in Asher and Aloth; 17Jehoshaphat the son of Paruah, in Issachar; 18Shimei the son of Elah, in Benjamin; 19Geber the son of Uri, in the land of Gilead, *in* the country of Sihon king of the Amorites, and of Og king of Bashan. *He was* the only governor who *was* in the land.

Prosperity and Wisdom of Solomon's Reign

20Judah and Israel *were* as numerous as the sand by the sea in multitude,

4:8 [a] Literally *Son of Hur* 4:9 [a] Literally *Son of Deker* 4:10 [a] Literally *Son of Hesed*
4:11 [a] Literally *Son of Abinadab* 4:13 [a] Literally *Son of Geber*

eating and drinking and rejoicing. 21So Solomon reigned over all kingdoms from the River[a] *to* the land of the Philistines, as far as the border of Egypt. *They* brought tribute and served Solomon all the days of his life.

22Now Solomon's provision for one day was thirty kors of fine flour, sixty kors of meal, 23ten fatted oxen, twenty oxen from the pastures, and one hundred sheep, besides deer, gazelles, roebucks, and fatted fowl.

24For he had dominion over all *the region* on this side of the River[a] from Tiphsah even to Gaza, namely over all the kings on this side of the River; and he had peace on every side all around him. 25And Judah and Israel dwelt safely, each man under his vine and his fig tree, from Dan as far as Beersheba, all the days of Solomon.

26Solomon had forty[a] thousand stalls of horses for his chariots, and twelve thousand horsemen. 27And these governors, each man in his month, provided food for King Solomon and for all who came to King Solomon's table. There was no lack in their supply. 28They also brought barley and straw to the proper place, for the horses and steeds, each man according to his charge.

29And God gave Solomon wisdom and exceedingly great understanding, and largeness of heart like the sand on the seashore. 30Thus Solomon's wisdom excelled the wisdom of all the men of the East and all the wisdom of Egypt. 31For he was wiser than all men—than Ethan the Ezrahite, and Heman, Chalcol, and Darda, the sons of Mahol; and his fame was in all the surrounding nations. 32He spoke three thousand proverbs, and his songs were one thousand and five. 33Also he spoke of trees, from the cedar tree of Lebanon even to the hyssop that springs out of the wall; he spoke also of animals, of birds, of creeping things, and of fish. 34And men of all nations, from all the kings of the earth who had heard of his wisdom, came to hear the wisdom of Solomon.

Solomon Prepares to Build the Temple

5 Now Hiram king of Tyre sent his servants to Solomon, because he heard that they had anointed him king in place of his father, for Hiram had always loved David. 2Then Solomon sent to Hiram, saying:

3 You know how my father David
could not build a house for
the name of the LORD his God
because of the wars which were
fought against him on every side,
until the LORD put *his foes*[a] under
the soles of his feet.
4 But now the LORD my God has
given me rest on every side; *there
is* neither adversary nor evil
occurrence.
5 And behold, I propose to build a
house for the name of the LORD
my God, as the LORD spoke to my
father David, saying, "Your son,
whom I will set on your throne
in your place, he shall build the
house for My name."
6 Now therefore, command that
they cut down cedars for me from
Lebanon; and my servants will
be with your servants, and I will
pay you wages for your servants
according to whatever you say.
For you know *there is* none among
us who has skill to cut timber like
the Sidonians.

7So it was, when Hiram heard the words of Solomon, that he rejoiced greatly and said,

Blessed *be* the LORD this day, for
He has given David a wise son
over this great people!

8Then Hiram sent to Solomon, saying:

I have considered *the message*
which you sent me, *and* I will do
all you desire concerning the
cedar and cypress logs.
9 My servants shall bring *them*
down from Lebanon to the sea;

4:21 [a] That is, the Euphrates **4:24** [a] That is, the Euphrates **4:26** [a] Following Masoretic Text and most other authorities; some manuscripts of the Septuagint read *four* (compare 2 Chronicles 9:25).
5:3 [a] Literally *them*

I will float them in rafts by sea
to the place you indicate to me,
and will have them broken apart
there; then you can take *them*
away. And you shall fulfill my
desire by giving food for my
household.

10Then Hiram gave Solomon cedar and cypress logs *according to* all his desire. 11And Solomon gave Hiram twenty thousand kors of wheat *as* food for his household, and twenty[a] kors of pressed oil. Thus Solomon gave to Hiram year by year.

12So the LORD gave Solomon wisdom, as He had promised him; and there was peace between Hiram and Solomon, and the two of them made a treaty together.

13Then King Solomon raised up a labor force out of all Israel; and the labor force was thirty thousand men. 14And he sent them to Lebanon, ten thousand a month in shifts: they were one month in Lebanon *and* two months at home; Adoniram *was* in charge of the labor force. 15Solomon had seventy thousand who carried burdens, and eighty thousand who quarried *stone* in the mountains, 16besides three thousand three hundred[a] from the chiefs of Solomon's deputies, who supervised the people who labored in the work. 17And the king commanded them to quarry large stones, costly stones, *and* hewn stones, to lay the foundation of the temple.[a] 18So Solomon's builders, Hiram's builders, and the Gebalites quarried *them;* and they prepared timber and stones to build the temple.

Solomon Builds the Temple

6 And it came to pass in the four hundred and eightieth[a] year after the children of Israel had come out of the land of Egypt, in the fourth year of Solomon's reign over Israel, in the month of Ziv, which *is* the second month, that he began to build the house of the LORD. 2Now the house which King Solomon built for the LORD, its length *was* sixty cubits, its width twenty, and its height thirty cubits. 3The vestibule in front of the sanctuary[a] of the house *was* twenty cubits long across the width of the house, *and* the width of *the vestibule*[b] *extended* ten cubits from the front of the house. 4And he made for the house windows with beveled frames.

5Against the wall of the temple he built chambers all around, *against* the walls of the temple, all around the sanctuary and the inner sanctuary.[a] Thus he made side chambers all around it. 6The lowest chamber *was* five cubits wide, the middle *was* six cubits wide, and the third *was* seven cubits wide; for he made narrow ledges around the outside of the temple, so that *the support beams* would not be fastened into the walls of the temple. 7And the temple, when it was being built, was built with stone finished at the quarry, so that no hammer or chisel *or* any iron tool was heard in the temple while it was being built. 8The doorway for the middle story[a] *was* on the right side of the temple. They went up by stairs to the middle *story,* and from the middle to the third.

9So he built the temple and finished it, and he paneled the temple with beams and boards of cedar. 10And he built side chambers against the entire temple, each five cubits high; they were attached to the temple with cedar beams.

11Then the word of the LORD came to Solomon, saying: 12"*Concerning* this temple which you are building, if you walk in My statutes, execute My judgments, keep all My commandments, and walk in them, then I will perform My word with you, which I spoke to your father David. 13And I will dwell among

5:11 [a] Following Masoretic Text, Targum, and Vulgate; Septuagint and Syriac read *twenty thousand.*
5:16 [a] Following Masoretic Text, Targum, and Vulgate; Septuagint reads *three thousand six hundred.*
5:17 [a] Literally *house,* and so frequently throughout this book 6:1 [a] Following Masoretic Text, Targum, and Vulgate; Septuagint reads *fortieth.* 6:3 [a] Hebrew *heykal;* here the main room of the temple, elsewhere called the holy place (compare Exodus 26:33 and Ezekiel 41:1) [b] Literally *it*
6:5 [a] Hebrew *debir;* here the inner room of the temple, elsewhere called the Most Holy Place (compare verse 16) 6:8 [a] Following Masoretic Text and Vulgate; Septuagint reads *upper story;* Targum reads *ground story.*

the children of Israel, and will not for-
sake My people Israel."
14 So Solomon built the temple and fin-
ished it. 15 And he built the inside walls
of the temple with cedar boards; from
the floor of the temple to the ceiling
he paneled the inside with wood; and
he covered the floor of the temple with
planks of cypress. 16 Then he built the
twenty-cubit room at the rear of the
temple, from floor to ceiling, with cedar
boards; he built *it* inside as the inner
sanctuary, as the Most Holy *Place*. 17 And
in front of it the temple sanctuary was
forty cubits *long*. 18 The inside of the tem-
ple was cedar, carved with ornamental
buds and open flowers. All *was* cedar;
there was no stone *to be* seen.
19 And he prepared the inner sanctu-
ary inside the temple, to set the ark of
the covenant of the LORD there. 20 The
inner sanctuary *was* twenty cubits long,
twenty cubits wide, and twenty cubits
high. He overlaid it with pure gold, and
overlaid the altar of cedar. 21 So Sol-
omon overlaid the inside of the temple
with pure gold. He stretched gold chains
across the front of the inner sanctuary,
and overlaid it with gold. 22 The whole
temple he overlaid with gold, until he
had finished all the temple; also he
overlaid with gold the entire altar that
was by the inner sanctuary.
23 Inside the inner sanctuary he made
two cherubim *of* olive wood, *each* ten
cubits high. 24 One wing of the cherub
was five cubits, and the other wing of
the cherub five cubits: ten cubits from
the tip of one wing to the tip of the other.
25 And the other cherub *was* ten cubits;
both cherubim *were* of the same size and
shape. 26 The height of one cherub *was*
ten cubits, and so *was* the other cherub.
27 Then he set the cherubim inside the
inner room;[a] and they stretched out
the wings of the cherubim so that the
wing of the one touched *one* wall, and
the wing of the other cherub touched the
other wall. And their wings touched each
other in the middle of the room. 28 Also
he overlaid the cherubim with gold.
29 Then he carved all the walls of the
temple all around, both the inner and
outer *sanctuaries*, with carved figures of
cherubim, palm trees, and open flow-
ers. 30 And the floor of the temple he
overlaid with gold, both the inner and
outer *sanctuaries*.
31 For the entrance of the inner sanc-
tuary he made doors *of* olive wood; the
lintel *and* doorposts *were* one-fifth *of
the wall*. 32 The two doors *were of* olive
wood; and he carved on them figures of
cherubim, palm trees, and open flowers,
and overlaid *them* with gold; and he
spread gold on the cherubim and on
the palm trees. 33 So for the door of the
sanctuary he also made doorposts *of*
olive wood, one-fourth *of the wall*. 34 And
the two doors *were of* cypress wood; two
panels *comprised* one folding door, and
two panels *comprised* the other folding
door. 35 Then he carved cherubim, palm
trees, and open flowers *on them*, and
overlaid *them* with gold applied evenly
on the carved work.
36 And he built the inner court with
three rows of hewn stone and a row of
cedar beams.
37 In the fourth year the foundation
of the house of the LORD was laid, in
the month of Ziv. 38 And in the eleventh
year, in the month of Bul, which is the
eighth month, the house was finished
in all its details and according to all its
plans. So he was seven years in build-
ing it.

Solomon's Other Buildings

7 But Solomon took thirteen years to
build his own house; so he finished
all his house.
2 He also built the House of the Forest
of Lebanon; its length *was* one hun-
dred cubits, its width fifty cubits, and its
height thirty cubits, with four rows of
cedar pillars, and cedar beams on the
pillars. 3 And *it was* paneled with cedar
above the beams that *were* on forty-
five pillars, fifteen *to* a row. 4 *There were*
windows *with beveled frames in* three
rows, and window *was* opposite window
in three tiers. 5 And all the doorways
and doorposts *had* rectangular frames;
and window *was* opposite window *in*
three tiers.

6:27 a Literally *house*

6He also made the Hall of Pillars: its
length *was* fifty cubits, and its width
thirty cubits; and in front of them *was*
a portico with pillars, and a canopy *was*
in front of them.
7Then he made a hall for the throne,
the Hall of Judgment, where he might
judge; and *it was* paneled with cedar
from floor to ceiling.[a]
8And the house where he dwelt *had*
another court inside the hall, of like
workmanship. Solomon also made a
house like this hall for Pharaoh's daugh-
ter, whom he had taken *as wife.*
9All these *were of* costly stones cut to
size, trimmed with saws, inside and out,
from the foundation to the eaves, and
also on the outside to the great court.
10The foundation *was of* costly stones,
large stones, some ten cubits and some
eight cubits. 11And above *were* costly
stones, hewn to size, and cedar wood.
12The great court *was* enclosed with
three rows of hewn stones and a row of
cedar beams. So were the inner court of
the house of the LORD and the vestibule
of the temple.

Hiram the Craftsman

13Now King Solomon sent and brought
Huram[a] from Tyre. 14He *was* the son of
a widow from the tribe of Naphtali, and
his father *was* a man of Tyre, a bronze
worker; he was filled with wisdom and
understanding and skill in working with
all kinds of bronze work. So he came
to King Solomon and did all his work.

The Bronze Pillars for the Temple

15And he cast two pillars of bronze,
each one eighteen cubits high, and a
line of twelve cubits measured the cir-
cumference of each. 16Then he made
two capitals *of* cast bronze, to set on
the tops of the pillars. The height of one
capital *was* five cubits, and the height
of the other capital *was* five cubits. 17*He
made* a lattice network, with wreaths
of chainwork, for the capitals which
were on top of the pillars: seven chains
for one capital and seven for the other
capital. 18So he made the pillars, and
two rows of pomegranates above the
network all around to cover the capitals
that *were* on top; and thus he did for the
other capital.
19The capitals which *were* on top of
the pillars in the hall *were* in the shape
of lilies, four cubits. 20The capitals on
the two pillars also *had pomegranates*
above, by the convex surface which *was*
next to the network; and there *were* two
hundred such pomegranates in rows on
each of the capitals all around.
21Then he set up the pillars by the ves-
tibule of the temple; he set up the pillar
on the right and called its name Jachin,
and he set up the pillar on the left and
called its name Boaz. 22The tops of the
pillars were in the shape of lilies. So the
work of the pillars was finished.

The Sea and the Oxen

23And he made the Sea of cast bronze,
ten cubits from one brim to the other;
it was completely round. Its height *was*
five cubits, and a line of thirty cubits
measured its circumference.
24Below its brim *were* ornamental
buds encircling it all around, ten to a
cubit, all the way around the Sea. The
ornamental buds *were* cast in two rows
when it was cast. 25It stood on twelve
oxen: three looking toward the north,
three looking toward the west, three
looking toward the south, and three
looking toward the east; the Sea *was
set* upon them, and all their back parts
pointed inward. 26It *was* a handbreadth
thick; and its brim was shaped like the
brim of a cup, *like* a lily blossom. It con-
tained two thousand[a] baths.

The Carts and the Lavers

27He also made ten carts of bronze;
four cubits *was* the length of each cart,
four cubits its width, and three cubits
its height. 28And this *was* the design
of the carts: They had panels, and the
panels *were* between frames; 29on the
panels that *were* between the frames
were lions, oxen, and cherubim. And
on the frames *was* a pedestal on top.
Below the lions and oxen *were* wreaths
of plaited work. 30Every cart had four
bronze wheels and axles of bronze, and

7:7 [a] Literally *floor,* that is, of the upper level **7:13** [a] Hebrew *Hiram* (compare 2 Chronicles 2:13, 14)
7:26 [a] Or *three thousand* (compare 2 Chronicles 4:5)

its four feet had supports. Under the
laver *were* supports of cast *bronze* be-
side each wreath. 31Its opening inside
the crown at the top *was* one cubit in
diameter; and the opening *was* round,
shaped *like* a pedestal, one and a half
cubits in outside diameter; and also on
the opening *were* engravings, but the
panels were square, not round. 32Under
the panels *were* the four wheels, and the
axles of the wheels *were joined* to the
cart. The height of a wheel *was* one and
a half cubits. 33The workmanship of the
wheels *was* like the workmanship of a
chariot wheel; their axle pins, their rims,
their spokes, and their hubs *were* all of
cast *bronze.* 34And *there were* four sup-
ports at the four corners of each cart;
its supports *were* part of the cart itself.
35On the top of the cart, at the height
of half a cubit, *it was* perfectly round.
And on the top of the cart, its flanges
and its panels *were* of the same casting.
36On the plates of its flanges and on its
panels he engraved cherubim, lions,
and palm trees, wherever there was a
clear space on each, with wreaths all
around. 37Thus he made the ten carts.
All of them were of the same mold, one
measure, *and* one shape.

38Then he made ten lavers of bronze;
each laver contained forty baths, *and*
each laver *was* four cubits. On each of
the ten carts *was* a laver. 39And he put
five carts on the right side of the house,
and five on the left side of the house.
He set the Sea on the right side of the
house, toward the southeast.

Furnishings of the Temple

40Huram[a] made the lavers and the
shovels and the bowls. So Huram fin-
ished doing all the work that he was
to do for King Solomon *for* the house
of the LORD: 41the two pillars, the *two*
bowl-shaped capitals that *were* on top
of the two pillars; the two networks
covering the two bowl-shaped capitals
which *were* on top of the pillars; 42four
hundred pomegranates for the two net-
works (two rows of pomegranates for
each network, to cover the two bowl-
shaped capitals that *were* on top of the
pillars); 43the ten carts, and ten lavers
on the carts; 44one Sea, and twelve oxen
under the Sea; 45the pots, the shovels,
and the bowls.

All these articles which Huram[a] made
for King Solomon *for* the house of the
LORD *were of* burnished bronze. 46In
the plain of Jordan the king had them
cast in clay molds, between Succoth
and Zaretan. 47And Solomon did not
weigh all the articles, because *there were*
so many; the weight of the bronze was
not determined.

48Thus Solomon had all the furnish-
ings made for the house of the LORD:
the altar of gold, and the table of gold
on which *was* the showbread; 49the
lampstands of pure gold, five on the
right *side* and five on the left in front
of the inner sanctuary, with the flowers
and the lamps and the wick-trimmers
of gold; 50the basins, the trimmers, the
bowls, the ladles, and the censers of
pure gold; and the hinges of gold, *both*
for the doors of the inner room (the
Most Holy *Place*) *and* for the doors of
the main hall of the temple.

51So all the work that King Solomon
had done for the house of the LORD
was finished; and Solomon brought
in the things which his father David
had dedicated: the silver and the gold
and the furnishings. He put them in
the treasuries of the house of the LORD.

The Ark Brought into the Temple

8 Now Solomon assembled the elders
of Israel and all the heads of the
tribes, the chief fathers of the children
of Israel, to King Solomon in Jerusalem,
that they might bring up the ark of the
covenant of the LORD from the City
of David, which *is* Zion. 2Therefore all
the men of Israel assembled with King
Solomon at the feast in the month of
Ethanim, which *is* the seventh month.
3So all the elders of Israel came, and
the priests took up the ark. 4Then they
brought up the ark of the LORD, the
tabernacle of meeting, and all the holy
furnishings that *were* in the taberna-
cle. The priests and the Levites brought
them up. 5Also King Solomon, and all

7:40 [a] Hebrew *Hiram* (compare 2 Chronicles 2:13, 14) **7:45** [a] Hebrew *Hiram* (compare 2 Chronicles 2:13, 14) the congregation of Israel who were assembled with him, *were* with him before the ark, sacrificing sheep and oxen that could not be counted or numbered for multitude. 6Then the priests brought in the ark of the covenant of the LORD to its place, into the inner sanctuary of the temple, to the Most Holy *Place,* under the wings of the cherubim. 7For the cherubim spread *their* two wings over the place of the ark, and the cherubim overshadowed the ark and its poles. 8The poles extended so that the ends of the poles could be seen from the holy *place,* in front of the inner sanctuary; but they could not be seen from outside. And they are there to this day. 9Nothing *was* in the ark except the two tablets of stone which Moses put there at Horeb, when the LORD made *a covenant* with the children of Israel, when they came out of the land of Egypt.

10And it came to pass, when the priests came out of the holy *place,* that the cloud filled the house of the LORD, 11so that the priests could not continue ministering because of the cloud; for the glory of the LORD filled the house of the LORD.

12Then Solomon spoke:

"The LORD said He would dwell in
 the dark cloud.
13 I have surely built You an exalted
 house,
And a place for You to dwell in
 forever."

Solomon's Speech at Completion of the Work

14Then the king turned around and blessed the whole assembly of Israel, while all the assembly of Israel was standing. 15And he said: "Blessed *be* the LORD God of Israel, who spoke with His mouth to my father David, and with His hand has fulfilled *it,* saying, 16'Since the day that I brought My people Israel out of Egypt, I have chosen no city from any tribe of Israel *in which* to build a house, that My name might be there; but I chose David to be over My people Israel.' 17Now it was in the heart of my father David to build a temple[a] for the name of the LORD God of Israel. 18But the LORD said to my father David, 'Whereas it was in your heart to build a temple for My name, you did well that it was in your heart. 19Nevertheless you shall not build the temple, but your son who will come from your body, he shall build the temple for My name.' 20So the LORD has fulfilled His word which He spoke; and I have filled the position of my father David, and sit on the throne of Israel, as the LORD promised; and I have built a temple for the name of the LORD God of Israel. 21And there I have made a place for the ark, in which *is* the covenant of the LORD which He made with our fathers, when He brought them out of the land of Egypt."

Solomon's Prayer of Dedication

22Then Solomon stood before the altar of the LORD in the presence of all the assembly of Israel, and spread out his hands toward heaven; 23and he said: "LORD God of Israel, *there is* no God in heaven above or on earth below like You, who keep *Your* covenant and mercy with Your servants who walk before You with all their hearts. 24You have kept what You promised Your servant David my father; You have both spoken with Your mouth and fulfilled *it* with Your hand, as *it is* this day. 25Therefore, LORD God of Israel, now keep what You promised Your servant David my father, saying, 'You shall not fail to have a man sit before Me on the throne of Israel, only if your sons take heed to their way, that they walk before Me as you have walked before Me.' 26And now I pray, O God of Israel, let Your word come true, which You have spoken to Your servant David my father.

27"But will God indeed dwell on the earth? Behold, heaven and the heaven of heavens cannot contain You. How much less this temple which I have built! 28Yet regard the prayer of Your servant and his supplication, O LORD my God, and listen to the cry and the prayer which Your servant is praying before You today: 29that Your eyes may be open toward this temple night and day,

8:17 a Literally *house,* and so in verses 18–20

toward the place of which You said, 'My
name shall be there,' that You may hear
the prayer which Your servant makes to-
ward this place. 30And may You hear the
supplication of Your servant and of Your
people Israel, when they pray toward
this place. Hear in heaven Your dwelling
place; and when You hear, forgive.

31"When anyone sins against his
neighbor, and is forced to take an oath,
and comes *and* takes an oath before
Your altar in this temple, 32then hear
in heaven, and act, and judge Your ser-
vants, condemning the wicked, bringing
his way on his head, and justifying the
righteous by giving him according to
his righteousness.

33"When Your people Israel are defeat-
ed before an enemy because they have
sinned against You, and when they turn
back to You and confess Your name, and
pray and make supplication to You in
this temple, 34then hear in heaven, and
forgive the sin of Your people Israel, and
bring them back to the land which You
gave to their fathers.

35"When the heavens are shut up and
there is no rain because they have sinned
against You, when they pray toward this
place and confess Your name, and turn
from their sin because You afflict them,
36then hear in heaven, and forgive the
sin of Your servants, Your people Israel,
that You may teach them the good way
in which they should walk; and send rain
on Your land which You have given to
Your people as an inheritance.

37"When there is famine in the land,
pestilence *or* blight *or* mildew, locusts
or grasshoppers; when their enemy
besieges them in the land of their cities;
whatever plague or whatever sickness
there is; 38whatever prayer, whatever
supplication is made by anyone, *or*
by all Your people Israel, when each
one knows the plague of his own heart,
and spreads out his hands toward this
temple: 39then hear in heaven Your
dwelling place, and forgive, and act,
and give to everyone according to all
his ways, whose heart You know (for You
alone know the hearts of all the sons of
men), 40that they may fear You all the
days that they live in the land which
You gave to our fathers.

41"Moreover, concerning a foreigner,
who *is* not of Your people Israel, but
has come from a far country for Your
name's sake 42(for they will hear of Your
great name and Your strong hand and
Your outstretched arm), when he comes
and prays toward this temple, 43hear
in heaven Your dwelling place, and do
according to all for which the foreigner
calls to You, that all peoples of the earth
may know Your name and fear You, as
do Your people Israel, and that they
may know that this temple which I have
built is called by Your name.

44"When Your people go out to battle
against their enemy, wherever You send
them, and when they pray to the LORD
toward the city which You have cho-
sen and the temple which I have built
for Your name, 45then hear in heaven
their prayer and their supplication, and
maintain their cause.

46"When they sin against You (for *there
is* no one who does not sin), and You
become angry with them and deliv-
er them to the enemy, and they take
them captive to the land of the enemy,
far or near; 47*yet* when they come to
themselves in the land where they were
carried captive, and repent, and make
supplication to You in the land of those
who took them captive, saying, 'We have
sinned and done wrong, we have com-
mitted wickedness'; 48and *when* they
return to You with all their heart and
with all their soul in the land of their
enemies who led them away captive,
and pray to You toward their land which
You gave to their fathers, the city which
You have chosen and the temple which I
have built for Your name: 49then hear in
heaven Your dwelling place their prayer
and their supplication, and maintain
their cause, 50and forgive Your people
who have sinned against You, and all
their transgressions which they have
transgressed against You; and grant
them compassion before those who
took them captive, that they may have
compassion on them 51(for they *are* Your
people and Your inheritance, whom You
brought out of Egypt, out of the iron
furnace), 52that Your eyes may be open
to the supplication of Your servant and
the supplication of Your people Israel,

to listen to them whenever they call to You. 53For You separated them from among all the peoples of the earth *to be* Your inheritance, as You spoke by Your servant Moses, when You brought our fathers out of Egypt, O Lord GOD."

Solomon Blesses the Assembly

54And so it was, when Solomon had finished praying all this prayer and supplication to the LORD, that he arose from before the altar of the LORD, from kneeling on his knees with his hands spread up to heaven. 55Then he stood and blessed all the assembly of Israel with a loud voice, saying: 56"Blessed *be* the LORD, who has given rest to His people Israel, according to all that He promised. There has not failed one word of all His good promise, which He promised through His servant Moses. 57May the LORD our God be with us, as He was with our fathers. May He not leave us nor forsake us, 58that He may incline our hearts to Himself, to walk in all His ways, and to keep His commandments and His statutes and His judgments, which He commanded our fathers. 59And may these words of mine, with which I have made supplication before the LORD, be near the LORD our God day and night, that He may maintain the cause of His servant and the cause of His people Israel, as each day may require, 60that all the peoples of the earth may know that the LORD *is* God; *there is* no other. 61Let your heart therefore be loyal to the LORD our God, to walk in His statutes and keep His commandments, as at this day."

Solomon Dedicates the Temple

62Then the king and all Israel with him offered sacrifices before the LORD. 63And Solomon offered a sacrifice of peace offerings, which he offered to the LORD, twenty-two thousand bulls and one hundred and twenty thousand sheep. So the king and all the children of Israel dedicated the house of the LORD. 64On the same day the king consecrated the middle of the court that *was* in front of the house of the LORD; for there he offered burnt offerings, grain offerings, and the fat of the peace offerings, because the bronze altar that *was* before the LORD *was* too small to receive the burnt offerings, the grain offerings, and the fat of the peace offerings.

65At that time Solomon held a feast, and all Israel with him, a great assembly from the entrance of Hamath to the Brook of Egypt, before the LORD our God, seven days and seven *more* days—fourteen days. 66On the eighth day he sent the people away; and they blessed the king, and went to their tents joyful and glad of heart for all the good that the LORD had done for His servant David, and for Israel His people.

God's Second Appearance to Solomon

9 And it came to pass, when Solomon had finished building the house of the LORD and the king's house, and all Solomon's desire which he wanted to do, 2that the LORD appeared to Solomon the second time, as He had appeared to him at Gibeon. 3And the LORD said to him: "I have heard your prayer and your supplication that you have made before Me; I have consecrated this house which you have built to put My name there forever, and My eyes and My heart will be there perpetually. 4Now if you walk before Me as your father David walked, in integrity of heart and in uprightness, to do according to all that I have commanded you, *and* if you keep My statutes and My judgments, 5then I will establish the throne of your kingdom over Israel forever, as I promised David your father, saying, 'You shall not fail to have a man on the throne of Israel.' 6*But* if you or your sons at all turn from following Me, and do not keep My commandments *and* My statutes which I have set before you, but go and serve other gods and worship them, 7then I will cut off Israel from the land which I have given them; and this house which I have consecrated for My name I will cast out of My sight. Israel will be a proverb and a byword among all peoples. 8And *as for* this house, *which* is exalted, everyone who passes by it will be astonished and will hiss, and say, 'Why has the LORD done thus to this land and to this house?' 9Then they will answer, 'Because they forsook the LORD

their God, who brought their fathers out
of the land of Egypt, and have embraced
other gods, and worshiped them and
served them; therefore the LORD has
brought all this calamity on them.' "

Solomon and Hiram Exchange Gifts

10 Now it happened at the end of twenty
years, when Solomon had built the two
houses, the house of the LORD and the
king's house 11 (Hiram the king of Tyre
had supplied Solomon with cedar and
cypress and gold, as much as he desired),
that King Solomon then gave Hiram
twenty cities in the land of Galilee. 12 Then
Hiram went from Tyre to see the cities
which Solomon had given him, but they
did not please him. 13 So he said, "What
kind of cities *are* these which you have
given me, my brother?" And he called
them the land of Cabul,[a] as they are to
this day. 14 Then Hiram sent the king
one hundred and twenty talents of gold.

Solomon's Additional Achievements

15 And this *is* the reason for the labor
force which King Solomon raised: to
build the house of the LORD, his own
house, the Millo,[a] the wall of Jerusalem,
Hazor, Megiddo, and Gezer. 16 (Phar-
aoh king of Egypt had gone up and
taken Gezer and burned it with fire, had
killed the Canaanites who dwelt in the
city, and had given it *as* a dowry to his
daughter, Solomon's wife.) 17 And Sol-
omon built Gezer, Lower Beth Horon,
18 Baalath, and Tadmor in the wilder-
ness, in the land *of Judah,* 19 all the stor-
age cities that Solomon had, cities for
his chariots and cities for his cavalry,
and whatever Solomon desired to build
in Jerusalem, in Lebanon, and in all the
land of his dominion.

20 All the people *who were* left of the
Amorites, Hittites, Perizzites, Hivites,
and Jebusites, who *were* not of the chil-
dren of Israel— 21 that is, their descen-
dants who were left in the land after
them, whom the children of Israel had
not been able to destroy completely—
from these Solomon raised forced labor,
as it is to this day. 22 But of the chil-
dren of Israel Solomon made no forced
laborers, because they *were* men of
war and his servants: his officers, his
captains, commanders of his chariots,
and his cavalry.

23 Others *were* chiefs of the officials
who *were* over Solomon's work: five
hundred and fifty, who ruled over the
people who did the work.

24 But Pharaoh's daughter came up
from the City of David to her house
which *Solomon*[a] had built for her. Then
he built the Millo.

25 Now three times a year Solomon
offered burnt offerings and peace of-
ferings on the altar which he had built
for the LORD, and he burned incense
with them *on the altar* that *was* before
the LORD. So he finished the temple.

26 King Solomon also built a fleet of
ships at Ezion Geber, which *is* near
Elath[a] on the shore of the Red Sea, in
the land of Edom. 27 Then Hiram sent
his servants with the fleet, seamen who
knew the sea, to work with the servants
of Solomon. 28 And they went to Ophir,
and acquired four hundred and twenty
talents of gold from there, and brought
it to King Solomon.

The Queen of Sheba's Praise of Solomon

10 Now when the queen of Sheba
heard of the fame of Solomon
concerning the name of the LORD, she
came to test him with hard questions.
2 She came to Jerusalem with a very
great retinue, with camels that bore
spices, very much gold, and precious
stones; and when she came to Solomon,
she spoke with him about all that was in
her heart. 3 So Solomon answered all her
questions; there was nothing so difficult
for the king that he could not explain *it*
to her. 4 And when the queen of Sheba
had seen all the wisdom of Solomon,
the house that he had built, 5 the food on
his table, the seating of his servants, the
service of his waiters and their apparel,
his cupbearers, and his entryway by
which he went up to the house of the
LORD, there was no more spirit in her.
6 Then she said to the king: "It was a true
report which I heard in my own land
about your words and your wisdom.

9:13 [a] Literally *Good for Nothing* **9:15** [a] Literally *The Landfill* **9:24** [a] Literally *he* (compare 2 Chronicles 8:11) **9:26** [a] Hebrew *Eloth* (compare 2 Kings 14:22)

7However I did not believe the words
until I came and saw with my own eyes;
and indeed the half was not told me.
Your wisdom and prosperity exceed
the fame of which I heard. 8Happy *are*
your men and happy *are* these your
servants, who stand continually before
you *and* hear your wisdom! 9Blessed be
the LORD your God, who delighted in
you, setting you on the throne of Isra-
el! Because the LORD has loved Israel
forever, therefore He made you king, to
do justice and righteousness."

10Then she gave the king one hundred
and twenty talents of gold, spices in
great quantity, and precious stones.
There never again came such abun-
dance of spices as the queen of Sheba
gave to King Solomon. 11Also, the ships
of Hiram, which brought gold from
Ophir, brought great quantities of al-
mug[a] wood and precious stones from
Ophir. 12And the king made steps of the
almug wood for the house of the LORD
and for the king's house, also harps and
stringed instruments for singers. There
never again came such almug wood,
nor has the like been seen to this day.

13Now King Solomon gave the queen
of Sheba all she desired, whatever she
asked, besides what Solomon had given
her according to the royal generosi-
ty. So she turned and went to her own
country, she and her servants.

Solomon's Great Wealth

14The weight of gold that came to Sol-
omon yearly was six hundred and sixty-
six talents of gold, 15besides *that* from the
traveling merchants, from the income
of traders, from all the kings of Arabia,
and from the governors of the country.

16And King Solomon made two hun-
dred large shields *of* hammered gold;
six hundred *shekels* of gold went into
each shield. 17He also *made* three hun-
dred shields *of* hammered gold; three
minas of gold went into each shield.
The king put them in the House of the
Forest of Lebanon.

18Moreover the king made a great
throne of ivory, and overlaid it with
pure gold. 19The throne had six steps,
and the top of the throne *was* round at
the back; *there were* armrests on either
side of the place of the seat, and two li-
ons stood beside the armrests. 20Twelve
lions stood there, one on each side of
the six steps; nothing like *this* had been
made for any *other* kingdom.

21All King Solomon's drinking ves-
sels *were* gold, and all the vessels of
the House of the Forest of Lebanon
were pure gold. Not *one was* silver, for
this was accounted as nothing in the
days of Solomon. 22For the king had
merchant ships[a] at sea with the fleet
of Hiram. Once every three years the
merchant ships came bringing gold,
silver, ivory, apes, and monkeys.[b] 23So
King Solomon surpassed all the kings
of the earth in riches and wisdom.

24Now all the earth sought the presence
of Solomon to hear his wisdom, which
God had put in his heart. 25Each man
brought his present: articles of silver and
gold, garments, armor, spices, horses,
and mules, at a set rate year by year.

26And Solomon gathered chariots and
horsemen; he had one thousand four
hundred chariots and twelve thousand
horsemen, whom he stationed[a] in the
chariot cities and with the king at Jeru-
salem. 27The king made silver *as com-*
mon in Jerusalem as stones, and he
made cedar trees as abundant as the
sycamores which *are* in the lowland.

28Also Solomon had horses import-
ed from Egypt and Keveh; the king's
merchants bought them in Keveh at
the *current* price. 29Now a chariot that
was imported from Egypt cost six hun-
dred *shekels* of silver, and a horse one
hundred and fifty; and thus, through
their agents,[a] they exported *them* to all
the kings of the Hittites and the kings
of Syria.

Solomon's Heart Turns from the LORD

11 But King Solomon loved many
foreign women, as well as the
daughter of Pharaoh: women of the Mo-
abites, Ammonites, Edomites, Sidoni-
ans, *and* Hittites— 2from the nations of

10:11 [a] Or *algum* (compare 2 Chronicles 9:10, 11) **10:22** [a] Literally *ships of Tarshish,* deep-sea vessels [b] Or *peacocks* **10:26** [a] Following Septuagint, Syriac, Targum, and Vulgate (compare 2 Chronicles 9:25); Masoretic Text reads *led.* **10:29** [a] Literally *by their hands*

whom the LORD had said to the children
of Israel, "You shall not intermarry with
them, nor they with you. Surely they will
turn away your hearts after their gods."
Solomon clung to these in love. 3And he
had seven hundred wives, princesses,
and three hundred concubines; and
his wives turned away his heart. 4For
it was so, when Solomon was old, that
his wives turned his heart after other
gods; and his heart was not loyal to the
LORD his God, as *was* the heart of his
father David. 5For Solomon went after
Ashtoreth the goddess of the Sidonians,
and after Milcom the abomination of
the Ammonites. 6Solomon did evil in
the sight of the LORD, and did not fully
follow the LORD, as *did* his father David.
7Then Solomon built a high place for
Chemosh the abomination of Moab, on
the hill that *is* east of Jerusalem, and for
Molech the abomination of the people
of Ammon. 8And he did likewise for all
his foreign wives, who burned incense
and sacrificed to their gods.

9So the LORD became angry with Sol-
omon, because his heart had turned
from the LORD God of Israel, who had
appeared to him twice, 10and had com-
manded him concerning this thing, that
he should not go after other gods; but he
did not keep what the LORD had com-
manded. 11Therefore the LORD said to
Solomon, "Because you have done this,
and have not kept My covenant and My
statutes, which I have commanded you,
I will surely tear the kingdom away from
you and give it to your servant. 12Never-
theless I will not do it in your days, for
the sake of your father David; I will tear
it out of the hand of your son. 13However
I will not tear away the whole kingdom;
I will give one tribe to your son for the
sake of My servant David, and for the
sake of Jerusalem which I have chosen."

Adversaries of Solomon

14Now the LORD raised up an ad-
versary against Solomon, Hadad the
Edomite; he *was* a descendant of the
king in Edom. 15For it happened, when
David was in Edom, and Joab the com-
mander of the army had gone up to
bury the slain, after he had killed every
male in Edom 16(because for six months
Joab remained there with all Israel,
until he had cut down every male in
Edom), 17that Hadad fled to go to Egypt,
he and certain Edomites of his father's
servants with him. Hadad *was* still a
little child. 18Then they arose from Mid-
ian and came to Paran; and they took
men with them from Paran and came
to Egypt, to Pharaoh king of Egypt, who
gave him a house, apportioned food for
him, and gave him land. 19And Hadad
found great favor in the sight of Phar-
aoh, so that he gave him as wife the
sister of his own wife, that is, the sister
of Queen Tahpenes. 20Then the sister of
Tahpenes bore him Genubath his son,
whom Tahpenes weaned in Pharaoh's
house. And Genubath was in Pharaoh's
household among the sons of Pharaoh.

21So when Hadad heard in Egypt that
David rested with his fathers, and that
Joab the commander of the army was
dead, Hadad said to Pharaoh, "Let me de-
part, that I may go to my own country."
22Then Pharaoh said to him, "But what
have you lacked with me, that suddenly
you seek to go to your own country?"

So he answered, "Nothing, but do let
me go anyway."

23And God raised up *another* adversary
against him, Rezon the son of Eliadah,
who had fled from his lord, Hadadezer
king of Zobah. 24So he gathered men to
him and became captain over a band
of raiders, when David killed those *of
Zobah.* And they went to Damascus and
dwelt there, and reigned in Damascus.
25He was an adversary of Israel all the
days of Solomon (besides the trouble
that Hadad *caused*); and he abhorred
Israel, and reigned over Syria.

Jeroboam's Rebellion

26Then Solomon's servant, Jeroboam
the son of Nebat, an Ephraimite from
Zereda, whose mother's name *was* Ze-
ruah, a widow, also rebelled against
the king.

27And this *is* what caused him to rebel
against the king: Solomon had built
the Millo *and* repaired the damages to
the City of David his father. 28The man
Jeroboam *was* a mighty man of valor;
and Solomon, seeing that the young
man was industrious, made him the

officer over all the labor force of the house of Joseph.

29Now it happened at that time, when Jeroboam went out of Jerusalem, that the prophet Ahijah the Shilonite met him on the way; and he had clothed himself with a new garment, and the two *were* alone in the field. 30Then Ahijah took hold of the new garment that *was* on him, and tore it *into* twelve pieces. 31And he said to Jeroboam, "Take for yourself ten pieces, for thus says the LORD, the God of Israel: 'Behold, I will tear the kingdom out of the hand of Solomon and will give ten tribes to you 32(but he shall have one tribe for the sake of My servant David, and for the sake of Jerusalem, the city which I have chosen out of all the tribes of Israel), 33because they have[a] forsaken Me, and worshiped Ashtoreth the goddess of the Sidonians, Chemosh the god of the Moabites, and Milcom the god of the people of Ammon, and have not walked in My ways to do *what is* right in My eyes and *keep* My statutes and My judgments, as *did* his father David. 34However I will not take the whole kingdom out of his hand, because I have made him ruler all the days of his life for the sake of My servant David, whom I chose because he kept My commandments and My statutes. 35But I will take the kingdom out of his son's hand and give it to you—ten tribes. 36And to his son I will give one tribe, that My servant David may always have a lamp before Me in Jerusalem, the city which I have chosen for Myself, to put My name there. 37So I will take you, and you shall reign over all your heart desires, and you shall be king over Israel. 38Then it shall be, if you heed all that I command you, walk in My ways, and do *what is* right in My sight, to keep My statutes and My commandments, as My servant David did, then I will be with you and build for you an enduring house, as I built for David, and will give Israel to you. 39And I will afflict the descendants of David because of this, but not forever.' "

40Solomon therefore sought to kill Jeroboam. But Jeroboam arose and fled to Egypt, to Shishak king of Egypt, and was in Egypt until the death of Solomon.

Death of Solomon

41Now the rest of the acts of Solomon, all that he did, and his wisdom, *are* they not written in the book of the acts of Solomon? 42And the period that Solomon reigned in Jerusalem over all Israel *was* forty years. 43Then Solomon rested with his fathers, and was buried in the City of David his father. And Rehoboam his son reigned in his place.

The Revolt Against Rehoboam

12 And Rehoboam went to Shechem, for all Israel had gone to Shechem to make him king. 2So it happened, when Jeroboam the son of Nebat heard *it* (he was still in Egypt, for he had fled from the presence of King Solomon and had been dwelling in Egypt), 3that they sent and called him. Then Jeroboam and the whole assembly of Israel came and spoke to Rehoboam, saying, 4"Your father made our yoke heavy; now therefore, lighten the burdensome service of your father, and his heavy yoke which he put on us, and we will serve you."

5So he said to them, "Depart *for* three days, then come back to me." And the people departed.

6Then King Rehoboam consulted the elders who stood before his father Solomon while he still lived, and he said, "How do you advise *me* to answer these people?"

7And they spoke to him, saying, "If you will be a servant to these people today, and serve them, and answer them, and speak good words to them, then they will be your servants forever."

8But he rejected the advice which the elders had given him, and consulted the young men who had grown up with him, who stood before him. 9And he said to them, "What advice do you give? How should we answer this people who have spoken to me, saying, 'Lighten the yoke which your father put on us'?"

10Then the young men who had grown up with him spoke to him, saying, "Thus

11:33 [a] Following Masoretic Text and Targum; Septuagint, Syriac, and Vulgate read *he has.*

you should speak to this people who
have spoken to you, saying, 'Your father
made our yoke heavy, but you make
it lighter on us'—thus you shall say to
them: 'My little *finger* shall be thick-
er than my father's waist! 11And now,
whereas my father put a heavy yoke
on you, I will add to your yoke; my fa-
ther chastised you with whips, but I will
chastise you with scourges!' "[a]
12So Jeroboam and all the people
came to Rehoboam the third day, as
the king had directed, saying, "Come
back to me the third day." 13Then the
king answered the people roughly, and
rejected the advice which the elders
had given him; 14and he spoke to them
according to the advice of the young
men, saying, "My father made your
yoke heavy, but I will add to your yoke;
my father chastised you with whips, but
I will chastise you with scourges!"[a] 15So
the king did not listen to the people; for
the turn *of events* was from the LORD,
that He might fulfill His word, which
the LORD had spoken by Ahijah the Shi-
lonite to Jeroboam the son of Nebat.
16Now when all Israel saw that the
king did not listen to them, the people
answered the king, saying:

"What share have we in David?
We have no inheritance in the son
of Jesse.
To your tents, O Israel!
Now, see to your own house,
O David!"

So Israel departed to their tents. 17But
Rehoboam reigned over the children of
Israel who dwelt in the cities of Judah.
18Then King Rehoboam sent Adoram,
who *was* in charge of the revenue; but
all Israel stoned him with stones, and
he died. Therefore King Rehoboam
mounted his chariot in haste to flee
to Jerusalem. 19So Israel has been in
rebellion against the house of David
to this day.
20Now it came to pass when all Israel
heard that Jeroboam had come back,
they sent for him and called him to
the congregation, and made him king
over all Israel. There was none who fol-
lowed the house of David, but the tribe
of Judah only.
21And when Rehoboam came to Jeru-
salem, he assembled all the house of
Judah with the tribe of Benjamin, one
hundred and eighty thousand chosen
men who were warriors, to fight against
the house of Israel, that he might re-
store the kingdom to Rehoboam the
son of Solomon. 22But the word of God
came to Shemaiah the man of God,
saying, 23"Speak to Rehoboam the son
of Solomon, king of Judah, to all the
house of Judah and Benjamin, and to
the rest of the people, saying, 24'Thus
says the LORD: "You shall not go up nor
fight against your brethren the chil-
dren of Israel. Let every man return to
his house, for this thing is from Me." ' "
Therefore they obeyed the word of the
LORD, and turned back, according to
the word of the LORD.

Jeroboam's Gold Calves

25Then Jeroboam built Shechem in
the mountains of Ephraim, and dwelt
there. Also he went out from there and
built Penuel. 26And Jeroboam said in
his heart, "Now the kingdom may re-
turn to the house of David: 27If these
people go up to offer sacrifices in the
house of the LORD at Jerusalem, then
the heart of this people will turn back
to their lord, Rehoboam king of Judah,
and they will kill me and go back to
Rehoboam king of Judah."
28Therefore the king asked advice,
made two calves of gold, and said to
the people, "It is too much for you to
go up to Jerusalem. Here are your gods,
O Israel, which brought you up from
the land of Egypt!" 29And he set up one
in Bethel, and the other he put in Dan.
30Now this thing became a sin, for the
people went *to worship* before the one
as far as Dan. 31He made shrines[a] on
the high places, and made priests from
every class of people, who were not of
the sons of Levi.
32Jeroboam ordained a feast on the
fifteenth day of the eighth month, like
the feast that *was* in Judah, and offered

12:11 [a] Literally *scorpions* **12:14** [a] Literally *scorpions* **12:31** [a] Literally *a house*

sacrifices on the altar. So he did at Bethel, sacrificing to the calves that he had made. And at Bethel he installed the priests of the high places which he had made. 33 So he made offerings on the altar which he had made at Bethel on the fifteenth day of the eighth month, in the month which he had devised in his own heart. And he ordained a feast for the children of Israel, and offered sacrifices on the altar and burned incense.

The Message of the Man of God

13 And behold, a man of God went from Judah to Bethel by the word of the LORD, and Jeroboam stood by the altar to burn incense. 2 Then he cried out against the altar by the word of the LORD, and said, "O altar, altar! Thus says the LORD: 'Behold, a child, Josiah by name, shall be born to the house of David; and on you he shall sacrifice the priests of the high places who burn incense on you, and men's bones shall be burned on you.' " 3 And he gave a sign the same day, saying, "This *is* the sign which the LORD has spoken: Surely the altar shall split apart, and the ashes on it shall be poured out."

4 So it came to pass when King Jeroboam heard the saying of the man of God, who cried out against the altar in Bethel, that he stretched out his hand from the altar, saying, "Arrest him!" Then his hand, which he stretched out toward him, withered, so that he could not pull it back to himself. 5 The altar also was split apart, and the ashes poured out from the altar, according to the sign which the man of God had given by the word of the LORD. 6 Then the king answered and said to the man of God, "Please entreat the favor of the LORD your God, and pray for me, that my hand may be restored to me."

So the man of God entreated the LORD, and the king's hand was restored to him, and became as before. 7 Then the king said to the man of God, "Come home with me and refresh yourself, and I will give you a reward."

8 But the man of God said to the king, "If you were to give me half your house, I would not go in with you; nor would I eat bread nor drink water in this place. 9 For so it was commanded me by the word of the LORD, saying, 'You shall not eat bread, nor drink water, nor return by the same way you came.' " 10 So he went another way and did not return by the way he came to Bethel.

Death of the Man of God

11 Now an old prophet dwelt in Bethel, and his sons came and told him all the works that the man of God had done that day in Bethel; they also told their father the words which he had spoken to the king. 12 And their father said to them, "Which way did he go?" For his sons had seen[a] which way the man of God went who came from Judah. 13 Then he said to his sons, "Saddle the donkey for me." So they saddled the donkey for him; and he rode on it, 14 and went after the man of God, and found him sitting under an oak. Then he said to him, "*Are* you the man of God who came from Judah?"

And he said, "I *am*."

15 Then he said to him, "Come home with me and eat bread."

16 And he said, "I cannot return with you nor go in with you; neither can I eat bread nor drink water with you in this place. 17 For I have been told by the word of the LORD, 'You shall not eat bread nor drink water there, nor return by going the way you came.' "

18 He said to him, "I too *am* a prophet as you *are*, and an angel spoke to me by the word of the LORD, saying, 'Bring him back with you to your house, that he may eat bread and drink water.' " (He was lying to him.)

19 So he went back with him, and ate bread in his house, and drank water.

20 Now it happened, as they sat at the table, that the word of the LORD came to the prophet who had brought him back; 21 and he cried out to the man of God who came from Judah, saying, "Thus says the LORD: 'Because you have disobeyed the word of the LORD, and have not kept the commandment which the LORD your God commanded you, 22 but you came back, ate bread, and drank

13:12 [a] Septuagint, Syriac, Targum, and Vulgate read *showed him.*

water in the place of which *the* LORD
said to you, "Eat no bread and drink
no water," your corpse shall not come
to the tomb of your fathers.' "
23So it was, after he had eaten bread
and after he had drunk, that he saddled
the donkey for him, the prophet whom
he had brought back. 24When he was
gone, a lion met him on the road and
killed him. And his corpse was thrown
on the road, and the donkey stood by
it. The lion also stood by the corpse.
25And there, men passed by and saw
the corpse thrown on the road, and the
lion standing by the corpse. Then they
went and told *it* in the city where the
old prophet dwelt.
26Now when the prophet who had
brought him back from the way heard
it, he said, "It *is* the man of God who was
disobedient to the word of the LORD.
Therefore the LORD has delivered him
to the lion, which has torn him and killed
him, according to the word of the LORD
which He spoke to him." 27And he spoke
to his sons, saying, "Saddle the donkey
for me." So they saddled *it.* 28Then he
went and found his corpse thrown on
the road, and the donkey and the lion
standing by the corpse. The lion had not
eaten the corpse nor torn the donkey.
29And the prophet took up the corpse
of the man of God, laid it on the donkey,
and brought it back. So the old prophet
came to the city to mourn, and to bury
him. 30Then he laid the corpse in his own
tomb; and they mourned over him, *say-
ing,* "Alas, my brother!" 31So it was, after
he had buried him, that he spoke to his
sons, saying, "When I am dead, then bury
me in the tomb where the man of God *is*
buried; lay my bones beside his bones.
32For the saying which he cried out by
the word of the LORD against the altar in
Bethel, and against all the shrines[a] on
the high places which *are* in the cities of
Samaria, will surely come to pass."
33After this event Jeroboam did not
turn from his evil way, but again he
made priests from every class of people
for the high places; whoever wished, he
consecrated him, and he became *one*
of the priests of the high places. 34And
this thing was the sin of the house of
Jeroboam, so as to exterminate and
destroy *it* from the face of the earth.

Judgment on the House of Jeroboam

14 At that time Abijah the son of
Jeroboam became sick. 2And
Jeroboam said to his wife, "Please arise,
and disguise yourself, that they may
not recognize you as the wife of Jero-
boam, and go to Shiloh. Indeed, Ahijah
the prophet *is* there, who told me that
I would be king over this people. 3Also
take with you ten loaves, *some* cakes,
and a jar of honey, and go to him; he
will tell you what will become of the
child." 4And Jeroboam's wife did so; she
arose and went to Shiloh, and came to
the house of Ahijah. But Ahijah could
not see, for his eyes were glazed by rea-
son of his age.
5Now the LORD had said to Ahijah,
"Here is the wife of Jeroboam, coming
to ask you something about her son,
for he *is* sick. Thus and thus you shall
say to her; for it will be, when she comes
in, that she will pretend *to be* another
woman."
6And so it was, when Ahijah heard
the sound of her footsteps as she came
through the door, he said, "Come in, wife
of Jeroboam. Why do you pretend *to be*
another *person?* For I *have been* sent
to you *with* bad *news.* 7Go, tell Jerobo-
am, 'Thus says the LORD God of Israel:
"Because I exalted you from among the
people, and made you ruler over My
people Israel, 8and tore the kingdom
away from the house of David, and gave
it to you; and *yet* you have not been as
My servant David, who kept My com-
mandments and who followed Me with
all his heart, to do only *what was* right in
My eyes; 9but you have done more evil
than all who were before you, for you
have gone and made for yourself other
gods and molded images to provoke
Me to anger, and have cast Me behind
your back— 10therefore behold! I will
bring disaster on the house of Jerobo-
am, and will cut off from Jeroboam
every male in Israel, bond and free; I
will take away the remnant of the house

13:32 [a] Literally *houses*

of Jeroboam, as one takes away refuse
until it is all gone. 11The dogs shall eat
whoever belongs to Jeroboam and dies
in the city, and the birds of the air shall
eat whoever dies in the field; for the
LORD has spoken!"' 12Arise therefore,
go to your own house. When your feet
enter the city, the child shall die. 13And
all Israel shall mourn for him and bury
him, for he is the only one of Jeroboam
who shall come to the grave, because
in him there is found something good
toward the LORD God of Israel in the
house of Jeroboam.
14"Moreover the LORD will raise up for
Himself a king over Israel who shall cut
off the house of Jeroboam; this is the
day. What? Even now! 15For the LORD
will strike Israel, as a reed is shaken in
the water. He will uproot Israel from
this good land which He gave to their
fathers, and will scatter them beyond
the River,[a] because they have made
their wooden images,[b] provoking the
LORD to anger. 16And He will give Isra-
el up because of the sins of Jeroboam,
who sinned and who made Israel sin."
17Then Jeroboam's wife arose and de-
parted, and came to Tirzah. When she
came to the threshold of the house, the
child died. 18And they buried him; and
all Israel mourned for him, according
to the word of the LORD which He spoke
through His servant Ahijah the prophet.

Death of Jeroboam

19Now the rest of the acts of Jeroboam,
how he made war and how he reigned,
indeed they *are* written in the book of
the chronicles of the kings of Israel.
20The period that Jeroboam reigned
was twenty-two years. So he rested with
his fathers. Then Nadab his son reigned
in his place.

Rehoboam Reigns in Judah

21And Rehoboam the son of Solomon
reigned in Judah. Rehoboam *was* forty-
one years old when he became king. He
reigned seventeen years in Jerusalem,
the city which the LORD had chosen
out of all the tribes of Israel, to put His
name there. His mother's name *was*
Naamah, an Ammonitess. 22Now Judah
did evil in the sight of the LORD, and
they provoked Him to jealousy with
their sins which they committed, more
than all that their fathers had done.
23For they also built for themselves
high places, *sacred* pillars, and wooden
images on every high hill and under
every green tree. 24And there were also
perverted persons[a] in the land. They
did according to all the abominations
of the nations which the LORD had cast
out before the children of Israel.
25It happened in the fifth year of King
Rehoboam *that* Shishak king of Egypt
came up against Jerusalem. 26And he
took away the treasures of the house of
the LORD and the treasures of the king's
house; he took away everything. He also
took away all the gold shields which Sol-
omon had made. 27Then King Rehobo-
am made bronze shields in their place,
and committed *them* to the hands of
the captains of the guard, who guarded
the doorway of the king's house. 28And
whenever the king entered the house of
the LORD, the guards carried them, then
brought them back into the guardroom.
29Now the rest of the acts of Rehoboam,
and all that he did, *are* they not written
in the book of the chronicles of the kings
of Judah? 30And there was war between
Rehoboam and Jeroboam all *their* days.
31So Rehoboam rested with his fathers,
and was buried with his fathers in the
City of David. His mother's name *was*
Naamah, an Ammonitess. Then Abijam[a]
his son reigned in his place.

Abijam Reigns in Judah

15 In the eighteenth year of King
Jeroboam the son of Nebat,
Abijam became king over Judah. 2He
reigned three years in Jerusalem.
His mother's name *was* Maachah the
granddaughter of Abishalom. 3And he
walked in all the sins of his father, which
he had done before him; his heart was
not loyal to the LORD his God, as was the
heart of his father David. 4Nevertheless
for David's sake the LORD his God gave

14:15 [a] That is, the Euphrates [b] Hebrew *Asherim,* Canaanite deities **14:24** [a] Hebrew *qadesh,* that is, one practicing sodomy and prostitution in religious rituals **14:31** [a] Spelled *Abijah* in 2 Chronicles 12:16ff

him a lamp in Jerusalem, by setting up
his son after him and by establishing
Jerusalem; 5because David did *what*
was right in the eyes of the LORD, and
had not turned aside from anything
that He commanded him all the days
of his life, except in the matter of Uriah
the Hittite. 6And there was war between
Rehoboam[a] and Jeroboam all the days
of his life. 7Now the rest of the acts of
Abijam, and all that he did, *are* they not
written in the book of the chronicles of
the kings of Judah? And there was war
between Abijam and Jeroboam.
8So Abijam rested with his fathers, and
they buried him in the City of David.
Then Asa his son reigned in his place.

Asa Reigns in Judah

9In the twentieth year of Jeroboam
king of Israel, Asa became king over
Judah. 10And he reigned forty-one
years in Jerusalem. His grandmother's
name *was* Maachah the granddaughter
of Abishalom. 11Asa did *what was* right
in the eyes of the LORD, as *did* his father
David. 12And he banished the perverted
persons[a] from the land, and removed
all the idols that his fathers had made.
13Also he removed Maachah his grand-
mother from *being* queen mother, be-
cause she had made an obscene image
of Asherah.[a] And Asa cut down her ob-
scene image and burned *it* by the Brook
Kidron. 14But the high places were not
removed. Nevertheless Asa's heart was
loyal to the LORD all his days. 15He also
brought into the house of the LORD the
things which his father had dedicated,
and the things which he himself had
dedicated: silver and gold and utensils.
16Now there was war between Asa and
Baasha king of Israel all their days.
17And Baasha king of Israel came up
against Judah, and built Ramah, that
he might let none go out or come in
to Asa king of Judah. 18Then Asa took
all the silver and gold *that was* left in
the treasuries of the house of the LORD
and the treasuries of the king's house,
and delivered them into the hand of his
servants. And King Asa sent them to
Ben-Hadad the son of Tabrimmon, the
son of Hezion, king of Syria, who dwelt
in Damascus, saying, 19"*Let there be* a
treaty between you and me, as there
was between my father and your father.
See, I have sent you a present of silver
and gold. Come and break your treaty
with Baasha king of Israel, so that he
will withdraw from me."
20So Ben-Hadad heeded King Asa, and
sent the captains of his armies against
the cities of Israel. He attacked Ijon,
Dan, Abel Beth Maachah, and all Chin-
neroth, with all the land of Naphtali.
21Now it happened, when Baasha heard
it, that he stopped building Ramah, and
remained in Tirzah.
22Then King Asa made a proclamation
throughout all Judah; none *was* exempt-
ed. And they took away the stones and
timber of Ramah, which Baasha had
used for building; and with them King
Asa built Geba of Benjamin, and Mizpah.
23The rest of all the acts of Asa, all his
might, all that he did, and the cities
which he built, *are* they not written in
the book of the chronicles of the kings
of Judah? But in the time of his old age
he was diseased in his feet. 24So Asa
rested with his fathers, and was buried
with his fathers in the City of David
his father. Then Jehoshaphat his son
reigned in his place.

Nadab Reigns in Israel

25Now Nadab the son of Jeroboam be-
came king over Israel in the second year
of Asa king of Judah, and he reigned
over Israel two years. 26And he did evil
in the sight of the LORD, and walked in
the way of his father, and in his sin by
which he had made Israel sin.
27Then Baasha the son of Ahijah, of the
house of Issachar, conspired against
him. And Baasha killed him at Gibbe-
thon, which *belonged* to the Philistines,
while Nadab and all Israel laid siege to
Gibbethon. 28Baasha killed him in the
third year of Asa king of Judah, and
reigned in his place. 29And it was so,
when he became king, *that* he killed all
the house of Jeroboam. He did not leave

15:6 [a] Following Masoretic Text, Septuagint, Targum, and Vulgate; some Hebrew manuscripts and Syriac read *Abijam.* 15:12 [a] Hebrew *qedeshim,* that is, those practicing sodomy and prostitution in religious rituals 15:13 [a] A Canaanite goddess

to Jeroboam anyone that breathed,
until he had destroyed him, according
to the word of the LORD which He had
spoken by His servant Ahijah the Shi-
lonite, 30because of the sins of Jerobo-
am, which he had sinned and by which
he had made Israel sin, because of his
provocation with which he had pro-
voked the LORD God of Israel to anger.
31Now the rest of the acts of Nadab,
and all that he did, *are* they not writ-
ten in the book of the chronicles of the
kings of Israel? 32And there was war
between Asa and Baasha king of Israel
all their days.

Baasha Reigns in Israel

33In the third year of Asa king of
Judah, Baasha the son of Ahijah be-
came king over all Israel in Tirzah, and
reigned twenty-four years. 34He did evil
in the sight of the LORD, and walked in
the way of Jeroboam, and in his sin by
which he had made Israel sin.

16 Then the word of the LORD
came to Jehu the son of Hana-
ni, against Baasha, saying: 2"Inasmuch
as I lifted you out of the dust and made
you ruler over My people Israel, and
you have walked in the way of Jerobo-
am, and have made My people Israel
sin, to provoke Me to anger with their
sins, 3surely I will take away the pos-
terity of Baasha and the posterity of his
house, and I will make your house like
the house of Jeroboam the son of Nebat.
4The dogs shall eat whoever belongs
to Baasha and dies in the city, and the
birds of the air shall eat whoever dies
in the fields."
5Now the rest of the acts of Baasha,
what he did, and his might, *are* they
not written in the book of the chroni-
cles of the kings of Israel? 6So Baasha
rested with his fathers and was buried
in Tirzah. Then Elah his son reigned in
his place.
7And also the word of the LORD came
by the prophet Jehu the son of Hanani
against Baasha and his house, because
of all the evil that he did in the sight of
the LORD in provoking Him to anger
with the work of his hands, in being like
the house of Jeroboam, and because he
killed them.

Elah Reigns in Israel

8In the twenty-sixth year of Asa king of
Judah, Elah the son of Baasha became
king over Israel, *and reigned* two years
in Tirzah. 9Now his servant Zimri, com-
mander of half *his* chariots, conspired
against him as he was in Tirzah drink-
ing himself drunk in the house of Arza,
steward of *his* house in Tirzah. 10And
Zimri went in and struck him and killed
him in the twenty-seventh year of Asa
king of Judah, and reigned in his place.
11Then it came to pass, when he began
to reign, as soon as he was seated on
his throne, *that* he killed all the house-
hold of Baasha; he did not leave him
one male, neither of his relatives nor of
his friends. 12Thus Zimri destroyed all
the household of Baasha, according to
the word of the LORD, which He spoke
against Baasha by Jehu the prophet,
13for all the sins of Baasha and the
sins of Elah his son, by which they had
sinned and by which they had made
Israel sin, in provoking the LORD God
of Israel to anger with their idols.
14Now the rest of the acts of Elah, and all
that he did, *are* they not written in the book
of the chronicles of the kings of Israel?

Zimri Reigns in Israel

15In the twenty-seventh year of Asa king
of Judah, Zimri had reigned in Tirzah sev-
en days. And the people *were* encamped
against Gibbethon, which *belonged* to
the Philistines. 16Now the people *who*
were encamped heard it said, "Zimri has
conspired and also has killed the king."
So all Israel made Omri, the commander
of the army, king over Israel that day in
the camp. 17Then Omri and all Israel with
him went up from Gibbethon, and they
besieged Tirzah. 18And it happened, when
Zimri saw that the city was taken, that he
went into the citadel of the king's house
and burned the king's house down upon
himself with fire, and died, 19because of
the sins which he had committed in doing
evil in the sight of the LORD, in walking in
the way of Jeroboam, and in his sin which
he had committed to make Israel sin.
20Now the rest of the acts of Zimri, and
the treason he committed, *are* they not
written in the book of the chronicles of
the kings of Israel?

Omri Reigns in Israel

21 Then the people of Israel were divid-
ed into two parts: half of the people fol-
lowed Tibni the son of Ginath, to make
him king, and half followed Omri. 22 But
the people who followed Omri prevailed
over the people who followed Tibni the
son of Ginath. So Tibni died and Omri
reigned. 23 In the thirty-first year of Asa
king of Judah, Omri became king over
Israel, *and reigned* twelve years. Six
years he reigned in Tirzah. 24 And he
bought the hill of Samaria from She-
mer for two talents of silver; then he
built on the hill, and called the name of
the city which he built, Samaria, after
the name of Shemer, owner of the hill.
25 Omri did evil in the eyes of the LORD,
and did worse than all who *were* before
him. 26 For he walked in all the ways of
Jeroboam the son of Nebat, and in his
sin by which he had made Israel sin,
provoking the LORD God of Israel to
anger with their idols.

27 Now the rest of the acts of Omri
which he did, and the might that he
showed, *are* they not written in the book
of the chronicles of the kings of Israel?
28 So Omri rested with his fathers and
was buried in Samaria. Then Ahab his
son reigned in his place.

Ahab Reigns in Israel

29 In the thirty-eighth year of Asa king
of Judah, Ahab the son of Omri became
king over Israel; and Ahab the son of
Omri reigned over Israel in Samar-
ia twenty-two years. 30 Now Ahab the
son of Omri did evil in the sight of the
LORD, more than all who *were* before
him. 31 And it came to pass, as though
it had been a trivial thing for him to
walk in the sins of Jeroboam the son
of Nebat, that he took as wife Jezebel
the daughter of Ethbaal, king of the Si-
donians; and he went and served Baal
and worshiped him. 32 Then he set up
an altar for Baal in the temple of Baal,
which he had built in Samaria. 33 And
Ahab made a wooden image.[a] Ahab
did more to provoke the LORD God of
Israel to anger than all the kings of Is-
rael who were before him. 34 In his days
Hiel of Bethel built Jericho. He laid its
foundation with Abiram his firstborn,
and with his youngest *son* Segub he set
up its gates, according to the word of the
LORD, which He had spoken through
Joshua the son of Nun.[a]

Elijah Proclaims a Drought

17 And Elijah the Tishbite, of the
inhabitants of Gilead, said to
Ahab, "*As* the LORD God of Israel lives,
before whom I stand, there shall not
be dew nor rain these years, except at
my word."

2 Then the word of the LORD came to
him, saying, 3 "Get away from here and
turn eastward, and hide by the Brook
Cherith, which flows into the Jordan.
4 And it will be *that* you shall drink from
the brook, and I have commanded the
ravens to feed you there."

5 So he went and did according to
the word of the LORD, for he went and
stayed by the Brook Cherith, which
flows into the Jordan. 6 The ravens
brought him bread and meat in the
morning, and bread and meat in the
evening; and he drank from the brook.
7 And it happened after a while that the
brook dried up, because there had been
no rain in the land.

Elijah and the Widow

8 Then the word of the LORD came to
him, saying, 9 "Arise, go to Zarephath,
which *belongs* to Sidon, and dwell there.
See, I have commanded a widow there
to provide for you." 10 So he arose and
went to Zarephath. And when he came
to the gate of the city, indeed a wid-
ow *was* there gathering sticks. And he
called to her and said, "Please bring
me a little water in a cup, that I may
drink." 11 And as she was going to get *it,*
he called to her and said, "Please bring
me a morsel of bread in your hand."

12 So she said, "As the LORD your God
lives, I do not have bread, only a hand-
ful of flour in a bin, and a little oil in a
jar; and see, I *am* gathering a couple
of sticks that I may go in and prepare
it for myself and my son, that we may
eat it, and die."

16:33 [a] Hebrew *Asherah,* a Canaanite goddess **16:34** [a] Compare Joshua 6:26

13And Elijah said to her, "Do not fear; go *and* do as you have said, but make me a small cake from it first, and bring *it* to me; and afterward make *some* for yourself and your son. 14For thus says the LORD God of Israel: 'The bin of flour shall not be used up, nor shall the jar of oil run dry, until the day the LORD sends rain on the earth.' "

15So she went away and did according to the word of Elijah; and she and he and her household ate for *many* days. 16The bin of flour was not used up, nor did the jar of oil run dry, according to the word of the LORD which He spoke by Elijah.

Elijah Revives the Widow's Son

17Now it happened after these things *that* the son of the woman who owned the house became sick. And his sickness was so serious that there was no breath left in him. 18So she said to Elijah, "What have I to do with you, O man of God? Have you come to me to bring my sin to remembrance, and to kill my son?"

19And he said to her, "Give me your son." So he took him out of her arms and carried him to the upper room where he was staying, and laid him on his own bed. 20Then he cried out to the LORD and said, "O LORD my God, have You also brought tragedy on the widow with whom I lodge, by killing her son?" 21And he stretched himself out on the child three times, and cried out to the LORD and said, "O LORD my God, I pray, let this child's soul come back to him." 22Then the LORD heard the voice of Elijah; and the soul of the child came back to him, and he revived.

23And Elijah took the child and brought him down from the upper room into the house, and gave him to his mother. And Elijah said, "See, your son lives!"

24Then the woman said to Elijah, "Now by this I know that you *are* a man of God, *and* that the word of the LORD in your mouth *is* the truth."

Elijah's Message to Ahab

18 And it came to pass *after* many days that the word of the LORD came to Elijah, in the third year, saying, "Go, present yourself to Ahab, and I will send rain on the earth."

2So Elijah went to present himself to Ahab; and *there was* a severe famine in Samaria. 3And Ahab had called Obadiah, who *was* in charge of *his* house. (Now Obadiah feared the LORD greatly. 4For so it was, while Jezebel massacred the prophets of the LORD, that Obadiah had taken one hundred prophets and hidden them, fifty to a cave, and had fed them with bread and water.) 5And Ahab had said to Obadiah, "Go into the land to all the springs of water and to all the brooks; perhaps we may find grass to keep the horses and mules alive, so that we will not have to kill any livestock." 6So they divided the land between them to explore it; Ahab went one way by himself, and Obadiah went another way by himself.

7Now as Obadiah was on his way, suddenly Elijah met him; and he recognized him, and fell on his face, and said, "*Is* that you, my lord Elijah?"

8And he answered him, "*It is* I. Go, tell your master, 'Elijah *is here.*' "

9So he said, "How have I sinned, that you are delivering your servant into the hand of Ahab, to kill me? 10*As* the LORD your God lives, there is no nation or kingdom where my master has not sent someone to hunt for you; and when they said, '*He is* not *here,*' he took an oath from the kingdom or nation that they could not find you. 11And now you say, 'Go, tell your master, "Elijah *is here*" '! 12And it shall come to pass, *as soon as* I am gone from you, that the Spirit of the LORD will carry you to a place I do not know; so when I go and tell Ahab, and he cannot find you, he will kill me. But I your servant have feared the LORD from my youth. 13Was it not reported to my lord what I did when Jezebel killed the prophets of the LORD, how I hid one hundred men of the LORD's prophets, fifty to a cave, and fed them with bread and water? 14And now you say, 'Go, tell your master, "Elijah *is here.*" ' He will kill me!"

15Then Elijah said, "As the LORD of hosts lives, before whom I stand, I will surely present myself to him today."

16So Obadiah went to meet Ahab, and told him; and Ahab went to meet Elijah.

17Then it happened, when Ahab saw Elijah, that Ahab said to him, "*Is that* you, O troubler of Israel?"

18 And he answered, "I have not trou-
bled Israel, but you and your father's
house *have,* in that you have forsaken
the commandments of the LORD and
have followed the Baals. 19 Now there-
fore, send *and* gather all Israel to me
on Mount Carmel, the four hundred
and fifty prophets of Baal, and the four
hundred prophets of Asherah,[a] who eat
at Jezebel's table."

Elijah's Mount Carmel Victory

20 So Ahab sent for all the children
of Israel, and gathered the prophets
together on Mount Carmel. 21 And Elijah
came to all the people, and said, "How
long will you falter between two opin-
ions? If the LORD *is* God, follow Him;
but if Baal, follow him." But the peo-
ple answered him not a word. 22 Then
Elijah said to the people, "I alone am
left a prophet of the LORD; but Baal's
prophets *are* four hundred and fifty
men. 23 Therefore let them give us two
bulls; and let them choose one bull for
themselves, cut it in pieces, and lay *it* on
the wood, but put no fire *under it;* and I
will prepare the other bull, and lay *it* on
the wood, but put no fire *under it.* 24 Then
you call on the name of your gods, and
I will call on the name of the LORD; and
the God who answers by fire, He is God."
So all the people answered and said,
"It is well spoken."
25 Now Elijah said to the prophets of
Baal, "Choose one bull for yourselves
and prepare *it* first, for you *are* many;
and call on the name of your god, but
put no fire *under it.*"
26 So they took the bull which was given
them, and they prepared *it,* and called
on the name of Baal from morning even
till noon, saying, "O Baal, hear us!" But
there was no voice; no one answered.
Then they leaped about the altar which
they had made.
27 And so it was, at noon, that Elijah
mocked them and said, "Cry aloud, for
he *is* a god; either he is meditating, or he
is busy, or he is on a journey, *or* perhaps
he is sleeping and must be awakened."
28 So they cried aloud, and cut them-
selves, as was their custom, with knives
and lances, until the blood gushed out
on them. 29 And when midday was past,
they prophesied until the *time* of the
offering of the *evening* sacrifice. But
there was no voice; no one answered,
no one paid attention.
30 Then Elijah said to all the people,
"Come near to me." So all the people
came near to him. And he repaired
the altar of the LORD *that was* broken
down. 31 And Elijah took twelve stones,
according to the number of the tribes
of the sons of Jacob, to whom the word
of the LORD had come, saying, "Israel
shall be your name."[a] 32 Then with the
stones he built an altar in the name
of the LORD; and he made a trench
around the altar large enough to hold
two seahs of seed. 33 And he put the
wood in order, cut the bull in pieces,
and laid *it* on the wood, and said, "Fill
four waterpots with water, and pour *it*
on the burnt sacrifice and on the wood."
34 Then he said, "Do *it* a second time,"
and they did *it* a second time; and he
said, "Do *it* a third time," and they did
it a third time. 35 So the water ran all
around the altar; and he also filled the
trench with water.
36 And it came to pass, at *the time of*
the offering of the *evening* sacrifice,
that Elijah the prophet came near and
said, "LORD God of Abraham, Isaac, and
Israel, let it be known this day that You
are God in Israel and I *am* Your servant,
and *that* I have done all these things at
Your word. 37 Hear me, O LORD, hear me,
that this people may know that You *are*
the LORD God, and *that* You have turned
their hearts back *to You* again."
38 Then the fire of the LORD fell and
consumed the burnt sacrifice, and the
wood and the stones and the dust, and
it licked up the water that *was* in the
trench. 39 Now when all the people saw
it, they fell on their faces; and they said,
"The LORD, He *is* God! The LORD, He *is*
God!"
40 And Elijah said to them, "Seize the
prophets of Baal! Do not let one of them
escape!" So they seized them; and Elijah
brought them down to the Brook Kishon
and executed them there.

18:19 [a] A Canaanite goddess **18:31** [a] Genesis 32:28

The Drought Ends

41Then Elijah said to Ahab, "Go up,
eat and drink; for *there is* the sound of
abundance of rain." 42So Ahab went up
to eat and drink. And Elijah went up to
the top of Carmel; then he bowed down
on the ground, and put his face between
his knees, 43and said to his servant, "Go
up now, look toward the sea."

So he went up and looked, and said,
"*There is* nothing." And seven times he
said, "Go again."

44Then it came to pass the seventh
time, that he said, "There is a cloud, as
small as a man's hand, rising out of the
sea!" So he said, "Go up, say to Ahab,
'Prepare *your chariot,* and go down be-
fore the rain stops you.' "

45Now it happened in the meantime
that the sky became black with clouds
and wind, and there was a heavy rain.
So Ahab rode away and went to Jezreel.
46Then the hand of the LORD came upon
Elijah; and he girded up his loins and ran
ahead of Ahab to the entrance of Jezreel.

Elijah Escapes from Jezebel

19 And Ahab told Jezebel all that
Elijah had done, also how he
had executed all the prophets with the
sword. 2Then Jezebel sent a messenger
to Elijah, saying, "So let the gods do *to
me,* and more also, if I do not make
your life as the life of one of them by
tomorrow about this time." 3And when
he saw *that,* he arose and ran for his life,
and went to Beersheba, which *belongs* to
Judah, and left his servant there.

4But he himself went a day's journey
into the wilderness, and came and
sat down under a broom tree. And he
prayed that he might die, and said, "It
is enough! Now, LORD, take my life, for
I *am* no better than my fathers!"

5Then as he lay and slept under a broom
tree, suddenly an angel[a] touched him,
and said to him, "Arise *and* eat." 6Then
he looked, and there by his head *was* a
cake baked on coals, and a jar of water.
So he ate and drank, and lay down again.
7And the angel[a] of the LORD came back
the second time, and touched him, and
said, "Arise *and* eat, because the journey
is too great for you." 8So he arose, and ate
and drank; and he went in the strength
of that food forty days and forty nights
as far as Horeb, the mountain of God.

9And there he went into a cave, and
spent the night in that place; and be-
hold, the word of the LORD *came* to him,
and He said to him, "What are you do-
ing here, Elijah?"

10So he said, "I have been very zealous
for the LORD God of hosts; for the chil-
dren of Israel have forsaken Your cov-
enant, torn down Your altars, and killed
Your prophets with the sword. I alone
am left; and they seek to take my life."

God's Revelation to Elijah

11Then He said, "Go out, and stand
on the mountain before the LORD."
And behold, the LORD passed by, and
a great and strong wind tore into the
mountains and broke the rocks in piec-
es before the LORD, *but* the LORD *was*
not in the wind; and after the wind an
earthquake, *but* the LORD *was* not in the
earthquake; 12and after the earthquake
a fire, *but* the LORD *was* not in the fire;
and after the fire a still small voice.

13So it was, when Elijah heard *it,* that
he wrapped his face in his mantle and
went out and stood in the entrance of the
cave. Suddenly a voice *came* to him, and
said, "What are you doing here, Elijah?"

14And he said, "I have been very zealous
for the LORD God of hosts; because the
children of Israel have forsaken Your cov-
enant, torn down Your altars, and killed
Your prophets with the sword. I alone
am left; and they seek to take my life."

15Then the LORD said to him: "Go, return
on your way to the Wilderness of Damas-
cus; and when you arrive, anoint Haz-
ael *as* king over Syria. 16Also you shall
anoint Jehu the son of Nimshi *as* king
over Israel. And Elisha the son of Sha-
phat of Abel Meholah you shall anoint
as prophet in your place. 17It shall be *that*
whoever escapes the sword of Hazael,
Jehu will kill; and whoever escapes the
sword of Jehu, Elisha will kill. 18Yet I have
reserved seven thousand in Israel, all
whose knees have not bowed to Baal, and
every mouth that has not kissed him."

19:5 [a] Or *Angel* 19:7 [a] Or *Angel*

Elisha Follows Elijah

19So he departed from there, and
found Elisha the son of Shaphat, who
was plowing *with* twelve yoke *of oxen*
before him, and he was with the twelfth.
Then Elijah passed by him and threw his
mantle on him. 20And he left the oxen
and ran after Elijah, and said, "Please
let me kiss my father and my mother,
and *then* I will follow you."
And he said to him, "Go back again,
for what have I done to you?"
21So *Elisha* turned back from him, and
took a yoke of oxen and slaughtered
them and boiled their flesh, using the
oxen's equipment, and gave it to the
people, and they ate. Then he arose and
followed Elijah, and became his servant.

Ahab Defeats the Syrians

20 Now Ben-Hadad the king of Syria
gathered all his forces together;
thirty-two kings *were* with him, with
horses and chariots. And he went up
and besieged Samaria, and made war
against it. 2Then he sent messengers
into the city to Ahab king of Israel, and
said to him, "Thus says Ben-Hadad:
3'Your silver and your gold *are* mine;
your loveliest wives and children are
mine.' "
4And the king of Israel answered and
said, "My lord, O king, just as you say, I
and all that I have *are* yours."
5Then the messengers came back and
said, "Thus speaks Ben-Hadad, saying,
'Indeed I have sent to you, saying, "You
shall deliver to me your silver and your
gold, your wives and your children";
6but I will send my servants to you
tomorrow about this time, and they
shall search your house and the houses
of your servants. And it shall be, *that*
whatever is pleasant in your eyes, they
will put *it* in their hands and take *it.*' "
7So the king of Israel called all the
elders of the land, and said, "Notice,
please, and see how this *man* seeks trou-
ble, for he sent to me for my wives, my
children, my silver, and my gold; and
I did not deny him."
8And all the elders and all the people
said to him, "Do not listen or consent."
9Therefore he said to the messengers
of Ben-Hadad, "Tell my lord the king,
'All that you sent for to your servant
the first time I will do, but this thing I
cannot do.' "
And the messengers departed and
brought back word to him.
10Then Ben-Hadad sent to him and
said, "The gods do so to me, and more
also, if enough dust is left of Samaria
for a handful for each of the people
who follow me."
11So the king of Israel answered and
said, "Tell *him,* 'Let not the one who
puts on *his armor* boast like the one
who takes *it off.*' "
12And it happened when *Ben-Hadad*
heard this message, as he and the kings
were drinking at the command post,
that he said to his servants, "Get ready."
And they got ready to attack the city.
13Suddenly a prophet approached
Ahab king of Israel, saying, "Thus says
the LORD: 'Have you seen all this great
multitude? Behold, I will deliver it into
your hand today, and you shall know
that I *am* the LORD.' "
14So Ahab said, "By whom?"
And he said, "Thus says the LORD: 'By
the young leaders of the provinces.' "
Then he said, "Who will set the battle
in order?"
And he answered, "You."
15Then he mustered the young lead-
ers of the provinces, and there were
two hundred and thirty-two; and after
them he mustered all the people, all
the children of Israel—seven thousand.
16So they went out at noon. Meanwhile
Ben-Hadad and the thirty-two kings
helping him were getting drunk at the
command post. 17The young leaders of
the provinces went out first. And Ben-
Hadad sent out *a patrol,* and they told
him, saying, "Men are coming out of
Samaria!" 18So he said, "If they have
come out for peace, take them alive;
and if they have come out for war, take
them alive."
19Then these young leaders of the
provinces went out of the city with
the army which followed them. 20And
each one killed his man; so the Syri-
ans fled, and Israel pursued them; and
Ben-Hadad the king of Syria escaped
on a horse with the cavalry. 21Then the
king of Israel went out and attacked

the horses and chariots, and killed the
Syrians with a great slaughter.
22And the prophet came to the king of
Israel and said to him, "Go, strengthen
yourself; take note, and see what you
should do, for in the spring of the year the
king of Syria will come up against you."

The Syrians Again Defeated

23Then the servants of the king of Syria
said to him, "Their gods *are* gods of the
hills. Therefore they were stronger than
we; but if we fight against them in the
plain, surely we will be stronger than
they. 24So do this thing: Dismiss the
kings, each from his position, and put
captains in their places; 25and you shall
muster an army like the army that you
have lost, horse for horse and chariot
for chariot. Then we will fight against
them in the plain; surely we will be
stronger than they."
And he listened to their voice and did so.
26So it was, in the spring of the year,
that Ben-Hadad mustered the Syrians
and went up to Aphek to fight against
Israel. 27And the children of Israel were
mustered and given provisions, and
they went against them. Now the chil-
dren of Israel encamped before them
like two little flocks of goats, while the
Syrians filled the countryside.
28Then a man of God came and spoke
to the king of Israel, and said, "Thus
says the LORD: 'Because the Syrians
have said, "The LORD *is* God of the hills,
but He *is* not God of the valleys," there-
fore I will deliver all this great multitude
into your hand, and you shall know that
I *am* the LORD.' " 29And they encamped
opposite each other for seven days. So it
was that on the seventh day the battle
was joined; and the children of Israel
killed one hundred thousand foot sol-
diers *of* the Syrians in one day. 30But
the rest fled to Aphek, into the city; then
a wall fell on twenty-seven thousand of
the men *who were* left.
And Ben-Hadad fled and went into the
city, into an inner chamber.

Ahab's Treaty with Ben-Hadad

31Then his servants said to him, "Look
now, we have heard that the kings of
the house of Israel *are* merciful kings.
Please, let us put sackcloth around our
waists and ropes around our heads,
and go out to the king of Israel; perhaps
he will spare your life." 32So they wore
sackcloth around their waists and *put*
ropes around their heads, and came to
the king of Israel and said, "Your servant
Ben-Hadad says, 'Please let me live.' "
And he said, "*Is* he still alive? He *is*
my brother."
33Now the men were watching closely
to see whether *any sign of mercy would
come* from him; and they quickly
grasped *at this word* and said, "Your
brother Ben-Hadad."
So he said, "Go, bring him." Then Ben-
Hadad came out to him; and he had
him come up into the chariot.
34So *Ben-Hadad* said to him, "The cities
which my father took from your father
I will restore; and you may set up mar-
ketplaces for yourself in Damascus, as
my father did in Samaria."
Then *Ahab said,* "I will send you away
with this treaty." So he made a treaty
with him and sent him away.

Ahab Condemned

35Now a certain man of the sons of the
prophets said to his neighbor by the
word of the LORD, "Strike me, please."
And the man refused to strike him.
36Then he said to him, "Because you
have not obeyed the voice of the LORD,
surely, as soon as you depart from me, a
lion shall kill you." And as soon as he left
him, a lion found him and killed him.
37And he found another man, and
said, "Strike me, please." So the man
struck him, inflicting a wound. 38Then
the prophet departed and waited for the
king by the road, and disguised himself
with a bandage over his eyes. 39Now as
the king passed by, he cried out to the
king and said, "Your servant went out
into the midst of the battle; and there,
a man came over and brought a man
to me, and said, 'Guard this man; if by
any means he is missing, your life shall
be for his life, or else you shall pay a
talent of silver.' 40While your servant
was busy here and there, he was gone."
Then the king of Israel said to him, "So
shall your judgment *be;* you yourself
have decided *it.*"

41 And he hastened to take the ban-
dage away from his eyes; and the king
of Israel recognized him as one of the
prophets. 42 Then he said to him, "Thus
says the LORD: 'Because you have let
slip out of *your* hand a man whom I ap-
pointed to utter destruction, therefore
your life shall go for his life, and your
people for his people.' "
43 So the king of Israel went to his
house sullen and displeased, and came
to Samaria.

Naboth Is Murdered for His Vineyard

21 And it came to pass after these
things *that* Naboth the Jezreel-
ite had a vineyard which *was* in Jezre-
el, next to the palace of Ahab king of
Samaria. 2 So Ahab spoke to Naboth,
saying, "Give me your vineyard, that
I may have it for a vegetable garden,
because it *is* near, next to my house; and
for it I will give you a vineyard better
than it. *Or,* if it seems good to you, I will
give you its worth in money."
3 But Naboth said to Ahab, "The LORD
forbid that I should give the inheritance
of my fathers to you!"
4 So Ahab went into his house sullen
and displeased because of the word
which Naboth the Jezreelite had spoken
to him; for he had said, "I will not give
you the inheritance of my fathers." And
he lay down on his bed, and turned
away his face, and would eat no food.
5 But Jezebel his wife came to him, and
said to him, "Why is your spirit so sullen
that you eat no food?"
6 He said to her, "Because I spoke to
Naboth the Jezreelite, and said to him,
'Give me your vineyard for money; or
else, if it pleases you, I will give you *an-
other* vineyard for it.' And he answered,
'I will not give you my vineyard.' "
7 Then Jezebel his wife said to him,
"You now exercise authority over Is-
rael! Arise, eat food, and let your heart
be cheerful; I will give you the vineyard
of Naboth the Jezreelite."
8 And she wrote letters in Ahab's
name, sealed *them* with his seal, and
sent the letters to the elders and the
nobles who *were* dwelling in the city
with Naboth. 9 She wrote in the letters,
saying,

Proclaim a fast, and seat Naboth
with high honor among the
people; 10 and seat two men,
scoundrels, before him to bear
witness against him, saying,
"You have blasphemed God and
the king." *Then* take him out, and
stone him, that he may die.

11 So the men of his city, the elders and
nobles who were inhabitants of his city,
did as Jezebel had sent to them, as it
was written in the letters which she had
sent to them. 12 They proclaimed a fast,
and seated Naboth with high honor
among the people. 13 And two men,
scoundrels, came in and sat before him;
and the scoundrels witnessed against
him, against Naboth, in the presence of
the people, saying, "Naboth has blas-
phemed God and the king!" Then they
took him outside the city and stoned
him with stones, so that he died. 14 Then
they sent to Jezebel, saying, "Naboth
has been stoned and is dead."
15 And it came to pass, when Jezebel
heard that Naboth had been stoned
and was dead, that Jezebel said to Ahab,
"Arise, take possession of the vineyard
of Naboth the Jezreelite, which he re-
fused to give you for money; for Naboth
is not alive, but dead." 16 So it was, when
Ahab heard that Naboth was dead, that
Ahab got up and went down to take
possession of the vineyard of Naboth
the Jezreelite.

The LORD Condemns Ahab

17 Then the word of the LORD came to
Elijah the Tishbite, saying, 18 "Arise,
go down to meet Ahab king of Israel,
who *lives* in Samaria. There *he is,* in the
vineyard of Naboth, where he has gone
down to take possession of it. 19 You
shall speak to him, saying, 'Thus says
the LORD: "Have you murdered and
also taken possession?" ' And you shall
speak to him, saying, 'Thus says the
LORD: "In the place where dogs licked
the blood of Naboth, dogs shall lick your
blood, even yours." ' "
20 So Ahab said to Elijah, "Have you
found me, O my enemy?"
And he answered, "I have found *you,*
because you have sold yourself to do

evil in the sight of the LORD: 21'Behold,
I will bring calamity on you. I will take
away your posterity, and will cut off
from Ahab every male in Israel, both
bond and free. 22I will make your house
like the house of Jeroboam the son of
Nebat, and like the house of Baasha the
son of Ahijah, because of the provoca-
tion with which you have provoked *Me*
to anger, and made Israel sin.' 23And
concerning Jezebel the LORD also spoke,
saying, 'The dogs shall eat Jezebel by
the wall[a] of Jezreel.' 24The dogs shall
eat whoever belongs to Ahab and dies
in the city, and the birds of the air shall
eat whoever dies in the field."
25But there was no one like Ahab who
sold himself to do wickedness in the
sight of the LORD, because Jezebel his
wife stirred him up. 26And he behaved
very abominably in following idols,
according to all *that* the Amorites had
done, whom the LORD had cast out be-
fore the children of Israel.
27So it was, when Ahab heard those
words, that he tore his clothes and
put sackcloth on his body, and fasted
and lay in sackcloth, and went about
mourning.
28And the word of the LORD came to
Elijah the Tishbite, saying, 29"See how
Ahab has humbled himself before Me?
Because he has humbled himself before
Me, I will not bring the calamity in his
days. In the days of his son I will bring
the calamity on his house."

Micaiah Warns Ahab

22 Now three years passed without
war between Syria and Israel.
2Then it came to pass, in the third year,
that Jehoshaphat the king of Judah
went down to *visit* the king of Israel.
3And the king of Israel said to his ser-
vants, "Do you know that Ramoth in
Gilead *is* ours, but we hesitate to take
it out of the hand of the king of Syria?"
4So he said to Jehoshaphat, "Will you
go with me to fight at Ramoth Gilead?"
Jehoshaphat said to the king of Is-
rael, "I *am* as you *are,* my people as
your people, my horses as your horses."
5Also Jehoshaphat said to the king of
Israel, "Please inquire for the word of
the LORD today."
6Then the king of Israel gathered the
prophets together, about four hun-
dred men, and said to them, "Shall I
go against Ramoth Gilead to fight, or
shall I refrain?"
So they said, "Go up, for the Lord will
deliver *it* into the hand of the king."
7And Jehoshaphat said, "*Is there* not
still a prophet of the LORD here, that we
may inquire of Him?"[a]
8So the king of Israel said to Jehosha-
phat, "*There is* still one man, Micaiah the
son of Imlah, by whom we may inquire
of the LORD; but I hate him, because he
does not prophesy good concerning
me, but evil."
And Jehoshaphat said, "Let not the
king say such things!"
9Then the king of Israel called an of-
ficer and said, "Bring Micaiah the son
of Imlah quickly!"
10The king of Israel and Jehosha-
phat the king of Judah, having put on
their robes, sat each on his throne, at a
threshing floor at the entrance of the
gate of Samaria; and all the prophets
prophesied before them. 11Now Zede-
kiah the son of Chenaanah had made
horns of iron for himself; and he said,
"Thus says the LORD: 'With these you
shall gore the Syrians until they are
destroyed.' " 12And all the prophets
prophesied so, saying, "Go up to Ra-
moth Gilead and prosper, for the LORD
will deliver *it* into the king's hand."
13Then the messenger who had gone to
call Micaiah spoke to him, saying, "Now
listen, the words of the prophets with
one accord encourage the king. Please,
let your word be like the word of one
of them, and speak encouragement."
14And Micaiah said, "*As* the LORD lives,
whatever the LORD says to me, that I
will speak."
15Then he came to the king; and the
king said to him, "Micaiah, shall we go
to war against Ramoth Gilead, or shall
we refrain?"
And he answered him, "Go and pros-
per, for the LORD will deliver *it* into the
hand of the king!"

21:23 [a] Following Masoretic Text and Septuagint; some Hebrew manuscripts, Syriac, Targum, and Vulgate read *plot of ground* (compare 2 Kings 9:36). **22:7** [a] Or *him*

16So the king said to him, "How many
times shall I make you swear that you
tell me nothing but the truth in the
name of the LORD?"
17Then he said, "I saw all Israel scat-
tered on the mountains, as sheep that
have no shepherd. And the LORD said,
'These have no master. Let each return
to his house in peace.' "
18And the king of Israel said to Jehosh-
aphat, "Did I not tell you he would not
prophesy good concerning me, but evil?"
19Then *Micaiah* said, "Therefore hear the
word of the LORD: I saw the LORD sitting
on His throne, and all the host of heaven
standing by, on His right hand and on
His left. 20And the LORD said, 'Who will
persuade Ahab to go up, that he may
fall at Ramoth Gilead?' So one spoke in
this manner, and another spoke in that
manner. 21Then a spirit came forward
and stood before the LORD, and said, 'I
will persuade him.' 22The LORD said to
him, 'In what way?' So he said, 'I will go
out and be a lying spirit in the mouth
of all his prophets.' And the LORD said,
'You shall persuade *him,* and also prevail.
Go out and do so.' 23Therefore look! The
LORD has put a lying spirit in the mouth
of all these prophets of yours, and the
LORD has declared disaster against you."
24Now Zedekiah the son of Chenaanah
went near and struck Micaiah on the
cheek, and said, "Which way did the
spirit from the LORD go from me to
speak to you?"
25And Micaiah said, "Indeed, you shall
see on that day when you go into an
inner chamber to hide!"
26So the king of Israel said, "Take Mi-
caiah, and return him to Amon the gov-
ernor of the city and to Joash the king's
son; 27and say, 'Thus says the king: "Put
this *fellow* in prison, and feed him with
bread of affliction and water of affliction,
until I come in peace." ' "
28But Micaiah said, "If you ever return
in peace, the LORD has not spoken by me."
And he said, "Take heed, all you people!"

Ahab Dies in Battle

29So the king of Israel and Jehosh-
aphat the king of Judah went up to
Ramoth Gilead. 30And the king of Is-
rael said to Jehoshaphat, "I will disguise
myself and go into battle; but you put
on your robes." So the king of Israel
disguised himself and went into battle.
31Now the king of Syria had command-
ed the thirty-two captains of his chari-
ots, saying, "Fight with no one small or
great, but only with the king of Israel."
32So it was, when the captains of the
chariots saw Jehoshaphat, that they
said, "Surely it *is* the king of Israel!"
Therefore they turned aside to fight
against him, and Jehoshaphat cried
out. 33And it happened, when the cap-
tains of the chariots saw that it *was* not
the king of Israel, that they turned back
from pursuing him. 34Now a *certain*
man drew a bow at random, and struck
the king of Israel between the joints of
his armor. So he said to the driver of his
chariot, "Turn around and take me out
of the battle, for I am wounded."
35The battle increased that day; and
the king was propped up in his chariot,
facing the Syrians, and died at eve-
ning. The blood ran out from the wound
onto the floor of the chariot. 36Then, as
the sun was going down, a shout went
throughout the army, saying, "Every
man to his city, and every man to his
own country!"
37So the king died, and was brought
to Samaria. And they buried the king
in Samaria. 38Then *someone* washed
the chariot at a pool in Samaria, and
the dogs licked up his blood while the
harlots bathed,[a] according to the word
of the LORD which He had spoken.
39Now the rest of the acts of Ahab, and
all that he did, the ivory house which
he built and all the cities that he built,
are they not written in the book of the
chronicles of the kings of Israel? 40So
Ahab rested with his fathers. Then Aha-
ziah his son reigned in his place.

Jehoshaphat Reigns in Judah

41Jehoshaphat the son of Asa had be-
come king over Judah in the fourth year
of Ahab king of Israel. 42Jehoshaphat
was thirty-five years old when he be-
came king, and he reigned twenty-five

22:38 [a] Syriac and Targum read *they washed his armor.*

years in Jerusalem. His mother's name
was Azubah the daughter of Shilhi.
43And he walked in all the ways of his
father Asa. He did not turn aside from
them, doing *what was* right in the eyes
of the LORD. Nevertheless the high plac-
es were not taken away, *for* the people
offered sacrifices and burned incense
on the high places. 44Also Jehoshaphat
made peace with the king of Israel.
45Now the rest of the acts of Jehosh-
aphat, the might that he showed, and
how he made war, *are* they not written in
the book of the chronicles of the kings of
Judah? 46And the rest of the perverted
persons,[a] who remained in the days of
his father Asa, he banished from the
land. 47*There was* then no king in Edom,
only a deputy of the king.
48Jehoshaphat made merchant ships[a]
to go to Ophir for gold; but they never
sailed, for the ships were wrecked at
Ezion Geber. 49Then Ahaziah the son
of Ahab said to Jehoshaphat, "Let my
servants go with your servants in the
ships." But Jehoshaphat would not.
50And Jehoshaphat rested with his
fathers, and was buried with his fathers
in the City of David his father. Then
Jehoram his son reigned in his place.

Ahaziah Reigns in Israel

51Ahaziah the son of Ahab became king
over Israel in Samaria in the seventeenth
year of Jehoshaphat king of Judah, and
reigned two years over Israel. 52He did
evil in the sight of the LORD, and walked
in the way of his father and in the way of
his mother and in the way of Jeroboam
the son of Nebat, who had made Israel
sin; 53for he served Baal and worshiped
him, and provoked the LORD God of Is-
rael to anger, according to all that his
father had done.

22:46 [a] Hebrew *qadesh,* that is, one practicing sodomy and prostitution in religious rituals
22:48 [a] Or *ships of Tarshish*

THE SECOND BOOK OF THE

KINGS

The Book of 2 Kings continues the stories of the evil kings of Israel and evil and good kings of Judah. Despite God's warning through the prophet Elijah, His people continue to disobey Him and worship idols. God sends another prophet named Elisha who also performs miracles and warns the people. But they still do not listen. God is patient, but time is running out for His people to turn from their sin and avoid discipline. In time, the northern kingdom of Israel is defeated by the Assyrians and many of the people are taken into a foreign land. The southern kingdom of Judah lasts longer, but it fails to learn from what happened to Israel. They are defeated by the Babylonians and taken captive, too.

- **GENRE:** History
- **AUTHOR:** Jeremiah, possibly
- **TIME:** c. 851–565 BC (written c. 565–538 BC)
- **PURPOSE:** To show what happened when God's people would not obey Him, did not listen to His prophets, and refused to follow His rules. God is patent, but He will discipline the disobedient.

God Judges Ahaziah

1 Moab rebelled against Israel after
the death of Ahab.
2Now Ahaziah fell through the lattice
of his upper room in Samaria, and was
injured; so he sent messengers and said
to them, "Go, inquire of Baal-Zebub, the
god of Ekron, whether I shall recover
from this injury." 3But the angel[a] of the
LORD said to Elijah the Tishbite, "Arise,
go up to meet the messengers of the
king of Samaria, and say to them, '*Is
it* because *there is* no God in Israel *that*
you are going to inquire of Baal-Zebub,
the god of Ekron?' 4Now therefore, thus
says the LORD: 'You shall not come
down from the bed to which you have
gone up, but you shall surely die.'" So
Elijah departed.
5And when the messengers returned
to him, he said to them, "Why have you
come back?"
6So they said to him, "A man came up
to meet us, and said to us, 'Go, return to
the king who sent you, and say to him,
"Thus says the LORD: '*Is it* because *there
is* no God in Israel *that* you are sending
to inquire of Baal-Zebub, the god of
Ekron? Therefore you shall not come
down from the bed to which you have
gone up, but you shall surely die.'"'"
7Then he said to them, "What kind of
man *was it* who came up to meet you
and told you these words?"
8So they answered him, "A hairy man
wearing a leather belt around his waist."
And he said, "It *is* Elijah the Tishbite."
9Then the king sent to him a captain
of fifty with his fifty men. So he went up
to him; and there he was, sitting on the
top of a hill. And he spoke to him: "Man
of God, the king has said, 'Come down!'"
10So Elijah answered and said to the
captain of fifty, "If I *am* a man of God,
then let fire come down from heaven and
consume you and your fifty men." And fire
came down from heaven and consumed
him and his fifty. 11Then he sent to him
another captain of fifty with his fifty men.
And he answered and said to him:
"Man of God, thus has the king said,
'Come down quickly!'"
12So Elijah answered and said to them,
"If I *am* a man of God, let fire come down
from heaven and consume you and
your fifty men." And the fire of God
came down from heaven and consumed
him and his fifty.

1:3 a Or *Angel*

13Again, he sent a third captain of fifty
with his fifty men. And the third captain
of fifty went up, and came and fell on
his knees before Elijah, and pleaded
with him, and said to him: "Man of God,
please let my life and the life of these
fifty servants of yours be precious in
your sight. 14Look, fire has come down
from heaven and burned up the first two
captains of fifties with their fifties. But let
my life now be precious in your sight."

15And the angel[a] of the LORD said to
Elijah, "Go down with him; do not be
afraid of him." So he arose and went
down with him to the king. 16Then he
said to him, "Thus says the LORD: 'Be-
cause you have sent messengers to in-
quire of Baal-Zebub, the god of Ekron,
is it because *there is* no God in Israel
to inquire of His word? Therefore you
shall not come down from the bed to
which you have gone up, but you shall
surely die.' "

17So *Ahaziah* died according to the
word of the LORD which Elijah had spo-
ken. Because he had no son, Jehoram[a]
became king in his place, in the second
year of Jehoram the son of Jehosha-
phat, king of Judah.

18Now the rest of the acts of Ahaziah
which he did, *are* they not written in
the book of the chronicles of the kings
of Israel?

Elijah Ascends to Heaven

2 And it came to pass, when the LORD
was about to take up Elijah into
heaven by a whirlwind, that Elijah went
with Elisha from Gilgal. 2Then Elijah
said to Elisha, "Stay here, please, for the
LORD has sent me on to Bethel."

But Elisha said, "*As* the LORD lives, and
as your soul lives, I will not leave you!"
So they went down to Bethel.

3Now the sons of the prophets who
were at Bethel came out to Elisha, and
said to him, "Do you know that the LORD
will take away your master from over
you today?"

And he said, "Yes, I know; keep silent!"
4Then Elijah said to him, "Elisha, stay
here, please, for the LORD has sent me
on to Jericho."

But he said, "*As* the LORD lives, and *as*
your soul lives, I will not leave you!" So
they came to Jericho.

5Now the sons of the prophets who
were at Jericho came to Elisha and said
to him, "Do you know that the LORD
will take away your master from over
you today?"

So he answered, "Yes, I know; keep
silent!"

6Then Elijah said to him, "Stay here,
please, for the LORD has sent me on to
the Jordan."

But he said, "*As* the LORD lives, and *as*
your soul lives, I will not leave you!" So
the two of them went on. 7And fifty men
of the sons of the prophets went and
stood facing *them* at a distance, while
the two of them stood by the Jordan.
8Now Elijah took his mantle, rolled *it*
up, and struck the water; and it was
divided this way and that, so that the
two of them crossed over on dry ground.

9And so it was, when they had crossed
over, that Elijah said to Elisha, "Ask!
What may I do for you, before I am
taken away from you?"

Elisha said, "Please let a double por-
tion of your spirit be upon me."

10So he said, "You have asked a hard
thing. *Nevertheless,* if you see me *when
I am* taken from you, it shall be so for
you; but if not, it shall not be *so.*" 11Then
it happened, as they continued on and
talked, that suddenly a chariot of fire
appeared with horses of fire, and sepa-
rated the two of them; and Elijah went
up by a whirlwind into heaven.

12And Elisha saw *it,* and he cried out,
"My father, my father, the chariot of
Israel and its horsemen!" So he saw
him no more. And he took hold of his
own clothes and tore them into two
pieces. 13He also took up the mantle
of Elijah that had fallen from him, and
went back and stood by the bank of the
Jordan. 14Then he took the mantle of
Elijah that had fallen from him, and
struck the water, and said, "Where *is*
the LORD God of Elijah?" And when
he also had struck the water, it was
divided this way and that; and Elisha
crossed over.

1:15 [a] Or *Angel* 1:17 [a] The son of Ahab king of Israel (compare 3:1)

15Now when the sons of the prophets
who *were* from Jericho saw him, they
said, "The spirit of Elijah rests on Elisha."
And they came to meet him, and bowed
to the ground before him. 16Then they
said to him, "Look now, there are fifty
strong men with your servants. Please
let them go and search for your master,
lest perhaps the Spirit of the LORD has
taken him up and cast him upon some
mountain or into some valley."

And he said, "You shall not send any-
one."

17But when they urged him till he
was ashamed, he said, "Send *them!*"
Therefore they sent fifty men, and they
searched for three days but did not find
him. 18And when they came back to
him, for he had stayed in Jericho, he
said to them, "Did I not say to you, 'Do
not go'?"

Elisha Performs Miracles

19Then the men of the city said to Eli-
sha, "Please notice, the situation of this
city *is* pleasant, as my lord sees; but the
water *is* bad, and the ground barren."

20And he said, "Bring me a new bowl,
and put salt in it." So they brought *it* to
him. 21Then he went out to the source of
the water, and cast in the salt there, and
said, "Thus says the LORD: 'I have healed
this water; from it there shall be no more
death or barrenness.' " 22So the water
remains healed to this day, according
to the word of Elisha which he spoke.

23Then he went up from there to Beth-
el; and as he was going up the road,
some youths came from the city and
mocked him, and said to him, "Go up,
you baldhead! Go up, you baldhead!"

24So he turned around and looked
at them, and pronounced a curse on
them in the name of the LORD. And two
female bears came out of the woods and
mauled forty-two of the youths.

25Then he went from there to Mount
Carmel, and from there he returned to
Samaria.

Moab Rebels Against Israel

3 Now Jehoram the son of Ahab be-
came king over Israel at Samaria
in the eighteenth year of Jehoshaphat
king of Judah, and reigned twelve years.
2And he did evil in the sight of the LORD,
but not like his father and mother; for
he put away the *sacred* pillar of Baal
that his father had made. 3Nevertheless
he persisted in the sins of Jeroboam the
son of Nebat, who had made Israel sin;
he did not depart from them.

4Now Mesha king of Moab was a sheep-
breeder, and he regularly paid the king
of Israel one hundred thousand lambs
and the wool of one hundred thousand
rams. 5But it happened, when Ahab
died, that the king of Moab rebelled
against the king of Israel.

6So King Jehoram went out of Sa-
maria at that time and mustered all
Israel. 7Then he went and sent to Je-
hoshaphat king of Judah, saying, "The
king of Moab has rebelled against me.
Will you go with me to fight against
Moab?"

And he said, "I will go up; I *am* as you
are, my people as your people, my
horses as your horses." 8Then he said,
"Which way shall we go up?"

And he answered, "By way of the Wil-
derness of Edom."

9So the king of Israel went with the
king of Judah and the king of Edom, and
they marched on that roundabout route
seven days; and there was no water
for the army, nor for the animals that
followed them. 10And the king of Isra-
el said, "Alas! For the LORD has called
these three kings together to deliver
them into the hand of Moab."

11But Jehoshaphat said, "*Is there* no
prophet of the LORD here, that we may
inquire of the LORD by him?"

So one of the servants of the king of Is-
rael answered and said, "Elisha the son
of Shaphat *is* here, who poured water
on the hands of Elijah."

12And Jehoshaphat said, "The word
of the LORD is with him." So the king of
Israel and Jehoshaphat and the king
of Edom went down to him.

13Then Elisha said to the king of Is-
rael, "What have I to do with you? Go
to the prophets of your father and the
prophets of your mother."

But the king of Israel said to him, "No,
for the LORD has called these three
kings *together* to deliver them into the
hand of Moab."

14And Elisha said, "As the LORD of
hosts lives, before whom I stand, surely
were it not that I regard the presence
of Jehoshaphat king of Judah, I would
not look at you, nor see you. 15But now
bring me a musician."
Then it happened, when the musician
played, that the hand of the LORD came
upon him. 16And he said, "Thus says the
LORD: 'Make this valley full of ditches.'
17For thus says the LORD: 'You shall not
see wind, nor shall you see rain; yet that
valley shall be filled with water, so that
you, your cattle, and your animals may
drink.' 18And this is a simple matter
in the sight of the LORD; He will also
deliver the Moabites into your hand.
19Also you shall attack every fortified
city and every choice city, and shall
cut down every good tree, and stop up
every spring of water, and ruin every
good piece of land with stones."
20Now it happened in the morning,
when the grain offering was offered,
that suddenly water came by way of
Edom, and the land was filled with wa-
ter.
21And when all the Moabites heard
that the kings had come up to fight
against them, all who were able to bear
arms and older were gathered; and they
stood at the border. 22Then they rose up
early in the morning, and the sun was
shining on the water; and the Moabites
saw the water on the other side *as* red as
blood. 23And they said, "This is blood;
the kings have surely struck swords and
have killed one another; now therefore,
Moab, to the spoil!"
24So when they came to the camp of
Israel, Israel rose up and attacked the
Moabites, so that they fled before them;
and they entered *their* land, killing the
Moabites. 25Then they destroyed the
cities, and each man threw a stone on
every good piece of land and filled it;
and they stopped up all the springs of
water and cut down all the good trees.
But they left the stones of Kir Haraseth
intact. However the slingers surrounded
and attacked it.
26And when the king of Moab saw that
the battle was too fierce for him, he took
with him seven hundred men who drew
swords, to break through to the king
of Edom, but they could not. 27Then
he took his eldest son who would have
reigned in his place, and offered him
as a burnt offering upon the wall; and
there was great indignation against
Israel. So they departed from him and
returned to *their own* land.

Elisha and the Widow's Oil

4 A certain woman of the wives of
the sons of the prophets cried out
to Elisha, saying, "Your servant my
husband is dead, and you know that
your servant feared the LORD. And the
creditor is coming to take my two sons
to be his slaves."
2So Elisha said to her, "What shall I do
for you? Tell me, what do you have in
the house?" And she said, "Your maid-
servant has nothing in the house but
a jar of oil."
3Then he said, "Go, borrow vessels from
everywhere, from all your neighbors—
empty vessels; do not gather just a few.
4And when you have come in, you shall
shut the door behind you and your sons;
then pour it into all those vessels, and
set aside the full ones."
5So she went from him and shut the
door behind her and her sons, who
brought *the vessels* to her; and she
poured *it* out. 6Now it came to pass,
when the vessels were full, that she said
to her son, "Bring me another vessel."
And he said to her, "*There is* not anoth-
er vessel." So the oil ceased. 7Then she
came and told the man of God. And he
said, "Go, sell the oil and pay your debt;
and you *and* your sons live on the rest."

Elisha Raises the Shunammite's Son

8Now it happened one day that Eli-
sha went to Shunem, where there *was*
a notable woman, and she persuaded
him to eat some food. So it was, as often
as he passed by, he would turn in there
to eat some food. 9And she said to her
husband, "Look now, I know that this
is a holy man of God, who passes by
us regularly. 10Please, let us make a
small upper room on the wall; and let
us put a bed for him there, and a table
and a chair and a lampstand; so it will
be, whenever he comes to us, he can
turn in there."

11And it happened one day that he
came there, and he turned in to the
upper room and lay down there. 12Then
he said to Gehazi his servant, "Call this
Shunammite woman." When he had
called her, she stood before him. 13And
he said to him, "Say now to her, 'Look,
you have been concerned for us with
all this care. What *can I* do for you? Do
you want me to speak on your behalf
to the king or to the commander of the
army?' "
She answered, "I dwell among my own
people."
14So he said, "What then *is* to be done
for her?"
And Gehazi answered, "Actually, she
has no son, and her husband is old."
15So he said, "Call her." When he had
called her, she stood in the doorway.
16Then he said, "About this time next
year you shall embrace a son."
And she said, "No, my lord. Man of
God, do not lie to your maidservant!"
17But the woman conceived, and bore a
son when the appointed time had come,
of which Elisha had told her.
18And the child grew. Now it happened
one day that he went out to his father, to
the reapers. 19And he said to his father,
"My head, my head!"
So he said to a servant, "Carry him to
his mother." 20When he had taken him
and brought him to his mother, he sat
on her knees till noon, and *then* died.
21And she went up and laid him on the
bed of the man of God, shut *the door*
upon him, and went out. 22Then she
called to her husband, and said, "Please
send me one of the young men and one
of the donkeys, that I may run to the
man of God and come back."
23So he said, "Why are you going to
him today? *It is* neither the New Moon
nor the Sabbath."
And she said, "*It is* well." 24Then she
saddled a donkey, and said to her ser-
vant, "Drive, and go forward; do not
slacken the pace for me unless I tell
you." 25And so she departed, and went
to the man of God at Mount Carmel.
So it was, when the man of God saw
her afar off, that he said to his servant
Gehazi, "Look, the Shunammite woman!
26Please run now to meet her, and say
to her, '*Is it* well with you? *Is it* well with
your husband? *Is it* well with the child?' "
And she answered, "*It is* well." 27Now
when she came to the man of God at the
hill, she caught him by the feet, but Geha-
zi came near to push her away. But the
man of God said, "Let her alone; for her
soul *is* in deep distress, and the LORD has
hidden *it* from me, and has not told me."
28So she said, "Did I ask a son of my
lord? Did I not say, 'Do not deceive me'?"
29Then he said to Gehazi, "Get yourself
ready, and take my staff in your hand,
and be on your way. If you meet any-
one, do not greet him; and if anyone
greets you, do not answer him; but lay
my staff on the face of the child."
30And the mother of the child said,
"*As* the LORD lives, and *as* your soul
lives, I will not leave you." So he arose
and followed her. 31Now Gehazi went
on ahead of them, and laid the staff
on the face of the child; but *there was*
neither voice nor hearing. Therefore he
went back to meet him, and told him,
saying, "The child has not awakened."
32When Elisha came into the house,
there was the child, lying dead on his
bed. 33He went in therefore, shut the
door behind the two of them, and prayed
to the LORD. 34And he went up and lay
on the child, and put his mouth on his
mouth, his eyes on his eyes, and his
hands on his hands; and he stretched
himself out on the child, and the flesh of
the child became warm. 35He returned
and walked back and forth in the house,
and again went up and stretched himself
out on him; then the child sneezed seven
times, and the child opened his eyes.
36And he called Gehazi and said, "Call
this Shunammite woman." So he called
her. And when she came in to him, he
said, "Pick up your son." 37So she went in,
fell at his feet, and bowed to the ground;
then she picked up her son and went out.

Elisha Purifies the Pot of Stew

38And Elisha returned to Gilgal, and
there was a famine in the land. Now the
sons of the prophets *were* sitting before
him; and he said to his servant, "Put on
the large pot, and boil stew for the sons
of the prophets." 39So one went out into
the field to gather herbs, and found a

wild vine, and gathered from it a lapful
of wild gourds, and came and sliced
them into the pot of stew, though they
did not know *what they were.* 40Then
they served it to the men to eat. Now
it happened, as they were eating the
stew, that they cried out and said, "Man
of God, *there is* death in the pot!" And
they could not eat *it.*
41So he said, "Then bring some flour."
And he put *it* into the pot, and said,
"Serve *it* to the people, that they may
eat." And there was nothing harmful
in the pot.

Elisha Feeds One Hundred Men

42Then a man came from Baal Shali-
sha, and brought the man of God bread
of the firstfruits, twenty loaves of barley
bread, and newly ripened grain in his
knapsack. And he said, "Give *it* to the
people, that they may eat."
43But his servant said, "What? Shall
I set this before one hundred men?"
He said again, "Give it to the people,
that they may eat; for thus says the
LORD: 'They shall eat and have *some*
left over.' " 44So he set *it* before them;
and they ate and had *some* left over,
according to the word of the LORD.

Naaman's Leprosy Healed

5 Now Naaman, commander of the
army of the king of Syria, was a
great and honorable man in the eyes
of his master, because by him the LORD
had given victory to Syria. He was also
a mighty man of valor, *but* a leper. 2And
the Syrians had gone out on raids, and
had brought back captive a young girl
from the land of Israel. She waited on
Naaman's wife. 3Then she said to her
mistress, "If only my master *were* with
the prophet who *is* in Samaria! For he
would heal him of his leprosy." 4And
Naaman went in and told his master,
saying, "Thus and thus said the girl who
is from the land of Israel."
5Then the king of Syria said, "Go now,
and I will send a letter to the king of
Israel."
So he departed and took with him ten
talents of silver, six thousand *shekels*
of gold, and ten changes of clothing.
6Then he brought the letter to the king
of Israel, which said,

> Now be advised, when this letter
> comes to you, that I have sent
> Naaman my servant to you, that
> you may heal him of his leprosy.

7And it happened, when the king of Isra-
el read the letter, that he tore his clothes
and said, "*Am* I God, to kill and make
alive, that this man sends a man to me
to heal him of his leprosy? Therefore
please consider, and see how he seeks
a quarrel with me."
8So it was, when Elisha the man of God
heard that the king of Israel had torn
his clothes, that he sent to the king, say-
ing, "Why have you torn your clothes?
Please let him come to me, and he shall
know that there is a prophet in Israel."
9Then Naaman went with his horses
and chariot, and he stood at the door of
Elisha's house. 10And Elisha sent a mes-
senger to him, saying, "Go and wash in
the Jordan seven times, and your flesh
shall be restored to you, and *you shall* be
clean." 11But Naaman became furious,
and went away and said, "Indeed, I said
to myself, 'He will surely come out *to me,*
and stand and call on the name of the
LORD his God, and wave his hand over
the place, and heal the leprosy.' 12*Are*
not the Abanah[a] and the Pharpar, the
rivers of Damascus, better than all the
waters of Israel? Could I not wash in
them and be clean?" So he turned and
went away in a rage. 13And his servants
came near and spoke to him, and said,
"My father, *if* the prophet had told you
to do something great, would you not
have done *it?* How much more then,
when he says to you, 'Wash, and be
clean'?" 14So he went down and dipped
seven times in the Jordan, according
to the saying of the man of God; and
his flesh was restored like the flesh of
a little child, and he was clean.
15And he returned to the man of God,
he and all his aides, and came and stood
before him; and he said, "Indeed, now
I know that *there is* no God in all the

5:12 [a] Following Kethib, Septuagint, and Vulgate; Qere, Syriac, and Targum read *Amanah.*

earth, except in Israel; now therefore,
please take a gift from your servant."
16But he said, "*As* the LORD lives, before
whom I stand, I will receive nothing." And
he urged him to take *it,* but he refused.
17So Naaman said, "Then, if not, please
let your servant be given two mule-
loads of earth; for your servant will no
longer offer either burnt offering or
sacrifice to other gods, but to the LORD.
18Yet in this thing may the LORD pardon
your servant: when my master goes into
the temple of Rimmon to worship there,
and he leans on my hand, and I bow
down in the temple of Rimmon—when
I bow down in the temple of Rimmon,
may the LORD please pardon your ser-
vant in this thing."
19Then he said to him, "Go in peace." So
he departed from him a short distance.

Gehazi's Greed

20But Gehazi, the servant of Elisha
the man of God, said, "Look, my master
has spared Naaman this Syrian, while
not receiving from his hands what he
brought; but *as* the LORD lives, I will
run after him and take something from
him." 21So Gehazi pursued Naaman.
When Naaman saw *him* running after
him, he got down from the chariot to
meet him, and said, "*Is* all well?"
22And he said, "All *is* well. My mas-
ter has sent me, saying, 'Indeed, just
now two young men of the sons of the
prophets have come to me from the
mountains of Ephraim. Please give
them a talent of silver and two changes
of garments.' "
23So Naaman said, "Please, take two
talents." And he urged him, and bound
two talents of silver in two bags, with
two changes of garments, and handed
them to two of his servants; and they
carried *them* on ahead of him. 24When
he came to the citadel, he took *them*
from their hand, and stored *them* away
in the house; then he let the men go, and
they departed. 25Now he went in and
stood before his master. Elisha said to
him, "Where *did you go,* Gehazi?"
And he said, "Your servant did not go
anywhere."
26Then he said to him, "Did not my heart
go *with you* when the man turned back
from his chariot to meet you? *Is it* time
to receive money and to receive cloth-
ing, olive groves and vineyards, sheep
and oxen, male and female servants?
27Therefore the leprosy of Naaman shall
cling to you and your descendants for-
ever." And he went out from his presence
leprous, *as white* as snow.

The Floating Ax Head

6 And the sons of the prophets said to
Elisha, "See now, the place where we
dwell with you is too small for us. 2Please,
let us go to the Jordan, and let every man
take a beam from there, and let us make
there a place where we may dwell."
So he answered, "Go."
3Then one said, "Please consent to go
with your servants."
And he answered, "I will go." 4So he
went with them. And when they came
to the Jordan, they cut down trees. 5But
as one was cutting down a tree, the iron
ax head fell into the water; and he cried
out and said, "Alas, master! For it was
borrowed."
6So the man of God said, "Where did it
fall?" And he showed him the place. So
he cut off a stick, and threw *it* in there;
and he made the iron float. 7Therefore
he said, "Pick *it* up for yourself." So he
reached out his hand and took it.

The Blinded Syrians Captured

8Now the king of Syria was making
war against Israel; and he consulted
with his servants, saying, "My camp *will
be* in such and such a place." 9And the
man of God sent to the king of Israel,
saying, "Beware that you do not pass
this place, for the Syrians are coming
down there." 10Then the king of Isra-
el sent *someone* to the place of which
the man of God had told him. Thus he
warned him, and he was watchful there,
not just once or twice.
11Therefore the heart of the king of
Syria was greatly troubled by this thing;
and he called his servants and said to
them, "Will you not show me which of
us *is* for the king of Israel?"
12And one of his servants said, "None,
my lord, O king; but Elisha, the prophet
who *is* in Israel, tells the king of Israel the
words that you speak in your bedroom."

13So he said, "Go and see where he *is,*
that I may send and get him."
And it was told him, saying, "Surely *he*
is in Dothan."
14Therefore he sent horses and char-
iots and a great army there, and they
came by night and surrounded the city.
15And when the servant of the man of
God arose early and went out, there
was an army, surrounding the city with
horses and chariots. And his servant
said to him, "Alas, my master! What
shall we do?"
16So he answered, "Do not fear, for those
who *are* with us *are* more than those who
are with them." 17And Elisha prayed, and
said, "LORD, I pray, open his eyes that he
may see." Then the LORD opened the eyes
of the young man, and he saw. And be-
hold, the mountain *was* full of horses and
chariots of fire all around Elisha. 18So
when *the Syrians* came down to him, Eli-
sha prayed to the LORD, and said, "Strike
this people, I pray, with blindness." And
He struck them with blindness according
to the word of Elisha.
19Now Elisha said to them, "This *is* not
the way, nor *is* this the city. Follow me,
and I will bring you to the man whom
you seek." But he led them to Samaria.
20So it was, when they had come to Sa-
maria, that Elisha said, "LORD, open the
eyes of these *men,* that they may see."
And the LORD opened their eyes, and they
saw; and there *they were,* inside Samaria!
21Now when the king of Israel saw
them, he said to Elisha, "My father, shall
I kill *them?* Shall I kill *them?*"
22But he answered, "You shall not kill
them. Would you kill those whom you
have taken captive with your sword and
your bow? Set food and water before
them, that they may eat and drink and
go to their master." 23Then he prepared
a great feast for them; and after they
ate and drank, he sent them away and
they went to their master. So the bands
of Syrian *raiders* came no more into the
land of Israel.

Syria Besieges Samaria in Famine

24And it happened after this that Ben-
Hadad king of Syria gathered all his
army, and went up and besieged Sa-
maria. 25And there was a great famine
in Samaria; and indeed they besieged it
until a donkey's head was *sold* for eighty
shekels of silver, and one-fourth of a kab
of dove droppings for five *shekels* of silver.
26Then, as the king of Israel was pass-
ing by on the wall, a woman cried out
to him, saying, "Help, my lord, O king!"
27And he said, "If the LORD does not
help you, where can I find help for you?
From the threshing floor or from the
winepress?" 28Then the king said to her,
"What is troubling you?"
And she answered, "This woman said
to me, 'Give your son, that we may eat
him today, and we will eat my son to-
morrow.' 29So we boiled my son, and ate
him. And I said to her on the next day,
'Give your son, that we may eat him';
but she has hidden her son."
30Now it happened, when the king
heard the words of the woman, that he
tore his clothes; and as he passed by on
the wall, the people looked, and there
underneath *he had* sackcloth on his
body. 31Then he said, "God do so to me
and more also, if the head of Elisha the
son of Shaphat remains on him today!"
32But Elisha was sitting in his house,
and the elders were sitting with him. And
the king sent a man ahead of him, but be-
fore the messenger came to him, he said
to the elders, "Do you see how this son
of a murderer has sent someone to take
away my head? Look, when the messen-
ger comes, shut the door, and hold him
fast at the door. *Is* not the sound of his
master's feet behind him?" 33And while
he was still talking with them, there was
the messenger, coming down to him; and
then *the king* said, "Surely this calamity
is from the LORD; why should I wait for
the LORD any longer?"

7 Then Elisha said, "Hear the word
of the LORD. Thus says the LORD:
'Tomorrow about this time a seah of
fine flour *shall be sold* for a shekel, and
two seahs of barley for a shekel, at the
gate of Samaria.' "
2So an officer on whose hand the king
leaned answered the man of God and
said, "Look, *if* the LORD would make
windows in heaven, could this thing
be?"
And he said, "In fact, you shall see *it*
with your eyes, but you shall not eat of it."

The Syrians Flee

3Now there were four leprous men at
the entrance of the gate; and they said
to one another, "Why are we sitting here
until we die? 4If we say, 'We will enter the
city,' the famine *is* in the city, and we shall
die there. And if we sit here, we die also.
Now therefore, come, let us surrender to
the army of the Syrians. If they keep us
alive, we shall live; and if they kill us, we
shall only die." 5And they rose at twilight
to go to the camp of the Syrians; and
when they had come to the outskirts of
the Syrian camp, to their surprise no one
was there. 6For the Lord had caused the
army of the Syrians to hear the noise of
chariots and the noise of horses—the
noise of a great army; so they said to
one another, "Look, the king of Israel has
hired against us the kings of the Hittites
and the kings of the Egyptians to attack
us!" 7Therefore they arose and fled at
twilight, and left the camp intact—their
tents, their horses, and their donkeys—
and they fled for their lives. 8And when
these lepers came to the outskirts of the
camp, they went into one tent and ate
and drank, and carried from it silver
and gold and clothing, and went and hid
them; then they came back and entered
another tent, and carried *some* from
there *also,* and went and hid *it.*

9Then they said to one another, "We
are not doing right. This day *is* a day of
good news, and we remain silent. If we
wait until morning light, some punish-
ment will come upon us. Now therefore,
come, let us go and tell the king's house-
hold." 10So they went and called to the
gatekeepers of the city, and told them,
saying, "We went to the Syrian camp,
and surprisingly no one *was* there, not
a human sound—only horses and don-
keys tied, and the tents intact." 11And the
gatekeepers called out, and they told *it*
to the king's household inside.

12So the king arose in the night and
said to his servants, "Let me now tell you
what the Syrians have done to us. They
know that we *are* hungry; therefore
they have gone out of the camp to hide
themselves in the field, saying, 'When
they come out of the city, we shall catch
them alive, and get into the city.' "

13And one of his servants answered
and said, "Please, let several *men* take
five of the remaining horses which are
left in the city. Look, they *may either
become* like all the multitude of Israel
that are left in it; or indeed, *I say,* they
may become like all the multitude of Is-
rael left from those who are consumed;
so let us send them and see." 14Therefore
they took two chariots with horses; and
the king sent them in the direction of
the Syrian army, saying, "Go and see."
15And they went after them to the Jor-
dan; and indeed all the road *was* full of
garments and weapons which the Syri-
ans had thrown away in their haste. So
the messengers returned and told the
king. 16Then the people went out and
plundered the tents of the Syrians. So a
seah of fine flour was *sold* for a shekel,
and two seahs of barley for a shekel,
according to the word of the LORD.

17Now the king had appointed the of-
ficer on whose hand he leaned to have
charge of the gate. But the people tram-
pled him in the gate, and he died, just
as the man of God had said, who spoke
when the king came down to him. 18So
it happened just as the man of God had
spoken to the king, saying, "Two seahs
of barley for a shekel, and a seah of fine
flour for a shekel, shall be *sold* tomorrow
about this time in the gate of Samaria."

19Then that officer had answered the
man of God, and said, "Now look, *if* the
LORD would make windows in heaven,
could such a thing be?"

And he had said, "In fact, you shall see
it with your eyes, but you shall not eat
of it." 20And so it happened to him, for
the people trampled him in the gate,
and he died.

The King Restores the Shunammite's Land

8 Then Elisha spoke to the woman
whose son he had restored to life,
saying, "Arise and go, you and your
household, and stay wherever you can;
for the LORD has called for a famine,
and furthermore, it will come upon the
land for seven years." 2So the woman
arose and did according to the saying
of the man of God, and she went with
her household and dwelt in the land of
the Philistines seven years.

3It came to pass, at the end of seven
years, that the woman returned from
the land of the Philistines; and she went
to make an appeal to the king for her
house and for her land. 4Then the king
talked with Gehazi, the servant of the
man of God, saying, "Tell me, please, all
the great things Elisha has done." 5Now
it happened, as he was telling the king
how he had restored the dead to life,
that there was the woman whose son
he had restored to life, appealing to
the king for her house and for her land.
And Gehazi said, "My lord, O king, this
is the woman, and this *is* her son whom
Elisha restored to life." 6And when the
king asked the woman, she told him.

So the king appointed a certain of-
ficer for her, saying, "Restore all that
was hers, and all the proceeds of the
field from the day that she left the land
until now."

Death of Ben-Hadad

7Then Elisha went to Damascus, and
Ben-Hadad king of Syria was sick; and
it was told him, saying, "The man of God
has come here." 8And the king said to
Hazael, "Take a present in your hand, and
go to meet the man of God, and inquire of
the LORD by him, saying, 'Shall I recover
from this disease?' " 9So Hazael went to
meet him and took a present with him,
of every good thing of Damascus, forty
camel-loads; and he came and stood be-
fore him, and said, "Your son Ben-Hadad
king of Syria has sent me to you, saying,
'Shall I recover from this disease?' "

10And Elisha said to him, "Go, say to
him, 'You shall certainly recover.' How-
ever the LORD has shown me that he
will really die." 11Then he set his counte-
nance in a stare until he was ashamed;
and the man of God wept. 12And Hazael
said, "Why is my lord weeping?"

He answered, "Because I know the
evil that you will do to the children of
Israel: Their strongholds you will set on
fire, and their young men you will kill
with the sword; and you will dash their
children, and rip open their women
with child."

13So Hazael said, "But what *is* your
servant—a dog, that he should do this
gross thing?"

And Elisha answered, "The LORD has
shown me that you *will become* king
over Syria."

14Then he departed from Elisha, and
came to his master, who said to him,
"What did Elisha say to you?" And he
answered, "He told me you would sure-
ly recover." 15But it happened on the
next day that he took a thick cloth and
dipped *it* in water, and spread *it* over his
face so that he died; and Hazael reigned
in his place.

Jehoram Reigns in Judah

16Now in the fifth year of Joram the
son of Ahab, king of Israel, Jehoshaphat
having been king of Judah, Jehoram
the son of Jehoshaphat began to reign
as king of Judah. 17He was thirty-two
years old when he became king, and
he reigned eight years in Jerusalem.
18And he walked in the way of the kings
of Israel, just as the house of Ahab had
done, for the daughter of Ahab was his
wife; and he did evil in the sight of the
LORD. 19Yet the LORD would not destroy
Judah, for the sake of His servant David,
as He promised him to give a lamp to
him *and* his sons forever.

20In his days Edom revolted against
Judah's authority, and made a king
over themselves. 21So Joram[a] went
to Zair, and all his chariots with him.
Then he rose by night and attacked the
Edomites who had surrounded him and
the captains of the chariots; and the
troops fled to their tents. 22Thus Edom
has been in revolt against Judah's au-
thority to this day. And Libnah revolted
at that time.

23Now the rest of the acts of Joram,
and all that he did, *are* they not written
in the book of the chronicles of the kings
of Judah? 24So Joram rested with his
fathers, and was buried with his fathers
in the City of David. Then Ahaziah his
son reigned in his place.

Ahaziah Reigns in Judah

25In the twelfth year of Joram the son
of Ahab, king of Israel, Ahaziah the

8:21 [a] Spelled *Jehoram* in verse 16

son of Jehoram, king of Judah, began
to reign. 26Ahaziah *was* twenty-two
years old when he became king, and
he reigned one year in Jerusalem. His
mother's name *was* Athaliah the grand-
daughter of Omri, king of Israel. 27And
he walked in the way of the house of
Ahab, and did evil in the sight of the
LORD, like the house of Ahab, for he *was*
the son-in-law of the house of Ahab.
28Now he went with Joram the son
of Ahab to war against Hazael king of
Syria at Ramoth Gilead; and the Syrians
wounded Joram. 29Then King Joram
went back to Jezreel to recover from the
wounds which the Syrians had inflict-
ed on him at Ramah, when he fought
against Hazael king of Syria. And Aha-
ziah the son of Jehoram, king of Judah,
went down to see Joram the son of Ahab
in Jezreel, because he was sick.

Jehu Anointed King of Israel

9 And Elisha the prophet called one
of the sons of the prophets, and said
to him, "Get yourself ready, take this
flask of oil in your hand, and go to Ra-
moth Gilead. 2Now when you arrive
at that place, look there for Jehu the
son of Jehoshaphat, the son of Nimshi,
and go in and make him rise up from
among his associates, and take him to
an inner room. 3Then take the flask of
oil, and pour *it* on his head, and say,
'Thus says the LORD: "I have anointed
you king over Israel." ' Then open the
door and flee, and do not delay."
4So the young man, the servant of the
prophet, went to Ramoth Gilead. 5And
when he arrived, there *were* the cap-
tains of the army sitting; and he said, "I
have a message for you, Commander."
Jehu said, "For which *one* of us?"
And he said, "For you, Commander."
6Then he arose and went into the house.
And he poured the oil on his head, and
said to him, "Thus says the LORD God
of Israel: 'I have anointed you king
over the people of the LORD, over Isra-
el. 7You shall strike down the house of
Ahab your master, that I may avenge
the blood of My servants the prophets,
and the blood of all the servants of the
LORD, at the hand of Jezebel. 8For the
whole house of Ahab shall perish; and
I will cut off from Ahab all the males
in Israel, both bond and free. 9So I will
make the house of Ahab like the house
of Jeroboam the son of Nebat, and like
the house of Baasha the son of Ahijah.
10The dogs shall eat Jezebel on the plot
of ground at Jezreel, and *there shall be*
none to bury *her*.' " And he opened the
door and fled.
11Then Jehu came out to the servants
of his master, and *one* said to him, "*Is*
all well? Why did this madman come
to you?"
And he said to them, "You know the
man and his babble."
12And they said, "A lie! Tell us now."
So he said, "Thus and thus he spoke
to me, saying, 'Thus says the LORD: "I
have anointed you king over Israel." ' "
13Then each man hastened to take his
garment and put *it* under him on the
top of the steps; and they blew trumpets,
saying, "Jehu is king!"

Joram of Israel Killed

14So Jehu the son of Jehoshaphat,
the son of Nimshi, conspired against
Joram. (Now Joram had been defend-
ing Ramoth Gilead, he and all Isra-
el, against Hazael king of Syria. 15But
King Joram had returned to Jezreel
to recover from the wounds which the
Syrians had inflicted on him when he
fought with Hazael king of Syria.) And
Jehu said, "If you are so minded, let no
one leave *or* escape from the city to go
and tell *it* in Jezreel." 16So Jehu rode in
a chariot and went to Jezreel, for Joram
was laid up there; and Ahaziah king of
Judah had come down to see Joram.
17Now a watchman stood on the tower
in Jezreel, and he saw the company
of Jehu as he came, and said, "I see a
company of men."
And Joram said, "Get a horseman and
send him to meet them, and let him say,
'*Is it* peace?' "
18So the horseman went to meet him,
and said, "Thus says the king: '*Is it*
peace?' "
And Jehu said, "What have you to do
with peace? Turn around and follow me."
So the watchman reported, saying,
"The messenger went to them, but is
not coming back."

19Then he sent out a second horseman
who came to them, and said, "Thus says
the king: '*Is it* peace?' "
And Jehu answered, "What have you
to do with peace? Turn around and fol-
low me."
20So the watchman reported, saying,
"He went up to them and is not coming
back; and the driving *is* like the driving
of Jehu the son of Nimshi, for he drives
furiously!"
21Then Joram said, "Make ready."
And his chariot was made ready. Then
Joram king of Israel and Ahaziah king
of Judah went out, each in his chariot;
and they went out to meet Jehu, and
met him on the property of Naboth the
Jezreelite. 22Now it happened, when
Joram saw Jehu, that he said, "*Is it*
peace, Jehu?"
So he answered, "What peace, as long
as the harlotries of your mother Jezebel
and her witchcraft *are so* many?"
23Then Joram turned around and fled,
and said to Ahaziah, "Treachery, Ahazi-
ah!" 24Now Jehu drew his bow with full
strength and shot Jehoram between his
arms; and the arrow came out at his
heart, and he sank down in his chariot.
25Then *Jehu* said to Bidkar his captain,
"Pick *him* up, *and* throw him into the
tract of the field of Naboth the Jezreel-
ite; for remember, when you and I were
riding together behind Ahab his father,
that the LORD laid this burden upon him:
26'Surely I saw yesterday the blood of
Naboth and the blood of his sons,' says
the LORD, 'and I will repay you in this
plot,' says the LORD. Now therefore, take
and throw him on the plot *of ground,*
according to the word of the LORD."

Ahaziah of Judah Killed

27But when Ahaziah king of Judah saw
this, he fled by the road to Beth Hag-
gan.[a] So Jehu pursued him, and said,
"Shoot him also in the chariot." *And they
shot him* at the Ascent of Gur, which is
by Ibleam. Then he fled to Megiddo, and
died there. 28And his servants carried
him in the chariot to Jerusalem, and
buried him in his tomb with his fathers
in the City of David. 29In the eleventh
year of Joram the son of Ahab, Ahaziah
had become king over Judah.

Jezebel's Violent Death

30Now when Jehu had come to Jezreel,
Jezebel heard *of it;* and she put paint
on her eyes and adorned her head, and
looked through a window. 31Then, as
Jehu entered at the gate, she said, "*Is it*
peace, Zimri, murderer of your master?"
32And he looked up at the window, and
said, "Who *is* on my side? Who?" So two *or*
three eunuchs looked out at him. 33Then
he said, "Throw her down." So they threw
her down, and *some* of her blood spattered
on the wall and on the horses; and he
trampled her underfoot. 34And when he
had gone in, he ate and drank. Then
he said, "Go now, see to this accursed
woman, and bury her, for she was a king's
daughter." 35So they went to bury her,
but they found no more of her than the
skull and the feet and the palms of *her*
hands. 36Therefore they came back and
told him. And he said, "This *is* the word of
the LORD, which He spoke by His servant
Elijah the Tishbite, saying, 'On the plot *of
ground* at Jezreel dogs shall eat the flesh
of Jezebel;[a] 37and the corpse of Jezebel
shall be as refuse on the surface of the
field, in the plot at Jezreel, so that they
shall not say, "Here *lies* Jezebel." ' "

Ahab's Seventy Sons Killed

10 Now Ahab had seventy sons in
Samaria. And Jehu wrote and
sent letters to Samaria, to the rulers of
Jezreel,[a] to the elders, and to those who
reared Ahab's *sons,* saying:

2 Now as soon as this letter comes
to you, since your master's sons
are with you, and you have
chariots and horses, a fortified
city also, and weapons, 3choose
the best qualified of your
master's sons, set *him* on his
father's throne, and fight for your
master's house.

4But they were exceedingly afraid, and
said, "Look, two kings could not stand
up to him; how then can we stand?"

9:27 [a] Literally *The Garden House* 9:36 [a] 1 Kings 21:23 10:1 [a] Following Masoretic Text, Syriac, and Targum; Septuagint reads *Samaria;* Vulgate reads *city.*

5And he who *was* in charge of the house,
and he who *was* in charge of the city,
the elders also, and those who reared
the sons, sent to Jehu, saying, "We *are*
your servants, we will do all you tell us;
but we will not make anyone king. Do
what is good in your sight." 6Then he
wrote a second letter to them, saying:

> If you *are* for me and will obey
> my voice, take the heads of the
> men, your master's sons, and
> come to me at Jezreel by this time
> tomorrow.

Now the king's sons, seventy persons,
were with the great men of the city, *who*
were rearing them. 7So it was, when the
letter came to them, that they took the
king's sons and slaughtered seventy
persons, put their heads in baskets and
sent *them* to him at Jezreel.
8Then a messenger came and told him,
saying, "They have brought the heads
of the king's sons."
And he said, "Lay them in two heaps at
the entrance of the gate until morning."
9So it was, in the morning, that he went
out and stood, and said to all the people,
"You *are* righteous. Indeed I conspired
against my master and killed him; but
who killed all these? 10Know now that
nothing shall fall to the earth of the
word of the LORD which the LORD spoke
concerning the house of Ahab; for the
LORD has done what He spoke by His
servant Elijah." 11So Jehu killed all who
remained of the house of Ahab in Jez-
reel, and all his great men and his close
acquaintances and his priests, until he
left him none remaining.

Ahaziah's Forty-two Brothers Killed

12And he arose and departed and went
to Samaria. On the way, at Beth Eked[a]
of the Shepherds, 13Jehu met with the
brothers of Ahaziah king of Judah, and
said, "Who *are* you?"
So they answered, "We *are* the brothers
of Ahaziah; we have come down to greet
the sons of the king and the sons of the
queen mother."
14And he said, "Take them alive!" So
they took them alive, and killed them
at the well of Beth Eked, forty-two men;
and he left none of them.

The Rest of Ahab's Family Killed

15Now when he departed from there,
he met Jehonadab the son of Rechab,
coming to meet him; and he greeted him
and said to him, "Is your heart right, as
my heart *is* toward your heart?"
And Jehonadab answered, "It is."
Jehu said, "If it is, give *me* your hand."
So he gave *him* his hand, and he took
him up to him into the chariot. 16Then
he said, "Come with me, and see my
zeal for the LORD." So they had him ride
in his chariot. 17And when he came to
Samaria, he killed all who remained to
Ahab in Samaria, till he had destroyed
them, according to the word of the LORD
which He spoke to Elijah.

Worshipers of Baal Killed

18Then Jehu gathered all the people
together, and said to them, "Ahab
served Baal a little, Jehu will serve him
much. 19Now therefore, call to me all
the prophets of Baal, all his servants,
and all his priests. Let no one be miss-
ing, for I have a great sacrifice for Baal.
Whoever is missing shall not live." But
Jehu acted deceptively, with the intent
of destroying the worshipers of Baal.
20And Jehu said, "Proclaim a solemn
assembly for Baal." So they proclaimed
it. 21Then Jehu sent throughout all Is-
rael; and all the worshipers of Baal
came, so that there was not a man left
who did not come. So they came into
the temple[a] of Baal, and the temple of
Baal was full from one end to the other.
22And he said to the one in charge of
the wardrobe, "Bring out vestments
for all the worshipers of Baal." So he
brought out vestments for them. 23Then
Jehu and Jehonadab the son of Rechab
went into the temple of Baal, and said
to the worshipers of Baal, "Search and
see that no servants of the LORD are
here with you, but only the worshipers
of Baal." 24So they went in to offer sac-
rifices and burnt offerings. Now Jehu
had appointed for himself eighty men

10:12 [a] Or *The Shearing House* 10:21 [a] Literally *house,* and so elsewhere in this chapter

on the outside, and had said, "*If* any
of the men whom I have brought into
your hands escapes, *whoever lets him
escape, it shall be* his life for the life of
the other."
25Now it happened, as soon as he had
made an end of offering the burnt of-
fering, that Jehu said to the guard and
to the captains, "Go in *and* kill them;
let no one come out!" And they killed
them with the edge of the sword; then
the guards and the officers threw *them*
out, and went into the inner room of
the temple of Baal. 26And they brought
the *sacred* pillars out of the temple of
Baal and burned them. 27Then they
broke down the *sacred* pillar of Baal,
and tore down the temple of Baal and
made it a refuse dump to this day.
28Thus Jehu destroyed Baal from Is-
rael.
29However Jehu did not turn away
from the sins of Jeroboam the son of
Nebat, who had made Israel sin, *that
is,* from the golden calves that *were* at
Bethel and Dan. 30And the LORD said
to Jehu, "Because you have done well
in doing *what is* right in My sight, *and*
have done to the house of Ahab all that
was in My heart, your sons shall sit
on the throne of Israel to the fourth
generation." 31But Jehu took no heed
to walk in the law of the LORD God of
Israel with all his heart; for he did not
depart from the sins of Jeroboam, who
had made Israel sin.

Death of Jehu

32In those days the LORD began to
cut off *parts* of Israel; and Hazael con-
quered them in all the territory of Is-
rael 33from the Jordan eastward: all
the land of Gilead—Gad, Reuben, and
Manasseh—from Aroer, which *is* by
the River Arnon, including Gilead and
Bashan.
34Now the rest of the acts of Jehu, all
that he did, and all his might, *are* they
not written in the book of the chron-
icles of the kings of Israel? 35So Jehu
rested with his fathers, and they buried
him in Samaria. Then Jehoahaz his son
reigned in his place. 36And the period
that Jehu reigned over Israel in Samar-
ia *was* twenty-eight years.

Athaliah Reigns in Judah

11 When Athaliah the mother of
Ahaziah saw that her son was
dead, she arose and destroyed all the
royal heirs. 2But Jehosheba, the daugh-
ter of King Joram, sister of Ahaziah,
took Joash the son of Ahaziah, and stole
him away from among the king's sons
who were being murdered; and they hid
him and his nurse in the bedroom, from
Athaliah, so that he was not killed. 3So
he was hidden with her in the house of
the LORD for six years, while Athaliah
reigned over the land.

Joash Crowned King of Judah

4In the seventh year Jehoiada
sent and brought the captains of
hundreds—of the bodyguards and
the escorts—and brought them into
the house of the LORD to him. And he
made a covenant with them and took
an oath from them in the house of the
LORD, and showed them the king's son.
5Then he commanded them, saying,
"This *is* what you shall do: One-third of
you who come on duty on the Sabbath
shall be keeping watch over the king's
house, 6one-third *shall be* at the gate of
Sur, and one-third at the gate behind
the escorts. You shall keep the watch of
the house, lest it be broken down. 7The
two contingents of you who go off duty
on the Sabbath shall keep the watch
of the house of the LORD for the king.
8But you shall surround the king on all
sides, every man with his weapons in
his hand; and whoever comes within
range, let him be put to death. You are
to be with the king as he goes out and
as he comes in."
9So the captains of the hundreds
did according to all that Jehoiada
the priest commanded. Each of them
took his men who were to be on duty
on the Sabbath, with those who were
going off duty on the Sabbath, and
came to Jehoiada the priest. 10And the
priest gave the captains of hundreds
the spears and shields which *had be-
longed* to King David, that were in the
temple of the LORD. 11Then the escorts
stood, every man with his weapons in
his hand, all around the king, from
the right side of the temple to the left

side of the temple, by the altar and
the house. 12And he brought out the
king's son, put the crown on him, and
gave him the Testimony;[a] they made
him king and anointed him, and they
clapped their hands and said, "Long
live the king!"

Death of Athaliah

13Now when Athaliah heard the noise
of the escorts *and* the people, she came
to the people *in* the temple of the LORD.
14When she looked, there was the king
standing by a pillar according to cus-
tom; and the leaders and the trumpet-
ers were by the king. All the people of
the land were rejoicing and blowing
trumpets. So Athaliah tore her clothes
and cried out, "Treason! Treason!"

15And Jehoiada the priest command-
ed the captains of the hundreds, the
officers of the army, and said to them,
"Take her outside under guard, and
slay with the sword whoever follows
her." For the priest had said, "Do not
let her be killed in the house of the
LORD." 16So they seized her; and she
went by way of the horses' entrance
into the king's house, and there she
was killed.

17Then Jehoiada made a covenant
between the LORD, the king, and the
people, that they should be the LORD's
people, and *also* between the king and
the people. 18And all the people of the
land went to the temple of Baal, and
tore it down. They thoroughly broke in
pieces its altars and images, and killed
Mattan the priest of Baal before the
altars. And the priest appointed offi-
cers over the house of the LORD. 19Then
he took the captains of hundreds, the
bodyguards, the escorts, and all the
people of the land; and they brought
the king down from the house of the
LORD, and went by way of the gate of
the escorts to the king's house. Then
he sat on the throne of the kings. 20So
all the people of the land rejoiced; and
the city was quiet, for they had slain
Athaliah with the sword *in* the king's
house. 21Jehoash *was* seven years old
when he became king.

Jehoash Repairs the Temple

12 In the seventh year of Jehu, Je-
hoash[a] became king, and he
reigned forty years in Jerusalem. His
mother's name *was* Zibiah of Beershe-
ba. 2Jehoash did *what was* right in the
sight of the LORD all the days in which
Jehoiada the priest instructed him. 3But
the high places were not taken away;
the people still sacrificed and burned
incense on the high places.

4And Jehoash said to the priests,
"All the money of the dedicated gifts
that are brought into the house of the
LORD—each man's census money, each
man's assessment money[a]—*and* all the
money that a man purposes in his heart
to bring into the house of the LORD, 5let
the priests take *it* themselves, each from
his constituency; and let them repair
the damages of the temple, wherever
any dilapidation is found."

6Now it was so, by the twenty-third year
of King Jehoash, *that* the priests had not
repaired the damages of the temple.
7So King Jehoash called Jehoiada the
priest and the *other* priests, and said to
them, "Why have you not repaired the
damages of the temple? Now therefore,
do not take *more* money from your con-
stituency, but deliver it for repairing the
damages of the temple." 8And the priests
agreed that they would neither receive
more money from the people, nor repair
the damages of the temple.

9Then Jehoiada the priest took a chest,
bored a hole in its lid, and set it beside the
altar, on the right side as one comes into
the house of the LORD; and the priests
who kept the door put there all the money
brought into the house of the LORD. 10So
it was, whenever they saw that *there was*
much money in the chest, that the king's
scribe and the high priest came up and
put it in bags, and counted the money
that was found in the house of the LORD.
11Then they gave the money, which had
been apportioned, into the hands of those
who did the work, who had the oversight
of the house of the LORD; and they paid
it out to the carpenters and builders who
worked on the house of the LORD, 12and to
masons and stonecutters, and for buying

11:12 [a] That is, the Law (compare Exodus 25:16, 21 and Deuteronomy 31:9) **12:1** [a] Spelled *Joash* in 11:2ff **12:4** [a] Compare Leviticus 27:2ff

timber and hewn stone, to repair the
damage of the house of the LORD, and
for all that was paid out to repair the
temple. 13However there were not made
for the house of the LORD basins of silver,
trimmers, sprinkling-bowls, trumpets,
any articles of gold or articles of silver,
from the money brought into the house
of the LORD. 14But they gave that to the
workmen, and they repaired the house
of the LORD with it. 15Moreover they did
not require an account from the men into
whose hand they delivered the money
to be paid to workmen, for they dealt
faithfully. 16The money from the trespass
offerings and the money from the sin
offerings was not brought into the house
of the LORD. It belonged to the priests.

Hazael Threatens Jerusalem

17Hazael king of Syria went up and
fought against Gath, and took it; then
Hazael set his face to go up to Jerusa-
lem. 18And Jehoash king of Judah took
all the sacred things that his fathers,
Jehoshaphat and Jehoram and Ahazi-
ah, kings of Judah, had dedicated, and
his own sacred things, and all the gold
found in the treasuries of the house of
the LORD and in the king's house, and
sent *them* to Hazael king of Syria. Then
he went away from Jerusalem.

Death of Joash

19Now the rest of the acts of Joash,[a]
and all that he did, *are* they not written
in the book of the chronicles of the kings
of Judah?
20And his servants arose and formed
a conspiracy, and killed Joash in the
house of the Millo,[a] which goes down to
Silla. 21For Jozachar[a] the son of Shime-
ath and Jehozabad the son of Shomer,[b]
his servants, struck him. So he died, and
they buried him with his fathers in the
City of David. Then Amaziah his son
reigned in his place.

Jehoahaz Reigns in Israel

13 In the twenty-third year of Joash[a]
the son of Ahaziah, king of Judah,
Jehoahaz the son of Jehu became king
over Israel in Samaria, *and reigned* sev-
enteen years. 2And he did evil in the sight
of the LORD, and followed the sins of Jer-
oboam the son of Nebat, who had made
Israel sin. He did not depart from them.
3Then the anger of the LORD was
aroused against Israel, and He delivered
them into the hand of Hazael king of
Syria, and into the hand of Ben-Hadad
the son of Hazael, all *their* days. 4So
Jehoahaz pleaded with the LORD, and
the LORD listened to him; for He saw
the oppression of Israel, because the
king of Syria oppressed them. 5Then the
LORD gave Israel a deliverer, so that they
escaped from under the hand of the Syr-
ians; and the children of Israel dwelt in
their tents as before. 6Nevertheless they
did not depart from the sins of the house
of Jeroboam, who had made Israel sin,
but walked in them; and the wooden
image[a] also remained in Samaria. 7For
He left of the army of Jehoahaz only
fifty horsemen, ten chariots, and ten
thousand foot soldiers; for the king of
Syria had destroyed them and made
them like the dust at threshing.
8Now the rest of the acts of Jehoahaz,
all that he did, and his might, *are* they
not written in the book of the chroni-
cles of the kings of Israel? 9So Jehoahaz
rested with his fathers, and they buried
him in Samaria. Then Joash his son
reigned in his place.

Jehoash Reigns in Israel

10In the thirty-seventh year of Joash
king of Judah, Jehoash[a] the son of Je-
hoahaz became king over Israel in Sa-
maria, *and reigned* sixteen years. 11And
he did evil in the sight of the LORD. He
did not depart from all the sins of Jero-
boam the son of Nebat, who made Israel
sin, *but* walked in them.
12Now the rest of the acts of Joash, all
that he did, and his might with which he
fought against Amaziah king of Judah,
are they not written in the book of the
chronicles of the kings of Israel? 13So
Joash rested with his fathers. Then Jero-
boam sat on his throne. And Joash was
buried in Samaria with the kings of Israel.

12:19 [a] Spelled *Jehoash* in 12:1ff **12:20** [a] Literally *The Landfill* **12:21** [a] Called *Zabad* in 2 Chronicles 24:26 [b] Called *Shimrith* in 2 Chronicles 24:26 **13:1** [a] Spelled *Jehoash* in 12:1ff **13:6** [a] Hebrew *Asherah,* a Canaanite goddess **13:10** [a] Spelled *Joash* in verse 9

Death of Elisha

14Elisha had become sick with the ill-
ness of which he would die. Then Joash
the king of Israel came down to him,
and wept over his face, and said, "O my
father, my father, the chariots of Israel
and their horsemen!"
15And Elisha said to him, "Take a bow
and some arrows." So he took himself a
bow and some arrows. 16Then he said to
the king of Israel, "Put your hand on the
bow." So he put his hand *on it,* and Elisha
put his hands on the king's hands. 17And
he said, "Open the east window"; and
he opened *it.* Then Elisha said, "Shoot";
and he shot. And he said, "The arrow of
the LORD's deliverance and the arrow
of deliverance from Syria; for you must
strike the Syrians at Aphek till you have
destroyed *them.*" 18Then he said, "Take
the arrows"; so he took *them.* And he
said to the king of Israel, "Strike the
ground"; so he struck three times, and
stopped. 19And the man of God was
angry with him, and said, "You should
have struck five or six times; then you
would have struck Syria till you had
destroyed *it!* But now you will strike
Syria *only* three times."
20Then Elisha died, and they buried
him. And the *raiding* bands from Moab
invaded the land in the spring of the
year. 21So it was, as they were burying
a man, that suddenly they spied a band
of raiders; and they put the man in the
tomb of Elisha; and when the man was
let down and touched the bones of Eli-
sha, he revived and stood on his feet.

Israel Recaptures Cities from Syria

22And Hazael king of Syria oppressed
Israel all the days of Jehoahaz. 23But
the LORD was gracious to them, had
compassion on them, and regarded
them, because of His covenant with
Abraham, Isaac, and Jacob, and would
not yet destroy them or cast them from
His presence.
24Now Hazael king of Syria died. Then
Ben-Hadad his son reigned in his place.
25And Jehoash[a] the son of Jehoahaz re-
captured from the hand of Ben-Hadad,
the son of Hazael, the cities which he
had taken out of the hand of Jehoahaz
his father by war. Three times Joash
defeated him and recaptured the cities
of Israel.

Amaziah Reigns in Judah

14 In the second year of Joash the
son of Jehoahaz, king of Isra-
el, Amaziah the son of Joash, king of
Judah, became king. 2He was twenty-
five years old when he became king,
and he reigned twenty-nine years in
Jerusalem. His mother's name was Je-
hoaddan of Jerusalem. 3And he did
what was right in the sight of the LORD,
yet not like his father David; he did ev-
erything as his father Joash had done.
4However the high places were not tak-
en away, and the people still sacrificed
and burned incense on the high places.
5Now it happened, as soon as the
kingdom was established in his hand,
that he executed his servants who had
murdered his father the king. 6But the
children of the murderers he did not
execute, according to what is written in
the Book of the Law of Moses, in which
the LORD commanded, saying, "Fathers
shall not be put to death for their chil-
dren, nor shall children be put to death
for their fathers; but a person shall be
put to death for his own sin."[a]
7He killed ten thousand Edomites in
the Valley of Salt, and took Sela by war,
and called its name Joktheel to this day.
8Then Amaziah sent messengers to
Jehoash[a] the son of Jehoahaz, the son
of Jehu, king of Israel, saying, "Come,
let us face one another *in battle.*" 9And
Jehoash king of Israel sent to Amazi-
ah king of Judah, saying, "The thistle
that *was* in Lebanon sent to the cedar
that *was* in Lebanon, saying, 'Give your
daughter to my son as wife'; and a wild
beast that *was* in Lebanon passed by
and trampled the thistle. 10You have
indeed defeated Edom, and your heart
has lifted you up. Glory *in that,* and stay
at home; for why should you meddle
with trouble so that you fall—you and
Judah with you?"
11But Amaziah would not heed. There-
fore Jehoash king of Israel went out; so

13:25 [a] Spelled *Joash* in verses 12–14, 25 and 2 Chronicles 25:17ff **14:6** [a] Deuteronomy 24:16 **14:8** [a] Spelled *Joash* in 13:12ff

he and Amaziah king of Judah faced one
another at Beth Shemesh, which *belongs*
to Judah. 12And Judah was defeated by
Israel, and every man fled to his tent.
13Then Jehoash king of Israel captured
Amaziah king of Judah, the son of Je-
hoash, the son of Ahaziah, at Beth She-
mesh; and he went to Jerusalem, and
broke down the wall of Jerusalem from
the Gate of Ephraim to the Corner Gate—
four hundred cubits. 14And he took all
the gold and silver, all the articles that
were found in the house of the LORD
and in the treasuries of the king's house,
and hostages, and returned to Samaria.
15Now the rest of the acts of Jeho-
ash which he did—his might, and
how he fought with Amaziah king of
Judah—*are* they not written in the book
of the chronicles of the kings of Israel?
16So Jehoash rested with his fathers,
and was buried in Samaria with the
kings of Israel. Then Jeroboam his son
reigned in his place.
17Amaziah the son of Joash, king of
Judah, lived fifteen years after the death
of Jehoash the son of Jehoahaz, king
of Israel. 18Now the rest of the acts of
Amaziah, *are* they not written in the
book of the chronicles of the kings of
Judah? 19And they formed a conspiracy
against him in Jerusalem, and he fled
to Lachish; but they sent after him to
Lachish and killed him there. 20Then
they brought him on horses, and he was
buried at Jerusalem with his fathers in
the City of David.
21And all the people of Judah took Az-
ariah,[a] who *was* sixteen years old, and
made him king instead of his father
Amaziah. 22He built Elath and restored
it to Judah, after the king rested with
his fathers.

Jeroboam II Reigns in Israel

23In the fifteenth year of Amaziah the
son of Joash, king of Judah, Jeroboam
the son of Joash, king of Israel, became
king in Samaria, *and reigned* forty-one
years. 24And he did evil in the sight of
the LORD; he did not depart from all the
sins of Jeroboam the son of Nebat, who
had made Israel sin. 25He restored the
territory of Israel from the entrance
of Hamath to the Sea of the Arabah,
according to the word of the LORD God
of Israel, which He had spoken through
His servant Jonah the son of Amittai,
the prophet who *was* from Gath Hepher.
26For the LORD saw *that* the affliction
of Israel *was* very bitter; and whether
bond or free, there was no helper for Is-
rael. 27And the LORD did not say that He
would blot out the name of Israel from
under heaven; but He saved them by
the hand of Jeroboam the son of Joash.
28Now the rest of the acts of Jeroboam,
and all that he did—his might, how he
made war, and how he recaptured for Is-
rael, from Damascus and Hamath, *what
had belonged* to Judah—*are* they not
written in the book of the chronicles of
the kings of Israel? 29So Jeroboam rested
with his fathers, the kings of Israel. Then
Zechariah his son reigned in his place.

Azariah Reigns in Judah

15 In the twenty-seventh year of
Jeroboam king of Israel, Azari-
ah the son of Amaziah, king of Judah,
became king. 2He was sixteen years old
when he became king, and he reigned
fifty-two years in Jerusalem. His
mother's name *was* Jecholiah of Jeru-
salem. 3And he did *what was* right in the
sight of the LORD, according to all that
his father Amaziah had done, 4except
that the high places were not removed;
the people still sacrificed and burned
incense on the high places. 5Then the
LORD struck the king, so that he was a
leper until the day of his death; so he
dwelt in an isolated house. And Jotham
the king's son *was* over the *royal* house,
judging the people of the land.
6Now the rest of the acts of Azariah,
and all that he did, *are* they not writ-
ten in the book of the chronicles of the
kings of Judah? 7So Azariah rested with
his fathers, and they buried him with
his fathers in the City of David. Then
Jotham his son reigned in his place.

Zechariah Reigns in Israel

8In the thirty-eighth year of Azari-
ah king of Judah, Zechariah the son

14:21 [a] Called *Uzziah* in 2 Chronicles 26:1ff, Isaiah 6:1, and elsewhere

of Jeroboam reigned over Israel in
Samaria six months. 9And he did evil
in the sight of the LORD, as his fathers
had done; he did not depart from the
sins of Jeroboam the son of Nebat, who
had made Israel sin. 10Then Shallum
the son of Jabesh conspired against
him, and struck and killed him in front
of the people; and he reigned in his
place.
11Now the rest of the acts of Zechari-
ah, indeed they *are* written in the book
of the chronicles of the kings of Israel.
12This *was* the word of the LORD which
He spoke to Jehu, saying, "Your sons
shall sit on the throne of Israel to the
fourth *generation*."[a] And so it was.

Shallum Reigns in Israel

13Shallum the son of Jabesh became
king in the thirty-ninth year of Uzziah[a]
king of Judah; and he reigned a full
month in Samaria. 14For Menahem the
son of Gadi went up from Tirzah, came
to Samaria, and struck Shallum the son
of Jabesh in Samaria and killed him;
and he reigned in his place.
15Now the rest of the acts of Shallum,
and the conspiracy which he led, in-
deed they *are* written in the book of the
chronicles of the kings of Israel. 16Then
from Tirzah, Menahem attacked Tiph-
sah, all who *were* there, and its territory.
Because they did not surrender, there-
fore he attacked *it*. All the women there
who were with child he ripped open.

Menahem Reigns in Israel

17In the thirty-ninth year of Azariah
king of Judah, Menahem the son of Gadi
became king over Israel, *and reigned* ten
years in Samaria. 18And he did evil in
the sight of the LORD; he did not depart
all his days from the sins of Jeroboam
the son of Nebat, who had made Is-
rael sin. 19Pul[a] king of Assyria came
against the land; and Menahem gave
Pul a thousand talents of silver, that his
hand might be with him to strengthen
the kingdom under his control. 20And
Menahem exacted the money from Is-
rael, from all the very wealthy, from
each man fifty shekels of silver, to give
to the king of Assyria. So the king of
Assyria turned back, and did not stay
there in the land.
21Now the rest of the acts of Menahem,
and all that he did, *are* they not written
in the book of the chronicles of the kings
of Israel? 22So Menahem rested with his
fathers. Then Pekahiah his son reigned
in his place.

Pekahiah Reigns in Israel

23In the fiftieth year of Azariah king of
Judah, Pekahiah the son of Menahem
became king over Israel in Samaria,
and reigned two years. 24And he did
evil in the sight of the LORD; he did not
depart from the sins of Jeroboam the
son of Nebat, who had made Israel sin.
25Then Pekah the son of Remaliah, an
officer of his, conspired against him and
killed him in Samaria, in the citadel of
the king's house, along with Argob and
Arieh; and with him were fifty men of
Gilead. He killed him and reigned in
his place.
26Now the rest of the acts of Pekahi-
ah, and all that he did, indeed they *are*
written in the book of the chronicles of
the kings of Israel.

Pekah Reigns in Israel

27In the fifty-second year of Azariah
king of Judah, Pekah the son of Remali-
ah became king over Israel in Samaria,
and reigned twenty years. 28And he did
evil in the sight of the LORD; he did not
depart from the sins of Jeroboam the
son of Nebat, who had made Israel sin.
29In the days of Pekah king of Israel,
Tiglath-Pileser king of Assyria came
and took Ijon, Abel Beth Maachah, Ja-
noah, Kedesh, Hazor, Gilead, and Gal-
ilee, all the land of Naphtali; and he
carried them captive to Assyria. 30Then
Hoshea the son of Elah led a conspiracy
against Pekah the son of Remaliah, and
struck and killed him; so he reigned in
his place in the twentieth year of Jo-
tham the son of Uzziah.
31Now the rest of the acts of Pekah, and
all that he did, indeed they *are* written in
the book of the chronicles of the kings
of Israel.

15:12 [a] 2 Kings 10:30 (compare verse 29) **15:13** [a] Called *Azariah* in 14:21ff and 15:1ff **15:19** [a] That is, Tiglath-Pileser III

Jotham Reigns in Judah

32 In the second year of Pekah the son of Remaliah, king of Israel, Jotham the son of Uzziah, king of Judah, began to reign. 33 He was twenty-five years old when he became king, and he reigned sixteen years in Jerusalem. His mother's name *was* Jerusha[a] the daughter of Zadok. 34 And he did *what was* right in the sight of the LORD; he did according to all that his father Uzziah had done. 35 However the high places were not removed; the people still sacrificed and burned incense on the high places. He built the Upper Gate of the house of the LORD.

36 Now the rest of the acts of Jotham, and all that he did, *are* they not written in the book of the chronicles of the kings of Judah? 37 In those days the LORD began to send Rezin king of Syria and Pekah the son of Remaliah against Judah. 38 So Jotham rested with his fathers, and was buried with his fathers in the City of David his father. Then Ahaz his son reigned in his place.

Ahaz Reigns in Judah

16 In the seventeenth year of Pekah the son of Remaliah, Ahaz the son of Jotham, king of Judah, began to reign. 2 Ahaz *was* twenty years old when he became king, and he reigned sixteen years in Jerusalem; and he did not do *what was* right in the sight of the LORD his God, as his father David *had done.* 3 But he walked in the way of the kings of Israel; indeed he made his son pass through the fire, according to the abominations of the nations whom the LORD had cast out from before the children of Israel. 4 And he sacrificed and burned incense on the high places, on the hills, and under every green tree.

5 Then Rezin king of Syria and Pekah the son of Remaliah, king of Israel, came up to Jerusalem to *make* war; and they besieged Ahaz but could not overcome *him.* 6 At that time Rezin king of Syria captured Elath for Syria, and drove the men of Judah from Elath. Then the Edomites[a] went to Elath, and dwell there to this day.

7 So Ahaz sent messengers to Tiglath-Pileser king of Assyria, saying, "I *am* your servant and your son. Come up and save me from the hand of the king of Syria and from the hand of the king of Israel, who rise up against me." 8 And Ahaz took the silver and gold that was found in the house of the LORD, and in the treasuries of the king's house, and sent *it as* a present to the king of Assyria. 9 So the king of Assyria heeded him; for the king of Assyria went up against Damascus and took it, carried *its people* captive to Kir, and killed Rezin.

10 Now King Ahaz went to Damascus to meet Tiglath-Pileser king of Assyria, and saw an altar that *was* at Damascus; and King Ahaz sent to Urijah the priest the design of the altar and its pattern, according to all its workmanship. 11 Then Urijah the priest built an altar according to all that King Ahaz had sent from Damascus. So Urijah the priest made *it* before King Ahaz came back from Damascus. 12 And when the king came back from Damascus, the king saw the altar; and the king approached the altar and made offerings on it. 13 So he burned his burnt offering and his grain offering; and he poured his drink offering and sprinkled the blood of his peace offerings on the altar. 14 He also brought the bronze altar which *was* before the LORD, from the front of the temple—from between the *new* altar and the house of the LORD—and put it on the north side of the *new* altar. 15 Then King Ahaz commanded Urijah the priest, saying, "On the great *new* altar burn the morning burnt offering, the evening grain offering, the king's burnt sacrifice, and his grain offering, with the burnt offering of all the people of the land, their grain offering, and their drink offerings; and sprinkle on it all the blood of the burnt offering and all the blood of the sacrifice. And the bronze altar shall be for me to inquire *by.*" 16 Thus did Urijah the priest, according to all that King Ahaz commanded.

17 And King Ahaz cut off the panels of the carts, and removed the lavers from them; and he took down the Sea

15:33 [a] Spelled *Jerushah* in 2 Chronicles 27:1 16:6 [a] Some ancient authorities read *Syrians.*

from the bronze oxen that *were* under
it, and put it on a pavement of stones.
18Also he removed the Sabbath pavilion
which they had built in the temple, and
he removed the king's outer entrance
from the house of the LORD, on account
of the king of Assyria.
19Now the rest of the acts of Ahaz
which he did, *are* they not written in
the book of the chronicles of the kings
of Judah? 20So Ahaz rested with his
fathers, and was buried with his fathers
in the City of David. Then Hezekiah his
son reigned in his place.

Hoshea Reigns in Israel

17 In the twelfth year of Ahaz king
of Judah, Hoshea the son of Elah
became king of Israel in Samaria, *and
he reigned* nine years. 2And he did evil
in the sight of the LORD, but not as the
kings of Israel who were before him.
3Shalmaneser king of Assyria came up
against him; and Hoshea became his
vassal, and paid him tribute money.
4And the king of Assyria uncovered
a conspiracy by Hoshea; for he had
sent messengers to So, king of Egypt,
and brought no tribute to the king of
Assyria, as *he had done* year by year.
Therefore the king of Assyria shut him
up, and bound him in prison.

Israel Carried Captive to Assyria

5Now the king of Assyria went through-
out all the land, and went up to Samaria
and besieged it for three years. 6In the
ninth year of Hoshea, the king of As-
syria took Samaria and carried Israel
away to Assyria, and placed them in
Halah and by the Habor, the River of
Gozan, and in the cities of the Medes.
7For so it was that the children of Is-
rael had sinned against the LORD their
God, who had brought them up out of
the land of Egypt, from under the hand
of Pharaoh king of Egypt; and they had
feared other gods, 8and had walked in
the statutes of the nations whom the
LORD had cast out from before the chil-
dren of Israel, and of the kings of Israel,
which they had made. 9Also the children
of Israel secretly did against the LORD
their God things that *were* not right, and
they built for themselves high places in
all their cities, from watchtower to for-
tified city. 10They set up for themselves
sacred pillars and wooden images[a] on
every high hill and under every green
tree. 11There they burned incense on all
the high places, like the nations whom
the LORD had carried away before them;
and they did wicked things to provoke
the LORD to anger, 12for they served
idols, of which the LORD had said to
them, "You shall not do this thing."
13Yet the LORD testified against Is-
rael and against Judah, by all of His
prophets, every seer, saying, "Turn from
your evil ways, and keep My command-
ments *and* My statutes, according to
all the law which I commanded your
fathers, and which I sent to you by My
servants the prophets." 14Nevertheless
they would not hear, but stiffened their
necks, like the necks of their fathers,
who did not believe in the LORD their
God. 15And they rejected His statutes
and His covenant that He had made
with their fathers, and His testimonies
which He had testified against them;
they followed idols, became idolaters,
and *went* after the nations who *were*
all around them, *concerning* whom
the LORD had charged them that they
should not do like them. 16So they left all
the commandments of the LORD their
God, made for themselves a molded
image *and* two calves, made a wooden
image and worshiped all the host of
heaven, and served Baal. 17And they
caused their sons and daughters to pass
through the fire, practiced witchcraft
and soothsaying, and sold themselves
to do evil in the sight of the LORD, to
provoke Him to anger. 18Therefore the
LORD was very angry with Israel, and
removed them from His sight; there was
none left but the tribe of Judah alone.
19Also Judah did not keep the com-
mandments of the LORD their God, but
walked in the statutes of Israel which
they made. 20And the LORD rejected
all the descendants of Israel, afflicted
them, and delivered them into the hand
of plunderers, until He had cast them

17:10 [a] Hebrew *Asherim*, Canaanite deities

from His sight. 21For He tore Israel from
the house of David, and they made Jer-
oboam the son of Nebat king. Then Jer-
oboam drove Israel from following the
LORD, and made them commit a great
sin. 22For the children of Israel walked
in all the sins of Jeroboam which he
did; they did not depart from them,
23until the LORD removed Israel out
of His sight, as He had said by all His
servants the prophets. So Israel was
carried away from their own land to
Assyria, *as it is* to this day.

Assyria Resettles Samaria

24Then the king of Assyria brought
people from Babylon, Cuthah, Ava,
Hamath, and from Sepharvaim, and
placed *them* in the cities of Samaria
instead of the children of Israel; and
they took possession of Samaria and
dwelt in its cities. 25And it was so, at the
beginning of their dwelling there, *that*
they did not fear the LORD; therefore
the LORD sent lions among them, which
killed *some* of them. 26So they spoke to
the king of Assyria, saying, "The nations
whom you have removed and placed in
the cities of Samaria do not know the
rituals of the God of the land; therefore
He has sent lions among them, and in-
deed, they are killing them because they
do not know the rituals of the God of the
land." 27Then the king of Assyria com-
manded, saying, "Send there one of the
priests whom you brought from there;
let him go and dwell there, and let him
teach them the rituals of the God of the
land." 28Then one of the priests whom
they had carried away from Samaria
came and dwelt in Bethel, and taught
them how they should fear the LORD.

29However every nation continued to
make gods of its own, and put *them* in
the shrines on the high places which the
Samaritans had made, *every* nation in
the cities where they dwelt. 30The men
of Babylon made Succoth Benoth, the
men of Cuth made Nergal, the men of
Hamath made Ashima, 31and the Avites
made Nibhaz and Tartak; and the Se-
pharvites burned their children in fire
to Adrammelech and Anammelech, the
gods of Sepharvaim. 32So they feared
the LORD, and from every class they
appointed for themselves priests of the
high places, who sacrificed for them in
the shrines of the high places. 33They
feared the LORD, yet served their own
gods—according to the rituals of the
nations from among whom they were
carried away.

34To this day they continue prac-
ticing the former rituals; they do not
fear the LORD, nor do they follow their
statutes or their ordinances, or the law
and commandment which the LORD
had commanded the children of Jacob,
whom He named Israel, 35with whom
the LORD had made a covenant and
charged them, saying: "You shall not
fear other gods, nor bow down to them
nor serve them nor sacrifice to them;
36but the LORD, who brought you up
from the land of Egypt with great pow-
er and an outstretched arm, Him you
shall fear, Him you shall worship, and to
Him you shall offer sacrifice. 37And the
statutes, the ordinances, the law, and the
commandment which He wrote for you,
you shall be careful to observe forever;
you shall not fear other gods. 38And the
covenant that I have made with you, you
shall not forget, nor shall you fear other
gods. 39But the LORD your God you shall
fear; and He will deliver you from the
hand of all your enemies." 40However
they did not obey, but they followed
their former rituals. 41So these nations
feared the LORD, yet served their carved
images; also their children and their
children's children have continued doing
as their fathers did, even to this day.

Hezekiah Reigns in Judah

18 Now it came to pass in the third
year of Hoshea the son of Elah,
king of Israel, *that* Hezekiah the son
of Ahaz, king of Judah, began to reign.
2He was twenty-five years old when he
became king, and he reigned twenty-
nine years in Jerusalem. His mother's
name *was* Abi[a] the daughter of Zecha-
riah. 3And he did *what was* right in the
sight of the LORD, according to all that
his father David had done.

18:2 [a] Called *Abijah* in 2 Chronicles 29:1ff

4He removed the high places and broke
the *sacred* pillars, cut down the wooden
image[a] and broke in pieces the bronze
serpent that Moses had made; for until
those days the children of Israel burned
incense to it, and called it Nehushtan.[b]
5He trusted in the LORD God of Israel, so
that after him was none like him among
all the kings of Judah, nor who were be-
fore him. 6For he held fast to the LORD;
he did not depart from following Him,
but kept His commandments, which
the LORD had commanded Moses. 7The
LORD was with him; he prospered wher-
ever he went. And he rebelled against
the king of Assyria and did not serve
him. 8He subdued the Philistines, as far
as Gaza and its territory, from watch-
tower to fortified city.

9Now it came to pass in the fourth
year of King Hezekiah, which *was* the
seventh year of Hoshea the son of Elah,
king of Israel, *that* Shalmaneser king of
Assyria came up against Samaria and
besieged it. 10And at the end of three
years they took it. In the sixth year of
Hezekiah, that *is,* the ninth year of Ho-
shea king of Israel, Samaria was taken.
11Then the king of Assyria carried Israel
away captive to Assyria, and put them
in Halah and by the Habor, the River of
Gozan, and in the cities of the Medes,
12because they did not obey the voice
of the LORD their God, but transgressed
His covenant *and* all that Moses the ser-
vant of the LORD had commanded; and
they would neither hear nor do *them.*

13And in the fourteenth year of King
Hezekiah, Sennacherib king of Assyria
came up against all the fortified cities of
Judah and took them. 14Then Hezekiah
king of Judah sent to the king of Assyria
at Lachish, saying, "I have done wrong;
turn away from me; whatever you im-
pose on me I will pay." And the king of
Assyria assessed Hezekiah king of Judah
three hundred talents of silver and thirty
talents of gold. 15So Hezekiah gave *him*
all the silver that was found in the house
of the LORD and in the treasuries of the
king's house. 16At that time Hezekiah
stripped *the gold from* the doors of the
temple of the LORD, and *from* the pillars
which Hezekiah king of Judah had over-
laid, and gave it to the king of Assyria.

Sennacherib Boasts Against the LORD

17Then the king of Assyria sent *the* Tar-
tan,[a] *the* Rabsaris,[b] *and the* Rabshakeh[c]
from Lachish, with a great army against
Jerusalem, to King Hezekiah. And they
went up and came to Jerusalem. When
they had come up, they went and stood
by the aqueduct from the upper pool,
which *was* on the highway to the Ful-
ler's Field. 18And when they had called
to the king, Eliakim the son of Hilkiah,
who *was* over the household, Shebna the
scribe, and Joah the son of Asaph, the
recorder, came out to them. 19Then
the Rabshakeh said to them, "Say now
to Hezekiah, 'Thus says the great king,
the king of Assyria: "What confidence *is*
this in which you trust? 20You speak of
having plans and power for war; but *they*
are mere words. And in whom do you
trust, that you rebel against me? 21Now
look! You are trusting in the staff of this
broken reed, Egypt, on which if a man
leans, it will go into his hand and pierce
it. So *is* Pharaoh king of Egypt to all who
trust in him. 22But if you say to me, 'We
trust in the LORD our God,' *is* it not He
whose high places and whose altars
Hezekiah has taken away, and said to
Judah and Jerusalem, 'You shall worship
before this altar in Jerusalem'?"' 23Now
therefore, I urge you, give a pledge to
my master the king of Assyria, and I
will give you two thousand horses—if
you are able on your part to put riders
on them! 24How then will you repel one
captain of the least of my master's ser-
vants, and put your trust in Egypt for
chariots and horsemen? 25Have I now
come up without the LORD against this
place to destroy it? The LORD said to me,
'Go up against this land, and destroy it.'"

26Then Eliakim the son of Hilkiah,
Shebna, and Joah said to *the* Rab-
shakeh, "Please speak to your servants
in Aramaic, for we understand *it;* and do
not speak to us in Hebrew[a] in the hear-
ing of the people who *are* on the wall."

18:4 [a] Hebrew *Asherah,* a Canaanite goddess [b] Literally *Bronze Thing* **18:17** [a] A title, probably *Commander in Chief* [b] A title, probably *Chief Officer* [c] A title, probably *Chief of Staff* or *Governor*
18:26 [a] Literally *Judean*

27But *the* Rabshakeh said to them,
"Has my master sent me to your mas-
ter and to you to speak these words,
and not to the men who sit on the wall,
who will eat and drink their own waste
with you?"
28Then *the* Rabshakeh stood and called
out with a loud voice in Hebrew, and
spoke, saying, "Hear the word of the
great king, the king of Assyria! 29Thus
says the king: 'Do not let Hezekiah de-
ceive you, for he shall not be able to deliv-
er you from his hand; 30nor let Hezekiah
make you trust in the LORD, saying, "The
LORD will surely deliver us; this city shall
not be given into the hand of the king of
Assyria." ' 31Do not listen to Hezekiah; for
thus says the king of Assyria: 'Make *peace*
with me by a present and come out to me;
and every one of you eat from his own
vine and every one from his own fig tree,
and every one of you drink the waters of
his own cistern; 32until I come and take
you away to a land like your own land,
a land of grain and new wine, a land
of bread and vineyards, a land of olive
groves and honey, that you may live and
not die. But do not listen to Hezekiah, lest
he persuade you, saying, "The LORD will
deliver us." 33Has any of the gods of the
nations at all delivered its land from the
hand of the king of Assyria? 34Where *are*
the gods of Hamath and Arpad? Where
are the gods of Sepharvaim and Hena
and Ivah? Indeed, have they delivered
Samaria from my hand? 35Who among
all the gods of the lands have delivered
their countries from my hand, that the
LORD should deliver Jerusalem from
my hand?' "
36But the people held their peace and
answered him not a word; for the king's
commandment was, "Do not answer
him." 37Then Eliakim the son of Hilkiah,
who *was* over the household, Shebna the
scribe, and Joah the son of Asaph, the
recorder, came to Hezekiah with *their*
clothes torn, and told him the words of
the Rabshakeh.

Isaiah Assures Deliverance

19 And so it was, when King Hez-
ekiah heard *it,* that he tore his
clothes, covered himself with sackcloth,
and went into the house of the LORD.
2Then he sent Eliakim, who *was* over
the household, Shebna the scribe, and
the elders of the priests, covered with
sackcloth, to Isaiah the prophet, the
son of Amoz. 3And they said to him,
"Thus says Hezekiah: 'This day *is* a day
of trouble, and rebuke, and blasphemy;
for the children have come to birth, but
there is no strength to bring them forth.
4It may be that the LORD your God will
hear all the words of *the* Rabshakeh,
whom his master the king of Assyria
has sent to reproach the living God,
and will rebuke the words which the
LORD your God has heard. Therefore
lift up *your* prayer for the remnant that
is left.' "
5So the servants of King Hezeki-
ah came to Isaiah. 6And Isaiah said
to them, "Thus you shall say to your
master, 'Thus says the LORD: "Do not
be afraid of the words which you have
heard, with which the servants of the
king of Assyria have blasphemed Me.
7Surely I will send a spirit upon him,
and he shall hear a rumor and return
to his own land; and I will cause him
to fall by the sword in his own land." ' "

Sennacherib's Threat and Hezekiah's Prayer

8Then *the* Rabshakeh returned and
found the king of Assyria warring
against Libnah, for he heard that he
had departed from Lachish. 9And the
king heard concerning Tirhakah king
of Ethiopia, "Look, he has come out
to make war with you." So he again
sent messengers to Hezekiah, saying,
10"Thus you shall speak to Hezekiah
king of Judah, saying: 'Do not let your
God in whom you trust deceive you,
saying, "Jerusalem shall not be given
into the hand of the king of Assyria."
11Look! You have heard what the kings
of Assyria have done to all lands by
utterly destroying them; and shall you
be delivered? 12Have the gods of the na-
tions delivered those whom my fathers
have destroyed, Gozan and Haran and
Rezeph, and the people of Eden who
were in Telassar? 13Where *is* the king
of Hamath, the king of Arpad, and the
king of the city of Sepharvaim, Hena,
and Ivah?' "

14And Hezekiah received the letter from
the hand of the messengers, and read it;
and Hezekiah went up to the house of
the LORD, and spread it before the LORD.
15Then Hezekiah prayed before the LORD,
and said: "O LORD God of Israel, *the One*
who dwells *between* the cherubim, You
are God, You alone, of all the kingdoms
of the earth. You have made heaven
and earth. 16Incline Your ear, O LORD,
and hear; open Your eyes, O LORD, and
see; and hear the words of Sennacherib,
which he has sent to reproach the living
God. 17Truly, LORD, the kings of Assyria
have laid waste the nations and their
lands, 18and have cast their gods into
the fire; for they *were* not gods, but the
work of men's hands—wood and stone.
Therefore they destroyed them. 19Now
therefore, O LORD our God, I pray, save
us from his hand, that all the kingdoms
of the earth may know that You *are* the
LORD God, You alone."

The Word of the LORD Concerning Sennacherib

20Then Isaiah the son of Amoz sent to
Hezekiah, saying, "Thus says the LORD
God of Israel: 'Because you have prayed
to Me against Sennacherib king of As-
syria, I have heard.' 21This *is* the word
which the LORD has spoken concerning
him:

'The virgin, the daughter of Zion,
Has despised you, laughed you to scorn;
The daughter of Jerusalem
Has shaken *her* head behind your back!

22 'Whom have you reproached and blasphemed?
Against whom have you raised *your* voice,
And lifted up your eyes on high?
Against the Holy *One* of Israel.
23 By your messengers you have reproached the Lord,
And said: "By the multitude of my chariots
I have come up to the height of the mountains,
To the limits of Lebanon;
I will cut down its tall cedars
And its choice cypress trees;
I will enter the extremity of its borders,
To its fruitful forest.
24 I have dug and drunk strange water,
And with the soles of my feet I have dried up
All the brooks of defense."

25 'Did you not hear long ago
How I made it,
From ancient times that I formed it?
Now I have brought it to pass,
That you should be
For crushing fortified cities *into* heaps of ruins.
26 Therefore their inhabitants had little power;
They were dismayed and confounded;
They were *as* the grass of the field
And the green herb,
As the grass on the housetops
And *grain* blighted before it is grown.

27 'But I know your dwelling place,
Your going out and your coming in,
And your rage against Me.
28 Because your rage against Me and your tumult
Have come up to My ears,
Therefore I will put My hook in your nose
And My bridle in your lips,
And I will turn you back
By the way which you came.

29'This *shall be* a sign to you:

'You shall eat this year such as grows of itself,
And in the second year what springs from the same;
Also in the third year sow and reap,
Plant vineyards and eat the fruit of them.
30 And the remnant who have escaped of the house of Judah
Shall again take root downward,
And bear fruit upward.

31 For out of Jerusalem shall go a
remnant,
And those who escape from
Mount Zion.
The zeal of the LORD of hosts[a] will
do this.'

32"Therefore thus says the LORD con-
cerning the king of Assyria:

'He shall not come into this city,
Nor shoot an arrow there,
Nor come before it with shield,
Nor build a siege mound against it.
33 By the way that he came,
By the same shall he return;
And he shall not come into this
city,'
Says the LORD.
34 'For I will defend this city, to save it
For My own sake and for My
servant David's sake.' "

Sennacherib's Defeat and Death

35And it came to pass on a certain night
that the angel[a] of the LORD went out, and
killed in the camp of the Assyrians one
hundred and eighty-five thousand; and
when *people* arose early in the morning,
there were the corpses—all dead. 36So
Sennacherib king of Assyria departed
and went away, returned *home*, and re-
mained at Nineveh. 37Now it came to
pass, as he was worshiping in the temple
of Nisroch his god, that his sons Adram-
melech and Sharezer struck him down
with the sword; and they escaped into
the land of Ararat. Then Esarhaddon his
son reigned in his place.

Hezekiah's Life Extended

20 In those days Hezekiah was sick
and near death. And Isaiah the
prophet, the son of Amoz, went to him
and said to him, "Thus says the LORD:
'Set your house in order, for you shall
die, and not live.' "

2Then he turned his face toward the
wall, and prayed to the LORD, saying,
3"Remember now, O LORD, I pray, how
I have walked before You in truth and
with a loyal heart, and have done *what*
was good in Your sight." And Hezekiah
wept bitterly.

4And it happened, before Isaiah had
gone out into the middle court, that the
word of the LORD came to him, saying,
5"Return and tell Hezekiah the leader of
My people, 'Thus says the LORD, the God
of David your father: "I have heard your
prayer, I have seen your tears; surely I
will heal you. On the third day you shall
go up to the house of the LORD. 6And
I will add to your days fifteen years. I
will deliver you and this city from the
hand of the king of Assyria; and I will
defend this city for My own sake, and
for the sake of My servant David." ' "

7Then Isaiah said, "Take a lump of
figs." So they took and laid *it* on the
boil, and he recovered.

8And Hezekiah said to Isaiah, "What
is the sign that the LORD will heal me,
and that I shall go up to the house of
the LORD the third day?"

9Then Isaiah said, "This is the sign to
you from the LORD, that the LORD will
do the thing which He has spoken: *shall*
the shadow go forward ten degrees or
go backward ten degrees?"

10And Hezekiah answered, "It is an
easy thing for the shadow to go down
ten degrees; no, but let the shadow go
backward ten degrees."

11So Isaiah the prophet cried out to the
LORD, and He brought the shadow ten
degrees backward, by which it had gone
down on the sundial of Ahaz.

The Babylonian Envoys

12At that time Berodach-Baladan[a] the
son of Baladan, king of Babylon, sent
letters and a present to Hezekiah, for
he heard that Hezekiah had been sick.
13And Hezekiah was attentive to them,
and showed them all the house of his
treasures—the silver and gold, the spic-
es and precious ointment, and all[a] his
armory—all that was found among
his treasures. There was nothing in his
house or in all his dominion that Hez-
ekiah did not show them.

14Then Isaiah the prophet went to King
Hezekiah, and said to him, "What did

19:31 [a] Following many Hebrew manuscripts and ancient versions (compare Isaiah 37:32); Masoretic Text omits *of hosts*. **19:35** [a] Or *Angel* **20:12** [a] Spelled *Merodach-Baladan* in Isaiah 39:1
20:13 [a] Following many Hebrew manuscripts, Syriac, and Targum; Masoretic Text omits *all*.

these men say, and from where did they
come to you?"
So Hezekiah said, "They came from a
far country, from Babylon."
15And he said, "What have they seen
in your house?"
So Hezekiah answered, "They have
seen all that *is* in my house; there is
nothing among my treasures that I
have not shown them."
16Then Isaiah said to Hezekiah, "Hear
the word of the LORD: 17'Behold, the
days are coming when all that *is* in
your house, and what your fathers have
accumulated until this day, shall be
carried to Babylon; nothing shall be
left,' says the LORD. 18'And they shall
take away some of your sons who will
descend from you, whom you will beget;
and they shall be eunuchs in the palace
of the king of Babylon.' "
19So Hezekiah said to Isaiah, "The
word of the LORD which you have spo-
ken *is* good!" For he said, "Will there not
be peace and truth at least in my days?"

Death of Hezekiah

20Now the rest of the acts of Hezeki-
ah—all his might, and how he made a
pool and a tunnel and brought water
into the city—*are* they not written in
the book of the chronicles of the kings
of Judah? 21So Hezekiah rested with his
fathers. Then Manasseh his son reigned
in his place.

Manasseh Reigns in Judah

21 Manasseh *was* twelve years old
when he became king, and he
reigned fifty-five years in Jerusalem. His
mother's name *was* Hephzibah. 2And he
did evil in the sight of the LORD, accord-
ing to the abominations of the nations
whom the LORD had cast out before the
children of Israel. 3For he rebuilt the
high places which Hezekiah his father
had destroyed; he raised up altars for
Baal, and made a wooden image,[a] as
Ahab king of Israel had done; and he
worshiped all the host of heaven[b] and
served them. 4He also built altars in the
house of the LORD, of which the LORD
had said, "In Jerusalem I will put My
name." 5And he built altars for all the
host of heaven in the two courts of the
house of the LORD. 6Also he made his son
pass through the fire, practiced sooth-
saying, used witchcraft, and consulted
spiritists and mediums. He did much evil
in the sight of the LORD, to provoke *Him*
to anger. 7He even set a carved image of
Asherah[a] that he had made, in the house
of which the LORD had said to David
and to Solomon his son, "In this house
and in Jerusalem, which I have chosen
out of all the tribes of Israel, I will put
My name forever; 8and I will not make
the feet of Israel wander anymore from
the land which I gave their fathers—
only if they are careful to do according
to all that I have commanded them,
and according to all the law that My
servant Moses commanded them." 9But
they paid no attention, and Manasseh
seduced them to do more evil than the
nations whom the LORD had destroyed
before the children of Israel.
10And the LORD spoke by His servants
the prophets, saying, 11"Because Ma-
nasseh king of Judah has done these
abominations (he has acted more wick-
edly than all the Amorites who *were*
before him, and has also made Judah
sin with his idols), 12therefore thus says
the LORD God of Israel: 'Behold, *I* am
bringing *such* calamity upon Jerusa-
lem and Judah, that whoever hears of
it, both his ears will tingle. 13And I will
stretch over Jerusalem the measuring
line of Samaria and the plummet of the
house of Ahab; I will wipe Jerusalem as
one wipes a dish, wiping *it* and turning
it upside down. 14So I will forsake the
remnant of My inheritance and deliver
them into the hand of their enemies;
and they shall become victims of plun-
der to all their enemies, 15because they
have done evil in My sight, and have
provoked Me to anger since the day
their fathers came out of Egypt, even
to this day.' "
16Moreover Manasseh shed very much
innocent blood, till he had filled Jeru-
salem from one end to another, besides
his sin by which he made Judah sin, in
doing evil in the sight of the LORD.

21:3 [a] Hebrew *Asherah,* a Canaanite goddess [b] The gods of the Assyrians **21:7** [a] A Canaanite goddess

17Now the rest of the acts of Manas-
seh—all that he did, and the sin that
he committed—*are* they not written in
the book of the chronicles of the kings
of Judah? 18So Manasseh rested with his
fathers, and was buried in the garden
of his own house, in the garden of Uzza.
Then his son Amon reigned in his place.

Amon's Reign and Death

19Amon *was* twenty-two years old
when he became king, and he reigned
two years in Jerusalem. His mother's
name *was* Meshullemeth the daughter
of Haruz of Jotbah. 20And he did evil
in the sight of the LORD, as his father
Manasseh had done. 21So he walked in
all the ways that his father had walked;
and he served the idols that his father
had served, and worshiped them. 22He
forsook the LORD God of his fathers, and
did not walk in the way of the LORD.

23Then the servants of Amon con-
spired against him, and killed the king
in his own house. 24But the people of
the land executed all those who had
conspired against King Amon. Then the
people of the land made his son Josiah
king in his place.

25Now the rest of the acts of Amon
which he did, *are* they not written in
the book of the chronicles of the kings
of Judah? 26And he was buried in his
tomb in the garden of Uzza. Then Josiah
his son reigned in his place.

Josiah Reigns in Judah

22 Josiah *was* eight years old
when he became king, and he
reigned thirty-one years in Jerusalem.
His mother's name *was* Jedidah the
daughter of Adaiah of Bozkath. 2And
he did *what was* right in the sight of the
LORD, and walked in all the ways of his
father David; he did not turn aside to
the right hand or to the left.

Hilkiah Finds the Book of the Law

3Now it came to pass, in the eighteenth
year of King Josiah, *that* the king sent
Shaphan the scribe, the son of Azaliah,
the son of Meshullam, to the house of
the LORD, saying: 4"Go up to Hilkiah
the high priest, that he may count the
money which has been brought into
the house of the LORD, which the door-
keepers have gathered from the people.
5And let them deliver it into the hand
of those doing the work, who are the
overseers in the house of the LORD;
let them give it to those who *are* in the
house of the LORD doing the work, to
repair the damages of the house— 6to
carpenters and builders and masons—
and to buy timber and hewn stone to
repair the house. 7However there need
be no accounting made with them of
the money delivered into their hand,
because they deal faithfully."

8Then Hilkiah the high priest said to
Shaphan the scribe, "I have found the
Book of the Law in the house of the LORD."
And Hilkiah gave the book to Shaphan,
and he read it. 9So Shaphan the scribe
went to the king, bringing the king word,
saying, "Your servants have gathered the
money that was found in the house, and
have delivered it into the hand of those
who do the work, who oversee the house
of the LORD." 10Then Shaphan the scribe
showed the king, saying, "Hilkiah the
priest has given me a book." And Sha-
phan read it before the king.

11Now it happened, when the king
heard the words of the Book of the Law,
that he tore his clothes. 12Then the king
commanded Hilkiah the priest, Ahikam
the son of Shaphan, Achbor[a] the son
of Michaiah, Shaphan the scribe, and
Asaiah a servant of the king, saying,
13"Go, inquire of the LORD for me, for the
people and for all Judah, concerning
the words of this book that has been
found; for great *is* the wrath of the LORD
that is aroused against us, because our
fathers have not obeyed the words of
this book, to do according to all that is
written concerning us."

14So Hilkiah the priest, Ahikam, Ach-
bor, Shaphan, and Asaiah went to Hul-
dah the prophetess, the wife of Shallum
the son of Tikvah, the son of Harhas,
keeper of the wardrobe. (She dwelt in
Jerusalem in the Second Quarter.) And
they spoke with her. 15Then she said
to them, "Thus says the LORD God of

22:12 [a] *Abdon the son of Micah* in 2 Chronicles 34:20

Israel, 'Tell the man who sent you to
Me, 16"Thus says the LORD: 'Behold, I
will bring calamity on this place and
on its inhabitants—all the words of the
book which the king of Judah has read—
17because they have forsaken Me and
burned incense to other gods, that they
might provoke Me to anger with all the
works of their hands. Therefore My wrath
shall be aroused against this place and
shall not be quenched.' " ' 18But as for the
king of Judah, who sent you to inquire
of the LORD, in this manner you shall
speak to him, 'Thus says the LORD God
of Israel: "*Concerning* the words which
you have heard— 19because your heart
was tender, and you humbled yourself
before the LORD when you heard what
I spoke against this place and against
its inhabitants, that they would become
a desolation and a curse, and you tore
your clothes and wept before Me, I also
have heard *you*," says the LORD. 20"Sure-
ly, therefore, I will gather you to your
fathers, and you shall be gathered to
your grave in peace; and your eyes shall
not see all the calamity which I will bring
on this place." ' " So they brought back
word to the king.

Josiah Restores True Worship

23 Now the king sent them to gather
all the elders of Judah and Je-
rusalem to him. 2The king went up to
the house of the LORD with all the men
of Judah, and with him all the inhab-
itants of Jerusalem—the priests and
the prophets and all the people, both
small and great. And he read in their
hearing all the words of the Book of the
Covenant which had been found in the
house of the LORD.

3Then the king stood by a pillar and
made a covenant before the LORD, to
follow the LORD and to keep His com-
mandments and His testimonies and
His statutes, with all *his* heart and all
his soul, to perform the words of this
covenant that were written in this book.
And all the people took a stand for the
covenant. 4And the king commanded
Hilkiah the high priest, the priests of
the second order, and the doorkeepers,
to bring out of the temple of the LORD
all the articles that were made for Baal,
for Asherah,[a] and for all the host of
heaven;[b] and he burned them outside
Jerusalem in the fields of Kidron, and
carried their ashes to Bethel. 5Then he
removed the idolatrous priests whom
the kings of Judah had ordained to burn
incense on the high places in the cities
of Judah and in the places all around
Jerusalem, and those who burned in-
cense to Baal, to the sun, to the moon, to
the constellations, and to all the host of
heaven. 6And he brought out the wood-
en image[a] from the house of the LORD,
to the Brook Kidron outside Jerusa-
lem, burned it at the Brook Kidron and
ground *it* to ashes, and threw its ashes
on the graves of the common people.
7Then he tore down the *ritual* booths of
the perverted persons[a] that *were* in the
house of the LORD, where the women
wove hangings for the wooden image.
8And he brought all the priests from
the cities of Judah, and defiled the high
places where the priests had burned
incense, from Geba to Beersheba; also
he broke down the high places at the
gates which *were* at the entrance of the
Gate of Joshua the governor of the city,
which *were* to the left of the city gate.
9Nevertheless the priests of the high
places did not come up to the altar of
the LORD in Jerusalem, but they ate un-
leavened bread among their brethren.

10And he defiled Topheth, which *is*
in the Valley of the Son[a] of Hinnom,
that no man might make his son or
his daughter pass through the fire to
Molech. 11Then he removed the horses
that the kings of Judah had dedicat-
ed to the sun, at the entrance to the
house of the LORD, by the chamber of
Nathan-Melech, the officer who *was* in
the court; and he burned the chariots
of the sun with fire. 12The altars that
were on the roof, the upper chamber
of Ahaz, which the kings of Judah had
made, and the altars which Manasseh
had made in the two courts of the house
of the LORD, the king broke down and

23:4 [a] A Canaanite goddess [b] The gods of the Assyrians **23:6** [a] Hebrew *Asherah,* a Canaanite goddess **23:7** [a] Hebrew *qedeshim,* that is, those practicing sodomy and prostitution in religious rituals **23:10** [a] Kethib reads *Sons.*

pulverized there, and threw their dust
into the Brook Kidron. [13]Then the king
defiled the high places that *were* east
of Jerusalem, which *were* on the south
of the Mount of Corruption, which Sol-
omon king of Israel had built for Ashto-
reth the abomination of the Sidonians,
for Chemosh the abomination of the
Moabites, and for Milcom the abomi-
nation of the people of Ammon. [14]And
he broke in pieces the *sacred* pillars and
cut down the wooden images, and filled
their places with the bones of men.
[15]Moreover the altar that *was* at Beth-
el, *and* the high place which Jeroboam
the son of Nebat, who made Israel sin,
had made, both that altar and the high
place he broke down; and he burned the
high place *and* crushed *it* to powder, and
burned the wooden image. [16]As Josi-
ah turned, he saw the tombs that *were*
there on the mountain. And he sent and
took the bones out of the tombs and
burned *them* on the altar, and defiled
it according to the word of the LORD
which the man of God proclaimed, who
proclaimed these words. [17]Then he said,
"What gravestone *is* this that I see?"
So the men of the city told him, "*It is*
the tomb of the man of God who came
from Judah and proclaimed these
things which you have done against
the altar of Bethel."
[18]And he said, "Let him alone; let
no one move his bones." So they let
his bones alone, with the bones of the
prophet who came from Samaria.
[19]Now Josiah also took away all the
shrines of the high places that *were* in
the cities of Samaria, which the kings of
Israel had made to provoke the LORD[a]
to anger; and he did to them according
to all the deeds he had done in Bethel.
[20]He executed all the priests of the high
places who *were* there, on the altars,
and burned men's bones on them; and
he returned to Jerusalem.
[21]Then the king commanded all the
people, saying, "Keep the Passover to
the LORD your God, as *it is* written in
this Book of the Covenant." [22]Such a
Passover surely had never been held
since the days of the judges who judged
Israel, nor in all the days of the kings
of Israel and the kings of Judah. [23]But
in the eighteenth year of King Josiah
this Passover was held before the LORD
in Jerusalem. [24]Moreover Josiah put
away those who consulted mediums
and spiritists, the household gods and
idols, all the abominations that were
seen in the land of Judah and in Je-
rusalem, that he might perform the
words of the law which were written in
the book that Hilkiah the priest found
in the house of the LORD. [25]Now before
him there was no king like him, who
turned to the LORD with all his heart,
with all his soul, and with all his might,
according to all the Law of Moses; nor
after him did *any* arise like him.

Impending Judgment on Judah

[26]Nevertheless the LORD did not turn
from the fierceness of His great wrath,
with which His anger was aroused
against Judah, because of all the prov-
ocations with which Manasseh had pro-
voked Him. [27]And the LORD said, "I will
also remove Judah from My sight, as I
have removed Israel, and will cast off
this city Jerusalem which I have chosen,
and the house of which I said, 'My name
shall be there.' "[a]

Josiah Dies in Battle

[28]Now the rest of the acts of Josiah,
and all that he did, *are* they not writ-
ten in the book of the chronicles of the
kings of Judah? [29]In his days Pharaoh
Necho king of Egypt went to the aid of
the king of Assyria, to the River Euphra-
tes; and King Josiah went against him.
And *Pharaoh Necho* killed him at Megid-
do when he confronted him. [30]Then his
servants moved his body in a chariot
from Megiddo, brought him to Jerusa-
lem, and buried him in his own tomb.
And the people of the land took Jeho-
ahaz the son of Josiah, anointed him,
and made him king in his father's place.

The Reign and Captivity of Jehoahaz

[31]Jehoahaz *was* twenty-three years
old when he became king, and he
reigned three months in Jerusalem.

23:19 [a] Following Septuagint, Syriac, and Vulgate; Masoretic Text and Targum omit *the LORD*.
23:27 [a] 1 Kings 8:29

His mother's name *was* Hamutal the
daughter of Jeremiah of Libnah. 32And
he did evil in the sight of the LORD, ac-
cording to all that his fathers had done.
33Now Pharaoh Necho put him in prison
at Riblah in the land of Hamath, that
he might not reign in Jerusalem; and
he imposed on the land a tribute of one
hundred talents of silver and a talent
of gold. 34Then Pharaoh Necho made
Eliakim the son of Josiah king in place
of his father Josiah, and changed his
name to Jehoiakim. And *Pharaoh* took
Jehoahaz and went to Egypt, and he[a]
died there.

Jehoiakim Reigns in Judah

35So Jehoiakim gave the silver and
gold to Pharaoh; but he taxed the land
to give money according to the com-
mand of Pharaoh; he exacted the silver
and gold from the people of the land,
from every one according to his as-
sessment, to give *it* to Pharaoh Necho.
36Jehoiakim *was* twenty-five years old
when he became king, and he reigned
eleven years in Jerusalem. His mother's
name *was* Zebudah the daughter of
Pedaiah of Rumah. 37And he did evil
in the sight of the LORD, according to
all that his fathers had done.

Judah Overrun by Enemies

24 In his days Nebuchadnez-
zar king of Babylon came up,
and Jehoiakim became his vassal *for*
three years. Then he turned and re-
belled against him. 2And the LORD
sent against him *raiding* bands of
Chaldeans, bands of Syrians, bands
of Moabites, and bands of the people of
Ammon; He sent them against Judah
to destroy it, according to the word of
the LORD which He had spoken by His
servants the prophets. 3Surely at the
commandment of the LORD *this* came
upon Judah, to remove *them* from His
sight because of the sins of Manasseh,
according to all that he had done, 4and
also because of the innocent blood that
he had shed; for he had filled Jerusalem
with innocent blood, which the LORD
would not pardon.

5Now the rest of the acts of Jehoiakim,
and all that he did, *are* they not written
in the book of the chronicles of the kings
of Judah? 6So Jehoiakim rested with
his fathers. Then Jehoiachin his son
reigned in his place.
7And the king of Egypt did not come
out of his land anymore, for the king
of Babylon had taken all that belonged
to the king of Egypt from the Brook of
Egypt to the River Euphrates.

The Reign and Captivity of Jehoiachin

8Jehoiachin *was* eighteen years old
when he became king, and he reigned in
Jerusalem three months. His mother's
name *was* Nehushta the daughter of
Elnathan of Jerusalem. 9And he did evil
in the sight of the LORD, according to
all that his father had done.
10At that time the servants of Nebu-
chadnezzar king of Babylon came up
against Jerusalem, and the city was
besieged. 11And Nebuchadnezzar king
of Babylon came against the city, as
his servants were besieging it. 12Then
Jehoiachin king of Judah, his mother,
his servants, his princes, and his officers
went out to the king of Babylon; and the
king of Babylon, in the eighth year of
his reign, took him prisoner.

The Captivity of Jerusalem

13And he carried out from there all the
treasures of the house of the LORD and
the treasures of the king's house, and he
cut in pieces all the articles of gold which
Solomon king of Israel had made in the
temple of the LORD, as the LORD had said.
14Also he carried into captivity all Jerusa-
lem: all the captains and all the mighty
men of valor, ten thousand captives, and
all the craftsmen and smiths. None re-
mained except the poorest people of the
land. 15And he carried Jehoiachin captive
to Babylon. The king's mother, the king's
wives, his officers, and the mighty of
the land he carried into captivity from
Jerusalem to Babylon. 16All the valiant
men, seven thousand, and craftsmen
and smiths, one thousand, all *who were*
strong *and* fit for war, these the king of
Babylon brought captive to Babylon.

23:34 [a] That is, Jehoahaz

Zedekiah Reigns in Judah

17Then the king of Babylon made Mat-
taniah, *Jehoiachin's*[a] uncle, king in his
place, and changed his name to Zed-
ekiah.

18Zedekiah *was* twenty-one years old
when he became king, and he reigned
eleven years in Jerusalem. His mother's
name *was* Hamutal the daughter of Jer-
emiah of Libnah. 19He also did evil in
the sight of the LORD, according to all
that Jehoiakim had done. 20For because
of the anger of the LORD *this* happened
in Jerusalem and Judah, that He finally
cast them out from His presence. Then
Zedekiah rebelled against the king of
Babylon.

The Fall and Captivity of Judah

25 Now it came to pass in the ninth
year of his reign, in the tenth
month, on the tenth *day* of the month,
that Nebuchadnezzar king of Babylon
and all his army came against Jeru-
salem and encamped against it; and
they built a siege wall against it all
around. 2So the city was besieged un-
til the eleventh year of King Zedekiah.
3By the ninth *day* of the *fourth* month
the famine had become so severe in
the city that there was no food for the
people of the land.

4Then the city wall was broken
through, and all the men of war *fled* at
night by way of the gate between two
walls, which was by the king's garden,
even though the Chaldeans *were* still
encamped all around against the city.
And *the king*[a] went by way of the plain.[b]
5But the army of the Chaldeans pur-
sued the king, and they overtook him
in the plains of Jericho. All his army
was scattered from him. 6So they took
the king and brought him up to the
king of Babylon at Riblah, and they
pronounced judgment on him. 7Then
they killed the sons of Zedekiah before
his eyes, put out the eyes of Zedekiah,
bound him with bronze fetters, and took
him to Babylon.

8And in the fifth month, on the seventh
day of the month (which *was* the nine-
teenth year of King Nebuchadnezzar
king of Babylon), Nebuzaradan the
captain of the guard, a servant of the
king of Babylon, came to Jerusalem.
9He burned the house of the LORD and
the king's house; all the houses of Je-
rusalem, that is, all the houses of the
great, he burned with fire. 10And all the
army of the Chaldeans who *were with*
the captain of the guard broke down the
walls of Jerusalem all around.

11Then Nebuzaradan the captain of
the guard carried away captive the rest
of the people *who* remained in the city
and the defectors who had deserted to
the king of Babylon, with the rest of
the multitude. 12But the captain of the
guard left *some* of the poor of the land as
vinedressers and farmers. 13The bronze
pillars that *were* in the house of the
LORD, and the carts and the bronze Sea
that *were* in the house of the LORD, the
Chaldeans broke in pieces, and carried
their bronze to Babylon. 14They also
took away the pots, the shovels, the
trimmers, the spoons, and all the bronze
utensils with which the priests minis-
tered. 15The firepans and the basins, the
things of solid gold and solid silver, the
captain of the guard took away. 16The
two pillars, one Sea, and the carts, which
Solomon had made for the house of the
LORD, the bronze of all these articles
was beyond measure. 17The height of
one pillar *was* eighteen cubits, and the
capital on it *was* of bronze. The height
of the capital was three cubits, and the
network and pomegranates all around
the capital were all of bronze. The sec-
ond pillar was the same, with a network.

18And the captain of the guard took
Seraiah the chief priest, Zephaniah
the second priest, and the three door-
keepers. 19He also took out of the city
an officer who had charge of the men
of war, five men of the king's close as-
sociates who were found in the city,
the chief recruiting officer of the army,
who mustered the people of the land,
and sixty men of the people of the land
who were found in the city. 20So Neb-
uzaradan, captain of the guard, took
these and brought them to the king of
Babylon at Riblah. 21Then the king of

24:17 [a] Literally *his* 25:4 [a] Literally *he* [b] Or *Arabah,* that is, the Jordan Valley

Babylon struck them and put them to death at Riblah in the land of Hamath. Thus Judah was carried away captive from its own land.

Gedaliah Made Governor of Judah

22Then he made Gedaliah the son of
Ahikam, the son of Shaphan, governor
over the people who remained in the
land of Judah, whom Nebuchadnezzar
king of Babylon had left. 23Now when
all the captains of the armies, they and
their men, heard that the king of Babylon had made Gedaliah governor, they
came to Gedaliah at Mizpah—Ishmael
the son of Nethaniah, Johanan the son
of Careah, Seraiah the son of Tanhumeth the Netophathite, and Jaazaniah[a] the son of a Maachathite, they and
their men. 24And Gedaliah took an oath
before them and their men, and said to
them, "Do not be afraid of the servants
of the Chaldeans. Dwell in the land and
serve the king of Babylon, and it shall
be well with you."
25But it happened in the seventh month
that Ishmael the son of Nethaniah, the
son of Elishama, of the royal family,
came with ten men and struck and killed
Gedaliah, the Jews, as well as the Chaldeans who were with him at Mizpah.
26And all the people, small and great,
and the captains of the armies, arose
and went to Egypt; for they were afraid
of the Chaldeans.

Jehoiachin Released from Prison

27Now it came to pass in the thirty-
seventh year of the captivity of Jehoiachin king of Judah, in the twelfth
month, on the twenty-seventh *day* of
the month, *that* Evil-Merodach[a] king
of Babylon, in the year that he began
to reign, released Jehoiachin king of
Judah from prison. 28He spoke kindly
to him, and gave him a more prominent
seat than those of the kings who *were*
with him in Babylon. 29So Jehoiachin
changed from his prison garments, and
he ate bread regularly before the king
all the days of his life. 30And as for his
provisions, *there was* a regular ration
given him by the king, a portion for
each day, all the days of his life.

25:23 [a] Spelled *Jezaniah* in Jeremiah 40:8 25:27 [a] Literally *Man of Marduk*

THE FIRST BOOK OF THE

CHRONICLES

The Book of 1 Chronicles tells much of the same story that 2 Samuel and 1 Kings tells. But this book is not just a repeat of what was shared earlier. First Chronicles was written after God's people returned to their land after being in foreign captivity. It was written, then, to remind the Israelites of the good times before they were defeated by the Assyrians and Babylonians. God's people needed to remember that He is always faithful to all His promises and even though they had gone through a hard time, good times were coming once again.

- **GENRE:** History
- **AUTHOR:** Ezra
- **TIME:** 1004–971 BC (written c. 450–400 BC)
- **PURPOSE:** To remind the people who had come back to a destroyed Jerusalem that they were from the royal line of David and were God's chosen people. God had not forgotten His promises to them.

The Family of Adam—Seth to Abraham

1 Adam, Seth, Enosh, 2Cainan,[a] Ma-
halalel, Jared, 3Enoch, Methuse-
lah, Lamech, 4Noah,[a] Shem, Ham, and
Japheth.

5The sons of Japheth *were* Gomer,
Magog, Madai, Javan, Tubal, Meshech,
and Tiras. 6The sons of Gomer *were*
Ashkenaz, Diphath,[a] and Togarmah.
7The sons of Javan *were* Elishah, Tar-
shishah,[a] Kittim, and Rodanim.[b]

8The sons of Ham *were* Cush, Mizra-
im, Put, and Canaan. 9The sons of Cush
were Seba, Havilah, Sabta,[a] Raama,[b]
and Sabtecha. The sons of Raama *were*
Sheba and Dedan. 10Cush begot Nim-
rod; he began to be a mighty one on the
earth. 11Mizraim begot Ludim, Anamim,
Lehabim, Naphtuhim, 12Pathrusim,
Casluhim (from whom came the Phi-
listines and the Caphtorim). 13Canaan
begot Sidon, his firstborn, and Heth;
14the Jebusite, the Amorite, and the Gir-
gashite; 15the Hivite, the Arkite, and the
Sinite; 16the Arvadite, the Zemarite, and
the Hamathite.

17The sons of Shem *were* Elam, Asshur,
Arphaxad, Lud, Aram, Uz, Hul, Gether,
and Meshech.[a] 18Arphaxad begot She-
lah, and Shelah begot Eber. 19To Eber
were born two sons: the name of one
was Peleg,[a] for in his days the earth was
divided; and his brother's name *was*
Joktan. 20Joktan begot Almodad, She-
leph, Hazarmaveth, Jerah, 21Hadoram,
Uzal, Diklah, 22Ebal,[a] Abimael, Sheba,
23Ophir, Havilah, and Jobab. All these
were the sons of Joktan.

24Shem, Arphaxad, Shelah, 25Eber,
Peleg, Reu, 26Serug, Nahor, Terah, 27and
Abram, who *is* Abraham. 28The sons
of Abraham *were* Isaac and Ishmael.

The Family of Ishmael

29These *are* their genealogies: The
firstborn of Ishmael *was* Nebajoth;
then Kedar, Adbeel, Mibsam, 30Mish-
ma, Dumah, Massa, Hadad,[a] Tema,
31Jetur, Naphish, and Kedemah. These
were the sons of Ishmael.

The Family of Keturah

32Now the sons born to Keturah, Abra-
ham's concubine, *were* Zimran, Jokshan,
Medan, Midian, Ishbak, and Shuah. The
sons of Jokshan *were* Sheba and Dedan.

1:2 [a] Hebrew *Qenan* **1:4** [a] Following Masoretic Text and Vulgate; Septuagint adds *the sons of Noah.* **1:6** [a] Spelled *Riphath* in Genesis 10:3 **1:7** [a] Spelled *Tarshish* in Genesis 10:4 [b] Spelled *Dodanim* in Genesis 10:4 **1:9** [a] Spelled *Sabtah* in Genesis 10:7 [b] Spelled *Raamah* in Genesis 10:7 **1:17** [a] Spelled *Mash* in Genesis 10:23 **1:19** [a] Literally *Division* **1:22** [a] Spelled *Obal* in Genesis 10:28 **1:30** [a] Spelled *Hadar* in Genesis 25:15

33The sons of Midian *were* Ephah, Epher, Hanoch, Abida, and Eldaah. All these were the children of Keturah.

The Family of Isaac

34And Abraham begot Isaac. The sons of Isaac *were* Esau and Israel. 35The sons of Esau *were* Eliphaz, Reuel, Jeush, Jaalam, and Korah. 36And the sons of Eliphaz *were* Teman, Omar, Zephi,[a] Gatam, *and* Kenaz; and *by* Timna,[b] Amalek. 37The sons of Reuel *were* Nahath, Zerah, Shammah, and Mizzah.

The Family of Seir

38The sons of Seir *were* Lotan, Shobal, Zibeon, Anah, Dishon, Ezer, and Dishan. 39And the sons of Lotan *were* Hori and Homam; Lotan's sister *was* Timna. 40The sons of Shobal *were* Alian,[a] Manahath, Ebal, Shephi,[b] and Onam. The sons of Zibeon *were* Ajah and Anah. 41The son of Anah *was* Dishon. The sons of Dishon *were* Hamran,[a] Eshban, Ithran, and Cheran. 42The sons of Ezer *were* Bilhan, Zaavan, *and* Jaakan.[a] The sons of Dishan *were* Uz and Aran.

The Kings of Edom

43Now these *were* the kings who reigned in the land of Edom before a king reigned over the children of Israel: Bela the son of Beor, and the name of his city was Dinhabah. 44And when Bela died, Jobab the son of Zerah of Bozrah reigned in his place. 45When Jobab died, Husham of the land of the Temanites reigned in his place. 46And when Husham died, Hadad the son of Bedad, who attacked Midian in the field of Moab, reigned in his place. The name of his city *was* Avith. 47When Hadad died, Samlah of Masrekah reigned in his place. 48And when Samlah died, Saul of Rehoboth-by-the-River reigned in his place. 49When Saul died, Baal-Hanan the son of Achbor reigned in his place. 50And when Baal-Hanan died, Hadad[a] reigned in his place; and the name of his city was Pai.[b] His wife's name was Mehetabel the daughter of Matred, the daughter of Mezahab. 51Hadad died also. And the chiefs of Edom were Chief Timnah, Chief Aliah,[a] Chief Jetheth, 52Chief Aholibamah, Chief Elah, Chief Pinon, 53Chief Kenaz, Chief Teman, Chief Mibzar, 54Chief Magdiel, and Chief Iram. These *were* the chiefs of Edom.

The Family of Israel

2 These *were* the sons of Israel: Reuben, Simeon, Levi, Judah, Issachar, Zebulun, 2Dan, Joseph, Benjamin, Naphtali, Gad, and Asher.

From Judah to David

3The sons of Judah *were* Er, Onan, and Shelah. *These* three were born to him by the daughter of Shua, the Canaanitess. Er, the firstborn of Judah, was wicked in the sight of the LORD; so He killed him. 4And Tamar, his daughter-in-law, bore him Perez and Zerah. All the sons of Judah *were* five.

5The sons of Perez *were* Hezron and Hamul. 6The sons of Zerah *were* Zimri, Ethan, Heman, Calcol, and Dara—five of them in all.

7The son of Carmi *was* Achar,[a] the troubler of Israel, who transgressed in the accursed thing.

8The son of Ethan *was* Azariah.

9Also the sons of Hezron who were born to him *were* Jerahmeel, Ram, and Chelubai.[a] 10Ram begot Amminadab, and Amminadab begot Nahshon, leader of the children of Judah; 11Nahshon begot Salma,[a] and Salma begot Boaz; 12Boaz begot Obed, and Obed begot Jesse; 13Jesse begot Eliab his firstborn, Abinadab the second, Shimea[a] the third, 14Nethanel the fourth, Raddai the fifth, 15Ozem the sixth, *and* David the seventh.

16Now their sisters *were* Zeruiah and Abigail. And the sons of Zeruiah *were* Abishai, Joab, and Asahel—three. 17Abigail bore Amasa; and the father of Amasa *was* Jether the Ishmaelite.[a]

1:36 [a] Spelled *Zepho* in Genesis 36:11 [b] Compare Genesis 36:12 **1:40** [a] Spelled *Alvan* in Genesis 36:23 [b] Spelled *Shepho* in Genesis 36:23 **1:41** [a] Spelled *Hemdan* in Genesis 36:26 **1:42** [a] Spelled *Akan* in Genesis 36:27 **1:50** [a] Spelled *Hadar* in Genesis 36:39 [b] Spelled *Pau* in Genesis 36:39 **1:51** [a] Spelled *Alvah* in Genesis 36:40 **2:7** [a] Spelled *Achan* in Joshua 7:1 and elsewhere **2:9** [a] Spelled *Caleb* in 2:18, 42 **2:11** [a] Spelled *Salmon* in Ruth 4:21 and Luke 3:32 **2:13** [a] Spelled *Shammah* in 1 Samuel 16:9 and elsewhere **2:17** [a] Compare 2 Samuel 17:25

The Family of Hezron

18Caleb the son of Hezron had children by Azubah, *his* wife, and by Jerioth. Now these were her sons: Jesher, Shobab, and Ardon. 19When Azubah died, Caleb took Ephrath[a] as his wife, who bore him Hur. 20And Hur begot Uri, and Uri begot Bezalel.

21Now afterward Hezron went in to the daughter of Machir the father of Gilead, whom he married when he *was* sixty years old; and she bore him Segub. 22Segub begot Jair, who had twenty-three cities in the land of Gilead. 23(Geshur and Syria took from them the towns of Jair, with Kenath and its towns—sixty towns.) All these *belonged to* the sons of Machir the father of Gilead. 24After Hezron died in Caleb Ephrathah, Hezron's wife Abijah bore him Ashhur the father of Tekoa.

The Family of Jerahmeel

25The sons of Jerahmeel, the firstborn of Hezron, *were* Ram, the firstborn, and Bunah, Oren, Ozem, *and* Ahijah. 26Jerahmeel had another wife, whose name was Atarah; she was the mother of Onam. 27The sons of Ram, the firstborn of Jerahmeel, were Maaz, Jamin, and Eker. 28The sons of Onam were Shammai and Jada. The sons of Shammai *were* Nadab and Abishur.

29And the name of the wife of Abishur *was* Abihail, and she bore him Ahban and Molid. 30The sons of Nadab *were* Seled and Appaim; Seled died without children. 31The son of Appaim *was* Ishi, the son of Ishi *was* Sheshan, and Sheshan's son *was* Ahlai. 32The sons of Jada, the brother of Shammai, *were* Jether and Jonathan; Jether died without children. 33The sons of Jonathan *were* Peleth and Zaza. These were the sons of Jerahmeel.

34Now Sheshan had no sons, only daughters. And Sheshan had an Egyptian servant whose name *was* Jarha. 35Sheshan gave his daughter to Jarha his servant as wife, and she bore him Attai. 36Attai begot Nathan, and Nathan begot Zabad; 37Zabad begot Ephlal, and Ephlal begot Obed; 38Obed begot Jehu, and Jehu begot Azariah; 39Azariah begot Helez, and Helez begot Eleasah; 40Eleasah begot Sismai, and Sismai begot Shallum; 41Shallum begot Jekamiah, and Jekamiah begot Elishama.

The Family of Caleb

42The descendants of Caleb the brother of Jerahmeel *were* Mesha, his firstborn, who was the father of Ziph, and the sons of Mareshah the father of Hebron. 43The sons of Hebron *were* Korah, Tappuah, Rekem, and Shema. 44Shema begot Raham the father of Jorkoam, and Rekem begot Shammai. 45And the son of Shammai *was* Maon, and Maon *was* the father of Beth Zur.

46Ephah, Caleb's concubine, bore Haran, Moza, and Gazez; and Haran begot Gazez. 47And the sons of Jahdai *were* Regem, Jotham, Geshan, Pelet, Ephah, and Shaaph.

48Maachah, Caleb's concubine, bore Sheber and Tirhanah. 49She also bore Shaaph the father of Madmannah, Sheva the father of Machbenah and the father of Gibea. And the daughter of Caleb *was* Achsah.

50These were the descendants of Caleb: The sons of Hur, the firstborn of Ephrathah, *were* Shobal the father of Kirjath Jearim, 51Salma the father of Bethlehem, *and* Hareph the father of Beth Gader.

52And Shobal the father of Kirjath Jearim had descendants: Haroeh, *and* half of the *families of* Manuhoth.[a] 53The families of Kirjath Jearim *were* the Ithrites, the Puthites, the Shumathites, and the Mishraites. From these came the Zorathites and the Eshtaolites.

54The sons of Salma *were* Bethlehem, the Netophathites, Atroth Beth Joab, half of the Manahethites, and the Zorites.

55And the families of the scribes who dwelt at Jabez *were* the Tirathites, the Shimeathites, *and* the Suchathites. These *were* the Kenites who came from Hammath, the father of the house of Rechab.

The Family of David

3 Now these were the sons of David who were born to him in Hebron: The firstborn *was* Amnon, by Ahinoam the Jezreelitess; the second, Daniel,[a] by

2:19 [a] Spelled *Ephrathah* elsewhere in 2 Samuel 3:3 2:52 [a] Same as *the Manahethites,* verse 54 3:1 [a] Called *Chileab*

Abigail the Carmelitess; 2the third, Absalom the son of Maacah, the daughter of Talmai, king of Geshur; the fourth, Adonijah the son of Haggith; 3the fifth, Shephatiah, by Abital; the sixth, Ithream, by his wife Eglah.

4*These* six were born to him in Hebron. There he reigned seven years and six months, and in Jerusalem he reigned thirty-three years. 5And these were born to him in Jerusalem: Shimea,[a] Shobab, Nathan, and Solomon—four by Bathshua[b] the daughter of Ammiel.[c] 6Also *there* were Ibhar, Elishama,[a] Eliphelet,[b] 7Nogah, Nepheg, Japhia, 8Elishama, Eliada,[a] and Eliphelet—nine *in all.* 9*These were* all the sons of David, besides the sons of the concubines, and Tamar their sister.

The Family of Solomon

10Solomon's son *was* Rehoboam; Abijah[a] *was* his son, Asa his son, Jehoshaphat his son, 11Joram[a] his son, Ahaziah his son, Joash[b] his son, 12Amaziah his son, Azariah[a] his son, Jotham his son, 13Ahaz his son, Hezekiah his son, Manasseh his son, 14Amon his son, *and* Josiah his son. 15The sons of Josiah *were* Johanan the firstborn, the second Jehoiakim, the third Zedekiah, and the fourth Shallum.[a] 16The sons of Jehoiakim *were* Jeconiah his son *and* Zedekiah[a] his son.

The Family of Jeconiah

17And the sons of Jeconiah[a] *were* Assir,[b] Shealtiel his son, 18*and* Malchiram, Pedaiah, Shenazzar, Jecamiah, Hoshama, and Nedabiah. 19The sons of Pedaiah *were* Zerubbabel and Shimei. The sons of Zerubbabel *were* Meshullam, Hananiah, Shelomith their sister, 20and Hashubah, Ohel, Berechiah, Hasadiah, and Jushab-Hesed—five *in all.*

21The sons of Hananiah *were* Pelatiah and Jeshaiah, the sons of Rephaiah, the sons of Arnan, the sons of Obadiah, and the sons of Shechaniah. 22The son of Shechaniah was Shemaiah. The sons of Shemaiah *were* Hattush, Igal, Bariah, Neariah, and Shaphat—six *in all.* 23The sons of Neariah *were* Elioenai, Hezekiah, and Azrikam—three *in all.* 24The sons of Elioenai *were* Hodaviah, Eliashib, Pelaiah, Akkub, Johanan, Delaiah, and Anani—seven *in all.*

The Family of Judah

4 The sons of Judah *were* Perez, Hezron, Carmi, Hur, and Shobal. 2And Reaiah the son of Shobal begot Jahath, and Jahath begot Ahumai and Lahad. These *were* the families of the Zorathites. 3These *were the sons of* the father of Etam: Jezreel, Ishma, and Idbash; and the name of their sister *was* Hazelelponi; 4and Penuel *was* the father of Gedor, and Ezer *was the* father of Hushah.

These *were* the sons of Hur, the firstborn of Ephrathah the father of Bethlehem.

5And Ashhur the father of Tekoa had two wives, Helah and Naarah. 6Naarah bore him Ahuzzam, Hepher, Temeni, and Haahashtari. These *were* the sons of Naarah. 7The sons of Helah *were* Zereth, Zohar, and Ethnan; 8and Koz begot Anub, Zobebah, and the families of Aharhel the son of Harum.

9Now Jabez was more honorable than his brothers, and his mother called his name Jabez,[a] saying, "Because I bore *him* in pain." 10And Jabez called on the God of Israel saying, "Oh, that You would bless me indeed, and enlarge my territory, that Your hand would be with me, and that You would keep *me* from evil, that I may not cause pain!" So God granted him what he requested.

11Chelub the brother of Shuhah begot Mehir, who *was* the father of Eshton. 12And Eshton begot Beth-Rapha, Paseah, and Tehinnah the father of Ir-Nahash. These *were* the men of Rechah.

3:5 [a] Spelled *Shammua* in 14:4 and 2 Samuel 5:14 [b] Spelled *Bathsheba* in 2 Samuel 11:3 [c] Called *Eliam* in 2 Samuel 11:3 **3:6** [a] Spelled *Elishua* in 14:5 and 2 Samuel 5:15 [b] Spelled *Elpelet* in 14:5 **3:8** [a] Spelled *Beeliada* in 14:7 **3:10** [a] Spelled *Abijam* in 1 Kings 15:1 **3:11** [a] Spelled *Jehoram* in 2 Kings 1:17 and 8:16 [b] Spelled *Jehoash* in 2 Kings 12:1 **3:12** [a] Called *Uzziah* in Isaiah 6:1 **3:15** [a] Called *Jehoahaz* in 2 Kings 23:31 **3:16** [a] Compare 2 Kings 24:17 **3:17** [a] Also called *Coniah* in Jeremiah 22:24 and *Jehoiachin* in 2 Kings 24:8 [b] Or *Jeconiah the captive were* **4:9** [a] Literally *He Will Cause Pain*

13 The sons of Kenaz *were* Othniel and Seraiah. The sons of Othniel *were* Hathath,[a] 14 and Meonothai *who* begot Ophrah. Seraiah begot Joab the father of Ge Harashim,[a] for they were craftsmen. 15 The sons of Caleb the son of Jephunneh *were* Iru, Elah, and Naam. The son of Elah *was* Kenaz. 16 The sons of Jehallelel *were* Ziph, Ziphah, Tiria, and Asarel. 17 The sons of Ezrah *were* Jether, Mered, Epher, and Jalon. And *Mered's wife*[a] bore Miriam, Shammai, and Ishbah the father of Eshtemoa. 18 (His wife Jehudijah[a] bore Jered the father of Gedor, Heber the father of Sochoh, and Jekuthiel the father of Zanoah.) And these were the sons of Bithiah the daughter of Pharaoh, whom Mered took.

19 The sons of Hodiah's wife, the sister of Naham, *were* the fathers of Keilah the Garmite and of Eshtemoa the Maachathite. 20 And the sons of Shimon *were* Amnon, Rinnah, Ben-Hanan, and Tilon. And the sons of Ishi *were* Zoheth and Ben-Zoheth.

21 The sons of Shelah the son of Judah *were* Er the father of Lecah, Laadah the father of Mareshah, and the families of the house of the linen workers of the house of Ashbea; 22 also Jokim, the men of Chozeba, and Joash; Saraph, who ruled in Moab, and Jashubi-Lehem. Now the records are ancient. 23 These *were* the potters and those who dwell at Netaim[a] and Gederah;[b] there they dwelt with the king for his work.

The Family of Simeon

24 The sons of Simeon *were* Nemuel, Jamin, Jarib,[a] Zerah,[b] *and* Shaul, 25 Shallum his son, Mibsam his son, and Mishma his son. 26 And the sons of Mishma *were* Hamuel his son, Zacchur his son, and Shimei his son. 27 Shimei had sixteen sons and six daughters; but his brothers did not have many children, nor did any of their families multiply as much as the children of Judah.

28 They dwelt at Beersheba, Moladah, Hazar Shual, 29 Bilhah, Ezem, Tolad, 30 Bethuel, Hormah, Ziklag, 31 Beth Marcaboth, Hazar Susim, Beth Biri, and at Shaaraim. These *were* their cities until the reign of David. 32 And their villages *were* Etam, Ain, Rimmon, Tochen, and Ashan—five cities— 33 and all the villages that *were* around these cities as far as Baal.[a] These *were* their dwelling places, and they maintained their genealogy: 34 Meshobab, Jamlech, and Joshah the son of Amaziah; 35 Joel, and Jehu the son of Joshibiah, the son of Seraiah, the son of Asiel; 36 Elioenai, Jaakobah, Jeshohaiah, Asaiah, Adiel, Jesimiel, and Benaiah; 37 Ziza the son of Shiphi, the son of Allon, the son of Jedaiah, the son of Shimri, the son of Shemaiah— 38 these mentioned by name *were* leaders in their families, and their father's house increased greatly.

39 So they went to the entrance of Gedor, as far as the east side of the valley, to seek pasture for their flocks. 40 And they found rich, good pasture, and the land *was* broad, quiet, and peaceful; for some Hamites formerly lived there.

41 These recorded by name came in the days of Hezekiah king of Judah; and they attacked their tents and the Meunites who were found there, and utterly destroyed them, as it is to this day. So they dwelt in their place, because *there was* pasture for their flocks there. 42 Now *some* of them, five hundred men of the sons of Simeon, went to Mount Seir, having as their captains Pelatiah, Neariah, Rephaiah, and Uzziel, the sons of Ishi. 43 And they defeated the rest of the Amalekites who had escaped. They have dwelt there to this day.

The Family of Reuben

5 Now the sons of Reuben the firstborn of Israel—he *was* indeed the firstborn, but because he defiled his father's bed, his birthright was given to the sons of Joseph, the son of Israel, so that the genealogy is not listed according to the birthright; 2 yet Judah prevailed over his brothers, and from him *came* a ruler, although the birthright

4:13 [a] Septuagint and Vulgate add *and Meonothai.* **4:14** [a] Literally *Valley of Craftsmen*
4:17 [a] Literally *she* **4:18** [a] Or *His Judean wife* **4:23** [a] Literally *Plants* [b] Literally *Hedges*
4:24 [a] Called *Jachin* in Genesis 46:10 [b] Called *Zohar* in Genesis 46:10 **4:33** [a] Or *Baalath Beer* (compare Joshua 19:8)

was Joseph's— 3the sons of Reuben the firstborn of Israel were Hanoch, Pallu, Hezron, and Carmi.

4The sons of Joel *were* Shemaiah his son, Gog his son, Shimei his son, 5Micah his son, Reaiah his son, Baal his son, 6and Beerah his son, whom Tiglath-Pileser[a] king of Assyria carried into captivity. He *was* leader of the Reubenites. 7And his brethren by their families, when the genealogy of their generations was registered: the chief, Jeiel, and Zechariah, 8and Bela the son of Azaz, the son of Shema, the son of Joel, who dwelt in Aroer, as far as Nebo and Baal Meon. 9Eastward they settled as far as the entrance of the wilderness this side of the River Euphrates, because their cattle had multiplied in the land of Gilead.

10Now in the days of Saul they made war with the Hagrites, who fell by their hand; and they dwelt in their tents throughout the entire *area* east of Gilead.

The Family of Gad

11And the children of Gad dwelt next to them in the land of Bashan as far as Salcah: 12Joel *was* the chief, Shapham the next, then Jaanai and Shaphat in Bashan, 13and their brethren of their father's house: Michael, Meshullam, Sheba, Jorai, Jachan, Zia, and Eber—seven *in all.* 14These *were* the children of Abihail the son of Huri, the son of Jaroah, the son of Gilead, the son of Michael, the son of Jeshishai, the son of Jahdo, the son of Buz; 15Ahi the son of Abdiel, the son of Guni, *was* chief of their father's house. 16And *the Gadites* dwelt in Gilead, in Bashan and in its villages, and in all the common-lands of Sharon within their borders. 17All these were registered by genealogies in the days of Jotham king of Judah, and in the days of Jeroboam king of Israel.

18The sons of Reuben, the Gadites, and half the tribe of Manasseh *had* forty-four thousand seven hundred and sixty valiant men, men able to bear shield and sword, to shoot with the bow, and skillful in war, who went to war. 19They made war with the Hagrites, Jetur, Naphish, and Nodab. 20And they were helped against them, and the Hagrites were delivered into their hand, and all who *were* with them, for they cried out to God in the battle. He heeded their prayer, because they put their trust in Him. 21Then they took away their livestock—fifty thousand of their camels, two hundred and fifty thousand of their sheep, and two thousand of their donkeys—also one hundred thousand of their men; 22for many fell dead, because the war *was* God's. And they dwelt in their place until the captivity.

The Family of Manasseh (East)

23So the children of the half-tribe of Manasseh dwelt in the land. Their *numbers* increased from Bashan to Baal Hermon, that is, to Senir, or Mount Hermon. 24These *were* the heads of their fathers' houses: Epher, Ishi, Eliel, Azriel, Jeremiah, Hodaviah, and Jahdiel. They were mighty men of valor, famous men, *and* heads of their fathers' houses.

25And they were unfaithful to the God of their fathers, and played the harlot after the gods of the peoples of the land, whom God had destroyed before them. 26So the God of Israel stirred up the spirit of Pul king of Assyria, that is, Tiglath-Pileser[a] king of Assyria. He carried the Reubenites, the Gadites, and the half-tribe of Manasseh into captivity. He took them to Halah, Habor, Hara, and the river of Gozan to this day.

The Family of Levi

6 The sons of Levi *were* Gershon, Kohath, and Merari. 2The sons of Kohath *were* Amram, Izhar, Hebron, and Uzziel. 3The children of Amram *were* Aaron, Moses, and Miriam. And the sons of Aaron *were* Nadab, Abihu, Eleazar, and Ithamar. 4Eleazar begot Phinehas, *and* Phinehas begot Abishua; 5Abishua begot Bukki, and Bukki begot Uzzi; 6Uzzi begot Zerahiah, and Zerahiah begot Meraioth; 7Meraioth begot Amariah, and Amariah begot Ahitub; 8Ahitub begot Zadok, and Zadok begot Ahimaaz; 9Ahimaaz begot Azariah, and

5:6 [a] Hebrew *Tilgath-Pilneser* 5:26 [a] Hebrew *Tilgath-Pilneser*

Azariah begot Johanan; 10Johanan begot Azariah (it was he who ministered as priest in the temple that Solomon built in Jerusalem); 11Azariah begot Amariah, and Amariah begot Ahitub; 12Ahitub begot Zadok, and Zadok begot Shallum; 13Shallum begot Hilkiah, and Hilkiah begot Azariah; 14Azariah begot Seraiah, and Seraiah begot Jehozadak. 15Jehozadak went *into captivity* when the LORD carried Judah and Jerusalem into captivity by the hand of Nebuchadnezzar.

16The sons of Levi *were* Gershon,[a] Kohath, and Merari. 17These are the names of the sons of Gershon: Libni and Shimei. 18The sons of Kohath *were* Amram, Izhar, Hebron, and Uzziel. 19The sons of Merari *were* Mahli and Mushi. Now these *are* the families of the Levites according to their fathers: 20Of Gershon *were* Libni his son, Jahath his son, Zimmah his son, 21Joah his son, Iddo his son, Zerah his son, *and* Jeatherai his son. 22The sons of Kohath *were* Amminadab his son, Korah his son, Assir his son, 23Elkanah his son, Ebiasaph his son, Assir his son, 24Tahath his son, Uriel his son, Uzziah his son, and Shaul his son. 25The sons of Elkanah *were* Amasai and Ahimoth. 26*As for* Elkanah,[a] the sons of Elkanah *were* Zophai[b] his son, Nahath[c] his son, 27Eliab[a] his son, Jeroham his son, *and* Elkanah his son. 28The sons of Samuel *were Joel*[a] the firstborn, and Abijah the second.[b] 29The sons of Merari *were* Mahli, Libni his son, Shimei his son, Uzzah his son, 30Shimea his son, Haggiah his son, *and* Asaiah his son.

Musicians in the House of the LORD

31Now these are the men whom David appointed over the service of song in the house of the LORD, after the ark came to rest. 32They were ministering with music before the dwelling place of the tabernacle of meeting, until Solomon had built the house of the LORD in Jerusalem, and they served in their office according to their order.

33And these *are* the ones who ministered with their sons: Of the sons of the Kohathites *were* Heman the singer, the son of Joel, the son of Samuel, 34the son of Elkanah, the son of Jeroham, the son of Eliel,[a] the son of Toah,[b] 35the son of Zuph, the son of Elkanah, the son of Mahath, the son of Amasai, 36the son of Elkanah, the son of Joel, the son of Azariah, the son of Zephaniah, 37the son of Tahath, the son of Assir, the son of Ebiasaph, the son of Korah, 38the son of Izhar, the son of Kohath, the son of Levi, the son of Israel. 39And his brother Asaph, who stood at his right hand, *was* Asaph the son of Berachiah, the son of Shimea, 40the son of Michael, the son of Baaseiah, the son of Malchijah, 41the son of Ethni, the son of Zerah, the son of Adaiah, 42the son of Ethan, the son of Zimmah, the son of Shimei, 43the son of Jahath, the son of Gershon, the son of Levi.

44Their brethren, the sons of Merari, on the left hand, *were* Ethan the son of Kishi, the son of Abdi, the son of Malluch, 45the son of Hashabiah, the son of Amaziah, the son of Hilkiah, 46the son of Amzi, the son of Bani, the son of Shamer, 47the son of Mahli, the son of Mushi, the son of Merari, the son of Levi.

48And their brethren, the Levites, *were* appointed to every kind of service of the tabernacle of the house of God.

The Family of Aaron

49But Aaron and his sons offered sacrifices on the altar of burnt offering and on the altar of incense, for all the work of the Most Holy *Place,* and to make atonement for Israel, according to all that Moses the servant of God had commanded. 50Now these *are* the sons of Aaron: Eleazar his son, Phinehas his son, Abishua his son, 51Bukki his son, Uzzi his son, Zerahiah his son, 52Meraioth his son, Amariah his son, Ahitub his son, 53Zadok his son, *and* Ahimaaz his son.

Dwelling Places of the Levites

54Now these *are* their dwelling places throughout their settlements in their

6:16 [a] Hebrew *Gershom* (alternate spelling of *Gershon,* as in verses 1, 17, 20, 43, 62, and 71) **6:26** [a] Compare verse 35 [b] Spelled *Zuph* in verse 35 and 1 Samuel 1:1 [c] Compare verse 34 **6:27** [a] Compare verse 34 **6:28** [a] Following Septuagint, Syriac, and Arabic (compare verse 33 and 1 Samuel 8:2) [b] Hebrew *Vasheni* **6:34** [a] Spelled *Elihu* in 1 Samuel 1:1 [b] Spelled *Tohu* in 1 Samuel 1:1

territory, for they were *given* by lot to the sons of Aaron, of the family of the Kohathites: 55They gave them Hebron in the land of Judah, with its surrounding common-lands. 56But the fields of the city and its villages they gave to Caleb the son of Jephunneh. 57And to the sons of Aaron they gave *one of* the cities of refuge, Hebron; also Libnah with its common-lands, Jattir, Eshtemoa with its common-lands, 58Hilen[a] with its common-lands, Debir with its common-lands, 59Ashan[a] with its common-lands, and Beth Shemesh with its common-lands. 60And from the tribe of Benjamin: Geba with its common-lands, Alemeth[a] with its common-lands, and Anathoth with its common-lands. All their cities among their families *were* thirteen.

61To the rest of the family of the tribe of the Kohathites *they gave* by lot ten cities from half the tribe of Manasseh. 62And to the sons of Gershon, throughout their families, *they gave* thirteen cities from the tribe of Issachar, from the tribe of Asher, from the tribe of Naphtali, and from the tribe of Manasseh in Bashan. 63To the sons of Merari, throughout their families, *they gave* twelve cities from the tribe of Reuben, from the tribe of Gad, and from the tribe of Zebulun. 64So the children of Israel gave *these* cities with their common-lands to the Levites. 65And they gave by lot from the tribe of the children of Judah, from the tribe of the children of Simeon, and from the tribe of the children of Benjamin these cities which are called by *their* names.

66Now some of the families of the sons of Kohath *were given* cities as their territory from the tribe of Ephraim. 67And they gave them *one of* the cities of refuge, Shechem with its common-lands, in the mountains of Ephraim, also Gezer with its common-lands, 68Jokmeam with its common-lands, Beth Horon with its common-lands, 69Aijalon with its common-lands, and Gath Rimmon with its common-lands. 70And from the half-tribe of Manasseh: Aner with its common-lands and Bileam with its common-lands, for the rest of the family of the sons of Kohath.

71From the family of the half-tribe of Manasseh the sons of Gershon *were given* Golan in Bashan with its common-lands and Ashtaroth with its common-lands. 72And from the tribe of Issachar: Kedesh with its common-lands, Daberath with its common-lands, 73Ramoth with its common-lands, and Anem with its common-lands. 74And from the tribe of Asher: Mashal with its common-lands, Abdon with its common-lands, 75Hukok with its common-lands, and Rehob with its common-lands. 76And from the tribe of Naphtali: Kedesh in Galilee with its common-lands, Hammon with its common-lands, and Kirjathaim with its common-lands.

77From the tribe of Zebulun the rest of the children of Merari *were given* Rimmon[a] with its common-lands and Tabor with its common-lands. 78And on the other side of the Jordan, across from Jericho, on the east side of the Jordan, *they were given* from the tribe of Reuben: Bezer in the wilderness with its common-lands, Jahzah with its common-lands, 79Kedemoth with its common-lands, and Mephaath with its common-lands. 80And from the tribe of Gad: Ramoth in Gilead with its common-lands, Mahanaim with its common-lands, 81Heshbon with its common-lands, and Jazer with its common-lands.

The Family of Issachar

7 The sons of Issachar *were* Tola, Puah,[a] Jashub, and Shimron—four *in all.* 2The sons of Tola *were* Uzzi, Rephaiah, Jeriel, Jahmai, Jibsam, and Shemuel, heads of their father's house. *The sons* of Tola *were* mighty men of valor in their generations; their number in the days of David *was* twenty-two thousand six hundred. 3The son of Uzzi *was* Izrahiah, and the sons of Izrahiah *were* Michael, Obadiah, Joel, and Ishiah. All five of them *were* chief men. 4And with them, by their generations, according to their fathers' houses, *were* thirty-six

6:58 [a] Spelled *Holon* in Joshua 21:15 **6:59** [a] Spelled *Ain* in Joshua 21:16 **6:60** [a] Spelled *Almon* in Joshua 21:18 **6:77** [a] Hebrew *Rimmono,* alternate spelling of *Rimmon;* see 4:32 **7:1** [a] Spelled *Puvah* in Genesis 46:13

thousand troops ready for war; for they
had many wives and sons.
5Now their brethren among all the
families of Issachar *were* mighty men
of valor, listed by their genealogies,
eighty-seven thousand in all.

The Family of Benjamin

6*The sons* of Benjamin *were* Bela, Be-
cher, and Jediael—three *in all.* 7The sons
of Bela were Ezbon, Uzzi, Uzziel, Jer-
imoth, and Iri—five *in all.* They *were*
heads of *their* fathers' houses, and they
were listed by their genealogies, twenty-
two thousand and thirty-four mighty
men of valor.
8The sons of Becher *were* Zemirah,
Joash, Eliezer, Elioenai, Omri, Jeri-
moth, Abijah, Anathoth, and Alemeth.
All these *are* the sons of Becher. 9And
they were recorded by genealogy ac-
cording to their generations, heads of
their fathers' houses, twenty thousand
two hundred mighty men of valor. 10The
son of Jediael *was* Bilhan, and the sons
of Bilhan *were* Jeush, Benjamin, Ehud,
Chenaanah, Zethan, Tharshish, and
Ahishahar.
11All these sons of Jediael *were* heads of
their fathers' houses; *there were* seven-
teen thousand two hundred mighty men
of valor fit to go out for war *and* battle.
12Shuppim and Huppim[a] *were* the sons
of Ir, *and* Hushim *was* the son of Aher.

The Family of Naphtali

13The sons of Naphtali *were* Jahziel,[a]
Guni, Jezer, and Shallum,[b] the sons of
Bilhah.

The Family of Manasseh (West)

14The descendants of Manasseh: his
Syrian concubine bore him Machir
the father of Gilead, the father of As-
riel.[a] 15Machir took as his wife *the sis-
ter* of Huppim and Shuppim,[a] whose
name *was* Maachah. The name of
Gilead's grandson[b] *was* Zelophehad,[c]
but Zelophehad begot only daughters.
16(Maachah the wife of Machir bore a
son, and she called his name Peresh.
The name of his brother *was* Sheresh,
and his sons *were* Ulam and Rakem.
17The son of Ulam *was* Bedan.) These
were the descendants of Gilead the son
of Machir, the son of Manasseh.
18His sister Hammoleketh bore Ish-
hod, Abiezer, and Mahlah.
19And the sons of Shemida were Ahian,
Shechem, Likhi, and Aniam.

The Family of Ephraim

20The sons of Ephraim *were* Shuthe-
lah, Bered his son, Tahath his son, Ela-
dah his son, Tahath his son, 21Zabad his
son, Shuthelah his son, and Ezer and
Elead. The men of Gath who were born
in *that* land killed *them* because they
came down to take away their cattle.
22Then Ephraim their father mourned
many days, and his brethren came to
comfort him.
23And when he went in to his wife, she
conceived and bore a son; and he called
his name Beriah,[a] because tragedy had
come upon his house. 24Now his daugh-
ter *was* Sheerah, who built Lower and
Upper Beth Horon and Uzzen Sheerah;
25and Rephah *was* his son, *as well* as
Resheph, and Telah his son, Tahan his
son, 26Laadan his son, Ammihud his
son, Elishama his son, 27Nun[a] his son,
and Joshua his son.
28Now their possessions and dwelling
places *were* Bethel and its towns: to the
east Naaran, to the west Gezer and its
towns, and Shechem and its towns, as
far as Ayyah[a] and its towns; 29and by
the borders of the children of Manasseh
were Beth Shean and its towns, Taanach
and its towns, Megiddo and its towns,
Dor and its towns. In these dwelt the
children of Joseph, the son of Israel.

The Family of Asher

30The sons of Asher *were* Imnah,
Ishvah, Ishvi, Beriah, and their sister
Serah. 31The sons of Beriah *were* Heber
and Malchiel, who was the father of
Birzaith.[a] 32And Heber begot Japhlet,

7:12 [a] Called *Hupham* in Numbers 26:39 **7:13** [a] Spelled *Jahzeel* in Genesis 46:24 [b] Spelled *Shillem* in Genesis 46:24 **7:14** [a] The son of Gilead (compare Numbers 26:30, 31) **7:15** [a] Compare verse 12 [b] Literally *the second* [c] Compare Numbers 26:30–33 **7:23** [a] Literally *In Tragedy* **7:27** [a] Hebrew *Non* **7:28** [a] Many Hebrew manuscripts, Bomberg, Septuagint, Targum, and Vulgate read *Gazza.* **7:31** [a] Or *Birzavith* or *Birzoth*

Shomer,[a] Hotham,[b] and their sister Shua. 33The sons of Japhlet *were* Pasach, Bimhal, and Ashvath. These *were* the children of Japhlet. 34The sons of Shemer *were* Ahi, Rohgah, Jehubbah, and Aram. 35And the sons of his brother Helem *were* Zophah, Imna, Shelesh, and Amal. 36The sons of Zophah *were* Suah, Harnepher, Shual, Beri, Imrah, 37Bezer, Hod, Shamma, Shilshah, Jithran,[a] and Beera. 38The sons of Jether *were* Jephunneh, Pispah, and Ara. 39The sons of Ulla *were* Arah, Haniel, and Rizia.

40All these *were* the children of Asher, heads of *their* fathers' houses, choice men, mighty men of valor, chief leaders. And they were recorded by genealogies among the army fit for battle; their number *was* twenty-six thousand.

The Family Tree of King Saul of Benjamin

8 Now Benjamin begot Bela his firstborn, Ashbel the second, Aharah[a] the third, 2Nohah the fourth, and Rapha the fifth. 3The sons of Bela *were* Addar,[a] Gera, Abihud, 4Abishua, Naaman, Ahoah, 5Gera, Shephuphan, and Huram.

6These *are* the sons of Ehud, who were the heads of the fathers' *houses* of the inhabitants of Geba, and who forced them to move to Manahath: 7Naaman, Ahijah, and Gera who forced them to move. He begot Uzza and Ahihud.

8Also Shaharaim had children in the country of Moab, after he had sent away Hushim and Baara his wives. 9By Hodesh his wife he begot Jobab, Zibia, Mesha, Malcam, 10Jeuz, Sachiah, and Mirmah. These *were* his sons, heads of their fathers' *houses*.

11And by Hushim he begot Abitub and Elpaal. 12The sons of Elpaal *were* Eber, Misham, and Shemed, who built Ono and Lod with its towns; 13and Beriah and Shema, who *were* heads of their fathers' *houses* of the inhabitants of Aijalon, who drove out the inhabitants of Gath. 14Ahio, Shashak, Jeremoth, 15Zebadiah, Arad, Eder, 16Michael, Ispah, and Joha *were* the sons of Beriah. 17Zebadiah, Meshullam, Hizki, Heber, 18Ishmerai, Jizliah, and Jobab *were* the sons of Elpaal. 19Jakim, Zichri, Zabdi, 20Elienai, Zillethai, Eliel, 21Adaiah, Beraiah, and Shimrath *were* the sons of Shimei. 22Ishpan, Eber, Eliel, 23Abdon, Zichri, Hanan, 24Hananiah, Elam, Antothijah, 25Iphdeiah, and Penuel *were* the sons of Shashak. 26Shamsherai, Shehariah, Athaliah, 27Jaareshiah, Elijah, and Zichri *were* the sons of Jeroham.

28These *were* heads of the fathers' *houses* by their generations, chief men. These dwelt in Jerusalem.

29Now the father of Gibeon, whose wife's name *was* Maacah, dwelt at Gibeon. 30And his firstborn son *was* Abdon, then Zur, Kish, Baal, Nadab, 31Gedor, Ahio, Zecher, 32and Mikloth, *who* begot Shimeah.[a] They also dwelt alongside their relatives in Jerusalem, with their brethren. 33Ner[a] begot Kish, Kish begot Saul, and Saul begot Jonathan, Malchishua, Abinadab,[b] and Esh-Baal.[c] 34The son of Jonathan *was* Merib-Baal,[a] and Merib-Baal begot Micah. 35The sons of Micah *were* Pithon, Melech, Tarea, and Ahaz. 36And Ahaz begot Jehoaddah;[a] Jehoaddah begot Alemeth, Azmaveth, and Zimri; and Zimri begot Moza. 37Moza begot Binea, Raphah[a] his son, Eleasah his son, *and* Azel his son.

38Azel had six sons whose names *were* these: Azrikam, Bocheru, Ishmael, Sheariah, Obadiah, and Hanan. All these *were* the sons of Azel. 39And the sons of Eshek his brother *were* Ulam his firstborn, Jeush the second, and Eliphelet the third.

40The sons of Ulam were mighty men of valor—archers. *They* had many sons and grandsons, one hundred and fifty *in all*. These *were* all sons of Benjamin.

9 So all Israel was recorded by genealogies, and indeed, they *were* inscribed in the book of the kings of Israel. But Judah was carried away captive to Babylon because of their unfaithfulness. 2And the first inhabitants

7:32 [a] Spelled *Shemer* in verse 34 [b] Spelled *Helem* in verse 35 **7:37** [a] Spelled *Jether* in verse 38 **8:1** [a] Spelled *Ahiram* in Numbers 26:38 **8:3** [a] Called *Ard* in Numbers 26:40 **8:32** [a] Spelled *Shimeam* in 9:38 **8:33** [a] Also the son of Gibeon (compare 9:36, 39) [b] Called *Jishui* in 1 Samuel 14:49 [c] Called *Ishbosheth* in 2 Samuel 2:8 and elsewhere **8:34** [a] Called *Mephibosheth* in 2 Samuel 4:4 **8:36** [a] Spelled *Jarah* in 9:42 **8:37** [a] Spelled *Rephaiah* in 9:43

who *dwelt* in their possessions in their
cities *were* Israelites, priests, Levites,
and the Nethinim.

Dwellers in Jerusalem

3Now in Jerusalem the children of
Judah dwelt, and some of the children
of Benjamin, and of the children of
Ephraim and Manasseh: 4Uthai the
son of Ammihud, the son of Omri, the
son of Imri, the son of Bani, of the de-
scendants of Perez, the son of Judah.
5Of the Shilonites: Asaiah the firstborn
and his sons. 6Of the sons of Zerah:
Jeuel, and their brethren—six hundred
and ninety. 7Of the sons of Benjamin:
Sallu the son of Meshullam, the son of
Hodaviah, the son of Hassenuah; 8Ib-
neiah the son of Jeroham; Elah the son
of Uzzi, the son of Michri; Meshullam
the son of Shephatiah, the son of Reuel,
the son of Ibnijah; 9and their brethren,
according to their generations—nine
hundred and fifty-six. All these men
were heads of a father's *house* in their
fathers' houses.

The Priests at Jerusalem

10Of the priests: Jedaiah, Jehoiarib,
and Jachin; 11Azariah the son of Hil-
kiah, the son of Meshullam, the son
of Zadok, the son of Meraioth, the son
of Ahitub, the officer over the house of
God; 12Adaiah the son of Jeroham, the
son of Pashur, the son of Malchijah;
Maasai the son of Adiel, the son of Jah-
zerah, the son of Meshullam, the son of
Meshillemith, the son of Immer; 13and
their brethren, heads of their fathers'
houses—one thousand seven hundred
and sixty. *They were* very able men for
the work of the service of the house
of God.

The Levites at Jerusalem

14Of the Levites: Shemaiah the son of
Hasshub, the son of Azrikam, the son
of Hashabiah, of the sons of Merari;
15Bakbakkar, Heresh, Galal, and Matta-
niah the son of Micah, the son of Zichri,
the son of Asaph; 16Obadiah the son
of Shemaiah, the son of Galal, the son
of Jeduthun; and Berechiah the son of
Asa, the son of Elkanah, who lived in the
villages of the Netophathites.

The Levite Gatekeepers

17And the gatekeepers *were* Shallum,
Akkub, Talmon, Ahiman, and their
brethren. Shallum *was* the chief. 18Un-
til then *they had been* gatekeepers for
the camps of the children of Levi at the
King's Gate on the east.

19Shallum the son of Kore, the son of
Ebiasaph, the son of Korah, and his
brethren, from his father's house, the
Korahites, *were* in charge of the work
of the service, gatekeepers of the taber-
nacle. Their fathers had been keepers of
the entrance to the camp of the LORD.
20And Phinehas the son of Eleazar had
been the officer over them in time past;
the LORD *was* with him. 21Zechariah the
son of Meshelemiah *was* keeper of the
door of the tabernacle of meeting.

22All those chosen as gatekeepers *were*
two hundred and twelve. They were
recorded by their genealogy, in their vil-
lages. David and Samuel the seer had ap-
pointed them to their trusted office. 23So
they and their children *were* in charge of
the gates of the house of the LORD, the
house of the tabernacle, by assignment.
24The gatekeepers were assigned to the
four directions: the east, west, north, and
south. 25And their brethren in their vil-
lages *had* to come with them from time to
time for seven days. 26For in this trusted
office *were* four chief gatekeepers; they
were Levites. And they had charge over
the chambers and treasuries of the house
of God. 27And they lodged *all* around
the house of God because they *had* the
responsibility, and they *were* in charge
of opening *it* every morning.

Other Levite Responsibilities

28Now *some* of them were in charge
of the serving vessels, for they brought
them in and took them out by count.
29*Some* of them *were* appointed over
the furnishings and over all the im-
plements of the sanctuary, and over
the fine flour and the wine and the oil
and the incense and the spices. 30And
some of the sons of the priests made the
ointment of the spices.

31Mattithiah of the Levites, the first-
born of Shallum the Korahite, had the
trusted office over the things that were
baked in the pans. 32And some of their

brethren of the sons of the Kohathites *were* in charge of preparing the showbread for every Sabbath.

33These are the singers, heads of the fathers' *houses* of the Levites, *who lodged* in the chambers, *and were* free *from other duties;* for they were employed in *that* work day and night. 34These heads of the fathers' *houses* of the Levites *were* heads throughout their generations. They dwelt at Jerusalem.

The Family of King Saul

35Jeiel the father of Gibeon, whose wife's name *was* Maacah, dwelt at Gibeon. 36His firstborn son *was* Abdon, then Zur, Kish, Baal, Ner, Nadab, 37Gedor, Ahio, Zechariah,[a] and Mikloth. 38And Mikloth begot Shimeam.[a] They also dwelt alongside their relatives in Jerusalem, with their brethren. 39Ner begot Kish, Kish begot Saul, and Saul begot Jonathan, Malchishua, Abinadab, and Esh-Baal. 40The son of Jonathan *was* Merib-Baal, and Merib-Baal begot Micah. 41The sons of Micah *were* Pithon, Melech, Tahrea,[a] and Ahaz.[b] 42And Ahaz begot Jarah;[a] Jarah begot Alemeth, Azmaveth, and Zimri; and Zimri begot Moza; 43Moza begot Binea, Rephaiah[a] his son, Eleasah his son, and Azel his son.

44And Azel had six sons whose names *were* these: Azrikam, Bocheru, Ishmael, Sheariah, Obadiah, and Hanan; these *were* the sons of Azel.

Tragic End of Saul and His Sons

10 Now the Philistines fought against Israel; and the men of Israel fled from before the Philistines, and fell slain on Mount Gilboa. 2Then the Philistines followed hard after Saul and his sons. And the Philistines killed Jonathan, Abinadab, and Malchishua, Saul's sons. 3The battle became fierce against Saul. The archers hit him, and he was wounded by the archers. 4Then Saul said to his armorbearer, "Draw your sword, and thrust me through with it, lest these uncircumcised men come and abuse me." But his armorbearer would not, for he was greatly afraid. Therefore Saul took a sword and fell on it. 5And when his armorbearer saw that Saul was dead, he also fell on his sword and died. 6So Saul and his three sons died, and all his house died together. 7And when all the men of Israel who *were* in the valley saw that they had fled and that Saul and his sons were dead, they forsook their cities and fled; then the Philistines came and dwelt in them.

8So it happened the next day, when the Philistines came to strip the slain, that they found Saul and his sons fallen on Mount Gilboa. 9And they stripped him and took his head and his armor, and sent word throughout the land of the Philistines to proclaim the news *in the temple* of their idols and among the people. 10Then they put his armor in the temple of their gods, and fastened his head in the temple of Dagon.

11And when all Jabesh Gilead heard all that the Philistines had done to Saul, 12all the valiant men arose and took the body of Saul and the bodies of his sons; and they brought them to Jabesh, and buried their bones under the tamarisk tree at Jabesh, and fasted seven days.

13So Saul died for his unfaithfulness which he had committed against the LORD, because he did not keep the word of the LORD, and also because he consulted a medium for guidance. 14But *he* did not inquire of the LORD; therefore He killed him, and turned the kingdom over to David the son of Jesse.

David Made King over All Israel

11 Then all Israel came together to David at Hebron, saying, "Indeed we *are* your bone and your flesh. 2Also, in time past, even when Saul was king, you *were* the one who led Israel out and brought them in; and the LORD your God said to you, 'You shall shepherd My people Israel, and be ruler over My people Israel.' " 3Therefore all the elders of Israel came to the king at Hebron, and David made a covenant with them at Hebron before the LORD. And they anointed David king over Israel, according to the word of the LORD by Samuel.

9:37 [a] Called *Zecher* in 8:31 **9:38** [a] Spelled *Shimeah* in 8:32 **9:41** [a] Spelled *Tarea* in 8:35 [b] Following Arabic, Syriac, Targum, and Vulgate (compare 8:35); Masoretic Text and Septuagint omit *and Ahaz.* **9:42** [a] Spelled *Jehoaddah* in 8:36 **9:43** [a] Spelled *Raphah* in 8:37

The City of David

4And David and all Israel went to Jerusalem, which is Jebus, where the Jebusites *were,* the inhabitants of the land. 5But the inhabitants of Jebus said to David, "You shall not come in here!" Nevertheless David took the stronghold of Zion (that is, the City of David). 6Now David said, "Whoever attacks the Jebusites first shall be chief and captain." And Joab the son of Zeruiah went up first, and became chief. 7Then David dwelt in the stronghold; therefore they called it the City of David. 8And he built the city around it, from the Millo[a] to the surrounding area. Joab repaired the rest of the city. 9So David went on and became great, and the LORD of hosts *was* with him.

The Mighty Men of David

10Now these *were* the heads of the mighty men whom David had, who strengthened themselves with him in his kingdom, with all Israel, to make him king, according to the word of the LORD concerning Israel.

11And this *is* the number of the mighty men whom David had: Jashobeam the son of a Hachmonite, chief of the captains;[a] he had lifted up his spear against three hundred, killed *by him* at one time.

12After him *was* Eleazar the son of Dodo, the Ahohite, who *was one* of the three mighty men. 13He was with David at Pasdammim. Now there the Philistines were gathered for battle, and there was a piece of ground full of barley. So the people fled from the Philistines. 14But they stationed themselves in the middle of *that* field, defended it, and killed the Philistines. So the LORD brought about a great victory.

15Now three of the thirty chief men went down to the rock to David, into the cave of Adullam; and the army of the Philistines encamped in the Valley of Rephaim. 16David *was* then in the stronghold, and the garrison of the Philistines *was* then in Bethlehem. 17And David said with longing, "Oh, that someone would give me a drink of water from the well of Bethlehem, which is by the gate!" 18So the three broke through the camp of the Philistines, drew water from the well of Bethlehem that *was* by the gate, and took *it* and brought *it* to David. Nevertheless David would not drink it, but poured it out to the LORD. 19And he said, "Far be it from me, O my God, that I should do this! Shall I drink the blood of these men *who have put* their lives *in jeopardy?* For at the risk of their lives they brought it." Therefore he would not drink it. These things were done by the three mighty men.

20Abishai the brother of Joab was chief of *another* three.[a] He had lifted up his spear against three hundred *men,* killed *them,* and won a name among *these* three. 21Of the three he was more honored than the other two men. Therefore he became their captain. However he did not attain to the *first* three.

22Benaiah was the son of Jehoiada, the son of a valiant man from Kabzeel, who had done many deeds. He had killed two lion-like heroes of Moab. He also had gone down and killed a lion in the midst of a pit on a snowy day. 23And he killed an Egyptian, a man of *great* height, five cubits tall. In the Egyptian's hand *there was* a spear like a weaver's beam; and he went down to him with a staff, wrested the spear out of the Egyptian's hand, and killed him with his own spear. 24These *things* Benaiah the son of Jehoiada did, and won a name among three mighty men. 25Indeed he was more honored than the thirty, but he did not attain to the *first* three. And David appointed him over his guard.

26Also the mighty warriors *were* Asahel the brother of Joab, Elhanan the son of Dodo of Bethlehem, 27Shammoth the Harorite,[a] Helez the Pelonite,[b] 28Ira the son of Ikkesh the Tekoite, Abiezer the Anathothite, 29Sibbechai the Hushathite, Ilai the Ahohite, 30Maharai the Netophathite, Heled[a] the son of Baanah the Netophathite, 31Ithai[a] the son of

11:8 [a] Literally *The Landfill* **11:11** [a] Following Qere; Kethib, Septuagint, and Vulgate read *the thirty* (compare 2 Samuel 23:8). **11:20** [a] Following Masoretic Text, Septuagint, and Vulgate; Syriac reads *thirty*. **11:27** [a] Spelled *Harodite* in 2 Samuel 23:25 [b] Called *Paltite* in 2 Samuel 23:26 **11:30** [a] Spelled *Heleb* in 2 Samuel 23:29 and *Heldai* in 1 Chronicles 27:15 **11:31** [a] Spelled *Ittai* in 2 Samuel 23:29

Ribai of Gibeah, of the sons of Benjamin,
Benaiah the Pirathonite, 32 Hurai[a] of
the brooks of Gaash, Abiel[b] the Arba-
thite, 33 Azmaveth the Baharumite,[a]
Eliahba the Shaalbonite, 34 the sons of
Hashem the Gizonite, Jonathan the son
of Shageh the Hararite, 35 Ahiam the son
of Sacar the Hararite, Eliphal the son of
Ur, 36 Hepher the Mecherathite, Ahijah
the Pelonite, 37 Hezro the Carmelite, Na-
arai the son of Ezbai, 38 Joel the brother
of Nathan, Mibhar the son of Hagri,
39 Zelek the Ammonite, Naharai the Be-
rothite[a] (the armorbearer of Joab the
son of Zeruiah), 40 Ira the Ithrite, Gareb
the Ithrite, 41 Uriah the Hittite, Zabad the
son of Ahlai, 42 Adina the son of Shiza
the Reubenite (a chief of the Reubenites)
and thirty with him, 43 Hanan the son
of Maachah, Joshaphat the Mithnite,
44 Uzzia the Ashterathite, Shama and
Jeiel the sons of Hotham the Aroerite,
45 Jediael the son of Shimri, and Joha his
brother, the Tizite, 46 Eliel the Mahavite,
Jeribai and Joshaviah the sons of Elna-
am, Ithmah the Moabite, 47 Eliel, Obed,
and Jaasiel the Mezobaite.

The Growth of David's Army

12 Now these *were* the men who
came to David at Ziklag while he
was still a fugitive from Saul the son of
Kish; and they *were* among the mighty
men, helpers in the war, 2 armed with
bows, using both the right hand and
the left in *hurling* stones and *shooting*
arrows with the bow. *They were* of Ben-
jamin, Saul's brethren.

3 The chief *was* Ahiezer, then Joash,
the sons of Shemaah the Gibeathite;
Jeziel and Pelet the sons of Azmaveth;
Berachah, and Jehu the Anathothite;
4 Ishmaiah the Gibeonite, a mighty man
among the thirty, and over the thirty;
Jeremiah, Jahaziel, Johanan, and Joza-
bad the Gederathite; 5 Eluzai, Jerimoth,
Bealiah, Shemariah, and Shephatiah
the Haruphite; 6 Elkanah, Jisshiah, Aza-
rel, Joezer, and Jashobeam, the Korah-
ites; 7 and Joelah and Zebadiah the sons
of Jeroham of Gedor.

8 *Some* Gadites joined David at the
stronghold in the wilderness, mighty
men of valor, men trained for battle,
who could handle shield and spear,
whose faces *were like* the faces of lions,
and *were* as swift as gazelles on the
mountains: 9 Ezer the first, Obadiah the
second, Eliab the third, 10 Mishmannah
the fourth, Jeremiah the fifth, 11 Attai the
sixth, Eliel the seventh, 12 Johanan the
eighth, Elzabad the ninth, 13 Jeremiah
the tenth, and Machbanai the eleventh.
14 These *were* from the sons of Gad, cap-
tains of the army; the least was over
a hundred, and the greatest was over
a thousand. 15 These *are* the ones who
crossed the Jordan in the first month,
when it had overflowed all its banks;
and they put to flight all *those* in the
valleys, to the east and to the west.

16 Then some of the sons of Benja-
min and Judah came to David at the
stronghold. 17 And David went out to
meet them, and answered and said
to them, "If you have come peaceably
to me to help me, my heart will be unit-
ed with you; but if to betray me to my
enemies, since *there is* no wrong in my
hands, may the God of our fathers look
and bring judgment." 18 Then the Spirit
came upon Amasai, chief of the cap-
tains, *and he said:*

"*We are* yours, O David;
We *are* on your side, O son of
Jesse!
Peace, peace to you,
And peace to your helpers!
For your God helps you."

So David received them, and made
them captains of the troop.

19 And *some* from Manasseh defected to
David when he was going with the Philis-
tines to battle against Saul; but they did
not help them, for the lords of the Philis-
tines sent him away by agreement, say-
ing, "He may defect to his master Saul
and endanger our heads." 20 When he
went to Ziklag, those of Manasseh who
defected to him were Adnah, Jozabad,
Jediael, Michael, Jozabad, Elihu, and
Zillethai, captains of the thousands who
were from Manasseh. 21 And they helped
David against the bands *of raiders,* for

11:32 [a] Spelled *Hiddai* in 2 Samuel 23:30 [b] Spelled *Abi-Albon* in 2 Samuel 23:31 **11:33** [a] Spelled *Barhumite* in 2 Samuel 23:31 **11:39** [a] Spelled *Beerothite* in 2 Samuel 23:37

they *were* all mighty men of valor, and they were captains in the army. 22For at *that* time they came to David day by day to help him, until *it was* a great army, like the army of God.

David's Army at Hebron

23Now these *were* the numbers of the divisions *that were* equipped for war, *and* came to David at Hebron to turn *over* the kingdom of Saul to him, according to the word of the LORD: 24of the sons of Judah bearing shield and spear, six thousand eight hundred armed for war; 25of the sons of Simeon, mighty men of valor fit for war, seven thousand one hundred; 26of the sons of Levi four thousand six hundred; 27Jehoiada, the leader of the Aaronites, and with him three thousand seven hundred; 28Zadok, a young man, a valiant warrior, and from his father's house twenty-two captains; 29of the sons of Benjamin, relatives of Saul, three thousand (until then the greatest part of them had remained loyal to the house of Saul); 30of the sons of Ephraim twenty thousand eight hundred, mighty men of valor, famous men throughout their father's house; 31of the half-tribe of Manasseh eighteen thousand, who were designated by name to come and make David king; 32of the sons of Issachar who had understanding of the times, to know what Israel ought to do, their chiefs were two hundred; and all their brethren were at their command; 33of Zebulun there were fifty thousand who went out to battle, expert in war with all weapons of war, stouthearted men who could keep ranks; 34of Naphtali one thousand captains, and with them thirty-seven thousand with shield and spear; 35of the Danites who could keep battle formation, twenty-eight thousand six hundred; 36of Asher, those who could go out to war, able to keep battle formation, forty thousand; 37of the Reubenites and the Gadites and the half-tribe of Manasseh, from the other side of the Jordan, one hundred and twenty thousand armed for battle with every *kind* of weapon of war.

38All these men of war, who could keep ranks, came to Hebron with a loyal heart, to make David king over all Israel; and all the rest of Israel *were* of one mind to make David king. 39And they were there with David three days, eating and drinking, for their brethren had prepared for them. 40Moreover those who were near to them, from as far away as Issachar and Zebulun and Naphtali, were bringing food on donkeys and camels, on mules and oxen—provisions of flour and cakes of figs and cakes of raisins, wine and oil and oxen and sheep abundantly, for *there was* joy in Israel.

The Ark Brought from Kirjath Jearim

13 Then David consulted with the captains of thousands and hundreds, *and* with every leader. 2And David said to all the assembly of Israel, "If *it seems* good to you, and if it is of the LORD our God, let us send out to our brethren everywhere *who are* left in all the land of Israel, and with them to the priests and Levites *who are* in their cities *and* their common-lands, that they may gather together to us; 3and let us bring the ark of our God back to us, for we have not inquired at it since the days of Saul." 4Then all the assembly said that they would do so, for the thing was right in the eyes of all the people.

5So David gathered all Israel together, from Shihor in Egypt to as far as the entrance of Hamath, to bring the ark of God from Kirjath Jearim. 6And David and all Israel went up to Baalah,[a] to Kirjath Jearim, which belonged to Judah, to bring up from there the ark of God the LORD, who dwells *between* the cherubim, where *His* name is proclaimed. 7So they carried the ark of God on a new cart from the house of Abinadab, and Uzza and Ahio drove the cart. 8Then David and all Israel played *music* before God with all *their* might, with singing, on harps, on stringed instruments, on tambourines, on cymbals, and with trumpets.

9And when they came to Chidon's[a] threshing floor, Uzza put out his hand to hold the ark, for the oxen stumbled.

13:6 [a] Called *Baale Judah* in 2 Samuel 6:2 13:9 [a] Called *Nachon* in 2 Samuel 6:6

10Then the anger of the LORD was
aroused against Uzza, and He struck him
because he put his hand to the ark; and
he died there before God. 11And David
became angry because of the LORD's out-
break against Uzza; therefore that place
is called Perez Uzza[a] to this day. 12David
was afraid of God that day, saying, "How
can I bring the ark of God to me?"
13So David would not move the ark
with him into the City of David, but took
it aside into the house of Obed-Edom the
Gittite. 14The ark of God remained with
the family of Obed-Edom in his house
three months. And the LORD blessed
the house of Obed-Edom and all that
he had.

David Established at Jerusalem

14 Now Hiram king of Tyre sent
messengers to David, and cedar
trees, with masons and carpenters, to
build him a house. 2So David knew that
the LORD had established him as king
over Israel, for his kingdom was highly
exalted for the sake of His people Israel.
3Then David took more wives in Jeru-
salem, and David begot more sons and
daughters. 4And these are the names of
his children whom he had in Jerusalem:
Shammua,[a] Shobab, Nathan, Solomon,
5Ibhar, Elishua,[a] Elpelet,[b] 6Nogah, Ne-
pheg, Japhia, 7Elishama, Beeliada,[a]
and Eliphelet.

The Philistines Defeated

8Now when the Philistines heard that
David had been anointed king over
all Israel, all the Philistines went up to
search for David. And David heard *of it*
and went out against them. 9Then the
Philistines went and made a raid on
the Valley of Rephaim. 10And David
inquired of God, saying, "Shall I go up
against the Philistines? Will You deliver
them into my hand?"
The LORD said to him, "Go up, for I will
deliver them into your hand."
11So they went up to Baal Perazim,
and David defeated them there. Then
David said, "God has broken through
my enemies by my hand like a break-
through of water." Therefore they called
the name of that place Baal Perazim.[a]
12And when they left their gods there,
David gave a commandment, and they
were burned with fire.
13Then the Philistines once again
made a raid on the valley. 14Therefore
David inquired again of God, and God
said to him, "You shall not go up after
them; circle around them, and come
upon them in front of the mulberry
trees. 15And it shall be, when you hear
a sound of marching in the tops of the
mulberry trees, then you shall go out to
battle, for God has gone out before you
to strike the camp of the Philistines."
16So David did as God commanded him,
and they drove back the army of the
Philistines from Gibeon as far as Gezer.
17Then the fame of David went out into
all lands, and the LORD brought the fear
of him upon all nations.

The Ark Brought to Jerusalem

15 *David* built houses for himself
in the City of David; and he pre-
pared a place for the ark of God, and
pitched a tent for it. 2Then David said,
"No one may carry the ark of God but the
Levites, for the LORD has chosen them
to carry the ark of God and to minister
before Him forever." 3And David gath-
ered all Israel together at Jerusalem, to
bring up the ark of the LORD to its place,
which he had prepared for it. 4Then Da-
vid assembled the children of Aaron and
the Levites: 5of the sons of Kohath, Uriel
the chief, and one hundred and twenty
of his brethren; 6of the sons of Merari,
Asaiah the chief, and two hundred and
twenty of his brethren; 7of the sons of
Gershom, Joel the chief, and one hun-
dred and thirty of his brethren; 8of the
sons of Elizaphan, Shemaiah the chief,
and two hundred of his brethren; 9of
the sons of Hebron, Eliel the chief, and
eighty of his brethren; 10of the sons of
Uzziel, Amminadab the chief, and one
hundred and twelve of his brethren.
11And David called for Zadok and Abi-
athar the priests, and for the Levites: for
Uriel, Asaiah, Joel, Shemaiah, Eliel, and
Amminadab. 12He said to them, "You *are*
the heads of the fathers' *houses* of the

13:11 [a] Literally *Outburst Against Uzza* 14:4 [a] Spelled *Shimea* in 3:5 14:5 [a] Spelled *Elishama* in 3:6 [b] Spelled *Eliphelet* in 3:6 14:7 [a] Spelled *Eliada* in 3:8 14:11 [a] Literally *Master of Breakthroughs*

Levites; sanctify yourselves, you and your brethren, that you may bring up the ark of the LORD God of Israel to *the place* I have prepared for it. 13For because you *did* not *do it* the first *time,* the LORD our God broke out against us, because we did not consult Him about the proper order."

14So the priests and the Levites sanctified themselves to bring up the ark of the LORD God of Israel. 15And the children of the Levites bore the ark of God on their shoulders, by its poles, as Moses had commanded according to the word of the LORD.

16Then David spoke to the leaders of the Levites to appoint their brethren *to be* the singers accompanied by instruments of music, stringed instruments, harps, and cymbals, by raising the voice with resounding joy. 17So the Levites appointed Heman the son of Joel; and of his brethren, Asaph the son of Berechiah; and of their brethren, the sons of Merari, Ethan the son of Kushaiah; 18and with them their brethren of the second *rank:* Zechariah, Ben,[a] Jaaziel, Shemiramoth, Jehiel, Unni, Eliab, Benaiah, Maaseiah, Mattithiah, Elipheleh, Mikneiah, Obed-Edom, and Jeiel, the gatekeepers; 19the singers, Heman, Asaph, and Ethan, *were* to sound the cymbals of bronze; 20Zechariah, Aziel, Shemiramoth, Jehiel, Unni, Eliab, Maaseiah, and Benaiah, with strings according to Alamoth; 21Mattithiah, Elipheleh, Mikneiah, Obed-Edom, Jeiel, and Azaziah, to direct with harps on the Sheminith; 22Chenaniah, leader of the Levites, was instructor *in charge of* the music, because he *was* skillful; 23Berechiah and Elkanah *were* doorkeepers for the ark; 24Shebaniah, Joshaphat, Nethanel, Amasai, Zechariah, Benaiah, and Eliezer, the priests, were to blow the trumpets before the ark of God; and Obed-Edom and Jehiah, doorkeepers for the ark.

25So David, the elders of Israel, and the captains over thousands went to bring up the ark of the covenant of the LORD from the house of Obed-Edom with joy. 26And so it was, when God helped the Levites who bore the ark of the covenant of the LORD, that they offered seven bulls and seven rams. 27David was clothed with a robe of fine linen, as were all the Levites who bore the ark, the singers, and Chenaniah the music master *with* the singers. David also wore a linen ephod. 28Thus all Israel brought up the ark of the covenant of the LORD with shouting and with the sound of the horn, with trumpets and with cymbals, making music with stringed instruments and harps.

29And it happened, *as* the ark of the covenant of the LORD came to the City of David, that Michal, Saul's daughter, looked through a window and saw King David whirling and playing music; and she despised him in her heart.

The Ark Placed in the Tabernacle

16 So they brought the ark of God, and set it in the midst of the tabernacle that David had erected for it. Then they offered burnt offerings and peace offerings before God. 2And when David had finished offering the burnt offerings and the peace offerings, he blessed the people in the name of the LORD. 3Then he distributed to everyone of Israel, both man and woman, to everyone a loaf of bread, a piece *of meat,* and a cake of raisins.

4And he appointed some of the Levites to minister before the ark of the LORD, to commemorate, to thank, and to praise the LORD God of Israel: 5Asaph the chief, and next to him Zechariah, *then* Jeiel, Shemiramoth, Jehiel, Mattithiah, Eliab, Benaiah, and Obed-Edom: Jeiel with stringed instruments and harps, but Asaph made music with cymbals; 6Benaiah and Jahaziel the priests regularly *blew* the trumpets before the ark of the covenant of God.

David's Song of Thanksgiving

7On that day David first delivered *this psalm* into the hand of Asaph and his brethren, to thank the LORD:

8 Oh, give thanks to the LORD!
Call upon His name;
Make known His deeds among
the peoples!

15:18 [a] Following Masoretic Text and Vulgate; Septuagint omits *Ben.*

9 Sing to Him, sing psalms to Him;
Talk of all His wondrous works!
10 Glory in His holy name;
Let the hearts of those rejoice who seek the LORD!
11 Seek the LORD and His strength;
Seek His face evermore!
12 Remember His marvelous works which He has done,
His wonders, and the judgments of His mouth,
13 O seed of Israel His servant,
You children of Jacob, His chosen ones!

14 He *is* the LORD our God;
His judgments *are* in all the earth.
15 Remember His covenant forever,
The word which He commanded, for a thousand generations,
16 *The covenant which* He made with Abraham,
And His oath to Isaac,
17 And confirmed it to Jacob for a statute,
To Israel *for* an everlasting covenant,
18 Saying, "To you I will give the land of Canaan
As the allotment of your inheritance,"
19 When you were few in number,
Indeed very few, and strangers in it.

20 When they went from one nation to another,
And from *one* kingdom to another people,
21 He permitted no man to do them wrong;
Yes, He rebuked kings for their sakes,
22 *Saying,* "Do not touch My anointed ones,
And do My prophets no harm."[a]

23 Sing to the LORD, all the earth;
Proclaim the good news of His salvation from day to day.
24 Declare His glory among the nations,
His wonders among all peoples.
25 For the LORD *is* great and greatly to be praised;
He *is* also to be feared above all gods.
26 For all the gods of the peoples *are* idols,
But the LORD made the heavens.
27 Honor and majesty *are* before Him;
Strength and gladness are in His place.

28 Give to the LORD, O families of the peoples,
Give to the LORD glory and strength.
29 Give to the LORD the glory *due* His name;
Bring an offering, and come before Him.
Oh, worship the LORD in the beauty of holiness!
30 Tremble before Him, all the earth.
The world also is firmly established,
It shall not be moved.

31 Let the heavens rejoice, and let the earth be glad;
And let them say among the nations, "The LORD reigns."
32 Let the sea roar, and all its fullness;
Let the field rejoice, and all that *is* in it.
33 Then the trees of the woods shall rejoice before the LORD,
For He is coming to judge the earth.[a]

34 Oh, give thanks to the LORD, for *He is* good!
For His mercy *endures* forever.[a]
35 And say, "Save us, O God of our salvation;
Gather us together, and deliver us from the Gentiles,
To give thanks to Your holy name,
To triumph in Your praise."

36 Blessed *be* the LORD God of Israel
From everlasting to everlasting![a]

And all the people said, "Amen!" and praised the LORD.

16:22 [a] Compare verses 8–22 with Psalm 105:1–15 **16:33** [a] Compare verses 23–33 with Psalm 96:1–13
16:34 [a] Compare verse 34 with Psalm 106:1 **16:36** [a] Compare verses 35, 36 with Psalm 106:47, 48

Regular Worship Maintained

37So he left Asaph and his brothers
there before the ark of the covenant
of the LORD to minister before the ark
regularly, as every day's work required;
38and Obed-Edom with his sixty-eight
brethren, including Obed-Edom the
son of Jeduthun, and Hosah, *to be* gate-
keepers; 39and Zadok the priest and his
brethren the priests, before the taber-
nacle of the LORD at the high place that
was at Gibeon, 40to offer burnt offerings
to the LORD on the altar of burnt offer-
ing regularly morning and evening,
and *to do* according to all that is written
in the Law of the LORD which He com-
manded Israel; 41and with them Heman
and Jeduthun and the rest who were
chosen, who were designated by name,
to give thanks to the LORD, because
His mercy *endures* forever; 42and with
them Heman and Jeduthun, to sound
aloud with trumpets and cymbals and
the musical instruments of God. Now
the sons of Jeduthun *were* gatekeepers.
43Then all the people departed, every
man to his house; and David returned
to bless his house.

God's Covenant with David

17 Now it came to pass, when David
was dwelling in his house, that
David said to Nathan the prophet, "See
now, I dwell in a house of cedar, but the
ark of the covenant of the LORD *is* under
tent curtains."
2Then Nathan said to David, "Do all
that *is* in your heart, for God *is* with you."
3But it happened that night that the
word of God came to Nathan, saying,
4"Go and tell My servant David, 'Thus
says the LORD: "You shall not build
Me a house to dwell in. 5For I have not
dwelt in a house since the time that I
brought up Israel, even to this day, but
have gone from tent to tent, and from
one tabernacle *to another.* 6Wherever I
have moved about with all Israel, have
I ever spoken a word to any of the judg-
es of Israel, whom I commanded to
shepherd My people, saying, 'Why have
you not built Me a house of cedar?' " '
7Now therefore, thus shall you say to My
servant David, 'Thus says the LORD of
hosts: "I took you from the sheepfold,
from following the sheep, to be ruler
over My people Israel. 8And I have been
with you wherever you have gone, and
have cut off all your enemies from be-
fore you, and have made you a name
like the name of the great men who *are*
on the earth. 9Moreover I will appoint
a place for My people Israel, and will
plant them, that they may dwell in a
place of their own and move no more;
nor shall the sons of wickedness oppress
them anymore, as previously, 10since
the time that I commanded judges *to be*
over My people Israel. Also I will subdue
all your enemies. Furthermore I tell you
that the LORD will build you a house.[a]
11And it shall be, when your days are
fulfilled, when you must go *to be* with
your fathers, that I will set up your seed
after you, who will be of your sons; and
I will establish his kingdom. 12He shall
build Me a house, and I will establish his
throne forever. 13I will be his Father, and
he shall be My son; and I will not take
My mercy away from him, as I took *it*
from *him* who was before you. 14And I
will establish him in My house and in
My kingdom forever; and his throne
shall be established forever." ' "
15According to all these words and
according to all this vision, so Nathan
spoke to David.
16Then King David went in and sat be-
fore the LORD; and he said: "Who *am* I,
O LORD God? And what is my house, that
You have brought me this far? 17And
yet this was a small thing in Your sight,
O God; and You have *also* spoken of
Your servant's house for a great while
to come, and have regarded me accord-
ing to the rank of a man of high degree,
O LORD God. 18What more can David *say*
to You for the honor of Your servant? For
You know Your servant. 19O LORD, for
Your servant's sake, and according to
Your own heart, You have done all this
greatness, in making known all these
great things. 20O LORD, *there is* none like
You, nor *is there any* God besides You,
according to all that we have heard with
our ears. 21And who *is* like Your people

17:10 [a] That is, a royal dynasty

Israel, the one nation on the earth whom God went to redeem for Himself *as* a people—to make for Yourself a name by great and awesome deeds, by driving out nations from before Your people whom You redeemed from Egypt? 22For You have made Your people Israel Your very own people forever; and You, LORD, have become their God.

23"And now, O LORD, the word which You have spoken concerning Your servant and concerning his house, *let it* be established forever, and do as You have said. 24So let it be established, that Your name may be magnified forever, saying, 'The LORD of hosts, the God of Israel, *is* Israel's God.' And let the house of Your servant David be established before You. 25For You, O my God, have revealed to Your servant that You will build him a house. Therefore Your servant has found it *in his heart* to pray before You. 26And now, LORD, You are God, and have promised this goodness to Your servant. 27Now You have been pleased to bless the house of Your servant, that it may continue before You forever; for You have blessed it, O LORD, and *it shall be* blessed forever."

David's Further Conquests

18 After this it came to pass that David attacked the Philistines, subdued them, and took Gath and its towns from the hand of the Philistines. 2Then he defeated Moab, and the Moabites became David's servants, *and* brought tribute.

3And David defeated Hadadezer[a] king of Zobah *as far as* Hamath, as he went to establish his power by the River Euphrates. 4David took from him one thousand chariots, seven thousand[a] horsemen, and twenty thousand foot soldiers. Also David hamstrung all the chariot *horses,* except that he spared enough of them for one hundred chariots.

5When the Syrians of Damascus came to help Hadadezer king of Zobah, David killed twenty-two thousand of the Syrians. 6Then David put *garrisons* in Syria of Damascus; and the Syrians became David's servants, *and* brought tribute. So the LORD preserved David wherever he went. 7And David took the shields of gold that were on the servants of Hadadezer, and brought them to Jerusalem. 8Also from Tibhath[a] and from Chun, cities of Hadadezer, David brought a large amount of bronze, with which Solomon made the bronze Sea, the pillars, and the articles of bronze.

9Now when Tou[a] king of Hamath heard that David had defeated all the army of Hadadezer king of Zobah, 10he sent Hadoram[a] his son to King David, to greet him and bless him, because he had fought against Hadadezer and defeated him (for Hadadezer had been at war with Tou); and *Hadoram brought with him* all kinds of articles of gold, silver, and bronze. 11King David also dedicated these to the LORD, along with the silver and gold that he had brought from all *these* nations—from Edom, from Moab, from the people of Ammon, from the Philistines, and from Amalek.

12Moreover Abishai the son of Zeruiah killed eighteen thousand Edomites[a] in the Valley of Salt. 13He also put garrisons in Edom, and all the Edomites became David's servants. And the LORD preserved David wherever he went.

David's Administration

14So David reigned over all Israel, and administered judgment and justice to all his people. 15Joab the son of Zeruiah *was* over the army; Jehoshaphat the son of Ahilud *was* recorder; 16Zadok the son of Ahitub and Abimelech the son of Abiathar *were* the priests; Shavsha[a] *was* the scribe; 17Benaiah the son of Jehoiada *was* over the Cherethites and the Pelethites; and David's sons *were* chief ministers at the king's side.

The Ammonites and Syrians Defeated

19 It happened after this that Nahash the king of the people of Ammon died, and his son reigned in his place. 2Then David said, "I will show

18:3 [a] Hebrew *Hadarezer,* and so throughout chapters 18 and 19 **18:4** [a] Or *seven hundred* (compare 2 Samuel 8:4) **18:8** [a] Spelled *Betah* in 2 Samuel 8:8 **18:9** [a] Spelled *Toi* in 2 Samuel 8:9, 10 **18:10** [a] Spelled *Joram* in 2 Samuel 8:10 **18:12** [a] Or *Syrians* (compare 2 Samuel 8:13) **18:16** [a] Spelled *Seraiah* in 2 Samuel 8:17

kindness to Hanun the son of Nahash, because his father showed kindness to me." So David sent messengers to comfort him concerning his father. And David's servants came to Hanun in the land of the people of Ammon to comfort him.

3 And the princes of the people of Ammon said to Hanun, "Do you think that David really honors your father because he has sent comforters to you? Did his servants not come to you to search and to overthrow and to spy out the land?"

4 Therefore Hanun took David's servants, shaved them, and cut off their garments in the middle, at their buttocks, and sent them away. 5 Then *some* went and told David about the men; and he sent to meet them, because the men were greatly ashamed. And the king said, "Wait at Jericho until your beards have grown, and *then* return."

6 When the people of Ammon saw that they had made themselves repulsive to David, Hanun and the people of Ammon sent a thousand talents of silver to hire for themselves chariots and horsemen from Mesopotamia,[a] from Syrian Maacah, and from Zobah.[b] 7 So they hired for themselves thirty-two thousand chariots, with the king of Maacah and his people, who came and encamped before Medeba. Also the people of Ammon gathered together from their cities, and came to battle.

8 Now when David heard *of it,* he sent Joab and all the army of the mighty men. 9 Then the people of Ammon came out and put themselves in battle array before the gate of the city, and the kings who had come *were* by themselves in the field.

10 When Joab saw that the battle line was against him before and behind, he chose some of Israel's best and put *them* in battle array against the Syrians. 11 And the rest of the people he put under the command of Abishai his brother, and they set *themselves* in battle array against the people of Ammon. 12 Then he said, "If the Syrians are too strong for me, then you shall help me; but if the people of Ammon are too strong for you, then I will help you. 13 Be of good courage, and let us be strong for our people and for the cities of our God. And may the LORD do *what is* good in His sight."

14 So Joab and the people who *were* with him drew near for the battle against the Syrians, and they fled before him. 15 When the people of Ammon saw that the Syrians were fleeing, they also fled before Abishai his brother, and entered the city. So Joab went to Jerusalem.

16 Now when the Syrians saw that they had been defeated by Israel, they sent messengers and brought the Syrians who were beyond the River,[a] and Shophach[b] the commander of Hadadezer's army *went* before them. 17 When it was told David, he gathered all Israel, crossed over the Jordan and came upon them, and set up in battle array against them. So when David had set up in battle array against the Syrians, they fought with him. 18 Then the Syrians fled before Israel; and David killed seven thousand[a] charioteers and forty thousand foot soldiers[b] of the Syrians, and killed Shophach the commander of the army. 19 And when the servants of Hadadezer saw that they were defeated by Israel, they made peace with David and became his servants. So the Syrians were not willing to help the people of Ammon anymore.

Rabbah Is Conquered

20 It happened in the spring of the year, at the time kings go out *to battle,* that Joab led out the armed forces and ravaged the country of the people of Ammon, and came and besieged Rabbah. But David stayed at Jerusalem. And Joab defeated Rabbah and overthrew it. 2 Then David took their king's crown from his head, and found it to weigh a talent of gold, and *there were* precious stones in it. And it was set on David's head. Also he brought out the spoil of the city in great abundance. 3 And he brought out the people who *were* in it, and put *them* to work[a] with saws, with iron picks, and with axes. So

19:6 [a] Hebrew *Aram Naharaim* [b] Spelled *Zoba* in 2 Samuel 10:6 **19:16** [a] That is, the Euphrates [b] Spelled *Shobach* in 2 Samuel 10:16 **19:18** [a] Or *seven hundred* (compare 2 Samuel 10:18) [b] Or *horsemen* (compare 2 Samuel 10:18) **20:3** [a] Septuagint reads *cut them.*

David did to all the cities of the people of
Ammon. Then David and all the people
returned *to* Jerusalem.

Philistine Giants Destroyed

4Now it happened afterward that war
broke out at Gezer with the Philistines,
at which time Sibbechai the Hushathite
killed Sippai,[a] *who was one* of the sons
of the giant. And they were subdued.
5Again there was war with the Phi-
listines, and Elhanan the son of Jair[a]
killed Lahmi the brother of Goliath the
Gittite, the shaft of whose spear *was* like
a weaver's beam.
6Yet again there was war at Gath,
where there was a man of *great* stat-
ure, with twenty-four fingers and toes,
six *on each hand* and six *on each foot;*
and he also was born to the giant. 7So
when he defied Israel, Jonathan the son
of Shimea,[a] David's brother, killed him.
8These were born to the giant in Gath,
and they fell by the hand of David and
by the hand of his servants.

The Census of Israel and Judah

21 Now Satan stood up against Is-
rael, and moved David to num-
ber Israel. 2So David said to Joab and to
the leaders of the people, "Go, number
Israel from Beersheba to Dan, and bring
the number of them to me that I may
know *it.*"
3And Joab answered, "May the LORD
make His people a hundred times more
than they are. But, my lord the king, *are*
they not all my lord's servants? Why
then does my lord require this thing?
Why should he be a cause of guilt in
Israel?"
4Nevertheless the king's word pre-
vailed against Joab. Therefore Joab
departed and went throughout all Isra-
el and came to Jerusalem. 5Then Joab
gave the sum of the number of the peo-
ple to David. All Israel *had* one million
one hundred thousand men who drew
the sword, and Judah *had* four hundred
and seventy thousand men who drew
the sword. 6But he did not count Levi
and Benjamin among them, for the
king's word was abominable to Joab.
7And God was displeased with this
thing; therefore He struck Israel. 8So Da-
vid said to God, "I have sinned greatly,
because I have done this thing; but now,
I pray, take away the iniquity of Your
servant, for I have done very foolishly."
9Then the LORD spoke to Gad, David's
seer, saying, 10"Go and tell David, say-
ing, 'Thus says the LORD: "I offer you
three *things;* choose one of them for
yourself, that I may do *it* to you." ' "
11So Gad came to David and said to
him, "Thus says the LORD: 'Choose for
yourself, 12either three[a] years of fam-
ine, or three months to be defeated by
your foes with the sword of your ene-
mies overtaking *you,* or else for three
days the sword of the LORD—the plague
in the land, with the angel[b] of the LORD
destroying throughout all the territory
of Israel.' Now consider what answer I
should take back to Him who sent me."
13And David said to Gad, "I am in great
distress. Please let me fall into the hand
of the LORD, for His mercies *are* very
great; but do not let me fall into the hand
of man."
14So the LORD sent a plague upon Isra-
el, and seventy thousand men of Israel
fell. 15And God sent an angel to Jerusa-
lem to destroy it. As he[a] was destroying,
the LORD looked and relented of the
disaster, and said to the angel who was
destroying, "It is enough; now restrain
your[b] hand." And the angel of the LORD
stood by the threshing floor of Ornan[c]
the Jebusite.
16Then David lifted his eyes and saw
the angel of the LORD standing between
earth and heaven, having in his hand
a drawn sword stretched out over Jeru-
salem. So David and the elders, clothed
in sackcloth, fell on their faces. 17And
David said to God, "Was it not I who
commanded the people to be num-
bered? I am the one who has sinned and
done evil indeed; but these sheep, what
have they done? Let Your hand, I pray,
O LORD my God, be against me and my

20:4 [a] Spelled *Saph* in 2 Samuel 21:18 **20:5** [a] Spelled *Jaare-Oregim* in 2 Samuel 21:19 **20:7** [a] Spelled *Shimeah* in 2 Samuel 21:21 and *Shammah* in 1 Samuel 16:9 **21:12** [a] Or *seven* (compare 2 Samuel 24:13) [b] Or *Angel,* and so elsewhere in this chapter **21:15** [a] Or *He* [b] Or *Your* [c] Spelled *Araunah* in 2 Samuel 24:16

father's house, but not against Your people that they should be plagued."

18Therefore, the angel of the LORD commanded Gad to say to David that David should go and erect an altar to the LORD on the threshing floor of Ornan the Jebusite. 19So David went up at the word of Gad, which he had spoken in the name of the LORD. 20Now Ornan turned and saw the angel; and his four sons *who were* with him hid themselves, but Ornan continued threshing wheat. 21So David came to Ornan, and Ornan looked and saw David. And he went out from the threshing floor, and bowed before David with *his* face to the ground. 22Then David said to Ornan, "Grant me the place of *this* threshing floor, that I may build an altar on it to the LORD. You shall grant it to me at the full price, that the plague may be withdrawn from the people."

23But Ornan said to David, "Take *it* to yourself, and let my lord the king do *what is* good in his eyes. Look, I *also* give *you* the oxen for burnt offerings, the threshing implements for wood, and the wheat for the grain offering; I give *it* all."

24Then King David said to Ornan, "No, but I will surely buy *it* for the full price, for I will not take what is yours for the LORD, nor offer burnt offerings with *that which* costs *me* nothing." 25So David gave Ornan six hundred shekels of gold by weight for the place. 26And David built there an altar to the LORD, and offered burnt offerings and peace offerings, and called on the LORD; and He answered him from heaven by fire on the altar of burnt offering.

27So the LORD commanded the angel, and he returned his sword to its sheath.

28At that time, when David saw that the LORD had answered him on the threshing floor of Ornan the Jebusite, he sacrificed there. 29For the tabernacle of the LORD and the altar of the burnt offering, which Moses had made in the wilderness, *were* at that time at the high place in Gibeon. 30But David could not go before it to inquire of God, for he was afraid of the sword of the angel of the LORD.

David Prepares to Build the Temple

22 Then David said, "This *is* the house of the LORD God, and this *is* the altar of burnt offering for Israel." 2So David commanded to gather the aliens who *were* in the land of Israel; and he appointed masons to cut hewn stones to build the house of God. 3And David prepared iron in abundance for the nails of the doors of the gates and for the joints, and bronze in abundance beyond measure, 4and cedar trees in abundance; for the Sidonians and those from Tyre brought much cedar wood to David.

5Now David said, "Solomon my son *is* young and inexperienced, and the house to be built for the LORD *must be* exceedingly magnificent, famous and glorious throughout all countries. I will now make preparation for it." So David made abundant preparations before his death.

6Then he called for his son Solomon, and charged him to build a house for the LORD God of Israel. 7And David said to Solomon: "My son, as for me, it was in my mind to build a house to the name of the LORD my God; 8but the word of the LORD came to me, saying, 'You have shed much blood and have made great wars; you shall not build a house for My name, because you have shed much blood on the earth in My sight. 9Behold, a son shall be born to you, who shall be a man of rest; and I will give him rest from all his enemies all around. His name shall be Solomon,[a] for I will give peace and quietness to Israel in his days. 10He shall build a house for My name, and he shall be My son, and I *will be* his Father; and I will establish the throne of his kingdom over Israel forever.' 11Now, my son, may the LORD be with you; and may you prosper, and build the house of the LORD your God, as He has said to you. 12Only may the LORD give you wisdom and understanding, and give you charge concerning Israel, that you may keep the law of the LORD your God. 13Then you will prosper, if you take care to fulfill the statutes and judgments with which the LORD charged Moses concerning Israel. Be

22:9 [a] Literally *Peaceful*

GOD SIN JESUS SALVATION LOVE

strong and of good courage; do not
fear nor be dismayed. 14Indeed I have
taken much trouble to prepare for the
house of the LORD one hundred thou-
sand talents of gold and one million
talents of silver, and bronze and iron
beyond measure, for it is so abundant.
I have prepared timber and stone also,
and you may add to them. 15Moreover
there are workmen with you in abun-
dance: woodsmen and stonecutters,
and all types of skillful men for every
kind of work. 16Of gold and silver and
bronze and iron *there is* no limit. Arise
and begin working, and the LORD be
with you."
17David also commanded all the lead-
ers of Israel to help Solomon his son,
saying, 18"*Is* not the LORD your God with
you? And has He *not* given you rest on
every side? For He has given the inhab-
itants of the land into my hand, and
the land is subdued before the LORD
and before His people. 19Now set your
heart and your soul to seek the LORD
your God. Therefore arise and build the
sanctuary of the LORD God, to bring
the ark of the covenant of the LORD and
the holy articles of God into the house that
is to be built for the name of the LORD."

The Divisions of the Levites

23 So when David was old and full
of days, he made his son Sol-
omon king over Israel.
2And he gathered together all the lead-
ers of Israel, with the priests and the Le-
vites. 3Now the Levites were numbered
from the age of thirty years and above;
and the number of individual males
was thirty-eight thousand. 4Of these,
twenty-four thousand *were* to look af-
ter the work of the house of the LORD,
six thousand *were* officers and judges,
5four thousand *were* gatekeepers, and
four thousand praised the LORD with
musical instruments, "which I made,"
said David, "for giving praise."
6Also David separated them into divi-
sions among the sons of Levi: Gershon,
Kohath, and Merari.
7Of the Gershonites: Laadan[a] and
Shimei. 8The sons of Laadan: the first
Jehiel, then Zetham and Joel—three
in all. 9The sons of Shimei: Shelomith,
Haziel, and Haran—three *in all.* These
were the heads of the fathers' *houses*
of Laadan. 10And the sons of Shimei:
Jahath, Zina,[a] Jeush, and Beriah. These
were the four sons of Shimei. 11Jahath
was the first and Zizah the second. But
Jeush and Beriah did not have many
sons; therefore they were assigned as
one father's house.
12The sons of Kohath: Amram, Izhar,
Hebron, and Uzziel—four *in all.* 13The
sons of Amram: Aaron and Moses; and
Aaron was set apart, he and his sons
forever, that he should sanctify the most
holy things, to burn incense before the
LORD, to minister to Him, and to give
the blessing in His name forever. 14Now
the sons of Moses the man of God were
reckoned to the tribe of Levi. 15The sons
of Moses *were* Gershon[a] and Eliezer.
16Of the sons of Gershon, Shebuel[a] *was*
the first. 17Of the descendants of Eliezer,
Rehabiah was the first. And Eliezer had
no other sons, but the sons of Rehabiah
were very many. 18Of the sons of Izhar,
Shelomith *was* the first. 19Of the sons
of Hebron, Jeriah *was* the first, Amari-
ah the second, Jahaziel the third, and
Jekameam the fourth. 20Of the sons of
Uzziel, Michah *was* the first and Jesshi-
ah the second.
21The sons of Merari *were* Mahli and
Mushi. The sons of Mahli *were* Eleazar
and Kish. 22And Eleazar died, and had
no sons, but only daughters; and their
brethren, the sons of Kish, took them *as*
wives. 23The sons of Mushi *were* Mahli,
Eder, and Jeremoth—three *in all.*
24These *were* the sons of Levi by their
fathers' houses—the heads of the fa-
thers' *houses* as they were counted
individually by the number of their
names, who did the work for the service
of the house of the LORD, from the age
of twenty years and above.
25For David said, "The LORD God of
Israel has given rest to His people, that
they may dwell in Jerusalem forever";
26and also to the Levites, "They shall
no longer carry the tabernacle, or any
of the articles for its service." 27For by

23:7 [a] Spelled *Libni* in Exodus 6:17 **23:10** [a] Septuagint and Vulgate read *Zizah* (compare verse 11).
23:15 [a] Hebrew *Gershom* (compare 6:16) **23:16** [a] Spelled *Shubael* in 24:20

the last words of David the Levites *were*
numbered from twenty years old and
above; 28because their duty *was* to help
the sons of Aaron in the service of the
house of the LORD, in the courts and in
the chambers, in the purifying of all
holy things and the work of the service
of the house of God, 29both with the
showbread and the fine flour for the
grain offering, with the unleavened
cakes and *what is baked in* the pan,
with what is mixed and with all kinds
of measures and sizes; 30to stand every
morning to thank and praise the LORD,
and likewise at evening; 31and at every
presentation of a burnt offering to the
LORD on the Sabbaths and on the New
Moons and on the set feasts, by number
according to the ordinance governing
them, regularly before the LORD; 32and
that they should attend to the needs of
the tabernacle of meeting, the needs of
the holy *place,* and the needs of the sons
of Aaron their brethren in the work of
the house of the LORD.

The Divisions of the Priests

24 Now *these are* the divisions of
the sons of Aaron. The sons of
Aaron *were* Nadab, Abihu, Eleazar, and
Ithamar. 2And Nadab and Abihu died
before their father, and had no children;
therefore Eleazar and Ithamar minis-
tered as priests. 3Then David with Zadok
of the sons of Eleazar, and Ahimelech of
the sons of Ithamar, divided them ac-
cording to the schedule of their service.
4There were more leaders found of
the sons of Eleazar than of the sons of
Ithamar, and *thus* they were divided.
Among the sons of Eleazar *were* sixteen
heads of *their* fathers' houses, and eight
heads of their fathers' houses among
the sons of Ithamar. 5Thus they were
divided by lot, one group as another,
for there were officials of the sanctuary
and officials *of the house* of God, from
the sons of Eleazar and from the sons
of Ithamar. 6And the scribe, Shemaiah
the son of Nethanel, *one of* the Levites,
wrote them down before the king, the
leaders, Zadok the priest, Ahimelech
the son of Abiathar, and the heads of
the fathers' *houses* of the priests and
Levites, one father's house taken for
Eleazar and *one* for Ithamar.
7Now the first lot fell to Jehoiarib,
the second to Jedaiah, 8the third to
Harim, the fourth to Seorim, 9the fifth
to Malchijah, the sixth to Mijamin, 10the
seventh to Hakkoz, the eighth to Abi-
jah, 11the ninth to Jeshua, the tenth to
Shecaniah, 12the eleventh to Eliashib,
the twelfth to Jakim, 13the thirteenth to
Huppah, the fourteenth to Jeshebeab,
14the fifteenth to Bilgah, the sixteenth to
Immer, 15the seventeenth to Hezir, the
eighteenth to Happizzez,[a] 16the nine-
teenth to Pethahiah, the twentieth to Je-
hezekel,[a] 17the twenty-first to Jachin, the
twenty-second to Gamul, 18the twenty-
third to Delaiah, the twenty-fourth to
Maaziah.
19This *was* the schedule of their service
for coming into the house of the LORD
according to their ordinance by the
hand of Aaron their father, as the LORD
God of Israel had commanded him.

Other Levites

20And the rest of the sons of Levi: of
the sons of Amram, Shubael;[a] of the
sons of Shubael, Jehdeiah. 21Concern-
ing Rehabiah, of the sons of Rehabiah,
the first *was* Isshiah. 22Of the Izharites,
Shelomoth;[a] of the sons of Shelomoth,
Jahath. 23Of the sons *of Hebron,*[a] Jeriah
was the first,[b] Amariah the second, Jaha-
ziel the third, *and* Jekameam the fourth.
24*Of* the sons of Uzziel, Michah; of the
sons of Michah, Shamir. 25The brother of
Michah, Isshiah; of the sons of Isshiah,
Zechariah. 26The sons of Merari *were*
Mahli and Mushi; the son of Jaaziah,
Beno. 27The sons of Merari by Jaaziah
were Beno, Shoham, Zaccur, and Ibri.
28Of Mahli: Eleazar, who had no sons.
29Of Kish: the son of Kish, Jerahmeel.
30Also the sons of Mushi *were* Mahli,
Eder, and Jerimoth. These *were* the sons
of the Levites according to their fathers'
houses.

24:15 [a] Septuagint and Vulgate read *Aphses.* **24:16** [a] Masoretic Text reads *Jehezkel.*
24:20 [a] Spelled *Shebuel* in 23:16 **24:22** [a] Spelled *Shelomith* in 23:18 **24:23** [a] Supplied from 23:19 (following some Hebrew manuscripts and Septuagint manuscripts) [b] Supplied from 23:19 (following some Hebrew manuscripts and Septuagint manuscripts)

31These also cast lots just as their
brothers the sons of Aaron did, in the
presence of King David, Zadok, Ahim-
elech, and the heads of the fathers'
houses of the priests and Levites. The
chief fathers *did* just as their younger
brethren.

The Musicians

25 Moreover David and the cap-
tains of the army separated for
the service *some* of the sons of Asaph,
of Heman, and of Jeduthun, who *should*
prophesy with harps, stringed instru-
ments, and cymbals. And the number of
the skilled men performing their service
was: 2Of the sons of Asaph: Zaccur, Jo-
seph, Nethaniah, and Asharelah;[a] the
sons of Asaph *were* under the direction
of Asaph, who prophesied according
to the order of the king. 3Of Jeduthun,
the sons of Jeduthun: Gedaliah, Zeri,[a]
Jeshaiah, *Shimei*, Hashabiah, and Mat-
tithiah, six,[b] under the direction of their
father Jeduthun, who prophesied with
a harp to give thanks and to praise the
LORD. 4Of Heman, the sons of Heman:
Bukkiah, Mattaniah, Uzziel,[a] Shebuel,[b]
Jerimoth,[c] Hananiah, Hanani, Eliathah,
Giddalti, Romamti-Ezer, Joshbekashah,
Mallothi, Hothir, *and* Mahazioth. 5All
these *were* the sons of Heman the king's
seer in the words of God, to exalt his
horn.[a] For God gave Heman fourteen
sons and three daughters.

6All these *were* under the direction of
their father for the music *in* the house
of the LORD, with cymbals, stringed
instruments, and harps, for the service
of the house of God. Asaph, Jeduthun,
and Heman *were* under the authority of
the king. 7So the number of them, with
their brethren who were instructed in
the songs of the LORD, all who were skill-
ful, *was* two hundred and eighty-eight.

8And they cast lots for their duty, the
small as well as the great, the teacher
with the student.

9Now the first lot for Asaph came out
for Joseph; the second for Gedaliah, him
with his brethren and sons, twelve; 10the
third for Zaccur, his sons and his breth-
ren, twelve; 11the fourth for Jizri,[a] his
sons and his brethren, twelve; 12the fifth
for Nethaniah, his sons and his brethren,
twelve; 13the sixth for Bukkiah, his sons
and his brethren, twelve; 14the seventh
for Jesharelah,[a] his sons and his breth-
ren, twelve; 15the eighth for Jeshaiah,
his sons and his brethren, twelve; 16the
ninth for Mattaniah, his sons and his
brethren, twelve; 17the tenth for Shim-
ei, his sons and his brethren, twelve;
18the eleventh for Azarel,[a] his sons and
his brethren, twelve; 19the twelfth for
Hashabiah, his sons and his brethren,
twelve; 20the thirteenth for Shubael,[a]
his sons and his brethren, twelve; 21the
fourteenth for Mattithiah, his sons and
his brethren, twelve; 22the fifteenth for
Jeremoth,[a] his sons and his brethren,
twelve; 23the sixteenth for Hananiah, his
sons and his brethren, twelve; 24the sev-
enteenth for Joshbekashah, his sons and
his brethren, twelve; 25the eighteenth
for Hanani, his sons and his brethren,
twelve; 26the nineteenth for Mallothi,
his sons and his brethren, twelve; 27the
twentieth for Eliathah, his sons and
his brethren, twelve; 28the twenty-first
for Hothir, his sons and his brethren,
twelve; 29the twenty-second for Giddalti,
his sons and his brethren, twelve; 30the
twenty-third for Mahazioth, his sons
and his brethren, twelve; 31the twenty-
fourth for Romamti-Ezer, his sons and
his brethren, twelve.

The Gatekeepers

26 Concerning the divisions of the
gatekeepers: of the Korahites,
Meshelemiah the son of Kore, of the
sons of Asaph. 2And the sons of Me-
shelemiah *were* Zechariah the first-
born, Jediael the second, Zebadiah the
third, Jathniel the fourth, 3Elam the
fifth, Jehohanan the sixth, Eliehoenai
the seventh.

25:2 [a] Spelled *Jesharelah* in verse 14 **25:3** [a] Spelled *Jizri* in verse 11 [b] *Shimei*, appearing in one Hebrew and several Septuagint manuscripts, completes the total of six sons (compare verse 17). **25:4** [a] Spelled *Azarel* in verse 18 [b] Spelled *Shubael* in verse 20 [c] Spelled *Jeremoth* in verse 22 **25:5** [a] That is, to increase his power or influence **25:11** [a] Spelled *Zeri* in verse 3 **25:14** [a] Spelled *Asharelah* in verse 2 **25:18** [a] Spelled *Uzziel* in verse 4 **25:20** [a] Spelled *Shebuel* in verse 4 **25:22** [a] Spelled *Jerimoth* in verse 4

4 Moreover the sons of Obed-Edom
were Shemaiah the firstborn, Jehoza-
bad the second, Joah the third, Sacar the
fourth, Nethanel the fifth, 5 Ammiel the
sixth, Issachar the seventh, Peulthai
the eighth; for God blessed him.
6 Also to Shemaiah his son were sons
born who governed their fathers' houses,
because they *were* men of great ability.
7 The sons of Shemaiah *were* Othni, Re-
phael, Obed, and Elzabad, whose brothers
Elihu and Semachiah *were* able men.
8 All these *were* of the sons of Obed-
Edom, they and their sons and their
brethren, able men with strength for the
work: sixty-two of Obed-Edom.
9 And Meshelemiah had sons and
brethren, eighteen able men.
10 Also Hosah, of the children of Merari,
had sons: Shimri the first (for *though* he
was not the firstborn, his father made him
the first), 11 Hilkiah the second, Tebaliah
the third, Zechariah the fourth; all the
sons and brethren of Hosah *were* thirteen.
12 Among these *were* the divisions of
the gatekeepers, among the chief men,
having duties just like their brethren, to
serve in the house of the LORD. 13 And
they cast lots for each gate, the small
as well as the great, according to their
father's house. 14 The lot for the East *Gate*
fell to Shelemiah. Then they cast lots
for his son Zechariah, a wise counselor,
and his lot came out for the North Gate;
15 to Obed-Edom the South Gate, and to
his sons the storehouse.[a] 16 To Shuppim
and Hosah *the lot came out* for the West
Gate, with the Shallecheth Gate on the
ascending highway—watchman op-
posite watchman. 17 On the east *were*
six Levites, on the north four each day,
on the south four each day, and for the
storehouse[a] two by two. 18 As for the
Parbar[a] on the west, *there were* four
on the highway *and* two at the Parbar.
19 These were the divisions of the gate-
keepers among the sons of Korah and
among the sons of Merari.

The Treasuries and Other Duties

20 Of the Levites, Ahijah *was* over the
treasuries of the house of God and over
the treasuries of the dedicated things.
21 The sons of Laadan, the descendants
of the Gershonites of Laadan, heads of
their fathers' *houses,* of Laadan the Ger-
shonite: Jehieli. 22 The sons of Jehieli, Ze-
tham and Joel his brother, *were* over the
treasuries of the house of the LORD. 23 Of
the Amramites, the Izharites, the He-
bronites, and the Uzzielites: 24 Shebuel
the son of Gershom, the son of Moses,
was overseer of the treasuries. 25 And
his brethren by Eliezer *were* Rehabiah
his son, Jeshaiah his son, Joram his son,
Zichri his son, and Shelomith his son.
26 This Shelomith and his brethren *were*
over all the treasuries of the dedicated
things which King David and the heads
of fathers' *houses,* the captains over thou-
sands and hundreds, and the captains of
the army, had dedicated. 27 Some of the
spoils won in battles they dedicated to
maintain the house of the LORD. 28 And
all that Samuel the seer, Saul the son
of Kish, Abner the son of Ner, and Joab
the son of Zeruiah had dedicated, every
dedicated *thing,* was under the hand of
Shelomith and his brethren.
29 Of the Izharites, Chenaniah and his
sons *performed* duties as officials and
judges over Israel outside Jerusalem.
30 Of the Hebronites, Hashabiah and
his brethren, one thousand seven hun-
dred able men, had the oversight of Is-
rael on the west side of the Jordan for
all the business of the LORD, and in the
service of the king. 31 Among the Hebron-
ites, Jerijah *was* head of the Hebronites
according to his genealogy of the fa-
thers. In the fortieth year of the reign
of David they were sought, and there
were found among them capable men
at Jazer of Gilead. 32 And his brethren
were two thousand seven hundred able
men, heads of fathers' *houses,* whom
King David made officials over the Reu-
benites, the Gadites, and the half-tribe of
Manasseh, for every matter pertaining
to God and the affairs of the king.

The Military Divisions

27 And the children of Israel, ac-
cording to their number, the
heads of fathers' *houses,* the captains
of thousands and hundreds and their

26:15 [a] Hebrew *asuppim* **26:17** [a] Hebrew *asuppim* **26:18** [a] Probably a court or colonnade extending west of the temple

officers, served the king in every matter of the *military* divisions. *These divisions* came in and went out month by month throughout all the months of the year, each division *having* twenty-four thousand.

2Over the first division for the first month *was* Jashobeam the son of Zabdiel, and in his division *were* twenty-four thousand; 3*he was* of the children of Perez, and the chief of all the captains of the army for the first month. 4Over the division of the second month *was* Dodai[a] an Ahohite, and of his division Mikloth also *was* the leader; in his division *were* twenty-four thousand. 5The third captain of the army for the third month *was* Benaiah, the son of Jehoiada the priest, who was chief; in his division *were* twenty-four thousand. 6This was the Benaiah *who was* mighty *among* the thirty, and was over the thirty; in his division *was* Ammizabad his son. 7The fourth *captain* for the fourth month *was* Asahel the brother of Joab, and Zebadiah his son after him; in his division *were* twenty-four thousand. 8The fifth captain for the fifth month *was* Shamhuth[a] the Izrahite; in his division were twenty-four thousand. 9The sixth *captain* for the sixth month *was* Ira the son of Ikkesh the Tekoite; in his division *were* twenty-four thousand. 10The seventh *captain* for the seventh month *was* Helez the Pelonite, of the children of Ephraim; in his division *were* twenty-four thousand. 11The eighth *captain* for the eighth month *was* Sibbechai the Hushathite, of the Zarhites; in his division *were* twenty-four thousand. 12The ninth *captain* for the ninth month *was* Abiezer the Anathothite, of the Benjamites; in his division *were* twenty-four thousand. 13The tenth *captain* for the tenth month *was* Maharai the Netophathite, of the Zarhites; in his division *were* twenty-four thousand. 14The eleventh *captain* for the eleventh month *was* Benaiah the Pirathonite, of the children of Ephraim; in his division *were* twenty-four thousand. 15The twelfth *captain* for the twelfth month *was* Heldai[a] the Netophathite, of Othniel; in his division *were* twenty-four thousand.

Leaders of Tribes

16Furthermore, over the tribes of Israel: the officer over the Reubenites *was* Eliezer the son of Zichri; over the Simeonites, Shephatiah the son of Maachah; 17*over* the Levites, Hashabiah the son of Kemuel; over the Aaronites, Zadok; 18*over* Judah, Elihu, *one* of David's brothers; *over* Issachar, Omri the son of Michael; 19*over* Zebulun, Ishmaiah the son of Obadiah; *over* Naphtali, Jerimoth the son of Azriel; 20*over* the children of Ephraim, Hoshea the son of Azaziah; *over* the half-tribe of Manasseh, Joel the son of Pedaiah; 21*over* the half-*tribe* of Manasseh in Gilead, Iddo the son of Zechariah; *over* Benjamin, Jaasiel the son of Abner; 22*over* Dan, Azarel the son of Jeroham. These *were* the leaders of the tribes of Israel.

23But David did not take the number of those twenty years old and under, because the LORD had said He would multiply Israel like the stars of the heavens. 24Joab the son of Zeruiah began a census, but he did not finish, for wrath came upon Israel because of this census; nor was the number recorded in the account of the chronicles of King David.

Other State Officials

25And Azmaveth the son of Adiel *was* over the king's treasuries; and Jehonathan the son of Uzziah was over the storehouses in the field, in the cities, in the villages, and in the fortresses. 26Ezri the son of Chelub was over those who did the work of the field for tilling the ground. 27And Shimei the Ramathite *was* over the vineyards, and Zabdi the Shiphmite was over the produce of the vineyards for the supply of wine. 28Baal-Hanan the Gederite was over the olive trees and the sycamore trees that *were* in the lowlands, and Joash *was* over the store of oil. 29And Shitrai the Sharonite *was* over the herds that fed in Sharon, and Shaphat the son of Adlai was over the herds *that were* in the valleys. 30Obil the Ishmaelite *was* over the camels, Jehdeiah the Meronothite *was* over the donkeys, 31and Jaziz the Hagrite *was* over the flocks.

27:4 [a] Hebrew *Dodai,* usually spelled *Dodo* (compare 2 Samuel 23:9) 27:8 [a] Spelled *Shammoth* in 11:27 and *Shammah* in 2 Samuel 23:11 27:15 [a] Spelled *Heled* in 11:30 and *Heleb* in 2 Samuel 23:29

All these *were* the officials over King
David's property.
32Also Jehonathan, David's uncle, *was*
a counselor, a wise man, and a scribe;
and Jehiel the son of Hachmoni *was*
with the king's sons. 33Ahithophel *was*
the king's counselor, and Hushai the Ar-
chite *was* the king's companion. 34After
Ahithophel *was* Jehoiada the son of Be-
naiah, then Abiathar. And the general
of the king's army *was* Joab.

Solomon Instructed to Build the Temple

28 Now David assembled at Jerusa-
lem all the leaders of Israel: the
officers of the tribes and the captains of
the divisions who served the king, the
captains over thousands and captains
over hundreds, and the stewards over
all the substance and possessions of the
king and of his sons, with the officials,
the valiant men, and all the mighty
men of valor.
2Then King David rose to his feet and
said, "Hear me, my brethren and my
people: I *had* it in my heart to build a
house of rest for the ark of the covenant
of the LORD, and for the footstool of our
God, and had made preparations to
build it. 3But God said to me, 'You shall
not build a house for My name, because
you *have been* a man of war and have
shed blood.' 4However the LORD God of
Israel chose me above all the house of
my father to be king over Israel forever,
for He has chosen Judah *to be* the ruler.
And of the house of Judah, the house of
my father, and among the sons of my
father, He was pleased with me to make
me king over all Israel. 5And of all my
sons (for the LORD has given me many
sons) He has chosen my son Solomon
to sit on the throne of the kingdom of
the LORD over Israel. 6Now He said to
me, 'It is your son Solomon *who* shall
build My house and My courts; for I
have chosen him *to be* My son, and I will
be his Father. 7Moreover I will establish
his kingdom forever, if he is steadfast
to observe My commandments and
My judgments, as it is this day.' 8Now
therefore, in the sight of all Israel, the
assembly of the LORD, and in the hear-
ing of our God, be careful to seek out all
the commandments of the LORD your
God, that you may possess this good
land, and leave *it* as an inheritance for
your children after you forever.
9"As for you, my son Solomon, know
the God of your father, and serve Him
with a loyal heart and with a willing
mind; for the LORD searches all hearts
and understands all the intent of the
thoughts. If you seek Him, He will be
found by you; but if you forsake Him,
He will cast you off forever. 10Consid-
er now, for the LORD has chosen you
to build a house for the sanctuary; be
strong, and do it."
11Then David gave his son Solomon
the plans for the vestibule, its houses, its
treasuries, its upper chambers, its inner
chambers, and the place of the mercy
seat; 12and the plans for all that he had
by the Spirit, of the courts of the house of
the LORD, of all the chambers all around,
of the treasuries of the house of God, and
of the treasuries for the dedicated things;
13also for the division of the priests and
the Levites, for all the work of the service
of the house of the LORD, and for all the
articles of service in the house of the
LORD. 14*He gave* gold by weight for *things*
of gold, for all articles used in every kind
of service; also *silver* for all articles of
silver by weight, for all articles used in
every kind of service; 15the weight for
the lampstands of gold, and their lamps
of gold, by weight for each lampstand
and its lamps; for the lampstands of
silver by weight, for the lampstand and
its lamps, according to the use of each
lampstand. 16And by weight *he gave* gold
for the tables of the showbread, for each
table, and silver for the tables of silver;
17also pure gold for the forks, the basins,
the pitchers of pure gold, and the golden
bowls—*he gave gold* by weight for every
bowl; and for the silver bowls, *silver* by
weight for every bowl; 18and refined gold
by weight for the altar of incense, and
for the construction of the chariot, that
is, the gold cherubim that spread *their*
wings and overshadowed the ark of the
covenant of the LORD. 19"All *this,*" *said*
David, "the LORD made me understand
in writing, by *His* hand upon me, all the
works of these plans."
20And David said to his son Solomon,
"Be strong and of good courage, and do

it; do not fear nor be dismayed, for the
LORD God—my God—*will be* with you.
He will not leave you nor forsake you,
until you have finished all the work for
the service of the house of the LORD.
21 *Here are* the divisions of the priests
and the Levites for all the service of the
house of God; and every willing crafts-
man *will be* with you for all manner of
workmanship, for every kind of service;
also the leaders and all the people *will
be* completely at your command."

Offerings for Building the Temple

29 Furthermore King David said to
all the assembly: "My son Sol-
omon, whom alone God has chosen, *is*
young and inexperienced; and the work
is great, because the temple[a] *is* not for
man but for the LORD God. 2 Now for
the house of my God I have prepared
with all my might: gold for *things to be
made of* gold, silver for *things of* silver,
bronze for *things of* bronze, iron for *things
of* iron, wood for *things of* wood, onyx
stones, *stones* to be set, glistening stones
of various colors, all kinds of precious
stones, and marble slabs in abundance.
3 Moreover, because I have set my af-
fection on the house of my God, I have
given to the house of my God, over and
above all that I have prepared for the
holy house, my own special treasure of
gold and silver: 4 three thousand talents
of gold, of the gold of Ophir, and seven
thousand talents of refined silver, to
overlay the walls of the houses; 5 the gold
for *things of* gold and the silver for *things
of* silver, and for all kinds of work *to be
done* by the hands of craftsmen. Who
then is willing to consecrate himself this
day to the LORD?"

6 Then the leaders of the fathers' *hous-
es,* leaders of the tribes of Israel, the
captains of thousands and of hundreds,
with the officers over the king's work,
offered willingly. 7 They gave for the
work of the house of God five thousand
talents and ten thousand darics of gold,
ten thousand talents of silver, eighteen
thousand talents of bronze, and one
hundred thousand talents of iron. 8 And
whoever had *precious* stones gave *them*
to the treasury of the house of the LORD,
into the hand of Jehiel[a] the Gershonite.
9 Then the people rejoiced, for they had
offered willingly, because with a loyal
heart they had offered willingly to the
LORD; and King David also rejoiced
greatly.

David's Praise to God

10 Therefore David blessed the LORD
before all the assembly; and David said:

"Blessed are You, LORD God of
Israel, our Father, forever
and ever.
11 Yours, O LORD, *is* the greatness,
The power and the glory,
The victory and the majesty;
For all *that is* in heaven and in
earth *is Yours;*
Yours *is* the kingdom, O LORD,
And You are exalted as head
over all.
12 Both riches and honor *come* from
You,
And You reign over all.
In Your hand *is* power and might;
In Your hand *it is* to make great
And to give strength to all.

13 "Now therefore, our God,
We thank You
And praise Your glorious name.
14 But who *am* I, and who *are* my
people,
That we should be able to offer so
willingly as this?
For all things *come* from You,
And of Your own we have given
You.
15 For we *are* aliens and pilgrims
before You,
As *were* all our fathers;
Our days on earth *are* as a
shadow,
And without hope.

16 "O LORD our God, all this abundance
that we have prepared to build You a
house for Your holy name is from Your
hand, and *is* all Your own. 17 I know also,
my God, that You test the heart and
have pleasure in uprightness. As for me,

29:1 a Literally *palace* 29:8 a Possibly the same as *Jehieli* (compare 26:21, 22)

in the uprightness of my heart I have
willingly offered all these *things;* and
now with joy I have seen Your people,
who are present here to offer willing-
ly to You. 18O LORD God of Abraham,
Isaac, and Israel, our fathers, keep this
forever in the intent of the thoughts of
the heart of Your people, and fix their
heart toward You. 19And give my son
Solomon a loyal heart to keep Your
commandments and Your testimonies
and Your statutes, to do all *these things,*
and to build the temple[a] for which I
have made provision."
20Then David said to all the assembly,
"Now bless the LORD your God." So all
the assembly blessed the LORD God of
their fathers, and bowed their heads
and prostrated themselves before the
LORD and the king.

Solomon Anointed King

21And they made sacrifices to the LORD
and offered burnt offerings to the LORD
on the next day: a thousand bulls, a
thousand rams, a thousand lambs, with
their drink offerings, and sacrifices in
abundance for all Israel. 22So they ate
and drank before the LORD with great
gladness on that day. And they made
Solomon the son of David king the
second time, and anointed *him* before
the LORD *to be* the leader, and Zadok
to be priest. 23Then Solomon sat on the
throne of the LORD as king instead of
David his father, and prospered; and all
Israel obeyed him. 24All the leaders and
the mighty men, and also all the sons
of King David, submitted themselves to
King Solomon. 25So the LORD exalted
Solomon exceedingly in the sight of all
Israel, and bestowed on him *such* royal
majesty as had not been on any king
before him in Israel.

The Close of David's Reign

26Thus David the son of Jesse reigned
over all Israel. 27And the period that
he reigned over Israel *was* forty years;
seven years he reigned in Hebron, and
thirty-three *years* he reigned in Jeru-
salem. 28So he died in a good old age,
full of days and riches and honor; and
Solomon his son reigned in his place.
29Now the acts of King David, first and
last, indeed they *are* written in the book
of Samuel the seer, in the book of Na-
than the prophet, and in the book of
Gad the seer, 30with all his reign and his
might, and the events that happened to
him, to Israel, and to all the kingdoms
of the lands.

29:19 [a] Literally *palace*

THE SECOND BOOK OF THE

CHRONICLES

Like 1 Chronicles, the Book of 2 Chronicles focuses on the good events of Israel's past and tells much of the same story as 1 and 2 Kings. The book begins with Solomon's reign as king. Then it traces the good kings of Judah, showing how they tried to help the Judahites turn from their sins. The evil reigns of the northern kings of Israel are ignored. The temple is central to the book. Second Chronicles begins with Solomon building the temple and it ends with Cyrus ordering the temple to be rebuilt four hundred years later.

- **GENRE:** History
- **AUTHOR:** Ezra
- **TIME:** 971–538 BC (written c. 450–400 BC)
- **PURPOSE:** To remind the Israelites who had returned from captivity of God's goodness to them in the past so they would have hope that God would be faithful to them still.

Solomon Requests Wisdom

1 Now Solomon the son of David was
strengthened in his kingdom, and
the LORD his God *was* with him and
exalted him exceedingly.
2And Solomon spoke to all Israel,
to the captains of thousands and of
hundreds, to the judges, and to every
leader in all Israel, the heads of the
fathers' *houses.* 3Then Solomon, and
all the assembly with him, went to the
high place that *was* at Gibeon; for the
tabernacle of meeting with God was
there, which Moses the servant of the
LORD had made in the wilderness. 4But
David had brought up the ark of God
from Kirjath Jearim to *the place* David
had prepared for it, for he had pitched a
tent for it at Jerusalem. 5Now the bronze
altar that Bezalel the son of Uri, the son
of Hur, had made, he put[a] before the
tabernacle of the LORD; Solomon and
the assembly sought Him *there.* 6And
Solomon went up there to the bronze
altar before the LORD, which *was* at the
tabernacle of meeting, and offered a
thousand burnt offerings on it.
7On that night God appeared to Sol-
omon, and said to him, "Ask! What shall
I give you?"
8And Solomon said to God: "You have
shown great mercy to David my father,
and have made me king in his place.
9Now, O LORD God, let Your promise
to David my father be established, for
You have made me king over a people
like the dust of the earth in multitude.
10Now give me wisdom and knowledge,
that I may go out and come in before
this people; for who can judge this great
people of Yours?"
11Then God said to Solomon: "Because
this was in your heart, and you have not
asked riches or wealth or honor or the
life of your enemies, nor have you asked
long life—but have asked wisdom and
knowledge for yourself, that you may
judge My people over whom I have made
you king— 12wisdom and knowledge *are*
granted to you; and I will give you riches
and wealth and honor, such as none of
the kings have had who *were* before you,
nor shall any after you have the like."

Solomon's Military and Economic Power

13So Solomon came to Jerusalem from
the high place that *was* at Gibeon, from
before the tabernacle of meeting, and
reigned over Israel. 14And Solomon
gathered chariots and horsemen; he had
one thousand four hundred chariots and
twelve thousand horsemen, whom he
stationed in the chariot cities and with
the king in Jerusalem. 15Also the king

1:5 [a] Some authorities read *it was there.*

made silver and gold as common in Jerusalem as stones, and he made cedars as abundant as the sycamores which *are* in the lowland. 16And Solomon had horses imported from Egypt and Keveh; the king's merchants bought them in Keveh at the *current* price. 17They also acquired and imported from Egypt a chariot for six hundred *shekels* of silver, and a horse for one hundred and fifty; thus, through their agents,[a] they exported them to all the kings of the Hittites and the kings of Syria.

Solomon Prepares to Build the Temple

2 Then Solomon determined to build a temple for the name of the LORD, and a royal house for himself. 2Solomon selected seventy thousand men to bear burdens, eighty thousand to quarry *stone* in the mountains, and three thousand six hundred to oversee them.

3Then Solomon sent to Hiram[a] king of Tyre, saying:

As you have dealt with David my
father, and sent him cedars to
build himself a house to dwell
in, *so deal with me.* 4Behold, I
am building a temple for the
name of the LORD my God,
to dedicate *it* to Him, to burn
before Him sweet incense, for
the continual showbread, for the
burnt offerings morning and
evening, on the Sabbaths, on the
New Moons, and on the set feasts
of the LORD our God. This *is an*
ordinance forever to Israel.

5 And the temple which I build *will*
be great, for our God is greater
than all gods. 6But who is able to
build Him a temple, since heaven
and the heaven of heavens
cannot contain Him? Who *am* I
then, that I should build Him a
temple, except to burn sacrifice
before Him?

7 Therefore send me at once a man
skillful to work in gold and silver,
in bronze and iron, in purple
and crimson and blue, who has
skill to engrave with the skillful
men who are with me in Judah
and Jerusalem, whom David my
father provided. 8Also send me
cedar and cypress and algum logs
from Lebanon, for I know that
your servants have skill to cut
timber in Lebanon; and indeed
my servants *will be* with your
servants, 9to prepare timber for
me in abundance, for the temple
which I am about to build *shall be*
great and wonderful.

10 And indeed I will give to your
servants, the woodsmen who cut
timber, twenty thousand kors of
ground wheat, twenty thousand
kors of barley, twenty thousand
baths of wine, and twenty
thousand baths of oil.

11Then Hiram king of Tyre answered in writing, which he sent to Solomon:

Because the LORD loves His
people, He has made you king
over them.

12Hiram[a] also said:

Blessed *be* the LORD God of Israel,
who made heaven and earth, for
He has given King David a wise
son, endowed with prudence and
understanding, who will build a
temple for the LORD and a royal
house for himself!

13 And now I have sent a skillful man,
endowed with understanding,
Huram[a] my master[b] *craftsman*
14(the son of a woman of the
daughters of Dan, and his father
was a man of Tyre), skilled to work
in gold and silver, bronze and
iron, stone and wood, purple and
blue, fine linen and crimson, and
to make any engraving and to
accomplish any plan which may
be given to him, with your skillful

1:17 [a] Literally *by their hands* 2:3 [a] Hebrew *Huram* (compare 1 Kings 5:1) 2:12 [a] Hebrew *Huram* (compare 1 Kings 5:1) 2:13 [a] Spelled *Hiram* in 1 Kings 7:13 [b] Literally *father* (compare 1 Kings 7:13, 14)

men and with the skillful men of
my lord David your father.

15 Now therefore, the wheat, the
barley, the oil, and the wine which
my lord has spoken of, let him
send to his servants. 16And we will
cut wood from Lebanon, as much
as you need; we will bring it to
you in rafts by sea to Joppa, and
you will carry it up to Jerusalem.

17Then Solomon numbered all the aliens who *were* in the land of Israel, after the census in which David his father had numbered them; and there were found to be one hundred and fifty-three thousand six hundred. 18And he made seventy thousand of them bearers of burdens, eighty thousand stonecutters in the mountain, and three thousand six hundred overseers to make the people work.

Solomon Builds the Temple

3 Now Solomon began to build the house of the LORD at Jerusalem on Mount Moriah, where *the LORD*[a] had appeared to his father David, at the place that David had prepared on the threshing floor of Ornan[b] the Jebusite. 2And he began to build on the second *day* of the second month in the fourth year of his reign.

3This is the foundation which Solomon laid for building the house of God: The length *was* sixty cubits (by cubits according to the former measure) and the width twenty cubits. 4And the vestibule that *was* in front *of the sanctuary*[a] was twenty cubits long across the width of the house, and the height *was* one hundred and[b] twenty. He overlaid the inside with pure gold. 5The larger room[a] he paneled with cypress which he overlaid with fine gold, and he carved palm trees and chainwork on it. 6And he decorated the house with precious stones for beauty, and the gold *was* gold from Parvaim. 7He also overlaid the house—the beams and doorposts, its walls and doors—with gold; and he carved cherubim on the walls.

8And he made the Most Holy Place. Its length was according to the width of the house, twenty cubits, and its width twenty cubits. He overlaid it with six hundred talents of fine gold. 9The weight of the nails *was* fifty shekels of gold; and he overlaid the upper area with gold. 10In the Most Holy Place he made two cherubim, fashioned by carving, and overlaid them with gold. 11The wings of the cherubim *were* twenty cubits in *overall* length: one wing *of the one cherub was* five cubits, touching the wall of the room, and the other wing *was* five cubits, touching the wing of the other cherub; 12*one* wing of the other cherub *was* five cubits, touching the wall of the room, and the other wing *also was* five cubits, touching the wing of the other cherub. 13The wings of these cherubim spanned twenty cubits overall. They stood on their feet, and they faced inward. 14And he made the veil of blue, purple, crimson, and fine linen, and wove cherubim into it.

15Also he made in front of the temple[a] two pillars thirty-five[b] cubits high, and the capital that *was* on the top of each of *them* was five cubits. 16He made wreaths of chainwork, as in the inner sanctuary, and put *them* on top of the pillars; and he made one hundred pomegranates, and put *them* on the wreaths of chainwork. 17Then he set up the pillars before the temple, one on the right hand and the other on the left; he called the name of the one on the right hand Jachin, and the name of the one on the left Boaz.

Furnishings of the Temple

4 Moreover he made a bronze altar: twenty cubits was its length, twenty cubits its width, and ten cubits its height.

2Then he made the Sea of cast *bronze*, ten cubits from one brim to the other;

3:1 [a] Literally *He,* following Masoretic Text and Vulgate; Septuagint reads *the LORD;* Targum reads *the Angel of the LORD.* [b] Spelled *Araunah* in 2 Samuel 24:16ff **3:4** [a] The main room of the temple; elsewhere called the holy place (compare 1 Kings 6:3) [b] Following Masoretic Text, Septuagint, and Vulgate; Arabic, some manuscripts of the Septuagint, and Syriac omit *one hundred and.* **3:5** [a] Literally *house* **3:15** [a] Literally *house* [b] Or *eighteen* (compare 1 Kings 7:15; 2 Kings 25:17; and Jeremiah 52:21)

it was completely round. Its height *was*
five cubits, and a line of thirty cubits
measured its circumference. 3And un-
der it *was* the likeness of oxen encircling
it all around, ten to a cubit, all the way
around the Sea. The oxen *were* cast in
two rows, when it was cast. 4It stood on
twelve oxen: three looking toward the
north, three looking toward the west,
three looking toward the south, and
three looking toward the east; the Sea
was set upon them, and all their back
parts *pointed* inward. 5It *was* a hand-
breadth thick; and its brim was shaped
like the brim of a cup, *like* a lily blossom.
It contained three thousand[a] baths.

6He also made ten lavers, and put five
on the right side and five on the left, to
wash in them; such things as they of-
fered for the burnt offering they would
wash in them, but the Sea *was* for the
priests to wash in. 7And he made ten
lampstands of gold according to their
design, and set *them* in the temple, five
on the right side and five on the left.
8He also made ten tables, and placed
them in the temple, five on the right side
and five on the left. And he made one
hundred bowls of gold.

9Furthermore he made the court of the
priests, and the great court and doors
for the court; and he overlaid these
doors with bronze. 10He set the Sea on
the right side, toward the southeast.

11Then Huram made the pots and the
shovels and the bowls. So Huram fin-
ished doing the work that he was to do
for King Solomon for the house of God:
12the two pillars and the bowl-shaped
capitals *that were* on top of the two pil-
lars; the two networks covering the two
bowl-shaped capitals which *were* on top
of the pillars; 13four hundred pomegran-
ates for the two networks (two rows of
pomegranates for each network, to cover
the two bowl-shaped capitals that *were*
on the pillars); 14he also made carts and
the lavers on the carts; 15one Sea and
twelve oxen under it; 16also the pots, the
shovels, the forks—and all their articles
Huram his master[a] *craftsman* made of
burnished bronze for King Solomon for
the house of the LORD.

17In the plain of Jordan the king had
them cast in clay molds, between Suc-
coth and Zeredah.[a] 18And Solomon
had all these articles made in such
great abundance that the weight of
the bronze was not determined.

19Thus Solomon had all the furnish-
ings made for the house of God: the
altar of gold and the tables on which
was the showbread; 20the lampstands
with their lamps of pure gold, to burn
in the prescribed manner in front of
the inner sanctuary, 21with the flowers
and the lamps and the wick-trimmers
of gold, of purest gold; 22the trimmers,
the bowls, the ladles, and the censers of
pure gold. As for the entry of the sanc-
tuary, its inner doors to the Most Holy
Place, and the doors of the main hall of
the temple, *were* gold.

5 So all the work that Solomon had
done for the house of the LORD was
finished; and Solomon brought in the
things which his father David had ded-
icated: the silver and the gold and all
the furnishings. And he put *them* in the
treasuries of the house of God.

The Ark Brought into the Temple

2Now Solomon assembled the elders
of Israel and all the heads of the tribes,
the chief fathers of the children of Isra-
el, in Jerusalem, that they might bring
the ark of the covenant of the LORD up
from the City of David, which *is* Zion.
3Therefore all the men of Israel assem-
bled with the king at the feast, which *was*
in the seventh month. 4So all the elders of
Israel came, and the Levites took up the
ark. 5Then they brought up the ark, the
tabernacle of meeting, and all the holy
furnishings that *were* in the tabernacle.
The priests and the Levites brought them
up. 6Also King Solomon, and all the con-
gregation of Israel who were assembled
with him before the ark, were sacrificing
sheep and oxen that could not be counted
or numbered for multitude. 7Then the
priests brought in the ark of the cov-
enant of the LORD to its place, into the
inner sanctuary of the temple,[a] to
the Most Holy *Place*, under the wings of
the cherubim. 8For the cherubim spread

4:5 [a] Or *two thousand* (compare 1 Kings 7:26) 4:16 [a] Literally *father* 4:17 [a] Spelled *Zaretan* in
1 Kings 7:46 5:7 [a] Literally *house*

their wings over the place of the ark, and the cherubim overshadowed the ark and its poles. 9The poles extended so that the ends of the poles of the ark could be seen from *the holy place,* in front of the inner sanctuary; but they could not be seen from outside. And they are there to this day. 10Nothing was in the ark except the two tablets which Moses put *there* at Horeb, when the LORD made *a covenant* with the children of Israel, when they had come out of Egypt.

11And it came to pass when the priests came out of the *Most* Holy *Place* (for all the priests who *were* present had sanctified themselves, without keeping to their divisions), 12and the Levites *who were* the singers, all those of Asaph and Heman and Jeduthun, with their sons and their brethren, stood at the east end of the altar, clothed in white linen, having cymbals, stringed instruments and harps, and with them one hundred and twenty priests sounding with trumpets— 13indeed it came to pass, when the trumpeters and singers *were* as one, to make one sound to be heard in praising and thanking the LORD, and when they lifted up their voice with the trumpets and cymbals and instruments of music, and praised the LORD, *saying:*

> "*For He is* good,
> For His mercy *endures* forever,"[a]

that the house, the house of the LORD, was filled with a cloud, 14so that the priests could not continue ministering because of the cloud; for the glory of the LORD filled the house of God.

6 Then Solomon spoke:

> "The LORD said He would dwell in
> the dark cloud.
> 2 I have surely built You an exalted
> house,
> And a place for You to dwell in
> forever."

Solomon's Speech upon Completion of the Work

3Then the king turned around and blessed the whole assembly of Israel, while all the assembly of Israel was standing. 4And he said: "Blessed *be* the LORD God of Israel, who has fulfilled with His hands *what* He spoke with His mouth to my father David, saying, 5'Since the day that I brought My people out of the land of Egypt, I have chosen no city from any tribe of Israel *in which* to build a house, that My name might be there, nor did I choose any man to be a ruler over My people Israel. 6Yet I have chosen Jerusalem, that My name may be there, and I have chosen David to be over My people Israel.' 7Now it was in the heart of my father David to build a temple[a] for the name of the LORD God of Israel. 8But the LORD said to my father David, 'Whereas it was in your heart to build a temple for My name, you did well in that it was in your heart. 9Nevertheless you shall not build the temple, but your son who will come from your body, he shall build the temple for My name.' 10So the LORD has fulfilled His word which He spoke, and I have filled the position of my father David, and sit on the throne of Israel, as the LORD promised; and I have built the temple for the name of the LORD God of Israel. 11And there I have put the ark, in which *is* the covenant of the LORD which He made with the children of Israel."

Solomon's Prayer of Dedication

12Then *Solomon*[a] stood before the altar of the LORD in the presence of all the assembly of Israel, and spread out his hands 13(for Solomon had made a bronze platform five cubits long, five cubits wide, and three cubits high, and had set it in the midst of the court; and he stood on it, knelt down on his knees before all the assembly of Israel, and spread out his hands toward heaven); 14and he said: "LORD God of Israel, *there is* no God in heaven or on earth like You, who keep *Your* covenant and mercy with Your servants who walk before You with all their hearts. 15You have kept what You promised Your servant David my father; You have both spoken with Your mouth and fulfilled *it* with Your hand, as *it is* this day. 16Therefore, LORD God

5:13 [a] Compare Psalm 106:1 6:7 [a] Literally *house,* and so in verses 8–10 6:12 [a] Literally *he* (compare 1 Kings 8:22)

of Israel, now keep what You promised
Your servant David my father, saying,
'You shall not fail to have a man sit
before Me on the throne of Israel, only
if your sons take heed to their way, that
they walk in My law as you have walked
before Me.' 17And now, O LORD God of
Israel, let Your word come true, which
You have spoken to Your servant David.
18"But will God indeed dwell with men
on the earth? Behold, heaven and the
heaven of heavens cannot contain You.
How much less this temple[a] which I
have built! 19Yet regard the prayer of
Your servant and his supplication,
O LORD my God, and listen to the cry
and the prayer which Your servant is
praying before You: 20that Your eyes
may be open toward this temple day
and night, toward the place where *You*
said *You would* put Your name, that
You may hear the prayer which Your
servant makes toward this place. 21And
may You hear the supplications of Your
servant and of Your people Israel, when
they pray toward this place. Hear from
heaven Your dwelling place, and when
You hear, forgive.
22"If anyone sins against his neighbor,
and is forced to take an oath, and comes
and takes an oath before Your altar in
this temple, 23then hear from heav-
en, and act, and judge Your servants,
bringing retribution on the wicked by
bringing his way on his own head, and
justifying the righteous by giving him
according to his righteousness.
24"Or if Your people Israel are defeated
before an enemy because they have
sinned against You, and return and
confess Your name, and pray and make
supplication before You in this temple,
25then hear from heaven and forgive
the sin of Your people Israel, and bring
them back to the land which You gave
to them and their fathers.
26"When the heavens are shut up
and there is no rain because they have
sinned against You, when they pray to-
ward this place and confess Your name,
and turn from their sin because You
afflict them, 27then hear *in* heaven,
and forgive the sin of Your servants,
Your people Israel, that You may teach
them the good way in which they should
walk; and send rain on Your land which
You have given to Your people as an
inheritance.
28"When there is famine in the land,
pestilence or blight or mildew, locusts
or grasshoppers; when their enemies
besiege them in the land of their cities;
whatever plague or whatever sickness
there is; 29whatever prayer, whatever
supplication is *made* by anyone, or by
all Your people Israel, when each one
knows his own burden and his own
grief, and spreads out his hands to this
temple: 30then hear from heaven Your
dwelling place, and forgive, and give
to everyone according to all his ways,
whose heart You know (for You alone
know the hearts of the sons of men),
31that they may fear You, to walk in
Your ways as long as they live in the
land which You gave to our fathers.
32"Moreover, concerning a foreigner,
who is not of Your people Israel, but has
come from a far country for the sake of
Your great name and Your mighty hand
and Your outstretched arm, when they
come and pray in this temple; 33then
hear from heaven Your dwelling place,
and do according to all for which the
foreigner calls to You, that all peoples of
the earth may know Your name and fear
You, as *do* Your people Israel, and that
they may know that this temple which I
have built is called by Your name.
34"When Your people go out to battle
against their enemies, wherever You
send them, and when they pray to You
toward this city which You have chosen
and the temple which I have built for
Your name, 35then hear from heaven
their prayer and their supplication, and
maintain their cause.
36"When they sin against You (for *there
is* no one who does not sin), and You
become angry with them and deliver
them to the enemy, and they take them
captive to a land far or near; 37*yet* when
they come to themselves in the land
where they were carried captive, and
repent, and make supplication to You
in the land of their captivity, saying,

6:18 [a] Literally *house*

GOD SIN JESUS SALVATION LOVE

'We have sinned, we have done wrong,
and have committed wickedness'; 38and
when they return to You with all their
heart and with all their soul in the land
of their captivity, where they have been
carried captive, and pray toward their
land which You gave to their fathers,
the city which You have chosen, and
toward the temple which I have built for
Your name: 39then hear from heaven
Your dwelling place their prayer and
their supplications, and maintain their
cause, and forgive Your people who
have sinned against You. 40Now, my
God, I pray, let Your eyes be open and
let Your ears *be* attentive to the prayer
made in this place.

41 "Now therefore,
Arise, O LORD God, to Your resting place,
You and the ark of Your strength.
Let Your priests, O LORD God, be clothed with salvation,
And let Your saints rejoice in goodness.

42 "O LORD God, do not turn away the face of Your Anointed;
Remember the mercies of Your servant David."[a]

Solomon Dedicates the Temple

7 When Solomon had finished pray-
ing, fire came down from heaven
and consumed the burnt offering and
the sacrifices; and the glory of the LORD
filled the temple.[a] 2And the priests could
not enter the house of the LORD, because
the glory of the LORD had filled the
LORD's house. 3When all the children
of Israel saw how the fire came down,
and the glory of the LORD on the temple,
they bowed their faces to the ground
on the pavement, and worshiped and
praised the LORD, *saying:*

"For *He is* good,
For His mercy *endures* forever."[a]

4Then the king and all the people
offered sacrifices before the LORD.
5King Solomon offered a sacrifice of
twenty-two thousand bulls and one
hundred and twenty thousand sheep.
So the king and all the people dedicat-
ed the house of God. 6And the priests
attended to their services; the Levites
also with instruments of the music of
the LORD, which King David had made
to praise the LORD, saying, "For His
mercy *endures* forever,"[a] whenever Da-
vid offered praise by their ministry.
The priests sounded trumpets opposite
them, while all Israel stood.

7Furthermore Solomon consecrated
the middle of the court that *was* in front
of the house of the LORD; for there he
offered burnt offerings and the fat of
the peace offerings, because the bronze
altar which Solomon had made was not
able to receive the burnt offerings, the
grain offerings, and the fat.
8At that time Solomon kept the feast
seven days, and all Israel with him, a
very great assembly from the entrance
of Hamath to the Brook of Egypt.[a] 9And
on the eighth day they held a sacred
assembly, for they observed the dedi-
cation of the altar seven days, and the
feast seven days. 10On the twenty-third
day of the seventh month he sent the
people away to their tents, joyful and
glad of heart for the good that the LORD
had done for David, for Solomon, and
for His people Israel. 11Thus Solomon
finished the house of the LORD and the
king's house; and Solomon successfully
accomplished all that came into his
heart to make in the house of the LORD
and in his own house.

God's Second Appearance to Solomon

12Then the LORD appeared to Solomon
by night, and said to him: "I have heard
your prayer, and have chosen this place
for Myself as a house of sacrifice. 13When
I shut up heaven and there is no rain, or
command the locusts to devour the land,
or send pestilence among My people,
14if My people who are called by My
name will humble themselves, and pray
and seek My face, and turn from their
wicked ways, then I will hear from heav-
en, and will forgive their sin and heal
their land. 15Now My eyes will be open

6:42 [a] Compare Psalm 132:8–10 7:1 [a] Literally *house* 7:3 [a] Compare Psalm 106:1 7:6 [a] Compare Psalm 106:1 7:8 [a] That is, the Shihor (compare 1 Chronicles 13:5)

and My ears attentive to prayer *made*
in this place. 16For now I have chosen
and sanctified this house, that My name
may be there forever; and My eyes and
My heart will be there perpetually. 17As
for you, if you walk before Me as your
father David walked, and do according
to all that I have commanded you, and if
you keep My statutes and My judgments,
18then I will establish the throne of your
kingdom, as I covenanted with David
your father, saying, 'You shall not fail
to have a man as ruler in Israel.'

19"But if you turn away and forsake My
statutes and My commandments which
I have set before you, and go and serve
other gods, and worship them, 20then I
will uproot them from My land which I
have given them; and this house which
I have sanctified for My name I will cast
out of My sight, and will make it a prov-
erb and a byword among all peoples.

21"And *as for* this house, which is ex-
alted, everyone who passes by it will
be astonished and say, 'Why has the
LORD done thus to this land and this
house?' 22Then they will answer, 'Be-
cause they forsook the LORD God of
their fathers, who brought them out of
the land of Egypt, and embraced other
gods, and worshiped them and served
them; therefore He has brought all this
calamity on them.' "

Solomon's Additional Achievements

8 It came to pass at the end of twenty
years, when Solomon had built the
house of the LORD and his own house,
2that the cities which Hiram[a] had given
to Solomon, Solomon built them; and
he settled the children of Israel there.
3And Solomon went to Hamath Zobah
and seized it. 4He also built Tadmor
in the wilderness, and all the storage
cities which he built in Hamath. 5He
built Upper Beth Horon and Lower Beth
Horon, fortified cities *with* walls, gates,
and bars, 6also Baalath and all the stor-
age cities that Solomon had, and all
the chariot cities and the cities of the
cavalry, and all that Solomon desired
to build in Jerusalem, in Lebanon, and
in all the land of his dominion.

7All the people *who were* left of the Hit-
tites, Amorites, Perizzites, Hivites, and
Jebusites, who *were* not of Israel— 8that
is, their descendants who were left in the
land after them, whom the children of
Israel did not destroy—from these Sol-
omon raised forced labor, as it is to this
day. 9But Solomon did not make the
children of Israel servants for his work.
Some *were* men of war, captains of his
officers, captains of his chariots, and his
cavalry. 10And others *were* chiefs of the
officials of King Solomon: two hundred
and fifty, who ruled over the people.

11Now Solomon brought the daughter
of Pharaoh up from the City of David
to the house he had built for her, for
he said, "My wife shall not dwell in the
house of David king of Israel, because
the places to which the ark of the LORD
has come are holy."

12Then Solomon offered burnt offer-
ings to the LORD on the altar of the
LORD which he had built before the
vestibule, 13according to the daily rate,
offering according to the command-
ment of Moses, for the Sabbaths, the
New Moons, and the three appointed
yearly feasts—the Feast of Unleavened
Bread, the Feast of Weeks, and the Feast
of Tabernacles. 14And, according to the
order of David his father, he appoint-
ed the divisions of the priests for their
service, the Levites for their duties (to
praise and serve before the priests) as
the duty of each day required, and the
gatekeepers by their divisions at each
gate; for so David the man of God had
commanded. 15They did not depart
from the command of the king to the
priests and Levites concerning any
matter or concerning the treasuries.

16Now all the work of Solomon was
well-ordered from[a] the day of the foun-
dation of the house of the LORD until it
was finished. So the house of the LORD
was completed.

17Then Solomon went to Ezion Geber
and Elath[a] on the seacoast, in the land
of Edom. 18And Hiram sent him ships
by the hand of his servants, and ser-
vants who knew the sea. They went with
the servants of Solomon to Ophir, and

8:2 [a] Hebrew *Huram* (compare 2 Chronicles 2:3) **8:16** [a] Following Septuagint, Syriac, and Vulgate; Masoretic Text reads *as far as*. **8:17** [a] Hebrew *Eloth* (compare 2 Kings 14:22)

acquired four hundred and fifty talents
of gold from there, and brought it to
King Solomon.

The Queen of Sheba's Praise of Solomon

9 Now when the queen of Sheba heard
of the fame of Solomon, she came
to Jerusalem to test Solomon with hard
questions, *having* a very great retinue,
camels that bore spices, gold in abun-
dance, and precious stones; and when
she came to Solomon, she spoke with
him about all that was in her heart. 2So
Solomon answered all her questions;
there was nothing so difficult for Sol-
omon that he could not explain it to her.
3And when the queen of Sheba had seen
the wisdom of Solomon, the house that
he had built, 4the food on his table, the
seating of his servants, the service of his
waiters and their apparel, his cupbearers
and their apparel, and his entryway by
which he went up to the house of the
LORD, there was no more spirit in her.
5Then she said to the king: "*It was* a
true report which I heard in my own
land about your words and your wis-
dom. 6However I did not believe their
words until I came and saw with my
own eyes; and indeed the half of the
greatness of your wisdom was not told
me. You exceed the fame of which I
heard. 7Happy *are* your men and hap-
py *are* these your servants, who stand
continually before you and hear your
wisdom! 8Blessed be the LORD your God,
who delighted in you, setting you on
His throne *to be* king for the LORD your
God! Because your God has loved Israel,
to establish them forever, therefore He
made you king over them, to do justice
and righteousness."
9And she gave the king one hundred
and twenty talents of gold, spices in
great abundance, and precious stones;
there never were any spices such as
those the queen of Sheba gave to King
Solomon.
10Also, the servants of Hiram and the
servants of Solomon, who brought gold
from Ophir, brought algum[a] wood and
precious stones. 11And the king made
walkways *of* the algum[a] wood for the
house of the LORD and for the king's
house, also harps and stringed instru-
ments for singers; and there were none
such *as these* seen before in the land
of Judah.
12Now King Solomon gave to the queen
of Sheba all she desired, whatever she
asked, *much more* than she had brought
to the king. So she turned and went to
her own country, she and her servants.

Solomon's Great Wealth

13The weight of gold that came to
Solomon yearly was six hundred and
sixty-six talents of gold, 14besides *what*
the traveling merchants and traders
brought. And all the kings of Arabia and
governors of the country brought gold
and silver to Solomon. 15And King Sol-
omon made two hundred large shields
of hammered gold; six hundred *shek-
els* of hammered gold went into each
shield. 16*He* also *made* three hundred
shields of hammered gold; three hun-
dred *shekels*[a] of gold went into each
shield. The king put them in the House
of the Forest of Lebanon.
17Moreover the king made a great
throne of ivory, and overlaid it with
pure gold. 18The throne *had* six steps,
with a footstool of gold, *which were* fas-
tened to the throne; there were armrests
on either side of the place of the seat,
and two lions stood beside the armrests.
19Twelve lions stood there, one on each
side of the six steps; nothing like *this*
had been made for any *other* kingdom.
20All King Solomon's drinking ves-
sels *were* gold, and all the vessels of the
House of the Forest of Lebanon *were*
pure gold. Not *one was* silver, for this
was accounted as nothing in the days
of Solomon. 21For the king's ships went
to Tarshish with the servants of Hiram.[a]
Once every three years the merchant
ships[b] came, bringing gold, silver, ivory,
apes, and monkeys.[c]
22So King Solomon surpassed all the
kings of the earth in riches and wis-
dom. 23And all the kings of the earth
sought the presence of Solomon to hear

9:10 [a] Or *almug* (compare 1 Kings 10:11, 12) **9:11** [a] Or *almug* (compare 1 Kings 10:11, 12) **9:16** [a] Or *three minas* (compare 1 Kings 10:17) **9:21** [a] Hebrew *Huram* (compare 1 Kings 10:22) [b] Literally *ships of Tarshish* (deep-sea vessels) [c] Or *peacocks*

his wisdom, which God had put in his heart. 24 Each man brought his present: articles of silver and gold, garments, armor, spices, horses, and mules, at a set rate year by year.

25 Solomon had four thousand stalls for horses and chariots, and twelve thousand horsemen whom he stationed in the chariot cities and with the king at Jerusalem.

26 So he reigned over all the kings from the River[a] to the land of the Philistines, as far as the border of Egypt. 27 The king made silver *as common* in Jerusalem as stones, and he made cedar trees as abundant as the sycamores which *are* in the lowland. 28 And they brought horses to Solomon from Egypt and from all lands.

Death of Solomon

29 Now the rest of the acts of Solomon, first and last, *are* they not written in the book of Nathan the prophet, in the prophecy of Ahijah the Shilonite, and in the visions of Iddo the seer concerning Jeroboam the son of Nebat? 30 Solomon reigned in Jerusalem over all Israel forty years. 31 Then Solomon rested with his fathers, and was buried in the City of David his father. And Rehoboam his son reigned in his place.

The Revolt Against Rehoboam

10 And Rehoboam went to Shechem, for all Israel had gone to Shechem to make him king. 2 So it happened, when Jeroboam the son of Nebat heard *it* (he was in Egypt, where he had fled from the presence of King Solomon), that Jeroboam returned from Egypt. 3 Then they sent for him and called him. And Jeroboam and all Israel came and spoke to Rehoboam, saying, 4 "Your father made our yoke heavy; now therefore, lighten the burdensome service of your father and his heavy yoke which he put on us, and we will serve you."

5 So he said to them, "Come back to me after three days." And the people departed.

6 Then King Rehoboam consulted the elders who stood before his father Solomon while he still lived, saying, "How do you advise *me* to answer these people?"

7 And they spoke to him, saying, "If you are kind to these people, and please them, and speak good words to them, they will be your servants forever."

8 But he rejected the advice which the elders had given him, and consulted the young men who had grown up with him, who stood before him. 9 And he said to them, "What advice do you give? How should we answer this people who have spoken to me, saying, 'Lighten the yoke which your father put on us'?"

10 Then the young men who had grown up with him spoke to him, saying, "Thus you should speak to the people who have spoken to you, saying, 'Your father made our yoke heavy, but you make *it* lighter on us'—thus you shall say to them: 'My little *finger* shall be thicker than my father's waist! 11 And now, whereas my father put a heavy yoke on you, I will add to your yoke; my father chastised you with whips, but I *will chastise you* with scourges!'"[a]

12 So Jeroboam and all the people came to Rehoboam on the third day, as the king had directed, saying, "Come back to me the third day." 13 Then the king answered them roughly. King Rehoboam rejected the advice of the elders, 14 and he spoke to them according to the advice of the young men, saying, "My father[a] made your yoke heavy, but I will add to it; my father chastised you with whips, but I *will chastise you* with scourges!"[b] 15 So the king did not listen to the people; for the turn *of events* was from God, that the LORD might fulfill His word, which He had spoken by the hand of Ahijah the Shilonite to Jeroboam the son of Nebat.

16 Now when all Israel *saw* that the king did not listen to them, the people answered the king, saying:

"What share have we in David?
We have no inheritance in the son
of Jesse.

9:26 [a] That is, the Euphrates 10:11 [a] Literally *scorpions* 10:14 [a] Following many Hebrew manuscripts, Septuagint, Syriac, and Vulgate (compare verse 10 and 1 Kings 12:14); Masoretic Text reads *I.* [b] Literally *scorpions*

Every man to your tents, O Israel!
Now see to your own house,
O David!"

So all Israel departed to their tents. 17But Rehoboam reigned over the children of Israel who dwelt in the cities of Judah.

18Then King Rehoboam sent Hadoram, who *was* in charge of revenue; but the children of Israel stoned him with stones, and he died. Therefore King Rehoboam mounted *his* chariot in haste to flee to Jerusalem. 19So Israel has been in rebellion against the house of David to this day.

11 Now when Rehoboam came to Jerusalem, he assembled from the house of Judah and Benjamin one hundred and eighty thousand chosen *men* who were warriors, to fight against Israel, that he might restore the kingdom to Rehoboam.

2But the word of the LORD came to Shemaiah the man of God, saying, 3"Speak to Rehoboam the son of Solomon, king of Judah, and to all Israel in Judah and Benjamin, saying, 4'Thus says the LORD: "You shall not go up or fight against your brethren! Let every man return to his house, for this thing is from Me." ' " Therefore they obeyed the words of the LORD, and turned back from attacking Jeroboam.

Rehoboam Fortifies the Cities

5So Rehoboam dwelt in Jerusalem, and built cities for defense in Judah. 6And he built Bethlehem, Etam, Tekoa, 7Beth Zur, Sochoh, Adullam, 8Gath, Mareshah, Ziph, 9Adoraim, Lachish, Azekah, 10Zorah, Aijalon, and Hebron, which are in Judah and Benjamin, fortified cities. 11And he fortified the strongholds, and put captains in them, and stores of food, oil, and wine. 12Also in every city *he put* shields and spears, and made them very strong, having Judah and Benjamin on his side.

Priests and Levites Move to Judah

13And from all their territories the priests and the Levites who *were* in all Israel took their stand with him. 14For the Levites left their common-lands and their possessions and came to Judah and Jerusalem, for Jeroboam and his sons had rejected them from serving as priests to the LORD. 15Then he appointed for himself priests for the high places, for the demons, and the calf idols which he had made. 16And after *the* Levites *left,*[a] those from all the tribes of Israel, such as set their heart to seek the LORD God of Israel, came to Jerusalem to sacrifice to the LORD God of their fathers. 17So they strengthened the kingdom of Judah, and made Rehoboam the son of Solomon strong for three years, because they walked in the way of David and Solomon for three years.

The Family of Rehoboam

18Then Rehoboam took for himself as wife Mahalath the daughter of Jerimoth the son of David, *and of* Abihail the daughter of Eliah the son of Jesse. 19And she bore him children: Jeush, Shamariah, and Zaham. 20After her he took Maachah the granddaughter[a] of Absalom; and she bore him Abijah, Attai, Ziza, and Shelomith. 21Now Rehoboam loved Maachah the granddaughter of Absalom more than all his wives and his concubines; for he took eighteen wives and sixty concubines, and begot twenty-eight sons and sixty daughters. 22And Rehoboam appointed Abijah the son of Maachah as chief, *to be* leader among his brothers; for he *intended* to make him king. 23He dealt wisely, and dispersed some of his sons throughout all the territories of Judah and Benjamin, to every fortified city; and he gave them provisions in abundance. He also sought many wives *for them.*

Egypt Attacks Judah

12 Now it came to pass, when Rehoboam had established the kingdom and had strengthened himself, that he forsook the law of the LORD, and all Israel along with him. 2And it happened in the fifth year of King Rehoboam *that* Shishak king of Egypt came

11:16 [a] Literally *after them* **11:20** [a] Literally *daughter,* but in the broader sense of granddaughter (compare 2 Chronicles 13:2)

up against Jerusalem, because they had transgressed against the LORD, 3with twelve hundred chariots, sixty thousand horsemen, and people without number who came with him out of Egypt—the Lubim and the Sukkiim and the Ethiopians. 4And he took the fortified cities of Judah and came to Jerusalem.

5Then Shemaiah the prophet came to Rehoboam and the leaders of Judah, who were gathered together in Jerusalem because of Shishak, and said to them, "Thus says the LORD: 'You have forsaken Me, and therefore I also have left you in the hand of Shishak.'"

6So the leaders of Israel and the king humbled themselves; and they said, "The LORD *is* righteous."

7Now when the LORD saw that they humbled themselves, the word of the LORD came to Shemaiah, saying, "They have humbled themselves; *therefore* I will not destroy them, but I will grant them some deliverance. My wrath shall not be poured out on Jerusalem by the hand of Shishak. 8Nevertheless they will be his servants, that they may distinguish My service from the service of the kingdoms of the nations."

9So Shishak king of Egypt came up against Jerusalem, and took away the treasures of the house of the LORD and the treasures of the king's house; he took everything. He also carried away the gold shields which Solomon had made. 10Then King Rehoboam made bronze shields in their place, and committed *them* to the hands of the captains of the guard, who guarded the doorway of the king's house. 11And whenever the king entered the house of the LORD, the guard would go and bring them out; then they would take them back into the guardroom. 12When he humbled himself, the wrath of the LORD turned from him, so as not to destroy *him* completely; and things also went well in Judah.

The End of Rehoboam's Reign

13Thus King Rehoboam strengthened himself in Jerusalem and reigned. Now Rehoboam *was* forty-one years old when he became king; and he reigned seventeen years in Jerusalem, the city which the LORD had chosen out of all the tribes of Israel, to put His name there. His mother's name *was* Naamah, an Ammonitess. 14And he did evil, because he did not prepare his heart to seek the LORD.

15The acts of Rehoboam, first and last, *are* they not written in the book of Shemaiah the prophet, and of Iddo the seer concerning genealogies? And *there were* wars between Rehoboam and Jeroboam all their days. 16So Rehoboam rested with his fathers, and was buried in the City of David. Then Abijah[a] his son reigned in his place.

Abijah Reigns in Judah

13 In the eighteenth year of King Jeroboam, Abijah became king over Judah. 2He reigned three years in Jerusalem. His mother's name *was* Michaiah[a] the daughter of Uriel of Gibeah.

And there was war between Abijah and Jeroboam. 3Abijah set the battle in order with an army of valiant warriors, four hundred thousand choice men. Jeroboam also drew up in battle formation against him with eight hundred thousand choice men, mighty men of valor.

4Then Abijah stood on Mount Zemaraim, which *is* in the mountains of Ephraim, and said, "Hear me, Jeroboam and all Israel: 5Should you not know that the LORD God of Israel gave the dominion over Israel to David forever, to him and his sons, by a covenant of salt? 6Yet Jeroboam the son of Nebat, the servant of Solomon the son of David, rose up and rebelled against his lord. 7Then worthless rogues gathered to him, and strengthened themselves against Rehoboam the son of Solomon, when Rehoboam was young and inexperienced and could not withstand them. 8And now you think to withstand the kingdom of the LORD, which is in the hand of the sons of David; and you *are* a great multitude, and with you are the gold calves which Jeroboam made for you as gods. 9Have you not cast out the priests of the LORD, the sons of Aaron, and the Levites, and made

12:16 [a] Spelled *Abijam* in 1 Kings 14:31 13:2 [a] Spelled *Maachah* in 11:20, 21 and 1 Kings 15:2

for yourselves priests, like the peoples
of *other* lands, so that whoever comes
to consecrate himself with a young
bull and seven rams may be a priest
of *things that are* not gods? 10But as for
us, the LORD *is* our God, and we have
not forsaken Him; and the priests who
minister to the LORD *are* the sons of
Aaron, and the Levites *attend* to *their*
duties. 11And they burn to the LORD
every morning and every evening burnt
sacrifices and sweet incense; *they* also
set the showbread *in order on* the pure
gold table, and the lampstand of gold
with its lamps to burn every evening;
for we keep the command of the LORD
our God, but you have forsaken Him.
12Now look, God Himself is with us as
our head, and His priests with sounding
trumpets to sound the alarm against
you. O children of Israel, do not fight
against the LORD God of your fathers,
for you shall not prosper!"
13But Jeroboam caused an ambush to
go around behind them; so they were
in front of Judah, and the ambush *was*
behind them. 14And when Judah looked
around, to their surprise the battle line
was at both front and rear; and they
cried out to the LORD, and the priests
sounded the trumpets. 15Then the men
of Judah gave a shout; and as the men
of Judah shouted, it happened that God
struck Jeroboam and all Israel before
Abijah and Judah. 16And the children of
Israel fled before Judah, and God deliv-
ered them into their hand. 17Then Abijah
and his people struck them with a great
slaughter; so five hundred thousand
choice men of Israel fell slain. 18Thus
the children of Israel were subdued at
that time; and the children of Judah
prevailed, because they relied on the
LORD God of their fathers.
19And Abijah pursued Jeroboam and
took cities from him: Bethel with its
villages, Jeshanah with its villages, and
Ephrain[a] with its villages. 20So Jerobo-
am did not recover strength again in
the days of Abijah; and the LORD struck
him, and he died.
21But Abijah grew mighty, married
fourteen wives, and begot twenty-two
sons and sixteen daughters. 22Now the
rest of the acts of Abijah, his ways, and
his sayings *are* written in the annals of
the prophet Iddo.

14 So Abijah rested with his fathers,
and they buried him in the City
of David. Then Asa his son reigned in
his place. In his days the land was quiet
for ten years.

Asa Reigns in Judah

2Asa did *what was* good and right in
the eyes of the LORD his God, 3for he
removed the altars of the foreign *gods*
and the high places, and broke down the
sacred pillars and cut down the wooden
images. 4He commanded Judah to seek
the LORD God of their fathers, and to
observe the law and the commandment.
5He also removed the high places and
the incense altars from all the cities
of Judah, and the kingdom was quiet
under him. 6And he built fortified cities
in Judah, for the land had rest; he had
no war in those years, because the LORD
had given him rest. 7Therefore he said
to Judah, "Let us build these cities and
make walls around *them,* and towers,
gates, and bars, *while* the land *is* yet
before us, because we have sought the
LORD our God; we have sought *Him,* and
He has given us rest on every side." So
they built and prospered. 8And Asa had
an army of three hundred thousand
from Judah who carried shields and
spears, and from Benjamin two hun-
dred and eighty thousand men who
carried shields and drew bows; all these
were mighty men of valor.
9Then Zerah the Ethiopian came out
against them with an army of a million
men and three hundred chariots, and
he came to Mareshah. 10So Asa went out
against him, and they set the troops in
battle array in the Valley of Zephathah
at Mareshah. 11And Asa cried out to
the LORD his God, and said, "LORD, *it is*
nothing for You to help, whether with
many or with those who have no power;
help us, O LORD our God, for we rest on
You, and in Your name we go against
this multitude. O LORD, You *are* our God;
do not let man prevail against You!"

13:19 [a] Or *Ephron*

12So the LORD struck the Ethiopians
before Asa and Judah, and the Ethio-
pians fled. 13And Asa and the people
who *were* with him pursued them to
Gerar. So the Ethiopians were over-
thrown, and they could not recover,
for they were broken before the LORD
and His army. And they carried away
very much spoil. 14Then they defeated
all the cities around Gerar, for the fear
of the LORD came upon them; and they
plundered all the cities, for there was
exceedingly much spoil in them. 15They
also attacked the livestock enclosures,
and carried off sheep and camels in
abundance, and returned to Jerusalem.

The Reforms of Asa

15 Now the Spirit of God came upon
Azariah the son of Oded. 2And he
went out to meet Asa, and said to him:
"Hear me, Asa, and all Judah and Ben-
jamin. The LORD *is* with you while you
are with Him. If you seek Him, He will be
found by you; but if you forsake Him, He
will forsake you. 3For a long time Israel
has been without the true God, without
a teaching priest, and without law; 4but
when in their trouble they turned to the
LORD God of Israel, and sought Him, He
was found by them. 5And in those times
there was no peace to the one who went
out, nor to the one who came in, but
great turmoil *was* on all the inhabitants
of the lands. 6So nation was destroyed by
nation, and city by city, for God troubled
them with every adversity. 7But you,
be strong and do not let your hands be
weak, for your work shall be rewarded!"
8And when Asa heard these words
and the prophecy of Oded[a] the proph-
et, he took courage, and removed the
abominable idols from all the land of
Judah and Benjamin and from the cities
which he had taken in the mountains of
Ephraim; and he restored the altar of
the LORD that *was* before the vestibule
of the LORD. 9Then he gathered all Judah
and Benjamin, and those who dwelt with
them from Ephraim, Manasseh, and
Simeon, for they came over to him in
great numbers from Israel when they
saw that the LORD his God was with him.
10So they gathered together at Jerusa-
lem in the third month, in the fifteenth
year of the reign of Asa. 11And they of-
fered to the LORD at that time seven
hundred bulls and seven thousand
sheep from the spoil they had brought.
12Then they entered into a covenant
to seek the LORD God of their fathers
with all their heart and with all their
soul; 13and whoever would not seek
the LORD God of Israel was to be put to
death, whether small or great, whether
man or woman. 14Then they took an
oath before the LORD with a loud voice,
with shouting and trumpets and rams'
horns. 15And all Judah rejoiced at the
oath, for they had sworn with all their
heart and sought Him with all their
soul; and He was found by them, and
the LORD gave them rest all around.
16Also he removed Maachah, the
mother of Asa the king, from *being*
queen mother, because she had made
an obscene image of Asherah;[a] and
Asa cut down her obscene image, then
crushed and burned *it* by the Brook
Kidron. 17But the high places were not
removed from Israel. Nevertheless the
heart of Asa was loyal all his days.
18He also brought into the house of
God the things that his father had dedi-
cated and that he himself had dedicat-
ed: silver and gold and utensils. 19And
there was no war until the thirty-fifth
year of the reign of Asa.

Asa's Treaty with Syria

16 In the thirty-sixth year of the
reign of Asa, Baasha king of Is-
rael came up against Judah and built
Ramah, that he might let none go out or
come in to Asa king of Judah. 2Then Asa
brought silver and gold from the trea-
suries of the house of the LORD and of
the king's house, and sent to Ben-Hadad
king of Syria, who dwelt in Damascus,
saying, 3"*Let there be* a treaty between
you and me, as there was between my
father and your father. See, I have sent
you silver and gold; come, break your
treaty with Baasha king of Israel, so
that he will withdraw from me."
4So Ben-Hadad heeded King Asa, and

15:8 [a] Following Masoretic Text and Septuagint; Syriac and Vulgate read *Azariah the son of Oded* (compare verse 1). **15:16** [a] A Canaanite deity

sent the captains of his armies against
the cities of Israel. They attacked Ijon,
Dan, Abel Maim, and all the storage
cities of Naphtali. 5Now it happened,
when Baasha heard *it,* that he stopped
building Ramah and ceased his work.
6Then King Asa took all Judah, and they
carried away the stones and timber of
Ramah, which Baasha had used for
building; and with them he built Geba
and Mizpah.

Hanani's Message to Asa

7And at that time Hanani the seer
came to Asa king of Judah, and said
to him: "Because you have relied on the
king of Syria, and have not relied on the
LORD your God, therefore the army of
the king of Syria has escaped from your
hand. 8Were the Ethiopians and the
Lubim not a huge army with very many
chariots and horsemen? Yet, because
you relied on the LORD, He delivered
them into your hand. 9For the eyes of
the LORD run to and fro throughout the
whole earth, to show Himself strong on
behalf of *those* whose heart *is* loyal to
Him. In this you have done foolishly;
therefore from now on you shall have
wars." 10Then Asa was angry with the
seer, and put him in prison, for *he was*
enraged at him because of this. And
Asa oppressed *some* of the people at
that time.

Illness and Death of Asa

11Note that the acts of Asa, first and
last, are indeed written in the book of
the kings of Judah and Israel. 12And
in the thirty-ninth year of his reign,
Asa became diseased in his feet, and
his malady was severe; yet in his dis-
ease he did not seek the LORD, but the
physicians.

13So Asa rested with his fathers; he
died in the forty-first year of his reign.
14They buried him in his own tomb,
which he had made for himself in the
City of David; and they laid him in the
bed which was filled with spices and var-
ious ingredients prepared in a mixture
of ointments. They made a very great
burning for him.

Jehoshaphat Reigns in Judah

17 Then Jehoshaphat his son
reigned in his place, and
strengthened himself against Israel.
2And he placed troops in all the forti-
fied cities of Judah, and set garrisons
in the land of Judah and in the cities of
Ephraim which Asa his father had taken.
3Now the LORD was with Jehoshaphat,
because he walked in the former ways
of his father David; he did not seek the
Baals, 4but sought the God[a] of his fa-
ther, and walked in His commandments
and not according to the acts of Israel.
5Therefore the LORD established the
kingdom in his hand; and all Judah gave
presents to Jehoshaphat, and he had
riches and honor in abundance. 6And
his heart took delight in the ways of the
LORD; moreover he removed the high
places and wooden images from Judah.

7Also in the third year of his reign he
sent his leaders, Ben-Hail, Obadiah,
Zechariah, Nethanel, and Michaiah,
to teach in the cities of Judah. 8And
with them *he sent* Levites: Shemaiah,
Nethaniah, Zebadiah, Asahel, Shemir-
amoth, Jehonathan, Adonijah, Tobi-
jah, and Tobadonijah—the Levites; and
with them Elishama and Jehoram, the
priests. 9So they taught in Judah, and
had the Book of the Law of the LORD
with them; they went throughout all the
cities of Judah and taught the people.

10And the fear of the LORD fell on all
the kingdoms of the lands that *were*
around Judah, so that they did not make
war against Jehoshaphat. 11Also *some*
of the Philistines brought Jehoshaphat
presents and silver as tribute; and the
Arabians brought him flocks, seven
thousand seven hundred rams and sev-
en thousand seven hundred male goats.

12So Jehoshaphat became increasing-
ly powerful, and he built fortresses and
storage cities in Judah. 13He had much
property in the cities of Judah; and the
men of war, mighty men of valor, *were*
in Jerusalem.

14These *are* their numbers, accord-
ing to their fathers' houses. Of Judah,
the captains of thousands: Adnah the
captain, and with him three hundred

17:4 [a] Septuagint reads *LORD God.*

thousand mighty men of valor; 15and
next to him *was* Jehohanan the cap-
tain, and with him two hundred and
eighty thousand; 16and next to him
was Amasiah the son of Zichri, who
willingly offered himself to the LORD,
and with him two hundred thousand
mighty men of valor. 17Of Benjamin:
Eliada a mighty man of valor, and with
him two hundred thousand men armed
with bow and shield; 18and next to him
was Jehozabad, and with him one hun-
dred and eighty thousand prepared for
war. 19These served the king, besides
those the king put in the fortified cities
throughout all Judah.

Micaiah Warns Ahab

18 Jehoshaphat had riches and
honor in abundance; and by
marriage he allied himself with Ahab.
2After some years he went down to *visit*
Ahab in Samaria; and Ahab killed sheep
and oxen in abundance for him and
the people who were with him, and per-
suaded him to go up *with him* to Ramoth
Gilead. 3So Ahab king of Israel said to
Jehoshaphat king of Judah, "Will you
go with me *against* Ramoth Gilead?"
And he answered him, "I *am* as you
are, and my people as your people; *we
will be* with you in the war."
4Also Jehoshaphat said to the king of
Israel, "Please inquire for the word of
the LORD today."
5Then the king of Israel gathered the
prophets together, four hundred men,
and said to them, "Shall we go to war
against Ramoth Gilead, or shall I re-
frain?"
So they said, "Go up, for God will deliver
it into the king's hand."
6But Jehoshaphat said, "*Is there* not
still a prophet of the LORD here, that
we may inquire of Him?"[a]
7So the king of Israel said to Jehosh-
aphat, "*There is* still one man by whom
we may inquire of the LORD; but I hate
him, because he never prophesies good
concerning me, but always evil. He *is*
Micaiah the son of Imla."
And Jehoshaphat said, "Let not the
king say such things!"
8Then the king of Israel called one *of
his* officers and said, "Bring Micaiah the
son of Imla quickly!"
9The king of Israel and Jehoshaphat
king of Judah, clothed in *their* robes,
sat each on his throne; and they sat at
a threshing floor at the entrance of the
gate of Samaria; and all the prophets
prophesied before them. 10Now Zede-
kiah the son of Chenaanah had made
horns of iron for himself; and he said,
"Thus says the LORD: 'With these you
shall gore the Syrians until they are
destroyed.' "
11And all the prophets prophesied so,
saying, "Go up to Ramoth Gilead and
prosper, for the LORD will deliver *it* into
the king's hand."
12Then the messenger who had gone
to call Micaiah spoke to him, saying,
"Now listen, the words of the prophets
with one accord encourage the king.
Therefore please let your word be like
the word of one of them, and speak en-
couragement."
13And Micaiah said, "As the LORD lives,
whatever my God says, that I will speak."
14Then he came to the king; and the
king said to him, "Micaiah, shall we go
to war against Ramoth Gilead, or shall
I refrain?"
And he said, "Go and prosper, and they
shall be delivered into your hand!"
15So the king said to him, "How many
times shall I make you swear that you
tell me nothing but the truth in the
name of the LORD?"
16Then he said, "I saw all Israel scat-
tered on the mountains, as sheep that
have no shepherd. And the LORD said,
'These have no master. Let each return
to his house in peace.' "
17And the king of Israel said to Jehosh-
aphat, "Did I not tell you he would not
prophesy good concerning me, but evil?"
18Then *Micaiah* said, "Therefore hear
the word of the LORD: I saw the LORD
sitting on His throne, and all the host
of heaven standing on His right hand
and His left. 19And the LORD said, 'Who
will persuade Ahab king of Israel to
go up, that he may fall at Ramoth Gil-
ead?' So one spoke in this manner, and

18:6 [a] Or *him*

another spoke in that manner. 20Then
a spirit came forward and stood before
the LORD, and said, 'I will persuade him.'
The LORD said to him, 'In what way?'
21So he said, 'I will go out and be a lying
spirit in the mouth of all his prophets.'
And *the LORD* said, 'You shall persuade
him and also prevail; go out and do so.'
22Therefore look! The LORD has put a
lying spirit in the mouth of these proph-
ets of yours, and the LORD has declared
disaster against you."
23Then Zedekiah the son of Che-
naanah went near and struck Micaiah
on the cheek, and said, "Which way did
the spirit from the LORD go from me to
speak to you?"
24And Micaiah said, "Indeed you shall
see on that day when you go into an
inner chamber to hide!"
25Then the king of Israel said, "Take
Micaiah, and return him to Amon
the governor of the city and to Joash
the king's son; 26and say, 'Thus says the
king: "Put this *fellow* in prison, and feed
him with bread of affliction and water
of affliction, until I return in peace." ' "
27But Micaiah said, "If you ever return in
peace, the LORD has not spoken by me."
And he said, "Take heed, all you people!"

Ahab Dies in Battle

28So the king of Israel and Jehosha-
phat the king of Judah went up to Ra-
moth Gilead. 29And the king of Israel
said to Jehoshaphat, "I will disguise
myself and go into battle; but you put
on your robes." So the king of Israel
disguised himself, and they went into
battle.
30Now the king of Syria had com-
manded the captains of the chariots
who *were* with him, saying, "Fight with
no one small or great, but only with the
king of Israel."
31So it was, when the captains of the
chariots saw Jehoshaphat, that they
said, "It *is* the king of Israel!" There-
fore they surrounded him to attack;
but Jehoshaphat cried out, and the
LORD helped him, and God diverted
them from him. 32For so it was, when
the captains of the chariots saw that
it was not the king of Israel, that they
turned back from pursuing him. 33Now
a certain man drew a bow at random,
and struck the king of Israel between
the joints of his armor. So he said to
the driver of his chariot, "Turn around
and take me out of the battle, for I am
wounded." 34The battle increased that
day, and the king of Israel propped
himself up in *his* chariot facing the Syr-
ians until evening; and about the time
of sunset he died.

19 Then Jehoshaphat the king of
Judah returned safely to his
house in Jerusalem. 2And Jehu the son
of Hanani the seer went out to meet
him, and said to King Jehoshaphat,
"Should you help the wicked and love
those who hate the LORD? Therefore the
wrath of the LORD *is* upon you. 3Never-
theless good things are found in you,
in that you have removed the wooden
images from the land, and have pre-
pared your heart to seek God."

The Reforms of Jehoshaphat

4So Jehoshaphat dwelt at Jerusalem;
and he went out again among the peo-
ple from Beersheba to the mountains
of Ephraim, and brought them back
to the LORD God of their fathers. 5Then
he set judges in the land throughout
all the fortified cities of Judah, city by
city, 6and said to the judges, "Take heed
to what you are doing, for you do not
judge for man but for the LORD, who *is*
with you in the judgment. 7Now there-
fore, let the fear of the LORD be upon
you; take care and do *it*, for *there is* no
iniquity with the LORD our God, no par-
tiality, nor taking of bribes."
8Moreover in Jerusalem, for the judg-
ment of the LORD and for controversies,
Jehoshaphat appointed some of the Le-
vites and priests, and some of the chief
fathers of Israel, when they returned to
Jerusalem.[a] 9And he commanded them,
saying, "Thus you shall act in the fear
of the LORD, faithfully and with a loyal
heart: 10Whatever case comes to you
from your brethren who dwell in their
cities, whether of bloodshed or offenses
against law or commandment, against

19:8 [a] Septuagint and Vulgate read *for the inhabitants of Jerusalem*.

statutes or ordinances, you shall warn
them, lest they trespass against the
LORD and wrath come upon you and
your brethren. Do this, and you will
not be guilty. 11And take notice: Am-
ariah the chief priest *is* over you in all
matters of the LORD; and Zebadiah the
son of Ishmael, the ruler of the house
of Judah, for all the king's matters; also
the Levites *will be* officials before you.
Behave courageously, and the LORD
will be with the good."

Ammon, Moab, and Mount Seir Defeated

20 It happened after this *that* the
people of Moab with the people
of Ammon, and *others* with them be-
sides the Ammonites,[a] came to battle
against Jehoshaphat. 2Then some came
and told Jehoshaphat, saying, "A great
multitude is coming against you from
beyond the sea, from Syria;[a] and they
are in Hazazon Tamar" (which *is* En
Gedi). 3And Jehoshaphat feared, and
set himself to seek the LORD, and pro-
claimed a fast throughout all Judah.
4So Judah gathered together to ask *help*
from the LORD; and from all the cities
of Judah they came to seek the LORD.
5Then Jehoshaphat stood in the as-
sembly of Judah and Jerusalem, in the
house of the LORD, before the new court,
6and said: "O LORD God of our fathers,
are You not God in heaven, and do You
not rule over all the kingdoms of the
nations, and in Your hand *is there not*
power and might, so that no one is able
to withstand You? 7*Are* You not our God,
who drove out the inhabitants of this
land before Your people Israel, and gave
it to the descendants of Abraham Your
friend forever? 8And they dwell in it,
and have built You a sanctuary in it for
Your name, saying, 9'If disaster comes
upon us—sword, judgment, pestilence,
or famine—we will stand before this
temple and in Your presence (for Your
name *is* in this temple), and cry out
to You in our affliction, and You will
hear and save.' 10And now, here are the
people of Ammon, Moab, and Mount
Seir—whom You would not let Israel
invade when they came out of the land
of Egypt, but they turned from them
and did not destroy them— 11here they
are, rewarding us by coming to throw
us out of Your possession which You
have given us to inherit. 12O our God,
will You not judge them? For we have no
power against this great multitude that
is coming against us; nor do we know
what to do, but our eyes *are* upon You."
13Now all Judah, with their little ones,
their wives, and their children, stood
before the LORD.
14Then the Spirit of the LORD came
upon Jahaziel the son of Zechariah,
the son of Benaiah, the son of Jeiel, the
son of Mattaniah, a Levite of the sons
of Asaph, in the midst of the assembly.
15And he said, "Listen, all you of Judah
and you inhabitants of Jerusalem, and
you, King Jehoshaphat! Thus says the
LORD to you: 'Do not be afraid nor dis-
mayed because of this great multitude,
for the battle *is* not yours, but God's. 16To-
morrow go down against them. They
will surely come up by the Ascent of Ziz,
and you will find them at the end of the
brook before the Wilderness of Jeruel.
17You will not *need* to fight in this *battle*.
Position yourselves, stand still and see
the salvation of the LORD, who is with
you, O Judah and Jerusalem!' Do not
fear or be dismayed; tomorrow go out
against them, for the LORD *is* with you."
18And Jehoshaphat bowed his head
with *his* face to the ground, and all Judah
and the inhabitants of Jerusalem bowed
before the LORD, worshiping the LORD.
19Then the Levites of the children of the
Kohathites and of the children of the
Korahites stood up to praise the LORD
God of Israel with voices loud and high.
20So they rose early in the morning
and went out into the Wilderness of
Tekoa; and as they went out, Jehosha-
phat stood and said, "Hear me, O Judah
and you inhabitants of Jerusalem: Be-
lieve in the LORD your God, and you
shall be established; believe His proph-
ets, and you shall prosper." 21And when
he had consulted with the people, he
appointed those who should sing to the

20:1 [a] Following Masoretic Text and Vulgate; Septuagint reads *Meunites* (compare 26:7).
20:2 [a] Following Masoretic Text, Septuagint, and Vulgate; some Hebrew manuscripts and Old Latin read *Edom*.

LORD, and who should praise the beauty
of holiness, as they went out before the
army and were saying:

"Praise the LORD,
For His mercy *endures* forever."[a]

22Now when they began to sing and to
praise, the LORD set ambushes against
the people of Ammon, Moab, and Mount
Seir, who had come against Judah; and
they were defeated. 23For the people of
Ammon and Moab stood up against the
inhabitants of Mount Seir to utterly kill
and destroy *them.* And when they had
made an end of the inhabitants of Seir,
they helped to destroy one another.
24So when Judah came to a place over-
looking the wilderness, they looked
toward the multitude; and there *were*
their dead bodies, fallen on the earth.
No one had escaped.
25When Jehoshaphat and his peo-
ple came to take away their spoil, they
found among them an abundance of
valuables on the dead bodies,[a] and pre-
cious jewelry, which they stripped off
for themselves, more than they could
carry away; and they were three days
gathering the spoil because there was
so much. 26And on the fourth day they
assembled in the Valley of Berachah,
for there they blessed the LORD; there-
fore the name of that place was called
The Valley of Berachah[a] until this day.
27Then they returned, every man of
Judah and Jerusalem, with Jehosha-
phat in front of them, to go back to Jeru-
salem with joy, for the LORD had made
them rejoice over their enemies. 28So
they came to Jerusalem, with stringed
instruments and harps and trumpets,
to the house of the LORD. 29And the
fear of God was on all the kingdoms of
those countries when they heard that
the LORD had fought against the ene-
mies of Israel. 30Then the realm of Je-
hoshaphat was quiet, for his God gave
him rest all around.

The End of Jehoshaphat's Reign

31So Jehoshaphat was king over Judah.
He was thirty-five years old when he
became king, and he reigned twenty-
five years in Jerusalem. His mother's
name *was* Azubah the daughter of Shil-
hi. 32And he walked in the way of his
father Asa, and did not turn aside from
it, doing *what was* right in the sight of
the LORD. 33Nevertheless the high plac-
es were not taken away, for as yet the
people had not directed their hearts to
the God of their fathers.
34Now the rest of the acts of Jehosh-
aphat, first and last, indeed they *are*
written in the book of Jehu the son of
Hanani, which *is* mentioned in the book
of the kings of Israel.
35After this Jehoshaphat king of Judah
allied himself with Ahaziah king of Is-
rael, who acted very wickedly. 36And he
allied himself with him to make ships to
go to Tarshish, and they made the ships
in Ezion Geber. 37But Eliezer the son
of Dodavah of Mareshah prophesied
against Jehoshaphat, saying, "Because
you have allied yourself with Ahaziah,
the LORD has destroyed your works."
Then the ships were wrecked, so that
they were not able to go to Tarshish.

Jehoram Reigns in Judah

21 And Jehoshaphat rested with his
fathers, and was buried with his
fathers in the City of David. Then Jeho-
ram his son reigned in his place. 2He
had brothers, the sons of Jehoshaphat:
Azariah, Jehiel, Zechariah, Azaryahu,
Michael, and Shephatiah; all these *were*
the sons of Jehoshaphat king of Israel.
3Their father gave them great gifts of
silver and gold and precious things,
with fortified cities in Judah; but he
gave the kingdom to Jehoram, because
he *was* the firstborn.
4Now when Jehoram was established
over the kingdom of his father, he
strengthened himself and killed all his
brothers with the sword, and also *others*
of the princes of Israel.
5Jehoram *was* thirty-two years old
when he became king, and he reigned
eight years in Jerusalem. 6And he
walked in the way of the kings of Isra-
el, just as the house of Ahab had done,
for he had the daughter of Ahab as a

20:21 [a] Compare Psalm 106:1 **20:25** [a] A few Hebrew manuscripts, Old Latin, and Vulgate read *garments;* Septuagint reads *armor.* **20:26** [a] Literally *Blessing*

wife; and he did evil in the sight of the LORD. 7Yet the LORD would not destroy the house of David, because of the covenant that He had made with David, and since He had promised to give a lamp to him and to his sons forever.

8In his days Edom revolted against Judah's authority, and made a king over themselves. 9So Jehoram went out with his officers, and all his chariots with him. And he rose by night and attacked the Edomites who had surrounded him and the captains of the chariots. 10Thus Edom has been in revolt against Judah's authority to this day. At that time Libnah revolted against his rule, because he had forsaken the LORD God of his fathers. 11Moreover he made high places in the mountains of Judah, and caused the inhabitants of Jerusalem to commit harlotry, and led Judah astray.

12And a letter came to him from Elijah the prophet, saying,

> Thus says the LORD God of your father David:
> Because you have not walked in the ways of Jehoshaphat your father, or in the ways of Asa king of Judah, 13but have walked in the way of the kings of Israel, and have made Judah and the inhabitants of Jerusalem to play the harlot like the harlotry of the house of Ahab, and also have killed your brothers, those of your father's household, *who were* better than yourself, 14behold, the LORD will strike your people with a serious affliction—your children, your wives, and all your possessions; 15and you *will become* very sick with a disease of your intestines, until your intestines come out by reason of the sickness, day by day.

16Moreover the LORD stirred up against Jehoram the spirit of the Philistines and the Arabians who *were* near the Ethiopians. 17And they came up into Judah and invaded it, and carried away all the possessions that were found in the king's house, and also his sons and his wives, so that there was not a son left to him except Jehoahaz,[a] the youngest of his sons.

18After all this the LORD struck him in his intestines with an incurable disease. 19Then it happened in the course of time, after the end of two years, that his intestines came out because of his sickness; so he died in severe pain. And his people made no burning for him, like the burning for his fathers.

20He was thirty-two years old when he became king. He reigned in Jerusalem eight years and, to no one's sorrow, departed. However they buried him in the City of David, but not in the tombs of the kings.

Ahaziah Reigns in Judah

22 Then the inhabitants of Jerusalem made Ahaziah his youngest son king in his place, for the raiders who came with the Arabians into the camp had killed all the older *sons*. So Ahaziah the son of Jehoram, king of Judah, reigned. 2Ahaziah *was* forty-two[a] years old when he became king, and he reigned one year in Jerusalem. His mother's name *was* Athaliah the granddaughter of Omri. 3He also walked in the ways of the house of Ahab, for his mother advised him to do wickedly. 4Therefore he did evil in the sight of the LORD, like the house of Ahab; for they were his counselors after the death of his father, to his destruction. 5He also followed their advice, and went with Jehoram[a] the son of Ahab king of Israel to war against Hazael king of Syria at Ramoth Gilead; and the Syrians wounded Joram. 6Then he returned to Jezreel to recover from the wounds which he had received at Ramah, when he fought against Hazael king of Syria. And Azariah[a] the son of Jehoram, king of Judah, went down to see Jehoram the son of Ahab in Jezreel, because he was sick.

7His going to Joram was God's occasion for Ahaziah's downfall; for when he arrived, he went out with Jehoram against Jehu the son of Nimshi, whom

21:17 [a] Elsewhere called *Ahaziah* (compare 2 Chronicles 22:1) **22:2** [a] Or *twenty-two* (compare 2 Kings 8:26) **22:5** [a] Also spelled *Joram* (compare verses 5 and 7; 2 Kings 8:28; and elsewhere) **22:6** [a] Some Hebrew manuscripts, Septuagint, Syriac, Vulgate, and 2 Kings 8:29 read *Ahaziah.*

the LORD had anointed to cut off the
house of Ahab. 8And it happened, when
Jehu was executing judgment on the
house of Ahab, and found the princ-
es of Judah and the sons of Ahaziah's
brothers who served Ahaziah, that he
killed them. 9Then he searched for Aha-
ziah; and they caught him (he was hid-
ing in Samaria), and brought him to
Jehu. When they had killed him, they
buried him, "because," they said, "he
is the son of Jehoshaphat, who sought
the LORD with all his heart."
So the house of Ahaziah had no one
to assume power over the kingdom.

Athaliah Reigns in Judah

10Now when Athaliah the mother of
Ahaziah saw that her son was dead,
she arose and destroyed all the roy-
al heirs of the house of Judah. 11But
Jehoshabeath,[a] the daughter of the
king, took Joash the son of Ahaziah, and
stole him away from among the king's
sons who were being murdered, and
put him and his nurse in a bedroom.
So Jehoshabeath, the daughter of King
Jehoram, the wife of Jehoiada the priest
(for she was the sister of Ahaziah), hid
him from Athaliah so that she did not
kill him. 12And he was hidden with them
in the house of God for six years, while
Athaliah reigned over the land.

Joash Crowned King of Judah

23 In the seventh year Jehoiada
strengthened himself, *and made
a* covenant with the captains of hun-
dreds: Azariah the son of Jeroham, Ish-
mael the son of Jehohanan, Azariah the
son of Obed, Maaseiah the son of Ada-
iah, and Elishaphat the son of Zichri.
2And they went throughout Judah and
gathered the Levites from all the cities
of Judah, and the chief fathers of Israel,
and they came to Jerusalem.
3Then all the assembly made a cov-
enant with the king in the house of
God. And he said to them, "Behold, the
king's son shall reign, as the LORD has
said of the sons of David. 4This *is* what
you shall do: One-third of you entering
on the Sabbath, of the priests and the
Levites, *shall be* keeping watch over the
doors; 5one-third *shall be* at the king's
house; and one-third at the Gate of the
Foundation. All the people *shall be* in
the courts of the house of the LORD.
6But let no one come into the house of
the LORD except the priests and those
of the Levites who serve. They may go
in, for they *are* holy; but all the people
shall keep the watch of the LORD. 7And
the Levites shall surround the king on
all sides, every man with his weapons
in his hand; and whoever comes into
the house, let him be put to death. You
are to be with the king when he comes
in and when he goes out."
8So the Levites and all Judah did ac-
cording to all that Jehoiada the priest
commanded. And each man took his
men who were to be on duty on the
Sabbath, with those who were going
off duty on the Sabbath; for Jehoiada the
priest had not dismissed the divisions.
9And Jehoiada the priest gave to the
captains of hundreds the spears and
the large and small shields which *had
belonged* to King David, that *were* in the
temple of God. 10Then he set all the peo-
ple, every man with his weapon in his
hand, from the right side of the temple
to the left side of the temple, along by
the altar and by the temple, all around
the king. 11And they brought out the
king's son, put the crown on him, *gave
him* the Testimony,[a] and made him king.
Then Jehoiada and his sons anointed
him, and said, "*Long* live the king!"

Death of Athaliah

12Now when Athaliah heard the noise
of the people running and praising
the king, she came to the people *in* the
temple of the LORD. 13*When* she looked,
there was the king standing by his pillar
at the entrance; and the leaders and
the trumpeters *were* by the king. All the
people of the land were rejoicing and
blowing trumpets, also the singers with
musical instruments, and those who led
in praise. So Athaliah tore her clothes
and said, "Treason! Treason!"
14And Jehoiada the priest brought out
the captains of hundreds who were set

22:11 [a] Spelled *Jehosheba* in 2 Kings 11:2 **23:11** [a] That is, the Law (compare Exodus 25:16, 21; 31:18)

over the army, and said to them, "Take her outside under guard, and slay with the sword whoever follows her." For the priest had said, "Do not kill her in the house of the LORD."

15 So they seized her; and she went by way of the entrance of the Horse Gate *into* the king's house, and they killed her there.

16 Then Jehoiada made a covenant between himself, the people, and the king, that they should be the LORD's people. 17 And all the people went to the temple[a] of Baal, and tore it down. They broke in pieces its altars and images, and killed Mattan the priest of Baal before the altars. 18 Also Jehoiada appointed the oversight of the house of the LORD to the hand of the priests, the Levites, whom David had assigned in the house of the LORD, to offer the burnt offerings of the LORD, as *it is* written in the Law of Moses, with rejoicing and with singing, *as it was established* by David. 19 And he set the gatekeepers at the gates of the house of the LORD, so that no one *who was* in any way unclean should enter.

20 Then he took the captains of hundreds, the nobles, the governors of the people, and all the people of the land, and brought the king down from the house of the LORD; and they went through the Upper Gate to the king's house, and set the king on the throne of the kingdom. 21 So all the people of the land rejoiced; and the city was quiet, for they had slain Athaliah with the sword.

Joash Repairs the Temple

24 Joash *was* seven years old when he became king, and he reigned forty years in Jerusalem. His mother's name *was* Zibiah of Beersheba. 2 Joash did *what was* right in the sight of the LORD all the days of Jehoiada the priest. 3 And Jehoiada took two wives for him, and he had sons and daughters.

4 Now it happened after this *that* Joash set his heart on repairing the house of the LORD. 5 Then he gathered the priests and the Levites, and said to them, "Go out to the cities of Judah, and gather from all Israel money to repair the house of your God from year to year, and see that you do it quickly."

However the Levites did not do it quickly. 6 So the king called Jehoiada the chief *priest,* and said to him, "Why have you not required the Levites to bring in from Judah and from Jerusalem the collection, *according to the commandment* of Moses the servant of the LORD and of the assembly of Israel, for the tabernacle of witness?" 7 For the sons of Athaliah, that wicked woman, had broken into the house of God, and had also presented all the dedicated things of the house of the LORD to the Baals.

8 Then at the king's command they made a chest, and set it outside at the gate of the house of the LORD. 9 And they made a proclamation throughout Judah and Jerusalem to bring to the LORD the collection *that* Moses the servant of God *had imposed* on Israel in the wilderness. 10 Then all the leaders and all the people rejoiced, brought their contributions, and put *them* into the chest until all had given. 11 So it was, at that time, when the chest was brought to the king's official by the hand of the Levites, and when they saw that *there was* much money, that the king's scribe and the high priest's officer came and emptied the chest, and took it and returned it to its place. Thus they did day by day, and gathered money in abundance.

12 The king and Jehoiada gave it to those who did the work of the service of the house of the LORD; and they hired masons and carpenters to repair the house of the LORD, and also those who worked in iron and bronze to restore the house of the LORD. 13 So the workmen labored, and the work was completed by them; they restored the house of God to its original condition and reinforced it. 14 When they had finished, they brought the rest of the money before the king and Jehoiada; they made from it articles for the house of the LORD, articles for serving and offering, spoons and vessels of gold and silver. And they offered burnt offerings in the house of the LORD continually all the days of Jehoiada.

23:17 [a] Literally *house*

Apostasy of Joash

15But Jehoiada grew old and was full
of days, and he died; *he was* one hun-
dred and thirty years old when he died.
16And they buried him in the City of
David among the kings, because he
had done good in Israel, both toward
God and His house.

17Now after the death of Jehoiada the
leaders of Judah came and bowed down
to the king. And the king listened to
them. 18Therefore they left the house
of the LORD God of their fathers, and
served wooden images and idols; and
wrath came upon Judah and Jerusalem
because of their trespass. 19Yet He sent
prophets to them, to bring them back
to the LORD; and they testified against
them, but they would not listen.

20Then the Spirit of God came upon
Zechariah the son of Jehoiada the
priest, who stood above the people, and
said to them, "Thus says God: 'Why do
you transgress the commandments of
the LORD, so that you cannot prosper?
Because you have forsaken the LORD,
He also has forsaken you.' " 21So they
conspired against him, and at the com-
mand of the king they stoned him with
stones in the court of the house of the
LORD. 22Thus Joash the king did not
remember the kindness which Jehoiada
his father had done to him, but killed
his son; and as he died, he said, "The
LORD look on *it,* and repay!"

Death of Joash

23So it happened in the spring of the
year *that* the army of Syria came up
against him; and they came to Judah
and Jerusalem, and destroyed all the
leaders of the people from among the
people, and sent all their spoil to the king
of Damascus. 24For the army of the Syri-
ans came with a small company of men;
but the LORD delivered a very great army
into their hand, because they had forsak-
en the LORD God of their fathers. So they
executed judgment against Joash. 25And
when they had withdrawn from him (for
they left him severely wounded), his own
servants conspired against him because
of the blood of the sons[a] of Jehoiada the
priest, and killed him on his bed. So he
died. And they buried him in the City of
David, but they did not bury him in the
tombs of the kings.

26These are the ones who conspired
against him: Zabad[a] the son of Shime-
ath the Ammonitess, and Jehozabad the
son of Shimrith[b] the Moabitess. 27Now
concerning his sons, and the many ora-
cles about him, and the repairing of the
house of God, indeed they *are* written in
the annals of the book of the kings. Then
Amaziah his son reigned in his place.

Amaziah Reigns in Judah

25 Amaziah *was* twenty-five years
old *when* he became king, and
he reigned twenty-nine years in Jerusa-
lem. His mother's name *was* Jehoaddan
of Jerusalem. 2And he did *what was*
right in the sight of the LORD, but not
with a loyal heart.

3Now it happened, as soon as the king-
dom was established for him, that he ex-
ecuted his servants who had murdered
his father the king. 4However he did not
execute their children, but *did* as *it is*
written in the Law in the Book of Moses,
where the LORD commanded, saying,
"The fathers shall not be put to death
for their children, nor shall the children
be put to death for their fathers; but a
person shall die for his own sin."[a]

The War Against Edom

5Moreover Amaziah gathered Judah
together and set over them captains of
thousands and captains of hundreds,
according to *their* fathers' houses,
throughout all Judah and Benjamin;
and he numbered them from twenty
years old and above, and found them
to be three hundred thousand choice
men, able to go to war, who could handle
spear and shield. 6He also hired one
hundred thousand mighty men of valor
from Israel for one hundred talents of
silver. 7But a man of God came to him,
saying, "O king, do not let the army of
Israel go with you, for the LORD *is* not
with Israel—*not with* any of the children
of Ephraim. 8But if you go, be gone! Be
strong in battle! *Even so,* God shall make

24:25 [a] Septuagint and Vulgate read *son* (compare verses 20–22). **24:26** [a] Or *Jozachar* (compare 2 Kings 12:21) [b] Or *Shomer* (compare 2 Kings 12:21) **25:4** [a] Deuteronomy 24:16

you fall before the enemy; for God has
power to help and to overthrow."
9Then Amaziah said to the man of
God, "But what *shall we* do about the
hundred talents which I have given to
the troops of Israel?"
And the man of God answered, "The
LORD is able to give you much more than
this." 10So Amaziah discharged the troops
that had come to him from Ephraim, to
go back home. Therefore their anger was
greatly aroused against Judah, and they
returned home in great anger.
11Then Amaziah strengthened himself,
and leading his people, he went to the
Valley of Salt and killed ten thousand of
the people of Seir. 12Also the children of
Judah took captive ten thousand alive,
brought them to the top of the rock, and
cast them down from the top of the rock,
so that they all were dashed in pieces.
13But as for the soldiers of the army
which Amaziah had discharged, so that
they would not go with him to battle,
they raided the cities of Judah from
Samaria to Beth Horon, killed three
thousand in them, and took much spoil.
14Now it was so, after Amaziah came
from the slaughter of the Edomites,
that he brought the gods of the people
of Seir, set them up *to be* his gods, and
bowed down before them and burned
incense to them. 15Therefore the anger
of the LORD was aroused against Am-
aziah, and He sent him a prophet who
said to him, "Why have you sought the
gods of the people, which could not res-
cue their own people from your hand?"
16So it was, as he talked with him, that
the king said to him, "Have we made
you the king's counselor? Cease! Why
should you be killed?"
Then the prophet ceased, and said,
"I know that God has determined to
destroy you, because you have done
this and have not heeded my advice."

Israel Defeats Judah

17Now Amaziah king of Judah asked
advice and sent to Joash[a] the son of Je-
hoahaz, the son of Jehu, king of Israel,
saying, "Come, let us face one another
in battle."
18And Joash king of Israel sent to Amazi-
ah king of Judah, saying, "The thistle that
was in Lebanon sent to the cedar that was
in Lebanon, saying, 'Give your daughter
to my son as wife'; and a wild beast that
was in Lebanon passed by and trampled
the thistle. 19Indeed you say that you have
defeated the Edomites, and your heart is
lifted up to boast. Stay at home now; why
should you meddle with trouble, that you
should fall—you and Judah with you?"
20But Amaziah would not heed, for it
came from God, that He might give them
into the hand *of their enemies,* because
they sought the gods of Edom. 21So Joash
king of Israel went out; and he and Ama-
ziah king of Judah faced one another at
Beth Shemesh, which *belongs* to Judah.
22And Judah was defeated by Israel,
and every man fled to his tent. 23Then
Joash the king of Israel captured Am-
aziah king of Judah, the son of Joash,
the son of Jehoahaz, at Beth Shemesh;
and he brought him to Jerusalem, and
broke down the wall of Jerusalem from
the Gate of Ephraim to the Corner Gate—
four hundred cubits. 24And *he took* all the
gold and silver, all the articles that were
found in the house of God with Obed-
Edom, the treasures of the king's house,
and hostages, and returned to Samaria.

Death of Amaziah

25Amaziah the son of Joash, king of
Judah, lived fifteen years after the death
of Joash the son of Jehoahaz, king of
Israel. 26Now the rest of the acts of Am-
aziah, from first to last, indeed *are* they
not written in the book of the kings of
Judah and Israel? 27After the time that
Amaziah turned away from follow-
ing the LORD, they made a conspiracy
against him in Jerusalem, and he fled
to Lachish; but they sent after him to
Lachish and killed him there. 28Then
they brought him on horses and buried
him with his fathers in the City of Judah.

Uzziah Reigns in Judah

26 Now all the people of Judah took
Uzziah,[a] who *was* sixteen years
old, and made him king instead of his
father Amaziah. 2He built Elath[a] and

25:17 [a] Spelled *Jehoash* in 2 Kings 14:8ff 26:1 [a] Called *Azariah* in 2 Kings 14:21ff 26:2 [a] Hebrew *Eloth*

restored it to Judah, after the king rested
with his fathers.
3Uzziah *was* sixteen years old when he
became king, and he reigned fifty-two
years in Jerusalem. His mother's name
was Jecholiah of Jerusalem. 4And he did
what was right in the sight of the LORD,
according to all that his father Amaziah
had done. 5He sought God in the days
of Zechariah, who had understanding
in the visions[a] of God; and as long as he
sought the LORD, God made him prosper.
6Now he went out and made war
against the Philistines, and broke down
the wall of Gath, the wall of Jabneh,
and the wall of Ashdod; and he built
cities *around* Ashdod and among the
Philistines. 7God helped him against
the Philistines, against the Arabians
who lived in Gur Baal, and against the
Meunites. 8Also the Ammonites brought
tribute to Uzziah. His fame spread as far
as the entrance of Egypt, for he became
exceedingly strong.
9And Uzziah built towers in Jerusa-
lem at the Corner Gate, at the Valley
Gate, and at the corner buttress of the
wall; then he fortified them. 10Also he
built towers in the desert. He dug many
wells, for he had much livestock, both
in the lowlands and in the plains; *he
also had* farmers and vinedressers in
the mountains and in Carmel, for he
loved the soil.
11Moreover Uzziah had an army of
fighting men who went out to war by
companies, according to the number
on their roll as prepared by Jeiel the
scribe and Maaseiah the officer, under
the hand of Hananiah, *one* of the king's
captains. 12The total number of chief offi-
cers[a] of the mighty men of valor *was* two
thousand six hundred. 13And under their
authority *was* an army of three hundred
and seven thousand five hundred, that
made war with mighty power, to help the
king against the enemy. 14Then Uzziah
prepared for them, for the entire army,
shields, spears, helmets, body armor,
bows, and slings *to cast* stones. 15And
he made devices in Jerusalem, invented
by skillful men, to be on the towers and
the corners, to shoot arrows and large
stones. So his fame spread far and wide,
for he was marvelously helped till he
became strong.

The Penalty for Uzziah's Pride

16But when he was strong his heart
was lifted up, to *his* destruction, for he
transgressed against the LORD his God
by entering the temple of the LORD to
burn incense on the altar of incense.
17So Azariah the priest went in after
him, and with him were eighty priests
of the LORD—valiant men. 18And they
withstood King Uzziah, and said to him,
"*It is* not for you, Uzziah, to burn incense
to the LORD, but for the priests, the sons
of Aaron, who are consecrated to burn
incense. Get out of the sanctuary, for
you have trespassed! You *shall have* no
honor from the LORD God."
19Then Uzziah became furious; and
he *had* a censer in his hand to burn
incense. And while he was angry with
the priests, leprosy broke out on his
forehead, before the priests in the house
of the LORD, beside the incense altar.
20And Azariah the chief priest and all
the priests looked at him, and there, on
his forehead, he *was* leprous; so they
thrust him out of that place. Indeed
he also hurried to get out, because the
LORD had struck him.
21King Uzziah was a leper until the
day of his death. He dwelt in an isolated
house, because he was a leper; for he
was cut off from the house of the LORD.
Then Jotham his son *was* over the king's
house, judging the people of the land.
22Now the rest of the acts of Uzziah,
from first to last, the prophet Isaiah the
son of Amoz wrote. 23So Uzziah rested
with his fathers, and they buried him
with his fathers in the field of burial
which *belonged* to the kings, for they
said, "He is a leper." Then Jotham his
son reigned in his place.

Jotham Reigns in Judah

27 Jotham *was* twenty-five years
old when he became king, and
he reigned sixteen years in Jerusalem.
His mother's name *was* Jerushah[a] the
daughter of Zadok. 2And he did *what*

26:5 [a] Several Hebrew manuscripts, Septuagint, Syriac, Targum, and Arabic read *fear.*
26:12 [a] Literally *chief fathers* **27:1** [a] Spelled *Jerusha* in 2 Kings 15:33

was right in the sight of the LORD, according to all that his father Uzziah had done (although he did not enter the temple of the LORD). But still the people acted corruptly.

3 He built the Upper Gate of the house of the LORD, and he built extensively on the wall of Ophel. 4 Moreover he built cities in the mountains of Judah, and in the forests he built fortresses and towers. 5 He also fought with the king of the Ammonites and defeated them. And the people of Ammon gave him in that year one hundred talents of silver, ten thousand kors of wheat, and ten thousand of barley. The people of Ammon paid this to him in the second and third years also. 6 So Jotham became mighty, because he prepared his ways before the LORD his God.

7 Now the rest of the acts of Jotham, and all his wars and his ways, indeed they *are* written in the book of the kings of Israel and Judah. 8 He was twenty-five years old when he became king, and he reigned sixteen years in Jerusalem. 9 So Jotham rested with his fathers, and they buried him in the City of David. Then Ahaz his son reigned in his place.

Ahaz Reigns in Judah

28 Ahaz *was* twenty years old when he became king, and he reigned sixteen years in Jerusalem; and he did not do *what was* right in the sight of the LORD, as his father David *had done.* 2 For he walked in the ways of the kings of Israel, and made molded images for the Baals. 3 He burned incense in the Valley of the Son of Hinnom, and burned his children in the fire, according to the abominations of the nations whom the LORD had cast out before the children of Israel. 4 And he sacrificed and burned incense on the high places, on the hills, and under every green tree.

Syria and Israel Defeat Judah

5 Therefore the LORD his God delivered him into the hand of the king of Syria. They defeated him, and carried away a great multitude of them as captives, and brought *them* to Damascus. Then he was also delivered into the hand of the king of Israel, who defeated him with a great slaughter. 6 For Pekah the son of Remaliah killed one hundred and twenty thousand in Judah in one day, all valiant men, because they had forsaken the LORD God of their fathers. 7 Zichri, a mighty man of Ephraim, killed Maaseiah the king's son, Azrikam the officer over the house, and Elkanah *who was* second to the king. 8 And the children of Israel carried away captive of their brethren two hundred thousand women, sons, and daughters; and they also took away much spoil from them, and brought the spoil to Samaria.

Israel Returns the Captives

9 But a prophet of the LORD was there, whose name *was* Oded; and he went out before the army that came to Samaria, and said to them: "Look, because the LORD God of your fathers was angry with Judah, He has delivered them into your hand; but you have killed them in a rage *that* reaches up to heaven. 10 And now you propose to force the children of Judah and Jerusalem to be your male and female slaves; *but are* you not also guilty before the LORD your God? 11 Now hear me, therefore, and return the captives, whom you have taken captive from your brethren, for the fierce wrath of the LORD *is* upon you."

12 Then some of the heads of the children of Ephraim, Azariah the son of Johanan, Berechiah the son of Meshillemoth, Jehizkiah the son of Shallum, and Amasa the son of Hadlai, stood up against those who came from the war, 13 and said to them, "You shall not bring the captives here, for we *already* have offended the LORD. You intend to add to our sins and to our guilt; for our guilt is great, and *there is* fierce wrath against Israel." 14 So the armed men left the captives and the spoil before the leaders and all the assembly. 15 Then the men who were designated by name rose up and took the captives, and from the spoil they clothed all who were naked among them, dressed them and gave them sandals, gave them food and drink, and anointed them; and they let all the feeble ones ride on donkeys. So they brought them to their brethren at Jericho, the city of palm trees. Then they returned to Samaria.

Assyria Refuses to Help Judah

16At the same time King Ahaz sent to the kings[a] of Assyria to help him. 17For again the Edomites had come, attacked Judah, and carried away captives. 18The Philistines also had invaded the cities of the lowland and of the South of Judah, and had taken Beth Shemesh, Aijalon, Gederoth, Sochoh with its villages, Timnah with its villages, and Gimzo with its villages; and they dwelt there. 19For the LORD brought Judah low because of Ahaz king of Israel, for he had encouraged moral decline in Judah and had been continually unfaithful to the LORD. 20Also Tiglath-Pileser[a] king of Assyria came to him and distressed him, and did not assist him. 21For Ahaz took part *of the treasures* from the house of the LORD, from the house of the king, and from the leaders, and he gave *it* to the king of Assyria; but he did not help him.

Apostasy and Death of Ahaz

22Now in the time of his distress King Ahaz became increasingly unfaithful to the LORD. This *is that* King Ahaz. 23For he sacrificed to the gods of Damascus which had defeated him, saying, "Because the gods of the kings of Syria help them, I will sacrifice to them that they may help me." But they were the ruin of him and of all Israel. 24So Ahaz gathered the articles of the house of God, cut in pieces the articles of the house of God, shut up the doors of the house of the LORD, and made for himself altars in every corner of Jerusalem. 25And in every single city of Judah he made high places to burn incense to other gods, and provoked to anger the LORD God of his fathers.

26Now the rest of his acts and all his ways, from first to last, indeed they *are* written in the book of the kings of Judah and Israel. 27So Ahaz rested with his fathers, and they buried him in the city, in Jerusalem; but they did not bring him into the tombs of the kings of Israel. Then Hezekiah his son reigned in his place.

Hezekiah Reigns in Judah

29 Hezekiah became king *when he was* twenty-five years old, and he reigned twenty-nine years in Jerusalem. His mother's name *was* Abijah[a] the daughter of Zechariah. 2And he did *what was* right in the sight of the LORD, according to all that his father David had done.

Hezekiah Cleanses the Temple

3In the first year of his reign, in the first month, he opened the doors of the house of the LORD and repaired them. 4Then he brought in the priests and the Levites, and gathered them in the East Square, 5and said to them: "Hear me, Levites! Now sanctify yourselves, sanctify the house of the LORD God of your fathers, and carry out the rubbish from the holy *place.* 6For our fathers have trespassed and done evil in the eyes of the LORD our God; they have forsaken Him, have turned their faces away from the dwelling place of the LORD, and turned *their* backs *on Him.* 7They have also shut up the doors of the vestibule, put out the lamps, and have not burned incense or offered burnt offerings in the holy *place* to the God of Israel. 8Therefore the wrath of the LORD fell upon Judah and Jerusalem, and He has given them up to trouble, to desolation, and to jeering, as you see with your eyes. 9For indeed, because of this our fathers have fallen by the sword; and our sons, our daughters, and our wives *are* in captivity.

10"Now *it is* in my heart to make a covenant with the LORD God of Israel, that His fierce wrath may turn away from us. 11My sons, do not be negligent now, for the LORD has chosen you to stand before Him, to serve Him, and that you should minister to Him and burn incense."

12Then these Levites arose: Mahath the son of Amasai and Joel the son of Azariah, of the sons of the Kohathites; of the sons of Merari, Kish the son of Abdi and Azariah the son of Jehallelel; of the Gershonites, Joah the son of Zimmah and Eden the son of Joah;

28:16 [a] Septuagint, Syriac, and Vulgate read *king* (compare verse 20). **28:20** [a] Hebrew *Tilgath-Pilneser* **29:1** [a] Spelled *Abi* in 2 Kings 18:2

13of the sons of Elizaphan, Shimri and
Jeiel; of the sons of Asaph, Zechariah
and Mattaniah; 14of the sons of Heman,
Jehiel and Shimei; and of the sons of
Jeduthun, Shemaiah and Uzziel.
15And they gathered their brethren,
sanctified themselves, and went accord-
ing to the commandment of the king,
at the words of the LORD, to cleanse the
house of the LORD. 16Then the priests
went into the inner part of the house
of the LORD to cleanse *it,* and brought
out all the debris that they found in the
temple of the LORD to the court of the
house of the LORD. And the Levites took
it out and carried *it* to the Brook Kidron.
17Now they began to sanctify on the
first *day* of the first month, and on the
eighth day of the month they came
to the vestibule of the LORD. So they
sanctified the house of the LORD in eight
days, and on the sixteenth day of the
first month they finished.
18Then they went in to King Hezeki-
ah and said, "We have cleansed all the
house of the LORD, the altar of burnt
offerings with all its articles, and the
table of the showbread with all its ar-
ticles. 19Moreover all the articles which
King Ahaz in his reign had cast aside in
his transgression we have prepared and
sanctified; and there they *are,* before
the altar of the LORD."

Hezekiah Restores Temple Worship

20Then King Hezekiah rose early,
gathered the rulers of the city, and
went up to the house of the LORD. 21And
they brought seven bulls, seven rams,
seven lambs, and seven male goats
for a sin offering for the kingdom, for
the sanctuary, and for Judah. Then he
commanded the priests, the sons of
Aaron, to offer *them* on the altar of the
LORD. 22So they killed the bulls, and the
priests received the blood and sprinkled
it on the altar. Likewise they killed the
rams and sprinkled the blood on the
altar. They also killed the lambs and
sprinkled the blood on the altar. 23Then
they brought out the male goats *for* the
sin offering before the king and the
assembly, and they laid their hands on
them. 24And the priests killed them; and
they presented their blood on the altar
as a sin offering to make an atonement
for all Israel, for the king commanded
that the burnt offering and the sin of-
fering *be made* for all Israel.
25And he stationed the Levites in the
house of the LORD with cymbals, with
stringed instruments, and with harps,
according to the commandment of Da-
vid, of Gad the king's seer, and of Nathan
the prophet; for thus *was* the command-
ment of the LORD by His prophets. 26The
Levites stood with the instruments of
David, and the priests with the trumpets.
27Then Hezekiah commanded *them* to
offer the burnt offering on the altar.
And when the burnt offering began, the
song of the LORD *also* began, with the
trumpets and with the instruments of
David king of Israel. 28So all the assem-
bly worshiped, the singers sang, and the
trumpeters sounded; all *this continued*
until the burnt offering was finished.
29And when they had finished offering,
the king and all who were present with
him bowed and worshiped. 30Moreover
King Hezekiah and the leaders com-
manded the Levites to sing praise to
the LORD with the words of David and
of Asaph the seer. So they sang praises
with gladness, and they bowed their
heads and worshiped.
31Then Hezekiah answered and said,
"Now *that* you have consecrated your-
selves to the LORD, come near, and
bring sacrifices and thank offerings
into the house of the LORD." So the as-
sembly brought in sacrifices and thank
offerings, and as many as were of a
willing heart *brought* burnt offerings.
32And the number of the burnt offer-
ings which the assembly brought was
seventy bulls, one hundred rams, *and*
two hundred lambs; all these *were* for a
burnt offering to the LORD. 33The con-
secrated things *were* six hundred bulls
and three thousand sheep. 34But the
priests were too few, so that they could
not skin all the burnt offerings; there-
fore their brethren the Levites helped
them until the work was ended and
until the *other* priests had sanctified
themselves, for the Levites were more
diligent in sanctifying themselves than
the priests. 35Also the burnt offerings
were in abundance, with the fat of the

peace offerings and *with* the drink of-
ferings for *every* burnt offering.
So the service of the house of the LORD
was set in order. 36Then Hezekiah and
all the people rejoiced that God had
prepared the people, since the events
took place so suddenly.

Hezekiah Keeps the Passover

30 And Hezekiah sent to all Isra-
el and Judah, and also wrote
letters to Ephraim and Manasseh, that
they should come to the house of the
LORD at Jerusalem, to keep the Passover
to the LORD God of Israel. 2For the king
and his leaders and all the assembly
in Jerusalem had agreed to keep the
Passover in the second month. 3For they
could not keep it at the regular time,[a]
because a sufficient number of priests
had not consecrated themselves, nor
had the people gathered together at
Jerusalem. 4And the matter pleased
the king and all the assembly. 5So
they resolved to make a proclamation
throughout all Israel, from Beersheba
to Dan, that they should come to keep
the Passover to the LORD God of Israel
at Jerusalem, since they had not done *it*
for a long *time* in the *prescribed* manner.
6Then the runners went throughout all
Israel and Judah with the letters from
the king and his leaders, and spoke
according to the command of the king:
"Children of Israel, return to the LORD
God of Abraham, Isaac, and Israel; then
He will return to the remnant of you
who have escaped from the hand of
the kings of Assyria. 7And do not be
like your fathers and your brethren,
who trespassed against the LORD God
of their fathers, so that He gave them up
to desolation, as you see. 8Now do not
be stiff-necked, as your fathers *were, but*
yield yourselves to the LORD; and enter
His sanctuary, which He has sanctified
forever, and serve the LORD your God,
that the fierceness of His wrath may
turn away from you. 9For if you return
to the LORD, your brethren and your
children *will be treated* with compassion
by those who lead them captive, so that
they may come back to this land; for the
LORD your God *is* gracious and merciful,
and will not turn *His* face from you if
you return to Him."
10So the runners passed from city to
city through the country of Ephraim
and Manasseh, as far as Zebulun; but
they laughed at them and mocked
them. 11Nevertheless some from Asher,
Manasseh, and Zebulun humbled them-
selves and came to Jerusalem. 12Also
the hand of God was on Judah to give
them singleness of heart to obey the
command of the king and the leaders,
at the word of the LORD.
13Now many people, a very great
assembly, gathered at Jerusalem to
keep the Feast of Unleavened Bread in
the second month. 14They arose and
took away the altars that *were* in Je-
rusalem, and they took away all the
incense altars and cast *them* into the
Brook Kidron. 15Then they slaughtered
the Passover *lambs* on the fourteenth
day of the second month. The priests
and the Levites were ashamed, and
sanctified themselves, and brought the
burnt offerings to the house of the LORD.
16They stood in their place according
to their custom, according to the Law
of Moses the man of God; the priests
sprinkled the blood *received* from the
hand of the Levites. 17For *there were*
many in the assembly who had not
sanctified themselves; therefore the
Levites had charge of the slaughter of
the Passover *lambs* for everyone *who*
was not clean, to sanctify *them* to the
LORD. 18For a multitude of the people,
many from Ephraim, Manasseh, Issa-
char, and Zebulun, had not cleansed
themselves, yet they ate the Passover
contrary to what was written. But Hez-
ekiah prayed for them, saying, "May
the good LORD provide atonement for
everyone 19*who* prepares his heart to
seek God, the LORD God of his fathers,
though *he is* not *cleansed* according
to the purification of the sanctuary."
20And the LORD listened to Hezekiah
and healed the people.
21So the children of Israel who were
present at Jerusalem kept the Feast
of Unleavened Bread seven days with

30:3 [a] That is, the first month (compare Leviticus 23:5); literally *at that time*

great gladness; and the Levites and
the priests praised the LORD day by
day, *singing* to the LORD, accompanied
by loud instruments. 22And Hezekiah
gave encouragement to all the Levites
who taught the good knowledge of the
LORD; and they ate throughout the feast
seven days, offering peace offerings
and making confession to the LORD
God of their fathers.
23Then the whole assembly agreed to
keep *the feast* another seven days, and
they kept it *another* seven days with
gladness. 24For Hezekiah king of Judah
gave to the assembly a thousand bulls
and seven thousand sheep, and the
leaders gave to the assembly a thou-
sand bulls and ten thousand sheep;
and a great number of priests sanctified
themselves. 25The whole assembly of
Judah rejoiced, also the priests and Le-
vites, all the assembly that came from
Israel, the sojourners who came from
the land of Israel, and those who dwelt
in Judah. 26So there was great joy in Je-
rusalem, for since the time of Solomon
the son of David, king of Israel, *there
had* been nothing like this in Jerusalem.
27Then the priests, the Levites, arose and
blessed the people, and their voice was
heard; and their prayer came *up* to His
holy dwelling place, to heaven.

The Reforms of Hezekiah

31 Now when all this was finished,
all Israel who were present went
out to the cities of Judah and broke
the *sacred* pillars in pieces, cut down
the wooden images, and threw down the
high places and the altars—from all
Judah, Benjamin, Ephraim, and Manas-
seh—until they had utterly destroyed
them all. Then all the children of Israel
returned to their own cities, every man
to his possession.
2And Hezekiah appointed the divi-
sions of the priests and the Levites ac-
cording to their divisions, each man
according to his service, the priests and
Levites for burnt offerings and peace
offerings, to serve, to give thanks, and
to praise in the gates of the camp[a] of
the LORD. 3The king also *appointed* a
portion of his possessions for the burnt
offerings: for the morning and evening
burnt offerings, the burnt offerings for
the Sabbaths and the New Moons and
the set feasts, as *it is* written in the Law
of the LORD.
4Moreover he commanded the people
who dwelt in Jerusalem to contribute
support for the priests and the Levites,
that they might devote themselves to
the Law of the LORD.
5As soon as the commandment
was circulated, the children of Israel
brought in abundance the firstfruits
of grain and wine, oil and honey, and
of all the produce of the field; and they
brought in abundantly the tithe of ev-
erything. 6And the children of Israel
and Judah, who dwelt in the cities of
Judah, brought the tithe of oxen and
sheep; also the tithe of holy things
which were consecrated to the LORD
their God they laid in heaps.
7In the third month they began laying
them in heaps, and they finished in the
seventh month. 8And when Hezeki-
ah and the leaders came and saw the
heaps, they blessed the LORD and His
people Israel. 9Then Hezekiah ques-
tioned the priests and the Levites con-
cerning the heaps. 10And Azariah the
chief priest, from the house of Zadok,
answered him and said, "Since *the peo-
ple* began to bring the offerings into the
house of the LORD, we have had enough
to eat and have plenty left, for the LORD
has blessed His people; and what is left
is this great abundance."
11Now Hezekiah commanded *them*
to prepare rooms in the house of the
LORD, and they prepared them. 12Then
they faithfully brought in the offerings,
the tithes, and the dedicated things;
Cononiah the Levite had charge of
them, and Shimei his brother *was* the
next. 13Jehiel, Azaziah, Nahath, Asahel,
Jerimoth, Jozabad, Eliel, Ismachiah,
Mahath, and Benaiah *were* overseers
under the hand of Cononiah and Shim-
ei his brother, at the commandment of
Hezekiah the king and Azariah the ruler
of the house of God. 14Kore the son of
Imnah the Levite, the keeper of the East

31:2 [a] That is, the temple

Gate, *was* over the freewill offerings to God, to distribute the offerings of the LORD and the most holy things. 15And under him *were* Eden, Miniamin, Jeshua, Shemaiah, Amariah, and Shecaniah, *his* faithful assistants in the cities of the priests, to distribute allotments to their brethren by divisions, to the great as well as the small.

16Besides those males from three years old and up who were written in the genealogy, they distributed to everyone who entered the house of the LORD his daily portion for the work of his service, by his division, 17and to the priests who were written in the genealogy according to their father's house, and to the Levites from twenty years old and up according to their work, by their divisions, 18and to all who were written in the genealogy—their little ones and their wives, their sons and daughters, the whole company of them—for in their faithfulness they sanctified themselves in holiness.

19Also for the sons of Aaron the priests, *who were* in the fields of the common-lands of their cities, in every single city, *there were* men who were designated by name to distribute portions to all the males among the priests and to all who were listed by genealogies among the Levites.

20Thus Hezekiah did throughout all Judah, and he did what *was* good and right and true before the LORD his God. 21And in every work that he began in the service of the house of God, in the law and in the commandment, to seek his God, he did *it* with all his heart. So he prospered.

Sennacherib Boasts Against the LORD

32 After these deeds of faithfulness, Sennacherib king of Assyria came and entered Judah; he encamped against the fortified cities, thinking to win them over to himself. 2And when Hezekiah saw that Sennacherib had come, and that his purpose was to make war against Jerusalem, 3he consulted with his leaders and commanders[a] to stop the water from the springs which *were* outside the city; and they helped him. 4Thus many people gathered together who stopped all the springs and the brook that ran through the land, saying, "Why should the kings[a] of Assyria come and find much water?" 5And he strengthened himself, built up all the wall that was broken, raised *it* up to the towers, and *built* another wall outside; also he repaired the Millo[a] *in* the City of David, and made weapons and shields in abundance. 6Then he set military captains over the people, gathered them together to him in the open square of the city gate, and gave them encouragement, saying, 7"Be strong and courageous; do not be afraid nor dismayed before the king of Assyria, nor before all the multitude that *is* with him; for *there are* more with us than with him. 8With him *is* an arm of flesh; but with us *is* the LORD our God, to help us and to fight our battles." And the people were strengthened by the words of Hezekiah king of Judah.

9After this Sennacherib king of Assyria sent his servants to Jerusalem (but he and all the forces with him *laid siege* against Lachish), to Hezekiah king of Judah, and to all Judah who *were* in Jerusalem, saying, 10"Thus says Sennacherib king of Assyria: 'In what do you trust, that you remain under siege in Jerusalem? 11Does not Hezekiah persuade you to give yourselves over to die by famine and by thirst, saying, "The LORD our God will deliver us from the hand of the king of Assyria"? 12Has not the same Hezekiah taken away His high places and His altars, and commanded Judah and Jerusalem, saying, "You shall worship before one altar and burn incense on it"? 13Do you not know what I and my fathers have done to all the peoples of *other* lands? Were the gods of the nations of those lands in any way able to deliver their lands out of my hand? 14Who *was there* among all the gods of those nations that my fathers utterly destroyed that could deliver his people from my hand, that your God should be able to deliver you from my hand? 15Now therefore, do not

32:3 [a] Literally *mighty men* 32:4 [a] Following Masoretic Text and Vulgate; Arabic, Septuagint, and Syriac read *king.* 32:5 [a] Literally *The Landfill*

let Hezekiah deceive you or persuade you like this, and do not believe him; for no god of any nation or kingdom was able to deliver his people from my hand or the hand of my fathers. How much less will your God deliver you from my hand?' "

16Furthermore, his servants spoke against the LORD God and against His servant Hezekiah.

17He also wrote letters to revile the LORD God of Israel, and to speak against Him, saying, "As the gods of the nations of *other* lands have not delivered their people from my hand, so the God of Hezekiah will not deliver His people from my hand." 18Then they called out with a loud voice in Hebrew[a] to the people of Jerusalem who *were* on the wall, to frighten them and trouble them, that they might take the city. 19And they spoke against the God of Jerusalem, as against the gods of the people of the earth—the work of men's hands.

Sennacherib's Defeat and Death

20Now because of this King Hezekiah and the prophet Isaiah, the son of Amoz, prayed and cried out to heaven. 21Then the LORD sent an angel who cut down every mighty man of valor, leader, and captain in the camp of the king of Assyria. So he returned shamefaced to his own land. And when he had gone into the temple of his god, some of his own offspring struck him down with the sword there.

22Thus the LORD saved Hezekiah and the inhabitants of Jerusalem from the hand of Sennacherib the king of Assyria, and from the hand of all *others,* and guided them[a] on every side. 23And many brought gifts to the LORD at Jerusalem, and presents to Hezekiah king of Judah, so that he was exalted in the sight of all nations thereafter.

Hezekiah Humbles Himself

24In those days Hezekiah was sick and near death, and he prayed to the LORD; and He spoke to him and gave him a sign. 25But Hezekiah did not repay according to the favor *shown* him, for his heart was lifted up; therefore wrath was looming over him and over Judah and Jerusalem. 26Then Hezekiah humbled himself for the pride of his heart, he and the inhabitants of Jerusalem, so that the wrath of the LORD did not come upon them in the days of Hezekiah.

Hezekiah's Wealth and Honor

27Hezekiah had very great riches and honor. And he made himself treasuries for silver, for gold, for precious stones, for spices, for shields, and for all kinds of desirable items; 28storehouses for the harvest of grain, wine, and oil; and stalls for all kinds of livestock, and folds for flocks.[a] 29Moreover he provided cities for himself, and possessions of flocks and herds in abundance; for God had given him very much property. 30This same Hezekiah also stopped the water outlet of Upper Gihon, and brought the water by tunnel[a] to the west side of the City of David. Hezekiah prospered in all his works.

31However, *regarding* the ambassadors of the princes of Babylon, whom they sent to him to inquire about the wonder that was *done* in the land, God withdrew from him, in order to test him, that He might know all *that was* in his heart.

Death of Hezekiah

32Now the rest of the acts of Hezekiah, and his goodness, indeed they *are* written in the vision of Isaiah the prophet, the son of Amoz, *and* in the book of the kings of Judah and Israel. 33So Hezekiah rested with his fathers, and they buried him in the upper tombs of the sons of David; and all Judah and the inhabitants of Jerusalem honored him at his death. Then Manasseh his son reigned in his place.

Manasseh Reigns in Judah

33 Manasseh *was* twelve years old when he became king, and he reigned fifty-five years in Jerusalem. 2But he did evil in the sight of the LORD, according to the abominations of the

32:18 [a] Literally *Judean* 32:22 [a] Septuagint reads *gave them rest;* Vulgate reads *gave them treasures.* 32:28 [a] Following Septuagint and Vulgate; Arabic and Syriac omit *folds for flocks;* Masoretic Text reads *flocks for sheepfolds.* 32:30 [a] Literally *brought it straight* (compare 2 Kings 20:20)

nations whom the LORD had cast out
before the children of Israel. 3For he re-
built the high places which Hezekiah his
father had broken down; he raised up
altars for the Baals, and made wooden
images; and he worshiped all the host of
heaven[a] and served them. 4He also built
altars in the house of the LORD, of which
the LORD had said, "In Jerusalem shall
My name be forever." 5And he built al-
tars for all the host of heaven in the two
courts of the house of the LORD. 6Also he
caused his sons to pass through the fire
in the Valley of the Son of Hinnom; he
practiced soothsaying, used witchcraft
and sorcery, and consulted mediums
and spiritists. He did much evil in the
sight of the LORD, to provoke Him to
anger. 7He even set a carved image, the
idol which he had made, in the house of
God, of which God had said to David and
to Solomon his son, "In this house and
in Jerusalem, which I have chosen out of
all the tribes of Israel, I will put My name
forever; 8and I will not again remove
the foot of Israel from the land which
I have appointed for your fathers—
only if they are careful to do all that
I have commanded them, according
to the whole law and the statutes and
the ordinances by the hand of Moses."
9So Manasseh seduced Judah and the
inhabitants of Jerusalem to do more evil
than the nations whom the LORD had
destroyed before the children of Israel.

Manasseh Restored After Repentance

10And the LORD spoke to Manasseh
and his people, but they would not lis-
ten. 11Therefore the LORD brought upon
them the captains of the army of the
king of Assyria, who took Manasseh
with hooks,[a] bound him with bronze
fetters, and carried him off to Babylon.
12Now when he was in affliction, he im-
plored the LORD his God, and humbled
himself greatly before the God of his
fathers, 13and prayed to Him; and He
received his entreaty, heard his suppli-
cation, and brought him back to Jerusa-
lem into his kingdom. Then Manasseh
knew that the LORD *was* God.
14After this he built a wall outside the
City of David on the west side of Gihon,
in the valley, as far as the entrance of
the Fish Gate; and *it* enclosed Ophel,
and he raised it to a very great height.
Then he put military captains in all the
fortified cities of Judah. 15He took away
the foreign gods and the idol from the
house of the LORD, and all the altars that
he had built in the mount of the house of
the LORD and in Jerusalem; and he cast
them out of the city. 16He also repaired
the altar of the LORD, sacrificed peace
offerings and thank offerings on it, and
commanded Judah to serve the LORD
God of Israel. 17Nevertheless the people
still sacrificed on the high places, *but*
only to the LORD their God.

Death of Manasseh

18Now the rest of the acts of Manasseh,
his prayer to his God, and the words of
the seers who spoke to him in the name
of the LORD God of Israel, indeed they
are written in the book[a] of the kings of
Israel. 19Also his prayer and *how God*
received his entreaty, and all his sin
and trespass, and the sites where he
built high places and set up wooden
images and carved images, before he
was humbled, indeed they *are* written
among the sayings of Hozai.[a] 20So Ma-
nasseh rested with his fathers, and they
buried him in his own house. Then his
son Amon reigned in his place.

Amon's Reign and Death

21Amon *was* twenty-two years old
when he became king, and he reigned
two years in Jerusalem. 22But he did evil
in the sight of the LORD, as his father
Manasseh had done; for Amon sacri-
ficed to all the carved images which
his father Manasseh had made, and
served them. 23And he did not humble
himself before the LORD, as his father
Manasseh had humbled himself; but
Amon trespassed more and more.
24Then his servants conspired against
him, and killed him in his own house.
25But the people of the land executed
all those who had conspired against
King Amon. Then the people of the land
made his son Josiah king in his place.

33:3 [a] The gods of the Assyrians **33:11** [a] That is, nose hooks (compare 2 Kings 19:28)
33:18 [a] Literally *words* **33:19** [a] Septuagint reads *the seers.*

Josiah Reigns in Judah

34 Josiah *was* eight years old when he became king, and he reigned thirty-one years in Jerusalem. 2And he did *what was* right in the sight of the LORD, and walked in the ways of his father David; *he* did *not* turn aside to the right hand or to the left.

3For in the eighth year of his reign, while he was still young, he began to seek the God of his father David; and in the twelfth year he began to purge Judah and Jerusalem of the high places, the wooden images, the carved images, and the molded images. 4They broke down the altars of the Baals in his presence, and the incense altars which *were* above them he cut down; and the wooden images, the carved images, and the molded images he broke in pieces, and made dust of them and scattered *it* on the graves of those who had sacrificed to them. 5He also burned the bones of the priests on their altars, and cleansed Judah and Jerusalem. 6And *so he did* in the cities of Manasseh, Ephraim, and Simeon, as far as Naphtali and all around, with axes.[a] 7When he had broken down the altars and the wooden images, had beaten the carved images into powder, and cut down all the incense altars throughout all the land of Israel, he returned to Jerusalem.

Hilkiah Finds the Book of the Law

8In the eighteenth year of his reign, when he had purged the land and the temple,[a] he sent Shaphan the son of Azaliah, Maaseiah the governor of the city, and Joah the son of Joahaz the recorder, to repair the house of the LORD his God. 9When they came to Hilkiah the high priest, they delivered the money that was brought into the house of God, which the Levites who kept the doors had gathered from the hand of Manasseh and Ephraim, from all the remnant of Israel, from all Judah and Benjamin, and *which* they had brought back to Jerusalem. 10Then they put *it* in the hand of the foremen who had the oversight of the house of the LORD; and they gave it to the workmen who worked in the house of the LORD, to repair and restore the house. 11They gave *it* to the craftsmen and builders to buy hewn stone and timber for beams, and to floor the houses which the kings of Judah had destroyed. 12And the men did the work faithfully. Their overseers *were* Jahath and Obadiah the Levites, of the sons of Merari, and Zechariah and Meshullam, of the sons of the Kohathites, to supervise. *Others of* the Levites, all of whom were skillful with instruments of music, 13*were* over the burden bearers and *were* overseers of all who did work in any kind of service. And *some* of the Levites *were* scribes, officers, and gatekeepers.

14Now when they brought out the money that was brought into the house of the LORD, Hilkiah the priest found the Book of the Law of the LORD *given* by Moses. 15Then Hilkiah answered and said to Shaphan the scribe, "I have found the Book of the Law in the house of the LORD." And Hilkiah gave the book to Shaphan. 16So Shaphan carried the book to the king, bringing the king word, saying, "All that was committed to your servants they are doing. 17And they have gathered the money that was found in the house of the LORD, and have delivered it into the hand of the overseers and the workmen." 18Then Shaphan the scribe told the king, saying, "Hilkiah the priest has given me a book." And Shaphan read it before the king.

19Thus it happened, when the king heard the words of the Law, that he tore his clothes. 20Then the king commanded Hilkiah, Ahikam the son of Shaphan, Abdon[a] the son of Micah, Shaphan the scribe, and Asaiah a servant of the king, saying, 21"Go, inquire of the LORD for me, and for those who are left in Israel and Judah, concerning the words of the book that is found; for great *is* the wrath of the LORD that is poured out on us, because our fathers have not kept the word of the LORD, to do according to all that is written in this book."

22So Hilkiah and those the king *had appointed* went to Huldah the prophetess, the wife of Shallum the son of Tokhath,[a] the son of Hasrah,[b] keeper of

34:6 [a] Literally *swords* **34:8** [a] Literally *house* **34:20** [a] *Achbor the son of Michaiah* in 2 Kings 22:12
34:22 [a] Spelled *Tikvah* in 2 Kings 22:14 [b] Spelled *Harhas* in 2 Kings 22:14

the wardrobe. (She dwelt in Jerusalem
in the Second Quarter.) And they spoke
to her to that *effect.*
23Then she answered them, "Thus says
the LORD God of Israel, 'Tell the man
who sent you to Me, 24"Thus says the
LORD: 'Behold, I will bring calamity
on this place and on its inhabitants, all
the curses that are written in the book
which they have read before the king
of Judah, 25because they have forsaken
Me and burned incense to other gods,
that they might provoke Me to anger
with all the works of their hands. There-
fore My wrath will be poured out on this
place, and not be quenched.' " ' 26But
as for the king of Judah, who sent you
to inquire of the LORD, in this manner
you shall speak to him, 'Thus says the
LORD God of Israel: "*Concerning* the
words which you have heard— 27be-
cause your heart was tender, and you
humbled yourself before God when
you heard His words against this place
and against its inhabitants, and you
humbled yourself before Me, and you
tore your clothes and wept before Me,
I also have heard *you,*" says the LORD.
28"Surely I will gather you to your fa-
thers, and you shall be gathered to your
grave in peace; and your eyes shall not
see all the calamity which I will bring
on this place and its inhabitants." ' "
So they brought back word to the king.

Josiah Restores True Worship

29Then the king sent and gathered all
the elders of Judah and Jerusalem. 30The
king went up to the house of the LORD,
with all the men of Judah and the inhab-
itants of Jerusalem—the priests and the
Levites, and all the people, great and
small. And he read in their hearing all
the words of the Book of the Covenant
which had been found in the house of
the LORD. 31Then the king stood in his
place and made a covenant before the
LORD, to follow the LORD, and to keep
His commandments and His testimo-
nies and His statutes with all his heart
and all his soul, to perform the words of
the covenant that were written in this
book. 32And he made all who were pres-
ent in Jerusalem and Benjamin take a
stand. So the inhabitants of Jerusalem
did according to the covenant of God,
the God of their fathers. 33Thus Josiah
removed all the abominations from all
the country that *belonged* to the children
of Israel, and made all who were present
in Israel diligently serve the LORD their
God. All his days they did not depart from
following the LORD God of their fathers.

Josiah Keeps the Passover

35 Now Josiah kept a Passover to
the LORD in Jerusalem, and they
slaughtered the Passover *lambs* on the
fourteenth *day* of the first month. 2And
he set the priests in their duties and
encouraged them for the service of the
house of the LORD. 3Then he said to the
Levites who taught all Israel, who were
holy to the LORD: "Put the holy ark in the
house which Solomon the son of David,
king of Israel, built. *It shall* no longer *be* a
burden on *your* shoulders. Now serve the
LORD your God and His people Israel.
4Prepare *yourselves* according to your
fathers' houses, according to your divi-
sions, following the written instruction
of David king of Israel and the written
instruction of Solomon his son. 5And
stand in the holy *place* according to the
divisions of the fathers' houses of your
brethren the *lay* people, and *according
to* the division of the father's house of
the Levites. 6So slaughter the Passover
offerings, consecrate yourselves, and
prepare *them* for your brethren, that
they may do according to the word of
the LORD by the hand of Moses."
7Then Josiah gave the *lay* people lambs
and young goats from the flock, all for
Passover *offerings* for all who were pres-
ent, to the number of thirty thousand,
as well as three thousand cattle; these
were from the king's possessions. 8And
his leaders gave willingly to the people,
to the priests, and to the Levites. Hilki-
ah, Zechariah, and Jehiel, rulers of the
house of God, gave to the priests for
the Passover *offerings* two thousand
six hundred *from the flock,* and three
hundred cattle. 9Also Conaniah, his
brothers Shemaiah and Nethanel, and
Hashabiah and Jeiel and Jozabad, chief
of the Levites, gave to the Levites for
Passover *offerings* five thousand *from
the flock* and five hundred cattle.

10 So the service was prepared, and the priests stood in their places, and the Levites in their divisions, according to the king's command. 11 And they slaughtered the Passover *offerings;* and the priests sprinkled *the blood* with their hands, while the Levites skinned *the animals.* 12 Then they removed the burnt offerings that *they* might give them to the divisions of the fathers' houses of the *lay* people, to offer to the LORD, as *it is* written in the Book of Moses. And so *they did* with the cattle. 13 Also they roasted the Passover *offerings* with fire according to the ordinance; but the *other* holy *offerings* they boiled in pots, in caldrons, and in pans, and divided *them* quickly among all the *lay* people. 14 Then afterward they prepared portions for themselves and for the priests, because the priests, the sons of Aaron, *were busy* in offering burnt offerings and fat until night; therefore the Levites prepared portions for themselves and for the priests, the sons of Aaron. 15 And the singers, the sons of Asaph, *were* in their places, according to the command of David, Asaph, Heman, and Jeduthun the king's seer. Also the gatekeepers were at each gate; they did not have to leave their position, because their brethren the Levites prepared portions for them.

16 So all the service of the LORD was prepared the same day, to keep the Passover and to offer burnt offerings on the altar of the LORD, according to the command of King Josiah. 17 And the children of Israel who were present kept the Passover at that time, and the Feast of Unleavened Bread for seven days. 18 There had been no Passover kept in Israel like that since the days of Samuel the prophet; and none of the kings of Israel had kept such a Passover as Josiah kept, with the priests and the Levites, all Judah and Israel who were present, and the inhabitants of Jerusalem. 19 In the eighteenth year of the reign of Josiah this Passover was kept.

Josiah Dies in Battle

20 After all this, when Josiah had prepared the temple, Necho king of Egypt came up to fight against Carchemish by the Euphrates; and Josiah went out against him. 21 But he sent messengers to him, saying, "What have I to do with you, king of Judah? *I have* not *come* against you this day, but against the house with which I have war; for God commanded me to make haste. Refrain *from meddling with* God, who *is* with me, lest He destroy you." 22 Nevertheless Josiah would not turn his face from him, but disguised himself so that he might fight with him, and did not heed the words of Necho from the mouth of God. So he came to fight in the Valley of Megiddo.

23 And the archers shot King Josiah; and the king said to his servants, "Take me away, for I am severely wounded." 24 His servants therefore took him out of that chariot and put him in the second chariot that he had, and they brought him to Jerusalem. So he died, and was buried in *one of* the tombs of his fathers. And all Judah and Jerusalem mourned for Josiah.

25 Jeremiah also lamented for Josiah. And to this day all the singing men and the singing women speak of Josiah in their lamentations. They made it a custom in Israel; and indeed they *are* written in the Laments.

26 Now the rest of the acts of Josiah and his goodness, according to *what was* written in the Law of the LORD, 27 and his deeds from first to last, indeed they *are* written in the book of the kings of Israel and Judah.

The Reign and Captivity of Jehoahaz

36 Then the people of the land took Jehoahaz the son of Josiah, and made him king in his father's place in Jerusalem. 2 Jehoahaz[a] *was* twenty-three years old when he became king, and he reigned three months in Jerusalem. 3 Now the king of Egypt deposed him at Jerusalem; and he imposed on the land a tribute of one hundred talents of silver and a talent of gold. 4 Then the king of Egypt made *Jehoahaz's*[a] brother Eliakim king over Judah and Jerusalem, and changed his name to Jehoiakim. And Necho took Jehoahaz[b] his brother and carried him off to Egypt.

36:2 [a] Masoretic Text reads *Joahaz.* 36:4 [a] Literally *his* [b] Masoretic Text reads *Joahaz.*

The Reign and Captivity of Jehoiakim

5Jehoiakim *was* twenty-five years old
when he became king, and he reigned
eleven years in Jerusalem. And he did
evil in the sight of the LORD his God.
6Nebuchadnezzar king of Babylon
came up against him, and bound him
in bronze *fetters* to carry him off to Bab-
ylon. 7Nebuchadnezzar also carried off
some of the articles from the house of
the LORD to Babylon, and put them in
his temple at Babylon. 8Now the rest
of the acts of Jehoiakim, the abomina-
tions which he did, and what was found
against him, indeed they *are* written
in the book of the kings of Israel and
Judah. Then Jehoiachin his son reigned
in his place.

The Reign and Captivity of Jehoiachin

9Jehoiachin *was* eight[a] years old when
he became king, and he reigned in Jeru-
salem three months and ten days. And
he did evil in the sight of the LORD. 10At
the turn of the year King Nebuchadnez-
zar summoned *him* and took him to
Babylon, with the costly articles from
the house of the LORD, and made Zed-
ekiah, *Jehoiakim's*[a] brother, king over
Judah and Jerusalem.

Zedekiah Reigns in Judah

11Zedekiah *was* twenty-one years old
when he became king, and he reigned
eleven years in Jerusalem. 12He did
evil in the sight of the LORD his God,
and did not humble himself before
Jeremiah the prophet, *who spoke* from
the mouth of the LORD. 13And he also
rebelled against King Nebuchadnez-
zar, who had made him swear *an oath*
by God; but he stiffened his neck and
hardened his heart against turning to
the LORD God of Israel. 14Moreover all
the leaders of the priests and the people
transgressed more and more, *according*
to all the abominations of the nations,
and defiled the house of the LORD which
He had consecrated in Jerusalem.

The Fall of Jerusalem

15And the LORD God of their fa-
thers sent *warnings* to them by His
messengers, rising up early and send-
ing *them,* because He had compassion
on His people and on His dwelling
place. 16But they mocked the messen-
gers of God, despised His words, and
scoffed at His prophets, until the wrath
of the LORD arose against His people,
till *there was* no remedy.
17Therefore He brought against them
the king of the Chaldeans, who killed
their young men with the sword in the
house of their sanctuary, and had no
compassion on young man or virgin,
on the aged or the weak; He gave *them*
all into his hand. 18And all the articles
from the house of God, great and small,
the treasures of the house of the LORD,
and the treasures of the king and of
his leaders, all *these* he took to Bab-
ylon. 19Then they burned the house
of God, broke down the wall of Jeru-
salem, burned all its palaces with fire,
and destroyed all its precious posses-
sions. 20And those who escaped from
the sword he carried away to Babylon,
where they became servants to him and
his sons until the rule of the kingdom of
Persia, 21to fulfill the word of the LORD
by the mouth of Jeremiah, until the land
had enjoyed her Sabbaths. As long as
she lay desolate she kept Sabbath, to
fulfill seventy years.

The Proclamation of Cyrus

22Now in the first year of Cyrus king
of Persia, that the word of the LORD
by the mouth of Jeremiah might be
fulfilled, the LORD stirred up the spir-
it of Cyrus king of Persia, so that he
made a proclamation throughout all
his kingdom, and also *put it* in writing,
saying,

23 Thus says Cyrus king of Persia:
All the kingdoms of the earth
the LORD God of heaven
has given me. And He has
commanded me to build Him a
house at Jerusalem which is in
Judah. Who *is* among you of all
His people? May the LORD his
God *be* with him, and let him
go up!

36:9 [a] Some Hebrew manuscripts, Septuagint, Syriac, and 2 Kings 24:8 read *eighteen.*
36:10 [a] Literally *his* (compare 2 Kings 24:17)

THE BOOK OF
EZRA

The Book of Ezra tells the story of coming home. After living in a faraway country for seventy years, some of the Jewish exiles return to Jerusalem. God had promised that He would bring His people home, and He does. This is the story of how the Israelites started over. They first rebuild God's altar and begin rebuilding the temple. But when the neighboring nations get angry, the Israelites stop their work. Then, after eighteen years, they resume and complete the temple. They then begin to worship God as He had instructed in Leviticus once again.

- **GENRE:** History
- **AUTHOR:** Ezra
- **TIME:** c. 538–516 / c. 458–457 BC (written c. 457–444 BC)
- **PURPOSE:** To tell the story of God's people coming home. God had disciplined the Israelites because of their sin, but He also kept His promise to bring them home again.

End of the Babylonian Captivity

1 Now in the first year of Cyrus king
of Persia, that the word of the LORD
by the mouth of Jeremiah might be
fulfilled, the LORD stirred up the spirit
of Cyrus king of Persia, so that he made
a proclamation throughout all his king-
dom, and also *put it* in writing, saying,

2 Thus says Cyrus king of Persia:
All the kingdoms of the earth the
LORD God of heaven has given me.
And He has commanded me to
build Him a house at Jerusalem
which *is* in Judah. 3Who *is* among
you of all His people? May his God
be with him, and let him go up
to Jerusalem which *is* in Judah,
and build the house of the LORD
God of Israel (He *is* God), which
is in Jerusalem. 4And whoever is
left in any place where he dwells,
let the men of his place help him
with silver and gold, with goods
and livestock, besides the freewill
offerings for the house of God
which *is* in Jerusalem.

5Then the heads of the fathers' *houses*
of Judah and Benjamin, and the priests
and the Levites, with all whose spirits
God had moved, arose to go up and
build the house of the LORD which *is*
in Jerusalem. 6And all those who *were*
around them encouraged them with
articles of silver and gold, with goods
and livestock, and with precious things,
besides all *that* was willingly offered.

7King Cyrus also brought out the arti-
cles of the house of the LORD, which Neb-
uchadnezzar had taken from Jerusalem
and put in the temple of his gods; 8and
Cyrus king of Persia brought them out
by the hand of Mithredath the treasurer,
and counted them out to Sheshbazzar
the prince of Judah. 9This *is* the number
of them: thirty gold platters, one thou-
sand silver platters, twenty-nine knives,
10thirty gold basins, four hundred and
ten silver basins of a similar *kind, and*
one thousand other articles. 11All the
articles of gold and silver *were* five thou-
sand four hundred. All *these* Sheshbazzar
took with the captives who were brought
from Babylon to Jerusalem.

The Captives Who Returned to Jerusalem

2 Now[a] these *are* the people of the
province who came back from the
captivity, of those who had been car-
ried away, whom Nebuchadnezzar the
king of Babylon had carried away to

2:1 [a] Compare this chapter with Nehemiah 7:6–73.

Babylon, and who returned to Jerusalem and Judah, everyone to his *own* city.

2 *Those* who came with Zerubbabel *were* Jeshua, Nehemiah, Seraiah, Reelaiah, Mordecai, Bilshan, Mispar,[a] Bigvai, Rehum,[b] *and* Baanah. The number of the men of the people of Israel: 3 the people of Parosh, two thousand one hundred and seventy-two; 4 the people of Shephatiah, three hundred and seventy-two; 5 the people of Arah, seven hundred and seventy-five; 6 the people of Pahath-Moab, of the people of Jeshua *and* Joab, two thousand eight hundred and twelve; 7 the people of Elam, one thousand two hundred and fifty-four; 8 the people of Zattu, nine hundred and forty-five; 9 the people of Zaccai, seven hundred and sixty; 10 the people of Bani,[a] six hundred and forty-two; 11 the people of Bebai, six hundred and twenty-three; 12 the people of Azgad, one thousand two hundred and twenty-two; 13 the people of Adonikam, six hundred and sixty-six; 14 the people of Bigvai, two thousand and fifty-six; 15 the people of Adin, four hundred and fifty-four; 16 the people of Ater of Hezekiah, ninety-eight; 17 the people of Bezai, three hundred and twenty-three; 18 the people of Jorah,[a] one hundred and twelve; 19 the people of Hashum, two hundred and twenty-three; 20 the people of Gibbar,[a] ninety-five; 21 the people of Bethlehem, one hundred and twenty-three; 22 the men of Netophah, fifty-six; 23 the men of Anathoth, one hundred and twenty-eight; 24 the people of Azmaveth,[a] forty-two; 25 the people of Kirjath Arim,[a] Chephirah, and Beeroth, seven hundred and forty-three; 26 the people of Ramah and Geba, six hundred and twenty-one; 27 the men of Michmas, one hundred and twenty-two; 28 the men of Bethel and Ai, two hundred and twenty-three; 29 the people of Nebo, fifty-two; 30 the people of Magbish, one hundred and fifty-six; 31 the people of the other Elam, one thousand two hundred and fifty-four; 32 the people of Harim, three hundred and twenty; 33 the people of Lod, Hadid, and Ono, seven hundred and twenty-five; 34 the people of Jericho, three hundred and forty-five; 35 the people of Senaah, three thousand six hundred and thirty.

36 The priests: the sons of Jedaiah, of the house of Jeshua, nine hundred and seventy-three; 37 the sons of Immer, one thousand and fifty-two; 38 the sons of Pashhur, one thousand two hundred and forty-seven; 39 the sons of Harim, one thousand and seventeen.

40 The Levites: the sons of Jeshua and Kadmiel, of the sons of Hodaviah,[a] seventy-four.

41 The singers: the sons of Asaph, one hundred and twenty-eight.

42 The sons of the gatekeepers: the sons of Shallum, the sons of Ater, the sons of Talmon, the sons of Akkub, the sons of Hatita, and the sons of Shobai, one hundred and thirty-nine *in* all.

43 The Nethinim: the sons of Ziha, the sons of Hasupha, the sons of Tabbaoth, 44 the sons of Keros, the sons of Siaha,[a] the sons of Padon, 45 the sons of Lebanah, the sons of Hagabah, the sons of Akkub, 46 the sons of Hagab, the sons of Shalmai, the sons of Hanan, 47 the sons of Giddel, the sons of Gahar, the sons of Reaiah, 48 the sons of Rezin, the sons of Nekoda, the sons of Gazzam, 49 the sons of Uzza, the sons of Paseah, the sons of Besai, 50 the sons of Asnah, the sons of Meunim, the sons of Nephusim,[a] 51 the sons of Bakbuk, the sons of Hakupha, the sons of Harhur, 52 the sons of Bazluth,[a] the sons of Mehida, the sons of Harsha, 53 the sons of Barkos, the sons of Sisera, the sons of Tamah, 54 the sons of Neziah, and the sons of Hatipha.

55 The sons of Solomon's servants: the sons of Sotai, the sons of Sophereth, the sons of Peruda,[a] 56 the sons of Jaala, the sons of Darkon, the sons of Giddel, 57 the sons of Shephatiah, the sons of Hattil, the sons of Pochereth of Zebaim, and the sons of Ami.[a] 58 All the Nethinim

2:2 [a] Spelled *Mispereth* in Nehemiah 7:7 [b] Spelled *Nehum* in Nehemiah 7:7 **2:10** [a] Spelled *Binnui* in Nehemiah 7:15 **2:18** [a] Called *Hariph* in Nehemiah 7:24 **2:20** [a] Called *Gibeon* in Nehemiah 7:25 **2:24** [a] Called *Beth Azmaveth* in Nehemiah 7:28 **2:25** [a] Called *Kirjath Jearim* in Nehemiah 7:29 **2:40** [a] Spelled *Hodevah* in Nehemiah 7:43 **2:44** [a] Spelled *Sia* in Nehemiah 7:47 **2:50** [a] Spelled *Nephishesim* in Nehemiah 7:52 **2:52** [a] Spelled *Bazlith* in Nehemiah 7:54 **2:55** [a] Spelled *Perida* in Nehemiah 7:57 **2:57** [a] Spelled *Amon* in Nehemiah 7:59

and the children of Solomon's servants
were three hundred and ninety-two.
59And these *were* the ones who came
up from Tel Melah, Tel Harsha, Cherub,
Addan,[a] and Immer; but they could not
identify their father's house or their ge-
nealogy,[b] whether they *were* of Israel:
60the sons of Delaiah, the sons of Tobi-
ah, and the sons of Nekoda, six hundred
and fifty-two; 61and of the sons of the
priests: the sons of Habaiah, the sons of
Koz,[a] and the sons of Barzillai, who took
a wife of the daughters of Barzillai the
Gileadite, and was called by their name.
62These sought their listing *among* those
who were registered by genealogy, but
they were not found; therefore they *were*
excluded from the priesthood as defiled.
63And the governor[a] said to them that
they should not eat of the most holy
things till a priest could consult with
the Urim and Thummim.
64The whole assembly together *was*
forty-two thousand three hundred *and*
sixty, 65besides their male and female
servants, of whom *there were* seven
thousand three hundred and thirty-
seven; and they had two hundred men
and women singers. 66Their horses
were seven hundred and thirty-six,
their mules two hundred and forty-
five, 67their camels four hundred and
thirty-five, and *their* donkeys six thou-
sand seven hundred and twenty.
68*Some* of the heads of the fathers'
houses, when they came to the house of
the LORD which *is* in Jerusalem, offered
freely for the house of God, to erect it in
its place: 69According to their ability,
they gave to the treasury for the work
sixty-one thousand gold drachmas,
five thousand minas of silver, and one
hundred priestly garments.
70So the priests and the Levites, *some*
of the people, the singers, the gate-
keepers, and the Nethinim, dwelt in
their cities, and all Israel in their cities.

Worship Restored at Jerusalem

3 And when the seventh month had
come, and the children of Israel
were in the cities, the people gathered
together as one man to Jerusalem.
2Then Jeshua the son of Jozadak[a] and
his brethren the priests, and Zerubba-
bel the son of Shealtiel and his breth-
ren, arose and built the altar of the God
of Israel, to offer burnt offerings on it,
as *it is* written in the Law of Moses the
man of God. 3Though fear *had come*
upon them because of the people of
those countries, they set the altar on its
bases; and they offered burnt offerings
on it to the LORD, *both* the morning
and evening burnt offerings. 4They
also kept the Feast of Tabernacles, as
it is written, and *offered* the daily burnt
offerings in the number required by
ordinance for each day. 5Afterwards
they offered the regular burnt offering,
and *those* for New Moons and for all
the appointed feasts of the LORD that
were consecrated, and *those* of every-
one who willingly offered a freewill
offering to the LORD. 6From the first
day of the seventh month they began
to offer burnt offerings to the LORD,
although the foundation of the temple
of the LORD had not been laid. 7They
also gave money to the masons and
the carpenters, and food, drink, and
oil to the people of Sidon and Tyre to
bring cedar logs from Lebanon to the
sea, to Joppa, according to the per-
mission which they had from Cyrus
king of Persia.

Restoration of the Temple Begins

8Now in the second month of the sec-
ond year of their coming to the house
of God at Jerusalem, Zerubbabel the son
of Shealtiel, Jeshua the son of Jozadak,[a]
and the rest of their brethren the priests
and the Levites, and all those who had
come out of the captivity to Jerusalem,
began *work* and appointed the Levites
from twenty years old and above to
oversee the work of the house of the
LORD. 9Then Jeshua *with* his sons and
brothers, Kadmiel *with* his sons, and the
sons of Judah,[a] arose as one to oversee
those working on the house of God: the
sons of Henadad *with* their sons and
their brethren the Levites.

2:59 [a] Spelled *Addon* in Nehemiah 7:61 [b] Literally *seed* **2:61** [a] Or *Hakkoz* **2:63** [a] Hebrew *Tirshatha* **3:2** [a] Spelled *Jehozadak* in 1 Chronicles 6:14 **3:8** [a] Spelled *Jehozadak* in 1 Chronicles 6:14 **3:9** [a] Or *Hodaviah* (compare 2:40)

10When the builders laid the founda-
tion of the temple of the LORD, the priests
stood[a] in their apparel with trumpets,
and the Levites, the sons of Asaph, with
cymbals, to praise the LORD, according
to the ordinance of David king of Israel.
11And they sang responsively, praising
and giving thanks to the LORD:

"For *He is* good,
For His mercy *endures* forever
toward Israel."[a]

Then all the people shouted with a great
shout, when they praised the LORD, be-
cause the foundation of the house of
the LORD was laid.
12But many of the priests and Levites
and heads of the fathers' *houses,* old
men who had seen the first temple, wept
with a loud voice when the foundation
of this temple was laid before their eyes.
Yet many shouted aloud for joy, 13so
that the people could not discern the
noise of the shout of joy from the noise
of the weeping of the people, for the
people shouted with a loud shout, and
the sound was heard afar off.

Resistance to Rebuilding the Temple

4 Now when the adversaries of Judah
and Benjamin heard that the de-
scendants of the captivity were building
the temple of the LORD God of Israel,
2they came to Zerubbabel and the heads
of the fathers' *houses,* and said to them,
"Let us build with you, for we seek your
God as you *do;* and we have sacrificed to
Him since the days of Esarhaddon king
of Assyria, who brought us here." 3But
Zerubbabel and Jeshua and the rest of
the heads of the fathers' *houses* of Israel
said to them, "You may do nothing with
us to build a house for our God; but we
alone will build to the LORD God of Isra-
el, as King Cyrus the king of Persia has
commanded us." 4Then the people of the
land tried to discourage the people of
Judah. They troubled them in building,
5and hired counselors against them to
frustrate their purpose all the days of
Cyrus king of Persia, even until the reign
of Darius king of Persia.

Rebuilding of Jerusalem Opposed

6In the reign of Ahasuerus, in the
beginning of his reign, they wrote an
accusation against the inhabitants of
Judah and Jerusalem.
7In the days of Artaxerxes also, Bish-
lam, Mithredath, Tabel, and the rest of
their companions wrote to Artaxerxes
king of Persia; and the letter *was* written
in Aramaic script, and translated into
the Aramaic language. 8Rehum[a] the
commander and Shimshai the scribe
wrote a letter against Jerusalem to King
Artaxerxes in this fashion:

9 From[a] Rehum the commander,
Shimshai the scribe, and the
rest of their companions—
representatives of the Dinaites, the
Apharsathchites, the Tarpelites,
the people of Persia and Erech
and Babylon and Shushan,[b] the
Dehavites, the Elamites, 10and
the rest of the nations whom the
great and noble Osnapper took
captive and settled in the cities
of Samaria and the remainder
beyond the River[a]—and so forth.[b]

11(This *is* a copy of the letter that they
sent him.)

To King Artaxerxes from your
servants, the men *of the region*
beyond the River, and so forth:[a]

12 Let it be known to the king that
the Jews who came up from you
have come to us at Jerusalem,
and are building the rebellious
and evil city, and are finishing
its walls and repairing the
foundations. 13Let it now be
known to the king that, if this city
is built and the walls completed,
they will not pay tax, tribute, or
custom, and the king's treasury
will be diminished. 14Now because

3:10 [a] Following Septuagint, Syriac, and Vulgate; Masoretic Text reads *they stationed the priests.*
3:11 [a] Compare Psalm 136:1 4:8 [a] The original language of Ezra 4:8 through 6:18 is Aramaic.
4:9 [a] Literally *Then* [b] Or *Susa* 4:10 [a] That is, the Euphrates [b] Literally *and now* 4:11 [a] Literally *and now*

we receive support from the
palace, it was not proper for us to
see the king's dishonor; therefore
we have sent and informed the
king, 15 that search may be made
in the book of the records of your
fathers. And you will find in the
book of the records and know
that this city *is* a rebellious city,
harmful to kings and provinces,
and that they have incited
sedition within the city in former
times, for which cause this city
was destroyed.

16 We inform the king that if this
city is rebuilt and its walls are
completed, the result will be
that you will have no dominion
beyond the River.

17 The king sent an answer:

To Rehum the commander, *to*
Shimshai the scribe, *to* the rest of
their companions who dwell in
Samaria, and *to* the remainder
beyond the River:

Peace, and so forth.[a]

18 The letter which you sent to us
has been clearly read before me.
19 And I gave the command, and
a search has been made, and it
was found that this city in former
times has revolted against kings,
and rebellion and sedition have
been fostered in it. 20 There have
also been mighty kings over
Jerusalem, who have ruled over
all *the region* beyond the River;
and tax, tribute, and custom
were paid to them. 21 Now give the
command to make these men
cease, that this city may not be
built until the command is given
by me.

22 Take heed now that you do
not fail to do this. Why should
damage increase to the hurt of
the kings?

23 Now when the copy of King Arta-
xerxes' letter *was* read before Rehum,
Shimshai the scribe, and their compan-
ions, they went up in haste to Jerusalem
against the Jews, and by force of arms
made them cease. 24 Thus the work of
the house of God which *is* at Jerusalem
ceased, and it was discontinued until
the second year of the reign of Darius
king of Persia.

Restoration of the Temple Resumed

5 Then the prophet Haggai and Zech-
ariah the son of Iddo, prophets,
prophesied to the Jews who *were* in
Judah and Jerusalem, in the name of
the God of Israel, *who was* over them.
2 So Zerubbabel the son of Shealtiel and
Jeshua the son of Jozadak[a] rose up and
began to build the house of God which *is*
in Jerusalem; and the prophets of God
were with them, helping them.
3 At the same time Tattenai the gover-
nor of *the region* beyond the River[a] and
Shethar-Boznai and their companions
came to them and spoke thus to them:
"Who has commanded you to build this
temple and finish this wall?" 4 Then, ac-
cordingly, we told them the names of the
men who were constructing this build-
ing. 5 But the eye of their God was upon
the elders of the Jews, so that they could
not make them cease till a report could
go to Darius. Then a written answer was
returned concerning this *matter.* 6 This
is a copy of the letter that Tattenai sent:

The governor of *the region* beyond
the River, and Shethar-Boznai,
and his companions, the Persians
who *were in the region* beyond the
River, to Darius the king.

7 (They sent a letter to him, in which was
written thus.)

To Darius the king:

All peace.

8 Let it be known to the king that we
went into the province of Judea,
to the temple of the great God,

4:17 [a] Literally *and now* 5:2 [a] Spelled *Jehozadak* in 1 Chronicles 6:14 5:3 [a] That is, the Euphrates

which is being built with heavy
stones, and timber is being laid in
the walls; and this work goes on
diligently and prospers in their
hands.

9 Then we asked those elders,
and spoke thus to them: "Who
commanded you to build this
temple and to finish these walls?"
10We also asked them their names
to inform you, that we might
write the names of the men who
were chief among them.

11 And thus they returned us an
answer, saying: "We are the
servants of the God of heaven
and earth, and we are rebuilding
the temple that was built many
years ago, which a great king of
Israel built and completed. 12But
because our fathers provoked
the God of heaven to wrath,
He gave them into the hand of
Nebuchadnezzar king of Babylon,
the Chaldean, *who* destroyed this
temple and carried the people
away to Babylon. 13However,
in the first year of Cyrus king
of Babylon, King Cyrus issued
a decree to build this house of
God. 14Also, the gold and silver
articles of the house of God, which
Nebuchadnezzar had taken from
the temple that *was* in Jerusalem
and carried into the temple of
Babylon—those King Cyrus took
from the temple of Babylon, and
they were given to one named
Sheshbazzar, whom he had made
governor. 15And he said to him,
'Take these articles; go, carry
them to the temple *site* that *is* in
Jerusalem, and let the house of
God be rebuilt on its former site.'
16Then the same Sheshbazzar
came *and* laid the foundation
of the house of God which *is*
in Jerusalem; but from that
time even until now it has been
under construction, and it is not
finished."

17 Now therefore, if *it seems* good to
the king, let a search be made in
the king's treasure house, which
is there in Babylon, whether it
is *so* that a decree was issued by
King Cyrus to build this house of
God at Jerusalem, and let the king
send us his pleasure concerning
this *matter.*

The Decree of Darius

6 Then King Darius issued a decree,
and a search was made in the ar-
chives,[a] where the treasures were stored
in Babylon. 2And at Achmetha,[a] in the
palace that *is* in the province of Media,
a scroll was found, and in it a record
was written thus:

3 In the first year of King Cyrus,
King Cyrus issued a decree
concerning the house of God at
Jerusalem: "Let the house be
rebuilt, the place where they
offered sacrifices; and let the
foundations of it be firmly laid, its
height sixty cubits *and* its width
sixty cubits, 4*with* three rows
of heavy stones and one row of
new timber. Let the expenses be
paid from the king's treasury.
5Also let the gold and silver
articles of the house of God, which
Nebuchadnezzar took from the
temple which *is* in Jerusalem and
brought to Babylon, be restored
and taken back to the temple
which *is* in Jerusalem, *each* to its
place; and deposit *them* in the
house of God"—

6 Now *therefore,* Tattenai, governor
of *the region* beyond the River,
and Shethar-Boznai, and your
companions the Persians who *are*
beyond the River, keep yourselves
far from there. 7Let the work of
this house of God alone; let the
governor of the Jews and the
elders of the Jews build this house
of God on its site.

8 Moreover I issue a decree *as to*

6:1 [a] Literally *house of the scrolls* **6:2** [a] Probably *Ecbatana,* the ancient capital of Media

what you shall do for the elders of
these Jews, for the building of this
house of God: Let the cost be paid
at the king's expense from taxes
on the region beyond the River;
this is to be given immediately to
these men, so that they are not
hindered. 9And whatever they
need—young bulls, rams, and
lambs for the burnt offerings of
the God of heaven, wheat, salt,
wine, and oil, according to the
request of the priests who *are* in
Jerusalem—let it be given them
day by day without fail, 10that
they may offer sacrifices of sweet
aroma to the God of heaven, and
pray for the life of the king and
his sons.

11 Also I issue a decree that whoever
alters this edict, let a timber
be pulled from his house and
erected, and let him be hanged
on it; and let his house be made a
refuse heap because of this. 12And
may the God who causes His
name to dwell there destroy any
king or people who put their hand
to alter it, or to destroy this house
of God which is in Jerusalem. I
Darius issue a decree; let it be
done diligently.

The Temple Completed and Dedicated

13Then Tattenai, governor of *the region* beyond the River, Shethar-Boznai, and their companions diligently did according to what King Darius had sent. 14So the elders of the Jews built, and they prospered through the prophesying of Haggai the prophet and Zechariah the son of Iddo. And they built and finished *it,* according to the commandment of the God of Israel, and according to the command of Cyrus, Darius, and Artaxerxes king of Persia. 15Now the temple was finished on the third day of the month of Adar, which was in the sixth year of the reign of King Darius. 16Then the children of Israel, the priests and the Levites and the rest of the descendants of the captivity, celebrated the dedication of this house of God with joy. 17And they offered sacrifices at the dedication of this house of God, one hundred bulls, two hundred rams, four hundred lambs, and as a sin offering for all Israel twelve male goats, according to the number of the tribes of Israel. 18They assigned the priests to their divisions and the Levites to their divisions, over the service of God in Jerusalem, as it is written in the Book of Moses.

The Passover Celebrated

19And the descendants of the captivity kept the Passover on the fourteenth *day* of the first month. 20For the priests and the Levites had purified themselves; all of them *were ritually* clean. And they slaughtered the Passover *lambs* for all the descendants of the captivity, for their brethren the priests, and for themselves. 21Then the children of Israel who had returned from the captivity ate together with all who had separated themselves from the filth of the nations of the land in order to seek the LORD God of Israel. 22And they kept the Feast of Unleavened Bread seven days with joy; for the LORD made them joyful, and turned the heart of the king of Assyria toward them, to strengthen their hands in the work of the house of God, the God of Israel.

The Arrival of Ezra

7 Now after these things, in the reign of Artaxerxes king of Persia, Ezra the son of Seraiah, the son of Azariah, the son of Hilkiah, 2the son of Shallum, the son of Zadok, the son of Ahitub, 3the son of Amariah, the son of Azariah, the son of Meraioth, 4the son of Zerahiah, the son of Uzzi, the son of Bukki, 5the son of Abishua, the son of Phinehas, the son of Eleazar, the son of Aaron the chief priest— 6this Ezra came up from Babylon; and he *was* a skilled scribe in the Law of Moses, which the LORD God of Israel had given. The king granted him all his request, according to the hand of the LORD his God upon him. 7*Some* of the children of Israel, the priests, the Levites, the singers, the gatekeepers, and the Nethinim came up to Jerusalem in the seventh year of King Artaxerxes. 8And Ezra came to Jerusalem in the fifth month, which *was* in the seventh

year of the king. 9On the first *day* of the
first month he began *his* journey from
Babylon, and on the first *day* of the fifth
month he came to Jerusalem, according
to the good hand of his God upon him.
10For Ezra had prepared his heart to seek
the Law of the LORD, and to do *it*, and to
teach statutes and ordinances in Israel.

The Letter of Artaxerxes to Ezra

11This *is* a copy of the letter that King
Artaxerxes gave Ezra the priest, the
scribe, expert in the words of the com-
mandments of the LORD, and of His
statutes to Israel:

12 Artaxerxes,[a] king of kings,

To Ezra the priest, a scribe of the
Law of the God of heaven:

Perfect *peace*, and so forth.[b]

13 I issue a decree that all those of
the people of Israel and the priests
and Levites in my realm, who
volunteer to go up to Jerusalem,
may go with you. 14And whereas
you are being sent by the king and
his seven counselors to inquire
concerning Judah and Jerusalem,
with regard to the Law of your
God which *is* in your hand; 15and
whereas you are to carry the silver
and gold which the king and his
counselors have freely offered to
the God of Israel, whose dwelling
is in Jerusalem; 16and *whereas* all
the silver and gold that you may
find in all the province of Babylon,
along with the freewill offering of
the people and the priests, *are to
be* freely offered for the house of
their God in Jerusalem— 17now
therefore, be careful to buy with
this money bulls, rams, and
lambs, with their grain offerings
and their drink offerings, and offer
them on the altar of the house of
your God in Jerusalem.

18 And whatever seems good to you
and your brethren to do with the
rest of the silver and the gold, do it
according to the will of your God.
19Also the articles that are given
to you for the service of the house
of your God, deliver in full before
the God of Jerusalem. 20And
whatever more may be needed for
the house of your God, which you
may have occasion to provide,
pay *for it* from the king's treasury.

21 And I, *even* I, Artaxerxes the
king, issue a decree to all the
treasurers who *are in the region*
beyond the River, that whatever
Ezra the priest, the scribe of the
Law of the God of heaven, may
require of you, let it be done
diligently, 22up to one hundred
talents of silver, one hundred kors
of wheat, one hundred baths of
wine, one hundred baths of oil,
and salt without prescribed limit.
23Whatever is commanded by the
God of heaven, let it diligently be
done for the house of the God of
heaven. For why should there be
wrath against the realm of the
king and his sons?

24 Also we inform you that it
shall not be lawful to impose
tax, tribute, or custom on any
of the priests, Levites, singers,
gatekeepers, Nethinim, or
servants of this house of God.
25And you, Ezra, according to
your God-given wisdom, set
magistrates and judges who
may judge all the people who *are
in the region* beyond the River,
all such as know the laws of
your God; and teach those who
do not know *them*. 26Whoever
will not observe the law of your
God and the law of the king, let
judgment be executed speedily
on him, whether *it be* death, or
banishment, or confiscation of
goods, or imprisonment.

27Blessed *be* the LORD God of our fa-
thers, who has put *such a thing* as this in

7:12 [a] The original language of Ezra 7:12–26 is Aramaic. [b] Literally *and now*

the king's heart, to beautify the house of
the LORD which *is* in Jerusalem, 28and
has extended mercy to me before the
king and his counselors, and before all
the king's mighty princes.

So I was encouraged, as the hand of
the LORD my God *was* upon me; and I
gathered leading men of Israel to go
up with me.

Heads of Families Who Returned with Ezra

8 These *are* the heads of their fathers'
houses, and *this is* the genealogy of
those who went up with me from Bab-
ylon, in the reign of King Artaxerxes: 2of
the sons of Phinehas, Gershom; of the
sons of Ithamar, Daniel; of the sons of
David, Hattush; 3of the sons of Shecani-
ah, of the sons of Parosh, Zechariah; and
registered with him *were* one hundred
and fifty males; 4of the sons of Pahath-
Moab, Eliehoenai the son of Zerahiah,
and with him two hundred males; 5of the
sons of Shechaniah,[a] Ben-Jahaziel, and
with him three hundred males; 6of the
sons of Adin, Ebed the son of Jonathan,
and with him fifty males; 7of the sons of
Elam, Jeshaiah the son of Athaliah, and
with him seventy males; 8of the sons of
Shephatiah, Zebadiah the son of Michael,
and with him eighty males; 9of the sons of
Joab, Obadiah the son of Jehiel, and with
him two hundred and eighteen males;
10of the sons of Shelomith,[a] Ben-Josiphi-
ah, and with him one hundred and sixty
males; 11of the sons of Bebai, Zechariah
the son of Bebai, and with him twenty-
eight males; 12of the sons of Azgad, Jo-
hanan the son of Hakkatan, and with
him one hundred and ten males; 13of the
last sons of Adonikam, whose names *are*
these—Eliphelet, Jeiel, and Shemaiah—
and with them sixty males; 14also of the
sons of Bigvai, Uthai and Zabbud, and
with them seventy males.

Servants for the Temple

15Now I gathered them by the river that
flows to Ahava, and we camped there
three days. And I looked among the
people and the priests, and found none
of the sons of Levi there. 16Then I sent
for Eliezer, Ariel, Shemaiah, Elnathan,
Jarib, Elnathan, Nathan, Zechariah, and
Meshullam, leaders; also for Joiarib and
Elnathan, men of understanding. 17And I
gave them a command for Iddo the chief
man at the place Casiphia, and I told
them what they should say to Iddo *and*
his brethren[a] the Nethinim at the place
Casiphia—that they should bring us ser-
vants for the house of our God. 18Then,
by the good hand of our God upon us,
they brought us a man of understanding,
of the sons of Mahli the son of Levi, the
son of Israel, namely Sherebiah, with his
sons and brothers, eighteen men; 19and
Hashabiah, and with him Jeshaiah of
the sons of Merari, his brothers and their
sons, twenty men; 20also of the Nethi-
nim, whom David and the leaders had
appointed for the service of the Levites,
two hundred and twenty Nethinim. All of
them were designated by name.

Fasting and Prayer for Protection

21Then I proclaimed a fast there at the
river of Ahava, that we might humble
ourselves before our God, to seek from
Him the right way for us and our little
ones and all our possessions. 22For I
was ashamed to request of the king
an escort of soldiers and horsemen to
help us against the enemy on the road,
because we had spoken to the king, say-
ing, "The hand of our God *is* upon all
those for good who seek Him, but His
power and His wrath *are* against all
those who forsake Him." 23So we fasted
and entreated our God for this, and He
answered our prayer.

Gifts for the Temple

24And I separated twelve of the leaders
of the priests—Sherebiah, Hashabiah,
and ten of their brethren with them—
25and weighed out to them the silver,
the gold, and the articles, the offering
for the house of our God which the king
and his counselors and his princes, and
all Israel *who were* present, had offered.
26I weighed into their hand six hundred
and fifty talents of silver, silver articles

8:5 [a] Following Masoretic Text and Vulgate; Septuagint reads *the sons of Zatho, Shechaniah.*
8:10 [a] Following Masoretic Text and Vulgate; Septuagint reads *the sons of Banni, Shelomith.*
8:17 [a] Following Vulgate; Masoretic Text reads *to Iddo his brother;* Septuagint reads *to their brethren.*

weighing one hundred talents, one
hundred talents of gold, 27twenty gold
basins *worth* a thousand drachmas,
and two vessels of fine polished bronze,
precious as gold. 28And I said to them,
"You *are* holy to the LORD; the articles
are holy also; and the silver and the gold
are a freewill offering to the LORD God
of your fathers. 29Watch and keep *them*
until you weigh *them* before the leaders
of the priests and the Levites and heads
of the fathers' *houses* of Israel in Jeru-
salem, *in* the chambers of the house
of the LORD." 30So the priests and the
Levites received the silver and the gold
and the articles by weight, to bring *them*
to Jerusalem to the house of our God.

The Return to Jerusalem

31Then we departed from the river of
Ahava on the twelfth *day* of the first
month, to go to Jerusalem. And the
hand of our God was upon us, and He
delivered us from the hand of the ene-
my and from ambush along the road.
32So we came to Jerusalem, and stayed
there three days.

33Now on the fourth day the silver and
the gold and the articles were weighed
in the house of our God by the hand of
Meremoth the son of Uriah the priest,
and with him *was* Eleazar the son of
Phinehas; with them *were* the Levites,
Jozabad the son of Jeshua and Noadiah
the son of Binnui, 34with the number
and weight of everything. All the weight
was written down at that time.

35The children of those who had been
carried away captive, who had come
from the captivity, offered burnt offer-
ings to the God of Israel: twelve bulls
for all Israel, ninety-six rams, seventy-
seven lambs, and twelve male goats
as a sin offering. All *this was* a burnt
offering to the LORD.

36And they delivered the king's orders
to the king's satraps and the governors
in the region beyond the River. So they
gave support to the people and the
house of God.

Intermarriage with Pagans

9 When these things were done, the
leaders came to me, saying, "The
people of Israel and the priests and the
Levites have not separated themselves
from the peoples of the lands, with re-
spect to the abominations of the Ca-
naanites, the Hittites, the Perizzites, the
Jebusites, the Ammonites, the Moabites,
the Egyptians, and the Amorites. 2For
they have taken some of their daugh-
ters *as wives* for themselves and their
sons, so that the holy seed is mixed with
the peoples of *those* lands. Indeed, the
hand of the leaders and rulers has been
foremost in this trespass." 3So when
I heard this thing, I tore my garment
and my robe, and plucked out some of
the hair of my head and beard, and sat
down astonished. 4Then everyone who
trembled at the words of the God of Is-
rael assembled to me, because of the
transgression of those who had been
carried away captive, and I sat aston-
ished until the evening sacrifice.

5At the evening sacrifice I arose from
my fasting; and having torn my gar-
ment and my robe, I fell on my knees
and spread out my hands to the LORD
my God. 6And I said: "O my God, I am
too ashamed and humiliated to lift up
my face to You, my God; for our iniqui-
ties have risen higher than *our* heads,
and our guilt has grown up to the heav-
ens. 7Since the days of our fathers to
this day we *have been* very guilty, and
for our iniquities we, our kings, *and*
our priests have been delivered into
the hand of the kings of the lands, to
the sword, to captivity, to plunder, and
to humiliation, as *it is* this day. 8And
now for a little while grace has been
shown from the LORD our God, to leave
us a remnant to escape, and to give us
a peg in His holy place, that our God
may enlighten our eyes and give us
a measure of revival in our bondage.
9For we *were* slaves. Yet our God did
not forsake us in our bondage; but He
extended mercy to us in the sight of
the kings of Persia, to revive us, to re-
pair the house of our God, to rebuild
its ruins, and to give us a wall in Judah
and Jerusalem. 10And now, O our God,
what shall we say after this? For we have
forsaken Your commandments, 11which
You commanded by Your servants the
prophets, saying, 'The land which you
are entering to possess is an unclean

land, with the uncleanness of the peo-
ples of the lands, with their abomina-
tions which have filled it from one end
to another with their impurity. 12Now
therefore, do not give your daughters
as wives for their sons, nor take their
daughters to your sons; and never seek
their peace or prosperity, that you may
be strong and eat the good of the land,
and leave *it* as an inheritance to your
children forever.' 13And after all that
has come upon us for our evil deeds
and for our great guilt, since You our
God have punished us less than our in-
iquities *deserve,* and have given us *such*
deliverance as this, 14should we again
break Your commandments, and join
in marriage with the people *committing*
these abominations? Would You not be
angry with us until You had consumed
us, so that *there would be* no remnant
or survivor? 15O LORD God of Israel,
You *are* righteous, for we are left as a
remnant, as *it is* this day. Here we *are*
before You, in our guilt, though no one
can stand before You because of this!"

Confession of Improper Marriages

10 Now while Ezra was praying,
and while he was confessing,
weeping, and bowing down before the
house of God, a very large assembly of
men, women, and children gathered to
him from Israel; for the people wept
very bitterly. 2And Shechaniah the
son of Jehiel, *one* of the sons of Elam,
spoke up and said to Ezra, "We have
trespassed against our God, and have
taken pagan wives from the peoples
of the land; yet now there is hope in
Israel in spite of this. 3Now therefore,
let us make a covenant with our God to
put away all these wives and those who
have been born to them, according to
the advice of my master and of those
who tremble at the commandment of
our God; and let it be done according
to the law. 4Arise, for *this* matter *is* your
responsibility. We also *are* with you. Be
of good courage, and do *it.*"

5Then Ezra arose, and made the lead-
ers of the priests, the Levites, and all
Israel swear an oath that they would do
according to this word. So they swore
an oath. 6Then Ezra rose up from before
the house of God, and went into the
chamber of Jehohanan the son of Eli-
ashib; and *when* he came there, he ate
no bread and drank no water, for he
mourned because of the guilt of those
from the captivity.

7And they issued a proclamation
throughout Judah and Jerusalem to
all the descendants of the captivity, that
they must gather at Jerusalem, 8and
that whoever would not come within
three days, according to the instruc-
tions of the leaders and elders, all his
property would be confiscated, and he
himself would be separated from the
assembly of those from the captivity.

9So all the men of Judah and Ben-
jamin gathered at Jerusalem within
three days. It *was* the ninth month, on
the twentieth of the month; and all the
people sat in the open square of the
house of God, trembling because of
this matter and because of heavy rain.
10Then Ezra the priest stood up and
said to them, "You have transgressed
and have taken pagan wives, adding
to the guilt of Israel. 11Now therefore,
make confession to the LORD God of
your fathers, and do His will; separate
yourselves from the peoples of the land,
and from the pagan wives."

12Then all the assembly answered
and said with a loud voice, "Yes! As you
have said, so we must do. 13But *there are*
many people; *it is* the season for heavy
rain, and we are not able to stand out-
side. Nor *is this* the work of one or two
days, for *there are* many of us who have
transgressed in this matter. 14Please,
let the leaders of our entire assembly
stand; and let all those in our cities who
have taken pagan wives come at ap-
pointed times, together with the elders
and judges of their cities, until the fierce
wrath of our God is turned away from
us in this matter." 15Only Jonathan the
son of Asahel and Jahaziah the son of
Tikvah opposed this, and Meshullam
and Shabbethai the Levite gave them
support.

16Then the descendants of the cap-
tivity did so. And Ezra the priest, *with*
certain heads of the fathers' *households,*
were set apart by the fathers' house-
holds, each of them by name; and they

sat down on the first day of the tenth
month to examine the matter. 17By the
first day of the first month they finished
questioning all the men who had taken
pagan wives.

Pagan Wives Put Away

18And among the sons of the priests
who had taken pagan wives *the follow-*
ing were found of the sons of Jeshua
the son of Jozadak,[a] and his brothers:
Maaseiah, Eliezer, Jarib, and Gedaliah.
19And they gave their promise that they
would put away their wives; and *being*
guilty, *they presented* a ram of the flock
as their trespass offering.
20Also of the sons of Immer: Hanani
and Zebadiah; 21of the sons of Harim:
Maaseiah, Elijah, Shemaiah, Jehiel,
and Uzziah; 22of the sons of Pashhur:
Elioenai, Maaseiah, Ishmael, Nethanel,
Jozabad, and Elasah.
23Also of the Levites: Jozabad, Shimei,
Kelaiah (the same *is* Kelita), Pethahiah,
Judah, and Eliezer.
24Also of the singers: Eliashib; and
of the gatekeepers: Shallum, Telem,
and Uri.
25And others of Israel: of the sons
of Parosh: Ramiah, Jeziah, Malchiah,
Mijamin, Eleazar, Malchijah, and Bena-
iah; 26of the sons of Elam: Mattaniah,
Zechariah, Jehiel, Abdi, Jeremoth, and
Eliah; 27of the sons of Zattu: Elioenai, Eli-
ashib, Mattaniah, Jeremoth, Zabad, and
Aziza; 28of the sons of Bebai: Jehoha-
nan, Hananiah, Zabbai, *and* Athlai; 29of
the sons of Bani: Meshullam, Malluch,
Adaiah, Jashub, Sheal, *and* Ramoth;[a]
30of the sons of Pahath-Moab: Adna,
Chelal, Benaiah, Maaseiah, Mattaniah,
Bezalel, Binnui, and Manasseh; 31*of* the
sons of Harim: Eliezer, Ishijah, Malchi-
jah, Shemaiah, Shimeon, 32Benjamin,
Malluch, *and* Shemariah; 33of the sons
of Hashum: Mattenai, Mattattah, Zabad,
Eliphelet, Jeremai, Manasseh, *and* Shim-
ei; 34of the sons of Bani: Maadai, Amram,
Uel, 35Benaiah, Bedeiah, Cheluh,[a] 36Va-
niah, Meremoth, Eliashib, 37Mattani-
ah, Mattenai, Jaasai,[a] 38Bani, Binnui,
Shimei, 39Shelemiah, Nathan, Adaiah,
40Machnadebai, Shashai, Sharai, 41Az-
arel, Shelemiah, Shemariah, 42Shallum,
Amariah, *and* Joseph; 43of the sons of
Nebo: Jeiel, Mattithiah, Zabad, Zebina,
Jaddai,[a] Joel, *and* Benaiah.
44All these had taken pagan wives,
and *some* of them had wives *by whom*
they had children.

10:18 [a] Spelled *Jehozadak* in 1 Chronicles 6:14 **10:29** [a] Or *Jeremoth* **10:35** [a] Or *Cheluhi*, or *Cheluhu*
10:37 [a] Or *Jaasu* **10:43** [a] Or *Jaddu*

THE BOOK OF

NEHEMIAH

The Book of Nehemiah continues telling the history of the Israelites who returned to their homes from captivity in Babylon. When Nehemiah hears that Jerusalem's walls are still torn down, he asks the foreign king he serves if he can return to Jerusalem to repair them. The king agrees, and even provides materials for the project. Nehemiah then helps organize the people to rebuild the walls. Even though the neighboring nations try to stop the work, the Israelites finish building the walls in just fifty-two days. Jerusalem is protected from any enemies once again.

- **GENRE:** History
- **AUTHOR:** Nehemiah
- **TIME:** c. 444–425 BC
- **PURPOSE:** To record the history of God's people rebuilding the walls of Jerusalem showing that God was still providing for His people and protecting them.

Nehemiah Prays for His People

1 The words of Nehemiah the son of Hachaliah.

It came to pass in the month of Chislev, *in* the twentieth year, as I was in Shushan[a] the citadel, 2that Hanani one of my brethren came with men from Judah; and I asked them concerning the Jews who had escaped, who had survived the captivity, and concerning Jerusalem. 3And they said to me, "The survivors who are left from the captivity in the province *are* there in great distress and reproach. The wall of Jerusalem *is* also broken down, and its gates are burned with fire."

4So it was, when I heard these words, that I sat down and wept, and mourned *for many* days; I was fasting and praying before the God of heaven.

5And I said: "I pray, LORD God of heaven, O great and awesome God, *You* who keep *Your* covenant and mercy with those who love You[a] and observe Your[b] commandments, 6please let Your ear be attentive and Your eyes open, that You may hear the prayer of Your servant which I pray before You now, day and night, for the children of Israel Your servants, and confess the sins of the children of Israel which we have sinned against You. Both my father's house and I have sinned. 7We have acted very corruptly against You, and have not kept the commandments, the statutes, nor the ordinances which You commanded Your servant Moses. 8Remember, I pray, the word that You commanded Your servant Moses, saying, '*If* you are unfaithful, I will scatter you among the nations;[a] 9but *if* you return to Me, and keep My commandments and do them, though some of you were cast out to the farthest part of the heavens, *yet* I will gather them from there, and bring them to the place which I have chosen as a dwelling for My name.'[a] 10Now these *are* Your servants and Your people, whom You have redeemed by Your great power, and by Your strong hand. 11O Lord, I pray, please let Your ear be attentive to the prayer of Your servant, and to the prayer of Your servants who desire to fear Your name; and let Your servant prosper this day, I pray, and grant him mercy in the sight of this man."

For I was the king's cupbearer.

Nehemiah Sent to Judah

2 And it came to pass in the month of Nisan, in the twentieth year of King Artaxerxes, *when* wine *was* before him, that I took the wine and gave it to the king. Now I had never been sad

1:1 [a] Or *Susa* 1:5 [a] Literally *Him* [b] Literally *His* 1:8 [a] Leviticus 26:33 1:9 [a] Deuteronomy 30:2–5

GOD SIN JESUS SALVATION LOVE

in his presence before. 2Therefore the
king said to me, "Why *is* your face sad,
since you *are* not sick? This *is* nothing
but sorrow of heart."

So I became dreadfully afraid, 3and
said to the king, "May the king live
forever! Why should my face not be
sad, when the city, the place of my fathers' tombs, *lies* waste, and its gates
are burned with fire?"

4Then the king said to me, "What do
you request?"

So I prayed to the God of heaven. 5And
I said to the king, "If it pleases the king,
and if your servant has found favor in
your sight, I ask that you send me to
Judah, to the city of my fathers' tombs,
that I may rebuild it."

6Then the king said to me (the queen
also sitting beside him), "How long will
your journey be? And when will you
return?" So it pleased the king to send
me; and I set him a time.

7Furthermore I said to the king, "If it
pleases the king, let letters be given to
me for the governors *of the region* beyond the River,[a] that they must permit
me to pass through till I come to Judah,
8and a letter to Asaph the keeper of the
king's forest, that he must give me timber to make beams for the gates of the
citadel which *pertains* to the temple,[a] for
the city wall, and for the house that I will
occupy." And the king granted *them* to
me according to the good hand of my
God upon me.

9Then I went to the governors *in the region* beyond the River, and gave them
the king's letters. Now the king had sent
captains of the army and horsemen
with me. 10When Sanballat the Horonite and Tobiah the Ammonite official[a]
heard *of it*, they were deeply disturbed
that a man had come to seek the well-being of the children of Israel.

Nehemiah Views the Wall of Jerusalem

11So I came to Jerusalem and was there
three days. 12Then I arose in the night,
I and a few men with me; I told no one
what my God had put in my heart to do
at Jerusalem; nor was there any animal
with me, except the one on which I rode.
13And I went out by night through the
Valley Gate to the Serpent Well and the
Refuse Gate, and viewed the walls of Jerusalem which were broken down and
its gates which were burned with fire.
14Then I went on to the Fountain Gate
and to the King's Pool, but *there was* no
room for the animal under me to pass.
15So I went up in the night by the valley,
and viewed the wall; then I turned back
and entered by the Valley Gate, and so
returned. 16And the officials did not
know where I had gone or what I had
done; I had not yet told the Jews, the
priests, the nobles, the officials, or the
others who did the work.

17Then I said to them, "You see the
distress that we *are* in, how Jerusalem
lies waste, and its gates are burned with
fire. Come and let us build the wall of
Jerusalem, that we may no longer be
a reproach." 18And I told them of the
hand of my God which had been good
upon me, and also of the king's words
that he had spoken to me.

So they said, "Let us rise up and build."
Then they set their hands to *this* good
work.

19But when Sanballat the Horonite,
Tobiah the Ammonite official, and Geshem the Arab heard *of it*, they laughed
at us and despised us, and said, "What
is this thing that you are doing? Will
you rebel against the king?"

20So I answered them, and said to
them, "The God of heaven Himself will
prosper us; therefore we His servants
will arise and build, but you have no
heritage or right or memorial in Jerusalem."

Rebuilding the Wall

3 Then Eliashib the high priest rose
up with his brethren the priests and
built the Sheep Gate; they consecrated
it and hung its doors. They built as far
as the Tower of the Hundred,[a] *and* consecrated it, then as far as the Tower of
Hananel. 2Next to *Eliashib*[a] the men of
Jericho built. And next to them Zaccur
the son of Imri built.

2:7 [a] That is, the Euphrates, and so elsewhere in this book 2:8 [a] Literally *house* 2:10 [a] Literally *servant*, and so elsewhere in this book 3:1 [a] Hebrew *Hammeah*, also at 12:39 3:2 [a] Literally *On his hand*

3Also the sons of Hassenaah built the
Fish Gate; they laid its beams and hung
its doors with its bolts and bars. 4And
next to them Meremoth the son of Urijah,
the son of Koz,[a] made repairs. Next to
them Meshullam the son of Berechiah,
the son of Meshezabel, made repairs.
Next to them Zadok the son of Baana
made repairs. 5Next to them the Tekoites
made repairs; but their nobles did not put
their shoulders[a] to the work of their Lord.

6Moreover Jehoiada the son of Paseah
and Meshullam the son of Besodeiah re-
paired the Old Gate; they laid its beams
and hung its doors, with its bolts and
bars. 7And next to them Melatiah the
Gibeonite, Jadon the Meronothite, the
men of Gibeon and Mizpah, repaired
the residence[a] of the governor *of the
region* beyond the River. 8Next to him
Uzziel the son of Harhaiah, one of the
goldsmiths, made repairs. Also next to
him Hananiah, one[a] of the perfumers,
made repairs; and they fortified Jerusa-
lem as far as the Broad Wall. 9And next
to them Rephaiah the son of Hur, leader
of half the district of Jerusalem, made
repairs. 10Next to them Jedaiah the son
of Harumaph made repairs in front of
his house. And next to him Hattush the
son of Hashabniah made repairs.

11Malchijah the son of Harim and
Hashub the son of Pahath-Moab re-
paired another section, as well as the
Tower of the Ovens. 12And next to him
was Shallum the son of Hallohesh, lead-
er of half the district of Jerusalem; he
and his daughters made repairs.

13Hanun and the inhabitants of Zano-
ah repaired the Valley Gate. They built
it, hung its doors with its bolts and bars,
and *repaired* a thousand cubits of the
wall as far as the Refuse Gate.

14Malchijah the son of Rechab, leader
of the district of Beth Haccerem, re-
paired the Refuse Gate; he built it and
hung its doors with its bolts and bars.

15Shallun the son of Col-Hozeh, leader
of the district of Mizpah, repaired the
Fountain Gate; he built it, covered it,
hung its doors with its bolts and bars, and
repaired the wall of the Pool of Shelah by
the King's Garden, as far as the stairs that
go down from the City of David. 16After
him Nehemiah the son of Azbuk, lead-
er of half the district of Beth Zur, made
repairs as far as *the place* in front of the
tombs[a] of David, to the man-made pool,
and as far as the House of the Mighty.

17After him the Levites, *under* Rehum
the son of Bani, made repairs. Next
to him Hashabiah, leader of half the
district of Keilah, made repairs for his
district. 18After him their brethren, *under*
Bavai[a] the son of Henadad, leader of the
other half of the district of Keilah, made
repairs. 19And next to him Ezer the son
of Jeshua, the leader of Mizpah, repaired
another section in front of the Ascent
to the Armory at the buttress. 20After
him Baruch the son of Zabbai[a] care-
fully repaired the other section, from
the buttress to the door of the house
of Eliashib the high priest. 21After him
Meremoth the son of Urijah, the son of
Koz,[a] repaired another section, from the
door of the house of Eliashib to the end
of the house of Eliashib.

22And after him the priests, the men
of the plain, made repairs. 23After him
Benjamin and Hasshub made repairs
opposite their house. After them Aza-
riah the son of Maaseiah, the son of
Ananiah, made repairs by his house.
24After him Binnui the son of Hena-
dad repaired another section, from the
house of Azariah to the buttress, even
as far as the corner. 25Palal the son of
Uzai *made repairs* opposite the buttress,
and on the tower which projects from
the king's upper house that *was* by the
court of the prison. After him Pedaiah
the son of Parosh *made repairs.*
26Moreover the Nethinim who dwelt in
Ophel *made repairs* as far as *the place* in
front of the Water Gate toward the east,
and on the projecting tower. 27After
them the Tekoites repaired another
section, next to the great projecting
tower, and as far as the wall of Ophel.

28Beyond the Horse Gate the priests
made repairs, each in front of his *own*

3:4 [a] Or *Hakkoz* **3:5** [a] Literally *necks* **3:7** [a] Literally *throne* **3:8** [a] Literally *the son*
3:16 [a] Septuagint, Syriac, and Vulgate read *tomb.* **3:18** [a] Following Masoretic Text and Vulgate; some Hebrew manuscripts, Septuagint, and Syriac read *Binnui* (compare verse 24). **3:20** [a] A few Hebrew manuscripts, Syriac, and Vulgate read *Zaccai.* **3:21** [a] Or *Hakkoz*

house. 29After them Zadok the son of
Immer made repairs in front of his *own*
house. After him Shemaiah the son of
Shechaniah, the keeper of the East Gate,
made repairs. 30After him Hananiah the
son of Shelemiah, and Hanun, the sixth
son of Zalaph, repaired another section.
After him Meshullam the son of Berechi-
ah made repairs in front of his dwelling.
31After him Malchijah, one of the gold-
smiths, made repairs as far as the house
of the Nethinim and of the merchants,
in front of the Miphkad[a] Gate, and as far
as the upper room at the corner. 32And
between the upper room at the corner,
as far as the Sheep Gate, the goldsmiths
and the merchants made repairs.

The Wall Defended Against Enemies

4 But it so happened, when Sanbal-
lat heard that we were rebuilding
the wall, that he was furious and very
indignant, and mocked the Jews. 2And
he spoke before his brethren and the
army of Samaria, and said, "What are
these feeble Jews doing? Will they for-
tify themselves? Will they offer sacrific-
es? Will they complete it in a day? Will
they revive the stones from the heaps
of rubbish—*stones* that are burned?"
3Now Tobiah the Ammonite *was* beside
him, and he said, "Whatever they build,
if even a fox goes up *on it,* he will break
down their stone wall."
4Hear, O our God, for we are despised;
turn their reproach on their own heads,
and give them as plunder to a land of
captivity! 5Do not cover their iniquity,
and do not let their sin be blotted out
from before You; for they have provoked
You to anger before the builders.
6So we built the wall, and the entire wall
was joined together up to half its *height,*
for the people had a mind to work.
7Now it happened, when Sanballat,
Tobiah, the Arabs, the Ammonites, and
the Ashdodites heard that the walls of
Jerusalem were being restored and the
gaps were beginning to be closed, that
they became very angry, 8and all of
them conspired together to come *and*
attack Jerusalem and create confusion.
9Nevertheless we made our prayer to
our God, and because of them we set
a watch against them day and night.
10Then Judah said, "The strength of
the laborers is failing, and *there is* so
much rubbish that we are not able to
build the wall."
11And our adversaries said, "They will
neither know nor see anything, till we
come into their midst and kill them and
cause the work to cease."
12So it was, when the Jews who dwelt
near them came, that they told us ten
times, "From whatever place you turn,
they will be upon us."
13Therefore I positioned *men* behind
the lower parts of the wall, at the open-
ings; and I set the people according to
their families, with their swords, their
spears, and their bows. 14And I looked,
and arose and said to the nobles, to the
leaders, and to the rest of the people, "Do
not be afraid of them. Remember the
Lord, great and awesome, and fight for
your brethren, your sons, your daugh-
ters, your wives, and your houses."
15And it happened, when our enemies
heard that it was known to us, and *that*
God had brought their plot to nothing,
that all of us returned to the wall, every-
one to his work. 16So it was, from that
time on, *that* half of my servants worked
at construction, while the other half held
the spears, the shields, the bows, and
wore armor; and the leaders *were* behind
all the house of Judah. 17Those who built
on the wall, and those who carried bur-
dens, loaded themselves so that with one
hand they worked at construction, and
with the other held a weapon. 18Every
one of the builders had his sword girded
at his side as he built. And the one who
sounded the trumpet *was* beside me.
19Then I said to the nobles, the rulers,
and the rest of the people, "The work *is*
great and extensive, and we are sepa-
rated far from one another on the wall.
20Wherever you hear the sound of the
trumpet, rally to us there. Our God will
fight for us."
21So we labored in the work, and half
of *the men*[a] held the spears from day-
break until the stars appeared. 22At
the same time I also said to the people,

3:31 [a] Literally *Inspection* or *Recruiting* **4:21** [a] Literally *them*

"Let each man and his servant stay at night in Jerusalem, that they may be our guard by night and a working party by day." 23So neither I, my brethren, my servants, nor the men of the guard who followed me took off our clothes, *except* that everyone took them off for washing.

Nehemiah Deals with Oppression

5 And there was a great outcry of the people and their wives against their Jewish brethren. 2For there were those who said, "We, our sons, and our daughters *are* many; therefore let us get grain, that we may eat and live."

3There were also *some* who said, "We have mortgaged our lands and vineyards and houses, that we might buy grain because of the famine."

4There were also those who said, "We have borrowed money for the king's tax *on* our lands and vineyards. 5Yet now our flesh *is* as the flesh of our brethren, our children as their children; and indeed we are forcing our sons and our daughters to be slaves, and *some* of our daughters have been brought into slavery. *It is* not in our power *to redeem them,* for other men have our lands and vineyards."

6And I became very angry when I heard their outcry and these words. 7After serious thought, I rebuked the nobles and rulers, and said to them, "Each of you is exacting usury from his brother." So I called a great assembly against them. 8And I said to them, "According to our ability we have redeemed our Jewish brethren who were sold to the nations. Now indeed, will you even sell your brethren? Or should they be sold to us?"

Then they were silenced and found nothing *to say.* 9Then I said, "What you are doing *is* not good. Should you not walk in the fear of our God because of the reproach of the nations, our enemies? 10I also, *with* my brethren and my servants, am lending them money and grain. Please, let us stop this usury! 11Restore now to them, even this day, their lands, their vineyards, their olive groves, and their houses, also a hundredth of the money and the grain, the new wine and the oil, that you have charged them."

12So they said, "We will restore *it,* and will require nothing from them; we will do as you say."

Then I called the priests, and required an oath from them that they would do according to this promise. 13Then I shook out the fold of my garment[a] and said, "So may God shake out each man from his house, and from his property, who does not perform this promise. Even thus may he be shaken out and emptied."

And all the assembly said, "Amen!" and praised the LORD. Then the people did according to this promise.

The Generosity of Nehemiah

14Moreover, from the time that I was appointed to be their governor in the land of Judah, from the twentieth year until the thirty-second year of King Artaxerxes, twelve years, neither I nor my brothers ate the governor's provisions. 15But the former governors who *were* before me laid burdens on the people, and took from them bread and wine, besides forty shekels of silver. Yes, even their servants bore rule over the people, but I did not do so, because of the fear of God. 16Indeed, I also continued the work on this wall, and we[a] did not buy any land. All my servants *were* gathered there for the work.

17And at my table *were* one hundred and fifty Jews and rulers, besides those who came to us from the nations around us. 18Now *that* which was prepared daily *was* one ox *and* six choice sheep. Also fowl were prepared for me, and once every ten days an abundance of all kinds of wine. Yet in spite of this I did not demand the governor's provisions, because the bondage was heavy on this people.

19Remember me, my God, for good, *according to* all that I have done for this people.

Conspiracy Against Nehemiah

6 Now it happened when Sanballat, Tobiah, Geshem the Arab, and the rest of our enemies heard that I had rebuilt the wall, and *that* there were no

5:13 [a] Literally *my lap* 5:16 [a] Following Masoretic Text; Septuagint, Syriac, and Vulgate read *I.*

breaks left in it (though at that time I
had not hung the doors in the gates),
2that Sanballat and Geshem sent to
me, saying, "Come, let us meet together
among the villages in the plain of Ono."
But they thought to do me harm.
3So I sent messengers to them, saying,
"I *am* doing a great work, so that I cannot
come down. Why should the work cease
while I leave it and go down to you?"
4But they sent me this message four
times, and I answered them in the same
manner.
5Then Sanballat sent his servant to me
as before, the fifth time, with an open
letter in his hand. 6In it *was* written:

> It is reported among the nations,
> and Geshem[a] says, *that* you and
> the Jews plan to rebel; therefore,
> according to these rumors, you are
> rebuilding the wall, that you may
> be their king. 7And you have also
> appointed prophets to proclaim
> concerning you at Jerusalem,
> saying, "*There is* a king in Judah!"
> Now these matters will be reported
> to the king. So come, therefore,
> and let us consult together.

8Then I sent to him, saying, "No such
things as you say are being done, but
you invent them in your own heart."
9For they all *were trying to* make us
afraid, saying, "Their hands will be weak-
ened in the work, and it will not be done."
Now therefore, *O God,* strengthen my
hands.
10Afterward I came to the house of
Shemaiah the son of Delaiah, the son of
Mehetabel, who *was* a secret informer;
and he said, "Let us meet together in the
house of God, within the temple, and
let us close the doors of the temple, for
they are coming to kill you; indeed, at
night they will come to kill you."
11And I said, "Should such a man as
I flee? And who *is there* such as I who
would go into the temple to save his life?
I will not go in!" 12Then I perceived that
God had not sent him at all, but that
he pronounced *this* prophecy against
me because Tobiah and Sanballat had
hired him. 13For this reason he *was*
hired, that I should be afraid and act
that way and sin, so *that* they might
have *cause* for an evil report, that they
might reproach me.
14My God, remember Tobiah and San-
ballat, according to these their works,
and the prophetess Noadiah and the
rest of the prophets who would have
made me afraid.

The Wall Completed

15So the wall was finished on the
twenty-fifth *day* of Elul, in fifty-two
days. 16And it happened, when all our
enemies heard *of it,* and all the nations
around us saw *these things,* that they
were very disheartened in their own
eyes; for they perceived that this work
was done by our God.
17Also in those days the nobles of
Judah sent many letters to Tobiah,
and *the letters of* Tobiah came to them.
18For many in Judah were pledged to
him, because he was the son-in-law of
Shechaniah the son of Arah, and his son
Jehohanan had married the daughter
of Meshullam the son of Berechiah.
19Also they reported his good deeds
before me, and reported my words to
him. Tobiah sent letters to frighten me.
7 Then it was, when the wall was built
and I had hung the doors, when the
gatekeepers, the singers, and the Le-
vites had been appointed, 2that I gave
the charge of Jerusalem to my brother
Hanani, and Hananiah the leader of the
citadel, for he *was* a faithful man and
feared God more than many.
3And I said to them, "Do not let the
gates of Jerusalem be opened until
the sun is hot; and while they stand
guard, let them shut and bar the doors;
and appoint guards from among the
inhabitants of Jerusalem, one at his
watch station and another in front of
his own house."

The Captives Who Returned to Jerusalem

4Now the city *was* large and spacious,
but the people in it *were* few, and the
houses *were* not rebuilt. 5Then my God

6:6 [a] Hebrew *Gashmu*

put it into my heart to gather the nobles, the rulers, and the people, that they might be registered by genealogy. And I found a register of the genealogy of those who had come up in the first *return,* and found written in it:

6 These[a] *are* the people of the province who came back from the captivity, of those who had been carried away, whom Nebuchadnezzar the king of Babylon had carried away, and who returned to Jerusalem and Judah, everyone to his city.

7 Those who came with Zerubbabel *were* Jeshua, Nehemiah, Azariah, Raamiah, Nahamani, Mordecai, Bilshan, Mispereth,[a] Bigvai, Nehum, and Baanah.

The number of the men of the
people of Israel: 8the sons of Pa-
rosh, two thousand one hundred and seventy-two;
9the sons of Shephatiah, three hundred and seventy-two;
10the sons of Arah, six hundred and fifty-two;
11the sons of Pahath-Moab, of the sons of Jeshua and Joab, two thousand eight hundred and eighteen;
12the sons of Elam, one thousand two hundred and fifty-four;
13the sons of Zattu, eight hundred and forty-five;
14the sons of Zaccai, seven hundred and sixty;
15the sons of Binnui,[a] six hundred and forty-eight;
16the sons of Bebai, six hundred and twenty-eight;
17the sons of Azgad, two thousand three hundred and twenty-two;
18the sons of Adonikam, six hundred and sixty-seven;
19the sons of Bigvai, two thousand and sixty-seven;
20the sons of Adin, six hundred and fifty-five;
21the sons of Ater of Hezekiah, ninety-eight;
22the sons of Hashum, three hundred and twenty-eight;
23the sons of Bezai, three hundred and twenty-four;
24the sons of Hariph,[a] one hundred and twelve;
25the sons of Gibeon,[a] ninety-five;
26the men of Bethlehem and Netophah, one hundred and eighty-eight;
27the men of Anathoth, one hundred and twenty-eight;
28the men of Beth Azmaveth,[a] forty-two;
29the men of Kirjath Jearim, Chephirah, and Beeroth, seven hundred and forty-three;
30the men of Ramah and Geba, six hundred and twenty-one;
31the men of Michmas, one hundred and twenty-two;
32the men of Bethel and Ai, one hundred and twenty-three;
33the men of the other Nebo, fifty-two;
34the sons of the other Elam, one thousand two hundred and fifty-four;
35the sons of Harim, three hundred and twenty;
36the sons of Jericho, three hundred and forty-five;
37the sons of Lod, Hadid, and Ono, seven hundred and twenty-one;
38the sons of Senaah, three thousand nine hundred and thirty.

39 The priests: the sons of Jedaiah, of the house of Jeshua, nine hundred and seventy-three;
40the sons of Immer, one thousand and fifty-two;
41the sons of Pashhur, one thousand two hundred and forty-seven;
42the sons of Harim, one thousand and seventeen.

7:6 [a] Compare verses 6–72 with Ezra 2:1–70 7:7 [a] Spelled *Mispar* in Ezra 2:2 7:15 [a] Spelled *Bani* in Ezra 2:10 7:24 [a] Called *Jorah* in Ezra 2:18 7:25 [a] Called *Gibbar* in Ezra 2:20 7:28 [a] Called *Azmaveth* in Ezra 2:24

43 The Levites: the sons of Jeshua, of
Kadmiel,
and of the sons of Hodevah,[a]
seventy-four.

44 The singers: the sons of Asaph,
one hundred and forty-eight.

45 The gatekeepers: the sons of Shallum,
the sons of Ater,
the sons of Talmon,
the sons of Akkub,
the sons of Hatita,
the sons of Shobai, one hundred
and thirty-eight.

46 The Nethinim: the sons of
Ziha,
the sons of Hasupha,
the sons of Tabbaoth,
47the sons of Keros,
the sons of Sia,[a]
the sons of Padon,
48the sons of Lebana,[a]
the sons of Hagaba,[b]
the sons of Salmai,[c]
49the sons of Hanan,
the sons of Giddel,
the sons of Gahar,
50the sons of Reaiah,
the sons of Rezin,
the sons of Nekoda,
51the sons of Gazzam,
the sons of Uzza,
the sons of Paseah,
52the sons of Besai,
the sons of Meunim,
the sons of Nephishesim,[a]
53the sons of Bakbuk,
the sons of Hakupha,
the sons of Harhur,
54the sons of Bazlith,[a]
the sons of Mehida,
the sons of Harsha,
55the sons of Barkos,
the sons of Sisera,
the sons of Tamah,
56the sons of Neziah,
and the sons of Hatipha.

57 The sons of Solomon's servants:
the sons of Sotai,
the sons of Sophereth,
the sons of Perida,[a]
58the sons of Jaala,
the sons of Darkon,
the sons of Giddel,
59the sons of Shephatiah,
the sons of Hattil,
the sons of Pochereth of Zebaim,
and the sons of Amon.[a]
60All the Nethinim, and the sons
of Solomon's servants, *were* three
hundred and ninety-two.

61 And these *were* the ones who
came up from Tel Melah, Tel Harsha, Cherub, Addon,[a] and Immer,
but they could not identify their
father's house nor their lineage,
whether they *were* of Israel: 62the
sons of Delaiah,
the sons of Tobiah,
the sons of Nekoda, six hundred
and forty-two;
63and of the priests: the sons of
Habaiah,
the sons of Koz,[a]
the sons of Barzillai, who took a
wife of the daughters of Barzillai
the Gileadite, and was called by
their name.
64These sought their listing *among*
those who were registered by
genealogy, but it was not found;
therefore they were excluded from
the priesthood as defiled. 65And the
governor[a] said to them that they
should not eat of the most holy
things till a priest could consult
with the Urim and Thummim.

66 Altogether the whole assembly
was forty-two thousand three
hundred and sixty, 67besides their
male and female servants, of
whom *there were* seven thousand
three hundred and thirty-seven;
and they had two hundred and
forty-five men and women singers.

7:43 [a] Spelled *Hodaviah* in Ezra 2:40 **7:47** [a] Spelled *Siaha* in Ezra 2:44 **7:48** [a] Masoretic Text reads *Lebanah.* [b] Masoretic Text reads *Hogabah.* [c] Or *Shalmai,* or *Shamlai* **7:52** [a] Spelled *Nephusim* in Ezra 2:50 **7:54** [a] Spelled *Bazluth* in Ezra 2:52 **7:57** [a] Spelled *Peruda* in Ezra 2:55 **7:59** [a] Spelled *Ami* in Ezra 2:57 **7:61** [a] Spelled *Addan* in Ezra 2:59 **7:63** [a] Or *Hakkoz* **7:65** [a] Hebrew *Tirshatha*

68Their horses were seven hundred
and thirty-six, their mules two
hundred and forty-five, 69*their*
camels four hundred and thirty-
five, *and* donkeys six thousand
seven hundred and twenty.

70 And some of the heads of the
fathers' *houses* gave to the
work. The governor[a] gave to
the treasury one thousand gold
drachmas, fifty basins, and five
hundred and thirty priestly
garments. 71Some of the heads
of the fathers' *houses* gave to
the treasury of the work twenty
thousand gold drachmas, and
two thousand two hundred silver
minas. 72And that which the rest
of the people gave *was* twenty
thousand gold drachmas, two
thousand silver minas, and sixty-
seven priestly garments.

73So the priests, the Levites, the gate-
keepers, the singers, *some* of the people,
the Nethinim, and all Israel dwelt in
their cities.

Ezra Reads the Law

When the seventh month came, the
children of Israel *were* in their cities.

8 Now all the people gathered togeth-
er as one man in the open square
that *was* in front of the Water Gate; and
they told Ezra the scribe to bring the
Book of the Law of Moses, which the
LORD had commanded Israel. 2So Ezra
the priest brought the Law before the
assembly of men and women and all
who *could* hear with understanding
on the first day of the seventh month.
3Then he read from it in the open square
that *was* in front of the Water Gate from
morning until midday, before the men
and women and those who could under-
stand; and the ears of all the people
were attentive to the Book of the Law.

4So Ezra the scribe stood on a platform
of wood which they had made for the
purpose; and beside him, at his right
hand, stood Mattithiah, Shema, Anaiah,
Urijah, Hilkiah, and Maaseiah; and at
his left hand Pedaiah, Mishael, Malchi-
jah, Hashum, Hashbadana, Zechariah,
and Meshullam. 5And Ezra opened the
book in the sight of all the people, for
he was *standing* above all the people;
and when he opened it, all the people
stood up. 6And Ezra blessed the LORD,
the great God.

Then all the people answered, "Amen,
Amen!" while lifting up their hands. And
they bowed their heads and worshiped
the LORD with *their* faces to the ground.

7Also Jeshua, Bani, Sherebiah, Jamin,
Akkub, Shabbethai, Hodijah, Maaseiah,
Kelita, Azariah, Jozabad, Hanan, Pela-
iah, and the Levites, helped the people
to understand the Law; and the people
stood in their place. 8So they read dis-
tinctly from the book, in the Law of God;
and they gave the sense, and helped
them to understand the reading.

9And Nehemiah, who *was* the gover-
nor,[a] Ezra the priest *and* scribe, and the
Levites who taught the people said to all
the people, "This day *is* holy to the LORD
your God; do not mourn nor weep." For
all the people wept, when they heard
the words of the Law.

10Then he said to them, "Go your way,
eat the fat, drink the sweet, and send
portions to those for whom nothing
is prepared; for *this* day *is* holy to our
Lord. Do not sorrow, for the joy of the
LORD is your strength."

11So the Levites quieted all the people,
saying, "Be still, for the day *is* holy; do
not be grieved." 12And all the people
went their way to eat and drink, to send
portions and rejoice greatly, because
they understood the words that were
declared to them.

The Feast of Tabernacles

13Now on the second day the heads of
the fathers' *houses* of all the people, with
the priests and Levites, were gathered to
Ezra the scribe, in order to understand
the words of the Law. 14And they found
written in the Law, which the LORD had
commanded by Moses, that the chil-
dren of Israel should dwell in booths
during the feast of the seventh month,
15and that they should announce and

7:70 [a] Hebrew *Tirshatha* **8:9** [a] Hebrew *Tirshatha* proclaim in all their cities and in Jerusalem, saying, "Go out to the mountain, and bring olive branches, branches of oil trees, myrtle branches, palm branches, and branches of leafy trees, to make booths, as *it is* written."

16Then the people went out and brought *them* and made themselves booths, each one on the roof of his house, or in their courtyards or the courts of the house of God, and in the open square of the Water Gate and in the open square of the Gate of Ephraim. 17So the whole assembly of those who had returned from the captivity made booths and sat under the booths; for since the days of Joshua the son of Nun until that day the children of Israel had not done so. And there was very great gladness. 18Also day by day, from the first day until the last day, he read from the Book of the Law of God. And they kept the feast seven days; and on the eighth day *there was* a sacred assembly, according to the *prescribed* manner.

The People Confess Their Sins

9 Now on the twenty-fourth day of this month the children of Israel were assembled with fasting, in sackcloth, and with dust on their heads.[a] 2Then those of Israelite lineage separated themselves from all foreigners; and they stood and confessed their sins and the iniquities of their fathers. 3And they stood up in their place and read from the Book of the Law of the LORD their God *for one*-fourth of the day; and *for another* fourth they confessed and worshiped the LORD their God.

4Then Jeshua, Bani, Kadmiel, Shebaniah, Bunni, Sherebiah, Bani, *and* Chenani stood on the stairs of the Levites and cried out with a loud voice to the LORD their God. 5And the Levites, Jeshua, Kadmiel, Bani, Hashabniah, Sherebiah, Hodijah, Shebaniah, *and* Pethahiah, said:

"Stand up *and* bless the LORD your God
Forever and ever!

"Blessed be Your glorious name,
Which is exalted above all blessing and praise!
6 You alone *are* the LORD;
You have made heaven,
The heaven of heavens, with all their host,
The earth and everything on it,
The seas and all that is in them,
And You preserve them all.
The host of heaven worships You.

7 "You *are* the LORD God,
Who chose Abram,
And brought him out of Ur of the Chaldeans,
And gave him the name Abraham;
8 You found his heart faithful before You,
And made a covenant with him
To give the land of the Canaanites,
The Hittites, the Amorites,
The Perizzites, the Jebusites,
And the Girgashites—
To give *it* to his descendants.
You have performed Your words,
For You *are* righteous.

9 "You saw the affliction of our fathers in Egypt,
And heard their cry by the Red Sea.
10 You showed signs and wonders against Pharaoh,
Against all his servants,
And against all the people of his land.
For You knew that they acted proudly against them.
So You made a name for Yourself, as *it is* this day.
11 And You divided the sea before them,
So that they went through the midst of the sea on the dry land;
And their persecutors You threw into the deep,
As a stone into the mighty waters.
12 Moreover You led them by day with a cloudy pillar,

9:1 [a] Literally *earth on them*

And by night with a pillar of fire,
To give them light on the road
Which they should travel.

13 "You came down also on Mount
Sinai,
And spoke with them from heaven,
And gave them just ordinances
and true laws,
Good statutes and commandments.
14 You made known to them Your
holy Sabbath,
And commanded them precepts,
statutes and laws,
By the hand of Moses Your servant.
15 You gave them bread from
heaven for their hunger,
And brought them water out of
the rock for their thirst,
And told them to go in to possess
the land
Which You had sworn to give
them.

16 "But they and our fathers acted
proudly,
Hardened their necks,
And did not heed Your
commandments.
17 They refused to obey,
And they were not mindful of
Your wonders
That You did among them.
But they hardened their necks,
And in their rebellion[a]
They appointed a leader
To return to their bondage.
But You *are* God,
Ready to pardon,
Gracious and merciful,
Slow to anger,
Abundant in kindness,
And did not forsake them.

18 "Even when they made a molded
calf for themselves,
And said, 'This *is* your god
That brought you up out of Egypt,'
And worked great provocations,
19 Yet in Your manifold mercies
You did not forsake them in the
wilderness.
The pillar of the cloud did not
depart from them by day,
To lead them on the road;
Nor the pillar of fire by night,
To show them light,
And the way they should go.
20 You also gave Your good Spirit to
instruct them,
And did not withhold Your manna
from their mouth,
And gave them water for their
thirst.
21 Forty years You sustained them
in the wilderness;
They lacked nothing;
Their clothes did not wear out[a]
And their feet did not swell.

22 "Moreover You gave them
kingdoms and nations,
And divided them into districts.[a]
So they took possession of the
land of Sihon,
The land of[b] the king of Heshbon,
And the land of Og king of
Bashan.
23 You also multiplied their children
as the stars of heaven,
And brought them into the land
Which You had told their fathers
To go in and possess.
24 So the people went in
And possessed the land;
You subdued before them the
inhabitants of the land,
The Canaanites,
And gave them into their hands,
With their kings
And the people of the land,
That they might do with them as
they wished.
25 And they took strong cities and a
rich land,
And possessed houses full of all
goods,
Cisterns *already* dug, vineyards,
olive groves,
And fruit trees in abundance.
So they ate and were filled and
grew fat,
And delighted themselves in Your
great goodness.

9:17 [a] Following Masoretic Text and Vulgate; Septuagint reads *in Egypt.* **9:21** [a] Compare Deuteronomy 29:5 **9:22** [a] Literally *corners* [b] Following Masoretic Text and Vulgate; Septuagint omits *The land of.*

26 "Nevertheless they were
disobedient
And rebelled against You,
Cast Your law behind their backs
And killed Your prophets, who
testified against them
To turn them to Yourself;
And they worked great
provocations.
27 Therefore You delivered them into
the hand of their enemies,
Who oppressed them;
And in the time of their trouble,
When they cried to You,
You heard from heaven;
And according to Your abundant
mercies
You gave them deliverers who
saved them
From the hand of their enemies.

28 "But after they had rest,
They again did evil before You.
Therefore You left them in the
hand of their enemies,
So that they had dominion over
them;
Yet when they returned and cried
out to You,
You heard from heaven;
And many times You delivered them
according to Your mercies,
29 And testified against them,
That You might bring them back
to Your law.
Yet they acted proudly,
And did not heed Your
commandments,
But sinned against Your judgments,
'Which if a man does, he shall live
by them.'[a]
And they shrugged their
shoulders,
Stiffened their necks,
And would not hear.
30 Yet for many years You had
patience with them,
And testified against them by
Your Spirit in Your prophets.
Yet they would not listen;
Therefore You gave them into the
hand of the peoples of the
lands.
31 Nevertheless in Your great mercy
You did not utterly consume them
nor forsake them;
For You *are* God, gracious and
merciful.

32 "Now therefore, our God,
The great, the mighty, and
awesome God,
Who keeps covenant and mercy:
Do not let all the trouble seem
small before You
That has come upon us,
Our kings and our princes,
Our priests and our prophets,
Our fathers and on all Your
people,
From the days of the kings of
Assyria until this day.
33 However You *are* just in all that
has befallen us;
For You have dealt faithfully,
But we have done wickedly.
34 Neither our kings nor our
princes,
Our priests nor our fathers,
Have kept Your law,
Nor heeded Your commandments
and Your testimonies,
With which You testified against
them.
35 For they have not served You in
their kingdom,
Or in the many good *things* that
You gave them,
Or in the large and rich land
which You set before them;
Nor did they turn from their
wicked works.

36 "Here we *are*, servants today!
And the land that You gave to our
fathers,
To eat its fruit and its bounty,
Here we *are*, servants in it!
37 And it yields much increase to the
kings
You have set over us,
Because of our sins;
Also they have dominion over our
bodies and our cattle
At their pleasure;
And we *are* in great distress.

9:29 [a] Leviticus 18:5

38 "And because of all this,
We make a sure *covenant* and
write *it;*
Our leaders, our Levites, *and* our
priests seal *it.*"

The People Who Sealed the Covenant

10 Now those who placed *their* seal
on *the document were:*
Nehemiah the governor, the son of
Hacaliah, and Zedekiah, 2Seraiah,
Azariah, Jeremiah, 3Pashhur, Amari-
ah, Malchijah, 4Hattush, Shebaniah,
Malluch, 5Harim, Meremoth, Obadiah,
6Daniel, Ginnethon, Baruch, 7Meshul-
lam, Abijah, Mijamin, 8Maaziah, Bilgai,
and Shemaiah. These *were* the priests.
9The Levites: Jeshua the son of Aza-
niah, Binnui of the sons of Henadad,
and Kadmiel.
10Their brethren: Shebaniah, Hodijah,
Kelita, Pelaiah, Hanan, 11Micha, Rehob,
Hashabiah, 12Zaccur, Sherebiah, Sheb-
aniah, 13Hodijah, Bani, *and* Beninu.
14The leaders of the people: Parosh, Pa-
hath-Moab, Elam, Zattu, Bani, 15Bunni,
Azgad, Bebai, 16Adonijah, Bigvai, Adin,
17Ater, Hezekiah, Azzur, 18Hodijah, Ha-
shum, Bezai, 19Hariph, Anathoth, Nebai,
20Magpiash, Meshullam, Hezir, 21Me-
shezabel, Zadok, Jaddua, 22Pelatiah,
Hanan, Anaiah, 23Hoshea, Hanani-
ah, Hasshub, 24Hallohesh, Pilha, Sho-
bek, 25Rehum, Hashabnah, Maaseiah,
26Ahijah, Hanan, Anan, 27Malluch,
Harim, *and* Baanah.

The Covenant That Was Sealed

28Now the rest of the people—the
priests, the Levites, the gatekeepers,
the singers, the Nethinim, and all those
who had separated themselves from
the peoples of the lands to the Law of
God, their wives, their sons, and their
daughters, everyone who had knowl-
edge and understanding— 29these
joined with their brethren, their nobles,
and entered into a curse and an oath
to walk in God's Law, which was given
by Moses the servant of God, and to ob-
serve and do all the commandments of
the LORD our Lord, and His ordinances
and His statutes: 30We would not give
our daughters as wives to the peoples
of the land, nor take their daughters
for our sons; 31*if* the peoples of the land
brought wares or any grain to sell on
the Sabbath day, we would not buy it
from them on the Sabbath, or on a holy
day; and we would forego the seventh
year's *produce* and the exacting of ev-
ery debt.
32Also we made ordinances for our-
selves, to exact from ourselves yearly
one-third of a shekel for the service of
the house of our God: 33for the show-
bread, for the regular grain offering,
for the regular burnt offering of the
Sabbaths, the New Moons, and the set
feasts; for the holy things, for the sin
offerings to make atonement for Isra-
el, and all the work of the house of our
God. 34We cast lots among the priests,
the Levites, and the people, for bringing
the wood offering into the house of our
God, according to our fathers' houses,
at the appointed times year by year, to
burn on the altar of the LORD our God
as *it is* written in the Law.
35And *we made ordinances* to bring
the firstfruits of our ground and the
firstfruits of all fruit of all trees, year
by year, to the house of the LORD; 36to
bring the firstborn of our sons and our
cattle, as *it is* written in the Law, and the
firstborn of our herds and our flocks,
to the house of our God, to the priests
who minister in the house of our God;
37to bring the firstfruits of our dough,
our offerings, the fruit from all kinds
of trees, *the* new wine and oil, to the
priests, to the storerooms of the house
of our God; and to bring the tithes of
our land to the Levites, for the Le-
vites should receive the tithes in all
our farming communities. 38And the
priest, the descendant of Aaron, shall
be with the Levites when the Levites
receive tithes; and the Levites shall
bring up a tenth of the tithes to the
house of our God, to the rooms of the
storehouse.
39For the children of Israel and the
children of Levi shall bring the offering
of the grain, of the new wine and the oil,
to the storerooms where the articles of
the sanctuary *are, where* the priests who
minister and the gatekeepers and the
singers *are;* and we will not neglect the
house of our God.

The People Dwelling in Jerusalem

11 Now the leaders of the people dwelt at Jerusalem; the rest of the people cast lots to bring one out of ten to dwell in Jerusalem, the holy city, and nine-tenths *were to dwell* in *other* cities. 2And the people blessed all the men who willingly offered themselves to dwell at Jerusalem.

3These *are* the heads of the province who dwelt in Jerusalem. (But in the cities of Judah everyone dwelt in his own possession in their cities—Israelites, priests, Levites, Nethinim, and descendants of Solomon's servants.) 4Also in Jerusalem dwelt *some* of the children of Judah and of the children of Benjamin.

The children of Judah: Athaiah the son of Uzziah, the son of Zechariah, the son of Amariah, the son of Shephatiah, the son of Mahalalel, of the children of Perez; 5and Maaseiah the son of Baruch, the son of Col-Hozeh, the son of Hazaiah, the son of Adaiah, the son of Joiarib, the son of Zechariah, the son of Shiloni. 6All the sons of Perez who dwelt at Jerusalem *were* four hundred and sixty-eight valiant men.

7And these are the sons of Benjamin: Sallu the son of Meshullam, the son of Joed, the son of Pedaiah, the son of Kolaiah, the son of Maaseiah, the son of Ithiel, the son of Jeshaiah; 8and after him Gabbai *and* Sallai, nine hundred and twenty-eight. 9Joel the son of Zichri *was* their overseer, and Judah the son of Senuah[a] *was* second over the city.

10Of the priests: Jedaiah the son of Joiarib, and Jachin; 11Seraiah the son of Hilkiah, the son of Meshullam, the son of Zadok, the son of Meraioth, the son of Ahitub, *was* the leader of the house of God. 12Their brethren who did the work of the house *were* eight hundred and twenty-two; and Adaiah the son of Jeroham, the son of Pelaliah, the son of Amzi, the son of Zechariah, the son of Pashhur, the son of Malchijah, 13and his brethren, heads of the fathers' *houses, were* two hundred and forty-two; and Amashai the son of Azarel, the son of Ahzai, the son of Meshillemoth, the son of Immer, 14and their brethren, mighty men of valor, *were* one hundred and twenty-eight. Their overseer *was* Zabdiel the son of *one of* the great men.[a]

15Also of the Levites: Shemaiah the son of Hasshub, the son of Azrikam, the son of Hashabiah, the son of Bunni; 16Shabbethai and Jozabad, of the heads of the Levites, *had* the oversight of the business outside of the house of God; 17Mattaniah the son of Micha,[a] the son of Zabdi, the son of Asaph, the leader *who* began the thanksgiving with prayer; Bakbukiah, the second among his brethren; and Abda the son of Shammua, the son of Galal, the son of Jeduthun. 18All the Levites in the holy city *were* two hundred and eighty-four.

19Moreover the gatekeepers, Akkub, Talmon, and their brethren who kept the gates, *were* one hundred and seventy-two.

20And the rest of Israel, of the priests *and* Levites, *were* in all the cities of Judah, everyone in his inheritance. 21But the Nethinim dwelt in Ophel. And Ziha and Gishpa *were* over the Nethinim.

22Also the overseer of the Levites at Jerusalem *was* Uzzi the son of Bani, the son of Hashabiah, the son of Mattaniah, the son of Micha, of the sons of Asaph, the singers in charge of the service of the house of God. 23For *it was* the king's command concerning them that a certain portion should be for the singers, a quota day by day. 24Pethahiah the son of Meshezabel, of the children of Zerah the son of Judah, *was* the king's deputy[a] in all matters concerning the people.

The People Dwelling Outside Jerusalem

25And as for the villages with their fields, *some* of the children of Judah dwelt in Kirjath Arba and its villages, Dibon and its villages, Jekabzeel and its villages; 26in Jeshua, Moladah, Beth Pelet, 27Hazar Shual, and Beersheba and its villages; 28in Ziklag and Meconah and its villages; 29in En Rimmon, Zorah, Jarmuth, 30Zanoah, Adullam, and their villages; in Lachish and its fields; in Azekah and its villages. They dwelt from Beersheba to the Valley of Hinnom.

11:9 [a] Or *Hassenuah* **11:14** [a] Or *the son of Haggedolim* **11:17** [a] Or *Michah* **11:24** [a] Literally *at the king's hand*

31Also the children of Benjamin from Geba *dwelt* in Michmash, Aija, and Bethel, and their villages; 32in Anathoth, Nob, Ananiah; 33in Hazor, Ramah, Gittaim; 34in Hadid, Zeboim, Neballat; 35in Lod, Ono, *and* the Valley of Craftsmen. 36Some of the Judean divisions of Levites *were* in Benjamin.

The Priests and Levites

12 Now these *are* the priests and the Levites who came up with Zerubbabel the son of Shealtiel, and Jeshua: Seraiah, Jeremiah, Ezra, 2Amariah, Malluch, Hattush, 3Shechaniah, Rehum, Meremoth, 4Iddo, Ginnethoi,[a] Abijah, 5Mijamin, Maadiah, Bilgah, 6Shemaiah, Joiarib, Jedaiah, 7Sallu, Amok, Hilkiah, *and* Jedaiah.

These *were* the heads of the priests and their brethren in the days of Jeshua.

8Moreover the Levites *were* Jeshua, Binnui, Kadmiel, Sherebiah, Judah, *and* Mattaniah *who led* the thanksgiving *psalms,* he and his brethren. 9Also Bakbukiah and Unni, their brethren, *stood* across from them in *their* duties.

10Jeshua begot Joiakim, Joiakim begot Eliashib, Eliashib begot Joiada, 11Joiada begot Jonathan, and Jonathan begot Jaddua.

12Now in the days of Joiakim, the priests, the heads of the fathers' *houses were:* of Seraiah, Meraiah; of Jeremiah, Hananiah; 13of Ezra, Meshullam; of Amariah, Jehohanan; 14of Melichu,[a] Jonathan; of Shebaniah,[b] Joseph; 15of Harim,[a] Adna; of Meraioth,[b] Helkai; 16of Iddo, Zechariah; of Ginnethon, Meshullam; 17of Abijah, Zichri; *the son* of Minjamin;[a] of Moadiah,[b] Piltai; 18of Bilgah, Shammua; of Shemaiah, Jehonathan; 19of Joiarib, Mattenai; of Jedaiah, Uzzi; 20of Sallai,[a] Kallai; of Amok, Eber; 21of Hilkiah, Hashabiah; *and* of Jedaiah, Nethanel.

22During the reign of Darius the Persian, a record *was also kept* of the Levites and priests *who had been* heads of their fathers' *houses* in the days of Eliashib, Joiada, Johanan, and Jaddua. 23The sons of Levi, the heads of the fathers' *houses* until the days of Johanan the son of Eliashib, *were* written in the book of the chronicles.

24And the heads of the Levites *were* Hashabiah, Sherebiah, and Jeshua the son of Kadmiel, with their brothers across from them, to praise *and* give thanks, group alternating with group, according to the command of David the man of God. 25Mattaniah, Bakbukiah, Obadiah, Meshullam, Talmon, and Akkub *were* gatekeepers keeping the watch at the storerooms of the gates. 26These *lived* in the days of Joiakim the son of Jeshua, the son of Jozadak,[a] and in the days of Nehemiah the governor, and of Ezra the priest, the scribe.

Nehemiah Dedicates the Wall

27Now at the dedication of the wall of Jerusalem they sought out the Levites in all their places, to bring them to Jerusalem to celebrate the dedication with gladness, both with thanksgivings and singing, *with* cymbals and stringed instruments and harps. 28And the sons of the singers gathered together from the countryside around Jerusalem, from the villages of the Netophathites, 29from the house of Gilgal, and from the fields of Geba and Azmaveth; for the singers had built themselves villages all around Jerusalem. 30Then the priests and Levites purified themselves, and purified the people, the gates, and the wall.

31So I brought the leaders of Judah up on the wall, and appointed two large thanksgiving choirs. *One* went to the right hand on the wall toward the Refuse Gate. 32After them went Hoshaiah and half of the leaders of Judah, 33and Azariah, Ezra, Meshullam, 34Judah, Benjamin, Shemaiah, Jeremiah, 35and some of the priests' sons with trumpets—Zechariah the son of Jonathan, the son of Shemaiah, the son of Mattaniah, the son of Michaiah, the son of Zaccur, the son of Asaph, 36and his brethren, Shemaiah, Azarel, Milalai, Gilalai, Maai, Nethanel, Judah, *and* Hanani, with the

12:4 [a] Or *Ginnethon* (compare verse 16) **12:14** [a] Or *Malluch* (compare verse 2) [b] Or *Shechaniah* (compare verse 3) **12:15** [a] Or *Rehum* (compare verse 3) [b] Or *Meremoth* (compare verse 3) **12:17** [a] Or *Mijamin* (compare verse 5) [b] Or *Maadiah* (compare verse 5) **12:20** [a] Or *Sallu* (compare verse 7) **12:26** [a] Spelled *Jehozadak* in 1 Chronicles 6:14

musical instruments of David the man
of God. And Ezra the scribe *went* before
them. 37By the Fountain Gate, in front
of them, they went up the stairs of the
City of David, on the stairway of the
wall, beyond the house of David, as far
as the Water Gate eastward.
38The other thanksgiving choir went
the opposite *way,* and I *was* behind
them with half of the people on the wall,
going past the Tower of the Ovens as
far as the Broad Wall, 39and above the
Gate of Ephraim, above the Old Gate,
above the Fish Gate, the Tower of Han-
anel, the Tower of the Hundred, as far
as the Sheep Gate; and they stopped by
the Gate of the Prison.
40So the two thanksgiving choirs stood
in the house of God, likewise I and the
half of the rulers with me; 41and the
priests, Eliakim, Maaseiah, Minja-
min,[a] Michaiah, Elioenai, Zechariah,
and Hananiah, with trumpets; 42also
Maaseiah, Shemaiah, Eleazar, Uzzi,
Jehohanan, Malchijah, Elam, and Ezer.
The singers sang loudly with Jezrahiah
the director.
43Also that day they offered great sac-
rifices, and rejoiced, for God had made
them rejoice with great joy; the women
and the children also rejoiced, so that
the joy of Jerusalem was heard afar off.

Temple Responsibilities

44And at the same time some were
appointed over the rooms of the store-
house for the offerings, the firstfruits,
and the tithes, to gather into them from
the fields of the cities the portions spec-
ified by the Law for the priests and Le-
vites; for Judah rejoiced over the priests
and Levites who ministered. 45Both the
singers and the gatekeepers kept the
charge of their God and the charge of
the purification, according to the com-
mand of David *and* Solomon his son.
46For in the days of David and Asaph
of old *there were* chiefs of the singers,
and songs of praise and thanksgiving
to God. 47In the days of Zerubbabel and
in the days of Nehemiah all Israel gave
the portions for the singers and the
gatekeepers, a portion for each day.
They also consecrated *holy things* for
the Levites, and the Levites consecrated
them for the children of Aaron.

Principles of Separation

13 On that day they read from the
Book of Moses in the hearing of
the people, and in it was found written
that no Ammonite or Moabite should
ever come into the assembly of God,
2because they had not met the children
of Israel with bread and water, but hired
Balaam against them to curse them.
However, our God turned the curse into
a blessing. 3So it was, when they had
heard the Law, that they separated all
the mixed multitude from Israel.

The Reforms of Nehemiah

4Now before this, Eliashib the priest,
having authority over the storerooms
of the house of our God, *was* allied with
Tobiah. 5And he had prepared for him
a large room, where previously they
had stored the grain offerings, the
frankincense, the articles, the tithes of
grain, the new wine and oil, which were
commanded *to be given* to the Levites
and singers and gatekeepers, and the
offerings for the priests. 6But during
all this I was not in Jerusalem, for in
the thirty-second year of Artaxerxes
king of Babylon I had returned to the
king. Then after certain days I obtained
leave from the king, 7and I came to Je-
rusalem and discovered the evil that
Eliashib had done for Tobiah, in pre-
paring a room for him in the courts
of the house of God. 8And it grieved
me bitterly; therefore I threw all the
household goods of Tobiah out of the
room. 9Then I commanded them to
cleanse the rooms; and I brought back
into them the articles of the house of
God, with the grain offering and the
frankincense.
10I also realized that the portions for
the Levites had not been given *them;* for
each of the Levites and the singers who
did the work had gone back to his field.
11So I contended with the rulers, and
said, "Why is the house of God forsak-
en?" And I gathered them together and

12:41 [a] Or *Mijamin* (compare verse 5)

set them in their place. 12Then all Judah
brought the tithe of the grain and the
new wine and the oil to the storehouse.
13And I appointed as treasurers over the
storehouse Shelemiah the priest and
Zadok the scribe, and of the Levites, Pe-
daiah; and next to them *was* Hanan the
son of Zaccur, the son of Mattaniah; for
they were considered faithful, and their
task *was* to distribute to their brethren.

14Remember me, O my God, concern-
ing this, and do not wipe out my good
deeds that I have done for the house of
my God, and for its services!

15In those days I saw *people* in Judah
treading winepresses on the Sabbath,
and bringing in sheaves, and loading
donkeys with wine, grapes, figs, and all
kinds of burdens, which they brought
into Jerusalem on the Sabbath day. And
I warned *them* about the day on which
they were selling provisions. 16Men of
Tyre dwelt there also, who brought in
fish and all kinds of goods, and sold
them on the Sabbath to the children of
Judah, and in Jerusalem.

17Then I contended with the nobles
of Judah, and said to them, "What evil
thing *is* this that you do, by which you
profane the Sabbath day? 18Did not
your fathers do thus, and did not our
God bring all this disaster on us and on
this city? Yet you bring added wrath on
Israel by profaning the Sabbath."

19So it was, at the gates of Jerusalem,
as it began to be dark before the Sab-
bath, that I commanded the gates to
be shut, and charged that they must
not be opened till after the Sabbath.
Then I posted *some* of my servants at
the gates, *so that* no burdens would be
brought in on the Sabbath day. 20Now
the merchants and sellers of all kinds
of wares lodged outside Jerusalem once
or twice.

21Then I warned them, and said to
them, "Why do you spend the night
around the wall? If you do *so* again, I
will lay hands on you!" From that time
on they came no *more* on the Sabbath.
22And I commanded the Levites that
they should cleanse themselves, and
that they should go and guard the gates,
to sanctify the Sabbath day.

Remember me, O my God, *concerning*
this also, and spare me according to
the greatness of Your mercy!

23In those days I also saw Jews
who had married women of Ashdod,
Ammon, *and* Moab. 24And half of their
children spoke the language of Ash-
dod, and could not speak the language
of Judah, but spoke according to the
language of one or the other people.

25So I contended with them and cursed
them, struck some of them and pulled
out their hair, and made them swear
by God, *saying,* "You shall not give your
daughters as wives to their sons, nor
take their daughters for your sons or
yourselves. 26Did not Solomon king of
Israel sin by these things? Yet among
many nations there was no king like
him, who was beloved of his God; and
God made him king over all Israel. Nev-
ertheless pagan women caused even
him to sin. 27Should we then hear of
your doing all this great evil, trans-
gressing against our God by marrying
pagan women?"

28And *one* of the sons of Joiada, the
son of Eliashib the high priest, *was* a
son-in-law of Sanballat the Horonite;
therefore I drove him from me.

29Remember them, O my God, because
they have defiled the priesthood and
the covenant of the priesthood and the
Levites.

30Thus I cleansed them of everything
pagan. I also assigned duties to the
priests and the Levites, each to his ser-
vice, 31and *to bringing* the wood offering
and the firstfruits at appointed times.

Remember me, O my God, for good!

THE BOOK OF
ESTHER

The Book of Esther teaches that God is active, even when we might not be able to tell. Esther is a Jewish woman who becomes queen of Persia. But when a royal official named Haman becomes angry with Esther's cousin Mordecai, he plans to have all the Jews killed. Mordecai learns of the plan and encourages Esther to do something to save her people. At risk to her own life, Esther goes to the king, and he passes a law to save the Jews. Haman is punished and the Jews celebrate their rescue in a feast that becomes known as Purim.

- **GENRE:** History
- **AUTHOR:** Unknown, possibly Mordecai, Ezra, or Nehemiah
- **TIME:** c. 483–473 BC (written c. 470–424 BC)
- **PURPOSE:** To tell an important event that happened to the Jews who remained in Persia and to teach that God is in control and always working to protect His people.

The King Dethrones Queen Vashti

1 Now it came to pass in the days
of Ahasuerus[a] (this *was* the Ahas-
uerus who reigned over one hundred
and twenty-seven provinces, from In-
dia to Ethiopia), 2in those days when
King Ahasuerus sat on the throne of
his kingdom, which *was* in Shushan[a]
the citadel, 3*that* in the third year of
his reign he made a feast for all his
officials and servants—the powers of
Persia and Media, the nobles, and the
princes of the provinces *being* before
him— 4when he showed the riches of
his glorious kingdom and the splendor
of his excellent majesty for many days,
one hundred and eighty days *in all.*
5And when these days were complet-
ed, the king made a feast lasting seven
days for all the people who were present
in Shushan the citadel, from great to
small, in the court of the garden of the
king's palace. 6*There were* white and
blue linen *curtains* fastened with cords
of fine linen and purple on silver rods
and marble pillars; *and the* couches *were*
of gold and silver on a *mosaic* pavement
of alabaster, turquoise, and white and
black marble. 7And they served drinks
in golden vessels, each vessel being dif-
ferent from the other, with royal wine in
abundance, according to the generosity
of the king. 8In accordance with the law,
the drinking was not compulsory; for
so the king had ordered all the officers
of his household, that they should do
according to each man's pleasure.
9Queen Vashti also made a feast for
the women *in* the royal palace which
belonged to King Ahasuerus.
10On the seventh day, when the heart
of the king was merry with wine, he
commanded Mehuman, Biztha, Har-
bona, Bigtha, Abagtha, Zethar, and
Carcas, seven eunuchs who served in
the presence of King Ahasuerus, 11to
bring Queen Vashti before the king,
wearing her royal crown, in order to
show her beauty to the people and the
officials, for she *was* beautiful to behold.
12But Queen Vashti refused to come
at the king's command *brought* by *his*
eunuchs; therefore the king was furious,
and his anger burned within him.
13Then the king said to the wise men
who understood the times (for this *was*
the king's manner toward all who knew
law and justice, 14those closest to him
being Carshena, Shethar, Admatha, Tar-
shish, Meres, Marsena, and Memucan,
the seven princes of Persia and Media,
who had access to the king's presence,
and who ranked highest in the king-
dom): 15"What *shall we* do to Queen

1:1 [a] Generally identified with Xerxes I (485–464 BC)

1:2 [a] Or *Susa,* and so throughout this book

Vashti, according to law, because she did
not obey the command of King Ahas-
uerus *brought to her* by the eunuchs?"
16And Memucan answered before the
king and the princes: "Queen Vashti has
not only wronged the king, but also all
the princes, and all the people who *are* in
all the provinces of King Ahasuerus. 17For
the queen's behavior will become known
to all women, so that they will despise
their husbands in their eyes, when they
report, 'King Ahasuerus commanded
Queen Vashti to be brought in before
him, but she did not come.' 18This very
day the *noble* ladies of Persia and Media
will say to all the king's officials that they
have heard of the behavior of the queen.
Thus *there will be* excessive contempt and
wrath. 19If it pleases the king, let a royal
decree go out from him, and let it be re-
corded in the laws of the Persians and the
Medes, so that it will not be altered, that
Vashti shall come no more before King
Ahasuerus; and let the king give her royal
position to another who is better than she.
20When the king's decree which he will
make is proclaimed throughout all his
empire (for it is great), all wives will honor
their husbands, both great and small."
21And the reply pleased the king and
the princes, and the king did according
to the word of Memucan. 22Then he
sent letters to all the king's provinces,
to each province in its own script, and
to every people in their own language,
that each man should be master in his
own house, and speak in the language
of his own people.

Esther Becomes Queen

2 After these things, when the wrath
of King Ahasuerus subsided, he re-
membered Vashti, what she had done,
and what had been decreed against her.
2Then the king's servants who attended
him said: "Let beautiful young virgins
be sought for the king; 3and let the king
appoint officers in all the provinces of
his kingdom, that they may gather all
the beautiful young virgins to Shushan
the citadel, into the women's quarters,
under the custody of Hegai[a] the king's
eunuch, custodian of the women. And
let beauty preparations be given *them.*
4Then let the young woman who pleases
the king be queen instead of Vashti."
This thing pleased the king, and he
did so.
5In Shushan the citadel there was a
certain Jew whose name *was* Mordecai
the son of Jair, the son of Shimei, the
son of Kish, a Benjamite. 6*Kish*[a] had
been carried away from Jerusalem with
the captives who had been captured
with Jeconiah[b] king of Judah, whom
Nebuchadnezzar the king of Babylon
had carried away. 7And *Mordecai* had
brought up Hadassah, that *is,* Esther,
his uncle's daughter, for she had neither
father nor mother. The young woman
was lovely and beautiful. When her fa-
ther and mother died, Mordecai took
her as his own daughter.
8So it was, when the king's command
and decree were heard, and when
many young women were gathered at
Shushan the citadel, *under* the custody
of Hegai, that Esther also was taken to
the king's palace, into the care of Hegai
the custodian of the women. 9Now the
young woman pleased him, and she
obtained his favor; so he readily gave
beauty preparations to her, besides her
allowance. Then seven choice maid-
servants were provided for her from
the king's palace, and he moved her
and her maidservants to the best *place*
in the house of the women.
10Esther had not revealed her people
or family, for Mordecai had charged her
not to reveal *it.* 11And every day Mor-
decai paced in front of the court of the
women's quarters, to learn of Esther's
welfare and what was happening to her.
12Each young woman's turn came to
go in to King Ahasuerus after she had
completed twelve months' preparation,
according to the regulations for the
women, for thus were the days of their
preparation apportioned: six months
with oil of myrrh, and six months with
perfumes and preparations for beau-
tifying women. 13Thus *prepared, each*
young woman went to the king, and she
was given whatever she desired to take
with her from the women's quarters to

2:3 [a] Hebrew *Hege* 2:6 [a] Literally *Who* [b] Same as *Jehoiachin,* 2 Kings 24:6 and elsewhere

GOD SIN JESUS SALVATION LOVE

the king's palace. 14In the evening she
went, and in the morning she returned
to the second house of the women, to
the custody of Shaashgaz, the king's
eunuch who kept the concubines. She
would not go in to the king again unless
the king delighted in her and called for
her by name.

15Now when the turn came for Esther
the daughter of Abihail the uncle of
Mordecai, who had taken her as his
daughter, to go in to the king, she re-
quested nothing but what Hegai the
king's eunuch, the custodian of the
women, advised. And Esther obtained
favor in the sight of all who saw her.
16So Esther was taken to King Ahasue-
rus, into his royal palace, in the tenth
month, which *is* the month of Tebeth,
in the seventh year of his reign. 17The
king loved Esther more than all the
other women, and she obtained grace
and favor in his sight more than all the
virgins; so he set the royal crown upon
her head and made her queen instead
of Vashti. 18Then the king made a great
feast, the Feast of Esther, for all his offi-
cials and servants; and he proclaimed a
holiday in the provinces and gave gifts
according to the generosity of a king.

Mordecai Discovers a Plot

19When virgins were gathered togeth-
er a second time, Mordecai sat within
the king's gate. 20*Now* Esther had not
revealed her family and her people, just
as Mordecai had charged her, for Esther
obeyed the command of Mordecai as
when she was brought up by him.

21In those days, while Mordecai sat
within the king's gate, two of the king's
eunuchs, Bigthan and Teresh, door-
keepers, became furious and sought
to lay hands on King Ahasuerus. 22So
the matter became known to Morde-
cai, who told Queen Esther, and Esther
informed the king in Mordecai's name.
23And when an inquiry was made into
the matter, it was confirmed, and both
were hanged on a gallows; and it was
written in the book of the chronicles in
the presence of the king.

Haman's Conspiracy Against the Jews

3 After these things King Ahasuerus
promoted Haman, the son of Ham-
medatha the Agagite, and advanced him
and set his seat above all the princes
who *were* with him. 2And all the king's
servants who *were* within the king's gate
bowed and paid homage to Haman, for
so the king had commanded concern-
ing him. But Mordecai would not bow or
pay homage. 3Then the king's servants
who *were* within the king's gate said to
Mordecai, "Why do you transgress the
king's command?" 4Now it happened,
when they spoke to him daily and he
would not listen to them, that they told
it to Haman, to see whether Mordecai's
words would stand; for *Mordecai* had told
them that he *was* a Jew. 5When Haman
saw that Mordecai did not bow or pay
him homage, Haman was filled with
wrath. 6But he disdained to lay hands
on Mordecai alone, for they had told
him of the people of Mordecai. Instead,
Haman sought to destroy all the Jews
who *were* throughout the whole kingdom
of Ahasuerus—the people of Mordecai.

7In the first month, which is the month
of Nisan, in the twelfth year of King
Ahasuerus, they cast Pur (that *is,* the
lot), before Haman to determine the day
and the month,[a] until *it fell on the* twelfth
month,[b] which *is* the month of Adar.

8Then Haman said to King Ahasuerus,
"There is a certain people scattered and
dispersed among the people in all the
provinces of your kingdom; their laws *are*
different from all *other* people's, and they
do not keep the king's laws. Therefore it
is not fitting for the king to let them re-
main. 9If it pleases the king, let *a decree*
be written that they be destroyed, and
I will pay ten thousand talents of silver
into the hands of those who do the work,
to bring *it* into the king's treasuries."

10So the king took his signet ring from
his hand and gave it to Haman, the
son of Hammedatha the Agagite, the
enemy of the Jews. 11And the king said
to Haman, "The money and the people
are given to you, to do with them as
seems good to you."

3:7 [a] Septuagint adds *to destroy the people of Mordecai in one day;* Vulgate adds *the nation of the Jews should be destroyed.* [b] Following Masoretic Text and Vulgate; Septuagint reads *and the lot fell on the fourteenth of the month.*

12 Then the king's scribes were called on the thirteenth day of the first month, and *a decree* was written according to all that Haman commanded—to the king's satraps, to the governors who *were* over each province, to the officials of all people, to every province according to its script, and to every people in their language. In the name of King Ahasuerus it was written, and sealed with the king's signet ring. 13 And the letters were sent by couriers into all the king's provinces, to destroy, to kill, and to annihilate all the Jews, both young and old, little children and women, in one day, on the thirteenth *day* of the twelfth month, which *is* the month of Adar, and to plunder their possessions.[a] 14 A copy of the document was to be issued as law in every province, being published for all people, that they should be ready for that day. 15 The couriers went out, hastened by the king's command; and the decree was proclaimed in Shushan the citadel. So the king and Haman sat down to drink, but the city of Shushan was perplexed.

Esther Agrees to Help the Jews

4 When Mordecai learned all that had happened, he tore his clothes and put on sackcloth and ashes, and went out into the midst of the city. He cried out with a loud and bitter cry. 2 He went as far as the front of the king's gate, for no one *might* enter the king's gate clothed with sackcloth. 3 And in every province where the king's command and decree arrived, *there was* great mourning among the Jews, with fasting, weeping, and wailing; and many lay in sackcloth and ashes.

4 So Esther's maids and eunuchs came and told her, and the queen was deeply distressed. Then she sent garments to clothe Mordecai and take his sackcloth away from him, but he would not accept *them.* 5 Then Esther called Hathach, *one* of the king's eunuchs whom he had appointed to attend her, and she gave him a command concerning Mordecai, to learn what and why this *was.* 6 So Hathach went out to Mordecai in the city square that *was* in front of the king's gate. 7 And Mordecai told him all that had happened to him, and the sum of money that Haman had promised to pay into the king's treasuries to destroy the Jews. 8 He also gave him a copy of the written decree for their destruction, which was given at Shushan, that he might show it to Esther and explain it to her, and that he might command her to go in to the king to make supplication to him and plead before him for her people. 9 So Hathach returned and told Esther the words of Mordecai.

10 Then Esther spoke to Hathach, and gave him a command for Mordecai: 11 "All the king's servants and the people of the king's provinces know that any man or woman who goes into the inner court to the king, who has not been called, *he has* but one law: put *all* to death, except the one to whom the king holds out the golden scepter, that he may live. Yet I myself have not been called to go in to the king these thirty days." 12 So they told Mordecai Esther's words.

13 And Mordecai told *them* to answer Esther: "Do not think in your heart that you will escape in the king's palace any more than all the other Jews. 14 For if you remain completely silent at this time, relief and deliverance will arise for the Jews from another place, but you and your father's house will perish. Yet who knows whether you have come to the kingdom for *such* a time as this?"

15 Then Esther told *them* to reply to Mordecai: 16 "Go, gather all the Jews who are present in Shushan, and fast for me; neither eat nor drink for three days, night or day. My maids and I will fast likewise. And so I will go to the king, which *is* against the law; and if I perish, I perish!"

17 So Mordecai went his way and did according to all that Esther commanded him.[a]

Esther's Banquet

5 Now it happened on the third day that Esther put on *her* royal *robes* and stood in the inner court of the king's palace, across from the king's house, while the king sat on his royal throne in the royal house, facing the entrance of the house.[a] 2 So it was, when the king saw Queen Esther standing in the court, *that*

3:13 [a] Septuagint adds the text of the letter here. 4:17 [a] Septuagint adds a prayer of Mordecai here. 5:1 [a] Septuagint adds many extra details in verses 1 and 2.

she found favor in his sight, and the king
held out to Esther the golden scepter
that *was* in his hand. Then Esther went
near and touched the top of the scepter.
3And the king said to her, "What do
you wish, Queen Esther? What *is* your
request? It shall be given to you—up to
half the kingdom!"
4So Esther answered, "If it pleases the
king, let the king and Haman come
today to the banquet that I have pre-
pared for him."
5Then the king said, "Bring Haman
quickly, that he may do as Esther has
said." So the king and Haman went to
the banquet that Esther had prepared.
6At the banquet of wine the king said
to Esther, "What *is* your petition? It shall
be granted you. What *is* your request, up
to half the kingdom? It shall be done!"
7Then Esther answered and said, "My
petition and request *is this:* 8If I have
found favor in the sight of the king,
and if it pleases the king to grant my
petition and fulfill my request, then let
the king and Haman come to the ban-
quet which I will prepare for them, and
tomorrow I will do as the king has said."

Haman's Plot Against Mordecai

9So Haman went out that day joyful
and with a glad heart; but when Haman
saw Mordecai in the king's gate, and
that he did not stand or tremble be-
fore him, he was filled with indigna-
tion against Mordecai. 10Nevertheless
Haman restrained himself and went
home, and he sent and called for his
friends and his wife Zeresh. 11Then
Haman told them of his great riches, the
multitude of his children, everything
in which the king had promoted him,
and how he had advanced him above
the officials and servants of the king.
12Moreover Haman said, "Besides,
Queen Esther invited no one but me to
come in with the king to the banquet that
she prepared; and tomorrow I am again
invited by her, along with the king. 13Yet
all this avails me nothing, so long as I see
Mordecai the Jew sitting at the king's gate."
14Then his wife Zeresh and all his friends
said to him, "Let a gallows be made, fifty
cubits high, and in the morning suggest
to the king that Mordecai be hanged on
it; then go merrily with the king to the
banquet."
And the thing pleased Haman; so he
had the gallows made.

The King Honors Mordecai

6 That night the king could not sleep.
So one was commanded to bring the
book of the records of the chronicles;
and they were read before the king.
2And it was found written that Mordecai
had told of Bigthana and Teresh, two
of the king's eunuchs, the doorkeepers
who had sought to lay hands on King
Ahasuerus. 3Then the king said, "What
honor or dignity has been bestowed on
Mordecai for this?"
And the king's servants who attended
him said, "Nothing has been done for
him."
4So the king said, "Who *is* in the court?"
Now Haman had *just* entered the outer
court of the king's palace to suggest that
the king hang Mordecai on the gallows
that he had prepared for him.
5The king's servants said to him,
"Haman is there, standing in the court."
And the king said, "Let him come in."
6So Haman came in, and the king
asked him, "What shall be done for the
man whom the king delights to honor?"
Now Haman thought in his heart,
"Whom would the king delight to honor
more than me?" 7And Haman answered
the king, "*For* the man whom the king
delights to honor, 8let a royal robe be
brought which the king has worn, and
a horse on which the king has ridden,
which has a royal crest placed on its
head. 9Then let this robe and horse be
delivered to the hand of one of the king's
most noble princes, that he may ar-
ray the man whom the king delights to
honor. Then parade him on horseback
through the city square, and proclaim
before him: 'Thus shall it be done to the
man whom the king delights to honor!' "
10Then the king said to Haman, "Hur-
ry, take the robe and the horse, as you
have suggested, and do so for Mordecai
the Jew who sits within the king's gate!
Leave nothing undone of all that you
have spoken."
11So Haman took the robe and the
horse, arrayed Mordecai and led him

on horseback through the city square,
and proclaimed before him, "Thus shall
it be done to the man whom the king
delights to honor!"
12Afterward Mordecai went back to
the king's gate. But Haman hurried to
his house, mourning and with his head
covered. 13When Haman told his wife
Zeresh and all his friends everything
that had happened to him, his wise men
and his wife Zeresh said to him, "If Mor-
decai, before whom you have begun to
fall, is of Jewish descent, you will not
prevail against him but will surely fall
before him."
14While they *were* still talking with
him, the king's eunuchs came, and has-
tened to bring Haman to the banquet
which Esther had prepared.

Haman Hanged Instead of Mordecai

7 So the king and Haman went to dine
with Queen Esther. 2And on the sec-
ond day, at the banquet of wine, the king
again said to Esther, "What *is* your peti-
tion, Queen Esther? It shall be granted
you. And what *is* your request, up to half
the kingdom? It shall be done!"
3Then Queen Esther answered and
said, "If I have found favor in your sight,
O king, and if it pleases the king, let my
life be given me at my petition, and my
people at my request. 4For we have been
sold, my people and I, to be destroyed,
to be killed, and to be annihilated. Had
we been sold as male and female slaves,
I would have held my tongue, although
the enemy could never compensate for
the king's loss."
5So King Ahasuerus answered and
said to Queen Esther, "Who is he, and
where is he, who would dare presume
in his heart to do such a thing?"
6And Esther said, "The adversary and
enemy *is* this wicked Haman!"
So Haman was terrified before the
king and queen.
7Then the king arose in his wrath from
the banquet of wine *and went* into the
palace garden; but Haman stood before
Queen Esther, pleading for his life, for he
saw that evil was determined against
him by the king. 8When the king re-
turned from the palace garden to the
place of the banquet of wine, Haman
had fallen across the couch where Esther
was. Then the king said, "Will he also as-
sault the queen while I *am* in the house?"
As the word left the king's mouth, they
covered Haman's face. 9Now Harbo-
nah, one of the eunuchs, said to the
king, "Look! The gallows, fifty cubits
high, which Haman made for Mordecai,
who spoke good on the king's behalf, is
standing at the house of Haman."
Then the king said, "Hang him on it!"
10So they hanged Haman on the gal-
lows that he had prepared for Mordecai.
Then the king's wrath subsided.

Esther Saves the Jews

8 On that day King Ahasuerus gave
Queen Esther the house of Haman,
the enemy of the Jews. And Mordecai
came before the king, for Esther had
told how he *was related* to her. 2So the
king took off his signet ring, which he
had taken from Haman, and gave it to
Mordecai; and Esther appointed Mor-
decai over the house of Haman.
3Now Esther spoke again to the king,
fell down at his feet, and implored
him with tears to counteract the evil
of Haman the Agagite, and the scheme
which he had devised against the Jews.
4And the king held out the golden scep-
ter toward Esther. So Esther arose and
stood before the king, 5and said, "If it
pleases the king, and if I have found
favor in his sight and the thing *seems*
right to the king and I am pleasing in
his eyes, let it be written to revoke the
letters devised by Haman, the son of
Hammedatha the Agagite, which he
wrote to annihilate the Jews who *are* in
all the king's provinces. 6For how can I
endure to see the evil that will come to
my people? Or how can I endure to see
the destruction of my countrymen?"
7Then King Ahasuerus said to Queen
Esther and Mordecai the Jew, "Indeed, I
have given Esther the house of Haman,
and they have hanged him on the gal-
lows because he *tried to* lay his hand on
the Jews. 8You yourselves write *a decree*
concerning the Jews, as you please, in
the king's name, and seal *it* with the
king's signet ring; for whatever is written
in the king's name and sealed with the
king's signet ring no one can revoke."

9So the king's scribes were called at
that time, in the third month, which *is*
the month of Sivan, on the twenty-third
day; and it was written, according to
all that Mordecai commanded, to the
Jews, the satraps, the governors, and the
princes of the provinces from India to
Ethiopia, one hundred and twenty-seven
provinces *in all,* to every province in its
own script, to every people in their own
language, and to the Jews in their own
script and language. 10And he wrote in
the name of King Ahasuerus, sealed
it with the king's signet ring, and sent
letters by couriers on horseback, riding
on royal horses bred from swift steeds.[a]
11By these letters the king permitted
the Jews who *were* in every city to gather
together and protect their lives—to de-
stroy, kill, and annihilate all the forces
of any people or province that would as-
sault them, *both* little children and wom-
en, and to plunder their possessions,
12on one day in all the provinces of King
Ahasuerus, on the thirteenth *day* of the
twelfth month, which *is* the month of
Adar.[a] 13A copy of the document was to
be issued as a decree in every province
and published for all people, so that
the Jews would be ready on that day to
avenge themselves on their enemies.
14The couriers who rode on royal horses
went out, hastened and pressed on by
the king's command. And the decree was
issued in Shushan the citadel.
15So Mordecai went out from the pres-
ence of the king in royal apparel of
blue and white, with a great crown of
gold and a garment of fine linen and
purple; and the city of Shushan rejoiced
and was glad. 16The Jews had light and
gladness, joy and honor. 17And in every
province and city, wherever the king's
command and decree came, the Jews
had joy and gladness, a feast and a
holiday. Then many of the people of
the land became Jews, because fear of
the Jews fell upon them.

The Jews Destroy Their Tormentors

9 Now in the twelfth month, that *is,*
the month of Adar, on the thir-
teenth day, *the time* came for the king's
command and his decree to be execut-
ed. On the day that the enemies of the
Jews had hoped to overpower them,
the opposite occurred, in that the Jews
themselves overpowered those who hat-
ed them. 2The Jews gathered together in
their cities throughout all the provinces
of King Ahasuerus to lay hands on those
who sought their harm. And no one
could withstand them, because fear of
them fell upon all people. 3And all the
officials of the provinces, the satraps,
the governors, and all those doing the
king's work, helped the Jews, because
the fear of Mordecai fell upon them.
4For Mordecai *was* great in the king's
palace, and his fame spread throughout
all the provinces; for this man Mordecai
became increasingly prominent. 5Thus
the Jews defeated all their enemies with
the stroke of the sword, with slaugh-
ter and destruction, and did what they
pleased with those who hated them.
6And in Shushan the citadel the Jews
killed and destroyed five hundred men.
7Also Parshandatha, Dalphon, Aspatha,
8Poratha, Adalia, Aridatha, 9Parmash-
ta, Arisai, Aridai, and Vajezatha— 10the
ten sons of Haman the son of Hamme-
datha, the enemy of the Jews—they
killed; but they did not lay a hand on
the plunder.
11On that day the number of those
who were killed in Shushan the citadel
was brought to the king. 12And the king
said to Queen Esther, "The Jews have
killed and destroyed five hundred men
in Shushan the citadel, and the ten sons
of Haman. What have they done in the
rest of the king's provinces? Now what
is your petition? It shall be granted to
you. Or what *is* your further request? It
shall be done."
13Then Esther said, "If it pleases the
king, let it be granted to the Jews who
are in Shushan to do again tomorrow
according to today's decree, and let
Haman's ten sons be hanged on the
gallows."
14So the king commanded this to be
done; the decree was issued in Shushan,
and they hanged Haman's ten sons.
15And the Jews who *were* in Shushan

8:10 [a] Literally *sons of the swift horses* **8:12** [a] Septuagint adds the text of the letter here.

gathered together again on the four-
teenth day of the month of Adar and
killed three hundred men at Shushan;
but they did not lay a hand on the
plunder.
16 The remainder of the Jews in the
king's provinces gathered together and
protected their lives, had rest from their
enemies, and killed seventy-five thou-
sand of their enemies; but they did not
lay a hand on the plunder. 17 *This was*
on the thirteenth day of the month
of Adar. And on the fourteenth of *the*
month[a] they rested and made it a day
of feasting and gladness.

The Feast of Purim

18 But the Jews who *were* at Shushan
assembled together on the thirteenth
day, as well as on the fourteenth; and
on the fifteenth of *the month*[a] they
rested, and made it a day of feasting
and gladness. 19 Therefore the Jews of
the villages who dwelt in the unwalled
towns celebrated the fourteenth day of
the month of Adar *with* gladness and
feasting, as a holiday, and for sending
presents to one another.
20 And Mordecai wrote these things
and sent letters to all the Jews, near
and far, who *were* in all the provinces of
King Ahasuerus, 21 to establish among
them that they should celebrate yearly
the fourteenth and fifteenth days of
the month of Adar, 22 as the days on
which the Jews had rest from their en-
emies, as the month which was turned
from sorrow to joy for them, and from
mourning to a holiday; that they should
make them days of feasting and joy, of
sending presents to one another and
gifts to the poor. 23 So the Jews accepted
the custom which they had begun, as
Mordecai had written to them, 24 be-
cause Haman, the son of Hammedatha
the Agagite, the enemy of all the Jews,
had plotted against the Jews to anni-
hilate them, and had cast Pur (that *is,*
the lot), to consume them and destroy
them; 25 but when *Esther*[a] came before
the king, he commanded by letter that
this[b] wicked plot which *Haman* had
devised against the Jews should return
on his own head, and that he and his
sons should be hanged on the gallows.
26 So they called these days Purim, after
the name Pur. Therefore, because of all
the words of this letter, what they had
seen concerning this matter, and what
had happened to them, 27 the Jews estab-
lished and imposed it upon themselves
and their descendants and all who would
join them, that without fail they should
celebrate these two days every year,
according to the written *instructions* and
according to the *prescribed* time, 28 *that*
these days *should be* remembered and
kept throughout every generation, every
family, every province, and every city,
that these days of Purim should not fail
to be observed among the Jews, and *that*
the memory of them should not perish
among their descendants.
29 Then Queen Esther, the daughter of
Abihail, with Mordecai the Jew, wrote
with full authority to confirm this sec-
ond letter about Purim. 30 And *Mordecai*
sent letters to all the Jews, to the one
hundred and twenty-seven provinc-
es of the kingdom of Ahasuerus, *with*
words of peace and truth, 31 to confirm
these days of Purim at their *appointed*
time, as Mordecai the Jew and Queen
Esther had prescribed for them, and as
they had decreed for themselves and
their descendants concerning matters
of their fasting and lamenting. 32 So
the decree of Esther confirmed these
matters of Purim, and it was written
in the book.

Mordecai's Advancement

10 And King Ahasuerus imposed
tribute on the land and *on* the
islands of the sea. 2 Now all the acts of
his power and his might, and the ac-
count of the greatness of Mordecai, to
which the king advanced him, *are* they
not written in the book of the chronicles
of the kings of Media and Persia? 3 For
Mordecai the Jew *was* second to King
Ahasuerus, and was great among the
Jews and well received by the multitude
of his brethren, seeking the good of his
people and speaking peace to all his
countrymen.[a]

9:17 [a] Literally *it* 9:18 [a] Literally *it* 9:25 [a] Literally *she* or *it* [b] Literally *his* 10:3 [a] Literally *seed.* Septuagint and Vulgate add a dream of Mordecai here; Vulgate adds six more chapters.

THE BOOK OF

JOB

The Book of Job might tell one of the earliest stories of the Bible and may have been written early, too. Job may have lived during the time of Abraham, Isaac, Jacob, or Joseph. Job is a wealthy man who loves God but when he loses everything he had, he cannot understand why. What has he done to deserve this suffering? He has not done wrong, so maybe God has made a mistake. If only Job could talk with God and clear up the misunderstanding. When some of his friends show up, they try to convince Job that he had to have done something wrong to bring this suffering into his life. Finally, God speaks with Job. Job comes to see that God's ways are too great and wonderful for us to understand at times. All we are to do is trust Him.

- **GENRE:** Wisdom and Poetry
- **AUTHOR:** Unknown, possibly Moses
- **TIME:** c. 2100–1900 BC
- **PURPOSE:** To teach us that God is in control of everything and that there is a reason for everything, even when we go through hard times.

Job and His Family in Uz

1 There was a man in the land of Uz,
whose name *was* Job; and that man
was blameless and upright, and one
who feared God and shunned evil. 2And
seven sons and three daughters were
born to him. 3Also, his possessions were
seven thousand sheep, three thousand
camels, five hundred yoke of oxen, five
hundred female donkeys, and a very
large household, so that this man was
the greatest of all the people of the East.
4And his sons would go and feast *in*
their houses, each on his *appointed* day,
and would send and invite their three
sisters to eat and drink with them. 5So
it was, when the days of feasting had
run their course, that Job would send
and sanctify them, and he would rise
early in the morning and offer burnt
offerings *according to* the number of
them all. For Job said, "It may be that
my sons have sinned and cursed[a] God
in their hearts." Thus Job did regularly.

Satan Attacks Job's Character

6Now there was a day when the sons
of God came to present themselves be-
fore the LORD, and Satan[a] also came
among them. 7And the LORD said to
Satan, "From where do you come?"
So Satan answered the LORD and said,
"From going to and fro on the earth,
and from walking back and forth on it."
8Then the LORD said to Satan, "Have
you considered My servant Job, that
there is none like him on the earth, a
blameless and upright man, one who
fears God and shuns evil?"
9So Satan answered the LORD and
said, "Does Job fear God for nothing?
10Have You not made a hedge around
him, around his household, and around
all that he has on every side? You have
blessed the work of his hands, and his
possessions have increased in the land.
11But now, stretch out Your hand and
touch all that he has, and he will surely
curse You to Your face!"
12And the LORD said to Satan, "Behold,
all that he has *is* in your power; only do
not lay a hand on his *person*."
So Satan went out from the presence
of the LORD.

Job Loses His Property and Children

13Now there was a day when his sons
and daughters *were* eating and drinking

1:5 [a] Literally *blessed,* but used here in the evil sense, and so in verse 11 and 2:5, 9 **1:6** [a] Literally *the Adversary,* and so throughout this book

wine in their oldest brother's house;
14and a messenger came to Job and
said, "The oxen were plowing and the
donkeys feeding beside them, 15when
the Sabeans[a] raided *them* and took
them away—indeed they have killed
the servants with the edge of the sword;
and I alone have escaped to tell you!"
16While he *was* still speaking, another
also came and said, "The fire of God fell
from heaven and burned up the sheep
and the servants, and consumed them;
and I alone have escaped to tell you!"
17While he *was* still speaking, another
also came and said, "The Chaldeans
formed three bands, raided the camels
and took them away, yes, and killed the
servants with the edge of the sword;
and I alone have escaped to tell you!"
18While he *was* still speaking, another
also came and said, "Your sons and
daughters *were* eating and drinking
wine in their oldest brother's house,
19and suddenly a great wind came from
across[a] the wilderness and struck the
four corners of the house, and it fell on
the young people, and they are dead;
and I alone have escaped to tell you!"
20Then Job arose, tore his robe, and
shaved his head; and he fell to the
ground and worshiped. 21And he said:

"Naked I came from my mother's
womb,
And naked shall I return there.
The LORD gave, and the LORD has
taken away;
Blessed be the name of the LORD."

22In all this Job did not sin nor charge
God with wrong.

Satan Attacks Job's Health

2 Again there was a day when the
sons of God came to present them-
selves before the LORD, and Satan came
also among them to present himself
before the LORD. 2And the LORD said
to Satan, "From where do you come?"
Satan answered the LORD and said,
"From going to and fro on the earth,
and from walking back and forth on it."
3Then the LORD said to Satan, "Have you
considered My servant Job, that *there is*
none like him on the earth, a blameless
and upright man, one who fears God and
shuns evil? And still he holds fast to his in-
tegrity, although you incited Me against
him, to destroy him without cause."
4So Satan answered the LORD and
said, "Skin for skin! Yes, all that a man
has he will give for his life. 5But stretch
out Your hand now, and touch his bone
and his flesh, and he will surely curse
You to Your face!"
6And the LORD said to Satan, "Behold,
he *is* in your hand, but spare his life."
7So Satan went out from the presence
of the LORD, and struck Job with painful
boils from the sole of his foot to the
crown of his head. 8And he took for
himself a potsherd with which to scrape
himself while he sat in the midst of the
ashes.
9Then his wife said to him, "Do you
still hold fast to your integrity? Curse
God and die!"
10But he said to her, "You speak as one
of the foolish women speaks. Shall we
indeed accept good from God, and shall
we not accept adversity?" In all this Job
did not sin with his lips.

Job's Three Friends

11Now when Job's three friends heard
of all this adversity that had come
upon him, each one came from his own
place—Eliphaz the Temanite, Bildad the
Shuhite, and Zophar the Naamathite.
For they had made an appointment
together to come and mourn with him,
and to comfort him. 12And when they
raised their eyes from afar, and did not
recognize him, they lifted their voices
and wept; and each one tore his robe
and sprinkled dust on his head toward
heaven. 13So they sat down with him
on the ground seven days and sev-
en nights, and no one spoke a word
to him, for they saw that *his* grief was
very great.

Job Deplores His Birth

3 After this Job opened his mouth and
cursed the day of his *birth*. 2And Job
spoke, and said:

1:15 [a] Literally *Sheba* (compare 6:19) 1:19 [a] Septuagint omits *across*.

3 "May the day perish on which I was born,
And the night *in which* it was said,
'A male child is conceived.'
4 May that day be darkness;
May God above not seek it,
Nor the light shine upon it.
5 May darkness and the shadow of death claim it;
May a cloud settle on it;
May the blackness of the day terrify it.
6 *As for* that night, may darkness seize it;
May it not rejoice[a] among the days of the year,
May it not come into the number of the months.
7 Oh, may that night be barren!
May no joyful shout come into it!
8 May those curse it who curse the day,
Those who are ready to arouse Leviathan.
9 May the stars of its morning be dark;
May it look for light, but *have* none,
And not see the dawning of the day;
10 Because it did not shut up the doors of my *mother's* womb,
Nor hide sorrow from my eyes.

11 "Why did I not die at birth?
Why did I *not* perish when I came from the womb?
12 Why did the knees receive me?
Or why the breasts, that I should nurse?
13 For now I would have lain still and been quiet,
I would have been asleep;
Then I would have been at rest
14 With kings and counselors of the earth,
Who built ruins for themselves,
15 Or with princes who had gold,
Who filled their houses *with* silver;
16 Or *why* was I not hidden like a stillborn child,
Like infants who never saw light?
17 There the wicked cease *from* troubling,
And there the weary are at rest.
18 *There* the prisoners rest together;
They do not hear the voice of the oppressor.
19 The small and great are there,
And the servant *is* free from his master.

20 "Why is light given to him who is in misery,
And life to the bitter of soul,
21 Who long for death, but it does not *come*,
And search for it more than hidden treasures;
22 Who rejoice exceedingly,
And are glad when they can find the grave?
23 *Why is light given* to a man whose way is hidden,
And whom God has hedged in?
24 For my sighing comes before I eat,[a]
And my groanings pour out like water.
25 For the thing I greatly feared has come upon me,
And what I dreaded has happened to me.
26 I am not at ease, nor am I quiet;
I have no rest, for trouble comes."

Eliphaz: Job Has Sinned

4 Then Eliphaz the Temanite answered and said:

2 "*If* one attempts a word with you, will you become weary?
But who can withhold himself from speaking?
3 Surely you have instructed many,
And you have strengthened weak hands.
4 Your words have upheld him who was stumbling,
And you have strengthened the feeble knees;
5 But now it comes upon you, and you are weary;
It touches you, and you are troubled.

3:6 [a] Septuagint, Syriac, Targum, and Vulgate read *be joined.* 3:24 [a] Literally *my bread*

6 *Is* not your reverence your
confidence?
And the integrity of your ways
your hope?
7 "Remember now, who *ever* perished
being innocent?
Or where were the upright *ever* cut
off?
8 Even as I have seen,
Those who plow iniquity
And sow trouble reap the same.
9 By the blast of God they perish,
And by the breath of His anger
they are consumed.
10 The roaring of the lion,
The voice of the fierce lion,
And the teeth of the young lions
are broken.
11 The old lion perishes for lack of
prey,
And the cubs of the lioness are
scattered.

12 "Now a word was secretly brought
to me,
And my ear received a whisper of
it.
13 In disquieting thoughts from the
visions of the night,
When deep sleep falls on men,
14 Fear came upon me, and
trembling,
Which made all my bones shake.
15 Then a spirit passed before my
face;
The hair on my body stood up.
16 It stood still,
But I could not discern its
appearance.
A form *was* before my eyes;
There was silence;
Then I heard a voice *saying:*
17 'Can a mortal be more righteous
than God?
Can a man be more pure than his
Maker?
18 If He puts no trust in His servants,
If He charges His angels with
error,
19 How much more those who dwell
in houses of clay,
Whose foundation is in the dust,
Who are crushed before a moth?
20 They are broken in pieces from
morning till evening;
They perish forever, with no one
regarding.
21 Does not their own excellence go
away?
They die, even without wisdom.'

Eliphaz: Job Is Chastened by God

5 "Call out now;
Is there anyone who will answer
you?
And to which of the holy ones will
you turn?
2 For wrath kills a foolish man,
And envy slays a simple one.
3 I have seen the foolish taking
root,
But suddenly I cursed his
dwelling place.
4 His sons are far from safety,
They are crushed in the gate,
And *there is* no deliverer.
5 Because the hungry eat up his
harvest,
Taking it even from the thorns,[a]
And a snare snatches their
substance.[b]
6 For affliction does not come from
the dust,
Nor does trouble spring from the
ground;
7 Yet man is born to trouble,
As the sparks fly upward.

8 "But as for me, I would seek God,
And to God I would commit my
cause—
9 Who does great things, and
unsearchable,
Marvelous things without
number.
10 He gives rain on the earth,
And sends waters on the fields.
11 He sets on high those who are
lowly,
And those who mourn are lifted to
safety.
12 He frustrates the devices of the
crafty,

5:5 [a] Septuagint reads *They shall not be taken from evil men;* Vulgate reads *And the armed man shall take him by violence.* [b] Septuagint reads *The might shall draw them off;* Vulgate reads *And the thirsty shall drink up their riches.*

So that their hands cannot carry
out their plans.
13 He catches the wise in their own
craftiness,
And the counsel of the cunning
comes quickly upon them.
14 They meet with darkness in the
daytime,
And grope at noontime as in the
night.
15 But He saves the needy from the
sword,
From the mouth of the mighty,
And from their hand.
16 So the poor have hope,
And injustice shuts her mouth.

17 "Behold, happy *is* the man whom
God corrects;
Therefore do not despise the
chastening of the Almighty.
18 For He bruises, but He binds up;
He wounds, but His hands make
whole.
19 He shall deliver you in six troubles,
Yes, in seven no evil shall touch
you.
20 In famine He shall redeem you
from death,
And in war from the power of the
sword.
21 You shall be hidden from the
scourge of the tongue,
And you shall not be afraid of
destruction when it comes.
22 You shall laugh at destruction
and famine,
And you shall not be afraid of the
beasts of the earth.
23 For you shall have a covenant
with the stones of the field,
And the beasts of the field shall be
at peace with you.
24 You shall know that your tent *is* in
peace;
You shall visit your dwelling and
find nothing amiss.
25 You shall also know that your
descendants *shall be* many,
And your offspring like the grass
of the earth.
26 You shall come to the grave at a
full age,
As a sheaf of grain ripens in its
season.
27 Behold, this we have searched
out;
It *is* true.
Hear it, and know for yourself."

Job: My Complaint Is Just

6 Then Job answered and said:
2 "Oh, that my grief were fully
weighed,
And my calamity laid with it on
the scales!
3 For then it would be heavier than
the sand of the sea—
Therefore my words have been
rash.
4 For the arrows of the Almighty
are within me;
My spirit drinks in their poison;
The terrors of God are arrayed
against me.
5 Does the wild donkey bray when
it has grass,
Or does the ox low over its
fodder?
6 Can flavorless food be eaten
without salt?
Or is there *any* taste in the white
of an egg?
7 My soul refuses to touch them;
They *are* as loathsome food to me.

8 "Oh, that I might have my
request,
That God would grant *me* the
thing that I long for!
9 That it would please God to
crush me,
That He would loose His hand and
cut me off!
10 Then I would still have comfort;
Though in anguish I would exult,
He will not spare;
For I have not concealed the
words of the Holy One.

11 "What strength do I have, that I
should hope?
And what *is* my end, that I should
prolong my life?
12 *Is* my strength the strength of
stones?
Or is my flesh bronze?
13 *Is* my help not within me?
And is success driven from me?

14 "To him who is afflicted, kindness
should be shown by his
friend,
Even though he forsakes the fear
of the Almighty.
15 My brothers have dealt deceitfully
like a brook,
Like the streams of the brooks
that pass away,
16 Which are dark because of the ice,
And into which the snow vanishes.
17 When it is warm, they cease to flow;
When it is hot, they vanish from
their place.
18 The paths of their way turn aside,
They go nowhere and perish.
19 The caravans of Tema look,
The travelers of Sheba hope for
them.
20 They are disappointed because
they were confident;
They come there and are
confused.
21 For now you are nothing,
You see terror and are afraid.
22 Did I ever say, 'Bring *something* to
me'?
Or, 'Offer a bribe for me from your
wealth'?
23 Or, 'Deliver me from the enemy's
hand'?
Or, 'Redeem me from the hand of
oppressors'?

24 "Teach me, and I will hold my
tongue;
Cause me to understand wherein
I have erred.
25 How forceful are right words!
But what does your arguing
prove?
26 Do you intend to rebuke *my*
words,
And the speeches of a desperate
one, *which are* as wind?
27 Yes, you overwhelm the
fatherless,
And you undermine your friend.
28 Now therefore, be pleased to look
at me;
For I would never lie to your face.
29 Yield now, let there be no
injustice!
Yes, concede, my righteousness
still stands!
30 Is there injustice on my tongue?
Cannot my taste discern the
unsavory?

Job: My Suffering Is Comfortless

7 "*Is there* not a time of hard service
for man on earth?
Are not his days also like the days
of a hired man?
2 Like a servant who earnestly
desires the shade,
And like a hired man who eagerly
looks for his wages,
3 So I have been allotted months of
futility,
And wearisome nights have been
appointed to me.
4 When I lie down, I say, 'When
shall I arise,
And the night be ended?'
For I have had my fill of tossing
till dawn.
5 My flesh is caked with worms and
dust,
My skin is cracked and breaks out
afresh.

6 "My days are swifter than a
weaver's shuttle,
And are spent without hope.
7 Oh, remember that my life *is* a
breath!
My eye will never again see good.
8 The eye of him who sees me will
see me no *more;*
While your eyes *are* upon me, I
shall no longer *be.*
9 *As* the cloud disappears and
vanishes away,
So he who goes down to the grave
does not come up.
10 He shall never return to his house,
Nor shall his place know him
anymore.

11 "Therefore I will not restrain my
mouth;
I will speak in the anguish of my
spirit;
I will complain in the bitterness of
my soul.
12 *Am* I a sea, or a sea serpent,
That You set a guard over me?
13 When I say, 'My bed will
comfort me,

My couch will ease my complaint,'
14 Then You scare me with dreams
And terrify me with visions,
15 So that my soul chooses strangling
And death rather than my body.[a]
16 I loathe *my life;*
I would not live forever.
Let me alone,
For my days *are but* a breath.

17 "What *is* man, that You should exalt him,
That You should set Your heart on him,
18 That You should visit him every morning,
And test him every moment?
19 How long?
Will You not look away from me,
And let me alone till I swallow my saliva?
20 Have I sinned?
What have I done to You,
O watcher of men?
Why have You set me as Your target,
So that I am a burden to myself?[a]
21 Why then do You not pardon my transgression,
And take away my iniquity?
For now I will lie down in the dust,
And You will seek me diligently,
But I *will* no longer *be.*"

Bildad: Job Should Repent

8 Then Bildad the Shuhite answered and said:

2 "How long will you speak these *things,*
And the words of your mouth *be like* a strong wind?
3 Does God subvert judgment?
Or does the Almighty pervert justice?
4 If your sons have sinned against Him,
He has cast them away for their transgression.
5 If you would earnestly seek God
And make your supplication to the Almighty,
6 If you *were* pure and upright,
Surely now He would awake for you,
And prosper your rightful dwelling place.
7 Though your beginning was small,
Yet your latter end would increase abundantly.

8 "For inquire, please, of the former age,
And consider the things discovered by their fathers;
9 For we *were born* yesterday, and know nothing,
Because our days on earth *are* a shadow.
10 Will they not teach you and tell you,
And utter words from their heart?

11 "Can the papyrus grow up without a marsh?
Can the reeds flourish without water?
12 While it *is* yet green *and* not cut down,
It withers before any *other* plant.
13 So *are* the paths of all who forget God;
And the hope of the hypocrite shall perish,
14 Whose confidence shall be cut off,
And whose trust *is* a spider's web.
15 He leans on his house, but it does not stand.
He holds it fast, but it does not endure.
16 He grows green in the sun,
And his branches spread out in his garden.
17 His roots wrap around the rock heap,
And look for a place in the stones.
18 If he is destroyed from his place,
Then *it* will deny him, *saying,* 'I have not seen you.'

19 "Behold, this is the joy of His way,
And out of the earth others will grow.
20 Behold, God will not cast away the blameless,
Nor will He uphold the evildoers.

7:15 [a] Literally *my bones* 7:20 [a] Following Masoretic Text, Targum, and Vulgate; Septuagint and Jewish tradition read *to You.*

21 He will yet fill your mouth with laughing,
And your lips with rejoicing.
22 Those who hate you will be clothed with shame,
And the dwelling place of the wicked will come to nothing."[a]

Job: There Is No Mediator

9 Then Job answered and said:
2 "Truly I know *it is* so,
But how can a man be righteous before God?
3 If one wished to contend with Him,
He could not answer Him one time out of a thousand.
4 *God is* wise in heart and mighty in strength.
Who has hardened *himself* against Him and prospered?
5 He removes the mountains, and they do not know
When He overturns them in His anger;
6 He shakes the earth out of its place,
And its pillars tremble;
7 He commands the sun, and it does not rise;
He seals off the stars;
8 He alone spreads out the heavens,
And treads on the waves of the sea;
9 He made the Bear, Orion, and the Pleiades,
And the chambers of the south;
10 He does great things past finding out,
Yes, wonders without number.
11 If He goes by me, I do not see *Him;*
If He moves past, I do not perceive Him;
12 If He takes away, who can hinder Him?
Who can say to Him, 'What are You doing?'
13 God will not withdraw His anger,
The allies of the proud[a] lie prostrate beneath Him.

14 "How then can I answer Him,
And choose my words *to reason* with Him?
15 For though I were righteous, I could not answer Him;
I would beg mercy of my Judge.
16 If I called and He answered me,
I would not believe that He was listening to my voice.
17 For He crushes me with a tempest,
And multiplies my wounds without cause.
18 He will not allow me to catch my breath,
But fills me with bitterness.
19 If *it is a matter* of strength, indeed *He is* strong;
And if of justice, who will appoint my day *in court?*
20 Though I were righteous, my own mouth would condemn me;
Though I *were* blameless, it would prove me perverse.

21 "I am blameless, yet I do not know myself;
I despise my life.
22 It *is* all one *thing;*
Therefore I say, 'He destroys the blameless and the wicked.'
23 If the scourge slays suddenly,
He laughs at the plight of the innocent.
24 The earth is given into the hand of the wicked.
He covers the faces of its judges.
If it is not *He,* who else could it be?

25 "Now my days are swifter than a runner;
They flee away, they see no good.
26 They pass by like swift ships,
Like an eagle swooping on its prey.
27 If I say, 'I will forget my complaint,
I will put off my sad face and wear a smile,'
28 I am afraid of all my sufferings;
I know that You will not hold me innocent.
29 *If* I am condemned,
Why then do I labor in vain?

8:22 [a] Literally *will not be* 9:13 [a] Hebrew *rahab*

30 If I wash myself with snow water,
And cleanse my hands with soap,
31 Yet You will plunge me into the pit,
And my own clothes will abhor me.

32 "For *He is* not a man, as I *am,*
That I may answer Him,
And that we should go to court together.
33 Nor is there any mediator between us,
Who may lay his hand on us both.
34 Let Him take His rod away from me,
And do not let dread of Him terrify me.
35 *Then* I would speak and not fear Him,
But it is not so with me.

Job: I Would Plead with God

10 "My soul loathes my life;
I will give free course to my complaint,
I will speak in the bitterness of my soul.
2 I will say to God, 'Do not condemn me;
Show me why You contend with me.
3 *Does it* seem good to You that You should oppress,
That You should despise the work of Your hands,
And smile on the counsel of the wicked?
4 Do You have eyes of flesh?
Or do You see as man sees?
5 *Are* Your days like the days of a mortal man?
Are Your years like the days of a mighty man,
6 That You should seek for my iniquity
And search out my sin,
7 Although You know that I am not wicked,
And *there is* no one who can deliver from Your hand?

8 'Your hands have made me and fashioned me,
An intricate unity;
Yet You would destroy me.
9 Remember, I pray, that You have made me like clay.
And will You turn me into dust again?
10 Did You not pour me out like milk,
And curdle me like cheese,
11 Clothe me with skin and flesh,
And knit me together with bones and sinews?
12 You have granted me life and favor,
And Your care has preserved my spirit.

13 'And these *things* You have hidden in Your heart;
I know that this *was* with You:
14 If I sin, then You mark me,
And will not acquit me of my iniquity.
15 If I am wicked, woe to me;
Even *if* I am righteous, I cannot lift up my head.
I am full of disgrace;
See my misery!
16 If *my head* is exalted,
You hunt me like a fierce lion,
And again You show Yourself awesome against me.
17 You renew Your witnesses against me,
And increase Your indignation toward me;
Changes and war are *ever* with me.

18 'Why then have You brought me out of the womb?
Oh, that I had perished and no eye had seen me!
19 I would have been as though I had not been.
I would have been carried from the womb to the grave.
20 Are not my days few?
Cease! Leave me alone, that I may take a little comfort,
21 Before I go *to the place from which* I shall not return,
To the land of darkness and the shadow of death,
22 A land as dark as darkness *itself,*
As the shadow of death, without any order,
Where even the light *is* like darkness.' "

Zophar Urges Job to Repent

11 Then Zophar the Naamathite
answered and said:

2 "Should not the multitude of words
be answered?
And should a man full of talk be
vindicated?
3 Should your empty talk make
men hold their peace?
And when you mock, should no
one rebuke you?
4 For you have said,
'My doctrine *is* pure,
And I am clean in your eyes.'
5 But oh, that God would speak,
And open His lips against you,
6 That He would show you the
secrets of wisdom!
For *they would* double *your*
prudence.
Know therefore that God exacts
from you
Less than your iniquity *deserves*.

7 "Can you search out the deep
things of God?
Can you find out the limits of the
Almighty?
8 *They are* higher than heaven—
what can you do?
Deeper than Sheol—what can you
know?
9 Their measure *is* longer than the
earth
And broader than the sea.

10 "If He passes by, imprisons, and
gathers *to judgment*,
Then who can hinder Him?
11 For He knows deceitful men;
He sees wickedness also.
Will He not then consider *it*?
12 For an empty-headed man will be
wise,
When a wild donkey's colt is born
a man.

13 "If you would prepare your heart,
And stretch out your hands
toward Him;
14 If iniquity *were* in your hand, *and*
you put it far away,
And would not let wickedness
dwell in your tents;
15 Then surely you could lift up your
face without spot;
Yes, you could be steadfast, and
not fear;
16 Because you would forget *your*
misery,
And remember *it* as waters *that*
have passed away,
17 And *your* life would be brighter
than noonday.
Though you were dark, you would
be like the morning.
18 And you would be secure, because
there is hope;
Yes, you would dig *around you*,
and take your rest in safety.
19 You would also lie down, and no
one would make *you* afraid;
Yes, many would court your favor.
20 But the eyes of the wicked will fail,
And they shall not escape,
And their hope—loss of life!"

Job Answers His Critics

12 Then Job answered and said:

2 "No doubt you *are* the people,
And wisdom will die with you!
3 But I have understanding as well
as you;
I *am* not inferior to you.
Indeed, who does not *know* such
things as these?

4 "I am one mocked by his friends,
Who called on God, and He
answered him,
The just and blameless *who is*
ridiculed.
5 A lamp[a] is despised in the thought
of one who is at ease;
It is made ready for those whose
feet slip.
6 The tents of robbers prosper,
And those who provoke God are
secure—
In what God provides by His
hand.

7 "But now ask the beasts, and they
will teach you;

12:5 [a] Or *disaster*

And the birds of the air, and they will tell you;
8 Or speak to the earth, and it will teach you;
And the fish of the sea will explain to you.
9 Who among all these does not know
That the hand of the LORD has done this,
10 In whose hand *is* the life of every living thing,
And the breath of all mankind?
11 Does not the ear test words
And the mouth taste its food?
12 Wisdom *is* with aged men,
And with length of days, understanding.

13 "With Him *are* wisdom and strength,
He has counsel and understanding.
14 If He breaks *a thing* down, it cannot be rebuilt;
If He imprisons a man, there can be no release.
15 If He withholds the waters, they dry up;
If He sends them out, they overwhelm the earth.
16 With Him *are* strength and prudence.
The deceived and the deceiver *are* His.
17 He leads counselors away plundered,
And makes fools of the judges.
18 He loosens the bonds of kings,
And binds their waist with a belt.
19 He leads princes[a] away plundered,
And overthrows the mighty.
20 He deprives the trusted ones of speech,
And takes away the discernment of the elders.
21 He pours contempt on princes,
And disarms the mighty.
22 He uncovers deep things out of darkness,
And brings the shadow of death to light.
23 He makes nations great, and destroys them;
He enlarges nations, and guides them.
24 He takes away the understanding[a] of the chiefs of the people of the earth,
And makes them wander in a pathless wilderness.
25 They grope in the dark without light,
And He makes them stagger like a drunken *man*.

13

"Behold, my eye has seen all *this*,
My ear has heard and understood it.
2 What you know, I also know;
I *am* not inferior to you.
3 But I would speak to the Almighty,
And I desire to reason with God.
4 But you forgers of lies,
You *are* all worthless physicians.
5 Oh, that you would be silent,
And it would be your wisdom!
6 Now hear my reasoning,
And heed the pleadings of my lips.
7 Will you speak wickedly for God,
And talk deceitfully for Him?
8 Will you show partiality for Him?
Will you contend for God?
9 Will it be well when He searches you out?
Or can you mock Him as one mocks a man?
10 He will surely rebuke you
If you secretly show partiality.
11 Will not His excellence make you afraid,
And the dread of Him fall upon you?
12 Your platitudes *are* proverbs of ashes,
Your defenses are defenses of clay.

13 "Hold your peace with me, and let me speak,
Then let come on me what *may!*
14 Why do I take my flesh in my teeth,
And put my life in my hands?

12:19 [a] Literally *priests*, but not in a technical sense 12:24 [a] Literally *heart*

15 Though He slay me, yet will I trust Him.
Even so, I will defend my own ways before Him.
16 He also *shall* be my salvation,
For a hypocrite could not come before Him.
17 Listen carefully to my speech,
And to my declaration with your ears.
18 See now, I have prepared *my* case,
I know that I shall be vindicated.
19 Who *is* he *who* will contend with me?
If now I hold my tongue, I perish.

Job's Despondent Prayer

20 "Only two *things* do not do to me,
Then I will not hide myself from You:
21 Withdraw Your hand far from me,
And let not the dread of You make me afraid.
22 Then call, and I will answer;
Or let me speak, then You respond to me.
23 How many *are* my iniquities and sins?
Make me know my transgression and my sin.
24 Why do You hide Your face,
And regard me as Your enemy?
25 Will You frighten a leaf driven to and fro?
And will You pursue dry stubble?
26 For You write bitter things against me,
And make me inherit the iniquities of my youth.
27 You put my feet in the stocks,
And watch closely all my paths.
You set a limit[a] for the soles of my feet.

28 "*Man*[a] decays like a rotten thing,
Like a garment that is moth-eaten.

14

"Man *who is* born of woman
Is of few days and full of trouble.
2 He comes forth like a flower and fades away;
He flees like a shadow and does not continue.
3 And do You open Your eyes on such a one,
And bring me[a] to judgment with Yourself?
4 Who can bring a clean *thing* out of an unclean?
No one!
5 Since his days *are* determined,
The number of his months *is* with You;
You have appointed his limits, so that he cannot pass.
6 Look away from him that he may rest,
Till like a hired man he finishes his day.

7 "For there is hope for a tree,
If it is cut down, that it will sprout again,
And that its tender shoots will not cease.
8 Though its root may grow old in the earth,
And its stump may die in the ground,
9 *Yet* at the scent of water it will bud
And bring forth branches like a plant.
10 But man dies and is laid away;
Indeed he breathes his last
And where *is* he?
11 *As* water disappears from the sea,
And a river becomes parched and dries up,
12 So man lies down and does not rise.
Till the heavens *are* no more,
They will not awake
Nor be roused from their sleep.

13 "Oh, that You would hide me in the grave,
That You would conceal me until Your wrath is past,
That You would appoint me a set time, and remember me!
14 If a man dies, shall he live *again?*
All the days of my hard service I will wait,
Till my change comes.
15 You shall call, and I will answer You;

13:27 [a] Literally *inscribe a print* 13:28 [a] Literally *He* 14:3 [a] Septuagint, Syriac, and Vulgate read *him.*

You shall desire the work of Your hands.
16 For now You number my steps,
But do not watch over my sin.
17 My transgression *is* sealed up in a bag,
And You cover[a] my iniquity.

18 "But *as* a mountain falls *and* crumbles away,
And *as* a rock is moved from its place;
19 *As* water wears away stones,
And as torrents wash away the soil of the earth;
So You destroy the hope of man.
20 You prevail forever against him, and he passes on;
You change his countenance and send him away.
21 His sons come to honor, and he does not know *it;*
They are brought low, and he does not perceive *it.*
22 But his flesh will be in pain over it,
And his soul will mourn over it."

Eliphaz Accuses Job of Folly

15 Then Eliphaz the Temanite answered and said:

2 "Should a wise man answer with empty knowledge,
And fill himself with the east wind?
3 Should he reason with unprofitable talk,
Or by speeches with which he can do no good?
4 Yes, you cast off fear,
And restrain prayer before God.
5 For your iniquity teaches your mouth,
And you choose the tongue of the crafty.
6 Your own mouth condemns you, and not I;
Yes, your own lips testify against you.

7 "*Are* you the first man *who* was born?
Or were you made before the hills?
8 Have you heard the counsel of God?
Do you limit wisdom to yourself?
9 What do you know that we do not know?
What do you understand that *is* not in us?
10 Both the gray-haired and the aged *are* among us,
Much older than your father.
11 *Are* the consolations of God too small for you,
And the word *spoken* gently[a] with you?
12 Why does your heart carry you away,
And what do your eyes wink at,
13 That you turn your spirit against God,
And let *such* words go out of your mouth?

14 "What *is* man, that he could be pure?
And *he who is* born of a woman, that he could be righteous?
15 If *God* puts no trust in His saints,
And the heavens are not pure in His sight,
16 How much less man, *who is* abominable and filthy,
Who drinks iniquity like water!

17 "I will tell you, hear me;
What I have seen I will declare,
18 What wise men have told,
Not hiding *anything received* from their fathers,
19 To whom alone the land was given,
And no alien passed among them:
20 The wicked man writhes with pain all *his* days,
And the number of years is hidden from the oppressor.
21 Dreadful sounds *are* in his ears;
In prosperity the destroyer comes upon him.
22 He does not believe that he will return from darkness,
For a sword is waiting for him.
23 He wanders about for bread, *saying,* 'Where *is it?*'

14:17 [a] Literally *plaster over* 15:11 [a] Septuagint reads *a secret thing.*

He knows that a day of darkness
is ready at his hand.
24 Trouble and anguish make him
afraid;
They overpower him, like a king
ready for battle.
25 For he stretches out his hand
against God,
And acts defiantly against the
Almighty,
26 Running stubbornly against Him
With his strong, embossed shield.
27 "Though he has covered his face
with his fatness,
And made *his* waist heavy
with fat,
28 He dwells in desolate cities,
In houses which no one inhabits,
Which are destined to become
ruins.
29 He will not be rich,
Nor will his wealth continue,
Nor will his possessions
overspread the earth.
30 He will not depart from darkness;
The flame will dry out his
branches,
And by the breath of His mouth
he will go away.
31 Let him not trust in futile *things,*
deceiving himself,
For futility will be his reward.
32 It will be accomplished before his
time,
And his branch will not be green.
33 He will shake off his unripe grape
like a vine,
And cast off his blossom like an
olive tree.
34 For the company of hypocrites
will be barren,
And fire will consume the tents of
bribery.
35 They conceive trouble and bring
forth futility;
Their womb prepares deceit."

Job Reproaches His Pitiless Friends

16 Then Job answered and said:
2 "I have heard many such things;
Miserable comforters *are* you all!
3 Shall words of wind have an end?
Or what provokes you that you
answer?
4 I also could speak as you *do,*
If your soul were in my soul's
place.
I could heap up words against
you,
And shake my head at you;
5 *But* I would strengthen you with
my mouth,
And the comfort of my lips would
relieve *your grief.*
6 "Though I speak, my grief is not
relieved;
And *if* I remain silent, how am I
eased?
7 But now He has worn me out;
You have made desolate all my
company.
8 You have shriveled me up,
And it is a witness *against me;*
My leanness rises up against me
And bears witness to my face.
9 He tears *me* in His wrath, and
hates me;
He gnashes at me with His
teeth;
My adversary sharpens His gaze
on me.
10 They gape at me with their
mouth,
They strike me reproachfully on
the cheek,
They gather together against me.
11 God has delivered me to the
ungodly,
And turned me over to the hands
of the wicked.
12 I was at ease, but He has
shattered me;
He also has taken *me* by my neck,
and shaken me to pieces;
He has set me up for His target,
13 His archers surround me.
He pierces my heart[a] and does
not pity;
He pours out my gall on the
ground.
14 He breaks me with wound upon
wound;
He runs at me like a warrior.[a]

16:13 [a] Literally *kidneys* 16:14 [a] Vulgate reads *giant.*

15 "I have sewn sackcloth over my
skin,
And laid my head[a] in the dust.
16 My face is flushed from weeping,
And on my eyelids *is* the shadow
of death;
17 Although no violence *is* in my
hands,
And my prayer *is* pure.

18 "O earth, do not cover my blood,
And let my cry have no *resting*
place!
19 Surely even now my witness *is* in
heaven,
And my evidence *is* on high.
20 My friends scorn me;
My eyes pour out *tears* to God.
21 Oh, that one might plead for a
man with God,
As a man *pleads* for his neighbor!
22 For when a few years are finished,
I shall go the way of no return.

Job Prays for Relief

17 "My spirit is broken,
My days are extinguished,
The grave *is ready* for me.
2 *Are* not mockers with me?
And does not my eye dwell on
their provocation?

3 "Now put down a pledge for me with
Yourself.
Who *is* he *who* will shake hands
with me?
4 For You have hidden their heart
from understanding;
Therefore You will not exalt *them.*
5 He who speaks flattery to *his*
friends,
Even the eyes of his children will
fail.

6 "But He has made me a byword of
the people,
And I have become one in whose
face men spit.
7 My eye has also grown dim
because of sorrow,
And all my members *are* like
shadows.
8 Upright *men* are astonished at this,
And the innocent stirs himself up
against the hypocrite.
9 Yet the righteous will hold to his
way,
And he who has clean hands will
be stronger and stronger.

10 "But please, come back again, all of
you,[a]
For I shall not find *one* wise *man*
among you.
11 My days are past,
My purposes are broken off,
Even the thoughts of my heart.
12 They change the night into day;
'The light *is* near,' *they say,* in the
face of darkness.
13 If I wait *for* the grave *as* my
house,
If I make my bed in the
darkness,
14 If I say to corruption, 'You *are* my
father,'
And to the worm, 'You *are* my
mother and my sister,'
15 Where then *is* my hope?
As for my hope, who can see it?
16 *Will* they go down to the gates of
Sheol?
Shall *we have* rest together in the
dust?"

Bildad: The Wicked Are Punished

18 Then Bildad the Shuhite answered and said:

2 "How long *till* you put an end to
words?
Gain understanding, and
afterward we will speak.
3 Why are we counted as beasts,
And regarded as stupid in your
sight?
4 You who tear yourself in anger,
Shall the earth be forsaken for
you?
Or shall the rock be removed from
its place?

5 "The light of the wicked indeed goes
out,
And the flame of his fire does not
shine.

16:15 [a] Literally *horn* 17:10 [a] Following some Hebrew manuscripts, Septuagint, Syriac, and Vulgate; Masoretic Text and Targum read *all of them.*

6 The light is dark in his tent,
And his lamp beside him is put out.
7 The steps of his strength are shortened,
And his own counsel casts him down.
8 For he is cast into a net by his own feet,
And he walks into a snare.
9 The net takes *him* by the heel,
And a snare lays hold of him.
10 A noose *is* hidden for him on the ground,
And a trap for him in the road.
11 Terrors frighten him on every side,
And drive him to his feet.
12 His strength is starved,
And destruction *is* ready at his side.
13 It devours patches of his skin;
The firstborn of death devours his limbs.
14 He is uprooted from the shelter of his tent,
And they parade him before the king of terrors.
15 They dwell in his tent *who are* none of his;
Brimstone is scattered on his dwelling.
16 His roots are dried out below,
And his branch withers above.
17 The memory of him perishes from the earth,
And he has no name among the renowned.[a]
18 He is driven from light into darkness,
And chased out of the world.
19 He has neither son nor posterity among his people,
Nor any remaining in his dwellings.
20 Those in the west are astonished at his day,
As those in the east are frightened.
21 Surely such *are* the dwellings of the wicked,
And this *is* the place *of him who* does not know God."

Job Trusts in His Redeemer

19 Then Job answered and said:
2 "How long will you torment my soul,
And break me in pieces with words?
3 These ten times you have reproached me;
You are not ashamed *that* you have wronged me.[a]
4 And if indeed I have erred,
My error remains with me.
5 If indeed you exalt *yourselves* against me,
And plead my disgrace against me,
6 Know then that God has wronged me,
And has surrounded me with His net.

7 "If I cry out concerning wrong, I am not heard.
If I cry aloud, *there is* no justice.
8 He has fenced up my way, so that I cannot pass;
And He has set darkness in my paths.
9 He has stripped me of my glory,
And taken the crown *from* my head.
10 He breaks me down on every side,
And I am gone;
My hope He has uprooted like a tree.
11 He has also kindled His wrath against me,
And He counts me as *one of* His enemies.
12 His troops come together
And build up their road against me;
They encamp all around my tent.

13 "He has removed my brothers far from me,
And my acquaintances are completely estranged from me.
14 My relatives have failed,
And my close friends have forgotten me.

18:17 [a] Literally *before the outside,* meaning distinguished, famous 19:3 [a] A Jewish tradition reads *make yourselves strange to me.*

15 Those who dwell in my house, and my maidservants,
Count me as a stranger;
I am an alien in their sight.
16 I call my servant, but he gives no answer;
I beg him with my mouth.
17 My breath is offensive to my wife,
And I am repulsive to the children of my own body.
18 Even young children despise me;
I arise, and they speak against me.
19 All my close friends abhor me,
And those whom I love have turned against me.
20 My bone clings to my skin and to my flesh,
And I have escaped by the skin of my teeth.

21 "Have pity on me, have pity on me, O you my friends,
For the hand of God has struck me!
22 Why do you persecute me as God *does,*
And are not satisfied with my flesh?

23 "Oh, that my words were written!
Oh, that they were inscribed in a book!
24 That they were engraved on a rock
With an iron pen and lead, forever!
25 For I know *that* my Redeemer lives,
And He shall stand at last on the earth;
26 And after my skin is destroyed, this *I know,*
That in my flesh I shall see God,
27 Whom I shall see for myself,
And my eyes shall behold, and not another.
How my heart yearns within me!
28 If you should say, 'How shall we persecute him?'—
Since the root of the matter is found in me,
29 Be afraid of the sword for yourselves;
For wrath *brings* the punishment of the sword,
That you may know *there is* a judgment."

Zophar's Sermon on the Wicked Man

20 Then Zophar the Naamathite answered and said:

2 "Therefore my anxious thoughts make me answer,
Because of the turmoil within me.
3 I have heard the rebuke that reproaches me,
And the spirit of my understanding causes me to answer.

4 "Do you *not* know this of old,
Since man was placed on earth,
5 That the triumphing of the wicked is short,
And the joy of the hypocrite is *but* for a moment?
6 Though his haughtiness mounts up to the heavens,
And his head reaches to the clouds,
7 *Yet* he will perish forever like his own refuse;
Those who have seen him will say, 'Where is he?'
8 He will fly away like a dream, and not be found;
Yes, he will be chased away like a vision of the night.
9 The eye *that* saw him will *see him* no more,
Nor will his place behold him anymore.
10 His children will seek the favor of the poor,
And his hands will restore his wealth.
11 His bones are full of his youthful vigor,
But it will lie down with him in the dust.

12 "Though evil is sweet in his mouth,
And he hides it under his tongue,
13 *Though* he spares it and does not forsake it,
But still keeps it in his mouth,

14 *Yet* his food in his stomach turns sour;
It becomes cobra venom within him.
15 He swallows down riches
And vomits them up again;
God casts them out of his belly.
16 He will suck the poison of cobras;
The viper's tongue will slay him.
17 He will not see the streams,
The rivers flowing with honey and cream.
18 He will restore that for which he labored,
And will not swallow *it* down;
From the proceeds of business
He will get no enjoyment.
19 For he has oppressed *and* forsaken the poor,
He has violently seized a house which he did not build.

20 "Because he knows no quietness in his heart,[a]
He will not save anything he desires.
21 Nothing is left for him to eat;
Therefore his well-being will not last.
22 In his self-sufficiency he will be in distress;
Every hand of misery will come against him.
23 *When* he is about to fill his stomach,
God will cast on him the fury of His wrath,
And will rain *it* on him while he is eating.
24 He will flee from the iron weapon;
A bronze bow will pierce him through.
25 It is drawn, and comes out of the body;
Yes, the glittering *point comes* out of his gall.
Terrors *come* upon him;
26 Total darkness *is* reserved for his treasures.
An unfanned fire will consume him;
It shall go ill with him who is left in his tent.
27 The heavens will reveal his iniquity,
And the earth will rise up against him.
28 The increase of his house will depart,
And his goods will flow away in the day of His wrath.
29 This *is* the portion from God for a wicked man,
The heritage appointed to him by God."

Job's Discourse on the Wicked

21 Then Job answered and said:

2 "Listen carefully to my speech,
And let this be your consolation.
3 Bear with me that I may speak,
And after I have spoken, keep mocking.

4 "As for me, *is* my complaint against man?
And if *it were,* why should I not be impatient?
5 Look at me and be astonished;
Put *your* hand over *your* mouth.
6 Even when I remember I am terrified,
And trembling takes hold of my flesh.
7 Why do the wicked live *and* become old,
Yes, become mighty in power?
8 Their descendants are established with them in their sight,
And their offspring before their eyes.
9 Their houses *are* safe from fear,
Neither *is* the rod of God upon them.
10 Their bull breeds without failure;
Their cow calves without miscarriage.
11 They send forth their little ones like a flock,
And their children dance.
12 They sing to the tambourine and harp,
And rejoice to the sound of the flute.
13 They spend their days in wealth,
And in a moment go down to the grave.[a]

20:20 [a] Literally *belly* 21:13 [a] Or *Sheol*

14 Yet they say to God, 'Depart
from us,
For we do not desire the
knowledge of Your ways.
15 Who *is* the Almighty, that we
should serve Him?
And what profit do we have if we
pray to Him?'
16 Indeed their prosperity *is* not in
their hand;
The counsel of the wicked is far
from me.

17 "How often is the lamp of the
wicked put out?
How often does their destruction
come upon them,
The sorrows *God* distributes in His
anger?
18 They are like straw before the
wind,
And like chaff that a storm carries
away.
19 *They say,* 'God lays up one's[a]
iniquity for his children';
Let Him recompense him, that he
may know *it.*
20 Let his eyes see his destruction,
And let him drink of the wrath of
the Almighty.
21 For what does he care about his
household after him,
When the number of his months
is cut in half?

22 "Can *anyone* teach God knowledge,
Since He judges those on high?
23 One dies in his full strength,
Being wholly at ease and secure;
24 His pails[a] are full of milk,
And the marrow of his bones is
moist.
25 Another man dies in the
bitterness of his soul,
Never having eaten with pleasure.
26 They lie down alike in the dust,
And worms cover them.

27 "Look, I know your thoughts,
And the schemes *with which* you
would wrong me.
28 For you say,
'Where *is* the house of the prince?
And where *is* the tent,[a]
The dwelling place of the wicked?'
29 Have you not asked those who
travel the road?
And do you not know their
signs?
30 For the wicked are reserved for
the day of doom;
They shall be brought out on the
day of wrath.
31 Who condemns his way to his
face?
And who repays him *for what* he
has done?
32 Yet he shall be brought to the
grave,
And a vigil kept over the tomb.
33 The clods of the valley shall be
sweet to him;
Everyone shall follow him,
As countless *have gone* before
him.
34 How then can you comfort me
with empty words,
Since falsehood remains in your
answers?"

Eliphaz Accuses Job of Wickedness

22 Then Eliphaz the Temanite answered and said:

2 "Can a man be profitable to God,
Though he who is wise may be
profitable to himself?
3 *Is it* any pleasure to the Almighty
that you are righteous?
Or *is it* gain *to Him* that you make
your ways blameless?

4 "Is it because of your fear of Him
that He corrects you,
And enters into judgment with
you?
5 *Is* not your wickedness great,
And your iniquity without end?
6 For you have taken pledges from
your brother for no reason,
And stripped the naked of their
clothing.
7 You have not given the weary
water to drink,
And you have withheld bread
from the hungry.

21:19 [a] Literally *his* 21:24 [a] Septuagint and Vulgate read *bowels;* Syriac reads *sides;* Targum reads *breasts.* 21:28 [a] Vulgate omits *the tent.*

8 But the mighty man possessed
the land,
And the honorable man dwelt
in it.
9 You have sent widows away
empty,
And the strength of the fatherless
was crushed.
10 Therefore snares *are* all around
you,
And sudden fear troubles you,
11 Or darkness *so that* you cannot
see;
And an abundance of water
covers you.

12 "Is not God in the height of heaven?
And see the highest stars, how
lofty they are!
13 And you say, 'What does God
know?
Can He judge through the deep
darkness?
14 Thick clouds cover Him, so that
He cannot see,
And He walks above the circle of
heaven.'
15 Will you keep to the old way
Which wicked men have trod,
16 Who were cut down before their
time,
Whose foundations were swept
away by a flood?
17 They said to God, 'Depart from us!
What can the Almighty do to
them?'[a]
18 Yet He filled their houses with
good *things;*
But the counsel of the wicked is
far from me.

19 "The righteous see *it* and are glad,
And the innocent laugh at them:
20 'Surely our adversaries[a] are cut
down,
And the fire consumes their
remnant.'

21 "Now acquaint yourself with Him,
and be at peace;
Thereby good will come to you.
22 Receive, please, instruction from
His mouth,
And lay up His words in your
heart.
23 If you return to the Almighty, you
will be built up;
You will remove iniquity far from
your tents.
24 Then you will lay your gold in the
dust,
And the *gold* of Ophir among the
stones of the brooks.
25 Yes, the Almighty will be your
gold[a]
And your precious silver;
26 For then you will have your
delight in the Almighty,
And lift up your face to God.
27 You will make your prayer to
Him,
He will hear you,
And you will pay your vows.
28 You will also declare a thing,
And it will be established for you;
So light will shine on your ways.
29 When they cast *you* down, and
you say, 'Exaltation *will*
come!'
Then He will save the humble
person.
30 He will *even* deliver one who is not
innocent;
Yes, he will be delivered by the
purity of your hands."

Job Proclaims God's Righteous Judgments

23 Then Job answered and said:
2 "Even today my complaint is
bitter;
My[a] hand is listless because of
my groaning.
3 Oh, that I knew where I might find
Him,
That I might come to His seat!
4 I would present *my* case before
Him,
And fill my mouth with arguments.
5 I would know the words *which* He
would answer me,

22:17 [a] Septuagint and Syriac read *us.* **22:20** [a] Septuagint reads *substance.* **22:25** [a] The ancient versions suggest *defense;* Hebrew reads *gold* as in verse 24. **23:2** [a] Following Masoretic Text, Targum, and Vulgate; Septuagint and Syriac read *His.*

And understand what He would
say to me.
6 Would He contend with me in His
great power?
No! But He would take *note* of me.
7 There the upright could reason
with Him,
And I would be delivered forever
from my Judge.

8 "Look, I go forward, but He is not
there,
And backward, but I cannot
perceive Him;
9 When He works on the left hand, I
cannot behold *Him;*
When He turns to the right hand,
I cannot see *Him.*
10 But He knows the way that I take;
When He has tested me, I shall
come forth as gold.
11 My foot has held fast to His
steps;
I have kept His way and not
turned aside.
12 I have not departed from the
commandment of His lips;
I have treasured the words of His
mouth
More than my necessary *food.*

13 "But He *is* unique, and who can
make Him change?
And *whatever* His soul desires,
that He does.
14 For He performs *what is*
appointed for me,
And many such *things are* with
Him.
15 Therefore I am terrified at His
presence;
When I consider *this,* I am afraid
of Him.
16 For God made my heart weak,
And the Almighty terrifies me;
17 Because I was not cut off from the
presence of darkness,
And He did *not* hide deep
darkness from my face.

Job Complains of Violence on the Earth

24 "*Since* times are not hidden
from the Almighty,
Why do those who know Him see
not His days?
2 "*Some* remove landmarks;
They seize flocks violently and
feed *on them;*
3 They drive away the donkey of
the fatherless;
They take the widow's ox as a
pledge.
4 They push the needy off the road;
All the poor of the land are forced
to hide.
5 Indeed, *like* wild donkeys in the
desert,
They go out to their work,
searching for food.
The wilderness *yields* food for
them *and* for *their* children.
6 They gather their fodder in the
field
And glean in the vineyard of the
wicked.
7 They spend the night naked,
without clothing,
And have no covering in the cold.
8 They are wet with the showers of
the mountains,
And huddle around the rock for
want of shelter.

9 "*Some* snatch the fatherless from
the breast,
And take a pledge from the poor.
10 They cause *the poor* to go naked,
without clothing;
And they take away the sheaves
from the hungry.
11 They press out oil within their walls,
And tread winepresses, yet suffer
thirst.
12 The dying groan in the city,
And the souls of the wounded cry
out;
Yet God does not charge *them*
with wrong.

13 "There are those who rebel against
the light;
They do not know its ways
Nor abide in its paths.
14 The murderer rises with the light;
He kills the poor and needy;
And in the night he is like a thief.
15 The eye of the adulterer waits for
the twilight,
Saying, 'No eye will see me';
And he disguises *his* face.

16 In the dark they break into houses
Which they marked for themselves in the daytime;
They do not know the light.
17 For the morning is the same to them as the shadow of death;
If *someone* recognizes *them,*
They are in the terrors of the shadow of death.

18 "They *should be* swift on the face of the waters,
Their portion *should be* cursed in the earth,
So that no *one would* turn into the way of their vineyards.
19 As drought and heat consume the snow waters,
So the grave[a] *consumes those who* have sinned.
20 The womb *should* forget him,
The worm *should* feed sweetly on him;
He *should* be remembered no more,
And wickedness *should* be broken like a tree.
21 For he preys on the barren *who* do not bear,
And does no good for the widow.

22 "But *God* draws the mighty away with His power;
He rises up, but no *man* is sure of life.
23 He gives them security, and they rely *on it;*
Yet His eyes *are* on their ways.
24 They are exalted for a little while,
Then they are gone.
They are brought low;
They are taken out of the way like all *others;*
They dry out like the heads of grain.

25 "Now if *it is* not *so,* who will prove me a liar,
And make my speech worth nothing?"

Bildad: How Can Man Be Righteous?

25 Then Bildad the Shuhite answered and said:

2 "Dominion and fear *belong* to Him;
He makes peace in His high places.
3 Is there any number to His armies?
Upon whom does His light not rise?
4 How then can man be righteous before God?
Or how can he be pure *who is* born of a woman?
5 If even the moon does not shine,
And the stars are not pure in His sight,
6 How much less man, *who is* a maggot,
And a son of man, *who is* a worm?"

Job: Man's Frailty and God's Majesty

26 But Job answered and said:

2 "How have you helped *him who is* without power?
How have you saved the arm *that has* no strength?
3 How have you counseled *one who has* no wisdom?
And *how* have you declared sound advice to many?
4 To whom have you uttered words?
And whose spirit came from you?

5 "The dead tremble,
Those under the waters and those inhabiting them.
6 Sheol *is* naked before Him,
And Destruction has no covering.
7 He stretches out the north over empty space;
He hangs the earth on nothing.
8 He binds up the water in His thick clouds,
Yet the clouds are not broken under it.
9 He covers the face of *His* throne,
And spreads His cloud over it.
10 He drew a circular horizon on the face of the waters,
At the boundary of light and darkness.

24:19 [a] Or *Sheol*

11 The pillars of heaven tremble,
And are astonished at His rebuke.
12 He stirs up the sea with His power,
And by His understanding He
breaks up the storm.
13 By His Spirit He adorned the
heavens;
His hand pierced the fleeing
serpent.
14 Indeed these *are* the mere edges
of His ways,
And how small a whisper we hear
of Him!
But the thunder of His power who
can understand?"

Job Maintains His Integrity

27 Moreover Job continued his discourse, and said:

2 "As God lives, *who* has taken away
my justice,
And the Almighty, *who* has made
my soul bitter,
3 As long as my breath *is* in me,
And the breath of God in my nostrils,
4 My lips will not speak wickedness,
Nor my tongue utter deceit.
5 Far be it from me
That I should say you are right;
Till I die I will not put away my
integrity from me.
6 My righteousness I hold fast, and
will not let it go;
My heart shall not reproach *me* as
long as I live.

7 "May my enemy be like the wicked,
And he who rises up against me
like the unrighteous.
8 For what is the hope of the
hypocrite,
Though he may gain *much,*
If God takes away his life?
9 Will God hear his cry
When trouble comes upon him?
10 Will he delight himself in the
Almighty?
Will he always call on God?

11 "I will teach you about the hand of
God;
What *is* with the Almighty I will
not conceal.
12 Surely all of you have seen *it;*
Why then do you behave with
complete nonsense?

13 "This is the portion of a wicked man
with God,
And the heritage of oppressors,
received from the Almighty:
14 If his children are multiplied, *it is*
for the sword;
And his offspring shall not be
satisfied with bread.
15 Those who survive him shall be
buried in death,
And their[a] widows shall not weep,
16 Though he heaps up silver like dust,
And piles up clothing like clay—
17 He may pile *it* up, but the just will
wear *it,*
And the innocent will divide the
silver.
18 He builds his house like a moth,[a]
Like a booth *which* a watchman
makes.
19 The rich man will lie down,
But not be gathered *up;*[a]
He opens his eyes,
And he *is* no more.
20 Terrors overtake him like a flood;
A tempest steals him away in the
night.
21 The east wind carries him away,
and he is gone;
It sweeps him out of his place.
22 It hurls against him and does not
spare;
He flees desperately from its
power.
23 *Men* shall clap their hands at him,
And shall hiss him out of his
place.

Job's Discourse on Wisdom

28 "Surely there is a mine for
silver,
And a place *where* gold is refined.
2 Iron is taken from the earth,
And copper *is* smelted *from* ore.
3 *Man* puts an end to darkness,
And searches every recess

27:15 [a] Literally *his* **27:18** [a] Following Masoretic Text and Vulgate; Septuagint and Syriac read *spider* (compare 8:14); Targum reads *decay.* **27:19** [a] Following Masoretic Text and Targum; Septuagint and Syriac read *But shall not add* (that is, do it again); Vulgate reads *But take away nothing.*

For ore in the darkness and the
shadow of death.
4 He breaks open a shaft away
from people;
In places forgotten by feet
They hang far away from men;
They swing to and fro.
5 *As for* the earth, from it comes
bread,
But underneath it is turned up as
by fire;
6 Its stones *are* the source of
sapphires,
And it contains gold dust.
7 *That* path no bird knows,
Nor has the falcon's eye seen it.
8 The proud lions[a] have not
trodden it,
Nor has the fierce lion passed
over it.
9 He puts his hand on the flint;
He overturns the mountains at
the roots.
10 He cuts out channels in the rocks,
And his eye sees every precious
thing.
11 He dams up the streams from
trickling;
What is hidden he brings forth to
light.

12 "But where can wisdom be found?
And where *is* the place of
understanding?
13 Man does not know its value,
Nor is it found in the land of the
living.
14 The deep says, '*It is* not in me';
And the sea says, '*It is* not with me.'
15 It cannot be purchased for gold,
Nor can silver be weighed *for* its
price.
16 It cannot be valued in the gold of
Ophir,
In precious onyx or sapphire.
17 Neither gold nor crystal can
equal it,
Nor can it be exchanged for
jewelry of fine gold.
18 No mention shall be made of
coral or quartz,
For the price of wisdom *is* above
rubies.
19 The topaz of Ethiopia cannot
equal it,
Nor can it be valued in pure gold.

20 "From where then does wisdom
come?
And where *is* the place of
understanding?
21 It is hidden from the eyes of all
living,
And concealed from the birds of
the air.
22 Destruction and Death say,
'We have heard a report about it
with our ears.'
23 God understands its way,
And He knows its place.
24 For He looks to the ends of the
earth,
And sees under the whole
heavens,
25 To establish a weight for the wind,
And apportion the waters by
measure.
26 When He made a law for the rain,
And a path for the thunderbolt,
27 Then He saw *wisdom*[a] and
declared it;
He prepared it, indeed, He
searched it out.
28 And to man He said,
'Behold, the fear of the Lord, that *is*
wisdom,
And to depart from evil *is*
understanding.' "

Job's Summary Defense

29 Job further continued his discourse, and said:

2 "Oh, that I were as *in* months past,
As *in* the days *when* God watched
over me;
3 When His lamp shone upon my
head,
And when by His light I walked
through darkness;
4 Just as I was in the days of my
prime,
When the friendly counsel of God
was over my tent;
5 When the Almighty *was* yet
with me,

28:8 [a] Literally *sons of pride,* figurative of the great lions 28:27 [a] Literally *it*

When my children *were* around me;
6 When my steps were bathed with cream,[a]
And the rock poured out rivers of oil for me!

7 "When I went out to the gate by the city,
When I took my seat in the open square,
8 The young men saw me and hid,
And the aged arose *and* stood;
9 The princes refrained from talking,
And put *their* hand on their mouth;
10 The voice of nobles was hushed,
And their tongue stuck to the roof of their mouth.
11 When the ear heard, then it blessed me,
And when the eye saw, then it approved me;
12 Because I delivered the poor who cried out,
The fatherless and *the one who* had no helper.
13 The blessing of a perishing *man* came upon me,
And I caused the widow's heart to sing for joy.
14 I put on righteousness, and it clothed me;
My justice *was* like a robe and a turban.
15 I *was* eyes to the blind,
And I *was* feet to the lame.
16 I *was* a father to the poor,
And I searched out the case *that* I did not know.
17 I broke the fangs of the wicked,
And plucked the victim from his teeth.

18 "Then I said, 'I shall die in my nest,
And multiply *my* days as the sand.
19 My root *is* spread out to the waters,
And the dew lies all night on my branch.
20 My glory *is* fresh within me,
And my bow is renewed in my hand.'
21 "*Men* listened to me and waited,
And kept silence for my counsel.
22 After my words they did not speak again,
And my speech settled on them *as* dew.
23 They waited for me *as* for the rain,
And they opened their mouth wide *as* for the spring rain.
24 *If* I mocked at them, they did not believe *it*,
And the light of my countenance they did not cast down.
25 I chose the way for them, and sat as chief;
So I dwelt as a king in the army,
As one *who* comforts mourners.

30 "But now they mock at me, *men* younger than I,
Whose fathers I disdained to put with the dogs of my flock.
2 Indeed, what *profit* is the strength of their hands to me?
Their vigor has perished.
3 *They are* gaunt from want and famine,
Fleeing late to the wilderness, desolate and waste,
4 Who pluck mallow by the bushes,
And broom tree roots *for* their food.
5 They were driven out from among *men*,
They shouted at them as *at* a thief.
6 *They had* to live in the clefts of the valleys,
In caves of the earth and the rocks.
7 Among the bushes they brayed,
Under the nettles they nestled.
8 *They were* sons of fools,
Yes, sons of vile men;
They were scourged from the land.

9 "And now I am their taunting song;
Yes, I am their byword.
10 They abhor me, they keep far from me;
They do not hesitate to spit in my face.

29:6 [a] Masoretic Text reads *wrath;* ancient versions and some Hebrew manuscripts read *cream* (compare 20:17).

11 Because He has loosed my[a] bowstring and afflicted me,
They have cast off restraint before me.
12 At *my* right *hand* the rabble arises;
They push away my feet,
And they raise against me their ways of destruction.
13 They break up my path,
They promote my calamity;
They have no helper.
14 They come as broad breakers;
Under the ruinous storm they roll along.
15 Terrors are turned upon me;
They pursue my honor as the wind,
And my prosperity has passed like a cloud.

16 "And now my soul is poured out because of my *plight;*
The days of affliction take hold of me.
17 My bones are pierced in me at night,
And my gnawing pains take no rest.
18 By great force my garment is disfigured;
It binds me about as the collar of my coat.
19 He has cast me into the mire,
And I have become like dust and ashes.

20 "I cry out to You, but You do not answer me;
I stand up, and You regard me.
21 *But* You have become cruel to me;
With the strength of Your hand You oppose me.
22 You lift me up to the wind and cause me to ride *on it;*
You spoil my success.
23 For I know *that* You will bring me *to* death,
And *to* the house appointed for all living.

24 "Surely He would not stretch out *His* hand against a heap of ruins,
If they cry out when He destroys *it.*
25 Have I not wept for him who was in trouble?
Has *not* my soul grieved for the poor?
26 But when I looked for good, evil came *to me;*
And when I waited for light, then came darkness.
27 My heart is in turmoil and cannot rest;
Days of affliction confront me.
28 I go about mourning, but not in the sun;
I stand up in the assembly *and* cry out for help.
29 I am a brother of jackals,
And a companion of ostriches.
30 My skin grows black and falls from me;
My bones burn with fever.
31 My harp is *turned* to mourning,
And my flute to the voice of those who weep.

31 "I have made a covenant with my eyes;
Why then should I look upon a young woman?
2 For what *is* the allotment of God from above,
And the inheritance of the Almighty from on high?
3 *Is* it not destruction for the wicked,
And disaster for the workers of iniquity?
4 Does He not see my ways,
And count all my steps?

5 "If I have walked with falsehood,
Or if my foot has hastened to deceit,
6 Let me be weighed on honest scales,
That God may know my integrity.
7 If my step has turned from the way,
Or my heart walked after my eyes,
Or if any spot adheres to my hands,

30:11 [a] Following Masoretic Text, Syriac, and Targum; Septuagint and Vulgate read *His.*

8 *Then* let me sow, and another eat;
Yes, let my harvest be rooted out.

9 "If my heart has been enticed by a woman,
Or *if* I have lurked at my neighbor's door,
10 *Then* let my wife grind for another,
And let others bow down over her.
11 For that *would be* wickedness;
Yes, it *would be* iniquity *deserving of* judgment.
12 For that *would be* a fire *that* consumes to destruction,
And would root out all my increase.

13 "If I have despised the cause of my male or female servant
When they complained against me,
14 What then shall I do when God rises up?
When He punishes, how shall I answer Him?
15 Did not He who made me in the womb make them?
Did not the same One fashion us in the womb?

16 "If I have kept the poor from *their* desire,
Or caused the eyes of the widow to fail,
17 Or eaten my morsel by myself,
So that the fatherless could not eat of it
18 (But from my youth I reared him as a father,
And from my mother's womb I guided *the widow*[a]);
19 If I have seen anyone perish for lack of clothing,
Or any poor *man* without covering;
20 If his heart[a] has not blessed me,
And *if* he was *not* warmed with the fleece of my sheep;
21 If I have raised my hand against the fatherless,
When I saw I had help in the gate;
22 *Then* let my arm fall from my shoulder,
Let my arm be torn from the socket.
23 For destruction *from* God *is* a terror to me,
And because of His magnificence I cannot endure.

24 "If I have made gold my hope,
Or said to fine gold, '*You are* my confidence';
25 If I have rejoiced because my wealth *was* great,
And because my hand had gained much;
26 If I have observed the sun[a] when it shines,
Or the moon moving *in* brightness,
27 So that my heart has been secretly enticed,
And my mouth has kissed my hand;
28 This also *would be* an iniquity *deserving of* judgment,
For I would have denied God *who is* above.

29 "If I have rejoiced at the destruction of him who hated me,
Or lifted myself up when evil found him
30 (Indeed I have not allowed my mouth to sin
By asking for a curse on his soul);
31 If the men of my tent have not said,
'Who is there that has not been satisfied with his meat?'
32 (*But* no sojourner had to lodge in the street,
For I have opened my doors to the traveler[a]);
33 If I have covered my transgressions as Adam,
By hiding my iniquity in my bosom,
34 Because I feared the great multitude,
And dreaded the contempt of families,
So that I kept silence
And did not go out of the door—

31:18 [a] Literally *her* (compare verse 16) **31:20** [a] Literally *loins* **31:26** [a] Literally *light*
31:32 [a] Following Septuagint, Syriac, Targum, and Vulgate; Masoretic Text reads *road*.

35 Oh, that I had one to hear me!
Here is my mark.
Oh, that the Almighty would answer me,
That my Prosecutor had written a book!
36 Surely I would carry it on my shoulder,
And bind it on me *like* a crown;
37 I would declare to Him the number of my steps;
Like a prince I would approach Him.

38 "If my land cries out against me,
And its furrows weep together;
39 If I have eaten its fruit[a] without money,
Or caused its owners to lose their lives;
40 *Then* let thistles grow instead of wheat,
And weeds instead of barley."

The words of Job are ended.

Elihu Contradicts Job's Friends

32 So these three men ceased an-
swering Job, because he *was*
righteous in his own eyes. 2Then the
wrath of Elihu, the son of Barachel
the Buzite, of the family of Ram, was
aroused against Job; his wrath was
aroused because he justified himself
rather than God. 3Also against his three
friends his wrath was aroused, because
they had found no answer, and *yet* had
condemned Job.
4Now because they *were* years older
than he, Elihu had waited to speak to
Job.[a] 5When Elihu saw that *there was*
no answer in the mouth of these three
men, his wrath was aroused.
6So Elihu, the son of Barachel the Bu-
zite, answered and said:

"I *am* young in years, and you *are* very old;
Therefore I was afraid,
And dared not declare my opinion to you.
7 I said, 'Age[a] should speak,
And multitude of years should teach wisdom.'
8 But *there is* a spirit in man,
And the breath of the Almighty gives him understanding.
9 Great men[a] are not *always* wise,
Nor do the aged *always* understand justice.

10 "Therefore I say, 'Listen to me,
I also will declare my opinion.'
11 Indeed I waited for your words,
I listened to your reasonings, while you searched out what to say.
12 I paid close attention to you;
And surely not one of you convinced Job,
Or answered his words—
13 Lest you say,
'We have found wisdom';
God will vanquish him, not man.
14 Now he has not directed *his* words against me;
So I will not answer him with your words.

15 "They are dismayed and answer no more;
Words escape them.
16 And I have waited, because they did not speak,
Because they stood still *and* answered no more.
17 I also will answer my part,
I too will declare my opinion.
18 For I am full of words;
The spirit within me compels me.
19 Indeed my belly *is* like wine *that* has no vent;
It is ready to burst like new wineskins.
20 I will speak, that I may find relief;
I must open my lips and answer.
21 Let me not, I pray, show partiality to anyone;
Nor let me flatter any man.
22 For I do not know how to flatter,
Else my Maker would soon take me away.

31:39 [a] Literally *its strength* 32:4 [a] Vulgate reads *till Job had spoken.* 32:7 [a] Literally *Days,* that is, years 32:9 [a] Or *Men of many years*

Elihu Contradicts Job

33 "But please, Job, hear my
speech,
And listen to all my words.
2 Now, I open my mouth;
My tongue speaks in my mouth.
3 My words *come* from my upright
heart;
My lips utter pure knowledge.
4 The Spirit of God has made me,
And the breath of the Almighty
gives me life.
5 If you can answer me,
Set *your words* in order before me;
Take your stand.
6 Truly I *am* as your spokesman[a]
before God;
I also have been formed out of
clay.
7 Surely no fear of me will terrify
you,
Nor will my hand be heavy on you.

8 "Surely you have spoken in my
hearing,
And I have heard the sound of
your words, *saying,*
9 'I *am* pure, without transgression;
I *am* innocent, and *there is* no
iniquity in me.
10 Yet He finds occasions against
me,
He counts me as His enemy;
11 He puts my feet in the stocks,
He watches all my paths.'

12 "Look, *in* this you are not
righteous.
I will answer you,
For God is greater than man.
13 Why do you contend with Him?
For He does not give an
accounting of any of His
words.
14 For God may speak in one way, or
in another,
Yet man does not perceive it.
15 In a dream, in a vision of the
night,
When deep sleep falls upon men,
While slumbering on their beds,
16 Then He opens the ears of men,
And seals their instruction.
17 In order to turn man *from his*
deed,
And conceal pride from man,
18 He keeps back his soul from the
Pit,
And his life from perishing by the
sword.

19 "*Man* is also chastened with pain on
his bed,
And with strong *pain* in many of
his bones,
20 So that his life abhors bread,
And his soul succulent food.
21 His flesh wastes away from sight,
And his bones stick out *which
once* were not seen.
22 Yes, his soul draws near the Pit,
And his life to the executioners.

23 "If there is a messenger for him,
A mediator, one among a
thousand,
To show man His uprightness,
24 Then He is gracious to him, and
says,
'Deliver him from going down to
the Pit;
I have found a ransom';
25 His flesh shall be young like a
child's,
He shall return to the days of his
youth.
26 He shall pray to God, and He will
delight in him,
He shall see His face with joy,
For He restores to man His
righteousness.
27 Then he looks at men and says,
'I have sinned, and perverted *what
was* right,
And it did not profit me.'
28 He will redeem his[a] soul from
going down to the Pit,
And his[b] life shall see the light.

29 "Behold, God works all these *things,*
Twice, *in fact,* three *times* with a
man,
30 To bring back his soul from the
Pit,
That he may be enlightened with
the light of life.

33:6 [a] Literally *as your mouth* **33:28** [a] Or *my* (Kethib) [b] Or *my* (Kethib)

31 "Give ear, Job, listen to me;
Hold your peace, and I will speak.
32 If you have anything to say, answer me;
Speak, for I desire to justify you.
33 If not, listen to me;
Hold your peace, and I will teach you wisdom."

Elihu Proclaims God's Justice

34 Elihu further answered and said:

2 "Hear my words, you wise *men;*
Give ear to me, you who have knowledge.
3 For the ear tests words
As the palate tastes food.
4 Let us choose justice for ourselves;
Let us know among ourselves what *is* good.

5 "For Job has said, 'I am righteous,
But God has taken away my justice;
6 Should I lie concerning my right?
My wound *is* incurable, *though I am* without transgression.'
7 What man *is* like Job,
Who drinks scorn like water,
8 Who goes in company with the workers of iniquity,
And walks with wicked men?
9 For he has said, 'It profits a man nothing
That he should delight in God.'

10 "Therefore listen to me, you men of understanding:
Far be it from God *to do* wickedness,
And *from* the Almighty to *commit* iniquity.
11 For He repays man *according to* his work,
And makes man to find a reward according to *his* way.
12 Surely God will never do wickedly,
Nor will the Almighty pervert justice.
13 Who gave Him charge over the earth?
Or who appointed *Him over* the whole world?
14 If He should set His heart on it,
If He should gather to Himself His Spirit and His breath,
15 All flesh would perish together,
And man would return to dust.

16 "If *you have* understanding, hear this;
Listen to the sound of my words:
17 Should one who hates justice govern?
Will you condemn *Him who is* most just?
18 *Is it fitting* to say to a king, '*You are* worthless,'
And to nobles, '*You are* wicked'?
19 Yet He is not partial to princes,
Nor does He regard the rich more than the poor;
For they *are* all the work of His hands.
20 In a moment they die, in the middle of the night;
The people are shaken and pass away;
The mighty are taken away without a hand.

21 "For His eyes *are* on the ways of man,
And He sees all his steps.
22 There is no darkness nor shadow of death
Where the workers of iniquity may hide themselves.
23 For He need not further consider a man,
That he should go before God in judgment.
24 He breaks in pieces mighty men without inquiry,
And sets others in their place.
25 Therefore He knows their works;
He overthrows *them* in the night,
And they are crushed.
26 He strikes them as wicked *men*
In the open sight of others,
27 Because they turned back from Him,
And would not consider any of His ways,
28 So that they caused the cry of the poor to come to Him;
For He hears the cry of the afflicted.
29 When He gives quietness, who then can make trouble?

And when He hides *His* face, who then can see Him,
Whether *it is* against a nation or a man alone?—
30 That the hypocrite should not reign,
Lest the people be ensnared.

31 "For has *anyone* said to God,
'I have borne *chastening;*
I will offend no more;
32 Teach me *what* I do not see;
If I have done iniquity, I will do no more'?
33 Should He repay *it* according to your *terms,*
Just because you disavow it?
You must choose, and not I;
Therefore speak what you know.

34 "Men of understanding say to me,
Wise men who listen to me:
35 'Job speaks without knowledge,
His words *are* without wisdom.'
36 Oh, that Job were tried to the utmost,
Because *his* answers *are like* those of wicked men!
37 For he adds rebellion to his sin;
He claps *his hands* among us,
And multiplies his words against God."

Elihu Condemns Self-Righteousness

35 Moreover Elihu answered and said:

2 "Do you think this is right?
Do you say,
'My righteousness is more than God's'?
3 For you say,
'What advantage will it be to You?
What profit shall I have, more than *if* I had sinned?'

4 "I will answer you,
And your companions with you.
5 Look to the heavens and see;
And behold the clouds—
They are higher than you.
6 If you sin, what do you accomplish against Him?
Or, *if* your transgressions are multiplied, what do you do to Him?
7 If you are righteous, what do you give Him?
Or what does He receive from your hand?
8 Your wickedness affects a man such as you,
And your righteousness a son of man.

9 "Because of the multitude of oppressions they cry out;
They cry out for help because of the arm of the mighty.
10 But no one says, 'Where *is* God my Maker,
Who gives songs in the night,
11 Who teaches us more than the beasts of the earth,
And makes us wiser than the birds of heaven?'
12 There they cry out, but He does not answer,
Because of the pride of evil men.
13 Surely God will not listen to empty *talk,*
Nor will the Almighty regard it.
14 Although you say you do not see Him,
Yet justice *is* before Him, and you must wait for Him.
15 And now, because He has not punished in His anger,
Nor taken much notice of folly,
16 Therefore Job opens his mouth in vain;
He multiplies words without knowledge."

Elihu Proclaims God's Goodness

36 Elihu also proceeded and said:

2 "Bear with me a little, and I will show you
That *there are* yet words to speak on God's behalf.
3 I will fetch my knowledge from afar;
I will ascribe righteousness to my Maker.
4 For truly my words *are* not false;
One who is perfect in knowledge *is* with you.

5 "Behold, God *is* mighty, but despises *no one;*

He is mighty in strength of
understanding.
6 He does not preserve the life of
the wicked,
But gives justice to the oppressed.
7 He does not withdraw His eyes
from the righteous;
But *they are* on the throne with
kings,
For He has seated them forever,
And they are exalted.
8 And if *they are* bound in fetters,
Held in the cords of affliction,
9 Then He tells them their work and
their transgressions—
That they have acted defiantly.
10 He also opens their ear to
instruction,
And commands that they turn
from iniquity.
11 If they obey and serve *Him,*
They shall spend their days in
prosperity,
And their years in pleasures.
12 But if they do not obey,
They shall perish by the sword,
And they shall die without
knowledge.[a]

13 "But the hypocrites in heart store
up wrath;
They do not cry for help when He
binds them.
14 They die in youth,
And their life *ends* among the
perverted persons.[a]
15 He delivers the poor in their
affliction,
And opens their ears in oppression.

16 "Indeed He would have brought
you out of dire distress,
Into a broad place where *there is*
no restraint;
And what is set on your table
would be full of richness.
17 But you are filled with the
judgment due the wicked;
Judgment and justice take hold *of*
you.
18 Because *there is* wrath, *beware* lest
He take you away with *one*
blow;
For a large ransom would not
help you avoid *it.*
19 Will your riches,
Or all the mighty forces,
Keep you from distress?
20 Do not desire the night,
When people are cut off in their
place.
21 Take heed, do not turn to iniquity,
For you have chosen this rather
than affliction.

22 "Behold, God is exalted by His
power;
Who teaches like Him?
23 Who has assigned Him His way,
Or who has said, 'You have done
wrong'?

Elihu Proclaims God's Majesty

24 "Remember to magnify His work,
Of which men have sung.
25 Everyone has seen it;
Man looks on *it* from afar.

26 "Behold, God *is* great, and we do not
know *Him;*
Nor can the number of His years
be discovered.
27 For He draws up drops of water,
Which distill as rain from the
mist,
28 Which the clouds drop down
And pour abundantly on man.
29 Indeed, can *anyone* understand
the spreading of clouds,
The thunder from His canopy?
30 Look, He scatters His light
upon it,
And covers the depths of the sea.
31 For by these He judges the
peoples;
He gives food in abundance.
32 He covers *His* hands with
lightning,
And commands it to strike.
33 His thunder declares it,
The cattle also, concerning the
rising *storm.*

37 "At this also my heart
trembles,
And leaps from its place.

36:12 [a] Masoretic Text reads *as one without knowledge.*

36:14 [a] Hebrew *qedeshim,* that is, those practicing sodomy and prostitution in religious rituals

2 Hear attentively the thunder of
His voice,
And the rumbling *that* comes
from His mouth.
3 He sends it forth under the whole
heaven,
His lightning to the ends of the
earth.
4 After it a voice roars;
He thunders with His majestic
voice,
And He does not restrain them
when His voice is heard.
5 God thunders marvelously with
His voice;
He does great things which we
cannot comprehend.
6 For He says to the snow, 'Fall *on*
the earth';
Likewise to the gentle rain
and the heavy rain of His
strength.
7 He seals the hand of every man,
That all men may know His
work.
8 The beasts go into dens,
And remain in their lairs.
9 From the chamber *of the south*
comes the whirlwind,
And cold from the scattering
winds *of the north.*
10 By the breath of God ice is given,
And the broad waters are frozen.
11 Also with moisture He saturates
the thick clouds;
He scatters His bright clouds.
12 And they swirl about, being
turned by His guidance,
That they may do whatever He
commands them
On the face of the whole earth.[a]
13 He causes it to come,
Whether for correction,
Or for His land,
Or for mercy.

14 "Listen to this, O Job;
Stand still and consider the
wondrous works of God.
15 Do you know when God
dispatches them,
And causes the light of His cloud
to shine?
16 Do you know how the clouds are
balanced,
Those wondrous works of
Him who is perfect in
knowledge?
17 Why *are* your garments hot,
When He quiets the earth by the
south *wind?*
18 With Him, have you spread out
the skies,
Strong as a cast metal mirror?

19 "Teach us what we should say
to Him,
For we can prepare nothing
because of the darkness.
20 Should He be told that I *wish to*
speak?
If a man were to speak, surely he
would be swallowed up.
21 Even now *men* cannot look at the
light *when it is* bright in the
skies,
When the wind has passed and
cleared them.
22 He comes from the north *as*
golden *splendor;*
With God *is* awesome majesty.
23 *As for* the Almighty, we cannot
find Him;
He is excellent in power,
In judgment and abundant
justice;
He does not oppress.
24 Therefore men fear Him;
He shows no partiality to any *who
are* wise of heart."

The LORD Reveals His Omnipotence to Job

38 Then the LORD answered Job
out of the whirlwind, and said:

2 "Who *is* this who darkens counsel
By words without knowledge?
3 Now prepare yourself like a man;
I will question you, and you shall
answer Me.

4 "Where were you when I laid the
foundations of the earth?
Tell *Me,* if you have
understanding.

37:12 [a] Literally *the world of the earth*

5 Who determined its measurements?
Surely you know!
Or who stretched the line upon it?
6 To what were its foundations
fastened?
Or who laid its cornerstone,
7 When the morning stars sang
together,
And all the sons of God shouted
for joy?

8 "Or *who* shut in the sea with doors,
When it burst forth *and* issued
from the womb;
9 When I made the clouds its
garment,
And thick darkness its swaddling
band;
10 When I fixed My limit for it,
And set bars and doors;
11 When I said,
'This far you may come, but no
farther,
And here your proud waves must
stop!'

12 "Have you commanded the
morning since your days
began,
And caused the dawn to know its
place,
13 That it might take hold of the ends
of the earth,
And the wicked be shaken out of
it?
14 It takes on form like clay *under* a
seal,
And stands out like a garment.
15 From the wicked their light is
withheld,
And the upraised arm is broken.

16 "Have you entered the springs of
the sea?
Or have you walked in search of
the depths?
17 Have the gates of death been
revealed to you?
Or have you seen the doors of the
shadow of death?
18 Have you comprehended the
breadth of the earth?
Tell *Me,* if you know all this.

19 "Where *is* the way *to* the dwelling of
light?
And darkness, where *is* its place,
20 That you may take it to its territory,
That you may know the paths *to*
its home?
21 Do you know *it,* because you were
born then,
Or *because* the number of your
days *is* great?

22 "Have you entered the treasury of
snow,
Or have you seen the treasury of
hail,
23 Which I have reserved for the
time of trouble,
For the day of battle and war?
24 By what way is light diffused,
Or the east wind scattered over
the earth?

25 "Who has divided a channel for the
overflowing *water,*
Or a path for the thunderbolt,
26 To cause it to rain on a land *where*
there is no one,
A wilderness in which *there is* no
man;
27 To satisfy the desolate waste,
And cause to spring forth the
growth of tender grass?
28 Has the rain a father?
Or who has begotten the drops of
dew?
29 From whose womb comes the ice?
And the frost of heaven, who gives
it birth?
30 The waters harden like stone,
And the surface of the deep is
frozen.

31 "Can you bind the cluster of the
Pleiades,
Or loose the belt of Orion?
32 Can you bring out Mazzaroth[a] in
its season?
Or can you guide the Great Bear
with its cubs?
33 Do you know the ordinances of
the heavens?
Can you set their dominion over
the earth?

38:32 [a] Literally *Constellations*

34 "Can you lift up your voice to the clouds,
That an abundance of water may cover you?
35 Can you send out lightnings, that they may go,
And say to you, 'Here we *are!*'?
36 Who has put wisdom in the mind?[a]
Or who has given understanding to the heart?
37 Who can number the clouds by wisdom?
Or who can pour out the bottles of heaven,
38 When the dust hardens in clumps,
And the clods cling together?

39 "Can you hunt the prey for the lion,
Or satisfy the appetite of the young lions,
40 When they crouch in *their* dens,
Or lurk in their lairs to lie in wait?
41 Who provides food for the raven,
When its young ones cry to God,
And wander about for lack of food?

39 "Do you know the time when the wild mountain goats bear young?
Or can you mark when the deer gives birth?
2 Can you number the months *that* they fulfill?
Or do you know the time when they bear young?
3 They bow down,
They bring forth their young,
They deliver their offspring.[a]
4 Their young ones are healthy,
They grow strong with grain;
They depart and do not return to them.

5 "Who set the wild donkey free?
Who loosed the bonds of the onager,
6 Whose home I have made the wilderness,
And the barren land his dwelling?
7 He scorns the tumult of the city;
He does not heed the shouts of the driver.
8 The range of the mountains *is* his pasture,
And he searches after every green thing.

9 "Will the wild ox be willing to serve you?
Will he bed by your manger?
10 Can you bind the wild ox in the furrow with ropes?
Or will he plow the valleys behind you?
11 Will you trust him because his strength *is* great?
Or will you leave your labor to him?
12 Will you trust him to bring home your grain,
And gather it to your threshing floor?

13 "The wings of the ostrich wave proudly,
But are her wings and pinions *like the* kindly stork's?
14 For she leaves her eggs on the ground,
And warms them in the dust;
15 She forgets that a foot may crush them,
Or that a wild beast may break them.
16 She treats her young harshly, as though *they were* not hers;
Her labor is in vain, without concern,
17 Because God deprived her of wisdom,
And did not endow her with understanding.
18 When she lifts herself on high,
She scorns the horse and its rider.

19 "Have you given the horse strength?
Have you clothed his neck with thunder?[a]
20 Can you frighten him like a locust?
His majestic snorting strikes terror.

38:36 [a] Literally *inward parts* **39:3** [a] Literally *pangs*, figurative of offspring **39:19** [a] Or *a mane*

21 He paws in the valley, and
rejoices in *his* strength;
He gallops into the clash of arms.
22 He mocks at fear, and is not
frightened;
Nor does he turn back from the
sword.
23 The quiver rattles against him,
The glittering spear and javelin.
24 He devours the distance with
fierceness and rage;
Nor does he come to a halt because
the trumpet *has* sounded.
25 At *the blast of* the trumpet he says,
'Aha!'
He smells the battle from afar,
The thunder of captains and
shouting.

26 "Does the hawk fly by your
wisdom,
And spread its wings toward the
south?
27 Does the eagle mount up at your
command,
And make its nest on high?
28 On the rock it dwells and resides,
On the crag of the rock and the
stronghold.
29 From there it spies out the prey;
Its eyes observe from afar.
30 Its young ones suck up blood;
And where the slain *are,* there it *is.*"

40 Moreover the LORD answered
Job, and said:

2 "Shall the one who contends with
the Almighty correct *Him?*
He who rebukes God, let him
answer it."

Job's Response to God

3Then Job answered the LORD and
said:

4 "Behold, I am vile;
What shall I answer You?
I lay my hand over my mouth.
5 Once I have spoken, but I will not
answer;
Yes, twice, but I will proceed no
further."

God's Challenge to Job

6Then the LORD answered Job out of
the whirlwind, and said:

7 "Now prepare yourself like a man;
I will question you, and you shall
answer Me:

8 "Would you indeed annul My
judgment?
Would you condemn Me that you
may be justified?
9 Have you an arm like God?
Or can you thunder with a voice
like His?
10 Then adorn yourself *with* majesty
and splendor,
And array yourself with glory
and beauty.
11 Disperse the rage of your wrath;
Look on everyone *who is* proud,
and humble him.
12 Look on everyone *who is* proud,
and bring him low;
Tread down the wicked in their
place.
13 Hide them in the dust together,
Bind their faces in hidden
darkness.
14 Then I will also confess to you
That your own right hand can
save you.

15 "Look now at the behemoth,[a]
which I made *along* with
you;
He eats grass like an ox.
16 See now, his strength *is* in his hips,
And his power *is* in his stomach
muscles.
17 He moves his tail like a cedar;
The sinews of his thighs are
tightly knit.
18 His bones *are like* beams of
bronze,
His ribs like bars of iron.
19 He *is* the first of the ways of God;
Only He who made him can bring
near His sword.
20 Surely the mountains yield food
for him,
And all the beasts of the field play
there.

40:15 [a] A large animal, exact identity unknown

21 He lies under the lotus trees,
In a covert of reeds and marsh.
22 The lotus trees cover him *with* their shade;
The willows by the brook surround him.
23 Indeed the river may rage,
Yet he is not disturbed;
He is confident, though the Jordan gushes into his mouth,
24 *Though* he takes it in his eyes,
Or one pierces *his* nose with a snare.

41 "Can you draw out Leviathan[a] with a hook,
Or *snare* his tongue with a line *which* you lower?
2 Can you put a reed through his nose,
Or pierce his jaw with a hook?
3 Will he make many supplications to you?
Will he speak softly to you?
4 Will he make a covenant with you?
Will you take him as a servant forever?
5 Will you play with him as *with* a bird,
Or will you leash him for your maidens?
6 Will *your* companions make a banquet[a] of him?
Will they apportion him among the merchants?
7 Can you fill his skin with harpoons,
Or his head with fishing spears?
8 Lay your hand on him;
Remember the battle—
Never do it again!
9 Indeed, *any* hope of *overcoming* him is false;
Shall *one not* be overwhelmed at the sight of him?
10 No one *is so* fierce that he would dare stir him up.
Who then is able to stand against Me?
11 Who has preceded Me, that I should pay *him?*
Everything under heaven is Mine.

12 "I will not conceal[a] his limbs,
His mighty power, or his graceful proportions.
13 Who can remove his outer coat?
Who can approach *him* with a double bridle?
14 Who can open the doors of his face,
With his terrible teeth all around?
15 *His* rows of scales are *his* pride,
Shut up tightly *as with* a seal;
16 One is so near another
That no air can come between them;
17 They are joined one to another,
They stick together and cannot be parted.
18 His sneezings flash forth light,
And his eyes *are* like the eyelids of the morning.
19 Out of his mouth go burning lights;
Sparks of fire shoot out.
20 Smoke goes out of his nostrils,
As *from* a boiling pot and burning rushes.
21 His breath kindles coals,
And a flame goes out of his mouth.
22 Strength dwells in his neck,
And sorrow dances before him.
23 The folds of his flesh are joined together;
They are firm on him and cannot be moved.
24 His heart is as hard as stone,
Even as hard as the lower *millstone.*
25 When he raises himself up, the mighty are afraid;
Because of his crashings they are beside[a] themselves.
26 *Though* the sword reaches him, it cannot avail;
Nor does spear, dart, or javelin.
27 He regards iron as straw,
And bronze as rotten wood.
28 The arrow cannot make him flee;
Slingstones become like stubble to him.
29 Darts are regarded as straw;
He laughs at the threat of javelins.

41:1 [a] A large sea creature, exact identity unknown **41:6** [a] Or *bargain over him* **41:12** [a] Literally *keep silent about* **41:25** [a] Or *purify themselves*

30 His undersides *are* like sharp potsherds;
He spreads pointed *marks* in the mire.
31 He makes the deep boil like a pot;
He makes the sea like a pot of ointment.
32 He leaves a shining wake behind him;
One would think the deep had white hair.
33 On earth there is nothing like him,
Which is made without fear.
34 He beholds every high *thing;*
He *is* king over all the children of pride."

Job's Repentance and Restoration

42 Then Job answered the LORD and said:

2 "I know that You can do everything,
And that no purpose *of Yours* can be withheld from You.
3 *You asked,* 'Who *is* this who hides counsel without knowledge?'
Therefore I have uttered what I did not understand,
Things too wonderful for me, which I did not know.
4 Listen, please, and let me speak;
You said, 'I will question you, and you shall answer Me.'

5 "I have heard of You by the hearing of the ear,
But now my eye sees You.
6 Therefore I abhor *myself,*
And repent in dust and ashes."

7And so it was, after the LORD had spo-
ken these words to Job, that the LORD
said to Eliphaz the Temanite, "My wrath
is aroused against you and your two
friends, for you have not spoken of Me
what is right, as My servant Job *has.*
8Now therefore, take for yourselves
seven bulls and seven rams, go to My
servant Job, and offer up for yourselves
a burnt offering; and My servant Job
shall pray for you. For I will accept him,
lest I deal with you *according to your*
folly; because you have not spoken of
Me *what is* right, as My servant Job *has.*"
9So Eliphaz the Temanite and Bildad
the Shuhite *and* Zophar the Naamathite
went and did as the LORD commanded
them; for the LORD had accepted Job.
10And the LORD restored Job's losses[a]
when he prayed for his friends. Indeed
the LORD gave Job twice as much as he
had before. 11Then all his brothers, all
his sisters, and all those who had been
his acquaintances before, came to him
and ate food with him in his house; and
they consoled him and comforted him
for all the adversity that the LORD had
brought upon him. Each one gave him
a piece of silver and each a ring of gold.
12Now the LORD blessed the latter *days*
of Job more than his beginning; for
he had fourteen thousand sheep, six
thousand camels, one thousand yoke
of oxen, and one thousand female don-
keys. 13He also had seven sons and three
daughters. 14And he called the name
of the first Jemimah, the name of the
second Keziah, and the name of the
third Keren-Happuch. 15In all the land
were found no women *so* beautiful as
the daughters of Job; and their father
gave them an inheritance among their
brothers.
16After this Job lived one hundred and
forty years, and saw his children and
grandchildren *for* four generations. 17So
Job died, old and full of days.

42:10 [a] Literally *Job's captivity,* that is, what was captured from Job

THE BOOK OF

PSALMS

The Book of Psalms is a collection of songs used by God's people to worship Him. These one hundred and fifty songs express a variety of feelings and experiences. Some are full of happiness and joy, and others are filled with sadness and sorrow. Some were written in times of worry, and others in times of celebration. Psalms teaches us how to pray, how to grieve, how to trust, how to rejoice, and how to worship.

- **GENRE:** Wisdom and Poetry
- **AUTHORS:** David, Asaph, the sons of Korah, Solomon, Moses, Ethan, Heman, and others
- **TIME:** c. 1410–430 BC
- **PURPOSE:** To be used by God's people to worship Him and to show the different feelings that people can have when following God.

BOOK ONE
Psalms 1–41

PSALM 1
The Way of the Righteous and the End of the Ungodly

1 Blessed *is* the man
Who walks not in the counsel of the ungodly,
Nor stands in the path of sinners,
Nor sits in the seat of the scornful;
2 But his delight *is* in the law of the LORD,
And in His law he meditates day and night.
3 He shall be like a tree
Planted by the rivers of water,
That brings forth its fruit in its season,
Whose leaf also shall not wither;
And whatever he does shall prosper.

4 The ungodly *are* not so,
But *are* like the chaff which the wind drives away.
5 Therefore the ungodly shall not stand in the judgment,
Nor sinners in the congregation of the righteous.
6 For the LORD knows the way of the righteous,
But the way of the ungodly shall perish.

PSALM 2
The Messiah's Triumph and Kingdom

1 Why do the nations rage,
And the people plot a vain thing?
2 The kings of the earth set themselves,
And the rulers take counsel together,
Against the LORD and against His Anointed, *saying,*
3 "Let us break Their bonds in pieces
And cast away Their cords from us."

4 He who sits in the heavens shall laugh;
The Lord shall hold them in derision.
5 Then He shall speak to them in His wrath,
And distress them in His deep displeasure:
6 "Yet I have set My King
On My holy hill of Zion."

7 "I will declare the decree:
The LORD has said to Me,
'You *are* My Son,
Today I have begotten You.
8 Ask of Me, and I will give *You*
The nations *for* Your inheritance,

And the ends of the earth *for* Your
possession.
9 You shall break[a] them with a rod
of iron;
You shall dash them to pieces like
a potter's vessel.' "

10 Now therefore, be wise, O kings;
Be instructed, you judges of the
earth.
11 Serve the LORD with fear,
And rejoice with trembling.
12 Kiss the Son,[a] lest He[b] be angry,
And you perish *in* the way,
When His wrath is kindled but a
little.
Blessed *are* all those who put their
trust in Him.

PSALM 3

The LORD Helps His Troubled People

A Psalm of David when he fled from Absalom his son.

1 LORD, how they have increased
who trouble me!
Many *are* they who rise up
against me.
2 Many *are* they who say of me,
"*There is* no help for him in God."
Selah

3 But You, O LORD, *are* a shield for
me,
My glory and the One who lifts up
my head.
4 I cried to the LORD with my voice,
And He heard me from His holy
hill. *Selah*

5 I lay down and slept;
I awoke, for the LORD sustained
me.
6 I will not be afraid of ten
thousands of people
Who have set *themselves* against
me all around.

7 Arise, O LORD;
Save me, O my God!
For You have struck all my
enemies on the cheekbone;
You have broken the teeth of the
ungodly.
8 Salvation *belongs* to the LORD.
Your blessing *is* upon Your
people. *Selah*

PSALM 4

The Safety of the Faithful

To the Chief Musician. With stringed instruments. A Psalm of David.

1 Hear me when I call, O God of my
righteousness!
You have relieved me in *my*
distress;
Have mercy on me, and hear my
prayer.

2 How long, O you sons of men,
Will you turn my glory to shame?
How long will you love
worthlessness
And seek falsehood? *Selah*
3 But know that the LORD has set
apart[a] for Himself him who
is godly;
The LORD will hear when I call to
Him.

4 Be angry, and do not sin.
Meditate within your heart on
your bed, and be still. *Selah*
5 Offer the sacrifices of
righteousness,
And put your trust in the LORD.

6 *There are* many who say,
"Who will show us *any* good?"
LORD, lift up the light of Your
countenance upon us.
7 You have put gladness in my
heart,
More than in the season that their
grain and wine increased.
8 I will both lie down in peace, and
sleep;
For You alone, O LORD, make me
dwell in safety.

2:9 [a] Following Masoretic Text and Targum; Septuagint, Syriac, and Vulgate read *rule* (compare Revelation 2:27). **2:12** [a] Septuagint and Vulgate read *Embrace discipline;* Targum reads *Receive instruction.* [b] Septuagint reads *the LORD.* **4:3** [a] Many Hebrew manuscripts, Septuagint, Targum, and Vulgate read *made wonderful.*

GOD SIN JESUS SALVATION LOVE

PSALM 5
A Prayer for Guidance

To the Chief Musician. With flutes.[a] *A Psalm of David.*

1 Give ear to my words, O LORD,
Consider my meditation.
2 Give heed to the voice of my cry,
My King and my God,
For to You I will pray.
3 My voice You shall hear in the morning, O LORD;
In the morning I will direct *it* to You,
And I will look up.

4 For You *are* not a God who takes pleasure in wickedness,
Nor shall evil dwell with You.
5 The boastful shall not stand in Your sight;
You hate all workers of iniquity.
6 You shall destroy those who speak falsehood;
The LORD abhors the bloodthirsty and deceitful man.

7 But as for me, I will come into Your house in the multitude of Your mercy;
In fear of You I will worship toward Your holy temple.
8 Lead me, O LORD, in Your righteousness because of my enemies;
Make Your way straight before my face.

9 For *there is* no faithfulness in their mouth;
Their inward part *is* destruction;
Their throat *is* an open tomb;
They flatter with their tongue.
10 Pronounce them guilty, O God!
Let them fall by their own counsels;
Cast them out in the multitude of their transgressions,
For they have rebelled against You.

11 But let all those rejoice who put their trust in You;
Let them ever shout for joy, because You defend them;
Let those also who love Your name
Be joyful in You.
12 For You, O LORD, will bless the righteous;
With favor You will surround him as *with* a shield.

PSALM 6
A Prayer of Faith in Time of Distress

To the Chief Musician. With stringed instruments. On an eight-stringed harp.[a] *A Psalm of David.*

1 O LORD, do not rebuke me in Your anger,
Nor chasten me in Your hot displeasure.
2 Have mercy on me, O LORD, for I *am* weak;
O LORD, heal me, for my bones are troubled.
3 My soul also is greatly troubled;
But You, O LORD—how long?

4 Return, O LORD, deliver me!
Oh, save me for Your mercies' sake!
5 For in death *there is* no remembrance of You;
In the grave who will give You thanks?

6 I am weary with my groaning;
All night I make my bed swim;
I drench my couch with my tears.
7 My eye wastes away because of grief;
It grows old because of all my enemies.

8 Depart from me, all you workers of iniquity;
For the LORD has heard the voice of my weeping.
9 The LORD has heard my supplication;
The LORD will receive my prayer.
10 Let all my enemies be ashamed and greatly troubled;
Let them turn back *and* be ashamed suddenly.

5:title [a] Hebrew *nehiloth* **6:title** [a] Hebrew *Sheminith*

PSALM 7

Prayer and Praise for Deliverance from Enemies

A Meditation[a] of David, which he sang to the LORD concerning the words of Cush, a Benjamite.

1 O LORD my God, in You I put my trust;
Save me from all those who persecute me;
And deliver me,
2 Lest they tear me like a lion,
Rending *me* in pieces, while *there is* none to deliver.

3 O LORD my God, if I have done this:
If there is iniquity in my hands,
4 If I have repaid evil to him who was at peace with me,
Or have plundered my enemy without cause,
5 Let the enemy pursue me and overtake *me;*
Yes, let him trample my life to the earth,
And lay my honor in the dust. *Selah*

6 Arise, O LORD, in Your anger;
Lift Yourself up because of the rage of my enemies;
Rise up for me[a] *to* the judgment You have commanded!
7 So the congregation of the peoples shall surround You;
For their sakes, therefore, return on high.
8 The LORD shall judge the peoples;
Judge me, O LORD, according to my righteousness,
And according to my integrity within me.

9 Oh, let the wickedness of the wicked come to an end,
But establish the just;
For the righteous God tests the hearts and minds.
10 My defense *is* of God,
Who saves the upright in heart.
11 God *is* a just judge,
And God is angry *with the wicked* every day.
12 If he does not turn back,
He will sharpen His sword;
He bends His bow and makes it ready.
13 He also prepares for Himself instruments of death;
He makes His arrows into fiery shafts.

14 Behold, *the wicked* brings forth iniquity;
Yes, he conceives trouble and brings forth falsehood.
15 He made a pit and dug it out,
And has fallen into the ditch *which* he made.
16 His trouble shall return upon his own head,
And his violent dealing shall come down on his own crown.

17 I will praise the LORD according to His righteousness,
And will sing praise to the name of the LORD Most High.

PSALM 8

The Glory of the LORD in Creation

To the Chief Musician. On the instrument of Gath.[a] A Psalm of David.

1 O LORD, our Lord,
How excellent *is* Your name in all the earth,
Who have set Your glory above the heavens!

2 Out of the mouth of babes and nursing infants
You have ordained strength,
Because of Your enemies,
That You may silence the enemy and the avenger.

3 When I consider Your heavens, the work of Your fingers,
The moon and the stars, which You have ordained,

7:title [a] Hebrew *Shiggaion* 7:6 [a] Following Masoretic Text, Targum, and Vulgate; Septuagint reads *O LORD my God.* 8:title [a] Hebrew *Al Gittith*

4 What is man that You are mindful
of him,
And the son of man that You visit
him?
5 For You have made him a little
lower than the angels,[a]
And You have crowned him with
glory and honor.

6 You have made him to have
dominion over the works of
Your hands;
You have put all *things* under his
feet,
7 All sheep and oxen—
Even the beasts of the field,
8 The birds of the air,
And the fish of the sea
That pass through the paths of
the seas.

9 O LORD, our Lord,
How excellent *is* Your name in all
the earth!

PSALM 9

Prayer and Thanksgiving for the LORD's Righteous Judgments

To the Chief Musician. To the tune of "Death of the Son."[a] A Psalm of David.

1 I will praise *You,* O LORD, with my
whole heart;
I will tell of all Your marvelous
works.
2 I will be glad and rejoice in You;
I will sing praise to Your name,
O Most High.

3 When my enemies turn back,
They shall fall and perish at Your
presence.
4 For You have maintained my
right and my cause;
You sat on the throne judging in
righteousness.
5 You have rebuked the nations,
You have destroyed the wicked;
You have blotted out their name
forever and ever.

6 O enemy, destructions are
finished forever!
And you have destroyed cities;
Even their memory has perished.
7 But the LORD shall endure
forever;
He has prepared His throne for
judgment.
8 He shall judge the world in
righteousness,
And He shall administer
judgment for the peoples in
uprightness.

9 The LORD also will be a refuge for
the oppressed,
A refuge in times of trouble.
10 And those who know Your name
will put their trust in You;
For You, LORD, have not forsaken
those who seek You.

11 Sing praises to the LORD, who
dwells in Zion!
Declare His deeds among the
people.
12 When He avenges blood, He
remembers them;
He does not forget the cry of the
humble.

13 Have mercy on me, O LORD!
Consider my trouble from those
who hate me,
You who lift me up from the gates
of death,
14 That I may tell of all Your praise
In the gates of the daughter of
Zion.
I will rejoice in Your salvation.

15 The nations have sunk down in
the pit *which* they made;
In the net which they hid, their
own foot is caught.
16 The LORD is known *by* the
judgment He executes;
The wicked is snared in the work
of his own hands.
Meditation.[a] *Selah*

17 The wicked shall be turned into
hell,
And all the nations that forget
God.

8:5 [a] Hebrew *Elohim, God;* Septuagint, Syriac, Targum, and Jewish tradition translate as *angels.*
9:title [a] Hebrew *Muth Labben* 9:16 [a] Hebrew *Higgaion*

18 For the needy shall not always be
forgotten;
The expectation of the poor shall
not perish forever.
19 Arise, O LORD,
Do not let man prevail;
Let the nations be judged in Your
sight.
20 Put them in fear, O LORD,
That the nations may know
themselves *to be but* men.
Selah

PSALM 10

A Song of Confidence in God's Triumph over Evil

1 Why do You stand afar off, O LORD?
Why do You hide in times of
trouble?
2 The wicked in *his* pride persecutes
the poor;
Let them be caught in the plots
which they have devised.

3 For the wicked boasts of his
heart's desire;
He blesses the greedy *and*
renounces the LORD.
4 The wicked in his proud
countenance does not seek
God;
God *is* in none of his thoughts.

5 His ways are always prospering;
Your judgments *are* far above, out
of his sight;
As for all his enemies, he sneers at
them.
6 He has said in his heart, "I shall
not be moved;
I shall never be in adversity."
7 His mouth is full of cursing and
deceit and oppression;
Under his tongue *is* trouble and
iniquity.

8 He sits in the lurking places of the
villages;
In the secret places he murders
the innocent;
His eyes are secretly fixed on the
helpless.
9 He lies in wait secretly, as a lion
in his den;
He lies in wait to catch the poor;
He catches the poor when he
draws him into his net.
10 So he crouches, he lies low,
That the helpless may fall by his
strength.
11 He has said in his heart,
"God has forgotten;
He hides His face;
He will never see."

12 Arise, O LORD!
O God, lift up Your hand!
Do not forget the humble.
13 Why do the wicked renounce God?
He has said in his heart,
"You will not require *an account.*"

14 But You have seen, for You
observe trouble and grief,
To repay *it* by Your hand.
The helpless commits himself to
You;
You are the helper of the
fatherless.
15 Break the arm of the wicked and
the evil *man;*
Seek out his wickedness *until* You
find none.

16 The LORD *is* King forever and ever;
The nations have perished out of
His land.
17 LORD, You have heard the desire
of the humble;
You will prepare their heart;
You will cause Your ear to hear,
18 To do justice to the fatherless and
the oppressed,
That the man of the earth may
oppress no more.

PSALM 11

Faith in the LORD's Righteousness

To the Chief Musician. A Psalm of David.

1 In the LORD I put my trust;
How can you say to my soul,
"Flee *as* a bird to your mountain"?
2 For look! The wicked bend *their*
bow,
They make ready their arrow on
the string,
That they may shoot secretly at
the upright in heart.

3 If the foundations are destroyed,
What can the righteous do?

4 The LORD *is* in His holy temple,
The LORD's throne *is* in heaven;
His eyes behold,
His eyelids test the sons of men.
5 The LORD tests the righteous,
But the wicked and the one who loves violence His soul hates.
6 Upon the wicked He will rain coals;
Fire and brimstone and a burning wind
Shall be the portion of their cup.

7 For the LORD *is* righteous,
He loves righteousness;
His countenance beholds the upright.[a]

PSALM 12

Man's Treachery and God's Constancy

To the Chief Musician. On an eight-stringed harp.[a] A Psalm of David.

1 Help, LORD, for the godly man ceases!
For the faithful disappear from among the sons of men.
2 They speak idly everyone with his neighbor;
With flattering lips *and* a double heart they speak.

3 May the LORD cut off all flattering lips,
And the tongue that speaks proud things,
4 Who have said,
"With our tongue we will prevail;
Our lips *are* our own;
Who *is* lord over us?"

5 "For the oppression of the poor, for the sighing of the needy,
Now I will arise," says the LORD;
"I will set *him* in the safety for which he yearns."

6 The words of the LORD *are* pure words,
Like silver tried in a furnace of earth,
Purified seven times.
7 You shall keep them, O LORD,
You shall preserve them from this generation forever.

8 The wicked prowl on every side,
When vileness is exalted among the sons of men.

PSALM 13

Trust in the Salvation of the LORD

To the Chief Musician. A Psalm of David.

1 How long, O LORD? Will You forget me forever?
How long will You hide Your face from me?
2 How long shall I take counsel in my soul,
Having sorrow in my heart daily?
How long will my enemy be exalted over me?

3 Consider *and* hear me, O LORD my God;
Enlighten my eyes,
Lest I sleep the *sleep of* death;
4 Lest my enemy say,
"I have prevailed against him";
Lest those who trouble me rejoice when I am moved.

5 But I have trusted in Your mercy;
My heart shall rejoice in Your salvation.
6 I will sing to the LORD,
Because He has dealt bountifully with me.

PSALM 14

Folly of the Godless, and God's Final Triumph

To the Chief Musician. A Psalm of David.

1 The fool has said in his heart,
"*There is* no God."
They are corrupt,
They have done abominable works,
There is none who does good.

2 The LORD looks down from heaven upon the children of men,
To see if there are any who understand, who seek God.

11:7 [a] Or *The upright beholds His countenance* 12:title [a] Hebrew *Sheminith*

3 They have all turned aside,
They have together become corrupt;
There is none who does good,
No, not one.

4 Have all the workers of iniquity no knowledge,
Who eat up my people *as* they eat bread,
And do not call on the LORD?
5 There they are in great fear,
For God *is* with the generation of the righteous.
6 You shame the counsel of the poor,
But the LORD *is* his refuge.

7 Oh, that the salvation of Israel *would come* out of Zion!
When the LORD brings back the captivity of His people,
Let Jacob rejoice *and* Israel be glad.

PSALM 15

The Character of Those Who May Dwell with the LORD

A Psalm of David.

1 LORD, who may abide in Your tabernacle?
Who may dwell in Your holy hill?

2 He who walks uprightly,
And works righteousness,
And speaks the truth in his heart;
3 He *who* does not backbite with his tongue,
Nor does evil to his neighbor,
Nor does he take up a reproach against his friend;
4 In whose eyes a vile person is despised,
But he honors those who fear the LORD;
He *who* swears to his own hurt and does not change;
5 He *who* does not put out his money at usury,
Nor does he take a bribe against the innocent.

He who does these *things* shall never be moved.

PSALM 16

The Hope of the Faithful, and the Messiah's Victory

A Michtam of David.

1 Preserve me, O God, for in You I put my trust.

2 *O my soul,* you have said to the LORD,
"You *are* my Lord,
My goodness is nothing apart from You."
3 As for the saints who *are* on the earth,
"They are the excellent ones, in whom is all my delight."

4 Their sorrows shall be multiplied who hasten *after* another *god;*
Their drink offerings of blood I will not offer,
Nor take up their names on my lips.

5 O LORD, *You are* the portion of my inheritance and my cup;
You maintain my lot.
6 The lines have fallen to me in pleasant *places;*
Yes, I have a good inheritance.

7 I will bless the LORD who has given me counsel;
My heart also instructs me in the night seasons.
8 I have set the LORD always before me;
Because *He is* at my right hand I shall not be moved.

9 Therefore my heart is glad, and my glory rejoices;
My flesh also will rest in hope.
10 For You will not leave my soul in Sheol,
Nor will You allow Your Holy One to see corruption.
11 You will show me the path of life;
In Your presence *is* fullness of joy;
At Your right hand *are* pleasures forevermore.

PSALM 17

Prayer with Confidence in Final Salvation

A Prayer of David.

1 Hear a just cause, O LORD,
Attend to my cry;
Give ear to my prayer *which is* not
from deceitful lips.
2 Let my vindication come from
Your presence;
Let Your eyes look on the things
that are upright.

3 You have tested my heart;
You have visited *me* in the night;
You have tried me and have
found nothing;
I have purposed that my mouth
shall not transgress.
4 Concerning the works of men,
By the word of Your lips,
I have kept away from the paths
of the destroyer.
5 Uphold my steps in Your paths,
That my footsteps may not slip.

6 I have called upon You, for You
will hear me, O God;
Incline Your ear to me, *and* hear
my speech.
7 Show Your marvelous
lovingkindness by Your right
hand,
O You who save those who trust *in
You*
From those who rise up *against
them.*
8 Keep me as the apple of Your eye;
Hide me under the shadow of
Your wings,
9 From the wicked who oppress me,
From my deadly enemies who
surround me.

10 They have closed up their fat *hearts;*
With their mouths they speak
proudly.
11 They have now surrounded us in
our steps;
They have set their eyes,
crouching down to the earth,
12 As a lion is eager to tear his prey,
And like a young lion lurking in
secret places.

13 Arise, O LORD,
Confront him, cast him
down;
Deliver my life from the wicked
with Your sword,
14 With Your hand from men,
O LORD,
From men of the world *who have*
their portion in *this* life,
And whose belly You fill with Your
hidden treasure.
They are satisfied with children,
And leave the rest of their
possession for their babes.

15 As for me, I will see Your face in
righteousness;
I shall be satisfied when I awake
in Your likeness.

PSALM 18

God the Sovereign Savior

To the Chief Musician. A Psalm of David the servant of the LORD, who spoke to the LORD the words of this song on the day that the LORD delivered him from the hand of all his enemies and from the hand of Saul. And he said:

1 I will love You, O LORD, my
strength.
2 The LORD is my rock and my
fortress and my deliverer;
My God, my strength, in whom I
will trust;
My shield and the horn of my
salvation, my stronghold.
3 I will call upon the LORD, *who is
worthy* to be praised;
So shall I be saved from my
enemies.

4 The pangs of death surrounded me,
And the floods of ungodliness
made me afraid.
5 The sorrows of Sheol
surrounded me;
The snares of death confronted me.
6 In my distress I called upon the
LORD,
And cried out to my God;
He heard my voice from His
temple,
And my cry came before Him,
even to His ears.

7 Then the earth shook and trembled;
The foundations of the hills also quaked and were shaken,
Because He was angry.
8 Smoke went up from His nostrils,
And devouring fire from His mouth;
Coals were kindled by it.
9 He bowed the heavens also, and came down
With darkness under His feet.
10 And He rode upon a cherub, and flew;
He flew upon the wings of the wind.
11 He made darkness His secret place;
His canopy around Him *was* dark waters
And thick clouds of the skies.
12 From the brightness before Him,
His thick clouds passed with hailstones and coals of fire.

13 The LORD thundered from heaven,
And the Most High uttered His voice,
Hailstones and coals of fire.[a]
14 He sent out His arrows and scattered the foe,
Lightnings in abundance, and He vanquished them.
15 Then the channels of the sea were seen,
The foundations of the world were uncovered
At Your rebuke, O LORD,
At the blast of the breath of Your nostrils.

16 He sent from above, He took me;
He drew me out of many waters.
17 He delivered me from my strong enemy,
From those who hated me,
For they were too strong for me.
18 They confronted me in the day of my calamity,
But the LORD was my support.
19 He also brought me out into a broad place;
He delivered me because He delighted in me.

20 The LORD rewarded me according to my righteousness;
According to the cleanness of my hands
He has recompensed me.
21 For I have kept the ways of the LORD,
And have not wickedly departed from my God.
22 For all His judgments *were* before me,
And I did not put away His statutes from me.
23 I was also blameless before Him,
And I kept myself from my iniquity.
24 Therefore the LORD has recompensed me according to my righteousness,
According to the cleanness of my hands in His sight.

25 With the merciful You will show Yourself merciful;
With a blameless man You will show Yourself blameless;
26 With the pure You will show Yourself pure;
And with the devious You will show Yourself shrewd.
27 For You will save the humble people,
But will bring down haughty looks.

28 For You will light my lamp;
The LORD my God will enlighten my darkness.
29 For by You I can run against a troop,
By my God I can leap over a wall.
30 *As for* God, His way *is* perfect;
The word of the LORD is proven;
He *is* a shield to all who trust in Him.

31 For who *is* God, except the LORD?
And who *is* a rock, except our God?
32 *It is* God who arms me with strength,
And makes my way perfect.

18:13 [a] Following Masoretic Text, Targum, and Vulgate; a few Hebrew manuscripts and Septuagint omit *Hailstones and coals of fire.*

33 He makes my feet like the *feet of* deer,
And sets me on my high places.
34 He teaches my hands to make war,
So that my arms can bend a bow of bronze.

35 You have also given me the shield of Your salvation;
Your right hand has held me up,
Your gentleness has made me great.
36 You enlarged my path under me,
So my feet did not slip.

37 I have pursued my enemies and overtaken them;
Neither did I turn back again till they were destroyed.
38 I have wounded them,
So that they could not rise;
They have fallen under my feet.
39 For You have armed me with strength for the battle;
You have subdued under me those who rose up against me.
40 You have also given me the necks of my enemies,
So that I destroyed those who hated me.
41 They cried out, but *there was* none to save;
Even to the LORD, but He did not answer them.
42 Then I beat them as fine as the dust before the wind;
I cast them out like dirt in the streets.

43 You have delivered me from the strivings of the people;
You have made me the head of the nations;
A people I have not known shall serve me.
44 As soon as they hear of me they obey me;
The foreigners submit to me.
45 The foreigners fade away,
And come frightened from their hideouts.

46 The LORD lives!
Blessed *be* my Rock!
Let the God of my salvation be exalted.
47 *It is* God who avenges me,
And subdues the peoples under me;
48 He delivers me from my enemies.
You also lift me up above those who rise against me;
You have delivered me from the violent man.
49 Therefore I will give thanks to You, O LORD, among the Gentiles,
And sing praises to Your name.

50 Great deliverance He gives to His king,
And shows mercy to His anointed,
To David and his descendants forevermore.

PSALM 19

The Perfect Revelation of the LORD

To the Chief Musician. A Psalm of David.

1 The heavens declare the glory of God;
And the firmament shows His handiwork.
2 Day unto day utters speech,
And night unto night reveals knowledge.
3 *There is* no speech nor language
Where their voice is not heard.
4 Their line[a] has gone out through all the earth,
And their words to the end of the world.

In them He has set a tabernacle for the sun,
5 Which *is* like a bridegroom coming out of his chamber,
And rejoices like a strong man to run its race.
6 Its rising *is* from one end of heaven,
And its circuit to the other end;
And there is nothing hidden from its heat.

7 The law of the LORD *is* perfect, converting the soul;

19:4 [a] Septuagint, Syriac, and Vulgate read *sound;* Targum reads *business.*

The testimony of the LORD *is* sure,
making wise the simple;
8 The statutes of the LORD *are* right,
rejoicing the heart;
The commandment of the LORD *is*
pure, enlightening the eyes;
9 The fear of the LORD *is* clean,
enduring forever;
The judgments of the LORD *are*
true *and* righteous altogether.
10 More to be desired *are they* than
gold,
Yea, than much fine gold;
Sweeter also than honey and the
honeycomb.
11 Moreover by them Your servant is
warned,
And in keeping them *there is* great
reward.

12 Who can understand *his* errors?
Cleanse me from secret *faults.*
13 Keep back Your servant also from
presumptuous *sins;*
Let them not have dominion
over me.
Then I shall be blameless,
And I shall be innocent of great
transgression.

14 Let the words of my mouth and
the meditation of my heart
Be acceptable in Your sight,
O LORD, my strength and my
Redeemer.

PSALM 20

The Assurance of God's Saving Work

To the Chief Musician. A Psalm of David.

1 May the LORD answer you in the
day of trouble;
May the name of the God of Jacob
defend you;
2 May He send you help from the
sanctuary,
And strengthen you out of Zion;
3 May He remember all your
offerings,
And accept your burnt sacrifice.
Selah

4 May He grant you according to
your heart's *desire,*
And fulfill all your purpose.
5 We will rejoice in your salvation,
And in the name of our God we
will set up *our* banners!
May the LORD fulfill all your
petitions.

6 Now I know that the LORD saves
His anointed;
He will answer him from His holy
heaven
With the saving strength of His
right hand.

7 Some *trust* in chariots, and some
in horses;
But we will remember the name
of the LORD our God.
8 They have bowed down and
fallen;
But we have risen and stand
upright.

9 Save, LORD!
May the King answer us when we
call.

PSALM 21

Joy in the Salvation of the LORD

To the Chief Musician. A Psalm of David.

1 The king shall have joy in Your
strength, O LORD;
And in Your salvation how greatly
shall he rejoice!
2 You have given him his heart's
desire,
And have not withheld the
request of his lips. *Selah*

3 For You meet him with the
blessings of goodness;
You set a crown of pure gold upon
his head.
4 He asked life from You, *and* You
gave *it* to him—
Length of days forever and ever.
5 His glory *is* great in Your
salvation;
Honor and majesty You have
placed upon him.
6 For You have made him most
blessed forever;
You have made him exceedingly
glad with Your presence.
7 For the king trusts in the LORD,

And through the mercy of the
Most High he shall not be
moved.
8 Your hand will find all Your
enemies;
Your right hand will find those
who hate You.
9 You shall make them as a fiery
oven in the time of Your
anger;
The LORD shall swallow them up
in His wrath,
And the fire shall devour them.
10 Their offspring You shall destroy
from the earth,
And their descendants from
among the sons of men.
11 For they intended evil against
You;
They devised a plot *which* they
are not able *to perform*.
12 Therefore You will make them
turn their back;
You will make ready *Your arrows*
on Your string toward their
faces.

13 Be exalted, O LORD, in Your own
strength!
We will sing and praise Your
power.

PSALM 22

The Suffering, Praise, and Posterity of the Messiah

To the Chief Musician. Set to "The Deer of the Dawn."[a] *A Psalm of David.*

1 My God, My God, why have You
forsaken Me?
Why are You so far from
helping Me,
And from the words of My
groaning?
2 O My God, I cry in the daytime,
but You do not hear;
And in the night season, and am
not silent.

3 But You *are* holy,
Enthroned in the praises of Israel.
4 Our fathers trusted in You;
They trusted, and You delivered
them.
5 They cried to You, and were
delivered;
They trusted in You, and were not
ashamed.

6 But I *am* a worm, and no man;
A reproach of men, and despised
by the people.
7 All those who see Me ridicule Me;
They shoot out the lip, they shake
the head, *saying,*
8 "He trusted[a] in the LORD, let Him
rescue Him;
Let Him deliver Him, since He
delights in Him!"

9 But You *are* He who took Me out of
the womb;
You made Me trust *while* on My
mother's breasts.
10 I was cast upon You from birth.
From My mother's womb
You *have been* My God.
11 Be not far from Me,
For trouble *is* near;
For *there is* none to help.

12 Many bulls have surrounded Me;
Strong *bulls* of Bashan have
encircled Me.
13 They gape at Me *with* their
mouths,
Like a raging and roaring lion.

14 I am poured out like water,
And all My bones are out of joint;
My heart is like wax;
It has melted within Me.
15 My strength is dried up like a
potsherd,
And My tongue clings to My jaws;
You have brought Me to the dust
of death.

16 For dogs have surrounded Me;
The congregation of the wicked
has enclosed Me.
They pierced[a] My hands and My
feet;

22:title [a] Hebrew *Aijeleth Hashahar* **22:8** [a] Septuagint, Syriac, and Vulgate read *hoped;* Targum reads *praised.* **22:16** [a] Following some Hebrew manuscripts, Septuagint, Syriac, Vulgate; Masoretic Text reads *Like a lion.*

17 I can count all My bones.
They look *and* stare at Me.
18 They divide My garments among them,
And for My clothing they cast lots.

19 But You, O LORD, do not be far from Me;
O My Strength, hasten to help Me!
20 Deliver Me from the sword,
My precious *life* from the power of the dog.
21 Save Me from the lion's mouth
And from the horns of the wild oxen!

You have answered Me.

22 I will declare Your name to My brethren;
In the midst of the assembly I will praise You.
23 You who fear the LORD, praise Him!
All you descendants of Jacob, glorify Him,
And fear Him, all you offspring of Israel!
24 For He has not despised nor abhorred the affliction of the afflicted;
Nor has He hidden His face from Him;
But when He cried to Him, He heard.

25 My praise *shall be* of You in the great assembly;
I will pay My vows before those who fear Him.
26 The poor shall eat and be satisfied;
Those who seek Him will praise the LORD.
Let your heart live forever!

27 All the ends of the world
Shall remember and turn to the LORD,
And all the families of the nations
Shall worship before You.[a]

28 For the kingdom *is* the LORD's,
And He rules over the nations.

29 All the prosperous of the earth
Shall eat and worship;
All those who go down to the dust
Shall bow before Him,
Even he who cannot keep himself alive.

30 A posterity shall serve Him.
It will be recounted of the Lord to the *next* generation,
31 They will come and declare His righteousness to a people who will be born,
That He has done *this*.

PSALM 23

The LORD the Shepherd of His People

A Psalm of David.

1 The LORD *is* my shepherd;
I shall not want.
2 He makes me to lie down in green pastures;
He leads me beside the still waters.
3 He restores my soul;
He leads me in the paths of righteousness
For His name's sake.

4 Yea, though I walk through the valley of the shadow of death,
I will fear no evil;
For You *are* with me;
Your rod and Your staff, they comfort me.

5 You prepare a table before me in the presence of my enemies;
You anoint my head with oil;
My cup runs over.
6 Surely goodness and mercy shall follow me
All the days of my life;
And I will dwell[a] in the house of the LORD
Forever.

22:27 [a] Following Masoretic Text, Septuagint, and Targum; Arabic, Syriac, and Vulgate read *Him.*
23:6 [a] Following Septuagint, Syriac, Targum, and Vulgate; Masoretic Text reads *return.*

PSALM 24

The King of Glory and His Kingdom

A Psalm of David.

1 The earth *is* the LORD's, and all its fullness,
The world and those who dwell therein.
2 For He has founded it upon the seas,
And established it upon the waters.

3 Who may ascend into the hill of the LORD?
Or who may stand in His holy place?
4 He who has clean hands and a pure heart,
Who has not lifted up his soul to an idol,
Nor sworn deceitfully.
5 He shall receive blessing from the LORD,
And righteousness from the God of his salvation.
6 This *is* Jacob, the generation of those who seek Him,
Who seek Your face. *Selah*

7 Lift up your heads, O you gates!
And be lifted up, you everlasting doors!
And the King of glory shall come in.
8 Who *is* this King of glory?
The LORD strong and mighty,
The LORD mighty in battle.
9 Lift up your heads, O you gates!
Lift up, you everlasting doors!
And the King of glory shall come in.
10 Who is this King of glory?
The LORD of hosts,
He *is* the King of glory. *Selah*

PSALM 25

A Plea for Deliverance and Forgiveness

A Psalm of David.

1 To You, O LORD, I lift up my soul.
2 O my God, I trust in You;
Let me not be ashamed;
Let not my enemies triumph over me.
3 Indeed, let no one who waits on You be ashamed;
Let those be ashamed who deal treacherously without cause.

4 Show me Your ways, O LORD;
Teach me Your paths.
5 Lead me in Your truth and teach me,
For You *are* the God of my salvation;
On You I wait all the day.

6 Remember, O LORD, Your tender mercies and Your lovingkindnesses,
For they *are* from of old.
7 Do not remember the sins of my youth, nor my transgressions;
According to Your mercy remember me,
For Your goodness' sake, O LORD.

8 Good and upright *is* the LORD;
Therefore He teaches sinners in the way.
9 The humble He guides in justice,
And the humble He teaches His way.
10 All the paths of the LORD *are* mercy and truth,
To such as keep His covenant and His testimonies.
11 For Your name's sake, O LORD,
Pardon my iniquity, for it *is* great.

12 Who *is* the man that fears the LORD?
Him shall He[a] teach in the way He[b] chooses.
13 He himself shall dwell in prosperity,
And his descendants shall inherit the earth.
14 The secret of the LORD *is* with those who fear Him,
And He will show them His covenant.
15 My eyes *are* ever toward the LORD,
For He shall pluck my feet out of the net.

25:12 [a] Or *he* [b] Or *he*

16 Turn Yourself to me, and have mercy on me,
For I *am* desolate and afflicted.
17 The troubles of my heart have enlarged;
Bring me out of my distresses!
18 Look on my affliction and my pain,
And forgive all my sins.
19 Consider my enemies, for they are many;
And they hate me with cruel hatred.
20 Keep my soul, and deliver me;
Let me not be ashamed, for I put my trust in You.
21 Let integrity and uprightness preserve me,
For I wait for You.

22 Redeem Israel, O God,
Out of all their troubles!

PSALM 26

A Prayer for Divine Scrutiny and Redemption

A Psalm of David.

1 Vindicate me, O LORD,
For I have walked in my integrity.
I have also trusted in the LORD;
I shall not slip.
2 Examine me, O LORD, and prove me;
Try my mind and my heart.
3 For Your lovingkindness *is* before my eyes,
And I have walked in Your truth.
4 I have not sat with idolatrous mortals,
Nor will I go in with hypocrites.
5 I have hated the assembly of evildoers,
And will not sit with the wicked.

6 I will wash my hands in innocence;
So I will go about Your altar, O LORD,
7 That I may proclaim with the voice of thanksgiving,
And tell of all Your wondrous works.
8 LORD, I have loved the habitation of Your house,
And the place where Your glory dwells.

9 Do not gather my soul with sinners,
Nor my life with bloodthirsty men,
10 In whose hands *is* a sinister scheme,
And whose right hand is full of bribes.

11 But as for me, I will walk in my integrity;
Redeem me and be merciful to me.
12 My foot stands in an even place;
In the congregations I will bless the LORD.

PSALM 27

An Exuberant Declaration of Faith

A Psalm of David.

1 The LORD *is* my light and my salvation;
Whom shall I fear?
The LORD *is* the strength of my life;
Of whom shall I be afraid?
2 When the wicked came against me
To eat up my flesh,
My enemies and foes,
They stumbled and fell.
3 Though an army may encamp against me,
My heart shall not fear;
Though war may rise against me,
In this I *will be* confident.

4 One *thing* I have desired of the LORD,
That will I seek:
That I may dwell in the house of the LORD
All the days of my life,
To behold the beauty of the LORD,
And to inquire in His temple.
5 For in the time of trouble
He shall hide me in His pavilion;
In the secret place of His tabernacle
He shall hide me;
He shall set me high upon a rock.

6 And now my head shall be lifted
up above my enemies all
around me;
Therefore I will offer sacrifices of
joy in His tabernacle;
I will sing, yes, I will sing praises
to the LORD.

7 Hear, O LORD, *when* I cry with my
voice!
Have mercy also upon me, and
answer me.
8 *When You said,* "Seek My face,"
My heart said to You, "Your face,
LORD, I will seek."
9 Do not hide Your face from me;
Do not turn Your servant away in
anger;
You have been my help;
Do not leave me nor forsake me,
O God of my salvation.
10 When my father and my mother
forsake me,
Then the LORD will take care of me.

11 Teach me Your way, O LORD,
And lead me in a smooth path,
because of my enemies.
12 Do not deliver me to the will of
my adversaries;
For false witnesses have risen
against me,
And such as breathe out violence.
13 *I would have lost heart,* unless I
had believed
That I would see the goodness of
the LORD
In the land of the living.

14 Wait on the LORD;
Be of good courage,
And He shall strengthen your heart;
Wait, I say, on the LORD!

PSALM 28

Rejoicing in Answered Prayer

A Psalm of David.

1 To You I will cry, O LORD my Rock:
Do not be silent to me,
Lest, if You *are* silent to me,
I become like those who go down
to the pit.

2 Hear the voice of my supplications
When I cry to You,
When I lift up my hands toward
Your holy sanctuary.

3 Do not take me away with the
wicked
And with the workers of iniquity,
Who speak peace to their
neighbors,
But evil *is* in their hearts.
4 Give them according to their
deeds,
And according to the wickedness
of their endeavors;
Give them according to the work
of their hands;
Render to them what they
deserve.
5 Because they do not regard the
works of the LORD,
Nor the operation of His hands,
He shall destroy them
And not build them up.

6 Blessed *be* the LORD,
Because He has heard the voice of
my supplications!
7 The LORD *is* my strength and my
shield;
My heart trusted in Him, and I
am helped;
Therefore my heart greatly
rejoices,
And with my song I will praise
Him.

8 The LORD *is* their strength,[a]
And He *is* the saving refuge of His
anointed.
9 Save Your people,
And bless Your inheritance;
Shepherd them also,
And bear them up forever.

PSALM 29

Praise to God in His Holiness and Majesty

A Psalm of David.

1 Give unto the LORD, O you mighty
ones,
Give unto the LORD glory and
strength.

28:8 [a] Following Masoretic Text and Targum; Septuagint, Syriac, and Vulgate read *the strength of His people.*

WORSHIP GROWTH HEAVEN FAMILY

2 Give unto the LORD the glory due
to His name;
Worship the LORD in the beauty
of holiness.

3 The voice of the LORD *is* over the
waters;
The God of glory thunders;
The LORD *is* over many waters.
4 The voice of the LORD *is* powerful;
The voice of the LORD *is* full of
majesty.

5 The voice of the LORD breaks the
cedars,
Yes, the LORD splinters the cedars
of Lebanon.
6 He makes them also skip like a
calf,
Lebanon and Sirion like a young
wild ox.
7 The voice of the LORD divides the
flames of fire.

8 The voice of the LORD shakes the
wilderness;
The LORD shakes the Wilderness
of Kadesh.
9 The voice of the LORD makes the
deer give birth,
And strips the forests bare;
And in His temple everyone says,
"Glory!"

10 The LORD sat *enthroned* at the
Flood,
And the LORD sits as King forever.
11 The LORD will give strength to His
people;
The LORD will bless His people
with peace.

PSALM 30

The Blessedness of Answered Prayer

A Psalm. A Song at the dedication of the house of David.

1 I will extol You, O LORD, for You
have lifted me up,
And have not let my foes rejoice
over me.
2 O LORD my God, I cried out to You,
And You healed me.
3 O LORD, You brought my soul up
from the grave;
You have kept me alive, that I
should not go down to the pit.[a]

4 Sing praise to the LORD, you
saints of His,
And give thanks at the
remembrance of His holy
name.[a]
5 For His anger *is but for* a moment,
His favor *is for* life;
Weeping may endure for a night,
But joy *comes* in the morning.

6 Now in my prosperity I said,
"I shall never be moved."
7 LORD, by Your favor You have made
my mountain stand strong;
You hid Your face, *and* I was
troubled.

8 I cried out to You, O LORD;
And to the LORD I made
supplication:
9 "What profit *is there* in my blood,
When I go down to the pit?
Will the dust praise You?
Will it declare Your truth?
10 Hear, O LORD, and have mercy
on me;
LORD, be my helper!"

11 You have turned for me my
mourning into dancing;
You have put off my sackcloth
and clothed me with
gladness,
12 To the end that *my* glory may
sing praise to You and not be
silent.
O LORD my God, I will give thanks
to You forever.

PSALM 31

The LORD a Fortress in Adversity

To the Chief Musician. A Psalm of David.

1 In You, O LORD, I put my trust;
Let me never be ashamed;
Deliver me in Your righteousness.
2 Bow down Your ear to me,
Deliver me speedily;

30:3 [a] Following Qere and Targum; Kethib, Septuagint, Syriac, and Vulgate read *from those who descend to the pit.* 30:4 [a] Or *His holiness*

Be my rock of refuge,
A fortress of defense to save me.

3 For You *are* my rock and my fortress;
Therefore, for Your name's sake,
Lead me and guide me.
4 Pull me out of the net which they have secretly laid for me,
For You *are* my strength.
5 Into Your hand I commit my spirit;
You have redeemed me, O LORD God of truth.

6 I have hated those who regard useless idols;
But I trust in the LORD.
7 I will be glad and rejoice in Your mercy,
For You have considered my trouble;
You have known my soul in adversities,
8 And have not shut me up into the hand of the enemy;
You have set my feet in a wide place.

9 Have mercy on me, O LORD, for I am in trouble;
My eye wastes away with grief,
Yes, my soul and my body!
10 For my life is spent with grief,
And my years with sighing;
My strength fails because of my iniquity,
And my bones waste away.
11 I am a reproach among all my enemies,
But especially among my neighbors,
And *am* repulsive to my acquaintances;
Those who see me outside flee from me.
12 I am forgotten like a dead man, out of mind;
I am like a broken vessel.
13 For I hear the slander of many;
Fear *is* on every side;
While they take counsel together against me,
They scheme to take away my life.

14 But as for me, I trust in You, O LORD;
I say, "You *are* my God."
15 My times *are* in Your hand;
Deliver me from the hand of my enemies,
And from those who persecute me.
16 Make Your face shine upon Your servant;
Save me for Your mercies' sake.
17 Do not let me be ashamed, O LORD, for I have called upon You;
Let the wicked be ashamed;
Let them be silent in the grave.
18 Let the lying lips be put to silence,
Which speak insolent things proudly and contemptuously against the righteous.

19 Oh, how great *is* Your goodness,
Which You have laid up for those who fear You,
Which You have prepared for those who trust in You
In the presence of the sons of men!
20 You shall hide them in the secret place of Your presence
From the plots of man;
You shall keep them secretly in a pavilion
From the strife of tongues.

21 Blessed *be* the LORD,
For He has shown me His marvelous kindness in a strong city!
22 For I said in my haste,
"I am cut off from before Your eyes";
Nevertheless You heard the voice of my supplications
When I cried out to You.

23 Oh, love the LORD, all you His saints!
For the LORD preserves the faithful,
And fully repays the proud person.
24 Be of good courage,
And He shall strengthen your heart,
All you who hope in the LORD.

PSALM 32
The Joy of Forgiveness
A Psalm *of David. A Contemplation.*[a]

1 Blessed *is he whose* transgression
is forgiven,
Whose sin *is* covered.
2 Blessed *is* the man to whom
the LORD does not impute
iniquity,
And in whose spirit *there is* no
deceit.

3 When I kept silent, my bones
grew old
Through my groaning all the day
long.
4 For day and night Your hand was
heavy upon me;
My vitality was turned into the
drought of summer. *Selah*
5 I acknowledged my sin to You,
And my iniquity I have not
hidden.
I said, "I will confess my
transgressions to the LORD,"
And You forgave the iniquity of
my sin. *Selah*

6 For this cause everyone who is
godly shall pray to You
In a time when You may be found;
Surely in a flood of great waters
They shall not come near him.
7 You *are* my hiding place;
You shall preserve me from trouble;
You shall surround me with songs
of deliverance. *Selah*

8 I will instruct you and teach you
in the way you should go;
I will guide you with My eye.
9 Do not be like the horse *or* like the
mule,
Which have no understanding,
Which must be harnessed with bit
and bridle,
Else they will not come near you.

10 Many sorrows *shall be* to the
wicked;
But he who trusts in the LORD,
mercy shall surround him.
11 Be glad in the LORD and rejoice,
you righteous;
And shout for joy, all *you* upright
in heart!

PSALM 33
The Sovereignty of the LORD in Creation and History
1 Rejoice in the LORD, O you
righteous!
For praise from the upright is
beautiful.
2 Praise the LORD with the harp;
Make melody to Him with an
instrument of ten strings.
3 Sing to Him a new song;
Play skillfully with a shout of joy.

4 For the word of the LORD *is* right,
And all His work *is done* in truth.
5 He loves righteousness and
justice;
The earth is full of the goodness of
the LORD.

6 By the word of the LORD the
heavens were made,
And all the host of them by the
breath of His mouth.
7 He gathers the waters of the sea
together as a heap;[a]
He lays up the deep in
storehouses.

8 Let all the earth fear the LORD;
Let all the inhabitants of the
world stand in awe of Him.
9 For He spoke, and it was *done;*
He commanded, and it stood
fast.

10 The LORD brings the counsel of
the nations to nothing;
He makes the plans of the peoples
of no effect.
11 The counsel of the LORD stands
forever,
The plans of His heart to all
generations.
12 Blessed *is* the nation whose God *is*
the LORD,
The people He has chosen as His
own inheritance.

32:title [a] Hebrew *Maschil* **33:7** [a] Septuagint, Targum, and Vulgate read *in a vessel.*

13 The LORD looks from heaven;
He sees all the sons of men.
14 From the place of His dwelling He looks
On all the inhabitants of the earth;
15 He fashions their hearts individually;
He considers all their works.

16 No king *is* saved by the multitude of an army;
A mighty man is not delivered by great strength.
17 A horse *is* a vain hope for safety;
Neither shall it deliver *any* by its great strength.

18 Behold, the eye of the LORD *is* on those who fear Him,
On those who hope in His mercy,
19 To deliver their soul from death,
And to keep them alive in famine.

20 Our soul waits for the LORD;
He *is* our help and our shield.
21 For our heart shall rejoice in Him,
Because we have trusted in His holy name.
22 Let Your mercy, O LORD, be upon us,
Just as we hope in You.

PSALM 34

The Happiness of Those Who Trust in God

A Psalm of David when he pretended madness before Abimelech, who drove him away, and he departed.

1 I will bless the LORD at all times;
His praise *shall* continually *be* in my mouth.
2 My soul shall make its boast in the LORD;
The humble shall hear *of it* and be glad.
3 Oh, magnify the LORD with me,
And let us exalt His name together.

4 I sought the LORD, and He heard me,
And delivered me from all my fears.
5 They looked to Him and were radiant,
And their faces were not ashamed.
6 This poor man cried out, and the LORD heard *him,*
And saved him out of all his troubles.
7 The angel[a] of the LORD encamps all around those who fear Him,
And delivers them.
8 Oh, taste and see that the LORD *is* good;
Blessed *is* the man *who* trusts in Him!
9 Oh, fear the LORD, you His saints!
There is no want to those who fear Him.
10 The young lions lack and suffer hunger;
But those who seek the LORD shall not lack any good *thing.*

11 Come, you children, listen to me;
I will teach you the fear of the LORD.
12 Who *is* the man *who* desires life,
And loves *many* days, that he may see good?
13 Keep your tongue from evil,
And your lips from speaking deceit.
14 Depart from evil and do good;
Seek peace and pursue it.

15 The eyes of the LORD *are* on the righteous,
And His ears *are open* to their cry.
16 The face of the LORD *is* against those who do evil,
To cut off the remembrance of them from the earth.

17 *The righteous* cry out, and the LORD hears,
And delivers them out of all their troubles.
18 The LORD *is* near to those who have a broken heart,
And saves such as have a contrite spirit.

34:7 [a] Or *Angel*

19 Many *are* the afflictions of the righteous,
But the LORD delivers him out of them all.
20 He guards all his bones;
Not one of them is broken.
21 Evil shall slay the wicked,
And those who hate the righteous shall be condemned.
22 The LORD redeems the soul of His servants,
And none of those who trust in Him shall be condemned.

PSALM 35

The LORD the Avenger of His People

A Psalm of David.

1 Plead *my cause,* O LORD, with those who strive with me;
Fight against those who fight against me.
2 Take hold of shield and buckler,
And stand up for my help.
3 Also draw out the spear,
And stop those who pursue me.
Say to my soul,
"I *am* your salvation."

4 Let those be put to shame and brought to dishonor
Who seek after my life;
Let those be turned back and brought to confusion
Who plot my hurt.
5 Let them be like chaff before the wind,
And let the angel[a] of the LORD chase *them.*
6 Let their way be dark and slippery,
And let the angel of the LORD pursue them.
7 For without cause they have hidden their net for me *in* a pit,
Which they have dug without cause for my life.
8 Let destruction come upon him unexpectedly,
And let his net that he has hidden catch himself;
Into that very destruction let him fall.
9 And my soul shall be joyful in the LORD;
It shall rejoice in His salvation.
10 All my bones shall say,
"LORD, who *is* like You,
Delivering the poor from him who is too strong for him,
Yes, the poor and the needy from him who plunders him?"

11 Fierce witnesses rise up;
They ask me *things* that I do not know.
12 They reward me evil for good,
To the sorrow of my soul.
13 But as for me, when they were sick,
My clothing *was* sackcloth;
I humbled myself with fasting;
And my prayer would return to my own heart.
14 I paced about as though *he were* my friend *or* brother;
I bowed down heavily, as one who mourns *for his* mother.

15 But in my adversity they rejoiced
And gathered together;
Attackers gathered against me,
And I did not know *it;*
They tore *at me* and did not cease;
16 With ungodly mockers at feasts
They gnashed at me with their teeth.

17 Lord, how long will You look on?
Rescue me from their destructions,
My precious *life* from the lions.
18 I will give You thanks in the great assembly;
I will praise You among many people.

19 Let them not rejoice over me who are wrongfully my enemies;
Nor let them wink with the eye who hate me without a cause.
20 For they do not speak peace,
But they devise deceitful matters
Against *the* quiet ones in the land.

35:5 [a] Or *Angel*

21 They also opened their mouth
wide against me,
And said, "Aha, aha!
Our eyes have seen *it*."

22 *This* You have seen, O LORD;
Do not keep silence.
O Lord, do not be far from me.
23 Stir up Yourself, and awake to my
vindication,
To my cause, my God and my
Lord.
24 Vindicate me, O LORD my
God, according to Your
righteousness;
And let them not rejoice over me.
25 Let them not say in their hearts,
"Ah, so we would have it!"
Let them not say, "We have
swallowed him up."

26 Let them be ashamed and
brought to mutual confusion
Who rejoice at my hurt;
Let them be clothed with shame
and dishonor
Who exalt themselves against me.

27 Let them shout for joy and be
glad,
Who favor my righteous cause;
And let them say continually,
"Let the LORD be magnified,
Who has pleasure in the
prosperity of His servant."
28 And my tongue shall speak of
Your righteousness
And of Your praise all the day
long.

PSALM 36

Man's Wickedness and God's Perfections

To the Chief Musician. A Psalm of David the servant of the LORD.

1 An oracle within my
heart concerning the
transgression of the wicked:
There is no fear of God before his
eyes.
2 For he flatters himself in his own
eyes,
When he finds out his iniquity
and when he hates.
3 The words of his mouth *are*
wickedness and deceit;
He has ceased to be wise *and* to do
good.
4 He devises wickedness on his bed;
He sets himself in a way *that is*
not good;
He does not abhor evil.

5 Your mercy, O LORD, *is* in the
heavens;
Your faithfulness *reaches* to the
clouds.
6 Your righteousness *is* like the
great mountains;
Your judgments *are* a great deep;
O LORD, You preserve man and
beast.

7 How precious *is* Your
lovingkindness, O God!
Therefore the children of men put
their trust under the shadow
of Your wings.
8 They are abundantly satisfied with
the fullness of Your house,
And You give them drink from the
river of Your pleasures.
9 For with You *is* the fountain of life;
In Your light we see light.

10 Oh, continue Your lovingkindness
to those who know You,
And Your righteousness to the
upright in heart.
11 Let not the foot of pride come
against me,
And let not the hand of the wicked
drive me away.
12 There the workers of iniquity have
fallen;
They have been cast down and
are not able to rise.

PSALM 37

The Heritage of the Righteous and the Calamity of the Wicked

A Psalm of David.

1 Do not fret because of evildoers,
Nor be envious of the workers of
iniquity.
2 For they shall soon be cut down
like the grass,
And wither as the green herb.

3 Trust in the LORD, and do good;
Dwell in the land, and feed on His faithfulness.
4 Delight yourself also in the LORD,
And He shall give you the desires of your heart.

5 Commit your way to the LORD,
Trust also in Him,
And He shall bring *it* to pass.
6 He shall bring forth your righteousness as the light,
And your justice as the noonday.

7 Rest in the LORD, and wait patiently for Him;
Do not fret because of him who prospers in his way,
Because of the man who brings wicked schemes to pass.
8 Cease from anger, and forsake wrath;
Do not fret—*it* only *causes* harm.

9 For evildoers shall be cut off;
But those who wait on the LORD,
They shall inherit the earth.
10 For yet a little while and the wicked *shall be* no *more;*
Indeed, you will look carefully for his place,
But it *shall be* no *more.*
11 But the meek shall inherit the earth,
And shall delight themselves in the abundance of peace.

12 The wicked plots against the just,
And gnashes at him with his teeth.
13 The Lord laughs at him,
For He sees that his day is coming.
14 The wicked have drawn the sword
And have bent their bow,
To cast down the poor and needy,
To slay those who are of upright conduct.
15 Their sword shall enter their own heart,
And their bows shall be broken.

16 A little that a righteous man has
Is better than the riches of many wicked.
17 For the arms of the wicked shall be broken,
But the LORD upholds the righteous.

18 The LORD knows the days of the upright,
And their inheritance shall be forever.
19 They shall not be ashamed in the evil time,
And in the days of famine they shall be satisfied.
20 But the wicked shall perish;
And the enemies of the LORD,
Like the splendor of the meadows, shall vanish.
Into smoke they shall vanish away.

21 The wicked borrows and does not repay,
But the righteous shows mercy and gives.
22 For *those* blessed by Him shall inherit the earth,
But *those* cursed by Him shall be cut off.

23 The steps of a *good* man are ordered by the LORD,
And He delights in his way.
24 Though he fall, he shall not be utterly cast down;
For the LORD upholds *him with* His hand.

25 I have been young, and *now* am old;
Yet I have not seen the righteous forsaken,
Nor his descendants begging bread.
26 *He is* ever merciful, and lends;
And his descendants *are* blessed.

27 Depart from evil, and do good;
And dwell forevermore.
28 For the LORD loves justice,
And does not forsake His saints;
They are preserved forever,
But the descendants of the wicked shall be cut off.
29 The righteous shall inherit the land,
And dwell in it forever.

30 The mouth of the righteous speaks wisdom,
And his tongue talks of justice.
31 The law of his God *is* in his heart;
None of his steps shall slide.

32 The wicked watches the righteous,
And seeks to slay him.
33 The LORD will not leave him in his hand,
Nor condemn him when he is judged.

34 Wait on the LORD,
And keep His way,
And He shall exalt you to inherit the land;
When the wicked are cut off, you shall see *it.*
35 I have seen the wicked in great power,
And spreading himself like a native green tree.
36 Yet he passed away,[a] and behold, he *was* no *more;*
Indeed I sought him, but he could not be found.

37 Mark the blameless *man,* and observe the upright;
For the future of *that* man *is* peace.
38 But the transgressors shall be destroyed together;
The future of the wicked shall be cut off.

39 But the salvation of the righteous *is* from the LORD;
He is their strength in the time of trouble.
40 And the LORD shall help them and deliver them;
He shall deliver them from the wicked,
And save them,
Because they trust in Him.

PSALM 38

Prayer in Time of Chastening

A Psalm of David. To bring to remembrance.

1 O LORD, do not rebuke me in Your wrath,
Nor chasten me in Your hot displeasure!
2 For Your arrows pierce me deeply,
And Your hand presses me down.

3 *There is* no soundness in my flesh
Because of Your anger,
Nor *any* health in my bones
Because of my sin.
4 For my iniquities have gone over my head;
Like a heavy burden they are too heavy for me.
5 My wounds are foul *and* festering
Because of my foolishness.

6 I am troubled, I am bowed down greatly;
I go mourning all the day long.
7 For my loins are full of inflammation,
And *there is* no soundness in my flesh.
8 I am feeble and severely broken;
I groan because of the turmoil of my heart.

9 Lord, all my desire *is* before You;
And my sighing is not hidden from You.
10 My heart pants, my strength fails me;
As for the light of my eyes, it also has gone from me.

11 My loved ones and my friends stand aloof from my plague,
And my relatives stand afar off.
12 Those also who seek my life lay snares *for me;*
Those who seek my hurt speak of destruction,
And plan deception all the day long.

13 But I, like a deaf *man,* do not hear;
And *I am* like a mute *who* does not open his mouth.
14 Thus I am like a man who does not hear,
And in whose mouth *is* no response.

15 For in You, O LORD, I hope;
You will hear, O Lord my God.
16 For I said, "*Hear me,* lest they rejoice over me,
Lest, when my foot slips, they exalt *themselves* against me."

37:36 [a] Following Masoretic Text, Septuagint, and Targum; Syriac and Vulgate read *I passed by.*

17 For I *am* ready to fall,
And my sorrow *is* continually
before me.
18 For I will declare my iniquity;
I will be in anguish over my sin.
19 But my enemies *are* vigorous, *and*
they are strong;
And those who hate me
wrongfully have multiplied.
20 Those also who render evil for
good,
They are my adversaries, because
I follow *what is* good.

21 Do not forsake me, O LORD;
O my God, be not far from me!
22 Make haste to help me,
O Lord, my salvation!

PSALM 39

Prayer for Wisdom and Forgiveness

*To the Chief Musician. To Jeduthun.
A Psalm of David.*

1 I said, "I will guard my ways,
Lest I sin with my tongue;
I will restrain my mouth with a
muzzle,
While the wicked are
before me."
2 I was mute with silence,
I held my peace *even* from good;
And my sorrow was stirred up.
3 My heart was hot within me;
While I was musing, the fire
burned.
Then I spoke with my tongue:

4 "LORD, make me to know my end,
And what *is* the measure of my
days,
That I may know how frail I *am*.
5 Indeed, You have made my days
as handbreadths,
And my age *is* as nothing before
You;
Certainly every man at his best
state *is* but vapor. *Selah*
6 Surely every man walks about
like a shadow;
Surely they busy themselves in
vain;
He heaps up *riches*,
And does not know who will
gather them.

7 "And now, Lord, what do I wait for?
My hope *is* in You.
8 Deliver me from all my
transgressions;
Do not make me the reproach of
the foolish.
9 I was mute, I did not open my
mouth,
Because it was You who did *it*.
10 Remove Your plague from me;
I am consumed by the blow of
Your hand.
11 When with rebukes You correct
man for iniquity,
You make his beauty melt away
like a moth;
Surely every man *is* vapor. *Selah*

12 "Hear my prayer, O LORD,
And give ear to my cry;
Do not be silent at my tears;
For I *am* a stranger with You,
A sojourner, as all my fathers
were.
13 Remove Your gaze from me, that I
may regain strength,
Before I go away and am no
more."

PSALM 40

Faith Persevering in Trial

To the Chief Musician. A Psalm of David.

1 I waited patiently for the LORD;
And He inclined to me,
And heard my cry.
2 He also brought me up out of a
horrible pit,
Out of the miry clay,
And set my feet upon a rock,
And established my steps.
3 He has put a new song in my
mouth—
Praise to our God;
Many will see *it* and fear,
And will trust in the LORD.

4 Blessed *is* that man who makes
the LORD his trust,
And does not respect the proud,
nor such as turn aside to lies.
5 Many, O LORD my God, *are* Your
wonderful works
Which You have done;
And Your thoughts toward us

Cannot be recounted to You in order;
If I would declare and speak *of them,*
They are more than can be numbered.

6 Sacrifice and offering You did not desire;
My ears You have opened.
Burnt offering and sin offering You did not require.
7 Then I said, "Behold, I come;
In the scroll of the book *it is* written of me.
8 I delight to do Your will, O my God,
And Your law *is* within my heart."

9 I have proclaimed the good news of righteousness
In the great assembly;
Indeed, I do not restrain my lips,
O LORD, You Yourself know.
10 I have not hidden Your righteousness within my heart;
I have declared Your faithfulness and Your salvation;
I have not concealed Your lovingkindness and Your truth
From the great assembly.

11 Do not withhold Your tender mercies from me, O LORD;
Let Your lovingkindness and Your truth continually preserve me.
12 For innumerable evils have surrounded me;
My iniquities have overtaken me, so that I am not able to look up;
They are more than the hairs of my head;
Therefore my heart fails me.

13 Be pleased, O LORD, to deliver me;
O LORD, make haste to help me!
14 Let them be ashamed and brought to mutual confusion
Who seek to destroy my life;
Let them be driven backward and brought to dishonor
Who wish me evil.
15 Let them be confounded because of their shame,
Who say to me, "Aha, aha!"

16 Let all those who seek You rejoice and be glad in You;
Let such as love Your salvation say continually,
"The LORD be magnified!"
17 But I *am* poor and needy;
Yet the LORD thinks upon me.
You *are* my help and my deliverer;
Do not delay, O my God.

PSALM 41

The Blessing and Suffering of the Godly

To the Chief Musician. A Psalm of David.

1 Blessed *is* he who considers the poor;
The LORD will deliver him in time of trouble.
2 The LORD will preserve him and keep him alive,
And he will be blessed on the earth;
You will not deliver him to the will of his enemies.
3 The LORD will strengthen him on his bed of illness;
You will sustain him on his sickbed.

4 I said, "LORD, be merciful to me;
Heal my soul, for I have sinned against You."
5 My enemies speak evil of me:
"When will he die, and his name perish?"
6 And if he comes to see *me,* he speaks lies;
His heart gathers iniquity to itself;
When he goes out, he tells *it.*

7 All who hate me whisper together against me;
Against me they devise my hurt.
8 "An evil disease," *they say,* "clings to him.
And *now* that he lies down, he will rise up no more."
9 Even my own familiar friend in whom I trusted,
Who ate my bread,
Has lifted up *his* heel against me.

10 But You, O LORD, be merciful to
me, and raise me up,
That I may repay them.
11 By this I know that You are well
pleased with me,
Because my enemy does not
triumph over me.
12 As for me, You uphold me in my
integrity,
And set me before Your face
forever.

13 Blessed *be* the LORD God of Israel
From everlasting to everlasting!
Amen and Amen.

BOOK TWO
Psalms 42–72

PSALM 42
Yearning for God in the Midst of Distresses

To the Chief Musician. A Contemplation[a] *of the sons of Korah.*

1 As the deer pants for the water
brooks,
So pants my soul for You, O God.
2 My soul thirsts for God, for the
living God.
When shall I come and appear
before God?[a]
3 My tears have been my food day
and night,
While they continually say to me,
"Where *is* your God?"

4 When I remember these *things,*
I pour out my soul within me.
For I used to go with the
multitude;
I went with them to the house of
God,
With the voice of joy and praise,
With a multitude that kept a
pilgrim feast.

5 Why are you cast down, O my
soul?
And *why* are you disquieted
within me?
Hope in God, for I shall yet praise
Him
For the help of His countenance.[a]

6 O my God,[a] my soul is cast down
within me;
Therefore I will remember You
from the land of the Jordan,
And from the heights of
Hermon,
From the Hill Mizar.
7 Deep calls unto deep at the noise
of Your waterfalls;
All Your waves and billows have
gone over me.
8 The LORD will command His
lovingkindness in the
daytime,
And in the night His song *shall be*
with me—
A prayer to the God of my life.

9 I will say to God my Rock,
"Why have You forgotten me?
Why do I go mourning because
of the oppression of the
enemy?"
10 *As* with a breaking of my bones,
My enemies reproach me,
While they say to me all day long,
"Where *is* your God?"

11 Why are you cast down, O my
soul?
And why are you disquieted
within me?
Hope in God;
For I shall yet praise Him,
The help of my countenance and
my God.

PSALM 43
Prayer to God in Time of Trouble

1 Vindicate me, O God,
And plead my cause against an
ungodly nation;
Oh, deliver me from the deceitful
and unjust man!

42:title [a] Hebrew *Maschil* **42:2** [a] Following Masoretic Text and Vulgate; some Hebrew manuscripts, Septuagint, Syriac, and Targum read *I see the face of God.* **42:5** [a] Following Masoretic Text and Targum; a few Hebrew manuscripts, Septuagint, Syriac, and Vulgate read *The help of my countenance, my God.* **42:6** [a] Following Masoretic Text and Targum; a few Hebrew manuscripts, Septuagint, Syriac, and Vulgate put *my God* at the end of verse 5.

2 For You *are* the God of my strength;
Why do You cast me off?
Why do I go mourning because
of the oppression of the
enemy?

3 Oh, send out Your light and Your
truth!
Let them lead me;
Let them bring me to Your holy
hill
And to Your tabernacle.
4 Then I will go to the altar of God,
To God my exceeding joy;
And on the harp I will praise You,
O God, my God.

5 Why are you cast down, O my soul?
And why are you disquieted
within me?
Hope in God;
For I shall yet praise Him,
The help of my countenance and
my God.

PSALM 44

Redemption Remembered in Present Dishonor

To the Chief Musician. A Contemplation[a] of the sons of Korah.

1 We have heard with our ears,
O God,
Our fathers have told us,
The deeds You did in their days,
In days of old:
2 You drove out the nations with
Your hand,
But them You planted;
You afflicted the peoples, and cast
them out.
3 For they did not gain possession
of the land by their own
sword,
Nor did their own arm save them;
But it was Your right hand, Your
arm, and the light of Your
countenance,
Because You favored them.

4 You are my King, O God;[a]
Command[b] victories for Jacob.
5 Through You we will push down
our enemies;
Through Your name we will trample
those who rise up against us.
6 For I will not trust in my bow,
Nor shall my sword save me.
7 But You have saved us from our
enemies,
And have put to shame those who
hated us.
8 In God we boast all day long,
And praise Your name forever.
Selah

9 But You have cast *us* off and put
us to shame,
And You do not go out with our
armies.
10 You make us turn back from the
enemy,
And those who hate us have taken
spoil for themselves.
11 You have given us up like sheep
intended for food,
And have scattered us among the
nations.
12 You sell Your people for *next to*
nothing,
And are not enriched by selling
them.

13 You make us a reproach to our
neighbors,
A scorn and a derision to those all
around us.
14 You make us a byword among the
nations,
A shaking of the head among the
peoples.
15 My dishonor *is* continually
before me,
And the shame of my face has
covered me,
16 Because of the voice of him who
reproaches and reviles,
Because of the enemy and the
avenger.

17 All this has come upon us;
But we have not forgotten You,
Nor have we dealt falsely with
Your covenant.

44:title [a] Hebrew *Maschil* 44:4 [a] Following Masoretic Text and Targum; Septuagint and Vulgate read *and my God.* [b] Following Masoretic Text and Targum; Septuagint, Syriac, and Vulgate read *Who commands.*

18 Our heart has not turned back,
Nor have our steps departed from
Your way;
19 But You have severely broken us
in the place of jackals,
And covered us with the shadow
of death.

20 If we had forgotten the name of
our God,
Or stretched out our hands to a
foreign god,
21 Would not God search this out?
For He knows the secrets of the
heart.
22 Yet for Your sake we are killed all
day long;
We are accounted as sheep for the
slaughter.

23 Awake! Why do You sleep, O Lord?
Arise! Do not cast *us* off forever.
24 Why do You hide Your face,
And forget our affliction and our
oppression?
25 For our soul is bowed down to the
dust;
Our body clings to the ground.
26 Arise for our help,
And redeem us for Your mercies'
sake.

PSALM 45

The Glories of the Messiah and His Bride

To the Chief Musician. Set to "The Lilies."[a] *A Contemplation*[b] *of the sons of Korah. A Song of Love.*

1 My heart is overflowing with a
good theme;
I recite my composition
concerning the King;
My tongue *is* the pen of a ready
writer.

2 You are fairer than the sons of men;
Grace is poured upon Your lips;
Therefore God has blessed You
forever.
3 Gird Your sword upon *Your* thigh,
O Mighty One,
With Your glory and Your majesty.
4 And in Your majesty ride
prosperously because of truth,
humility, *and* righteousness;
And Your right hand shall teach
You awesome things.
5 Your arrows *are* sharp in the
heart of the King's enemies;
The peoples fall under You.

6 Your throne, O God, *is* forever and
ever;
A scepter of righteousness *is* the
scepter of Your kingdom.
7 You love righteousness and hate
wickedness;
Therefore God, Your God, has
anointed You
With the oil of gladness more
than Your companions.
8 All Your garments *are scented*
with myrrh and aloes *and*
cassia,
Out of the ivory palaces, by which
they have made You glad.
9 Kings' daughters *are* among Your
honorable women;
At Your right hand stands the
queen in gold from Ophir.

10 Listen, O daughter,
Consider and incline your ear;
Forget your own people also, and
your father's house;
11 So the King will greatly desire
your beauty;
Because He *is* your Lord, worship
Him.
12 And the daughter of Tyre *will
come* with a gift;
The rich among the people will
seek your favor.

13 The royal daughter *is* all glorious
within *the palace;*
Her clothing *is* woven with gold.
14 She shall be brought to the King
in robes of many colors;
The virgins, her companions who
follow her, shall be brought
to You.
15 With gladness and rejoicing they
shall be brought;
They shall enter the King's palace.

45:title [a] Hebrew *Shoshannim* [b] Hebrew *Maschil*

16 Instead of Your fathers shall be
Your sons,
Whom You shall make princes in
all the earth.
17 I will make Your name to
be remembered in all
generations;
Therefore the people shall praise
You forever and ever.

PSALM 46

God the Refuge of His People and Conqueror of the Nations

To the Chief Musician. A Psalm of the sons of Korah. A Song for Alamoth.

1 God *is* our refuge and strength,
A very present help in trouble.
2 Therefore we will not fear,
Even though the earth be
removed,
And though the mountains be
carried into the midst of the
sea;
3 *Though* its waters roar *and* be
troubled,
Though the mountains shake with
its swelling. *Selah*

4 *There is* a river whose streams shall
make glad the city of God,
The holy *place* of the tabernacle of
the Most High.
5 God *is* in the midst of her, she
shall not be moved;
God shall help her, just at the
break of dawn.
6 The nations raged, the kingdoms
were moved;
He uttered His voice, the earth
melted.

7 The LORD of hosts *is* with us;
The God of Jacob *is* our refuge.
Selah

8 Come, behold the works of the
LORD,
Who has made desolations in the
earth.
9 He makes wars cease to the end of
the earth;
He breaks the bow and cuts the
spear in two;
He burns the chariot in the fire.
10 Be still, and know that I *am* God;
I will be exalted among the nations,
I will be exalted in the earth!

11 The LORD of hosts *is* with us;
The God of Jacob *is* our refuge.
Selah

PSALM 47

Praise to God, the Ruler of the Earth

To the Chief Musician. A Psalm of the sons of Korah.

1 Oh, clap your hands, all you
peoples!
Shout to God with the voice of
triumph!
2 For the LORD Most High *is*
awesome;
He is a great King over all the
earth.
3 He will subdue the peoples
under us,
And the nations under our feet.
4 He will choose our inheritance
for us,
The excellence of Jacob whom He
loves. *Selah*

5 God has gone up with a shout,
The LORD with the sound of a
trumpet.
6 Sing praises to God, sing praises!
Sing praises to our King, sing
praises!
7 For God *is* the King of all the earth;
Sing praises with understanding.

8 God reigns over the nations;
God sits on His holy throne.
9 The princes of the people have
gathered together,
The people of the God of Abraham.
For the shields of the earth *belong*
to God;
He is greatly exalted.

PSALM 48

The Glory of God in Zion

A Song. A Psalm of the sons of Korah.

1 Great *is* the LORD, and greatly to
be praised
In the city of our God,
In His holy mountain.

2 Beautiful in elevation,
The joy of the whole earth,
Is Mount Zion *on* the sides of the north,
The city of the great King.
3 God *is* in her palaces;
He is known as her refuge.

4 For behold, the kings assembled,
They passed by together.
5 They saw *it, and* so they marveled;
They were troubled, they hastened away.
6 Fear took hold of them there,
And pain, as of a woman in birth pangs,
7 *As when* You break the ships of Tarshish
With an east wind.

8 As we have heard,
So we have seen
In the city of the LORD of hosts,
In the city of our God:
God will establish it forever. *Selah*

9 We have thought, O God, on Your lovingkindness,
In the midst of Your temple.
10 According to Your name, O God,
So *is* Your praise to the ends of the earth;
Your right hand is full of righteousness.
11 Let Mount Zion rejoice,
Let the daughters of Judah be glad,
Because of Your judgments.

12 Walk about Zion,
And go all around her.
Count her towers;
13 Mark well her bulwarks;
Consider her palaces;
That you may tell *it* to the generation following.
14 For this *is* God,
Our God forever and ever;
He will be our guide
Even to death.[a]

PSALM 49

The Confidence of the Foolish

To the Chief Musician. A Psalm of the sons of Korah.

1 Hear this, all peoples;
Give ear, all inhabitants of the world,
2 Both low and high,
Rich and poor together.
3 My mouth shall speak wisdom,
And the meditation of my heart *shall give* understanding.
4 I will incline my ear to a proverb;
I will disclose my dark saying on the harp.

5 Why should I fear in the days of evil,
When the iniquity at my heels surrounds me?
6 Those who trust in their wealth
And boast in the multitude of their riches,
7 None *of them* can by any means redeem *his* brother,
Nor give to God a ransom for him—
8 For the redemption of their souls *is* costly,
And it shall cease forever—
9 That he should continue to live eternally,
And not see the Pit.

10 For he sees wise men die;
Likewise the fool and the senseless person perish,
And leave their wealth to others.
11 Their inner thought *is that* their houses *will last* forever,[a]
Their dwelling places to all generations;
They call *their* lands after their own names.
12 Nevertheless man, *though* in honor, does not remain;[a]
He is like the beasts *that* perish.

13 This is the way of those who *are* foolish,

48:14 [a] Following Masoretic Text and Syriac; Septuagint and Vulgate read *Forever.*
49:11 [a] Septuagint, Syriac, Targum, and Vulgate read *Their graves shall be their houses forever.*
49:12 [a] Following Masoretic Text and Targum; Septuagint, Syriac, and Vulgate read *understand* (compare verse 20).

And of their posterity who
approve their sayings. *Selah*
14 Like sheep they are laid in the
grave;
Death shall feed on them;
The upright shall have dominion
over them in the morning;
And their beauty shall be
consumed in the grave, far
from their dwelling.
15 But God will redeem my soul from
the power of the grave,
For He shall receive me. *Selah*

16 Do not be afraid when one
becomes rich,
When the glory of his house is
increased;
17 For when he dies he shall carry
nothing away;
His glory shall not descend after
him.
18 Though while he lives he blesses
himself
(For *men* will praise you when you
do well for yourself),
19 He shall go to the generation of
his fathers;
They shall never see light.
20 A man *who is* in honor, yet does
not understand,
Is like the beasts *that* perish.

PSALM 50

God the Righteous Judge

A Psalm of Asaph.

1 The Mighty One, God the LORD,
Has spoken and called the earth
From the rising of the sun to its
going down.
2 Out of Zion, the perfection of beauty,
God will shine forth.
3 Our God shall come, and shall not
keep silent;
A fire shall devour before Him,
And it shall be very tempestuous
all around Him.

4 He shall call to the heavens from
above,
And to the earth, that He may
judge His people:
5 "Gather My saints together to Me,
Those who have made a covenant
with Me by sacrifice."
6 Let the heavens declare His
righteousness,
For God Himself *is* Judge. *Selah*

7 "Hear, O My people, and I will
speak,
O Israel, and I will testify against
you;
I *am* God, your God!
8 I will not rebuke you for your
sacrifices
Or your burnt offerings,
Which are continually before Me.
9 I will not take a bull from your
house,
Nor goats out of your folds.
10 For every beast of the forest *is*
Mine,
And the cattle on a thousand hills.
11 I know all the birds of the mountains,
And the wild beasts of the field *are*
Mine.

12 "If I were hungry, I would not tell
you;
For the world *is* Mine, and all its
fullness.
13 Will I eat the flesh of bulls,
Or drink the blood of goats?
14 Offer to God thanksgiving,
And pay your vows to the Most
High.
15 Call upon Me in the day of
trouble;
I will deliver you, and you shall
glorify Me."

16 But to the wicked God says:
"What *right* have you to declare My
statutes,
Or take My covenant in your
mouth,
17 Seeing you hate instruction
And cast My words behind you?
18 When you saw a thief, you
consented[a] with him,
And have been a partaker with
adulterers.
19 You give your mouth to evil,
And your tongue frames deceit.

50:18 [a] Septuagint, Syriac, Targum, and Vulgate read *ran.*

20 You sit *and* speak against your
brother;
You slander your own mother's
son.
21 These *things* you have done, and I
kept silent;
You thought that I was altogether
like you;
But I will rebuke you,
And set *them* in order before your
eyes.

22 "Now consider this, you who forget
God,
Lest I tear *you* in pieces,
And *there be* none to deliver:
23 Whoever offers praise glorifies Me;
And to him who orders *his*
conduct *aright*
I will show the salvation of God."

PSALM 51

A Prayer of Repentance

To the Chief Musician. A Psalm of David when Nathan the prophet went to him, after he had gone in to Bathsheba.

1 Have mercy upon me, O God,
According to Your lovingkindness;
According to the multitude of
Your tender mercies,
Blot out my transgressions.
2 Wash me thoroughly from my
iniquity,
And cleanse me from my sin.

3 For I acknowledge my
transgressions,
And my sin *is* always before me.
4 Against You, You only, have I
sinned,
And done *this* evil in Your sight—
That You may be found just when
You speak,[a]
And blameless when You judge.

5 Behold, I was brought forth in
iniquity,
And in sin my mother conceived me.
6 Behold, You desire truth in the
inward parts,
And in the hidden *part* You will
make me to know wisdom.

7 Purge me with hyssop, and I shall
be clean;
Wash me, and I shall be whiter
than snow.
8 Make me hear joy and gladness,
That the bones You have broken
may rejoice.
9 Hide Your face from my sins,
And blot out all my iniquities.

10 Create in me a clean heart, O God,
And renew a steadfast spirit
within me.
11 Do not cast me away from Your
presence,
And do not take Your Holy Spirit
from me.

12 Restore to me the joy of Your
salvation,
And uphold me *by Your* generous
Spirit.
13 *Then* I will teach transgressors
Your ways,
And sinners shall be converted to
You.

14 Deliver me from the guilt of
bloodshed, O God,
The God of my salvation,
And my tongue shall sing aloud
of Your righteousness.
15 O Lord, open my lips,
And my mouth shall show forth
Your praise.
16 For You do not desire sacrifice, or
else I would give *it;*
You do not delight in burnt
offering.
17 The sacrifices of God *are* a broken
spirit,
A broken and a contrite heart—
These, O God, You will not despise.

18 Do good in Your good pleasure to
Zion;
Build the walls of Jerusalem.
19 Then You shall be pleased with the
sacrifices of righteousness,
With burnt offering and whole
burnt offering;
Then they shall offer bulls on Your
altar.

51:4 [a] Septuagint, Targum, and Vulgate read *in Your words.*

PSALM 52

The End of the Wicked and the Peace of the Godly

To the Chief Musician. A Contemplation[a] of David when Doeg the Edomite went and told Saul, and said to him, "David has gone to the house of Ahimelech."

1 Why do you boast in evil,
O mighty man?
The goodness of God *endures* continually.
2 Your tongue devises destruction,
Like a sharp razor, working deceitfully.
3 You love evil more than good,
Lying rather than speaking righteousness. *Selah*
4 You love all devouring words,
You deceitful tongue.

5 God shall likewise destroy you forever;
He shall take you away, and pluck you out of *your* dwelling place,
And uproot you from the land of the living. *Selah*
6 The righteous also shall see and fear,
And shall laugh at him, *saying,*
7 "Here is the man *who* did not make God his strength,
But trusted in the abundance of his riches,
And strengthened himself in his wickedness."

8 But I *am* like a green olive tree in the house of God;
I trust in the mercy of God forever and ever.
9 I will praise You forever,
Because You have done *it;*
And in the presence of Your saints
I will wait on Your name, for *it is* good.

PSALM 53

Folly of the Godless, and the Restoration of Israel

To the Chief Musician. Set to "Mahalath." A Contemplation[a] of David.

1 The fool has said in his heart,
"*There is* no God."
They are corrupt, and have done abominable iniquity;
There is none who does good.

2 God looks down from heaven upon the children of men,
To see if there are *any* who understand, who seek God.
3 Every one of them has turned aside;
They have together become corrupt;
There is none who does good,
No, not one.

4 Have the workers of iniquity no knowledge,
Who eat up my people *as* they eat bread,
And do not call upon God?
5 There they are in great fear
Where no fear was,
For God has scattered the bones of him who encamps against you;
You have put *them* to shame,
Because God has despised them.

6 Oh, that the salvation of Israel would come out of Zion!
When God brings back the captivity of His people,
Let Jacob rejoice *and* Israel be glad.

PSALM 54

Answered Prayer for Deliverance from Adversaries

To the Chief Musician. With stringed instruments.[a] A Contemplation[b] of David when the Ziphites went and said to Saul, "Is David not hiding with us?"

1 Save me, O God, by Your name,
And vindicate me by Your strength.

52:title a Hebrew *Maschil* **53:title** a Hebrew *Maschil* **54:title** a Hebrew *neginoth* b Hebrew *Maschil*

2 Hear my prayer, O God;
Give ear to the words of my mouth.
3 For strangers have risen up against me,
And oppressors have sought after my life;
They have not set God before them. *Selah*

4 Behold, God *is* my helper;
The Lord *is* with those who uphold my life.
5 He will repay my enemies for their evil.
Cut them off in Your truth.

6 I will freely sacrifice to You;
I will praise Your name, O LORD, for *it is* good.
7 For He has delivered me out of all trouble;
And my eye has seen *its desire* upon my enemies.

PSALM 55

Trust in God Concerning the Treachery of Friends

To the Chief Musician. With stringed instruments.[a] A Contemplation[b] of David.

1 Give ear to my prayer, O God,
And do not hide Yourself from my supplication.
2 Attend to me, and hear me;
I am restless in my complaint, and moan noisily,
3 Because of the voice of the enemy,
Because of the oppression of the wicked;
For they bring down trouble upon me,
And in wrath they hate me.

4 My heart is severely pained within me,
And the terrors of death have fallen upon me.
5 Fearfulness and trembling have come upon me,
And horror has overwhelmed me.
6 So I said, "Oh, that I had wings like a dove!
I would fly away and be at rest.
7 Indeed, I would wander far off,
And remain in the wilderness. *Selah*
8 I would hasten my escape
From the windy storm *and* tempest."

9 Destroy, O Lord, *and* divide their tongues,
For I have seen violence and strife in the city.
10 Day and night they go around it on its walls;
Iniquity and trouble *are* also in the midst of it.
11 Destruction *is* in its midst;
Oppression and deceit do not depart from its streets.

12 For *it is* not an enemy *who* reproaches me;
Then I could bear *it.*
Nor *is it* one *who* hates me who has exalted *himself* against me;
Then I could hide from him.
13 But *it was* you, a man my equal,
My companion and my acquaintance.
14 We took sweet counsel together,
And walked to the house of God in the throng.

15 Let death seize them;
Let them go down alive into hell,
For wickedness *is* in their dwellings *and* among them.

16 As for me, I will call upon God,
And the LORD shall save me.
17 Evening and morning and at noon
I will pray, and cry aloud,
And He shall hear my voice.
18 He has redeemed my soul in peace from the battle *that was* against me,
For there were many against me.
19 God will hear, and afflict them,
Even He who abides from of old. *Selah*
Because they do not change,
Therefore they do not fear God.

55:title [a] Hebrew *neginoth* [b] Hebrew *Maschil*

20 He has put forth his hands
against those who were at
peace with him;
He has broken his covenant.
21 *The words* of his mouth were
smoother than butter,
But war *was* in his heart;
His words were softer than oil,
Yet they *were* drawn swords.

22 Cast your burden on the LORD,
And He shall sustain you;
He shall never permit the
righteous to be moved.

23 But You, O God, shall bring them
down to the pit of destruction;
Bloodthirsty and deceitful men
shall not live out half their
days;
But I will trust in You.

PSALM 56

Prayer for Relief from Tormentors

To the Chief Musician. Set to "The Silent Dove in Distant Lands."[a] A Michtam of David when the Philistines captured him in Gath.

1 Be merciful to me, O God, for man
would swallow me up;
Fighting all day he oppresses me.
2 My enemies would hound *me* all
day,
For *there are* many who fight
against me, O Most High.

3 Whenever I am afraid,
I will trust in You.
4 In God (I will praise His word),
In God I have put my trust;
I will not fear.
What can flesh do to me?

5 All day they twist my words;
All their thoughts *are* against me
for evil.
6 They gather together,
They hide, they mark my steps,
When they lie in wait for my life.
7 Shall they escape by iniquity?
In anger cast down the peoples,
O God!
8 You number my wanderings;
Put my tears into Your bottle;
Are they not in Your book?
9 When I cry out *to You,*
Then my enemies will turn back;
This I know, because God *is* for
me.
10 In God (I will praise *His* word),
In the LORD (I will praise *His*
word),
11 In God I have put my trust;
I will not be afraid.
What can man do to me?

12 Vows *made* to You *are binding*
upon me, O God;
I will render praises to You,
13 For You have delivered my soul
from death.
Have You not *kept* my feet from
falling,
That I may walk before God
In the light of the living?

PSALM 57

Prayer for Safety from Enemies

To the Chief Musician. Set to "Do Not Destroy."[a] A Michtam of David when he fled from Saul into the cave.

1 Be merciful to me, O God, be
merciful to me!
For my soul trusts in You;
And in the shadow of Your wings I
will make my refuge,
Until *these* calamities have
passed by.

2 I will cry out to God Most High,
To God who performs *all things* for
me.
3 He shall send from heaven and
save me;
He reproaches the one who would
swallow me up. *Selah*
God shall send forth His mercy
and His truth.

4 My soul *is* among lions;
I lie *among* the sons of men
Who are set on fire,
Whose teeth *are* spears and arrows,
And their tongue a sharp sword.

56:title [a] Hebrew *Jonath Elem Rechokim* **57:title** [a] Hebrew *Al Tashcheth*

5 Be exalted, O God, above the
heavens;
Let Your glory *be* above all the
earth.

6 They have prepared a net for my
steps;
My soul is bowed down;
They have dug a pit before me;
Into the midst of it they
themselves have fallen. *Selah*

7 My heart is steadfast, O God, my
heart is steadfast;
I will sing and give praise.
8 Awake, my glory!
Awake, lute and harp!
I will awaken the dawn.

9 I will praise You, O Lord, among
the peoples;
I will sing to You among the
nations.
10 For Your mercy reaches unto the
heavens,
And Your truth unto the clouds.

11 Be exalted, O God, above the
heavens;
Let Your glory *be* above all the
earth.

PSALM 58

The Just Judgment of the Wicked

To the Chief Musician. Set to "Do Not Destroy."[a] A Michtam of David.

1 Do you indeed speak righteousness,
you silent ones?
Do you judge uprightly, you sons
of men?
2 No, in heart you work wickedness;
You weigh out the violence of
your hands in the earth.

3 The wicked are estranged from
the womb;
They go astray as soon as they
are born, speaking lies.
4 Their poison *is* like the poison of a
serpent;
They are like the deaf cobra *that*
stops its ear,
5 Which will not heed the voice of
charmers,
Charming ever so skillfully.

6 Break their teeth in their mouth,
O God!
Break out the fangs of the young
lions, O LORD!
7 Let them flow away as waters
which run continually;
When he bends *his bow,*
Let his arrows be as if cut in
pieces.
8 *Let them be* like a snail which
melts away as it goes,
Like a stillborn child of a woman,
that they may not see the sun.

9 Before your pots can feel *the*
burning thorns,
He shall take them away as with a
whirlwind,
As in His living and burning
wrath.
10 The righteous shall rejoice when
he sees the vengeance;
He shall wash his feet in the blood
of the wicked,
11 So that men will say,
"Surely *there is* a reward for the
righteous;
Surely He is God who judges in
the earth."

PSALM 59

The Assured Judgment of the Wicked

To the Chief Musician. Set to "Do Not Destroy."[a] A Michtam of David when Saul sent men, and they watched the house in order to kill him.

1 Deliver me from my enemies,
O my God;
Defend me from those who rise
up against me.
2 Deliver me from the workers of
iniquity,
And save me from bloodthirsty
men.

3 For look, they lie in wait for my
life;
The mighty gather against me,

58:title [a] Hebrew *Al Taschcheth* 59:title [a] Hebrew *Al Taschcheth*

Not *for* my transgression nor *for* my sin, O LORD.
4 They run and prepare themselves through no fault *of mine.*

Awake to help me, and behold!
5 You therefore, O LORD God of hosts, the God of Israel,
Awake to punish all the nations;
Do not be merciful to any wicked transgressors. *Selah*

6 At evening they return,
They growl like a dog,
And go all around the city.
7 Indeed, they belch with their mouth;
Swords *are* in their lips;
For *they say,* "Who hears?"

8 But You, O LORD, shall laugh at them;
You shall have all the nations in derision.
9 I will wait for You, O You his Strength;[a]
For God *is* my defense.
10 My God of mercy[a] shall come to meet me;
God shall let me see *my desire* on my enemies.

11 Do not slay them, lest my people forget;
Scatter them by Your power,
And bring them down,
O Lord our shield.
12 *For* the sin of their mouth *and* the words of their lips,
Let them even be taken in their pride,
And for the cursing and lying *which* they speak.
13 Consume *them* in wrath, consume *them,*
That they *may* not *be;*
And let them know that God rules in Jacob
To the ends of the earth. *Selah*

14 And at evening they return,
They growl like a dog,
And go all around the city.
15 They wander up and down for food,
And howl[a] if they are not satisfied.

16 But I will sing of Your power;
Yes, I will sing aloud of Your mercy in the morning;
For You have been my defense
And refuge in the day of my trouble.
17 To You, O my Strength, I will sing praises;
For God *is* my defense,
My God of mercy.

PSALM 60

Urgent Prayer for the Restored Favor of God

To the Chief Musician. Set to "Lily of the Testimony."[a] A Michtam of David. For teaching. When he fought against Mesopotamia and Syria of Zobah, and Joab returned and killed twelve thousand Edomites in the Valley of Salt.

1 O God, You have cast us off;
You have broken us down;
You have been displeased;
Oh, restore us again!
2 You have made the earth tremble;
You have broken it;
Heal its breaches, for it is shaking.
3 You have shown Your people hard things;
You have made us drink the wine of confusion.

4 You have given a banner to those who fear You,
That it may be displayed because of the truth. *Selah*
5 That Your beloved may be delivered,
Save *with* Your right hand, and hear me.

59:9 [a] Following Masoretic Text and Syriac; some Hebrew manuscripts, Septuagint, Targum, and Vulgate read *my Strength.* **59:10** [a] Following Qere; some Hebrew manuscripts, Septuagint, and Vulgate read *My God, His mercy;* Kethib, some Hebrew manuscripts and Targum read *O God, my mercy;* Syriac reads *O God, Your mercy.* **59:15** [a] Following Septuagint and Vulgate; Masoretic Text, Syriac, and Targum read *spend the night.* **60:title** [a] Hebrew *Shushan Eduth*

6 God has spoken in His holiness:
"I will rejoice;
I will divide Shechem
And measure out the Valley of
Succoth.
7 Gilead *is* Mine, and Manasseh *is*
Mine;
Ephraim also *is* the helmet for My
head;
Judah *is* My lawgiver.
8 Moab *is* My washpot;
Over Edom I will cast My shoe;
Philistia, shout in triumph
because of Me."

9 Who will bring me *to* the strong
city?
Who will lead me to Edom?
10 *Is it* not You, O God, *who* cast us
off?
And You, O God, *who* did not go
out with our armies?
11 Give us help from trouble,
For the help of man *is* useless.
12 Through God we will do valiantly,
For *it is* He *who* shall tread down
our enemies.[a]

PSALM 61

Assurance of God's Eternal Protection

To the Chief Musician. On a stringed instrument.[a] *A Psalm of David.*

1 Hear my cry, O God;
Attend to my prayer.
2 From the end of the earth I will
cry to You,
When my heart is overwhelmed;
Lead me to the rock that is higher
than I.

3 For You have been a shelter for me,
A strong tower from the enemy.
4 I will abide in Your tabernacle
forever;
I will trust in the shelter of Your
wings. *Selah*

5 For You, O God, have heard my vows;
You have given *me* the heritage of
those who fear Your name.
6 You will prolong the king's life,
His years as many generations.
7 He shall abide before God forever.
Oh, prepare mercy and truth,
which may preserve him!

8 So I will sing praise to Your name
forever,
That I may daily perform my vows.

PSALM 62

A Calm Resolve to Wait for the Salvation of God

To the Chief Musician. To Jeduthun. A Psalm of David.

1 Truly my soul silently *waits* for
God;
From Him *comes* my salvation.
2 He only *is* my rock and my
salvation;
He is my defense;
I shall not be greatly moved.

3 How long will you attack a man?
You shall be slain, all of you,
Like a leaning wall and a tottering
fence.
4 They only consult to cast *him*
down from his high position;
They delight in lies;
They bless with their mouth,
But they curse inwardly. *Selah*

5 My soul, wait silently for God alone,
For my expectation *is* from Him.
6 He only *is* my rock and my
salvation;
He is my defense;
I shall not be moved.
7 In God *is* my salvation and my
glory;
The rock of my strength,
And my refuge, *is* in God.

8 Trust in Him at all times, you people;
Pour out your heart before Him;
God *is* a refuge for us. *Selah*

9 Surely men of low degree *are* a
vapor,
Men of high degree *are* a lie;
If they are weighed on the scales,
They *are* altogether *lighter* than
vapor.

60:12 [a] Compare verses 5–12 with 108:6–13 61:title [a] Hebrew *neginah*

10 Do not trust in oppression,
Nor vainly hope in robbery;
If riches increase,
Do not set *your* heart *on them.*

11 God has spoken once,
Twice I have heard this:
That power *belongs* to God.
12 Also to You, O Lord, *belongs* mercy;
For You render to each one according to his work.

PSALM 63

Joy in the Fellowship of God

A Psalm of David when he was in the wilderness of Judah.

1 O God, You *are* my God;
Early will I seek You;
My soul thirsts for You;
My flesh longs for You
In a dry and thirsty land
Where there is no water.
2 So I have looked for You in the sanctuary,
To see Your power and Your glory.

3 Because Your lovingkindness *is* better than life,
My lips shall praise You.
4 Thus I will bless You while I live;
I will lift up my hands in Your name.
5 My soul shall be satisfied as with marrow and fatness,
And my mouth shall praise *You* with joyful lips.

6 When I remember You on my bed,
I meditate on You in the *night* watches.
7 Because You have been my help,
Therefore in the shadow of Your wings I will rejoice.
8 My soul follows close behind You;
Your right hand upholds me.

9 But those *who* seek my life, to destroy *it,*
Shall go into the lower parts of the earth.
10 They shall fall by the sword;
They shall be a portion for jackals.

11 But the king shall rejoice in God;
Everyone who swears by Him shall glory;
But the mouth of those who speak lies shall be stopped.

PSALM 64

Oppressed by the Wicked but Rejoicing in the LORD

To the Chief Musician. A Psalm of David.

1 Hear my voice, O God, in my meditation;
Preserve my life from fear of the enemy.
2 Hide me from the secret plots of the wicked,
From the rebellion of the workers of iniquity,
3 Who sharpen their tongue like a sword,
And bend *their bows to shoot* their arrows—bitter words,
4 That they may shoot in secret at the blameless;
Suddenly they shoot at him and do not fear.

5 They encourage themselves *in* an evil matter;
They talk of laying snares secretly;
They say, "Who will see them?"
6 They devise iniquities:
"We have perfected a shrewd scheme."
Both the inward thought and the heart of man are deep.

7 But God shall shoot at them *with* an arrow;
Suddenly they shall be wounded.
8 So He will make them stumble over their own tongue;
All who see them shall flee away.
9 All men shall fear,
And shall declare the work of God;
For they shall wisely consider His doing.

10 The righteous shall be glad in the LORD, and trust in Him.
And all the upright in heart shall glory.

PSALM 65

Praise to God for His Salvation and Providence

To the Chief Musician. A Psalm of David. A Song.

1 Praise is awaiting You, O God, in Zion;
And to You the vow shall be performed.
2 O You who hear prayer,
To You all flesh will come.
3 Iniquities prevail against me;
As for our transgressions,
You will provide atonement for them.

4 Blessed *is the man* You choose,
And cause to approach *You,*
That he may dwell in Your courts.
We shall be satisfied with the goodness of Your house,
Of Your holy temple.

5 *By* awesome deeds in righteousness You will answer us,
O God of our salvation,
You who are the confidence of all the ends of the earth,
And of the far-off seas;
6 Who established the mountains by His strength,
Being clothed with power;
7 You who still the noise of the seas,
The noise of their waves,
And the tumult of the peoples.
8 They also who dwell in the farthest parts are afraid of Your signs;
You make the outgoings of the morning and evening rejoice.

9 You visit the earth and water it,
You greatly enrich it;
The river of God is full of water;
You provide their grain,
For so You have prepared it.
10 You water its ridges abundantly,
You settle its furrows;
You make it soft with showers,
You bless its growth.
11 You crown the year with Your goodness,
And Your paths drip *with* abundance.
12 They drop *on* the pastures of the wilderness,
And the little hills rejoice on every side.
13 The pastures are clothed with flocks;
The valleys also are covered with grain;
They shout for joy, they also sing.

PSALM 66

Praise to God for His Awesome Works

To the Chief Musician. A Song. A Psalm.

1 Make a joyful shout to God, all the earth!
2 Sing out the honor of His name;
Make His praise glorious.
3 Say to God,
"How awesome are Your works!
Through the greatness of Your power
Your enemies shall submit themselves to You.
4 All the earth shall worship You
And sing praises to You;
They shall sing praises *to* Your name." *Selah*

5 Come and see the works of God;
He is awesome *in His* doing toward the sons of men.
6 He turned the sea into dry *land;*
They went through the river on foot.
There we will rejoice in Him.
7 He rules by His power forever;
His eyes observe the nations;
Do not let the rebellious exalt themselves. *Selah*

8 Oh, bless our God, you peoples!
And make the voice of His praise to be heard,
9 Who keeps our soul among the living,
And does not allow our feet to be moved.
10 For You, O God, have tested us;
You have refined us as silver is refined.

11 You brought us into the net;
You laid affliction on our backs.
12 You have caused men to ride over our heads;
We went through fire and through water;
But You brought us out to rich *fulfillment.*

13 I will go into Your house with burnt offerings;
I will pay You my vows,
14 Which my lips have uttered
And my mouth has spoken when I was in trouble.
15 I will offer You burnt sacrifices of fat animals,
With the sweet aroma of rams;
I will offer bulls with goats. *Selah*

16 Come *and* hear, all you who fear God,
And I will declare what He has done for my soul.
17 I cried to Him with my mouth,
And He was extolled with my tongue.
18 If I regard iniquity in my heart,
The Lord will not hear.
19 *But* certainly God has heard *me;*
He has attended to the voice of my prayer.

20 Blessed *be* God,
Who has not turned away my prayer,
Nor His mercy from me!

PSALM 67

An Invocation and a Doxology

To the Chief Musician. On stringed instruments.[a] *A Psalm. A Song.*

1 God be merciful to us and bless us,
And cause His face to shine upon us, *Selah*
2 That Your way may be known on earth,
Your salvation among all nations.

3 Let the peoples praise You, O God;
Let all the peoples praise You.
4 Oh, let the nations be glad and sing for joy!
For You shall judge the people righteously,
And govern the nations on earth. *Selah*

5 Let the peoples praise You, O God;
Let all the peoples praise You.
6 *Then* the earth shall yield her increase;
God, our own God, shall bless us.
7 God shall bless us,
And all the ends of the earth shall fear Him.

PSALM 68

The Glory of God in His Goodness to Israel

To the Chief Musician. A Psalm of David. A Song.

1 Let God arise,
Let His enemies be scattered;
Let those also who hate Him flee before Him.
2 As smoke is driven away,
So drive *them* away;
As wax melts before the fire,
So let the wicked perish at the presence of God.
3 But let the righteous be glad;
Let them rejoice before God;
Yes, let them rejoice exceedingly.

4 Sing to God, sing praises to His name;
Extol Him who rides on the clouds,[a]
By His name YAH,
And rejoice before Him.

5 A father of the fatherless, a defender of widows,
Is God in His holy habitation.
6 God sets the solitary in families;
He brings out those who are bound into prosperity;
But the rebellious dwell in a dry *land.*

7 O God, when You went out before Your people,
When You marched through the wilderness, *Selah*

67:title [a] Hebrew *neginoth* **68:4** [a] Masoretic Text reads *deserts;* Targum reads *heavens* (compare verse 34 and Isaiah 19:1).

8 The earth shook;
The heavens also dropped *rain* at the presence of God;
Sinai itself *was moved* at the presence of God, the God of Israel.
9 You, O God, sent a plentiful rain,
Whereby You confirmed Your inheritance,
When it was weary.
10 Your congregation dwelt in it;
You, O God, provided from Your goodness for the poor.

11 The Lord gave the word;
Great *was* the company of those who proclaimed *it:*
12 "Kings of armies flee, they flee,
And she who remains at home divides the spoil.
13 Though you lie down among the sheepfolds,
You will be like the wings of a dove covered with silver,
And her feathers with yellow gold."
14 When the Almighty scattered kings in it,
It was *white* as snow in Zalmon.

15 A mountain of God *is* the mountain of Bashan;
A mountain *of many* peaks *is* the mountain of Bashan.
16 Why do you fume with envy, you mountains of *many* peaks?
This is the mountain *which* God desires to dwell in;
Yes, the LORD will dwell *in it* forever.

17 The chariots of God *are* twenty thousand,
Even thousands of thousands;
The Lord is among them *as in* Sinai, in the Holy *Place.*
18 You have ascended on high,
You have led captivity captive;
You have received gifts among men,
Even *from* the rebellious,
That the LORD God might dwell *there.*

19 Blessed *be* the Lord,
Who daily loads us *with benefits,*
The God of our salvation! *Selah*
20 Our God *is* the God of salvation;
And to GOD the Lord *belong* escapes from death.

21 But God will wound the head of His enemies,
The hairy scalp of the one who still goes on in his trespasses.
22 The Lord said, "I will bring back from Bashan,
I will bring *them* back from the depths of the sea,
23 That your foot may crush *them*[a] in blood,
And the tongues of your dogs *may have* their portion from *your* enemies."

24 They have seen Your procession, O God,
The procession of my God, my King, into the sanctuary.
25 The singers went before, the players on instruments *followed* after;
Among *them were* the maidens playing timbrels.
26 Bless God in the congregations,
The Lord, from the fountain of Israel.
27 There *is* little Benjamin, their leader,
The princes of Judah *and* their company,
The princes of Zebulun *and* the princes of Naphtali.

28 Your God has commanded[a] your strength;
Strengthen, O God, what You have done for us.
29 Because of Your temple at Jerusalem,
Kings will bring presents to You.
30 Rebuke the beasts of the reeds,
The herd of bulls with the calves of the peoples,
Till everyone submits himself with pieces of silver.
Scatter the peoples *who* delight in war.

68:23 [a] Septuagint, Syriac, Targum, and Vulgate read *you may dip your foot.* **68:28** [a] Septuagint, Syriac, Targum, and Vulgate read *Command, O God.*

31 Envoys will come out of Egypt;
Ethiopia will quickly stretch out her hands to God.

32 Sing to God, you kingdoms of the earth;
Oh, sing praises to the Lord, *Selah*
33 To Him who rides on the heaven of heavens, *which were* of old!
Indeed, He sends out His voice, a mighty voice.
34 Ascribe strength to God;
His excellence *is* over Israel,
And His strength *is* in the clouds.
35 O God, *You are* more awesome than Your holy places.
The God of Israel *is* He who gives strength and power to *His* people.

Blessed *be* God!

PSALM 69

An Urgent Plea for Help in Trouble

To the Chief Musician. Set to "The Lilies."[a] *A Psalm of David.*

1 Save me, O God!
For the waters have come up to *my* neck.
2 I sink in deep mire,
Where *there is* no standing;
I have come into deep waters,
Where the floods overflow me.
3 I am weary with my crying;
My throat is dry;
My eyes fail while I wait for my God.

4 Those who hate me without a cause
Are more than the hairs of my head;
They are mighty who would destroy me,
Being my enemies wrongfully;
Though I have stolen nothing,
I *still* must restore *it*.

5 O God, You know my foolishness;
And my sins are not hidden from You.
6 Let not those who wait for You, O Lord GOD of hosts, be ashamed because of me;
Let not those who seek You be confounded because of me, O God of Israel.
7 Because for Your sake I have borne reproach;
Shame has covered my face.
8 I have become a stranger to my brothers,
And an alien to my mother's children;
9 Because zeal for Your house has eaten me up,
And the reproaches of those who reproach You have fallen on me.
10 When I wept *and chastened* my soul with fasting,
That became my reproach.
11 I also made sackcloth my garment;
I became a byword to them.
12 Those who sit in the gate speak against me,
And I *am* the song of the drunkards.

13 But as for me, my prayer *is* to You,
O LORD, *in* the acceptable time;
O God, in the multitude of Your mercy,
Hear me in the truth of Your salvation.
14 Deliver me out of the mire,
And let me not sink;
Let me be delivered from those who hate me,
And out of the deep waters.
15 Let not the floodwater overflow me,
Nor let the deep swallow me up;
And let not the pit shut its mouth on me.

16 Hear me, O LORD, for Your lovingkindness *is* good;
Turn to me according to the multitude of Your tender mercies.
17 And do not hide Your face from Your servant,
For I am in trouble;
Hear me speedily.

69:title [a] Hebrew *Shoshannim*

18 Draw near to my soul, *and* redeem it;
Deliver me because of my enemies.

19 You know my reproach, my shame, and my dishonor;
My adversaries *are* all before You.
20 Reproach has broken my heart,
And I am full of heaviness;
I looked *for someone* to take pity, but *there was* none;
And for comforters, but I found none.
21 They also gave me gall for my food,
And for my thirst they gave me vinegar to drink.

22 Let their table become a snare before them,
And their well-being a trap.
23 Let their eyes be darkened, so that they do not see;
And make their loins shake continually.
24 Pour out Your indignation upon them,
And let Your wrathful anger take hold of them.
25 Let their dwelling place be desolate;
Let no one live in their tents.
26 For they persecute the *ones* You have struck,
And talk of the grief of those You have wounded.
27 Add iniquity to their iniquity,
And let them not come into Your righteousness.
28 Let them be blotted out of the book of the living,
And not be written with the righteous.

29 But I *am* poor and sorrowful;
Let Your salvation, O God, set me up on high.
30 I will praise the name of God with a song,
And will magnify Him with thanksgiving.
31 *This* also shall please the LORD better than an ox *or* bull,
Which has horns and hooves.
32 The humble shall see *this and* be glad;
And you who seek God, your hearts shall live.
33 For the LORD hears the poor,
And does not despise His prisoners.

34 Let heaven and earth praise Him,
The seas and everything that moves in them.
35 For God will save Zion
And build the cities of Judah,
That they may dwell there and possess it.
36 Also, the descendants of His servants shall inherit it,
And those who love His name shall dwell in it.

PSALM 70

Prayer for Relief from Adversaries

To the Chief Musician. A Psalm of David. To bring to remembrance.

1 *Make haste*, O God, to deliver me!
Make haste to help me, O LORD!

2 Let them be ashamed and confounded
Who seek my life;
Let them be turned back[a] and confused
Who desire my hurt.
3 Let them be turned back because of their shame,
Who say, "Aha, aha!"

4 Let all those who seek You rejoice and be glad in You;
And let those who love Your salvation say continually,
"Let God be magnified!"
5 But I *am* poor and needy;
Make haste to me, O God!
You *are* my help and my deliverer;
O LORD, do not delay.

70:2 [a] Following Masoretic Text, Septuagint, Targum, and Vulgate; some Hebrew manuscripts and Syriac read *be appalled* (compare 40:15).

PSALM 71

God the Rock of Salvation

1 In You, O LORD, I put my trust;
Let me never be put to shame.
2 Deliver me in Your righteousness, and cause me to escape;
Incline Your ear to me, and save me.
3 Be my strong refuge,
To which I may resort continually;
You have given the commandment to save me,
For You *are* my rock and my fortress.

4 Deliver me, O my God, out of the hand of the wicked,
Out of the hand of the unrighteous and cruel man.
5 For You are my hope, O Lord GOD;
You are my trust from my youth.
6 By You I have been upheld from birth;
You are He who took me out of my mother's womb.
My praise *shall be* continually of You.

7 I have become as a wonder to many,
But You *are* my strong refuge.
8 Let my mouth be filled *with* Your praise
And with Your glory all the day.

9 Do not cast me off in the time of old age;
Do not forsake me when my strength fails.
10 For my enemies speak against me;
And those who lie in wait for my life take counsel together,
11 Saying, "God has forsaken him;
Pursue and take him, for *there is* none to deliver *him*."

12 O God, do not be far from me;
O my God, make haste to help me!
13 Let them be confounded *and* consumed
Who are adversaries of my life;
Let them be covered *with* reproach and dishonor
Who seek my hurt.
14 But I will hope continually,
And will praise You yet more and more.
15 My mouth shall tell of Your righteousness
And Your salvation all the day,
For I do not know *their* limits.
16 I will go in the strength of the Lord GOD;
I will make mention of Your righteousness, of Yours only.

17 O God, You have taught me from my youth;
And to this *day* I declare Your wondrous works.
18 Now also when *I am* old and grayheaded,
O God, do not forsake me,
Until I declare Your strength to *this* generation,
Your power to everyone *who* is to come.

19 Also Your righteousness, O God, *is* very high,
You who have done great things;
O God, who *is* like You?
20 *You,* who have shown me great and severe troubles,
Shall revive me again,
And bring me up again from the depths of the earth.
21 You shall increase my greatness,
And comfort me on every side.

22 Also with the lute I will praise You—
And Your faithfulness, O my God!
To You I will sing with the harp,
O Holy One of Israel.
23 My lips shall greatly rejoice when I sing to You,
And my soul, which You have redeemed.
24 My tongue also shall talk of Your righteousness all the day long;
For they are confounded,
For they are brought to shame
Who seek my hurt.

PSALM 72

Glory and Universality of the Messiah's Reign

A Psalm of Solomon.

1 Give the king Your judgments, O God,
And Your righteousness to the king's Son.
2 He will judge Your people with righteousness,
And Your poor with justice.
3 The mountains will bring peace to the people,
And the little hills, by righteousness.
4 He will bring justice to the poor of the people;
He will save the children of the needy,
And will break in pieces the oppressor.

5 They shall fear You[a]
As long as the sun and moon endure,
Throughout all generations.
6 He shall come down like rain upon the grass before mowing,
Like showers *that* water the earth.
7 In His days the righteous shall flourish,
And abundance of peace,
Until the moon is no more.

8 He shall have dominion also from sea to sea,
And from the River to the ends of the earth.
9 Those who dwell in the wilderness will bow before Him,
And His enemies will lick the dust.
10 The kings of Tarshish and of the isles
Will bring presents;
The kings of Sheba and Seba
Will offer gifts.
11 Yes, all kings shall fall down before Him;
All nations shall serve Him.

12 For He will deliver the needy when he cries,
The poor also, and *him* who has no helper.
13 He will spare the poor and needy,
And will save the souls of the needy.
14 He will redeem their life from oppression and violence;
And precious shall be their blood in His sight.

15 And He shall live;
And the gold of Sheba will be given to Him;
Prayer also will be made for Him continually,
And daily He shall be praised.

16 There will be an abundance of grain in the earth,
On the top of the mountains;
Its fruit shall wave like Lebanon;
And *those* of the city shall flourish like grass of the earth.

17 His name shall endure forever;
His name shall continue as long as the sun.
And *men* shall be blessed in Him;
All nations shall call Him blessed.

18 Blessed *be* the LORD God, the God of Israel,
Who only does wondrous things!
19 And blessed *be* His glorious name forever!
And let the whole earth be filled *with* His glory.
Amen and Amen.

20 The prayers of David the son of Jesse are ended.

BOOK THREE

Psalms 73–89

PSALM 73

The Tragedy of the Wicked, and the Blessedness of Trust in God

A Psalm of Asaph.

1 Truly God *is* good to Israel,
To such as are pure in heart.
2 But as for me, my feet had almost stumbled;

72:5 [a] Following Masoretic Text and Targum; Septuagint and Vulgate read *They shall continue.*

My steps had nearly slipped.
3 For I *was* envious of the boastful,
When I saw the prosperity of the wicked.

4 For *there are* no pangs in their death,
But their strength *is* firm.
5 They *are* not in trouble *as other* men,
Nor are they plagued like *other* men.
6 Therefore pride serves as their necklace;
Violence covers them *like* a garment.
7 Their eyes bulge[a] with abundance;
They have more than heart could wish.
8 They scoff and speak wickedly *concerning* oppression;
They speak loftily.
9 They set their mouth against the heavens,
And their tongue walks through the earth.

10 Therefore his people return here,
And waters of a full *cup* are drained by them.
11 And they say, "How does God know?
And is there knowledge in the Most High?"
12 Behold, these *are* the ungodly,
Who are always at ease;
They increase *in* riches.
13 Surely I have cleansed my heart *in* vain,
And washed my hands in innocence.
14 For all day long I have been plagued,
And chastened every morning.

15 If I had said, "I will speak thus,"
Behold, I would have been untrue to the generation of Your children.
16 When I thought *how* to understand this,
It *was* too painful for me—
17 Until I went into the sanctuary of God;
Then I understood their end.
18 Surely You set them in slippery places;
You cast them down to destruction.
19 Oh, how they are *brought* to desolation, as in a moment!
They are utterly consumed with terrors.
20 As a dream when *one* awakes,
So, Lord, when You awake,
You shall despise their image.

21 Thus my heart was grieved,
And I was vexed in my mind.
22 I *was* so foolish and ignorant;
I was *like* a beast before You.
23 Nevertheless I *am* continually with You;
You hold *me* by my right hand.
24 You will guide me with Your counsel,
And afterward receive me *to* glory.

25 Whom have I in heaven *but You?*
And *there is* none upon earth *that* I desire besides You.
26 My flesh and my heart fail;
But God *is* the strength of my heart and my portion forever.

27 For indeed, those who are far from You shall perish;
You have destroyed all those who desert You for harlotry.
28 But *it is* good for me to draw near to God;
I have put my trust in the Lord GOD,
That I may declare all Your works.

PSALM 74

A Plea for Relief from Oppressors

A Contemplation[a] of Asaph.

1 O God, why have You cast *us* off forever?
Why does Your anger smoke against the sheep of Your pasture?

73:7 [a] Targum reads *face bulges;* Septuagint, Syriac, and Vulgate read *iniquity bulges.*
74:title [a] Hebrew *Maschil*

2 Remember Your congregation,
which You have purchased of old,
The tribe of Your inheritance,
which You have redeemed—
This Mount Zion where You have dwelt.
3 Lift up Your feet to the perpetual desolations.
The enemy has damaged everything in the sanctuary.
4 Your enemies roar in the midst of Your meeting place;
They set up their banners *for* signs.
5 They seem like men who lift up
Axes among the thick trees.
6 And now they break down its carved work, all at once,
With axes and hammers.
7 They have set fire to Your sanctuary;
They have defiled the dwelling place of Your name to the ground.
8 They said in their hearts,
"Let us destroy them altogether."
They have burned up all the meeting places of God in the land.

9 We do not see our signs;
There is no longer any prophet;
Nor *is there* any among us who knows how long.
10 O God, how long will the adversary reproach?
Will the enemy blaspheme Your name forever?
11 Why do You withdraw Your hand, even Your right hand?
Take it out of Your bosom and destroy *them*.
12 For God *is* my King from of old,
Working salvation in the midst of the earth.
13 You divided the sea by Your strength;
You broke the heads of the sea serpents in the waters.
14 You broke the heads of Leviathan in pieces,
And gave him *as* food to the people inhabiting the wilderness.
15 You broke open the fountain and the flood;
You dried up mighty rivers.
16 The day *is* Yours, the night also *is* Yours;
You have prepared the light and the sun.
17 You have set all the borders of the earth;
You have made summer and winter.

18 Remember this, *that* the enemy has reproached, O LORD,
And *that* a foolish people has blasphemed Your name.
19 Oh, do not deliver the life of Your turtledove to the wild beast!
Do not forget the life of Your poor forever.
20 Have respect to the covenant;
For the dark places of the earth are full of the haunts of cruelty.
21 Oh, do not let the oppressed return ashamed!
Let the poor and needy praise Your name.

22 Arise, O God, plead Your own cause;
Remember how the foolish man reproaches You daily.
23 Do not forget the voice of Your enemies;
The tumult of those who rise up against You increases continually.

PSALM 75

Thanksgiving for God's Righteous Judgment

To the Chief Musician. Set to "Do Not Destroy."[a] A Psalm of Asaph. A Song.

1 We give thanks to You, O God, we give thanks!
For Your wondrous works declare *that* Your name is near.

2 "When I choose the proper time,
I will judge uprightly.
3 The earth and all its inhabitants are dissolved;
I set up its pillars firmly. *Selah*

75:title [a] Hebrew *Al Tashcheth*

4 "I said to the boastful, 'Do not deal boastfully,'
And to the wicked, 'Do not lift up the horn.
5 Do not lift up your horn on high;
Do *not* speak with a stiff neck.' "

6 For exaltation *comes* neither from the east
Nor from the west nor from the south.
7 But God *is* the Judge:
He puts down one,
And exalts another.
8 For in the hand of the LORD *there is* a cup,
And the wine is red;
It is fully mixed, and He pours it out;
Surely its dregs shall all the wicked of the earth
Drain *and* drink down.

9 But I will declare forever,
I will sing praises to the God of Jacob.

10 "All the horns of the wicked I will also cut off,
But the horns of the righteous shall be exalted."

PSALM 76

The Majesty of God in Judgment

To the Chief Musician. On stringed instruments.[a] A Psalm of Asaph. A Song.

1 In Judah God *is* known;
His name *is* great in Israel.
2 In Salem[a] also is His tabernacle,
And His dwelling place in Zion.
3 There He broke the arrows of the bow,
The shield and sword of battle. *Selah*

4 You *are* more glorious and excellent
Than the mountains of prey.
5 The stouthearted were plundered;
They have sunk into their sleep;
And none of the mighty men have found the use of their hands.
6 At Your rebuke, O God of Jacob,
Both the chariot and horse were cast into a dead sleep.

7 You, Yourself, *are* to be feared;
And who may stand in Your presence
When once You are angry?
8 You caused judgment to be heard from heaven;
The earth feared and was still,
9 When God arose to judgment,
To deliver all the oppressed of the earth. *Selah*

10 Surely the wrath of man shall praise You;
With the remainder of wrath You shall gird Yourself.

11 Make vows to the LORD your God, and pay *them;*
Let all who are around Him bring presents to Him who ought to be feared.
12 He shall cut off the spirit of princes;
He is awesome to the kings of the earth.

PSALM 77

The Consoling Memory of God's Redemptive Works

To the Chief Musician. To Jeduthun. A Psalm of Asaph.

1 I cried out to God with my voice—
To God with my voice;
And He gave ear to me.
2 In the day of my trouble I sought the Lord;
My hand was stretched out in the night without ceasing;
My soul refused to be comforted.
3 I remembered God, and was troubled;
I complained, and my spirit was overwhelmed. *Selah*

4 You hold my eyelids *open;*
I am so troubled that I cannot speak.
5 I have considered the days of old,
The years of ancient times.

76:title [a] Hebrew *neginoth* **76:2** [a] That is, Jerusalem

6 I call to remembrance my song in the night;
I meditate within my heart,
And my spirit makes diligent search.
7 Will the Lord cast off forever?
And will He be favorable no more?
8 Has His mercy ceased forever?
Has *His* promise failed forevermore?
9 Has God forgotten to be gracious?
Has He in anger shut up His tender mercies? *Selah*

10 And I said, "This *is* my anguish;
But I will remember the years of the right hand of the Most High."
11 I will remember the works of the LORD;
Surely I will remember Your wonders of old.
12 I will also meditate on all Your work,
And talk of Your deeds.
13 Your way, O God, *is* in the sanctuary;
Who *is* so great a God as *our* God?
14 You *are* the God who does wonders;
You have declared Your strength among the peoples.
15 You have with *Your* arm redeemed Your people,
The sons of Jacob and Joseph. *Selah*

16 The waters saw You, O God;
The waters saw You, they were afraid;
The depths also trembled.
17 The clouds poured out water;
The skies sent out a sound;
Your arrows also flashed about.
18 The voice of Your thunder *was* in the whirlwind;
The lightnings lit up the world;
The earth trembled and shook.
19 Your way *was* in the sea,
Your path in the great waters,
And Your footsteps were not known.
20 You led Your people like a flock
By the hand of Moses and Aaron.

PSALM 78

God's Kindness to Rebellious Israel

A Contemplation[a] of Asaph.

1 Give ear, O my people, *to* my law;
Incline your ears to the words of my mouth.
2 I will open my mouth in a parable;
I will utter dark sayings of old,
3 Which we have heard and known,
And our fathers have told us.
4 We will not hide *them* from their children,
Telling to the generation to come the praises of the LORD,
And His strength and His wonderful works that He has done.

5 For He established a testimony in Jacob,
And appointed a law in Israel,
Which He commanded our fathers,
That they should make them known to their children;
6 That the generation to come might know *them*,
The children *who* would be born,
That they may arise and declare *them* to their children,
7 That they may set their hope in God,
And not forget the works of God,
But keep His commandments;
8 And may not be like their fathers,
A stubborn and rebellious generation,
A generation *that* did not set its heart aright,
And whose spirit was not faithful to God.

9 The children of Ephraim, *being* armed *and* carrying bows,
Turned back in the day of battle.
10 They did not keep the covenant of God;
They refused to walk in His law,
11 And forgot His works
And His wonders that He had shown them.

78:title [a] Hebrew *Maschil*

12 Marvelous things He did in the
sight of their fathers,
In the land of Egypt, *in* the field of
Zoan.
13 He divided the sea and caused
them to pass through;
And He made the waters stand up
like a heap.
14 In the daytime also He led them
with the cloud,
And all the night with a light of
fire.
15 He split the rocks in the wilderness,
And gave *them* drink in
abundance like the depths.
16 He also brought streams out of
the rock,
And caused waters to run down
like rivers.

17 But they sinned even more
against Him
By rebelling against the Most
High in the wilderness.
18 And they tested God in their heart
By asking for the food of their
fancy.
19 Yes, they spoke against God:
They said, "Can God prepare a
table in the wilderness?
20 Behold, He struck the rock,
So that the waters gushed out,
And the streams overflowed.
Can He give bread also?
Can He provide meat for His
people?"

21 Therefore the LORD heard *this* and
was furious;
So a fire was kindled against
Jacob,
And anger also came up against
Israel,
22 Because they did not believe in
God,
And did not trust in His salvation.
23 Yet He had commanded the
clouds above,
And opened the doors of heaven,
24 Had rained down manna on them
to eat,
And given them of the bread of
heaven.
25 Men ate angels' food;
He sent them food to the full.
26 He caused an east wind to blow in
the heavens;
And by His power He brought in
the south wind.
27 He also rained meat on them like
the dust,
Feathered fowl like the sand of
the seas;
28 And He let *them* fall in the midst
of their camp,
All around their dwellings.
29 So they ate and were well filled,
For He gave them their own desire.
30 They were not deprived of their
craving;
But while their food *was* still in
their mouths,
31 The wrath of God came against them,
And slew the stoutest of them,
And struck down the choice *men*
of Israel.

32 In spite of this they still sinned,
And did not believe in His
wondrous works.
33 Therefore their days He
consumed in futility,
And their years in fear.

34 When He slew them, then they
sought Him;
And they returned and sought
earnestly for God.
35 Then they remembered that God
was their rock,
And the Most High God their
Redeemer.
36 Nevertheless they flattered Him
with their mouth,
And they lied to Him with their
tongue;
37 For their heart was not steadfast
with Him,
Nor were they faithful in His
covenant.
38 But He, *being* full of compassion,
forgave *their* iniquity,
And did not destroy *them*.
Yes, many a time He turned His
anger away,
And did not stir up all His wrath;
39 For He remembered that they
were but flesh,
A breath that passes away and
does not come again.

40 How often they provoked Him in the wilderness,
And grieved Him in the desert!
41 Yes, again and again they tempted God,
And limited the Holy One of Israel.
42 They did not remember His power:
The day when He redeemed them from the enemy,
43 When He worked His signs in Egypt,
And His wonders in the field of Zoan;
44 Turned their rivers into blood,
And their streams, that they could not drink.
45 He sent swarms of flies among them, which devoured them,
And frogs, which destroyed them.
46 He also gave their crops to the caterpillar,
And their labor to the locust.
47 He destroyed their vines with hail,
And their sycamore trees with frost.
48 He also gave up their cattle to the hail,
And their flocks to fiery lightning.
49 He cast on them the fierceness of His anger,
Wrath, indignation, and trouble,
By sending angels of destruction *among them.*
50 He made a path for His anger;
He did not spare their soul from death,
But gave their life over to the plague,
51 And destroyed all the firstborn in Egypt,
The first of *their* strength in the tents of Ham.
52 But He made His own people go forth like sheep,
And guided them in the wilderness like a flock;
53 And He led them on safely, so that they did not fear;
But the sea overwhelmed their enemies.
54 And He brought them to His holy border,
This mountain *which* His right hand had acquired.
55 He also drove out the nations before them,
Allotted them an inheritance by survey,
And made the tribes of Israel dwell in their tents.

56 Yet they tested and provoked the Most High God,
And did not keep His testimonies,
57 But turned back and acted unfaithfully like their fathers;
They were turned aside like a deceitful bow.
58 For they provoked Him to anger with their high places,
And moved Him to jealousy with their carved images.
59 When God heard *this,* He was furious,
And greatly abhorred Israel,
60 So that He forsook the tabernacle of Shiloh,
The tent He had placed among men,
61 And delivered His strength into captivity,
And His glory into the enemy's hand.
62 He also gave His people over to the sword,
And was furious with His inheritance.
63 The fire consumed their young men,
And their maidens were not given in marriage.
64 Their priests fell by the sword,
And their widows made no lamentation.

65 Then the Lord awoke as *from* sleep,
Like a mighty man who shouts because of wine.
66 And He beat back His enemies;
He put them to a perpetual reproach.

67 Moreover He rejected the tent of Joseph,
And did not choose the tribe of Ephraim,
68 But chose the tribe of Judah,
Mount Zion which He loved.

69 And He built His sanctuary like the heights,
Like the earth which He has established forever.
70 He also chose David His servant,
And took him from the sheepfolds;
71 From following the ewes that had young He brought him,
To shepherd Jacob His people,
And Israel His inheritance.
72 So he shepherded them according to the integrity of his heart,
And guided them by the skillfulness of his hands.

PSALM 79

A Dirge and a Prayer for Israel, Destroyed by Enemies

A Psalm of Asaph.

1 O God, the nations have come into Your inheritance;
Your holy temple they have defiled;
They have laid Jerusalem in heaps.
2 The dead bodies of Your servants
They have given *as* food for the birds of the heavens,
The flesh of Your saints to the beasts of the earth.
3 Their blood they have shed like water all around Jerusalem,
And *there was* no one to bury *them.*
4 We have become a reproach to our neighbors,
A scorn and derision to those who are around us.

5 How long, LORD?
Will You be angry forever?
Will Your jealousy burn like fire?
6 Pour out Your wrath on the nations that do not know You,
And on the kingdoms that do not call on Your name.
7 For they have devoured Jacob,
And laid waste his dwelling place.

8 Oh, do not remember former iniquities against us!
Let Your tender mercies come speedily to meet us,
For we have been brought very low.
9 Help us, O God of our salvation,
For the glory of Your name;
And deliver us, and provide atonement for our sins,
For Your name's sake!
10 Why should the nations say,
"Where *is* their God?"
Let there be known among the nations in our sight
The avenging of the blood of Your servants *which has been* shed.

11 Let the groaning of the prisoner come before You;
According to the greatness of Your power
Preserve those who are appointed to die;
12 And return to our neighbors sevenfold into their bosom
Their reproach with which they have reproached You, O Lord.

13 So we, Your people and sheep of Your pasture,
Will give You thanks forever;
We will show forth Your praise to all generations.

PSALM 80

Prayer for Israel's Restoration

To the Chief Musician. Set to "The Lilies."[a]
A Testimony[b] *of Asaph. A Psalm.*

1 Give ear, O Shepherd of Israel,
You who lead Joseph like a flock;
You who dwell *between* the cherubim, shine forth!
2 Before Ephraim, Benjamin, and Manasseh,
Stir up Your strength,
And come *and* save us!

3 Restore us, O God;
Cause Your face to shine,
And we shall be saved!

4 O LORD God of hosts,
How long will You be angry
Against the prayer of Your people?

80:title [a] Hebrew *Shoshannim* [b] Hebrew *Eduth*

5 You have fed them with the bread of tears,
And given them tears to drink in great measure.
6 You have made us a strife to our neighbors,
And our enemies laugh among themselves.

7 Restore us, O God of hosts;
Cause Your face to shine,
And we shall be saved!

8 You have brought a vine out of Egypt;
You have cast out the nations, and planted it.
9 You prepared *room* for it,
And caused it to take deep root,
And it filled the land.
10 The hills were covered with its shadow,
And the mighty cedars with its boughs.
11 She sent out her boughs to the Sea,[a]
And her branches to the River.[b]

12 Why have You broken down her hedges,
So that all who pass by the way pluck her *fruit?*
13 The boar out of the woods uproots it,
And the wild beast of the field devours it.

14 Return, we beseech You, O God of hosts;
Look down from heaven and see,
And visit this vine
15 And the vineyard which Your right hand has planted,
And the branch *that* You made strong for Yourself.
16 *It is* burned with fire, *it is* cut down;
They perish at the rebuke of Your countenance.
17 Let Your hand be upon the man of Your right hand,
Upon the son of man *whom* You made strong for Yourself.
18 Then we will not turn back from You;
Revive us, and we will call upon Your name.

19 Restore us, O LORD God of hosts;
Cause Your face to shine,
And we shall be saved!

PSALM 81

An Appeal for Israel's Repentance

To the Chief Musician. On an instrument of Gath.[a] *A Psalm of Asaph.*

1 Sing aloud to God our strength;
Make a joyful shout to the God of Jacob.
2 Raise a song and strike the timbrel,
The pleasant harp with the lute.

3 Blow the trumpet at the time of the New Moon,
At the full moon, on our solemn feast day.
4 For this *is* a statute for Israel,
A law of the God of Jacob.
5 This He established in Joseph *as* a testimony,
When He went throughout the land of Egypt,
Where I heard a language I did not understand.

6 "I removed his shoulder from the burden;
His hands were freed from the baskets.
7 You called in trouble, and I delivered you;
I answered you in the secret place of thunder;
I tested you at the waters of Meribah. *Selah*

8 "Hear, O My people, and I will admonish you!
O Israel, if you will listen to Me!
9 There shall be no foreign god among you;
Nor shall you worship any foreign god.

80:11 [a] That is, the Mediterranean [b] That is, the Euphrates **81:title** [a] Hebrew *Al Gittith*

10 I *am* the LORD your God,
Who brought you out of the land of Egypt;
Open your mouth wide, and I will fill it.

11 "But My people would not heed My voice,
And Israel would *have* none of Me.
12 So I gave them over to their own stubborn heart,
To walk in their own counsels.

13 "Oh, that My people would listen to Me,
That Israel would walk in My ways!
14 I would soon subdue their enemies,
And turn My hand against their adversaries.
15 The haters of the LORD would pretend submission to Him,
But their fate would endure forever.
16 He would have fed them also with the finest of wheat;
And with honey from the rock I would have satisfied you."

PSALM 82

A Plea for Justice

A Psalm of Asaph.

1 God stands in the congregation of the mighty;
He judges among the gods.[a]
2 How long will you judge unjustly,
And show partiality to the wicked? *Selah*
3 Defend the poor and fatherless;
Do justice to the afflicted and needy.
4 Deliver the poor and needy;
Free *them* from the hand of the wicked.

5 They do not know, nor do they understand;
They walk about in darkness;
All the foundations of the earth are unstable.

6 I said, "You *are* gods,[a]
And all of you *are* children of the Most High.
7 But you shall die like men,
And fall like one of the princes."

8 Arise, O God, judge the earth;
For You shall inherit all nations.

PSALM 83

Prayer to Frustrate Conspiracy Against Israel

A Song. A Psalm of Asaph.

1 Do not keep silent, O God!
Do not hold Your peace,
And do not be still, O God!
2 For behold, Your enemies make a tumult;
And those who hate You have lifted up their head.
3 They have taken crafty counsel against Your people,
And consulted together against Your sheltered ones.
4 They have said, "Come, and let us cut them off from *being* a nation,
That the name of Israel may be remembered no more."

5 For they have consulted together with one consent;
They form a confederacy against You:
6 The tents of Edom and the Ishmaelites;
Moab and the Hagrites;
7 Gebal, Ammon, and Amalek;
Philistia with the inhabitants of Tyre;
8 Assyria also has joined with them;
They have helped the children of Lot. *Selah*

9 Deal with them as *with* Midian,
As *with* Sisera,
As *with* Jabin at the Brook Kishon,
10 Who perished at En Dor,
Who became *as* refuse on the earth.

82:1 [a] Hebrew *elohim, mighty ones;* that is, the judges

82:6 [a] Hebrew *elohim, mighty ones;* that is, the judges

11 Make their nobles like Oreb and
like Zeeb,
Yes, all their princes like Zebah
and Zalmunna,
12 Who said, "Let us take for ourselves
The pastures of God for a
possession."

13 O my God, make them like the
whirling dust,
Like the chaff before the wind!
14 As the fire burns the woods,
And as the flame sets the
mountains on fire,
15 So pursue them with Your
tempest,
And frighten them with Your
storm.
16 Fill their faces with shame,
That they may seek Your name,
O LORD.
17 Let them be confounded and
dismayed forever;
Yes, let them be put to shame and
perish,
18 That they may know that You,
whose name alone *is* the
LORD,
Are the Most High over all the earth.

PSALM 84

The Blessedness of Dwelling in the House of God

To the Chief Musician. On an instrument of Gath.[a] *A Psalm of the sons of Korah.*

1 How lovely *is* Your tabernacle,
O LORD of hosts!
2 My soul longs, yes, even faints
For the courts of the LORD;
My heart and my flesh cry out for
the living God.

3 Even the sparrow has found a
home,
And the swallow a nest for herself,
Where she may lay her young—
Even Your altars, O LORD of hosts,
My King and my God.
4 Blessed *are* those who dwell in
Your house;
They will still be praising
You. *Selah*

5 Blessed *is* the man whose strength
is in You,
Whose heart *is* set on pilgrimage.
6 *As they* pass through the Valley of
Baca,
They make it a spring;
The rain also covers it with pools.
7 They go from strength to
strength;
Each one appears before God in
Zion.[a]

8 O LORD God of hosts, hear my
prayer;
Give ear, O God of Jacob! *Selah*
9 O God, behold our shield,
And look upon the face of Your
anointed.

10 For a day in Your courts *is* better
than a thousand.
I would rather be a doorkeeper in
the house of my God
Than dwell in the tents of
wickedness.
11 For the LORD God *is* a sun and
shield;
The LORD will give grace and glory;
No good *thing* will He withhold
From those who walk uprightly.

12 O LORD of hosts,
Blessed *is* the man who trusts in
You!

PSALM 85

Prayer that the LORD Will Restore Favor to the Land

To the Chief Musician. A Psalm of the sons of Korah.

1 LORD, You have been favorable to
Your land;
You have brought back the
captivity of Jacob.
2 You have forgiven the iniquity of
Your people;
You have covered all their sin.
Selah
3 You have taken away all Your
wrath;
You have turned from the
fierceness of Your anger.

84:title [a] Hebrew *Al Gittith* 84:7 [a] Septuagint, Syriac, and Vulgate read *The God of gods shall be seen.*

4 Restore us, O God of our salvation,
And cause Your anger toward us to cease.
5 Will You be angry with us forever?
Will You prolong Your anger to all generations?
6 Will You not revive us again,
That Your people may rejoice in You?
7 Show us Your mercy, LORD,
And grant us Your salvation.

8 I will hear what God the LORD will speak,
For He will speak peace
To His people and to His saints;
But let them not turn back to folly.
9 Surely His salvation *is* near to those who fear Him,
That glory may dwell in our land.

10 Mercy and truth have met together;
Righteousness and peace have kissed.
11 Truth shall spring out of the earth,
And righteousness shall look down from heaven.
12 Yes, the LORD will give *what is* good;
And our land will yield its increase.
13 Righteousness will go before Him,
And shall make His footsteps *our* pathway.

PSALM 86

Prayer for Mercy, with Meditation on the Excellencies of the LORD

A Prayer of David.

1 Bow down Your ear, O LORD, hear me;
For I *am* poor and needy.
2 Preserve my life, for I *am* holy;
You are my God;
Save Your servant who trusts in You!
3 Be merciful to me, O Lord,
For I cry to You all day long.
4 Rejoice the soul of Your servant,
For to You, O Lord, I lift up my soul.
5 For You, Lord, *are* good, and ready to forgive,
And abundant in mercy to all those who call upon You.

6 Give ear, O LORD, to my prayer;
And attend to the voice of my supplications.
7 In the day of my trouble I will call upon You,
For You will answer me.

8 Among the gods *there is* none like You, O Lord;
Nor *are there any works* like Your works.
9 All nations whom You have made
Shall come and worship before You, O Lord,
And shall glorify Your name.
10 For You *are* great, and do wondrous things;
You alone *are* God.

11 Teach me Your way, O LORD;
I will walk in Your truth;
Unite my heart to fear Your name.
12 I will praise You, O Lord my God, with all my heart,
And I will glorify Your name forevermore.
13 For great *is* Your mercy toward me,
And You have delivered my soul from the depths of Sheol.

14 O God, the proud have risen against me,
And a mob of violent *men* have sought my life,
And have not set You before them.
15 But You, O Lord, *are* a God full of compassion, and gracious,
Longsuffering and abundant in mercy and truth.

16 Oh, turn to me, and have mercy on me!
Give Your strength to Your servant,
And save the son of Your maidservant.
17 Show me a sign for good,
That those who hate me may see *it* and be ashamed,
Because You, LORD, have helped me and comforted me.

PSALM 87

The Glories of the City of God

A Psalm of the sons of Korah. A Song.

1 His foundation *is* in the holy
mountains.
2 The LORD loves the gates of Zion
More than all the dwellings of
Jacob.
3 Glorious things are spoken of you,
O city of God! *Selah*

4 "I will make mention of Rahab
and Babylon to those who
know Me;
Behold, O Philistia and Tyre, with
Ethiopia:
'This *one* was born there.' "

5 And of Zion it will be said,
"This *one* and that *one* were born in
her;
And the Most High Himself shall
establish her."
6 The LORD will record,
When He registers the
peoples:
"This *one* was born there." *Selah*

7 Both the singers and the players
on instruments *say,*
"All my springs *are* in you."

PSALM 88

A Prayer for Help in Despondency

A Song. A Psalm of the sons of Korah. To the Chief Musician. Set to "Mahalath Leannoth." A Contemplation[a] of Heman the Ezrahite.

1 O LORD, God of my salvation,
I have cried out day and night
before You.
2 Let my prayer come before You;
Incline Your ear to my cry.

3 For my soul is full of troubles,
And my life draws near to the
grave.
4 I am counted with those who go
down to the pit;
I am like a man *who has* no
strength,
5 Adrift among the dead,
Like the slain who lie in the
grave,
Whom You remember no more,
And who are cut off from Your
hand.

6 You have laid me in the lowest pit,
In darkness, in the depths.
7 Your wrath lies heavy upon me,
And You have afflicted *me* with all
Your waves. *Selah*
8 You have put away my
acquaintances far from me;
You have made me an
abomination to them;
I am shut up, and I cannot get
out;
9 My eye wastes away because of
affliction.

LORD, I have called daily upon
You;
I have stretched out my hands to
You.
10 Will You work wonders for the
dead?
Shall the dead arise *and* praise
You? *Selah*
11 Shall Your lovingkindness be
declared in the grave?
Or Your faithfulness in the place
of destruction?
12 Shall Your wonders be known in
the dark?
And Your righteousness in the
land of forgetfulness?

13 But to You I have cried out,
O LORD,
And in the morning my prayer
comes before You.
14 LORD, why do You cast off my
soul?
Why do You hide Your face from
me?
15 I *have been* afflicted and ready to
die from *my* youth;
I suffer Your terrors;
I am distraught.
16 Your fierce wrath has gone over
me;
Your terrors have cut me off.

88:title a Hebrew *Maschil*

17 They came around me all day
long like water;
They engulfed me altogether.
18 Loved one and friend You have
put far from me,
And my acquaintances into
darkness.

PSALM 89

Remembering the Covenant with David, and Sorrow for Lost Blessings

A Contemplation[a] of Ethan the Ezrahite.

1 I will sing of the mercies of the
LORD forever;
With my mouth will I make
known Your faithfulness to
all generations.
2 For I have said, "Mercy shall be
built up forever;
Your faithfulness You shall
establish in the very
heavens."

3 "I have made a covenant with My
chosen,
I have sworn to My servant David:
4 'Your seed I will establish forever,
And build up your throne to all
generations.' " *Selah*

5 And the heavens will praise Your
wonders, O LORD;
Your faithfulness also in the
assembly of the saints.
6 For who in the heavens can be
compared to the LORD?
Who among the sons of the mighty
can be likened to the LORD?
7 God is greatly to be feared in the
assembly of the saints,
And to be held in reverence by all
those around Him.
8 O LORD God of hosts,
Who *is* mighty like You, O LORD?
Your faithfulness also surrounds
You.
9 You rule the raging of the sea;
When its waves rise, You still them.
10 You have broken Rahab in pieces,
as one who is slain;
You have scattered Your enemies
with Your mighty arm.
11 The heavens *are* Yours, the earth
also *is* Yours;
The world and all its fullness, You
have founded them.
12 The north and the south, You have
created them;
Tabor and Hermon rejoice in Your
name.
13 You have a mighty arm;
Strong is Your hand, *and* high is
Your right hand.
14 Righteousness and justice
are the foundation of Your
throne;
Mercy and truth go before Your
face.
15 Blessed *are* the people who know
the joyful sound!
They walk, O LORD, in the light of
Your countenance.
16 In Your name they rejoice all day
long,
And in Your righteousness they
are exalted.
17 For You *are* the glory of their
strength,
And in Your favor our horn is
exalted.
18 For our shield *belongs* to
the LORD,
And our king to the Holy One of
Israel.

19 Then You spoke in a vision to Your
holy one,[a]
And said: "I have given help to
one who is mighty;
I have exalted one chosen from
the people.
20 I have found My servant David;
With My holy oil I have anointed
him,
21 With whom My hand shall be
established;
Also My arm shall strengthen
him.
22 The enemy shall not outwit
him,
Nor the son of wickedness afflict
him.
23 I will beat down his foes before
his face,
And plague those who hate him.

89:title [a] Hebrew *Maschil* 89:19 [a] Following many Hebrew manuscripts; Masoretic Text, Septuagint, Targum, and Vulgate read *holy ones*.

24 "But My faithfulness and My mercy *shall be* with him,
And in My name his horn shall be exalted.
25 Also I will set his hand over the sea,
And his right hand over the rivers.
26 He shall cry to Me, 'You *are* my Father,
My God, and the rock of my salvation.'
27 Also I will make him *My* firstborn,
The highest of the kings of the earth.
28 My mercy I will keep for him forever,
And My covenant shall stand firm with him.
29 His seed also I will make *to endure* forever,
And his throne as the days of heaven.

30 "If his sons forsake My law
And do not walk in My judgments,
31 If they break My statutes
And do not keep My commandments,
32 Then I will punish their transgression with the rod,
And their iniquity with stripes.
33 Nevertheless My lovingkindness I will not utterly take from him,
Nor allow My faithfulness to fail.
34 My covenant I will not break,
Nor alter the word that has gone out of My lips.
35 Once I have sworn by My holiness;
I will not lie to David:
36 His seed shall endure forever,
And his throne as the sun before Me;
37 It shall be established forever like the moon,
Even *like* the faithful witness in the sky." *Selah*

38 But You have cast off and abhorred,
You have been furious with Your anointed.
39 You have renounced the covenant of Your servant;
You have profaned his crown *by casting it* to the ground.
40 You have broken down all his hedges;
You have brought his strongholds to ruin.
41 All who pass by the way plunder him;
He is a reproach to his neighbors.
42 You have exalted the right hand of his adversaries;
You have made all his enemies rejoice.
43 You have also turned back the edge of his sword,
And have not sustained him in the battle.
44 You have made his glory cease,
And cast his throne down to the ground.
45 The days of his youth You have shortened;
You have covered him with shame. *Selah*

46 How long, LORD?
Will You hide Yourself forever?
Will Your wrath burn like fire?
47 Remember how short my time is;
For what futility have You created all the children of men?
48 What man can live and not see death?
Can he deliver his life from the power of the grave? *Selah*

49 Lord, where *are* Your former lovingkindnesses,
Which You swore to David in Your truth?
50 Remember, Lord, the reproach of Your servants—
How I bear in my bosom *the reproach of* all the many peoples,
51 With which Your enemies have reproached, O LORD,
With which they have reproached the footsteps of Your anointed.

52 Blessed *be* the LORD forevermore!
Amen and Amen.

BOOK FOUR
Psalms 90–106

PSALM 90
The Eternity of God, and Man's Frailty

A Prayer of Moses the man of God.

1 Lord, You have been our dwelling
place[a] in all generations.
2 Before the mountains were
brought forth,
Or ever You had formed the earth
and the world,
Even from everlasting to
everlasting, You *are* God.

3 You turn man to destruction,
And say, "Return, O children of men."
4 For a thousand years in Your sight
Are like yesterday when it is past,
And *like* a watch in the night.
5 You carry them away *like* a flood;
They are like a sleep.
In the morning they are like grass
which grows up:
6 In the morning it flourishes and
grows up;
In the evening it is cut down and
withers.

7 For we have been consumed by
Your anger,
And by Your wrath we are terrified.
8 You have set our iniquities before
You,
Our secret *sins* in the light of Your
countenance.
9 For all our days have passed
away in Your wrath;
We finish our years like a sigh.
10 The days of our lives *are* seventy
years;
And if by reason of strength *they
are* eighty years,
Yet their boast *is* only labor and
sorrow;
For it is soon cut off, and we fly
away.
11 Who knows the power of Your
anger?
For as the fear of You, *so is* Your
wrath.
12 So teach *us* to number our days,
That we may gain a heart of
wisdom.

13 Return, O LORD!
How long?
And have compassion on Your
servants.
14 Oh, satisfy us early with Your
mercy,
That we may rejoice and be glad
all our days!
15 Make us glad according to the
days *in which* You have
afflicted us,
The years *in which* we have seen
evil.
16 Let Your work appear to Your
servants,
And Your glory to their children.
17 And let the beauty of the LORD
our God be upon us,
And establish the work of our
hands for us;
Yes, establish the work of our hands.

PSALM 91
Safety of Abiding in the Presence of God

1 He who dwells in the secret place
of the Most High
Shall abide under the shadow of
the Almighty.
2 I will say of the LORD, "*He is* my
refuge and my fortress;
My God, in Him I will trust."

3 Surely He shall deliver you from
the snare of the fowler[a]
And from the perilous pestilence.
4 He shall cover you with His
feathers,
And under His wings you shall
take refuge;
His truth *shall be your* shield and
buckler.
5 You shall not be afraid of the
terror by night,
Nor of the arrow *that* flies by day,
6 *Nor* of the pestilence *that* walks in
darkness,
Nor of the destruction *that* lays
waste at noonday.

90:1 [a] Septuagint, Targum, and Vulgate read *refuge*. **91:3** [a] That is, one who catches birds in a trap or snare

7 A thousand may fall at your side,
And ten thousand at your right
hand;
But it shall not come near you.
8 Only with your eyes shall you
look,
And see the reward of the wicked.

9 Because you have made the
LORD, *who is* my refuge,
Even the Most High, your dwelling
place,
10 No evil shall befall you,
Nor shall any plague come near
your dwelling;
11 For He shall give His angels
charge over you,
To keep you in all your ways.
12 In *their* hands they shall bear
you up,
Lest you dash your foot against a
stone.
13 You shall tread upon the lion and
the cobra,
The young lion and the serpent
you shall trample underfoot.

14 "Because he has set his love upon
Me, therefore I will deliver
him;
I will set him on high, because he
has known My name.
15 He shall call upon Me, and I will
answer him;
I *will be* with him in trouble;
I will deliver him and honor him.
16 With long life I will satisfy him,
And show him My salvation."

PSALM 92

Praise to the LORD for His Love and Faithfulness

A Psalm. A Song for the Sabbath day.

1 *It is* good to give thanks to the
LORD,
And to sing praises to Your name,
O Most High;
2 To declare Your lovingkindness in
the morning,
And Your faithfulness every night,
3 On an instrument of ten strings,
On the lute,
And on the harp,
With harmonious sound.
4 For You, LORD, have made me
glad through Your work;
I will triumph in the works of Your
hands.

5 O LORD, how great are Your
works!
Your thoughts are very deep.
6 A senseless man does not know,
Nor does a fool understand this.
7 When the wicked spring up like
grass,
And when all the workers of
iniquity flourish,
It is that they may be destroyed
forever.

8 But You, LORD, *are* on high
forevermore.
9 For behold, Your enemies, O LORD,
For behold, Your enemies shall
perish;
All the workers of iniquity shall be
scattered.

10 But my horn You have exalted
like a wild ox;
I have been anointed with fresh
oil.
11 My eye also has seen *my desire* on
my enemies;
My ears hear *my desire* on the
wicked
Who rise up against me.

12 The righteous shall flourish like a
palm tree,
He shall grow like a cedar in
Lebanon.
13 Those who are planted in the
house of the LORD
Shall flourish in the courts of our
God.
14 They shall still bear fruit in old age;
They shall be fresh and flourishing,
15 To declare that the LORD is
upright;
He is my rock, and *there is* no
unrighteousness in Him.

PSALM 93

The Eternal Reign of the LORD

1 The LORD reigns, He is clothed
with majesty;
The LORD is clothed,

He has girded Himself with
strength.
Surely the world is established, so
that it cannot be moved.
2 Your throne *is* established from of
old;
You *are* from everlasting.

3 The floods have lifted up, O LORD,
The floods have lifted up their
voice;
The floods lift up their waves.
4 The LORD on high *is* mightier
Than the noise of many waters,
Than the mighty waves of the sea.

5 Your testimonies are very sure;
Holiness adorns Your house,
O LORD, forever.

PSALM 94

God the Refuge of the Righteous

1 O LORD God, to whom vengeance
belongs—
O God, to whom vengeance
belongs, shine forth!
2 Rise up, O Judge of the earth;
Render punishment to the proud.
3 LORD, how long will the wicked,
How long will the wicked
triumph?

4 They utter speech, *and* speak
insolent things;
All the workers of iniquity boast
in themselves.
5 They break in pieces Your people,
O LORD,
And afflict Your heritage.
6 They slay the widow and the
stranger,
And murder the fatherless.
7 Yet they say, "The LORD does not
see,
Nor does the God of Jacob
understand."

8 Understand, you senseless
among the people;
And *you* fools, when will you be
wise?
9 He who planted the ear, shall He
not hear?
He who formed the eye, shall He
not see?
10 He who instructs the nations,
shall He not correct,
He who teaches man
knowledge?
11 The LORD knows the thoughts of
man,
That they *are* futile.

12 Blessed *is* the man whom You
instruct, O LORD,
And teach out of Your law,
13 That You may give him rest from
the days of adversity,
Until the pit is dug for the
wicked.
14 For the LORD will not cast off His
people,
Nor will He forsake His
inheritance.
15 But judgment will return to
righteousness,
And all the upright in heart will
follow it.

16 Who will rise up for me against
the evildoers?
Who will stand up for me against
the workers of iniquity?
17 Unless the LORD *had been* my
help,
My soul would soon have settled
in silence.
18 If I say, "My foot slips,"
Your mercy, O LORD, will hold
me up.
19 In the multitude of my anxieties
within me,
Your comforts delight my soul.

20 Shall the throne of iniquity, which
devises evil by law,
Have fellowship with You?
21 They gather together against the
life of the righteous,
And condemn innocent blood.
22 But the LORD has been my
defense,
And my God the rock of my
refuge.
23 He has brought on them their
own iniquity,
And shall cut them off in their
own wickedness;
The LORD our God shall cut them
off.

PSALM 95

A Call to Worship and Obedience

1 Oh come, let us sing to the LORD!
Let us shout joyfully to the Rock of our salvation.
2 Let us come before His presence with thanksgiving;
Let us shout joyfully to Him with psalms.
3 For the LORD *is* the great God,
And the great King above all gods.
4 In His hand *are* the deep places of the earth;
The heights of the hills *are* His also.
5 The sea *is* His, for He made it;
And His hands formed the dry *land.*

6 Oh come, let us worship and bow down;
Let us kneel before the LORD our Maker.
7 For He *is* our God,
And we *are* the people of His pasture,
And the sheep of His hand.

Today, if you will hear His voice:
8 "Do not harden your hearts, as in the rebellion,[a]
As *in* the day of trial[b] in the wilderness,
9 When your fathers tested Me;
They tried Me, though they saw My work.
10 For forty years I was grieved with *that* generation,
And said, 'It *is* a people who go astray in their hearts,
And they do not know My ways.'
11 So I swore in My wrath,
'They shall not enter My rest.' "

PSALM 96

A Song of Praise to God Coming in Judgment

1 Oh, sing to the LORD a new song!
Sing to the LORD, all the earth.
2 Sing to the LORD, bless His name;
Proclaim the good news of His salvation from day to day.
3 Declare His glory among the nations,
His wonders among all peoples.

4 For the LORD *is* great and greatly to be praised;
He *is* to be feared above all gods.
5 For all the gods of the peoples *are* idols,
But the LORD made the heavens.
6 Honor and majesty *are* before Him;
Strength and beauty *are* in His sanctuary.

7 Give to the LORD, O families of the peoples,
Give to the LORD glory and strength.
8 Give to the LORD the glory *due* His name;
Bring an offering, and come into His courts.
9 Oh, worship the LORD in the beauty of holiness!
Tremble before Him, all the earth.

10 Say among the nations, "The LORD reigns;
The world also is firmly established,
It shall not be moved;
He shall judge the peoples righteously."

11 Let the heavens rejoice, and let the earth be glad;
Let the sea roar, and all its fullness;
12 Let the field be joyful, and all that *is* in it.
Then all the trees of the woods will rejoice
13 before the LORD.
For He is coming, for He is coming to judge the earth.
He shall judge the world with righteousness,
And the peoples with His truth.

PSALM 97

A Song of Praise to the Sovereign LORD

1 The LORD reigns;
Let the earth rejoice;
Let the multitude of isles be glad!

95:8 [a] Or *Meribah* [b] Or *Massah*

2 Clouds and darkness surround
Him;
Righteousness and justice *are* the
foundation of His throne.
3 A fire goes before Him,
And burns up His enemies round
about.
4 His lightnings light the world;
The earth sees and trembles.
5 The mountains melt like wax at
the presence of the LORD,
At the presence of the Lord of the
whole earth.
6 The heavens declare His
righteousness,
And all the peoples see His glory.

7 Let all be put to shame who serve
carved images,
Who boast of idols.
Worship Him, all *you* gods.
8 Zion hears and is glad,
And the daughters of Judah rejoice
Because of Your judgments,
O LORD.
9 For You, LORD, *are* most high
above all the earth;
You are exalted far above all gods.

10 You who love the LORD, hate evil!
He preserves the souls of His
saints;
He delivers them out of the hand
of the wicked.
11 Light is sown for the righteous,
And gladness for the upright in
heart.
12 Rejoice in the LORD, you
righteous,
And give thanks at the
remembrance of His holy
name.[a]

PSALM 98

A Song of Praise to the LORD for His Salvation and Judgment

A Psalm.

1 Oh, sing to the LORD a new song!
For He has done marvelous
things;
His right hand and His holy arm
have gained Him the victory.
2 The LORD has made known His
salvation;
His righteousness He has
revealed in the sight of the
nations.
3 He has remembered His mercy
and His faithfulness to the
house of Israel;
All the ends of the earth have seen
the salvation of our God.

4 Shout joyfully to the LORD, all the
earth;
Break forth in song, rejoice, and
sing praises.
5 Sing to the LORD with the harp,
With the harp and the sound of a
psalm,
6 With trumpets and the sound of a
horn;
Shout joyfully before the LORD,
the King.

7 Let the sea roar, and all its
fullness,
The world and those who dwell in it;
8 Let the rivers clap *their* hands;
Let the hills be joyful together
9 before the LORD,
For He is coming to judge the
earth.
With righteousness He shall judge
the world,
And the peoples with equity.

PSALM 99

Praise to the LORD for His Holiness

1 The LORD reigns;
Let the peoples tremble!
He dwells *between* the cherubim;
Let the earth be moved!
2 The LORD *is* great in Zion,
And He *is* high above all the
peoples.
3 Let them praise Your great and
awesome name—
He *is* holy.

4 The King's strength also loves
justice;
You have established equity;
You have executed justice and
righteousness in Jacob.

97:12 [a] Or *His holiness*

5 Exalt the LORD our God,
And worship at His footstool—
He *is* holy.

6 Moses and Aaron were among His priests,
And Samuel was among those who called upon His name;
They called upon the LORD, and He answered them.
7 He spoke to them in the cloudy pillar;
They kept His testimonies
and the ordinance He gave them.

8 You answered them, O LORD our God;
You were to them God-Who-Forgives,
Though You took vengeance on their deeds.
9 Exalt the LORD our God,
And worship at His holy hill;
For the LORD our God
is holy.

PSALM 100

A Song of Praise for the LORD's Faithfulness to His People

A Psalm of Thanksgiving.

1 Make a joyful shout to the LORD, all you lands!
2 Serve the LORD with gladness;
Come before His presence with singing.
3 Know that the LORD, He
is God;
It is He *who* has made us, and not we ourselves;[a]
We are His people and the sheep of His pasture.

4 Enter into His gates with thanksgiving,
And into His courts with praise.
Be thankful to Him, *and* bless His name.
5 For the LORD *is* good;
His mercy *is* everlasting,
And His truth *endures* to all generations.

PSALM 101

Promised Faithfulness to the LORD

A Psalm of David.

1 I will sing of mercy and justice;
To You, O LORD, I will sing praises.

2 I will behave wisely in a perfect way.
Oh, when will You come to me?
I will walk within my house with a perfect heart.

3 I will set nothing wicked before my eyes;
I hate the work of those who fall away;
It shall not cling to me.
4 A perverse heart shall depart from me;
I will not know wickedness.

5 Whoever secretly slanders his neighbor,
Him I will destroy;
The one who has a haughty look and a proud heart,
Him I will not endure.

6 My eyes *shall be* on the faithful of the land,
That they may dwell with me;
He who walks in a perfect way,
He shall serve me.
7 He who works deceit shall not dwell within my house;
He who tells lies shall not continue in my presence.
8 Early I will destroy all the wicked of the land,
That I may cut off all the evildoers from the city of the LORD.

PSALM 102

The LORD's Eternal Love

A Prayer of the afflicted, when he is overwhelmed and pours out his complaint before the LORD.

1 Hear my prayer, O LORD,
And let my cry come to You.
2 Do not hide Your face from me in the day of my trouble;

100:3 a Following Kethib, Septuagint, and Vulgate; Qere, many Hebrew manuscripts, and Targum read *we are His*.

Incline Your ear to me;
In the day that I call, answer me speedily.

3 For my days are consumed like smoke,
And my bones are burned like a hearth.
4 My heart is stricken and withered like grass,
So that I forget to eat my bread.
5 Because of the sound of my groaning
My bones cling to my skin.
6 I am like a pelican of the wilderness;
I am like an owl of the desert.
7 I lie awake,
And am like a sparrow alone on the housetop.

8 My enemies reproach me all day long;
Those who deride me swear an oath against me.
9 For I have eaten ashes like bread,
And mingled my drink with weeping,
10 Because of Your indignation and Your wrath;
For You have lifted me up and cast me away.
11 My days *are* like a shadow that lengthens,
And I wither away like grass.

12 But You, O LORD, shall endure forever,
And the remembrance of Your name to all generations.
13 You will arise *and* have mercy on Zion;
For the time to favor her,
Yes, the set time, has come.
14 For Your servants take pleasure in her stones,
And show favor to her dust.
15 So the nations shall fear the name of the LORD,
And all the kings of the earth Your glory.
16 For the LORD shall build up Zion;
He shall appear in His glory.
17 He shall regard the prayer of the destitute,
And shall not despise their prayer.
18 This will be written for the generation to come,
That a people yet to be created may praise the LORD.
19 For He looked down from the height of His sanctuary;
From heaven the LORD viewed the earth,
20 To hear the groaning of the prisoner,
To release those appointed to death,
21 To declare the name of the LORD in Zion,
And His praise in Jerusalem,
22 When the peoples are gathered together,
And the kingdoms, to serve the LORD.

23 He weakened my strength in the way;
He shortened my days.
24 I said, "O my God,
Do not take me away in the midst of my days;
Your years *are* throughout all generations.
25 Of old You laid the foundation of the earth,
And the heavens *are* the work of Your hands.
26 They will perish, but You will endure;
Yes, they will all grow old like a garment;
Like a cloak You will change them,
And they will be changed.
27 But You *are* the same,
And Your years will have no end.
28 The children of Your servants will continue,
And their descendants will be established before You."

PSALM 103

Praise for the LORD's Mercies

A Psalm of David.

1 Bless the LORD, O my soul;
And all that is within me, *bless* His holy name!
2 Bless the LORD, O my soul,
And forget not all His benefits:
3 Who forgives all your iniquities,
Who heals all your diseases,

4 Who redeems your life from destruction,
Who crowns you with lovingkindness and tender mercies,
5 Who satisfies your mouth with good *things,*
So that your youth is renewed like the eagle's.

6 The LORD executes righteousness
And justice for all who are oppressed.
7 He made known His ways to Moses,
His acts to the children of Israel.
8 The LORD *is* merciful and gracious,
Slow to anger, and abounding in mercy.
9 He will not always strive *with us,*
Nor will He keep *His anger* forever.
10 He has not dealt with us according to our sins,
Nor punished us according to our iniquities.

11 For as the heavens are high above the earth,
So great is His mercy toward those who fear Him;
12 As far as the east is from the west,
So far has He removed our transgressions from us.
13 As a father pities *his* children,
So the LORD pities those who fear Him.
14 For He knows our frame;
He remembers that we *are* dust.
15 *As for* man, his days *are* like grass;
As a flower of the field, so he flourishes.
16 For the wind passes over it, and it is gone,
And its place remembers it no more.[a]
17 But the mercy of the LORD *is* from everlasting to everlasting
On those who fear Him,
And His righteousness to children's children,
18 To such as keep His covenant,
And to those who remember His commandments to do them.

19 The LORD has established His throne in heaven,
And His kingdom rules over all.

20 Bless the LORD, you His angels,
Who excel in strength, who do His word,
Heeding the voice of His word.
21 Bless the LORD, all *you* His hosts,
You ministers of His, who do His pleasure.
22 Bless the LORD, all His works,
In all places of His dominion.

Bless the LORD, O my soul!

PSALM 104

Praise to the Sovereign LORD for His Creation and Providence

1 Bless the LORD, O my soul!

O LORD my God, You are very great:
You are clothed with honor and majesty,
2 Who cover *Yourself* with light as *with* a garment,
Who stretch out the heavens like a curtain.

3 He lays the beams of His upper chambers in the waters,
Who makes the clouds His chariot,
Who walks on the wings of the wind,
4 Who makes His angels spirits,
His ministers a flame of fire.

5 *You who* laid the foundations of the earth,
So *that* it should not be moved forever,
6 You covered it with the deep as *with* a garment;
The waters stood above the mountains.
7 At Your rebuke they fled;
At the voice of Your thunder they hastened away.
8 They went up over the mountains;
They went down into the valleys,
To the place which You founded for them.

103:16 [a] Compare Job 7:10

9 You have set a boundary that
they may not pass over,
That they may not return to cover
the earth.

10 He sends the springs into the
valleys;
They flow among the hills.
11 They give drink to every beast of
the field;
The wild donkeys quench their
thirst.
12 By them the birds of the heavens
have their home;
They sing among the branches.
13 He waters the hills from His upper
chambers;
The earth is satisfied with the fruit
of Your works.

14 He causes the grass to grow for
the cattle,
And vegetation for the service of
man,
That he may bring forth food
from the earth,
15 And wine *that* makes glad the
heart of man,
Oil to make *his* face shine,
And bread *which* strengthens
man's heart.
16 The trees of the LORD are full *of
sap,*
The cedars of Lebanon which He
planted,
17 Where the birds make their nests;
The stork has her home in the fir
trees.
18 The high hills *are* for the wild
goats;
The cliffs are a refuge for the rock
badgers.[a]

19 He appointed the moon for
seasons;
The sun knows its going down.
20 You make darkness, and it is
night,
In which all the beasts of the
forest creep about.
21 The young lions roar after their
prey,
And seek their food from God.
22 *When* the sun rises, they gather
together
And lie down in their dens.
23 Man goes out to his work
And to his labor until the
evening.

24 O LORD, how manifold are Your
works!
In wisdom You have made them
all.
The earth is full of Your
possessions—
25 This great and wide sea,
In which *are* innumerable
teeming things,
Living things both small and
great.
26 There the ships sail about;
There is that Leviathan
Which You have made to play
there.

27 These all wait for You,
That You may give *them* their food
in due season.
28 *What* You give them they gather
in;
You open Your hand, they are
filled with good.
29 You hide Your face, they are
troubled;
You take away their breath,
they die and return to their
dust.
30 You send forth Your Spirit, they
are created;
And You renew the face of the
earth.

31 May the glory of the LORD endure
forever;
May the LORD rejoice in His
works.
32 He looks on the earth, and it
trembles;
He touches the hills, and they
smoke.

33 I will sing to the LORD as long as I
live;
I will sing praise to my God while
I have my being.

104:18 [a] Or *rock hyrax* (compare Leviticus 11:5)

34 May my meditation be sweet to
Him;
I will be glad in the LORD.
35 May sinners be consumed from
the earth,
And the wicked be no more.

Bless the LORD, O my soul!
Praise the LORD!

PSALM 105

The Eternal Faithfulness of the LORD

1 Oh, give thanks to the LORD!
Call upon His name;
Make known His deeds among
the peoples!
2 Sing to Him, sing psalms to Him;
Talk of all His wondrous works!
3 Glory in His holy name;
Let the hearts of those rejoice who
seek the LORD!
4 Seek the LORD and His strength;
Seek His face evermore!
5 Remember His marvelous works
which He has done,
His wonders, and the judgments
of His mouth,
6 O seed of Abraham His servant,
You children of Jacob, His chosen
ones!

7 He *is* the LORD our God;
His judgments *are* in all the earth.
8 He remembers His covenant
forever,
The word *which* He commanded,
for a thousand generations,
9 *The covenant* which He made with
Abraham,
And His oath to Isaac,
10 And confirmed it to Jacob for a
statute,
To Israel *as* an everlasting covenant,
11 Saying, "To you I will give the
land of Canaan
As the allotment of your
inheritance,"
12 When they were few in number,
Indeed very few, and strangers
in it.

13 When they went from one nation
to another,
From *one* kingdom to another
people,
14 He permitted no one to do them
wrong;
Yes, He rebuked kings for their
sakes,
15 *Saying,* "Do not touch My
anointed ones,
And do My prophets no harm."

16 Moreover He called for a famine
in the land;
He destroyed all the provision of
bread.
17 He sent a man before them—
Joseph—*who* was sold as a slave.
18 They hurt his feet with fetters,
He was laid in irons.
19 Until the time that his word came
to pass,
The word of the LORD tested him.
20 The king sent and released him,
The ruler of the people let him go
free.
21 He made him lord of his house,
And ruler of all his possessions,
22 To bind his princes at his pleasure,
And teach his elders wisdom.

23 Israel also came into Egypt,
And Jacob dwelt in the land of
Ham.
24 He increased His people greatly,
And made them stronger than
their enemies.
25 He turned their heart to hate His
people,
To deal craftily with His servants.

26 He sent Moses His servant,
And Aaron whom He had chosen.
27 They performed His signs among
them,
And wonders in the land of Ham.
28 He sent darkness, and made *it*
dark;
And they did not rebel against
His word.
29 He turned their waters into blood,
And killed their fish.
30 Their land abounded with frogs,
Even in the chambers of their kings.
31 He spoke, and there came swarms
of flies,
And lice in all their territory.
32 He gave them hail for rain,
And flaming fire in their land.

33 He struck their vines also, and
their fig trees,
And splintered the trees of their
territory.
34 He spoke, and locusts came,
Young locusts without number,
35 And ate up all the vegetation in
their land,
And devoured the fruit of their
ground.
36 He also destroyed all the firstborn
in their land,
The first of all their strength.

37 He also brought them out with
silver and gold,
And *there was* none feeble among
His tribes.
38 Egypt was glad when they departed,
For the fear of them had fallen
upon them.
39 He spread a cloud for a covering,
And fire to give light in the night.
40 *The people* asked, and He brought
quail,
And satisfied them with the bread
of heaven.
41 He opened the rock, and water
gushed out;
It ran in the dry places *like* a river.

42 For He remembered His holy
promise,
And Abraham His servant.
43 He brought out His people with joy,
His chosen ones with gladness.
44 He gave them the lands of the
Gentiles,
And they inherited the labor of
the nations,
45 That they might observe His
statutes
And keep His laws.

Praise the LORD!

PSALM 106

Joy in Forgiveness of Israel's Sins

1 Praise the LORD!

Oh, give thanks to the LORD, for
He is good!
For His mercy *endures* forever.
2 Who can utter the mighty acts of
the LORD?
Who can declare all His praise?
3 Blessed *are* those who keep
justice,
And he who does[a] righteousness
at all times!

4 Remember me, O LORD, with the
favor *You have toward* Your
people.
Oh, visit me with Your salvation,
5 That I may see the benefit of Your
chosen ones,
That I may rejoice in the gladness
of Your nation,
That I may glory with Your
inheritance.

6 We have sinned with our fathers,
We have committed iniquity,
We have done wickedly.
7 Our fathers in Egypt did not
understand Your wonders;
They did not remember the
multitude of Your mercies,
But rebelled by the sea—the Red
Sea.

8 Nevertheless He saved them for
His name's sake,
That He might make His mighty
power known.
9 He rebuked the Red Sea also, and
it dried up;
So He led them through the depths,
As through the wilderness.
10 He saved them from the hand of
him who hated *them*,
And redeemed them from the
hand of the enemy.
11 The waters covered their enemies;
There was not one of them left.
12 Then they believed His words;
They sang His praise.

13 They soon forgot His works;
They did not wait for His counsel,
14 But lusted exceedingly in the
wilderness,
And tested God in the desert.
15 And He gave them their request,
But sent leanness into their soul.

106:3 [a] Septuagint, Syriac, Targum, and Vulgate read *those who do*.

16 When they envied Moses in the camp,
And Aaron the saint of the LORD,
17 The earth opened up and swallowed Dathan,
And covered the faction of Abiram.
18 A fire was kindled in their company;
The flame burned up the wicked.

19 They made a calf in Horeb,
And worshiped the molded image.
20 Thus they changed their glory
Into the image of an ox that eats grass.
21 They forgot God their Savior,
Who had done great things in Egypt,
22 Wondrous works in the land of Ham,
Awesome things by the Red Sea.
23 Therefore He said that He would destroy them,
Had not Moses His chosen one stood before Him in the breach,
To turn away His wrath, lest He destroy *them.*

24 Then they despised the pleasant land;
They did not believe His word,
25 But complained in their tents,
And did not heed the voice of the LORD.
26 Therefore He raised His hand *in an oath* against them,
To overthrow them in the wilderness,
27 To overthrow their descendants among the nations,
And to scatter them in the lands.

28 They joined themselves also to Baal of Peor,
And ate sacrifices made to the dead.
29 Thus they provoked *Him* to anger with their deeds,
And the plague broke out among them.
30 Then Phinehas stood up and intervened,
And the plague was stopped.
31 And that was accounted to him for righteousness
To all generations forevermore.

32 They angered *Him* also at the waters of strife,[a]
So that it went ill with Moses on account of them;
33 Because they rebelled against His Spirit,
So that he spoke rashly with his lips.

34 They did not destroy the peoples,
Concerning whom the LORD had commanded them,
35 But they mingled with the Gentiles
And learned their works;
36 They served their idols,
Which became a snare to them.
37 They even sacrificed their sons
And their daughters to demons,
38 And shed innocent blood,
The blood of their sons and daughters,
Whom they sacrificed to the idols of Canaan;
And the land was polluted with blood.
39 Thus they were defiled by their own works,
And played the harlot by their own deeds.

40 Therefore the wrath of the LORD was kindled against His people,
So that He abhorred His own inheritance.
41 And He gave them into the hand of the Gentiles,
And those who hated them ruled over them.
42 Their enemies also oppressed them,
And they were brought into subjection under their hand.
43 Many times He delivered them;
But they rebelled in their counsel,
And were brought low for their iniquity.

44 Nevertheless He regarded their affliction,
When He heard their cry;

106:32 [a] Or *Meribah*

45 And for their sake He
remembered His covenant,
And relented according to the
multitude of His mercies.
46 He also made them to be pitied
By all those who carried them
away captive.

47 Save us, O LORD our God,
And gather us from among the
Gentiles,
To give thanks to Your holy name,
To triumph in Your praise.

48 Blessed *be* the LORD God of Israel
From everlasting to everlasting!
And let all the people say, "Amen!"

Praise the LORD!

BOOK FIVE
Psalms 107–150

PSALM 107
Thanksgiving to the LORD for His Great Works of Deliverance

1 Oh, give thanks to the LORD, for
He is good!
For His mercy *endures* forever.
2 Let the redeemed of the LORD
say *so,*
Whom He has redeemed from the
hand of the enemy,
3 And gathered out of the lands,
From the east and from the west,
From the north and from the south.

4 They wandered in the wilderness
in a desolate way;
They found no city to dwell in.
5 Hungry and thirsty,
Their soul fainted in them.
6 Then they cried out to the LORD in
their trouble,
And He delivered them out of
their distresses.
7 And He led them forth by the
right way,
That they might go to a city for a
dwelling place.
8 Oh, that *men* would give thanks to
the LORD *for* His goodness,
And *for* His wonderful works to
the children of men!
9 For He satisfies the longing soul,
And fills the hungry soul with
goodness.

10 Those who sat in darkness and in
the shadow of death,
Bound in affliction and irons—
11 Because they rebelled against the
words of God,
And despised the counsel of the
Most High,
12 Therefore He brought down their
heart with labor;
They fell down, and *there was*
none to help.
13 Then they cried out to the LORD in
their trouble,
And He saved them out of their
distresses.
14 He brought them out of darkness
and the shadow of death,
And broke their chains in pieces.
15 Oh, that *men* would give thanks
to the LORD *for* His
goodness,
And *for* His wonderful works to
the children of men!
16 For He has broken the gates of
bronze,
And cut the bars of iron in two.

17 Fools, because of their
transgression,
And because of their iniquities,
were afflicted.
18 Their soul abhorred all manner of
food,
And they drew near to the gates
of death.
19 Then they cried out to the LORD in
their trouble,
And He saved them out of their
distresses.
20 He sent His word and healed
them,
And delivered *them* from their
destructions.
21 Oh, that *men* would give thanks to
the LORD *for* His goodness,
And *for* His wonderful works to
the children of men!
22 Let them sacrifice the sacrifices of
thanksgiving,
And declare His works with
rejoicing.

23 Those who go down to the sea in ships,
Who do business on great waters,
24 They see the works of the LORD,
And His wonders in the deep.
25 For He commands and raises the stormy wind,
Which lifts up the waves of the sea.
26 They mount up to the heavens,
They go down again to the depths;
Their soul melts because of trouble.
27 They reel to and fro, and stagger like a drunken man,
And are at their wits' end.
28 Then they cry out to the LORD in their trouble,
And He brings them out of their distresses.
29 He calms the storm,
So that its waves are still.
30 Then they are glad because they are quiet;
So He guides them to their desired haven.
31 Oh, that *men* would give thanks to the LORD *for* His goodness,
And *for* His wonderful works to the children of men!
32 Let them exalt Him also in the assembly of the people,
And praise Him in the company of the elders.

33 He turns rivers into a wilderness,
And the watersprings into dry ground;
34 A fruitful land into barrenness,
For the wickedness of those who dwell in it.
35 He turns a wilderness into pools of water,
And dry land into watersprings.
36 There He makes the hungry dwell,
That they may establish a city for a dwelling place,
37 And sow fields and plant vineyards,
That they may yield a fruitful harvest.
38 He also blesses them, and they multiply greatly;
And He does not let their cattle decrease.
39 When they are diminished and brought low
Through oppression, affliction, and sorrow,
40 He pours contempt on princes,
And causes them to wander in the wilderness *where there is* no way;
41 Yet He sets the poor on high, far from affliction,
And makes *their* families like a flock.
42 The righteous see *it* and rejoice,
And all iniquity stops its mouth.

43 Whoever *is* wise will observe these *things*,
And they will understand the lovingkindness of the LORD.

PSALM 108

Assurance of God's Victory over Enemies

A Song. A Psalm of David.

1 O God, my heart is steadfast;
I will sing and give praise, even with my glory.
2 Awake, lute and harp!
I will awaken the dawn.
3 I will praise You, O LORD, among the peoples,
And I will sing praises to You among the nations.
4 For Your mercy *is* great above the heavens,
And Your truth *reaches* to the clouds.

5 Be exalted, O God, above the heavens,
And Your glory above all the earth;
6 That Your beloved may be delivered,
Save *with* Your right hand, and hear me.

7 God has spoken in His holiness:
"I will rejoice;
I will divide Shechem

And measure out the Valley of
Succoth.
8 Gilead *is* Mine; Manasseh *is* Mine;
Ephraim also *is* the helmet for My
head;
Judah *is* My lawgiver.
9 Moab *is* My washpot;
Over Edom I will cast My shoe;
Over Philistia I will triumph."

10 Who will bring me *into* the strong
city?
Who will lead me to Edom?
11 *Is it* not *You,* O God, *who* cast us
off?
And *You,* O God, *who* did not go
out with our armies?
12 Give us help from trouble,
For the help of man is useless.
13 Through God we will do valiantly,
For *it is* He *who* shall tread down
our enemies.[a]

PSALM 109

Plea for Judgment of False Accusers

To the Chief Musician. A Psalm of David.

1 Do not keep silent,
O God of my praise!
2 For the mouth of the wicked and
the mouth of the deceitful
Have opened against me;
They have spoken against me
with a lying tongue.
3 They have also surrounded me
with words of hatred,
And fought against me without a
cause.
4 In return for my love they are my
accusers,
But I *give myself to* prayer.
5 Thus they have rewarded me evil
for good,
And hatred for my love.

6 Set a wicked man over him,
And let an accuser[a] stand at his
right hand.
7 When he is judged, let him be
found guilty,
And let his prayer become sin.
8 Let his days be few,
And let another take his office.
9 Let his children be fatherless,
And his wife a widow.
10 Let his children continually be
vagabonds, and beg;
Let them seek *their bread*[a] also
from their desolate places.
11 Let the creditor seize all that he
has,
And let strangers plunder his
labor.
12 Let there be none to extend mercy
to him,
Nor let there be any to favor his
fatherless children.
13 Let his posterity be cut off,
And in the generation following
let their name be blotted out.

14 Let the iniquity of his fathers be
remembered before the LORD,
And let not the sin of his mother
be blotted out.
15 Let them be continually before
the LORD,
That He may cut off the memory
of them from the earth;
16 Because he did not remember to
show mercy,
But persecuted the poor and
needy man,
That he might even slay the
broken in heart.
17 As he loved cursing, so let it come
to him;
As he did not delight in blessing,
so let it be far from him.
18 As he clothed himself with
cursing as with his garment,
So let it enter his body like water,
And like oil into his bones.
19 Let it be to him like the garment
which covers him,
And for a belt with which he girds
himself continually.
20 *Let this be* the LORD's reward to
my accusers,
And to those who speak evil
against my person.

21 But You, O GOD the Lord,
Deal with me for Your name's sake;
Because Your mercy *is* good,
deliver me.

108:13 [a] Compare verses 6–13 with 60:5–12 **109:6** [a] Hebrew *satan* **109:10** [a] Following Masoretic Text and Targum; Septuagint and Vulgate read *be cast out.*

22 For I *am* poor and needy,
And my heart is wounded within me.
23 I am gone like a shadow when it lengthens;
I am shaken off like a locust.
24 My knees are weak through fasting,
And my flesh is feeble from lack of fatness.
25 I also have become a reproach to them;
When they look at me, they shake their heads.

26 Help me, O LORD my God!
Oh, save me according to Your mercy,
27 That they may know that this *is* Your hand—
That You, LORD, have done it!
28 Let them curse, but You bless;
When they arise, let them be ashamed,
But let Your servant rejoice.
29 Let my accusers be clothed with shame,
And let them cover themselves with their own disgrace as with a mantle.

30 I will greatly praise the LORD with my mouth;
Yes, I will praise Him among the multitude.
31 For He shall stand at the right hand of the poor,
To save *him* from those who condemn him.

PSALM 110

Announcement of the Messiah's Reign

A Psalm of David.

1 The LORD said to my Lord,
"Sit at My right hand,
Till I make Your enemies Your footstool."
2 The LORD shall send the rod of Your strength out of Zion.
Rule in the midst of Your enemies!

3 Your people *shall be* volunteers
In the day of Your power;
In the beauties of holiness, from the womb of the morning,
You have the dew of Your youth.
4 The LORD has sworn
And will not relent,
"You *are* a priest forever
According to the order of Melchizedek."

5 The Lord *is* at Your right hand;
He shall execute kings in the day of His wrath.
6 He shall judge among the nations,
He shall fill *the places* with dead bodies,
He shall execute the heads of many countries.
7 He shall drink of the brook by the wayside;
Therefore He shall lift up the head.

PSALM 111

Praise to God for His Faithfulness and Justice

1 Praise the LORD!

I will praise the LORD with *my* whole heart,
In the assembly of the upright and *in* the congregation.

2 The works of the LORD *are* great,
Studied by all who have pleasure in them.
3 His work *is* honorable and glorious,
And His righteousness endures forever.
4 He has made His wonderful works to be remembered;
The LORD *is* gracious and full of compassion.
5 He has given food to those who fear Him;
He will ever be mindful of His covenant.
6 He has declared to His people the power of His works,
In giving them the heritage of the nations.

7 The works of His hands *are* verity and justice;
All His precepts *are* sure.

GOD SIN JESUS SALVATION LOVE

8 They stand fast forever and ever,
And are done in truth and uprightness.
9 He has sent redemption to His people;
He has commanded His covenant forever:
Holy and awesome *is* His name.

10 The fear of the LORD *is* the beginning of wisdom;
A good understanding have all those who do *His commandments.*
His praise endures forever.

PSALM 112

The Blessed State of the Righteous

1 Praise the LORD!

Blessed *is* the man *who* fears the LORD,
Who delights greatly in His commandments.

2 His descendants will be mighty on earth;
The generation of the upright will be blessed.
3 Wealth and riches *will be* in his house,
And his righteousness endures forever.
4 Unto the upright there arises light in the darkness;
He is gracious, and full of compassion, and righteous.
5 A good man deals graciously and lends;
He will guide his affairs with discretion.
6 Surely he will never be shaken;
The righteous will be in everlasting remembrance.
7 He will not be afraid of evil tidings;
His heart is steadfast, trusting in the LORD.
8 His heart *is* established;
He will not be afraid,
Until he sees *his desire* upon his enemies.

9 He has dispersed abroad,
He has given to the poor;
His righteousness endures forever;
His horn will be exalted with honor.
10 The wicked will see *it* and be grieved;
He will gnash his teeth and melt away;
The desire of the wicked shall perish.

PSALM 113

The Majesty and Condescension of God

1 Praise the LORD!

Praise, O servants of the LORD,
Praise the name of the LORD!
2 Blessed be the name of the LORD
From this time forth and forevermore!
3 From the rising of the sun to its going down
The LORD's name *is* to be praised.

4 The LORD *is* high above all nations,
His glory above the heavens.
5 Who *is* like the LORD our God,
Who dwells on high,
6 Who humbles Himself to behold
The things that are in the heavens and in the earth?

7 He raises the poor out of the dust,
And lifts the needy out of the ash heap,
8 That He may seat *him* with princes—
With the princes of His people.
9 He grants the barren woman a home,
Like a joyful mother of children.

Praise the LORD!

PSALM 114

The Power of God in His Deliverance of Israel

1 When Israel went out of Egypt,
The house of Jacob from a people of strange language,
2 Judah became His sanctuary,
And Israel His dominion.

3 The sea saw *it* and fled;
Jordan turned back.
4 The mountains skipped like rams,
The little hills like lambs.

5 What ails you, O sea, that you fled?
O Jordan, *that* you turned back?
6 O mountains, *that* you skipped like rams?
O little hills, like lambs?

7 Tremble, O earth, at the presence of the Lord,
At the presence of the God of Jacob,
8 Who turned the rock *into* a pool of water,
The flint into a fountain of waters.

PSALM 115

The Futility of Idols and the Trustworthiness of God

1 Not unto us, O LORD, not unto us,
But to Your name give glory,
Because of Your mercy,
Because of Your truth.
2 Why should the Gentiles say,
"So where *is* their God?"

3 But our God *is* in heaven;
He does whatever He pleases.
4 Their idols *are* silver and gold,
The work of men's hands.
5 They have mouths, but they do not speak;
Eyes they have, but they do not see;
6 They have ears, but they do not hear;
Noses they have, but they do not smell;
7 They have hands, but they do not handle;
Feet they have, but they do not walk;
Nor do they mutter through their throat.
8 Those who make them are like them;
So is everyone who trusts in them.

9 O Israel, trust in the LORD;
He *is* their help and their shield.
10 O house of Aaron, trust in the LORD;
He *is* their help and their shield.
11 You who fear the LORD, trust in the LORD;
He *is* their help and their shield.

12 The LORD has been mindful of *us;*
He will bless us;
He will bless the house of Israel;
He will bless the house of Aaron.
13 He will bless those who fear the LORD,
Both small and great.

14 May the LORD give you increase more and more,
You and your children.
15 *May* you *be* blessed by the LORD,
Who made heaven and earth.

16 The heaven, *even* the heavens, *are* the LORD's;
But the earth He has given to the children of men.
17 The dead do not praise the LORD,
Nor any who go down into silence.
18 But we will bless the LORD
From this time forth and forevermore.

Praise the LORD!

PSALM 116

Thanksgiving for Deliverance from Death

1 I love the LORD, because He has heard
My voice *and* my supplications.
2 Because He has inclined His ear to me,
Therefore I will call *upon Him* as long as I live.

3 The pains of death surrounded me,
And the pangs of Sheol laid hold of me;
I found trouble and sorrow.
4 Then I called upon the name of the LORD:
"O LORD, I implore You, deliver my soul!"

5 Gracious *is* the LORD, and righteous;
Yes, our God *is* merciful.
6 The LORD preserves the simple;
I was brought low, and He saved me.
7 Return to your rest, O my soul,
For the LORD has dealt bountifully with you.

8 For You have delivered my soul
from death,
My eyes from tears,
And my feet from falling.
9 I will walk before the LORD
In the land of the living.
10 I believed, therefore I spoke,
"I am greatly afflicted."
11 I said in my haste,
"All men *are* liars."

12 What shall I render to the
LORD
For all His benefits toward me?
13 I will take up the cup of
salvation,
And call upon the name of the
LORD.
14 I will pay my vows to the LORD
Now in the presence of all His
people.

15 Precious in the sight of the LORD
Is the death of His saints.

16 O LORD, truly I *am* Your servant;
I *am* Your servant, the son of Your
maidservant;
You have loosed my bonds.
17 I will offer to You the sacrifice of
thanksgiving,
And will call upon the name of
the LORD.

18 I will pay my vows to the LORD
Now in the presence of all His
people,
19 In the courts of the LORD's house,
In the midst of you, O Jerusalem.

Praise the LORD!

PSALM 117

Let All Peoples Praise the LORD

1 Praise the LORD, all you
Gentiles!
Laud Him, all you peoples!
2 For His merciful kindness is great
toward us,
And the truth of the LORD *endures*
forever.

Praise the LORD!

PSALM 118

Praise to God for His Everlasting Mercy

1 Oh, give thanks to the LORD, for
He is good!
For His mercy *endures* forever.

2 Let Israel now say,
"His mercy *endures* forever."
3 Let the house of Aaron now say,
"His mercy *endures* forever."
4 Let those who fear the LORD now
say,
"His mercy *endures* forever."

5 I called on the LORD in distress;
The LORD answered me *and set me*
in a broad place.
6 The LORD *is* on my side;
I will not fear.
What can man do to me?
7 The LORD is for me among those
who help me;
Therefore I shall see *my desire* on
those who hate me.
8 *It is* better to trust in the LORD
Than to put confidence in man.
9 *It is* better to trust in the LORD
Than to put confidence in princes.

10 All nations surrounded me,
But in the name of the LORD I will
destroy them.
11 They surrounded me,
Yes, they surrounded me;
But in the name of the LORD I will
destroy them.
12 They surrounded me like bees;
They were quenched like a fire of
thorns;
For in the name of the LORD I will
destroy them.
13 You pushed me violently, that I
might fall,
But the LORD helped me.
14 The LORD *is* my strength and song,
And He has become my
salvation.[a]

15 The voice of rejoicing and
salvation
Is in the tents of the righteous;
The right hand of the LORD does
valiantly.

118:14 [a] Compare Exodus 15:2

16 The right hand of the LORD is exalted;
The right hand of the LORD does valiantly.
17 I shall not die, but live,
And declare the works of the LORD.
18 The LORD has chastened me severely,
But He has not given me over to death.

19 Open to me the gates of righteousness;
I will go through them,
And I will praise the LORD.
20 This is the gate of the LORD,
Through which the righteous shall enter.

21 I will praise You,
For You have answered me,
And have become my salvation.

22 The stone *which* the builders rejected
Has become the chief cornerstone.
23 This was the LORD's doing;
It *is* marvelous in our eyes.
24 This *is* the day the LORD has made;
We will rejoice and be glad in it.

25 Save now, I pray, O LORD;
O LORD, I pray, send now prosperity.
26 Blessed *is* he who comes in the name of the LORD!
We have blessed you from the house of the LORD.
27 God *is* the LORD,
And He has given us light;
Bind the sacrifice with cords to the horns of the altar.
28 You *are* my God, and I will praise You;
You are my God, I will exalt You.

29 Oh, give thanks to the LORD, for *He is* good!
For His mercy *endures* forever.

PSALM 119

Meditations on the Excellencies of the Word of God

א ALEPH

1 Blessed *are* the undefiled in the way,
Who walk in the law of the LORD!
2 Blessed *are* those who keep His testimonies,
Who seek Him with the whole heart!
3 They also do no iniquity;
They walk in His ways.
4 You have commanded *us*
To keep Your precepts diligently.
5 Oh, that my ways were directed
To keep Your statutes!
6 Then I would not be ashamed,
When I look into all Your commandments.
7 I will praise You with uprightness of heart,
When I learn Your righteous judgments.
8 I will keep Your statutes;
Oh, do not forsake me utterly!

ב BETH

9 How can a young man cleanse his way?
By taking heed according to Your word.
10 With my whole heart I have sought You;
Oh, let me not wander from Your commandments!
11 Your word I have hidden in my heart,
That I might not sin against You.
12 Blessed *are* You, O LORD!
Teach me Your statutes.
13 With my lips I have declared
All the judgments of Your mouth.
14 I have rejoiced in the way of Your testimonies,
As *much as* in all riches.
15 I will meditate on Your precepts,
And contemplate Your ways.
16 I will delight myself in Your statutes;
I will not forget Your word.

ג GIMEL

17 Deal bountifully with Your servant,
That I may live and keep Your word.
18 Open my eyes, that I may see
Wondrous things from Your law.
19 I *am* a stranger in the earth;
Do not hide Your commandments from me.

20 My soul breaks with longing
For Your judgments at all times.
21 You rebuke the proud—the cursed,
Who stray from Your commandments.
22 Remove from me reproach and contempt,
For I have kept Your testimonies.
23 Princes also sit *and* speak against me,
But Your servant meditates on Your statutes.
24 Your testimonies also *are* my delight
And my counselors.

ד DALETH

25 My soul clings to the dust;
Revive me according to Your word.
26 I have declared my ways, and You answered me;
Teach me Your statutes.
27 Make me understand the way of Your precepts;
So shall I meditate on Your wonderful works.
28 My soul melts from heaviness;
Strengthen me according to Your word.
29 Remove from me the way of lying,
And grant me Your law graciously.
30 I have chosen the way of truth;
Your judgments I have laid *before me.*
31 I cling to Your testimonies;
O LORD, do not put me to shame!
32 I will run the course of Your commandments,
For You shall enlarge my heart.

ה HE

33 Teach me, O LORD, the way of Your statutes,
And I shall keep it *to* the end.
34 Give me understanding, and I shall keep Your law;
Indeed, I shall observe it with *my* whole heart.
35 Make me walk in the path of Your commandments,
For I delight in it.
36 Incline my heart to Your testimonies,
And not to covetousness.
37 Turn away my eyes from looking at worthless things,
And revive me in Your way.[a]
38 Establish Your word to Your servant,
Who *is devoted* to fearing You.
39 Turn away my reproach which I dread,
For Your judgments *are* good.
40 Behold, I long for Your precepts;
Revive me in Your righteousness.

ו WAW

41 Let Your mercies come also to me, O LORD—
Your salvation according to Your word.
42 So shall I have an answer for him who reproaches me,
For I trust in Your word.
43 And take not the word of truth utterly out of my mouth,
For I have hoped in Your ordinances.
44 So shall I keep Your law continually,
Forever and ever.
45 And I will walk at liberty,
For I seek Your precepts.
46 I will speak of Your testimonies also before kings,
And will not be ashamed.
47 And I will delight myself in Your commandments,
Which I love.
48 My hands also I will lift up to Your commandments,
Which I love,
And I will meditate on Your statutes.

ז ZAYIN

49 Remember the word to Your servant,
Upon which You have caused me to hope.
50 This *is* my comfort in my affliction,
For Your word has given me life.
51 The proud have me in great derision,
Yet I do not turn aside from Your law.

119:37 [a] Following Masoretic Text, Septuagint, and Vulgate; Targum reads *Your words.*

52 I remembered Your judgments of old, O LORD,
And have comforted myself.
53 Indignation has taken hold of me
Because of the wicked, who forsake Your law.
54 Your statutes have been my songs
In the house of my pilgrimage.
55 I remember Your name in the night, O LORD,
And I keep Your law.
56 This has become mine,
Because I kept Your precepts.

ח HETH

57 *You are* my portion, O LORD;
I have said that I would keep Your words.
58 I entreated Your favor with *my* whole heart;
Be merciful to me according to Your word.
59 I thought about my ways,
And turned my feet to Your testimonies.
60 I made haste, and did not delay
To keep Your commandments.
61 The cords of the wicked have bound me,
But I have not forgotten Your law.
62 At midnight I will rise to give thanks to You,
Because of Your righteous judgments.
63 I *am* a companion of all who fear You,
And of those who keep Your precepts.
64 The earth, O LORD, is full of Your mercy;
Teach me Your statutes.

ט TETH

65 You have dealt well with Your servant,
O LORD, according to Your word.
66 Teach me good judgment and knowledge,
For I believe Your commandments.
67 Before I was afflicted I went astray,
But now I keep Your word.
68 You *are* good, and do good;
Teach me Your statutes.
69 The proud have forged a lie against me,
But I will keep Your precepts with *my* whole heart.
70 Their heart is as fat as grease,
But I delight in Your law.
71 *It is* good for me that I have been afflicted,
That I may learn Your statutes.
72 The law of Your mouth *is* better to me
Than thousands of *coins of* gold and silver.

י YOD

73 Your hands have made me and fashioned me;
Give me understanding, that I may learn Your commandments.
74 Those who fear You will be glad when they see me,
Because I have hoped in Your word.
75 I know, O LORD, that Your judgments *are* right,
And *that* in faithfulness You have afflicted me.
76 Let, I pray, Your merciful kindness be for my comfort,
According to Your word to Your servant.
77 Let Your tender mercies come to me, that I may live;
For Your law *is* my delight.
78 Let the proud be ashamed,
For they treated me wrongfully with falsehood;
But I will meditate on Your precepts.
79 Let those who fear You turn to me,
Those who know Your testimonies.
80 Let my heart be blameless regarding Your statutes,
That I may not be ashamed.

כ KAPH

81 My soul faints for Your salvation,
But I hope in Your word.
82 My eyes fail *from searching* Your word,
Saying, "When will You comfort me?"
83 For I have become like a wineskin in smoke,
Yet I do not forget Your statutes.

84 How many *are* the days of Your servant?
When will You execute judgment on those who persecute me?
85 The proud have dug pits for me,
Which *is* not according to Your law.
86 All Your commandments *are* faithful;
They persecute me wrongfully;
Help me!
87 They almost made an end of me on earth,
But I did not forsake Your precepts.
88 Revive me according to Your lovingkindness,
So that I may keep the testimony of Your mouth.

ל LAMED

89 Forever, O LORD,
Your word is settled in heaven.
90 Your faithfulness *endures* to all generations;
You established the earth, and it abides.
91 They continue this day according to Your ordinances,
For all *are* Your servants.
92 Unless Your law *had been* my delight,
I would then have perished in my affliction.
93 I will never forget Your precepts,
For by them You have given me life.
94 I *am* Yours, save me;
For I have sought Your precepts.
95 The wicked wait for me to destroy me,
But I will consider Your testimonies.
96 I have seen the consummation of all perfection,
But Your commandment *is* exceedingly broad.

מ MEM

97 Oh, how I love Your law!
It *is* my meditation all the day.
98 You, through Your commandments, make me wiser than my enemies;
For they *are* ever with me.
99 I have more understanding than all my teachers,
For Your testimonies *are* my meditation.
100 I understand more than the ancients,
Because I keep Your precepts.
101 I have restrained my feet from every evil way,
That I may keep Your word.
102 I have not departed from Your judgments,
For You Yourself have taught me.
103 How sweet are Your words to my taste,
Sweeter than honey to my mouth!
104 Through Your precepts I get understanding;
Therefore I hate every false way.

נ NUN

105 Your word *is* a lamp to my feet
And a light to my path.
106 I have sworn and confirmed
That I will keep Your righteous judgments.
107 I am afflicted very much;
Revive me, O LORD, according to Your word.
108 Accept, I pray, the freewill offerings of my mouth, O LORD,
And teach me Your judgments.
109 My life *is* continually in my hand,
Yet I do not forget Your law.
110 The wicked have laid a snare for me,
Yet I have not strayed from Your precepts.
111 Your testimonies I have taken as a heritage forever,
For they *are* the rejoicing of my heart.
112 I have inclined my heart to perform Your statutes
Forever, to the very end.

ס SAMEK

113 I hate the double-minded,
But I love Your law.
114 You *are* my hiding place and my shield;
I hope in Your word.
115 Depart from me, you evildoers,
For I will keep the commandments of my God!

116 Uphold me according to Your
word, that I may live;
And do not let me be ashamed of
my hope.
117 Hold me up, and I shall be safe,
And I shall observe Your statutes
continually.
118 You reject all those who stray
from Your statutes,
For their deceit *is* falsehood.
119 You put away all the wicked of the
earth *like* dross;
Therefore I love Your testimonies.
120 My flesh trembles for fear of You,
And I am afraid of Your
judgments.

ע AYIN

121 I have done justice and
righteousness;
Do not leave me to my oppressors.
122 Be surety for Your servant for
good;
Do not let the proud oppress me.
123 My eyes fail *from seeking* Your
salvation
And Your righteous word.
124 Deal with Your servant according
to Your mercy,
And teach me Your statutes.
125 I *am* Your servant;
Give me understanding,
That I may know Your
testimonies.
126 *It is* time for *You* to act, O LORD,
For they have regarded Your law
as void.
127 Therefore I love Your
commandments
More than gold, yes, than fine gold!
128 Therefore all *Your* precepts
concerning all *things*
I consider *to be* right;
I hate every false way.

פ PE

129 Your testimonies are wonderful;
Therefore my soul keeps them.
130 The entrance of Your words gives
light;
It gives understanding to the
simple.
131 I opened my mouth and panted,
For I longed for Your
commandments.
132 Look upon me and be merciful to me,
As Your custom *is* toward those
who love Your name.
133 Direct my steps by Your word,
And let no iniquity have
dominion over me.
134 Redeem me from the oppression
of man,
That I may keep Your precepts.
135 Make Your face shine upon Your
servant,
And teach me Your statutes.
136 Rivers of water run down from
my eyes,
Because *men* do not keep Your law.

צ TSADDE

137 Righteous *are* You, O LORD,
And upright *are* Your judgments.
138 Your testimonies, *which* You have
commanded,
Are righteous and very faithful.
139 My zeal has consumed me,
Because my enemies have
forgotten Your words.
140 Your word *is* very pure;
Therefore Your servant loves it.
141 I *am* small and despised,
Yet I do not forget Your precepts.
142 Your righteousness *is* an
everlasting righteousness,
And Your law *is* truth.
143 Trouble and anguish have
overtaken me,
Yet Your commandments *are* my
delights.
144 The righteousness of Your
testimonies *is* everlasting;
Give me understanding, and I
shall live.

ק QOPH

145 I cry out with *my* whole heart;
Hear me, O LORD!
I will keep Your statutes.
146 I cry out to You;
Save me, and I will keep Your
testimonies.
147 I rise before the dawning of the
morning,
And cry for help;
I hope in Your word.
148 My eyes are awake through the
night watches,
That I may meditate on Your word.

149 Hear my voice according to Your lovingkindness;
O LORD, revive me according to Your justice.
150 They draw near who follow after wickedness;
They are far from Your law.
151 You *are* near, O LORD,
And all Your commandments *are* truth.
152 Concerning Your testimonies,
I have known of old that You have founded them forever.

ר RESH

153 Consider my affliction and deliver me,
For I do not forget Your law.
154 Plead my cause and redeem me;
Revive me according to Your word.
155 Salvation *is* far from the wicked,
For they do not seek Your statutes.
156 Great *are* Your tender mercies, O LORD;
Revive me according to Your judgments.
157 Many *are* my persecutors and my enemies,
Yet I do not turn from Your testimonies.
158 I see the treacherous, and am disgusted,
Because they do not keep Your word.
159 Consider how I love Your precepts;
Revive me, O LORD, according to Your lovingkindness.
160 The entirety of Your word *is* truth,
And every one of Your righteous judgments *endures* forever.

ש SHIN

161 Princes persecute me without a cause,
But my heart stands in awe of Your word.
162 I rejoice at Your word
As one who finds great treasure.
163 I hate and abhor lying,
But I love Your law.
164 Seven times a day I praise You,
Because of Your righteous judgments.
165 Great peace have those who love Your law,
And nothing causes them to stumble.
166 LORD, I hope for Your salvation,
And I do Your commandments.
167 My soul keeps Your testimonies,
And I love them exceedingly.
168 I keep Your precepts and Your testimonies,
For all my ways *are* before You.

ת TAU

169 Let my cry come before You, O LORD;
Give me understanding according to Your word.
170 Let my supplication come before You;
Deliver me according to Your word.
171 My lips shall utter praise,
For You teach me Your statutes.
172 My tongue shall speak of Your word,
For all Your commandments *are* righteousness.
173 Let Your hand become my help,
For I have chosen Your precepts.
174 I long for Your salvation, O LORD,
And Your law *is* my delight.
175 Let my soul live, and it shall praise You;
And let Your judgments help me.
176 I have gone astray like a lost sheep;
Seek Your servant,
For I do not forget Your commandments.

PSALM 120

Plea for Relief from Bitter Foes

A Song of Ascents.

1 In my distress I cried to the LORD,
And He heard me.
2 Deliver my soul, O LORD, from lying lips
And from a deceitful tongue.

3 What shall be given to you,
Or what shall be done to you,
You false tongue?
4 Sharp arrows of the warrior,
With coals of the broom tree!

5 Woe is me, that I dwell in Meshech,
That I dwell among the tents of Kedar!
6 My soul has dwelt too long
With one who hates peace.
7 I *am for* peace;
But when I speak, they *are* for war.

PSALM 121

God the Help of Those Who Seek Him

A Song of Ascents.

1 I will lift up my eyes to the hills—
From whence comes my help?
2 My help *comes* from the LORD,
Who made heaven and earth.

3 He will not allow your foot to be moved;
He who keeps you will not slumber.
4 Behold, He who keeps Israel
Shall neither slumber nor sleep.

5 The LORD *is* your keeper;
The LORD *is* your shade at your right hand.
6 The sun shall not strike you by day,
Nor the moon by night.

7 The LORD shall preserve you from all evil;
He shall preserve your soul.
8 The LORD shall preserve your going out and your coming in
From this time forth, and even forevermore.

PSALM 122

The Joy of Going to the House of the LORD

A Song of Ascents. Of David.

1 I was glad when they said to me,
"Let us go into the house of the LORD."
2 Our feet have been standing
Within your gates, O Jerusalem!

3 Jerusalem is built
As a city that is compact together,
4 Where the tribes go up,
The tribes of the LORD,
To the Testimony of Israel,
To give thanks to the name of the LORD.
5 For thrones are set there for judgment,
The thrones of the house of David.

6 Pray for the peace of Jerusalem:
"May they prosper who love you.
7 Peace be within your walls,
Prosperity within your palaces."
8 For the sake of my brethren and companions,
I will now say, "Peace *be* within you."
9 Because of the house of the LORD our God
I will seek your good.

PSALM 123

Prayer for Relief from Contempt

A Song of Ascents.

1 Unto You I lift up my eyes,
O You who dwell in the heavens.
2 Behold, as the eyes of servants *look* to the hand of their masters,
As the eyes of a maid to the hand of her mistress,
So our eyes *look* to the LORD our God,
Until He has mercy on us.

3 Have mercy on us, O LORD, have mercy on us!
For we are exceedingly filled with contempt.
4 Our soul is exceedingly filled
With the scorn of those who are at ease,
With the contempt of the proud.

PSALM 124

The LORD the Defense of His People

A Song of Ascents. Of David.

1 "If it had not been the LORD who was on our side,"
Let Israel now say—
2 "If it had not been the LORD who was on our side,
When men rose up against us,
3 Then they would have swallowed us alive,

When their wrath was kindled
against us;
4 Then the waters would have
overwhelmed us,
The stream would have gone over
our soul;
5 Then the swollen waters
Would have gone over our soul."

6 Blessed *be* the LORD,
Who has not given us *as* prey to
their teeth.
7 Our soul has escaped as a bird
from the snare of the
fowlers;[a]
The snare is broken, and we have
escaped.
8 Our help *is* in the name of the
LORD,
Who made heaven and earth.

PSALM 125

The LORD the Strength of His People

A Song of Ascents.

1 Those who trust in the LORD
Are like Mount Zion,
Which cannot be moved, *but*
abides forever.
2 As the mountains surround
Jerusalem,
So the LORD surrounds His
people
From this time forth and forever.

3 For the scepter of wickedness
shall not rest
On the land allotted to the
righteous,
Lest the righteous reach out their
hands to iniquity.

4 Do good, O LORD, to *those who are*
good,
And to *those who are* upright in
their hearts.
5 As for such as turn aside to their
crooked ways,
The LORD shall lead them away
With the workers of iniquity.

Peace *be* upon Israel!

PSALM 126

A Joyful Return to Zion

A Song of Ascents.

1 When the LORD brought back the
captivity of Zion,
We were like those who dream.
2 Then our mouth was filled with
laughter,
And our tongue with singing.
Then they said among the nations,
"The LORD has done great things
for them."
3 The LORD has done great things
for us,
And we are glad.

4 Bring back our captivity, O LORD,
As the streams in the South.

5 Those who sow in tears
Shall reap in joy.
6 He who continually goes forth
weeping,
Bearing seed for sowing,
Shall doubtless come again with
rejoicing,
Bringing his sheaves *with him.*

PSALM 127

Laboring and Prospering with the LORD

A Song of Ascents. Of Solomon.

1 Unless the LORD builds the house,
They labor in vain who build it;
Unless the LORD guards the city,
The watchman stays awake in vain.
2 *It is* vain for you to rise up early,
To sit up late,
To eat the bread of sorrows;
For so He gives His beloved sleep.

3 Behold, children *are* a heritage
from the LORD,
The fruit of the womb *is* a reward.
4 Like arrows in the hand of a
warrior,
So *are* the children of one's youth.
5 Happy *is* the man who has his
quiver full of them;
They shall not be ashamed,
But shall speak with their
enemies in the gate.

124:7 [a] That is, persons who catch birds in a trap or snare

PSALM 128
Blessings of Those Who Fear the LORD

A Song of Ascents.

1 Blessed *is* every one who fears the LORD,
Who walks in His ways.

2 When you eat the labor of your hands,
You *shall be* happy, and *it shall be* well with you.
3 Your wife *shall be* like a fruitful vine
In the very heart of your house,
Your children like olive plants
All around your table.
4 Behold, thus shall the man be blessed
Who fears the LORD.

5 The LORD bless you out of Zion,
And may you see the good of Jerusalem
All the days of your life.
6 Yes, may you see your children's children.

Peace *be* upon Israel!

PSALM 129
Song of Victory over Zion's Enemies

A Song of Ascents.

1 "Many a time they have afflicted me from my youth,"
Let Israel now say—
2 "Many a time they have afflicted me from my youth;
Yet they have not prevailed against me.
3 The plowers plowed on my back;
They made their furrows long."
4 The LORD *is* righteous;
He has cut in pieces the cords of the wicked.

5 Let all those who hate Zion
Be put to shame and turned back.
6 Let them be as the grass *on* the housetops,
Which withers before it grows up,
7 With which the reaper does not fill his hand,
Nor he who binds sheaves, his arms.
8 Neither let those who pass by them say,
"The blessing of the LORD *be* upon you;
We bless you in the name of the LORD!"

PSALM 130
Waiting for the Redemption of the LORD

A Song of Ascents.

1 Out of the depths I have cried to You, O LORD;
2 Lord, hear my voice!
Let Your ears be attentive
To the voice of my supplications.

3 If You, LORD, should mark iniquities,
O Lord, who could stand?
4 But *there is* forgiveness with You,
That You may be feared.

5 I wait for the LORD, my soul waits,
And in His word I do hope.
6 My soul *waits* for the Lord
More than those who watch for the morning—
Yes, more than those who watch for the morning.

7 O Israel, hope in the LORD;
For with the LORD *there is* mercy,
And with Him *is* abundant redemption.
8 And He shall redeem Israel
From all his iniquities.

PSALM 131
Simple Trust in the LORD

A Song of Ascents. Of David.

1 LORD, my heart is not haughty,
Nor my eyes lofty.
Neither do I concern myself with great matters,
Nor with things too profound for me.

2 Surely I have calmed and quieted my soul,
Like a weaned child with his mother;
Like a weaned child *is* my soul within me.

3 O Israel, hope in the LORD
From this time forth and forever.

PSALM 132

The Eternal Dwelling of God in Zion

A Song of Ascents.

1 LORD, remember David
And all his afflictions;
2 How he swore to the LORD,
And vowed to the Mighty One of Jacob:
3 "Surely I will not go into the chamber of my house,
Or go up to the comfort of my bed;
4 I will not give sleep to my eyes
Or slumber to my eyelids,
5 Until I find a place for the LORD,
A dwelling place for the Mighty One of Jacob."

6 Behold, we heard of it in Ephrathah;
We found it in the fields of the woods.[a]
7 Let us go into His tabernacle;
Let us worship at His footstool.
8 Arise, O LORD, to Your resting place,
You and the ark of Your strength.
9 Let Your priests be clothed with righteousness,
And let Your saints shout for joy.

10 For Your servant David's sake,
Do not turn away the face of Your Anointed.

11 The LORD has sworn *in* truth to David;
He will not turn from it:
"I will set upon your throne the fruit of your body.
12 If your sons will keep My covenant
And My testimony which I shall teach them,
Their sons also shall sit upon your throne forevermore."

13 For the LORD has chosen Zion;
He has desired *it* for His dwelling place:
14 "This *is* My resting place forever;
Here I will dwell, for I have desired it.
15 I will abundantly bless her provision;
I will satisfy her poor with bread.
16 I will also clothe her priests with salvation,
And her saints shall shout aloud for joy.
17 There I will make the horn of David grow;
I will prepare a lamp for My Anointed.
18 His enemies I will clothe with shame,
But upon Himself His crown shall flourish."

PSALM 133

Blessed Unity of the People of God

A Song of Ascents. Of David.

1 Behold, how good and how pleasant *it is*
For brethren to dwell together in unity!

2 *It is* like the precious oil upon the head,
Running down on the beard,
The beard of Aaron,
Running down on the edge of his garments.
3 *It is* like the dew of Hermon,
Descending upon the mountains of Zion;
For there the LORD commanded the blessing—
Life forevermore.

PSALM 134

Praising the LORD in His House at Night

A Song of Ascents.

1 Behold, bless the LORD,
All *you* servants of the LORD,
Who by night stand in the house of the LORD!
2 Lift up your hands *in* the sanctuary,
And bless the LORD.

3 The LORD who made heaven and earth
Bless you from Zion!

132:6 [a] Hebrew *Jaar*

PSALM 135

Praise to God in Creation and Redemption

1 Praise the LORD!

Praise the name of the LORD;
Praise *Him,* O you servants of the LORD!
2 You who stand in the house of the LORD,
In the courts of the house of our God,
3 Praise the LORD, for the LORD *is* good;
Sing praises to His name, for *it is* pleasant.
4 For the LORD has chosen Jacob for Himself,
Israel for His special treasure.

5 For I know that the LORD *is* great,
And our Lord *is* above all gods.
6 Whatever the LORD pleases He does,
In heaven and in earth,
In the seas and in all deep places.
7 He causes the vapors to ascend from the ends of the earth;
He makes lightning for the rain;
He brings the wind out of His treasuries.

8 He destroyed the firstborn of Egypt,
Both of man and beast.
9 He sent signs and wonders into the midst of you, O Egypt,
Upon Pharaoh and all his servants.
10 He defeated many nations
And slew mighty kings—
11 Sihon king of the Amorites,
Og king of Bashan,
And all the kingdoms of Canaan—
12 And gave their land *as* a heritage,
A heritage to Israel His people.

13 Your name, O LORD, *endures* forever,
Your fame, O LORD, throughout all generations.
14 For the LORD will judge His people,
And He will have compassion on His servants.

15 The idols of the nations *are* silver and gold,
The work of men's hands.
16 They have mouths, but they do not speak;
Eyes they have, but they do not see;
17 They have ears, but they do not hear;
Nor is there *any* breath in their mouths.
18 Those who make them are like them;
So is everyone who trusts in them.

19 Bless the LORD, O house of Israel!
Bless the LORD, O house of Aaron!
20 Bless the LORD, O house of Levi!
You who fear the LORD, bless the LORD!
21 Blessed be the LORD out of Zion,
Who dwells in Jerusalem!

Praise the LORD!

PSALM 136

Thanksgiving to God for His Enduring Mercy

1 Oh, give thanks to the LORD, for *He is* good!
For His mercy *endures* forever.
2 Oh, give thanks to the God of gods!
For His mercy *endures* forever.
3 Oh, give thanks to the Lord of lords!
For His mercy *endures* forever:

4 To Him who alone does great wonders,
For His mercy *endures* forever;
5 To Him who by wisdom made the heavens,
For His mercy *endures* forever;
6 To Him who laid out the earth above the waters,
For His mercy *endures* forever;
7 To Him who made great lights,
For His mercy *endures* forever—
8 The sun to rule by day,
For His mercy *endures* forever;
9 The moon and stars to rule by night,
For His mercy *endures* forever.

10 To Him who struck Egypt in their
firstborn,
For His mercy *endures* forever;
11 And brought out Israel from
among them,
For His mercy *endures* forever;
12 With a strong hand, and with an
outstretched arm,
For His mercy *endures* forever;
13 To Him who divided the Red Sea
in two,
For His mercy *endures* forever;
14 And made Israel pass through the
midst of it,
For His mercy *endures* forever;
15 But overthrew Pharaoh and his
army in the Red Sea,
For His mercy *endures* forever;
16 To Him who led His people
through the wilderness,
For His mercy *endures* forever;
17 To Him who struck down great
kings,
For His mercy *endures* forever;
18 And slew famous kings,
For His mercy *endures*
forever—
19 Sihon king of the Amorites,
For His mercy *endures* forever;
20 And Og king of Bashan,
For His mercy *endures* forever—
21 And gave their land as a heritage,
For His mercy *endures* forever;
22 A heritage to Israel His servant,
For His mercy *endures* forever.

23 Who remembered us in our lowly
state,
For His mercy *endures* forever;
24 And rescued us from our enemies,
For His mercy *endures* forever;
25 Who gives food to all flesh,
For His mercy *endures* forever.

26 Oh, give thanks to the God of
heaven!
For His mercy *endures* forever.

PSALM 137

Longing for Zion in a Foreign Land

1 By the rivers of Babylon,
There we sat down, yea, we wept
When we remembered Zion.
2 We hung our harps
Upon the willows in the midst of it.
3 For there those who carried us away
captive asked of us a song,
And those who plundered us
requested mirth,
Saying, "Sing us *one* of the songs
of Zion!"

4 How shall we sing the LORD's song
In a foreign land?
5 If I forget you, O Jerusalem,
Let my right hand forget *its skill!*
6 If I do not remember you,
Let my tongue cling to the roof of
my mouth—
If I do not exalt Jerusalem
Above my chief joy.

7 Remember, O LORD, against the
sons of Edom
The day of Jerusalem,
Who said, "Raze *it,* raze *it,*
To its very foundation!"

8 O daughter of Babylon, who are
to be destroyed,
Happy the one who repays you as
you have served us!
9 Happy the one who takes and
dashes
Your little ones against the rock!

PSALM 138

The LORD's Goodness to the Faithful

A Psalm *of David.*

1 I will praise You with my whole
heart;
Before the gods I will sing praises
to You.
2 I will worship toward Your holy
temple,
And praise Your name
For Your lovingkindness and Your
truth;
For You have magnified Your
word above all Your name.
3 In the day when I cried out, You
answered me,
And made me bold *with* strength
in my soul.

4 All the kings of the earth shall
praise You, O LORD,
When they hear the words of Your
mouth.

5 Yes, they shall sing of the ways of
the LORD,
For great *is* the glory of the LORD.
6 Though the LORD *is* on high,
Yet He regards the lowly;
But the proud He knows from
afar.

7 Though I walk in the midst of
trouble, You will revive me;
You will stretch out Your hand
Against the wrath of my enemies,
And Your right hand will save me.
8 The LORD will perfect *that which*
concerns me;
Your mercy, O LORD, *endures*
forever;
Do not forsake the works of Your
hands.

PSALM 139

God's Perfect Knowledge of Man

For the Chief Musician. A Psalm of David.

1 O LORD, You have searched me
and known *me.*
2 You know my sitting down and
my rising up;
You understand my thought afar
off.
3 You comprehend my path and
my lying down,
And are acquainted with all my
ways.
4 For *there is* not a word on my
tongue,
But behold, O LORD, You know it
altogether.
5 You have hedged me behind and
before,
And laid Your hand upon me.
6 *Such* knowledge *is* too wonderful
for me;
It is high, I cannot *attain* it.

7 Where can I go from Your Spirit?
Or where can I flee from Your
presence?
8 If I ascend into heaven, You *are*
there;
If I make my bed in hell, behold,
You *are there.*
9 *If* I take the wings of the morning,
And dwell in the uttermost parts
of the sea,
10 Even there Your hand shall lead me,
And Your right hand shall hold me.
11 If I say, "Surely the darkness shall
fall[a] on me,"
Even the night shall be light
about me;
12 Indeed, the darkness shall not
hide from You,
But the night shines as the day;
The darkness and the light *are*
both alike *to You.*

13 For You formed my inward parts;
You covered me in my mother's
womb.
14 I will praise You, for I am fearfully
and wonderfully made;[a]
Marvelous are Your works,
And *that* my soul knows very well.
15 My frame was not hidden from
You,
When I was made in secret,
And skillfully wrought in the
lowest parts of the earth.
16 Your eyes saw my substance,
being yet unformed.
And in Your book they all were
written,
The days fashioned for me,
When *as yet there were* none of
them.

17 How precious also are Your
thoughts to me, O God!
How great is the sum of them!
18 *If* I should count them, they
would be more in number
than the sand;
When I awake, I am still with
You.

19 Oh, that You would slay the
wicked, O God!
Depart from me, therefore, you
bloodthirsty men.
20 For they speak against You
wickedly;
Your enemies take *Your name* in
vain.[a]

139:11 [a] Vulgate and Symmachus read *cover.* **139:14** [a] Following Masoretic Text and Targum; Septuagint, Syriac, and Vulgate read *You are fearfully wonderful.* **139:20** [a] Septuagint and Vulgate read *They take Your cities in vain.*

21 Do I not hate them, O LORD, who
hate You?
And do I not loathe those who rise
up against You?
22 I hate them with perfect hatred;
I count them my enemies.

23 Search me, O God, and know my
heart;
Try me, and know my anxieties;
24 And see if *there is any* wicked way
in me,
And lead me in the way
everlasting.

PSALM 140

Prayer for Deliverance from Evil Men

To the Chief Musician.
A Psalm of David.

1 Deliver me, O LORD, from evil
men;
Preserve me from violent men,
2 Who plan evil things in *their*
hearts;
They continually gather together
for war.
3 They sharpen their tongues like a
serpent;
The poison of asps *is* under their
lips. *Selah*

4 Keep me, O LORD, from the hands
of the wicked;
Preserve me from violent men,
Who have purposed to make my
steps stumble.
5 The proud have hidden a snare
for me, and cords;
They have spread a net by the
wayside;
They have set traps for me. *Selah*

6 I said to the LORD: "You *are* my
God;
Hear the voice of my
supplications, O LORD.
7 O GOD the Lord, the strength of
my salvation,
You have covered my head in the
day of battle.
8 Do not grant, O LORD, the desires
of the wicked;
Do not further his *wicked* scheme,
Lest they be exalted. *Selah*

9 "*As for* the head of those who
surround me,
Let the evil of their lips cover them;
10 Let burning coals fall upon them;
Let them be cast into the fire,
Into deep pits, that they rise not
up again.
11 Let not a slanderer be established
in the earth;
Let evil hunt the violent man to
overthrow *him*."

12 I know that the LORD will maintain
The cause of the afflicted,
And justice for the poor.
13 Surely the righteous shall give
thanks to Your name;
The upright shall dwell in Your
presence.

PSALM 141

Prayer for Safekeeping from Wickedness

A Psalm of David.

1 LORD, I cry out to You;
Make haste to me!
Give ear to my voice when I cry
out to You.
2 Let my prayer be set before You
as incense,
The lifting up of my hands *as* the
evening sacrifice.

3 Set a guard, O LORD, over my
mouth;
Keep watch over the door of my
lips.
4 Do not incline my heart to any
evil thing,
To practice wicked works
With men who work iniquity;
And do not let me eat of their
delicacies.

5 Let the righteous strike me;
It shall be a kindness.
And let him rebuke me;
It shall be as excellent oil;
Let my head not refuse it.

For still my prayer *is* against the
deeds of the wicked.
6 Their judges are overthrown by
the sides of the cliff,

And they hear my words, for they are sweet.
7 Our bones are scattered at the mouth of the grave,
As when one plows and breaks up the earth.

8 But my eyes *are* upon You, O GOD the Lord;
In You I take refuge;
Do not leave my soul destitute.
9 Keep me from the snares they have laid for me,
And from the traps of the workers of iniquity.
10 Let the wicked fall into their own nets,
While I escape safely.

PSALM 142

A Plea for Relief from Persecutors

A Contemplation[a] of David. A Prayer when he was in the cave.

1 I cry out to the LORD with my voice;
With my voice to the LORD I make my supplication.
2 I pour out my complaint before Him;
I declare before Him my trouble.

3 When my spirit was overwhelmed within me,
Then You knew my path.
In the way in which I walk
They have secretly set a snare for me.
4 Look on *my* right hand and see,
For *there is* no one who acknowledges me;
Refuge has failed me;
No one cares for my soul.

5 I cried out to You, O LORD:
I said, "You *are* my refuge,
My portion in the land of the living.
6 Attend to my cry,
For I am brought very low;
Deliver me from my persecutors,
For they are stronger than I.
7 Bring my soul out of prison,
That I may praise Your name;
The righteous shall surround me,
For You shall deal bountifully with me."

PSALM 143

An Earnest Appeal for Guidance and Deliverance

A Psalm of David.

1 Hear my prayer, O LORD,
Give ear to my supplications!
In Your faithfulness answer me,
And in Your righteousness.
2 Do not enter into judgment with Your servant,
For in Your sight no one living is righteous.

3 For the enemy has persecuted my soul;
He has crushed my life to the ground;
He has made me dwell in darkness,
Like those who have long been dead.
4 Therefore my spirit is overwhelmed within me;
My heart within me is distressed.

5 I remember the days of old;
I meditate on all Your works;
I muse on the work of Your hands.
6 I spread out my hands to You;
My soul *longs* for You like a thirsty land. *Selah*

7 Answer me speedily, O LORD;
My spirit fails!
Do not hide Your face from me,
Lest I be like those who go down into the pit.
8 Cause me to hear Your lovingkindness in the morning,
For in You do I trust;
Cause me to know the way in which I should walk,
For I lift up my soul to You.

9 Deliver me, O LORD, from my enemies;
In You I take shelter.[a]

142:title [a] Hebrew *Maschil* 143:9 [a] Septuagint and Vulgate read *To You I flee.*

10 Teach me to do Your will,
For You *are* my God;
Your Spirit *is* good.
Lead me in the land of
uprightness.

11 Revive me, O LORD, for Your
name's sake!
For Your righteousness' sake
bring my soul out of trouble.
12 In Your mercy cut off my
enemies,
And destroy all those who afflict
my soul;
For I *am* Your servant.

PSALM 144

A Song to the LORD Who Preserves and Prospers His People

A Psalm of David.

1 Blessed *be* the LORD my Rock,
Who trains my hands for war,
And my fingers for battle—
2 My lovingkindness and my
fortress,
My high tower and my deliverer,
My shield and *the One* in whom I
take refuge,
Who subdues my people[a] under
me.

3 LORD, what *is* man, that You take
knowledge of him?
Or the son of man, that You are
mindful of him?
4 Man is like a breath;
His days *are* like a passing
shadow.

5 Bow down Your heavens, O LORD,
and come down;
Touch the mountains, and they
shall smoke.
6 Flash forth lightning and scatter
them;
Shoot out Your arrows and
destroy them.
7 Stretch out Your hand from
above;
Rescue me and deliver me out of
great waters,
From the hand of foreigners,
8 Whose mouth speaks lying words,
And whose right hand *is* a right
hand of falsehood.

9 I will sing a new song to You,
O God;
On a harp of ten strings I will sing
praises to You,
10 *The One* who gives salvation to
kings,
Who delivers David His servant
From the deadly sword.

11 Rescue me and deliver me from
the hand of foreigners,
Whose mouth speaks lying
words,
And whose right hand *is* a right
hand of falsehood—
12 That our sons *may be* as plants
grown up in their youth;
That our daughters *may be* as
pillars,
Sculptured in palace style;
13 *That* our barns *may be* full,
Supplying all kinds of produce;
That our sheep may bring forth
thousands
And ten thousands in our fields;
14 *That* our oxen *may be* well laden;
That there be no breaking in or
going out;
That there be no outcry in our
streets.
15 Happy *are* the people who are in
such a state;
Happy *are* the people whose God
is the LORD!

PSALM 145

A Song of God's Majesty and Love

A Praise of David.

1 I will extol You, my God, O King;
And I will bless Your name forever
and ever.
2 Every day I will bless You,
And I will praise Your name
forever and ever.
3 Great *is* the LORD, and greatly to
be praised;
And His greatness *is*
unsearchable.

144:2 [a] Following Masoretic Text, Septuagint, and Vulgate; Syriac and Targum read *the peoples* (compare 18:47).

4 One generation shall praise Your
works to another,
And shall declare Your mighty
acts.
5 I[a] will meditate on the glorious
splendor of Your majesty,
And on Your wondrous works.[b]
6 *Men* shall speak of the might of
Your awesome acts,
And I will declare Your greatness.
7 They shall utter the memory of
Your great goodness,
And shall sing of Your
righteousness.

8 The LORD *is* gracious and full of
compassion,
Slow to anger and great in mercy.
9 The LORD *is* good to all,
And His tender mercies *are* over
all His works.

10 All Your works shall praise You,
O LORD,
And Your saints shall bless You.
11 They shall speak of the glory of
Your kingdom,
And talk of Your power,
12 To make known to the sons of
men His mighty acts,
And the glorious majesty of His
kingdom.
13 Your kingdom *is* an everlasting
kingdom,
And Your dominion *endures*
throughout all generations.[a]

14 The LORD upholds all who fall,
And raises up all *who are* bowed
down.
15 The eyes of all look expectantly to
You,
And You give them their food in
due season.
16 You open Your hand
And satisfy the desire of every
living thing.

17 The LORD *is* righteous in all His
ways,
Gracious in all His works.
18 The LORD *is* near to all who call
upon Him,
To all who call upon Him in truth.
19 He will fulfill the desire of those
who fear Him;
He also will hear their cry and
save them.
20 The LORD preserves all who love
Him,
But all the wicked He will destroy.
21 My mouth shall speak the praise
of the LORD,
And all flesh shall bless His holy
name
Forever and ever.

PSALM 146

The Happiness of Those Whose Help Is the LORD

1 Praise the LORD!

Praise the LORD, O my soul!
2 While I live I will praise the LORD;
I will sing praises to my God while
I have my being.

3 Do not put your trust in princes,
Nor in a son of man, in whom
there is no help.
4 His spirit departs, he returns to
his earth;
In that very day his plans perish.

5 Happy *is he* who *has* the God of
Jacob for his help,
Whose hope *is* in the LORD his
God,
6 Who made heaven and earth,
The sea, and all that *is* in them;
Who keeps truth forever,
7 Who executes justice for the
oppressed,
Who gives food to the hungry.
The LORD gives freedom to the
prisoners.

8 The LORD opens *the eyes of* the
blind;
The LORD raises those who are
bowed down;
The LORD loves the righteous.

145:5 [a] Following Masoretic Text and Targum; Dead Sea Scrolls, Septuagint, Syriac, and Vulgate read *They*. [b] Literally *on the words of Your wondrous works* 145:13 [a] Following Masoretic Text and Targum; Dead Sea Scrolls, Septuagint, Syriac, and Vulgate add *The LORD is faithful in all His words, And holy in all His works.*

9 The LORD watches over the
strangers;
He relieves the fatherless and
widow;
But the way of the wicked He
turns upside down.

10 The LORD shall reign forever—
Your God, O Zion, to all
generations.

Praise the LORD!

PSALM 147

Praise to God for His Word and Providence

1 Praise the LORD!
For *it is* good to sing praises to
our God;
For *it is* pleasant, *and* praise is
beautiful.

2 The LORD builds up Jerusalem;
He gathers together the outcasts
of Israel.
3 He heals the brokenhearted
And binds up their wounds.
4 He counts the number of the stars;
He calls them all by name.
5 Great *is* our Lord, and mighty in
power;
His understanding *is* infinite.
6 The LORD lifts up the humble;
He casts the wicked down to the
ground.

7 Sing to the LORD with
thanksgiving;
Sing praises on the harp to our
God,
8 Who covers the heavens with
clouds,
Who prepares rain for the earth,
Who makes grass to grow on the
mountains.
9 He gives to the beast its food,
And to the young ravens that cry.

10 He does not delight in the
strength of the horse;
He takes no pleasure in the legs of
a man.
11 The LORD takes pleasure in those
who fear Him,
In those who hope in His mercy.

12 Praise the LORD, O Jerusalem!
Praise your God, O Zion!
13 For He has strengthened the bars
of your gates;
He has blessed your children
within you.
14 He makes peace *in* your borders,
And fills you with the finest wheat.

15 He sends out His command *to the*
earth;
His word runs very swiftly.
16 He gives snow like wool;
He scatters the frost like ashes;
17 He casts out His hail like morsels;
Who can stand before His cold?
18 He sends out His word and melts
them;
He causes His wind to blow, *and*
the waters flow.

19 He declares His word to Jacob,
His statutes and His judgments to
Israel.
20 He has not dealt thus with any
nation;
And *as for His* judgments, they
have not known them.

Praise the LORD!

PSALM 148

Praise to the LORD from Creation

1 Praise the LORD!

Praise the LORD from the
heavens;
Praise Him in the heights!
2 Praise Him, all His angels;
Praise Him, all His hosts!
3 Praise Him, sun and moon;
Praise Him, all you stars of light!
4 Praise Him, you heavens of
heavens,
And you waters above the
heavens!

5 Let them praise the name of the
LORD,
For He commanded and they
were created.
6 He also established them forever
and ever;
He made a decree which shall not
pass away.

7 Praise the LORD from the earth,
You great sea creatures and all the depths;
8 Fire and hail, snow and clouds;
Stormy wind, fulfilling His word;
9 Mountains and all hills;
Fruitful trees and all cedars;
10 Beasts and all cattle;
Creeping things and flying fowl;
11 Kings of the earth and all peoples;
Princes and all judges of the earth;
12 Both young men and maidens;
Old men and children.
13 Let them praise the name of the LORD,
For His name alone is exalted;
His glory *is* above the earth and heaven.
14 And He has exalted the horn of His people,
The praise of all His saints—
Of the children of Israel,
A people near to Him.

Praise the LORD!

PSALM 149

Praise to God for His Salvation and Judgment

1 Praise the LORD!

Sing to the LORD a new song,
And His praise in the assembly of saints.

2 Let Israel rejoice in their Maker;
Let the children of Zion be joyful in their King.
3 Let them praise His name with the dance;
Let them sing praises to Him with the timbrel and harp.
4 For the LORD takes pleasure in His people;
He will beautify the humble with salvation.
5 Let the saints be joyful in glory;
Let them sing aloud on their beds.
6 *Let* the high praises of God *be* in their mouth,
And a two-edged sword in their hand,
7 To execute vengeance on the nations,
And punishments on the peoples;
8 To bind their kings with chains,
And their nobles with fetters of iron;
9 To execute on them the written judgment—
This honor have all His saints.

Praise the LORD!

PSALM 150

Let All Things Praise the LORD

1 Praise the LORD!

Praise God in His sanctuary;
Praise Him in His mighty firmament!

2 Praise Him for His mighty acts;
Praise Him according to His excellent greatness!

3 Praise Him with the sound of the trumpet;
Praise Him with the lute and harp!
4 Praise Him with the timbrel and dance;
Praise Him with stringed instruments and flutes!
5 Praise Him with loud cymbals;
Praise Him with clashing cymbals!

6 Let everything that has breath praise the LORD.

Praise the LORD!

THE BOOK OF
PROVERBS

Wisdom is more than just knowing something; it is living differently because of what you know. The Book of Proverbs provides godly wisdom that helps us live in a way that pleases God and that is best for us, too. The short sayings in this book cover many different everyday subjects like friendship, justice, wealth, family, work, and even laziness.

- **GENRE:** Wisdom and Poetry
- **AUTHORS:** Solomon, Agur, Lemuel, and others
- **TIME:** c. 950–700 BC (compiled c. 700 BC)
- **PURPOSE:** To teach God's people how to please Him and live a joyful and meaningful life by following His plan for living.

The Beginning of Knowledge

1 The proverbs of Solomon the son of David, king of Israel:

2 To know wisdom and instruction,
To perceive the words of understanding,
3 To receive the instruction of wisdom,
Justice, judgment, and equity;
4 To give prudence to the simple,
To the young man knowledge and discretion—
5 A wise *man* will hear and increase learning,
And a man of understanding will attain wise counsel,
6 To understand a proverb and an enigma,
The words of the wise and their riddles.

7 The fear of the LORD *is* the beginning of knowledge,
But fools despise wisdom and instruction.

Shun Evil Counsel

8 My son, hear the instruction of your father,
And do not forsake the law of your mother;
9 For they *will be* a graceful ornament on your head,
And chains about your neck.

10 My son, if sinners entice you,
Do not consent.
11 If they say, "Come with us,
Let us lie in wait to *shed* blood;
Let us lurk secretly for the innocent without cause;
12 Let us swallow them alive like Sheol,[a]
And whole, like those who go down to the Pit;
13 We shall find all *kinds* of precious possessions,
We shall fill our houses with spoil;
14 Cast in your lot among us,
Let us all have one purse"—
15 My son, do not walk in the way with them,
Keep your foot from their path;
16 For their feet run to evil,
And they make haste to shed blood.
17 Surely, in vain the net is spread
In the sight of any bird;
18 But they lie in wait for their *own* blood,
They lurk secretly for their *own* lives.
19 So *are* the ways of everyone who is greedy for gain;
It takes away the life of its owners.

The Call of Wisdom

20 Wisdom calls aloud outside;
She raises her voice in the open squares.

1:12 [a] Or *the grave*

21 She cries out in the chief
concourses,[a]
At the openings of the gates in the
city
She speaks her words:
22 "How long, you simple ones, will
you love simplicity?
For scorners delight in their
scorning,
And fools hate knowledge.
23 Turn at my rebuke;
Surely I will pour out my spirit on
you;
I will make my words known to you.
24 Because I have called and you
refused,
I have stretched out my hand and
no one regarded,
25 Because you disdained all my
counsel,
And would have none of my
rebuke,
26 I also will laugh at your calamity;
I will mock when your terror comes,
27 When your terror comes like a
storm,
And your destruction comes like
a whirlwind,
When distress and anguish come
upon you.

28 "Then they will call on me, but I will
not answer;
They will seek me diligently, but
they will not find me.
29 Because they hated knowledge
And did not choose the fear of the
LORD,
30 They would have none of my
counsel
And despised my every rebuke.
31 Therefore they shall eat the fruit
of their own way,
And be filled to the full with their
own fancies.
32 For the turning away of the
simple will slay them,
And the complacency of fools will
destroy them;
33 But whoever listens to me will
dwell safely,
And will be secure, without fear of
evil."

The Value of Wisdom

2 My son, if you receive my words,
And treasure my commands
within you,
2 So that you incline your ear to
wisdom,
And apply your heart to
understanding;
3 Yes, if you cry out for discernment,
And lift up your voice for
understanding,
4 If you seek her as silver,
And search for her as *for* hidden
treasures;
5 Then you will understand the fear
of the LORD,
And find the knowledge of God.
6 For the LORD gives wisdom;
From His mouth *come* knowledge
and understanding;
7 He stores up sound wisdom for
the upright;
He is a shield to those who walk
uprightly;
8 He guards the paths of justice,
And preserves the way of His
saints.
9 Then you will understand
righteousness and justice,
Equity *and* every good path.

10 When wisdom enters your heart,
And knowledge is pleasant to
your soul,
11 Discretion will preserve you;
Understanding will keep you,
12 To deliver you from the way of
evil,
From the man who speaks
perverse things,
13 From those who leave the paths
of uprightness
To walk in the ways of darkness;
14 Who rejoice in doing evil,
And delight in the perversity of
the wicked;
15 Whose ways *are* crooked,
And *who are* devious in their
paths;
16 To deliver you from the immoral
woman,
From the seductress *who* flatters
with her words,

1:21 [a] Septuagint, Syriac, and Targum read *top of the walls;* Vulgate reads *the head of multitudes.*

17 Who forsakes the companion of her youth,
And forgets the covenant of her God.
18 For her house leads down to death,
And her paths to the dead;
19 None who go to her return,
Nor do they regain the paths of life—
20 So you may walk in the way of goodness,
And keep *to* the paths of righteousness.
21 For the upright will dwell in the land,
And the blameless will remain in it;
22 But the wicked will be cut off from the earth,
And the unfaithful will be uprooted from it.

Guidance for the Young

3 My son, do not forget my law,
But let your heart keep my commands;
2 For length of days and long life
And peace they will add to you.

3 Let not mercy and truth forsake you;
Bind them around your neck,
Write them on the tablet of your heart,
4 *And* so find favor and high esteem
In the sight of God and man.

5 Trust in the LORD with all your heart,
And lean not on your own understanding;
6 In all your ways acknowledge Him,
And He shall direct[a] your paths.

7 Do not be wise in your own eyes;
Fear the LORD and depart from evil.
8 It will be health to your flesh,[a]
And strength[b] to your bones.

9 Honor the LORD with your possessions,
And with the firstfruits of all your increase;
10 So your barns will be filled with plenty,
And your vats will overflow with new wine.

11 My son, do not despise the chastening of the LORD,
Nor detest His correction;
12 For whom the LORD loves He corrects,
Just as a father the son *in whom* he delights.

13 Happy *is* the man *who* finds wisdom,
And the man *who* gains understanding;
14 For her proceeds *are* better than the profits of silver,
And her gain than fine gold.
15 She *is* more precious than rubies,
And all the things you may desire cannot compare with her.
16 Length of days *is* in her right hand,
In her left hand riches and honor.
17 Her ways *are* ways of pleasantness,
And all her paths *are* peace.
18 She *is* a tree of life to those who take hold of her,
And happy *are all* who retain her.

19 The LORD by wisdom founded the earth;
By understanding He established the heavens;
20 By His knowledge the depths were broken up,
And clouds drop down the dew.

21 My son, let them not depart from your eyes—
Keep sound wisdom and discretion;
22 So they will be life to your soul
And grace to your neck.
23 Then you will walk safely in your way,
And your foot will not stumble.

3:6 [a] Or *make smooth* or *straight* **3:8** [a] Literally *navel,* figurative of the body [b] Literally *drink* or *refreshment*

24 When you lie down, you will not
be afraid;
Yes, you will lie down and your
sleep will be sweet.
25 Do not be afraid of sudden terror,
Nor of trouble from the wicked
when it comes;
26 For the LORD will be your confidence,
And will keep your foot from
being caught.

27 Do not withhold good from those
to whom it is due,
When it is in the power of your
hand to do *so.*
28 Do not say to your neighbor,
"Go, and come back,
And tomorrow I will give *it,*"
When you have it with you.
29 Do not devise evil against your
neighbor,
For he dwells by you for safety's
sake.
30 Do not strive with a man without
cause,
If he has done you no harm.

31 Do not envy the oppressor,
And choose none of his ways;
32 For the perverse *person is* an
abomination to the LORD,
But His secret counsel *is* with the
upright.
33 The curse of the LORD *is* on the
house of the wicked,
But He blesses the home of the
just.
34 Surely He scorns the scornful,
But gives grace to the humble.
35 The wise shall inherit glory,
But shame shall be the legacy of
fools.

Security in Wisdom

4 Hear, *my* children, the instruction
of a father,
And give attention to know
understanding;
2 For I give you good doctrine:
Do not forsake my law.
3 When I was my father's son,
Tender and the only one in the
sight of my mother,
4 He also taught me, and said to me:
"Let your heart retain my words;
Keep my commands, and live.
5 Get wisdom! Get understanding!
Do not forget, nor turn away from
the words of my mouth.
6 Do not forsake her, and she will
preserve you;
Love her, and she will keep you.
7 Wisdom *is* the principal thing;
Therefore get wisdom.
And in all your getting, get
understanding.
8 Exalt her, and she will promote you;
She will bring you honor, when
you embrace her.
9 She will place on your head an
ornament of grace;
A crown of glory she will deliver
to you."

10 Hear, my son, and receive my
sayings,
And the years of your life will be
many.
11 I have taught you in the way of
wisdom;
I have led you in right paths.
12 When you walk, your steps will
not be hindered,
And when you run, you will not
stumble.
13 Take firm hold of instruction, do
not let go;
Keep her, for she *is* your life.
14 Do not enter the path of the wicked,
And do not walk in the way of evil.
15 Avoid it, do not travel on it;
Turn away from it and pass on.
16 For they do not sleep unless they
have done evil;
And their sleep is taken away
unless they make *someone*
fall.
17 For they eat the bread of
wickedness,
And drink the wine of violence.

18 But the path of the just *is* like the
shining sun,[a]
That shines ever brighter unto the
perfect day.

4:18 [a] Literally *light*

19 The way of the wicked *is* like
darkness;
They do not know what makes
them stumble.

20 My son, give attention to my words;
Incline your ear to my sayings.
21 Do not let them depart from your
eyes;
Keep them in the midst of your
heart;
22 For they *are* life to those who find
them,
And health to all their flesh.
23 Keep your heart with all diligence,
For out of it *spring* the issues of
life.
24 Put away from you a deceitful
mouth,
And put perverse lips far from you.
25 Let your eyes look straight ahead,
And your eyelids look right before
you.
26 Ponder the path of your feet,
And let all your ways be
established.
27 Do not turn to the right or the left;
Remove your foot from evil.

The Peril of Adultery

5 My son, pay attention to my
wisdom;
Lend your ear to my
understanding,
2 That you may preserve discretion,
And your lips may keep
knowledge.
3 For the lips of an immoral woman
drip honey,
And her mouth *is* smoother than
oil;
4 But in the end she is bitter as
wormwood,
Sharp as a two-edged sword.
5 Her feet go down to death,
Her steps lay hold of hell.[a]
6 Lest you ponder *her* path of life—
Her ways are unstable;
You do not know *them.*

7 Therefore hear me now, *my* children,
And do not depart from the words
of my mouth.
8 Remove your way far from her,
And do not go near the door of
her house,
9 Lest you give your honor to
others,
And your years to the cruel *one;*
10 Lest aliens be filled with your
wealth,
And your labors *go* to the house
of a foreigner;
11 And you mourn at last,
When your flesh and your body
are consumed,
12 And say:
"How I have hated instruction,
And my heart despised
correction!
13 I have not obeyed the voice of my
teachers,
Nor inclined my ear to those who
instructed me!
14 I was on the verge of total ruin,
In the midst of the assembly and
congregation."

15 Drink water from your own
cistern,
And running water from your
own well.
16 Should your fountains be
dispersed abroad,
Streams of water in the streets?
17 Let them be only your own,
And not for strangers with
you.
18 Let your fountain be blessed,
And rejoice with the wife of your
youth.
19 *As a* loving deer and a graceful
doe,
Let her breasts satisfy you at all
times;
And always be enraptured with
her love.
20 For why should you, my son, be
enraptured by an immoral
woman,
And be embraced in the arms of a
seductress?

21 For the ways of man *are* before
the eyes of the LORD,
And He ponders all his paths.

5:5 [a] Or *Sheol*

22 His own iniquities entrap the
wicked *man,*
And he is caught in the cords of
his sin.
23 He shall die for lack of instruction,
And in the greatness of his folly
he shall go astray.

Dangerous Promises

6 My son, if you become surety for
your friend,
If you have shaken hands in
pledge for a stranger,
2 You are snared by the words of
your mouth;
You are taken by the words of
your mouth.
3 So do this, my son, and deliver
yourself;
For you have come into the hand
of your friend:
Go and humble yourself;
Plead with your friend.
4 Give no sleep to your eyes,
Nor slumber to your eyelids.
5 Deliver yourself like a gazelle
from the hand *of the hunter,*
And like a bird from the hand of
the fowler.[a]

The Folly of Indolence

6 Go to the ant, you sluggard!
Consider her ways and be wise,
7 Which, having no captain,
Overseer or ruler,
8 Provides her supplies in the
summer,
And gathers her food in the
harvest.
9 How long will you slumber,
O sluggard?
When will you rise from your
sleep?
10 A little sleep, a little slumber,
A little folding of the hands to
sleep—
11 So shall your poverty come on
you like a prowler,
And your need like an armed man.

The Wicked Man

12 A worthless person, a wicked man,
Walks with a perverse mouth;
13 He winks with his eyes,
He shuffles his feet,
He points with his fingers;
14 Perversity *is* in his heart,
He devises evil continually,
He sows discord.
15 Therefore his calamity shall come
suddenly;
Suddenly he shall be broken
without remedy.

16 These six *things* the LORD hates,
Yes, seven *are* an abomination to
Him:
17 A proud look,
A lying tongue,
Hands that shed innocent blood,
18 A heart that devises wicked plans,
Feet that are swift in running to
evil,
19 A false witness *who* speaks lies,
And one who sows discord among
brethren.

Beware of Adultery

20 My son, keep your father's
command,
And do not forsake the law of
your mother.
21 Bind them continually upon your
heart;
Tie them around your neck.
22 When you roam, they[a] will lead
you;
When you sleep, they will keep
you;
And *when* you awake, they will
speak with you.
23 For the commandment *is* a lamp,
And the law a light;
Reproofs of instruction *are* the
way of life,
24 To keep you from the evil woman,
From the flattering tongue of a
seductress.
25 Do not lust after her beauty in
your heart,
Nor let her allure you with her
eyelids.
26 For by means of a harlot
A man is reduced to a crust of bread;
And an adulteress[a] will prey upon
his precious life.

6:5 [a] That is, one who catches birds in a trap or snare **6:22** [a] Literally *it* **6:26** [a] Literally *a man's wife,* that is, of another

27 Can a man take fire to his bosom,
And his clothes not be burned?
28 Can one walk on hot coals,
And his feet not be seared?
29 So *is* he who goes in to his neighbor's wife;
Whoever touches her shall not be innocent.

30 *People* do not despise a thief
If he steals to satisfy himself when he is starving.
31 Yet *when* he is found, he must restore sevenfold;
He may have to give up all the substance of his house.
32 Whoever commits adultery with a woman lacks understanding;
He *who* does so destroys his own soul.
33 Wounds and dishonor he will get,
And his reproach will not be wiped away.
34 For jealousy *is* a husband's fury;
Therefore he will not spare in the day of vengeance.
35 He will accept no recompense,
Nor will he be appeased though you give many gifts.

7 My son, keep my words,
And treasure my commands within you.
2 Keep my commands and live,
And my law as the apple of your eye.
3 Bind them on your fingers;
Write them on the tablet of your heart.
4 Say to wisdom, "You *are* my sister,"
And call understanding *your* nearest kin,
5 That they may keep you from the immoral woman,
From the seductress *who* flatters with her words.

The Crafty Harlot

6 For at the window of my house
I looked through my lattice,
7 And saw among the simple,
I perceived among the youths,
A young man devoid of understanding,
8 Passing along the street near her corner;
And he took the path to her house
9 In the twilight, in the evening,
In the black and dark night.

10 And there a woman met him,
With the attire of a harlot, and a crafty heart.
11 She *was* loud and rebellious,
Her feet would not stay at home.
12 At times *she was* outside, at times in the open square,
Lurking at every corner.
13 So she caught him and kissed him;
With an impudent face she said to him:
14 "*I have* peace offerings with me;
Today I have paid my vows.
15 So I came out to meet you,
Diligently to seek your face,
And I have found you.
16 I have spread my bed with tapestry,
Colored coverings of Egyptian linen.
17 I have perfumed my bed
With myrrh, aloes, and cinnamon.
18 Come, let us take our fill of love until morning;
Let us delight ourselves with love.
19 For my husband *is* not at home;
He has gone on a long journey;
20 He has taken a bag of money with him,
And will come home on the appointed day."

21 With her enticing speech she caused him to yield,
With her flattering lips she seduced him.
22 Immediately he went after her, as an ox goes to the slaughter,
Or as a fool to the correction of the stocks,[a]
23 Till an arrow struck his liver.
As a bird hastens to the snare,
He did not know it *would cost* his life.

7:22 [a] Septuagint, Syriac, and Targum read *as a dog to bonds;* Vulgate reads *as a lamb . . . to bonds.*

24 Now therefore, listen to me, *my* children;
Pay attention to the words of my mouth:
25 Do not let your heart turn aside to her ways,
Do not stray into her paths;
26 For she has cast down many wounded,
And all who were slain by her were strong *men.*
27 Her house *is* the way to hell,[a]
Descending to the chambers of death.

The Excellence of Wisdom

8 Does not wisdom cry out,
And understanding lift up her voice?
2 She takes her stand on the top of the high hill,
Beside the way, where the paths meet.
3 She cries out by the gates, at the entry of the city,
At the entrance of the doors:
4 "To you, O men, I call,
And my voice *is* to the sons of men.
5 O you simple ones, understand prudence,
And you fools, be of an understanding heart.
6 Listen, for I will speak of excellent things,
And from the opening of my lips *will come* right things;
7 For my mouth will speak truth;
Wickedness *is* an abomination to my lips.
8 All the words of my mouth *are* with righteousness;
Nothing crooked or perverse *is* in them.
9 They *are* all plain to him who understands,
And right to those who find knowledge.
10 Receive my instruction, and not silver,
And knowledge rather than choice gold;
11 For wisdom *is* better than rubies,
And all the things one may desire cannot be compared with her.

12 "I, wisdom, dwell with prudence,
And find out knowledge *and* discretion.
13 The fear of the LORD *is* to hate evil;
Pride and arrogance and the evil way
And the perverse mouth I hate.
14 Counsel *is* mine, and sound wisdom;
I *am* understanding, I have strength.
15 By me kings reign,
And rulers decree justice.
16 By me princes rule, and nobles,
All the judges of the earth.[a]
17 I love those who love me,
And those who seek me diligently will find me.
18 Riches and honor *are* with me,
Enduring riches and righteousness.
19 My fruit *is* better than gold, yes, than fine gold,
And my revenue than choice silver.
20 I traverse the way of righteousness,
In the midst of the paths of justice,
21 That I may cause those who love me to inherit wealth,
That I may fill their treasuries.

22 "The LORD possessed me at the beginning of His way,
Before His works of old.
23 I have been established from everlasting,
From the beginning, before there was ever an earth.
24 When *there were* no depths I was brought forth,
When *there were* no fountains abounding with water.
25 Before the mountains were settled,
Before the hills, I was brought forth;
26 While as yet He had not made the earth or the fields,
Or the primal dust of the world.

7:27 [a] Or *Sheol* 8:16 [a] Masoretic Text, Syriac, Targum, and Vulgate read *righteousness;* Septuagint, Bomberg, and some manuscripts and editions read *earth.*

27 When He prepared the heavens, I *was* there,
When He drew a circle on the face of the deep,
28 When He established the clouds above,
When He strengthened the fountains of the deep,
29 When He assigned to the sea its limit,
So that the waters would not transgress His command,
When He marked out the foundations of the earth,
30 Then I was beside Him *as* a master craftsman;[a]
And I was daily *His* delight,
Rejoicing always before Him,
31 Rejoicing in His inhabited world,
And my delight *was* with the sons of men.

32 "Now therefore, listen to me, *my* children,
For blessed *are those who* keep my ways.
33 Hear instruction and be wise,
And do not disdain *it*.
34 Blessed is the man who listens to me,
Watching daily at my gates,
Waiting at the posts of my doors.
35 For whoever finds me finds life,
And obtains favor from the LORD;
36 But he who sins against me wrongs his own soul;
All those who hate me love death."

The Way of Wisdom

9 Wisdom has built her house,
She has hewn out her seven pillars;
2 She has slaughtered her meat,
She has mixed her wine,
She has also furnished her table.
3 She has sent out her maidens,
She cries out from the highest places of the city,
4 "Whoever *is* simple, let him turn in here!"
As for him who lacks understanding, she says to him,
5 "Come, eat of my bread
And drink of the wine I have mixed.
6 Forsake foolishness and live,
And go in the way of understanding.

7 "He who corrects a scoffer gets shame for himself,
And he who rebukes a wicked *man* *only* harms himself.
8 Do not correct a scoffer, lest he hate you;
Rebuke a wise *man*, and he will love you.
9 Give *instruction* to a wise *man*, and he will be still wiser;
Teach a just *man*, and he will increase in learning.

10 "The fear of the LORD *is* the beginning of wisdom,
And the knowledge of the Holy One *is* understanding.
11 For by me your days will be multiplied,
And years of life will be added to you.
12 If you are wise, you are wise for yourself,
And *if* you scoff, you will bear *it* alone."

The Way of Folly

13 A foolish woman is clamorous;
She is simple, and knows nothing.
14 For she sits at the door of her house,
On a seat *by* the highest places of the city,
15 To call to those who pass by,
Who go straight on their way:
16 "Whoever *is* simple, let him turn in here";
And *as for* him who lacks understanding, she says to him,
17 "Stolen water is sweet,
And bread *eaten* in secret is pleasant."
18 But he does not know that the dead *are* there,
That her guests *are* in the depths of hell.[a]

8:30 [a] A Jewish tradition reads *one brought up*. 9:18 [a] Or *Sheol*

Wise Sayings of Solomon

10 The proverbs of Solomon:

A wise son makes a glad father,
But a foolish son *is* the grief of his mother.

2 Treasures of wickedness profit nothing,
But righteousness delivers from death.
3 The LORD will not allow the righteous soul to famish,
But He casts away the desire of the wicked.

4 He who has a slack hand becomes poor,
But the hand of the diligent makes rich.
5 He who gathers in summer *is* a wise son;
He who sleeps in harvest *is* a son who causes shame.

6 Blessings *are* on the head of the righteous,
But violence covers the mouth of the wicked.
7 The memory of the righteous *is* blessed,
But the name of the wicked will rot.

8 The wise in heart will receive commands,
But a prating fool will fall.

9 He who walks with integrity walks securely,
But he who perverts his ways will become known.

10 He who winks with the eye causes trouble,
But a prating fool will fall.

11 The mouth of the righteous *is* a well of life,
But violence covers the mouth of the wicked.

12 Hatred stirs up strife,
But love covers all sins.

13 Wisdom is found on the lips of him who has understanding,
But a rod *is* for the back of him who is devoid of understanding.

14 Wise *people* store up knowledge,
But the mouth of the foolish *is* near destruction.

15 The rich man's wealth *is* his strong city;
The destruction of the poor *is* their poverty.

16 The labor of the righteous *leads* to life,
The wages of the wicked to sin.

17 He who keeps instruction *is in* the way of life,
But he who refuses correction goes astray.

18 Whoever hides hatred *has* lying lips,
And whoever spreads slander *is* a fool.

19 In the multitude of words sin is not lacking,
But he who restrains his lips *is* wise.
20 The tongue of the righteous *is* choice silver;
The heart of the wicked *is worth* little.
21 The lips of the righteous feed many,
But fools die for lack of wisdom.[a]

22 The blessing of the LORD makes *one* rich,
And He adds no sorrow with it.

23 To do evil *is* like sport to a fool,
But a man of understanding has wisdom.
24 The fear of the wicked will come upon him,
And the desire of the righteous will be granted.
25 When the whirlwind passes by, the wicked *is* no *more*,
But the righteous *has* an everlasting foundation.

10:21 [a] Literally *heart*

26 As vinegar to the teeth and smoke
to the eyes,
So *is* the lazy *man* to those who
send him.

27 The fear of the LORD prolongs
days,
But the years of the wicked will be
shortened.
28 The hope of the righteous *will be*
gladness,
But the expectation of the wicked
will perish.
29 The way of the LORD *is* strength
for the upright,
But destruction *will come* to the
workers of iniquity.

30 The righteous will never be
removed,
But the wicked will not inhabit the
earth.
31 The mouth of the righteous brings
forth wisdom,
But the perverse tongue will be
cut out.
32 The lips of the righteous know
what is acceptable,
But the mouth of the wicked *what*
is perverse.

11 Dishonest scales *are* an
abomination to the LORD,
But a just weight *is* His delight.

2 When pride comes, then comes
shame;
But with the humble *is* wisdom.

3 The integrity of the upright will
guide them,
But the perversity of the
unfaithful will destroy
them.
4 Riches do not profit in the day of
wrath,
But righteousness delivers from
death.
5 The righteousness of the
blameless will direct[a] his
way aright,
But the wicked will fall by his own
wickedness.
6 The righteousness of the upright
will deliver them,
But the unfaithful will be caught
by *their* lust.

7 When a wicked man dies, *his*
expectation will perish,
And the hope of the unjust perishes.
8 The righteous is delivered from
trouble,
And it comes to the wicked instead.
9 The hypocrite with *his* mouth
destroys his neighbor,
But through knowledge the
righteous will be delivered.
10 When it goes well with the
righteous, the city rejoices;
And when the wicked perish, *there*
is jubilation.
11 By the blessing of the upright the
city is exalted,
But it is overthrown by the mouth
of the wicked.

12 He who is devoid of wisdom
despises his neighbor,
But a man of understanding
holds his peace.

13 A talebearer reveals secrets,
But he who is of a faithful spirit
conceals a matter.

14 Where *there is* no counsel, the
people fall;
But in the multitude of counselors
there is safety.

15 He who is surety for a stranger
will suffer,
But one who hates being surety is
secure.

16 A gracious woman retains honor,
But ruthless *men* retain riches.
17 The merciful man does good for
his own soul,
But *he who is* cruel troubles his
own flesh.
18 The wicked *man* does deceptive
work,
But he who sows righteousness
will have a sure reward.

11:5 [a] Or *make smooth* or *straight*

19 As righteousness *leads* to life,
So he who pursues evil *pursues it* to his own death.
20 Those who are of a perverse heart *are* an abomination to the LORD,
But *the* blameless in their ways *are* His delight.
21 *Though they join* forces,[a] the wicked will not go unpunished;
But the posterity of the righteous will be delivered.

22 *As* a ring of gold in a swine's snout,
So is a lovely woman who lacks discretion.

23 The desire of the righteous *is* only good,
But the expectation of the wicked *is* wrath.

24 There is *one* who scatters, yet increases more;
And there is *one* who withholds more than is right,
But it *leads* to poverty.
25 The generous soul will be made rich,
And he who waters will also be watered himself.
26 The people will curse him who withholds grain,
But blessing *will be* on the head of him who sells *it*.

27 He who earnestly seeks good finds favor,
But trouble will come to him who seeks *evil*.

28 He who trusts in his riches will fall,
But the righteous will flourish like foliage.

29 He who troubles his own house will inherit the wind,
And the fool *will be* servant to the wise of heart.

30 The fruit of the righteous *is a* tree of life,
And he who wins souls *is* wise.

31 If the righteous will be recompensed on the earth,
How much more the ungodly and the sinner.

12

Whoever loves instruction loves knowledge,
But he who hates correction *is* stupid.

2 A good *man* obtains favor from the LORD,
But a man of wicked intentions He will condemn.

3 A man is not established by wickedness,
But the root of the righteous cannot be moved.

4 An excellent[a] wife *is* the crown of her husband,
But she who causes shame *is* like rottenness in his bones.

5 The thoughts of the righteous *are* right,
But the counsels of the wicked *are* deceitful.
6 The words of the wicked *are*, "Lie in wait for blood,"
But the mouth of the upright will deliver them.

7 The wicked are overthrown and *are* no more,
But the house of the righteous will stand.

8 A man will be commended according to his wisdom,
But he who is of a perverse heart will be despised.

9 Better *is the one* who is slighted but has a servant,
Than he who honors himself but lacks bread.

10 A righteous *man* regards the life of his animal,
But the tender mercies of the wicked *are* cruel.

11:21 [a] Literally *hand to hand* **12:4** [a] Literally *A wife of valor*

11 He who tills his land will be
satisfied with bread,
But he who follows frivolity *is*
devoid of understanding.[a]

12 The wicked covet the catch of evil
men,
But the root of the righteous
yields *fruit.*
13 The wicked is ensnared by the
transgression of *his* lips,
But the righteous will come
through trouble.
14 A man will be satisfied with
good by the fruit of *his*
mouth,
And the recompense of a man's
hands will be rendered to
him.

15 The way of a fool *is* right in his
own eyes,
But he who heeds counsel *is* wise.
16 A fool's wrath is known at once,
But a prudent *man* covers shame.

17 He *who* speaks truth declares
righteousness,
But a false witness, deceit.
18 There is one who speaks like the
piercings of a sword,
But the tongue of the wise
promotes health.
19 The truthful lip shall be
established forever,
But a lying tongue *is* but for a
moment.
20 Deceit is in the heart of those who
devise evil,
But counselors of peace have joy.
21 No grave trouble will overtake the
righteous,
But the wicked shall be filled with
evil.
22 Lying lips *are* an abomination to
the LORD,
But those who deal truthfully *are*
His delight.

23 A prudent man conceals
knowledge,
But the heart of fools proclaims
foolishness.

24 The hand of the diligent will rule,
But the lazy *man* will be put to
forced labor.

25 Anxiety in the heart of man
causes depression,
But a good word makes it glad.

26 The righteous should choose his
friends carefully,
For the way of the wicked leads
them astray.

27 The lazy *man* does not roast what
he took in hunting,
But diligence *is* man's precious
possession.

28 In the way of righteousness *is* life,
And in *its* pathway *there is* no
death.

13 A wise son *heeds* his father's
instruction,
But a scoffer does not listen to
rebuke.

2 A man shall eat well by the fruit
of *his* mouth,
But the soul of the unfaithful
feeds on violence.
3 He who guards his mouth
preserves his life,
But he who opens wide his lips
shall have destruction.

4 The soul of a lazy *man* desires,
and *has* nothing;
But the soul of the diligent shall
be made rich.

5 A righteous *man* hates lying,
But a wicked *man* is loathsome
and comes to shame.
6 Righteousness guards *him whose*
way is blameless,
But wickedness overthrows the
sinner.

7 There is one who makes himself
rich, yet *has* nothing;
And one who makes himself poor,
yet *has* great riches.

12:11 [a] Literally *heart*

8 The ransom of a man's life *is* his
riches,
But the poor does not hear rebuke.

9 The light of the righteous rejoices,
But the lamp of the wicked will be
put out.

10 By pride comes nothing but strife,
But with the well-advised *is*
wisdom.

11 Wealth *gained by* dishonesty will
be diminished,
But he who gathers by labor will
increase.

12 Hope deferred makes the heart
sick,
But *when* the desire comes, *it is* a
tree of life.

13 He who despises the word will be
destroyed,
But he who fears the
commandment will be
rewarded.
14 The law of the wise *is* a fountain of
life,
To turn *one* away from the snares
of death.

15 Good understanding gains favor,
But the way of the unfaithful *is*
hard.
16 Every prudent *man* acts with
knowledge,
But a fool lays open *his* folly.

17 A wicked messenger falls into
trouble,
But a faithful ambassador *brings*
health.

18 Poverty and shame *will come* to
him who disdains correction,
But he who regards a rebuke will
be honored.

19 A desire accomplished is sweet to
the soul,
But *it is* an abomination to fools
to depart from evil.

20 He who walks with wise *men* will
be wise,
But the companion of fools will be
destroyed.

21 Evil pursues sinners,
But to the righteous, good shall be
repaid.

22 A good *man* leaves an inheritance
to his children's children,
But the wealth of the sinner is
stored up for the righteous.

23 Much food *is in* the fallow *ground*
of the poor,
And for lack of justice there is
waste.[a]

24 He who spares his rod hates his son,
But he who loves him disciplines
him promptly.

25 The righteous eats to the
satisfying of his soul,
But the stomach of the wicked
shall be in want.

14 The wise woman builds her
house,
But the foolish pulls it down with
her hands.

2 He who walks in his uprightness
fears the LORD,
But *he who is* perverse in his ways
despises Him.

3 In the mouth of a fool *is* a rod of
pride,
But the lips of the wise will
preserve them.

4 Where no oxen *are,* the trough *is*
clean;
But much increase *comes* by the
strength of an ox.

5 A faithful witness does not lie,
But a false witness will utter lies.

6 A scoffer seeks wisdom and does
not *find it,*

13:23 [a] Literally *what is swept away*

But knowledge *is* easy to him who
understands.
7 Go from the presence of a foolish
man,
When you do not perceive *in him*
the lips of knowledge.
8 The wisdom of the prudent *is* to
understand his way,
But the folly of fools *is* deceit.

9 Fools mock at sin,
But among the upright *there is*
favor.

10 The heart knows its own bitterness,
And a stranger does not share its
joy.

11 The house of the wicked will be
overthrown,
But the tent of the upright will
flourish.

12 There is a way *that seems* right to
a man,
But its end *is* the way of death.

13 Even in laughter the heart may
sorrow,
And the end of mirth *may be* grief.

14 The backslider in heart will be
filled with his own ways,
But a good man *will be satisfied*
from above.[a]

15 The simple believes every word,
But the prudent considers well his
steps.
16 A wise *man* fears and departs
from evil,
But a fool rages and is self-
confident.
17 A quick-tempered *man* acts
foolishly,
And a man of wicked intentions is
hated.
18 The simple inherit folly,
But the prudent are crowned with
knowledge.
19 The evil will bow before the good,
And the wicked at the gates of the
righteous.
20 The poor *man* is hated even by his
own neighbor,
But the rich *has* many friends.
21 He who despises his neighbor
sins;
But he who has mercy on the
poor, happy *is* he.

22 Do they not go astray who devise
evil?
But mercy and truth *belong* to
those who devise good.

23 In all labor there is profit,
But idle chatter[a] *leads* only to
poverty.

24 The crown of the wise is their riches,
But the foolishness of fools *is* folly.

25 A true witness delivers souls,
But a deceitful *witness* speaks lies.

26 In the fear of the LORD *there is*
strong confidence,
And His children will have a place
of refuge.
27 The fear of the LORD *is* a fountain
of life,
To turn *one* away from the snares
of death.

28 In a multitude of people *is* a
king's honor,
But in the lack of people *is* the
downfall of a prince.

29 *He who is* slow to wrath has great
understanding,
But *he who is* impulsive[a] exalts folly.

30 A sound heart *is* life to the body,
But envy *is* rottenness to the bones.

31 He who oppresses the poor
reproaches his Maker,
But he who honors Him has
mercy on the needy.

32 The wicked is banished in his
wickedness,
But the righteous has a refuge in
his death.

14:14 [a] Literally *from above himself* **14:23** [a] Literally *talk of the lips* **14:29** [a] Literally *short of spirit*

33 Wisdom rests in the heart of him
who has understanding,
But *what is* in the heart of fools is
made known.

34 Righteousness exalts a nation,
But sin *is* a reproach to *any* people.

35 The king's favor *is* toward a wise
servant,
But his wrath *is against* him who
causes shame.

15 A soft answer turns away wrath,
But a harsh word stirs up anger.
2 The tongue of the wise uses
knowledge rightly,
But the mouth of fools pours forth
foolishness.

3 The eyes of the LORD *are* in every
place,
Keeping watch on the evil and the
good.

4 A wholesome tongue *is* a tree of
life,
But perverseness in it breaks the
spirit.

5 A fool despises his father's
instruction,
But he who receives correction is
prudent.

6 *In* the house of the righteous *there
is* much treasure,
But in the revenue of the wicked is
trouble.

7 The lips of the wise disperse
knowledge,
But the heart of the fool *does* not
do so.

8 The sacrifice of the wicked *is* an
abomination to the LORD,
But the prayer of the upright *is*
His delight.
9 The way of the wicked *is* an
abomination to the LORD,
But He loves him who follows
righteousness.

10 Harsh discipline *is* for him who
forsakes the way,
And he who hates correction will
die.

11 Hell[a] and Destruction[b] *are* before
the LORD;
So how much more the hearts of
the sons of men.

12 A scoffer does not love one who
corrects him,
Nor will he go to the wise.

13 A merry heart makes a cheerful
countenance,
But by sorrow of the heart the
spirit is broken.

14 The heart of him who has
understanding seeks
knowledge,
But the mouth of fools feeds on
foolishness.

15 All the days of the afflicted *are* evil,
But he who is of a merry heart *has*
a continual feast.

16 Better *is* a little with the fear of the
LORD,
Than great treasure with trouble.
17 Better *is* a dinner of herbs[a] where
love is,
Than a fatted calf with hatred.

18 A wrathful man stirs up strife,
But *he who is* slow to anger allays
contention.

19 The way of the lazy *man is* like a
hedge of thorns,
But the way of the upright *is* a
highway.

20 A wise son makes a father glad,
But a foolish man despises his
mother.

21 Folly *is* joy *to him who is* destitute
of discernment,
But a man of understanding
walks uprightly.

15:11 [a] Or *Sheol* [b] Hebrew *Abaddon* 15:17 [a] Or *vegetables*

22 Without counsel, plans go awry,
But in the multitude of counselors
they are established.

23 A man has joy by the answer of
his mouth,
And a word *spoken* in due season,
how good *it is!*

24 The way of life *winds* upward for
the wise,
That he may turn away from hell[a]
below.

25 The LORD will destroy the house
of the proud,
But He will establish the
boundary of the widow.

26 The thoughts of the wicked *are* an
abomination to the LORD,
But the words of the pure *are*
pleasant.

27 He who is greedy for gain troubles
his own house,
But he who hates bribes will live.

28 The heart of the righteous studies
how to answer,
But the mouth of the wicked
pours forth evil.

29 The LORD *is* far from the wicked,
But He hears the prayer of the
righteous.

30 The light of the eyes rejoices the
heart,
And a good report makes the
bones healthy.[a]

31 The ear that hears the rebukes of
life
Will abide among the wise.
32 He who disdains instruction
despises his own soul,
But he who heeds rebuke gets
understanding.
33 The fear of the LORD *is* the
instruction of wisdom,
And before honor *is*
humility.

16

The preparations of the heart
belong to man,
But the answer of the tongue *is*
from the LORD.

2 All the ways of a man *are* pure in
his own eyes,
But the LORD weighs the spirits.

3 Commit your works to the LORD,
And your thoughts will be
established.

4 The LORD has made all for Himself,
Yes, even the wicked for the day of
doom.

5 Everyone proud in heart *is* an
abomination to the LORD;
Though they join forces,[a] none will
go unpunished.

6 In mercy and truth
Atonement is provided for
iniquity;
And by the fear of the LORD *one*
departs from evil.

7 When a man's ways please the
LORD,
He makes even his enemies to be
at peace with him.

8 Better *is* a little with
righteousness,
Than vast revenues without
justice.

9 A man's heart plans his way,
But the LORD directs his steps.

10 Divination *is* on the lips of the
king;
His mouth must not transgress in
judgment.
11 Honest weights and scales *are* the
LORD's;
All the weights in the bag *are* His
work.
12 *It is* an abomination for kings to
commit wickedness,
For a throne is established by
righteousness.

15:24 [a] Or *Sheol* 15:30 [a] Literally *fat* 16:5 [a] Literally *hand to hand*

13 Righteous lips *are* the delight of
kings,
And they love him who speaks
what is right.
14 As messengers of death *is* the
king's wrath,
But a wise man will
appease it.
15 In the light of the king's face *is*
life,
And his favor *is* like a cloud of the
latter rain.

16 How much better to get wisdom
than gold!
And to get understanding is to be
chosen rather than silver.

17 The highway of the upright *is* to
depart from evil;
He who keeps his way preserves
his soul.

18 Pride *goes* before destruction,
And a haughty spirit before
a fall.
19 Better *to be* of a humble spirit with
the lowly,
Than to divide the spoil with the
proud.

20 He who heeds the word wisely will
find good,
And whoever trusts in the LORD,
happy *is* he.

21 The wise in heart will be called
prudent,
And sweetness of the lips
increases learning.

22 Understanding *is* a wellspring of
life to him who has it.
But the correction of fools *is* folly.

23 The heart of the wise teaches his
mouth,
And adds learning to his lips.

24 Pleasant words *are like* a
honeycomb,
Sweetness to the soul and health
to the bones.

25 There is a way *that seems* right to
a man,
But its end *is* the way of death.

26 The person who labors, labors for
himself,
For his *hungry* mouth drives him *on.*

27 An ungodly man digs up evil,
And *it is* on his lips like a burning
fire.
28 A perverse man sows strife,
And a whisperer separates the
best of friends.
29 A violent man entices his neighbor,
And leads him in a way *that is* not
good.
30 He winks his eye to devise
perverse things;
He purses his lips *and* brings
about evil.

31 The silver-haired head *is* a crown
of glory,
If it is found in the way of
righteousness.

32 *He who is* slow to anger *is* better
than the mighty,
And he who rules his spirit than
he who takes a city.

33 The lot is cast into the lap,
But its every decision *is* from the
LORD.

17

1 Better *is* a dry morsel with
quietness,
Than a house full of feasting[a]
with strife.

2 A wise servant will rule over a son
who causes shame,
And will share an inheritance
among the brothers.

3 The refining pot *is* for silver and
the furnace for gold,
But the LORD tests the hearts.

4 An evildoer gives heed to false lips;
A liar listens eagerly to a spiteful
tongue.

17:1 [a] Or *sacrificial meals*

5 He who mocks the poor
reproaches his Maker;
He who is glad at calamity will
not go unpunished.

6 Children's children *are* the crown
of old men,
And the glory of children *is* their
father.

7 Excellent speech is not becoming
to a fool,
Much less lying lips to a prince.

8 A present *is* a precious stone in
the eyes of its possessor;
Wherever he turns, he prospers.

9 He who covers a transgression
seeks love,
But he who repeats a matter
separates friends.

10 Rebuke is more effective for a
wise *man*
Than a hundred blows on a fool.

11 An evil *man* seeks only rebellion;
Therefore a cruel messenger will
be sent against him.

12 Let a man meet a bear robbed of
her cubs,
Rather than a fool in his folly.

13 Whoever rewards evil for good,
Evil will not depart from his
house.

14 The beginning of strife *is like*
releasing water;
Therefore stop contention before
a quarrel starts.

15 He who justifies the wicked, and
he who condemns the just,
Both of them alike *are* an
abomination to the LORD.

16 Why *is there* in the hand of a
fool the purchase price of
wisdom,
Since *he has* no heart *for it?*

17 A friend loves at all times,
And a brother is born for
adversity.

18 A man devoid of understanding
shakes hands in a pledge,
And becomes surety for his friend.

19 He who loves transgression loves
strife,
And he who exalts his gate seeks
destruction.

20 He who has a deceitful heart finds
no good,
And he who has a perverse
tongue falls into evil.

21 He who begets a scoffer *does so* to
his sorrow,
And the father of a fool has no joy.

22 A merry heart does good, *like*
medicine,[a]
But a broken spirit dries the
bones.

23 A wicked *man* accepts a bribe
behind the back[a]
To pervert the ways of justice.

24 Wisdom *is* in the sight of him who
has understanding,
But the eyes of a fool *are* on the
ends of the earth.

25 A foolish son *is* a grief to his
father,
And bitterness to her who bore him.

26 Also, to punish the righteous *is*
not good,
Nor to strike princes for *their*
uprightness.

27 He who has knowledge spares his
words,
And a man of understanding is of
a calm spirit.

28 Even a fool is counted wise when
he holds his peace;
When he shuts his lips, *he is*
considered perceptive.

17:22 [a] Or *makes medicine even better* **17:23** [a] Literally *from the bosom*

18 A man who isolates himself
seeks his own desire;
He rages against all wise judgment.

2 A fool has no delight in
understanding,
But in expressing his own heart.

3 When the wicked comes,
contempt comes also;
And with dishonor *comes*
reproach.

4 The words of a man's mouth *are*
deep waters;
The wellspring of wisdom *is* a
flowing brook.

5 *It is* not good to show partiality to
the wicked,
Or to overthrow the righteous in
judgment.

6 A fool's lips enter into contention,
And his mouth calls for blows.
7 A fool's mouth *is* his destruction,
And his lips *are* the snare of his
soul.
8 The words of a talebearer *are* like
tasty trifles,[a]
And they go down into the inmost
body.

9 He who is slothful in his work
Is a brother to him who is a great
destroyer.

10 The name of the LORD *is* a strong
tower;
The righteous run to it and are
safe.
11 The rich man's wealth *is* his strong
city,
And like a high wall in his own
esteem.

12 Before destruction the heart of a
man is haughty,
And before honor *is* humility.

13 He who answers a matter before
he hears *it*,
It *is* folly and shame to him.

14 The spirit of a man will sustain
him in sickness,
But who can bear a broken spirit?

15 The heart of the prudent acquires
knowledge,
And the ear of the wise seeks
knowledge.

16 A man's gift makes room for him,
And brings him before great men.

17 The first *one* to plead his cause
seems right,
Until his neighbor comes and
examines him.

18 Casting lots causes contentions to
cease,
And keeps the mighty apart.

19 A brother offended *is harder to
win* than a strong city,
And contentions *are* like the bars
of a castle.

20 A man's stomach shall be
satisfied from the fruit of his
mouth;
From the produce of his lips he
shall be filled.

21 Death and life *are* in the power of
the tongue,
And those who love it will eat its
fruit.

22 *He who* finds a wife finds a good
thing,
And obtains favor from the LORD.

23 The poor *man* uses entreaties,
But the rich answers roughly.

24 A man *who has* friends must
himself be friendly,[a]
But there is a friend *who* sticks
closer than a brother.

19 Better *is* the poor who walks in
his integrity
Than *one who is* perverse in his
lips, and is a fool.

18:8 [a] A Jewish tradition reads *wounds*. 18:24 [a] Following Greek manuscripts, Syriac, Targum, and Vulgate; Masoretic Text reads *may come to ruin*.

2 Also it is not good *for* a soul *to be*
without knowledge,
And he sins who hastens with *his*
feet.

3 The foolishness of a man twists
his way,
And his heart frets against the
LORD.

4 Wealth makes many friends,
But the poor is separated from his
friend.

5 A false witness will not go
unpunished,
And *he who* speaks lies will not
escape.

6 Many entreat the favor of the
nobility,
And every man *is* a friend to one
who gives gifts.
7 All the brothers of the poor hate
him;
How much more do his friends go
far from him!
He may pursue *them with* words,
yet they abandon *him.*

8 He who gets wisdom loves his own
soul;
He who keeps understanding will
find good.

9 A false witness will not go
unpunished,
And *he who* speaks lies shall
perish.

10 Luxury is not fitting for a fool,
Much less for a servant to rule
over princes.

11 The discretion of a man makes
him slow to anger,
And his glory *is* to overlook a
transgression.

12 The king's wrath *is* like the roaring
of a lion,
But his favor *is* like dew on the
grass.

13 A foolish son *is* the ruin of his
father,
And the contentions of a wife *are*
a continual dripping.

14 Houses and riches *are* an
inheritance from fathers,
But a prudent wife *is* from the LORD.

15 Laziness casts *one* into a deep
sleep,
And an idle person will suffer
hunger.

16 He who keeps the commandment
keeps his soul,
But he who is careless[a] of his
ways will die.

17 He who has pity on the poor lends
to the LORD,
And He will pay back what he has
given.

18 Chasten your son while there is
hope,
And do not set your heart on his
destruction.[a]

19 *A man of* great wrath will suffer
punishment;
For if you rescue *him,* you will
have to do it again.

20 Listen to counsel and receive
instruction,
That you may be wise in your
latter days.

21 There are many plans in a man's
heart,
Nevertheless the LORD's counsel—
that will stand.

22 What is desired in a man is
kindness,
And a poor man is better than a
liar.

23 The fear of the LORD *leads* to life,
And *he who has it* will abide in
satisfaction;
He will not be visited with evil.

19:16 [a] Literally *despises,* figurative of recklessness or carelessness **19:18** [a] Literally *to put him to death;* a Jewish tradition reads *on his crying.*

24 A lazy *man* buries his hand in the bowl,[a]
And will not so much as bring it to his mouth again.

25 Strike a scoffer, and the simple will become wary;
Rebuke one who has understanding, *and* he will discern knowledge.

26 He who mistreats *his* father *and* chases away *his* mother
Is a son who causes shame and brings reproach.

27 Cease listening to instruction, my son,
And you will stray from the words of knowledge.

28 A disreputable witness scorns justice,
And the mouth of the wicked devours iniquity.

29 Judgments are prepared for scoffers,
And beatings for the backs of fools.

20 Wine *is* a mocker,
Strong drink *is* a brawler,
And whoever is led astray by it is not wise.

2 The wrath[a] of a king *is* like the roaring of a lion;
Whoever provokes him to anger sins *against* his own life.

3 *It is* honorable for a man to stop striving,
Since any fool can start a quarrel.

4 The lazy *man* will not plow because of winter;
He will beg during harvest and *have* nothing.

5 Counsel in the heart of man *is like* deep water,
But a man of understanding will draw it out.

6 Most men will proclaim each his own goodness,
But who can find a faithful man?

7 The righteous *man* walks in his integrity;
His children *are* blessed after him.

8 A king who sits on the throne of judgment
Scatters all evil with his eyes.

9 Who can say, "I have made my heart clean,
I am pure from my sin"?

10 Diverse weights *and* diverse measures,
They *are* both alike, an abomination to the LORD.

11 Even a child is known by his deeds,
Whether what he does *is* pure and right.

12 The hearing ear and the seeing eye,
The LORD has made them both.

13 Do not love sleep, lest you come to poverty;
Open your eyes, *and* you will be satisfied with bread.

14 "*It is* good for nothing,"[a] cries the buyer;
But when he has gone his way, then he boasts.

15 There is gold and a multitude of rubies,
But the lips of knowledge *are* a precious jewel.

16 Take the garment of one who is surety *for* a stranger,
And hold it as a pledge *when it* is for a seductress.

17 Bread gained by deceit *is* sweet to a man,
But afterward his mouth will be filled with gravel.

19:24 [a] Septuagint and Syriac read *bosom;* Targum and Vulgate read *armpit.* **20:2** [a] Literally *fear* or *terror* which is produced by the king's wrath **20:14** [a] Literally *evil, evil*

18 Plans are established by counsel;
By wise counsel wage war.

19 He who goes about *as* a talebearer reveals secrets;
Therefore do not associate with one who flatters with his lips.

20 Whoever curses his father or his mother,
His lamp will be put out in deep darkness.

21 An inheritance gained hastily at the beginning
Will not be blessed at the end.

22 Do not say, "I will recompense evil";
Wait for the LORD, and He will save you.

23 Diverse weights *are* an abomination to the LORD,
And dishonest scales *are* not good.

24 A man's steps *are* of the LORD;
How then can a man understand his own way?

25 *It is* a snare for a man to devote rashly *something as* holy,
And afterward to reconsider *his* vows.

26 A wise king sifts out the wicked,
And brings the threshing wheel over them.

27 The spirit of a man *is* the lamp of the LORD,
Searching all the inner depths of his heart.[a]

28 Mercy and truth preserve the king,
And by lovingkindness he upholds his throne.

29 The glory of young men *is* their strength,
And the splendor of old men *is* their gray head.

30 Blows that hurt cleanse away evil,
As *do* stripes the inner depths of the heart.[a]

21 The king's heart *is* in the hand of the LORD,
Like the rivers of water;
He turns it wherever He wishes.

2 Every way of a man *is* right in his own eyes,
But the LORD weighs the hearts.

3 To do righteousness and justice
Is more acceptable to the LORD than sacrifice.

4 A haughty look, a proud heart,
And the plowing[a] of the wicked *are* sin.

5 The plans of the diligent *lead* surely to plenty,
But *those of* everyone *who is* hasty, surely to poverty.

6 Getting treasures by a lying tongue
Is the fleeting fantasy of those who seek death.[a]

7 The violence of the wicked will destroy them,[a]
Because they refuse to do justice.

8 The way of a guilty man *is* perverse;[a]
But *as for* the pure, his work *is* right.

9 Better to dwell in a corner of a housetop,
Than in a house shared with a contentious woman.

10 The soul of the wicked desires evil;
His neighbor finds no favor in his eyes.

11 When the scoffer is punished, the simple is made wise;
But when the wise is instructed, he receives knowledge.

20:27 [a] Literally *the rooms of the belly* **20:30** [a] Literally *the rooms of the belly* **21:4** [a] Or *lamp* **21:6** [a] Septuagint reads *Pursue vanity on the snares of death;* Vulgate reads *Is vain and foolish, and shall stumble on the snares of death;* Targum reads *They shall be destroyed, and they shall fall who seek death.* **21:7** [a] Literally *drag them away* **21:8** [a] Or *The way of a man is perverse and strange*

12 The righteous *God* wisely
considers the house of the
wicked,
Overthrowing the wicked for *their*
wickedness.

13 Whoever shuts his ears to the cry
of the poor
Will also cry himself and not be
heard.

14 A gift in secret pacifies anger,
And a bribe behind the back,[a]
strong wrath.

15 *It is* a joy for the just to do justice,
But destruction *will come* to the
workers of iniquity.

16 A man who wanders from the way
of understanding
Will rest in the assembly of the dead.

17 He who loves pleasure *will be* a
poor man;
He who loves wine and oil will not
be rich.

18 The wicked *shall be* a ransom for
the righteous,
And the unfaithful for the upright.

19 Better to dwell in the wilderness,
Than with a contentious and
angry woman.

20 *There is* desirable treasure,
And oil in the dwelling of the wise,
But a foolish man squanders it.

21 He who follows righteousness and
mercy
Finds life, righteousness, and
honor.

22 A wise *man* scales the city of the
mighty,
And brings down the trusted
stronghold.

23 Whoever guards his mouth and
tongue
Keeps his soul from troubles.

24 A proud *and* haughty *man*—
"Scoffer" *is* his name;
He acts with arrogant pride.

25 The desire of the lazy *man* kills him,
For his hands refuse to labor.

26 He covets greedily all day long,
But the righteous gives and does
not spare.

27 The sacrifice of the wicked *is* an
abomination;
How much more *when* he brings it
with wicked intent!

28 A false witness shall perish,
But the man who hears *him* will
speak endlessly.

29 A wicked man hardens his face,
But *as for* the upright, he
establishes[a] his way.

30 *There is* no wisdom or
understanding
Or counsel against the LORD.

31 The horse *is* prepared for the day
of battle,
But deliverance *is* of the LORD.

22

A *good* name is to be chosen
rather than great riches,
Loving favor rather than silver
and gold.

2 The rich and the poor have this in
common,
The LORD *is* the maker of them all.

3 A prudent *man* foresees evil and
hides himself,
But the simple pass on and are
punished.

4 By humility *and* the fear of the
LORD
Are riches and honor and life.

5 Thorns *and* snares *are* in the way
of the perverse;
He who guards his soul will be far
from them.

21:14 [a] Literally *in the bosom* 21:29 [a] Qere and Septuagint read *understands*.

6 Train up a child in the way he
should go,
And when he is old he will not
depart from it.

7 The rich rules over the poor,
And the borrower *is* servant to the
lender.

8 He who sows iniquity will reap
sorrow,
And the rod of his anger will fail.

9 He who has a generous eye will be
blessed,
For he gives of his bread to the
poor.

10 Cast out the scoffer, and
contention will leave;
Yes, strife and reproach will cease.

11 He who loves purity of heart
And has grace on his lips,
The king *will be* his friend.

12 The eyes of the LORD preserve
knowledge,
But He overthrows the words of
the faithless.

13 The lazy *man* says, "*There is* a lion
outside!
I shall be slain in the streets!"

14 The mouth of an immoral woman
is a deep pit;
He who is abhorred by the LORD
will fall there.

15 Foolishness *is* bound up in the
heart of a child;
The rod of correction will drive it
far from him.

16 He who oppresses the poor to
increase his *riches,*
And he who gives to the rich, *will*
surely *come* to poverty.

Sayings of the Wise

17 Incline your ear and hear the
words of the wise,
And apply your heart to my
knowledge;

18 For *it is* a pleasant thing if you
keep them within you;
Let them all be fixed upon your
lips,

19 So that your trust may be in the
LORD;
I have instructed you today, even
you.

20 Have I not written to you
excellent things
Of counsels and knowledge,

21 That I may make you know the
certainty of the words of truth,
That you may answer words of
truth
To those who send to you?

22 Do not rob the poor because he *is*
poor,
Nor oppress the afflicted at the
gate;

23 For the LORD will plead their
cause,
And plunder the soul of those who
plunder them.

24 Make no friendship with an angry
man,
And with a furious man do not go,

25 Lest you learn his ways
And set a snare for your soul.

26 Do not be one of those who
shakes hands in a pledge,
One of those who is surety for
debts;

27 If you have nothing *with which* to
pay,
Why should he take away your
bed from under you?

28 Do not remove the ancient
landmark
Which your fathers have set.

29 Do you see a man *who* excels in
his work?
He will stand before kings;
He will not stand before unknown
men.

23 When you sit down to eat with
a ruler,
Consider carefully what *is* before
you;

2 And put a knife to your throat
If you *are* a man given to appetite.
3 Do not desire his delicacies,
For they *are* deceptive food.

4 Do not overwork to be rich;
Because of your own understanding, cease!
5 Will you set your eyes on that which is not?
For *riches* certainly make themselves wings;
They fly away like an eagle *toward* heaven.

6 Do not eat the bread of a miser,[a]
Nor desire his delicacies;
7 For as he thinks in his heart, so *is* he.
"Eat and drink!" he says to you,
But his heart is not with you.
8 The morsel you have eaten, you will vomit up,
And waste your pleasant words.

9 Do not speak in the hearing of a fool,
For he will despise the wisdom of your words.

10 Do not remove the ancient landmark,
Nor enter the fields of the fatherless;
11 For their Redeemer *is* mighty;
He will plead their cause against you.

12 Apply your heart to instruction,
And your ears to words of knowledge.

13 Do not withhold correction from a child,
For *if* you beat him with a rod, he will not die.
14 You shall beat him with a rod,
And deliver his soul from hell.[a]

15 My son, if your heart is wise,
My heart will rejoice—indeed, I myself;
16 Yes, my inmost being will rejoice
When your lips speak right things.

17 Do not let your heart envy sinners,
But *be zealous* for the fear of the LORD all the day;
18 For surely there is a hereafter,
And your hope will not be cut off.

19 Hear, my son, and be wise;
And guide your heart in the way.
20 Do not mix with winebibbers,
Or with gluttonous eaters of meat;
21 For the drunkard and the glutton will come to poverty,
And drowsiness will clothe *a man* with rags.

22 Listen to your father who begot you,
And do not despise your mother when she is old.

23 Buy the truth, and do not sell *it,*
Also wisdom and instruction and understanding.

24 The father of the righteous will greatly rejoice,
And he who begets a wise *child* will delight in him.
25 Let your father and your mother be glad,
And let her who bore you rejoice.

26 My son, give me your heart,
And let your eyes observe my ways.
27 For a harlot *is* a deep pit,
And a seductress *is* a narrow well.
28 She also lies in wait as *for* a victim,
And increases the unfaithful among men.

29 Who has woe?
Who has sorrow?
Who has contentions?
Who has complaints?
Who has wounds without cause?
Who has redness of eyes?

23:6 [a] Literally *one who has an evil eye* 23:14 [a] Or *Sheol*

30 Those who linger long at the wine,
Those who go in search of mixed wine.
31 Do not look on the wine when it is red,
When it sparkles in the cup,
When it swirls around smoothly;
32 At the last it bites like a serpent,
And stings like a viper.
33 Your eyes will see strange things,
And your heart will utter perverse things.
34 Yes, you will be like one who lies down in the midst of the sea,
Or like one who lies at the top of the mast, *saying:*
35 "They have struck me, *but* I was not hurt;
They have beaten me, but I did not feel *it*.
When shall I awake, that I may seek another *drink?*"

24 Do not be envious of evil men,
Nor desire to be with them;
2 For their heart devises violence,
And their lips talk of troublemaking.

3 Through wisdom a house is built,
And by understanding it is established;
4 By knowledge the rooms are filled
With all precious and pleasant riches.

5 A wise man *is* strong,
Yes, a man of knowledge increases strength;
6 For by wise counsel you will wage your own war,
And in a multitude of counselors *there is* safety.

7 Wisdom *is* too lofty for a fool;
He does not open his mouth in the gate.

8 He who plots to do evil
Will be called a schemer.
9 The devising of foolishness *is* sin,
And the scoffer *is* an abomination to men.

10 *If* you faint in the day of adversity,
Your strength *is* small.

11 Deliver *those who* are drawn toward death,
And hold back *those* stumbling to the slaughter.
12 If you say, "Surely we did not know this,"
Does not He who weighs the hearts consider *it?*
He who keeps your soul, does He *not* know *it?*
And will He *not* render to *each* man according to his deeds?

13 My son, eat honey because *it is* good,
And the honeycomb *which is* sweet to your taste;
14 So *shall* the knowledge of wisdom *be* to your soul;
If you have found *it*, there is a prospect,
And your hope will not be cut off.

15 Do not lie in wait, O wicked *man*, against the dwelling of the righteous;
Do not plunder his resting place;
16 For a righteous *man* may fall seven times
And rise again,
But the wicked shall fall by calamity.

17 Do not rejoice when your enemy falls,
And do not let your heart be glad when he stumbles;
18 Lest the LORD see *it*, and it displease Him,
And He turn away His wrath from him.

19 Do not fret because of evildoers,
Nor be envious of the wicked;
20 For there will be no prospect for the evil *man;*
The lamp of the wicked will be put out.

21 My son, fear the LORD and the king;
Do not associate with those given to change;
22 For their calamity will rise suddenly,
And who knows the ruin those two can bring?

Further Sayings of the Wise

23These *things* also *belong* to the wise:

It is not good to show partiality in
judgment.
24 He who says to the wicked, "You
are righteous,"
Him the people will curse;
Nations will abhor him.
25 But those who rebuke *the wicked*
will have delight,
And a good blessing will come
upon them.

26 He who gives a right answer
kisses the lips.

27 Prepare your outside work,
Make it fit for yourself in the field;
And afterward build your house.

28 Do not be a witness against your
neighbor without cause,
For would you deceive[a] with your lips?
29 Do not say, "I will do to him just
as he has done to me;
I will render to the man according
to his work."

30 I went by the field of the lazy *man*,
And by the vineyard of the man
devoid of understanding;
31 And there it was, all overgrown
with thorns;
Its surface was covered with nettles;
Its stone wall was broken down.
32 When I saw *it*, I considered *it* well;
I looked on *it and* received instruction:
33 A little sleep, a little slumber,
A little folding of the hands to rest;
34 So shall your poverty come *like* a
prowler,
And your need like an armed man.

Further Wise Sayings of Solomon

25 These also *are* proverbs of Sol-
omon which the men of Hezeki-
ah king of Judah copied:

2 *It is* the glory of God to conceal a
matter,
But the glory of kings *is* to search
out a matter.
3 *As* the heavens for height and the
earth for depth,
So the heart of kings *is* unsearchable.
4 Take away the dross from silver,
And it will go to the silversmith
for jewelry.
5 Take away the wicked from before
the king,
And his throne will be established
in righteousness.

6 Do not exalt yourself in the
presence of the king,
And do not stand in the place of
the great;
7 For *it is* better that he say to you,
"Come up here,"
Than that you should be put lower
in the presence of the prince,
Whom your eyes have seen.

8 Do not go hastily to court;
For what will you do in the end,
When your neighbor has put you
to shame?
9 Debate your case with your neighbor,
And do not disclose the secret to
another;
10 Lest he who hears *it* expose your
shame,
And your reputation be ruined.

11 A word fitly spoken *is like* apples
of gold
In settings of silver.
12 *Like* an earring of gold and an
ornament of fine gold
Is a wise rebuker to an obedient ear.

13 Like the cold of snow in time of
harvest
Is a faithful messenger to those
who send him,
For he refreshes the soul of his
masters.

14 Whoever falsely boasts of giving
Is like clouds and wind without rain.

15 By long forbearance a ruler is
persuaded,
And a gentle tongue breaks a bone.

24:28 a Septuagint and Vulgate read *Do not deceive.*

16 Have you found honey?
Eat only as much as you need,
Lest you be filled with it and vomit.

17 Seldom set foot in your neighbor's house,
Lest he become weary of you and hate you.

18 A man who bears false witness against his neighbor
Is like a club, a sword, and a sharp arrow.

19 Confidence in an unfaithful *man* in time of trouble
Is like a bad tooth and a foot out of joint.

20 *Like* one who takes away a garment in cold weather,
And like vinegar on soda,
Is one who sings songs to a heavy heart.

21 If your enemy is hungry, give him bread to eat;
And if he is thirsty, give him water to drink;
22 For *so* you will heap coals of fire on his head,
And the LORD will reward you.

23 The north wind brings forth rain,
And a backbiting tongue an angry countenance.

24 *It is* better to dwell in a corner of a housetop,
Than in a house shared with a contentious woman.

25 *As* cold water to a weary soul,
So *is* good news from a far country.

26 A righteous *man* who falters before the wicked
Is like a murky spring and a polluted well.

27 *It is* not good to eat much honey;
So to seek one's own glory *is not* glory.

28 Whoever *has* no rule over his own spirit
Is like a city broken down, without walls.

26

As snow in summer and rain in harvest,
So honor is not fitting for a fool.

2 Like a flitting sparrow, like a flying swallow,
So a curse without cause shall not alight.

3 A whip for the horse,
A bridle for the donkey,
And a rod for the fool's back.
4 Do not answer a fool according to his folly,
Lest you also be like him.
5 Answer a fool according to his folly,
Lest he be wise in his own eyes.
6 He who sends a message by the hand of a fool
Cuts off *his own* feet *and* drinks violence.
7 *Like* the legs of the lame that hang limp
Is a proverb in the mouth of fools.
8 Like one who binds a stone in a sling
Is he who gives honor to a fool.
9 *Like* a thorn *that* goes into the hand of a drunkard
Is a proverb in the mouth of fools.
10 The great *God* who formed everything
Gives the fool *his* hire and the transgressor *his* wages.[a]
11 As a dog returns to his own vomit,
So a fool repeats his folly.
12 Do you see a man wise in his own eyes?
There is more hope for a fool than for him.

13 The lazy *man* says, "*There is* a lion in the road!
A fierce lion *is* in the streets!"
14 *As* a door turns on its hinges,
So *does* the lazy *man* on his bed.

26:10 [a] The Hebrew is difficult; ancient and modern translators differ greatly.

15 The lazy *man* buries his hand in the bowl;[a]
It wearies him to bring it back to his mouth.
16 The lazy *man is* wiser in his own eyes
Than seven men who can answer sensibly.

17 He who passes by *and* meddles in a quarrel not his own
Is like one who takes a dog by the ears.

18 Like a madman who throws firebrands, arrows, and death,
19 *Is* the man *who* deceives his neighbor,
And says, "I was only joking!"

20 Where *there is* no wood, the fire goes out;
And where *there is* no talebearer, strife ceases.
21 *As* charcoal *is* to burning coals, and wood to fire,
So *is* a contentious man to kindle strife.
22 The words of a talebearer *are* like tasty trifles,
And they go down into the inmost body.

23 Fervent lips with a wicked heart
Are like earthenware covered with silver dross.

24 He who hates, disguises *it* with his lips,
And lays up deceit within himself;
25 When he speaks kindly, do not believe him,
For *there are* seven abominations in his heart;
26 *Though his* hatred is covered by deceit,
His wickedness will be revealed before the assembly.

27 Whoever digs a pit will fall into it,
And he who rolls a stone will have it roll back on him.

28 A lying tongue hates *those who are* crushed by it,
And a flattering mouth works ruin.

27 Do not boast about tomorrow,
For you do not know what a day may bring forth.

2 Let another man praise you, and not your own mouth;
A stranger, and not your own lips.

3 A stone *is* heavy and sand *is* weighty,
But a fool's wrath *is* heavier than both of them.

4 Wrath *is* cruel and anger a torrent,
But who *is* able to stand before jealousy?

5 Open rebuke *is* better
Than love carefully concealed.

6 Faithful *are* the wounds of a friend,
But the kisses of an enemy *are* deceitful.

7 A satisfied soul loathes the honeycomb,
But to a hungry soul every bitter thing *is* sweet.

8 Like a bird that wanders from its nest
Is a man who wanders from his place.

9 Ointment and perfume delight the heart,
And the sweetness of a man's friend *gives delight* by hearty counsel.

10 Do not forsake your own friend or your father's friend,
Nor go to your brother's house in the day of your calamity;
Better *is* a neighbor nearby than a brother far away.

26:15 [a] Compare 19:24

11 My son, be wise, and make my heart glad,
That I may answer him who reproaches me.

12 A prudent *man* foresees evil *and* hides himself;
The simple pass on *and* are punished.

13 Take the garment of him who is surety for a stranger,
And hold it in pledge *when* he is surety for a seductress.

14 He who blesses his friend with a loud voice, rising early in the morning,
It will be counted a curse to him.

15 A continual dripping on a very rainy day
And a contentious woman are alike;
16 Whoever restrains her restrains the wind,
And grasps oil with his right hand.

17 *As* iron sharpens iron,
So a man sharpens the countenance of his friend.

18 Whoever keeps the fig tree will eat its fruit;
So he who waits on his master will be honored.

19 As in water face *reflects* face,
So a man's heart *reveals* the man.

20 Hell[a] and Destruction[b] are never full;
So the eyes of man are never satisfied.

21 The refining pot *is* for silver and the furnace for gold,
And a man *is valued* by what others say of him.

22 Though you grind a fool in a mortar with a pestle along with crushed grain,
Yet his foolishness will not depart from him.

23 Be diligent to know the state of your flocks,
And attend to your herds;
24 For riches *are* not forever,
Nor does a crown *endure* to all generations.
25 *When* the hay is removed, and the tender grass shows itself,
And the herbs of the mountains are gathered in,
26 The lambs *will provide* your clothing,
And the goats the price of a field;
27 *You shall have* enough goats' milk for your food,
For the food of your household,
And the nourishment of your maidservants.

28 The wicked flee when no one pursues,
But the righteous are bold as a lion.

2 Because of the transgression of a land, many *are* its princes;
But by a man of understanding *and* knowledge
Right will be prolonged.

3 A poor man who oppresses the poor
Is like a driving rain which leaves no food.

4 Those who forsake the law praise the wicked,
But such as keep the law contend with them.

5 Evil men do not understand justice,
But those who seek the LORD understand all.

6 Better *is* the poor who walks in his integrity
Than one perverse *in his* ways, though he *be* rich.

27:20 [a] Or *Sheol* [b] Hebrew *Abaddon*

7 Whoever keeps the law *is* a discerning son,
But a companion of gluttons shames his father.

8 One who increases his possessions by usury and extortion
Gathers it for him who will pity the poor.

9 One who turns away his ear from hearing the law,
Even his prayer *is* an abomination.

10 Whoever causes the upright to go astray in an evil way,
He himself will fall into his own pit;
But the blameless will inherit good.

11 The rich man *is* wise in his own eyes,
But the poor who has understanding searches him out.

12 When the righteous rejoice, *there is* great glory;
But when the wicked arise, men hide themselves.

13 He who covers his sins will not prosper,
But whoever confesses and forsakes *them* will have mercy.

14 Happy *is* the man who is always reverent,
But he who hardens his heart will fall into calamity.

15 *Like* a roaring lion and a charging bear
Is a wicked ruler over poor people.

16 A ruler who lacks understanding *is* a great oppressor,
But he who hates covetousness will prolong *his* days.

17 A man burdened with bloodshed will flee into a pit;
Let no one help him.

18 Whoever walks blamelessly will be saved,
But *he who is* perverse *in his* ways will suddenly fall.

19 He who tills his land will have plenty of bread,
But he who follows frivolity will have poverty enough!

20 A faithful man will abound with blessings,
But he who hastens to be rich will not go unpunished.

21 To show partiality *is* not good,
Because for a piece of bread a man will transgress.

22 A man with an evil eye hastens after riches,
And does not consider that poverty will come upon him.

23 He who rebukes a man will find more favor afterward
Than he who flatters with the tongue.

24 Whoever robs his father or his mother,
And says, "*It is* no transgression,"
The same *is* companion to a destroyer.

25 He who is of a proud heart stirs up strife,
But he who trusts in the LORD will be prospered.

26 He who trusts in his own heart is a fool,
But whoever walks wisely will be delivered.

27 He who gives to the poor will not lack,
But he who hides his eyes will have many curses.

28 When the wicked arise, men hide themselves;
But when they perish, the righteous increase.

29 He who is often rebuked, *and* hardens *his* neck,
Will suddenly be destroyed, and that without remedy.

2 When the righteous are in authority, the people rejoice;
But when a wicked *man* rules, the people groan.

3 Whoever loves wisdom makes his father rejoice,
But a companion of harlots wastes *his* wealth.

4 The king establishes the land by justice,
But he who receives bribes overthrows it.

5 A man who flatters his neighbor
Spreads a net for his feet.

6 By transgression an evil man is snared,
But the righteous sings and rejoices.

7 The righteous considers the cause of the poor,
But the wicked does not understand *such* knowledge.

8 Scoffers set a city aflame,
But wise *men* turn away wrath.

9 *If* a wise man contends with a foolish man,
Whether *the fool* rages or laughs, *there is* no peace.

10 The bloodthirsty hate the blameless,
But the upright seek his well-being.[a]

11 A fool vents all his feelings,[a]
But a wise *man* holds them back.

12 If a ruler pays attention to lies,
All his servants *become* wicked.

13 The poor *man* and the oppressor have this in common:
The LORD gives light to the eyes of both.

14 The king who judges the poor with truth,
His throne will be established forever.

15 The rod and rebuke give wisdom,
But a child left *to himself* brings shame to his mother.

16 When the wicked are multiplied, transgression increases;
But the righteous will see their fall.

17 Correct your son, and he will give you rest;
Yes, he will give delight to your soul.

18 Where *there is* no revelation,[a] the people cast off restraint;
But happy *is* he who keeps the law.

19 A servant will not be corrected by mere words;
For though he understands, he will not respond.

20 Do you see a man hasty in his words?
There is more hope for a fool than for him.

21 He who pampers his servant from childhood
Will have him as a son in the end.

22 An angry man stirs up strife,
And a furious man abounds in transgression.

23 A man's pride will bring him low,
But the humble in spirit will retain honor.

24 Whoever is a partner with a thief hates his own life;
He swears to tell the truth,[a] but reveals nothing.

29:10 [a] Literally *soul* **29:11** [a] Literally *spirit* **29:18** [a] Or *prophetic vision* **29:24** [a] Literally *hears the adjuration*

25 The fear of man brings a snare,
But whoever trusts in the LORD
shall be safe.

26 Many seek the ruler's favor,
But justice for man *comes* from
the LORD.

27 An unjust man *is* an abomination
to the righteous,
And *he who is* upright in the way
is an abomination to the
wicked.

The Wisdom of Agur

30 The words of Agur the son of
Jakeh, *his* utterance. This man
declared to Ithiel—to Ithiel and Ucal:

2 Surely I *am* more stupid than *any*
man,
And do not have the
understanding of a man.
3 I neither learned wisdom
Nor have knowledge of the Holy
One.

4 Who has ascended into heaven,
or descended?
Who has gathered the wind in His
fists?
Who has bound the waters in a
garment?
Who has established all the ends
of the earth?
What *is* His name, and what *is* His
Son's name,
If you know?

5 Every word of God *is* pure;
He *is* a shield to those who put
their trust in Him.
6 Do not add to His words,
Lest He rebuke you, and you be
found a liar.

7 Two *things* I request of You
(Deprive me not before I die):
8 Remove falsehood and lies far
from me;
Give me neither poverty nor riches—
Feed me with the food allotted
to me;
9 Lest I be full and deny *You,*
And say, "Who *is* the LORD?"
Or lest I be poor and steal,
And profane the name of my God.

10 Do not malign a servant to his
master,
Lest he curse you, and you be
found guilty.

11 *There is* a generation *that* curses
its father,
And does not bless its mother.
12 *There is* a generation *that is* pure
in its own eyes,
Yet is not washed from its
filthiness.
13 *There is* a generation—oh, how
lofty are their eyes!
And their eyelids are lifted up.
14 *There is* a generation whose teeth
are like swords,
And whose fangs *are like* knives,
To devour the poor from off the
earth,
And the needy from *among* men.

15 The leech has two daughters—
Give *and* Give!

There are three *things that* are
never satisfied,
Four never say, "Enough!":
16 The grave,[a]
The barren womb,
The earth *that* is not satisfied with
water—
And the fire never says, "Enough!"

17 The eye *that* mocks *his* father,
And scorns obedience to *his*
mother,
The ravens of the valley will pick
it out,
And the young eagles will eat it.

18 There are three *things which* are
too wonderful for me,
Yes, four *which* I do not
understand:
19 The way of an eagle in the air,
The way of a serpent on
a rock,

30:16 [a] Or *Sheol*

The way of a ship in the midst of the sea,
And the way of a man with a virgin.

20 This *is* the way of an adulterous woman:
She eats and wipes her mouth,
And says, "I have done no wickedness."

21 For three *things* the earth is perturbed,
Yes, for four it cannot bear up:
22 For a servant when he reigns,
A fool when he is filled with food,
23 A hateful *woman* when she is married,
And a maidservant who succeeds her mistress.

24 There are four *things which* are little on the earth,
But they *are* exceedingly wise:
25 The ants *are* a people not strong,
Yet they prepare their food in the summer;
26 The rock badgers[a] are a feeble folk,
Yet they make their homes in the crags;
27 The locusts have no king,
Yet they all advance in ranks;
28 The spider[a] skillfully grasps with its hands,
And it is in kings' palaces.

29 There are three *things which* are majestic in pace,
Yes, four *which* are stately in walk:
30 A lion, *which is* mighty among beasts
And does not turn away from any;
31 A greyhound,[a]
A male goat also,
And a king *whose* troops *are* with him.[b]

32 If you have been foolish in exalting yourself,
Or if you have devised evil, *put your* hand on *your* mouth.
33 For *as* the churning of milk produces butter,
And wringing the nose produces blood,
So the forcing of wrath produces strife.

The Words of King Lemuel's Mother

31 The words of King Lemuel, the utterance which his mother taught him:

2 What, my son?
And what, son of my womb?
And what, son of my vows?
3 Do not give your strength to women,
Nor your ways to that which destroys kings.

4 *It is* not for kings, O Lemuel,
It is not for kings to drink wine,
Nor for princes intoxicating drink;
5 Lest they drink and forget the law,
And pervert the justice of all the afflicted.
6 Give strong drink to him who is perishing,
And wine to those who are bitter of heart.
7 Let him drink and forget his poverty,
And remember his misery no more.

8 Open your mouth for the speechless,
In the cause of all *who are* appointed to die.[a]
9 Open your mouth, judge righteously,
And plead the cause of the poor and needy.

The Virtuous Wife

10 Who[a] can find a virtuous[b] wife?
For her worth *is* far above rubies.
11 The heart of her husband safely trusts her;
So he will have no lack of gain.

30:26 [a] Or *hyraxes* **30:28** [a] Or *lizard* **30:31** [a] Exact identity unknown [b] A Jewish tradition reads *a king against whom there is no uprising.* **31:8** [a] Literally *sons of passing away* **31:10** [a] Verses 10 through 31 are an alphabetic acrostic in Hebrew (compare Psalm 119). [b] Literally *a wife of valor,* in the sense of all forms of excellence

12 She does him good and not evil
All the days of her life.
13 She seeks wool and flax,
And willingly works with her hands.
14 She is like the merchant ships,
She brings her food from afar.
15 She also rises while it is yet night,
And provides food for her household,
And a portion for her maidservants.
16 She considers a field and buys it;
From her profits she plants a vineyard.
17 She girds herself with strength,
And strengthens her arms.
18 She perceives that her merchandise *is* good,
And her lamp does not go out by night.
19 She stretches out her hands to the distaff,
And her hand holds the spindle.
20 She extends her hand to the poor,
Yes, she reaches out her hands to the needy.
21 She is not afraid of snow for her household,
For all her household *is* clothed with scarlet.
22 She makes tapestry for herself;
Her clothing *is* fine linen and purple.
23 Her husband is known in the gates,
When he sits among the elders of the land.
24 She makes linen garments and sells *them*,
And supplies sashes for the merchants.
25 Strength and honor *are* her clothing;
She shall rejoice in time to come.
26 She opens her mouth with wisdom,
And on her tongue *is* the law of kindness.
27 She watches over the ways of her household,
And does not eat the bread of idleness.
28 Her children rise up and call her blessed;
Her husband *also*, and he praises her:
29 "Many daughters have done well,
But you excel them all."
30 Charm *is* deceitful and beauty *is* passing,
But a woman *who* fears the LORD, she shall be praised.
31 Give her of the fruit of her hands,
And let her own works praise her in the gates.

THE BOOK OF
ECCLESIASTES

The Book of Ecclesiastes talks about the meaning of life. Why do we exist and what is the point of our lives? These are the questions Solomon wanted to answer, so he set out to find meaning in different ways like power, wealth, and pleasure. But Solomon learned that none of these things were of lasting value on their own. The key, he discovered, is to have God at the center of life. When you place Him there, He gives all of those other things meaning and purpose. Loving God and wanting to serve Him is what gives life meaning.

- **GENRE:** Wisdom and Poetry
- **AUTHOR:** Solomon
- **TIME:** c. 935 BC
- **PURPOSE:** To explain that life has incredible meaning because of God and how to enjoy life properly.

The Vanity of Life

1 The words of the Preacher, the son of David, king in Jerusalem.

2 "Vanity[a] of vanities," says the Preacher;
"Vanity of vanities, all *is* vanity."

3 What profit has a man from all his labor
In which he toils under the sun?
4 *One* generation passes away, and *another* generation comes;
But the earth abides forever.
5 The sun also rises, and the sun goes down,
And hastens to the place where it arose.
6 The wind goes toward the south,
And turns around to the north;
The wind whirls about continually,
And comes again on its circuit.
7 All the rivers run into the sea,
Yet the sea *is* not full;
To the place from which the rivers come,
There they return again.
8 All things *are* full of labor;
Man cannot express *it*.
The eye is not satisfied with seeing,
Nor the ear filled with hearing.

9 That which has been *is* what will be,
That which *is* done is what will be done,
And *there is* nothing new under the sun.
10 Is there anything of which it may be said,
"See, this *is* new"?
It has already been in ancient times before us.
11 *There is* no remembrance of former *things,*
Nor will there be any remembrance of *things* that are to come
By *those* who will come after.

The Grief of Wisdom

12I, the Preacher, was king over Israel
in Jerusalem. 13And I set my heart to
seek and search out by wisdom con-
cerning all that is done under heaven;
this burdensome task God has given to
the sons of man, by which they may be
exercised. 14I have seen all the works
that are done under the sun; and indeed,
all *is* vanity and grasping for the wind.

1:2 a Or *Absurdity, Frustration, Futility, Nonsense;* and so throughout this book

15 *What is* crooked cannot be made
straight,
And what is lacking cannot be
numbered.

16I communed with my heart, say-
ing, "Look, I have attained greatness,
and have gained more wisdom than all
who were before me in Jerusalem. My
heart has understood great wisdom
and knowledge." 17And I set my heart
to know wisdom and to know madness
and folly. I perceived that this also is
grasping for the wind.

18 For in much wisdom *is* much grief,
And he who increases knowledge
increases sorrow.

The Vanity of Pleasure

2 I said in my heart, "Come now, I will
test you with mirth; therefore enjoy
pleasure"; but surely, this also *was* vani-
ty. 2I said of laughter—"Madness!"; and
of mirth, "What does it accomplish?"
3I searched in my heart *how* to gratify
my flesh with wine, while guiding my
heart with wisdom, and how to lay hold
on folly, till I might see what *was* good
for the sons of men to do under heaven
all the days of their lives.
4I made my works great, I built myself
houses, and planted myself vineyards.
5I made myself gardens and orchards,
and I planted all *kinds* of fruit trees in
them. 6I made myself water pools from
which to water the growing trees of the
grove. 7I acquired male and female
servants, and had servants born in my
house. Yes, I had greater possessions of
herds and flocks than all who were in Je-
rusalem before me. 8I also gathered for
myself silver and gold and the special
treasures of kings and of the provinces.
I acquired male and female singers, the
delights of the sons of men, *and* musical
instruments[a] of all kinds.
9So I became great and excelled more
than all who were before me in Jerusa-
lem. Also my wisdom remained with me.

10 Whatever my eyes desired I did
not keep from them.
I did not withhold my heart from
any pleasure,
For my heart rejoiced in all my
labor;
And this was my reward from all
my labor.
11 Then I looked on all the works
that my hands had done
And on the labor in which I had
toiled;
And indeed all *was* vanity and
grasping for the wind.
There was no profit under the sun.

The End of the Wise and the Fool

12 Then I turned myself to consider
wisdom and madness and
folly;
For what *can* the man *do* who
succeeds the king?—
Only what he has already done.
13 Then I saw that wisdom excels
folly
As light excels darkness.
14 The wise man's eyes *are* in his
head,
But the fool walks in darkness.
Yet I myself perceived
That the same event happens to
them all.

15 So I said in my heart,
"As it happens to the fool,
It also happens to me,
And why was I then more wise?"
Then I said in my heart,
"This also *is* vanity."
16 For *there is* no more
remembrance of the wise
than of the fool forever,
Since all that now *is* will be
forgotten in the days to come.
And how does a wise *man* die?
As the fool!

17Therefore I hated life because the
work that was done under the sun *was*
distressing to me, for all *is* vanity and
grasping for the wind.
18Then I hated all my labor in which
I had toiled under the sun, because I
must leave it to the man who will come
after me. 19And who knows whether he

2:8 a Exact meaning unknown

will be wise or a fool? Yet he will rule
over all my labor in which I toiled and in
which I have shown myself wise under
the sun. This also *is* vanity. [20]Therefore
I turned my heart and despaired of all
the labor in which I had toiled under the
sun. [21]For there is a man whose labor *is*
with wisdom, knowledge, and skill; yet
he must leave his heritage to a man who
has not labored for it. This also *is* vanity
and a great evil. [22]For what has man for
all his labor, and for the striving of his
heart with which he has toiled under the
sun? [23]For all his days *are* sorrowful,
and his work burdensome; even in the
night his heart takes no rest. This also
is vanity.

[24]Nothing *is* better for a man *than* that
he should eat and drink, and *that* his
soul should enjoy good in his labor.
This also, I saw, was from the hand of
God. [25]For who can eat, or who can
have enjoyment, more than I?[a] [26]For
God gives wisdom and knowledge and
joy to a man who *is* good in His sight;
but to the sinner He gives the work of
gathering and collecting, that he may
give to *him who is* good before God. This
also *is* vanity and grasping for the wind.

Everything Has Its Time

3 To everything *there is* a season,
A time for every purpose under
heaven:

2 A time to be born,
And a time to die;
A time to plant,
And a time to pluck *what is*
planted;
3 A time to kill,
And a time to heal;
A time to break down,
And a time to build up;
4 A time to weep,
And a time to laugh;
A time to mourn,
And a time to dance;
5 A time to cast away stones,
And a time to gather stones;
A time to embrace,
And a time to refrain from
embracing;
6 A time to gain,
And a time to lose;
A time to keep,
And a time to throw away;
7 A time to tear,
And a time to sew;
A time to keep silence,
And a time to speak;
8 A time to love,
And a time to hate;
A time of war,
And a time of peace.

The God-Given Task

[9]What profit has the worker from that
in which he labors? [10]I have seen the
God-given task with which the sons of
men are to be occupied. [11]He has made
everything beautiful in its time. Also He
has put eternity in their hearts, except
that no one can find out the work that
God does from beginning to end.

[12]I know that nothing *is* better for them
than to rejoice, and to do good in their
lives, [13]and also that every man should
eat and drink and enjoy the good of all
his labor—it *is* the gift of God.

14 I know that whatever God does,
It shall be forever.
Nothing can be added to it,
And nothing taken from it.
God does *it,* that men should fear
before Him.
15 That which is has already been,
And what is to be has already
been;
And God requires an account of
what is past.

Injustice Seems to Prevail

[16]Moreover I saw under the sun:

In the place of judgment,
Wickedness *was* there;
And *in* the place of
righteousness,
Iniquity *was* there.

[17]I said in my heart,

"God shall judge the righteous and
the wicked,

2:25 [a] Following Masoretic Text, Targum, and Vulgate; some Hebrew manuscripts, Septuagint, and Syriac read *without Him.*

For *there is* a time there for every
purpose and for every work."

18I said in my heart, "Concerning the
condition of the sons of men, God tests
them, that they may see that they them-
selves are *like* animals." 19For what hap-
pens to the sons of men also happens
to animals; one thing befalls them: as
one dies, so dies the other. Surely, they
all have one breath; man has no advan-
tage over animals, for all *is* vanity. 20All
go to one place: all are from the dust,
and all return to dust. 21Who knows the
spirit of the sons of men, which goes
upward, and the spirit of the animal,
which goes down to the earth?[a] 22So
I perceived that nothing *is* better than
that a man should rejoice in his own
works, for that *is* his heritage. For who
can bring him to see what will happen
after him?

4 Then I returned and considered all
the oppression that is done under
the sun:

And look! The tears of the
oppressed,
But they have no comforter—
On the side of their oppressors
there is power,
But they have no comforter.
2 Therefore I praised the dead who
were already dead,
More than the living who are still
alive.
3 Yet, better than both *is he* who has
never existed,
Who has not seen the evil work
that is done under the sun.

The Vanity of Selfish Toil

4Again, I saw that for all toil and ev-
ery skillful work a man is envied by
his neighbor. This also *is* vanity and
grasping for the wind.

5 The fool folds his hands
And consumes his own flesh.
6 Better a handful *with* quietness
Than both hands full, *together
with* toil and grasping for the
wind.

7Then I returned, and I saw vanity
under the sun:

8 There is one alone, without
companion:
He has neither son nor brother.
Yet *there is* no end to all his
labors,
Nor is his eye satisfied with riches.
But he never asks,
"For whom do I toil and deprive
myself of good?"
This also *is* vanity and a grave
misfortune.

The Value of a Friend

9 Two *are* better than one,
Because they have a good reward
for their labor.
10 For if they fall, one will lift up his
companion.
But woe to him *who is* alone when
he falls,
For *he has* no one to help him up.
11 Again, if two lie down together,
they will keep warm;
But how can one be warm *alone?*
12 Though one may be overpowered
by another, two can
withstand him.
And a threefold cord is not
quickly broken.

Popularity Passes Away

13 Better a poor and wise youth
Than an old and foolish king who
will be admonished no more.
14 For he comes out of prison to be
king,
Although he was born poor in his
kingdom.
15 I saw all the living who walk
under the sun;
They were with the second youth
who stands in his place.
16 *There was* no end of all the people
over whom he was made
king;
Yet those who come afterward will
not rejoice in him.
Surely this also *is* vanity and
grasping for the wind.

3:21 [a] Septuagint, Syriac, Targum, and Vulgate read *Who knows whether the spirit . . . goes upward, and whether . . . goes downward to the earth?*

Fear God, Keep Your Vows

5 Walk prudently when you go to the house of God; and draw near to hear rather than to give the sacrifice of fools, for they do not know that they do evil.

2 Do not be rash with your mouth,
And let not your heart utter anything hastily before God.
For God *is* in heaven, and you on earth;
Therefore let your words be few.
3 For a dream comes through much activity,
And a fool's voice *is known* by *his* many words.

4 When you make a vow to God, do not delay to pay it;
For *He has* no pleasure in fools.
Pay what you have vowed—
5 Better not to vow than to vow and not pay.

6Do not let your mouth cause your
flesh to sin, nor say before the mes-
senger *of God* that it *was* an error. Why
should God be angry at your excuse[a]
and destroy the work of your hands?
7For in the multitude of dreams and
many words *there is* also vanity. But fear
God.

The Vanity of Gain and Honor

8If you see the oppression of the poor,
and the violent perversion of justice
and righteousness in a province, do not
marvel at the matter; for high official
watches over high official, and higher
officials are over them.
9Moreover the profit of the land is for
all; *even* the king is served from the field.

10 He who loves silver will not be satisfied with silver;
Nor he who loves abundance, with increase.
This also *is* vanity.

11 When goods increase,
They increase who eat them;
So what profit have the owners
Except to see *them* with their eyes?

12 The sleep of a laboring man *is* sweet,
Whether he eats little or much;
But the abundance of the rich will not permit him to sleep.

13 There is a severe evil *which* I have seen under the sun:
Riches kept for their owner to his hurt.
14 But those riches perish through misfortune;
When he begets a son, *there is* nothing in his hand.
15 As he came from his mother's womb, naked shall he return,
To go as he came;
And he shall take nothing from his labor
Which he may carry away in his hand.
16 And this also *is* a severe evil—
Just exactly as he came, so shall he go.
And what profit has he who has labored for the wind?
17 All his days he also eats in darkness,
And *he has* much sorrow and sickness and anger.

18Here is what I have seen: *It is* good
and fitting *for one* to eat and drink,
and to enjoy the good of all his labor
in which he toils under the sun all the
days of his life which God gives him; for
it *is* his heritage. 19As for every man to
whom God has given riches and wealth,
and given him power to eat of it, to re-
ceive his heritage and rejoice in his
labor—this *is* the gift of God. 20For he
will not dwell unduly on the days of his
life, because God keeps *him* busy with
the joy of his heart.

6 There is an evil which I have seen
under the sun, and it *is* common
among men: 2A man to whom God has
given riches and wealth and honor, so
that he lacks nothing for himself of all he
desires; yet God does not give him power
to eat of it, but a foreigner consumes it.
This *is* vanity, and it *is* an evil affliction.

5:6 [a] Literally *voice*

3If a man begets a hundred *children*
and lives many years, so that the days
of his years are many, but his soul is not
satisfied with goodness, or indeed he has
no burial, I say *that* a stillborn child *is*
better than he— 4for it comes in vanity
and departs in darkness, and its name
is covered with darkness. 5Though it has
not seen the sun or known *anything,* this
has more rest than that man, 6even if he
lives a thousand years twice—but has not
seen goodness. Do not all go to one place?

7 All the labor of man *is* for his
mouth,
And yet the soul is not satisfied.
8 For what more has the wise *man*
than the fool?
What does the poor man have,
Who knows *how* to walk before
the living?
9 Better *is* the sight of the eyes than
the wandering of desire.
This also *is* vanity and grasping
for the wind.

10 Whatever one is, he has been
named already,
For it is known that he *is* man;
And he cannot contend with Him
who is mightier than he.
11 Since there are many things that
increase vanity,
How *is* man the better?

12For who knows what *is* good for man
in life, all the days of his vain life which
he passes like a shadow? Who can tell a
man what will happen after him under
the sun?

The Value of Practical Wisdom

7 A good name *is* better than
precious ointment,
And the day of death than the
day of one's birth;
2 Better to go to the house of
mourning
Than to go to the house of
feasting,
For that *is* the end of all men;
And the living will take *it* to heart.
3 Sorrow *is* better than laughter,
For by a sad countenance the
heart is made better.
4 The heart of the wise *is* in the
house of mourning,
But the heart of fools *is* in the
house of mirth.
5 *It is* better to hear the rebuke of
the wise
Than for a man to hear the song
of fools.
6 For like the crackling of thorns
under a pot,
So *is* the laughter of the fool.
This also is vanity.
7 Surely oppression destroys a wise
man's reason,
And a bribe debases the heart.

8 The end of a thing *is* better than
its beginning;
The patient in spirit *is* better than
the proud in spirit.
9 Do not hasten in your spirit to be
angry,
For anger rests in the bosom of
fools.
10 Do not say,
"Why were the former days better
than these?"
For you do not inquire wisely
concerning this.

11 Wisdom *is* good with an
inheritance,
And profitable to those who see
the sun.
12 For wisdom *is* a defense *as* money
is a defense,
But the excellence of knowledge
is that wisdom gives life to
those who have it.

13 Consider the work of God;
For who can make straight what
He has made crooked?
14 In the day of prosperity be
joyful,
But in the day of adversity
consider:
Surely God has appointed the one
as well as the other,
So that man can find out nothing
that will come after him.

15I have seen everything in my days
of vanity:

There is a just *man* who perishes
in his righteousness,
And there is a wicked *man*
who prolongs *life* in his
wickedness.

16 Do not be overly righteous,
Nor be overly wise:
Why should you destroy
yourself?
17 Do not be overly wicked,
Nor be foolish:
Why should you die before your
time?
18 *It is* good that you grasp this,
And also not remove your hand
from the other;
For he who fears God will escape
them all.

19 Wisdom strengthens the wise
More than ten rulers of the city.

20 For *there is* not a just man on
earth who does good
And does not sin.

21 Also do not take to heart
everything people say,
Lest you hear your servant
cursing you.
22 For many times, also, your own
heart has known
That even you have cursed
others.

23 All this I have proved by wisdom.
I said, "I will be wise";
But it *was* far from me.
24 As for that which is far off and
exceedingly deep,
Who can find it out?
25 I applied my heart to know,
To search and seek out wisdom
and the reason *of things,*
To know the wickedness of folly,
Even of foolishness *and* madness.
26 And I find more bitter than death
The woman whose heart *is* snares
and nets,
Whose hands *are* fetters.
He who pleases God shall escape
from her,
But the sinner shall be trapped
by her.

27 "Here is what I have found," says
the Preacher,
"*Adding* one thing to the other to
find out the reason,
28 Which my soul still seeks but I
cannot find:
One man among a thousand I
have found,
But a woman among all these I
have not found.
29 Truly, this only I have found:
That God made man upright,
But they have sought out many
schemes."

8 Who *is* like a wise *man?*
And who knows the interpretation
of a thing?
A man's wisdom makes his face
shine,
And the sternness of his face is
changed.

Obey Authorities for God's Sake

2 I *say,* "Keep the king's commandment
for the sake of your oath to God. 3 Do not
be hasty to go from his presence. Do not
take your stand for an evil thing, for he
does whatever pleases him."

4 Where the word of a king *is, there*
is power;
And who may say to him, "What
are you doing?"
5 He who keeps his command will
experience nothing harmful;
And a wise man's heart discerns
both time and judgment,
6 Because for every matter there is
a time and judgment,
Though the misery of man
increases greatly.
7 For he does not know what will
happen;
So who can tell him when it will
occur?
8 No one has power over the spirit
to retain the spirit,
And no one has power in the day
of death.
There is no release from that
war,
And wickedness will not
deliver those who are given
to it.

9All this I have seen, and applied my
heart to every work that is done under
the sun: *There is* a time in which one
man rules over another to his own hurt.

Death Comes to All

10Then I saw the wicked buried, who
had come and gone from the place of
holiness, and they were forgotten[a] in the
city where they had so done. This also *is*
vanity. 11Because the sentence against
an evil work is not executed speedily,
therefore the heart of the sons of men
is fully set in them to do evil. 12Though
a sinner does evil a hundred *times,* and
his *days* are prolonged, yet I surely know
that it will be well with those who fear
God, who fear before Him. 13But it will
not be well with the wicked; nor will he
prolong *his* days, *which are* as a shadow,
because he does not fear before God.
14There is a vanity which occurs on earth,
that there are just *men* to whom it hap-
pens according to the work of the wicked;
again, there are wicked *men* to whom it
happens according to the work of the
righteous. I said that this also *is* vanity.
15So I commended enjoyment, be-
cause a man has nothing better under
the sun than to eat, drink, and be merry;
for this will remain with him in his labor
all the days of his life which God gives
him under the sun.
16When I applied my heart to know
wisdom and to see the business that is
done on earth, even though one sees
no sleep day or night, 17then I saw all
the work of God, that a man cannot find
out the work that is done under the sun.
For though a man labors to discover *it,*
yet he will not find *it;* moreover, though
a wise *man* attempts to know *it,* he will
not be able to find *it.*

9 For I considered all this in my heart,
so that I could declare it all: that the
righteous and the wise and their works
are in the hand of God. People know
neither love nor hatred *by* anything
they see before them. 2All things *come*
alike to all:

One event *happens* to the
righteous and the wicked;
To the good,[a] the clean, and the
unclean;
To him who sacrifices and him
who does not sacrifice.
As is the good, so *is* the sinner;
He who takes an oath as *he* who
fears an oath.

3This *is* an evil in all that is done under
the sun: that one thing *happens* to all.
Truly the hearts of the sons of men are
full of evil; madness *is* in their hearts
while they live, and after that *they go* to
the dead. 4But for him who is joined to
all the living there is hope, for a living
dog is better than a dead lion.

5 For the living know that they will
die;
But the dead know nothing,
And they have no more reward,
For the memory of them is
forgotten.
6 Also their love, their hatred,
and their envy have now
perished;
Nevermore will they have a share
In anything done under the sun.

7 Go, eat your bread with joy,
And drink your wine with a merry
heart;
For God has already accepted
your works.
8 Let your garments always be
white,
And let your head lack no oil.

9Live joyfully with the wife whom you
love all the days of your vain life which
He has given you under the sun, all
your days of vanity; for that *is* your
portion in life, and in the labor which
you perform under the sun.
10Whatever your hand finds to do, do
it with your might; for *there is* no work
or device or knowledge or wisdom in
the grave where you are going.
11I returned and saw under the sun
that—

The race *is* not to the swift,
Nor the battle to the strong,

8:10 [a] Some Hebrew manuscripts, Septuagint, and Vulgate read *praised.* **9:2** [a] Septuagint, Syriac, and Vulgate read *good and bad.*

Nor bread to the wise,
Nor riches to men of understanding,
Nor favor to men of skill;
But time and chance happen to them all.
12 For man also does not know his time:
Like fish taken in a cruel net,
Like birds caught in a snare,
So the sons of men *are* snared in an evil time,
When it falls suddenly upon them.

Wisdom Superior to Folly

13This wisdom I have also seen un-
der the sun, and it *seemed* great to me:
14*There was* a little city with few men
in it; and a great king came against
it, besieged it, and built great snares[a]
around it. 15Now there was found in it
a poor wise man, and he by his wisdom
delivered the city. Yet no one remem-
bered that same poor man.
16Then I said:

"Wisdom *is* better than strength.
Nevertheless the poor man's wisdom *is* despised,
And his words are not heard.
17 Words of the wise, *spoken* quietly, *should be* heard
Rather than the shout of a ruler of fools.
18 Wisdom *is* better than weapons of war;
But one sinner destroys much good."

10

Dead flies putrefy[a] the perfumer's ointment,
And cause it to give off a foul odor;
So does a little folly to one respected for wisdom *and* honor.
2 A wise man's heart *is* at his right hand,
But a fool's heart at his left.
3 Even when a fool walks along the way,
He lacks wisdom,
And he shows everyone *that* he *is* a fool.
4 If the spirit of the ruler rises against you,
Do not leave your post;
For conciliation pacifies great offenses.
5 There is an evil I have seen under the sun,
As an error proceeding from the ruler:
6 Folly is set in great dignity,
While the rich sit in a lowly place.
7 I have seen servants on horses,
While princes walk on the ground like servants.
8 He who digs a pit will fall into it,
And whoever breaks through a wall will be bitten by a serpent.
9 He who quarries stones may be hurt by them,
And he who splits wood may be endangered by it.
10 If the ax is dull,
And one does not sharpen the edge,
Then he must use more strength;
But wisdom brings success.
11 A serpent may bite when *it is* not charmed;
The babbler is no different.
12 The words of a wise man's mouth *are* gracious,
But the lips of a fool shall swallow him up;
13 The words of his mouth begin with foolishness,
And the end of his talk *is* raving madness.
14 A fool also multiplies words.
No man knows what is to be;
Who can tell him what will be after him?
15 The labor of fools wearies them,
For they do not even know how to go to the city!
16 Woe to you, O land, when your king *is* a child,
And your princes feast in the morning!

9:14 [a] Septuagint, Syriac, and Vulgate read *bulwarks*. 10:1 [a] Targum and Vulgate omit *putrefy*.

17 Blessed *are* you, O land, when your king *is* the son of nobles,
And your princes feast at the proper time—
For strength and not for drunkenness!
18 Because of laziness the building decays,
And through idleness of hands the house leaks.
19 A feast is made for laughter,
And wine makes merry;
But money answers everything.

20 Do not curse the king, even in your thought;
Do not curse the rich, even in your bedroom;
For a bird of the air may carry your voice,
And a bird in flight may tell the matter.

The Value of Diligence

11 Cast your bread upon the waters,
For you will find it after many days.
2 Give a serving to seven, and also to eight,
For you do not know what evil will be on the earth.

3 If the clouds are full of rain,
They empty *themselves* upon the earth;
And if a tree falls to the south or the north,
In the place where the tree falls, there it shall lie.
4 He who observes the wind will not sow,
And he who regards the clouds will not reap.

5 As you do not know what *is* the way of the wind,[a]
Or how the bones *grow* in the womb of her who is with child,
So you do not know the works of God who makes everything.
6 In the morning sow your seed,
And in the evening do not withhold your hand;
For you do not know which will prosper,
Either this or that,
Or whether both alike *will be* good.

7 Truly the light is sweet,
And *it is* pleasant for the eyes to behold the sun;
8 But if a man lives many years
And rejoices in them all,
Yet let him remember the days of darkness,
For they will be many.
All that is coming *is* vanity.

Seek God in Early Life

9 Rejoice, O young man, in your youth,
And let your heart cheer you in the days of your youth;
Walk in the ways of your heart,
And in the sight of your eyes;
But know that for all these
God will bring you into judgment.
10 Therefore remove sorrow from your heart,
And put away evil from your flesh,
For childhood and youth *are* vanity.

12 Remember now your Creator in the days of your youth,
Before the difficult days come,
And the years draw near when you say,
"I have no pleasure in them":
2 While the sun and the light,
The moon and the stars,
Are not darkened,
And the clouds do not return after the rain;
3 In the day when the keepers of the house tremble,
And the strong men bow down;
When the grinders cease because they are few,
And those that look through the windows grow dim;

11:5 [a] Or *spirit*

4 When the doors are shut in the streets,
And the sound of grinding is low;
When one rises up at the sound of a bird,
And all the daughters of music are brought low.
5 Also they are afraid of height,
And of terrors in the way;
When the almond tree blossoms,
The grasshopper is a burden,
And desire fails.
For man goes to his eternal home,
And the mourners go about the streets.

6 *Remember your Creator* before the silver cord is loosed,[a]
Or the golden bowl is broken,
Or the pitcher shattered at the fountain,
Or the wheel broken at the well.
7 Then the dust will return to the earth as it was,
And the spirit will return to God who gave it.

8 "Vanity of vanities," says the Preacher,
"All *is* vanity."

The Whole Duty of Man

9And moreover, because the Preach-
er was wise, he still taught the people
knowledge; yes, he pondered and sought
out *and* set in order many proverbs.
10The Preacher sought to find accept-
able words; and *what was* written *was*
upright—words of truth. 11The words of
the wise are like goads, and the words
of scholars[a] are like well-driven nails,
given by one Shepherd. 12And further,
my son, be admonished by these. Of
making many books *there is* no end, and
much study *is* wearisome to the flesh.
13Let us hear the conclusion of the
whole matter:

Fear God and keep His commandments,
For this is man's all.
14 For God will bring every work into judgment,
Including every secret thing,
Whether good or evil.

12:6 a Following Qere and Targum; Kethib reads *removed;* Septuagint and Vulgate read *broken.*
12:11 a Literally *masters of the assemblies*

THE SONG OF SOLOMON

The Song of Solomon is a poem that tells the story of God's gift of marriage. The story takes place in three main scenes: a couple preparing for their wedding, the couple celebrating their wedding, and then the couple living in marriage. Four main characters are featured in the song: the woman, the man, the woman's friends, and the woman's brothers.

- **GENRE:** Wisdom and Poetry
- **AUTHOR:** Solomon
- **TIME:** c. 971–931 BC
- **PURPOSE:** To celebrate God's gift of marriage.

---

1 The song of songs, which *is* Solomon's.

The Banquet

The Shulamite[a]

2 Let him kiss me with the kisses of his mouth—
For your[b] love *is* better than wine.
3 Because of the fragrance of your good ointments,
Your name *is* ointment poured forth;
Therefore the virgins love you.
4 Draw me away!

The Daughters of Jerusalem

We will run after you.[a]

The Shulamite

The king has brought me into his chambers.

The Daughters of Jerusalem

We will be glad and rejoice in you.[b]

We will remember your[c] love more than wine.

The Shulamite

Rightly do they love you.[d]

5 I *am* dark, but lovely,
O daughters of Jerusalem,
Like the tents of Kedar,
Like the curtains of Solomon.
6 Do not look upon me, because I *am* dark,
Because the sun has tanned me.
My mother's sons were angry with me;
They made me the keeper of the vineyards,
But my own vineyard I have not kept.

(To Her Beloved)

7 Tell me, O you whom I love,
Where you feed *your flock,*
Where you make *it* rest at noon.
For why should I be as one who veils herself[a]
By the flocks of your companions?

The Beloved

8 If you do not know, O fairest among women,
Follow in the footsteps of the flock,

1:2 [a] A young woman from the town of Shulam or Shunem (compare 6:13). The speaker and audience are identified according to the number, gender, and person of the Hebrew words. Occasionally the identity is not certain. [b] Masculine singular, that is, the Beloved
1:4 [a] Masculine singular, that is, the Beloved [b] Feminine singular, that is, the Shulamite [c] Masculine singular, that is, the Beloved [d] Masculine singular, that is, the Beloved
1:7 [a] Septuagint, Syriac, and Vulgate read *wanders.*

And feed your little goats
Beside the shepherds' tents.
9 I have compared you, my love,
To my filly among Pharaoh's
chariots.
10 Your cheeks are lovely with
ornaments,
Your neck with chains *of gold*.

The Daughters of Jerusalem
11 We will make you[a] ornaments of
gold
With studs of silver.

The Shulamite
12 While the king *is* at his table,
My spikenard sends forth its
fragrance.
13 A bundle of myrrh *is* my beloved
to me,
That lies all night between my
breasts.
14 My beloved *is* to me a cluster of
henna *blooms*
In the vineyards of En Gedi.

The Beloved
15 Behold, you *are* fair, my love!
Behold, you *are* fair!
You *have* dove's eyes.

The Shulamite
16 Behold, you *are* handsome, my
beloved!
Yes, pleasant!
Also our bed *is* green.
17 The beams of our houses *are* cedar,
And our rafters of fir.

2 I *am* the rose of Sharon,
And the lily of the valleys.

The Beloved
2 Like a lily among thorns,
So is my love among the daughters.

The Shulamite
3 Like an apple tree among the
trees of the woods,
So *is* my beloved among the sons.
I sat down in his shade with great
delight,
And his fruit *was* sweet to my
taste.

The Shulamite to the Daughters of Jerusalem
4 He brought me to the banqueting
house,
And his banner over me *was* love.
5 Sustain me with cakes of raisins,
Refresh me with apples,
For I *am* lovesick.

6 His left hand *is* under my head,
And his right hand embraces me.
7 I charge you, O daughters of
Jerusalem,
By the gazelles or by the does of
the field,
Do not stir up nor awaken love
Until it pleases.

The Beloved's Request
The Shulamite
8 The voice of my beloved!
Behold, he comes
Leaping upon the mountains,
Skipping upon the hills.
9 My beloved is like a gazelle or a
young stag.
Behold, he stands behind our wall;
He is looking through the windows,
Gazing through the lattice.

10 My beloved spoke, and said to me:
"Rise up, my love, my fair one,
And come away.
11 For lo, the winter is past,
The rain is over *and* gone.
12 The flowers appear on the earth;
The time of singing has come,
And the voice of the turtledove
Is heard in our land.
13 The fig tree puts forth her green
figs,
And the vines *with* the tender
grapes
Give a *good* smell.
Rise up, my love, my fair one,
And come away!

14 " O my dove, in the clefts of the rock,
In the secret *places* of the cliff,
Let me see your face,
Let me hear your voice;
For your voice *is* sweet,
And your face *is* lovely."

1:11 [a] Feminine singular, that is, the Shulamite

Her Brothers

15 Catch us the foxes,
The little foxes that spoil the vines,
For our vines *have* tender grapes.

The Shulamite

16 My beloved *is* mine, and I *am* his.
He feeds *his flock* among the lilies.

(To Her Beloved)

17 Until the day breaks
And the shadows flee away,
Turn, my beloved,
And be like a gazelle
Or a young stag
Upon the mountains of Bether.[a]

A Troubled Night

The Shulamite

3 By night on my bed I sought the one I love;
I sought him, but I did not find him.
2 "I will rise now," *I said,*
"And go about the city;
In the streets and in the squares
I will seek the one I love."
I sought him, but I did not find him.
3 The watchmen who go about the city found me;
I said,
"Have you seen the one I love?"

4 Scarcely had I passed by them,
When I found the one I love.
I held him and would not let him go,
Until I had brought him to the house of my mother,
And into the chamber of her who conceived me.

5 I charge you, O daughters of Jerusalem,
By the gazelles or by the does of the field,
Do not stir up nor awaken love
Until it pleases.

The Coming of Solomon

The Shulamite

6 Who *is* this coming out of the wilderness
Like pillars of smoke,
Perfumed with myrrh and frankincense,
With all the merchant's fragrant powders?
7 Behold, it *is* Solomon's couch,
With sixty valiant men around it,
Of the valiant of Israel.
8 They all hold swords,
Being expert in war.
Every man *has* his sword on his thigh
Because of fear in the night.

9 Of the wood of Lebanon
Solomon the King
Made himself a palanquin:[a]
10 He made its pillars *of* silver,
Its support *of* gold,
Its seat *of* purple,
Its interior paved *with* love
By the daughters of Jerusalem.
11 Go forth, O daughters of Zion,
And see King Solomon with the crown
With which his mother crowned him
On the day of his wedding,
The day of the gladness of his heart.

The Bridegroom Praises the Bride

The Beloved

4 Behold, you *are* fair, my love!
Behold, you *are* fair!
You *have* dove's eyes behind your veil.
Your hair *is* like a flock of goats,
Going down from Mount Gilead.
2 Your teeth *are* like a flock of shorn *sheep*
Which have come up from the washing,
Every one of which bears twins,
And none *is* barren among them.
3 Your lips *are* like a strand of scarlet,
And your mouth is lovely.
Your temples behind your veil
Are like a piece of pomegranate.
4 Your neck *is* like the tower of David,
Built for an armory,
On which hang a thousand bucklers,
All shields of mighty men.

2:17 [a] Literally *Separation* 3:9 [a] A portable enclosed chair

5 Your two breasts *are* like two fawns,
Twins of a gazelle,
Which feed among the lilies.

6 Until the day breaks
And the shadows flee away,
I will go my way to the mountain
of myrrh
And to the hill of frankincense.

7 You *are* all fair, my love,
And *there is* no spot in you.
8 Come with me from Lebanon, *my*
spouse,
With me from Lebanon.
Look from the top of Amana,
From the top of Senir and Hermon,
From the lions' dens,
From the mountains of the
leopards.

9 You have ravished my heart,
My sister, *my* spouse;
You have ravished my heart
With one *look* of your eyes,
With one link of your necklace.
10 How fair is your love,
My sister, *my* spouse!
How much better than wine is
your love,
And the scent of your perfumes
Than all spices!
11 Your lips, O *my* spouse,
Drip as the honeycomb;
Honey and milk *are* under your
tongue;
And the fragrance of your garments
Is like the fragrance of Lebanon.

12 A garden enclosed
Is my sister, *my* spouse,
A spring shut up,
A fountain sealed.
13 Your plants *are* an orchard of
pomegranates
With pleasant fruits,
Fragrant henna with spikenard,
14 Spikenard and saffron,
Calamus and cinnamon,
With all trees of frankincense,
Myrrh and aloes,
With all the chief spices—
15 A fountain of gardens,
A well of living waters,
And streams from Lebanon.

The Shulamite

16 Awake, O north *wind,*
And come, O south!
Blow upon my garden,
That its spices may flow out.
Let my beloved come to his garden
And eat its pleasant fruits.

The Beloved

5 I have come to my garden, my
sister, *my* spouse;
I have gathered my myrrh with
my spice;
I have eaten my honeycomb with
my honey;
I have drunk my wine with my
milk.

(To His Friends)

Eat, O friends!
Drink, yes, drink deeply,
O beloved ones!

The Shulamite's Troubled Evening

The Shulamite

2 I sleep, but my heart is awake;
It is the voice of my beloved!
He knocks, *saying,*
"Open for me, my sister, my love,
My dove, my perfect one;
For my head is covered with dew,
My locks with the drops of the
night."

3 I have taken off my robe;
How can I put it on *again?*
I have washed my feet;
How can I defile them?
4 My beloved put his hand
By the latch *of the door,*
And my heart yearned for him.
5 I arose to open for my beloved,
And my hands dripped *with*
myrrh,
My fingers with liquid myrrh,
On the handles of the lock.

6 I opened for my beloved,
But my beloved had turned away
and was gone.
My heart leaped up when he spoke.
I sought him, but I could not find
him;
I called him, but he gave me no
answer.

7 The watchmen who went about
the city found me.
They struck me, they
wounded me;
The keepers of the walls
Took my veil away from me.
8 I charge you, O daughters of
Jerusalem,
If you find my beloved,
That you tell him I *am* lovesick!

The Daughters of Jerusalem

9 What *is* your beloved
More than *another* beloved,
O fairest among women?
What *is* your beloved
More than *another* beloved,
That you so charge us?

The Shulamite

10 My beloved *is* white and ruddy,
Chief among ten thousand.
11 His head *is like* the finest gold;
His locks *are* wavy,
And black as a raven.
12 His eyes *are* like doves
By the rivers of waters,
Washed with milk,
And fitly set.
13 His cheeks *are* like a bed of
spices,
Banks of scented herbs.
His lips *are* lilies,
Dripping liquid myrrh.

14 His hands *are* rods of gold
Set with beryl.
His body *is* carved ivory
Inlaid *with* sapphires.
15 His legs *are* pillars of marble
Set on bases of fine gold.
His countenance *is* like Lebanon,
Excellent as the cedars.
16 His mouth *is* most sweet,
Yes, he *is* altogether lovely.
This *is* my beloved,
And this *is* my friend,
O daughters of Jerusalem!

The Daughters of Jerusalem

6 Where has your beloved gone,
O fairest among women?
Where has your beloved turned
aside,
That we may seek him with you?

The Shulamite

2 My beloved has gone to his
garden,
To the beds of spices,
To feed *his flock* in the gardens,
And to gather lilies.
3 I *am* my beloved's,
And my beloved *is* mine.
He feeds *his flock* among the lilies.

Praise of the Shulamite's Beauty

The Beloved

4 O my love, you *are as* beautiful as
Tirzah,
Lovely as Jerusalem,
Awesome as *an army* with banners!
5 Turn your eyes away from me,
For they have overcome me.
Your hair *is* like a flock of goats
Going down from Gilead.
6 Your teeth *are* like a flock of sheep
Which have come up from the
washing;
Every one bears twins,
And none *is* barren among them.
7 Like a piece of pomegranate
Are your temples behind your
veil.

8 There are sixty queens
And eighty concubines,
And virgins without number.
9 My dove, my perfect one,
Is the only one,
The only one of her mother,
The favorite of the one who bore
her.
The daughters saw her
And called her blessed,
The queens and the concubines,
And they praised her.

10 Who is she who looks forth as the
morning,
Fair as the moon,
Clear as the sun,
Awesome as *an army* with banners?

The Shulamite

11 I went down to the garden of nuts
To see the verdure of the valley,
To see whether the vine had
budded
And the pomegranates had
bloomed.

12 Before I was even aware,
My soul had made me
As the chariots of my noble people.[a]

The Beloved and His Friends

13 Return, return, O Shulamite;
Return, return, that we may look
upon you!

The Shulamite

What would you see in the
Shulamite—
As it were, the dance of the two
camps?[a]

Expressions of Praise

The Beloved

7 How beautiful are your feet in
sandals,
O prince's daughter!
The curves of your thighs *are* like
jewels,
The work of the hands of a skillful
workman.
2 Your navel *is* a rounded goblet;
It lacks no blended beverage.
Your waist *is* a heap of wheat
Set about with lilies.
3 Your two breasts *are* like two fawns,
Twins of a gazelle.
4 Your neck *is* like an ivory tower,
Your eyes *like* the pools in
Heshbon
By the gate of Bath Rabbim.
Your nose *is* like the tower of
Lebanon
Which looks toward Damascus.
5 Your head *crowns* you like *Mount*
Carmel,
And the hair of your head *is* like
purple;
A king *is* held captive by *your*
tresses.

6 How fair and how pleasant you
are,
O love, with your delights!
7 This stature of yours is like a palm
tree,
And your breasts *like* its clusters.
8 I said, "I will go up to the palm
tree,
I will take hold of its branches."
Let now your breasts be like
clusters of the vine,
The fragrance of your breath like
apples,
9 And the roof of your mouth like
the best wine.

The Shulamite

The wine goes *down* smoothly for
my beloved,
Moving gently the lips of sleepers.[a]
10 I *am* my beloved's,
And his desire *is* toward me.

11 Come, my beloved,
Let us go forth to the field;
Let us lodge in the villages.
12 Let us get up early to the
vineyards;
Let us see if the vine has budded,
Whether the grape blossoms are
open,
And the pomegranates are in
bloom.
There I will give you my love.
13 The mandrakes give off a
fragrance,
And at our gates *are* pleasant
fruits,
All manner, new and old,
Which I have laid up for you, my
beloved.

8 Oh, that you were like my brother,
Who nursed at my mother's
breasts!
If I should find you outside,
I would kiss you;
I would not be despised.
2 I would lead you *and* bring you
Into the house of my mother,
She *who* used to instruct me.
I would cause you to drink of
spiced wine,
Of the juice of my pomegranate.

(To the Daughters of Jerusalem)

3 His left hand *is* under my head,
And his right hand embraces me.
4 I charge you, O daughters of
Jerusalem,
Do not stir up nor awaken love
Until it pleases.

6:12 [a] Hebrew *Ammi Nadib* **6:13** [a] Hebrew *Mahanaim* **7:9** [a] Septuagint, Syriac, and Vulgate read *lips and teeth.*

Love Renewed in Lebanon

A Relative

5 Who *is* this coming up from the wilderness,
Leaning upon her beloved?

I awakened you under the apple tree.
There your mother brought you forth;
There she *who* bore you brought *you* forth.

The Shulamite to Her Beloved

6 Set me as a seal upon your heart,
As a seal upon your arm;
For love *is as* strong as death,
Jealousy *as* cruel as the grave;[a]
Its flames *are* flames of fire,
A most vehement flame.[b]

7 Many waters cannot quench love,
Nor can the floods drown it.
If a man would give for love
All the wealth of his house,
It would be utterly despised.

The Shulamite's Brothers

8 We have a little sister,
And she has no breasts.
What shall we do for our sister
In the day when she is spoken for?
9 If she *is* a wall,
We will build upon her
A battlement of silver;
And if she *is* a door,
We will enclose her
With boards of cedar.

The Shulamite

10 I *am* a wall,
And my breasts like towers;
Then I became in his eyes
As one who found peace.
11 Solomon had a vineyard at Baal Hamon;
He leased the vineyard to keepers;
Everyone was to bring for its fruit
A thousand silver *coins*.

(To Solomon)

12 My own vineyard *is* before me.
You, O Solomon, *may have* a thousand,
And those who tend its fruit two hundred.

The Beloved

13 You who dwell in the gardens,
The companions listen for your voice—
Let me hear it!

The Shulamite

14 Make haste, my beloved,
And be like a gazelle
Or a young stag
On the mountains of spices.

8:6 [a] Or *Sheol* [b] Literally *A flame of* YAH (a poetic form of *YHWH, the* LORD)

THE BOOK OF ISAIAH

The Book of Isaiah records the prophet's warnings that Jerusalem and Judah would be judged because of the people's wickedness. Halfway through the book, Isaiah predicts that the people would be carried off to Babylon. But he also shared the hope that the kingdom would exist again. The book is much like the Bible in miniature. The first thirty-nine chapters are filled with God's judgment on an idolatrous people, much like the thirty-nine books of the Old Testament. The final twenty-seven chapters declare a message of hope and forgiveness that would come through the Messiah, much like the twenty-seven books of the New Testament.

- **GENRE:** Major Prophet
- **AUTHOR:** Isaiah
- **TIME:** c. 739–680 BC
- **PURPOSE:** To warn the people that God would punish them if they didn't change their ways. After the punishment, though, God would heal and save them.

---

1 The vision of Isaiah the son of Amoz, which he saw concerning Judah and Jerusalem in the days of Uzziah, Jotham, Ahaz, *and* Hezekiah, kings of Judah.

The Wickedness of Judah

2 Hear, O heavens, and give ear, O earth!
For the LORD has spoken:
"I have nourished and brought up children,
And they have rebelled against Me;
3 The ox knows its owner
And the donkey its master's crib;
But Israel does not know,
My people do not consider."

4 Alas, sinful nation,
A people laden with iniquity,
A brood of evildoers,
Children who are corrupters!
They have forsaken the LORD,
They have provoked to anger
The Holy One of Israel,
They have turned away backward.

5 Why should you be stricken again?
You will revolt more and more.
The whole head is sick,
And the whole heart faints.
6 From the sole of the foot even to the head,
There is no soundness in it,
But wounds and bruises and putrefying sores;
They have not been closed or bound up,
Or soothed with ointment.

7 Your country *is* desolate,
Your cities *are* burned with fire;
Strangers devour your land in your presence;
And *it is* desolate, as overthrown by strangers.
8 So the daughter of Zion is left as a booth in a vineyard,
As a hut in a garden of cucumbers,
As a besieged city.
9 Unless the LORD of hosts
Had left to us a very small remnant,
We would have become like Sodom,
We would have been made like Gomorrah.

10 Hear the word of the LORD,
You rulers of Sodom;
Give ear to the law of our God,
You people of Gomorrah:

11 "To what purpose *is* the multitude
of your sacrifices to Me?"
Says the LORD.
"I have had enough of burnt
offerings of rams
And the fat of fed cattle.
I do not delight in the blood of
bulls,
Or of lambs or goats.

12 "When you come to appear
before Me,
Who has required this from your
hand,
To trample My courts?
13 Bring no more futile sacrifices;
Incense is an abomination to Me.
The New Moons, the Sabbaths, and
the calling of assemblies—
I cannot endure iniquity and the
sacred meeting.
14 Your New Moons and your
appointed feasts
My soul hates;
They are a trouble to Me,
I am weary of bearing *them*.
15 When you spread out your hands,
I will hide My eyes from you;
Even though you make many
prayers,
I will not hear.
Your hands are full of blood.

16 "Wash yourselves, make yourselves
clean;
Put away the evil of your doings
from before My eyes.
Cease to do evil,
17 Learn to do good;
Seek justice,
Rebuke the oppressor;[a]
Defend the fatherless,
Plead for the widow.

18 "Come now, and let us reason
together,"
Says the LORD,
"Though your sins are like scarlet,
They shall be as white as snow;
Though they are red like crimson,
They shall be as wool.
19 If you are willing and obedient,
You shall eat the good of the land;
20 But if you refuse and rebel,
You shall be devoured by the
sword";
For the mouth of the LORD has
spoken.

The Degenerate City

21 How the faithful city has become
a harlot!
It was full of justice;
Righteousness lodged in it,
But now murderers.
22 Your silver has become dross,
Your wine mixed with water.
23 Your princes *are* rebellious,
And companions of thieves;
Everyone loves bribes,
And follows after rewards.
They do not defend the fatherless,
Nor does the cause of the widow
come before them.

24 Therefore the Lord says,
The LORD of hosts, the Mighty
One of Israel,
"Ah, I will rid Myself of My
adversaries,
And take vengeance on My
enemies.
25 I will turn My hand against you,
And thoroughly purge away your
dross,
And take away all your alloy.
26 I will restore your judges as at the
first,
And your counselors as at the
beginning.
Afterward you shall be called the
city of righteousness, the
faithful city."

27 Zion shall be redeemed with
justice,
And her penitents with
righteousness.
28 The destruction of transgressors
and of sinners *shall be*
together,
And those who forsake the LORD
shall be consumed.
29 For they[a] shall be ashamed of the
terebinth trees
Which you have desired;

1:17 [a] Some ancient versions read *the oppressed*. 1:29 [a] Following Masoretic Text, Septuagint, and Vulgate; some Hebrew manuscripts and Targum read *you*.

And you shall be embarrassed
because of the gardens
Which you have chosen.
30 For you shall be as a terebinth
whose leaf fades,
And as a garden that has no
water.
31 The strong shall be as tinder,
And the work of it as a spark;
Both will burn together,
And no one shall quench *them.*

The Future House of God

2 The word that Isaiah the son of Amoz saw concerning Judah and Jerusalem.

2 Now it shall come to pass in the
latter days
That the mountain of the LORD's
house
Shall be established on the top of
the mountains,
And shall be exalted above the
hills;
And all nations shall flow to it.
3 Many people shall come and say,
"Come, and let us go up to the
mountain of the LORD,
To the house of the God of Jacob;
He will teach us His ways,
And we shall walk in His paths."
For out of Zion shall go forth the
law,
And the word of the LORD from
Jerusalem.
4 He shall judge between the
nations,
And rebuke many people;
They shall beat their swords into
plowshares,
And their spears into pruning
hooks;
Nation shall not lift up sword
against nation,
Neither shall they learn war
anymore.

The Day of the LORD

5 O house of Jacob, come and let us
walk
In the light of the LORD.

6 For You have forsaken Your
people, the house of Jacob,
Because they are filled with
eastern ways;
They *are* soothsayers like the
Philistines,
And they are pleased with the
children of foreigners.
7 Their land is also full of silver and
gold,
And there is no end to their
treasures;
Their land is also full of horses,
And there is no end to their
chariots.
8 Their land is also full of idols;
They worship the work of their
own hands,
That which their own fingers have
made.
9 People bow down,
And each man humbles himself;
Therefore do not forgive them.

10 Enter into the rock, and hide in
the dust,
From the terror of the LORD
And the glory of His majesty.
11 The lofty looks of man shall be
humbled,
The haughtiness of men shall be
bowed down,
And the LORD alone shall be
exalted in that day.

12 For the day of the LORD of hosts
Shall come upon everything proud
and lofty,
Upon everything lifted up—
And it shall be brought low—
13 Upon all the cedars of Lebanon
that are high and lifted up,
And upon all the oaks of Bashan;
14 Upon all the high mountains,
And upon all the hills *that are*
lifted up;
15 Upon every high tower,
And upon every fortified wall;
16 Upon all the ships of Tarshish,
And upon all the beautiful
sloops.
17 The loftiness of man shall be
bowed down,
And the haughtiness of men shall
be brought low;
The LORD alone will be exalted in
that day,

18 But the idols He shall utterly
abolish.

19 They shall go into the holes of the
rocks,
And into the caves of the earth,
From the terror of the LORD
And the glory of His majesty,
When He arises to shake the earth
mightily.

20 In that day a man will cast away
his idols of silver
And his idols of gold,
Which they made, *each* for
himself to worship,
To the moles and bats,
21 To go into the clefts of the rocks,
And into the crags of the rugged
rocks,
From the terror of the LORD
And the glory of His majesty,
When He arises to shake the earth
mightily.

22 Sever yourselves from such a man,
Whose breath *is* in his nostrils;
For of what account is he?

Judgment on Judah and Jerusalem

3 For behold, the Lord, the LORD of
hosts,
Takes away from Jerusalem and
from Judah
The stock and the store,
The whole supply of bread and
the whole supply of water;
2 The mighty man and the man of
war,
The judge and the prophet,
And the diviner and the elder;
3 The captain of fifty and the
honorable man,
The counselor and the skillful
artisan,
And the expert enchanter.

4 "I will give children *to be* their
princes,
And babes shall rule over them.
5 The people will be oppressed,
Every one by another and every
one by his neighbor;
The child will be insolent toward
the elder,
And the base toward the
honorable."

6 When a man takes hold of his
brother
In the house of his father, *saying,*
"You have clothing;
You be our ruler,
And *let* these ruins *be* under your
power,"[a]
7 In that day he will protest, saying,
"I cannot cure *your* ills,
For in my house *is* neither food
nor clothing;
Do not make me a ruler of the
people."

8 For Jerusalem stumbled,
And Judah is fallen,
Because their tongue and their
doings
Are against the LORD,
To provoke the eyes of His glory.
9 The look on their countenance
witnesses against them,
And they declare their sin as
Sodom;
They do not hide *it.*
Woe to their soul!
For they have brought evil upon
themselves.

10 "Say to the righteous that *it shall be*
well *with them,*
For they shall eat the fruit of their
doings.
11 Woe to the wicked! *It shall be* ill
with him,
For the reward of his hands shall
be given him.
12 *As for* My people, children *are*
their oppressors,
And women rule over them.
O My people! Those who lead you
cause *you* to err,
And destroy the way of your
paths."

Oppression and Luxury Condemned

13 The LORD stands up to plead,
And stands to judge the people.

3:6 [a] Literally *hand*

14 The LORD will enter into judgment
With the elders of His people
And His princes:
"For you have eaten up the vineyard;
The plunder of the poor *is* in your houses.
15 What do you mean by crushing My people
And grinding the faces of the poor?"
Says the Lord GOD of hosts.

16Moreover the LORD says:

"Because the daughters of Zion are haughty,
And walk with outstretched necks
And wanton eyes,
Walking and mincing *as* they go,
Making a jingling with their feet,
17 Therefore the Lord will strike with a scab
The crown of the head of the daughters of Zion,
And the LORD will uncover their secret parts."

18 In that day the Lord will take away the finery:
The jingling anklets, the scarves, and the crescents;
19 The pendants, the bracelets, and the veils;
20 The headdresses, the leg ornaments, and the headbands;
The perfume boxes, the charms,
21 and the rings;
The nose jewels,
22 the festal apparel, and the mantles;
The outer garments, the purses,
23 and the mirrors;
The fine linen, the turbans, and the robes.

24And so it shall be:

Instead of a sweet smell there will be a stench;
Instead of a sash, a rope;
Instead of well-set hair, baldness;
Instead of a rich robe, a girding of sackcloth;
And branding instead of beauty.
25 Your men shall fall by the sword,
And your mighty in the war.

26 Her gates shall lament and mourn,
And she *being* desolate shall sit on the ground.

4 And in that day seven women shall take hold of one man, saying,
"We will eat our own food and wear our own apparel;
Only let us be called by your name,
To take away our reproach."

The Renewal of Zion

2 In that day the Branch of the LORD shall be beautiful and glorious;
And the fruit of the earth *shall be* excellent and appealing
For those of Israel who have escaped.

3And it shall come to pass that *he who*
is left in Zion and remains in Jerusalem
will be called holy—everyone who is
recorded among the living in Jerusa-
lem. 4When the Lord has washed away
the filth of the daughters of Zion, and
purged the blood of Jerusalem from
her midst, by the spirit of judgment
and by the spirit of burning, 5then the
LORD will create above every dwelling
place of Mount Zion, and above her
assemblies, a cloud and smoke by day
and the shining of a flaming fire by
night. For over all the glory there *will*
be a covering. 6And there will be a tab-
ernacle for shade in the daytime from
the heat, for a place of refuge, and for
a shelter from storm and rain.

God's Disappointing Vineyard

5 Now let me sing to my Well-beloved
A song of my Beloved regarding His vineyard:

My Well-beloved has a vineyard
On a very fruitful hill.
2 He dug it up and cleared out its stones,

And planted it with the choicest
vine.
He built a tower in its midst,
And also made a winepress in it;
So He expected *it* to bring forth
good grapes,
But it brought forth wild grapes.

3 "And now, O inhabitants of
Jerusalem and men of
Judah,
Judge, please, between Me and
My vineyard.
4 What more could have been done
to My vineyard
That I have not done in it?
Why then, when I expected *it* to
bring forth *good* grapes,
Did it bring forth wild grapes?
5 And now, please let Me tell
you what I will do to My
vineyard:
I will take away its hedge, and it
shall be burned;
And break down its wall, and it
shall be trampled down.
6 I will lay it waste;
It shall not be pruned or dug,
But there shall come up briers
and thorns.
I will also command the clouds
That they rain no rain on it."

7 For the vineyard of the LORD of
hosts *is* the house of Israel,
And the men of Judah are His
pleasant plant.
He looked for justice, but behold,
oppression;
For righteousness, but behold, a
cry *for help.*

Impending Judgment on Excesses

8 Woe to those who join house to
house;
They add field to field,
Till *there is* no place
Where they may dwell alone in
the midst of the land!
9 In my hearing the LORD of hosts
said,
"Truly, many houses shall be
desolate,
Great and beautiful ones, without
inhabitant.
10 For ten acres of vineyard shall
yield one bath,
And a homer of seed shall yield
one ephah."

11 Woe to those who rise early in the
morning,
That they may follow intoxicating
drink;
Who continue until night, *till* wine
inflames them!
12 The harp and the strings,
The tambourine and flute,
And wine are in their feasts;
But they do not regard the work
of the LORD,
Nor consider the operation of His
hands.

13 Therefore my people have gone
into captivity,
Because *they have* no knowledge;
Their honorable men *are* famished,
And their multitude dried up with
thirst.
14 Therefore Sheol has enlarged itself
And opened its mouth beyond
measure;
Their glory and their multitude
and their pomp,
And he who is jubilant, shall
descend into it.
15 People shall be brought down,
Each man shall be humbled,
And the eyes of the lofty shall be
humbled.
16 But the LORD of hosts shall be
exalted in judgment,
And God who is holy shall be
hallowed in righteousness.
17 Then the lambs shall feed in their
pasture,
And in the waste places of the fat
ones strangers shall eat.

18 Woe to those who draw iniquity
with cords of vanity,
And sin as if with a cart rope;
19 That say, "Let Him make speed
and hasten His work,
That we may see *it;*
And let the counsel of the Holy
One of Israel draw near and
come,
That we may know *it.*"

20 Woe to those who call evil good,
and good evil;
Who put darkness for light, and
light for darkness;
Who put bitter for sweet, and
sweet for bitter!

21 Woe to *those who are* wise in their
own eyes,
And prudent in their own sight!

22 Woe to men mighty at drinking
wine,
Woe to men valiant for mixing
intoxicating drink,
23 Who justify the wicked for a bribe,
And take away justice from the
righteous man!

24 Therefore, as the fire devours the
stubble,
And the flame consumes the
chaff,
So their root will be as rottenness,
And their blossom will ascend like
dust;
Because they have rejected the
law of the LORD of hosts,
And despised the word of the Holy
One of Israel.
25 Therefore the anger of the
LORD is aroused against
His people;
He has stretched out His hand
against them
And stricken them,
And the hills trembled.
Their carcasses *were* as refuse in
the midst of the streets.

For all this His anger is not turned
away,
But His hand *is* stretched out still.

26 He will lift up a banner to the
nations from afar,
And will whistle to them from the
end of the earth;
Surely they shall come with
speed, swiftly.
27 No one will be weary or stumble
among them,
No one will slumber or sleep;
Nor will the belt on their loins be
loosed,
Nor the strap of their sandals be
broken;
28 Whose arrows *are* sharp,
And all their bows bent;
Their horses' hooves will seem like
flint,
And their wheels like a
whirlwind.
29 Their roaring *will be* like a lion,
They will roar like young lions;
Yes, they will roar
And lay hold of the prey;
They will carry *it* away safely,
And no one will deliver.
30 In that day they will roar against
them
Like the roaring of the sea.
And if *one* looks to the land,
Behold, darkness *and* sorrow;
And the light is darkened by the
clouds.

Isaiah Called to Be a Prophet

6 In the year that King Uzziah died,
I saw the Lord sitting on a throne,
high and lifted up, and the train of His
robe filled the temple. 2Above it stood
seraphim; each one had six wings: with
two he covered his face, with two he
covered his feet, and with two he flew.
3And one cried to another and said:

"Holy, holy, holy *is* the LORD of
hosts;
The whole earth *is* full of His
glory!"

4And the posts of the door were shaken
by the voice of him who cried out, and
the house was filled with smoke.
5So I said:

"Woe *is* me, for I am undone!
Because I *am* a man of unclean
lips,
And I dwell in the midst of a
people of unclean lips;
For my eyes have seen the King,
The LORD of hosts."

6Then one of the seraphim flew to me,
having in his hand a live coal *which*
he had taken with the tongs from the
altar. 7And he touched my mouth *with*
it, and said:

"Behold, this has touched your lips;
Your iniquity is taken away,
And your sin purged."

8Also I heard the voice of the Lord, saying:

"Whom shall I send,
And who will go for Us?"

Then I said, "Here *am* I! Send me."
9And He said, "Go, and tell this people:

'Keep on hearing, but do not
understand;
Keep on seeing, but do not
perceive.'

10 "Make the heart of this people dull,
And their ears heavy,
And shut their eyes;
Lest they see with their eyes,
And hear with their ears,
And understand with their heart,
And return and be healed."

11Then I said, "Lord, how long?"
And He answered:

"Until the cities are laid waste and
without inhabitant,
The houses are without a man,
The land is utterly desolate,
12 The LORD has removed men far
away,
And the forsaken places *are* many
in the midst of the land.
13 But yet a tenth *will be* in it,
And will return and be for
consuming,
As a terebinth tree or as an oak,
Whose stump *remains* when it is
cut down.
So the holy seed *shall be* its stump."

Isaiah Sent to King Ahaz

7 Now it came to pass in the days of Ahaz the son of Jotham, the son of Uzziah, king of Judah, *that* Rezin king of Syria and Pekah the son of Remaliah, king of Israel, went up to Jerusalem to *make* war against it, but could not prevail against it. 2And it was told to the house of David, saying, "Syria's forces are deployed in Ephraim." So his heart and the heart of his people were moved as the trees of the woods are moved with the wind.

3Then the LORD said to Isaiah, "Go out now to meet Ahaz, you and Shear-Jashub[a] your son, at the end of the aqueduct from the upper pool, on the highway to the Fuller's Field, 4and say to him: 'Take heed, and be quiet; do not fear or be fainthearted for these two stubs of smoking firebrands, for the fierce anger of Rezin and Syria, and the son of Remaliah. 5Because Syria, Ephraim, and the son of Remaliah have plotted evil against you, saying, 6"Let us go up against Judah and trouble it, and let us make a gap in its wall for ourselves, and set a king over them, the son of Tabel"— 7thus says the Lord GOD:

"It shall not stand,
Nor shall it come to pass.
8 For the head of Syria *is* Damascus,
And the head of Damascus *is*
Rezin.
Within sixty-five years Ephraim
will be broken,
So that it will not *be* a people.
9 The head of Ephraim *is* Samaria,
And the head of Samaria *is*
Remaliah's son.
If you will not believe,
Surely you shall not be
established."'"

The Immanuel Prophecy

10Moreover the LORD spoke again to Ahaz, saying, 11"Ask a sign for yourself from the LORD your God; ask it either in the depth or in the height above."

12But Ahaz said, "I will not ask, nor will I test the LORD!"

13Then he said, "Hear now, O house of David! *Is it* a small thing for you to weary men, but will you weary my God also? 14Therefore the Lord Himself will give you a sign: Behold, the virgin shall conceive and bear a Son, and shall call His name Immanuel.[a] 15Curds and honey He shall eat, that He may know to refuse the evil and choose the good.

7:3 [a] Literally *A Remnant Shall Return* 7:14 [a] Literally *God-With-Us*

16For before the Child shall know to
refuse the evil and choose the good, the
land that you dread will be forsaken by
both her kings. 17The LORD will bring
the king of Assyria upon you and your
people and your father's house—days
that have not come since the day that
Ephraim departed from Judah."

18 And it shall come to pass in that
day
That the LORD will whistle for the
fly
That *is* in the farthest part of the
rivers of Egypt,
And for the bee that *is* in the land
of Assyria.
19 They will come, and all of them
will rest
In the desolate valleys and in the
clefts of the rocks,
And on all thorns and in all
pastures.

20 In the same day the Lord will
shave with a hired razor,
With those from beyond the
River,[a] with the king of
Assyria,
The head and the hair of the legs,
And will also remove the beard.

21 It shall be in that day
That a man will keep alive a
young cow and two sheep;
22 So it shall be, from the abundance
of milk they give,
That he will eat curds;
For curds and honey everyone will
eat who is left in the land.

23 It shall happen in that day,
That wherever there could be a
thousand vines
Worth a thousand *shekels* of silver,
It will be for briers and thorns.
24 With arrows and bows *men* will
come there,
Because all the land will become
briers and thorns.

25 And to any hill which could be
dug with the hoe,
You will not go there for fear of
briers and thorns;
But it will become a range for
oxen
And a place for sheep to roam.

Assyria Will Invade the Land

8 Moreover the LORD said to me,
"Take a large scroll, and write
on it with a man's pen concerning
Maher-Shalal-Hash-Baz.[a] 2And I will
take for Myself faithful witnesses to
record, Uriah the priest and Zechariah
the son of Jeberechiah."
3Then I went to the prophetess, and
she conceived and bore a son. Then
the LORD said to me, "Call his name
Maher-Shalal-Hash-Baz; 4for before
the child shall have knowledge to cry
'My father' and 'My mother,' the riches
of Damascus and the spoil of Samaria
will be taken away before the king of
Assyria."
5The LORD also spoke to me again,
saying:

6 "Inasmuch as these people refused
The waters of Shiloah that flow
softly,
And rejoice in Rezin and in
Remaliah's son;
7 Now therefore, behold, the Lord
brings up over them
The waters of the River,[a] strong
and mighty—
The king of Assyria and all his
glory;
He will go up over all his channels
And go over all his banks.
8 He will pass through Judah,
He will overflow and pass over,
He will reach up to the neck;
And the stretching out of his
wings
Will fill the breadth of Your land,
O Immanuel.[a]

9 "Be shattered, O you peoples, and
be broken in pieces!
Give ear, all you from far
countries.
Gird yourselves, but be broken in
pieces;

7:20 [a] That is, the Euphrates 8:1 [a] Literally *Speed the Spoil, Hasten the Booty* 8:7 [a] That is, the Euphrates 8:8 [a] Literally *God-With-Us*

Gird yourselves, but be broken in
pieces.
10 Take counsel together, but it will
come to nothing;
Speak the word, but it will not
stand,
For God *is* with us."[a]

Fear God, Heed His Word

11For the LORD spoke thus to me with
a strong hand, and instructed me that I
should not walk in the way of this peo-
ple, saying:

12 "Do not say, 'A conspiracy,'
Concerning all that this people
call a conspiracy,
Nor be afraid of their threats, nor
be troubled.
13 The LORD of hosts, Him you shall
hallow;
Let Him *be* your fear,
And *let* Him *be* your dread.
14 He will be as a sanctuary,
But a stone of stumbling and a
rock of offense
To both the houses of Israel,
As a trap and a snare to the
inhabitants of Jerusalem.
15 And many among them shall
stumble;
They shall fall and be broken,
Be snared and taken."

16 Bind up the testimony,
Seal the law among my disciples.
17 And I will wait on the LORD,
Who hides His face from the
house of Jacob;
And I will hope in Him.
18 Here am I and the children whom
the LORD has given me!
We are for signs and wonders in
Israel
From the LORD of hosts,
Who dwells in Mount Zion.

19And when they say to you, "Seek
those who are mediums and wizards,
who whisper and mutter," should not a
people seek their God? *Should they seek*
the dead on behalf of the living? 20To
the law and to the testimony! If they do
not speak according to this word, *it is*
because *there is* no light in them.
21They will pass through it hard-
pressed and hungry; and it shall hap-
pen, when they are hungry, that they
will be enraged and curse their king and
their God, and look upward. 22Then they
will look to the earth, and see trouble
and darkness, gloom of anguish; and
they will be driven into darkness.

The Government of the Promised Son

9 Nevertheless the gloom *will* not *be*
upon her who *is* distressed,
As when at first He lightly
esteemed
The land of Zebulun and the land
of Naphtali,
And afterward more heavily
oppressed *her*,
By the way of the sea, beyond the
Jordan,
In Galilee of the Gentiles.
2 The people who walked in
darkness
Have seen a great light;
Those who dwelt in the land of the
shadow of death,
Upon them a light has shined.

3 You have multiplied the nation
And increased its joy;[a]
They rejoice before You
According to the joy of harvest,
As *men* rejoice when they divide
the spoil.
4 For You have broken the yoke of
his burden
And the staff of his shoulder,
The rod of his oppressor,
As in the day of Midian.
5 For every warrior's sandal from
the noisy battle,
And garments rolled in blood,
Will be used for burning *and* fuel
of fire.

6 For unto us a Child is born,
Unto us a Son is given;
And the government will be upon
His shoulder.
And His name will be called
Wonderful, Counselor, Mighty God,

8:10 [a] Hebrew *Immanuel* 9:3 [a] Following Qere and Targum; Kethib and Vulgate read *not increased joy;* Septuagint reads *Most of the people You brought down in Your joy.*

Everlasting Father, Prince of
Peace.
7 Of the increase of *His* government
and peace
There will be no end,
Upon the throne of David and
over His kingdom,
To order it and establish it with
judgment and justice
From that time forward, even
forever.
The zeal of the LORD of hosts will
perform this.

The Punishment of Samaria

8 The Lord sent a word against
Jacob,
And it has fallen on Israel.
9 All the people will know—
Ephraim and the inhabitant of
Samaria—
Who say in pride and arrogance
of heart:
10 "The bricks have fallen down,
But we will rebuild with hewn
stones;
The sycamores are cut down,
But we will replace *them* with
cedars."
11 Therefore the LORD shall set up
The adversaries of Rezin against
him,
And spur his enemies on,
12 The Syrians before and the
Philistines behind;
And they shall devour Israel with
an open mouth.

For all this His anger is not turned
away,
But His hand *is* stretched out still.

13 For the people do not turn to Him
who strikes them,
Nor do they seek the LORD of hosts.
14 Therefore the LORD will cut off
head and tail from Israel,
Palm branch and bulrush in one
day.
15 The elder and honorable, he *is* the
head;
The prophet who teaches lies, he *is*
the tail.
16 For the leaders of this people
cause *them* to err,
And *those who are* led by them are
destroyed.
17 Therefore the Lord will have no
joy in their young men,
Nor have mercy on their
fatherless and widows;
For everyone *is* a hypocrite and
an evildoer,
And every mouth speaks folly.

For all this His anger is not turned
away,
But His hand *is* stretched out still.

18 For wickedness burns as the fire;
It shall devour the briers and
thorns,
And kindle in the thickets of the
forest;
They shall mount up *like* rising
smoke.
19 Through the wrath of the LORD of
hosts
The land is burned up,
And the people shall be as fuel for
the fire;
No man shall spare his brother.
20 And he shall snatch on the right
hand
And be hungry;
He shall devour on the left hand
And not be satisfied;
Every man shall eat the flesh of
his own arm.
21 Manasseh *shall devour* Ephraim,
and Ephraim Manasseh;
Together they *shall be* against
Judah.

For all this His anger is not turned
away,
But His hand *is* stretched out still.

10 "Woe to those who decree
unrighteous decrees,
Who write misfortune,
Which they have prescribed
2 To rob the needy of justice,
And to take what is right from the
poor of My people,
That widows may be their prey,
And *that* they may rob the
fatherless.
3 What will you do in the day of
punishment,

And in the desolation *which* will come from afar?
To whom will you flee for help?
And where will you leave your glory?
4 Without Me they shall bow down among the prisoners,
And they shall fall among the slain."

For all this His anger is not turned away,
But His hand *is* stretched out still.

Arrogant Assyria Also Judged

5 "Woe to Assyria, the rod of My anger
And the staff in whose hand is My indignation.
6 I will send him against an ungodly nation,
And against the people of My wrath
I will give him charge,
To seize the spoil, to take the prey,
And to tread them down like the mire of the streets.
7 Yet he does not mean so,
Nor does his heart think so;
But *it is* in his heart to destroy,
And cut off not a few nations.
8 For he says,
'*Are* not my princes altogether kings?
9 *Is* not Calno like Carchemish?
Is not Hamath like Arpad?
Is not Samaria like Damascus?
10 As my hand has found the kingdoms of the idols,
Whose carved images excelled those of Jerusalem and Samaria,
11 As I have done to Samaria and her idols,
Shall I not do also to Jerusalem and her idols?' "

12Therefore it shall come to pass, when
the Lord has performed all His work on
Mount Zion and on Jerusalem, *that He*
will say, "I will punish the fruit of the
arrogant heart of the king of Assyria,
and the glory of his haughty looks."

13For he says:

"By the strength of my hand I have done *it,*
And by my wisdom, for I am prudent;
Also I have removed the boundaries of the people,
And have robbed their treasuries;
So I have put down the inhabitants like a valiant *man.*
14 My hand has found like a nest the riches of the people,
And as one gathers eggs *that are* left,
I have gathered all the earth;
And there was no one who moved *his* wing,
Nor opened *his* mouth with even a peep."

15 Shall the ax boast itself against him who chops with it?
Or shall the saw exalt itself against him who saws with it?
As if a rod could wield *itself* against those who lift it up,
Or as if a staff could lift up, *as if it were* not wood!
16 Therefore the Lord, the Lord[a] of hosts,
Will send leanness among his fat ones;
And under his glory
He will kindle a burning
Like the burning of a fire.
17 So the Light of Israel will be for a fire,
And his Holy One for a flame;
It will burn and devour
His thorns and his briers in one day.
18 And it will consume the glory of his forest and of his fruitful field,
Both soul and body;
And they will be as when a sick man wastes away.
19 Then the rest of the trees of his forest
Will be so few in number
That a child may write them.

10:16 [a] Following Bomberg; Masoretic Text and Dead Sea Scrolls read *YHWH* (*the* LORD).

The Returning Remnant of Israel

20 And it shall come to pass in that day
That the remnant of Israel,
And such as have escaped of the house of Jacob,
Will never again depend on him who defeated them,
But will depend on the LORD, the Holy One of Israel, in truth.
21 The remnant will return, the remnant of Jacob,
To the Mighty God.
22 For though your people, O Israel, be as the sand of the sea,
A remnant of them will return;
The destruction decreed shall overflow with righteousness.
23 For the Lord GOD of hosts
Will make a determined end
In the midst of all the land.

24Therefore thus says the Lord GOD
of hosts: "O My people, who dwell in
Zion, do not be afraid of the Assyrian.
He shall strike you with a rod and lift
up his staff against you, in the manner
of Egypt. 25For yet a very little while
and the indignation will cease, as will
My anger in their destruction." 26And
the LORD of hosts will stir up a scourge
for him like the slaughter of Midian at
the rock of Oreb; *as* His rod was on the
sea, so will He lift it up in the manner
of Egypt.

27 It shall come to pass in that day
That his burden will be taken away from your shoulder,
And his yoke from your neck,
And the yoke will be destroyed because of the anointing oil.

28 He has come to Aiath,
He has passed Migron;
At Michmash he has attended to his equipment.
29 They have gone along the ridge,
They have taken up lodging at Geba.
Ramah is afraid,
Gibeah of Saul has fled.
30 Lift up your voice,
O daughter of Gallim!
Cause it to be heard as far as Laish—
O poor Anathoth![a]
31 Madmenah has fled,
The inhabitants of Gebim seek refuge.
32 As yet he will remain at Nob that day;
He will shake his fist at the mount of the daughter of Zion,
The hill of Jerusalem.

33 Behold, the Lord,
The LORD of hosts,
Will lop off the bough with terror;
Those of high stature *will be* hewn down,
And the haughty will be humbled.
34 He will cut down the thickets of the forest with iron,
And Lebanon will fall by the Mighty One.

The Reign of Jesse's Offspring

11 There shall come forth a Rod from the stem of Jesse,
And a Branch shall grow out of his roots.
2 The Spirit of the LORD shall rest upon Him,
The Spirit of wisdom and understanding,
The Spirit of counsel and might,
The Spirit of knowledge and of the fear of the LORD.

3 His delight *is* in the fear of the LORD,
And He shall not judge by the sight of His eyes,
Nor decide by the hearing of His ears;
4 But with righteousness He shall judge the poor,
And decide with equity for the meek of the earth;
He shall strike the earth with the rod of His mouth,
And with the breath of His lips He shall slay the wicked.
5 Righteousness shall be the belt of His loins,

10:30 [a] Following Masoretic Text, Targum, and Vulgate; Septuagint and Syriac read *Listen to her, O Anathoth.*

And faithfulness the belt of His
waist.

6 "The wolf also shall dwell with the
lamb,
The leopard shall lie down with
the young goat,
The calf and the young lion and
the fatling together;
And a little child shall lead them.
7 The cow and the bear shall graze;
Their young ones shall lie down
together;
And the lion shall eat straw like
the ox.
8 The nursing child shall play by
the cobra's hole,
And the weaned child shall put
his hand in the viper's den.
9 They shall not hurt nor destroy in
all My holy mountain,
For the earth shall be full of the
knowledge of the LORD
As the waters cover the sea.

10 "And in that day there shall be a
Root of Jesse,
Who shall stand as a banner to
the people;
For the Gentiles shall seek Him,
And His resting place shall be
glorious."

11 It shall come to pass in that day
That the Lord shall set His hand
again the second time
To recover the remnant of His
people who are left,
From Assyria and Egypt,
From Pathros and Cush,
From Elam and Shinar,
From Hamath and the islands of
the sea.

12 He will set up a banner for the
nations,
And will assemble the outcasts of
Israel,
And gather together the dispersed
of Judah
From the four corners of the earth.
13 Also the envy of Ephraim shall
depart,
And the adversaries of Judah
shall be cut off;
Ephraim shall not envy Judah,
And Judah shall not harass
Ephraim.
14 But they shall fly down upon the
shoulder of the Philistines
toward the west;
Together they shall plunder the
people of the East;
They shall lay their hand on
Edom and Moab;
And the people of Ammon shall
obey them.
15 The LORD will utterly destroy[a]
the tongue of the Sea of
Egypt;
With His mighty wind He will
shake His fist over the River,[b]
And strike it in the seven streams,
And make *men* cross over
dry-shod.
16 There will be a highway for the
remnant of His people
Who will be left from Assyria,
As it was for Israel
In the day that he came up from
the land of Egypt.

A Hymn of Praise

12 And in that day you will say:

"O LORD, I will praise You;
Though You were angry with me,
Your anger is turned away, and
You comfort me.
2 Behold, God *is* my salvation,
I will trust and not be afraid;
'For YAH, the LORD, *is* my strength
and song;
He also has become my
salvation.' "[a]

3 Therefore with joy you will draw
water
From the wells of salvation.

4 And in that day you will say:

"Praise the LORD, call upon His
name;
Declare His deeds among the
peoples,

11:15 [a] Following Masoretic Text and Vulgate; Septuagint, Syriac, and Targum read *dry up.* [b] That is, the Euphrates 12:2 [a] Exodus 15:2

Make mention that His name is exalted.
5 Sing to the LORD,
For He has done excellent things;
This *is* known in all the earth.
6 Cry out and shout, O inhabitant of Zion,
For great *is* the Holy One of Israel in your midst!"

Proclamation Against Babylon

13 The burden against Babylon which Isaiah the son of Amoz saw.

2 "Lift up a banner on the high mountain,
Raise your voice to them;
Wave your hand, that they may enter the gates of the nobles.
3 I have commanded My sanctified ones;
I have also called My mighty ones for My anger—
Those who rejoice in My exaltation."

4 The noise of a multitude in the mountains,
Like that of many people!
A tumultuous noise of the kingdoms of nations gathered together!
The LORD of hosts musters
The army for battle.
5 They come from a far country,
From the end of heaven—
The LORD and His weapons of indignation,
To destroy the whole land.

6 Wail, for the day of the LORD *is* at hand!
It will come as destruction from the Almighty.
7 Therefore all hands will be limp,
Every man's heart will melt,
8 And they will be afraid.
Pangs and sorrows will take hold of *them;*
They will be in pain as a woman in childbirth;
They will be amazed at one another;
Their faces *will be like* flames.

9 Behold, the day of the LORD comes,
Cruel, with both wrath and fierce anger,
To lay the land desolate;
And He will destroy its sinners from it.
10 For the stars of heaven and their constellations
Will not give their light;
The sun will be darkened in its going forth,
And the moon will not cause its light to shine.

11 "I will punish the world for *its* evil,
And the wicked for their iniquity;
I will halt the arrogance of the proud,
And will lay low the haughtiness of the terrible.
12 I will make a mortal more rare than fine gold,
A man more than the golden wedge of Ophir.
13 Therefore I will shake the heavens,
And the earth will move out of her place,
In the wrath of the LORD of hosts
And in the day of His fierce anger.
14 It shall be as the hunted gazelle,
And as a sheep that no man takes up;
Every man will turn to his own people,
And everyone will flee to his own land.
15 Everyone who is found will be thrust through,
And everyone who is captured will fall by the sword.
16 Their children also will be dashed to pieces before their eyes;
Their houses will be plundered
And their wives ravished.

17 "Behold, I will stir up the Medes against them,
Who will not regard silver;
And *as for* gold, they will not delight in it.
18 Also *their* bows will dash the young men to pieces,

And they will have no pity on the
fruit of the womb;
Their eye will not spare children.
19 And Babylon, the glory of
kingdoms,
The beauty of the Chaldeans'
pride,
Will be as when God overthrew
Sodom and Gomorrah.
20 It will never be inhabited,
Nor will it be settled from
generation to generation;
Nor will the Arabian pitch tents
there,
Nor will the shepherds make their
sheepfolds there.
21 But wild beasts of the desert will
lie there,
And their houses will be full of
owls;
Ostriches will dwell there,
And wild goats will caper there.
22 The hyenas will howl in their
citadels,
And jackals in their pleasant
palaces.
Her time *is* near to come,
And her days will not be
prolonged."

Mercy on Jacob

14 For the LORD will have mercy
on Jacob, and will still choose
Israel, and settle them in their own land.
The strangers will be joined with them,
and they will cling to the house of Jacob.
2Then people will take them and bring
them to their place, and the house of Is-
rael will possess them for servants and
maids in the land of the LORD; they will
take them captive whose captives they
were, and rule over their oppressors.

Fall of the King of Babylon

3It shall come to pass in the day the
LORD gives you rest from your sorrow,
and from your fear and the hard bond-
age in which you were made to serve,
4that you will take up this proverb
against the king of Babylon, and say:

"How the oppressor has ceased,
The golden[a] city ceased!
5 The LORD has broken the staff of
the wicked,
The scepter of the rulers;
6 He who struck the people in wrath
with a continual stroke,
He who ruled the nations in anger,
Is persecuted *and* no one hinders.
7 The whole earth is at rest *and*
quiet;
They break forth into singing.
8 Indeed the cypress trees rejoice
over you,
And the cedars of Lebanon,
Saying, 'Since you were cut down,
No woodsman has come up
against us.'

9 "Hell from beneath is excited about
you,
To meet *you* at your coming;
It stirs up the dead for you,
All the chief ones of the earth;
It has raised up from their
thrones
All the kings of the nations.
10 They all shall speak and say to
you:
'Have you also become as weak
as we?
Have you become like us?
11 Your pomp is brought down to
Sheol,
And the sound of your stringed
instruments;
The maggot is spread under you,
And worms cover you.'

The Fall of Lucifer

12 "How you are fallen from heaven,
O Lucifer,[a] son of the morning!
How you are cut down to the
ground,
You who weakened the nations!
13 For you have said in your heart:
'I will ascend into heaven,
I will exalt my throne above the
stars of God;
I will also sit on the mount of the
congregation
On the farthest sides of the north;
14 I will ascend above the heights of
the clouds,
I will be like the Most High.'

14:4 [a] Or *insolent* 14:12 [a] Literally *Day Star*

15 Yet you shall be brought down to
Sheol,
To the lowest depths of the Pit.

16 "Those who see you will gaze at you,
And consider you, *saying:*
'*Is* this the man who made the
earth tremble,
Who shook kingdoms,
17 Who made the world as a
wilderness
And destroyed its cities,
Who did not open the house of his
prisoners?'

18 "All the kings of the nations,
All of them, sleep in glory,
Everyone in his own house;
19 But you are cast out of
your grave
Like an abominable branch,
Like the garment of those who are
slain,
Thrust through with a sword,
Who go down to the stones of the
pit,
Like a corpse trodden underfoot.
20 You will not be joined with them
in burial,
Because you have destroyed your
land
And slain your people.
The brood of evildoers shall never
be named.
21 Prepare slaughter for his children
Because of the iniquity of their
fathers,
Lest they rise up and possess the
land,
And fill the face of the world with
cities."

Babylon Destroyed

22 "For I will rise up against them,"
says the LORD of hosts,
"And cut off from Babylon the
name and remnant,
And offspring and posterity," says
the LORD.
23 "I will also make it a possession for
the porcupine,
And marshes of muddy water;
I will sweep it with the broom of
destruction," says the LORD
of hosts.

Assyria Destroyed

24 The LORD of hosts has sworn,
saying,
"Surely, as I have thought, so it
shall come to pass,
And as I have purposed, *so* it shall
stand:
25 That I will break the Assyrian in
My land,
And on My mountains tread him
underfoot.
Then his yoke shall be removed
from them,
And his burden removed from
their shoulders.
26 This *is* the purpose that is
purposed against the whole
earth,
And this *is* the hand that is
stretched out over all the
nations.
27 For the LORD of hosts has
purposed,
And who will annul *it?*
His hand *is* stretched out,
And who will turn it back?"

Philistia Destroyed

28This is the burden which came in the
year that King Ahaz died.

29 "Do not rejoice, all you of Philistia,
Because the rod that struck you is
broken;
For out of the serpent's roots will
come forth a viper,
And its offspring *will be* a fiery
flying serpent.
30 The firstborn of the poor will feed,
And the needy will lie down in
safety;
I will kill your roots with famine,
And it will slay your remnant.
31 Wail, O gate! Cry, O city!
All you of Philistia *are* dissolved;
For smoke will come from the
north,
And no one *will be* alone in his
appointed times."

32 What will they answer the
messengers of the nation?
That the LORD has founded Zion,
And the poor of His people shall
take refuge in it.

Proclamation Against Moab

15 The burden against Moab.

Because in the night Ar of Moab is
laid waste
And destroyed,
Because in the night Kir of Moab
is laid waste
And destroyed,
2 He has gone up to the temple[a]
and Dibon,
To the high places to weep.
Moab will wail over Nebo and over
Medeba;
On all their heads *will be* baldness,
And every beard cut off.
3 In their streets they will clothe
themselves with sackcloth;
On the tops of their houses
And in their streets
Everyone will wail, weeping
bitterly.
4 Heshbon and Elealeh will cry out,
Their voice shall be heard as far
as Jahaz;
Therefore the armed soldiers[a] of
Moab will cry out;
His life will be burdensome to him.

5 "My heart will cry out for Moab;
His fugitives *shall flee* to Zoar,
Like a three-year-old heifer.[a]
For by the Ascent of Luhith
They will go up with weeping;
For in the way of Horonaim
They will raise up a cry of
destruction,
6 For the waters of Nimrim will be
desolate,
For the green grass has withered
away;
The grass fails, there is nothing
green.
7 Therefore the abundance they
have gained,
And what they have laid up,
They will carry away to the Brook
of the Willows.
8 For the cry has gone all around
the borders of Moab,
Its wailing to Eglaim
And its wailing to Beer Elim.
9 For the waters of Dimon[a] will be
full of blood;
Because I will bring more upon
Dimon,[b]
Lions upon him who escapes from
Moab,
And on the remnant of the land."

Moab Destroyed

16 Send the lamb to the ruler of
the land,
From Sela to the wilderness,
To the mount of the daughter of
Zion.
2 For it shall be as a wandering bird
thrown out of the nest;
So shall be the daughters of Moab
at the fords of the Arnon.

3 "Take counsel, execute judgment;
Make your shadow like the night
in the middle of the day;
Hide the outcasts,
Do not betray him who escapes.
4 Let My outcasts dwell with you,
O Moab;
Be a shelter to them from the face
of the spoiler.
For the extortioner is at an end,
Devastation ceases,
The oppressors are consumed out
of the land.
5 In mercy the throne will be
established;
And One will sit on it in truth, in
the tabernacle of David,
Judging and seeking justice and
hastening righteousness."

6 We have heard of the pride of
Moab—
He is very proud—
Of his haughtiness and his pride
and his wrath;
But his lies *shall* not *be* so.
7 Therefore Moab shall wail for
Moab;
Everyone shall wail.

15:2 [a] Hebrew *bayith,* literally *house* 15:4 [a] Following Masoretic Text, Targum, and Vulgate; Septuagint and Syriac read *loins.* 15:5 [a] Or *The Third Eglath,* an unknown city (compare Jeremiah 48:34) 15:9 [a] Following Masoretic Text and Targum; Dead Sea Scrolls and Vulgate read *Dibon;* Septuagint reads *Rimon.* [b] Following Masoretic Text and Targum; Dead Sea Scrolls and Vulgate read *Dibon;* Septuagint reads *Rimon.*

For the foundations of Kir
Hareseth you shall mourn;
Surely *they are* stricken.

8 For the fields of Heshbon
languish,
And the vine of Sibmah;
The lords of the nations have
broken down its choice
plants,
Which have reached to Jazer
And wandered through the
wilderness.
Her branches are stretched out,
They are gone over the sea.
9 Therefore I will bewail the vine of
Sibmah,
With the weeping of Jazer;
I will drench you with my tears,
O Heshbon and Elealeh;
For battle cries have fallen
Over your summer fruits and
your harvest.

10 Gladness is taken away,
And joy from the plentiful field;
In the vineyards there will be no
singing,
Nor will there be shouting;
No treaders will tread out wine in
the presses;
I have made their shouting cease.
11 Therefore my heart shall resound
like a harp for Moab,
And my inner being for Kir Heres.

12 And it shall come to pass,
When it is seen that Moab is
weary on the high place,
That he will come to his sanctuary
to pray;
But he will not prevail.

13This *is* the word which the LORD has
spoken concerning Moab since that
time. 14But now the LORD has spoken,
saying, "Within three years, as the years
of a hired man, the glory of Moab will be
despised with all that great multitude,
and the remnant *will be* very small *and*
feeble."

Proclamation Against Syria and Israel

17 The burden against Damascus.

"Behold, Damascus will cease from
being a city,
And it will be a ruinous heap.
2 The cities of Aroer *are* forsaken;[a]
They will be for flocks
Which lie down, and no one will
make *them* afraid.
3 The fortress also will cease from
Ephraim,
The kingdom from Damascus,
And the remnant of Syria;
They will be as the glory of the
children of Israel,"
Says the LORD of hosts.

4 "In that day it shall come to pass
That the glory of Jacob will wane,
And the fatness of his flesh grow
lean.
5 It shall be as when the harvester
gathers the grain,
And reaps the heads with his arm;
It shall be as he who gathers
heads of grain
In the Valley of Rephaim.
6 Yet gleaning grapes will be left
in it,
Like the shaking of an olive tree,
Two *or* three olives at the top of
the uppermost bough,
Four *or* five in its most fruitful
branches,"
Says the LORD God of Israel.

7 In that day a man will look to his
Maker,
And his eyes will have respect for
the Holy One of Israel.
8 He will not look to the altars,
The work of his hands;
He will not respect what his
fingers have made,
Nor the wooden images[a] nor the
incense altars.

9 In that day his strong cities will
be as a forsaken bough[a]
And an uppermost branch,[b]

17:2 [a] Following Masoretic Text and Vulgate; Septuagint reads *It shall be forsaken forever;* Targum reads *Its cities shall be forsaken and desolate.* **17:8** [a] Hebrew *Asherim,* Canaanite deities **17:9** [a] Septuagint reads *Hivites;* Targum reads *laid waste;* Vulgate reads *as the plows.* [b] Septuagint reads *Amorites;* Targum reads *in ruins;* Vulgate reads *corn.*

Which they left because of the
children of Israel;
And there will be desolation.

10 Because you have forgotten the
God of your salvation,
And have not been mindful of the
Rock of your stronghold,
Therefore you will plant pleasant
plants
And set out foreign seedlings;
11 In the day you will make your
plant to grow,
And in the morning you will
make your seed to flourish;
But the harvest *will be* a heap of
ruins
In the day of grief and desperate
sorrow.

12 Woe to the multitude of many
people
Who make a noise like the roar of
the seas,
And to the rushing of nations
That make a rushing like the
rushing of mighty waters!
13 The nations will rush like the
rushing of many waters;
But *God* will rebuke them and
they will flee far away,
And be chased like the chaff
of the mountains before
the wind,
Like a rolling thing before the
whirlwind.
14 Then behold, at eventide, trouble!
And before the morning, he *is* no
more.
This *is* the portion of those who
plunder us,
And the lot of those who rob us.

Proclamation Against Ethiopia

18 Woe to the land shadowed
with buzzing wings,
Which *is* beyond the rivers of
Ethiopia,
2 Which sends ambassadors by sea,
Even in vessels of reed on the
waters, *saying,*
"Go, swift messengers, to a nation
tall and smooth *of skin,*
To a people terrible from their
beginning onward,
A nation powerful and treading
down,
Whose land the rivers divide."

3 All inhabitants of the world and
dwellers on the earth:
When he lifts up a banner on the
mountains, you see *it;*
And when he blows a trumpet,
you hear *it.*
4 For so the LORD said to me,
"I will take My rest,
And I will look from My dwelling
place
Like clear heat in sunshine,
Like a cloud of dew in the heat of
harvest."
5 For before the harvest, when the
bud is perfect
And the sour grape is ripening in
the flower,
He will both cut off the sprigs with
pruning hooks
And take away *and* cut down the
branches.
6 They will be left together for the
mountain birds of prey
And for the beasts of the earth;
The birds of prey will summer on
them,
And all the beasts of the earth will
winter on them.

7 In that time a present will be
brought to the LORD of hosts
From[a] a people tall and smooth *of
skin,*
And from a people terrible from
their beginning onward,
A nation powerful and treading
down,
Whose land the rivers divide—
To the place of the name of the
LORD of hosts,
To Mount Zion.

Proclamation Against Egypt

19 The burden against Egypt.

Behold, the LORD rides on a swift
cloud,

18:7 a Following Dead Sea Scrolls, Septuagint, and Vulgate; Masoretic Text omits *From;* Targum reads *To.*

And will come into Egypt;
The idols of Egypt will totter at His presence,
And the heart of Egypt will melt in its midst.

2 "I will set Egyptians against Egyptians;
Everyone will fight against his brother,
And everyone against his neighbor,
City against city, kingdom against kingdom.
3 The spirit of Egypt will fail in its midst;
I will destroy their counsel,
And they will consult the idols and the charmers,
The mediums and the sorcerers.
4 And the Egyptians I will give
Into the hand of a cruel master,
And a fierce king will rule over them,"
Says the Lord, the LORD of hosts.

5 The waters will fail from the sea,
And the river will be wasted and dried up.
6 The rivers will turn foul;
The brooks of defense will be emptied and dried up;
The reeds and rushes will wither.
7 The papyrus reeds by the River,[a] by the mouth of the River,
And everything sown by the River,
Will wither, be driven away, and be no more.
8 The fishermen also will mourn;
All those will lament who cast hooks into the River,
And they will languish who spread nets on the waters.
9 Moreover those who work in fine flax
And those who weave fine fabric will be ashamed;
10 And its foundations will be broken.
All who make wages *will be* troubled of soul.

11 Surely the princes of Zoan *are* fools;
Pharaoh's wise counselors give foolish counsel.
How do you say to Pharaoh, "I *am* the son of the wise,
The son of ancient kings?"
12 Where *are* they?
Where are your wise men?
Let them tell you now,
And let them know what the LORD of hosts has purposed against Egypt.
13 The princes of Zoan have become fools;
The princes of Noph[a] are deceived;
They have also deluded Egypt,
Those who are the mainstay of its tribes.
14 The LORD has mingled a perverse spirit in her midst;
And they have caused Egypt to err in all her work,
As a drunken man staggers in his vomit.
15 Neither will there be *any* work for Egypt,
Which the head or tail,
Palm branch or bulrush,
may do.[a]

16In that day Egypt will be like women,
and will be afraid and fear because of
the waving of the hand of the LORD of
hosts, which He waves over it. 17And
the land of Judah will be a terror to
Egypt; everyone who makes mention
of it will be afraid in himself, because of
the counsel of the LORD of hosts which
He has determined against it.

Egypt, Assyria, and Israel Blessed

18In that day five cities in the land of
Egypt will speak the language of Canaan and swear by the LORD of hosts;
one will be called the City of Destruction.[a]
19In that day there will be an altar to
the LORD in the midst of the land of
Egypt, and a pillar to the LORD at its
border. 20And it will be for a sign and

19:7 [a] That is, the Nile **19:13** [a] That is, ancient Memphis **19:15** [a] Compare Isaiah 9:14–16
19:18 [a] Some Hebrew manuscripts, Arabic, Dead Sea Scrolls, Targum, and Vulgate read *Sun*; Septuagint reads *Asedek* (literally *Righteousness*).

for a witness to the LORD of hosts in the land of Egypt; for they will cry to the LORD because of the oppressors, and He will send them a Savior and a Mighty One, and He will deliver them. 21 Then the LORD will be known to Egypt, and the Egyptians will know the LORD in that day, and will make sacrifice and offering; yes, they will make a vow to the LORD and perform *it.* 22 And the LORD will strike Egypt, He will strike and heal *it;* they will return to the LORD, and He will be entreated by them and heal them.

23 In that day there will be a highway from Egypt to Assyria, and the Assyrian will come into Egypt and the Egyptian into Assyria, and the Egyptians will serve with the Assyrians.

24 In that day Israel will be one of three with Egypt and Assyria—a blessing in the midst of the land, 25 whom the LORD of hosts shall bless, saying, "Blessed *is* Egypt My people, and Assyria the work of My hands, and Israel My inheritance."

The Sign Against Egypt and Ethiopia

20 In the year that Tartan[a] came to Ashdod, when Sargon the king of Assyria sent him, and he fought against Ashdod and took it, 2 at the same time the LORD spoke by Isaiah the son of Amoz, saying, "Go, and remove the sackcloth from your body, and take your sandals off your feet." And he did so, walking naked and barefoot.

3 Then the LORD said, "Just as My servant Isaiah has walked naked and barefoot three years *for* a sign and a wonder against Egypt and Ethiopia, 4 so shall the king of Assyria lead away the Egyptians as prisoners and the Ethiopians as captives, young and old, naked and barefoot, with their buttocks uncovered, to the shame of Egypt. 5 Then they shall be afraid and ashamed of Ethiopia their expectation and Egypt their glory. 6 And the inhabitant of this territory will say in that day, 'Surely such *is* our expectation, wherever we flee for help to be delivered from the king of Assyria; and how shall we escape?' "

The Fall of Babylon Proclaimed

21 The burden against the Wilderness of the Sea.

As whirlwinds in the South pass
through,
So it comes from the desert, from
a terrible land.
2 A distressing vision is declared
to me;
The treacherous dealer deals
treacherously,
And the plunderer plunders.
Go up, O Elam!
Besiege, O Media!
All its sighing I have made to
cease.

3 Therefore my loins are filled with
pain;
Pangs have taken hold of me, like
the pangs of a woman in
labor.
I was distressed when *I* heard *it;*
I was dismayed when *I* saw *it.*
4 My heart wavered, fearfulness
frightened me;
The night for which I longed He
turned into fear for me.
5 Prepare the table,
Set a watchman in the tower,
Eat and drink.
Arise, you princes,
Anoint the shield!

6 For thus has the Lord said to me:
"Go, set a watchman,
Let him declare what he sees."
7 And he saw a chariot *with* a pair
of horsemen,
A chariot of donkeys, *and* a
chariot of camels,
And he listened earnestly with
great care.
8 Then he cried, "A lion,[a] my Lord!
I stand continually on the
watchtower in the daytime;
I have sat at my post every night.
9 And look, here comes a chariot
of men *with* a pair of
horsemen!"
Then he answered and said,
"Babylon is fallen, is fallen!

20:1 [a] Or *the Commander in Chief* 21:8 [a] Dead Sea Scrolls read *Then the observer cried.*

And all the carved images of her gods
He has broken to the ground."
10 Oh, my threshing and the grain of my floor!
That which I have heard from the LORD of hosts,
The God of Israel,
I have declared to you.

Proclamation Against Edom

11The burden against Dumah.

He calls to me out of Seir,
"Watchman, what of the night?
Watchman, what of the night?"
12 The watchman said,
"The morning comes, and also the night.
If you will inquire, inquire;
Return! Come back!"

Proclamation Against Arabia

13The burden against Arabia.

In the forest in Arabia you will lodge,
O you traveling companies of Dedanites.
14 O inhabitants of the land of Tema,
Bring water to him who is thirsty;
With their bread they met him who fled.
15 For they fled from the swords, from the drawn sword,
From the bent bow, and from the distress of war.

16For thus the LORD has said to me:
"Within a year, according to the year of
a hired man, all the glory of Kedar will
fail; 17and the remainder of the num-
ber of archers, the mighty men of the
people of Kedar, will be diminished; for
the LORD God of Israel has spoken *it*."

Proclamation Against Jerusalem

22 The burden against the Valley of Vision.

What ails you now, that you have all gone up to the housetops,
2 You who are full of noise,
A tumultuous city, a joyous city?
Your slain *men are* not slain with the sword,
Nor dead in battle.
3 All your rulers have fled together;
They are captured by the archers.
All who are found in you are bound together;
They have fled from afar.
4 Therefore I said, "Look away from me,
I will weep bitterly;
Do not labor to comfort me
Because of the plundering of the daughter of my people."

5 For *it is* a day of trouble and treading down and perplexity
By the Lord GOD of hosts
In the Valley of Vision—
Breaking down the walls
And of crying to the mountain.
6 Elam bore the quiver
With chariots of men *and* horsemen,
And Kir uncovered the shield.
7 It shall come to pass *that* your choicest valleys
Shall be full of chariots,
And the horsemen shall set themselves in array at the gate.

8 He removed the protection of Judah.
You looked in that day to the armor of the House of the Forest;
9 You also saw the damage to the city of David,
That it was great;
And you gathered together the waters of the lower pool.
10 You numbered the houses of Jerusalem,
And the houses you broke down
To fortify the wall.
11 You also made a reservoir between the two walls
For the water of the old pool.
But you did not look to its Maker,
Nor did you have respect for Him who fashioned it long ago.

12 And in that day the Lord GOD of hosts

Called for weeping and for mourning,
For baldness and for girding with sackcloth.
13 But instead, joy and gladness,
Slaying oxen and killing sheep,
Eating meat and drinking wine:
"Let us eat and drink, for tomorrow we die!"

14 Then it was revealed in my hearing by the LORD of hosts,
"Surely for this iniquity there will be no atonement for you,
Even to your death," says the Lord GOD of hosts.

The Judgment on Shebna

15Thus says the Lord GOD of hosts:

"Go, proceed to this steward,
To Shebna, who *is* over the house, *and say:*
16 'What have you here, and whom have you here,
That you have hewn a sepulcher here,
As he who hews himself a sepulcher on high,
Who carves a tomb for himself in a rock?
17 Indeed, the LORD will throw you away violently,
O mighty man,
And will surely seize you.
18 He will surely turn violently and toss you like a ball
Into a large country;
There you shall die, and there your glorious chariots
Shall be the shame of your master's house.
19 So I will drive you out of your office,
And from your position he will pull you down.[a]

20 'Then it shall be in that day,
That I will call My servant Eliakim the son of Hilkiah;
21 I will clothe him with your robe
And strengthen him with your belt;
I will commit your responsibility into his hand.
He shall be a father to the inhabitants of Jerusalem
And to the house of Judah.
22 The key of the house of David
I will lay on his shoulder;
So he shall open, and no one shall shut;
And he shall shut, and no one shall open.
23 I will fasten him *as* a peg in a secure place,
And he will become a glorious throne to his father's house.

24'They will hang on him all the glo-
ry of his father's house, the offspring
and the posterity, all vessels of small
quantity, from the cups to all the pitch-
ers. 25In that day,' says the LORD of
hosts, 'the peg that is fastened in the
secure place will be removed and be
cut down and fall, and the burden that
was on it will be cut off; for the LORD
has spoken.' "

Proclamation Against Tyre

23 The burden against Tyre.

Wail, you ships of Tarshish!
For it is laid waste,
So that there is no house, no harbor;
From the land of Cyprus[a] it is revealed to them.

2 Be still, you inhabitants of the coastland,
You merchants of Sidon,
Whom those who cross the sea have filled.[a]
3 And on great waters the grain of Shihor,
The harvest of the River,[a] *is* her revenue;
And she is a marketplace for the nations.

22:19 [a] Septuagint omits *he will pull you down;* Syriac, Targum, and Vulgate read *I will pull you down.*
23:1 [a] Hebrew *Kittim,* western lands, especially Cyprus 23:2 [a] Following Masoretic Text and Vulgate; Septuagint and Targum read *Passing over the water;* Dead Sea Scrolls read *Your messengers passing over the sea.* 23:3 [a] That is, the Nile

4 Be ashamed, O Sidon;
For the sea has spoken,
The strength of the sea, saying,
"I do not labor, nor bring forth children;
Neither do I rear young men,
Nor bring up virgins."
5 When the report *reaches* Egypt,
They also will be in agony at the report of Tyre.

6 Cross over to Tarshish;
Wail, you inhabitants of the coastland!
7 *Is* this your joyous *city,*
Whose antiquity *is* from ancient days,
Whose feet carried her far off to dwell?
8 Who has taken this counsel against Tyre, the crowning *city,*
Whose merchants *are* princes,
Whose traders *are* the honorable of the earth?
9 The LORD of hosts has purposed it,
To bring to dishonor the pride of all glory,
To bring into contempt all the honorable of the earth.

10 Overflow through your land like the River,[a]
O daughter of Tarshish;
There is no more strength.
11 He stretched out His hand over the sea,
He shook the kingdoms;
The LORD has given a commandment against Canaan
To destroy its strongholds.
12 And He said, "You will rejoice no more,
O you oppressed virgin daughter of Sidon.
Arise, cross over to Cyprus;
There also you will have no rest."

13 Behold, the land of the Chaldeans,
This people *which* was not;
Assyria founded it for wild beasts of the desert.
They set up its towers,
They raised up its palaces,
And brought it to ruin.

14 Wail, you ships of Tarshish!
For your strength is laid waste.

15Now it shall come to pass in that
day that Tyre will be forgotten seventy
years, according to the days of one king.
At the end of seventy years it will hap-
pen to Tyre as *in* the song of the harlot:

16 "Take a harp, go about the city,
You forgotten harlot;
Make sweet melody, sing many songs,
That you may be remembered."

17And it shall be, at the end of seventy
years, that the LORD will deal with Tyre.
She will return to her hire, and commit
fornication with all the kingdoms of the
world on the face of the earth. 18Her
gain and her pay will be set apart for
the LORD; it will not be treasured nor
laid up, for her gain will be for those
who dwell before the LORD, to eat suf-
ficiently, and for fine clothing.

Impending Judgment on the Earth

24 Behold, the LORD makes the earth empty and makes it waste,
Distorts its surface
And scatters abroad its inhabitants.
2 And it shall be:
As with the people, so with the priest;
As with the servant, so with his master;
As with the maid, so with her mistress;
As with the buyer, so with the seller;
As with the lender, so with the borrower;
As with the creditor, so with the debtor.
3 The land shall be entirely emptied and utterly plundered,
For the LORD has spoken this word.

23:10 [a] That is, the Nile

4 The earth mourns *and* fades away,
The world languishes *and* fades away;
The haughty people of the earth languish.
5 The earth is also defiled under its inhabitants,
Because they have transgressed the laws,
Changed the ordinance,
Broken the everlasting covenant.
6 Therefore the curse has devoured the earth,
And those who dwell in it are desolate.
Therefore the inhabitants of the earth are burned,
And few men *are* left.

7 The new wine fails, the vine languishes,
All the merry-hearted sigh.
8 The mirth of the tambourine ceases,
The noise of the jubilant ends,
The joy of the harp ceases.
9 They shall not drink wine with a song;
Strong drink is bitter to those who drink it.
10 The city of confusion is broken down;
Every house is shut up, so that none may go in.
11 *There is* a cry for wine in the streets,
All joy is darkened,
The mirth of the land is gone.
12 In the city desolation is left,
And the gate is stricken with destruction.
13 When it shall be thus in the midst of the land among the people,
It shall be like the shaking of an olive tree,
Like the gleaning of grapes when the vintage is done.

14 They shall lift up their voice, they shall sing;
For the majesty of the LORD
They shall cry aloud from the sea.
15 Therefore glorify the LORD in the dawning light,
The name of the LORD God of Israel in the coastlands of the sea.
16 From the ends of the earth we have heard songs:
"Glory to the righteous!"
But I said, "I am ruined, ruined!
Woe to me!
The treacherous dealers have dealt treacherously,
Indeed, the treacherous dealers have dealt very treacherously."

17 Fear and the pit and the snare
Are upon you, O inhabitant of the earth.
18 And it shall be
That he who flees from the noise of the fear
Shall fall into the pit,
And he who comes up from the midst of the pit
Shall be caught in the snare;
For the windows from on high are open,
And the foundations of the earth are shaken.

19 The earth is violently broken,
The earth is split open,
The earth is shaken exceedingly.
20 The earth shall reel to and fro like a drunkard,
And shall totter like a hut;
Its transgression shall be heavy upon it,
And it will fall, and not rise again.

21 It shall come to pass in that day
That the LORD will punish on high the host of exalted ones,
And on the earth the kings of the earth.
22 They will be gathered together,
As prisoners are gathered in the pit,
And will be shut up in the prison;
After many days they will be punished.
23 Then the moon will be disgraced
And the sun ashamed;
For the LORD of hosts will reign
On Mount Zion and in Jerusalem
And before His elders, gloriously.

Praise to God

25 O LORD, You *are* my God.
I will exalt You,
I will praise Your name,
For You have done wonderful *things;*
Your counsels of old *are* faithfulness *and* truth.
2 For You have made a city a ruin,
A fortified city a ruin,
A palace of foreigners to be a city no more;
It will never be rebuilt.
3 Therefore the strong people will glorify You;
The city of the terrible nations will fear You.
4 For You have been a strength to the poor,
A strength to the needy in his distress,
A refuge from the storm,
A shade from the heat;
For the blast of the terrible ones *is* as a storm *against* the wall.
5 You will reduce the noise of aliens,
As heat in a dry place;
As heat in the shadow of a cloud,
The song of the terrible ones will be diminished.

6 And in this mountain
The LORD of hosts will make for all people
A feast of choice pieces,
A feast of wines on the lees,
Of fat things full of marrow,
Of well-refined wines on the lees.
7 And He will destroy on this mountain
The surface of the covering cast over all people,
And the veil that is spread over all nations.
8 He will swallow up death forever,
And the Lord GOD will wipe away tears from all faces;
The rebuke of His people
He will take away from all the earth;
For the LORD has spoken.

9 And it will be said in that day:
"Behold, this *is* our God;
We have waited for Him, and He will save us.
This *is* the LORD;
We have waited for Him;
We will be glad and rejoice in His salvation."
10 For on this mountain the hand of the LORD will rest,
And Moab shall be trampled down under Him,
As straw is trampled down for the refuse heap.
11 And He will spread out His hands in their midst
As a swimmer reaches out to swim,
And He will bring down their pride
Together with the trickery of their hands.
12 The fortress of the high fort of your walls
He will bring down, lay low,
And bring to the ground, down to the dust.

A Song of Salvation

26 In that day this song will be sung in the land of Judah:

"We have a strong city;
God will appoint salvation *for* walls and bulwarks.
2 Open the gates,
That the righteous nation which keeps the truth may enter in.
3 You will keep *him* in perfect peace,
Whose mind *is* stayed *on You,*
Because he trusts in You.
4 Trust in the LORD forever,
For in YAH, the LORD, *is* everlasting strength.[a]
5 For He brings down those who dwell on high,
The lofty city;
He lays it low,
He lays it low to the ground,
He brings it down to the dust.
6 The foot shall tread it down—
The feet of the poor
And the steps of the needy."

26:4 [a] Or *Rock of Ages*

7 The way of the just *is* uprightness;
O Most Upright,
You weigh the path of the just.
8 Yes, in the way of Your judgments,
O LORD, we have waited for You;
The desire of *our* soul *is* for Your name
And for the remembrance of You.
9 With my soul I have desired You in the night,
Yes, by my spirit within me I will seek You early;
For when Your judgments *are* in the earth,
The inhabitants of the world will learn righteousness.

10 Let grace be shown to the wicked,
Yet he will not learn righteousness;
In the land of uprightness he will deal unjustly,
And will not behold the majesty of the LORD.
11 LORD, *when* Your hand is lifted up, they will not see.
But they will see and be ashamed
For *their* envy of people;
Yes, the fire of Your enemies shall devour them.

12 LORD, You will establish peace for us,
For You have also done all our works in us.
13 O LORD our God, masters besides You
Have had dominion over us;
But by You only we make mention of Your name.
14 *They are* dead, they will not live;
They are deceased, they will not rise.
Therefore You have punished and destroyed them,
And made all their memory to perish.
15 You have increased the nation, O LORD,
You have increased the nation;
You are glorified;
You have expanded all the borders of the land.
16 LORD, in trouble they have visited You,
They poured out a prayer *when* Your chastening *was* upon them.
17 As a woman with child
Is in pain and cries out in her pangs,
When she draws near the time of her delivery,
So have we been in Your sight, O LORD.
18 We have been with child, we have been in pain;
We have, as it were, brought forth wind;
We have not accomplished any deliverance in the earth,
Nor have the inhabitants of the world fallen.

19 Your dead shall live;
Together with my dead body[a] they shall arise.
Awake and sing, you who dwell in dust;
For your dew *is like* the dew of herbs,
And the earth shall cast out the dead.

Take Refuge from the Coming Judgment

20 Come, my people, enter your chambers,
And shut your doors behind you;
Hide yourself, as it were, for a little moment,
Until the indignation is past.
21 For behold, the LORD comes out of His place
To punish the inhabitants of the earth for their iniquity;
The earth will also disclose her blood,
And will no more cover her slain.

27 In that day the LORD with His severe sword, great and strong,
Will punish Leviathan the fleeing serpent,
Leviathan that twisted serpent;

26:19 [a] Following Masoretic Text and Vulgate; Syriac and Targum read *their dead bodies;* Septuagint reads *those in the tombs.*

And He will slay the reptile that *is*
in the sea.

The Restoration of Israel

2 In that day sing to her,
"A vineyard of red wine![a]
3 I, the LORD, keep it,
I water it every moment;
Lest any hurt it,
I keep it night and day.
4 Fury *is* not in Me.
Who would set briers *and* thorns
Against Me in battle?
I would go through them,
I would burn them together.
5 Or let him take hold of My
strength,
That he may make peace with Me;
And he shall make peace with Me."

6 Those who come He shall cause to
take root in Jacob;
Israel shall blossom and bud,
And fill the face of the world with
fruit.

7 Has He struck Israel as He struck
those who struck him?
Or has He been slain according to
the slaughter of those who
were slain by Him?
8 In measure, by sending it away,
You contended with it.
He removes *it* by His rough wind
In the day of the east wind.
9 Therefore by this the iniquity of
Jacob will be covered;
And this *is* all the fruit of taking
away his sin:
When he makes all the stones of
the altar
Like chalkstones that are beaten
to dust,
Wooden images[a] and incense
altars shall not stand.

10 Yet the fortified city *will be*
desolate,
The habitation forsaken and left
like a wilderness;
There the calf will feed, and there
it will lie down
And consume its branches.
11 When its boughs are withered,
they will be broken off;
The women come *and* set them on
fire.
For it *is* a people of no
understanding;
Therefore He who made them will
not have mercy on them,
And He who formed them will
show them no favor.

12 And it shall come to pass in that
day
That the LORD will thresh,
From the channel of the River[a] to
the Brook of Egypt;
And you will be gathered one by
one,
O you children of Israel.

13 So it shall be in that day:
The great trumpet will be blown;
They will come, who are about
to perish in the land of
Assyria,
And they who are outcasts in the
land of Egypt,
And shall worship the LORD in the
holy mount at Jerusalem.

Woe to Ephraim and Jerusalem

28 Woe to the crown of pride,
to the drunkards of
Ephraim,
Whose glorious beauty *is* a fading
flower
Which *is* at the head of the
verdant valleys,
To those who are overcome with
wine!
2 Behold, the Lord has a mighty
and strong one,
Like a tempest of hail and a
destroying storm,
Like a flood of mighty waters
overflowing,
Who will bring *them* down to the
earth with *His* hand.
3 The crown of pride, the drunkards
of Ephraim,
Will be trampled underfoot;

27:2 [a] Following Masoretic Text (Kittel's *Biblia Hebraica*), Bomberg, and Vulgate; Masoretic Text (*Biblia Hebraica Stuttgartensia*), some Hebrew manuscripts, and Septuagint read *delight;* Targum reads *choice vineyard.* **27:9** [a] Hebrew *Asherim,* Canaanite deities **27:12** [a] That is, the Euphrates

4 And the glorious beauty is a fading flower
Which *is* at the head of the verdant valley,
Like the first fruit before the summer,
Which an observer sees;
He eats it up while it is still in his hand.

5 In that day the LORD of hosts will be
For a crown of glory and a diadem of beauty
To the remnant of His people,
6 For a spirit of justice to him who sits in judgment,
And for strength to those who turn back the battle at the gate.

7 But they also have erred through wine,
And through intoxicating drink are out of the way;
The priest and the prophet have erred through intoxicating drink,
They are swallowed up by wine,
They are out of the way through intoxicating drink;
They err in vision, they stumble *in* judgment.
8 For all tables are full of vomit *and* filth;
No place *is clean.*

9 "Whom will he teach knowledge?
And whom will he make to understand the message?
Those *just* weaned from milk?
Those *just* drawn from the breasts?
10 For precept *must be* upon precept, precept upon precept,
Line upon line, line upon line,
Here a little, there a little."

11 For with stammering lips and another tongue
He will speak to this people,
12 To whom He said, "This *is* the rest *with which*
You may cause the weary to rest,"
And, "This *is* the refreshing";
Yet they would not hear.
13 But the word of the LORD was to them,
"Precept upon precept, precept upon precept,
Line upon line, line upon line,
Here a little, there a little,"
That they might go and fall backward, and be broken
And snared and caught.

14 Therefore hear the word of the LORD, you scornful men,
Who rule this people who *are* in Jerusalem,
15 Because you have said, "We have made a covenant with death,
And with Sheol we are in agreement.
When the overflowing scourge passes through,
It will not come to us,
For we have made lies our refuge,
And under falsehood we have hidden ourselves."

A Cornerstone in Zion

16 Therefore thus says the Lord GOD:

"Behold, I lay in Zion a stone for a foundation,
A tried stone, a precious cornerstone, a sure foundation;
Whoever believes will not act hastily.
17 Also I will make justice the measuring line,
And righteousness the plummet;
The hail will sweep away the refuge of lies,
And the waters will overflow the hiding place.
18 Your covenant with death will be annulled,
And your agreement with Sheol will not stand;
When the overflowing scourge passes through,
Then you will be trampled down by it.
19 As often as it goes out it will take you;

For morning by morning it will
pass over,
And by day and by night;
It will be a terror just to
understand the report."

20 For the bed is too short to stretch
out *on,*
And the covering so narrow that
one cannot wrap himself *in*
it.
21 For the LORD will rise up as *at*
Mount Perazim,
He will be angry as in the Valley
of Gibeon—
That He may do His work, His
awesome work,
And bring to pass His act, His
unusual act.
22 Now therefore, do not be mockers,
Lest your bonds be made strong;
For I have heard from the Lord
GOD of hosts,
A destruction determined even
upon the whole earth.

Listen to the Teaching of God

23 Give ear and hear my voice,
Listen and hear my speech.
24 Does the plowman keep plowing
all day to sow?
Does he keep turning his soil and
breaking the clods?
25 When he has leveled its surface,
Does he not sow the black
cummin
And scatter the cummin,
Plant the wheat in rows,
The barley in the appointed place,
And the spelt in its place?
26 For He instructs him in right
judgment,
His God teaches him.

27 For the black cummin is not
threshed with a threshing
sledge,
Nor is a cartwheel rolled over the
cummin;
But the black cummin is beaten
out with a stick,
And the cummin with a rod.
28 Bread *flour* must be ground;
Therefore he does not thresh it
forever,
Break *it with* his cartwheel,
Or crush it *with* his horsemen.
29 This also comes from the LORD of
hosts,
Who is wonderful in counsel *and*
excellent in guidance.

Woe to Jerusalem

29 "Woe to Ariel,[a] to Ariel, the city
where David dwelt!
Add year to year;
Let feasts come around.
2 Yet I will distress Ariel;
There shall be heaviness and
sorrow,
And it shall be to Me as Ariel.
3 I will encamp against you all
around,
I will lay siege against you with a
mound,
And I will raise siegeworks
against you.
4 You shall be brought down,
You shall speak out of the
ground;
Your speech shall be low, out of
the dust;
Your voice shall be like a
medium's, out of the ground;
And your speech shall whisper
out of the dust.

5 "Moreover the multitude of your
foes
Shall be like fine dust,
And the multitude of the terrible
ones
Like chaff that passes away;
Yes, it shall be in an instant,
suddenly.
6 You will be punished by the LORD
of hosts
With thunder and earthquake
and great noise,
With storm and tempest
And the flame of devouring fire.
7 The multitude of all the nations
who fight against Ariel,
Even all who fight against her and
her fortress,
And distress her,

29:1 [a] That is, Jerusalem

Shall be as a dream of a night
vision.
8 It shall even be as when a hungry
man dreams,
And look—he eats;
But he awakes, and his soul is still
empty;
Or as when a thirsty man dreams,
And look—he drinks;
But he awakes, and indeed *he is*
faint,
And his soul still craves:
So the multitude of all the nations
shall be,
Who fight against Mount Zion."

The Blindness of Disobedience

9 Pause and wonder!
Blind yourselves and be blind!
They are drunk, but not with
wine;
They stagger, but not with
intoxicating drink.
10 For the LORD has poured out on
you
The spirit of deep sleep,
And has closed your eyes,
namely, the prophets;
And He has covered your heads,
namely, the seers.

11The whole vision has become to you
like the words of a book that is sealed,
which *men* deliver to one who is literate,
saying, "Read this, please."
And he says, "I cannot, for it *is* sealed."
12Then the book is delivered to one who
is illiterate, saying, "Read this, please."
And he says, "I am not literate."
13Therefore the Lord said:

"Inasmuch as these people draw
near with their mouths
And honor Me with their lips,
But have removed their hearts far
from Me,
And their fear toward
Me is taught by the
commandment of men,
14 Therefore, behold, I will again do
a marvelous work
Among this people,
A marvelous work and a wonder;
For the wisdom of their wise *men*
shall perish,
And the understanding of their
prudent *men* shall be
hidden."
15 Woe to those who seek deep to
hide their counsel far from
the LORD,
And their works are in the dark;
They say, "Who sees us?" and,
"Who knows us?"
16 Surely you have things turned
around!
Shall the potter be esteemed as
the clay;
For shall the thing made say of
him who made it,
"He did not make me"?
Or shall the thing formed say of
him who formed it,
"He has no understanding"?

Future Recovery of Wisdom

17 *Is* it not yet a very little while
Till Lebanon shall be turned into
a fruitful field,
And the fruitful field be esteemed
as a forest?
18 In that day the deaf shall hear the
words of the book,
And the eyes of the blind shall see
out of obscurity and out of
darkness.
19 The humble also shall increase
their joy in the LORD,
And the poor among men shall
rejoice
In the Holy One of Israel.
20 For the terrible one is brought to
nothing,
The scornful one is consumed,
And all who watch for iniquity are
cut off—
21 Who make a man an offender by
a word,
And lay a snare for him who
reproves in the gate,
And turn aside the just by empty
words.

22Therefore thus says the LORD, who
redeemed Abraham, concerning the
house of Jacob:

"Jacob shall not now be ashamed,
Nor shall his face now grow pale;

23 But when he sees his children,
The work of My hands, in his midst,
They will hallow My name,
And hallow the Holy One of Jacob,
And fear the God of Israel.
24 These also who erred in spirit will come to understanding,
And those who complained will learn doctrine."

Futile Confidence in Egypt

30 "Woe to the rebellious children," says the LORD,
"Who take counsel, but not of Me,
And who devise plans, but not of My Spirit,
That they may add sin to sin;
2 Who walk to go down to Egypt,
And have not asked My advice,
To strengthen themselves in the strength of Pharaoh,
And to trust in the shadow of Egypt!
3 Therefore the strength of Pharaoh
Shall be your shame,
And trust in the shadow of Egypt
Shall be *your* humiliation.
4 For his princes were at Zoan,
And his ambassadors came to Hanes.
5 They were all ashamed of a people *who* could not benefit them,
Or be help or benefit,
But a shame and also a reproach."

6The burden against the beasts of the
South.

Through a land of trouble and anguish,
From which *came* the lioness and lion,
The viper and fiery flying serpent,
They will carry their riches on the backs of young donkeys,
And their treasures on the humps of camels,
To a people *who* shall not profit;
7 For the Egyptians shall help in vain and to no purpose.
Therefore I have called her
Rahab-Hem-Shebeth.[a]

A Rebellious People

8 Now go, write it before them on a tablet,
And note it on a scroll,
That it may be for time to come,
Forever and ever:
9 That this *is* a rebellious people,
Lying children,
Children *who* will not hear the law of the LORD;
10 Who say to the seers, "Do not see,"
And to the prophets, "Do not prophesy to us right things;
Speak to us smooth things, prophesy deceits.
11 Get out of the way,
Turn aside from the path,
Cause the Holy One of Israel
To cease from before us."

12Therefore thus says the Holy One
of Israel:

"Because you despise this word,
And trust in oppression and perversity,
And rely on them,
13 Therefore this iniquity shall be to you
Like a breach ready to fall,
A bulge in a high wall,
Whose breaking comes suddenly, in an instant.
14 And He shall break it like the breaking of the potter's vessel,
Which is broken in pieces;
He shall not spare.
So there shall not be found among its fragments
A shard to take fire from the hearth,
Or to take water from the cistern."

15For thus says the Lord GOD, the Holy
One of Israel:

"In returning and rest you shall be saved;
In quietness and confidence shall be your strength."

30:7 [a] Literally *Rahab Sits Idle*

But you would not,
16 And you said, "No, for we will flee
on horses"—
Therefore you shall flee!
And, "We will ride on swift
horses"—
Therefore those who pursue you
shall be swift!

17 One thousand *shall flee* at the
threat of one,
At the threat of five you
shall flee,
Till you are left as a pole on top of
a mountain
And as a banner on a hill.

God Will Be Gracious

18 Therefore the LORD will wait, that
He may be gracious to you;
And therefore He will be exalted,
that He may have mercy on
you.
For the LORD *is* a God of justice;
Blessed *are* all those who wait for
Him.

19 For the people shall dwell in Zion
at Jerusalem;
You shall weep no more.
He will be very gracious to you at
the sound of your cry;
When He hears it, He will answer
you.
20 And *though* the Lord gives you
The bread of adversity and the
water of affliction,
Yet your teachers will not
be moved into a corner
anymore,
But your eyes shall see your
teachers.
21 Your ears shall hear a word
behind you, saying,
"This *is* the way, walk in it,"
Whenever you turn to the right
hand
Or whenever you turn to the left.
22 You will also defile the covering of
your images of silver,
And the ornament of your
molded images of gold.
You will throw them away as an
unclean thing;
You will say to them, "Get away!"

23 Then He will give the rain for your
seed
With which you sow the ground,
And bread of the increase of the
earth;
It will be fat and plentiful.
In that day your cattle will feed
In large pastures.
24 Likewise the oxen and the young
donkeys that work the
ground
Will eat cured fodder,
Which has been winnowed with
the shovel and fan.
25 There will be on every high
mountain
And on every high hill
Rivers *and* streams of waters,
In the day of the great slaughter,
When the towers fall.
26 Moreover the light of the moon
will be as the light of the sun,
And the light of the sun will be
sevenfold,
As the light of seven days,
In the day that the LORD binds up
the bruise of His people
And heals the stroke of their
wound.

Judgment on Assyria

27 Behold, the name of the LORD
comes from afar,
Burning *with* His anger,
And *His* burden *is* heavy;
His lips are full of indignation,
And His tongue like a devouring
fire.
28 His breath is like an overflowing
stream,
Which reaches up to the neck,
To sift the nations with the sieve
of futility;
And *there shall be* a bridle in the
jaws of the people,
Causing *them* to err.

29 You shall have a song
As in the night *when* a holy
festival is kept,
And gladness of heart as when
one goes with a flute,
To come into the mountain of the
LORD,
To the Mighty One of Israel.

30 The LORD will cause His glorious
voice to be heard,
And show the descent of His arm,
With the indignation of *His* anger
And the flame of a devouring
fire,
With scattering, tempest, and
hailstones.
31 For through the voice of the LORD
Assyria will be beaten down,
As He strikes with the rod.
32 And *in* every place where the staff
of punishment passes,
Which the LORD lays on him,
It will be with tambourines and
harps;
And in battles of brandishing He
will fight with it.
33 For Tophet *was* established
of old,
Yes, for the king it is prepared.
He has made *it* deep and large;
Its pyre *is* fire with much wood;
The breath of the LORD, like a
stream of brimstone,
Kindles it.

The Folly of Not Trusting God

31 Woe to those who go down to
Egypt for help,
And rely on horses,
Who trust in chariots because
they are many,
And in horsemen because they
are very strong,
But who do not look to the Holy
One of Israel,
Nor seek the LORD!
2 Yet He also *is* wise and will bring
disaster,
And will not call back His words,
But will arise against the house of
evildoers,
And against the help of those who
work iniquity.
3 Now the Egyptians *are* men, and
not God;
And their horses are flesh, and
not spirit.
When the LORD stretches out His
hand,
Both he who helps will fall,
And he who is helped will fall
down;
They all will perish together.

God Will Deliver Jerusalem

4For thus the LORD has spoken to me:

"As a lion roars,
And a young lion over his prey
(When a multitude of shepherds
is summoned against him,
He will not be afraid of their
voice
Nor be disturbed by their noise),
So the LORD of hosts will come
down
To fight for Mount Zion and for its
hill.
5 Like birds flying about,
So will the LORD of hosts defend
Jerusalem.
Defending, He will also deliver *it;*
Passing over, He will preserve *it.*"

6Return *to Him* against whom the chil-
dren of Israel have deeply revolted.
7For in that day every man shall throw
away his idols of silver and his idols of
gold—sin, which your own hands have
made for yourselves.

8 "Then Assyria shall fall by a sword
not of man,
And a sword not of mankind shall
devour him.
But he shall flee from the sword,
And his young men shall become
forced labor.
9 He shall cross over to his
stronghold for fear,
And his princes shall be afraid of
the banner,"
Says the LORD,
Whose fire *is* in Zion
And whose furnace *is* in
Jerusalem.

A Reign of Righteousness

32 Behold, a king will reign in
righteousness,
And princes will rule with justice.
2 A man will be as a hiding place
from the wind,
And a cover from the tempest,
As rivers of water in a dry place,
As the shadow of a great rock in a
weary land.
3 The eyes of those who see will not
be dim,

And the ears of those who hear
will listen.
4 Also the heart of the rash will
understand knowledge,
And the tongue of the
stammerers will be ready to
speak plainly.

5 The foolish person will no longer
be called generous,
Nor the miser said *to be* bountiful;
6 For the foolish person will speak
foolishness,
And his heart will work iniquity:
To practice ungodliness,
To utter error against the LORD,
To keep the hungry unsatisfied,
And he will cause the drink of the
thirsty to fail.
7 Also the schemes of the schemer
are evil;
He devises wicked plans
To destroy the poor with lying
words,
Even when the needy speaks
justice.
8 But a generous man devises
generous things,
And by generosity he shall stand.

Consequences of Complacency

9 Rise up, you women who are at
ease,
Hear my voice;
You complacent daughters,
Give ear to my speech.
10 In a year and *some* days
You will be troubled, you
complacent women;
For the vintage will fail,
The gathering will not come.
11 Tremble, you *women* who are at
ease;
Be troubled, you complacent
ones;
Strip yourselves, make yourselves
bare,
And gird *sackcloth* on *your* waists.

12 People shall mourn upon their
breasts
For the pleasant fields, for the
fruitful vine.
13 On the land of my people will
come up thorns *and* briers,
Yes, on all the happy homes *in* the
joyous city;
14 Because the palaces will be
forsaken,
The bustling city will be
deserted.
The forts and towers will become
lairs forever,
A joy of wild donkeys, a pasture of
flocks—
15 Until the Spirit is poured upon us
from on high,
And the wilderness becomes a
fruitful field,
And the fruitful field is counted as
a forest.

The Peace of God's Reign

16 Then justice will dwell in the
wilderness,
And righteousness remain in the
fruitful field.
17 The work of righteousness will be
peace,
And the effect of righteousness,
quietness and assurance
forever.
18 My people will dwell in a peaceful
habitation,
In secure dwellings, and in quiet
resting places,
19 Though hail comes down on the
forest,
And the city is brought low in
humiliation.

20 Blessed *are* you who sow beside
all waters,
Who send out freely the feet of
the ox and the donkey.

A Prayer in Deep Distress

33 Woe to you who plunder,
though you *have* not *been*
plundered;
And you who deal treacherously,
though they have not
dealt treacherously with
you!
When you cease plundering,
You will be plundered;
When you make an end of
dealing treacherously,
They will deal treacherously with
you.

2 O LORD, be gracious to us;
We have waited for You.
Be their[a] arm every morning,
Our salvation also in the time of trouble.
3 At the noise of the tumult the people shall flee;
When You lift Yourself up, the nations shall be scattered;
4 And Your plunder shall be gathered
Like the gathering of the caterpillar;
As the running to and fro of locusts,
He shall run upon them.

5 The LORD is exalted, for He dwells on high;
He has filled Zion with justice and righteousness.
6 Wisdom and knowledge will be the stability of your times,
And the strength of salvation;
The fear of the LORD *is* His treasure.

7 Surely their valiant ones shall cry outside,
The ambassadors of peace shall weep bitterly.
8 The highways lie waste,
The traveling man ceases.
He has broken the covenant,
He has despised the cities,[a]
He regards no man.
9 The earth mourns *and* languishes,
Lebanon is shamed *and* shriveled;
Sharon is like a wilderness,
And Bashan and Carmel shake off *their fruits.*

Impending Judgment on Zion

10 "Now I will rise," says the LORD;
"Now I will be exalted,
Now I will lift Myself up.
11 You shall conceive chaff,
You shall bring forth stubble;
Your breath, *as* fire, shall devour you.
12 And the people shall be *like* the burnings of lime;
Like thorns cut up they shall be burned in the fire.
13 Hear, you *who are* afar off, what I have done;
And you *who are* near, acknowledge My might."

14 The sinners in Zion are afraid;
Fearfulness has seized the hypocrites:
"Who among us shall dwell with the devouring fire?
Who among us shall dwell with everlasting burnings?"
15 He who walks righteously and speaks uprightly,
He who despises the gain of oppressions,
Who gestures with his hands, refusing bribes,
Who stops his ears from hearing of bloodshed,
And shuts his eyes from seeing evil:
16 He will dwell on high;
His place of defense *will be* the fortress of rocks;
Bread will be given him,
His water *will be* sure.

The Land of the Majestic King

17 Your eyes will see the King in His beauty;
They will see the land that is very far off.
18 Your heart will meditate on terror:
"Where *is* the scribe?
Where *is* he who weighs?
Where *is* he who counts the towers?"
19 You will not see a fierce people,
A people of obscure speech, beyond perception,
Of a stammering tongue *that you* cannot understand.

20 Look upon Zion, the city of our appointed feasts;
Your eyes will see Jerusalem, a quiet home,

33:2 [a] Septuagint omits *their;* Syriac, Targum, and Vulgate read *our.* 33:8 [a] Following Masoretic Text and Vulgate; Dead Sea Scrolls read *witnesses;* Septuagint omits *cities;* Targum reads *They have been removed from their cities.*

A tabernacle *that* will not be taken down;
Not one of its stakes will ever be removed,
Nor will any of its cords be broken.
21 But there the majestic LORD *will be* for us
A place of broad rivers *and* streams,
In which no galley with oars will sail,
Nor majestic ships pass by
22 (For the LORD *is* our Judge,
The LORD *is* our Lawgiver,
The LORD *is* our King;
He will save us);
23 Your tackle is loosed,
They could not strengthen their mast,
They could not spread the sail.

Then the prey of great plunder is divided;
The lame take the prey.
24 And the inhabitant will not say, "I am sick";
The people who dwell in it *will be* forgiven *their* iniquity.

Judgment on the Nations

34 Come near, you nations, to hear;
And heed, you people!
Let the earth hear, and all that is in it,
The world and all things that come forth from it.
2 For the indignation of the LORD *is* against all nations,
And *His* fury against all their armies;
He has utterly destroyed them,
He has given them over to the slaughter.
3 Also their slain shall be thrown out;
Their stench shall rise from their corpses,
And the mountains shall be melted with their blood.
4 All the host of heaven shall be dissolved,
And the heavens shall be rolled up like a scroll;
All their host shall fall down
As the leaf falls from the vine,
And as *fruit* falling from a fig tree.

5 "For My sword shall be bathed in heaven;
Indeed it shall come down on Edom,
And on the people of My curse, for judgment.
6 The sword of the LORD is filled with blood,
It is made overflowing with fatness,
With the blood of lambs and goats,
With the fat of the kidneys of rams.
For the LORD has a sacrifice in Bozrah,
And a great slaughter in the land of Edom.
7 The wild oxen shall come down with them,
And the young bulls with the mighty bulls;
Their land shall be soaked with blood,
And their dust saturated with fatness."

8 For *it is* the day of the LORD's vengeance,
The year of recompense for the cause of Zion.
9 Its streams shall be turned into pitch,
And its dust into brimstone;
Its land shall become burning pitch.
10 It shall not be quenched night or day;
Its smoke shall ascend forever.
From generation to generation it shall lie waste;
No one shall pass through it forever and ever.
11 But the pelican and the porcupine shall possess it,
Also the owl and the raven shall dwell in it.
And He shall stretch out over it
The line of confusion and the stones of emptiness.
12 They shall call its nobles to the kingdom,
But none *shall be* there, and all its princes shall be nothing.

13 And thorns shall come up in its
palaces,
Nettles and brambles in its
fortresses;
It shall be a habitation of jackals,
A courtyard for ostriches.
14 The wild beasts of the desert shall
also meet with the jackals,
And the wild goat shall bleat to its
companion;
Also the night creature shall rest
there,
And find for herself a place of rest.
15 There the arrow snake shall make
her nest and lay *eggs*
And hatch, and gather *them*
under her shadow;
There also shall the hawks be
gathered,
Every one with her mate.

16 "Search from the book of the LORD,
and read:
Not one of these shall fail;
Not one shall lack her mate.
For My mouth has commanded it,
and His Spirit has gathered
them.
17 He has cast the lot for them,
And His hand has divided
it among them with a
measuring line.
They shall possess it forever;
From generation to generation
they shall dwell in it."

The Future Glory of Zion

35 The wilderness and the
wasteland shall be glad
for them,
And the desert shall rejoice and
blossom as the rose;
2 It shall blossom abundantly and
rejoice,
Even with joy and singing.
The glory of Lebanon shall be
given to it,
The excellence of Carmel and
Sharon.
They shall see the glory of the
LORD,
The excellency of our God.

3 Strengthen the weak hands,
And make firm the feeble knees.
4 Say to those *who are*
fearful-hearted,
"Be strong, do not fear!
Behold, your God will come *with*
vengeance,
With the recompense of God;
He will come and save you."

5 Then the eyes of the blind shall be
opened,
And the ears of the deaf shall be
unstopped.
6 Then the lame shall leap like a
deer,
And the tongue of the dumb sing.
For waters shall burst forth in the
wilderness,
And streams in the desert.
7 The parched ground shall become
a pool,
And the thirsty land springs of
water;
In the habitation of jackals, where
each lay,
There shall be grass with reeds and
rushes.

8 A highway shall be there, and a
road,
And it shall be called the Highway
of Holiness.
The unclean shall not pass over it,
But it *shall be* for others.
Whoever walks the road, although
a fool,
Shall not go astray.
9 No lion shall be there,
Nor shall *any* ravenous beast go
up on it;
It shall not be found there.
But the redeemed shall walk *there*,
10 And the ransomed of the LORD
shall return,
And come to Zion with singing,
With everlasting joy on their
heads.
They shall obtain joy and
gladness,
And sorrow and sighing shall flee
away.

Sennacherib Boasts Against the LORD

36 Now it came to pass in the
fourteenth year of King Heze-
kiah *that* Sennacherib king of Assyria

came up against all the fortified cities
of Judah and took them. 2Then the king
of Assyria sent *the* Rabshakeh[a] with a
great army from Lachish to King Heze-
kiah at Jerusalem. And he stood by the
aqueduct from the upper pool, on the
highway to the Fuller's Field. 3And Eli-
akim the son of Hilkiah, who was over
the household, Shebna the scribe, and
Joah the son of Asaph, the recorder,
came out to him.

4Then *the* Rabshakeh said to them,
"Say now to Hezekiah, 'Thus says the
great king, the king of Assyria: "What
confidence is this in which you trust?
5I say you speak of having plans and
power for war; but *they are* mere words.
Now in whom do you trust, that you re-
bel against me? 6Look! You are trusting
in the staff of this broken reed, Egypt,
on which if a man leans, it will go into
his hand and pierce it. So *is* Pharaoh
king of Egypt to all who trust in him.

7"But if you say to me, 'We trust in the
LORD our God,' *is it* not He whose high
places and whose altars Hezekiah has
taken away, and said to Judah and Je-
rusalem, 'You shall worship before this
altar'?" ' 8Now therefore, I urge you,
give a pledge to my master the king of
Assyria, and I will give you two thou-
sand horses—if you are able on your
part to put riders on them! 9How then
will you repel one captain of the least
of my master's servants, and put your
trust in Egypt for chariots and horse-
men? 10Have I now come up without
the LORD against this land to destroy
it? The LORD said to me, 'Go up against
this land, and destroy it.' "

11Then Eliakim, Shebna, and Joah said
to *the* Rabshakeh, "Please speak to your
servants in Aramaic, for we understand
it; and do not speak to us in Hebrew[a]
in the hearing of the people who *are*
on the wall."

12But *the* Rabshakeh said, "Has my
master sent me to your master and to
you to speak these words, and not to the
men who sit on the wall, who will eat
and drink their own waste with you?"

13Then *the* Rabshakeh stood and called
out with a loud voice in Hebrew, and
said, "Hear the words of the great king,
the king of Assyria! 14Thus says the king:
'Do not let Hezekiah deceive you, for he
will not be able to deliver you; 15nor let
Hezekiah make you trust in the LORD,
saying, "The LORD will surely deliver us;
this city will not be given into the hand
of the king of Assyria." ' 16Do not listen
to Hezekiah; for thus says the king of As-
syria: 'Make *peace* with me *by a* present
and come out to me; and every one of
you eat from his own vine and every one
from his own fig tree, and every one of
you drink the waters of his own cistern;
17until I come and take you away to a
land like your own land, a land of grain
and new wine, a land of bread and vine-
yards. 18*Beware* lest Hezekiah persuade
you, saying, "The LORD will deliver us."
Has any one of the gods of the nations
delivered its land from the hand of the
king of Assyria? 19Where *are* the gods of
Hamath and Arpad? Where *are* the gods
of Sepharvaim? Indeed, have they de-
livered Samaria from my hand? 20Who
among all the gods of these lands have
delivered their countries from my hand,
that the LORD should deliver Jerusalem
from my hand?' "

21But they held their peace and an-
swered him not a word; for the king's
commandment was, "Do not answer
him." 22Then Eliakim the son of Hilkiah,
who *was* over the household, Shebna the
scribe, and Joah the son of Asaph, the
recorder, came to Hezekiah with *their*
clothes torn, and told him the words of
the Rabshakeh.

Isaiah Assures Deliverance

37 And so it was, when King Hez-
ekiah heard *it,* that he tore his
clothes, covered himself with sackcloth,
and went into the house of the LORD.
2Then he sent Eliakim, who *was* over
the household, Shebna the scribe, and
the elders of the priests, covered with
sackcloth, to Isaiah the prophet, the
son of Amoz. 3And they said to him,
"Thus says Hezekiah: 'This day *is* a day
of trouble and rebuke and blasphemy;
for the children have come to birth, but
there is no strength to bring them forth.

36:2 [a] A title, probably *Chief of Staff* or *Governor* 36:11 [a] Literally *Judean*

4It may be that the LORD your God will
hear the words of *the* Rabshakeh, whom
his master the king of Assyria has sent
to reproach the living God, and will re-
buke the words which the LORD your
God has heard. Therefore lift up *your*
prayer for the remnant that is left.' "

5So the servants of King Hezeki-
ah came to Isaiah. 6And Isaiah said
to them, "Thus you shall say to your
master, 'Thus says the LORD: "Do not
be afraid of the words which you have
heard, with which the servants of the
king of Assyria have blasphemed Me.
7Surely I will send a spirit upon him,
and he shall hear a rumor and return
to his own land; and I will cause him
to fall by the sword in his own land." ' "

Sennacherib's Threat and Hezekiah's Prayer

8Then *the* Rabshakeh returned, and
found the king of Assyria warring
against Libnah, for he heard that he
had departed from Lachish. 9And the
king heard concerning Tirhakah king
of Ethiopia, "He has come out to make
war with you." So when he heard *it,* he
sent messengers to Hezekiah, saying,
10"Thus you shall speak to Hezekiah king
of Judah, saying: 'Do not let your God in
whom you trust deceive you, saying, "Je-
rusalem shall not be given into the hand
of the king of Assyria." 11Look! You have
heard what the kings of Assyria have
done to all lands by utterly destroying
them; and shall you be delivered? 12Have
the gods of the nations delivered those
whom my fathers have destroyed, Gozan
and Haran and Rezeph, and the people
of Eden who *were* in Telassar? 13Where *is*
the king of Hamath, the king of Arpad,
and the king of the city of Sepharvaim,
Hena, and Ivah?' "

14And Hezekiah received the letter
from the hand of the messengers, and
read it; and Hezekiah went up to the
house of the LORD, and spread it before
the LORD. 15Then Hezekiah prayed to the
LORD, saying: 16"O LORD of hosts, God of
Israel, *the One* who dwells *between* the
cherubim, You *are* God, You alone, of
all the kingdoms of the earth. You have
made heaven and earth. 17Incline Your
ear, O LORD, and hear; open Your eyes,
O LORD, and see; and hear all the words
of Sennacherib, which he has sent to
reproach the living God. 18Truly, LORD,
the kings of Assyria have laid waste all
the nations and their lands, 19and have
cast their gods into the fire; for they
were not gods, but the work of men's
hands—wood and stone. Therefore
they destroyed them. 20Now therefore,
O LORD our God, save us from his hand,
that all the kingdoms of the earth may
know that You *are* the LORD, You alone."

The Word of the LORD Concerning Sennacherib

21Then Isaiah the son of Amoz sent to
Hezekiah, saying, "Thus says the LORD
God of Israel, 'Because you have prayed
to Me against Sennacherib king of As-
syria, 22this *is* the word which the LORD
has spoken concerning him:

"The virgin, the daughter of Zion,
Has despised you, laughed you to scorn;
The daughter of Jerusalem
Has shaken *her* head behind your back!

23 "Whom have you reproached and blasphemed?
Against whom have you raised *your* voice,
And lifted up your eyes on high?
Against the Holy One of Israel.
24 By your servants you have reproached the Lord,
And said, 'By the multitude of my chariots
I have come up to the height of the mountains,
To the limits of Lebanon;
I will cut down its tall cedars
And its choice cypress trees;
I will enter its farthest height,
To its fruitful forest.
25 I have dug and drunk water,
And with the soles of my feet I have dried up
All the brooks of defense.'

26 "Did you not hear long ago
How I made it,
From ancient times that I formed it?

Now I have brought it to pass,
That you should be
For crushing fortified cities *into*
heaps of ruins.
27 Therefore their inhabitants *had*
little power;
They were dismayed and
confounded;
They were *as* the grass of the field
And the green herb,
As the grass on the housetops
And *grain* blighted before it is
grown.

28 "But I know your dwelling place,
Your going out and your
coming in,
And your rage against Me.
29 Because your rage against Me
and your tumult
Have come up to My ears,
Therefore I will put My hook in
your nose
And My bridle in your lips,
And I will turn you back
By the way which you came." '

30"This *shall be* a sign to you:

You shall eat this year such as
grows of itself,
And the second year what springs
from the same;
Also in the third year sow and
reap,
Plant vineyards and eat the fruit
of them.
31 And the remnant who have
escaped of the house of Judah
Shall again take root downward,
And bear fruit upward.
32 For out of Jerusalem shall go a
remnant,
And those who escape from
Mount Zion.
The zeal of the LORD of hosts will
do this.

33"Therefore thus says the LORD con-
cerning the king of Assyria:

'He shall not come into this city,
Nor shoot an arrow there,
Nor come before it with shield,
Nor build a siege mound against it.
34 By the way that he came,
By the same shall he return;
And he shall not come into this
city,'
Says the LORD.
35 'For I will defend this city, to save it
For My own sake and for My
servant David's sake.' "

Sennacherib's Defeat and Death

36Then the angel[a] of the LORD went
out, and killed in the camp of the As-
syrians one hundred and eighty-five
thousand; and when *people* arose early
in the morning, there were the corpses—
all dead. 37So Sennacherib king of As-
syria departed and went away, returned
home, and remained at Nineveh. 38Now it
came to pass, as he was worshiping in the
house of Nisroch his god, that his sons
Adrammelech and Sharezer struck him
down with the sword; and they escaped
into the land of Ararat. Then Esarhaddon
his son reigned in his place.

Hezekiah's Life Extended

38 In those days Hezekiah was sick
and near death. And Isaiah the
prophet, the son of Amoz, went to him
and said to him, "Thus says the LORD:
'Set your house in order, for you shall
die and not live.' "
2Then Hezekiah turned his face toward
the wall, and prayed to the LORD, 3and
said, "Remember now, O LORD, I pray,
how I have walked before You in truth
and with a loyal heart, and have done
what is good in Your sight." And Heze-
kiah wept bitterly.
4And the word of the LORD came to
Isaiah, saying, 5"Go and tell Hezekiah,
'Thus says the LORD, the God of David
your father: "I have heard your prayer,
I have seen your tears; surely I will add
to your days fifteen years. 6I will deliver
you and this city from the hand of the
king of Assyria, and I will defend this
city." ' 7And this *is* the sign to you from
the LORD, that the LORD will do this
thing which He has spoken: 8Behold,
I will bring the shadow on the sundial,

37:36 [a] Or *Angel*

which has gone down with the sun on
the sundial of Ahaz, ten degrees back-
ward." So the sun returned ten degrees
on the dial by which it had gone down.
9This is the writing of Hezekiah king of
Judah, when he had been sick and had
recovered from his sickness:

10 I said,
"In the prime of my life
I shall go to the gates of Sheol;
I am deprived of the remainder of
my years."
11 I said,
"I shall not see YAH,
The LORD[a] in the land of the living;
I shall observe man no more
among the inhabitants of
the world.[b]
12 My life span is gone,
Taken from me like a shepherd's
tent;
I have cut off my life like a weaver.
He cuts me off from the loom;
From day until night You make
an end of me.
13 I have considered until morning—
Like a lion,
So He breaks all my bones;
From day until night You make
an end of me.
14 Like a crane *or* a swallow, so I
chattered;
I mourned like a dove;
My eyes fail *from looking* upward.
O LORD,[a] I am oppressed;
Undertake for me!

15 "What shall I say?
He has both spoken to me,[a]
And He Himself has done *it*.
I shall walk carefully all my years
In the bitterness of my soul.
16 O Lord, by these *things men* live;
And in all these *things is* the life of
my spirit;
So You will restore me and make
me live.
17 Indeed *it was* for *my own* peace
That I had great bitterness;
But You have lovingly *delivered*
my soul from the pit of
corruption,
For You have cast all my sins
behind Your back.
18 For Sheol cannot thank You,
Death cannot praise You;
Those who go down to the pit
cannot hope for Your truth.
19 The living, the living man, he
shall praise You,
As I *do* this day;
The father shall make known Your
truth to the children.

20 "The LORD *was ready* to save me;
Therefore we will sing my songs
with stringed instruments
All the days of our life, in the
house of the LORD."

21Now Isaiah had said, "Let them take
a lump of figs, and apply *it* as a poultice
on the boil, and he shall recover."
22And Hezekiah had said, "What *is*
the sign that I shall go up to the house
of the LORD?"

The Babylonian Envoys

39 At that time Merodach-Bala-
dan[a] the son of Baladan, king
of Babylon, sent letters and a present to
Hezekiah, for he heard that he had been
sick and had recovered. 2And Hezekiah
was pleased with them, and showed
them the house of his treasures—the
silver and gold, the spices and precious
ointment, and all his armory—all that
was found among his treasures. There
was nothing in his house or in all his
dominion that Hezekiah did not show
them.
3Then Isaiah the prophet went to King
Hezekiah, and said to him, "What did
these men say, and from where did they
come to you?"
So Hezekiah said, "They came to me
from a far country, from Babylon."
4And he said, "What have they seen
in your house?"

38:11 [a] Hebrew *YAH, YAH* [b] Following some Hebrew manuscripts; Masoretic Text and Vulgate read *rest;* Septuagint omits *among the inhabitants of the world;* Targum reads *land.* 38:14 [a] Following Bomberg; Masoretic Text and Dead Sea Scrolls read *Lord.* 38:15 [a] Following Masoretic Text and Vulgate; Dead Sea Scrolls and Targum read *And shall I say to Him;* Septuagint omits first half of this verse. 39:1 [a] Spelled *Berodach-Baladan* in 2 Kings 20:12

So Hezekiah answered, "They have
seen all that *is* in my house; there is
nothing among my treasures that I
have not shown them."
5Then Isaiah said to Hezekiah, "Hear
the word of the LORD of hosts: 6'Behold,
the days are coming when all that *is*
in your house, and what your fathers
have accumulated until this day, shall
be carried to Babylon; nothing shall be
left,' says the LORD. 7'And they shall take
away *some* of your sons who will descend
from you, whom you will beget; and they
shall be eunuchs in the palace of the king
of Babylon.' "
8So Hezekiah said to Isaiah, "The word
of the LORD which you have spoken *is*
good!" For he said, "At least there will
be peace and truth in my days."

God's People Are Comforted

40 "Comfort, yes, comfort My people!"
Says your God.
2 "Speak comfort to Jerusalem, and cry out to her,
That her warfare is ended,
That her iniquity is pardoned;
For she has received from the LORD's hand
Double for all her sins."

3 The voice of one crying in the wilderness:
"Prepare the way of the LORD;
Make straight in the desert[a]
A highway for our God.
4 Every valley shall be exalted
And every mountain and hill brought low;
The crooked places shall be made straight
And the rough places smooth;
5 The glory of the LORD shall be revealed,
And all flesh shall see *it* together;
For the mouth of the LORD has spoken."

6 The voice said, "Cry out!"
And he[a] said, "What shall I cry?"
"All flesh *is* grass,
And all its loveliness *is* like the flower of the field.
7 The grass withers, the flower fades,
Because the breath of the LORD blows upon it;
Surely the people *are* grass.
8 The grass withers, the flower fades,
But the word of our God stands forever."

9 O Zion,
You who bring good tidings,
Get up into the high mountain;
O Jerusalem,
You who bring good tidings,
Lift up your voice with strength,
Lift *it* up, be not afraid;
Say to the cities of Judah, "Behold your God!"

10 Behold, the Lord GOD shall come with a strong *hand*,
And His arm shall rule for Him;
Behold, His reward *is* with Him,
And His work before Him.
11 He will feed His flock like a shepherd;
He will gather the lambs with His arm,
And carry *them* in His bosom,
And gently lead those who are with young.

12 Who has measured the waters[a] in the hollow of His hand,
Measured heaven with a span
And calculated the dust of the earth in a measure?
Weighed the mountains in scales
And the hills in a balance?
13 Who has directed the Spirit of the LORD,
Or *as* His counselor has taught Him?
14 With whom did He take counsel, and *who* instructed Him,
And taught Him in the path of justice?

40:3 [a] Following Masoretic Text, Targum, and Vulgate; Septuagint omits *in the desert*.
40:6 [a] Following Masoretic Text and Targum; Dead Sea Scrolls, Septuagint, and Vulgate read *I*.
40:12 [a] Following Masoretic Text, Septuagint, and Vulgate; Dead Sea Scrolls read *waters of the sea;* Targum reads *waters of the world*.

Who taught Him knowledge,
And showed Him the way of
understanding?

15 Behold, the nations *are* as a drop
in a bucket,
And are counted as the small dust
on the scales;
Look, He lifts up the isles as a very
little thing.
16 And Lebanon *is* not sufficient to
burn,
Nor its beasts sufficient for a
burnt offering.
17 All nations before Him *are* as
nothing,
And they are counted by Him less
than nothing and worthless.

18 To whom then will you liken God?
Or what likeness will you compare
to Him?
19 The workman molds an image,
The goldsmith overspreads it with
gold,
And the silversmith casts silver
chains.
20 Whoever *is* too impoverished for
such a contribution
Chooses a tree *that* will not rot;
He seeks for himself a skillful
workman
To prepare a carved image *that*
will not totter.

21 Have you not known?
Have you not heard?
Has it not been told you from the
beginning?
Have you not understood from
the foundations of the earth?
22 *It is* He who sits above the circle of
the earth,
And its inhabitants *are* like
grasshoppers,
Who stretches out the heavens
like a curtain,
And spreads them out like a tent
to dwell in.
23 He brings the princes to nothing;
He makes the judges of the earth
useless.

24 Scarcely shall they be planted,
Scarcely shall they be sown,
Scarcely shall their stock take
root in the earth,
When He will also blow on them,
And they will wither,
And the whirlwind will take them
away like stubble.

25 "To whom then will you liken Me,
Or *to whom* shall I be equal?" says
the Holy One.
26 Lift up your eyes on high,
And see who has created these
things,
Who brings out their host by
number;
He calls them all by name,
By the greatness of His might
And the strength of *His* power;
Not one is missing.

27 Why do you say, O Jacob,
And speak, O Israel:
"My way is hidden from the LORD,
And my just claim is passed over
by my God"?
28 Have you not known?
Have you not heard?
The everlasting God, the LORD,
The Creator of the ends of the earth,
Neither faints nor is weary.
His understanding is
unsearchable.
29 He gives power to the weak,
And to *those who have* no might
He increases strength.
30 Even the youths shall faint and be
weary,
And the young men shall utterly
fall,
31 But those who wait on the LORD
Shall renew *their* strength;
They shall mount up with wings
like eagles,
They shall run and not be weary,
They shall walk and not faint.

Israel Assured of God's Help

41 "Keep silence before Me,
O coastlands,
And let the people renew *their*
strength!
Let them come near, then let
them speak;
Let us come near together for
judgment.

2 "Who raised up one from the east?
Who in righteousness called him to His feet?
Who gave the nations before him,
And made *him* rule over kings?
Who gave *them* as the dust *to* his sword,
As driven stubble to his bow?
3 Who pursued them, *and* passed safely
By the way *that* he had not gone with his feet?
4 Who has performed and done *it,*
Calling the generations from the beginning?
'I, the LORD, am the first;
And with the last I *am* He.' "

5 The coastlands saw *it* and feared,
The ends of the earth were afraid;
They drew near and came.
6 Everyone helped his neighbor,
And said to his brother,
"Be of good courage!"
7 So the craftsman encouraged the goldsmith;
He who smooths *with* the hammer *inspired* him who strikes the anvil,
Saying, "It *is* ready for the soldering";
Then he fastened it with pegs,
That it might not totter.

8 "But you, Israel, *are* My servant,
Jacob whom I have chosen,
The descendants of Abraham My friend.
9 *You* whom I have taken from the ends of the earth,
And called from its farthest regions,
And said to you,
'You *are* My servant,
I have chosen you and have not cast you away:
10 Fear not, for I *am* with you;
Be not dismayed, for I *am* your God.
I will strengthen you,
Yes, I will help you,
I will uphold you with My righteous right hand.'

11 "Behold, all those who were incensed against you
Shall be ashamed and disgraced;
They shall be as nothing,
And those who strive with you shall perish.
12 You shall seek them and not find them—
Those who contended with you.
Those who war against you
Shall be as nothing,
As a nonexistent thing.
13 For I, the LORD your God, will hold your right hand,
Saying to you, 'Fear not, I will help you.'

14 "Fear not, you worm Jacob,
You men of Israel!
I will help you," says the LORD
And your Redeemer, the Holy One of Israel.
15 "Behold, I will make you into a new threshing sledge with sharp teeth;
You shall thresh the mountains and beat *them* small,
And make the hills like chaff.
16 You shall winnow them, the wind shall carry them away,
And the whirlwind shall scatter them;
You shall rejoice in the LORD,
And glory in the Holy One of Israel.

17 "The poor and needy seek water, but *there is* none,
Their tongues fail for thirst.
I, the LORD, will hear them;
I, the God of Israel, will not forsake them.
18 I will open rivers in desolate heights,
And fountains in the midst of the valleys;
I will make the wilderness a pool of water,
And the dry land springs of water.
19 I will plant in the wilderness the cedar and the acacia tree,
The myrtle and the oil tree;
I will set in the desert the cypress tree *and* the pine
And the box tree together,

20 That they may see and know,
And consider and understand
together,
That the hand of the LORD has
done this,
And the Holy One of Israel has
created it.

The Futility of Idols

21 "Present your case," says the LORD.
"Bring forth your strong *reasons,*"
says the King of Jacob.
22 "Let them bring forth and show us
what will happen;
Let them show the former things,
what they *were,*
That we may consider them,
And know the latter end of them;
Or declare to us things to come.
23 Show the things that are to come
hereafter,
That we may know that you *are*
gods;
Yes, do good or do evil,
That we may be dismayed and see
it together.
24 Indeed you *are* nothing,
And your work *is* nothing;
He who chooses you *is* an
abomination.

25 "I have raised up one from the
north,
And he shall come;
From the rising of the sun he shall
call on My name;
And he shall come against
princes as *though* mortar,
As the potter treads clay.
26 Who has declared from the
beginning, that we may
know?
And former times, that we may
say, '*He is* righteous'?
Surely *there is* no one who shows,
Surely *there is* no one who
declares,
Surely *there is* no one who hears
your words.
27 The first time *I said* to Zion,
'Look, there they are!'
And I will give to Jerusalem one
who brings good tidings.
28 For I looked, and *there was* no
man;
I looked among them, but *there*
was no counselor,
Who, when I asked of them, could
answer a word.
29 Indeed they *are* all worthless;[a]
Their works *are* nothing;
Their molded images *are* wind
and confusion.

The Servant of the LORD

42 "Behold! My Servant whom I
uphold,
My Elect One *in whom* My soul
delights!
I have put My Spirit upon Him;
He will bring forth justice to the
Gentiles.
2 He will not cry out, nor raise *His*
voice,
Nor cause His voice to be heard in
the street.
3 A bruised reed He will not break,
And smoking flax He will not
quench;
He will bring forth justice for truth.
4 He will not fail nor be
discouraged,
Till He has established justice in
the earth;
And the coastlands shall wait for
His law."

5 Thus says God the LORD,
Who created the heavens and
stretched them out,
Who spread forth the earth and
that which comes from it,
Who gives breath to the people
on it,
And spirit to those who walk on it:
6 "I, the LORD, have called You in
righteousness,
And will hold Your hand;
I will keep You and give You as a
covenant to the people,
As a light to the Gentiles,
7 To open blind eyes,
To bring out prisoners from the
prison,
Those who sit in darkness from
the prison house.

41:29 [a] Following Masoretic Text and Vulgate; Dead Sea Scrolls, Syriac, and Targum read *nothing;* Septuagint omits the first line.

8 I *am* the LORD, that *is* My name;
And My glory I will not give to another,
Nor My praise to carved images.
9 Behold, the former things have come to pass,
And new things I declare;
Before they spring forth I tell you of them."

Praise to the LORD

10 Sing to the LORD a new song,
And His praise from the ends of the earth,
You who go down to the sea, and all that is in it,
You coastlands and you inhabitants of them!
11 Let the wilderness and its cities lift up *their voice,*
The villages *that* Kedar inhabits.
Let the inhabitants of Sela sing,
Let them shout from the top of the mountains.
12 Let them give glory to the LORD,
And declare His praise in the coastlands.
13 The LORD shall go forth like a mighty man;
He shall stir up *His* zeal like a man of war.
He shall cry out, yes, shout aloud;
He shall prevail against His enemies.

Promise of the LORD's Help

14 "I have held My peace a long time,
I have been still and restrained Myself.
Now I will cry like a woman in labor,
I will pant and gasp at once.
15 I will lay waste the mountains and hills,
And dry up all their vegetation;
I will make the rivers coastlands,
And I will dry up the pools.
16 I will bring the blind by a way they did not know;
I will lead them in paths they have not known.
I will make darkness light before them,
And crooked places straight.
These things I will do for them,
And not forsake them.
17 They shall be turned back,
They shall be greatly ashamed,
Who trust in carved images,
Who say to the molded images,
'You *are* our gods.'

18 "Hear, you deaf;
And look, you blind, that you may see.
19 Who *is* blind but My servant,
Or deaf as My messenger *whom* I send?
Who *is* blind as *he who is* perfect,
And blind as the LORD's servant?
20 Seeing many things, but you do not observe;
Opening the ears, but he does not hear."

Israel's Obstinate Disobedience

21 The LORD is well pleased for His righteousness' sake;
He will exalt the law and make *it* honorable.
22 But this *is* a people robbed and plundered;
All of them are snared in holes,
And they are hidden in prison houses;
They are for prey, and no one delivers;
For plunder, and no one says, "Restore!"

23 Who among you will give ear to this?
Who will listen and hear for the time to come?
24 Who gave Jacob for plunder, and Israel to the robbers?
Was it not the LORD,
He against whom we have sinned?
For they would not walk in His ways,
Nor were they obedient to His law.
25 Therefore He has poured on him the fury of His anger
And the strength of battle;
It has set him on fire all around,
Yet he did not know;
And it burned him,
Yet he did not take *it* to heart.

The Redeemer of Israel

43 But now, thus says the LORD,
who created you, O Jacob,
And He who formed you, O Israel:
"Fear not, for I have redeemed you;
I have called *you* by your name;
You *are* Mine.
2 When you pass through the waters, I *will be* with you;
And through the rivers, they shall not overflow you.
When you walk through the fire, you shall not be burned,
Nor shall the flame scorch you.
3 For I *am* the LORD your God,
The Holy One of Israel, your Savior;
I gave Egypt for your ransom,
Ethiopia and Seba in your place.
4 Since you were precious in My sight,
You have been honored,
And I have loved you;
Therefore I will give men for you,
And people for your life.
5 Fear not, for I *am* with you;
I will bring your descendants from the east,
And gather you from the west;
6 I will say to the north, 'Give them up!'
And to the south, 'Do not keep them back!'
Bring My sons from afar,
And My daughters from the ends of the earth—
7 Everyone who is called by My name,
Whom I have created for My glory;
I have formed him, yes, I have made him."

8 Bring out the blind people who have eyes,
And the deaf who have ears.
9 Let all the nations be gathered together,
And let the people be assembled.
Who among them can declare this,
And show us former things?
Let them bring out their witnesses, that they may be justified;
Or let them hear and say, "*It is* truth."
10 "You *are* My witnesses," says the LORD,
"And My servant whom I have chosen,
That you may know and believe Me,
And understand that I *am* He.
Before Me there was no God formed,
Nor shall there be after Me.
11 I, *even* I, *am* the LORD,
And besides Me *there is* no savior.
12 I have declared and saved,
I have proclaimed,
And *there was* no foreign *god* among you;
Therefore you *are* My witnesses,"
Says the LORD, "that I *am* God.
13 Indeed before the day *was*, I *am* He;
And *there is* no one who can deliver out of My hand;
I work, and who will reverse it?"

14 Thus says the LORD, your Redeemer,
The Holy One of Israel:
"For your sake I will send to Babylon,
And bring them all down as fugitives—
The Chaldeans, who rejoice in their ships.
15 I *am* the LORD, your Holy One,
The Creator of Israel, your King."

16 Thus says the LORD, who makes a way in the sea
And a path through the mighty waters,
17 Who brings forth the chariot and horse,
The army and the power
(They shall lie down together, they shall not rise;
They are extinguished, they are quenched like a wick):
18 "Do not remember the former things,
Nor consider the things of old.
19 Behold, I will do a new thing,
Now it shall spring forth;
Shall you not know it?

I will even make a road in the
wilderness
And rivers in the desert.
20 The beast of the field will honor Me,
The jackals and the ostriches,
Because I give waters in the
wilderness
And rivers in the desert,
To give drink to My people, My
chosen.
21 This people I have formed for
Myself;
They shall declare My praise.

Pleading with Unfaithful Israel

22 "But you have not called upon Me,
O Jacob;
And you have been weary of Me,
O Israel.
23 You have not brought Me the sheep
for your burnt offerings,
Nor have you honored Me with
your sacrifices.
I have not caused you to serve
with grain offerings,
Nor wearied you with incense.
24 You have bought Me no sweet
cane with money,
Nor have you satisfied Me with
the fat of your sacrifices;
But you have burdened Me with
your sins,
You have wearied Me with your
iniquities.

25 "I, *even* I, *am* He who blots out your
transgressions for My own
sake;
And I will not remember your sins.
26 Put Me in remembrance;
Let us contend together;
State your *case*, that you may be
acquitted.
27 Your first father sinned,
And your mediators have
transgressed against Me.
28 Therefore I will profane the
princes of the sanctuary;
I will give Jacob to the curse,
And Israel to reproaches.

God's Blessing on Israel

44 "Yet hear now, O Jacob My
servant,
And Israel whom I have chosen.
2 Thus says the LORD who made you
And formed you from the womb,
who will help you:
'Fear not, O Jacob My servant;
And you, Jeshurun, whom I have
chosen.
3 For I will pour water on him who
is thirsty,
And floods on the dry ground;
I will pour My Spirit on your
descendants,
And My blessing on your
offspring;
4 They will spring up among the
grass
Like willows by the watercourses.'
5 One will say, 'I *am* the LORD's';
Another will call *himself* by the
name of Jacob;
Another will write *with* his hand,
'The LORD's,'
And name *himself* by the name of
Israel.

There Is No Other God

6 "Thus says the LORD, the King of
Israel,
And his Redeemer, the LORD of
hosts:
'I *am* the First and I *am* the Last;
Besides Me *there is* no God.
7 And who can proclaim as I do?
Then let him declare it and set it
in order for Me,
Since I appointed the ancient
people.
And the things that are coming
and shall come,
Let them show these to them.
8 Do not fear, nor be afraid;
Have I not told you from that
time, and declared *it?*
You *are* My witnesses.
Is there a God besides Me?
Indeed *there is* no other Rock;
I know not *one.*' "

Idolatry Is Foolishness

9 Those who make an image, all of
them *are* useless,
And their precious things shall
not profit;
They *are* their own witnesses;
They neither see nor know, that
they may be ashamed.

10 Who would form a god or mold
an image
That profits him nothing?
11 Surely all his companions would
be ashamed;
And the workmen, they *are* mere
men.
Let them all be gathered together,
Let them stand up;
Yet they shall fear,
They shall be ashamed together.

12 The blacksmith with the tongs
works one in the coals,
Fashions it with hammers,
And works it with the strength of
his arms.
Even so, he is hungry, and his
strength fails;
He drinks no water and is faint.

13 The craftsman stretches out *his*
rule,
He marks one out with chalk;
He fashions it with a plane,
He marks it out with the compass,
And makes it like the figure of a
man,
According to the beauty of a man,
that it may remain in the
house.
14 He cuts down cedars for himself,
And takes the cypress and the
oak;
He secures *it* for himself among
the trees of the forest.
He plants a pine, and the rain
nourishes *it.*

15 Then it shall be for a man to burn,
For he will take some of it and
warm himself;
Yes, he kindles *it* and bakes bread;
Indeed he makes a god and
worships *it;*
He makes it a carved image, and
falls down to it.
16 He burns half of it in the fire;
With this half he eats meat;
He roasts a roast, and is satisfied.
He even warms *himself* and says,
"Ah! I am warm,
I have seen the fire."
17 And the rest of it he makes into a
god,
His carved image.
He falls down before it and
worships *it,*
Prays to it and says,
"Deliver me, for you *are* my god!"

18 They do not know nor
understand;
For He has shut their eyes, so that
they cannot see,
And their hearts, so that they
cannot understand.
19 And no one considers in his
heart,
Nor *is there* knowledge nor
understanding to say,
"I have burned half of it in the fire,
Yes, I have also baked bread on its
coals;
I have roasted meat and eaten *it;*
And shall I make the rest of it an
abomination?
Shall I fall down before a block of
wood?"
20 He feeds on ashes;
A deceived heart has turned him
aside;
And he cannot deliver his soul,
Nor say, "*Is there* not a lie in my
right hand?"

Israel Is Not Forgotten

21 "Remember these, O Jacob,
And Israel, for you *are* My
servant;
I have formed you, you *are* My
servant;
O Israel, you will not be forgotten
by Me!
22 I have blotted out, like a thick
cloud, your transgressions,
And like a cloud, your sins.
Return to Me, for I have redeemed
you."

23 Sing, O heavens, for the LORD has
done *it!*
Shout, you lower parts of the
earth;
Break forth into singing, you
mountains,
O forest, and every tree in it!
For the LORD has redeemed
Jacob,
And glorified Himself in Israel.

Judah Will Be Restored

24 Thus says the LORD, your Redeemer,
And He who formed you from the womb:
"I *am* the LORD, who makes all *things,*
Who stretches out the heavens all alone,
Who spreads abroad the earth by Myself;
25 Who frustrates the signs of the babblers,
And drives diviners mad;
Who turns wise men backward,
And makes their knowledge foolishness;
26 Who confirms the word of His servant,
And performs the counsel of His messengers;
Who says to Jerusalem, 'You shall be inhabited,'
To the cities of Judah, 'You shall be built,'
And I will raise up her waste places;
27 Who says to the deep, 'Be dry!
And I will dry up your rivers';
28 Who says of Cyrus, '*He is* My shepherd,
And he shall perform all My pleasure,
Saying to Jerusalem, "You shall be built,"
And to the temple, "Your foundation shall be laid." '

Cyrus, God's Instrument

45 "Thus says the LORD to His anointed,
To Cyrus, whose right hand I have held—
To subdue nations before him
And loose the armor of kings,
To open before him the double doors,
So that the gates will not be shut:
2 'I will go before you
And make the crooked places[a] straight;
I will break in pieces the gates of bronze
And cut the bars of iron.
3 I will give you the treasures of darkness
And hidden riches of secret places,
That you may know that I, the LORD,
Who call *you* by your name,
Am the God of Israel.
4 For Jacob My servant's sake,
And Israel My elect,
I have even called you by your name;
I have named you, though you have not known Me.
5 I *am* the LORD, and *there is* no other;
There is no God besides Me.
I will gird you, though you have not known Me,
6 That they may know from the rising of the sun to its setting
That *there is* none besides Me.
I *am* the LORD, and *there is* no other;
7 I form the light and create darkness,
I make peace and create calamity;
I, the LORD, do all these *things.'*

8 "Rain down, you heavens, from above,
And let the skies pour down righteousness;
Let the earth open, let them bring forth salvation,
And let righteousness spring up together.
I, the LORD, have created it.

9 "Woe to him who strives with his Maker!
Let the potsherd *strive* with the potsherds of the earth!
Shall the clay say to him who forms it, 'What are you making?'
Or shall your handiwork *say,* 'He has no hands'?
10 Woe to him who says to *his* father, 'What are you begetting?'
Or to the woman, 'What have you brought forth?' "

45:2 [a] Dead Sea Scrolls and Septuagint read *mountains;* Targum reads *I will trample down the walls;* Vulgate reads *I will humble the great ones of the earth.*

11 Thus says the LORD,
The Holy One of Israel, and his
Maker:
"Ask Me of things to come
concerning My sons;
And concerning the work of My
hands, you command Me.
12 I have made the earth,
And created man on it.
I—My hands—stretched out the
heavens,
And all their host I have
commanded.
13 I have raised him up in
righteousness,
And I will direct all his ways;
He shall build My city
And let My exiles go free,
Not for price nor reward,"
Says the LORD of hosts.

The LORD, the Only Savior

14 Thus says the LORD:

"The labor of Egypt and
merchandise of Cush
And of the Sabeans, men of stature,
Shall come over to you, and they
shall be yours;
They shall walk behind you,
They shall come over in chains;
And they shall bow down to you.
They will make supplication to
you, *saying,* 'Surely God *is* in
you,
And *there is* no other;
There is no other God.' "

15 Truly You *are* God, who hide
Yourself,
O God of Israel, the Savior!
16 They shall be ashamed
And also disgraced, all of them;
They shall go in confusion
together,
Who are makers of idols.
17 *But* Israel shall be saved by the
LORD
With an everlasting salvation;
You shall not be ashamed or
disgraced
Forever and ever.

18 For thus says the LORD,
Who created the heavens,
Who is God,
Who formed the earth and
made it,
Who has established it,
Who did not create it in vain,
Who formed it to be inhabited:
"I *am* the LORD, and *there is* no
other.
19 I have not spoken in secret,
In a dark place of the earth;
I did not say to the seed of Jacob,
'Seek Me in vain';
I, the LORD, speak righteousness,
I declare things that are right.

20 "Assemble yourselves and come;
Draw near together,
You *who have* escaped from the
nations.
They have no knowledge,
Who carry the wood of their
carved image,
And pray to a god *that* cannot
save.
21 Tell and bring forth *your case;*
Yes, let them take counsel
together.
Who has declared this from
ancient time?
Who has told it from that time?
Have not I, the LORD?
And *there is* no other God
besides Me,
A just God and a Savior;
There is none besides Me.

22 "Look to Me, and be saved,
All you ends of the earth!
For I *am* God, and *there is* no other.
23 I have sworn by Myself;
The word has gone out of My
mouth *in* righteousness,
And shall not return,
That to Me every knee shall bow,
Every tongue shall take an oath.
24 He shall say,
'Surely in the LORD I have
righteousness and strength.
To Him *men* shall come,
And all shall be ashamed
Who are incensed against Him.
25 In the LORD all the descendants
of Israel
Shall be justified, and shall
glory.' "

Dead Idols and the Living God

46 Bel bows down, Nebo stoops;
Their idols were on the beasts
and on the cattle.
Your carriages *were* heavily
loaded,
A burden to the weary *beast.*
2 They stoop, they bow down
together;
They could not deliver the burden,
But have themselves gone into
captivity.

3 "Listen to Me, O house of Jacob,
And all the remnant of the house
of Israel,
Who have been upheld *by Me*
from birth,
Who have been carried from the
womb:
4 Even to *your* old age, I *am* He,
And *even* to gray hairs I will carry
you!
I have made, and I will bear;
Even I will carry, and will deliver
you.

5 "To whom will you liken Me, and
make *Me* equal
And compare Me, that we should
be alike?
6 They lavish gold out of the bag,
And weigh silver on the scales;
They hire a goldsmith, and he
makes it a god;
They prostrate themselves, yes,
they worship.
7 They bear it on the shoulder, they
carry it
And set it in its place, and it
stands;
From its place it shall not move.
Though *one* cries out to it, yet it
cannot answer
Nor save him out of his trouble.

8 "Remember this, and show
yourselves men;
Recall to mind, O you
transgressors.
9 Remember the former things of
old,
For I *am* God, and *there is* no other;
I am God, and *there is* none
like Me,
10 Declaring the end from the
beginning,
And from ancient times *things*
that are not *yet* done,
Saying, 'My counsel shall stand,
And I will do all My pleasure,'
11 Calling a bird of prey from the
east,
The man who executes My
counsel, from a far country.
Indeed I have spoken *it;*
I will also bring it to pass.
I have purposed *it;*
I will also do it.

12 "Listen to Me, you
stubborn-hearted,
Who *are* far from righteousness:
13 I bring My righteousness near, it
shall not be far off;
My salvation shall not linger.
And I will place salvation in Zion,
For Israel My glory.

The Humiliation of Babylon

47 "Come down and sit in the
dust,
O virgin daughter of Babylon;
Sit on the ground without a
throne,
O daughter of the Chaldeans!
For you shall no more be called
Tender and delicate.
2 Take the millstones and grind
meal.
Remove your veil,
Take off the skirt,
Uncover the thigh,
Pass through the rivers.
3 Your nakedness shall be
uncovered,
Yes, your shame will be seen;
I will take vengeance,
And I will not arbitrate with a
man."

4 *As for* our Redeemer, the LORD of
hosts *is* His name,
The Holy One of Israel.

5 "Sit in silence, and go into darkness,
O daughter of the Chaldeans;
For you shall no longer be called
The Lady of Kingdoms.
6 I was angry with My people;

I have profaned My inheritance,
And given them into your hand.
You showed them no mercy;
On the elderly you laid your yoke very heavily.
7 And you said, 'I shall be a lady forever,'
So that you did not take these *things* to heart,
Nor remember the latter end of them.

8 "Therefore hear this now, *you who are* given to pleasures,
Who dwell securely,
Who say in your heart, 'I *am*, and *there is* no one else besides me;
I shall not sit *as* a widow,
Nor shall I know the loss of children';
9 But these two *things* shall come to you
In a moment, in one day:
The loss of children, and widowhood.
They shall come upon you in their fullness
Because of the multitude of your sorceries,
For the great abundance of your enchantments.

10 "For you have trusted in your wickedness;
You have said, 'No one sees me';
Your wisdom and your knowledge have warped you;
And you have said in your heart,
'I *am*, and *there is* no one else besides me.'
11 Therefore evil shall come upon you;
You shall not know from where it arises.
And trouble shall fall upon you;
You will not be able to put it off.
And desolation shall come upon you suddenly,
Which you shall not know.

12 "Stand now with your enchantments
And the multitude of your sorceries,
In which you have labored from your youth—
Perhaps you will be able to profit,
Perhaps you will prevail.
13 You are wearied in the multitude of your counsels;
Let now the astrologers, the stargazers,
And the monthly prognosticators
Stand up and save you
From what shall come upon you.
14 Behold, they shall be as stubble,
The fire shall burn them;
They shall not deliver themselves
From the power of the flame;
It shall not *be* a coal to be warmed by,
Nor a fire to sit before!
15 Thus shall they be to you
With whom you have labored,
Your merchants from your youth;
They shall wander each one to his quarter.
No one shall save you.

Israel Refined for God's Glory

48 "Hear this, O house of Jacob,
Who are called by the name of Israel,
And have come forth from the wellsprings of Judah;
Who swear by the name of the LORD,
And make mention of the God of Israel,
But not in truth or in righteousness;
2 For they call themselves after the holy city,
And lean on the God of Israel;
The LORD of hosts *is* His name:

3 "I have declared the former things from the beginning;
They went forth from My mouth, and I caused them to hear it.
Suddenly I did *them*, and they came to pass.
4 Because I knew that you *were* obstinate,
And your neck *was* an iron sinew,
And your brow bronze,
5 Even from the beginning I have declared *it* to you;

Before it came to pass I
proclaimed *it* to you,
Lest you should say, 'My idol has
done them,
And my carved image and my
molded image
Have commanded them.'

6 "You have heard;
See all this.
And will you not declare *it?*
I have made you hear new things
from this time,
Even hidden things, and you did
not know them.
7 They are created now and not
from the beginning;
And before this day you have not
heard them,
Lest you should say, 'Of course I
knew them.'
8 Surely you did not hear,
Surely you did not know;
Surely from long ago your ear
was not opened.
For I knew that you would deal
very treacherously,
And were called a transgressor
from the womb.

9 "For My name's sake I will defer My
anger,
And *for* My praise I will restrain it
from you,
So that I do not cut you off.
10 Behold, I have refined you, but
not as silver;
I have tested you in the furnace of
affliction.
11 For My own sake, for My own
sake, I will do *it;*
For how should *My name* be
profaned?
And I will not give My glory to
another.

God's Ancient Plan to Redeem Israel

12 "Listen to Me, O Jacob,
And Israel, My called:
I *am* He, I *am* the First,
I *am* also the Last.
13 Indeed My hand has laid the
foundation of the earth,
And My right hand has stretched
out the heavens;
When I call to them,
They stand up together.

14 "All of you, assemble yourselves,
and hear!
Who among them has declared
these *things?*
The LORD loves him;
He shall do His pleasure on
Babylon,
And His arm *shall be against* the
Chaldeans.
15 I, *even* I, have spoken;
Yes, I have called him,
I have brought him, and his way
will prosper.

16 "Come near to Me, hear this:
I have not spoken in secret from
the beginning;
From the time that it was, I *was*
there.
And now the Lord GOD and His
Spirit
Have[a] sent Me."

17 Thus says the LORD, your
Redeemer,
The Holy One of Israel:
"I *am* the LORD your God,
Who teaches you to profit,
Who leads you by the way you
should go.
18 Oh, that you had heeded My
commandments!
Then your peace would have been
like a river,
And your righteousness like the
waves of the sea.
19 Your descendants also would
have been like the sand,
And the offspring of your body
like the grains of sand;
His name would not have been
cut off
Nor destroyed from before Me."

20 Go forth from Babylon!
Flee from the Chaldeans!
With a voice of singing,
Declare, proclaim this,

48:16 [a] The Hebrew verb is singular.

Utter it to the end of the earth;
Say, "The LORD has redeemed
His servant Jacob!"
21 And they did not thirst
When He led them through the deserts;
He caused the waters to flow from the rock for them;
He also split the rock, and the waters gushed out.

22 "*There is* no peace," says the LORD, "for the wicked."

The Servant, the Light to the Gentiles

49 "Listen, O coastlands, to Me,
And take heed, you peoples from afar!
The LORD has called Me from the womb;
From the matrix of My mother
He has made mention of My name.
2 And He has made My mouth like a sharp sword;
In the shadow of His hand He has hidden Me,
And made Me a polished shaft;
In His quiver He has hidden Me."

3 "And He said to me,
'You *are* My servant, O Israel,
In whom I will be glorified.'
4 Then I said, 'I have labored in vain,
I have spent my strength for nothing and in vain;
Yet surely my just reward *is* with the LORD,
And my work with my God.' "

5 "And now the LORD says,
Who formed Me from the womb *to be* His Servant,
To bring Jacob back to Him,
So that Israel is gathered to Him[a]
(For I shall be glorious in the eyes of the LORD,
And My God shall be My strength),
6 Indeed He says,
'It is too small a thing that You should be My Servant
To raise up the tribes of Jacob,
And to restore the preserved ones of Israel;
I will also give You as a light to the Gentiles,
That You should be My salvation to the ends of the earth.' "

7 Thus says the LORD,
The Redeemer of Israel, their Holy One,
To Him whom man despises,
To Him whom the nation abhors,
To the Servant of rulers:
"Kings shall see and arise,
Princes also shall worship,
Because of the LORD who is faithful,
The Holy One of Israel;
And He has chosen You."

8 Thus says the LORD:

"In an acceptable time I have heard You,
And in the day of salvation I have helped You;
I will preserve You and give You
As a covenant to the people,
To restore the earth,
To cause them to inherit the desolate heritages;
9 That You may say to the prisoners, 'Go forth,'
To those who *are* in darkness, 'Show yourselves.'

"They shall feed along the roads,
And their pastures *shall be* on all desolate heights.
10 They shall neither hunger nor thirst,
Neither heat nor sun shall strike them;
For He who has mercy on them will lead them,
Even by the springs of water He will guide them.
11 I will make each of My mountains a road,
And My highways shall be elevated.
12 Surely these shall come from afar;

49:5 [a] Qere, Dead Sea Scrolls, and Septuagint read *is gathered to Him;* Kethib reads *is not gathered.*

Look! Those from the north and
the west,
And these from the land of
Sinim."

13 Sing, O heavens!
Be joyful, O earth!
And break out in singing,
O mountains!
For the LORD has comforted His
people,
And will have mercy on His
afflicted.

God Will Remember Zion

14 But Zion said, "The LORD has
forsaken me,
And my Lord has forgotten me."

15 "Can a woman forget her nursing
child,
And not have compassion on the
son of her womb?
Surely they may forget,
Yet I will not forget you.
16 See, I have inscribed you on the
palms *of My hands;*
Your walls *are* continually
before Me.
17 Your sons[a] shall make haste;
Your destroyers and those who
laid you waste
Shall go away from you.
18 Lift up your eyes, look around
and see;
All these gather together *and*
come to you.
As I live," says the LORD,
"You shall surely clothe yourselves
with them all as an
ornament,
And bind them *on you* as a bride
does.

19 "For your waste and desolate
places,
And the land of your destruction,
Will even now be too small for the
inhabitants;
And those who swallowed you up
will be far away.
20 The children you will have,
After you have lost the others,
Will say again in your ears,
'The place *is* too small for me;
Give me a place where I may
dwell.'
21 Then you will say in your heart,
'Who has begotten these for me,
Since I have lost my children and
am desolate,
A captive, and wandering to and
fro?
And who has brought these up?
There I was, left alone;
But these, where *were* they?' "

22 Thus says the Lord GOD:

"Behold, I will lift My hand in an
oath to the nations,
And set up My standard for the
peoples;
They shall bring your sons in *their*
arms,
And your daughters shall be
carried on *their* shoulders;
23 Kings shall be your foster fathers,
And their queens your nursing
mothers;
They shall bow down to you with
their faces to the earth,
And lick up the dust of your feet.
Then you will know that I *am* the
LORD,
For they shall not be ashamed
who wait for Me."

24 Shall the prey be taken from the
mighty,
Or the captives of the righteous[a]
be delivered?

25 But thus says the LORD:

"Even the captives of the mighty
shall be taken away,
And the prey of the terrible be
delivered;
For I will contend with him who
contends with you,
And I will save your children.
26 I will feed those who oppress you
with their own flesh,

49:17 [a] Dead Sea Scrolls, Septuagint, Targum, and Vulgate read *builders.* **49:24** [a] Following Masoretic Text and Targum; Dead Sea Scrolls, Syriac, and Vulgate read *the mighty;* Septuagint reads *unjustly.*

And they shall be drunk with their
own blood as with sweet wine.
All flesh shall know
That I, the LORD, *am* your Savior,
And your Redeemer, the Mighty
One of Jacob."

The Servant, Israel's Hope

50 Thus says the LORD:

"Where *is* the certificate of your
mother's divorce,
Whom I have put away?
Or which of My creditors *is it* to
whom I have sold you?
For your iniquities you have sold
yourselves,
And for your transgressions your
mother has been put away.
2 Why, when I came, *was there* no
man?
Why, when I called, *was there*
none to answer?
Is My hand shortened at all that it
cannot redeem?
Or have I no power to deliver?
Indeed with My rebuke I dry up
the sea,
I make the rivers a wilderness;
Their fish stink because *there is* no
water,
And die of thirst.
3 I clothe the heavens with
blackness,
And I make sackcloth their
covering."

4 "The Lord GOD has given Me
The tongue of the learned,
That I should know how to speak
A word in season to *him who is*
weary.
He awakens Me morning by
morning,
He awakens My ear
To hear as the learned.
5 The Lord GOD has opened My ear;
And I was not rebellious,
Nor did I turn away.
6 I gave My back to those who
struck *Me*,
And My cheeks to those who
plucked out the beard;
I did not hide My face from
shame and spitting.
7 "For the Lord GOD will help Me;
Therefore I will not be disgraced;
Therefore I have set My face like a
flint,
And I know that I will not be
ashamed.
8 *He is* near who justifies Me;
Who will contend with Me?
Let us stand together.
Who *is* My adversary?
Let him come near Me.
9 Surely the Lord GOD will
help Me;
Who *is* he *who* will condemn Me?
Indeed they will all grow old like a
garment;
The moth will eat them up.

10 "Who among you fears the LORD?
Who obeys the voice of His
Servant?
Who walks in darkness
And has no light?
Let him trust in the name of the
LORD
And rely upon his God.
11 Look, all you who kindle a fire,
Who encircle *yourselves* with
sparks:
Walk in the light of your fire
and in the sparks you have
kindled—
This you shall have from My
hand:
You shall lie down in torment.

The LORD Comforts Zion

51 "Listen to Me, you who follow
after righteousness,
You who seek the LORD:
Look to the rock *from which* you
were hewn,
And to the hole of the pit *from
which* you were dug.
2 Look to Abraham your father,
And to Sarah *who* bore you;
For I called him alone,
And blessed him and increased
him."

3 For the LORD will comfort Zion,
He will comfort all her waste
places;
He will make her wilderness like
Eden,

And her desert like the garden of the LORD;
Joy and gladness will be found in it,
Thanksgiving and the voice of melody.

4 "Listen to Me, My people;
And give ear to Me, O My nation:
For law will proceed from Me,
And I will make My justice rest
As a light of the peoples.
5 My righteousness *is* near,
My salvation has gone forth,
And My arms will judge the peoples;
The coastlands will wait upon Me,
And on My arm they will trust.
6 Lift up your eyes to the heavens,
And look on the earth beneath.
For the heavens will vanish away like smoke,
The earth will grow old like a garment,
And those who dwell in it will die in like manner;
But My salvation will be forever,
And My righteousness will not be abolished.

7 "Listen to Me, you who know righteousness,
You people in whose heart *is* My law:
Do not fear the reproach of men,
Nor be afraid of their insults.
8 For the moth will eat them up like a garment,
And the worm will eat them like wool;
But My righteousness will be forever,
And My salvation from generation to generation."

9 Awake, awake, put on strength,
O arm of the LORD!
Awake as in the ancient days,
In the generations of old.
Are You not *the arm* that cut Rahab apart,
And wounded the serpent?
10 *Are* You not *the One* who dried up the sea,
The waters of the great deep;
That made the depths of the sea a road
For the redeemed to cross over?
11 So the ransomed of the LORD shall return,
And come to Zion with singing,
With everlasting joy on their heads.
They shall obtain joy and gladness;
Sorrow and sighing shall flee away.

12 "I, *even* I, *am* He who comforts you.
Who *are* you that you should be afraid
Of a man *who* will die,
And of the son of a man *who* will be made like grass?
13 And you forget the LORD your Maker,
Who stretched out the heavens
And laid the foundations of the earth;
You have feared continually every day
Because of the fury of the oppressor,
When *he has* prepared to destroy.
And where *is* the fury of the oppressor?
14 The captive exile hastens, that he may be loosed,
That he should not die in the pit,
And that his bread should not fail.
15 But I *am* the LORD your God,
Who divided the sea whose waves roared—
The LORD of hosts *is* His name.
16 And I have put My words in your mouth;
I have covered you with the shadow of My hand,
That I may plant the heavens,
Lay the foundations of the earth,
And say to Zion, 'You *are* My people.' "

God's Fury Removed

17 Awake, awake!
Stand up, O Jerusalem,
You who have drunk at the hand of the LORD
The cup of His fury;

You have drunk the dregs of the cup of trembling,
And drained *it* out.
18 *There is* no one to guide her
Among all the sons she has brought forth;
Nor *is there any* who takes her by the hand
Among all the sons she has brought up.
19 These two *things* have come to you;
Who will be sorry for you?—
Desolation and destruction, famine and sword—
By whom will I comfort you?
20 Your sons have fainted,
They lie at the head of all the streets,
Like an antelope in a net;
They are full of the fury of the LORD,
The rebuke of your God.

21 Therefore please hear this, you afflicted,
And drunk but not with wine.
22 Thus says your Lord,
The LORD and your God,
Who pleads the cause of His people:
"See, I have taken out of your hand
The cup of trembling,
The dregs of the cup of My fury;
You shall no longer drink it.
23 But I will put it into the hand of those who afflict you,
Who have said to you,[a]
'Lie down, that we may walk over you.'
And you have laid your body like the ground,
And as the street, for those who walk over."

God Redeems Jerusalem

52 Awake, awake!
Put on your strength, O Zion;
Put on your beautiful garments,
O Jerusalem, the holy city!
For the uncircumcised and the unclean
Shall no longer come to you.
2 Shake yourself from the dust, arise;
Sit down, O Jerusalem!
Loose yourself from the bonds of your neck,
O captive daughter of Zion!

3For thus says the LORD:

"You have sold yourselves for nothing,
And you shall be redeemed without money."

4For thus says the Lord GOD:

"My people went down at first
Into Egypt to dwell there;
Then the Assyrian oppressed them without cause.
5 Now therefore, what have I here," says the LORD,
"That My people are taken away for nothing?
Those who rule over them
Make them wail,"[a] says the LORD,
"And My name *is* blasphemed continually every day.
6 Therefore My people shall know My name;
Therefore *they shall know* in that day
That I *am* He who speaks:
'Behold, *it is* I.' "

7 How beautiful upon the mountains
Are the feet of him who brings good news,
Who proclaims peace,
Who brings glad tidings of good *things*,
Who proclaims salvation,
Who says to Zion,
"Your God reigns!"
8 Your watchmen shall lift up *their* voices,
With their voices they shall sing together;
For they shall see eye to eye
When the LORD brings back Zion.
9 Break forth into joy, sing together,

51:23 [a] Literally *your soul* **52:5** [a] Dead Sea Scrolls read *Mock;* Septuagint reads *Marvel and wail;* Targum reads *Boast themselves;* Vulgate reads *Treat them unjustly.*

You waste places of Jerusalem!
For the LORD has comforted His people,
He has redeemed Jerusalem.
10 The LORD has made bare His holy arm
In the eyes of all the nations;
And all the ends of the earth shall see
The salvation of our God.

11 Depart! Depart! Go out from there,
Touch no unclean *thing;*
Go out from the midst of her,
Be clean,
You who bear the vessels of the LORD.
12 For you shall not go out with haste,
Nor go by flight;
For the LORD will go before you,
And the God of Israel *will be* your rear guard.

The Sin-Bearing Servant

13 Behold, My Servant shall deal prudently;
He shall be exalted and extolled and be very high.
14 Just as many were astonished at you,
So His visage was marred more than any man,
And His form more than the sons of men;
15 So shall He sprinkle[a] many nations.
Kings shall shut their mouths at Him;
For what had not been told them they shall see,
And what they had not heard they shall consider.

53 Who has believed our report?
And to whom has the arm of the LORD been revealed?
2 For He shall grow up before Him as a tender plant,
And as a root out of dry ground.
He has no form or comeliness;
And when we see Him,
There is no beauty that we should desire Him.
3 He is despised and rejected by men,
A Man of sorrows and acquainted with grief.
And we hid, as it were, *our* faces from Him;
He was despised, and we did not esteem Him.

4 Surely He has borne our griefs
And carried our sorrows;
Yet we esteemed Him stricken,
Smitten by God, and afflicted.
5 But He *was* wounded for our transgressions,
He was bruised for our iniquities;
The chastisement for our peace *was* upon Him,
And by His stripes we are healed.
6 All we like sheep have gone astray;
We have turned, every one, to his own way;
And the LORD has laid on Him the iniquity of us all.

7 He was oppressed and He was afflicted,
Yet He opened not His mouth;
He was led as a lamb to the slaughter,
And as a sheep before its shearers is silent,
So He opened not His mouth.
8 He was taken from prison and from judgment,
And who will declare His generation?
For He was cut off from the land of the living;
For the transgressions of My people He was stricken.
9 And they[a] made His grave with the wicked—
But with the rich at His death,
Because He had done no violence,
Nor *was any* deceit in His mouth.

10 Yet it pleased the LORD to bruise Him;
He has put *Him* to grief.

52:15 [a] Or *startle* 53:9 [a] Literally *he* or *He*

When You make His soul an
offering for sin,
He shall see *His* seed, He shall
prolong *His* days,
And the pleasure of the LORD
shall prosper in His hand.
11 He shall see the labor of His soul,[a]
and be satisfied.
By His knowledge My righteous
Servant shall justify many,
For He shall bear their iniquities.
12 Therefore I will divide Him a
portion with the great,
And He shall divide the spoil with
the strong,
Because He poured out His soul
unto death,
And He was numbered with the
transgressors,
And He bore the sin of many,
And made intercession for the
transgressors.

A Perpetual Covenant of Peace

54 "Sing, O barren,
You *who* have not borne!
Break forth into singing, and cry
aloud,
You *who* have not labored with
child!
For more *are* the children of the
desolate
Than the children of the married
woman," says the LORD.
2 "Enlarge the place of your tent,
And let them stretch out the
curtains of your dwellings;
Do not spare;
Lengthen your cords,
And strengthen your stakes.
3 For you shall expand to the right
and to the left,
And your descendants will inherit
the nations,
And make the desolate cities
inhabited.

4 "Do not fear, for you will not be
ashamed;
Neither be disgraced, for you will
not be put to shame;
For you will forget the shame of
your youth,
And will not remember the
reproach of your
widowhood anymore.
5 For your Maker *is* your
husband,
The LORD of hosts *is* His name;
And your Redeemer *is* the Holy
One of Israel;
He is called the God of the whole
earth.
6 For the LORD has called you
Like a woman forsaken and
grieved in spirit,
Like a youthful wife when you
were refused,"
Says your God.
7 "For a mere moment I have
forsaken you,
But with great mercies I will
gather you.
8 With a little wrath I hid My face
from you for a moment;
But with everlasting kindness I
will have mercy on you,"
Says the LORD, your Redeemer.

9 "For this *is* like the waters of Noah
to Me;
For as I have sworn
That the waters of Noah would no
longer cover the earth,
So have I sworn
That I would not be angry with
you, nor rebuke you.
10 For the mountains shall depart
And the hills be removed,
But My kindness shall not depart
from you,
Nor shall My covenant of peace
be removed,"
Says the LORD, who has mercy on
you.

11 "O you afflicted one,
Tossed with tempest, *and* not
comforted,
Behold, I will lay your stones with
colorful gems,
And lay your foundations with
sapphires.
12 I will make your pinnacles of
rubies,
Your gates of crystal,

53:11 [a] Following Masoretic Text, Targum, and Vulgate; Dead Sea Scrolls and Septuagint read *From the labor of His soul He shall see light.*

And all your walls of precious
stones.
13 All your children *shall be* taught
by the LORD,
And great *shall be* the peace of
your children.
14 In righteousness you shall be
established;
You shall be far from oppression,
for you shall not fear;
And from terror, for it shall not
come near you.
15 Indeed they shall surely assemble,
but not because of Me.
Whoever assembles against you
shall fall for your sake.

16 "Behold, I have created the
blacksmith
Who blows the coals in the fire,
Who brings forth an instrument
for his work;
And I have created the spoiler to
destroy.
17 No weapon formed against you
shall prosper,
And every tongue *which* rises
against you in judgment
You shall condemn.
This *is* the heritage of the servants
of the LORD,
And their righteousness *is*
from Me,"
Says the LORD.

An Invitation to Abundant Life

55 "Ho! Everyone who thirsts,
Come to the waters;
And you who have no money,
Come, buy and eat.
Yes, come, buy wine and milk
Without money and without price.
2 Why do you spend money for
what is not bread,
And your wages for *what* does not
satisfy?
Listen carefully to Me, and eat
what is good,
And let your soul delight itself in
abundance.
3 Incline your ear, and come to Me.
Hear, and your soul shall live;
And I will make an everlasting
covenant with you—
The sure mercies of David.
4 Indeed I have given him *as* a
witness to the people,
A leader and commander for the
people.
5 Surely you shall call a nation you
do not know,
And nations *who* do not know you
shall run to you,
Because of the LORD your God,
And the Holy One of Israel;
For He has glorified you."

6 Seek the LORD while He may be
found,
Call upon Him while He is near.
7 Let the wicked forsake his way,
And the unrighteous man his
thoughts;
Let him return to the LORD,
And He will have mercy on him;
And to our God,
For He will abundantly pardon.

8 "For My thoughts *are* not your
thoughts,
Nor *are* your ways My ways," says
the LORD.
9 "For *as* the heavens are higher than
the earth,
So are My ways higher than your
ways,
And My thoughts than your
thoughts.

10 "For as the rain comes down, and
the snow from heaven,
And do not return there,
But water the earth,
And make it bring forth and bud,
That it may give seed to the
sower
And bread to the eater,
11 So shall My word be that goes
forth from My mouth;
It shall not return to Me void,
But it shall accomplish what I
please,
And it shall prosper *in the thing*
for which I sent it.

12 "For you shall go out with joy,
And be led out with peace;
The mountains and the hills
Shall break forth into singing
before you,

And all the trees of the field shall
clap *their* hands.
13 Instead of the thorn shall come
up the cypress tree,
And instead of the brier shall
come up the myrtle tree;
And it shall be to the LORD for a
name,
For an everlasting sign *that* shall
not be cut off."

Salvation for the Gentiles

56 Thus says the LORD:
"Keep justice, and do
righteousness,
For My salvation *is* about to come,
And My righteousness to be
revealed.
2 Blessed *is* the man *who* does this,
And the son of man *who* lays hold
on it;
Who keeps from defiling the
Sabbath,
And keeps his hand from doing
any evil."

3 Do not let the son of the foreigner
Who has joined himself to the
LORD
Speak, saying,
"The LORD has utterly separated me
from His people";
Nor let the eunuch say,
"Here I am, a dry tree."
4 For thus says the LORD:
"To the eunuchs who keep My
Sabbaths,
And choose what pleases Me,
And hold fast My covenant,
5 Even to them I will give in My
house
And within My walls a place and a
name
Better than that of sons and
daughters;
I will give them[a] an everlasting
name
That shall not be cut off.

6 "Also the sons of the foreigner
Who join themselves to the LORD,
to serve Him,
And to love the name of the LORD,
to be His servants—
Everyone who keeps from defiling
the Sabbath,
And holds fast My covenant—
7 Even them I will bring to My holy
mountain,
And make them joyful in My
house of prayer.
Their burnt offerings and their
sacrifices
Will be accepted on My altar;
For My house shall be called
a house of prayer for all
nations."
8 The Lord GOD, who gathers the
outcasts of Israel, says,
"Yet I will gather to him
Others besides those who are
gathered to him."

Israel's Irresponsible Leaders

9 All you beasts of the field, come to
devour,
All you beasts in the forest.
10 His watchmen *are* blind,
They are all ignorant;
They *are* all dumb dogs,
They cannot bark;
Sleeping, lying down, loving to
slumber.
11 Yes, *they are* greedy dogs
Which never have enough.
And they *are* shepherds
Who cannot understand;
They all look to their own way,
Every one for his own gain,
From his *own* territory.
12 "Come," *one says,* "I will bring wine,
And we will fill ourselves with
intoxicating drink;
Tomorrow will be as today,
And much more abundant."

Israel's Futile Idolatry

57 The righteous perishes,
And no man takes *it* to heart;
Merciful men *are* taken away,
While no one considers
That the righteous is taken away
from evil.
2 He shall enter into peace;
They shall rest in their beds,

56:5 [a] Literally *him*

Each one walking *in* his
uprightness.

3 "But come here,
You sons of the sorceress,
You offspring of the adulterer and
the harlot!

4 Whom do you ridicule?
Against whom do you make a
wide mouth
And stick out the tongue?
Are you not children of
transgression,
Offspring of falsehood,

5 Inflaming yourselves with gods
under every green tree,
Slaying the children in the
valleys,
Under the clefts of the rocks?

6 Among the smooth *stones* of the
stream
Is your portion;
They, they, *are* your lot!
Even to them you have poured a
drink offering,
You have offered a grain offering.
Should I receive comfort
in these?

7 "On a lofty and high mountain
You have set your bed;
Even there you went up
To offer sacrifice.

8 Also behind the doors and their
posts
You have set up your
remembrance;
For you have uncovered yourself
to those other than Me,
And have gone up to them;
You have enlarged your bed
And made *a covenant* with them;
You have loved their bed,
Where you saw *their* nudity.[a]

9 You went to the king with
ointment,
And increased your perfumes;
You sent your messengers far off,
And *even* descended to Sheol.

10 You are wearied in the length of
your way;
Yet you did not say, 'There is no
hope.'
You have found the life of your
hand;
Therefore you were not grieved.

11 "And of whom have you been
afraid, or feared,
That you have lied
And not remembered Me,
Nor taken *it* to your heart?
Is it not because I have held My
peace from of old
That you do not fear Me?

12 I will declare your righteousness
And your works,
For they will not profit you.

13 When you cry out,
Let your collection *of idols* deliver
you.
But the wind will carry them all
away,
A breath will take *them*.
But he who puts his trust in Me
shall possess the land,
And shall inherit My holy
mountain."

Healing for the Backslider

14 And one shall say,
"Heap it up! Heap it up!
Prepare the way,
Take the stumbling block out of
the way of My people."

15 For thus says the High and Lofty
One
Who inhabits eternity, whose
name *is* Holy:
"I dwell in the high and holy *place*,
With him *who* has a contrite and
humble spirit,
To revive the spirit of the humble,
And to revive the heart of the
contrite ones.

16 For I will not contend forever,
Nor will I always be angry;
For the spirit would fail before Me,
And the souls *which* I have made.

17 For the iniquity of his
covetousness
I was angry and struck him;
I hid and was angry,
And he went on backsliding in the
way of his heart.

57:8 [a] Literally *hand*, a euphemism

18 I have seen his ways, and will heal
him;
I will also lead him,
And restore comforts to him
And to his mourners.

19 "I create the fruit of the lips:
Peace, peace to *him who is* far off
and to *him who is* near,"
Says the LORD,
"And I will heal him."
20 But the wicked *are* like the
troubled sea,
When it cannot rest,
Whose waters cast up mire and
dirt.

21 "*There is* no peace,"
Says my God, "for the wicked."

Fasting that Pleases God

58 "Cry aloud, spare not;
Lift up your voice like a
trumpet;
Tell My people their
transgression,
And the house of Jacob their sins.
2 Yet they seek Me daily,
And delight to know My ways,
As a nation that did
righteousness,
And did not forsake the ordinance
of their God.
They ask of Me the ordinances of
justice;
They take delight in approaching
God.
3 'Why have we fasted,' *they say,* 'and
You have not seen?
Why have we afflicted our souls,
and You take no notice?'

"In fact, in the day of your fast you
find pleasure,
And exploit all your laborers.
4 Indeed you fast for strife and
debate,
And to strike with the fist of
wickedness.
You will not fast as *you do* this
day,
To make your voice heard on
high.
5 Is it a fast that I have chosen,
A day for a man to afflict his soul?
Is it to bow down his head like a
bulrush,
And to spread out sackcloth and
ashes?
Would you call this a fast,
And an acceptable day to the
LORD?

6 "*Is* this not the fast that I have
chosen:
To loose the bonds of wickedness,
To undo the heavy burdens,
To let the oppressed go free,
And that you break every yoke?
7 *Is it* not to share your bread with
the hungry,
And that you bring to your house
the poor who are cast out;
When you see the naked, that you
cover him,
And not hide yourself from your
own flesh?
8 Then your light shall break forth
like the morning,
Your healing shall spring forth
speedily,
And your righteousness shall go
before you;
The glory of the LORD shall be
your rear guard.
9 Then you shall call, and the LORD
will answer;
You shall cry, and He will say,
'Here I *am.*'

"If you take away the yoke from
your midst,
The pointing of the finger, and
speaking wickedness,
10 *If* you extend your soul to the
hungry
And satisfy the afflicted soul,
Then your light shall dawn in the
darkness,
And your darkness shall *be* as the
noonday.
11 The LORD will guide you
continually,
And satisfy your soul in drought,
And strengthen your bones;
You shall be like a watered
garden,
And like a spring of water, whose
waters do not fail.
12 Those from among you

Shall build the old waste places;
You shall raise up the foundations
of many generations;
And you shall be called the
Repairer of the Breach,
The Restorer of Streets to Dwell In.

13 "If you turn away your foot from
the Sabbath,
From doing your pleasure on My
holy day,
And call the Sabbath a delight,
The holy *day* of the LORD
honorable,
And shall honor Him, not doing
your own ways,
Nor finding your own pleasure,
Nor speaking *your own* words,
14 Then you shall delight yourself in
the LORD;
And I will cause you to ride on the
high hills of the earth,
And feed you with the heritage of
Jacob your father.
The mouth of the LORD has
spoken."

Separated from God

59 Behold, the LORD's hand is not
shortened,
That it cannot save;
Nor His ear heavy,
That it cannot hear.
2 But your iniquities have
separated you from your
God;
And your sins have hidden *His*
face from you,
So that He will not hear.
3 For your hands are defiled with
blood,
And your fingers with iniquity;
Your lips have spoken lies,
Your tongue has muttered
perversity.

4 No one calls for justice,
Nor does *any* plead for truth.
They trust in empty words and
speak lies;
They conceive evil and bring forth
iniquity.
5 They hatch vipers' eggs and
weave the spider's web;
He who eats of their eggs dies,
And *from* that which is crushed a
viper breaks out.

6 Their webs will not become
garments,
Nor will they cover themselves
with their works;
Their works *are* works of iniquity,
And the act of violence *is* in their
hands.
7 Their feet run to evil,
And they make haste to shed
innocent blood;
Their thoughts *are* thoughts of
iniquity;
Wasting and destruction *are* in
their paths.
8 The way of peace they have not
known,
And *there is* no justice in their
ways;
They have made themselves
crooked paths;
Whoever takes that way shall not
know peace.

Sin Confessed

9 Therefore justice is far from us,
Nor does righteousness
overtake us;
We look for light, but there is
darkness!
For brightness, *but* we walk in
blackness!
10 We grope for the wall like the
blind,
And we grope as if *we had* no eyes;
We stumble at noonday as at
twilight;
We are as dead *men* in desolate
places.
11 We all growl like bears,
And moan sadly like doves;
We look for justice, but *there is*
none;
For salvation, *but* it is far from us.
12 For our transgressions are
multiplied before You,
And our sins testify against us;
For our transgressions *are*
with us,
And *as for* our iniquities, we know
them:
13 In transgressing and lying
against the LORD,

And departing from our God,
Speaking oppression and revolt,
Conceiving and uttering from the heart words of falsehood.
14 Justice is turned back,
And righteousness stands afar off;
For truth is fallen in the street,
And equity cannot enter.
15 So truth fails,
And he *who* departs from evil makes himself a prey.

The Redeemer of Zion

Then the LORD saw *it,* and it displeased Him
That *there was* no justice.
16 He saw that *there was* no man,
And wondered that *there was* no intercessor;
Therefore His own arm brought salvation for Him;
And His own righteousness, it sustained Him.
17 For He put on righteousness as a breastplate,
And a helmet of salvation on His head;
He put on the garments of vengeance for clothing,
And was clad with zeal as a cloak.
18 According to *their* deeds, accordingly He will repay,
Fury to His adversaries,
Recompense to His enemies;
The coastlands He will fully repay.
19 So shall they fear
The name of the LORD from the west,
And His glory from the rising of the sun;
When the enemy comes in like a flood,
The Spirit of the LORD will lift up a standard against him.

20 "The Redeemer will come to Zion,
And to those who turn from transgression in Jacob,"
Says the LORD.

21"As for Me," says the LORD, "this *is*
My covenant with them: My Spirit who
is upon you, and My words which I have
put in your mouth, shall not depart
from your mouth, nor from the mouth
of your descendants, nor from the
mouth of your descendants' descen-
dants," says the LORD, "from this time
and forevermore."

The Gentiles Bless Zion

60 Arise, shine;
For your light has come!
And the glory of the LORD is risen upon you.
2 For behold, the darkness shall cover the earth,
And deep darkness the people;
But the LORD will arise over you,
And His glory will be seen upon you.
3 The Gentiles shall come to your light,
And kings to the brightness of your rising.

4 "Lift up your eyes all around, and see:
They all gather together, they come to you;
Your sons shall come from afar,
And your daughters shall be nursed at *your* side.
5 Then you shall see and become radiant,
And your heart shall swell with joy;
Because the abundance of the sea shall be turned to you,
The wealth of the Gentiles shall come to you.
6 The multitude of camels shall cover your *land,*
The dromedaries of Midian and Ephah;
All those from Sheba shall come;
They shall bring gold and incense,
And they shall proclaim the praises of the LORD.
7 All the flocks of Kedar shall be gathered together to you,
The rams of Nebaioth shall minister to you;
They shall ascend with acceptance on My altar,
And I will glorify the house of My glory.

8 "Who *are* these *who* fly like a cloud,
And like doves to their roosts?
9 Surely the coastlands shall wait
for Me;
And the ships of Tarshish *will*
come first,
To bring your sons from afar,
Their silver and their gold with
them,
To the name of the LORD your
God,
And to the Holy One of Israel,
Because He has glorified you.

10 "The sons of foreigners shall build
up your walls,
And their kings shall minister to
you;
For in My wrath I struck you,
But in My favor I have had mercy
on you.
11 Therefore your gates shall be
open continually;
They shall not be shut day or
night,
That *men* may bring to you the
wealth of the Gentiles,
And their kings in procession.
12 For the nation and kingdom
which will not serve you
shall perish,
And *those* nations shall be utterly
ruined.

13 "The glory of Lebanon shall come
to you,
The cypress, the pine, and the box
tree together,
To beautify the place of My
sanctuary;
And I will make the place of My
feet glorious.
14 Also the sons of those who
afflicted you
Shall come bowing to you,
And all those who despised you
shall fall prostrate at the
soles of your feet;
And they shall call you The City of
the LORD,
Zion of the Holy One of Israel.

15 "Whereas you have been forsaken
and hated,
So that no one went through *you*,
I will make you an eternal
excellence,
A joy of many generations.
16 You shall drink the milk of the
Gentiles,
And milk the breast of kings;
You shall know that I, the LORD,
am your Savior
And your Redeemer, the Mighty
One of Jacob.

17 "Instead of bronze I will bring gold,
Instead of iron I will bring silver,
Instead of wood, bronze,
And instead of stones, iron.
I will also make your officers
peace,
And your magistrates
righteousness.
18 Violence shall no longer be heard
in your land,
Neither wasting nor destruction
within your borders;
But you shall call your walls
Salvation,
And your gates Praise.

God the Glory of His People

19 "The sun shall no longer be your
light by day,
Nor for brightness shall the moon
give light to you;
But the LORD will be to you an
everlasting light,
And your God your glory.
20 Your sun shall no longer
go down,
Nor shall your moon withdraw
itself;
For the LORD will be your
everlasting light,
And the days of your mourning
shall be ended.
21 Also your people *shall* all *be*
righteous;
They shall inherit the land
forever,
The branch of My planting,
The work of My hands,
That I may be glorified.
22 A little one shall become a
thousand,
And a small one a strong nation.
I, the LORD, will hasten it in its
time."

The Good News of Salvation

61 "The Spirit of the Lord GOD *is* upon Me,
Because the LORD has anointed Me
To preach good tidings to the poor;
He has sent Me to heal the brokenhearted,
To proclaim liberty to the captives,
And the opening of the prison to *those who are* bound;
2 To proclaim the acceptable year of the LORD,
And the day of vengeance of our God;
To comfort all who mourn,
3 To console those who mourn in Zion,
To give them beauty for ashes,
The oil of joy for mourning,
The garment of praise for the spirit of heaviness;
That they may be called trees of righteousness,
The planting of the LORD, that He may be glorified."

4 And they shall rebuild the old ruins,
They shall raise up the former desolations,
And they shall repair the ruined cities,
The desolations of many generations.
5 Strangers shall stand and feed your flocks,
And the sons of the foreigner
Shall be your plowmen and your vinedressers.
6 But you shall be named the priests of the LORD,
They shall call you the servants of our God.
You shall eat the riches of the Gentiles,
And in their glory you shall boast.
7 Instead of your shame *you shall have* double *honor,*
And *instead of* confusion they shall rejoice in their portion.
Therefore in their land they shall possess double;
Everlasting joy shall be theirs.
8 "For I, the LORD, love justice;
I hate robbery for burnt offering;
I will direct their work in truth,
And will make with them an everlasting covenant.
9 Their descendants shall be known among the Gentiles,
And their offspring among the people.
All who see them shall acknowledge them,
That they *are* the posterity *whom* the LORD has blessed."

10 I will greatly rejoice in the LORD,
My soul shall be joyful in my God;
For He has clothed me with the garments of salvation,
He has covered me with the robe of righteousness,
As a bridegroom decks *himself* with ornaments,
And as a bride adorns *herself* with her jewels.
11 For as the earth brings forth its bud,
As the garden causes the things that are sown in it to spring forth,
So the Lord GOD will cause righteousness and praise to spring forth before all the nations.

Assurance of Zion's Salvation

62 For Zion's sake I will not hold My peace,
And for Jerusalem's sake I will not rest,
Until her righteousness goes forth as brightness,
And her salvation as a lamp *that* burns.
2 The Gentiles shall see your righteousness,
And all kings your glory.
You shall be called by a new name,
Which the mouth of the LORD will name.
3 You shall also be a crown of glory
In the hand of the LORD,
And a royal diadem
In the hand of your God.
4 You shall no longer be termed Forsaken,

Nor shall your land any more be
termed Desolate;
But you shall be called
Hephzibah,[a] and your land
Beulah;[b]
For the LORD delights in you,
And your land shall be married.
5 For *as* a young man marries a
virgin,
So shall your sons marry you;
And *as* the bridegroom rejoices
over the bride,
So shall your God rejoice over
you.

6 I have set watchmen on your
walls, O Jerusalem;
They shall never hold their peace
day or night.
You who make mention of the
LORD, do not keep silent,
7 And give Him no rest till He
establishes
And till He makes Jerusalem a
praise in the earth.

8 The LORD has sworn by His right
hand
And by the arm of His strength:
"Surely I will no longer give your
grain
As food for your enemies;
And the sons of the foreigner
shall not drink your new
wine,
For which you have labored.
9 But those who have gathered it
shall eat it,
And praise the LORD;
Those who have brought it
together shall drink it in My
holy courts."

10 Go through,
Go through the gates!
Prepare the way for the people;
Build up,
Build up the highway!
Take out the stones,
Lift up a banner for the peoples!

11 Indeed the LORD has proclaimed
To the end of the world:
"Say to the daughter of Zion,
'Surely your salvation is coming;
Behold, His reward *is* with Him,
And His work before Him.' "
12 And they shall call them The Holy
People,
The Redeemed of the LORD;
And you shall be called Sought
Out,
A City Not Forsaken.

The LORD in Judgment and Salvation

63 Who *is* this who comes from
Edom,
With dyed garments from Bozrah,
This *One who is* glorious in His
apparel,
Traveling in the greatness of His
strength?—

"I who speak in righteousness,
mighty to save."

2 Why *is* Your apparel red,
And Your garments like one who
treads in the winepress?

3 "I have trodden the winepress
alone,
And from the peoples no one *was*
with Me.
For I have trodden them in My
anger,
And trampled them in My fury;
Their blood is sprinkled upon My
garments,
And I have stained all My robes.
4 For the day of vengeance *is* in My
heart,
And the year of My redeemed has
come.
5 I looked, but *there was* no one to
help,
And I wondered
That *there was* no one to uphold;
Therefore My own arm brought
salvation for Me;
And My own fury, it sustained Me.
6 I have trodden down the peoples
in My anger,
Made them drunk in My fury,
And brought down their strength
to the earth."

62:4 [a] Literally *My Delight Is in Her* [b] Literally *Married*

God's Mercy Remembered

7 I will mention the
lovingkindnesses of the
LORD
And the praises of the LORD,
According to all that the LORD has
bestowed on us,
And the great goodness toward
the house of Israel,
Which He has bestowed on them
according to His mercies,
According to the multitude of His
lovingkindnesses.
8 For He said, "Surely they *are* My
people,
Children *who* will not lie."
So He became their Savior.
9 In all their affliction He was
afflicted,
And the Angel of His Presence
saved them;
In His love and in His pity He
redeemed them;
And He bore them and carried
them
All the days of old.
10 But they rebelled and grieved His
Holy Spirit;
So He turned Himself against
them as an enemy,
And He fought against them.

11 Then he remembered the days of
old,
Moses *and* his people, *saying:*
"Where *is* He who brought them up
out of the sea
With the shepherd of His flock?
Where *is* He who put His Holy
Spirit within them,
12 Who led *them* by the right hand of
Moses,
With His glorious arm,
Dividing the water before them
To make for Himself an
everlasting name,
13 Who led them through the deep,
As a horse in the wilderness,
That they might not stumble?"

14 As a beast goes down into the
valley,
And the Spirit of the LORD causes
him to rest,
So You lead Your people,
To make Yourself a glorious
name.

A Prayer of Penitence

15 Look down from heaven,
And see from Your habitation,
holy and glorious.
Where *are* Your zeal and Your
strength,
The yearning of Your heart and
Your mercies toward me?
Are they restrained?
16 Doubtless You *are* our Father,
Though Abraham was ignorant
of us,
And Israel does not
acknowledge us.
You, O LORD, *are* our Father;
Our Redeemer from Everlasting *is*
Your name.
17 O LORD, why have You made us
stray from Your ways,
And hardened our heart from
Your fear?
Return for Your servants' sake,
The tribes of Your inheritance.
18 Your holy people have possessed
it but a little while;
Our adversaries have trodden
down Your sanctuary.
19 We have become *like* those of old,
over whom You never ruled,
Those who were never called by
Your name.

64 Oh, that You would rend the
heavens!
That You would come down!
That the mountains might shake
at Your presence—
2 As fire burns brushwood,
As fire causes water to boil—
To make Your name known to
Your adversaries,
That the nations may tremble at
Your presence!
3 When You did awesome things *for
which* we did not look,
You came down,
The mountains shook at Your
presence.
4 For since the beginning of the
world
Men have not heard nor perceived
by the ear,

Nor has the eye seen any God
besides You,
Who acts for the one who waits
for Him.
5 You meet him who rejoices and
does righteousness,
Who remembers You in Your ways.
You are indeed angry, for we have
sinned—
In these ways we continue;
And we need to be saved.

6 But we are all like an unclean
thing,
And all our righteousnesses *are*
like filthy rags;
We all fade as a leaf,
And our iniquities, like the wind,
Have taken us away.
7 And *there is* no one who calls on
Your name,
Who stirs himself up to take hold
of You;
For You have hidden Your face
from us,
And have consumed us because
of our iniquities.

8 But now, O LORD,
You *are* our Father;
We *are* the clay, and You our potter;
And all we *are* the work of Your
hand.
9 Do not be furious, O LORD,
Nor remember iniquity forever;
Indeed, please look—we all *are*
Your people!
10 Your holy cities are a wilderness,
Zion is a wilderness,
Jerusalem a desolation.
11 Our holy and beautiful temple,
Where our fathers praised You,
Is burned up with fire;
And all our pleasant things are
laid waste.
12 Will You restrain Yourself because
of these *things,* O LORD?
Will You hold Your peace, and
afflict us very severely?

The Righteousness of God's Judgment

65 "I was sought by *those who* did
not ask *for Me;*
I was found by *those who* did not
seek Me.
I said, 'Here I am, here I am,'
To a nation *that* was not called by
My name.
2 I have stretched out My hands
all day long to a rebellious
people,
Who walk in a way *that is* not
good,
According to their own thoughts;
3 A people who provoke Me to
anger continually to My
face;
Who sacrifice in gardens,
And burn incense on altars of
brick;
4 Who sit among the graves,
And spend the night in the tombs;
Who eat swine's flesh,
And the broth of abominable
things is *in* their vessels;
5 Who say, 'Keep to yourself,
Do not come near me,
For I am holier than you!'
These *are* smoke in My nostrils,
A fire that burns all the day.

6 "Behold, *it is* written before Me:
I will not keep silence, but will
repay—
Even repay into their bosom—
7 Your iniquities and the
iniquities of your fathers
together,"
Says the LORD,
"Who have burned incense on the
mountains
And blasphemed Me on the hills;
Therefore I will measure their
former work into their
bosom."

8 Thus says the LORD:

"As the new wine is found in the
cluster,
And *one* says, 'Do not destroy it,
For a blessing *is* in it,'
So will I do for My servants'
sake,
That I may not destroy them all.
9 I will bring forth descendants
from Jacob,
And from Judah an heir of My
mountains;
My elect shall inherit it,

And My servants shall dwell
there.
10 Sharon shall be a fold of flocks,
And the Valley of Achor a place
for herds to lie down,
For My people who have
sought Me.

11 "But you *are* those who forsake the
LORD,
Who forget My holy mountain,
Who prepare a table for Gad,[a]
And who furnish a drink offering
for Meni.[b]
12 Therefore I will number you for
the sword,
And you shall all bow down to the
slaughter;
Because, when I called, you did
not answer;
When I spoke, you did not hear,
But did evil before My eyes,
And chose *that* in which I do not
delight."

13 Therefore thus says the Lord GOD:

"Behold, My servants shall eat,
But you shall be hungry;
Behold, My servants shall drink,
But you shall be thirsty;
Behold, My servants shall rejoice,
But you shall be ashamed;
14 Behold, My servants shall sing for
joy of heart,
But you shall cry for sorrow of
heart,
And wail for grief of spirit.
15 You shall leave your name as a
curse to My chosen;
For the Lord GOD will slay you,
And call His servants by another
name;
16 So that he who blesses himself in
the earth
Shall bless himself in the God of
truth;
And he who swears in the earth
Shall swear by the God of truth;
Because the former troubles are
forgotten,
And because they are hidden
from My eyes.

The Glorious New Creation

17 "For behold, I create new heavens
and a new earth;
And the former shall not be
remembered or come to
mind.
18 But be glad and rejoice forever in
what I create;
For behold, I create Jerusalem *as*
a rejoicing,
And her people a joy.
19 I will rejoice in Jerusalem,
And joy in My people;
The voice of weeping shall no
longer be heard in her,
Nor the voice of crying.

20 "No more shall an infant from there
live but a few days,
Nor an old man who has not
fulfilled his days;
For the child shall die one
hundred years old,
But the sinner *being* one hundred
years old shall be accursed.
21 They shall build houses and
inhabit *them;*
They shall plant vineyards and
eat their fruit.
22 They shall not build and another
inhabit;
They shall not plant and another
eat;
For as the days of a tree, *so shall
be* the days of My people,
And My elect shall long enjoy the
work of their hands.
23 They shall not labor in vain,
Nor bring forth children for
trouble;
For they *shall be* the descendants
of the blessed of the LORD,
And their offspring with them.

24 "It shall come to pass
That before they call, I will answer;
And while they are still speaking,
I will hear.
25 The wolf and the lamb shall feed
together,
The lion shall eat straw like the ox,
And dust *shall be* the serpent's
food.

65:11 [a] Literally *Troop* or *Fortune,* a pagan deity [b] Literally *Number* or *Destiny,* a pagan deity

They shall not hurt nor destroy in
all My holy mountain,"
Says the LORD.

True Worship and False

66 Thus says the LORD:

"Heaven *is* My throne,
And earth *is* My footstool.
Where *is* the house that you will
build Me?
And where *is* the place of
My rest?
2 For all those *things* My hand has
made,
And all those *things* exist,"
Says the LORD.
"But on this *one* will I look:
On *him who is* poor and of a
contrite spirit,
And who trembles at My word.

3 "He who kills a bull *is as if* he slays a
man;
He who sacrifices a lamb, *as if* he
breaks a dog's neck;
He who offers a grain offering, *as
if he offers* swine's blood;
He who burns incense, *as if* he
blesses an idol.
Just as they have chosen their
own ways,
And their soul delights in their
abominations,
4 So will I choose their delusions,
And bring their fears on them;
Because, when I called, no one
answered,
When I spoke they did not hear;
But they did evil before My eyes,
And chose *that* in which I do not
delight."

The LORD Vindicates Zion

5 Hear the word of the LORD,
You who tremble at His word:
"Your brethren who hated you,
Who cast you out for My name's
sake, said,
'Let the LORD be glorified,
That we may see your joy.'
But they shall be ashamed."

6 The sound of noise from the city!
A voice from the temple!
The voice of the LORD,
Who fully repays His enemies!

7 "Before she was in labor, she gave
birth;
Before her pain came,
She delivered a male child.
8 Who has heard such a thing?
Who has seen such things?
Shall the earth be made to give
birth in one day?
Or shall a nation be born at once?
For as soon as Zion was in labor,
She gave birth to her children.
9 Shall I bring to the time of birth,
and not cause delivery?"
says the LORD.
"Shall I who cause delivery shut up
the womb?" says your God.
10 "Rejoice with Jerusalem,
And be glad with her, all you who
love her;
Rejoice for joy with her, all you
who mourn for her;
11 That you may feed and be
satisfied
With the consolation of her
bosom,
That you may drink deeply and
be delighted
With the abundance of her glory."

12 For thus says the LORD:

"Behold, I will extend peace to her
like a river,
And the glory of the Gentiles like
a flowing stream.
Then you shall feed;
On *her* sides shall you be carried,
And be dandled on *her* knees.
13 As one whom his mother comforts,
So I will comfort you;
And you shall be comforted in
Jerusalem."

The Reign and Indignation of God

14 When you see *this*, your heart
shall rejoice,
And your bones shall flourish like
grass;
The hand of the LORD shall be
known to His servants,
And *His* indignation to His
enemies.

15 For behold, the LORD will come
with fire
And with His chariots, like a
whirlwind,
To render His anger with fury,
And His rebuke with flames of
fire.
16 For by fire and by His sword
The LORD will judge all flesh;
And the slain of the LORD shall be
many.

17 "Those who sanctify themselves
and purify themselves,
To go to the gardens
After an *idol* in the midst,
Eating swine's flesh and the
abomination and the mouse,
Shall be consumed together," says
the LORD.

18"For I *know* their works and their
thoughts. It shall be that I will gather
all nations and tongues; and they shall
come and see My glory. 19I will set a
sign among them; and those among
them who escape I will send to the na-
tions: *to* Tarshish and Pul[a] and Lud, who
draw the bow, and Tubal and Javan, *to*
the coastlands afar off who have not
heard My fame nor seen My glory. And
they shall declare My glory among the
Gentiles. 20Then they shall bring all
your brethren for an offering to the
LORD out of all nations, on horses and
in chariots and in litters, on mules and
on camels, to My holy mountain Jerusa-
lem," says the LORD, "as the children of
Israel bring an offering in a clean vessel
into the house of the LORD. 21And I will
also take some of them for priests *and*
Levites," says the LORD.

22 "For as the new heavens and the
new earth
Which I will make shall remain
before Me," says the LORD,
"So shall your descendants and
your name remain.
23 And it shall come to pass
That from one New Moon to
another,
And from one Sabbath to another,
All flesh shall come to worship
before Me," says the LORD.

24 "And they shall go forth and look
Upon the corpses of the men
Who have transgressed
against Me.
For their worm does not die,
And their fire is not quenched.
They shall be an abhorrence to all
flesh."

66:19 [a] Following Masoretic Text and Targum; Septuagint reads *Put* (compare Jeremiah 46:9).

THE BOOK OF JEREMIAH

The Book of Jeremiah is the story of God telling Jeremiah to warn Judah about its wickedness. For forty years the determined and compassionate Jeremiah encourages the people to turn back to God. Sadly, they do not listen and reject Jeremiah's ministry and message instead. Because Jeremiah's ministry was so difficult, he is often called "the weeping prophet."

- **GENRE:** Major Prophet
- **AUTHOR:** Jeremiah, with Baruch
- **TIME:** c. 627–580 BC
- **PURPOSE:** To warn the people of their punishment and to give them hope for the future.

---

1 The words of Jeremiah the son of
Hilkiah, of the priests who *were*
in Anathoth in the land of Benjamin,
2to whom the word of the LORD came
in the days of Josiah the son of Amon,
king of Judah, in the thirteenth year of
his reign. 3It came also in the days of
Jehoiakim the son of Josiah, king
of Judah, until the end of the eleventh year of Zedekiah the son of Josiah, king of Judah, until the carrying away of Jerusalem captive in the fifth month.

The Prophet Is Called

4Then the word of the LORD came to me, saying:

5 "Before I formed you in the womb I knew you;
Before you were born I sanctified you;
I ordained you a prophet to the nations."

6Then said I:

"Ah, Lord GOD!
Behold, I cannot speak, for I *am* a youth."

7But the LORD said to me:

"Do not say, 'I *am* a youth,'
For you shall go to all to whom I send you,
And whatever I command you, you shall speak.
8 Do not be afraid of their faces,
For I *am* with you to deliver you," says the LORD.

9Then the LORD put forth His hand and touched my mouth, and the LORD said to me:

"Behold, I have put My words in your mouth.
10 See, I have this day set you over the nations and over the kingdoms,
To root out and to pull down,
To destroy and to throw down,
To build and to plant."

11Moreover the word of the LORD came
to me, saying, "Jeremiah, what do you
see?"
And I said, "I see a branch of an al-
mond tree."
12Then the LORD said to me, "You have
seen well, for I am ready to perform
My word."
13And the word of the LORD came to
me the second time, saying, "What do
you see?"
And I said, "I see a boiling pot, and it
is facing away from the north."

14Then the LORD said to me:

"Out of the north calamity shall
break forth
On all the inhabitants of the land.
15 For behold, I am calling
All the families of the kingdoms
of the north," says the LORD;
"They shall come and each one set
his throne
At the entrance of the gates of
Jerusalem,
Against all its walls all around,
And against all the cities of Judah.
16 I will utter My judgments
Against them concerning all their
wickedness,
Because they have forsaken Me,
Burned incense to other gods,
And worshiped the works of their
own hands.

17 "Therefore prepare yourself and
arise,
And speak to them all that I
command you.
Do not be dismayed before their
faces,
Lest I dismay you before them.
18 For behold, I have made you this
day
A fortified city and an iron pillar,
And bronze walls against the
whole land—
Against the kings of Judah,
Against its princes,
Against its priests,
And against the people of the land.
19 They will fight against you,
But they shall not prevail against
you.
For I *am* with you," says the LORD,
"to deliver you."

God's Case Against Israel

2 Moreover the word of the LORD
came to me, saying, 2"Go and cry
in the hearing of Jerusalem, saying,
'Thus says the LORD:

"I remember you,
The kindness of your youth,
The love of your betrothal,
When you went after Me in the
wilderness,
In a land not sown.
3 Israel *was* holiness to the LORD,
The firstfruits of His increase.
All that devour him will offend;
Disaster will come upon them,"
says the LORD.'"

4Hear the word of the LORD, O house of
Jacob and all the families of the house
of Israel. 5Thus says the LORD:

"What injustice have your fathers
found in Me,
That they have gone far from Me,
Have followed idols,
And have become idolaters?
6 Neither did they say, 'Where *is* the
LORD,
Who brought us up out of the
land of Egypt,
Who led us through the
wilderness,
Through a land of deserts and pits,
Through a land of drought and
the shadow of death,
Through a land that no one
crossed
And where no one dwelt?'
7 I brought you into a bountiful
country,
To eat its fruit and its goodness.
But when you entered, you defiled
My land
And made My heritage an
abomination.
8 The priests did not say, 'Where *is*
the LORD?'
And those who handle the law did
not know Me;
The rulers also transgressed
against Me;
The prophets prophesied by Baal,
And walked after *things that* do
not profit.

9 "Therefore I will yet bring charges
against you," says the LORD,
"And against your children's
children I will bring charges.
10 For pass beyond the coasts of
Cyprus[a] and see,

2:10 [a] Hebrew *Kittim*, western lands, especially Cyprus

Send to Kedar[b] and consider
diligently,
And see if there has been such *a*
thing.
11 Has a nation changed *its* gods,
Which *are* not gods?
But My people have changed
their Glory
For *what* does not profit.
12 Be astonished, O heavens,
at this,
And be horribly afraid;
Be very desolate," says the LORD.
13 "For My people have committed
two evils:
They have forsaken Me, the
fountain of living waters,
And hewn themselves cisterns—
broken cisterns that can hold
no water.

14 "*Is* Israel a servant?
Is he a homeborn *slave?*
Why is he plundered?
15 The young lions roared at him,
and growled;
They made his land waste;
His cities are burned, without
inhabitant.
16 Also the people of Noph[a] and
Tahpanhes
Have broken the crown of your
head.
17 Have you not brought this on
yourself,
In that you have forsaken the
LORD your God
When He led you in the way?
18 And now why take the road to
Egypt,
To drink the waters of Sihor?
Or why take the road to Assyria,
To drink the waters of the River?[a]
19 Your own wickedness will correct
you,
And your backslidings will rebuke
you.
Know therefore and see that *it is*
an evil and bitter *thing*
That you have forsaken the LORD
your God,
And the fear of Me *is* not in you,"
Says the Lord GOD of hosts.

20 "For of old I have broken your yoke
and burst your bonds;
And you said, 'I will not
transgress,'
When on every high hill and
under every green tree
You lay down, playing the harlot.
21 Yet I had planted you a noble vine,
a seed of highest quality.
How then have you turned
before Me
Into the degenerate plant of an
alien vine?
22 For though you wash yourself
with lye, and use much soap,
Yet your iniquity is marked before
Me," says the Lord GOD.

23 "How can you say, 'I am not
polluted,
I have not gone after the Baals'?
See your way in the valley;
Know what you have done:
You are a swift dromedary
breaking loose in her ways,
24 A wild donkey used to the
wilderness,
That sniffs at the wind in her
desire;
In her time of mating, who can
turn her away?
All those who seek her will not
weary themselves;
In her month they will find her.
25 Withhold your foot from being
unshod, and your throat
from thirst.
But you said, 'There is no hope.
No! For I have loved aliens, and
after them I will go.'

26 "As the thief is ashamed when he is
found out,
So is the house of Israel ashamed;
They and their kings and their
princes, and their priests and
their prophets,
27 Saying to a tree, 'You *are* my
father,'
And to a stone, 'You gave birth
to me.'
For they have turned *their* back to
Me, and not *their* face.

2:10 [b] In the northern Arabian desert, representative of the eastern cultures **2:16** [a] That is, Memphis in ancient Egypt **2:18** [a] That is, the Euphrates

But in the time of their trouble
They will say, 'Arise and save us.'
28 But where *are* your gods that you have made for yourselves?
Let them arise,
If they can save you in the time of your trouble;
For *according to* the number of your cities
Are your gods, O Judah.

29 "Why will you plead with Me?
You all have transgressed against Me," says the LORD.
30 "In vain I have chastened your children;
They received no correction.
Your sword has devoured your prophets
Like a destroying lion.

31 "O generation, see the word of the LORD!
Have I been a wilderness to Israel,
Or a land of darkness?
Why do My people say, 'We are lords;
We will come no more to You'?
32 Can a virgin forget her ornaments,
Or a bride her attire?
Yet My people have forgotten Me days without number.

33 "Why do you beautify your way to seek love?
Therefore you have also taught
The wicked women your ways.
34 Also on your skirts is found
The blood of the lives of the poor innocents.
I have not found it by secret search,
But plainly on all these things.
35 Yet you say, 'Because I am innocent,
Surely His anger shall turn from me.'
Behold, I will plead My case against you,
Because you say, 'I have not sinned.'
36 Why do you gad about so much to change your way?
Also you shall be ashamed of Egypt as you were ashamed of Assyria.
37 Indeed you will go forth from him
With your hands on your head;
For the LORD has rejected your trusted allies,
And you will not prosper by them.

Israel Is Shameless

3 "They say, 'If a man divorces his wife,
And she goes from him
And becomes another man's,
May he return to her again?'
Would not that land be greatly polluted?
But you have played the harlot with many lovers;
Yet return to Me," says the LORD.

2 "Lift up your eyes to the desolate heights and see:
Where have you not lain *with men?*
By the road you have sat for them
Like an Arabian in the wilderness;
And you have polluted the land
With your harlotries and your wickedness.
3 Therefore the showers have been withheld,
And there has been no latter rain.
You have had a harlot's forehead;
You refuse to be ashamed.
4 Will you not from this time cry to Me,
'My Father, You *are* the guide of my youth?
5 Will He remain angry forever?
Will He keep it to the end?'
Behold, you have spoken and done evil things,
As you were able."

A Call to Repentance

6The LORD said also to me in the days
of Josiah the king: "Have you seen
what backsliding Israel has done? She
has gone up on every high mountain
and under every green tree, and there
played the harlot. 7And I said, after
she had done all these *things,* 'Return
to Me.' But she did not return. And her
treacherous sister Judah saw it. 8Then

I saw that for all the causes for which
backsliding Israel had committed adul-
tery, I had put her away and given her a
certificate of divorce; yet her treacher-
ous sister Judah did not fear, but went
and played the harlot also. 9So it came
to pass, through her casual harlotry,
that she defiled the land and committed
adultery with stones and trees. 10And
yet for all this her treacherous sister
Judah has not turned to Me with her
whole heart, but in pretense," says the
LORD.
11Then the LORD said to me, "Back-
sliding Israel has shown herself more
righteous than treacherous Judah. 12Go
and proclaim these words toward the
north, and say:

'Return, backsliding Israel,' says
the LORD;
'I will not cause My anger to fall on
you.
For I *am* merciful,' says the LORD;
'I will not remain angry forever.
13 Only acknowledge your iniquity,
That you have transgressed
against the LORD your God,
And have scattered your charms
To alien deities under every green
tree,
And you have not obeyed My
voice,' says the LORD.

14"Return, O backsliding children,"
says the LORD; "for I am married to you.
I will take you, one from a city and two
from a family, and I will bring you to
Zion. 15And I will give you shepherds ac-
cording to My heart, who will feed you
with knowledge and understanding.
16"Then it shall come to pass, when
you are multiplied and increased in
the land in those days," says the LORD,
"that they will say no more, 'The ark of
the covenant of the LORD.' It shall not
come to mind, nor shall they remember
it, nor shall they visit *it,* nor shall it be
made anymore.
17"At that time Jerusalem shall be
called The Throne of the LORD, and all
the nations shall be gathered to it, to
the name of the LORD, to Jerusalem.
No more shall they follow the dictates
of their evil hearts.
18"In those days the house of Judah
shall walk with the house of Israel, and
they shall come together out of the land
of the north to the land that I have given
as an inheritance to your fathers.
19"But I said:

'How can I put you among the
children
And give you a pleasant land,
A beautiful heritage of the hosts
of nations?'

"And I said:

'You shall call Me, "My Father,"
And not turn away from Me.'
20 Surely, *as* a wife treacherously
departs from her husband,
So have you dealt treacherously
with Me,
O house of Israel," says the LORD.

21 A voice was heard on the desolate
heights,
Weeping *and* supplications of the
children of Israel.
For they have perverted their way;
They have forgotten the LORD
their God.

22 "Return, you backsliding children,
And I will heal your backslidings."

"Indeed we do come to You,
For You are the LORD our God.
23 Truly, in vain *is salvation hoped
for* from the hills,
And from the multitude of
mountains;
Truly, in the LORD our God
Is the salvation of Israel.
24 For shame has devoured
The labor of our fathers from our
youth—
Their flocks and their herds,
Their sons and their daughters.
25 We lie down in our shame,
And our reproach covers us.
For we have sinned against the
LORD our God,
We and our fathers,
From our youth even to this day,
And have not obeyed the voice of
the LORD our God."

4 "If you will return, O Israel," says
the LORD,
"Return to Me;
And if you will put away your
abominations out of My
sight,
Then you shall not be moved.
2 And you shall swear, 'The LORD
lives,'
In truth, in judgment, and in
righteousness;
The nations shall bless
themselves in Him,
And in Him they shall glory."

3For thus says the LORD to the men of
Judah and Jerusalem:

"Break up your fallow ground,
And do not sow among thorns.
4 Circumcise yourselves to the
LORD,
And take away the foreskins of
your hearts,
You men of Judah and
inhabitants of Jerusalem,
Lest My fury come forth like fire,
And burn so that no one can
quench *it,*
Because of the evil of your
doings."

An Imminent Invasion

5Declare in Judah and proclaim in
Jerusalem, and say:

"Blow the trumpet in the land;
Cry, 'Gather together,'
And say, 'Assemble yourselves,
And let us go into the fortified
cities.'
6 Set up the standard toward Zion.
Take refuge! Do not delay!
For I will bring disaster from the
north,
And great destruction."

7 The lion has come up from his
thicket,
And the destroyer of nations is on
his way.
He has gone forth from his place
To make your land desolate.
Your cities will be laid waste,
Without inhabitant.

8 For this, clothe yourself with
sackcloth,
Lament and wail.
For the fierce anger of the LORD
Has not turned back from us.

9 "And it shall come to pass in that
day," says the LORD,
"*That* the heart of the king shall
perish,
And the heart of the princes;
The priests shall be astonished,
And the prophets shall wonder."

10 Then I said, "Ah, Lord GOD!
Surely You have greatly deceived
this people and Jerusalem,
Saying, 'You shall have peace,'
Whereas the sword reaches to the
heart."

11 At that time it will be said
To this people and to Jerusalem,
"A dry wind of the desolate heights
blows in the wilderness
Toward the daughter of My
people—
Not to fan or to cleanse—
12 A wind too strong for these will
come for Me;
Now I will also speak judgment
against them."

13 "Behold, he shall come up like
clouds,
And his chariots like a whirlwind.
His horses are swifter than eagles.
Woe to us, for we are plundered!"

14 O Jerusalem, wash your heart
from wickedness,
That you may be saved.
How long shall your evil thoughts
lodge within you?
15 For a voice declares from Dan
And proclaims affliction from
Mount Ephraim:
16 "Make mention to the nations,
Yes, proclaim against Jerusalem,
That watchers come from a far
country
And raise their voice against the
cities of Judah.
17 Like keepers of a field they are
against her all around,

Because she has been rebellious
against Me," says the LORD.
18 "Your ways and your doings
Have procured these *things* for you.
This *is* your wickedness,
Because it is bitter,
Because it reaches to your heart."

Sorrow for the Doomed Nation

19 O my soul, my soul!
I am pained in my very heart!
My heart makes a noise in me;
I cannot hold my peace,
Because you have heard, O my
soul,
The sound of the trumpet,
The alarm of war.
20 Destruction upon destruction is
cried,
For the whole land is plundered.
Suddenly my tents are plundered,
And my curtains in a moment.
21 How long will I see the standard,
And hear the sound of the
trumpet?

22 "For My people *are* foolish,
They have not known Me.
They *are* silly children,
And they have no understanding.
They *are* wise to do evil,
But to do good they have no
knowledge."

23 I beheld the earth, and indeed *it*
was without form, and void;
And the heavens, they *had* no light.
24 I beheld the mountains, and
indeed they trembled,
And all the hills moved back and
forth.
25 I beheld, and indeed *there was* no
man,
And all the birds of the heavens
had fled.
26 I beheld, and indeed the fruitful
land *was* a wilderness,
And all its cities were broken down
At the presence of the LORD,
By His fierce anger.

27 For thus says the LORD:

"The whole land shall be desolate;
Yet I will not make a full end.
28 For this shall the earth mourn,
And the heavens above be black,
Because I have spoken.
I have purposed and will not
relent,
Nor will I turn back from it.
29 The whole city shall flee from the
noise of the horsemen and
bowmen.
They shall go into thickets and
climb up on the rocks.
Every city *shall be* forsaken,
And not a man shall dwell in it.

30 "And *when* you *are* plundered,
What will you do?
Though you clothe yourself with
crimson,
Though you adorn *yourself* with
ornaments of gold,
Though you enlarge your eyes
with paint,
In vain you will make yourself
fair;
Your lovers will despise you;
They will seek your life.

31 "For I have heard a voice as of a
woman in labor,
The anguish as of her who brings
forth her first child,
The voice of the daughter of Zion
bewailing herself;
She spreads her hands, *saying,*
'Woe *is* me now, for my soul is
weary
Because of murderers!'

The Justice of God's Judgment

5 "Run to and fro through the
streets of Jerusalem;
See now and know;
And seek in her open places
If you can find a man,
If there is *anyone* who executes
judgment,
Who seeks the truth,
And I will pardon her.
2 Though they say, '*As* the LORD
lives,'
Surely they swear falsely."

3 O LORD, *are* not Your eyes on the
truth?
You have stricken them,

But they have not grieved;
You have consumed them,
But they have refused to receive correction.
They have made their faces harder than rock;
They have refused to return.

4 Therefore I said, "Surely these *are* poor.
They are foolish;
For they do not know the way of the LORD,
The judgment of their God.
5 I will go to the great men and speak to them,
For they have known the way of the LORD,
The judgment of their God."

But these have altogether broken the yoke
And burst the bonds.
6 Therefore a lion from the forest shall slay them,
A wolf of the deserts shall destroy them;
A leopard will watch over their cities.
Everyone who goes out from there shall be torn in pieces,
Because their transgressions are many;
Their backslidings have increased.

7 "How shall I pardon you for this?
Your children have forsaken Me
And sworn by *those that are* not gods.
When I had fed them to the full,
Then they committed adultery
And assembled themselves by troops in the harlots' houses.
8 They were *like* well-fed lusty stallions;
Every one neighed after his neighbor's wife.
9 Shall I not punish *them* for these *things?*" says the LORD.
"And shall I not avenge Myself on such a nation as this?

10 "Go up on her walls and destroy,
But do not make a complete end.
Take away her branches,
For they *are* not the LORD's.
11 For the house of Israel and the house of Judah
Have dealt very treacherously with Me," says the LORD.

12 They have lied about the LORD,
And said, "*It is* not He.
Neither will evil come upon us,
Nor shall we see sword or famine.
13 And the prophets become wind,
For the word *is* not in them.
Thus shall it be done to them."

14 Therefore thus says the LORD God of hosts:

"Because you speak this word,
Behold, I will make My words in your mouth fire,
And this people wood,
And it shall devour them.
15 Behold, I will bring a nation against you from afar,
O house of Israel," says the LORD.
"It *is* a mighty nation,
It *is* an ancient nation,
A nation whose language you do not know,
Nor can you understand what they say.
16 Their quiver *is* like an open tomb;
They *are* all mighty men.
17 And they shall eat up your harvest and your bread,
Which your sons and daughters should eat.
They shall eat up your flocks and your herds;
They shall eat up your vines and your fig trees;
They shall destroy your fortified cities,
In which you trust, with the sword.

18 "Nevertheless in those days," says
the LORD, "I will not make a complete
end of you. 19 And it will be when you
say, 'Why does the LORD our God do
all these *things* to us?' then you shall
answer them, 'Just as you have forsaken
Me and served foreign gods in your
land, so you shall serve aliens in a land
that is not yours.'

20 "Declare this in the house of
Jacob
And proclaim it in Judah, saying,
21 'Hear this now, O foolish people,
Without understanding,
Who have eyes and see not,
And who have ears and hear not:
22 Do you not fear Me?' says the
LORD.
'Will you not tremble at My
presence,
Who have placed the sand as the
bound of the sea,
By a perpetual decree, that it
cannot pass beyond it?
And though its waves toss to and
fro,
Yet they cannot prevail;
Though they roar, yet they cannot
pass over it.
23 But this people has a defiant and
rebellious heart;
They have revolted and departed.
24 They do not say in their heart,
"Let us now fear the LORD our God,
Who gives rain, both the former
and the latter, in its season.
He reserves for us the appointed
weeks of the harvest."
25 Your iniquities have turned these
things away,
And your sins have withheld good
from you.

26 'For among My people are found
wicked *men;*
They lie in wait as one who sets
snares;
They set a trap;
They catch men.
27 As a cage is full of birds,
So their houses *are* full of deceit.
Therefore they have become great
and grown rich.
28 They have grown fat, they are
sleek;
Yes, they surpass the deeds of the
wicked;
They do not plead the cause,
The cause of the fatherless;
Yet they prosper,
And the right of the needy they
do not defend.
29 Shall I not punish *them* for these
things?' says the LORD.
'Shall I not avenge Myself on such
a nation as this?'

30 "An astonishing and horrible thing
Has been committed in the land:
31 The prophets prophesy falsely,
And the priests rule by their *own*
power;
And My people love *to have it* so.
But what will you do in the end?

Impending Destruction from the North

6 "O you children of Benjamin,
Gather yourselves to flee from
the midst of Jerusalem!
Blow the trumpet in Tekoa,
And set up a signal-fire in Beth
Haccerem;
For disaster appears out of the
north,
And great destruction.
2 I have likened the daughter of
Zion
To a lovely and delicate woman.
3 The shepherds with their flocks
shall come to her.
They shall pitch *their* tents
against her all around.
Each one shall pasture in his own
place."

4 "Prepare war against her;
Arise, and let us go up at noon.
Woe to us, for the day goes away,
For the shadows of the evening
are lengthening.
5 Arise, and let us go by night,
And let us destroy her palaces."

6 For thus has the LORD of hosts said:

"Cut down trees,
And build a mound against
Jerusalem.
This *is* the city to be punished.
She *is* full of oppression in her
midst.
7 As a fountain wells up with water,
So she wells up with her
wickedness.
Violence and plundering are
heard in her.
Before Me continually *are* grief
and wounds.
8 Be instructed, O Jerusalem,

Lest My soul depart from you;
Lest I make you desolate,
A land not inhabited."

9Thus says the LORD of hosts:

"They shall thoroughly glean as a vine the remnant of Israel;
As a grape-gatherer, put your hand back into the branches."

10 To whom shall I speak and give warning,
That they may hear?
Indeed their ear *is* uncircumcised,
And they cannot give heed.
Behold, the word of the LORD is a reproach to them;
They have no delight in it.
11 Therefore I am full of the fury of the LORD.
I am weary of holding *it* in.
"I will pour it out on the children outside,
And on the assembly of young men together;
For even the husband shall be taken with the wife,
The aged with *him who is* full of days.
12 And their houses shall be turned over to others,
Fields and wives together;
For I will stretch out My hand
Against the inhabitants of the land," says the LORD.
13 "Because from the least of them even to the greatest of them,
Everyone *is* given to covetousness;
And from the prophet even to the priest,
Everyone deals falsely.
14 They have also healed the hurt of My people slightly,
Saying, 'Peace, peace!'
When *there is* no peace.
15 Were they ashamed when they had committed abomination?
No! They were not at all ashamed;
Nor did they know how to blush.
Therefore they shall fall among those who fall;
At the time I punish them,
They shall be cast down," says the LORD.

16Thus says the LORD:

"Stand in the ways and see,
And ask for the old paths, where the good way *is*,
And walk in it;
Then you will find rest for your souls.
But they said, 'We will not walk *in it.*'
17 Also, I set watchmen over you, *saying*,
'Listen to the sound of the trumpet!'
But they said, 'We will not listen.'
18 Therefore hear, you nations,
And know, O congregation, what *is* among them.
19 Hear, O earth!
Behold, I will certainly bring calamity on this people—
The fruit of their thoughts,
Because they have not heeded My words
Nor My law, but rejected it.
20 For what purpose to Me
Comes frankincense from Sheba,
And sweet cane from a far country?
Your burnt offerings *are* not acceptable,
Nor your sacrifices sweet to Me."

21Therefore thus says the LORD:

"Behold, I will lay stumbling blocks before this people,
And the fathers and the sons together shall fall on them.
The neighbor and his friend shall perish."

22Thus says the LORD:

"Behold, a people comes from the north country,
And a great nation will be raised from the farthest parts of the earth.
23 They will lay hold on bow and spear;

They *are* cruel and have no mercy;
Their voice roars like the sea;
And they ride on horses,
As men of war set in array
against you, O daughter of
Zion."

24 We have heard the report of it;
Our hands grow feeble.
Anguish has taken hold of us,
Pain as of a woman in labor.
25 Do not go out into the field,
Nor walk by the way.
Because of the sword of the
enemy,
Fear *is* on every side.
26 O daughter of my people,
Dress in sackcloth
And roll about in ashes!
Make mourning *as for* an only
son, most bitter lamentation;
For the plunderer will suddenly
come upon us.

27 "I have set you *as* an assayer *and* a
fortress among My people,
That you may know and test their
way.
28 They *are* all stubborn rebels,
walking as slanderers.
They are bronze and iron,
They *are* all corrupters;
29 The bellows blow fiercely,
The lead is consumed by the fire;
The smelter refines in vain,
For the wicked are not drawn off.
30 *People* will call them rejected
silver,
Because the LORD has rejected
them."

Trusting in Lying Words

7 The word that came to Jeremiah
from the LORD, saying, 2"Stand in
the gate of the LORD's house, and pro-
claim there this word, and say, 'Hear the
word of the LORD, all *you of* Judah who
enter in at these gates to worship the
LORD!' " 3Thus says the LORD of hosts,
the God of Israel: "Amend your ways
and your doings, and I will cause you
to dwell in this place. 4Do not trust in
these lying words, saying, 'The temple
of the LORD, the temple of the LORD, the
temple of the LORD *are* these.'
5"For if you thoroughly amend your
ways and your doings, if you thorough-
ly execute judgment between a man
and his neighbor, 6*if* you do not oppress
the stranger, the fatherless, and the
widow, and do not shed innocent blood
in this place, or walk after other gods to
your hurt, 7then I will cause you to dwell
in this place, in the land that I gave to
your fathers forever and ever.
8"Behold, you trust in lying words that
cannot profit. 9Will you steal, murder,
commit adultery, swear falsely, burn
incense to Baal, and walk after other
gods whom you do not know, 10and
then come and stand before Me in this
house which is called by My name, and
say, 'We are delivered to do all these
abominations'? 11Has this house, which
is called by My name, become a den of
thieves in your eyes? Behold, I, even I,
have seen *it*," says the LORD.
12"But go now to My place which *was* in
Shiloh, where I set My name at the first,
and see what I did to it because of the
wickedness of My people Israel. 13And
now, because you have done all these
works," says the LORD, "and I spoke to
you, rising up early and speaking, but you
did not hear, and I called you, but you
did not answer, 14therefore I will do to
the house which is called by My name,
in which you trust, and to this place
which I gave to you and your fathers,
as I have done to Shiloh. 15And I will cast
you out of My sight, as I have cast out
all your brethren—the whole posterity
of Ephraim.
16"Therefore do not pray for this peo-
ple, nor lift up a cry or prayer for them,
nor make intercession to Me; for I will
not hear you. 17Do you not see what
they do in the cities of Judah and in
the streets of Jerusalem? 18The children
gather wood, the fathers kindle the fire,
and the women knead dough, to make
cakes for the queen of heaven; and *they*
pour out drink offerings to other gods,
that they may provoke Me to anger.
19Do they provoke Me to anger?" says
the LORD. "*Do they* not *provoke* them-
selves, to the shame of their own faces?"
20Therefore thus says the Lord GOD:
"Behold, My anger and My fury will be
poured out on this place—on man and

on beast, on the trees of the field and on the fruit of the ground. And it will burn and not be quenched."

21Thus says the LORD of hosts, the God of Israel: "Add your burnt offerings to your sacrifices and eat meat. 22For I did not speak to your fathers, or command them in the day that I brought them out of the land of Egypt, concerning burnt offerings or sacrifices. 23But this is what I commanded them, saying, 'Obey My voice, and I will be your God, and you shall be My people. And walk in all the ways that I have commanded you, that it may be well with you.' 24Yet they did not obey or incline their ear, but followed the counsels *and* the dictates of their evil hearts, and went backward and not forward. 25Since the day that your fathers came out of the land of Egypt until this day, I have even sent to you all My servants the prophets, daily rising up early and sending *them.* 26Yet they did not obey Me or incline their ear, but stiffened their neck. They did worse than their fathers.

27"Therefore you shall speak all these words to them, but they will not obey you. You shall also call to them, but they will not answer you.

Judgment on Obscene Religion

28"So you shall say to them, 'This *is* a nation that does not obey the voice of the LORD their God nor receive correction. Truth has perished and has been cut off from their mouth. 29Cut off your hair and cast *it* away, and take up a lamentation on the desolate heights; for the LORD has rejected and forsaken the generation of His wrath.' 30For the children of Judah have done evil in My sight," says the LORD. "They have set their abominations in the house which is called by My name, to pollute it. 31And they have built the high places of Tophet, which *is* in the Valley of the Son of Hinnom, to burn their sons and their daughters in the fire, which I did not command, nor did it come into My heart.

32"Therefore behold, the days are coming," says the LORD, "when it will no more be called Tophet, or the Valley of the Son of Hinnom, but the Valley of Slaughter; for they will bury in Tophet until there is no room. 33The corpses of this people will be food for the birds of the heaven and for the beasts of the earth. And no one will frighten *them away.* 34Then I will cause to cease from the cities of Judah and from the streets of Jerusalem the voice of mirth and the voice of gladness, the voice of the bridegroom and the voice of the bride. For the land shall be desolate.

8 "At that time," says the LORD, "they shall bring out the bones of the kings of Judah, and the bones of its princes, and the bones of the priests, and the bones of the prophets, and the bones of the inhabitants of Jerusalem, out of their graves. 2They shall spread them before the sun and the moon and all the host of heaven, which they have loved and which they have served and after which they have walked, which they have sought and which they have worshiped. They shall not be gathered nor buried; they shall be like refuse on the face of the earth. 3Then death shall be chosen rather than life by all the residue of those who remain of this evil family, who remain in all the places where I have driven them," says the LORD of hosts.

The Peril of False Teaching

4"Moreover you shall say to them, 'Thus says the LORD:

"Will they fall and not rise?
Will one turn away and not
return?
5 Why has this people slidden back,
Jerusalem, in a perpetual
backsliding?
They hold fast to deceit,
They refuse to return.
6 I listened and heard,
But they do not speak aright.
No man repented of his
wickedness,
Saying, 'What have I done?'
Everyone turned to his own
course,
As the horse rushes into the
battle.

7 "Even the stork in the heavens
Knows her appointed times;

And the turtledove, the swift, and
the swallow
Observe the time of their coming.
But My people do not know the
judgment of the LORD.

8 "How can you say, 'We *are* wise,
And the law of the LORD *is*
with us'?
Look, the false pen of the scribe
certainly works falsehood.
9 The wise men are ashamed,
They are dismayed and taken.
Behold, they have rejected the
word of the LORD;
So what wisdom do they have?
10 Therefore I will give their wives to
others,
And their fields to those who will
inherit *them;*
Because from the least even to the
greatest
Everyone is given to covetousness;
From the prophet even to the
priest
Everyone deals falsely.
11 For they have healed the hurt of
the daughter of My people
slightly,
Saying, 'Peace, peace!'
When *there is* no peace.
12 Were they ashamed when
they had committed
abomination?
No! They were not at all ashamed,
Nor did they know how to blush.
Therefore they shall fall among
those who fall;
In the time of their punishment
They shall be cast down," says the
LORD.

13 "I will surely consume them," says
the LORD.
"No grapes *shall be* on the vine,
Nor figs on the fig tree,
And the leaf shall fade;
And *the things* I have given
them shall pass away from
them." ' "

14 "Why do we sit still?
Assemble yourselves,
And let us enter the fortified
cities,
And let us be silent there.
For the LORD our God has put us
to silence
And given us water of gall to
drink,
Because we have sinned against
the LORD.
15 "*We* looked for peace, but no good
came;
And for a time of health, and
there was trouble!
16 The snorting of His horses was
heard from Dan.
The whole land trembled at the
sound of the neighing of His
strong ones;
For they have come and devoured
the land and all that is in it,
The city and those who dwell
in it."

17 "For behold, I will send serpents
among you,
Vipers which cannot be charmed,
And they shall bite you," says the
LORD.

The Prophet Mourns for the People

18 I would comfort myself in sorrow;
My heart *is* faint in me.
19 Listen! The voice,
The cry of the daughter of my
people
From a far country:
"*Is* not the LORD in Zion?
Is not her King in her?"

"Why have they provoked Me to
anger
With their carved images—
With foreign idols?"

20 "The harvest is past,
The summer is ended,
And we are not saved!"

21 For the hurt of the daughter of my
people I am hurt.
I am mourning;
Astonishment has taken hold
of me.
22 *Is there* no balm in Gilead,
Is there no physician there?
Why then is there no recovery

For the health of the daughter of
my people?

9 Oh, that my head were waters,
And my eyes a fountain of tears,
That I might weep day and night
For the slain of the daughter of
my people!
2 Oh, that I had in the wilderness
A lodging place for travelers;
That I might leave my people,
And go from them!
For they *are* all adulterers,
An assembly of treacherous men.

3 "And *like* their bow they have bent
their tongues *for* lies.
They are not valiant for the truth
on the earth.
For they proceed from evil to evil,
And they do not know Me," says
the LORD.
4 "Everyone take heed to his neighbor,
And do not trust any brother;
For every brother will utterly
supplant,
And every neighbor will walk with
slanderers.
5 Everyone will deceive his
neighbor,
And will not speak the truth;
They have taught their tongue to
speak lies;
They weary themselves to commit
iniquity.
6 Your dwelling place *is* in the midst
of deceit;
Through deceit they refuse to
know Me," says the LORD.

7Therefore thus says the LORD of hosts:

"Behold, I will refine them and try
them;
For how shall I deal with the
daughter of My people?
8 Their tongue *is* an arrow shot out;
It speaks deceit;
One speaks peaceably to his
neighbor with his mouth,
But in his heart he lies in wait.
9 Shall I not punish them for these
things?" says the LORD.
"Shall I not avenge Myself on such
a nation as this?"

10 I will take up a weeping and
wailing for the mountains,
And for the dwelling places of the
wilderness a lamentation,
Because they are burned up,
So that no one can pass through;
Nor can *men* hear the voice of the
cattle.
Both the birds of the heavens and
the beasts have fled;
They are gone.

11 "I will make Jerusalem a heap of
ruins, a den of jackals.
I will make the cities of Judah
desolate, without an
inhabitant."

12Who *is* the wise man who may under-
stand this? And *who is he* to whom the
mouth of the LORD has spoken, that
he may declare it? Why does the land
perish *and* burn up like a wilderness, so
that no one can pass through?
13And the LORD said, "Because they
have forsaken My law which I set be-
fore them, and have not obeyed My
voice, nor walked according to it, 14but
they have walked according to the dic-
tates of their own hearts and after the
Baals, which their fathers taught them,"
15therefore thus says the LORD of hosts,
the God of Israel: "Behold, I will feed
them, this people, with wormwood, and
give them water of gall to drink. 16I will
scatter them also among the Gentiles,
whom neither they nor their fathers
have known. And I will send a sword af-
ter them until I have consumed them."

The People Mourn in Judgment

17Thus says the LORD of hosts:

"Consider and call for the mourning
women,
That they may come;
And send for skillful *wailing*
women,
That they may come.
18 Let them make haste
And take up a wailing for us,
That our eyes may run with tears,
And our eyelids gush with water.
19 For a voice of wailing is heard
from Zion:

'How we are plundered!
We are greatly ashamed,
Because we have forsaken the land,
Because we have been cast out of our dwellings.' "

20 Yet hear the word of the LORD, O women,
And let your ear receive the word of His mouth;
Teach your daughters wailing,
And everyone her neighbor a lamentation.
21 For death has come through our windows,
Has entered our palaces,
To kill off the children—*no longer to be* outside!
And the young men—*no longer* on the streets!

22Speak, "Thus says the LORD:

'Even the carcasses of men shall fall as refuse on the open field,
Like cuttings after the harvester,
And no one shall gather *them*.' "

23Thus says the LORD:

"Let not the wise *man* glory in his wisdom,
Let not the mighty *man* glory in his might,
Nor let the rich *man* glory in his riches;
24 But let him who glories glory in this,
That he understands and knows Me,
That I *am* the LORD, exercising lovingkindness, judgment, and righteousness in the earth.
For in these I delight," says the LORD.

25"Behold, the days are coming," says
the LORD, "that I will punish all *who*
are circumcised with the uncircum-
cised— 26Egypt, Judah, Edom, the
people of Ammon, Moab, and all *who*
are in the farthest corners, who dwell
in the wilderness. For all *these* nations
are uncircumcised, and all the house of
Israel *are* uncircumcised in the heart."

Idols and the True God

10 Hear the word which the LORD speaks to you, O house of Israel.
2Thus says the LORD:

"Do not learn the way of the Gentiles;
Do not be dismayed at the signs of heaven,
For the Gentiles are dismayed at them.
3 For the customs of the peoples *are* futile;
For *one* cuts a tree from the forest,
The work of the hands of the workman, with the ax.
4 They decorate it with silver and gold;
They fasten it with nails and hammers
So that it will not topple.
5 They *are* upright, like a palm tree,
And they cannot speak;
They must be carried,
Because they cannot go *by themselves*.
Do not be afraid of them,
For they cannot do evil,
Nor can they do any good."

6 Inasmuch as *there is* none like You, O LORD
(You *are* great, and Your name *is* great in might),
7 Who would not fear You, O King of the nations?
For this is Your rightful due.
For among all the wise *men* of the nations,
And in all their kingdoms,
There is none like You.
8 But they are altogether dull-hearted and foolish;
A wooden idol *is* a worthless doctrine.
9 Silver is beaten into plates;
It is brought from Tarshish,
And gold from Uphaz,
The work of the craftsman
And of the hands of the metalsmith;

Blue and purple *are* their clothing;
They *are* all the work of skillful
men.
10 But the LORD *is* the true God;
He *is* the living God and the
everlasting King.
At His wrath the earth will
tremble,
And the nations will not be able to
endure His indignation.

11Thus you shall say to them: "The gods
that have not made the heavens and the
earth shall perish from the earth and
from under these heavens."

12 He has made the earth by His
power,
He has established the world by
His wisdom,
And has stretched out the
heavens at His discretion.
13 When He utters His voice,
There is a multitude of waters in
the heavens:
"And He causes the vapors to
ascend from the ends of the
earth.
He makes lightning for the rain,
He brings the wind out of His
treasuries."[a]

14 Everyone is dull-hearted, without
knowledge;
Every metalsmith is put to shame
by an image;
For his molded image *is*
falsehood,
And *there is* no breath in them.
15 They *are* futile, a work of errors;
In the time of their punishment
they shall perish.
16 The Portion of Jacob *is* not like
them,
For He *is* the Maker of all *things*,
And Israel *is* the tribe of His
inheritance;
The LORD of hosts *is* His name.

The Coming Captivity of Judah

17 Gather up your wares from the
land,
O inhabitant of the fortress!

18For thus says the LORD:

"Behold, I will throw out at this
time
The inhabitants of the land,
And will distress them,
That they may find *it so*."

19 Woe is me for my hurt!
My wound is severe.
But I say, "Truly this *is* an
infirmity,
And I must bear it."
20 My tent is plundered,
And all my cords are broken;
My children have gone from me,
And they *are* no more.
There is no one to pitch my tent
anymore,
Or set up my curtains.

21 For the shepherds have become
dull-hearted,
And have not sought the LORD;
Therefore they shall not
prosper,
And all their flocks shall be
scattered.
22 Behold, the noise of the report
has come,
And a great commotion out of the
north country,
To make the cities of Judah
desolate, a den of jackals.

23 O LORD, I know the way of man *is*
not in himself;
It is not in man who walks to
direct his own steps.
24 O LORD, correct me, but with
justice;
Not in Your anger, lest You bring
me to nothing.
25 Pour out Your fury on the
Gentiles, who do not know
You,
And on the families who do not
call on Your name;
For they have eaten up Jacob,
Devoured him and consumed
him,
And made his dwelling place
desolate.

10:13 [a] Psalm 135:7

The Broken Covenant

11 The word that came to Jeremiah from the LORD, saying, 2"Hear the words of this covenant, and speak to the men of Judah and to the inhabitants of Jerusalem; 3and say to them, 'Thus says the LORD God of Israel: "Cursed *is* the man who does not obey the words of this covenant 4which I commanded your fathers in the day I brought them out of the land of Egypt, from the iron furnace, saying, 'Obey My voice, and do according to all that I command you; so shall you be My people, and I will be your God,' 5that I may establish the oath which I have sworn to your fathers, to give them 'a land flowing with milk and honey,'[a] as *it is* this day." ' "

And I answered and said, "So be it, LORD."

6Then the LORD said to me, "Proclaim all these words in the cities of Judah and in the streets of Jerusalem, saying: 'Hear the words of this covenant and do them. 7For I earnestly exhorted your fathers in the day I brought them up out of the land of Egypt, until this day, rising early and exhorting, saying, "Obey My voice." 8Yet they did not obey or incline their ear, but everyone followed the dictates of his evil heart; therefore I will bring upon them all the words of this covenant, which I commanded *them* to do, but *which* they have not done.' "

9And the LORD said to me, "A conspiracy has been found among the men of Judah and among the inhabitants of Jerusalem. 10They have turned back to the iniquities of their forefathers who refused to hear My words, and they have gone after other gods to serve them; the house of Israel and the house of Judah have broken My covenant which I made with their fathers."

11Therefore thus says the LORD: "Behold, I will surely bring calamity on them which they will not be able to escape; and though they cry out to Me, I will not listen to them. 12Then the cities of Judah and the inhabitants of Jerusalem will go and cry out to the gods to whom they offer incense, but they will not save them at all in the time of their trouble. 13For *according to* the number of your cities were your gods, O Judah; and *according to* the number of the streets of Jerusalem you have set up altars to *that* shameful thing, altars to burn incense to Baal.

14"So do not pray for this people, or lift up a cry or prayer for them; for I will not hear *them* in the time that they cry out to Me because of their trouble.

15 "What has My beloved to do in My house,
Having done lewd deeds with many?
And the holy flesh has passed from you.
When you do evil, then you rejoice.
16 The LORD called your name,
Green Olive Tree, Lovely *and* of Good Fruit.
With the noise of a great tumult
He has kindled fire on it,
And its branches are broken.

17"For the LORD of hosts, who planted you, has pronounced doom against you for the evil of the house of Israel and of the house of Judah, which they have done against themselves to provoke Me to anger in offering incense to Baal."

Jeremiah's Life Threatened

18Now the LORD gave me knowledge *of it,* and I know *it;* for You showed me their doings. 19But I *was* like a docile lamb brought to the slaughter; and I did not know that they had devised schemes against me, *saying,* "Let us destroy the tree with its fruit, and let us cut him off from the land of the living, that his name may be remembered no more."

20 But, O LORD of hosts,
You who judge righteously,
Testing the mind and the heart,
Let me see Your vengeance on them,
For to You I have revealed my cause.

21"Therefore thus says the LORD concerning the men of Anathoth who seek

11:5 [a] Exodus 3:8

your life, saying, 'Do not prophesy in
the name of the LORD, lest you die by
our hand'— 22therefore thus says the
LORD of hosts: 'Behold, I will punish
them. The young men shall die by the
sword, their sons and their daughters
shall die by famine; 23and there shall
be no remnant of them, for I will bring
catastrophe on the men of Anathoth,
even the year of their punishment.' "

Jeremiah's Question

12 Righteous *are* You, O LORD, when I plead with You;
Yet let me talk with You about *Your* judgments.
Why does the way of the wicked prosper?
Why are those happy who deal so treacherously?
2 You have planted them, yes, they have taken root;
They grow, yes, they bear fruit.
You *are* near in their mouth
But far from their mind.

3 But You, O LORD, know me;
You have seen me,
And You have tested my heart toward You.
Pull them out like sheep for the slaughter,
And prepare them for the day of slaughter.
4 How long will the land mourn,
And the herbs of every field wither?
The beasts and birds are consumed,
For the wickedness of those who dwell there,
Because they said, "He will not see our final end."

The LORD Answers Jeremiah

5 "If you have run with the footmen, and they have wearied you,
Then how can you contend with horses?
And *if* in the land of peace,
In which you trusted, *they wearied you,*
Then how will you do in the floodplain[a] of the Jordan?
6 For even your brothers, the house of your father,
Even they have dealt treacherously with you;
Yes, they have called a multitude after you.
Do not believe them,
Even though they speak smooth words to you.

7 "I have forsaken My house, I have left My heritage;
I have given the dearly beloved of My soul into the hand of her enemies.
8 My heritage is to Me like a lion in the forest;
It cries out against Me;
Therefore I have hated it.
9 My heritage *is* to Me *like* a speckled vulture;
The vultures all around *are* against her.
Come, assemble all the beasts of the field,
Bring them to devour!

10 "Many rulers[a] have destroyed My vineyard,
They have trodden My portion underfoot;
They have made My pleasant portion a desolate wilderness.
11 They have made it desolate;
Desolate, it mourns to Me;
The whole land is made desolate,
Because no one takes *it* to heart.
12 The plunderers have come
On all the desolate heights in the wilderness,
For the sword of the LORD shall devour
From *one* end of the land to the *other* end of the land;
No flesh shall have peace.
13 They have sown wheat but reaped thorns;
They have put themselves to pain *but* do not profit.
But be ashamed of your harvest
Because of the fierce anger of the LORD."

12:5 [a] Or *thicket* 12:10 [a] Literally *shepherds* or *pastors*

14 Thus says the LORD: "Against all My
evil neighbors who touch the inheri-
tance which I have caused My people
Israel to inherit—behold, I will pluck
them out of their land and pluck out
the house of Judah from among them.
15 Then it shall be, after I have plucked
them out, that I will return and have
compassion on them and bring them
back, everyone to his heritage and ev-
eryone to his land. 16 And it shall be, if
they will learn carefully the ways of My
people, to swear by My name, 'As the
LORD lives,' as they taught My people to
swear by Baal, then they shall be estab-
lished in the midst of My people. 17 But if
they do not obey, I will utterly pluck up
and destroy that nation," says the LORD.

Symbol of the Linen Sash

13 Thus the LORD said to me: "Go
and get yourself a linen sash,
and put it around your waist, but do
not put it in water." 2 So I got a sash ac-
cording to the word of the LORD, and
put *it* around my waist.
3 And the word of the LORD came to me
the second time, saying, 4 "Take the sash
that you acquired, which *is* around your
waist, and arise, go to the Euphrates,[a]
and hide it there in a hole in the rock."
5 So I went and hid it by the Euphrates,
as the LORD commanded me.
6 Now it came to pass after many days
that the LORD said to me, "Arise, go to
the Euphrates, and take from there the
sash which I commanded you to hide
there." 7 Then I went to the Euphrates
and dug, and I took the sash from the
place where I had hidden it; and there
was the sash, ruined. It was profitable
for nothing.
8 Then the word of the LORD came
to me, saying, 9 "Thus says the LORD:
'In this manner I will ruin the pride of
Judah and the great pride of Jerusalem.
10 This evil people, who refuse to hear
My words, who follow the dictates of
their hearts, and walk after other gods
to serve them and worship them, shall
be just like this sash which is profitable
for nothing. 11 For as the sash clings to
the waist of a man, so I have caused
the whole house of Israel and the whole
house of Judah to cling to Me,' says
the LORD, 'that they may become My
people, for renown, for praise, and for
glory; but they would not hear.'

Symbol of the Wine Bottles

12 "Therefore you shall speak to them
this word: 'Thus says the LORD God of
Israel: "Every bottle shall be filled with
wine." '
"And they will say to you, 'Do we not
certainly know that every bottle will be
filled with wine?'
13 "Then you shall say to them, 'Thus
says the LORD: "Behold, I will fill all the
inhabitants of this land—even the kings
who sit on David's throne, the priests,
the prophets, and all the inhabitants of
Jerusalem—with drunkenness! 14 And
I will dash them one against another,
even the fathers and the sons togeth-
er," says the LORD. "I will not pity nor
spare nor have mercy, but will destroy
them." ' "

Pride Precedes Captivity

15 Hear and give ear:
Do not be proud,
For the LORD has spoken.
16 Give glory to the LORD your God
Before He causes darkness,
And before your feet stumble
On the dark mountains,
And while you are looking for
light,
He turns it into the shadow of
death
And makes *it* dense darkness.
17 But if you will not hear it,
My soul will weep in secret for
your pride;
My eyes will weep bitterly
And run down with tears,
Because the LORD's flock has been
taken captive.

18 Say to the king and to the queen
mother,
"Humble yourselves;
Sit down,
For your rule shall collapse, the
crown of your glory."

13:4 [a] Hebrew *Perath*

19 The cities of the South shall be
shut up,
And no one shall open *them;*
Judah shall be carried away
captive, all of it;
It shall be wholly carried away
captive.

20 Lift up your eyes and see
Those who come from the north.
Where *is* the flock *that* was given
to you,
Your beautiful sheep?
21 What will you say when He
punishes you?
For you have taught them
To be chieftains, to be head over
you.
Will not pangs seize you,
Like a woman in labor?
22 And if you say in your heart,
"Why have these things come
upon me?"
For the greatness of your iniquity
Your skirts have been uncovered,
Your heels made bare.
23 Can the Ethiopian change his skin
or the leopard its spots?
Then may you also do good who
are accustomed to do evil.

24 "Therefore I will scatter them like
stubble
That passes away by the wind of
the wilderness.
25 This is your lot,
The portion of your measures
from Me," says the LORD,
"Because you have forgotten Me
And trusted in falsehood.
26 Therefore I will uncover your
skirts over your face,
That your shame may appear.
27 I have seen your adulteries
And your *lustful* neighings,
The lewdness of your harlotry,
Your abominations on the hills in
the fields.
Woe to you, O Jerusalem!
Will you still not be made clean?"

Sword, Famine, and Pestilence

14 The word of the LORD that came
to Jeremiah concerning the
droughts.

2 "Judah mourns,
And her gates languish;
They mourn for the land,
And the cry of Jerusalem has
gone up.
3 Their nobles have sent their lads
for water;
They went to the cisterns *and*
found no water.
They returned with their vessels
empty;
They were ashamed and
confounded
And covered their heads.
4 Because the ground is parched,
For there was no rain in the land,
The plowmen were ashamed;
They covered their heads.
5 Yes, the deer also gave birth in the
field,
But left because there was no
grass.
6 And the wild donkeys stood in the
desolate heights;
They sniffed at the wind like
jackals;
Their eyes failed because *there
was* no grass."

7 O LORD, though our iniquities
testify against us,
Do it for Your name's sake;
For our backslidings are many,
We have sinned against You.
8 O the Hope of Israel, his Savior in
time of trouble,
Why should You be like a stranger
in the land,
And like a traveler *who* turns
aside to tarry for a night?
9 Why should You be like a man
astonished,
Like a mighty one *who* cannot
save?
Yet You, O LORD, *are* in our midst,
And we are called by Your name;
Do not leave us!

10 Thus says the LORD to this people:

"Thus they have loved to wander;
They have not restrained their
feet.
Therefore the LORD does not
accept them;

He will remember their iniquity
now,
And punish their sins."

11 Then the LORD said to me, "Do not
pray for this people, for *their* good.
12 When they fast, I will not hear their cry;
and when they offer burnt offering and
grain offering, I will not accept them.
But I will consume them by the sword,
by the famine, and by the pestilence."
13 Then I said, "Ah, Lord GOD! Behold,
the prophets say to them, 'You shall not
see the sword, nor shall you have fam-
ine, but I will give you assured peace
in this place.' "
14 And the LORD said to me, "The proph-
ets prophesy lies in My name. I have
not sent them, commanded them, nor
spoken to them; they prophesy to you
a false vision, divination, a worthless
thing, and the deceit of their heart.
15 Therefore thus says the LORD con-
cerning the prophets who prophesy in
My name, whom I did not send, and who
say, 'Sword and famine shall not be in
this land'—'By sword and famine those
prophets shall be consumed! 16 And the
people to whom they prophesy shall
be cast out in the streets of Jerusalem
because of the famine and the sword;
they will have no one to bury them—
them nor their wives, their sons nor
their daughters—for I will pour their
wickedness on them.'
17 "Therefore you shall say this word
to them:

'Let my eyes flow with tears night
and day,
And let them not cease;
For the virgin daughter of my
people
Has been broken with a mighty
stroke, with a very severe
blow.
18 If I go out to the field,
Then behold, those slain with the
sword!
And if I enter the city,
Then behold, those sick from
famine!
Yes, both prophet and priest go
about in a land they do not
know.' "

The People Plead for Mercy

19 Have You utterly rejected Judah?
Has Your soul loathed Zion?
Why have You stricken us so that
there is no healing for us?
We looked for peace, but *there was*
no good;
And for the time of healing, and
there was trouble.
20 We acknowledge, O LORD, our
wickedness
And the iniquity of our fathers,
For we have sinned against You.
21 Do not abhor *us*, for Your name's
sake;
Do not disgrace the throne of
Your glory.
Remember, do not break Your
covenant with us.
22 Are there any among the idols of
the nations that can cause
rain?
Or can the heavens give
showers?
Are You not He, O LORD our God?
Therefore we will wait for You,
Since You have made all these.

The LORD Will Not Relent

15 Then the LORD said to me, "*Even*
if Moses and Samuel stood be-
fore Me, My mind *would* not *be* favor-
able toward this people. Cast *them* out
of My sight, and let them go forth. 2 And
it shall be, if they say to you, 'Where
should we go?' then you shall tell them,
'Thus says the LORD:

"Such as *are* for death, to death;
And such as *are* for the sword, to
the sword;
And such as *are* for the famine, to
the famine;
And such as *are* for the captivity,
to the captivity." '

3 "And I will appoint over them four
forms *of destruction*," says the LORD:
"the sword to slay, the dogs to drag, the
birds of the heavens and the beasts of
the earth to devour and destroy. 4 I will
hand them over to trouble, to all king-
doms of the earth, because of Manasseh
the son of Hezekiah, king of Judah, for
what he did in Jerusalem.

5 "For who will have pity on you,
O Jerusalem?
Or who will bemoan you?
Or who will turn aside to ask how
you are doing?
6 You have forsaken Me," says the
LORD,
"You have gone backward.
Therefore I will stretch out My
hand against you and
destroy you;
I am weary of relenting!
7 And I will winnow them with a
winnowing fan in the gates
of the land;
I will bereave *them* of children;
I will destroy My people,
Since they do not return from
their ways.
8 Their widows will be increased to
Me more than the sand of
the seas;
I will bring against them,
Against the mother of the young
men,
A plunderer at noonday;
I will cause anguish and terror to
fall on them suddenly.

9 "She languishes who has borne
seven;
She has breathed her last;
Her sun has gone down
While *it was* yet day;
She has been ashamed and
confounded.
And the remnant of them I will
deliver to the sword
Before their enemies," says the
LORD.

Jeremiah's Dejection

10 Woe is me, my mother,
That you have borne me,
A man of strife and a man of
contention to the whole
earth!
I have neither lent for interest,
Nor have men lent to me for
interest.
Every one of them curses me.

11The LORD said:

"Surely it will be well with your
remnant;
Surely I will cause the enemy to
intercede with you
In the time of adversity and in the
time of affliction.
12 Can anyone break iron,
The northern iron and the bronze?
13 Your wealth and your treasures
I will give as plunder without
price,
Because of all your sins,
Throughout your territories.
14 And I will make *you* cross over
with[a] your enemies
Into a land *which* you do not
know;
For a fire is kindled in My anger,
Which shall burn upon you."

15 O LORD, You know;
Remember me and visit me,
And take vengeance for me on my
persecutors.
In Your enduring patience, do not
take me away.
Know that for Your sake I have
suffered rebuke.
16 Your words were found, and I ate
them,
And Your word was to me the joy
and rejoicing of my heart;
For I am called by Your name,
O LORD God of hosts.
17 I did not sit in the assembly of the
mockers,
Nor did I rejoice;
I sat alone because of Your hand,
For You have filled me with
indignation.
18 Why is my pain perpetual
And my wound incurable,
Which refuses to be healed?
Will You surely be to me like an
unreliable stream,
As waters *that* fail?

The LORD Reassures Jeremiah

19Therefore thus says the LORD:

"If you return,
Then I will bring you back;
You shall stand before Me;

15:14 [a] Following Masoretic Text and Vulgate; Septuagint, Syriac, and Targum read *cause you to serve* (compare 17:4).

If you take out the precious from
the vile,
You shall be as My mouth.
Let them return to you,
But you must not return to them.
20 And I will make you to this
people a fortified bronze
wall;
And they will fight against you,
But they shall not prevail against
you;
For I *am* with you to save you
And deliver you," says the LORD.
21 "I will deliver you from the hand of
the wicked,
And I will redeem you from the
grip of the terrible."

Jeremiah's Lifestyle and Message

16 The word of the LORD also came
to me, saying, 2"You shall not
take a wife, nor shall you have sons
or daughters in this place." 3For thus
says the LORD concerning the sons and
daughters who are born in this place,
and concerning their mothers who bore
them and their fathers who begot them
in this land: 4"They shall die gruesome
deaths; they shall not be lamented nor
shall they be buried, *but* they shall be
like refuse on the face of the earth. They
shall be consumed by the sword and
by famine, and their corpses shall be
meat for the birds of heaven and for
the beasts of the earth."
5For thus says the LORD: "Do not enter
the house of mourning, nor go to lament
or bemoan them; for I have taken away
My peace from this people," says the
LORD, "lovingkindness and mercies.
6Both the great and the small shall die
in this land. They shall not be buried;
neither shall men lament for them, cut
themselves, nor make themselves bald
for them. 7Nor shall *men* break *bread* in
mourning for them, to comfort them
for the dead; nor shall *men* give them
the cup of consolation to drink for their
father or their mother. 8Also you shall
not go into the house of feasting to sit
with them, to eat and drink."
9For thus says the LORD of hosts, the
God of Israel: "Behold, I will cause to
cease from this place, before your eyes
and in your days, the voice of mirth and
the voice of gladness, the voice of the
bridegroom and the voice of the bride.
10"And it shall be, when you show this
people all these words, and they say to
you, 'Why has the LORD pronounced all
this great disaster against us? Or what
is our iniquity? Or what *is* our sin that
we have committed against the LORD
our God?' 11then you shall say to them,
'Because your fathers have forsaken
Me,' says the LORD; 'they have walked
after other gods and have served them
and worshiped them, and have forsak-
en Me and not kept My law. 12And you
have done worse than your fathers, for
behold, each one follows the dictates of
his own evil heart, so that no one listens
to Me. 13Therefore I will cast you out of
this land into a land that you do not
know, neither you nor your fathers;
and there you shall serve other gods
day and night, where I will not show
you favor.'

God Will Restore Israel

14"Therefore behold, the days are
coming," says the LORD, "that it shall
no more be said, 'The LORD lives who
brought up the children of Israel from
the land of Egypt,' 15but, 'The LORD lives
who brought up the children of Israel
from the land of the north and from all
the lands where He had driven them.'
For I will bring them back into their land
which I gave to their fathers.
16"Behold, I will send for many
fishermen," says the LORD, "and they
shall fish them; and afterward I will
send for many hunters, and they shall
hunt them from every mountain and
every hill, and out of the holes of the
rocks. 17For My eyes *are* on all their
ways; they are not hidden from My
face, nor is their iniquity hidden from
My eyes. 18And first I will repay double
for their iniquity and their sin, because
they have defiled My land; they have
filled My inheritance with the carcass-
es of their detestable and abominable
idols."

19 O LORD, my strength and my
fortress,
My refuge in the day of affliction,
The Gentiles shall come to You

From the ends of the earth and say,
"Surely our fathers have inherited lies,
Worthlessness and unprofitable *things*."
20 Will a man make gods for himself,
Which *are* not gods?

21 "Therefore behold, I will this once cause them to know,
I will cause them to know
My hand and My might;
And they shall know that My name *is* the LORD.

Judah's Sin and Punishment

17 "The sin of Judah *is* written with a pen of iron;
With the point of a diamond *it is* engraved
On the tablet of their heart,
And on the horns of your altars,
2 While their children remember
Their altars and their wooden images[a]
By the green trees on the high hills.
3 O My mountain in the field,
I will give as plunder your wealth, all your treasures,
And your high places of sin within all your borders.
4 And you, even yourself,
Shall let go of your heritage which I gave you;
And I will cause you to serve your enemies
In the land which you do not know;
For you have kindled a fire in My anger *which* shall burn forever."

5 Thus says the LORD:

"Cursed *is* the man who trusts in man
And makes flesh his strength,
Whose heart departs from the LORD.
6 For he shall be like a shrub in the desert,
And shall not see when good comes,
But shall inhabit the parched places in the wilderness,
In a salt land *which is* not inhabited.

7 "Blessed *is* the man who trusts in the LORD,
And whose hope is the LORD.
8 For he shall be like a tree planted by the waters,
Which spreads out its roots by the river,
And will not fear[a] when heat comes;
But its leaf will be green,
And will not be anxious in the year of drought,
Nor will cease from yielding fruit.

9 "The heart *is* deceitful above all *things*,
And desperately wicked;
Who can know it?
10 I, the LORD, search the heart,
I test the mind,
Even to give every man according to his ways,
According to the fruit of his doings.

11 "*As* a partridge that broods but does not hatch,
So is he who gets riches, but not by right;
It will leave him in the midst of his days,
And at his end he will be a fool."

12 A glorious high throne from the beginning
Is the place of our sanctuary.
13 O LORD, the hope of Israel,
All who forsake You shall be ashamed.

"Those who depart from Me
Shall be written in the earth,
Because they have forsaken the LORD,
The fountain of living waters."

17:2 [a] Hebrew *Asherim*, Canaanite deities 17:8 [a] Qere and Targum read *see*.

WORSHIP GROWTH HEAVEN FAMILY

Jeremiah Prays for Deliverance

14 Heal me, O LORD, and I shall be healed;
Save me, and I shall be saved,
For You *are* my praise.
15 Indeed they say to me,
"Where *is* the word of the LORD?
Let it come now!"
16 As for me, I have not hurried away from *being* a shepherd *who* follows You,
Nor have I desired the woeful day;
You know what came out of my lips;
It was right there before You.
17 Do not be a terror to me;
You *are* my hope in the day of doom.
18 Let them be ashamed who persecute me,
But do not let me be put to shame;
Let them be dismayed,
But do not let me be dismayed.
Bring on them the day of doom,
And destroy them with double destruction!

Hallow the Sabbath Day

19Thus the LORD said to me: "Go and
stand in the gate of the children of the
people, by which the kings of Judah
come in and by which they go out, and
in all the gates of Jerusalem; 20and say
to them, 'Hear the word of the LORD,
you kings of Judah, and all Judah, and
all the inhabitants of Jerusalem, who
enter by these gates. 21Thus says the
LORD: "Take heed to yourselves, and
bear no burden on the Sabbath day,
nor bring *it* in by the gates of Jerusa-
lem; 22nor carry a burden out of your
houses on the Sabbath day, nor do any
work, but hallow the Sabbath day, as I
commanded your fathers. 23But they
did not obey nor incline their ear, but
made their neck stiff, that they might
not hear nor receive instruction.
24"And it shall be, if you heed Me care-
fully," says the LORD, "to bring no bur-
den through the gates of this city on the
Sabbath day, but hallow the Sabbath
day, to do no work in it, 25then shall
enter the gates of this city kings and
princes sitting on the throne of David,
riding in chariots and on horses, they
and their princes, accompanied by the
men of Judah and the inhabitants of
Jerusalem; and this city shall remain
forever. 26And they shall come from
the cities of Judah and from the places
around Jerusalem, from the land of Ben-
jamin and from the lowland, from the
mountains and from the South, bring-
ing burnt offerings and sacrifices, grain
offerings and incense, bringing sacri-
fices of praise to the house of the LORD.
27"But if you will not heed Me to hallow
the Sabbath day, such as not carrying
a burden when entering the gates of
Jerusalem on the Sabbath day, then I
will kindle a fire in its gates, and it shall
devour the palaces of Jerusalem, and
it shall not be quenched." ' "

The Potter and the Clay

18 The word which came to Jere-
miah from the LORD, saying:
2"Arise and go down to the potter's
house, and there I will cause you to
hear My words." 3Then I went down to
the potter's house, and there he was,
making something at the wheel. 4And
the vessel that he made of clay was
marred in the hand of the potter; so he
made it again into another vessel, as
it seemed good to the potter to make.
5Then the word of the LORD came to
me, saying: 6"O house of Israel, can I
not do with you as this potter?" says the
LORD. "Look, as the clay *is* in the potter's
hand, so *are* you in My hand, O house of
Israel! 7The instant I speak concerning
a nation and concerning a kingdom, to
pluck up, to pull down, and to destroy
it, 8if that nation against whom I have
spoken turns from its evil, I will relent of
the disaster that I thought to bring upon
it. 9And the instant I speak concerning
a nation and concerning a kingdom,
to build and to plant *it*, 10if it does evil
in My sight so that it does not obey My
voice, then I will relent concerning the
good with which I said I would benefit it.
11"Now therefore, speak to the men
of Judah and to the inhabitants of Je-
rusalem, saying, 'Thus says the LORD:
"Behold, I am fashioning a disaster and
devising a plan against you. Return now
every one from his evil way, and make
your ways and your doings good." ' "

God's Warning Rejected

12And they said, "That is hopeless! So we will walk according to our own plans, and we will every one obey the dictates of his evil heart."

13Therefore thus says the LORD:

"Ask now among the Gentiles,
Who has heard such things?
The virgin of Israel has done a very horrible thing.
14 Will *a man* leave the snow water of Lebanon,
Which comes from the rock of the field?
Will the cold flowing waters be forsaken for strange waters?

15 "Because My people have forgotten Me,
They have burned incense to worthless idols.
And they have caused themselves to stumble in their ways,
From the ancient paths,
To walk in pathways and not on a highway,
16 To make their land desolate *and* a perpetual hissing;
Everyone who passes by it will be astonished
And shake his head.
17 I will scatter them as with an east wind before the enemy;
I will show them[a] the back and not the face
In the day of their calamity."

Jeremiah Persecuted

18Then they said, "Come and let us devise plans against Jeremiah; for the law shall not perish from the priest, nor counsel from the wise, nor the word from the prophet. Come and let us attack him with the tongue, and let us not give heed to any of his words."

19 Give heed to me, O LORD,
And listen to the voice of those who contend with me!
20 Shall evil be repaid for good?
For they have dug a pit for my life.
Remember that I stood before You
To speak good for them,
To turn away Your wrath from them.
21 Therefore deliver up their children to the famine,
And pour out their *blood*
By the force of the sword;
Let their wives *become* widows
And bereaved of their children.
Let their men be put to death,
Their young men *be* slain
By the sword in battle.
22 Let a cry be heard from their houses,
When You bring a troop suddenly upon them;
For they have dug a pit to take me,
And hidden snares for my feet.
23 Yet, LORD, You know all their counsel
Which is against me, to slay *me*.
Provide no atonement for their iniquity,
Nor blot out their sin from Your sight;
But let them be overthrown before You.
Deal *thus* with them
In the time of Your anger.

The Sign of the Broken Flask

19 Thus says the LORD: "Go and
get a potter's earthen flask, and
take some of the elders of the people
and some of the elders of the priests.
2And go out to the Valley of the Son
of Hinnom, which *is* by the entry of
the Potsherd Gate; and proclaim there
the words that I will tell you, 3and say,
'Hear the word of the LORD, O kings of
Judah and inhabitants of Jerusalem.
Thus says the LORD of hosts, the God
of Israel: "Behold, I will bring such a
catastrophe on this place, that whoever
hears of it, his ears will tingle.
4"Because they have forsaken Me and
made this an alien place, because they
have burned incense in it to other gods
whom neither they, their fathers, nor
the kings of Judah have known, and
have filled this place with the blood of

18:17 [a] Following Septuagint, Syriac, Targum, and Vulgate; Masoretic Text reads *look them in*.

the innocents 5(they have also built the high places of Baal, to burn their sons with fire *for* burnt offerings to Baal, which I did not command or speak, nor did it come into My mind), 6therefore behold, the days are coming," says the LORD, "that this place shall no more be called Tophet or the Valley of the Son of Hinnom, but the Valley of Slaughter. 7And I will make void the counsel of Judah and Jerusalem in this place, and I will cause them to fall by the sword before their enemies and by the hands of those who seek their lives; their corpses I will give as meat for the birds of the heaven and for the beasts of the earth. 8I will make this city desolate and a hissing; everyone who passes by it will be astonished and hiss because of all its plagues. 9And I will cause them to eat the flesh of their sons and the flesh of their daughters, and everyone shall eat the flesh of his friend in the siege and in the desperation with which their enemies and those who seek their lives shall drive them to despair." '

10"Then you shall break the flask in the sight of the men who go with you, 11and say to them, 'Thus says the LORD of hosts: "Even so I will break this people and this city, as *one* breaks a potter's vessel, which cannot be made whole again; and they shall bury *them* in Tophet till *there is* no place to bury. 12Thus I will do to this place," says the LORD, "and to its inhabitants, and make this city like Tophet. 13And the houses of Jerusalem and the houses of the kings of Judah shall be defiled like the place of Tophet, because of all the houses on whose roofs they have burned incense to all the host of heaven, and poured out drink offerings to other gods." ' "

14Then Jeremiah came from Tophet, where the LORD had sent him to prophesy; and he stood in the court of the LORD's house and said to all the people, 15"Thus says the LORD of hosts, the God of Israel: 'Behold, I will bring on this city and on all her towns all the doom that I have pronounced against it, because they have stiffened their necks that they might not hear My words.' "

The Word of God to Pashhur

20 Now Pashhur the son of Immer, the priest who *was* also chief governor in the house of the LORD, heard that Jeremiah prophesied these things. 2Then Pashhur struck Jeremiah the prophet, and put him in the stocks that *were* in the high gate of Benjamin, which *was* by the house of the LORD.

3And it happened on the next day that Pashhur brought Jeremiah out of the stocks. Then Jeremiah said to him, "The LORD has not called your name Pashhur, but Magor-Missabib.[a] 4For thus says the LORD: 'Behold, I will make you a terror to yourself and to all your friends; and they shall fall by the sword of their enemies, and your eyes shall see *it*. I will give all Judah into the hand of the king of Babylon, and he shall carry them captive to Babylon and slay them with the sword. 5Moreover I will deliver all the wealth of this city, all its produce, and all its precious things; all the treasures of the kings of Judah I will give into the hand of their enemies, who will plunder them, seize them, and carry them to Babylon. 6And you, Pashhur, and all who dwell in your house, shall go into captivity. You shall go to Babylon, and there you shall die, and be buried there, you and all your friends, to whom you have prophesied lies.' "

Jeremiah's Unpopular Ministry

7 O LORD, You induced me, and I was persuaded;
You are stronger than I, and have prevailed.
I am in derision daily;
Everyone mocks me.
8 For when I spoke, I cried out;
I shouted, "Violence and plunder!"
Because the word of the LORD was made to me
A reproach and a derision daily.
9 Then I said, "I will not make mention of Him,
Nor speak anymore in His name."
But *His word* was in my heart like a burning fire
Shut up in my bones;

20:3 [a] Literally *Fear on Every Side*

I was weary of holding *it* back,
And I could not.
10 For I heard many mocking:
"Fear on every side!"
"Report," *they say,* "and we will report it!"
All my acquaintances watched for my stumbling, *saying,*
"Perhaps he can be induced;
Then we will prevail against him,
And we will take our revenge on him."

11 But the LORD *is* with me as a mighty, awesome One.
Therefore my persecutors will stumble, and will not prevail.
They will be greatly ashamed, for they will not prosper.
Their everlasting confusion will never be forgotten.
12 But, O LORD of hosts,
You who test the righteous,
And see the mind and heart,
Let me see Your vengeance on them;
For I have pleaded my cause before You.

13 Sing to the LORD! Praise the LORD!
For He has delivered the life of the poor
From the hand of evildoers.

14 Cursed *be* the day in which I was born!
Let the day not be blessed in which my mother bore me!
15 Let the man *be* cursed
Who brought news to my father, saying,
"A male child has been born to you!"
Making him very glad.
16 And let that man be like the cities
Which the LORD overthrew, and did not relent;
Let him hear the cry in the morning
And the shouting at noon,
17 Because he did not kill me from the womb,
That my mother might have been my grave,
And her womb always enlarged *with me.*
18 Why did I come forth from the womb to see labor and sorrow,
That my days should be consumed with shame?

Jerusalem's Doom Is Sealed

21 The word which came to Jere-
miah from the LORD when King
Zedekiah sent to him Pashhur the son
of Melchiah, and Zephaniah the son of
Maaseiah, the priest, saying, 2"Please
inquire of the LORD for us, for Nebu-
chadnezzar[a] king of Babylon makes
war against us. Perhaps the LORD will
deal with us according to all His won-
derful works, that *the king* may go away
from us."
3Then Jeremiah said to them, "Thus
you shall say to Zedekiah, 4'Thus says
the LORD God of Israel: "Behold, I will
turn back the weapons of war that *are*
in your hands, with which you fight
against the king of Babylon and the
Chaldeans[a] who besiege you outside
the walls; and I will assemble them in
the midst of this city. 5I Myself will fight
against you with an outstretched hand
and with a strong arm, even in anger
and fury and great wrath. 6I will strike
the inhabitants of this city, both man
and beast; they shall die of a great pes-
tilence. 7And afterward," says the LORD,
"I will deliver Zedekiah king of Judah,
his servants and the people, and such as
are left in this city from the pestilence
and the sword and the famine, into the
hand of Nebuchadnezzar king of Bab-
ylon, into the hand of their enemies,
and into the hand of those who seek
their life; and he shall strike them with
the edge of the sword. He shall not spare
them, or have pity or mercy." '
8"Now you shall say to this people,
'Thus says the LORD: "Behold, I set be-
fore you the way of life and the way
of death. 9He who remains in this city
shall die by the sword, by famine, and
by pestilence; but he who goes out and
defects to the Chaldeans who besiege
you, he shall live, and his life shall be

21:2 [a] Hebrew *Nebuchadrezzar,* and so elsewhere 21:4 [a] Or *Babylonians*

as a prize to him. 10For I have set My
face against this city for adversity and
not for good," says the LORD. "It shall
be given into the hand of the king of
Babylon, and he shall burn it with fire." '

Message to the House of David

11"And concerning the house of the
king of Judah, *say,* 'Hear the word of
the LORD, 12O house of David! Thus says
the LORD:

"Execute judgment in the morning;
And deliver *him who is* plundered
Out of the hand of the oppressor,
Lest My fury go forth like fire
And burn so that no one can
quench *it,*
Because of the evil of your doings.

13 "Behold, I *am* against you,
O inhabitant of the valley,
And rock of the plain," says the
LORD,
"Who say, 'Who shall come down
against us?
Or who shall enter our dwellings?'
14 But I will punish you according
to the fruit of your doings,"
says the LORD;
"I will kindle a fire in its forest,
And it shall devour all things
around it." ' "

22

Thus says the LORD: "Go down to
the house of the king of Judah,
and there speak this word, 2and say,
'Hear the word of the LORD, O king of
Judah, you who sit on the throne of
David, you and your servants and your
people who enter these gates! 3Thus says
the LORD: "Execute judgment and righ-
teousness, and deliver the plundered
out of the hand of the oppressor. Do
no wrong and do no violence to the
stranger, the fatherless, or the widow,
nor shed innocent blood in this place.
4For if you indeed do this thing, then
shall enter the gates of this house, rid-
ing on horses and in chariots, accom-
panied by servants and people, kings
who sit on the throne of David. 5But if
you will not hear these words, I swear
by Myself," says the LORD, "that this
house shall become a desolation." ' "
6For thus says the LORD to the house
of the king of Judah:

"You *are* Gilead to Me,
The head of Lebanon;
Yet I surely will make you a
wilderness,
Cities *which* are not inhabited.
7 I will prepare destroyers against
you,
Everyone with his weapons;
They shall cut down your choice
cedars
And cast *them* into the fire.

8And many nations will pass by this
city; and everyone will say to his neigh-
bor, 'Why has the LORD done so to this
great city?' 9Then they will answer, 'Be-
cause they have forsaken the covenant
of the LORD their God, and worshiped
other gods and served them.' "

10 Weep not for the dead, nor
bemoan him;
Weep bitterly for him who goes
away,
For he shall return no more,
Nor see his native country.

Message to the Sons of Josiah

11For thus says the LORD concerning
Shallum[a] the son of Josiah, king of
Judah, who reigned instead of Josiah
his father, who went from this place: "He
shall not return here anymore, 12but he
shall die in the place where they have
led him captive, and shall see this land
no more.

13 "Woe to him who builds his house
by unrighteousness
And his chambers by injustice,
Who uses his neighbor's service
without wages
And gives him nothing for his
work,
14 Who says, 'I will build myself a
wide house with spacious
chambers,
And cut out windows for it,

22:11 [a] Also called *Jehoahaz*

Paneling *it* with cedar
And painting *it* with vermilion.'

15 "Shall you reign because you
enclose *yourself* in cedar?
Did not your father eat and drink,
And do justice and righteousness?
Then *it was* well with him.
16 He judged the cause of the poor
and needy;
Then *it was* well.
Was not this knowing Me?" says
the LORD.
17 "Yet your eyes and your heart
are for nothing but your
covetousness,
For shedding innocent blood,
And practicing oppression and
violence."

18Therefore thus says the LORD con-
cerning Jehoiakim the son of Josiah,
king of Judah:

"They shall not lament for him,
Saying, 'Alas, my brother!' or 'Alas,
my sister!'

"They shall not lament for him,
Saying, 'Alas, master!' or 'Alas, his
glory!'
19 He shall be buried with the burial
of a donkey,
Dragged and cast out beyond the
gates of Jerusalem.

20 "Go up to Lebanon, and cry out,
And lift up your voice in Bashan;
Cry from Abarim,
For all your lovers are destroyed.
21 I spoke to you in your
prosperity,
But you said, 'I will not hear.'
This *has been* your manner from
your youth,
That you did not obey My voice.
22 The wind shall eat up all your
rulers,
And your lovers shall go into
captivity;
Surely then you will be ashamed
and humiliated
For all your wickedness.
23 O inhabitant of Lebanon,
Making your nest in the cedars,
How gracious will you be when
pangs come upon you,
Like the pain of a woman in
labor?

Message to Coniah

24"*As* I live," says the LORD, "though
Coniah[a] the son of Jehoiakim, king
of Judah, were the signet on My right
hand, yet I would pluck you off; 25and
I will give you into the hand of those
who seek your life, and into the hand *of*
those whose face you fear—the hand of
Nebuchadnezzar king of Babylon and
the hand of the Chaldeans. 26So I will
cast you out, and your mother who bore
you, into another country where you
were not born; and there you shall die.
27But to the land to which they desire
to return, there they shall not return.

28 "Is this man Coniah a despised,
broken idol—
A vessel in which *is* no pleasure?
Why are they cast out, he and his
descendants,
And cast into a land which they
do not know?
29 O earth, earth, earth,
Hear the word of the LORD!
30 Thus says the LORD:
'Write this man down as childless,
A man *who* shall not prosper in
his days;
For none of his descendants shall
prosper,
Sitting on the throne of David,
And ruling anymore in Judah.' "

The Branch of Righteousness

23 "Woe to the shepherds who de-
stroy and scatter the sheep of
My pasture!" says the LORD. 2There-
fore thus says the LORD God of Israel
against the shepherds who feed My
people: "You have scattered My flock,
driven them away, and not attended to
them. Behold, I will attend to you for
the evil of your doings," says the LORD.
3"But I will gather the remnant of My
flock out of all countries where I have

22:24 [a] Also called *Jeconiah* and *Jehoiachin*

driven them, and bring them back to
their folds; and they shall be fruitful and
increase. 4I will set up shepherds over
them who will feed them; and they shall
fear no more, nor be dismayed, nor
shall they be lacking," says the LORD.

5 "Behold, *the* days are coming," says
the LORD,
"That I will raise to David a Branch
of righteousness;
A King shall reign and prosper,
And execute judgment and
righteousness in the earth.
6 In His days Judah will be saved,
And Israel will dwell safely;
Now this *is* His name by which He
will be called:

THE LORD OUR
RIGHTEOUSNESS.[a]

7"Therefore, behold, *the* days are com-
ing," says the LORD, "that they shall
no longer say, 'As the LORD lives who
brought up the children of Israel from
the land of Egypt,' 8but, 'As the LORD
lives who brought up and led the de-
scendants of the house of Israel from
the north country and from all the
countries where I had driven them.'
And they shall dwell in their own land."

False Prophets and Empty Oracles

9 My heart within me is broken
Because of the prophets;
All my bones shake.
I am like a drunken man,
And like a man whom wine has
overcome,
Because of the LORD,
And because of His holy words.
10 For the land is full of
adulterers;
For because of a curse the land
mourns.
The pleasant places of the
wilderness are dried up.
Their course of life is evil,
And their might *is* not right.

11 "For both prophet and priest are
profane;
Yes, in My house I have found their
wickedness," says the LORD.
12 "Therefore their way shall be to
them
Like slippery *ways;*
In the darkness they shall be
driven on
And fall in them;
For I will bring disaster on them,
The year of their punishment,"
says the LORD.
13 "And I have seen folly in the
prophets of Samaria:
They prophesied by Baal
And caused My people Israel to
err.
14 Also I have seen a horrible thing
in the prophets of Jerusalem:
They commit adultery and walk
in lies;
They also strengthen the hands of
evildoers,
So that no one turns back from
his wickedness.
All of them are like Sodom to Me,
And her inhabitants like
Gomorrah.

15"Therefore thus says the LORD of
hosts concerning the prophets:

'Behold, I will feed them with
wormwood,
And make them drink the water
of gall;
For from the prophets of
Jerusalem
Profaneness has gone out into all
the land.' "

16Thus says the LORD of hosts:

"Do not listen to the words of the
prophets who prophesy to
you.
They make you worthless;
They speak a vision of their own
heart,
Not from the mouth of the LORD.
17 They continually say to those who
despise Me,
'The LORD has said, "You shall have
peace" ';

23:6 a Hebrew *YHWH Tsidkenu*

And *to* everyone who walks
according to the dictates of
his own heart, they say,
'No evil shall come upon you.' "

18 For who has stood in the counsel
of the LORD,
And has perceived and heard His
word?
Who has marked His word and
heard *it?*
19 Behold, a whirlwind of the LORD
has gone forth in fury—
A violent whirlwind!
It will fall violently on the head of
the wicked.
20 The anger of the LORD will not
turn back
Until He has executed and
performed the thoughts of
His heart.
In the latter days you will
understand it perfectly.

21 "I have not sent these prophets, yet
they ran.
I have not spoken to them, yet
they prophesied.
22 But if they had stood in My
counsel,
And had caused My people to
hear My words,
Then they would have turned
them from their evil way
And from the evil of their doings.

23 "*Am* I a God near at hand," says the
LORD,
"And not a God afar off?
24 Can anyone hide himself in secret
places,
So I shall not see him?" says the
LORD;
"Do I not fill heaven and earth?"
says the LORD.

25"I have heard what the prophets
have said who prophesy lies in My
name, saying, 'I have dreamed, I have
dreamed!' 26How long will *this* be in the
heart of the prophets who prophesy
lies? Indeed *they are* prophets of the
deceit of their own heart, 27who try to
make My people forget My name by
their dreams which everyone tells his
neighbor, as their fathers forgot My
name for Baal.

28 "The prophet who has a dream, let
him tell a dream;
And he who has My word, let him
speak My word faithfully.
What *is* the chaff to the wheat?"
says the LORD.
29 "*Is* not My word like a fire?" says the
LORD,
"And like a hammer *that* breaks the
rock in pieces?

30"Therefore behold, I *am* against the
prophets," says the LORD, "who steal
My words every one from his neigh-
bor. 31Behold, I *am* against the proph-
ets," says the LORD, "who use their
tongues and say, 'He says.' 32Behold, I
am against those who prophesy false
dreams," says the LORD, "and tell them,
and cause My people to err by their lies
and by their recklessness. Yet I did not
send them or command them; therefore
they shall not profit this people at all,"
says the LORD.
33"So when these people or the prophet
or the priest ask you, saying, 'What
is the oracle of the LORD?' you shall
then say to them, 'What oracle?'[a] I
will even forsake you," says the LORD.
34"And *as for* the prophet and the priest
and the people who say, 'The oracle
of the LORD!' I will even punish that
man and his house. 35Thus every one
of you shall say to his neighbor, and
every one to his brother, 'What has the
LORD answered?' and, 'What has the
LORD spoken?' 36And the oracle of
the LORD you shall mention no more.
For every man's word will be his oracle,
for you have perverted the words of the
living God, the LORD of hosts, our God.
37Thus you shall say to the prophet, 'What
has the LORD answered you?' and, 'What
has the LORD spoken?' 38But since you
say, 'The oracle of the LORD!' therefore
thus says the LORD: 'Because you say
this word, "The oracle of the LORD!" and
I have sent to you, saying, "Do not say,

23:33 [a] Septuagint, Targum, and Vulgate read '*You are the burden.*'

'The oracle of the LORD!' " 39therefore behold, I, even I, will utterly forget you and forsake you, and the city that I gave you and your fathers, and *will cast you* out of My presence. 40And I will bring an everlasting reproach upon you, and a perpetual shame, which shall not be forgotten.' "

The Sign of Two Baskets of Figs

24 The LORD showed me, and there were two baskets of figs set before the temple of the LORD, after Nebuchadnezzar king of Babylon had carried away captive Jeconiah the son of Jehoiakim, king of Judah, and the princes of Judah with the craftsmen and smiths, from Jerusalem, and had brought them to Babylon. 2One basket *had* very good figs, like the figs *that are* first ripe; and the other basket *had* very bad figs which could not be eaten, they were so bad. 3Then the LORD said to me, "What do you see, Jeremiah?"

And I said, "Figs, the good figs, very good; and the bad, very bad, which cannot be eaten, they are so bad."

4Again the word of the LORD came to me, saying, 5"Thus says the LORD, the God of Israel: 'Like these good figs, so will I acknowledge those who are carried away captive from Judah, whom I have sent out of this place for *their own* good, into the land of the Chaldeans. 6For I will set My eyes on them for good, and I will bring them back to this land; I will build them and not pull *them* down, and I will plant them and not pluck *them* up. 7Then I will give them a heart to know Me, that I *am* the LORD; and they shall be My people, and I will be their God, for they shall return to Me with their whole heart.

8'And as the bad figs which cannot be eaten, they are so bad'—surely thus says the LORD—'so will I give up Zedekiah the king of Judah, his princes, the residue of Jerusalem who remain in this land, and those who dwell in the land of Egypt. 9I will deliver them to trouble into all the kingdoms of the earth, for *their* harm, *to be* a reproach and a byword, a taunt and a curse, in all places where I shall drive them. 10And I will send the sword, the famine, and the pestilence among them, till they are consumed from the land that I gave to them and their fathers.' "

Seventy Years of Desolation

25 The word that came to Jeremiah concerning all the people of Judah, in the fourth year of Jehoiakim the son of Josiah, king of Judah (which *was* the first year of Nebuchadnezzar king of Babylon), 2which Jeremiah the prophet spoke to all the people of Judah and to all the inhabitants of Jerusalem, saying: 3"From the thirteenth year of Josiah the son of Amon, king of Judah, even to this day, this *is* the twenty-third year in which the word of the LORD has come to me; and I have spoken to you, rising early and speaking, but you have not listened. 4And the LORD has sent to you all His servants the prophets, rising early and sending *them,* but you have not listened nor inclined your ear to hear. 5They said, 'Repent now everyone of his evil way and his evil doings, and dwell in the land that the LORD has given to you and your fathers forever and ever. 6Do not go after other gods to serve them and worship them, and do not provoke Me to anger with the works of your hands; and I will not harm you.' 7Yet you have not listened to Me," says the LORD, "that you might provoke Me to anger with the works of your hands to your own hurt.

8"Therefore thus says the LORD of hosts: 'Because you have not heard My words, 9behold, I will send and take all the families of the north,' says the LORD, 'and Nebuchadnezzar the king of Babylon, My servant, and will bring them against this land, against its inhabitants, and against these nations all around, and will utterly destroy them, and make them an astonishment, a hissing, and perpetual desolations. 10Moreover I will take from them the voice of mirth and the voice of gladness, the voice of the bridegroom and the voice of the bride, the sound of the millstones and the light of the lamp. 11And this whole land shall be a desolation *and* an astonishment, and these nations shall serve the king of Babylon seventy years.

12'Then it will come to pass, when sev-
enty years are completed, *that* I will
punish the king of Babylon and that
nation, the land of the Chaldeans, for
their iniquity,' says the LORD; 'and I will
make it a perpetual desolation. 13So I
will bring on that land all My words
which I have pronounced against it,
all that is written in this book, which
Jeremiah has prophesied concerning
all the nations. 14(For many nations
and great kings shall be served by them
also; and I will repay them according to
their deeds and according to the works
of their own hands.)' "

Judgment on the Nations

15For thus says the LORD God of Israel to
me: "Take this wine cup of fury from My
hand, and cause all the nations, to whom
I send you, to drink it. 16And they will
drink and stagger and go mad because of
the sword that I will send among them."
17Then I took the cup from the LORD's
hand, and made all the nations drink,
to whom the LORD had sent me: 18Jeru-
salem and the cities of Judah, its kings
and its princes, to make them a desola-
tion, an astonishment, a hissing, and a
curse, as *it is* this day; 19Pharaoh king
of Egypt, his servants, his princes, and
all his people; 20all the mixed multi-
tude, all the kings of the land of Uz, all
the kings of the land of the Philistines
(namely, Ashkelon, Gaza, Ekron, and
the remnant of Ashdod); 21Edom, Moab,
and the people of Ammon; 22all the
kings of Tyre, all the kings of Sidon,
and the kings of the coastlands which
are across the sea; 23Dedan, Tema, Buz,
and all *who are* in the farthest corners;
24all the kings of Arabia and all the
kings of the mixed multitude who dwell
in the desert; 25all the kings of Zimri, all
the kings of Elam, and all the kings of the
Medes; 26all the kings of the north, far
and near, one with another; and all the
kingdoms of the world which *are* on the
face of the earth. Also the king of She-
shach[a] shall drink after them.
27"Therefore you shall say to them,
'Thus says the LORD of hosts, the God of
Israel: "Drink, be drunk, and vomit! Fall
and rise no more, because of the sword
which I will send among you." ' 28And
it shall be, if they refuse to take the cup
from your hand to drink, then you shall
say to them, 'Thus says the LORD of
hosts: "You shall certainly drink! 29For
behold, I begin to bring calamity on the
city which is called by My name, and
should you be utterly unpunished? You
shall not be unpunished, for I will call
for a sword on all the inhabitants of the
earth," says the LORD of hosts.'
30"Therefore prophesy against them
all these words, and say to them:

'The LORD will roar from on high,
And utter His voice from His holy
habitation;
He will roar mightily against His
fold.
He will give a shout, as those who
tread *the grapes,*
Against all the inhabitants of the
earth.
31 A noise will come to the ends of
the earth—
For the LORD has a controversy
with the nations;
He will plead His case with all
flesh.
He will give those *who are* wicked
to the sword,' says the LORD."

32Thus says the LORD of hosts:

"Behold, disaster shall go forth
From nation to nation,
And a great whirlwind shall be
raised up
From the farthest parts of the
earth.

33And at that day the slain of the LORD
shall be from *one* end of the earth even
to the *other* end of the earth. They shall
not be lamented, or gathered, or buried;
they shall become refuse on the ground.

34 "Wail, shepherds, and cry!
Roll about *in the ashes,*
You leaders of the flock!
For the days of your slaughter and
your dispersions are fulfilled;

25:26 [a] A code word for Babylon (compare 51:41)

You shall fall like a precious
vessel.
35 And the shepherds will have no
way to flee,
Nor the leaders of the flock to
escape.
36 A voice of the cry of the
shepherds,
And a wailing of the leaders to the
flock *will be heard.*
For the LORD has plundered their
pasture,
37 And the peaceful dwellings are
cut down
Because of the fierce anger of the
LORD.
38 He has left His lair like the lion;
For their land is desolate
Because of the fierceness of the
Oppressor,
And because of His fierce anger."

Jeremiah Saved from Death

26 In the beginning of the reign
of Jehoiakim the son of Josiah,
king of Judah, this word came from the
LORD, saying, 2"Thus says the LORD:
'Stand in the court of the LORD's house,
and speak to all the cities of Judah,
which come to worship *in* the LORD's
house, all the words that I command
you to speak to them. Do not diminish
a word. 3Perhaps everyone will listen
and turn from his evil way, that I may
relent concerning the calamity which
I purpose to bring on them because of
the evil of their doings.' 4And you shall
say to them, 'Thus says the LORD: "If you
will not listen to Me, to walk in My law
which I have set before you, 5to heed
the words of My servants the prophets
whom I sent to you, both rising up early
and sending *them* (but you have not
heeded), 6then I will make this house
like Shiloh, and will make this city a
curse to all the nations of the earth." ' "
7So the priests and the prophets and
all the people heard Jeremiah speaking
these words in the house of the LORD.
8Now it happened, when Jeremiah had
made an end of speaking all that the
LORD had commanded *him* to speak
to all the people, that the priests and
the prophets and all the people seized
him, saying, "You will surely die! 9Why
have you prophesied in the name of the
LORD, saying, 'This house shall be like
Shiloh, and this city shall be desolate,
without an inhabitant'?" And all the
people were gathered against Jeremiah
in the house of the LORD.
10When the princes of Judah heard
these things, they came up from the
king's house to the house of the LORD
and sat down in the entry of the New
Gate of the LORD's *house.* 11And the
priests and the prophets spoke to the
princes and all the people, saying, "This
man deserves to die! For he has prophe-
sied against this city, as you have heard
with your ears."
12Then Jeremiah spoke to all the princ-
es and all the people, saying: "The LORD
sent me to prophesy against this house
and against this city with all the words
that you have heard. 13Now therefore,
amend your ways and your doings, and
obey the voice of the LORD your God;
then the LORD will relent concerning the
doom that He has pronounced against
you. 14As for me, here I am, in your hand;
do with me as seems good and proper to
you. 15But know for certain that if you
put me to death, you will surely bring
innocent blood on yourselves, on this
city, and on its inhabitants; for truly
the LORD has sent me to you to speak
all these words in your hearing."
16So the princes and all the people
said to the priests and the prophets,
"This man does not deserve to die. For
he has spoken to us in the name of the
LORD our God."
17Then certain of the elders of the land
rose up and spoke to all the assembly
of the people, saying: 18"Micah of Mo-
resheth prophesied in the days of Heze-
kiah king of Judah, and spoke to all the
people of Judah, saying, 'Thus says the
LORD of hosts:

"Zion shall be plowed *like* a field,
Jerusalem shall become heaps of
ruins,
And the mountain of the temple[a]
Like the bare hills of the forest." '[b]

26:18 [a] Literally *house* [b] Compare Micah 3:12

19 Did Hezekiah king of Judah and all
Judah ever put him to death? Did he
not fear the LORD and seek the LORD's
favor? And the LORD relented concern-
ing the doom which He had pronounced
against them. But we are doing great
evil against ourselves."

20 Now there was also a man who
prophesied in the name of the LORD,
Urijah the son of Shemaiah of Kirjath
Jearim, who prophesied against this
city and against this land according
to all the words of Jeremiah. 21 And
when Jehoiakim the king, with all his
mighty men and all the princes, heard
his words, the king sought to put him
to death; but when Urijah heard *it,* he
was afraid and fled, and went to Egypt.
22 Then Jehoiakim the king sent men to
Egypt: Elnathan the son of Achbor, and
other men *who went* with him to Egypt.
23 And they brought Urijah from Egypt
and brought him to Jehoiakim the king,
who killed him with the sword and cast
his dead body into the graves of the
common people.

24 Nevertheless the hand of Ahikam the
son of Shaphan was with Jeremiah, so
that they should not give him into the
hand of the people to put him to death.

Symbol of the Bonds and Yokes

27 In the beginning of the reign
of Jehoiakim[a] the son of Jo-
siah, king of Judah, this word came
to Jeremiah from the LORD, saying,[b]
2 "Thus says the LORD to me: 'Make for
yourselves bonds and yokes, and put
them on your neck, 3 and send them
to the king of Edom, the king of Moab,
the king of the Ammonites, the king
of Tyre, and the king of Sidon, by the
hand of the messengers who come to
Jerusalem to Zedekiah king of Judah.
4 And command them to say to their
masters, "Thus says the LORD of hosts,
the God of Israel—thus you shall say to
your masters: 5 'I have made the earth,
the man and the beast that *are* on the
ground, by My great power and by My
outstretched arm, and have given it to
whom it seemed proper to Me. 6 And
now I have given all these lands into
the hand of Nebuchadnezzar the king
of Babylon, My servant; and the beasts
of the field I have also given him to
serve him. 7 So all nations shall serve
him and his son and his son's son, until
the time of his land comes; and then
many nations and great kings shall
make him serve them. 8 And it shall be,
that the nation and kingdom which will
not serve Nebuchadnezzar the king of
Babylon, and which will not put its neck
under the yoke of the king of Babylon,
that nation I will punish,' says the LORD,
'with the sword, the famine, and the
pestilence, until I have consumed them
by his hand. 9 Therefore do not listen
to your prophets, your diviners, your
dreamers, your soothsayers, or your
sorcerers, who speak to you, saying,
"You shall not serve the king of Bab-
ylon." 10 For they prophesy a lie to you,
to remove you far from your land; and
I will drive you out, and you will perish.
11 But the nations that bring their necks
under the yoke of the king of Babylon
and serve him, I will let them remain
in their own land,' says the LORD, 'and
they shall till it and dwell in it.' " ' "

12 I also spoke to Zedekiah king of
Judah according to all these words,
saying, "Bring your necks under the
yoke of the king of Babylon, and serve
him and his people, and live! 13 Why will
you die, you and your people, by the
sword, by the famine, and by the pes-
tilence, as the LORD has spoken against
the nation that will not serve the king
of Babylon? 14 Therefore do not listen
to the words of the prophets who speak
to you, saying, 'You shall not serve the
king of Babylon,' for they prophesy a
lie to you; 15 for I have not sent them,"
says the LORD, "yet they prophesy a lie
in My name, that I may drive you out,
and that you may perish, you and the
prophets who prophesy to you."

16 Also I spoke to the priests and to
all this people, saying, "Thus says the
LORD: 'Do not listen to the words of your
prophets who prophesy to you, saying,
"Behold, the vessels of the LORD's house
will now shortly be brought back from
Babylon"; for they prophesy a lie to you.

27:1 [a] Following Masoretic Text, Targum, and Vulgate; some Hebrew manuscripts, Arabic, and Syriac read *Zedekiah* (compare 27:3, 12; 28:1). [b] Septuagint omits verse 1.

17Do not listen to them; serve the king of
Babylon, and live! Why should this city
be laid waste? 18But if they *are* prophets,
and if the word of the LORD is with them,
let them now make intercession to the
LORD of hosts, that the vessels which
are left in the house of the LORD, *in* the
house of the king of Judah, and at Je-
rusalem, do not go to Babylon.'
19"For thus says the LORD of hosts con-
cerning the pillars, concerning the Sea,
concerning the carts, and concerning
the remainder of the vessels that re-
main in this city, 20which Nebuchad-
nezzar king of Babylon did not take,
when he carried away captive Jeconiah
the son of Jehoiakim, king of Judah,
from Jerusalem to Babylon, and all the
nobles of Judah and Jerusalem— 21yes,
thus says the LORD of hosts, the God
of Israel, concerning the vessels that
remain in the house of the LORD, and
in the house of the king of Judah and of
Jerusalem: 22'They shall be carried to
Babylon, and there they shall be until
the day that I visit them,' says the LORD.
'Then I will bring them up and restore
them to this place.' "

Hananiah's Falsehood and Doom

28 And it happened in the same
year, at the beginning of the
reign of Zedekiah king of Judah, in the
fourth year *and* in the fifth month, *that*
Hananiah the son of Azur the prophet,
who *was* from Gibeon, spoke to me in
the house of the LORD in the presence of
the priests and of all the people, saying,
2"Thus speaks the LORD of hosts, the
God of Israel, saying: 'I have broken the
yoke of the king of Babylon. 3Within two
full years I will bring back to this place
all the vessels of the LORD's house, that
Nebuchadnezzar king of Babylon took
away from this place and carried to
Babylon. 4And I will bring back to this
place Jeconiah the son of Jehoiakim,
king of Judah, with all the captives of
Judah who went to Babylon,' says the
LORD, 'for I will break the yoke of the
king of Babylon.' "
5Then the prophet Jeremiah spoke to
the prophet Hananiah in the presence
of the priests and in the presence of all
the people who stood in the house of
the LORD, 6and the prophet Jeremiah
said, "Amen! The LORD do so; the LORD
perform your words which you have
prophesied, to bring back the vessels of
the LORD's house and all who were car-
ried away captive, from Babylon to this
place. 7Nevertheless hear now this word
that I speak in your hearing and in the
hearing of all the people: 8The prophets
who have been before me and before you
of old prophesied against many coun-
tries and great kingdoms—of war and di-
saster and pestilence. 9As for the prophet
who prophesies of peace, when the
word of the prophet comes to pass, the
prophet will be known *as* one whom
the LORD has truly sent."
10Then Hananiah the prophet took the
yoke off the prophet Jeremiah's neck
and broke it. 11And Hananiah spoke
in the presence of all the people, say-
ing, "Thus says the LORD: 'Even so I will
break the yoke of Nebuchadnezzar king
of Babylon from the neck of all nations
within the space of two full years.' " And
the prophet Jeremiah went his way.
12Now the word of the LORD came to
Jeremiah, after Hananiah the prophet
had broken the yoke from the neck of
the prophet Jeremiah, saying, 13"Go
and tell Hananiah, saying, 'Thus says
the LORD: "You have broken the yokes
of wood, but you have made in their
place yokes of iron." 14For thus says
the LORD of hosts, the God of Israel: "I
have put a yoke of iron on the neck of
all these nations, that they may serve
Nebuchadnezzar king of Babylon; and
they shall serve him. I have given him
the beasts of the field also." ' "
15Then the prophet Jeremiah said
to Hananiah the prophet, "Hear now,
Hananiah, the LORD has not sent you,
but you make this people trust in a lie.
16Therefore thus says the LORD: 'Behold,
I will cast you from the face of the earth.
This year you shall die, because you have
taught rebellion against the LORD.' "
17So Hananiah the prophet died the
same year in the seventh month.

Jeremiah's Letter to the Captives

29 Now these *are* the words of the
letter that Jeremiah the prophet
sent from Jerusalem to the remainder

of the elders who were carried away
captive—to the priests, the prophets,
and all the people whom Nebuchadnez-
zar had carried away captive from Jeru-
salem to Babylon. 2(This happened after
Jeconiah the king, the queen mother,
the eunuchs, the princes of Judah and
Jerusalem, the craftsmen, and the
smiths had departed from Jerusalem.)
3*The letter was sent* by the hand of Ela-
sah the son of Shaphan, and Gemariah
the son of Hilkiah, whom Zedekiah king
of Judah sent to Babylon, to Nebuchad-
nezzar king of Babylon, saying,

4 Thus says the LORD of hosts, the
God of Israel, to all who were
carried away captive, whom I
have caused to be carried away
from Jerusalem to Babylon:

5 Build houses and dwell *in them;*
plant gardens and eat their
fruit. 6Take wives and beget
sons and daughters; and take
wives for your sons and give
your daughters to husbands,
so that they may bear sons
and daughters—that you may
be increased there, and not
diminished. 7And seek the peace
of the city where I have caused
you to be carried away captive,
and pray to the LORD for it; for
in its peace you will have peace.
8For thus says the LORD of hosts,
the God of Israel: Do not let your
prophets and your diviners who
are in your midst deceive you, nor
listen to your dreams which you
cause to be dreamed. 9For they
prophesy falsely to you in My
name; I have not sent them, says
the LORD.

10 For thus says the LORD: After
seventy years are completed
at Babylon, I will visit you and
perform My good word toward
you, and cause you to return
to this place. 11For I know the
thoughts that I think toward
you, says the LORD, thoughts of
peace and not of evil, to give you
a future and a hope. 12Then you
will call upon Me and go and
pray to Me, and I will listen to
you. 13And you will seek Me and
find *Me,* when you search for Me
with all your heart. 14I will be
found by you, says the LORD, and
I will bring you back from your
captivity; I will gather you from
all the nations and from all the
places where I have driven you,
says the LORD, and I will bring
you to the place from which I
cause you to be carried away
captive.

15 Because you have said, "The
LORD has raised up prophets
for us in Babylon"— 16therefore
thus says the LORD concerning
the king who sits on the throne
of David, concerning all the
people who dwell in this city,
and concerning your brethren
who have not gone out with you
into captivity— 17thus says the
LORD of hosts: Behold, I will
send on them the sword, the
famine, and the pestilence, and
will make them like rotten figs
that cannot be eaten, they are
so bad. 18And I will pursue them
with the sword, with famine, and
with pestilence; and I will deliver
them to trouble among all the
kingdoms of the earth—to be a
curse, an astonishment, a hissing,
and a reproach among all the
nations where I have driven them,
19because they have not heeded
My words, says the LORD, which
I sent to them by My servants
the prophets, rising up early and
sending *them;* neither would you
heed, says the LORD. 20Therefore
hear the word of the LORD, all you
of the captivity, whom I have sent
from Jerusalem to Babylon.

21 Thus says the LORD of hosts,
the God of Israel, concerning
Ahab the son of Kolaiah, and
Zedekiah the son of Maaseiah,
who prophesy a lie to you in My
name: Behold, I will deliver them
into the hand of Nebuchadnezzar

king of Babylon, and he shall slay
them before your eyes. 22And
because of them a curse shall
be taken up by all the captivity
of Judah who *are* in Babylon,
saying, "The LORD make you
like Zedekiah and Ahab, whom
the king of Babylon roasted in
the fire"; 23because they have
done disgraceful things in Israel,
have committed adultery with
their neighbors' wives, and have
spoken lying words in My name,
which I have not commanded
them. Indeed I know, and *am* a
witness, says the LORD.

24 You shall also speak to Shemaiah
the Nehelamite, saying, 25Thus
speaks the LORD of hosts, the God
of Israel, saying: You have sent
letters in your name to all the
people who *are* at Jerusalem, to
Zephaniah the son of Maaseiah
the priest, and to all the priests,
saying, 26"The LORD has made
you priest instead of Jehoiada
the priest, so that there should be
officers *in* the house of the LORD
over every man *who* is demented
and considers himself a prophet,
that you should put him in prison
and in the stocks. 27Now therefore,
why have you not rebuked
Jeremiah of Anathoth who makes
himself a prophet to you? 28For he
has sent to us *in* Babylon, saying,
'This *captivity is* long; build houses
and dwell *in them,* and plant
gardens and eat their fruit.' "

29Now Zephaniah the priest read this
letter in the hearing of Jeremiah the
prophet. 30Then the word of the LORD
came to Jeremiah, saying: 31Send to
all those in captivity, saying, Thus says
the LORD concerning Shemaiah the
Nehelamite: Because Shemaiah has
prophesied to you, and I have not sent
him, and he has caused you to trust
in a lie— 32therefore thus says the
LORD: Behold, I will punish Shemaiah
the Nehelamite and his family: he shall
not have anyone to dwell among this
people, nor shall he see the good that
I will do for My people, says the LORD,
because he has taught rebellion against
the LORD.

Restoration of Israel and Judah

30 The word that came to Jeremiah from the LORD, saying,
2"Thus speaks the LORD God of Israel,
saying: 'Write in a book for yourself all
the words that I have spoken to you.
3For behold, the days are coming,' says
the LORD, 'that I will bring back from
captivity My people Israel and Judah,'
says the LORD. 'And I will cause them
to return to the land that I gave to their
fathers, and they shall possess it.' "
4Now these *are* the words that the LORD
spoke concerning Israel and Judah.
5"For thus says the LORD:

'We have heard a voice of
trembling,
Of fear, and not of peace.
6 Ask now, and see,
Whether a man is ever in labor
with child?
So why do I see every man *with*
his hands on his loins
Like a woman in labor,
And all faces turned pale?
7 Alas! For that day *is* great,
So that none *is* like it;
And it *is* the time of Jacob's
trouble,
But he shall be saved out of it.

8 'For it shall come to pass in that
day,'
Says the LORD of hosts,
'*That* I will break his yoke from
your neck,
And will burst your bonds;
Foreigners shall no more enslave
them.
9 But they shall serve the LORD
their God,
And David their king,
Whom I will raise up for them.

10 'Therefore do not fear, O My
servant Jacob,' says the
LORD,
'Nor be dismayed, O Israel;
For behold, I will save you from
afar,

And your seed from the land of their captivity.
Jacob shall return, have rest and be quiet,
And no one shall make *him* afraid.
11 For I *am* with you,' says the LORD, 'to save you;
Though I make a full end of all nations where I have scattered you,
Yet I will not make a complete end of you.
But I will correct you in justice,
And will not let you go altogether unpunished.'

12"For thus says the LORD:

'Your affliction *is* incurable,
Your wound *is* severe.
13 *There is* no one to plead your cause,
That you may be bound up;
You have no healing medicines.
14 All your lovers have forgotten you;
They do not seek you;
For I have wounded you with the wound of an enemy,
With the chastisement of a cruel one,
For the multitude of your iniquities,
Because your sins have increased.
15 Why do you cry about your affliction?
Your sorrow *is* incurable.
Because of the multitude of your iniquities,
Because your sins have increased,
I have done these things to you.

16 'Therefore all those who devour you shall be devoured;
And all your adversaries, every one of them, shall go into captivity;
Those who plunder you shall become plunder,
And all who prey upon you I will make a prey.
17 For I will restore health to you
And heal you of your wounds,' says the LORD,
'Because they called you an outcast *saying:*
"This *is* Zion;
No one seeks her." '

18"Thus says the LORD:

'Behold, I will bring back the captivity of Jacob's tents,
And have mercy on his dwelling places;
The city shall be built upon its own mound,
And the palace shall remain according to its own plan.
19 Then out of them shall proceed thanksgiving
And the voice of those who make merry;
I will multiply them, and they shall not diminish;
I will also glorify them, and they shall not be small.
20 Their children also shall be as before,
And their congregation shall be established before Me;
And I will punish all who oppress them.
21 Their nobles shall be from among them,
And their governor shall come from their midst;
Then I will cause him to draw near,
And he shall approach Me;
For who *is* this who pledged his heart to approach Me?' says the LORD.
22 'You shall be My people,
And I will be your God.' "

23 Behold, the whirlwind of the LORD
Goes forth with fury,
A continuing whirlwind;
It will fall violently on the head of the wicked.
24 The fierce anger of the LORD will not return until He has done it,
And until He has performed the intents of His heart.

In the latter days you will consider it.

The Remnant of Israel Saved

31 "At the same time," says the LORD, "I will be the God of all the families of Israel, and they shall be My people."

2Thus says the LORD:

"The people who survived the sword
Found grace in the wilderness—
Israel, when I went to give him rest."

3 The LORD has appeared of old to me, *saying:*
"Yes, I have loved you with an everlasting love;
Therefore with lovingkindness I have drawn you.
4 Again I will build you, and you shall be rebuilt,
O virgin of Israel!
You shall again be adorned with your tambourines,
And shall go forth in the dances of those who rejoice.
5 You shall yet plant vines on the mountains of Samaria;
The planters shall plant and eat *them* as ordinary food.
6 For there shall be a day
When the watchmen will cry on Mount Ephraim,
'Arise, and let us go up *to* Zion,
To the LORD our God.' "

7For thus says the LORD:

"Sing with gladness for Jacob,
And shout among the chief of the nations;
Proclaim, give praise, and say,
'O LORD, save Your people,
The remnant of Israel!'
8 Behold, I will bring them from the north country,
And gather them from the ends of the earth,
Among them the blind and the lame,
The woman with child
And the one who labors with child, together;
A great throng shall return there.
9 They shall come with weeping,
And with supplications I will lead them.
I will cause them to walk by the rivers of waters,
In a straight way in which they shall not stumble;
For I am a Father to Israel,
And Ephraim *is* My firstborn.

10 "Hear the word of the LORD, O nations,
And declare *it* in the isles afar off, and say,
'He who scattered Israel will gather him,
And keep him as a shepherd *does* his flock.'
11 For the LORD has redeemed Jacob,
And ransomed him from the hand of one stronger than he.
12 Therefore they shall come and sing in the height of Zion,
Streaming to the goodness of the LORD—
For wheat and new wine and oil,
For the young of the flock and the herd;
Their souls shall be like a well-watered garden,
And they shall sorrow no more at all.

13 "Then shall the virgin rejoice in the dance,
And the young men and the old, together;
For I will turn their mourning to joy,
Will comfort them,
And make them rejoice rather than sorrow.
14 I will satiate the soul of the priests with abundance,
And My people shall be satisfied with My goodness, says the LORD."

Mercy on Ephraim

15Thus says the LORD:

"A voice was heard in Ramah,
Lamentation *and* bitter weeping,
Rachel weeping for her children,

Refusing to be comforted for her
children,
Because they *are* no more."

16Thus says the LORD:

"Refrain your voice from weeping,
And your eyes from tears;
For your work shall be rewarded,
says the LORD,
And they shall come back from
the land of the enemy.
17 There is hope in your future, says
the LORD,
That *your* children shall come
back to their own border.

18 "I have surely heard Ephraim
bemoaning himself:
'You have chastised me, and I was
chastised,
Like an untrained bull;
Restore me, and I will return,
For You *are* the LORD my God.
19 Surely, after my turning, I
repented;
And after I was instructed, I
struck myself on the thigh;
I was ashamed, yes, even
humiliated,
Because I bore the reproach of
my youth.'
20 *Is* Ephraim My dear son?
Is he a pleasant child?
For though I spoke against him,
I earnestly remember him still;
Therefore My heart yearns for him;
I will surely have mercy on him,
says the LORD.

21 "Set up signposts,
Make landmarks;
Set your heart toward the
highway,
The way in *which* you went.
Turn back, O virgin of Israel,
Turn back to these your cities.
22 How long will you gad about,
O you backsliding daughter?
For the LORD has created a new
thing in the earth—
A woman shall encompass a
man."

Future Prosperity of Judah

23Thus says the LORD of hosts, the
God of Israel: "They shall again use this
speech in the land of Judah and in its
cities, when I bring back their captivity:
'The LORD bless you, O home of justice,
and mountain of holiness!' 24And there
shall dwell in Judah itself, and in all its
cities together, farmers and those going
out with flocks. 25For I have satiated
the weary soul, and I have replenished
every sorrowful soul."
26After this I awoke and looked
around, and my sleep was sweet to me.
27"Behold, the days are coming, says
the LORD, that I will sow the house of
Israel and the house of Judah with
the seed of man and the seed of beast.
28And it shall come to pass, *that* as I
have watched over them to pluck up, to
break down, to throw down, to destroy,
and to afflict, so I will watch over them
to build and to plant, says the LORD.
29In those days they shall say no more:

'The fathers have eaten sour
grapes,
And the children's teeth are set on
edge.'

30But every one shall die for his own
iniquity; every man who eats the sour
grapes, his teeth shall be set on edge.

A New Covenant

31"Behold, the days are coming, says
the LORD, when I will make a new cov-
enant with the house of Israel and with
the house of Judah— 32not according
to the covenant that I made with their
fathers in the day *that* I took them by
the hand to lead them out of the land of
Egypt, My covenant which they broke,
though I was a husband to them,[a] says
the LORD. 33But this *is* the covenant
that I will make with the house of Israel
after those days, says the LORD: I will
put My law in their minds, and write it
on their hearts; and I will be their God,
and they shall be My people. 34No more
shall every man teach his neighbor, and
every man his brother, saying, 'Know
the LORD,' for they all shall know Me,

31:32 [a] Following Masoretic Text, Targum, and Vulgate; Septuagint and Syriac read *and I turned away from them.*

from the least of them to the greatest
of them, says the LORD. For I will for-
give their iniquity, and their sin I will
remember no more."

35 Thus says the LORD,
Who gives the sun for a light by
day,
The ordinances of the moon and
the stars for a light by night,
Who disturbs the sea,
And its waves roar
(The LORD of hosts *is* His name):

36 "If those ordinances depart
From before Me, says the LORD,
Then the seed of Israel shall also
cease
From being a nation before Me
forever."

37Thus says the LORD:

"If heaven above can be measured,
And the foundations of the earth
searched out beneath,
I will also cast off all the seed of
Israel
For all that they have done, says
the LORD.

38"Behold, the days are coming, says
the LORD, that the city shall be built for
the LORD from the Tower of Hananel
to the Corner Gate. 39The surveyor's line
shall again extend straight forward
over the hill Gareb; then it shall turn
toward Goath. 40And the whole valley
of the dead bodies and of the ashes, and
all the fields as far as the Brook Kidron,
to the corner of the Horse Gate toward
the east, *shall be* holy to the LORD. It
shall not be plucked up or thrown down
anymore forever."

Jeremiah Buys a Field

32 The word that came to Jeremi-
ah from the LORD in the tenth
year of Zedekiah king of Judah, which
was the eighteenth year of Nebuchad-
nezzar. 2For then the king of Babylon's
army besieged Jerusalem, and Jeremi-
ah the prophet was shut up in the court
of the prison, which *was in* the king of
Judah's house. 3For Zedekiah king of
Judah had shut him up, saying, "Why
do you prophesy and say, 'Thus says the
LORD: "Behold, I will give this city into
the hand of the king of Babylon, and
he shall take it; 4and Zedekiah king of
Judah shall not escape from the hand
of the Chaldeans, but shall surely be
delivered into the hand of the king of
Babylon, and shall speak with him face
to face,[a] and see him eye to eye; 5then
he shall lead Zedekiah to Babylon, and
there he shall be until I visit him," says
the LORD; "though you fight with the
Chaldeans, you shall not succeed" '?"

6And Jeremiah said, "The word of the
LORD came to me, saying, 7'Behold,
Hanamel the son of Shallum your uncle
will come to you, saying, "Buy my field
which *is* in Anathoth, for the right of
redemption *is* yours to buy *it*." ' 8Then
Hanamel my uncle's son came to me
in the court of the prison according to
the word of the LORD, and said to me,
'Please buy my field that *is* in Anathoth,
which *is* in the country of Benjamin;
for the right of inheritance *is* yours,
and the redemption yours; buy *it* for
yourself.' Then I knew that this was the
word of the LORD. 9So I bought the field
from Hanamel, the son of my uncle
who *was* in Anathoth, and weighed *out
to* him the money—seventeen shekels
of silver. 10And I signed the deed and
sealed *it,* took witnesses, and weighed
the money on the scales. 11So I took
the purchase deed, *both* that which was
sealed *according* to the law and custom,
and that which was open; 12and I gave
the purchase deed to Baruch the son of
Neriah, son of Mahseiah, in the pres-
ence of Hanamel my uncle's *son,* and
in the presence of the witnesses who
signed the purchase deed, before all the
Jews who sat in the court of the prison.

13"Then I charged Baruch before them,
saying, 14'Thus says the LORD of hosts,
the God of Israel: "Take these deeds,
both this purchase deed which is sealed
and this deed which is open, and put
them in an earthen vessel, that they
may last many days." 15For thus says

32:4 [a] Literally *mouth to mouth*

GOD SIN JESUS SALVATION LOVE

the LORD of hosts, the God of Israel: “Houses and fields and vineyards shall be possessed again in this land.” ’

Jeremiah Prays for Understanding

16“Now when I had delivered the purchase deed to Baruch the son of Neriah, I prayed to the LORD, saying: 17‘Ah, Lord GOD! Behold, You have made the heavens and the earth by Your great power and outstretched arm. There is nothing too hard for You. 18*You* show lovingkindness to thousands, and repay the iniquity of the fathers into the bosom of their children after them—the Great, the Mighty God, whose name *is* the LORD of hosts. 19*You are* great in counsel and mighty in work, for Your eyes *are* open to all the ways of the sons of men, to give everyone according to his ways and according to the fruit of his doings. 20You have set signs and wonders in the land of Egypt, to this day, and in Israel and among *other* men; and You have made Yourself a name, as it is this day. 21You have brought Your people Israel out of the land of Egypt with signs and wonders, with a strong hand and an outstretched arm, and with great terror; 22You have given them this land, of which You swore to their fathers to give them—“a land flowing with milk and honey.”[a] 23And they came in and took possession of it, but they have not obeyed Your voice or walked in Your law. They have done nothing of all that You commanded them to do; therefore You have caused all this calamity to come upon them.

24‘Look, the siege mounds! They have come to the city to take it; and the city has been given into the hand of the Chaldeans who fight against it, because of the sword and famine and pestilence. What You have spoken has happened; there You see *it!* 25And You have said to me, O Lord GOD, “Buy the field for money, and take witnesses”!—yet the city has been given into the hand of the Chaldeans.’ ”

God’s Assurance of the People’s Return

26Then the word of the LORD came to Jeremiah, saying, 27“Behold, I *am* the LORD, the God of all flesh. Is there anything too hard for Me? 28Therefore thus says the LORD: ‘Behold, I will give this city into the hand of the Chaldeans, into the hand of Nebuchadnezzar king of Babylon, and he shall take it. 29And the Chaldeans who fight against this city shall come and set fire to this city and burn it, with the houses on whose roofs they have offered incense to Baal and poured out drink offerings to other gods, to provoke Me to anger; 30because the children of Israel and the children of Judah have done only evil before Me from their youth. For the children of Israel have provoked Me only to anger with the work of their hands,’ says the LORD. 31‘For this city has been to Me *a provocation of* My anger and My fury from the day that they built it, even to this day; so I will remove it from before My face 32because of all the evil of the children of Israel and the children of Judah, which they have done to provoke Me to anger—they, their kings, their princes, their priests, their prophets, the men of Judah, and the inhabitants of Jerusalem. 33And they have turned to Me the back, and not the face; though I taught them, rising up early and teaching *them,* yet they have not listened to receive instruction. 34But they set their abominations in the house which is called by My name, to defile it. 35And they built the high places of Baal which *are* in the Valley of the Son of Hinnom, to cause their sons and their daughters to pass through *the fire* to Molech, which I did not command them, nor did it come into My mind that they should do this abomination, to cause Judah to sin.’

36“Now therefore, thus says the LORD, the God of Israel, concerning this city of which you say, ‘It shall be delivered into the hand of the king of Babylon by the sword, by the famine, and by the pestilence: 37Behold, I will gather them out of all countries where I have driven them in My anger, in My fury, and in great wrath; I will bring them back to this place, and I will cause them to dwell safely. 38They shall be My people, and I will be their God; 39then I will give them

32:22 [a] Exodus 3:8

one heart and one way, that they may
fear Me forever, for the good of them
and their children after them. 40And
I will make an everlasting covenant
with them, that I will not turn away
from doing them good; but I will put
My fear in their hearts so that they will
not depart from Me. 41Yes, I will rejoice
over them to do them good, and I will
assuredly plant them in this land, with
all My heart and with all My soul.'
42"For thus says the LORD: 'Just as I
have brought all this great calamity
on this people, so I will bring on them
all the good that I have promised them.
43And fields will be bought in this land
of which you say, "*It is* desolate, without
man or beast; it has been given into the
hand of the Chaldeans." 44Men will buy
fields for money, sign deeds and seal
them, and take witnesses, in the land
of Benjamin, in the places around Jerusalem, in the cities of Judah, in the
cities of the mountains, in the cities
of the lowland, and in the cities of the
South; for I will cause their captives to
return,' says the LORD."

Excellence of the Restored Nation

33 Moreover the word of the LORD
came to Jeremiah a second
time, while he was still shut up in the
court of the prison, saying, 2"Thus says
the LORD who made it, the LORD who
formed it to establish it (the LORD *is* His
name): 3'Call to Me, and I will answer
you, and show you great and mighty
things, which you do not know.'
4"For thus says the LORD, the God of
Israel, concerning the houses of this city
and the houses of the kings of Judah,
which have been pulled down *to fortify*[a] against the siege mounds and the
sword: 5'They come to fight with the
Chaldeans, but *only* to fill their places[a]
with the dead bodies of men whom I
will slay in My anger and My fury, all
for whose wickedness I have hidden My
face from this city. 6Behold, I will bring
it health and healing; I will heal them
and reveal to them the abundance of
peace and truth. 7And I will cause the
captives of Judah and the captives of
Israel to return, and will rebuild those
places as at the first. 8I will cleanse
them from all their iniquity by which
they have sinned against Me, and I will
pardon all their iniquities by which they
have sinned and by which they have
transgressed against Me. 9Then it shall
be to Me a name of joy, a praise, and an
honor before all nations of the earth,
who shall hear all the good that I do to
them; they shall fear and tremble for
all the goodness and all the prosperity
that I provide for it.'
10"Thus says the LORD: 'Again there
shall be heard in this place—of which
you say, "It *is* desolate, without man
and without beast"—in the cities of
Judah, in the streets of Jerusalem that
are desolate, without man and without inhabitant and without beast, 11the
voice of joy and the voice of gladness,
the voice of the bridegroom and the
voice of the bride, the voice of those
who will say:

"Praise the LORD of hosts,
For the LORD *is* good,
For His mercy *endures* forever"—

and of those *who will* bring the sacrifice
of praise into the house of the LORD. For
I will cause the captives of the land to
return as at the first,' says the LORD.
12"Thus says the LORD of hosts: 'In this
place which is desolate, without man
and without beast, and in all its cities,
there shall again be a dwelling place
of shepherds causing *their* flocks to lie
down. 13In the cities of the mountains,
in the cities of the lowland, in the cities
of the South, in the land of Benjamin,
in the places around Jerusalem, and
in the cities of Judah, the flocks shall
again pass under the hands of him who
counts *them,*' says the LORD.
14'Behold, the days are coming,' says
the LORD, 'that I will perform that
good thing which I have promised to
the house of Israel and to the house
of Judah:

15 'In those days and at that time
I will cause to grow up to David

33:4 [a] Compare Isaiah 22:10 33:5 [a] Compare 2 Kings 23:14

A Branch of righteousness;
He shall execute judgment and
righteousness in the earth.
16 In those days Judah will be saved,
And Jerusalem will dwell safely.
And this *is the name* by which she
will be called:

THE LORD OUR
RIGHTEOUSNESS.'[a]

17"For thus says the LORD: 'David shall
never lack a man to sit on the throne
of the house of Israel; 18nor shall the
priests, the Levites, lack a man to offer
burnt offerings before Me, to kindle
grain offerings, and to sacrifice con-
tinually.' "

The Permanence of God's Covenant

19And the word of the LORD came to
Jeremiah, saying, 20"Thus says the
LORD: 'If you can break My covenant
with the day and My covenant with the
night, so that there will not be day and
night in their season, 21then My cov-
enant may also be broken with David
My servant, so that he shall not have a
son to reign on his throne, and with the
Levites, the priests, My ministers. 22As
the host of heaven cannot be numbered,
nor the sand of the sea measured, so will
I multiply the descendants of David My
servant and the Levites who minister
to Me.' "

23Moreover the word of the LORD came
to Jeremiah, saying, 24"Have you not
considered what these people have spo-
ken, saying, 'The two families which
the LORD has chosen, He has also cast
them off'? Thus they have despised My
people, as if they should no more be a
nation before them.

25"Thus says the LORD: 'If My covenant
is not with day and night, *and if* I have
not appointed the ordinances of heaven
and earth, 26then I will cast away the
descendants of Jacob and David My
servant, *so* that I will not take *any* of
his descendants *to be* rulers over the
descendants of Abraham, Isaac, and
Jacob. For I will cause their captives to
return, and will have mercy on them.' "

Zedekiah Warned by God

34 The word which came to Jeremi-
ah from the LORD, when Nebu-
chadnezzar king of Babylon and all
his army, all the kingdoms of the earth
under his dominion, and all the people,
fought against Jerusalem and all its
cities, saying, 2"Thus says the LORD, the
God of Israel: 'Go and speak to Zedekiah
king of Judah and tell him, "Thus says
the LORD: 'Behold, I will give this city
into the hand of the king of Babylon,
and he shall burn it with fire. 3And you
shall not escape from his hand, but shall
surely be taken and delivered into his
hand; your eyes shall see the eyes of
the king of Babylon, he shall speak with
you face to face,[a] and you shall go to
Babylon.' " ' 4Yet hear the word of the
LORD, O Zedekiah king of Judah! Thus
says the LORD concerning you: 'You
shall not die by the sword. 5You shall die
in peace; as in the ceremonies of your
fathers, the former kings who were be-
fore you, so they shall burn *incense* for
you and lament for you, *saying,* "Alas,
lord!" For I have pronounced the word,
says the LORD.' "

6Then Jeremiah the prophet spoke all
these words to Zedekiah king of Judah
in Jerusalem, 7when the king of Bab-
ylon's army fought against Jerusalem
and all the cities of Judah that were
left, against Lachish and Azekah; for
only these fortified cities remained of
the cities of Judah.

Treacherous Treatment of Slaves

8*This is* the word that came to Jeremi-
ah from the LORD, after King Zedekiah
had made a covenant with all the peo-
ple who *were* at Jerusalem to proclaim
liberty to them: 9that every man should
set free his male and female slave—a
Hebrew man or woman—that no one
should keep a Jewish brother in bond-
age. 10Now when all the princes and all
the people, who had entered into the
covenant, heard that everyone should
set free his male and female slaves, that
no one should keep them in bondage
anymore, they obeyed and let *them*
go. 11But afterward they changed their

33:16 [a] Compare 23:5, 6 34:3 [a] Literally *mouth to mouth*

minds and made the male and female
slaves return, whom they had set free,
and brought them into subjection as
male and female slaves.
12Therefore the word of the LORD came
to Jeremiah from the LORD, saying,
13"Thus says the LORD, the God of Israel:
'I made a covenant with your fathers
in the day that I brought them out of
the land of Egypt, out of the house of
bondage, saying, 14"At the end of seven
years let every man set free his Hebrew
brother, who has been sold to him; and
when he has served you six years, you
shall let him go free from you." But your
fathers did not obey Me nor incline their
ear. 15Then you recently turned and
did what was right in My sight—every
man proclaiming liberty to his neigh-
bor; and you made a covenant before
Me in the house which is called by My
name. 16Then you turned around and
profaned My name, and every one of
you brought back his male and female
slaves, whom you had set at liberty, at
their pleasure, and brought them back
into subjection, to be your male and
female slaves.'
17"Therefore thus says the LORD: 'You
have not obeyed Me in proclaiming lib-
erty, every one to his brother and every
one to his neighbor. Behold, I proclaim
liberty to you,' says the LORD—'to the
sword, to pestilence, and to famine! And
I will deliver you to trouble among all
the kingdoms of the earth. 18And I will
give the men who have transgressed My
covenant, who have not performed the
words of the covenant which they made
before Me, when they cut the calf in two
and passed between the parts of it—
19the princes of Judah, the princes of
Jerusalem, the eunuchs, the priests, and
all the people of the land who passed
between the parts of the calf— 20I will
give them into the hand of their ene-
mies and into the hand of those who
seek their life. Their dead bodies shall be
for meat for the birds of the heaven and
the beasts of the earth. 21And I will give
Zedekiah king of Judah and his princes
into the hand of their enemies, into the
hand of those who seek their life, and
into the hand of the king of Babylon's
army which has gone back from you.
22Behold, I will command,' says the
LORD, 'and cause them to return to this
city. They will fight against it and take
it and burn it with fire; and I will make
the cities of Judah a desolation without
inhabitant.' "

The Obedient Rechabites

35 The word which came to Jere-
miah from the LORD in the days
of Jehoiakim the son of Josiah, king of
Judah, saying, 2"Go to the house of the
Rechabites, speak to them, and bring
them into the house of the LORD, into
one of the chambers, and give them
wine to drink."
3Then I took Jaazaniah the son of
Jeremiah, the son of Habazziniah, his
brothers and all his sons, and the whole
house of the Rechabites, 4and I brought
them into the house of the LORD, into
the chamber of the sons of Hanan the
son of Igdaliah, a man of God, which
was by the chamber of the princes,
above the chamber of Maaseiah the
son of Shallum, the keeper of the door.
5Then I set before the sons of the house
of the Rechabites bowls full of wine, and
cups; and I said to them, "Drink wine."
6But they said, "We will drink no wine,
for Jonadab the son of Rechab, our fa-
ther, commanded us, saying, 'You shall
drink no wine, you nor your sons, for-
ever. 7You shall not build a house, sow
seed, plant a vineyard, nor have *any of
these;* but all your days you shall dwell
in tents, that you may live many days
in the land where you are sojourners.'
8Thus we have obeyed the voice of Jon-
adab the son of Rechab, our father, in
all that he charged us, to drink no wine
all our days, we, our wives, our sons,
or our daughters, 9nor to build our-
selves houses to dwell in; nor do we
have vineyard, field, or seed. 10But we
have dwelt in tents, and have obeyed
and done according to all that Jonadab
our father commanded us. 11But it came
to pass, when Nebuchadnezzar king of
Babylon came up into the land, that we
said, 'Come, let us go to Jerusalem for
fear of the army of the Chaldeans and
for fear of the army of the Syrians.' So
we dwell at Jerusalem."
12Then came the word of the LORD to

Jeremiah, saying, 13"Thus says the LORD
of hosts, the God of Israel: 'Go and tell
the men of Judah and the inhabitants
of Jerusalem, "Will you not receive in-
struction to obey My words?" says the
LORD. 14"The words of Jonadab the son
of Rechab, which he commanded his
sons, not to drink wine, are performed;
for to this day they drink none, and
obey their father's commandment. But
although I have spoken to you, rising
early and speaking, you did not obey
Me. 15I have also sent to you all My
servants the prophets, rising up early
and sending *them,* saying, 'Turn now
everyone from his evil way, amend your
doings, and do not go after other gods
to serve them; then you will dwell in
the land which I have given you and
your fathers.' But you have not inclined
your ear, nor obeyed Me. 16Surely the
sons of Jonadab the son of Rechab have
performed the commandment of their
father, which he commanded them, but
this people has not obeyed Me." '

17"Therefore thus says the LORD God of
hosts, the God of Israel: 'Behold, I will
bring on Judah and on all the inhab-
itants of Jerusalem all the doom that
I have pronounced against them; be-
cause I have spoken to them but they
have not heard, and I have called to
them but they have not answered.' "

18And Jeremiah said to the house of
the Rechabites, "Thus says the LORD
of hosts, the God of Israel: 'Because
you have obeyed the commandment
of Jonadab your father, and kept all
his precepts and done according to all
that he commanded you, 19therefore
thus says the LORD of hosts, the God
of Israel: "Jonadab the son of Rechab
shall not lack a man to stand before
Me forever." ' "

The Scroll Read in the Temple

36 Now it came to pass in the fourth
year of Jehoiakim the son of Jo-
siah, king of Judah, *that* this word came
to Jeremiah from the LORD, saying:
2"Take a scroll of a book and write on
it all the words that I have spoken to
you against Israel, against Judah, and
against all the nations, from the day I
spoke to you, from the days of Josiah
even to this day. 3It may be that the
house of Judah will hear all the adver-
sities which I purpose to bring upon
them, that everyone may turn from
his evil way, that I may forgive their
iniquity and their sin."

4Then Jeremiah called Baruch the son
of Neriah; and Baruch wrote on a scroll
of a book, at the instruction of Jeremi-
ah,[a] all the words of the LORD which
He had spoken to him. 5And Jeremi-
ah commanded Baruch, saying, "I *am*
confined, I cannot go into the house
of the LORD. 6You go, therefore, and
read from the scroll which you have
written at my instruction,[a] the words
of the LORD, in the hearing of the peo-
ple in the LORD's house on the day of
fasting. And you shall also read them
in the hearing of all Judah who come
from their cities. 7It may be that they
will present their supplication before
the LORD, and everyone will turn from
his evil way. For great *is* the anger and
the fury that the LORD has pronounced
against this people." 8And Baruch the
son of Neriah did according to all that
Jeremiah the prophet commanded him,
reading from the book the words of the
LORD in the LORD's house.

9Now it came to pass in the fifth year
of Jehoiakim the son of Josiah, king of
Judah, in the ninth month, *that* they
proclaimed a fast before the LORD to
all the people in Jerusalem, and to all
the people who came from the cities
of Judah to Jerusalem. 10Then Baruch
read from the book the words of Jere-
miah in the house of the LORD, in the
chamber of Gemariah the son of Sha-
phan the scribe, in the upper court at
the entry of the New Gate of the LORD's
house, in the hearing of all the people.

The Scroll Read in the Palace

11When Michaiah the son of Gemari-
ah, the son of Shaphan, heard all the
words of the LORD from the book, 12he
then went down to the king's house,
into the scribe's chamber; and there all
the princes were sitting—Elishama the

36:4 [a] Literally *from Jeremiah's mouth* 36:6 [a] Literally *from my mouth*

scribe, Delaiah the son of Shemaiah,
Elnathan the son of Achbor, Gemari-
ah the son of Shaphan, Zedekiah the
son of Hananiah, and all the princes.
13Then Michaiah declared to them all
the words that he had heard when Bar-
uch read the book in the hearing of
the people. 14Therefore all the princes
sent Jehudi the son of Nethaniah, the
son of Shelemiah, the son of Cushi, to
Baruch, saying, "Take in your hand
the scroll from which you have read in
the hearing of the people, and come."
So Baruch the son of Neriah took the
scroll in his hand and came to them.
15And they said to him, "Sit down now,
and read it in our hearing." So Baruch
read *it* in their hearing.
16Now it happened, when they had
heard all the words, that they looked
in fear from one to another, and said
to Baruch, "We will surely tell the king
of all these words." 17And they asked
Baruch, saying, "Tell us now, how did
you write all these words—at his in-
struction?"[a]
18So Baruch answered them, "He pro-
claimed with his mouth all these words
to me, and I wrote *them* with ink in the
book."
19Then the princes said to Baruch, "Go
and hide, you and Jeremiah; and let no
one know where you are."

The King Destroys Jeremiah's Scroll

20And they went to the king, into the
court; but they stored the scroll in the
chamber of Elishama the scribe, and
told all the words in the hearing of the
king. 21So the king sent Jehudi to bring
the scroll, and he took it from Elisha-
ma the scribe's chamber. And Jehudi
read it in the hearing of the king and
in the hearing of all the princes who
stood beside the king. 22Now the king
was sitting in the winter house in the
ninth month, with *a fire* burning on the
hearth before him. 23And it happened,
when Jehudi had read three or four
columns, *that the king* cut it with the
scribe's knife and cast *it* into the fire
that *was* on the hearth, until all the
scroll was consumed in the fire that
was on the hearth. 24Yet they were not
afraid, nor did they tear their garments,
the king nor any of his servants who
heard all these words. 25Nevertheless
Elnathan, Delaiah, and Gemariah im-
plored the king not to burn the scroll;
but he would not listen to them. 26And
the king commanded Jerahmeel the
king's[a] son, Seraiah the son of Azriel,
and Shelemiah the son of Abdeel, to
seize Baruch the scribe and Jeremiah
the prophet, but the LORD hid them.

Jeremiah Rewrites the Scroll

27Now after the king had burned the
scroll with the words which Baruch had
written at the instruction of Jeremiah,[a]
the word of the LORD came to Jeremiah,
saying: 28"Take yet another scroll, and
write on it all the former words that were
in the first scroll which Jehoiakim the
king of Judah has burned. 29And you
shall say to Jehoiakim king of Judah,
'Thus says the LORD: "You have burned
this scroll, saying, 'Why have you writ-
ten in it that the king of Babylon will
certainly come and destroy this land,
and cause man and beast to cease from
here?' " 30Therefore thus says the LORD
concerning Jehoiakim king of Judah:
"He shall have no one to sit on the throne
of David, and his dead body shall be cast
out to the heat of the day and the frost of
the night. 31I will punish him, his family,
and his servants for their iniquity; and
I will bring on them, on the inhabitants
of Jerusalem, and on the men of Judah
all the doom that I have pronounced
against them; but they did not heed." ' "
32Then Jeremiah took another scroll
and gave it to Baruch the scribe, the
son of Neriah, who wrote on it at the
instruction of Jeremiah[a] all the words
of the book which Jehoiakim king of
Judah had burned in the fire. And be-
sides, there were added to them many
similar words.

Zedekiah's Vain Hope

37 Now King Zedekiah the son of
Josiah reigned instead of Coni-
ah the son of Jehoiakim, whom Neb-
uchadnezzar king of Babylon made

36:17 [a] Literally *with his mouth* 36:26 [a] Hebrew *Hammelech* 36:27 [a] Literally *from Jeremiah's mouth* 36:32 [a] Literally *from Jeremiah's mouth*

king in the land of Judah. 2But neither
he nor his servants nor the people of
the land gave heed to the words of the
LORD which He spoke by the prophet
Jeremiah.
3And Zedekiah the king sent Jehucal
the son of Shelemiah, and Zephaniah
the son of Maaseiah, the priest, to the
prophet Jeremiah, saying, "Pray now
to the LORD our God for us." 4Now Jer-
emiah was coming and going among
the people, for they had not *yet* put him
in prison. 5Then Pharaoh's army came
up from Egypt; and when the Chaldeans
who were besieging Jerusalem heard
news of them, they departed from Je-
rusalem.
6Then the word of the LORD came to
the prophet Jeremiah, saying, 7"Thus
says the LORD, the God of Israel, 'Thus
you shall say to the king of Judah, who
sent you to Me to inquire of Me: "Be-
hold, Pharaoh's army which has come
up to help you will return to Egypt, to
their own land. 8And the Chaldeans
shall come back and fight against this
city, and take it and burn it with fire." '
9Thus says the LORD: 'Do not deceive
yourselves, saying, "The Chaldeans will
surely depart from us," for they will not
depart. 10For though you had defeated
the whole army of the Chaldeans who
fight against you, and there remained
only wounded men among them, they
would rise up, every man in his tent,
and burn the city with fire.' "

Jeremiah Imprisoned

11And it happened, when the army of
the Chaldeans left *the siege* of Jerusa-
lem for fear of Pharaoh's army, 12that
Jeremiah went out of Jerusalem to go
into the land of Benjamin to claim his
property there among the people. 13And
when he was in the Gate of Benjamin, a
captain of the guard *was* there whose
name *was* Irijah the son of Shelemiah,
the son of Hananiah; and he seized
Jeremiah the prophet, saying, "You are
defecting to the Chaldeans!"
14Then Jeremiah said, "False! I am not
defecting to the Chaldeans." But he did
not listen to him.
So Irijah seized Jeremiah and brought
him to the princes. 15Therefore the
princes were angry with Jeremiah, and
they struck him and put him in prison
in the house of Jonathan the scribe. For
they had made that the prison.
16When Jeremiah entered the dun-
geon and the cells, and Jeremiah had
remained there many days, 17then Zede-
kiah the king sent and took him *out.* The
king asked him secretly in his house, and
said, "Is there *any* word from the LORD?"
And Jeremiah said, "There is." Then
he said, "You shall be delivered into the
hand of the king of Babylon!"
18Moreover Jeremiah said to King Zed-
ekiah, "What offense have I committed
against you, against your servants,
or against this people, that you have
put me in prison? 19Where now *are*
your prophets who prophesied to you,
saying, 'The king of Babylon will not
come against you or against this land'?
20Therefore please hear now, O my lord
the king. Please, let my petition be ac-
cepted before you, and do not make
me return to the house of Jonathan the
scribe, lest I die there."
21Then Zedekiah the king commanded
that they should commit Jeremiah to
the court of the prison, and that they
should give him daily a piece of bread
from the bakers' street, until all the
bread in the city was gone. Thus Jeremi-
ah remained in the court of the prison.

Jeremiah in the Dungeon

38 Now Shephatiah the son of Mat-
tan, Gedaliah the son of Pash-
hur, Jucal[a] the son of Shelemiah, and
Pashhur the son of Malchiah heard
the words that Jeremiah had spoken
to all the people, saying, 2"Thus says
the LORD: 'He who remains in this city
shall die by the sword, by famine, and
by pestilence; but he who goes over to
the Chaldeans shall live; his life shall
be as a prize to him, and he shall live.'[a]
3Thus says the LORD: 'This city shall
surely be given into the hand of the king
of Babylon's army, which shall take it.' "
4Therefore the princes said to the king,
"Please, let this man be put to death, for

38:1 [a] Same as *Jehucal* (compare 37:3) **38:2** [a] Compare 21:9

thus he weakens the hands of the men
of war who remain in this city, and the
hands of all the people, by speaking
such words to them. For this man does
not seek the welfare of this people, but
their harm."
5Then Zedekiah the king said, "Look,
he *is* in your hand. For the king can *do*
nothing against you." 6So they took Jer-
emiah and cast him into the dungeon
of Malchiah the king's[a] son, which *was*
in the court of the prison, and they let
Jeremiah down with ropes. And in the
dungeon *there was* no water, but mire.
So Jeremiah sank in the mire.
7Now Ebed-Melech the Ethiopian, one
of the eunuchs, who was in the king's
house, heard that they had put Jeremi-
ah in the dungeon. When the king was
sitting at the Gate of Benjamin, 8Ebed-
Melech went out of the king's house
and spoke to the king, saying: 9"My
lord the king, these men have done evil
in all that they have done to Jeremi-
ah the prophet, whom they have cast
into the dungeon, and he is likely to die
from hunger in the place where he is.
For *there is* no more bread in the city."
10Then the king commanded Ebed-Me-
lech the Ethiopian, saying, "Take from
here thirty men with you, and lift Jer-
emiah the prophet out of the dungeon
before he dies." 11So Ebed-Melech took
the men with him and went into the
house of the king under the treasury,
and took from there old clothes and old
rags, and let them down by ropes into
the dungeon to Jeremiah. 12Then Ebed-
Melech the Ethiopian said to Jeremiah,
"Please put these old clothes and rags
under your armpits, under the ropes."
And Jeremiah did so. 13So they pulled
Jeremiah up with ropes and lifted him
out of the dungeon. And Jeremiah re-
mained in the court of the prison.

Zedekiah's Fears and Jeremiah's Advice

14Then Zedekiah the king sent and
had Jeremiah the prophet brought to
him at the third entrance of the house
of the LORD. And the king said to Jere-
miah, "I will ask you something. Hide
nothing from me."
15Jeremiah said to Zedekiah, "If I de-
clare *it* to you, will you not surely put
me to death? And if I give you advice,
you will not listen to me."
16So Zedekiah the king swore secretly
to Jeremiah, saying, "*As* the LORD lives,
who made our very souls, I will not put
you to death, nor will I give you into the
hand of these men who seek your life."
17Then Jeremiah said to Zedekiah,
"Thus says the LORD, the God of hosts,
the God of Israel: 'If you surely surren-
der to the king of Babylon's princes,
then your soul shall live; this city shall
not be burned with fire, and you and
your house shall live. 18But if you do
not surrender to the king of Babylon's
princes, then this city shall be given
into the hand of the Chaldeans; they
shall burn it with fire, and you shall not
escape from their hand.' "
19And Zedekiah the king said to Jer-
emiah, "I am afraid of the Jews who
have defected to the Chaldeans, lest
they deliver me into their hand, and
they abuse me."
20But Jeremiah said, "They shall not
deliver *you.* Please, obey the voice of the
LORD which I speak to you. So it shall be
well with you, and your soul shall live.
21But if you refuse to surrender, this *is*
the word that the LORD has shown me:
22'Now behold, all the women who are
left in the king of Judah's house *shall
be* surrendered to the king of Babylon's
princes, and those *women* shall say:

"Your close friends have set upon
you
And prevailed against you;
Your feet have sunk in the mire,
And they have turned away
again."

23'So they shall surrender all your
wives and children to the Chaldeans.
You shall not escape from their hand,
but shall be taken by the hand of the
king of Babylon. And you shall cause
this city to be burned with fire.' "
24Then Zedekiah said to Jeremiah, "Let
no one know of these words, and you
shall not die. 25But if the princes hear

38:6 a Hebrew *Hammelech*

that I have talked with you, and they
come to you and say to you, 'Declare to
us now what you have said to the king,
and also what the king said to you; do
not hide *it* from us, and we will not put
you to death,' 26then you shall say to
them, 'I presented my request before
the king, that he would not make me re-
turn to Jonathan's house to die there.' "
27Then all the princes came to Jere-
miah and asked him. And he told them
according to all these words that the
king had commanded. So they stopped
speaking with him, for the conversation
had not been heard. 28Now Jeremiah
remained in the court of the prison until
the day that Jerusalem was taken. And
he was *there* when Jerusalem was taken.

The Fall of Jerusalem

39 In the ninth year of Zedeki-
ah king of Judah, in the tenth
month, Nebuchadnezzar king of Bab-
ylon and all his army came against
Jerusalem, and besieged it. 2In the elev-
enth year of Zedekiah, in the fourth
month, on the ninth *day* of the month,
the city was penetrated.
3Then all the princes of the king of
Babylon came in and sat in the Middle
Gate: Nergal-Sharezer, Samgar-Nebo,
Sarsechim, Rabsaris,[a] Nergal-Sarezer,
Rabmag,[b] with the rest of the princes
of the king of Babylon.
4So it was, when Zedekiah the king of
Judah and all the men of war saw them,
that they fled and went out of the city
by night, by way of the king's garden, by
the gate between the two walls. And he
went out by way of the plain.[a] 5But the
Chaldean army pursued them and over-
took Zedekiah in the plains of Jericho.
And when they had captured him, they
brought him up to Nebuchadnezzar
king of Babylon, to Riblah in the land
of Hamath, where he pronounced judg-
ment on him. 6Then the king of Babylon
killed the sons of Zedekiah before his
eyes in Riblah; the king of Babylon also
killed all the nobles of Judah. 7Moreover
he put out Zedekiah's eyes, and bound
him with bronze fetters to carry him off
to Babylon. 8And the Chaldeans burned
the king's house and the houses of the
people with fire, and broke down the
walls of Jerusalem. 9Then Nebuzara-
dan the captain of the guard carried
away captive to Babylon the remnant
of the people who remained in the city
and those who defected to him, with the
rest of the people who remained. 10But
Nebuzaradan the captain of the guard
left in the land of Judah the poor peo-
ple, who had nothing, and gave them
vineyards and fields at the same time.

Jeremiah Goes Free

11Now Nebuchadnezzar king of Bab-
ylon gave charge concerning Jeremi-
ah to Nebuzaradan the captain of the
guard, saying, 12"Take him and look
after him, and do him no harm; but
do to him just as he says to you." 13So
Nebuzaradan the captain of the guard
sent Nebushasban, Rabsaris, Nergal-
Sharezer, Rabmag, and all the king of
Babylon's chief officers; 14then they
sent *someone* to take Jeremiah from the
court of the prison, and committed him
to Gedaliah the son of Ahikam, the son
of Shaphan, that he should take him
home. So he dwelt among the people.
15Meanwhile the word of the LORD had
come to Jeremiah while he was shut up
in the court of the prison, saying, 16"Go
and speak to Ebed-Melech the Ethiopi-
an, saying, 'Thus says the LORD of hosts,
the God of Israel: "Behold, I will bring
My words upon this city for adversity
and not for good, and they shall be *per-
formed* in that day before you. 17But I
will deliver you in that day," says the
LORD, "and you shall not be given into
the hand of the men of whom you *are*
afraid. 18For I will surely deliver you,
and you shall not fall by the sword;
but your life shall be as a prize to you,
because you have put your trust in Me,"
says the LORD.' "

Jeremiah with Gedaliah the Governor

40 The word that came to Jeremi-
ah from the LORD after Nebu-
zaradan the captain of the guard had
let him go from Ramah, when he had
taken him bound in chains among all

39:3 [a] A title, probably *Chief Officer;* also verse 13 [b] A title, probably *Troop Commander;* also verse 13
39:4 [a] Or *the Arabah,* that is, the Jordan Valley

who were carried away captive from Jerusalem and Judah, who were carried away captive to Babylon.

2And the captain of the guard took Jeremiah and said to him: "The LORD your God has pronounced this doom on this place. 3Now the LORD has brought *it,* and has done just as He said. Because you *people* have sinned against the LORD, and not obeyed His voice, therefore this thing has come upon you. 4And now look, I free you this day from the chains that *were* on your hand. If it seems good to you to come with me to Babylon, come, and I will look after you. But if it seems wrong for you to come with me to Babylon, remain here. See, all the land *is* before you; wherever it seems good and convenient for you to go, go there."

5Now while Jeremiah had not yet gone back, *Nebuzaradan said,* "Go back to Gedaliah the son of Ahikam, the son of Shaphan, whom the king of Babylon has made governor over the cities of Judah, and dwell with him among the people. Or go wherever it seems convenient for you to go." So the captain of the guard gave him rations and a gift and let him go. 6Then Jeremiah went to Gedaliah the son of Ahikam, to Mizpah, and dwelt with him among the people who were left in the land.

7And when all the captains of the armies who *were* in the fields, they and their men, heard that the king of Babylon had made Gedaliah the son of Ahikam governor in the land, and had committed to him men, women, children, and the poorest of the land who had not been carried away captive to Babylon, 8then they came to Gedaliah at Mizpah—Ishmael the son of Nethaniah, Johanan and Jonathan the sons of Kareah, Seraiah the son of Tanhumeth, the sons of Ephai the Netophathite, and Jezaniah[a] the son of a Maachathite, they and their men. 9And Gedaliah the son of Ahikam, the son of Shaphan, took an oath before them and their men, saying, "Do not be afraid to serve the Chaldeans. Dwell in the land and serve the king of Babylon, and it shall be well with you. 10As for me, I will indeed dwell at Mizpah and serve the Chaldeans who come to us. But you, gather wine and summer fruit and oil, put *them* in your vessels, and dwell in your cities that you have taken." 11Likewise, when all the Jews who *were* in Moab, among the Ammonites, in Edom, and who *were* in all the countries, heard that the king of Babylon had left a remnant of Judah, and that he had set over them Gedaliah the son of Ahikam, the son of Shaphan, 12then all the Jews returned out of all places where they had been driven, and came to the land of Judah, to Gedaliah at Mizpah, and gathered wine and summer fruit in abundance.

13Moreover Johanan the son of Kareah and all the captains of the forces that *were* in the fields came to Gedaliah at Mizpah, 14and said to him, "Do you certainly know that Baalis the king of the Ammonites has sent Ishmael the son of Nethaniah to murder you?" But Gedaliah the son of Ahikam did not believe them.

15Then Johanan the son of Kareah spoke secretly to Gedaliah in Mizpah, saying, "Let me go, please, and I will kill Ishmael the son of Nethaniah, and no one will know *it.* Why should he murder you, so that all the Jews who are gathered to you would be scattered, and the remnant in Judah perish?"

16But Gedaliah the son of Ahikam said to Johanan the son of Kareah, "You shall not do this thing, for you speak falsely concerning Ishmael."

Insurrection Against Gedaliah

41 Now it came to pass in the seventh month *that* Ishmael the son of Nethaniah, the son of Elishama, of the royal family and of the officers of the king, came with ten men to Gedaliah the son of Ahikam, at Mizpah. And there they ate bread together in Mizpah. 2Then Ishmael the son of Nethaniah, and the ten men who were with him, arose and struck Gedaliah the son of Ahikam, the son of Shaphan, with the sword, and killed him whom the king of Babylon had made governor over the

40:8 [a] Spelled *Jaazaniah* in 2 Kings 25:23

land. 3Ishmael also struck down all the
Jews who were with him, *that is,* with
Gedaliah at Mizpah, and the Chaldeans
who were found there, the men of war.
4And it happened, on the second day
after he had killed Gedaliah, when as
yet no one knew *it,* 5that certain men
came from Shechem, from Shiloh, and
from Samaria, eighty men with their
beards shaved and their clothes torn,
having cut themselves, with offerings
and incense in their hand, to bring *them*
to the house of the LORD. 6Now Ishma-
el the son of Nethaniah went out from
Mizpah to meet them, weeping as he
went along; and it happened as he met
them that he said to them, "Come to
Gedaliah the son of Ahikam!" 7So it was,
when they came into the midst of the
city, that Ishmael the son of Nethaniah
killed them *and cast them* into the midst
of a pit, he and the men who were with
him. 8But ten men were found among
them who said to Ishmael, "Do not kill
us, for we have treasures of wheat, bar-
ley, oil, and honey in the field." So he
desisted and did not kill them among
their brethren. 9Now the pit into which
Ishmael had cast all the dead bodies of
the men whom he had slain, because
of Gedaliah, *was* the same one Asa the
king had made for fear of Baasha king
of Israel. Ishmael the son of Nethaniah
filled it with *the* slain. 10Then Ishmael
carried away captive all the rest of the
people who *were* in Mizpah, the king's
daughters and all the people who re-
mained in Mizpah, whom Nebuzaradan
the captain of the guard had committed
to Gedaliah the son of Ahikam. And
Ishmael the son of Nethaniah carried
them away captive and departed to go
over to the Ammonites.
11But when Johanan the son of Kare-
ah and all the captains of the forces
that *were* with him heard of all the evil
that Ishmael the son of Nethaniah had
done, 12they took all the men and went
to fight with Ishmael the son of Netha-
niah; and they found him by the great
pool that *is* in Gibeon. 13So it was, when
all the people who *were* with Ishmael
saw Johanan the son of Kareah, and
all the captains of the forces who *were*
with him, that they were glad. 14Then
all the people whom Ishmael had car-
ried away captive from Mizpah turned
around and came back, and went to
Johanan the son of Kareah. 15But Ish-
mael the son of Nethaniah escaped
from Johanan with eight men and went
to the Ammonites.
16Then Johanan the son of Kareah, and
all the captains of the forces that were
with him, took from Mizpah all the rest
of the people whom he had recovered
from Ishmael the son of Nethaniah
after he had murdered Gedaliah the son
of Ahikam—the mighty men of war and
the women and the children and the
eunuchs, whom he had brought back
from Gibeon. 17And they departed and
dwelt in the habitation of Chimham,
which is near Bethlehem, as they went
on their way to Egypt, 18because of the
Chaldeans; for they were afraid of them,
because Ishmael the son of Nethaniah
had murdered Gedaliah the son of Ahi-
kam, whom the king of Babylon had
made governor in the land.

The Flight to Egypt Forbidden

42 Now all the captains of the
forces, Johanan the son of Ka-
reah, Jezaniah the son of Hoshaiah,
and all the people, from the least to
the greatest, came near 2and said to
Jeremiah the prophet, "Please, let our
petition be acceptable to you, and pray
for us to the LORD your God, for all this
remnant (since we are left *but* a few
of many, as you can see), 3that the
LORD your God may show us the way
in which we should walk and the thing
we should do."
4Then Jeremiah the prophet said to
them, "I have heard. Indeed, I will pray
to the LORD your God according to your
words, and it shall be, *that* whatever the
LORD answers you, I will declare *it* to
you. I will keep nothing back from you."
5So they said to Jeremiah, "Let the
LORD be a true and faithful witness be-
tween us, if we do not do according to
everything which the LORD your God
sends us by you. 6Whether *it is* pleasing
or displeasing, we will obey the voice
of the LORD our God to whom we send
you, that it may be well with us when
we obey the voice of the LORD our God."

7And it happened after ten days that
the word of the LORD came to Jeremi-
ah. 8Then he called Johanan the son of
Kareah, all the captains of the forces
which *were* with him, and all the people
from the least even to the greatest, 9and
said to them, "Thus says the LORD, the
God of Israel, to whom you sent me to
present your petition before Him: 10'If
you will still remain in this land, then
I will build you and not pull *you* down,
and I will plant you and not pluck *you*
up. For I relent concerning the disas-
ter that I have brought upon you. 11Do
not be afraid of the king of Babylon, of
whom you are afraid; do not be afraid
of him,' says the LORD, 'for I *am* with
you, to save you and deliver you from
his hand. 12And I will show you mercy,
that he may have mercy on you and
cause you to return to your own land.'
13"But if you say, 'We will not dwell in
this land,' disobeying the voice of the
LORD your God, 14saying, 'No, but we
will go to the land of Egypt where we
shall see no war, nor hear the sound of
the trumpet, nor be hungry for bread,
and there we will dwell'— 15Then hear
now the word of the LORD, O remnant
of Judah! Thus says the LORD of hosts,
the God of Israel: 'If you wholly set your
faces to enter Egypt, and go to dwell
there, 16then it shall be *that* the sword
which you feared shall overtake you
there in the land of Egypt; the famine
of which you were afraid shall follow
close after you there *in* Egypt; and there
you shall die. 17So shall it be with all the
men who set their faces to go to Egypt to
dwell there. They shall die by the sword,
by famine, and by pestilence. And none
of them shall remain or escape from the
disaster that I will bring upon them.'
18"For thus says the LORD of hosts, the
God of Israel: 'As My anger and My fury
have been poured out on the inhab-
itants of Jerusalem, so will My fury
be poured out on you when you enter
Egypt. And you shall be an oath, an
astonishment, a curse, and a reproach;
and you shall see this place no more.'
19"The LORD has said concerning
you, O remnant of Judah, 'Do not go
to Egypt!' Know certainly that I have
admonished you this day. 20For you
were hypocrites in your hearts when
you sent me to the LORD your God, say-
ing, 'Pray for us to the LORD our God,
and according to all that the LORD your
God says, so declare to us and we will
do *it*.' 21And I have this day declared
it to you, but you have not obeyed the
voice of the LORD your God, or anything
which He has sent you by me. 22Now
therefore, know certainly that you shall
die by the sword, by famine, and by
pestilence in the place where you desire
to go to dwell."

Jeremiah Taken to Egypt

43 Now it happened, when Jeremi-
ah had stopped speaking to all
the people all the words of the LORD
their God, for which the LORD their God
had sent him to them, all these words,
2that Azariah the son of Hoshaiah, Jo-
hanan the son of Kareah, and all the
proud men spoke, saying to Jeremiah,
"You speak falsely! The LORD our God
has not sent you to say, 'Do not go to
Egypt to dwell there.' 3But Baruch the
son of Neriah has set you against us,
to deliver us into the hand of the Chal-
deans, that they may put us to death
or carry us away captive to Babylon."
4So Johanan the son of Kareah, all the
captains of the forces, and all the people
would not obey the voice of the LORD, to
remain in the land of Judah. 5But Joha-
nan the son of Kareah and all the cap-
tains of the forces took all the remnant
of Judah who had returned to dwell
in the land of Judah, from all nations
where they had been driven— 6men,
women, children, the king's daughters,
and every person whom Nebuzaradan
the captain of the guard had left with
Gedaliah the son of Ahikam, the son of
Shaphan, and Jeremiah the prophet
and Baruch the son of Neriah. 7So they
went to the land of Egypt, for they did
not obey the voice of the LORD. And they
went as far as Tahpanhes.
8Then the word of the LORD came to
Jeremiah in Tahpanhes, saying, 9"Take
large stones in your hand, and hide
them in the sight of the men of Judah,
in the clay in the brick courtyard which
is at the entrance to Pharaoh's house in
Tahpanhes; 10and say to them, 'Thus

says the LORD of hosts, the God of Israel: "Behold, I will send and bring Nebuchadnezzar the king of Babylon, My servant, and will set his throne above these stones that I have hidden. And he will spread his royal pavilion over them. 11When he comes, he shall strike the land of Egypt *and deliver* to death *those appointed* for death, and to captivity *those appointed* for captivity, and to the sword *those appointed* for the sword. 12I[a] will kindle a fire in the houses of the gods of Egypt, and he shall burn them and carry them away captive. And he shall array himself with the land of Egypt, as a shepherd puts on his garment, and he shall go out from there in peace. 13He shall also break the *sacred* pillars of Beth Shemesh[a] that *are* in the land of Egypt; and the houses of the gods of the Egyptians he shall burn with fire." ' "

Israelites Will Be Punished in Egypt

44 The word that came to Jeremiah concerning all the Jews who dwell in the land of Egypt, who dwell at Migdol, at Tahpanhes, at Noph,[a] and in the country of Pathros, saying, 2"Thus says the LORD of hosts, the God of Israel: 'You have seen all the calamity that I have brought on Jerusalem and on all the cities of Judah; and behold, this day they *are* a desolation, and no one dwells in them, 3because of their wickedness which they have committed to provoke Me to anger, in that they went to burn incense *and* to serve other gods whom they did not know, they nor you nor your fathers. 4However I have sent to you all My servants the prophets, rising early and sending *them,* saying, "Oh, do not do this abominable thing that I hate!" 5But they did not listen or incline their ear to turn from their wickedness, to burn no incense to other gods. 6So My fury and My anger were poured out and kindled in the cities of Judah and in the streets of Jerusalem; and they are wasted *and* desolate, as it is this day.'

7"Now therefore, thus says the LORD, the God of hosts, the God of Israel: 'Why do you commit *this* great evil against yourselves, to cut off from you man and woman, child and infant, out of Judah, leaving none to remain, 8in that you provoke Me to wrath with the works of your hands, burning incense to other gods in the land of Egypt where you have gone to dwell, that you may cut yourselves off and be a curse and a reproach among all the nations of the earth? 9Have you forgotten the wickedness of your fathers, the wickedness of the kings of Judah, the wickedness of their wives, your own wickedness, and the wickedness of your wives, which they committed in the land of Judah and in the streets of Jerusalem? 10They have not been humbled, to this day, nor have they feared; they have not walked in My law or in My statutes that I set before you and your fathers.'

11"Therefore thus says the LORD of hosts, the God of Israel: 'Behold, I will set My face against you for catastrophe and for cutting off all Judah. 12And I will take the remnant of Judah who have set their faces to go into the land of Egypt to dwell there, and they shall all be consumed *and* fall in the land of Egypt. They shall be consumed by the sword *and* by famine. They shall die, from the least to the greatest, by the sword and by famine; and they shall be an oath, an astonishment, a curse and a reproach! 13For I will punish those who dwell in the land of Egypt, as I have punished Jerusalem, by the sword, by famine, and by pestilence, 14so that none of the remnant of Judah who have gone into the land of Egypt to dwell there shall escape or survive, lest they return to the land of Judah, to which they desire to return and dwell. For none shall return except those who escape.' "

15Then all the men who knew that their wives had burned incense to other gods, with all the women who stood by, a great multitude, and all the people who dwelt in the land of Egypt, in Pathros, answered Jeremiah, saying: 16"*As for* the word that you have spoken to us in the name of the LORD, we will

43:12 [a] Following Masoretic Text and Targum; Septuagint, Syriac, and Vulgate read *He.*
43:13 [a] Literally *House of the Sun,* ancient On; later called Heliopolis **44:1** [a] That is, ancient Memphis

not listen to you! 17But we will certainly
do whatever has gone out of our own
mouth, to burn incense to the queen of
heaven and pour out drink offerings
to her, as we have done, we and our
fathers, our kings and our princes, in
the cities of Judah and in the streets of
Jerusalem. For *then* we had plenty of
food, were well-off, and saw no trouble.
18But since we stopped burning incense
to the queen of heaven and pouring out
drink offerings to her, we have lacked
everything and have been consumed
by the sword and by famine."
19*The women also said,* "And when we
burned incense to the queen of heaven
and poured out drink offerings to her,
did we make cakes for her, to worship
her, and pour out drink offerings to her
without our husbands' *permission?*"
20Then Jeremiah spoke to all the
people—the men, the women, and all
the people who had given him *that*
answer—saying: 21"The incense that
you burned in the cities of Judah and in
the streets of Jerusalem, you and your
fathers, your kings and your princes,
and the people of the land, did not the
LORD remember them, and did it *not*
come into His mind? 22So the LORD
could no longer bear *it,* because of the
evil of your doings *and* because of the
abominations which you committed.
Therefore your land is a desolation, an
astonishment, a curse, and without an
inhabitant, as *it is* this day. 23Because
you have burned incense and because
you have sinned against the LORD, and
have not obeyed the voice of the LORD
or walked in His law, in His statutes or in
His testimonies, therefore this calamity
has happened to you, as *at* this day."
24Moreover Jeremiah said to all the
people and to all the women, "Hear the
word of the LORD, all Judah who *are*
in the land of Egypt! 25Thus says the
LORD of hosts, the God of Israel, say-
ing: 'You and your wives have spoken
with your mouths and fulfilled with
your hands, saying, "We will surely keep
our vows that we have made, to burn
incense to the queen of heaven and
pour out drink offerings to her." You
will surely keep your vows and perform
your vows!' 26Therefore hear the word
of the LORD, all Judah who dwell in the
land of Egypt: 'Behold, I have sworn by
My great name,' says the LORD, 'that My
name shall no more be named in the
mouth of any man of Judah in all the
land of Egypt, saying, "The Lord GOD
lives." 27Behold, I will watch over them
for adversity and not for good. And all
the men of Judah who *are* in the land of
Egypt shall be consumed by the sword
and by famine, until there is an end to
them. 28Yet a small number who escape
the sword shall return from the land of
Egypt to the land of Judah; and all the
remnant of Judah, who have gone to
the land of Egypt to dwell there, shall
know whose words will stand, Mine or
theirs. 29And this *shall be* a sign to you,'
says the LORD, 'that I will punish you
in this place, that you may know that
My words will surely stand against you
for adversity.'
30"Thus says the LORD: 'Behold, I will
give Pharaoh Hophra king of Egypt
into the hand of his enemies and into
the hand of those who seek his life, as
I gave Zedekiah king of Judah into the
hand of Nebuchadnezzar king of Bab-
ylon, his enemy who sought his life.' "

Assurance to Baruch

45 The word that Jeremiah the
prophet spoke to Baruch the son
of Neriah, when he had written these
words in a book at the instruction of
Jeremiah,[a] in the fourth year of Jehoi-
akim the son of Josiah, king of Judah,
saying, 2"Thus says the LORD, the God
of Israel, to you, O Baruch: 3'You said,
"Woe is me now! For the LORD has add-
ed grief to my sorrow. I fainted in my
sighing, and I find no rest." '
4"Thus you shall say to him, 'Thus
says the LORD: "Behold, what I have
built I will break down, and what I have
planted I will pluck up, that is, this whole
land. 5And do you seek great things for
yourself? Do not seek *them;* for behold, I
will bring adversity on all flesh," says the
LORD. "But I will give your life to you as
a prize in all places, wherever you go." ' "

45:1 [a] Literally *from Jeremiah's mouth*

Judgment on Egypt

46 The word of the LORD which came to Jeremiah the prophet against the nations. 2Against Egypt.

Concerning the army of Pharaoh Necho, king of Egypt, which was by the River Euphrates in Carchemish, and which Nebuchadnezzar king of Babylon defeated in the fourth year of Jehoiakim the son of Josiah, king of Judah:

3 "Order the buckler and shield,
And draw near to battle!
4 Harness the horses,
And mount up, you horsemen!
Stand forth with *your* helmets,
Polish the spears,
Put on the armor!
5 Why have I seen them dismayed
and turned back?
Their mighty ones are beaten
down;
They have speedily fled,
And did not look back,
For fear *was* all around," says the
LORD.
6 "Do not let the swift flee away,
Nor the mighty man escape;
They will stumble and fall
Toward the north, by the River
Euphrates.

7 "Who *is* this coming up like a flood,
Whose waters move like the
rivers?
8 Egypt rises up like a flood,
And *its* waters move like the
rivers;
And he says, 'I will go up *and*
cover the earth,
I will destroy the city and its
inhabitants.'
9 Come up, O horses, and rage,
O chariots!
And let the mighty men come
forth:
The Ethiopians and the Libyans
who handle the shield,
And the Lydians who handle *and*
bend the bow.
10 For this *is* the day of the Lord GOD
of hosts,
A day of vengeance,
That He may avenge Himself on
His adversaries.
The sword shall devour;
It shall be satiated and made
drunk with their blood;
For the Lord GOD of hosts has a
sacrifice
In the north country by the River
Euphrates.

11 "Go up to Gilead and take balm,
O virgin, the daughter of Egypt;
In vain you will use many
medicines;
You shall not be cured.
12 The nations have heard of your
shame,
And your cry has filled the land;
For the mighty man has
stumbled against the
mighty;
They both have fallen together."

Babylonia Will Strike Egypt

13The word that the LORD spoke to Jeremiah the prophet, how Nebuchadnezzar king of Babylon would come *and* strike the land of Egypt.

14 "Declare in Egypt, and proclaim in
Migdol;
Proclaim in Noph[a] and in
Tahpanhes;
Say, 'Stand fast and prepare
yourselves,
For the sword devours all around
you.'
15 Why are your valiant *men* swept
away?
They did not stand
Because the LORD drove them
away.
16 He made many fall;
Yes, one fell upon another.
And they said, 'Arise!
Let us go back to our own people
And to the land of our nativity
From the oppressing sword.'
17 They cried there,
'Pharaoh, king of Egypt, *is but* a
noise.
He has passed by the appointed
time!'

46:14 [a] That is, ancient Memphis

18 "*As* I live," says the King,
Whose name *is* the LORD of hosts,
"Surely as Tabor *is* among the mountains
And as Carmel by the sea, *so* he shall come.
19 O you daughter dwelling in Egypt,
Prepare yourself to go into captivity!
For Noph[a] shall be waste and desolate, without inhabitant.

20 "Egypt *is* a very pretty heifer,
But destruction comes, it comes from the north.
21 Also her mercenaries are in her midst like fat bulls,
For they also are turned back,
They have fled away together.
They did not stand,
For the day of their calamity had come upon them,
The time of their punishment.
22 Her noise shall go like a serpent,
For they shall march with an army
And come against her with axes,
Like those who chop wood.

23 "They shall cut down her forest," says the LORD,
"Though it cannot be searched,
Because they *are* innumerable,
And more numerous than grasshoppers.
24 The daughter of Egypt shall be ashamed;
She shall be delivered into the hand
Of the people of the north."

25The LORD of hosts, the God of Isra-
el, says: "Behold, I will bring punish-
ment on Amon[a] of No,[b] and Pharaoh
and Egypt, with their gods and their
kings—Pharaoh and those who trust
in him. 26And I will deliver them into
the hand of those who seek their lives,
into the hand of Nebuchadnezzar king
of Babylon and the hand of his servants.
Afterward it shall be inhabited as in the
days of old," says the LORD.

God Will Preserve Israel

27 "But do not fear, O My servant Jacob,
And do not be dismayed, O Israel!
For behold, I will save you from afar,
And your offspring from the land of their captivity;
Jacob shall return, have rest and be at ease;
No one shall make *him* afraid.
28 Do not fear, O Jacob My servant," says the LORD,
"For I *am* with you;
For I will make a complete end of all the nations
To which I have driven you,
But I will not make a complete end of you.
I will rightly correct you,
For I will not leave you wholly unpunished."

Judgment on Philistia

47 The word of the LORD that came
to Jeremiah the prophet against
the Philistines, before Pharaoh attacked
Gaza.
2Thus says the LORD:

"Behold, waters rise out of the north,
And shall be an overflowing flood;
They shall overflow the land and all that is in it,
The city and those who dwell within;
Then the men shall cry,
And all the inhabitants of the land shall wail.
3 At the noise of the stamping hooves of his strong horses,
At the rushing of his chariots,
At the rumbling of his wheels,
The fathers will not look back for *their* children,
Lacking courage,
4 Because of the day that comes to plunder all the Philistines,
To cut off from Tyre and Sidon every helper who remains;
For the LORD shall plunder the Philistines,

46:19 [a] That is, ancient Memphis **46:25** [a] A sun god [b] That is, ancient Thebes

The remnant of the country of
Caphtor.
5 Baldness has come upon Gaza,
Ashkelon is cut off
With the remnant of their valley.
How long will you cut yourself?

6 "O you sword of the LORD,
How long until you are quiet?
Put yourself up into your
scabbard,
Rest and be still!
7 How can it be quiet,
Seeing the LORD has given it a
charge
Against Ashkelon and against the
seashore?
There He has appointed it."

Judgment on Moab

48 Against Moab.
Thus says the LORD of hosts, the
God of Israel:

"Woe to Nebo!
For it is plundered,
Kirjathaim is shamed *and* taken;
The high stronghold[a] is shamed
and dismayed—
2 No more praise of Moab.
In Heshbon they have devised
evil against her:
'Come, and let us cut her off as a
nation.'
You also shall be cut down,
O Madmen![a]
The sword shall pursue you;
3 A voice of crying *shall be* from
Horonaim:
'Plundering and great
destruction!'

4 "Moab is destroyed;
Her little ones have caused a cry
to be heard;[a]
5 For in the Ascent of Luhith they
ascend with continual
weeping;
For in the descent of Horonaim
the enemies have heard a
cry of destruction.

6 "Flee, save your lives!
And be like the juniper[a] in the
wilderness.
7 For because you have trusted
in your works and your
treasures,
You also shall be taken.
And Chemosh shall go forth into
captivity,
His priests and his princes
together.
8 And the plunderer shall come
against every city;
No one shall escape.
The valley also shall perish,
And the plain shall be destroyed,
As the LORD has spoken.

9 "Give wings to Moab,
That she may flee and get away;
For her cities shall be desolate,
Without any to dwell in them.
10 Cursed *is* he who does the work of
the LORD deceitfully,
And cursed *is* he who keeps back
his sword from blood.

11 "Moab has been at ease from his[a]
youth;
He has settled on his dregs,
And has not been emptied from
vessel to vessel,
Nor has he gone into captivity.
Therefore his taste remained in
him,
And his scent has not changed.

12 "Therefore behold, the days are
coming," says the LORD,
"That I shall send him wine-workers
Who will tip him over
And empty his vessels
And break the bottles.
13 Moab shall be ashamed of
Chemosh,
As the house of Israel was
ashamed of Bethel, their
confidence.

14 "How can you say, 'We *are* mighty
And strong men for the war'?

48:1 [a] Hebrew *Misgab* **48:2** [a] A city of Moab **48:4** [a] Following Masoretic Text, Targum, and Vulgate; Septuagint reads *Proclaim it in Zoar*. **48:6** [a] Or *Aroer*, a city of Moab **48:11** [a] The Hebrew uses masculine and feminine pronouns interchangeably in this chapter.

15 Moab is plundered and gone up
from her cities;
Her chosen young men have gone
down to the slaughter," says
the King,
Whose name *is* the LORD of hosts.

16 "The calamity of Moab *is* near at
hand,
And his affliction comes quickly.
17 Bemoan him, all you who are
around him;
And all you who know his name,
Say, 'How the strong staff is broken,
The beautiful rod!'

18 "O daughter inhabiting Dibon,
Come down from *your* glory,
And sit in thirst;
For the plunderer of Moab has
come against you,
He has destroyed your
strongholds.
19 O inhabitant of Aroer,
Stand by the way and watch;
Ask him who flees
And her who escapes;
Say, 'What has happened?'
20 Moab is shamed, for he is broken
down.
Wail and cry!
Tell it in Arnon, that Moab is
plundered.

21 "And judgment has come on the
plain country:
On Holon and Jahzah and
Mephaath,
22 On Dibon and Nebo and Beth
Diblathaim,
23 On Kirjathaim and Beth Gamul
and Beth Meon,
24 On Kerioth and Bozrah,
On all the cities of the land of
Moab,
Far or near.
25 The horn of Moab is cut off,
And his arm is broken," says the
LORD.

26 "Make him drunk,
Because he exalted *himself*
against the LORD.
Moab shall wallow in his vomit,
And he shall also be in derision.
27 For was not Israel a derision to
you?
Was he found among thieves?
For whenever you speak of him,
You shake *your head in scorn.*
28 You who dwell in Moab,
Leave the cities and dwell in the
rock,
And be like the dove *which* makes
her nest
In the sides of the cave's mouth.

29 "We have heard the pride of Moab
(He *is* exceedingly proud),
Of his loftiness and arrogance
and pride,
And of the haughtiness of his
heart."

30 "I know his wrath," says the LORD,
"But it *is* not right;
His lies have made nothing right.
31 Therefore I will wail for Moab,
And I will cry out for all Moab;
I[a] will mourn for the men of Kir
Heres.
32 O vine of Sibmah! I will weep for
you with the weeping of
Jazer.
Your plants have gone over the
sea,
They reach to the sea of Jazer.
The plunderer has fallen on your
summer fruit and your
vintage.
33 Joy and gladness are taken
From the plentiful field
And from the land of Moab;
I have caused wine to fail from
the winepresses;
No one will tread with joyous
shouting—
Not joyous shouting!

34 "From the cry of Heshbon to
Elealeh and to Jahaz
They have uttered their voice,
From Zoar to Horonaim,
Like a three-year-old heifer;[a]
For the waters of Nimrim also
shall be desolate.

48:31 [a] Following Dead Sea Scrolls, Septuagint, and Vulgate; Masoretic Text reads *He.* **48:34** [a] Or *The Third Eglath,* an unknown city (compare Isaiah 15:5)

35 “Moreover,” says the LORD,
“I will cause to cease in Moab
The one who offers *sacrifices* in the high places
And burns incense to his gods.
36 Therefore My heart shall wail like flutes for Moab,
And like flutes My heart shall wail
For the men of Kir Heres.
Therefore the riches they have acquired have perished.

37 “For every head *shall be* bald, and every beard clipped;
On all the hands *shall be* cuts, and on the loins sackcloth—
38 A general lamentation
On all the housetops of Moab,
And in its streets;
For I have broken Moab like a vessel in which *is* no pleasure,” says the LORD.
39 “They shall wail:
‘How she is broken down!
How Moab has turned her back with shame!’
So Moab shall be a derision
And a dismay to all those about her.”

40 For thus says the LORD:

“Behold, one shall fly like an eagle,
And spread his wings over Moab.
41 Kerioth is taken,
And the strongholds are surprised;
The mighty men’s hearts in Moab on that day shall be
Like the heart of a woman in birth pangs.
42 And Moab shall be destroyed as a people,
Because he exalted *himself* against the LORD.
43 Fear and the pit and the snare *shall be* upon you,
O inhabitant of Moab,” says the LORD.
44 “He who flees from the fear shall fall into the pit,
And he who gets out of the pit shall be caught in the snare.
For upon Moab, upon it I will bring
The year of their punishment,” says the LORD.

45 “Those who fled stood under the shadow of Heshbon
Because of exhaustion.
But a fire shall come out of Heshbon,
A flame from the midst of Sihon,
And shall devour the brow of Moab,
The crown of the head of the sons of tumult.
46 Woe to you, O Moab!
The people of Chemosh perish;
For your sons have been taken captive,
And your daughters captive.

47 “Yet I will bring back the captives of Moab
In the latter days,” says the LORD.

Thus far *is* the judgment of Moab.

Judgment on Ammon

49 Against the Ammonites.
Thus says the LORD:

“Has Israel no sons?
Has he no heir?
Why *then* does Milcom[a] inherit Gad,
And his people dwell in its cities?
2 Therefore behold, the days are coming,” says the LORD,
“That I will cause to be heard an alarm of war
In Rabbah of the Ammonites;
It shall be a desolate mound,
And her villages shall be burned with fire.
Then Israel shall take possession of his inheritance,” says the LORD.

3 “Wail, O Heshbon, for Ai is plundered!
Cry, you daughters of Rabbah,
Gird yourselves with sackcloth!
Lament and run to and fro by the walls;

49:1 [a] Hebrew *Malcam,* literally *their king,* a god of the Ammonites; also called *Molech* (compare verse 3)

For Milcom shall go into captivity
With his priests and his princes
together.
4 Why do you boast in the valleys,
Your flowing valley, O backsliding
daughter?
Who trusted in her treasures,
saying,
'Who will come against me?'
5 Behold, I will bring fear upon
you,"
Says the Lord GOD of hosts,
"From all those who are around
you;
You shall be driven out, everyone
headlong,
And no one will gather those who
wander off.
6 But afterward I will bring back
The captives of the people of
Ammon," says the LORD.

Judgment on Edom

7 Against Edom.
Thus says the LORD of hosts:

"*Is* wisdom no more in Teman?
Has counsel perished from the
prudent?
Has their wisdom vanished?
8 Flee, turn back, dwell in the
depths, O inhabitants of
Dedan!
For I will bring the calamity of
Esau upon him,
The time *that* I will punish him.
9 If grape-gatherers came to you,
Would they not leave *some*
gleaning grapes?
If thieves by night,
Would they not destroy until they
have enough?
10 But I have made Esau bare;
I have uncovered his secret
places,[a]
And he shall not be able to hide
himself.
His descendants are plundered,
His brethren and his neighbors,
And he *is* no more.
11 Leave your fatherless children,
I will preserve *them* alive;
And let your widows trust in Me."

12 For thus says the LORD: "Behold,
those whose judgment *was* not to drink
of the cup have assuredly drunk. And
are you the one who will altogether go
unpunished? You shall not go unpun-
ished, but you shall surely drink *of it.*
13 For I have sworn by Myself," says
the LORD, "that Bozrah shall become
a desolation, a reproach, a waste, and
a curse. And all its cities shall be per-
petual wastes."

14 I have heard a message from the
LORD,
And an ambassador has been
sent to the nations:
"Gather together, come against her,
And rise up to battle!

15 "For indeed, I will make you small
among nations,
Despised among men.
16 Your fierceness has deceived you,
The pride of your heart,
O you who dwell in the clefts of
the rock,
Who hold the height of the hill!
Though you make your nest as
high as the eagle,
I will bring you down from there,"
says the LORD.[a]

17 "Edom also shall be an
astonishment;
Everyone who goes by it will be
astonished
And will hiss at all its plagues.
18 As in the overthrow of Sodom and
Gomorrah
And their neighbors," says the
LORD,
"No one shall remain there,
Nor shall a son of man dwell in it.

19 "Behold, he shall come up like a
lion from the floodplain[a] of
the Jordan
Against the dwelling place of the
strong;
But I will suddenly make him run
away from her.
And who *is* a chosen *man that* I
may appoint over her?

49:10 [a] Compare Obadiah 5, 6 49:16 [a] Compare Obadiah 3, 4 49:19 [a] Or *thicket*

For who *is* like Me?
Who will arraign Me?
And who *is* that shepherd
Who will withstand Me?"

20 Therefore hear the counsel of the LORD that He has taken against Edom,
And His purposes that He has proposed against the inhabitants of Teman:
Surely the least of the flock shall draw them out;
Surely He shall make their dwelling places desolate with them.
21 The earth shakes at the noise of their fall;
At the cry its noise is heard at the Red Sea.
22 Behold, He shall come up and fly like the eagle,
And spread His wings over Bozrah;
The heart of the mighty men of Edom in that day shall be
Like the heart of a woman in birth pangs.

Judgment on Damascus

23Against Damascus.

"Hamath and Arpad are shamed,
For they have heard bad news.
They are fainthearted;
There is trouble on the sea;
It cannot be quiet.
24 Damascus has grown feeble;
She turns to flee,
And fear has seized *her.*
Anguish and sorrows have taken her like a woman in labor.
25 Why is the city of praise not deserted, the city of My joy?
26 Therefore her young men shall fall in her streets,
And all the men of war shall be cut off in that day," says the LORD of hosts.
27 "I will kindle a fire in the wall of Damascus,
And it shall consume the palaces of Ben-Hadad."[a]

Judgment on Kedar and Hazor

28Against Kedar and against the king-
doms of Hazor, which Nebuchadnezzar
king of Babylon shall strike.
Thus says the LORD:

"Arise, go up to Kedar,
And devastate the men of the East!
29 Their tents and their flocks they shall take away.
They shall take for themselves their curtains,
All their vessels and their camels;
And they shall cry out to them,
'Fear *is* on every side!'

30 "Flee, get far away! Dwell in the depths,
O inhabitants of Hazor!" says the LORD.
"For Nebuchadnezzar king of Babylon has taken counsel against you,
And has conceived a plan against you.

31 "Arise, go up to the wealthy nation that dwells securely," says the LORD,
"Which has neither gates nor bars,
Dwelling alone.
32 Their camels shall be for booty,
And the multitude of their cattle for plunder.
I will scatter to all winds those in the farthest corners,
And I will bring their calamity from all its sides," says the LORD.
33 "Hazor shall be a dwelling for jackals, a desolation forever;
No one shall reside there,
Nor son of man dwell in it."

Judgment on Elam

34The word of the LORD that came to
Jeremiah the prophet against Elam, in
the beginning of the reign of Zedekiah
king of Judah, saying, 35"Thus says the
LORD of hosts:

'Behold, I will break the bow of Elam,
The foremost of their might.

49:27 [a] Compare Amos 1:4

36 Against Elam I will bring the four winds
From the four quarters of heaven,
And scatter them toward all those winds;
There shall be no nations where the outcasts of Elam will not go.
37 For I will cause Elam to be dismayed before their enemies
And before those who seek their life.
I will bring disaster upon them,
My fierce anger,' says the LORD;
'And I will send the sword after them
Until I have consumed them.
38 I will set My throne in Elam,
And will destroy from there the king and the princes,' says the LORD.

39 'But it shall come to pass in the latter days:
I will bring back the captives of Elam,' says the LORD."

Judgment on Babylon and Babylonia

50 The word that the LORD spoke against Babylon *and* against the land of the Chaldeans by Jeremiah the prophet.

2 "Declare among the nations,
Proclaim, and set up a standard;
Proclaim—do not conceal *it*—
Say, 'Babylon is taken, Bel is shamed.
Merodach[a] is broken in pieces;
Her idols are humiliated,
Her images are broken in pieces.'
3 For out of the north a nation comes up against her,
Which shall make her land desolate,
And no one shall dwell therein.
They shall move, they shall depart,
Both man and beast.

4 "In those days and in that time," says the LORD,
"The children of Israel shall come,
They and the children of Judah together;
With continual weeping they shall come,
And seek the LORD their God.
5 They shall ask the way to Zion,
With their faces toward it, *saying,*
'Come and let us join ourselves to the LORD
In a perpetual covenant
That will not be forgotten.'

6 "My people have been lost sheep.
Their shepherds have led them astray;
They have turned them away *on* the mountains.
They have gone from mountain to hill;
They have forgotten their resting place.
7 All who found them have devoured them;
And their adversaries said, 'We have not offended,
Because they have sinned against the LORD, the habitation of justice,
The LORD, the hope of their fathers.'

8 "Move from the midst of Babylon,
Go out of the land of the Chaldeans;
And be like the rams before the flocks.
9 For behold, I will raise and cause to come up against Babylon
An assembly of great nations from the north country,
And they shall array themselves against her;
From there she shall be captured.
Their arrows *shall be* like *those* of an expert warrior;[a]
None shall return in vain.
10 And Chaldea shall become plunder;
All who plunder her shall be satisfied," says the LORD.

11 "Because you were glad, because you rejoiced,

50:2 [a] A Babylonian god; sometimes spelled *Marduk*

50:9 [a] Following some Hebrew manuscripts, Septuagint, and Syriac; Masoretic Text, Targum, and Vulgate read *a warrior who makes childless.*

You destroyers of My heritage,
Because you have grown fat like a heifer threshing grain,
And you bellow like bulls,
12 Your mother shall be deeply ashamed;
She who bore you shall be ashamed.
Behold, the least of the nations *shall be* a wilderness,
A dry land and a desert.
13 Because of the wrath of the LORD
She shall not be inhabited,
But she shall be wholly desolate.
Everyone who goes by Babylon shall be horrified
And hiss at all her plagues.

14 "Put yourselves in array against Babylon all around,
All you who bend the bow;
Shoot at her, spare no arrows,
For she has sinned against the LORD.
15 Shout against her all around;
She has given her hand,
Her foundations have fallen,
Her walls are thrown down;
For it *is* the vengeance of the LORD.
Take vengeance on her.
As she has done, so do to her.
16 Cut off the sower from Babylon,
And him who handles the sickle at harvest time.
For fear of the oppressing sword
Everyone shall turn to his own people,
And everyone shall flee to his own land.

17 "Israel *is* like scattered sheep;
The lions have driven *him* away.
First the king of Assyria devoured him;
Now at last this Nebuchadnezzar king of Babylon has broken his bones."

18Therefore thus says the LORD of
hosts, the God of Israel:

"Behold, I will punish the king of Babylon and his land,
As I have punished the king of Assyria.
19 But I will bring back Israel to his home,
And he shall feed on Carmel and Bashan;
His soul shall be satisfied on Mount Ephraim and Gilead.
20 In those days and in that time," says the LORD,
"The iniquity of Israel shall be sought, but *there shall be* none;
And the sins of Judah, but they shall not be found;
For I will pardon those whom I preserve.

21 "Go up against the land of Merathaim, against it,
And against the inhabitants of Pekod.
Waste and utterly destroy them," says the LORD,
"And do according to all that I have commanded you.
22 A sound of battle *is* in the land,
And of great destruction.
23 How the hammer of the whole earth has been cut apart and broken!
How Babylon has become a desolation among the nations!
24 I have laid a snare for you;
You have indeed been trapped, O Babylon,
And you were not aware;
You have been found and also caught,
Because you have contended against the LORD.
25 The LORD has opened His armory,
And has brought out the weapons of His indignation;
For this *is* the work of the Lord GOD of hosts
In the land of the Chaldeans.
26 Come against her from the farthest border;
Open her storehouses;
Cast her up as heaps of ruins,
And destroy her utterly;
Let nothing of her be left.
27 Slay all her bulls,
Let them go down to the slaughter.

Woe to them!
For their day has come, the time
of their punishment.
28 The voice of those who flee and
escape from the land of
Babylon
Declares in Zion the vengeance of
the LORD our God,
The vengeance of His temple.

29 "Call together the archers against
Babylon.
All you who bend the bow,
encamp against it all
around;
Let none of them escape.[a]
Repay her according to her work;
According to all she has done, do
to her;
For she has been proud against
the LORD,
Against the Holy One of Israel.
30 Therefore her young men shall
fall in the streets,
And all her men of war shall be
cut off in that day," says the
LORD.
31 "Behold, I *am* against you,
O most haughty one!" says the
Lord GOD of hosts;
"For your day has come,
The time *that* I will punish you.[a]
32 The most proud shall stumble and
fall,
And no one will raise him up;
I will kindle a fire in his cities,
And it will devour all around
him."

33 Thus says the LORD of hosts:

"The children of Israel *were*
oppressed,
Along with the children of Judah;
All who took them captive have
held them fast;
They have refused to let them go.
34 Their Redeemer *is* strong;
The LORD of hosts *is* His name.
He will thoroughly plead their
case,
That He may give rest to the land,
And disquiet the inhabitants of
Babylon.

35 "A sword *is* against the Chaldeans,"
says the LORD,
"Against the inhabitants of Babylon,
And against her princes and her
wise men.
36 A sword *is* against the
soothsayers, and they will be
fools.
A sword *is* against her mighty
men, and they will be
dismayed.
37 A sword *is* against their horses,
Against their chariots,
And against all the mixed peoples
who *are* in her midst;
And they will become like women.
A sword *is* against her treasures,
and they will be robbed.
38 A drought[a] *is* against her waters,
and they will be dried up.
For it *is* the land of carved images,
And they are insane with *their*
idols.

39 "Therefore the wild desert beasts
shall dwell *there* with the
jackals,
And the ostriches shall dwell in it.
It shall be inhabited no more
forever,
Nor shall it be dwelt in from
generation to generation.
40 As God overthrew Sodom and
Gomorrah
And their neighbors," says the
LORD,
"*So* no one shall reside there,
Nor son of man dwell in it.

41 "Behold, a people shall come from
the north,
And a great nation and many
kings
Shall be raised up from the ends
of the earth.
42 They shall hold the bow and the
lance;

50:29 [a] Qere, some Hebrew manuscripts, Septuagint, and Targum add *to her*. **50:31** [a] Following Masoretic Text and Targum; Septuagint and Vulgate read *The time of your punishment*.
50:38 [a] Following Masoretic Text, Targum, and Vulgate; Syriac reads *sword;* Septuagint omits *A drought is*.

They *are* cruel and shall not show mercy.
Their voice shall roar like the sea;
They shall ride on horses,
Set in array, like a man for the battle,
Against you, O daughter of Babylon.

43 "The king of Babylon has heard the report about them,
And his hands grow feeble;
Anguish has taken hold of him,
Pangs as of a woman in childbirth.

44 "Behold, he shall come up like a lion from the floodplain[a] of the Jordan
Against the dwelling place of the strong;
But I will make them suddenly run away from her.
And who *is* a chosen *man that* I may appoint over her?
For who *is* like Me?
Who will arraign Me?
And who *is* that shepherd
Who will withstand Me?"

45 Therefore hear the counsel of the LORD that He has taken against Babylon,
And His purposes that He has proposed against the land of the Chaldeans:
Surely the least of the flock shall draw them out;
Surely He will make their dwelling place desolate with them.
46 At the noise of the taking of Babylon
The earth trembles,
And the cry is heard among the nations.

The Utter Destruction of Babylon

51 Thus says the LORD:

"Behold, I will raise up against Babylon,
Against those who dwell in Leb Kamai,[a]
A destroying wind.
2 And I will send winnowers to Babylon,
Who shall winnow her and empty her land.
For in the day of doom
They shall be against her all around.
3 Against *her* let the archer bend his bow,
And lift himself up against *her* in his armor.
Do not spare her young men;
Utterly destroy all her army.
4 Thus the slain shall fall in the land of the Chaldeans,
And *those* thrust through in her streets.
5 For Israel is not forsaken, nor Judah,
By his God, the LORD of hosts,
Though their land was filled with sin against the Holy One of Israel."

6 Flee from the midst of Babylon,
And every one save his life!
Do not be cut off in her iniquity,
For this *is* the time of the LORD's vengeance;
He shall recompense her.
7 Babylon *was* a golden cup in the LORD's hand,
That made all the earth drunk.
The nations drank her wine;
Therefore the nations are deranged.
8 Babylon has suddenly fallen and been destroyed.
Wail for her!
Take balm for her pain;
Perhaps she may be healed.

9 We would have healed Babylon,
But she is not healed.
Forsake her, and let us go everyone to his own country;
For her judgment reaches to heaven and is lifted up to the skies.
10 The LORD has revealed our righteousness.
Come and let us declare in Zion the work of the LORD our God.

50:44 [a] Or *thicket* **51:1** [a] A code word for Chaldea (Babylonia); may be translated *The Midst of Those Who Rise Up Against Me*

11 Make the arrows bright!
Gather the shields!
The LORD has raised up the spirit
of the kings of the Medes.
For His plan *is* against Babylon to
destroy it,
Because it *is* the vengeance of the
LORD,
The vengeance for His temple.
12 Set up the standard on the walls
of Babylon;
Make the guard strong,
Set up the watchmen,
Prepare the ambushes.
For the LORD has both devised
and done
What He spoke against the
inhabitants of Babylon.
13 O you who dwell by many waters,
Abundant in treasures,
Your end has come,
The measure of your covetousness.
14 The LORD of hosts has sworn by
Himself:
"Surely I will fill you with men, as
with locusts,
And they shall lift up a shout
against you."

15 He has made the earth by His
power;
He has established the world by
His wisdom,
And stretched out the heaven by
His understanding.
16 When He utters *His* voice—
There is a multitude of waters in
the heavens:
"He causes the vapors to ascend
from the ends of the earth;
He makes lightnings for the rain;
He brings the wind out of His
treasures."[a]

17 Everyone is dull-hearted, without
knowledge;
Every metalsmith is put to shame
by the carved image;
For his molded image *is* falsehood,
And *there is* no breath in them.
18 They *are* futile, a work of errors;
In the time of their punishment
they shall perish.

19 The Portion of Jacob *is* not like
them,
For He *is* the Maker of all things;
And *Israel is* the tribe of His
inheritance.
The LORD of hosts *is* His name.

20 "You *are* My battle-ax *and* weapons
of war:
For with you I will break the
nation in pieces;
With you I will destroy kingdoms;
21 With you I will break in pieces the
horse and its rider;
With you I will break in pieces the
chariot and its rider;
22 With you also I will break in
pieces man and woman;
With you I will break in pieces old
and young;
With you I will break in pieces the
young man and the maiden;
23 With you also I will break in pieces
the shepherd and his flock;
With you I will break in pieces the
farmer and his yoke of oxen;
And with you I will break in pieces
governors and rulers.

24 "And I will repay Babylon
And all the inhabitants of Chaldea
For all the evil they have done
In Zion in your sight," says the
LORD.

25 "Behold, I *am* against you,
O destroying mountain,
Who destroys all the earth," says
the LORD.
"And I will stretch out My hand
against you,
Roll you down from the rocks,
And make you a burnt mountain.
26 They shall not take from you a
stone for a corner
Nor a stone for a foundation,
But you shall be desolate forever,"
says the LORD.

27 Set up a banner in the land,
Blow the trumpet among the
nations!
Prepare the nations against her,

51:16 [a] Psalm 135:7

Call the kingdoms together
against her:
Ararat, Minni, and Ashkenaz.
Appoint a general against her;
Cause the horses to come up like
the bristling locusts.
28 Prepare against her the nations,
With the kings of the Medes,
Its governors and all its rulers,
All the land of his dominion.
29 And the land will tremble and
sorrow;
For every purpose of the LORD
shall be performed against
Babylon,
To make the land of Babylon
a desolation without
inhabitant.
30 The mighty men of Babylon have
ceased fighting,
They have remained in their
strongholds;
Their might has failed,
They became *like* women;
They have burned her dwelling
places,
The bars of her *gate* are broken.
31 One runner will run to meet
another,
And one messenger to meet
another,
To show the king of Babylon that
his city is taken on *all* sides;
32 The passages are blocked,
The reeds they have burned with
fire,
And the men of war are terrified.

33For thus says the LORD of hosts, the
God of Israel:

"The daughter of Babylon *is* like a
threshing floor
When it is time to thresh her;
Yet a little while
And the time of her harvest will
come."

34 "Nebuchadnezzar the king of
Babylon
Has devoured me, he has
crushed me;
He has made me an empty vessel,
He has swallowed me up like a
monster;
He has filled his stomach with my
delicacies,
He has spit me out.
35 Let the violence *done* to me and
my flesh *be* upon Babylon,"
The inhabitant of Zion will say;
"And my blood be upon the
inhabitants of Chaldea!"
Jerusalem will say.

36Therefore thus says the LORD:

"Behold, I will plead your case and
take vengeance for you.
I will dry up her sea and make her
springs dry.
37 Babylon shall become a heap,
A dwelling place for jackals,
An astonishment and a hissing,
Without an inhabitant.
38 They shall roar together like lions,
They shall growl like lions' whelps.
39 In their excitement I will prepare
their feasts;
I will make them drunk,
That they may rejoice,
And sleep a perpetual sleep
And not awake," says the LORD.
40 "I will bring them down
Like lambs to the slaughter,
Like rams with male goats.

41 "Oh, how Sheshach[a] is taken!
Oh, how the praise of the whole
earth is seized!
How Babylon has become desolate
among the nations!
42 The sea has come up over Babylon;
She is covered with the multitude
of its waves.
43 Her cities are a desolation,
A dry land and a wilderness,
A land where no one dwells,
Through which no son of man
passes.
44 I will punish Bel in Babylon,
And I will bring out of his mouth
what he has swallowed;
And the nations shall not stream
to him anymore.
Yes, the wall of Babylon shall fall.

51:41 [a] A code word for Babylon (compare Jeremiah 25:26)

45 "My people, go out of the midst of her!
And let everyone deliver himself from the fierce anger of the LORD.
46 And lest your heart faint,
And you fear for the rumor that *will be* heard in the land
(A rumor will come *one* year,
And after that, in *another* year
A rumor *will come,*
And violence in the land,
Ruler against ruler),
47 Therefore behold, the days are coming
That I will bring judgment on the carved images of Babylon;
Her whole land shall be ashamed,
And all her slain shall fall in her midst.
48 Then the heavens and the earth and all that *is* in them
Shall sing joyously over Babylon;
For the plunderers shall come to her from the north," says the LORD.

49 As Babylon *has caused* the slain of Israel to fall,
So at Babylon the slain of all the earth shall fall.
50 You who have escaped the sword,
Get away! Do not stand still!
Remember the LORD afar off,
And let Jerusalem come to your mind.
51 We are ashamed because we have heard reproach.
Shame has covered our faces,
For strangers have come into the sanctuaries of the LORD's house.

52 "Therefore behold, the days are coming," says the LORD,
"That I will bring judgment on her carved images,
And throughout all her land the wounded shall groan.
53 Though Babylon were to mount up to heaven,
And though she were to fortify the height of her strength,
Yet from Me plunderers would come to her," says the LORD.

54 The sound of a cry *comes* from Babylon,
And great destruction from the land of the Chaldeans,
55 Because the LORD is plundering Babylon
And silencing her loud voice,
Though her waves roar like great waters,
And the noise of their voice is uttered,
56 Because the plunderer comes against her, against Babylon,
And her mighty men are taken.
Every one of their bows is broken;
For the LORD *is* the God of recompense,
He will surely repay.

57 "And I will make drunk
Her princes and wise men,
Her governors, her deputies, and her mighty men.
And they shall sleep a perpetual sleep
And not awake," says the King,
Whose name *is* the LORD of hosts.

58 Thus says the LORD of hosts:

"The broad walls of Babylon shall be utterly broken,
And her high gates shall be burned with fire;
The people will labor in vain,
And the nations, because of the fire;
And they shall be weary."

Jeremiah's Command to Seraiah

59 The word which Jeremiah the proph-
et commanded Seraiah the son of Neri-
ah, the son of Mahseiah, when he went
with Zedekiah the king of Judah to Bab-
ylon in the fourth year of his reign. And
Seraiah *was* the quartermaster. 60 So
Jeremiah wrote in a book all the evil
that would come upon Babylon, all
these words that are written against
Babylon. 61 And Jeremiah said to Sera-
iah, "When you arrive in Babylon and

see it, and read all these words, 62then you shall say, 'O LORD, You have spoken against this place to cut it off, so that none shall remain in it, neither man nor beast, but it shall be desolate forever.' 63Now it shall be, when you have finished reading this book, *that* you shall tie a stone to it and throw it out into the Euphrates. 64Then you shall say, 'Thus Babylon shall sink and not rise from the catastrophe that I will bring upon her. And they shall be weary.' "

Thus far *are* the words of Jeremiah.

The Fall of Jerusalem Reviewed

52 Zedekiah *was* twenty-one years old when he became king, and he reigned eleven years in Jerusalem. His mother's name *was* Hamutal the daughter of Jeremiah of Libnah. 2He also did evil in the sight of the LORD, according to all that Jehoiakim had done. 3For because of the anger of the LORD *this* happened in Jerusalem and Judah, till He finally cast them out from His presence. Then Zedekiah rebelled against the king of Babylon.

4Now it came to pass in the ninth year of his reign, in the tenth month, on the tenth *day* of the month, *that* Nebuchadnezzar king of Babylon and all his army came against Jerusalem and encamped against it; and *they* built a siege wall against it all around. 5So the city was besieged until the eleventh year of King Zedekiah. 6By the fourth month, on the ninth day of the month, the famine had become so severe in the city that there was no food for the people of the land. 7Then the city *wall* was broken through, and all the men of war fled and went out of the city at night by way of the gate between the two walls, which *was* by the king's garden, even though the Chaldeans *were* near the city all around. And they went by way of the plain.[a]

8But the army of the Chaldeans pursued the king, and they overtook Zedekiah in the plains of Jericho. All his army was scattered from him. 9So they took the king and brought him up to the king of Babylon at Riblah in the land of Hamath, and he pronounced judgment on him. 10Then the king of Babylon killed the sons of Zedekiah before his eyes. And he killed all the princes of Judah in Riblah. 11He also put out the eyes of Zedekiah; and the king of Babylon bound him in bronze fetters, took him to Babylon, and put him in prison till the day of his death.

The Temple and City Plundered and Burned

12Now in the fifth month, on the tenth *day* of the month (which *was* the nineteenth year of King Nebuchadnezzar king of Babylon), Nebuzaradan, the captain of the guard, *who* served the king of Babylon, came to Jerusalem. 13He burned the house of the LORD and the king's house; all the houses of Jerusalem, that is, all the houses of the great, he burned with fire. 14And all the army of the Chaldeans who *were* with the captain of the guard broke down all the walls of Jerusalem all around. 15Then Nebuzaradan the captain of the guard carried away captive *some* of the poor people, the rest of the people who remained in the city, the defectors who had deserted to the king of Babylon, and the rest of the craftsmen. 16But Nebuzaradan the captain of the guard left *some* of the poor of the land as vinedressers and farmers.

17The bronze pillars that *were* in the house of the LORD, and the carts and the bronze Sea that *were* in the house of the LORD, the Chaldeans broke in pieces, and carried all their bronze to Babylon. 18They also took away the pots, the shovels, the trimmers, the bowls, the spoons, and all the bronze utensils with which the *priests* ministered. 19The basins, the firepans, the bowls, the pots, the lampstands, the spoons, and the cups, whatever *was* solid gold and whatever *was* solid silver, the captain of the guard took away. 20The two pillars, one Sea, the twelve bronze bulls which *were* under *it, and* the carts, which King Solomon had made for the house of the LORD—the bronze of all these articles was beyond measure. 21Now *concerning* the pillars: the height of one

52:7 [a] Or *the Arabah,* that is, the Jordan Valley

pillar *was* eighteen cubits, a measuring
line of twelve cubits could measure its
circumference, and its thickness *was*
four fingers; *it was* hollow. 22A capital of
bronze *was* on it; and the height of one
capital *was* five cubits, with a network
and pomegranates all around the capi-
tal, all of bronze. The second pillar, with
pomegranates was the same. 23There
were ninety-six pomegranates on the
sides; all the pomegranates, all around
on the network, *were* one hundred.

The People Taken Captive to Babylonia

24The captain of the guard took Sera-
iah the chief priest, Zephaniah the sec-
ond priest, and the three doorkeepers.
25He also took out of the city an officer
who had charge of the men of war, seven
men of the king's close associates who
were found in the city, the principal
scribe of the army who mustered the
people of the land, and sixty men of
the people of the land who were found
in the midst of the city. 26And Nebu-
zaradan the captain of the guard took
these and brought them to the king of
Babylon at Riblah. 27Then the king of
Babylon struck them and put them to
death at Riblah in the land of Hamath.
Thus Judah was carried away captive
from its own land.

28These *are* the people whom Nebu-
chadnezzar carried away captive: in
the seventh year, three thousand and
twenty-three Jews; 29in the eighteenth
year of Nebuchadnezzar he carried
away captive from Jerusalem eight hun-
dred and thirty-two persons; 30in the
twenty-third year of Nebuchadnezzar,
Nebuzaradan the captain of the guard
carried away captive of the Jews seven
hundred and forty-five persons. All the
persons *were* four thousand six hundred.

Jehoiachin Released from Prison

31Now it came to pass in the thirty-
seventh year of the captivity of Jehoia-
chin king of Judah, in the twelfth month,
on the twenty-fifth *day* of the month,
that Evil-Merodach[a] king of Babylon,
in the *first* year of his reign, lifted up
the head of Jehoiachin king of Judah
and brought him out of prison. 32And
he spoke kindly to him and gave him a
more prominent seat than those of the
kings who *were* with him in Babylon.
33So Jehoiachin changed from his prison
garments, and he ate bread regularly
before the *king* all the days of his life.
34And as for his provisions, there was a
regular ration given him by the king of
Babylon, a portion for each day until the
day of his death, all the days of his life.

52:31 [a] Or *Awil-Marduk*

THE BOOK OF LAMENTATIONS

The Book of Lamentations is a collection of sad poems. Jeremiah writes these poems as he thinks about Jerusalem and the temple being destroyed. God's people seemed to have lost everything. But Jeremiah also recognizes that God's judgment of Jerusalem and the people was righteous. Jeremiah also knows that God is faithful. God had made promises to His people that He would keep. All seemed hopeless in the moment, but God would restore His people one day.

- **GENRE:** Major Prophet
- **AUTHOR:** Jeremiah
- **TIME:** 586 BC
- **PURPOSE:** To share the distress and despair of the destruction of God's holy city.

Jerusalem in Affliction

1 How lonely sits the city
That was full of people!
How like a widow is she,
Who *was* great among the nations!
The princess among the provinces
Has become a slave!

2 She weeps bitterly in the night,
Her tears *are* on her cheeks;
Among all her lovers
She has none to comfort *her*.
All her friends have dealt
treacherously with her;
They have become her enemies.

3 Judah has gone into captivity,
Under affliction and hard
servitude;
She dwells among the nations,
She finds no rest;
All her persecutors overtake her
in dire straits.

4 The roads to Zion mourn
Because no one comes to the set
feasts.
All her gates are desolate;
Her priests sigh,
Her virgins are afflicted,
And she *is* in bitterness.

5 Her adversaries have become the
master,
Her enemies prosper;
For the LORD has afflicted her
Because of the multitude of her
transgressions.
Her children have gone into
captivity before the enemy.

6 And from the daughter of Zion
All her splendor has departed.
Her princes have become like deer
That find no pasture,
That flee without strength
Before the pursuer.

7 In the days of her affliction and
roaming,
Jerusalem remembers all her
pleasant things
That she had in the days of old.
When her people fell into the
hand of the enemy,
With no one to help her,
The adversaries saw her
And mocked at her downfall.[a]

8 Jerusalem has sinned gravely,
Therefore she has become vile.[a]
All who honored her despise her
Because they have seen her
nakedness;
Yes, she sighs and turns away.

9 Her uncleanness *is* in her skirts;
She did not consider her destiny;

1:7 [a] Vulgate reads *her Sabbaths.* 1:8 [a] Septuagint and Vulgate read *moved* or *removed.*

Therefore her collapse was
awesome;
She had no comforter.
"O LORD, behold my affliction,
For *the* enemy is exalted!"

10 The adversary has spread his hand
Over all her pleasant things;
For she has seen the nations enter
her sanctuary,
Those whom You commanded
Not to enter Your assembly.

11 All her people sigh,
They seek bread;
They have given their valuables
for food to restore life.
"See, O LORD, and consider,
For I am scorned."

12 "*Is it* nothing to you, all you who
pass by?
Behold and see
If there is any sorrow like my
sorrow,
Which has been brought on me,
Which the LORD has inflicted
In the day of His fierce anger.

13 "From above He has sent fire into
my bones,
And it overpowered them;
He has spread a net for my feet
And turned me back;
He has made me desolate
And faint all the day.

14 "The yoke of my transgressions was
bound;[a]
They were woven together by His
hands,
And thrust upon my neck.
He made my strength fail;
The Lord delivered me into the
hands of *those whom* I am
not able to withstand.

15 "The Lord has trampled underfoot
all my mighty *men* in my
midst;
He has called an assembly
against me
To crush my young men;
The Lord trampled *as* in a
winepress
The virgin daughter of Judah.

16 "For these *things* I weep;
My eye, my eye overflows with
water;
Because the comforter, who
should restore my life,
Is far from me.
My children are desolate
Because the enemy prevailed."

17 Zion spreads out her hands,
But no one comforts her;
The LORD has commanded
concerning Jacob
That those around him *become* his
adversaries;
Jerusalem has become an
unclean thing among them.

18 "The LORD is righteous,
For I rebelled against His
commandment.
Hear now, all peoples,
And behold my sorrow;
My virgins and my young men
Have gone into captivity.

19 "I called for my lovers,
But they deceived me;
My priests and my elders
Breathed their last in the city,
While they sought food
To restore their life.

20 "See, O LORD, that I *am* in distress;
My soul is troubled;
My heart is overturned within me,
For I have been very rebellious.
Outside the sword bereaves,
At home *it is* like death.

21 "They have heard that I sigh,
But no one comforts me.
All my enemies have heard of my
trouble;
They are glad that You have
done *it*.
Bring on the day You have
announced,
That they may become like me.

1:14 [a] Following Masoretic Text and Targum; Septuagint, Syriac, and Vulgate read *watched over.*

22 "Let all their wickedness come
before You,
And do to them as You have done
to me
For all my transgressions;
For my sighs *are* many,
And my heart *is* faint."

God's Anger with Jerusalem

2 How the Lord has covered the
daughter of Zion
With a cloud in His anger!
He cast down from heaven to the
earth
The beauty of Israel,
And did not remember His
footstool
In the day of His anger.

2 The Lord has swallowed up and
has not pitied
All the dwelling places of Jacob.
He has thrown down in His wrath
The strongholds of the daughter
of Judah;
He has brought *them* down to the
ground;
He has profaned the kingdom
and its princes.

3 He has cut off in fierce anger
Every horn of Israel;
He has drawn back His right hand
From before the enemy.
He has blazed against Jacob like
a flaming fire
Devouring all around.

4 Standing like an enemy, He has
bent His bow;
With His right hand, like an
adversary,
He has slain all *who were* pleasing
to His eye;
On the tent of the daughter of Zion,
He has poured out His fury like fire.

5 The Lord was like an enemy.
He has swallowed up Israel,
He has swallowed up all her
palaces;
He has destroyed her strongholds,
And has increased mourning and
lamentation
In the daughter of Judah.

6 He has done violence to His
tabernacle,
As if it were a garden;
He has destroyed His place of
assembly;
The LORD has caused
The appointed feasts and
Sabbaths to be forgotten in
Zion.
In His burning indignation He
has spurned the king and the
priest.

7 The Lord has spurned His altar,
He has abandoned His sanctuary;
He has given up the walls of her
palaces
Into the hand of the enemy.
They have made a noise in the
house of the LORD
As on the day of a set feast.

8 The LORD has purposed to destroy
The wall of the daughter of Zion.
He has stretched out a line;
He has not withdrawn His hand
from destroying;
Therefore He has caused the
rampart and wall to lament;
They languished together.

9 Her gates have sunk into the
ground;
He has destroyed and broken her
bars.
Her king and her princes *are*
among the nations;
The Law *is* no *more*,
And her prophets find no vision
from the LORD.

10 The elders of the daughter of Zion
Sit on the ground *and* keep
silence;
They throw dust on their heads
And gird themselves with
sackcloth.
The virgins of Jerusalem
Bow their heads to the ground.

11 My eyes fail with tears,
My heart is troubled;
My bile is poured on the ground
Because of the destruction of the
daughter of my people,

Because the children and the
infants
Faint in the streets of the city.

12 They say to their mothers,
"Where *is* grain and wine?"
As they swoon like the wounded
In the streets of the city,
As their life is poured out
In their mothers' bosom.

13 How shall I console you?
To what shall I liken you,
O daughter of Jerusalem?
What shall I compare with you,
that I may comfort you,
O virgin daughter of Zion?
For your ruin *is* spread wide as
the sea;
Who can heal you?

14 Your prophets have seen for you
False and deceptive visions;
They have not uncovered your
iniquity,
To bring back your captives,
But have envisioned for you false
prophecies and delusions.

15 All who pass by clap *their* hands
at you;
They hiss and shake their heads
At the daughter of Jerusalem:
"*Is* this the city that is called
'The perfection of beauty,
The joy of the whole earth'?"

16 All your enemies have opened
their mouth against you;
They hiss and gnash *their* teeth.
They say, "We have swallowed *her*
up!
Surely this *is* the day we have
waited for;
We have found *it*, we have seen *it!*"

17 The LORD has done what He
purposed;
He has fulfilled His word
Which He commanded in days of
old.
He has thrown down and has not
pitied,
And He has caused an enemy to
rejoice over you;
He has exalted the horn of your
adversaries.

18 Their heart cried out to the Lord,
"O wall of the daughter of Zion,
Let tears run down like a river day
and night;
Give yourself no relief;
Give your eyes no rest.

19 "Arise, cry out in the night,
At the beginning of the watches;
Pour out your heart like water
before the face of the Lord.
Lift your hands toward Him
For the life of your young children,
Who faint from hunger at the
head of every street."

20 "See, O LORD, and consider!
To whom have You done this?
Should the women eat their
offspring,
The children they have cuddled?[a]
Should the priest and prophet be
slain
In the sanctuary of the Lord?

21 "Young and old lie
On the ground in the streets;
My virgins and my young men
Have fallen by the sword;
You have slain *them* in the day of
Your anger,
You have slaughtered *and* not
pitied.

22 "You have invited as to a feast day
The terrors that surround me.
In the day of the LORD's anger
There was no refugee or survivor.
Those whom I have borne and
brought up
My enemies have destroyed."

The Prophet's Anguish and Hope

3 I *am* the man *who* has seen
affliction by the rod of His
wrath.
2 He has led me and made *me* walk
In darkness and not *in* light.

2:20 [a] Vulgate reads *a span long.*

3 Surely He has turned His hand against me
Time and time again throughout the day.

4 He has aged my flesh and my skin,
And broken my bones.
5 He has besieged me
And surrounded *me* with bitterness and woe.
6 He has set me in dark places
Like the dead of long ago.

7 He has hedged me in so that I cannot get out;
He has made my chain heavy.
8 Even when I cry and shout,
He shuts out my prayer.
9 He has blocked my ways with hewn stone;
He has made my paths crooked.

10 He *has been* to me a bear lying in wait,
Like a lion in ambush.
11 He has turned aside my ways and torn me in pieces;
He has made me desolate.
12 He has bent His bow
And set me up as a target for the arrow.

13 He has caused the arrows of His quiver
To pierce my loins.[a]
14 I have become the ridicule of all my people—
Their taunting song all the day.
15 He has filled me with bitterness,
He has made me drink wormwood.

16 He has also broken my teeth with gravel,
And covered me with ashes.
17 You have moved my soul far from peace;
I have forgotten prosperity.
18 And I said, "My strength and my hope
Have perished from the LORD."

19 Remember my affliction and roaming,
The wormwood and the gall.
20 My soul still remembers
And sinks within me.
21 This I recall to my mind,
Therefore I have hope.

22 *Through* the LORD's mercies we are not consumed,
Because His compassions fail not.
23 *They are* new every morning;
Great *is* Your faithfulness.
24 "The LORD *is* my portion," says my soul,
"Therefore I hope in Him!"

25 The LORD *is* good to those who wait for Him,
To the soul *who* seeks Him.
26 *It is* good that *one* should hope and wait quietly
For the salvation of the LORD.
27 *It is* good for a man to bear
The yoke in his youth.

28 Let him sit alone and keep silent,
Because *God* has laid *it* on him;
29 Let him put his mouth in the dust—
There may yet be hope.
30 Let him give *his* cheek to the one who strikes him,
And be full of reproach.

31 For the Lord will not cast off forever.
32 Though He causes grief,
Yet He will show compassion
According to the multitude of His mercies.
33 For He does not afflict willingly,
Nor grieve the children of men.

34 To crush under one's feet
All the prisoners of the earth,
35 To turn aside the justice *due* a man
Before the face of the Most High,
36 Or subvert a man in his cause—
The Lord does not approve.

37 Who *is* he *who* speaks and it comes to pass,
When the Lord has not commanded *it?*

3:13 [a] Literally *kidneys*

38 *Is it* not from the mouth of the Most High
That woe and well-being proceed?
39 Why should a living man complain,
A man for the punishment of his sins?

40 Let us search out and examine our ways,
And turn back to the LORD;
41 Let us lift our hearts and hands
To God in heaven.
42 We have transgressed and rebelled;
You have not pardoned.

43 You have covered *Yourself* with anger
And pursued us;
You have slain *and* not pitied.
44 You have covered Yourself with a cloud,
That prayer should not pass through.
45 You have made us an offscouring and refuse
In the midst of the peoples.

46 All our enemies
Have opened their mouths against us.
47 Fear and a snare have come upon us,
Desolation and destruction.
48 My eyes overflow with rivers of water
For the destruction of the daughter of my people.

49 My eyes flow and do not cease,
Without interruption,
50 Till the LORD from heaven
Looks down and sees.
51 My eyes bring suffering to my soul
Because of all the daughters of my city.

52 My enemies without cause
Hunted me down like a bird.
53 They silenced[a] my life in the pit
And threw stones at me.
54 The waters flowed over my head;
I said, "I am cut off!"

55 I called on Your name, O LORD,
From the lowest pit.
56 You have heard my voice:
"Do not hide Your ear
From my sighing, from my cry for help."
57 You drew near on the day I called on You,
And said, "Do not fear!"

58 O Lord, You have pleaded the case for my soul;
You have redeemed my life.
59 O LORD, You have seen *how* I am wronged;
Judge my case.
60 You have seen all their vengeance,
All their schemes against me.

61 You have heard their reproach, O LORD,
All their schemes against me,
62 The lips of my enemies
And their whispering against me all the day.
63 Look at their sitting down and their rising up;
I *am* their taunting song.

64 Repay them, O LORD,
According to the work of their hands.
65 Give them a veiled[a] heart;
Your curse *be* upon them!
66 In Your anger,
Pursue and destroy them
From under the heavens of the LORD.

The Degradation of Zion

4 How the gold has become dim!
How changed the fine gold!
The stones of the sanctuary are scattered
At the head of every street.

2 The precious sons of Zion,
Valuable as fine gold,
How they are regarded as clay pots,

3:53 [a] Septuagint reads *put to death.* 3:65 [a] A Jewish tradition reads *sorrow of.*

The work of the hands of the
potter!

3 Even the jackals present their
breasts
To nurse their young;
But the daughter of my people *is*
cruel,
Like ostriches in the wilderness.

4 The tongue of the infant clings
To the roof of its mouth for thirst;
The young children ask for bread,
But no one breaks *it* for them.

5 Those who ate delicacies
Are desolate in the streets;
Those who were brought up in
scarlet
Embrace ash heaps.

6 The punishment of the iniquity of
the daughter of my people
Is greater than the punishment of
the sin of Sodom,
Which was overthrown in a
moment,
With no hand to help her!

7 Her Nazirites[a] were brighter than
snow
And whiter than milk;
They were more ruddy in body
than rubies,
Like sapphire in their appearance.

8 *Now* their appearance is blacker
than soot;
They go unrecognized in the
streets;
Their skin clings to their bones,
It has become as dry as wood.

9 *Those* slain by the sword are better
off
Than *those* who die of hunger;
For these pine away,
Stricken *for lack* of the fruits of the
field.

10 The hands of the compassionate
women
Have cooked their own children;
They became food for them
In the destruction of the daughter
of my people.

11 The LORD has fulfilled His fury,
He has poured out His fierce
anger.
He kindled a fire in Zion,
And it has devoured its
foundations.

12 The kings of the earth,
And all inhabitants of the world,
Would not have believed
That the adversary and the enemy
Could enter the gates of
Jerusalem—

13 Because of the sins of her prophets
And the iniquities of her priests,
Who shed in her midst
The blood of the just.

14 They wandered blind in the streets;
They have defiled themselves with
blood,
So that no one would touch their
garments.

15 They cried out to them,
"Go away, unclean!
Go away, go away,
Do not touch us!"
When they fled and wandered,
Those among the nations said,
"They shall no longer dwell *here.*"

16 The face[a] of the LORD scattered
them;
He no longer regards them.
The people do not respect the
priests
Nor show favor to the elders.

17 Still our eyes failed us,
Watching vainly for our help;
In our watching we watched
For a nation *that* could not
save *us.*

18 They tracked our steps
So that we could not walk in our
streets.

4:7 [a] Or *nobles* **4:16** [a] Targum reads *anger.*

Our end was near;
Our days were over,
For our end had come.

19 Our pursuers were swifter
Than the eagles of the heavens.
They pursued us on the mountains
And lay in wait for us in the wilderness.

20 The breath of our nostrils, the anointed of the LORD,
Was caught in their pits,
Of whom we said, "Under his shadow
We shall live among the nations."

21 Rejoice and be glad, O daughter of Edom,
You who dwell in the land of Uz!
The cup shall also pass over to you
And you shall become drunk and make yourself naked.

22 *The punishment of* your iniquity is accomplished,
O daughter of Zion;
He will no longer send you into captivity.
He will punish your iniquity,
O daughter of Edom;
He will uncover your sins!

Prayer for Restoration

5 Remember, O LORD, what has come upon us;
Look, and behold our reproach!
2 Our inheritance has been turned over to aliens,
And our houses to foreigners.
3 We have become orphans and waifs,
Our mothers *are* like widows.

4 We pay for the water we drink,
And our wood comes at a price.
5 *They* pursue at our heels;[a]
We labor *and* have no rest.
6 We have given our hand *to* the Egyptians
And the Assyrians, to be satisfied with bread.
7 Our fathers sinned *and are* no more,
But we bear their iniquities.
8 Servants rule over us;
There is none to deliver *us* from their hand.
9 We get our bread *at the risk* of our lives,
Because of the sword in the wilderness.

10 Our skin is hot as an oven,
Because of the fever of famine.
11 They ravished the women in Zion,
The maidens in the cities of Judah.
12 Princes were hung up by their hands,
And elders were not respected.
13 Young men ground at the millstones;
Boys staggered under *loads of* wood.
14 The elders have ceased *gathering at* the gate,
And the young men from their music.

15 The joy of our heart has ceased;
Our dance has turned into mourning.
16 The crown has fallen *from* our head.
Woe to us, for we have sinned!
17 Because of this our heart is faint;
Because of these *things* our eyes grow dim;
18 Because of Mount Zion which is desolate,
With foxes walking about on it.

19 You, O LORD, remain forever;
Your throne from generation to generation.
20 Why do You forget us forever,
And forsake us for so long a time?
21 Turn us back to You, O LORD, and we will be restored;
Renew our days as of old,
22 Unless You have utterly rejected us,
And are very angry with us!

5:5 [a] Literally *necks*

THE BOOK OF EZEKIEL

Ezekiel ministers to the Jews who had been captured and taken to live in Babylon. Ezekiel sees himself as a watchman or lookout who is in Babylon to warn God's people of still further coming danger. During the first part of his ministry, Ezekiel prophesies that Jerusalem and the temple would be destroyed. After that happens, Ezekiel tells the people about a future of hope and rebuilding.

- **GENRE:** Major Prophet
- **AUTHOR:** Ezekiel
- **TIME:** c. 592–570 BC
- **PURPOSE:** To preserve the history of Judah and to show that God loves and comforts His people even during terrible times.

Ezekiel's Vision of God

1 Now it came to pass in the thirtieth year, in the fourth *month,* on the fifth *day* of the month, as I *was* among the captives by the River Chebar, *that* the heavens were opened and I saw visions[a] of God. 2On the fifth *day* of the month, which *was* in the fifth year of King Jehoiachin's captivity, 3the word of the LORD came expressly to Ezekiel the priest, the son of Buzi, in the land of the Chaldeans[a] by the River Chebar; and the hand of the LORD was upon him there.

4Then I looked, and behold, a whirlwind was coming out of the north, a great cloud with raging fire engulfing itself; and brightness *was* all around it and radiating out of its midst like the color of amber, out of the midst of the fire. 5Also from within it *came* the likeness of four living creatures. And this *was* their appearance: they had the likeness of a man. 6Each one had four faces, and each one had four wings. 7Their legs *were* straight, and the soles of their feet *were* like the soles of calves' feet. They sparkled like the color of burnished bronze. 8The hands of a man *were* under their wings on their four sides; and each of the four had faces and wings. 9Their wings touched one another. *The creatures* did not turn when they went, but each one went straight forward.

10As for the likeness of their faces, *each* had the face of a man; each of the four had the face of a lion on the right side, each of the four had the face of an ox on the left side, and each of the four had the face of an eagle. 11Thus *were* their faces. Their wings stretched upward; two *wings* of each one touched one another, and two covered their bodies. 12And each one went straight forward; they went wherever the spirit wanted to go, and they did not turn when they went.

13As for the likeness of the living creatures, their appearance *was* like burning coals of fire, like the appearance of torches going back and forth among the living creatures. The fire was bright, and out of the fire went lightning. 14And the living creatures ran back and forth, in appearance like a flash of lightning.

15Now as I looked at the living creatures, behold, a wheel *was* on the earth beside each living creature with its four faces. 16The appearance of the wheels and their workings *was* like the color of beryl, and all four had the same likeness. The appearance of their workings *was,* as it were, a wheel in the middle of a wheel. 17When they moved, they went toward any one of four directions; they did not turn aside when they went. 18As for their rims, they were so high they were awesome; and their rims *were* full of eyes, all around the

1:1 [a] Following Masoretic Text, Septuagint, and Vulgate; Syriac and Targum read *a vision.* 1:3 [a] Or *Babylonians,* and so elsewhere in this book

four of them. 19When the living creatures
went, the wheels went beside them; and
when the living creatures were lifted up
from the earth, the wheels were lifted up.
20Wherever the spirit wanted to go, they
went, *because* there the spirit went; and
the wheels were lifted together with them,
for the spirit of the living creatures[a] *was*
in the wheels. 21When those went, *these*
went; when those stood, *these* stood; and
when those were lifted up from the earth,
the wheels were lifted up together with
them, for the spirit of the living creatures[a]
was in the wheels.

22The likeness of the firmament above
the heads of the living creatures[a] *was*
like the color of an awesome crystal,
stretched out over their heads. 23And
under the firmament their wings *spread
out* straight, one toward another. Each
one had two which covered one side,
and each one had two which covered
the other side of the body. 24When they
went, I heard the noise of their wings,
like the noise of many waters, like the
voice of the Almighty, a tumult like the
noise of an army; and when they stood
still, they let down their wings. 25A voice
came from above the firmament that
was over their heads; whenever they
stood, they let down their wings.

26And above the firmament over their
heads *was* the likeness of a throne, in
appearance like a sapphire stone; on
the likeness of the throne *was* a likeness
with the appearance of a man high
above it. 27Also from the appearance of
His waist and upward I saw, as it were,
the color of amber with the appearance
of fire all around within it; and from the
appearance of His waist and downward
I saw, as it were, the appearance of fire
with brightness all around. 28Like the
appearance of a rainbow in a cloud on
a rainy day, so *was* the appearance of
the brightness all around it. This *was*
the appearance of the likeness of the
glory of the LORD.

Ezekiel Sent to Rebellious Israel

So when I saw *it,* I fell on my face, and
I heard a voice of One speaking.

2 And He said to me, "Son of man,
stand on your feet, and I will speak
to you." 2Then the Spirit entered me
when He spoke to me, and set me on
my feet; and I heard Him who spoke to
me. 3And He said to me: "Son of man,
I am sending you to the children of
Israel, to a rebellious nation that has
rebelled against Me; they and their fa-
thers have transgressed against Me to
this very day. 4For *they are* impudent
and stubborn children. I am sending
you to them, and you shall say to
them, 'Thus says the Lord GOD.' 5As for
them, whether they hear or whether
they refuse—for they *are* a rebellious
house—yet they will know that a proph-
et has been among them.

6"And you, son of man, do not be
afraid of them nor be afraid of their
words, though briers and thorns *are*
with you and you dwell among scorpi-
ons; do not be afraid of their words or
dismayed by their looks, though they
are a rebellious house. 7You shall speak
My words to them, whether they hear or
whether they refuse, for they *are* rebel-
lious. 8But you, son of man, hear what
I say to you. Do not be rebellious like
that rebellious house; open your mouth
and eat what I give you."

9Now when I looked, there was a hand
stretched out to me; and behold, a scroll
of a book *was* in it. 10Then He spread it
before me; and *there was* writing on the
inside and on the outside, and written
on it *were* lamentations and mourning
and woe.

3 Moreover He said to me, "Son of
man, eat what you find; eat this
scroll, and go, speak to the house of
Israel." 2So I opened my mouth, and
He caused me to eat that scroll.

3And He said to me, "Son of man,
feed your belly, and fill your stomach
with this scroll that I give you." So I ate,
and it was in my mouth like honey in
sweetness.

4Then He said to me: "Son of man, go
to the house of Israel and speak with
My words to them. 5For you *are* not sent
to a people of unfamiliar speech and of

1:20 [a] Literally *living creature;* Septuagint and Vulgate read *spirit of life;* Targum reads *creatures.*
1:21 [a] Literally *living creature;* Septuagint and Vulgate read *spirit of life;* Targum reads *creatures.*
1:22 [a] Following Septuagint, Targum, and Vulgate; Masoretic Text reads *living creature.*

hard language, *but* to the house of Israel, 6not to many people of unfamiliar speech and of hard language, whose words you cannot understand. Surely, had I sent you to them, they would have listened to you. 7But the house of Israel will not listen to you, because they will not listen to Me; for all the house of Israel *are* impudent and hard-hearted. 8Behold, I have made your face strong against their faces, and your forehead strong against their foreheads. 9Like adamant stone, harder than flint, I have made your forehead; do not be afraid of them, nor be dismayed at their looks, though they *are* a rebellious house."

10Moreover He said to me: "Son of man, receive into your heart all My words that I speak to you, and hear with your ears. 11And go, get to the captives, to the children of your people, and speak to them and tell them, 'Thus says the Lord GOD,' whether they hear, or whether they refuse."

12Then the Spirit lifted me up, and I heard behind me a great thunderous voice: "Blessed *is* the glory of the LORD from His place!" 13*I* also *heard* the noise of the wings of the living creatures that touched one another, and the noise of the wheels beside them, and a great thunderous noise. 14So the Spirit lifted me up and took me away, and I went in bitterness, in the heat of my spirit; but the hand of the LORD was strong upon me. 15Then I came to the captives at Tel Abib, who dwelt by the River Chebar; and I sat where they sat, and remained there astonished among them seven days.

Ezekiel Is a Watchman

16Now it came to pass at the end of seven days that the word of the LORD came to me, saying, 17"Son of man, I have made you a watchman for the house of Israel; therefore hear a word from My mouth, and give them warning from Me: 18When I say to the wicked, 'You shall surely die,' and you give him no warning, nor speak to warn the wicked from his wicked way, to save his life, that same wicked *man* shall die in his iniquity; but his blood I will require at your hand. 19Yet, if you warn the wicked, and he does not turn from his wickedness, nor from his wicked way, he shall die in his iniquity; but you have delivered your soul.

20"Again, when a righteous *man* turns from his righteousness and commits iniquity, and I lay a stumbling block before him, he shall die; because you did not give him warning, he shall die in his sin, and his righteousness which he has done shall not be remembered; but his blood I will require at your hand. 21Nevertheless if you warn the righteous *man* that the righteous should not sin, and he does not sin, he shall surely live because he took warning; also you will have delivered your soul."

22Then the hand of the LORD was upon me there, and He said to me, "Arise, go out into the plain, and there I shall talk with you."

23So I arose and went out into the plain, and behold, the glory of the LORD stood there, like the glory which I saw by the River Chebar; and I fell on my face. 24Then the Spirit entered me and set me on my feet, and spoke with me and said to me: "Go, shut yourself inside your house. 25And you, O son of man, surely they will put ropes on you and bind you with them, so that you cannot go out among them. 26I will make your tongue cling to the roof of your mouth, so that you shall be mute and not be one to rebuke them, for they *are* a rebellious house. 27But when I speak with you, I will open your mouth, and you shall say to them, 'Thus says the Lord GOD.' He who hears, let him hear; and he who refuses, let him refuse; for they *are* a rebellious house.

The Siege of Jerusalem Portrayed

4 "You also, son of man, take a clay tablet and lay it before you, and portray on it a city, Jerusalem. 2Lay siege against it, build a siege wall against it, and heap up a mound against it; set camps against it also, and place battering rams against it all around. 3Moreover take for yourself an iron plate, and set it *as* an iron wall between you and the city. Set your face against it, and it shall be besieged, and you shall lay siege against it. This *will be* a sign to the house of Israel.

4“Lie also on your left side, and lay the iniquity of the house of Israel upon it. *According* to the number of the days that you lie on it, you shall bear their iniquity. 5For I have laid on you the years of their iniquity, according to the number of the days, three hundred and ninety days; so you shall bear the iniquity of the house of Israel. 6And when you have completed them, lie again on your right side; then you shall bear the iniquity of the house of Judah forty days. I have laid on you a day for each year.

7“Therefore you shall set your face toward the siege of Jerusalem; your arm *shall be* uncovered, and you shall prophesy against it. 8And surely I will restrain you so that you cannot turn from one side to another till you have ended the days of your siege.

9“Also take for yourself wheat, barley, beans, lentils, millet, and spelt; put them into one vessel, and make bread of them for yourself. *During* the number of days that you lie on your side, three hundred and ninety days, you shall eat it. 10And your food which you eat *shall be* by weight, twenty shekels a day; from time to time you shall eat it. 11You shall also drink water by measure, one-sixth of a hin; from time to time you shall drink. 12And you shall eat it *as* barley cakes; and bake it using fuel of human waste in their sight.”

13Then the LORD said, “So shall the children of Israel eat their defiled bread among the Gentiles, where I will drive them.”

14So I said, “Ah, Lord GOD! Indeed I have never defiled myself from my youth till now; I have never eaten what died of itself or was torn by beasts, nor has abominable flesh ever come into my mouth.”

15Then He said to me, “See, I am giving you cow dung instead of human waste, and you shall prepare your bread over it.”

16Moreover He said to me, “Son of man, surely I will cut off the supply of bread in Jerusalem; they shall eat bread by weight and with anxiety, and shall drink water by measure and with dread, 17that they may lack bread and water, and be dismayed with one another, and waste away because of their iniquity.

A Sword Against Jerusalem

5 “And you, son of man, take a sharp sword, take it as a barber’s razor, and pass *it* over your head and your beard; then take scales to weigh and divide the *hair*. 2You shall burn with fire one-third in the midst of the city, when the days of the siege are finished; then you shall take one-third and strike around *it* with the sword, and one-third you shall scatter in the wind: I will draw out a sword after them. 3You shall also take a small number of them and bind them in the edge of your *garment*. 4Then take some of them again and throw them into the midst of the fire, and burn them in the fire. From there a fire will go out into all the house of Israel.

5“Thus says the Lord GOD: ‘This *is* Jerusalem; I have set her in the midst of the nations and the countries all around her. 6She has rebelled against My judgments by doing wickedness more than the nations, and against My statutes more than the countries that *are* all around her; for they have refused My judgments, and they have not walked in My statutes.’ 7Therefore thus says the Lord GOD: ‘Because you have multiplied *disobedience* more than the nations that *are* all around you, have not walked in My statutes nor kept My judgments, nor even done[a] according to the judgments of the nations that *are* all around you’— 8therefore thus says the Lord GOD: ‘Indeed I, even I, *am* against you and will execute judgments in your midst in the sight of the nations. 9And I will do among you what I have never done, and the like of which I will never do again, because of all your abominations. 10Therefore fathers shall eat *their* sons in your midst, and sons shall eat their fathers; and I will execute judgments among you, and all of you who remain I will scatter to all the winds.

11‘Therefore, *as* I live,’ says the Lord GOD, ‘surely, because you have defiled

5:7 [a] Following Masoretic Text, Septuagint, Targum, and Vulgate; many Hebrew manuscripts and Syriac read *but have done* (compare 11:12).

My sanctuary with all your detestable
things and with all your abominations,
therefore I will also diminish *you;* My eye
will not spare, nor will I have any pity.
12One-third of you shall die of the pes-
tilence, and be consumed with famine
in your midst; and one-third shall fall
by the sword all around you; and I will
scatter another third to all the winds,
and I will draw out a sword after them.

13'Thus shall My anger be spent, and
I will cause My fury to rest upon them,
and I will be avenged; and they shall
know that I, the LORD, have spoken *it*
in My zeal, when I have spent My fury
upon them. 14Moreover I will make you
a waste and a reproach among the na-
tions that *are* all around you, in the
sight of all who pass by.

15'So it[a] shall be a reproach, a taunt,
a lesson, and an astonishment to the
nations that *are* all around you, when I
execute judgments among you in anger
and in fury and in furious rebukes. I,
the LORD, have spoken. 16When I send
against them the terrible arrows of
famine which shall be for destruction,
which I will send to destroy you, I will
increase the famine upon you and cut
off your supply of bread. 17So I will send
against you famine and wild beasts,
and they will bereave you. Pestilence
and blood shall pass through you, and
I will bring the sword against you. I, the
LORD, have spoken.' "

Judgment on Idolatrous Israel

6 Now the word of the LORD came to
me, saying: 2"Son of man, set your
face toward the mountains of Israel,
and prophesy against them, 3and say,
'O mountains of Israel, hear the word of
the Lord GOD! Thus says the Lord GOD
to the mountains, to the hills, to the ra-
vines, and to the valleys: "Indeed I, *even*
I, will bring a sword against you, and
I will destroy your high places. 4Then
your altars shall be desolate, your in-
cense altars shall be broken, and I will
cast down your slain *men* before your
idols. 5And I will lay the corpses of the
children of Israel before their idols, and
I will scatter your bones all around your
altars. 6In all your dwelling places the
cities shall be laid waste, and the high
places shall be desolate, so that your
altars may be laid waste and made deso-
late, your idols may be broken and made
to cease, your incense altars may be cut
down, and your works may be abolished.
7The slain shall fall in your midst, and
you shall know that I *am* the LORD.

8"Yet I will leave a remnant, so that
you may have *some* who escape the
sword among the nations, when you
are scattered through the countries.
9Then those of you who escape will re-
member Me among the nations where
they are carried captive, because I was
crushed by their adulterous heart which
has departed from Me, and by their
eyes which play the harlot after their
idols; they will loathe themselves for the
evils which they committed in all their
abominations. 10And they shall know
that I *am* the LORD; I have not said in
vain that I would bring this calamity
upon them."

11'Thus says the Lord GOD: "Pound
your fists and stamp your feet, and say,
'Alas, for all the evil abominations of the
house of Israel! For they shall fall by the
sword, by famine, and by pestilence.
12He who is far off shall die by the pes-
tilence, he who is near shall fall by the
sword, and he who remains and is be-
sieged shall die by the famine. Thus will
I spend My fury upon them. 13Then you
shall know that I *am* the LORD, when
their slain are among their idols all
around their altars, on every high hill,
on all the mountaintops, under every
green tree, and under every thick oak,
wherever they offered sweet incense to
all their idols. 14So I will stretch out My
hand against them and make the land
desolate, yes, more desolate than the
wilderness toward Diblah, in all their
dwelling places. Then they shall know
that I *am* the LORD.' " ' "

Judgment on Israel Is Near

7 Moreover the word of the LORD
came to me, saying, 2"And you, son
of man, thus says the Lord GOD to the
land of Israel:

5:15 a Septuagint, Syriac, Targum, and Vulgate read *you.*

'An end! The end has come upon
the four corners of the land.
3 Now the end *has come* upon you,
And I will send My anger against
you;
I will judge you according to your
ways,
And I will repay you for all your
abominations.
4 My eye will not spare you,
Nor will I have pity;
But I will repay your ways,
And your abominations will be in
your midst;
Then you shall know that I *am* the
LORD!'

5"Thus says the Lord GOD:

'A disaster, a singular disaster;
Behold, it has come!
6 An end has come,
The end has come;
It has dawned for you;
Behold, it has come!
7 Doom has come to you, you who
dwell in the land;
The time has come,
A day of trouble *is* near,
And not of rejoicing in the
mountains.
8 Now upon you I will soon pour
out My fury,
And spend My anger upon you;
I will judge you according to your
ways,
And I will repay you for all your
abominations.
9 'My eye will not spare,
Nor will I have pity;
I will repay you according to your
ways,
And your abominations will be in
your midst.
Then you shall know that I *am* the
LORD who strikes.

10 'Behold, the day!
Behold, it has come!
Doom has gone out;
The rod has blossomed,
Pride has budded.
11 Violence has risen up into a rod of
wickedness;
None of them *shall remain,*
None of their multitude,
None of them;
Nor *shall there be* wailing for them.
12 The time has come,
The day draws near.

'Let not the buyer rejoice,
Nor the seller mourn,
For wrath *is* on their whole
multitude.
13 For the seller shall not return to
what has been sold,
Though he may still be alive;
For the vision concerns the whole
multitude,
And it shall not turn back;
No one will strengthen himself
Who lives in iniquity.

14 'They have blown the trumpet and
made everyone ready,
But no one goes to battle;
For My wrath *is* on all their
multitude.
15 The sword *is* outside,
And the pestilence and famine
within.
Whoever *is* in the field
Will die by the sword;
And whoever *is* in the city,
Famine and pestilence will
devour him.

16 'Those who survive will escape and
be on the mountains
Like doves of the valleys,
All of them mourning,
Each for his iniquity.
17 Every hand will be feeble,
And every knee will be *as* weak *as*
water.
18 They will also be girded with
sackcloth;
Horror will cover them;
Shame *will be* on every face,
Baldness on all their heads.

19 'They will throw their silver into the
streets,
And their gold will be like refuse;
Their silver and their gold will not
be able to deliver them
In the day of the wrath of the
LORD;

They will not satisfy their souls,
Nor fill their stomachs,
Because it became their
stumbling block of iniquity.

20 'As for the beauty of his
ornaments,
He set it in majesty;
But they made from it
The images of their
abominations—
Their detestable things;
Therefore I have made it
Like refuse to them.
21 I will give it as plunder
Into the hands of strangers,
And to the wicked of the earth as
spoil;
And they shall defile it.
22 I will turn My face from them,
And they will defile My secret
place;
For robbers shall enter it and
defile it.

23 'Make a chain,
For the land is filled with crimes
of blood,
And the city is full of violence.
24 Therefore I will bring the worst of
the Gentiles,
And they will possess their
houses;
I will cause the pomp of the
strong to cease,
And their holy places shall be
defiled.
25 Destruction comes;
They will seek peace, but *there
shall be* none.
26 Disaster will come upon disaster,
And rumor will be upon rumor.
Then they will seek a vision from
a prophet;
But the law will perish from the
priest,
And counsel from the elders.

27 'The king will mourn,
The prince will be clothed with
desolation,
And the hands of the common
people will tremble.
I will do to them according to
their way,
And according to what they
deserve I will judge them;
Then they shall know that I *am*
the LORD!' "

Abominations in the Temple

8 And it came to pass in the sixth year,
in the sixth *month,* on the fifth *day*
of the month, as I sat in my house with
the elders of Judah sitting before me,
that the hand of the Lord GOD fell upon
me there. 2Then I looked, and there was
a likeness, like the appearance of fire—
from the appearance of His waist and
downward, fire; and from His waist
and upward, like the appearance of
brightness, like the color of amber. 3He
stretched out the form of a hand, and
took me by a lock of my hair; and the
Spirit lifted me up between earth and
heaven, and brought me in visions of
God to Jerusalem, to the door of the
north gate of the inner *court,* where the
seat of the image of jealousy *was,* which
provokes to jealousy. 4And behold, the
glory of the God of Israel *was* there, like
the vision that I saw in the plain.
5Then He said to me, "Son of man, lift
your eyes now toward the north." So I
lifted my eyes toward the north, and
there, north of the altar gate, was this
image of jealousy in the entrance.
6Furthermore He said to me, "Son of
man, do you see what they are doing,
the great abominations that the house
of Israel commits here, to make Me go
far away from My sanctuary? Now turn
again, you will see greater abomina-
tions." 7So He brought me to the door
of the court; and when I looked, there
was a hole in the wall. 8Then He said
to me, "Son of man, dig into the wall";
and when I dug into the wall, there was
a door.
9And He said to me, "Go in, and see
the wicked abominations which they
are doing there." 10So I went in and saw,
and there—every sort of creeping thing,
abominable beasts, and all the idols
of the house of Israel, portrayed all
around on the walls. 11And there stood
before them seventy men of the elders
of the house of Israel, and in their midst
stood Jaazaniah the son of Shaphan.
Each man had a censer in his hand,

and a thick cloud of incense went up. 12Then He said to me, "Son of man, have you seen what the elders of the house of Israel do in the dark, every man in the room of his idols? For they say, 'The LORD does not see us, the LORD has forsaken the land.' "

13And He said to me, "Turn again, *and* you will see greater abominations that they are doing." 14So He brought me to the door of the north gate of the LORD's house; and to my dismay, women were sitting there weeping for Tammuz.

15Then He said to me, "Have you seen *this,* O son of man? Turn again, you will see greater abominations than these." 16So He brought me into the inner court of the LORD's house; and there, at the door of the temple of the LORD, between the porch and the altar, *were* about twenty-five men with their backs toward the temple of the LORD and their faces toward the east, and they were worshiping the sun toward the east.

17And He said to me, "Have you seen *this,* O son of man? Is it a trivial thing to the house of Judah to commit the abominations which they commit here? For they have filled the land with violence; then they have returned to provoke Me to anger. Indeed they put the branch to their nose. 18Therefore I also will act in fury. My eye will not spare nor will I have pity; and though they cry in My ears with a loud voice, I will not hear them."

The Wicked Are Slain

9 Then He called out in my hearing with a loud voice, saying, "Let those who have charge over the city draw near, each *with* a deadly weapon in his hand." 2And suddenly six men came from the direction of the upper gate, which faces north, each with his battle-ax in his hand. One man among them *was* clothed with linen and had a writer's inkhorn at his side. They went in and stood beside the bronze altar.

3Now the glory of the God of Israel had gone up from the cherub, where it had been, to the threshold of the temple.[a] And He called to the man clothed with linen, who *had* the writer's inkhorn at his side; 4and the LORD said to him, "Go through the midst of the city, through the midst of Jerusalem, and put a mark on the foreheads of the men who sigh and cry over all the abominations that are done within it."

5To the others He said in my hearing, "Go after him through the city and kill; do not let your eye spare, nor have any pity. 6Utterly slay old *and* young men, maidens and little children and women; but do not come near anyone on whom *is* the mark; and begin at My sanctuary." So they began with the elders who *were* before the temple. 7Then He said to them, "Defile the temple, and fill the courts with the slain. Go out!" And they went out and killed in the city.

8So it was, that while they were killing them, I was left *alone;* and I fell on my face and cried out, and said, "Ah, Lord GOD! Will You destroy all the remnant of Israel in pouring out Your fury on Jerusalem?"

9Then He said to me, "The iniquity of the house of Israel and Judah *is* exceedingly great, and the land is full of bloodshed, and the city full of perversity; for they say, 'The LORD has forsaken the land, and the LORD does not see!' 10And as for Me also, My eye will neither spare, nor will I have pity, *but* I will recompense their deeds on their own head."

11Just then, the man clothed with linen, who *had* the inkhorn at his side, reported back and said, "I have done as You commanded me."

The Glory Departs from the Temple

10 And I looked, and there in the firmament that was above the head of the cherubim, there appeared something like a sapphire stone, having the appearance of the likeness of a throne. 2Then He spoke to the man clothed with linen, and said, "Go in among the wheels, under the cherub, fill your hands with coals of fire from among the cherubim, and scatter *them* over the city." And he went in as I watched.

9:3 [a] Literally *house*

3Now the cherubim were standing on the south side of the temple[a] when the man went in, and the cloud filled the inner court. 4Then the glory of the LORD went up from the cherub, *and paused* over the threshold of the temple; and the house was filled with the cloud, and the court was full of the brightness of the LORD's glory. 5And the sound of the wings of the cherubim was heard *even* in the outer court, like the voice of Almighty God when He speaks.

6Then it happened, when He commanded the man clothed in linen, saying, "Take fire from among the wheels, from among the cherubim," that he went in and stood beside the wheels. 7And the cherub stretched out his hand from among the cherubim to the fire that *was* among the cherubim, and took *some of it* and put *it* into the hands of the *man* clothed with linen, who took *it* and went out. 8The cherubim appeared to have the form of a man's hand under their wings.

9And when I looked, there were four wheels by the cherubim, one wheel by one cherub and another wheel by each other cherub; the wheels appeared *to have* the color of a beryl stone. 10*As for* their appearance, all four looked alike—as it were, a wheel in the middle of a wheel. 11When they went, they went toward *any of* their four directions; they did not turn aside when they went, but followed in the direction the head was facing. They did not turn aside when they went. 12And their whole body, with their back, their hands, their wings, and the wheels that the four had, *were* full of eyes all around. 13As for the wheels, they were called in my hearing, "Wheel."

14Each one had four faces: the first face *was* the face of a cherub, the second face the face of a man, the third the face of a lion, and the fourth the face of an eagle. 15And the cherubim were lifted up. This *was* the living creature I saw by the River Chebar. 16When the cherubim went, the wheels went beside them; and when the cherubim lifted their wings to mount up from the earth, the same wheels also did not turn from beside them. 17When *the cherubim*[a] stood still, *the wheels* stood still, and when *one*[b] was lifted up, *the other*[c] lifted itself up, for the spirit of the living creature *was* in them.

18Then the glory of the LORD departed from the threshold of the temple and stood over the cherubim. 19And the cherubim lifted their wings and mounted up from the earth in my sight. When they went out, the wheels *were* beside them; and they stood at the door of the east gate of the LORD's house, and the glory of the God of Israel *was* above them.

20This *is* the living creature I saw under the God of Israel by the River Chebar, and I knew they *were* cherubim. 21Each one had four faces and each one four wings, and the likeness of the hands of a man *was* under their wings. 22And the likeness of their faces *was* the same *as* the faces which I had seen by the River Chebar, their appearance and their persons. They each went straight forward.

Judgment on Wicked Counselors

11 Then the Spirit lifted me up and brought me to the East Gate of the LORD's house, which faces eastward; and there at the door of the gate were twenty-five men, among whom I saw Jaazaniah the son of Azzur, and Pelatiah the son of Benaiah, princes of the people. 2And He said to me: "Son of man, these *are* the men who devise iniquity and give wicked counsel in this city, 3who say, '*The time is* not near to build houses; this *city is* the caldron, and we *are* the meat.' 4Therefore prophesy against them, prophesy, O son of man!"

5Then the Spirit of the LORD fell upon me, and said to me, "Speak! 'Thus says the LORD: "Thus you have said, O house of Israel; for I know the things that come into your mind. 6You have multiplied your slain in this city, and you have filled its streets with the slain." 7Therefore thus says the Lord GOD: "Your slain whom you have laid in its midst, they *are* the meat, and this *city is* the caldron; but I shall bring you out of the midst of it. 8You have feared the sword; and I

10:3 [a] Literally *house,* also in verses 4 and 18 **10:17** [a] Literally *they* [b] Literally *they* [c] Literally *they*

will bring a sword upon you," says the
Lord GOD. 9"And I will bring you out of
its midst, and deliver you into the hands
of strangers, and execute judgments
on you. 10You shall fall by the sword. I
will judge you at the border of Israel.
Then you shall know that I *am* the LORD.
11This *city* shall not be your caldron, nor
shall you be the meat in its midst. I will
judge you at the border of Israel. 12And
you shall know that I *am* the LORD; for
you have not walked in My statutes nor
executed My judgments, but have done
according to the customs of the Gentiles
which *are* all around you." ' "

13Now it happened, while I was proph-
esying, that Pelatiah the son of Benaiah
died. Then I fell on my face and cried
with a loud voice, and said, "Ah, Lord
GOD! Will You make a complete end of
the remnant of Israel?"

God Will Restore Israel

14Again the word of the LORD came to
me, saying, 15"Son of man, your breth-
ren, your relatives, your countrymen,
and all the house of Israel in its entirety,
are those about whom the inhabitants
of Jerusalem have said, 'Get far away
from the LORD; this land has been given
to us as a possession.' 16Therefore say,
'Thus says the Lord GOD: "Although I
have cast them far off among the Gen-
tiles, and although I have scattered
them among the countries, yet I shall
be a little sanctuary for them in the
countries where they have gone." '
17Therefore say, 'Thus says the Lord
GOD: "I will gather you from the peo-
ples, assemble you from the countries
where you have been scattered, and I
will give you the land of Israel." ' 18And
they will go there, and they will take
away all its detestable things and all
its abominations from there. 19Then
I will give them one heart, and I will
put a new spirit within them,[a] and take
the stony heart out of their flesh, and
give them a heart of flesh, 20that they
may walk in My statutes and keep My
judgments and do them; and they shall
be My people, and I will be their God.
21But *as for those* whose hearts follow the
desire for their detestable things and
their abominations, I will recompense
their deeds on their own heads," says
the Lord GOD.

22So the cherubim lifted up their
wings, with the wheels beside them,
and the glory of the God of Israel *was*
high above them. 23And the glory of
the LORD went up from the midst of the
city and stood on the mountain, which
is on the east side of the city.

24Then the Spirit took me up and
brought me in a vision by the Spirit of
God into Chaldea,[a] to those in captivity.
And the vision that I had seen went
up from me. 25So I spoke to those in
captivity of all the things the LORD had
shown me.

Judah's Captivity Portrayed

12 Now the word of the LORD came
to me, saying: 2"Son of man, you
dwell in the midst of a rebellious house,
which has eyes to see but does not see,
and ears to hear but does not hear; for
they *are* a rebellious house.

3"Therefore, son of man, prepare your
belongings for captivity, and go into
captivity by day in their sight. You shall
go from your place into captivity to
another place in their sight. It may be
that they will consider, though they
are a rebellious house. 4By day you
shall bring out your belongings in their
sight, as though going into captivity;
and at evening you shall go in their
sight, like those who go into captivity.
5Dig through the wall in their sight, and
carry *your belongings* out through it. 6In
their sight you shall bear *them* on *your*
shoulders *and* carry *them* out at twi-
light; you shall cover your face, so that
you cannot see the ground, for I have
made you a sign to the house of Israel."

7So I did as I was commanded. I
brought out my belongings by day,
as though going into captivity, and at
evening I dug through the wall with
my hand. I brought *them* out at twi-
light, *and* I bore *them* on *my* shoulder
in their sight.

8And in the morning the word of the
LORD came to me, saying, 9"Son of man,

11:19 [a] Literally *you* **11:24** [a] Or *Babylon,* and so elsewhere in this book

has not the house of Israel, the rebel-
lious house, said to you, 'What are you
doing?' 10Say to them, 'Thus says the
Lord GOD: "This burden *concerns* the
prince in Jerusalem and all the house
of Israel who are among them." ' 11Say,
'I *am* a sign to you. As I have done, so
shall it be done to them; they shall be
carried away into captivity.' 12And the
prince who *is* among them shall bear
his belongings on *his* shoulder at twilight
and go out. They shall dig through the
wall to carry *them* out through it. He
shall cover his face, so that he cannot
see the ground with *his* eyes. 13I will also
spread My net over him, and he shall be
caught in My snare. I will bring him to
Babylon, *to* the land of the Chaldeans;
yet he shall not see it, though he shall
die there. 14I will scatter to every wind
all who *are* around him to help him,
and all his troops; and I will draw out
the sword after them.

15"Then they shall know that I *am* the
LORD, when I scatter them among the
nations and disperse them throughout
the countries. 16But I will spare a few of
their men from the sword, from famine,
and from pestilence, that they may
declare all their abominations among
the Gentiles wherever they go. Then they
shall know that I *am* the LORD."

Judgment Not Postponed

17Moreover the word of the LORD came
to me, saying, 18"Son of man, eat your
bread with quaking, and drink your wa-
ter with trembling and anxiety. 19And
say to the people of the land, 'Thus says
the Lord GOD to the inhabitants of Jeru-
salem *and* to the land of Israel: "They
shall eat their bread with anxiety, and
drink their water with dread, so that her
land may be emptied of all who are in
it, because of the violence of all those
who dwell in it. 20Then the cities that
are inhabited shall be laid waste, and
the land shall become desolate; and
you shall know that I *am* the LORD." ' "

21And the word of the LORD came to
me, saying, 22"Son of man, what *is* this
proverb *that* you *people* have about the
land of Israel, which says, 'The days are
prolonged, and every vision fails'? 23Tell
them therefore, 'Thus says the Lord
GOD: "I will lay this proverb to rest, and
they shall no more use it as a proverb
in Israel." ' But say to them, ' "The days
are at hand, and the fulfillment of every
vision. 24For no more shall there be
any false vision or flattering divina-
tion within the house of Israel. 25For
I *am* the LORD. I speak, and the word
which I speak will come to pass; it will
no more be postponed; for in your days,
O rebellious house, I will say the word
and perform it," says the Lord GOD.' "

26Again the word of the LORD came
to me, saying, 27"Son of man, look, the
house of Israel is saying, 'The vision that
he sees *is* for many days *from now,* and
he prophesies of times far off.' 28There-
fore say to them, 'Thus says the Lord
GOD: "None of My words will be post-
poned any more, but the word which I
speak will be done," says the Lord GOD.' "

Woe to Foolish Prophets

13 And the word of the LORD came
to me, saying, 2"Son of man,
prophesy against the prophets of Is-
rael who prophesy, and say to those
who prophesy out of their own heart,
'Hear the word of the LORD!' "

3Thus says the Lord GOD: "Woe to the
foolish prophets, who follow their own
spirit and have seen nothing! 4O Isra-
el, your prophets are like foxes in the
deserts. 5You have not gone up into
the gaps to build a wall for the house
of Israel to stand in battle on the day
of the LORD. 6They have envisioned
futility and false divination, saying,
'Thus says the LORD!' But the LORD has
not sent them; yet they hope that the
word may be confirmed. 7Have you
not seen a futile vision, and have you
not spoken false divination? You say,
'The LORD says,' but I have not spoken."

8Therefore thus says the Lord GOD:
"Because you have spoken nonsense
and envisioned lies, therefore I *am* in-
deed against you," says the Lord GOD.
9"My hand will be against the prophets
who envision futility and who divine
lies; they shall not be in the assembly
of My people, nor be written in the rec-
ord of the house of Israel, nor shall they
enter into the land of Israel. Then you
shall know that I *am* the Lord GOD.

10"Because, indeed, because they have
seduced My people, saying, 'Peace!'
when *there is* no peace—and one builds
a wall, and they plaster it with untem-
pered *mortar*— 11say to those who plas-
ter *it* with untempered *mortar*, that it
will fall. There will be flooding rain, and
you, O great hailstones, shall fall; and a
stormy wind shall tear *it* down. 12Surely,
when the wall has fallen, will it not be
said to you, 'Where *is* the mortar with
which you plastered *it*?' "
13Therefore thus says the Lord GOD: "I
will cause a stormy wind to break forth
in My fury; and there shall be a flooding
rain in My anger, and great hailstones
in fury to consume *it*. 14So I will break
down the wall you have plastered with
untempered *mortar*, and bring it down
to the ground, so that its foundation will
be uncovered; it will fall, and you shall
be consumed in the midst of it. Then you
shall know that I *am* the LORD.
15"Thus will I accomplish My wrath on
the wall and on those who have plas-
tered it with untempered *mortar*; and
I will say to you, 'The wall *is* no *more*,
nor those who plastered it, 16*that is*,
the prophets of Israel who prophesy
concerning Jerusalem, and who see
visions of peace for her when *there is*
no peace,' " says the Lord GOD.
17"Likewise, son of man, set your face
against the daughters of your people,
who prophesy out of their own heart;
prophesy against them, 18and say, 'Thus
says the Lord GOD: "Woe to the *women*
who sew *magic* charms on their sleeves[a]
and make veils for the heads of people
of every height to hunt souls! Will you
hunt the souls of My people, and keep
yourselves alive? 19And will you profane
Me among My people for handfuls of
barley and for pieces of bread, killing
people who should not die, and keeping
people alive who should not live, by your
lying to My people who listen to lies?"
20"Therefore thus says the Lord GOD:
"Behold, I *am* against your *magic*
charms by which you hunt souls there
like birds. I will tear them from your
arms, and let the souls go, the souls
you hunt like birds. 21I will also tear off
your veils and deliver My people out of
your hand, and they shall no longer be
as prey in your hand. Then you shall
know that I *am* the LORD.
22"Because with lies you have made
the heart of the righteous sad, whom
I have not made sad; and you have
strengthened the hands of the wicked,
so that he does not turn from his wicked
way to save his life. 23Therefore you
shall no longer envision futility nor
practice divination; for I will deliver My
people out of your hand, and you shall
know that I *am* the LORD." ' "

Idolatry Will Be Punished

14 Now some of the elders of Israel
came to me and sat before me.
2And the word of the LORD came to me,
saying, 3"Son of man, these men have
set up their idols in their hearts, and put
before them that which causes them
to stumble into iniquity. Should I let
Myself be inquired of at all by them?
4"Therefore speak to them, and say to
them, 'Thus says the Lord GOD: "Every-
one of the house of Israel who sets up
his idols in his heart, and puts before
him what causes him to stumble into
iniquity, and then comes to the prophet,
I the LORD will answer him who comes,
according to the multitude of his idols,
5that I may seize the house of Israel
by their heart, because they are all es-
tranged from Me by their idols." '
6"Therefore say to the house of Israel,
'Thus says the Lord GOD: "Repent, turn
away from your idols, and turn your
faces away from all your abominations.
7For anyone of the house of Israel, or
of the strangers who dwell in Israel,
who separates himself from Me and
sets up his idols in his heart and puts
before him what causes him to stumble
into iniquity, then comes to a prophet
to inquire of him concerning Me, I the
LORD will answer him by Myself. 8I will
set My face against that man and make
him a sign and a proverb, and I will cut
him off from the midst of My people.
Then you shall know that I *am* the LORD.

13:18 [a] Literally *over all the joints of My hands;* Vulgate reads *under every elbow;* Septuagint and Targum read *on all elbows of the hands.*

9“And if the prophet is induced to
speak anything, I the LORD have in-
duced that prophet, and I will stretch
out My hand against him and destroy
him from among My people Israel.
10And they shall bear their iniquity;
the punishment of the prophet shall
be the same as the punishment of the
one who inquired, 11that the house of
Israel may no longer stray from Me,
nor be profaned anymore with all their
transgressions, but that they may be My
people and I may be their God,” says
the Lord GOD.’ ”

Judgment on Persistent Unfaithfulness

12The word of the LORD came again
to me, saying: 13“Son of man, when a
land sins against Me by persistent un-
faithfulness, I will stretch out My hand
against it; I will cut off its supply of
bread, send famine on it, and cut off
man and beast from it. 14Even *if* these
three men, Noah, Daniel, and Job, were
in it, they would deliver *only* themselves
by their righteousness,” says the Lord
GOD.

15“If I cause wild beasts to pass through
the land, and they empty it, and make
it so desolate that no man may pass
through because of the beasts, 16*even
though* these three men *were* in it, *as* I
live,” says the Lord GOD, “they would
deliver neither sons nor daughters; only
they would be delivered, and the land
would be desolate.

17“Or *if* I bring a sword on that land,
and say, ‘Sword, go through the land,’
and I cut off man and beast from it,
18even *though* these three men *were* in
it, *as* I live,” says the Lord GOD, “they
would deliver neither sons nor daugh-
ters, but only they themselves would
be delivered.

19“Or *if* I send a pestilence into that
land and pour out My fury on it in
blood, and cut off from it man and
beast, 20even *though* Noah, Daniel, and
Job *were* in it, *as* I live,” says the Lord
GOD, “they would deliver neither son
nor daughter; they would deliver *only*
themselves by their righteousness.”

21For thus says the Lord GOD:
“How much more it shall be when I
send My four severe judgments on
Jerusalem—the sword and famine
and wild beasts and pestilence—to cut
off man and beast from it? 22Yet be-
hold, there shall be left in it a remnant
who will be brought out, *both* sons and
daughters; surely they will come out
to you, and you will see their ways and
their doings. Then you will be comfort-
ed concerning the disaster that I have
brought upon Jerusalem, all that I have
brought upon it. 23And they will com-
fort you, when you see their ways and
their doings; and you shall know that I
have done nothing without cause that
I have done in it,” says the Lord GOD.

The Outcast Vine

15 Then the word of the LORD came
to me, saying: 2“Son of man,
how is the wood of the vine *better* than
any other wood, the vine branch which
is among the trees of the forest? 3Is
wood taken from it to make any object?
Or can *men* make a peg from it to hang
any vessel on? 4Instead, it is thrown into
the fire for fuel; the fire devours both
ends of it, and its middle is burned. Is
it useful for *any* work? 5Indeed, when
it was whole, no object could be made
from it. How much less will it be useful
for *any* work when the fire has devoured
it, and it is burned?

6“Therefore thus says the Lord GOD:
‘Like the wood of the vine among the
trees of the forest, which I have given
to the fire for fuel, so I will give up the
inhabitants of Jerusalem; 7and I will
set My face against them. They will go
out from *one* fire, but *another* fire shall
devour them. Then you shall know that I
am the LORD, when I set My face against
them. 8Thus I will make the land des-
olate, because they have persisted in
unfaithfulness,’ says the Lord GOD.”

God’s Love for Jerusalem

16 Again the word of the LORD
came to me, saying, 2“Son of
man, cause Jerusalem to know her
abominations, 3and say, ‘Thus says
the Lord GOD to Jerusalem: “Your birth
and your nativity *are* from the land
of Canaan; your father *was* an Am-
orite and your mother a Hittite. 4*As
for* your nativity, on the day you were

born your navel cord was not cut, nor were you washed in water to cleanse *you;* you were not rubbed with salt nor wrapped in swaddling cloths. 5No eye pitied you, to do any of these things for you, to have compassion on you; but you were thrown out into the open field, when you yourself were loathed on the day you were born.

6"And when I passed by you and saw you struggling in your own blood, I said to you in your blood, 'Live!' Yes, I said to you in your blood, 'Live!' 7I made you thrive like a plant in the field; and you grew, matured, and became very beautiful. *Your* breasts were formed, your hair grew, but you *were* naked and bare.

8"When I passed by you again and looked upon you, indeed your time *was* the time of love; so I spread My wing over you and covered your nakedness. Yes, I swore an oath to you and entered into a covenant with you, and you became Mine," says the Lord GOD.

9"Then I washed you in water; yes, I thoroughly washed off your blood, and I anointed you with oil. 10I clothed you in embroidered cloth and gave you sandals of badger skin; I clothed you with fine linen and covered you with silk. 11I adorned you with ornaments, put bracelets on your wrists, and a chain on your neck. 12And I put a jewel in your nose, earrings in your ears, and a beautiful crown on your head. 13Thus you were adorned with gold and silver, and your clothing *was of* fine linen, silk, and embroidered cloth. You ate *pastry of* fine flour, honey, and oil. You were exceedingly beautiful, and succeeded to royalty. 14Your fame went out among the nations because of your beauty, for it *was* perfect through My splendor which I had bestowed on you," says the Lord GOD.

Jerusalem's Harlotry

15"But you trusted in your own beauty, played the harlot because of your fame, and poured out your harlotry on everyone passing by who *would have* it. 16You took some of your garments and adorned multicolored high places for yourself, and played the harlot on them. *Such* things should not happen, nor be. 17You have also taken your beautiful jewelry from My gold and My silver, which I had given you, and made for yourself male images and played the harlot with them. 18You took your embroidered garments and covered them, and you set My oil and My incense before them. 19Also My food which I gave you—the pastry of fine flour, oil, and honey *which* I fed you—you set it before them as sweet incense; and *so* it was," says the Lord GOD.

20"Moreover you took your sons and your daughters, whom you bore to Me, and these you sacrificed to them to be devoured. *Were* your *acts* of harlotry a small matter, 21that you have slain My children and offered them up to them by causing them to pass through *the fire?* 22And in all your abominations and acts of harlotry you did not remember the days of your youth, when you were naked and bare, struggling in your blood.

23"Then it was so, after all your wickedness—'Woe, woe to you!' says the Lord GOD— 24*that* you also built for yourself a shrine, and made a high place for yourself in every street. 25You built your high places at the head of every road, and made your beauty to be abhorred. You offered yourself to everyone who passed by, and multiplied your acts of harlotry. 26You also committed harlotry with the Egyptians, your very fleshly neighbors, and increased your acts of harlotry to provoke Me to anger.

27"Behold, therefore, I stretched out My hand against you, diminished your allotment, and gave you up to the will of those who hate you, the daughters of the Philistines, who were ashamed of your lewd behavior. 28You also played the harlot with the Assyrians, because you were insatiable; indeed you played the harlot with them and still were not satisfied. 29Moreover you multiplied your acts of harlotry as far as the land of the trader, Chaldea; and even then you were not satisfied.

30"How degenerate is your heart!" says the Lord GOD, "seeing you do all these *things,* the deeds of a brazen harlot.

Jerusalem's Adultery

31“You erected your shrine at the head
of every road, and built your high place
in every street. Yet you were not like a
harlot, because you scorned payment.
32*You are* an adulterous wife, *who* takes
strangers instead of her husband.
33Men make payment to all harlots,
but you made your payments to all
your lovers, and hired them to come to
you from all around for your harlotry.
34You are the opposite of *other* women
in your harlotry, because no one solic-
ited you to be a harlot. In that you gave
payment but no payment was given
you, therefore you are the opposite.”

Jerusalem's Lovers Will Abuse Her

35‘Now then, O harlot, hear the word
of the LORD! 36Thus says the Lord GOD:
“Because your filthiness was poured out
and your nakedness uncovered in your
harlotry with your lovers, and with all
your abominable idols, and because of
the blood of your children which you
gave to them, 37surely, therefore, I will
gather all your lovers with whom you
took pleasure, all those you loved, *and*
all those you hated; I will gather them
from all around against you and will
uncover your nakedness to them, that
they may see all your nakedness. 38And
I will judge you as women who break
wedlock or shed blood are judged; I
will bring blood upon you in fury and
jealousy. 39I will also give you into their
hand, and they shall throw down your
shrines and break down your high plac-
es. They shall also strip you of your
clothes, take your beautiful jewelry,
and leave you naked and bare.
40“They shall also bring up an as-
sembly against you, and they shall
stone you with stones and thrust you
through with their swords. 41They shall
burn your houses with fire, and execute
judgments on you in the sight of many
women; and I will make you cease play-
ing the harlot, and you shall no longer
hire lovers. 42So I will lay to rest My
fury toward you, and My jealousy shall
depart from you. I will be quiet, and be
angry no more. 43Because you did not
remember the days of your youth, but
agitated Me[a] with all these *things*, sure-
ly I will also recompense your deeds
on *your own* head,” says the Lord GOD.
“And you shall not commit lewdness
in addition to all your abominations.

More Wicked than Samaria and Sodom

44“Indeed everyone who quotes prov-
erbs will use *this* proverb against you:
‘Like mother, like daughter!’ 45You *are*
your mother's daughter, loathing hus-
band and children; and you *are* the
sister of your sisters, who loathed their
husbands and children; your mother
was a Hittite and your father an Am-
orite.
46“Your elder sister *is* Samaria, who
dwells with her daughters to the north
of you; and your younger sister, who
dwells to the south of you, *is* Sodom
and her daughters. 47You did not walk
in their ways nor act according to their
abominations; but, as *if that were* too
little, you became more corrupt than
they in all your ways.
48“As I live,” says the Lord GOD, “neither
your sister Sodom nor her daughters
have done as you and your daughters
have done. 49Look, this was the iniqui-
ty of your sister Sodom: She and her
daughter had pride, fullness of food,
and abundance of idleness; neither did
she strengthen the hand of the poor and
needy. 50And they were haughty and
committed abomination before Me;
therefore I took them away as I saw *fit*.[a]
51“Samaria did not commit half of
your sins; but you have multiplied
your abominations more than they,
and have justified your sisters by all
the abominations which you have done.
52You who judged your sisters, bear
your own shame also, because the sins
which you committed were more abom-
inable than theirs; they are more righ-
teous than you. Yes, be disgraced also,
and bear your own shame, because you
justified your sisters.
53“When I bring back their captives,
the captives of Sodom and her daugh-
ters, and the captives of Samaria and
her daughters, then *I will also bring back*

16:43 [a] Following Septuagint, Syriac, Targum, and Vulgate; Masoretic Text reads *were agitated with Me.* **16:50** [a] Vulgate reads *you saw;* Septuagint reads *he saw;* Targum reads *as was revealed to Me.*

the captives of your captivity among
them, 54that you may bear your own
shame and be disgraced by all that you
did when you comforted them. 55When
your sisters, Sodom and her daugh-
ters, return to their former state, and
Samaria and her daughters return to
their former state, then you and your
daughters will return to your former
state. 56For your sister Sodom was not
a byword in your mouth in the days of
your pride, 57before your wickedness
was uncovered. It was like the time of
the reproach of the daughters of Syria[a]
and all *those* around her, and of the
daughters of the Philistines, who de-
spise you everywhere. 58You have paid
for your lewdness and your abomina-
tions," says the LORD. 59For thus says
the Lord GOD: "I will deal with you as
you have done, who despised the oath
by breaking the covenant.

An Everlasting Covenant

60"Nevertheless I will remember My
covenant with you in the days of your
youth, and I will establish an everlast-
ing covenant with you. 61Then you will
remember your ways and be ashamed,
when you receive your older and your
younger sisters; for I will give them to
you for daughters, but not because of
My covenant with you. 62And I will es-
tablish My covenant with you. Then you
shall know that I *am* the LORD, 63that
you may remember and be ashamed,
and never open your mouth anymore
because of your shame, when I pro-
vide you an atonement for all you have
done," says the Lord GOD.' "

The Eagles and the Vine

17 And the word of the LORD came
to me, saying, 2"Son of man,
pose a riddle, and speak a parable to
the house of Israel, 3and say, 'Thus says
the Lord GOD:

"A great eagle with large wings and
long pinions,
Full of feathers of various colors,
Came to Lebanon
And took from the cedar the
highest branch.
4 He cropped off its topmost young
twig
And carried it to a land of trade;
He set it in a city of merchants.
5 Then he took some of the seed of
the land
And planted it in a fertile field;
He placed *it* by abundant waters
And set it like a willow tree.
6 And it grew and became a
spreading vine of low stature;
Its branches turned toward him,
But its roots were under it.
So it became a vine,
Brought forth branches,
And put forth shoots.

7 "But there was another[a] great eagle
with large wings and many
feathers;
And behold, this vine bent its
roots toward him,
And stretched its branches toward
him,
From the garden terrace where it
had been planted,
That he might water it.
8 It was planted in good soil by
many waters,
To bring forth branches, bear
fruit,
And become a majestic vine." '

9"Say, 'Thus says the Lord GOD:

"Will it thrive?
Will he not pull up its roots,
Cut off its fruit,
And leave it to wither?
All of its spring leaves will wither,
And no great power or many
people
Will be needed to pluck it up by its
roots.
10 Behold, *it is* planted,
Will it thrive?
Will it not utterly wither when the
east wind touches it?
It will wither in the garden terrace
where it grew." ' "

16:57 [a] Following Masoretic Text, Septuagint, Targum, and Vulgate; many Hebrew manuscripts and Syriac read *Edom*. **17:7** [a] Following Septuagint, Syriac, and Vulgate; Masoretic Text and Targum read *one*.

11Moreover the word of the LORD came
to me, saying, 12“Say now to the rebel-
lious house: ‘Do you not know what
these *things mean?*’ Tell *them,* ‘Indeed
the king of Babylon went to Jerusalem
and took its king and princes, and led
them with him to Babylon. 13And he
took the king’s offspring, made a cov-
enant with him, and put him under
oath. He also took away the mighty of
the land, 14that the kingdom might be
brought low and not lift itself up, *but*
that by keeping his covenant it might
stand. 15But he rebelled against him
by sending his ambassadors to Egypt,
that they might give him horses and
many people. Will he prosper? Will he
who does such *things* escape? Can he
break a covenant and still be delivered?
16‘*As* I live,’ says the Lord GOD, ‘surely
in the place *where* the king *dwells* who
made him king, whose oath he despised
and whose covenant he broke—with
him in the midst of Babylon he shall
die. 17Nor will Pharaoh with *his* mighty
army and great company do anything
in the war, when they heap up a siege
mound and build a wall to cut off many
persons. 18Since he despised the oath by
breaking the covenant, and in fact gave
his hand and still did all these *things,*
he shall not escape.’ ”
19Therefore thus says the Lord GOD:
“*As* I live, surely My oath which he
despised, and My covenant which he
broke, I will recompense on his own
head. 20I will spread My net over him,
and he shall be taken in My snare. I will
bring him to Babylon and try him there
for the treason which he committed
against Me. 21All his fugitives[a] with all
his troops shall fall by the sword, and
those who remain shall be scattered to
every wind; and you shall know that I,
the LORD, have spoken.”

Israel Exalted at Last

22Thus says the Lord GOD: “I will take
also *one* of the highest branches of the
high cedar and set *it* out. I will crop off
from the topmost of its young twigs a
tender one, and will plant *it* on a high
and prominent mountain. 23On the
mountain height of Israel I will plant it;
and it will bring forth boughs, and bear
fruit, and be a majestic cedar. Under
it will dwell birds of every sort; in the
shadow of its branches they will dwell.
24And all the trees of the field shall know
that I, the LORD, have brought down the
high tree and exalted the low tree, dried
up the green tree and made the dry tree
flourish; I, the LORD, have spoken and
have done *it.*”

A False Proverb Refuted

18 The word of the LORD came to
me again, saying, 2“What do
you mean when you use this proverb
concerning the land of Israel, saying:

‘The fathers have eaten sour
grapes,
And the children’s teeth are set on
edge’?

3“*As* I live,” says the Lord GOD, “you
shall no longer use this proverb in Is-
rael.

4 “Behold, all souls are Mine;
The soul of the father
As well as the soul of the son is
Mine;
The soul who sins shall die.
5 But if a man is just
And does what is lawful and right;
6 If he has not eaten on the
mountains,
Nor lifted up his eyes to the idols
of the house of Israel,
Nor defiled his neighbor’s wife,
Nor approached a woman during
her impurity;
7 If he has not oppressed anyone,
But has restored to the debtor his
pledge;
Has robbed no one by violence,
But has given his bread to the
hungry
And covered the naked with
clothing;
8 If he has not exacted usury
Nor taken any increase,
But has withdrawn his hand from
iniquity

17:21 [a] Following Masoretic Text and Vulgate; many Hebrew manuscripts and Syriac read *choice men;* Targum reads *mighty men;* Septuagint omits *All his fugitives.*

And executed true judgment
between man and man;
9 *If* he has walked in My statutes
And kept My judgments
faithfully—
He *is* just;
He shall surely live!"
Says the Lord GOD.

10 "If he begets a son *who is* a robber
Or a shedder of blood,
Who does any of these *things*
11 And does none of those *duties,*
But has eaten on the mountains
Or defiled his neighbor's wife;
12 If he has oppressed the poor and
needy,
Robbed by violence,
Not restored the pledge,
Lifted his eyes to the idols,
Or committed abomination;
13 If he has exacted usury
Or taken increase—
Shall he then live?
He shall not live!
If he has done any of these
abominations,
He shall surely die;
His blood shall be upon him.

14 "*If,* however, he begets a son
Who sees all the sins which his
father has done,
And considers but does not do
likewise;
15 *Who* has not eaten on the
mountains,
Nor lifted his eyes to the idols of
the house of Israel,
Nor defiled his neighbor's wife;
16 Has not oppressed anyone,
Nor withheld a pledge,
Nor robbed by violence,
But has given his bread to the
hungry
And covered the naked with
clothing;
17 *Who* has withdrawn his hand
from the poor[a]
And not received usury or
increase,
But has executed My judgments
And walked in My statutes—
He shall not die for the iniquity of
his father;
He shall surely live!

18 "*As for* his father,
Because he cruelly oppressed,
Robbed his brother by violence,
And did what *is* not good among
his people,
Behold, he shall die for his
iniquity.

Turn and Live

19"Yet you say, 'Why should the son
not bear the guilt of the father?' Be-
cause the son has done what is lawful
and right, and has kept all My statutes
and observed them, he shall surely live.
20The soul who sins shall die. The son
shall not bear the guilt of the father, nor
the father bear the guilt of the son. The
righteousness of the righteous shall be
upon himself, and the wickedness of the
wicked shall be upon himself.
21"But if a wicked man turns from all
his sins which he has committed, keeps
all My statutes, and does what is lawful
and right, he shall surely live; he shall
not die. 22None of the transgressions
which he has committed shall be re-
membered against him; because of
the righteousness which he has done,
he shall live. 23Do I have any pleasure
at all that the wicked should die?" says
the Lord GOD, "*and* not that he should
turn from his ways and live?
24"But when a righteous man turns
away from his righteousness and com-
mits iniquity, and does according to all
the abominations that the wicked *man*
does, shall he live? All the righteousness
which he has done shall not be remem-
bered; because of the unfaithfulness
of which he is guilty and the sin which
he has committed, because of them he
shall die.
25"Yet you say, 'The way of the Lord
is not fair.' Hear now, O house of Isra-
el, is it not My way which is fair, and
your ways which are not fair? 26When
a righteous *man* turns away from his
righteousness, commits iniquity, and
dies in it, it is because of the iniquity

18:17 [a] Following Masoretic Text, Targum, and Vulgate; Septuagint reads *iniquity* (compare verse 8).

which he has done that he dies. 27Again,
when a wicked *man* turns away from
the wickedness which he committed,
and does what is lawful and right, he
preserves himself alive. 28Because he
considers and turns away from all the
transgressions which he committed, he
shall surely live; he shall not die. 29Yet
the house of Israel says, 'The way of the
Lord is not fair.' O house of Israel, is it
not My ways which are fair, and your
ways which are not fair?

30"Therefore I will judge you, O house
of Israel, every one according to his
ways," says the Lord GOD. "Repent, and
turn from all your transgressions, so
that iniquity will not be your ruin. 31Cast
away from you all the transgressions
which you have committed, and get
yourselves a new heart and a new spir-
it. For why should you die, O house of
Israel? 32For I have no pleasure in the
death of one who dies," says the Lord
GOD. "Therefore turn and live!"

Israel Degraded

19 "Moreover take up a lamenta-
tion for the princes of Israel,
2and say:

'What *is* your mother? A lioness:
She lay down among the lions;
Among the young lions she
nourished her cubs.
3 She brought up one of her cubs,
And he became a young lion;
He learned to catch prey,
And he devoured men.
4 The nations also heard of him;
He was trapped in their pit,
And they brought him with
chains to the land of Egypt.

5 'When she saw that she waited, *that*
her hope was lost,
She took another of her cubs *and*
made him a young lion.
6 He roved among the lions,
And became a young lion;
He learned to catch prey;
He devoured men.
7 He knew their desolate places,[a]
And laid waste their cities;
The land with its fullness was
desolated
By the noise of his roaring.
8 Then the nations set against him
from the provinces on every
side,
And spread their net over him;
He was trapped in their pit.
9 They put him in a cage with
chains,
And brought him to the king of
Babylon;
They brought him in nets,
That his voice should no longer be
heard on the mountains of
Israel.

10 'Your mother *was* like a vine in
your bloodline,[a]
Planted by the waters,
Fruitful and full of branches
Because of many waters.
11 She had strong branches for
scepters of rulers.
She towered in stature above the
thick branches,
And was seen in her height amid
the dense foliage.
12 But she was plucked up in fury,
She was cast down to the ground,
And the east wind dried her fruit.
Her strong branches were broken
and withered;
The fire consumed them.
13 And now she *is* planted in the
wilderness,
In a dry and thirsty land.
14 Fire has come out from a rod of
her branches
And devoured her fruit,
So that she has no strong
branch—a scepter for
ruling.' "

This *is* a lamentation, and has become
a lamentation.

The Rebellions of Israel

20 It came to pass in the seventh
year, in the fifth *month,* on the
tenth *day* of the month, *that* certain of

19:7 [a] Septuagint reads *He stood in insolence;* Targum reads *He destroyed its palaces;* Vulgate reads *He learned to make widows.* 19:10 [a] Literally *blood,* following Masoretic Text, Syriac, and Vulgate; Septuagint reads *like a flower on a pomegranate tree;* Targum reads *in your likeness.*

the elders of Israel came to inquire of
the LORD, and sat before me. 2Then the
word of the LORD came to me, saying,
3"Son of man, speak to the elders of
Israel, and say to them, 'Thus says the
Lord GOD: "Have you come to inquire
of Me? *As* I live," says the Lord GOD, "I
will not be inquired of by you." ' 4Will
you judge them, son of man, will you
judge *them?* Then make known to them
the abominations of their fathers.

5"Say to them, 'Thus says the Lord
GOD: "On the day when I chose Israel
and raised My hand in an oath to the
descendants of the house of Jacob, and
made Myself known to them in the land
of Egypt, I raised My hand in an oath
to them, saying, 'I *am* the LORD your
God.' 6On that day I raised My hand
in an oath to them, to bring them out
of the land of Egypt into a land that
I had searched out for them, 'flowing
with milk and honey,'[a] the glory of all
lands. 7Then I said to them, 'Each of you,
throw away the abominations which
are before his eyes, and do not defile
yourselves with the idols of Egypt. I *am*
the LORD your God.' 8But they rebelled
against Me and would not obey Me.
They did not all cast away the abomina-
tions which were before their eyes, nor
did they forsake the idols of Egypt. Then
I said, 'I will pour out My fury on them
and fulfill My anger against them in the
midst of the land of Egypt.' 9But I acted
for My name's sake, that it should not
be profaned before the Gentiles among
whom they *were,* in whose sight I had
made Myself known to them, to bring
them out of the land of Egypt.

10"Therefore I made them go out of the
land of Egypt and brought them into the
wilderness. 11And I gave them My stat-
utes and showed them My judgments,
'which, *if* a man does, he shall live by
them.'[a] 12Moreover I also gave them My
Sabbaths, to be a sign between them
and Me, that they might know that I *am*
the LORD who sanctifies them. 13Yet the
house of Israel rebelled against Me in
the wilderness; they did not walk in My
statutes; they despised My judgments,
'which, *if* a man does, he shall live by
them';[a] and they greatly defiled My
Sabbaths. Then I said I would pour out
My fury on them in the wilderness, to
consume them. 14But I acted for My
name's sake, that it should not be pro-
faned before the Gentiles, in whose
sight I had brought them out. 15So I
also raised My hand in an oath to them
in the wilderness, that I would not bring
them into the land which I had given
them, 'flowing with milk and honey,'[a]
the glory of all lands, 16because they
despised My judgments and did not
walk in My statutes, but profaned My
Sabbaths; for their heart went after their
idols. 17Nevertheless My eye spared
them from destruction. I did not make
an end of them in the wilderness.

18"But I said to their children in the
wilderness, 'Do not walk in the statutes
of your fathers, nor observe their judg-
ments, nor defile yourselves with their
idols. 19I *am* the LORD your God: Walk
in My statutes, keep My judgments,
and do them; 20hallow My Sabbaths,
and they will be a sign between Me and
you, that you may know that I *am* the
LORD your God.'

21"Notwithstanding, the children re-
belled against Me; they did not walk
in My statutes, and were not careful to
observe My judgments, 'which, *if* a man
does, he shall live by them';[a] but they
profaned My Sabbaths. Then I said I
would pour out My fury on them and
fulfill My anger against them in the
wilderness. 22Nevertheless I withdrew
My hand and acted for My name's sake,
that it should not be profaned in the
sight of the Gentiles, in whose sight I
had brought them out. 23Also I raised
My hand in an oath to those in the
wilderness, that I would scatter them
among the Gentiles and disperse them
throughout the countries, 24because
they had not executed My judgments,
but had despised My statutes, profaned
My Sabbaths, and their eyes were fixed
on their fathers' idols.

25"Therefore I also gave them up to
statutes *that were* not good, and judg-
ments by which they could not live;
26and I pronounced them unclean

20:6 [a] Exodus 3:8 **20:11** [a] Leviticus 18:5 **20:13** [a] Leviticus 18:5 **20:15** [a] Exodus 3:8
20:21 [a] Leviticus 18:5

because of their ritual gifts, in that
they caused all their firstborn to pass
through *the fire,* that I might make them
desolate and that they might know that
I am the LORD." '
27"Therefore, son of man, speak to the
house of Israel, and say to them, 'Thus
says the Lord GOD: "In this too your fa-
thers have blasphemed Me, by being un-
faithful to Me. 28When I brought them
into the land *concerning* which I had
raised My hand in an oath to give them,
and they saw all the high hills and all
the thick trees, there they offered their
sacrifices and provoked Me with their
offerings. There they also sent up
their sweet aroma and poured out their
drink offerings. 29Then I said to them,
'What *is* this high place to which you
go?' So its name is called Bamah[a] to this
day." ' 30Therefore say to the house of
Israel, 'Thus says the Lord GOD: "Are you
defiling yourselves in the manner of
your fathers, and committing harlotry
according to their abominations? 31For
when you offer your gifts and make
your sons pass through the fire, you de-
file yourselves with all your idols, even
to this day. So shall I be inquired of by
you, O house of Israel? *As* I live," says
the Lord GOD, "I will not be inquired of
by you. 32What you have in your mind
shall never be, when you say, 'We will be
like the Gentiles, like the families in oth-
er countries, serving wood and stone.'

God Will Restore Israel

33"*As* I live," says the Lord GOD, "sure-
ly with a mighty hand, with an out-
stretched arm, and with fury poured
out, I will rule over you. 34I will bring
you out from the peoples and gather
you out of the countries where you are
scattered, with a mighty hand, with an
outstretched arm, and with fury poured
out. 35And I will bring you into the wil-
derness of the peoples, and there I will
plead My case with you face to face.
36Just as I pleaded My case with your
fathers in the wilderness of the land of
Egypt, so I will plead My case with you,"
says the Lord GOD.
37"I will make you pass under the rod,
and I will bring you into the bond of the
covenant; 38I will purge the rebels from
among you, and those who transgress
against Me; I will bring them out of the
country where they dwell, but they shall
not enter the land of Israel. Then you
will know that I *am* the LORD.
39"As for you, O house of Israel," thus
says the Lord GOD: "Go, serve every one
of you his idols—and hereafter—if you
will not obey Me; but profane My holy
name no more with your gifts and your
idols. 40For on My holy mountain, on
the mountain height of Israel," says the
Lord GOD, "there all the house of Isra-
el, all of them in the land, shall serve
Me; there I will accept them, and there
I will require your offerings and the
firstfruits of your sacrifices, together
with all your holy things. 41I will accept
you as a sweet aroma when I bring you
out from the peoples and gather you
out of the countries where you have
been scattered; and I will be hallowed
in you before the Gentiles. 42Then you
shall know that I *am* the LORD, when I
bring you into the land of Israel, into
the country *for* which I raised My hand
in an oath to give to your fathers. 43And
there you shall remember your ways
and all your doings with which you were
defiled; and you shall loathe yourselves
in your own sight because of all the evils
that you have committed. 44Then you
shall know that I *am* the LORD, when
I have dealt with you for My name's
sake, not according to your wicked ways
nor according to your corrupt doings,
O house of Israel," says the Lord GOD.' "

Fire in the Forest

45Furthermore the word of the LORD
came to me, saying, 46"Son of man,
set your face toward the south; preach
against the south and prophesy against
the forest land, the South,[a] 47and say to
the forest of the South, 'Hear the word
of the LORD! Thus says the Lord GOD:
"Behold, I will kindle a fire in you, and
it shall devour every green tree and
every dry tree in you; the blazing flame
shall not be quenched, and all faces
from the south to the north shall be

20:29 [a] Literally *High Place* **20:46** [a] Hebrew *Negev*

scorched by it. [48]All flesh shall see that
I, the LORD, have kindled it; it shall not
be quenched." ' "
[49]Then I said, "Ah, Lord GOD! They say
of me, 'Does he not speak parables?' "

Babylon, the Sword of God

21 And the word of the LORD came
to me, saying, [2]"Son of man, set
your face toward Jerusalem, preach
against the holy places, and prophesy
against the land of Israel; [3]and say to
the land of Israel, 'Thus says the LORD:
"Behold, I *am* against you, and I will
draw My sword out of its sheath and cut
off both righteous and wicked from you.
[4]Because I will cut off both righteous
and wicked from you, therefore My
sword shall go out of its sheath against
all flesh from south *to* north, [5]that all
flesh may know that I, the LORD, have
drawn My sword out of its sheath;
it shall not return anymore." ' [6]Sigh
therefore, son of man, with a breaking
heart, and sigh with bitterness before
their eyes. [7]And it shall be when they
say to you, 'Why are you sighing?' that
you shall answer, 'Because of the news;
when it comes, every heart will melt,
all hands will be feeble, every spirit
will faint, and all knees will be weak *as*
water. Behold, it is coming and shall be
brought to pass,' says the Lord GOD."
[8]Again the word of the LORD came to
me, saying, [9]"Son of man, prophesy and
say, 'Thus says the LORD!' Say:

'A sword, a sword is sharpened
And also polished!
10 Sharpened to make a dreadful
slaughter,
Polished to flash like lightning!
Should we then make mirth?
It despises the scepter of My son,
As it does all wood.
11 And He has given it to be
polished,
That it may be handled;
This sword is sharpened, and it is
polished
To be given into the hand of the
slayer.'

12 "Cry and wail, son of man;
For it will be against My people,
Against all the princes of Israel.
Terrors including the sword will
be against My people;
Therefore strike *your* thigh.

13 "Because *it is* a testing,
And what if *the sword* despises
even the scepter?
The scepter shall be no *more*,"

says the Lord GOD.

14 "You therefore, son of man,
prophesy,
And strike *your* hands together.
The third time let the sword do
double *damage*.
It *is* the sword *that* slays,
The sword that slays the great
men,
That enters their private
chambers.
15 I have set the point of the sword
against all their gates,
That the heart may melt and
many may stumble.
Ah! *It is* made bright;
It is grasped for slaughter:

16 "Swords at the ready!
Thrust right!
Set your blade!
Thrust left—
Wherever your edge is ordered!

17 "I also will beat My fists together,
And I will cause My fury to rest;
I, the LORD, have spoken."

[18]The word of the LORD came to me
again, saying: [19]"And son of man,
appoint for yourself two ways for the
sword of the king of Babylon to go; both
of them shall go from the same land.
Make a sign; put *it* at the head of the
road to the city. [20]Appoint a road for
the sword to go to Rabbah of the Am-
monites, and to Judah, into fortified
Jerusalem. [21]For the king of Babylon
stands at the parting of the road, at the
fork of the two roads, to use divination:
he shakes the arrows, he consults the
images, he looks at the liver. [22]In his
right hand is the divination for Jeru-
salem: to set up battering rams, to call

for a slaughter, to lift the voice with shouting, to set battering rams against the gates, to heap up a *siege* mound, and to build a wall. [23]And it will be to them like a false divination in the eyes of those who have sworn oaths with them; but he will bring their iniquity to remembrance, that they may be taken.

[24]"Therefore thus says the Lord GOD: 'Because you have made your iniquity to be remembered, in that your transgressions are uncovered, so that in all your doings your sins appear—because you have come to remembrance, you shall be taken in hand.

[25]'Now to you, O profane, wicked prince of Israel, whose day has come, whose iniquity *shall* end, [26]thus says the Lord GOD:

"Remove the turban, and take off
the crown;
Nothing *shall remain* the same.
Exalt the humble, and humble the
exalted.
27 Overthrown, overthrown,
I will make it overthrown!
It shall be no *longer*,
Until He comes whose right it is,
And I will give it *to Him.*" '

A Sword Against the Ammonites

[28]"And you, son of man, prophesy and say, 'Thus says the Lord GOD concerning the Ammonites and concerning their reproach,' and say:

'A sword, a sword *is* drawn,
Polished for slaughter,
For consuming, for flashing—
29 While they see false visions for
you,
While they divine a lie to you,
To bring you on the necks of the
wicked, the slain
Whose day has come,
Whose iniquity *shall* end.

30 'Return *it* to its sheath.
I will judge you
In the place where you were
created,
In the land of your nativity.
31 I will pour out My indignation on
you;
I will blow against you with the
fire of My wrath,
And deliver you into the hands of
brutal men *who are* skillful to
destroy.
32 You shall be fuel for the fire;
Your blood shall be in the midst of
the land.
You shall not be remembered,
For I the LORD have spoken.' "

Sins of Jerusalem

22 Moreover the word of the LORD
came to me, saying, [2]"Now, son
of man, will you judge, will you judge
the bloody city? Yes, show her all her
abominations! [3]Then say, 'Thus says
the Lord GOD: "The city sheds blood in
her own midst, that her time may come;
and she makes idols within herself to
defile herself. [4]You have become guilty
by the blood which you have shed, and
have defiled yourself with the idols
which you have made. You have caused
your days to draw near, and have come
to *the end of* your years; therefore I have
made you a reproach to the nations,
and a mockery to all countries. [5]*Those*
near and *those* far from you will mock
you as infamous *and* full of tumult.

[6]"Look, the princes of Israel: each one
has used his power to shed blood in
you. [7]In you they have made light of
father and mother; in your midst they
have oppressed the stranger; in you
they have mistreated the fatherless
and the widow. [8]You have despised My
holy things and profaned My Sabbaths.
[9]In you are men who slander to cause
bloodshed; in you are those who eat
on the mountains; in your midst they
commit lewdness. [10]In you men uncov-
er their fathers' nakedness; in you they
violate women who are set apart during
their impurity. [11]One commits abomi-
nation with his neighbor's wife; another
lewdly defiles his daughter-in-law; and
another in you violates his sister, his
father's daughter. [12]In you they take
bribes to shed blood; you take usury
and increase; you have made profit
from your neighbors by extortion, and
have forgotten Me," says the Lord GOD.

[13]"Behold, therefore, I beat My fists
at the dishonest profit which you have

made, and at the bloodshed which has been in your midst. 14Can your heart endure, or can your hands remain strong, in the days when I shall deal with you? I, the LORD, have spoken, and will do *it*. 15I will scatter you among the nations, disperse you throughout the countries, and remove your filthiness completely from you. 16You shall defile yourself in the sight of the nations; then you shall know that I *am* the LORD." ' "

Israel in the Furnace

17The word of the LORD came to me, saying, 18"Son of man, the house of Israel has become dross to Me; they *are* all bronze, tin, iron, and lead, in the midst of a furnace; they have become dross from silver. 19Therefore thus says the Lord GOD: 'Because you have all become dross, therefore behold, I will gather you into the midst of Jerusalem. 20*As men* gather silver, bronze, iron, lead, and tin into the midst of a furnace, to blow fire on it, to melt *it;* so I will gather *you* in My anger and in My fury, and I will leave *you there* and melt you. 21Yes, I will gather you and blow on you with the fire of My wrath, and you shall be melted in its midst. 22As silver is melted in the midst of a furnace, so shall you be melted in its midst; then you shall know that I, the LORD, have poured out My fury on you.' "

Israel's Wicked Leaders

23And the word of the LORD came to me, saying, 24"Son of man, say to her: 'You *are* a land that is not cleansed[a] or rained on in the day of indignation.' 25The conspiracy of her prophets[a] in her midst is like a roaring lion tearing the prey; they have devoured people; they have taken treasure and precious things; they have made many widows in her midst. 26Her priests have violated My law and profaned My holy things; they have not distinguished between the holy and unholy, nor have they made known *the difference* between the unclean and the clean; and they have hidden their eyes from My Sabbaths, so that I am profaned among them. 27Her princes in her midst *are* like wolves tearing the prey, to shed blood, to destroy people, and to get dishonest gain. 28Her prophets plastered them with untempered *mortar,* seeing false visions, and divining lies for them, saying, 'Thus says the Lord GOD,' when the LORD had not spoken. 29The people of the land have used oppressions, committed robbery, and mistreated the poor and needy; and they wrongfully oppress the stranger. 30So I sought for a man among them who would make a wall, and stand in the gap before Me on behalf of the land, that I should not destroy it; but I found no one. 31Therefore I have poured out My indignation on them; I have consumed them with the fire of My wrath; and I have recompensed their deeds on their own heads," says the Lord GOD.

Two Harlot Sisters

23 The word of the LORD came again to me, saying:

2 "Son of man, there were two women,
The daughters of one mother.
3 They committed harlotry in Egypt,
They committed harlotry in their youth;
Their breasts were there embraced,
Their virgin bosom was there pressed.
4 Their names: Oholah[a] the elder and Oholibah[b] her sister;
They were Mine,
And they bore sons and daughters.
As for their names,
Samaria *is* Oholah, and Jerusalem *is* Oholibah.

The Older Sister, Samaria

5 "Oholah played the harlot even though she was Mine;
And she lusted for her lovers, the neighboring Assyrians,

22:24 [a] Following Masoretic Text, Syriac, and Vulgate; Septuagint reads *showered upon.*
22:25 [a] Following Masoretic Text and Vulgate; Septuagint reads *princes;* Targum reads *scribes.*
23:4 [a] Literally *Her Own Tabernacle* [b] Literally *My Tabernacle Is in Her*

6 *Who were* clothed in purple,
Captains and rulers,
All of them desirable young men,
Horsemen riding on horses.
7 Thus she committed her harlotry
with them,
All of them choice men of
Assyria;
And with all for whom she lusted,
With all their idols, she defiled
herself.
8 She has never given up her
harlotry *brought* from Egypt,
For in her youth they had lain
with her,
Pressed her virgin bosom,
And poured out their immorality
upon her.

9 "Therefore I have delivered her
Into the hand of her lovers,
Into the hand of the Assyrians,
For whom she lusted.
10 They uncovered her nakedness,
Took away her sons and
daughters,
And slew her with the sword;
She became a byword among
women,
For they had executed judgment
on her.

The Younger Sister, Jerusalem

11"Now although her sister Oholibah
saw *this,* she became more corrupt in
her lust than she, and in her harlotry
more corrupt than her sister's harlotry.

12 "She lusted for the neighboring
Assyrians,
Captains and rulers,
Clothed most gorgeously,
Horsemen riding on horses,
All of them desirable young men.
13 Then I saw that she was defiled;
Both *took* the same way.
14 But she increased her harlotry;
She looked at men portrayed on
the wall,
Images of Chaldeans portrayed
in vermilion,
15 Girded with belts around their
waists,
Flowing turbans on their heads,
All of them looking like captains,
In the manner of the Babylonians
of Chaldea,
The land of their nativity.
16 As soon as her eyes saw them,
She lusted for them
And sent messengers to them in
Chaldea.

17 "Then the Babylonians came to her,
into the bed of love,
And they defiled her with their
immorality;
So she was defiled by them, and
alienated herself from them.
18 She revealed her harlotry and
uncovered her nakedness.
Then I alienated Myself from her,
As I had alienated Myself from
her sister.

19 "Yet she multiplied her harlotry
In calling to remembrance the
days of her youth,
When she had played the harlot
in the land of Egypt.
20 For she lusted for her paramours,
Whose flesh *is like* the flesh of
donkeys,
And whose issue *is like* the issue of
horses.
21 Thus you called to remembrance
the lewdness of your youth,
When the Egyptians pressed your
bosom
Because of your youthful breasts.

Judgment on Jerusalem

22"Therefore, Oholibah, thus says the
Lord GOD:

'Behold, I will stir up your lovers
against you,
From whom you have alienated
yourself,
And I will bring them against you
from every side:
23 The Babylonians,
All the Chaldeans,
Pekod, Shoa, Koa,
All the Assyrians with them,
All of them desirable young men,
Governors and rulers,
Captains and men of renown,
All of them riding on horses.
24 And they shall come against you

With chariots, wagons, and
war-horses,
With a horde of people.
They shall array against you
Buckler, shield, and helmet all
around.

'I will delegate judgment to them,
And they shall judge you
according to their judgments.
25 I will set My jealousy against you,
And they shall deal furiously with
you;
They shall remove your nose and
your ears,
And your remnant shall fall by
the sword;
They shall take your sons and
your daughters,
And your remnant shall be
devoured by fire.
26 They shall also strip you of your
clothes
And take away your beautiful
jewelry.

27 'Thus I will make you cease your
lewdness and your harlotry
Brought from the land of Egypt,
So that you will not lift your eyes
to them,
Nor remember Egypt anymore.'

28"For thus says the Lord GOD: 'Surely
I will deliver you into the hand of those
you hate, into the hand *of those* from
whom you alienated yourself. 29They
will deal hatefully with you, take away
all you have worked for, and leave you
naked and bare. The nakedness of your
harlotry shall be uncovered, both your
lewdness and your harlotry. 30I will do
these *things* to you because you have
gone as a harlot after the Gentiles, be-
cause you have become defiled by their
idols. 31You have walked in the way of
your sister; therefore I will put her cup
in your hand.'
32"Thus says the Lord GOD:

'You shall drink of your sister's cup,
The deep and wide one;
You shall be laughed to scorn
And held in derision;
It contains much.
33 You will be filled with
drunkenness and sorrow,
The cup of horror and desolation,
The cup of your sister Samaria.
34 You shall drink and drain it,
You shall break its shards,
And tear at your own breasts;
For I have spoken,'
Says the Lord GOD.

35"Therefore thus says the Lord GOD:

'Because you have forgotten Me
and cast Me behind your
back,
Therefore you shall bear the
penalty
Of your lewdness and your
harlotry.' "

Both Sisters Judged

36The LORD also said to me: "Son of
man, will you judge Oholah and Ohol-
ibah? Then declare to them their abom-
inations. 37For they have committed
adultery, and blood *is* on their hands.
They have committed adultery with
their idols, and even *sacrificed* their
sons whom they bore to Me, passing
them through *the fire,* to devour *them.*
38Moreover they have done this to Me:
They have defiled My sanctuary on the
same day and profaned My Sabbaths.
39For after they had slain their children
for their idols, on the same day they
came into My sanctuary to profane it;
and indeed thus they have done in the
midst of My house.
40"Furthermore you sent for men to
come from afar, to whom a messenger
was sent; and there they came. And
you washed yourself for them, paint-
ed your eyes, and adorned yourself
with ornaments. 41You sat on a stately
couch, with a table prepared before it,
on which you had set My incense and
My oil. 42The sound of a carefree mul-
titude *was* with her, and Sabeans *were*
brought from the wilderness with men
of the common sort, who put bracelets
on their wrists and beautiful crowns on
their heads. 43Then I said concerning
her who had grown old in adulteries,
'Will they commit harlotry with her now,
and she *with them?*' 44Yet they went in

to her, as men go in to a woman who
plays the harlot; thus they went in to
Oholah and Oholibah, the lewd women.
45But righteous men will judge them
after the manner of adulteresses, and
after the manner of women who shed
blood, because they *are* adulteresses,
and blood *is* on their hands.
46"For thus says the Lord GOD: 'Bring
up an assembly against them, give
them up to trouble and plunder. 47The
assembly shall stone them with stones
and execute them with their swords;
they shall slay their sons and their
daughters, and burn their houses with
fire. 48Thus I will cause lewdness to
cease from the land, that all women
may be taught not to practice your
lewdness. 49They shall repay you for
your lewdness, and you shall pay for
your idolatrous sins. Then you shall
know that I *am* the Lord GOD.' "

Symbol of the Cooking Pot

24 Again, in the ninth year, in the
tenth month, on the tenth *day* of
the month, the word of the LORD came
to me, saying, 2"Son of man, write down
the name of the day, this very day—the
king of Babylon started his siege against
Jerusalem this very day. 3And utter a
parable to the rebellious house, and
say to them, 'Thus says the Lord GOD:

"Put on a pot, set *it* on,
And also pour water into it.
4 Gather pieces *of meat* in it,
Every good piece,
The thigh and the shoulder.
Fill *it* with choice cuts;
5 Take the choice of the flock.
Also pile *fuel* bones under it,
Make it boil well,
And let the cuts simmer in it."

6'Therefore thus says the Lord GOD:

"Woe to the bloody city,
To the pot whose scum *is* in it,
And whose scum is not gone from it!
Bring it out piece by piece,
On which no lot has fallen.
7 For her blood is in her midst;
She set it on top of a rock;
She did not pour it on the ground,
To cover it with dust.
8 That it may raise up fury and take vengeance,
I have set her blood on top of a rock,
That it may not be covered."

9'Therefore thus says the Lord GOD:

"Woe to the bloody city!
I too will make the pyre great.
10 Heap on the wood,
Kindle the fire;
Cook the meat well,
Mix in the spices,
And let the cuts be burned up.

11 "Then set the pot empty on the coals,
That it may become hot and its bronze may burn,
That its filthiness may be melted in it,
That its scum may be consumed.
12 She has grown weary with lies,
And her great scum has not gone from her.
Let her scum *be* in the fire!
13 In your filthiness *is* lewdness.
Because I have cleansed you, and you were not cleansed,
You will not be cleansed of your filthiness anymore,
Till I have caused My fury to rest upon you.
14 I, the LORD, have spoken *it;*
It shall come to pass, and I will do *it;*
I will not hold back,
Nor will I spare,
Nor will I relent;
According to your ways
And according to your deeds
They[a] will judge you,"
Says the Lord GOD.' "

The Prophet's Wife Dies

15Also the word of the LORD came to
me, saying, 16"Son of man, behold, I
take away from you the desire of your

24:14 [a] Septuagint, Syriac, Targum, and Vulgate read *I*.

eyes with one stroke; yet you shall nei-
ther mourn nor weep, nor shall your
tears run down. 17Sigh in silence, make
no mourning for the dead; bind your
turban on your head, and put your san-
dals on your feet; do not cover *your* lips,
and do not eat man's bread *of sorrow*."
18So I spoke to the people in the morn-
ing, and at evening my wife died; and
the next morning I did as I was com-
manded.
19And the people said to me, "Will you
not tell us what these *things signify* to
us, that you behave so?"
20Then I answered them, "The word of
the LORD came to me, saying, 21'Speak
to the house of Israel, "Thus says the
Lord GOD: 'Behold, I will profane My
sanctuary, your arrogant boast, the
desire of your eyes, the delight of your
soul; and your sons and daughters
whom you left behind shall fall by the
sword. 22And you shall do as I have
done; you shall not cover *your* lips nor
eat man's bread *of sorrow*. 23Your tur-
bans shall be on your heads and your
sandals on your feet; you shall neither
mourn nor weep, but you shall pine
away in your iniquities and mourn with
one another. 24Thus Ezekiel is a sign to
you; according to all that he has done
you shall do; and when this comes, you
shall know that I *am* the Lord GOD.' "
25'And you, son of man—*will it* not *be*
in the day when I take from them their
stronghold, their joy and their glory,
the desire of their eyes, and that on
which they set their minds, their sons
and their daughters: 26*that* on that day
one who escapes will come to you to let
you hear *it* with *your* ears? 27On that
day your mouth will be opened to him
who has escaped; you shall speak and
no longer be mute. Thus you will be a
sign to them, and they shall know that
I *am* the LORD.' "

Proclamation Against Ammon

25 The word of the LORD came to
me, saying, 2"Son of man, set
your face against the Ammonites, and
prophesy against them. 3Say to the
Ammonites, 'Hear the word of the Lord
GOD! Thus says the Lord GOD: "Because
you said, 'Aha!' against My sanctuary
when it was profaned, and against the
land of Israel when it was desolate, and
against the house of Judah when they
went into captivity, 4indeed, therefore,
I will deliver you as a possession to the
men of the East, and they shall set their
encampments among you and make
their dwellings among you; they shall
eat your fruit, and they shall drink your
milk. 5And I will make Rabbah a stable
for camels and Ammon a resting place
for flocks. Then you shall know that I
am the LORD."
6'For thus says the Lord GOD: "Because
you clapped *your* hands, stamped your
feet, and rejoiced in heart with all your
disdain for the land of Israel, 7indeed,
therefore, I will stretch out My hand
against you, and give you as plunder to
the nations; I will cut you off from the
peoples, and I will cause you to perish
from the countries; I will destroy you,
and you shall know that I *am* the LORD."

Proclamation Against Moab

8'Thus says the Lord GOD: "Because
Moab and Seir say, 'Look! The house of
Judah *is* like all the nations,' 9therefore,
behold, I will clear the territory of Moab
of cities, of the cities on its frontier, the
glory of the country, Beth Jeshimoth,
Baal Meon, and Kirjathaim. 10To the
men of the East I will give it as a pos-
session, together with the Ammonites,
that the Ammonites may not be re-
membered among the nations. 11And
I will execute judgments upon Moab,
and they shall know that I *am* the LORD."

Proclamation Against Edom

12'Thus says the Lord GOD: "Because
of what Edom did against the house of
Judah by taking vengeance, and has
greatly offended by avenging itself on
them," 13therefore thus says the Lord
GOD: "I will also stretch out My hand
against Edom, cut off man and beast
from it, and make it desolate from
Teman; Dedan shall fall by the sword.
14I will lay My vengeance on Edom by
the hand of My people Israel, that they
may do in Edom according to My anger
and according to My fury; and they
shall know My vengeance," says the
Lord GOD.

Proclamation Against Philistia

15“Thus says the Lord GOD: “Because the Philistines dealt vengefully and took vengeance with a spiteful heart, to destroy because of the old hatred,” 16therefore thus says the Lord GOD: “I will stretch out My hand against the Philistines, and I will cut off the Cherethites and destroy the remnant of the seacoast. 17I will execute great vengeance on them with furious rebukes; and they shall know that I *am* the LORD, when I lay My vengeance upon them.” ’ ”

Proclamation Against Tyre

26 And it came to pass in the eleventh year, on the first *day* of the month, *that* the word of the LORD came to me, saying, 2“Son of man, because Tyre has said against Jerusalem, ‘Aha! She is broken who *was* the gateway of the peoples; now she is turned over to me; I shall be filled; she is laid waste.’

3“Therefore thus says the Lord GOD: ‘Behold, I *am* against you, O Tyre, and will cause many nations to come up against you, as the sea causes its waves to come up. 4And they shall destroy the walls of Tyre and break down her towers; I will also scrape her dust from her, and make her like the top of a rock. 5It shall be *a place for* spreading nets in the midst of the sea, for I have spoken,’ says the Lord GOD; ‘it shall become plunder for the nations. 6Also her daughter *villages* which *are* in the fields shall be slain by the sword. Then they shall know that I am the LORD.’

7“For thus says the Lord GOD: ‘Behold, I will bring against Tyre from the north Nebuchadnezzar[a] king of Babylon, king of kings, with horses, with chariots, and with horsemen, and an army with many people. 8He will slay with the sword your daughter *villages* in the fields; he will heap up a siege mound against you, build a wall against you, and raise a defense against you. 9He will direct his battering rams against your walls, and with his axes he will break down your towers. 10Because of the abundance of his horses, their dust will cover you; your walls will shake at the noise of the horsemen, the wagons, and the chariots, when he enters your gates, as men enter a city that has been breached. 11With the hooves of his horses he will trample all your streets; he will slay your people by the sword, and your strong pillars will fall to the ground. 12They will plunder your riches and pillage your merchandise; they will break down your walls and destroy your pleasant houses; they will lay your stones, your timber, and your soil in the midst of the water. 13I will put an end to the sound of your songs, and the sound of your harps shall be heard no more. 14I will make you like the top of a rock; you shall be *a place for* spreading nets, and you shall never be rebuilt, for I the LORD have spoken,’ says the Lord GOD.

15“Thus says the Lord GOD to Tyre: ‘Will the coastlands not shake at the sound of your fall, when the wounded cry, when slaughter is made in the midst of you? 16Then all the princes of the sea will come down from their thrones, lay aside their robes, and take off their embroidered garments; they will clothe themselves with trembling; they will sit on the ground, tremble *every* moment, and be astonished at you. 17And they will take up a lamentation for you, and say to you:

“How you have perished,
O one inhabited by seafaring
men,
O renowned city,
Who was strong at sea,
She and her inhabitants,
Who caused their terror *to be* on
all her inhabitants!
18 Now the coastlands tremble on
the day of your fall;
Yes, the coastlands by the sea are
troubled at your departure.” ’

19“For thus says the Lord GOD: ‘When I make you a desolate city, like cities that are not inhabited, when I bring the deep upon you, and great waters cover you, 20then I will bring you down with those who descend into the Pit, to

26:7 [a] Hebrew *Nebuchadrezzar,* and so elsewhere in this book

the people of old, and I will make you dwell in the lowest part of the earth, in places desolate from antiquity, with those who go down to the Pit, so that you may never be inhabited; and I shall establish glory in the land of the living.
21I will make you a terror, and you *shall be* no *more;* though you are sought for, you will never be found again,' says the Lord GOD."

Lamentation for Tyre

27 The word of the LORD came again to me, saying,
2"Now, son of man, take up a lamentation for Tyre,
3and say to Tyre, 'You who are situated at the entrance of the sea, merchant of the peoples on many coastlands, thus says the Lord GOD:

"O Tyre, you have said,
'I *am* perfect in beauty.'
4 Your borders *are* in the midst of the seas.
Your builders have perfected your beauty.
5 They made all *your* planks of fir trees from Senir;
They took a cedar from Lebanon to make you a mast.
6 *Of* oaks from Bashan they made your oars;
The company of Ashurites have inlaid your planks
With ivory from the coasts of Cyprus.[a]
7 Fine embroidered linen from Egypt was what you spread for your sail;
Blue and purple from the coasts of Elishah was what covered you.

8 "Inhabitants of Sidon and Arvad were your oarsmen;
Your wise men, O Tyre, were in you;
They became your pilots.
9 Elders of Gebal and its wise men
Were in you to caulk your seams;
All the ships of the sea
And their oarsmen were in you
To market your merchandise.

10 "Those from Persia, Lydia,[a] and Libya[b]
Were in your army as men of war;
They hung shield and helmet in you;
They gave splendor to you.
11 Men of Arvad with your army *were* on your walls *all* around,
And the men of Gammad were in your towers;
They hung their shields on your walls *all* around;
They made your beauty perfect.

12"Tarshish *was* your merchant be-
cause of your many luxury goods. They
gave you silver, iron, tin, and lead for
your goods. 13Javan, Tubal, and Me-
shech *were* your traders. They bartered
human lives and vessels of bronze for
your merchandise. 14Those from the
house of Togarmah traded for your
wares with horses, steeds, and mules.
15The men of Dedan *were* your traders;
many isles *were* the market of your
hand. They brought you ivory tusks
and ebony as payment. 16Syria *was*
your merchant because of the abun-
dance of goods you made. They gave
you for your wares emeralds, purple,
embroidery, fine linen, corals, and
rubies. 17Judah and the land of Isra-
el *were* your traders. They traded for
your merchandise wheat of Minnith,
millet, honey, oil, and balm. 18Damas-
cus *was* your merchant because of the
abundance of goods you made, because
of your many luxury items, with the
wine of Helbon and with white wool.
19Dan and Javan paid for your wares,
traversing back and forth. Wrought
iron, cassia, and cane were among your
merchandise. 20Dedan *was* your mer-
chant in saddlecloths for riding. 21Ara-
bia and all the princes of Kedar *were*
your regular merchants. They traded
with you in lambs, rams, and goats.
22The merchants of Sheba and Raamah
were your merchants. They traded for
your wares the choicest spices, all kinds
of precious stones, and gold. 23Haran,
Canneh, Eden, the merchants of Sheba,

27:6 [a] Hebrew *Kittim,* western lands, especially Cyprus 27:10 [a] Hebrew *Lud* [b] Hebrew *Put*

Assyria, *and* Chilmad *were* your merchants.
[24]These *were* your merchants
in choice items—in purple clothes, in
embroidered garments, in chests of
multicolored apparel, in sturdy woven
cords, which were in your marketplace.

25 "The ships of Tarshish were carriers
of your merchandise.
You were filled and very glorious
in the midst of the seas.
26 Your oarsmen brought you into
many waters,
But the east wind broke you in the
midst of the seas.

27 "Your riches, wares, and
merchandise,
Your mariners and pilots,
Your caulkers and merchandisers,
All your men of war who *are* in
you,
And the entire company which *is*
in your midst,
Will fall into the midst of the seas
on the day of your ruin.
28 The common-land will shake at
the sound of the cry of your
pilots.

29 "All who handle the oar,
The mariners,
All the pilots of the sea
Will come down from their ships
and stand on the shore.
30 They will make their voice heard
because of you;
They will cry bitterly and cast
dust on their heads;
They will roll about in ashes;
31 They will shave themselves
completely bald because of
you,
Gird themselves with sackcloth,
And weep for you
With bitterness of heart *and* bitter
wailing.
32 In their wailing for you
They will take up a lamentation,
And lament for you:
'What *city is* like Tyre,
Destroyed in the midst of the sea?

33 'When your wares went out by sea,
You satisfied many people;
You enriched the kings of the
earth
With your many luxury goods
and your merchandise.
34 But you are broken by the seas in
the depths of the waters;
Your merchandise and the entire
company will fall in your
midst.
35 All the inhabitants of the isles will
be astonished at you;
Their kings will be greatly afraid,
And *their* countenance will be
troubled.
36 The merchants among the
peoples will hiss at you;
You will become a horror, and *be*
no more forever.' " ' "

Proclamation Against the King of Tyre

28 The word of the LORD came to
me again, saying, [2]"Son of man,
say to the prince of Tyre, 'Thus says the
Lord GOD:

"Because your heart *is* lifted up,
And you say, 'I *am* a god,
I sit *in* the seat of gods,
In the midst of the seas,'
Yet you *are* a man, and not a god,
Though you set your heart as the
heart of a god
3 (Behold, you *are* wiser than
Daniel!
There is no secret that can be
hidden from you!
4 With your wisdom and your
understanding
You have gained riches for
yourself,
And gathered gold and silver into
your treasuries;
5 By your great wisdom in trade
you have increased your
riches,
And your heart is lifted up
because of your riches),"

[6]'Therefore thus says the Lord GOD:

"Because you have set your heart
as the heart of a god,
7 Behold, therefore, I will bring
strangers against you,
The most terrible of the nations;

And they shall draw their swords
against the beauty of your
wisdom,
And defile your splendor.
8 They shall throw you down into
the Pit,
And you shall die the death of the
slain
In the midst of the seas.

9 "Will you still say before him who
slays you,
'I *am* a god'?
But you *shall be* a man, and not a
god,
In the hand of him who slays you.
10 You shall die the death of the
uncircumcised
By the hand of aliens;
For I have spoken," says the Lord
GOD.'"

Lamentation for the King of Tyre

11Moreover the word of the LORD came
to me, saying, 12"Son of man, take up a
lamentation for the king of Tyre, and
say to him, 'Thus says the Lord GOD:

"You *were* the seal of perfection,
Full of wisdom and perfect in
beauty.
13 You were in Eden, the garden of
God;
Every precious stone *was* your
covering:
The sardius, topaz, and diamond,
Beryl, onyx, and jasper,
Sapphire, turquoise, and emerald
with gold.
The workmanship of your
timbrels and pipes
Was prepared for you on the day
you were created.

14 "You *were* the anointed cherub who
covers;
I established you;
You were on the holy mountain of
God;
You walked back and forth in the
midst of fiery stones.
15 You *were* perfect in your ways
from the day you were
created,
Till iniquity was found in you.

16 "By the abundance of your trading
You became filled with violence
within,
And you sinned;
Therefore I cast you as a profane
thing
Out of the mountain of God;
And I destroyed you, O covering
cherub,
From the midst of the fiery
stones.

17 "Your heart was lifted up because of
your beauty;
You corrupted your wisdom for
the sake of your splendor;
I cast you to the ground,
I laid you before kings,
That they might gaze at you.

18 "You defiled your sanctuaries
By the multitude of your
iniquities,
By the iniquity of your trading;
Therefore I brought fire from your
midst;
It devoured you,
And I turned you to ashes upon
the earth
In the sight of all who saw you.
19 All who knew you among the
peoples are astonished at
you;
You have become a horror,
And *shall be* no more forever."'"

Proclamation Against Sidon

20Then the word of the LORD came to
me, saying, 21"Son of man, set your face
toward Sidon, and prophesy against
her, 22and say, 'Thus says the Lord GOD:

"Behold, I *am* against you, O Sidon;
I will be glorified in your midst;
And they shall know that I *am* the
LORD,
When I execute judgments in her
and am hallowed in her.
23 For I will send pestilence upon
her,
And blood in her streets;
The wounded shall be judged in
her midst
By the sword against her on every
side;

Then they shall know that I *am*
the LORD.

24"And there shall no longer be a
pricking brier or a painful thorn for the
house of Israel from among all *who are*
around them, who despise them. Then
they shall know that I *am* the Lord GOD."

Israel's Future Blessing

25'Thus says the Lord GOD: "When I
have gathered the house of Israel from
the peoples among whom they are scat-
tered, and am hallowed in them in the
sight of the Gentiles, then they will dwell
in their own land which I gave to My ser-
vant Jacob. 26And they will dwell safely
there, build houses, and plant vineyards;
yes, they will dwell securely, when I ex-
ecute judgments on all those around
them who despise them. Then they shall
know that I *am* the LORD their God." ' "

Proclamation Against Egypt

29 In the tenth year, in the tenth
month, on the twelfth *day* of the
month, the word of the LORD came to
me, saying, 2"Son of man, set your face
against Pharaoh king of Egypt, and
prophesy against him, and against all
Egypt. 3Speak, and say, 'Thus says the
Lord GOD:

"Behold, I *am* against you,
O Pharaoh king of Egypt,
O great monster who lies in the
midst of his rivers,
Who has said, 'My River[a] *is* my
own;
I have made *it* for myself.'
4 But I will put hooks in your jaws,
And cause the fish of your rivers
to stick to your scales;
I will bring you up out of the
midst of your rivers,
And all the fish in your rivers will
stick to your scales.
5 I will leave you in the wilderness,
You and all the fish of your rivers;
You shall fall on the open field;
You shall not be picked up or
gathered.[a]
I have given you as food
To the beasts of the field
And to the birds of the heavens.

6 "Then all the inhabitants of Egypt
Shall know that I *am* the LORD,
Because they have been a staff of
reed to the house of Israel.
7 When they took hold of you with
the hand,
You broke and tore all their
shoulders;[a]
When they leaned on you,
You broke and made all their
backs quiver."

8'Therefore thus says the Lord GOD:
"Surely I will bring a sword upon you
and cut off from you man and beast.
9And the land of Egypt shall become
desolate and waste; then they will know
that I *am* the LORD, because he said,
'The River *is* mine, and I have made *it*.'
10Indeed, therefore, I *am* against you
and against your rivers, and I will make
the land of Egypt utterly waste and des-
olate, from Migdol[a] *to* Syene, as far as
the border of Ethiopia. 11Neither foot
of man shall pass through it nor foot
of beast pass through it, and it shall be
uninhabited forty years. 12I will make
the land of Egypt desolate in the midst
of the countries *that are* desolate; and
among the cities *that are* laid waste, her
cities shall be desolate forty years; and
I will scatter the Egyptians among the
nations and disperse them throughout
the countries."
13'Yet, thus says the Lord GOD: "At the
end of forty years I will gather the Egyp-
tians from the peoples among whom
they were scattered. 14I will bring back
the captives of Egypt and cause them to
return to the land of Pathros, to the land
of their origin, and there they shall be
a lowly kingdom. 15It shall be the low-
liest of kingdoms; it shall never again
exalt itself above the nations, for I will
diminish them so that they will not rule
over the nations anymore. 16No longer
shall it be the confidence of the house
of Israel, but will remind them of *their*

29:3 [a] That is, the Nile **29:5** [a] Following Masoretic Text, Septuagint, and Vulgate; some Hebrew manuscripts and Targum read *buried.* **29:7** [a] Following Masoretic Text and Vulgate; Septuagint and Syriac read *hand.* **29:10** [a] Or *tower*

iniquity when they turned to follow them. Then they shall know that I *am* the Lord GOD." ' "

Babylonia Will Plunder Egypt

17And it came to pass in the twenty-
seventh year, in the first *month,* on the
first *day* of the month, *that* the word of
the LORD came to me, saying, 18"Son of
man, Nebuchadnezzar king of Babylon
caused his army to labor strenuously
against Tyre; every head *was* made
bald, and every shoulder rubbed raw;
yet neither he nor his army received
wages from Tyre, for the labor which
they expended on it. 19Therefore thus
says the Lord GOD: 'Surely I will give
the land of Egypt to Nebuchadnezzar
king of Babylon; he shall take away her
wealth, carry off her spoil, and remove
her pillage; and that will be the wages
for his army. 20I have given him the
land of Egypt *for* his labor, because they
worked for Me,' says the Lord GOD.
21'In that day I will cause the horn of
the house of Israel to spring forth, and
I will open your mouth to speak in their
midst. Then they shall know that I *am*
the LORD.' "

Egypt and Her Allies Will Fall

30 The word of the LORD came to
me again, saying, 2"Son of man,
prophesy and say, 'Thus says the Lord
GOD:

"Wail, 'Woe to the day!'
3 For the day *is* near,
Even the day of the LORD *is* near;
It will be a day of clouds, the time of the Gentiles.
4 The sword shall come upon Egypt,
And great anguish shall be in Ethiopia,
When the slain fall in Egypt,
And they take away her wealth,
And her foundations are broken down.

5"Ethiopia, Libya,[a] Lydia,[b] all the min-
gled people, Chub, and the men of the
lands who are allied, shall fall with them
by the sword."

6"Thus says the LORD:

"Those who uphold Egypt shall fall,
And the pride of her power shall come down.
From Migdol *to* Syene
Those within her shall fall by the sword,"
Says the Lord GOD.

7 "They shall be desolate in the midst of the desolate countries,
And her cities shall be in the midst of the cities *that are* laid waste.
8 Then they will know that I *am* the LORD,
When I have set a fire in Egypt
And all her helpers are destroyed.
9 On that day messengers shall go forth from Me in ships
To make the careless Ethiopians afraid,
And great anguish shall come upon them,
As on the day of Egypt;
For indeed it is coming!"

10"Thus says the Lord GOD:

"I will also make a multitude of Egypt to cease
By the hand of Nebuchadnezzar king of Babylon.
11 He and his people with him, the most terrible of the nations,
Shall be brought to destroy the land;
They shall draw their swords against Egypt,
And fill the land with the slain.
12 I will make the rivers dry,
And sell the land into the hand of the wicked;
I will make the land waste, and all that is in it,
By the hand of aliens.
I, the LORD, have spoken."

13"Thus says the Lord GOD:

"I will also destroy the idols,
And cause the images to cease from Noph;[a]

30:5 [a] Hebrew *Put* [b] Hebrew *Lud* 30:13 [a] That is, ancient Memphis

There shall no longer be princes
from the land of Egypt;
I will put fear in the land of Egypt.
14 I will make Pathros desolate,
Set fire to Zoan,
And execute judgments in No.[a]
15 I will pour My fury on Sin,[a] the
strength of Egypt;
I will cut off the multitude of No,
16 And set a fire in Egypt;
Sin shall have great pain,
No shall be split open,
And Noph *shall be in* distress
daily.
17 The young men of Aven[a] and
Pi Beseth shall fall by the
sword,
And these *cities* shall go into
captivity.
18 At Tehaphnehes[a] the day shall
also be darkened,[b]
When I break the yokes of Egypt
there.
And her arrogant strength shall
cease in her;
As for her, a cloud shall cover her,
And her daughters shall go into
captivity.
19 Thus I will execute judgments on
Egypt,
Then they shall know that I *am*
the LORD." ' "

Proclamation Against Pharaoh

20 And it came to pass in the eleventh
year, in the first *month,* on the seventh
day of the month, *that* the word of the
LORD came to me, saying, 21 "Son of
man, I have broken the arm of Pharaoh
king of Egypt; and see, it has not been
bandaged for healing, nor a splint put
on to bind it, to make it strong enough
to hold a sword. 22 Therefore thus says
the Lord GOD: 'Surely I *am* against Phar-
aoh king of Egypt, and will break his
arms, both the strong one and the one
that was broken; and I will make the
sword fall out of his hand. 23 I will scatter
the Egyptians among the nations, and
disperse them throughout the coun-
tries. 24 I will strengthen the arms of
the king of Babylon and put My sword
in his hand; but I will break Pharaoh's
arms, and he will groan before him with
the groanings of a mortally wounded
man. 25 Thus I will strengthen the arms
of the king of Babylon, but the arms
of Pharaoh shall fall down; they shall
know that I *am* the LORD, when I put My
sword into the hand of the king of Bab-
ylon and he stretches it out against the
land of Egypt. 26 I will scatter the Egyp-
tians among the nations and disperse
them throughout the countries. Then
they shall know that I *am* the LORD.' "

Egypt Cut Down Like a Great Tree

31 Now it came to pass in the elev-
enth year, in the third *month,* on
the first *day* of the month, *that* the word
of the LORD came to me, saying, 2 "Son
of man, say to Pharaoh king of Egypt
and to his multitude:

'Whom are you like in your
greatness?
3 Indeed Assyria *was* a cedar in
Lebanon,
With fine branches that shaded
the forest,
And of high stature;
And its top was among the thick
boughs.
4 The waters made it grow;
Underground waters gave it
height,
With their rivers running around
the place where it was
planted,
And sent out rivulets to all the
trees of the field.

5 'Therefore its height was exalted
above all the trees of the field;
Its boughs were multiplied,
And its branches became long
because of the abundance of
water,
As it sent them out.
6 All the birds of the heavens made
their nests in its boughs;
Under its branches all the beasts
of the field brought forth
their young;

30:14 [a] That is, ancient Thebes 30:15 [a] That is, ancient Pelusium 30:17 [a] That is, ancient On (Heliopolis) 30:18 [a] Spelled *Tahpanhes* in Jeremiah 43:7 and elsewhere [b] Following many Hebrew manuscripts, Bomberg, Septuagint, Syriac, Targum, and Vulgate; Masoretic Text reads *refrained.*

And in its shadow all great
nations made their home.

7 'Thus it was beautiful in greatness
and in the length of its
branches,
Because its roots reached to
abundant waters.
8 The cedars in the garden of God
could not hide it;
The fir trees were not like its
boughs,
And the chestnut[a] trees were not
like its branches;
No tree in the garden of God was
like it in beauty.
9 I made it beautiful with a
multitude of branches,
So that all the trees of Eden
envied it,
That *were* in the garden of God.'

10"Therefore thus says the Lord GOD:
'Because you have increased in height,
and it set its top among the thick
boughs, and its heart was lifted up in
its height, 11therefore I will deliver it
into the hand of the mighty one of the
nations, and he shall surely deal with it;
I have driven it out for its wickedness.
12And aliens, the most terrible of the
nations, have cut it down and left it;
its branches have fallen on the moun-
tains and in all the valleys; its boughs
lie broken by all the rivers of the land;
and all the peoples of the earth have
gone from under its shadow and left it.

13 'On its ruin will remain all the birds
of the heavens,
And all the beasts of the field will
come to its branches—

14So that no trees by the waters may
ever again exalt themselves for their
height, nor set their tops among the
thick boughs, that no tree which drinks
water may ever be high enough to reach
up to them.

'For they have all been delivered to
death,
To the depths of the earth,
Among the children of men who
go down to the Pit.'

15"Thus says the Lord GOD: 'In the day
when it went down to hell, I caused
mourning. I covered the deep because
of it. I restrained its rivers, and the great
waters were held back. I caused Leba-
non to mourn for it, and all the trees of
the field wilted because of it. 16I made
the nations shake at the sound of its
fall, when I cast it down to hell together
with those who descend into the Pit;
and all the trees of Eden, the choice and
best of Lebanon, all that drink water,
were comforted in the depths of the
earth. 17They also went down to hell
with it, with those slain by the sword;
and *those who were* its *strong* arm dwelt
in its shadows among the nations.
18'To which of the trees in Eden will you
then be likened in glory and greatness?
Yet you shall be brought down with the
trees of Eden to the depths of the earth;
you shall lie in the midst of the uncir-
cumcised, with *those* slain by the sword.
This *is* Pharaoh and all his multitude,'
says the Lord GOD."

Lamentation for Pharaoh and Egypt

32 And it came to pass in the twelfth
year, in the twelfth *month,* on the
first *day* of the month, *that* the word of
the LORD came to me, saying, 2"Son of
man, take up a lamentation for Phar-
aoh king of Egypt, and say to him:

'You are like a young lion among
the nations,
And you *are* like a monster in the
seas,
Bursting forth in your rivers,
Troubling the waters with your
feet,
And fouling their rivers.

3'Thus says the Lord GOD:

"I will therefore spread My net
over you with a company of
many people,
And they will draw you up in My
net.

31:8 [a] Hebrew *armon*

4 Then I will leave you on the land;
I will cast you out on the open fields,
And cause to settle on you all the birds of the heavens.
And with you I will fill the beasts of the whole earth.
5 I will lay your flesh on the mountains,
And fill the valleys with your carcass.

6 "I will also water the land with the flow of your blood,
Even to the mountains;
And the riverbeds will be full of you.
7 When *I* put out your light,
I will cover the heavens, and make its stars dark;
I will cover the sun with a cloud,
And the moon shall not give her light.
8 All the bright lights of the heavens I will make dark over you,
And bring darkness upon your land,"
Says the Lord GOD.

9'I will also trouble the hearts of many
peoples, when I bring your destruction
among the nations, into the countries
which you have not known. 10Yes, I will
make many peoples astonished at you,
and their kings shall be horribly afraid
of you when I brandish My sword be-
fore them; and they shall tremble *every*
moment, every man for his own life, in
the day of your fall.
11"For thus says the Lord GOD: 'The
sword of the king of Babylon shall come
upon you. 12By the swords of the mighty
warriors, all of them the most terrible
of the nations, I will cause your multi-
tude to fall.

'They shall plunder the pomp of Egypt,
And all its multitude shall be destroyed.
13 Also I will destroy all its animals
From beside its great waters;
The foot of man shall muddy them no more,
Nor shall the hooves of animals muddy them.
14 Then I will make their waters clear,
And make their rivers run like oil,'
Says the Lord GOD.

15 'When I make the land of Egypt desolate,
And the country is destitute of all that once filled it,
When I strike all who dwell in it,
Then they shall know that I *am* the LORD.

16 'This *is* the lamentation
With which they shall lament her;
The daughters of the nations shall lament her;
They shall lament for her, for Egypt,
And for all her multitude,'
Says the Lord GOD."

Egypt and Others Consigned to the Pit

17It came to pass also in the twelfth
year, on the fifteenth *day* of the month,
that the word of the LORD came to me,
saying:

18 "Son of man, wail over the multitude of Egypt,
And cast them down to the depths of the earth,
Her and the daughters of the famous nations,
With those who go down to the Pit:
19 'Whom do you surpass in beauty?
Go down, be placed with the uncircumcised.'

20 "They shall fall in the midst of *those* slain by the sword;
She is delivered to the sword,
Drawing her and all her multitudes.
21 The strong among the mighty
Shall speak to him out of the midst of hell
With those who help him:
'They have gone down,
They lie with the uncircumcised, slain by the sword.'

22 "Assyria *is* there, and all her company,

With their graves all around her,
All of them slain, fallen by the sword.
23 Her graves are set in the recesses of the Pit,
And her company is all around her grave,
All of them slain, fallen by the sword,
Who caused terror in the land of the living.

24 "There *is* Elam and all her multitude,
All around her grave,
All of them slain, fallen by the sword,
Who have gone down uncircumcised to the lower parts of the earth,
Who caused their terror in the land of the living;
Now they bear their shame with those who go down to the Pit.
25 They have set her bed in the midst of the slain,
With all her multitude,
With her graves all around it,
All of them uncircumcised, slain by the sword;
Though their terror was caused
In the land of the living,
Yet they bear their shame
With those who go down to the Pit;
It was put in the midst of the slain.

26 "There *are* Meshech and Tubal and all their multitudes,
With all their graves around it,
All of them uncircumcised, slain by the sword,
Though they caused their terror in the land of the living.
27 They do not lie with the mighty
Who are fallen of the uncircumcised,
Who have gone down to hell with their weapons of war;
They have laid their swords under their heads,
But their iniquities will be on their bones,
Because of the terror of the mighty in the land of the living.
28 Yes, you shall be broken in the midst of the uncircumcised,
And lie with *those* slain by the sword.

29 "There *is* Edom,
Her kings and all her princes,
Who despite their might
Are laid beside *those* slain by the sword;
They shall lie with the uncircumcised,
And with those who go down to the Pit.
30 There *are* the princes of the north,
All of them, and all the Sidonians,
Who have gone down with the slain
In shame at the terror which they caused by their might;
They lie uncircumcised with *those* slain by the sword,
And bear their shame with those who go down to the Pit.

31 "Pharaoh will see them
And be comforted over all his multitude,
Pharaoh and all his army,
Slain by the sword,"
Says the Lord GOD.

32 "For I have caused My terror in the land of the living;
And he shall be placed in the midst of the uncircumcised
With *those* slain by the sword,
Pharaoh and all his multitude,"
Says the Lord GOD.

The Watchman and His Message

33 Again the word of the LORD
came to me, saying, 2"Son of
man, speak to the children of your peo-
ple, and say to them: 'When I bring the
sword upon a land, and the people of
the land take a man from their terri-
tory and make him their watchman,
3when he sees the sword coming upon
the land, if he blows the trumpet and
warns the people, 4then whoever hears
the sound of the trumpet and does not
take warning, if the sword comes and
takes him away, his blood shall be on
his *own* head. 5He heard the sound of

the trumpet, but did not take warning; his blood shall be upon himself. But he who takes warning will save his life.
6But if the watchman sees the sword coming and does not blow the trumpet, and the people are not warned, and the sword comes and takes *any* person from among them, he is taken away in his iniquity; but his blood I will require at the watchman's hand.'

7"So you, son of man: I have made you a watchman for the house of Israel; therefore you shall hear a word from My mouth and warn them for Me.
8When I say to the wicked, 'O wicked *man,* you shall surely die!' and you do not speak to warn the wicked from his way, that wicked *man* shall die in his iniquity; but his blood I will require at your hand.
9Nevertheless if you warn the wicked to turn from his way, and he does not turn from his way, he shall die in his iniquity; but you have delivered your soul.

10"Therefore you, O son of man, say to the house of Israel: 'Thus you say, "If our transgressions and our sins *lie* upon us, and we pine away in them, how can we then live?" '
11Say to them: '*As* I live,' says the Lord GOD, 'I have no pleasure in the death of the wicked, but that the wicked turn from his way and live. Turn, turn from your evil ways! For why should you die, O house of Israel?'

The Fairness of God's Judgment

12"Therefore you, O son of man, say to the children of your people: 'The righteousness of the righteous man shall not deliver him in the day of his transgression; as for the wickedness of the wicked, he shall not fall because of it in the day that he turns from his wickedness; nor shall the righteous be able to live because of *his righteousness* in the day that he sins.'
13When I say to the righteous *that* he shall surely live, but he trusts in his own righteousness and commits iniquity, none of his righteous works shall be remembered; but because of the iniquity that he has committed, he shall die.
14Again, when I say to the wicked, 'You shall surely die,' if he turns from his sin and does what is lawful and right,
15*if* the wicked restores the pledge, gives back what he has stolen, and walks in the statutes of life without committing iniquity, he shall surely live; he shall not die.
16None of his sins which he has committed shall be remembered against him; he has done what is lawful and right; he shall surely live.

17"Yet the children of your people say, 'The way of the Lord is not fair.' But it is their way which is not fair!
18When the righteous turns from his righteousness and commits iniquity, he shall die because of it.
19But when the wicked turns from his wickedness and does what is lawful and right, he shall live because of it.
20Yet you say, 'The way of the Lord is not fair.' O house of Israel, I will judge every one of you according to his own ways."

The Fall of Jerusalem

21And it came to pass in the twelfth year of our captivity, in the tenth *month,* on the fifth *day* of the month, *that* one who had escaped from Jerusalem came to me and said, "The city has been captured!"

22Now the hand of the LORD had been upon me the evening before the man came who had escaped. And He had opened my mouth; so when he came to me in the morning, my mouth was opened, and I was no longer mute.

The Cause of Judah's Ruin

23Then the word of the LORD came to me, saying:
24"Son of man, they who inhabit those ruins in the land of Israel are saying, 'Abraham was only one, and he inherited the land. But we *are* many; the land has been given to us as a possession.'

25"Therefore say to them, 'Thus says the Lord GOD: "You eat *meat* with blood, you lift up your eyes toward your idols, and shed blood. Should you then possess the land?
26You rely on your sword, you commit abominations, and you defile one another's wives. Should you then possess the land?" '

27"Say thus to them, 'Thus says the Lord GOD: "*As* I live, surely those who *are* in the ruins shall fall by the sword, and the one who *is* in the open field I will give to the beasts to be devoured, and those who *are* in the strongholds and

caves shall die of the pestilence. 28For
I will make the land most desolate, her
arrogant strength shall cease, and the
mountains of Israel shall be so desolate
that no one will pass through. 29Then
they shall know that I *am* the LORD,
when I have made the land most des-
olate because of all their abominations
which they have committed." '

Hearing and Not Doing

30"As for you, son of man, the children
of your people are talking about you
beside the walls and in the doors of the
houses; and they speak to one another,
everyone saying to his brother, 'Please
come and hear what the word is that
comes from the LORD.' 31So they come
to you as people do, they sit before you
as My people, and they hear your words,
but they do not do them; for with their
mouth they show much love, *but* their
hearts pursue their *own* gain. 32Indeed
you *are* to them as a very lovely song of
one who has a pleasant voice and can
play well on an instrument; for they
hear your words, but they do not do
them. 33And when this comes to pass—
surely it will come—then they will know
that a prophet has been among them."

Irresponsible Shepherds

34 And the word of the LORD came
to me, saying, 2"Son of man,
prophesy against the shepherds of Is-
rael, prophesy and say to them, 'Thus
says the Lord GOD to the shepherds:
"Woe to the shepherds of Israel who
feed themselves! Should not the shep-
herds feed the flocks? 3You eat the fat
and clothe yourselves with the wool;
you slaughter the fatlings, *but* you do
not feed the flock. 4The weak you have
not strengthened, nor have you healed
those who were sick, nor bound up the
broken, nor brought back what was driv-
en away, nor sought what was lost; but
with force and cruelty you have ruled
them. 5So they were scattered because
there was no shepherd; and they be-
came food for all the beasts of the field
when they were scattered. 6My sheep
wandered through all the mountains,
and on every high hill; yes, My flock
was scattered over the whole face of
the earth, and no one was seeking or
searching *for them.*"

7'Therefore, you shepherds, hear the
word of the LORD: 8"*As* I live," says the
Lord GOD, "surely because My flock be-
came a prey, and My flock became food
for every beast of the field, because *there*
was no shepherd, nor did My shepherds
search for My flock, but the shepherds
fed themselves and did not feed My
flock"— 9therefore, O shepherds, hear
the word of the LORD! 10Thus says the
Lord GOD: "Behold, I *am* against the
shepherds, and I will require My flock
at their hand; I will cause them to cease
feeding the sheep, and the shepherds
shall feed themselves no more; for I will
deliver My flock from their mouths, that
they may no longer be food for them."

God, the True Shepherd

11'For thus says the Lord GOD: "Indeed
I Myself will search for My sheep and
seek them out. 12As a shepherd seeks
out his flock on the day he is among
his scattered sheep, so will I seek out
My sheep and deliver them from all
the places where they were scattered
on a cloudy and dark day. 13And I will
bring them out from the peoples and
gather them from the countries, and
will bring them to their own land; I will
feed them on the mountains of Israel,
in the valleys and in all the inhabited
places of the country. 14I will feed them
in good pasture, and their fold shall be
on the high mountains of Israel. There
they shall lie down in a good fold and
feed in rich pasture on the mountains
of Israel. 15I will feed My flock, and I
will make them lie down," says the Lord
GOD. 16"I will seek what was lost and
bring back what was driven away, bind
up the broken and strengthen what was
sick; but I will destroy the fat and the
strong, and feed them in judgment."

17'And *as for* you, O My flock, thus says
the Lord GOD: "Behold, I shall judge be-
tween sheep and sheep, between rams
and goats. 18*Is it* too little for you to
have eaten up the good pasture, that
you must tread down with your feet the
residue of your pasture—and to have
drunk of the clear waters, that you must
foul the residue with your feet? 19And

as for My flock, they eat what you have
trampled with your feet, and they drink
what you have fouled with your feet."
20 "Therefore thus says the Lord GOD
to them: "Behold, I Myself will judge
between the fat and the lean sheep.
21 Because you have pushed with side
and shoulder, butted all the weak ones
with your horns, and scattered them
abroad, 22 therefore I will save My flock,
and they shall no longer be a prey; and I
will judge between sheep and sheep. 23 I
will establish one shepherd over them,
and he shall feed them—My servant
David. He shall feed them and be their
shepherd. 24 And I, the LORD, will be their
God, and My servant David a prince
among them; I, the LORD, have spoken.
25 "I will make a covenant of peace
with them, and cause wild beasts to
cease from the land; and they will dwell
safely in the wilderness and sleep in
the woods. 26 I will make them and the
places all around My hill a blessing;
and I will cause showers to come down
in their season; there shall be showers
of blessing. 27 Then the trees of the field
shall yield their fruit, and the earth shall
yield her increase. They shall be safe in
their land; and they shall know that I
am the LORD, when I have broken the
bands of their yoke and delivered them
from the hand of those who enslaved
them. 28 And they shall no longer be a
prey for the nations, nor shall beasts
of the land devour them; but they shall
dwell safely, and no one shall make
them afraid. 29 I will raise up for them
a garden of renown, and they shall no
longer be consumed with hunger in the
land, nor bear the shame of the Gentiles
anymore. 30 Thus they shall know that
I, the LORD their God, *am* with them,
and they, the house of Israel, *are* My
people," says the Lord GOD.'
31 "You are My flock, the flock of My
pasture; you *are* men, *and* I *am* your
God," says the Lord GOD.

Judgment on Mount Seir

35 Moreover the word of the LORD
came to me, saying, 2 "Son of
man, set your face against Mount Seir
and prophesy against it, 3 and say to it,
'Thus says the Lord GOD:

"Behold, O Mount Seir, I *am* against
you;
I will stretch out My hand against
you,
And make you most desolate;
4 I shall lay your cities waste,
And you shall be desolate.
Then you shall know that I *am* the
LORD.

5 "Because you have had an ancient
hatred, and have shed *the blood of* the
children of Israel by the power of the
sword at the time of their calamity,
when their iniquity *came to an* end,
6 therefore, *as* I live," says the Lord
GOD, "I will prepare you for blood, and
blood shall pursue you; since you have
not hated blood, therefore blood shall
pursue you. 7 Thus I will make Mount
Seir most desolate, and cut off from it
the one who leaves and the one who
returns. 8 And I will fill its mountains
with the slain; on your hills and in your
valleys and in all your ravines those
who are slain by the sword shall fall.
9 I will make you perpetually desolate,
and your cities shall be uninhabited;
then you shall know that I *am* the LORD.
10 "Because you have said, 'These two
nations and these two countries shall
be mine, and we will possess them,' al-
though the LORD was there, 11 therefore,
as I live," says the Lord GOD, "I will do
according to your anger and accord-
ing to the envy which you showed in
your hatred against them; and I will
make Myself known among them when
I judge you. 12 Then you shall know that
I *am* the LORD. I have heard all your
blasphemies which you have spoken
against the mountains of Israel, saying,
'They are desolate; they are given to us
to consume.' 13 Thus with your mouth
you have boasted against Me and mul-
tiplied your words against Me; I have
heard *them.*"
14 'Thus says the Lord GOD: "The whole
earth will rejoice when I make you des-
olate. 15 As you rejoiced because the
inheritance of the house of Israel was
desolate, so I will do to you; you shall
be desolate, O Mount Seir, as well as all
of Edom—all of it! Then they shall know
that I *am* the LORD." '

Blessing on Israel

36 "And you, son of man, prophesy to the mountains of Israel, and say, 'O mountains of Israel, hear the word of the LORD! 2 Thus says the Lord GOD: "Because the enemy has said of you, 'Aha! The ancient heights have become our possession,' " ' 3 therefore prophesy, and say, 'Thus says the Lord GOD: "Because they made *you* desolate and swallowed you up on every side, so that you became the possession of the rest of the nations, and you are taken up by the lips of talkers and slandered by the people"— 4 therefore, O mountains of Israel, hear the word of the Lord GOD! Thus says the Lord GOD to the mountains, the hills, the rivers, the valleys, the desolate wastes, and the cities that have been forsaken, which became plunder and mockery to the rest of the nations all around— 5 therefore thus says the Lord GOD: "Surely I have spoken in My burning jealousy against the rest of the nations and against all Edom, who gave My land to themselves as a possession, with wholehearted joy *and* spiteful minds, in order to plunder its open country." '

6 "Therefore prophesy concerning the land of Israel, and say to the mountains, the hills, the rivers, and the valleys, 'Thus says the Lord GOD: "Behold, I have spoken in My jealousy and My fury, because you have borne the shame of the nations." 7 Therefore thus says the Lord GOD: "I have raised My hand in an oath that surely the nations that *are* around you shall bear their own shame. 8 But you, O mountains of Israel, you shall shoot forth your branches and yield your fruit to My people Israel, for they are about to come. 9 For indeed I *am* for you, and I will turn to you, and you shall be tilled and sown. 10 I will multiply men upon you, all the house of Israel, all of it; and the cities shall be inhabited and the ruins rebuilt. 11 I will multiply upon you man and beast; and they shall increase and bear young; I will make you inhabited as in former times, and do better *for you* than at your beginnings. Then you shall know that I *am* the LORD. 12 Yes, I will cause men to walk on you, My people Israel; they shall take possession of you, and you shall be their inheritance; no more shall you bereave them *of children.*"

13 "Thus says the Lord GOD: "Because they say to you, 'You devour men and bereave your nation *of children,*' 14 therefore you shall devour men no more, nor bereave your nation anymore," says the Lord GOD. 15 "Nor will I let you hear the taunts of the nations anymore, nor bear the reproach of the peoples anymore, nor shall you cause your nation to stumble anymore," says the Lord GOD.' "

The Renewal of Israel

16 Moreover the word of the LORD came to me, saying: 17 "Son of man, when the house of Israel dwelt in their own land, they defiled it by their own ways and deeds; to Me their way was like the uncleanness of a woman in her customary impurity. 18 Therefore I poured out My fury on them for the blood they had shed on the land, and for their idols *with which* they had defiled it. 19 So I scattered them among the nations, and they were dispersed throughout the countries; I judged them according to their ways and their deeds. 20 When they came to the nations, wherever they went, they profaned My holy name—when they said of them, 'These *are* the people of the LORD, *and* yet they have gone out of His land.' 21 But I had concern for My holy name, which the house of Israel had profaned among the nations wherever they went.

22 "Therefore say to the house of Israel, 'Thus says the Lord GOD: "I do not do *this* for your sake, O house of Israel, but for My holy name's sake, which you have profaned among the nations wherever you went. 23 And I will sanctify My great name, which has been profaned among the nations, which you have profaned in their midst; and the nations shall know that I *am* the LORD," says the Lord GOD, "when I am hallowed in you before their eyes. 24 For I will take you from among the nations, gather you out of all countries, and bring you into your own land. 25 Then I will sprinkle clean water on you, and you shall be clean; I will cleanse you from all your filthiness and from all your idols. 26 I will give you a new

heart and put a new spirit within you;
I will take the heart of stone out of your
flesh and give you a heart of flesh. 27I
will put My Spirit within you and cause
you to walk in My statutes, and you
will keep My judgments and do *them.*
28Then you shall dwell in the land that
I gave to your fathers; you shall be My
people, and I will be your God. 29I will
deliver you from all your uncleannesses.
I will call for the grain and multiply it,
and bring no famine upon you. 30And I
will multiply the fruit of your trees and
the increase of your fields, so that you
need never again bear the reproach of
famine among the nations. 31Then you
will remember your evil ways and your
deeds that *were* not good; and you will
loathe yourselves in your own sight, for
your iniquities and your abominations.
32Not for your sake do I do *this,*" says
the Lord GOD, "let it be known to you.
Be ashamed and confounded for your
own ways, O house of Israel!"

33'Thus says the Lord GOD: "On the
day that I cleanse you from all your
iniquities, I will also enable *you* to
dwell in the cities, and the ruins shall
be rebuilt. 34The desolate land shall be
tilled instead of lying desolate in the
sight of all who pass by. 35So they will
say, 'This land that was desolate has
become like the garden of Eden; and
the wasted, desolate, and ruined cities
are now fortified *and* inhabited.' 36Then
the nations which are left all around
you shall know that I, the LORD, have
rebuilt the ruined places *and* planted
what was desolate. I, the LORD, have
spoken *it,* and I will do *it.*"

37'Thus says the Lord GOD: "I will also
let the house of Israel inquire of Me to
do this for them: I will increase their
men like a flock. 38Like a flock *offered as*
holy *sacrifices,* like the flock at Jerusa-
lem on its feast days, so shall the ruined
cities be filled with flocks of men. Then
they shall know that I *am* the LORD." ' "

The Dry Bones Live

37 The hand of the LORD came upon
me and brought me out in the
Spirit of the LORD, and set me down
in the midst of the valley; and it *was*
full of bones. 2Then He caused me to
pass by them all around, and behold,
there were very many in the open valley;
and indeed *they were* very dry. 3And
He said to me, "Son of man, can these
bones live?"

So I answered, "O Lord GOD, You know."

4Again He said to me, "Prophesy to
these bones, and say to them, 'O dry
bones, hear the word of the LORD! 5Thus
says the Lord GOD to these bones: "Sure-
ly I will cause breath to enter into you,
and you shall live. 6I will put sinews on
you and bring flesh upon you, cover
you with skin and put breath in you;
and you shall live. Then you shall know
that I *am* the LORD." ' "

7So I prophesied as I was commanded;
and as I prophesied, there was a noise,
and suddenly a rattling; and the bones
came together, bone to bone. 8Indeed,
as I looked, the sinews and the flesh
came upon them, and the skin covered
them over; but *there was* no breath in
them.

9Also He said to me, "Prophesy to the
breath, prophesy, son of man, and say
to the breath, 'Thus says the Lord GOD:
"Come from the four winds, O breath,
and breathe on these slain, that they
may live." ' " 10So I prophesied as He
commanded me, and breath came into
them, and they lived, and stood upon
their feet, an exceedingly great army.

11Then He said to me, "Son of man,
these bones are the whole house of Is-
rael. They indeed say, 'Our bones are
dry, our hope is lost, and we ourselves
are cut off!' 12Therefore prophesy and
say to them, 'Thus says the Lord GOD:
"Behold, O My people, I will open your
graves and cause you to come up from
your graves, and bring you into the land
of Israel. 13Then you shall know that I
am the LORD, when I have opened your
graves, O My people, and brought you up
from your graves. 14I will put My Spirit in
you, and you shall live, and I will place
you in your own land. Then you shall
know that I, the LORD, have spoken *it* and
performed *it,*" says the LORD.' "

One Kingdom, One King

15Again the word of the LORD came to
me, saying, 16"As for you, son of man,
take a stick for yourself and write on it:

'For Judah and for the children of Israel, his companions.' Then take another stick and write on it, 'For Joseph, the stick of Ephraim, and *for* all the house of Israel, his companions.' 17Then join them one to another for yourself into one stick, and they will become one in your hand.

18"And when the children of your people speak to you, saying, 'Will you not show us what you *mean* by these?'— 19say to them, 'Thus says the Lord GOD: "Surely I will take the stick of Joseph, which *is* in the hand of Ephraim, and the tribes of Israel, his companions; and I will join them with it, with the stick of Judah, and make them one stick, and they will be one in My hand." ' 20And the sticks on which you write will be in your hand before their eyes.

21"Then say to them, 'Thus says the Lord GOD: "Surely I will take the children of Israel from among the nations, wherever they have gone, and will gather them from every side and bring them into their own land; 22and I will make them one nation in the land, on the mountains of Israel; and one king shall be king over them all; they shall no longer be two nations, nor shall they ever be divided into two kingdoms again. 23They shall not defile themselves anymore with their idols, nor with their detestable things, nor with any of their transgressions; but I will deliver them from all their dwelling places in which they have sinned, and will cleanse them. Then they shall be My people, and I will be their God.

24"David My servant *shall be* king over them, and they shall all have one shepherd; they shall also walk in My judgments and observe My statutes, and do them. 25Then they shall dwell in the land that I have given to Jacob My servant, where your fathers dwelt; and they shall dwell there, they, their children, and their children's children, forever; and My servant David *shall be* their prince forever. 26Moreover I will make a covenant of peace with them, and it shall be an everlasting covenant with them; I will establish them and multiply them, and I will set My sanctuary in their midst forevermore. 27My tabernacle also shall be with them; indeed I will be their God, and they shall be My people. 28The nations also will know that I, the LORD, sanctify Israel, when My sanctuary is in their midst forevermore." ' "

Gog and Allies Attack Israel

38 Now the word of the LORD came to me, saying, 2"Son of man, set your face against Gog, of the land of Magog, the prince of Rosh,[a] Meshech, and Tubal, and prophesy against him, 3and say, 'Thus says the Lord GOD: "Behold, I *am* against you, O Gog, the prince of Rosh, Meshech, and Tubal. 4I will turn you around, put hooks into your jaws, and lead you out, with all your army, horses, and horsemen, all splendidly clothed, a great company *with* bucklers and shields, all of them handling swords. 5Persia, Ethiopia,[a] and Libya[b] are with them, all of them *with* shield and helmet; 6Gomer and all its troops; the house of Togarmah *from* the far north and all its troops—many people *are* with you.

7"Prepare yourself and be ready, you and all your companies that are gathered about you; and be a guard for them. 8After many days you will be visited. In the latter years you will come into the land of those brought back from the sword *and* gathered from many people on the mountains of Israel, which had long been desolate; they were brought out of the nations, and now all of them dwell safely. 9You will ascend, coming like a storm, covering the land like a cloud, you and all your troops and many peoples with you."

10'Thus says the Lord GOD: "On that day it shall come to pass *that* thoughts will arise in your mind, and you will make an evil plan: 11You will say, 'I will go up against a land of unwalled villages; I will go to a peaceful people, who dwell safely, all of them dwelling without walls, and having neither bars nor gates'— 12to take plunder and to take booty, to stretch out your hand against the waste places *that are again* inhabited, and against a people gathered from

38:2 a Targum, Vulgate, and Aquila read *chief prince of* (also verse 3). 38:5 a Hebrew *Cush* b Hebrew *Put*

the nations, who have acquired live-
stock and goods, who dwell in the midst
of the land. 13Sheba, Dedan, the mer-
chants of Tarshish, and all their young
lions will say to you, 'Have you come to
take plunder? Have you gathered your
army to take booty, to carry away silver
and gold, to take away livestock and
goods, to take great plunder?' " '
14"Therefore, son of man, prophesy
and say to Gog, 'Thus says the Lord GOD:
"On that day when My people Israel
dwell safely, will you not know *it?* 15Then
you will come from your place out of
the far north, you and many peoples
with you, all of them riding on horses,
a great company and a mighty army.
16You will come up against My people
Israel like a cloud, to cover the land.
It will be in the latter days that I will
bring you against My land, so that the
nations may know Me, when I am hal-
lowed in you, O Gog, before their eyes."
17Thus says the Lord GOD: "Are *you* he
of whom I have spoken in former days
by My servants the prophets of Israel,
who prophesied for years in those days
that I would bring you against them?

Judgment on Gog

18"And it will come to pass at the same
time, when Gog comes against the land
of Israel," says the Lord GOD, "*that* My
fury will show in My face. 19For in My
jealousy *and* in the fire of My wrath
I have spoken: 'Surely in that day
there shall be a great earthquake in
the land of Israel, 20so that the fish of
the sea, the birds of the heavens, the
beasts of the field, all creeping things
that creep on the earth, and all men
who *are* on the face of the earth shall
shake at My presence. The mountains
shall be thrown down, the steep places
shall fall, and every wall shall fall to the
ground.' 21I will call for a sword against
Gog throughout all My mountains,"
says the Lord GOD. "Every man's sword
will be against his brother. 22And I will
bring him to judgment with pestilence
and bloodshed; I will rain down on him,
on his troops, and on the many peoples
who *are* with him, flooding rain, great
hailstones, fire, and brimstone. 23Thus
I will magnify Myself and sanctify My-
self, and I will be known in the eyes of
many nations. Then they shall know
that I *am* the LORD." '

Gog's Armies Destroyed

39 "And you, son of man, prophesy
against Gog, and say, 'Thus says
the Lord GOD: "Behold, I *am* against
you, O Gog, the prince of Rosh,[a] Me-
shech, and Tubal; 2and I will turn you
around and lead you on, bringing
you up from the far north, and bring
you against the mountains of Israel.
3Then I will knock the bow out of your
left hand, and cause the arrows to fall
out of your right hand. 4You shall fall
upon the mountains of Israel, you and
all your troops and the peoples who *are*
with you; I will give you to birds of prey
of every sort and *to* the beasts of the
field to be devoured. 5You shall fall on
the open field; for I have spoken," says
the Lord GOD. 6"And I will send fire on
Magog and on those who live in security
in the coastlands. Then they shall know
that I *am* the LORD. 7So I will make My
holy name known in the midst of My
people Israel, and I will not *let them*
profane My holy name anymore. Then
the nations shall know that *I am* the
LORD, the Holy One in Israel. 8Surely
it is coming, and it shall be done," says
the Lord GOD. "This *is* the day of which
I have spoken.
9"Then those who dwell in the cities
of Israel will go out and set on fire and
burn the weapons, both the shields and
bucklers, the bows and arrows, the jav-
elins and spears; and they will make
fires with them for seven years. 10They
will not take wood from the field nor cut
down *any* from the forests, because they
will make fires with the weapons; and
they will plunder those who plundered
them, and pillage those who pillaged
them," says the Lord GOD.

The Burial of Gog

11"It will come to pass in that day *that*
I will give Gog a burial place there in Is-
rael, the valley of those who pass by east

39:1 [a] Targum, Vulgate and Aquila read *chief prince of.*

of the sea; and it will obstruct travelers,
because there they will bury Gog and all
his multitude. Therefore they will call *it*
the Valley of Hamon Gog.[a] 12For seven
months the house of Israel will be bury-
ing them, in order to cleanse the land.
13Indeed all the people of the land will
be burying, and they will gain renown
for it on the day that I am glorified,"
says the Lord GOD. 14"They will set apart
men regularly employed, with the help
of a search party,[a] to pass through the
land and bury those bodies remaining
on the ground, in order to cleanse it. At
the end of seven months they will make
a search. 15The search party will pass
through the land; and *when anyone* sees
a man's bone, he shall set up a marker
by it, till the buriers have buried it in
the Valley of Hamon Gog. 16*The* name
of *the* city *will* also *be* Hamonah. Thus
they shall cleanse the land." '

A Triumphant Festival

17"And as for you, son of man, thus
says the Lord GOD, 'Speak to every sort
of bird and to every beast of the field:

"Assemble yourselves and come;
Gather together from all sides to
My sacrificial meal
Which I am sacrificing for you,
A great sacrificial meal on the
mountains of Israel,
That you may eat flesh and drink
blood.
18 You shall eat the flesh of the
mighty,
Drink the blood of the princes of
the earth,
Of rams and lambs,
Of goats and bulls,
All of them fatlings of Bashan.
19 You shall eat fat till you are full,
And drink blood till you are
drunk,
At My sacrificial meal
Which I am sacrificing for you.
20 You shall be filled at My table
With horses and riders,
With mighty men
And with all the men of war," says
the Lord GOD.

Israel Restored to the Land

21"I will set My glory among the na-
tions; all the nations shall see My judg-
ment which I have executed, and My
hand which I have laid on them. 22So
the house of Israel shall know that I
am the LORD their God from that day
forward. 23The Gentiles shall know that
the house of Israel went into captivity
for their iniquity; because they were
unfaithful to Me, therefore I hid My face
from them. I gave them into the hand
of their enemies, and they all fell by the
sword. 24According to their uncleanness
and according to their transgressions
I have dealt with them, and hidden My
face from them." '

25"Therefore thus says the Lord GOD:
'Now I will bring back the captives of Ja-
cob, and have mercy on the whole house
of Israel; and I will be jealous for My
holy name— 26after they have borne
their shame, and all their unfaithful-
ness in which they were unfaithful to
Me, when they dwelt safely in their *own*
land and no one made *them* afraid.
27When I have brought them back from
the peoples and gathered them out of
their enemies' lands, and I am hallowed
in them in the sight of many nations,
28then they shall know that I *am* the
LORD their God, who sent them into
captivity among the nations, but also
brought them back to their land, and
left none of them captive any longer.
29And I will not hide My face from them
anymore; for I shall have poured out
My Spirit on the house of Israel,' says
the Lord GOD."

A New City, a New Temple

40 In the twenty-fifth year of our
captivity, at the beginning of the
year, on the tenth *day* of the month, in
the fourteenth year after the city was
captured, on the very same day the
hand of the LORD was upon me; and
He took me there. 2In the visions of God
He took me into the land of Israel and
set me on a very high mountain; on it
toward the south *was* something like the
structure of a city. 3He took me there,
and behold, *there was* a man whose

39:11 [a] Literally *The Multitude of Gog* 39:14 [a] Literally *those who pass through*

appearance *was* like the appearance of bronze. He had a line of flax and a measuring rod in his hand, and he stood in the gateway.

4And the man said to me, "Son of man, look with your eyes and hear with your ears, and fix your mind on everything I show you; for you *were* brought here so that I might show *them* to you. Declare to the house of Israel everything you see." 5Now there was a wall all around the outside of the temple.[a] In the man's hand was a measuring rod six cubits *long, each being a* cubit and a handbreadth; and he measured the width of the wall structure, one rod; and the height, one rod.

The Eastern Gateway of the Temple

6Then he went to the gateway which faced east; and he went up its stairs and measured the threshold of the gateway, *which was* one rod wide, and the other threshold *was* one rod wide. 7Each gate chamber *was* one rod long and one rod wide; between the gate chambers *was a space of* five cubits; and the threshold of the gateway by the vestibule of the inside gate *was* one rod. 8He also measured the vestibule of the inside gate, one rod. 9Then he measured the vestibule of the gateway, eight cubits; and the gateposts, two cubits. The vestibule of the gate *was* on the inside. 10In the eastern gateway *were* three gate chambers on one side and three on the other; the three *were* all the same size; also the gateposts were of the same size on this side and that side.

11He measured the width of the entrance to the gateway, ten cubits; *and* the length of the gate, thirteen cubits. 12*There was* a space in front of the gate chambers, one cubit *on this side* and one cubit on that side; the gate chambers *were* six cubits on this side and six cubits on that side. 13Then he measured the gateway from the roof of *one* gate chamber to the roof of the other; the width *was* twenty-five cubits, as door faces door. 14He measured the gateposts, sixty cubits high, and the court all around the gateway *extended* to the gatepost. 15*From* the front of the entrance gate to the front of the vestibule of the inner gate *was* fifty cubits. 16*There were* beveled window *frames* in the gate chambers and in their intervening archways on the inside of the gateway all around, and likewise in the vestibules. *There were* windows all around on the inside. And on each gatepost *were* palm trees.

The Outer Court

17Then he brought me into the outer court; and *there were* chambers and a pavement made all around the court; thirty chambers faced the pavement. 18The pavement was by the side of the gateways, corresponding to the length of the gateways; *this was* the lower pavement. 19Then he measured the width from the front of the lower gateway to the front of the inner court exterior, one hundred cubits toward the east and the north.

The Northern Gateway

20On the outer court was also a gateway facing north, and he measured its length and its width. 21Its gate chambers, three on this side and three on that side, its gateposts and its archways, had the same measurements as the first gate; its length *was* fifty cubits and its width twenty-five cubits. 22Its windows and those of its archways, and also its palm trees, *had* the same measurements as the gateway facing east; it was ascended by seven steps, and its archway *was* in front of it. 23A gate of the inner court was opposite the northern gateway, just as the eastern *gateway;* and he measured from gateway to gateway, one hundred cubits.

The Southern Gateway

24After that he brought me toward the south, and there a gateway was facing south; and he measured its gateposts and archways according to these same measurements. 25*There were* windows in it and in its archways all around like those windows; its length *was* fifty cubits and its width twenty-five cubits.

40:5 [a] Literally *house,* and so elsewhere in this book

26Seven steps led up to it, and its archway *was* in front of them; and it had palm trees on its gateposts, one on this side and one on that side. 27*There was* also a gateway on the inner court, facing south; and he measured from gateway to gateway toward the south, one hundred cubits.

Gateways of the Inner Court

28Then he brought me to the inner court through the southern gateway; he measured the southern gateway according to these same measurements. 29Also its gate chambers, its gateposts, and its archways *were* according to these same measurements; *there were* windows in it and in its archways all around; *it was* fifty cubits long and twenty-five cubits wide. 30*There were* archways all around, twenty-five cubits long and five cubits wide. 31Its archways faced the outer court, palm trees *were* on its gateposts, and going up to it *were* eight steps.

32And he brought me into the inner court facing east; he measured the gateway according to these same measurements. 33Also its gate chambers, its gateposts, and its archways *were* according to these same measurements; and *there were* windows in it and in its archways all around; *it was* fifty cubits long and twenty-five cubits wide. 34Its archways faced the outer court, and palm trees *were* on its gateposts on this side and on that side; and going up to it *were* eight steps.

35Then he brought me to the north gateway and measured *it* according to these same measurements— 36also its gate chambers, its gateposts, and its archways. It had windows all around; its length *was* fifty cubits and its width twenty-five cubits. 37Its gateposts faced the outer court, palm trees *were* on its gateposts on this side and on that side, and going up to it *were* eight steps.

Where Sacrifices Were Prepared

38*There was* a chamber and its entrance by the gateposts of the gateway, where they washed the burnt offering. 39In the vestibule of the gateway *were* two tables on this side and two tables on that side, on which to slay the burnt offering, the sin offering, and the trespass offering. 40At the outer side of the *vestibule,* as one goes up to the entrance of the northern gateway, *were* two tables; and on the other side of the vestibule of the gateway *were* two tables. 41Four tables *were* on this side and four tables on that side, by the side of the gateway, eight tables on which they slaughtered *the sacrifices.* 42*There were* also four tables of hewn stone for the burnt offering, one cubit and a half long, one cubit and a half wide, and one cubit high; on these they laid the instruments with which they slaughtered the burnt offering and the sacrifice. 43Inside *were* hooks, a handbreadth wide, fastened all around; and the flesh of the sacrifices *was* on the tables.

Chambers for Singers and Priests

44Outside the inner gate *were* the chambers for the singers in the inner court, one facing south at the side of the northern gateway, and the other facing north at the side of the southern[a] gateway. 45Then he said to me, "This chamber which faces south *is* for the priests who have charge of the temple. 46The chamber which faces north *is* for the priests who have charge of the altar; these *are* the sons of Zadok, from the sons of Levi, who come near the LORD to minister to Him."

Dimensions of the Inner Court and Vestibule

47And he measured the court, one hundred cubits long and one hundred cubits wide, foursquare. The altar *was* in front of the temple. 48Then he brought me to the vestibule of the temple and measured the doorposts of the vestibule, five cubits on this side and five cubits on that side; and the width of the gateway was three cubits on this side and three cubits on that side. 49The length of the vestibule *was* twenty cubits, and the width eleven cubits; and by the steps which led up to it *there were* pillars by the doorposts, one on this side and another on that side.

40:44 [a] Following Septuagint; Masoretic Text and Vulgate read *eastern.*

Dimensions of the Sanctuary

41 Then he brought me into the
sanctuary[a] and measured the
doorposts, six cubits wide on one side
and six cubits wide on the other side—
the width of the tabernacle. 2The width
of the entryway *was* ten cubits, and
the side walls of the entrance *were*
five cubits on this side and five cubits
on the other side; and he measured
its length, forty cubits, and its width,
twenty cubits.
3Also he went inside and measured
the doorposts, two cubits; and the en-
trance, six cubits *high;* and the width of
the entrance, seven cubits. 4He mea-
sured the length, twenty cubits; and
the width, twenty cubits, beyond the
sanctuary; and he said to me, "This *is*
the Most Holy *Place.*"

The Side Chambers on the Wall

5Next, he measured the wall of the tem-
ple, six cubits. The width of each side
chamber all around the temple *was* four
cubits on every side. 6The side chambers
were in three stories, one above the oth-
er, thirty chambers in each story; they
rested on ledges which *were* for the side
chambers all around, that they might be
supported, but not fastened to the wall
of the temple. 7As one went up from sto-
ry to story, the side chambers became
wider all around, because their sup-
porting ledges in the wall of the temple
ascended like steps; therefore the width
of the structure increased as one went
up *from* the lowest *story* to the highest
by way of the middle one. 8I also saw an
elevation all around the temple; it was
the foundation of the side chambers,
a full rod, *that is,* six cubits *high.* 9The
thickness of the outer wall of the side
chambers *was* five cubits, and so also
the remaining terrace by the place of
the side chambers of the temple. 10And
between *it and* the *wall* chambers was
a width of twenty cubits all around the
temple on every side. 11The doors of the
side chambers opened on the terrace,
one door toward the north and another
toward the south; and the width of the
terrace *was* five cubits all around.

The Building at the Western End

12The building that faced the sepa-
rating courtyard at its western end
was seventy cubits wide; the wall of
the building *was* five cubits thick all
around, and its length ninety cubits.

Dimensions and Design of the Temple Area

13So he measured the temple, one
hundred cubits long; and the separat-
ing courtyard with the building and
its walls *was* one hundred cubits long;
14also the width of the eastern face of
the temple, including the separating
courtyard, *was* one hundred cubits.
15He measured the length of the build-
ing behind it, facing the separating
courtyard, with its galleries on the one
side and on the other side, one hundred
cubits, as well as the inner temple and
the porches of the court, 16their door-
posts and the beveled window frames.
And the galleries all around their three
stories opposite the threshold were pan-
eled with wood from the ground to the
windows—the windows were covered—
17from the space above the door, even
to the inner room,[a] as well as outside,
and on every wall all around, inside
and outside, by measure.
18And *it was* made with cherubim and
palm trees, a palm tree between cherub
and cherub. *Each* cherub had two faces,
19so that the face of a man *was* toward
a palm tree on one side, and the face of
a young lion toward a palm tree on the
other side; thus *it was* made throughout
the temple all around. 20From the floor
to the space above the door, and on the
wall of the sanctuary, cherubim and
palm trees *were* carved.
21The doorposts of the temple *were*
square, *as was* the front of the sanctu-
ary; their appearance was similar. 22The
altar *was* of wood, three cubits high,
and its length two cubits. Its corners, its
length, and its sides *were* of wood; and
he said to me, "This *is* the table that *is*
before the LORD."
23The temple and the sanctuary had
two doors. 24The doors had two panels
apiece, two folding panels: two *panels*

41:1 [a] Hebrew *heykal,* here the main room of the temple, sometimes called the *holy place* (compare Exodus 26:33) **41:17** [a] Literally *house,* here *the Most Holy Place*

for one door and two panels for the
other *door.* 25Cherubim and palm trees
were carved on the doors of the temple
just as they *were* carved on the walls. A
wooden canopy *was* on the front of the
vestibule outside. 26*There were* beveled
window *frames* and palm trees on one
side and on the other, on the sides of the
vestibule—also on the side chambers of
the temple and on the canopies.

The Chambers for the Priests

42 Then he brought me out into
the outer court, by the way to-
ward the north; and he brought me
into the chamber which *was* opposite
the separating courtyard, and which
was opposite the building toward the
north. 2Facing the length, *which was*
one hundred cubits (the width was fifty
cubits), was the north door. 3Opposite
the inner court of twenty *cubits,* and
opposite the pavement of the outer
court, *was* gallery against gallery in
three *stories.* 4In front of the chambers,
toward the inside, *was* a walk ten cubits
wide, at a distance of one cubit; and
their doors faced north. 5Now the upper
chambers *were* shorter, because the gal-
leries took away *space* from them more
than from the lower and middle stories
of the building. 6For they *were* in three
stories and did not have pillars like the
pillars of the courts; therefore *the upper
level* was shortened more than the low-
er and middle levels from the ground
up. 7And a wall which *was* outside ran
parallel to the chambers, at the front of
the chambers, toward the outer court;
its length *was* fifty cubits. 8The length
of the chambers toward the outer court
was fifty cubits, whereas that facing the
temple *was* one hundred cubits. 9At
the lower chambers *was* the entrance
on the east side, as one goes into them
from the outer court.

10Also *there were* chambers in the
thickness of the wall of the court toward
the east, opposite the separating court-
yard and opposite the building. 11*There
was* a walk in front of them also, and
their appearance *was* like the chambers
which *were* toward the north; they *were*
as long and as wide as the others, and
all their exits and entrances *were* ac-
cording to plan. 12And corresponding
to the doors of the chambers that *were*
facing south, as one enters them, *there
was* a door in front of the walk, the way
directly in front of the wall toward the
east.

13Then he said to me, "The north cham-
bers *and* the south chambers, which *are*
opposite the separating courtyard, *are*
the holy chambers where the priests
who approach the LORD shall eat the
most holy offerings. There they shall lay
the most holy offerings—the grain of-
fering, the sin offering, and the trespass
offering—for the place *is* holy. 14When
the priests enter them, they shall not go
out of the holy *chamber* into the outer
court; but there they shall leave their
garments in which they minister, for
they *are* holy. They shall put on other
garments; then they may approach
that which *is* for the people."

Outer Dimensions of the Temple

15Now when he had finished measur-
ing the inner temple, he brought me
out through the gateway that faces
toward the east, and measured it all
around. 16He measured the east side
with the measuring rod,[a] five hundred
rods by the measuring rod all around.
17He measured the north side, five
hundred rods by the measuring rod all
around. 18He measured the south side,
five hundred rods by the measuring
rod. 19He came around to the west side
and measured five hundred rods by the
measuring rod. 20He measured it on the
four sides; it had a wall all around, five
hundred *cubits* long and five hundred
wide, to separate the holy areas from
the common.

The Temple, the LORD's Dwelling Place

43 Afterward he brought me to the
gate, the gate that faces toward
the east. 2And behold, the glory of the
God of Israel came from the way of the
east. His voice *was* like the sound of
many waters; and the earth shone with
His glory. 3*It was* like the appearance of

42:16 a Compare 40:5

the vision which I saw—like the vision
which I saw when I[a] came to destroy
the city. The visions *were* like the vision
which I saw by the River Chebar; and
I fell on my face. 4And the glory of the
LORD came into the temple by way of
the gate which faces toward the east.
5The Spirit lifted me up and brought
me into the inner court; and behold,
the glory of the LORD filled the temple.
6Then I heard *Him* speaking to me
from the temple, while a man stood
beside me. 7And He said to me, "Son
of man, *this is* the place of My throne
and the place of the soles of My feet,
where I will dwell in the midst of the
children of Israel forever. No more shall
the house of Israel defile My holy name,
they nor their kings, by their harlotry
or with the carcasses of their kings on
their high places. 8When they set their
threshold by My threshold, and their
doorpost by My doorpost, with a wall
between them and Me, they defiled My
holy name by the abominations which
they committed; therefore I have con-
sumed them in My anger. 9Now let them
put their harlotry and the carcasses of
their kings far away from Me, and I will
dwell in their midst forever.
10"Son of man, describe the temple
to the house of Israel, that they may
be ashamed of their iniquities; and let
them measure the pattern. 11And if they
are ashamed of all that they have done,
make known to them the design of the
temple and its arrangement, its exits
and its entrances, its entire design and
all its ordinances, all its forms and all
its laws. Write *it* down in their sight, so
that they may keep its whole design and
all its ordinances, and perform them.
12This *is* the law of the temple: The whole
area surrounding the mountaintop *is*
most holy. Behold, this *is* the law of
the temple.

Dimensions of the Altar

13"These are the measurements of the
altar in cubits (the cubit *is* one cubit
and a handbreadth): the base one cubit
high and one cubit wide, with a rim
all around its edge of one span. This *is*
the height of the altar: 14from the base
on the ground to the lower ledge, two
cubits; the width of the ledge, one cubit;
from the smaller ledge to the larger
ledge, four cubits; and the width of the
ledge, *one* cubit. 15The altar hearth *is*
four cubits high, with four horns ex-
tending upward from the hearth. 16The
altar hearth *is* twelve *cubits* long, twelve
wide, square at its four corners; 17the
ledge, fourteen *cubits* long and fourteen
wide on its four sides, with a rim of half
a cubit around it; its base, one cubit
all around; and its steps face toward
the east."

Consecrating the Altar

18And He said to me, "Son of man, thus
says the Lord GOD: 'These *are* the ordi-
nances for the altar on the day when it
is made, for sacrificing burnt offerings
on it, and for sprinkling blood on it.
19You shall give a young bull for a sin
offering to the priests, the Levites, who
are of the seed of Zadok, who approach
Me to minister to Me,' says the Lord GOD.
20'You shall take some of its blood and
put *it* on the four horns of the altar, on
the four corners of the ledge, and on the
rim around it; thus you shall cleanse it
and make atonement for it. 21Then you
shall also take the bull of the sin offer-
ing, and burn it in the appointed place
of the temple, outside the sanctuary.
22On the second day you shall offer a
kid of the goats without blemish for a
sin offering; and they shall cleanse the
altar, as they cleansed *it* with the bull.
23When you have finished cleansing
it, you shall offer a young bull without
blemish, and a ram from the flock with-
out blemish. 24When you offer them
before the LORD, the priests shall throw
salt on them, and they will offer them up
as a burnt offering to the LORD. 25Every
day for seven days you shall prepare a
goat *for* a sin offering; they shall also
prepare a young bull and a ram from
the flock, both without blemish. 26Seven
days they shall make atonement for the
altar and purify it, and so consecrate
it. 27When these days are over it shall
be, on the eighth day and thereafter,

43:3 [a] Some Hebrew manuscripts and Vulgate read *He.*

that the priests shall offer your burnt
offerings and your peace offerings on
the altar; and I will accept you,' says
the Lord GOD."

The East Gate and the Prince

44 Then He brought me back to
the outer gate of the sanctuary
which faces toward the east, but it *was*
shut. 2And the LORD said to me, "This
gate shall be shut; it shall not be opened,
and no man shall enter by it, because
the LORD God of Israel has entered by
it; therefore it shall be shut. 3*As for* the
prince, *because* he *is* the prince, he may
sit in it to eat bread before the LORD; he
shall enter by way of the vestibule of
the gateway, and go out the same way."

Those Admitted to the Temple

4Also He brought me by way of the
north gate to the front of the temple;
so I looked, and behold, the glory of
the LORD filled the house of the LORD;
and I fell on my face. 5And the LORD
said to me, "Son of man, mark well,
see with your eyes and hear with your
ears, all that I say to you concerning
all the ordinances of the house of the
LORD and all its laws. Mark well who
may enter the house and all who go
out from the sanctuary.

6"Now say to the rebellious, to the
house of Israel, 'Thus says the Lord GOD:
"O house of Israel, let Us have no more
of all your abominations. 7When you
brought in foreigners, uncircumcised
in heart and uncircumcised in flesh,
to be in My sanctuary to defile it—
My house—and when you offered My
food, the fat and the blood, then they
broke My covenant because of all your
abominations. 8And you have not kept
charge of My holy things, but you have
set *others* to keep charge of My sanctu-
ary for you." 9Thus says the Lord GOD:
"No foreigner, uncircumcised in heart
or uncircumcised in flesh, shall enter
My sanctuary, including any foreigner
who *is* among the children of Israel.

Laws Governing Priests

10"And the Levites who went far from
Me, when Israel went astray, who
strayed away from Me after their idols,
they shall bear their iniquity. 11Yet they
shall be ministers in My sanctuary, *as*
gatekeepers of the house and ministers
of the house; they shall slay the burnt
offering and the sacrifice for the peo-
ple, and they shall stand before them
to minister to them. 12Because they
ministered to them before their idols
and caused the house of Israel to fall
into iniquity, therefore I have raised
My hand in an oath against them," says
the Lord GOD, "that they shall bear their
iniquity. 13And they shall not come near
Me to minister to Me as priest, nor come
near any of My holy things, nor into the
Most Holy *Place;* but they shall bear
their shame and their abominations
which they have committed. 14Never-
theless I will make them keep charge
of the temple, for all its work, and for
all that has to be done in it.

15"But the priests, the Levites, the
sons of Zadok, who kept charge of My
sanctuary when the children of Israel
went astray from Me, they shall come
near Me to minister to Me; and they
shall stand before Me to offer to Me the
fat and the blood," says the Lord GOD.
16"They shall enter My sanctuary, and
they shall come near My table to minis-
ter to Me, and they shall keep My charge.
17And it shall be, whenever they enter
the gates of the inner court, that they
shall put on linen garments; no wool
shall come upon them while they min-
ister within the gates of the inner court
or within the house. 18They shall have
linen turbans on their heads and linen
trousers on their bodies; they shall not
clothe themselves with *anything that
causes* sweat. 19When they go out to the
outer court, to the outer court to the peo-
ple, they shall take off their garments in
which they have ministered, leave them
in the holy chambers, and put on other
garments; and in their holy garments
they shall not sanctify the people.

20"They shall neither shave their heads
nor let their hair grow long, but they
shall keep their hair well trimmed. 21No
priest shall drink wine when he enters
the inner court. 22They shall not take
as wife a widow or a divorced woman,
but take virgins of the descendants of
the house of Israel, or widows of priests.

23“And they shall teach My people
the difference between the holy and the
unholy, and cause them to discern be-
tween the unclean and the clean. 24In
controversy they shall stand as judges,
and judge it according to My judgments.
They shall keep My laws and My stat-
utes in all My appointed meetings, and
they shall hallow My Sabbaths.
25“They shall not defile *themselves* by
coming near a dead person. Only for
father or mother, for son or daughter,
for brother or unmarried sister may
they defile themselves. 26After he is
cleansed, they shall count seven days
for him. 27And on the day that he goes
to the sanctuary to minister in the sanc-
tuary, he must offer his sin offering in
the inner court,” says the Lord GOD.
28“It shall be, in regard to their inher-
itance, *that* I *am* their inheritance. You
shall give them no possession in Israel,
for I *am* their possession. 29They shall
eat the grain offering, the sin offering,
and the trespass offering; every ded-
icated thing in Israel shall be theirs.
30The best of all firstfruits of any kind,
and every sacrifice of any kind from all
your sacrifices, shall be the priest’s; also
you shall give to the priest the first of
your ground meal, to cause a blessing
to rest on your house. 31The priests shall
not eat anything, bird or beast, that died
naturally or was torn *by wild beasts.*

The Holy District

45 “Moreover, when you divide the
land by lot into inheritance, you
shall set apart a district for the LORD,
a holy section of the land; its length
shall be twenty-five thousand *cubits,* and
the width ten thousand. It *shall be* holy
throughout its territory all around. 2Of
this there shall be a square plot for the
sanctuary, five hundred by five hundred
rods, with fifty cubits around it for an
open space. 3So this is the district you
shall measure: twenty-five thousand
cubits long and ten thousand wide;
in it shall be the sanctuary, the Most
Holy *Place.* 4It shall be a holy *section*
of the land, belonging to the priests,
the ministers of the sanctuary, who
come near to minister to the LORD; it
shall be a place for their houses and a
holy place for the sanctuary. 5*An area*
twenty-five thousand *cubits* long and
ten thousand wide shall belong to the
Levites, the ministers of the temple;
they shall have twenty chambers as a
possession.[a]

Properties of the City and the Prince

6“You shall appoint as the property
of the city *an area* five thousand *cubits*
wide and twenty-five thousand long,
adjacent to the district of the holy *sec-
tion;* it shall belong to the whole house
of Israel.
7“The prince shall have *a section* on one
side and the other of the holy district
and the city’s property; and bordering
on the holy district and the city’s prop-
erty, extending westward on the west
side and eastward on the east side, the
length *shall be* side by side with one of
the *tribal* portions, from the west border
to the east border. 8The land shall be his
possession in Israel; and My princes
shall no more oppress My people, but
they shall give *the rest of* the land to
the house of Israel, according to their
tribes.”

Laws Governing the Prince

9‘Thus says the Lord GOD: “Enough,
O princes of Israel! Remove violence
and plundering, execute justice and
righteousness, and stop dispossessing
My people,” says the Lord GOD. 10“You
shall have honest scales, an honest
ephah, and an honest bath. 11The ephah
and the bath shall be of the same mea-
sure, so that the bath contains one-tenth
of a homer, and the ephah one-tenth
of a homer; their measure shall be
according to the homer. 12The shekel
shall be twenty gerahs; twenty shek-
els, twenty-five shekels, *and* fifteen
shekels shall be your mina.
13“This *is* the offering which you shall
offer: you shall give one-sixth of an
ephah from a homer of wheat, and
one-sixth of an ephah from a homer
of barley. 14The ordinance concerning
oil, the bath of oil, *is* one-tenth of a bath

45:5 [a] Following Masoretic Text, Targum, and Vulgate; Septuagint reads *a possession, cities of dwelling.*

from a kor. *A kor is* a homer or ten baths, for ten baths *are* a homer. 15And one lamb shall be given from a flock of two hundred, from the rich pastures of Israel. These shall be for grain offerings, burnt offerings, and peace offerings, to make atonement for them," says the Lord GOD. 16"All the people of the land shall give this offering for the prince in Israel. 17Then it shall be the prince's part *to give* burnt offerings, grain offerings, and drink offerings, at the feasts, the New Moons, the Sabbaths, and at all the appointed seasons of the house of Israel. He shall prepare the sin offering, the grain offering, the burnt offering, and the peace offerings to make atonement for the house of Israel."

Keeping the Feasts

18"Thus says the Lord GOD: "In the first *month,* on the first *day* of the month, you shall take a young bull without blemish and cleanse the sanctuary. 19The priest shall take some of the blood of the sin offering and put *it* on the doorposts of the temple, on the four corners of the ledge of the altar, and on the gateposts of the gate of the inner court. 20And so you shall do on the seventh *day* of the month for everyone who has sinned unintentionally or in ignorance. Thus you shall make atonement for the temple.

21"In the first *month,* on the fourteenth day of the month, you shall observe the Passover, a feast of seven days; unleavened bread shall be eaten. 22And on that day the prince shall prepare for himself and for all the people of the land a bull *for* a sin offering. 23On the seven days of the feast he shall prepare a burnt offering to the LORD, seven bulls and seven rams without blemish, daily for seven days, and a kid of the goats daily *for* a sin offering. 24And he shall prepare a grain offering of one ephah for each bull and one ephah for each ram, together with a hin of oil for each ephah.

25"In the seventh *month,* on the fifteenth day of the month, at the feast, he shall do likewise for seven days, according to the sin offering, the burnt offering, the grain offering, and the oil."

The Manner of Worship

46 "Thus says the Lord GOD: "The gateway of the inner court that faces toward the east shall be shut the six working days; but on the Sabbath it shall be opened, and on the day of the New Moon it shall be opened. 2The prince shall enter by way of the vestibule of the gateway from the outside, and stand by the gatepost. The priests shall prepare his burnt offering and his peace offerings. He shall worship at the threshold of the gate. Then he shall go out, but the gate shall not be shut until evening. 3Likewise the people of the land shall worship at the entrance to this gateway before the LORD on the Sabbaths and the New Moons. 4The burnt offering that the prince offers to the LORD on the Sabbath day *shall be* six lambs without blemish, and a ram without blemish; 5and the grain offering *shall be one* ephah for a ram, and the grain offering for the lambs, as much as he wants to give, as well as a hin of oil with every ephah. 6On the day of the New Moon *it shall be* a young bull without blemish, six lambs, and a ram; they shall be without blemish. 7He shall prepare a grain offering of an ephah for a bull, an ephah for a ram, as much as he wants to give for the lambs, and a hin of oil with every ephah. 8When the prince enters, he shall go in by way of the vestibule of the gateway, and go out the same way.

9"But when the people of the land come before the LORD on the appointed feast days, whoever enters by way of the north gate to worship shall go out by way of the south gate; and whoever enters by way of the south gate shall go out by way of the north gate. He shall not return by way of the gate through which he came, but shall go out through the opposite gate. 10The prince shall then be in their midst. When they go in, he shall go in; and when they go out, he shall go out. 11At the festivals and the appointed feast days the grain offering shall be an ephah for a bull, an ephah for a ram, as much as he wants to give for the lambs, and a hin of oil with every ephah.

12"Now when the prince makes a

voluntary burnt offering or voluntary
peace offering to the LORD, the gate
that faces toward the east shall then
be opened for him; and he shall pre-
pare his burnt offering and his peace
offerings as he did on the Sabbath day.
Then he shall go out, and after he goes
out the gate shall be shut.
13“You shall daily make a burnt of-
fering to the LORD *of* a lamb of the first
year without blemish; you shall pre-
pare it every morning. 14And you shall
prepare a grain offering with it every
morning, a sixth of an ephah, and a
third of a hin of oil to moisten the fine
flour. This grain offering is a perpetual
ordinance, to be made regularly to the
LORD. 15Thus they shall prepare the
lamb, the grain offering, and the oil, *as* a
regular burnt offering every morning.”

The Prince and Inheritance Laws

16‘Thus says the Lord GOD: “If the
prince gives a gift *of some* of his inher-
itance to any of his sons, it shall belong
to his sons; it is their possession by in-
heritance. 17But if he gives a gift of some
of his inheritance to one of his servants,
it shall be his until the year of liberty,
after which it shall return to the prince.
But his inheritance shall belong to his
sons; it shall become theirs. 18More-
over the prince shall not take any of the
people’s inheritance by evicting them
from their property; he shall provide an
inheritance for his sons from his own
property, so that none of My people
may be scattered from his property.” ’ ”

How the Offerings Were Prepared

19Now he brought me through the
entrance, which *was* at the side of
the gate, into the holy chambers of
the priests which face toward the north;
and there a place *was* situated at their
extreme western end. 20And he said to
me, “This *is* the place where the priests
shall boil the trespass offering and the
sin offering, *and* where they shall bake
the grain offering, so that they do not
bring *them* out into the outer court to
sanctify the people.”
21Then he brought me out into the out-
er court and caused me to pass by the
four corners of the court; and in fact, in
every corner of the court *there was an-
other* court. 22In the four corners of the
court *were* enclosed courts, forty *cubits*
long and thirty wide; all four corners
were the same size. 23*There was* a row
of building stones all around in them,
all around the four of them; and cook-
ing hearths were made under the rows
of stones all around. 24And he said to
me, “These *are* the kitchens where the
ministers of the temple shall boil the
sacrifices of the people.”

The Healing Waters and Trees

47 Then he brought me back to
the door of the temple; and
there was water, flowing from under
the threshold of the temple toward the
east, for the front of the temple faced
east; the water was flowing from under
the right side of the temple, south of the
altar. 2He brought me out by way of
the north gate, and led me around on
the outside to the outer gateway that
faces east; and there was water, running
out on the right side.
3And when the man went out to the
east with the line in his hand, he mea-
sured one thousand cubits, and he
brought me through the waters; the
water *came up to my* ankles. 4Again he
measured one thousand and brought
me through the waters; the water *came
up to my* knees. Again he measured one
thousand and brought me through; the
water *came up to my* waist. 5Again he
measured one thousand, *and it was* a
river that I could not cross; for the water
was too deep, water in which one must
swim, a river that could not be crossed.
6He said to me, “Son of man, have you
seen *this*?” Then he brought me and
returned me to the bank of the river.
7When I returned, there, along the bank
of the river, *were* very many trees on
one side and the other. 8Then he said to
me: “This water flows toward the east-
ern region, goes down into the valley,
and enters the sea. *When it* reaches the
sea, *its* waters are healed. 9And it shall
be *that* every living thing that moves,
wherever the rivers go, will live. There
will be a very great multitude of fish,
because these waters go there; for they
will be healed, and everything will live

wherever the river goes. 10 It shall be
that fishermen will stand by it from En
Gedi to En Eglaim; they will be *places*
for spreading their nets. Their fish will
be of the same kinds as the fish of the
Great Sea, exceedingly many. 11 But its
swamps and marshes will not be healed;
they will be given over to salt. 12 Along
the bank of the river, on this side and
that, will grow all *kinds of* trees used for
food; their leaves will not wither, and
their fruit will not fail. They will bear fruit
every month, because their water flows
from the sanctuary. Their fruit will be
for food, and their leaves for medicine."

Borders of the Land

13 Thus says the Lord GOD: "These *are*
the borders by which you shall divide
the land as an inheritance among the
twelve tribes of Israel. Joseph *shall
have two* portions. 14 You shall inherit
it equally with one another; for I raised
My hand in an oath to give it to your
fathers, and this land shall fall to you
as your inheritance.
15 "This *shall be* the border of the land
on the north: from the Great Sea, *by* the
road to Hethlon, as one goes to Zedad,
16 Hamath, Berothah, Sibraim (which *is*
between the border of Damascus and
the border of Hamath), to Hazar Hatti-
con (which *is* on the border of Hauran).
17 Thus the boundary shall be from the
Sea to Hazar Enan, the border of Da-
mascus; and as for the north, north-
ward, it is the border of Hamath. *This
is* the north side.
18 "On the east side you shall mark out
the border from between Hauran and
Damascus, and between Gilead and the
land of Israel, along the Jordan, and
along the eastern side of the sea. *This
is* the east side.
19 "The south side, toward the South,[a]
shall be from Tamar to the waters of
Meribah by Kadesh, along the brook
to the Great Sea. *This is* the south side,
toward the South.
20 "The west side *shall be* the Great Sea,
from the *southern* boundary until one
comes to a point opposite Hamath. This
is the west side.
21 "Thus you shall divide this land
among yourselves according to the
tribes of Israel. 22 It shall be that you
will divide it by lot as an inheritance
for yourselves, and for the strangers
who dwell among you and who bear
children among you. They shall be to
you as native-born among the children
of Israel; they shall have an inheritance
with you among the tribes of Israel.
23 And it shall be *that* in whatever tribe
the stranger dwells, there you shall give
him his inheritance," says the Lord GOD.

Division of the Land

48 "Now these *are* the names of
the tribes: From the northern
border along the road to Hethlon at the
entrance of Hamath, to Hazar Enan,
the border of Damascus northward, in
the direction of Hamath, *there shall be*
one *section for* Dan from its east to its
west side; 2 by the border of Dan, from
the east side to the west, one *section for*
Asher; 3 by the border of Asher, from
the east side to the west, one *section
for* Naphtali; 4 by the border of Naph-
tali, from the east side to the west, one
section for Manasseh; 5 by the border
of Manasseh, from the east side to the
west, one *section for* Ephraim; 6 by the
border of Ephraim, from the east side
to the west, one *section for* Reuben; 7 by
the border of Reuben, from the east
side to the west, one *section for* Judah;
8 by the border of Judah, from the east
side to the west, shall be the district
which you shall set apart, twenty-five
thousand *cubits* in width, and *in* length
the same as one of the *other* portions,
from the east side to the west, with the
sanctuary in the center.
9 "The district that you shall set apart
for the LORD *shall be* twenty-five thou-
sand *cubits* in length and ten thousand
in width. 10 To these—to the priests—the
holy district shall belong: on the north
twenty-five thousand *cubits in length,* on
the west ten thousand in width, on the
east ten thousand in width, and on the
south twenty-five thousand in length.
The sanctuary of the LORD shall be in
the center. 11 *It shall be* for the priests of

47:19 [a] Hebrew *Negev*

the sons of Zadok, who are sanctified,
who have kept My charge, who did not
go astray when the children of Israel
went astray, as the Levites went astray.
12And *this* district of land that is set
apart shall be to them a thing most holy
by the border of the Levites.

13"Opposite the border of the priests,
the Levites *shall have an area* twenty-
five thousand *cubits* in length and ten
thousand in width; its entire length *shall*
be twenty-five thousand and its width
ten thousand. 14And they shall not sell
or exchange any of it; they may not
alienate this best *part* of the land, for
it is holy to the LORD.

15"The five thousand *cubits* in width
that remain, along the edge of the
twenty-five thousand, shall be for gen-
eral use by the city, for dwellings and
common-land; and the city shall be in
the center. 16These *shall be* its measure-
ments: the north side four thousand five
hundred *cubits,* the south side four thou-
sand five hundred, the east side four
thousand five hundred, and the west
side four thousand five hundred. 17The
common-land of the city shall be: to the
north two hundred and fifty *cubits,* to
the south two hundred and fifty, to the
east two hundred and fifty, and to the
west two hundred and fifty. 18The rest of
the length, alongside the district of the
holy *section, shall be* ten thousand *cubits*
to the east and ten thousand to the west.
It shall be adjacent to the district of the
holy *section,* and its produce shall be
food for the workers of the city. 19The
workers of the city, from all the tribes
of Israel, shall cultivate it. 20The entire
district *shall be* twenty-five thousand
cubits by twenty-five thousand *cubits,*
foursquare. You shall set apart the holy
district with the property of the city.

21"The rest *shall belong* to the prince,
on one side and on the other of the holy
district and of the city's property, next
to the twenty-five thousand *cubits* of the
holy district as far as the eastern border,
and westward next to the twenty-five
thousand as far as the western border,
adjacent to the *tribal* portions; *it shall*
belong to the prince. It shall be the holy
district, and the sanctuary of the tem-
ple *shall be* in the center. 22Moreover,
apart from the possession of the Levites
and the possession of the city *which are*
in the midst of what *belongs* to the
prince, *the area* between the border of
Judah and the border of Benjamin shall
belong to the prince.

23"As for the rest of the tribes, from
the east side to the west, Benjamin *shall*
have one *section;* 24by the border of Ben-
jamin, from the east side to the west,
Simeon *shall have* one *section;* 25by the
border of Simeon, from the east side to
the west, Issachar *shall have* one *section;*
26by the border of Issachar, from the
east side to the west, Zebulun *shall have*
one *section;* 27by the border of Zebulun,
from the east side to the west, Gad *shall*
have one *section;* 28by the border of Gad,
on the south side, toward the South,[a]
the border shall be from Tamar *to* the
waters of Meribah *by* Kadesh, along
the brook to the Great Sea. 29This *is* the
land which you shall divide by lot as an
inheritance among the tribes of Israel,
and these *are* their portions," says the
Lord GOD.

The Gates of the City and Its Name

30"These *are* the exits of the city. On the
north side, measuring four thousand
five hundred *cubits* 31(the gates of the
city *shall be* named after the tribes of
Israel), the three gates northward: one
gate for Reuben, one gate for Judah,
and one gate for Levi; 32on the east side,
four thousand five hundred *cubits,* three
gates: one gate for Joseph, one gate for
Benjamin, and one gate for Dan; 33on
the south side, measuring four thou-
sand five hundred *cubits,* three gates:
one gate for Simeon, one gate for Issa-
char, and one gate for Zebulun; 34on the
west side, four thousand five hundred
cubits with their three gates: one gate
for Gad, one gate for Asher, and one
gate for Naphtali. 35All the way around
shall be eighteen thousand *cubits;* and
the name of the city from *that* day *shall*
be: THE LORD *IS* THERE."[a]

48:28 [a] Hebrew *Negev* **48:35** [a] Hebrew *YHWH Shammah*

THE BOOK OF
DANIEL

The Book of Daniel includes the experiences of Daniel and his friends while they live as captives in Babylon and Persia. Daniel was taken to Babylon as a sixteen-year-old and was chosen for government service. Nine of the twelve chapters of the book include dreams and visions, some of which show what would happen in the future. Through his prophecies and his example of depending on God even in challenging situations, Daniel helps us see how to trust in God no matter what.

- **GENRE:** Major Prophet
- **AUTHOR:** Daniel
- **TIME:** c. 605–536 BC
- **PURPOSE:** To encourage God's people to trust in Him. God controls rulers, nations, and history.

Daniel and His Friends Obey God

1 In the third year of the reign of
Jehoiakim king of Judah, Nebu-
chadnezzar king of Babylon came to
Jerusalem and besieged it. 2And the
Lord gave Jehoiakim king of Judah
into his hand, with some of the articles
of the house of God, which he carried
into the land of Shinar to the house of
his god; and he brought the articles into
the treasure house of his god.
3Then the king instructed Ashpenaz,
the master of his eunuchs, to bring
some of the children of Israel and some
of the king's descendants and some
of the nobles, 4young men in whom
there was no blemish, but good-looking,
gifted in all wisdom, possessing knowl-
edge and quick to understand, who *had*
ability to serve in the king's palace, and
whom they might teach the language
and literature of the Chaldeans. 5And
the king appointed for them a daily
provision of the king's delicacies and
of the wine which he drank, and three
years of training for them, so that at the
end of *that time* they might serve before
the king. 6Now from among those of
the sons of Judah were Daniel, Hana-
niah, Mishael, and Azariah. 7To them
the chief of the eunuchs gave names:
he gave Daniel *the name* Belteshazzar;
to Hananiah, Shadrach; to Mishael,
Meshach; and to Azariah, Abed-Nego.
8But Daniel purposed in his heart that
he would not defile himself with the
portion of the king's delicacies, nor with
the wine which he drank; therefore he
requested of the chief of the eunuchs
that he might not defile himself. 9Now
God had brought Daniel into the favor
and goodwill of the chief of the eunuchs.
10And the chief of the eunuchs said to
Daniel, "I fear my lord the king, who
has appointed your food and drink. For
why should he see your faces looking
worse than the young men who *are*
your age? Then you would endanger
my head before the king."
11So Daniel said to the steward[a] whom
the chief of the eunuchs had set over
Daniel, Hananiah, Mishael, and Azari-
ah, 12"Please test your servants for ten
days, and let them give us vegetables
to eat and water to drink. 13Then let
our appearance be examined before
you, and the appearance of the young
men who eat the portion of the king's
delicacies; and as you see fit, *so* deal
with your servants." 14So he consented
with them in this matter, and tested
them ten days.
15And at the end of ten days their fea-
tures appeared better and fatter in flesh

1:11 [a] Hebrew *Melzar,* also in verse 16

than all the young men who ate the portion of the king's delicacies. 16Thus the steward took away their portion of delicacies and the wine that they were to drink, and gave them vegetables.

17As for these four young men, God gave them knowledge and skill in all literature and wisdom; and Daniel had understanding in all visions and dreams.

18Now at the end of the days, when the king had said that they should be brought in, the chief of the eunuchs brought them in before Nebuchadnezzar. 19Then the king interviewed[a] them, and among them all none was found like Daniel, Hananiah, Mishael, and Azariah; therefore they served before the king. 20And in all matters of wisdom *and* understanding about which the king examined them, he found them ten times better than all the magicians *and* astrologers who *were* in all his realm. 21Thus Daniel continued until the first year of King Cyrus.

Nebuchadnezzar's Dream

2 Now in the second year of Nebuchadnezzar's reign, Nebuchadnezzar had dreams; and his spirit was *so* troubled that his sleep left him. 2Then the king gave the command to call the magicians, the astrologers, the sorcerers, and the Chaldeans to tell the king his dreams. So they came and stood before the king. 3And the king said to them, "I have had a dream, and my spirit is anxious to know the dream."

4Then the Chaldeans spoke to the king in Aramaic,[a] "O king, live forever! Tell your servants the dream, and we will give the interpretation."

5The king answered and said to the Chaldeans, "My decision is firm: if you do not make known the dream to me, and its interpretation, you shall be cut in pieces, and your houses shall be made an ash heap. 6However, if you tell the dream and its interpretation, you shall receive from me gifts, rewards, and great honor. Therefore tell me the dream and its interpretation."

7They answered again and said, "Let the king tell his servants the dream, and we will give its interpretation."

8The king answered and said, "I know for certain that you would gain time, because you see that my decision is firm: 9if you do not make known the dream to me, *there is only* one decree for you! For you have agreed to speak lying and corrupt words before me till the time has changed. Therefore tell me the dream, and I shall know that you can give me its interpretation."

10The Chaldeans answered the king, and said, "There is not a man on earth who can tell the king's matter; therefore no king, lord, or ruler has *ever* asked such things of any magician, astrologer, or Chaldean. 11*It is* a difficult thing that the king requests, and there is no other who can tell it to the king except the gods, whose dwelling is not with flesh."

12For this reason the king was angry and very furious, and gave the command to destroy all the wise *men* of Babylon. 13So the decree went out, and they began killing the wise *men;* and they sought Daniel and his companions, to kill *them.*

God Reveals Nebuchadnezzar's Dream

14Then with counsel and wisdom Daniel answered Arioch, the captain of the king's guard, who had gone out to kill the wise *men* of Babylon; 15he answered and said to Arioch the king's captain, "Why is the decree from the king so urgent?" Then Arioch made the decision known to Daniel.

16So Daniel went in and asked the king to give him time, that he might tell the king the interpretation. 17Then Daniel went to his house, and made the decision known to Hananiah, Mishael, and Azariah, his companions, 18that they might seek mercies from the God of heaven concerning this secret, so that Daniel and his companions might not perish with the rest of the wise *men* of Babylon. 19Then the secret was revealed to Daniel in a night vision. So Daniel blessed the God of heaven.

1:19 [a] Literally *talked with them* **2:4** [a] The original language of Daniel 2:4b through 7:28 is Aramaic.

20 Daniel answered and said:

"Blessed be the name of God forever
and ever,
For wisdom and might are His.
21 And He changes the times and
the seasons;
He removes kings and raises up
kings;
He gives wisdom to the wise
And knowledge to those who have
understanding.
22 He reveals deep and secret things;
He knows what *is* in the darkness,
And light dwells with Him.

23 "I thank You and praise You,
O God of my fathers;
You have given me wisdom and
might,
And have now made known to me
what we asked of You,
For You have made known to us
the king's demand."

Daniel Explains the Dream

24 Therefore Daniel went to Arioch,
whom the king had appointed to de-
stroy the wise *men* of Babylon. He went
and said thus to him: "Do not destroy
the wise *men* of Babylon; take me be-
fore the king, and I will tell the king the
interpretation."
25 Then Arioch quickly brought Daniel
before the king, and said thus to him,
"I have found a man of the captives[a]
of Judah, who will make known to the
king the interpretation."
26 The king answered and said to
Daniel, whose name *was* Belteshaz-
zar, "Are you able to make known to
me the dream which I have seen, and
its interpretation?"
27 Daniel answered in the presence of
the king, and said, "The secret which the
king has demanded, the wise *men,*
the astrologers, the magicians, and
the soothsayers cannot declare to the
king. 28 But there is a God in heaven
who reveals secrets, and He has made
known to King Nebuchadnezzar what
will be in the latter days. Your dream,
and the visions of your head upon your
bed, were these: 29 As for you, O king,
thoughts came *to* your *mind while* on
your bed, *about* what would come to
pass after this; and He who reveals se-
crets has made known to you what will
be. 30 But as for me, this secret has not
been revealed to me because I have
more wisdom than anyone living, but
for *our* sakes who make known the in-
terpretation to the king, and that you
may know the thoughts of your heart.
31 "You, O king, were watching; and
behold, a great image! This great image,
whose splendor *was* excellent, stood
before you; and its form *was* awesome.
32 This image's head *was* of fine gold, its
chest and arms of silver, its belly and
thighs[a] of bronze, 33 its legs of iron, its
feet partly of iron and partly of clay.[a]
34 You watched while a stone was cut out
without hands, which struck the image
on its feet of iron and clay, and broke
them in pieces. 35 Then the iron, the clay,
the bronze, the silver, and the gold were
crushed together, and became like chaff
from the summer threshing floors; the
wind carried them away so that no trace
of them was found. And the stone that
struck the image became a great moun-
tain and filled the whole earth.
36 "This *is* the dream. Now we will tell
the interpretation of it before the king.
37 You, O king, *are* a king of kings. For
the God of heaven has given you a king-
dom, power, strength, and glory; 38 and
wherever the children of men dwell,
or the beasts of the field and the birds
of the heaven, He has given *them* into
your hand, and has made you ruler
over them all—you *are* this head of
gold. 39 But after you shall arise an-
other kingdom inferior to yours; then
another, a third kingdom of bronze,
which shall rule over all the earth.
40 And the fourth kingdom shall be as
strong as iron, inasmuch as iron breaks
in pieces and shatters everything; and
like iron that crushes, *that kingdom* will
break in pieces and crush all the oth-
ers. 41 Whereas you saw the feet and
toes, partly of potter's clay and partly
of iron, the kingdom shall be divided;
yet the strength of the iron shall be in

2:25 [a] Literally *of the sons of the captivity* **2:32** [a] Or *sides* **2:33** [a] Or *baked clay,* and so in verses 34, 35, and 42

GOD SIN JESUS SALVATION LOVE

it, just as you saw the iron mixed with ceramic clay. 42And *as* the toes of the feet *were* partly of iron and partly of clay, *so* the kingdom shall be partly strong and partly fragile. 43As you saw iron mixed with ceramic clay, they will mingle with the seed of men; but they will not adhere to one another, just as iron does not mix with clay. 44And in the days of these kings the God of heaven will set up a kingdom which shall never be destroyed; and the kingdom shall not be left to other people; it shall break in pieces and consume all these kingdoms, and it shall stand forever. 45Inasmuch as you saw that the stone was cut out of the mountain without hands, and that it broke in pieces the iron, the bronze, the clay, the silver, and the gold—the great God has made known to the king what will come to pass after this. The dream is certain, and its interpretation is sure."

Daniel and His Friends Promoted

46Then King Nebuchadnezzar fell on his face, prostrate before Daniel, and commanded that they should present an offering and incense to him. 47The king answered Daniel, and said, "Truly your God *is* the God of gods, the Lord of kings, and a revealer of secrets, since you could reveal this secret." 48Then the king promoted Daniel and gave him many great gifts; and he made him ruler over the whole province of Babylon, and chief administrator over all the wise *men* of Babylon. 49Also Daniel petitioned the king, and he set Shadrach, Meshach, and Abed-Nego over the affairs of the province of Babylon; but Daniel *sat* in the gate[a] of the king.

The Image of Gold

3 Nebuchadnezzar the king made an image of gold, whose height *was* sixty cubits *and* its width six cubits. He set it up in the plain of Dura, in the province of Babylon. 2And King Nebuchadnezzar sent *word* to gather together the satraps, the administrators, the governors, the counselors, the treasurers, the judges, the magistrates, and all the officials of the provinces, to come to the dedication of the image which King Nebuchadnezzar had set up. 3So the satraps, the administrators, the governors, the counselors, the treasurers, the judges, the magistrates, and all the officials of the provinces gathered together for the dedication of the image that King Nebuchadnezzar had set up; and they stood before the image that Nebuchadnezzar had set up. 4Then a herald cried aloud: "To you it is commanded, O peoples, nations, and languages, 5*that* at the time you hear the sound of the horn, flute, harp, lyre, *and* psaltery, in symphony with all kinds of music, you shall fall down and worship the gold image that King Nebuchadnezzar has set up; 6and whoever does not fall down and worship shall be cast immediately into the midst of a burning fiery furnace."

7So at that time, when all the people heard the sound of the horn, flute, harp, *and* lyre, in symphony with all kinds of music, all the people, nations, and languages fell down *and* worshiped the gold image which King Nebuchadnezzar had set up.

Daniel's Friends Disobey the King

8Therefore at that time certain Chaldeans came forward and accused the Jews. 9They spoke and said to King Nebuchadnezzar, "O king, live forever! 10You, O king, have made a decree that everyone who hears the sound of the horn, flute, harp, lyre, *and* psaltery, in symphony with all kinds of music, shall fall down and worship the gold image; 11and whoever does not fall down and worship shall be cast into the midst of a burning fiery furnace. 12There are certain Jews whom you have set over the affairs of the province of Babylon: Shadrach, Meshach, and Abed-Nego; these men, O king, have not paid due regard to you. They do not serve your gods or worship the gold image which you have set up."

13Then Nebuchadnezzar, in rage and fury, gave the command to bring Shadrach, Meshach, and Abed-Nego. So they brought these men before the king. 14Nebuchadnezzar spoke, saying to them, "*Is it* true, Shadrach, Meshach,

2:49 [a] That is, the king's court

and Abed-Nego, *that* you do not serve
my gods or worship the gold image
which I have set up? 15 Now if you are
ready at the time you hear the sound of
the horn, flute, harp, lyre, *and* psaltery,
in symphony with all kinds of music,
and you fall down and worship the
image which I have made, *good!* But if
you do not worship, you shall be cast
immediately into the midst of a burning
fiery furnace. And who *is* the god who
will deliver you from my hands?"
16 Shadrach, Meshach, and Abed-Nego
answered and said to the king, "O Nebu-
chadnezzar, we have no need to answer
you in this matter. 17 If that *is the case,*
our God whom we serve is able to de-
liver us from the burning fiery furnace,
and He will deliver *us* from your hand,
O king. 18 But if not, let it be known to
you, O king, that we do not serve your
gods, nor will we worship the gold image
which you have set up."

Saved in Fiery Trial

19 Then Nebuchadnezzar was full of
fury, and the expression on his face
changed toward Shadrach, Meshach,
and Abed-Nego. He spoke and com-
manded that they heat the furnace
seven times more than it was usually
heated. 20 And he commanded certain
mighty men of valor who *were* in his
army to bind Shadrach, Meshach, and
Abed-Nego, *and* cast *them* into the burn-
ing fiery furnace. 21 Then these men were
bound in their coats, their trousers, their
turbans, and their *other* garments, and
were cast into the midst of the burning
fiery furnace. 22 Therefore, because the
king's command was urgent, and the
furnace exceedingly hot, the flame of
the fire killed those men who took up
Shadrach, Meshach, and Abed-Nego.
23 And these three men, Shadrach,
Meshach, and Abed-Nego, fell down
bound into the midst of the burning
fiery furnace.
24 Then King Nebuchadnezzar was
astonished; and he rose in haste *and*
spoke, saying to his counselors, "Did
we not cast three men bound into the
midst of the fire?"
They answered and said to the king,
"True, O king."
25 "Look!" he answered, "I see four men
loose, walking in the midst of the fire;
and they are not hurt, and the form of
the fourth is like the Son of God."[a]

Nebuchadnezzar Praises God

26 Then Nebuchadnezzar went near the
mouth of the burning fiery furnace *and*
spoke, saying, "Shadrach, Meshach, and
Abed-Nego, servants of the Most High
God, come out, and come *here.*" Then
Shadrach, Meshach, and Abed-Nego
came from the midst of the fire. 27 And
the satraps, administrators, governors,
and the king's counselors gathered
together, and they saw these men on
whose bodies the fire had no power; the
hair of their head was not singed nor
were their garments affected, and the
smell of fire was not on them.
28 Nebuchadnezzar spoke, saying,
"Blessed be the God of Shadrach, Me-
shach, and Abed-Nego, who sent His
Angel[a] and delivered His servants who
trusted in Him, and they have frustrated
the king's word, and yielded their bodies,
that they should not serve nor worship
any god except their own God! 29 There-
fore I make a decree that any people,
nation, or language which speaks any-
thing amiss against the God of Sha-
drach, Meshach, and Abed-Nego shall
be cut in pieces, and their houses shall
be made an ash heap; because there is
no other God who can deliver like this."
30 Then the king promoted Shadrach,
Meshach, and Abed-Nego in the prov-
ince of Babylon.

Nebuchadnezzar's Second Dream

4 Nebuchadnezzar the king,

To all peoples, nations, and
languages that dwell in all the
earth:

Peace be multiplied to you.

2 I thought it good to declare the
signs and wonders that the Most
High God has worked for me.

3:25 [a] Or *a son of the gods* **3:28** [a] Or *angel*

GOD | SIN | JESUS | SALVATION | LOVE

3 How great *are* His signs,
And how mighty His wonders!
His kingdom *is* an everlasting
kingdom,
And His dominion *is* from
generation to generation.

4 I, Nebuchadnezzar, was at rest
in my house, and flourishing in
my palace. 5I saw a dream which
made me afraid, and the thoughts
on my bed and the visions of my
head troubled me. 6Therefore I
issued a decree to bring in all the
wise *men* of Babylon before me,
that they might make known
to me the interpretation of the
dream. 7Then the magicians,
the astrologers, the Chaldeans,
and the soothsayers came in,
and I told them the dream; but
they did not make known to
me its interpretation. 8But at
last Daniel came before me (his
name *is* Belteshazzar, according
to the name of my god; in him
is the Spirit of the Holy God),
and I told the dream before him,
saying: 9"Belteshazzar, chief of the
magicians, because I know that
the Spirit of the Holy God *is* in you,
and no secret troubles you, explain
to me the visions of my dream that
I have seen, and its interpretation.

10 "These *were* the visions of my
head *while* on my bed:

I was looking, and behold,
A tree in the midst of the earth,
And its height was great.
11 The tree grew and became strong;
Its height reached to the heavens,
And it could be seen to the ends of
all the earth.
12 Its leaves *were* lovely,
Its fruit abundant,
And in it *was* food for all.
The beasts of the field found
shade under it,
The birds of the heavens dwelt in
its branches,
And all flesh was fed from it.

13 "I saw in the visions of my head
while on my bed, and there was a
watcher, a holy one, coming down
from heaven. 14He cried aloud
and said thus:

'Chop down the tree and cut off its
branches,
Strip off its leaves and scatter its
fruit.
Let the beasts get out from
under it,
And the birds from its branches.
15 Nevertheless leave the stump and
roots in the earth,
Bound with a band of iron and
bronze,
In the tender grass of the field.
Let it be wet with the dew of
heaven,
And *let* him graze with the beasts
On the grass of the earth.
16 Let his heart be changed from
that of a man,
Let him be given the heart of a
beast,
And let seven times[a] pass over
him.

17 'This decision *is* by the decree of the
watchers,
And the sentence by the word of
the holy ones,
In order that the living may know
That the Most High rules in the
kingdom of men,
Gives it to whomever He will,
And sets over it the lowest of men.'

18 "This dream I, King
Nebuchadnezzar, have seen.
Now you, Belteshazzar, declare
its interpretation, since all the
wise *men* of my kingdom are not
able to make known to me the
interpretation; but you *are* able,
for the Spirit of the Holy God *is* in
you."

Daniel Explains the Second Dream

19 Then Daniel, whose name *was*
Belteshazzar, was astonished for
a time, and his thoughts troubled

4:16 [a] Possibly *seven years,* and so in verses 23, 25, and 32

him. *So* the king spoke, and said,
"Belteshazzar, do not let the dream
or its interpretation trouble you."
Belteshazzar answered and
said, "My lord, *may* the dream
concern those who hate you, and
its interpretation concern your
enemies!

20 "The tree that you saw, which
grew and became strong, whose
height reached to the heavens
and which *could be* seen by all
the earth, 21whose leaves *were*
lovely and its fruit abundant,
in which *was* food for all, under
which the beasts of the field
dwelt, and in whose branches
the birds of the heaven had their
home— 22it *is* you, O king, who
have grown and become strong;
for your greatness has grown and
reaches to the heavens, and your
dominion to the end of the earth.
23 "And inasmuch as the king saw a
watcher, a holy one, coming down
from heaven and saying, 'Chop
down the tree and destroy it, but
leave its stump and roots in the
earth, *bound* with a band of iron
and bronze in the tender grass of
the field; let it be wet with the dew
of heaven, and let him graze with
the beasts of the field, till seven
times pass over him'; 24this is the
interpretation, O king, and this
is the decree of the Most High,
which has come upon my lord
the king: 25They shall drive you
from men, your dwelling shall be
with the beasts of the field, and
they shall make you eat grass like
oxen. They shall wet you with the
dew of heaven, and seven times
shall pass over you, till you know
that the Most High rules in the
kingdom of men, and gives it to
whomever He chooses.
26 "And inasmuch as they gave the
command to leave the stump *and*
roots of the tree, your kingdom
shall be assured to you, after you
come to know that Heaven rules.
27Therefore, O king, let my advice
be acceptable to you; break off
your sins by *being* righteous, and
your iniquities by showing mercy
to *the* poor. Perhaps there may be
a lengthening of your prosperity."

Nebuchadnezzar's Humiliation

28 All *this* came upon King
Nebuchadnezzar. 29At the end
of the twelve months he was
walking about the royal palace
of Babylon. 30The king spoke,
saying, "Is not this great Babylon,
that I have built for a royal
dwelling by my mighty power and
for the honor of my majesty?"
31 While the word *was still* in the
king's mouth, a voice fell from
heaven: "King Nebuchadnezzar,
to you it is spoken: the kingdom
has departed from you! 32And
they shall drive you from men,
and your dwelling *shall be* with
the beasts of the field. They shall
make you eat grass like oxen;
and seven times shall pass over
you, until you know that the Most
High rules in the kingdom of
men, and gives it to whomever He
chooses."
33 That very hour the word
was fulfilled concerning
Nebuchadnezzar; he was driven
from men and ate grass like oxen;
his body was wet with the dew of
heaven till his hair had grown like
eagles' *feathers* and his nails like
birds' *claws*.

Nebuchadnezzar Praises God

34 And at the end of the time[a] I,
Nebuchadnezzar, lifted my eyes
to heaven, and my understanding
returned to me; and I blessed
the Most High and praised and
honored Him who lives forever:

For His dominion *is* an
everlasting dominion,
And His kingdom *is* from
generation to generation.

4:34 [a] Literally *days*

35 All the inhabitants of the earth
are reputed as nothing;
He does according to His will in
the army of heaven
And *among* the inhabitants of the
earth.
No one can restrain His hand
Or say to Him, "What have You
done?"

36 At the same time my reason
returned to me, and for the glory
of my kingdom, my honor and
splendor returned to me. My
counselors and nobles resorted
to me, I was restored to my
kingdom, and excellent majesty
was added to me. 37Now I,
Nebuchadnezzar, praise and extol
and honor the King of heaven, all
of whose works *are* truth, and His
ways justice. And those who walk
in pride He is able to put down.

Belshazzar's Feast

5 Belshazzar the king made a great
feast for a thousand of his lords,
and drank wine in the presence of the
thousand. 2While he tasted the wine,
Belshazzar gave the command to bring
the gold and silver vessels which his
father Nebuchadnezzar had taken from
the temple which *had been* in Jerusa-
lem, that the king and his lords, his
wives, and his concubines might drink
from them. 3Then they brought the gold
vessels that had been taken from the
temple of the house of God which *had
been* in Jerusalem; and the king and
his lords, his wives, and his concubines
drank from them. 4They drank wine,
and praised the gods of gold and silver,
bronze and iron, wood and stone.
5In the same hour the fingers of a man's
hand appeared and wrote opposite the
lampstand on the plaster of the wall of
the king's palace; and the king saw the
part of the hand that wrote. 6Then the
king's countenance changed, and his
thoughts troubled him, so that the joints
of his hips were loosened and his knees
knocked against each other. 7The king
cried aloud to bring in the astrologers,
the Chaldeans, and the soothsayers. The
king spoke, saying to the wise *men* of
Babylon, "Whoever reads this writing,
and tells me its interpretation, shall be
clothed with purple and *have* a chain of
gold around his neck; and he shall be
the third ruler in the kingdom." 8Now all
the king's wise *men* came, but they could
not read the writing, or make known to
the king its interpretation. 9Then King
Belshazzar was greatly troubled, his
countenance was changed, and his lords
were astonished.
10The queen, because of the words
of the king and his lords, came to the
banquet hall. The queen spoke, saying,
"O king, live forever! Do not let your
thoughts trouble you, nor let your coun-
tenance change. 11There is a man in
your kingdom in whom *is* the Spirit of
the Holy God. And in the days of your
father, light and understanding and
wisdom, like the wisdom of the gods,
were found in him; and King Nebu-
chadnezzar your father—your father
the king—made him chief of the ma-
gicians, astrologers, Chaldeans, *and*
soothsayers. 12Inasmuch as an excel-
lent spirit, knowledge, understanding,
interpreting dreams, solving riddles,
and explaining enigmas[a] were found
in this Daniel, whom the king named
Belteshazzar, now let Daniel be called,
and he will give the interpretation."

The Writing on the Wall Explained

13Then Daniel was brought in before
the king. The king spoke, and said to
Daniel, "*Are* you that Daniel who is one
of the captives[a] from Judah, whom my
father the king brought from Judah? 14I
have heard of you, that the Spirit of God
is in you, and *that* light and understand-
ing and excellent wisdom are found in
you. 15Now the wise *men*, the astrolo-
gers, have been brought in before me,
that they should read this writing and
make known to me its interpretation,
but they could not give the interpreta-
tion of the thing. 16And I have heard of
you, that you can give interpretations
and explain enigmas. Now if you can
read the writing and make known to me

5:12 [a] Literally *untying knots*, and so in verse 16

5:13 [a] Literally *of the sons of the captivity*

its interpretation, you shall be clothed
with purple and *have* a chain of gold
around your neck, and shall be the third
ruler in the kingdom."
17Then Daniel answered, and said
before the king, "Let your gifts be for
yourself, and give your rewards to
another; yet I will read the writing to
the king, and make known to him the
interpretation. 18O king, the Most High
God gave Nebuchadnezzar your fa-
ther a kingdom and majesty, glory and
honor. 19And because of the majesty
that He gave him, all peoples, nations,
and languages trembled and feared
before him. Whomever he wished, he
executed; whomever he wished, he kept
alive; whomever he wished, he set up;
and whomever he wished, he put down.
20But when his heart was lifted up, and
his spirit was hardened in pride, he was
deposed from his kingly throne, and
they took his glory from him. 21Then
he was driven from the sons of men,
his heart was made like the beasts, and
his dwelling *was* with the wild donkeys.
They fed him with grass like oxen, and
his body was wet with the dew of heav-
en, till he knew that the Most High God
rules in the kingdom of men, and ap-
points over it whomever He chooses.
22"But you his son, Belshazzar, have
not humbled your heart, although you
knew all this. 23And you have lifted
yourself up against the Lord of heaven.
They have brought the vessels of His
house before you, and you and your
lords, your wives and your concubines,
have drunk wine from them. And you
have praised the gods of silver and gold,
bronze and iron, wood and stone, which
do not see or hear or know; and the God
who *holds* your breath in His hand and
owns all your ways, you have not glo-
rified. 24Then the fingers[a] of the hand
were sent from Him, and this writing
was written.
25"And this is the inscription that was
written:

MENE,[a] MENE, TEKEL,[b]
UPHARSIN.[c]

26This *is* the interpretation of *each*
word. MENE: God has numbered your
kingdom, and finished it; 27TEKEL: You
have been weighed in the balances,
and found wanting; 28PERES: Your
kingdom has been divided, and given
to the Medes and Persians."[a] 29Then
Belshazzar gave the command, and
they clothed Daniel with purple and
put a chain of gold around his neck,
and made a proclamation concerning
him that he should be the third ruler in
the kingdom.

Belshazzar's Fall

30That very night Belshazzar, king of
the Chaldeans, was slain. 31And Darius
the Mede received the kingdom, *being*
about sixty-two years old.

The Plot Against Daniel

6 It pleased Darius to set over the
kingdom one hundred and twenty
satraps, to be over the whole kingdom;
2and over these, three governors, of
whom Daniel *was* one, that the satraps
might give account to them, so that the
king would suffer no loss. 3Then this
Daniel distinguished himself above
the governors and satraps, because
an excellent spirit *was* in him; and the
king gave thought to setting him over
the whole realm. 4So the governors
and satraps sought to find *some* charge
against Daniel concerning the king-
dom; but they could find no charge or
fault, because he *was* faithful; nor was
there any error or fault found in him.
5Then these men said, "We shall not find
any charge against this Daniel unless
we find *it* against him concerning the
law of his God."
6So these governors and satraps
thronged before the king, and said
thus to him: "King Darius, live forever!
7All the governors of the kingdom, the
administrators and satraps, the coun-
selors and advisors, have consulted
together to establish a royal statute and
to make a firm decree, that whoever pe-
titions any god or man for thirty days,
except you, O king, shall be cast into the

5:24 [a] Literally *palm* **5:25** [a] Literally *a mina* (50 shekels) from the verb "to number" [b] Literally *a shekel* from the verb "to weigh" [c] Literally *and half-shekels* from the verb "to divide" **5:28** [a] Aramaic *Paras,* consonant with *Peres*

den of lions. 8Now, O king, establish the
decree and sign the writing, so that it
cannot be changed, according to the
law of the Medes and Persians, which
does not alter." 9Therefore King Darius
signed the written decree.

Daniel in the Lions' Den

10Now when Daniel knew that the writ-
ing was signed, he went home. And in
his upper room, with his windows open
toward Jerusalem, he knelt down on his
knees three times that day, and prayed
and gave thanks before his God, as was
his custom since early days.

11Then these men assembled and
found Daniel praying and making sup-
plication before his God. 12And they
went before the king, and spoke con-
cerning the king's decree: "Have you
not signed a decree that every man who
petitions any god or man within thirty
days, except you, O king, shall be cast
into the den of lions?"

The king answered and said, "The thing
is true, according to the law of the Medes
and Persians, which does not alter."

13So they answered and said before
the king, "That Daniel, who is one of the
captives[a] from Judah, does not show
due regard for you, O king, or for the
decree that you have signed, but makes
his petition three times a day."

14And the king, when he heard *these*
words, was greatly displeased with
himself, and set *his* heart on Daniel
to deliver him; and he labored till the
going down of the sun to deliver him.
15Then these men approached the king,
and said to the king, "Know, O king, that
it is the law of the Medes and Persians
that no decree or statute which the king
establishes may be changed."

16So the king gave the command, and
they brought Daniel and cast *him* into
the den of lions. *But* the king spoke, say-
ing to Daniel, "Your God, whom you serve
continually, He will deliver you." 17Then a
stone was brought and laid on the mouth
of the den, and the king sealed it with his
own signet ring and with the signets of
his lords, that the purpose concerning
Daniel might not be changed.

Daniel Saved from the Lions

18Now the king went to his palace and
spent the night fasting; and no musi-
cians[a] were brought before him. Also
his sleep went from him. 19Then the king
arose very early in the morning and
went in haste to the den of lions. 20And
when he came to the den, he cried out
with a lamenting voice to Daniel. The
king spoke, saying to Daniel, "Daniel,
servant of the living God, has your God,
whom you serve continually, been able
to deliver you from the lions?"

21Then Daniel said to the king, "O king,
live forever! 22My God sent His angel
and shut the lions' mouths, so that they
have not hurt me, because I was found
innocent before Him; and also, O king,
I have done no wrong before you."

23Now the king was exceedingly glad
for him, and commanded that they
should take Daniel up out of the den.
So Daniel was taken up out of the den,
and no injury whatever was found on
him, because he believed in his God.

Darius Honors God

24And the king gave the command, and
they brought those men who had accused
Daniel, and they cast *them* into the den
of lions—them, their children, and their
wives; and the lions overpowered them,
and broke all their bones in pieces before
they ever came to the bottom of the den.
25Then King Darius wrote:

> To all peoples, nations, and
> languages that dwell in all the
> earth:
>
> Peace be multiplied to you.
>
> 26 I make a decree that in every
> dominion of my kingdom *men*
> *must* tremble and fear before the
> God of Daniel.
>
> For He *is* the living God,
> And steadfast forever;
> His kingdom *is the one* which shall
> not be destroyed,
> And His dominion *shall endure* to
> the end.

6:13 [a] Literally *of the sons of the captivity* 6:18 [a] Exact meaning unknown

27 He delivers and rescues,
And He works signs and
wonders
In heaven and on earth,
Who has delivered Daniel from
the power of the lions.

28 So this Daniel prospered in the reign
of Darius and in the reign of Cyrus the
Persian.

Vision of the Four Beasts

7 In the first year of Belshazzar king
of Babylon, Daniel had a dream
and visions of his head *while* on his bed.
Then he wrote down the dream, telling
the main facts.[a]
2 Daniel spoke, saying, "I saw in my
vision by night, and behold, the four
winds of heaven were stirring up the
Great Sea.
3 And four great beasts came
up from the sea, each different from the
other.
4 The first *was* like a lion, and had
eagle's wings. I watched till its wings
were plucked off; and it was lifted up
from the earth and made to stand on
two feet like a man, and a man's heart
was given to it.
5 "And suddenly another beast, a sec-
ond, like a bear. It was raised up on one
side, and *had* three ribs in its mouth
between its teeth. And they said thus
to it: 'Arise, devour much flesh!'
6 "After this I looked, and there was
another, like a leopard, which had on
its back four wings of a bird. The beast
also had four heads, and dominion was
given to it.
7 "After this I saw in the night visions,
and behold, a fourth beast, dreadful
and terrible, exceedingly strong. It
had huge iron teeth; it was devouring,
breaking in pieces, and trampling the
residue with its feet. It *was* different
from all the beasts that *were* before it,
and it had ten horns.
8 I was consider-
ing the horns, and there was another
horn, a little one, coming up among
them, before whom three of the first
horns were plucked out by the roots.
And there, in this horn, *were* eyes like
the eyes of a man, and a mouth speak-
ing pompous words.

Vision of the Ancient of Days

9 "I watched till thrones were put in
place,
And the Ancient of Days was
seated;
His garment *was* white as snow,
And the hair of His head *was* like
pure wool.
His throne *was* a fiery flame,
Its wheels a burning fire;
10 A fiery stream issued
And came forth from before Him.
A thousand thousands ministered
to Him;
Ten thousand times ten thousand
stood before Him.
The court[a] was seated,
And the books were opened.

11 "I watched then because of the sound
of the pompous words which the horn
was speaking; I watched till the beast
was slain, and its body destroyed and
given to the burning flame.
12 As for
the rest of the beasts, they had their
dominion taken away, yet their lives
were prolonged for a season and a time.

13 "I was watching in the night visions,
And behold, *One* like the Son of
Man,
Coming with the clouds of heaven!
He came to the Ancient of Days,
And they brought Him near
before Him.
14 Then to Him was given dominion
and glory and a kingdom,
That all peoples, nations, and
languages should serve Him.
His dominion *is* an everlasting
dominion,
Which shall not pass away,
And His kingdom *the one*
Which shall not be destroyed.

Daniel's Visions Interpreted

15 "I, Daniel, was grieved in my spirit
within *my* body, and the visions of my
head troubled me.
16 I came near to one
of those who stood by, and asked him
the truth of all this. So he told me and
made known to me the interpretation
of these things:
17 'Those great beasts,

7:1 [a] Literally *the head* (or *chief*) *of the words* 7:10 [a] Or *judgment*

GOD SIN JESUS SALVATION LOVE

which are four, *are* four kings[a] *which*
arise out of the earth. 18But the saints
of the Most High shall receive the king-
dom, and possess the kingdom forever,
even forever and ever.'

19"Then I wished to know the truth
about the fourth beast, which was dif-
ferent from all the others, exceedingly
dreadful, *with* its teeth of iron and its
nails of bronze, *which* devoured, broke
in pieces, and trampled the residue with
its feet; 20and the ten horns that *were* on
its head, and the other *horn* which came
up, before which three fell, namely, that
horn which had eyes and a mouth which
spoke pompous words, whose appear-
ance *was* greater than his fellows.

21"I was watching; and the same horn
was making war against the saints, and
prevailing against them, 22until the
Ancient of Days came, and a judgment
was made *in favor* of the saints of the
Most High, and the time came for the
saints to possess the kingdom.

23"Thus he said:

'The fourth beast shall be
A fourth kingdom on earth,
Which shall be different from all
other kingdoms,
And shall devour the whole earth,
Trample it and break it in pieces.
24 The ten horns *are* ten kings
Who shall arise from this kingdom.
And another shall rise after them;
He shall be different from the first
ones,
And shall subdue three kings.
25 He shall speak *pompous* words
against the Most High,
Shall persecute[a] the saints of the
Most High,
And shall intend to change times
and law.
Then *the saints* shall be given into
his hand
For a time and times and half a
time.

26 'But the court shall be seated,
And they shall take away his
dominion,
To consume and destroy *it* forever.
27 Then the kingdom and dominion,
And the greatness of the
kingdoms under the whole
heaven,
Shall be given to the people, the
saints of the Most High.
His kingdom *is* an everlasting
kingdom,
And all dominions shall serve and
obey Him.'

28"This *is* the end of the account.[a] As for
me, Daniel, my thoughts greatly trou-
bled me, and my countenance changed;
but I kept the matter in my heart."

Vision of a Ram and a Goat

8 In the third year of the reign
of King Belshazzar a vision ap-
peared *to* me—to me, Daniel—after
the one that appeared to me the first
time. 2I saw in the vision, and it so
happened while I was looking, that
I *was* in Shushan, the citadel, which
is in the province of Elam; and I saw
in the vision that I was by the River
Ulai. 3Then I lifted my eyes and saw,
and there, standing beside the river,
was a ram which had two horns, and
the two horns *were* high; but one *was*
higher than the other, and the high-
er *one* came up last. 4I saw the ram
pushing westward, northward, and
southward, so that no animal could
withstand him; nor *was there any* that
could deliver from his hand, but he did
according to his will and became great.
5And as I was considering, suddenly a
male goat came from the west, across
the surface of the whole earth, without
touching the ground; and the goat *had*
a notable horn between his eyes. 6Then
he came to the ram that had two horns,
which I had seen standing beside the
river, and ran at him with furious power.
7And I saw him confronting the ram;
he was moved with rage against him,
attacked the ram, and broke his two
horns. There was no power in the ram
to withstand him, but he cast him down
to the ground and trampled him; and
there was no one that could deliver the
ram from his hand.

7:17 [a] Representing their kingdoms (compare verse 23) **7:25** [a] Literally *wear out* **7:28** [a] Literally *the word*

8 Therefore the male goat grew very
great; but when he became strong, the
large horn was broken, and in place
of it four notable ones came up to-
ward the four winds of heaven. 9 And
out of one of them came a little horn
which grew exceedingly great toward
the south, toward the east, and toward
the Glorious *Land.* 10 And it grew up to the
host of heaven; and it cast down *some*
of the host and *some* of the stars to the
ground, and trampled them. 11 He even
exalted *himself* as high as the Prince of
the host; and by him the daily *sacrifices*
were taken away, and the place of His
sanctuary was cast down. 12 Because of
transgression, an army was given over
to the horn to oppose the daily *sacrifices;*
and he cast truth down to the ground.
He did *all this* and prospered.

13 Then I heard a holy one speaking;
and *another* holy one said to that cer-
tain *one* who was speaking, "How long
will the vision *be, concerning* the daily
sacrifices and the transgression of deso-
lation, the giving of both the sanctuary
and the host to be trampled underfoot?"

14 And he said to me, "For two thousand
three hundred days;[a] then the sanctu-
ary shall be cleansed."

Gabriel Interprets the Vision

15 Then it happened, when I, Daniel,
had seen the vision and was seeking
the meaning, that suddenly there stood
before me one having the appearance
of a man. 16 And I heard a man's voice
between *the banks of* the Ulai, who
called, and said, "Gabriel, make this
man understand the vision." 17 So he
came near where I stood, and when he
came I was afraid and fell on my face;
but he said to me, "Understand, son of
man, that the vision *refers* to the time
of the end."

18 Now, as he was speaking with me, I
was in a deep sleep with my face to the
ground; but he touched me, and stood
me upright. 19 And he said, "Look, I am
making known to you what shall hap-
pen in the latter time of the indignation;
for at the appointed time the end *shall
be.* 20 The ram which you saw, having the
two horns—*they are* the kings of Media
and Persia. 21 And the male goat *is* the
kingdom[a] of Greece. The large horn that
is between its eyes *is* the first king. 22 As
for the broken *horn* and the four that
stood up in its place, four kingdoms
shall arise out of that nation, but not
with its power.

23 "And in the latter time of their
kingdom,
When the transgressors have
reached their fullness,
A king shall arise,
Having fierce features,
Who understands sinister
schemes.
24 His power shall be mighty, but
not by his own power;
He shall destroy fearfully,
And shall prosper and thrive;
He shall destroy the mighty, and
also the holy people.

25 "Through his cunning
He shall cause deceit to prosper
under his rule;[a]
And he shall exalt *himself* in his
heart.
He shall destroy many in *their*
prosperity.
He shall even rise against the
Prince of princes;
But he shall be broken without
human means.[b]

26 "And the vision of the evenings and
mornings
Which was told is true;
Therefore seal up the vision,
For *it refers* to many days *in the
future.*"

27 And I, Daniel, fainted and was sick
for days; afterward I arose and went
about the king's business. I was aston-
ished by the vision, but no one under-
stood it.

Daniel's Prayer for the People

9 In the first year of Darius the son
of Ahasuerus, of the lineage of
the Medes, who was made king over

8:14 [a] Literally *evening-mornings* 8:21 [a] Literally *king,* representing his kingdom (compare 7:17, 23)
8:25 [a] Literally *hand* [b] Literally *hand*

the realm of the Chaldeans— 2in the
first year of his reign I, Daniel, under-
stood by the books the number of the
years *specified* by the word of the LORD
through Jeremiah the prophet, that He
would accomplish seventy years in the
desolations of Jerusalem.
3Then I set my face toward the Lord
God to make request by prayer and
supplications, with fasting, sackcloth,
and ashes. 4And I prayed to the LORD
my God, and made confession, and said,
"O Lord, great and awesome God, who
keeps His covenant and mercy with
those who love Him, and with those
who keep His commandments, 5we
have sinned and committed iniquity,
we have done wickedly and rebelled,
even by departing from Your precepts
and Your judgments. 6Neither have we
heeded Your servants the prophets, who
spoke in Your name to our kings and
our princes, to our fathers and all the
people of the land. 7O Lord, righteous-
ness *belongs* to You, but to us shame
of face, as *it is* this day—to the men of
Judah, to the inhabitants of Jerusalem
and all Israel, those near and those far
off in all the countries to which You have
driven them, because of the unfaith-
fulness which they have committed
against You.
8"O Lord, to us *belongs* shame of face,
to our kings, our princes, and our fa-
thers, because we have sinned against
You. 9To the Lord our God *belong* mer-
cy and forgiveness, though we have
rebelled against Him. 10We have not
obeyed the voice of the LORD our God,
to walk in His laws, which He set before
us by His servants the prophets. 11Yes,
all Israel has transgressed Your law,
and has departed so as not to obey Your
voice; therefore the curse and the oath
written in the Law of Moses the servant
of God have been poured out on us,
because we have sinned against Him.
12And He has confirmed His words,
which He spoke against us and against
our judges who judged us, by bringing
upon us a great disaster; for under the
whole heaven such has never been done
as what has been done to Jerusalem.
13"As *it is* written in the Law of Moses,
all this disaster has come upon us; yet
we have not made our prayer before
the LORD our God, that we might turn
from our iniquities and understand
Your truth. 14Therefore the LORD has
kept the disaster in mind, and brought
it upon us; for the LORD our God *is* righ-
teous in all the works which He does,
though we have not obeyed His voice.
15And now, O Lord our God, who brought
Your people out of the land of Egypt
with a mighty hand, and made Your-
self a name, as *it is* this day—we have
sinned, we have done wickedly!
16"O Lord, according to all Your righ-
teousness, I pray, let Your anger and
Your fury be turned away from Your
city Jerusalem, Your holy mountain;
because for our sins, and for the in-
iquities of our fathers, Jerusalem and
Your people *are* a reproach to all *those*
around us. 17Now therefore, our God,
hear the prayer of Your servant, and his
supplications, and for the Lord's sake
cause Your face to shine on Your sanc-
tuary, which is desolate. 18O my God,
incline Your ear and hear; open Your
eyes and see our desolations, and the
city which is called by Your name; for we
do not present our supplications before
You because of our righteous deeds, but
because of Your great mercies. 19O Lord,
hear! O Lord, forgive! O Lord, listen and
act! Do not delay for Your own sake, my
God, for Your city and Your people are
called by Your name."

The Seventy-Weeks Prophecy

20Now while I *was* speaking, pray-
ing, and confessing my sin and the sin
of my people Israel, and presenting
my supplication before the LORD my
God for the holy mountain of my God,
21yes, while I *was* speaking in prayer,
the man Gabriel, whom I had seen in the
vision at the beginning, being caused
to fly swiftly, reached me about the
time of the evening offering. 22And he
informed *me,* and talked with me, and
said, "O Daniel, I have now come forth
to give you skill to understand. 23At
the beginning of your supplications
the command went out, and I have
come to tell *you,* for you *are* greatly
beloved; therefore consider the matter,
and understand the vision:

24 "Seventy weeks[a] are determined
For your people and for your holy
city,
To finish the transgression,
To make an end of[b] sins,
To make reconciliation for
iniquity,
To bring in everlasting
righteousness,
To seal up vision and prophecy,
And to anoint the Most Holy.

25 "Know therefore and understand,
That from the going forth of the
command
To restore and build Jerusalem
Until Messiah the Prince,
There shall be seven weeks and
sixty-two weeks;
The street[a] shall be built again,
and the wall,[b]
Even in troublesome times.

26 "And after the sixty-two weeks
Messiah shall be cut off, but not
for Himself;
And the people of the prince who
is to come
Shall destroy the city and the
sanctuary.
The end of it *shall be* with a flood,
And till the end of the war
desolations are determined.
27 Then he shall confirm a covenant
with many for one week;
But in the middle of the week
He shall bring an end to sacrifice
and offering.
And on the wing of abominations
shall be one who makes
desolate,
Even until the consummation,
which is determined,
Is poured out on the desolate."

Vision of the Glorious Man

10 In the third year of Cyrus king of
Persia a message was revealed
to Daniel, whose name was called Bel-
teshazzar. The message *was* true, but
the appointed time *was* long;[a] and
he understood the message, and had
understanding of the vision. 2In those
days I, Daniel, was mourning three full
weeks. 3I ate no pleasant food, no meat
or wine came into my mouth, nor did
I anoint myself at all, till three whole
weeks were fulfilled.
4Now on the twenty-fourth day of the
first month, as I was by the side of the
great river, that *is,* the Tigris,[a] 5I lifted my
eyes and looked, and behold, a certain
man clothed in linen, whose waist *was*
girded with gold of Uphaz! 6His body *was*
like beryl, his face like the appearance
of lightning, his eyes like torches of fire,
his arms and feet like burnished bronze
in color, and the sound of his words like
the voice of a multitude.
7And I, Daniel, alone saw the vision,
for the men who were with me did not
see the vision; but a great terror fell
upon them, so that they fled to hide
themselves. 8Therefore I was left alone
when I saw this great vision, and no
strength remained in me; for my vig-
or was turned to frailty in me, and I
retained no strength. 9Yet I heard the
sound of his words; and while I heard the
sound of his words I was in a deep sleep
on my face, with my face to the ground.

Prophecies Concerning Persia and Greece

10Suddenly, a hand touched me, which
made me tremble on my knees and *on*
the palms of my hands. 11And he said
to me, "O Daniel, man greatly beloved,
understand the words that I speak to
you, and stand upright, for I have now
been sent to you." While he was speak-
ing this word to me, I stood trembling.
12Then he said to me, "Do not fear,
Daniel, for from the first day that you
set your heart to understand, and to
humble yourself before your God, your
words were heard; and I have come be-
cause of your words. 13But the prince
of the kingdom of Persia withstood me
twenty-one days; and behold, Michael,
one of the chief princes, came to help
me, for I had been left alone there with
the kings of Persia. 14Now I have come to
make you understand what will happen

9:24 [a] Literally *sevens,* and so throughout the chapter [b] Following Qere, Septuagint, Syriac, and Vulgate; Kethib and Theodotion read *To seal up.* 9:25 [a] Or *open square* [b] Or *moat* 10:1 [a] Or *and of great conflict* 10:4 [a] Hebrew *Hiddekel*

to your people in the latter days, for the
vision *refers* to *many* days yet *to come.*"
15When he had spoken such words to
me, I turned my face toward the ground
and became speechless. 16And sud-
denly, *one* having the likeness of the
sons[a] of men touched my lips; then I
opened my mouth and spoke, saying
to him who stood before me, "My lord,
because of the vision my sorrows have
overwhelmed me, and I have retained
no strength. 17For how can this servant
of my lord talk with you, my lord? As
for me, no strength remains in me now,
nor is any breath left in me."
18Then again, *the one* having the like-
ness of a man touched me and strength-
ened me. 19And he said, "O man greatly
beloved, fear not! Peace *be* to you; be
strong, yes, be strong!"
So when he spoke to me I was strength-
ened, and said, "Let my lord speak, for
you have strengthened me."
20Then he said, "Do you know why
I have come to you? And now I must
return to fight with the prince of Persia;
and when I have gone forth, indeed the
prince of Greece will come. 21But I will
tell you what is noted in the Scripture
of Truth. (No one upholds me against
these, except Michael your prince.

11 "Also in the first year of Darius
the Mede, I, *even* I, stood up to
confirm and strengthen him.) 2And now
I will tell you the truth: Behold, three
more kings will arise in Persia, and the
fourth shall be far richer than *them* all;
by his strength, through his riches, he
shall stir up all against the realm of
Greece. 3Then a mighty king shall arise,
who shall rule with great dominion, and
do according to his will. 4And when he
has arisen, his kingdom shall be broken
up and divided toward the four winds
of heaven, but not among his posterity
nor according to his dominion with
which he ruled; for his kingdom shall be
uprooted, even for others besides these.

Warring Kings of North and South

5"Also the king of the South shall
become strong, as well as *one* of his
princes; and he shall gain power over
him and have dominion. His dominion
shall be a great dominion. 6And at the
end of *some* years they shall join forces,
for the daughter of the king of the South
shall go to the king of the North to make
an agreement; but she shall not retain
the power of her authority,[a] and neither
he nor his authority[b] shall stand; but
she shall be given up, with those who
brought her, and with him who begot
her, and with him who strengthened
her in *those* times. 7But from a branch
of her roots *one* shall arise in his place,
who shall come with an army, enter
the fortress of the king of the North,
and deal with them and prevail. 8And
he shall also carry their gods captive
to Egypt, with their princes[a] *and* their
precious articles of silver and gold; and
he shall continue *more* years than the
king of the North.
9"Also *the king of the North* shall come
to the kingdom of the king of the South,
but shall return to his own land. 10How-
ever his sons shall stir up strife, and
assemble a multitude of great forces;
and *one* shall certainly come and over-
whelm and pass through; then he shall
return to his fortress and stir up strife.
11"And the king of the South shall be
moved with rage, and go out and fight
with him, with the king of the North,
who shall muster a great multitude;
but the multitude shall be given into
the hand of his *enemy.* 12When he has
taken away the multitude, his heart will
be lifted up; and he will cast down tens
of thousands, but he will not prevail.
13For the king of the North will return
and muster a multitude greater than
the former, and shall certainly come
at the end of some years with a great
army and much equipment.
14"Now in those times many shall
rise up against the king of the South.
Also, violent men[a] of your people shall
exalt themselves in fulfillment of the
vision, but they shall fall. 15So the king
of the North shall come and build a
siege mound, and take a fortified city;
and the forces[a] of the South shall not

10:16 [a] Theodotion and Vulgate read *the son;* Septuagint reads *a hand.* **11:6** [a] Literally *arm* [b] Literally *arm* **11:8** [a] Or *molded images* **11:14** [a] Or *robbers,* literally *sons of breakage* **11:15** [a] Literally *arms*

withstand *him.* Even his choice troops *shall have* no strength to resist. 16But he who comes against him shall do according to his own will, and no one shall stand against him. He shall stand in the Glorious Land with destruction in his power.[a]

17"He shall also set his face to enter with the strength of his whole kingdom, and upright ones[a] with him; thus shall he do. And he shall give him the daughter of women to destroy it; but she shall not stand *with him,* or be for him. 18After this he shall turn his face to the coastlands, and shall take many. But a ruler shall bring the reproach against them to an end; and with the reproach removed, he shall turn back on him. 19Then he shall turn his face toward the fortress of his own land; but he shall stumble and fall, and not be found.

20"There shall arise in his place one who imposes taxes *on* the glorious kingdom; but within a few days he shall be destroyed, but not in anger or in battle. 21And in his place shall arise a vile person, to whom they will not give the honor of royalty; but he shall come in peaceably, and seize the kingdom by intrigue. 22With the force[a] of a flood they shall be swept away from before him and be broken, and also the prince of the covenant. 23And after the league *is made* with him he shall act deceitfully, for he shall come up and become strong with a small *number of* people. 24He shall enter peaceably, even into the richest places of the province; and he shall do *what* his fathers have not done, nor his forefathers: he shall disperse among them the plunder, spoil, and riches; and he shall devise his plans against the strongholds, but *only* for a time.

25"He shall stir up his power and his courage against the king of the South with a great army. And the king of the South shall be stirred up to battle with a very great and mighty army; but he shall not stand, for they shall devise plans against him. 26Yes, those who eat of the portion of his delicacies shall destroy him; his army shall be swept away, and many shall fall down slain. 27Both these kings' hearts *shall be* bent on evil, and they shall speak lies at the same table; but it shall not prosper, for the end *will* still *be* at the appointed time. 28While returning to his land with great riches, his heart shall be *moved* against the holy covenant; so he shall do *damage* and return to his own land.

The Northern King's Blasphemies

29"At the appointed time he shall return and go toward the south; but it shall not be like the former or the latter. 30For ships from Cyprus[a] shall come against him; therefore he shall be grieved, and return in rage against the holy covenant, and do *damage.*

"So he shall return and show regard for those who forsake the holy covenant. 31And forces[a] shall be mustered by him, and they shall defile the sanctuary fortress; then they shall take away the daily *sacrifices,* and place *there* the abomination of desolation. 32Those who do wickedly against the covenant he shall corrupt with flattery; but the people who know their God shall be strong, and carry out *great exploits.* 33And those of the people who understand shall instruct many; yet *for many* days they shall fall by sword and flame, by captivity and plundering. 34Now when they fall, they shall be aided with a little help; but many shall join with them by intrigue. 35And *some* of those of understanding shall fall, to refine them, purify *them,* and make *them* white, *until* the time of the end; because *it is* still for the appointed time.

36"Then the king shall do according to his own will: he shall exalt and magnify himself above every god, shall speak blasphemies against the God of gods, and shall prosper till the wrath has been accomplished; for what has been determined shall be done. 37He shall regard neither the God[a] of his fathers nor the desire of women, nor regard any god; for he shall exalt himself above *them* all. 38But in their place he shall honor a god of fortresses; and a god which his fathers did not know he shall honor with gold and silver, with precious stones and pleasant things. 39Thus he shall act

11:16 [a] Literally *hand* **11:17** [a] Or *bring equitable terms* **11:22** [a] Literally *arms* **11:30** [a] Hebrew *Kittim,* western lands, especially Cyprus **11:31** [a] Literally *arms* **11:37** [a] Or *gods*

against the strongest fortresses with a
foreign god, which he shall acknowl-
edge, *and* advance *its* glory; and he
shall cause them to rule over many,
and divide the land for gain.

The Northern King's Conquests

40“At the time of the end the king of the
South shall attack him; and the king of
the North shall come against him like
a whirlwind, with chariots, horsemen,
and with many ships; and he shall enter
the countries, overwhelm *them,* and
pass through. 41He shall also enter the
Glorious Land, and many *countries* shall
be overthrown; but these shall escape
from his hand: Edom, Moab, and the
prominent people of Ammon. 42He
shall stretch out his hand against the
countries, and the land of Egypt shall
not escape. 43He shall have power over
the treasures of gold and silver, and
over all the precious things of Egypt;
also the Libyans and Ethiopians *shall*
follow at his heels. 44But news from the
east and the north shall trouble him;
therefore he shall go out with great fury
to destroy and annihilate many. 45And
he shall plant the tents of his palace
between the seas and the glorious holy
mountain; yet he shall come to his end,
and no one will help him.

Prophecy of the End Time

12 “At that time Michael shall
stand up,
The great prince who stands *watch*
over the sons of your people;
And there shall be a time of
trouble,
Such as never was since there was
a nation,
Even to that time.
And at that time your people
shall be delivered,
Every one who is found written in
the book.
2 And many of those who sleep in
the dust of the earth shall
awake,
Some to everlasting life,
Some to shame *and* everlasting
contempt.
3 Those who are wise shall shine
Like the brightness of the
firmament,
And those who turn many to
righteousness
Like the stars forever and ever.

4“But you, Daniel, shut up the words,
and seal the book until the time of the
end; many shall run to and fro, and
knowledge shall increase.”
5Then I, Daniel, looked; and there
stood two others, one on this riverbank
and the other on that riverbank. 6And
one said to the man clothed in linen,
who *was* above the waters of the river,
“How long shall the fulfillment of these
wonders *be?*”
7Then I heard the man clothed in linen,
who *was* above the waters of the river,
when he held up his right hand and his
left hand to heaven, and swore by Him
who lives forever, that *it shall be* for a
time, times, and half *a time;* and when
the power of the holy people has been
completely shattered, all these *things*
shall be finished.
8Although I heard, I did not under-
stand. Then I said, “My lord, what *shall*
be the end of these *things?*”
9And he said, “Go *your way,* Daniel,
for the words *are* closed up and sealed
till the time of the end. 10Many shall be
purified, made white, and refined, but
the wicked shall do wickedly; and none
of the wicked shall understand, but the
wise shall understand.
11“And from the time *that* the daily
sacrifice is taken away, and the abom-
ination of desolation is set up, *there*
shall be one thousand two hundred and
ninety days. 12Blessed *is* he who waits,
and comes to the one thousand three
hundred and thirty-five days.
13“But you, go *your way* till the end;
for you shall rest, and will arise to your
inheritance at the end of the days.”

THE BOOK OF HOSEA

Hosea ministers at the same time as Isaiah, just before Assyria would conquer the northern kingdom of Israel. God uses Hosea's family as a picture of His relationship with His people. When Hosea's wife becomes unfaithful to the prophet and leaves, God tells Hosea to restore their marriage. Hosea finds her and pays to secure her freedom. In this, Israel was given a picture of how they, like Hosea's wife, had been unfaithful to God, but He, like Hosea, was still faithful to them and would do what it takes to restore their relationship.

- **GENRE:** Minor Prophet
- **AUTHOR:** Hosea
- **TIME:** c. 755–710 BC
- **PURPOSE:** To remind Israel that God continues to be faithful to them even when they are unfaithful to God.

---

1 The word of the LORD that came to
Hosea the son of Beeri, in the days
of Uzziah, Jotham, Ahaz, *and* Hezekiah,
kings of Judah, and in the days of Jer-
oboam the son of Joash, king of Israel.

The Family of Hosea

2When the LORD began to speak by
Hosea, the LORD said to Hosea:

"Go, take yourself a wife of harlotry
And children of harlotry,
For the land has committed great
harlotry
By departing from the LORD."

3So he went and took Gomer the daugh-
ter of Diblaim, and she conceived and
bore him a son. 4Then the LORD said
to him:

"Call his name Jezreel,
For in a little *while*
I will avenge the bloodshed
of Jezreel on the house
of Jehu,
And bring an end to the kingdom
of the house of Israel.
5 It shall come to pass in that day
That I will break the bow of
Israel in the Valley of
Jezreel."

6And she conceived again and bore a
daughter. Then *God* said to him:

"Call her name Lo-Ruhamah,[a]
For I will no longer have mercy on
the house of Israel,
But I will utterly take them away.[b]
7 Yet I will have mercy on the house
of Judah,
Will save them by the LORD their
God,
And will not save them by bow,
Nor by sword or battle,
By horses or horsemen."

8Now when she had weaned Lo-Ru-
hamah, she conceived and bore a son.
9Then *God* said:

"Call his name Lo-Ammi,[a]
For you *are* not My people,
And I will not be your *God*.

The Restoration of Israel

10 "Yet the number of the children of
Israel
Shall be as the sand of the sea,
Which cannot be measured or
numbered.
And it shall come to pass
In the place where it was said to
them,

1:6 [a] Literally *No-Mercy* [b] Or *That I may forgive them at all* 1:9 [a] Literally *Not-My-People*

'You *are* not My people,'[a]
There it shall be said to them,
'*You are* sons of the living God.'
11 Then the children of Judah and the children of Israel
Shall be gathered together,
And appoint for themselves one head;
And they shall come up out of the land,
For great *will be* the day of Jezreel!

2 Say to your brethren, 'My people,'[a]
And to your sisters, 'Mercy[b] *is shown*.'

God's Unfaithful People

2 "Bring charges against your mother, bring charges;
For she *is* not My wife, nor *am* I her Husband!
Let her put away her harlotries from her sight,
And her adulteries from between her breasts;
3 Lest I strip her naked
And expose her, as in the day she was born,
And make her like a wilderness,
And set her like a dry land,
And slay her with thirst.

4 "I will not have mercy on her children,
For they *are* the children of harlotry.
5 For their mother has played the harlot;
She who conceived them has behaved shamefully.
For she said, 'I will go after my lovers,
Who give *me* my bread and my water,
My wool and my linen,
My oil and my drink.'

6 "Therefore, behold,
I will hedge up your way with thorns,
And wall her in,
So that she cannot find her paths.
7 She will chase her lovers,
But not overtake them;
Yes, she will seek them, but not find *them*.
Then she will say,
'I will go and return to my first husband,
For then *it was* better for me than now.'
8 For she did not know
That I gave her grain, new wine, and oil,
And multiplied her silver and gold—
Which they prepared for Baal.

9 "Therefore I will return and take away
My grain in its time
And My new wine in its season,
And will take back My wool and My linen,
Given to cover her nakedness.
10 Now I will uncover her lewdness in the sight of her lovers,
And no one shall deliver her from My hand.
11 I will also cause all her mirth to cease,
Her feast days,
Her New Moons,
Her Sabbaths—
All her appointed feasts.

12 "And I will destroy her vines and her fig trees,
Of which she has said,
'These *are* my wages that my lovers have given me.'
So I will make them a forest,
And the beasts of the field shall eat them.
13 I will punish her
For the days of the Baals to which she burned incense.
She decked herself with her earrings and jewelry,
And went after her lovers;
But Me she forgot," says the LORD.

God's Mercy on His People

14 "Therefore, behold, I will allure her,
Will bring her into the wilderness,
And speak comfort to her.

1:10 [a] Hebrew *lo-ammi* (compare verse 9) 2:1 [a] Hebrew *Ammi* (compare 1:9, 10) [b] Hebrew *Ruhamah* (compare 1:6)

15 I will give her her vineyards from
there,
And the Valley of Achor as a door
of hope;
She shall sing there,
As in the days of her youth,
As in the day when she came up
from the land of Egypt.

16 "And it shall be, in that day,"
Says the LORD,
"*That* you will call Me 'My Husband,'[a]
And no longer call Me 'My Master,'[b]
17 For I will take from her mouth the
names of the Baals,
And they shall be remembered by
their name no more.
18 In that day I will make a covenant
for them
With the beasts of the field,
With the birds of the air,
And *with* the creeping things of
the ground.
Bow and sword of battle I will
shatter from the earth,
To make them lie down safely.

19 "I will betroth you to Me forever;
Yes, I will betroth you to Me
In righteousness and justice,
In lovingkindness and mercy;
20 I will betroth you to Me in
faithfulness,
And you shall know the LORD.

21 "It shall come to pass in that day
That I will answer," says the LORD;
"I will answer the heavens,
And they shall answer the earth.
22 The earth shall answer
With grain,
With new wine,
And with oil;
They shall answer Jezreel.[a]
23 Then I will sow her for Myself in
the earth,
And I will have mercy on *her who
had* not obtained mercy;[a]
Then I will say to *those who were*
not My people,[b]
'You *are* My people!'
And they shall say, '*You are* my
God!' "

Israel Will Return to God

3 Then the LORD said to me, "Go
again, love a woman *who is* loved
by a lover[a] and is committing adultery,
just like the love of the LORD for the chil-
dren of Israel, who look to other gods
and love *the* raisin cakes *of the pagans*."
2 So I bought her for myself for fifteen
shekels of silver, and one and one-half
homers of barley. 3 And I said to her, "You
shall stay with me many days; you shall
not play the harlot, nor shall you have
a man—so, too, *will* I *be* toward you."
4 For the children of Israel shall abide
many days without king or prince, with-
out sacrifice or *sacred* pillar, without
ephod or teraphim. 5 Afterward the chil-
dren of Israel shall return and seek the
LORD their God and David their king.
They shall fear the LORD and His good-
ness in the latter days.

God's Charge Against Israel

4 Hear the word of the LORD,
You children of Israel,
For the LORD *brings* a charge
against the inhabitants of
the land:

"There is no truth or mercy
Or knowledge of God in the land.
2 *By* swearing and lying,
Killing and stealing and
committing adultery,
They break all restraint,
With bloodshed upon bloodshed.
3 Therefore the land will mourn;
And everyone who dwells there
will waste away
With the beasts of the field
And the birds of the air;
Even the fish of the sea will be
taken away.

4 "Now let no man contend, or rebuke
another;
For your people *are* like those who
contend with the priest.
5 Therefore you shall stumble in the
day;
The prophet also shall stumble
with you in the night;
And I will destroy your mother.

2:16 [a] Hebrew *Ishi* [b] Hebrew *Baali* 2:22 [a] Literally *God Will Sow* 2:23 [a] Hebrew *lo-ruhamah* [b] Hebrew *lo-ammi* 3:1 [a] Literally *friend* or *husband*

6 My people are destroyed for lack of knowledge.
Because you have rejected knowledge,
I also will reject you from being priest for Me;
Because you have forgotten the law of your God,
I also will forget your children.

7 "The more they increased,
The more they sinned against Me;
I will change[a] their glory[b] into shame.
8 They eat up the sin of My people;
They set their heart on their iniquity.
9 And it shall be: like people, like priest.
So I will punish them for their ways,
And reward them for their deeds.
10 For they shall eat, but not have enough;
They shall commit harlotry, but not increase;
Because they have ceased obeying the LORD.

The Idolatry of Israel

11 "Harlotry, wine, and new wine enslave the heart.
12 My people ask counsel from their wooden *idols*,
And their staff informs them.
For the spirit of harlotry has caused *them* to stray,
And they have played the harlot against their God.
13 They offer sacrifices on the mountaintops,
And burn incense on the hills,
Under oaks, poplars, and terebinths,
Because their shade *is* good.
Therefore your daughters commit harlotry,
And your brides commit adultery.

14 "I will not punish your daughters when they commit harlotry,
Nor your brides when they commit adultery;
For *the men* themselves go apart with harlots,
And offer sacrifices with a ritual harlot.[a]
Therefore people *who* do not understand will be trampled.

15 "Though you, Israel, play the harlot,
Let not Judah offend.
Do not come up to Gilgal,
Nor go up to Beth Aven,
Nor swear an oath, *saying,* 'As the LORD lives'—

16 "For Israel is stubborn
Like a stubborn calf;
Now the LORD will let them forage
Like a lamb in open country.

17 "Ephraim *is* joined to idols,
Let him alone.
18 Their drink is rebellion,
They commit harlotry continually.
Her rulers dearly[a] love dishonor.
19 The wind has wrapped her up in its wings,
And they shall be ashamed because of their sacrifices.

Impending Judgment on Israel and Judah

5 "Hear this, O priests!
Take heed, O house of Israel!
Give ear, O house of the king!
For yours *is* the judgment,
Because you have been a snare to Mizpah
And a net spread on Tabor.
2 The revolters are deeply involved in slaughter,
Though I rebuke them all.
3 I know Ephraim,
And Israel is not hidden from Me;
For now, O Ephraim, you commit harlotry;
Israel is defiled.

4 "They do not direct their deeds
Toward turning to their God,

4:7 [a] Following Masoretic Text, Septuagint, and Vulgate; scribal tradition, Syriac, and Targum read *They will change.* [b] Following Masoretic Text, Septuagint, Syriac, Targum, and Vulgate; scribal tradition reads *My glory.* **4:14** [a] Compare Deuteronomy 23:18 **4:18** [a] Hebrew is difficult; a Jewish tradition reads *Her rulers shamefully love, 'Give!'*

For the spirit of harlotry is in their
midst,
And they do not know the LORD.
5 The pride of Israel testifies to his
face;
Therefore Israel and Ephraim
stumble in their iniquity;
Judah also stumbles with them.

6 "With their flocks and herds
They shall go to seek the LORD,
But they will not find *Him;*
He has withdrawn Himself from
them.
7 They have dealt treacherously
with the LORD,
For they have begotten pagan
children.
Now a New Moon shall devour
them and their heritage.

8 "Blow the ram's horn in Gibeah,
The trumpet in Ramah!
Cry aloud *at* Beth Aven,
'*Look* behind you, O Benjamin!'
9 Ephraim shall be desolate in the
day of rebuke;
Among the tribes of Israel I make
known what is sure.

10 "The princes of Judah are like those
who remove a landmark;
I will pour out My wrath on them
like water.
11 Ephraim is oppressed *and* broken
in judgment,
Because he willingly walked by
human precept.
12 Therefore I *will be* to Ephraim like
a moth,
And to the house of Judah like
rottenness.

13 "When Ephraim saw his sickness,
And Judah *saw* his wound,
Then Ephraim went to Assyria
And sent to King Jareb;
Yet he cannot cure you,
Nor heal you of your wound.
14 For I *will be* like a lion to
Ephraim,
And like a young lion to the
house of Judah.
I, *even* I, will tear *them* and go
away;
I will take *them* away, and no one
shall rescue.
15 I will return again to My place
Till they acknowledge their
offense.
Then they will seek My face;
In their affliction they will
earnestly seek Me."

A Call to Repentance

6 Come, and let us return to the
LORD;
For He has torn, but He will
heal us;
He has stricken, but He will bind
us up.
2 After two days He will revive us;
On the third day He will raise
us up,
That we may live in His sight.
3 Let us know,
Let us pursue the knowledge of
the LORD.
His going forth is established as
the morning;
He will come to us like the rain,
Like the latter *and* former rain to
the earth.

Impenitence of Israel and Judah

4 "O Ephraim, what shall I do to you?
O Judah, what shall I do to you?
For your faithfulness is like a
morning cloud,
And like the early dew it goes
away.
5 Therefore I have hewn *them* by
the prophets,
I have slain them by the words of
My mouth;
And your judgments *are like* light
that goes forth.
6 For I desire mercy and not
sacrifice,
And the knowledge of God more
than burnt offerings.

7 "But like men[a] they transgressed
the covenant;
There they dealt treacherously
with Me.

6:7 [a] Or *like Adam*

8 Gilead *is* a city of evildoers
And defiled with blood.
9 As bands of robbers lie in wait for a man,
So the company of priests murder on the way to Shechem;
Surely they commit lewdness.
10 I have seen a horrible thing in the house of Israel:
There *is* the harlotry of Ephraim;
Israel is defiled.
11 Also, O Judah, a harvest is appointed for you,
When I return the captives of My people.

7 "When I would have healed Israel,
Then the iniquity of Ephraim was uncovered,
And the wickedness of Samaria.
For they have committed fraud;
A thief comes in;
A band of robbers takes spoil outside.
2 They do not consider in their hearts
That I remember all their wickedness;
Now their own deeds have surrounded them;
They are before My face.
3 They make a king glad with their wickedness,
And princes with their lies.

4 "They *are* all adulterers.
Like an oven heated by a baker—
He ceases stirring *the fire* after kneading the dough,
Until it is leavened.
5 In the day of our king
Princes have made *him* sick, inflamed with wine;
He stretched out his hand with scoffers.
6 They prepare their heart like an oven,
While they lie in wait;
Their baker[a] sleeps all night;
In the morning it burns like a flaming fire.
7 They are all hot, like an oven,
And have devoured their judges;
All their kings have fallen.
None among them calls upon Me.

8 "Ephraim has mixed himself among the peoples;
Ephraim is a cake unturned.
9 Aliens have devoured his strength,
But he does not know *it;*
Yes, gray hairs are here and there on him,
Yet he does not know *it.*
10 And the pride of Israel testifies to his face,
But they do not return to the LORD their God,
Nor seek Him for all this.

Futile Reliance on the Nations

11 "Ephraim also is like a silly dove, without sense—
They call to Egypt,
They go to Assyria.
12 Wherever they go, I will spread My net on them;
I will bring them down like birds of the air;
I will chastise them
According to what their congregation has heard.

13 "Woe to them, for they have fled from Me!
Destruction to them,
Because they have transgressed against Me!
Though I redeemed them,
Yet they have spoken lies against Me.
14 They did not cry out to Me with their heart
When they wailed upon their beds.

"They assemble together for[a] grain and new wine,
They rebel against Me;[b]
15 Though I disciplined *and* strengthened their arms,
Yet they devise evil against Me;

7:6 [a] Following Masoretic Text and Vulgate; Syriac and Targum read *Their anger;* Septuagint reads *Ephraim.* 7:14 [a] Following Masoretic Text and Targum; Vulgate reads *thought upon;* Septuagint reads *slashed themselves for* (compare 1 Kings 18:28). [b] Following Masoretic Text, Syriac, and Targum; Septuagint omits *They rebel against Me;* Vulgate reads *They departed from Me.*

16 They return, *but* not to the Most
High;[a]
They are like a treacherous bow.
Their princes shall fall by the
sword
For the cursings of their tongue.
This *shall be* their derision in the
land of Egypt.

The Apostasy of Israel

8 "*Set* the trumpet[a] to your mouth!
He shall come like an eagle
against the house of the
LORD,
Because they have transgressed
My covenant
And rebelled against My law.
2 Israel will cry to Me,
'My God, we know You!'
3 Israel has rejected the good;
The enemy will pursue him.

4 "They set up kings, but not by Me;
They made princes, but I did not
acknowledge *them*.
From their silver and gold
They made idols for themselves—
That they might be cut off.
5 Your calf is rejected, O Samaria!
My anger is aroused against
them—
How long until they attain to
innocence?
6 For from Israel *is* even this:
A workman made it, and it *is* not
God;
But the calf of Samaria shall be
broken to pieces.

7 "They sow the wind,
And reap the whirlwind.
The stalk has no bud;
It shall never produce meal.
If it should produce,
Aliens would swallow it up.
8 Israel is swallowed up;
Now they are among the Gentiles
Like a vessel in which *is* no
pleasure.
9 For they have gone up to Assyria,
Like a wild donkey alone
by itself;
Ephraim has hired lovers.
10 Yes, though they have hired
among the nations,
Now I will gather them;
And they shall sorrow a little,[a]
Because of the burden[b] of the
king of princes.

11 "Because Ephraim has made many
altars for sin,
They have become for him altars
for sinning.
12 I have written for him the great
things of My law,
But they were considered a
strange thing.
13 *For* the sacrifices of My offerings
they sacrifice flesh and eat *it*,
But the LORD does not accept
them.
Now He will remember their
iniquity and punish their
sins.
They shall return to Egypt.

14 "For Israel has forgotten his Maker,
And has built temples;[a]
Judah also has multiplied
fortified cities;
But I will send fire upon his cities,
And it shall devour his palaces."

Judgment of Israel's Sin

9 Do not rejoice, O Israel, with joy
like *other* peoples,
For you have played the harlot
against your God.
You have made love *for* hire on
every threshing floor.
2 The threshing floor and the
winepress
Shall not feed them,
And the new wine shall fail in her.

3 They shall not dwell in the LORD's
land,
But Ephraim shall return to
Egypt,
And shall eat unclean *things* in
Assyria.
4 They shall not offer wine *offerings*
to the LORD,
Nor shall their sacrifices be
pleasing to Him.

7:16 [a] Or *upward* 8:1 [a] Hebrew *shophar*, ram's horn 8:10 [a] Or *begin to diminish* [b] Or *oracle*
8:14 [a] Or *palaces*

It shall be like bread of mourners
to them;
All who eat it shall be defiled.
For their bread *shall be* for their
own life;
It shall not come into the house of
the LORD.

5 What will you do in the appointed
day,
And in the day of the feast of the
LORD?
6 For indeed they are gone because
of destruction.
Egypt shall gather them up;
Memphis shall bury them.
Nettles shall possess their
valuables of silver;
Thorns *shall be* in their tents.

7 The days of punishment have
come;
The days of recompense have
come.
Israel knows!
The prophet *is* a fool,
The spiritual man *is* insane,
Because of the greatness of your
iniquity and great enmity.
8 The watchman of Ephraim *is* with
my God;
But the prophet *is* a fowler's[a]
snare in all his ways—
Enmity in the house of his God.
9 They are deeply corrupted,
As in the days of Gibeah.
He will remember their iniquity;
He will punish their sins.

10 "I found Israel
Like grapes in the wilderness;
I saw your fathers
As the firstfruits on the fig tree in
its first season.
But they went to Baal Peor,
And separated themselves *to that*
shame;
They became an abomination like
the thing they loved.
11 *As for* Ephraim, their glory shall
fly away like a bird—
No birth, no pregnancy, and no
conception!
12 Though they bring up their
children,
Yet I will bereave them to the last
man.
Yes, woe to them when I depart
from them!
13 Just as I saw Ephraim like Tyre,
planted in a pleasant place,
So Ephraim will bring out his
children to the murderer."

14 Give them, O LORD—
What will You give?
Give them a miscarrying womb
And dry breasts!

15 "All their wickedness *is* in Gilgal,
For there I hated them.
Because of the evil of their deeds
I will drive them from My house;
I will love them no more.
All their princes *are* rebellious.
16 Ephraim is stricken,
Their root is dried up;
They shall bear no fruit.
Yes, were they to bear children,
I would kill the darlings of their
womb."

17 My God will cast them away,
Because they did not obey Him;
And they shall be wanderers
among the nations.

Israel's Sin and Captivity

10 Israel empties *his* vine;
He brings forth fruit for
himself.
According to the multitude of his
fruit
He has increased the altars;
According to the bounty of his
land
They have embellished *his sacred*
pillars.
2 Their heart is divided;
Now they are held guilty.
He will break down their altars;
He will ruin their *sacred* pillars.

3 For now they say,
"We have no king,
Because we did not fear the LORD.

9:8 [a] That is, one who catches birds in a trap or snare

And as for a king, what would he
do for us?"
4 They have spoken words,
Swearing falsely in making a
covenant.
Thus judgment springs up like
hemlock in the furrows of
the field.

5 The inhabitants of Samaria fear
Because of the calf[a] of
Beth Aven.
For its people mourn for it,
And its priests shriek for it—
Because its glory has departed
from it.
6 *The idol* also shall be carried to
Assyria
As a present for King Jareb.
Ephraim shall receive shame,
And Israel shall be ashamed of
his own counsel.

7 *As for* Samaria, her king is cut off
Like a twig on the water.
8 Also the high places of Aven, the
sin of Israel,
Shall be destroyed.
The thorn and thistle shall grow
on their altars;
They shall say to the mountains,
"Cover us!"
And to the hills, "Fall on us!"

9 "O Israel, you have sinned from the
days of Gibeah;
There they stood.
The battle in Gibeah against the
children of iniquity[a]
Did not overtake them.
10 When *it is* My desire, I will
chasten them.
Peoples shall be gathered against
them
When I bind them for their two
transgressions.[a]
11 Ephraim *is* a trained heifer
That loves to thresh *grain;*
But I harnessed her fair neck,
I will make Ephraim pull *a plow.*
Judah shall plow;
Jacob shall break his clods."

12 Sow for yourselves righteousness;
Reap in mercy;
Break up your fallow ground,
For *it is* time to seek the LORD,
Till He comes and rains
righteousness on you.
13 You have plowed wickedness;
You have reaped iniquity.
You have eaten the fruit of lies,
Because you trusted in your own
way,
In the multitude of your mighty
men.
14 Therefore tumult shall arise
among your people,
And all your fortresses shall be
plundered
As Shalman plundered Beth Arbel
in the day of battle—
A mother dashed in pieces upon
her children.
15 Thus it shall be done to you,
O Bethel,
Because of your great wickedness.
At dawn the king of Israel
Shall be cut off utterly.

God's Continuing Love for Israel

11 "When Israel *was* a child, I
loved him,
And out of Egypt I called
My son.
2 *As* they called them,[a]
So they went from them;[b]
They sacrificed to the Baals,
And burned incense to carved
images.

3 "I taught Ephraim to walk,
Taking them by their arms;[a]
But they did not know that I
healed them.
4 I drew them with gentle cords,[a]
With bands of love,

10:5 [a] Literally *calves* **10:9** [a] So read many Hebrew manuscripts, Septuagint, and Vulgate; Masoretic Text reads *unruliness.* **10:10** [a] Or *in their two habitations* **11:2** [a] Following Masoretic Text and Vulgate; Septuagint reads *Just as I called them;* Targum interprets as *I sent prophets to a thousand of them.* [b] Following Masoretic Text, Targum, and Vulgate; Septuagint reads *from My face.* **11:3** [a] Some Hebrew manuscripts, Septuagint, Syriac, and Vulgate read *My arms.* **11:4** [a] Literally *cords of a man*

And I was to them as those who
take the yoke from their
neck.[b]
I stooped *and* fed them.

5 "He shall not return to the land of
Egypt;
But the Assyrian shall be his king,
Because they refused to repent.
6 And the sword shall slash in his
cities,
Devour his districts,
And consume *them,*
Because of their own counsels.
7 My people are bent on
backsliding from Me.
Though they call to the Most
High,[a]
None at all exalt *Him.*

8 "How can I give you up, Ephraim?
How can I hand you over, Israel?
How can I make you like Admah?
How can I set you like Zeboiim?
My heart churns within Me;
My sympathy is stirred.
9 I will not execute the fierceness of
My anger;
I will not again destroy Ephraim.
For I *am* God, and not man,
The Holy One in your midst;
And I will not come with terror.[a]

10 "They shall walk after the LORD.
He will roar like a lion.
When He roars,
Then *His* sons shall come
trembling from the west;
11 They shall come trembling like a
bird from Egypt,
Like a dove from the land of
Assyria.
And I will let them dwell in their
houses,"
Says the LORD.

God's Charge Against Ephraim

12 "Ephraim has encircled Me with
lies,
And the house of Israel with
deceit;
But Judah still walks with God,
Even with the Holy One[a] *who is*
faithful.

12 "Ephraim feeds on the wind,
And pursues the east wind;
He daily increases lies and
desolation.
Also they make a covenant with
the Assyrians,
And oil is carried to Egypt.

2 "The LORD also *brings* a charge
against Judah,
And will punish Jacob according
to his ways;
According to his deeds He will
recompense him.
3 He took his brother by the heel in
the womb,
And in his strength he struggled
with God.[a]
4 Yes, he struggled with the Angel
and prevailed;
He wept, and sought favor from
Him.
He found Him *in* Bethel,
And there He spoke to us—
5 That is, the LORD God of hosts.
The LORD *is* His memorable
name.
6 So you, by *the help of* your God,
return;
Observe mercy and justice,
And wait on your God
continually.

7 "A cunning Canaanite!
Deceitful scales *are* in his hand;
He loves to oppress.
8 And Ephraim said,
'Surely I have become rich,
I have found wealth for myself;
In all my labors
They shall find in me no iniquity
that *is* sin.'

9 "But I *am* the LORD your God,
Ever since the land of Egypt;
I will again make you dwell in
tents,
As in the days of the appointed
feast.

11:4 [b] Literally *jaws* 11:7 [a] Or *upward* 11:9 [a] Or *I will not enter a city* 11:12 [a] Or *holy ones*
12:3 [a] Compare Genesis 32:28

10 I have also spoken by the prophets,
And have multiplied visions;
I have given symbols through the witness of the prophets."

11 Though Gilead *has* idols—
Surely they are vanity—
Though they sacrifice bulls in Gilgal,
Indeed their altars *shall be* heaps in the furrows of the field.

12 Jacob fled to the country of Syria;
Israel served for a spouse,
And for a wife he tended *sheep.*
13 By a prophet the LORD brought Israel out of Egypt,
And by a prophet he was preserved.
14 Ephraim provoked *Him* to anger most bitterly;
Therefore his Lord will leave the guilt of his bloodshed upon him,
And return his reproach upon him.

Relentless Judgment on Israel

13 When Ephraim spoke, trembling,
He exalted *himself* in Israel;
But when he offended through Baal *worship,* he died.
2 Now they sin more and more,
And have made for themselves molded images,
Idols of their silver, according to their skill;
All of it *is* the work of craftsmen.
They say of them,
"Let the men who sacrifice[a] kiss the calves!"
3 Therefore they shall be like the morning cloud
And like the early dew that passes away,
Like chaff blown off from a threshing floor
And like smoke from a chimney.

4 "Yet I *am* the LORD your God
Ever since the land of Egypt,
And you shall know no God but Me;
For *there is* no savior besides Me.
5 I knew you in the wilderness,
In the land of great drought.
6 When they had pasture, they were filled;
They were filled and their heart was exalted;
Therefore they forgot Me.

7 "So I will be to them like a lion;
Like a leopard by the road I will lurk;
8 I will meet them like a bear deprived *of her cubs;*
I will tear open their rib cage,
And there I will devour them like a lion.
The wild beast shall tear them.

9 "O Israel, you are destroyed,[a]
But your help[b] *is* from Me.
10 I will be your King;[a]
Where *is any other,*
That he may save you in all your cities?
And your judges to whom you said,
'Give me a king and princes'?
11 I gave you a king in My anger,
And took *him* away in My wrath.

12 "The iniquity of Ephraim *is* bound up;
His sin *is* stored up.
13 The sorrows of a woman in childbirth shall come upon him.
He *is* an unwise son,
For he should not stay long where children are born.

14 "I will ransom them from the power of the grave;[a]
I will redeem them from death.
O Death, I will be your plagues![b]
O Grave,[c] I will be your destruction![d]
Pity is hidden from My eyes."

13:2 [a] Or *those who offer human sacrifice* 13:9 [a] Literally *it* or *he destroyed you* [b] Literally *in your help* 13:10 [a] Septuagint, Syriac, Targum, and Vulgate read *Where is your king?* 13:14 [a] Or *Sheol* [b] Septuagint reads *where is your punishment?* [c] Or *Sheol* [d] Septuagint reads *where is your sting?*

15 Though he is fruitful among *his* brethren,
An east wind shall come;
The wind of the LORD shall come up from the wilderness.
Then his spring shall become dry,
And his fountain shall be dried up.
He shall plunder the treasury of every desirable prize.
16 Samaria is held guilty,[a]
For she has rebelled against her God.
They shall fall by the sword,
Their infants shall be dashed in pieces,
And their women with child ripped open.

Israel Restored at Last

14 O Israel, return to the LORD your God,
For you have stumbled because of your iniquity;
2 Take words with you,
And return to the LORD.
Say to Him,
"Take away all iniquity;
Receive *us* graciously,
For we will offer the sacrifices[a] of our lips.
3 Assyria shall not save us,
We will not ride on horses,
Nor will we say anymore to the work of our hands, '*You are* our gods.'
For in You the fatherless finds mercy."

4 "I will heal their backsliding,
I will love them freely,
For My anger has turned away from him.
5 I will be like the dew to Israel;
He shall grow like the lily,
And lengthen his roots like Lebanon.
6 His branches shall spread;
His beauty shall be like an olive tree,
And his fragrance like Lebanon.
7 Those who dwell under his shadow shall return;
They shall be revived *like* grain,
And grow like a vine.
Their scent[a] *shall be* like the wine of Lebanon.

8 "Ephraim *shall say,* 'What have I to do anymore with idols?'
I have heard and observed him.
I *am* like a green cypress tree;
Your fruit is found in Me."

9 Who *is* wise?
Let him understand these things.
Who is prudent?
Let him know them.
For the ways of the LORD *are* right;
The righteous walk in them,
But transgressors stumble in them.

13:16 [a] Septuagint reads *shall be disfigured* **14:2** [a] Literally *bull calves;* Septuagint reads *fruit.*
14:7 [a] Literally *remembrance*

THE BOOK OF JOEL

The Book of Joel tells the story of a horrible locust plague in Judah. For a society that was so dependent on farming, crops are life itself. A locust plague like the one in Joel was a serious national disaster, which could lead to famine and death. In this plague, Joel sees a sign of God's final judgment that is to come. As bad as this plague was, it was not nearly as bad as that future day of judgment known as the "day of the LORD." God's people had to turn back to God and prepare for this day. It would be a day of judgment or a day of blessing depending on where one stands with God.

- **GENRE:** Minor Prophet
- **AUTHOR:** Joel
- **TIME:** c. 835–796 BC
- **PURPOSE:** To warn of the coming day of judgment, called the "day of the LORD."

---

1 The word of the LORD that came to Joel the son of Pethuel.

The Land Laid Waste

2 Hear this, you elders,
And give ear, all you inhabitants of the land!
Has *anything like* this happened in your days,
Or even in the days of your fathers?
3 Tell your children about it,
Let your children *tell* their children,
And their children another generation.

4 What the chewing locust[a] left, the swarming locust has eaten;
What the swarming locust left, the crawling locust has eaten;
And what the crawling locust left, the consuming locust has eaten.

5 Awake, you drunkards, and weep;
And wail, all you drinkers of wine,
Because of the new wine,
For it has been cut off from your mouth.
6 For a nation has come up against My land,
Strong, and without number;
His teeth *are* the teeth of a lion,
And he has the fangs of a fierce lion.
7 He has laid waste My vine,
And ruined My fig tree;
He has stripped it bare and thrown *it* away;
Its branches are made white.

8 Lament like a virgin girded with sackcloth
For the husband of her youth.
9 The grain offering and the drink offering
Have been cut off from the house of the LORD;
The priests mourn, who minister to the LORD.
10 The field is wasted,
The land mourns;
For the grain is ruined,
The new wine is dried up,
The oil fails.

11 Be ashamed, you farmers,
Wail, you vinedressers,
For the wheat and the barley;
Because the harvest of the field has perished.
12 The vine has dried up,
And the fig tree has withered;
The pomegranate tree,
The palm tree also,

1:4 [a] Exact identity of these locusts is unknown.

And the apple tree—
All the trees of the field are
withered;
Surely joy has withered away
from the sons of men.

Mourning for the Land

13 Gird yourselves and lament, you
priests;
Wail, you who minister before the
altar;
Come, lie all night in sackcloth,
You who minister to my God;
For the grain offering and the
drink offering
Are withheld from the house of
your God.
14 Consecrate a fast,
Call a sacred assembly;
Gather the elders
And all the inhabitants of the land
Into the house of the LORD your
God,
And cry out to the LORD.

15 Alas for the day!
For the day of the LORD *is* at hand;
It shall come as destruction from
the Almighty.
16 Is not the food cut off before our
eyes,
Joy and gladness from the house
of our God?
17 The seed shrivels under the clods,
Storehouses are in shambles;
Barns are broken down,
For the grain has withered.
18 How the animals groan!
The herds of cattle are restless,
Because they have no pasture;
Even the flocks of sheep suffer
punishment.[a]

19 O LORD, to You I cry out;
For fire has devoured the open
pastures,
And a flame has burned all the
trees of the field.
20 The beasts of the field also cry out
to You,
For the water brooks are dried up,
And fire has devoured the open
pastures.

The Day of the LORD

2 Blow the trumpet in Zion,
And sound an alarm in My holy
mountain!
Let all the inhabitants of the land
tremble;
For the day of the LORD is coming,
For it is at hand:
2 A day of darkness and
gloominess,
A day of clouds and thick
darkness,
Like the morning *clouds* spread
over the mountains.
A people *come,* great and strong,
The like of whom has never been;
Nor will there ever be any *such*
after them,
Even for many successive
generations.

3 A fire devours before them,
And behind them a flame burns;
The land *is* like the Garden of
Eden before them,
And behind them a desolate
wilderness;
Surely nothing shall escape them.
4 Their appearance is like the
appearance of horses;
And like swift steeds, so they run.
5 With a noise like chariots
Over mountaintops they leap,
Like the noise of a flaming fire
that devours the stubble,
Like a strong people set in battle
array.

6 Before them the people writhe in
pain;
All faces are drained of color.[a]
7 They run like mighty men,
They climb the wall like men of
war;
Every one marches in formation,
And they do not break ranks.
8 They do not push one another;
Every one marches in his own
column.[a]
Though they lunge between the
weapons,
They are not cut down.[b]
9 They run to and fro in the city,

1:18 [a] Septuagint and Vulgate read *are made desolate.* **2:6** [a] Septuagint, Targum, and Vulgate read *gather blackness.* **2:8** [a] Literally *his own highway* [b] That is, they are not halted by losses

They run on the wall;
They climb into the houses,
They enter at the windows like a thief.

10 The earth quakes before them,
The heavens tremble;
The sun and moon grow dark,
And the stars diminish their brightness.
11 The LORD gives voice before His army,
For His camp is very great;
For strong *is the One* who executes His word.
For the day of the LORD *is* great and very terrible;
Who can endure it?

A Call to Repentance

12 "Now, therefore," says the LORD,
"Turn to Me with all your heart,
With fasting, with weeping, and with mourning."
13 So rend your heart, and not your garments;
Return to the LORD your God,
For He *is* gracious and merciful,
Slow to anger, and of great kindness;
And He relents from doing harm.
14 Who knows *if* He will turn and relent,
And leave a blessing behind Him—
A grain offering and a drink offering
For the LORD your God?

15 Blow the trumpet in Zion,
Consecrate a fast,
Call a sacred assembly;
16 Gather the people,
Sanctify the congregation,
Assemble the elders,
Gather the children and nursing babes;
Let the bridegroom go out from his chamber,
And the bride from her dressing room.
17 Let the priests, who minister to the LORD,
Weep between the porch and the altar;
Let them say, "Spare Your people, O LORD,
And do not give Your heritage to reproach,
That the nations should rule over them.
Why should they say among the peoples,
'Where *is* their God?' "

The Land Refreshed

18 Then the LORD will be zealous for His land,
And pity His people.
19 The LORD will answer and say to His people,
"Behold, I will send you grain and new wine and oil,
And you will be satisfied by them;
I will no longer make you a reproach among the nations.

20 "But I will remove far from you the northern *army,*
And will drive him away into a barren and desolate land,
With his face toward the eastern sea
And his back toward the western sea;
His stench will come up,
And his foul odor will rise,
Because he has done monstrous things."

21 Fear not, O land;
Be glad and rejoice,
For the LORD has done marvelous things!
22 Do not be afraid, you beasts of the field;
For the open pastures are springing up,
And the tree bears its fruit;
The fig tree and the vine yield their strength.
23 Be glad then, you children of Zion,
And rejoice in the LORD your God;
For He has given you the former rain faithfully,[a]

2:23 [a] Or *the teacher of righteousness*

And He will cause the rain to
come down for you—
The former rain,
And the latter rain in the first
month.
24 The threshing floors shall be full
of wheat,
And the vats shall overflow with
new wine and oil.

25 "So I will restore to you the years
that the swarming locust has
eaten,
The crawling locust,
The consuming locust,
And the chewing locust,[a]
My great army which I sent
among you.
26 You shall eat in plenty and be
satisfied,
And praise the name of the LORD
your God,
Who has dealt wondrously with
you;
And My people shall never be put
to shame.
27 Then you shall know that I *am* in
the midst of Israel:
I *am* the LORD your God
And there is no other.
My people shall never be put to
shame.

God's Spirit Poured Out

28 "And it shall come to pass afterward
That I will pour out My Spirit on
all flesh;
Your sons and your daughters
shall prophesy,
Your old men shall dream
dreams,
Your young men shall see visions.
29 And also on *My* menservants and
on *My* maidservants
I will pour out My Spirit in those
days.

30 "And I will show wonders in the
heavens and in the earth:
Blood and fire and pillars of
smoke.
31 The sun shall be turned into
darkness,
And the moon into blood,
Before the coming of the great
and awesome day of the
LORD.
32 And it shall come to pass
That whoever calls on the name of
the LORD
Shall be saved.
For in Mount Zion and in
Jerusalem there shall be
deliverance,
As the LORD has said,
Among the remnant whom the
LORD calls.

God Judges the Nations

3 "For behold, in those days and at
that time,
When I bring back the captives of
Judah and Jerusalem,
2 I will also gather all nations,
And bring them down to the
Valley of Jehoshaphat;
And I will enter into judgment
with them there
On account of My people, My
heritage Israel,
Whom they have scattered
among the nations;
They have also divided up My
land.
3 They have cast lots for My people,
Have given a boy *as payment* for a
harlot,
And sold a girl for wine, that they
may drink.

4 "Indeed, what have you to do
with Me,
O Tyre and Sidon, and all the
coasts of Philistia?
Will you retaliate against Me?
But if you retaliate against Me,
Swiftly and speedily I will return
your retaliation upon your
own head;
5 Because you have taken My silver
and My gold,
And have carried into your
temples My prized
possessions.
6 Also the people of Judah and the
people of Jerusalem

2:25 [a] Compare 1:4

You have sold to the Greeks,
That you may remove them far
from their borders.

7 "Behold, I will raise them
Out of the place to which you
have sold them,
And will return your retaliation
upon your own head.
8 I will sell your sons and your
daughters
Into the hand of the people of
Judah,
And they will sell them to the
Sabeans,[a]
To a people far off;
For the LORD has spoken."

9 Proclaim this among the nations:
"Prepare for war!
Wake up the mighty men,
Let all the men of war draw near,
Let them come up.
10 Beat your plowshares into swords
And your pruning hooks into
spears;
Let the weak say, 'I *am* strong.' "
11 Assemble and come, all you
nations,
And gather together all around.
Cause Your mighty ones to go
down there, O LORD.
12 "Let the nations be wakened, and
come up to the Valley of
Jehoshaphat;
For there I will sit to judge all the
surrounding nations.
13 Put in the sickle, for the harvest is
ripe.
Come, go down;
For the winepress is full,
The vats overflow—
For their wickedness *is* great."

14 Multitudes, multitudes in the
valley of decision!
For the day of the LORD *is* near in
the valley of decision.
15 The sun and moon will grow dark,
And the stars will diminish their
brightness.
16 The LORD also will roar from Zion,
And utter His voice from
Jerusalem;
The heavens and earth will shake;
But the LORD will be a shelter for
His people,
And the strength of the children
of Israel.

17 "So you shall know that I *am* the
LORD your God,
Dwelling in Zion My holy
mountain.
Then Jerusalem shall be holy,
And no aliens shall ever pass
through her again."

God Blesses His People

18 And it will come to pass in that
day
That the mountains shall drip
with new wine,
The hills shall flow with milk,
And all the brooks of Judah shall
be flooded with water;
A fountain shall flow from the
house of the LORD
And water the Valley of Acacias.

19 "Egypt shall be a desolation,
And Edom a desolate wilderness,
Because of violence *against* the
people of Judah,
For they have shed innocent
blood in their land.
20 But Judah shall abide forever,
And Jerusalem from generation
to generation.
21 For I will acquit them of the guilt
of bloodshed, whom I had
not acquitted;
For the LORD dwells in Zion."

3:8 [a] Literally *Shebaites* (compare Isaiah 60:6 and Ezekiel 27:22)

THE BOOK OF

AMOS

Amos ministers at the same time as Isaiah and Hosea. He is a farmer from Judah who God sends to Israel. There, he warns the people against neglecting God, mistreating the poor, and practicing hollow worship. The nation of Israel was like a basket of rotting fruit, ready to be judged by God. For those who loved God, however, Amos offers hope. The day was coming when David's kingdom would come back, and God's people would live in safety.

- **GENRE:** Minor Prophet
- **AUTHOR:** Amos
- **TIME:** c. 760–755 BC
- **PURPOSE:** To warn of the grave dangers of forgetting about God and mistreating one another.

---

1 The words of Amos, who was among
the sheepbreeders[a] of Tekoa, which
he saw concerning Israel in the days of
Uzziah king of Judah, and in the days
of Jeroboam the son of Joash, king of
Israel, two years before the earthquake.
2 And he said:

"The LORD roars from Zion,
And utters His voice from Jerusalem;
The pastures of the shepherds mourn,
And the top of Carmel withers."

Judgment on the Nations

3 Thus says the LORD:

"For three transgressions of Damascus, and for four,
I will not turn away its *punishment*,
Because they have threshed Gilead with implements of iron.
4 But I will send a fire into the house of Hazael,
Which shall devour the palaces of Ben-Hadad.
5 I will also break the *gate* bar of Damascus,
And cut off the inhabitant from the Valley of Aven,
And the one who holds the scepter from Beth Eden.
The people of Syria shall go captive to Kir,"
Says the LORD.

6 Thus says the LORD:

"For three transgressions of Gaza, and for four,
I will not turn away its *punishment*,
Because they took captive the whole captivity
To deliver *them* up to Edom.
7 But I will send a fire upon the wall of Gaza,
Which shall devour its palaces.
8 I will cut off the inhabitant from Ashdod,
And the one who holds the scepter from Ashkelon;
I will turn My hand against Ekron,
And the remnant of the Philistines shall perish,"
Says the Lord GOD.

9 Thus says the LORD:

"For three transgressions of Tyre, and for four,
I will not turn away its *punishment*,

1:1 [a] Compare 2 Kings 3:4

Because they delivered up the
whole captivity to Edom,
And did not remember the
covenant of brotherhood.
10 But I will send a fire upon the wall
of Tyre,
Which shall devour its palaces."

11Thus says the LORD:

"For three transgressions of Edom,
and for four,
I will not turn away its
punishment,
Because he pursued his brother
with the sword,
And cast off all pity;
His anger tore perpetually,
And he kept his wrath forever.
12 But I will send a fire upon Teman,
Which shall devour the palaces of
Bozrah."

13Thus says the LORD:

"For three transgressions of the
people of Ammon, and for
four,
I will not turn away its
punishment,
Because they ripped open the
women with child in Gilead,
That they might enlarge their
territory.
14 But I will kindle a fire in the wall
of Rabbah,
And it shall devour its palaces,
Amid shouting in the day of
battle,
And a tempest in the day of the
whirlwind.
15 Their king shall go into captivity,
He and his princes together,"
Says the LORD.

2 Thus says the LORD:

"For three transgressions of Moab,
and for four,
I will not turn away its
punishment,
Because he burned the bones of
the king of Edom to lime.
2 But I will send a fire upon Moab,
And it shall devour the palaces of
Kerioth;
Moab shall die with tumult,
With shouting *and* trumpet sound.
3 And I will cut off the judge from
its midst,
And slay all its princes with him,"
Says the LORD.

Judgment on Judah

4Thus says the LORD:

"For three transgressions of Judah,
and for four,
I will not turn away its *punishment,*
Because they have despised the
law of the LORD,
And have not kept His
commandments.
Their lies lead them astray,
Lies which their fathers followed.
5 But I will send a fire upon Judah,
And it shall devour the palaces of
Jerusalem."

Judgment on Israel

6Thus says the LORD:

"For three transgressions of Israel,
and for four,
I will not turn away its *punishment,*
Because they sell the righteous
for silver,
And the poor for a pair of sandals.
7 They pant after[a] the dust of the
earth *which is* on the head of
the poor,
And pervert the way of the
humble.
A man and his father go in to the
same girl,
To defile My holy name.
8 They lie down by every altar on
clothes taken in pledge,
And drink the wine of the
condemned *in* the house of
their god.
9 "Yet *it was* I *who* destroyed the
Amorite before them,
Whose height *was* like the height
of the cedars,

2:7 [a] Or *trample on*

And he *was as* strong as the oaks;
Yet I destroyed his fruit above
And his roots beneath.
10 Also *it was* I *who* brought you up
from the land of Egypt,
And led you forty years through
the wilderness,
To possess the land of the
Amorite.
11 I raised up some of your sons as
prophets,
And some of your young men as
Nazirites.
Is it not so, O you children of
Israel?"
Says the LORD.
12 "But you gave the Nazirites wine to
drink,
And commanded the prophets
saying,
'Do not prophesy!'
13 "Behold, I am weighed down by
you,
As a cart full of sheaves is
weighed down.
14 Therefore flight shall perish from
the swift,
The strong shall not strengthen
his power,
Nor shall the mighty deliver
himself;
15 He shall not stand who handles
the bow,
The swift of foot shall not escape,
Nor shall he who rides a horse
deliver himself.
16 The most courageous men of
might
Shall flee naked in that day,"
Says the LORD.

Authority of the Prophet's Message

3 Hear this word that the LORD has
spoken against you, O children of
Israel, against the whole family which
I brought up from the land of Egypt,
saying:

2 "You only have I known of all the
families of the earth;
Therefore I will punish you for all
your iniquities."
3 Can two walk together, unless
they are agreed?
4 Will a lion roar in the forest, when
he has no prey?
Will a young lion cry out of
his den, if he has caught
nothing?
5 Will a bird fall into a snare on the
earth, where there is no trap
for it?
Will a snare spring up from
the earth, if it has caught
nothing at all?
6 If a trumpet is blown in a city, will
not the people be afraid?
If there is calamity in a city, will
not the LORD have done *it?*

7 Surely the Lord GOD does nothing,
Unless He reveals His secret to
His servants the prophets.
8 A lion has roared!
Who will not fear?
The Lord GOD has spoken!
Who can but prophesy?

Punishment of Israel's Sins

9 "Proclaim in the palaces at Ashdod,[a]
And in the palaces in the land of
Egypt, and say:
'Assemble on the mountains of
Samaria;
See great tumults in her midst,
And the oppressed within her.
10 For they do not know to do right,'
Says the LORD,
'Who store up violence and robbery
in their palaces.'"

11 Therefore thus says the Lord GOD:

"An adversary *shall be* all around
the land;
He shall sap your strength from
you,
And your palaces shall be
plundered."

12 Thus says the LORD:

"As a shepherd takes from the
mouth of a lion
Two legs or a piece of an ear,

3:9 [a] Following Masoretic Text; Septuagint reads *Assyria.*

So shall the children of Israel be
taken out
Who dwell in Samaria—
In the corner of a bed and on the
edge[a] of a couch!
13 Hear and testify against the
house of Jacob,"
Says the Lord GOD, the God of
hosts,
14 "That in the day I punish Israel for
their transgressions,
I will also visit *destruction* on the
altars of Bethel;
And the horns of the altar shall be
cut off
And fall to the ground.
15 I will destroy the winter house
along with the summer
house;
The houses of ivory shall perish,
And the great houses shall have
an end,"
Says the LORD.

4 Hear this word, you cows of
Bashan, who *are* on the
mountain of Samaria,
Who oppress the poor,
Who crush the needy,
Who say to your husbands,[a]
"Bring *wine*, let us drink!"
2 The Lord GOD has sworn by His
holiness:
"Behold, the days shall come upon
you
When He will take you away with
fishhooks,
And your posterity with fishhooks.
3 You will go out *through* broken
walls,
Each one straight ahead of her,
And you will be cast into Harmon,"
Says the LORD.

4 "Come to Bethel and transgress,
At Gilgal multiply transgression;
Bring your sacrifices every
morning,
Your tithes every three days.[a]
5 Offer a sacrifice of thanksgiving
with leaven,
Proclaim *and* announce the
freewill offerings;
For this you love,
You children of Israel!"
Says the Lord GOD.

Israel Did Not Accept Correction

6 "Also I gave you cleanness of teeth
in all your cities,
And lack of bread in all your
places;
Yet you have not returned to Me,"
Says the LORD.

7 "I also withheld rain from you,
When *there were* still three
months to the harvest.
I made it rain on one city,
I withheld rain from another city.
One part was rained upon,
And where it did not rain the part
withered.
8 So two *or* three cities wandered to
another city to drink water,
But they were not satisfied;
Yet you have not returned to Me,"
Says the LORD.

9 "I blasted you with blight and
mildew.
When your gardens increased,
Your vineyards,
Your fig trees,
And your olive trees,
The locust devoured *them*;
Yet you have not returned to Me,"
Says the LORD.

10 "I sent among you a plague after
the manner of Egypt;
Your young men I killed with a
sword,
Along with your captive horses;
I made the stench of your camps
come up into your nostrils;
Yet you have not returned to Me,"
Says the LORD.

11 "I overthrew *some* of you,
As God overthrew Sodom and
Gomorrah,
And you were like a firebrand
plucked from the burning;
Yet you have not returned to Me,"
Says the LORD.

3:12 [a] The Hebrew is uncertain. 4:1 [a] Literally *their lords* or *their masters* 4:4 [a] Or *years* (compare Deuteronomy 14:28)

12 "Therefore thus will I do to you,
O Israel;
Because I will do this to you,
Prepare to meet your God,
O Israel!"

13 For behold,
He who forms mountains,
And creates the wind,
Who declares to man what his[a]
thought *is,*
And makes the morning darkness,
Who treads the high places of the
earth—
The LORD God of hosts *is* His name.

A Lament for Israel

5 Hear this word which I take up against you, a lamentation, O house of Israel:

2 The virgin of Israel has fallen;
She will rise no more.
She lies forsaken on her land;
There is no one to raise her up.

3For thus says the Lord GOD:

"The city that goes out by a
thousand
Shall have a hundred left,
And that which goes out by a
hundred
Shall have ten left to the house of
Israel."

A Call to Repentance

4For thus says the LORD to the house of Israel:

"Seek Me and live;
5 But do not seek Bethel,
Nor enter Gilgal,
Nor pass over to Beersheba;
For Gilgal shall surely go into
captivity,
And Bethel shall come to nothing.
6 Seek the LORD and live,
Lest He break out like fire *in* the
house of Joseph,
And devour *it,*
With no one to quench *it* in
Bethel—
7 You who turn justice to
wormwood,
And lay righteousness to rest in
the earth!"

8 He made the Pleiades and Orion;
He turns the shadow of death into
morning
And makes the day dark as night;
He calls for the waters of the sea
And pours them out on the face of
the earth;
The LORD *is* His name.
9 He rains ruin upon the strong,
So that fury comes upon the
fortress.

10 They hate the one who rebukes in
the gate,
And they abhor the one who
speaks uprightly.
11 Therefore, because you tread
down the poor
And take grain taxes from him,
Though you have built houses of
hewn stone,
Yet you shall not dwell in them;
You have planted pleasant
vineyards,
But you shall not drink wine from
them.
12 For I know your manifold
transgressions
And your mighty sins:
Afflicting the just *and* taking
bribes;
Diverting the poor *from justice* at
the gate.
13 Therefore the prudent keep silent
at that time,
For it *is* an evil time.

14 Seek good and not evil,
That you may live;
So the LORD God of hosts will be
with you,
As you have spoken.
15 Hate evil, love good;
Establish justice in the gate.
It may be that the LORD God of
hosts
Will be gracious to the remnant of
Joseph.

4:13 [a] Or *His*

The Day of the LORD

16Therefore the LORD God of hosts, the Lord, says this:

"*There shall be* wailing in all streets,
And they shall say in all the highways,
'Alas! Alas!'
They shall call the farmer to mourning,
And skillful lamenters to wailing.
17 In all vineyards *there shall be* wailing,
For I will pass through you,"
Says the LORD.

18 Woe to you who desire the day of the LORD!
For what good *is* the day of the LORD to you?
It *will be* darkness, and not light.
19 It *will be* as though a man fled from a lion,
And a bear met him!
Or *as though* he went into the house,
Leaned his hand on the wall,
And a serpent bit him!
20 *Is* not the day of the LORD darkness, and not light?
Is it not very dark, with no brightness in it?

21 "I hate, I despise your feast days,
And I do not savor your sacred assemblies.
22 Though you offer Me burnt offerings and your grain offerings,
I will not accept *them*,
Nor will I regard your fattened peace offerings.
23 Take away from Me the noise of your songs,
For I will not hear the melody of your stringed instruments.
24 But let justice run down like water,
And righteousness like a mighty stream.

25 "Did you offer Me sacrifices and offerings
In the wilderness forty years,
O house of Israel?
26 You also carried Sikkuth[a] your king[b]
And Chiun,[c] your idols,
The star of your gods,
Which you made for yourselves.
27 Therefore I will send you into captivity beyond Damascus,"
Says the LORD, whose name *is* the God of hosts.

Warnings to Zion and Samaria

6 Woe to you *who are* at ease in Zion,
And trust in Mount Samaria,
Notable persons in the chief nation,
To whom the house of Israel comes!
2 Go over to Calneh and see;
And from there go to Hamath the great;
Then go down to Gath of the Philistines.
Are you better than these kingdoms?
Or is their territory greater than your territory?

3 *Woe to* you who put far off the day of doom,
Who cause the seat of violence to come near;
4 Who lie on beds of ivory,
Stretch out on your couches,
Eat lambs from the flock
And calves from the midst of the stall;
5 Who sing idly to the sound of stringed instruments,
And invent for yourselves musical instruments like David;
6 Who drink wine from bowls,
And anoint yourselves with the best ointments,
But are not grieved for the affliction of Joseph.
7 Therefore they shall now go captive as the first of the captives,
And those who recline at banquets shall be removed.

5:26 [a] A pagan deity [b] Septuagint and Vulgate read *tabernacle of Moloch.* [c] A pagan deity

8 The Lord GOD has sworn by
Himself,
The LORD God of hosts says:
"I abhor the pride of Jacob,
And hate his palaces;
Therefore I will deliver up *the* city
And all that is in it."

9Then it shall come to pass, that if ten
men remain in one house, they shall
die. 10And when a relative *of the dead,*
with one who will burn *the bodies,* picks
up the bodies[a] to take them out of the
house, he will say to one inside the
house, "*Are there* any more with you?"
Then someone will say, "None."
And he will say, "Hold your tongue!
For we dare not mention the name of
the LORD."

11 For behold, the LORD gives a
command:
He will break the great house into
bits,
And the little house into pieces.

12 Do horses run on rocks?
Does *one* plow *there* with oxen?
Yet you have turned justice into
gall,
And the fruit of righteousness
into wormwood,
13 You who rejoice over Lo Debar,[a]
Who say, "Have we not taken
Karnaim[b] for ourselves
By our own strength?"

14 "But, behold, I will raise up a nation
against you,
O house of Israel,"
Says the LORD God of hosts;
"And they will afflict you from the
entrance of Hamath
To the Valley of the Arabah."

Vision of the Locusts

7 Thus the Lord GOD showed me: Be-
hold, He formed locust swarms at
the beginning of the late crop; indeed *it*
was the late crop after the king's mow-
ings. 2And so it was, when they had
finished eating the grass of the land,
that I said:

"O Lord GOD, forgive, I pray!
Oh, that Jacob may stand,
For he *is* small!"
3 *So* the LORD relented concerning
this.
"It shall not be," said the LORD.

Vision of the Fire

4Thus the Lord GOD showed me: Be-
hold, the Lord GOD called for conflict
by fire, and it consumed the great deep
and devoured the territory. 5Then I said:

"O Lord GOD, cease, I pray!
Oh, that Jacob may stand,
For he *is* small!"
6 *So* the LORD relented concerning
this.
"This also shall not be," said the
Lord GOD.

Vision of the Plumb Line

7Thus He showed me: Behold, the Lord
stood on a wall *made* with a plumb line,
with a plumb line in His hand. 8And
the LORD said to me, "Amos, what do
you see?"
And I said, "A plumb line."
Then the Lord said:

"Behold, I am setting a plumb line
In the midst of My people Israel;
I will not pass by them anymore.
9 The high places of Isaac shall be
desolate,
And the sanctuaries of Israel
shall be laid waste.
I will rise with the sword
against the house of
Jeroboam."

Amaziah's Complaint

10Then Amaziah the priest of Bethel
sent to Jeroboam king of Israel, saying,
"Amos has conspired against you in the
midst of the house of Israel. The land is
not able to bear all his words. 11For thus
Amos has said:

'Jeroboam shall die by the sword,
And Israel shall surely be led
away captive
From their own land.' "

6:10 [a] Literally *bones* **6:13** [a] Literally *Nothing* [b] Literally *Horns,* symbol of strength

12Then Amaziah said to Amos:

"Go, you seer!
Flee to the land of Judah.
There eat bread,
And there prophesy.
13 But never again prophesy at
Bethel,
For it *is* the king's sanctuary,
And it *is* the royal residence."

14Then Amos answered, and said to
Amaziah:

"I *was* no prophet,
Nor *was* I a son of a prophet,
But I *was* a sheepbreeder[a]
And a tender of sycamore fruit.
15 Then the LORD took me as I
followed the flock,
And the LORD said to me,
'Go, prophesy to My people Israel.'
16 Now therefore, hear the word of
the LORD:
You say, 'Do not prophesy against
Israel,
And do not spout against the
house of Isaac.'

17"Therefore thus says the LORD:

'Your wife shall be a harlot in the
city;
Your sons and daughters shall fall
by the sword;
Your land shall be divided by
survey line;
You shall die in a defiled land;
And Israel shall surely be led
away captive
From his own land.' "

Vision of the Summer Fruit

8 Thus the Lord GOD showed me: Be-
hold, a basket of summer fruit. 2And
He said, "Amos, what do you see?"
So I said, "A basket of summer fruit."
Then the LORD said to me:

"The end has come upon My people
Israel;
I will not pass by them anymore.
3 And the songs of the temple
Shall be wailing in that day,"
Says the Lord GOD—
"Many dead bodies everywhere,
They shall be thrown out in
silence."
4 Hear this, you who swallow up[a]
the needy,
And make the poor of the land
fail,
5Saying:

"When will the New Moon be past,
That we may sell grain?
And the Sabbath,
That we may trade wheat?
Making the ephah small and the
shekel large,
Falsifying the scales by deceit,
6 That we may buy the poor for
silver,
And the needy for a pair of
sandals—
Even sell the bad wheat?"

7 The LORD has sworn by the pride
of Jacob:
"Surely I will never forget any of
their works.
8 Shall the land not tremble for this,
And everyone mourn who dwells
in it?
All of it shall swell like the River,[a]
Heave and subside
Like the River of Egypt.

9 "And it shall come to pass in that
day," says the Lord GOD,
"That I will make the sun go down
at noon,
And I will darken the earth in
broad daylight;
10 I will turn your feasts into
mourning,
And all your songs into
lamentation;
I will bring sackcloth on every
waist,
And baldness on every head;
I will make it like mourning for an
only *son*,
And its end like a bitter day.

7:14 [a] Compare 2 Kings 3:4 8:4 [a] Or *trample on* (compare 2:7) 8:8 [a] That is, the Nile; some Hebrew manuscripts, Septuagint, Syriac, Targum, and Vulgate read *River;* Masoretic Text reads *the light.*

11 "Behold, the days are coming," says
the Lord GOD,
"That I will send a famine on the
land,
Not a famine of bread,
Nor a thirst for water,
But of hearing the words of the
LORD.
12 They shall wander from sea to sea,
And from north to east;
They shall run to and fro, seeking
the word of the LORD,
But shall not find *it.*

13 "In that day the fair virgins
And strong young men
Shall faint from thirst.
14 Those who swear by the sin[a] of
Samaria,
Who say,
'As your god lives, O Dan!'
And, 'As the way of Beersheba
lives!'
They shall fall and never rise
again."

The Destruction of Israel

9 I saw the Lord standing by the altar, and He said:

"Strike the doorposts, that the
thresholds may shake,
And break them on the heads of
them all.
I will slay the last of them with
the sword.
He who flees from them shall not
get away,
And he who escapes from them
shall not be delivered.

2 "Though they dig into hell,[a]
From there My hand shall take
them;
Though they climb up to heaven,
From there I will bring them
down;
3 And though they hide themselves
on top of Carmel,
From there I will search and take
them;
Though they hide from My sight
at the bottom of the sea,
From there I will command the
serpent, and it shall bite
them;
4 Though they go into captivity
before their enemies,
From there I will command the
sword,
And it shall slay them.
I will set My eyes on them for
harm and not for good."

5 The Lord GOD of hosts,
He who touches the earth and it
melts,
And all who dwell there mourn;
All of it shall swell like the River,[a]
And subside like the River of
Egypt.
6 He who builds His layers in the
sky,
And has founded His strata in the
earth;
Who calls for the waters of the
sea,
And pours them out on the face of
the earth—
The LORD *is* His name.

7 "*Are* you not like the people of
Ethiopia to Me,
O children of Israel?" says the
LORD.
"Did I not bring up Israel from the
land of Egypt,
The Philistines from Caphtor,
And the Syrians from Kir?

8 "Behold, the eyes of the Lord GOD
are on the sinful kingdom,
And I will destroy it from the face
of the earth;
Yet I will not utterly destroy the
house of Jacob,"
Says the LORD.

9 "For surely I will command,
And will sift the house of Israel
among all nations,
As *grain* is sifted in a sieve;
Yet not the smallest grain shall
fall to the ground.
10 All the sinners of My people shall
die by the sword,

8:14 [a] Or *Ashima,* a Syrian goddess 9:2 [a] Or *Sheol* 9:5 [a] That is, the Nile

Who say, 'The calamity shall not
overtake nor confront us.'

Israel Will Be Restored

11 "On that day I will raise up
The tabernacle[a] of David, which
has fallen down,
And repair its damages;
I will raise up its ruins,
And rebuild it as in the days of
old;
12 That they may possess the
remnant of Edom,[a]
And all the Gentiles who are
called by My name,"
Says the LORD who does this
thing.

13 "Behold, the days are coming," says
the LORD,
"When the plowman shall overtake
the reaper,
And the treader of grapes him
who sows seed;
The mountains shall drip with
sweet wine,
And all the hills shall flow *with it.*
14 I will bring back the captives of
My people Israel;
They shall build the waste cities
and inhabit *them;*
They shall plant vineyards and
drink wine from them;
They shall also make gardens and
eat fruit from them.
15 I will plant them in their land,
And no longer shall they be
pulled up
From the land I have given them,"
Says the LORD your God.

9:11 [a] Literally *booth,* figure of a deposed dynasty **9:12** [a] Septuagint reads *mankind.*

THE BOOK OF

OBADIAH

Obadiah is a prophecy against Edom, the nation that descended from Jacob's brother, Esau. Throughout most of the Old Testament, whenever Edom is mentioned, it was always shown as doing harm to Israel. This friction started when the king of Edom refused to let the Israelites cross his territory as they journeyed towards the Promised Land in Numbers 20:14–21. When Israel and Judah were taken into exile, Edom stood by, watched, and even celebrated. The purpose of Obadiah is to encourage the Israelites. God will judge all of Israel's enemies and rescue His people.

- **GENRE:** Minor Prophet
- **AUTHOR:** Obadiah
- **TIME:** c. 848–840 BC
- **PURPOSE:** To tell God's people that they weren't the only ones being punished for disobeying God.

The Coming Judgment on Edom

The vision of Obadiah.

Thus says the Lord GOD concerning Edom
(We have heard a report from the LORD,
And a messenger has been sent among the nations, *saying,*
"Arise, and let us rise up against her for battle"):

2 "Behold, I will make you small among the nations;
You shall be greatly despised.
3 The pride of your heart has deceived you,
You who dwell in the clefts of the rock,
Whose habitation is high;
You who say in your heart, 'Who will bring me down to the ground?'
4 Though you ascend *as* high as the eagle,
And though you set your nest among the stars,
From there I will bring you down," says the LORD.

5 "If thieves had come to you,
If robbers by night—
Oh, how you will be cut off!—
Would they not have stolen till they had enough?
If grape-gatherers had come to you,
Would they not have left *some* gleanings?

6 "Oh, how Esau shall be searched out!
How his hidden treasures shall be sought after!
7 All the men in your confederacy
Shall force you to the border;
The men at peace with you
Shall deceive you *and* prevail against you.
Those who eat your bread shall lay a trap[a] for you.
No one is aware of it.

8 "Will I not in that day," says the LORD,
"Even destroy the wise *men* from Edom,
And understanding from the mountains of Esau?
9 Then your mighty men, O Teman, shall be dismayed,
To the end that everyone from the mountains of Esau
May be cut off by slaughter.

7 [a] Or *wound,* or *plot*

Edom Mistreated His Brother

10 "For violence against your brother Jacob,
Shame shall cover you,
And you shall be cut off forever.
11 In the day that you stood on the other side—
In the day that strangers carried captive his forces,
When foreigners entered his gates
And cast lots for Jerusalem—
Even you *were* as one of them.

12 "But you should not have gazed on the day of your brother
In the day of his captivity;[a]
Nor should you have rejoiced over the children of Judah
In the day of their destruction;
Nor should you have spoken proudly
In the day of distress.
13 You should not have entered the gate of My people
In the day of their calamity.
Indeed, you should not have gazed on their affliction
In the day of their calamity,
Nor laid *hands* on their substance
In the day of their calamity.
14 You should not have stood at the crossroads
To cut off those among them who escaped;
Nor should you have delivered up those among them who remained
In the day of distress.

15 "For the day of the LORD upon all the nations *is* near;
As you have done, it shall be done to you;
Your reprisal shall return upon your own head.
16 For as you drank on My holy mountain,
So shall all the nations drink continually;
Yes, they shall drink, and swallow,
And they shall be as though they had never been.

Israel's Final Triumph

17 "But on Mount Zion there shall be deliverance,
And there shall be holiness;
The house of Jacob shall possess their possessions.
18 The house of Jacob shall be a fire,
And the house of Joseph a flame;
But the house of Esau *shall be* stubble;
They shall kindle them and devour them,
And no survivor shall *remain* of the house of Esau,"
For the LORD has spoken.

19 The South[a] shall possess the mountains of Esau,
And the Lowland shall possess Philistia.
They shall possess the fields of Ephraim
And the fields of Samaria.
Benjamin *shall possess* Gilead.
20 And the captives of this host of the children of Israel
Shall possess the land of the Canaanites
As far as Zarephath.
The captives of Jerusalem who are in Sepharad
Shall possess the cities of the South.[a]
21 Then saviors[a] shall come to Mount Zion
To judge the mountains of Esau,
And the kingdom shall be the LORD's.

12 [a] Literally *On the day he became a foreigner* 19 [a] Hebrew *Negev* 20 [a] Hebrew *Negev* 21 [a] Or *deliverers*

THE BOOK OF JONAH

When God tells Jonah to go to the wicked city of Nineveh and tell them to repent and then He will forgive them, Jonah disobeys and runs in the opposite direction. Nineveh was the enemy of Israel, and Jonah did not want to help them in any way. But God does not allow Jonah to run very far. He gets Jonah's attention in a surprising way, and eventually Jonah goes to Nineveh and preaches. But when the people repent, Jonah becomes angry and wants God to destroy them anyway. Once again, God extends compassion to His disobedient and troubled prophet and teaches him that His love and forgiveness extends even to the most wicked of people who repent.

- **GENRE:** Minor Prophet
- **AUTHOR:** Jonah
- **TIME:** c. 760 BC
- **PURPOSE:** To teach that God will forgive even the most wicked of people if they repent of their sins.

Jonah's Disobedience

1 Now the word of the LORD came to
Jonah the son of Amittai, saying,
2"Arise, go to Nineveh, that great city,
and cry out against it; for their wick-
edness has come up before Me." 3But
Jonah arose to flee to Tarshish from
the presence of the LORD. He went down
to Joppa, and found a ship going to
Tarshish; so he paid the fare, and went
down into it, to go with them to Tarshish
from the presence of the LORD.

The Storm at Sea

4But the LORD sent out a great wind on
the sea, and there was a mighty tempest
on the sea, so that the ship was about
to be broken up.
5Then the mariners were afraid; and
every man cried out to his god, and
threw the cargo that *was* in the ship
into the sea, to lighten the load.[a] But
Jonah had gone down into the lowest
parts of the ship, had lain down, and
was fast asleep.
6So the captain came to him, and said
to him, "What do you mean, sleeper?
Arise, call on your God; perhaps your
God will consider us, so that we may
not perish."
7And they said to one another, "Come,
let us cast lots, that we may know for
whose cause this trouble *has come* upon
us." So they cast lots, and the lot fell on
Jonah. 8Then they said to him, "Please
tell us! For whose cause *is* this trouble
upon us? What is your occupation? And
where do you come from? What is your
country? And of what people are you?"
9So he said to them, "I *am* a Hebrew;
and I fear the LORD, the God of heaven,
who made the sea and the dry *land*."

Jonah Thrown into the Sea

10Then the men were exceedingly
afraid, and said to him, "Why have
you done this?" For the men knew that
he fled from the presence of the LORD,
because he had told them. 11Then they
said to him, "What shall we do to you
that the sea may be calm for us?"—for
the sea was growing more tempestuous.
12And he said to them, "Pick me up and
throw me into the sea; then the sea will
become calm for you. For I know that
this great tempest *is* because of me."
13Nevertheless the men rowed hard to
return to land, but they could not, for
the sea continued to grow more tempes-
tuous against them. 14Therefore they
cried out to the LORD and said, "We
pray, O LORD, please do not let us perish

1:5 [a] Literally *from upon them*

for this man's life, and do not charge us
with innocent blood; for You, O LORD,
have done as it pleased You." 15So they
picked up Jonah and threw him into
the sea, and the sea ceased from its
raging. 16Then the men feared the LORD
exceedingly, and offered a sacrifice to
the LORD and took vows.

Jonah's Prayer and Deliverance

17Now the LORD had prepared a great
fish to swallow Jonah. And Jonah was
in the belly of the fish three days and
three nights.

2 Then Jonah prayed to the LORD
his God from the fish's belly. 2And
he said:

"I cried out to the LORD because of
my affliction,
And He answered me.

"Out of the belly of Sheol I cried,
And You heard my voice.
3 For You cast me into the deep,
Into the heart of the seas,
And the floods surrounded me;
All Your billows and Your waves
passed over me.
4 Then I said, 'I have been cast out
of Your sight;
Yet I will look again toward Your
holy temple.'
5 The waters surrounded me, *even*
to my soul;
The deep closed around me;
Weeds were wrapped around my
head.
6 I went down to the moorings of
the mountains;
The earth with its bars *closed*
behind me forever;
Yet You have brought up my life
from the pit,
O LORD, my God.

7 "When my soul fainted within me,
I remembered the LORD;
And my prayer went *up* to You,
Into Your holy temple.

8 "Those who regard worthless idols
Forsake their own Mercy.
9 But I will sacrifice to You
With the voice of thanksgiving;
I will pay what I have vowed.
Salvation *is* of the LORD."

10So the LORD spoke to the fish, and it
vomited Jonah onto dry *land.*

Jonah Preaches at Nineveh

3 Now the word of the LORD came
to Jonah the second time, saying,
2"Arise, go to Nineveh, that great city,
and preach to it the message that I tell
you." 3So Jonah arose and went to Nine-
veh, according to the word of the LORD.
Now Nineveh was an exceedingly great
city, a three-day journey[a] *in extent.*
4And Jonah began to enter the city on
the first day's walk. Then he cried out
and said, "Yet forty days, and Nineveh
shall be overthrown!"

The People of Nineveh Believe

5So the people of Nineveh believed
God, proclaimed a fast, and put on
sackcloth, from the greatest to the
least of them. 6Then word came to the
king of Nineveh; and he arose from his
throne and laid aside his robe, covered
himself with sackcloth and sat in ashes.
7And he caused *it* to be proclaimed
and published throughout Nineveh by
the decree of the king and his nobles,
saying,

Let neither man nor beast, herd
nor flock, taste anything; do not
let them eat, or drink water. 8But
let man and beast be covered
with sackcloth, and cry mightily
to God; yes, let every one turn
from his evil way and from the
violence that is in his hands.
9Who can tell *if* God will turn and
relent, and turn away from His
fierce anger, so that we may not
perish?

10Then God saw their works, that they
turned from their evil way; and God
relented from the disaster that He had
said He would bring upon them, and
He did not do it.

3:3 [a] Exact meaning unknown

GOD SIN JESUS SALVATION LOVE

Jonah's Anger and God's Kindness

4 But it displeased Jonah exceed-
ingly, and he became angry. 2So
he prayed to the LORD, and said, "Ah,
LORD, was not this what I said when I
was still in my country? Therefore I fled
previously to Tarshish; for I know that
You *are* a gracious and merciful God,
slow to anger and abundant in loving-
kindness, One who relents from doing
harm. 3Therefore now, O LORD, please
take my life from me, for *it is* better for
me to die than to live!"

4Then the LORD said, "*Is it* right for
you to be angry?"

5So Jonah went out of the city and sat
on the east side of the city. There he
made himself a shelter and sat under
it in the shade, till he might see what
would become of the city. 6And the
LORD God prepared a plant[a] and made
it come up over Jonah, that it might be
shade for his head to deliver him from
his misery. So Jonah was very grateful
for the plant. 7But as morning dawned
the next day God prepared a worm, and
it *so* damaged the plant that it withered.
8And it happened, when the sun arose,
that God prepared a vehement east
wind; and the sun beat on Jonah's head,
so that he grew faint. Then he wished
death for himself, and said, "*It is* better
for me to die than to live."

9Then God said to Jonah, "*Is it* right
for you to be angry about the plant?"

And he said, "*It is* right for me to be
angry, even to death!"

10But the LORD said, "You have had pity
on the plant for which you have not la-
bored, nor made it grow, which came up
in a night and perished in a night. 11And
should I not pity Nineveh, that great city,
in which are more than one hundred and
twenty thousand persons who cannot
discern between their right hand and
their left—and much livestock?"

4:6 [a] Hebrew *kikayon,* exact identity unknown

THE BOOK OF MICAH

Micah, who was from a town in Judah, delivered a message to Samaria and Jerusalem. He was probably around when the Assyrians destroyed Samaria in 722 BC and may have lived through the later siege of Jerusalem. Micah was troubled by the abuse of the poor by the wealthy. His message was one calling on God's people to live rightly with one another so that they could please God.

- **GENRE:** Minor Prophet
- **AUTHOR:** Micah
- **TIME:** c. 735–710 BC
- **PURPOSE:** To show how God's people are to act and treat others.

1 The word of the LORD that came to
Micah of Moresheth in the days of
Jotham, Ahaz, *and* Hezekiah, kings of
Judah, which he saw concerning Samaria and Jerusalem.

The Coming Judgment on Israel

2 Hear, all you peoples!
Listen, O earth, and all that is in it!
Let the Lord GOD be a witness against you,
The Lord from His holy temple.

3 For behold, the LORD is coming out of His place;
He will come down
And tread on the high places of the earth.
4 The mountains will melt under Him,
And the valleys will split
Like wax before the fire,
Like waters poured down a steep place.
5 All this is for the transgression of Jacob
And for the sins of the house of Israel.
What *is* the transgression of Jacob?
Is it not Samaria?
And what *are* the high places of Judah?
Are they not Jerusalem?

6 "Therefore I will make Samaria a heap of ruins in the field,
Places for planting a vineyard;
I will pour down her stones into the valley,
And I will uncover her foundations.
7 All her carved images shall be beaten to pieces,
And all her pay as a harlot shall be burned with the fire;
All her idols I will lay desolate,
For she gathered *it* from the pay of a harlot,
And they shall return to the pay of a harlot."

Mourning for Israel and Judah

8 Therefore I will wail and howl,
I will go stripped and naked;
I will make a wailing like the jackals
And a mourning like the ostriches,
9 For her wounds *are* incurable.
For it has come to Judah;
It has come to the gate of My people—
To Jerusalem.

10 Tell *it* not in Gath,
Weep not at all;
In Beth Aphrah[a]
Roll yourself in the dust.
11 Pass by in naked shame, you inhabitant of Shaphir;

1:10 [a] Literally *House of Dust*

The inhabitant of Zaanan[a] does
not go out.
Beth Ezel mourns;
Its place to stand is taken away
from you.
12 For the inhabitant of Maroth
pined[a] for good,
But disaster came down from the
LORD
To the gate of Jerusalem.
13 O inhabitant of Lachish,
Harness the chariot to the swift
steeds
(She *was* the beginning of sin to
the daughter of Zion),
For the transgressions of Israel
were found in you.

14 Therefore you shall give presents
to Moresheth Gath;[a]
The houses of Achzib[b] *shall be* a lie
to the kings of Israel.
15 I will yet bring an heir to you,
O inhabitant of Mareshah;[a]
The glory of Israel shall come to
Adullam.
16 Make yourself bald and cut off
your hair,
Because of your precious children;
Enlarge your baldness like an
eagle,
For they shall go from you into
captivity.

Woe to Evildoers

2 Woe to those who devise iniquity,
And work out evil on their beds!
At morning light they practice it,
Because it is in the power of their
hand.
2 They covet fields and take *them* by
violence,
Also houses, and seize *them*.
So they oppress a man and his
house,
A man and his inheritance.

3 Therefore thus says the LORD:

"Behold, against this family I am
devising disaster,
From which you cannot remove
your necks;
Nor shall you walk haughtily,
For this *is* an evil time.
4 In that day *one* shall take up a
proverb against you,
And lament with a bitter
lamentation, saying:
'We are utterly destroyed!
He has changed the heritage of
my people;
How He has removed *it* from me!
To a turncoat He has divided our
fields.' "

5 Therefore you will have no one to
determine boundaries[a] by
lot
In the assembly of the LORD.

Lying Prophets

6 "Do not prattle," *you say to those*
who prophesy.
So they shall not prophesy to you;[a]
They shall not return insult for
insult.[b]
7 *You who are* named the house of
Jacob:
"Is the Spirit of the LORD restricted?
Are these His doings?
Do not My words do good
To him who walks uprightly?

8 "Lately My people have risen up as
an enemy—
You pull off the robe with the
garment
From those who trust *you*, as they
pass by,
Like men returned from war.
9 The women of My people you cast
out
From their pleasant houses;
From their children
You have taken away My glory
forever.

10 "Arise and depart,
For this *is* not *your* rest;
Because it is defiled, it shall
destroy,
Yes, with utter destruction.

1:11 [a] Literally *Going Out* 1:12 [a] Literally *was sick* 1:14 [a] Literally *Possession of Gath* [b] Literally *Lie* 1:15 [a] Literally *Inheritance* 2:5 [a] Literally *one casting a surveyor's line* 2:6 [a] Literally *to these* [b] Vulgate reads *He shall not take shame.*

11 If a man should walk in a false spirit
And speak a lie, *saying*,
'I will prophesy to you of wine and drink,'
Even he would be the prattler of this people.

Israel Restored

12 "I will surely assemble all of you, O Jacob,
I will surely gather the remnant of Israel;
I will put them together like sheep of the fold,[a]
Like a flock in the midst of their pasture;
They shall make a loud noise because of *so many* people.
13 The one who breaks open will come up before them;
They will break out,
Pass through the gate,
And go out by it;
Their king will pass before them,
With the LORD at their head."

Wicked Rulers and Prophets

3 And I said:
"Hear now, O heads of Jacob,
And you rulers of the house of Israel:
Is it not for you to know justice?
2 You who hate good and love evil;
Who strip the skin from My people,[a]
And the flesh from their bones;
3 Who also eat the flesh of My people,
Flay their skin from them,
Break their bones,
And chop *them* in pieces
Like *meat* for the pot,
Like flesh in the caldron."

4 Then they will cry to the LORD,
But He will not hear them;
He will even hide His face from them at that time,
Because they have been evil in their deeds.

5 Thus says the LORD concerning the prophets
Who make my people stray;
Who chant "Peace"
While they chew with their teeth,
But who prepare war against him
Who puts nothing into their mouths:
6 "Therefore you shall have night without vision,
And you shall have darkness without divination;
The sun shall go down on the prophets,
And the day shall be dark for them.
7 So the seers shall be ashamed,
And the diviners abashed;
Indeed they shall all cover their lips;
For *there is* no answer from God."

8 But truly I am full of power by the Spirit of the LORD,
And of justice and might,
To declare to Jacob his transgression
And to Israel his sin.
9 Now hear this,
You heads of the house of Jacob
And rulers of the house of Israel,
Who abhor justice
And pervert all equity,
10 Who build up Zion with bloodshed
And Jerusalem with iniquity:
11 Her heads judge for a bribe,
Her priests teach for pay,
And her prophets divine for money.
Yet they lean on the LORD, and say,
"Is not the LORD among us?
No harm can come upon us."
12 Therefore because of you
Zion shall be plowed *like* a field,
Jerusalem shall become heaps of ruins,
And the mountain of the temple[a]
Like the bare hills of the forest.

The LORD's Reign in Zion

4 Now it shall come to pass in the latter days
That the mountain of the LORD's house

2:12 [a] Hebrew *Bozrah* 3:2 [a] Literally *them* 3:12 [a] Literally *house*

Shall be established on the top of the mountains,
And shall be exalted above the hills;
And peoples shall flow to it.
2 Many nations shall come and say,
"Come, and let us go up to the mountain of the LORD,
To the house of the God of Jacob;
He will teach us His ways,
And we shall walk in His paths."
For out of Zion the law shall go forth,
And the word of the LORD from Jerusalem.
3 He shall judge between many peoples,
And rebuke strong nations afar off;
They shall beat their swords into plowshares,
And their spears into pruning hooks;
Nation shall not lift up sword against nation,
Neither shall they learn war anymore.[a]

4 But everyone shall sit under his vine and under his fig tree,
And no one shall make *them* afraid;
For the mouth of the LORD of hosts has spoken.
5 For all people walk each in the name of his god,
But we will walk in the name of the LORD our God
Forever and ever.

Zion's Future Triumph

6 "In that day," says the LORD,
"I will assemble the lame,
I will gather the outcast
And those whom I have afflicted;
7 I will make the lame a remnant,
And the outcast a strong nation;
So the LORD will reign over them in Mount Zion
From now on, even forever.
8 And you, O tower of the flock,
The stronghold of the daughter of Zion,
To you shall it come,
Even the former dominion shall come,
The kingdom of the daughter of Jerusalem."

9 Now why do you cry aloud?
Is there no king in your midst?
Has your counselor perished?
For pangs have seized you like a woman in labor.
10 Be in pain, and labor to bring forth,
O daughter of Zion,
Like a woman in birth pangs.
For now you shall go forth from the city,
You shall dwell in the field,
And to Babylon you shall go.
There you shall be delivered;
There the LORD will redeem you
From the hand of your enemies.

11 Now also many nations have gathered against you,
Who say, "Let her be defiled,
And let our eye look upon Zion."
12 But they do not know the thoughts of the LORD,
Nor do they understand His counsel;
For He will gather them like sheaves to the threshing floor.

13 "Arise and thresh, O daughter of Zion;
For I will make your horn iron,
And I will make your hooves bronze;
You shall beat in pieces many peoples;
I will consecrate their gain to the LORD,
And their substance to the Lord of the whole earth."

5 Now gather yourself in troops,
O daughter of troops;
He has laid siege against us;
They will strike the judge of Israel with a rod on the cheek.

4:3 [a] Compare Isaiah 2:2–4

The Coming Messiah

2 "But you, Bethlehem Ephrathah,
Though you are little among the thousands of Judah,
Yet out of you shall come forth to Me
The One to be Ruler in Israel,
Whose goings forth *are* from of old,
From everlasting."

3 Therefore He shall give them up,
Until the time *that* she who is in labor has given birth;
Then the remnant of His brethren
Shall return to the children of Israel.
4 And He shall stand and feed *His* flock
In the strength of the LORD,
In the majesty of the name of the LORD His God;
And they shall abide,
For now He shall be great
To the ends of the earth;
5 And this *One* shall be peace.

Judgment on Israel's Enemies

When the Assyrian comes into our land,
And when he treads in our palaces,
Then we will raise against him
Seven shepherds and eight princely men.
6 They shall waste with the sword the land of Assyria,
And the land of Nimrod at its entrances;
Thus He shall deliver *us* from the Assyrian,
When he comes into our land
And when he treads within our borders.

7 Then the remnant of Jacob
Shall be in the midst of many peoples,
Like dew from the LORD,
Like showers on the grass,
That tarry for no man
Nor wait for the sons of men.
8 And the remnant of Jacob
Shall be among the Gentiles,
In the midst of many peoples,
Like a lion among the beasts of the forest,
Like a young lion among flocks of sheep,
Who, if he passes through,
Both treads down and tears in pieces,
And none can deliver.
9 Your hand shall be lifted against your adversaries,
And all your enemies shall be cut off.

10 "And it shall be in that day," says the LORD,
"That I will cut off your horses from your midst
And destroy your chariots.
11 I will cut off the cities of your land
And throw down all your strongholds.
12 I will cut off sorceries from your hand,
And you shall have no soothsayers.
13 Your carved images I will also cut off,
And your *sacred* pillars from your midst;
You shall no more worship the work of your hands;
14 I will pluck your wooden images[a] from your midst;
Thus I will destroy your cities.
15 And I will execute vengeance in anger and fury
On the nations that have not heard."[a]

God Pleads with Israel

6 Hear now what the LORD says:

"Arise, plead your case before the mountains,
And let the hills hear your voice.
2 Hear, O you mountains, the LORD's complaint,
And you strong foundations of the earth;
For the LORD has a complaint against His people,
And He will contend with Israel.

5:14 [a] Hebrew *Asherim,* Canaanite deities 5:15 [a] Or *obeyed*

3 "O My people, what have I done to
you?
And how have I wearied you?
Testify against Me.
4 For I brought you up from the
land of Egypt,
I redeemed you from the house of
bondage;
And I sent before you Moses,
Aaron, and Miriam.
5 O My people, remember now
What Balak king of Moab
counseled,
And what Balaam the son of Beor
answered him,
From Acacia Grove[a] to Gilgal,
That you may know the
righteousness of the LORD."

6 With what shall I come before the
LORD,
And bow myself before the High
God?
Shall I come before Him with
burnt offerings,
With calves a year old?
7 Will the LORD be pleased with
thousands of rams,
Ten thousand rivers of oil?
Shall I give my firstborn *for* my
transgression,
The fruit of my body *for* the sin of
my soul?

8 He has shown you, O man, what *is*
good;
And what does the LORD require
of you
But to do justly,
To love mercy,
And to walk humbly with your
God?

Punishment of Israel's Injustice

9 The LORD's voice cries to the
city—
Wisdom shall see Your name:

"Hear the rod!
Who has appointed it?
10 Are there yet the treasures of
wickedness
In the house of the wicked,
And the short measure *that is* an
abomination?
11 Shall I count pure *those* with the
wicked scales,
And with the bag of deceitful
weights?
12 For her rich men are full of
violence,
Her inhabitants have spoken lies,
And their tongue is deceitful in
their mouth.

13 "Therefore I will also make *you* sick
by striking you,
By making *you* desolate because
of your sins.
14 You shall eat, but not be satisfied;
Hunger[a] *shall be* in your midst.
You may carry *some* away,[b] but
shall not save *them;*
And what you do rescue I will give
over to the sword.

15 "You shall sow, but not reap;
You shall tread the olives, but not
anoint yourselves with oil;
And *make* sweet wine, but not
drink wine.
16 For the statutes of Omri are kept;
All the works of Ahab's house *are*
done;
And you walk in their counsels,
That I may make you a
desolation,
And your inhabitants a hissing.
Therefore you shall bear the
reproach of My people."[a]

Sorrow for Israel's Sins

7 Woe is me!
For I am like those who gather
summer fruits,
Like those who glean vintage
grapes;
There is no cluster to eat
Of the first-ripe fruit *which* my
soul desires.
2 The faithful *man* has perished
from the earth,
And *there is* no one upright
among men.

6:5 [a] Hebrew *Shittim* (compare Numbers 25:1; Joshua 2:1; 3:1) 6:14 [a] Or *Emptiness* or *Humiliation* [b] Targum and Vulgate read *You shall take hold.* 6:16 [a] Following Masoretic Text, Targum, and Vulgate; Septuagint reads *of nations.*

They all lie in wait for blood;
Every man hunts his brother with a net.

3 That they may successfully do evil with both hands—
The prince asks *for gifts,*
The judge *seeks* a bribe,
And the great *man* utters his evil desire;
So they scheme together.
4 The best of them *is* like a brier;
The most upright *is sharper* than a thorn hedge;
The day of your watchman and your punishment comes;
Now shall be their perplexity.

5 Do not trust in a friend;
Do not put your confidence in a companion;
Guard the doors of your mouth
From her who lies in your bosom.
6 For son dishonors father,
Daughter rises against her mother,
Daughter-in-law against her mother-in-law;
A man's enemies *are* the men of his own household.
7 Therefore I will look to the LORD;
I will wait for the God of my salvation;
My God will hear me.

Israel's Confession and Comfort

8 Do not rejoice over me, my enemy;
When I fall, I will arise;
When I sit in darkness,
The LORD *will be* a light to me.
9 I will bear the indignation of the LORD,
Because I have sinned against Him,
Until He pleads my case
And executes justice for me.
He will bring me forth to the light;
I will see His righteousness.
10 Then *she who is* my enemy will see,
And shame will cover her who said to me,
"Where is the LORD your God?"
My eyes will see her;
Now she will be trampled down
Like mud in the streets.

11 *In* the day when your walls are to be built,
In that day the decree shall go far and wide.[a]
12 *In* that day they[a] shall come to you
From Assyria and the fortified cities,[b]
From the fortress[c] to the River,[d]
From sea to sea,
And mountain *to* mountain.
13 Yet the land shall be desolate
Because of those who dwell in it,
And for the fruit of their deeds.

God Will Forgive Israel

14 Shepherd Your people with Your staff,
The flock of Your heritage,
Who dwell solitarily *in* a woodland,
In the midst of Carmel;
Let them feed *in* Bashan and Gilead,
As in days of old.

15 "As in the days when you came out of the land of Egypt,
I will show them[a] wonders."

16 The nations shall see and be ashamed of all their might;
They shall put *their* hand over *their* mouth;
Their ears shall be deaf.
17 They shall lick the dust like a serpent;
They shall crawl from their holes like snakes of the earth.
They shall be afraid of the LORD our God,
And shall fear because of You.
18 Who *is* a God like You,
Pardoning iniquity

7:11 [a] Or *the boundary shall be extended* 7:12 [a] Literally *he,* collective of the captives [b] Hebrew *arey mazor,* possibly *cities of Egypt* [c] Hebrew *mazor,* possibly *Egypt* [d] That is, the Euphrates
7:15 [a] Literally *him,* collective for the captives

And passing over the
transgression of the
remnant of His heritage?

He does not retain His anger
forever,
Because He delights *in* mercy.
19 He will again have compassion
on us,
And will subdue our iniquities.

You will cast all our[a] sins
Into the depths of the sea.
20 You will give truth to Jacob
And mercy to Abraham,
Which You have sworn to our
fathers
From days of old.

7:19 [a] Literally *their*

THE BOOK OF

NAHUM

Under Jonah's preaching, Nineveh had repented of its sin, and God withheld judgment against it. Now, however, one hundred years later, the prophet Nahum declares the downfall of the city. The Assyrians had abandoned their revival and had returned to idolatry and violence. While Nineveh may be powerful, her day of destruction is coming. Nineveh is not invincible. The message is that God's standards apply to all nations, not just Israel and Judah. All people need to live by God's standards or face His judgment.

- **GENRE:** Minor Prophet
- **AUTHOR:** Nahum
- **TIME:** c. 660–650 BC
- **PURPOSE:** To show that God is in charge of the entire world; He judges not only His people for their sins, but all the nations for their sins, too.

---

1 The burden[a] against Nineveh. The book of the vision of Nahum the Elkoshite.

God's Wrath on His Enemies

2 God *is* jealous, and the LORD avenges;
The LORD avenges and *is* furious.
The LORD will take vengeance on His adversaries,
And He reserves *wrath* for His enemies;
3 The LORD *is* slow to anger and great in power,
And will not at all acquit *the wicked.*

The LORD has His way
In the whirlwind and in the storm,
And the clouds *are* the dust of His feet.
4 He rebukes the sea and makes it dry,
And dries up all the rivers.
Bashan and Carmel wither,
And the flower of Lebanon wilts.
5 The mountains quake before Him,
The hills melt,
And the earth heaves[a] at His presence,
Yes, the world and all who dwell in it.
6 Who can stand before His indignation?
And who can endure the fierceness of His anger?
His fury is poured out like fire,
And the rocks are thrown down by Him.

7 The LORD *is* good,
A stronghold in the day of trouble;
And He knows those who trust in Him.
8 But with an overflowing flood
He will make an utter end of its place,
And darkness will pursue His enemies.

9 What do you conspire against the LORD?
He will make an utter end *of it.*
Affliction will not rise up a second time.
10 For while tangled *like* thorns,
And while drunken *like* drunkards,
They shall be devoured like stubble fully dried.
11 From you comes forth *one*
Who plots evil against the LORD,
A wicked counselor.

1:1 [a] Or *oracle* 1:5 [a] Targum reads *burns.*

12 Thus says the LORD:

"Though *they are* safe, and likewise
many,
Yet in this manner they will be cut
down
When he passes through.
Though I have afflicted you,
I will afflict you no more;
13 For now I will break off his yoke
from you,
And burst your bonds apart."

14 The LORD has given a command
concerning you:
"Your name shall be perpetuated
no longer.
Out of the house of your gods
I will cut off the carved image and
the molded image.
I will dig your grave,
For you are vile."

15 Behold, on the mountains
The feet of him who brings good
tidings,
Who proclaims peace!
O Judah, keep your appointed
feasts,
Perform your vows.
For the wicked one shall no more
pass through you;
He is utterly cut off.

The Destruction of Nineveh

2 He who scatters[a] has come up
before your face.
Man the fort!
Watch the road!
Strengthen *your* flanks!
Fortify *your* power mightily.

2 For the LORD will restore the
excellence of Jacob
Like the excellence of Israel,
For the emptiers have emptied
them out
And ruined their vine branches.

3 The shields of his mighty men *are*
made red,
The valiant men *are* in scarlet.
The chariots *come* with flaming
torches
In the day of his preparation,
And the spears are brandished.[a]
4 The chariots rage in the streets,
They jostle one another in the
broad roads;
They seem like torches,
They run like lightning.

5 He remembers his nobles;
They stumble in their walk;
They make haste to her walls,
And the defense is prepared.
6 The gates of the rivers are opened,
And the palace is dissolved.
7 It is decreed:[a]
She shall be led away captive,
She shall be brought up;
And her maidservants shall
lead *her* as with the voice of
doves,
Beating their breasts.

8 Though Nineveh of old *was* like a
pool of water,
Now they flee away.
"Halt! Halt!" *they cry;*
But no one turns back.
9 Take spoil of silver!
Take spoil of gold!
There is no end of treasure,
Or wealth of every desirable
prize.
10 She is empty, desolate, and waste!
The heart melts, and the knees
shake;
Much pain *is* in every side,
And all their faces are drained of
color.[a]

11 Where *is* the dwelling of the lions,
And the feeding place of the
young lions,
Where the lion walked, the lioness
and lion's cub,
And no one made *them* afraid?
12 The lion tore in pieces enough for
his cubs,
Killed for his lionesses,
Filled his caves with prey,
And his dens with flesh.

2:1 [a] Vulgate reads *He who destroys.* **2:3** [a] Literally *the cypresses are shaken;* Septuagint and Syriac read *the horses rush about;* Vulgate reads *the drivers are stupefied.* **2:7** [a] Hebrew *Huzzab* **2:10** [a] Compare Joel 2:6

13"Behold, I *am* against you," says the
LORD of hosts, "I will burn your[a] chariots
in smoke, and the sword shall devour
your young lions; I will cut off your prey
from the earth, and the voice of your
messengers shall be heard no more."

The Woe of Nineveh

3 Woe to the bloody city!
It *is* all full of lies *and* robbery.
Its victim never departs.
2 The noise of a whip
And the noise of rattling wheels,
Of galloping horses,
Of clattering chariots!
3 Horsemen charge with bright
sword and glittering spear.
There is a multitude of slain,
A great number of bodies,
Countless corpses—
They stumble over the corpses—
4 Because of the multitude of
harlotries of the seductive
harlot,
The mistress of sorceries,
Who sells nations through her
harlotries,
And families through her
sorceries.

5 "Behold, I *am* against you," says the
LORD of hosts;
"I will lift your skirts over your face,
I will show the nations your
nakedness,
And the kingdoms your shame.
6 I will cast abominable filth upon
you,
Make you vile,
And make you a spectacle.
7 It shall come to pass *that* all who
look upon you
Will flee from you, and say,
'Nineveh is laid waste!
Who will bemoan her?'
Where shall I seek comforters for
you?"

8 Are you better than No Amon[a]
That was situated by the River,[b]
That had the waters around her,
Whose rampart *was* the sea,
Whose wall *was* the sea?
9 Ethiopia and Egypt *were* her
strength,
And *it was* boundless;
Put and Lubim were your[a]
helpers.
10 Yet she *was* carried away,
She went into captivity;
Her young children also were
dashed to pieces
At the head of every street;
They cast lots for her honorable
men,
And all her great men were bound
in chains.
11 You also will be drunk;
You will be hidden;
You also will seek refuge from the
enemy.

12 All your strongholds *are* fig trees
with ripened figs:
If they are shaken,
They fall into the mouth of the
eater.
13 Surely, your people in your midst
are women!
The gates of your land are wide
open for your enemies;
Fire shall devour the bars of your
gates.

14 Draw your water for the siege!
Fortify your strongholds!
Go into the clay and tread the
mortar!
Make strong the brick kiln!
15 There the fire will devour you,
The sword will cut you off;
It will eat you up like a locust.

Make yourself many—like the
locust!
Make yourself many—like the
swarming locusts!
16 You have multiplied your
merchants more than the
stars of heaven.
The locust plunders and flies
away.
17 Your commanders *are* like
swarming locusts,
And your generals like great
grasshoppers,

2:13 [a] Literally *her* 3:8 [a] That is, ancient Thebes; Targum and Vulgate read *populous Alexandria*.
[b] Literally *rivers*, that is, the Nile and the surrounding canals 3:9 [a] Septuagint reads *her*.

Which camp in the hedges on a
cold day;
When the sun rises they flee
away,
And the place where they *are* is
not known.

18 Your shepherds slumber, O king
of Assyria;
Your nobles rest *in the dust.*
Your people are scattered on the
mountains,
And no one gathers them.
19 Your injury *has* no healing,
Your wound is severe.
All who hear news of you
Will clap *their* hands over you,
For upon whom has not your
wickedness passed
continually?

THE BOOK OF HABAKKUK

Habakkuk ministered during the final days of Judah's kingdom right before it was conquered. He saw the leaders in Judah mistreating the poor and the ungodly nation of Babylon becoming more powerful, so he asked God why He allows wicked people to do so well in life. God tells Habakkuk that He was using Babylon to discipline His people, but Babylon would be disciplined too. It might be difficult for God's people to see what He is doing, which is why they must live by faith.

- **GENRE:** Minor Prophet
- **AUTHOR:** Habakkuk
- **TIME:** c. 607–604 BC
- **PURPOSE:** To affirm that God knows what is going on and that wicked people do not really succeed.

---

1 The burden[a] which the prophet Habakkuk saw.

The Prophet's Question

2 O LORD, how long shall I cry,
And You will not hear?
Even cry out to You, "Violence!"
And You will not save.
3 Why do You show me iniquity,
And cause *me* to see trouble?
For plundering and violence *are* before me;
There is strife, and contention arises.
4 Therefore the law is powerless,
And justice never goes forth.
For the wicked surround the righteous;
Therefore perverse judgment proceeds.

The LORD's Reply

5 "Look among the nations and watch—
Be utterly astounded!
For *I will* work a work in your days
Which you would not believe, though it were told *you*.
6 For indeed I am raising up the Chaldeans,
A bitter and hasty nation
Which marches through the breadth of the earth,
To possess dwelling places *that are* not theirs.
7 They are terrible and dreadful;
Their judgment and their dignity proceed from themselves.
8 Their horses also are swifter than leopards,
And more fierce than evening wolves.
Their chargers charge ahead;
Their cavalry comes from afar;
They fly as the eagle *that* hastens to eat.

9 "They all come for violence;
Their faces are set *like* the east wind.
They gather captives like sand.
10 They scoff at kings,
And princes are scorned by them.
They deride every stronghold,
For they heap up earthen *mounds* and seize it.
11 Then *his* mind[a] changes, and he transgresses;
He commits offense,
Ascribing this power to his god."

The Prophet's Second Question

12 Are You not from everlasting,
O LORD my God, my Holy One?
We shall not die.

1:1 [a] Or *oracle* 1:11 [a] Literally *spirit* or *wind*

O LORD, You have appointed them
for judgment;
O Rock, You have marked them
for correction.
13 *You are* of purer eyes than to
behold evil,
And cannot look on wickedness.
Why do You look on those who
deal treacherously,
And hold Your tongue when the
wicked devours
A *person* more righteous than he?
14 *Why* do You make men like fish of
the sea,
Like creeping things *that have* no
ruler over them?
15 They take up all of them with a
hook,
They catch them in their net,
And gather them in their dragnet.
Therefore they rejoice and are
glad.
16 Therefore they sacrifice to their
net,
And burn incense to their
dragnet;
Because by them their share *is*
sumptuous
And their food plentiful.
17 Shall they therefore empty their
net,
And continue to slay nations
without pity?

2 I will stand my watch
And set myself on the rampart,
And watch to see what He will say
to me,
And what I will answer when I am
corrected.

The Just Live by Faith

2Then the LORD answered me and said:

"Write the vision
And make *it* plain on tablets,
That he may run who reads it.
3 For the vision *is* yet for an
appointed time;
But at the end it will speak, and it
will not lie.
Though it tarries, wait for it;
Because it will surely come,
It will not tarry.

4 "Behold the proud,
His soul is not upright in him;
But the just shall live by his faith.

Woe to the Wicked

5 "Indeed, because he transgresses
by wine,
He is a proud man,
And he does not stay at home.
Because he enlarges his desire as
hell,[a]
And he *is* like death, and cannot
be satisfied,
He gathers to himself all nations
And heaps up for himself all
peoples.

6 "Will not all these take up a proverb
against him,
And a taunting riddle against
him, and say,
'Woe to him who increases
What is not his—how long?
And to him who loads himself
with many pledges'?[a]
7 Will not your creditors[a] rise up
suddenly?
Will they not awaken who oppress
you?
And you will become their booty.
8 Because you have plundered
many nations,
All the remnant of the people
shall plunder you,
Because of men's blood
And the violence of the land *and*
the city,
And of all who dwell in it.

9 "Woe to him who covets evil gain
for his house,
That he may set his nest on high,
That he may be delivered from
the power of disaster!
10 You give shameful counsel to
your house,
Cutting off many peoples,
And sin *against* your soul.
11 For the stone will cry out from the
wall,

2:5 [a] Or *Sheol* 2:6 [a] Syriac and Vulgate read *thick clay.* 2:7 [a] Literally *those who bite you*

And the beam from the timbers
will answer it.

12 "Woe to him who builds a town with
bloodshed,
Who establishes a city by iniquity!
13 Behold, *is it* not of the LORD of
hosts
That the peoples labor to feed the
fire,[a]
And nations weary themselves in
vain?
14 For the earth will be filled
With the knowledge of the glory
of the LORD,
As the waters cover the sea.

15 "Woe to him who gives drink to his
neighbor,
Pressing[a] *him to* your bottle,
Even to make *him* drunk,
That you may look on his
nakedness!
16 You are filled with shame instead
of glory.
You also—drink!
And be exposed as
uncircumcised![a]
The cup of the LORD's right hand
will be turned against you,
And utter shame will be on your
glory.
17 For the violence *done to* Lebanon
will cover you,
And the plunder of beasts *which*
made them afraid,
Because of men's blood
And the violence of the land *and*
the city,
And of all who dwell in it.

18 "What profit is the image, that its
maker should carve it,
The molded image, a teacher of
lies,
That the maker of its mold should
trust in it,
To make mute idols?
19 Woe to him who says to wood,
'Awake!'
To silent stone, 'Arise! It shall
teach!'
Behold, it is overlaid with gold
and silver,
Yet in it there is no breath at all.

20 "But the LORD is in His holy temple.
Let all the earth keep silence
before Him."

The Prophet's Prayer

3 A prayer of Habakkuk the prophet,
on Shigionoth.[a]

2 O LORD, I have heard Your speech
and was afraid;
O LORD, revive Your work in the
midst of the years!
In the midst of the years make *it*
known;
In wrath remember mercy.

3 God came from Teman,
The Holy One from Mount Paran.
Selah

His glory covered the heavens,
And the earth was full of His
praise.
4 *His* brightness was like the light;
He had rays *flashing* from His
hand,
And there His power *was* hidden.
5 Before Him went pestilence,
And fever followed at His feet.

6 He stood and measured the earth;
He looked and startled the
nations.
And the everlasting mountains
were scattered,
The perpetual hills bowed.
His ways *are* everlasting.
7 I saw the tents of Cushan in
affliction;
The curtains of the land of Midian
trembled.

8 O LORD, were *You* displeased with
the rivers,
Was Your anger against the rivers,
Was Your wrath against the sea,
That You rode on Your horses,
Your chariots of salvation?

2:13 [a] Literally *for what satisfies fire,* that is, for what is of no lasting value 2:15 [a] Literally *Attaching* or *Joining* 2:16 [a] Dead Sea Scrolls and Septuagint read *And reel!;* Syriac and Vulgate read *And fall fast asleep!* 3:1 [a] Exact meaning unknown

9 Your bow was made quite ready;
Oaths were sworn over *Your* arrows.[a] *Selah*

You divided the earth with rivers.
10 The mountains saw You *and* trembled;
The overflowing of the water passed by.
The deep uttered its voice,
And lifted its hands on high.
11 The sun and moon stood still in their habitation;
At the light of Your arrows they went,
At the shining of Your glittering spear.

12 You marched through the land in indignation;
You trampled the nations in anger.
13 You went forth for the salvation of Your people,
For salvation with Your Anointed.
You struck the head from the house of the wicked,
By laying bare from foundation to neck. *Selah*

14 You thrust through with his own arrows
The head of his villages.
They came out like a whirlwind to scatter me;
Their rejoicing was like feasting on the poor in secret.
15 You walked through the sea with Your horses,
Through the heap of great waters.

16 When I heard, my body trembled;
My lips quivered at *the* voice;
Rottenness entered my bones;
And I trembled in myself,
That I might rest in the day of trouble.
When he comes up to the people,
He will invade them with his troops.

A Hymn of Faith

17 Though the fig tree may not blossom,
Nor fruit be on the vines;
Though the labor of the olive may fail,
And the fields yield no food;
Though the flock may be cut off from the fold,
And there be no herd in the stalls—
18 Yet I will rejoice in the LORD,
I will joy in the God of my salvation.

19 The LORD God[a] is my strength;
He will make my feet like deer's *feet*,
And He will make me walk on my high hills.

To the Chief Musician. With my stringed instruments.

3:9 [a] Literally *rods* or *tribes* (compare verse 14) 3:19 [a] Hebrew *YHWH Adonai*

THE BOOK OF
ZEPHANIAH

Zephaniah ministered at the same time as Jeremiah, during the reign of Josiah, one of the good kings of Judah. But the revival God's people experienced during this time would not last, and they would return to their idolatry. The book follows the familiar pattern for the prophets. Zephaniah declares God's judgment on Judah as well as several surrounding nations. After the judgment of the first two chapters, the third promises that after the time of discipline is completed, blessings will come in the person of the Messiah.

- **GENRE:** Minor Prophet
- **AUTHOR:** Zephaniah
- **TIME:** c. 635–625 BC
- **PURPOSE:** To show that even though punishment comes, God's love continues forever.

---

1 The word of the LORD which came
to Zephaniah the son of Cushi, the
son of Gedaliah, the son of Amariah, the
son of Hezekiah, in the days of Josiah
the son of Amon, king of Judah.

The Great Day of the LORD

2 "I will utterly consume everything
From the face of the land,"
Says the LORD;
3 "I will consume man and beast;
I will consume the birds of the heavens,
The fish of the sea,
And the stumbling blocks[a] along with the wicked.
I will cut off man from the face of the land,"
Says the LORD.

4 "I will stretch out My hand against Judah,
And against all the inhabitants of Jerusalem.
I will cut off every trace of Baal from this place,
The names of the idolatrous priests[a] with the *pagan* priests—
5 Those who worship the host of heaven on the housetops;
Those who worship and swear *oaths* by the LORD,
But who *also* swear by Milcom;[a]
6 Those who have turned back from *following* the LORD,
And have not sought the LORD, nor inquired of Him."

7 Be silent in the presence of the Lord GOD;
For the day of the LORD *is* at hand,
For the LORD has prepared a sacrifice;
He has invited[a] His guests.
8 "And it shall be,
In the day of the LORD's sacrifice,
That I will punish the princes and the king's children,
And all such as are clothed with foreign apparel.
9 In the same day I will punish
All those who leap over the threshold,[a]
Who fill their masters' houses with violence and deceit.

10 "And there shall be on that day," says the LORD,
"The sound of a mournful cry from the Fish Gate,

1:3 [a] Figurative of idols 1:4 [a] Hebrew *chemarim* 1:5 [a] Or *Malcam*, an Ammonite god, also called *Molech* (compare Leviticus 18:21) 1:7 [a] Literally *set apart, consecrated* 1:9 [a] Compare 1 Samuel 5:5

A wailing from the Second
Quarter,
And a loud crashing from the hills.
11 Wail, you inhabitants of
Maktesh![a]
For all the merchant people are
cut down;
All those who handle money are
cut off.

12 "And it shall come to pass at that
time
That I will search Jerusalem with
lamps,
And punish the men
Who are settled in complacency,[a]
Who say in their heart,
'The LORD will not do good,
Nor will He do evil.'
13 Therefore their goods shall
become booty,
And their houses a desolation;
They shall build houses, but not
inhabit *them;*
They shall plant vineyards, but
not drink their wine."

14 The great day of the LORD *is* near;
It is near and hastens quickly.
The noise of the day of the LORD
is bitter;
There the mighty men shall cry
out.
15 That day *is* a day of wrath,
A day of trouble and distress,
A day of devastation and
desolation,
A day of darkness and
gloominess,
A day of clouds and thick
darkness,
16 A day of trumpet and alarm
Against the fortified cities
And against the high towers.

17 "I will bring distress upon men,
And they shall walk like blind
men,
Because they have sinned against
the LORD;
Their blood shall be poured out
like dust,
And their flesh like refuse."
18 Neither their silver nor their gold
Shall be able to deliver them
In the day of the LORD's wrath;
But the whole land shall be
devoured
By the fire of His jealousy,
For He will make speedy riddance
Of all those who dwell in the land.

A Call to Repentance

2 Gather yourselves together, yes,
gather together,
O undesirable[a] nation,
2 Before the decree is issued,
Or the day passes like chaff,
Before the LORD's fierce anger
comes upon you,
Before the day of the LORD's
anger comes upon you!
3 Seek the LORD, all you meek of
the earth,
Who have upheld His justice.
Seek righteousness, seek
humility.
It may be that you will be hidden
In the day of the LORD's anger.

Judgment on Nations

4 For Gaza shall be forsaken,
And Ashkelon desolate;
They shall drive out Ashdod at
noonday,
And Ekron shall be uprooted.
5 Woe to the inhabitants of the
seacoast,
The nation of the Cherethites!
The word of the LORD *is* against
you,
O Canaan, land of the Philistines:
"I will destroy you;
So there shall be no inhabitant."

6 The seacoast shall be pastures,
With shelters[a] for shepherds and
folds for flocks.
7 The coast shall be for the remnant
of the house of Judah;
They shall feed *their* flocks there;
In the houses of Ashkelon they
shall lie down at evening.
For the LORD their God will
intervene for them,
And return their captives.

1:11 [a] Literally *Mortar,* a market district of Jerusalem **1:12** [a] Literally *on their lees,* that is, settled like the dregs of wine **2:1** [a] Or *shameless* **2:6** [a] Literally *excavations,* either underground huts or cisterns

8 "I have heard the reproach of Moab,
And the insults of the people of Ammon,
With which they have reproached My people,
And made arrogant threats against their borders.
9 Therefore, as I live,"
Says the LORD of hosts, the God of Israel,
"Surely Moab shall be like Sodom,
And the people of Ammon like Gomorrah—
Overrun with weeds and saltpits,
And a perpetual desolation.
The residue of My people shall plunder them,
And the remnant of My people shall possess them."

10 This they shall have for their pride,
Because they have reproached and made arrogant threats
Against the people of the LORD of hosts.
11 The LORD *will be* awesome to them,
For He will reduce to nothing all the gods of the earth;
People shall worship Him,
Each one from his place,
Indeed all the shores of the nations.

12 "You Ethiopians also,
You shall be slain by My sword."

13 And He will stretch out His hand against the north,
Destroy Assyria,
And make Nineveh a desolation,
As dry as the wilderness.
14 The herds shall lie down in her midst,
Every beast of the nation.
Both the pelican and the bittern
Shall lodge on the capitals *of* her *pillars;*
Their voice shall sing in the windows;
Desolation *shall be* at the threshold;
For He will lay bare the cedar work.
15 This is the rejoicing city
That dwelt securely,
That said in her heart,
"I *am it,* and *there is* none besides me."
How has she become a desolation,
A place for beasts to lie down!
Everyone who passes by her
Shall hiss and shake his fist.

The Wickedness of Jerusalem

3 Woe to her who is rebellious and polluted,
To the oppressing city!
2 She has not obeyed *His* voice,
She has not received correction;
She has not trusted in the LORD,
She has not drawn near to her God.

3 Her princes in her midst *are* roaring lions;
Her judges *are* evening wolves
That leave not a bone till morning.
4 Her prophets are insolent, treacherous people;
Her priests have polluted the sanctuary,
They have done violence to the law.
5 The LORD *is* righteous in her midst,
He will do no unrighteousness.
Every morning He brings His justice to light;
He never fails,
But the unjust knows no shame.

6 "I have cut off nations,
Their fortresses are devastated;
I have made their streets desolate,
With none passing by.
Their cities are destroyed;
There is no one, no inhabitant.
7 I said, 'Surely you will fear Me,
You will receive instruction'—
So that her dwelling would not be cut off,
Despite everything for which I punished her.
But they rose early and corrupted all their deeds.

A Faithful Remnant

8 "Therefore wait for Me," says the LORD,
"Until the day I rise up for plunder;[a]
My determination *is* to gather the nations
To My assembly of kingdoms,
To pour on them My indignation,
All My fierce anger;
All the earth shall be devoured
With the fire of My jealousy.

9 "For then I will restore to the peoples a pure language,
That they all may call on the name of the LORD,
To serve Him with one accord.
10 From beyond the rivers of Ethiopia
My worshipers,
The daughter of My dispersed ones,
Shall bring My offering.
11 In that day you shall not be shamed for any of your deeds
In which you transgress against Me;
For then I will take away from your midst
Those who rejoice in your pride,
And you shall no longer be haughty
In My holy mountain.
12 I will leave in your midst
A meek and humble people,
And they shall trust in the name of the LORD.
13 The remnant of Israel shall do no unrighteousness
And speak no lies,
Nor shall a deceitful tongue be found in their mouth;
For they shall feed *their* flocks and lie down,
And no one shall make *them* afraid."

Joy in God's Faithfulness

14 Sing, O daughter of Zion!
Shout, O Israel!
Be glad and rejoice with all *your* heart,
O daughter of Jerusalem!
15 The LORD has taken away your judgments,
He has cast out your enemy.
The King of Israel, the LORD, *is* in your midst;
You shall see[a] disaster no more.

16 In that day it shall be said to Jerusalem:
"Do not fear;
Zion, let not your hands be weak.
17 The LORD your God in your midst,
The Mighty One, will save;
He will rejoice over you with gladness,
He will quiet *you* with His love,
He will rejoice over you with singing."

18 "I will gather those who sorrow over the appointed assembly,
Who are among you,
To whom its reproach *is* a burden.
19 Behold, at that time
I will deal with all who afflict you;
I will save the lame,
And gather those who were driven out;
I will appoint them for praise and fame
In every land where they were put to shame.
20 At that time I will bring you back,
Even at the time I gather you;
For I will give you fame and praise
Among all the peoples of the earth,
When I return your captives before your eyes,"
Says the LORD.

3:8 [a] Septuagint and Syriac read *for witness;* Targum reads *for the day of My revelation for judgment;* Vulgate reads *for the day of My resurrection that is to come.* **3:15** [a] Some Hebrew manuscripts, Septuagint, and Bomberg read *see;* Masoretic Text and Vulgate read *fear.*

THE BOOK OF

HAGGAI

Haggai is the first prophet to minister to God's people after the exile. Haggai addresses the immediate problem of the rebuilding of the temple. The people had returned about twenty years earlier and started this project but had failed to finish. Haggai's concern is that the people neglecting the temple is a symptom of a bigger problem. They have dropped God as their highest priority and are more concerned with building their lifestyles than their relationship with God. With Haggai's encouragement, the people rebuild the temple. Haggai tells them that this new temple might be smaller than the one Solomon built, but it is better because God would fill this house with His glory.

- **GENRE:** Minor Prophet
- **AUTHOR:** Haggai
- **TIME:** 520 BC
- **PURPOSE:** To encourage the people to stop thinking about themselves and to rebuild God's temple.

The Command to Build God's House

1 In the second year of King Darius, in the sixth month, on the first day of the month, the word of the LORD came by Haggai the prophet to Zerubbabel the son of Shealtiel, governor of Judah, and to Joshua the son of Jehozadak, the high priest, saying, 2"Thus speaks the LORD of hosts, saying: 'This people says, "The time has not come, the time that the LORD's house should be built." ' "

3Then the word of the LORD came by Haggai the prophet, saying, 4"*Is it* time for you yourselves to dwell in your paneled houses, and this temple[a] *to lie* in ruins?" 5Now therefore, thus says the LORD of hosts: "Consider your ways!

6 "You have sown much, and bring in little;
You eat, but do not have enough;
You drink, but you are not filled with drink;
You clothe yourselves, but no one is warm;
And he who earns wages,
Earns wages *to put* into a bag with holes."

7Thus says the LORD of hosts: "Consider your ways! 8Go up to the mountains and bring wood and build the temple, that I may take pleasure in it and be glorified," says the LORD. 9"You looked for much, but indeed *it came to* little; and when you brought it home, I blew it away. Why?" says the LORD of hosts. "Because of My house that *is in* ruins, while every one of you runs to his own house. 10Therefore the heavens above you withhold the dew, and the earth withholds its fruit. 11For I called for a drought on the land and the mountains, on the grain and the new wine and the oil, on whatever the ground brings forth, on men and livestock, and on all the labor of *your* hands."

The People's Obedience

12Then Zerubbabel the son of Shealtiel, and Joshua the son of Jehozadak, the high priest, with all the remnant of the people, obeyed the voice of the LORD their God, and the words of Haggai the prophet, as the LORD their God had sent him; and the people feared the presence of the LORD. 13Then Haggai, the LORD's messenger, spoke the LORD's message to the people, saying, "I *am* with you, says the LORD." 14So the LORD stirred up the spirit of Zerubbabel the son of Shealtiel, governor of Judah, and the spirit of Joshua the son of Jehozadak, the high priest, and the spirit of all the remnant of the people; and they came and worked on

1:4 [a] Literally *house,* and so in verse 8

the house of the LORD of hosts, their God, 15on the twenty-fourth day of the sixth month, in the second year of King Darius.

The Coming Glory of God's House

2 In the seventh *month,* on the twenty-first of the month, the word of the LORD came by Haggai the prophet, saying: 2"Speak now to Zerubbabel the son of Shealtiel, governor of Judah, and to Joshua the son of Jehozadak, the high priest, and to the remnant of the people, saying: 3'Who is left among you who saw this temple[a] in its former glory? And how do you see it now? In comparison with it, *is this* not in your eyes as nothing? 4Yet now be strong, Zerubbabel,' says the LORD; 'and be strong, Joshua, son of Jehozadak, the high priest; and be strong, all you people of the land,' says the LORD, 'and work; for I *am* with you,' says the LORD of hosts. 5'*According to* the word that I covenanted with you when you came out of Egypt, so My Spirit remains among you; do not fear!'

6"For thus says the LORD of hosts: 'Once more (it *is* a little while) I will shake heaven and earth, the sea and dry land; 7and I will shake all nations, and they shall come to the Desire of All Nations,[a] and I will fill this temple with glory,' says the LORD of hosts. 8'The silver *is* Mine, and the gold *is* Mine,' says the LORD of hosts. 9'The glory of this latter temple shall be greater than the former,' says the LORD of hosts. 'And in this place I will give peace,' says the LORD of hosts."

The People Are Defiled

10On the twenty-fourth *day* of the ninth *month,* in the second year of Darius, the word of the LORD came by Haggai the prophet, saying, 11"Thus says the LORD of hosts: 'Now, ask the priests *concerning the* law, saying, 12"If one carries holy meat in the fold of his garment, and with the edge he touches bread or stew, wine or oil, or any food, will it become holy?" ' "

Then the priests answered and said, "No."

13And Haggai said, "If *one who is* unclean *because* of a dead body touches any of these, will it be unclean?"

So the priests answered and said, "It shall be unclean."

14Then Haggai answered and said, " 'So is this people, and so is this nation before Me,' says the LORD, 'and so is every work of their hands; and what they offer there is unclean.

Promised Blessing

15'And now, carefully consider from this day forward: from before stone was laid upon stone in the temple of the LORD— 16since those *days,* when *one* came to a heap of twenty ephahs, there were *but* ten; when *one* came to the wine vat to draw out fifty baths from the press, there were *but* twenty. 17I struck you with blight and mildew and hail in all the labors of your hands; yet you did not *turn* to Me,' says the LORD. 18'Consider now from this day forward, from the twenty-fourth day of the ninth month, from the day that the foundation of the LORD's temple was laid—consider it: 19Is the seed still in the barn? As yet the vine, the fig tree, the pomegranate, and the olive tree have not yielded *fruit. But* from this day I will bless *you.*' "

Zerubbabel Chosen as a Signet

20And again the word of the LORD came to Haggai on the twenty-fourth day of the month, saying, 21"Speak to Zerubbabel, governor of Judah, saying:

'I will shake heaven and earth.
22 I will overthrow the throne of kingdoms;
I will destroy the strength of the Gentile kingdoms.
I will overthrow the chariots
And those who ride in them;
The horses and their riders shall come down,
Every one by the sword of his brother.

23'In that day,' says the LORD of hosts, 'I will take you, Zerubbabel My servant, the son of Shealtiel,' says the LORD, 'and will make you like a signet *ring;* for I have chosen you,' says the LORD of hosts."

2:3 [a] Literally *house,* and so in verses 7 and 9 2:7 [a] Or *the desire of all nations*

THE BOOK OF
ZECHARIAH

Zechariah's writings were designed to encourage the Jews and inspire energy, identity, and vision during the rebuilding of the temple. The people must build the temple because their future blessings depend on it. Like Isaiah, Daniel, and Ezekiel, his prophecies include visions of God and the future. Perhaps more than any of the other Old Testament books, Zechariah shares clear prophecies about Jesus, which are fulfilled in the New Testament.

- **GENRE:** Minor Prophet
- **AUTHOR:** Zechariah
- **TIME:** c. 520–518 BC / c. 480–470 BC
- **PURPOSE:** To encourage God's people and give them hope for the future.

A Call to Repentance

1 In the eighth month of the second
year of Darius, the word of the LORD
came to Zechariah the son of Berechiah,
the son of Iddo the prophet, saying,
2"The LORD has been very angry with
your fathers. 3Therefore say to them,
'Thus says the LORD of hosts: "Return
to Me," says the LORD of hosts, "and I
will return to you," says the LORD of
hosts. 4"Do not be like your fathers, to
whom the former prophets preached,
saying, 'Thus says the LORD of hosts:
"Turn now from your evil ways and your
evil deeds." ' But they did not hear nor
heed Me," says the LORD.

5 "Your fathers, where *are* they?
And the prophets, do they live
forever?
6 Yet surely My words and My
statutes,
Which I commanded My servants
the prophets,
Did they not overtake your
fathers?

"So they returned and said:

'Just as the LORD of hosts
determined to do to us,
According to our ways and
according to our
deeds,
So He has dealt with us.' " ' "

Vision of the Horses

7On the twenty-fourth day of the elev-
enth month, which is the month She-
bat, in the second year of Darius, the
word of the LORD came to Zechariah
the son of Berechiah, the son of Iddo the
prophet: 8I saw by night, and behold, a
man riding on a red horse, and it stood
among the myrtle trees in the hollow;
and behind him *were* horses: red, sorrel,
and white. 9Then I said, "My lord, what
are these?" So the angel who talked with
me said to me, "I will show you what
they *are*."
10And the man who stood among the
myrtle trees answered and said, "These
are the ones whom the LORD has sent to
walk to and fro throughout the earth."
11So they answered the Angel of the
LORD, who stood among the myrtle
trees, and said, "We have walked to and
fro throughout the earth, and behold,
all the earth is resting quietly."

The LORD Will Comfort Zion

12Then the Angel of the LORD answered
and said, "O LORD of hosts, how long will
You not have mercy on Jerusalem and
on the cities of Judah, against which
You were angry these seventy years?"
13And the LORD answered the angel
who talked to me, *with* good *and* com-
forting words. 14So the angel who spoke
with me said to me, "Proclaim, saying,
'Thus says the LORD of hosts:

"I am zealous for Jerusalem
And for Zion with great zeal.
15 I am exceedingly angry with the
nations at ease;
For I was a little angry,
And they helped—*but* with evil
intent."

16"Therefore thus says the LORD:

"I am returning to Jerusalem with
mercy;
My house shall be built in it," says
the LORD of hosts,
"And a *surveyor's* line shall
be stretched out over
Jerusalem." '

17"Again proclaim, saying, 'Thus says
the LORD of hosts:

"My cities shall again spread out
through prosperity;
The LORD will again comfort Zion,
And will again choose
Jerusalem." ' "

Vision of the Horns

18Then I raised my eyes and looked,
and there *were* four horns. 19And I said
to the angel who talked with me, "What
are these?"
So he answered me, "These *are* the
horns that have scattered Judah, Israel,
and Jerusalem."
20Then the LORD showed me four
craftsmen. 21And I said, "What are these
coming to do?"
So he said, "These *are* the horns that
scattered Judah, so that no one could lift
up his head; but the craftsmen[a] are com-
ing to terrify them, to cast out the horns
of the nations that lifted up *their* horn
against the land of Judah to scatter it."

Vision of the Measuring Line

2 Then I raised my eyes and looked,
and behold, a man with a measur-
ing line in his hand. 2So I said, "Where
are you going?"
And he said to me, "To measure Jeru-
salem, to see what *is* its width and what
is its length."
3And there *was* the angel who talked
with me, going out; and another angel
was coming out to meet him, 4who said
to him, "Run, speak to this young man,
saying: 'Jerusalem shall be inhabited
as towns without walls, because of the
multitude of men and livestock in it.
5For I,' says the LORD, 'will be a wall
of fire all around her, and I will be the
glory in her midst.' "

Future Joy of Zion and Many Nations

6"Up, up! Flee from the land of the
north," says the LORD; "for I have spread
you abroad like the four winds of heav-
en," says the LORD. 7"Up, Zion! Escape,
you who dwell with the daughter of
Babylon."
8For thus says the LORD of hosts: "He
sent Me after glory, to the nations which
plunder you; for he who touches you
touches the apple of His eye. 9For sure-
ly I will shake My hand against them,
and they shall become spoil for their
servants. Then you will know that the
LORD of hosts has sent Me.
10"Sing and rejoice, O daughter of
Zion! For behold, I am coming and I
will dwell in your midst," says the LORD.
11"Many nations shall be joined to the
LORD in that day, and they shall be-
come My people. And I will dwell in
your midst. Then you will know that the
LORD of hosts has sent Me to you. 12And
the LORD will take possession of Judah
as His inheritance in the Holy Land,
and will again choose Jerusalem. 13Be
silent, all flesh, before the LORD, for He
is aroused from His holy habitation!"

Vision of the High Priest

3 Then he showed me Joshua the high
priest standing before the Angel
of the LORD, and Satan standing at his
right hand to oppose him. 2And the
LORD said to Satan, "The LORD rebuke
you, Satan! The LORD who has chosen
Jerusalem rebuke you! *Is* this not a
brand plucked from the fire?"
3Now Joshua was clothed with filthy
garments, and was standing before
the Angel.
4Then He answered and spoke to those

1:21 [a] Literally *these*

who stood before Him, saying, "Take
away the filthy garments from him."
And to him He said, "See, I have removed your iniquity from you, and I
will clothe you with rich robes."
5And I said, "Let them put a clean tur-
ban on his head."
So they put a clean turban on his head,
and they put the clothes on him. And
the Angel of the LORD stood by.

The Coming Branch

6Then the Angel of the LORD admon-
ished Joshua, saying, 7"Thus says the
LORD of hosts:

'If you will walk in My ways,
And if you will keep My command,
Then you shall also judge My house,
And likewise have charge of My courts;
I will give you places to walk
Among these who stand here.

8 'Hear, O Joshua, the high priest,
You and your companions who sit before you,
For they are a wondrous sign;
For behold, I am bringing forth
My Servant the BRANCH.
9 For behold, the stone
That I have laid before Joshua:
Upon the stone *are* seven eyes.
Behold, I will engrave its inscription,'
Says the LORD of hosts,
'And I will remove the iniquity of that land in one day.
10 In that day,' says the LORD of hosts,
'Everyone will invite his neighbor
Under his vine and under his fig tree.' "

Vision of the Lampstand and Olive Trees

4 Now the angel who talked with me
came back and wakened me, as a
man who is wakened out of his sleep.
2And he said to me, "What do you see?"
So I said, "I am looking, and there *is*
a lampstand of solid gold with a bowl
on top of it, and on the *stand* seven
lamps with seven pipes to the seven
lamps. 3Two olive trees *are* by it, one
at the right of the bowl and the other
at its left." 4So I answered and spoke to
the angel who talked with me, saying,
"What *are* these, my lord?"
5Then the angel who talked with me
answered and said to me, "Do you not
know what these are?"
And I said, "No, my lord."
6So he answered and said to me:

"This *is* the word of the LORD to Zerubbabel:
'Not by might nor by power, but by My Spirit,'
Says the LORD of hosts.
7 'Who *are* you, O great mountain?
Before Zerubbabel *you shall become* a plain!
And he shall bring forth the capstone
With shouts of "Grace, grace to it!" ' "

8Moreover the word of the LORD came
to me, saying:

9 "The hands of Zerubbabel
Have laid the foundation of this temple;[a]
His hands shall also finish *it*.
Then you will know
That the LORD of hosts has sent Me to you.
10 For who has despised the day of small things?
For these seven rejoice to see
The plumb line in the hand of Zerubbabel.
They are the eyes of the LORD,
Which scan to and fro throughout the whole earth."

11Then I answered and said to him,
"What *are* these two olive trees—at the
right of the lampstand and at its left?"
12And I further answered and said to him,
"What *are these* two olive branches that
drip into the receptacles[a] of the two gold
pipes from which the golden *oil* drains?"

4:9 [a] Literally *house* 4:12 [a] Literally *into the hands of*

13Then he answered me and said, "Do
you not know what these *are?*"
And I said, "No, my lord."
14So he said, "These *are* the two anoint-
ed ones, who stand beside the Lord of
the whole earth."

Vision of the Flying Scroll

5 Then I turned and raised my eyes,
and saw there a flying scroll.
2And he said to me, "What do you see?"
So I answered, "I see a flying scroll.
Its length *is* twenty cubits and its width
ten cubits."
3Then he said to me, "This *is* the curse
that goes out over the face of the whole
earth: 'Every thief shall be expelled,'
according *to* this side of *the scroll;* and,
'Every perjurer shall be expelled,' ac-
cording *to* that side of it."

4 "I will send out *the curse,*" says the
LORD of hosts;
"It shall enter the house of the thief
And the house of the one who
swears falsely by My name.
It shall remain in the midst of his
house
And consume it, with its timber
and stones."

Vision of the Woman in a Basket

5Then the angel who talked with me
came out and said to me, "Lift your eyes
now, and see what this *is* that goes forth."
6So I asked, "What *is* it?" And he said,
"It *is* a basket[a] that is going forth."
He also said, "This *is* their resemblance
throughout the earth: 7Here *is* a lead
disc lifted up, and this *is* a woman sit-
ting inside the basket"; 8then he said,
"This *is* Wickedness!" And he thrust her
down into the basket, and threw the lead
cover[a] over its mouth. 9Then I raised my
eyes and looked, and there *were* two
women, coming with the wind in their
wings; for they had wings like the wings
of a stork, and they lifted up the basket
between earth and heaven.
10So I said to the angel who talked
with me, "Where are they carrying the
basket?"
11And he said to me, "To build a house
for it in the land of Shinar;[a] when it is
ready, *the basket* will be set there on
its base."

Vision of the Four Chariots

6 Then I turned and raised my eyes
and looked, and behold, four char-
iots *were* coming from between two
mountains, and the mountains *were*
mountains of bronze. 2With the first
chariot *were* red horses, with the sec-
ond chariot black horses, 3with the
third chariot white horses, and with
the fourth chariot dappled horses—
strong *steeds.* 4Then I answered and
said to the angel who talked with me,
"What *are* these, my lord?"
5And the angel answered and said to
me, "These *are* four spirits of heaven, who
go out from *their* station before the Lord
of all the earth. 6The one with the black
horses is going to the north country, the
white are going after them, and the dap-
pled are going toward the south country."
7Then the strong *steeds* went out, eager
to go, that they might walk to and fro
throughout the earth. And He said, "Go,
walk to and fro throughout the earth." So
they walked to and fro throughout the
earth. 8And He called to me, and spoke
to me, saying, "See, those who go toward
the north country have given rest to My
Spirit in the north country."

The Command to Crown Joshua

9Then the word of the LORD came to
me, saying: 10"Receive *the gift* from the
captives—from Heldai, Tobijah, and
Jedaiah, who have come from Bab-
ylon—and go the same day and enter
the house of Josiah the son of Zephani-
ah. 11Take the silver and gold, make an
elaborate crown, and set *it* on the head
of Joshua the son of Jehozadak, the
high priest. 12Then speak to him, saying,
'Thus says the LORD of hosts, saying:

"Behold, the Man whose name *is* the
BRANCH!
From His place He shall branch
out,
And He shall build the temple of
the LORD;

5:6 [a] Hebrew *ephah,* a measuring container, and so elsewhere 5:8 [a] Literally *stone* 5:11 [a] That is, Babylon

13 Yes, He shall build the temple of
the LORD.
He shall bear the glory,
And shall sit and rule on His
throne;
So He shall be a priest on His
throne,
And the counsel of peace shall be
between them both." '

14"Now the elaborate crown shall be for
a memorial in the temple of the LORD
for Helem,[a] Tobijah, Jedaiah, and Hen
the son of Zephaniah. 15Even those from
afar shall come and build the temple of
the LORD. Then you shall know that the
LORD of hosts has sent Me to you. And
this shall come to pass if you diligently
obey the voice of the LORD your God."

Obedience Better than Fasting

7 Now in the fourth year of King Da-
rius it came to pass *that* the word
of the LORD came to Zechariah, on the
fourth *day* of the ninth month, Chis-
lev, 2when *the people*[a] sent Sherezer,[b]
with Regem-Melech and his men, *to*
the house of God,[c] to pray before the
LORD, 3*and* to ask the priests who *were*
in the house of the LORD of hosts, and
the prophets, saying, "Should I weep in
the fifth month and fast as I have done
for so many years?"

4Then the word of the LORD of hosts
came to me, saying, 5"Say to all the peo-
ple of the land, and to the priests: 'When
you fasted and mourned in the fifth and
seventh *months* during those seventy
years, did you really fast for Me—for
Me? 6When you eat and when you drink,
do you not eat and drink *for yourselves?*
7*Should you* not *have obeyed* the words
which the LORD proclaimed through
the former prophets when Jerusalem
and the cities around it were inhabited
and prosperous, and the South[a] and the
Lowland were inhabited?' "

Disobedience Resulted in Captivity

8Then the word of the LORD came to
Zechariah, saying, 9"Thus says the LORD
of hosts:

'Execute true justice,
Show mercy and compassion
Everyone to his brother.
10 Do not oppress the widow or the
fatherless,
The alien or the poor.
Let none of you plan evil in his
heart
Against his brother.'

11"But they refused to heed, shrugged
their shoulders, and stopped their ears
so that they could not hear. 12Yes, they
made their hearts like flint, refusing to
hear the law and the words which the
LORD of hosts had sent by His Spirit
through the former prophets. Thus great
wrath came from the LORD of hosts.
13Therefore it happened, *that* just as He
proclaimed and they would not hear, so
they called out and I would not listen,"
says the LORD of hosts. 14"But I scattered
them with a whirlwind among all the na-
tions which they had not known. Thus the
land became desolate after them, so that
no one passed through or returned; for
they made the pleasant land desolate."

Jerusalem, Holy City of the Future

8 Again the word of the LORD of hosts
came, saying, 2"Thus says the LORD
of hosts:

'I am zealous for Zion with great
zeal;
With great fervor I am zealous for
her.'

3"Thus says the LORD:

'I will return to Zion,
And dwell in the midst of
Jerusalem.
Jerusalem shall be called the City
of Truth,
The Mountain of the LORD of hosts,
The Holy Mountain.'

4"Thus says the LORD of hosts:

'Old men and old women shall
again sit

6:14 [a] Following Masoretic Text, Targum, and Vulgate; Syriac reads *for Heldai* (compare verse 10); Septuagint reads *for the patient ones.* 7:2 [a] Literally *they* (compare verse 5) [b] Or *Sar-Ezer* [c] Hebrew *Bethel* 7:7 [a] Hebrew *Negev*

In the streets of Jerusalem,
Each one with his staff in his hand
Because of great age.
5 The streets of the city
Shall be full of boys and girls
Playing in its streets.'

6"Thus says the LORD of hosts:

'If it is marvelous in the eyes of the remnant of this people in these days,
Will it also be marvelous in My eyes?'
Says the LORD of hosts.

7"Thus says the LORD of hosts:

'Behold, I will save My people from the land of the east
And from the land of the west;
8 I will bring them *back*,
And they shall dwell in the midst of Jerusalem.
They shall be My people
And I will be their God,
In truth and righteousness.'

9"Thus says the LORD of hosts:

'Let your hands be strong,
You who have been hearing in these days
These words by the mouth of the prophets,
Who *spoke* in the day the foundation was laid
For the house of the LORD of hosts,
That the temple might be built.
10 For before these days
There were no wages for man nor any hire for beast;
There was no peace from the enemy for whoever went out or came in;
For I set all men, everyone, against his neighbor.

11But now I *will* not *treat* the remnant of
this people as in the former days,' says
the LORD of hosts.

12 'For the seed *shall be* prosperous,
The vine shall give its fruit,
The ground shall give her increase,
And the heavens shall give their dew—
I will cause the remnant of this people
To possess all these.
13 And it shall come to pass
That just as you were a curse among the nations,
O house of Judah and house of Israel,
So I will save you, and you shall be a blessing.
Do not fear,
Let your hands be strong.'

14"For thus says the LORD of hosts:

'Just as I determined to punish you
When your fathers provoked Me to wrath,'
Says the LORD of hosts,
'And I would not relent,
15 So again in these days
I am determined to do good
To Jerusalem and to the house of Judah.
Do not fear.
16 These *are* the things you shall do:
Speak each man the truth to his neighbor;
Give judgment in your gates for truth, justice, and peace;
17 Let none of you think evil in your[a] heart against your neighbor;
And do not love a false oath.
For all these *are things* that I hate,'
Says the LORD."

18Then the word of the LORD of hosts
came to me, saying, 19"Thus says the
LORD of hosts:

'The fast of the fourth *month*,
The fast of the fifth,
The fast of the seventh,
And the fast of the tenth,
Shall be joy and gladness and cheerful feasts

8:17 [a] Literally *his*

For the house of Judah.
Therefore love truth and peace.'

20"Thus says the LORD of hosts:

'Peoples shall yet come,
Inhabitants of many cities;
21 The inhabitants of one *city* shall go to another, saying,
"Let us continue to go and pray before the LORD,
And seek the LORD of hosts.
I myself will go also."
22 Yes, many peoples and strong nations
Shall come to seek the LORD of hosts in Jerusalem,
And to pray before the LORD.'

23"Thus says the LORD of hosts: 'In
those days ten men from every lan-
guage of the nations shall grasp the
sleeve of a Jewish man, saying, "Let us
go with you, for we have heard *that* God
is with you." ' "

Israel Defended Against Enemies

9 The burden[a] of the word of the LORD
Against the land of Hadrach,
And Damascus its resting place
(For the eyes of men
And all the tribes of Israel
Are on the LORD);
2 Also *against* Hamath, *which* borders on it,
And *against* Tyre and Sidon, though they are very wise.

3 For Tyre built herself a tower,
Heaped up silver like the dust,
And gold like the mire of the streets.
4 Behold, the Lord will cast her out;
He will destroy her power in the sea,
And she will be devoured by fire.

5 Ashkelon shall see *it* and fear;
Gaza also shall be very sorrowful;
And Ekron, for He dried up her expectation.
The king shall perish from Gaza,
And Ashkelon shall not be inhabited.

6 "A mixed race shall settle in Ashdod,
And I will cut off the pride of the Philistines.
7 I will take away the blood from his mouth,
And the abominations from between his teeth.
But he who remains, even he *shall be* for our God,
And shall be like a leader in Judah,
And Ekron like a Jebusite.
8 I will camp around My house
Because of the army,
Because of him who passes by and him who returns.
No more shall an oppressor pass through them,
For now I have seen with My eyes.

The Coming King

9 "Rejoice greatly, O daughter of Zion!
Shout, O daughter of Jerusalem!
Behold, your King is coming to you;
He *is* just and having salvation,
Lowly and riding on a donkey,
A colt, the foal of a donkey.
10 I will cut off the chariot from Ephraim
And the horse from Jerusalem;
The battle bow shall be cut off.
He shall speak peace to the nations;
His dominion *shall be* 'from sea to sea,
And from the River to the ends of the earth.'[a]

God Will Save His People

11 "As for you also,
Because of the blood of your covenant,
I will set your prisoners free from the waterless pit.
12 Return to the stronghold,
You prisoners of hope.
Even today I declare
That I will restore double to you.

9:1 [a] Or *oracle* 9:10 [a] Psalm 72:8

13 For I have bent Judah, My *bow*,
Fitted the bow with Ephraim,
And raised up your sons, O Zion,
Against your sons, O Greece,
And made you like the sword of a
mighty man."

14 Then the LORD will be seen over
them,
And His arrow will go forth like
lightning.
The Lord GOD will blow the
trumpet,
And go with whirlwinds from the
south.
15 The LORD of hosts will defend
them;
They shall devour and subdue
with slingstones.
They shall drink *and* roar as if
with wine;
They shall be filled *with blood* like
basins,
Like the corners of the altar.
16 The LORD their God will save them
in that day,
As the flock of His people.
For they *shall be like* the jewels of
a crown,
Lifted like a banner over His
land—
17 For how great is its[a] goodness
And how great its[b] beauty!
Grain shall make the young men
thrive,
And new wine the young women.

Restoration of Judah and Israel

10 Ask the LORD for rain
In the time of the latter rain.[a]
The LORD will make flashing
clouds;
He will give them showers of rain,
Grass in the field for everyone.

2 For the idols[a] speak delusion;
The diviners envision lies,
And tell false dreams;
They comfort in vain.
Therefore *the people* wend their
way like sheep;
They are in trouble because *there*
is no shepherd.

3 "My anger is kindled against the
shepherds,
And I will punish the goatherds.
For the LORD of hosts will visit His
flock,
The house of Judah,
And will make them as His royal
horse in the battle.
4 From him comes the cornerstone,
From him the tent peg,
From him the battle bow,
From him every ruler[a] together.
5 They shall be like mighty men,
Who tread down *their enemies*
In the mire of the streets in the
battle.
They shall fight because the LORD
is with them,
And the riders on horses shall be
put to shame.

6 "I will strengthen the house of
Judah,
And I will save the house of
Joseph.
I will bring them back,
Because I have mercy on them.
They shall be as though I had not
cast them aside;
For I *am* the LORD their God,
And I will hear them.
7 *Those of* Ephraim shall be like a
mighty man,
And their heart shall rejoice as if
with wine.
Yes, their children shall see *it* and
be glad;
Their heart shall rejoice in the
LORD.
8 I will whistle for them and gather
them,
For I will redeem them;
And they shall increase as they
once increased.

9 "I will sow them among the peoples,
And they shall remember Me in
far countries;
They shall live, together with their
children,
And they shall return.
10 I will also bring them back from
the land of Egypt,

9:17 [a] Or *His* [b] Or *His* 10:1 [a] That is, spring rain 10:2 [a] Hebrew *teraphim* 10:4 [a] Or *despot*

And gather them from Assyria.
I will bring them into the land of
Gilead and Lebanon,
Until no *more room* is found for
them.
11 He shall pass through the sea
with affliction,
And strike the waves of the sea:
All the depths of the River[a] shall
dry up.
Then the pride of Assyria shall be
brought down,
And the scepter of Egypt shall
depart.

12 "So I will strengthen them in the
LORD,
And they shall walk up and down
in His name,"
Says the LORD.

Desolation of Israel

11 Open your doors, O Lebanon,
That fire may devour your
cedars.
2 Wail, O cypress, for the cedar has
fallen,
Because the mighty *trees* are
ruined.
Wail, O oaks of Bashan,
For the thick forest has come
down.
3 *There is* the sound of wailing
shepherds!
For their glory is in ruins.
There is the sound of roaring lions!
For the pride[a] of the Jordan is in
ruins.

Prophecy of the Shepherds

4Thus says the LORD my God, "Feed
the flock for slaughter, 5whose owners
slaughter them and feel no guilt; those
who sell them say, 'Blessed be the LORD,
for I am rich'; and their shepherds do not
pity them. 6For I will no longer pity the
inhabitants of the land," says the LORD.
"But indeed I will give everyone into his
neighbor's hand and into the hand of his
king. They shall attack the land, and I
will not deliver *them* from their hand."
7So I fed the flock for slaughter, in par-
ticular the poor of the flock.[a] I took for
myself two staffs: the one I called Beau-
ty,[b] and the other I called Bonds;[c] and I
fed the flock. 8I dismissed the three shep-
herds in one month. My soul loathed
them, and their soul also abhorred me.
9Then I said, "I will not feed you. Let what
is dying die, and what is perishing perish.
Let those that are left eat each other's
flesh." 10And I took my staff, Beauty,
and cut it in two, that I might break the
covenant which I had made with all the
peoples. 11So it was broken on that day.
Thus the poor[a] of the flock, who were
watching me, knew that it *was* the word
of the LORD. 12Then I said to them, "If it
is agreeable to you, give *me* my wages;
and if not, refrain." So they weighed out
for my wages thirty *pieces* of silver.
13And the LORD said to me, "Throw it
to the potter"—that princely price they
set on me. So I took the thirty *pieces* of
silver and threw them into the house of
the LORD for the potter. 14Then I cut in
two my other staff, Bonds, that I might
break the brotherhood between Judah
and Israel.
15And the LORD said to me, "Next, take
for yourself the implements of a foolish
shepherd. 16For indeed I will raise up a
shepherd in the land *who* will not care
for those who are cut off, nor seek the
young, nor heal those that are broken,
nor feed those that still stand. But he
will eat the flesh of the fat and tear their
hooves in pieces.

17 "Woe to the worthless shepherd,
Who leaves the flock!
A sword *shall be* against his arm
And against his right eye;
His arm shall completely wither,
And his right eye shall be totally
blinded."

The Coming Deliverance of Judah

12 The burden[a] of the word of the
LORD against Israel. Thus says
the LORD, who stretches out the heav-
ens, lays the foundation of the earth,

10:11 [a] That is, the Nile 11:3 [a] Or *floodplain, thicket* 11:7 [a] Following Masoretic Text, Targum, and Vulgate; Septuagint reads *for the Canaanites.* [b] Or *Grace,* and so in verse 10 [c] Or *Unity,* and so in verse 14 11:11 [a] Following Masoretic Text, Targum, and Vulgate; Septuagint reads *the Canaanites.* 12:1 [a] Or *oracle*

and forms the spirit of man within him:
2"Behold, I will make Jerusalem a cup of
drunkenness to all the surrounding peo-
ples, when they lay siege against Judah
and Jerusalem. 3And it shall happen in
that day that I will make Jerusalem a
very heavy stone for all peoples; all who
would heave it away will surely be cut in
pieces, though all nations of the earth
are gathered against it. 4In that day,"
says the LORD, "I will strike every horse
with confusion, and its rider with mad-
ness; I will open My eyes on the house
of Judah, and will strike every horse of
the peoples with blindness. 5And the gov-
ernors of Judah shall say in their heart,
'The inhabitants of Jerusalem *are* my
strength in the LORD of hosts, their God.'
6In that day I will make the governors
of Judah like a firepan in the woodpile,
and like a fiery torch in the sheaves; they
shall devour all the surrounding peoples
on the right hand and on the left, but
Jerusalem shall be inhabited again in
her own place—Jerusalem.
7"The LORD will save the tents of Judah
first, so that the glory of the house of Da-
vid and the glory of the inhabitants of Je-
rusalem shall not become greater than
that of Judah. 8In that day the LORD will
defend the inhabitants of Jerusalem; the
one who is feeble among them in that
day shall be like David, and the house
of David *shall be* like God, like the Angel
of the LORD before them. 9It shall be in
that day *that* I will seek to destroy all the
nations that come against Jerusalem.

Mourning for the Pierced One

10"And I will pour on the house of Da-
vid and on the inhabitants of Jerusalem
the Spirit of grace and supplication;
then they will look on Me whom they
pierced. Yes, they will mourn for Him
as one mourns for *his* only *son,* and
grieve for Him as one grieves for a first-
born. 11In that day there shall be a great
mourning in Jerusalem, like the mourn-
ing at Hadad Rimmon in the plain of
Megiddo.[a] 12And the land shall mourn,
every family by itself: the family of the
house of David by itself, and their wives
by themselves; the family of the house
of Nathan by itself, and their wives by
themselves; 13the family of the house of
Levi by itself, and their wives by them-
selves; the family of Shimei by itself,
and their wives by themselves; 14all the
families that remain, every family by
itself, and their wives by themselves.

Idolatry Cut Off

13 "In that day a fountain shall be
opened for the house of David
and for the inhabitants of Jerusalem,
for sin and for uncleanness.
2"It shall be in that day," says the LORD
of hosts, "*that* I will cut off the names of
the idols from the land, and they shall
no longer be remembered. I will also
cause the prophets and the unclean
spirit to depart from the land. 3It shall
come to pass *that* if anyone still proph-
esies, then his father and mother who
begot him will say to him, 'You shall not
live, because you have spoken lies in the
name of the LORD.' And his father and
mother who begot him shall thrust him
through when he prophesies.
4"And it shall be in that day *that* every
prophet will be ashamed of his vision
when he prophesies; they will not wear a
robe of coarse hair to deceive. 5But he will
say, 'I *am* no prophet, I *am* a farmer; for
a man taught me to keep cattle from my
youth.' 6And *one* will say to him, 'What
are these wounds between your arms?'[a]
Then he will answer, '*Those* with which I
was wounded in the house of my friends.'

The Shepherd Savior

7 "Awake, O sword, against My
Shepherd,
Against the Man who is My
Companion,"
Says the LORD of hosts.
"Strike the Shepherd,
And the sheep will be scattered;
Then I will turn My hand against
the little ones.
8 And it shall come to pass in all
the land,"
Says the LORD,
"*That* two-thirds in it shall be cut off
and die,
But *one*-third shall be left in it:

12:11 [a] Hebrew *Megiddon* 13:6 [a] Or *hands*

9 I will bring the *one*-third through
the fire,
Will refine them as silver is
refined,
And test them as gold is tested.
They will call on My name,
And I will answer them.
I will say, 'This *is* My people';
And each one will say, 'The LORD
is my God.' "

The Day of the LORD

14 Behold, the day of the LORD is
coming,
And your spoil will be divided in
your midst.
2 For I will gather all the nations to
battle against Jerusalem;
The city shall be taken,
The houses rifled,
And the women ravished.
Half of the city shall go into
captivity,
But the remnant of the people
shall not be cut off from the
city.

3 Then the LORD will go forth
And fight against those nations,
As He fights in the day of battle.
4 And in that day His feet will stand
on the Mount of Olives,
Which faces Jerusalem on the
east.
And the Mount of Olives shall be
split in two,
From east to west,
Making a very large valley;
Half of the mountain shall move
toward the north
And half of it toward the south.

5 Then you shall flee *through* My
mountain valley,
For the mountain valley shall
reach to Azal.
Yes, you shall flee
As you fled from the earthquake
In the days of Uzziah king of
Judah.

Thus the LORD my God will come,
And all the saints with You.[a]

6 It shall come to pass in that day
That there will be no light;
The lights will diminish.
7 It shall be one day
Which is known to the LORD—
Neither day nor night.
But at evening time it shall
happen
That it will be light.

8 And in that day it shall be
That living waters shall flow from
Jerusalem,
Half of them toward the eastern
sea
And half of them toward the
western sea;
In both summer and winter it
shall occur.
9 And the LORD shall be King over
all the earth.
In that day it shall be—
"The LORD *is* one,"[a]
And His name one.

10 All the land shall be turned into a
plain from Geba to Rimmon south of Je-
rusalem. *Jerusalem*[a] shall be raised up
and inhabited in her place from Benja-
min's Gate to the place of the First Gate
and the Corner Gate, and *from* the Tower
of Hananel to the king's winepresses.

11 *The people* shall dwell in it;
And no longer shall there be utter
destruction,
But Jerusalem shall be safely
inhabited.

12 And this shall be the plague with
which the LORD will strike all the people
who fought against Jerusalem:

Their flesh shall dissolve while
they stand on their feet,
Their eyes shall dissolve in their
sockets,
And their tongues shall dissolve
in their mouths.

13 It shall come to pass in that day
That a great panic from the LORD
will be among them.

14:5 [a] Or *you;* Septuagint, Targum, and Vulgate read *Him.* 14:9 [a] Compare Deuteronomy 6:4
14:10 [a] Literally *She*

Everyone will seize the hand of
his neighbor,
And raise his hand against his
neighbor's hand;
14 Judah also will fight at Jerusalem.
And the wealth of all the
surrounding nations
Shall be gathered together:
Gold, silver, and apparel in great
abundance.

15 Such also shall be the plague
On the horse *and* the mule,
On the camel and the donkey,
And on all the cattle that will be in
those camps.
So *shall* this plague *be.*

The Nations Worship the King

16And it shall come to pass *that* every-
one who is left of all the nations which
came against Jerusalem shall go up
from year to year to worship the King,
the LORD of hosts, and to keep the Feast
of Tabernacles. 17And it shall be *that*
whichever of the families of the earth
do not come up to Jerusalem to worship
the King, the LORD of hosts, on them
there will be no rain. 18If the family
of Egypt will not come up and enter
in, they *shall have* no *rain;* they shall
receive the plague with which the LORD
strikes the nations who do not come up
to keep the Feast of Tabernacles. 19This
shall be the punishment of Egypt and
the punishment of all the nations that
do not come up to keep the Feast of
Tabernacles.

20In that day "HOLINESS TO THE
LORD" shall be *engraved* on the bells of
the horses. The pots in the LORD's house
shall be like the bowls before the altar.
21Yes, every pot in Jerusalem and Judah
shall be holiness to the LORD of hosts.[a]
Everyone who sacrifices shall come and
take them and cook in them. In that day
there shall no longer be a Canaanite in
the house of the LORD of hosts.

14:21 [a] Or *on every pot . . . shall be (engraved) "HOLINESS TO THE LORD OF HOSTS"*

THE BOOK OF

MALACHI

In Malachi, God's people have returned from exile and are mostly living in peace. Now, they are waiting for God to provide the Messiah and restore their nation to be like it was under David and Solomon. But while they wait for God to act, they act in defiance of Him. The people are not worshiping idols now as they had done before, but neither are they worshiping God rightly. Malachi calls the people back to genuine faith in God. If they did not return, the blessings they waited for would not come; judgment would come instead.

- **GENRE:** Minor Prophet
- **AUTHOR:** Malachi
- **TIME:** c. 450–420 BC
- **PURPOSE:** To encourage the proper reverence and worship of God.

---

1 The burden[a] of the word of the LORD
to Israel by Malachi.

Israel Beloved of God

2 "I have loved you," says the LORD.
"Yet you say, 'In what way have You loved us?'
Was not Esau Jacob's brother?"
Says the LORD.
"Yet Jacob I have loved;
3 But Esau I have hated,
And laid waste his mountains and his heritage
For the jackals of the wilderness."

4 Even though Edom has said,
"We have been impoverished,
But we will return and build the desolate places,"

Thus says the LORD of hosts:

"They may build, but I will throw down;
They shall be called the Territory of Wickedness,
And the people against whom the LORD will have indignation forever.
5 Your eyes shall see,
And you shall say,
'The LORD is magnified beyond the border of Israel.'

Polluted Offerings

6 "A son honors *his* father,
And a servant *his* master.
If then I am the Father,
Where *is* My honor?
And if I *am* a Master,
Where *is* My reverence?
Says the LORD of hosts
To you priests who despise My name.
Yet you say, 'In what way have we despised Your name?'

7 "You offer defiled food on My altar,
But say,
'In what way have we defiled You?'
By saying,
'The table of the LORD is contemptible.'
8 And when you offer the blind as a sacrifice,
Is it not evil?
And when you offer the lame and sick,
Is it not evil?
Offer it then to your governor!
Would he be pleased with you?
Would he accept you favorably?"
Says the LORD of hosts.

9 "But now entreat God's favor,
That He may be gracious to us.

1:1 a Or *oracle*

GOD SIN JESUS SALVATION LOVE

While this is being *done* by your
hands,
Will He accept you favorably?"
Says the LORD of hosts.
10 "Who *is there* even among you who
would shut the doors,
So that you would not kindle fire
on My altar in vain?
I have no pleasure in you,"
Says the LORD of hosts,
"Nor will I accept an offering from
your hands.
11 For from the rising of the sun,
even to its going down,
My name *shall be* great among
the Gentiles;
In every place incense *shall be*
offered to My name,
And a pure offering;
For My name shall be great
among the nations,"
Says the LORD of hosts.

12 "But you profane it,
In that you say,
'The table of the LORD[a] is defiled;
And its fruit, its food, *is*
contemptible.'
13 You also say,
'Oh, what a weariness!'
And you sneer at it,"
Says the LORD of hosts.
"And you bring the stolen, the lame,
and the sick;
Thus you bring an offering!
Should I accept this from your
hand?"
Says the LORD.
14 "But cursed *be* the deceiver
Who has in his flock a male,
And takes a vow,
But sacrifices to the Lord what is
blemished—
For I *am* a great King,"
Says the LORD of hosts,
"And My name *is to be* feared
among the nations.

Corrupt Priests

2 "And now, O priests, this
commandment is for you.
2 If you will not hear,
And if you will not take *it* to heart,
To give glory to My name,"
Says the LORD of hosts,
"I will send a curse upon you,
And I will curse your blessings.
Yes, I have cursed them already,
Because you do not take *it* to
heart.

3 "Behold, I will rebuke your
descendants
And spread refuse on your faces,
The refuse of your solemn feasts;
And *one* will take you away with it.
4 Then you shall know that I have
sent this commandment to
you,
That My covenant with Levi may
continue,"
Says the LORD of hosts.
5 "My covenant was with him, *one* of
life and peace,
And I gave them to him *that he
might* fear *Me;*
So he feared Me
And was reverent before My name.
6 The law of truth[a] was in his mouth,
And injustice was not found on
his lips.
He walked with Me in peace and
equity,
And turned many away from
iniquity.

7 "For the lips of a priest should keep
knowledge,
And *people* should seek the law
from his mouth;
For he is the messenger of the
LORD of hosts.
8 But you have departed from the
way;
You have caused many to
stumble at the law.
You have corrupted the covenant
of Levi,"
Says the LORD of hosts.
9 "Therefore I also have made you
contemptible and base
Before all the people,
Because you have not kept My
ways
But have shown partiality in the
law."

1:12 [a] Following Bomberg; Masoretic Text reads *Lord.* 2:6 [a] Or *true instruction*

Treachery of Infidelity

10 Have we not all one Father?
Has not one God created us?
Why do we deal treacherously
with one another
By profaning the covenant of the
fathers?
11 Judah has dealt treacherously,
And an abomination has been
committed in Israel and in
Jerusalem,
For Judah has profaned
The LORD's holy *institution* which
He loves:
He has married the daughter of a
foreign god.
12 May the LORD cut off from the
tents of Jacob
The man who does this, being
awake and aware,[a]
Yet who brings an offering to the
LORD of hosts!

13 And this is the second thing you
do:
You cover the altar of the LORD
with tears,
With weeping and crying;
So He does not regard the
offering anymore,
Nor receive *it* with goodwill from
your hands.
14 Yet you say, "For what reason?"
Because the LORD has been
witness
Between you and the wife of your
youth,
With whom you have dealt
treacherously;
Yet she is your companion
And your wife by covenant.
15 But did He not make *them* one,
Having a remnant of the Spirit?
And why one?
He seeks godly offspring.
Therefore take heed to your spirit,
And let none deal treacherously
with the wife of his youth.

16 "For the LORD God of Israel says
That He hates divorce,
For it covers one's garment with
violence,"
Says the LORD of hosts.
"Therefore take heed to your spirit,
That you do not deal
treacherously."

17 You have wearied the LORD with
your words;
Yet you say,
"In what way have we wearied
Him?"
In that you say,
"Everyone who does evil
Is good in the sight of the LORD,
And He delights in them,"
Or, "Where *is* the God of justice?"

The Coming Messenger

3 "Behold, I send My messenger,
And he will prepare the way
before Me.
And the Lord, whom you seek,
Will suddenly come to His temple,
Even the Messenger of the
covenant,
In whom you delight.
Behold, He is coming,"
Says the LORD of hosts.

2 "But who can endure the day of His
coming?
And who can stand when He
appears?
For He *is* like a refiner's fire
And like launderers' soap.
3 He will sit as a refiner and a
purifier of silver;
He will purify the sons of Levi,
And purge them as gold and
silver,
That they may offer to the LORD
An offering in righteousness.

4 "Then the offering of Judah and
Jerusalem
Will be pleasant to the LORD,
As in the days of old,
As in former years.
5 And I will come near you for
judgment;
I will be a swift witness
Against sorcerers,
Against adulterers,
Against perjurers,

2:12 [a] Talmud and Vulgate read *teacher and student*.

Against those who exploit wage earners and widows and orphans,
And against those who turn away an alien—
Because they do not fear Me,"
Says the LORD of hosts.

6 "For I *am* the LORD, I do not change;
Therefore you are not consumed, O sons of Jacob.
7 Yet from the days of your fathers
You have gone away from My ordinances
And have not kept *them*.
Return to Me, and I will return to you,"
Says the LORD of hosts.
"But you said,
'In what way shall we return?'

Do Not Rob God

8 "Will a man rob God?
Yet you have robbed Me!
But you say,
'In what way have we robbed You?'
In tithes and offerings.
9 You are cursed with a curse,
For you have robbed Me,
Even this whole nation.
10 Bring all the tithes into the storehouse,
That there may be food in My house,
And try Me now in this,"
Says the LORD of hosts,
"If I will not open for you the windows of heaven
And pour out for you *such* blessing
That *there will* not *be room* enough *to receive it.*

11 "And I will rebuke the devourer for your sakes,
So that he will not destroy the fruit of your ground,
Nor shall the vine fail to bear fruit for you in the field,"
Says the LORD of hosts;
12 "And all nations will call you blessed,
For you will be a delightful land,"
Says the LORD of hosts.

The People Complain Harshly

13 "Your words have been harsh against Me,"
Says the LORD,
"Yet you say,
'What have we spoken against You?'
14 You have said,
'It is useless to serve God;
What profit *is it* that we have kept His ordinance,
And that we have walked as mourners
Before the LORD of hosts?
15 So now we call the proud blessed,
For those who do wickedness are raised up;
They even tempt God and go free.' "

A Book of Remembrance

16 Then those who feared the LORD spoke to one another,
And the LORD listened and heard *them;*
So a book of remembrance was written before Him
For those who fear the LORD
And who meditate on His name.

17 "They shall be Mine," says the LORD of hosts,
"On the day that I make them My jewels.[a]
And I will spare them
As a man spares his own son who serves him."
18 Then you shall again discern
Between the righteous and the wicked,
Between one who serves God
And one who does not serve Him.

The Great Day of God

4 "For behold, the day is coming,
Burning like an oven,
And all the proud, yes, all who do wickedly will be stubble.
And the day which is coming shall burn them up,"
Says the LORD of hosts,
"That will leave them neither root nor branch.

3:17 [a] Literally *special treasure*

2 But to you who fear My name
The Sun of Righteousness shall arise
With healing in His wings;
And you shall go out
And grow fat like stall-fed calves.
3 You shall trample the wicked,
For they shall be ashes under the soles of your feet
On the day that I do *this*,"
Says the LORD of hosts.

4 "Remember the Law of Moses, My servant,
Which I commanded him in Horeb for all Israel,
With the statutes and judgments.
5 Behold, I will send you Elijah the prophet
Before the coming of the great and dreadful day of the LORD.
6 And he will turn
The hearts of the fathers to the children,
And the hearts of the children to their fathers,
Lest I come and strike the earth with a curse."

THE NEW TESTAMENT

THE GOSPEL ACCORDING TO

MATTHEW

Matthew is written by a Jew to tell the story of Jesus for the Jewish people. Because of this, Matthew contains more references to Jewish culture and the Old Testament than the other three Gospels. Matthew's purpose is to show that Jesus is the long-awaited Messiah who had been promised since the Book of Genesis. Matthew also provides the fullest account of Jesus' teachings: the Sermon on the Mount (chs. 5–7), the mission of the Twelve (ch. 10), the kingdom parables (ch. 13), the church (ch. 18), and the end times (chs. 23–25).

- **GENRE:** Gospel
- **AUTHOR:** Matthew
- **TIME:** c. 6 BC–AD 33 (written c. AD 50–60)
- **PURPOSE:** To tell the Jews about Jesus' life and teachings, and to prove that Jesus is the Messiah they had been waiting for.

The Genealogy of Jesus Christ

1 The book of the genealogy of Jesus Christ, the Son of David, the Son of Abraham:

2 Abraham begot Isaac, Isaac begot Jacob, and Jacob begot Judah and his brothers. 3 Judah begot Perez and Zerah by Tamar, Perez begot Hezron, and Hezron begot Ram. 4 Ram begot Amminadab, Amminadab begot Nahshon, and Nahshon begot Salmon. 5 Salmon begot Boaz by Rahab, Boaz begot Obed by Ruth, Obed begot Jesse, 6 and Jesse begot David the king.

David the king begot Solomon by her *who had been the wife*[a] of Uriah. 7 Solomon begot Rehoboam, Rehoboam begot Abijah, and Abijah begot Asa.[a] 8 Asa begot Jehoshaphat, Jehoshaphat begot Joram, and Joram begot Uzziah. 9 Uzziah begot Jotham, Jotham begot Ahaz, and Ahaz begot Hezekiah. 10 Hezekiah begot Manasseh, Manasseh begot Amon,[a] and Amon begot Josiah. 11 Josiah begot Jeconiah and his brothers about the time they were carried away to Babylon.

12 And after they were brought to Babylon, Jeconiah begot Shealtiel, and Shealtiel begot Zerubbabel. 13 Zerubbabel begot Abiud, Abiud begot Eliakim, and Eliakim begot Azor. 14 Azor begot Zadok, Zadok begot Achim, and Achim begot Eliud. 15 Eliud begot Eleazar, Eleazar begot Matthan, and Matthan begot Jacob. 16 And Jacob begot Joseph the husband of Mary, of whom was born Jesus who is called Christ.

17 So all the generations from Abraham to David *are* fourteen generations, from David until the captivity in Babylon *are* fourteen generations, and from the captivity in Babylon until the Christ *are* fourteen generations.

Christ Born of Mary

18 Now the birth of Jesus Christ was as follows: After His mother Mary was betrothed to Joseph, before they came together, she was found with child of the Holy Spirit. 19 Then Joseph her husband, being a just *man,* and not wanting to make her a public example, was minded to put her away secretly. 20 But while he thought about these things, behold, an angel of the Lord appeared to him in a dream, saying, "Joseph, son of David, do not be afraid to take to you Mary your wife, for that which is conceived in her is of the Holy Spirit. 21 And she will bring forth a Son, and you shall call His name JESUS, for He will save His people from their sins."

22 So all this was done that it might be

1:6 [a] Words in italic type have been added for clarity. They are not found in the original Greek.
1:7 [a] NU-Text reads *Asaph.* 1:10 [a] NU-Text reads *Amos.*

WORSHIP | GROWTH | HEAVEN | FAMILY

fulfilled which was spoken by the Lord
through the prophet, saying: 23"Behold,
the virgin shall be with child, and bear
a Son, and they shall call His name
Immanuel,"[a] which is translated, "God
with us."
24Then Joseph, being aroused from
sleep, did as the angel of the Lord com-
manded him and took to him his wife,
25and did not know her till she had
brought forth her firstborn Son.[a] And
he called His name JESUS.

Wise Men from the East

2 Now after Jesus was born in Bethle-
hem of Judea in the days of Herod
the king, behold, wise men from the East
came to Jerusalem, 2saying, "Where is
He who has been born King of the Jews?
For we have seen His star in the East and
have come to worship Him."
3When Herod the king heard *this,* he
was troubled, and all Jerusalem with
him. 4And when he had gathered all the
chief priests and scribes of the people
together, he inquired of them where the
Christ was to be born.
5So they said to him, "In Bethlehem
of Judea, for thus it is written by the
prophet:

6 'But you, Bethlehem, *in* the land
of Judah,
Are not the least among the
rulers of Judah;
For out of you shall come
a Ruler
Who will shepherd My people
Israel.' "[a]

7Then Herod, when he had secretly
called the wise men, determined from
them what time the star appeared. 8And
he sent them to Bethlehem and said,
"Go and search carefully for the young
Child, and when you have found *Him,*
bring back word to me, that I may come
and worship Him also."
9When they heard the king, they de-
parted; and behold, the star which they
had seen in the East went before them,
till it came and stood over where the
young Child was. 10When they saw the
star, they rejoiced with exceedingly
great joy. 11And when they had come
into the house, they saw the young Child
with Mary His mother, and fell down
and worshiped Him. And when they
had opened their treasures, they pre-
sented gifts to Him: gold, frankincense,
and myrrh.
12Then, being divinely warned in a
dream that they should not return to
Herod, they departed for their own
country another way.

The Flight into Egypt

13Now when they had departed, be-
hold, an angel of the Lord appeared to
Joseph in a dream, saying, "Arise, take
the young Child and His mother, flee to
Egypt, and stay there until I bring you
word; for Herod will seek the young
Child to destroy Him."
14When he arose, he took the young
Child and His mother by night and de-
parted for Egypt, 15and was there until
the death of Herod, that it might be
fulfilled which was spoken by the Lord
through the prophet, saying, "Out of
Egypt I called My Son."[a]

Massacre of the Innocents

16Then Herod, when he saw that he
was deceived by the wise men, was
exceedingly angry; and he sent forth
and put to death all the male children
who were in Bethlehem and in all its
districts, from two years old and under,
according to the time which he had
determined from the wise men. 17Then
was fulfilled what was spoken by Jere-
miah the prophet, saying:

18 "A voice was heard in Ramah,
Lamentation, weeping, and great
mourning,
Rachel weeping *for* her children,
Refusing to be comforted,
Because they are no more."[a]

The Home in Nazareth

19Now when Herod was dead, behold,
an angel of the Lord appeared in a
dream to Joseph in Egypt, 20saying,
"Arise, take the young Child and His

1:23 [a] Isaiah 7:14 1:25 [a] NU-Text reads *a Son.* 2:6 [a] Micah 5:2 2:15 [a] Hosea 11:1
2:18 [a] Jeremiah 31:15

mother, and go to the land of Israel, for those who sought the young Child's life are dead." 21Then he arose, took the young Child and His mother, and came into the land of Israel.

22But when he heard that Archelaus was reigning over Judea instead of his father Herod, he was afraid to go there. And being warned by God in a dream, he turned aside into the region of Galilee. 23And he came and dwelt in a city called Nazareth, that it might be fulfilled which was spoken by the prophets, "He shall be called a Nazarene."

John the Baptist Prepares the Way

3 In those days John the Baptist came preaching in the wilderness of Judea, 2and saying, "Repent, for the kingdom of heaven is at hand!" 3For this is he who was spoken of by the prophet Isaiah, saying:

> "The voice of one crying in the
> wilderness:
> 'Prepare the way of the LORD;
> Make His paths straight.' "[a]

4Now John himself was clothed in camel's hair, with a leather belt around his waist; and his food was locusts and wild honey. 5Then Jerusalem, all Judea, and all the region around the Jordan went out to him 6and were baptized by him in the Jordan, confessing their sins.

7But when he saw many of the Pharisees and Sadducees coming to his baptism, he said to them, "Brood of vipers! Who warned you to flee from the wrath to come? 8Therefore bear fruits worthy of repentance, 9and do not think to say to yourselves, 'We have Abraham as *our* father.' For I say to you that God is able to raise up children to Abraham from these stones. 10And even now the ax is laid to the root of the trees. Therefore every tree which does not bear good fruit is cut down and thrown into the fire. 11I indeed baptize you with water unto repentance, but He who is coming after me is mightier than I, whose sandals I am not worthy to carry. He will baptize you with the Holy Spirit and fire.[a] 12His winnowing fan *is* in His hand, and He will thoroughly clean out His threshing floor, and gather His wheat into the barn; but He will burn up the chaff with unquenchable fire."

John Baptizes Jesus

13Then Jesus came from Galilee to John at the Jordan to be baptized by him. 14And John *tried to* prevent Him, saying, "I need to be baptized by You, and are You coming to me?"

15But Jesus answered and said to him, "Permit *it to be so* now, for thus it is fitting for us to fulfill all righteousness." Then he allowed Him.

16When He had been baptized, Jesus came up immediately from the water; and behold, the heavens were opened to Him, and He[a] saw the Spirit of God descending like a dove and alighting upon Him. 17And suddenly a voice *came* from heaven, saying, "This is My beloved Son, in whom I am well pleased."

Satan Tempts Jesus

4 Then Jesus was led up by the Spirit into the wilderness to be tempted by the devil. 2And when He had fasted forty days and forty nights, afterward He was hungry. 3Now when the tempter came to Him, he said, "If You are the Son of God, command that these stones become bread."

4But He answered and said, "It is written, 'Man shall not live by bread alone, but by every word that proceeds from the mouth of God.' "[a]

5Then the devil took Him up into the holy city, set Him on the pinnacle of the temple, 6and said to Him, "If You are the Son of God, throw Yourself down. For it is written:

> 'He shall give His angels charge
> over you,'

and,

> 'In *their* hands they shall bear
> you up,
> Lest you dash your foot against a
> stone.' "[a]

3:3 [a] Isaiah 40:3 3:11 [a] M-Text omits *and fire.* 3:16 [a] Or *he* 4:4 [a] Deuteronomy 8:3
4:6 [a] Psalm 91:11, 12

7Jesus said to him, "It is written again,
'You shall not tempt the LORD your
God.' "[a]
8Again, the devil took Him up on
an exceedingly high mountain, and
showed Him all the kingdoms of the
world and their glory. 9And he said to
Him, "All these things I will give You
if You will fall down and worship me."
10Then Jesus said to him, "Away with
you,[a] Satan! For it is written, 'You shall
worship the LORD your God, and Him
only you shall serve.' "[b]
11Then the devil left Him, and behold,
angels came and ministered to Him.

Jesus Begins His Galilean Ministry

12Now when Jesus heard that John
had been put in prison, He departed
to Galilee. 13And leaving Nazareth, He
came and dwelt in Capernaum, which
is by the sea, in the regions of Zebulun
and Naphtali, 14that it might be ful-
filled which was spoken by Isaiah the
prophet, saying:

15 "The land of Zebulun and the land
of Naphtali,
By the way of the sea, beyond the
Jordan,
Galilee of the Gentiles:
16 The people who sat in darkness
have seen a great light,
And upon those who sat in the
region and shadow of death
Light has dawned."[a]

17From that time Jesus began to
preach and to say, "Repent, for the
kingdom of heaven is at hand."

Four Fishermen Called as Disciples

18And Jesus, walking by the Sea of
Galilee, saw two brothers, Simon called
Peter, and Andrew his brother, cast-
ing a net into the sea; for they were
fishermen. 19Then He said to them, "Fol-
low Me, and I will make you fishers of
men." 20They immediately left *their* nets
and followed Him.
21Going on from there, He saw two
other brothers, James *the son* of Zebe-
dee, and John his brother, in the boat
with Zebedee their father, mending their
nets. He called them, 22and immediate-
ly they left the boat and their father,
and followed Him.

Jesus Heals a Great Multitude

23And Jesus went about all Galilee,
teaching in their synagogues, preach-
ing the gospel of the kingdom, and
healing all kinds of sickness and all
kinds of disease among the people.
24Then His fame went throughout all
Syria; and they brought to Him all sick
people who were afflicted with various
diseases and torments, and those who
were demon-possessed, epileptics, and
paralytics; and He healed them. 25Great
multitudes followed Him—from Galilee,
and *from* Decapolis, Jerusalem, Judea,
and beyond the Jordan.

The Beatitudes

5 And seeing the multitudes, He went
up on a mountain, and when He
was seated His disciples came to Him.
2Then He opened His mouth and taught
them, saying:

3 "Blessed *are* the poor in spirit,
For theirs is the kingdom of
heaven.
4 Blessed *are* those who mourn,
For they shall be comforted.
5 Blessed *are* the meek,
For they shall inherit the earth.
6 Blessed *are* those who hunger and
thirst for righteousness,
For they shall be filled.
7 Blessed *are* the merciful,
For they shall obtain mercy.
8 Blessed *are* the pure in heart,
For they shall see God.
9 Blessed *are* the peacemakers,
For they shall be called sons of
God.
10 Blessed *are* those who
are persecuted for
righteousness' sake,
For theirs is the kingdom of
heaven.

11Blessed are you when they revile
and persecute you, and say all kinds

4:7 [a] Deuteronomy 6:16 4:10 [a] M-Text reads *Get behind Me.* [b] Deuteronomy 6:13 4:16 [a] Isaiah 9:1, 2

GOD SIN JESUS SALVATION LOVE

of evil against you falsely for My sake. 12Rejoice and be exceedingly glad, for great *is* your reward in heaven, for so they persecuted the prophets who were before you.

Believers Are Salt and Light

13"You are the salt of the earth; but if the salt loses its flavor, how shall it be seasoned? It is then good for nothing but to be thrown out and trampled underfoot by men.

14"You are the light of the world. A city that is set on a hill cannot be hidden. 15Nor do they light a lamp and put it under a basket, but on a lampstand, and it gives light to all *who are* in the house. 16Let your light so shine before men, that they may see your good works and glorify your Father in heaven.

Christ Fulfills the Law

17"Do not think that I came to destroy the Law or the Prophets. I did not come to destroy but to fulfill. 18For assuredly, I say to you, till heaven and earth pass away, one jot or one tittle will by no means pass from the law till all is fulfilled. 19Whoever therefore breaks one of the least of these commandments, and teaches men so, shall be called least in the kingdom of heaven; but whoever does and teaches *them,* he shall be called great in the kingdom of heaven. 20For I say to you, that unless your righteousness exceeds *the righteousness* of the scribes and Pharisees, you will by no means enter the kingdom of heaven.

Murder Begins in the Heart

21"You have heard that it was said to those of old, 'You shall not murder,[a] and whoever murders will be in danger of the judgment.' 22But I say to you that whoever is angry with his brother without a cause[a] shall be in danger of the judgment. And whoever says to his brother, 'Raca!' shall be in danger of the council. But whoever says, 'You fool!' shall be in danger of hell fire. 23Therefore if you bring your gift to the altar, and there remember that your brother has something against you, 24leave your gift there before the altar, and go your way. First be reconciled to your brother, and then come and offer your gift. 25Agree with your adversary quickly, while you are on the way with him, lest your adversary deliver you to the judge, the judge hand you over to the officer, and you be thrown into prison. 26Assuredly, I say to you, you will by no means get out of there till you have paid the last penny.

Adultery in the Heart

27"You have heard that it was said to those of old,[a] 'You shall not commit adultery.'[b] 28But I say to you that whoever looks at a woman to lust for her has already committed adultery with her in his heart. 29If your right eye causes you to sin, pluck it out and cast *it* from you; for it is more profitable for you that one of your members perish, than for your whole body to be cast into hell. 30And if your right hand causes you to sin, cut it off and cast *it* from you; for it is more profitable for you that one of your members perish, than for your whole body to be cast into hell.

Marriage Is Sacred and Binding

31"Furthermore it has been said, 'Whoever divorces his wife, let him give her a certificate of divorce.' 32But I say to you that whoever divorces his wife for any reason except sexual immorality[a] causes her to commit adultery; and whoever marries a woman who is divorced commits adultery.

Jesus Forbids Oaths

33"Again you have heard that it was said to those of old, 'You shall not swear falsely, but shall perform your oaths to the Lord.' 34But I say to you, do not swear at all: neither by heaven, for it is God's throne; 35nor by the earth, for it is His footstool; nor by Jerusalem, for it is the city of the great King. 36Nor shall you swear by your head, because you cannot make one hair white or black. 37But let your 'Yes' be 'Yes,' and your 'No,' 'No.' For whatever is more than these is from the evil one.

5:21 [a] Exodus 20:13; Deuteronomy 5:17 5:22 [a] NU-Text omits *without a cause.* 5:27 [a] NU-Text and M-Text omit *to those of old.* [b] Exodus 20:14; Deuteronomy 5:18 5:32 [a] Or *fornication*

Go the Second Mile

38"You have heard that it was said,
'An eye for an eye and a tooth for a
tooth.'[a] 39But I tell you not to resist an
evil person. But whoever slaps you on
your right cheek, turn the other to him
also. 40If anyone wants to sue you and
take away your tunic, let him have *your*
cloak also. 41And whoever compels you
to go one mile, go with him two. 42Give
to him who asks you, and from him
who wants to borrow from you do not
turn away.

Love Your Enemies

43"You have heard that it was said,
'You shall love your neighbor[a] and hate
your enemy.' 44But I say to you, love
your enemies, bless those who curse
you, do good to those who hate you, and
pray for those who spitefully use you
and persecute you,[a] 45that you may be
sons of your Father in heaven; for He
makes His sun rise on the evil and on
the good, and sends rain on the just and
on the unjust. 46For if you love those
who love you, what reward have you?
Do not even the tax collectors do the
same? 47And if you greet your brethren[a]
only, what do you do more *than others?*
Do not even the tax collectors[b] do so?
48Therefore you shall be perfect, just as
your Father in heaven is perfect.

Do Good to Please God

6 "Take heed that you do not do your
charitable deeds before men, to be
seen by them. Otherwise you have no
reward from your Father in heaven.
2Therefore, when you do a charitable
deed, do not sound a trumpet before
you as the hypocrites do in the syn-
agogues and in the streets, that they
may have glory from men. Assuredly, I
say to you, they have their reward. 3But
when you do a charitable deed, do not
let your left hand know what your right
hand is doing, 4that your charitable
deed may be in secret; and your Father
who sees in secret will Himself reward
you openly.[a]

The Model Prayer

5"And when you pray, you shall not
be like the hypocrites. For they love to
pray standing in the synagogues and
on the corners of the streets, that they
may be seen by men. Assuredly, I say to
you, they have their reward. 6But you,
when you pray, go into your room, and
when you have shut your door, pray to
your Father who *is* in the secret *place;*
and your Father who sees in secret will
reward you openly.[a] 7And when you
pray, do not use vain repetitions as the
heathen *do.* For they think that they will
be heard for their many words.
8"Therefore do not be like them. For
your Father knows the things you have
need of before you ask Him. 9In this
manner, therefore, pray:

Our Father in heaven,
Hallowed be Your name.
10 Your kingdom come.
Your will be done
On earth as *it is* in heaven.
11 Give us this day our daily bread.
12 And forgive us our debts,
As we forgive our debtors.
13 And do not lead us into
temptation,
But deliver us from the evil one.
For Yours is the kingdom and the
power and the glory forever.
Amen.[a]

14"For if you forgive men their tres-
passes, your heavenly Father will also
forgive you. 15But if you do not forgive
men their trespasses, neither will your
Father forgive your trespasses.

Fasting to Be Seen Only by God

16"Moreover, when you fast, do not be
like the hypocrites, with a sad counte-
nance. For they disfigure their faces
that they may appear to men to be fast-
ing. Assuredly, I say to you, they have
their reward. 17But you, when you fast,
anoint your head and wash your face,
18so that you do not appear to men to
be fasting, but to your Father who *is* in

5:38 [a] Exodus 21:24; Leviticus 24:20; Deuteronomy 19:21 **5:43** [a] Compare Leviticus 19:18
5:44 [a] NU-Text omits three clauses from this verse, leaving, *"But I say to you, love your enemies and pray for those who persecute you."* **5:47** [a] M-Text reads *friends.* [b] NU-Text reads *Gentiles.* **6:4** [a] NU-Text omits *openly.* **6:6** [a] NU-Text omits *openly.* **6:13** [a] NU-Text omits *For Yours* through *Amen.*

GOD SIN JESUS SALVATION LOVE

the secret *place;* and your Father who sees in secret will reward you openly.[a]

Lay Up Treasures in Heaven

19“Do not lay up for yourselves treasures on earth, where moth and rust destroy and where thieves break in and steal; 20but lay up for yourselves treasures in heaven, where neither moth nor rust destroys and where thieves do not break in and steal. 21For where your treasure is, there your heart will be also.

The Lamp of the Body

22“The lamp of the body is the eye. If therefore your eye is good, your whole body will be full of light. 23But if your eye is bad, your whole body will be full of darkness. If therefore the light that is in you is darkness, how great *is* that darkness!

You Cannot Serve God and Riches

24“No one can serve two masters; for either he will hate the one and love the other, or else he will be loyal to the one and despise the other. You cannot serve God and mammon.

Do Not Worry

25“Therefore I say to you, do not worry about your life, what you will eat or what you will drink; nor about your body, what you will put on. Is not life more than food and the body more than clothing? 26Look at the birds of the air, for they neither sow nor reap nor gather into barns; yet your heavenly Father feeds them. Are you not of more value than they? 27Which of you by worrying can add one cubit to his stature?

28“So why do you worry about clothing? Consider the lilies of the field, how they grow: they neither toil nor spin; 29and yet I say to you that even Solomon in all his glory was not arrayed like one of these. 30Now if God so clothes the grass of the field, which today is, and tomorrow is thrown into the oven, *will He* not much more *clothe* you, O you of little faith?

31“Therefore do not worry, saying, ‘What shall we eat?’ or ‘What shall we drink?’ or ‘What shall we wear?’ 32For after all these things the Gentiles seek. For your heavenly Father knows that you need all these things. 33But seek first the kingdom of God and His righteousness, and all these things shall be added to you. 34Therefore do not worry about tomorrow, for tomorrow will worry about its own things. Sufficient for the day *is* its own trouble.

Do Not Judge

7 “Judge not, that you be not judged. 2For with what judgment you judge, you will be judged; and with the measure you use, it will be measured back to you. 3And why do you look at the speck in your brother’s eye, but do not consider the plank in your own eye? 4Or how can you say to your brother, ‘Let me remove the speck from your eye’; and look, a plank *is* in your own eye? 5Hypocrite! First remove the plank from your own eye, and then you will see clearly to remove the speck from your brother’s eye.

6“Do not give what is holy to the dogs; nor cast your pearls before swine, lest they trample them under their feet, and turn and tear you in pieces.

Keep Asking, Seeking, Knocking

7“Ask, and it will be given to you; seek, and you will find; knock, and it will be opened to you. 8For everyone who asks receives, and he who seeks finds, and to him who knocks it will be opened. 9Or what man is there among you who, if his son asks for bread, will give him a stone? 10Or if he asks for a fish, will he give him a serpent? 11If you then, being evil, know how to give good gifts to your children, how much more will your Father who is in heaven give good things to those who ask Him! 12Therefore, whatever you want men to do to you, do also to them, for this is the Law and the Prophets.

The Narrow Way

13“Enter by the narrow gate; for wide *is* the gate and broad *is* the way that leads to destruction, and there are many who go in by it. 14Because[a] narrow *is* the gate and difficult *is* the way which leads to life, and there are few who find it.

6:18 [a] NU-Text and M-Text omit *openly.* **7:14** [a] NU-Text and M-Text read *How . . . !*

You Will Know Them by Their Fruits

15"Beware of false prophets, who come
to you in sheep's clothing, but inwardly
they are ravenous wolves. 16You will
know them by their fruits. Do men gath-
er grapes from thornbushes or figs from
thistles? 17Even so, every good tree bears
good fruit, but a bad tree bears bad fruit.
18A good tree cannot bear bad fruit, nor
can a bad tree bear good fruit. 19Every
tree that does not bear good fruit is cut
down and thrown into the fire. 20There-
fore by their fruits you will know them.

I Never Knew You

21"Not everyone who says to Me, 'Lord,
Lord,' shall enter the kingdom of heav-
en, but he who does the will of My Father
in heaven. 22Many will say to Me in that
day, 'Lord, Lord, have we not prophe-
sied in Your name, cast out demons in
Your name, and done many wonders in
Your name?' 23And then I will declare
to them, 'I never knew you; depart from
Me, you who practice lawlessness!'

Build on the Rock

24"Therefore whoever hears these say-
ings of Mine, and does them, I will liken
him to a wise man who built his house
on the rock: 25and the rain descended,
the floods came, and the winds blew and
beat on that house; and it did not fall,
for it was founded on the rock.

26"But everyone who hears these say-
ings of Mine, and does not do them, will
be like a foolish man who built his house
on the sand: 27and the rain descended,
the floods came, and the winds blew
and beat on that house; and it fell. And
great was its fall."

28And so it was, when Jesus had end-
ed these sayings, that the people were
astonished at His teaching, 29for He
taught them as one having authority,
and not as the scribes.

Jesus Cleanses a Leper

8 When He had come down from the
mountain, great multitudes fol-
lowed Him. 2And behold, a leper came
and worshiped Him, saying, "Lord, if
You are willing, You can make me clean."
3Then Jesus put out *His* hand and
touched him, saying, "I am willing; be
cleansed." Immediately his leprosy was
cleansed.

4And Jesus said to him, "See that you
tell no one; but go your way, show your-
self to the priest, and offer the gift that
Moses commanded, as a testimony to
them."

Jesus Heals a Centurion's Servant

5Now when Jesus had entered Ca-
pernaum, a centurion came to Him,
pleading with Him, 6saying, "Lord, my
servant is lying at home paralyzed,
dreadfully tormented."

7And Jesus said to him, "I will come
and heal him."

8The centurion answered and said,
"Lord, I am not worthy that You should
come under my roof. But only speak a
word, and my servant will be healed.
9For I also am a man under authority,
having soldiers under me. And I say
to this *one*, 'Go,' and he goes; and to
another, 'Come,' and he comes; and to
my servant, 'Do this,' and he does *it*."

10When Jesus heard *it*, He marveled,
and said to those who followed, "As-
suredly, I say to you, I have not found
such great faith, not even in Israel! 11And
I say to you that many will come from
east and west, and sit down with Abra-
ham, Isaac, and Jacob in the kingdom
of heaven. 12But the sons of the king-
dom will be cast out into outer darkness.
There will be weeping and gnashing of
teeth." 13Then Jesus said to the centu-
rion, "Go your way; and as you have
believed, *so* let it be done for you." And
his servant was healed that same hour.

Peter's Mother-in-Law Healed

14Now when Jesus had come into Pe-
ter's house, He saw his wife's mother
lying sick with a fever. 15So He touched
her hand, and the fever left her. And she
arose and served them.[a]

Many Healed in the Evening

16When evening had come, they
brought to Him many who were demon-
possessed. And He cast out the spirits

8:15 [a] NU-Text and M-Text read *Him*.

GOD SIN JESUS SALVATION LOVE

with a word, and healed all who were
sick, 17that it might be fulfilled which
was spoken by Isaiah the prophet,
saying:

"He Himself took our infirmities
And bore *our* sicknesses."[a]

The Cost of Discipleship

18And when Jesus saw great multi-
tudes about Him, He gave a command
to depart to the other side. 19Then a
certain scribe came and said to Him,
"Teacher, I will follow You wherever
You go."
20And Jesus said to him, "Foxes have
holes and birds of the air *have* nests,
but the Son of Man has nowhere to lay
His head."
21Then another of His disciples said
to Him, "Lord, let me first go and bury
my father."
22But Jesus said to him, "Follow Me,
and let the dead bury their own dead."

Wind and Wave Obey Jesus

23Now when He got into a boat, His
disciples followed Him. 24And suddenly
a great tempest arose on the sea, so that
the boat was covered with the waves.
But He was asleep. 25Then His disciples
came to *Him* and awoke Him, saying,
"Lord, save us! We are perishing!"
26But He said to them, "Why are you
fearful, O you of little faith?" Then He
arose and rebuked the winds and the
sea, and there was a great calm. 27So
the men marveled, saying, "Who can
this be, that even the winds and the sea
obey Him?"

Two Demon-Possessed Men Healed

28When He had come to the other side,
to the country of the Gergesenes,[a] there
met Him two demon-possessed *men*,
coming out of the tombs, exceedingly
fierce, so that no one could pass that
way. 29And suddenly they cried out,
saying, "What have we to do with You,
Jesus, You Son of God? Have You come
here to torment us before the time?"
30Now a good way off from them there
was a herd of many swine feeding. 31So
the demons begged Him, saying, "If You
cast us out, permit us to go away[a] into
the herd of swine."
32And He said to them, "Go." So when
they had come out, they went into the
herd of swine. And suddenly the whole
herd of swine ran violently down the
steep place into the sea, and perished
in the water.
33Then those who kept *them* fled; and
they went away into the city and told
everything, including what *had hap-
pened* to the demon-possessed *men*.
34And behold, the whole city came out
to meet Jesus. And when they saw Him,
they begged *Him* to depart from their
region.

Jesus Forgives and Heals a Paralytic

9 So He got into a boat, crossed over,
and came to His own city. 2Then
behold, they brought to Him a paralytic
lying on a bed. When Jesus saw their
faith, He said to the paralytic, "Son, be
of good cheer; your sins are forgiven
you."
3And at once some of the scribes said
within themselves, "This Man blas-
phemes!"
4But Jesus, knowing their thoughts,
said, "Why do you think evil in your
hearts? 5For which is easier, to say, '*Your*
sins are forgiven you,' or to say, 'Arise
and walk'? 6But that you may know
that the Son of Man has power on earth
to forgive sins"—then He said to the
paralytic, "Arise, take up your bed, and
go to your house." 7And he arose and
departed to his house.
8Now when the multitudes saw *it*, they
marveled[a] and glorified God, who had
given such power to men.

Matthew the Tax Collector

9As Jesus passed on from there, He
saw a man named Matthew sitting at
the tax office. And He said to him, "Fol-
low Me." So he arose and followed Him.
10Now it happened, as Jesus sat at the
table in the house, *that* behold, many
tax collectors and sinners came and sat
down with Him and His disciples. 11And
when the Pharisees saw *it*, they said to

8:17 [a] Isaiah 53:4 **8:28** [a] NU-Text reads *Gadarenes.* **8:31** [a] NU-Text reads *send us.* **9:8** [a] NU-Text reads *were afraid.*

His disciples, "Why does your Teacher
eat with tax collectors and sinners?"
12When Jesus heard *that,* He said to
them, "Those who are well have no need
of a physician, but those who are sick.
13But go and learn what *this* means: 'I
desire mercy and not sacrifice.'[a] For I
did not come to call the righteous, but
sinners, to repentance."[b]

Jesus Is Questioned About Fasting

14Then the disciples of John came to
Him, saying, "Why do we and the Phar-
isees fast often,[a] but Your disciples do
not fast?"
15And Jesus said to them, "Can the
friends of the bridegroom mourn as
long as the bridegroom is with them?
But the days will come when the bride-
groom will be taken away from them,
and then they will fast. 16No one puts a
piece of unshrunk cloth on an old gar-
ment; for the patch pulls away from the
garment, and the tear is made worse.
17Nor do they put new wine into old
wineskins, or else the wineskins break,
the wine is spilled, and the wineskins
are ruined. But they put new wine into
new wineskins, and both are preserved."

A Girl Restored to Life and a Woman Healed

18While He spoke these things to them,
behold, a ruler came and worshiped
Him, saying, "My daughter has just
died, but come and lay Your hand on her
and she will live." 19So Jesus arose and
followed him, and so *did* His disciples.
20And suddenly, a woman who had
a flow of blood for twelve years came
from behind and touched the hem of
His garment. 21For she said to herself,
"If only I may touch His garment, I
shall be made well." 22But Jesus turned
around, and when He saw her He said,
"Be of good cheer, daughter; your faith
has made you well." And the woman
was made well from that hour.
23When Jesus came into the ruler's
house, and saw the flute players and the
noisy crowd wailing, 24He said to them,
"Make room, for the girl is not dead,
but sleeping." And they ridiculed Him.
25But when the crowd was put outside,
He went in and took her by the hand,
and the girl arose. 26And the report of
this went out into all that land.

Two Blind Men Healed

27When Jesus departed from there,
two blind men followed Him, crying
out and saying, "Son of David, have
mercy on us!"
28And when He had come into the
house, the blind men came to Him. And
Jesus said to them, "Do you believe that
I am able to do this?"
They said to Him, "Yes, Lord."
29Then He touched their eyes, say-
ing, "According to your faith let it be
to you." 30And their eyes were opened.
And Jesus sternly warned them, say-
ing, "See *that* no one knows *it.*" 31But
when they had departed, they spread
the news about Him in all that country.

A Mute Man Speaks

32As they went out, behold, they
brought to Him a man, mute and
demon-possessed. 33And when the
demon was cast out, the mute spoke.
And the multitudes marveled, saying,
"It was never seen like this in Israel!"
34But the Pharisees said, "He casts out
demons by the ruler of the demons."

The Compassion of Jesus

35Then Jesus went about all the cities
and villages, teaching in their syna-
gogues, preaching the gospel of the
kingdom, and healing every sickness
and every disease among the people.[a]
36But when He saw the multitudes, He
was moved with compassion for them,
because they were weary[a] and scat-
tered, like sheep having no shepherd.
37Then He said to His disciples, "The
harvest truly *is* plentiful, but the labor-
ers *are* few. 38Therefore pray the Lord
of the harvest to send out laborers into
His harvest."

The Twelve Apostles

10 And when He had called His
twelve disciples to *Him,* He gave
them power *over* unclean spirits, to cast

9:13 [a] Hosea 6:6 [b] NU-Text omits *to repentance.* **9:14** [a] NU-Text brackets *often* as disputed.
9:35 [a] NU-Text omits *among the people.* **9:36** [a] NU-Text and M-Text read *harassed.*

GOD SIN JESUS SALVATION LOVE

them out, and to heal all kinds of sick-
ness and all kinds of disease. 2Now the
names of the twelve apostles are these:
first, Simon, who is called Peter, and An-
drew his brother; James the *son* of Zeb-
edee, and John his brother; 3Philip and
Bartholomew; Thomas and Matthew the
tax collector; James the *son* of Alphae-
us, and Lebbaeus, whose surname was[a]
Thaddaeus; 4Simon the Cananite,[a] and
Judas Iscariot, who also betrayed Him.

Sending Out the Twelve

5These twelve Jesus sent out and com-
manded them, saying: "Do not go into
the way of the Gentiles, and do not en-
ter a city of the Samaritans. 6But go
rather to the lost sheep of the house of
Israel. 7And as you go, preach, saying,
'The kingdom of heaven is at hand.'
8Heal the sick, cleanse the lepers, raise
the dead,[a] cast out demons. Freely you
have received, freely give. 9Provide nei-
ther gold nor silver nor copper in your
money belts, 10nor bag for *your* journey,
nor two tunics, nor sandals, nor staffs;
for a worker is worthy of his food.

11"Now whatever city or town you enter,
inquire who in it is worthy, and stay
there till you go out. 12And when you go
into a household, greet it. 13If the house-
hold is worthy, let your peace come upon
it. But if it is not worthy, let your peace
return to you. 14And whoever will not re-
ceive you nor hear your words, when you
depart from that house or city, shake off
the dust from your feet. 15Assuredly, I
say to you, it will be more tolerable for
the land of Sodom and Gomorrah in
the day of judgment than for that city!

Persecutions Are Coming

16"Behold, I send you out as sheep in
the midst of wolves. Therefore be wise as
serpents and harmless as doves. 17But
beware of men, for they will deliver you
up to councils and scourge you in their
synagogues. 18You will be brought be-
fore governors and kings for My sake, as
a testimony to them and to the Gentiles.
19But when they deliver you up, do not
worry about how or what you should
speak. For it will be given to you in that
hour what you should speak; 20for it is
not you who speak, but the Spirit of your
Father who speaks in you.

21"Now brother will deliver up brother
to death, and a father *his* child; and
children will rise up against parents and
cause them to be put to death. 22And
you will be hated by all for My name's
sake. But he who endures to the end will
be saved. 23When they persecute you in
this city, flee to another. For assuredly,
I say to you, you will not have gone
through the cities of Israel before the
Son of Man comes.

24"A disciple is not above *his* teacher,
nor a servant above his master. 25It is
enough for a disciple that he be like his
teacher, and a servant like his master. If
they have called the master of the house
Beelzebub,[a] how much more *will they*
call those of his household! 26Therefore
do not fear them. For there is nothing
covered that will not be revealed, and
hidden that will not be known.

Jesus Teaches the Fear of God

27"Whatever I tell you in the dark,
speak in the light; and what you hear in
the ear, preach on the housetops. 28And
do not fear those who kill the body but
cannot kill the soul. But rather fear Him
who is able to destroy both soul and
body in hell. 29Are not two sparrows
sold for a copper coin? And not one of
them falls to the ground apart from
your Father's will. 30But the very hairs
of your head are all numbered. 31Do not
fear therefore; you are of more value
than many sparrows.

Confess Christ Before Men

32"Therefore whoever confesses Me
before men, him I will also confess be-
fore My Father who is in heaven. 33But
whoever denies Me before men, him I
will also deny before My Father who is
in heaven.

Christ Brings Division

34"Do not think that I came to bring
peace on earth. I did not come to bring

10:3 [a] NU-Text omits *Lebbaeus, whose surname was.* **10:4** [a] NU-Text reads *Cananaean.*
10:8 [a] NU-Text reads *raise the dead, cleanse the lepers;* M-Text omits *raise the dead.* **10:25** [a] NU-Text and M-Text read *Beelzebul.*

peace but a sword. 35For I have come to
'set a man against his father, a daughter
against her mother, and a daughter-in-
law against her mother-in-law'; 36and 'a
man's enemies *will be* those of his *own*
household.'[a] 37He who loves father or
mother more than Me is not worthy of
Me. And he who loves son or daughter
more than Me is not worthy of Me. 38And
he who does not take his cross and fol-
low after Me is not worthy of Me. 39He
who finds his life will lose it, and he who
loses his life for My sake will find it.

A Cup of Cold Water

40"He who receives you receives Me,
and he who receives Me receives Him
who sent Me. 41He who receives a proph-
et in the name of a prophet shall receive
a prophet's reward. And he who receives
a righteous man in the name of a righ-
teous man shall receive a righteous
man's reward. 42And whoever gives
one of these little ones only a cup of
cold *water* in the name of a disciple,
assuredly, I say to you, he shall by no
means lose his reward."

John the Baptist Sends Messengers to Jesus

11 Now it came to pass, when
Jesus finished commanding
His twelve disciples, that He departed
from there to teach and to preach in
their cities.
2And when John had heard in prison
about the works of Christ, he sent two
of[a] his disciples 3and said to Him, "Are
You the Coming One, or do we look for
another?"
4Jesus answered and said to them, "Go
and tell John the things which you hear
and see: 5*The* blind see and *the* lame
walk; *the* lepers are cleansed and *the*
deaf hear; *the* dead are raised up and
the poor have the gospel preached to
them. 6And blessed is he who is not
offended because of Me."
7As they departed, Jesus began to
say to the multitudes concerning
John: "What did you go out into the
wilderness to see? A reed shaken by
the wind? 8But what did you go out to
see? A man clothed in soft garments?
Indeed, those who wear soft *clothing* are
in kings' houses. 9But what did you go
out to see? A prophet? Yes, I say to you,
and more than a prophet. 10For this is
he of whom it is written:

'Behold, I send My messenger
before Your face,
Who will prepare Your way before
You.'[a]

11"Assuredly, I say to you, among those
born of women there has not risen one
greater than John the Baptist; but he
who is least in the kingdom of heaven
is greater than he. 12And from the days
of John the Baptist until now the king-
dom of heaven suffers violence, and
the violent take it by force. 13For all the
prophets and the law prophesied until
John. 14And if you are willing to receive
it, he is Elijah who is to come. 15He who
has ears to hear, let him hear!
16"But to what shall I liken this gen-
eration? It is like children sitting in the
marketplaces and calling to their com-
panions, 17and saying:

'We played the flute for you,
And you did not dance;
We mourned to you,
And you did not lament.'

18For John came neither eating nor
drinking, and they say, 'He has a de-
mon.' 19The Son of Man came eating
and drinking, and they say, 'Look, a
glutton and a winebibber, a friend of
tax collectors and sinners!' But wisdom
is justified by her children."[a]

Woe to the Impenitent Cities

20Then He began to rebuke the cities
in which most of His mighty works had
been done, because they did not re-
pent: 21"Woe to you, Chorazin! Woe to
you, Bethsaida! For if the mighty works
which were done in you had been done
in Tyre and Sidon, they would have
repented long ago in sackcloth and
ashes. 22But I say to you, it will be more
tolerable for Tyre and Sidon in the day

10:36 [a] Micah 7:6 **11:2** [a] NU-Text reads *by* for *two of.* **11:10** [a] Malachi 3:1 **11:19** [a] NU-Text reads *works.*

of judgment than for you. 23And you,
Capernaum, who are exalted to heaven,
will be[a] brought down to Hades; for if
the mighty works which were done in
you had been done in Sodom, it would
have remained until this day. 24But I
say to you that it shall be more tolera-
ble for the land of Sodom in the day of
judgment than for you."

Jesus Gives True Rest

25At that time Jesus answered and said,
"I thank You, Father, Lord of heaven and
earth, that You have hidden these things
from *the* wise and prudent and have re-
vealed them to babes. 26Even so, Father,
for so it seemed good in Your sight. 27All
things have been delivered to Me by My
Father, and no one knows the Son except
the Father. Nor does anyone know the Fa-
ther except the Son, and *the one* to whom
the Son wills to reveal *Him.* 28Come to Me,
all *you* who labor and are heavy laden,
and I will give you rest. 29Take My yoke
upon you and learn from Me, for I am
gentle and lowly in heart, and you will
find rest for your souls. 30For My yoke *is*
easy and My burden is light."

Jesus Is Lord of the Sabbath

12 At that time Jesus went through
the grainfields on the Sabbath.
And His disciples were hungry, and
began to pluck heads of grain and to
eat. 2And when the Pharisees saw *it,*
they said to Him, "Look, Your disciples
are doing what is not lawful to do on
the Sabbath!"

3But He said to them, "Have you not
read what David did when he was hun-
gry, he and those who were with him:
4how he entered the house of God and
ate the showbread which was not lawful
for him to eat, nor for those who were
with him, but only for the priests? 5Or
have you not read in the law that on
the Sabbath the priests in the temple
profane the Sabbath, and are blame-
less? 6Yet I say to you that in this place
there is *One* greater than the temple.
7But if you had known what *this* means,
'I desire mercy and not sacrifice,'[a]
you would not have condemned the
guiltless. 8For the Son of Man is Lord
even[a] of the Sabbath."

Healing on the Sabbath

9Now when He had departed from
there, He went into their synagogue.
10And behold, there was a man who
had a withered hand. And they asked
Him, saying, "Is it lawful to heal on the
Sabbath?"—that they might accuse Him.
11Then He said to them, "What man is
there among you who has one sheep,
and if it falls into a pit on the Sabbath,
will not lay hold of it and lift *it* out? 12Of
how much more value then is a man
than a sheep? Therefore it is lawful to do
good on the Sabbath." 13Then He said to
the man, "Stretch out your hand." And
he stretched *it* out, and it was restored
as whole as the other. 14Then the Phari-
sees went out and plotted against Him,
how they might destroy Him.

Behold, My Servant

15But when Jesus knew *it,* He withdrew
from there. And great multitudes[a] fol-
lowed Him, and He healed them all.
16Yet He warned them not to make Him
known, 17that it might be fulfilled which
was spoken by Isaiah the prophet, say-
ing:

18 "Behold! My Servant whom I have
chosen,
My Beloved in whom My soul is
well pleased!
I will put My Spirit upon Him,
And He will declare justice to the
Gentiles.
19 He will not quarrel nor cry out,
Nor will anyone hear His voice in
the streets.
20 A bruised reed He will not break,
And smoking flax He will not
quench,
Till He sends forth justice to
victory;
21 And in His name Gentiles will
trust."[a]

A House Divided Cannot Stand

22Then one was brought to Him who
was demon-possessed, blind and mute;

11:23 [a] NU-Text reads *will you be exalted to heaven? No, you will be.* 12:7 [a] Hosea 6:6 12:8 [a] NU-Text and M-Text omit *even.* 12:15 [a] NU-Text brackets *multitudes* as disputed. 12:21 [a] Isaiah 42:1–4

and He healed him, so that the blind and[a] mute man both spoke and saw. 23And all the multitudes were amazed and said, "Could this be the Son of David?"

24Now when the Pharisees heard *it* they said, "This *fellow* does not cast out demons except by Beelzebub,[a] the ruler of the demons."

25But Jesus knew their thoughts, and said to them: "Every kingdom divided against itself is brought to desolation, and every city or house divided against itself will not stand. 26If Satan casts out Satan, he is divided against himself. How then will his kingdom stand? 27And if I cast out demons by Beelzebub, by whom do your sons cast *them* out? Therefore they shall be your judges. 28But if I cast out demons by the Spirit of God, surely the kingdom of God has come upon you. 29Or how can one enter a strong man's house and plunder his goods, unless he first binds the strong man? And then he will plunder his house. 30He who is not with Me is against Me, and he who does not gather with Me scatters abroad.

The Unpardonable Sin

31"Therefore I say to you, every sin and blasphemy will be forgiven men, but the blasphemy *against* the Spirit will not be forgiven men. 32Anyone who speaks a word against the Son of Man, it will be forgiven him; but whoever speaks against the Holy Spirit, it will not be forgiven him, either in this age or in the *age* to come.

A Tree Known by Its Fruit

33"Either make the tree good and its fruit good, or else make the tree bad and its fruit bad; for a tree is known by *its* fruit. 34Brood of vipers! How can you, being evil, speak good things? For out of the abundance of the heart the mouth speaks. 35A good man out of the good treasure of his heart[a] brings forth good things, and an evil man out of the evil treasure brings forth evil things. 36But I say to you that for every idle word men may speak, they will give account of it in the day of judgment. 37For by your words you will be justified, and by your words you will be condemned."

The Scribes and Pharisees Ask for a Sign

38Then some of the scribes and Pharisees answered, saying, "Teacher, we want to see a sign from You."

39But He answered and said to them, "An evil and adulterous generation seeks after a sign, and no sign will be given to it except the sign of the prophet Jonah. 40For as Jonah was three days and three nights in the belly of the great fish, so will the Son of Man be three days and three nights in the heart of the earth. 41The men of Nineveh will rise up in the judgment with this generation and condemn it, because they repented at the preaching of Jonah; and indeed a greater than Jonah *is* here. 42The queen of the South will rise up in the judgment with this generation and condemn it, for she came from the ends of the earth to hear the wisdom of Solomon; and indeed a greater than Solomon *is* here.

An Unclean Spirit Returns

43"When an unclean spirit goes out of a man, he goes through dry places, seeking rest, and finds none. 44Then he says, 'I will return to my house from which I came.' And when he comes, he finds *it* empty, swept, and put in order. 45Then he goes and takes with him seven other spirits more wicked than himself, and they enter and dwell there; and the last *state* of that man is worse than the first. So shall it also be with this wicked generation."

Jesus' Mother and Brothers Send for Him

46While He was still talking to the multitudes, behold, His mother and brothers stood outside, seeking to speak with Him. 47Then one said to Him, "Look, Your mother and Your brothers are standing outside, seeking to speak with You."

48But He answered and said to the one who told Him, "Who is My mother and who are My brothers?" 49And He

12:22 [a] NU-Text omits *blind and.* **12:24** [a] NU-Text and M-Text read *Beelzebul.* **12:35** [a] NU-Text and M-Text omit *of his heart.*

stretched out His hand toward His dis-
ciples and said, "Here are My mother
and My brothers! 50For whoever does
the will of My Father in heaven is My
brother and sister and mother."

The Parable of the Sower

13 On the same day Jesus went out
of the house and sat by the sea.
2And great multitudes were gathered
together to Him, so that He got into a
boat and sat; and the whole multitude
stood on the shore.
3Then He spoke many things to them
in parables, saying: "Behold, a sower
went out to sow. 4And as he sowed, some
seed fell by the wayside; and the birds
came and devoured them. 5Some fell
on stony places, where they did not
have much earth; and they immedi-
ately sprang up because they had no
depth of earth. 6But when the sun was
up they were scorched, and because
they had no root they withered away.
7And some fell among thorns, and the
thorns sprang up and choked them.
8But others fell on good ground and
yielded a crop: some a hundredfold,
some sixty, some thirty. 9He who has
ears to hear, let him hear!"

The Purpose of Parables

10And the disciples came and said to
Him, "Why do You speak to them in
parables?"
11He answered and said to them, "Be-
cause it has been given to you to know
the mysteries of the kingdom of heaven,
but to them it has not been given. 12For
whoever has, to him more will be given,
and he will have abundance; but whoev-
er does not have, even what he has will
be taken away from him. 13Therefore
I speak to them in parables, because
seeing they do not see, and hearing they
do not hear, nor do they understand.
14And in them the prophecy of Isaiah
is fulfilled, which says:

'Hearing you will hear and shall
not understand,
And seeing you will see and not
perceive;
15 For the hearts of this people have
grown dull.
Their ears are hard of hearing,
And their eyes they have closed,
Lest they should see with *their*
eyes and hear with *their* ears,
Lest they should understand with
their hearts and turn,
So that I should[a] heal them.'[b]

16But blessed *are* your eyes for they see,
and your ears for they hear; 17for as-
suredly, I say to you that many proph-
ets and righteous *men* desired to see
what you see, and did not see *it*, and to
hear what you hear, and did not hear *it*.

The Parable of the Sower Explained

18"Therefore hear the parable of the
sower: 19When anyone hears the word
of the kingdom, and does not under-
stand *it*, then the wicked *one* comes
and snatches away what was sown in
his heart. This is he who received seed
by the wayside. 20But he who received
the seed on stony places, this is he who
hears the word and immediately re-
ceives it with joy; 21yet he has no root
in himself, but endures only for a while.
For when tribulation or persecution
arises because of the word, immediately
he stumbles. 22Now he who received
seed among the thorns is he who hears
the word, and the cares of this world
and the deceitfulness of riches choke
the word, and he becomes unfruitful.
23But he who received seed on the good
ground is he who hears the word and
understands *it*, who indeed bears fruit
and produces: some a hundredfold,
some sixty, some thirty."

The Parable of the Wheat and the Tares

24Another parable He put forth to
them, saying: "The kingdom of heav-
en is like a man who sowed good seed
in his field; 25but while men slept, his
enemy came and sowed tares among
the wheat and went his way. 26But when
the grain had sprouted and produced
a crop, then the tares also appeared.
27So the servants of the owner came
and said to him, 'Sir, did you not sow

13:15 [a] NU-Text and M-Text read *would.* [b] Isaiah 6:9, 10

WORSHIP GROWTH HEAVEN FAMILY

good seed in your field? How then does
it have tares?' 28He said to them, 'An
enemy has done this.' The servants said
to him, 'Do you want us then to go and
gather them up?' 29But he said, 'No, lest
while you gather up the tares you also
uproot the wheat with them. 30Let both
grow together until the harvest, and
at the time of harvest I will say to the
reapers, "First gather together the tares
and bind them in bundles to burn them,
but gather the wheat into my barn." ' "

The Parable of the Mustard Seed

31Another parable He put forth to
them, saying: "The kingdom of heaven
is like a mustard seed, which a man took
and sowed in his field, 32which indeed
is the least of all the seeds; but when
it is grown it is greater than the herbs
and becomes a tree, so that the birds of
the air come and nest in its branches."

The Parable of the Leaven

33Another parable He spoke to them:
"The kingdom of heaven is like leaven,
which a woman took and hid in three
measures[a] of meal till it was all leav-
ened."

Prophecy and the Parables

34All these things Jesus spoke to the
multitude in parables; and without a
parable He did not speak to them, 35that
it might be fulfilled which was spoken
by the prophet, saying:

> "I will open My mouth in parables;
> I will utter things kept secret
> from the foundation of the
> world."[a]

The Parable of the Tares Explained

36Then Jesus sent the multitude away
and went into the house. And His disci-
ples came to Him, saying, "Explain to
us the parable of the tares of the field."
37He answered and said to them: "He
who sows the good seed is the Son of
Man. 38The field is the world, the good
seeds are the sons of the kingdom, but
the tares are the sons of the wicked
one. 39The enemy who sowed them is
the devil, the harvest is the end of the
age, and the reapers are the angels.
40Therefore as the tares are gathered
and burned in the fire, so it will be at
the end of this age. 41The Son of Man
will send out His angels, and they will
gather out of His kingdom all things
that offend, and those who practice
lawlessness, 42and will cast them into
the furnace of fire. There will be wailing
and gnashing of teeth. 43Then the righ-
teous will shine forth as the sun in the
kingdom of their Father. He who has
ears to hear, let him hear!

The Parable of the Hidden Treasure

44"Again, the kingdom of heaven is
like treasure hidden in a field, which
a man found and hid; and for joy over
it he goes and sells all that he has and
buys that field.

The Parable of the Pearl of Great Price

45"Again, the kingdom of heaven is like
a merchant seeking beautiful pearls,
46who, when he had found one pearl
of great price, went and sold all that
he had and bought it.

The Parable of the Dragnet

47"Again, the kingdom of heaven is like
a dragnet that was cast into the sea and
gathered some of every kind, 48which,
when it was full, they drew to shore; and
they sat down and gathered the good
into vessels, but threw the bad away.
49So it will be at the end of the age. The
angels will come forth, separate the
wicked from among the just, 50and cast
them into the furnace of fire. There will
be wailing and gnashing of teeth."
51Jesus said to them,[a] "Have you
understood all these things?"
They said to Him, "Yes, Lord."[b]
52Then He said to them, "Therefore
every scribe instructed concerning[a]
the kingdom of heaven is like a house-
holder who brings out of his treasure
things new and old."

Jesus Rejected at Nazareth

53Now it came to pass, when Jesus had
finished these parables, that He departed

13:33 [a] Greek *sata,* approximately two pecks in all **13:35** [a] Psalm 78:2 **13:51** [a] NU-Text omits *Jesus said to them.* [b] NU-Text omits *Lord.* **13:52** [a] Or *for*

from there. 54When He had come to His
own country, He taught them in their
synagogue, so that they were astonished
and said, "Where did this *Man* get this
wisdom and *these* mighty works? 55Is
this not the carpenter's son? Is not His
mother called Mary? And His brothers
James, Joses,[a] Simon, and Judas? 56And
His sisters, are they not all with us?
Where then did this *Man* get all these
things?" 57So they were offended at Him.
But Jesus said to them, "A prophet is
not without honor except in his own
country and in his own house." 58Now
He did not do many mighty works there
because of their unbelief.

John the Baptist Beheaded

14 At that time Herod the tetrarch
heard the report about Jesus
2and said to his servants, "This is John
the Baptist; he is risen from the dead,
and therefore these powers are at work
in him." 3For Herod had laid hold of John
and bound him, and put *him* in prison
for the sake of Herodias, his brother
Philip's wife. 4Because John had said
to him, "It is not lawful for you to have
her." 5And although he wanted to put
him to death, he feared the multitude,
because they counted him as a prophet.
6But when Herod's birthday was
celebrated, the daughter of Herodias
danced before them and pleased Herod.
7Therefore he promised with an oath to
give her whatever she might ask.
8So she, having been prompted by
her mother, said, "Give me John the
Baptist's head here on a platter."
9And the king was sorry; nevertheless,
because of the oaths and because of
those who sat with him, he commanded
it to be given to *her*. 10So he sent and
had John beheaded in prison. 11And
his head was brought on a platter and
given to the girl, and she brought *it* to
her mother. 12Then his disciples came
and took away the body and buried it,
and went and told Jesus.

Feeding the Five Thousand

13When Jesus heard *it*, He departed
from there by boat to a deserted place
by Himself. But when the multitudes
heard it, they followed Him on foot from
the cities. 14And when Jesus went out
He saw a great multitude; and He was
moved with compassion for them, and
healed their sick. 15When it was evening,
His disciples came to Him, saying, "This
is a deserted place, and the hour is al-
ready late. Send the multitudes away,
that they may go into the villages and
buy themselves food."
16But Jesus said to them, "They do not
need to go away. You give them some-
thing to eat."
17And they said to Him, "We have here
only five loaves and two fish."
18He said, "Bring them here to Me."
19Then He commanded the multitudes
to sit down on the grass. And He took
the five loaves and the two fish, and
looking up to heaven, He blessed and
broke and gave the loaves to the dis-
ciples; and the disciples gave to the
multitudes. 20So they all ate and were
filled, and they took up twelve baskets
full of the fragments that remained.
21Now those who had eaten were about
five thousand men, besides women and
children.

Jesus Walks on the Sea

22Immediately Jesus made His dis-
ciples get into the boat and go before
Him to the other side, while He sent the
multitudes away. 23And when He had
sent the multitudes away, He went up
on the mountain by Himself to pray.
Now when evening came, He was alone
there. 24But the boat was now in the
middle of the sea,[a] tossed by the waves,
for the wind was contrary.
25Now in the fourth watch of the night
Jesus went to them, walking on the sea.
26And when the disciples saw Him walk-
ing on the sea, they were troubled, say-
ing, "It is a ghost!" And they cried out
for fear.
27But immediately Jesus spoke to
them, saying, "Be of good cheer! It is
I; do not be afraid."
28And Peter answered Him and said,
"Lord, if it is You, command me to come
to You on the water."

13:55 [a] NU-Text reads *Joseph*. 14:24 [a] NU-Text reads *many furlongs away from the land.*

29So He said, "Come." And when Peter
had come down out of the boat, he
walked on the water to go to Jesus. 30But
when he saw that the wind *was* boister-
ous,[a] he was afraid; and beginning to
sink he cried out, saying, "Lord, save me!"
31And immediately Jesus stretched out
His hand and caught him, and said to
him, "O you of little faith, why did you
doubt?" 32And when they got into the
boat, the wind ceased.
33Then those who were in the boat
came and[a] worshiped Him, saying,
"Truly You are the Son of God."

Many Touch Him and Are Made Well

34When they had crossed over, they
came to the land of[a] Gennesaret. 35And
when the men of that place recognized
Him, they sent out into all that sur-
rounding region, brought to Him all
who were sick, 36and begged Him that
they might only touch the hem of His
garment. And as many as touched *it*
were made perfectly well.

Defilement Comes from Within

15 Then the scribes and Pharisees
who were from Jerusalem came
to Jesus, saying, 2"Why do Your dis-
ciples transgress the tradition of the
elders? For they do not wash their hands
when they eat bread."
3He answered and said to them, "Why
do you also transgress the command-
ment of God because of your tradition?
4For God commanded, saying, 'Honor
your father and your mother';[a] and, 'He
who curses father or mother, let him be
put to death.'[b] 5But you say, 'Whoever
says to his father or mother, "Whatever
profit you might have received from me
is a gift *to God*"— 6then he need not honor
his father or mother.'[a] Thus you have
made the commandment[b] of God of no
effect by your tradition. 7Hypocrites! Well
did Isaiah prophesy about you, saying:

8 'These people draw near to Me with
their mouth,
And[a] honor Me with *their* lips,
But their heart is far from Me.
9 And in vain they worship Me,
Teaching *as* doctrines the
commandments of men.' "[a]

10When He had called the multitude
to *Himself,* He said to them, "Hear and
understand: 11Not what goes into the
mouth defiles a man; but what comes
out of the mouth, this defiles a man."
12Then His disciples came and said to
Him, "Do You know that the Pharisees
were offended when they heard this
saying?"
13But He answered and said, "Every
plant which My heavenly Father has
not planted will be uprooted. 14Let them
alone. They are blind leaders of the
blind. And if the blind leads the blind,
both will fall into a ditch."
15Then Peter answered and said to
Him, "Explain this parable to us."
16So Jesus said, "Are you also still with-
out understanding? 17Do you not yet
understand that whatever enters the
mouth goes into the stomach and is
eliminated? 18But those things which
proceed out of the mouth come from the
heart, and they defile a man. 19For out
of the heart proceed evil thoughts, mur-
ders, adulteries, fornications, thefts,
false witness, blasphemies. 20These
are *the things* which defile a man, but
to eat with unwashed hands does not
defile a man."

A Gentile Shows Her Faith

21Then Jesus went out from there and
departed to the region of Tyre and
Sidon. 22And behold, a woman of Ca-
naan came from that region and cried
out to Him, saying, "Have mercy on me,
O Lord, Son of David! My daughter is
severely demon-possessed."
23But He answered her not a word.
And His disciples came and urged
Him, saying, "Send her away, for she
cries out after us."
24But He answered and said, "I was
not sent except to the lost sheep of the
house of Israel."

14:30 [a] NU-Text brackets *that* and *boisterous* as disputed. **14:33** [a] NU-Text omits *came and.*
14:34 [a] NU-Text reads *came to land at.* **15:4** [a] Exodus 20:12; Deuteronomy 5:16 [b] Exodus 21:17
15:6 [a] NU-Text omits *or mother.* [b] NU-Text reads *word.* **15:8** [a] NU-Text omits *draw near to Me with their mouth, And.* **15:9** [a] Isaiah 29:13

25Then she came and worshiped Him,
saying, "Lord, help me!"
26But He answered and said, "It is not
good to take the children's bread and
throw *it* to the little dogs."
27And she said, "Yes, Lord, yet even
the little dogs eat the crumbs which fall
from their masters' table."
28Then Jesus answered and said to her,
"O woman, great *is* your faith! Let it be
to you as you desire." And her daughter
was healed from that very hour.

Jesus Heals Great Multitudes

29Jesus departed from there, skirted
the Sea of Galilee, and went up on the
mountain and sat down there. 30Then
great multitudes came to Him, hav-
ing with them *the* lame, blind, mute,
maimed, and many others; and they
laid them down at Jesus' feet, and He
healed them. 31So the multitude mar-
veled when they saw *the* mute speak-
ing, *the* maimed made whole, *the* lame
walking, and *the* blind seeing; and they
glorified the God of Israel.

Feeding the Four Thousand

32Now Jesus called His disciples to
Himself and said, "I have compassion
on the multitude, because they have
now continued with Me three days and
have nothing to eat. And I do not want
to send them away hungry, lest they
faint on the way."
33Then His disciples said to Him,
"Where could we get enough bread in
the wilderness to fill such a great mul-
titude?"
34Jesus said to them, "How many
loaves do you have?"
And they said, "Seven, and a few little
fish."
35So He commanded the multitude to
sit down on the ground. 36And He took
the seven loaves and the fish and gave
thanks, broke *them* and gave *them* to
His disciples; and the disciples *gave* to
the multitude. 37So they all ate and were
filled, and they took up seven large bas-
kets full of the fragments that were left.
38Now those who ate were four thou-
sand men, besides women and children.
39And He sent away the multitude, got
into the boat, and came to the region
of Magdala.[a]

The Pharisees and Sadducees Seek a Sign

16 Then the Pharisees and Sad-
ducees came, and testing Him
asked that He would show them a sign
from heaven. 2He answered and said
to them, "When it is evening you say,
'*It will be* fair weather, for the sky is
red'; 3and in the morning, '*It will be* foul
weather today, for the sky is red and
threatening.' Hypocrites![a] You know
how to discern the face of the sky, but
you cannot *discern* the signs of the
times. 4A wicked and adulterous gen-
eration seeks after a sign, and no sign
shall be given to it except the sign of
the prophet[a] Jonah." And He left them
and departed.

The Leaven of the Pharisees and Sadducees

5Now when His disciples had come to
the other side, they had forgotten to
take bread. 6Then Jesus said to them,
"Take heed and beware of the leaven
of the Pharisees and the Sadducees."
7And they reasoned among them-
selves, saying, "*It is* because we have
taken no bread."
8But Jesus, being aware of *it,* said to
them, "O you of little faith, why do you
reason among yourselves because you
have brought no bread?[a] 9Do you not yet
understand, or remember the five loaves
of the five thousand and how many bas-
kets you took up? 10Nor the seven loaves
of the four thousand and how many
large baskets you took up? 11How is it
you do not understand that I did not
speak to you concerning bread?—*but*
to beware of the leaven of the Pharisees
and Sadducees." 12Then they understood
that He did not tell *them* to beware of the
leaven of bread, but of the doctrine of
the Pharisees and Sadducees.

Peter Confesses Jesus as the Christ

13When Jesus came into the region
of Caesarea Philippi, He asked His

15:39 [a] NU-Text reads *Magadan.* **16:3** [a] NU-Text omits *Hypocrites.* **16:4** [a] NU-Text omits *the prophet.* **16:8** [a] NU-Text reads *you have no bread.*

disciples, saying, "Who do men say
that I, the Son of Man, am?"
14So they said, "Some *say* John the
Baptist, some Elijah, and others Jere-
miah or one of the prophets."
15He said to them, "But who do you
say that I am?"
16Simon Peter answered and said, "You
are the Christ, the Son of the living God."
17Jesus answered and said to him,
"Blessed are you, Simon Bar-Jonah, for
flesh and blood has not revealed *this* to
you, but My Father who is in heaven.
18And I also say to you that you are
Peter, and on this rock I will build My
church, and the gates of Hades shall
not prevail against it. 19And I will give
you the keys of the kingdom of heaven,
and whatever you bind on earth will
be bound in heaven, and whatever you
loose on earth will be loosed[a] in heaven."
20Then He commanded His disciples
that they should tell no one that He was
Jesus the Christ.

Jesus Predicts His Death and Resurrection

21From that time Jesus began to show
to His disciples that He must go to Jeru-
salem, and suffer many things from the
elders and chief priests and scribes, and
be killed, and be raised the third day.
22Then Peter took Him aside and be-
gan to rebuke Him, saying, "Far be it
from You, Lord; this shall not happen
to You!"
23But He turned and said to Peter, "Get
behind Me, Satan! You are an offense
to Me, for you are not mindful of the
things of God, but the things of men."

Take Up the Cross and Follow Him

24Then Jesus said to His disciples, "If
anyone desires to come after Me, let him
deny himself, and take up his cross, and
follow Me. 25For whoever desires to save
his life will lose it, but whoever loses his
life for My sake will find it. 26For what
profit is it to a man if he gains the whole
world, and loses his own soul? Or what
will a man give in exchange for his soul?
27For the Son of Man will come in the
glory of His Father with His angels, and
then He will reward each according to
his works. 28Assuredly, I say to you,
there are some standing here who shall
not taste death till they see the Son of
Man coming in His kingdom."

Jesus Transfigured on the Mount

17 Now after six days Jesus took
Peter, James, and John his
brother, led them up on a high moun-
tain by themselves; 2and He was trans-
figured before them. His face shone
like the sun, and His clothes became as
white as the light. 3And behold, Moses
and Elijah appeared to them, talking
with Him. 4Then Peter answered and
said to Jesus, "Lord, it is good for us to
be here; if You wish, let us[a] make here
three tabernacles: one for You, one for
Moses, and one for Elijah."
5While he was still speaking, behold,
a bright cloud overshadowed them;
and suddenly a voice came out of the
cloud, saying, "This is My beloved Son,
in whom I am well pleased. Hear Him!"
6And when the disciples heard *it,* they
fell on their faces and were greatly
afraid. 7But Jesus came and touched
them and said, "Arise, and do not be
afraid." 8When they had lifted up their
eyes, they saw no one but Jesus only.
9Now as they came down from the
mountain, Jesus commanded them,
saying, "Tell the vision to no one until
the Son of Man is risen from the dead."
10And His disciples asked Him, saying,
"Why then do the scribes say that Elijah
must come first?"
11Jesus answered and said to them,
"Indeed, Elijah is coming first[a] and will
restore all things. 12But I say to you that
Elijah has come already, and they did
not know him but did to him whatever
they wished. Likewise the Son of Man
is also about to suffer at their hands."
13Then the disciples understood that
He spoke to them of John the Baptist.

A Boy Is Healed

14And when they had come to the mul-
titude, a man came to Him, kneeling
down to Him and saying, 15"Lord, have
mercy on my son, for he is an epileptic[a]

16:19 [a] Or *will have been bound . . . will have been loosed* **17:4** [a] NU-Text reads *I will.* **17:11** [a] NU-Text omits *first.* **17:15** [a] Literally *moonstruck*

and suffers severely; for he often falls
into the fire and often into the water.
16So I brought him to Your disciples,
but they could not cure him."
17Then Jesus answered and said,
"O faithless and perverse generation,
how long shall I be with you? How long
shall I bear with you? Bring him here
to Me." 18And Jesus rebuked the demon,
and it came out of him; and the child
was cured from that very hour.
19Then the disciples came to Jesus
privately and said, "Why could we not
cast it out?"
20So Jesus said to them, "Because of
your unbelief;[a] for assuredly, I say to
you, if you have faith as a mustard seed,
you will say to this mountain, 'Move
from here to there,' and it will move;
and nothing will be impossible for you.
21However, this kind does not go out
except by prayer and fasting."[a]

Jesus Again Predicts His Death and Resurrection

22Now while they were staying[a] in
Galilee, Jesus said to them, "The Son
of Man is about to be betrayed into the
hands of men, 23and they will kill Him,
and the third day He will be raised up."
And they were exceedingly sorrowful.

Peter and His Master Pay Their Taxes

24When they had come to Caperna-
um,[a] those who received the *temple*
tax came to Peter and said, "Does your
Teacher not pay the *temple* tax?"
25He said, "Yes."
And when he had come into the house,
Jesus anticipated him, saying, "What do
you think, Simon? From whom do the
kings of the earth take customs or taxes,
from their sons or from strangers?"
26Peter said to Him, "From strangers."
Jesus said to him, "Then the sons are
free. 27Nevertheless, lest we offend
them, go to the sea, cast in a hook, and
take the fish that comes up first. And
when you have opened its mouth, you
will find a piece of money;[a] take that
and give it to them for Me and you."

Who Is the Greatest?

18 At that time the disciples came
to Jesus, saying, "Who then is
greatest in the kingdom of heaven?"
2Then Jesus called a little child to Him,
set him in the midst of them, 3and said,
"Assuredly, I say to you, unless you are
converted and become as little children,
you will by no means enter the kingdom
of heaven. 4Therefore whoever humbles
himself as this little child is the greatest
in the kingdom of heaven. 5Whoever
receives one little child like this in My
name receives Me.

Jesus Warns of Offenses

6"But whoever causes one of these
little ones who believe in Me to sin, it
would be better for him if a millstone
were hung around his neck, and he were
drowned in the depth of the sea. 7Woe
to the world because of offenses! For
offenses must come, but woe to that
man by whom the offense comes!
8"If your hand or foot causes you to
sin, cut it off and cast *it* from you. It is
better for you to enter into life lame or
maimed, rather than having two hands
or two feet, to be cast into the everlast-
ing fire. 9And if your eye causes you to
sin, pluck it out and cast *it* from you. It
is better for you to enter into life with
one eye, rather than having two eyes,
to be cast into hell fire.

The Parable of the Lost Sheep

10"Take heed that you do not despise
one of these little ones, for I say to you
that in heaven their angels always see
the face of My Father who is in heaven.
11For the Son of Man has come to save
that which was lost.[a]
12"What do you think? If a man has a
hundred sheep, and one of them goes
astray, does he not leave the ninety-
nine and go to the mountains to seek
the one that is straying? 13And if he
should find it, assuredly, I say to you, he
rejoices more over that *sheep* than over
the ninety-nine that did not go astray.
14Even so it is not the will of your Father

17:20 [a] NU-Text reads *little faith.* **17:21** [a] NU-Text omits this verse. **17:22** [a] NU-Text reads *gathering together.* **17:24** [a] NU-Text reads *Capharnaum* (here and elsewhere). **17:27** [a] Greek *stater,* the exact amount to pay the temple tax (didrachma) for two **18:11** [a] NU-Text omits this verse.

who is in heaven that one of these little ones should perish.

Dealing with a Sinning Brother

15"Moreover if your brother sins against you, go and tell him his fault between you and him alone. If he hears you, you have gained your brother. 16But if he will not hear, take with you one or two more, that 'by the mouth of two or three witnesses every word may be established.'[a] 17And if he refuses to hear them, tell *it* to the church. But if he refuses even to hear the church, let him be to you like a heathen and a tax collector.

18"Assuredly, I say to you, whatever you bind on earth will be bound in heaven, and whatever you loose on earth will be loosed in heaven.

19"Again I say[a] to you that if two of you agree on earth concerning anything that they ask, it will be done for them by My Father in heaven. 20For where two or three are gathered together in My name, I am there in the midst of them."

The Parable of the Unforgiving Servant

21Then Peter came to Him and said, "Lord, how often shall my brother sin against me, and I forgive him? Up to seven times?"

22Jesus said to him, "I do not say to you, up to seven times, but up to seventy times seven. 23Therefore the kingdom of heaven is like a certain king who wanted to settle accounts with his servants. 24And when he had begun to settle accounts, one was brought to him who owed him ten thousand talents. 25But as he was not able to pay, his master commanded that he be sold, with his wife and children and all that he had, and that payment be made. 26The servant therefore fell down before him, saying, 'Master, have patience with me, and I will pay you all.' 27Then the master of that servant was moved with compassion, released him, and forgave him the debt.

28"But that servant went out and found one of his fellow servants who owed him a hundred denarii; and he laid hands on him and took *him* by the throat, saying, 'Pay me what you owe!' 29So his fellow servant fell down at his feet[a] and begged him, saying, 'Have patience with me, and I will pay you all.'[b] 30And he would not, but went and threw him into prison till he should pay the debt. 31So when his fellow servants saw what had been done, they were very grieved, and came and told their master all that had been done. 32Then his master, after he had called him, said to him, 'You wicked servant! I forgave you all that debt because you begged me. 33Should you not also have had compassion on your fellow servant, just as I had pity on you?' 34And his master was angry, and delivered him to the torturers until he should pay all that was due to him.

35"So My heavenly Father also will do to you if each of you, from his heart, does not forgive his brother his trespasses."[a]

Marriage and Divorce

19 Now it came to pass, when Jesus had finished these sayings, *that* He departed from Galilee and came to the region of Judea beyond the Jordan. 2And great multitudes followed Him, and He healed them there.

3The Pharisees also came to Him, testing Him, and saying to Him, "Is it lawful for a man to divorce his wife for *just* any reason?"

4And He answered and said to them, "Have you not read that He who made[a] *them* at the beginning 'made them male and female,'[b] 5and said, 'For this reason a man shall leave his father and mother and be joined to his wife, and the two shall become one flesh'?[a] 6So then, they are no longer two but one flesh. Therefore what God has joined together, let not man separate."

7They said to Him, "Why then did Moses command to give a certificate of divorce, and to put her away?"

8He said to them, "Moses, because of

18:16 [a] Deuteronomy 19:15 **18:19** [a] NU-Text and M-Text read *Again, assuredly, I say.* **18:29** [a] NU-Text omits *at his feet.* [b] NU-Text and M-Text omit *all.* **18:35** [a] NU-Text omits *his trespasses.* **19:4** [a] NU-Text reads *created.* [b] Genesis 1:27; 5:2 **19:5** [a] Genesis 2:24

the hardness of your hearts, permitted you to divorce your wives, but from the beginning it was not so. 9And I say to you, whoever divorces his wife, except for sexual immorality,[a] and marries another, commits adultery; and whoever marries her who is divorced commits adultery."

10His disciples said to Him, "If such is the case of the man with *his* wife, it is better not to marry."

Jesus Teaches on Celibacy

11But He said to them, "All cannot accept this saying, but only *those* to whom it has been given: 12For there are eunuchs who were born thus from *their* mother's womb, and there are eunuchs who were made eunuchs by men, and there are eunuchs who have made themselves eunuchs for the kingdom of heaven's sake. He who is able to accept *it,* let him accept *it.*"

Jesus Blesses Little Children

13Then little children were brought to Him that He might put *His* hands on them and pray, but the disciples rebuked them. 14But Jesus said, "Let the little children come to Me, and do not forbid them; for of such is the kingdom of heaven." 15And He laid *His* hands on them and departed from there.

Jesus Counsels the Rich Young Ruler

16Now behold, one came and said to Him, "Good[a] Teacher, what good thing shall I do that I may have eternal life?"

17So He said to him, "Why do you call Me good?[a] No one *is* good but One, *that is,* God.[b] But if you want to enter into life, keep the commandments."

18He said to Him, "Which ones?"

Jesus said, " 'You shall not murder,' 'You shall not commit adultery,' 'You shall not steal,' 'You shall not bear false witness,' 19'Honor your father and *your* mother,'[a] and, 'You shall love your neighbor as yourself.' "[b]

20The young man said to Him, "All these things I have kept from my youth.[a] What do I still lack?"

21Jesus said to him, "If you want to be perfect, go, sell what you have and give to the poor, and you will have treasure in heaven; and come, follow Me."

22But when the young man heard that saying, he went away sorrowful, for he had great possessions.

With God All Things Are Possible

23Then Jesus said to His disciples, "Assuredly, I say to you that it is hard for a rich man to enter the kingdom of heaven. 24And again I say to you, it is easier for a camel to go through the eye of a needle than for a rich man to enter the kingdom of God."

25When His disciples heard *it,* they were greatly astonished, saying, "Who then can be saved?"

26But Jesus looked at *them* and said to them, "With men this is impossible, but with God all things are possible."

27Then Peter answered and said to Him, "See, we have left all and followed You. Therefore what shall we have?"

28So Jesus said to them, "Assuredly I say to you, that in the regeneration, when the Son of Man sits on the throne of His glory, you who have followed Me will also sit on twelve thrones, judging the twelve tribes of Israel. 29And everyone who has left houses or brothers or sisters or father or mother or wife[a] or children or lands, for My name's sake, shall receive a hundredfold, and inherit eternal life. 30But many *who are* first will be last, and the last first.

The Parable of the Workers in the Vineyard

20 "For the kingdom of heaven is like a landowner who went out early in the morning to hire laborers for his vineyard. 2Now when he had agreed with the laborers for a denarius a day, he sent them into his vineyard. 3And he went out about the third hour and saw others standing idle in the marketplace, 4and said to them, 'You also go into the vineyard, and whatever is right I will give you.' So they went. 5Again he went out about the sixth and the ninth

19:9 [a] Or *fornication* **19:16** [a] NU-Text omits *Good.* **19:17** [a] NU-Text reads *Why do you ask Me about what is good?* [b] NU-Text reads *There is One who is good.* **19:19** [a] Exodus 20:12–16; Deuteronomy 5:16–20 [b] Leviticus 19:18 **19:20** [a] NU-Text omits *from my youth.* **19:29** [a] NU-Text omits *or wife.*

WORSHIP GROWTH HEAVEN FAMILY

hour, and did likewise. 6And about the
eleventh hour he went out and found
others standing idle,[a] and said to them,
'Why have you been standing here idle
all day?' 7They said to him, 'Because no
one hired us.' He said to them, 'You also
go into the vineyard, and whatever is
right you will receive.'[a]
8"So when evening had come, the own-
er of the vineyard said to his steward,
'Call the laborers and give them *their*
wages, beginning with the last to the
first.' 9And when those came who *were*
hired about the eleventh hour, they
each received a denarius. 10But when
the first came, they supposed that they
would receive more; and they likewise
received each a denarius. 11And when
they had received *it,* they complained
against the landowner, 12saying, 'These
last *men* have worked *only* one hour,
and you made them equal to us who
have borne the burden and the heat
of the day.' 13But he answered one of
them and said, 'Friend, I am doing you
no wrong. Did you not agree with me
for a denarius? 14Take *what is* yours
and go your way. I wish to give to this
last man *the same* as to you. 15Is it not
lawful for me to do what I wish with my
own things? Or is your eye evil because
I am good?' 16So the last will be first,
and the first last. For many are called,
but few chosen."[a]

Jesus a Third Time Predicts His Death and Resurrection

17Now Jesus, going up to Jerusalem,
took the twelve disciples aside on the
road and said to them, 18"Behold, we are
going up to Jerusalem, and the Son of
Man will be betrayed to the chief priests
and to the scribes; and they will con-
demn Him to death, 19and deliver Him
to the Gentiles to mock and to scourge
and to crucify. And the third day He
will rise again."

Greatness Is Serving

20Then the mother of Zebedee's sons
came to Him with her sons, kneeling
down and asking something from Him.
21And He said to her, "What do you
wish?"
She said to Him, "Grant that these two
sons of mine may sit, one on Your right
hand and the other on the left, in Your
kingdom."
22But Jesus answered and said, "You
do not know what you ask. Are you
able to drink the cup that I am about to
drink, and be baptized with the baptism
that I am baptized with?"[a]
They said to Him, "We are able."
23So He said to them, "You will indeed
drink My cup, and be baptized with the
baptism that I am baptized with;[a] but
to sit on My right hand and on My left
is not Mine to give, but *it is for those*
for whom it is prepared by My Father."
24And when the ten heard *it,* they
were greatly displeased with the two
brothers. 25But Jesus called them to
Himself and said, "You know that the
rulers of the Gentiles lord it over them,
and those who are great exercise au-
thority over them. 26Yet it shall not be
so among you; but whoever desires to
become great among you, let him be
your servant. 27And whoever desires
to be first among you, let him be your
slave—28just as the Son of Man did not
come to be served, but to serve, and to
give His life a ransom for many."

Two Blind Men Receive Their Sight

29Now as they went out of Jericho, a
great multitude followed Him. 30And
behold, two blind men sitting by the
road, when they heard that Jesus was
passing by, cried out, saying, "Have
mercy on us, O Lord, Son of David!"
31Then the multitude warned them
that they should be quiet; but they cried
out all the more, saying, "Have mercy
on us, O Lord, Son of David!"
32So Jesus stood still and called them,
and said, "What do you want Me to do
for you?"
33They said to Him, "Lord, that our
eyes may be opened." 34So Jesus had
compassion and touched their eyes.
And immediately their eyes received
sight, and they followed Him.

20:6 [a] NU-Text omits *idle.* **20:7** [a] NU-Text omits the last clause of this verse. **20:16** [a] NU-Text omits the last sentence of this verse. **20:22** [a] NU-Text omits *and be baptized with the baptism that I am baptized with.* **20:23** [a] NU-Text omits *and be baptized with the baptism that I am baptized with.*

The Triumphal Entry

21 Now when they drew near Jeru-
salem, and came to Bethphage,[a]
at the Mount of Olives, then Jesus sent
two disciples, 2saying to them, "Go into
the village opposite you, and immedi-
ately you will find a donkey tied, and
a colt with her. Loose *them* and bring
them to Me. 3And if anyone says any-
thing to you, you shall say, 'The Lord
has need of them,' and immediately he
will send them."
4All[a] this was done that it might be
fulfilled which was spoken by the proph-
et, saying:

5 "Tell the daughter of Zion,
'Behold, your King is coming to you,
Lowly, and sitting on a donkey,
A colt, the foal of a donkey.'"[a]

6So the disciples went and did as Jesus
commanded them. 7They brought the
donkey and the colt, laid their clothes
on them, and set *Him*[a] on them. 8And
a very great multitude spread their
clothes on the road; others cut down
branches from the trees and spread
them on the road. 9Then the multitudes
who went before and those who fol-
lowed cried out, saying:

"Hosanna to the Son of David!
'Blessed *is* He who comes in the
name of the LORD!'[a]
Hosanna in the highest!"

10And when He had come into Jeru-
salem, all the city was moved, saying,
"Who is this?"
11So the multitudes said, "This is Jesus,
the prophet from Nazareth of Galilee."

Jesus Cleanses the Temple

12Then Jesus went into the temple of
God[a] and drove out all those who bought
and sold in the temple, and overturned
the tables of the money changers and
the seats of those who sold doves. 13And
He said to them, "It is written, 'My house
shall be called a house of prayer,'[a] but
you have made it a 'den of thieves.'"[b]

14Then *the* blind and *the* lame came
to Him in the temple, and He healed
them. 15But when the chief priests and
scribes saw the wonderful things that
He did, and the children crying out in
the temple and saying, "Hosanna to
the Son of David!" they were indignant
16and said to Him, "Do You hear what
these are saying?"
And Jesus said to them, "Yes. Have
you never read,

'Out of the mouth of babes and
nursing infants
You have perfected praise'?"[a]

17Then He left them and went out of the
city to Bethany, and He lodged there.

The Fig Tree Withered

18Now in the morning, as He returned
to the city, He was hungry. 19And see-
ing a fig tree by the road, He came to
it and found nothing on it but leaves,
and said to it, "Let no fruit grow on you
ever again." Immediately the fig tree
withered away.

The Lesson of the Withered Fig Tree

20And when the disciples saw *it,* they
marveled, saying, "How did the fig tree
wither away so soon?"
21So Jesus answered and said to them,
"Assuredly, I say to you, if you have
faith and do not doubt, you will not
only do what was done to the fig tree,
but also if you say to this mountain, 'Be
removed and be cast into the sea,' it will
be done. 22And whatever things you ask
in prayer, believing, you will receive."

Jesus' Authority Questioned

23Now when He came into the tem-
ple, the chief priests and the elders of
the people confronted Him as He was
teaching, and said, "By what authority
are You doing these things? And who
gave You this authority?"
24But Jesus answered and said to
them, "I also will ask you one thing,
which if you tell Me, I likewise will tell
you by what authority I do these things:

21:1 [a] M-Text reads *Bethsphage.* **21:4** [a] NU-Text omits *All.* **21:5** [a] Zechariah 9:9 **21:7** [a] NU-Text reads *and He sat.* **21:9** [a] Psalm 118:26 **21:12** [a] NU-Text omits *of God.* **21:13** [a] Isaiah 56:7 [b] Jeremiah 7:11 **21:16** [a] Psalm 8:2

25 The baptism of John—where was it
from? From heaven or from men?"
And they reasoned among them-
selves, saying, "If we say, 'From heav-
en,' He will say to us, 'Why then did you
not believe him?' 26 But if we say, 'From
men,' we fear the multitude, for all count
John as a prophet." 27 So they answered
Jesus and said, "We do not know."
And He said to them, "Neither will I tell
you by what authority I do these things.

The Parable of the Two Sons

28 "But what do you think? A man had
two sons, and he came to the first and
said, 'Son, go, work today in my vine-
yard.' 29 He answered and said, 'I will
not,' but afterward he regretted it and
went. 30 Then he came to the second
and said likewise. And he answered and
said, 'I *go,* sir,' but he did not go. 31 Which
of the two did the will of *his* father?"
They said to Him, "The first."
Jesus said to them, "Assuredly, I say
to you that tax collectors and harlots
enter the kingdom of God before you.
32 For John came to you in the way of
righteousness, and you did not believe
him; but tax collectors and harlots be-
lieved him; and when you saw *it,* you did
not afterward relent and believe him.

The Parable of the Wicked Vinedressers

33 "Hear another parable: There was a
certain landowner who planted a vine-
yard and set a hedge around it, dug a
winepress in it and built a tower. And he
leased it to vinedressers and went into a
far country. 34 Now when vintage-time
drew near, he sent his servants to the
vinedressers, that they might receive
its fruit. 35 And the vinedressers took
his servants, beat one, killed one, and
stoned another. 36 Again he sent other
servants, more than the first, and they
did likewise to them. 37 Then last of all he
sent his son to them, saying, 'They will
respect my son.' 38 But when the vine-
dressers saw the son, they said among
themselves, 'This is the heir. Come, let
us kill him and seize his inheritance.'
39 So they took him and cast *him* out of
the vineyard and killed *him.*

40 "Therefore, when the owner of the
vineyard comes, what will he do to those
vinedressers?"
41 They said to Him, "He will destroy
those wicked men miserably, and lease
his vineyard to other vinedressers who
will render to him the fruits in their
seasons."
42 Jesus said to them, "Have you never
read in the Scriptures:

'The stone which the builders
rejected
Has become the chief cornerstone.
This was the LORD's doing,
And it is marvelous in our eyes'?[a]

43 "Therefore I say to you, the kingdom
of God will be taken from you and giv-
en to a nation bearing the fruits of it.
44 And whoever falls on this stone will
be broken; but on whomever it falls, it
will grind him to powder."
45 Now when the chief priests and Phar-
isees heard His parables, they perceived
that He was speaking of them. 46 But
when they sought to lay hands on Him,
they feared the multitudes, because
they took Him for a prophet.

The Parable of the Wedding Feast

22 And Jesus answered and spoke
to them again by parables and
said: 2 "The kingdom of heaven is like a
certain king who arranged a marriage
for his son, 3 and sent out his servants
to call those who were invited to the
wedding; and they were not willing to
come. 4 Again, he sent out other ser-
vants, saying, 'Tell those who are in-
vited, "See, I have prepared my dinner;
my oxen and fatted cattle *are* killed,
and all things *are* ready. Come to the
wedding." ' 5 But they made light of it
and went their ways, one to his own
farm, another to his business. 6 And the
rest seized his servants, treated *them*
spitefully, and killed *them.* 7 But when
the king heard *about it,* he was furious.
And he sent out his armies, destroyed
those murderers, and burned up their
city. 8 Then he said to his servants, 'The
wedding is ready, but those who were

21:42 [a] Psalm 118:22, 23

invited were not worthy. 9Therefore go
into the highways, and as many as you
find, invite to the wedding.' 10So those
servants went out into the highways
and gathered together all whom they
found, both bad and good. And the wed-
ding *hall* was filled with guests.
11"But when the king came in to see
the guests, he saw a man there who did
not have on a wedding garment. 12So he
said to him, 'Friend, how did you come
in here without a wedding garment?'
And he was speechless. 13Then the king
said to the servants, 'Bind him hand and
foot, take him away, and[a] cast *him* into
outer darkness; there will be weeping
and gnashing of teeth.'
14"For many are called, but few *are*
chosen."

The Pharisees: Is It Lawful to Pay Taxes to Caesar?

15Then the Pharisees went and plot-
ted how they might entangle Him in
His talk. 16And they sent to Him their
disciples with the Herodians, saying,
"Teacher, we know that You are true,
and teach the way of God in truth; nor
do You care about anyone, for You do
not regard the person of men. 17Tell us,
therefore, what do You think? Is it lawful
to pay taxes to Caesar, or not?"
18But Jesus perceived their wicked-
ness, and said, "Why do you test Me, *you*
hypocrites? 19Show Me the tax money."
So they brought Him a denarius.
20And He said to them, "Whose image
and inscription *is* this?"
21They said to Him, "Caesar's."
And He said to them, "Render there-
fore to Caesar the things that are Cae-
sar's, and to God the things that are
God's." 22When they had heard *these
words,* they marveled, and left Him and
went their way.

The Sadducees: What About the Resurrection?

23The same day the Sadducees, who
say there is no resurrection, came to
Him and asked Him, 24saying: "Teacher,
Moses said that if a man dies, having no
children, his brother shall marry his wife
and raise up offspring for his brother.
25Now there were with us seven brothers.
The first died after he had married, and
having no offspring, left his wife to his
brother. 26Likewise the second also, and
the third, even to the seventh. 27Last of
all the woman died also. 28Therefore,
in the resurrection, whose wife of the
seven will she be? For they all had her."
29Jesus answered and said to them,
"You are mistaken, not knowing the
Scriptures nor the power of God. 30For
in the resurrection they neither marry
nor are given in marriage, but are like
angels of God[a] in heaven. 31But con-
cerning the resurrection of the dead,
have you not read what was spoken
to you by God, saying, 32'I am the God
of Abraham, the God of Isaac, and the
God of Jacob'?[a] God is not the God of
the dead, but of the living." 33And when
the multitudes heard *this,* they were
astonished at His teaching.

The Scribes: Which Is the First Commandment of All?

34But when the Pharisees heard that
He had silenced the Sadducees, they
gathered together. 35Then one of them,
a lawyer, asked *Him a question,* testing
Him, and saying, 36"Teacher, which *is*
the great commandment in the law?"
37Jesus said to him, " 'You shall love
the LORD your God with all your heart,
with all your soul, and with all your
mind.'[a] 38This is *the* first and great com-
mandment. 39And *the* second *is* like it:
'You shall love your neighbor as your-
self.'[a] 40On these two commandments
hang all the Law and the Prophets."

Jesus: How Can David Call His Descendant "Lord"?

41While the Pharisees were gathered
together, Jesus asked them, 42saying,
"What do you think about the Christ?
Whose Son is He?"
They said to Him, "*The Son* of David."
43He said to them, "How then does Da-
vid in the Spirit call Him 'Lord,' saying:

44 'The LORD said to my Lord,
"Sit at My right hand,

22:13 [a] NU-Text omits *take him away, and.* **22:30** [a] NU-Text omits *of God.* **22:32** [a] Exodus 3:6, 15
22:37 [a] Deuteronomy 6:5 **22:39** [a] Leviticus 19:18

Till I make Your enemies Your
footstool" '?[a]

45If David then calls Him 'Lord,' how
is He his Son?" 46And no one was able
to answer Him a word, nor from that
day on did anyone dare question Him
anymore.

Woe to the Scribes and Pharisees

23 Then Jesus spoke to the multi-
tudes and to His disciples, 2say-
ing: "The scribes and the Pharisees sit in
Moses' seat. 3Therefore whatever they
tell you to observe,[a] *that* observe and
do, but do not do according to their
works; for they say, and do not do. 4For
they bind heavy burdens, hard to bear,
and lay *them* on men's shoulders; but
they *themselves* will not move them with
one of their fingers. 5But all their works
they do to be seen by men. They make
their phylacteries broad and enlarge
the borders of their garments. 6They
love the best places at feasts, the best
seats in the synagogues, 7greetings in
the marketplaces, and to be called by
men, 'Rabbi, Rabbi.' 8But you, do not be
called 'Rabbi'; for One is your Teacher,
the Christ,[a] and you are all brethren.
9Do not call anyone on earth your fa-
ther; for One is your Father, He who is in
heaven. 10And do not be called teachers;
for One is your Teacher, the Christ. 11But
he who is greatest among you shall
be your servant. 12And whoever exalts
himself will be humbled, and he who
humbles himself will be exalted.

13"But woe to you, scribes and Phar-
isees, hypocrites! For you shut up the
kingdom of heaven against men; for you
neither go in *yourselves,* nor do you allow
those who are entering to go in. 14Woe to
you, scribes and Pharisees, hypocrites!
For you devour widows' houses, and for
a pretense make long prayers. Therefore
you will receive greater condemnation.[a]

15"Woe to you, scribes and Pharisees,
hypocrites! For you travel land and
sea to win one proselyte, and when he
is won, you make him twice as much a
son of hell as yourselves.

16"Woe to you, blind guides, who say,
'Whoever swears by the temple, it is
nothing; but whoever swears by the
gold of the temple, he is obliged *to per-*
form it.' 17Fools and blind! For which
is greater, the gold or the temple that
sanctifies[a] the gold? 18And, 'Whoever
swears by the altar, it is nothing; but
whoever swears by the gift that is on it,
he is obliged *to perform it.'* 19Fools and
blind! For which is greater, the gift or the
altar that sanctifies the gift? 20Therefore
he who swears by the altar, swears by it
and by all things on it. 21He who swears
by the temple, swears by it and by Him
who dwells[a] in it. 22And he who swears
by heaven, swears by the throne of God
and by Him who sits on it.

23"Woe to you, scribes and Pharisees,
hypocrites! For you pay tithe of mint
and anise and cummin, and have ne-
glected the weightier *matters* of the law:
justice and mercy and faith. These you
ought to have done, without leaving
the others undone. 24Blind guides, who
strain out a gnat and swallow a camel!

25"Woe to you, scribes and Pharisees,
hypocrites! For you cleanse the outside
of the cup and dish, but inside they are
full of extortion and self-indulgence.[a]
26Blind Pharisee, first cleanse the inside
of the cup and dish, that the outside of
them may be clean also.

27"Woe to you, scribes and Pharisees,
hypocrites! For you are like white-
washed tombs which indeed appear
beautiful outwardly, but inside are full
of dead *men's* bones and all unclean-
ness. 28Even so you also outwardly ap-
pear righteous to men, but inside you
are full of hypocrisy and lawlessness.

29"Woe to you, scribes and Phari-
sees, hypocrites! Because you build
the tombs of the prophets and adorn
the monuments of the righteous, 30and
say, 'If we had lived in the days of our
fathers, we would not have been par-
takers with them in the blood of the
prophets.'

31"Therefore you are witnesses against
yourselves that you are sons of those
who murdered the prophets. 32Fill up,

22:44 [a] Psalm 110:1 **23:3** [a] NU-Text omits *to observe.* **23:8** [a] NU-Text omits *the Christ.*
23:14 [a] NU-Text omits this verse. **23:17** [a] NU-Text reads *sanctified.* **23:21** [a] M-Text reads *dwelt.*
23:25 [a] M-Text reads *unrighteousness.*

then, the measure of your fathers' *guilt.*
33Serpents, brood of vipers! How can
you escape the condemnation of hell?
34Therefore, indeed, I send you proph-
ets, wise men, and scribes: *some* of them
you will kill and crucify, and *some* of
them you will scourge in your syna-
gogues and persecute from city to city,
35that on you may come all the righ-
teous blood shed on the earth, from the
blood of righteous Abel to the blood of
Zechariah, son of Berechiah, whom you
murdered between the temple and the
altar. 36Assuredly, I say to you, all these
things will come upon this generation.

Jesus Laments over Jerusalem

37"O Jerusalem, Jerusalem, the one
who kills the prophets and stones those
who are sent to her! How often I wanted
to gather your children together, as a
hen gathers her chicks under *her* wings,
but you were not willing! 38See! Your
house is left to you desolate; 39for I
say to you, you shall see Me no more
till you say, 'Blessed *is* He who comes
in the name of the LORD!' "[a]

Jesus Predicts the Destruction of the Temple

24 Then Jesus went out and de-
parted from the temple, and
His disciples came up to show Him
the buildings of the temple. 2And Jesus
said to them, "Do you not see all these
things? Assuredly, I say to you, not *one*
stone shall be left here upon another,
that shall not be thrown down."

The Signs of the Times and the End of the Age

3Now as He sat on the Mount of Olives,
the disciples came to Him privately,
saying, "Tell us, when will these things
be? And what *will be* the sign of Your
coming, and of the end of the age?"
4And Jesus answered and said to
them: "Take heed that no one deceives
you. 5For many will come in My name,
saying, 'I am the Christ,' and will de-
ceive many. 6And you will hear of wars
and rumors of wars. See that you are
not troubled; for all[a] *these things* must
come to pass, but the end is not yet.
7For nation will rise against nation, and
kingdom against kingdom. And there
will be famines, pestilences,[a] and earth-
quakes in various places. 8All these *are*
the beginning of sorrows.
9"Then they will deliver you up to trib-
ulation and kill you, and you will be
hated by all nations for My name's sake.
10And then many will be offended, will
betray one another, and will hate one
another. 11Then many false prophets
will rise up and deceive many. 12And
because lawlessness will abound, the
love of many will grow cold. 13But he
who endures to the end shall be saved.
14And this gospel of the kingdom will
be preached in all the world as a wit-
ness to all the nations, and then the
end will come.

The Great Tribulation

15"Therefore when you see the 'abom-
ination of desolation,'[a] spoken of by
Daniel the prophet, standing in the holy
place" (whoever reads, let him under-
stand), 16"then let those who are in
Judea flee to the mountains. 17Let him
who is on the housetop not go down to
take anything out of his house. 18And let
him who is in the field not go back to get
his clothes. 19But woe to those who are
pregnant and to those who are nursing
babies in those days! 20And pray that
your flight may not be in winter or on
the Sabbath. 21For then there will be
great tribulation, such as has not been
since the beginning of the world until
this time, no, nor ever shall be. 22And
unless those days were shortened, no
flesh would be saved; but for the elect's
sake those days will be shortened.
23"Then if anyone says to you, 'Look,
here *is* the Christ!' or 'There!' do not
believe *it.* 24For false christs and false
prophets will rise and show great signs
and wonders to deceive, if possible, even
the elect. 25See, I have told you before-
hand.
26"Therefore if they say to you, 'Look,
He is in the desert!' do not go out; *or*
'Look, *He is* in the inner rooms!' do not
believe *it.* 27For as the lightning comes

23:39 [a] Psalm 118:26 **24:6** [a] NU-Text omits *all.* **24:7** [a] NU-Text omits *pestilences.* **24:15** [a] Daniel 11:31; 12:11

from the east and flashes to the west, so
also will the coming of the Son of Man
be. 28For wherever the carcass is, there
the eagles will be gathered together.

The Coming of the Son of Man

29"Immediately after the tribulation
of those days the sun will be darkened,
and the moon will not give its light;
the stars will fall from heaven, and the
powers of the heavens will be shak-
en. 30Then the sign of the Son of Man
will appear in heaven, and then all the
tribes of the earth will mourn, and they
will see the Son of Man coming on the
clouds of heaven with power and great
glory. 31And He will send His angels
with a great sound of a trumpet, and
they will gather together His elect from
the four winds, from one end of heaven
to the other.

The Parable of the Fig Tree

32"Now learn this parable from the
fig tree: When its branch has already
become tender and puts forth leaves,
you know that summer *is* near. 33So
you also, when you see all these things,
know that it[a] is near—at the doors!
34Assuredly, I say to you, this genera-
tion will by no means pass away till all
these things take place. 35Heaven and
earth will pass away, but My words will
by no means pass away.

No One Knows the Day or Hour

36"But of that day and hour no one
knows, not even the angels of heaven,[a]
but My Father only. 37But as the days
of Noah *were,* so also will the coming of
the Son of Man be. 38For as in the days
before the flood, they were eating and
drinking, marrying and giving in mar-
riage, until the day that Noah entered
the ark, 39and did not know until the
flood came and took them all away,
so also will the coming of the Son of
Man be. 40Then two *men* will be in the
field: one will be taken and the other
left. 41Two *women will be* grinding at
the mill: one will be taken and the other
left. 42Watch therefore, for you do not
know what hour[a] your Lord is coming.
43But know this, that if the master of the
house had known what hour the thief
would come, he would have watched
and not allowed his house to be broken
into. 44Therefore you also be ready, for
the Son of Man is coming at an hour
you do not expect.

The Faithful Servant and the Evil Servant

45"Who then is a faithful and wise ser-
vant, whom his master made ruler over
his household, to give them food in due
season? 46Blessed *is* that servant whom
his master, when he comes, will find so
doing. 47Assuredly, I say to you that he
will make him ruler over all his goods.
48But if that evil servant says in his heart,
'My master is delaying his coming,'[a]
49and begins to beat *his* fellow servants,
and to eat and drink with the drunkards,
50the master of that servant will come on
a day when he is not looking for *him* and
at an hour that he is not aware of, 51and
will cut him in two and appoint *him* his
portion with the hypocrites. There shall
be weeping and gnashing of teeth.

The Parable of the Wise and Foolish Virgins

25 "Then the kingdom of heaven
shall be likened to ten virgins
who took their lamps and went out to
meet the bridegroom. 2Now five of them
were wise, and five *were* foolish. 3Those
who *were* foolish took their lamps and
took no oil with them, 4but the wise took
oil in their vessels with their lamps. 5But
while the bridegroom was delayed, they
all slumbered and slept.

6"And at midnight a cry was *heard:*
'Behold, the bridegroom is coming;[a] go
out to meet him!' 7Then all those virgins
arose and trimmed their lamps. 8And
the foolish said to the wise, 'Give us *some*
of your oil, for our lamps are going out.'
9But the wise answered, saying, '*No,* lest
there should not be enough for us and
you; but go rather to those who sell, and
buy for yourselves.' 10And while they
went to buy, the bridegroom came, and
those who were ready went in with him
to the wedding; and the door was shut.

24:33 [a] Or *He* **24:36** [a] NU-Text adds *nor the Son.* **24:42** [a] NU-Text reads *day.* **24:48** [a] NU-Text omits *his coming.* **25:6** [a] NU-Text omits *is coming.*

11“Afterward the other virgins came
also, saying, ‘Lord, Lord, open to us!’
12But he answered and said, ‘Assuredly,
I say to you, I do not know you.’
13“Watch therefore, for you know neither the day nor the hour[a] in which the
Son of Man is coming.

The Parable of the Talents

14“For *the kingdom of heaven is* like a
man traveling to a far country, *who*
called his own servants and delivered
his goods to them. 15And to one he gave
five talents, to another two, and to another one, to each according to his own
ability; and immediately he went on a
journey. 16Then he who had received
the five talents went and traded with
them, and made another five talents.
17And likewise he who *had received* two
gained two more also. 18But he who
had received one went and dug in the
ground, and hid his lord’s money. 19After a long time the lord of those servants
came and settled accounts with them.
20“So he who had received five talents
came and brought five other talents,
saying, ‘Lord, you delivered to me five
talents; look, I have gained five more
talents besides them.’ 21His lord said
to him, ‘Well *done,* good and faithful
servant; you were faithful over a few
things, I will make you ruler over many
things. Enter into the joy of your lord.’
22He also who had received two talents
came and said, ‘Lord, you delivered
to me two talents; look, I have gained
two more talents besides them.’ 23His
lord said to him, ‘Well *done,* good and
faithful servant; you have been faithful
over a few things, I will make you ruler
over many things. Enter into the joy of
your lord.’
24“Then he who had received the one
talent came and said, ‘Lord, I knew you
to be a hard man, reaping where you
have not sown, and gathering where
you have not scattered seed. 25And I
was afraid, and went and hid your talent in the ground. Look, *there* you have
what is yours.’
26“But his lord answered and said to
him, ‘You wicked and lazy servant, you
knew that I reap where I have not sown,
and gather where I have not scattered
seed. 27So you ought to have deposited
my money with the bankers, and at my
coming I would have received back my
own with interest. 28So take the talent
from him, and give *it* to him who has
ten talents.
29‘For to everyone who has, more will
be given, and he will have abundance;
but from him who does not have, even
what he has will be taken away. 30And
cast the unprofitable servant into the
outer darkness. There will be weeping
and gnashing of teeth.’

The Son of Man Will Judge the Nations

31“When the Son of Man comes in His
glory, and all the holy[a] angels with
Him, then He will sit on the throne of
His glory. 32All the nations will be gathered before Him, and He will separate
them one from another, as a shepherd
divides *his* sheep from the goats. 33And
He will set the sheep on His right hand,
but the goats on the left. 34Then the
King will say to those on His right hand,
‘Come, you blessed of My Father, inherit the kingdom prepared for you
from the foundation of the world: 35for
I was hungry and you gave Me food; I
was thirsty and you gave Me drink;
I was a stranger and you took Me in;
36I *was* naked and you clothed Me; I
was sick and you visited Me; I was in
prison and you came to Me.’
37“Then the righteous will answer Him,
saying, ‘Lord, when did we see You hungry and feed *You,* or thirsty and give *You*
drink? 38When did we see You a stranger
and take *You* in, or naked and clothe
You? 39Or when did we see You sick,
or in prison, and come to You?’ 40And
the King will answer and say to them,
‘Assuredly, I say to you, inasmuch as
you did *it* to one of the least of these My
brethren, you did *it* to Me.’
41“Then He will also say to those on the
left hand, ‘Depart from Me, you cursed,
into the everlasting fire prepared for the
devil and his angels: 42for I was hungry
and you gave Me no food; I was thirsty

25:13 [a] NU-Text omits the rest of this verse. **25:31** [a] NU-Text omits *holy.*

and you gave Me no drink; 43 I was a
stranger and you did not take Me in,
naked and you did not clothe Me, sick
and in prison and you did not visit Me.'
44 "Then they also will answer Him,[a]
saying, 'Lord, when did we see You hun-
gry or thirsty or a stranger or naked or
sick or in prison, and did not minister
to You?' 45 Then He will answer them,
saying, 'Assuredly, I say to you, inas-
much as you did not do *it* to one of the
least of these, you did not do *it* to Me.'
46 And these will go away into everlast-
ing punishment, but the righteous into
eternal life."

The Plot to Kill Jesus

26 Now it came to pass, when Jesus
had finished all these sayings,
that He said to His disciples, 2 "You know
that after two days is the Passover, and
the Son of Man will be delivered up to
be crucified."
3 Then the chief priests, the scribes,[a]
and the elders of the people assembled
at the palace of the high priest, who was
called Caiaphas, 4 and plotted to take
Jesus by trickery and kill *Him.* 5 But they
said, "Not during the feast, lest there be
an uproar among the people."

The Anointing at Bethany

6 And when Jesus was in Bethany at
the house of Simon the leper, 7 a wom-
an came to Him having an alabaster
flask of very costly fragrant oil, and
she poured *it* on His head as He sat *at
the table.* 8 But when His disciples saw
it, they were indignant, saying, "Why
this waste? 9 For this fragrant oil might
have been sold for much and given to
the poor."
10 But when Jesus was aware of *it,* He
said to them, "Why do you trouble the
woman? For she has done a good work
for Me. 11 For you have the poor with
you always, but Me you do not have
always. 12 For in pouring this fragrant
oil on My body, she did *it* for My burial.
13 Assuredly, I say to you, wherever this
gospel is preached in the whole world,
what this woman has done will also be
told as a memorial to her."

Judas Agrees to Betray Jesus

14 Then one of the twelve, called Judas
Iscariot, went to the chief priests 15 and
said, "What are you willing to give me if
I deliver Him to you?" And they counted
out to him thirty pieces of silver. 16 So
from that time he sought opportunity
to betray Him.

Jesus Celebrates Passover with His Disciples

17 Now on the first *day of the Feast* of the
Unleavened Bread the disciples came
to Jesus, saying to Him, "Where do You
want us to prepare for You to eat the
Passover?"
18 And He said, "Go into the city to
a certain man, and say to him, 'The
Teacher says, "My time is at hand; I will
keep the Passover at your house with
My disciples." ' "
19 So the disciples did as Jesus had di-
rected them; and they prepared the
Passover.
20 When evening had come, He sat
down with the twelve. 21 Now as they
were eating, He said, "Assuredly, I say
to you, one of you will betray Me."
22 And they were exceedingly sorrow-
ful, and each of them began to say to
Him, "Lord, is it I?"
23 He answered and said, "He who
dipped *his* hand with Me in the dish
will betray Me. 24 The Son of Man indeed
goes just as it is written of Him, but woe
to that man by whom the Son of Man
is betrayed! It would have been good
for that man if he had not been born."
25 Then Judas, who was betraying Him,
answered and said, "Rabbi, is it I?"
He said to him, "You have said it."

Jesus Institutes the Lord's Supper

26 And as they were eating, Jesus took
bread, blessed[a] and broke *it,* and gave
it to the disciples and said, "Take, eat;
this is My body."
27 Then He took the cup, and gave
thanks, and gave *it* to them, saying,
"Drink from it, all of you. 28 For this is
My blood of the new[a] covenant, which
is shed for many for the remission of
sins. 29 But I say to you, I will not drink

25:44 [a] NU-Text and M-Text omit *Him.* **26:3** [a] NU-Text omits *the scribes.* **26:26** [a] M-Text reads *gave thanks for.* **26:28** [a] NU-Text omits *new.*

of this fruit of the vine from now on
until that day when I drink it new with
you in My Father's kingdom."
30And when they had sung a hymn,
they went out to the Mount of Olives.

Jesus Predicts Peter's Denial

31Then Jesus said to them, "All of you
will be made to stumble because of Me
this night, for it is written:

'I will strike the Shepherd,
And the sheep of the flock will be
scattered.'[a]

32But after I have been raised, I will go
before you to Galilee."
33Peter answered and said to Him,
"Even if all are made to stumble be-
cause of You, I will never be made to
stumble."
34Jesus said to him, "Assuredly, I say
to you that this night, before the rooster
crows, you will deny Me three times."
35Peter said to Him, "Even if I have to
die with You, I will not deny You!"
And so said all the disciples.

The Prayer in the Garden

36Then Jesus came with them to a
place called Gethsemane, and said to
the disciples, "Sit here while I go and
pray over there." 37And He took with
Him Peter and the two sons of Zebedee,
and He began to be sorrowful and deep-
ly distressed. 38Then He said to them,
"My soul is exceedingly sorrowful, even
to death. Stay here and watch with Me."
39He went a little farther and fell on
His face, and prayed, saying, "O My
Father, if it is possible, let this cup pass
from Me; nevertheless, not as I will, but
as You *will*."
40Then He came to the disciples and
found them sleeping, and said to Peter,
"What! Could you not watch with Me
one hour? 41Watch and pray, lest you
enter into temptation. The spirit indeed
is willing, but the flesh *is* weak."
42Again, a second time, He went away
and prayed, saying, "O My Father, if this
cup cannot pass away from Me unless[a]
I drink it, Your will be done." 43And He
came and found them asleep again, for
their eyes were heavy.
44So He left them, went away again,
and prayed the third time, saying the
same words. 45Then He came to His
disciples and said to them, "Are *you*
still sleeping and resting? Behold, the
hour is at hand, and the Son of Man is
being betrayed into the hands of sin-
ners. 46Rise, let us be going. See, My
betrayer is at hand."

Betrayal and Arrest in Gethsemane

47And while He was still speaking, be-
hold, Judas, one of the twelve, with a
great multitude with swords and clubs,
came from the chief priests and elders
of the people.
48Now His betrayer had given them
a sign, saying, "Whomever I kiss, He is
the One; seize Him." 49Immediately he
went up to Jesus and said, "Greetings,
Rabbi!" and kissed Him.
50But Jesus said to him, "Friend, why
have you come?"
Then they came and laid hands on
Jesus and took Him. 51And sudden-
ly, one of those *who were* with Jesus
stretched out *his* hand and drew his
sword, struck the servant of the high
priest, and cut off his ear.
52But Jesus said to him, "Put your
sword in its place, for all who take the
sword will perish[a] by the sword. 53Or
do you think that I cannot now pray
to My Father, and He will provide Me
with more than twelve legions of an-
gels? 54How then could the Scriptures
be fulfilled, that it must happen thus?"
55In that hour Jesus said to the multi-
tudes, "Have you come out, as against
a robber, with swords and clubs to take
Me? I sat daily with you, teaching in the
temple, and you did not seize Me. 56But
all this was done that the Scriptures of
the prophets might be fulfilled."
Then all the disciples forsook Him
and fled.

Jesus Faces the Sanhedrin

57And those who had laid hold of Jesus
led *Him* away to Caiaphas the high
priest, where the scribes and the elders

26:31 [a] Zechariah 13:7 **26:42** [a] NU-Text reads *if this may not pass away unless.* **26:52** [a] M-Text reads *die.*

were assembled. 58But Peter followed
Him at a distance to the high priest's
courtyard. And he went in and sat with
the servants to see the end.
59Now the chief priests, the elders,[a] and
all the council sought false testimony
against Jesus to put Him to death, 60but
found none. Even though many false
witnesses came forward, they found
none.[a] But at last two false witnesses[b]
came forward 61and said, "This *fellow*
said, 'I am able to destroy the temple
of God and to build it in three days.' "
62And the high priest arose and said to
Him, "Do You answer nothing? What *is*
it these men testify against You?" 63But
Jesus kept silent. And the high priest
answered and said to Him, "I put You
under oath by the living God: Tell us
if You are the Christ, the Son of God!"
64Jesus said to him, "*It is as* you said.
Nevertheless, I say to you, hereafter you
will see the Son of Man sitting at the
right hand of the Power, and coming
on the clouds of heaven."
65Then the high priest tore his clothes,
saying, "He has spoken blasphemy!
What further need do we have of wit-
nesses? Look, now you have heard His
blasphemy! 66What do you think?"
They answered and said, "He is de-
serving of death."
67Then they spat in His face and beat
Him; and others struck *Him* with the
palms of their hands, 68saying, "Proph-
esy to us, Christ! Who is the one who
struck You?"

Peter Denies Jesus, and Weeps Bitterly

69Now Peter sat outside in the court-
yard. And a servant girl came to him,
saying, "You also were with Jesus of
Galilee."
70But he denied it before *them* all,
saying, "I do not know what you are
saying."
71And when he had gone out to the
gateway, another *girl* saw him and said
to those *who were* there, "This *fellow* also
was with Jesus of Nazareth."
72But again he denied with an oath,
"I do not know the Man!"
73And a little later those who stood by
came up and said to Peter, "Surely you
also are *one* of them, for your speech
betrays you."
74Then he began to curse and swear,
saying, "I do not know the Man!"
Immediately a rooster crowed. 75And
Peter remembered the word of Jesus
who had said to him, "Before the rooster
crows, you will deny Me three times." So
he went out and wept bitterly.

Jesus Handed Over to Pontius Pilate

27 When morning came, all the
chief priests and elders of the
people plotted against Jesus to put Him
to death. 2And when they had bound
Him, they led Him away and delivered
Him to Pontius[a] Pilate the governor.

Judas Hangs Himself

3Then Judas, His betrayer, seeing that
He had been condemned, was remorse-
ful and brought back the thirty pieces
of silver to the chief priests and elders,
4saying, "I have sinned by betraying
innocent blood."
And they said, "What *is that* to us?
You see *to it!*"
5Then he threw down the pieces of
silver in the temple and departed, and
went and hanged himself.
6But the chief priests took the silver
pieces and said, "It is not lawful to put
them into the treasury, because they
are the price of blood." 7And they con-
sulted together and bought with them
the potter's field, to bury strangers in.
8Therefore that field has been called
the Field of Blood to this day.
9Then was fulfilled what was spoken
by Jeremiah the prophet, saying, "And
they took the thirty pieces of silver, the
value of Him who was priced, whom
they of the children of Israel priced,
10and gave them for the potter's field,
as the LORD directed me."[a]

Jesus Faces Pilate

11Now Jesus stood before the governor.
And the governor asked Him, saying,
"Are You the King of the Jews?"

26:59 [a] NU-Text omits *the elders.* **26:60** [a] NU-Text puts a comma after *but found none,* does not capitalize *Even,* and omits *they found none.* [b] NU-Text omits *false witnesses.* **27:2** [a] NU-Text omits *Pontius.* **27:10** [a] Jeremiah 32:6–9

Jesus said to him, "*It is as* you say."
12And while He was being accused by
the chief priests and elders, He an-
swered nothing.
13Then Pilate said to Him, "Do You
not hear how many things they testify
against You?" 14But He answered him
not one word, so that the governor mar-
veled greatly.

Taking the Place of Barabbas

15Now at the feast the governor was
accustomed to releasing to the multi-
tude one prisoner whom they wished.
16And at that time they had a notorious
prisoner called Barabbas.[a] 17Therefore,
when they had gathered together, Pilate
said to them, "Whom do you want me to
release to you? Barabbas, or Jesus who
is called Christ?" 18For he knew that they
had handed Him over because of envy.
19While he was sitting on the judgment
seat, his wife sent to him, saying, "Have
nothing to do with that just Man, for I
have suffered many things today in a
dream because of Him."
20But the chief priests and elders per-
suaded the multitudes that they should
ask for Barabbas and destroy Jesus.
21The governor answered and said to
them, "Which of the two do you want
me to release to you?"
They said, "Barabbas!"
22Pilate said to them, "What then shall
I do with Jesus who is called Christ?"
They all said to him, "Let Him be cru-
cified!"
23Then the governor said, "Why, what
evil has He done?"
But they cried out all the more, saying,
"Let Him be crucified!"
24When Pilate saw that he could not
prevail at all, but rather *that* a tumult
was rising, he took water and washed
his hands before the multitude, saying,
"I am innocent of the blood of this just
Person.[a] You see *to it.*"
25And all the people answered and
said, "His blood *be* on us and on our
children."
26Then he released Barabbas to them;
and when he had scourged Jesus, he
delivered *Him* to be crucified.

The Soldiers Mock Jesus

27Then the soldiers of the governor
took Jesus into the Praetorium and
gathered the whole garrison around
Him. 28And they stripped Him and put
a scarlet robe on Him. 29When they had
twisted a crown of thorns, they put *it* on
His head, and a reed in His right hand.
And they bowed the knee before Him
and mocked Him, saying, "Hail, King
of the Jews!" 30Then they spat on Him,
and took the reed and struck Him on
the head. 31And when they had mocked
Him, they took the robe off Him, put His
own clothes on Him, and led Him away
to be crucified.

The King on a Cross

32Now as they came out, they found
a man of Cyrene, Simon by name. Him
they compelled to bear His cross. 33And
when they had come to a place called
Golgotha, that is to say, Place of a Skull,
34they gave Him sour[a] wine mingled
with gall to drink. But when He had
tasted *it,* He would not drink.
35Then they crucified Him, and divid-
ed His garments, casting lots,[a] that it
might be fulfilled which was spoken by
the prophet:

> "They divided My garments among
> them,
> And for My clothing they cast
> lots."[b]

36Sitting down, they kept watch over
Him there. 37And they put up over His
head the accusation written against
Him:

THIS IS JESUS
THE KING OF THE JEWS.

38Then two robbers were crucified with
Him, one on the right and another on
the left.
39And those who passed by blas-
phemed Him, wagging their heads
40and saying, "You who destroy the
temple and build *it* in three days, save
Yourself! If You are the Son of God, come
down from the cross."

27:16 [a] NU-Text reads *Jesus Barabbas.* **27:24** [a] NU-Text omits *just.* **27:34** [a] NU-Text omits *sour.*
27:35 [a] NU-Text and M-Text omit the rest of this verse. [b] Psalm 22:18

41Likewise the chief priests also, mocking with the scribes and elders,[a] said, 42"He saved others; Himself He cannot save. If He is the King of Israel,[a] let Him now come down from the cross, and we will believe Him.[b] 43He trusted in God; let Him deliver Him now if He will have Him; for He said, 'I am the Son of God.' "

44Even the robbers who were crucified with Him reviled Him with the same thing.

Jesus Dies on the Cross

45Now from the sixth hour until the ninth hour there was darkness over all the land. 46And about the ninth hour Jesus cried out with a loud voice, saying, "Eli, Eli, lama sabachthani?" that is, "My God, My God, why have You forsaken Me?"[a]

47Some of those who stood there, when they heard *that,* said, "This Man is calling for Elijah!" 48Immediately one of them ran and took a sponge, filled *it* with sour wine and put *it* on a reed, and offered it to Him to drink.

49The rest said, "Let Him alone; let us see if Elijah will come to save Him."

50And Jesus cried out again with a loud voice, and yielded up His spirit.

51Then, behold, the veil of the temple was torn in two from top to bottom; and the earth quaked, and the rocks were split, 52and the graves were opened; and many bodies of the saints who had fallen asleep were raised; 53and coming out of the graves after His resurrection, they went into the holy city and appeared to many.

54So when the centurion and those with him, who were guarding Jesus, saw the earthquake and the things that had happened, they feared greatly, saying, "Truly this was the Son of God!"

55And many women who followed Jesus from Galilee, ministering to Him, were there looking on from afar, 56among whom were Mary Magdalene, Mary the mother of James and Joses,[a] and the mother of Zebedee's sons.

Jesus Buried in Joseph's Tomb

57Now when evening had come, there came a rich man from Arimathea, named Joseph, who himself had also become a disciple of Jesus. 58This man went to Pilate and asked for the body of Jesus. Then Pilate commanded the body to be given to him. 59When Joseph had taken the body, he wrapped it in a clean linen cloth, 60and laid it in his new tomb which he had hewn out of the rock; and he rolled a large stone against the door of the tomb, and departed. 61And Mary Magdalene was there, and the other Mary, sitting opposite the tomb.

Pilate Sets a Guard

62On the next day, which followed the Day of Preparation, the chief priests and Pharisees gathered together to Pilate, 63saying, "Sir, we remember, while He was still alive, how that deceiver said, 'After three days I will rise.' 64Therefore command that the tomb be made secure until the third day, lest His disciples come by night[a] and steal Him *away,* and say to the people, 'He has risen from the dead.' So the last deception will be worse than the first."

65Pilate said to them, "You have a guard; go your way, make *it* as secure as you know how." 66So they went and made the tomb secure, sealing the stone and setting the guard.

He Is Risen

28 Now after the Sabbath, as the first *day* of the week began to dawn, Mary Magdalene and the other Mary came to see the tomb. 2And behold, there was a great earthquake; for an angel of the Lord descended from heaven, and came and rolled back the stone from the door,[a] and sat on it. 3His countenance was like lightning, and his clothing as white as snow. 4And the guards shook for fear of him, and became like dead *men.*

5But the angel answered and said to the women, "Do not be afraid, for I know that you seek Jesus who was crucified. 6He is not here; for He is risen, as He

27:41 a M-Text reads *with the scribes, the Pharisees, and the elders.* **27:42** a NU-Text reads *He is the King of Israel!* b NU-Text and M-Text read *we will believe in Him.* **27:46** a Psalm 22:1 **27:56** a NU-Text reads *Joseph.* **27:64** a NU-Text omits *by night.* **28:2** a NU-Text omits *from the door.*

GOD SIN JESUS SALVATION LOVE

said. Come, see the place where the
Lord lay. 7And go quickly and tell His
disciples that He is risen from the dead,
and indeed He is going before you into
Galilee; there you will see Him. Behold,
I have told you."
8So they went out quickly from the
tomb with fear and great joy, and ran
to bring His disciples word.

The Women Worship the Risen Lord

9And as they went to tell His disci-
ples,[a] behold, Jesus met them, saying,
"Rejoice!" So they came and held Him
by the feet and worshiped Him. 10Then
Jesus said to them, "Do not be afraid.
Go *and* tell My brethren to go to Galilee,
and there they will see Me."

The Soldiers Are Bribed

11Now while they were going, behold,
some of the guard came into the city
and reported to the chief priests all the
things that had happened. 12When they
had assembled with the elders and con-
sulted together, they gave a large sum
of money to the soldiers, 13saying, "Tell
them, 'His disciples came at night and
stole Him *away* while we slept.' 14And
if this comes to the governor's ears, we
will appease him and make you secure."
15So they took the money and did as
they were instructed; and this saying
is commonly reported among the Jews
until this day.

The Great Commission

16Then the eleven disciples went away
into Galilee, to the mountain which
Jesus had appointed for them. 17When
they saw Him, they worshiped Him; but
some doubted.
18And Jesus came and spoke to them,
saying, "All authority has been giv-
en to Me in heaven and on earth. 19Go
therefore[a] and make disciples of all the
nations, baptizing them in the name
of the Father and of the Son and of the
Holy Spirit, 20teaching them to observe
all things that I have commanded you;
and lo, I am with you always, *even* to
the end of the age." Amen.[a]

28:9 [a] NU-Text omits the first clause of this verse. **28:19** [a] M-Text omits *therefore.*
28:20 [a] NU-Text omits *Amen.*

THE GOSPEL ACCORDING TO

MARK

Mark is the shortest of the Gospels, written primarily to a Roman audience. Unlike Matthew and Luke, Mark does not provide any details of the birth and childhood of Jesus. Instead, he begins with Jesus' ministry itself. Mark's purpose is to show Jesus as the Suffering Servant sent by God. As such, Mark shows Jesus in constant action. One of the most common terms in the book is "immediately." Mark's quickly paced Gospel is often confrontational, as he tells the story of Jesus as clearly as possible. He wants the reader to respond, and almost seems to be saying, "Here is the truth, believe it, and get on with following Jesus."

- **GENRE:** Gospel
- **AUTHOR:** Mark
- **TIME:** c. AD 29–33 (written c. AD 50–60)
- **PURPOSE:** To tell the Gentiles the story of Jesus and present Him as the Servant of God.

John the Baptist Prepares the Way

1 The beginning of the gospel of Jesus
Christ, the Son of God. 2As it is writ-
ten in the Prophets:[a]

"Behold, I send My messenger
before Your face,
Who will prepare Your way before
You."[b]
3 "The voice of one crying in the
wilderness:
'Prepare the way of the LORD;
Make His paths straight.' "[a]

4John came baptizing in the wilder-
ness and preaching a baptism of repen-
tance for the remission of sins. 5Then
all the land of Judea, and those from
Jerusalem, went out to him and were
all baptized by him in the Jordan River,
confessing their sins.
6Now John was clothed with camel's
hair and with a leather belt around his
waist, and he ate locusts and wild hon-
ey. 7And he preached, saying, "There
comes One after me who is mightier
than I, whose sandal strap I am not
worthy to stoop down and loose. 8I in-
deed baptized you with water, but He
will baptize you with the Holy Spirit."

John Baptizes Jesus

9It came to pass in those days *that*
Jesus came from Nazareth of Galilee,
and was baptized by John in the Jordan.
10And immediately, coming up from[a]
the water, He saw the heavens parting
and the Spirit descending upon Him
like a dove. 11Then a voice came from
heaven, "You are My beloved Son, in
whom I am well pleased."

Satan Tempts Jesus

12Immediately the Spirit drove Him
into the wilderness. 13And He was there
in the wilderness forty days, tempted
by Satan, and was with the wild beasts;
and the angels ministered to Him.

Jesus Begins His Galilean Ministry

14Now after John was put in prison,
Jesus came to Galilee, preaching the
gospel of the kingdom[a] of God, 15and
saying, "The time is fulfilled, and the
kingdom of God is at hand. Repent, and
believe in the gospel."

Four Fishermen Called as Disciples

16And as He walked by the Sea of
Galilee, He saw Simon and Andrew his
brother casting a net into the sea; for

1:2 [a] NU-Text reads *Isaiah the prophet.* [b] Malachi 3:1 **1:3** [a] Isaiah 40:3 **1:10** [a] NU-Text reads *out of.*
1:14 [a] NU-Text omits *of the kingdom.*

GOD | SIN | JESUS | SALVATION | LOVE

they were fishermen. 17Then Jesus said
to them, "Follow Me, and I will make you
become fishers of men." 18They imme-
diately left their nets and followed Him.
19When He had gone a little farther
from there, He saw James the *son* of Zeb-
edee, and John his brother, who also *were*
in the boat mending their nets. 20And
immediately He called them, and they
left their father Zebedee in the boat with
the hired servants, and went after Him.

Jesus Casts Out an Unclean Spirit

21Then they went into Capernaum, and
immediately on the Sabbath He entered
the synagogue and taught. 22And they
were astonished at His teaching, for He
taught them as one having authority,
and not as the scribes.
23Now there was a man in their syn-
agogue with an unclean spirit. And he
cried out, 24saying, "Let *us* alone! What
have we to do with You, Jesus of Naza-
reth? Did You come to destroy us? I know
who You are—the Holy One of God!"
25But Jesus rebuked him, saying, "Be
quiet, and come out of him!" 26And
when the unclean spirit had convulsed
him and cried out with a loud voice, he
came out of him. 27Then they were all
amazed, so that they questioned among
themselves, saying, "What is this? What
new doctrine *is* this? For with authority[a]
He commands even the unclean spirits,
and they obey Him." 28And immediate-
ly His fame spread throughout all the
region around Galilee.

Peter's Mother-in-Law Healed

29Now as soon as they had come out of
the synagogue, they entered the house
of Simon and Andrew, with James and
John. 30But Simon's wife's mother lay
sick with a fever, and they told Him
about her at once. 31So He came and
took her by the hand and lifted her up,
and immediately the fever left her. And
she served them.

Many Healed After Sabbath Sunset

32At evening, when the sun had set,
they brought to Him all who were sick
and those who were demon-possessed.
33And the whole city was gathered to-
gether at the door. 34Then He healed
many who were sick with various dis-
eases, and cast out many demons; and
He did not allow the demons to speak,
because they knew Him.

Preaching in Galilee

35Now in the morning, having risen
a long while before daylight, He went
out and departed to a solitary place;
and there He prayed. 36And Simon and
those *who were* with Him searched for
Him. 37When they found Him, they said
to Him, "Everyone is looking for You."
38But He said to them, "Let us go into
the next towns, that I may preach there
also, because for this purpose I have
come forth."
39And He was preaching in their syn-
agogues throughout all Galilee, and
casting out demons.

Jesus Cleanses a Leper

40Now a leper came to Him, imploring
Him, kneeling down to Him and say-
ing to Him, "If You are willing, You can
make me clean."
41Then Jesus, moved with compassion,
stretched out *His* hand and touched
him, and said to him, "I am willing; be
cleansed." 42As soon as He had spoken,
immediately the leprosy left him, and he
was cleansed. 43And He strictly warned
him and sent him away at once, 44and
said to him, "See that you say noth-
ing to anyone; but go your way, show
yourself to the priest, and offer for your
cleansing those things which Moses
commanded, as a testimony to them."
45However, he went out and began to
proclaim *it* freely, and to spread the
matter, so that Jesus could no longer
openly enter the city, but was outside
in deserted places; and they came to
Him from every direction.

Jesus Forgives and Heals a Paralytic

2 And again He entered Capernaum
after *some* days, and it was heard
that He was in the house. 2Immediate-
ly[a] many gathered together, so that
there was no longer room to receive

1:27 [a] NU-Text reads *What is this? A new doctrine with authority.* 2:2 [a] NU-Text omits *Immediately.*

them, not even near the door. And He
preached the word to them. 3Then they
came to Him, bringing a paralytic who
was carried by four *men.* 4And when
they could not come near Him because
of the crowd, they uncovered the roof
where He was. So when they had broken
through, they let down the bed on which
the paralytic was lying.
5When Jesus saw their faith, He said
to the paralytic, "Son, your sins are
forgiven you."
6And some of the scribes were sitting
there and reasoning in their hearts,
7"Why does this *Man* speak blasphemies
like this? Who can forgive sins but God
alone?"
8But immediately, when Jesus per-
ceived in His spirit that they reasoned
thus within themselves, He said to them,
"Why do you reason about these things
in your hearts? 9Which is easier, to say
to the paralytic, '*Your* sins are forgiven
you,' or to say, 'Arise, take up your bed
and walk'? 10But that you may know
that the Son of Man has power on earth
to forgive sins"—He said to the paralyt-
ic, 11"I say to you, arise, take up your
bed, and go to your house." 12Imme-
diately he arose, took up the bed, and
went out in the presence of them all,
so that all were amazed and glorified
God, saying, "We never saw *anything*
like this!"

Matthew the Tax Collector

13Then He went out again by the sea;
and all the multitude came to Him, and
He taught them. 14As He passed by, He
saw Levi the *son* of Alphaeus sitting at
the tax office. And He said to him, "Fol-
low Me." So he arose and followed Him.
15Now it happened, as He was dining
in *Levi's* house, that many tax collec-
tors and sinners also sat together with
Jesus and His disciples; for there were
many, and they followed Him. 16And
when the scribes and[a] Pharisees saw
Him eating with the tax collectors and
sinners, they said to His disciples, "How
is it that He eats and drinks with tax
collectors and sinners?"
17When Jesus heard *it,* He said to them,
"Those who are well have no need of
a physician, but those who are sick. I
did not come to call *the* righteous, but
sinners, to repentance."[a]

Jesus Is Questioned About Fasting

18The disciples of John and of the Phar-
isees were fasting. Then they came and
said to Him, "Why do the disciples of
John and of the Pharisees fast, but Your
disciples do not fast?"
19And Jesus said to them, "Can the
friends of the bridegroom fast while
the bridegroom is with them? As long
as they have the bridegroom with them
they cannot fast. 20But the days will
come when the bridegroom will be tak-
en away from them, and then they will
fast in those days. 21No one sews a piece
of unshrunk cloth on an old garment;
or else the new piece pulls away from
the old, and the tear is made worse.
22And no one puts new wine into old
wineskins; or else the new wine bursts
the wineskins, the wine is spilled, and
the wineskins are ruined. But new wine
must be put into new wineskins."

Jesus Is Lord of the Sabbath

23Now it happened that He went
through the grainfields on the Sabbath;
and as they went His disciples began to
pluck the heads of grain. 24And the Phar-
isees said to Him, "Look, why do they
do what is not lawful on the Sabbath?"
25But He said to them, "Have you nev-
er read what David did when he was in
need and hungry, he and those with
him: 26how he went into the house of
God *in the days* of Abiathar the high
priest, and ate the showbread, which is
not lawful to eat except for the priests,
and also gave some to those who were
with him?"
27And He said to them, "The Sabbath
was made for man, and not man for the
Sabbath. 28Therefore the Son of Man is
also Lord of the Sabbath."

Healing on the Sabbath

3 And He entered the synagogue
again, and a man was there who
had a withered hand. 2So they watched

2:16 [a] NU-Text reads *of the.* 2:17 [a] NU-Text omits *to repentance.*

Him closely, whether He would heal him on the Sabbath, so that they might accuse Him. 3And He said to the man who had the withered hand, "Step forward." 4Then He said to them, "Is it lawful on the Sabbath to do good or to do evil, to save life or to kill?" But they kept silent. 5And when He had looked around at them with anger, being grieved by the hardness of their hearts, He said to the man, "Stretch out your hand." And he stretched *it* out, and his hand was restored as whole as the other.[a] 6Then the Pharisees went out and immediately plotted with the Herodians against Him, how they might destroy Him.

A Great Multitude Follows Jesus

7But Jesus withdrew with His disciples to the sea. And a great multitude from Galilee followed Him, and from Judea 8and Jerusalem and Idumea and beyond the Jordan; and those from Tyre and Sidon, a great multitude, when they heard how many things He was doing, came to Him. 9So He told His disciples that a small boat should be kept ready for Him because of the multitude, lest they should crush Him. 10For He healed many, so that as many as had afflictions pressed about Him to touch Him. 11And the unclean spirits, whenever they saw Him, fell down before Him and cried out, saying, "You are the Son of God." 12But He sternly warned them that they should not make Him known.

The Twelve Apostles

13And He went up on the mountain and called to *Him* those He Himself wanted. And they came to Him. 14Then He appointed twelve,[a] that they might be with Him and that He might send them out to preach, 15and to have power to heal sicknesses and[a] to cast out demons: 16Simon,[a] to whom He gave the name Peter; 17James the *son* of Zebedee and John the brother of James, to whom He gave the name Boanerges, that is, "Sons of Thunder"; 18Andrew, Philip, Bartholomew, Matthew, Thomas, James the *son* of Alphaeus, Thaddaeus, Simon the Cananite; 19and Judas Iscariot, who also betrayed Him. And they went into a house.

A House Divided Cannot Stand

20Then the multitude came together again, so that they could not so much as eat bread. 21But when His own people heard *about this,* they went out to lay hold of Him, for they said, "He is out of His mind."

22And the scribes who came down from Jerusalem said, "He has Beelzebub," and, "By the ruler of the demons He casts out demons."

23So He called them to *Himself* and said to them in parables: "How can Satan cast out Satan? 24If a kingdom is divided against itself, that kingdom cannot stand. 25And if a house is divided against itself, that house cannot stand. 26And if Satan has risen up against himself, and is divided, he cannot stand, but has an end. 27No one can enter a strong man's house and plunder his goods, unless he first binds the strong man. And then he will plunder his house.

The Unpardonable Sin

28"Assuredly, I say to you, all sins will be forgiven the sons of men, and whatever blasphemies they may utter; 29but he who blasphemes against the Holy Spirit never has forgiveness, but is subject to eternal condemnation"— 30because they said, "He has an unclean spirit."

Jesus' Mother and Brothers Send for Him

31Then His brothers and His mother came, and standing outside they sent to Him, calling Him. 32And a multitude was sitting around Him; and they said to Him, "Look, Your mother and Your brothers[a] are outside seeking You."

33But He answered them, saying, "Who is My mother, or My brothers?" 34And He looked around in a circle at those who sat about Him, and said, "Here are My mother and My brothers! 35For whoever does the will of God is My brother and My sister and mother."

3:5 [a] NU-Text omits *as whole as the other.* 3:14 [a] NU-Text adds *whom He also named apostles.* 3:15 [a] NU-Text omits *to heal sicknesses and.* 3:16 [a] NU-Text reads *and He appointed the twelve: Simon....* 3:32 [a] NU-Text and M-Text add *and Your sisters.*

The Parable of the Sower

4 And again He began to teach by the sea. And a great multitude was gathered to Him, so that He got into a boat and sat *in it* on the sea; and the whole multitude was on the land facing the sea. 2 Then He taught them many things by parables, and said to them in His teaching:

3 "Listen! Behold, a sower went out to sow. 4 And it happened, as he sowed, *that* some *seed* fell by the wayside; and the birds of the air[a] came and devoured it. 5 Some fell on stony ground, where it did not have much earth; and immediately it sprang up because it had no depth of earth. 6 But when the sun was up it was scorched, and because it had no root it withered away. 7 And some *seed* fell among thorns; and the thorns grew up and choked it, and it yielded no crop. 8 But other *seed* fell on good ground and yielded a crop that sprang up, increased and produced: some thirtyfold, some sixty, and some a hundred."

9 And He said to them,[a] "He who has ears to hear, let him hear!"

The Purpose of Parables

10 But when He was alone, those around Him with the twelve asked Him about the parable. 11 And He said to them, "To you it has been given to know the mystery of the kingdom of God; but to those who are outside, all things come in parables, 12 so that

'Seeing they may see and not
perceive,
And hearing they may hear and
not understand;
Lest they should turn,
And *their* sins be forgiven them.' "[a]

The Parable of the Sower Explained

13 And He said to them, "Do you not understand this parable? How then will you understand all the parables? 14 The sower sows the word. 15 And these are the ones by the wayside where the word is sown. When they hear, Satan comes immediately and takes away the word that was sown in their hearts. 16 These likewise are the ones sown on stony ground who, when they hear the word, immediately receive it with gladness; 17 and they have no root in themselves, and so endure only for a time. Afterward, when tribulation or persecution arises for the word's sake, immediately they stumble. 18 Now these are the ones sown among thorns; *they are* the ones who hear the word, 19 and the cares of this world, the deceitfulness of riches, and the desires for other things entering in choke the word, and it becomes unfruitful. 20 But these are the ones sown on good ground, those who hear the word, accept *it,* and bear fruit: some thirtyfold, some sixty, and some a hundred."

Light Under a Basket

21 Also He said to them, "Is a lamp brought to be put under a basket or under a bed? Is it not to be set on a lampstand? 22 For there is nothing hidden which will not be revealed, nor has anything been kept secret but that it should come to light. 23 If anyone has ears to hear, let him hear."

24 Then He said to them, "Take heed what you hear. With the same measure you use, it will be measured to you; and to you who hear, more will be given. 25 For whoever has, to him more will be given; but whoever does not have, even what he has will be taken away from him."

The Parable of the Growing Seed

26 And He said, "The kingdom of God is as if a man should scatter seed on the ground, 27 and should sleep by night and rise by day, and the seed should sprout and grow, he himself does not know how. 28 For the earth yields crops by itself: first the blade, then the head, after that the full grain in the head. 29 But when the grain ripens, immediately he puts in the sickle, because the harvest has come."

The Parable of the Mustard Seed

30 Then He said, "To what shall we liken the kingdom of God? Or with what parable shall we picture it? 31 *It is* like a mustard seed which, when it is sown on the ground, is smaller than all the

4:4 [a] NU-Text and M-Text omit *of the air.* **4:9** [a] NU-Text and M-Text omit *to them.* **4:12** [a] Isaiah 6:9, 10

seeds on earth; 32but when it is sown, it grows up and becomes greater than all herbs, and shoots out large branches, so that the birds of the air may nest under its shade."

Jesus' Use of Parables

33And with many such parables He spoke the word to them as they were able to hear *it.* 34But without a parable He did not speak to them. And when they were alone, He explained all things to His disciples.

Wind and Wave Obey Jesus

35On the same day, when evening had come, He said to them, "Let us cross over to the other side." 36Now when they had left the multitude, they took Him along in the boat as He was. And other little boats were also with Him. 37And a great windstorm arose, and the waves beat into the boat, so that it was already filling. 38But He was in the stern, asleep on a pillow. And they awoke Him and said to Him, "Teacher, do You not care that we are perishing?"

39Then He arose and rebuked the wind, and said to the sea, "Peace, be still!" And the wind ceased and there was a great calm. 40But He said to them, "Why are you so fearful? How *is it* that you have no faith?"[a] 41And they feared exceedingly, and said to one another, "Who can this be, that even the wind and the sea obey Him!"

A Demon-Possessed Man Healed

5 Then they came to the other side of the sea, to the country of the Gadarenes.[a] 2And when He had come out of the boat, immediately there met Him out of the tombs a man with an unclean spirit, 3who had *his* dwelling among the tombs; and no one could bind him,[a] not even with chains, 4because he had often been bound with shackles and chains. And the chains had been pulled apart by him, and the shackles broken in pieces; neither could anyone tame him. 5And always, night and day, he was in the mountains and in the tombs, crying out and cutting himself with stones.

6When he saw Jesus from afar, he ran and worshiped Him. 7And he cried out with a loud voice and said, "What have I to do with You, Jesus, Son of the Most High God? I implore You by God that You do not torment me."

8For He said to him, "Come out of the man, unclean spirit!" 9Then He asked him, "What *is* your name?"

And he answered, saying, "My name *is* Legion; for we are many." 10Also he begged Him earnestly that He would not send them out of the country.

11Now a large herd of swine was feeding there near the mountains. 12So all the demons begged Him, saying, "Send us to the swine, that we may enter them." 13And at once Jesus[a] gave them permission. Then the unclean spirits went out and entered the swine (there were about two thousand); and the herd ran violently down the steep place into the sea, and drowned in the sea.

14So those who fed the swine fled, and they told *it* in the city and in the country. And they went out to see what it was that had happened. 15Then they came to Jesus, and saw the one *who had been* demon-possessed and had the legion, sitting and clothed and in his right mind. And they were afraid. 16And those who saw it told them how it happened to him *who had been* demon-possessed, and about the swine. 17Then they began to plead with Him to depart from their region.

18And when He got into the boat, he who had been demon-possessed begged Him that he might be with Him. 19However, Jesus did not permit him, but said to him, "Go home to your friends, and tell them what great things the Lord has done for you, and how He has had compassion on you." 20And he departed and began to proclaim in Decapolis all that Jesus had done for him; and all marveled.

A Girl Restored to Life and a Woman Healed

21Now when Jesus had crossed over again by boat to the other side, a great multitude gathered to Him; and He was by the sea. 22And behold, one of the

4:40 [a] NU-Text reads *Have you still no faith?* **5:1** [a] NU-Text reads *Gerasenes.* **5:3** [a] NU-Text adds *anymore.* **5:13** [a] NU-Text reads *And He gave.*

rulers of the synagogue came, Jairus by name. And when he saw Him, he fell at His feet 23and begged Him earnestly, saying, "My little daughter lies at the point of death. Come and lay Your hands on her, that she may be healed, and she will live." 24So *Jesus* went with him, and a great multitude followed Him and thronged Him.

25Now a certain woman had a flow of blood for twelve years, 26and had suffered many things from many physicians. She had spent all that she had and was no better, but rather grew worse. 27When she heard about Jesus, she came behind *Him* in the crowd and touched His garment. 28For she said, "If only I may touch His clothes, I shall be made well."

29Immediately the fountain of her blood was dried up, and she felt in *her* body that she was healed of the affliction. 30And Jesus, immediately knowing in Himself that power had gone out of Him, turned around in the crowd and said, "Who touched My clothes?"

31But His disciples said to Him, "You see the multitude thronging You, and You say, 'Who touched Me?' "

32And He looked around to see her who had done this thing. 33But the woman, fearing and trembling, knowing what had happened to her, came and fell down before Him and told Him the whole truth. 34And He said to her, "Daughter, your faith has made you well. Go in peace, and be healed of your affliction."

35While He was still speaking, *some* came from the ruler of the synagogue's *house* who said, "Your daughter is dead. Why trouble the Teacher any further?"

36As soon as Jesus heard the word that was spoken, He said to the ruler of the synagogue, "Do not be afraid; only believe." 37And He permitted no one to follow Him except Peter, James, and John the brother of James. 38Then He came to the house of the ruler of the synagogue, and saw a tumult and those who wept and wailed loudly. 39When He came in, He said to them, "Why make this commotion and weep? The child is not dead, but sleeping."

40And they ridiculed Him. But when He had put them all outside, He took the father and the mother of the child, and those *who were* with Him, and entered where the child was lying. 41Then He took the child by the hand, and said to her, "Talitha, cumi," which is translated, "Little girl, I say to you, arise." 42Immediately the girl arose and walked, for she was twelve years *of age.* And they were overcome with great amazement. 43But He commanded them strictly that no one should know it, and said that *something* should be given her to eat.

Jesus Rejected at Nazareth

6 Then He went out from there and came to His own country, and His disciples followed Him. 2And when the Sabbath had come, He began to teach in the synagogue. And many hearing *Him* were astonished, saying, "Where *did* this Man *get* these things? And what wisdom *is* this which is given to Him, that such mighty works are performed by His hands! 3Is this not the carpenter, the Son of Mary, and brother of James, Joses, Judas, and Simon? And are not His sisters here with us?" So they were offended at Him.

4But Jesus said to them, "A prophet is not without honor except in his own country, among his own relatives, and in his own house." 5Now He could do no mighty work there, except that He laid His hands on a few sick people and healed *them.* 6And He marveled because of their unbelief. Then He went about the villages in a circuit, teaching.

Sending Out the Twelve

7And He called the twelve to *Himself,* and began to send them out two *by* two, and gave them power over unclean spirits. 8He commanded them to take nothing for the journey except a staff—no bag, no bread, no copper in *their* money belts— 9but to wear sandals, and not to put on two tunics.

10Also He said to them, "In whatever place you enter a house, stay there till you depart from that place. 11And whoever[a] will not receive you nor hear you,

6:11 [a] NU-Text reads *whatever place.*

when you depart from there, shake off
the dust under your feet as a testimony
against them.[b] Assuredly, I say to you,
it will be more tolerable for Sodom and
Gomorrah in the day of judgment than
for that city!"
12So they went out and preached that
people should repent. 13And they cast
out many demons, and anointed with
oil many who were sick, and healed
them.

John the Baptist Beheaded

14Now King Herod heard *of Him,* for
His name had become well known. And
he said, "John the Baptist is risen from
the dead, and therefore these powers
are at work in him."
15Others said, "It is Elijah."
And others said, "It is the Prophet, or[a]
like one of the prophets."
16But when Herod heard, he said, "This
is John, whom I beheaded; he has been
raised from the dead!" 17For Herod him-
self had sent and laid hold of John, and
bound him in prison for the sake of He-
rodias, his brother Philip's wife; for he
had married her. 18Because John had
said to Herod, "It is not lawful for you
to have your brother's wife."
19Therefore Herodias held it against
him and wanted to kill him, but she
could not; 20for Herod feared John,
knowing that he *was* a just and holy
man, and he protected him. And when
he heard him, he did many things, and
heard him gladly.
21Then an opportune day came when
Herod on his birthday gave a feast for
his nobles, the high officers, and the
chief *men* of Galilee. 22And when He-
rodias' daughter herself came in and
danced, and pleased Herod and those
who sat with him, the king said to the
girl, "Ask me whatever you want, and I
will give *it* to you." 23He also swore to
her, "Whatever you ask me, I will give
you, up to half my kingdom."
24So she went out and said to her
mother, "What shall I ask?"
And she said, "The head of John the
Baptist!"
25Immediately she came in with haste
to the king and asked, saying, "I want
you to give me at once the head of John
the Baptist on a platter."
26And the king was exceedingly sorry;
yet, because of the oaths and because of
those who sat with him, he did not want
to refuse her. 27Immediately the king
sent an executioner and commanded
his head to be brought. And he went
and beheaded him in prison, 28brought
his head on a platter, and gave it to the
girl; and the girl gave it to her mother.
29When his disciples heard *of it,* they
came and took away his corpse and
laid it in a tomb.

Feeding the Five Thousand

30Then the apostles gathered to Jesus
and told Him all things, both what they
had done and what they had taught.
31And He said to them, "Come aside by
yourselves to a deserted place and rest a
while." For there were many coming and
going, and they did not even have time
to eat. 32So they departed to a deserted
place in the boat by themselves.
33But the multitudes[a] saw them de-
parting, and many knew Him and
ran there on foot from all the cities.
They arrived before them and came
together to Him. 34And Jesus, when He
came out, saw a great multitude and
was moved with compassion for them,
because they were like sheep not hav-
ing a shepherd. So He began to teach
them many things. 35When the day was
now far spent, His disciples came to
Him and said, "This is a deserted place,
and already the hour *is* late. 36Send
them away, that they may go into the
surrounding country and villages and
buy themselves bread;[a] for they have
nothing to eat."
37But He answered and said to them,
"You give them something to eat."
And they said to Him, "Shall we go
and buy two hundred denarii worth of
bread and give them *something* to eat?"
38But He said to them, "How many
loaves do you have? Go and see."
And when they found out they said,
"Five, and two fish."
39Then He commanded them to make

6:11 [b] NU-Text omits the rest of this verse. **6:15** [a] NU-Text and M-Text omit *or.* **6:33** [a] NU-Text and M-Text read *they.* **6:36** [a] NU-Text reads *something to eat* and omits the rest of this verse.

them all sit down in groups on the green
grass. 40So they sat down in ranks, in
hundreds and in fifties. 41And when He
had taken the five loaves and the two
fish, He looked up to heaven, blessed
and broke the loaves, and gave *them*
to His disciples to set before them; and
the two fish He divided among *them* all.
42So they all ate and were filled. 43And
they took up twelve baskets full of frag-
ments and of the fish. 44Now those who
had eaten the loaves were about[a] five
thousand men.

Jesus Walks on the Sea

45Immediately He made His disciples
get into the boat and go before Him to
the other side, to Bethsaida, while He
sent the multitude away. 46And when
He had sent them away, He departed
to the mountain to pray. 47Now when
evening came, the boat was in the mid-
dle of the sea; and He *was* alone on the
land. 48Then He saw them straining at
rowing, for the wind was against them.
Now about the fourth watch of the night
He came to them, walking on the sea,
and would have passed them by. 49And
when they saw Him walking on the sea,
they supposed it was a ghost, and cried
out; 50for they all saw Him and were
troubled. But immediately He talked
with them and said to them, "Be of good
cheer! It is I; do not be afraid." 51Then
He went up into the boat to them, and
the wind ceased. And they were greatly
amazed in themselves beyond mea-
sure, and marveled. 52For they had not
understood about the loaves, because
their heart was hardened.

Many Touch Him and Are Made Well

53When they had crossed over, they
came to the land of Gennesaret and
anchored there. 54And when they came
out of the boat, immediately the people
recognized Him, 55ran through that
whole surrounding region, and began
to carry about on beds those who were
sick to wherever they heard He was.
56Wherever He entered, into villages,
cities, or the country, they laid the sick
in the marketplaces, and begged Him
that they might just touch the hem of
His garment. And as many as touched
Him were made well.

Defilement Comes from Within

7 Then the Pharisees and some of
the scribes came together to Him,
having come from Jerusalem. 2Now
when[a] they saw some of His disciples
eat bread with defiled, that is, with un-
washed hands, they found fault. 3For
the Pharisees and all the Jews do not
eat unless they wash *their* hands in a
special way, holding the tradition of
the elders. 4*When they come* from the
marketplace, they do not eat unless
they wash. And there are many other
things which they have received and
hold, *like* the washing of cups, pitchers,
copper vessels, and couches.

5Then the Pharisees and scribes asked
Him, "Why do Your disciples not walk
according to the tradition of the elders,
but eat bread with unwashed hands?"

6He answered and said to them, "Well
did Isaiah prophesy of you hypocrites,
as it is written:

'This people honors Me with *their*
lips,
But their heart is far from Me.
7 And in vain they worship Me,
Teaching *as* doctrines the
commandments of men.'[a]

8For laying aside the commandment
of God, you hold the tradition of
men[a]—the washing of pitchers and
cups, and many other such things
you do."

9He said to them, "*All too* well you re-
ject the commandment of God, that
you may keep your tradition. 10For
Moses said, 'Honor your father and your
mother';[a] and, 'He who curses father or
mother, let him be put to death.'[b] 11But
you say, 'If a man says to his father or
mother, "Whatever profit you might
have received from me *is* Corban"—'
(that is, a gift *to God*), 12then you no lon-
ger let him do anything for his father or

6:44 [a] NU-Text and M-Text omit *about.* **7:2** [a] NU-Text omits *when* and *they found fault.*
7:7 [a] Isaiah 29:13 **7:8** [a] NU-Text omits the rest of this verse. **7:10** [a] Exodus 20:12; Deuteronomy 5:16 [b] Exodus 21:17

his mother, 13making the word of God of
no effect through your tradition which
you have handed down. And many such
things you do."
14When He had called all the multitude
to *Himself,* He said to them, "Hear Me,
everyone, and understand: 15There is
nothing that enters a man from outside
which can defile him; but the things
which come out of him, those are the
things that defile a man. 16If anyone
has ears to hear, let him hear!"[a]
17When He had entered a house away
from the crowd, His disciples asked Him
concerning the parable. 18So He said
to them, "Are you thus without under-
standing also? Do you not perceive that
whatever enters a man from outside
cannot defile him, 19because it does not
enter his heart but his stomach, and is
eliminated, *thus* purifying all foods?"[a]
20And He said, "What comes out of a
man, that defiles a man. 21For from
within, out of the heart of men, proceed
evil thoughts, adulteries, fornications,
murders, 22thefts, covetousness, wick-
edness, deceit, lewdness, an evil eye,
blasphemy, pride, foolishness. 23All
these evil things come from within and
defile a man."

A Gentile Shows Her Faith

24From there He arose and went to
the region of Tyre and Sidon.[a] And He
entered a house and wanted no one to
know *it,* but He could not be hidden.
25For a woman whose young daughter
had an unclean spirit heard about Him,
and she came and fell at His feet. 26The
woman was a Greek, a Syro-Phoenician
by birth, and she kept asking Him to
cast the demon out of her daughter.
27But Jesus said to her, "Let the children
be filled first, for it is not good to take
the children's bread and throw *it* to the
little dogs."
28And she answered and said to Him,
"Yes, Lord, yet even the little dogs un-
der the table eat from the children's
crumbs."
29Then He said to her, "For this saying
go your way; the demon has gone out
of your daughter."
30And when she had come to her
house, she found the demon gone out,
and her daughter lying on the bed.

Jesus Heals a Deaf-Mute

31Again, departing from the region
of Tyre and Sidon, He came through
the midst of the region of Decapolis to
the Sea of Galilee. 32Then they brought
to Him one who was deaf and had an
impediment in his speech, and they
begged Him to put His hand on him.
33And He took him aside from the mul-
titude, and put His fingers in his ears,
and He spat and touched his tongue.
34Then, looking up to heaven, He sighed,
and said to him, "Ephphatha," that is,
"Be opened."
35Immediately his ears were opened,
and the impediment of his tongue was
loosed, and he spoke plainly. 36Then He
commanded them that they should tell
no one; but the more He commanded
them, the more widely they proclaimed
it. 37And they were astonished beyond
measure, saying, "He has done all
things well. He makes both the deaf to
hear and the mute to speak."

Feeding the Four Thousand

8 In those days, the multitude being
very great and having nothing to
eat, Jesus called His disciples *to Him*
and said to them, 2"I have compassion
on the multitude, because they have
now continued with Me three days and
have nothing to eat. 3And if I send them
away hungry to their own houses, they
will faint on the way; for some of them
have come from afar."
4Then His disciples answered Him,
"How can one satisfy these people with
bread here in the wilderness?"
5He asked them, "How many loaves
do you have?"
And they said, "Seven."
6So He commanded the multitude to
sit down on the ground. And He took
the seven loaves and gave thanks, broke
them and gave *them* to His disciples
to set before *them;* and they set *them*
before the multitude. 7They also had a
few small fish; and having blessed them,

7:16 [a] NU-Text omits this verse. **7:19** [a] NU-Text ends quotation with *eliminated,* setting off the final clause as Mark's comment that Jesus has declared all foods clean. **7:24** [a] NU-Text omits *and Sidon.*

He said to set them also before *them.*
8So they ate and were filled, and they
took up seven large baskets of leftover
fragments. 9Now those who had eaten
were about four thousand. And He sent
them away, 10immediately got into the
boat with His disciples, and came to the
region of Dalmanutha.

The Pharisees Seek a Sign

11Then the Pharisees came out and be-
gan to dispute with Him, seeking from
Him a sign from heaven, testing Him.
12But He sighed deeply in His spirit,
and said, "Why does this generation
seek a sign? Assuredly, I say to you, no
sign shall be given to this generation."

Beware of the Leaven of the Pharisees and Herod

13And He left them, and getting into
the boat again, departed to the other
side. 14Now the disciples[a] had forgotten
to take bread, and they did not have
more than one loaf with them in the
boat. 15Then He charged them, saying,
"Take heed, beware of the leaven of the
Pharisees and the leaven of Herod."
16And they reasoned among them-
selves, saying, "*It is* because we have
no bread."
17But Jesus, being aware of *it,* said to
them, "Why do you reason because you
have no bread? Do you not yet perceive
nor understand? Is your heart still[a]
hardened? 18Having eyes, do you not
see? And having ears, do you not hear?
And do you not remember? 19When I
broke the five loaves for the five thou-
sand, how many baskets full of frag-
ments did you take up?"
They said to Him, "Twelve."
20"Also, when I broke the seven for the
four thousand, how many large baskets
full of fragments did you take up?"
And they said, "Seven."
21So He said to them, "How *is it* you do
not understand?"

A Blind Man Healed at Bethsaida

22Then He came to Bethsaida; and
they brought a blind man to Him, and
begged Him to touch him. 23So He took
the blind man by the hand and led him
out of the town. And when He had spit
on his eyes and put His hands on him,
He asked him if he saw anything.
24And he looked up and said, "I see
men like trees, walking."
25Then He put *His* hands on his eyes
again and made him look up. And he
was restored and saw everyone clearly.
26Then He sent him away to his house,
saying, "Neither go into the town, nor
tell anyone in the town."[a]

Peter Confesses Jesus as the Christ

27Now Jesus and His disciples went
out to the towns of Caesarea Philippi;
and on the road He asked His disciples,
saying to them, "Who do men say that
I am?"
28So they answered, "John the Baptist;
but some *say,* Elijah; and others, one of
the prophets."
29He said to them, "But who do you
say that I am?"
Peter answered and said to Him, "You
are the Christ."
30Then He strictly warned them that
they should tell no one about Him.

Jesus Predicts His Death and Resurrection

31And He began to teach them that the
Son of Man must suffer many things,
and be rejected by the elders and chief
priests and scribes, and be killed, and
after three days rise again. 32He spoke
this word openly. Then Peter took Him
aside and began to rebuke Him. 33But
when He had turned around and looked
at His disciples, He rebuked Peter, say-
ing, "Get behind Me, Satan! For you are
not mindful of the things of God, but the
things of men."

Take Up the Cross and Follow Him

34When He had called the people to
Himself, with His disciples also, He said
to them, "Whoever desires to come after
Me, let him deny himself, and take up
his cross, and follow Me. 35For whoever
desires to save his life will lose it, but
whoever loses his life for My sake and
the gospel's will save it. 36For what will

8:14 [a] NU-Text and M-Text read *they.* 8:17 [a] NU-Text omits *still.* 8:26 [a] NU-Text reads *"Do not even go into the town."*

it profit a man if he gains the whole
world, and loses his own soul? 37Or
what will a man give in exchange for
his soul? 38For whoever is ashamed of
Me and My words in this adulterous
and sinful generation, of him the Son
of Man also will be ashamed when He
comes in the glory of His Father with
the holy angels."

9 And He said to them, "Assuredly,
I say to you that there are some
standing here who will not taste death
till they see the kingdom of God present
with power."

Jesus Transfigured on the Mount

2Now after six days Jesus took Peter,
James, and John, and led them up on
a high mountain apart by themselves;
and He was transfigured before them.
3His clothes became shining, exceed-
ingly white, like snow, such as no laun-
derer on earth can whiten them. 4And
Elijah appeared to them with Moses,
and they were talking with Jesus. 5Then
Peter answered and said to Jesus, "Rab-
bi, it is good for us to be here; and let
us make three tabernacles: one for You,
one for Moses, and one for Elijah"—
6because he did not know what to say,
for they were greatly afraid.

7And a cloud came and overshadowed
them; and a voice came out of the cloud,
saying, "This is My beloved Son. Hear
Him!" 8Suddenly, when they had looked
around, they saw no one anymore, but
only Jesus with themselves.

9Now as they came down from the
mountain, He commanded them that
they should tell no one the things they
had seen, till the Son of Man had risen
from the dead. 10So they kept this word
to themselves, questioning what the
rising from the dead meant.

11And they asked Him, saying, "Why
do the scribes say that Elijah must come
first?"

12Then He answered and told them,
"Indeed, Elijah is coming first and re-
stores all things. And how is it written
concerning the Son of Man, that He
must suffer many things and be treat-
ed with contempt? 13But I say to you
that Elijah has also come, and they
did to him whatever they wished, as it
is written of him."

A Boy Is Healed

14And when He came to the disci-
ples, He saw a great multitude around
them, and scribes disputing with them.
15Immediately, when they saw Him, all
the people were greatly amazed, and
running to *Him,* greeted Him. 16And
He asked the scribes, "What are you
discussing with them?"

17Then one of the crowd answered and
said, "Teacher, I brought You my son,
who has a mute spirit. 18And wherever
it seizes him, it throws him down; he
foams at the mouth, gnashes his teeth,
and becomes rigid. So I spoke to Your
disciples, that they should cast it out,
but they could not."

19He answered him and said, "O faith-
less generation, how long shall I be with
you? How long shall I bear with you?
Bring him to Me." 20Then they brought
him to Him. And when he saw Him,
immediately the spirit convulsed him,
and he fell on the ground and wallowed,
foaming at the mouth.

21So He asked his father, "How long
has this been happening to him?"

And he said, "From childhood. 22And
often he has thrown him both into the
fire and into the water to destroy him.
But if You can do anything, have com-
passion on us and help us."

23Jesus said to him, "If you can be-
lieve,[a] all things *are* possible to him
who believes."

24Immediately the father of the child
cried out and said with tears, "Lord, I
believe; help my unbelief!"

25When Jesus saw that the people
came running together, He rebuked
the unclean spirit, saying to it, "Deaf
and dumb spirit, I command you, come
out of him and enter him no more!"
26Then *the spirit* cried out, convulsed
him greatly, and came out of him. And
he became as one dead, so that many
said, "He is dead." 27But Jesus took him
by the hand and lifted him up, and he
arose.

9:23 [a] NU-Text reads "*'If You can!' All things . . . .*"

28And when He had come into the
house, His disciples asked Him private-
ly, "Why could we not cast it out?"
29So He said to them, "This kind can
come out by nothing but prayer and
fasting."[a]

Jesus Again Predicts His Death and Resurrection

30Then they departed from there and
passed through Galilee, and He did not
want anyone to know *it.* 31For He taught
His disciples and said to them, "The Son
of Man is being betrayed into the hands
of men, and they will kill Him. And after
He is killed, He will rise the third day."
32But they did not understand this say-
ing, and were afraid to ask Him.

Who Is the Greatest?

33Then He came to Capernaum. And
when He was in the house He asked
them, "What was it you disputed among
yourselves on the road?" 34But they kept
silent, for on the road they had disputed
among themselves who *would be the*
greatest. 35And He sat down, called the
twelve, and said to them, "If anyone
desires to be first, he shall be last of all
and servant of all." 36Then He took a little
child and set him in the midst of them.
And when He had taken him in His arms,
He said to them, 37"Whoever receives
one of these little children in My name
receives Me; and whoever receives Me,
receives not Me but Him who sent Me."

Jesus Forbids Sectarianism

38Now John answered Him, saying,
"Teacher, we saw someone who does not
follow us casting out demons in Your
name, and we forbade him because he
does not follow us."
39But Jesus said, "Do not forbid him,
for no one who works a miracle in My
name can soon afterward speak evil
of Me. 40For he who is not against us is
on our[a] side. 41For whoever gives you
a cup of water to drink in My name,
because you belong to Christ, assuredly,
I say to you, he will by no means lose
his reward.

Jesus Warns of Offenses

42"But whoever causes one of these
little ones who believe in Me to stum-
ble, it would be better for him if a mill-
stone were hung around his neck, and
he were thrown into the sea. 43If your
hand causes you to sin, cut it off. It is
better for you to enter into life maimed,
rather than having two hands, to go
to hell, into the fire that shall never be
quenched— 44where

'Their worm does not die,
And the fire is not quenched.'[a]

45And if your foot causes you to sin,
cut it off. It is better for you to enter life
lame, rather than having two feet, to
be cast into hell, into the fire that shall
never be quenched— 46where

'Their worm does not die
And the fire is not quenched.'[a]

47And if your eye causes you to sin,
pluck it out. It is better for you to enter
the kingdom of God with one eye, rather
than having two eyes, to be cast into
hell fire— 48where

'Their worm does not die,
And the fire is not quenched.'[a]

Tasteless Salt Is Worthless

49"For everyone will be seasoned with
fire,[a] and every sacrifice will be sea-
soned with salt. 50Salt *is* good, but if
the salt loses its flavor, how will you
season it? Have salt in yourselves, and
have peace with one another."

Marriage and Divorce

10 Then He arose from there and
came to the region of Judea by
the other side of the Jordan. And multi-
tudes gathered to Him again, and as He
was accustomed, He taught them again.
2The Pharisees came and asked Him,
"Is it lawful for a man to divorce *his*
wife?" testing Him.
3And He answered and said to them,
"What did Moses command you?"

9:29 [a] NU-Text omits *and fasting.* **9:40** [a] M-Text reads *against you is on your side.* **9:44** [a] NU-Text omits this verse. **9:46** [a] NU-Text omits the last clause of verse 45 and all of verse 46. **9:48** [a] Isaiah 66:24 **9:49** [a] NU-Text omits the rest of this verse.

4They said, "Moses permitted *a man*
to write a certificate of divorce, and to
dismiss *her.*"
5And Jesus answered and said to them,
"Because of the hardness of your heart
he wrote you this precept. 6But from the
beginning of the creation, God 'made
them male and female.'[a] 7'For this rea-
son a man shall leave his father and
mother and be joined to his wife, 8and
the two shall become one flesh';[a] so
then they are no longer two, but one
flesh. 9Therefore what God has joined
together, let not man separate."
10In the house His disciples also asked
Him again about the same *matter.* 11So
He said to them, "Whoever divorces
his wife and marries another commits
adultery against her. 12And if a woman
divorces her husband and marries an-
other, she commits adultery."

Jesus Blesses Little Children

13Then they brought little children to
Him, that He might touch them; but the
disciples rebuked those who brought
them. 14But when Jesus saw *it,* He was
greatly displeased and said to them,
"Let the little children come to Me, and
do not forbid them; for of such is the
kingdom of God. 15Assuredly, I say to
you, whoever does not receive the king-
dom of God as a little child will by no
means enter it." 16And He took them up
in His arms, laid *His* hands on them,
and blessed them.

Jesus Counsels the Rich Young Ruler

17Now as He was going out on the road,
one came running, knelt before Him,
and asked Him, "Good Teacher, what
shall I do that I may inherit eternal
life?"
18So Jesus said to him, "Why do you
call Me good? No one *is* good but One,
that is, God. 19You know the command-
ments: 'Do not commit adultery,' 'Do
not murder,' 'Do not steal,' 'Do not bear
false witness,' 'Do not defraud,' 'Honor
your father and your mother.' "[a]
20And he answered and said to Him,
"Teacher, all these things I have kept
from my youth."
21Then Jesus, looking at him, loved
him, and said to him, "One thing you
lack: Go your way, sell whatever you
have and give to the poor, and you will
have treasure in heaven; and come, take
up the cross, and follow Me."
22But he was sad at this word, and
went away sorrowful, for he had great
possessions.

With God All Things Are Possible

23Then Jesus looked around and said
to His disciples, "How hard it is for those
who have riches to enter the kingdom
of God!" 24And the disciples were aston-
ished at His words. But Jesus answered
again and said to them, "Children, how
hard it is for those who trust in riches[a] to
enter the kingdom of God! 25It is easier
for a camel to go through the eye of a
needle than for a rich man to enter the
kingdom of God."
26And they were greatly astonished,
saying among themselves, "Who then
can be saved?"
27But Jesus looked at them and said,
"With men *it is* impossible, but not with
God; for with God all things are pos-
sible."
28Then Peter began to say to Him, "See,
we have left all and followed You."
29So Jesus answered and said, "As-
suredly, I say to you, there is no one
who has left house or brothers or sisters
or father or mother or wife[a] or children
or lands, for My sake and the gospel's,
30who shall not receive a hundredfold
now in this time—houses and brothers
and sisters and mothers and children
and lands, with persecutions—and
in the age to come, eternal life. 31But
many *who are* first will be last, and the
last first."

Jesus a Third Time Predicts His Death and Resurrection

32Now they were on the road, going
up to Jerusalem, and Jesus was going
before them; and they were amazed.
And as they followed they were afraid.
Then He took the twelve aside again and
began to tell them the things that would
happen to Him: 33"Behold, we are going

10:6 [a] Genesis 1:27; 5:2 **10:8** [a] Genesis 2:24 **10:19** [a] Exodus 20:12–16; Deuteronomy 5:16–20
10:24 [a] NU-Text omits *for those who trust in riches.* **10:29** [a] NU-Text omits *or wife.*

up to Jerusalem, and the Son of Man will
be betrayed to the chief priests and to
the scribes; and they will condemn Him
to death and deliver Him to the Gentiles;
34 and they will mock Him, and scourge
Him, and spit on Him, and kill Him. And
the third day He will rise again."

Greatness Is Serving

35 Then James and John, the sons of Zeb-
edee, came to Him, saying, "Teacher, we
want You to do for us whatever we ask."
36 And He said to them, "What do you
want Me to do for you?"
37 They said to Him, "Grant us that we
may sit, one on Your right hand and
the other on Your left, in Your glory."
38 But Jesus said to them, "You do
not know what you ask. Are you able
to drink the cup that I drink, and be
baptized with the baptism that I am
baptized with?"
39 They said to Him, "We are able."
So Jesus said to them, "You will indeed
drink the cup that I drink, and with the
baptism I am baptized with you will be
baptized; 40 but to sit on My right hand
and on My left is not Mine to give, but
it is for those for whom it is prepared."
41 And when the ten heard *it,* they be-
gan to be greatly displeased with James
and John. 42 But Jesus called them to
Himself and said to them, "You know
that those who are considered rulers
over the Gentiles lord it over them, and
their great ones exercise authority over
them. 43 Yet it shall not be so among you;
but whoever desires to become great
among you shall be your servant. 44 And
whoever of you desires to be first shall
be slave of all. 45 For even the Son of Man
did not come to be served, but to serve,
and to give His life a ransom for many."

Jesus Heals Blind Bartimaeus

46 Now they came to Jericho. As He went
out of Jericho with His disciples and a
great multitude, blind Bartimaeus, the
son of Timaeus, sat by the road begging.
47 And when he heard that it was Jesus of
Nazareth, he began to cry out and say,
"Jesus, Son of David, have mercy on me!"
48 Then many warned him to be quiet;
but he cried out all the more, "Son of
David, have mercy on me!"
49 So Jesus stood still and commanded
him to be called.
Then they called the blind man, saying
to him, "Be of good cheer. Rise, He is
calling you."
50 And throwing aside his garment, he
rose and came to Jesus.
51 So Jesus answered and said to him,
"What do you want Me to do for you?"
The blind man said to Him, "Rabboni,
that I may receive my sight."
52 Then Jesus said to him, "Go your
way; your faith has made you well." And
immediately he received his sight and
followed Jesus on the road.

The Triumphal Entry

11 Now when they drew near Je-
rusalem, to Bethphage[a] and
Bethany, at the Mount of Olives, He
sent two of His disciples; 2 and He said
to them, "Go into the village opposite
you; and as soon as you have entered
it you will find a colt tied, on which no
one has sat. Loose it and bring *it.* 3 And
if anyone says to you, 'Why are you
doing this?' say, 'The Lord has need of
it,' and immediately he will send it here."
4 So they went their way, and found
the[a] colt tied by the door outside on
the street, and they loosed it. 5 But some
of those who stood there said to them,
"What are you doing, loosing the colt?"
6 And they spoke to them just as Jesus
had commanded. So they let them go.
7 Then they brought the colt to Jesus and
threw their clothes on it, and He sat on it.
8 And many spread their clothes on the
road, and others cut down leafy branch-
es from the trees and spread *them* on the
road. 9 Then those who went before and
those who followed cried out, saying:

"Hosanna!
'Blessed *is* He who comes in the
name of the LORD!'[a]
10 Blessed *is* the kingdom of our
father David
That comes in the name of the
Lord![a]
Hosanna in the highest!"

11:1 [a] M-Text reads *Bethsphage.* 11:4 [a] NU-Text and M-Text read *a.* 11:9 [a] Psalm 118:26
11:10 [a] NU-Text omits *in the name of the Lord.*

11And Jesus went into Jerusalem and into the temple. So when He had looked around at all things, as the hour was already late, He went out to Bethany with the twelve.

The Fig Tree Withered

12Now the next day, when they had come out from Bethany, He was hungry. 13And seeing from afar a fig tree having leaves, He went to see if perhaps He would find something on it. When He came to it, He found nothing but leaves, for it was not the season for figs. 14In response Jesus said to it, "Let no one eat fruit from you ever again."

And His disciples heard *it.*

Jesus Cleanses the Temple

15So they came to Jerusalem. Then Jesus went into the temple and began to drive out those who bought and sold in the temple, and overturned the tables of the money changers and the seats of those who sold doves. 16And He would not allow anyone to carry wares through the temple. 17Then He taught, saying to them, "Is it not written, 'My house shall be called a house of prayer for all nations'?[a] But you have made it a 'den of thieves.' "[b]

18And the scribes and chief priests heard it and sought how they might destroy Him; for they feared Him, because all the people were astonished at His teaching. 19When evening had come, He went out of the city.

The Lesson of the Withered Fig Tree

20Now in the morning, as they passed by, they saw the fig tree dried up from the roots. 21And Peter, remembering, said to Him, "Rabbi, look! The fig tree which You cursed has withered away."

22So Jesus answered and said to them, "Have faith in God. 23For assuredly, I say to you, whoever says to this mountain, 'Be removed and be cast into the sea,' and does not doubt in his heart, but believes that those things he says will be done, he will have whatever he says. 24Therefore I say to you, whatever things you ask when you pray, believe that you receive *them,* and you will have *them.*

Forgiveness and Prayer

25"And whenever you stand praying, if you have anything against anyone, forgive him, that your Father in heaven may also forgive you your trespasses. 26But if you do not forgive, neither will your Father in heaven forgive your trespasses."[a]

Jesus' Authority Questioned

27Then they came again to Jerusalem. And as He was walking in the temple, the chief priests, the scribes, and the elders came to Him. 28And they said to Him, "By what authority are You doing these things? And who gave You this authority to do these things?"

29But Jesus answered and said to them, "I also will ask you one question; then answer Me, and I will tell you by what authority I do these things: 30The baptism of John—was it from heaven or from men? Answer Me."

31And they reasoned among themselves, saying, "If we say, 'From heaven,' He will say, 'Why then did you not believe him?' 32But if we say, 'From men' "—they feared the people, for all counted John to have been a prophet indeed. 33So they answered and said to Jesus, "We do not know."

And Jesus answered and said to them, "Neither will I tell you by what authority I do these things."

The Parable of the Wicked Vinedressers

12 Then He began to speak to them in parables: "A man planted a vineyard and set a hedge around *it,* dug *a place for* the wine vat and built a tower. And he leased it to vinedressers and went into a far country. 2Now at vintage-time he sent a servant to the vinedressers, that he might receive some of the fruit of the vineyard from the vinedressers. 3And they took *him* and beat him and sent *him* away empty-handed. 4Again he sent them another servant, and at him they threw stones,[a] wounded *him* in the head, and sent *him*

11:17 [a] Isaiah 56:7 [b] Jeremiah 7:11 **11:26** [a] NU-Text omits this verse. **12:4** [a] NU-Text omits *and at him they threw stones.*

away shamefully treated. 5And again
he sent another, and him they killed;
and many others, beating some and
killing some. 6Therefore still having
one son, his beloved, he also sent him
to them last, saying, 'They will respect
my son.' 7But those vinedressers said
among themselves, 'This is the heir.
Come, let us kill him, and the inheri-
tance will be ours.' 8So they took him
and killed *him* and cast *him* out of the
vineyard.

9"Therefore what will the owner of the
vineyard do? He will come and destroy
the vinedressers, and give the vineyard
to others. 10Have you not even read
this Scripture:

> 'The stone which the builders
> rejected
> Has become the chief
> cornerstone.
> 11 This was the LORD's doing,
> And it is marvelous in our eyes'?"[a]

12And they sought to lay hands on Him,
but feared the multitude, for they knew
He had spoken the parable against
them. So they left Him and went away.

The Pharisees: Is It Lawful to Pay Taxes to Caesar?

13Then they sent to Him some of the
Pharisees and the Herodians, to catch
Him in *His* words. 14When they had
come, they said to Him, "Teacher, we
know that You are true, and care about
no one; for You do not regard the person
of men, but teach the way of God in truth.
Is it lawful to pay taxes to Caesar, or not?
15Shall we pay, or shall we not pay?"

But He, knowing their hypocrisy, said
to them, "Why do you test Me? Bring
Me a denarius that I may see *it.*" 16So
they brought *it.*

And He said to them, "Whose image
and inscription *is* this?" They said to
Him, "Caesar's."

17And Jesus answered and said to
them, "Render to Caesar the things that
are Caesar's, and to God the things that
are God's."

And they marveled at Him.

The Sadducees: What About the Resurrection?

18Then *some* Sadducees, who say there
is no resurrection, came to Him; and
they asked Him, saying: 19"Teacher,
Moses wrote to us that if a man's brother
dies, and leaves *his* wife behind, and
leaves no children, his brother should
take his wife and raise up offspring
for his brother. 20Now there were sev-
en brothers. The first took a wife; and
dying, he left no offspring. 21And the
second took her, and he died; nor did
he leave any offspring. And the third
likewise. 22So the seven had her and left
no offspring. Last of all the woman died
also. 23Therefore, in the resurrection,
when they rise, whose wife will she be?
For all seven had her as wife."

24Jesus answered and said to them,
"Are you not therefore mistaken, be-
cause you do not know the Scriptures
nor the power of God? 25For when they
rise from the dead, they neither marry
nor are given in marriage, but are like
angels in heaven. 26But concerning the
dead, that they rise, have you not read
in the book of Moses, in the *burning* bush
passage, how God spoke to him, saying,
'I *am* the God of Abraham, the God of
Isaac, and the God of Jacob'?[a] 27He is
not the God of the dead, but the God of
the living. You are therefore greatly
mistaken."

The Scribes: Which Is the First Commandment of All?

28Then one of the scribes came, and
having heard them reasoning togeth-
er, perceiving[a] that He had answered
them well, asked Him, "Which is the
first commandment of all?"

29Jesus answered him, "The first of all
the commandments *is:* 'Hear, O Isra-
el, the LORD our God, the LORD is one.
30And you shall love the LORD your God
with all your heart, with all your soul,
with all your mind, and with all your
strength.'[a] This *is* the first command-
ment.[b] 31And the second, like *it, is* this:
'You shall love your neighbor as your-
self.'[a] There is no other commandment
greater than these."

12:11 [a] Psalm 118:22, 23 **12:26** [a] Exodus 3:6, 15 **12:28** [a] NU-Text reads *seeing.*
12:30 [a] Deuteronomy 6:4, 5 [b] NU-Text omits this sentence. **12:31** [a] Leviticus 19:18

GOD SIN JESUS SALVATION LOVE

32So the scribe said to Him, "Well *said,*
Teacher. You have spoken the truth, for
there is one God, and there is no other
but He. 33And to love Him with all the
heart, with all the understanding, with
all the soul,[a] and with all the strength,
and to love one's neighbor as oneself, is
more than all the whole burnt offerings
and sacrifices."
34Now when Jesus saw that he an-
swered wisely, He said to him, "You
are not far from the kingdom of God."
But after that no one dared question
Him.

Jesus: How Can David Call His Descendant "Lord"?

35Then Jesus answered and said, while
He taught in the temple, "How *is it* that
the scribes say that the Christ is the Son
of David? 36For David himself said by
the Holy Spirit:

> 'The LORD said to my Lord,
> "Sit at My right hand,
> Till I make Your enemies Your
> footstool." '[a]

37Therefore David himself calls Him
'Lord'; how is He *then* his Son?"
And the common people heard Him
gladly.

Beware of the Scribes

38Then He said to them in His teaching,
"Beware of the scribes, who desire to go
around in long robes, *love* greetings in
the marketplaces, 39the best seats in the
synagogues, and the best places at feasts,
40who devour widows' houses, and for a
pretense make long prayers. These will
receive greater condemnation."

The Widow's Two Mites

41Now Jesus sat opposite the treasury
and saw how the people put money into
the treasury. And many *who were* rich
put in much. 42Then one poor widow
came and threw in two mites,[a] which
make a quadrans. 43So He called His
disciples to *Himself* and said to them,
"Assuredly, I say to you that this poor
widow has put in more than all those
who have given to the treasury; 44for
they all put in out of their abundance,
but she out of her poverty put in all that
she had, her whole livelihood."

Jesus Predicts the Destruction of the Temple

13 Then as He went out of the tem-
ple, one of His disciples said to
Him, "Teacher, see what manner of
stones and what buildings *are here!*"
2And Jesus answered and said to him,
"Do you see these great buildings? Not
one stone shall be left upon another,
that shall not be thrown down."

The Signs of the Times and the End of the Age

3Now as He sat on the Mount of Olives
opposite the temple, Peter, James, John,
and Andrew asked Him privately, 4"Tell
us, when will these things be? And what
will be the sign when all these things
will be fulfilled?"
5And Jesus, answering them, began
to say: "Take heed that no one deceives
you. 6For many will come in My name,
saying, 'I am *He,*' and will deceive many.
7But when you hear of wars and rumors
of wars, do not be troubled; for *such things*
must happen, but the end *is* not yet. 8For
nation will rise against nation, and king-
dom against kingdom. And there will be
earthquakes in various places, and there
will be famines and troubles.[a] These *are*
the beginnings of sorrows.
9"But watch out for yourselves, for they
will deliver you up to councils, and you
will be beaten in the synagogues. You will
be brought[a] before rulers and kings for
My sake, for a testimony to them. 10And
the gospel must first be preached to
all the nations. 11But when they arrest
you and deliver you up, do not worry
beforehand, or premeditate[a] what you
will speak. But whatever is given you in
that hour, speak that; for it is not you
who speak, but the Holy Spirit. 12Now
brother will betray brother to death, and
a father *his* child; and children will rise
up against parents and cause them to

12:33 [a] NU-Text omits *with all the soul.* **12:36** [a] Psalm 110:1 **12:42** [a] Greek *lepta,* very small copper coins worth a fraction of a penny **13:8** [a] NU-Text omits *and troubles.* **13:9** [a] NU-Text and M-Text read *will stand.* **13:11** [a] NU-Text omits *or premeditate.*

be put to death. 13And you will be hated
by all for My name's sake. But he who
endures to the end shall be saved.

The Great Tribulation

14"So when you see the 'abomination
of desolation,'[a] spoken of by Daniel the
prophet,[b] standing where it ought not"
(let the reader understand), "then let
those who are in Judea flee to the moun-
tains. 15Let him who is on the housetop
not go down into the house, nor enter to
take anything out of his house. 16And let
him who is in the field not go back to get
his clothes. 17But woe to those who are
pregnant and to those who are nursing
babies in those days! 18And pray that
your flight may not be in winter. 19For *in*
those days there will be tribulation, such
as has not been since the beginning of
the creation which God created until this
time, nor ever shall be. 20And unless the
Lord had shortened those days, no flesh
would be saved; but for the elect's sake,
whom He chose, He shortened the days.
21"Then if anyone says to you, 'Look,
here *is* the Christ!' or, 'Look, *He is* there!'
do not believe it. 22For false christs and
false prophets will rise and show signs
and wonders to deceive, if possible, even
the elect. 23But take heed; see, I have
told you all things beforehand.

The Coming of the Son of Man

24"But in those days, after that trib-
ulation, the sun will be darkened, and
the moon will not give its light; 25the
stars of heaven will fall, and the powers
in the heavens will be shaken. 26Then
they will see the Son of Man coming in
the clouds with great power and glory.
27And then He will send His angels, and
gather together His elect from the four
winds, from the farthest part of earth
to the farthest part of heaven.

The Parable of the Fig Tree

28"Now learn this parable from the
fig tree: When its branch has already
become tender, and puts forth leaves,
you know that summer is near. 29So
you also, when you see these things
happening, know that it[a] is near—at
the doors! 30Assuredly, I say to you, this
generation will by no means pass away
till all these things take place. 31Heaven
and earth will pass away, but My words
will by no means pass away.

No One Knows the Day or Hour

32"But of that day and hour no one
knows, not even the angels in heaven,
nor the Son, but only the Father. 33Take
heed, watch and pray; for you do not
know when the time is. 34*It is* like a man
going to a far country, who left his house
and gave authority to his servants, and
to each his work, and commanded the
doorkeeper to watch. 35Watch therefore,
for you do not know when the master of
the house is coming—in the evening, at
midnight, at the crowing of the roost-
er, or in the morning— 36lest, coming
suddenly, he find you sleeping. 37And
what I say to you, I say to all: Watch!"

The Plot to Kill Jesus

14 After two days it was the Pass-
over and *the Feast* of Unleav-
ened Bread. And the chief priests and
the scribes sought how they might take
Him by trickery and put *Him* to death.
2But they said, "Not during the feast,
lest there be an uproar of the people."

The Anointing at Bethany

3And being in Bethany at the house of
Simon the leper, as He sat at the table, a
woman came having an alabaster flask
of very costly oil of spikenard. Then she
broke the flask and poured *it* on His
head. 4But there were some who were
indignant among themselves, and said,
"Why was this fragrant oil wasted? 5For
it might have been sold for more than
three hundred denarii and given to the
poor." And they criticized her sharply.
6But Jesus said, "Let her alone. Why do
you trouble her? She has done a good
work for Me. 7For you have the poor with
you always, and whenever you wish
you may do them good; but Me you do
not have always. 8She has done what
she could. She has come beforehand to
anoint My body for burial. 9Assuredly,
I say to you, wherever this gospel is

13:14 [a] Daniel 11:31; 12:11 [b] NU-Text omits *spoken of by Daniel the prophet.* 13:29 [a] Or *He*

preached in the whole world, what this
woman has done will also be told as a
memorial to her."

Judas Agrees to Betray Jesus

10Then Judas Iscariot, one of the
twelve, went to the chief priests to be-
tray Him to them. 11And when they
heard *it,* they were glad, and promised
to give him money. So he sought how he
might conveniently betray Him.

Jesus Celebrates the Passover with His Disciples

12Now on the first day of Unleavened
Bread, when they killed the Passover
lamb, His disciples said to Him, "Where
do You want us to go and prepare, that
You may eat the Passover?"
13And He sent out two of His disciples
and said to them, "Go into the city, and
a man will meet you carrying a pitcher
of water; follow him. 14Wherever he
goes in, say to the master of the house,
'The Teacher says, "Where is the guest
room in which I may eat the Passover
with My disciples?"' 15Then he will show
you a large upper room, furnished *and*
prepared; there make ready for us."
16So His disciples went out, and came
into the city, and found it just as He
had said to them; and they prepared
the Passover.
17In the evening He came with the
twelve. 18Now as they sat and ate, Jesus
said, "Assuredly, I say to you, one of
you who eats with Me will betray Me."
19And they began to be sorrowful, and
to say to Him one by one, "*Is* it I?" And
another *said,* "*Is* it I?"[a]
20He answered and said to them, "*It is*
one of the twelve, who dips with Me in
the dish. 21The Son of Man indeed goes
just as it is written of Him, but woe to
that man by whom the Son of Man is
betrayed! It would have been good for
that man if he had never been born."

Jesus Institutes the Lord's Supper

22And as they were eating, Jesus took
bread, blessed and broke *it,* and gave
it to them and said, "Take, eat;[a] this is
My body."
23Then He took the cup, and when He
had given thanks He gave *it* to them,
and they all drank from it. 24And He
said to them, "This is My blood of the
new[a] covenant, which is shed for many.
25Assuredly, I say to you, I will no lon-
ger drink of the fruit of the vine until
that day when I drink it new in the king-
dom of God."
26And when they had sung a hymn,
they went out to the Mount of Olives.

Jesus Predicts Peter's Denial

27Then Jesus said to them, "All of you
will be made to stumble because of Me
this night,[a] for it is written:

'I will strike the Shepherd,
And the sheep will be scattered.'[b]

28"But after I have been raised, I will
go before you to Galilee."
29Peter said to Him, "Even if all are
made to stumble, yet I *will* not *be.*"
30Jesus said to him, "Assuredly, I say
to you that today, *even* this night, before
the rooster crows twice, you will deny
Me three times."
31But he spoke more vehemently, "If
I have to die with You, I will not deny
You!"
And they all said likewise.

The Prayer in the Garden

32Then they came to a place which
was named Gethsemane; and He said
to His disciples, "Sit here while I pray."
33And He took Peter, James, and John
with Him, and He began to be troubled
and deeply distressed. 34Then He said to
them, "My soul is exceedingly sorrow-
ful, *even* to death. Stay here and watch."
35He went a little farther, and fell on
the ground, and prayed that if it were
possible, the hour might pass from Him.
36And He said, "Abba, Father, all things
are possible for You. Take this cup away
from Me; nevertheless, not what I will,
but what You *will.*"
37Then He came and found them
sleeping, and said to Peter, "Simon, are
you sleeping? Could you not watch one
hour? 38Watch and pray, lest you enter

14:19 [a] NU-Text omits this sentence. **14:22** [a] NU-Text omits *eat.* **14:24** [a] NU-Text omits *new.*
14:27 [a] NU-Text omits *because of Me this night.* [b] Zechariah 13:7

into temptation. The spirit indeed *is*
willing, but the flesh *is* weak."
39 Again He went away and prayed,
and spoke the same words. 40 And when
He returned, He found them asleep
again, for their eyes were heavy; and
they did not know what to answer Him.
41 Then He came the third time and
said to them, "Are you still sleeping
and resting? It is enough! The hour has
come; behold, the Son of Man is being
betrayed into the hands of sinners.
42 Rise, let us be going. See, My betray-
er is at hand."

Betrayal and Arrest in Gethsemane

43 And immediately, while He was
still speaking, Judas, one of the twelve,
with a great multitude with swords and
clubs, came from the chief priests and
the scribes and the elders. 44 Now His
betrayer had given them a signal, say-
ing, "Whomever I kiss, He is the One;
seize Him and lead *Him* away safely."
45 As soon as he had come, immediate-
ly he went up to Him and said to Him,
"Rabbi, Rabbi!" and kissed Him.
46 Then they laid their hands on Him
and took Him. 47 And one of those who
stood by drew his sword and struck the
servant of the high priest, and cut off
his ear.
48 Then Jesus answered and said to
them, "Have you come out, as against
a robber, with swords and clubs to take
Me? 49 I was daily with you in the temple
teaching, and you did not seize Me. But
the Scriptures must be fulfilled."
50 Then they all forsook Him and fled.

A Young Man Flees Naked

51 Now a certain young man followed
Him, having a linen cloth thrown
around *his* naked *body*. And the young
men laid hold of him, 52 and he left the
linen cloth and fled from them naked.

Jesus Faces the Sanhedrin

53 And they led Jesus away to the high
priest; and with him were assembled
all the chief priests, the elders, and the
scribes. 54 But Peter followed Him at a
distance, right into the courtyard of the
high priest. And he sat with the servants
and warmed himself at the fire.
55 Now the chief priests and all the
council sought testimony against Jesus
to put Him to death, but found none.
56 For many bore false witness against
Him, but their testimonies did not agree.
57 Then some rose up and bore false
witness against Him, saying, 58 "We
heard Him say, 'I will destroy this tem-
ple made with hands, and within three
days I will build another made without
hands.' " 59 But not even then did their
testimony agree.
60 And the high priest stood up in the
midst and asked Jesus, saying, "Do You
answer nothing? What *is it* these men
testify against You?" 61 But He kept silent
and answered nothing.
Again the high priest asked Him, say-
ing to Him, "Are You the Christ, the Son
of the Blessed?"
62 Jesus said, "I am. And you will see
the Son of Man sitting at the right
hand of the Power, and coming with
the clouds of heaven."
63 Then the high priest tore his clothes
and said, "What further need do we
have of witnesses? 64 You have heard
the blasphemy! What do you think?"
And they all condemned Him to be
deserving of death.
65 Then some began to spit on Him,
and to blindfold Him, and to beat Him,
and to say to Him, "Prophesy!" And the
officers struck Him with the palms of
their hands.[a]

Peter Denies Jesus, and Weeps

66 Now as Peter was below in the court-
yard, one of the servant girls of the high
priest came. 67 And when she saw Peter
warming himself, she looked at him
and said, "You also were with Jesus of
Nazareth."
68 But he denied it, saying, "I neither
know nor understand what you are say-
ing." And he went out on the porch, and
a rooster crowed.
69 And the servant girl saw him again,
and began to say to those who stood by,
"This is *one* of them." 70 But he denied
it again.

14:65 [a] NU-Text reads *received Him with slaps.*

And a little later those who stood by
said to Peter again, "Surely you are *one*
of them; for you are a Galilean, and
your speech shows *it*."[a]
71Then he began to curse and swear,
"I do not know this Man of whom you
speak!"
72A second time *the* rooster crowed.
Then Peter called to mind the word that
Jesus had said to him, "Before the roost-
er crows twice, you will deny Me three
times." And when he thought about it,
he wept.

Jesus Faces Pilate

15 Immediately, in the morning,
the chief priests held a consulta-
tion with the elders and scribes and the
whole council; and they bound Jesus,
led *Him* away, and delivered *Him* to
Pilate. 2Then Pilate asked Him, "Are
You the King of the Jews?"
He answered and said to him, "*It is*
as you say."
3And the chief priests accused Him of
many things, but He answered nothing.
4Then Pilate asked Him again, saying,
"Do You answer nothing? See how many
things they testify against You!"[a] 5But
Jesus still answered nothing, so that
Pilate marveled.

Taking the Place of Barabbas

6Now at the feast he was accustomed
to releasing one prisoner to them,
whomever they requested. 7And there
was one named Barabbas, *who was*
chained with his fellow rebels; they had
committed murder in the rebellion.
8Then the multitude, crying aloud,[a]
began to ask *him to do* just as he had
always done for them. 9But Pilate an-
swered them, saying, "Do you want me
to release to you the King of the Jews?"
10For he knew that the chief priests had
handed Him over because of envy.
11But the chief priests stirred up the
crowd, so that he should rather release
Barabbas to them. 12Pilate answered
and said to them again, "What then do
you want me to do *with Him* whom you
call the King of the Jews?"
13So they cried out again, "Crucify Him!"
14Then Pilate said to them, "Why, what
evil has He done?"
But they cried out all the more, "Cru-
cify Him!"
15So Pilate, wanting to gratify the
crowd, released Barabbas to them;
and he delivered Jesus, after he had
scourged *Him*, to be crucified.

The Soldiers Mock Jesus

16Then the soldiers led Him away into
the hall called Praetorium, and they
called together the whole garrison.
17And they clothed Him with purple;
and they twisted a crown of thorns, put
it on His *head*, 18and began to salute
Him, "Hail, King of the Jews!" 19Then
they struck Him on the head with a reed
and spat on Him; and bowing the knee,
they worshiped Him. 20And when they
had mocked Him, they took the purple
off Him, put His own clothes on Him,
and led Him out to crucify Him.

The King on a Cross

21Then they compelled a certain man,
Simon a Cyrenian, the father of Alex-
ander and Rufus, as he was coming out
of the country and passing by, to bear
His cross. 22And they brought Him to
the place Golgotha, which is translated,
Place of a Skull. 23Then they gave Him
wine mingled with myrrh to drink, but
He did not take *it*. 24And when they cru-
cified Him, they divided His garments,
casting lots for them *to determine* what
every man should take.
25Now it was the third hour, and they
crucified Him. 26And the inscription
of His accusation was written above:

THE KING OF THE JEWS.

27With Him they also crucified two rob-
bers, one on His right and the other on
His left. 28So the Scripture was fulfilled[a]
which says, "And He was numbered with
the transgressors."[b]
29And those who passed by blas-
phemed Him, wagging their heads and
saying, "Aha! *You* who destroy the temple
and build *it* in three days, 30save Your-
self, and come down from the cross!"

14:70 [a] NU-Text omits *and your speech shows it.* **15:4** [a] NU-Text reads *of which they accuse You.*
15:8 [a] NU-Text reads *going up.* **15:28** [a] Isaiah 53:12 [b] NU-Text omits this verse.

31Likewise the chief priests also, mock-
ing among themselves with the scribes,
said, "He saved others; Himself He can-
not save. 32Let the Christ, the King of
Israel, descend now from the cross, that
we may see and believe."[a]
Even those who were crucified with
Him reviled Him.

Jesus Dies on the Cross

33Now when the sixth hour had come,
there was darkness over the whole land
until the ninth hour. 34And at the ninth
hour Jesus cried out with a loud voice,
saying, "Eloi, Eloi, lama sabachthani?"
which is translated, "My God, My God,
why have You forsaken Me?"[a]
35Some of those who stood by, when
they heard *that,* said, "Look, He is call-
ing for Elijah!" 36Then someone ran
and filled a sponge full of sour wine,
put *it* on a reed, and offered *it* to Him to
drink, saying, "Let Him alone; let us see
if Elijah will come to take Him down."
37And Jesus cried out with a loud voice,
and breathed His last.
38Then the veil of the temple was torn
in two from top to bottom. 39So when
the centurion, who stood opposite Him,
saw that He cried out like this and
breathed His last,[a] he said, "Truly this
Man was the Son of God!"
40There were also women looking on
from afar, among whom were Mary
Magdalene, Mary the mother of James
the Less and of Joses, and Salome,
41who also followed Him and minis-
tered to Him when He was in Galilee,
and many other women who came up
with Him to Jerusalem.

Jesus Buried in Joseph's Tomb

42Now when evening had come, be-
cause it was the Preparation Day, that
is, the day before the Sabbath, 43Jo-
seph of Arimathea, a prominent council
member, who was himself waiting for
the kingdom of God, coming and taking
courage, went in to Pilate and asked for
the body of Jesus. 44Pilate marveled
that He was already dead; and sum-
moning the centurion, he asked him if
He had been dead for some time. 45So
when he found out from the centurion,
he granted the body to Joseph. 46Then
he bought fine linen, took Him down,
and wrapped Him in the linen. And he
laid Him in a tomb which had been
hewn out of the rock, and rolled a stone
against the door of the tomb. 47And
Mary Magdalene and Mary *the mother*
of Joses observed where He was laid.

He Is Risen

16 Now when the Sabbath was
past, Mary Magdalene, Mary *the*
mother of James, and Salome bought
spices, that they might come and anoint
Him. 2Very early in the morning, on
the first *day* of the week, they came to
the tomb when the sun had risen. 3And
they said among themselves, "Who will
roll away the stone from the door of the
tomb for us?" 4But when they looked up,
they saw that the stone had been rolled
away—for it was very large. 5And en-
tering the tomb, they saw a young man
clothed in a long white robe sitting on
the right side; and they were alarmed.
6But he said to them, "Do not be
alarmed. You seek Jesus of Nazareth,
who was crucified. He is risen! He is
not here. See the place where they laid
Him. 7But go, tell His disciples—and
Peter—that He is going before you into
Galilee; there you will see Him, as He
said to you."
8So they went out quickly[a] and fled
from the tomb, for they trembled and
were amazed. And they said nothing to
anyone, for they were afraid.

Mary Magdalene Sees the Risen Lord

9Now when *He* rose early on the first
day of the week, He appeared first to
Mary Magdalene, out of whom He had
cast seven demons. 10She went and told
those who had been with Him, as they
mourned and wept. 11And when they
heard that He was alive and had been
seen by her, they did not believe.

Jesus Appears to Two Disciples

12After that, He appeared in another
form to two of them as they walked and
went into the country. 13And they went

15:32 [a] M-Text reads *believe Him.* **15:34** [a] Psalm 22:1 **15:39** [a] NU-Text reads *that He thus breathed His last.* **16:8** [a] NU-Text and M-Text omit *quickly.*

and told *it* to the rest, *but* they did not
believe them either.

The Great Commission

14 Later He appeared to the eleven as
they sat at the table; and He rebuked
their unbelief and hardness of heart,
because they did not believe those who
had seen Him after He had risen. 15 And
He said to them, "Go into all the world
and preach the gospel to every creature.
16 He who believes and is baptized will
be saved; but he who does not believe
will be condemned. 17 And these signs
will follow those who believe: In My
name they will cast out demons; they
will speak with new tongues; 18 they[a]
will take up serpents; and if they drink
anything deadly, it will by no means
hurt them; they will lay hands on the
sick, and they will recover."

Christ Ascends to God's Right Hand

19 So then, after the Lord had spoken
to them, He was received up into heav-
en, and sat down at the right hand of
God. 20 And they went out and preached
everywhere, the Lord working with *them*
and confirming the word through the
accompanying signs. Amen.[a]

16:18 [a] NU-Text reads *and in their hands they will.* **16:20** [a] Verses 9–20 are bracketed in NU-Text as not original. They are lacking in Codex Sinaiticus and Codex Vaticanus, although nearly all other manuscripts of Mark contain them.

THE GOSPEL ACCORDING TO
LUKE

Luke, a physician, writes his Gospel with great precision and detail. His goal is to show that Jesus is the Son of Man who came not just for Israel, but for the entire world. This goal is seen in how Luke shows Jesus loving and reaching out to all sorts of people. Luke focuses more on the women who took part in Jesus' story, as well as the poor, outsiders, and even children. As Luke shows that Jesus came for all sorts of people, he also shows how people responded differently to Him. While some grew in belief of Jesus, others grew in opposition. This opposition would continue until Jesus was placed on a cross.

- **GENRE:** Gospel
- **AUTHOR:** Luke
- **TIME:** c. 6 BC–AD 33 (written c. AD 60–61)
- **PURPOSE:** To show a primarily Greek audience that Jesus is the Son of Man.

Dedication to Theophilus

1 Inasmuch as many have taken in
hand to set in order a narrative of
those things which have been fulfilled[a]
among us, 2just as those who from the
beginning were eyewitnesses and min-
isters of the word delivered them to
us, 3it seemed good to me also, hav-
ing had perfect understanding of all
things from the very first, to write to
you an orderly account, most excellent
Theophilus, 4that you may know the
certainty of those things in which you
were instructed.

John's Birth Announced to Zacharias

5There was in the days of Herod, the
king of Judea, a certain priest named
Zacharias, of the division of Abijah. His
wife *was* of the daughters of Aaron, and
her name *was* Elizabeth. 6And they were
both righteous before God, walking in
all the commandments and ordinances
of the Lord blameless. 7But they had no
child, because Elizabeth was barren,
and they were both well advanced in
years.

8So it was, that while he was serving
as priest before God in the order of his
division, 9according to the custom of
the priesthood, his lot fell to burn in-
cense when he went into the temple of
the Lord. 10And the whole multitude
of the people was praying outside at
the hour of incense. 11Then an angel
of the Lord appeared to him, standing
on the right side of the altar of incense.
12And when Zacharias saw *him,* he was
troubled, and fear fell upon him.

13But the angel said to him, "Do not
be afraid, Zacharias, for your prayer
is heard; and your wife Elizabeth will
bear you a son, and you shall call his
name John. 14And you will have joy
and gladness, and many will rejoice
at his birth. 15For he will be great in
the sight of the Lord, and shall drink
neither wine nor strong drink. He will
also be filled with the Holy Spirit, even
from his mother's womb. 16And he will
turn many of the children of Israel to
the Lord their God. 17He will also go
before Him in the spirit and power of
Elijah, 'to turn the hearts of the fathers
to the children,'[a] and the disobedient to
the wisdom of the just, to make ready a
people prepared for the Lord."

18And Zacharias said to the angel,
"How shall I know this? For I am an
old man, and my wife is well advanced
in years."

19And the angel answered and said to
him, "I am Gabriel, who stands in the
presence of God, and was sent to speak
to you and bring you these glad tidings.
20But behold, you will be mute and not

1:1 [a] Or *are most surely believed* 1:17 [a] Malachi 4:5, 6

able to speak until the day these things
take place, because you did not believe
my words which will be fulfilled in their
own time."

21And the people waited for Zacharias,
and marveled that he lingered so long
in the temple. 22But when he came out,
he could not speak to them; and they
perceived that he had seen a vision in
the temple, for he beckoned to them
and remained speechless.

23So it was, as soon as the days of his
service were completed, that he depart-
ed to his own house. 24Now after those
days his wife Elizabeth conceived; and
she hid herself five months, saying,
25"Thus the Lord has dealt with me, in
the days when He looked on *me,* to take
away my reproach among people."

Christ's Birth Announced to Mary

26Now in the sixth month the angel Ga-
briel was sent by God to a city of Galilee
named Nazareth, 27to a virgin betrothed
to a man whose name was Joseph, of the
house of David. The virgin's name *was*
Mary. 28And having come in, the angel
said to her, "Rejoice, highly favored *one,*
the Lord *is* with you; blessed *are* you
among women!"[a]

29But when she saw *him,*[a] she was trou-
bled at his saying, and considered what
manner of greeting this was. 30Then
the angel said to her, "Do not be afraid,
Mary, for you have found favor with
God. 31And behold, you will conceive in
your womb and bring forth a Son, and
shall call His name JESUS. 32He will be
great, and will be called the Son of the
Highest; and the Lord God will give Him
the throne of His father David. 33And He
will reign over the house of Jacob forever,
and of His kingdom there will be no end."

34Then Mary said to the angel, "How
can this be, since I do not know a man?"

35And the angel answered and said to
her, "*The* Holy Spirit will come upon you,
and the power of the Highest will over-
shadow you; therefore, also, that Holy
One who is to be born will be called the
Son of God. 36Now indeed, Elizabeth your
relative has also conceived a son in her
old age; and this is now the sixth month
for her who was called barren. 37For with
God nothing will be impossible."

38Then Mary said, "Behold the maid-
servant of the Lord! Let it be to me ac-
cording to your word." And the angel
departed from her.

Mary Visits Elizabeth

39Now Mary arose in those days and
went into the hill country with haste, to a
city of Judah, 40and entered the house of
Zacharias and greeted Elizabeth. 41And
it happened, when Elizabeth heard the
greeting of Mary, that the babe leaped in
her womb; and Elizabeth was filled with
the Holy Spirit. 42Then she spoke out with
a loud voice and said, "Blessed *are* you
among women, and blessed *is* the fruit of
your womb! 43But why *is* this *granted* to
me, that the mother of my Lord should
come to me? 44For indeed, as soon as
the voice of your greeting sounded in
my ears, the babe leaped in my womb
for joy. 45Blessed *is* she who believed, for
there will be a fulfillment of those things
which were told her from the Lord."

The Song of Mary

46And Mary said:

"My soul magnifies the Lord,
47 And my spirit has rejoiced in God
my Savior.
48 For He has regarded the lowly
state of His maidservant;
For behold, henceforth all
generations will call me
blessed.
49 For He who is mighty has done
great things for me,
And holy *is* His name.
50 And His mercy *is* on those who
fear Him
From generation to generation.
51 He has shown strength with His
arm;
He has scattered *the* proud in the
imagination of their hearts.
52 He has put down the mighty from
their thrones,
And exalted *the* lowly.
53 He has filled *the* hungry with
good things,

1:28 [a] NU-Text omits *blessed are you among women.* 1:29 [a] NU-Text omits *when she saw him.*

And *the* rich He has sent away
empty.
54 He has helped His servant Israel,
In remembrance of *His* mercy,
55 As He spoke to our fathers,
To Abraham and to his seed
forever."

56And Mary remained with her about
three months, and returned to her
house.

Birth of John the Baptist

57Now Elizabeth's full time came for her
to be delivered, and she brought forth a
son. 58When her neighbors and relatives
heard how the Lord had shown great
mercy to her, they rejoiced with her.

Circumcision of John the Baptist

59So it was, on the eighth day, that
they came to circumcise the child; and
they would have called him by the name
of his father, Zacharias. 60His mother
answered and said, "No; he shall be
called John."

61But they said to her, "There is no one
among your relatives who is called by
this name." 62So they made signs to his
father—what he would have him called.

63And he asked for a writing tablet,
and wrote, saying, "His name is John."
So they all marveled. 64Immediately
his mouth was opened and his tongue
loosed, and he spoke, praising God.
65Then fear came on all who dwelt
around them; and all these sayings
were discussed throughout all the hill
country of Judea. 66And all those who
heard *them* kept *them* in their hearts,
saying, "What kind of child will this be?"
And the hand of the Lord was with him.

Zacharias' Prophecy

67Now his father Zacharias was filled
with the Holy Spirit, and prophesied,
saying:

68 "Blessed *is* the Lord God of Israel,
For He has visited and redeemed
His people,
69 And has raised up a horn of
salvation for us
In the house of His servant David,
70 As He spoke by the mouth of His
holy prophets,
Who *have been* since the world
began,
71 That we should be saved from our
enemies
And from the hand of all who
hate us,
72 To perform the mercy *promised* to
our fathers
And to remember His holy
covenant,
73 The oath which He swore to our
father Abraham:
74 To grant us that we,
Being delivered from the hand of
our enemies,
Might serve Him without fear,
75 In holiness and righteousness
before Him all the days of
our life.

76 "And you, child, will be called the
prophet of the Highest;
For you will go before the face of
the Lord to prepare His ways,
77 To give knowledge of salvation to
His people
By the remission of their sins,
78 Through the tender mercy of our
God,
With which the Dayspring from
on high has visited[a] us;
79 To give light to those who sit in
darkness and the shadow of
death,
To guide our feet into the way of
peace."

80So the child grew and became strong
in spirit, and was in the deserts till the
day of his manifestation to Israel.

Christ Born of Mary

2 And it came to pass in those days
that a decree went out from Caesar
Augustus that all the world should be
registered. 2This census first took place
while Quirinius was governing Syria.
3So all went to be registered, everyone
to his own city.
4Joseph also went up from Galilee, out

1:78 [a] NU-Text reads *shall visit.*

of the city of Nazareth, into Judea, to
the city of David, which is called Beth-
lehem, because he was of the house and
lineage of David, 5to be registered with
Mary, his betrothed wife,[a] who was with
child. 6So it was, that while they were
there, the days were completed for her
to be delivered. 7And she brought forth
her firstborn Son, and wrapped Him
in swaddling cloths, and laid Him in
a manger, because there was no room
for them in the inn.

Glory in the Highest

8Now there were in the same country
shepherds living out in the fields, keep-
ing watch over their flock by night. 9And
behold,[a] an angel of the Lord stood be-
fore them, and the glory of the Lord
shone around them, and they were
greatly afraid. 10Then the angel said
to them, "Do not be afraid, for behold,
I bring you good tidings of great joy
which will be to all people. 11For there
is born to you this day in the city of
David a Savior, who is Christ the Lord.
12And this *will be* the sign to you: You
will find a Babe wrapped in swaddling
cloths, lying in a manger."
13And suddenly there was with the
angel a multitude of the heavenly host
praising God and saying:

14 "Glory to God in the highest,
And on earth peace, goodwill
toward men!"[a]

15So it was, when the angels had gone
away from them into heaven, that the
shepherds said to one another, "Let us
now go to Bethlehem and see this thing
that has come to pass, which the Lord
has made known to us." 16And they came
with haste and found Mary and Joseph,
and the Babe lying in a manger. 17Now
when they had seen *Him,* they made
widely[a] known the saying which was
told them concerning this Child. 18And
all those who heard *it* marveled at those
things which were told them by the shep-
herds. 19But Mary kept all these things
and pondered *them* in her heart. 20Then
the shepherds returned, glorifying and
praising God for all the things that they
had heard and seen, as it was told them.

Circumcision of Jesus

21And when eight days were completed
for the circumcision of the Child,[a] His
name was called JESUS, the name given
by the angel before He was conceived
in the womb.

Jesus Presented in the Temple

22Now when the days of her purifi-
cation according to the law of Moses
were completed, they brought Him to
Jerusalem to present *Him* to the Lord
23(as it is written in the law of the Lord,
"Every male who opens the womb shall
be called holy to the LORD"),[a] 24and to
offer a sacrifice according to what is
said in the law of the Lord, "A pair of
turtledoves or two young pigeons."[a]

Simeon Sees God's Salvation

25And behold, there was a man in Je-
rusalem whose name *was* Simeon, and
this man *was* just and devout, waiting
for the Consolation of Israel, and the
Holy Spirit was upon him. 26And it had
been revealed to him by the Holy Spirit
that he would not see death before he
had seen the Lord's Christ. 27So he came
by the Spirit into the temple. And when
the parents brought in the Child Jesus,
to do for Him according to the custom
of the law, 28he took Him up in his arms
and blessed God and said:

29 "Lord, now You are letting Your
servant depart in peace,
According to Your word;
30 For my eyes have seen Your
salvation
31 Which You have prepared before
the face of all peoples,
32 A light to *bring* revelation to the
Gentiles,
And the glory of Your people
Israel."

33And Joseph and His mother[a] mar-
veled at those things which were spoken

2:5 [a] NU-Text omits *wife.* 2:9 [a] NU-Text omits *behold.* 2:14 [a] NU-Text reads *toward men of goodwill.* 2:17 [a] NU-Text omits *widely.* 2:21 [a] NU-Text reads *for His circumcision.* 2:23 [a] Exodus 13:2, 12, 15 2:24 [a] Leviticus 12:8 2:33 [a] NU-Text reads *And His father and mother.*

of Him. 34Then Simeon blessed them, and said to Mary His mother, "Behold, this *Child* is destined for the fall and rising of many in Israel, and for a sign which will be spoken against 35(yes, a sword will pierce through your own soul also), that the thoughts of many hearts may be revealed."

Anna Bears Witness to the Redeemer

36Now there was one, Anna, a prophetess, the daughter of Phanuel, of the tribe of Asher. She was of a great age, and had lived with a husband seven years from her virginity; 37and this woman *was* a widow of about eighty-four years,[a] who did not depart from the temple, but served *God* with fastings and prayers night and day. 38And coming in that instant she gave thanks to the Lord,[a] and spoke of Him to all those who looked for redemption in Jerusalem.

The Family Returns to Nazareth

39So when they had performed all things according to the law of the Lord, they returned to Galilee, to their *own* city, Nazareth. 40And the Child grew and became strong in spirit,[a] filled with wisdom; and the grace of God was upon Him.

The Boy Jesus Amazes the Scholars

41His parents went to Jerusalem every year at the Feast of the Passover. 42And when He was twelve years old, they went up to Jerusalem according to the custom of the feast. 43When they had finished the days, as they returned, the Boy Jesus lingered behind in Jerusalem. And Joseph and His mother[a] did not know *it;* 44but supposing Him to have been in the company, they went a day's journey, and sought Him among *their* relatives and acquaintances. 45So when they did not find Him, they returned to Jerusalem, seeking Him. 46Now so it was *that* after three days they found Him in the temple, sitting in the midst of the teachers, both listening to them and asking them questions. 47And all who heard Him were astonished at His understanding and answers. 48So when they saw Him, they were amazed; and His mother said to Him, "Son, why have You done this to us? Look, Your father and I have sought You anxiously."

49And He said to them, "Why did you seek Me? Did you not know that I must be about My Father's business?" 50But they did not understand the statement which He spoke to them.

Jesus Advances in Wisdom and Favor

51Then He went down with them and came to Nazareth, and was subject to them, but His mother kept all these things in her heart. 52And Jesus increased in wisdom and stature, and in favor with God and men.

John the Baptist Prepares the Way

3 Now in the fifteenth year of the reign of Tiberius Caesar, Pontius Pilate being governor of Judea, Herod being tetrarch of Galilee, his brother Philip tetrarch of Iturea and the region of Trachonitis, and Lysanias tetrarch of Abilene, 2while Annas and Caiaphas were high priests,[a] the word of God came to John the son of Zacharias in the wilderness. 3And he went into all the region around the Jordan, preaching a baptism of repentance for the remission of sins, 4as it is written in the book of the words of Isaiah the prophet, saying:

"The voice of one crying in the
 wilderness:
'Prepare the way of the LORD;
Make His paths straight.
5 Every valley shall be filled
And every mountain and hill
 brought low;
The crooked places shall be made
 straight
And the rough ways smooth;
6 And all flesh shall see the
 salvation of God.' "[a]

John Preaches to the People

7Then he said to the multitudes that came out to be baptized by him, "Brood of vipers! Who warned you to flee from

2:37 [a] NU-Text reads *a widow until she was eighty-four.* 2:38 [a] NU-Text reads *to God.* 2:40 [a] NU-Text omits *in spirit.* 2:43 [a] NU-Text reads *And His parents.* 3:2 [a] NU-Text and M-Text read *in the high priesthood of Annas and Caiaphas.* 3:6 [a] Isaiah 40:3–5

the wrath to come? 8Therefore bear
fruits worthy of repentance, and do
not begin to say to yourselves, 'We have
Abraham as *our* father.' For I say to you
that God is able to raise up children
to Abraham from these stones. 9And
even now the ax is laid to the root of
the trees. Therefore every tree which
does not bear good fruit is cut down
and thrown into the fire."
10So the people asked him, saying,
"What shall we do then?"
11He answered and said to them, "He
who has two tunics, let him give to him
who has none; and he who has food, let
him do likewise."
12Then tax collectors also came to be
baptized, and said to him, "Teacher,
what shall we do?"
13And he said to them, "Collect no
more than what is appointed for you."
14Likewise the soldiers asked him, say-
ing, "And what shall we do?"
So he said to them, "Do not intimidate
anyone or accuse falsely, and be con-
tent with your wages."
15Now as the people were in expecta-
tion, and all reasoned in their hearts
about John, whether he was the Christ
or not, 16John answered, saying to all,
"I indeed baptize you with water; but
One mightier than I is coming, whose
sandal strap I am not worthy to loose.
He will baptize you with the Holy Spirit
and fire. 17His winnowing fan *is* in His
hand, and He will thoroughly clean
out His threshing floor, and gather the
wheat into His barn; but the chaff He
will burn with unquenchable fire."
18And with many other exhortations
he preached to the people. 19But Herod
the tetrarch, being rebuked by him con-
cerning Herodias, his brother Philip's
wife,[a] and for all the evils which Herod
had done, 20also added this, above all,
that he shut John up in prison.

John Baptizes Jesus

21When all the people were baptized,
it came to pass that Jesus also was bap-
tized; and while He prayed, the heaven
was opened. 22And the Holy Spirit de-
scended in bodily form like a dove upon
Him, and a voice came from heaven
which said, "You are My beloved Son;
in You I am well pleased."

The Genealogy of Jesus Christ

23Now Jesus Himself began *His minis-
try at* about thirty years of age, being (as
was supposed) *the* son of Joseph, *the son*
of Heli, 24*the son* of Matthat,[a] *the son* of
Levi, *the son* of Melchi, *the son* of Janna,
the son of Joseph, 25*the son* of Mattathi-
ah, *the son* of Amos, *the son* of Nahum,
the son of Esli, *the son* of Naggai, 26*the
son* of Maath, *the son* of Mattathiah, *the
son* of Semei, *the son* of Joseph, *the son*
of Judah, 27*the son* of Joannas, *the son*
of Rhesa, *the son* of Zerubbabel, *the
son* of Shealtiel, *the son* of Neri, 28*the
son* of Melchi, *the son* of Addi, *the son* of
Cosam, *the son* of Elmodam, *the son* of
Er, 29*the son* of Jose, *the son* of Eliezer,
the son of Jorim, *the son* of Matthat, *the
son* of Levi, 30*the son* of Simeon, *the
son* of Judah, *the son* of Joseph, *the son*
of Jonan, *the son* of Eliakim, 31*the son*
of Melea, *the son* of Menan, *the son* of
Mattathah, *the son* of Nathan, *the son* of
David, 32*the son* of Jesse, *the son* of Obed,
the son of Boaz, *the son* of Salmon, *the
son* of Nahshon, 33*the son* of Ammina-
dab, *the son* of Ram, *the son* of Hezron,
the son of Perez, *the son* of Judah, 34*the
son* of Jacob, *the son* of Isaac, *the son*
of Abraham, *the son* of Terah, *the son*
of Nahor, 35*the son* of Serug, *the son* of
Reu, *the son* of Peleg, *the son* of Eber, *the
son* of Shelah, 36*the son* of Cainan, *the
son* of Arphaxad, *the son* of Shem,
the son of Noah, *the son* of Lamech, 37*the
son* of Methuselah, *the son* of Enoch, *the
son* of Jared, *the son* of Mahalalel, *the son*
of Cainan, 38*the son* of Enosh, *the son* of
Seth, *the son* of Adam, *the son* of God.

Satan Tempts Jesus

4 Then Jesus, being filled with the
Holy Spirit, returned from the Jor-
dan and was led by the Spirit into[a] the
wilderness, 2being tempted for forty

3:19 [a] NU-Text reads *his brother's wife.* **3:24** [a] This and several other names in the genealogy are spelled somewhat differently in the NU-Text. Since the New King James Version uses the Old Testament spelling for persons mentioned in the New Testament, these variations, which come from the Greek, have not been footnoted. **4:1** [a] NU-Text reads *in.*

days by the devil. And in those days He
ate nothing, and afterward, when they
had ended, He was hungry.
3And the devil said to Him, "If You are
the Son of God, command this stone to
become bread."
4But Jesus answered him, saying,[a] "It
is written, 'Man shall not live by bread
alone, but by every word of God.' "[b]
5Then the devil, taking Him up on a
high mountain, showed Him[a] all the
kingdoms of the world in a moment
of time. 6And the devil said to Him,
"All this authority I will give You, and
their glory; for *this* has been delivered
to me, and I give it to whomever I wish.
7Therefore, if You will worship before
me, all will be Yours."
8And Jesus answered and said to him,
"Get behind Me, Satan![a] For[b] it is writ-
ten, 'You shall worship the LORD your
God, and Him only you shall serve.' "[c]
9Then he brought Him to Jerusalem,
set Him on the pinnacle of the temple,
and said to Him, "If You are the Son of
God, throw Yourself down from here.
10For it is written:

'He shall give His angels charge
over you,
To keep you,'

11and,

'In *their* hands they shall bear
you up,
Lest you dash your foot against a
stone.' "[a]

12And Jesus answered and said to him,
"It has been said, 'You shall not tempt
the LORD your God.' "[a]
13Now when the devil had ended every
temptation, he departed from Him until
an opportune time.

Jesus Begins His Galilean Ministry

14Then Jesus returned in the power of
the Spirit to Galilee, and news of Him
went out through all the surrounding
region. 15And He taught in their syna-
gogues, being glorified by all.

Jesus Rejected at Nazareth

16So He came to Nazareth, where He
had been brought up. And as His cus-
tom was, He went into the synagogue
on the Sabbath day, and stood up to
read. 17And He was handed the book of
the prophet Isaiah. And when He had
opened the book, He found the place
where it was written:

18 "The Spirit of the LORD *is* upon Me,
Because He has anointed Me
To preach the gospel to *the* poor;
He has sent Me to heal the
brokenhearted,[a]
To proclaim liberty to *the* captives
And recovery of sight to *the* blind,
To set at liberty those who are
oppressed;
19 To proclaim the acceptable year
of the LORD."[a]

20Then He closed the book, and gave
it back to the attendant and sat down.
And the eyes of all who were in the syn-
agogue were fixed on Him. 21And He
began to say to them, "Today this Scrip-
ture is fulfilled in your hearing." 22So
all bore witness to Him, and marveled
at the gracious words which proceeded
out of His mouth. And they said, "Is this
not Joseph's son?"
23He said to them, "You will surely
say this proverb to Me, 'Physician, heal
yourself! Whatever we have heard done
in Capernaum,[a] do also here in Your
country.' " 24Then He said, "Assuredly,
I say to you, no prophet is accepted in
his own country. 25But I tell you truly,
many widows were in Israel in the days
of Elijah, when the heaven was shut up
three years and six months, and there
was a great famine throughout all the
land; 26but to none of them was Elijah
sent except to Zarephath,[a] *in the region*
of Sidon, to a woman *who was* a widow.
27And many lepers were in Israel in the

4:4 [a] Deuteronomy 8:3 [b] NU-Text omits *but by every word of God.* **4:5** [a] NU-Text reads *And taking Him up, he showed Him.* **4:8** [a] NU-Text omits *Get behind Me, Satan.* [b] NU-Text and M-Text omit *For.* [c] Deuteronomy 6:13 **4:11** [a] Psalm 91:11, 12 **4:12** [a] Deuteronomy 6:16 **4:18** [a] NU-Text omits *to heal the brokenhearted.* **4:19** [a] Isaiah 61:1, 2 **4:23** [a] Here and elsewhere the NU-Text spelling is *Capharnaum.* **4:26** [a] Greek *Sarepta*

time of Elisha the prophet, and none
of them was cleansed except Naaman
the Syrian."
28So all those in the synagogue, when
they heard these things, were filled with
wrath, 29and rose up and thrust Him
out of the city; and they led Him to the
brow of the hill on which their city was
built, that they might throw Him down
over the cliff. 30Then passing through
the midst of them, He went His way.

Jesus Casts Out an Unclean Spirit

31Then He went down to Capernaum, a
city of Galilee, and was teaching them
on the Sabbaths. 32And they were as-
tonished at His teaching, for His word
was with authority. 33Now in the syn-
agogue there was a man who had a
spirit of an unclean demon. And he
cried out with a loud voice, 34saying,
"Let *us* alone! What have we to do with
You, Jesus of Nazareth? Did You come
to destroy us? I know who You are—the
Holy One of God!"
35But Jesus rebuked him, saying, "Be
quiet, and come out of him!" And when
the demon had thrown him in *their*
midst, it came out of him and did not
hurt him. 36Then they were all amazed
and spoke among themselves, saying,
"What a word this *is!* For with authority
and power He commands the unclean
spirits, and they come out." 37And the
report about Him went out into every
place in the surrounding region.

Peter's Mother-in-Law Healed

38Now He arose from the synagogue
and entered Simon's house. But Si-
mon's wife's mother was sick with a
high fever, and they made request of
Him concerning her. 39So He stood over
her and rebuked the fever, and it left
her. And immediately she arose and
served them.

Many Healed After Sabbath Sunset

40When the sun was setting, all those
who had any that were sick with various
diseases brought them to Him; and He
laid His hands on every one of them and
healed them. 41And demons also came
out of many, crying out and saying,
"You are the Christ,[a] the Son of God!"
And He, rebuking *them,* did not allow
them to speak, for they knew that He
was the Christ.

Jesus Preaches in Galilee

42Now when it was day, He departed
and went into a deserted place. And the
crowd sought Him and came to Him,
and tried to keep Him from leaving
them; 43but He said to them, "I must
preach the kingdom of God to the other
cities also, because for this purpose I
have been sent." 44And He was preach-
ing in the synagogues of Galilee.[a]

Four Fishermen Called as Disciples

5 So it was, as the multitude pressed
about Him to hear the word of God,
that He stood by the Lake of Gennesaret,
2and saw two boats standing by the lake;
but the fishermen had gone from them
and were washing *their* nets. 3Then He
got into one of the boats, which was Si-
mon's, and asked him to put out a little
from the land. And He sat down and
taught the multitudes from the boat.
4When He had stopped speaking, He
said to Simon, "Launch out into the
deep and let down your nets for a catch."
5But Simon answered and said to
Him, "Master, we have toiled all night
and caught nothing; nevertheless at
Your word I will let down the net." 6And
when they had done this, they caught
a great number of fish, and their net
was breaking. 7So they signaled to *their*
partners in the other boat to come and
help them. And they came and filled
both the boats, so that they began to
sink. 8When Simon Peter saw *it,* he fell
down at Jesus' knees, saying, "Depart
from me, for I am a sinful man, O Lord!"
9For he and all who were with him
were astonished at the catch of fish
which they had taken; 10and so also
were James and John, the sons of Zebe-
dee, who were partners with Simon. And
Jesus said to Simon, "Do not be afraid.
From now on you will catch men." 11So
when they had brought their boats to
land, they forsook all and followed Him.

4:41 [a] NU-Text omits *the Christ.* **4:44** [a] NU-Text reads *Judea.*

Jesus Cleanses a Leper

12 And it happened when He was in a
certain city, that behold, a man who
was full of leprosy saw Jesus; and he fell
on *his* face and implored Him, saying,
"Lord, if You are willing, You can make
me clean."
13 Then He put out *His* hand and
touched him, saying, "I am willing; be
cleansed." Immediately the leprosy left
him. 14 And He charged him to tell no
one, "But go and show yourself to the
priest, and make an offering for your
cleansing, as a testimony to them, just
as Moses commanded."
15 However, the report went around
concerning Him all the more; and great
multitudes came together to hear, and
to be healed by Him of their infirmities.
16 So He Himself *often* withdrew into the
wilderness and prayed.

Jesus Forgives and Heals a Paralytic

17 Now it happened on a certain day, as
He was teaching, that there were Phar-
isees and teachers of the law sitting
by, who had come out of every town of
Galilee, Judea, and Jerusalem. And the
power of the Lord was *present* to heal
them.[a] 18 Then behold, men brought
on a bed a man who was paralyzed,
whom they sought to bring in and lay
before Him. 19 And when they could
not find how they might bring him in,
because of the crowd, they went up on
the housetop and let him down with *his*
bed through the tiling into the midst
before Jesus.
20 When He saw their faith, He said to
him, "Man, your sins are forgiven you."
21 And the scribes and the Pharisees
began to reason, saying, "Who is this
who speaks blasphemies? Who can for-
give sins but God alone?"
22 But when Jesus perceived their
thoughts, He answered and said to
them, "Why are you reasoning in your
hearts? 23 Which is easier, to say, 'Your
sins are forgiven you,' or to say, 'Rise
up and walk'? 24 But that you may know
that the Son of Man has power on earth
to forgive sins"—He said to the man who
was paralyzed, "I say to you, arise, take
up your bed, and go to your house."
25 Immediately he rose up before them,
took up what he had been lying on, and
departed to his own house, glorifying
God. 26 And they were all amazed, and
they glorified God and were filled with
fear, saying, "We have seen strange
things today!"

Matthew the Tax Collector

27 After these things He went out and
saw a tax collector named Levi, sitting
at the tax office. And He said to him,
"Follow Me." 28 So he left all, rose up,
and followed Him.
29 Then Levi gave Him a great feast in
his own house. And there were a great
number of tax collectors and others
who sat down with them. 30 And their
scribes and the Pharisees[a] complained
against His disciples, saying, "Why do
You eat and drink with tax collectors
and sinners?"
31 Jesus answered and said to them,
"Those who are well have no need of a
physician, but those who are sick. 32 I
have not come to call *the* righteous, but
sinners, to repentance."

Jesus Is Questioned About Fasting

33 Then they said to Him, "Why do[a] the
disciples of John fast often and make
prayers, and likewise those of the Phar-
isees, but Yours eat and drink?"
34 And He said to them, "Can you make
the friends of the bridegroom fast while
the bridegroom is with them? 35 But the
days will come when the bridegroom
will be taken away from them; then
they will fast in those days."
36 Then He spoke a parable to them:
"No one puts a piece from a new gar-
ment on an old one;[a] otherwise the
new makes a tear, and also the piece
that was *taken* out of the new does not
match the old. 37 And no one puts new
wine into old wineskins; or else the new
wine will burst the wineskins and be
spilled, and the wineskins will be ruined.
38 But new wine must be put into new
wineskins, and both are preserved.[a]

5:17 [a] NU-Text reads *present with Him to heal.* **5:30** [a] NU-Text reads *But the Pharisees and their scribes.* **5:33** [a] NU-Text omits *Why do,* making the verse a statement. **5:36** [a] NU-Text reads *No one tears a piece from a new garment and puts it on an old one.* **5:38** [a] NU-Text omits *and both are preserved.*

39And no one, having drunk old *wine,*
immediately[a] desires new; for he says,
'The old is better.' "[b]

Jesus Is Lord of the Sabbath

6 Now it happened on the second Sab-
bath after the first[a] that He went
through the grainfields. And His disci-
ples plucked the heads of grain and ate
them, rubbing *them* in *their* hands. 2And
some of the Pharisees said to them,
"Why are you doing what is not lawful
to do on the Sabbath?"
3But Jesus answering them said, "Have
you not even read this, what David did
when he was hungry, he and those who
were with him: 4how he went into the
house of God, took and ate the show-
bread, and also gave some to those
with him, which is not lawful for any
but the priests to eat?" 5And He said to
them, "The Son of Man is also Lord of
the Sabbath."

Healing on the Sabbath

6Now it happened on another Sab-
bath, also, that He entered the syn-
agogue and taught. And a man was
there whose right hand was withered.
7So the scribes and Pharisees watched
Him closely, whether He would heal on
the Sabbath, that they might find an
accusation against Him. 8But He knew
their thoughts, and said to the man who
had the withered hand, "Arise and stand
here." And he arose and stood. 9Then
Jesus said to them, "I will ask you one
thing: Is it lawful on the Sabbath to
do good or to do evil, to save life or to
destroy?"[a] 10And when He had looked
around at them all, He said to the man,[a]
"Stretch out your hand." And he did so,
and his hand was restored as whole as
the other.[b] 11But they were filled with
rage, and discussed with one another
what they might do to Jesus.

The Twelve Apostles

12Now it came to pass in those days
that He went out to the mountain to
pray, and continued all night in prayer
to God. 13And when it was day, He called
His disciples to *Himself;* and from them
He chose twelve whom He also named
apostles: 14Simon, whom He also named
Peter, and Andrew his brother; James
and John; Philip and Bartholomew;
15Matthew and Thomas; James the *son*
of Alphaeus, and Simon called the Zeal-
ot; 16Judas *the son* of James, and Judas
Iscariot who also became a traitor.

Jesus Heals a Great Multitude

17And He came down with them and
stood on a level place with a crowd of
His disciples and a great multitude of
people from all Judea and Jerusalem,
and from the seacoast of Tyre and
Sidon, who came to hear Him and be
healed of their diseases, 18as well as
those who were tormented with unclean
spirits. And they were healed. 19And
the whole multitude sought to touch
Him, for power went out from Him and
healed *them* all.

The Beatitudes

20Then He lifted up His eyes toward
His disciples, and said:

"Blessed *are you* poor,
For yours is the kingdom of
God.
21 Blessed *are you* who hunger now,
For you shall be filled.
Blessed *are you* who weep now,
For you shall laugh.
22 Blessed are you when men hate
you,
And when they exclude you,
And revile *you,* and cast out
your name as evil,
For the Son of Man's sake.
23 Rejoice in that day and leap for
joy!
For indeed your reward *is* great
in heaven,
For in like manner their fathers
did to the prophets.

Jesus Pronounces Woes

24 "But woe to you who are rich,
For you have received your
consolation.

5:39 [a] NU-Text omits *immediately.* [b] NU-Text reads *good.* **6:1** [a] NU-Text reads *on a Sabbath.*
6:9 [a] M-Text reads *to kill.* **6:10** [a] NU-Text and M-Text read *to him.* [b] NU-Text omits *as whole as the other.*

25 Woe to you who are full,
For you shall hunger.
Woe to you who laugh now,
For you shall mourn and weep.
26 Woe to you[a] when all[b] men speak
well of you,
For so did their fathers to the
false prophets.

Love Your Enemies

27"But I say to you who hear: Love
your enemies, do good to those who
hate you, 28bless those who curse you,
and pray for those who spitefully use
you. 29To him who strikes you on the
one cheek, offer the other also. And from
him who takes away your cloak, do not
withhold *your* tunic either. 30Give to
everyone who asks of you. And from
him who takes away your goods do
not ask *them* back. 31And just as you
want men to do to you, you also do to
them likewise.
32"But if you love those who love you,
what credit is that to you? For even sin-
ners love those who love them. 33And
if you do good to those who do good to
you, what credit is that to you? For even
sinners do the same. 34And if you lend
to those from whom you hope to receive
back, what credit is that to you? For
even sinners lend to sinners to receive
as much back. 35But love your enemies,
do good, and lend, hoping for nothing
in return; and your reward will be great,
and you will be sons of the Most High.
For He is kind to the unthankful and
evil. 36Therefore be merciful, just as
your Father also is merciful.

Do Not Judge

37"Judge not, and you shall not be
judged. Condemn not, and you shall
not be condemned. Forgive, and you
will be forgiven. 38Give, and it will be
given to you: good measure, pressed
down, shaken together, and running
over will be put into your bosom. For
with the same measure that you use, it
will be measured back to you."
39And He spoke a parable to them:
"Can the blind lead the blind? Will they
not both fall into the ditch? 40A disciple
is not above his teacher, but everyone
who is perfectly trained will be like his
teacher. 41And why do you look at the
speck in your brother's eye, but do not
perceive the plank in your own eye?
42Or how can you say to your brother,
'Brother, let me remove the speck that
is in your eye,' when you yourself do
not see the plank that *is* in your own
eye? Hypocrite! First remove the plank
from your own eye, and then you will
see clearly to remove the speck that is
in your brother's eye.

A Tree Is Known by Its Fruit

43"For a good tree does not bear bad
fruit, nor does a bad tree bear good
fruit. 44For every tree is known by its
own fruit. For *men* do not gather figs
from thorns, nor do they gather grapes
from a bramble bush. 45A good man out
of the good treasure of his heart brings
forth good; and an evil man out of the
evil treasure of his heart[a] brings forth
evil. For out of the abundance of the
heart his mouth speaks.

Build on the Rock

46"But why do you call Me 'Lord,
Lord,' and not do the things which I
say? 47Whoever comes to Me, and hears
My sayings and does them, I will show
you whom he is like: 48He is like a man
building a house, who dug deep and
laid the foundation on the rock. And
when the flood arose, the stream beat
vehemently against that house, and
could not shake it, for it was founded
on the rock.[a] 49But he who heard and
did nothing is like a man who built a
house on the earth without a founda-
tion, against which the stream beat
vehemently; and immediately it fell.[a]
And the ruin of that house was great."

Jesus Heals a Centurion's Servant

7 Now when He concluded all His say-
ings in the hearing of the people,
He entered Capernaum. 2And a certain
centurion's servant, who was dear to
him, was sick and ready to die. 3So when
he heard about Jesus, he sent elders of
the Jews to Him, pleading with Him to

6:26 [a] NU-Text and M-Text omit *to you.* [b] M-Text omits *all.* 6:45 [a] NU-Text omits *treasure of his heart.* 6:48 [a] NU-Text reads *for it was well built.* 6:49 [a] NU-Text reads *collapsed.*

come and heal his servant. 4And when
they came to Jesus, they begged Him
earnestly, saying that the one for whom
He should do this was deserving, 5"for
he loves our nation, and has built us a
synagogue."
6Then Jesus went with them. And when
He was already not far from the house,
the centurion sent friends to Him,
saying to Him, "Lord, do not trouble
Yourself, for I am not worthy that You
should enter under my roof. 7Therefore
I did not even think myself worthy to
come to You. But say the word, and my
servant will be healed. 8For I also am
a man placed under authority, having
soldiers under me. And I say to one, 'Go,'
and he goes; and to another, 'Come,' and
he comes; and to my servant, 'Do this,'
and he does *it*."
9When Jesus heard these things, He
marveled at him, and turned around
and said to the crowd that followed
Him, "I say to you, I have not found
such great faith, not even in Israel!"
10And those who were sent, returning to
the house, found the servant well who
had been sick.[a]

Jesus Raises the Son of the Widow of Nain

11Now it happened, the day after, *that*
He went into a city called Nain; and
many of His disciples went with Him,
and a large crowd. 12And when He came
near the gate of the city, behold, a dead
man was being carried out, the only son
of his mother; and she was a widow. And
a large crowd from the city was with
her. 13When the Lord saw her, He had
compassion on her and said to her, "Do
not weep." 14Then He came and touched
the open coffin, and those who carried
him stood still. And He said, "Young
man, I say to you, arise." 15So he who
was dead sat up and began to speak.
And He presented him to his mother.
16Then fear came upon all, and they
glorified God, saying, "A great prophet
has risen up among us"; and, "God has
visited His people." 17And this report
about Him went throughout all Judea
and all the surrounding region.

John the Baptist Sends Messengers to Jesus

18Then the disciples of John reported to
him concerning all these things. 19And
John, calling two of his disciples to *him*,
sent *them* to Jesus,[a] saying, "Are You the
Coming One, or do we look for another?"
20When the men had come to Him,
they said, "John the Baptist has sent us
to You, saying, 'Are You the Coming One,
or do we look for another?' " 21And that
very hour He cured many of infirmities,
afflictions, and evil spirits; and to many
blind He gave sight.
22Jesus answered and said to them,
"Go and tell John the things you have
seen and heard: that *the* blind see, *the*
lame walk, *the* lepers are cleansed,
the deaf hear, *the* dead are raised, *the*
poor have the gospel preached to them.
23And blessed is *he* who is not offended
because of Me."
24When the messengers of John had
departed, He began to speak to the mul-
titudes concerning John: "What did
you go out into the wilderness to see?
A reed shaken by the wind? 25But what
did you go out to see? A man clothed
in soft garments? Indeed those who
are gorgeously appareled and live in
luxury are in kings' courts. 26But what
did you go out to see? A prophet? Yes, I
say to you, and more than a prophet.
27This is *he* of whom it is written:

> 'Behold, I send My messenger
> before Your face,
> Who will prepare Your way before
> You.'[a]

28For I say to you, among those born of
women there is not a greater prophet
than John the Baptist;[a] but he who is
least in the kingdom of God is greater
than he."
29And when all the people heard *Him*,
even the tax collectors justified God,
having been baptized with the bap-
tism of John. 30But the Pharisees and
lawyers rejected the will of God for
themselves, not having been baptized
by him.
31And the Lord said,[a] "To what then

7:10 [a] NU-Text omits *who had been sick.* **7:19** [a] NU-Text reads *the Lord.* **7:27** [a] Malachi 3:1
7:28 [a] NU-Text reads *there is none greater than John.* **7:31** [a] NU-Text and M-Text omit *And the Lord said.*

shall I liken the men of this generation,
and what are they like? 32They are like
children sitting in the marketplace and
calling to one another, saying:

'We played the flute for you,
And you did not dance;
We mourned to you,
And you did not weep.'

33For John the Baptist came neither
eating bread nor drinking wine, and
you say, 'He has a demon.' 34The Son
of Man has come eating and drinking,
and you say, 'Look, a glutton and a
winebibber, a friend of tax collectors
and sinners!' 35But wisdom is justified
by all her children."

A Sinful Woman Forgiven

36Then one of the Pharisees asked Him
to eat with him. And He went to the
Pharisee's house, and sat down to eat.
37And behold, a woman in the city who
was a sinner, when she knew that *Jesus*
sat at the table in the Pharisee's house,
brought an alabaster flask of fragrant
oil, 38and stood at His feet behind *Him*
weeping; and she began to wash His feet
with her tears, and wiped *them* with the
hair of her head; and she kissed His feet
and anointed *them* with the fragrant oil.
39Now when the Pharisee who had in-
vited Him saw *this*, he spoke to himself,
saying, "This Man, if He were a prophet,
would know who and what manner of
woman *this is* who is touching Him, for
she is a sinner."

40And Jesus answered and said to
him, "Simon, I have something to say
to you."

So he said, "Teacher, say it."

41"There was a certain creditor who
had two debtors. One owed five hundred
denarii, and the other fifty. 42And when
they had nothing with which to repay,
he freely forgave them both. Tell Me,
therefore, which of them will love him
more?"

43Simon answered and said, "I sup-
pose the *one* whom he forgave more."

And He said to him, "You have right-
ly judged." 44Then He turned to the
woman and said to Simon, "Do you
see this woman? I entered your house;
you gave Me no water for My feet, but
she has washed My feet with her tears
and wiped *them* with the hair of her
head. 45You gave Me no kiss, but this
woman has not ceased to kiss My feet
since the time I came in. 46You did not
anoint My head with oil, but this woman
has anointed My feet with fragrant oil.
47Therefore I say to you, her sins, which
are many, are forgiven, for she loved
much. But to whom little is forgiven,
the same loves little."

48Then He said to her, "Your sins are
forgiven."

49And those who sat at the table with
Him began to say to themselves, "Who
is this who even forgives sins?"

50Then He said to the woman, "Your
faith has saved you. Go in peace."

Many Women Minister to Jesus

8 Now it came to pass, afterward,
that He went through every city
and village, preaching and bringing
the glad tidings of the kingdom of God.
And the twelve *were* with Him, 2and
certain women who had been healed
of evil spirits and infirmities—Mary
called Magdalene, out of whom had
come seven demons, 3and Joanna the
wife of Chuza, Herod's steward, and Su-
sanna, and many others who provided
for Him[a] from their substance.

The Parable of the Sower

4And when a great multitude had
gathered, and they had come to Him
from every city, He spoke by a para-
ble: 5"A sower went out to sow his seed.
And as he sowed, some fell by the
wayside; and it was trampled down,
and the birds of the air devoured it.
6Some fell on rock; and as soon as it
sprang up, it withered away because
it lacked moisture. 7And some fell
among thorns, and the thorns sprang
up with it and choked it. 8But others fell
on good ground, sprang up, and yielded
a crop a hundredfold." When He had
said these things He cried, "He who has
ears to hear, let him hear!"

8:3 [a] NU-Text and M-Text read *them*.

The Purpose of Parables

9Then His disciples asked Him, saying,
"What does this parable mean?"
10And He said, "To you it has been
given to know the mysteries of the king-
dom of God, but to the rest *it is given* in
parables, that

'Seeing they may not see,
And hearing they may not
understand.'[a]

The Parable of the Sower Explained

11"Now the parable is this: The seed is
the word of God. 12Those by the wayside
are the ones who hear; then the devil
comes and takes away the word out of
their hearts, lest they should believe and
be saved. 13But the ones on the rock *are*
those who, when they hear, receive the
word with joy; and these have no root,
who believe for a while and in time of
temptation fall away. 14Now the ones
that fell among thorns are those who,
when they have heard, go out and are
choked with cares, riches, and pleasures
of life, and bring no fruit to maturi-
ty. 15But the ones *that* fell on the good
ground are those who, having heard the
word with a noble and good heart, keep
it and bear fruit with patience.

The Parable of the Revealed Light

16"No one, when he has lit a lamp, cov-
ers it with a vessel or puts *it* under a bed,
but sets *it* on a lampstand, that those
who enter may see the light. 17For noth-
ing is secret that will not be revealed,
nor *anything* hidden that will not be
known and come to light. 18Therefore
take heed how you hear. For whoev-
er has, to him *more* will be given; and
whoever does not have, even what he
seems to have will be taken from him."

Jesus' Mother and Brothers Come to Him

19Then His mother and brothers came
to Him, and could not approach Him
because of the crowd. 20And it was told
Him *by some,* who said, "Your mother
and Your brothers are standing outside,
desiring to see You."
21But He answered and said to them,
"My mother and My brothers are these
who hear the word of God and do it."

Wind and Wave Obey Jesus

22Now it happened, on a certain day,
that He got into a boat with His disci-
ples. And He said to them, "Let us cross
over to the other side of the lake." And
they launched out. 23But as they sailed
He fell asleep. And a windstorm came
down on the lake, and they were filling
with water, and were in jeopardy. 24And
they came to Him and awoke Him, say-
ing, "Master, Master, we are perishing!"
Then He arose and rebuked the wind
and the raging of the water. And they
ceased, and there was a calm. 25But
He said to them, "Where is your faith?"
And they were afraid, and marveled,
saying to one another, "Who can this
be? For He commands even the winds
and water, and they obey Him!"

A Demon-Possessed Man Healed

26Then they sailed to the country
of the Gadarenes,[a] which is opposite
Galilee. 27And when He stepped out
on the land, there met Him a certain
man from the city who had demons for
a long time. And he wore no clothes,[a]
nor did he live in a house but in the
tombs. 28When he saw Jesus, he cried
out, fell down before Him, and with a
loud voice said, "What have I to do with
You, Jesus, Son of the Most High God?
I beg You, do not torment me!" 29For
He had commanded the unclean spirit
to come out of the man. For it had of-
ten seized him, and he was kept under
guard, bound with chains and shackles;
and he broke the bonds and was driven
by the demon into the wilderness.
30Jesus asked him, saying, "What is
your name?"
And he said, "Legion," because many
demons had entered him. 31And they
begged Him that He would not com-
mand them to go out into the abyss.
32Now a herd of many swine was
feeding there on the mountain. So they
begged Him that He would permit them
to enter them. And He permitted them.

8:10 [a] Isaiah 6:9 **8:26** [a] NU-Text reads *Gerasenes.* **8:27** [a] NU-Text reads *who had demons and for a long time wore no clothes.*

33Then the demons went out of the man
and entered the swine, and the herd ran
violently down the steep place into the
lake and drowned.
34When those who fed *them* saw what
had happened, they fled and told *it* in
the city and in the country. 35Then they
went out to see what had happened,
and came to Jesus, and found the man
from whom the demons had depart-
ed, sitting at the feet of Jesus, clothed
and in his right mind. And they were
afraid. 36They also who had seen *it* told
them by what means he who had been
demon-possessed was healed. 37Then
the whole multitude of the surrounding
region of the Gadarenes[a] asked Him to
depart from them, for they were seized
with great fear. And He got into the boat
and returned.
38Now the man from whom the de-
mons had departed begged Him that
he might be with Him. But Jesus sent
him away, saying, 39"Return to your
own house, and tell what great things
God has done for you." And he went his
way and proclaimed throughout the
whole city what great things Jesus had
done for him.

A Girl Restored to Life and a Woman Healed

40So it was, when Jesus returned, that
the multitude welcomed Him, for they
were all waiting for Him. 41And behold,
there came a man named Jairus, and
he was a ruler of the synagogue. And
he fell down at Jesus' feet and begged
Him to come to his house, 42for he had
an only daughter about twelve years of
age, and she was dying.
But as He went, the multitudes
thronged Him. 43Now a woman, having
a flow of blood for twelve years, who had
spent all her livelihood on physicians
and could not be healed by any, 44came
from behind and touched the border of
His garment. And immediately her flow
of blood stopped.
45And Jesus said, "Who touched Me?"
When all denied it, Peter and those
with him[a] said, "Master, the multitudes
throng and press You, and You say,
'Who touched Me?' "[b]
46But Jesus said, "Somebody touched
Me, for I perceived power going out
from Me." 47Now when the woman saw
that she was not hidden, she came trem-
bling; and falling down before Him,
she declared to Him in the presence
of all the people the reason she had
touched Him and how she was healed
immediately.
48And He said to her, "Daughter, be of
good cheer;[a] your faith has made you
well. Go in peace."
49While He was still speaking, some-
one came from the ruler of the syn-
agogue's *house,* saying to him, "Your
daughter is dead. Do not trouble the
Teacher."[a]
50But when Jesus heard *it,* He an-
swered him, saying, "Do not be afraid;
only believe, and she will be made well."
51When He came into the house, He
permitted no one to go in[a] except Peter,
James, and John,[b] and the father and
mother of the girl. 52Now all wept and
mourned for her; but He said, "Do not
weep; she is not dead, but sleeping."
53And they ridiculed Him, knowing
that she was dead.
54But He put them all outside,[a] took
her by the hand and called, saying,
"Little girl, arise." 55Then her spirit re-
turned, and she arose immediately.
And He commanded that she be given
something to eat. 56And her parents
were astonished, but He charged them
to tell no one what had happened.

Sending Out the Twelve

9 Then He called His twelve disciples
together and gave them power and
authority over all demons, and to cure
diseases. 2He sent them to preach the
kingdom of God and to heal the sick.
3And He said to them, "Take nothing
for the journey, neither staffs nor bag
nor bread nor money; and do not have
two tunics apiece.
4"Whatever house you enter, stay

8:37 [a] NU-Text reads *Gerasenes.* **8:45** [a] NU-Text omits *and those with him.* [b] NU-Text omits *and You say, 'Who touched Me?'* **8:48** [a] NU-Text omits *be of good cheer.* **8:49** [a] NU-Text adds *anymore.* **8:51** [a] NU-Text adds *with Him.* [b] NU-Text and M-Text read *Peter, John, and James.* **8:54** [a] NU-Text omits *put them all outside.*

there, and from there depart. 5And who-
ever will not receive you, when you go
out of that city, shake off the very dust
from your feet as a testimony against
them."
6So they departed and went through
the towns, preaching the gospel and
healing everywhere.

Herod Seeks to See Jesus

7Now Herod the tetrarch heard of all
that was done by Him; and he was per-
plexed, because it was said by some that
John had risen from the dead, 8and by
some that Elijah had appeared, and by
others that one of the old prophets had
risen again. 9Herod said, "John I have
beheaded, but who is this of whom I
hear such things?" So he sought to see
Him.

Feeding the Five Thousand

10And the apostles, when they had re-
turned, told Him all that they had done.
Then He took them and went aside pri-
vately into a deserted place belonging
to the city called Bethsaida. 11But when
the multitudes knew *it,* they followed
Him; and He received them and spoke
to them about the kingdom of God, and
healed those who had need of healing.
12When the day began to wear away, the
twelve came and said to Him, "Send the
multitude away, that they may go into
the surrounding towns and country,
and lodge and get provisions; for we
are in a deserted place here."
13But He said to them, "You give them
something to eat."
And they said, "We have no more than
five loaves and two fish, unless we go
and buy food for all these people." 14For
there were about five thousand men.
Then He said to His disciples, "Make
them sit down in groups of fifty." 15And
they did so, and made them all sit down.
16Then He took the five loaves and
the two fish, and looking up to heaven,
He blessed and broke them, and gave
them to the disciples to set before the
multitude. 17So they all ate and were
filled, and twelve baskets of the leftover
fragments were taken up by them.

Peter Confesses Jesus as the Christ

18And it happened, as He was alone
praying, *that* His disciples joined Him,
and He asked them, saying, "Who do
the crowds say that I am?"
19So they answered and said, "John
the Baptist, but some *say* Elijah; and
others *say* that one of the old prophets
has risen again."
20He said to them, "But who do you
say that I am?"
Peter answered and said, "The Christ
of God."

Jesus Predicts His Death and Resurrection

21And He strictly warned and com-
manded them to tell this to no one,
22saying, "The Son of Man must suffer
many things, and be rejected by the
elders and chief priests and scribes, and
be killed, and be raised the third day."

Take Up the Cross and Follow Him

23Then He said to *them* all, "If anyone
desires to come after Me, let him deny
himself, and take up his cross daily,[a] and
follow Me. 24For whoever desires to save
his life will lose it, but whoever loses his
life for My sake will save it. 25For what
profit is it to a man if he gains the whole
world, and is himself destroyed or lost?
26For whoever is ashamed of Me and
My words, of him the Son of Man will
be ashamed when He comes in His *own*
glory, and *in His* Father's, and of the holy
angels. 27But I tell you truly, there are
some standing here who shall not taste
death till they see the kingdom of God."

Jesus Transfigured on the Mount

28Now it came to pass, about eight
days after these sayings, that He took
Peter, John, and James and went up on
the mountain to pray. 29As He prayed,
the appearance of His face was altered,
and His robe *became* white *and* glis-
tening. 30And behold, two men talked
with Him, who were Moses and Elijah,
31who appeared in glory and spoke of
His decease which He was about to ac-
complish at Jerusalem. 32But Peter and
those with him were heavy with sleep;

9:23 [a] M-Text omits *daily.*

and when they were fully awake, they
saw His glory and the two men who
stood with Him. 33Then it happened, as
they were parting from Him, *that* Peter
said to Jesus, "Master, it is good for us to
be here; and let us make three taberna-
cles: one for You, one for Moses, and one
for Elijah"—not knowing what he said.
34While he was saying this, a cloud
came and overshadowed them; and
they were fearful as they entered the
cloud. 35And a voice came out of the
cloud, saying, "This is My beloved
Son.[a] Hear Him!" 36When the voice
had ceased, Jesus was found alone. But
they kept quiet, and told no one in those
days any of the things they had seen.

A Boy Is Healed

37Now it happened on the next day,
when they had come down from the
mountain, that a great multitude
met Him. 38Suddenly a man from the
multitude cried out, saying, "Teacher,
I implore You, look on my son, for he
is my only child. 39And behold, a spirit
seizes him, and he suddenly cries out;
it convulses him so that he foams *at the
mouth;* and it departs from him with
great difficulty, bruising him. 40So I
implored Your disciples to cast it out,
but they could not."
41Then Jesus answered and said,
"O faithless and perverse generation,
how long shall I be with you and bear
with you? Bring your son here." 42And
as he was still coming, the demon
threw him down and convulsed *him.*
Then Jesus rebuked the unclean spirit,
healed the child, and gave him back
to his father.

Jesus Again Predicts His Death

43And they were all amazed at the
majesty of God.

But while everyone marveled at all
the things which Jesus did, He said to
His disciples, 44"Let these words sink
down into your ears, for the Son of Man
is about to be betrayed into the hands of
men." 45But they did not understand this
saying, and it was hidden from them so
that they did not perceive it; and they
were afraid to ask Him about this saying.

Who Is the Greatest?

46Then a dispute arose among them
as to which of them would be greatest.
47And Jesus, perceiving the thought of
their heart, took a little child and set
him by Him, 48and said to them, "Who-
ever receives this little child in My name
receives Me; and whoever receives Me
receives Him who sent Me. For he who
is least among you all will be great."

Jesus Forbids Sectarianism

49Now John answered and said, "Mas-
ter, we saw someone casting out de-
mons in Your name, and we forbade
him because he does not follow with us."
50But Jesus said to him, "Do not forbid
him, for he who is not against us[a] is on
our[b] side."

A Samaritan Village Rejects the Savior

51Now it came to pass, when the time
had come for Him to be received up,
that He steadfastly set His face to go
to Jerusalem, 52and sent messengers
before His face. And as they went, they
entered a village of the Samaritans, to
prepare for Him. 53But they did not re-
ceive Him, because His face was *set* for
the journey to Jerusalem. 54And when
His disciples James and John saw *this,*
they said, "Lord, do You want us to com-
mand fire to come down from heaven
and consume them, just as Elijah did?"[a]
55But He turned and rebuked them,[a]
and said, "You do not know what man-
ner of spirit you are of. 56For the Son
of Man did not come to destroy men's
lives but to save *them.*"[a] And they went
to another village.

The Cost of Discipleship

57Now it happened as they journeyed
on the road, *that* someone said to Him,
"Lord, I will follow You wherever You go."
58And Jesus said to him, "Foxes have
holes and birds of the air *have* nests,
but the Son of Man has nowhere to lay
His head."

9:35 [a] NU-Text reads *This is My Son, the Chosen One.* **9:50** [a] NU-Text reads *you.* [b] NU-Text reads *your.* **9:54** [a] NU-Text omits *just as Elijah did.* **9:55** [a] NU-Text omits the rest of this verse. **9:56** [a] NU-Text omits the first sentence of this verse.

59Then He said to another, "Follow Me."
But he said, "Lord, let me first go and
bury my father."
60Jesus said to him, "Let the dead bury
their own dead, but you go and preach
the kingdom of God."
61And another also said, "Lord, I will
follow You, but let me first go *and* bid
them farewell who are at my house."
62But Jesus said to him, "No one, hav-
ing put his hand to the plow, and look-
ing back, is fit for the kingdom of God."

The Seventy Sent Out

10 After these things the Lord ap-
pointed seventy others also,[a]
and sent them two by two before His
face into every city and place where He
Himself was about to go. 2Then He said
to them, "The harvest truly *is* great, but
the laborers *are* few; therefore pray the
Lord of the harvest to send out laborers
into His harvest. 3Go your way; behold,
I send you out as lambs among wolves.
4Carry neither money bag, knapsack,
nor sandals; and greet no one along the
road. 5But whatever house you enter, first
say, 'Peace to this house.' 6And if a son of
peace is there, your peace will rest on it;
if not, it will return to you. 7And remain
in the same house, eating and drinking
such things as they give, for the laborer
is worthy of his wages. Do not go from
house to house. 8Whatever city you en-
ter, and they receive you, eat such things
as are set before you. 9And heal the sick
there, and say to them, 'The kingdom of
God has come near to you.' 10But whatev-
er city you enter, and they do not receive
you, go out into its streets and say, 11'The
very dust of your city which clings to us[a]
we wipe off against you. Nevertheless
know this, that the kingdom of God has
come near you.' 12But[a] I say to you that
it will be more tolerable in that Day for
Sodom than for that city.

Woe to the Impenitent Cities

13"Woe to you, Chorazin! Woe to you,
Bethsaida! For if the mighty works
which were done in you had been done
in Tyre and Sidon, they would have
repented long ago, sitting in sackcloth
and ashes. 14But it will be more tolerable
for Tyre and Sidon at the judgment than
for you. 15And you, Capernaum, who
are exalted to heaven, will be brought
down to Hades.[a] 16He who hears you
hears Me, he who rejects you rejects
Me, and he who rejects Me rejects Him
who sent Me."

The Seventy Return with Joy

17Then the seventy[a] returned with joy,
saying, "Lord, even the demons are
subject to us in Your name."
18And He said to them, "I saw Satan
fall like lightning from heaven. 19Be-
hold, I give you the authority to trample
on serpents and scorpions, and over all
the power of the enemy, and nothing
shall by any means hurt you. 20Never-
theless do not rejoice in this, that the
spirits are subject to you, but rather[a]
rejoice because your names are written
in heaven."

Jesus Rejoices in the Spirit

21In that hour Jesus rejoiced in the
Spirit and said, "I thank You, Father,
Lord of heaven and earth, that You have
hidden these things from *the* wise and
prudent and revealed them to babes.
Even so, Father, for so it seemed good
in Your sight. 22All[a] things have been
delivered to Me by My Father, and no
one knows who the Son is except the
Father, and who the Father is except
the Son, and *the one* to whom the Son
wills to reveal *Him.*"
23Then He turned to *His* disciples and
said privately, "Blessed *are* the eyes
which see the things you see; 24for I
tell you that many prophets and kings
have desired to see what you see, and
have not seen *it,* and to hear what you
hear, and have not heard *it.*"

The Parable of the Good Samaritan

25And behold, a certain lawyer stood
up and tested Him, saying, "Teacher,
what shall I do to inherit eternal life?"

10:1 a NU-Text reads *seventy-two others.* **10:11** a NU-Text reads *our feet.* **10:12** a NU-Text and M-Text omit *But.* **10:15** a NU-Text reads *will you be exalted to heaven? You will be thrust down to Hades!* **10:17** a NU-Text reads *seventy-two.* **10:20** a NU-Text and M-Text omit *rather.* **10:22** a M-Text reads *And turning to the disciples He said, "All . . . .*

26He said to him, "What is written in the law? What is your reading *of it?*"

27So he answered and said, " 'You shall love the LORD your God with all your heart, with all your soul, with all your strength, and with all your mind,'[a] and 'your neighbor as yourself.' "[b]

28And He said to him, "You have answered rightly; do this and you will live."

29But he, wanting to justify himself, said to Jesus, "And who is my neighbor?"

30Then Jesus answered and said: "A certain *man* went down from Jerusalem to Jericho, and fell among thieves, who stripped him of his clothing, wounded *him,* and departed, leaving *him* half dead. 31Now by chance a certain priest came down that road. And when he saw him, he passed by on the other side. 32Likewise a Levite, when he arrived at the place, came and looked, and passed by on the other side. 33But a certain Samaritan, as he journeyed, came where he was. And when he saw him, he had compassion. 34So he went to *him* and bandaged his wounds, pouring on oil and wine; and he set him on his own animal, brought him to an inn, and took care of him. 35On the next day, when he departed,[a] he took out two denarii, gave *them* to the innkeeper, and said to him, 'Take care of him; and whatever more you spend, when I come again, I will repay you.' 36So which of these three do you think was neighbor to him who fell among the thieves?"

37And he said, "He who showed mercy on him."

Then Jesus said to him, "Go and do likewise."

Mary and Martha Worship and Serve

38Now it happened as they went that He entered a certain village; and a certain woman named Martha welcomed Him into her house. 39And she had a sister called Mary, who also sat at Jesus'[a] feet and heard His word. 40But Martha was distracted with much serving, and she approached Him and said, "Lord, do You not care that my sister has left me to serve alone? Therefore tell her to help me."

41And Jesus[a] answered and said to her, "Martha, Martha, you are worried and troubled about many things. 42But one thing is needed, and Mary has chosen that good part, which will not be taken away from her."

The Model Prayer

11 Now it came to pass, as He was praying in a certain place, when He ceased, *that* one of His disciples said to Him, "Lord, teach us to pray, as John also taught his disciples."

2So He said to them, "When you pray, say:

Our Father in heaven,[a]
Hallowed be Your name.
Your kingdom come.[b]
Your will be done
On earth as *it is* in heaven.
3 Give us day by day our daily
bread.
4 And forgive us our sins,
For we also forgive everyone who
is indebted to us.
And do not lead us into
temptation,
But deliver us from the evil one."[a]

A Friend Comes at Midnight

5And He said to them, "Which of you shall have a friend, and go to him at midnight and say to him, 'Friend, lend me three loaves; 6for a friend of mine has come to me on his journey, and I have nothing to set before him'; 7and he will answer from within and say, 'Do not trouble me; the door is now shut, and my children are with me in bed; I cannot rise and give to you'? 8I say to you, though he will not rise and give to him because he is his friend, yet because of his persistence he will rise and give him as many as he needs.

Keep Asking, Seeking, Knocking

9"So I say to you, ask, and it will be given to you; seek, and you will find; knock, and it will be opened to you.

10:27 [a] Deuteronomy 6:5 [b] Leviticus 19:18 **10:35** [a] NU-Text omits *when he departed.* **10:39** [a] NU-Text reads *the Lord's.* **10:41** [a] NU-Text reads *the Lord.* **11:2** [a] NU-Text omits *Our* and *in heaven.* [b] NU-Text omits the rest of this verse. **11:4** [a] NU-Text omits *But deliver us from the evil one.*

10For everyone who asks receives, and
he who seeks finds, and to him who
knocks it will be opened. 11If a son asks
for bread[a] from any father among you,
will he give him a stone? Or if *he asks*
for a fish, will he give him a serpent
instead of a fish? 12Or if he asks for an
egg, will he offer him a scorpion? 13If
you then, being evil, know how to give
good gifts to your children, how much
more will *your* heavenly Father give
the Holy Spirit to those who ask Him!"

A House Divided Cannot Stand

14And He was casting out a demon,
and it was mute. So it was, when the
demon had gone out, that the mute
spoke; and the multitudes marveled.
15But some of them said, "He casts out
demons by Beelzebub,[a] the ruler of the
demons."

16Others, testing *Him,* sought from
Him a sign from heaven. 17But He,
knowing their thoughts, said to them:
"Every kingdom divided against itself
is brought to desolation, and a house
divided against a house falls. 18If Satan
also is divided against himself, how
will his kingdom stand? Because you
say I cast out demons by Beelzebub.
19And if I cast out demons by Beelze-
bub, by whom do your sons cast *them*
out? Therefore they will be your judges.
20But if I cast out demons with the fin-
ger of God, surely the kingdom of God
has come upon you. 21When a strong
man, fully armed, guards his own pal-
ace, his goods are in peace. 22But when
a stronger than he comes upon him
and overcomes him, he takes from him
all his armor in which he trusted, and
divides his spoils. 23He who is not with
Me is against Me, and he who does not
gather with Me scatters.

An Unclean Spirit Returns

24"When an unclean spirit goes out
of a man, he goes through dry places,
seeking rest; and finding none, he says,
'I will return to my house from which I
came.' 25And when he comes, he finds
it swept and put in order. 26Then he
goes and takes with *him* seven other
spirits more wicked than himself, and
they enter and dwell there; and the last
state of that man is worse than the first."

Keeping the Word

27And it happened, as He spoke these
things, that a certain woman from the
crowd raised her voice and said to Him,
"Blessed *is* the womb that bore You, and
the breasts which nursed You!"

28But He said, "More than that, blessed
are those who hear the word of God and
keep it!"

Seeking a Sign

29And while the crowds were thickly
gathered together, He began to say,
"This is an evil generation. It seeks a
sign, and no sign will be given to it ex-
cept the sign of Jonah the prophet.[a]
30For as Jonah became a sign to the
Ninevites, so also the Son of Man will
be to this generation. 31The queen of
the South will rise up in the judgment
with the men of this generation and
condemn them, for she came from the
ends of the earth to hear the wisdom
of Solomon; and indeed a greater than
Solomon *is* here. 32The men of Nineveh
will rise up in the judgment with this
generation and condemn it, for they
repented at the preaching of Jonah;
and indeed a greater than Jonah *is* here.

The Lamp of the Body

33"No one, when he has lit a lamp, puts
it in a secret place or under a basket, but
on a lampstand, that those who come
in may see the light. 34The lamp of the
body is the eye. Therefore, when your
eye is good, your whole body also is full
of light. But when *your eye* is bad, your
body also *is* full of darkness. 35There-
fore take heed that the light which is
in you is not darkness. 36If then your
whole body *is* full of light, having no
part dark, *the* whole *body* will be full of
light, as when the bright shining of a
lamp gives you light."

Woe to the Pharisees and Lawyers

37And as He spoke, a certain Phari-
see asked Him to dine with him. So He

11:11 [a] NU-Text omits the words from *bread* through *for* in the next sentence. **11:15** [a] NU-Text and M-Text read *Beelzebul.* **11:29** [a] NU-Text omits *the prophet.*

went in and sat down to eat. 38When the Pharisee saw *it,* he marveled that He had not first washed before dinner.

39Then the Lord said to him, "Now you Pharisees make the outside of the cup and dish clean, but your inward part is full of greed and wickedness. 40Foolish ones! Did not He who made the outside make the inside also? 41But rather give alms of such things as you have; then indeed all things are clean to you.

42"But woe to you Pharisees! For you tithe the mint and rue and all manner of herbs, and pass by justice and the love of God. These you ought to have done, without leaving the others undone. 43Woe to you Pharisees! For you love the best seats in the synagogues and greetings in the marketplaces. 44Woe to you, scribes and Pharisees, hypocrites![a] For you are like graves which are not seen, and the men who walk over *them* are not aware *of them.*"

45Then one of the lawyers answered and said to Him, "Teacher, by saying these things You reproach us also."

46And He said, "Woe to you also, lawyers! For you load men with burdens hard to bear, and you yourselves do not touch the burdens with one of your fingers. 47Woe to you! For you build the tombs of the prophets, and your fathers killed them. 48In fact, you bear witness that you approve the deeds of your fathers; for they indeed killed them, and you build their tombs. 49Therefore the wisdom of God also said, 'I will send them prophets and apostles, and *some* of them they will kill and persecute,' 50that the blood of all the prophets which was shed from the foundation of the world may be required of this generation, 51from the blood of Abel to the blood of Zechariah who perished between the altar and the temple. Yes, I say to you, it shall be required of this generation.

52"Woe to you lawyers! For you have taken away the key of knowledge. You did not enter in yourselves, and those who were entering in you hindered."

53And as He said these things to them,[a] the scribes and the Pharisees began to assail *Him* vehemently, and to cross-examine Him about many things, 54lying in wait for Him, and seeking to catch Him in something He might say, that they might accuse Him.[a]

Beware of Hypocrisy

12 In the meantime, when an innumerable multitude of people had gathered together, so that they trampled one another, He began to say to His disciples first *of all,* "Beware of the leaven of the Pharisees, which is hypocrisy. 2For there is nothing covered that will not be revealed, nor hidden that will not be known. 3Therefore whatever you have spoken in the dark will be heard in the light, and what you have spoken in the ear in inner rooms will be proclaimed on the housetops.

Jesus Teaches the Fear of God

4"And I say to you, My friends, do not be afraid of those who kill the body, and after that have no more that they can do. 5But I will show you whom you should fear: Fear Him who, after He has killed, has power to cast into hell; yes, I say to you, fear Him!

6"Are not five sparrows sold for two copper coins?[a] And not one of them is forgotten before God. 7But the very hairs of your head are all numbered. Do not fear therefore; you are of more value than many sparrows.

Confess Christ Before Men

8"Also I say to you, whoever confesses Me before men, him the Son of Man also will confess before the angels of God. 9But he who denies Me before men will be denied before the angels of God.

10"And anyone who speaks a word against the Son of Man, it will be forgiven him; but to him who blasphemes against the Holy Spirit, it will not be forgiven.

11"Now when they bring you to the synagogues and magistrates and authorities, do not worry about how or what you should answer, or what you

11:44 [a] NU-Text omits *scribes and Pharisees, hypocrites.* **11:53** [a] NU-Text reads *And when He left there.* **11:54** [a] NU-Text omits *and seeking* and *that they might accuse Him.* **12:6** [a] Greek *assarion,* a coin of very small value

should say. 12For the Holy Spirit will teach you in that very hour what you ought to say."

The Parable of the Rich Fool

13Then one from the crowd said to Him, "Teacher, tell my brother to divide the inheritance with me."

14But He said to him, "Man, who made Me a judge or an arbitrator over you?" 15And He said to them, "Take heed and beware of covetousness,[a] for one's life does not consist in the abundance of the things he possesses."

16Then He spoke a parable to them, saying: "The ground of a certain rich man yielded plentifully. 17And he thought within himself, saying, 'What shall I do, since I have no room to store my crops?' 18So he said, 'I will do this: I will pull down my barns and build greater, and there I will store all my crops and my goods. 19And I will say to my soul, "Soul, you have many goods laid up for many years; take your ease; eat, drink, *and* be merry." ' 20But God said to him, 'Fool! This night your soul will be required of you; then whose will those things be which you have provided?'

21"So *is* he who lays up treasure for himself, and is not rich toward God."

Do Not Worry

22Then He said to His disciples, "Therefore I say to you, do not worry about your life, what you will eat; nor about the body, what you will put on. 23Life is more than food, and the body *is more* than clothing. 24Consider the ravens, for they neither sow nor reap, which have neither storehouse nor barn; and God feeds them. Of how much more value are you than the birds? 25And which of you by worrying can add one cubit to his stature? 26If you then are not able to do *the* least, why are you anxious for the rest? 27Consider the lilies, how they grow: they neither toil nor spin; and yet I say to you, even Solomon in all his glory was not arrayed like one of these. 28If then God so clothes the grass, which today is in the field and tomorrow is thrown into the oven, how much more *will He clothe* you, O *you* of little faith?

29"And do not seek what you should eat or what you should drink, nor have an anxious mind. 30For all these things the nations of the world seek after, and your Father knows that you need these things. 31But seek the kingdom of God, and all these things[a] shall be added to you.

32"Do not fear, little flock, for it is your Father's good pleasure to give you the kingdom. 33Sell what you have and give alms; provide yourselves money bags which do not grow old, a treasure in the heavens that does not fail, where no thief approaches nor moth destroys. 34For where your treasure is, there your heart will be also.

The Faithful Servant and the Evil Servant

35"Let your waist be girded and *your* lamps burning; 36and you yourselves be like men who wait for their master, when he will return from the wedding, that when he comes and knocks they may open to him immediately. 37Blessed *are* those servants whom the master, when he comes, will find watching. Assuredly, I say to you that he will gird himself and have them sit down *to eat,* and will come and serve them. 38And if he should come in the second watch, or come in the third watch, and find *them* so, blessed are those servants. 39But know this, that if the master of the house had known what hour the thief would come, he would have watched and[a] not allowed his house to be broken into. 40Therefore you also be ready, for the Son of Man is coming at an hour you do not expect."

41Then Peter said to Him, "Lord, do You speak this parable *only* to us, or to all *people?*"

42And the Lord said, "Who then is that faithful and wise steward, whom *his* master will make ruler over his household, to give *them their* portion of food in due season? 43Blessed *is* that servant whom his master will find so doing when

12:15 [a] NU-Text reads *all covetousness.* **12:31** [a] NU-Text reads *His kingdom, and these things.*
12:39 [a] NU-Text reads *he would not have allowed.*

he comes. 44Truly, I say to you that
he will make him ruler over all that he
has. 45But if that servant says in his
heart, 'My master is delaying his com-
ing,' and begins to beat the male and
female servants, and to eat and drink
and be drunk, 46the master of that ser-
vant will come on a day when he is not
looking for *him,* and at an hour when
he is not aware, and will cut him in two
and appoint *him* his portion with the un-
believers. 47And that servant who knew
his master's will, and did not prepare
himself or do according to his will, shall
be beaten with many *stripes.* 48But he
who did not know, yet committed things
deserving of stripes, shall be beaten with
few. For everyone to whom much is giv-
en, from him much will be required; and
to whom much has been committed, of
him they will ask the more.

Christ Brings Division

49"I came to send fire on the earth,
and how I wish it were already kindled!
50But I have a baptism to be baptized
with, and how distressed I am till it is
accomplished! 51Do *you* suppose that
I came to give peace on earth? I tell
you, not at all, but rather division. 52For
from now on five in one house will be
divided: three against two, and two
against three. 53Father will be divided
against son and son against father,
mother against daughter and daughter
against mother, mother-in-law against
her daughter-in-law and daughter-in-
law against her mother-in-law."

Discern the Time

54Then He also said to the multitudes,
"Whenever you see a cloud rising out
of the west, immediately you say, 'A
shower is coming'; and so it is. 55And
when *you see* the south wind blow, you
say, 'There will be hot weather'; and
there is. 56Hypocrites! You can discern
the face of the sky and of the earth, but
how *is it* you do not discern this time?

Make Peace with Your Adversary

57"Yes, and why, even of yourselves, do
you not judge what is right? 58When you
go with your adversary to the magis-
trate, make every effort along the way
to settle with him, lest he drag you to
the judge, the judge deliver you to the
officer, and the officer throw you into
prison. 59I tell you, you shall not depart
from there till you have paid the very
last mite."

Repent or Perish

13 There were present at that sea-
son some who told Him about
the Galileans whose blood Pilate had
mingled with their sacrifices. 2And
Jesus answered and said to them, "Do
you suppose that these Galileans were
worse sinners than all *other* Galileans,
because they suffered such things? 3I
tell you, no; but unless you repent you
will all likewise perish. 4Or those eigh-
teen on whom the tower in Siloam fell
and killed them, do you think that they
were worse sinners than all *other* men
who dwelt in Jerusalem? 5I tell you,
no; but unless you repent you will all
likewise perish."

The Parable of the Barren Fig Tree

6He also spoke this parable: "A certain
man had a fig tree planted in his vine-
yard, and he came seeking fruit on it
and found none. 7Then he said to the
keeper of his vineyard, 'Look, for three
years I have come seeking fruit on this
fig tree and find none. Cut it down; why
does it use up the ground?' 8But he an-
swered and said to him, 'Sir, let it alone
this year also, until I dig around it and
fertilize *it.* 9And if it bears fruit, *well.* But
if not, after that[a] you can cut it down.'"

A Spirit of Infirmity

10Now He was teaching in one of the
synagogues on the Sabbath. 11And be-
hold, there was a woman who had a
spirit of infirmity eighteen years, and
was bent over and could in no way raise
herself up. 12But when Jesus saw her,
He called *her* to *Him* and said to her,
"Woman, you are loosed from your
infirmity." 13And He laid *His* hands on
her, and immediately she was made
straight, and glorified God.

13:9 [a] NU-Text reads *And if it bears fruit after that, well. But if not, you can cut it down.*

14But the ruler of the synagogue an-
swered with indignation, because Jesus
had healed on the Sabbath; and he said
to the crowd, "There are six days on
which men ought to work; therefore
come and be healed on them, and not
on the Sabbath day."
15The Lord then answered him and
said, "Hypocrite![a] Does not each one
of you on the Sabbath loose his ox or
donkey from the stall, and lead *it* away
to water it? 16So ought not this woman,
being a daughter of Abraham, whom
Satan has bound—think of it—for eigh-
teen years, be loosed from this bond on
the Sabbath?" 17And when He said these
things, all His adversaries were put to
shame; and all the multitude rejoiced
for all the glorious things that were
done by Him.

The Parable of the Mustard Seed

18Then He said, "What is the kingdom
of God like? And to what shall I compare
it? 19It is like a mustard seed, which a
man took and put in his garden; and it
grew and became a large[a] tree, and the
birds of the air nested in its branches."

The Parable of the Leaven

20And again He said, "To what shall
I liken the kingdom of God? 21It is like
leaven, which a woman took and hid
in three measures[a] of meal till it was
all leavened."

The Narrow Way

22And He went through the cities
and villages, teaching, and journey-
ing toward Jerusalem. 23Then one said
to Him, "Lord, are there few who are
saved?"
And He said to them, 24"Strive to enter
through the narrow gate, for many, I
say to you, will seek to enter and will not
be able. 25When once the Master of the
house has risen up and shut the door,
and you begin to stand outside and
knock at the door, saying, 'Lord, Lord,
open for us,' and He will answer and say
to you, 'I do not know you, where you
are from,' 26then you will begin to say,
'We ate and drank in Your presence,
and You taught in our streets.' 27But He
will say, 'I tell you I do not know you,
where you are from. Depart from Me,
all you workers of iniquity.' 28There will
be weeping and gnashing of teeth, when
you see Abraham and Isaac and Jacob
and all the prophets in the kingdom of
God, and yourselves thrust out. 29They
will come from the east and the west,
from the north and the south, and sit
down in the kingdom of God. 30And
indeed there are last who will be first,
and there are first who will be last."
31On that very day[a] some Pharisees
came, saying to Him, "Get out and de-
part from here, for Herod wants to kill
You."
32And He said to them, "Go, tell that
fox, 'Behold, I cast out demons and
perform cures today and tomorrow,
and the third *day* I shall be perfected.'
33Nevertheless I must journey today,
tomorrow, and the *day* following; for it
cannot be that a prophet should perish
outside of Jerusalem.

Jesus Laments over Jerusalem

34"O Jerusalem, Jerusalem, the one
who kills the prophets and stones those
who are sent to her! How often I want-
ed to gather your children together,
as a hen *gathers* her brood under *her*
wings, but you were not willing! 35See!
Your house is left to you desolate; and
assuredly,[a] I say to you, you shall not
see Me until *the time* comes when you
say, 'Blessed is He who comes in the
name of the LORD!' "[b]

A Man with Dropsy Healed on the Sabbath

14 Now it happened, as He went
into the house of one of the rul-
ers of the Pharisees to eat bread on the
Sabbath, that they watched Him close-
ly. 2And behold, there was a certain
man before Him who had dropsy. 3And
Jesus, answering, spoke to the lawyers
and Pharisees, saying, "Is it lawful to
heal on the Sabbath?"[a]
4But they kept silent. And He took *him*

13:15 [a] NU-Text and M-Text read *Hypocrites*. 13:19 [a] NU-Text omits *large*. 13:21 [a] Greek *sata*, approximately two pecks in all 13:31 [a] NU-Text reads *In that very hour*. 13:35 [a] NU-Text and M-Text omit *assuredly*. [b] Psalm 118:26 14:3 [a] NU-Text adds *or not*.

and healed him, and let him go. 5Then
He answered them, saying, "Which of
you, having a donkey[a] or an ox that has
fallen into a pit, will not immediately
pull him out on the Sabbath day?" 6And
they could not answer Him regarding
these things.

Take the Lowly Place

7So He told a parable to those who were
invited, when He noted how they chose
the best places, saying to them: 8"When
you are invited by anyone to a wedding
feast, do not sit down in the best place,
lest one more honorable than you be
invited by him; 9and he who invited
you and him come and say to you, 'Give
place to this man,' and then you begin
with shame to take the lowest place.
10But when you are invited, go and sit
down in the lowest place, so that when
he who invited you comes he may say to
you, 'Friend, go up higher.' Then you will
have glory in the presence of those who
sit at the table with you. 11For whoever
exalts himself will be humbled, and he
who humbles himself will be exalted."

12Then He also said to him who in-
vited Him, "When you give a dinner
or a supper, do not ask your friends,
your brothers, your relatives, nor rich
neighbors, lest they also invite you
back, and you be repaid. 13But when
you give a feast, invite *the* poor, *the*
maimed, *the* lame, *the* blind. 14And you
will be blessed, because they cannot
repay you; for you shall be repaid at
the resurrection of the just."

The Parable of the Great Supper

15Now when one of those who sat at the
table with Him heard these things, he
said to Him, "Blessed *is* he who shall eat
bread[a] in the kingdom of God!"

16Then He said to him, "A certain man
gave a great supper and invited many,
17and sent his servant at supper time to
say to those who were invited, 'Come, for
all things are now ready.' 18But they all
with one *accord* began to make excuses.
The first said to him, 'I have bought a
piece of ground, and I must go and see
it. I ask you to have me excused.' 19And
another said, 'I have bought five yoke of
oxen, and I am going to test them. I ask
you to have me excused.' 20Still another
said, 'I have married a wife, and there-
fore I cannot come.' 21So that servant
came and reported these things to his
master. Then the master of the house,
being angry, said to his servant, 'Go
out quickly into the streets and lanes
of the city, and bring in here *the* poor
and *the* maimed and *the* lame and *the*
blind.' 22And the servant said, 'Master,
it is done as you commanded, and still
there is room.' 23Then the master said to
the servant, 'Go out into the highways
and hedges, and compel *them* to come
in, that my house may be filled. 24For I
say to you that none of those men who
were invited shall taste my supper.' "

Leaving All to Follow Christ

25Now great multitudes went with Him.
And He turned and said to them, 26"If
anyone comes to Me and does not hate
his father and mother, wife and children,
brothers and sisters, yes, and his own
life also, he cannot be My disciple. 27And
whoever does not bear his cross and
come after Me cannot be My disciple.
28For which of you, intending to build a
tower, does not sit down first and count
the cost, whether he has *enough* to finish
it— 29lest, after he has laid the founda-
tion, and is not able to finish, all who
see *it* begin to mock him, 30saying, 'This
man began to build and was not able to
finish'? 31Or what king, going to make
war against another king, does not sit
down first and consider whether he is
able with ten thousand to meet him who
comes against him with twenty thou-
sand? 32Or else, while the other is still a
great way off, he sends a delegation and
asks conditions of peace. 33So likewise,
whoever of you does not forsake all that
he has cannot be My disciple.

Tasteless Salt Is Worthless

34"Salt *is* good; but if the salt has lost
its flavor, how shall it be seasoned? 35It
is neither fit for the land nor for the
dunghill, *but* men throw it out. He who
has ears to hear, let him hear!"

14:5 [a] NU-Text and M-Text read *son.* **14:15** [a] M-Text reads *dinner.*

The Parable of the Lost Sheep

15 Then all the tax collectors and
the sinners drew near to Him
to hear Him. 2And the Pharisees and
scribes complained, saying, "This Man
receives sinners and eats with them." 3So
He spoke this parable to them, saying:
4"What man of you, having a hundred
sheep, if he loses one of them, does not
leave the ninety-nine in the wilderness,
and go after the one which is lost until
he finds it? 5And when he has found *it,*
he lays *it* on his shoulders, rejoicing.
6And when he comes home, he calls
together *his* friends and neighbors,
saying to them, 'Rejoice with me, for I
have found my sheep which was lost!'
7I say to you that likewise there will
be more joy in heaven over one sinner
who repents than over ninety-nine just
persons who need no repentance.

The Parable of the Lost Coin

8"Or what woman, having ten silver
coins,[a] if she loses one coin, does not
light a lamp, sweep the house, and
search carefully until she finds *it?*
9And when she has found *it,* she calls
her friends and neighbors together, saying,
'Rejoice with me, for I have found
the piece which I lost!' 10Likewise, I say
to you, there is joy in the presence of
the angels of God over one sinner who
repents."

The Parable of the Lost Son

11Then He said: "A certain man had two
sons. 12And the younger of them said to
his father, 'Father, give me the portion
of goods that falls *to me.*' So he divided
to them *his* livelihood. 13And not many
days after, the younger son gathered all
together, journeyed to a far country,
and there wasted his possessions with
prodigal living. 14But when he had spent
all, there arose a severe famine in that
land, and he began to be in want. 15Then
he went and joined himself to a citizen
of that country, and he sent him into
his fields to feed swine. 16And he would
gladly have filled his stomach with the
pods that the swine ate, and no one gave
him *anything.*

17"But when he came to himself, he
said, 'How many of my father's hired
servants have bread enough and to
spare, and I perish with hunger! 18I will
arise and go to my father, and will say
to him, "Father, I have sinned against
heaven and before you, 19and I am no
longer worthy to be called your son.
Make me like one of your hired servants." '

20"And he arose and came to his father.
But when he was still a great way
off, his father saw him and had compassion,
and ran and fell on his neck and
kissed him. 21And the son said to him,
'Father, I have sinned against heaven
and in your sight, and am no longer
worthy to be called your son.'

22"But the father said to his servants,
'Bring[a] out the best robe and put *it* on
him, and put a ring on his hand and
sandals on *his* feet. 23And bring the
fatted calf here and kill *it,* and let us
eat and be merry; 24for this my son was
dead and is alive again; he was lost and
is found.' And they began to be merry.

25"Now his older son was in the field.
And as he came and drew near to the
house, he heard music and dancing.
26So he called one of the servants and
asked what these things meant. 27And
he said to him, 'Your brother has come,
and because he has received him safe
and sound, your father has killed the
fatted calf.'

28"But he was angry and would not go
in. Therefore his father came out and
pleaded with him. 29So he answered
and said to *his* father, 'Lo, these many
years I have been serving you; I never
transgressed your commandment at
any time; and yet you never gave me
a young goat, that I might make merry
with my friends. 30But as soon as this
son of yours came, who has devoured
your livelihood with harlots, you killed
the fatted calf for him.'

31"And he said to him, 'Son, you are
always with me, and all that I have is
yours. 32It was right that we should
make merry and be glad, for your
brother was dead and is alive again,
and was lost and is found.' "

15:8 [a] Greek *drachma,* a valuable coin often worn in a ten-piece garland by married women
15:22 [a] NU-Text reads *Quickly bring.*

WORSHIP GROWTH HEAVEN FAMILY

The Parable of the Unjust Steward

16 He also said to His disciples:
"There was a certain rich man
who had a steward, and an accusation
was brought to him that this man was
wasting his goods. 2So he called him
and said to him, 'What is this I hear
about you? Give an account of your
stewardship, for you can no longer be
steward.'
3"Then the steward said within him-
self, 'What shall I do? For my master is
taking the stewardship away from me.
I cannot dig; I am ashamed to beg. 4I
have resolved what to do, that when
I am put out of the stewardship, they
may receive me into their houses.'
5"So he called every one of his master's
debtors to *him,* and said to the first, 'How
much do you owe my master?' 6And
he said, 'A hundred measures[a] of oil.'
So he said to him, 'Take your bill, and
sit down quickly and write fifty.' 7Then
he said to another, 'And how much do
you owe?' So he said, 'A hundred mea-
sures[a] of wheat.' And he said to him,
'Take your bill, and write eighty.' 8So the
master commended the unjust steward
because he had dealt shrewdly. For the
sons of this world are more shrewd in
their generation than the sons of light.
9"And I say to you, make friends for
yourselves by unrighteous mammon,
that when you fail,[a] they may receive
you into an everlasting home. 10He who
is faithful in *what is* least is faithful also
in much; and he who is unjust in *what is*
least is unjust also in much. 11Therefore
if you have not been faithful in the un-
righteous mammon, who will commit
to your trust the true *riches?* 12And if
you have not been faithful in what is
another man's, who will give you what
is your own?
13"No servant can serve two masters;
for either he will hate the one and love
the other, or else he will be loyal to the
one and despise the other. You cannot
serve God and mammon."

The Law, the Prophets, and the Kingdom

14Now the Pharisees, who were lovers of
money, also heard all these things, and
they derided Him. 15And He said to them,
"You are those who justify yourselves
before men, but God knows your hearts.
For what is highly esteemed among men
is an abomination in the sight of God.
16"The law and the prophets *were* until
John. Since that time the kingdom of
God has been preached, and everyone
is pressing into it. 17And it is easier for
heaven and earth to pass away than
for one tittle of the law to fail.
18"Whoever divorces his wife and mar-
ries another commits adultery; and
whoever marries her who is divorced
from *her* husband commits adultery.

The Rich Man and Lazarus

19"There was a certain rich man who
was clothed in purple and fine linen and
fared sumptuously every day. 20But
there was a certain beggar named
Lazarus, full of sores, who was laid
at his gate, 21desiring to be fed with
the crumbs which fell[a] from the rich
man's table. Moreover the dogs came
and licked his sores. 22So it was that
the beggar died, and was carried by the
angels to Abraham's bosom. The rich
man also died and was buried. 23And
being in torments in Hades, he lifted
up his eyes and saw Abraham afar off,
and Lazarus in his bosom.
24"Then he cried and said, 'Father
Abraham, have mercy on me, and send
Lazarus that he may dip the tip of his
finger in water and cool my tongue; for
I am tormented in this flame.' 25But
Abraham said, 'Son, remember that in
your lifetime you received your good
things, and likewise Lazarus evil things;
but now he is comforted and you are
tormented. 26And besides all this, be-
tween us and you there is a great gulf
fixed, so that those who want to pass
from here to you cannot, nor can those
from there pass to us.'
27"Then he said, 'I beg you therefore,
father, that you would send him to my
father's house, 28for I have five brothers,
that he may testify to them, lest they
also come to this place of torment.'
29Abraham said to him, 'They have
Moses and the prophets; let them hear

16:6 [a] Greek *batos,* eight or nine gallons each (Old Testament *bath*) **16:7** [a] Greek *koros,* ten or twelve bushels each (Old Testament *kor*) **16:9** [a] NU-Text reads *it fails.* **16:21** [a] NU-Text reads *with what fell.*

GOD SIN JESUS SALVATION LOVE

them.' 30And he said, 'No, father Abra-
ham; but if one goes to them from the
dead, they will repent.' 31But he said to
him, 'If they do not hear Moses and the
prophets, neither will they be persuaded
though one rise from the dead.' "

Jesus Warns of Offenses

17 Then He said to the disciples, "It
is impossible that no offenses
should come, but woe *to him* through
whom they do come! 2It would be better
for him if a millstone were hung around
his neck, and he were thrown into the
sea, than that he should offend one of
these little ones. 3Take heed to your-
selves. If your brother sins against you,[a]
rebuke him; and if he repents, forgive
him. 4And if he sins against you seven
times in a day, and seven times in a day
returns to you,[a] saying, 'I repent,' you
shall forgive him."

Faith and Duty

5And the apostles said to the Lord,
"Increase our faith."

6So the Lord said, "If you have faith
as a mustard seed, you can say to this
mulberry tree, 'Be pulled up by the roots
and be planted in the sea,' and it would
obey you. 7And which of you, having a
servant plowing or tending sheep, will
say to him when he has come in from
the field, 'Come at once and sit down to
eat'? 8But will he not rather say to him,
'Prepare something for my supper, and
gird yourself and serve me till I have
eaten and drunk, and afterward you
will eat and drink'? 9Does he thank that
servant because he did the things that
were commanded him? I think not.[a] 10So
likewise you, when you have done all
those things which you are commanded,
say, 'We are unprofitable servants. We
have done what was our duty to do.' "

Ten Lepers Cleansed

11Now it happened as He went to Je-
rusalem that He passed through the
midst of Samaria and Galilee. 12Then
as He entered a certain village, there
met Him ten men who were lepers, who
stood afar off. 13And they lifted up *their*
voices and said, "Jesus, Master, have
mercy on us!"

14So when He saw *them,* He said to
them, "Go, show yourselves to the
priests." And so it was that as they went,
they were cleansed.

15And one of them, when he saw that
he was healed, returned, and with a loud
voice glorified God, 16and fell down on
his face at His feet, giving Him thanks.
And he was a Samaritan.

17So Jesus answered and said, "Were
there not ten cleansed? But where *are*
the nine? 18Were there not any found
who returned to give glory to God ex-
cept this foreigner?" 19And He said to
him, "Arise, go your way. Your faith has
made you well."

The Coming of the Kingdom

20Now when He was asked by the Phar-
isees when the kingdom of God would
come, He answered them and said, "The
kingdom of God does not come with
observation; 21nor will they say, 'See
here!' or 'See there!'[a] For indeed, the
kingdom of God is within you."

22Then He said to the disciples, "The
days will come when you will desire to
see one of the days of the Son of Man,
and you will not see *it.* 23And they will
say to you, 'Look here!' or 'Look there!'[a]
Do not go after *them* or follow *them.*
24For as the lightning that flashes out
of one *part* under heaven shines to the
other *part* under heaven, so also the
Son of Man will be in His day. 25But
first He must suffer many things and
be rejected by this generation. 26And
as it was in the days of Noah, so it will
be also in the days of the Son of Man:
27They ate, they drank, they married
wives, they were given in marriage,
until the day that Noah entered the
ark, and the flood came and destroyed
them all. 28Likewise as it was also in the
days of Lot: They ate, they drank, they
bought, they sold, they planted, they
built; 29but on the day that Lot went out
of Sodom it rained fire and brimstone
from heaven and destroyed *them* all.

17:3 [a] NU-Text omits *against you.* **17:4** [a] M-Text omits *to you.* **17:9** [a] NU-Text ends verse with *commanded;* M-Text omits *him.* **17:21** [a] NU-Text reverses *here* and *there.* **17:23** [a] NU-Text reverses *here* and *there.*

30 Even so will it be in the day when the Son of Man is revealed.

31 "In that day, he who is on the housetop, and his goods *are* in the house, let him not come down to take them away. And likewise the one who is in the field, let him not turn back. 32 Remember Lot's wife. 33 Whoever seeks to save his life will lose it, and whoever loses his life will preserve it. 34 I tell you, in that night there will be two *men* in one bed: the one will be taken and the other will be left. 35 Two *women* will be grinding together: the one will be taken and the other left. 36 Two *men* will be in the field: the one will be taken and the other left."[a]

37 And they answered and said to Him, "Where, Lord?"

So He said to them, "Wherever the body is, there the eagles will be gathered together."

The Parable of the Persistent Widow

18 Then He spoke a parable to them, that men always ought to pray and not lose heart, 2 saying: "There was in a certain city a judge who did not fear God nor regard man. 3 Now there was a widow in that city; and she came to him, saying, 'Get justice for me from my adversary.' 4 And he would not for a while; but afterward he said within himself, 'Though I do not fear God nor regard man, 5 yet because this widow troubles me I will avenge her, lest by her continual coming she weary me.' "

6 Then the Lord said, "Hear what the unjust judge said. 7 And shall God not avenge His own elect who cry out day and night to Him, though He bears long with them? 8 I tell you that He will avenge them speedily. Nevertheless, when the Son of Man comes, will He really find faith on the earth?"

The Parable of the Pharisee and the Tax Collector

9 Also He spoke this parable to some who trusted in themselves that they were righteous, and despised others: 10 "Two men went up to the temple to pray, one a Pharisee and the other a tax collector. 11 The Pharisee stood and prayed thus with himself, 'God, I thank You that I am not like other men—extortioners, unjust, adulterers, or even as this tax collector. 12 I fast twice a week; I give tithes of all that I possess.' 13 And the tax collector, standing afar off, would not so much as raise *his* eyes to heaven, but beat his breast, saying, 'God, be merciful to me a sinner!' 14 I tell you, this man went down to his house justified *rather* than the other; for everyone who exalts himself will be humbled, and he who humbles himself will be exalted."

Jesus Blesses Little Children

15 Then they also brought infants to Him that He might touch them; but when the disciples saw *it,* they rebuked them. 16 But Jesus called them to *Him* and said, "Let the little children come to Me, and do not forbid them; for of such is the kingdom of God. 17 Assuredly, I say to you, whoever does not receive the kingdom of God as a little child will by no means enter it."

Jesus Counsels the Rich Young Ruler

18 Now a certain ruler asked Him, saying, "Good Teacher, what shall I do to inherit eternal life?"

19 So Jesus said to him, "Why do you call Me good? No one *is* good but One, *that is,* God. 20 You know the commandments: 'Do not commit adultery,' 'Do not murder,' 'Do not steal,' 'Do not bear false witness,' 'Honor your father and your mother.' "[a]

21 And he said, "All these things I have kept from my youth."

22 So when Jesus heard these things, He said to him, "You still lack one thing. Sell all that you have and distribute to the poor, and you will have treasure in heaven; and come, follow Me."

23 But when he heard this, he became very sorrowful, for he was very rich.

With God All Things Are Possible

24 And when Jesus saw that he became very sorrowful, He said, "How hard it is for those who have riches to enter the kingdom of God! 25 For it is easier for a camel to go through the eye of a

17:36 [a] NU-Text and M-Text omit verse 36. **18:20** [a] Exodus 20:12–16; Deuteronomy 5:16–20

GOD SIN JESUS SALVATION LOVE

needle than for a rich man to enter the
kingdom of God."
26And those who heard it said, "Who
then can be saved?"
27But He said, "The things which are im-
possible with men are possible with God."
28Then Peter said, "See, we have left
all[a] and followed You."
29So He said to them, "Assuredly, I
say to you, there is no one who has left
house or parents or brothers or wife or
children, for the sake of the kingdom
of God, 30who shall not receive many
times more in this present time, and in
the age to come eternal life."

Jesus a Third Time Predicts His Death and Resurrection

31Then He took the twelve aside and
said to them, "Behold, we are going up to
Jerusalem, and all things that are writ-
ten by the prophets concerning the Son
of Man will be accomplished. 32For He
will be delivered to the Gentiles and will
be mocked and insulted and spit upon.
33They will scourge *Him* and kill Him.
And the third day He will rise again."
34But they understood none of these
things; this saying was hidden from
them, and they did not know the things
which were spoken.

A Blind Man Receives His Sight

35Then it happened, as He was coming
near Jericho, that a certain blind man
sat by the road begging. 36And hearing
a multitude passing by, he asked what
it meant. 37So they told him that Jesus
of Nazareth was passing by. 38And he
cried out, saying, "Jesus, Son of David,
have mercy on me!"
39Then those who went before warned
him that he should be quiet; but he cried
out all the more, "Son of David, have
mercy on me!"
40So Jesus stood still and commanded
him to be brought to Him. And when he
had come near, He asked him, 41saying,
"What do you want Me to do for you?"
He said, "Lord, that I may receive my
sight."
42Then Jesus said to him, "Receive
your sight; your faith has made you
well." 43And immediately he received
his sight, and followed Him, glorifying
God. And all the people, when they saw
it, gave praise to God.

Jesus Comes to Zacchaeus' House

19 Then *Jesus* entered and passed
through Jericho. 2Now behold,
there was a man named Zacchaeus who
was a chief tax collector, and he was
rich. 3And he sought to see who Jesus
was, but could not because of the crowd,
for he was of short stature. 4So he ran
ahead and climbed up into a sycamore
tree to see Him, for He was going to pass
that *way*. 5And when Jesus came to the
place, He looked up and saw him,[a] and
said to him, "Zacchaeus, make haste
and come down, for today I must stay
at your house." 6So he made haste and
came down, and received Him joyfully.
7But when they saw *it*, they all com-
plained, saying, "He has gone to be a
guest with a man who is a sinner."
8Then Zacchaeus stood and said to
the Lord, "Look, Lord, I give half of my
goods to the poor; and if I have taken
anything from anyone by false accu-
sation, I restore fourfold."
9And Jesus said to him, "Today salva-
tion has come to this house, because he
also is a son of Abraham; 10for the Son
of Man has come to seek and to save
that which was lost."

The Parable of the Minas

11Now as they heard these things, He
spoke another parable, because He
was near Jerusalem and because they
thought the kingdom of God would ap-
pear immediately. 12Therefore He said:
"A certain nobleman went into a far
country to receive for himself a kingdom
and to return. 13So he called ten of his
servants, delivered to them ten minas,[a]
and said to them, 'Do business till I come.'
14But his citizens hated him, and sent a
delegation after him, saying, 'We will not
have this *man* to reign over us.'
15"And so it was that when he returned,
having received the kingdom, he then
commanded these servants, to whom
he had given the money, to be called to

18:28 [a] NU-Text reads *our own*. **19:5** [a] NU-Text omits *and saw him*. **19:13** [a] The *mina* (Greek *mna*, Hebrew *minah*) was worth about three months' salary.

him, that he might know how much ev-
ery man had gained by trading. 16Then
came the first, saying, 'Master, your
mina has earned ten minas.' 17And he
said to him, 'Well *done,* good servant;
because you were faithful in a very little,
have authority over ten cities.' 18And
the second came, saying, 'Master, your
mina has earned five minas.' 19Likewise
he said to him, 'You also be over five
cities.'
20"Then another came, saying, 'Mas-
ter, here is your mina, which I have
kept put away in a handkerchief. 21For
I feared you, because you are an aus-
tere man. You collect what you did not
deposit, and reap what you did not sow.'
22And he said to him, 'Out of your own
mouth I will judge you, *you* wicked ser-
vant. You knew that I was an austere
man, collecting what I did not deposit
and reaping what I did not sow. 23Why
then did you not put my money in the
bank, that at my coming I might have
collected it with interest?'
24"And he said to those who stood by,
'Take the mina from him, and give *it*
to him who has ten minas.' 25(But they
said to him, 'Master, he has ten minas.')
26'For I say to you, that to everyone who
has will be given; and from him who
does not have, even what he has will
be taken away from him. 27But bring
here those enemies of mine, who did
not want me to reign over them, and
slay *them* before me.' "

The Triumphal Entry

28When He had said this, He went on
ahead, going up to Jerusalem. 29And
it came to pass, when He drew near
to Bethphage[a] and Bethany, at the
mountain called Olivet, *that* He sent
two of His disciples, 30saying, "Go into
the village opposite *you,* where as you
enter you will find a colt tied, on which
no one has ever sat. Loose it and bring
it here. 31And if anyone asks you, 'Why
are you loosing *it?'* thus you shall say to
him, 'Because the Lord has need of it.' "
32So those who were sent went their
way and found *it* just as He had said
to them. 33But as they were loosing the
colt, the owners of it said to them, "Why
are you loosing the colt?"
34And they said, "The Lord has need of
him." 35Then they brought him to Jesus.
And they threw their own clothes on the
colt, and they set Jesus on him. 36And
as He went, *many* spread their clothes
on the road.
37Then, as He was now drawing near
the descent of the Mount of Olives, the
whole multitude of the disciples began
to rejoice and praise God with a loud
voice for all the mighty works they had
seen, 38saying:

" 'Blessed *is* the King who comes in
the name of the LORD!'[a]
Peace in heaven and glory in the
highest!"

39And some of the Pharisees called to
Him from the crowd, "Teacher, rebuke
Your disciples."
40But He answered and said to them, "I
tell you that if these should keep silent,
the stones would immediately cry out."

Jesus Weeps over Jerusalem

41Now as He drew near, He saw the
city and wept over it, 42saying, "If you
had known, even you, especially in this
your day, the things *that make* for your
peace! But now they are hidden from
your eyes. 43For days will come upon
you when your enemies will build an
embankment around you, surround
you and close you in on every side,
44and level you, and your children with-
in you, to the ground; and they will not
leave in you one stone upon another,
because you did not know the time of
your visitation."

Jesus Cleanses the Temple

45Then He went into the temple and be-
gan to drive out those who bought and
sold in it,[a] 46saying to them, "It is writ-
ten, 'My house is[a] a house of prayer,'[b]
but you have made it a 'den of thieves.' "[c]
47And He was teaching daily in the
temple. But the chief priests, the scribes,
and the leaders of the people sought to
destroy Him, 48and were unable to do

19:29 [a] M-Text reads *Bethsphage.* **19:38** [a] Psalm 118:26 **19:45** [a] NU-Text reads *those who were selling.* **19:46** [a] NU-Text reads *shall be.* [b] Isaiah 56:7 [c] Jeremiah 7:11

anything; for all the people were very
attentive to hear Him.

Jesus' Authority Questioned

20 Now it happened on one of those
days, as He taught the people in
the temple and preached the gospel, *that*
the chief priests and the scribes, together
with the elders, confronted *Him* 2and
spoke to Him, saying, "Tell us, by what
authority are You doing these things? Or
who is he who gave You this authority?"
3But He answered and said to them, "I
also will ask you one thing, and answer
Me: 4The baptism of John—was it from
heaven or from men?"
5And they reasoned among themselves,
saying, "If we say, 'From heaven,' He will
say, 'Why then[a] did you not believe him?'
6But if we say, 'From men,' all the people
will stone us, for they are persuaded that
John was a prophet." 7So they answered
that they did not know where *it was* from.
8And Jesus said to them, "Neither will
I tell you by what authority I do these
things."

The Parable of the Wicked Vinedressers

9Then He began to tell the people this
parable: "A certain man planted a vine-
yard, leased it to vinedressers, and went
into a far country for a long time. 10Now
at vintage-time he sent a servant to the
vinedressers, that they might give him
some of the fruit of the vineyard. But
the vinedressers beat him and sent *him*
away empty-handed. 11Again he sent
another servant; and they beat him
also, treated *him* shamefully, and sent
him away empty-handed. 12And again
he sent a third; and they wounded him
also and cast *him* out.
13"Then the owner of the vineyard
said, 'What shall I do? I will send my
beloved son. Probably they will respect
him when they see him.' 14But when the
vinedressers saw him, they reasoned
among themselves, saying, 'This is the
heir. Come, let us kill him, that the in-
heritance may be ours.' 15So they cast
him out of the vineyard and killed *him*.
Therefore what will the owner of the
vineyard do to them? 16He will come
and destroy those vinedressers and
give the vineyard to others."
And when they heard *it* they said,
"Certainly not!"
17Then He looked at them and said,
"What then is this that is written:

'The stone which the builders
rejected
Has become the chief
cornerstone'?[a]

18Whoever falls on that stone will be
broken; but on whomever it falls, it will
grind him to powder."
19And the chief priests and the scribes
that very hour sought to lay hands on
Him, but they feared the people[a]—for
they knew He had spoken this parable
against them.

The Pharisees: Is It Lawful to Pay Taxes to Caesar?

20So they watched *Him*, and sent spies
who pretended to be righteous, that
they might seize on His words, in order
to deliver Him to the power and the
authority of the governor.
21Then they asked Him, saying,
"Teacher, we know that You say and
teach rightly, and You do not show per-
sonal favoritism, but teach the way of
God in truth: 22Is it lawful for us to pay
taxes to Caesar or not?"
23But He perceived their craftiness,
and said to them, "Why do you test Me?[a]
24Show Me a denarius. Whose image
and inscription does it have?"
They answered and said, "Caesar's."
25And He said to them, "Render there-
fore to Caesar the things that are Cae-
sar's, and to God the things that are
God's."
26But they could not catch Him in His
words in the presence of the people.
And they marveled at His answer and
kept silent.

The Sadducees: What About the Resurrection?

27Then some of the Sadducees, who
deny that there is a resurrection, came
to *Him* and asked Him, 28saying:

20:5 [a] NU-Text and M-Text omit *then*. **20:17** [a] Psalm 118:22 **20:19** [a] M-Text reads *but they were afraid*. **20:23** [a] NU-Text omits *Why do you test Me?*

"Teacher, Moses wrote to us *that* if a
man's brother dies, having a wife, and
he dies without children, his brother
should take his wife and raise up off-
spring for his brother. 29Now there were
seven brothers. And the first took a wife,
and died without children. 30And the
second[a] took her as wife, and he died
childless. 31Then the third took her, and
in like manner the seven also; and they
left no children,[a] and died. 32Last of all
the woman died also. 33Therefore, in
the resurrection, whose wife does she
become? For all seven had her as wife."

34Jesus answered and said to them,
"The sons of this age marry and are
given in marriage. 35But those who are
counted worthy to attain that age, and
the resurrection from the dead, nei-
ther marry nor are given in marriage;
36nor can they die anymore, for they are
equal to the angels and are sons of God,
being sons of the resurrection. 37But
even Moses showed in the *burning* bush
passage that the dead are raised, when
he called the Lord 'the God of Abraham,
the God of Isaac, and the God of Jacob.'[a]
38For He is not the God of the dead but
of the living, for all live to Him."

39Then some of the scribes answered
and said, "Teacher, You have spoken
well." 40But after that they dared not
question Him anymore.

Jesus: How Can David Call His Descendant Lord?

41And He said to them, "How can they
say that the Christ is the Son of David?
42Now David himself said in the Book
of Psalms:

> 'The LORD said to my Lord,
> "Sit at My right hand,
> 43 Till I make Your enemies Your
> footstool." '[a]

44Therefore David calls Him 'Lord'; how
is He then his Son?"

Beware of the Scribes

45Then, in the hearing of all the people,
He said to His disciples, 46"Beware of
the scribes, who desire to go around in
long robes, love greetings in the mar-
ketplaces, the best seats in the syna-
gogues, and the best places at feasts,
47who devour widows' houses, and for a
pretense make long prayers. These will
receive greater condemnation."

The Widow's Two Mites

21 And He looked up and saw the
rich putting their gifts into the
treasury, 2and He saw also a certain
poor widow putting in two mites. 3So He
said, "Truly I say to you that this poor
widow has put in more than all; 4for
all these out of their abundance have
put in offerings for God,[a] but she out
of her poverty put in all the livelihood
that she had."

Jesus Predicts the Destruction of the Temple

5Then, as some spoke of the temple,
how it was adorned with beautiful stones
and donations, He said, 6"These things
which you see—the days will come in
which not *one* stone shall be left upon
another that shall not be thrown down."

The Signs of the Times and the End of the Age

7So they asked Him, saying, "Teacher,
but when will these things be? And what
sign *will there be* when these things are
about to take place?"

8And He said: "Take heed that you not
be deceived. For many will come in My
name, saying, 'I am *He*,' and, 'The time
has drawn near.' Therefore[a] do not go
after them. 9But when you hear of wars
and commotions, do not be terrified; for
these things must come to pass first,
but the end *will* not *come* immediately."

10Then He said to them, "Nation will rise
against nation, and kingdom against
kingdom. 11And there will be great earth-
quakes in various places, and famines
and pestilences; and there will be fear-
ful sights and great signs from heaven.
12But before all these things, they will lay
their hands on you and persecute *you*,
delivering *you* up to the synagogues and

20:30 [a] NU-Text ends verse 30 here. **20:31** [a] NU-Text and M-Text read *the seven also left no children.* **20:37** [a] Exodus 3:6, 15 **20:43** [a] Psalm 110:1 **21:4** [a] NU-Text omits *for God.* **21:8** [a] NU-Text omits *Therefore.*

prisons. You will be brought before kings
and rulers for My name's sake. 13But it
will turn out for you as an occasion for
testimony. 14Therefore settle *it* in your
hearts not to meditate beforehand on
what you will answer; 15for I will give
you a mouth and wisdom which all your
adversaries will not be able to contradict
or resist. 16You will be betrayed even
by parents and brothers, relatives and
friends; and they will put *some* of you to
death. 17And you will be hated by all for
My name's sake. 18But not a hair of your
head shall be lost. 19By your patience
possess your souls.

The Destruction of Jerusalem

20"But when you see Jerusalem sur-
rounded by armies, then know that its
desolation is near. 21Then let those who
are in Judea flee to the mountains, let
those who are in the midst of her depart,
and let not those who are in the country
enter her. 22For these are the days of ven-
geance, that all things which are written
may be fulfilled. 23But woe to those who
are pregnant and to those who are nurs-
ing babies in those days! For there will
be great distress in the land and wrath
upon this people. 24And they will fall by
the edge of the sword, and be led away
captive into all nations. And Jerusalem
will be trampled by Gentiles until the
times of the Gentiles are fulfilled.

The Coming of the Son of Man

25"And there will be signs in the sun,
in the moon, and in the stars; and on
the earth distress of nations, with per-
plexity, the sea and the waves roaring;
26men's hearts failing them from fear
and the expectation of those things
which are coming on the earth, for the
powers of the heavens will be shaken.
27Then they will see the Son of Man com-
ing in a cloud with power and great
glory. 28Now when these things begin to
happen, look up and lift up your heads,
because your redemption draws near."

The Parable of the Fig Tree

29Then He spoke to them a parable:
"Look at the fig tree, and all the trees.
30When they are already budding, you
see and know for yourselves that sum-
mer is now near. 31So you also, when
you see these things happening, know
that the kingdom of God is near. 32As-
suredly, I say to you, this generation
will by no means pass away till all
things take place. 33Heaven and earth
will pass away, but My words will by no
means pass away.

The Importance of Watching

34"But take heed to yourselves, lest
your hearts be weighed down with ca-
rousing, drunkenness, and cares of this
life, and that Day come on you unex-
pectedly. 35For it will come as a snare
on all those who dwell on the face of
the whole earth. 36Watch therefore, and
pray always that you may be counted
worthy[a] to escape all these things that
will come to pass, and to stand before
the Son of Man."

37And in the daytime He was teach-
ing in the temple, but at night He went
out and stayed on the mountain called
Olivet. 38Then early in the morning all
the people came to Him in the temple
to hear Him.

The Plot to Kill Jesus

22 Now the Feast of Unleavened
Bread drew near, which is called
Passover. 2And the chief priests and the
scribes sought how they might kill Him,
for they feared the people.

3Then Satan entered Judas, surnamed
Iscariot, who was numbered among
the twelve. 4So he went his way and
conferred with the chief priests and
captains, how he might betray Him to
them. 5And they were glad, and agreed
to give him money. 6So he promised
and sought opportunity to betray Him
to them in the absence of the multitude.

Jesus and His Disciples Prepare the Passover

7Then came the Day of Unleavened
Bread, when the Passover must be
killed. 8And He sent Peter and John,
saying, "Go and prepare the Passover
for us, that we may eat."

21:36 [a] NU-Text reads *may have strength.*

WORSHIP GROWTH HEAVEN FAMILY

9So they said to Him, "Where do You
want us to prepare?"
10And He said to them, "Behold, when
you have entered the city, a man will
meet you carrying a pitcher of water;
follow him into the house which he en-
ters. 11Then you shall say to the master
of the house, 'The Teacher says to you,
"Where is the guest room where I may
eat the Passover with My disciples?"'
12Then he will show you a large, fur-
nished upper room; there make ready."
13So they went and found it just as He
had said to them, and they prepared
the Passover.

Jesus Institutes the Lord's Supper

14When the hour had come, He sat
down, and the twelve[a] apostles with
Him. 15Then He said to them, "With
fervent desire I have desired to eat this
Passover with you before I suffer; 16for I
say to you, I will no longer eat of it until
it is fulfilled in the kingdom of God."
17Then He took the cup, and gave
thanks, and said, "Take this and divide
it among yourselves; 18for I say to you,[a]
I will not drink of the fruit of the vine
until the kingdom of God comes."
19And He took bread, gave thanks and
broke *it*, and gave *it* to them, saying,
"This is My body which is given for you;
do this in remembrance of Me."
20Likewise He also *took* the cup af-
ter supper, saying, "This cup *is* the new
covenant in My blood, which is shed
for you. 21But behold, the hand of My
betrayer *is* with Me on the table. 22And
truly the Son of Man goes as it has been
determined, but woe to that man by
whom He is betrayed!"
23Then they began to question among
themselves, which of them it was who
would do this thing.

The Disciples Argue About Greatness

24Now there was also a dispute among
them, as to which of them should be
considered the greatest. 25And He said
to them, "The kings of the Gentiles ex-
ercise lordship over them, and those
who exercise authority over them are
called 'benefactors.' 26But not so *among*
you; on the contrary, he who is greatest
among you, let him be as the younger,
and he who governs as he who serves.
27For who *is* greater, he who sits at the
table, or he who serves? *Is* it not he who
sits at the table? Yet I am among you
as the One who serves.
28"But you are those who have con-
tinued with Me in My trials. 29And I
bestow upon you a kingdom, just as My
Father bestowed *one* upon Me, 30that
you may eat and drink at My table in
My kingdom, and sit on thrones judging
the twelve tribes of Israel."

Jesus Predicts Peter's Denial

31And the Lord said,[a] "Simon, Simon!
Indeed, Satan has asked for you, that
he may sift *you* as wheat. 32But I have
prayed for you, that your faith should
not fail; and when you have returned to
Me, strengthen your brethren."
33But he said to Him, "Lord, I am ready
to go with You, both to prison and to
death."
34Then He said, "I tell you, Peter, the
rooster shall not crow this day before
you will deny three times that you
know Me."

Supplies for the Road

35And He said to them, "When I sent
you without money bag, knapsack, and
sandals, did you lack anything?"
So they said, "Nothing."
36Then He said to them, "But now, he
who has a money bag, let him take *it*,
and likewise a knapsack; and he who
has no sword, let him sell his garment
and buy one. 37For I say to you that this
which is written must still be accom-
plished in Me: 'And He was numbered
with the transgressors.'[a] For the things
concerning Me have an end."
38So they said, "Lord, look, here *are*
two swords."
And He said to them, "It is enough."

The Prayer in the Garden

39Coming out, He went to the Mount
of Olives, as He was accustomed, and
His disciples also followed Him. 40When

22:14 [a] NU-Text omits *twelve.* **22:18** [a] NU-Text adds *from now on.* **22:31** [a] NU-Text omits *And the Lord said.* **22:37** [a] Isaiah 53:12

He came to the place, He said to them,
"Pray that you may not enter into temp-
tation."
41And He was withdrawn from them
about a stone's throw, and He knelt
down and prayed, 42saying, "Father, if
it is Your will, take this cup away from
Me; nevertheless not My will, but Yours,
be done." 43Then an angel appeared to
Him from heaven, strengthening Him.
44And being in agony, He prayed more
earnestly. Then His sweat became like
great drops of blood falling down to
the ground.[a]
45When He rose up from prayer, and
had come to His disciples, He found
them sleeping from sorrow. 46Then He
said to them, "Why do you sleep? Rise
and pray, lest you enter into tempta-
tion."

Betrayal and Arrest in Gethsemane

47And while He was still speaking,
behold, a multitude; and he who was
called Judas, one of the twelve, went
before them and drew near to Jesus
to kiss Him. 48But Jesus said to him,
"Judas, are you betraying the Son of
Man with a kiss?"
49When those around Him saw what
was going to happen, they said to Him,
"Lord, shall we strike with the sword?"
50And one of them struck the servant of
the high priest and cut off his right ear.
51But Jesus answered and said, "Permit
even this." And He touched his ear and
healed him.
52Then Jesus said to the chief priests,
captains of the temple, and the elders
who had come to Him, "Have you come
out, as against a robber, with swords
and clubs? 53When I was with you daily
in the temple, you did not try to seize
Me. But this is your hour, and the power
of darkness."

Peter Denies Jesus, and Weeps Bitterly

54Having arrested Him, they led *Him*
and brought Him into the high priest's
house. But Peter followed at a distance.
55Now when they had kindled a fire in
the midst of the courtyard and sat down
together, Peter sat among them. 56And
a certain servant girl, seeing him as he
sat by the fire, looked intently at him
and said, "This man was also with Him."
57But he denied Him,[a] saying, "Wom-
an, I do not know Him."
58And after a little while another saw
him and said, "You also are of them."
But Peter said, "Man, I am not!"
59Then after about an hour had
passed, another confidently affirmed,
saying, "Surely this *fellow* also was with
Him, for he is a Galilean."
60But Peter said, "Man, I do not know
what you are saying!"
Immediately, while he was still speak-
ing, the rooster[a] crowed. 61And the Lord
turned and looked at Peter. Then Peter
remembered the word of the Lord, how
He had said to him, "Before the rooster
crows,[a] you will deny Me three times."
62So Peter went out and wept bitterly.

Jesus Mocked and Beaten

63Now the men who held Jesus mocked
Him and beat Him. 64And having blind-
folded Him, they struck Him on the face
and asked Him,[a] saying, "Prophesy!
Who is the one who struck You?" 65And
many other things they blasphemously
spoke against Him.

Jesus Faces the Sanhedrin

66As soon as it was day, the elders
of the people, both chief priests and
scribes, came together and led Him into
their council, saying, 67"If You are the
Christ, tell us."
But He said to them, "If I tell you, you
will by no means believe. 68And if I also
ask *you,* you will by no means answer
Me or let *Me* go.[a] 69Hereafter the Son
of Man will sit on the right hand of the
power of God."
70Then they all said, "Are You then the
Son of God?"
So He said to them, "You *rightly* say
that I am."
71And they said, "What further testi-
mony do we need? For we have heard it
ourselves from His own mouth."

22:44 [a] NU-Text brackets verses 43 and 44 as not in the original text. **22:57** [a] NU-Text reads *denied it.* **22:60** [a] NU-Text and M-Text read *a rooster.* **22:61** [a] NU-Text adds *today.* **22:64** [a] NU-Text reads *And having blindfolded Him, they asked Him.* **22:68** [a] NU-Text omits *also* and *Me or let Me go.*

Jesus Handed Over to Pontius Pilate

23 Then the whole multitude of them arose and led Him to Pilate. 2And they began to accuse Him, saying, "We found this *fellow* perverting the[a] nation, and forbidding to pay taxes to Caesar, saying that He Himself is Christ, a King."

3Then Pilate asked Him, saying, "Are You the King of the Jews?"

He answered him and said, "*It is as you say.*"

4So Pilate said to the chief priests and the crowd, "I find no fault in this Man."

5But they were the more fierce, saying, "He stirs up the people, teaching throughout all Judea, beginning from Galilee to this place."

Jesus Faces Herod

6When Pilate heard of Galilee,[a] he asked if the Man were a Galilean. 7And as soon as he knew that He belonged to Herod's jurisdiction, he sent Him to Herod, who was also in Jerusalem at that time. 8Now when Herod saw Jesus, he was exceedingly glad; for he had desired for a long *time* to see Him, because he had heard many things about Him, and he hoped to see some miracle done by Him. 9Then he questioned Him with many words, but He answered him nothing. 10And the chief priests and scribes stood and vehemently accused Him. 11Then Herod, with his men of war, treated Him with contempt and mocked *Him,* arrayed Him in a gorgeous robe, and sent Him back to Pilate. 12That very day Pilate and Herod became friends with each other, for previously they had been at enmity with each other.

Taking the Place of Barabbas

13Then Pilate, when he had called together the chief priests, the rulers, and the people, 14said to them, "You have brought this Man to me, as one who misleads the people. And indeed, having examined *Him* in your presence, I have found no fault in this Man concerning those things of which you accuse Him; 15no, neither did Herod, for I sent you back to him;[a] and indeed nothing deserving of death has been done by Him. 16I will therefore chastise Him and release *Him*" 17(for it was necessary for him to release one to them at the feast).[a]

18And they all cried out at once, saying, "Away with this *Man,* and release to us Barabbas"— 19who had been thrown into prison for a certain rebellion made in the city, and for murder.

20Pilate, therefore, wishing to release Jesus, again called out to them. 21But they shouted, saying, "Crucify *Him,* crucify Him!"

22Then he said to them the third time, "Why, what evil has He done? I have found no reason for death in Him. I will therefore chastise Him and let *Him* go."

23But they were insistent, demanding with loud voices that He be crucified. And the voices of these men and of the chief priests prevailed.[a] 24So Pilate gave sentence that it should be as they requested. 25And he released to them[a] the one they requested, who for rebellion and murder had been thrown into prison; but he delivered Jesus to their will.

The King on a Cross

26Now as they led Him away, they laid hold of a certain man, Simon a Cyrenian, who was coming from the country, and on him they laid the cross that he might bear *it* after Jesus.

27And a great multitude of the people followed Him, and women who also mourned and lamented Him. 28But Jesus, turning to them, said, "Daughters of Jerusalem, do not weep for Me, but weep for yourselves and for your children. 29For indeed the days are coming in which they will say, 'Blessed *are* the barren, wombs that never bore, and breasts which never nursed!' 30Then they will begin 'to say to the mountains, "Fall on us!" and to the hills, "Cover us!" '[a] 31For if they do these things in the green wood, what will be done in the dry?"

32There were also two others, criminals, led with Him to be put to death.

23:2 [a] NU-Text reads *our.* **23:6** [a] NU-Text omits *of Galilee.* **23:15** [a] NU-Text reads *for he sent Him back to us.* **23:17** [a] NU-Text omits verse 17. **23:23** [a] NU-Text omits *and of the chief priests.* **23:25** [a] NU-Text and M-Text omit *to them.* **23:30** [a] Hosea 10:8

33And when they had come to the place
called Calvary, there they crucified Him,
and the criminals, one on the right hand
and the other on the left. 34Then Jesus
said, "Father, forgive them, for they do
not know what they do."[a]

And they divided His garments and
cast lots. 35And the people stood look-
ing on. But even the rulers with them
sneered, saying, "He saved others; let
Him save Himself if He is the Christ, the
chosen of God."

36The soldiers also mocked Him, com-
ing and offering Him sour wine, 37and
saying, "If You are the King of the Jews,
save Yourself."

38And an inscription also was written
over Him in letters of Greek, Latin, and
Hebrew:[a]

THIS IS THE KING OF THE JEWS.

39Then one of the criminals who were
hanged blasphemed Him, saying,
"If You are the Christ,[a] save Yourself
and us."

40But the other, answering, rebuked
him, saying, "Do you not even fear God,
seeing you are under the same con-
demnation? 41And we indeed justly,
for we receive the due reward of our
deeds; but this Man has done nothing
wrong." 42Then he said to Jesus, "Lord,[a]
remember me when You come into Your
kingdom."

43And Jesus said to him, "Assuredly,
I say to you, today you will be with Me
in Paradise."

Jesus Dies on the Cross

44Now it was[a] about the sixth hour,
and there was darkness over all the
earth until the ninth hour. 45Then
the sun was darkened,[a] and the veil
of the temple was torn in two. 46And
when Jesus had cried out with a loud
voice, He said, "Father, 'into Your hands
I commit My spirit.' "[a] Having said this,
He breathed His last.

47So when the centurion saw what had
happened, he glorified God, saying,
"Certainly this was a righteous Man!"

48And the whole crowd who came to-
gether to that sight, seeing what had
been done, beat their breasts and re-
turned. 49But all His acquaintances,
and the women who followed Him from
Galilee, stood at a distance, watching
these things.

Jesus Buried in Joseph's Tomb

50Now behold, *there was* a man named
Joseph, a council member, a good and
just man. 51He had not consented to
their decision and deed. *He was* from
Arimathea, a city of the Jews, who him-
self was also waiting[a] for the kingdom
of God. 52This man went to Pilate and
asked for the body of Jesus. 53Then he
took it down, wrapped it in linen, and
laid it in a tomb *that was* hewn out of
the rock, where no one had ever lain
before. 54That day was the Preparation,
and the Sabbath drew near.

55And the women who had come with
Him from Galilee followed after, and
they observed the tomb and how His
body was laid. 56Then they returned and
prepared spices and fragrant oils. And
they rested on the Sabbath according
to the commandment.

He Is Risen

24 Now on the first *day* of the week,
very early in the morning, they,
and certain *other women* with them,[a]
came to the tomb bringing the spices
which they had prepared. 2But they
found the stone rolled away from the
tomb. 3Then they went in and did not
find the body of the Lord Jesus. 4And it
happened, as they were greatly[a] per-
plexed about this, that behold, two men
stood by them in shining garments.
5Then, as they were afraid and bowed
their faces to the earth, they said to
them, "Why do you seek the living
among the dead? 6He is not here, but
is risen! Remember how He spoke to you
when He was still in Galilee, 7saying,

23:34 [a] NU-Text brackets the first sentence as a later addition. **23:38** [a] NU-Text omits *written* and *in letters of Greek, Latin, and Hebrew.* **23:39** [a] NU-Text reads *Are You not the Christ?* **23:42** [a] NU-Text reads *And he said, "Jesus, remember me.* **23:44** [a] NU-Text adds *already.* **23:45** [a] NU-Text reads *obscured.* **23:46** [a] Psalm 31:5 **23:51** [a] NU-Text reads *who was waiting.* **24:1** [a] NU-Text omits *and certain other women with them.* **24:4** [a] NU-Text omits *greatly.*

'The Son of Man must be delivered into the hands of sinful men, and be crucified, and the third day rise again.' "

8And they remembered His words. 9Then they returned from the tomb and told all these things to the eleven and to all the rest. 10It was Mary Magdalene, Joanna, Mary *the mother* of James, and the other *women* with them, who told these things to the apostles. 11And their words seemed to them like idle tales, and they did not believe them. 12But Peter arose and ran to the tomb; and stooping down, he saw the linen cloths lying[a] by themselves; and he departed, marveling to himself at what had happened.

The Road to Emmaus

13Now behold, two of them were traveling that same day to a village called Emmaus, which was seven miles[a] from Jerusalem. 14And they talked together of all these things which had happened. 15So it was, while they conversed and reasoned, that Jesus Himself drew near and went with them. 16But their eyes were restrained, so that they did not know Him.

17And He said to them, "What kind of conversation *is* this that you have with one another as you walk and are sad?"[a]

18Then the one whose name was Cleopas answered and said to Him, "Are You the only stranger in Jerusalem, and have You not known the things which happened there in these days?"

19And He said to them, "What things?"

So they said to Him, "The things concerning Jesus of Nazareth, who was a Prophet mighty in deed and word before God and all the people, 20and how the chief priests and our rulers delivered Him to be condemned to death, and crucified Him. 21But we were hoping that it was He who was going to redeem Israel. Indeed, besides all this, today is the third day since these things happened. 22Yes, and certain women of our company, who arrived at the tomb early, astonished us. 23When they did not find His body, they came saying that they had also seen a vision of angels who said He was alive. 24And certain of those *who were* with us went to the tomb and found *it* just as the women had said; but Him they did not see."

25Then He said to them, "O foolish ones, and slow of heart to believe in all that the prophets have spoken! 26Ought not the Christ to have suffered these things and to enter into His glory?" 27And beginning at Moses and all the Prophets, He expounded to them in all the Scriptures the things concerning Himself.

The Disciples' Eyes Opened

28Then they drew near to the village where they were going, and He indicated that He would have gone farther. 29But they constrained Him, saying, "Abide with us, for it is toward evening, and the day is far spent." And He went in to stay with them.

30Now it came to pass, as He sat at the table with them, that He took bread, blessed and broke *it,* and gave it to them. 31Then their eyes were opened and they knew Him; and He vanished from their sight.

32And they said to one another, "Did not our heart burn within us while He talked with us on the road, and while He opened the Scriptures to us?" 33So they rose up that very hour and returned to Jerusalem, and found the eleven and those *who were* with them gathered together, 34saying, "The Lord is risen indeed, and has appeared to Simon!" 35And they told about the things *that had happened* on the road, and how He was known to them in the breaking of bread.

Jesus Appears to His Disciples

36Now as they said these things, Jesus Himself stood in the midst of them, and said to them, "Peace to you." 37But they were terrified and frightened, and supposed they had seen a spirit. 38And He said to them, "Why are you troubled? And why do doubts arise in your hearts? 39Behold My hands and My feet, that it is I Myself. Handle Me and see, for a spirit does not have flesh and bones as you see I have."

24:12 [a] NU-Text omits *lying.* **24:13** [a] Literally *sixty stadia* **24:17** [a] NU-Text reads *as you walk? And they stood still, looking sad.*

40When He had said this, He showed
them His hands and His feet.[a] 41But
while they still did not believe for joy,
and marveled, He said to them, "Have
you any food here?" 42So they gave
Him a piece of a broiled fish and some
honeycomb.[a] 43And He took *it* and ate
in their presence.

The Scriptures Opened

44Then He said to them, "These *are*
the words which I spoke to you while I
was still with you, that all things must
be fulfilled which were written in the
Law of Moses and *the* Prophets and
the Psalms concerning Me." 45And He
opened their understanding, that they
might comprehend the Scriptures.
46Then He said to them, "Thus it is writ-
ten, and thus it was necessary for the
Christ to suffer and to rise[a] from the dead
the third day, 47and that repentance and
remission of sins should be preached
in His name to all nations, beginning
at Jerusalem. 48And you are witness-
es of these things. 49Behold, I send the
Promise of My Father upon you; but
tarry in the city of Jerusalem[a] until you
are endued with power from on high."

The Ascension

50And He led them out as far as Beth-
any, and He lifted up His hands and
blessed them. 51Now it came to pass,
while He blessed them, that He was
parted from them and carried up into
heaven. 52And they worshiped Him, and
returned to Jerusalem with great joy,
53and were continually in the temple
praising and[a] blessing God. Amen.[b]

24:40 [a] Some printed New Testaments omit this verse. It is found in nearly all Greek manuscripts.
24:42 [a] NU-Text omits *and some honeycomb.* **24:46** [a] NU-Text reads *written, that the Christ should suffer and rise.* **24:49** [a] NU-Text omits *of Jerusalem.* **24:53** [a] NU-Text omits *praising and.*
[b] NU-Text omits *Amen.*

THE GOSPEL ACCORDING TO

JOHN

John's purpose is to show that Jesus is the Son of God who became human so that He could pay the sin penalty humans owe. As such, John focuses on what Jesus said and did to prove He is God. John chooses seven of Jesus' miracles, also called signs, and seven "I am" claims of Jesus to make his point. Jesus is not simply a nice moral teacher. He claimed to be much more than that, and what He did that no one else can do supports what He claimed. John leaves no room for indecision. Like the many people Jesus encounters in the Gospel, the reader must either reject or accept Jesus.

- **GENRE:** Gospel
- **AUTHOR:** John
- **TIME:** c. AD 29–33 (written c. AD 80–90)
- **PURPOSE:** To show that Jesus is the Son of God who came in the flesh to save the world.

The Eternal Word

1 In the beginning was the Word, and
the Word was with God, and the
Word was God. 2He was in the beginning
with God. 3All things were made through
Him, and without Him nothing was
made that was made. 4In Him was life,
and the life was the light of men. 5And
the light shines in the darkness, and
the darkness did not comprehend[a] it.

John's Witness: The True Light

6There was a man sent from God,
whose name *was* John. 7This man
came for a witness, to bear witness of
the Light, that all through him might
believe. 8He was not that Light, but *was
sent* to bear witness of that Light. 9That
was the true Light which gives light to
every man coming into the world.[a]

10He was in the world, and the world
was made through Him, and the world
did not know Him. 11He came to His
own,[a] and His own[b] did not receive Him.
12But as many as received Him, to them
He gave the right to become children of
God, to those who believe in His name:
13who were born, not of blood, nor of
the will of the flesh, nor of the will of
man, but of God.

The Word Becomes Flesh

14And the Word became flesh and
dwelt among us, and we beheld His
glory, the glory as of the only begotten
of the Father, full of grace and truth.

15John bore witness of Him and cried
out, saying, "This was He of whom I said,
'He who comes after me is preferred
before me, for He was before me.' "

16And[a] of His fullness we have all re-
ceived, and grace for grace. 17For the law
was given through Moses, *but* grace and
truth came through Jesus Christ. 18No
one has seen God at any time. The only
begotten Son,[a] who is in the bosom of
the Father, He has declared *Him*.

A Voice in the Wilderness

19Now this is the testimony of John,
when the Jews sent priests and Levites
from Jerusalem to ask him, "Who are
you?"

20He confessed, and did not deny, but
confessed, "I am not the Christ."

21And they asked him, "What then?
Are you Elijah?"

He said, "I am not."

"Are you the Prophet?"

And he answered, "No."

22Then they said to him, "Who are you,

1:5 [a] Or *overcome* **1:9** [a] Or *That was the true Light which, coming into the world, gives light to every man.* **1:11** [a] That is, His own things or domain [b] That is, His own people **1:16** [a] NU-Text reads *For.* **1:18** [a] NU-Text reads *only begotten God.*

GOD | SIN | JESUS | SALVATION | LOVE

that we may give an answer to those
who sent us? What do you say about
yourself?"
23He said: "I *am*

'The voice of one crying in the
wilderness:
"Make straight the way of the
LORD," '[a]

as the prophet Isaiah said."
24Now those who were sent were from
the Pharisees. 25And they asked him,
saying, "Why then do you baptize if
you are not the Christ, nor Elijah, nor
the Prophet?"
26John answered them, saying, "I bap-
tize with water, but there stands One
among you whom you do not know. 27It
is He who, coming after me, is preferred
before me, whose sandal strap I am not
worthy to loose."
28These things were done in Bethaba-
ra[a] beyond the Jordan, where John was
baptizing.

The Lamb of God

29The next day John saw Jesus com-
ing toward him, and said, "Behold! The
Lamb of God who takes away the sin of
the world! 30This is He of whom I said,
'After me comes a Man who is preferred
before me, for He was before me.' 31I
did not know Him; but that He should
be revealed to Israel, therefore I came
baptizing with water."
32And John bore witness, saying, "I saw
the Spirit descending from heaven like
a dove, and He remained upon Him. 33I
did not know Him, but He who sent me
to baptize with water said to me, 'Upon
whom you see the Spirit descending, and
remaining on Him, this is He who baptizes
with the Holy Spirit.' 34And I have seen
and testified that this is the Son of God."

The First Disciples

35Again, the next day, John stood with
two of his disciples. 36And looking at
Jesus as He walked, he said, "Behold
the Lamb of God!"
37The two disciples heard him speak,
and they followed Jesus. 38Then Jesus
turned, and seeing them following, said
to them, "What do you seek?"
They said to Him, "Rabbi" (which is to
say, when translated, Teacher), "where
are You staying?"
39He said to them, "Come and see."
They came and saw where He was stay-
ing, and remained with Him that day
(now it was about the tenth hour).
40One of the two who heard John
speak, and followed Him, was Andrew,
Simon Peter's brother. 41He first found
his own brother Simon, and said to him,
"We have found the Messiah" (which
is translated, the Christ). 42And he
brought him to Jesus.
Now when Jesus looked at him, He
said, "You are Simon the son of Jonah.[a]
You shall be called Cephas" (which is
translated, A Stone).

Philip and Nathanael

43The following day Jesus wanted to
go to Galilee, and He found Philip and
said to him, "Follow Me." 44Now Philip
was from Bethsaida, the city of Andrew
and Peter. 45Philip found Nathanael
and said to him, "We have found Him
of whom Moses in the law, and also the
prophets, wrote—Jesus of Nazareth, the
son of Joseph."
46And Nathanael said to him, "Can
anything good come out of Nazareth?"
Philip said to him, "Come and see."
47Jesus saw Nathanael coming toward
Him, and said of him, "Behold, an Is-
raelite indeed, in whom is no deceit!"
48Nathanael said to Him, "How do
You know me?"
Jesus answered and said to him, "Be-
fore Philip called you, when you were
under the fig tree, I saw you."
49Nathanael answered and said to
Him, "Rabbi, You are the Son of God!
You are the King of Israel!"
50Jesus answered and said to him,
"Because I said to you, 'I saw you under
the fig tree,' do you believe? You will
see greater things than these." 51And
He said to him, "Most assuredly, I say
to you, hereafter[a] you shall see heaven
open, and the angels of God ascending
and descending upon the Son of Man."

1:23 [a] Isaiah 40:3 **1:28** [a] NU-Text and M-Text read *Bethany.* **1:42** [a] NU-Text reads *John.*
1:51 [a] NU-Text omits *hereafter.*

Water Turned to Wine

2 On the third day there was a wedding in Cana of Galilee, and the mother of Jesus was there. 2Now both Jesus and His disciples were invited to the wedding. 3And when they ran out of wine, the mother of Jesus said to Him, "They have no wine."

4Jesus said to her, "Woman, what does your concern have to do with Me? My hour has not yet come."

5His mother said to the servants, "Whatever He says to you, do *it*."

6Now there were set there six waterpots of stone, according to the manner of purification of the Jews, containing twenty or thirty gallons apiece. 7Jesus said to them, "Fill the waterpots with water." And they filled them up to the brim. 8And He said to them, "Draw *some* out now, and take *it* to the master of the feast." And they took *it*. 9When the master of the feast had tasted the water that was made wine, and did not know where it came from (but the servants who had drawn the water knew), the master of the feast called the bridegroom. 10And he said to him, "Every man at the beginning sets out the good wine, and when the *guests* have well drunk, then the inferior. You have kept the good wine until now!"

11This beginning of signs Jesus did in Cana of Galilee, and manifested His glory; and His disciples believed in Him.

12After this He went down to Capernaum, He, His mother, His brothers, and His disciples; and they did not stay there many days.

Jesus Cleanses the Temple

13Now the Passover of the Jews was at hand, and Jesus went up to Jerusalem. 14And He found in the temple those who sold oxen and sheep and doves, and the money changers doing business. 15When He had made a whip of cords, He drove them all out of the temple, with the sheep and the oxen, and poured out the changers' money and overturned the tables. 16And He said to those who sold doves, "Take these things away! Do not make My Father's house a house of merchandise!" 17Then His disciples remembered that it was written, "Zeal for Your house has eaten[a] Me up."[b]

18So the Jews answered and said to Him, "What sign do You show to us, since You do these things?"

19Jesus answered and said to them, "Destroy this temple, and in three days I will raise it up."

20Then the Jews said, "It has taken forty-six years to build this temple, and will You raise it up in three days?"

21But He was speaking of the temple of His body. 22Therefore, when He had risen from the dead, His disciples remembered that He had said this to them;[a] and they believed the Scripture and the word which Jesus had said.

The Discerner of Hearts

23Now when He was in Jerusalem at the Passover, during the feast, many believed in His name when they saw the signs which He did. 24But Jesus did not commit Himself to them, because He knew all *men*, 25and had no need that anyone should testify of man, for He knew what was in man.

The New Birth

3 There was a man of the Pharisees named Nicodemus, a ruler of the Jews. 2This man came to Jesus by night and said to Him, "Rabbi, we know that You are a teacher come from God; for no one can do these signs that You do unless God is with him."

3Jesus answered and said to him, "Most assuredly, I say to you, unless one is born again, he cannot see the kingdom of God."

4Nicodemus said to Him, "How can a man be born when he is old? Can he enter a second time into his mother's womb and be born?"

5Jesus answered, "Most assuredly, I say to you, unless one is born of water and the Spirit, he cannot enter the kingdom of God. 6That which is born of the flesh is flesh, and that which is born of the Spirit is spirit. 7Do not marvel that

2:17 [a] NU-Text and M-Text read *will eat.* [b] Psalm 69:9 2:22 [a] NU-Text and M-Text omit *to them.*

GOD SIN JESUS SALVATION LOVE

I said to you, 'You must be born again.'
8The wind blows where it wishes, and
you hear the sound of it, but cannot tell
where it comes from and where it goes.
So is everyone who is born of the Spirit."
9Nicodemus answered and said to
Him, "How can these things be?"
10Jesus answered and said to him, "Are
you the teacher of Israel, and do not
know these things? 11Most assuredly,
I say to you, We speak what We know
and testify what We have seen, and
you do not receive Our witness. 12If I
have told you earthly things and you
do not believe, how will you believe if I
tell you heavenly things? 13No one has
ascended to heaven but He who came
down from heaven, *that is,* the Son of
Man who is in heaven.[a] 14And as Moses
lifted up the serpent in the wilderness,
even so must the Son of Man be lifted up,
15that whoever believes in Him should
not perish but[a] have eternal life. 16For
God so loved the world that He gave
His only begotten Son, that whoever
believes in Him should not perish but
have everlasting life. 17For God did not
send His Son into the world to condemn
the world, but that the world through
Him might be saved.
18"He who believes in Him is not con-
demned; but he who does not believe
is condemned already, because he has
not believed in the name of the only
begotten Son of God. 19And this is the
condemnation, that the light has come
into the world, and men loved darkness
rather than light, because their deeds
were evil. 20For everyone practicing
evil hates the light and does not come
to the light, lest his deeds should be
exposed. 21But he who does the truth
comes to the light, that his deeds may
be clearly seen, that they have been
done in God."

John the Baptist Exalts Christ

22After these things Jesus and His
disciples came into the land of Judea,
and there He remained with them and
baptized. 23Now John also was baptiz-
ing in Aenon near Salim, because there
was much water there. And they came
and were baptized. 24For John had not
yet been thrown into prison.
25Then there arose a dispute between
some of John's disciples and the Jews
about purification. 26And they came to
John and said to him, "Rabbi, He who
was with you beyond the Jordan, to
whom you have testified—behold, He is
baptizing, and all are coming to Him!"
27John answered and said, "A man
can receive nothing unless it has been
given to him from heaven. 28You your-
selves bear me witness, that I said, 'I am
not the Christ,' but, 'I have been sent
before Him.' 29He who has the bride
is the bridegroom; but the friend of
the bridegroom, who stands and hears
him, rejoices greatly because of the
bridegroom's voice. Therefore this joy
of mine is fulfilled. 30He must increase,
but I *must* decrease. 31He who comes
from above is above all; he who is of the
earth is earthly and speaks of the earth.
He who comes from heaven is above all.
32And what He has seen and heard, that
He testifies; and no one receives His
testimony. 33He who has received His
testimony has certified that God is true.
34For He whom God has sent speaks the
words of God, for God does not give the
Spirit by measure. 35The Father loves
the Son, and has given all things into
His hand. 36He who believes in the Son
has everlasting life; and he who does
not believe the Son shall not see life,
but the wrath of God abides on him."

A Samaritan Woman Meets Her Messiah

4 Therefore, when the Lord knew
that the Pharisees had heard that
Jesus made and baptized more disciples
than John 2(though Jesus Himself did
not baptize, but His disciples), 3He left
Judea and departed again to Galilee.
4But He needed to go through Samaria.
5So He came to a city of Samaria which
is called Sychar, near the plot of ground
that Jacob gave to his son Joseph. 6Now
Jacob's well was there. Jesus therefore,
being wearied from *His* journey, sat
thus by the well. It was about the sixth
hour.

3:13 [a] NU-Text omits *who is in heaven.* **3:15** [a] NU-Text omits *not perish but.*

7A woman of Samaria came to draw
water. Jesus said to her, "Give Me a
drink." 8For His disciples had gone away
into the city to buy food.
9Then the woman of Samaria said to
Him, "How is it that You, being a Jew,
ask a drink from me, a Samaritan wom-
an?" For Jews have no dealings with
Samaritans.
10Jesus answered and said to her, "If
you knew the gift of God, and who it is
who says to you, 'Give Me a drink,' you
would have asked Him, and He would
have given you living water."
11The woman said to Him, "Sir, You
have nothing to draw with, and the well
is deep. Where then do You get that
living water? 12Are You greater than
our father Jacob, who gave us the well,
and drank from it himself, as well as
his sons and his livestock?"
13Jesus answered and said to her,
"Whoever drinks of this water will thirst
again, 14but whoever drinks of the water
that I shall give him will never thirst.
But the water that I shall give him will
become in him a fountain of water
springing up into everlasting life."
15The woman said to Him, "Sir, give
me this water, that I may not thirst, nor
come here to draw."
16Jesus said to her, "Go, call your hus-
band, and come here."
17The woman answered and said, "I
have no husband."
Jesus said to her, "You have well said,
'I have no husband,' 18for you have had
five husbands, and the one whom you
now have is not your husband; in that
you spoke truly."
19The woman said to Him, "Sir, I per-
ceive that You are a prophet. 20Our
fathers worshiped on this mountain,
and you *Jews* say that in Jerusalem is
the place where one ought to worship."
21Jesus said to her, "Woman, believe
Me, the hour is coming when you will
neither on this mountain, nor in Jerusa-
lem, worship the Father. 22You worship
what you do not know; we know what
we worship, for salvation is of the Jews.
23But the hour is coming, and now is,
when the true worshipers will worship
the Father in spirit and truth; for the
Father is seeking such to worship Him.
24God *is* Spirit, and those who worship
Him must worship in spirit and truth."
25The woman said to Him, "I know
that Messiah is coming" (who is called
Christ). "When He comes, He will tell
us all things."
26Jesus said to her, "I who speak to
you am *He*."

The Whitened Harvest

27And at this *point* His disciples came,
and they marveled that He talked with
a woman; yet no one said, "What do
You seek?" or, "Why are You talking
with her?"
28The woman then left her waterpot,
went her way into the city, and said to
the men, 29"Come, see a Man who told
me all things that I ever did. Could this
be the Christ?" 30Then they went out of
the city and came to Him.
31In the meantime His disciples urged
Him, saying, "Rabbi, eat."
32But He said to them, "I have food to
eat of which you do not know."
33Therefore the disciples said to one
another, "Has anyone brought Him
anything to eat?"
34Jesus said to them, "My food is to
do the will of Him who sent Me, and
to finish His work. 35Do you not say,
'There are still four months and *then*
comes the harvest'? Behold, I say to you,
lift up your eyes and look at the fields,
for they are already white for harvest!
36And he who reaps receives wages, and
gathers fruit for eternal life, that both
he who sows and he who reaps may
rejoice together. 37For in this the saying
is true: 'One sows and another reaps.'
38I sent you to reap that for which you
have not labored; others have labored,
and you have entered into their labors."

The Savior of the World

39And many of the Samaritans of
that city believed in Him because of
the word of the woman who testified,
"He told me all that I *ever* did." 40So
when the Samaritans had come to Him,
they urged Him to stay with them; and
He stayed there two days. 41And many
more believed because of His own word.
42Then they said to the woman, "Now
we believe, not because of what you

said, for we ourselves have heard *Him*
and we know that this is indeed the
Christ,[a] the Savior of the world."

Welcome at Galilee

43Now after the two days He departed
from there and went to Galilee. 44For
Jesus Himself testified that a prophet
has no honor in his own country. 45So
when He came to Galilee, the Galileans
received Him, having seen all the things
He did in Jerusalem at the feast; for they
also had gone to the feast.

A Nobleman's Son Healed

46So Jesus came again to Cana of
Galilee where He had made the water
wine. And there was a certain noble-
man whose son was sick at Capernaum.
47When he heard that Jesus had come
out of Judea into Galilee, he went to Him
and implored Him to come down and
heal his son, for he was at the point of
death. 48Then Jesus said to him, "Unless
you *people* see signs and wonders, you
will by no means believe."

49The nobleman said to Him, "Sir,
come down before my child dies!"

50Jesus said to him, "Go your way;
your son lives." So the man believed
the word that Jesus spoke to him, and
he went his way. 51And as he was now
going down, his servants met him and
told *him,* saying, "Your son lives!"

52Then he inquired of them the hour
when he got better. And they said to
him, "Yesterday at the seventh hour the
fever left him." 53So the father knew that
it was at the same hour in which Jesus
said to him, "Your son lives." And he
himself believed, and his whole house-
hold.

54This again *is* the second sign Jesus
did when He had come out of Judea
into Galilee.

A Man Healed at the Pool of Bethesda

5 After this there was a feast of the
Jews, and Jesus went up to Jerusa-
lem. 2Now there is in Jerusalem by the
Sheep *Gate* a pool, which is called in
Hebrew, Bethesda,[a] having five porches.
3In these lay a great multitude of sick
people, blind, lame, paralyzed, wait-
ing for the moving of the water. 4For
an angel went down at a certain time
into the pool and stirred up the water;
then whoever stepped in first, after the
stirring of the water, was made well
of whatever disease he had.[a] 5Now a
certain man was there who had an in-
firmity thirty-eight years. 6When Jesus
saw him lying there, and knew that he
already had been *in that condition* a
long time, He said to him, "Do you want
to be made well?"

7The sick man answered Him, "Sir, I
have no man to put me into the pool
when the water is stirred up; but while
I am coming, another steps down be-
fore me."

8Jesus said to him, "Rise, take up your
bed and walk." 9And immediately the
man was made well, took up his bed,
and walked.

And that day was the Sabbath. 10The
Jews therefore said to him who was
cured, "It is the Sabbath; it is not lawful
for you to carry your bed."

11He answered them, "He who made
me well said to me, 'Take up your bed
and walk.' "

12Then they asked him, "Who is the
Man who said to you, 'Take up your
bed and walk'?" 13But the one who
was healed did not know who it was,
for Jesus had withdrawn, a multitude
being in *that* place. 14Afterward Jesus
found him in the temple, and said to
him, "See, you have been made well.
Sin no more, lest a worse thing come
upon you."

15The man departed and told the Jews
that it was Jesus who had made him
well.

Honor the Father and the Son

16For this reason the Jews persecuted
Jesus, and sought to kill Him,[a] because
He had done these things on the Sab-
bath. 17But Jesus answered them, "My
Father has been working until now, and
I have been working."

18Therefore the Jews sought all the

4:42 [a] NU-Text omits *the Christ.* **5:2** [a] NU-Text reads *Bethzatha.* **5:4** [a] NU-Text omits *waiting for the moving of the water* at the end of verse 3, and all of verse 4. **5:16** [a] NU-Text omits *and sought to kill Him.*

more to kill Him, because He not only broke the Sabbath, but also said that God was His Father, making Himself equal with God. 19Then Jesus answered and said to them, "Most assuredly, I say to you, the Son can do nothing of Himself, but what He sees the Father do; for whatever He does, the Son also does in like manner. 20For the Father loves the Son, and shows Him all things that He Himself does; and He will show Him greater works than these, that you may marvel. 21For as the Father raises the dead and gives life to *them,* even so the Son gives life to whom He will. 22For the Father judges no one, but has committed all judgment to the Son, 23that all should honor the Son just as they honor the Father. He who does not honor the Son does not honor the Father who sent Him.

Life and Judgment Are Through the Son

24"Most assuredly, I say to you, he who hears My word and believes in Him who sent Me has everlasting life, and shall not come into judgment, but has passed from death into life. 25Most assuredly, I say to you, the hour is coming, and now is, when the dead will hear the voice of the Son of God; and those who hear will live. 26For as the Father has life in Himself, so He has granted the Son to have life in Himself, 27and has given Him authority to execute judgment also, because He is the Son of Man. 28Do not marvel at this; for the hour is coming in which all who are in the graves will hear His voice 29and come forth—those who have done good, to the resurrection of life, and those who have done evil, to the resurrection of condemnation. 30I can of Myself do nothing. As I hear, I judge; and My judgment is righteous, because I do not seek My own will but the will of the Father who sent Me.

The Fourfold Witness

31"If I bear witness of Myself, My witness is not true. 32There is another who bears witness of Me, and I know that the witness which He witnesses of Me is true. 33You have sent to John, and he has borne witness to the truth. 34Yet I do not receive testimony from man, but I say these things that you may be saved. 35He was the burning and shining lamp, and you were willing for a time to rejoice in his light. 36But I have a greater witness than John's; for the works which the Father has given Me to finish—the very works that I do—bear witness of Me, that the Father has sent Me. 37And the Father Himself, who sent Me, has testified of Me. You have neither heard His voice at any time, nor seen His form. 38But you do not have His word abiding in you, because whom He sent, Him you do not believe. 39You search the Scriptures, for in them you think you have eternal life; and these are they which testify of Me. 40But you are not willing to come to Me that you may have life.

41"I do not receive honor from men. 42But I know you, that you do not have the love of God in you. 43I have come in My Father's name, and you do not receive Me; if another comes in his own name, him you will receive. 44How can you believe, who receive honor from one another, and do not seek the honor that *comes* from the only God? 45Do not think that I shall accuse you to the Father; there is *one* who accuses you—Moses, in whom you trust. 46For if you believed Moses, you would believe Me; for he wrote about Me. 47But if you do not believe his writings, how will you believe My words?"

Feeding the Five Thousand

6 After these things Jesus went over the Sea of Galilee, which is *the Sea* of Tiberias. 2Then a great multitude followed Him, because they saw His signs which He performed on those who were diseased. 3And Jesus went up on the mountain, and there He sat with His disciples.

4Now the Passover, a feast of the Jews, was near. 5Then Jesus lifted up *His* eyes, and seeing a great multitude coming toward Him, He said to Philip, "Where shall we buy bread, that these may eat?" 6But this He said to test him, for He Himself knew what He would do.

7Philip answered Him, "Two hundred denarii worth of bread is not sufficient for them, that every one of them may have a little."

8One of His disciples, Andrew, Simon Peter's brother, said to Him, 9"There is a lad here who has five barley loaves and two small fish, but what are they among so many?"

10Then Jesus said, "Make the people sit down." Now there was much grass in the place. So the men sat down, in number about five thousand. 11And Jesus took the loaves, and when He had given thanks He distributed *them* to the disciples, and the disciples[a] to those sitting down; and likewise of the fish, as much as they wanted. 12So when they were filled, He said to His disciples, "Gather up the fragments that remain, so that nothing is lost." 13Therefore they gathered *them* up, and filled twelve baskets with the fragments of the five barley loaves which were left over by those who had eaten. 14Then those men, when they had seen the sign that Jesus did, said, "This is truly the Prophet who is to come into the world."

Jesus Walks on the Sea

15Therefore when Jesus perceived that they were about to come and take Him by force to make Him king, He departed again to the mountain by Himself alone.

16Now when evening came, His disciples went down to the sea, 17got into the boat, and went over the sea toward Capernaum. And it was already dark, and Jesus had not come to them. 18Then the sea arose because a great wind was blowing. 19So when they had rowed about three or four miles,[a] they saw Jesus walking on the sea and drawing near the boat; and they were afraid. 20But He said to them, "It is I; do not be afraid." 21Then they willingly received Him into the boat, and immediately the boat was at the land where they were going.

The Bread from Heaven

22On the following day, when the people who were standing on the other side of the sea saw that there was no other boat there, except that one which His disciples had entered,[a] and that Jesus had not entered the boat with His disciples, but His disciples had gone away alone— 23however, other boats came from Tiberias, near the place where they ate bread after the Lord had given thanks— 24when the people therefore saw that Jesus was not there, nor His disciples, they also got into boats and came to Capernaum, seeking Jesus. 25And when they found Him on the other side of the sea, they said to Him, "Rabbi, when did You come here?"

26Jesus answered them and said, "Most assuredly, I say to you, you seek Me, not because you saw the signs, but because you ate of the loaves and were filled. 27Do not labor for the food which perishes, but for the food which endures to everlasting life, which the Son of Man will give you, because God the Father has set His seal on Him."

28Then they said to Him, "What shall we do, that we may work the works of God?"

29Jesus answered and said to them, "This is the work of God, that you believe in Him whom He sent."

30Therefore they said to Him, "What sign will You perform then, that we may see it and believe You? What work will You do? 31Our fathers ate the manna in the desert; as it is written, 'He gave them bread from heaven to eat.' "[a]

32Then Jesus said to them, "Most assuredly, I say to you, Moses did not give you the bread from heaven, but My Father gives you the true bread from heaven. 33For the bread of God is He who comes down from heaven and gives life to the world."

34Then they said to Him, "Lord, give us this bread always."

35And Jesus said to them, "I am the bread of life. He who comes to Me shall never hunger, and he who believes in Me shall never thirst. 36But I said to you that you have seen Me and yet do not believe. 37All that the Father gives Me will come to Me, and the one who comes to Me I will by no means cast out. 38For I have come down from heaven, not to

6:11 [a] NU-Text omits *to the disciples, and the disciples.* **6:19** [a] Literally *twenty-five or thirty stadia* **6:22** [a] NU-Text omits *that* and *which His disciples had entered.* **6:31** [a] Exodus 16:4; Nehemiah 9:15; Psalm 78:24

do My own will, but the will of Him who
sent Me. 39This is the will of the Father
who sent Me, that of all He has given Me
I should lose nothing, but should raise
it up at the last day. 40And this is the
will of Him who sent Me, that everyone
who sees the Son and believes in Him
may have everlasting life; and I will
raise him up at the last day."

Rejected by His Own

41The Jews then complained about
Him, because He said, "I am the bread
which came down from heaven." 42And
they said, "Is not this Jesus, the son of
Joseph, whose father and mother we
know? How is it then that He says, 'I
have come down from heaven'?"

43Jesus therefore answered and said
to them, "Do not murmur among your-
selves. 44No one can come to Me unless
the Father who sent Me draws him; and
I will raise him up at the last day. 45It
is written in the prophets, 'And they
shall all be taught by God.'[a] Therefore
everyone who has heard and learned[b]
from the Father comes to Me. 46Not
that anyone has seen the Father, except
He who is from God; He has seen the
Father. 47Most assuredly, I say to you,
he who believes in Me[a] has everlasting
life. 48I am the bread of life. 49Your fa-
thers ate the manna in the wilderness,
and are dead. 50This is the bread which
comes down from heaven, that one may
eat of it and not die. 51I am the living
bread which came down from heaven.
If anyone eats of this bread, he will live
forever; and the bread that I shall give
is My flesh, which I shall give for the
life of the world."

52The Jews therefore quarreled among
themselves, saying, "How can this Man
give us *His* flesh to eat?"

53Then Jesus said to them, "Most as-
suredly, I say to you, unless you eat the
flesh of the Son of Man and drink His
blood, you have no life in you. 54Who-
ever eats My flesh and drinks My blood
has eternal life, and I will raise him up
at the last day. 55For My flesh is food
indeed,[a] and My blood is drink indeed.
56He who eats My flesh and drinks My
blood abides in Me, and I in him. 57As
the living Father sent Me, and I live
because of the Father, so he who feeds
on Me will live because of Me. 58This
is the bread which came down from
heaven—not as your fathers ate the
manna, and are dead. He who eats this
bread will live forever."

59These things He said in the syna-
gogue as He taught in Capernaum.

Many Disciples Turn Away

60Therefore many of His disciples,
when they heard *this,* said, "This is a
hard saying; who can understand it?"

61When Jesus knew in Himself that
His disciples complained about this,
He said to them, "Does this offend you?
62*What* then if you should see the Son of
Man ascend where He was before? 63It is
the Spirit who gives life; the flesh profits
nothing. The words that I speak to you
are spirit, and *they* are life. 64But there
are some of you who do not believe."
For Jesus knew from the beginning
who they were who did not believe, and
who would betray Him. 65And He said,
"Therefore I have said to you that no
one can come to Me unless it has been
granted to him by My Father."

66From that *time* many of His disci-
ples went back and walked with Him no
more. 67Then Jesus said to the twelve,
"Do you also want to go away?"

68But Simon Peter answered Him,
"Lord, to whom shall we go? You have
the words of eternal life. 69Also we have
come to believe and know that You are
the Christ, the Son of the living God."[a]

70Jesus answered them, "Did I not
choose you, the twelve, and one of you
is a devil?" 71He spoke of Judas Iscariot,
the son of Simon, for it was he who would
betray Him, being one of the twelve.

Jesus' Brothers Disbelieve

7 After these things Jesus walked in
Galilee; for He did not want to walk
in Judea, because the Jews[a] sought to
kill Him. 2Now the Jews' Feast of Tab-
ernacles was at hand. 3His brothers

6:45 [a] Isaiah 54:13 [b] M-Text reads *hears and has learned.* **6:47** [a] NU-Text omits *in Me.*
6:55 [a] NU-Text reads *true food* and *true drink.* **6:69** [a] NU-Text reads *You are the Holy One of God.*
7:1 [a] That is, the ruling authorities

therefore said to Him, "Depart from
here and go into Judea, that Your dis-
ciples also may see the works that You
are doing. 4For no one does anything
in secret while he himself seeks to be
known openly. If You do these things,
show Yourself to the world." 5For even
His brothers did not believe in Him.
6Then Jesus said to them, "My time has
not yet come, but your time is always
ready. 7The world cannot hate you, but
it hates Me because I testify of it that its
works are evil. 8You go up to this feast.
I am not yet[a] going up to this feast, for
My time has not yet fully come." 9When
He had said these things to them, He
remained in Galilee.

The Heavenly Scholar

10But when His brothers had gone up,
then He also went up to the feast, not
openly, but as it were in secret. 11Then
the Jews sought Him at the feast, and
said, "Where is He?" 12And there was
much complaining among the peo-
ple concerning Him. Some said, "He is
good"; others said, "No, on the contrary,
He deceives the people." 13However,
no one spoke openly of Him for fear
of the Jews.
14Now about the middle of the feast
Jesus went up into the temple and
taught. 15And the Jews marveled, say-
ing, "How does this Man know letters,
having never studied?"
16Jesus[a] answered them and said, "My
doctrine is not Mine, but His who sent
Me. 17If anyone wills to do His will, he
shall know concerning the doctrine,
whether it is from God or *whether* I
speak on My own *authority*. 18He who
speaks from himself seeks his own
glory; but He who seeks the glory of
the One who sent Him is true, and no
unrighteousness is in Him. 19Did not
Moses give you the law, yet none of
you keeps the law? Why do you seek
to kill Me?"
20The people answered and said, "You
have a demon. Who is seeking to kill
You?"
21Jesus answered and said to them,
"I did one work, and you all marvel.
22Moses therefore gave you circum-
cision (not that it is from Moses, but
from the fathers), and you circumcise
a man on the Sabbath. 23If a man re-
ceives circumcision on the Sabbath,
so that the law of Moses should not be
broken, are you angry with Me because
I made a man completely well on the
Sabbath? 24Do not judge according to
appearance, but judge with righteous
judgment."

Could This Be the Christ?

25Now some of them from Jerusalem
said, "Is this not He whom they seek
to kill? 26But look! He speaks boldly,
and they say nothing to Him. Do the
rulers know indeed that this is truly[a]
the Christ? 27However, we know where
this Man is from; but when the Christ
comes, no one knows where He is from."
28Then Jesus cried out, as He taught
in the temple, saying, "You both know
Me, and you know where I am from;
and I have not come of Myself, but He
who sent Me is true, whom you do not
know. 29But[a] I know Him, for I am from
Him, and He sent Me."
30Therefore they sought to take Him;
but no one laid a hand on Him, because
His hour had not yet come. 31And many
of the people believed in Him, and said,
"When the Christ comes, will He do
more signs than these which this *Man*
has done?"

Jesus and the Religious Leaders

32The Pharisees heard the crowd mur-
muring these things concerning Him,
and the Pharisees and the chief priests
sent officers to take Him. 33Then Jesus
said to them,[a] "I shall be with you a little
while longer, and *then* I go to Him who
sent Me. 34You will seek Me and not find
Me, and where I am you cannot come."
35Then the Jews said among them-
selves, "Where does He intend to go that
we shall not find Him? Does He intend to
go to the Dispersion among the Greeks
and teach the Greeks? 36What is this
thing that He said, 'You will seek Me
and not find Me, and where I am you
cannot come'?"

7:8 [a] NU-Text omits *yet.* **7:16** [a] NU-Text and M-Text read *So Jesus.* **7:26** [a] NU-Text omits *truly.*
7:29 [a] NU-Text and M-Text omit *But.* **7:33** [a] NU-Text and M-Text omit *to them.*

The Promise of the Holy Spirit

37On the last day, that great *day* of the
feast, Jesus stood and cried out, saying,
"If anyone thirsts, let him come to Me
and drink. 38He who believes in Me, as
the Scripture has said, out of his heart
will flow rivers of living water." 39But
this He spoke concerning the Spirit,
whom those believing[a] in Him would
receive; for the Holy[b] Spirit was not
yet *given,* because Jesus was not yet
glorified.

Who Is He?

40Therefore many[a] from the crowd,
when they heard this saying, said, "Tru-
ly this is the Prophet." 41Others said,
"This is the Christ."
But some said, "Will the Christ come
out of Galilee? 42Has not the Scripture
said that the Christ comes from the
seed of David and from the town of
Bethlehem, where David was?" 43So
there was a division among the people
because of Him. 44Now some of them
wanted to take Him, but no one laid
hands on Him.

Rejected by the Authorities

45Then the officers came to the chief
priests and Pharisees, who said to them,
"Why have you not brought Him?"
46The officers answered, "No man ever
spoke like this Man!"
47Then the Pharisees answered them,
"Are you also deceived? 48Have any of
the rulers or the Pharisees believed in
Him? 49But this crowd that does not
know the law is accursed."
50Nicodemus (he who came to Jesus by
night,[a] being one of them) said to them,
51"Does our law judge a man before it
hears him and knows what he is doing?"
52They answered and said to him, "Are
you also from Galilee? Search and look,
for no prophet has arisen[a] out of Gal-
ilee."

An Adulteress Faces the Light of the World

53And everyone went to his *own*
house.[a]

8 But Jesus went to the Mount of Olives.
2Now early[a] in the morning He
came again into the temple, and all the
people came to Him; and He sat down
and taught them. 3Then the scribes and
Pharisees brought to Him a woman
caught in adultery. And when they had
set her in the midst, 4they said to Him,
"Teacher, this woman was caught[a] in
adultery, in the very act. 5Now Moses,
in the law, commanded[a] us that such
should be stoned.[b] But what do You
say?"[c] 6This they said, testing Him, that
they might have *something* of which to
accuse Him. But Jesus stooped down
and wrote on the ground with *His* finger,
as though He did not hear.[a]
7So when they continued asking Him,
He raised Himself up[a] and said to them,
"He who is without sin among you, let
him throw a stone at her first." 8And
again He stooped down and wrote on the
ground. 9Then those who heard *it,* being
convicted by *their* conscience,[a] went out
one by one, beginning with the oldest
even to the last. And Jesus was left alone,
and the woman standing in the midst.
10When Jesus had raised Himself up and
saw no one but the woman, He said to
her,[a] "Woman, where are those accusers
of yours?[b] Has no one condemned you?"
11She said, "No one, Lord."
And Jesus said to her, "Neither do I
condemn you; go and[a] sin no more."
12Then Jesus spoke to them again, say-
ing, "I am the light of the world. He who
follows Me shall not walk in darkness,
but have the light of life."

Jesus Defends His Self-Witness

13The Pharisees therefore said to Him,
"You bear witness of Yourself; Your wit-
ness is not true."

7:39 [a] NU-Text reads *who believed.* [b] NU-Text omits *Holy.* **7:40** [a] NU-Text reads *some.* **7:50** [a] NU-Text reads *before.* **7:52** [a] NU-Text reads *is to rise.* **7:53** [a] The words *And everyone* through *sin no more* (8:11) are bracketed by NU-Text as not original. They are present in over 900 manuscripts. **8:2** [a] M-Text reads *very early.* **8:4** [a] M-Text reads *we found this woman.* **8:5** [a] M-Text reads *in our law Moses commanded.* [b] NU-Text and M-Text read *to stone such.* [c] M-Text adds *about her.* **8:6** [a] NU-Text and M-Text omit *as though He did not hear.* **8:7** [a] M-Text reads *He looked up.* **8:9** [a] NU-Text and M-Text omit *being convicted by their conscience.* **8:10** [a] NU-Text omits *and saw no one but the woman;* M-Text reads *He saw her and said.* [b] NU-Text and M-Text omit *of yours.* **8:11** [a] NU-Text and M-Text add *from now on.*

14Jesus answered and said to them,
"Even if I bear witness of Myself, My
witness is true, for I know where I came
from and where I am going; but you do
not know where I come from and where
I am going. 15You judge according to
the flesh; I judge no one. 16And yet if
I do judge, My judgment is true; for I
am not alone, but I *am* with the Father
who sent Me. 17It is also written in your
law that the testimony of two men is
true. 18I am One who bears witness of
Myself, and the Father who sent Me
bears witness of Me."
19Then they said to Him, "Where is
Your Father?"
Jesus answered, "You know neither Me
nor My Father. If you had known Me,
you would have known My Father also."
20These words Jesus spoke in the trea-
sury, as He taught in the temple; and
no one laid hands on Him, for His hour
had not yet come.

Jesus Predicts His Departure

21Then Jesus said to them again, "I
am going away, and you will seek Me,
and will die in your sin. Where I go you
cannot come."
22So the Jews said, "Will He kill Him-
self, because He says, 'Where I go you
cannot come'?"
23And He said to them, "You are from
beneath; I am from above. You are
of this world; I am not of this world.
24Therefore I said to you that you will
die in your sins; for if you do not believe
that I am *He,* you will die in your sins."
25Then they said to Him, "Who are
You?"
And Jesus said to them, "Just what I
have been saying to you from the begin-
ning. 26I have many things to say and
to judge concerning you, but He who
sent Me is true; and I speak to the world
those things which I heard from Him."
27They did not understand that He
spoke to them of the Father.
28Then Jesus said to them, "When you
lift up the Son of Man, then you will
know that I am *He,* and *that* I do nothing
of Myself; but as My Father taught Me, I
speak these things. 29And He who sent
Me is with Me. The Father has not left
Me alone, for I always do those things
that please Him." 30As He spoke these
words, many believed in Him.

The Truth Shall Make You Free

31Then Jesus said to those Jews who
believed Him, "If you abide in My word,
you are My disciples indeed. 32And you
shall know the truth, and the truth shall
make you free."
33They answered Him, "We are Abra-
ham's descendants, and have never
been in bondage to anyone. How *can*
You say, 'You will be made free'?"
34Jesus answered them, "Most as-
suredly, I say to you, whoever commits
sin is a slave of sin. 35And a slave does
not abide in the house forever, *but* a
son abides forever. 36Therefore if the
Son makes you free, you shall be free
indeed.

Abraham's Seed and Satan's

37"I know that you are Abraham's de-
scendants, but you seek to kill Me, be-
cause My word has no place in you. 38I
speak what I have seen with My Father,
and you do what you have seen with[a]
your father."
39They answered and said to Him,
"Abraham is our father."
Jesus said to them, "If you were Abra-
ham's children, you would do the works
of Abraham. 40But now you seek to kill
Me, a Man who has told you the truth
which I heard from God. Abraham did
not do this. 41You do the deeds of your
father."
Then they said to Him, "We were
not born of fornication; we have one
Father—God."
42Jesus said to them, "If God were
your Father, you would love Me, for I
proceeded forth and came from God;
nor have I come of Myself, but He sent
Me. 43Why do you not understand My
speech? Because you are not able to lis-
ten to My word. 44You are of *your* father
the devil, and the desires of your father
you want to do. He was a murderer from
the beginning, and does not stand in the
truth, because there is no truth in him.

8:38 [a] NU-Text reads *heard from.*

When he speaks a lie, he speaks from
his own *resources,* for he is a liar and
the father of it. 45But because I tell the
truth, you do not believe Me. 46Which
of you convicts Me of sin? And if I tell
the truth, why do you not believe Me?
47He who is of God hears God's words;
therefore you do not hear, because you
are not of God."

Before Abraham Was, I AM

48Then the Jews answered and said to
Him, "Do we not say rightly that You
are a Samaritan and have a demon?"
49Jesus answered, "I do not have a
demon; but I honor My Father, and you
dishonor Me. 50And I do not seek My
own glory; there is One who seeks and
judges. 51Most assuredly, I say to you,
if anyone keeps My word he shall never
see death."
52Then the Jews said to Him, "Now we
know that You have a demon! Abraham
is dead, and the prophets; and You say,
'If anyone keeps My word he shall never
taste death.' 53Are You greater than our
father Abraham, who is dead? And the
prophets are dead. Who do You make
Yourself out to be?"
54Jesus answered, "If I honor Myself,
My honor is nothing. It is My Father who
honors Me, of whom you say that He is
your[a] God. 55Yet you have not known
Him, but I know Him. And if I say, 'I do
not know Him,' I shall be a liar like you;
but I do know Him and keep His word.
56Your father Abraham rejoiced to see
My day, and he saw *it* and was glad."
57Then the Jews said to Him, "You are
not yet fifty years old, and have You
seen Abraham?"
58Jesus said to them, "Most assuredly,
I say to you, before Abraham was, I AM."
59Then they took up stones to throw
at Him; but Jesus hid Himself and went
out of the temple,[a] going through the
midst of them, and so passed by.

A Man Born Blind Receives Sight

9 Now as *Jesus* passed by, He saw a
man who was blind from birth. 2And
His disciples asked Him, saying, "Rabbi,
who sinned, this man or his parents,
that he was born blind?"
3Jesus answered, "Neither this man
nor his parents sinned, but that the
works of God should be revealed in
him. 4I[a] must work the works of Him
who sent Me while it is day; *the* night
is coming when no one can work. 5As
long as I am in the world, I am the light
of the world."
6When He had said these things, He
spat on the ground and made clay with
the saliva; and He anointed the eyes of
the blind man with the clay. 7And He
said to him, "Go, wash in the pool of
Siloam" (which is translated, Sent). So
he went and washed, and came back
seeing.
8Therefore the neighbors and those
who previously had seen that he was
blind[a] said, "Is not this he who sat and
begged?"
9Some said, "This is he." Others *said,*
"He is like him."[a]
He said, "I am *he.*"
10Therefore they said to him, "How
were your eyes opened?"
11He answered and said, "A Man called
Jesus made clay and anointed my eyes
and said to me, 'Go to the pool of[a] Silo-
am and wash.' So I went and washed,
and I received sight."
12Then they said to him, "Where is He?"
He said, "I do not know."

The Pharisees Excommunicate the Healed Man

13They brought him who formerly was
blind to the Pharisees. 14Now it was a
Sabbath when Jesus made the clay and
opened his eyes. 15Then the Pharisees
also asked him again how he had re-
ceived his sight. He said to them, "He
put clay on my eyes, and I washed, and
I see."
16Therefore some of the Pharisees said,
"This Man is not from God, because He
does not keep the Sabbath."
Others said, "How can a man who is a
sinner do such signs?" And there was a
division among them.
17They said to the blind man again,

8:54 [a] NU-Text and M-Text read *our.* **8:59** [a] NU-Text omits the rest of this verse. **9:4** [a] NU-Text reads *We.* **9:8** [a] NU-Text reads *a beggar.* **9:9** [a] NU-Text reads *"No, but he is like him."* **9:11** [a] NU-Text omits *the pool of.*

"What do you say about Him because
He opened your eyes?"
He said, "He is a prophet."
18But the Jews did not believe concern-
ing him, that he had been blind and
received his sight, until they called the
parents of him who had received his
sight. 19And they asked them, saying,
"Is this your son, who you say was born
blind? How then does he now see?"
20His parents answered them and said,
"We know that this is our son, and that
he was born blind; 21but by what means
he now sees we do not know, or who
opened his eyes we do not know. He is of
age; ask him. He will speak for himself."
22His parents said these *things* because
they feared the Jews, for the Jews had
agreed already that if anyone confessed
that He *was* Christ, he would be put out of
the synagogue. 23Therefore his parents
said, "He is of age; ask him."
24So they again called the man who
was blind, and said to him, "Give God
the glory! We know that this Man is a
sinner."
25He answered and said, "Whether
He is a sinner *or not* I do not know. One
thing I know: that though I was blind,
now I see."
26Then they said to him again, "What
did He do to you? How did He open your
eyes?"
27He answered them, "I told you al-
ready, and you did not listen. Why do
you want to hear *it* again? Do you also
want to become His disciples?"
28Then they reviled him and said, "You
are His disciple, but we are Moses' dis-
ciples. 29We know that God spoke to
Moses; *as for* this *fellow,* we do not know
where He is from."
30The man answered and said to them,
"Why, this is a marvelous thing, that
you do not know where He is from; yet
He has opened my eyes! 31Now we know
that God does not hear sinners; but if
anyone is a worshiper of God and does
His will, He hears him. 32Since the world
began it has been unheard of that any-
one opened the eyes of one who was
born blind. 33If this Man were not from
God, He could do nothing."
34They answered and said to him, "You
were completely born in sins, and are
you teaching us?" And they cast him
out.

True Vision and True Blindness

35Jesus heard that they had cast him
out; and when He had found him, He
said to him, "Do you believe in the Son
of God?"[a]
36He answered and said, "Who is He,
Lord, that I may believe in Him?"
37And Jesus said to him, "You have
both seen Him and it is He who is
talking with you."
38Then he said, "Lord, I believe!" And
he worshiped Him.
39And Jesus said, "For judgment I have
come into this world, that those who do
not see may see, and that those who see
may be made blind."
40Then *some* of the Pharisees who were
with Him heard these words, and said
to Him, "Are we blind also?"
41Jesus said to them, "If you were
blind, you would have no sin; but now
you say, 'We see.' Therefore your sin
remains.

Jesus the True Shepherd

10 "Most assuredly, I say to you, he
who does not enter the sheep-
fold by the door, but climbs up some
other way, the same is a thief and a
robber. 2But he who enters by the door
is the shepherd of the sheep. 3To him the
doorkeeper opens, and the sheep hear
his voice; and he calls his own sheep by
name and leads them out. 4And when
he brings out his own sheep, he goes
before them; and the sheep follow him,
for they know his voice. 5Yet they will
by no means follow a stranger, but will
flee from him, for they do not know the
voice of strangers." 6Jesus used this il-
lustration, but they did not understand
the things which He spoke to them.

Jesus the Good Shepherd

7Then Jesus said to them again, "Most
assuredly, I say to you, I am the door
of the sheep. 8All who *ever* came be-
fore Me[a] are thieves and robbers, but

9:35 [a] NU-Text reads *Son of Man.* **10:8** [a] M-Text omits *before Me.*

the sheep did not hear them. 9I am the
door. If anyone enters by Me, he will be
saved, and will go in and out and find
pasture. 10The thief does not come ex-
cept to steal, and to kill, and to destroy. I
have come that they may have life, and
that they may have *it* more abundantly.
11"I am the good shepherd. The good
shepherd gives His life for the sheep.
12But a hireling, *he who is* not the shep-
herd, one who does not own the sheep,
sees the wolf coming and leaves the
sheep and flees; and the wolf catch-
es the sheep and scatters them. 13The
hireling flees because he is a hireling
and does not care about the sheep. 14I
am the good shepherd; and I know My
sheep, and am known by My own. 15As
the Father knows Me, even so I know the
Father; and I lay down My life for the
sheep. 16And other sheep I have which
are not of this fold; them also I must
bring, and they will hear My voice; and
there will be one flock *and* one shep-
herd.

17"Therefore My Father loves Me, be-
cause I lay down My life that I may take
it again. 18No one takes it from Me, but
I lay it down of Myself. I have power to
lay it down, and I have power to take it
again. This command I have received
from My Father."

19Therefore there was a division again
among the Jews because of these say-
ings. 20And many of them said, "He
has a demon and is mad. Why do you
listen to Him?"

21Others said, "These are not the words
of one who has a demon. Can a demon
open the eyes of the blind?"

The Shepherd Knows His Sheep

22Now it was the Feast of Dedication
in Jerusalem, and it was winter. 23And
Jesus walked in the temple, in Solomon's
porch. 24Then the Jews surrounded Him
and said to Him, "How long do You keep
us in doubt? If You are the Christ, tell
us plainly."

25Jesus answered them, "I told you,
and you do not believe. The works that
I do in My Father's name, they bear
witness of Me. 26But you do not believe,
because you are not of My sheep, as I
said to you.[a] 27My sheep hear My voice,
and I know them, and they follow Me.
28And I give them eternal life, and they
shall never perish; neither shall any-
one snatch them out of My hand. 29My
Father, who has given *them* to Me, is
greater than all; and no one is able to
snatch *them* out of My Father's hand.
30I and *My* Father are one."

Renewed Efforts to Stone Jesus

31Then the Jews took up stones again
to stone Him. 32Jesus answered them,
"Many good works I have shown you
from My Father. For which of those
works do you stone Me?"

33The Jews answered Him, saying, "For
a good work we do not stone You, but
for blasphemy, and because You, being
a Man, make Yourself God."

34Jesus answered them, "Is it not
written in your law, 'I said, "You are
gods" '?[a] 35If He called them gods, to
whom the word of God came (and the
Scripture cannot be broken), 36do you
say of Him whom the Father sancti-
fied and sent into the world, 'You are
blaspheming,' because I said, 'I am the
Son of God'? 37If I do not do the works
of My Father, do not believe Me; 38but
if I do, though you do not believe Me,
believe the works, that you may know
and believe[a] that the Father *is* in Me,
and I in Him." 39Therefore they sought
again to seize Him, but He escaped out
of their hand.

The Believers Beyond Jordan

40And He went away again beyond
the Jordan to the place where John was
baptizing at first, and there He stayed.
41Then many came to Him and said,
"John performed no sign, but all the
things that John spoke about this Man
were true." 42And many believed in Him
there.

The Death of Lazarus

11 Now a certain *man* was sick,
Lazarus of Bethany, the town
of Mary and her sister Martha. 2It was
that Mary who anointed the Lord with

10:26 [a] NU-Text omits *as I said to you.* 10:34 [a] Psalm 82:6 10:38 [a] NU-Text reads *understand.*

fragrant oil and wiped His feet with
her hair, whose brother Lazarus was
sick. 3Therefore the sisters sent to Him,
saying, "Lord, behold, he whom You
love is sick."

4When Jesus heard *that,* He said, "This
sickness is not unto death, but for the
glory of God, that the Son of God may
be glorified through it."

5Now Jesus loved Martha and her sis-
ter and Lazarus. 6So, when He heard
that he was sick, He stayed two more
days in the place where He was. 7Then
after this He said to *the* disciples, "Let
us go to Judea again."

8*The* disciples said to Him, "Rabbi,
lately the Jews sought to stone You, and
are You going there again?"

9Jesus answered, "Are there not twelve
hours in the day? If anyone walks in the
day, he does not stumble, because he
sees the light of this world. 10But if one
walks in the night, he stumbles, because
the light is not in him." 11These things
He said, and after that He said to them,
"Our friend Lazarus sleeps, but I go that
I may wake him up."

12Then His disciples said, "Lord, if he
sleeps he will get well." 13However, Jesus
spoke of his death, but they thought
that He was speaking about taking rest
in sleep.

14Then Jesus said to them plainly, "Laz-
arus is dead. 15And I am glad for your
sakes that I was not there, that you may
believe. Nevertheless let us go to him."

16Then Thomas, who is called the Twin,
said to his fellow disciples, "Let us also
go, that we may die with Him."

I Am the Resurrection and the Life

17So when Jesus came, He found that
he had already been in the tomb four
days. 18Now Bethany was near Jeru-
salem, about two miles[a] away. 19And
many of the Jews had joined the women
around Martha and Mary, to comfort
them concerning their brother.

20Then Martha, as soon as she heard
that Jesus was coming, went and met
Him, but Mary was sitting in the house.
21Now Martha said to Jesus, "Lord, if
You had been here, my brother would
not have died. 22But even now I know
that whatever You ask of God, God will
give You."

23Jesus said to her, "Your brother will
rise again."

24Martha said to Him, "I know that
he will rise again in the resurrection
at the last day."

25Jesus said to her, "I am the resurrec-
tion and the life. He who believes in Me,
though he may die, he shall live. 26And
whoever lives and believes in Me shall
never die. Do you believe this?"

27She said to Him, "Yes, Lord, I believe
that You are the Christ, the Son of God,
who is to come into the world."

Jesus and Death, the Last Enemy

28And when she had said these things,
she went her way and secretly called
Mary her sister, saying, "The Teacher
has come and is calling for you." 29As
soon as she heard *that,* she arose quick-
ly and came to Him. 30Now Jesus had
not yet come into the town, but was[a]
in the place where Martha met Him.
31Then the Jews who were with her in the
house, and comforting her, when they
saw that Mary rose up quickly and went
out, followed her, saying, "She is going
to the tomb to weep there."[a]

32Then, when Mary came where Jesus
was, and saw Him, she fell down at His
feet, saying to Him, "Lord, if You had
been here, my brother would not have
died."

33Therefore, when Jesus saw her weep-
ing, and the Jews who came with her
weeping, He groaned in the spirit and
was troubled. 34And He said, "Where
have you laid him?"

They said to Him, "Lord, come and
see."

35Jesus wept. 36Then the Jews said,
"See how He loved him!"

37And some of them said, "Could not
this Man, who opened the eyes of the
blind, also have kept this man from
dying?"

Lazarus Raised from the Dead

38Then Jesus, again groaning in Him-
self, came to the tomb. It was a cave,

11:18 [a] Literally *fifteen stadia* **11:30** [a] NU-Text adds *still.* **11:31** [a] NU-Text reads *supposing that she was going to the tomb to weep there.*

and a stone lay against it. 39Jesus said, "Take away the stone."

Martha, the sister of him who was dead, said to Him, "Lord, by this time there is a stench, for he has been *dead* four days."

40Jesus said to her, "Did I not say to you that if you would believe you would see the glory of God?" 41Then they took away the stone *from the place* where the dead man was lying.[a] And Jesus lifted up *His* eyes and said, "Father, I thank You that You have heard Me. 42And I know that You always hear Me, but because of the people who are standing by I said *this,* that they may believe that You sent Me." 43Now when He had said these things, He cried with a loud voice, "Lazarus, come forth!" 44And he who had died came out bound hand and foot with graveclothes, and his face was wrapped with a cloth. Jesus said to them, "Loose him, and let him go."

The Plot to Kill Jesus

45Then many of the Jews who had come to Mary, and had seen the things Jesus did, believed in Him. 46But some of them went away to the Pharisees and told them the things Jesus did. 47Then the chief priests and the Pharisees gathered a council and said, "What shall we do? For this Man works many signs. 48If we let Him alone like this, everyone will believe in Him, and the Romans will come and take away both our place and nation."

49And one of them, Caiaphas, being high priest that year, said to them, "You know nothing at all, 50nor do you consider that it is expedient for us[a] that one man should die for the people, and not that the whole nation should perish." 51Now this he did not say on his own *authority;* but being high priest that year he prophesied that Jesus would die for the nation, 52and not for that nation only, but also that He would gather together in one the children of God who were scattered abroad.

53Then, from that day on, they plotted to put Him to death. 54Therefore Jesus no longer walked openly among the Jews, but went from there into the country near the wilderness, to a city called Ephraim, and there remained with His disciples.

55And the Passover of the Jews was near, and many went from the country up to Jerusalem before the Passover, to purify themselves. 56Then they sought Jesus, and spoke among themselves as they stood in the temple, "What do you think—that He will not come to the feast?" 57Now both the chief priests and the Pharisees had given a command, that if anyone knew where He was, he should report *it,* that they might seize Him.

The Anointing at Bethany

12 Then, six days before the Passover, Jesus came to Bethany, where Lazarus was who had been dead,[a] whom He had raised from the dead. 2There they made Him a supper; and Martha served, but Lazarus was one of those who sat at the table with Him. 3Then Mary took a pound of very costly oil of spikenard, anointed the feet of Jesus, and wiped His feet with her hair. And the house was filled with the fragrance of the oil.

4But one of His disciples, Judas Iscariot, Simon's *son,* who would betray Him, said, 5"Why was this fragrant oil not sold for three hundred denarii[a] and given to the poor?" 6This he said, not that he cared for the poor, but because he was a thief, and had the money box; and he used to take what was put in it.

7But Jesus said, "Let her alone; she has kept[a] this for the day of My burial. 8For the poor you have with you always, but Me you do not have always."

The Plot to Kill Lazarus

9Now a great many of the Jews knew that He was there; and they came, not for Jesus' sake only, but that they might also see Lazarus, whom He had raised from the dead. 10But the chief priests plotted to put Lazarus to death also, 11because on account of him many of the Jews went away and believed in Jesus.

11:41 [a] NU-Text omits *from the place where the dead man was lying.* **11:50** [a] NU-Text reads *you.* **12:1** [a] NU-Text omits *who had been dead.* **12:5** [a] About one year's wages for a worker **12:7** [a] NU-Text reads *that she may keep.*

The Triumphal Entry
12 The next day a great multitude that
had come to the feast, when they heard
that Jesus was coming to Jerusalem,
13 took branches of palm trees and went
out to meet Him, and cried out:

"Hosanna!
'Blessed *is* He who comes in the
name of the LORD!'[a]
The King of Israel!"

14 Then Jesus, when He had found a
young donkey, sat on it; as it is written:

15 "Fear not, daughter of Zion;
Behold, your King is coming,
Sitting on a donkey's colt."[a]

16 His disciples did not understand
these things at first; but when Jesus was
glorified, then they remembered that
these things were written about Him
and *that* they had done these things
to Him.
17 Therefore the people, who were with
Him when He called Lazarus out of his
tomb and raised him from the dead,
bore witness. 18 For this reason the peo-
ple also met Him, because they heard
that He had done this sign. 19 The Phar-
isees therefore said among themselves,
"You see that you are accomplishing
nothing. Look, the world has gone after
Him!"

The Fruitful Grain of Wheat
20 Now there were certain Greeks
among those who came up to worship
at the feast. 21 Then they came to Phil-
ip, who was from Bethsaida of Galilee,
and asked him, saying, "Sir, we wish to
see Jesus."
22 Philip came and told Andrew, and
in turn Andrew and Philip told Jesus.
23 But Jesus answered them, saying,
"The hour has come that the Son of Man
should be glorified. 24 Most assuredly, I
say to you, unless a grain of wheat falls
into the ground and dies, it remains
alone; but if it dies, it produces much
grain. 25 He who loves his life will lose it,
and he who hates his life in this world will
keep it for eternal life. 26 If anyone serves
Me, let him follow Me; and where I am,
there My servant will be also. If anyone
serves Me, him *My* Father will honor.

Jesus Predicts His Death on the Cross
27 "Now My soul is troubled, and what
shall I say? 'Father, save Me from this
hour'? But for this purpose I came to
this hour. 28 Father, glorify Your name."
Then a voice came from heaven, *say-
ing,* "I have both glorified *it* and will
glorify *it* again."
29 Therefore the people who stood by
and heard *it* said that it had thundered.
Others said, "An angel has spoken to
Him."
30 Jesus answered and said, "This voice
did not come because of Me, but for
your sake. 31 Now is the judgment of
this world; now the ruler of this world
will be cast out. 32 And I, if I am lifted
up from the earth, will draw all *peoples*
to Myself." 33 This He said, signifying by
what death He would die.
34 The people answered Him, "We have
heard from the law that the Christ re-
mains forever; and how *can* You say,
'The Son of Man must be lifted up'? Who
is this Son of Man?"
35 Then Jesus said to them, "A little
while longer the light is with you. Walk
while you have the light, lest darkness
overtake you; he who walks in dark-
ness does not know where he is going.
36 While you have the light, believe in
the light, that you may become sons
of light." These things Jesus spoke, and
departed, and was hidden from them.

Who Has Believed Our Report?
37 But although He had done so many
signs before them, they did not believe
in Him, 38 that the word of Isaiah the
prophet might be fulfilled, which he
spoke:

"Lord, who has believed our report?
And to whom has the arm of the
LORD been revealed?"[a]

39 Therefore they could not believe,
because Isaiah said again:

12:13 [a] Psalm 118:26 **12:15** [a] Zechariah 9:9 **12:38** [a] Isaiah 53:1

40 "He has blinded their eyes and
hardened their hearts,
Lest they should see with *their*
eyes,
Lest they should understand with
their hearts and turn,
So that I should heal them."[a]

41 These things Isaiah said when[a] he saw
His glory and spoke of Him.

Walk in the Light

42 Nevertheless even among the rulers
many believed in Him, but because
of the Pharisees they did not confess
Him, lest they should be put out of the
synagogue; 43 for they loved the praise
of men more than the praise of God.
44 Then Jesus cried out and said, "He
who believes in Me, believes not in Me
but in Him who sent Me. 45 And he who
sees Me sees Him who sent Me. 46 I have
come *as* a light into the world, that who-
ever believes in Me should not abide in
darkness. 47 And if anyone hears My
words and does not believe,[a] I do not
judge him; for I did not come to judge the
world but to save the world. 48 He who re-
jects Me, and does not receive My words,
has that which judges him—the word
that I have spoken will judge him in the
last day. 49 For I have not spoken on My
own *authority;* but the Father who sent
Me gave Me a command, what I should
say and what I should speak. 50 And I
know that His command is everlasting
life. Therefore, whatever I speak, just as
the Father has told Me, so I speak."

Jesus Washes the Disciples' Feet

13 Now before the Feast of the Pass-
over, when Jesus knew that His
hour had come that He should depart
from this world to the Father, having
loved His own who were in the world,
He loved them to the end.
2 And supper being ended,[a] the devil
having already put it into the heart of
Judas Iscariot, Simon's *son,* to betray
Him, 3 Jesus, knowing that the Father
had given all things into His hands,
and that He had come from God and
was going to God, 4 rose from supper
and laid aside His garments, took a
towel and girded Himself. 5 After that,
He poured water into a basin and began
to wash the disciples' feet, and to wipe
them with the towel with which He was
girded. 6 Then He came to Simon Peter.
And *Peter* said to Him, "Lord, are You
washing my feet?"
7 Jesus answered and said to him,
"What I am doing you do not under-
stand now, but you will know after this."
8 Peter said to Him, "You shall never
wash my feet!"
Jesus answered him, "If I do not wash
you, you have no part with Me."
9 Simon Peter said to Him, "Lord, not
my feet only, but also *my* hands and
my head!"
10 Jesus said to him, "He who is bathed
needs only to wash *his* feet, but is com-
pletely clean; and you are clean, but not
all of you." 11 For He knew who would
betray Him; therefore He said, "You
are not all clean."
12 So when He had washed their feet,
taken His garments, and sat down
again, He said to them, "Do you know
what I have done to you? 13 You call Me
Teacher and Lord, and you say well,
for *so* I am. 14 If I then, *your* Lord and
Teacher, have washed your feet, you
also ought to wash one another's feet.
15 For I have given you an example, that
you should do as I have done to you.
16 Most assuredly, I say to you, a servant
is not greater than his master; nor is he
who is sent greater than he who sent
him. 17 If you know these things, blessed
are you if you do them.

Jesus Identifies His Betrayer

18 "I do not speak concerning all of
you. I know whom I have chosen; but
that the Scripture may be fulfilled, 'He
who eats bread with Me[a] has lifted up
his heel against Me.'[b] 19 Now I tell you
before it comes, that when it does come
to pass, you may believe that I am *He.*
20 Most assuredly, I say to you, he who
receives whomever I send receives Me;
and he who receives Me receives Him
who sent Me."
21 When Jesus had said these things,

12:40 [a] Isaiah 6:10 **12:41** [a] NU-Text reads *because.* **12:47** [a] NU-Text reads *keep them.*
13:2 [a] NU-Text reads *And during supper.* **13:18** [a] NU-Text reads *My bread.* [b] Psalm 41:9

He was troubled in spirit, and testified
and said, "Most assuredly, I say to you,
one of you will betray Me." 22Then the
disciples looked at one another, per-
plexed about whom He spoke.
23Now there was leaning on Jesus'
bosom one of His disciples, whom
Jesus loved. 24Simon Peter therefore
motioned to him to ask who it was of
whom He spoke.
25Then, leaning back[a] on Jesus' breast,
he said to Him, "Lord, who is it?"
26Jesus answered, "It is he to whom I
shall give a piece of bread when I have
dipped *it*." And having dipped the bread,
He gave *it* to Judas Iscariot, *the son* of
Simon. 27Now after the piece of bread,
Satan entered him. Then Jesus said to
him, "What you do, do quickly." 28But
no one at the table knew for what reason
He said this to him. 29For some thought,
because Judas had the money box, that
Jesus had said to him, "Buy *those things*
we need for the feast," or that he should
give something to the poor.
30Having received the piece of bread,
he then went out immediately. And it
was night.

The New Commandment

31So, when he had gone out, Jesus said,
"Now the Son of Man is glorified, and
God is glorified in Him. 32If God is glori-
fied in Him, God will also glorify Him in
Himself, and glorify Him immediately.
33Little children, I shall be with you a
little while longer. You will seek Me;
and as I said to the Jews, 'Where I am
going, you cannot come,' so now I say
to you. 34A new commandment I give
to you, that you love one another; as I
have loved you, that you also love one
another. 35By this all will know that
you are My disciples, if you have love
for one another."

Jesus Predicts Peter's Denial

36Simon Peter said to Him, "Lord,
where are You going?"
Jesus answered him, "Where I am go-
ing you cannot follow Me now, but you
shall follow Me afterward."
37Peter said to Him, "Lord, why can I
not follow You now? I will lay down my
life for Your sake."
38Jesus answered him, "Will you lay
down your life for My sake? Most as-
suredly, I say to you, the rooster shall
not crow till you have denied Me three
times.

The Way, the Truth, and the Life

14 "Let not your heart be troubled;
you believe in God, believe also
in Me. 2In My Father's house are many
mansions;[a] if *it were* not *so,* I would
have told you. I go to prepare a place for
you.[b] 3And if I go and prepare a place
for you, I will come again and receive
you to Myself; that where I am, *there*
you may be also. 4And where I go you
know, and the way you know."
5Thomas said to Him, "Lord, we do not
know where You are going, and how can
we know the way?"
6Jesus said to him, "I am the way, the
truth, and the life. No one comes to the
Father except through Me.

The Father Revealed

7"If you had known Me, you would
have known My Father also; and from
now on you know Him and have seen
Him."
8Philip said to Him, "Lord, show us
the Father, and it is sufficient for us."
9Jesus said to him, "Have I been with
you so long, and yet you have not
known Me, Philip? He who has seen
Me has seen the Father; so how can you
say, 'Show us the Father'? 10Do you not
believe that I am in the Father, and the
Father in Me? The words that I speak to
you I do not speak on My own *authority;*
but the Father who dwells in Me does
the works. 11Believe Me that I *am* in the
Father and the Father in Me, or else
believe Me for the sake of the works
themselves.

The Answered Prayer

12"Most assuredly, I say to you, he
who believes in Me, the works that I
do he will do also; and greater *works*

13:25 [a] NU-Text and M-Text add *thus.* 14:2 [a] Literally *dwellings* [b] NU-Text adds a word which would cause the text to read either *if it were not so, would I have told you that I go to prepare a place for you?* or *if it were not so I would have told you; for I go to prepare a place for you.*

than these he will do, because I go to
My Father. 13And whatever you ask in
My name, that I will do, that the Father
may be glorified in the Son. 14If you
ask[a] anything in My name, I will do *it*.

Jesus Promises Another Helper

15"If you love Me, keep[a] My command-
ments. 16And I will pray the Father, and
He will give you another Helper, that
He may abide with you forever— 17the
Spirit of truth, whom the world cannot
receive, because it neither sees Him
nor knows Him; but you know Him,
for He dwells with you and will be in
you. 18I will not leave you orphans; I
will come to you.

Indwelling of the Father and the Son

19"A little while longer and the world
will see Me no more, but you will see
Me. Because I live, you will live also.
20At that day you will know that I *am*
in My Father, and you in Me, and I in
you. 21He who has My commandments
and keeps them, it is he who loves Me.
And he who loves Me will be loved by My
Father, and I will love him and manifest
Myself to him."

22Judas (not Iscariot) said to Him,
"Lord, how is it that You will manifest
Yourself to us, and not to the world?"

23Jesus answered and said to him, "If
anyone loves Me, he will keep My word;
and My Father will love him, and We will
come to him and make Our home with
him. 24He who does not love Me does
not keep My words; and the word which
you hear is not Mine but the Father's
who sent Me.

The Gift of His Peace

25"These things I have spoken to you
while being present with you. 26But
the Helper, the Holy Spirit, whom the
Father will send in My name, He will
teach you all things, and bring to your
remembrance all things that I said to
you. 27Peace I leave with you, My peace
I give to you; not as the world gives
do I give to you. Let not your heart be
troubled, neither let it be afraid. 28You
have heard Me say to you, 'I am going
away and coming *back* to you.' If you
loved Me, you would rejoice because I
said,[a] 'I am going to the Father,' for My
Father is greater than I.

29"And now I have told you before it
comes, that when it does come to pass,
you may believe. 30I will no longer talk
much with you, for the ruler of this
world is coming, and he has nothing
in Me. 31But that the world may know
that I love the Father, and as the Father
gave Me commandment, so I do. Arise,
let us go from here.

The True Vine

15 "I am the true vine, and My Fa-
ther is the vinedresser. 2Every
branch in Me that does not bear fruit
He takes away;[a] and every *branch* that
bears fruit He prunes, that it may bear
more fruit. 3You are already clean be-
cause of the word which I have spoken
to you. 4Abide in Me, and I in you. As
the branch cannot bear fruit of itself,
unless it abides in the vine, neither can
you, unless you abide in Me.

5"I am the vine, you *are* the branch-
es. He who abides in Me, and I in him,
bears much fruit; for without Me you
can do nothing. 6If anyone does not
abide in Me, he is cast out as a branch
and is withered; and they gather them
and throw *them* into the fire, and they
are burned. 7If you abide in Me, and
My words abide in you, you will[a] ask
what you desire, and it shall be done
for you. 8By this My Father is glorified,
that you bear much fruit; so you will be
My disciples.

Love and Joy Perfected

9"As the Father loved Me, I also have
loved you; abide in My love. 10If you
keep My commandments, you will
abide in My love, just as I have kept
My Father's commandments and abide
in His love.

11"These things I have spoken to you,
that My joy may remain in you, and
that your joy may be full. 12This is My
commandment, that you love one an-
other as I have loved you. 13Greater love
has no one than this, than to lay down

14:14 [a] NU-Text adds *Me*. 14:15 [a] NU-Text reads *you will keep*. 14:28 [a] NU-Text omits *I said*.
15:2 [a] Or *lifts up* 15:7 [a] NU-Text omits *you will*.

one's life for his friends. 14You are My friends if you do whatever I command you. 15No longer do I call you servants, for a servant does not know what his master is doing; but I have called you friends, for all things that I heard from My Father I have made known to you. 16You did not choose Me, but I chose you and appointed you that you should go and bear fruit, and *that* your fruit should remain, that whatever you ask the Father in My name He may give you. 17These things I command you, that you love one another.

The World's Hatred

18"If the world hates you, you know that it hated Me before *it hated* you. 19If you were of the world, the world would love its own. Yet because you are not of the world, but I chose you out of the world, therefore the world hates you. 20Remember the word that I said to you, 'A servant is not greater than his master.' If they persecuted Me, they will also persecute you. If they kept My word, they will keep yours also. 21But all these things they will do to you for My name's sake, because they do not know Him who sent Me. 22If I had not come and spoken to them, they would have no sin, but now they have no excuse for their sin. 23He who hates Me hates My Father also. 24If I had not done among them the works which no one else did, they would have no sin; but now they have seen and also hated both Me and My Father. 25But *this happened* that the word might be fulfilled which is written in their law, 'They hated Me without a cause.'[a]

The Coming Rejection

26"But when the Helper comes, whom I shall send to you from the Father, the Spirit of truth who proceeds from the Father, He will testify of Me. 27And you also will bear witness, because you have been with Me from the beginning.

16 "These things I have spoken to you, that you should not be made to stumble. 2They will put you out of the synagogues; yes, the time is coming that whoever kills you will think that he offers God service. 3And these things they will do to you[a] because they have not known the Father nor Me. 4But these things I have told you, that when the[a] time comes, you may remember that I told you of them.

"And these things I did not say to you at the beginning, because I was with you.

The Work of the Holy Spirit

5"But now I go away to Him who sent Me, and none of you asks Me, 'Where are You going?' 6But because I have said these things to you, sorrow has filled your heart. 7Nevertheless I tell you the truth. It is to your advantage that I go away; for if I do not go away, the Helper will not come to you; but if I depart, I will send Him to you. 8And when He has come, He will convict the world of sin, and of righteousness, and of judgment: 9of sin, because they do not believe in Me; 10of righteousness, because I go to My Father and you see Me no more; 11of judgment, because the ruler of this world is judged.

12"I still have many things to say to you, but you cannot bear *them* now. 13However, when He, the Spirit of truth, has come, He will guide you into all truth; for He will not speak on His own *authority,* but whatever He hears He will speak; and He will tell you things to come. 14He will glorify Me, for He will take of what is Mine and declare *it* to you. 15All things that the Father has are Mine. Therefore I said that He will take of Mine and declare *it* to you.[a]

Sorrow Will Turn to Joy

16"A little while, and you will not see Me; and again a little while, and you will see Me, because I go to the Father."

17Then *some* of His disciples said among themselves, "What is this that He says to us, 'A little while, and you will not see Me; and again a little while, and you will see Me'; and, 'because I go to the Father'?" 18They said therefore, "What is this that He says, 'A little while'? We do not know what He is saying."

15:25 [a] Psalm 69:4 **16:3** [a] NU-Text and M-Text omit *to you.* **16:4** [a] NU-Text reads *their.* **16:15** [a] NU-Text and M-Text read *He takes of Mine and will declare it to you.*

19Now Jesus knew that they desired
to ask Him, and He said to them, "Are
you inquiring among yourselves about
what I said, 'A little while, and you will
not see Me; and again a little while, and
you will see Me'? 20Most assuredly, I say
to you that you will weep and lament,
but the world will rejoice; and you will be
sorrowful, but your sorrow will be turned
into joy. 21A woman, when she is in labor,
has sorrow because her hour has come;
but as soon as she has given birth to
the child, she no longer remembers the
anguish, for joy that a human being has
been born into the world. 22Therefore
you now have sorrow; but I will see you
again and your heart will rejoice, and
your joy no one will take from you.
23"And in that day you will ask Me
nothing. Most assuredly, I say to you,
whatever you ask the Father in My
name He will give you. 24Until now
you have asked nothing in My name.
Ask, and you will receive, that your joy
may be full.

Jesus Christ Has Overcome the World

25"These things I have spoken to you in
figurative language; but the time is com-
ing when I will no longer speak to you
in figurative language, but I will tell you
plainly about the Father. 26In that day
you will ask in My name, and I do not
say to you that I shall pray the Father
for you; 27for the Father Himself loves
you, because you have loved Me, and
have believed that I came forth from
God. 28I came forth from the Father
and have come into the world. Again,
I leave the world and go to the Father."
29His disciples said to Him, "See, now
You are speaking plainly, and using
no figure of speech! 30Now we are sure
that You know all things, and have no
need that anyone should question You.
By this we believe that You came forth
from God."
31Jesus answered them, "Do you now
believe? 32Indeed the hour is coming,
yes, has now come, that you will be scat-
tered, each to his own, and will leave Me
alone. And yet I am not alone, because
the Father is with Me. 33These things I
have spoken to you, that in Me you may
have peace. In the world you will[a] have
tribulation; but be of good cheer, I have
overcome the world."

Jesus Prays for Himself

17 Jesus spoke these words, lifted
up His eyes to heaven, and said:
"Father, the hour has come. Glorify Your
Son, that Your Son also may glorify You,
2as You have given Him authority over
all flesh, that He should[a] give eternal
life to as many as You have given Him.
3And this is eternal life, that they may
know You, the only true God, and Jesus
Christ whom You have sent. 4I have glo-
rified You on the earth. I have finished
the work which You have given Me to do.
5And now, O Father, glorify Me together
with Yourself, with the glory which I had
with You before the world was.

Jesus Prays for His Disciples

6"I have manifested Your name to the
men whom You have given Me out of the
world. They were Yours, You gave them
to Me, and they have kept Your word.
7Now they have known that all things
which You have given Me are from You.
8For I have given to them the words
which You have given Me; and they have
received *them,* and have known surely
that I came forth from You; and they
have believed that You sent Me.
9"I pray for them. I do not pray for
the world but for those whom You have
given Me, for they are Yours. 10And all
Mine are Yours, and Yours are Mine, and
I am glorified in them. 11Now I am no
longer in the world, but these are in the
world, and I come to You. Holy Father,
keep through Your name those whom
You have given Me,[a] that they may be
one as We *are.* 12While I was with them
in the world,[a] I kept them in Your name.
Those whom You gave Me I have kept;[b]
and none of them is lost except the son
of perdition, that the Scripture might
be fulfilled. 13But now I come to You,
and these things I speak in the world,
that they may have My joy fulfilled in

16:33 [a] NU-Text and M-Text omit *will.* **17:2** [a] M-Text reads *shall.* **17:11** [a] NU-Text and M-Text read *keep them through Your name which You have given Me.* **17:12** [a] NU-Text omits *in the world.* [b] NU-Text reads *in Your name which You gave Me. And I guarded them;* (or *it;*).

themselves. 14I have given them Your
word; and the world has hated them be-
cause they are not of the world, just as I
am not of the world. 15I do not pray that
You should take them out of the world,
but that You should keep them from the
evil one. 16They are not of the world, just
as I am not of the world. 17Sanctify them
by Your truth. Your word is truth. 18As
You sent Me into the world, I also have
sent them into the world. 19And for their
sakes I sanctify Myself, that they also
may be sanctified by the truth.

Jesus Prays for All Believers

20"I do not pray for these alone, but
also for those who will[a] believe in Me
through their word; 21that they all may
be one, as You, Father, *are* in Me, and
I in You; that they also may be one in
Us, that the world may believe that You
sent Me. 22And the glory which You gave
Me I have given them, that they may
be one just as We are one: 23I in them,
and You in Me; that they may be made
perfect in one, and that the world may
know that You have sent Me, and have
loved them as You have loved Me.

24"Father, I desire that they also whom
You gave Me may be with Me where
I am, that they may behold My glo-
ry which You have given Me; for You
loved Me before the foundation of the
world. 25O righteous Father! The world
has not known You, but I have known
You; and these have known that You
sent Me. 26And I have declared to them
Your name, and will declare *it,* that the
love with which You loved Me may be
in them, and I in them."

Betrayal and Arrest in Gethsemane

18 When Jesus had spoken these
words, He went out with His dis-
ciples over the Brook Kidron, where
there was a garden, which He and His
disciples entered. 2And Judas, who
betrayed Him, also knew the place;
for Jesus often met there with His dis-
ciples. 3Then Judas, having received
a detachment *of troops,* and officers
from the chief priests and Pharisees,
came there with lanterns, torches, and
weapons. 4Jesus therefore, knowing all
things that would come upon Him, went
forward and said to them, "Whom are
you seeking?"

5They answered Him, "Jesus of Naz-
areth."

Jesus said to them, "I am *He.*" And
Judas, who betrayed Him, also stood
with them. 6Now when He said to them,
"I am *He,*" they drew back and fell to
the ground.

7Then He asked them again, "Whom
are you seeking?"

And they said, "Jesus of Nazareth."

8Jesus answered, "I have told you that
I am *He.* Therefore, if you seek Me, let
these go their way," 9that the saying
might be fulfilled which He spoke, "Of
those whom You gave Me I have lost
none."

10Then Simon Peter, having a sword,
drew it and struck the high priest's
servant, and cut off his right ear. The
servant's name was Malchus.

11So Jesus said to Peter, "Put your
sword into the sheath. Shall I not drink
the cup which My Father has given Me?"

Before the High Priest

12Then the detachment *of troops* and
the captain and the officers of the Jews
arrested Jesus and bound Him. 13And
they led Him away to Annas first, for he
was the father-in-law of Caiaphas who
was high priest that year. 14Now it was
Caiaphas who advised the Jews that it
was expedient that one man should die
for the people.

Peter Denies Jesus

15And Simon Peter followed Jesus,
and so *did* another[a] disciple. Now that
disciple was known to the high priest,
and went with Jesus into the courtyard
of the high priest. 16But Peter stood at
the door outside. Then the other disci-
ple, who was known to the high priest,
went out and spoke to her who kept the
door, and brought Peter in. 17Then the
servant girl who kept the door said to
Peter, "You are not also *one* of this Man's
disciples, are you?"

He said, "I am not."

17:20 [a] NU-Text and M-Text omit *will.* 18:15 [a] M-Text reads *the other.*

18Now the servants and officers who had made a fire of coals stood there, for it was cold, and they warmed themselves. And Peter stood with them and warmed himself.

Jesus Questioned by the High Priest

19The high priest then asked Jesus about His disciples and His doctrine.

20Jesus answered him, "I spoke openly to the world. I always taught in synagogues and in the temple, where the Jews always meet,[a] and in secret I have said nothing. 21Why do you ask Me? Ask those who have heard Me what I said to them. Indeed they know what I said."

22And when He had said these things, one of the officers who stood by struck Jesus with the palm of his hand, saying, "Do You answer the high priest like that?"

23Jesus answered him, "If I have spoken evil, bear witness of the evil; but if well, why do you strike Me?"

24Then Annas sent Him bound to Caiaphas the high priest.

Peter Denies Twice More

25Now Simon Peter stood and warmed himself. Therefore they said to him, "You are not also *one* of His disciples, are you?"

He denied *it* and said, "I am not!"

26One of the servants of the high priest, a relative *of him* whose ear Peter cut off, said, "Did I not see you in the garden with Him?" 27Peter then denied again; and immediately a rooster crowed.

In Pilate's Court

28Then they led Jesus from Caiaphas to the Praetorium, and it was early morning. But they themselves did not go into the Praetorium, lest they should be defiled, but that they might eat the Passover. 29Pilate then went out to them and said, "What accusation do you bring against this Man?"

30They answered and said to him, "If He were not an evildoer, we would not have delivered Him up to you."

31Then Pilate said to them, "You take Him and judge Him according to your law."

Therefore the Jews said to him, "It is not lawful for us to put anyone to death," 32that the saying of Jesus might be fulfilled which He spoke, signifying by what death He would die.

33Then Pilate entered the Praetorium again, called Jesus, and said to Him, "Are You the King of the Jews?"

34Jesus answered him, "Are you speaking for yourself about this, or did others tell you this concerning Me?"

35Pilate answered, "Am I a Jew? Your own nation and the chief priests have delivered You to me. What have You done?"

36Jesus answered, "My kingdom is not of this world. If My kingdom were of this world, My servants would fight, so that I should not be delivered to the Jews; but now My kingdom is not from here."

37Pilate therefore said to Him, "Are You a king then?"

Jesus answered, "You say *rightly* that I am a king. For this cause I was born, and for this cause I have come into the world, that I should bear witness to the truth. Everyone who is of the truth hears My voice."

38Pilate said to Him, "What is truth?" And when he had said this, he went out again to the Jews, and said to them, "I find no fault in Him at all.

Taking the Place of Barabbas

39"But you have a custom that I should release someone to you at the Passover. Do you therefore want me to release to you the King of the Jews?"

40Then they all cried again, saying, "Not this Man, but Barabbas!" Now Barabbas was a robber.

The Soldiers Mock Jesus

19 So then Pilate took Jesus and scourged *Him.* 2And the soldiers twisted a crown of thorns and put *it* on His head, and they put on Him a purple robe. 3Then they said,[a] "Hail, King of the Jews!" And they struck Him with their hands.

4Pilate then went out again, and said to them, "Behold, I am bringing Him out to you, that you may know that I find no fault in Him."

18:20 [a] NU-Text reads *where all the Jews meet.* 19:3 [a] NU-Text reads *And they came up to Him and said.*

GOD SIN JESUS SALVATION LOVE

Pilate's Decision

5Then Jesus came out, wearing the
crown of thorns and the purple robe. And
Pilate said to them, "Behold the Man!"
6Therefore, when the chief priests and
officers saw Him, they cried out, saying,
"Crucify *Him,* crucify *Him!*"
Pilate said to them, "You take Him and
crucify *Him,* for I find no fault in Him."
7The Jews answered him, "We have a
law, and according to our[a] law He ought
to die, because He made Himself the
Son of God."
8Therefore, when Pilate heard that
saying, he was the more afraid, 9and
went again into the Praetorium, and
said to Jesus, "Where are You from?"
But Jesus gave him no answer.
10Then Pilate said to Him, "Are You not
speaking to me? Do You not know that
I have power to crucify You, and power
to release You?"
11Jesus answered, "You could have no
power at all against Me unless it had
been given you from above. Therefore
the one who delivered Me to you has
the greater sin."
12From then on Pilate sought to re-
lease Him, but the Jews cried out, say-
ing, "If you let this Man go, you are not
Caesar's friend. Whoever makes himself
a king speaks against Caesar."
13When Pilate therefore heard that
saying, he brought Jesus out and sat
down in the judgment seat in a place
that is called *The* Pavement, but in He-
brew, Gabbatha. 14Now it was the Prepa-
ration Day of the Passover, and about
the sixth hour. And he said to the Jews,
"Behold your King!"
15But they cried out, "Away with *Him,*
away with *Him!* Crucify Him!"
Pilate said to them, "Shall I crucify
your King?"
The chief priests answered, "We have
no king but Caesar!"
16Then he delivered Him to them to
be crucified. Then they took Jesus and
led *Him* away.[a]

The King on a Cross

17And He, bearing His cross, went out
to a place called *the Place* of a Skull,
which is called in Hebrew, Golgotha,
18where they crucified Him, and two
others with Him, one on either side, and
Jesus in the center. 19Now Pilate wrote
a title and put *it* on the cross. And the
writing was:

JESUS OF NAZARETH,
THE KING OF THE JEWS.

20Then many of the Jews read this title,
for the place where Jesus was crucified
was near the city; and it was written in
Hebrew, Greek, *and* Latin.
21Therefore the chief priests of the Jews
said to Pilate, "Do not write, 'The King of
the Jews,' but, 'He said, "I am the King
of the Jews." ' "
22Pilate answered, "What I have writ-
ten, I have written."
23Then the soldiers, when they had
crucified Jesus, took His garments and
made four parts, to each soldier a part,
and also the tunic. Now the tunic was
without seam, woven from the top in
one piece. 24They said therefore among
themselves, "Let us not tear it, but cast
lots for it, whose it shall be," that the
Scripture might be fulfilled which says:

"They divided My garments among
them,
And for My clothing they cast
lots."[a]

Therefore the soldiers did these things.

Behold Your Mother

25Now there stood by the cross of Jesus
His mother, and His mother's sister,
Mary the *wife* of Clopas, and Mary
Magdalene. 26When Jesus therefore
saw His mother, and the disciple whom
He loved standing by, He said to His
mother, "Woman, behold your son!"
27Then He said to the disciple, "Behold
your mother!" And from that hour that
disciple took her to his own *home.*

It Is Finished

28After this, Jesus, knowing[a] that all
things were now accomplished, that
the Scripture might be fulfilled, said,

19:7 [a] NU-Text reads *the law.* **19:16** [a] NU-Text omits *and led Him away.* **19:24** [a] Psalm 22:18
19:28 [a] M-Text reads *seeing.*

"I thirst!" 29Now a vessel full of sour
wine was sitting there; and they filled a
sponge with sour wine, put *it* on hyssop,
and put *it* to His mouth. 30So when Jesus
had received the sour wine, He said, "It
is finished!" And bowing His head, He
gave up His spirit.

Jesus' Side Is Pierced

31Therefore, because it was the Prepa-
ration *Day*, that the bodies should not
remain on the cross on the Sabbath
(for that Sabbath was a high day), the
Jews asked Pilate that their legs might
be broken, and *that* they might be tak-
en away. 32Then the soldiers came
and broke the legs of the first and of
the other who was crucified with Him.
33But when they came to Jesus and saw
that He was already dead, they did not
break His legs. 34But one of the soldiers
pierced His side with a spear, and im-
mediately blood and water came out.
35And he who has seen has testified, and
his testimony is true; and he knows that
he is telling the truth, so that you may
believe. 36For these things were done
that the Scripture should be fulfilled,
"Not *one* of His bones shall be broken."[a]
37And again another Scripture says,
"They shall look on Him whom they
pierced."[a]

Jesus Buried in Joseph's Tomb

38After this, Joseph of Arimathea,
being a disciple of Jesus, but secretly,
for fear of the Jews, asked Pilate that
he might take away the body of Jesus;
and Pilate gave *him* permission. So
he came and took the body of Jesus.
39And Nicodemus, who at first came
to Jesus by night, also came, bringing
a mixture of myrrh and aloes, about a
hundred pounds. 40Then they took the
body of Jesus, and bound it in strips of
linen with the spices, as the custom of
the Jews is to bury. 41Now in the place
where He was crucified there was a gar-
den, and in the garden a new tomb in
which no one had yet been laid. 42So
there they laid Jesus, because of the
Jews' Preparation *Day*, for the tomb
was nearby.

The Empty Tomb

20 Now the first *day* of the week
Mary Magdalene went to the
tomb early, while it was still dark, and
saw *that* the stone had been taken away
from the tomb. 2Then she ran and came
to Simon Peter, and to the other disciple,
whom Jesus loved, and said to them,
"They have taken away the Lord out of
the tomb, and we do not know where
they have laid Him."
3Peter therefore went out, and the oth-
er disciple, and were going to the tomb.
4So they both ran together, and the
other disciple outran Peter and came to
the tomb first. 5And he, stooping down
and looking in, saw the linen cloths
lying *there;* yet he did not go in. 6Then
Simon Peter came, following him, and
went into the tomb; and he saw the linen
cloths lying *there,* 7and the handker-
chief that had been around His head,
not lying with the linen cloths, but fold-
ed together in a place by itself. 8Then
the other disciple, who came to the tomb
first, went in also; and he saw and be-
lieved. 9For as yet they did not know
the Scripture, that He must rise again
from the dead. 10Then the disciples went
away again to their own homes.

Mary Magdalene Sees the Risen Lord

11But Mary stood outside by the tomb
weeping, and as she wept she stooped
down *and looked* into the tomb. 12And
she saw two angels in white sitting, one
at the head and the other at the feet,
where the body of Jesus had lain. 13Then
they said to her, "Woman, why are you
weeping?"
She said to them, "Because they have
taken away my Lord, and I do not know
where they have laid Him."
14Now when she had said this, she
turned around and saw Jesus standing
there, and did not know that it was Jesus.
15Jesus said to her, "Woman, why are
you weeping? Whom are you seeking?"
She, supposing Him to be the garden-
er, said to Him, "Sir, if You have carried
Him away, tell me where You have laid
Him, and I will take Him away."
16Jesus said to her, "Mary!"

19:36 [a] Exodus 12:46; Numbers 9:12; Psalm 34:20 **19:37** [a] Zechariah 12:10

She turned and said to Him,[a] "Rabbo-
ni!" (which is to say, Teacher).
17Jesus said to her, "Do not cling to Me,
for I have not yet ascended to My Father;
but go to My brethren and say to them,
'I am ascending to My Father and your
Father, and *to* My God and your God.'"
18Mary Magdalene came and told the
disciples that she had seen the Lord,[a]
and *that* He had spoken these things
to her.

The Apostles Commissioned

19Then, the same day at evening, being
the first *day* of the week, when the doors
were shut where the disciples were as-
sembled,[a] for fear of the Jews, Jesus
came and stood in the midst, and said
to them, "Peace *be* with you." 20When
He had said this, He showed them *His*
hands and His side. Then the disciples
were glad when they saw the Lord.
21So Jesus said to them again, "Peace
to you! As the Father has sent Me, I also
send you." 22And when He had said
this, He breathed on *them,* and said to
them, "Receive the Holy Spirit. 23If you
forgive the sins of any, they are forgiven
them; if you retain the *sins* of any, they
are retained."

Seeing and Believing

24Now Thomas, called the Twin, one
of the twelve, was not with them when
Jesus came. 25The other disciples
therefore said to him, "We have seen
the Lord."
So he said to them, "Unless I see in His
hands the print of the nails, and put my
finger into the print of the nails, and put
my hand into His side, I will not believe."
26And after eight days His disciples
were again inside, and Thomas with
them. Jesus came, the doors being
shut, and stood in the midst, and said,
"Peace to you!" 27Then He said to Thom-
as, "Reach your finger here, and look at
My hands; and reach your hand *here,*
and put *it* into My side. Do not be un-
believing, but believing."
28And Thomas answered and said to
Him, "My Lord and my God!"
29Jesus said to him, "Thomas,[a] be-
cause you have seen Me, you have be-
lieved. Blessed *are* those who have not
seen and *yet* have believed."

That You May Believe

30And truly Jesus did many other
signs in the presence of His disciples,
which are not written in this book; 31but
these are written that you may believe
that Jesus is the Christ, the Son of God,
and that believing you may have life
in His name.

Breakfast by the Sea

21 After these things Jesus showed
Himself again to the disciples at
the Sea of Tiberias, and in this way He
showed *Himself:* 2Simon Peter, Thomas
called the Twin, Nathanael of Cana in
Galilee, the *sons* of Zebedee, and two
others of His disciples were together.
3Simon Peter said to them, "I am going
fishing."
They said to him, "We are going with
you also." They went out and immedi-
ately[a] got into the boat, and that night
they caught nothing. 4But when the
morning had now come, Jesus stood
on the shore; yet the disciples did not
know that it was Jesus. 5Then Jesus said
to them, "Children, have you any food?"
They answered Him, "No."
6And He said to them, "Cast the net on
the right side of the boat, and you will
find *some.*" So they cast, and now they
were not able to draw it in because of
the multitude of fish.
7Therefore that disciple whom Jesus
loved said to Peter, "It is the Lord!" Now
when Simon Peter heard that it was the
Lord, he put on *his* outer garment (for
he had removed it), and plunged into
the sea. 8But the other disciples came
in the little boat (for they were not far
from land, but about two hundred cu-
bits), dragging the net with fish. 9Then,
as soon as they had come to land, they
saw a fire of coals there, and fish laid
on it, and bread. 10Jesus said to them,
"Bring some of the fish which you have
just caught."

20:16 [a] NU-Text adds *in Hebrew.* **20:18** [a] NU-Text reads *disciples, "I have seen the Lord,"* . . . . **20:19** [a] NU-Text omits *assembled.* **20:29** [a] NU-Text and M-Text omit *Thomas.* **21:3** [a] NU-Text omits *immediately.*

11 Simon Peter went up and dragged
the net to land, full of large fish, one
hundred and fifty-three; and although
there were so many, the net was not
broken. 12 Jesus said to them, "Come
and eat breakfast." Yet none of the dis-
ciples dared ask Him, "Who are You?"—
knowing that it was the Lord. 13 Jesus
then came and took the bread and gave
it to them, and likewise the fish.
14 This *is* now the third time Jesus
showed Himself to His disciples after
He was raised from the dead.

Jesus Restores Peter

15 So when they had eaten breakfast,
Jesus said to Simon Peter, "Simon, *son*
of Jonah,[a] do you love Me more than
these?"

He said to Him, "Yes, Lord; You know
that I love You."

He said to him, "Feed My lambs."
16 He said to him again a second time,
"Simon, *son* of Jonah,[a] do you love Me?"

He said to Him, "Yes, Lord; You know
that I love You."

He said to him, "Tend My sheep."
17 He said to him the third time, "Simon,
son of Jonah,[a] do you love Me?" Peter
was grieved because He said to him the
third time, "Do you love Me?"

And he said to Him, "Lord, You know
all things; You know that I love You."

Jesus said to him, "Feed My sheep.
18 Most assuredly, I say to you, when
you were younger, you girded yourself
and walked where you wished; but when
you are old, you will stretch out your
hands, and another will gird you and
carry *you* where you do not wish." 19 This
He spoke, signifying by what death he
would glorify God. And when He had
spoken this, He said to him, "Follow Me."

The Beloved Disciple and His Book

20 Then Peter, turning around, saw the
disciple whom Jesus loved following,
who also had leaned on His breast at
the supper, and said, "Lord, who is the
one who betrays You?" 21 Peter, seeing
him, said to Jesus, "But Lord, what *about*
this man?"

22 Jesus said to him, "If I will that he
remain till I come, what *is that* to you?
You follow Me."

23 Then this saying went out among
the brethren that this disciple would
not die. Yet Jesus did not say to him that
he would not die, but, "If I will that he
remain till I come, what *is that* to you?"
24 This is the disciple who testifies of
these things, and wrote these things;
and we know that his testimony is true.
25 And there are also many other
things that Jesus did, which if they were
written one by one, I suppose that even
the world itself could not contain the
books that would be written. Amen.

21:15 [a] NU-Text reads *John.* 21:16 [a] NU-Text reads *John.* 21:17 [a] NU-Text reads *John.*

GOD SIN JESUS SALVATION LOVE

THE ACTS OF THE APOSTLES

Jesus' earthly ministry was rather brief—only about three years—but it did not end with His ascension. Before He left, Jesus commanded His followers to continue what He started. The Book of Acts tells the story of how they were obedient to that mission and how the church began as a result. The beginning of Acts overlaps with the ending of the Gospels with the believers gathered in Jerusalem and Jesus ascending to return to the Father. Just about forty days after Jesus died on the cross and rose again, the disciples boldly proclaim Him in Jerusalem and 3,000 people believe. From there, the gospel spread throughout Jerusalem, Judea, Samaria, and toward the ends of the earth, thanks in large part to the disciples like Peter, Stephen, Philip, Paul, and Barnabas.

- **GENRE:** History
- **AUTHOR:** Luke
- **TIME:** c. AD 33–62 (written c. AD 62)
- **PURPOSE:** To record the history of the early church and show how it was continuing the mission that Jesus had begun.

Prologue

1 The former account I made, O The-
ophilus, of all that Jesus began both
to do and teach, 2until the day in which
He was taken up, after He through the
Holy Spirit had given commandments
to the apostles whom He had chosen,
3to whom He also presented Himself
alive after His suffering by many infal-
lible proofs, being seen by them during
forty days and speaking of the things
pertaining to the kingdom of God.

The Holy Spirit Promised

4And being assembled together with
them, He commanded them not to de-
part from Jerusalem, but to wait for
the Promise of the Father, "which," *He*
said, "you have heard from Me; 5for
John truly baptized with water, but you
shall be baptized with the Holy Spirit
not many days from now." 6Therefore,
when they had come together, they
asked Him, saying, "Lord, will You at
this time restore the kingdom to Isra-
el?" 7And He said to them, "It is not for
you to know times or seasons which the
Father has put in His own authority.
8But you shall receive power when the
Holy Spirit has come upon you; and you
shall be witnesses to Me[a] in Jerusalem,
and in all Judea and Samaria, and to
the end of the earth."

Jesus Ascends to Heaven

9Now when He had spoken these things,
while they watched, He was taken up,
and a cloud received Him out of their
sight. 10And while they looked steadfast-
ly toward heaven as He went up, behold,
two men stood by them in white apparel,
11who also said, "Men of Galilee, why do
you stand gazing up into heaven? This
same Jesus, who was taken up from you
into heaven, will so come in like manner
as you saw Him go into heaven."

The Upper Room Prayer Meeting

12Then they returned to Jerusalem
from the mount called Olivet, which is
near Jerusalem, a Sabbath day's jour-
ney. 13And when they had entered, they
went up into the upper room where they
were staying: Peter, James, John, and
Andrew; Philip and Thomas; Bartholo-
mew and Matthew; James *the son* of Al-
phaeus and Simon the Zealot; and Judas
the son of James. 14These all continued

1:8 [a] NU-Text reads *My witnesses.*

WORSHIP | GROWTH | HEAVEN | FAMILY

with one accord in prayer and suppli-
cation,[a] with the women and Mary the
mother of Jesus, and with His brothers.

Matthias Chosen

15 And in those days Peter stood up in
the midst of the disciples[a] (altogeth-
er the number of names was about a
hundred and twenty), and said, 16 "Men
and brethren, this Scripture had to be
fulfilled, which the Holy Spirit spoke
before by the mouth of David concern-
ing Judas, who became a guide to those
who arrested Jesus; 17 for he was num-
bered with us and obtained a part in
this ministry."

18 (Now this man purchased a field
with the wages of iniquity; and falling
headlong, he burst open in the middle
and all his entrails gushed out. 19 And
it became known to all those dwelling
in Jerusalem; so that field is called in
their own language, Akel Dama, that
is, Field of Blood.)

20 "For it is written in the Book of
Psalms:

'Let his dwelling place be desolate,
And let no one live in it';[a]

and,

'Let[b] another take his office.'[c]

21 "Therefore, of these men who have
accompanied us all the time that the
Lord Jesus went in and out among us,
22 beginning from the baptism of John
to that day when He was taken up from
us, one of these must become a witness
with us of His resurrection."

23 And they proposed two: Joseph
called Barsabas, who was surnamed
Justus, and Matthias. 24 And they
prayed and said, "You, O Lord, who
know the hearts of all, show which of
these two You have chosen 25 to take
part in this ministry and apostleship
from which Judas by transgression
fell, that he might go to his own place."
26 And they cast their lots, and the lot
fell on Matthias. And he was numbered
with the eleven apostles.

Coming of the Holy Spirit

2 When the Day of Pentecost had
fully come, they were all with one
accord[a] in one place. 2 And suddenly
there came a sound from heaven, as of
a rushing mighty wind, and it filled the
whole house where they were sitting.
3 Then there appeared to them divided
tongues, as of fire, and *one* sat upon
each of them. 4 And they were all filled
with the Holy Spirit and began to speak
with other tongues, as the Spirit gave
them utterance.

The Crowd's Response

5 And there were dwelling in Jeru-
salem Jews, devout men, from every
nation under heaven. 6 And when this
sound occurred, the multitude came
together, and were confused, because
everyone heard them speak in his own
language. 7 Then they were all amazed
and marveled, saying to one another,
"Look, are not all these who speak Gali-
leans? 8 And how *is it that* we hear, each
in our own language in which we were
born? 9 Parthians and Medes and Elam-
ites, those dwelling in Mesopotamia,
Judea and Cappadocia, Pontus and
Asia, 10 Phrygia and Pamphylia, Egypt
and the parts of Libya adjoining Cyre-
ne, visitors from Rome, both Jews and
proselytes, 11 Cretans and Arabs—we
hear them speaking in our own tongues
the wonderful works of God." 12 So they
were all amazed and perplexed, saying
to one another, "Whatever could this
mean?"

13 Others mocking said, "They are full
of new wine."

Peter's Sermon

14 But Peter, standing up with the elev-
en, raised his voice and said to them,
"Men of Judea and all who dwell in
Jerusalem, let this be known to you,
and heed my words. 15 For these are not
drunk, as you suppose, since it is *only*
the third hour of the day. 16 But this is
what was spoken by the prophet Joel:

17 'And it shall come to pass in the
last days, says God,

1:14 [a] NU-Text omits *and supplication.* 1:15 [a] NU-Text reads *brethren.* 1:20 [a] Psalm 69:25 [b] Psalm 109:8 [c] Greek *episkopen*, position of overseer 2:1 [a] NU-Text reads *together.*

That I will pour out of My Spirit
on all flesh;
Your sons and your daughters
shall prophesy,
Your young men shall see visions,
Your old men shall dream dreams.
18 And on My menservants and on
My maidservants
I will pour out My Spirit in those
days;
And they shall prophesy.
19 I will show wonders in heaven
above
And signs in the earth beneath:
Blood and fire and vapor of
smoke.
20 The sun shall be turned into
darkness,
And the moon into blood,
Before the coming of the great and
awesome day of the LORD.
21 And it shall come to pass
That whoever calls on the name of
the LORD
Shall be saved.'[a]

22"Men of Israel, hear these words:
Jesus of Nazareth, a Man attested by
God to you by miracles, wonders, and
signs which God did through Him in
your midst, as you yourselves also
know— 23Him, being delivered by the
determined purpose and foreknowl-
edge of God, you have taken[a] by lawless
hands, have crucified, and put to death;
24whom God raised up, having loosed
the pains of death, because it was not
possible that He should be held by it.
25For David says concerning Him:

'I foresaw the LORD always before
my face,
For He is at my right hand, that I
may not be shaken.
26 Therefore my heart rejoiced, and
my tongue was glad;
Moreover my flesh also will rest in
hope.
27 For You will not leave my soul in
Hades,
Nor will You allow Your Holy One
to see corruption.
28 You have made known to me the
ways of life;
You will make me full of joy in
Your presence.'[a]

29"Men *and* brethren, let *me* speak
freely to you of the patriarch David,
that he is both dead and buried, and his
tomb is with us to this day. 30Therefore,
being a prophet, and knowing that God
had sworn with an oath to him that of
the fruit of his body, according to the
flesh, He would raise up the Christ to
sit on his throne,[a] 31he, foreseeing this,
spoke concerning the resurrection of
the Christ, that His soul was not left in
Hades, nor did His flesh see corruption.
32This Jesus God has raised up, of which
we are all witnesses. 33Therefore being
exalted to the right hand of God, and
having received from the Father the
promise of the Holy Spirit, He poured
out this which you now see and hear.
34"For David did not ascend into the
heavens, but he says himself:

'The LORD said to my Lord,
"Sit at My right hand,
35 Till I make Your enemies Your
footstool." '[a]

36"Therefore let all the house of Israel
know assuredly that God has made this
Jesus, whom you crucified, both Lord
and Christ."
37Now when they heard *this,* they were
cut to the heart, and said to Peter and
the rest of the apostles, "Men *and* breth-
ren, what shall we do?"
38Then Peter said to them, "Repent,
and let every one of you be baptized in
the name of Jesus Christ for the remis-
sion of sins; and you shall receive the
gift of the Holy Spirit. 39For the promise
is to you and to your children, and to all
who are afar off, as many as the Lord
our God will call."

A Vital Church Grows

40And with many other words he tes-
tified and exhorted them, saying, "Be
saved from this perverse generation."

2:21 [a] Joel 2:28–32 **2:23** [a] NU-Text omits *have taken.* **2:28** [a] Psalm 16:8–11 **2:30** [a] NU-Text omits *according to the flesh, He would raise up the Christ* and completes the verse with *He would seat one on his throne.* **2:35** [a] Psalm 110:1

41Then those who gladly[a] received his
word were baptized; and that day about
three thousand souls were added *to
them.* 42And they continued steadfastly
in the apostles' doctrine and fellow-
ship, in the breaking of bread, and in
prayers. 43Then fear came upon every
soul, and many wonders and signs were
done through the apostles. 44Now all
who believed were together, and had
all things in common, 45and sold their
possessions and goods, and divided
them among all, as anyone had need.

46So continuing daily with one ac-
cord in the temple, and breaking bread
from house to house, they ate their food
with gladness and simplicity of heart,
47praising God and having favor with
all the people. And the Lord added to
the church[a] daily those who were being
saved.

A Lame Man Healed

3 Now Peter and John went up to-
gether to the temple at the hour of
prayer, the ninth *hour.* 2And a certain
man lame from his mother's womb
was carried, whom they laid daily at
the gate of the temple which is called
Beautiful, to ask alms from those who
entered the temple; 3who, seeing Peter
and John about to go into the temple,
asked for alms. 4And fixing his eyes
on him, with John, Peter said, "Look
at us." 5So he gave them his attention,
expecting to receive something from
them. 6Then Peter said, "Silver and
gold I do not have, but what I do have
I give you: In the name of Jesus Christ
of Nazareth, rise up and walk." 7And he
took him by the right hand and lifted
him up, and immediately his feet and
ankle bones received strength. 8So he,
leaping up, stood and walked and en-
tered the temple with them—walking,
leaping, and praising God. 9And all the
people saw him walking and praising
God. 10Then they knew that it was he
who sat begging alms at the Beautiful
Gate of the temple; and they were filled
with wonder and amazement at what
had happened to him.

Preaching in Solomon's Portico

11Now as the lame man who was healed
held on to Peter and John, all the people
ran together to them in the porch which
is called Solomon's, greatly amazed.
12So when Peter saw *it,* he responded to
the people: "Men of Israel, why do you
marvel at this? Or why look so intently
at us, as though by our own power or
godliness we had made this man walk?
13The God of Abraham, Isaac, and Ja-
cob, the God of our fathers, glorified His
Servant Jesus, whom you delivered up
and denied in the presence of Pilate,
when he was determined to let *Him* go.
14But you denied the Holy One and the
Just, and asked for a murderer to be
granted to you, 15and killed the Prince
of life, whom God raised from the dead,
of which we are witnesses. 16And His
name, through faith in His name, has
made this man strong, whom you see
and know. Yes, the faith which *comes*
through Him has given him this perfect
soundness in the presence of you all.

17"Yet now, brethren, I know that you
did *it* in ignorance, as *did* also your rul-
ers. 18But those things which God fore-
told by the mouth of all His prophets,
that the Christ would suffer, He has thus
fulfilled. 19Repent therefore and be con-
verted, that your sins may be blotted out,
so that times of refreshing may come
from the presence of the Lord, 20and
that He may send Jesus Christ, who
was preached to you before,[a] 21whom
heaven must receive until the times
of restoration of all things, which God
has spoken by the mouth of all His holy
prophets since the world began. 22For
Moses truly said to the fathers, 'The LORD
your God will raise up for you a Prophet
like me from your brethren. Him you
shall hear in all things, whatever He says
to you. 23And it shall be *that* every soul
who will not hear that Prophet shall be
utterly destroyed from among the peo-
ple.'[a] 24Yes, and all the prophets, from
Samuel and those who follow, as many
as have spoken, have also foretold[a] these
days. 25You are sons of the prophets,
and of the covenant which God made

2:41 [a] NU-Text omits *gladly.* **2:47** [a] NU-Text omits *to the church.* **3:20** [a] NU-Text and M-Text read *Christ Jesus, who was ordained for you before.* **3:23** [a] Deuteronomy 18:15, 18, 19 **3:24** [a] NU-Text and M-Text read *proclaimed.*

with our fathers, saying to Abraham, 'And in your seed all the families of the earth shall be blessed.'[a] 26To you first, God, having raised up His Servant Jesus, sent Him to bless you, in turning away every one *of you* from your iniquities."

Peter and John Arrested

4 Now as they spoke to the people, the priests, the captain of the temple, and the Sadducees came upon them, 2being greatly disturbed that they taught the people and preached in Jesus the resurrection from the dead. 3And they laid hands on them, and put *them* in custody until the next day, for it was already evening. 4However, many of those who heard the word believed; and the number of the men came to be about five thousand.

Addressing the Sanhedrin

5And it came to pass, on the next day, that their rulers, elders, and scribes, 6as well as Annas the high priest, Caiaphas, John, and Alexander, and as many as were of the family of the high priest, were gathered together at Jerusalem. 7And when they had set them in the midst, they asked, "By what power or by what name have you done this?"

8Then Peter, filled with the Holy Spirit, said to them, "Rulers of the people and elders of Israel: 9If we this day are judged for a good deed *done* to a helpless man, by what means he has been made well, 10let it be known to you all, and to all the people of Israel, that by the name of Jesus Christ of Nazareth, whom you crucified, whom God raised from the dead, by Him this man stands here before you whole. 11This is the 'stone which was rejected by you builders, which has become the chief cornerstone.'[a] 12Nor is there salvation in any other, for there is no other name under heaven given among men by which we must be saved."

The Name of Jesus Forbidden

13Now when they saw the boldness of Peter and John, and perceived that they were uneducated and untrained men, they marveled. And they realized that they had been with Jesus. 14And seeing the man who had been healed standing with them, they could say nothing against it. 15But when they had commanded them to go aside out of the council, they conferred among themselves, 16saying, "What shall we do to these men? For, indeed, that a notable miracle has been done through them *is* evident to all who dwell in Jerusalem, and we cannot deny *it.* 17But so that it spreads no further among the people, let us severely threaten them, that from now on they speak to no man in this name."

18So they called them and commanded them not to speak at all nor teach in the name of Jesus. 19But Peter and John answered and said to them, "Whether it is right in the sight of God to listen to you more than to God, you judge. 20For we cannot but speak the things which we have seen and heard." 21So when they had further threatened them, they let them go, finding no way of punishing them, because of the people, since they all glorified God for what had been done. 22For the man was over forty years old on whom this miracle of healing had been performed.

Prayer for Boldness

23And being let go, they went to their own *companions* and reported all that the chief priests and elders had said to them. 24So when they heard that, they raised their voice to God with one accord and said: "Lord, You *are* God, who made heaven and earth and the sea, and all that is in them, 25who by the mouth of Your servant David[a] have said:

'Why did the nations rage,
And the people plot vain things?
26 The kings of the earth took their
stand,
And the rulers were gathered
together
Against the LORD and against His
Christ.'[a]

27"For truly against Your holy Servant Jesus, whom You anointed, both Herod and Pontius Pilate, with the Gentiles

3:25 [a] Genesis 22:18; 26:4; 28:14 **4:11** [a] Psalm 118:22 **4:25** [a] NU-Text reads *who through the Holy Spirit, by the mouth of our father, Your servant David.* **4:26** [a] Psalm 2:1, 2

and the people of Israel, were gathered together 28to do whatever Your hand and Your purpose determined before to be done. 29Now, Lord, look on their threats, and grant to Your servants that with all boldness they may speak Your word, 30by stretching out Your hand to heal, and that signs and wonders may be done through the name of Your holy Servant Jesus."

31And when they had prayed, the place where they were assembled together was shaken; and they were all filled with the Holy Spirit, and they spoke the word of God with boldness.

Sharing in All Things

32Now the multitude of those who believed were of one heart and one soul; neither did anyone say that any of the things he possessed was his own, but they had all things in common. 33And with great power the apostles gave witness to the resurrection of the Lord Jesus. And great grace was upon them all. 34Nor was there anyone among them who lacked; for all who were possessors of lands or houses sold them, and brought the proceeds of the things that were sold, 35and laid *them* at the apostles' feet; and they distributed to each as anyone had need.

36And Joses,[a] who was also named Barnabas by the apostles (which is translated Son of Encouragement), a Levite of the country of Cyprus, 37having land, sold *it,* and brought the money and laid *it* at the apostles' feet.

Lying to the Holy Spirit

5 But a certain man named Ananias, with Sapphira his wife, sold a possession. 2And he kept back *part* of the proceeds, his wife also being aware *of it,* and brought a certain part and laid *it* at the apostles' feet. 3But Peter said, "Ananias, why has Satan filled your heart to lie to the Holy Spirit and keep back *part* of the price of the land for yourself? 4While it remained, was it not your own? And after it was sold, was it not in your own control? Why have you conceived this thing in your heart? You have not lied to men but to God."

5Then Ananias, hearing these words, fell down and breathed his last. So great fear came upon all those who heard these things. 6And the young men arose and wrapped him up, carried *him* out, and buried *him.*

7Now it was about three hours later when his wife came in, not knowing what had happened. 8And Peter answered her, "Tell me whether you sold the land for so much?"

She said, "Yes, for so much."

9Then Peter said to her, "How is it that you have agreed together to test the Spirit of the Lord? Look, the feet of those who have buried your husband *are* at the door, and they will carry you out." 10Then immediately she fell down at his feet and breathed her last. And the young men came in and found her dead, and carrying *her* out, buried *her* by her husband. 11So great fear came upon all the church and upon all who heard these things.

Continuing Power in the Church

12And through the hands of the apostles many signs and wonders were done among the people. And they were all with one accord in Solomon's Porch. 13Yet none of the rest dared join them, but the people esteemed them highly. 14And believers were increasingly added to the Lord, multitudes of both men and women, 15so that they brought the sick out into the streets and laid *them* on beds and couches, that at least the shadow of Peter passing by might fall on some of them. 16Also a multitude gathered from the surrounding cities to Jerusalem, bringing sick people and those who were tormented by unclean spirits, and they were all healed.

Imprisoned Apostles Freed

17Then the high priest rose up, and all those who *were* with him (which is the sect of the Sadducees), and they were filled with indignation, 18and laid their hands on the apostles and put them in the common prison. 19But at night an angel of the Lord opened the prison doors and brought them out, and said,

4:36 [a] NU-Text reads *Joseph.*

GOD | SIN | JESUS | SALVATION | LOVE

20“Go, stand in the temple and speak to the people all the words of this life.”

21And when they heard *that,* they entered the temple early in the morning and taught. But the high priest and those with him came and called the council together, with all the elders of the children of Israel, and sent to the prison to have them brought.

Apostles on Trial Again

22But when the officers came and did not find them in the prison, they returned and reported, 23saying, “Indeed we found the prison shut securely, and the guards standing outside[a] before the doors; but when we opened them, we found no one inside!” 24Now when the high priest,[a] the captain of the temple, and the chief priests heard these things, they wondered what the outcome would be. 25So one came and told them, saying,[a] “Look, the men whom you put in prison are standing in the temple and teaching the people!”

26Then the captain went with the officers and brought them without violence, for they feared the people, lest they should be stoned. 27And when they had brought them, they set *them* before the council. And the high priest asked them, 28saying, “Did we not strictly command you not to teach in this name? And look, you have filled Jerusalem with your doctrine, and intend to bring this Man’s blood on us!”

29But Peter and the *other* apostles answered and said: “We ought to obey God rather than men. 30The God of our fathers raised up Jesus whom you murdered by hanging on a tree. 31Him God has exalted to His right hand *to be* Prince and Savior, to give repentance to Israel and forgiveness of sins. 32And we are His witnesses to these things, and *so* also *is* the Holy Spirit whom God has given to those who obey Him.”

Gamaliel’s Advice

33When they heard *this,* they were furious and plotted to kill them. 34Then one in the council stood up, a Pharisee named Gamaliel, a teacher of the law held in respect by all the people, and commanded them to put the apostles outside for a little while. 35And he said to them: “Men of Israel, take heed to yourselves what you intend to do regarding these men. 36For some time ago Theudas rose up, claiming to be somebody. A number of men, about four hundred, joined him. He was slain, and all who obeyed him were scattered and came to nothing. 37After this man, Judas of Galilee rose up in the days of the census, and drew away many people after him. He also perished, and all who obeyed him were dispersed. 38And now I say to you, keep away from these men and let them alone; for if this plan or this work is of men, it will come to nothing; 39but if it is of God, you cannot overthrow it—lest you even be found to fight against God.”

40And they agreed with him, and when they had called for the apostles and beaten *them,* they commanded that they should not speak in the name of Jesus, and let them go. 41So they departed from the presence of the council, rejoicing that they were counted worthy to suffer shame for His[a] name. 42And daily in the temple, and in every house, they did not cease teaching and preaching Jesus *as* the Christ.

Seven Chosen to Serve

6 Now in those days, when *the number of* the disciples was multiplying, there arose a complaint against the Hebrews by the Hellenists,[a] because their widows were neglected in the daily distribution. 2Then the twelve summoned the multitude of the disciples and said, “It is not desirable that we should leave the word of God and serve tables. 3Therefore, brethren, seek out from among you seven men of *good* reputation, full of the Holy Spirit and wisdom, whom we may appoint over this business; 4but we will give ourselves continually to prayer and to the ministry of the word.”

5And the saying pleased the whole

5:23 [a] NU-Text and M-Text omit *outside.* 5:24 [a] NU-Text omits *the high priest.* 5:25 [a] NU-Text and M-Text omit *saying.* 5:41 [a] NU-Text reads *the name;* M-Text reads *the name of Jesus.* 6:1 [a] That is, Greek-speaking Jews

multitude. And they chose Stephen, a man full of faith and the Holy Spirit, and Philip, Prochorus, Nicanor, Timon, Parmenas, and Nicolas, a proselyte from Antioch, 6whom they set before the apostles; and when they had prayed, they laid hands on them.

7Then the word of God spread, and the number of the disciples multiplied greatly in Jerusalem, and a great many of the priests were obedient to the faith.

Stephen Accused of Blasphemy

8And Stephen, full of faith[a] and power, did great wonders and signs among the people. 9Then there arose some from what is called the Synagogue of the Freedmen (Cyrenians, Alexandrians, and those from Cilicia and Asia), disputing with Stephen. 10And they were not able to resist the wisdom and the Spirit by which he spoke. 11Then they secretly induced men to say, "We have heard him speak blasphemous words against Moses and God." 12And they stirred up the people, the elders, and the scribes; and they came upon *him*, seized him, and brought *him* to the council. 13They also set up false witnesses who said, "This man does not cease to speak blasphemous[a] words against this holy place and the law; 14for we have heard him say that this Jesus of Nazareth will destroy this place and change the customs which Moses delivered to us." 15And all who sat in the council, looking steadfastly at him, saw his face as the face of an angel.

Stephen's Address: The Call of Abraham

7 Then the high priest said, "Are these things so?"

2And he said, "Brethren and fathers, listen: The God of glory appeared to our father Abraham when he was in Mesopotamia, before he dwelt in Haran, 3and said to him, 'Get out of your country and from your relatives, and come to a land that I will show you.'[a] 4Then he came out of the land of the Chaldeans and dwelt in Haran. And from there, when his father was dead, He moved him to this land in which you now dwell. 5And *God* gave him no inheritance in it, not even *enough* to set his foot on. But even when *Abraham* had no child, He promised to give it to him for a possession, and to his descendants after him. 6But God spoke in this way: that his descendants would dwell in a foreign land, and that they would bring them into bondage and oppress *them* four hundred years. 7'And the nation to whom they will be in bondage I will judge,'[a] said God, 'and after that they shall come out and serve Me in this place.'[b] 8Then He gave him the covenant of circumcision; and so *Abraham* begot Isaac and circumcised him on the eighth day; and Isaac *begot* Jacob, and Jacob *begot* the twelve patriarchs.

The Patriarchs in Egypt

9"And the patriarchs, becoming envious, sold Joseph into Egypt. But God was with him 10and delivered him out of all his troubles, and gave him favor and wisdom in the presence of Pharaoh, king of Egypt; and he made him governor over Egypt and all his house. 11Now a famine and great trouble came over all the land of Egypt and Canaan, and our fathers found no sustenance. 12But when Jacob heard that there was grain in Egypt, he sent out our fathers first. 13And the second *time* Joseph was made known to his brothers, and Joseph's family became known to the Pharaoh. 14Then Joseph sent and called his father Jacob and all his relatives to *him*, seventy-five[a] people. 15So Jacob went down to Egypt; and he died, he and our fathers. 16And they were carried back to Shechem and laid in the tomb that Abraham bought for a sum of money from the sons of Hamor, *the father* of Shechem.

God Delivers Israel by Moses

17"But when the time of the promise drew near which God had sworn to Abraham, the people grew and multiplied in Egypt 18till another king arose who did not know Joseph. 19This man dealt treacherously with our people, and oppressed our forefathers, making

6:8 [a] NU-Text reads *grace.* **6:13** [a] NU-Text omits *blasphemous.* **7:3** [a] Genesis 12:1 **7:7** [a] Genesis 15:14 [b] Exodus 3:12 **7:14** [a] Or *seventy* (compare Exodus 1:5)

them expose their babies, so that they might not live. 20At this time Moses was born, and was well pleasing to God; and he was brought up in his father's house for three months. 21But when he was set out, Pharaoh's daughter took him away and brought him up as her own son. 22And Moses was learned in all the wisdom of the Egyptians, and was mighty in words and deeds.

23"Now when he was forty years old, it came into his heart to visit his brethren, the children of Israel. 24And seeing one of *them* suffer wrong, he defended and avenged him who was oppressed, and struck down the Egyptian. 25For he supposed that his brethren would have understood that God would deliver them by his hand, but they did not understand. 26And the next day he appeared to *two of* them as they were fighting, and *tried to* reconcile them, saying, 'Men, you are brethren; why do you wrong one another?' 27But he who did his neighbor wrong pushed him away, saying, 'Who made you a ruler and a judge over us? 28Do you want to kill me as you did the Egyptian yesterday?'[a] 29Then, at this saying, Moses fled and became a dweller in the land of Midian, where he had two sons.

30"And when forty years had passed, an Angel of the Lord[a] appeared to him in a flame of fire in a bush, in the wilderness of Mount Sinai. 31When Moses saw *it*, he marveled at the sight; and as he drew near to observe, the voice of the Lord came to him, 32*saying*, 'I *am* the God of your fathers—the God of Abraham, the God of Isaac, and the God of Jacob.'[a] And Moses trembled and dared not look. 33'Then the LORD said to him, "Take your sandals off your feet, for the place where you stand is holy ground. 34I have surely seen the oppression of My people who are in Egypt; I have heard their groaning and have come down to deliver them. And now come, I will send you to Egypt." '[a]

35"This Moses whom they rejected, saying, 'Who made you a ruler and a judge?'[a] is the one God sent *to be* a ruler and a deliverer by the hand of the Angel who appeared to him in the bush. 36He brought them out, after he had shown wonders and signs in the land of Egypt, and in the Red Sea, and in the wilderness forty years.

Israel Rebels Against God

37"This is that Moses who said to the children of Israel,[a] 'The LORD your God will raise up for you a Prophet like me from your brethren. Him you shall hear.'[b]

38"This is he who was in the congregation in the wilderness with the Angel who spoke to him on Mount Sinai, and *with* our fathers, the one who received the living oracles to give to us, 39whom our fathers would not obey, but rejected. And in their hearts they turned back to Egypt, 40saying to Aaron, 'Make us gods to go before us; *as for* this Moses who brought us out of the land of Egypt, we do not know what has become of him.'[a] 41And they made a calf in those days, offered sacrifices to the idol, and rejoiced in the works of their own hands. 42Then God turned and gave them up to worship the host of heaven, as it is written in the book of the Prophets:

'Did you offer Me slaughtered
animals and sacrifices
during forty years in the
wilderness,
O house of Israel?
43 You also took up the tabernacle of
Moloch,
And the star of your god
Remphan,
Images which you made to
worship;
And I will carry you away beyond
Babylon.'[a]

God's True Tabernacle

44"Our fathers had the tabernacle of witness in the wilderness, as He appointed, instructing Moses to make it according to the pattern that he had seen, 45which our fathers, having received it in turn, also brought with

7:28 [a] Exodus 2:14 **7:30** [a] NU-Text omits *of the Lord.* **7:32** [a] Exodus 3:6, 15 **7:34** [a] Exodus 3:5, 7, 8, 10 **7:35** [a] Exodus 2:14 **7:37** [a] Deuteronomy 18:15 [b] NU-Text and M-Text omit *Him you shall hear.* **7:40** [a] Exodus 32:1, 23 **7:43** [a] Amos 5:25–27

Joshua into the land possessed by the
Gentiles, whom God drove out before
the face of our fathers until the days
of David, 46who found favor before
God and asked to find a dwelling for
the God of Jacob. 47But Solomon built
Him a house.
48"However, the Most High does not
dwell in temples made with hands, as
the prophet says:

49 'Heaven *is* My throne,
And earth *is* My footstool.
What house will you build for Me? says the LORD,
Or what *is* the place of My rest?
50 Has My hand not made all these things?'[a]

Israel Resists the Holy Spirit

51"*You* stiff-necked and uncircumcised
in heart and ears! You always resist
the Holy Spirit; as your fathers *did*, so
do you. 52Which of the prophets did
your fathers not persecute? And they
killed those who foretold the coming
of the Just One, of whom you now have
become the betrayers and murderers,
53who have received the law by the direction
of angels and have not kept *it*."

Stephen the Martyr

54When they heard these things they
were cut to the heart, and they gnashed
at him with *their* teeth. 55But he, being
full of the Holy Spirit, gazed into heaven
and saw the glory of God, and Jesus
standing at the right hand of God, 56and
said, "Look! I see the heavens opened
and the Son of Man standing at the right
hand of God!"
57Then they cried out with a loud voice,
stopped their ears, and ran at him with
one accord; 58and they cast *him* out of
the city and stoned *him*. And the witnesses
laid down their clothes at the
feet of a young man named Saul. 59And
they stoned Stephen as he was calling
on *God* and saying, "Lord Jesus, receive
my spirit." 60Then he knelt down and
cried out with a loud voice, "Lord, do not
charge them with this sin." And when
he had said this, he fell asleep.

Saul Persecutes the Church

8 Now Saul was consenting to his
death.
At that time a great persecution arose
against the church which was at Jerusalem;
and they were all scattered
throughout the regions of Judea and
Samaria, except the apostles. 2And devout
men carried Stephen *to his burial*,
and made great lamentation over him.
3As for Saul, he made havoc of the
church, entering every house, and dragging
off men and women, committing
them to prison.

Christ Is Preached in Samaria

4Therefore those who were scattered
went everywhere preaching the word.
5Then Philip went down to the[a] city of
Samaria and preached Christ to them.
6And the multitudes with one accord
heeded the things spoken by Philip,
hearing and seeing the miracles which
he did. 7For unclean spirits, crying with
a loud voice, came out of many who
were possessed; and many who were
paralyzed and lame were healed. 8And
there was great joy in that city.

The Sorcerer's Profession of Faith

9But there was a certain man called
Simon, who previously practiced sorcery
in the city and astonished the
people of Samaria, claiming that he
was someone great, 10to whom they all
gave heed, from the least to the greatest,
saying, "This man is the great power of
God." 11And they heeded him because he
had astonished them with his sorceries
for a long time. 12But when they believed
Philip as he preached the things
concerning the kingdom of God and the
name of Jesus Christ, both men and
women were baptized. 13Then Simon
himself also believed; and when he was
baptized he continued with Philip, and
was amazed, seeing the miracles and
signs which were done.

The Sorcerer's Sin

14Now when the apostles who were at
Jerusalem heard that Samaria had received
the word of God, they sent Peter

7:50 [a] Isaiah 66:1, 2 8:5 [a] Or *a*

and John to them, 15who, when they had
come down, prayed for them that they
might receive the Holy Spirit. 16For as yet
He had fallen upon none of them. They
had only been baptized in the name of
the Lord Jesus. 17Then they laid hands on
them, and they received the Holy Spirit.
18And when Simon saw that through
the laying on of the apostles' hands the
Holy Spirit was given, he offered them
money, 19saying, "Give me this power
also, that anyone on whom I lay hands
may receive the Holy Spirit."
20But Peter said to him, "Your money
perish with you, because you thought
that the gift of God could be purchased
with money! 21You have neither part
nor portion in this matter, for your
heart is not right in the sight of God.
22Repent therefore of this your wick-
edness, and pray God if perhaps the
thought of your heart may be forgiven
you. 23For I see that you are poisoned
by bitterness and bound by iniquity."
24Then Simon answered and said,
"Pray to the Lord for me, that none of
the things which you have spoken may
come upon me."
25So when they had testified and
preached the word of the Lord, they re-
turned to Jerusalem, preaching the gos-
pel in many villages of the Samaritans.

Christ Is Preached to an Ethiopian

26Now an angel of the Lord spoke to
Philip, saying, "Arise and go toward the
south along the road which goes down
from Jerusalem to Gaza." This is desert.
27So he arose and went. And behold, a
man of Ethiopia, a eunuch of great au-
thority under Candace the queen of the
Ethiopians, who had charge of all her
treasury, and had come to Jerusalem to
worship, 28was returning. And sitting in
his chariot, he was reading Isaiah the
prophet. 29Then the Spirit said to Phil-
ip, "Go near and overtake this chariot."
30So Philip ran to him, and heard
him reading the prophet Isaiah, and
said, "Do you understand what you
are reading?"
31And he said, "How can I, unless
someone guides me?" And he asked
Philip to come up and sit with him.
32The place in the Scripture which he
read was this:

"He was led as a sheep to the
slaughter;
And as a lamb before its shearer
is silent,
So He opened not His mouth.
33 In His humiliation His justice was
taken away,
And who will declare His
generation?
For His life is taken from the
earth."[a]

34So the eunuch answered Philip
and said, "I ask you, of whom does the
prophet say this, of himself or of some
other man?" 35Then Philip opened his
mouth, and beginning at this Scripture,
preached Jesus to him. 36Now as they
went down the road, they came to some
water. And the eunuch said, "See, *here*
is water. What hinders me from being
baptized?"
37Then Philip said, "If you believe with
all your heart, you may."
And he answered and said, "I believe
that Jesus Christ is the Son of God."[a]
38So he commanded the chariot to
stand still. And both Philip and the eu-
nuch went down into the water, and he
baptized him. 39Now when they came
up out of the water, the Spirit of the Lord
caught Philip away, so that the eunuch
saw him no more; and he went on his way
rejoicing. 40But Philip was found at Azo-
tus. And passing through, he preached
in all the cities till he came to Caesarea.

The Damascus Road: Saul Converted

9 Then Saul, still breathing threats
and murder against the disciples of
the Lord, went to the high priest 2and
asked letters from him to the syna-
gogues of Damascus, so that if he found
any who were of the Way, whether men
or women, he might bring them bound
to Jerusalem.
3As he journeyed he came near Da-
mascus, and suddenly a light shone
around him from heaven. 4Then he fell

8:33 [a] Isaiah 53:7, 8 8:37 [a] NU-Text and M-Text omit this verse. It is found in Western texts, including the Latin tradition.

to the ground, and heard a voice saying
to him, "Saul, Saul, why are you perse-
cuting Me?"
5 And he said, "Who are You, Lord?"
Then the Lord said, "I am Jesus, whom
you are persecuting.[a] It *is* hard for you
to kick against the goads."
6 So he, trembling and astonished,
said, "Lord, what do You want me to do?"
Then the Lord *said* to him, "Arise and
go into the city, and you will be told
what you must do."
7 And the men who journeyed with him
stood speechless, hearing a voice but
seeing no one. 8 Then Saul arose from
the ground, and when his eyes were
opened he saw no one. But they led him
by the hand and brought *him* into Da-
mascus. 9 And he was three days without
sight, and neither ate nor drank.

Ananias Baptizes Saul

10 Now there was a certain disciple at
Damascus named Ananias; and to him
the Lord said in a vision, "Ananias."
And he said, "Here I am, Lord."
11 So the Lord *said* to him, "Arise and
go to the street called Straight, and
inquire at the house of Judas for *one*
called Saul of Tarsus, for behold, he is
praying. 12 And in a vision he has seen
a man named Ananias coming in and
putting *his* hand on him, so that he
might receive his sight."
13 Then Ananias answered, "Lord, I
have heard from many about this man,
how much harm he has done to Your
saints in Jerusalem. 14 And here he has
authority from the chief priests to bind
all who call on Your name."
15 But the Lord said to him, "Go, for he
is a chosen vessel of Mine to bear My
name before Gentiles, kings, and the
children of Israel. 16 For I will show him
how many things he must suffer for My
name's sake."
17 And Ananias went his way and en-
tered the house; and laying his hands
on him he said, "Brother Saul, the Lord
Jesus,[a] who appeared to you on the road
as you came, has sent me that you may
receive your sight and be filled with
the Holy Spirit." 18 Immediately there
fell from his eyes *something* like scales,
and he received his sight at once; and
he arose and was baptized.
19 So when he had received food, he was
strengthened. Then Saul spent some
days with the disciples at Damascus.

Saul Preaches Christ

20 Immediately he preached the
Christ[a] in the synagogues, that He is
the Son of God.
21 Then all who heard were amazed,
and said, "Is this not he who destroyed
those who called on this name in Je-
rusalem, and has come here for that
purpose, so that he might bring them
bound to the chief priests?"
22 But Saul increased all the more in
strength, and confounded the Jews who
dwelt in Damascus, proving that this
Jesus is the Christ.

Saul Escapes Death

23 Now after many days were past,
the Jews plotted to kill him. 24 But their
plot became known to Saul. And they
watched the gates day and night, to
kill him. 25 Then the disciples took him
by night and let *him* down through the
wall in a large basket.

Saul at Jerusalem

26 And when Saul had come to Jeru-
salem, he tried to join the disciples; but
they were all afraid of him, and did not
believe that he was a disciple. 27 But Bar-
nabas took him and brought *him* to the
apostles. And he declared to them how
he had seen the Lord on the road, and
that He had spoken to him, and how
he had preached boldly at Damascus
in the name of Jesus. 28 So he was with
them at Jerusalem, coming in and going
out. 29 And he spoke boldly in the name
of the Lord Jesus and disputed against
the Hellenists, but they attempted to kill
him. 30 When the brethren found out,
they brought him down to Caesarea
and sent him out to Tarsus.

The Church Prospers

31 Then the churches[a] throughout all
Judea, Galilee, and Samaria had peace

9:5 [a] NU-Text and M-Text omit the last sentence of verse 5 and begin verse 6 with *But arise and go.*
9:17 [a] M-Text omits *Jesus.* **9:20** [a] NU-Text reads *Jesus.* **9:31** [a] NU-Text reads *church . . . was edified.*

and were edified. And walking in the fear of the Lord and in the comfort of the Holy Spirit, they were multiplied.

Aeneas Healed

32Now it came to pass, as Peter went through all *parts of the country,* that he also came down to the saints who dwelt in Lydda. 33There he found a certain man named Aeneas, who had been bedridden eight years and was paralyzed. 34And Peter said to him, "Aeneas, Jesus the Christ heals you. Arise and make your bed." Then he arose immediately. 35So all who dwelt at Lydda and Sharon saw him and turned to the Lord.

Dorcas Restored to Life

36At Joppa there was a certain disciple named Tabitha, which is translated Dorcas. This woman was full of good works and charitable deeds which she did. 37But it happened in those days that she became sick and died. When they had washed her, they laid *her* in an upper room. 38And since Lydda was near Joppa, and the disciples had heard that Peter was there, they sent two men to him, imploring *him* not to delay in coming to them. 39Then Peter arose and went with them. When he had come, they brought *him* to the upper room. And all the widows stood by him weeping, showing the tunics and garments which Dorcas had made while she was with them. 40But Peter put them all out, and knelt down and prayed. And turning to the body he said, "Tabitha, arise." And she opened her eyes, and when she saw Peter she sat up. 41Then he gave her *his* hand and lifted her up; and when he had called the saints and widows, he presented her alive. 42And it became known throughout all Joppa, and many believed on the Lord. 43So it was that he stayed many days in Joppa with Simon, a tanner.

Cornelius Sends a Delegation

10 There was a certain man in Caesarea called Cornelius, a centurion of what was called the Italian Regiment, 2a devout *man* and one who feared God with all his household, who gave alms generously to the people, and prayed to God always. 3About the ninth hour of the day he saw clearly in a vision an angel of God coming in and saying to him, "Cornelius!"

4And when he observed him, he was afraid, and said, "What is it, lord?"

So he said to him, "Your prayers and your alms have come up for a memorial before God. 5Now send men to Joppa, and send for Simon whose surname is Peter. 6He is lodging with Simon, a tanner, whose house is by the sea.[a] He will tell you what you must do." 7And when the angel who spoke to him had departed, Cornelius called two of his household servants and a devout soldier from among those who waited on him continually. 8So when he had explained all *these* things to them, he sent them to Joppa.

Peter's Vision

9The next day, as they went on their journey and drew near the city, Peter went up on the housetop to pray, about the sixth hour. 10Then he became very hungry and wanted to eat; but while they made ready, he fell into a trance 11and saw heaven opened and an object like a great sheet bound at the four corners, descending to him and let down to the earth. 12In it were all kinds of four-footed animals of the earth, wild beasts, creeping things, and birds of the air. 13And a voice came to him, "Rise, Peter; kill and eat."

14But Peter said, "Not so, Lord! For I have never eaten anything common or unclean."

15And a voice *spoke* to him again the second time, "What God has cleansed you must not call common." 16This was done three times. And the object was taken up into heaven again.

Summoned to Caesarea

17Now while Peter wondered within himself what this vision which he had seen meant, behold, the men who had been sent from Cornelius had made inquiry for Simon's house, and stood

10:6 a NU-Text and M-Text omit the last sentence of this verse.

before the gate. 18And they called and
asked whether Simon, whose surname
was Peter, was lodging there.
19While Peter thought about the vision,
the Spirit said to him, "Behold, three
men are seeking you. 20Arise therefore,
go down and go with them, doubting
nothing; for I have sent them."
21Then Peter went down to the men
who had been sent to him from Cornel-
ius,[a] and said, "Yes, I am he whom you
seek. For what reason have you come?"
22And they said, "Cornelius *the* cen-
turion, a just man, one who fears God
and has a good reputation among all
the nation of the Jews, was divinely
instructed by a holy angel to summon
you to his house, and to hear words
from you." 23Then he invited them in
and lodged *them*.
On the next day Peter went away with
them, and some brethren from Joppa
accompanied him.

Peter Meets Cornelius

24And the following day they entered
Caesarea. Now Cornelius was waiting
for them, and had called together his
relatives and close friends. 25As Peter
was coming in, Cornelius met him and
fell down at his feet and worshiped *him*.
26But Peter lifted him up, saying, "Stand
up; I myself am also a man." 27And
as he talked with him, he went in and
found many who had come together.
28Then he said to them, "You know how
unlawful it is for a Jewish man to keep
company with or go to one of another
nation. But God has shown me that I
should not call any man common or
unclean. 29Therefore I came without
objection as soon as I was sent for. I
ask, then, for what reason have you
sent for me?"
30So Cornelius said, "Four days ago
I was fasting until this hour; and at
the ninth hour[a] I prayed in my house,
and behold, a man stood before me in
bright clothing, 31and said, 'Cornelius,
your prayer has been heard, and your
alms are remembered in the sight of
God. 32Send therefore to Joppa and call
Simon here, whose surname is Peter.
He is lodging in the house of Simon,
a tanner, by the sea.[a] When he comes,
he will speak to you.' 33So I sent to you
immediately, and you have done well
to come. Now therefore, we are all pres-
ent before God, to hear all the things
commanded you by God."

Preaching to Cornelius' Household

34Then Peter opened *his* mouth and
said: "In truth I perceive that God shows
no partiality. 35But in every nation who-
ever fears Him and works righteous-
ness is accepted by Him. 36The word
which *God* sent to the children of Israel,
preaching peace through Jesus Christ—
He is Lord of all— 37that word you know,
which was proclaimed throughout all
Judea, and began from Galilee after the
baptism which John preached: 38how
God anointed Jesus of Nazareth with the
Holy Spirit and with power, who went
about doing good and healing all who
were oppressed by the devil, for God
was with Him. 39And we are witness-
es of all things which He did both in
the land of the Jews and in Jerusalem,
whom they[a] killed by hanging on a tree.
40Him God raised up on the third day,
and showed Him openly, 41not to all the
people, but to witnesses chosen before
by God, *even* to us who ate and drank
with Him after He arose from the dead.
42And He commanded us to preach to
the people, and to testify that it is He
who was ordained by God *to be* Judge
of the living and the dead. 43To Him
all the prophets witness that, through
His name, whoever believes in Him will
receive remission of sins."

The Holy Spirit Falls on the Gentiles

44While Peter was still speaking these
words, the Holy Spirit fell upon all those
who heard the word. 45And those of the
circumcision who believed were as-
tonished, as many as came with Peter,
because the gift of the Holy Spirit had
been poured out on the Gentiles also.
46For they heard them speak with
tongues and magnify God.

10:21 [a] NU-Text and M-Text omit *who had been sent to him from Cornelius.* **10:30** [a] NU-Text reads *Four days ago to this hour, at the ninth hour.* **10:32** [a] NU-Text omits the last sentence of this verse. **10:39** [a] NU-Text and M-Text add *also.*

Then Peter answered, 47 "Can anyone forbid water, that these should not be baptized who have received the Holy Spirit just as we *have?*" 48 And he commanded them to be baptized in the name of the Lord. Then they asked him to stay a few days.

Peter Defends God's Grace

11 Now the apostles and brethren who were in Judea heard that the Gentiles had also received the word of God. 2 And when Peter came up to Jerusalem, those of the circumcision contended with him, 3 saying, "You went in to uncircumcised men and ate with them!"

4 But Peter explained *it* to them in order from the beginning, saying: 5 "I was in the city of Joppa praying; and in a trance I saw a vision, an object descending like a great sheet, let down from heaven by four corners; and it came to me. 6 When I observed it intently and considered, I saw four-footed animals of the earth, wild beasts, creeping things, and birds of the air. 7 And I heard a voice saying to me, 'Rise, Peter; kill and eat.' 8 But I said, 'Not so, Lord! For nothing common or unclean has at any time entered my mouth.' 9 But the voice answered me again from heaven, 'What God has cleansed you must not call common.' 10 Now this was done three times, and all were drawn up again into heaven. 11 At that very moment, three men stood before the house where I was, having been sent to me from Caesarea. 12 Then the Spirit told me to go with them, doubting nothing. Moreover these six brethren accompanied me, and we entered the man's house. 13 And he told us how he had seen an angel standing in his house, who said to him, 'Send men to Joppa, and call for Simon whose surname is Peter, 14 who will tell you words by which you and all your household will be saved.' 15 And as I began to speak, the Holy Spirit fell upon them, as upon us at the beginning. 16 Then I remembered the word of the Lord, how He said, 'John indeed baptized with water, but you shall be baptized with the Holy Spirit.' 17 If therefore God gave them the same gift as *He gave* us when we believed on the Lord Jesus Christ, who was I that I could withstand God?"

18 When they heard these things they became silent; and they glorified God, saying, "Then God has also granted to the Gentiles repentance to life."

Barnabas and Saul at Antioch

19 Now those who were scattered after the persecution that arose over Stephen traveled as far as Phoenicia, Cyprus, and Antioch, preaching the word to no one but the Jews only. 20 But some of them were men from Cyprus and Cyrene, who, when they had come to Antioch, spoke to the Hellenists, preaching the Lord Jesus. 21 And the hand of the Lord was with them, and a great number believed and turned to the Lord.

22 Then news of these things came to the ears of the church in Jerusalem, and they sent out Barnabas to go as far as Antioch. 23 When he came and had seen the grace of God, he was glad, and encouraged them all that with purpose of heart they should continue with the Lord. 24 For he was a good man, full of the Holy Spirit and of faith. And a great many people were added to the Lord.

25 Then Barnabas departed for Tarsus to seek Saul. 26 And when he had found him, he brought him to Antioch. So it was that for a whole year they assembled with the church and taught a great many people. And the disciples were first called Christians in Antioch.

Relief to Judea

27 And in these days prophets came from Jerusalem to Antioch. 28 Then one of them, named Agabus, stood up and showed by the Spirit that there was going to be a great famine throughout all the world, which also happened in the days of Claudius Caesar. 29 Then the disciples, each according to his ability, determined to send relief to the brethren dwelling in Judea. 30 This they also did, and sent it to the elders by the hands of Barnabas and Saul.

Herod's Violence to the Church

12 Now about that time Herod the king stretched out *his* hand to harass some from the church. 2 Then he

killed James the brother of John with the sword. 3And because he saw that it pleased the Jews, he proceeded further to seize Peter also. Now it was *during* the Days of Unleavened Bread. 4So when he had arrested him, he put *him* in prison, and delivered *him* to four squads of soldiers to keep him, intending to bring him before the people after Passover.

Peter Freed from Prison

5Peter was therefore kept in prison, but constant[a] prayer was offered to God for him by the church. 6And when Herod was about to bring him out, that night Peter was sleeping, bound with two chains between two soldiers; and the guards before the door were keeping the prison. 7Now behold, an angel of the Lord stood by *him,* and a light shone in the prison; and he struck Peter on the side and raised him up, saying, "Arise quickly!" And his chains fell off *his* hands. 8Then the angel said to him, "Gird yourself and tie on your sandals"; and so he did. And he said to him, "Put on your garment and follow me." 9So he went out and followed him, and did not know that what was done by the angel was real, but thought he was seeing a vision. 10When they were past the first and the second guard posts, they came to the iron gate that leads to the city, which opened to them of its own accord; and they went out and went down one street, and immediately the angel departed from him.

11And when Peter had come to himself, he said, "Now I know for certain that the Lord has sent His angel, and has delivered me from the hand of Herod and *from* all the expectation of the Jewish people."

12So, when he had considered *this,* he came to the house of Mary, the mother of John whose surname was Mark, where many were gathered together praying. 13And as Peter knocked at the door of the gate, a girl named Rhoda came to answer. 14When she recognized Peter's voice, because of *her* gladness she did not open the gate, but ran in and announced that Peter stood before the gate. 15But they said to her, "You are beside yourself!" Yet she kept insisting that it was so. So they said, "It is his angel."

16Now Peter continued knocking; and when they opened *the door* and saw him, they were astonished. 17But motioning to them with his hand to keep silent, he declared to them how the Lord had brought him out of the prison. And he said, "Go, tell these things to James and to the brethren." And he departed and went to another place.

18Then, as soon as it was day, there was no small stir among the soldiers about what had become of Peter. 19But when Herod had searched for him and not found him, he examined the guards and commanded that *they* should be put to death.

And he went down from Judea to Caesarea, and stayed *there.*

Herod's Violent Death

20Now Herod had been very angry with the people of Tyre and Sidon; but they came to him with one accord, and having made Blastus the king's personal aide their friend, they asked for peace, because their country was supplied with food by the king's *country.* 21So on a set day Herod, arrayed in royal apparel, sat on his throne and gave an oration to them. 22And the people kept shouting, "The voice of a god and not of a man!" 23Then immediately an angel of the Lord struck him, because he did not give glory to God. And he was eaten by worms and died.

24But the word of God grew and multiplied.

Barnabas and Saul Appointed

25And Barnabas and Saul returned from[a] Jerusalem when they had fulfilled *their* ministry, and they also took with them John whose surname was Mark.

13 Now in the church that was at Antioch there were certain prophets and teachers: Barnabas, Simeon who was called Niger, Lucius of Cyrene, Manaen who had been brought up with Herod the tetrarch, and Saul. 2As they ministered to the Lord and fasted,

12:5 [a] NU-Text reads *constantly* (or *earnestly*). 12:25 [a] NU-Text and M-Text read *to.*

the Holy Spirit said, "Now separate to
Me Barnabas and Saul for the work to
which I have called them." 3Then, hav-
ing fasted and prayed, and laid hands
on them, they sent *them* away.

Preaching in Cyprus

4So, being sent out by the Holy Spirit,
they went down to Seleucia, and from
there they sailed to Cyprus. 5And when
they arrived in Salamis, they preached
the word of God in the synagogues of
the Jews. They also had John as *their*
assistant.

6Now when they had gone through the
island[a] to Paphos, they found a certain
sorcerer, a false prophet, a Jew whose
name *was* Bar-Jesus, 7who was with the
proconsul, Sergius Paulus, an intelligent
man. This man called for Barnabas and
Saul and sought to hear the word of
God. 8But Elymas the sorcerer (for so
his name is translated) withstood them,
seeking to turn the proconsul away from
the faith. 9Then Saul, who also *is called*
Paul, filled with the Holy Spirit, looked
intently at him 10and said, "O full of all
deceit and all fraud, *you* son of the devil,
you enemy of all righteousness, will you
not cease perverting the straight ways
of the Lord? 11And now, indeed, the hand
of the Lord *is* upon you, and you shall
be blind, not seeing the sun for a time."

And immediately a dark mist fell on
him, and he went around seeking some-
one to lead him by the hand. 12Then the
proconsul believed, when he saw what
had been done, being astonished at the
teaching of the Lord.

At Antioch in Pisidia

13Now when Paul and his party set sail
from Paphos, they came to Perga in
Pamphylia; and John, departing from
them, returned to Jerusalem. 14But when
they departed from Perga, they came
to Antioch in Pisidia, and went into the
synagogue on the Sabbath day and sat
down. 15And after the reading of the
Law and the Prophets, the rulers of the
synagogue sent to them, saying, "Men
and brethren, if you have any word of
exhortation for the people, say on."

16Then Paul stood up, and motioning
with *his* hand said, "Men of Israel, and
you who fear God, listen: 17The God of
this people Israel[a] chose our fathers,
and exalted the people when they dwelt
as strangers in the land of Egypt, and
with an uplifted arm He brought them
out of it. 18Now for a time of about for-
ty years He put up with their ways in
the wilderness. 19And when He had
destroyed seven nations in the land of
Canaan, He distributed their land to
them by allotment.

20"After that He gave *them* judges for
about four hundred and fifty years, until
Samuel the prophet. 21And afterward
they asked for a king; so God gave them
Saul the son of Kish, a man of the tribe of
Benjamin, for forty years. 22And when
He had removed him, He raised up for
them David as king, to whom also He
gave testimony and said, 'I have found
David[a] the *son* of Jesse, a man after
My *own* heart, who will do all My will.'[b]
23From this man's seed, according to
the promise, God raised up for Israel a
Savior—Jesus—[a] 24after John had first
preached, before His coming, the bap-
tism of repentance to all the people of
Israel. 25And as John was finishing his
course, he said, 'Who do you think I am?
I am not *He*. But behold, there comes
One after me, the sandals of whose feet
I am not worthy to loose.'

26"Men *and* brethren, sons of the fam-
ily of Abraham, and those among you
who fear God, to you the word of this
salvation has been sent. 27For those who
dwell in Jerusalem, and their rulers, be-
cause they did not know Him, nor even
the voices of the Prophets which are
read every Sabbath, have fulfilled *them*
in condemning *Him*. 28And though they
found no cause for death *in Him*, they
asked Pilate that He should be put to
death. 29Now when they had fulfilled
all that was written concerning Him,
they took *Him* down from the tree and
laid *Him* in a tomb. 30But God raised
Him from the dead. 31He was seen for
many days by those who came up with
Him from Galilee to Jerusalem, who
are His witnesses to the people. 32And

13:6 [a] NU-Text reads *the whole island.* **13:17** [a] M-Text omits *Israel.* **13:22** [a] Psalm 89:20
[b] 1 Samuel 13:14 **13:23** [a] M-Text reads *for Israel salvation.*

we declare to you glad tidings—that
promise which was made to the fathers.
33God has fulfilled this for us their chil-
dren, in that He has raised up Jesus. As
it is also written in the second Psalm:

'You are My Son,
Today I have begotten You.'[a]

34And that He raised Him from the
dead, no more to return to corruption,
He has spoken thus:

'I will give you the sure mercies of
David.'[a]

35Therefore He also says in another
Psalm:

'You will not allow Your Holy One
to see corruption.'[a]

36"For David, after he had served his
own generation by the will of God, fell
asleep, was buried with his fathers, and
saw corruption; 37but He whom God
raised up saw no corruption. 38There-
fore let it be known to you, brethren,
that through this Man is preached to
you the forgiveness of sins; 39and by
Him everyone who believes is justified
from all things from which you could
not be justified by the law of Moses.
40Beware therefore, lest what has been
spoken in the prophets come upon you:

41 'Behold, you despisers,
Marvel and perish!
For I work a work in your days,
A work which you will by no
means believe,
Though one were to declare it to
you.'"[a]

Blessing and Conflict at Antioch

42So when the Jews went out of the
synagogue,[a] the Gentiles begged that
these words might be preached to them
the next Sabbath. 43Now when the con-
gregation had broken up, many of the
Jews and devout proselytes followed
Paul and Barnabas, who, speaking to
them, persuaded them to continue in
the grace of God.
44On the next Sabbath almost the
whole city came together to hear the
word of God. 45But when the Jews saw
the multitudes, they were filled with
envy; and contradicting and blasphem-
ing, they opposed the things spoken by
Paul. 46Then Paul and Barnabas grew
bold and said, "It was necessary that the
word of God should be spoken to you
first; but since you reject it, and judge
yourselves unworthy of everlasting life,
behold, we turn to the Gentiles. 47For so
the Lord has commanded us:

'I have set you as a light to the
Gentiles,
That you should be for salvation
to the ends of the earth.'"[a]

48Now when the Gentiles heard this,
they were glad and glorified the word
of the Lord. And as many as had been
appointed to eternal life believed.
49And the word of the Lord was being
spread throughout all the region. 50But
the Jews stirred up the devout and prom-
inent women and the chief men of the
city, raised up persecution against Paul
and Barnabas, and expelled them from
their region. 51But they shook off the dust
from their feet against them, and came
to Iconium. 52And the disciples were
filled with joy and with the Holy Spirit.

At Iconium

14 Now it happened in Iconium
that they went together to the
synagogue of the Jews, and so spoke
that a great multitude both of the Jews
and of the Greeks believed. 2But the
unbelieving Jews stirred up the Gentiles
and poisoned their minds against the
brethren. 3Therefore they stayed there a
long time, speaking boldly in the Lord,
who was bearing witness to the word of
His grace, granting signs and wonders
to be done by their hands.
4But the multitude of the city was di-
vided: part sided with the Jews, and part
with the apostles. 5And when a violent

13:33 [a] Psalm 2:7 13:34 [a] Isaiah 55:3 13:35 [a] Psalm 16:10 13:41 [a] Habakkuk 1:5 13:42 [a] Or *And when they went out of the synagogue of the Jews;* NU-Text reads *And when they went out, they begged.* 13:47 [a] Isaiah 49:6

GOD SIN JESUS SALVATION LOVE

attempt was made by both the Gentiles
and Jews, with their rulers, to abuse
and stone them, 6they became aware
of it and fled to Lystra and Derbe, cities
of Lycaonia, and to the surrounding
region. 7And they were preaching the
gospel there.

Idolatry at Lystra

8And in Lystra a certain man without
strength in his feet was sitting, a crip-
ple from his mother's womb, who had
never walked. 9*This* man heard Paul
speaking. Paul, observing him intent-
ly and seeing that he had faith to be
healed, 10said with a loud voice, "Stand
up straight on your feet!" And he leaped
and walked. 11Now when the people saw
what Paul had done, they raised their
voices, saying in the Lycaonian *lan-
guage,* "The gods have come down to
us in the likeness of men!" 12And Bar-
nabas they called Zeus, and Paul, Her-
mes, because he was the chief speaker.
13Then the priest of Zeus, whose temple
was in front of their city, brought oxen
and garlands to the gates, intending to
sacrifice with the multitudes.

14But when the apostles Barnabas and
Paul heard this, they tore their clothes
and ran in among the multitude, cry-
ing out 15and saying, "Men, why are
you doing these things? We also are
men with the same nature as you, and
preach to you that you should turn from
these useless things to the living God,
who made the heaven, the earth, the
sea, and all things that are in them,
16who in bygone generations allowed
all nations to walk in their own ways.
17Nevertheless He did not leave Himself
without witness, in that He did good,
gave us rain from heaven and fruitful
seasons, filling our hearts with food
and gladness." 18And with these say-
ings they could scarcely restrain the
multitudes from sacrificing to them.

Stoning, Escape to Derbe

19Then Jews from Antioch and Iconi-
um came there; and having persuaded
the multitudes, they stoned Paul *and*
dragged *him* out of the city, suppos-
ing him to be dead. 20However, when
the disciples gathered around him, he
rose up and went into the city. And the
next day he departed with Barnabas
to Derbe.

Strengthening the Converts

21And when they had preached the
gospel to that city and made many dis-
ciples, they returned to Lystra, Iconium,
and Antioch, 22strengthening the souls
of the disciples, exhorting *them* to con-
tinue in the faith, and *saying,* "We must
through many tribulations enter the
kingdom of God." 23So when they had
appointed elders in every church, and
prayed with fasting, they commended
them to the Lord in whom they had
believed. 24And after they had passed
through Pisidia, they came to Pam-
phylia. 25Now when they had preached
the word in Perga, they went down to
Attalia. 26From there they sailed to An-
tioch, where they had been commended
to the grace of God for the work which
they had completed.

27Now when they had come and gath-
ered the church together, they reported
all that God had done with them, and
that He had opened the door of faith to
the Gentiles. 28So they stayed there a
long time with the disciples.

Conflict over Circumcision

15 And certain *men* came down from
Judea and taught the brethren,
"Unless you are circumcised accord-
ing to the custom of Moses, you cannot
be saved." 2Therefore, when Paul and
Barnabas had no small dissension and
dispute with them, they determined that
Paul and Barnabas and certain others of
them should go up to Jerusalem, to the
apostles and elders, about this question.

3So, being sent on their way by the
church, they passed through Phoenicia
and Samaria, describing the conversion
of the Gentiles; and they caused great
joy to all the brethren. 4And when they
had come to Jerusalem, they were re-
ceived by the church and the apostles
and the elders; and they reported all
things that God had done with them.
5But some of the sect of the Pharisees
who believed rose up, saying, "It is nec-
essary to circumcise them, and to com-
mand *them* to keep the law of Moses."

The Jerusalem Council

6Now the apostles and elders came together to consider this matter. 7And when there had been much dispute, Peter rose up *and* said to them: "Men *and* brethren, you know that a good while ago God chose among us, that by my mouth the Gentiles should hear the word of the gospel and believe. 8So God, who knows the heart, acknowledged them by giving them the Holy Spirit, just as *He did* to us, 9and made no distinction between us and them, purifying their hearts by faith. 10Now therefore, why do you test God by putting a yoke on the neck of the disciples which neither our fathers nor we were able to bear? 11But we believe that through the grace of the Lord Jesus Christ[a] we shall be saved in the same manner as they."

12Then all the multitude kept silent and listened to Barnabas and Paul declaring how many miracles and wonders God had worked through them among the Gentiles. 13And after they had become silent, James answered, saying, "Men *and* brethren, listen to me: 14Simon has declared how God at the first visited the Gentiles to take out of them a people for His name. 15And with this the words of the prophets agree, just as it is written:

16 'After this I will return
And will rebuild the tabernacle of
David, which has fallen down;
I will rebuild its ruins,
And I will set it up;
17 So that the rest of mankind may
seek the LORD,
Even all the Gentiles who are
called by My name,
Says the LORD who does all these
things.'[a]

18"Known to God from eternity are all His works.[a] 19Therefore I judge that we should not trouble those from among the Gentiles who are turning to God, 20but that we write to them to abstain from things polluted by idols, *from* sexual immorality,[a] *from* things strangled, and *from* blood. 21For Moses has had throughout many generations those who preach him in every city, being read in the synagogues every Sabbath."

The Jerusalem Decree

22Then it pleased the apostles and elders, with the whole church, to send chosen men of their own company to Antioch with Paul and Barnabas, *namely,* Judas who was also named Barsabas,[a] and Silas, leading men among the brethren.

23They wrote this *letter* by them:

The apostles, the elders, and the brethren,

To the brethren who are of the Gentiles in Antioch, Syria, and Cilicia:

Greetings.

24 Since we have heard that some who went out from us have troubled you with words, unsettling your souls, saying, "*You must* be circumcised and keep the law"[a]—to whom we gave no *such* commandment— 25it seemed good to us, being assembled with one accord, to send chosen men to you with our beloved Barnabas and Paul, 26men who have risked their lives for the name of our Lord Jesus Christ. 27We have therefore sent Judas and Silas, who will also report the same things by word of mouth. 28For it seemed good to the Holy Spirit, and to us, to lay upon you no greater burden than these necessary things: 29that you abstain from things offered to idols, from blood, from things strangled, and from sexual immorality.[a] If you keep yourselves from these, you will do well.

Farewell.

15:11 [a] NU-Text and M-Text omit *Christ.* **15:17** [a] Amos 9:11, 12 **15:18** [a] NU-Text (combining with verse 17) reads *Says the Lord, who makes these things known from eternity (of old).* **15:20** [a] Or *fornication* **15:22** [a] NU-Text and M-Text read *Barsabbas.* **15:24** [a] NU-Text omits *saying, "You must be circumcised and keep the law."* **15:29** [a] Or *fornication*

Continuing Ministry in Syria

30So when they were sent off, they
came to Antioch; and when they had
gathered the multitude together, they
delivered the letter. 31When they had
read it, they rejoiced over its encour-
agement. 32Now Judas and Silas, them-
selves being prophets also, exhorted
and strengthened the brethren with
many words. 33And after they had
stayed *there* for a time, they were sent
back with greetings from the brethren
to the apostles.[a]

34However, it seemed good to Silas to
remain there.[a] 35Paul and Barnabas
also remained in Antioch, teaching and
preaching the word of the Lord, with
many others also.

Division over John Mark

36Then after some days Paul said to
Barnabas, "Let us now go back and visit
our brethren in every city where we
have preached the word of the Lord, *and*
see how they are doing." 37Now Barna-
bas was determined to take with them
John called Mark. 38But Paul insisted
that they should not take with them
the one who had departed from them
in Pamphylia, and had not gone with
them to the work. 39Then the contention
became so sharp that they parted from
one another. And so Barnabas took
Mark and sailed to Cyprus; 40but Paul
chose Silas and departed, being com-
mended by the brethren to the grace of
God. 41And he went through Syria and
Cilicia, strengthening the churches.

Timothy Joins Paul and Silas

16 Then he came to Derbe and
Lystra. And behold, a certain
disciple was there, named Timothy, *the*
son of a certain Jewish woman who be-
lieved, but his father *was* Greek. 2He was
well spoken of by the brethren who were
at Lystra and Iconium. 3Paul wanted to
have him go on with him. And he took
him and circumcised him because of
the Jews who were in that region, for
they all knew that his father was Greek.
4And as they went through the cities,
they delivered to them the decrees to
keep, which were determined by the
apostles and elders at Jerusalem. 5So
the churches were strengthened in the
faith, and increased in number daily.

The Macedonian Call

6Now when they had gone through
Phrygia and the region of Galatia, they
were forbidden by the Holy Spirit to
preach the word in Asia. 7After they
had come to Mysia, they tried to go
into Bithynia, but the Spirit[a] did not
permit them. 8So passing by Mysia,
they came down to Troas. 9And a vision
appeared to Paul in the night. A man
of Macedonia stood and pleaded with
him, saying, "Come over to Macedonia
and help us." 10Now after he had seen
the vision, immediately we sought to
go to Macedonia, concluding that the
Lord had called us to preach the gospel
to them.

Lydia Baptized at Philippi

11Therefore, sailing from Troas, we
ran a straight course to Samothrace,
and the next *day* came to Neapolis,
12and from there to Philippi, which is
the foremost city of that part of Mace-
donia, a colony. And we were staying
in that city for some days. 13And on the
Sabbath day we went out of the city to
the riverside, where prayer was custom-
arily made; and we sat down and spoke
to the women who met *there*. 14Now a
certain woman named Lydia heard
us. She was a seller of purple from the
city of Thyatira, who worshiped God.
The Lord opened her heart to heed the
things spoken by Paul. 15And when she
and her household were baptized, she
begged *us*, saying, "If you have judged
me to be faithful to the Lord, come to my
house and stay." So she persuaded us.

Paul and Silas Imprisoned

16Now it happened, as we went to
prayer, that a certain slave girl pos-
sessed with a spirit of divination met
us, who brought her masters much
profit by fortune-telling. 17This girl
followed Paul and us, and cried out,
saying, "These men are the servants

15:33 [a] NU-Text reads *to those who had sent them.*
16:7 [a] NU-Text adds *of Jesus.*
15:34 [a] NU-Text and M-Text omit this verse.

of the Most High God, who proclaim to
us the way of salvation." 18And this she
did for many days.
But Paul, greatly annoyed, turned and
said to the spirit, "I command you in
the name of Jesus Christ to come out of
her." And he came out that very hour.
19But when her masters saw that their
hope of profit was gone, they seized
Paul and Silas and dragged *them* into
the marketplace to the authorities.
20And they brought them to the magis-
trates, and said, "These men, being Jews,
exceedingly trouble our city; 21and they
teach customs which are not lawful for
us, being Romans, to receive or observe."
22Then the multitude rose up together
against them; and the magistrates tore
off their clothes and commanded *them*
to be beaten with rods. 23And when they
had laid many stripes on them, they
threw *them* into prison, commanding
the jailer to keep them securely. 24Hav-
ing received such a charge, he put them
into the inner prison and fastened their
feet in the stocks.

The Philippian Jailer Saved

25But at midnight Paul and Silas were
praying and singing hymns to God,
and the prisoners were listening to
them. 26Suddenly there was a great
earthquake, so that the foundations
of the prison were shaken; and imme-
diately all the doors were opened and
everyone's chains were loosed. 27And
the keeper of the prison, awaking from
sleep and seeing the prison doors open,
supposing the prisoners had fled, drew
his sword and was about to kill himself.
28But Paul called with a loud voice, say-
ing, "Do yourself no harm, for we are
all here."
29Then he called for a light, ran in, and
fell down trembling before Paul and Silas.
30And he brought them out and said,
"Sirs, what must I do to be saved?"
31So they said, "Believe on the Lord
Jesus Christ, and you will be saved, you
and your household." 32Then they spoke
the word of the Lord to him and to all
who were in his house. 33And he took
them the same hour of the night and
washed *their* stripes. And immediate-
ly he and all his *family* were baptized.
34Now when he had brought them into
his house, he set food before them; and
he rejoiced, having believed in God with
all his household.

Paul Refuses to Depart Secretly

35And when it was day, the magis-
trates sent the officers, saying, "Let
those men go."
36So the keeper of the prison report-
ed these words to Paul, saying, "The
magistrates have sent to let you go.
Now therefore depart, and go in peace."
37But Paul said to them, "They have
beaten us openly, uncondemned Ro-
mans, *and* have thrown *us* into prison.
And now do they put us out secretly?
No indeed! Let them come themselves
and get us out."
38And the officers told these words to
the magistrates, and they were afraid
when they heard that they were Ro-
mans. 39Then they came and pleaded
with them and brought *them* out, and
asked *them* to depart from the city. 40So
they went out of the prison and entered
the house of Lydia; and when they had
seen the brethren, they encouraged
them and departed.

Preaching Christ at Thessalonica

17 Now when they had passed
through Amphipolis and Apol-
lonia, they came to Thessalonica, where
there was a synagogue of the Jews.
2Then Paul, as his custom was, went in
to them, and for three Sabbaths rea-
soned with them from the Scriptures,
3explaining and demonstrating that
the Christ had to suffer and rise again
from the dead, and *saying,* "This Jesus
whom I preach to you is the Christ."
4And some of them were persuaded;
and a great multitude of the devout
Greeks, and not a few of the leading
women, joined Paul and Silas.

Assault on Jason's House

5But the Jews who were not persuad-
ed, becoming envious,[a] took some of
the evil men from the marketplace,

17:5 [a] NU-Text omits *who were not persuaded;* M-Text omits *becoming envious.*

and gathering a mob, set all the city
in an uproar and attacked the house
of Jason, and sought to bring them
out to the people. 6 But when they did
not find them, they dragged Jason and
some brethren to the rulers of the city,
crying out, "These who have turned the
world upside down have come here too.
7 Jason has harbored them, and these
are all acting contrary to the decrees of
Caesar, saying there is another king—
Jesus." 8 And they troubled the crowd
and the rulers of the city when they
heard these things. 9 So when they had
taken security from Jason and the rest,
they let them go.

Ministering at Berea

10 Then the brethren immediately
sent Paul and Silas away by night to
Berea. When they arrived, they went
into the synagogue of the Jews. 11 These
were more fair-minded than those in
Thessalonica, in that they received the
word with all readiness, and searched
the Scriptures daily *to find out* whether
these things were so. 12 Therefore many
of them believed, and also not a few of
the Greeks, prominent women as well as
men. 13 But when the Jews from Thessa-
lonica learned that the word of God was
preached by Paul at Berea, they came
there also and stirred up the crowds.
14 Then immediately the brethren sent
Paul away, to go to the sea; but both
Silas and Timothy remained there. 15 So
those who conducted Paul brought him
to Athens; and receiving a command
for Silas and Timothy to come to him
with all speed, they departed.

The Philosophers at Athens

16 Now while Paul waited for them at
Athens, his spirit was provoked within
him when he saw that the city was given
over to idols. 17 Therefore he reasoned in
the synagogue with the Jews and with
the *Gentile* worshipers, and in the mar-
ketplace daily with those who happened
to be there. 18 Then[a] certain Epicurean
and Stoic philosophers encountered
him. And some said, "What does this
babbler want to say?"
Others said, "He seems to be a pro-
claimer of foreign gods," because he
preached to them Jesus and the res-
urrection.
19 And they took him and brought him
to the Areopagus, saying, "May we know
what this new doctrine *is* of which you
speak? 20 For you are bringing some
strange things to our ears. Therefore we
want to know what these things mean."
21 For all the Athenians and the foreign-
ers who were there spent their time in
nothing else but either to tell or to hear
some new thing.

Addressing the Areopagus

22 Then Paul stood in the midst of the
Areopagus and said, "Men of Athens, I
perceive that in all things you are very
religious; 23 for as I was passing through
and considering the objects of your
worship, I even found an altar with this
inscription:

TO THE UNKNOWN GOD.

Therefore, the One whom you worship
without knowing, Him I proclaim to
you: 24 God, who made the world and
everything in it, since He is Lord of
heaven and earth, does not dwell in
temples made with hands. 25 Nor is He
worshiped with men's hands, as though
He needed anything, since He gives to
all life, breath, and all things. 26 And
He has made from one blood[a] every
nation of men to dwell on all the face
of the earth, and has determined their
preappointed times and the bound-
aries of their dwellings, 27 so that they
should seek the Lord, in the hope that
they might grope for Him and find Him,
though He is not far from each one of
us; 28 for in Him we live and move and
have our being, as also some of your
own poets have said, 'For we are also His
offspring.' 29 Therefore, since we are the
offspring of God, we ought not to think
that the Divine Nature is like gold or
silver or stone, something shaped by
art and man's devising. 30 Truly, these
times of ignorance God overlooked, but
now commands all men everywhere to

17:18 [a] NU-Text and M-Text add *also*. 17:26 [a] NU-Text omits *blood*.

repent, 31because He has appointed a
day on which He will judge the world in
righteousness by the Man whom He has
ordained. He has given assurance of this
to all by raising Him from the dead."
32And when they heard of the resur-
rection of the dead, some mocked, while
others said, "We will hear you again on
this *matter.*" 33So Paul departed from
among them. 34However, some men
joined him and believed, among them
Dionysius the Areopagite, a woman
named Damaris, and others with them.

Ministering at Corinth

18 After these things Paul depart-
ed from Athens and went to
Corinth. 2And he found a certain Jew
named Aquila, born in Pontus, who
had recently come from Italy with his
wife Priscilla (because Claudius had
commanded all the Jews to depart
from Rome); and he came to them.
3So, because he was of the same trade,
he stayed with them and worked; for
by occupation they were tentmakers.
4And he reasoned in the synagogue
every Sabbath, and persuaded both
Jews and Greeks.
5When Silas and Timothy had come
from Macedonia, Paul was compelled
by the Spirit, and testified to the Jews
that Jesus *is* the Christ. 6But when they
opposed him and blasphemed, he
shook *his* garments and said to them,
"Your blood *be* upon your *own* heads; I
am clean. From now on I will go to the
Gentiles." 7And he departed from there
and entered the house of a certain *man*
named Justus,[a] *one* who worshiped God,
whose house was next door to the syn-
agogue. 8Then Crispus, the ruler of the
synagogue, believed on the Lord with all
his household. And many of the Corinthi-
ans, hearing, believed and were baptized.
9Now the Lord spoke to Paul in the
night by a vision, "Do not be afraid, but
speak, and do not keep silent; 10for I am
with you, and no one will attack you to
hurt you; for I have many people in this
city." 11And he continued *there* a year
and six months, teaching the word of
God among them.
12When Gallio was proconsul of Acha-
ia, the Jews with one accord rose up
against Paul and brought him to the
judgment seat, 13saying, "This *fellow*
persuades men to worship God contrary
to the law."
14And when Paul was about to open
his mouth, Gallio said to the Jews, "If it
were a matter of wrongdoing or wicked
crimes, O Jews, there would be reason
why I should bear with you. 15But if
it is a question of words and names
and your own law, look *to it* yourselves;
for I do not want to be a judge of such
matters." 16And he drove them from the
judgment seat. 17Then all the Greeks[a]
took Sosthenes, the ruler of the syna-
gogue, and beat *him* before the judg-
ment seat. But Gallio took no notice of
these things.

Paul Returns to Antioch

18So Paul still remained a good while.
Then he took leave of the brethren and
sailed for Syria, and Priscilla and Aquila
were with him. He had *his* hair cut off at
Cenchrea, for he had taken a vow. 19And
he came to Ephesus, and left them there;
but he himself entered the synagogue
and reasoned with the Jews. 20When
they asked *him* to stay a longer time
with them, he did not consent, 21but
took leave of them, saying, "I must by all
means keep this coming feast in Jerusa-
lem;[a] but I will return again to you, God
willing." And he sailed from Ephesus.
22And when he had landed at Caes-
area, and gone up and greeted the
church, he went down to Antioch. 23Af-
ter he had spent some time *there,* he
departed and went over the region of
Galatia and Phrygia in order, strength-
ening all the disciples.

Ministry of Apollos

24Now a certain Jew named Apollos,
born at Alexandria, an eloquent man
and mighty in the Scriptures, came
to Ephesus. 25This man had been in-
structed in the way of the Lord; and
being fervent in spirit, he spoke and
taught accurately the things of the Lord,
though he knew only the baptism of

18:7 [a] NU-Text reads *Titius Justus.* **18:17** [a] NU-Text reads *they all.* **18:21** [a] NU-Text omits *I must through Jerusalem.*

John. 26So he began to speak boldly in the synagogue. When Aquila and Priscilla heard him, they took him aside and explained to him the way of God more accurately. 27And when he desired to cross to Achaia, the brethren wrote, exhorting the disciples to receive him; and when he arrived, he greatly helped those who had believed through grace; 28for he vigorously refuted the Jews publicly, showing from the Scriptures that Jesus is the Christ.

Paul at Ephesus

19 And it happened, while Apollos was at Corinth, that Paul, having passed through the upper regions, came to Ephesus. And finding some disciples 2he said to them, "Did you receive the Holy Spirit when you believed?"

So they said to him, "We have not so much as heard whether there is a Holy Spirit."

3And he said to them, "Into what then were you baptized?"

So they said, "Into John's baptism."

4Then Paul said, "John indeed baptized with a baptism of repentance, saying to the people that they should believe on Him who would come after him, that is, on Christ Jesus."

5When they heard *this,* they were baptized in the name of the Lord Jesus. 6And when Paul had laid hands on them, the Holy Spirit came upon them, and they spoke with tongues and prophesied. 7Now the men were about twelve in all.

8And he went into the synagogue and spoke boldly for three months, reasoning and persuading concerning the things of the kingdom of God. 9But when some were hardened and did not believe, but spoke evil of the Way before the multitude, he departed from them and withdrew the disciples, reasoning daily in the school of Tyrannus. 10And this continued for two years, so that all who dwelt in Asia heard the word of the Lord Jesus, both Jews and Greeks.

Miracles Glorify Christ

11Now God worked unusual miracles by the hands of Paul, 12so that even handkerchiefs or aprons were brought from his body to the sick, and the diseases left them and the evil spirits went out of them. 13Then some of the itinerant Jewish exorcists took it upon themselves to call the name of the Lord Jesus over those who had evil spirits, saying, "We[a] exorcise you by the Jesus whom Paul preaches." 14Also there were seven sons of Sceva, a Jewish chief priest, who did so.

15And the evil spirit answered and said, "Jesus I know, and Paul I know; but who are you?"

16Then the man in whom the evil spirit was leaped on them, overpowered[a] them, and prevailed against them,[b] so that they fled out of that house naked and wounded. 17This became known both to all Jews and Greeks dwelling in Ephesus; and fear fell on them all, and the name of the Lord Jesus was magnified. 18And many who had believed came confessing and telling their deeds. 19Also, many of those who had practiced magic brought their books together and burned *them* in the sight of all. And they counted up the value of them, and *it* totaled fifty thousand *pieces* of silver. 20So the word of the Lord grew mightily and prevailed.

The Riot at Ephesus

21When these things were accomplished, Paul purposed in the Spirit, when he had passed through Macedonia and Achaia, to go to Jerusalem, saying, "After I have been there, I must also see Rome." 22So he sent into Macedonia two of those who ministered to him, Timothy and Erastus, but he himself stayed in Asia for a time.

23And about that time there arose a great commotion about the Way. 24For a certain man named Demetrius, a silversmith, who made silver shrines of Diana,[a] brought no small profit to the craftsmen. 25He called them together with the workers of similar occupation, and said: "Men, you know that we have our prosperity by this trade. 26Moreover you see and hear that not only at Ephesus, but throughout almost all Asia, this

19:13 [a] NU-Text reads *I.* **19:16** [a] M-Text reads *and they overpowered.* [b] NU-Text reads *both of them.*
19:24 [a] Greek *Artemis*

Paul has persuaded and turned away
many people, saying that they are not
gods which are made with hands. 27So
not only is this trade of ours in danger
of falling into disrepute, but also the
temple of the great goddess Diana may
be despised and her magnificence de-
stroyed,[a] whom all Asia and the world
worship."
28Now when they heard *this,* they
were full of wrath and cried out, saying,
"Great *is* Diana of the Ephesians!" 29So
the whole city was filled with confusion,
and rushed into the theater with one
accord, having seized Gaius and Aristar-
chus, Macedonians, Paul's travel com-
panions. 30And when Paul wanted to go
in to the people, the disciples would not
allow him. 31Then some of the officials
of Asia, who were his friends, sent to
him pleading that he would not venture
into the theater. 32Some therefore cried
one thing and some another, for the
assembly was confused, and most of
them did not know why they had come
together. 33And they drew Alexander
out of the multitude, the Jews putting
him forward. And Alexander motioned
with his hand, and wanted to make his
defense to the people. 34But when they
found out that he was a Jew, all with
one voice cried out for about two hours,
"Great *is* Diana of the Ephesians!"
35And when the city clerk had quieted
the crowd, he said: "Men of Ephesus,
what man is there who does not know
that the city of the Ephesians is temple
guardian of the great goddess Diana,
and of the *image* which fell down from
Zeus? 36Therefore, since these things
cannot be denied, you ought to be quiet
and do nothing rashly. 37For you have
brought these men here who are neither
robbers of temples nor blasphemers of
your[a] goddess. 38Therefore, if Deme-
trius and his fellow craftsmen have a
case against anyone, the courts are
open and there are proconsuls. Let
them bring charges against one an-
other. 39But if you have any other in-
quiry to make, it shall be determined
in the lawful assembly. 40For we are in
danger of being called in question for
today's uproar, there being no reason
which we may give to account for this
disorderly gathering." 41And when he
had said these things, he dismissed
the assembly.

Journeys in Greece

20 After the uproar had ceased, Paul
called the disciples to *himself,*
embraced *them,* and departed to go to
Macedonia. 2Now when he had gone
over that region and encouraged them
with many words, he came to Greece
3and stayed three months. And when
the Jews plotted against him as he was
about to sail to Syria, he decided to re-
turn through Macedonia. 4And Sopater
of Berea accompanied him to Asia—
also Aristarchus and Secundus of the
Thessalonians, and Gaius of Derbe, and
Timothy, and Tychicus and Trophimus
of Asia. 5These men, going ahead, waited
for us at Troas. 6But we sailed away from
Philippi after the Days of Unleavened
Bread, and in five days joined them at
Troas, where we stayed seven days.

Ministering at Troas

7Now on the first *day* of the week, when
the disciples came together to break
bread, Paul, ready to depart the next
day, spoke to them and continued his
message until midnight. 8There were
many lamps in the upper room where
they[a] were gathered together. 9And
in a window sat a certain young man
named Eutychus, who was sinking into
a deep sleep. He was overcome by sleep;
and as Paul continued speaking, he
fell down from the third story and was
taken up dead. 10But Paul went down,
fell on him, and embracing *him* said,
"Do not trouble yourselves, for his life
is in him." 11Now when he had come
up, had broken bread and eaten, and
talked a long while, even till daybreak,
he departed. 12And they brought the
young man in alive, and they were not
a little comforted.

From Troas to Miletus

13Then we went ahead to the ship and
sailed to Assos, there intending to take

19:27 [a] NU-Text reads *she be deposed from her magnificence.* **19:37** [a] NU-Text reads *our.*
20:8 [a] NU-Text and M-Text read *we.*

Paul on board; for so he had given orders, intending himself to go on foot. 14And when he met us at Assos, we took him on board and came to Mitylene. 15We sailed from there, and the next *day* came opposite Chios. The following *day* we arrived at Samos and stayed at Trogyllium. The next *day* we came to Miletus. 16For Paul had decided to sail past Ephesus, so that he would not have to spend time in Asia; for he was hurrying to be at Jerusalem, if possible, on the Day of Pentecost.

The Ephesian Elders Exhorted

17From Miletus he sent to Ephesus and called for the elders of the church. 18And when they had come to him, he said to them: "You know, from the first day that I came to Asia, in what manner I always lived among you, 19serving the Lord with all humility, with many tears and trials which happened to me by the plotting of the Jews; 20how I kept back nothing that was helpful, but proclaimed it to you, and taught you publicly and from house to house, 21testifying to Jews, and also to Greeks, repentance toward God and faith toward our Lord Jesus Christ. 22And see, now I go bound in the spirit to Jerusalem, not knowing the things that will happen to me there, 23except that the Holy Spirit testifies in every city, saying that chains and tribulations await me. 24But none of these things move me; nor do I count my life dear to myself,[a] so that I may finish my race with joy, and the ministry which I received from the Lord Jesus, to testify to the gospel of the grace of God.

25"And indeed, now I know that you all, among whom I have gone preaching the kingdom of God, will see my face no more. 26Therefore I testify to you this day that I *am* innocent of the blood of all *men*. 27For I have not shunned to declare to you the whole counsel of God. 28Therefore take heed to yourselves and to all the flock, among which the Holy Spirit has made you overseers, to shepherd the church of God[a] which He purchased with His own blood. 29For I know this, that after my departure savage wolves will come in among you, not sparing the flock. 30Also from among yourselves men will rise up, speaking perverse things, to draw away the disciples after themselves. 31Therefore watch, and remember that for three years I did not cease to warn everyone night and day with tears.

32"So now, brethren, I commend you to God and to the word of His grace, which is able to build you up and give you an inheritance among all those who are sanctified. 33I have coveted no one's silver or gold or apparel. 34Yes,[a] you yourselves know that these hands have provided for my necessities, and for those who were with me. 35I have shown you in every way, by laboring like this, that you must support the weak. And remember the words of the Lord Jesus, that He said, 'It is more blessed to give than to receive.' "

36And when he had said these things, he knelt down and prayed with them all. 37Then they all wept freely, and fell on Paul's neck and kissed him, 38sorrowing most of all for the words which he spoke, that they would see his face no more. And they accompanied him to the ship.

Warnings on the Journey to Jerusalem

21 Now it came to pass, that when we had departed from them and set sail, running a straight course we came to Cos, the following *day* to Rhodes, and from there to Patara. 2And finding a ship sailing over to Phoenicia, we went aboard and set sail. 3When we had sighted Cyprus, we passed it on the left, sailed to Syria, and landed at Tyre; for there the ship was to unload her cargo. 4And finding disciples,[a] we stayed there seven days. They told Paul through the Spirit not to go up to Jerusalem. 5When we had come to the end of those days, we departed and went on our way; and they all accompanied us, with wives and children, till *we were* out of the city. And we knelt down on the shore and prayed. 6When we had taken our leave of one another, we boarded the ship, and they returned home.

20:24 [a] NU-Text reads *But I do not count my life of any value or dear to myself.* 20:28 [a] M-Text reads *of the Lord and God.* 20:34 [a] NU-Text and M-Text omit *Yes.* 21:4 [a] NU-Text reads *the disciples.*

7And when we had finished *our* voyage from Tyre, we came to Ptolemais, greeted the brethren, and stayed with them one day. 8On the next *day* we who were Paul's companions[a] departed and came to Caesarea, and entered the house of Philip the evangelist, who was *one* of the seven, and stayed with him. 9Now this man had four virgin daughters who prophesied. 10And as we stayed many days, a certain prophet named Agabus came down from Judea. 11When he had come to us, he took Paul's belt, bound his *own* hands and feet, and said, "Thus says the Holy Spirit, 'So shall the Jews at Jerusalem bind the man who owns this belt, and deliver *him* into the hands of the Gentiles.' "

12Now when we heard these things, both we and those from that place pleaded with him not to go up to Jerusalem. 13Then Paul answered, "What do you mean by weeping and breaking my heart? For I am ready not only to be bound, but also to die at Jerusalem for the name of the Lord Jesus."

14So when he would not be persuaded, we ceased, saying, "The will of the Lord be done."

Paul Urged to Make Peace

15And after those days we packed and went up to Jerusalem. 16Also some of the disciples from Caesarea went with us and brought with them a certain Mnason of Cyprus, an early disciple, with whom we were to lodge.

17And when we had come to Jerusalem, the brethren received us gladly. 18On the following *day* Paul went in with us to James, and all the elders were present. 19When he had greeted them, he told in detail those things which God had done among the Gentiles through his ministry. 20And when they heard *it*, they glorified the Lord. And they said to him, "You see, brother, how many myriads of Jews there are who have believed, and they are all zealous for the law; 21but they have been informed about you that you teach all the Jews who are among the Gentiles to forsake Moses, saying that they ought not to circumcise *their* children nor to walk according to the customs. 22What then? The assembly must certainly meet, for they will[a] hear that you have come. 23Therefore do what we tell you: We have four men who have taken a vow. 24Take them and be purified with them, and pay their expenses so that they may shave *their* heads, and that all may know that those things of which they were informed concerning you are nothing, but *that* you yourself also walk orderly and keep the law. 25But concerning the Gentiles who believe, we have written *and* decided that they should observe no such thing, except[a] that they should keep themselves from *things* offered to idols, from blood, from things strangled, and from sexual immorality."

Arrested in the Temple

26Then Paul took the men, and the next day, having been purified with them, entered the temple to announce the expiration of the days of purification, at which time an offering should be made for each one of them.

27Now when the seven days were almost ended, the Jews from Asia, seeing him in the temple, stirred up the whole crowd and laid hands on him, 28crying out, "Men of Israel, help! This is the man who teaches all *men* everywhere against the people, the law, and this place; and furthermore he also brought Greeks into the temple and has defiled this holy place." 29(For they had previously[a] seen Trophimus the Ephesian with him in the city, whom they supposed that Paul had brought into the temple.)

30And all the city was disturbed; and the people ran together, seized Paul, and dragged him out of the temple; and immediately the doors were shut. 31Now as they were seeking to kill him, news came to the commander of the garrison that all Jerusalem was in an uproar. 32He immediately took soldiers and centurions, and ran down to them. And when they saw the commander and the soldiers, they stopped beating

21:8 [a] NU-Text omits *who were Paul's companions.* **21:22** [a] NU-Text reads *What then is to be done? They will certainly.* **21:25** [a] NU-Text omits *that they should observe no such thing, except.* **21:29** [a] M-Text omits *previously.*

Paul. 33Then the commander came near and took him, and commanded *him* to be bound with two chains; and he asked who he was and what he had done. 34And some among the multitude cried one thing and some another.

So when he could not ascertain the truth because of the tumult, he commanded him to be taken into the barracks. 35When he reached the stairs, he had to be carried by the soldiers because of the violence of the mob. 36For the multitude of the people followed after, crying out, "Away with him!"

Addressing the Jerusalem Mob

37Then as Paul was about to be led into the barracks, he said to the commander, "May I speak to you?"

He replied, "Can you speak Greek? 38Are you not the Egyptian who some time ago stirred up a rebellion and led the four thousand assassins out into the wilderness?"

39But Paul said, "I am a Jew from Tarsus, in Cilicia, a citizen of no mean city; and I implore you, permit me to speak to the people."

40So when he had given him permission, Paul stood on the stairs and motioned with his hand to the people. And when there was a great silence, he spoke to *them* in the Hebrew language, saying,

22 "Brethren and fathers, hear my defense before you now." 2And when they heard that he spoke to them in the Hebrew language, they kept all the more silent.

Then he said: 3"I am indeed a Jew, born in Tarsus of Cilicia, but brought up in this city at the feet of Gamaliel, taught according to the strictness of our fathers' law, and was zealous toward God as you all are today. 4I persecuted this Way to the death, binding and delivering into prisons both men and women, 5as also the high priest bears me witness, and all the council of the elders, from whom I also received letters to the brethren, and went to Damascus to bring in chains even those who were there to Jerusalem to be punished.

6"Now it happened, as I journeyed and came near Damascus at about noon, suddenly a great light from heaven shone around me. 7And I fell to the ground and heard a voice saying to me, 'Saul, Saul, why are you persecuting Me?' 8So I answered, 'Who are You, Lord?' And He said to me, 'I am Jesus of Nazareth, whom you are persecuting.'

9"And those who were with me indeed saw the light and were afraid,[a] but they did not hear the voice of Him who spoke to me. 10So I said, 'What shall I do, Lord?' And the Lord said to me, 'Arise and go into Damascus, and there you will be told all things which are appointed for you to do.' 11And since I could not see for the glory of that light, being led by the hand of those who were with me, I came into Damascus.

12"Then a certain Ananias, a devout man according to the law, having a good testimony with all the Jews who dwelt *there,* 13came to me; and he stood and said to me, 'Brother Saul, receive your sight.' And at that same hour I looked up at him. 14Then he said, 'The God of our fathers has chosen you that you should know His will, and see the Just One, and hear the voice of His mouth. 15For you will be His witness to all men of what you have seen and heard. 16And now why are you waiting? Arise and be baptized, and wash away your sins, calling on the name of the Lord.'

17"Now it happened, when I returned to Jerusalem and was praying in the temple, that I was in a trance 18and saw Him saying to me, 'Make haste and get out of Jerusalem quickly, for they will not receive your testimony concerning Me.' 19So I said, 'Lord, they know that in every synagogue I imprisoned and beat those who believe on You. 20And when the blood of Your martyr Stephen was shed, I also was standing by consenting to his death,[a] and guarding the clothes of those who were killing him.' 21Then He said to me, 'Depart, for I will send you far from here to the Gentiles.' "

Paul's Roman Citizenship

22And they listened to him until this word, and *then* they raised their

22:9 [a] NU-Text omits *and were afraid.* **22:20** [a] NU-Text omits *to his death.*

voices and said, "Away with such a *fel-*
low from the earth, for he is not fit to
live!" 23Then, as they cried out and tore
off *their* clothes and threw dust into the
air, 24the commander ordered him to be
brought into the barracks, and said that
he should be examined under scourg-
ing, so that he might know why they
shouted so against him. 25And as they
bound him with thongs, Paul said to the
centurion who stood by, "Is it lawful for
you to scourge a man who is a Roman,
and uncondemned?"

26When the centurion heard *that,* he
went and told the commander, saying,
"Take care what you do, for this man is
a Roman."

27Then the commander came and said
to him, "Tell me, are you a Roman?"

He said, "Yes."

28The commander answered, "With a
large sum I obtained this citizenship."

And Paul said, "But I was born *a cit-*
izen."

29Then immediately those who were
about to examine him withdrew from
him; and the commander was also
afraid after he found out that he was a
Roman, and because he had bound him.

The Sanhedrin Divided

30The next day, because he wanted to
know for certain why he was accused
by the Jews, he released him from
his bonds, and commanded the chief
priests and all their council to appear,
and brought Paul down and set him
before them.

23 Then Paul, looking earnestly
at the council, said, "Men *and*
brethren, I have lived in all good con-
science before God until this day." 2And
the high priest Ananias commanded
those who stood by him to strike him
on the mouth. 3Then Paul said to him,
"God will strike you, *you* whitewashed
wall! For you sit to judge me according
to the law, and do you command me to
be struck contrary to the law?"

4And those who stood by said, "Do you
revile God's high priest?"

5Then Paul said, "I did not know, breth-
ren, that he was the high priest; for it
is written, 'You shall not speak evil of
a ruler of your people.' "[a]

6But when Paul perceived that one
part were Sadducees and the other
Pharisees, he cried out in the council,
"Men *and* brethren, I am a Pharisee,
the son of a Pharisee; concerning the
hope and resurrection of the dead I am
being judged!"

7And when he had said this, a dissen-
sion arose between the Pharisees and
the Sadducees; and the assembly was
divided. 8For Sadducees say that there
is no resurrection—and no angel or
spirit; but the Pharisees confess both.
9Then there arose a loud outcry. And
the scribes of the Pharisees' party arose
and protested, saying, "We find no evil
in this man; but if a spirit or an an-
gel has spoken to him, let us not fight
against God."[a]

10Now when there arose a great dis-
sension, the commander, fearing lest
Paul might be pulled to pieces by them,
commanded the soldiers to go down
and take him by force from among
them, and bring *him* into the barracks.

The Plot Against Paul

11But the following night the Lord
stood by him and said, "Be of good
cheer, Paul; for as you have testified
for Me in Jerusalem, so you must also
bear witness at Rome."

12And when it was day, some of the
Jews banded together and bound them-
selves under an oath, saying that they
would neither eat nor drink till they had
killed Paul. 13Now there were more than
forty who had formed this conspiracy.
14They came to the chief priests and
elders, and said, "We have bound our-
selves under a great oath that we will
eat nothing until we have killed Paul.
15Now you, therefore, together with the
council, suggest to the commander that
he be brought down to you tomorrow,[a]
as though you were going to make fur-
ther inquiries concerning him; but we
are ready to kill him before he comes
near."

16So when Paul's sister's son heard
of their ambush, he went and entered

23:5 [a] Exodus 22:28 **23:9** [a] NU-Text omits last clause and reads *what if a spirit or an angel has spoken to him?* **23:15** [a] NU-Text omits *tomorrow.*

the barracks and told Paul. 17Then Paul
called one of the centurions to *him* and
said, "Take this young man to the com-
mander, for he has something to tell
him." 18So he took him and brought *him*
to the commander and said, "Paul the
prisoner called me to *him* and asked *me*
to bring this young man to you. He has
something to say to you."
19Then the commander took him by
the hand, went aside, and asked private-
ly, "What is it that you have to tell me?"
20And he said, "The Jews have agreed
to ask that you bring Paul down to the
council tomorrow, as though they were
going to inquire more fully about him.
21But do not yield to them, for more
than forty of them lie in wait for him,
men who have bound themselves by
an oath that they will neither eat nor
drink till they have killed him; and now
they are ready, waiting for the promise
from you."
22So the commander let the young
man depart, and commanded *him*, "Tell
no one that you have revealed these
things to me."

Sent to Felix

23And he called for two centurions,
saying, "Prepare two hundred soldiers,
seventy horsemen, and two hundred
spearmen to go to Caesarea at the third
hour of the night; 24and provide mounts
to set Paul on, and bring *him* safely to
Felix the governor." 25He wrote a letter
in the following manner:

26 Claudius Lysias,

To the most excellent governor
Felix:

Greetings.

27 This man was seized by the Jews
and was about to be killed by
them. Coming with the troops I
rescued him, having learned that
he was a Roman. 28And when
I wanted to know the reason
they accused him, I brought
him before their council. 29I
found out that he was accused
concerning questions of their
law, but had nothing charged
against him deserving of death
or chains. 30And when it was told
me that the Jews lay in wait for
the man,[a] I sent him immediately
to you, and also commanded his
accusers to state before you the
charges against him.

Farewell.

31Then the soldiers, as they were com-
manded, took Paul and brought *him* by
night to Antipatris. 32The next day they
left the horsemen to go on with him, and
returned to the barracks. 33When they
came to Caesarea and had delivered the
letter to the governor, they also present-
ed Paul to him. 34And when the gover-
nor had read *it*, he asked what province
he was from. And when he understood
that *he was* from Cilicia, 35he said, "I
will hear you when your accusers also
have come." And he commanded him
to be kept in Herod's Praetorium.

Accused of Sedition

24 Now after five days Ananias the
high priest came down with the
elders and a certain orator *named* Ter-
tullus. These gave evidence to the gov-
ernor against Paul.
2And when he was called upon, Ter-
tullus began his accusation, saying:
"Seeing that through you we enjoy great
peace, and prosperity is being brought
to this nation by your foresight, 3we
accept *it* always and in all places, most
noble Felix, with all thankfulness. 4Nev-
ertheless, not to be tedious to you any
further, I beg you to hear, by your cour-
tesy, a few words from us. 5For we have
found this man a plague, a creator of
dissension among all the Jews through-
out the world, and a ringleader of the
sect of the Nazarenes. 6He even tried to
profane the temple, and we seized him,[a]
and wanted to judge him according to
our law. 7But the commander Lysias
came by and with great violence took
him out of our hands, 8commanding his

23:30 [a] NU-Text reads *there would be a plot against the man.* 24:6 [a] NU-Text ends the sentence here and omits the rest of verse 6, all of verse 7, and the first clause of verse 8.

accusers to come to you. By examining
him yourself you may ascertain all
these things of which we accuse him."
9And the Jews also assented,[a] maintain-
ing that these things were so.

The Defense Before Felix

10Then Paul, after the governor had
nodded to him to speak, answered: "In-
asmuch as I know that you have been
for many years a judge of this nation, I
do the more cheerfully answer for my-
self, 11because you may ascertain that
it is no more than twelve days since I
went up to Jerusalem to worship. 12And
they neither found me in the temple
disputing with anyone nor inciting the
crowd, either in the synagogues or in
the city. 13Nor can they prove the things
of which they now accuse me. 14But this
I confess to you, that according to the
Way which they call a sect, so I wor-
ship the God of my fathers, believing
all things which are written in the Law
and in the Prophets. 15I have hope in
God, which they themselves also accept,
that there will be a resurrection of *the*
dead,[a] both of *the* just and *the* unjust.
16This *being* so, I myself always strive
to have a conscience without offense
toward God and men.

17"Now after many years I came to
bring alms and offerings to my nation,
18in the midst of which some Jews from
Asia found me purified in the temple,
neither with a mob nor with tumult.
19They ought to have been here before
you to object if they had anything
against me. 20Or else let those who are
here themselves say if they found any
wrongdoing[a] in me while I stood before
the council, 21unless *it is* for this one
statement which I cried out, standing
among them, 'Concerning the resurrec-
tion of the dead I am being judged by
you this day.' "

Felix Procrastinates

22But when Felix heard these things,
having more accurate knowledge of
the Way, he adjourned the proceedings
and said, "When Lysias the commander
comes down, I will make a decision on
your case." 23So he commanded the cen-
turion to keep Paul and to let *him* have
liberty, and told him not to forbid any
of his friends to provide for or visit him.

24And after some days, when Felix
came with his wife Drusilla, who was
Jewish, he sent for Paul and heard him
concerning the faith in Christ. 25Now as
he reasoned about righteousness, self-
control, and the judgment to come, Felix
was afraid and answered, "Go away for
now; when I have a convenient time I
will call for you." 26Meanwhile he also
hoped that money would be given him
by Paul, that he might release him.[a]
Therefore he sent for him more often
and conversed with him.

27But after two years Porcius Festus
succeeded Felix; and Felix, wanting to
do the Jews a favor, left Paul bound.

Paul Appeals to Caesar

25 Now when Festus had come to
the province, after three days he
went up from Caesarea to Jerusalem.
2Then the high priest[a] and the chief
men of the Jews informed him against
Paul; and they petitioned him, 3asking
a favor against him, that he would sum-
mon him to Jerusalem—while *they* lay
in ambush along the road to kill him.
4But Festus answered that Paul should
be kept at Caesarea, and that he himself
was going *there* shortly. 5"Therefore,"
he said, "let those who have authori-
ty among you go down with *me* and
accuse this man, to see if there is any
fault in him."

6And when he had remained among
them more than ten days, he went down
to Caesarea. And the next day, sitting on
the judgment seat, he commanded Paul
to be brought. 7When he had come, the
Jews who had come down from Jerusa-
lem stood about and laid many serious
complaints against Paul, which they
could not prove, 8while he answered
for himself, "Neither against the law
of the Jews, nor against the temple,
nor against Caesar have I offended in
anything at all."

24:9 [a] NU-Text and M-Text read *joined the attack.* **24:15** [a] NU-Text omits *of the dead.*
24:20 [a] NU-Text and M-Text read *say what wrongdoing they found.* **24:26** [a] NU-Text omits *that he might release him.* **25:2** [a] NU-Text reads *chief priests.*

9But Festus, wanting to do the Jews
a favor, answered Paul and said, "Are
you willing to go up to Jerusalem and
there be judged before me concerning
these things?"
10So Paul said, "I stand at Caesar's
judgment seat, where I ought to be
judged. To the Jews I have done no
wrong, as you very well know. 11For if
I am an offender, or have committed
anything deserving of death, I do not
object to dying; but if there is nothing in
these things of which these men accuse
me, no one can deliver me to them. I
appeal to Caesar."
12Then Festus, when he had conferred
with the council, answered, "You have
appealed to Caesar? To Caesar you
shall go!"

Paul Before Agrippa

13And after some days King Agrippa
and Bernice came to Caesarea to greet
Festus. 14When they had been there
many days, Festus laid Paul's case before
the king, saying: "There is a certain man
left a prisoner by Felix, 15about whom the
chief priests and the elders of the Jews
informed *me,* when I was in Jerusalem,
asking for a judgment against him. 16To
them I answered, 'It is not the custom of
the Romans to deliver any man to de-
struction[a] before the accused meets the
accusers face to face, and has opportuni-
ty to answer for himself concerning the
charge against him.' 17Therefore when
they had come together, without any
delay, the next day I sat on the judgment
seat and commanded the man to be
brought in. 18When the accusers stood
up, they brought no accusation against
him of such things as I supposed, 19but
had some questions against him about
their own religion and about a certain
Jesus, who had died, whom Paul affirmed
to be alive. 20And because I was uncer-
tain of such questions, I asked whether
he was willing to go to Jerusalem and
there be judged concerning these mat-
ters. 21But when Paul appealed to be
reserved for the decision of Augustus, I
commanded him to be kept till I could
send him to Caesar."
22Then Agrippa said to Festus, "I also
would like to hear the man myself."
"Tomorrow," he said, "you shall hear
him."
23So the next day, when Agrippa and
Bernice had come with great pomp,
and had entered the auditorium with
the commanders and the prominent
men of the city, at Festus' command
Paul was brought in. 24And Festus said:
"King Agrippa and all the men who are
here present with us, you see this man
about whom the whole assembly of the
Jews petitioned me, both at Jerusalem
and here, crying out that he was not fit
to live any longer. 25But when I found
that he had committed nothing deserv-
ing of death, and that he himself had
appealed to Augustus, I decided to send
him. 26I have nothing certain to write
to my lord concerning him. Therefore I
have brought him out before you, and
especially before you, King Agrippa, so
that after the examination has taken
place I may have something to write.
27For it seems to me unreasonable to
send a prisoner and not to specify the
charges against him."

Paul's Early Life

26 Then Agrippa said to Paul, "You
are permitted to speak for your-
self."
So Paul stretched out his hand and
answered for himself: 2"I think myself
happy, King Agrippa, because today
I shall answer for myself before you
concerning all the things of which I
am accused by the Jews, 3especially
because you are expert in all customs
and questions which have to do with
the Jews. Therefore I beg you to hear
me patiently.
4"My manner of life from my youth,
which was spent from the beginning
among my own nation at Jerusalem,
all the Jews know. 5They knew me from
the first, if they were willing to testify,
that according to the strictest sect of our
religion I lived a Pharisee. 6And now I
stand and am judged for the hope of the
promise made by God to our fathers. 7To
this *promise* our twelve tribes, earnestly

25:16 [a] NU-Text omits *to destruction,* although it is implied.

serving *God* night and day, hope to at-
tain. For this hope's sake, King Agrippa,
I am accused by the Jews. 8 Why should
it be thought incredible by you that God
raises the dead?
9 "Indeed, I myself thought I must do
many things contrary to the name of
Jesus of Nazareth. 10 This I also did in Je-
rusalem, and many of the saints I shut
up in prison, having received authority
from the chief priests; and when they
were put to death, I cast my vote against
them. 11 And I punished them often in
every synagogue and compelled *them*
to blaspheme; and being exceedingly
enraged against them, I persecuted
them even to foreign cities.

Paul Recounts His Conversion

12 "While thus occupied, as I journeyed
to Damascus with authority and com-
mission from the chief priests, 13 at
midday, O king, along the road I saw
a light from heaven, brighter than the
sun, shining around me and those who
journeyed with me. 14 And when we all
had fallen to the ground, I heard a voice
speaking to me and saying in the He-
brew language, 'Saul, Saul, why are
you persecuting Me? *It is* hard for you
to kick against the goads.' 15 So I said,
'Who are You, Lord?' And He said, 'I
am Jesus, whom you are persecuting.
16 But rise and stand on your feet; for I
have appeared to you for this purpose,
to make you a minister and a witness
both of the things which you have seen
and of the things which I will yet reveal
to you. 17 I will deliver you from the *Jew-
ish* people, as well as *from* the Gentiles,
to whom I now[a] send you, 18 to open
their eyes, *in order* to turn *them* from
darkness to light, and *from* the power
of Satan to God, that they may receive
forgiveness of sins and an inheritance
among those who are sanctified by faith
in Me.'

Paul's Post-Conversion Life

19 "Therefore, King Agrippa, I was not
disobedient to the heavenly vision,
20 but declared first to those in Damas-
cus and in Jerusalem, and throughout
all the region of Judea, and *then* to the
Gentiles, that they should repent, turn
to God, and do works befitting repen-
tance. 21 For these reasons the Jews
seized me in the temple and tried to
kill *me.* 22 Therefore, having obtained
help from God, to this day I stand, wit-
nessing both to small and great, saying
no other things than those which the
prophets and Moses said would come—
23 that the Christ would suffer, that He
would be the first to rise from the dead,
and would proclaim light to the *Jewish*
people and to the Gentiles."

Agrippa Parries Paul's Challenge

24 Now as he thus made his defense,
Festus said with a loud voice, "Paul, you
are beside yourself! Much learning is
driving you mad!"
25 But he said, "I am not mad, most
noble Festus, but speak the words of
truth and reason. 26 For the king, before
whom I also speak freely, knows these
things; for I am convinced that none
of these things escapes his attention,
since this thing was not done in a cor-
ner. 27 King Agrippa, do you believe the
prophets? I know that you do believe."
28 Then Agrippa said to Paul, "You al-
most persuade me to become a Chris-
tian."
29 And Paul said, "I would to God that
not only you, but also all who hear me
today, might become both almost and
altogether such as I am, except for these
chains."
30 When he had said these things, the
king stood up, as well as the governor
and Bernice and those who sat with
them; 31 and when they had gone aside,
they talked among themselves, saying,
"This man is doing nothing deserving
of death or chains."
32 Then Agrippa said to Festus, "This
man might have been set free if he had
not appealed to Caesar."

The Voyage to Rome Begins

27 And when it was decided that
we should sail to Italy, they de-
livered Paul and some other prisoners
to *one* named Julius, a centurion of the

26:17 [a] NU-Text and M-Text omit *now.*

Augustan Regiment. 2So, entering a ship of Adramyttium, we put to sea, meaning to sail along the coasts of Asia. Aristarchus, a Macedonian of Thessalonica, was with us. 3And the next *day* we landed at Sidon. And Julius treated Paul kindly and gave *him* liberty to go to his friends and receive care. 4When we had put to sea from there, we sailed under *the shelter of* Cyprus, because the winds were contrary. 5And when we had sailed over the sea which is off Cilicia and Pamphylia, we came to Myra, *a city* of Lycia. 6There the centurion found an Alexandrian ship sailing to Italy, and he put us on board.

7When we had sailed slowly many days, and arrived with difficulty off Cnidus, the wind not permitting us to proceed, we sailed under *the shelter of* Crete off Salmone. 8Passing it with difficulty, we came to a place called Fair Havens, near the city *of* Lasea.

Paul's Warning Ignored

9Now when much time had been spent, and sailing was now dangerous because the Fast was already over, Paul advised them, 10saying, "Men, I perceive that this voyage will end with disaster and much loss, not only of the cargo and ship, but also our lives." 11Nevertheless the centurion was more persuaded by the helmsman and the owner of the ship than by the things spoken by Paul. 12And because the harbor was not suitable to winter in, the majority advised to set sail from there also, if by any means they could reach Phoenix, a harbor of Crete opening toward the southwest and northwest, *and* winter *there.*

In the Tempest

13When the south wind blew softly, supposing that they had obtained *their* desire, putting out to sea, they sailed close by Crete. 14But not long after, a tempestuous head wind arose, called Euroclydon.[a] 15So when the ship was caught, and could not head into the wind, we let *her* drive. 16And running under *the shelter of* an island called Clauda,[a] we secured the skiff with difficulty. 17When they had taken it on board, they used cables to undergird the ship; and fearing lest they should run aground on the Syrtis[a] *Sands,* they struck sail and so were driven. 18And because we were exceedingly tempest-tossed, the next *day* they lightened the ship. 19On the third *day* we threw the ship's tackle overboard with our own hands. 20Now when neither sun nor stars appeared for many days, and no small tempest beat on *us,* all hope that we would be saved was finally given up.

21But after long abstinence from food, then Paul stood in the midst of them and said, "Men, you should have listened to me, and not have sailed from Crete and incurred this disaster and loss. 22And now I urge you to take heart, for there will be no loss of life among you, but only of the ship. 23For there stood by me this night an angel of the God to whom I belong and whom I serve, 24saying, 'Do not be afraid, Paul; you must be brought before Caesar; and indeed God has granted you all those who sail with you.' 25Therefore take heart, men, for I believe God that it will be just as it was told me. 26However, we must run aground on a certain island."

27Now when the fourteenth night had come, as we were driven up and down in the Adriatic *Sea,* about midnight the sailors sensed that they were drawing near some land. 28And they took soundings and found *it* to be twenty fathoms; and when they had gone a little farther, they took soundings again and found *it* to be fifteen fathoms. 29Then, fearing lest we should run aground on the rocks, they dropped four anchors from the stern, and prayed for day to come. 30And as the sailors were seeking to escape from the ship, when they had let down the skiff into the sea, under pretense of putting out anchors from the prow, 31Paul said to the centurion and the soldiers, "Unless these men stay in the ship, you cannot be saved." 32Then the soldiers cut away the ropes of the skiff and let it fall off.

33And as day was about to dawn, Paul implored *them* all to take food, saying,

27:14 [a] NU-Text reads *Euraquilon.* **27:16** [a] NU-Text reads *Cauda.* **27:17** [a] M-Text reads *Syrtes.*

"Today is the fourteenth day you have
waited and continued without food,
and eaten nothing. 34Therefore I urge
you to take nourishment, for this is for
your survival, since not a hair will fall
from the head of any of you." 35And
when he had said these things, he took
bread and gave thanks to God in the
presence of them all; and when he had
broken *it* he began to eat. 36Then they
were all encouraged, and also took food
themselves. 37And in all we were two
hundred and seventy-six persons on the
ship. 38So when they had eaten enough,
they lightened the ship and threw out
the wheat into the sea.

Shipwrecked on Malta

39When it was day, they did not recog-
nize the land; but they observed a bay
with a beach, onto which they planned
to run the ship if possible. 40And they let
go the anchors and left *them* in the sea,
meanwhile loosing the rudder ropes;
and they hoisted the mainsail to the
wind and made for shore. 41But striking
a place where two seas met, they ran the
ship aground; and the prow stuck fast
and remained immovable, but the stern
was being broken up by the violence of
the waves.

42And the soldiers' plan was to kill the
prisoners, lest any of them should swim
away and escape. 43But the centurion,
wanting to save Paul, kept them from
their purpose, and commanded that
those who could swim should jump
overboard first and get to land, 44and
the rest, some on boards and some on
parts of the ship. And so it was that they
all escaped safely to land.

Paul's Ministry on Malta

28 Now when they had escaped,
they then found out that the is-
land was called Malta. 2And the natives
showed us unusual kindness; for they
kindled a fire and made us all welcome,
because of the rain that was falling
and because of the cold. 3But when
Paul had gathered a bundle of sticks
and laid *them* on the fire, a viper came
out because of the heat, and fastened
on his hand. 4So when the natives saw
the creature hanging from his hand,
they said to one another, "No doubt
this man is a murderer, whom, though
he has escaped the sea, yet justice does
not allow to live." 5But he shook off the
creature into the fire and suffered no
harm. 6However, they were expecting
that he would swell up or suddenly fall
down dead. But after they had looked
for a long time and saw no harm come
to him, they changed their minds and
said that he was a god.

7In that region there was an estate of
the leading citizen of the island, whose
name was Publius, who received us and
entertained us courteously for three
days. 8And it happened that the father
of Publius lay sick of a fever and dysen-
tery. Paul went in to him and prayed,
and he laid his hands on him and
healed him. 9So when this was done,
the rest of those on the island who had
diseases also came and were healed.
10They also honored us in many ways;
and when we departed, they provided
such things as were necessary.

Arrival at Rome

11After three months we sailed in an
Alexandrian ship whose figurehead was
the Twin Brothers, which had wintered
at the island. 12And landing at Syracuse,
we stayed three days. 13From there we
circled round and reached Rhegium.
And after one day the south wind blew;
and the next day we came to Puteoli,
14where we found brethren, and were
invited to stay with them seven days.
And so we went toward Rome. 15And
from there, when the brethren heard
about us, they came to meet us as far
as Appii Forum and Three Inns. When
Paul saw them, he thanked God and
took courage.

16Now when we came to Rome, the
centurion delivered the prisoners to
the captain of the guard; but Paul was
permitted to dwell by himself with the
soldier who guarded him.

Paul's Ministry at Rome

17And it came to pass after three days
that Paul called the leaders of the Jews
together. So when they had come to-
gether, he said to them: "Men *and*
brethren, though I have done nothing

against our people or the customs of
our fathers, yet I was delivered as a
prisoner from Jerusalem into the hands
of the Romans, 18 who, when they had
examined me, wanted to let *me* go, be-
cause there was no cause for putting me
to death. 19 But when the Jews[a] spoke
against *it,* I was compelled to appeal
to Caesar, not that I had anything of
which to accuse my nation. 20 For this
reason therefore I have called for you,
to see *you* and speak with *you,* because
for the hope of Israel I am bound with
this chain."

21 Then they said to him, "We neither
received letters from Judea concerning
you, nor have any of the brethren who
came reported or spoken any evil of
you. 22 But we desire to hear from you
what you think; for concerning this
sect, we know that it is spoken against
everywhere."

23 So when they had appointed him a
day, many came to him at *his* lodging,
to whom he explained and solemnly
testified of the kingdom of God, per-
suading them concerning Jesus from
both the Law of Moses and the Prophets,
from morning till evening. 24 And some
were persuaded by the things which
were spoken, and some disbelieved.
25 So when they did not agree among
themselves, they departed after Paul
had said one word: "The Holy Spirit
spoke rightly through Isaiah the proph-
et to our[a] fathers, 26 saying,

'Go to this people and say:
"Hearing you will hear, and shall
not understand;
And seeing you will see, and not
perceive;
27 For the hearts of this people have
grown dull.
Their ears are hard of hearing,
And their eyes they have closed,
Lest they should see with *their*
eyes and hear with *their* ears,
Lest they should understand with
their hearts and turn,
So that I should heal them." '[a]

28 "Therefore let it be known to you
that the salvation of God has been sent
to the Gentiles, and they will hear it!"
29 And when he had said these words,
the Jews departed and had a great dis-
pute among themselves.[a]

30 Then Paul dwelt two whole years
in his own rented house, and received
all who came to him, 31 preaching the
kingdom of God and teaching the things
which concern the Lord Jesus Christ with
all confidence, no one forbidding him.

28:19 [a] That is, the ruling authorities **28:25** [a] NU-Text reads *your.* **28:27** [a] Isaiah 6:9, 10
28:29 [a] NU-Text omits this verse.

THE LETTER OF PAUL TO THE

ROMANS

The church in Rome was formed several years before Paul wrote this letter to it. This church was fairly large and located at the center of the Roman Empire, making it strategic for taking the gospel farther into the world. Paul, however, wanted to be sure that the church was growing on the foundation of the true gospel of Jesus Christ. While he wanted to visit the church, he would not be able to for a while, so he wrote this letter instead. In Romans, Paul clearly presents the basics of the Christian faith: sin, salvation, and service. Paul explains that everyone has sinned, but Jesus came to earth to save us. Salvation is God's gift to us. We cannot work for it or earn it; we receive it by faith. We then serve Jesus because we love Him and are thankful for what He did.

- **GENRE:** Epistle
- **AUTHOR:** Paul
- **TIME:** c. AD 56–57
- **PURPOSE:** To tell the Good News to the Christians in Rome and prepare them for Paul's visit.

Greeting

1 Paul, a bondservant of Jesus Christ,
called *to be* an apostle, separated to
the gospel of God 2which He promised
before through His prophets in the Holy
Scriptures, 3concerning His Son Jesus
Christ our Lord, who was born of the
seed of David according to the flesh, 4*and*
declared *to be* the Son of God with power
according to the Spirit of holiness, by the
resurrection from the dead. 5Through
Him we have received grace and apos-
tleship for obedience to the faith among
all nations for His name, 6among whom
you also are the called of Jesus Christ;

7To all who are in Rome, beloved of
God, called *to be* saints:

Grace to you and peace from God our
Father and the Lord Jesus Christ.

Desire to Visit Rome

8First, I thank my God through Jesus
Christ for you all, that your faith is spo-
ken of throughout the whole world. 9For
God is my witness, whom I serve with
my spirit in the gospel of His Son, that
without ceasing I make mention of you
always in my prayers, 10making request
if, by some means, now at last I may
find a way in the will of God to come to
you. 11For I long to see you, that I may
impart to you some spiritual gift, so that
you may be established— 12that is, that
I may be encouraged together with you
by the mutual faith both of you and me.
13Now I do not want you to be unaware,
brethren, that I often planned to come
to you (but was hindered until now),
that I might have some fruit among you
also, just as among the other Gentiles.
14I am a debtor both to Greeks and to
barbarians, both to wise and to unwise.
15So, as much as is in me, *I am* ready
to preach the gospel to you who are in
Rome also.

The Just Live by Faith

16For I am not ashamed of the gospel
of Christ,[a] for it is the power of God to
salvation for everyone who believes, for
the Jew first and also for the Greek. 17For
in it the righteousness of God is revealed
from faith to faith; as it is written, "The
just shall live by faith."[a]

God's Wrath on Unrighteousness

18For the wrath of God is revealed from
heaven against all ungodliness and

1:16 [a] NU-Text omits *of Christ.* 1:17 [a] Habakkuk 2:4

unrighteousness of men, who suppress the truth in unrighteousness, 19because what may be known of God is manifest in them, for God has shown *it* to them. 20For since the creation of the world His invisible *attributes* are clearly seen, being understood by the things that are made, *even* His eternal power and Godhead, so that they are without excuse, 21because, although they knew God, they did not glorify *Him* as God, nor were thankful, but became futile in their thoughts, and their foolish hearts were darkened. 22Professing to be wise, they became fools, 23and changed the glory of the incorruptible God into an image made like corruptible man—and birds and four-footed animals and creeping things.

24Therefore God also gave them up to uncleanness, in the lusts of their hearts, to dishonor their bodies among themselves, 25who exchanged the truth of God for the lie, and worshiped and served the creature rather than the Creator, who is blessed forever. Amen.

26For this reason God gave them up to vile passions. For even their women exchanged the natural use for what is against nature. 27Likewise also the men, leaving the natural use of the woman, burned in their lust for one another, men with men committing what is shameful, and receiving in themselves the penalty of their error which was due.

28And even as they did not like to retain God in *their* knowledge, God gave them over to a debased mind, to do those things which are not fitting; 29being filled with all unrighteousness, sexual immorality,[a] wickedness, covetousness, maliciousness; full of envy, murder, strife, deceit, evil-mindedness; *they are* whisperers, 30backbiters, haters of God, violent, proud, boasters, inventors of evil things, disobedient to parents, 31undiscerning, untrustworthy, unloving, unforgiving,[a] unmerciful; 32who, knowing the righteous judgment of God, that those who practice such things are deserving of death, not only do the same but also approve of those who practice them.

God's Righteous Judgment

2 Therefore you are inexcusable, O man, whoever you are who judge, for in whatever you judge another you condemn yourself; for you who judge practice the same things. 2But we know that the judgment of God is according to truth against those who practice such things. 3And do you think this, O man, you who judge those practicing such things, and doing the same, that you will escape the judgment of God? 4Or do you despise the riches of His goodness, forbearance, and longsuffering, not knowing that the goodness of God leads you to repentance? 5But in accordance with your hardness and your impenitent heart you are treasuring up for yourself wrath in the day of wrath and revelation of the righteous judgment of God, 6who "will render to each one according to his deeds":[a] 7eternal life to those who by patient continuance in doing good seek for glory, honor, and immortality; 8but to those who are self-seeking and do not obey the truth, but obey unrighteousness—indignation and wrath, 9tribulation and anguish, on every soul of man who does evil, of the Jew first and also of the Greek; 10but glory, honor, and peace to everyone who works what is good, to the Jew first and also to the Greek. 11For there is no partiality with God.

12For as many as have sinned without law will also perish without law, and as many as have sinned in the law will be judged by the law 13(for not the hearers of the law *are* just in the sight of God, but the doers of the law will be justified; 14for when Gentiles, who do not have the law, by nature do the things in the law, these, although not having the law, are a law to themselves, 15who show the work of the law written in their hearts, their conscience also bearing witness, and between themselves *their* thoughts accusing or else excusing *them*) 16in the day when God will judge the secrets of men by Jesus Christ, according to my gospel.

The Jews Guilty as the Gentiles

17Indeed[a] you are called a Jew, and rest on the law, and make your boast in

1:29 [a] NU-Text omits *sexual immorality.* **1:31** [a] NU-Text omits *unforgiving.* **2:6** [a] Psalm 62:12; Proverbs 24:12 **2:17** [a] NU-Text reads *But if.*

God, 18 and know *His* will, and approve
the things that are excellent, being in-
structed out of the law, 19 and are con-
fident that you yourself are a guide to
the blind, a light to those who are in
darkness, 20 an instructor of the foolish,
a teacher of babes, having the form of
knowledge and truth in the law. 21 You,
therefore, who teach another, do you
not teach yourself? You who preach
that a man should not steal, do you
steal? 22 You who say, "Do not commit
adultery," do you commit adultery? You
who abhor idols, do you rob temples?
23 You who make your boast in the law,
do you dishonor God through breaking
the law? 24 For "the name of God is blas-
phemed among the Gentiles because of
you,"[a] as it is written.

Circumcision of No Avail

25 For circumcision is indeed profitable
if you keep the law; but if you are a
breaker of the law, your circumcision
has become uncircumcision. 26 There-
fore, if an uncircumcised man keeps
the righteous requirements of the law,
will not his uncircumcision be count-
ed as circumcision? 27 And will not the
physically uncircumcised, if he fulfills
the law, judge you who, *even* with *your*
written *code* and circumcision, *are* a
transgressor of the law? 28 For he is not a
Jew who *is one* outwardly, nor *is* circum-
cision that which *is* outward in the flesh;
29 but *he is* a Jew who *is one* inwardly;
and circumcision *is that* of the heart, in
the Spirit, not in the letter; whose praise
is not from men but from God.

God's Judgment Defended

3 What advantage then has the Jew,
or what *is* the profit of circumcision?
2 Much in every way! Chiefly because
to them were committed the oracles of
God. 3 For what if some did not believe?
Will their unbelief make the faithfulness
of God without effect? 4 Certainly not!
Indeed, let God be true but every man
a liar. As it is written:

"That You may be justified in Your
words,
And may overcome when You are
judged."[a]

5 But if our unrighteousness dem-
onstrates the righteousness of God,
what shall we say? *Is* God unjust who
inflicts wrath? (I speak as a man.) 6 Cer-
tainly not! For then how will God judge
the world?
7 For if the truth of God has increased
through my lie to His glory, why am
I also still judged as a sinner? 8 And
why not *say*, "Let us do evil that good
may come"?—as we are slanderously
reported and as some affirm that we
say. Their condemnation is just.

All Have Sinned

9 What then? Are we better *than they?*
Not at all. For we have previously
charged both Jews and Greeks that they
are all under sin.
10 As it is written:

"There is none righteous, no, not
one;
11 There is none who understands;
There is none who seeks after God.
12 They have all turned aside;
They have together become
unprofitable;
There is none who does good, no,
not one."[a]
13 "Their throat *is* an open tomb;
With their tongues they have
practiced deceit";[a]
"The poison of asps *is* under their
lips";[b]
14 "Whose mouth *is* full of cursing and
bitterness."[a]
15 "Their feet *are* swift to shed blood;
16 Destruction and misery *are* in
their ways;
17 And the way of peace they have
not known."[a]
18 "There is no fear of God before their
eyes."[a]

19 Now we know that whatever the law
says, it says to those who are under the
law, that every mouth may be stopped,
and all the world may become guilty be-
fore God. 20 Therefore by the deeds of the

2:24 [a] Isaiah 52:5; Ezekiel 36:22 3:4 [a] Psalm 51:4 3:12 [a] Psalms 14:1–3; 53:1–3; Ecclesiastes 7:20
3:13 [a] Psalm 5:9 [b] Psalm 140:3 3:14 [a] Psalm 10:7 3:17 [a] Isaiah 59:7, 8 3:18 [a] Psalm 36:1

law no flesh will be justified in His sight, for by the law *is* the knowledge of sin.

God's Righteousness Through Faith

21But now the righteousness of God apart from the law is revealed, being witnessed by the Law and the Prophets, 22even the righteousness of God, through faith in Jesus Christ, to all and on all[a] who believe. For there is no difference; 23for all have sinned and fall short of the glory of God, 24being justified freely by His grace through the redemption that is in Christ Jesus, 25whom God set forth *as* a propitiation by His blood, through faith, to demonstrate His righteousness, because in His forbearance God had passed over the sins that were previously committed, 26to demonstrate at the present time His righteousness, that He might be just and the justifier of the one who has faith in Jesus.

Boasting Excluded

27Where *is* boasting then? It is excluded. By what law? Of works? No, but by the law of faith. 28Therefore we conclude that a man is justified by faith apart from the deeds of the law. 29Or *is He* the God of the Jews only? *Is He* not also the God of the Gentiles? Yes, of the Gentiles also, 30since *there is* one God who will justify the circumcised by faith and the uncircumcised through faith. 31Do we then make void the law through faith? Certainly not! On the contrary, we establish the law.

Abraham Justified by Faith

4 What then shall we say that Abraham our father has found according to the flesh?[a] 2For if Abraham was justified by works, he has *something* to boast about, but not before God. 3For what does the Scripture say? "Abraham believed God, and it was accounted to him for righteousness."[a] 4Now to him who works, the wages are not counted as grace but as debt.

David Celebrates the Same Truth

5But to him who does not work but believes on Him who justifies the ungodly, his faith is accounted for righteousness, 6just as David also describes the blessedness of the man to whom God imputes righteousness apart from works:

7 "Blessed *are those* whose lawless
deeds are forgiven,
And whose sins are covered;
8 Blessed *is the* man to whom the
LORD shall not impute sin."[a]

Abraham Justified Before Circumcision

9*Does* this blessedness then *come* upon the circumcised *only*, or upon the uncircumcised also? For we say that faith was accounted to Abraham for righteousness. 10How then was it accounted? While he was circumcised, or uncircumcised? Not while circumcised, but while uncircumcised. 11And he received the sign of circumcision, a seal of the righteousness of the faith which *he had while still* uncircumcised, that he might be the father of all those who believe, though they are uncircumcised, that righteousness might be imputed to them also, 12and the father of circumcision to those who not only *are* of the circumcision, but who also walk in the steps of the faith which our father Abraham *had while still* uncircumcised.

The Promise Granted Through Faith

13For the promise that he would be the heir of the world *was* not to Abraham or to his seed through the law, but through the righteousness of faith. 14For if those who are of the law *are* heirs, faith is made void and the promise made of no effect, 15because the law brings about wrath; for where there is no law *there is* no transgression.

16Therefore *it is* of faith that *it might be* according to grace, so that the promise might be sure to all the seed, not only to those who are of the law, but also to those who are of the faith of Abraham, who is the father of us all 17(as it is written, "I have made you a father of many nations"[a]) in the presence of Him whom he believed—God, who gives life to the dead and calls those things which do not exist as though they did; 18who, contrary to hope, in hope believed, so that

3:22 [a] NU-Text omits *and on all.* **4:1** [a] Or *Abraham our (fore)father according to the flesh has found?*
4:3 [a] Genesis 15:6 **4:8** [a] Psalm 32:1, 2 **4:17** [a] Genesis 17:5

he became the father of many nations,
according to what was spoken, "So shall
your descendants be."[a] 19And not being
weak in faith, he did not consider his own
body, already dead (since he was about
a hundred years old), and the deadness
of Sarah's womb. 20He did not waver at
the promise of God through unbelief,
but was strengthened in faith, giving
glory to God, 21and being fully convinced
that what He had promised He was also
able to perform. 22And therefore "it was
accounted to him for righteousness."[a]
23Now it was not written for his sake
alone that it was imputed to him, 24but
also for us. It shall be imputed to us who
believe in Him who raised up Jesus our
Lord from the dead, 25who was deliv-
ered up because of our offenses, and
was raised because of our justification.

Faith Triumphs in Trouble

5 Therefore, having been justified
by faith, we have[a] peace with God
through our Lord Jesus Christ, 2through
whom also we have access by faith into
this grace in which we stand, and rejoice
in hope of the glory of God. 3And not
only *that,* but we also glory in tribula-
tions, knowing that tribulation produces
perseverance; 4and perseverance, char-
acter; and character, hope. 5Now hope
does not disappoint, because the love of
God has been poured out in our hearts
by the Holy Spirit who was given to us.

Christ in Our Place

6For when we were still without
strength, in due time Christ died for
the ungodly. 7For scarcely for a righ-
teous man will one die; yet perhaps for
a good man someone would even dare
to die. 8But God demonstrates His own
love toward us, in that while we were
still sinners, Christ died for us. 9Much
more then, having now been justified
by His blood, we shall be saved from
wrath through Him. 10For if when we
were enemies we were reconciled to
God through the death of His Son, much
more, having been reconciled, we shall
be saved by His life. 11And not only *that,*
but we also rejoice in God through our
Lord Jesus Christ, through whom we
have now received the reconciliation.

Death in Adam, Life in Christ

12Therefore, just as through one
man sin entered the world, and death
through sin, and thus death spread to
all men, because all sinned— 13(For until
the law sin was in the world, but sin is
not imputed when there is no law. 14Nev-
ertheless death reigned from Adam to
Moses, even over those who had not
sinned according to the likeness of the
transgression of Adam, who is a type of
Him who was to come. 15But the free gift
is not like the offense. For if by the one
man's offense many died, much more
the grace of God and the gift by the grace
of the one Man, Jesus Christ, abounded
to many. 16And the gift *is* not like *that*
which came through the one who sinned.
For the judgment *which came* from one
offense resulted in condemnation, but
the free gift *which came* from many of-
fenses *resulted* in justification. 17For if
by the one man's offense death reigned
through the one, much more those who
receive abundance of grace and of the
gift of righteousness will reign in life
through the One, Jesus Christ.)
18Therefore, as through one man's of-
fense *judgment came* to all men, result-
ing in condemnation, even so through
one Man's righteous act *the free gift came*
to all men, resulting in justification of
life. 19For as by one man's disobedience
many were made sinners, so also by one
Man's obedience many will be made
righteous.
20Moreover the law entered that the
offense might abound. But where sin
abounded, grace abounded much more,
21so that as sin reigned in death, even so
grace might reign through righteous-
ness to eternal life through Jesus Christ
our Lord.

Dead to Sin, Alive to God

6 What shall we say then? Shall we
continue in sin that grace may
abound? 2Certainly not! How shall we
who died to sin live any longer in it?
3Or do you not know that as many of

4:18 [a] Genesis 15:5 4:22 [a] Genesis 15:6 5:1 [a] Another ancient reading is, *let us have peace.*

GOD SIN JESUS SALVATION LOVE

us as were baptized into Christ Jesus
were baptized into His death? 4Therefore
fore we were buried with Him through
baptism into death, that just as Christ
was raised from the dead by the glory
of the Father, even so we also should
walk in newness of life.
5For if we have been united together in
the likeness of His death, certainly we
also shall be *in the likeness* of *His* resur-
rection, 6knowing this, that our old man
was crucified with *Him,* that the body of
sin might be done away with, that we
should no longer be slaves of sin. 7For
he who has died has been freed from sin.
8Now if we died with Christ, we believe
that we shall also live with Him, 9know-
ing that Christ, having been raised from
the dead, dies no more. Death no longer
has dominion over Him. 10For *the death*
that He died, He died to sin once for all;
but *the life* that He lives, He lives to God.
11Likewise you also, reckon yourselves
to be dead indeed to sin, but alive to God
in Christ Jesus our Lord.
12Therefore do not let sin reign in your
mortal body, that you should obey it
in its lusts. 13And do not present your
members *as* instruments of unrigh-
teousness to sin, but present yourselves
to God as being alive from the dead,
and your members *as* instruments of
righteousness to God. 14For sin shall not
have dominion over you, for you are
not under law but under grace.

From Slaves of Sin to Slaves of God

15What then? Shall we sin because we
are not under law but under grace? Cer-
tainly not! 16Do you not know that to
whom you present yourselves slaves
to obey, you are that one's slaves whom
you obey, whether of sin *leading* to
death, or of obedience *leading* to righ-
teousness? 17But God be thanked that
though you were slaves of sin, yet you
obeyed from the heart that form of doc-
trine to which you were delivered. 18And
having been set free from sin, you be-
came slaves of righteousness. 19I speak
in human *terms* because of the weakness
of your flesh. For just as you presented
your members *as* slaves of uncleanness,
and of lawlessness *leading* to *more* law-
lessness, so now present your members
as slaves *of* righteousness for holiness.
20For when you were slaves of sin, you
were free in regard to righteousness.
21What fruit did you have then in the
things of which you are now ashamed?
For the end of those things *is* death.
22But now having been set free from
sin, and having become slaves of God,
you have your fruit to holiness, and the
end, everlasting life. 23For the wages of
sin *is* death, but the gift of God *is* eternal
life in Christ Jesus our Lord.

Freed from the Law

7 Or do you not know, brethren (for I
speak to those who know the law),
that the law has dominion over a man
as long as he lives? 2For the woman who
has a husband is bound by the law to
her husband as long as he lives. But if
the husband dies, she is released from
the law of *her* husband. 3So then if, while
her husband lives, she marries another
man, she will be called an adulteress;
but if her husband dies, she is free from
that law, so that she is no adulteress,
though she has married another man.
4Therefore, my brethren, you also have
become dead to the law through the
body of Christ, that you may be mar-
ried to another—to Him who was raised
from the dead, that we should bear fruit
to God. 5For when we were in the flesh,
the sinful passions which were aroused
by the law were at work in our members
to bear fruit to death. 6But now we have
been delivered from the law, having
died to what we were held by, so that
we should serve in the newness of the
Spirit and not *in* the oldness of the letter.

Sin's Advantage in the Law

7What shall we say then? *Is* the law sin?
Certainly not! On the contrary, I would
not have known sin except through
the law. For I would not have known
covetousness unless the law had said,
"You shall not covet."[a] 8But sin, taking
opportunity by the commandment,
produced in me all *manner of evil* desire.
For apart from the law sin *was* dead. 9I

7:7 [a] Exodus 20:17; Deuteronomy 5:21

was alive once without the law, but when
the commandment came, sin revived
and I died. 10And the commandment,
which *was* to *bring* life, I found to *bring*
death. 11For sin, taking occasion by the
commandment, deceived me, and by it
killed *me.* 12Therefore the law *is* holy,
and the commandment holy and just
and good.

Law Cannot Save from Sin

13Has then what is good become death
to me? Certainly not! But sin, that it
might appear sin, was producing death
in me through what is good, so that sin
through the commandment might be-
come exceedingly sinful. 14For we know
that the law is spiritual, but I am carnal,
sold under sin. 15For what I am doing, I
do not understand. For what I will to do,
that I do not practice; but what I hate,
that I do. 16If, then, I do what I will not
to do, I agree with the law that *it is* good.
17But now, *it is* no longer I who do it, but
sin that dwells in me. 18For I know that
in me (that is, in my flesh) nothing good
dwells; for to will is present with me,
but *how* to perform what is good I do
not find. 19For the good that I will *to do,*
I do not do; but the evil I will not *to
do,* that I practice. 20Now if I do what
I will not *to do,* it is no longer I who do
it, but sin that dwells in me.

21I find then a law, that evil is present
with me, the one who wills to do good.
22For I delight in the law of God ac-
cording to the inward man. 23But I see
another law in my members, warring
against the law of my mind, and bring-
ing me into captivity to the law of sin
which is in my members. 24O wretched
man that I am! Who will deliver me
from this body of death? 25I thank
God—through Jesus Christ our Lord!

So then, with the mind I myself serve
the law of God, but with the flesh the
law of sin.

Free from Indwelling Sin

8 *There is* therefore now no condem-
nation to those who are in Christ
Jesus,[a] who do not walk according to
the flesh, but according to the Spirit.
2For the law of the Spirit of life in Christ
Jesus has made me free from the law of
sin and death. 3For what the law could
not do in that it was weak through the
flesh, God *did* by sending His own Son in
the likeness of sinful flesh, on account of
sin: He condemned sin in the flesh, 4that
the righteous requirement of the law
might be fulfilled in us who do not walk
according to the flesh but according to
the Spirit. 5For those who live according
to the flesh set their minds on the things
of the flesh, but those *who live* according
to the Spirit, the things of the Spirit. 6For
to be carnally minded *is* death, but to be
spiritually minded *is* life and peace. 7Be-
cause the carnal mind *is* enmity against
God; for it is not subject to the law of
God, nor indeed can be. 8So then, those
who are in the flesh cannot please God.

9But you are not in the flesh but in the
Spirit, if indeed the Spirit of God dwells
in you. Now if anyone does not have the
Spirit of Christ, he is not His. 10And if
Christ *is* in you, the body *is* dead because
of sin, but the Spirit *is* life because of
righteousness. 11But if the Spirit of Him
who raised Jesus from the dead dwells in
you, He who raised Christ from the dead
will also give life to your mortal bodies
through His Spirit who dwells in you.

Sonship Through the Spirit

12Therefore, brethren, we are debtors—
not to the flesh, to live according to the
flesh. 13For if you live according to the
flesh you will die; but if by the Spirit you
put to death the deeds of the body, you
will live. 14For as many as are led by
the Spirit of God, these are sons of God.
15For you did not receive the spirit of
bondage again to fear, but you received
the Spirit of adoption by whom we cry
out, "Abba, Father." 16The Spirit Himself
bears witness with our spirit that we are
children of God, 17and if children, then
heirs—heirs of God and joint heirs with
Christ, if indeed we suffer with *Him,* that
we may also be glorified together.

From Suffering to Glory

18For I consider that the sufferings of
this present time are not worthy *to be*

8:1 [a] NU-Text omits the rest of this verse.

compared with the glory which shall be revealed in us. 19For the earnest expectation of the creation eagerly waits for the revealing of the sons of God. 20For the creation was subjected to futility, not willingly, but because of Him who subjected *it* in hope; 21because the creation itself also will be delivered from the bondage of corruption into the glorious liberty of the children of God. 22For we know that the whole creation groans and labors with birth pangs together until now. 23Not only *that,* but we also who have the firstfruits of the Spirit, even we ourselves groan within ourselves, eagerly waiting for the adoption, the redemption of our body. 24For we were saved in this hope, but hope that is seen is not hope; for why does one still hope for what he sees? 25But if we hope for what we do not see, we eagerly wait for *it* with perseverance.

26Likewise the Spirit also helps in our weaknesses. For we do not know what we should pray for as we ought, but the Spirit Himself makes intercession for us[a] with groanings which cannot be uttered. 27Now He who searches the hearts knows what the mind of the Spirit *is,* because He makes intercession for the saints according to *the will of* God.

28And we know that all things work together for good to those who love God, to those who are the called according to *His* purpose. 29For whom He foreknew, He also predestined *to be* conformed to the image of His Son, that He might be the firstborn among many brethren. 30Moreover whom He predestined, these He also called; whom He called, these He also justified; and whom He justified, these He also glorified.

God's Everlasting Love

31What then shall we say to these things? If God *is* for us, who *can be* against us? 32He who did not spare His own Son, but delivered Him up for us all, how shall He not with Him also freely give us all things? 33Who shall bring a charge against God's elect? *It is* God who justifies. 34Who *is* he who condemns? *It is* Christ who died, and furthermore is also risen, who is even at the right hand of God, who also makes intercession for us. 35Who shall separate us from the love of Christ? *Shall* tribulation, or distress, or persecution, or famine, or nakedness, or peril, or sword? 36As it is written:

> "For Your sake we are killed all day long;
> We are accounted as sheep for the slaughter."[a]

37Yet in all these things we are more than conquerors through Him who loved us. 38For I am persuaded that neither death nor life, nor angels nor principalities nor powers, nor things present nor things to come, 39nor height nor depth, nor any other created thing, shall be able to separate us from the love of God which is in Christ Jesus our Lord.

Israel's Rejection of Christ

9 I tell the truth in Christ, I am not lying, my conscience also bearing me witness in the Holy Spirit, 2that I have great sorrow and continual grief in my heart. 3For I could wish that I myself were accursed from Christ for my brethren, my countrymen[a] according to the flesh, 4who are Israelites, to whom *pertain* the adoption, the glory, the covenants, the giving of the law, the service *of God,* and the promises; 5of whom *are* the fathers and from whom, according to the flesh, Christ *came,* who is over all, *the* eternally blessed God. Amen.

Israel's Rejection and God's Purpose

6But it is not that the word of God has taken no effect. For they *are* not all Israel who *are* of Israel, 7nor *are they* all children because they are the seed of Abraham; but, "In Isaac your seed shall be called."[a] 8That is, those who *are* the children of the flesh, these *are* not the children of God; but the children of the promise are counted as the seed. 9For this *is* the word of promise: "At this time I will come and Sarah shall have a son."[a]

8:26 [a] NU-Text omits *for us.* **8:36** [a] Psalm 44:22 **9:3** [a] Or *relatives* **9:7** [a] Genesis 21:12
9:9 [a] Genesis 18:10, 14

10And not only *this,* but when Rebecca
also had conceived by one man, *even*
by our father Isaac 11(for *the children*
not yet being born, nor having done
any good or evil, that the purpose of
God according to election might stand,
not of works but of Him who calls), 12it
was said to her, "The older shall serve
the younger."[a] 13As it is written, "Jacob
I have loved, but Esau I have hated."[a]

Israel's Rejection and God's Justice

14What shall we say then? *Is there* un-
righteousness with God? Certainly not!
15For He says to Moses, "I will have mer-
cy on whomever I will have mercy, and
I will have compassion on whomever I
will have compassion."[a] 16So then *it is*
not of him who wills, nor of him who
runs, but of God who shows mercy. 17For
the Scripture says to the Pharaoh, "For
this very purpose I have raised you up,
that I may show My power in you, and
that My name may be declared in all
the earth."[a] 18Therefore He has mercy
on whom He wills, and whom He wills
He hardens.
19You will say to me then, "Why does
He still find fault? For who has resisted
His will?" 20But indeed, O man, who
are you to reply against God? Will the
thing formed say to him who formed
it, "Why have you made me like this?"
21Does not the potter have power over
the clay, from the same lump to make
one vessel for honor and another for
dishonor?
22*What* if God, wanting to show *His*
wrath and to make His power known,
endured with much longsuffering the
vessels of wrath prepared for destruc-
tion, 23and that He might make known
the riches of His glory on the vessels
of mercy, which He had prepared be-
forehand for glory, 24even us whom He
called, not of the Jews only, but also of
the Gentiles?
25As He says also in Hosea:

"I will call them My people, who
were not My people,
And her beloved, who was not
beloved."[a]
26 "And it shall come to pass in the
place where it was said to
them,
'*You are* not My people,'
There they shall be called sons of
the living God."[a]

27Isaiah also cries out concerning Is-
rael:[a]

"Though the number of the children
of Israel be as the sand of
the sea,
The remnant will be saved.
28 For He will finish the work and cut
it short in righteousness,
Because the LORD will make a
short work upon the earth."[a]

29And as Isaiah said before:

"Unless the LORD of Sabaoth[a] had
left us a seed,
We would have become like
Sodom,
And we would have been made
like Gomorrah."[b]

Present Condition of Israel

30What shall we say then? That Gen-
tiles, who did not pursue righteousness,
have attained to righteousness, even
the righteousness of faith; 31but Israel,
pursuing the law of righteousness, has
not attained to the law of righteous-
ness.[a] 32Why? Because *they did* not *seek*
it by faith, but as it were, by the works
of the law.[a] For they stumbled at that
stumbling stone. 33As it is written:

"Behold, I lay in Zion a stumbling
stone and rock of offense,
And whoever believes on Him will
not be put to shame."[a]

Israel Needs the Gospel

10 Brethren, my heart's desire and
prayer to God for Israel[a] is that
they may be saved. 2For I bear them

9:12 [a] Genesis 25:23 9:13 [a] Malachi 1:2, 3 9:15 [a] Exodus 33:19 9:17 [a] Exodus 9:16 9:25 [a] Hosea 2:23 9:26 [a] Hosea 1:10 9:27 [a] Isaiah 10:22, 23 9:28 [a] NU-Text reads *For the LORD will finish the work and cut it short upon the earth.* 9:29 [a] Literally, in Hebrew, *Hosts* [b] Isaiah 1:9 9:31 [a] NU-Text omits *of righteousness.* 9:32 [a] NU-Text reads *by works.* 9:33 [a] Isaiah 8:14; 28:16 10:1 [a] NU-Text reads *them.*

witness that they have a zeal for God,
but not according to knowledge. 3For
they being ignorant of God's righteous-
ness, and seeking to establish their own
righteousness, have not submitted to
the righteousness of God. 4For Christ
is the end of the law for righteousness
to everyone who believes.
5For Moses writes about the righteous-
ness which is of the law, "The man who
does those things shall live by them."[a]
6But the righteousness of faith speaks in
this way, "Do not say in your heart, 'Who
will ascend into heaven?' "[a] (that is, to
bring Christ down *from above*) 7or, " 'Who
will descend into the abyss?' "[a] (that is,
to bring Christ up from the dead). 8But
what does it say? "The word is near you,
in your mouth and in your heart"[a] (that
is, the word of faith which we preach):
9that if you confess with your mouth the
Lord Jesus and believe in your heart that
God has raised Him from the dead, you
will be saved. 10For with the heart one
believes unto righteousness, and with
the mouth confession is made unto sal-
vation. 11For the Scripture says, "Who-
ever believes on Him will not be put to
shame."[a] 12For there is no distinction
between Jew and Greek, for the same
Lord over all is rich to all who call upon
Him. 13For "whoever calls on the name
of the LORD shall be saved."[a]

Israel Rejects the Gospel

14How then shall they call on Him in
whom they have not believed? And how
shall they believe in Him of whom they
have not heard? And how shall they
hear without a preacher? 15And how
shall they preach unless they are sent?
As it is written:

"How beautiful are the feet of those
who preach the gospel of
peace,[a]
Who bring glad tidings of good
things!"[b]

16But they have not all obeyed the gos-
pel. For Isaiah says, "LORD, who has
believed our report?"[a] 17So then faith
comes by hearing, and hearing by the
word of God.
18But I say, have they not heard? Yes
indeed:

"Their sound has gone out to all the
earth,
And their words to the ends of the
world."[a]

19But I say, did Israel not know? First
Moses says:

"I will provoke you to jealousy by
those who are not a nation,
I will move you to anger by a
foolish nation."[a]

20But Isaiah is very bold and says:

"I was found by those who did not
seek Me;
I was made manifest to those who
did not ask for Me."[a]

21But to Israel he says:

"All day long I have stretched out
My hands
To a disobedient and contrary
people."[a]

Israel's Rejection Not Total

11 I say then, has God cast away
His people? Certainly not! For
I also am an Israelite, of the seed of
Abraham, *of* the tribe of Benjamin. 2God
has not cast away His people whom He
foreknew. Or do you not know what the
Scripture says of Elijah, how he pleads
with God against Israel, saying, 3"LORD,
they have killed Your prophets and torn
down Your altars, and I alone am left,
and they seek my life"?[a] 4But what does
the divine response say to him? "I have
reserved for Myself seven thousand
men who have not bowed the knee to
Baal."[a] 5Even so then, at this present
time there is a remnant according to
the election of grace. 6And if by grace,

10:5 [a] Leviticus 18:5 **10:6** [a] Deuteronomy 30:12 **10:7** [a] Deuteronomy 30:13 **10:8** [a] Deuteronomy 30:14 **10:11** [a] Isaiah 28:16 **10:13** [a] Joel 2:32 **10:15** [a] NU-Text omits *preach the gospel of peace, Who.* [b] Isaiah 52:7; Nahum 1:15 **10:16** [a] Isaiah 53:1 **10:18** [a] Psalm 19:4 **10:19** [a] Deuteronomy 32:21 **10:20** [a] Isaiah 65:1 **10:21** [a] Isaiah 65:2 **11:3** [a] 1 Kings 19:10, 14 **11:4** [a] 1 Kings 19:18

then *it is* no longer of works; otherwise
grace is no longer grace.[a] But if *it is* of
works, it is no longer grace; otherwise
work is no longer work.
7What then? Israel has not obtained
what it seeks; but the elect have ob-
tained it, and the rest were blinded.
8Just as it is written:

"God has given them a spirit of
stupor,
Eyes that they should not see
And ears that they should not
hear,
To this very day."[a]

9And David says:

"Let their table become a snare and
a trap,
A stumbling block and a
recompense to them.
10 Let their eyes be darkened, so that
they do not see,
And bow down their back
always."[a]

Israel's Rejection Not Final

11I say then, have they stumbled that
they should fall? Certainly not! But
through their fall, to provoke them to
jealousy, salvation *has come* to the Gen-
tiles. 12Now if their fall *is* riches for the
world, and their failure riches for the
Gentiles, how much more their fullness!
13For I speak to you Gentiles; inas-
much as I am an apostle to the Gen-
tiles, I magnify my ministry, 14if by
any means I may provoke to jealousy
those who are my flesh and save some
of them. 15For if their being cast away
is the reconciling of the world, what
will their acceptance *be* but life from
the dead?
16For if the firstfruit *is* holy, the lump
is also *holy;* and if the root *is* holy, so
are the branches. 17And if some of the
branches were broken off, and you,
being a wild olive tree, were grafted in
among them, and with them became a
partaker of the root and fatness of the
olive tree, 18do not boast against the
branches. But if you do boast, *remember*
that you do not support the root, but the
root *supports* you.
19You will say then, "Branches were
broken off that I might be grafted in."
20Well *said.* Because of unbelief they
were broken off, and you stand by faith.
Do not be haughty, but fear. 21For if God
did not spare the natural branches, He
may not spare you either. 22Therefore
consider the goodness and severity of
God: on those who fell, severity; but
toward you, goodness,[a] if you continue
in *His* goodness. Otherwise you also will
be cut off. 23And they also, if they do
not continue in unbelief, will be graft-
ed in, for God is able to graft them in
again. 24For if you were cut out of the
olive tree which is wild by nature, and
were grafted contrary to nature into a
cultivated olive tree, how much more
will these, who *are* natural *branches,* be
grafted into their own olive tree?
25For I do not desire, brethren, that
you should be ignorant of this mys-
tery, lest you should be wise in your
own opinion, that blindness in part has
happened to Israel until the fullness of
the Gentiles has come in. 26And so all
Israel will be saved,[a] as it is written:

"The Deliverer will come out of Zion,
And He will turn away
ungodliness from Jacob;
27 For this *is* My covenant with them,
When I take away their sins."[a]

28Concerning the gospel *they are* ene-
mies for your sake, but concerning the
election *they are* beloved for the sake
of the fathers. 29For the gifts and the
calling of God *are* irrevocable. 30For as
you were once disobedient to God, yet
have now obtained mercy through their
disobedience, 31even so these also have
now been disobedient, that through the
mercy shown you they also may obtain
mercy. 32For God has committed them
all to disobedience, that He might have
mercy on all.
33Oh, the depth of the riches both of
the wisdom and knowledge of God! How
unsearchable *are* His judgments and
His ways past finding out!

11:6 [a] NU-Text omits the rest of this verse. **11:8** [a] Deuteronomy 29:4; Isaiah 29:10 **11:10** [a] Psalm 69:22, 23 **11:22** [a] NU-Text adds *of God.* **11:26** [a] Or *delivered* **11:27** [a] Isaiah 59:20, 21

34 "For who has known the mind of the
LORD?
Or who has become His
counselor?"[a]
35 "Or who has first given to Him
And it shall be repaid to him?"[a]

36For of Him and through Him and
to Him *are* all things, to whom *be* glory
forever. Amen.

Living Sacrifices to God

12 I beseech you therefore, brethren, by the mercies of God, that
you present your bodies a living sac-
rifice, holy, acceptable to God, *which*
is your reasonable service. 2And do
not be conformed to this world, but be
transformed by the renewing of your
mind, that you may prove what *is* that
good and acceptable and perfect will
of God.

Serve God with Spiritual Gifts

3For I say, through the grace given to
me, to everyone who is among you, not
to think *of himself* more highly than he
ought to think, but to think soberly, as
God has dealt to each one a measure of
faith. 4For as we have many members
in one body, but all the members do
not have the same function, 5so we,
being many, are one body in Christ, and
individually members of one another.
6Having then gifts differing according
to the grace that is given to us, *let us*
use them: if prophecy, *let us prophesy*
in proportion to our faith; 7or ministry,
let us use it in *our* ministering; he who
teaches, in teaching; 8he who exhorts,
in exhortation; he who gives, with lib-
erality; he who leads, with diligence; he
who shows mercy, with cheerfulness.

Behave Like a Christian

9*Let* love *be* without hypocrisy. Abhor
what is evil. Cling to what is good. 10*Be*
kindly affectionate to one another with
brotherly love, in honor giving prefer-
ence to one another; 11not lagging in
diligence, fervent in spirit, serving the
Lord; 12rejoicing in hope, patient in
tribulation, continuing steadfastly in
prayer; 13distributing to the needs of
the saints, given to hospitality.
14Bless those who persecute you; bless
and do not curse. 15Rejoice with those
who rejoice, and weep with those who
weep. 16Be of the same mind toward one
another. Do not set your mind on high
things, but associate with the humble.
Do not be wise in your own opinion.
17Repay no one evil for evil. Have
regard for good things in the sight of
all men. 18If it is possible, as much as
depends on you, live peaceably with
all men. 19Beloved, do not avenge your-
selves, but *rather* give place to wrath;
for it is written, "Vengeance *is* Mine, I
will repay,"[a] says the Lord. 20Therefore

"If your enemy is hungry,
feed him;
If he is thirsty, give him a drink;
For in so doing you will heap
coals of fire on his head."[a]

21Do not be overcome by evil, but over-
come evil with good.

Submit to Government

13 Let every soul be subject to the governing authorities. For there
is no authority except from God, and
the authorities that exist are appointed
by God. 2Therefore whoever resists the
authority resists the ordinance of God,
and those who resist will bring judg-
ment on themselves. 3For rulers are not
a terror to good works, but to evil. Do
you want to be unafraid of the author-
ity? Do what is good, and you will have
praise from the same. 4For he is God's
minister to you for good. But if you do
evil, be afraid; for he does not bear the
sword in vain; for he is God's minister,
an avenger to *execute* wrath on him who
practices evil. 5Therefore *you* must be
subject, not only because of wrath but
also for conscience' sake. 6For because
of this you also pay taxes, for they are
God's ministers attending continually
to this very thing. 7Render therefore to
all their due: taxes to whom taxes *are*
due, customs to whom customs, fear
to whom fear, honor to whom honor.

11:34 [a] Isaiah 40:13; Jeremiah 23:18 **11:35** [a] Job 41:11 **12:19** [a] Deuteronomy 32:35
12:20 [a] Proverbs 25:21, 22

Love Your Neighbor

8Owe no one anything except to love one another, for he who loves another has fulfilled the law. 9For the commandments, "You shall not commit adultery," "You shall not murder," "You shall not steal," "You shall not bear false witness,"[a] "You shall not covet,"[b] and if *there is* any other commandment, are *all* summed up in this saying, namely, "You shall love your neighbor as yourself."[c] 10Love does no harm to a neighbor; therefore love *is* the fulfillment of the law.

Put on Christ

11And *do* this, knowing the time, that now *it is* high time to awake out of sleep; for now our salvation *is* nearer than when we *first* believed. 12The night is far spent, the day is at hand. Therefore let us cast off the works of darkness, and let us put on the armor of light. 13Let us walk properly, as in the day, not in revelry and drunkenness, not in lewdness and lust, not in strife and envy. 14But put on the Lord Jesus Christ, and make no provision for the flesh, to *fulfill its* lusts.

The Law of Liberty

14 Receive one who is weak in the faith, *but* not to disputes over doubtful things. 2For one believes he may eat all things, but he who is weak eats *only* vegetables. 3Let not him who eats despise him who does not eat, and let not him who does not eat judge him who eats; for God has received him. 4Who are you to judge another's servant? To his own master he stands or falls. Indeed, he will be made to stand, for God is able to make him stand.

5One person esteems *one* day above another; another esteems every day *alike.* Let each be fully convinced in his own mind. 6He who observes the day, observes *it* to the Lord;[a] and he who does not observe the day, to the Lord he does not observe *it.* He who eats, eats to the Lord, for he gives God thanks; and he who does not eat, to the Lord he does not eat, and gives God thanks. 7For none of us lives to himself, and no one dies to himself. 8For if we live, we live to the Lord; and if we die, we die to the Lord. Therefore, whether we live or die, we are the Lord's. 9For to this end Christ died and rose[a] and lived again, that He might be Lord of both the dead and the living. 10But why do you judge your brother? Or why do you show contempt for your brother? For we shall all stand before the judgment seat of Christ.[a] 11For it is written:

"*As* I live, says the LORD,
Every knee shall bow to Me,
And every tongue shall confess to
God."[a]

12So then each of us shall give account of himself to God. 13Therefore let us not judge one another anymore, but rather resolve this, not to put a stumbling block or a cause to fall in *our* brother's way.

The Law of Love

14I know and am convinced by the Lord Jesus that *there is* nothing unclean of itself; but to him who considers anything to be unclean, to him *it is* unclean. 15Yet if your brother is grieved because of *your* food, you are no longer walking in love. Do not destroy with your food the one for whom Christ died. 16Therefore do not let your good be spoken of as evil; 17for the kingdom of God is not eating and drinking, but righteousness and peace and joy in the Holy Spirit. 18For he who serves Christ in these things[a] *is* acceptable to God and approved by men.

19Therefore let us pursue the things *which make* for peace and the things by which one may edify another. 20Do not destroy the work of God for the sake of food. All things indeed *are* pure, but *it is* evil for the man who eats with offense. 21*It is* good neither to eat meat nor drink wine nor *do anything* by which your brother stumbles or is offended or is made weak.[a] 22Do you have faith?

13:9 [a] NU-Text omits *"You shall not bear false witness."* [b] Exodus 20:13–15, 17; Deuteronomy 5:17–19, 21 [c] Leviticus 19:18 **14:6** [a] NU-Text omits the rest of this sentence. **14:9** [a] NU-Text omits *and rose.* **14:10** [a] NU-Text reads *of God.* **14:11** [a] Isaiah 45:23 **14:18** [a] NU-Text reads *this.* **14:21** [a] NU-Text omits *or is offended or is made weak.*

Have[a] *it* to yourself before God. Happy
is he who does not condemn himself in
what he approves. 23But he who doubts
is condemned if he eats, because *he does*
not *eat* from faith; for whatever *is* not
from faith is sin.[a]

Bearing Others' Burdens

15 We then who are strong ought
to bear with the scruples of the
weak, and not to please ourselves. 2Let
each of us please *his* neighbor for *his*
good, leading to edification. 3For even
Christ did not please Himself; but as
it is written, "The reproaches of those
who reproached You fell on Me."[a] 4For
whatever things were written before
were written for our learning, that we
through the patience and comfort of
the Scriptures might have hope. 5Now
may the God of patience and comfort
grant you to be like-minded toward one
another, according to Christ Jesus, 6that
you may with one mind *and* one mouth
glorify the God and Father of our Lord
Jesus Christ.

Glorify God Together

7Therefore receive one another, just
as Christ also received us,[a] to the glory
of God. 8Now I say that Jesus Christ
has become a servant to the circum-
cision for the truth of God, to confirm
the promises *made* to the fathers, 9and
that the Gentiles might glorify God for
His mercy, as it is written:

"For this reason I will confess to You
among the Gentiles,
And sing to Your name."[a]

10And again he says:

"Rejoice, O Gentiles, with His
people!"[a]

11And again:

"Praise the LORD, all you
Gentiles!
Laud Him, all you peoples!"[a]

12And again, Isaiah says:

"There shall be a root of Jesse;
And He who shall rise to reign
over the Gentiles,
In Him the Gentiles shall hope."[a]

13Now may the God of hope fill you
with all joy and peace in believing, that
you may abound in hope by the power
of the Holy Spirit.

From Jerusalem to Illyricum

14Now I myself am confident con-
cerning you, my brethren, that you
also are full of goodness, filled with all
knowledge, able also to admonish one
another.[a] 15Nevertheless, brethren, I
have written more boldly to you on
some points, as reminding you, because
of the grace given to me by God, 16that
I might be a minister of Jesus Christ to
the Gentiles, ministering the gospel of
God, that the offering of the Gentiles
might be acceptable, sanctified by the
Holy Spirit. 17Therefore I have reason to
glory in Christ Jesus in the things *which
pertain* to God. 18For I will not dare to
speak of any of those things which
Christ has not accomplished through
me, in word and deed, to make the
Gentiles obedient— 19in mighty signs
and wonders, by the power of the Spirit
of God, so that from Jerusalem and
round about to Illyricum I have fully
preached the gospel of Christ. 20And
so I have made it my aim to preach the
gospel, not where Christ was named,
lest I should build on another man's
foundation, 21but as it is written:

"To whom He was not announced,
they shall see;
And those who have not heard
shall understand."[a]

Plan to Visit Rome

22For this reason I also have been
much hindered from coming to you.
23But now no longer having a place in
these parts, and having a great desire

14:22 [a] NU-Text reads *The faith which you have—have.* **14:23** [a] M-Text puts Romans 16:25–27 here. **15:3** [a] Psalm 69:9 **15:7** [a] NU-Text and M-Text read *you.* **15:9** [a] 2 Samuel 22:50; Psalm 18:49 **15:10** [a] Deuteronomy 32:43 **15:11** [a] Psalm 117:1 **15:12** [a] Isaiah 11:10 **15:14** [a] M-Text reads *others.* **15:21** [a] Isaiah 52:15

these many years to come to you,
24whenever I journey to Spain, I shall
come to you.[a] For I hope to see you on
my journey, and to be helped on my
way there by you, if first I may enjoy
your *company* for a while. 25But now I
am going to Jerusalem to minister to
the saints. 26For it pleased those from
Macedonia and Achaia to make a cer-
tain contribution for the poor among
the saints who are in Jerusalem. 27It
pleased them indeed, and they are
their debtors. For if the Gentiles have
been partakers of their spiritual things,
their duty is also to minister to them
in material things. 28Therefore, when
I have performed this and have sealed
to them this fruit, I shall go by way of
you to Spain. 29But I know that when I
come to you, I shall come in the fullness
of the blessing of the gospel[a] of Christ.
30Now I beg you, brethren, through the
Lord Jesus Christ, and through the love
of the Spirit, that you strive together
with me in prayers to God for me, 31that
I may be delivered from those in Judea
who do not believe, and that my service
for Jerusalem may be acceptable to
the saints, 32that I may come to you
with joy by the will of God, and may
be refreshed together with you. 33Now
the God of peace *be* with you all. Amen.

Sister Phoebe Commended

16 I commend to you Phoebe our
sister, who is a servant of the
church in Cenchrea, 2that you may
receive her in the Lord in a manner
worthy of the saints, and assist her
in whatever business she has need of
you; for indeed she has been a helper
of many and of myself also.

Greeting Roman Saints

3Greet Priscilla and Aquila, my fellow
workers in Christ Jesus, 4who risked
their own necks for my life, to whom
not only I give thanks, but also all the
churches of the Gentiles. 5Likewise *greet*
the church that is in their house.
Greet my beloved Epaenetus, who
is the firstfruits of Achaia[a] to Christ.
6Greet Mary, who labored much for
us. 7Greet Andronicus and Junia, my
countrymen and my fellow prisoners,
who are of note among the apostles,
who also were in Christ before me.
8Greet Amplias, my beloved in the Lord.
9Greet Urbanus, our fellow worker in
Christ, and Stachys, my beloved. 10Greet
Apelles, approved in Christ. Greet those
who are of the *household* of Aristobu-
lus. 11Greet Herodion, my countryman.[a]
Greet those who are of the *household* of
Narcissus who are in the Lord.
12Greet Tryphena and Tryphosa, who
have labored in the Lord. Greet the
beloved Persis, who labored much in
the Lord. 13Greet Rufus, chosen in the
Lord, and his mother and mine. 14Greet
Asyncritus, Phlegon, Hermas, Patrobas,
Hermes, and the brethren who are with
them. 15Greet Philologus and Julia, Ne-
reus and his sister, and Olympas, and
all the saints who are with them.
16Greet one another with a holy kiss.
The[a] churches of Christ greet you.

Avoid Divisive Persons

17Now I urge you, brethren, note those
who cause divisions and offenses, con-
trary to the doctrine which you learned,
and avoid them. 18For those who are
such do not serve our Lord Jesus[a] Christ,
but their own belly, and by smooth
words and flattering speech deceive
the hearts of the simple. 19For your
obedience has become known to all.
Therefore I am glad on your behalf; but
I want you to be wise in what is good,
and simple concerning evil. 20And the
God of peace will crush Satan under
your feet shortly.
The grace of our Lord Jesus Christ *be*
with you. Amen.

Greetings from Paul's Friends

21Timothy, my fellow worker, and Lu-
cius, Jason, and Sosipater, my country-
men, greet you.
22I, Tertius, who wrote *this* epistle,
greet you in the Lord.
23Gaius, my host and *the host* of the
whole church, greets you. Erastus, the

15:24 [a] NU-Text omits *I shall come to you* (and joins *Spain* with the next sentence). **15:29** [a] NU-Text omits *of the gospel.* **16:5** [a] NU-Text reads *Asia.* **16:11** [a] Or *relative* **16:16** [a] NU-Text reads *All the churches.* **16:18** [a] NU-Text and M-Text omit *Jesus.*

treasurer of the city, greets you, and
Quartus, a brother. 24The grace of our
Lord Jesus Christ *be* with you all. Amen.[a]

Benediction

25Now to Him who is able to establish
you according to my gospel and the
preaching of Jesus Christ, according
to the revelation of the mystery kept
secret since the world began 26but now
made manifest, and by the prophetic
Scriptures made known to all nations,
according to the commandment of the
everlasting God, for obedience to the
faith— 27to God, alone wise, *be* glory
through Jesus Christ forever. Amen.[a]

16:24 [a] NU-Text omits this verse. **16:27** [a] M-Text puts Romans 16:25–27 after Romans 14:23.

THE FIRST LETTER OF PAUL TO THE

CORINTHIANS

Corinth was an important city in Greece, but it was also a place of widespread sin and idolatry. Paul had shared the gospel in this city for about eighteen months and then left Apollos to continue the work there. Paul later heard that the church was struggling with several problems, so he wrote this letter to address those issues and answer some questions he had been asked. Paul addressed division in the church, lawsuits, immorality, misunderstandings and abuse of the Lord's Supper, and misused spiritual gifts. The Corinthian church was experiencing these problems because it was living like its surrounding community rather than living like Christ.

- **GENRE:** Epistle
- **AUTHOR:** Paul
- **TIME:** c. AD 55–56
- **PURPOSE:** To address some of the problems in the church in Corinth and give them instructions in how to live as followers of Jesus.

Greeting

1 Paul, called *to be* an apostle of Jesus
Christ through the will of God, and
Sosthenes *our* brother,

2To the church of God which is at Cor-
inth, to those who are sanctified in Christ
Jesus, called *to be* saints, with all who in
every place call on the name of Jesus
Christ our Lord, both theirs and ours:

3Grace to you and peace from God our
Father and the Lord Jesus Christ.

Spiritual Gifts at Corinth

4I thank my God always concerning
you for the grace of God which was giv-
en to you by Christ Jesus, 5that you were
enriched in everything by Him in all
utterance and all knowledge, 6even as
the testimony of Christ was confirmed
in you, 7so that you come short in no
gift, eagerly waiting for the revelation
of our Lord Jesus Christ, 8who will also
confirm you to the end, *that you may be*
blameless in the day of our Lord Jesus
Christ. 9God *is* faithful, by whom you
were called into the fellowship of His
Son, Jesus Christ our Lord.

Sectarianism Is Sin

10Now I plead with you, brethren, by
the name of our Lord Jesus Christ, that
you all speak the same thing, and *that*
there be no divisions among you, but
that you be perfectly joined together in
the same mind and in the same judg-
ment. 11For it has been declared to me
concerning you, my brethren, by those
of Chloe's *household,* that there are con-
tentions among you. 12Now I say this,
that each of you says, "I am of Paul," or
"I am of Apollos," or "I am of Cephas,"
or "I am of Christ." 13Is Christ divided?
Was Paul crucified for you? Or were you
baptized in the name of Paul?
14I thank God that I baptized none of
you except Crispus and Gaius, 15lest
anyone should say that I had baptized
in my own name. 16Yes, I also baptized
the household of Stephanas. Besides,
I do not know whether I baptized any
other. 17For Christ did not send me to
baptize, but to preach the gospel, not
with wisdom of words, lest the cross
of Christ should be made of no effect.

Christ the Power and Wisdom of God

18For the message of the cross is fool-
ishness to those who are perishing, but
to us who are being saved it is the power
of God. 19For it is written:

> "I will destroy the wisdom of the
> wise,

And bring to nothing the
understanding of the
prudent."[a]

20Where *is* the wise? Where *is* the
scribe? Where *is* the disputer of this age?
Has not God made foolish the wisdom of
this world? 21For since, in the wisdom of
God, the world through wisdom did not
know God, it pleased God through the
foolishness of the message preached
to save those who believe. 22For Jews
request a sign, and Greeks seek after
wisdom; 23but we preach Christ cru-
cified, to the Jews a stumbling block
and to the Greeks[a] foolishness, 24but
to those who are called, both Jews and
Greeks, Christ the power of God and the
wisdom of God. 25Because the foolish-
ness of God is wiser than men, and the
weakness of God is stronger than men.

Glory Only in the Lord

26For you see your calling, brethren,
that not many wise according to the
flesh, not many mighty, not many no-
ble, *are called.* 27But God has chosen
the foolish things of the world to put to
shame the wise, and God has chosen the
weak things of the world to put to shame
the things which are mighty; 28and the
base things of the world and the things
which are despised God has chosen,
and the things which are not, to bring
to nothing the things that are, 29that no
flesh should glory in His presence. 30But
of Him you are in Christ Jesus, who be-
came for us wisdom from God—and
righteousness and sanctification and
redemption— 31that, as it is written, "He
who glories, let him glory in the LORD."[a]

Christ Crucified

2 And I, brethren, when I came to
you, did not come with excellence
of speech or of wisdom declaring to you
the testimony[a] of God. 2For I determined
not to know anything among you except
Jesus Christ and Him crucified. 3I was
with you in weakness, in fear, and in
much trembling. 4And my speech and
my preaching *were* not with persua-
sive words of human[a] wisdom, but in
demonstration of the Spirit and of pow-
er, 5that your faith should not be in the
wisdom of men but in the power of God.

Spiritual Wisdom

6However, we speak wisdom among
those who are mature, yet not the wis-
dom of this age, nor of the rulers of this
age, who are coming to nothing. 7But we
speak the wisdom of God in a mystery,
the hidden *wisdom* which God ordained
before the ages for our glory, 8which
none of the rulers of this age knew; for
had they known, they would not have
crucified the Lord of glory.
9But as it is written:

"Eye has not seen, nor ear heard,
Nor have entered into the heart of
man
The things which God has
prepared for those who love
Him."[a]

10But God has revealed *them* to us
through His Spirit. For the Spirit search-
es all things, yes, the deep things of God.
11For what man knows the things of a
man except the spirit of the man which
is in him? Even so no one knows the
things of God except the Spirit of God.
12Now we have received, not the spirit
of the world, but the Spirit who is from
God, that we might know the things that
have been freely given to us by God.
13These things we also speak, not in
words which man's wisdom teaches but
which the Holy[a] Spirit teaches, com-
paring spiritual things with spiritual.
14But the natural man does not receive
the things of the Spirit of God, for they
are foolishness to him; nor can he know
them, because they are spiritually dis-
cerned. 15But he who is spiritual judges
all things, yet he himself is *rightly* judged
by no one. 16For "who has known the
mind of the LORD that he may instruct
Him?"[a] But we have the mind of Christ.

Sectarianism Is Carnal

3 And I, brethren, could not speak to
you as to spiritual *people* but as to
carnal, as to babes in Christ. 2I fed you

1:19 [a] Isaiah 29:14 1:23 [a] NU-Text reads *Gentiles.* 1:31 [a] Jeremiah 9:24 2:1 [a] NU-Text reads *mystery.*
2:4 [a] NU-Text omits *human.* 2:9 [a] Isaiah 64:4 2:13 [a] NU-Text omits *Holy.* 2:16 [a] Isaiah 40:13

with milk and not with solid food; for until now you were not able *to receive it,* and even now you are still not able; 3for you are still carnal. For where *there are* envy, strife, and divisions among you, are you not carnal and behaving like *mere* men? 4For when one says, "I am of Paul," and another, "I *am* of Apollos," are you not carnal?

Watering, Working, Warning

5Who then is Paul, and who *is* Apollos, but ministers through whom you believed, as the Lord gave to each one? 6I planted, Apollos watered, but God gave the increase. 7So then neither he who plants is anything, nor he who waters, but God who gives the increase. 8Now he who plants and he who waters are one, and each one will receive his own reward according to his own labor.

9For we are God's fellow workers; you are God's field, *you are* God's building. 10According to the grace of God which was given to me, as a wise master builder I have laid the foundation, and another builds on it. But let each one take heed how he builds on it. 11For no other foundation can anyone lay than that which is laid, which is Jesus Christ. 12Now if anyone builds on this foundation *with* gold, silver, precious stones, wood, hay, straw, 13each one's work will become clear; for the Day will declare it, because it will be revealed by fire; and the fire will test each one's work, of what sort it is. 14If anyone's work which he has built on *it* endures, he will receive a reward. 15If anyone's work is burned, he will suffer loss; but he himself will be saved, yet so as through fire.

16Do you not know that you are the temple of God and *that* the Spirit of God dwells in you? 17If anyone defiles the temple of God, God will destroy him. For the temple of God is holy, which *temple* you are.

Avoid Worldly Wisdom

18Let no one deceive himself. If anyone among you seems to be wise in this age, let him become a fool that he may become wise. 19For the wisdom of this world is foolishness with God. For it is written, "He catches the wise in their *own* craftiness";[a] 20and again, "The LORD knows the thoughts of the wise, that they are futile."[a] 21Therefore let no one boast in men. For all things are yours: 22whether Paul or Apollos or Cephas, or the world or life or death, or things present or things to come—all are yours. 23And you *are* Christ's, and Christ *is* God's.

Stewards of the Mysteries of God

4 Let a man so consider us, as servants of Christ and stewards of the mysteries of God. 2Moreover it is required in stewards that one be found faithful. 3But with me it is a very small thing that I should be judged by you or by a human court.[a] In fact, I do not even judge myself. 4For I know of nothing against myself, yet I am not justified by this; but He who judges me is the Lord. 5Therefore judge nothing before the time, until the Lord comes, who will both bring to light the hidden things of darkness and reveal the counsels of the hearts. Then each one's praise will come from God.

Fools for Christ's Sake

6Now these things, brethren, I have figuratively transferred to myself and Apollos for your sakes, that you may learn in us not to think beyond what is written, that none of you may be puffed up on behalf of one against the other. 7For who makes you differ *from another?* And what do you have that you did not receive? Now if you did indeed receive *it,* why do you boast as if you had not received *it?*

8You are already full! You are already rich! You have reigned as kings without us—and indeed I could wish you did reign, that we also might reign with you! 9For I think that God has displayed us, the apostles, last, as men condemned to death; for we have been made a spectacle to the world, both to angels and to men. 10We *are* fools for Christ's sake, but you *are* wise in Christ! We *are* weak, but you *are* strong! You *are* distinguished,

3:19 [a] Job 5:13 3:20 [a] Psalm 94:11 4:3 [a] Literally *day*

GOD SIN JESUS SALVATION LOVE

but we *are* dishonored! 11To the present hour we both hunger and thirst, and we are poorly clothed, and beaten, and homeless. 12And we labor, working with our own hands. Being reviled, we bless; being persecuted, we endure; 13being defamed, we entreat. We have been made as the filth of the world, the offscouring of all things until now.

Paul's Paternal Care

14I do not write these things to shame you, but as my beloved children I warn *you.* 15For though you might have ten thousand instructors in Christ, yet *you do* not *have* many fathers; for in Christ Jesus I have begotten you through the gospel. 16Therefore I urge you, imitate me. 17For this reason I have sent Timothy to you, who is my beloved and faithful son in the Lord, who will remind you of my ways in Christ, as I teach everywhere in every church.

18Now some are puffed up, as though I were not coming to you. 19But I will come to you shortly, if the Lord wills, and I will know, not the word of those who are puffed up, but the power. 20For the kingdom of God *is* not in word but in power. 21What do you want? Shall I come to you with a rod, or in love and a spirit of gentleness?

Immorality Defiles the Church

5 It is actually reported *that there is* sexual immorality among you, and such sexual immorality as is not even named[a] among the Gentiles—that a man has his father's wife! 2And you are puffed up, and have not rather mourned, that he who has done this deed might be taken away from among you. 3For I indeed, as absent in body but present in spirit, have already judged (as though I were present) him who has so done this deed. 4In the name of our Lord Jesus Christ, when you are gathered together, along with my spirit, with the power of our Lord Jesus Christ, 5deliver such a one to Satan for the destruction of the flesh, that his spirit may be saved in the day of the Lord Jesus.[a]

6Your glorying *is* not good. Do you not know that a little leaven leavens the whole lump? 7Therefore purge out the old leaven, that you may be a new lump, since you truly are unleavened. For indeed Christ, our Passover, was sacrificed for us.[a] 8Therefore let us keep the feast, not with old leaven, nor with the leaven of malice and wickedness, but with the unleavened *bread* of sincerity and truth.

Immorality Must Be Judged

9I wrote to you in my epistle not to keep company with sexually immoral people. 10Yet *I* certainly *did* not *mean* with the sexually immoral people of this world, or with the covetous, or extortioners, or idolaters, since then you would need to go out of the world. 11But now I have written to you not to keep company with anyone named a brother, who is sexually immoral, or covetous, or an idolater, or a reviler, or a drunkard, or an extortioner—not even to eat with such a person.

12For what *have* I *to do* with judging those also who are outside? Do you not judge those who are inside? 13But those who are outside God judges. Therefore "put away from yourselves the evil person."[a]

Do Not Sue the Brethren

6 Dare any of you, having a matter against another, go to law before the unrighteous, and not before the saints? 2Do you not know that the saints will judge the world? And if the world will be judged by you, are you unworthy to judge the smallest matters? 3Do you not know that we shall judge angels? How much more, things that pertain to this life? 4If then you have judgments concerning things pertaining to this life, do you appoint those who are least esteemed by the church to judge? 5I say this to your shame. Is it so, that there is not a wise man among you, not even one, who will be able to judge between his brethren? 6But brother goes to law against brother, and that before unbelievers!

7Now therefore, it is already an utter failure for you that you go to law

5:1 [a] NU-Text omits *named.* 5:5 [a] NU-Text omits *Jesus.* 5:7 [a] NU-Text omits *for us.*
5:13 [a] Deuteronomy 17:7; 19:19; 22:21, 24; 24:7

against one another. Why do you not
rather accept wrong? Why do you not
rather *let yourselves* be cheated? 8No,
you yourselves do wrong and cheat, and
you do these things *to your* brethren!
9Do you not know that the unrighteous
will not inherit the kingdom of God? Do
not be deceived. Neither fornicators, nor
idolaters, nor adulterers, nor homosex-
uals,[a] nor sodomites, 10nor thieves, nor
covetous, nor drunkards, nor revilers,
nor extortioners will inherit the king-
dom of God. 11And such were some of
you. But you were washed, but you were
sanctified, but you were justified in the
name of the Lord Jesus and by the Spirit
of our God.

Glorify God in Body and Spirit

12All things are lawful for me, but all
things are not helpful. All things are
lawful for me, but I will not be brought
under the power of any. 13Foods for the
stomach and the stomach for foods, but
God will destroy both it and them. Now
the body *is* not for sexual immorality
but for the Lord, and the Lord for the
body. 14And God both raised up the Lord
and will also raise us up by His power.
15Do you not know that your bodies
are members of Christ? Shall I then
take the members of Christ and make
them members of a harlot? Certainly
not! 16Or do you not know that he who is
joined to a harlot is one body *with her?*
For "the two," He says, "shall become
one flesh."[a] 17But he who is joined to
the Lord is one spirit *with Him.*
18Flee sexual immorality. Every sin
that a man does is outside the body, but
he who commits sexual immorality sins
against his own body. 19Or do you not
know that your body is the temple of
the Holy Spirit *who is* in you, whom you
have from God, and you are not your
own? 20For you were bought at a price;
therefore glorify God in your body[a] and
in your spirit, which are God's.

Principles of Marriage

7 Now concerning the things of which
you wrote to me:
It is good for a man not to touch a
woman. 2Nevertheless, because of sex-
ual immorality, let each man have his
own wife, and let each woman have her
own husband. 3Let the husband render
to his wife the affection due her, and
likewise also the wife to her husband.
4The wife does not have authority over
her own body, but the husband *does.*
And likewise the husband does not have
authority over his own body, but the wife
does. 5Do not deprive one another except
with consent for a time, that you may
give yourselves to fasting and prayer;
and come together again so that Satan
does not tempt you because of your lack
of self-control. 6But I say this as a con-
cession, not as a commandment. 7For I
wish that all men were even as I myself.
But each one has his own gift from God,
one in this manner and another in that.
8But I say to the unmarried and to
the widows: It is good for them if they
remain even as I am; 9but if they cannot
exercise self-control, let them marry.
For it is better to marry than to burn
with passion.

Keep Your Marriage Vows

10Now to the married I command, *yet*
not I but the Lord: A wife is not to depart
from *her* husband. 11But even if she does
depart, let her remain unmarried or be
reconciled to *her* husband. And a hus-
band is not to divorce *his* wife.
12But to the rest I, not the Lord, say:
If any brother has a wife who does not
believe, and she is willing to live with
him, let him not divorce her. 13And a
woman who has a husband who does
not believe, if he is willing to live with
her, let her not divorce him. 14For the
unbelieving husband is sanctified by
the wife, and the unbelieving wife is
sanctified by the husband; otherwise
your children would be unclean, but
now they are holy. 15But if the unbeliev-
er departs, let him depart; a brother or
a sister is not under bondage in such
cases. But God has called us to peace.
16For how do you know, O wife, whether
you will save *your* husband? Or how do
you know, O husband, whether you will
save *your* wife?

6:9 [a] That is, catamites **6:16** [a] Genesis 2:24 **6:20** [a] NU-Text ends the verse at *body.*

Live as You Are Called

17But as God has distributed to each one, as the Lord has called each one, so let him walk. And so I ordain in all the churches. 18Was anyone called while circumcised? Let him not become uncircumcised. Was anyone called while uncircumcised? Let him not be circumcised. 19Circumcision is nothing and uncircumcision is nothing, but keeping the commandments of God *is what matters.* 20Let each one remain in the same calling in which he was called. 21Were you called *while* a slave? Do not be concerned about it; but if you can be made free, rather use *it.* 22For he who is called in the Lord *while* a slave is the Lord's freedman. Likewise he who is called *while* free is Christ's slave. 23You were bought at a price; do not become slaves of men. 24Brethren, let each one remain with God in that *state* in which he was called.

To the Unmarried and Widows

25Now concerning virgins: I have no commandment from the Lord; yet I give judgment as one whom the Lord in His mercy has made trustworthy. 26I suppose therefore that this is good because of the present distress—that *it is* good for a man to remain as he is: 27Are you bound to a wife? Do not seek to be loosed. Are you loosed from a wife? Do not seek a wife. 28But even if you do marry, you have not sinned; and if a virgin marries, she has not sinned. Nevertheless such will have trouble in the flesh, but I would spare you.

29But this I say, brethren, the time *is* short, so that from now on even those who have wives should be as though they had none, 30those who weep as though they did not weep, those who rejoice as though they did not rejoice, those who buy as though they did not possess, 31and those who use this world as not misusing *it.* For the form of this world is passing away.

32But I want you to be without care. He who is unmarried cares for the things of the Lord—how he may please the Lord. 33But he who is married cares about the things of the world—how he may please *his* wife. 34There is[a] a difference between a wife and a virgin. The unmarried woman cares about the things of the Lord, that she may be holy both in body and in spirit. But she who is married cares about the things of the world—how she may please *her* husband. 35And this I say for your own profit, not that I may put a leash on you, but for what is proper, and that you may serve the Lord without distraction.

36But if any man thinks he is behaving improperly toward his virgin, if she is past the flower of youth, and thus it must be, let him do what he wishes. He does not sin; let them marry. 37Nevertheless he who stands steadfast in his heart, having no necessity, but has power over his own will, and has so determined in his heart that he will keep his virgin,[a] does well. 38So then he who gives *her*[a] in marriage does well, but he who does not give *her* in marriage does better.

39A wife is bound by law as long as her husband lives; but if her husband dies, she is at liberty to be married to whom she wishes, only in the Lord. 40But she is happier if she remains as she is, according to my judgment—and I think I also have the Spirit of God.

Be Sensitive to Conscience

8 Now concerning things offered to idols: We know that we all have knowledge. Knowledge puffs up, but love edifies. 2And if anyone thinks that he knows anything, he knows nothing yet as he ought to know. 3But if anyone loves God, this one is known by Him.

4Therefore concerning the eating of things offered to idols, we know that an idol *is* nothing in the world, and that *there is* no other God but one. 5For even if there are so-called gods, whether in heaven or on earth (as there are many gods and many lords), 6yet for us *there is* one God, the Father, of whom *are* all things, and we for Him; and one Lord Jesus Christ, through whom *are* all things, and through whom we *live.*

7However, *there is* not in everyone that knowledge; for some, with

7:34 [a] M-Text adds *also.* **7:37** [a] Or *virgin daughter* **7:38** [a] NU-Text reads *his own virgin.*

consciousness of the idol, until now eat *it* as a thing offered to an idol; and their conscience, being weak, is defiled. 8But food does not commend us to God; for neither if we eat are we the better, nor if we do not eat are we the worse.

9But beware lest somehow this liberty of yours become a stumbling block to those who are weak. 10For if anyone sees you who have knowledge eating in an idol's temple, will not the conscience of him who is weak be emboldened to eat those things offered to idols? 11And because of your knowledge shall the weak brother perish, for whom Christ died? 12But when you thus sin against the brethren, and wound their weak conscience, you sin against Christ. 13Therefore, if food makes my brother stumble, I will never again eat meat, lest I make my brother stumble.

A Pattern of Self-Denial

9 Am I not an apostle? Am I not free? Have I not seen Jesus Christ our Lord? Are you not my work in the Lord? 2If I am not an apostle to others, yet doubtless I am to you. For you are the seal of my apostleship in the Lord.

3My defense to those who examine me is this: 4Do we have no right to eat and drink? 5Do we have no right to take along a believing wife, as *do* also the other apostles, the brothers of the Lord, and Cephas? 6Or *is it* only Barnabas and I *who* have no right to refrain from working? 7Who ever goes to war at his own expense? Who plants a vineyard and does not eat of its fruit? Or who tends a flock and does not drink of the milk of the flock?

8Do I say these things as a *mere* man? Or does not the law say the same also? 9For it is written in the law of Moses, "You shall not muzzle an ox while it treads out the grain."[a] Is it oxen God is concerned about? 10Or does He say *it* altogether for our sakes? For our sakes, no doubt, *this* is written, that he who plows should plow in hope, and he who threshes in hope should be partaker of his hope. 11If we have sown spiritual things for you, *is it* a great thing if we reap your material things? 12If others are partakers of *this* right over you, *are* we not even more?

Nevertheless we have not used this right, but endure all things lest we hinder the gospel of Christ. 13Do you not know that those who minister the holy things eat *of the things* of the temple, and those who serve at the altar partake of *the offerings of* the altar? 14Even so the Lord has commanded that those who preach the gospel should live from the gospel.

15But I have used none of these things, nor have I written these things that it should be done so to me; for it *would be* better for me to die than that anyone should make my boasting void. 16For if I preach the gospel, I have nothing to boast of, for necessity is laid upon me; yes, woe is me if I do not preach the gospel! 17For if I do this willingly, I have a reward; but if against my will, I have been entrusted with a stewardship. 18What is my reward then? That when I preach the gospel, I may present the gospel of Christ[a] without charge, that I may not abuse my authority in the gospel.

Serving All Men

19For though I am free from all *men,* I have made myself a servant to all, that I might win the more; 20and to the Jews I became as a Jew, that I might win Jews; to those *who are* under the law, as under the law,[a] that I might win those *who are* under the law; 21to those *who are* without law, as without law (not being without law toward God,[a] but under law toward Christ[b]), that I might win those *who are* without law; 22to the weak I became as[a] weak, that I might win the weak. I have become all things to all *men,* that I might by all means save some. 23Now this I do for the gospel's sake, that I may be partaker of it with *you.*

Striving for a Crown

24Do you not know that those who run in a race all run, but one receives the prize? Run in such a way that you may obtain *it.* 25And everyone who

9:9 a Deuteronomy 25:4 **9:18** a NU-Text omits *of Christ.* **9:20** a NU-Text adds *though not being myself under the law.* **9:21** a NU-Text reads *God's law.* b NU-Text reads *Christ's law.* **9:22** a NU-Text omits *as.*

competes *for the prize* is temperate in all things. Now they *do it* to obtain a perishable crown, but we *for* an imperishable *crown*. 26Therefore I run thus: not with uncertainty. Thus I fight: not as *one who* beats the air. 27But I discipline my body and bring *it* into subjection, lest, when I have preached to others, I myself should become disqualified.

Old Testament Examples

10 Moreover, brethren, I do not want you to be unaware that all our fathers were under the cloud, all passed through the sea, 2all were baptized into Moses in the cloud and in the sea, 3all ate the same spiritual food, 4and all drank the same spiritual drink. For they drank of that spiritual Rock that followed them, and that Rock was Christ. 5But with most of them God was not well pleased, for *their bodies* were scattered in the wilderness.

6Now these things became our examples, to the intent that we should not lust after evil things as they also lusted. 7And do not become idolaters as *were* some of them. As it is written, "The people sat down to eat and drink, and rose up to play."[a] 8Nor let us commit sexual immorality, as some of them did, and in one day twenty-three thousand fell; 9nor let us tempt Christ, as some of them also tempted, and were destroyed by serpents; 10nor complain, as some of them also complained, and were destroyed by the destroyer. 11Now all[a] these things happened to them as examples, and they were written for our admonition, upon whom the ends of the ages have come.

12Therefore let him who thinks he stands take heed lest he fall. 13No temptation has overtaken you except such as is common to man; but God *is* faithful, who will not allow you to be tempted beyond what you are able, but with the temptation will also make the way of escape, that you may be able to bear *it*.

Flee from Idolatry

14Therefore, my beloved, flee from idolatry. 15I speak as to wise men; judge for yourselves what I say. 16The cup of blessing which we bless, is it not the communion of the blood of Christ? The bread which we break, is it not the communion of the body of Christ? 17For we, *though* many, are one bread *and* one body; for we all partake of that one bread.

18Observe Israel after the flesh: Are not those who eat of the sacrifices partakers of the altar? 19What am I saying then? That an idol is anything, or what is offered to idols is anything? 20Rather, that the things which the Gentiles sacrifice they sacrifice to demons and not to God, and I do not want you to have fellowship with demons. 21You cannot drink the cup of the Lord and the cup of demons; you cannot partake of the Lord's table and of the table of demons. 22Or do we provoke the Lord to jealousy? Are we stronger than He?

All to the Glory of God

23All things are lawful for me,[a] but not all things are helpful; all things are lawful for me,[b] but not all things edify. 24Let no one seek his own, but each one the other's *well-being*.

25Eat whatever is sold in the meat market, asking no questions for conscience' sake; 26for "the earth *is* the LORD's, and all its fullness."[a]

27If any of those who do not believe invites you *to dinner*, and you desire to go, eat whatever is set before you, asking no question for conscience' sake. 28But if anyone says to you, "This was offered to idols," do not eat it for the sake of the one who told you, and for conscience' sake;[a] for "the earth *is* the LORD's, and all its fullness."[b] 29"Conscience," I say, not your own, but that of the other. For why is my liberty judged by another *man's* conscience? 30But if I partake with thanks, why am I evil spoken of for *the food* over which I give thanks?

31Therefore, whether you eat or drink, or whatever you do, do all to the glory of God. 32Give no offense, either to the Jews or to the Greeks or to the church of God, 33just as I also please all *men* in all *things*, not seeking my own profit, but the *profit* of many, that they may be saved.

10:7 [a] Exodus 32:6 **10:11** [a] NU-Text omits *all*. **10:23** [a] NU-Text omits *for me*. [b] NU-Text omits *for me*. **10:26** [a] Psalm 24:1 **10:28** [a] NU-Text omits the rest of this verse. [b] Psalm 24:1

11 Imitate me, just as I also *imitate* Christ.

Head Coverings

2Now I praise you, brethren, that you remember me in all things and keep the traditions just as I delivered *them* to you. 3But I want you to know that the head of every man is Christ, the head of woman *is* man, and the head of Christ *is* God. 4Every man praying or prophesying, having *his* head covered, dishonors his head. 5But every woman who prays or prophesies with *her* head uncovered dishonors her head, for that is one and the same as if her head were shaved. 6For if a woman is not covered, let her also be shorn. But if it is shameful for a woman to be shorn or shaved, let her be covered. 7For a man indeed ought not to cover *his* head, since he is the image and glory of God; but woman is the glory of man. 8For man is not from woman, but woman from man. 9Nor was man created for the woman, but woman for the man. 10For this reason the woman ought to have *a symbol of* authority on *her* head, because of the angels. 11Nevertheless, neither *is* man independent of woman, nor woman independent of man, in the Lord. 12For as woman *came* from man, even so man also *comes* through woman; but all things are from God.

13Judge among yourselves. Is it proper for a woman to pray to God with her head uncovered? 14Does not even nature itself teach you that if a man has long hair, it is a dishonor to him? 15But if a woman has long hair, it is a glory to her; for *her* hair is given to her[a] for a covering. 16But if anyone seems to be contentious, we have no such custom, nor *do* the churches of God.

Conduct at the Lord's Supper

17Now in giving these instructions I do not praise *you,* since you come together not for the better but for the worse. 18For first of all, when you come together as a church, I hear that there are divisions among you, and in part I believe it. 19For there must also be factions among you, that those who are approved may be recognized among you. 20Therefore when you come together in one place, it is not to eat the Lord's Supper. 21For in eating, each one takes his own supper ahead of *others;* and one is hungry and another is drunk. 22What! Do you not have houses to eat and drink in? Or do you despise the church of God and shame those who have nothing? What shall I say to you? Shall I praise you in this? I do not praise *you.*

Institution of the Lord's Supper

23For I received from the Lord that which I also delivered to you: that the Lord Jesus on the *same* night in which He was betrayed took bread; 24and when He had given thanks, He broke *it* and said, "Take, eat;[a] this is My body which is broken[b] for you; do this in remembrance of Me." 25In the same manner *He* also *took* the cup after supper, saying, "This cup is the new covenant in My blood. This do, as often as you drink *it,* in remembrance of Me."

26For as often as you eat this bread and drink this cup, you proclaim the Lord's death till He comes.

Examine Yourself

27Therefore whoever eats this bread or drinks *this* cup of the Lord in an unworthy manner will be guilty of the body and blood[a] of the Lord. 28But let a man examine himself, and so let him eat of the bread and drink of the cup. 29For he who eats and drinks in an unworthy manner[a] eats and drinks judgment to himself, not discerning the Lord's[b] body. 30For this reason many *are* weak and sick among you, and many sleep. 31For if we would judge ourselves, we would not be judged. 32But when we are judged, we are chastened by the Lord, that we may not be condemned with the world.

33Therefore, my brethren, when you come together to eat, wait for one another. 34But if anyone is hungry, let him eat at home, lest you come together for judgment. And the rest I will set in order when I come.

11:15 [a] M-Text omits *to her.* 11:24 [a] NU-Text omits *Take, eat.* [b] NU-Text omits *broken.*
11:27 [a] NU-Text and M-Text read *the blood.* 11:29 [a] NU-Text omits *in an unworthy manner.*
[b] NU-Text omits *Lord's.*

Spiritual Gifts: Unity in Diversity

12 Now concerning spiritual *gifts,*
brethren, I do not want you to
be ignorant: 2You know that[a] you were
Gentiles, carried away to these dumb
idols, however you were led. 3There-
fore I make known to you that no one
speaking by the Spirit of God calls Jesus
accursed, and no one can say that Jesus
is Lord except by the Holy Spirit.

4There are diversities of gifts, but the
same Spirit. 5There are differences of
ministries, but the same Lord. 6And
there are diversities of activities, but
it is the same God who works all in all.
7But the manifestation of the Spirit is
given to each one for the profit *of all:*
8for to one is given the word of wisdom
through the Spirit, to another the word
of knowledge through the same Spirit,
9to another faith by the same Spirit, to
another gifts of healings by the same[a]
Spirit, 10to another the working of mir-
acles, to another prophecy, to another
discerning of spirits, to another *differ-
ent* kinds of tongues, to another the
interpretation of tongues. 11But one and
the same Spirit works all these things,
distributing to each one individually
as He wills.

Unity and Diversity in One Body

12For as the body is one and has many
members, but all the members of that
one body, being many, are one body, so
also *is* Christ. 13For by one Spirit we were
all baptized into one body—whether
Jews or Greeks, whether slaves or free—
and have all been made to drink into[a]
one Spirit. 14For in fact the body is not
one member but many.

15If the foot should say, "Because I am
not a hand, I am not of the body," is it
therefore not of the body? 16And if the
ear should say, "Because I am not an
eye, I am not of the body," is it therefore
not of the body? 17If the whole body *were*
an eye, where *would be* the hearing? If
the whole *were* hearing, where *would be*
the smelling? 18But now God has set the
members, each one of them, in the body
just as He pleased. 19And if they were all
one member, where *would* the body *be?*

20But now indeed *there are* many
members, yet one body. 21And the eye
cannot say to the hand, "I have no need
of you"; nor again the head to the feet,
"I have no need of you." 22No, much
rather, those members of the body
which seem to be weaker are neces-
sary. 23And those *members* of the body
which we think to be less honorable, on
these we bestow greater honor; and our
unpresentable *parts* have greater mod-
esty, 24but our presentable *parts* have
no need. But God composed the body,
having given greater honor to that *part*
which lacks it, 25that there should be no
schism in the body, but *that* the mem-
bers should have the same care for one
another. 26And if one member suffers,
all the members suffer with *it;* or if one
member is honored, all the members
rejoice with *it.*

27Now you are the body of Christ, and
members individually. 28And God has
appointed these in the church: first
apostles, second prophets, third teach-
ers, after that miracles, then gifts of
healings, helps, administrations, vari-
eties of tongues. 29*Are* all apostles? *Are*
all prophets? *Are* all teachers? *Are* all
workers of miracles? 30Do all have gifts
of healings? Do all speak with tongues?
Do all interpret? 31But earnestly desire
the best[a] gifts. And yet I show you a
more excellent way.

The Greatest Gift

13 Though I speak with the tongues
of men and of angels, but have
not love, I have become sounding brass
or a clanging cymbal. 2And though I
have *the gift of* prophecy, and under-
stand all mysteries and all knowledge,
and though I have all faith, so that I
could remove mountains, but have not
love, I am nothing. 3And though I be-
stow all my goods to feed *the poor,* and
though I give my body to be burned,[a]
but have not love, it profits me nothing.

4Love suffers long *and* is kind; love
does not envy; love does not parade
itself, is not puffed up; 5does not behave
rudely, does not seek its own, is not pro-
voked, thinks no evil; 6does not rejoice

12:2 [a] NU-Text and M-Text add *when.* 12:9 [a] NU-Text reads *one.* 12:13 [a] NU-Text omits *into.*
12:31 [a] NU-Text reads *greater.* 13:3 [a] NU-Text reads *so I may boast.*

in iniquity, but rejoices in the truth; 7bears all things, believes all things, hopes all things, endures all things.

8Love never fails. But whether *there are* prophecies, they will fail; whether *there are* tongues, they will cease; whether *there is* knowledge, it will vanish away. 9For we know in part and we prophesy in part. 10But when that which is perfect has come, then that which is in part will be done away.

11When I was a child, I spoke as a child, I understood as a child, I thought as a child; but when I became a man, I put away childish things. 12For now we see in a mirror, dimly, but then face to face. Now I know in part, but then I shall know just as I also am known.

13And now abide faith, hope, love, these three; but the greatest of these *is* love.

Prophecy and Tongues

14 Pursue love, and desire spiritual *gifts,* but especially that you may prophesy. 2For he who speaks in a tongue does not speak to men but to God, for no one understands *him;* however, in the spirit he speaks mysteries. 3But he who prophesies speaks edification and exhortation and comfort to men. 4He who speaks in a tongue edifies himself, but he who prophesies edifies the church. 5I wish you all spoke with tongues, but even more that you prophesied; for[a] he who prophesies *is* greater than he who speaks with tongues, unless indeed he interprets, that the church may receive edification.

Tongues Must Be Interpreted

6But now, brethren, if I come to you speaking with tongues, what shall I profit you unless I speak to you either by revelation, by knowledge, by prophesying, or by teaching? 7Even things without life, whether flute or harp, when they make a sound, unless they make a distinction in the sounds, how will it be known what is piped or played? 8For if the trumpet makes an uncertain sound, who will prepare for battle? 9So likewise you, unless you utter by the tongue words easy to understand, how will it be known what is spoken? For you will be speaking into the air. 10There are, it may be, so many kinds of languages in the world, and none of them *is* without significance. 11Therefore, if I do not know the meaning of the language, I shall be a foreigner to him who speaks, and he who speaks *will be* a foreigner to me. 12Even so you, since you are zealous for spiritual *gifts, let it be* for the edification of the church *that* you seek to excel.

13Therefore let him who speaks in a tongue pray that he may interpret. 14For if I pray in a tongue, my spirit prays, but my understanding is unfruitful. 15What is *the conclusion* then? I will pray with the spirit, and I will also pray with the understanding. I will sing with the spirit, and I will also sing with the understanding. 16Otherwise, if you bless with the spirit, how will he who occupies the place of the uninformed say "Amen" at your giving of thanks, since he does not understand what you say? 17For you indeed give thanks well, but the other is not edified.

18I thank my God I speak with tongues more than you all; 19yet in the church I would rather speak five words with my understanding, that I may teach others also, than ten thousand words in a tongue.

Tongues a Sign to Unbelievers

20Brethren, do not be children in understanding; however, in malice be babes, but in understanding be mature.

21In the law it is written:

> "With *men of* other tongues and
> other lips
> I will speak to this people;
> And yet, for all that, they will not
> hear Me,"[a]

says the Lord.

22Therefore tongues are for a sign, not to those who believe but to unbelievers; but prophesying is not for unbelievers but for those who believe. 23Therefore

14:5 [a] NU-Text reads *and.* 14:21 [a] Isaiah 28:11, 12

if the whole church comes together in
one place, and all speak with tongues,
and there come in *those who are* unin-
formed or unbelievers, will they not say
that you are out of your mind? 24But
if all prophesy, and an unbeliever or
an uninformed person comes in, he is
convinced by all, he is convicted by all.
25And thus[a] the secrets of his heart are
revealed; and so, falling down on *his*
face, he will worship God and report
that God is truly among you.

Order in Church Meetings

26How is it then, brethren? Whenever
you come together, each of you has a
psalm, has a teaching, has a tongue, has
a revelation, has an interpretation. Let
all things be done for edification. 27If
anyone speaks in a tongue, *let there be*
two or at the most three, *each* in turn,
and let one interpret. 28But if there is
no interpreter, let him keep silent in
church, and let him speak to himself
and to God. 29Let two or three prophets
speak, and let the others judge. 30But if
anything is revealed to another who sits
by, let the first keep silent. 31For you can
all prophesy one by one, that all may
learn and all may be encouraged. 32And
the spirits of the prophets are subject to
the prophets. 33For God is not *the author*
of confusion but of peace, as in all the
churches of the saints.

34Let your[a] women keep silent in the
churches, for they are not permitted to
speak; but *they are* to be submissive, as
the law also says. 35And if they want to
learn something, let them ask their own
husbands at home; for it is shameful for
women to speak in church.

36Or did the word of God come *origi-*
nally from you? Or *was it* you only that
it reached? 37If anyone thinks himself
to be a prophet or spiritual, let him ac-
knowledge that the things which I write
to you are the commandments of the
Lord. 38But if anyone is ignorant, let
him be ignorant.[a]

39Therefore, brethren, desire earnestly
to prophesy, and do not forbid to speak
with tongues. 40Let all things be done
decently and in order.

The Risen Christ, Faith's Reality

15 Moreover, brethren, I declare to
you the gospel which I preached
to you, which also you received and in
which you stand, 2by which also you
are saved, if you hold fast that word
which I preached to you—unless you
believed in vain.

3For I delivered to you first of all that
which I also received: that Christ died
for our sins according to the Scriptures,
4and that He was buried, and that He
rose again the third day according to
the Scriptures, 5and that He was seen
by Cephas, then by the twelve. 6After
that He was seen by over five hundred
brethren at once, of whom the greater
part remain to the present, but some
have fallen asleep. 7After that He was
seen by James, then by all the apostles.
8Then last of all He was seen by me also,
as by one born out of due time.

9For I am the least of the apostles, who
am not worthy to be called an apostle,
because I persecuted the church of God.
10But by the grace of God I am what I
am, and His grace toward me was not
in vain; but I labored more abundantly
than they all, yet not I, but the grace
of God *which was* with me. 11Therefore,
whether *it was* I or they, so we preach
and so you believed.

The Risen Christ, Our Hope

12Now if Christ is preached that He
has been raised from the dead, how do
some among you say that there is no
resurrection of the dead? 13But if there is
no resurrection of the dead, then Christ
is not risen. 14And if Christ is not risen,
then our preaching *is* empty and your
faith *is* also empty. 15Yes, and we are
found false witnesses of God, because
we have testified of God that He raised
up Christ, whom He did not raise up—if
in fact the dead do not rise. 16For if *the*
dead do not rise, then Christ is not risen.
17And if Christ is not risen, your faith *is*
futile; you are still in your sins! 18Then
also those who have fallen asleep in
Christ have perished. 19If in this life
only we have hope in Christ, we are of
all men the most pitiable.

14:25 [a] NU-Text omits *And thus.* **14:34** [a] NU-Text omits *your.* **14:38** [a] NU-Text reads *if anyone does not recognize this, he is not recognized.*

The Last Enemy Destroyed

20But now Christ is risen from the
dead, *and* has become the firstfruits
of those who have fallen asleep. 21For
since by man *came* death, by Man also
came the resurrection of the dead. 22For
as in Adam all die, even so in Christ all
shall be made alive. 23But each one
in his own order: Christ the firstfruits,
afterward those *who are* Christ's at His
coming. 24Then *comes* the end, when He
delivers the kingdom to God the Father,
when He puts an end to all rule and all
authority and power. 25For He must
reign till He has put all enemies under
His feet. 26The last enemy *that* will be
destroyed *is* death. 27For "He has put
all things under His feet."[a] But when
He says "all things are put under *Him*,"
it is evident that He who put all things
under Him is excepted. 28Now when all
things are made subject to Him, then
the Son Himself will also be subject to
Him who put all things under Him, that
God may be all in all.

Effects of Denying the Resurrection

29Otherwise, what will they do who are
baptized for the dead, if the dead do not
rise at all? Why then are they baptized
for the dead? 30And why do we stand
in jeopardy every hour? 31I affirm, by
the boasting in you which I have in
Christ Jesus our Lord, I die daily. 32If, in
the manner of men, I have fought with
beasts at Ephesus, what advantage *is it*
to me? If *the* dead do not rise, "Let us
eat and drink, for tomorrow we die!"[a]
33Do not be deceived: "Evil company
corrupts good habits." 34Awake to righ-
teousness, and do not sin; for some do
not have the knowledge of God. I speak
this to your shame.

A Glorious Body

35But someone will say, "How are the
dead raised up? And with what body
do they come?" 36Foolish one, what
you sow is not made alive unless it
dies. 37And what you sow, you do not
sow that body that shall be, but mere
grain—perhaps wheat or some other
grain. 38But God gives it a body as He
pleases, and to each seed its own body.
39All flesh *is* not the same flesh, but
there is one *kind of* flesh[a] of men, an-
other flesh of animals, another of fish,
and another of birds.
40*There are* also celestial bodies and
terrestrial bodies; but the glory of the
celestial *is* one, and the *glory* of the ter-
restrial *is* another. 41*There is* one glory
of the sun, another glory of the moon,
and another glory of the stars; for *one*
star differs from *another* star in glory.
42So also *is* the resurrection of the
dead. *The body* is sown in corruption,
it is raised in incorruption. 43It is sown
in dishonor, it is raised in glory. It is
sown in weakness, it is raised in power.
44It is sown a natural body, it is raised a
spiritual body. There is a natural body,
and there is a spiritual body. 45And so it
is written, "The first man Adam became
a living being."[a] The last Adam *became*
a life-giving spirit.
46However, the spiritual is not first, but
the natural, and afterward the spiritual.
47The first man *was* of the earth, *made*
of dust; the second Man *is* the Lord[a]
from heaven. 48As *was* the *man* of dust,
so also *are* those *who are made* of dust;
and as *is* the heavenly *Man*, so also *are*
those *who are* heavenly. 49And as we
have borne the image of the *man* of
dust, we shall also bear[a] the image of
the heavenly *Man*.

Our Final Victory

50Now this I say, brethren, that flesh
and blood cannot inherit the kingdom
of God; nor does corruption inherit in-
corruption. 51Behold, I tell you a mys-
tery: We shall not all sleep, but we shall
all be changed— 52in a moment, in the
twinkling of an eye, at the last trumpet.
For the trumpet will sound, and the
dead will be raised incorruptible, and
we shall be changed. 53For this cor-
ruptible must put on incorruption, and
this mortal *must* put on immortality.
54So when this corruptible has put on
incorruption, and this mortal has put
on immortality, then shall be brought to

15:27 [a] Psalm 8:6 15:32 [a] Isaiah 22:13 15:39 [a] NU-Text and M-Text omit *of flesh*. 15:45 [a] Genesis 2:7 15:47 [a] NU-Text omits *the Lord*. 15:49 [a] M-Text reads *let us also bear*.

pass the saying that is written: "Death
is swallowed up in victory."[a]

55 "O Death, where *is* your sting?[a]
O Hades, where *is* your victory?"[b]

56The sting of death *is* sin, and the
strength of sin *is* the law. 57But thanks *be*
to God, who gives us the victory through
our Lord Jesus Christ.
58Therefore, my beloved brethren, be
steadfast, immovable, always abound-
ing in the work of the Lord, knowing
that your labor is not in vain in the Lord.

Collection for the Saints

16 Now concerning the collection
for the saints, as I have given
orders to the churches of Galatia, so you
must do also: 2On the first *day* of the
week let each one of you lay something
aside, storing up as he may prosper, that
there be no collections when I come.
3And when I come, whomever you ap-
prove by *your* letters I will send to bear
your gift to Jerusalem. 4But if it is fitting
that I go also, they will go with me.

Personal Plans

5Now I will come to you when I pass
through Macedonia (for I am passing
through Macedonia). 6And it may be
that I will remain, or even spend the
winter with you, that you may send me
on my journey, wherever I go. 7For I do
not wish to see you now on the way; but
I hope to stay a while with you, if the
Lord permits.
8But I will tarry in Ephesus until Pen-
tecost. 9For a great and effective door
has opened to me, and *there are* many
adversaries.
10And if Timothy comes, see that he
may be with you without fear; for he
does the work of the Lord, as I also *do*.
11Therefore let no one despise him. But
send him on his journey in peace, that
he may come to me; for I am waiting
for him with the brethren.
12Now concerning *our* brother Apol-
los, I strongly urged him to come to
you with the brethren, but he was quite
unwilling to come at this time; however,
he will come when he has a convenient
time.

Final Exhortations

13Watch, stand fast in the faith, be
brave, be strong. 14Let all *that* you *do*
be done with love.
15I urge you, brethren—you know the
household of Stephanas, that it is the
firstfruits of Achaia, and *that* they have
devoted themselves to the ministry of
the saints— 16that you also submit to
such, and to everyone who works and
labors with *us*.
17I am glad about the coming of Steph-
anas, Fortunatus, and Achaicus, for
what was lacking on your part they
supplied. 18For they refreshed my spir-
it and yours. Therefore acknowledge
such men.

Greetings and a Solemn Farewell

19The churches of Asia greet you. Aq-
uila and Priscilla greet you heartily in
the Lord, with the church that is in their
house. 20All the brethren greet you.
Greet one another with a holy kiss.
21The salutation with my own hand—
Paul's.
22If anyone does not love the Lord
Jesus Christ, let him be accursed.[a]
O Lord, come![b]
23The grace of our Lord Jesus Christ
be with you. 24My love *be* with you all
in Christ Jesus. Amen.

15:54 [a] Isaiah 25:8 **15:55** [a] Hosea 13:14 [b] NU-Text reads *O Death, where is your victory? O Death, where is your sting?* **16:22** [a] Greek *anathema* [b] Aramaic *Maranatha*

THE SECOND LETTER OF PAUL TO THE

CORINTHIANS

Since Paul's first letter to the church in Corinth, false teachers had stirred the church against Paul. They claimed that Paul was arrogant, unimpressive, and unqualified to be an apostle of Jesus Christ. Paul then made a difficult visit to the church and followed it up by a letter that has since been lost. He then sent Titus to Corinth. When Titus returned, he reported that the church had a change of heart. Upon hearing this good news, Paul wrote another letter, what we know as 2 Corinthians, to express thanksgiving for the church but also to appeal to a small number of people in the church who still rejected his authority.

- **GENRE:** Epistle
- **AUTHOR:** Paul
- **TIME:** c. AD 55–56
- **PURPOSE:** To comfort the Corinthians, instruct them in church issues, and defend Paul's position as a leader and apostle.

Greeting

1 Paul, an apostle of Jesus Christ by
the will of God, and Timothy *our*
brother,

To the church of God which is at Cor-
inth, with all the saints who are in all
Achaia:

2Grace to you and peace from God our
Father and the Lord Jesus Christ.

Comfort in Suffering

3Blessed *be* the God and Father of our
Lord Jesus Christ, the Father of mercies
and God of all comfort, 4who comforts
us in all our tribulation, that we may be
able to comfort those who are in any
trouble, with the comfort with which
we ourselves are comforted by God.
5For as the sufferings of Christ abound
in us, so our consolation also abounds
through Christ. 6Now if we are afflicted,
it is for your consolation and salvation,
which is effective for enduring the same
sufferings which we also suffer. Or if we
are comforted, *it is* for your consolation
and salvation. 7And our hope for you
is steadfast, because we know that as
you are partakers of the sufferings, so
also *you will partake* of the consolation.

Delivered from Suffering

8For we do not want you to be ignorant,
brethren, of our trouble which came
to us in Asia: that we were burdened
beyond measure, above strength, so
that we despaired even of life. 9Yes, we
had the sentence of death in ourselves,
that we should not trust in ourselves
but in God who raises the dead, 10who
delivered us from so great a death, and
does[a] deliver us; in whom we trust that
He will still deliver *us,* 11you also helping
together in prayer for us, that thanks
may be given by many persons on our[a]
behalf for the gift *granted* to us through
many.

Paul's Sincerity

12For our boasting is this: the testimo-
ny of our conscience that we conducted
ourselves in the world in simplicity
and godly sincerity, not with fleshly
wisdom but by the grace of God, and
more abundantly toward you. 13For
we are not writing any other things to
you than what you read or understand.
Now I trust you will understand, even
to the end 14(as also you have under-
stood us in part), that we are your boast
as you also *are* ours, in the day of the
Lord Jesus.

1:10 [a] NU-Text reads *shall.* **1:11** [a] M-Text reads *your behalf.*

GOD SIN JESUS SALVATION LOVE

Sparing the Church

15And in this confidence I intended
to come to you before, that you might
have a second benefit— 16to pass by
way of you to Macedonia, to come
again from Macedonia to you, and be
helped by you on my way to Judea.
17Therefore, when I was planning this,
did I do it lightly? Or the things I plan,
do I plan according to the flesh, that
with me there should be Yes, Yes, and
No, No? 18But *as* God *is* faithful, our word
to you was not Yes and No. 19For the Son
of God, Jesus Christ, who was preached
among you by us—by me, Silvanus, and
Timothy—was not Yes and No, but in
Him was Yes. 20For all the promises of
God in Him *are* Yes, and in Him Amen,
to the glory of God through us. 21Now
He who establishes us with you in Christ
and has anointed us *is* God, 22who also
has sealed us and given us the Spirit in
our hearts as a guarantee.

23Moreover I call God as witness
against my soul, that to spare you I
came no more to Corinth. 24Not that
we have dominion over your faith, but
are fellow workers for your joy; for by
faith you stand.

2 But I determined this within myself,
that I would not come again to you
in sorrow. 2For if I make you sorrowful,
then who is he who makes me glad but
the one who is made sorrowful by me?

Forgive the Offender

3And I wrote this very thing to you,
lest, when I came, I should have sorrow
over those from whom I ought to have
joy, having confidence in you all that
my joy is *the joy* of you all. 4For out of
much affliction and anguish of heart
I wrote to you, with many tears, not
that you should be grieved, but that
you might know the love which I have
so abundantly for you.

5But if anyone has caused grief, he
has not grieved me, but all of you to
some extent—not to be too severe. 6This
punishment which *was inflicted* by the
majority *is* sufficient for such a man, 7so
that, on the contrary, you *ought* rather
to forgive and comfort *him*, lest perhaps
such a one be swallowed up with too
much sorrow. 8Therefore I urge you to
reaffirm *your* love to him. 9For to this
end I also wrote, that I might put you
to the test, whether you are obedient
in all things. 10Now whom you forgive
anything, I also *forgive*. For if indeed I
have forgiven anything, I have forgiven
that one[a] for your sakes in the presence
of Christ, 11lest Satan should take ad-
vantage of us; for we are not ignorant
of his devices.

Triumph in Christ

12Furthermore, when I came to Troas
to *preach* Christ's gospel, and a door was
opened to me by the Lord, 13I had no
rest in my spirit, because I did not find
Titus my brother; but taking my leave
of them, I departed for Macedonia.

14Now thanks *be* to God who always
leads us in triumph in Christ, and
through us diffuses the fragrance of His
knowledge in every place. 15For we are
to God the fragrance of Christ among
those who are being saved and among
those who are perishing. 16To the one
we are the aroma of death *leading* to
death, and to the other the aroma of
life *leading* to life. And who *is* sufficient
for these things? 17For we are not, as so
many,[a] peddling the word of God; but as
of sincerity, but as from God, we speak
in the sight of God in Christ.

Christ's Epistle

3 Do we begin again to commend
ourselves? Or do we need, as some
others, epistles of commendation to
you or *letters* of commendation from
you? 2You are our epistle written in
our hearts, known and read by all men;
3clearly you are an epistle of Christ,
ministered by us, written not with ink
but by the Spirit of the living God, not on
tablets of stone but on tablets of flesh,
that is, of the heart.

The Spirit, Not the Letter

4And we have such trust through
Christ toward God. 5Not that we are
sufficient of ourselves to think of any-
thing as *being* from ourselves, but our

2:10 [a] NU-Text reads *For indeed, what I have forgiven, if I have forgiven anything, I did it.*
2:17 [a] M-Text reads *the rest.*

sufficiency *is* from God, 6who also made
us sufficient as ministers of the new
covenant, not of the letter but of the
Spirit;[a] for the letter kills, but the Spirit
gives life.

Glory of the New Covenant

7But if the ministry of death, written
and engraved on stones, was glorious,
so that the children of Israel could not
look steadily at the face of Moses be-
cause of the glory of his countenance,
which *glory* was passing away, 8how
will the ministry of the Spirit not be
more glorious? 9For if the ministry of
condemnation *had* glory, the ministry
of righteousness exceeds much more
in glory. 10For even what was made
glorious had no glory in this respect,
because of the glory that excels. 11For
if what is passing away *was* glorious,
what remains *is* much more glorious.
12Therefore, since we have such hope,
we use great boldness of speech— 13un-
like Moses, *who* put a veil over his face
so that the children of Israel could not
look steadily at the end of what was
passing away. 14But their minds were
blinded. For until this day the same
veil remains unlifted in the reading
of the Old Testament, because the *veil*
is taken away in Christ. 15But even to
this day, when Moses is read, a veil lies
on their heart. 16Nevertheless when
one turns to the Lord, the veil is taken
away. 17Now the Lord is the Spirit; and
where the Spirit of the Lord *is*, there *is*
liberty. 18But we all, with unveiled face,
beholding as in a mirror the glory of
the Lord, are being transformed into
the same image from glory to glory,
just as by the Spirit of the Lord.

The Light of Christ's Gospel

4 Therefore, since we have this min-
istry, as we have received mercy,
we do not lose heart. 2But we have re-
nounced the hidden things of shame,
not walking in craftiness nor handling
the word of God deceitfully, but by man-
ifestation of the truth commending
ourselves to every man's conscience in
the sight of God. 3But even if our gospel
is veiled, it is veiled to those who are
perishing, 4whose minds the god of this
age has blinded, who do not believe, lest
the light of the gospel of the glory of
Christ, who is the image of God, should
shine on them. 5For we do not preach
ourselves, but Christ Jesus the Lord, and
ourselves your bondservants for Jesus'
sake. 6For it is the God who commanded
light to shine out of darkness, who has
shone in our hearts to *give* the light of
the knowledge of the glory of God in
the face of Jesus Christ.

Cast Down but Unconquered

7But we have this treasure in earthen
vessels, that the excellence of the pow-
er may be of God and not of us. 8*We
are* hard-pressed on every side, yet not
crushed; *we are* perplexed, but not in
despair; 9persecuted, but not forsak-
en; struck down, but not destroyed—
10always carrying about in the body
the dying of the Lord Jesus, that the
life of Jesus also may be manifested in
our body. 11For we who live are always
delivered to death for Jesus' sake, that
the life of Jesus also may be manifested
in our mortal flesh. 12So then death is
working in us, but life in you.
13And since we have the same spirit
of faith, according to what is written, "I
believed and therefore I spoke,"[a] we also
believe and therefore speak, 14knowing
that He who raised up the Lord Jesus
will also raise us up with Jesus, and will
present *us* with you. 15For all things *are*
for your sakes, that grace, having spread
through the many, may cause thanks-
giving to abound to the glory of God.

Seeing the Invisible

16Therefore we do not lose heart. Even
though our outward man is perishing,
yet the inward *man* is being renewed
day by day. 17For our light affliction,
which is but for a moment, is working
for us a far more exceeding *and* eternal
weight of glory, 18while we do not look
at the things which are seen, but at the
things which are not seen. For the things
which are seen *are* temporary, but the
things which are not seen *are* eternal.

3:6 [a] Or *spirit* 4:13 [a] Psalm 116:10

Assurance of the Resurrection

5 For we know that if our earthly
house, *this* tent, is destroyed, we
have a building from God, a house not
made with hands, eternal in the heav-
ens. 2For in this we groan, earnestly de-
siring to be clothed with our habitation
which is from heaven, 3if indeed, having
been clothed, we shall not be found na-
ked. 4For we who are in *this* tent groan,
being burdened, not because we want to
be unclothed, but further clothed, that
mortality may be swallowed up by life.
5Now He who has prepared us for this
very thing *is* God, who also has given
us the Spirit as a guarantee.

6So *we are* always confident, know-
ing that while we are at home in the
body we are absent from the Lord. 7For
we walk by faith, not by sight. 8We are
confident, yes, well pleased rather to be
absent from the body and to be present
with the Lord.

The Judgment Seat of Christ

9Therefore we make it our aim, whether
present or absent, to be well pleasing to
Him. 10For we must all appear before the
judgment seat of Christ, that each one
may receive the things *done* in the body,
according to what he has done, whether
good or bad. 11Knowing, therefore, the
terror of the Lord, we persuade men;
but we are well known to God, and I also
trust are well known in your consciences.

Be Reconciled to God

12For we do not commend ourselves
again to you, but give you opportunity
to boast on our behalf, that you may
have *an answer* for those who boast in
appearance and not in heart. 13For if we
are beside ourselves, *it is* for God; or if
we are of sound mind, *it is* for you. 14For
the love of Christ compels us, because
we judge thus: that if One died for all,
then all died; 15and He died for all, that
those who live should live no longer for
themselves, but for Him who died for
them and rose again.

16Therefore, from now on, we regard no
one according to the flesh. Even though
we have known Christ according to the
flesh, yet now we know *Him thus* no lon-
ger. 17Therefore, if anyone *is* in Christ,
he is a new creation; old things have
passed away; behold, all things have
become new. 18Now all things *are* of
God, who has reconciled us to Himself
through Jesus Christ, and has given us
the ministry of reconciliation, 19that is,
that God was in Christ reconciling the
world to Himself, not imputing their
trespasses to them, and has committed
to us the word of reconciliation.

20Now then, we are ambassadors for
Christ, as though God were pleading
through us: we implore *you* on Christ's
behalf, be reconciled to God. 21For He
made Him who knew no sin *to be* sin
for us, that we might become the righ-
teousness of God in Him.

Marks of the Ministry

6 We then, *as* workers together *with*
Him also plead with *you* not to re-
ceive the grace of God in vain. 2For He
says:

> "In an acceptable time I have heard
> you,
> And in the day of salvation I have
> helped you."[a]

Behold, now *is* the accepted time; be-
hold, now *is* the day of salvation.

3We give no offense in anything, that
our ministry may not be blamed. 4But
in all *things* we commend ourselves as
ministers of God: in much patience, in
tribulations, in needs, in distresses, 5in
stripes, in imprisonments, in tumults,
in labors, in sleeplessness, in fastings;
6by purity, by knowledge, by longsuf-
fering, by kindness, by the Holy Spirit,
by sincere love, 7by the word of truth,
by the power of God, by the armor of
righteousness on the right hand and
on the left, 8by honor and dishonor, by
evil report and good report; as deceiv-
ers, and *yet* true; 9as unknown, and *yet*
well known; as dying, and behold we
live; as chastened, and *yet* not killed;
10as sorrowful, yet always rejoicing; as
poor, yet making many rich; as having
nothing, and *yet* possessing all things.

6:2 [a] Isaiah 49:8

Be Holy

11O Corinthians! We have spoken open-
ly to you, our heart is wide open. 12You
are not restricted by us, but you are
restricted by your *own* affections. 13Now
in return for the same (I speak as to
children), you also be open.

14Do not be unequally yoked together
with unbelievers. For what fellowship
has righteousness with lawlessness?
And what communion has light with
darkness? 15And what accord has Christ
with Belial? Or what part has a believer
with an unbeliever? 16And what agree-
ment has the temple of God with idols?
For you[a] are the temple of the living
God. As God has said:

"I will dwell in them
And walk among *them.*
I will be their God,
And they shall be My people."[b]

17Therefore

"Come out from among them
And be separate, says the Lord.
Do not touch what is unclean,
And I will receive you."[a]
18 "I will be a Father to you,
And you shall be My sons and
daughters,
Says the LORD Almighty."[a]

7 Therefore, having these promises,
beloved, let us cleanse ourselves
from all filthiness of the flesh and spirit,
perfecting holiness in the fear of God.

The Corinthians' Repentance

2Open *your hearts* to us. We have
wronged no one, we have corrupted
no one, we have cheated no one. 3I do
not say *this* to condemn; for I have said
before that you are in our hearts, to die
together and to live together. 4Great
is my boldness of speech toward you,
great *is* my boldness on your behalf. I
am filled with comfort. I am exceeding-
ly joyful in all our tribulation.

5For indeed, when we came to Macedo-
nia, our bodies had no rest, but we were
troubled on every side. Outside *were*
conflicts, inside *were* fears. 6Neverthe-
less God, who comforts the downcast,
comforted us by the coming of Titus,
7and not only by his coming, but also by
the consolation with which he was com-
forted in you, when he told us of your
earnest desire, your mourning, your
zeal for me, so that I rejoiced even more.

8For even if I made you sorry with my
letter, I do not regret it; though I did
regret it. For I perceive that the same
epistle made you sorry, though only for
a while. 9Now I rejoice, not that you were
made sorry, but that your sorrow led to
repentance. For you were made sorry in a
godly manner, that you might suffer loss
from us in nothing. 10For godly sorrow
produces repentance *leading* to salva-
tion, not to be regretted; but the sorrow of
the world produces death. 11For observe
this very thing, that you sorrowed in a
godly manner: What diligence it pro-
duced in you, *what* clearing *of yourselves,*
what indignation, *what* fear, *what* vehe-
ment desire, *what* zeal, *what* vindication!
In all *things* you proved yourselves to be
clear in this matter. 12Therefore, although
I wrote to you, *I did* not *do it* for the sake
of him who had done the wrong, nor for
the sake of him who suffered wrong, but
that our care for you in the sight of God
might appear to you.

The Joy of Titus

13Therefore we have been comforted in
your comfort. And we rejoiced exceed-
ingly more for the joy of Titus, because
his spirit has been refreshed by you all.
14For if in anything I have boasted to
him about you, I am not ashamed. But
as we spoke all things to you in truth,
even so our boasting to Titus was found
true. 15And his affections are greater for
you as he remembers the obedience of
you all, how with fear and trembling you
received him. 16Therefore I rejoice that
I have confidence in you in everything.

Excel in Giving

8 Moreover, brethren, we make known
to you the grace of God bestowed on
the churches of Macedonia: 2that in a
great trial of affliction the abundance

6:16 [a] NU-Text reads *we.* [b] Leviticus 26:12; Jeremiah 32:38; Ezekiel 37:27 6:17 [a] Isaiah 52:11; Ezekiel 20:34, 41 6:18 [a] 2 Samuel 7:14

of their joy and their deep poverty abounded in the riches of their liberality. 3For I bear witness that according to *their* ability, yes, and beyond *their* ability, *they were* freely willing, 4imploring us with much urgency that we would receive[a] the gift and the fellowship of the ministering to the saints. 5And not *only* as we had hoped, but they first gave themselves to the Lord, and *then* to us by the will of God. 6So we urged Titus, that as he had begun, so he would also complete this grace in you as well. 7But as you abound in everything—in faith, in speech, in knowledge, in all diligence, and in your love for us—*see* that you abound in this grace also.

Christ Our Pattern

8I speak not by commandment, but I am testing the sincerity of your love by the diligence of others. 9For you know the grace of our Lord Jesus Christ, that though He was rich, yet for your sakes He became poor, that you through His poverty might become rich.

10And in this I give advice: It is to your advantage not only to be doing what you began and were desiring to do a year ago; 11but now you also must complete the doing *of it;* that as *there was* a readiness to desire *it,* so *there* also *may be* a completion out of what *you* have. 12For if there is first a willing mind, *it is* accepted according to what one has, *and* not according to what he does not have.

13For *I do* not *mean* that others should be eased and you burdened; 14but by an equality, *that* now at this time your abundance *may supply* their lack, that their abundance also may *supply* your lack—that there may be equality. 15As it is written, "He who *gathered* much had nothing left over, and he who *gathered* little had no lack."[a]

Collection for the Judean Saints

16But thanks *be* to God who puts[a] the same earnest care for you into the heart of Titus. 17For he not only accepted the exhortation, but being more diligent, he went to you of his own accord. 18And we have sent with him the brother whose praise *is* in the gospel throughout all the churches, 19and not only *that,* but who was also chosen by the churches to travel with us with this gift, which is administered by us to the glory of the Lord Himself and *to show* your ready mind, 20avoiding this: that anyone should blame us in this lavish gift which is administered by us— 21providing honorable things, not only in the sight of the Lord, but also in the sight of men.

22And we have sent with them our brother whom we have often proved diligent in many things, but now much more diligent, because of the great confidence which *we have* in you. 23If *anyone inquires* about Titus, *he is* my partner and fellow worker concerning you. Or if our brethren *are inquired about, they are* messengers of the churches, the glory of Christ. 24Therefore show to them, and[a] before the churches, the proof of your love and of our boasting on your behalf.

Administering the Gift

9 Now concerning the ministering to the saints, it is superfluous for me to write to you; 2for I know your willingness, about which I boast of you to the Macedonians, that Achaia was ready a year ago; and your zeal has stirred up the majority. 3Yet I have sent the brethren, lest our boasting of you should be in vain in this respect, that, as I said, you may be ready; 4lest if *some* Macedonians come with me and find you unprepared, we (not to mention you!) should be ashamed of this confident boasting.[a] 5Therefore I thought it necessary to exhort the brethren to go to you ahead of time, and prepare your generous gift beforehand, which *you had* previously promised, that it may be ready as *a matter of* generosity and not as a grudging obligation.

The Cheerful Giver

6But this *I say:* He who sows sparingly will also reap sparingly, and he who sows bountifully will also reap bountifully. 7*So let* each one *give* as he purposes in his heart, not grudgingly or

8:4 [a] NU-Text and M-Text omit *that we would receive,* thus changing text to *urgency for the favor and fellowship* . . . . **8:15** [a] Exodus 16:18 **8:16** [a] NU-Text reads *has put.* **8:24** [a] NU-Text and M-Text omit *and.* **9:4** [a] NU-Text reads *this confidence.*

of necessity; for God loves a cheerful giver. 8And God *is* able to make all grace abound toward you, that you, always having all sufficiency in all *things,* may have an abundance for every good work. 9As it is written:

"He has dispersed abroad,
He has given to the poor;
His righteousness endures
forever."[a]

10Now may[a] He who supplies seed to the sower, and bread for food, supply and multiply the seed you have *sown* and increase the fruits of your righteousness, 11while *you are* enriched in everything for all liberality, which causes thanksgiving through us to God. 12For the administration of this service not only supplies the needs of the saints, but also is abounding through many thanksgivings to God, 13while, through the proof of this ministry, they glorify God for the obedience of your confession to the gospel of Christ, and for *your* liberal sharing with them and all *men,* 14and by their prayer for you, who long for you because of the exceeding grace of God in you. 15Thanks *be* to God for His indescribable gift!

The Spiritual War

10 Now I, Paul, myself am pleading with you by the meekness and gentleness of Christ—who in presence *am* lowly among you, but being absent am bold toward you. 2But I beg *you* that when I am present I may not be bold with that confidence by which I intend to be bold against some, who think of us as if we walked according to the flesh. 3For though we walk in the flesh, we do not war according to the flesh. 4For the weapons of our warfare *are* not carnal but mighty in God for pulling down strongholds, 5casting down arguments and every high thing that exalts itself against the knowledge of God, bringing every thought into captivity to the obedience of Christ, 6and being ready to punish all disobedience when your obedience is fulfilled.

Reality of Paul's Authority

7Do you look at things according to the outward appearance? If anyone is convinced in himself that he is Christ's, let him again consider this in himself, that just as he *is* Christ's, even so we *are* Christ's.[a] 8For even if I should boast somewhat more about our authority, which the Lord gave us[a] for edification and not for your destruction, I shall not be ashamed— 9lest I seem to terrify you by letters. 10"For *his* letters," they say, "*are* weighty and powerful, but *his* bodily presence *is* weak, and *his* speech contemptible." 11Let such a person consider this, that what we are in word by letters when we are absent, such *we will* also *be* in deed when we are present.

Limits of Paul's Authority

12For we dare not class ourselves or compare ourselves with those who commend themselves. But they, measuring themselves by themselves, and comparing themselves among themselves, are not wise. 13We, however, will not boast beyond measure, but within the limits of the sphere which God appointed us—a sphere which especially includes you. 14For we are not overextending ourselves (as though *our authority* did not extend to you), for it was to you that we came with the gospel of Christ; 15not boasting of things beyond measure, *that is,* in other men's labors, but having hope, *that* as your faith is increased, we shall be greatly enlarged by you in our sphere, 16to preach the gospel in the *regions* beyond you, *and* not to boast in another man's sphere of accomplishment.

17But "he who glories, let him glory in the LORD."[a] 18For not he who commends himself is approved, but whom the Lord commends.

Concern for Their Faithfulness

11 Oh, that you would bear with me in a little folly—and indeed you do bear with me. 2For I am jealous for you with godly jealousy. For I have betrothed you to one husband, that I may present *you as* a chaste virgin to Christ. 3But I fear, lest somehow, as the

9:9 [a] Psalm 112:9 9:10 [a] NU-Text reads *Now He who supplies . . . will supply . . . .* 10:7 [a] NU-Text reads *even as we are.* 10:8 [a] NU-Text omits *us.* 10:17 [a] Jeremiah 9:24

GOD SIN JESUS SALVATION LOVE

serpent deceived Eve by his craftiness,
so your minds may be corrupted from
the simplicity[a] that is in Christ. 4For if
he who comes preaches another Jesus
whom we have not preached, or *if* you
receive a different spirit which you have
not received, or a different gospel which
you have not accepted—you may well
put up with it!

Paul and False Apostles

5For I consider that I am not at all
inferior to the most eminent apostles.
6Even though *I am* untrained in speech,
yet *I am* not in knowledge. But we have
been thoroughly manifested[a] among
you in all things.

7Did I commit sin in humbling myself
that you might be exalted, because I
preached the gospel of God to you free
of charge? 8I robbed other churches,
taking wages *from them* to minister
to you. 9And when I was present with
you, and in need, I was a burden to no
one, for what I lacked the brethren who
came from Macedonia supplied. And
in everything I kept myself from being
burdensome to you, and so I will keep
myself. 10As the truth of Christ is in me,
no one shall stop me from this boast-
ing in the regions of Achaia. 11Why?
Because I do not love you? God knows!

12But what I do, I will also continue to
do, that I may cut off the opportunity
from those who desire an opportunity to
be regarded just as we are in the things
of which they boast. 13For such *are* false
apostles, deceitful workers, transform-
ing themselves into apostles of Christ.
14And no wonder! For Satan himself
transforms himself into an angel of
light. 15Therefore *it is* no great thing if
his ministers also transform themselves
into ministers of righteousness, whose
end will be according to their works.

Reluctant Boasting

16I say again, let no one think me a
fool. If otherwise, at least receive me
as a fool, that I also may boast a little.
17What I speak, I speak not according
to the Lord, but as it were, foolishly, in
this confidence of boasting. 18Seeing
that many boast according to the flesh,
I also will boast. 19For you put up with
fools gladly, since you *yourselves* are
wise! 20For you put up with it if one
brings you into bondage, if one devours
you, if one takes *from you*, if one exalts
himself, if one strikes you on the face.
21To *our* shame I say that we were too
weak for that! But in whatever anyone is
bold—I speak foolishly—I am bold also.

Suffering for Christ

22Are they Hebrews? So *am* I. Are they
Israelites? So *am* I. Are they the seed
of Abraham? So *am* I. 23Are they min-
isters of Christ?—I speak as a fool—I
am more: in labors more abundant, in
stripes above measure, in prisons more
frequently, in deaths often. 24From the
Jews five times I received forty *stripes*
minus one. 25Three times I was beaten
with rods; once I was stoned; three times
I was shipwrecked; a night and a day
I have been in the deep; 26*in* journeys
often, *in* perils of waters, *in* perils of rob-
bers, *in* perils of *my own* countrymen, *in*
perils of the Gentiles, *in* perils in the city,
in perils in the wilderness, *in* perils in
the sea, *in* perils among false brethren;
27in weariness and toil, in sleeplessness
often, in hunger and thirst, in fastings
often, in cold and nakedness— 28be-
sides the other things, what comes upon
me daily: my deep concern for all the
churches. 29Who is weak, and I am not
weak? Who is made to stumble, and I
do not burn *with indignation?*

30If I must boast, I will boast in the
things which concern my infirmity. 31The
God and Father of our Lord Jesus Christ,
who is blessed forever, knows that I am
not lying. 32In Damascus the governor,
under Aretas the king, was guarding the
city of the Damascenes with a garrison,
desiring to arrest me; 33but I was let
down in a basket through a window in
the wall, and escaped from his hands.

The Vision of Paradise

12 It is doubtless[a] not profitable
for me to boast. I will come to
visions and revelations of the Lord:
2I know a man in Christ who fourteen

11:3 [a] NU-Text adds *and purity.* 11:6 [a] NU-Text omits *been.* 12:1 [a] NU-Text reads *necessary, though not profitable, to boast.*

years ago—whether in the body I do
not know, or whether out of the body I
do not know, God knows—such a one
was caught up to the third heaven. 3And
I know such a man—whether in the
body or out of the body I do not know,
God knows— 4how he was caught up
into Paradise and heard inexpressible
words, which it is not lawful for a man
to utter. 5Of such a one I will boast; yet
of myself I will not boast, except in my
infirmities. 6For though I might desire
to boast, I will not be a fool; for I will
speak the truth. But I refrain, lest any-
one should think of me above what he
sees me *to be* or hears from me.

The Thorn in the Flesh

7And lest I should be exalted above
measure by the abundance of the rev-
elations, a thorn in the flesh was given
to me, a messenger of Satan to buffet
me, lest I be exalted above measure.
8Concerning this thing I pleaded with
the Lord three times that it might depart
from me. 9And He said to me, "My grace
is sufficient for you, for My strength is
made perfect in weakness." Therefore
most gladly I will rather boast in my
infirmities, that the power of Christ
may rest upon me. 10Therefore I take
pleasure in infirmities, in reproaches,
in needs, in persecutions, in distresses,
for Christ's sake. For when I am weak,
then I am strong.

Signs of an Apostle

11I have become a fool in boasting;[a]
you have compelled me. For I ought to
have been commended by you; for in
nothing was I behind the most eminent
apostles, though I am nothing. 12Truly
the signs of an apostle were accom-
plished among you with all persever-
ance, in signs and wonders and mighty
deeds. 13For what is it in which you were
inferior to other churches, except that
I myself was not burdensome to you?
Forgive me this wrong!

Love for the Church

14Now *for* the third time I am ready
to come to you. And I will not be
burdensome to you; for I do not seek
yours, but you. For the children ought
not to lay up for the parents, but the
parents for the children. 15And I will
very gladly spend and be spent for your
souls; though the more abundantly I
love you, the less I am loved.

16But be that *as it may,* I did not burden
you. Nevertheless, being crafty, I caught
you by cunning! 17Did I take advantage
of you by any of those whom I sent to
you? 18I urged Titus, and sent our brother
with *him.* Did Titus take advantage of
you? Did we not walk in the same spirit?
Did *we* not *walk* in the same steps?

19Again, do you think[a] that we excuse
ourselves to you? We speak before God
in Christ. But *we do* all things, beloved,
for your edification. 20For I fear lest,
when I come, I shall not find you such
as I wish, and *that* I shall be found by
you such as you do not wish; lest *there
be* contentions, jealousies, outbursts of
wrath, selfish ambitions, backbitings,
whisperings, conceits, tumults; 21lest,
when I come again, my God will hum-
ble me among you, and I shall mourn
for many who have sinned before and
have not repented of the uncleanness,
fornication, and lewdness which they
have practiced.

Coming with Authority

13 This *will be* the third *time* I am
coming to you. "By the mouth
of two or three witnesses every word
shall be established."[a] 2I have told you
before, and foretell as if I were present
the second time, and now being absent
I write[a] to those who have sinned be-
fore, and to all the rest, that if I come
again I will not spare— 3since you seek
a proof of Christ speaking in me, who
is not weak toward you, but mighty in
you. 4For though He was crucified in
weakness, yet He lives by the power of
God. For we also are weak in Him, but
we shall live with Him by the power of
God toward you.

5Examine yourselves *as to* whether
you are in the faith. Test yourselves.
Do you not know yourselves, that Jesus
Christ is in you?—unless indeed you

12:11 [a] NU-Text omits *in boasting.* **12:19** [a] NU-Text reads *You have been thinking for a long time . . . .*
13:1 [a] Deuteronomy 19:15 **13:2** [a] NU-Text omits *I write.*

are disqualified. 6But I trust that you
will know that we are not disqualified.

Paul Prefers Gentleness

7Now I[a] pray to God that you do no
evil, not that we should appear ap-
proved, but that you should do what
is honorable, though we may seem
disqualified. 8For we can do nothing
against the truth, but for the truth. 9For
we are glad when we are weak and you
are strong. And this also we pray, that
you may be made complete. 10Therefore
I write these things being absent, lest
being present I should use sharpness,
according to the authority which the
Lord has given me for edification and
not for destruction.

Greetings and Benediction

11Finally, brethren, farewell. Become
complete. Be of good comfort, be of one
mind, live in peace; and the God of love
and peace will be with you.
12Greet one another with a holy kiss.
13All the saints greet you.
14The grace of the Lord Jesus Christ,
and the love of God, and the commu-
nion of the Holy Spirit *be* with you all.
Amen.

13:7 a NU-Text reads *we*.

THE LETTER OF PAUL TO THE
GALATIANS

A big question the early church asked was, "Does a person have to become a Jew before they can be a Christian?" Many Jewish believers in Galatia thought this was the case. Furthermore, many also believed that Christians had to keep the Jewish law to keep their salvation. In response, Paul wrote to them to remind them that they had been saved by God's grace through faith in Jesus, not by what they had done. Just as they did nothing to earn salvation, they could do nothing to maintain that salvation. From start to finish, salvation is given and maintained by God's grace.

- **GENRE:** Epistle
- **AUTHOR:** Paul
- **TIME:** c. AD 40–56
- **PURPOSE:** To explain to the Galatians that they were saved by God's grace, not by keeping the law.

Greeting

1 Paul, an apostle (not from men nor
through man, but through Jesus
Christ and God the Father who raised
Him from the dead), 2and all the breth-
ren who are with me,

To the churches of Galatia:

3Grace to you and peace from God
the Father and our Lord Jesus Christ,
4who gave Himself for our sins, that He
might deliver us from this present evil
age, according to the will of our God
and Father, 5to whom *be* glory forever
and ever. Amen.

Only One Gospel

6I marvel that you are turning away
so soon from Him who called you in
the grace of Christ, to a different gos-
pel, 7which is not another; but there
are some who trouble you and want
to pervert the gospel of Christ. 8But
even if we, or an angel from heaven,
preach any other gospel to you than
what we have preached to you, let him
be accursed. 9As we have said before,
so now I say again, if anyone preaches
any other gospel to you than what you
have received, let him be accursed.
10For do I now persuade men, or God?
Or do I seek to please men? For if I still
pleased men, I would not be a bond-
servant of Christ.

Call to Apostleship

11But I make known to you, brethren,
that the gospel which was preached
by me is not according to man. 12For I
neither received it from man, nor was
I taught *it,* but *it came* through the rev-
elation of Jesus Christ.
13For you have heard of my former
conduct in Judaism, how I persecuted
the church of God beyond measure and
tried to destroy it. 14And I advanced in
Judaism beyond many of my contem-
poraries in my own nation, being more
exceedingly zealous for the traditions
of my fathers.
15But when it pleased God, who sepa-
rated me from my mother's womb and
called *me* through His grace, 16to reveal
His Son in me, that I might preach Him
among the Gentiles, I did not immediate-
ly confer with flesh and blood, 17nor did
I go up to Jerusalem to those *who were*
apostles before me; but I went to Arabia,
and returned again to Damascus.

Contacts at Jerusalem

18Then after three years I went up to
Jerusalem to see Peter,[a] and remained

1:18 [a] NU-Text reads *Cephas.*

GOD | SIN | JESUS | SALVATION | LOVE

with him fifteen days. 19But I saw none
of the other apostles except James, the
Lord's brother. 20(Now *concerning* the
things which I write to you, indeed, be-
fore God, I do not lie.)
21Afterward I went into the regions of
Syria and Cilicia. 22And I was unknown
by face to the churches of Judea which
were in Christ. 23But they were hearing
only, "He who formerly persecuted us
now preaches the faith which he once
tried to destroy." 24And they glorified
God in me.

Defending the Gospel

2 Then after fourteen years I went up
again to Jerusalem with Barnabas,
and also took Titus with *me.* 2And I went
up by revelation, and communicated
to them that gospel which I preach
among the Gentiles, but privately to
those who were of reputation, lest by
any means I might run, or had run, in
vain. 3Yet not even Titus who *was* with
me, being a Greek, was compelled to be
circumcised. 4And *this occurred* because
of false brethren secretly brought in
(who came in by stealth to spy out our
liberty which we have in Christ Jesus,
that they might bring us into bondage),
5to whom we did not yield submission
even for an hour, that the truth of the
gospel might continue with you.
6But from those who seemed to be
something—whatever they were, it
makes no difference to me; God shows
personal favoritism to no man—for
those who seemed *to be something* add-
ed nothing to me. 7But on the contrary,
when they saw that the gospel for the
uncircumcised had been committed to
me, as *the gospel* for the circumcised
was to Peter 8(for He who worked ef-
fectively in Peter for the apostleship to
the circumcised also worked effectively
in me toward the Gentiles), 9and when
James, Cephas, and John, who seemed
to be pillars, perceived the grace that
had been given to me, they gave me
and Barnabas the right hand of fellow-
ship, that we *should go* to the Gentiles
and they to the circumcised. 10*They
desired* only that we should remember
the poor, the very thing which I also
was eager to do.

No Return to the Law

11Now when Peter[a] had come to Anti-
och, I withstood him to his face, because
he was to be blamed; 12for before certain
men came from James, he would eat
with the Gentiles; but when they came,
he withdrew and separated himself,
fearing those who were of the circum-
cision. 13And the rest of the Jews also
played the hypocrite with him, so that
even Barnabas was carried away with
their hypocrisy.
14But when I saw that they were not
straightforward about the truth of the
gospel, I said to Peter before *them* all, "If
you, being a Jew, live in the manner of
Gentiles and not as the Jews, why do you[a]
compel Gentiles to live as Jews?[b] 15We
who are Jews by nature, and not sinners
of the Gentiles, 16knowing that a man is
not justified by the works of the law but
by faith in Jesus Christ, even we have
believed in Christ Jesus, that we might
be justified by faith in Christ and not by
the works of the law; for by the works of
the law no flesh shall be justified.
17"But if, while we seek to be justified by
Christ, we ourselves also are found sin-
ners, *is* Christ therefore a minister of sin?
Certainly not! 18For if I build again those
things which I destroyed, I make myself
a transgressor. 19For I through the law
died to the law that I might live to God.
20I have been crucified with Christ; it is
no longer I who live, but Christ lives in
me; and the *life* which I now live in the
flesh I live by faith in the Son of God,
who loved me and gave Himself for me.
21I do not set aside the grace of God; for
if righteousness *comes* through the law,
then Christ died in vain."

Justification by Faith

3 O foolish Galatians! Who has be-
witched you that you should not
obey the truth,[a] before whose eyes Jesus
Christ was clearly portrayed among
you[b] as crucified? 2This only I want to
learn from you: Did you receive the
Spirit by the works of the law, or by the

2:11 [a] NU-Text reads *Cephas.* 2:14 [a] NU-Text reads *how can you.* [b] Some interpreters stop the quotation here. 3:1 [a] NU-Text omits *that you should not obey the truth.* [b] NU-Text omits *among you.*

hearing of faith? 3Are you so foolish? Having begun in the Spirit, are you now being made perfect by the flesh? 4Have you suffered so many things in vain—if indeed *it was* in vain?

5Therefore He who supplies the Spirit to you and works miracles among you, *does He do it* by the works of the law, or by the hearing of faith?— 6just as Abraham "believed God, and it was accounted to him for righteousness."[a] 7Therefore know that *only* those who are of faith are sons of Abraham. 8And the Scripture, foreseeing that God would justify the Gentiles by faith, preached the gospel to Abraham beforehand, *saying,* "In you all the nations shall be blessed."[a] 9So then those who *are* of faith are blessed with believing Abraham.

The Law Brings a Curse

10For as many as are of the works of the law are under the curse; for it is written, "Cursed *is* everyone who does not continue in all things which are written in the book of the law, to do them."[a] 11But that no one is justified by the law in the sight of God *is* evident, for "the just shall live by faith."[a] 12Yet the law is not of faith, but "the man who does them shall live by them."[a]

13Christ has redeemed us from the curse of the law, having become a curse for us (for it is written, "Cursed *is* everyone who hangs on a tree"[a]), 14that the blessing of Abraham might come upon the Gentiles in Christ Jesus, that we might receive the promise of the Spirit through faith.

The Changeless Promise

15Brethren, I speak in the manner of men: Though *it is* only a man's covenant, yet *if it is* confirmed, no one annuls or adds to it. 16Now to Abraham and his Seed were the promises made. He does not say, "And to seeds," as of many, but as of one, "And to your Seed,"[a] who is Christ. 17And this I say, *that* the law, which was four hundred and thirty years later, cannot annul the covenant that was confirmed before by God in Christ,[a] that it should make the promise of no effect. 18For if the inheritance *is* of the law, *it is* no longer of promise; but God gave *it* to Abraham by promise.

Purpose of the Law

19What purpose then *does* the law *serve?* It was added because of transgressions, till the Seed should come to whom the promise was made; *and it was* appointed through angels by the hand of a mediator. 20Now a mediator does not *mediate* for one *only,* but God is one.

21*Is* the law then against the promises of God? Certainly not! For if there had been a law given which could have given life, truly righteousness would have been by the law. 22But the Scripture has confined all under sin, that the promise by faith in Jesus Christ might be given to those who believe. 23But before faith came, we were kept under guard by the law, kept for the faith which would afterward be revealed. 24Therefore the law was our tutor *to bring us* to Christ, that we might be justified by faith. 25But after faith has come, we are no longer under a tutor.

Sons and Heirs

26For you are all sons of God through faith in Christ Jesus. 27For as many of you as were baptized into Christ have put on Christ. 28There is neither Jew nor Greek, there is neither slave nor free, there is neither male nor female; for you are all one in Christ Jesus. 29And if you *are* Christ's, then you are Abraham's seed, and heirs according to the promise.

4 Now I say *that* the heir, as long as he is a child, does not differ at all from a slave, though he is master of all, 2but is under guardians and stewards until the time appointed by the father. 3Even so we, when we were children, were in bondage under the elements of the world. 4But when the fullness of the time had come, God sent forth His Son, born[a] of a woman, born under the law, 5to redeem those who were under the law, that we might receive the adoption as sons.

3:6 [a] Genesis 15:6 **3:8** [a] Genesis 12:3; 18:18; 22:18; 26:4; 28:14 **3:10** [a] Deuteronomy 27:26
3:11 [a] Habakkuk 2:4 **3:12** [a] Leviticus 18:5 **3:13** [a] Deuteronomy 21:23 **3:16** [a] Genesis 12:7; 13:15; 24:7 **3:17** [a] NU-Text omits *in Christ.* **4:4** [a] Or *made*

6And because you are sons, God has
sent forth the Spirit of His Son into
your hearts, crying out, "Abba, Father!"
7Therefore you are no longer a slave but
a son, and if a son, then an heir of[a] God
through Christ.

Fears for the Church

8But then, indeed, when you did not
know God, you served those which by
nature are not gods. 9But now after you
have known God, or rather are known
by God, how *is it that* you turn again
to the weak and beggarly elements, to
which you desire again to be in bond-
age? 10You observe days and months
and seasons and years. 11I am afraid for
you, lest I have labored for you in vain.
12Brethren, I urge you to become like
me, for I *became* like you. You have not
injured me at all. 13You know that be-
cause of physical infirmity I preached
the gospel to you at the first. 14And my
trial which was in my flesh you did not
despise or reject, but you received me
as an angel of God, *even* as Christ Jesus.
15What[a] then was the blessing you *en-*
joyed? For I bear you witness that, if
possible, you would have plucked out
your own eyes and given them to me.
16Have I therefore become your enemy
because I tell you the truth?
17They zealously court you, *but* for no
good; yes, they want to exclude you,
that you may be zealous for them. 18But
it is good to be zealous in a good thing
always, and not only when I am pres-
ent with you. 19My little children, for
whom I labor in birth again until Christ
is formed in you, 20I would like to be
present with you now and to change
my tone; for I have doubts about you.

Two Covenants

21Tell me, you who desire to be under
the law, do you not hear the law? 22For
it is written that Abraham had two sons:
the one by a bondwoman, the other by
a freewoman. 23But he *who was* of the
bondwoman was born according to the
flesh, and he of the freewoman through
promise, 24which things are symbolic.
For these are the[a] two covenants: the
one from Mount Sinai which gives birth
to bondage, which is Hagar— 25for this
Hagar is Mount Sinai in Arabia, and
corresponds to Jerusalem which now is,
and is in bondage with her children—
26but the Jerusalem above is free, which
is the mother of us all. 27For it is written:

"Rejoice, O barren,
You who do not bear!
Break forth and shout,
You who are not in labor!
For the desolate has many more
children
Than she who has a husband."[a]

28Now we, brethren, as Isaac *was,* are
children of promise. 29But, as he who
was born according to the flesh then
persecuted him *who was born* according
to the Spirit, even so *it is* now. 30Never-
theless what does the Scripture say?
"Cast out the bondwoman and her son,
for the son of the bondwoman shall not
be heir with the son of the freewoman."[a]
31So then, brethren, we are not children
of the bondwoman but of the free.

Christian Liberty

5 Stand fast therefore in the liberty by
which Christ has made us free,[a] and
do not be entangled again with a yoke
of bondage. 2Indeed I, Paul, say to you
that if you become circumcised, Christ
will profit you nothing. 3And I testify
again to every man who becomes cir-
cumcised that he is a debtor to keep the
whole law. 4You have become estranged
from Christ, you who *attempt to* be justi-
fied by law; you have fallen from grace.
5For we through the Spirit eagerly wait
for the hope of righteousness by faith.
6For in Christ Jesus neither circumci-
sion nor uncircumcision avails any-
thing, but faith working through love.

Love Fulfills the Law

7You ran well. Who hindered you from
obeying the truth? 8This persuasion
does not *come* from Him who calls you.
9A little leaven leavens the whole lump.

4:7 [a] NU-Text reads *through God* and omits *through Christ.* 4:15 [a] NU-Text reads *Where.* 4:24 [a] NU-Text and M-Text omit *the.* 4:27 [a] Isaiah 54:1 4:30 [a] Genesis 21:10 5:1 [a] NU-Text reads *For freedom Christ has made us free; stand fast therefore.*

10 I have confidence in you, in the Lord, that you will have no other mind; but he who troubles you shall bear his judgment, whoever he is.

11 And I, brethren, if I still preach circumcision, why do I still suffer persecution? Then the offense of the cross has ceased. 12 I could wish that those who trouble you would even cut themselves off!

13 For you, brethren, have been called to liberty; only do not *use* liberty as an opportunity for the flesh, but through love serve one another. 14 For all the law is fulfilled in one word, *even* in this: "You shall love your neighbor as yourself."[a] 15 But if you bite and devour one another, beware lest you be consumed by one another!

Walking in the Spirit

16 I say then: Walk in the Spirit, and you shall not fulfill the lust of the flesh. 17 For the flesh lusts against the Spirit, and the Spirit against the flesh; and these are contrary to one another, so that you do not do the things that you wish. 18 But if you are led by the Spirit, you are not under the law.

19 Now the works of the flesh are evident, which are: adultery,[a] fornication, uncleanness, lewdness, 20 idolatry, sorcery, hatred, contentions, jealousies, outbursts of wrath, selfish ambitions, dissensions, heresies, 21 envy, murders,[a] drunkenness, revelries, and the like; of which I tell you beforehand, just as I also told *you* in time past, that those who practice such things will not inherit the kingdom of God.

22 But the fruit of the Spirit is love, joy, peace, longsuffering, kindness, goodness, faithfulness, 23 gentleness, self-control. Against such there is no law. 24 And those *who are* Christ's have crucified the flesh with its passions and desires. 25 If we live in the Spirit, let us also walk in the Spirit. 26 Let us not become conceited, provoking one another, envying one another.

Bear and Share Burdens

6 Brethren, if a man is overtaken in any trespass, you who *are* spiritual restore such a one in a spirit of gentleness, considering yourself lest you also be tempted. 2 Bear one another's burdens, and so fulfill the law of Christ. 3 For if anyone thinks himself to be something, when he is nothing, he deceives himself. 4 But let each one examine his own work, and then he will have rejoicing in himself alone, and not in another. 5 For each one shall bear his own load.

Be Generous and Do Good

6 Let him who is taught the word share in all good things with him who teaches.

7 Do not be deceived, God is not mocked; for whatever a man sows, that he will also reap. 8 For he who sows to his flesh will of the flesh reap corruption, but he who sows to the Spirit will of the Spirit reap everlasting life. 9 And let us not grow weary while doing good, for in due season we shall reap if we do not lose heart. 10 Therefore, as we have opportunity, let us do good to all, especially to those who are of the household of faith.

Glory Only in the Cross

11 See with what large letters I have written to you with my own hand! 12 As many as desire to make a good showing in the flesh, these *would* compel you to be circumcised, only that they may not suffer persecution for the cross of Christ. 13 For not even those who are circumcised keep the law, but they desire to have you circumcised that they may boast in your flesh. 14 But God forbid that I should boast except in the cross of our Lord Jesus Christ, by whom[a] the world has been crucified to me, and I to the world. 15 For in Christ Jesus neither circumcision nor uncircumcision avails anything, but a new creation.

Blessing and a Plea

16 And as many as walk according to this rule, peace and mercy *be* upon them, and upon the Israel of God.

17 From now on let no one trouble me, for I bear in my body the marks of the Lord Jesus.

18 Brethren, the grace of our Lord Jesus Christ *be* with your spirit. Amen.

5:14 [a] Leviticus 19:18 **5:19** [a] NU-Text omits *adultery.* **5:21** [a] NU-Text omits *murders.* **6:14** [a] Or *by which* (the cross)

THE LETTER OF PAUL TO THE

EPHESIANS

In the Book of Ephesians, Paul wrote to believers who were rich in Jesus Christ but who were living like beggars. What God had said was true of them in Christ had not carried over to how they lived each day. In the first three chapters, Paul described the heavenly "bank account" that each believer has, such as being adopted and accepted by God, redeemed and forgiven in Christ, and sealed and empowered by the Holy Spirit. Then, in the final three chapters, Paul described what it looks like to live in light of this spiritual wealth.

- **GENRE:** Epistle
- **AUTHOR:** Paul
- **TIME:** c. AD 60–62
- **PURPOSE:** To remind the Ephesians of their spiritual blessings and instruct them to be holy.

Greeting

1 Paul, an apostle of Jesus Christ by
the will of God,

To the saints who are in Ephesus, and
faithful in Christ Jesus:

2Grace to you and peace from God our
Father and the Lord Jesus Christ.

Redemption in Christ

3Blessed *be* the God and Father of
our Lord Jesus Christ, who has blessed
us with every spiritual blessing in the
heavenly *places* in Christ, 4just as He
chose us in Him before the foundation
of the world, that we should be holy
and without blame before Him in love,
5having predestined us to adoption
as sons by Jesus Christ to Himself, ac-
cording to the good pleasure of His
will, 6to the praise of the glory of His
grace, by which He made us accepted
in the Beloved.
7In Him we have redemption through
His blood, the forgiveness of sins,
according to the riches of His grace
8which He made to abound toward us
in all wisdom and prudence, 9having
made known to us the mystery of His
will, according to His good pleasure
which He purposed in Himself, 10that
in the dispensation of the fullness of
the times He might gather together in
one all things in Christ, both[a] which are
in heaven and which are on earth—in
Him. 11In Him also we have obtained an
inheritance, being predestined accord-
ing to the purpose of Him who works all
things according to the counsel of His
will, 12that we who first trusted in Christ
should be to the praise of His glory.
13In Him you also *trusted,* after you
heard the word of truth, the gospel of
your salvation; in whom also, having
believed, you were sealed with the Holy
Spirit of promise, 14who[a] is the guaran-
tee of our inheritance until the redemp-
tion of the purchased possession, to the
praise of His glory.

Prayer for Spiritual Wisdom

15Therefore I also, after I heard of your
faith in the Lord Jesus and your love
for all the saints, 16do not cease to give
thanks for you, making mention of you
in my prayers: 17that the God of our
Lord Jesus Christ, the Father of glory,
may give to you the spirit of wisdom
and revelation in the knowledge of
Him, 18the eyes of your understand-
ing[a] being enlightened; that you may

1:10 [a] NU-Text and M-Text omit *both.* **1:14** [a] NU-Text reads *which.* **1:18** [a] NU-Text and M-Text read *hearts.*

know what is the hope of His calling,
what are the riches of the glory of His
inheritance in the saints, 19and what *is*
the exceeding greatness of His power
toward us who believe, according to the
working of His mighty power 20which
He worked in Christ when He raised
Him from the dead and seated *Him* at
His right hand in the heavenly *places,*
21far above all principality and power
and might and dominion, and every
name that is named, not only in this
age but also in that which is to come.
22And He put all *things* under His feet,
and gave Him *to be* head over all *things*
to the church, 23which is His body, the
fullness of Him who fills all in all.

By Grace Through Faith

2 And you *He made alive,* who were
dead in trespasses and sins, 2in
which you once walked according to
the course of this world, according to
the prince of the power of the air, the
spirit who now works in the sons of dis-
obedience, 3among whom also we all
once conducted ourselves in the lusts
of our flesh, fulfilling the desires of the
flesh and of the mind, and were by na-
ture children of wrath, just as the others.
4But God, who is rich in mercy, because
of His great love with which He loved us,
5even when we were dead in trespasses,
made us alive together with Christ (by
grace you have been saved), 6and raised
us up together, and made *us* sit together
in the heavenly *places* in Christ Jesus,
7that in the ages to come He might show
the exceeding riches of His grace in *His*
kindness toward us in Christ Jesus. 8For
by grace you have been saved through
faith, and that not of yourselves; *it is* the
gift of God, 9not of works, lest anyone
should boast. 10For we are His workman-
ship, created in Christ Jesus for good
works, which God prepared beforehand
that we should walk in them.

Brought Near by His Blood

11Therefore remember that you, once
Gentiles in the flesh—who are called
Uncircumcision by what is called the
Circumcision made in the flesh by
hands— 12that at that time you were
without Christ, being aliens from the
commonwealth of Israel and strangers
from the covenants of promise, having
no hope and without God in the world.
13But now in Christ Jesus you who once
were far off have been brought near by
the blood of Christ.

Christ Our Peace

14For He Himself is our peace, who has
made both one, and has broken down
the middle wall of separation, 15having
abolished in His flesh the enmity, *that*
is, the law of commandments *contained*
in ordinances, so as to create in Himself
one new man *from* the two, *thus* making
peace, 16and that He might reconcile
them both to God in one body through
the cross, thereby putting to death the
enmity. 17And He came and preached
peace to you who were afar off and to
those who were near. 18For through Him
we both have access by one Spirit to
the Father.

Christ Our Cornerstone

19Now, therefore, you are no longer
strangers and foreigners, but fellow citi-
zens with the saints and members of the
household of God, 20having been built
on the foundation of the apostles and
prophets, Jesus Christ Himself being
the chief corner*stone,* 21in whom the
whole building, being fitted together,
grows into a holy temple in the Lord, 22in
whom you also are being built together
for a dwelling place of God in the Spirit.

The Mystery Revealed

3 For this reason I, Paul, the prisoner
of Christ Jesus for you Gentiles— 2if
indeed you have heard of the dispensa-
tion of the grace of God which was given
to me for you, 3how that by revelation
He made known to me the mystery
(as I have briefly written already, 4by
which, when you read, you may under-
stand my knowledge in the mystery of
Christ), 5which in other ages was not
made known to the sons of men, as it
has now been revealed by the Spirit to
His holy apostles and prophets: 6that
the Gentiles should be fellow heirs, of
the same body, and partakers of His
promise in Christ through the gospel, 7of
which I became a minister according to

the gift of the grace of God given to me by the effective working of His power.

Purpose of the Mystery

8To me, who am less than the least of all the saints, this grace was given, that I should preach among the Gentiles the unsearchable riches of Christ, 9and to make all see what *is* the fellowship[a] of the mystery, which from the beginning of the ages has been hidden in God who created all things through Jesus Christ;[b] 10to the intent that now the manifold wisdom of God might be made known by the church to the principalities and powers in the heavenly *places,* 11according to the eternal purpose which He accomplished in Christ Jesus our Lord, 12in whom we have boldness and access with confidence through faith in Him. 13Therefore I ask that you do not lose heart at my tribulations for you, which is your glory.

Appreciation of the Mystery

14For this reason I bow my knees to the Father of our Lord Jesus Christ,[a] 15from whom the whole family in heaven and earth is named, 16that He would grant you, according to the riches of His glory, to be strengthened with might through His Spirit in the inner man, 17that Christ may dwell in your hearts through faith; that you, being rooted and grounded in love, 18may be able to comprehend with all the saints what *is* the width and length and depth and height— 19to know the love of Christ which passes knowledge; that you may be filled with all the fullness of God.

20Now to Him who is able to do exceedingly abundantly above all that we ask or think, according to the power that works in us, 21to Him *be* glory in the church by Christ Jesus to all generations, forever and ever. Amen.

Walk in Unity

4 I, therefore, the prisoner of the Lord, beseech you to walk worthy of the calling with which you were called, 2with all lowliness and gentleness, with longsuffering, bearing with one another in love, 3endeavoring to keep the unity of the Spirit in the bond of peace. 4*There is* one body and one Spirit, just as you were called in one hope of your calling; 5one Lord, one faith, one baptism; 6one God and Father of all, who *is* above all, and through all, and in you[a] all.

Spiritual Gifts

7But to each one of us grace was given according to the measure of Christ's gift. 8Therefore He says:

"When He ascended on high,
He led captivity captive,
And gave gifts to men."[a]

9(Now this, "He ascended"—what does it mean but that He also first[a] descended into the lower parts of the earth? 10He who descended is also the One who ascended far above all the heavens, that He might fill all things.)

11And He Himself gave some *to be* apostles, some prophets, some evangelists, and some pastors and teachers, 12for the equipping of the saints for the work of ministry, for the edifying of the body of Christ, 13till we all come to the unity of the faith and of the knowledge of the Son of God, to a perfect man, to the measure of the stature of the fullness of Christ; 14that we should no longer be children, tossed to and fro and carried about with every wind of doctrine, by the trickery of men, in the cunning craftiness of deceitful plotting, 15but, speaking the truth in love, may grow up in all things into Him who is the head—Christ— 16from whom the whole body, joined and knit together by what every joint supplies, according to the effective working by which every part does its share, causes growth of the body for the edifying of itself in love.

The New Man

17This I say, therefore, and testify in the Lord, that you should no longer walk as the rest of[a] the Gentiles walk, in the futility of their mind, 18having their understanding darkened, being

3:9 [a] NU-Text and M-Text read *stewardship* (dispensation). [b] NU-Text omits *through Jesus Christ.* **3:14** [a] NU-Text omits *of our Lord Jesus Christ.* **4:6** [a] NU-Text omits *you;* M-Text reads *us.* **4:8** [a] Psalm 68:18 **4:9** [a] NU-Text omits *first.* **4:17** [a] NU-Text omits *the rest of.*

WORSHIP GROWTH HEAVEN FAMILY

alienated from the life of God, because
of the ignorance that is in them, be-
cause of the blindness of their heart;
19who, being past feeling, have given
themselves over to lewdness, to work
all uncleanness with greediness.
20But you have not so learned Christ,
21if indeed you have heard Him and
have been taught by Him, as the truth
is in Jesus: 22that you put off, concern-
ing your former conduct, the old man
which grows corrupt according to the
deceitful lusts, 23and be renewed in
the spirit of your mind, 24and that you
put on the new man which was created
according to God, in true righteousness
and holiness.

Do Not Grieve the Spirit

25Therefore, putting away lying, "*Let
each one of you speak truth with his
neighbor,*"[a] for we are members of
one another. 26"Be angry, and do not
sin":[a] do not let the sun go down on
your wrath, 27nor give place to the devil.
28Let him who stole steal no longer,
but rather let him labor, working with
his hands what is good, that he may
have something to give him who has
need. 29Let no corrupt word proceed
out of your mouth, but what is good
for necessary edification, that it may
impart grace to the hearers. 30And do
not grieve the Holy Spirit of God, by
whom you were sealed for the day of
redemption. 31Let all bitterness, wrath,
anger, clamor, and evil speaking be put
away from you, with all malice. 32And
be kind to one another, tenderhearted,
forgiving one another, even as God in
Christ forgave you.

Walk in Love

5 Therefore be imitators of God as
dear children. 2And walk in love,
as Christ also has loved us and given
Himself for us, an offering and a sacri-
fice to God for a sweet-smelling aroma.
3But fornication and all unclean-
ness or covetousness, let it not even
be named among you, as is fitting for
saints; 4neither filthiness, nor foolish
talking, nor coarse jesting, which are
not fitting, but rather giving of thanks.
5For this you know,[a] that no fornicator,
unclean person, nor covetous man, who
is an idolater, has any inheritance in
the kingdom of Christ and God. 6Let
no one deceive you with empty words,
for because of these things the wrath
of God comes upon the sons of disobe-
dience. 7Therefore do not be partakers
with them.

Walk in Light

8For you were once darkness, but
now *you are* light in the Lord. Walk as
children of light 9(for the fruit of the
Spirit[a] *is* in all goodness, righteous-
ness, and truth), 10finding out what is
acceptable to the Lord. 11And have no
fellowship with the unfruitful works
of darkness, but rather expose *them*.
12For it is shameful even to speak of
those things which are done by them
in secret. 13But all things that are ex-
posed are made manifest by the light,
for whatever makes manifest is light.
14Therefore He says:

"Awake, you who sleep,
Arise from the dead,
And Christ will give you light."

Walk in Wisdom

15See then that you walk circumspect-
ly, not as fools but as wise, 16redeeming
the time, because the days are evil.
17Therefore do not be unwise, but
understand what the will of the Lord
is. 18And do not be drunk with wine, in
which is dissipation; but be filled with
the Spirit, 19speaking to one another in
psalms and hymns and spiritual songs,
singing and making melody in your
heart to the Lord, 20giving thanks always
for all things to God the Father in the
name of our Lord Jesus Christ, 21submit-
ting to one another in the fear of God.[a]

Marriage—Christ and the Church

22Wives, submit to your own hus-
bands, as to the Lord. 23For the husband
is head of the wife, as also Christ is head
of the church; and He is the Savior of
the body. 24Therefore, just as the church

4:25 [a] Zechariah 8:16 4:26 [a] Psalm 4:4 5:5 [a] NU-Text reads *For know this.* 5:9 [a] NU-Text reads *light.* 5:21 [a] NU-Text reads *Christ.*

GOD SIN JESUS SALVATION LOVE

is subject to Christ, so *let* the wives *be*
to their own husbands in everything.
25 Husbands, love your wives, just as
Christ also loved the church and gave
Himself for her, 26 that He might sanc-
tify and cleanse her with the washing of
water by the word, 27 that He might pre-
sent her to Himself a glorious church,
not having spot or wrinkle or any such
thing, but that she should be holy and
without blemish. 28 So husbands ought
to love their own wives as their own bod-
ies; he who loves his wife loves himself.
29 For no one ever hated his own flesh,
but nourishes and cherishes it, just as
the Lord *does* the church. 30 For we are
members of His body,[a] of His flesh and
of His bones. 31 "For this reason a man
shall leave his father and mother and
be joined to his wife, and the two shall
become one flesh."[a] 32 This is a great
mystery, but I speak concerning Christ
and the church. 33 Nevertheless let each
one of you in particular so love his own
wife as himself, and let the wife *see* that
she respects *her* husband.

Children and Parents

6 Children, obey your parents in the
Lord, for this is right. 2 "Honor your
father and mother," which is the first
commandment with promise: 3 "that
it may be well with you and you may
live long on the earth."[a]
4 And you, fathers, do not provoke your
children to wrath, but bring them up
in the training and admonition of the
Lord.

Bondservants and Masters

5 Bondservants, be obedient to those
who are your masters according to the
flesh, with fear and trembling, in sin-
cerity of heart, as to Christ; 6 not with
eyeservice, as men-pleasers, but as
bondservants of Christ, doing the will
of God from the heart, 7 with goodwill
doing service, as to the Lord, and not to
men, 8 knowing that whatever good any-
one does, he will receive the same from
the Lord, whether *he is* a slave or free.
9 And you, masters, do the same things
to them, giving up threatening, knowing
that your own Master also[a] is in heaven,
and there is no partiality with Him.

The Whole Armor of God

10 Finally, my brethren, be strong in
the Lord and in the power of His might.
11 Put on the whole armor of God, that
you may be able to stand against the
wiles of the devil. 12 For we do not wrestle
against flesh and blood, but against
principalities, against powers, against
the rulers of the darkness of this age,[a]
against spiritual *hosts* of wickedness in
the heavenly *places*. 13 Therefore take up
the whole armor of God, that you may
be able to withstand in the evil day, and
having done all, to stand.
14 Stand therefore, having girded
your waist with truth, having put on
the breastplate of righteousness, 15 and
having shod your feet with the prepara-
tion of the gospel of peace; 16 above all,
taking the shield of faith with which you
will be able to quench all the fiery darts
of the wicked one. 17 And take the helmet
of salvation, and the sword of the Spirit,
which is the word of God; 18 praying al-
ways with all prayer and supplication
in the Spirit, being watchful to this end
with all perseverance and supplication
for all the saints— 19 and for me, that ut-
terance may be given to me, that I may
open my mouth boldly to make known
the mystery of the gospel, 20 for which I
am an ambassador in chains; that in it
I may speak boldly, as I ought to speak.

A Gracious Greeting

21 But that you also may know my af-
fairs *and* how I am doing, Tychicus, a
beloved brother and faithful minister
in the Lord, will make all things known
to you; 22 whom I have sent to you for
this very purpose, that you may know
our affairs, and *that* he may comfort
your hearts.
23 Peace to the brethren, and love with
faith, from God the Father and the Lord
Jesus Christ. 24 Grace *be* with all those
who love our Lord Jesus Christ in sin-
cerity. Amen.

5:30 [a] NU-Text omits the rest of this verse. **5:31** [a] Genesis 2:24 **6:3** [a] Deuteronomy 5:16
6:9 [a] NU-Text reads *He who is both their Master and yours.* **6:12** [a] NU-Text reads *rulers of this darkness.*

THE LETTER OF PAUL TO THE

PHILIPPIANS

Paul had helped found a church in the Greek city of Philippi. Later when Paul was in a time of need, this church stepped up to help provide for him. In response, Paul wrote this letter to them. Even though Paul was writing from prison, his letter is full of joy. His situation was difficult, but his joy was not based on it but rather in his relationship with Christ and his fellow believers. Paul told the church to watch out for false teachers, to live in unity with one another, and to obey God.

- **GENRE:** Epistle
- **AUTHOR:** Paul
- **TIME:** c. AD 60–62
- **PURPOSE:** To thank the Philippians for their support and tell them how to live as Christians.

Greeting

1 Paul and Timothy, bondservants
of Jesus Christ,

To all the saints in Christ Jesus who
are in Philippi, with the bishops[a] and
deacons:

2 Grace to you and peace from God our
Father and the Lord Jesus Christ.

Thankfulness and Prayer

3 I thank my God upon every remem-
brance of you, 4 always in every prayer
of mine making request for you all with
joy, 5 for your fellowship in the gospel
from the first day until now, 6 being
confident of this very thing, that He
who has begun a good work in you will
complete *it* until the day of Jesus Christ;
7 just as it is right for me to think this
of you all, because I have you in my
heart, inasmuch as both in my chains
and in the defense and confirmation of
the gospel, you all are partakers with
me of grace. 8 For God is my witness,
how greatly I long for you all with the
affection of Jesus Christ.

9 And this I pray, that your love may
abound still more and more in knowl-
edge and all discernment, 10 that you
may approve the things that are ex-
cellent, that you may be sincere and
without offense till the day of Christ,
11 being filled with the fruits of righ-
teousness which *are* by Jesus Christ, to
the glory and praise of God.

Christ Is Preached

12 But I want you to know, brethren,
that the things *which happened* to me
have actually turned out for the fur-
therance of the gospel, 13 so that it has
become evident to the whole palace
guard, and to all the rest, that my chains
are in Christ; 14 and most of the brethren
in the Lord, having become confident
by my chains, are much more bold to
speak the word without fear.

15 Some indeed preach Christ even
from envy and strife, and some also
from goodwill: 16 The former[a] preach
Christ from selfish ambition, not sin-
cerely, supposing to add affliction to
my chains; 17 but the latter out of love,
knowing that I am appointed for the de-
fense of the gospel. 18 What then? Only
that in every way, whether in pretense
or in truth, Christ is preached; and in
this I rejoice, yes, and will rejoice.

To Live Is Christ

19 For I know that this will turn out for
my deliverance through your prayer
and the supply of the Spirit of Jesus
Christ, 20 according to my earnest

1:1 [a] Literally *overseers* 1:16 [a] NU-Text reverses the contents of verses 16 and 17.

expectation and hope that in nothing I
shall be ashamed, but with all boldness,
as always, so now also Christ will be
magnified in my body, whether by life
or by death. 21For to me, to live *is* Christ,
and to die *is* gain. 22But if *I* live on in
the flesh, this *will mean* fruit from *my*
labor; yet what I shall choose I cannot
tell. 23For[a] I am hard-pressed between
the two, having a desire to depart and
be with Christ, *which is* far better. 24Nev-
ertheless to remain in the flesh *is* more
needful for you. 25And being confident
of this, I know that I shall remain and
continue with you all for your progress
and joy of faith, 26that your rejoicing
for me may be more abundant in Jesus
Christ by my coming to you again.

Striving and Suffering for Christ

27Only let your conduct be worthy of
the gospel of Christ, so that whether I
come and see you or am absent, I may
hear of your affairs, that you stand
fast in one spirit, with one mind striv-
ing together for the faith of the gospel,
28and not in any way terrified by your
adversaries, which is to them a proof of
perdition, but to you of salvation,[a] and
that from God. 29For to you it has been
granted on behalf of Christ, not only to
believe in Him, but also to suffer for His
sake, 30having the same conflict which
you saw in me and now hear *is* in me.

Unity Through Humility

2 Therefore if *there is* any consolation
in Christ, if any comfort of love,
if any fellowship of the Spirit, if any
affection and mercy, 2fulfill my joy by
being like-minded, having the same
love, *being* of one accord, of one mind.
3*Let* nothing *be done* through selfish
ambition or conceit, but in lowliness
of mind let each esteem others better
than himself. 4Let each of you look out
not only for his own interests, but also
for the interests of others.

The Humbled and Exalted Christ

5Let this mind be in you which was also
in Christ Jesus, 6who, being in the form
of God, did not consider it robbery to be
equal with God, 7but made Himself of no
reputation, taking the form of a bond-
servant, *and* coming in the likeness of
men. 8And being found in appearance
as a man, He humbled Himself and
became obedient to *the point of* death,
even the death of the cross. 9Therefore
God also has highly exalted Him and
given Him the name which is above
every name, 10that at the name of Jesus
every knee should bow, of those in heav-
en, and of those on earth, and of those
under the earth, 11and *that* every tongue
should confess that Jesus Christ *is* Lord,
to the glory of God the Father.

Light Bearers

12Therefore, my beloved, as you have
always obeyed, not as in my presence
only, but now much more in my ab-
sence, work out your own salvation with
fear and trembling; 13for it is God who
works in you both to will and to do for
His good pleasure.

14Do all things without complaining
and disputing, 15that you may become
blameless and harmless, children of God
without fault in the midst of a crooked
and perverse generation, among whom
you shine as lights in the world, 16hold-
ing fast the word of life, so that I may
rejoice in the day of Christ that I have
not run in vain or labored in vain.

17Yes, and if I am being poured out *as
a drink offering* on the sacrifice and ser-
vice of your faith, I am glad and rejoice
with you all. 18For the same reason you
also be glad and rejoice with me.

Timothy Commended

19But I trust in the Lord Jesus to send
Timothy to you shortly, that I also may
be encouraged when I know your state.
20For I have no one like-minded, who
will sincerely care for your state. 21For
all seek their own, not the things which
are of Christ Jesus. 22But you know his
proven character, that as a son with *his*
father he served with me in the gospel.
23Therefore I hope to send him at once,
as soon as I see how it goes with me.
24But I trust in the Lord that I myself
shall also come shortly.

1:23 [a] NU-Text and M-Text read *But.* **1:28** [a] NU-Text reads *of your salvation.*

Epaphroditus Praised

25Yet I considered it necessary to send to you Epaphroditus, my brother, fellow worker, and fellow soldier, but your messenger and the one who ministered to my need; 26since he was longing for you all, and was distressed because you had heard that he was sick. 27For indeed he was sick almost unto death; but God had mercy on him, and not only on him but on me also, lest I should have sorrow upon sorrow. 28Therefore I sent him the more eagerly, that when you see him again you may rejoice, and I may be less sorrowful. 29Receive him therefore in the Lord with all gladness, and hold such men in esteem; 30because for the work of Christ he came close to death, not regarding his life, to supply what was lacking in your service toward me.

All for Christ

3 Finally, my brethren, rejoice in the Lord. For me to write the same things to you *is* not tedious, but for you *it is* safe.

2Beware of dogs, beware of evil workers, beware of the mutilation! 3For we are the circumcision, who worship God in the Spirit,[a] rejoice in Christ Jesus, and have no confidence in the flesh, 4though I also might have confidence in the flesh. If anyone else thinks he may have confidence in the flesh, I more so: 5circumcised the eighth day, of the stock of Israel, *of* the tribe of Benjamin, a Hebrew of the Hebrews; concerning the law, a Pharisee; 6concerning zeal, persecuting the church; concerning the righteousness which is in the law, blameless.

7But what things were gain to me, these I have counted loss for Christ. 8Yet indeed I also count all things loss for the excellence of the knowledge of Christ Jesus my Lord, for whom I have suffered the loss of all things, and count them as rubbish, that I may gain Christ 9and be found in Him, not having my own righteousness, which *is* from the law, but that which *is* through faith in Christ, the righteousness which is from God by faith; 10that I may know Him and the power of His resurrection, and the fellowship of His sufferings, being conformed to His death, 11if, by any means, I may attain to the resurrection from the dead.

Pressing Toward the Goal

12Not that I have already attained, or am already perfected; but I press on, that I may lay hold of that for which Christ Jesus has also laid hold of me. 13Brethren, I do not count myself to have apprehended; but one thing *I do,* forgetting those things which are behind and reaching forward to those things which are ahead, 14I press toward the goal for the prize of the upward call of God in Christ Jesus.

15Therefore let us, as many as are mature, have this mind; and if in anything you think otherwise, God will reveal even this to you. 16Nevertheless, to *the degree* that we have already attained, let us walk by the same rule,[a] let us be of the same mind.

Our Citizenship in Heaven

17Brethren, join in following my example, and note those who so walk, as you have us for a pattern. 18For many walk, of whom I have told you often, and now tell you even weeping, *that they are* the enemies of the cross of Christ: 19whose end *is* destruction, whose god *is their* belly, and *whose* glory *is* in their shame—who set their mind on earthly things. 20For our citizenship is in heaven, from which we also eagerly wait for the Savior, the Lord Jesus Christ, 21who will transform our lowly body that it may be conformed to His glorious body, according to the working by which He is able even to subdue all things to Himself.

4 Therefore, my beloved and longed-for brethren, my joy and crown, so stand fast in the Lord, beloved.

Be United, Joyful, and in Prayer

2I implore Euodia and I implore Syntyche to be of the same mind in the Lord. 3And[a] I urge you also, true companion, help these women who labored

3:3 [a] NU-Text and M-Text read *who worship in the Spirit of God.* **3:16** [a] NU-Text omits *rule* and the rest of the verse. **4:3** [a] NU-Text and M-Text read *Yes.*

with me in the gospel, with Clement
also, and the rest of my fellow workers,
whose names *are* in the Book of Life.
4Rejoice in the Lord always. Again I
will say, rejoice!
5Let your gentleness be known to all
men. The Lord *is* at hand.
6Be anxious for nothing, but in every-
thing by prayer and supplication, with
thanksgiving, let your requests be made
known to God; 7and the peace of God,
which surpasses all understanding, will
guard your hearts and minds through
Christ Jesus.

Meditate on These Things

8Finally, brethren, whatever things are
true, whatever things *are* noble, what-
ever things *are* just, whatever things
are pure, whatever things *are* lovely,
whatever things *are* of good report, if
there is any virtue and if *there is* any-
thing praiseworthy—meditate on these
things. 9The things which you learned
and received and heard and saw in me,
these do, and the God of peace will be
with you.

Philippian Generosity

10But I rejoiced in the Lord greatly
that now at last your care for me has
flourished again; though you surely
did care, but you lacked opportunity.
11Not that I speak in regard to need, for I
have learned in whatever state I am, to
be content: 12I know how to be abased,
and I know how to abound. Everywhere
and in all things I have learned both to
be full and to be hungry, both to abound
and to suffer need. 13I can do all things
through Christ[a] who strengthens me.
14Nevertheless you have done well that
you shared in my distress. 15Now you
Philippians know also that in the be-
ginning of the gospel, when I departed
from Macedonia, no church shared with
me concerning giving and receiving
but you only. 16For even in Thessalo-
nica you sent *aid* once and again for
my necessities. 17Not that I seek the
gift, but I seek the fruit that abounds to
your account. 18Indeed I have all and
abound. I am full, having received from
Epaphroditus the things *sent* from you,
a sweet-smelling aroma, an acceptable
sacrifice, well pleasing to God. 19And
my God shall supply all your need ac-
cording to His riches in glory by Christ
Jesus. 20Now to our God and Father *be*
glory forever and ever. Amen.

Greeting and Blessing

21Greet every saint in Christ Jesus. The
brethren who are with me greet you.
22All the saints greet you, but especially
those who are of Caesar's household.
23The grace of our Lord Jesus Christ
be with you all.[a] Amen.

4:13 [a] NU-Text reads *Him who.* **4:23** [a] NU-Text reads *your spirit.*

THE LETTER OF PAUL TO THE

COLOSSIANS

The problem of the Colossian church was similar to what many churches experience today. The Colossian believers wanted to believe biblical truth, but they also had a difficult time letting go of some other beliefs, and some false teachers were making it more challenging. Paul was in prison, but he wanted to help the Colossians, so he wrote this letter. In it, Paul reminds the church of the basics of the Christian faith and emphasizes that Jesus is superior to everything else. Jesus needs to be at the center of the believer's beliefs and practices. If the Colossians did this, they would see how foolish it is to hold on to other beliefs and distortions of the gospel that the false teachers were sharing.

- **GENRE:** Epistle
- **AUTHOR:** Paul
- **TIME:** c. AD 60–62
- **PURPOSE:** To explain that Christ is superior to every ruler, power, and authority in heaven and earth, and that He alone saves us.

Greeting

1 Paul, an apostle of Jesus Christ by
the will of God, and Timothy our
brother,

2To the saints and faithful brethren in
Christ *who are* in Colosse:

Grace to you and peace from God our
Father and the Lord Jesus Christ.[a]

Their Faith in Christ

3We give thanks to the God and Father
of our Lord Jesus Christ, praying always
for you, 4since we heard of your faith
in Christ Jesus and of your love for all
the saints; 5because of the hope which is
laid up for you in heaven, of which you
heard before in the word of the truth of
the gospel, 6which has come to you, as *it*
has also in all the world, and is bringing
forth fruit,[a] as *it is* also among you since
the day you heard and knew the grace
of God in truth; 7as you also learned
from Epaphras, our dear fellow servant,
who is a faithful minister of Christ on
your behalf, 8who also declared to us
your love in the Spirit.

Preeminence of Christ

9For this reason we also, since the day
we heard it, do not cease to pray for you,
and to ask that you may be filled with
the knowledge of His will in all wisdom
and spiritual understanding; 10that
you may walk worthy of the Lord, fully
pleasing *Him,* being fruitful in every
good work and increasing in the knowl-
edge of God; 11strengthened with all
might, according to His glorious power,
for all patience and longsuffering with
joy; 12giving thanks to the Father who
has qualified us to be partakers of the
inheritance of the saints in the light.
13He has delivered us from the power
of darkness and conveyed *us* into the
kingdom of the Son of His love, 14in
whom we have redemption through His
blood,[a] the forgiveness of sins.

15He is the image of the invisible God,
the firstborn over all creation. 16For by
Him all things were created that are in
heaven and that are on earth, visible
and invisible, whether thrones or do-
minions or principalities or powers. All
things were created through Him and
for Him. 17And He is before all things,

1:2 a NU-Text omits *and the Lord Jesus Christ.* **1:6** a NU-Text and M-Text add *and growing.*
1:14 a NU-Text and M-Text omit *through His blood.*

GOD | SIN | JESUS | SALVATION | LOVE

and in Him all things consist. 18And He is the head of the body, the church, who is the beginning, the firstborn from the dead, that in all things He may have the preeminence.

Reconciled in Christ

19For it pleased *the Father that* in Him all the fullness should dwell, 20and by Him to reconcile all things to Himself, by Him, whether things on earth or things in heaven, having made peace through the blood of His cross.

21And you, who once were alienated and enemies in your mind by wicked works, yet now He has reconciled 22in the body of His flesh through death, to present you holy, and blameless, and above reproach in His sight— 23if indeed you continue in the faith, grounded and steadfast, and are not moved away from the hope of the gospel which you heard, which was preached to every creature under heaven, of which I, Paul, became a minister.

Sacrificial Service for Christ

24I now rejoice in my sufferings for you, and fill up in my flesh what is lacking in the afflictions of Christ, for the sake of His body, which is the church, 25of which I became a minister according to the stewardship from God which was given to me for you, to fulfill the word of God, 26the mystery which has been hidden from ages and from generations, but now has been revealed to His saints. 27To them God willed to make known what are the riches of the glory of this mystery among the Gentiles: which[a] is Christ in you, the hope of glory. 28Him we preach, warning every man and teaching every man in all wisdom, that we may present every man perfect in Christ Jesus. 29To this *end* I also labor, striving according to His working which works in me mightily.

Not Philosophy but Christ

2 For I want you to know what a great conflict I have for you and those in Laodicea, and *for* as many as have not seen my face in the flesh, 2that their hearts may be encouraged, being knit together in love, and *attaining* to all riches of the full assurance of understanding, to the knowledge of the mystery of God, both of the Father and[a] of Christ, 3in whom are hidden all the treasures of wisdom and knowledge.

4Now this I say lest anyone should deceive you with persuasive words. 5For though I am absent in the flesh, yet I am with you in spirit, rejoicing to see your *good* order and the steadfastness of your faith in Christ.

6As you therefore have received Christ Jesus the Lord, so walk in Him, 7rooted and built up in Him and established in the faith, as you have been taught, abounding in it[a] with thanksgiving.

8Beware lest anyone cheat you through philosophy and empty deceit, according to the tradition of men, according to the basic principles of the world, and not according to Christ. 9For in Him dwells all the fullness of the Godhead bodily; 10and you are complete in Him, who is the head of all principality and power.

Not Legalism but Christ

11In Him you were also circumcised with the circumcision made without hands, by putting off the body of the sins[a] of the flesh, by the circumcision of Christ, 12buried with Him in baptism, in which you also were raised with *Him* through faith in the working of God, who raised Him from the dead. 13And you, being dead in your trespasses and the uncircumcision of your flesh, He has made alive together with Him, having forgiven you all trespasses, 14having wiped out the handwriting of requirements that was against us, which was contrary to us. And He has taken it out of the way, having nailed it to the cross. 15Having disarmed principalities and powers, He made a public spectacle of them, triumphing over them in it.

16So let no one judge you in food or in drink, or regarding a festival or a new moon or sabbaths, 17which are a shadow

1:27 [a] M-Text reads *who*. **2:2** [a] NU-Text omits *both of the Father and*. **2:7** [a] NU-Text omits *in it*. **2:11** [a] NU-Text omits *of the sins*.

of things to come, but the substance is of Christ. 18Let no one cheat you of your reward, taking delight in *false* humility and worship of angels, intruding into those things which he has not[a] seen, vainly puffed up by his fleshly mind, 19and not holding fast to the Head, from whom all the body, nourished and knit together by joints and ligaments, grows with the increase *that is* from God.

20Therefore,[a] if you died with Christ from the basic principles of the world, why, as *though* living in the world, do you subject yourselves to regulations— 21"Do not touch, do not taste, do not handle," 22which all concern things which perish with the using—according to the commandments and doctrines of men? 23These things indeed have an appearance of wisdom in self-imposed religion, *false* humility, and neglect of the body, *but are* of no value against the indulgence of the flesh.

Not Carnality but Christ

3 If then you were raised with Christ, seek those things which are above, where Christ is, sitting at the right hand of God. 2Set your mind on things above, not on things on the earth. 3For you died, and your life is hidden with Christ in God. 4When Christ *who is* our life appears, then you also will appear with Him in glory.

5Therefore put to death your members which are on the earth: fornication, uncleanness, passion, evil desire, and covetousness, which is idolatry. 6Because of these things the wrath of God is coming upon the sons of disobedience, 7in which you yourselves once walked when you lived in them.

8But now you yourselves are to put off all these: anger, wrath, malice, blasphemy, filthy language out of your mouth. 9Do not lie to one another, since you have put off the old man with his deeds, 10and have put on the new *man* who is renewed in knowledge according to the image of Him who created him, 11where there is neither Greek nor Jew, circumcised nor uncircumcised, barbarian, Scythian, slave *nor* free, but Christ *is* all and in all.

Character of the New Man

12Therefore, as *the* elect of God, holy and beloved, put on tender mercies, kindness, humility, meekness, longsuffering; 13bearing with one another, and forgiving one another, if anyone has a complaint against another; even as Christ forgave you, so you also *must do.* 14But above all these things put on love, which is the bond of perfection. 15And let the peace of God rule in your hearts, to which also you were called in one body; and be thankful. 16Let the word of Christ dwell in you richly in all wisdom, teaching and admonishing one another in psalms and hymns and spiritual songs, singing with grace in your hearts to the Lord. 17And whatever you do in word or deed, *do* all in the name of the Lord Jesus, giving thanks to God the Father through Him.

The Christian Home

18Wives, submit to your own husbands, as is fitting in the Lord.

19Husbands, love your wives and do not be bitter toward them.

20Children, obey your parents in all things, for this is well pleasing to the Lord.

21Fathers, do not provoke your children, lest they become discouraged.

22Bondservants, obey in all things your masters according to the flesh, not with eyeservice, as men-pleasers, but in sincerity of heart, fearing God. 23And whatever you do, do it heartily, as to the Lord and not to men, 24knowing that from the Lord you will receive the reward of the inheritance; for[a] you serve the Lord Christ. 25But he who does wrong will be repaid for what he has done, and there is no partiality.

4 Masters, give your bondservants what is just and fair, knowing that you also have a Master in heaven.

Christian Graces

2Continue earnestly in prayer, being vigilant in it with thanksgiving; 3meanwhile praying also for us, that God would open to us a door for the word, to speak the mystery of Christ, for

2:18 [a] NU-Text omits *not.* **2:20** [a] NU-Text and M-Text omit *Therefore.* **3:24** [a] NU-Text omits *for.*

which I am also in chains, 4that I may
make it manifest, as I ought to speak.
5Walk in wisdom toward those *who are*
outside, redeeming the time. 6*Let* your
speech always *be* with grace, seasoned
with salt, that you may know how you
ought to answer each one.

Final Greetings

7Tychicus, a beloved brother, faithful
minister, and fellow servant in the Lord,
will tell you all the news about me. 8I
am sending him to you for this very
purpose, that he[a] may know your cir-
cumstances and comfort your hearts,
9with Onesimus, a faithful and beloved
brother, who is *one* of you. They will
make known to you all things which
are happening here.
10Aristarchus my fellow prisoner
greets you, with Mark the cousin of
Barnabas (about whom you received
instructions: if he comes to you, wel-
come him), 11and Jesus who is called
Justus. These *are my* only fellow workers
for the kingdom of God who are of the
circumcision; they have proved to be a
comfort to me.
12Epaphras, who is *one* of you, a bond-
servant of Christ, greets you, always
laboring fervently for you in prayers,
that you may stand perfect and com-
plete[a] in all the will of God. 13For I bear
him witness that he has a great zeal[a]
for you, and those who are in Laodicea,
and those in Hierapolis. 14Luke the be-
loved physician and Demas greet you.
15Greet the brethren who are in Laodi-
cea, and Nymphas and the church that
is in his[a] house.

Closing Exhortations and Blessing

16Now when this epistle is read among
you, see that it is read also in the church
of the Laodiceans, and that you like-
wise read the *epistle* from Laodicea.
17And say to Archippus, "Take heed to
the ministry which you have received in
the Lord, that you may fulfill it."
18This salutation by my own hand—
Paul. Remember my chains. Grace *be*
with you. Amen.

4:8 [a] NU-Text reads *you may know our circumstances and he may.* 4:12 [a] NU-Text reads *fully assured.* 4:13 [a] NU-Text reads *concern.* 4:15 [a] NU-Text reads *Nympha . . . her house.*

THE FIRST LETTER OF PAUL TO THE

THESSALONIANS

Paul planted the Thessalonian church in Greece during his second missionary journey. Overall, this church was doing quite well, but they did have one problem: they were unclear about what happened when believers die before Christ returns. In response, Paul wrote this letter to them. Paul's main point was that Jesus' return should bring hope and comfort to them. Believers who have died are with Christ, so there is no need to be concerned about them. The Thessalonians were to wait patiently for the Lord's return and to keep living as they had been—with faith and love.

- **GENRE:** Epistle
- **AUTHOR:** Paul
- **TIME:** c. AD 50–54
- **PURPOSE:** To instruct the Thessalonians on how to live in a way that pleases God and encourage them that Jesus will come again.

Greeting

1 Paul, Silvanus, and Timothy,

To the church of the Thessalonians
in God the Father and the Lord Jesus
Christ:

Grace to you and peace from God our
Father and the Lord Jesus Christ.[a]

Their Good Example

2We give thanks to God always for
you all, making mention of you in our
prayers, 3remembering without ceasing
your work of faith, labor of love, and pa-
tience of hope in our Lord Jesus Christ in
the sight of our God and Father, 4know-
ing, beloved brethren, your election by
God. 5For our gospel did not come to you
in word only, but also in power, and in
the Holy Spirit and in much assurance,
as you know what kind of men we were
among you for your sake.
6And you became followers of us and
of the Lord, having received the word
in much affliction, with joy of the Holy
Spirit, 7so that you became examples
to all in Macedonia and Achaia who be-
lieve. 8For from you the word of the Lord
has sounded forth, not only in Macedo-
nia and Achaia, but also in every place.
Your faith toward God has gone out, so
that we do not need to say anything. 9For
they themselves declare concerning us
what manner of entry we had to you,
and how you turned to God from idols
to serve the living and true God, 10and
to wait for His Son from heaven, whom
He raised from the dead, *even* Jesus who
delivers us from the wrath to come.

Paul's Conduct

2 For you yourselves know, brethren,
that our coming to you was not in
vain. 2But even[a] after we had suffered
before and were spitefully treated at
Philippi, as you know, we were bold in
our God to speak to you the gospel of
God in much conflict. 3For our exhor-
tation *did* not *come* from error or un-
cleanness, nor *was it* in deceit.
4But as we have been approved by God
to be entrusted with the gospel, even so
we speak, not as pleasing men, but God
who tests our hearts. 5For neither at any
time did we use flattering words, as you
know, nor a cloak for covetousness—
God *is* witness. 6Nor did we seek glory
from men, either from you or from oth-
ers, when we might have made demands
as apostles of Christ. 7But we were gentle
among you, just as a nursing *mother*

1:1 [a] NU-Text omits *from God our Father and the Lord Jesus Christ.* **2:2** [a] NU-Text and M-Text omit *even.*

cherishes her own children. 8So, affectionately longing for you, we were well pleased to impart to you not only the gospel of God, but also our own lives, because you had become dear to us. 9For you remember, brethren, our labor and toil; for laboring night and day, that we might not be a burden to any of you, we preached to you the gospel of God.

10You *are* witnesses, and God *also,* how devoutly and justly and blamelessly we behaved ourselves among you who believe; 11as you know how we exhorted, and comforted, and charged[a] every one of you, as a father *does* his own children, 12that you would walk worthy of God who calls you into His own kingdom and glory.

Their Conversion

13For this reason we also thank God without ceasing, because when you received the word of God which you heard from us, you welcomed *it* not *as* the word of men, but as it is in truth, the word of God, which also effectively works in you who believe. 14For you, brethren, became imitators of the churches of God which are in Judea in Christ Jesus. For you also suffered the same things from your own countrymen, just as they *did* from the Judeans, 15who killed both the Lord Jesus and their own prophets, and have persecuted us; and they do not please God and are contrary to all men, 16forbidding us to speak to the Gentiles that they may be saved, so as always to fill up *the measure of* their sins; but wrath has come upon them to the uttermost.

Longing to See Them

17But we, brethren, having been taken away from you for a short time in presence, not in heart, endeavored more eagerly to see your face with great desire. 18Therefore we wanted to come to you—even I, Paul, time and again—but Satan hindered us. 19For what *is* our hope, or joy, or crown of rejoicing? *Is it* not even you in the presence of our Lord Jesus Christ at His coming? 20For you are our glory and joy.

Concern for Their Faith

3 Therefore, when we could no longer endure it, we thought it good to be left in Athens alone, 2and sent Timothy, our brother and minister of God, and our fellow laborer in the gospel of Christ, to establish you and encourage you concerning your faith, 3that no one should be shaken by these afflictions; for you yourselves know that we are appointed to this. 4For, in fact, we told you before when we were with you that we would suffer tribulation, just as it happened, and you know. 5For this reason, when I could no longer endure it, I sent to know your faith, lest by some means the tempter had tempted you, and our labor might be in vain.

Encouraged by Timothy

6But now that Timothy has come to us from you, and brought us good news of your faith and love, and that you always have good remembrance of us, greatly desiring to see us, as we also *to see* you— 7therefore, brethren, in all our affliction and distress we were comforted concerning you by your faith. 8For now we live, if you stand fast in the Lord.

9For what thanks can we render to God for you, for all the joy with which we rejoice for your sake before our God, 10night and day praying exceedingly that we may see your face and perfect what is lacking in your faith?

Prayer for the Church

11Now may our God and Father Himself, and our Lord Jesus Christ, direct our way to you. 12And may the Lord make you increase and abound in love to one another and to all, just as we *do* to you, 13so that He may establish your hearts blameless in holiness before our God and Father at the coming of our Lord Jesus Christ with all His saints.

Plea for Purity

4 Finally then, brethren, we urge and exhort in the Lord Jesus that you should abound more and more, just as you received from us how you ought to walk and to please God; 2for you know

2:11 [a] NU-Text and M-Text read *implored.*

what commandments we gave you through the Lord Jesus.

3For this is the will of God, your sanctification: that you should abstain from sexual immorality; 4that each of you should know how to possess his own vessel in sanctification and honor, 5not in passion of lust, like the Gentiles who do not know God; 6that no one should take advantage of and defraud his brother in this matter, because the Lord *is* the avenger of all such, as we also forewarned you and testified. 7For God did not call us to uncleanness, but in holiness. 8Therefore he who rejects *this* does not reject man, but God, who has also given[a] us His Holy Spirit.

A Brotherly and Orderly Life

9But concerning brotherly love you have no need that I should write to you, for you yourselves are taught by God to love one another; 10and indeed you do so toward all the brethren who are in all Macedonia. But we urge you, brethren, that you increase more and more; 11that you also aspire to lead a quiet life, to mind your own business, and to work with your own hands, as we commanded you, 12that you may walk properly toward those who are outside, and *that* you may lack nothing.

The Comfort of Christ's Coming

13But I do not want you to be ignorant, brethren, concerning those who have fallen asleep, lest you sorrow as others who have no hope. 14For if we believe that Jesus died and rose again, even so God will bring with Him those who sleep in Jesus.[a]

15For this we say to you by the word of the Lord, that we who are alive *and* remain until the coming of the Lord will by no means precede those who are asleep. 16For the Lord Himself will descend from heaven with a shout, with the voice of an archangel, and with the trumpet of God. And the dead in Christ will rise first. 17Then we who are alive *and* remain shall be caught up together with them in the clouds to meet the Lord in the air. And thus we shall always be with the Lord. 18Therefore comfort one another with these words.

The Day of the Lord

5 But concerning the times and the seasons, brethren, you have no need that I should write to you. 2For you yourselves know perfectly that the day of the Lord so comes as a thief in the night. 3For when they say, "Peace and safety!" then sudden destruction comes upon them, as labor pains upon a pregnant woman. And they shall not escape. 4But you, brethren, are not in darkness, so that this Day should overtake you as a thief. 5You are all sons of light and sons of the day. We are not of the night nor of darkness. 6Therefore let us not sleep, as others *do*, but let us watch and be sober. 7For those who sleep, sleep at night, and those who get drunk are drunk at night. 8But let us who are of the day be sober, putting on the breastplate of faith and love, and *as* a helmet the hope of salvation. 9For God did not appoint us to wrath, but to obtain salvation through our Lord Jesus Christ, 10who died for us, that whether we wake or sleep, we should live together with Him.

11Therefore comfort each other and edify one another, just as you also are doing.

Various Exhortations

12And we urge you, brethren, to recognize those who labor among you, and are over you in the Lord and admonish you, 13and to esteem them very highly in love for their work's sake. Be at peace among yourselves.

14Now we exhort you, brethren, warn those who are unruly, comfort the fainthearted, uphold the weak, be patient with all. 15See that no one renders evil for evil to anyone, but always pursue what is good both for yourselves and for all.

16Rejoice always, 17pray without ceasing, 18in everything give thanks; for this is the will of God in Christ Jesus for you.

19Do not quench the Spirit. 20Do not despise prophecies. 21Test all things; hold fast what is good. 22Abstain from every form of evil.

4:8 [a] NU-Text reads *who also gives.* **4:14** [a] Or *those who through Jesus sleep*

GOD SIN JESUS SALVATION LOVE

Blessing and Admonition

[23]Now may the God of peace Him-
self sanctify you completely; and may
your whole spirit, soul, and body be
preserved blameless at the coming of
our Lord Jesus Christ. [24]He who calls
you *is* faithful, who also will do *it*.

[25]Brethren, pray for us.
[26]Greet all the brethren with a holy
kiss.
[27]I charge you by the Lord that this
epistle be read to all the holy[a] brethren.
[28]The grace of our Lord Jesus Christ
be with you. Amen.

5:27 [a] NU-Text omits *holy*.

THE SECOND LETTER OF PAUL TO THE

THESSALONIANS

Since Paul's first letter to the Thessalonians, misunderstandings and false teachings about what he had said spread through the church. Some thought that the return of Christ had already happened and that they had missed it. Paul wrote this letter to correct that error. Jesus had not returned yet. They had not missed it. And they would not miss it when He does. No one will. Jesus' return will happen after other things take place. These signs will help them be watchful and recognize that day. Meanwhile, Paul encouraged the Thessalonians to be disciplined, work hard, and focus on the hope for eternity.

- **GENRE:** Epistle
- **AUTHOR:** Paul
- **TIME:** c. AD 50–54
- **PURPOSE:** To encourage the Thessalonians to work hard while they wait for Jesus to come again.

Greeting

1 Paul, Silvanus, and Timothy,

To the church of the Thessalonians
in God our Father and the Lord Jesus
Christ:

2Grace to you and peace from God our
Father and the Lord Jesus Christ.

God's Final Judgment and Glory

3We are bound to thank God always
for you, brethren, as it is fitting, because
your faith grows exceedingly, and the
love of every one of you all abounds
toward each other, 4so that we ourselves
boast of you among the churches of God
for your patience and faith in all your
persecutions and tribulations that you
endure, 5*which is* manifest evidence of
the righteous judgment of God, that you
may be counted worthy of the kingdom
of God, for which you also suffer; 6since
it is a righteous thing with God to repay
with tribulation those who trouble you,
7and to *give* you who are troubled rest
with us when the Lord Jesus is revealed
from heaven with His mighty angels,
8in flaming fire taking vengeance on
those who do not know God, and on
those who do not obey the gospel of our
Lord Jesus Christ. 9These shall be pun-
ished with everlasting destruction from
the presence of the Lord and from the
glory of His power, 10when He comes,
in that Day, to be glorified in His saints
and to be admired among all those who
believe,[a] because our testimony among
you was believed.

11Therefore we also pray always for you
that our God would count you worthy
of *this* calling, and fulfill all the good
pleasure of *His* goodness and the work of
faith with power, 12that the name of our
Lord Jesus Christ may be glorified in you,
and you in Him, according to the grace
of our God and the Lord Jesus Christ.

The Great Apostasy

2 Now, brethren, concerning the com-
ing of our Lord Jesus Christ and
our gathering together to Him, we ask
you, 2not to be soon shaken in mind or
troubled, either by spirit or by word or
by letter, as if from us, as though the day
of Christ[a] had come. 3Let no one deceive
you by any means; for *that Day will not
come* unless the falling away comes
first, and the man of sin[a] is revealed,
the son of perdition, 4who opposes and
exalts himself above all that is called
God or that is worshiped, so that he sits

1:10 [a] NU-Text and M-Text read *have believed.* 2:2 [a] NU-Text reads *the Lord.* 2:3 [a] NU-Text reads *lawlessness.*

GOD SIN JESUS SALVATION LOVE

as God[a] in the temple of God, showing himself that he is God.

5Do you not remember that when I was still with you I told you these things? 6And now you know what is restraining, that he may be revealed in his own time. 7For the mystery of lawlessness is already at work; only He[a] who now restrains *will do so* until He[b] is taken out of the way. 8And then the lawless one will be revealed, whom the Lord will consume with the breath of His mouth and destroy with the brightness of His coming. 9The coming of the *lawless one* is according to the working of Satan, with all power, signs, and lying wonders, 10and with all unrighteous deception among those who perish, because they did not receive the love of the truth, that they might be saved. 11And for this reason God will send them strong delusion, that they should believe the lie, 12that they all may be condemned who did not believe the truth but had pleasure in unrighteousness.

Stand Fast

13But we are bound to give thanks to God always for you, brethren beloved by the Lord, because God from the beginning chose you for salvation through sanctification by the Spirit and belief in the truth, 14to which He called you by our gospel, for the obtaining of the glory of our Lord Jesus Christ. 15Therefore, brethren, stand fast and hold the traditions which you were taught, whether by word or our epistle.

16Now may our Lord Jesus Christ Himself, and our God and Father, who has loved us and given *us* everlasting consolation and good hope by grace, 17comfort your hearts and establish you in every good word and work.

Pray for Us

3 Finally, brethren, pray for us, that the word of the Lord may run *swiftly* and be glorified, just as *it is* with you, 2and that we may be delivered from unreasonable and wicked men; for not all have faith.

3But the Lord is faithful, who will establish you and guard *you* from the evil one. 4And we have confidence in the Lord concerning you, both that you do and will do the things we command you.

5Now may the Lord direct your hearts into the love of God and into the patience of Christ.

Warning Against Idleness

6But we command you, brethren, in the name of our Lord Jesus Christ, that you withdraw from every brother who walks disorderly and not according to the tradition which he[a] received from us. 7For you yourselves know how you ought to follow us, for we were not disorderly among you; 8nor did we eat anyone's bread free of charge, but worked with labor and toil night and day, that we might not be a burden to any of you, 9not because we do not have authority, but to make ourselves an example of how you should follow us.

10For even when we were with you, we commanded you this: If anyone will not work, neither shall he eat. 11For we hear that there are some who walk among you in a disorderly manner, not working at all, but are busybodies. 12Now those who are such we command and exhort through our Lord Jesus Christ that they work in quietness and eat their own bread.

13But *as for* you, brethren, do not grow weary *in* doing good. 14And if anyone does not obey our word in this epistle, note that person and do not keep company with him, that he may be ashamed. 15Yet do not count *him* as an enemy, but admonish *him* as a brother.

Benediction

16Now may the Lord of peace Himself give you peace always in every way. The Lord *be* with you all.

17The salutation of Paul with my own hand, which is a sign in every epistle; so I write.

18The grace of our Lord Jesus Christ *be* with you all. Amen.

2:4 [a] NU-Text omits *as God.* 2:7 [a] Or *he* [b] Or *he* 3:6 [a] NU-Text and M-Text read *they.*

THE FIRST LETTER OF PAUL TO

TIMOTHY

Timothy was one of Paul's traveling companions on his missionary journeys and became one of the apostle's most trusted coworkers. Paul would often send Timothy to churches as his representative to serve in struggling and strategic churches. Timothy spent time in Philippi before going to Ephesus to be pastor of that church. The church Timothy found had several challenges. False teachings had to be removed, proper worship protected, and leadership developed. Added to these challenges was that Timothy was young. Paul wrote this letter to Timothy to encourage him and guide him in how best to serve the church.

- **GENRE:** Epistle
- **AUTHOR:** Paul
- **TIME:** c. AD 62–66
- **PURPOSE:** To encourage Timothy in his pastoral ministry and help him know how to minister better.

Greeting

1 Paul, an apostle of Jesus Christ, by the commandment of God our Savior and the Lord Jesus Christ, our hope,

2To Timothy, a true son in the faith:

Grace, mercy, *and* peace from God our Father and Jesus Christ our Lord.

No Other Doctrine

3As I urged you when I went into Macedonia—remain in Ephesus that you may charge some that they teach no other doctrine, 4nor give heed to fables and endless genealogies, which cause disputes rather than godly edification which is in faith. 5Now the purpose of the commandment is love from a pure heart, *from* a good conscience, and *from* sincere faith, 6from which some, having strayed, have turned aside to idle talk, 7desiring to be teachers of the law, understanding neither what they say nor the things which they affirm.

8But we know that the law *is* good if one uses it lawfully, 9knowing this: that the law is not made for a righteous person, but for *the* lawless and insubordinate, for *the* ungodly and for sinners, for *the* unholy and profane, for murderers of fathers and murderers of mothers, for manslayers, 10for fornicators, for sodomites, for kidnappers, for liars, for perjurers, and if there is any other thing that is contrary to sound doctrine, 11according to the glorious gospel of the blessed God which was committed to my trust.

Glory to God for His Grace

12And I thank Christ Jesus our Lord who has enabled me, because He counted me faithful, putting *me* into the ministry, 13although I was formerly a blasphemer, a persecutor, and an insolent man; but I obtained mercy because I did *it* ignorantly in unbelief. 14And the grace of our Lord was exceedingly abundant, with faith and love which are in Christ Jesus. 15This *is* a faithful saying and worthy of all acceptance, that Christ Jesus came into the world to save sinners, of whom I am chief. 16However, for this reason I obtained mercy, that in me first Jesus Christ might show all longsuffering, as a pattern to those who are going to believe on Him for everlasting life. 17Now to the King eternal, immortal, invisible, to God who alone is wise,[a] *be* honor and glory forever and ever. Amen.

1:17 [a] NU-Text reads *to the only God.*

GOD | SIN | JESUS | SALVATION | LOVE

Fight the Good Fight

18This charge I commit to you, son Timothy, according to the prophecies previously made concerning you, that by them you may wage the good warfare, 19having faith and a good conscience, which some having rejected, concerning the faith have suffered shipwreck, 20of whom are Hymenaeus and Alexander, whom I delivered to Satan that they may learn not to blaspheme.

Pray for All Men

2 Therefore I exhort first of all that supplications, prayers, intercessions, *and* giving of thanks be made for all men, 2for kings and all who are in authority, that we may lead a quiet and peaceable life in all godliness and reverence. 3For this *is* good and acceptable in the sight of God our Savior, 4who desires all men to be saved and to come to the knowledge of the truth. 5For *there is* one God and one Mediator between God and men, *the* Man Christ Jesus, 6who gave Himself a ransom for all, to be testified in due time, 7for which I was appointed a preacher and an apostle—I am speaking the truth in Christ[a] *and* not lying—a teacher of the Gentiles in faith and truth.

Men and Women in the Church

8I desire therefore that the men pray everywhere, lifting up holy hands, without wrath and doubting; 9in like manner also, that the women adorn themselves in modest apparel, with propriety and moderation, not with braided hair or gold or pearls or costly clothing, 10but, which is proper for women professing godliness, with good works. 11Let a woman learn in silence with all submission. 12And I do not permit a woman to teach or to have authority over a man, but to be in silence. 13For Adam was formed first, then Eve. 14And Adam was not deceived, but the woman being deceived, fell into transgression. 15Nevertheless she will be saved in childbearing if they continue in faith, love, and holiness, with self-control.

Qualifications of Overseers

3 This *is* a faithful saying: If a man desires the position of a bishop,[a] he desires a good work. 2A bishop then must be blameless, the husband of one wife, temperate, sober-minded, of good behavior, hospitable, able to teach; 3not given to wine, not violent, not greedy for money,[a] but gentle, not quarrelsome, not covetous; 4one who rules his own house well, having *his* children in submission with all reverence 5(for if a man does not know how to rule his own house, how will he take care of the church of God?); 6not a novice, lest being puffed up with pride he fall into the *same* condemnation as the devil. 7Moreover he must have a good testimony among those who are outside, lest he fall into reproach and the snare of the devil.

Qualifications of Deacons

8Likewise deacons *must be* reverent, not double-tongued, not given to much wine, not greedy for money, 9holding the mystery of the faith with a pure conscience. 10But let these also first be tested; then let them serve as deacons, being *found* blameless. 11Likewise, *their* wives *must be* reverent, not slanderers, temperate, faithful in all things. 12Let deacons be the husbands of one wife, ruling *their* children and their own houses well. 13For those who have served well as deacons obtain for themselves a good standing and great boldness in the faith which is in Christ Jesus.

The Great Mystery

14These things I write to you, though I hope to come to you shortly; 15but if I am delayed, *I write* so that you may know how you ought to conduct yourself in the house of God, which is the church of the living God, the pillar and ground of the truth. 16And without controversy great is the mystery of godliness:

God[a] was manifested in the flesh,
Justified in the Spirit,

2:7 [a] NU-Text omits *in Christ.* 3:1 [a] Literally *overseer* 3:3 [a] NU-Text omits *not greedy for money.* 3:16 [a] NU-Text reads *Who.*

Seen by angels,
Preached among the Gentiles,
Believed on in the world,
Received up in glory.

The Great Apostasy

4 Now the Spirit expressly says that in
latter times some will depart from
the faith, giving heed to deceiving spir-
its and doctrines of demons, 2speaking
lies in hypocrisy, having their own con-
science seared with a hot iron, 3for-
bidding to marry, *and commanding* to
abstain from foods which God created
to be received with thanksgiving by
those who believe and know the truth.
4For every creature of God *is* good, and
nothing is to be refused if it is received
with thanksgiving; 5for it is sanctified
by the word of God and prayer.

A Good Servant of Jesus Christ

6If you instruct the brethren in these
things, you will be a good minister of
Jesus Christ, nourished in the words of
faith and of the good doctrine which
you have carefully followed. 7But reject
profane and old wives' fables, and ex-
ercise yourself toward godliness. 8For
bodily exercise profits a little, but god-
liness is profitable for all things, having
promise of the life that now is and of
that which is to come. 9This *is* a faithful
saying and worthy of all acceptance.
10For to this *end* we both labor and suf-
fer reproach,[a] because we trust in the
living God, who is *the* Savior of all men,
especially of those who believe. 11These
things command and teach.

Take Heed to Your Ministry

12Let no one despise your youth, but
be an example to the believers in word,
in conduct, in love, in spirit,[a] in faith,
in purity. 13Till I come, give attention
to reading, to exhortation, to doctrine.
14Do not neglect the gift that is in you,
which was given to you by prophecy
with the laying on of the hands of the
eldership. 15Meditate on these things;
give yourself entirely to them, that your
progress may be evident to all. 16Take
heed to yourself and to the doctrine.
Continue in them, for in doing this you
will save both yourself and those who
hear you.

Treatment of Church Members

5 Do not rebuke an older man, but
exhort *him* as a father, younger
men as brothers, 2older women as
mothers, younger women as sisters,
with all purity.

Honor True Widows

3Honor widows who are really wid-
ows. 4But if any widow has children
or grandchildren, let them first learn
to show piety at home and to repay
their parents; for this is good and[a] ac-
ceptable before God. 5Now she who is
really a widow, and left alone, trusts
in God and continues in supplications
and prayers night and day. 6But she
who lives in pleasure is dead while she
lives. 7And these things command, that
they may be blameless. 8But if anyone
does not provide for his own, and es-
pecially for those of his household, he
has denied the faith and is worse than
an unbeliever.

9Do not let a widow under sixty years
old be taken into the number, *and not
unless* she has been the wife of one
man, 10well reported for good works:
if she has brought up children, if she
has lodged strangers, if she has washed
the saints' feet, if she has relieved the
afflicted, if she has diligently followed
every good work.

11But refuse *the* younger widows; for
when they have begun to grow wanton
against Christ, they desire to marry,
12having condemnation because they
have cast off their first faith. 13And be-
sides they learn *to be* idle, wandering
about from house to house, and not
only idle but also gossips and busy-
bodies, saying things which they ought
not. 14Therefore I desire that *the* youn-
ger *widows* marry, bear children, man-
age the house, give no opportunity to
the adversary to speak reproachfully.
15For some have already turned aside
after Satan. 16If any believing man or[a]
woman has widows, let them relieve

4:10 [a] NU-Text reads *we labor and strive.* **4:12** [a] NU-Text omits *in spirit.* **5:4** [a] NU-Text and M-Text omit *good and.* **5:16** [a] NU-Text omits *man or.*

them, and do not let the church be bur-
dened, that it may relieve those who are
really widows.

Honor the Elders

17Let the elders who rule well be count-
ed worthy of double honor, especially
those who labor in the word and doc-
trine. 18For the Scripture says, "You
shall not muzzle an ox while it treads
out the grain,"[a] and, "The laborer *is* wor-
thy of his wages."[b] 19Do not receive an
accusation against an elder except from
two or three witnesses. 20Those who are
sinning rebuke in the presence of all,
that the rest also may fear.

21I charge *you* before God and the Lord
Jesus Christ and the elect angels that
you observe these things without prej-
udice, doing nothing with partiality.
22Do not lay hands on anyone hastily,
nor share in other people's sins; keep
yourself pure.

23No longer drink only water, but use a
little wine for your stomach's sake and
your frequent infirmities.

24Some men's sins are clearly evident,
preceding *them* to judgment, but those
of some *men* follow later. 25Likewise, the
good works *of some* are clearly evident,
and those that are otherwise cannot
be hidden.

Honor Masters

6 Let as many bondservants as are
under the yoke count their own
masters worthy of all honor, so that the
name of God and *His* doctrine may not
be blasphemed. 2And those who have
believing masters, let them not despise
them because they are brethren, but
rather serve *them* because those who
are benefited are believers and beloved.
Teach and exhort these things.

Error and Greed

3If anyone teaches otherwise and does
not consent to wholesome words, *even*
the words of our Lord Jesus Christ, and
to the doctrine which accords with god-
liness, 4he is proud, knowing nothing,
but is obsessed with disputes and ar-
guments over words, from which come
envy, strife, reviling, evil suspicions,
5useless wranglings[a] of men of corrupt
minds and destitute of the truth, who
suppose that godliness is a *means of*
gain. From such withdraw yourself.[b]

6Now godliness with contentment is
great gain. 7For we brought nothing
into *this* world, *and it is* certain[a] we can
carry nothing out. 8And having food
and clothing, with these we shall be
content. 9But those who desire to be rich
fall into temptation and a snare, and
into many foolish and harmful lusts
which drown men in destruction and
perdition. 10For the love of money is a
root of all *kinds of* evil, for which some
have strayed from the faith in their
greediness, and pierced themselves
through with many sorrows.

The Good Confession

11But you, O man of God, flee these
things and pursue righteousness, god-
liness, faith, love, patience, gentleness.
12Fight the good fight of faith, lay hold
on eternal life, to which you were also
called and have confessed the good
confession in the presence of many
witnesses. 13I urge you in the sight of
God who gives life to all things, and
before Christ Jesus who witnessed the
good confession before Pontius Pilate,
14that you keep *this* commandment
without spot, blameless until our Lord
Jesus Christ's appearing, 15which He
will manifest in His own time, *He who*
is the blessed and only Potentate, the
King of kings and Lord of lords, 16who
alone has immortality, dwelling in un-
approachable light, whom no man has
seen or can see, to whom *be* honor and
everlasting power. Amen.

Instructions to the Rich

17Command those who are rich in this
present age not to be haughty, nor to
trust in uncertain riches but in the living
God, who gives us richly all things to
enjoy. 18*Let them* do good, that they be
rich in good works, ready to give, willing
to share, 19storing up for themselves a
good foundation for the time to come,
that they may lay hold on eternal life.

5:18 [a] Deuteronomy 25:4 [b] Luke 10:7 **6:5** [a] NU-Text and M-Text read *constant friction.* [b] NU-Text omits this sentence. **6:7** [a] NU-Text omits *and it is certain.*

Guard the Faith

[20]O Timothy! Guard what was commit-
ted to your trust, avoiding the profane
and idle babblings and contradictions
of what is falsely called knowledge—
[21]by professing it some have strayed
concerning the faith.

Grace *be* with you. Amen.

THE SECOND LETTER OF PAUL TO

TIMOTHY

Second Timothy is likely the last of Paul's writings that we have. He wote this letter from a cold Roman prison where he is being kept like a common criminal. He knows that his work on earth is nearing its conclusion, and he wanted to share some final words of counsel to Timothy, his trusted companion in ministry. Despite what was before him, Paul wrote not with gloom and despair but with conviction and hope. He encouraged Timothy as a minister so he would be better able to continue Paul's missionary work after Paul's death. Paul also gave Timothy instructions for leading the church. He warned him to stay away from false teachers and be faithful to true Christian teachings.

- **GENRE:** Epistle
- **AUTHOR:** Paul
- **TIME:** c. AD 66–67
- **PURPOSE:** To encourage Timothy to continue Paul's ministry work after Paul's death.

Greeting

1 Paul, an apostle of Jesus Christ[a] by the will of God, according to the promise of life which is in Christ Jesus,

2To Timothy, a beloved son:

Grace, mercy, *and* peace from God the Father and Christ Jesus our Lord.

Timothy's Faith and Heritage

3I thank God, whom I serve with a pure conscience, as *my* forefathers *did,* as without ceasing I remember you in my prayers night and day, 4greatly desiring to see you, being mindful of your tears, that I may be filled with joy, 5when I call to remembrance the genuine faith that is in you, which dwelt first in your grandmother Lois and your mother Eunice, and I am persuaded is in you also. 6Therefore I remind you to stir up the gift of God which is in you through the laying on of my hands. 7For God has not given us a spirit of fear, but of power and of love and of a sound mind.

Not Ashamed of the Gospel

8Therefore do not be ashamed of the testimony of our Lord, nor of me His prisoner, but share with me in the sufferings for the gospel according to the power of God, 9who has saved us and called *us* with a holy calling, not according to our works, but according to His own purpose and grace which was given to us in Christ Jesus before time began, 10but has now been revealed by the appearing of our Savior Jesus Christ, *who* has abolished death and brought life and immortality to light through the gospel, 11to which I was appointed a preacher, an apostle, and a teacher of the Gentiles.[a] 12For this reason I also suffer these things; nevertheless I am not ashamed, for I know whom I have believed and am persuaded that He is able to keep what I have committed to Him until that Day.

Be Loyal to the Faith

13Hold fast the pattern of sound words which you have heard from me, in faith and love which are in Christ Jesus. 14That good thing which was committed to you, keep by the Holy Spirit who dwells in us.

15This you know, that all those in Asia have turned away from me, among whom are Phygellus and Hermogenes. 16The Lord grant mercy to the household of Onesiphorus, for he often refreshed me, and was not ashamed of my chain; 17but when he arrived in Rome, he sought

1:1 [a] NU-Text and M-Text read *Christ Jesus.* 1:11 [a] NU-Text omits *of the Gentiles.*

me out very zealously and found *me.*
18The Lord grant to him that he may find
mercy from the Lord in that Day—and
you know very well how many ways he
ministered *to me*[a] at Ephesus.

Be Strong in Grace

2 You therefore, my son, be strong
in the grace that is in Christ Jesus.
2And the things that you have heard
from me among many witnesses, com-
mit these to faithful men who will be
able to teach others also. 3You therefore
must endure[a] hardship as a good soldier
of Jesus Christ. 4No one engaged in war-
fare entangles himself with the affairs
of *this* life, that he may please him who
enlisted him as a soldier. 5And also if
anyone competes in athletics, he is not
crowned unless he competes according
to the rules. 6The hardworking farmer
must be first to partake of the crops.
7Consider what I say, and may[a] the Lord
give you understanding in all things.
8Remember that Jesus Christ, of the
seed of David, was raised from the dead
according to my gospel, 9for which I
suffer trouble as an evildoer, *even* to
the point of chains; but the word of God
is not chained. 10Therefore I endure all
things for the sake of the elect, that they
also may obtain the salvation which is
in Christ Jesus with eternal glory.
11*This is* a faithful saying:

For if we died with *Him,*
We shall also live with *Him.*
12 If we endure,
We shall also reign with *Him.*
If we deny *Him,*
He also will deny us.
13 If we are faithless,
He remains faithful;
He cannot deny Himself.

Approved and Disapproved Workers

14Remind *them* of these things,
charging *them* before the Lord not to
strive about words to no profit, to the
ruin of the hearers. 15Be diligent to pre-
sent yourself approved to God, a worker
who does not need to be ashamed, right-
ly dividing the word of truth. 16But shun
profane *and* idle babblings, for they will
increase to more ungodliness. 17And
their message will spread like cancer.
Hymenaeus and Philetus are of this
sort, 18who have strayed concerning
the truth, saying that the resurrection
is already past; and they overthrow the
faith of some. 19Nevertheless the solid
foundation of God stands, having this
seal: "The Lord knows those who are
His," and, "Let everyone who names the
name of Christ[a] depart from iniquity."
20But in a great house there are not
only vessels of gold and silver, but also
of wood and clay, some for honor and
some for dishonor. 21Therefore if any-
one cleanses himself from the latter, he
will be a vessel for honor, sanctified and
useful for the Master, prepared for every
good work. 22Flee also youthful lusts; but
pursue righteousness, faith, love, peace
with those who call on the Lord out of
a pure heart. 23But avoid foolish and
ignorant disputes, knowing that they
generate strife. 24And a servant of the
Lord must not quarrel but be gentle to
all, able to teach, patient, 25in humility
correcting those who are in opposition, if
God perhaps will grant them repentance,
so that they may know the truth, 26and
that they may come to their senses *and
escape* the snare of the devil, having
been taken captive by him to *do* his will.

Perilous Times and Perilous Men

3 But know this, that in the last days
perilous times will come: 2For men
will be lovers of themselves, lovers of
money, boasters, proud, blasphemers,
disobedient to parents, unthankful,
unholy, 3unloving, unforgiving, slan-
derers, without self-control, brutal, de-
spisers of good, 4traitors, headstrong,
haughty, lovers of pleasure rather than
lovers of God, 5having a form of godli-
ness but denying its power. And from
such people turn away! 6For of this sort
are those who creep into households
and make captives of gullible women
loaded down with sins, led away by var-
ious lusts, 7always learning and never
able to come to the knowledge of the
truth. 8Now as Jannes and Jambres

1:18 [a] *To me* is from the Vulgate and a few Greek manuscripts. 2:3 [a] NU-Text reads *You must share.* 2:7 [a] NU-Text reads *the Lord will give you.* 2:19 [a] NU-Text and M-Text read *the Lord.*

resisted Moses, so do these also resist the truth: men of corrupt minds, disapproved concerning the faith; 9but they will progress no further, for their folly will be manifest to all, as theirs also was.

The Man of God and the Word of God

10But you have carefully followed my doctrine, manner of life, purpose, faith, longsuffering, love, perseverance, 11persecutions, afflictions, which happened to me at Antioch, at Iconium, at Lystra—what persecutions I endured. And out of *them* all the Lord delivered me. 12Yes, and all who desire to live godly in Christ Jesus will suffer persecution. 13But evil men and impostors will grow worse and worse, deceiving and being deceived. 14But you must continue in the things which you have learned and been assured of, knowing from whom you have learned *them,* 15and that from childhood you have known the Holy Scriptures, which are able to make you wise for salvation through faith which is in Christ Jesus.

16All Scripture *is* given by inspiration of God, and *is* profitable for doctrine, for reproof, for correction, for instruction in righteousness, 17that the man of God may be complete, thoroughly equipped for every good work.

Preach the Word

4 I charge *you* therefore before God and the Lord Jesus Christ, who will judge the living and the dead at[a] His appearing and His kingdom: 2Preach the word! Be ready in season *and* out of season. Convince, rebuke, exhort, with all longsuffering and teaching. 3For the time will come when they will not endure sound doctrine, but according to their own desires, *because* they have itching ears, they will heap up for themselves teachers; 4and they will turn *their* ears away from the truth, and be turned aside to fables. 5But you be watchful in all things, endure afflictions, do the work of an evangelist, fulfill your ministry.

Paul's Valedictory

6For I am already being poured out as a drink offering, and the time of my departure is at hand. 7I have fought the good fight, I have finished the race, I have kept the faith. 8Finally, there is laid up for me the crown of righteousness, which the Lord, the righteous Judge, will give to me on that Day, and not to me only but also to all who have loved His appearing.

The Abandoned Apostle

9Be diligent to come to me quickly; 10for Demas has forsaken me, having loved this present world, and has departed for Thessalonica—Crescens for Galatia, Titus for Dalmatia. 11Only Luke is with me. Get Mark and bring him with you, for he is useful to me for ministry. 12And Tychicus I have sent to Ephesus. 13Bring the cloak that I left with Carpus at Troas when you come—and the books, especially the parchments.

14Alexander the coppersmith did me much harm. May the Lord repay him according to his works. 15You also must beware of him, for he has greatly resisted our words.

16At my first defense no one stood with me, but all forsook me. May it not be charged against them.

The Lord Is Faithful

17But the Lord stood with me and strengthened me, so that the message might be preached fully through me, and *that* all the Gentiles might hear. Also I was delivered out of the mouth of the lion. 18And the Lord will deliver me from every evil work and preserve *me* for His heavenly kingdom. To Him *be* glory forever and ever. Amen!

Come Before Winter

19Greet Prisca and Aquila, and the household of Onesiphorus. 20Erastus stayed in Corinth, but Trophimus I have left in Miletus sick.

21Do your utmost to come before winter.

Eubulus greets you, as well as Pudens, Linus, Claudia, and all the brethren.

Farewell

22The Lord Jesus Christ[a] be with your spirit. Grace be with you. Amen.

4:1 [a] NU-Text omits *therefore* and reads *and by* for *at.* 4:22 [a] NU-Text omits *Jesus Christ.*

THE LETTER OF PAUL TO
TITUS

Like Timothy, Titus was one of Paul's most trusted coworkers. Paul gave Titus the difficult task of representing him in Corinth to help resolve problems there and then left him on the island of Crete to pastor the church there. This church faced many challenges, most notably that Crete was quite a sinful place. Paul wrote this letter to Titus to help him know what to do for this church. Paul advised Titus to focus on developing godly leaders in the church. Beyond that, Titus would need to deal with opponents who would challenge him and contradict his teachings. In addition, Paul reminded Titus that the people of Crete needed to see the church living their faith in Christ.

- **GENRE:** Epistle
- **AUTHOR:** Paul
- **TIME:** c. AD 62–66
- **PURPOSE:** To instruct Titus on how to be a good pastor in the church.

Greeting

1 Paul, a bondservant of God and an
apostle of Jesus Christ, according to
the faith of God's elect and the acknowl-
edgment of the truth which accords with
godliness, 2in hope of eternal life which
God, who cannot lie, promised before
time began, 3but has in due time man-
ifested His word through preaching,
which was committed to me according
to the commandment of God our Savior;

4To Titus, a true son in *our* common
faith:

Grace, mercy, *and* peace from God
the Father and the Lord Jesus Christ[a]
our Savior.

Qualified Elders

5For this reason I left you in Crete, that
you should set in order the things that
are lacking, and appoint elders in every
city as I commanded you— 6if a man is
blameless, the husband of one wife, hav-
ing faithful children not accused of dissi-
pation or insubordination. 7For a bishop[a]
must be blameless, as a steward of God,
not self-willed, not quick-tempered, not
given to wine, not violent, not greedy
for money, 8but hospitable, a lover of
what is good, sober-minded, just, holy,
self-controlled, 9holding fast the faithful
word as he has been taught, that he may
be able, by sound doctrine, both to exhort
and convict those who contradict.

The Elders' Task

10For there are many insubordi-
nate, both idle talkers and deceivers,
especially those of the circumcision,
11whose mouths must be stopped, who
subvert whole households, teaching
things which they ought not, for the
sake of dishonest gain. 12One of them,
a prophet of their own, said, "Cretans
are always liars, evil beasts, lazy glut-
tons." 13This testimony is true. Therefore
rebuke them sharply, that they may be
sound in the faith, 14not giving heed to
Jewish fables and commandments of
men who turn from the truth. 15To the
pure all things are pure, but to those
who are defiled and unbelieving noth-
ing is pure; but even their mind and
conscience are defiled. 16They profess
to know God, but in works they deny
Him, being abominable, disobedient,
and disqualified for every good work.

Qualities of a Sound Church

2 But as for you, speak the things
which are proper for sound doc-
trine: 2that the older men be sober,

1:4 [a] NU-Text reads *and Christ Jesus.* 1:7 [a] Literally *overseer*

reverent, temperate, sound in faith, in
love, in patience; 3the older women like-
wise, that they be reverent in behavior,
not slanderers, not given to much wine,
teachers of good things— 4that they
admonish the young women to love
their husbands, to love their children, 5*to
be* discreet, chaste, homemakers, good,
obedient to their own husbands, that the
word of God may not be blasphemed.

6Likewise, exhort the young men to
be sober-minded, 7in all things showing
yourself *to be* a pattern of good works;
in doctrine *showing* integrity, reverence,
incorruptibility,[a] 8sound speech that
cannot be condemned, that one who is
an opponent may be ashamed, having
nothing evil to say of you.[a]

9*Exhort* bondservants to be obedient
to their own masters, to be well pleasing
in all *things,* not answering back, 10not
pilfering, but showing all good fidelity,
that they may adorn the doctrine of
God our Savior in all things.

Trained by Saving Grace

11For the grace of God that brings sal-
vation has appeared to all men, 12teach-
ing us that, denying ungodliness and
worldly lusts, we should live soberly,
righteously, and godly in the present
age, 13looking for the blessed hope and
glorious appearing of our great God
and Savior Jesus Christ, 14who gave
Himself for us, that He might redeem us
from every lawless deed and purify for
Himself *His* own special people, zealous
for good works.

15Speak these things, exhort, and
rebuke with all authority. Let no one
despise you.

Graces of the Heirs of Grace

3 Remind them to be subject to rul-
ers and authorities, to obey, to be
ready for every good work, 2to speak
evil of no one, to be peaceable, gentle,
showing all humility to all men. 3For
we ourselves were also once foolish,
disobedient, deceived, serving various
lusts and pleasures, living in malice and
envy, hateful and hating one another.
4But when the kindness and the love of
God our Savior toward man appeared,
5not by works of righteousness which
we have done, but according to His mer-
cy He saved us, through the washing
of regeneration and renewing of the
Holy Spirit, 6whom He poured out on
us abundantly through Jesus Christ
our Savior, 7that having been justified
by His grace we should become heirs
according to the hope of eternal life.

8This is a faithful saying, and these
things I want you to affirm constantly,
that those who have believed in God
should be careful to maintain good
works. These things are good and prof-
itable to men.

Avoid Dissension

9But avoid foolish disputes, genealo-
gies, contentions, and strivings about
the law; for they are unprofitable and
useless. 10Reject a divisive man after the
first and second admonition, 11knowing
that such a person is warped and sin-
ning, being self-condemned.

Final Messages

12When I send Artemas to you, or
Tychicus, be diligent to come to me at
Nicopolis, for I have decided to spend
the winter there. 13Send Zenas the
lawyer and Apollos on their journey
with haste, that they may lack noth-
ing. 14And let our *people* also learn to
maintain good works, to *meet* urgent
needs, that they may not be unfruitful.

Farewell

15All who *are* with me greet you. Greet
those who love us in the faith.

Grace *be* with you all. Amen.

2:7 [a] NU-Text omits *incorruptibility.* 2:8 [a] NU-Text and M-Text read *us.*

THE LETTER OF PAUL TO

PHILEMON

Onesimus had been a slave in Philemon's house until he fled to Rome. There, he met Paul and became a follower of Jesus. Paul wanted to keep Onesimus with him in Rome, but he knew that the way Onesimus had left Philemon may have caused problems. So Paul sent Onesimus back to Philemon with this letter that he was to give to his former master. In this letter, Paul asked Philemon to receive Onesimus with the same gentleness that he would receive Paul. Paul explained that Onesimus may have left as a slave, but he was returning as a brother in Christ. If Onesimus caused Philemon to lose any money because of what he had done, Paul promised to pay that debt for him. Paul told Philemon he was confident that brotherly love and unity would carry the day.

- **GENRE:** Epistle
- **AUTHOR:** Paul
- **TIME:** c. AD 60–62
- **PURPOSE:** To encourage Philemon to accept his former slave as an equal brother in Christ.

Greeting

Paul, a prisoner of Christ Jesus, and
Timothy *our* brother,

To Philemon our beloved *friend* and
fellow laborer, 2to the beloved[a] Apphia,
Archippus our fellow soldier, and to the
church in your house:

3Grace to you and peace from God our
Father and the Lord Jesus Christ.

Philemon's Love and Faith

4I thank my God, making mention of
you always in my prayers, 5hearing of
your love and faith which you have to-
ward the Lord Jesus and toward all the
saints, 6that the sharing of your faith
may become effective by the acknowl-
edgment of every good thing which is
in you[a] in Christ Jesus. 7For we have[a]
great joy[b] and consolation in your love,
because the hearts of the saints have
been refreshed by you, brother.

The Plea for Onesimus

8Therefore, though I might be very
bold in Christ to command you what
is fitting, 9*yet* for love's sake I rather
appeal *to you*—being such a one as
Paul, the aged, and now also a prisoner
of Jesus Christ— 10I appeal to you for
my son Onesimus, whom I have begot-
ten *while* in my chains, 11who once was
unprofitable to you, but now is profit-
able to you and to me.

12I am sending him back.[a] You there-
fore receive him, that is, my own heart,
13whom I wished to keep with me, that on
your behalf he might minister to me in
my chains for the gospel. 14But without
your consent I wanted to do nothing,
that your good deed might not be by
compulsion, as it were, but voluntary.

15For perhaps he departed for a while
for this *purpose,* that you might receive
him forever, 16no longer as a slave but
more than a slave—a beloved brother,
especially to me but how much more to
you, both in the flesh and in the Lord.

Philemon's Obedience Encouraged

17If then you count me as a partner,
receive him as *you would* me. 18But if he
has wronged you or owes anything, put
that on my account. 19I, Paul, am writ-
ing with my own hand. I will repay—not
to mention to you that you owe me even

2 [a] NU-Text reads *to our sister Apphia.* 6 [a] NU-Text and M-Text read *us.* 7 [a] NU-Text reads *had.* [b] M-Text reads *thanksgiving.* 12 [a] NU-Text reads *back to you in person, that is, my own heart.*

GOD SIN JESUS SALVATION LOVE

your own self besides. [20]Yes, brother,
let me have joy from you in the Lord;
refresh my heart in the Lord.
[21]Having confidence in your obedi-
ence, I write to you, knowing that you
will do even more than I say. [22]But,
meanwhile, also prepare a guest room
for me, for I trust that through your
prayers I shall be granted to you.

Farewell

[23]Epaphras, my fellow prisoner in
Christ Jesus, greets you, [24]*as do* Mark,
Aristarchus, Demas, Luke, my fellow
laborers.
[25]The grace of our Lord Jesus Christ
be with your spirit. Amen.

THE LETTER TO THE

HEBREWS

When faced with hardship and opposition, many Jewish Christians who had left the Jewish faith to follow Jesus were tempted to give up on Jesus and return to what they had believed before. The writer of this letter was troubled by this and wanted to help these believers hold on to Jesus. His main reasoning was that everything in the Jewish faith points to Jesus. He is the fulfillment of it all. The Old Testament law pointed to Jesus. The temple pointed to Jesus. The priesthood pointed to Jesus. The animal sacrifices pointed to Jesus. Jesus was superior to all these parts of Jewish faith. Why would someone want to give up what is better? There is much more to be gained than lost by following Christ. The challenges they faced were real, but the answer was not to give up but to press on in faith like so many before them had done.

- **GENRE:** Epistle
- **AUTHOR:** Unknown, perhaps Paul, Barnabas, Luke, or Clement
- **TIME:** c. AD 67–69
- **PURPOSE:** To explain that Jesus is superior to Old Testament worship and that faith in Him is a greater way to live.

God's Supreme Revelation

1 God, who at various times and in
various ways spoke in time past
to the fathers by the prophets, 2has
in these last days spoken to us by *His*
Son, whom He has appointed heir of all
things, through whom also He made
the worlds; 3who being the brightness
of *His* glory and the express image of
His person, and upholding all things by
the word of His power, when He had by
Himself[a] purged our[b] sins, sat down at
the right hand of the Majesty on high,
4having become so much better than
the angels, as He has by inheritance ob-
tained a more excellent name than they.

The Son Exalted Above Angels

5For to which of the angels did He ever
say:

> "You are My Son,
> Today I have begotten You"?[a]

And again:

> "I will be to Him a Father,
> And He shall be to Me a Son"?[b]

6But when He again brings the first-
born into the world, He says:

> "Let all the angels of God worship
> Him."[a]

7And of the angels He says:

> "Who makes His angels spirits
> And His ministers a flame of fire."[a]

8But to the Son *He says:*

> "Your throne, O God, *is* forever and
> ever;
> A scepter of righteousness *is* the
> scepter of Your kingdom.
> 9 You have loved righteousness and
> hated lawlessness;
> Therefore God, Your God, has
> anointed You
> With the oil of gladness more
> than Your companions."[a]

10And:

> "You, LORD, in the beginning laid
> the foundation of the earth,

1:3 [a] NU-Text omits *by Himself.* [b] NU-Text omits *our.* 1:5 [a] Psalm 2:7 [b] 2 Samuel 7:14
1:6 [a] Deuteronomy 32:43 (Septuagint, Dead Sea Scrolls); Psalm 97:7 1:7 [a] Psalm 104:4 1:9 [a] Psalm 45:6, 7

GOD | SIN | JESUS | SALVATION | LOVE

And the heavens are the work of
Your hands.
11 They will perish, but You remain;
And they will all grow old like a
garment;
12 Like a cloak You will fold them up,
And they will be changed.
But You are the same,
And Your years will not fail."[a]

13But to which of the angels has He
ever said:

"Sit at My right hand,
Till I make Your enemies Your
footstool"?[a]

14Are they not all ministering spirits
sent forth to minister for those who will
inherit salvation?

Do Not Neglect Salvation

2 Therefore we must give the more
earnest heed to the things we have
heard, lest we drift away. 2For if the
word spoken through angels proved
steadfast, and every transgression and
disobedience received a just reward,
3how shall we escape if we neglect so
great a salvation, which at the first be-
gan to be spoken by the Lord, and was
confirmed to us by those who heard
Him, 4God also bearing witness both
with signs and wonders, with various
miracles, and gifts of the Holy Spirit,
according to His own will?

The Son Made Lower than Angels

5For He has not put the world to come,
of which we speak, in subjection to
angels. 6But one testified in a certain
place, saying:

"What is man that You are mindful
of him,
Or the son of man that You take
care of him?
7 You have made him a little lower
than the angels;
You have crowned him with glory
and honor,[a]
And set him over the works of
Your hands.
8 You have put all things in
subjection under his feet."[a]

For in that He put all in subjection un-
der him, He left nothing *that is* not put
under him. But now we do not yet see
all things put under him. 9But we see
Jesus, who was made a little lower than
the angels, for the suffering of death
crowned with glory and honor, that He,
by the grace of God, might taste death
for everyone.

Bringing Many Sons to Glory

10For it was fitting for Him, for whom
are all things and by whom *are* all
things, in bringing many sons to glory,
to make the captain of their salvation
perfect through sufferings. 11For both
He who sanctifies and those who are
being sanctified *are* all of one, for which
reason He is not ashamed to call them
brethren, 12saying:

"I will declare Your name to My
brethren;
In the midst of the assembly I will
sing praise to You."[a]

13And again:

"I will put My trust in Him."[a]

And again:

"Here am I and the children whom
God has given Me."[b]

14Inasmuch then as the children have
partaken of flesh and blood, He Him-
self likewise shared in the same, that
through death He might destroy him
who had the power of death, that is, the
devil, 15and release those who through
fear of death were all their lifetime sub-
ject to bondage. 16For indeed He does
not give aid to angels, but He does give
aid to the seed of Abraham. 17Therefore,
in all things He had to be made like *His*
brethren, that He might be a merciful
and faithful High Priest in things *per-*
taining to God, to make propitiation for
the sins of the people. 18For in that He

1:12 [a] Psalm 102:25–27 1:13 [a] Psalm 110:1 2:7 [a] NU-Text and M-Text omit the rest of verse 7.
2:8 [a] Psalm 8:4–6 2:12 [a] Psalm 22:22 2:13 [a] 2 Samuel 22:3; Isaiah 8:17 [b] Isaiah 8:18

Himself has suffered, being tempted, He is able to aid those who are tempted.

The Son Was Faithful

3 Therefore, holy brethren, partakers of the heavenly calling, consider the Apostle and High Priest of our confession, Christ Jesus, 2who was faithful to Him who appointed Him, as Moses also *was faithful* in all His house. 3For this One has been counted worthy of more glory than Moses, inasmuch as He who built the house has more honor than the house. 4For every house is built by someone, but He who built all things *is* God. 5And Moses indeed *was* faithful in all His house as a servant, for a testimony of those things which would be spoken *afterward,* 6but Christ as a Son over His own house, whose house we are if we hold fast the confidence and the rejoicing of the hope firm to the end.[a]

Be Faithful

7Therefore, as the Holy Spirit says:

"Today, if you will hear His voice,
8 Do not harden your hearts as in
the rebellion,
In the day of trial in the
wilderness,
9 Where your fathers tested Me,
tried Me,
And saw My works forty years.
10 Therefore I was angry with that
generation,
And said, 'They always go astray
in *their* heart,
And they have not known My
ways.'
11 So I swore in My wrath,
'They shall not enter My rest.' "[a]

12Beware, brethren, lest there be in any of you an evil heart of unbelief in departing from the living God; 13but exhort one another daily, while it is called "Today," lest any of you be hardened through the deceitfulness of sin. 14For we have become partakers of Christ if we hold the beginning of our confidence steadfast to the end, 15while it is said:

"Today, if you will hear His voice,
Do not harden your hearts as in
the rebellion."[a]

Failure of the Wilderness Wanderers

16For who, having heard, rebelled? Indeed, *was it* not all who came out of Egypt, *led* by Moses? 17Now with whom was He angry forty years? *Was it* not with those who sinned, whose corpses fell in the wilderness? 18And to whom did He swear that they would not enter His rest, but to those who did not obey? 19So we see that they could not enter in because of unbelief.

The Promise of Rest

4 Therefore, since a promise remains of entering His rest, let us fear lest any of you seem to have come short of it. 2For indeed the gospel was preached to us as well as to them; but the word which they heard did not profit them,[a] not being mixed with faith in those who heard *it.* 3For we who have believed do enter that rest, as He has said:

"So I swore in My wrath,
'They shall not enter My rest,' "[a]

although the works were finished from the foundation of the world. 4For He has spoken in a certain place of the seventh *day* in this way: "And God rested on the seventh day from all His works";[a] 5and again in this *place:* "They shall not enter My rest."[a]

6Since therefore it remains that some *must* enter it, and those to whom it was first preached did not enter because of disobedience, 7again He designates a certain day, saying in David, "Today," after such a long time, as it has been said:

"Today, if you will hear His voice,
Do not harden your hearts."[a]

8For if Joshua had given them rest, then He would not afterward have spoken of another day. 9There remains therefore a rest for the people of God.

3:6 [a] NU-Text omits *firm to the end.* **3:11** [a] Psalm 95:7–11 **3:15** [a] Psalm 95:7, 8 **4:2** [a] NU-Text and M-Text read *profit them, since they were not united by faith with those who heeded it.* **4:3** [a] Psalm 95:11 **4:4** [a] Genesis 2:2 **4:5** [a] Psalm 95:11 **4:7** [a] Psalm 95:7, 8

GOD | SIN | JESUS | SALVATION | LOVE

10For he who has entered His rest has
himself also ceased from his works as
God *did* from His.

The Word Discovers Our Condition

11Let us therefore be diligent to enter
that rest, lest anyone fall according
to the same example of disobedience.
12For the word of God *is* living and pow-
erful, and sharper than any two-edged
sword, piercing even to the division of
soul and spirit, and of joints and mar-
row, and is a discerner of the thoughts
and intents of the heart. 13And there
is no creature hidden from His sight,
but all things *are* naked and open to
the eyes of Him to whom we *must give*
account.

Our Compassionate High Priest

14Seeing then that we have a great
High Priest who has passed through
the heavens, Jesus the Son of God, let
us hold fast *our* confession. 15For we
do not have a High Priest who cannot
sympathize with our weaknesses, but
was in all *points* tempted as *we are, yet*
without sin. 16Let us therefore come
boldly to the throne of grace, that we
may obtain mercy and find grace to
help in time of need.

Qualifications for High Priesthood

5 For every high priest taken from
among men is appointed for men
in things *pertaining* to God, that he may
offer both gifts and sacrifices for sins.
2He can have compassion on those who
are ignorant and going astray, since
he himself is also subject to weakness.
3Because of this he is required as for the
people, so also for himself, to offer *sac-*
rifices for sins. 4And no man takes this
honor to himself, but he who is called
by God, just as Aaron *was.*

A Priest Forever

5So also Christ did not glorify Himself
to become High Priest, but *it was* He
who said to Him:

> "You are My Son,
> Today I have begotten You."[a]

6As *He* also says in another *place:*

> "You *are* a priest forever
> According to the order of
> Melchizedek";[a]

7who, in the days of His flesh, when He
had offered up prayers and supplica-
tions, with vehement cries and tears
to Him who was able to save Him from
death, and was heard because of His
godly fear, 8though He was a Son, *yet* He
learned obedience by the things which
He suffered. 9And having been perfect-
ed, He became the author of eternal
salvation to all who obey Him, 10called
by God as High Priest "according to the
order of Melchizedek," 11of whom we
have much to say, and hard to explain,
since you have become dull of hearing.

Spiritual Immaturity

12For though by this time you ought
to be teachers, you need *someone* to
teach you again the first principles of
the oracles of God; and you have come
to need milk and not solid food. 13For
everyone who partakes *only* of milk *is*
unskilled in the word of righteousness,
for he is a babe. 14But solid food belongs
to those who are of full age, *that is,* those
who by reason of use have their senses
exercised to discern both good and evil.

The Peril of Not Progressing

6 Therefore, leaving the discussion of
the elementary *principles* of Christ,
let us go on to perfection, not laying
again the foundation of repentance
from dead works and of faith toward
God, 2of the doctrine of baptisms, of
laying on of hands, of resurrection of
the dead, and of eternal judgment. 3And
this we will[a] do if God permits.
4For *it is* impossible for those who were
once enlightened, and have tasted the
heavenly gift, and have become partak-
ers of the Holy Spirit, 5and have tasted
the good word of God and the powers of
the age to come, 6if they fall away,[a] to
renew them again to repentance, since
they crucify again for themselves the Son
of God, and put *Him* to an open shame.

5:5 [a] Psalm 2:7 5:6 [a] Psalm 110:4 6:3 [a] M-Text reads *let us do.* 6:6 [a] Or *and have fallen away*

7For the earth which drinks in the rain
that often comes upon it, and bears
herbs useful for those by whom it is
cultivated, receives blessing from God;
8but if it bears thorns and briers, *it is* re-
jected and near to being cursed, whose
end *is* to be burned.

A Better Estimate

9But, beloved, we are confident of bet-
ter things concerning you, yes, things
that accompany salvation, though we
speak in this manner. 10For God *is* not
unjust to forget your work and labor of[a]
love which you have shown toward His
name, *in that* you have ministered to the
saints, and do minister. 11And we desire
that each one of you show the same
diligence to the full assurance of hope
until the end, 12that you do not become
sluggish, but imitate those who through
faith and patience inherit the promises.

God's Infallible Purpose in Christ

13For when God made a promise to
Abraham, because He could swear by
no one greater, He swore by Himself,
14saying, "Surely blessing I will bless
you, and multiplying I will multiply
you."[a] 15And so, after he had patiently
endured, he obtained the promise. 16For
men indeed swear by the greater, and an
oath for confirmation *is* for them an end
of all dispute. 17Thus God, determining
to show more abundantly to the heirs of
promise the immutability of His counsel,
confirmed *it* by an oath, 18that by two
immutable things, in which it *is* impossi-
ble for God to lie, we might[a] have strong
consolation, who have fled for refuge to
lay hold of the hope set before *us.*

19This *hope* we have as an anchor of
the soul, both sure and steadfast, and
which enters the *Presence* behind the
veil, 20where the forerunner has entered
for us, *even* Jesus, having become High
Priest forever according to the order of
Melchizedek.

The King of Righteousness

7 For this Melchizedek, king of Salem,
priest of the Most High God, who
met Abraham returning from the
slaughter of the kings and blessed him,
2to whom also Abraham gave a tenth
part of all, first being translated "king
of righteousness," and then also king
of Salem, meaning "king of peace,"
3without father, without mother, with-
out genealogy, having neither begin-
ning of days nor end of life, but made
like the Son of God, remains a priest
continually.

4Now consider how great this man
was, to whom even the patriarch Abra-
ham gave a tenth of the spoils. 5And
indeed those who are of the sons of
Levi, who receive the priesthood, have
a commandment to receive tithes from
the people according to the law, that is,
from their brethren, though they have
come from the loins of Abraham; 6but
he whose genealogy is not derived from
them received tithes from Abraham
and blessed him who had the promis-
es. 7Now beyond all contradiction the
lesser is blessed by the better. 8Here
mortal men receive tithes, but there he
receives them, of whom it is witnessed
that he lives. 9Even Levi, who receives
tithes, paid tithes through Abraham, so
to speak, 10for he was still in the loins of
his father when Melchizedek met him.

Need for a New Priesthood

11Therefore, if perfection were through
the Levitical priesthood (for under it
the people received the law), what
further need *was there* that another
priest should rise according to the or-
der of Melchizedek, and not be called
according to the order of Aaron? 12For
the priesthood being changed, of ne-
cessity there is also a change of the
law. 13For He of whom these things are
spoken belongs to another tribe, from
which no man has officiated at the altar.
14For *it is* evident that our Lord arose
from Judah, of which tribe Moses spoke
nothing concerning priesthood.[a] 15And
it is yet far more evident if, in the like-
ness of Melchizedek, there arises anoth-
er priest 16who has come, not according
to the law of a fleshly commandment,
but according to the power of an endless
life. 17For He testifies:[a]

6:10 [a] NU-Text omits *labor of.* **6:14** [a] Genesis 22:17 **6:18** [a] M-Text omits *might.* **7:14** [a] NU-Text reads *priests.* **7:17** [a] NU-Text reads *it is testified.*

GOD SIN JESUS SALVATION LOVE

"You *are* a priest forever
According to the order of
Melchizedek."[b]

18For on the one hand there is an an-
nulling of the former commandment
because of its weakness and unprofit-
ableness, 19for the law made nothing
perfect; on the other hand, *there is the*
bringing in of a better hope, through
which we draw near to God.

Greatness of the New Priest

20And inasmuch as *He was* not *made*
priest without an oath 21(for they have
become priests without an oath, but He
with an oath by Him who said to Him:

"The LORD has sworn
And will not relent,
'You *are* a priest forever[a]
According to the order of
Melchizedek' "),[b]

22by so much more Jesus has become
a surety of a better covenant.
23Also there were many priests, be-
cause they were prevented by death
from continuing. 24But He, because He
continues forever, has an unchangeable
priesthood. 25Therefore He is also able
to save to the uttermost those who come
to God through Him, since He always
lives to make intercession for them.
26For such a High Priest was fitting
for us, *who is* holy, harmless, undefiled,
separate from sinners, and has become
higher than the heavens; 27who does
not need daily, as those high priests,
to offer up sacrifices, first for His own
sins and then for the people's, for this
He did once for all when He offered up
Himself. 28For the law appoints as high
priests men who have weakness, but
the word of the oath, which came after
the law, *appoints* the Son who has been
perfected forever.

The New Priestly Service

8 Now *this is* the main point of the
things we are saying: We have such
a High Priest, who is seated at the right
hand of the throne of the Majesty in the
heavens, 2a Minister of the sanctuary
and of the true tabernacle which the
Lord erected, and not man.
3For every high priest is appointed to
offer both gifts and sacrifices. Therefore
it is necessary that this One also have
something to offer. 4For if He were on
earth, He would not be a priest, since
there are priests who offer the gifts ac-
cording to the law; 5who serve the copy
and shadow of the heavenly things, as
Moses was divinely instructed when he
was about to make the tabernacle. For
He said, "See *that* you make all things
according to the pattern shown you
on the mountain."[a] 6But now He has
obtained a more excellent ministry,
inasmuch as He is also Mediator of a
better covenant, which was established
on better promises.

A New Covenant

7For if that first *covenant* had been
faultless, then no place would have
been sought for a second. 8Because
finding fault with them, He says: "Be-
hold, the days are coming, says the
LORD, when I will make a new covenant
with the house of Israel and with the
house of Judah— 9not according to
the covenant that I made with their
fathers in the day when I took them by
the hand to lead them out of the land of
Egypt; because they did not continue in
My covenant, and I disregarded them,
says the LORD. 10For this *is* the cov-
enant that I will make with the house
of Israel after those days, says the
LORD: I will put My laws in their mind
and write them on their hearts; and I
will be their God, and they shall be My
people. 11None of them shall teach his
neighbor, and none his brother, saying,
'Know the LORD,' for all shall know Me,
from the least of them to the greatest
of them. 12For I will be merciful to their
unrighteousness, and their sins and
their lawless deeds[a] I will remember
no more."[b]
13In that He says, "A new *covenant*," He
has made the first obsolete. Now what
is becoming obsolete and growing old
is ready to vanish away.

7:17 [b] Psalm 110:4 7:21 [a] NU-Text ends the quotation here. [b] Psalm 110:4 8:5 [a] Exodus 25:40
8:12 [a] NU-Text omits *and their lawless deeds.* [b] Jeremiah 31:31–34

The Earthly Sanctuary

9 Then indeed, even the first *covenant* had ordinances of divine service and the earthly sanctuary. 2For a tabernacle was prepared: the first *part,* in which *was* the lampstand, the table, and the showbread, which is called the sanctuary; 3and behind the second veil, the part of the tabernacle which is called the Holiest of All, 4which had the golden censer and the ark of the covenant overlaid on all sides with gold, in which *were* the golden pot that had the manna, Aaron's rod that budded, and the tablets of the covenant; 5and above it were the cherubim of glory overshadowing the mercy seat. Of these things we cannot now speak in detail.

Limitations of the Earthly Service

6Now when these things had been thus prepared, the priests always went into the first part of the tabernacle, performing the services. 7But into the second part the high priest *went* alone once a year, not without blood, which he offered for himself and *for* the people's sins *committed* in ignorance; 8the Holy Spirit indicating this, that the way into the Holiest of All was not yet made manifest while the first tabernacle was still standing. 9It *was* symbolic for the present time in which both gifts and sacrifices are offered which cannot make him who performed the service perfect in regard to the conscience— 10*concerned* only with foods and drinks, various washings, and fleshly ordinances imposed until the time of reformation.

The Heavenly Sanctuary

11But Christ came *as* High Priest of the good things to come,[a] with the greater and more perfect tabernacle not made with hands, that is, not of this creation. 12Not with the blood of goats and calves, but with His own blood He entered the Most Holy Place once for all, having obtained eternal redemption. 13For if the blood of bulls and goats and the ashes of a heifer, sprinkling the unclean, sanctifies for the purifying of the flesh, 14how much more shall the blood of Christ, who through the eternal Spirit offered Himself without spot to God, cleanse your conscience from dead works to serve the living God? 15And for this reason He is the Mediator of the new covenant, by means of death, for the redemption of the transgressions under the first covenant, that those who are called may receive the promise of the eternal inheritance.

The Mediator's Death Necessary

16For where there *is* a testament, there must also of necessity be the death of the testator. 17For a testament *is* in force after men are dead, since it has no power at all while the testator lives. 18Therefore not even the first *covenant* was dedicated without blood. 19For when Moses had spoken every precept to all the people according to the law, he took the blood of calves and goats, with water, scarlet wool, and hyssop, and sprinkled both the book itself and all the people, 20saying, "This *is* the blood of the covenant which God has commanded you."[a] 21Then likewise he sprinkled with blood both the tabernacle and all the vessels of the ministry. 22And according to the law almost all things are purified with blood, and without shedding of blood there is no remission.

Greatness of Christ's Sacrifice

23Therefore *it was* necessary that the copies of the things in the heavens should be purified with these, but the heavenly things themselves with better sacrifices than these. 24For Christ has not entered the holy places made with hands, *which are* copies of the true, but into heaven itself, now to appear in the presence of God for us; 25not that He should offer Himself often, as the high priest enters the Most Holy Place every year with blood of another— 26He then would have had to suffer often since the foundation of the world; but now, once at the end of the ages, He has appeared to put away sin by the sacrifice of Himself. 27And as it is appointed for men to

9:11 [a] NU-Text reads *that have come.* 9:20 [a] Exodus 24:8

die once, but after this the judgment,
28so Christ was offered once to bear the
sins of many. To those who eagerly wait
for Him He will appear a second time,
apart from sin, for salvation.

Animal Sacrifices Insufficient

10 For the law, having a shadow of
the good things to come, *and* not
the very image of the things, can never
with these same sacrifices, which they
offer continually year by year, make
those who approach perfect. 2For then
would they not have ceased to be of-
fered? For the worshipers, once purified,
would have had no more consciousness
of sins. 3But in those *sacrifices there is*
a reminder of sins every year. 4For *it is*
not possible that the blood of bulls and
goats could take away sins.

Christ's Death Fulfills God's Will

5Therefore, when He came into the
world, He said:

"Sacrifice and offering You did not
desire,
But a body You have prepared
for Me.
6 In burnt offerings and *sacrifices*
for sin
You had no pleasure.
7 Then I said, 'Behold, I have
come—
In the volume of the book it is
written of Me—
To do Your will, O God.' "[a]

8Previously saying, "Sacrifice and offer-
ing, burnt offerings, and *offerings* for sin
You did not desire, nor had pleasure *in
them*" (which are offered according to
the law), 9then He said, "Behold, I have
come to do Your will, O God."[a] He takes
away the first that He may establish
the second. 10By that will we have been
sanctified through the offering of the
body of Jesus Christ once *for all.*

Christ's Death Perfects the Sanctified

11And every priest stands ministering
daily and offering repeatedly the same
sacrifices, which can never take away
sins. 12But this Man, after He had of-
fered one sacrifice for sins forever, sat
down at the right hand of God, 13from
that time waiting till His enemies are
made His footstool. 14For by one offer-
ing He has perfected forever those who
are being sanctified.

15But the Holy Spirit also witnesses to
us; for after He had said before,
16"This *is* the covenant that I will
make with them after those days, says
the LORD: I will put My laws into their
hearts, and in their minds I will write
them,"[a] 17*then He adds,* "Their sins and
their lawless deeds I will remember no
more."[a] 18Now where there is remission
of these, *there is* no longer an offering
for sin.

Hold Fast Your Confession

19Therefore, brethren, having bold-
ness to enter the Holiest by the blood of
Jesus, 20by a new and living way which
He consecrated for us, through the veil,
that is, His flesh, 21and *having* a High
Priest over the house of God, 22let us
draw near with a true heart in full assur-
ance of faith, having our hearts sprin-
kled from an evil conscience and our
bodies washed with pure water. 23Let
us hold fast the confession of *our* hope
without wavering, for He who promised
is faithful. 24And let us consider one
another in order to stir up love and good
works, 25not forsaking the assembling
of ourselves together, as *is* the manner
of some, but exhorting *one another,* and
so much the more as you see the Day
approaching.

The Just Live by Faith

26For if we sin willfully after we have
received the knowledge of the truth,
there no longer remains a sacrifice for
sins, 27but a certain fearful expecta-
tion of judgment, and fiery indigna-
tion which will devour the adversaries.
28Anyone who has rejected Moses' law
dies without mercy on *the testimony of*
two or three witnesses. 29Of how much
worse punishment, do you suppose, will
he be thought worthy who has trampled
the Son of God underfoot, counted the

10:7 [a] Psalm 40:6–8 **10:9** [a] NU-Text and M-Text omit *O God.* **10:16** [a] Jeremiah 31:33
10:17 [a] Jeremiah 31:34

blood of the covenant by which he was
sanctified a common thing, and insult-
ed the Spirit of grace? 30For we know
Him who said, "Vengeance is Mine, I
will repay,"[a] says the Lord.[b] And again,
"The LORD will judge His people."[c] 31It
is a fearful thing to fall into the hands
of the living God.

32But recall the former days in which,
after you were illuminated, you endured
a great struggle with sufferings: 33part-
ly while you were made a spectacle both
by reproaches and tribulations, and
partly while you became companions
of those who were so treated; 34for you
had compassion on me[a] in my chains,
and joyfully accepted the plundering of
your goods, knowing that you have a
better and an enduring possession for
yourselves in heaven.[b] 35Therefore do
not cast away your confidence, which
has great reward. 36For you have need
of endurance, so that after you have
done the will of God, you may receive
the promise:

37 "For yet a little while,
And He[a] who is coming will come
and will not tarry.
38 Now the[a] just shall live by faith;
But if *anyone* draws back,
My soul has no pleasure in him."[b]

39But we are not of those who draw back
to perdition, but of those who believe to
the saving of the soul.

By Faith We Understand

11 Now faith is the substance of
things hoped for, the evidence
of things not seen. 2For by it the elders
obtained a *good* testimony.

3By faith we understand that the
worlds were framed by the word of God,
so that the things which are seen were
not made of things which are visible.

Faith at the Dawn of History

4By faith Abel offered to God a more
excellent sacrifice than Cain, through
which he obtained witness that he was
righteous, God testifying of his gifts; and
through it he being dead still speaks.

5By faith Enoch was taken away so
that he did not see death, "and was not
found, because God had taken him";[a]
for before he was taken he had this tes-
timony, that he pleased God. 6But with-
out faith *it is* impossible to please *Him,*
for he who comes to God must believe
that He is, and *that* He is a rewarder of
those who diligently seek Him.

7By faith Noah, being divinely warned
of things not yet seen, moved with godly
fear, prepared an ark for the saving of
his household, by which he condemned
the world and became heir of the righ-
teousness which is according to faith.

Faithful Abraham

8By faith Abraham obeyed when he
was called to go out to the place which
he would receive as an inheritance.
And he went out, not knowing where
he was going. 9By faith he dwelt in the
land of promise as *in* a foreign country,
dwelling in tents with Isaac and Jacob,
the heirs with him of the same prom-
ise; 10for he waited for the city which
has foundations, whose builder and
maker *is* God.

11By faith Sarah herself also received
strength to conceive seed, and she bore
a child[a] when she was past the age,
because she judged Him faithful who
had promised. 12Therefore from one
man, and him as good as dead, were
born *as many* as the stars of the sky in
multitude—innumerable as the sand
which is by the seashore.

The Heavenly Hope

13These all died in faith, not having
received the promises, but having seen
them afar off were assured of them,[a]
embraced *them* and confessed that
they were strangers and pilgrims on
the earth. 14For those who say such
things declare plainly that they seek
a homeland. 15And truly if they had
called to mind that *country* from which
they had come out, they would have

10:30 [a] Deuteronomy 32:35 [b] NU-Text omits *says the Lord.* [c] Deuteronomy 32:36 **10:34** [a] NU-Text reads *the prisoners* instead of *me in my chains.* [b] NU-Text omits *in heaven.* **10:37** [a] Or *that which* **10:38** [a] NU-Text reads *My just one.* [b] Habakkuk 2:3, 4 **11:5** [a] Genesis 5:24 **11:11** [a] NU-Text omits *she bore a child.* **11:13** [a] NU-Text and M-Text omit *were assured of them.*

had opportunity to return. 16But now
they desire a better, that is, a heavenly
country. Therefore God is not ashamed
to be called their God, for He has pre-
pared a city for them.

The Faith of the Patriarchs

17By faith Abraham, when he was test-
ed, offered up Isaac, and he who had re-
ceived the promises offered up his only
begotten *son*, 18of whom it was said, "In
Isaac your seed shall be called,"[a] 19con-
cluding that God *was* able to raise *him*
up, even from the dead, from which he
also received him in a figurative sense.
20By faith Isaac blessed Jacob and
Esau concerning things to come.
21By faith Jacob, when he was dying,
blessed each of the sons of Joseph, and
worshiped, *leaning* on the top of his staff.
22By faith Joseph, when he was dying,
made mention of the departure of the
children of Israel, and gave instructions
concerning his bones.

The Faith of Moses

23By faith Moses, when he was born,
was hidden three months by his par-
ents, because they saw *he was* a beau-
tiful child; and they were not afraid of
the king's command.
24By faith Moses, when he became of
age, refused to be called the son of Phar-
aoh's daughter, 25choosing rather to
suffer affliction with the people of God
than to enjoy the passing pleasures of
sin, 26esteeming the reproach of Christ
greater riches than the treasures in[a]
Egypt; for he looked to the reward.
27By faith he forsook Egypt, not fear-
ing the wrath of the king; for he endured
as seeing Him who is invisible. 28By
faith he kept the Passover and the sprin-
kling of blood, lest he who destroyed the
firstborn should touch them.
29By faith they passed through the
Red Sea as by dry *land, whereas* the
Egyptians, attempting to do so, were
drowned.

By Faith They Overcame

30By faith the walls of Jericho fell
down after they were encircled for seven
days. 31By faith the harlot Rahab did
not perish with those who did not be-
lieve, when she had received the spies
with peace.
32And what more shall I say? For the
time would fail me to tell of Gideon and
Barak and Samson and Jephthah, also
of David and Samuel and the proph-
ets: 33who through faith subdued king-
doms, worked righteousness, obtained
promises, stopped the mouths of lions,
34quenched the violence of fire, escaped
the edge of the sword, out of weakness
were made strong, became valiant in
battle, turned to flight the armies of the
aliens. 35Women received their dead
raised to life again.
Others were tortured, not accepting
deliverance, that they might obtain
a better resurrection. 36Still others
had trial of mockings and scourgings,
yes, and of chains and imprisonment.
37They were stoned, they were sawn in
two, were tempted,[a] were slain with the
sword. They wandered about in sheep-
skins and goatskins, being destitute,
afflicted, tormented— 38of whom the
world was not worthy. They wandered
in deserts and mountains, *in* dens and
caves of the earth.
39And all these, having obtained a
good testimony through faith, did not
receive the promise, 40God having
provided something better for us, that
they should not be made perfect apart
from us.

The Race of Faith

12 Therefore we also, since we
are surrounded by so great a
cloud of witnesses, let us lay aside every
weight, and the sin which so easily en-
snares *us*, and let us run with endurance
the race that is set before us, 2looking
unto Jesus, the author and finisher of
our faith, who for the joy that was set
before Him endured the cross, despising
the shame, and has sat down at the
right hand of the throne of God.

The Discipline of God

3For consider Him who endured such
hostility from sinners against Himself,

11:18 [a] Genesis 21:12 11:26 [a] NU-Text and M-Text read *of*. 11:37 [a] NU-Text omits *were tempted*.

lest you become weary and discouraged
in your souls. 4You have not yet resisted
to bloodshed, striving against sin. 5And
you have forgotten the exhortation
which speaks to you as to sons:

"My son, do not despise the
chastening of the LORD,
Nor be discouraged when you are
rebuked by Him;
6 For whom the LORD loves He
chastens,
And scourges every son whom He
receives."[a]

7If[a] you endure chastening, God deals
with you as with sons; for what son is
there whom a father does not chas-
ten? 8But if you are without chastening,
of which all have become partakers,
then you are illegitimate and not sons.
9Furthermore, we have had human
fathers who corrected *us,* and we paid
them respect. Shall we not much more
readily be in subjection to the Father of
spirits and live? 10For they indeed for a
few days chastened *us* as seemed *best*
to them, but He for *our* profit, that *we*
may be partakers of His holiness. 11Now
no chastening seems to be joyful for
the present, but painful; nevertheless,
afterward it yields the peaceable fruit of
righteousness to those who have been
trained by it.

Renew Your Spiritual Vitality

12Therefore strengthen the hands
which hang down, and the feeble knees,
13and make straight paths for your feet,
so that what is lame may not be dislo-
cated, but rather be healed.
14Pursue peace with all *people,* and ho-
liness, without which no one will see the
Lord: 15looking carefully lest anyone
fall short of the grace of God; lest any
root of bitterness springing up cause
trouble, and by this many become
defiled; 16lest there *be* any fornicator
or profane person like Esau, who for
one morsel of food sold his birthright.
17For you know that afterward, when
he wanted to inherit the blessing, he
was rejected, for he found no place for
repentance, though he sought it dili-
gently with tears.

The Glorious Company

18For you have not come to the moun-
tain that[a] may be touched and that
burned with fire, and to blackness and
darkness[b] and tempest, 19and the sound
of a trumpet and the voice of words,
so that those who heard *it* begged that
the word should not be spoken to them
anymore. 20(For they could not endure
what was commanded: "And if so much
as a beast touches the mountain, it shall
be stoned[a] or shot with an arrow."[b]
21And so terrifying was the sight *that*
Moses said, "I am exceedingly afraid
and trembling."[a])
22But you have come to Mount Zion
and to the city of the living God, the
heavenly Jerusalem, to an innumerable
company of angels, 23to the general
assembly and church of the firstborn
who are registered in heaven, to God the
Judge of all, to the spirits of just men
made perfect, 24to Jesus the Mediator
of the new covenant, and to the blood
of sprinkling that speaks better things
than *that of* Abel.

Hear the Heavenly Voice

25See that you do not refuse Him who
speaks. For if they did not escape who
refused Him who spoke on earth, much
more *shall we not escape* if we turn away
from Him who *speaks* from heaven,
26whose voice then shook the earth;
but now He has promised, saying, "Yet
once more I shake[a] not only the earth,
but also heaven."[b] 27Now this, "Yet once
more," indicates the removal of those
things that are being shaken, as of
things that are made, that the things
which cannot be shaken may remain.
28Therefore, since we are receiving a
kingdom which cannot be shaken, let us
have grace, by which we may[a] serve God
acceptably with reverence and godly
fear. 29For our God *is* a consuming fire.

12:6 [a] Proverbs 3:11, 12 **12:7** [a] NU-Text and M-Text read *It is for discipline that you endure; God . . . .* **12:18** [a] NU-Text reads *to that which.* [b] NU-Text reads *gloom.* **12:20** [a] NU-Text and M-Text omit the rest of this verse. [b] Exodus 19:12, 13 **12:21** [a] Deuteronomy 9:19 **12:26** [a] NU-Text reads *will shake.* [b] Haggai 2:6 **12:28** [a] M-Text omits *may.*

GOD SIN JESUS SALVATION LOVE

Concluding Moral Directions

13 Let brotherly love continue. 2Do
not forget to entertain strang-
ers, for by so *doing* some have unwit-
tingly entertained angels. 3Remember
the prisoners as if chained with them—
those who are mistreated—since you
yourselves are in the body also.
4Marriage *is* honorable among all,
and the bed undefiled; but fornicators
and adulterers God will judge.
5*Let your* conduct *be* without covet-
ousness; *be* content with such things as
you have. For He Himself has said, "I
will never leave you nor forsake you."[a]
6So we may boldly say:

> "The LORD *is* my helper;
> I will not fear.
> What can man do to me?"[a]

Concluding Religious Directions

7Remember those who rule over you,
who have spoken the word of God to
you, whose faith follow, considering
the outcome of *their* conduct. 8Jesus
Christ *is* the same yesterday, today, and
forever. 9Do not be carried about[a] with
various and strange doctrines. For *it is*
good that the heart be established by
grace, not with foods which have not
profited those who have been occupied
with them.
10We have an altar from which those
who serve the tabernacle have no right
to eat. 11For the bodies of those ani-
mals, whose blood is brought into the
sanctuary by the high priest for sin, are
burned outside the camp. 12Therefore
Jesus also, that He might sanctify the
people with His own blood, suffered
outside the gate. 13Therefore let us go
forth to Him, outside the camp, bearing
His reproach. 14For here we have no
continuing city, but we seek the one to
come. 15Therefore by Him let us con-
tinually offer the sacrifice of praise to
God, that is, the fruit of *our* lips, giving
thanks to His name. 16But do not forget
to do good and to share, for with such
sacrifices God is well pleased.
17Obey those who rule over you, and be
submissive, for they watch out for your
souls, as those who must give account.
Let them do so with joy and not with
grief, for that would be unprofitable
for you.

Prayer Requested

18Pray for us; for we are confident that
we have a good conscience, in all things
desiring to live honorably. 19But I espe-
cially urge *you* to do this, that I may be
restored to you the sooner.

Benediction, Final Exhortation, Farewell

20Now may the God of peace who
brought up our Lord Jesus from the
dead, that great Shepherd of the sheep,
through the blood of the everlasting
covenant, 21make you complete in ev-
ery good work to do His will, working in
you[a] what is well pleasing in His sight,
through Jesus Christ, to whom *be* glory
forever and ever. Amen.
22And I appeal to you, brethren, bear
with the word of exhortation, for I have
written to you in few words. 23Know
that *our* brother Timothy has been set
free, with whom I shall see you if he
comes shortly.
24Greet all those who rule over you,
and all the saints. Those from Italy
greet you.
25Grace *be* with you all. Amen.

13:5 [a] Deuteronomy 31:6, 8; Joshua 1:5 13:6 [a] Psalm 118:6 13:9 [a] NU-Text and M-Text read *away*.
13:21 [a] NU-Text and M-Text read *us*.

THE LETTER OF

JAMES

Most of the first Christians were Jewish men, women, and children who had spent their entire lives believing they had to work to please God. The gospel, though, is not about what people can do for God but what He has done for them through Jesus. The gospel is by grace through faith, not by works through effort. Living in grace is freeing. But some of these early Christians took this too far and failed to understand that while they were not saved by works, once they were saved, God expected them to do good works. James, the half brother of Jesus and a leader in the Jerusalem church, wrote this letter to explain that real faith requires that believers live what they believe. A person cannot say he or she has faith if their life does not show it.

- **GENRE:** Epistle
- **AUTHOR:** James
- **TIME:** c. AD 44–49
- **PURPOSE:** To help the early Christians understand that true faith in Jesus results in changed living.

Greeting to the Twelve Tribes

1 James, a bondservant of God and
of the Lord Jesus Christ,

To the twelve tribes which are scattered abroad:

Greetings.

Profiting from Trials

2My brethren, count it all joy when you
fall into various trials, 3knowing that the
testing of your faith produces patience.
4But let patience have *its* perfect work,
that you may be perfect and complete,
lacking nothing. 5If any of you lacks
wisdom, let him ask of God, who gives to
all liberally and without reproach, and
it will be given to him. 6But let him ask
in faith, with no doubting, for he who
doubts is like a wave of the sea driven and tossed by the wind. 7For let not
that man suppose that he will receive
anything from the Lord; 8*he is* a double-minded man, unstable in all his ways.

The Perspective of Rich and Poor

9Let the lowly brother glory in his exaltation, 10but the rich in his humiliation,
because as a flower of the field he will
pass away. 11For no sooner has the sun
risen with a burning heat than it withers
the grass; its flower falls, and its beautiful appearance perishes. So the rich
man also will fade away in his pursuits.

Loving God Under Trials

12Blessed *is* the man who endures
temptation; for when he has been approved, he will receive the crown of life
which the Lord has promised to those
who love Him. 13Let no one say when
he is tempted, "I am tempted by God";
for God cannot be tempted by evil, nor
does He Himself tempt anyone. 14But
each one is tempted when he is drawn
away by his own desires and enticed.
15Then, when desire has conceived, it
gives birth to sin; and sin, when it is
full-grown, brings forth death.
16Do not be deceived, my beloved
brethren. 17Every good gift and every
perfect gift is from above, and comes
down from the Father of lights, with
whom there is no variation or shadow of
turning. 18Of His own will He brought us
forth by the word of truth, that we might
be a kind of firstfruits of His creatures.

Qualities Needed in Trials

19So then,[a] my beloved brethren, let every man be swift to hear, slow to speak,

1:19 [a] NU-Text reads *Know this* or *This you know.*

GOD SIN JESUS SALVATION LOVE

slow to wrath; 20for the wrath of man
does not produce the righteousness
of God.

Doers—Not Hearers Only

21Therefore lay aside all filthiness and
overflow of wickedness, and receive with
meekness the implanted word, which is
able to save your souls.
22But be doers of the word, and not
hearers only, deceiving yourselves. 23For
if anyone is a hearer of the word and
not a doer, he is like a man observing
his natural face in a mirror; 24for he
observes himself, goes away, and imme-
diately forgets what kind of man he was.
25But he who looks into the perfect law
of liberty and continues *in it,* and is not
a forgetful hearer but a doer of the work,
this one will be blessed in what he does.
26If anyone among you[a] thinks he is
religious, and does not bridle his tongue
but deceives his own heart, this one's
religion *is* useless. 27Pure and undefiled
religion before God and the Father is
this: to visit orphans and widows in
their trouble, *and* to keep oneself un-
spotted from the world.

Beware of Personal Favoritism

2 My brethren, do not hold the faith of
our Lord Jesus Christ, *the Lord* of glo-
ry, with partiality. 2For if there should
come into your assembly a man with
gold rings, in fine apparel, and there
should also come in a poor man in filthy
clothes, 3and you pay attention to the
one wearing the fine clothes and say to
him, "You sit here in a good place," and
say to the poor man, "You stand there,"
or, "Sit here at my footstool," 4have you
not shown partiality among yourselves,
and become judges with evil thoughts?
5Listen, my beloved brethren: Has God
not chosen the poor of this world *to
be* rich in faith and heirs of the king-
dom which He promised to those who
love Him? 6But you have dishonored
the poor man. Do not the rich oppress
you and drag you into the courts? 7Do
they not blaspheme that noble name
by which you are called?
8If you really fulfill *the* royal law ac-
cording to the Scripture, "You shall love
your neighbor as yourself,"[a] you do
well; 9but if you show partiality, you
commit sin, and are convicted by the
law as transgressors. 10For whoev-
er shall keep the whole law, and yet
stumble in one *point,* he is guilty of
all. 11For He who said, "Do not commit
adultery,"[a] also said, "Do not murder."[b]
Now if you do not commit adultery, but
you do murder, you have become a
transgressor of the law. 12So speak and
so do as those who will be judged by the
law of liberty. 13For judgment is without
mercy to the one who has shown no
mercy. Mercy triumphs over judgment.

Faith Without Works Is Dead

14What *does it* profit, my brethren, if
someone says he has faith but does not
have works? Can faith save him? 15If a
brother or sister is naked and destitute
of daily food, 16and one of you says to
them, "Depart in peace, be warmed and
filled," but you do not give them the
things which are needed for the body,
what *does it* profit? 17Thus also faith by
itself, if it does not have works, is dead.
18But someone will say, "You have
faith, and I have works." Show me your
faith without your[a] works, and I will
show you my faith by my[b] works. 19You
believe that there is one God. You do
well. Even the demons believe—and
tremble! 20But do you want to know,
O foolish man, that faith without works
is dead?[a] 21Was not Abraham our fa-
ther justified by works when he offered
Isaac his son on the altar? 22Do you see
that faith was working together with his
works, and by works faith was made
perfect? 23And the Scripture was fulfilled
which says, "Abraham believed God, and
it was accounted to him for righteous-
ness."[a] And he was called the friend of
God. 24You see then that a man is jus-
tified by works, and not by faith only.
25Likewise, was not Rahab the harlot
also justified by works when she re-
ceived the messengers and sent *them*
out another way?

1:26 [a] NU-Text omits *among you.* **2:8** [a] Leviticus 19:18 **2:11** [a] Exodus 20:14; Deuteronomy 5:18 [b] Exodus 20:13; Deuteronomy 5:17 **2:18** [a] NU-Text omits *your.* [b] NU-Text omits *my.* **2:20** [a] NU-Text reads *useless.* **2:23** [a] Genesis 15:6

26For as the body without the spirit is
dead, so faith without works is dead also.

The Untamable Tongue

3 My brethren, let not many of you
become teachers, knowing that
we shall receive a stricter judgment.
2For we all stumble in many things.
If anyone does not stumble in word,
he *is* a perfect man, able also to bridle
the whole body. 3Indeed,[a] we put bits
in horses' mouths that they may obey
us, and we turn their whole body. 4Look
also at ships: although they are so large
and are driven by fierce winds, they are
turned by a very small rudder wherever
the pilot desires. 5Even so the tongue is
a little member and boasts great things.
See how great a forest a little fire kin-
dles! 6And the tongue *is* a fire, a world of
iniquity. The tongue is so set among our
members that it defiles the whole body,
and sets on fire the course of nature;
and it is set on fire by hell. 7For every
kind of beast and bird, of reptile and
creature of the sea, is tamed and has
been tamed by mankind. 8But no man
can tame the tongue. *It is* an unruly
evil, full of deadly poison. 9With it we
bless our God and Father, and with it
we curse men, who have been made in
the similitude of God. 10Out of the same
mouth proceed blessing and cursing.
My brethren, these things ought not to
be so. 11Does a spring send forth fresh
water and bitter from the same open-
ing? 12Can a fig tree, my brethren, bear
olives, or a grapevine bear figs? Thus no
spring yields both salt water and fresh.[a]

Heavenly Versus Demonic Wisdom

13Who *is* wise and understanding
among you? Let him show by good
conduct *that* his works *are done* in the
meekness of wisdom. 14But if you have
bitter envy and self-seeking in your
hearts, do not boast and lie against the
truth. 15This wisdom does not descend
from above, but *is* earthly, sensual,
demonic. 16For where envy and self-
seeking *exist*, confusion and every evil
thing *are* there. 17But the wisdom that is
from above is first pure, then peaceable,
gentle, willing to yield, full of mercy
and good fruits, without partiality and
without hypocrisy. 18Now the fruit of
righteousness is sown in peace by those
who make peace.

Pride Promotes Strife

4 Where do wars and fights *come* from
among you? Do *they* not *come* from
your *desires for* pleasure that war in
your members? 2You lust and do not
have. You murder and covet and can-
not obtain. You fight and war. Yet[a] you
do not have because you do not ask.
3You ask and do not receive, because
you ask amiss, that you may spend *it*
on your pleasures. 4Adulterers and[a]
adulteresses! Do you not know that
friendship with the world is enmity with
God? Whoever therefore wants to be a
friend of the world makes himself an
enemy of God. 5Or do you think that the
Scripture says in vain, "The Spirit who
dwells in us yearns jealously"?
6But He gives more grace. Therefore
He says:

"God resists the proud,
But gives grace to the humble."[a]

Humility Cures Worldliness

7Therefore submit to God. Resist the
devil and he will flee from you. 8Draw
near to God and He will draw near to
you. Cleanse *your* hands, *you* sinners;
and purify *your* hearts, *you* double-
minded. 9Lament and mourn and weep!
Let your laughter be turned to mourn-
ing and *your* joy to gloom. 10Humble
yourselves in the sight of the Lord, and
He will lift you up.

Do Not Judge a Brother

11Do not speak evil of one anoth-
er, brethren. He who speaks evil of a
brother and judges his brother, speaks
evil of the law and judges the law. But if
you judge the law, you are not a doer of
the law but a judge. 12There is one Law-
giver,[a] who is able to save and to destroy.
Who[b] are you to judge another?[c]

3:3 [a] NU-Text reads *Now if.* **3:12** [a] NU-Text reads *Neither can a salty spring produce fresh water.*
4:2 [a] NU-Text and M-Text omit *Yet.* **4:4** [a] NU-Text omits *Adulterers and.* **4:6** [a] Proverbs 3:34
4:12 [a] NU-Text adds *and Judge.* [b] NU-Text and M-Text read *But who.* [c] NU-Text reads *a neighbor.*

Do Not Boast About Tomorrow

13Come now, you who say, "Today or
tomorrow we will[a] go to such and such
a city, spend a year there, buy and sell,
and make a profit"; 14whereas you do
not know what *will happen* tomorrow.
For what *is* your life? It is even a vapor
that appears for a little time and then
vanishes away. 15Instead you *ought* to
say, "If the Lord wills, we shall live and
do this or that." 16But now you boast
in your arrogance. All such boasting
is evil.

17Therefore, to him who knows to do
good and does not do *it,* to him it is sin.

Rich Oppressors Will Be Judged

5 Come now, *you* rich, weep and howl
for your miseries that are coming
upon *you!* 2Your riches are corrupted,
and your garments are moth-eaten.
3Your gold and silver are corroded, and
their corrosion will be a witness against
you and will eat your flesh like fire. You
have heaped up treasure in the last
days. 4Indeed the wages of the laborers
who mowed your fields, which you kept
back by fraud, cry out; and the cries of
the reapers have reached the ears of the
Lord of Sabaoth.[a] 5You have lived on
the earth in pleasure and luxury; you
have fattened your hearts as[a] in a day
of slaughter. 6You have condemned,
you have murdered the just; he does
not resist you.

Be Patient and Persevering

7Therefore be patient, brethren, until
the coming of the Lord. See *how* the
farmer waits for the precious fruit of
the earth, waiting patiently for it until it
receives the early and latter rain. 8You
also be patient. Establish your hearts,
for the coming of the Lord is at hand.

9Do not grumble against one another,
brethren, lest you be condemned.[a] Be-
hold, the Judge is standing at the door!
10My brethren, take the prophets, who
spoke in the name of the Lord, as an
example of suffering and patience.
11Indeed we count them blessed who
endure. You have heard of the persever-
ance of Job and seen the end *intended
by* the Lord—that the Lord is very com-
passionate and merciful.

12But above all, my brethren, do not
swear, either by heaven or by earth or
with any other oath. But let your "Yes"
be "Yes," and *your* "No," "No," lest you
fall into judgment.[a]

Meeting Specific Needs

13Is anyone among you suffering? Let
him pray. Is anyone cheerful? Let him
sing psalms. 14Is anyone among you
sick? Let him call for the elders of the
church, and let them pray over him,
anointing him with oil in the name of
the Lord. 15And the prayer of faith will
save the sick, and the Lord will raise him
up. And if he has committed sins, he will
be forgiven. 16Confess *your* trespass-
es[a] to one another, and pray for one
another, that you may be healed. The
effective, fervent prayer of a righteous
man avails much. 17Elijah was a man
with a nature like ours, and he prayed
earnestly that it would not rain; and it
did not rain on the land for three years
and six months. 18And he prayed again,
and the heaven gave rain, and the earth
produced its fruit.

Bring Back the Erring One

19Brethren, if anyone among you wan-
ders from the truth, and someone turns
him back, 20let him know that he who
turns a sinner from the error of his way
will save a soul[a] from death and cover
a multitude of sins.

4:13 [a] M-Text reads *let us.* **5:4** [a] Literally, in Hebrew, *Hosts* **5:5** [a] NU-Text omits *as.* **5:9** [a] NU-Text and M-Text read *judged.* **5:12** [a] M-Text reads *hypocrisy.* **5:16** [a] NU-Text reads *Therefore confess your sins.* **5:20** [a] NU-Text reads *his soul.*

THE FIRST LETTER OF PETER

First Peter was probably written to Christians living in the Roman provinces of Turkey at the beginning of Emperor Nero's persecutions of Christians. Peter wrote to give these believers comfort, hope, and encouragement. He asked them to hold fast to the faith in the midst of the coming hardships, with Jesus as their example. If they endured the challenges ahead of them with grace, love, and humility, they would show the power of the gospel.

- **GENRE:** Epistle
- **AUTHOR:** Peter
- **TIME:** c. AD 64–65
- **PURPOSE:** To encourage the Christians who faced persecution for their faith and instruct them to be holy.

Greeting to the Elect Pilgrims

1 Peter, an apostle of Jesus Christ,
To the pilgrims of the Dispersion in
Pontus, Galatia, Cappadocia, Asia, and
Bithynia, 2elect according to the fore-
knowledge of God the Father, in sancti-
fication of the Spirit, for obedience and
sprinkling of the blood of Jesus Christ:
Grace to you and peace be multiplied.

A Heavenly Inheritance

3Blessed *be* the God and Father of our
Lord Jesus Christ, who according to His
abundant mercy has begotten us again
to a living hope through the resurrection
of Jesus Christ from the dead, 4to an
inheritance incorruptible and undefiled
and that does not fade away, reserved
in heaven for you, 5who are kept by the
power of God through faith for salvation
ready to be revealed in the last time.
6In this you greatly rejoice, though
now for a little while, if need be, you
have been grieved by various trials,
7that the genuineness of your faith, *be-
ing* much more precious than gold that
perishes, though it is tested by fire, may
be found to praise, honor, and glory at
the revelation of Jesus Christ, 8whom
having not seen[a] you love. Though now
you do not see *Him,* yet believing, you
rejoice with joy inexpressible and full of
glory, 9receiving the end of your faith—
the salvation of *your* souls.
10Of this salvation the prophets have
inquired and searched carefully, who
prophesied of the grace *that would
come* to you, 11searching what, or what
manner of time, the Spirit of Christ who
was in them was indicating when He
testified beforehand the sufferings of
Christ and the glories that would follow.
12To them it was revealed that, not to
themselves, but to us[a] they were minis-
tering the things which now have been
reported to you through those who have
preached the gospel to you by the Holy
Spirit sent from heaven—things which
angels desire to look into.

Living Before God Our Father

13Therefore gird up the loins of your
mind, be sober, and rest *your* hope fully
upon the grace that is to be brought to
you at the revelation of Jesus Christ;
14as obedient children, not conforming
yourselves to the former lusts, *as* in your
ignorance; 15but as He who called you
is holy, you also be holy in all *your* con-
duct, 16because it is written, "Be holy,
for I am holy."[a]
17And if you call on the Father, who
without partiality judges according to
each one's work, conduct yourselves

1:8 [a] M-Text reads *known.* 1:12 [a] NU-Text and M-Text read *you.* 1:16 [a] Leviticus 11:44, 45; 19:2; 20:7

GOD | SIN | JESUS | SALVATION | LOVE

throughout the time of your stay *here*
in fear; 18knowing that you were not
redeemed with corruptible things, *like*
silver or gold, from your aimless con-
duct *received* by tradition from your
fathers, 19but with the precious blood
of Christ, as of a lamb without blem-
ish and without spot. 20He indeed was
foreordained before the foundation of
the world, but was manifest in these
last times for you 21who through Him
believe in God, who raised Him from the
dead and gave Him glory, so that your
faith and hope are in God.

The Enduring Word

22Since you have purified your souls
in obeying the truth through the Spirit[a]
in sincere love of the brethren, love one
another fervently with a pure heart,
23having been born again, not of cor-
ruptible seed but incorruptible, through
the word of God which lives and abides
forever,[a] 24because

"All flesh *is* as grass,
And all the glory of man[a] as the
flower of the grass.
The grass withers,
And its flower falls away,
25 But the word of the LORD endures
forever."[a]

Now this is the word which by the gospel
was preached to you.

2 Therefore, laying aside all malice,
all deceit, hypocrisy, envy, and all
evil speaking, 2as newborn babes, de-
sire the pure milk of the word, that you
may grow thereby,[a] 3if indeed you have
tasted that the Lord *is* gracious.

The Chosen Stone and His Chosen People

4Coming to Him *as to* a living stone,
rejected indeed by men, but chosen by
God *and* precious, 5you also, as living
stones, are being built up a spiritual
house, a holy priesthood, to offer up
spiritual sacrifices acceptable to God
through Jesus Christ. 6Therefore it is
also contained in the Scripture,

"Behold, I lay in Zion
A chief cornerstone, elect,
precious,
And he who believes on Him
will by no means be put to
shame."[a]

7Therefore, to you who believe, *He is*
precious; but to those who are disobe-
dient,[a]

"The stone which the builders
rejected
Has become the chief
cornerstone,"[b]

8and

"A stone of stumbling
And a rock of offense."[a]

They stumble, being disobedient to the
word, to which they also were appoint-
ed.

9But you *are* a chosen generation, a
royal priesthood, a holy nation, His own
special people, that you may proclaim
the praises of Him who called you out
of darkness into His marvelous light;
10who once *were* not a people but *are*
now the people of God, who had not
obtained mercy but now have obtained
mercy.

Living Before the World

11Beloved, I beg *you* as sojourners and
pilgrims, abstain from fleshly lusts
which war against the soul, 12having
your conduct honorable among the
Gentiles, that when they speak against
you as evildoers, they may, by *your*
good works which they observe, glorify
God in the day of visitation.

Submission to Government

13Therefore submit yourselves to ev-
ery ordinance of man for the Lord's
sake, whether to the king as supreme,
14or to governors, as to those who are
sent by him for the punishment of evil-
doers and *for the* praise of those who do
good. 15For this is the will of God, that by

1:22 [a] NU-Text omits *through the Spirit.* **1:23** [a] NU-Text omits *forever.* **1:24** [a] NU-Text reads *all its glory.* **1:25** [a] Isaiah 40:6–8 **2:2** [a] NU-Text adds *up to salvation.* **2:6** [a] Isaiah 28:16 **2:7** [a] NU-Text reads *to those who disbelieve.* [b] Psalm 118:22 **2:8** [a] Isaiah 8:14

doing good you may put to silence the ignorance of foolish men— 16as free, yet not using liberty as a cloak for vice, but as bondservants of God. 17Honor all *people.* Love the brotherhood. Fear God. Honor the king.

Submission to Masters

18Servants, *be* submissive to *your* masters with all fear, not only to the good and gentle, but also to the harsh. 19For this *is* commendable, if because of conscience toward God one endures grief, suffering wrongfully. 20For what credit *is it* if, when you are beaten for your faults, you take it patiently? But when you do good and suffer, if you take it patiently, this *is* commendable before God. 21For to this you were called, because Christ also suffered for us,[a] leaving us[b] an example, that you should follow His steps:

22 "Who committed no sin,
Nor was deceit found in His mouth";[a]

23who, when He was reviled, did not revile in return; when He suffered, He did not threaten, but committed *Himself* to Him who judges righteously; 24who Himself bore our sins in His own body on the tree, that we, having died to sins, might live for righteousness—by whose stripes you were healed. 25For you were like sheep going astray, but have now returned to the Shepherd and Overseer[a] of your souls.

Submission to Husbands

3 Wives, likewise, *be* submissive to your own husbands, that even if some do not obey the word, they, without a word, may be won by the conduct of their wives, 2when they observe your chaste conduct *accompanied* by fear. 3Do not let your adornment be *merely* outward—arranging the hair, wearing gold, or putting on *fine* apparel— 4rather *let it be* the hidden person of the heart, with the incorruptible *beauty* of a gentle and quiet spirit, which is very precious in the sight of God. 5For in this manner, in former times, the holy women who trusted in God also adorned themselves, being submissive to their own husbands, 6as Sarah obeyed Abraham, calling him lord, whose daughters you are if you do good and are not afraid with any terror.

A Word to Husbands

7Husbands, likewise, dwell with *them* with understanding, giving honor to the wife, as to the weaker vessel, and as *being* heirs together of the grace of life, that your prayers may not be hindered.

Called to Blessing

8Finally, all *of you be* of one mind, having compassion for one another; love as brothers, *be* tenderhearted, *be* courteous;[a] 9not returning evil for evil or reviling for reviling, but on the contrary blessing, knowing that you were called to this, that you may inherit a blessing. 10For

"He who would love life
And see good days,
Let him refrain his tongue from evil,
And his lips from speaking deceit.
11 Let him turn away from evil and do good;
Let him seek peace and pursue it.
12 For the eyes of the LORD *are* on the righteous,
And His ears *are open* to their prayers;
But the face of the LORD *is* against those who do evil."[a]

Suffering for Right and Wrong

13And who *is* he who will harm you if you become followers of what is good? 14But even if you should suffer for righteousness' sake, *you are* blessed. "And do not be afraid of their threats, nor be troubled."[a] 15But sanctify the Lord God[a] in your hearts, and always *be* ready to *give* a defense to everyone who asks you a reason for the hope that is in you, with meekness and fear; 16having a good conscience, that when they defame you

2:21 [a] NU-Text reads *you.* [b] NU-Text and M-Text read *you.* **2:22** [a] Isaiah 53:9 **2:25** [a] Greek *Episkopos* **3:8** [a] NU-Text reads *humble.* **3:12** [a] Psalm 34:12–16 **3:14** [a] Isaiah 8:12 **3:15** [a] NU-Text reads *Christ as Lord.*

as evildoers, those who revile your good conduct in Christ may be ashamed. 17For *it is* better, if it is the will of God, to suffer for doing good than for doing evil.

Christ's Suffering and Ours

18For Christ also suffered once for sins, the just for the unjust, that He might bring us[a] to God, being put to death in the flesh but made alive by the Spirit, 19by whom also He went and preached to the spirits in prison, 20who formerly were disobedient, when once the Divine longsuffering waited[a] in the days of Noah, while *the* ark was being prepared, in which a few, that is, eight souls, were saved through water. 21There is also an antitype which now saves us—baptism (not the removal of the filth of the flesh, but the answer of a good conscience toward God), through the resurrection of Jesus Christ, 22who has gone into heaven and is at the right hand of God, angels and authorities and powers having been made subject to Him.

4 Therefore, since Christ suffered for us[a] in the flesh, arm yourselves also with the same mind, for he who has suffered in the flesh has ceased from sin, 2that he no longer should live the rest of *his* time in the flesh for the lusts of men, but for the will of God. 3For we *have spent* enough of our past lifetime[a] in doing the will of the Gentiles—when we walked in lewdness, lusts, drunkenness, revelries, drinking parties, and abominable idolatries. 4In regard to these, they think it strange that you do not run with *them* in the same flood of dissipation, speaking evil of *you*. 5They will give an account to Him who is ready to judge the living and the dead. 6For this reason the gospel was preached also to those who are dead, that they might be judged according to men in the flesh, but live according to God in the spirit.

Serving for God's Glory

7But the end of all things is at hand; therefore be serious and watchful in your prayers. 8And above all things have fervent love for one another, for "love will cover a multitude of sins."[a] 9*Be* hospitable to one another without grumbling. 10As each one has received a gift, minister it to one another, as good stewards of the manifold grace of God. 11If anyone speaks, *let him speak* as the oracles of God. If anyone ministers, *let him do it* as with the ability which God supplies, that in all things God may be glorified through Jesus Christ, to whom belong the glory and the dominion forever and ever. Amen.

Suffering for God's Glory

12Beloved, do not think it strange concerning the fiery trial which is to try you, as though some strange thing happened to you; 13but rejoice to the extent that you partake of Christ's sufferings, that when His glory is revealed, you may also be glad with exceeding joy. 14If you are reproached for the name of Christ, blessed *are you,* for the Spirit of glory and of God rests upon you.[a] On their part He is blasphemed, but on your part He is glorified. 15But let none of you suffer as a murderer, a thief, an evildoer, or as a busybody in other people's matters. 16Yet if *anyone suffers* as a Christian, let him not be ashamed, but let him glorify God in this matter.[a]

17For the time *has come* for judgment to begin at the house of God; and if *it begins* with us first, what will *be* the end of those who do not obey the gospel of God? 18Now

"If the righteous one is scarcely
saved,
Where will the ungodly and the
sinner appear?"[a]

19Therefore let those who suffer according to the will of God commit their souls *to Him* in doing good, as to a faithful Creator.

Shepherd the Flock

5 The elders who are among you I exhort, I who am a fellow elder and a witness of the sufferings of Christ, and also a partaker of the glory that

3:18 [a] NU-Text and M-Text read *you.* 3:20 [a] NU-Text and M-Text read *when the longsuffering of God waited patiently.* 4:1 [a] NU-Text omits *for us.* 4:3 [a] NU-Text reads *time.* 4:8 [a] Proverbs 10:12 4:14 [a] NU-Text omits the rest of this verse. 4:16 [a] NU-Text reads *name.* 4:18 [a] Proverbs 11:31

will be revealed: 2 Shepherd the flock of God which is among you, serving as overseers, not by compulsion but willingly,[a] not for dishonest gain but eagerly; 3 nor as being lords over those entrusted to you, but being examples to the flock; 4 and when the Chief Shepherd appears, you will receive the crown of glory that does not fade away.

Submit to God, Resist the Devil

5 Likewise you younger people, submit yourselves to *your* elders. Yes, all of *you* be submissive to one another, and be clothed with humility, for

> "God resists the proud,
> But gives grace to the humble."[a]

6 Therefore humble yourselves under the mighty hand of God, that He may exalt you in due time, 7 casting all your care upon Him, for He cares for you.

8 Be sober, be vigilant; because[a] your adversary the devil walks about like a roaring lion, seeking whom he may devour. 9 Resist him, steadfast in the faith, knowing that the same sufferings are experienced by your brotherhood in the world. 10 But may[a] the God of all grace, who called us[b] to His eternal glory by Christ Jesus, after you have suffered a while, perfect, establish, strengthen, and settle *you*. 11 To Him *be* the glory and the dominion forever and ever. Amen.

Farewell and Peace

12 By Silvanus, our faithful brother as I consider him, I have written to you briefly, exhorting and testifying that this is the true grace of God in which you stand.

13 She who is in Babylon, elect together with *you*, greets you; and *so does* Mark my son. 14 Greet one another with a kiss of love.

Peace to you all who are in Christ Jesus. Amen.

5:2 [a] NU-Text adds *according to God.* 5:5 [a] Proverbs 3:34 5:8 [a] NU-Text and M-Text omit *because.*
5:10 [a] NU-Text reads *But the God of all grace . . . will perfect, establish, strengthen, and settle you.*
[b] NU-Text and M-Text read *you.*

GOD SIN JESUS SALVATION LOVE

THE SECOND LETTER OF

PETER

While 1 Peter deals with problems from outside the church, 2 Peter deals more with a problem from inside it: false teachers. Peter wrote this letter to teach how to recognize false teachings and stand against them. Peter warned the believers that they needed to keep a close watch on their lives so they could not be tricked by false teachers. They needed to be knowledgeable of the gospel, self-controlled, kind, and loving. This was also how they could recognize false teachers who did not live this way. He guaranteed that God would judge these false teachers, but he also warned them to be patient.

- **GENRE:** Epistle
- **AUTHOR:** Peter
- **TIME:** c. AD 67–68
- **PURPOSE:** To warn the church about false teachers who were twisting the truth.

Greeting the Faithful

1 Simon Peter, a bondservant and
apostle of Jesus Christ,

To those who have obtained like pre-
cious faith with us by the righteousness
of our God and Savior Jesus Christ:

2Grace and peace be multiplied to you
in the knowledge of God and of Jesus our
Lord, 3as His divine power has given to
us all things that *pertain* to life and godli-
ness, through the knowledge of Him who
called us by glory and virtue, 4by which
have been given to us exceedingly great
and precious promises, that through
these you may be partakers of the divine
nature, having escaped the corruption
that is in the world through lust.

Fruitful Growth in the Faith

5But also for this very reason, giving
all diligence, add to your faith virtue, to
virtue knowledge, 6to knowledge self-
control, to self-control perseverance, to
perseverance godliness, 7to godliness
brotherly kindness, and to brotherly
kindness love. 8For if these things are
yours and abound, *you* will be neither
barren nor unfruitful in the knowledge
of our Lord Jesus Christ. 9For he who
lacks these things is shortsighted, even
to blindness, and has forgotten that he
was cleansed from his old sins.

10Therefore, brethren, be even more
diligent to make your call and election
sure, for if you do these things you will
never stumble; 11for so an entrance will
be supplied to you abundantly into the
everlasting kingdom of our Lord and
Savior Jesus Christ.

Peter's Approaching Death

12For this reason I will not be negligent
to remind you always of these things,
though you know and are established
in the present truth. 13Yes, I think it is
right, as long as I am in this tent, to stir
you up by reminding *you*, 14knowing
that shortly I *must* put off my tent, just
as our Lord Jesus Christ showed me.
15Moreover I will be careful to ensure
that you always have a reminder of
these things after my decease.

The Trustworthy Prophetic Word

16For we did not follow cunningly de-
vised fables when we made known to
you the power and coming of our Lord
Jesus Christ, but were eyewitnesses of
His majesty. 17For He received from God
the Father honor and glory when such
a voice came to Him from the Excellent
Glory: "This is My beloved Son, in whom
I am well pleased." 18And we heard this
voice which came from heaven when we
were with Him on the holy mountain.
19And so we have the prophetic word

WORSHIP | GROWTH | HEAVEN | FAMILY

confirmed,[a] which you do well to heed
as a light that shines in a dark place,
until the day dawns and the morning
star rises in your hearts; 20knowing
this first, that no prophecy of Scrip-
ture is of any private interpretation,[a]
21for prophecy never came by the will
of man, but holy men of God[a] spoke
as they were moved by the Holy Spirit.

Destructive Doctrines

2 But there were also false prophets
among the people, even as there
will be false teachers among you, who
will secretly bring in destructive here-
sies, even denying the Lord who bought
them, *and* bring on themselves swift
destruction. 2And many will follow their
destructive ways, because of whom the
way of truth will be blasphemed. 3By
covetousness they will exploit you with
deceptive words; for a long time their
judgment has not been idle, and their
destruction does[a] not slumber.

Doom of False Teachers

4For if God did not spare the angels
who sinned, but cast *them* down to
hell and delivered *them* into chains of
darkness, to be reserved for judgment;
5and did not spare the ancient world,
but saved Noah, *one of* eight *people,* a
preacher of righteousness, bringing in
the flood on the world of the ungodly;
6and turning the cities of Sodom and
Gomorrah into ashes, condemned *them*
to destruction, making *them* an exam-
ple to those who afterward would live
ungodly; 7and delivered righteous Lot,
who was oppressed by the filthy conduct
of the wicked 8(for that righteous man,
dwelling among them, tormented *his*
righteous soul from day to day by see-
ing and hearing *their* lawless deeds)—
9*then* the Lord knows how to deliver
the godly out of temptations and to
reserve the unjust under punishment
for the day of judgment, 10and espe-
cially those who walk according to the
flesh in the lust of uncleanness and de-
spise authority. *They are* presumptuous,
self-willed. They are not afraid to speak
evil of dignitaries, 11whereas angels,
who are greater in power and might, do
not bring a reviling accusation against
them before the Lord.

Depravity of False Teachers

12But these, like natural brute beasts
made to be caught and destroyed, speak
evil of the things they do not understand,
and will utterly perish in their own cor-
ruption, 13*and* will receive the wages of
unrighteousness, *as* those who count it
pleasure to carouse in the daytime. *They*
are spots and blemishes, carousing in
their own deceptions while they feast
with you, 14having eyes full of adultery
and that cannot cease from sin, enticing
unstable souls. They have a heart trained
in covetous practices, *and are* accursed
children. 15They have forsaken the right
way and gone astray, following the way
of Balaam the *son* of Beor, who loved the
wages of unrighteousness; 16but he was
rebuked for his iniquity: a dumb donkey
speaking with a man's voice restrained
the madness of the prophet.
17These are wells without water,
clouds[a] carried by a tempest, for whom
is reserved the blackness of darkness
forever.[b]

Deceptions of False Teachers

18For when they speak great swelling
words of emptiness, they allure through
the lusts of the flesh, through lewdness,
the ones who have actually escaped[a]
from those who live in error. 19While
they promise them liberty, they them-
selves are slaves of corruption; for by
whom a person is overcome, by him
also he is brought into bondage. 20For if,
after they have escaped the pollutions
of the world through the knowledge of
the Lord and Savior Jesus Christ, they
are again entangled in them and over-
come, the latter end is worse for them
than the beginning. 21For it would have
been better for them not to have known
the way of righteousness, than having
known *it,* to turn from the holy com-
mandment delivered to them. 22But it
has happened to them according to the

1:19 [a] Or *We also have the more sure prophetic word.* **1:20** [a] Or *origin* **1:21** [a] NU-Text reads *but men spoke from God.* **2:3** [a] M-Text reads *will not.* **2:17** [a] NU-Text reads *and mists.* [b] NU-Text omits *forever.* **2:18** [a] NU-Text reads *are barely escaping.*

true proverb: "A dog returns to his own
vomit,"[a] and, "a sow, having washed, to
her wallowing in the mire."

God's Promise Is Not Slack

3 Beloved, I now write to you this sec-
ond epistle (in *both of* which I stir up
your pure minds by way of reminder),
2that you may be mindful of the words
which were spoken before by the holy
prophets, and of the commandment of
us,[a] the apostles of the Lord and Savior,
3knowing this first: that scoffers will
come in the last days, walking according
to their own lusts, 4and saying, "Where
is the promise of His coming? For since
the fathers fell asleep, all things contin-
ue as *they were* from the beginning of
creation." 5For this they willfully forget:
that by the word of God the heavens
were of old, and the earth standing out
of water and in the water, 6by which the
world *that* then existed perished, being
flooded with water. 7But the heavens
and the earth *which* are now preserved
by the same word, are reserved for fire
until the day of judgment and perdition
of ungodly men.
8But, beloved, do not forget this one
thing, that with the Lord one day *is* as a
thousand years, and a thousand years
as one day. 9The Lord is not slack con-
cerning *His* promise, as some count
slackness, but is longsuffering toward
us,[a] not willing that any should perish
but that all should come to repentance.

The Day of the Lord

10But the day of the Lord will come
as a thief in the night, in which the
heavens will pass away with a great
noise, and the elements will melt with
fervent heat; both the earth and the
works that are in it will be burned up.[a]
11Therefore, since all these things will
be dissolved, what manner *of persons*
ought you to be in holy conduct and
godliness, 12looking for and hastening
the coming of the day of God, because
of which the heavens will be dissolved,
being on fire, and the elements will melt
with fervent heat? 13Nevertheless we,
according to His promise, look for new
heavens and a new earth in which righ-
teousness dwells.

Be Steadfast

14Therefore, beloved, looking for-
ward to these things, be diligent to
be found by Him in peace, without
spot and blameless; 15and consider
that the longsuffering of our Lord *is*
salvation—as also our beloved brother
Paul, according to the wisdom given
to him, has written to you, 16as also
in all his epistles, speaking in them of
these things, in which are some things
hard to understand, which untaught
and unstable *people* twist to their own
destruction, as *they do* also the rest of
the Scriptures.
17You therefore, beloved, since you
know *this* beforehand, beware lest you
also fall from your own steadfastness,
being led away with the error of the
wicked; 18but grow in the grace and
knowledge of our Lord and Savior Jesus
Christ.
To Him *be* the glory both now and
forever. Amen.

2:22 [a] Proverbs 26:11 **3:2** [a] NU-Text and M-Text read *commandment of the apostles of your Lord and Savior* or *commandment of your apostles of the Lord and Savior.* **3:9** [a] NU-Text reads *you.* **3:10** [a] NU-Text reads *laid bare* (literally *found*).

THE FIRST LETTER OF

JOHN

False teachers who denied Jesus were confusing and worrying many people within the church. Some wondered if they had even been saved. The disciple John, by now an older man, wrote this letter to comfort and encourage these believers. There was no need to doubt. Christ had come as God in the flesh and lived a sinless life. He died and rose again. John knew this because he had been there with Jesus. All one must do is trust in Jesus to be saved. John also provided several tests to identify false teachers. Do they view Jesus and sin properly? Are they part of Christian fellowship? Do they live in love? Do they hope in Jesus? John encouraged the believers to keep their faith strong and love one another. Christians can know they are God's children if they love one another and obey God's commands.

- **GENRE:** Epistle
- **AUTHOR:** John
- **TIME:** c. AD 90–95
- **PURPOSE:** To encourage believers that they can be sure of their salvation and that they can know the truth and live in love for God.

What Was Heard, Seen, and Touched

1 That which was from the begin-
ning, which we have heard, which
we have seen with our eyes, which we
have looked upon, and our hands have
handled, concerning the Word of life—
2the life was manifested, and we have
seen, and bear witness, and declare to
you that eternal life which was with
the Father and was manifested to us—
3that which we have seen and heard we
declare to you, that you also may have
fellowship with us; and truly our fel-
lowship *is* with the Father and with His
Son Jesus Christ. 4And these things we
write to you that your[a] joy may be full.

Fellowship with Him and One Another

5This is the message which we have
heard from Him and declare to you,
that God is light and in Him is no dark-
ness at all. 6If we say that we have fel-
lowship with Him, and walk in darkness,
we lie and do not practice the truth.
7But if we walk in the light as He is in
the light, we have fellowship with one
another, and the blood of Jesus Christ
His Son cleanses us from all sin.
8If we say that we have no sin, we
deceive ourselves, and the truth is not
in us. 9If we confess our sins, He is faith-
ful and just to forgive us *our* sins and to
cleanse us from all unrighteousness. 10If
we say that we have not sinned, we make
Him a liar, and His word is not in us.

2 My little children, these things I
write to you, so that you may not
sin. And if anyone sins, we have an
Advocate with the Father, Jesus Christ
the righteous. 2And He Himself is the
propitiation for our sins, and not for
ours only but also for the whole world.

The Test of Knowing Him

3Now by this we know that we know
Him, if we keep His commandments.
4He who says, "I know Him," and does
not keep His commandments, is a liar,
and the truth is not in him. 5But whoev-
er keeps His word, truly the love of God
is perfected in him. By this we know that
we are in Him. 6He who says he abides
in Him ought himself also to walk just
as He walked.

7Brethren,[a] I write no new command-
ment to you, but an old commandment
which you have had from the begin-
ning. The old commandment is the word

1:4 [a] NU-Text and M-Text read *our*. 2:7 [a] NU-Text reads *Beloved*.

GOD SIN JESUS SALVATION LOVE

which you heard from the beginning.[b]
8Again, a new commandment I write
to you, which thing is true in Him and
in you, because the darkness is pass-
ing away, and the true light is already
shining.
9He who says he is in the light, and
hates his brother, is in darkness until
now. 10He who loves his brother abides
in the light, and there is no cause for
stumbling in him. 11But he who hates
his brother is in darkness and walks
in darkness, and does not know where
he is going, because the darkness has
blinded his eyes.

Their Spiritual State

12 I write to you, little children,
Because your sins are forgiven
you for His name's sake.
13 I write to you, fathers,
Because you have known Him
who is from the beginning.
I write to you, young men,
Because you have overcome
the wicked one.
I write to you, little children,
Because you have known the
Father.
14 I have written to you, fathers,
Because you have known Him
who is from the beginning.
I have written to you, young men,
Because you are strong, and the
word of God abides in you,
And you have overcome the
wicked one.

Do Not Love the World

15Do not love the world or the things
in the world. If anyone loves the world,
the love of the Father is not in him. 16For
all that *is* in the world—the lust of the
flesh, the lust of the eyes, and the pride
of life—is not of the Father but is of the
world. 17And the world is passing away,
and the lust of it; but he who does the
will of God abides forever.

Deceptions of the Last Hour

18Little children, it is the last hour; and
as you have heard that the[a] Antichrist
is coming, even now many antichrists
have come, by which we know that it is
the last hour. 19They went out from us,
but they were not of us; for if they had
been of us, they would have continued
with us; but *they went out* that they
might be made manifest, that none of
them were of us.
20But you have an anointing from the
Holy One, and you know all things.[a] 21I
have not written to you because you do
not know the truth, but because you
know it, and that no lie is of the truth.
22Who is a liar but he who denies that
Jesus is the Christ? He is antichrist who
denies the Father and the Son. 23Who-
ever denies the Son does not have the
Father either; he who acknowledges the
Son has the Father also.

Let Truth Abide in You

24Therefore let that abide in you which
you heard from the beginning. If what you
heard from the beginning abides in you,
you also will abide in the Son and in the
Father. 25And this is the promise that He
has promised us—eternal life.
26These things I have written to you
concerning those who *try to* deceive
you. 27But the anointing which you
have received from Him abides in you,
and you do not need that anyone teach
you; but as the same anointing teaches
you concerning all things, and is true,
and is not a lie, and just as it has taught
you, you will[a] abide in Him.

The Children of God

28And now, little children, abide in
Him, that when[a] He appears, we may
have confidence and not be ashamed
before Him at His coming. 29If you
know that He is righteous, you know
that everyone who practices righteous-
ness is born of Him.

3 Behold what manner of love the
Father has bestowed on us, that
we should be called children of God![a]
Therefore the world does not know us,[b]
because it did not know Him. 2Beloved,
now we are children of God; and it has
not yet been revealed what we shall be,

2:7 [b] NU-Text omits *from the beginning.* 2:18 [a] NU-Text omits *the.* 2:20 [a] NU-Text reads *you all know.* 2:27 [a] NU-Text reads *you abide.* 2:28 [a] NU-Text reads *if.* 3:1 [a] NU-Text adds *And we are.* [b] M-Text reads *you.*

but we know that when He is revealed, we shall be like Him, for we shall see Him as He is. 3And everyone who has this hope in Him purifies himself, just as He is pure.

Sin and the Child of God

4Whoever commits sin also commits lawlessness, and sin is lawlessness. 5And you know that He was manifested to take away our sins, and in Him there is no sin. 6Whoever abides in Him does not sin. Whoever sins has neither seen Him nor known Him.

7Little children, let no one deceive you. He who practices righteousness is righteous, just as He is righteous. 8He who sins is of the devil, for the devil has sinned from the beginning. For this purpose the Son of God was manifested, that He might destroy the works of the devil. 9Whoever has been born of God does not sin, for His seed remains in him; and he cannot sin, because he has been born of God.

The Imperative of Love

10In this the children of God and the children of the devil are manifest: Whoever does not practice righteousness is not of God, nor *is* he who does not love his brother. 11For this is the message that you heard from the beginning, that we should love one another, 12not as Cain *who* was of the wicked one and murdered his brother. And why did he murder him? Because his works were evil and his brother's righteous.

13Do not marvel, my brethren, if the world hates you. 14We know that we have passed from death to life, because we love the brethren. He who does not love *his* brother[a] abides in death. 15Whoever hates his brother is a murderer, and you know that no murderer has eternal life abiding in him.

The Outworking of Love

16By this we know love, because He laid down His life for us. And we also ought to lay down *our* lives for the brethren. 17But whoever has this world's goods, and sees his brother in need, and shuts up his heart from him, how does the love of God abide in him?

18My little children, let us not love in word or in tongue, but in deed and in truth. 19And by this we know[a] that we are of the truth, and shall assure our hearts before Him. 20For if our heart condemns us, God is greater than our heart, and knows all things. 21Beloved, if our heart does not condemn us, we have confidence toward God. 22And whatever we ask we receive from Him, because we keep His commandments and do those things that are pleasing in His sight. 23And this is His commandment: that we should believe on the name of His Son Jesus Christ and love one another, as He gave us[a] commandment.

The Spirit of Truth and the Spirit of Error

24Now he who keeps His commandments abides in Him, and He in him. And by this we know that He abides in us, by the Spirit whom He has given us.

4 Beloved, do not believe every spirit, but test the spirits, whether they are of God; because many false prophets have gone out into the world. 2By this you know the Spirit of God: Every spirit that confesses that Jesus Christ has come in the flesh is of God, 3and every spirit that does not confess that[a] Jesus Christ has come in the flesh is not of God. And this is the *spirit* of the Antichrist, which you have heard was coming, and is now already in the world.

4You are of God, little children, and have overcome them, because He who is in you is greater than he who is in the world. 5They are of the world. Therefore they speak *as* of the world, and the world hears them. 6We are of God. He who knows God hears us; he who is not of God does not hear us. By this we know the spirit of truth and the spirit of error.

Knowing God Through Love

7Beloved, let us love one another, for love is of God; and everyone who loves is born of God and knows God. 8He who does not love does not know God, for God is love. 9In this the love of God was manifested toward us, that God has sent

3:14 [a] NU-Text omits *his brother.* 3:19 [a] NU-Text reads *we shall know.* 3:23 [a] M-Text omits *us.*
4:3 [a] NU-Text omits *that* and *Christ has come in the flesh.*

GOD SIN JESUS SALVATION LOVE

His only begotten Son into the world, that we might live through Him. [10]In this is love, not that we loved God, but that He loved us and sent His Son *to be* the propitiation for our sins. [11]Beloved, if God so loved us, we also ought to love one another.

Seeing God Through Love

[12]No one has seen God at any time. If we love one another, God abides in us, and His love has been perfected in us. [13]By this we know that we abide in Him, and He in us, because He has given us of His Spirit. [14]And we have seen and testify that the Father has sent the Son *as* Savior of the world. [15]Whoever confesses that Jesus is the Son of God, God abides in him, and he in God. [16]And we have known and believed the love that God has for us. God is love, and he who abides in love abides in God, and God in him.

The Consummation of Love

[17]Love has been perfected among us in this: that we may have boldness in the day of judgment; because as He is, so are we in this world. [18]There is no fear in love; but perfect love casts out fear, because fear involves torment. But he who fears has not been made perfect in love. [19]We love Him[a] because He first loved us.

Obedience by Faith

[20]If someone says, "I love God," and hates his brother, he is a liar; for he who does not love his brother whom he has seen, how can[a] he love God whom he has not seen? [21]And this commandment we have from Him: that he who loves God *must* love his brother also.

5 Whoever believes that Jesus is the Christ is born of God, and everyone who loves Him who begot also loves him who is begotten of Him. [2]By this we know that we love the children of God, when we love God and keep His commandments. [3]For this is the love of God, that we keep His commandments. And His commandments are not burdensome. [4]For whatever is born of God overcomes the world. And this is the victory that has overcome the world—our[a] faith. [5]Who is he who overcomes the world, but he who believes that Jesus is the Son of God?

The Certainty of God's Witness

[6]This is He who came by water and blood—Jesus Christ; not only by water, but by water and blood. And it is the Spirit who bears witness, because the Spirit is truth. [7]For there are three that bear witness in heaven: the Father, the Word, and the Holy Spirit; and these three are one. [8]And there are three that bear witness on earth:[a] the Spirit, the water, and the blood; and these three agree as one.

[9]If we receive the witness of men, the witness of God is greater; for this is the witness of God which[a] He has testified of His Son. [10]He who believes in the Son of God has the witness in himself; he who does not believe God has made Him a liar, because he has not believed the testimony that God has given of His Son. [11]And this is the testimony: that God has given us eternal life, and this life is in His Son. [12]He who has the Son has life; he who does not have the Son of God does not have life. [13]These things I have written to you who believe in the name of the Son of God, that you may know that you have eternal life,[a] and that you may *continue to* believe in the name of the Son of God.

Confidence and Compassion in Prayer

[14]Now this is the confidence that we have in Him, that if we ask anything according to His will, He hears us. [15]And if we know that He hears us, whatever we ask, we know that we have the petitions that we have asked of Him.

[16]If anyone sees his brother sinning a sin *which does* not *lead* to death, he will ask, and He will give him life for those who commit sin not *leading* to death. There is sin *leading* to death. I do not

4:19 [a] NU-Text omits *Him.* **4:20** [a] NU-Text reads *he cannot.* **5:4** [a] M-Text reads *your.*
5:8 [a] NU-Text and M-Text omit the words from *in heaven* (verse 7) through *on earth* (verse 8). Only four or five very late manuscripts contain these words in Greek. **5:9** [a] NU-Text reads *God, that.*
5:13 [a] NU-Text omits the rest of this verse.

say that he should pray about that.
17All unrighteousness is sin, and there
is sin not *leading* to death.

Knowing the True—Rejecting the False

18We know that whoever is born of God
does not sin; but he who has been born
of God keeps himself,[a] and the wicked
one does not touch him.
19We know that we are of God, and the
whole world lies *under the sway of* the
wicked one.
20And we know that the Son of God
has come and has given us an under-
standing, that we may know Him who
is true; and we are in Him who is true,
in His Son Jesus Christ. This is the true
God and eternal life.
21Little children, keep yourselves from
idols. Amen.

5:18 [a] NU-Text reads *him*.

THE SECOND LETTER OF

JOHN

John wrote this letter to warn believers about showing hospitality to false teachers. It is important for Christians to love one another and obey God's commands, but they should not make the mistake of giving charity to false teachers. Doing this would only help the false teachers' cause of sowing seeds of error in the church.

- **GENRE:** Epistle
- **AUTHOR:** John
- **TIME:** c. AD 90–95
- **PURPOSE:** To warn Christians not to help false teachers.

Greeting the Elect Lady

The Elder,

To the elect lady and her children,
whom I love in truth, and not only I, but
also all those who have known the truth,
2because of the truth which abides in
us and will be with us forever:

3Grace, mercy, *and* peace will be with
you[a] from God the Father and from the
Lord Jesus Christ, the Son of the Father,
in truth and love.

Walk in Christ's Commandments

4I rejoiced greatly that I have found
some of your children walking in truth,
as we received commandment from
the Father. 5And now I plead with you,
lady, not as though I wrote a new com-
mandment to you, but that which we
have had from the beginning: that
we love one another. 6This is love, that
we walk according to His command-
ments. This is the commandment, that
as you have heard from the beginning,
you should walk in it.

Beware of Antichrist Deceivers

7For many deceivers have gone out
into the world who do not confess Jesus
Christ *as* coming in the flesh. This is a
deceiver and an antichrist. 8Look to
yourselves, that we[a] do not lose those
things we worked for, but *that* we[b] may
receive a full reward.

9Whoever transgresses[a] and does not
abide in the doctrine of Christ does not
have God. He who abides in the doctrine
of Christ has both the Father and the
Son. 10If anyone comes to you and does
not bring this doctrine, do not receive
him into your house nor greet him;
11for he who greets him shares in his
evil deeds.

John's Farewell Greeting

12Having many things to write to you,
I did not wish *to do so* with paper and
ink; but I hope to come to you and speak
face to face, that our joy may be full.
13The children of your elect sister greet
you. Amen.

3 [a] NU-Text and M-Text read *us.* 8 [a] NU-Text reads *you.* [b] NU-Text reads *you.* 9 [a] NU-Text reads *goes ahead.*

THE THIRD LETTER OF
JOHN

John wrote this letter for two reasons. First, he praised Gaius for being hospitable to traveling missionaries. By doing this, Gaius was helping to advance the gospel. Second, John warned about Diotrephes, a man in the church who refused to help the same kind of missionaries and who even made it difficult for others to help them.

- **GENRE:** Epistle
- **AUTHOR:** John
- **TIME:** c. AD 90–95
- **PURPOSE:** To encourage Christians to show hospitality to visitors and strangers.

Greeting to Gaius

The Elder,

To the beloved Gaius, whom I love in truth:

2 Beloved, I pray that you may prosper in all things and be in health, just as your soul prospers. 3 For I rejoiced greatly when brethren came and testified of the truth *that is* in you, just as you walk in the truth. 4 I have no greater joy than to hear that my children walk in truth.[a]

Gaius Commended for Generosity

5 Beloved, you do faithfully whatever you do for the brethren and[a] for strangers, 6 who have borne witness of your love before the church. *If* you send them forward on their journey in a manner worthy of God, you will do well, 7 because they went forth for His name's sake, taking nothing from the Gentiles. 8 We therefore ought to receive[a] such, that we may become fellow workers for the truth.

Diotrephes and Demetrius

9 I wrote to the church, but Diotrephes, who loves to have the preeminence among them, does not receive us. 10 Therefore, if I come, I will call to mind his deeds which he does, prating against us with malicious words. And not content with that, he himself does not receive the brethren, and forbids those who wish to, putting *them* out of the church.

11 Beloved, do not imitate what is evil, but what is good. He who does good is of God, but[a] he who does evil has not seen God.

12 Demetrius has a *good* testimony from all, and from the truth itself. And we also bear witness, and you know that our testimony is true.

Farewell Greeting

13 I had many things to write, but I do not wish to write to you with pen and ink; 14 but I hope to see you shortly, and we shall speak face to face.

Peace to you. Our friends greet you. Greet the friends by name.

4 [a] NU-Text reads *the truth.* 5 [a] NU-Text adds *especially.* 8 [a] NU-Text reads *support.* 11 [a] NU-Text and M-Text omit *but.*

THE LETTER OF

JUDE

Jude wanted to write to the church to encourage them, but as he began he was moved to warn them of their need to contend for the faith. False teachers were on the loose in the church and Jude wanted to make sure his readers understood the harm of their teaching. He urged Christians to resist these false teachers and to defend the faith that they had come to know and believe. Jude guaranteed that God would punish and destroy the false teachers like he punished sinners in the Old Testament. He finished by reminding them of the hope they have in knowing Christ is coming again.

- **GENRE:** Epistle
- **AUTHOR:** Jude
- **TIME:** c. AD 68–70
- **PURPOSE:** To warn Christians about false teachers who were trying to destroy the church.

Greeting to the Called

Jude, a bondservant of Jesus Christ, and brother of James,

To those who are called, sanctified[a] by God the Father, and preserved in Jesus Christ:

2 Mercy, peace, and love be multiplied to you.

Contend for the Faith

3 Beloved, while I was very diligent to write to you concerning our common salvation, I found it necessary to write to you exhorting you to contend earnestly for the faith which was once for all delivered to the saints. 4 For certain men have crept in unnoticed, who long ago were marked out for this condemnation, ungodly men, who turn the grace of our God into lewdness and deny the only Lord God[a] and our Lord Jesus Christ.

Old and New Apostates

5 But I want to remind you, though you once knew this, that the Lord, having saved the people out of the land of Egypt, afterward destroyed those who did not believe. 6 And the angels who did not keep their proper domain, but left their own abode, He has reserved in everlasting chains under darkness for the judgment of the great day; 7 as Sodom and Gomorrah, and the cities around them in a similar manner to these, having given themselves over to sexual immorality and gone after strange flesh, are set forth as an example, suffering the vengeance of eternal fire.

8 Likewise also these dreamers defile the flesh, reject authority, and speak evil of dignitaries. 9 Yet Michael the archangel, in contending with the devil, when he disputed about the body of Moses, dared not bring against him a reviling accusation, but said, "The Lord rebuke you!" 10 But these speak evil of whatever they do not know; and whatever they know naturally, like brute beasts, in these things they corrupt themselves. 11 Woe to them! For they have gone in the way of Cain, have run greedily in the error of Balaam for profit, and perished in the rebellion of Korah.

Apostates Depraved and Doomed

12 These are spots in your love feasts, while they feast with you without fear, serving *only* themselves. *They are* clouds without water, carried about[a] by the

1 [a] NU-Text reads *beloved.* 4 [a] NU-Text omits *God.* 12 [a] NU-Text and M-Text read *along.*

winds; late autumn trees without fruit,
twice dead, pulled up by the roots;
13 raging waves of the sea, foaming up
their own shame; wandering stars for
whom is reserved the blackness of dark-
ness forever.
14 Now Enoch, the seventh from Adam,
prophesied about these men also, say-
ing, "Behold, the Lord comes with ten
thousands of His saints, 15 to execute
judgment on all, to convict all who are
ungodly among them of all their un-
godly deeds which they have committed
in an ungodly way, and of all the harsh
things which ungodly sinners have spo-
ken against Him."

Apostates Predicted

16 These are grumblers, complainers,
walking according to their own lusts;
and they mouth great swelling *words*,
flattering people to gain advantage.
17 But you, beloved, remember the words
which were spoken before by the apos-
tles of our Lord Jesus Christ: 18 how they
told you that there would be mockers in
the last time who would walk according
to their own ungodly lusts. 19 These are
sensual persons, who cause divisions,
not having the Spirit.

Maintain Your Life with God

20 But you, beloved, building your-
selves up on your most holy faith, pray-
ing in the Holy Spirit, 21 keep yourselves
in the love of God, looking for the mercy
of our Lord Jesus Christ unto eternal
life.
22 And on some have compassion,
making a distinction;[a] 23 but others
save with fear, pulling *them* out of the
fire,[a] hating even the garment defiled
by the flesh.

Glory to God

24 Now to Him who is able to keep
you[a] from stumbling,
And to present *you* faultless
Before the presence of His glory
with exceeding joy,
25 To God our Savior,[a]
Who alone is wise,[b]
Be glory and majesty,
Dominion and power,[c]
Both now and forever.
Amen.

22 [a] NU-Text reads *who are doubting* (or *making distinctions*). 23 [a] NU-Text adds *and on some have mercy with fear* and omits *with fear* in first clause. 24 [a] M-Text reads *them.* 25 [a] NU-Text reads *To the only God our Savior.* [b] NU-Text omits *Who . . . is wise* and adds *Through Jesus Christ our Lord.* [c] NU-Text adds *Before all time.*

THE REVELATION OF JESUS CHRIST

Just as Genesis is the book of beginnings, Revelation is the book about completion. In Genesis, God's plan of forgiveness begins. In Revelation that plan is fulfilled entirely. John wrote this book while he was exiled on the island of Patmos off the coast of Turkey. While there, Jesus appeared to him in a vision that described how He will return. In this vision, John saw symbols and images that can be difficult to understand, but one thing is clear: Jesus Christ is Lord, ruler of everything, and He will return one day in victory.

- **GENRE:** Apocalyptic
- **AUTHOR:** John
- **TIME:** c. AD 94–96
- **PURPOSE:** To report the vision that Jesus gave to John describing His ultimate victory.

Introduction and Benediction

1 The Revelation of Jesus Christ,
which God gave Him to show His
servants—things which must shortly
take place. And He sent and signified *it*
by His angel to His servant John, 2who
bore witness to the word of God, and to
the testimony of Jesus Christ, to all things
that he saw. 3Blessed *is* he who reads
and those who hear the words of this
prophecy, and keep those things which
are written in it; for the time *is* near.

Greeting the Seven Churches

4John, to the seven churches which
are in Asia:

Grace to you and peace from Him who
is and who was and who is to come, and
from the seven Spirits who are before
His throne, 5and from Jesus Christ, the
faithful witness, the firstborn from the
dead, and the ruler over the kings of
the earth.

To Him who loved us and washed[a] us
from our sins in His own blood, 6and
has made us kings[a] and priests to His
God and Father, to Him *be* glory and
dominion forever and ever. Amen.

7Behold, He is coming with clouds,
and every eye will see Him, even they
who pierced Him. And all the tribes of
the earth will mourn because of Him.
Even so, Amen.

8"I am the Alpha and the Omega,
the Beginning and *the* End,"[a] says the
Lord,[b] "who is and who was and who is
to come, the Almighty."

Vision of the Son of Man

9I, John, both[a] your brother and com-
panion in the tribulation and kingdom
and patience of Jesus Christ, was on
the island that is called Patmos for the
word of God and for the testimony of
Jesus Christ. 10I was in the Spirit on
the Lord's Day, and I heard behind me
a loud voice, as of a trumpet, 11saying,
"I am the Alpha and the Omega, the
First and the Last," and,[a] "What you
see, write in a book and send *it* to the
seven churches which are in Asia:[b] to
Ephesus, to Smyrna, to Pergamos, to
Thyatira, to Sardis, to Philadelphia,
and to Laodicea."

12Then I turned to see the voice that
spoke with me. And having turned I saw
seven golden lampstands, 13and in the

1:5 [a] NU-Text reads *loves us and freed;* M-Text reads *loves us and washed.* 1:6 [a] NU-Text and M-Text read *a kingdom.* 1:8 [a] NU-Text and M-Text omit *the Beginning and the End.* [b] NU-Text and M-Text add *God.* 1:9 [a] NU-Text and M-Text omit *both.* 1:11 [a] NU-Text and M-Text omit *I am* through third *and.* [b] NU-Text and M-Text omit *which are in Asia.*

WORSHIP | GROWTH | HEAVEN | FAMILY

midst of the seven lampstands *One* like
the Son of Man, clothed with a garment
down to the feet and girded about the
chest with a golden band. 14His head
and hair *were* white like wool, as white
as snow, and His eyes like a flame of
fire; 15His feet *were* like fine brass, as if
refined in a furnace, and His voice as the
sound of many waters; 16He had in His
right hand seven stars, out of His mouth
went a sharp two-edged sword, and His
countenance *was* like the sun shining
in its strength. 17And when I saw Him, I
fell at His feet as dead. But He laid His
right hand on me, saying to me,[a] "Do
not be afraid; I am the First and the Last.
18I *am* He who lives, and was dead, and
behold, I am alive forevermore. Amen.
And I have the keys of Hades and of
Death. 19Write[a] the things which you
have seen, and the things which are,
and the things which will take place
after this. 20The mystery of the seven
stars which you saw in My right hand,
and the seven golden lampstands: The
seven stars are the angels of the seven
churches, and the seven lampstands
which you saw[a] are the seven churches.

The Loveless Church

2 "To the angel of the church of Eph-
esus write,
'These things says He who holds the
seven stars in His right hand, who walks
in the midst of the seven golden lamp-
stands: 2"I know your works, your labor,
your patience, and that you cannot bear
those who are evil. And you have tested
those who say they are apostles and are
not, and have found them liars; 3and
you have persevered and have patience,
and have labored for My name's sake
and have not become weary. 4Never-
theless I have *this* against you, that you
have left your first love. 5Remember
therefore from where you have fallen;
repent and do the first works, or else I
will come to you quickly and remove
your lampstand from its place—unless
you repent. 6But this you have, that
you hate the deeds of the Nicolaitans,
which I also hate.

7"He who has an ear, let him hear what
the Spirit says to the churches. To him
who overcomes I will give to eat from
the tree of life, which is in the midst of
the Paradise of God." '

The Persecuted Church

8"And to the angel of the church in
Smyrna write,
'These things says the First and the
Last, who was dead, and came to life: 9"I
know your works, tribulation, and pov-
erty (but you are rich); and *I know* the
blasphemy of those who say they are
Jews and are not, but *are* a synagogue
of Satan. 10Do not fear any of those
things which you are about to suffer.
Indeed, the devil is about to throw *some*
of you into prison, that you may be
tested, and you will have tribulation
ten days. Be faithful until death, and I
will give you the crown of life.
11"He who has an ear, let him hear
what the Spirit says to the churches. He
who overcomes shall not be hurt by the
second death." '

The Compromising Church

12"And to the angel of the church in
Pergamos write,
'These things says He who has the
sharp two-edged sword: 13"I know your
works, and where you dwell, where Sa-
tan's throne *is*. And you hold fast to My
name, and did not deny My faith even
in the days in which Antipas *was* My
faithful martyr, who was killed among
you, where Satan dwells. 14But I have
a few things against you, because you
have there those who hold the doctrine
of Balaam, who taught Balak to put a
stumbling block before the children of
Israel, to eat things sacrificed to idols,
and to commit sexual immorality.
15Thus you also have those who hold the
doctrine of the Nicolaitans, which thing
I hate.[a] 16Repent, or else I will come to
you quickly and will fight against them
with the sword of My mouth.
17"He who has an ear, let him hear
what the Spirit says to the churches. To
him who overcomes I will give some of

1:17 [a] NU-Text and M-Text omit *to me*. 1:19 [a] NU-Text and M-Text read *Therefore, write*. 1:20 [a] NU-Text and M-Text omit *which you saw*. 2:15 [a] NU-Text and M-Text read *likewise* for *which thing I hate*.

the hidden manna to eat. And I will give
him a white stone, and on the stone a
new name written which no one knows
except him who receives *it*." '

The Corrupt Church

18"And to the angel of the church in
Thyatira write,
'These things says the Son of God, who
has eyes like a flame of fire, and His feet
like fine brass: 19"I know your works,
love, service, faith,[a] and your patience;
and *as* for your works, the last *are* more
than the first. 20Nevertheless I have a few
things against you, because you allow[a]
that woman[b] Jezebel, who calls herself
a prophetess, to teach and seduce[c] My
servants to commit sexual immorality
and eat things sacrificed to idols. 21And
I gave her time to repent of her sexual
immorality, and she did not repent.[a]
22Indeed I will cast her into a sickbed,
and those who commit adultery with
her into great tribulation, unless they
repent of their[a] deeds. 23I will kill her
children with death, and all the churches
shall know that I am He who searches
the minds and hearts. And I will give to
each one of you according to your works.
24"Now to you I say, and[a] to the rest
in Thyatira, as many as do not have
this doctrine, who have not known the
depths of Satan, as they say, I will[b] put
on you no other burden. 25But hold fast
what you have till I come. 26And he who
overcomes, and keeps My works until
the end, to him I will give power over
the nations—

27 'He shall rule them with a rod of
iron;
They shall be dashed to pieces like
the potter's vessels'[a]—

as I also have received from My Father;
28and I will give him the morning star.
29"He who has an ear, let him hear
what the Spirit says to the churches." '

The Dead Church

3 "And to the angel of the church in
Sardis write,
'These things says He who has the sev-
en Spirits of God and the seven stars:
"I know your works, that you have a
name that you are alive, but you are
dead. 2Be watchful, and strengthen the
things which remain, that are ready
to die, for I have not found your works
perfect before God.[a] 3Remember there-
fore how you have received and heard;
hold fast and repent. Therefore if you
will not watch, I will come upon you
as a thief, and you will not know what
hour I will come upon you. 4You[a] have
a few names even in Sardis who have
not defiled their garments; and they
shall walk with Me in white, for they
are worthy. 5He who overcomes shall
be clothed in white garments, and I will
not blot out his name from the Book of
Life; but I will confess his name before
My Father and before His angels.
6"He who has an ear, let him hear what
the Spirit says to the churches." '

The Faithful Church

7"And to the angel of the church in
Philadelphia write,
'These things says He who is holy,
He who is true, "He who has the key
of David, He who opens and no one
shuts, and shuts and no one opens":[a]
8"I know your works. See, I have set be-
fore you an open door, and no one can
shut it;[a] for you have a little strength,
have kept My word, and have not denied
My name. 9Indeed I will make *those* of
the synagogue of Satan, who say they
are Jews and are not, but lie—indeed I
will make them come and worship be-
fore your feet, and to know that I have
loved you. 10Because you have kept
My command to persevere, I also will
keep you from the hour of trial which
shall come upon the whole world, to test
those who dwell on the earth. 11Behold,[a]

2:19 [a] NU-Text and M-Text read *faith, service.* **2:20** [a] NU-Text and M-Text read *I have against you that you tolerate.* [b] M-Text reads *your wife Jezebel.* [c] NU-Text and M-Text read *and teaches and seduces.* **2:21** [a] NU-Text and M-Text read *time to repent, and she does not want to repent of her sexual immorality.* **2:22** [a] NU-Text and M-Text read *her.* **2:24** [a] NU-Text and M-Text omit *and.* [b] NU-Text and M-Text omit *will.* **2:27** [a] Psalm 2:9 **3:2** [a] NU-Text and M-Text read *My God.* **3:4** [a] NU-Text and M-Text read *Nevertheless you have a few names in Sardis.* **3:7** [a] Isaiah 22:22 **3:8** [a] NU-Text and M-Text read *which no one can shut.* **3:11** [a] NU-Text and M-Text omit *Behold.*

I am coming quickly! Hold fast what
you have, that no one may take your
crown. 12He who overcomes, I will make
him a pillar in the temple of My God,
and he shall go out no more. I will write
on him the name of My God and the
name of the city of My God, the New
Jerusalem, which comes down out of
heaven from My God. And *I will write*
on him My new name.
13"He who has an ear, let him hear
what the Spirit says to the churches."'

The Lukewarm Church

14"And to the angel of the church of
the Laodiceans[a] write,
'These things says the Amen, the Faith-
ful and True Witness, the Beginning
of the creation of God: 15"I know your
works, that you are neither cold nor
hot. I could wish you were cold or hot.
16So then, because you are lukewarm,
and neither cold nor hot,[a] I will vomit
you out of My mouth. 17Because you
say, 'I am rich, have become wealthy,
and have need of nothing'—and do not
know that you are wretched, miserable,
poor, blind, and naked— 18I counsel
you to buy from Me gold refined in the
fire, that you may be rich; and white
garments, that you may be clothed, *that*
the shame of your nakedness may not
be revealed; and anoint your eyes with
eye salve, that you may see. 19As many
as I love, I rebuke and chasten. There-
fore be zealous and repent. 20Behold, I
stand at the door and knock. If anyone
hears My voice and opens the door, I will
come in to him and dine with him, and
he with Me. 21To him who overcomes I
will grant to sit with Me on My throne,
as I also overcame and sat down with
My Father on His throne.
22"He who has an ear, let him hear
what the Spirit says to the churches."'"

The Throne Room of Heaven

4 After these things I looked, and be-
hold, a door *standing* open in heav-
en. And the first voice which I heard
was like a trumpet speaking with me,
saying, "Come up here, and I will show
you things which must take place after
this."
2Immediately I was in the Spirit; and
behold, a throne set in heaven, and *One*
sat on the throne. 3And He who sat there
was[a] like a jasper and a sardius stone in
appearance; and *there was* a rainbow
around the throne, in appearance like
an emerald. 4Around the throne *were*
twenty-four thrones, and on the thrones
I saw twenty-four elders sitting, clothed
in white robes; and they had crowns[a]
of gold on their heads. 5And from the
throne proceeded lightnings, thunder-
ings, and voices.[a] Seven lamps of fire
were burning before the throne, which
are the[b] seven Spirits of God.
6Before the throne *there was*[a] a sea
of glass, like crystal. And in the midst
of the throne, and around the throne,
were four living creatures full of eyes
in front and in back. 7The first living
creature *was* like a lion, the second liv-
ing creature like a calf, the third living
creature had a face like a man, and
the fourth living creature *was* like a
flying eagle. 8*The* four living creatures,
each having six wings, were full of eyes
around and within. And they do not rest
day or night, saying:

"Holy, holy, holy,[a]
Lord God Almighty,
Who was and is and is to come!"

9Whenever the living creatures give
glory and honor and thanks to Him
who sits on the throne, who lives forever
and ever, 10the twenty-four elders fall
down before Him who sits on the throne
and worship Him who lives forever and
ever, and cast their crowns before the
throne, saying:

11 "You are worthy, O Lord,[a]
To receive glory and honor and
power;
For You created all things,

3:14 [a] NU-Text and M-Text read *in Laodicea.* **3:16** [a] NU-Text and M-Text read *hot nor cold.* **4:3** [a] M-Text omits *And He who sat there was* (which makes the description in verse 3 modify the throne rather than God). **4:4** [a] NU-Text and M-Text read *robes, with crowns.* **4:5** [a] NU-Text and M-Text read *voices, and thunderings.* [b] M-Text omits *the.* **4:6** [a] NU-Text and M-Text add *something like.* **4:8** [a] M-Text has *holy* nine times. **4:11** [a] NU-Text and M-Text read *our Lord and God.*

GOD SIN JESUS SALVATION LOVE

And by Your will they exist[b] and
were created."

The Lamb Takes the Scroll

5 And I saw in the right *hand* of Him
who sat on the throne a scroll writ-
ten inside and on the back, sealed with
seven seals. 2 Then I saw a strong angel
proclaiming with a loud voice, "Who is
worthy to open the scroll and to loose
its seals?" 3 And no one in heaven or on
the earth or under the earth was able to
open the scroll, or to look at it.
4 So I wept much, because no one was
found worthy to open and read[a] the
scroll, or to look at it. 5 But one of the
elders said to me, "Do not weep. Be-
hold, the Lion of the tribe of Judah, the
Root of David, has prevailed to open
the scroll and to loose[a] its seven seals."
6 And I looked, and behold,[a] in the
midst of the throne and of the four liv-
ing creatures, and in the midst of the
elders, stood a Lamb as though it had
been slain, having seven horns and sev-
en eyes, which are the seven Spirits of
God sent out into all the earth. 7 Then He
came and took the scroll out of the right
hand of Him who sat on the throne.

Worthy Is the Lamb

8 Now when He had taken the scroll, the
four living creatures and the twenty-
four elders fell down before the Lamb,
each having a harp, and golden bowls
full of incense, which are the prayers
of the saints. 9 And they sang a new
song, saying:

"You are worthy to take the scroll,
And to open its seals;
For You were slain,
And have redeemed us to God by
Your blood
Out of every tribe and tongue and
people and nation,
10 And have made us[a] kings[b] and
priests to our God;
And we[c] shall reign on the earth."

11 Then I looked, and I heard the voice
of many angels around the throne, the
living creatures, and the elders; and
the number of them was ten thousand
times ten thousand, and thousands of
thousands, 12 saying with a loud voice:

"Worthy is the Lamb who
was slain
To receive power and riches and
wisdom,
And strength and honor and
glory and blessing!"

13 And every creature which is in heav-
en and on the earth and under the earth
and such as are in the sea, and all that
are in them, I heard saying:

"Blessing and honor and glory and
power
Be to Him who sits on the throne,
And to the Lamb, forever and
ever!"[a]

14 Then the four living creatures said,
"Amen!" And the twenty-four[a] elders
fell down and worshiped Him who lives
forever and ever.[b]

First Seal: The Conqueror

6 Now I saw when the Lamb opened
one of the seals;[a] and I heard one of
the four living creatures saying with a
voice like thunder, "Come and see." 2 And
I looked, and behold, a white horse. He
who sat on it had a bow; and a crown
was given to him, and he went out con-
quering and to conquer.

Second Seal: Conflict on Earth

3 When He opened the second seal, I
heard the second living creature saying,
"Come and see."[a] 4 Another horse, fiery
red, went out. And it was granted to the
one who sat on it to take peace from the
earth, and that *people* should kill one
another; and there was given to him a
great sword.

4:11 [b] NU-Text and M-Text read *existed.* 5:4 [a] NU-Text and M-Text omit *and read.* 5:5 [a] NU-Text and M-Text omit *to loose.* 5:6 [a] NU-Text and M-Text read *I saw in the midst . . . a Lamb standing.* 5:10 [a] NU-Text and M-Text read *them.* [b] NU-Text reads *a kingdom.* [c] NU-Text and M-Text read *they.* 5:13 [a] M-Text adds *Amen.* 5:14 [a] NU-Text and M-Text omit *twenty-four.* [b] NU-Text and M-Text omit *Him who lives forever and ever.* 6:1 [a] NU-Text and M-Text read *seven seals.* 6:3 [a] NU-Text and M-Text omit *and see.*

Third Seal: Scarcity on Earth

5When He opened the third seal, I heard
the third living creature say, "Come and
see." So I looked, and behold, a black
horse, and he who sat on it had a pair of
scales in his hand. 6And I heard a voice in
the midst of the four living creatures say-
ing, "A quart[a] of wheat for a denarius,[b]
and three quarts of barley for a denarius;
and do not harm the oil and the wine."

Fourth Seal: Widespread Death on Earth

7When He opened the fourth seal,
I heard the voice of the fourth living
creature saying, "Come and see." 8So I
looked, and behold, a pale horse. And
the name of him who sat on it was
Death, and Hades followed with him.
And power was given to them over a
fourth of the earth, to kill with sword,
with hunger, with death, and by the
beasts of the earth.

Fifth Seal: The Cry of the Martyrs

9When He opened the fifth seal, I
saw under the altar the souls of those
who had been slain for the word of
God and for the testimony which they
held. 10And they cried with a loud voice,
saying, "How long, O Lord, holy and
true, until You judge and avenge our
blood on those who dwell on the earth?"
11Then a white robe was given to each of
them; and it was said to them that they
should rest a little while longer, until
both *the number of* their fellow servants
and their brethren, who would be killed
as they *were,* was completed.

Sixth Seal: Cosmic Disturbances

12I looked when He opened the sixth
seal, and behold,[a] there was a great
earthquake; and the sun became black as
sackcloth of hair, and the moon[b] became
like blood. 13And the stars of heaven fell
to the earth, as a fig tree drops its late
figs when it is shaken by a mighty wind.
14Then the sky receded as a scroll when
it is rolled up, and every mountain and
island was moved out of its place. 15And
the kings of the earth, the great men, the
rich men, the commanders,[a] the mighty
men, every slave and every free man,
hid themselves in the caves and in the
rocks of the mountains, 16and said to the
mountains and rocks, "Fall on us and
hide us from the face of Him who sits
on the throne and from the wrath of the
Lamb! 17For the great day of His wrath
has come, and who is able to stand?"

The Sealed of Israel

7 After these things I saw four angels
standing at the four corners of the
earth, holding the four winds of the
earth, that the wind should not blow
on the earth, on the sea, or on any tree.
2Then I saw another angel ascending
from the east, having the seal of the
living God. And he cried with a loud
voice to the four angels to whom it was
granted to harm the earth and the sea,
3saying, "Do not harm the earth, the
sea, or the trees till we have sealed the
servants of our God on their foreheads."
4And I heard the number of those who
were sealed. One hundred *and* forty-
four thousand of all the tribes of the
children of Israel *were* sealed:

5 of the tribe of Judah twelve
thousand *were* sealed;[a]
of the tribe of Reuben twelve
thousand *were* sealed;
of the tribe of Gad twelve
thousand *were* sealed;
6 of the tribe of Asher twelve
thousand *were* sealed;
of the tribe of Naphtali twelve
thousand *were* sealed;
of the tribe of Manasseh twelve
thousand *were* sealed;
7 of the tribe of Simeon twelve
thousand *were* sealed;
of the tribe of Levi twelve
thousand *were* sealed;
of the tribe of Issachar twelve
thousand *were* sealed;
8 of the tribe of Zebulun twelve
thousand *were* sealed;
of the tribe of Joseph twelve
thousand *were* sealed;

6:6 [a] Greek *choinix;* that is, approximately one quart [b] This was approximately one day's wage for a worker. 6:12 [a] NU-Text and M-Text omit *behold.* [b] NU-Text and M-Text read *the whole moon.* 6:15 [a] NU-Text and M-Text read *the commanders, the rich men.* 7:5 [a] In NU-Text and M-Text *were sealed* is stated only in verses 5a and 8c; the words are understood in the remainder of the passage.

of the tribe of Benjamin twelve
thousand *were* sealed.

A Multitude from the Great Tribulation

9After these things I looked, and behold, a great multitude which no one could number, of all nations, tribes, peoples, and tongues, standing before the throne and before the Lamb, clothed with white robes, with palm branches in their hands, 10and crying out with a loud voice, saying, "Salvation *belongs* to our God who sits on the throne, and to the Lamb!" 11All the angels stood around the throne and the elders and the four living creatures, and fell on their faces before the throne and worshiped God, 12saying:

"Amen! Blessing and glory and
wisdom,
Thanksgiving and honor and
power and might,
Be to our God forever and ever.
Amen."

13Then one of the elders answered, saying to me, "Who are these arrayed in white robes, and where did they come from?"

14And I said to him, "Sir,[a] you know."

So he said to me, "These are the ones who come out of the great tribulation, and washed their robes and made them white in the blood of the Lamb. 15Therefore they are before the throne of God, and serve Him day and night in His temple. And He who sits on the throne will dwell among them. 16They shall neither hunger anymore nor thirst anymore; the sun shall not strike them, nor any heat; 17for the Lamb who is in the midst of the throne will shepherd them and lead them to living fountains of waters.[a] And God will wipe away every tear from their eyes."

Seventh Seal: Prelude to the Seven Trumpets

8 When He opened the seventh seal, there was silence in heaven for about half an hour. 2And I saw the seven angels who stand before God, and to them were given seven trumpets. 3Then another angel, having a golden censer, came and stood at the altar. He was given much incense, that he should offer *it* with the prayers of all the saints upon the golden altar which was before the throne. 4And the smoke of the incense, with the prayers of the saints, ascended before God from the angel's hand. 5Then the angel took the censer, filled it with fire from the altar, and threw *it* to the earth. And there were noises, thunderings, lightnings, and an earthquake.

6So the seven angels who had the seven trumpets prepared themselves to sound.

First Trumpet: Vegetation Struck

7The first angel sounded: And hail and fire followed, mingled with blood, and they were thrown to the earth.[a] And a third of the trees were burned up, and all green grass was burned up.

Second Trumpet: The Seas Struck

8Then the second angel sounded: And *something* like a great mountain burning with fire was thrown into the sea, and a third of the sea became blood. 9And a third of the living creatures in the sea died, and a third of the ships were destroyed.

Third Trumpet: The Waters Struck

10Then the third angel sounded: And a great star fell from heaven, burning like a torch, and it fell on a third of the rivers and on the springs of water. 11The name of the star is Wormwood. A third of the waters became wormwood, and many men died from the water, because it was made bitter.

Fourth Trumpet: The Heavens Struck

12Then the fourth angel sounded: And a third of the sun was struck, a third of the moon, and a third of the stars, so that a third of them were darkened. A third of the day did not shine, and likewise the night.

13And I looked, and I heard an angel[a] flying through the midst of heaven,

7:14 [a] NU-Text and M-Text read *My lord.* **7:17** [a] NU-Text and M-Text read *to fountains of the waters of life.* **8:7** [a] NU-Text and M-Text add *and a third of the earth was burned up.* **8:13** [a] NU-Text and M-Text read *eagle.*

saying with a loud voice, "Woe, woe, woe to the inhabitants of the earth, because of the remaining blasts of the trumpet of the three angels who are about to sound!"

Fifth Trumpet: The Locusts from the Bottomless Pit

9 Then the fifth angel sounded: And I saw a star fallen from heaven to the earth. To him was given the key to the bottomless pit. 2And he opened the bottomless pit, and smoke arose out of the pit like the smoke of a great furnace. So the sun and the air were darkened because of the smoke of the pit. 3Then out of the smoke locusts came upon the earth. And to them was given power, as the scorpions of the earth have power. 4They were commanded not to harm the grass of the earth, or any green thing, or any tree, but only those men who do not have the seal of God on their foreheads. 5And they were not given *authority* to kill them, but to torment them *for* five months. Their torment *was* like the torment of a scorpion when it strikes a man. 6In those days men will seek death and will not find it; they will desire to die, and death will flee from them.

7The shape of the locusts was like horses prepared for battle. On their heads were crowns of something like gold, and their faces *were* like the faces of men. 8They had hair like women's hair, and their teeth were like lions' *teeth.* 9And they had breastplates like breastplates of iron, and the sound of their wings *was* like the sound of chariots with many horses running into battle. 10They had tails like scorpions, and there were stings in their tails. Their power *was* to hurt men five months. 11And they had as king over them the angel of the bottomless pit, whose name in Hebrew *is* Abaddon, but in Greek he has the name Apollyon.

12One woe is past. Behold, still two more woes are coming after these things.

Sixth Trumpet: The Angels from the Euphrates

13Then the sixth angel sounded: And I heard a voice from the four horns of the golden altar which is before God, 14saying to the sixth angel who had the trumpet, "Release the four angels who are bound at the great river Euphrates." 15So the four angels, who had been prepared for the hour and day and month and year, were released to kill a third of mankind. 16Now the number of the army of the horsemen *was* two hundred million; I heard the number of them. 17And thus I saw the horses in the vision: those who sat on them had breastplates of fiery red, hyacinth blue, and sulfur yellow; and the heads of the horses *were* like the heads of lions; and out of their mouths came fire, smoke, and brimstone. 18By these three *plagues* a third of mankind was killed—by the fire and the smoke and the brimstone which came out of their mouths. 19For their power[a] is in their mouth and in their tails; for their tails *are* like serpents, having heads; and with them they do harm.

20But the rest of mankind, who were not killed by these plagues, did not repent of the works of their hands, that they should not worship demons, and idols of gold, silver, brass, stone, and wood, which can neither see nor hear nor walk. 21And they did not repent of their murders or their sorceries[a] or their sexual immorality or their thefts.

The Mighty Angel with the Little Book

10 I saw still another mighty angel coming down from heaven, clothed with a cloud. And a rainbow *was* on his head, his face *was* like the sun, and his feet like pillars of fire. 2He had a little book open in his hand. And he set his right foot on the sea and *his* left *foot* on the land, 3and cried with a loud voice, as *when* a lion roars. When he cried out, seven thunders uttered their voices. 4Now when the seven thunders uttered their voices,[a] I was about to write; but I heard a voice from heaven saying to me,[b] "Seal up the things which the seven thunders uttered, and do not write them."

5The angel whom I saw standing on the sea and on the land raised up his

9:19 [a] NU-Text and M-Text read *the power of the horses.* **9:21** [a] NU-Text and M-Text read *drugs.*
10:4 [a] NU-Text and M-Text read *sounded.* [b] NU-Text and M-Text omit *to me.*

hand[a] to heaven 6and swore by Him
who lives forever and ever, who created
heaven and the things that are in it, the
earth and the things that are in it, and
the sea and the things that are in it, that
there should be delay no longer, 7but in
the days of the sounding of the seventh
angel, when he is about to sound, the
mystery of God would be finished, as He
declared to His servants the prophets.

John Eats the Little Book

8Then the voice which I heard from
heaven spoke to me again and said,
"Go, take the little book which is open
in the hand of the angel who stands on
the sea and on the earth."

9So I went to the angel and said to him,
"Give me the little book."

And he said to me, "Take and eat it; and
it will make your stomach bitter, but it
will be as sweet as honey in your mouth."

10Then I took the little book out of the
angel's hand and ate it, and it was as
sweet as honey in my mouth. But when
I had eaten it, my stomach became
bitter. 11And he[a] said to me, "You must
prophesy again about many peoples,
nations, tongues, and kings."

The Two Witnesses

11 Then I was given a reed like a
measuring rod. And the angel
stood,[a] saying, "Rise and measure the
temple of God, the altar, and those who
worship there. 2But leave out the court
which is outside the temple, and do
not measure it, for it has been given
to the Gentiles. And they will tread
the holy city underfoot *for* forty-two
months. 3And I will give *power* to my
two witnesses, and they will prophesy
one thousand two hundred and sixty
days, clothed in sackcloth."

4These are the two olive trees and the
two lampstands standing before the
God[a] of the earth. 5And if anyone wants
to harm them, fire proceeds from their
mouth and devours their enemies. And
if anyone wants to harm them, he must
be killed in this manner. 6These have
power to shut heaven, so that no rain
falls in the days of their prophecy; and
they have power over waters to turn
them to blood, and to strike the earth
with all plagues, as often as they desire.

The Witnesses Killed

7When they finish their testimony, the
beast that ascends out of the bottomless
pit will make war against them, over-
come them, and kill them. 8And their
dead bodies *will lie* in the street of the
great city which spiritually is called
Sodom and Egypt, where also our[a] Lord
was crucified. 9Then *those* from the peo-
ples, tribes, tongues, and nations will see
their dead bodies three-and-a-half days,
and not allow[a] their dead bodies to be
put into graves. 10And those who dwell
on the earth will rejoice over them, make
merry, and send gifts to one another,
because these two prophets tormented
those who dwell on the earth.

The Witnesses Resurrected

11Now after the three-and-a-half days
the breath of life from God entered
them, and they stood on their feet,
and great fear fell on those who saw
them. 12And they[a] heard a loud voice
from heaven saying to them, "Come up
here." And they ascended to heaven in
a cloud, and their enemies saw them.
13In the same hour there was a great
earthquake, and a tenth of the city fell.
In the earthquake seven thousand peo-
ple were killed, and the rest were afraid
and gave glory to the God of heaven.

14The second woe is past. Behold, the
third woe is coming quickly.

Seventh Trumpet: The Kingdom Proclaimed

15Then the seventh angel sounded: And
there were loud voices in heaven, saying,
"The kingdoms[a] of this world have be-
come *the kingdoms* of our Lord and of His
Christ, and He shall reign forever and
ever!" 16And the twenty-four elders who
sat before God on their thrones fell on
their faces and worshiped God, 17saying:

10:5 [a] NU-Text and M-Text read *right hand.* **10:11** [a] NU-Text and M-Text read *they.* **11:1** [a] NU-Text and M-Text omit *And the angel stood.* **11:4** [a] NU-Text and M-Text read *Lord.* **11:8** [a] NU-Text and M-Text read *their.* **11:9** [a] NU-Text and M-Text read *nations see . . . and will not allow.* **11:12** [a] M-Text reads *I.* **11:15** [a] NU-Text and M-Text read *kingdom . . . has become.*

"We give You thanks, O Lord God
Almighty,
The One who is and who was and
who is to come,[a]
Because You have taken Your
great power and reigned.
18 The nations were angry, and Your
wrath has come,
And the time of the dead, that
they should be judged,
And that You should reward Your
servants the prophets and
the saints,
And those who fear Your name,
small and great,
And should destroy those who
destroy the earth."

19Then the temple of God was opened
in heaven, and the ark of His covenant[a]
was seen in His temple. And there were
lightnings, noises, thunderings, an
earthquake, and great hail.

The Woman, the Child, and the Dragon

12 Now a great sign appeared in
heaven: a woman clothed with
the sun, with the moon under her feet,
and on her head a garland of twelve
stars. 2Then being with child, she cried
out in labor and in pain to give birth.
3And another sign appeared in heav-
en: behold, a great, fiery red dragon
having seven heads and ten horns, and
seven diadems on his heads. 4His tail
drew a third of the stars of heaven and
threw them to the earth. And the dragon
stood before the woman who was ready
to give birth, to devour her Child as soon
as it was born. 5She bore a male Child
who was to rule all nations with a rod
of iron. And her Child was caught up to
God and His throne. 6Then the wom-
an fled into the wilderness, where she
has a place prepared by God, that they
should feed her there one thousand two
hundred and sixty days.

Satan Thrown Out of Heaven

7And war broke out in heaven: Mi-
chael and his angels fought with the
dragon; and the dragon and his angels
fought, 8but they did not prevail, nor
was a place found for them[a] in heaven
any longer. 9So the great dragon was
cast out, that serpent of old, called the
Devil and Satan, who deceives the whole
world; he was cast to the earth, and his
angels were cast out with him.
10Then I heard a loud voice saying in
heaven, "Now salvation, and strength,
and the kingdom of our God, and the
power of His Christ have come, for the
accuser of our brethren, who accused
them before our God day and night, has
been cast down. 11And they overcame
him by the blood of the Lamb and by
the word of their testimony, and they
did not love their lives to the death.
12Therefore rejoice, O heavens, and you
who dwell in them! Woe to the inhab-
itants of the earth and the sea! For the
devil has come down to you, having
great wrath, because he knows that he
has a short time."

The Woman Persecuted

13Now when the dragon saw that he
had been cast to the earth, he perse-
cuted the woman who gave birth to
the male *Child*. 14But the woman was
given two wings of a great eagle, that
she might fly into the wilderness to
her place, where she is nourished for a
time and times and half a time, from
the presence of the serpent. 15So the
serpent spewed water out of his mouth
like a flood after the woman, that he
might cause her to be carried away by
the flood. 16But the earth helped the
woman, and the earth opened its mouth
and swallowed up the flood which the
dragon had spewed out of his mouth.
17And the dragon was enraged with the
woman, and he went to make war with
the rest of her offspring, who keep the
commandments of God and have the
testimony of Jesus Christ.[a]

The Beast from the Sea

13 Then I[a] stood on the sand of the
sea. And I saw a beast rising up
out of the sea, having seven heads and
ten horns,[b] and on his horns ten crowns,

11:17 [a] NU-Text and M-Text omit *and who is to come.* **11:19** [a] M-Text reads *the covenant of the Lord.*
12:8 [a] M-Text reads *him.* **12:17** [a] NU-Text and M-Text omit *Christ.* **13:1** [a] NU-Text reads *he.*
[b] NU-Text and M-Text read *ten horns and seven heads.*

and on his heads a blasphemous name.
2Now the beast which I saw was like a
leopard, his feet were like *the feet of*
a bear, and his mouth like the mouth of a
lion. The dragon gave him his power, his
throne, and great authority. 3And I saw
one of his heads as if it had been mortal-
ly wounded, and his deadly wound was
healed. And all the world marveled and
followed the beast. 4So they worshiped
the dragon who gave authority to the
beast; and they worshiped the beast,
saying, "Who *is* like the beast? Who is
able to make war with him?"

5And he was given a mouth speaking
great things and blasphemies, and he
was given authority to continue[a] for
forty-two months. 6Then he opened
his mouth in blasphemy against God,
to blaspheme His name, His taberna-
cle, and those who dwell in heaven. 7It
was granted to him to make war with
the saints and to overcome them. And
authority was given him over every
tribe,[a] tongue, and nation. 8All who
dwell on the earth will worship him,
whose names have not been written in
the Book of Life of the Lamb slain from
the foundation of the world.

9If anyone has an ear, let him hear.
10He who leads into captivity shall go
into captivity; he who kills with the
sword must be killed with the sword.
Here is the patience and the faith of
the saints.

The Beast from the Earth

11Then I saw another beast coming up
out of the earth, and he had two horns
like a lamb and spoke like a dragon.
12And he exercises all the authority of
the first beast in his presence, and caus-
es the earth and those who dwell in it
to worship the first beast, whose deadly
wound was healed. 13He performs great
signs, so that he even makes fire come
down from heaven on the earth in the
sight of men. 14And he deceives those[a]
who dwell on the earth by those signs
which he was granted to do in the sight
of the beast, telling those who dwell
on the earth to make an image to the
beast who was wounded by the sword
and lived. 15He was granted *power* to
give breath to the image of the beast,
that the image of the beast should both
speak and cause as many as would not
worship the image of the beast to be
killed. 16He causes all, both small and
great, rich and poor, free and slave, to
receive a mark on their right hand or
on their foreheads, 17and that no one
may buy or sell except one who has the
mark or[a] the name of the beast, or the
number of his name.

18Here is wisdom. Let him who has
understanding calculate the number
of the beast, for it is the number of a
man: His number *is* 666.

The Lamb and the 144,000

14 Then I looked, and behold, a[a]
Lamb standing on Mount Zion,
and with Him one hundred *and* forty-
four thousand, having[b] His Father's
name written on their foreheads. 2And
I heard a voice from heaven, like the
voice of many waters, and like the voice
of loud thunder. And I heard the sound
of harpists playing their harps. 3They
sang as it were a new song before the
throne, before the four living creatures,
and the elders; and no one could learn
that song except the hundred *and* forty-
four thousand who were redeemed from
the earth. 4These are the ones who were
not defiled with women, for they are
virgins. These are the ones who follow
the Lamb wherever He goes. These were
redeemed[a] from *among* men, *being* first-
fruits to God and to the Lamb. 5And
in their mouth was found no deceit,[a]
for they are without fault before the
throne of God.[b]

The Proclamations of Three Angels

6Then I saw another angel flying in the
midst of heaven, having the everlasting
gospel to preach to those who dwell on
the earth—to every nation, tribe, tongue,
and people— 7saying with a loud voice,
"Fear God and give glory to Him, for the

13:5 [a] M-Text reads *make war.* **13:7** [a] NU-Text and M-Text add *and people.* **13:14** [a] M-Text reads *my own people.* **13:17** [a] NU-Text and M-Text omit *or.* **14:1** [a] NU-Text and M-Text read *the.* [b] NU-Text and M-Text add *His name and.* **14:4** [a] M-Text adds *by Jesus.* **14:5** [a] NU-Text and M-Text read *falsehood.* [b] NU-Text and M-Text omit *before the throne of God.*

hour of His judgment has come; and worship Him who made heaven and earth, the sea and springs of water."

8 And another angel followed, saying, "Babylon[a] is fallen, is fallen, that great city, because she has made all nations drink of the wine of the wrath of her fornication."

9 Then a third angel followed them, saying with a loud voice, "If anyone worships the beast and his image, and receives *his* mark on his forehead or on his hand, 10 he himself shall also drink of the wine of the wrath of God, which is poured out full strength into the cup of His indignation. He shall be tormented with fire and brimstone in the presence of the holy angels and in the presence of the Lamb. 11 And the smoke of their torment ascends forever and ever; and they have no rest day or night, who worship the beast and his image, and whoever receives the mark of his name."

12 Here is the patience of the saints; here *are* those[a] who keep the commandments of God and the faith of Jesus.

13 Then I heard a voice from heaven saying to me,[a] "Write: 'Blessed *are* the dead who die in the Lord from now on.'"

"Yes," says the Spirit, "that they may rest from their labors, and their works follow them."

Reaping the Earth's Harvest

14 Then I looked, and behold, a white cloud, and on the cloud sat *One* like the Son of Man, having on His head a golden crown, and in His hand a sharp sickle. 15 And another angel came out of the temple, crying with a loud voice to Him who sat on the cloud, "Thrust in Your sickle and reap, for the time has come for You[a] to reap, for the harvest of the earth is ripe." 16 So He who sat on the cloud thrust in His sickle on the earth, and the earth was reaped.

Reaping the Grapes of Wrath

17 Then another angel came out of the temple which is in heaven, he also having a sharp sickle.

18 And another angel came out from the altar, who had power over fire, and he cried with a loud cry to him who had the sharp sickle, saying, "Thrust in your sharp sickle and gather the clusters of the vine of the earth, for her grapes are fully ripe." 19 So the angel thrust his sickle into the earth and gathered the vine of the earth, and threw *it* into the great winepress of the wrath of God. 20 And the winepress was trampled outside the city, and blood came out of the winepress, up to the horses' bridles, for one thousand six hundred furlongs.

Prelude to the Bowl Judgments

15 Then I saw another sign in heaven, great and marvelous: seven angels having the seven last plagues, for in them the wrath of God is complete.

2 And I saw *something* like a sea of glass mingled with fire, and those who have the victory over the beast, over his image and over his mark[a] *and* over the number of his name, standing on the sea of glass, having harps of God. 3 They sing the song of Moses, the servant of God, and the song of the Lamb, saying:

"Great and marvelous *are* Your works,
Lord God Almighty!
Just and true *are* Your ways,
O King of the saints![a]
4 Who shall not fear You, O Lord,
and glorify Your name?
For *You* alone *are* holy.
For all nations shall come and worship before You,
For Your judgments have been manifested."

5 After these things I looked, and behold,[a] the temple of the tabernacle of the testimony in heaven was opened. 6 And out of the temple came the seven angels having the seven plagues, clothed in pure bright linen, and having their chests girded with golden bands. 7 Then one of the four living creatures

14:8 [a] NU-Text reads *Babylon the great is fallen, is fallen, which has made;* M-Text reads *Babylon the great is fallen. She has made.* **14:12** [a] NU-Text and M-Text omit *here are those.* **14:13** [a] NU-Text and M-Text omit *to me.* **14:15** [a] NU-Text and M-Text omit *for You.* **15:2** [a] NU-Text and M-Text omit *over his mark.* **15:3** [a] NU-Text and M-Text read *nations.* **15:5** [a] NU-Text and M-Text omit *behold.*

gave to the seven angels seven golden
bowls full of the wrath of God who lives
forever and ever. 8The temple was filled
with smoke from the glory of God and
from His power, and no one was able to
enter the temple till the seven plagues
of the seven angels were completed.

16 Then I heard a loud voice from
the temple saying to the seven
angels, "Go and pour out the bowls[a] of
the wrath of God on the earth."

First Bowl: Loathsome Sores

2So the first went and poured out his
bowl upon the earth, and a foul and
loathsome sore came upon the men
who had the mark of the beast and
those who worshiped his image.

Second Bowl: The Sea Turns to Blood

3Then the second angel poured out his
bowl on the sea, and it became blood as
of a dead *man;* and every living creature
in the sea died.

Third Bowl: The Waters Turn to Blood

4Then the third angel poured out his
bowl on the rivers and springs of water,
and they became blood. 5And I heard
the angel of the waters saying:

"You are righteous, O Lord,[a]
The One who is and who was and
who is to be,[b]
Because You have judged these
things.
6 For they have shed the blood of
saints and prophets,
And You have given them blood
to drink.
For[a] it is their just due."

7And I heard another from[a] the altar
saying, "Even so, Lord God Almighty,
true and righteous *are* Your judgments."

Fourth Bowl: Men Are Scorched

8Then the fourth angel poured out his
bowl on the sun, and power was given to
him to scorch men with fire. 9And men
were scorched with great heat, and they
blasphemed the name of God who has
power over these plagues; and they did
not repent and give Him glory.

Fifth Bowl: Darkness and Pain

10Then the fifth angel poured out his
bowl on the throne of the beast, and his
kingdom became full of darkness; and
they gnawed their tongues because of
the pain. 11They blasphemed the God of
heaven because of their pains and their
sores, and did not repent of their deeds.

Sixth Bowl: Euphrates Dried Up

12Then the sixth angel poured out his
bowl on the great river Euphrates, and
its water was dried up, so that the way
of the kings from the east might be pre-
pared. 13And I saw three unclean spirits
like frogs *coming* out of the mouth of
the dragon, out of the mouth of the
beast, and out of the mouth of the false
prophet. 14For they are spirits of de-
mons, performing signs, *which* go out to
the kings of the earth and[a] of the whole
world, to gather them to the battle of
that great day of God Almighty.
15"Behold, I am coming as a thief.
Blessed *is* he who watches, and keeps
his garments, lest he walk naked and
they see his shame."
16And they gathered them together
to the place called in Hebrew, Arma-
geddon.[a]

Seventh Bowl: The Earth Utterly Shaken

17Then the seventh angel poured out
his bowl into the air, and a loud voice
came out of the temple of heaven, from
the throne, saying, "It is done!" 18And
there were noises and thunderings
and lightnings; and there was a great
earthquake, such a mighty and great
earthquake as had not occurred since
men were on the earth. 19Now the great
city was divided into three parts, and
the cities of the nations fell. And great
Babylon was remembered before God,
to give her the cup of the wine of the
fierceness of His wrath. 20Then every
island fled away, and the mountains

16:1 [a] NU-Text and M-Text read *seven bowls.* **16:5** [a] NU-Text and M-Text omit *O Lord.* [b] NU-Text and M-Text read *who was, the Holy One.* **16:6** [a] NU-Text and M-Text omit *For.* **16:7** [a] NU-Text and M-Text omit *another from.* **16:14** [a] NU-Text and M-Text omit *of the earth and.* **16:16** [a] M-Text reads *Megiddo.*

WORSHIP GROWTH HEAVEN FAMILY

were not found. 21And great hail from
heaven fell upon men, *each hailstone*
about the weight of a talent. Men blas-
phemed God because of the plague of
the hail, since that plague was exceed-
ingly great.

The Scarlet Woman and the Scarlet Beast

17 Then one of the seven angels
who had the seven bowls came
and talked with me, saying to me,[a]
"Come, I will show you the judgment
of the great harlot who sits on many
waters, 2with whom the kings of the
earth committed fornication, and the
inhabitants of the earth were made
drunk with the wine of her fornication."
3So he carried me away in the Spirit
into the wilderness. And I saw a wom-
an sitting on a scarlet beast *which was*
full of names of blasphemy, having
seven heads and ten horns. 4The wom-
an was arrayed in purple and scarlet,
and adorned with gold and precious
stones and pearls, having in her hand
a golden cup full of abominations and
the filthiness of her fornication.[a] 5And
on her forehead a name *was* written:

MYSTERY, BABYLON THE GREAT,
THE MOTHER OF HARLOTS
AND OF THE ABOMINATIONS
OF THE EARTH.

6I saw the woman, drunk with the blood
of the saints and with the blood of the
martyrs of Jesus. And when I saw her, I
marveled with great amazement.

The Meaning of the Woman and the Beast

7But the angel said to me, "Why did
you marvel? I will tell you the mystery
of the woman and of the beast that car-
ries her, which has the seven heads and
the ten horns. 8The beast that you saw
was, and is not, and will ascend out of
the bottomless pit and go to perdition.
And those who dwell on the earth will
marvel, whose names are not written in
the Book of Life from the foundation of
the world, when they see the beast that
was, and is not, and yet is.[a]
9"Here *is* the mind which has wisdom:
The seven heads are seven mountains
on which the woman sits. 10There are
also seven kings. Five have fallen, one
is, *and* the other has not yet come. And
when he comes, he must continue a
short time. 11The beast that was, and is
not, is himself also the eighth, and is
of the seven, and is going to perdition.
12"The ten horns which you saw are
ten kings who have received no king-
dom as yet, but they receive authority
for one hour as kings with the beast.
13These are of one mind, and they will
give their power and authority to the
beast. 14These will make war with the
Lamb, and the Lamb will overcome
them, for He is Lord of lords and King
of kings; and those *who are* with Him
are called, chosen, and faithful."
15Then he said to me, "The waters
which you saw, where the harlot sits,
are peoples, multitudes, nations, and
tongues. 16And the ten horns which you
saw on[a] the beast, these will hate the
harlot, make her desolate and naked,
eat her flesh and burn her with fire. 17For
God has put it into their hearts to fulfill
His purpose, to be of one mind, and to
give their kingdom to the beast, until
the words of God are fulfilled. 18And
the woman whom you saw is that great
city which reigns over the kings of the
earth."

The Fall of Babylon the Great

18 After these things I saw another
angel coming down from heav-
en, having great authority, and the
earth was illuminated with his glory.
2And he cried mightily[a] with a loud
voice, saying, "Babylon the great is fall-
en, is fallen, and has become a dwelling
place of demons, a prison for every foul
spirit, and a cage for every unclean
and hated bird! 3For all the nations
have drunk of the wine of the wrath of
her fornication, the kings of the earth
have committed fornication with her,
and the merchants of the earth have

17:1 [a] NU-Text and M-Text omit *to me.* 17:4 [a] M-Text reads *the filthiness of the fornication of the earth.* 17:8 [a] NU-Text and M-Text read *and shall be present.* 17:16 [a] NU-Text and M-Text read *saw, and the beast.* 18:2 [a] NU-Text and M-Text omit *mightily.*

become rich through the abundance of her luxury."

4And I heard another voice from heaven saying, "Come out of her, my people, lest you share in her sins, and lest you receive of her plagues. 5For her sins have reached[a] to heaven, and God has remembered her iniquities. 6Render to her just as she rendered to you,[a] and repay her double according to her works; in the cup which she has mixed, mix double for her. 7In the measure that she glorified herself and lived luxuriously, in the same measure give her torment and sorrow; for she says in her heart, 'I sit *as* queen, and am no widow, and will not see sorrow.' 8Therefore her plagues will come in one day—death and mourning and famine. And she will be utterly burned with fire, for strong *is* the Lord God who judges[a] her.

The World Mourns Babylon's Fall

9"The kings of the earth who committed fornication and lived luxuriously with her will weep and lament for her, when they see the smoke of her burning, 10standing at a distance for fear of her torment, saying, 'Alas, alas, that great city Babylon, that mighty city! For in one hour your judgment has come.'

11"And the merchants of the earth will weep and mourn over her, for no one buys their merchandise anymore: 12merchandise of gold and silver, precious stones and pearls, fine linen and purple, silk and scarlet, every kind of citron wood, every kind of object of ivory, every kind of object of most precious wood, bronze, iron, and marble; 13and cinnamon and incense, fragrant oil and frankincense, wine and oil, fine flour and wheat, cattle and sheep, horses and chariots, and bodies and souls of men. 14The fruit that your soul longed for has gone from you, and all the things which are rich and splendid have gone from you,[a] and you shall find them no more at all. 15The merchants of these things, who became rich by her, will stand at a distance for fear of her torment, weeping and wailing, 16and saying, 'Alas, alas, that great city that was clothed in fine linen, purple, and scarlet, and adorned with gold and precious stones and pearls! 17For in one hour such great riches came to nothing.' Every shipmaster, all who travel by ship, sailors, and as many as trade on the sea, stood at a distance 18and cried out when they saw the smoke of her burning, saying, 'What *is* like this great city?'

19"They threw dust on their heads and cried out, weeping and wailing, and saying, 'Alas, alas, that great city, in which all who had ships on the sea became rich by her wealth! For in one hour she is made desolate.'

20"Rejoice over her, O heaven, and *you* holy apostles[a] and prophets, for God has avenged you on her!"

Finality of Babylon's Fall

21Then a mighty angel took up a stone like a great millstone and threw *it* into the sea, saying, "Thus with violence the great city Babylon shall be thrown down, and shall not be found anymore. 22The sound of harpists, musicians, flutists, and trumpeters shall not be heard in you anymore. No craftsman of any craft shall be found in you anymore, and the sound of a millstone shall not be heard in you anymore. 23The light of a lamp shall not shine in you anymore, and the voice of bridegroom and bride shall not be heard in you anymore. For your merchants were the great men of the earth, for by your sorcery all the nations were deceived. 24And in her was found the blood of prophets and saints, and of all who were slain on the earth."

Heaven Exults over Babylon

19 After these things I heard[a] a loud voice of a great multitude in heaven, saying, "Alleluia! Salvation and glory and honor and power *belong* to the Lord[b] our God! 2For true and righteous *are* His judgments, because He

18:5 [a] NU-Text and M-Text read *have been heaped up.* **18:6** [a] NU-Text and M-Text omit *to you.* **18:8** [a] NU-Text and M-Text read *has judged.* **18:14** [a] NU-Text and M-Text read *been lost to you.* **18:20** [a] NU-Text and M-Text read *saints and apostles.* **19:1** [a] NU-Text and M-Text add *something like.* [b] NU-Text and M-Text omit *the Lord.*

has judged the great harlot who cor-
rupted the earth with her fornication;
and He has avenged on her the blood
of His servants *shed* by her." 3 Again
they said, "Alleluia! Her smoke rises up
forever and ever!" 4 And the twenty-four
elders and the four living creatures fell
down and worshiped God who sat on the
throne, saying, "Amen! Alleluia!" 5 Then
a voice came from the throne, saying,
"Praise our God, all you His servants
and those who fear Him, both[a] small
and great!"
6 And I heard, as it were, the voice of a
great multitude, as the sound of many
waters and as the sound of mighty
thunderings, saying, "Alleluia! For the[a]
Lord God Omnipotent reigns! 7 Let us
be glad and rejoice and give Him glo-
ry, for the marriage of the Lamb has
come, and His wife has made herself
ready." 8 And to her it was granted to be
arrayed in fine linen, clean and bright,
for the fine linen is the righteous acts
of the saints.
9 Then he said to me, "Write: 'Blessed
are those who are called to the marriage
supper of the Lamb!' " And he said to
me, "These are the true sayings of God."
10 And I fell at his feet to worship him.
But he said to me, "See *that you do* not
do that! I am your fellow servant, and of
your brethren who have the testimony
of Jesus. Worship God! For the testimo-
ny of Jesus is the spirit of prophecy."

Christ on a White Horse

11 Now I saw heaven opened, and be-
hold, a white horse. And He who sat on
him *was* called Faithful and True, and
in righteousness He judges and makes
war. 12 His eyes *were* like a flame of fire,
and on His head *were* many crowns. He
had[a] a name written that no one knew
except Himself. 13 He *was* clothed with
a robe dipped in blood, and His name
is called The Word of God. 14 And the
armies in heaven, clothed in fine linen,
white and clean,[a] followed Him on white
horses. 15 Now out of His mouth goes a
sharp[a] sword, that with it He should
strike the nations. And He Himself will
rule them with a rod of iron. He Himself
treads the winepress of the fierceness
and wrath of Almighty God. 16 And He
has on *His* robe and on His thigh a
name written:

KING OF KINGS AND
LORD OF LORDS.

The Beast and His Armies Defeated

17 Then I saw an angel standing in the
sun; and he cried with a loud voice, say-
ing to all the birds that fly in the midst
of heaven, "Come and gather together
for the supper of the great God,[a] 18 that
you may eat the flesh of kings, the flesh
of captains, the flesh of mighty men,
the flesh of horses and of those who
sit on them, and the flesh of all *people,*
free[a] and slave, both small and great."
19 And I saw the beast, the kings of the
earth, and their armies, gathered to-
gether to make war against Him who
sat on the horse and against His army.
20 Then the beast was captured, and
with him the false prophet who worked
signs in his presence, by which he de-
ceived those who received the mark of
the beast and those who worshiped his
image. These two were cast alive into
the lake of fire burning with brimstone.
21 And the rest were killed with the sword
which proceeded from the mouth of
Him who sat on the horse. And all the
birds were filled with their flesh.

Satan Bound 1,000 Years

20 Then I saw an angel coming
down from heaven, having the
key to the bottomless pit and a great
chain in his hand. 2 He laid hold of the
dragon, that serpent of old, who is *the*
Devil and Satan, and bound him for
a thousand years; 3 and he cast him
into the bottomless pit, and shut him
up, and set a seal on him, so that he
should deceive the nations no more till
the thousand years were finished. But
after these things he must be released
for a little while.

19:5 [a] NU-Text and M-Text omit *both.* 19:6 [a] NU-Text and M-Text read *our.* 19:12 [a] M-Text adds *names written, and.* 19:14 [a] NU-Text and M-Text read *pure white linen.* 19:15 [a] M-Text adds *two-edged.* 19:17 [a] NU-Text and M-Text read *the great supper of God.* 19:18 [a] NU-Text and M-Text read *both free.*

The Saints Reign with Christ 1,000 Years

4And I saw thrones, and they sat on
them, and judgment was committed
to them. Then *I saw* the souls of those
who had been beheaded for their wit-
ness to Jesus and for the word of God,
who had not worshiped the beast or his
image, and had not received *his* mark
on their foreheads or on their hands.
And they lived and reigned with Christ
for a[a] thousand years. 5But the rest of
the dead did not live again until the
thousand years were finished. This *is*
the first resurrection. 6Blessed and holy
is he who has part in the first resurrec-
tion. Over such the second death has
no power, but they shall be priests of
God and of Christ, and shall reign with
Him a thousand years.

Satanic Rebellion Crushed

7Now when the thousand years have
expired, Satan will be released from his
prison 8and will go out to deceive the
nations which are in the four corners
of the earth, Gog and Magog, to gather
them together to battle, whose number
is as the sand of the sea. 9They went up
on the breadth of the earth and sur-
rounded the camp of the saints and the
beloved city. And fire came down from
God out of heaven and devoured them.
10The devil, who deceived them, was
cast into the lake of fire and brimstone
where[a] the beast and the false prophet
are. And they will be tormented day and
night forever and ever.

The Great White Throne Judgment

11Then I saw a great white throne and
Him who sat on it, from whose face
the earth and the heaven fled away.
And there was found no place for them.
12And I saw the dead, small and great,
standing before God,[a] and books were
opened. And another book was opened,
which is *the Book* of Life. And the dead
were judged according to their works,
by the things which were written in the
books. 13The sea gave up the dead who
were in it, and Death and Hades deliv-
ered up the dead who were in them. And
they were judged, each one according
to his works. 14Then Death and Hades
were cast into the lake of fire. This is the
second death.[a] 15And anyone not found
written in the Book of Life was cast into
the lake of fire.

All Things Made New

21 Now I saw a new heaven and a
new earth, for the first heaven
and the first earth had passed away.
Also there was no more sea. 2Then I,
John,[a] saw the holy city, New Jerusa-
lem, coming down out of heaven from
God, prepared as a bride adorned for
her husband. 3And I heard a loud voice
from heaven saying, "Behold, the tab-
ernacle of God *is* with men, and He will
dwell with them, and they shall be His
people. God Himself will be with them
and be their God. 4And God will wipe
away every tear from their eyes; there
shall be no more death, nor sorrow, nor
crying. There shall be no more pain, for
the former things have passed away."
5Then He who sat on the throne said,
"Behold, I make all things new." And He
said to me,[a] "Write, for these words are
true and faithful."
6And He said to me, "It is done![a] I am
the Alpha and the Omega, the Begin-
ning and the End. I will give of the foun-
tain of the water of life freely to him who
thirsts. 7He who overcomes shall inherit
all things,[a] and I will be his God and
he shall be My son. 8But the cowardly,
unbelieving,[a] abominable, murderers,
sexually immoral, sorcerers, idolaters,
and all liars shall have their part in the
lake which burns with fire and brim-
stone, which is the second death."

The New Jerusalem

9Then one of the seven angels who had
the seven bowls filled with the seven
last plagues came to me[a] and talked
with me, saying, "Come, I will show you
the bride, the Lamb's wife."[b] 10And he

20:4 [a] M-Text reads *the.* **20:10** [a] NU-Text and M-Text add *also.* **20:12** [a] NU-Text and M-Text read *the throne.* **20:14** [a] NU-Text and M-Text add *the lake of fire.* **21:2** [a] NU-Text and M-Text omit *John.* **21:5** [a] NU-Text and M-Text omit *to me.* **21:6** [a] M-Text omits *It is done.* **21:7** [a] M-Text reads *overcomes, I shall give him these things.* **21:8** [a] M-Text adds *and sinners.* **21:9** [a] NU-Text and M-Text omit *to me.* [b] M-Text reads *I will show you the woman, the Lamb's bride.*

carried me away in the Spirit to a great
and high mountain, and showed me
the great city, the holy[a] Jerusalem, de-
scending out of heaven from God, 11hav-
ing the glory of God. Her light *was* like a
most precious stone, like a jasper stone,
clear as crystal. 12Also she had a great
and high wall with twelve gates, and
twelve angels at the gates, and names
written on them, which are *the names*
of the twelve tribes of the children of
Israel: 13three gates on the east, three
gates on the north, three gates on the
south, and three gates on the west.
14Now the wall of the city had twelve
foundations, and on them were the
names[a] of the twelve apostles of the
Lamb. 15And he who talked with me
had a gold reed to measure the city, its
gates, and its wall. 16The city is laid out
as a square; its length is as great as its
breadth. And he measured the city with
the reed: twelve thousand furlongs. Its
length, breadth, and height are equal.
17Then he measured its wall: one hun-
dred *and* forty-four cubits, *according*
to the measure of a man, that is, of an
angel. 18The construction of its wall was
of jasper; and the city *was* pure gold,
like clear glass. 19The foundations of
the wall of the city *were* adorned with
all kinds of precious stones: the first
foundation *was* jasper, the second
sapphire, the third chalcedony, the
fourth emerald, 20the fifth sardonyx,
the sixth sardius, the seventh chryso-
lite, the eighth beryl, the ninth topaz,
the tenth chrysoprase, the eleventh
jacinth, and the twelfth amethyst. 21The
twelve gates *were* twelve pearls: each
individual gate was of one pearl. And
the street of the city *was* pure gold, like
transparent glass.

The Glory of the New Jerusalem

22But I saw no temple in it, for the
Lord God Almighty and the Lamb are
its temple. 23The city had no need of the
sun or of the moon to shine in it,[a] for the
glory[b] of God illuminated it. The Lamb *is*
its light. 24And the nations of those who
are saved[a] shall walk in its light, and
the kings of the earth bring their glory
and honor into it.[b] 25Its gates shall not
be shut at all by day (there shall be no
night there). 26And they shall bring the
glory and the honor of the nations into
it.[a] 27But there shall by no means enter
it anything that defiles, or causes[a] an
abomination or a lie, but only those who
are written in the Lamb's Book of Life.

The River of Life

22 And he showed me a pure[a] river
of water of life, clear as crystal,
proceeding from the throne of God and
of the Lamb. 2In the middle of its street,
and on either side of the river, *was* the
tree of life, which bore twelve fruits, each
tree yielding its fruit every month. The
leaves of the tree *were* for the healing
of the nations. 3And there shall be no
more curse, but the throne of God and of
the Lamb shall be in it, and His servants
shall serve Him. 4They shall see His face,
and His name *shall be* on their fore-
heads. 5There shall be no night there:
They need no lamp nor light of the sun,
for the Lord God gives them light. And
they shall reign forever and ever.

The Time Is Near

6Then he said to me, "These words *are*
faithful and true." And the Lord God
of the holy[a] prophets sent His angel
to show His servants the things which
must shortly take place.
7"Behold, I am coming quickly!
Blessed *is* he who keeps the words of
the prophecy of this book."
8Now I, John, saw and heard[a] these
things. And when I heard and saw, I
fell down to worship before the feet of
the angel who showed me these things.
9Then he said to me, "See *that you do* not
do that. For[a] I am your fellow servant,

21:10 [a] NU-Text and M-Text omit *the great* and read *the holy city, Jerusalem.* **21:14** [a] NU-Text and M-Text read *twelve names.* **21:23** [a] NU-Text and M-Text omit *in it.* [b] M-Text reads *the very glory.* **21:24** [a] NU-Text and M-Text omit *of those who are saved.* [b] M-Text reads *the glory and honor of the nations to Him.* **21:26** [a] M-Text adds *that they may enter in.* **21:27** [a] NU-Text and M-Text read *anything profane, nor one who causes.* **22:1** [a] NU-Text and M-Text omit *pure.* **22:6** [a] NU-Text and M-Text read *spirits of the prophets.* **22:8** [a] NU-Text and M-Text read *am the one who heard and saw.* **22:9** [a] NU-Text and M-Text omit *For.*

and of your brethren the prophets, and
of those who keep the words of this book.
Worship God." 10And he said to me, "Do
not seal the words of the prophecy of this
book, for the time is at hand. 11He who
is unjust, let him be unjust still; he who
is filthy, let him be filthy still; he who is
righteous, let him be righteous[a] still; he
who is holy, let him be holy still."

Jesus Testifies to the Churches

12"And behold, I am coming quickly,
and My reward *is* with Me, to give to ev-
ery one according to his work. 13I am the
Alpha and the Omega, *the* Beginning
and *the* End, the First and the Last."[a]
14Blessed *are* those who do His com-
mandments,[a] that they may have the
right to the tree of life, and may enter
through the gates into the city. 15But[a]
outside *are* dogs and sorcerers and
sexually immoral and murderers and
idolaters, and whoever loves and prac-
tices a lie.
16"I, Jesus, have sent My angel to testi-
fy to you these things in the churches. I
am the Root and the Offspring of David,
the Bright and Morning Star."
17And the Spirit and the bride say,
"Come!" And let him who hears say,
"Come!" And let him who thirsts come.
Whoever desires, let him take the water
of life freely.

A Warning

18For[a] I testify to everyone who hears
the words of the prophecy of this book:
If anyone adds to these things, God
will add[b] to him the plagues that are
written in this book; 19and if anyone
takes away from the words of the book
of this prophecy, God shall take away[a]
his part from the Book[b] of Life, from the
holy city, and *from* the things which are
written in this book.

I Am Coming Quickly

20He who testifies to these things says,
"Surely I am coming quickly."
Amen. Even so, come, Lord Jesus!
21The grace of our Lord Jesus Christ *be*
with you all.[a] Amen.

22:11 [a] NU-Text and M-Text read *do right.* **22:13** [a] NU-Text and M-Text read *the First and the Last, the Beginning and the End.* **22:14** [a] NU-Text reads *wash their robes.* **22:15** [a] NU-Text and M-Text omit *But.* **22:18** [a] NU-Text and M-Text omit *For.* [b] M-Text reads *may God add.* **22:19** [a] M-Text reads *may God take away.* [b] NU-Text and M-Text read *tree of life.* **22:21** [a] NU-Text reads *with all;* M-Text reads *with all the saints.*

WORSHIP GROWTH HEAVEN FAMILY

365 DAYS THROUGH THE BIBLE

DAY	READING	DATE READ
☐ 1	Genesis 1–3	
☐ 2	Genesis 4–5	
☐ 3	Genesis 6:1—9:19	
☐ 4	Genesis 9:20—12:9	
☐ 5	Genesis 12:10—16:16	
☐ 6	Genesis 17:1—19:29	
☐ 7	Genesis 19:30—22:24	
☐ 8	Genesis 23–24	
☐ 9	Genesis 25–26	
☐ 10	Genesis 27:1—29:14	
☐ 11	Genesis 29:15—31:21	
☐ 12	Genesis 31:22—33:20	
☐ 13	Genesis 34:1—36:30	
☐ 14	Genesis 36:31—38:30	
☐ 15	Genesis 39:1—41:36	
☐ 16	Genesis 41:37—43:34	
☐ 17	Genesis 44–45	
☐ 18	Genesis 46–48	
☐ 19	Genesis 49–Exodus 1	
☐ 20	Exodus 2–4	
☐ 21	Exodus 5–7	
☐ 22	Exodus 8:1—10:20	
☐ 23	Exodus 10:21—13:16	
☐ 24	Exodus 13:17—16:36	
☐ 25	Exodus 17–20	
☐ 26	Exodus 21:1—23:13	
☐ 27	Exodus 23:14—25:40	
☐ 28	Exodus 26–28	
☐ 29	Exodus 29–30	
☐ 30	Exodus 31:1—33:10	
☐ 31	Exodus 33:11—36:7	
☐ 32	Exodus 36:8—38:20	
☐ 33	Exodus 38:21—40:38	
☐ 34	Leviticus 1:1—5:13	
☐ 35	Leviticus 5:14—7:38	
☐ 36	Leviticus 8–10	
☐ 37	Leviticus 11:1—13:46	
☐ 38	Leviticus 13:47—14:57	
☐ 39	Leviticus 15–17	
☐ 40	Leviticus 18–20	
☐ 41	Leviticus 21:1—23:25	
☐ 42	Leviticus 23:26—25:55	
☐ 43	Leviticus 26–27	
☐ 44	Numbers 1–2	
☐ 45	Numbers 3:1—4:33	
☐ 46	Numbers 4:34—6:27	
☐ 47	Numbers 7	
☐ 48	Numbers 8–10	
☐ 49	Numbers 11–13	
☐ 50	Numbers 14–15	
☐ 51	Numbers 16–18	
☐ 52	Numbers 19–21	
☐ 53	Numbers 22–24	
☐ 54	Numbers 25–26	
☐ 55	Numbers 27–29	
☐ 56	Numbers 30–31	
☐ 57	Numbers 32–33	
☐ 58	Numbers 34–36	
☐ 59	Deuteronomy 1:1—3:7	
☐ 60	Deuteronomy 3:8—5:33	
☐ 61	Deuteronomy 6:1—9:6	
☐ 62	Deuteronomy 9:7—11:32	
☐ 63	Deuteronomy 12–14	
☐ 64	Deuteronomy 15–18	
☐ 65	Deuteronomy 19–21	
☐ 66	Deuteronomy 22–25	
☐ 67	Deuteronomy 26:1—28:14	
☐ 68	Deuteronomy 28:15—29:29	
☐ 69	Deuteronomy 30:1—32:47	
☐ 70	Deuteronomy 32:48—Joshua 2:24	
☐ 71	Joshua 3–6	
☐ 72	Joshua 7–9	
☐ 73	Joshua 10–12	
☐ 74	Joshua 13–15	
☐ 75	Joshua 16:1—19:31	
☐ 76	Joshua 19:32—21:45	
☐ 77	Joshua 22–24	
☐ 78	Judges 1–3	
☐ 79	Judges 4–6	
☐ 80	Judges 7–8	
☐ 81	Judges 9–10	
☐ 82	Judges 11–13	
☐ 83	Judges 14–17	
☐ 84	Judges 18–19	
☐ 85	Judges 20–Ruth 1	
☐ 86	Ruth 2–4	
☐ 87	1 Samuel 1–4	
☐ 88	1 Samuel 5–8	
☐ 89	1 Samuel 9–12	
☐ 90	1 Samuel 13–14	
☐ 91	1 Samuel 15–16	
☐ 92	1 Samuel 17–18	
☐ 93	1 Samuel 19–21	
☐ 94	1 Samuel 22–24	
☐ 95	1 Samuel 25–27	

- [ ] 96 1 Samuel 28–31
- [ ] 97 2 Samuel 1:1—3:21
- [ ] 98 2 Samuel 3:22—6:23
- [ ] 99 2 Samuel 7–10
- [ ] 100 2 Samuel 11:1—13:22
- [ ] 101 2 Samuel 13:23—15:37
- [ ] 102 2 Samuel 16:1—19:8
- [ ] 103 2 Samuel 19:9—21:22
- [ ] 104 2 Samuel 22–23
- [ ] 105 2 Samuel 24:1—1 Kings 2:11
- [ ] 106 1 Kings 2:12—4:21
- [ ] 107 1 Kings 4:22—7:14
- [ ] 108 1 Kings 7:15—8:66
- [ ] 109 1 Kings 9–11
- [ ] 110 1 Kings 12–13
- [ ] 111 1 Kings 14:1—16:20
- [ ] 112 1 Kings 16:21—18:46
- [ ] 113 1 Kings 19–21
- [ ] 114 1 Kings 22–2 Kings 2
- [ ] 115 2 Kings 3–4
- [ ] 116 2 Kings 5–7
- [ ] 117 2 Kings 8:1—10:17
- [ ] 118 2 Kings 10:18—13:25
- [ ] 119 2 Kings 14–16
- [ ] 120 2 Kings 17–19
- [ ] 121 2 Kings 20–22
- [ ] 122 2 Kings 23–25
- [ ] 123 1 Chronicles 1:1—2:2
- [ ] 124 1 Chronicles 2:3—4:23
- [ ] 125 1 Chronicles 4:24—5:26
- [ ] 126 1 Chronicles 6:1—7:5
- [ ] 127 1 Chronicles 7:6—8:40
- [ ] 128 1 Chronicles 9:1—11:14
- [ ] 129 1 Chronicles 11:15—13:14
- [ ] 130 1 Chronicles 14–16
- [ ] 131 1 Chronicles 17–20
- [ ] 132 1 Chronicles 21–23
- [ ] 133 1 Chronicles 24–26
- [ ] 134 1 Chronicles 27–29
- [ ] 135 2 Chronicles 1–4
- [ ] 136 2 Chronicles 5–7
- [ ] 137 2 Chronicles 8–11
- [ ] 138 2 Chronicles 12–16
- [ ] 139 2 Chronicles 17–20
- [ ] 140 2 Chronicles 21–24
- [ ] 141 2 Chronicles 25–28
- [ ] 142 2 Chronicles 29–31
- [ ] 143 2 Chronicles 32–34
- [ ] 144 2 Chronicles 35–36
- [ ] 145 Ezra 1–3
- [ ] 146 Ezra 4–7
- [ ] 147 Ezra 8–10
- [ ] 148 Nehemiah 1–4
- [ ] 149 Nehemiah 5–7
- [ ] 150 Nehemiah 8–10
- [ ] 151 Nehemiah 11–13
- [ ] 152 Esther 1–4
- [ ] 153 Esther 5–10
- [ ] 154 Job 1–3
- [ ] 155 Job 4–7
- [ ] 156 Job 8–10
- [ ] 157 Job 11–14
- [ ] 158 Job 15–18
- [ ] 159 Job 19–21
- [ ] 160 Job 22–25
- [ ] 161 Job 26–31
- [ ] 162 Job 32–37
- [ ] 163 Job 38–42
- [ ] 164 Psalms 1–7
- [ ] 165 Psalms 8–15
- [ ] 166 Psalms 16–19
- [ ] 167 Psalms 20–25
- [ ] 168 Psalms 26–31
- [ ] 169 Psalms 32–35
- [ ] 170 Psalms 36–39
- [ ] 171 Psalms 40–45
- [ ] 172 Psalms 46–50
- [ ] 173 Psalms 51–57
- [ ] 174 Psalms 58–64
- [ ] 175 Psalms 65–68
- [ ] 176 Psalms 69–72
- [ ] 177 Psalms 73–77
- [ ] 178 Psalms 78–79
- [ ] 179 Psalms 80–85
- [ ] 180 Psalms 86–89
- [ ] 181 Psalms 90–95
- [ ] 182 Psalms 96–102
- [ ] 183 Psalms 103–105
- [ ] 184 Psalms 106–107
- [ ] 185 Psalms 108–114
- [ ] 186 Psalms 115–118
- [ ] 187 Psalm 119:1–88
- [ ] 188 Psalm 119:89–176
- [ ] 189 Psalms 120–131
- [ ] 190 Psalms 132–138
- [ ] 191 Psalms 139–144
- [ ] 192 Psalms 145–150
- [ ] 193 Proverbs 1–3
- [ ] 194 Proverbs 4–6
- [ ] 195 Proverbs 7–9
- [ ] 196 Proverbs 10–12
- [ ] 197 Proverbs 13–15
- [ ] 198 Proverbs 16–18
- [ ] 199 Proverbs 19–21
- [ ] 200 Proverbs 22–24
- [ ] 201 Proverbs 25–27
- [ ] 202 Proverbs 28–31
- [ ] 203 Ecclesiastes 1–3
- [ ] 204 Ecclesiastes 4–7
- [ ] 205 Ecclesiastes 8–12

- [ ] 206 Song of Solomon 1–8
- [ ] 207 Isaiah 1–4
- [ ] 208 Isaiah 5–8
- [ ] 209 Isaiah 9–12
- [ ] 210 Isaiah 13–17
- [ ] 211 Isaiah 18–22
- [ ] 212 Isaiah 23–27
- [ ] 213 Isaiah 28–30
- [ ] 214 Isaiah 31–35
- [ ] 215 Isaiah 36–38
- [ ] 216 Isaiah 39–42
- [ ] 217 Isaiah 43–45
- [ ] 218 Isaiah 46–50
- [ ] 219 Isaiah 51–56
- [ ] 220 Isaiah 57–61
- [ ] 221 Isaiah 62–66
- [ ] 222 Jeremiah 1–3
- [ ] 223 Jeremiah 4–5
- [ ] 224 Jeremiah 6–8
- [ ] 225 Jeremiah 9–11
- [ ] 226 Jeremiah 12–15
- [ ] 227 Jeremiah 16–19
- [ ] 228 Jeremiah 20–23
- [ ] 229 Jeremiah 24–26
- [ ] 230 Jeremiah 27–29
- [ ] 231 Jeremiah 30–31
- [ ] 232 Jeremiah 32:1—34:7
- [ ] 233 Jeremiah 34:8—37:21
- [ ] 234 Jeremiah 38–41
- [ ] 235 Jeremiah 42–45
- [ ] 236 Jeremiah 46–48
- [ ] 237 Jeremiah 49
- [ ] 238 Jeremiah 50–51
- [ ] 239 Jeremiah 52
- [ ] 240 Lamentations 1–5
- [ ] 241 Ezekiel 1–5
- [ ] 242 Ezekiel 6–10
- [ ] 243 Ezekiel 11–13
- [ ] 244 Ezekiel 14–16
- [ ] 245 Ezekiel 17–19
- [ ] 246 Ezekiel 20–21
- [ ] 247 Ezekiel 22–23
- [ ] 248 Ezekiel 24–27
- [ ] 249 Ezekiel 28–31
- [ ] 250 Ezekiel 32–34
- [ ] 251 Ezekiel 35–37
- [ ] 252 Ezekiel 38–40
- [ ] 253 Ezekiel 41–43
- [ ] 254 Ezekiel 44–46
- [ ] 255 Ezekiel 47–48
- [ ] 256 Daniel 1–3
- [ ] 257 Daniel 4–6
- [ ] 258 Daniel 7–9
- [ ] 259 Daniel 10–12
- [ ] 260 Hosea 1–5
- [ ] 261 Hosea 6–10
- [ ] 262 Hosea 11–14
- [ ] 263 Joel 1–3
- [ ] 264 Amos 1–4
- [ ] 265 Amos 5–Obadiah 1
- [ ] 266 Jonah 1–Micah 4
- [ ] 267 Micah 5–Nahum 3
- [ ] 268 Habakkuk 1–Zephaniah 3
- [ ] 269 Haggai 1–Zechariah 3
- [ ] 270 Zechariah 4–10
- [ ] 271 Zechariah 11–Malachi 4
- [ ] 272 Matthew 1–2
- [ ] 273 Matthew 3–4
- [ ] 274 Matthew 5–7
- [ ] 275 Matthew 8–9
- [ ] 276 Matthew 10–11
- [ ] 277 Matthew 12–13
- [ ] 278 Matthew 14–15
- [ ] 279 Matthew 16–18
- [ ] 280 Matthew 19–20
- [ ] 281 Matthew 21–22
- [ ] 282 Matthew 23–24
- [ ] 283 Matthew 25–26
- [ ] 284 Matthew 27–28
- [ ] 285 Mark 1–2
- [ ] 286 Mark 3–4
- [ ] 287 Mark 5–6
- [ ] 288 Mark 7–8
- [ ] 289 Mark 9–10
- [ ] 290 Mark 11–12
- [ ] 291 Mark 13–14
- [ ] 292 Mark 15–16
- [ ] 293 Luke 1
- [ ] 294 Luke 2
- [ ] 295 Luke 3–4
- [ ] 296 Luke 5–6
- [ ] 297 Luke 7–8
- [ ] 298 Luke 9
- [ ] 299 Luke 10–11
- [ ] 300 Luke 12–13
- [ ] 301 Luke 14–15
- [ ] 302 Luke 16–17
- [ ] 303 Luke 18–19
- [ ] 304 Luke 20–21
- [ ] 305 Luke 22:1—23:25
- [ ] 306 Luke 23:26—24:53
- [ ] 307 John 1–2
- [ ] 308 John 3–4
- [ ] 309 John 5–6
- [ ] 310 John 7
- [ ] 311 John 8–9
- [ ] 312 John 10:1—11:44
- [ ] 313 John 11:45—12:50
- [ ] 314 John 13–14
- [ ] 315 John 15–17

- [ ] 316 John 18–19
- [ ] 317 John 20–21
- [ ] 318 Acts 1–3
- [ ] 319 Acts 4–6
- [ ] 320 Acts 7–8
- [ ] 321 Acts 9–10
- [ ] 322 Acts 11:1—13:12
- [ ] 323 Acts 13:13—14:28
- [ ] 324 Acts 15–16
- [ ] 325 Acts 17–19
- [ ] 326 Acts 20–21
- [ ] 327 Acts 22–24
- [ ] 328 Acts 25–26
- [ ] 329 Acts 27–28
- [ ] 330 Romans 1–4
- [ ] 331 Romans 5–8
- [ ] 332 Romans 9–11
- [ ] 333 Romans 12–14
- [ ] 334 Romans 15–16
- [ ] 335 1 Corinthians 1–4
- [ ] 336 1 Corinthians 5–9
- [ ] 337 1 Corinthians 10–12
- [ ] 338 1 Corinthians 13–16
- [ ] 339 2 Corinthians 1–3
- [ ] 340 2 Corinthians 4–6
- [ ] 341 2 Corinthians 7–9
- [ ] 342 2 Corinthians 10–13
- [ ] 343 Galatians 1–3
- [ ] 344 Galatians 4–6
- [ ] 345 Ephesians 1–3
- [ ] 346 Ephesians 4–6
- [ ] 347 Philippians 1–4
- [ ] 348 Colossians 1–4
- [ ] 349 1 Thessalonians 1–5
- [ ] 350 2 Thessalonians 1–3
- [ ] 351 1 Timothy 1–6
- [ ] 352 2 Timothy 1–4
- [ ] 353 Titus 1–Philemon 1
- [ ] 354 Hebrews 1–6
- [ ] 355 Hebrews 7–13
- [ ] 356 James 1–3
- [ ] 357 James 4–5
- [ ] 358 1 Peter 1–5
- [ ] 359 2 Peter 1–3
- [ ] 360 1 John 1–Jude 1
- [ ] 361 Revelation 1–3
- [ ] 362 Revelation 4–9
- [ ] 363 Revelation 10–13
- [ ] 364 Revelation 14–18
- [ ] 365 Revelation 19–22

60 DAYS THROUGH THE STORY OF SCRIPTURE

In about fifteen minutes a day, you will be able to read through the highlights of the Bible's main story of God's plan to provide forgiveness through Jesus Christ.

DAY	READING	PASSAGE
1	God Creates the World	Gen. 1–2
2	Sin Enters the World	Gen. 3
3	Sin Spreads	Gen. 4–5
4	God Spares Noah	Gen. 6–10
5	God Makes a Covenant with Abraham	Gen. 12; 15
6	God Provides Isaac	Gen. 21–22
7	God Delivers His People	Ex. 1–4; 12
8	God Parts the Red Sea	Ex. 13–15
9	God Gives the Ten Commandments	Ex. 19–20
10	The People Build the Tabernacle	Ex. 35–40
11	The Sacrificial System Is Established	Lev. 1–4
12	The People Return to the Land	Josh. 2–4
13	God Defeats Jericho	Josh. 2; 6
14	The People Continue to Sin	Judg. 2

DAY	READING	PASSAGE
15	The People Demand a King	1 Sam. 8–10
16	God Makes Saul King	1 Sam. 11
17	Saul Sins and Is Rejected	1 Sam. 13
18	God Chooses David as King	1 Sam. 16
19	God Makes a Covenant with David	2 Sam. 6–7
20	God Gives Solomon Wisdom	1 Kin. 2–3
21	Solomon Builds the Temple	1 Kin. 6–9
22	Solomon's Sin Divides the Kingdom	1 Kin. 10–12
23	Jeroboam Disobeys God	1 Kin. 12–13
24	Elijah Serves as a Prophet	1 Kin. 16–18
25	Elisha Serves as a Prophet	2 Kin. 4–6
26	God's People Are Taken Captive	2 Chr. 36
27	Daniel Is Faithful	Dan. 1
28	God Returns His People	Ezra 1
29	The People Rebuild the Temple	Ezra 2, 4–6

DAY	READING	PASSAGE
30	Esther Saves Her People	Esth. 1–10
31	Nehemiah Rebuilds the Walls	Neh. 1–7
32	Ezra Reads the Law	Ezra 7–10; Neh. 8
33	Jesus Is Born	John 1:1–18; Luke 2
34	Jesus Is Baptized and Tempted	Luke 3:21—4:13
35	Jesus Calls His Disciples	John 1:29–51
36	Jesus' Miracles Prove He Is God	John 14
37	Jesus Teaches about God's Kingdom	Matt. 13:1–53
38	Jesus Is Rejected	Luke 13:22–35; John 11:45–57
39	Jesus Raises Lazarus	John 11:1–44
40	People Welcome Jesus as King	Matt. 21:1–11
41	The Leaders Want to Trap Jesus	Matt. 25:15–46
42	Jesus Is Anointed	John 12:1–8
43	Jesus Shares a Last Meal	Matt. 26:17–30
44	Jesus Is Arrested	Matt. 26:31–56

DAY	READING	PASSAGE
45	Jesus Is Put on Trial	Matt. 26:57—27:26
46	Jesus Is Crucified	Matt. 27:27–56
47	Jesus Is Raised	Matt. 27:57—28:15
48	Jesus Appears to the Disciples	Luke 24:1–43
49	Jesus Gives His Followers a Mission	Matt. 28:18–20; Acts 1:1–11
50	The Holy Spirit Comes	Acts 2:1–13
51	Peter Preaches Jesus	Acts 2:14–47
52	Stephen Is Martyred	Acts 6:8—7:60
53	The Church Spreads Out	Acts 8
54	Paul Becomes a Disciple	Acts 9:1–30
55	Gentiles Become Part of the Church	Acts 11:1–18
56	Paul Goes on Mission	Acts 13–14
57	The Church Clarifies the Gospel	Acts 15:1–35
58	Paul and Silas Plant Churches	Acts 15:36—18:22
59	Jesus Will Return	Rev. 19–20
60	The New Heaven and Earth to Come	Rev. 21–22

30 DAYS OF GETTING TO KNOW JESUS

In less than ten minutes a day, you will be able to read through the highlights of Jesus' life and ministry. The average daily reading takes about four minutes.

DAY	READING	PASSAGE
1	Jesus is the eternal Son of God	John 1:1–18
2	Jesus is the fulfillment of prophecy	Is. 7:14; 9:6–7; 61:1–2; Mic. 5:2; Zech. 9:9; Mal. 3:1
3	Jesus is the suffering servant	Is. 52:13—53:12
4	Jesus is born and is a child	Luke 2:1–52
5	Jesus is baptized and tempted	Matt. 3:13—4:11
6	Jesus calls His disciples	John 1:29–51
7	Jesus shows His power over creation	John 6:1–24
8	Jesus shows His power over sickness	Matt. 9:1–38
9	Jesus shows His power over death	John 11:1–44
10	Jesus teaches about character	Matt. 5:1–48
11	Jesus teaches about conduct	Matt. 6:1—7:29
12	Jesus teaches about Himself	John 10:1–42
13	Jesus tells parables of the kingdom	Matt. 13:1–58
14	Jesus tells parables of His mission	Luke 15:1–32
15	Jesus came for the affluent	John 3:1–36
16	Jesus came for the rejected	John 4:1–42
17	Jesus came for the outcast	Luke 19:1–10
18	Jesus is opposed	John 5:1–47
19	Jesus tells of His death	Matt. 16:1–28
20	Jesus enters Jerusalem	Matt. 21:1–17
21	Jesus is challenged	Mark 11:27—12:44
22	Jesus rebukes the religious leaders	Matt. 23:1–36
23	Jesus shares the Lord's Supper	John 13:1–38
24	Jesus prays	Mark 14:26–42; John 17:1–26
25	Jesus is arrested and put on trial	Mark 14:43—15:20
26	Jesus is crucified and buried	Luke 23:26–56
27	Jesus raises from the dead	Luke 24:1–8; John 20:1–18
28	Jesus appears to His followers	Luke 24:13–43; John 21:1–25; 1 Cor. 15:5–6
29	Jesus sends out His followers	Matt. 28:16–20; Acts 1:3–11
30	Jesus will return as conquering King	Rev. 19:1–21

THE MIRACLES OF JESUS

MIRACLE	MATTHEW	MARK	LUKE	JOHN
1. Man with Leprosy	8:2–4	1:40–42	5:12–13	
2. Centurion's Servant	8:5–13		7:1–10	
3. Peter's Mother-in-Law	8:14–15	1:30–31	4:38–39	
4. Calming the Storm	8:23–27	4:37–41	8:22–25	
5. Gadarenes Demoniac	8:28–34	5:1–15	8:27–35	
6. Paralyzed Man	9:2–7	2:3–12	5:18–25	
7. Raising of Jairus's Daughter	9:18–19, 23–25	5:22–24, 35–42	8:41–42, 49–56	
8. Hemorrhaging Woman	9:20–22	5:25–34	8:43–48	
9. Two Blind Men	9:27–31			
10. Mute and Possessed Man	9:32–34			
11. Man with a Withered Hand	12:9–14	3:1–6	6:6–11	
12. Blind, Mute, and Possessed Man	12:22–32		11:14–23	
13. Feeding of over Five Thousand	14:15–21	6:35–44	9:12–17	6:5–14
14. Walking on Water	14:25–32	6:48–51		6:19–21
15. Gentile Woman's Daughter	15:21–28	7:24–30		
16. Feeding of over Four Thousand	15:32–38	8:1–9		
17. Demon-Possessed Boy	17:14–18	9:14–29	9:38–43	
18. Coin in Fish's Mouth	17:24–27			
19. The Blind Men	20:29–34	10:46–52	18:35–43	
20. Fig Tree Withered	21:18–22	11:12–14, 20–25		
21. Possessed Man in Synagogue		1:23–26	4:33–35	

MIRACLE	MATTHEW	MARK	LUKE	JOHN
22. Deaf and Mute		7:31–37		
23. Blind Man at Bethsaida		8:22–26		
24. First Catch of Fish			5:1–11	
25. Raising Widow's Son at Nain			7:11–15	
26. Crippled Woman			13:10–13	
27. Man with Dropsy			14:1–4	
28. Ten Lepers			17:11–19	
29. High Priest's Servant			22:50–51	
30. Water to Wine				2:1–11
31. Nobleman's Son				4:46–54
32. Sick Man at Pool of Bethesda				5:1–9
33. Man Born Blind				9:1–41
34. Raising of Lazarus				11:1–44
35. Second Catch of Fish				21:1–14

THE PARABLES OF JESUS

PARABLE	MATTHEW	MARK	LUKE
1. Lamp Under a Basket	5:14–16	4:21–22	8:16–17, 11:33–36
2. The House Built on Rock and the House Built on Sand	7:24–27		6:47–49
3. New Cloth on an Old Garment	9:16	2:21	5:36
4. New Wine in Old Wineskins	9:17	2:22	5:37–38
5. The Sower	13:3–9, 18–23	4:3–9, 14–20	8:4–9, 11–15
6. The Tares	13:24–30, 36–43		
7. The Mustard Seed	13:31–32	4:30–32	13:18–19
8. The Leaven	13:33		13:20–21
9. The Hidden Treasure	13:44		
10. The Pearl of Great Price	13:45–46		
11. The Dragnet	13:47–50		
12. The Lost Sheep	18:12–14		15:3–7
13. The Unforgiving Servant	18:23–35		
14. The Laborers in the Vineyard	20:1–16		
15. The Two Sons	21:28–32		
16. The Wicked Vinedressers	21:33–45	12:1–12	20:9–19
17. The Wedding Feast	22:2–14		
18. The Fig Tree	24:32–36	13:28–32	21:29–33
19. The Wise and Foolish Virgins	25:1–13		
20. The Talents	25:14–30		
21. The Growing Seed		4:26–29	

PARABLE	MATTHEW	MARK	LUKE
22. The Absent Householder		13:33–37	
23. The Creditor and the Two Debtors			7:41–43
24. The Good Samaritan			10:30–37
25. A Friend in Need			11:5–13
26. The Rich Fool			12:16–21
27. The Faithful Servant			12:35–40
28. The Faithful and Wise Steward			12:42–48
29. The Barren Fig Tree			13:6–9
30. The Great Supper			14:16–24
31. Building a Tower and a King Making War			14:25–35
32. The Lost Coin			15:8–10
33. The Prodigal Son			15:11–32
34. The Unjust Steward			16:1–13
35. The Rich Man and Lazarus			16:19–31
36. Unprofitable Servants			17:7–10
37. The Persistent Widow			18:1–8
38. The Pharisee and the Tax Collector			18:9–14
39. The Minas			19:11–27

MY BIBLE JOURNAL

WHAT I'M LEARNING ABOUT GOD:

WHAT I'M LEARNING ABOUT GOD:

WHAT I'M LEARNING ABOUT GOD:

WHAT I'M LEARNING ABOUT GOD:

WHAT I'M LEARNING ABOUT MYSELF:

WHAT I'M LEARNING ABOUT MYSELF:

WHAT I'M LEARNING ABOUT MYSELF:

WHAT I'M LEARNING ABOUT MYSELF:

WHAT I'M LEARNING ABOUT THE GOOD NEWS:

WHAT I'M LEARNING ABOUT THE GOOD NEWS:

WHAT I'M LEARNING ABOUT THE GOOD NEWS:

WHAT I'M LEARNING ABOUT THE GOOD NEWS:

MY FAVORITE BIBLE VERSES:

MY FAVORITE BIBLE VERSES:

MY FAVORITE BIBLE VERSES:

MY FAVORITE BIBLE VERSES:

MY FAVORITE BIBLE STORIES:

MY FAVORITE BIBLE STORIES:

MY FAVORITE BIBLE STORIES:

MY FAVORITE BIBLE STORIES:

MY PRAYER REQUESTS:

MY PRAYER REQUESTS:

MY PRAYER REQUESTS:

MY PRAYER REQUESTS:

MY PRAYER REQUESTS:

MY PRAYER REQUESTS:

A NOTE REGARDING THE TYPE

This Bible was set in the Thomas Nelson NKJV Typeface, commissioned by Thomas Nelson Publishers and designed in Aarhus by Klaus Krogh and Heidi Rand Sørensen of 2K/DENMARK. The letter forms take inspiration from a distinctive typeface found in an early Thomas Nelson *Novum Testamentum*, printed in 1844 in Edinburgh—which in turn reflects the Scotch Roman typefaces created by the celebrated English punchcutter Richard Austin for the type foundry of William Miller, circa 1808–1813.

Just as the NKJV translation inherits the tradition and literary beauty of the King James Bible while updating the language for today's readers, so Thomas Nelson's custom NKJV font family builds on classic letter forms of the past while reflecting cutting-edge typographical design. The result is a type design that is at once beautiful and efficient, traditional and modern—ideal for presenting the sacred words of ancient Scripture to readers today.

INDEX TO MAPS

References are to the map number in **BOLD**, followed by the letter and number coordinates that correspond to the margin markings.

Map 1: WORLD OF THE PATRIARCHS

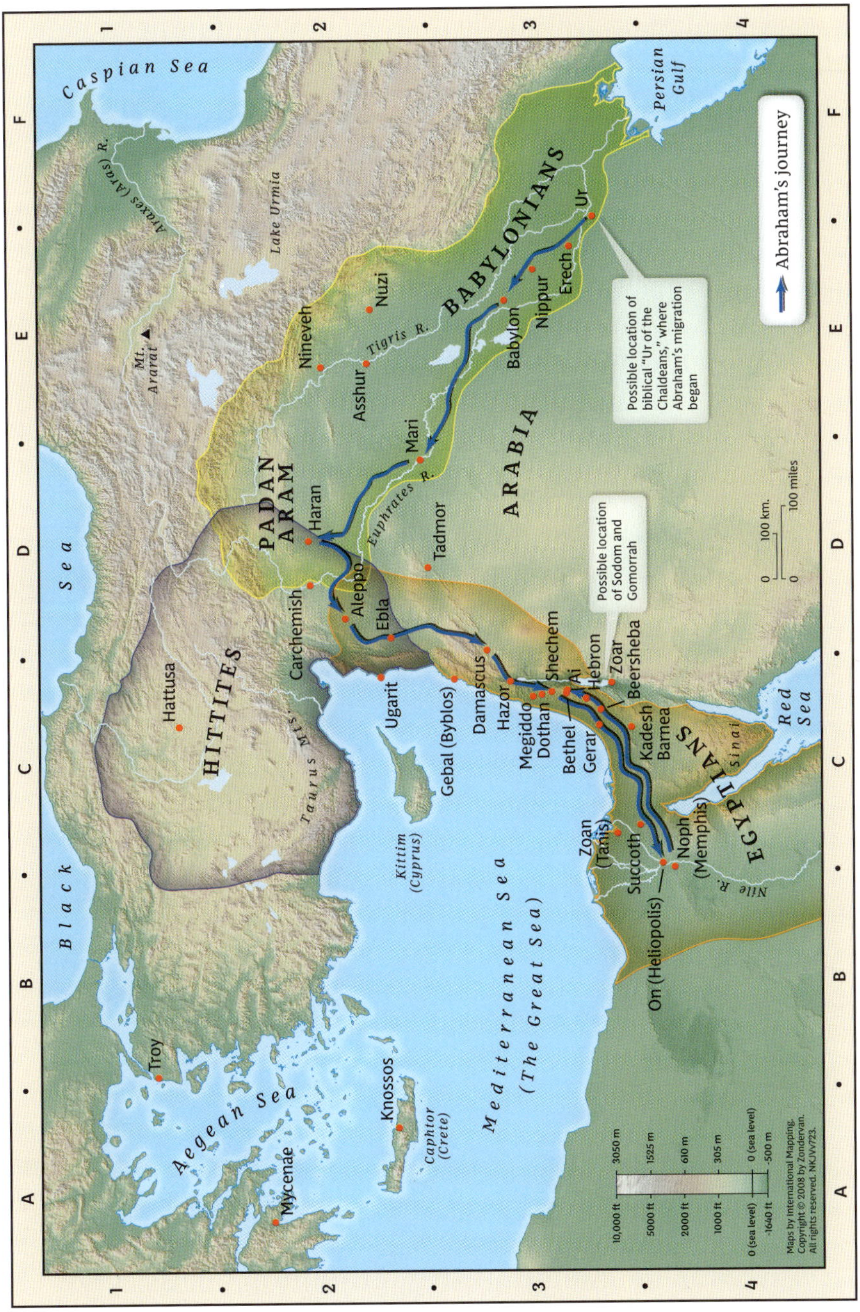

Map 2: EXODUS AND CONQUEST OF CANAAN

Map 3: LAND OF THE TWELVE TRIBES

Map 4: KINGDOM OF DAVID AND SOLOMON

Map 5: JESUS' MINISTRY

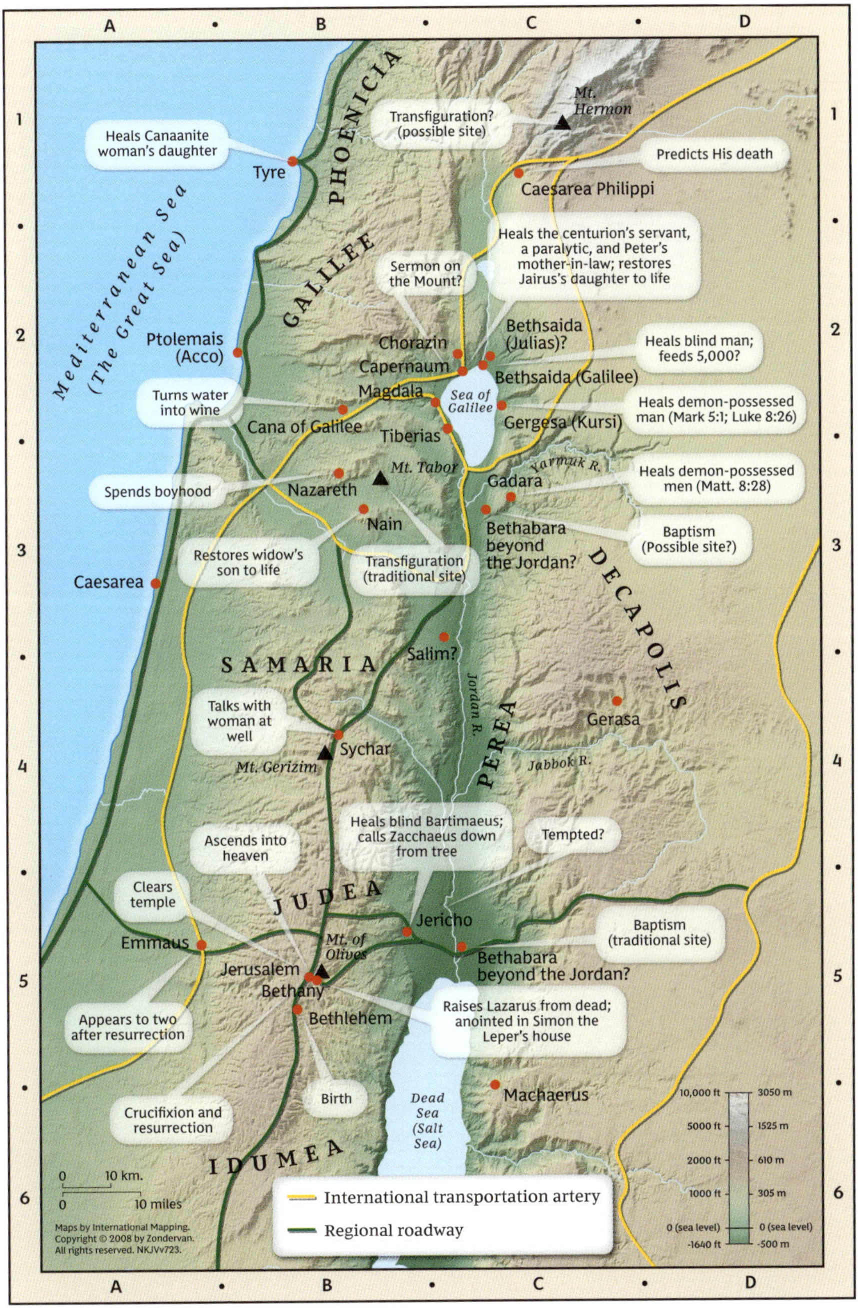

Map 6: PAUL'S MISSIONARY JOURNEYS

5
6
7
8
A
B
C
D
E
F
DACIA
MOESIA
THRACE
Black Sea
10,000 ft
5000 ft
2000 ft
1000 ft
0 (sea level)
-1640 ft
3050 m
1525 m
610 m
305 m
0 (sea level)
-500 m
ONIA
Amphipolis
Thessalonica
Philippi
Neapolis
Samothrace
Apollonia?
BITHYNIA & PONTUS
Mt. Olympus
Aegean Sea
Troas
Assos
Mitylene
Chios
MYSIA
ASIA
Pergamos
Thyatira
Sardis
LYDIA
GALATIA
CAPPADOCIA
LYCAONIA
Antioch (Pisidian)
PISIDIA
COMMAGENE
Delphi
Athens
Smyrna
Ephesus
Philadelphia
Iconium
Samos
Laodicea
Colosse
Euphrates R.
Cenchrea
Corinth
Sparta
Miletus
PAMPHYLIA
Derbe
Lystra
CILICIA
Patmos
LYCIA
Attalia
Tarsus
Issus
SYRIA
Cos
Cnidus
Seleucia Pieria
Aleppo
Patara
Myra
Perga
Antioch (Syrian)
Crete
Rhodes
Salmone
Phoenix
Lasea
Cyprus
Salamis
Claudа
Fair Havens
Paphos
PHOENICIA
ABILENE
Sidon
Mediterranean Sea
(The Great Sea)
Tyre
Ptolemais
Damascus
Caesarea
JUDEA
Jordan R.
Jerusalem
Dead Sea
(Salt Sea)
ENAICA
ARABIA
EGYPT
Nile R.
Red Sea
0
200 km.
0
200 miles

Map 7: JERUSALEM IN THE TIME OF JESUS

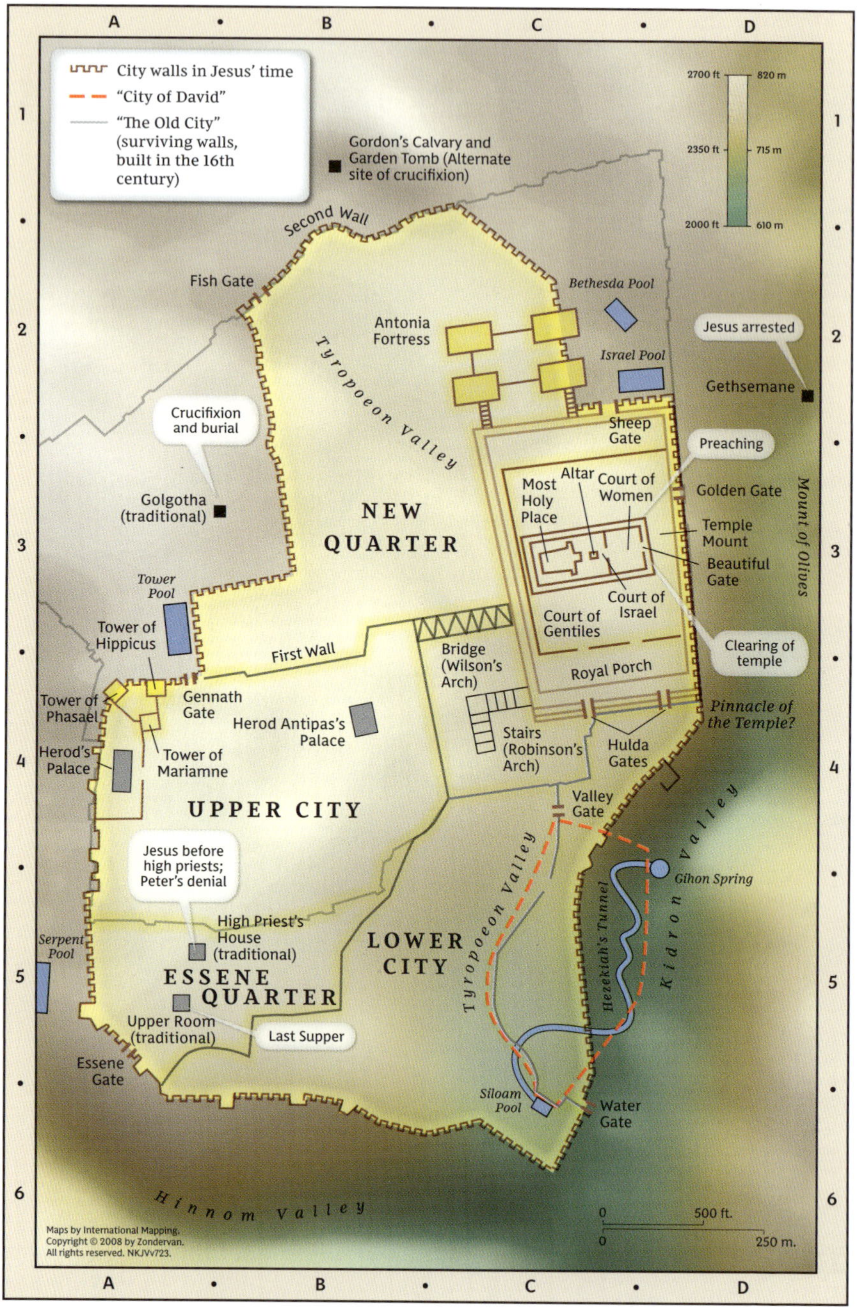